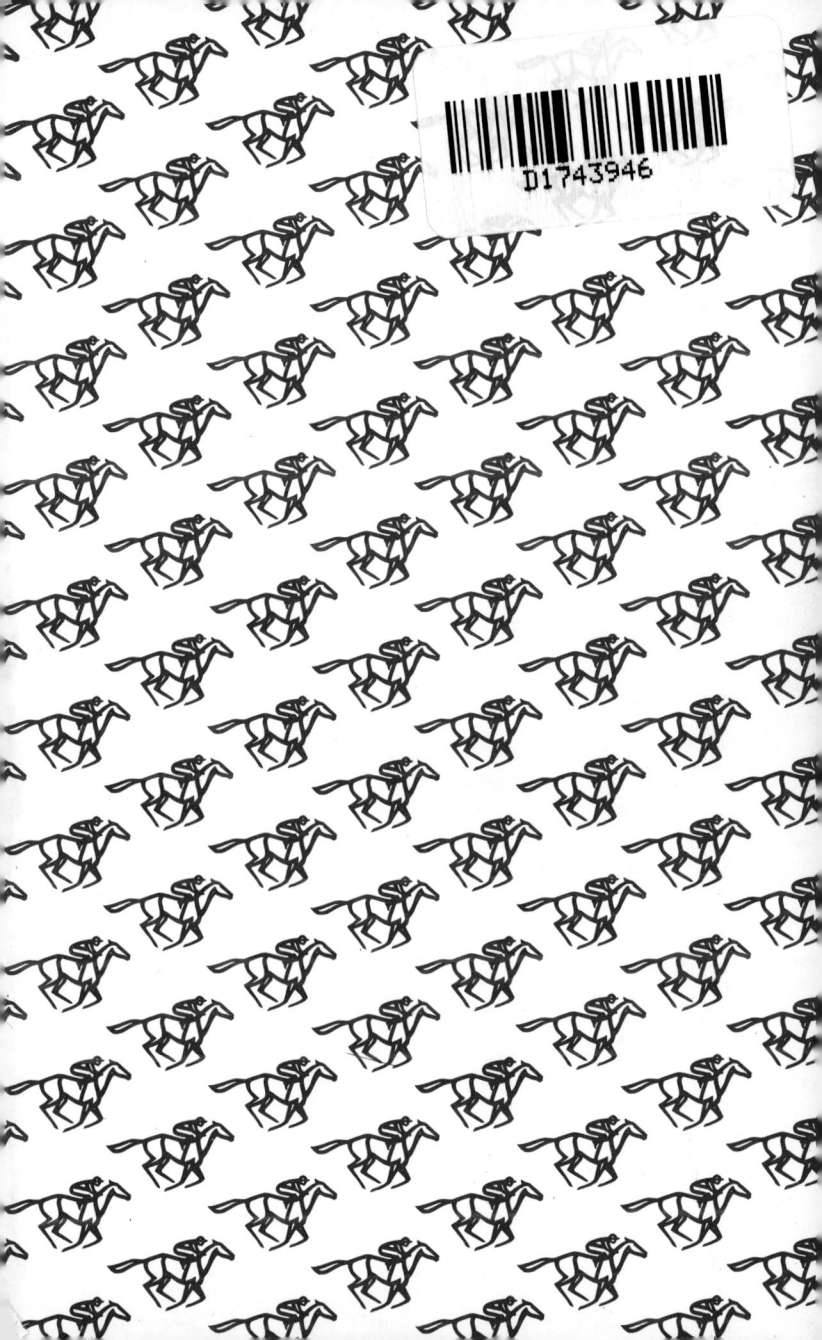

RACEHORSES
OF 1991

A Timeform Publication   Price £68.00

A Timeform Publication

Compiled and produced under the direction of
Reg Griffin

by members of the Timeform Organisation

G. Greetham, B.A., G. F. Walton, Dip.A.D.
(Directors), J. D. Newton, B.A. (Editor-in-Chief), R. J.
C. Austen, B.A. (Editor), D. P. Adams, S. N.
Copeland, G. Crowther, G. J. Cunningham, LL.B., P.
R. Entwistle, B.Sc., W. Hughes, G. M. Johnstone, G. J.
North, B.Sc., O. C. Pennant Jones, B.A., C. S.
Williams, and D. N. Yates, B.A.

© Portway Press Limited 1992

ISBN 0 900599 56 1

CONTENTS

AGE, WEIGHT & DISTANCE TABLE

Timeform's scale of weight-for-age for the flat

Dist	Age	Jan 1-16	Jan 17-31	Feb 1-16	Feb 17-28	Mar 1-16	Mar 17-31	Apr 1-16	Apr 17-30	May 1-16	May 17-31	June 1-16	June 17-30
5f	4	10-0	10-0	10-0	10-0	10-0	10-0	10-0	10-0	10-0	10-0	10-0	10-0
	3	9-5	9-5	9-6	9-7	9-7	9-8	9-8	9-9	9-9	9-10	9-10	9-11
	2						8-0	8-1	8-3	8-4	8-5	8-6	8-7
6f	4	10-0	10-0	10-0	10-0	10-0	10-0	10-0	10-0	10-0	10-0	10-0	10-0
	3	9-2	9-3	9-4	9-5	9-5	9-6	9-7	9-7	9-8	9-8	9-9	9-9
	2								8-0	8-2		8-3	8-4
7f	4	9-13	9-13	10-0	10-0	10-0	10-0	10-0	10-0	10-0	10-0	10-0	10-0
	3	9-0	9-1	9-2	9-3	9-4	9-4	9-5	9-6	9-6	9-7	9-8	9-8
	2											7-13	8-1
1m	4	9-13	9-13	9-13	9-13	10-0	10-0	10-0	10-0	10-0	10-0	10-0	10-0
	3	8-12	8-13	9-0	9-1	9-2	9-2	9-3	9-4	9-5	9-5	9-6	9-7
	2												
9f	4	9-12	9-12	9-12	9-13	9-13	9-13	9-13	10-0	10-0	10-0	10-0	10-0
	3	8-10	8-11	8-12	8-13	9-0	9-1	9-2	9-2	9-3	9-4	9-5	9-5
	2												
1¼m	4	9-11	9-12	9-12	9-12	9-13	9-13	9-13	9-13	9-13	10-0	10-0	10-0
	3	8-8	8-9	8-10	8-11	8-12	8-13	9-0	9-1	9-2	9-2	9-3	9-4
	2												
11f	4	9-10	9-11	9-11	9-12	9-12	9-12	9-13	9-13	9-13	9-13	9-13	10-0
	3	8-6	8-7	8-8	8-9	8-10	8-11	8-12	8-13	9-0	9-1	9-2	9-2
1½m	4	9-10	9-10	9-10	9-11	9-11	9-12	9-12	9-12	9-13	9-13	9-13	9-13
	3	8-4	8-5	8-6	8-7	8-8	8-9	8-10	8-11	8-12	8-13	9-0	9-1
13f	4	9-9	9-9	9-10	9-10	9-11	9-11	9-11	9-12	9-12	9-12	9-13	9-13
	3	8-2	8-3	8-4	8-5	8-7	8-8	8-9	8-10	8-11	8-12	8-13	9-0
1¾m	4	9-8	9-8	9-9	9-9	9-10	9-10	9-11	9-11	9-12	9-12	9-12	9-13
	3	8-0	8-2	8-3	8-4	8-5	8-6	8-7	8-8	8-9	8-10	8-11	8-12
15f	4	9-7	9-8	9-8	9-9	9-9	9-10	9-10	9-11	9-11	9-11	9-12	9-12
	3	7-13	8-0	8-1	8-2	8-4	8-5	8-6	8-7	8-8	8-9	8-10	8-11
2m	4	9-6	9-7	9-7	9-8	9-9	9-9	9-10	9-10	9-11	9-11	9-11	9-12
	3	7-11	7-12	7-13	8-1	8-2	8-3	8-4	8-5	8-6	8-7	8-8	8-9
2¼m	4	9-5	9-5	9-6	9-7	9-7	9-8	9-9	9-9	9-10	9-10	9-10	9-11
	3	7-8	7-9	7-11	7-12	7-13	8-0	8-2	8-3	8-4	8-5	8-6	8-7
2½m	4	9-3	9-4	9-5	9-6	9-6	9-7	9-7	9-8	9-9	9-9	9-10	9-10
	3	7-5	7-7	7-8	7-9	7-11	7-12	7-13	8-1	8-2	8-3	8-4	8-5

For 5-y-o's and older, use 10-0 in all cases
Race distances in the above tables are shown only at 1 furlong intervals.
For races over odd distances, the nearest distance shown in the table should be used:
thus for races of 1m to 1m 109 yards, use the table weights for 1m;
for 1m 110 yards to 1m 219 yards use the 9f table

4

AGE, WEIGHT & DISTANCE TABLE

Timeform's scale of weight-for-age for the flat

Dist	Age	July 1-16	July 17-31	Aug 1-16	Aug 17-31	Sept 1-16	Sept 17-30	Oct 1-16	Oct 17-31	Nov 1-16	Nov 17-30	Dec 1-16	Dec 17-31
5f	4	10-0	10-0	10-0	10-0	10-0	10-0	10-0	10-0	10-0	10-0	10-0	10-0
	3	9-11	9-12	9-12	9-12	9-13	9-13	9-13	9-13	10-0	10-0	10-0	10-0
	2	8-8	8-9	8-10	8-11	8-12	8-13	9-0	9-1	9-2	9-2	9-3	9-4
6f	4	10-0	10-0	10-0	10-0	10-0	10-0	10-0	10-0	10-0	10-0	10-0	10-0
	3	9-10	9-10	9-11	9-11	9-12	9-12	9-12	9-13	9-13	9-13	9-13	9-13
	2	8-5	8-6	8-7	8-8	8-9	8-10	8-11	8-12	8-13	9-0	9-1	9-2
7f	4	10-0	10-0	10-0	10-0	10-0	10-0	10-0	10-0	10-0	10-0	10-0	10-0
	3	9-9	9-9	9-10	9-10	9-11	9-11	9-11	9-12	9-12	9-12	9-13	9-13
	2	8-2	8-3	8-4	8-5	8-6	8-7	8-9	8-10	8-11	8-12	8-13	9-0
1m	4	10-0	10-0	10-0	10-0	10-0	10-0	10-0	10-0	10-0	10-0	10-0	10-0
	3	9-7	9-8	9-8	9-9	9-9	9-10	9-10	9-11	9-11	9-12	9-12	9-12
	2			8-2	8-3	8-4	8-5	8-6	8-7	8-8	8-9	8-10	8-11
9f	4	10-0	10-0	10-0	10-0	10-0	10-0	10-0	10-0	10-0	10-0	10-0	10-0
	3	9-6	9-7	9-7	9-8	9-8	9-9	9-9	9-10	9-10	9-11	9-11	9-12
	2					8-1	8-3	8-4	8-5	8-6	8-7	8-8	8-9
1¼m	4	10-0	10-0	10-0	10-0	10-0	10-0	10-0	10-0	10-0	10-0	10-0	10-0
	3	9-5	9-5	9-6	9-7	9-7	9-8	9-8	9-9	9-9	9-10	9-10	9-11
	2							8-1	8-2	8-4	8-5	8-6	8-7
11f	4	10-0	10-0	10-0	10-0	10-0	10-0	10-0	10-0	10-0	10-0	10-0	10-0
	3	9-3	9-4	9-5	9-5	9-6	9-7	9-7	9-8	9-8	9-9	9-9	9-10
1½m	4	10-0	10-0	10-0	10-0	10-0	10-0	10-0	10-0	10-0	10-0	10-0	10-0
	3	9-2	9-2	9-3	9-4	9-5	9-5	9-6	9-7	9-7	9-8	9-9	9-9
13f	4	9-13	9-13	10-0	10-0	10-0	10-0	10-0	10-0	10-0	10-0	10-0	10-0
	3	9-0	9-1	9-2	9-3	9-4	9-4	9-5	9-6	9-6	9-7	9-8	9-8
1¾m	4	9-13	9-13	9-13	10-0	10-0	10-0	10-0	10-0	10-0	10-0	10-0	10-0
	3	8-13	9-0	9-1	9-2	9-3	9-3	9-4	9-5	9-5	9-6	9-7	9-7
15f	4	9-12	9-13	9-13	9-13	9-13	10-0	10-0	10-0	10-0	10-0	10-0	10-0
	3	8-12	8-13	9-0	9-1	9-1	9-2	9-3	9-4	9-4	9-5	9-6	9-6
2m	4	9-12	9-12	9-13	9-13	9-13	9-13	10-0	10-0	10-0	10-0	10-0	10-0
	3	8-10	8-11	8-12	8-13	9-0	9-1	9-2	9-3	9-3	9-4	9-5	9-5
2¼m	4	9-11	9-12	9-12	9-12	9-13	9-13	9-13	9-13	10-0	10-0	10-0	10-0
	3	8-8	8-9	8-10	8-11	8-12	8-13	9-0	9-1	9-2	9-2	9-3	9-4
2½m	4	9-10	9-11	9-11	9-12	9-11	9-12	9-13	9-13	9-13	9-13	10-0	10-0
	3	8-6	8-7	8-8	8-9	8-10	8-11	8-12	8-13	9-0	9-1	9-2	9-3

For 5-y-o's and older, use 10-0 in all cases
Race distances in the above tables are shown only at 1 furlong intervals.
For races over odd distances, the nearest distance shown in the table should be used:
thus for races of 1m to 1m 109 yards, use the table weights for 1m;
for 1m 110 yards to 1m 219 yards use the 9f table

The Sporting Life

BEST RUNNER OF ALL EVERY YEAR

YOU'RE LIFELESS WITHOUT IT

ETALONS
1992

- **Stallion review**
- **Racing and breeding chronicles**
- **Statistics and results of the main sales of the year**
- **Results of the 1991 Group Races**
- **Register of all stallions standing in France in 1991 and their fees**
- **Register of all French stud farms with stallions**

NAME ....

ADDRESS ....

TOWN ....

COUNTRY ....

would like to receive (   ) copy(ies) of ETALONS 1992
at the unit price of 180 FF + 40 FF for p & p

Kindly complete and mail to:
ETALONS, 6 rond-point des Champs-Elysées, 75008 Paris, France
Tel: (1) 43 59 94 14   Fax: (1) 43 59 94 41

☐ attached payment by cheque in Fr. Francs at the order of **ETALONS**
☐ wishes to pay by charge card
☐ Visa   ☐ Mastercard

Card number ....

Expiration date ....   Signature

8

FOREWORD

"Racehorses of 1991" deals individually, in alphabetical sequence, with every horse that ran under Jockey Club Rules (including on the all-weather tracks) in 1991, plus a number of foreign-trained horses that did not race here. For each of these horses is given (1) its age, colour and sex, (2) its breeding, (3) a form summary giving details of all its performances during the past two seasons, (4) a rating of its merit, (5) a commentary upon its racing or general characteristics as a racehorse, with some suggestions, perhaps, regarding its prospects for 1992 and (6) the name of the trainer in whose charge it was on the last occasion it ran. For each two-year-old the foaling date is also given.

The book is published with a twofold purpose. Firstly, the book is intended to have permanent value as a review of the exploits and achievements of the more notable of our thoroughbreds in 1991. Thus, while the commentaries upon the vast majority of the horses are, of necessity, in note form, the best horses are more critically examined, and the short essays upon them are illustrated by half-tone portraits and photographs of the finishes of some of the races in which they were successful; and secondly, the book is designed to provide data for practical use in analysing the racing programmes from day to day, and instructions as to its use in that capacity will be found in the Explanatory Notes.

The attention of foreign buyers of British bloodstock, and others who are concerned with Timeform Ratings as a measure of absolute racing class in terms of a standard scale, is drawn to the section headed "The Level of the Ratings" in the Explanatory Notes.

February, 1992

INDEX TO PHOTOGRAPHS

PORTRAITS & SNAPSHOTS

11

RACE PHOTOGRAPHS

Ciga Prix Dollar (Longchamp)	*P. Bertrand*	956
Ciga Prix du Cadran (Longchamp)	*P. Bertrand*	936
Ciga Prix Marcel Boussac (Longchamp)	*P. Bertrand*	198
C. L. Weld EBF Park Stakes (the Curragh)	*Caroline Norris*	873
Coalite Handicap (Doncaster)	*Alec Russell*	805
Coalite St Leger Stakes (Doncaster)	*Alec Russell*	911
Coral-Eclipse Stakes (Sandown)	*John Crofts*	265
Cork And Orrery Stakes (Ascot)	*Alec Russell*	651
Cornwallis Stakes (Ascot)	*George Selwyn*	494
Coronation Stakes (Ascot)	*Alec Russell*	441
Courage Stakes (Limited Handicap) (Newbury)	*George Selwyn*	615
Coventry Stakes (Ascot)	*John Crofts*	223
Crawley Warren Handicap (York)	*Alec Russell*	324
Criterium de Maisons-Laffitte (Maisons-Laffitte)	*P. Bertrand*	140
Criterium de Saint-Cloud (Saint-Cloud)	*P. Bertrand*	328
Dalham Chester Vase (Chester)	*Alec Russell*	910
Daniel Prenn Royal Yorkshire Stakes (York)	*Alec Russell*	801
Derrinstown Stud Derby Trial (Leopardstown)	*Caroline Norris*	727
Desmond Stakes (the Curragh)	*Caroline Norris*	831
Diadem Stakes (Ascot)	*Alec Russell*	773
Dickins & Jones Goodwood Cup (Goodwood)	*John Crofts*	310
Doncaster Cup (Doncaster)	*Alec Russell*	343
Doonside Cup (Ayr)	*Alec Russell*	77
Dubai Champion Stakes (Newmarket)	*Ed Byrne*	878
Dubai Poule d'Essai des Poulains (Longchamp)	*P. Bertrand*	368
Dubai Poule d'Essai des Pouliches (Longchamp)	*John Crofts*	205
Duchess of Kent Stakes (York)	*Alec Russell*	414
Duke of York Stakes (York)	*Alec Russell*	349
EBF Anglesey Stakes (the Curragh)	*Caroline Norris*	837
EBF Granville Maiden Stakes (Ascot)	*George Selwyn*	755
EBF Leopardstown Stakes (Leopardstown)	*Caroline Norris*	865
EBF Theale Maiden Stakes (Newbury)	*John Crofts*	425
Emirates Prix du Moulin de Longchamp (Longchamp)	*John Crofts*	670
Ever Ready Derby (Epsom)	*John Crofts*	318
F. H. Lee 25th Anniversary Lymm Stakes (Haydock)	*Alec Russell*	943
Flying Childers Stakes (Doncaster)	*Alec Russell*	619
Gainsborough Stud Fred Darling Stakes (Newbury)	*John Crofts*	768
Galtres Stakes (York)	*John Crofts*	583
General Accident Jockey Club Stakes (Newmarket)	*John Crofts*	708
General Accident One Thousand Guineas (Newmarket)	*John Crofts*	769
General Accident Two Thousand Guineas (Newmarket)	*John Crofts*	573
Goffs Irish One Thousand Guineas (the Curragh)	*Caroline Norris*	440
Goffs Million (the Curragh)	*Caroline Norris*	277
Goffs Premier Challenge (the Curragh)	*Caroline Norris*	174
Gold Cup (Ascot)	*Alec Russell*	391
Gold Seal Oaks (Epsom)	*John Crofts*	411
Grand Prix de Deauville Lancel (Deauville)	*P. Bertrand*	810
Grand Prix de Saint-Cloud (Saint-Cloud)	*P. Bertrand*	266
Great Voltigeur Stakes (York)	*George Selwyn*	182
Greenlands Stakes (the Curragh)	*Caroline Norris*	65
Hackwood Stakes (Newbury)	*John Crofts*	429
Hanson Coronation Cup (Epsom)	*George Selwyn*	398
Hardwicke Stakes (Ascot)	*Alec Russell*	708
Heinz 57 Phoenix Stakes (Leopardstown)	*Caroline Norris*	118
Hillsdown Cherry Hinton Stakes (Newmarket)	*John Crofts*	564
Hoover Cumberland Lodge Stakes (Ascot)	*John Crofts*	241
Insulpak Sagaro EBF Stakes (Ascot)	*John Crofts*	876
Jefferson Smurfit Memorial Irish St Leger (the Curragh)	*Caroline Norris*	921
Jersey Stakes (Ascot)	*Alec Russell*	746
John Roarty Memorial International (the Curragh)	*Caroline Norris*	560
Juddmonte EBF Beresford Stakes (the Curragh)	*Caroline Norris*	257
Juddmonte International Stakes (York)	*Alec Russell*	882
Juddmonte Lockinge Stakes (Newbury)	*John Crofts*	648
Keeneland Nunthorpe Stakes (York)	*Ed Byrne*	783
Kensington Palace Stakes (Ascot)	*George Selwyn*	691

Queen Mary Stakes (Ascot)	*John Crofts*	514
Queen Mother's Cup (York)	*Alec Russell*	460
Queensberry Fillies Stakes (Newmarket)	*Alec Russell*	233
Queen's Vase (Ascot)	*Alec Russell*	409
Racecall Gold Trophy (Redcar)	*Alec Russell*	147
Racing Post Trophy (Doncaster)	*Alec Russell*	756
Radley Stakes (Newbury)	*John Crofts*	813
Reference Point Sceptre Stakes (Doncaster)	*Alec Russell*	962
Ribblesdale Stakes (Ascot)	*John Crofts*	890
ROA Foundation Stakes (Goodwood)	*John Crofts*	632
Rockfel Stakes (Newmarket)	*John Crofts*	565
Rockingham Stakes (York)	*Alec Russell*	545
Rokeby Farms Mill Reef Stakes (Newbury)	*George Selwyn*	790
Roses Stakes (York)	*John Crofts*	53
Rous Stakes (Newmarket)	*John Crofts*	107
Royal Hunt Cup (Ascot)	*John Crofts*	271
Royal Lodge William Hill Stakes (Ascot)	*John Crofts*	487
Sandringham Handicap (Ascot)	*George Selwyn*	387
Schroders Glorious Stakes (Goodwood)	*John Crofts*	297
Schweppes Golden Mile (Handicap) (Goodwood)	*John Crofts*	804
Scottish Equitable Gimcrack Stakes (York)	*George Selwyn*	703
Scottish Equitable Richmond Stakes (Goodwood)	*John Crofts*	224
Sea World Pretty Polly Stakes (the Curragh)	*Caroline Norris*	723
Shadwell Stud Nell Gwyn Stakes (Newmarket)	*John Crofts*	193
Singer & Friedlander Greenham Stakes (Newbury)	*George Selwyn*	109
Solario Stakes (Sandown)	*John Crofts*	158
Somerville Tattersall Stakes (Newmarket)	*John Crofts*	884
Southern Comfort Stakes (Ascot)	*W. Everitt*	667
Sporting Life Zetland Stakes (Newmarket)	*John Crofts*	114
St James's Palace Stakes (Ascot)	*George Selwyn*	512
St Simon Stakes (Newbury)	*John Crofts*	311
Sun Princess Graduation Guaranteed Sweepstakes (Doncaster)	*John Crofts*	219
Sussex Stakes (Goodwood)	*John Crofts*	759
Tap And Spile Handicap (Ascot)	*George Selwyn*	587
Tattersalls Cheveley Park Stakes (Newmarket)	*John Crofts*	515
Tattersalls Musidora Stakes (York)	*Alec Russell*	354
Tattersalls Rogers Gold Cup (the Curragh)	*Caroline Norris*	971
Tattersalls Tiffany Highflyer Stakes (Newmarket)	*John Crofts*	966
Three Chimneys Dewhurst Stakes (Newmarket)	*John Crofts*	237
Timeform Futurity (Pontefract)	*Alec Russell*	870
Timeform Handicap (Pontefract)	*Alec Russell*	651
Timeform Nursery Handicap (Pontefract)	*Alec Russell*	87
Timeform Perspective Handicap (Pontefract)	*Alec Russell*	880
Tote Cesarewitch (Newmarket)	*John Crofts*	329
Tote Credit Silver Bowl Handicap (Haydock)	*Alec Russell*	869
Tote Ebor (Handicap) (York)	*Alec Russell*	216
Tote Gold Trophy Stakes (Handicap) (Goodwood)	*George Selwyn*	895
Tote Great St Wilfrid Handicap (Ripon)	*Alec Russell*	662
Tote-Portland Handicap (Doncaster)	*Alec Russell*	743
Trafalgar House Sprint Stakes (Sandown)	*John Crofts*	145
Tricity Bendix Series Six Chester Stakes (Chester)	*Alec Russell*	64
Trusthouse Forte Mile (Sandown)	*George Selwyn*	397
Van Geest Criterion Stakes (Newmarket)	*John Crofts*	449
Vodafone Horris Hill Stakes (Newbury)	*John Crofts*	464
Vodafone Nassau Stakes (Goodwood)	*John Crofts*	724
Whatcombe Stakes (Newbury)	*John Crofts*	39
William Hill Cambridgeshire Handicap (Newmarket)	*John Crofts*	525
William Hill Dante Stakes (York)	*George Selwyn*	264
William Hill Lincoln Handicap (Doncaster)	*Alec Russell*	46
William Hill November Handicap (Doncaster)	*Alec Russell*	374
William Hill Stewards' Cup (Goodwood)	*John Crofts*	599
William Hill Golden Spurs Trophy (Handicap) (York)	*Alec Russell*	782
Wokingham Handicap (Ascot)	*John Crofts*	48
Zetland Gold Cup (Redcar)	*Alec Russell*	579

EXPLANATORY NOTES

To assess the prospects of any horse in a race it is necessary to know two things about him: first, how good he is; and second, what sort of horse he is. In this book the merit of each horse is expressed in the form of a *rating* (printed on the right) and the *racing character* of the horse is given in the commentary.

TIMEFORM RATINGS

The Timeform Rating of a horse is simply the merit of the horse expressed in pounds and is arrived at by careful examination of its running against other horses using a scale of weight for distance beaten which ranges from 3 lb a length at five furlongs and 2 lb a length at a mile and a quarter at two miles. We maintain a "running" handicap of all horses in training throughout the season, or, to be strictly accurate, two handicaps, one for horses aged three years and over, and one for two-year-olds.

THE LEVEL OF THE RATINGS

At the close of each season all the horses that have raced are re-handicapped from scratch, and each horse's rating is revised. It is also necessary to adjust the general level of the handicap, so that all the ratings are kept at the same standard level from year to year. Left to itself, the general level of the ratings, in each succeeding issue of Timeform, tends to rise steadily. For technical reasons it is desirable to allow it to do so during the season: but, in winter, when the complete re-handicap is done, the ratings must, of course, be put back on their proper level again.

This explains why, in this book, the ratings are in general, different from those in the final issue of the 1991 Timeform series.

RATINGS AND WEIGHT-FOR-AGE

These matters, however, are by the way. What concerns the reader is that he has, in the ratings in this book, a universal handicap embracing all the horses in training it is possible to weigh up, ranging from tip-top classic performers, with ratings from 130 to 145, down to the meanest selling platers, rated around the 20 mark. What we now have to explain is the practical use of these ratings in the business of weighing up a race.

Before doing so, it is important to mention that all ratings are at weight-for-age, so that equal ratings mean horses of equal merit: perhaps it would be clearer if we said that the universal rating handicap is really not a single handicap, but four handicaps side by side: one for 2-y-o's, one for 3-y-o's, one for 4-y-o's and one for older horses. Thus, a 3-y-o rated, for argument's sake, at 117 is deemed to be identical in point of "merit" with a 4-y-o also rated at 117: but for them to have equal chances in, say, a mile race in May, the 3-y-o would need to be receiving 9 lb from the 4-y-o, which is the weight difference specified by the Age, Weight and Distance Tables on pages 4 and 5.

USING THE RATINGS

In using Timeform Ratings with a view to discovering which horses in any race have the best chances at the weights, we have two distinct cases, according to whether the horses taking part are of the same age or of different ages. Here is the procedure in each case:-

A. Horses of the Same Age

If the horses all carry the same weight there are no adjustments to be made, and the horses with the highest ratings have the best chances. If the horses carry different weights, jot down their ratings, and to the rating of each horse add one point for every pound the horse is set to carry less than 10 st, or subtract one point for every pound it has to carry more than 10 st. When the ratings have been adjusted in this way the highest resultant figure indicates the horse with the best chance at the weights.

Example (any distance: any week of the season)

2 Good Girl (9-6)	. . . .	Rating 119	. . . .	add 8 127
2 Paulinus (9-4)	. . . .	Rating 113	. . . .	add 10 123
2 Abilene (8-11)	. . . .	Rating 107	. . . .	add 17 124
2 Bob's Joy (8-7)	. . . .	Rating 108	. . . .	add 21 129
2 Time Warp (8-2)	. . . .	Rating 100	. . . .	add 26 126
2 Eagle Eye (7-7)	. . . .	Rating 92	. . . .	add 35 127

Bob's Joy (129) has the best chance; Good Girl (127) and Eagle Eye (127) are the next best.

B. Horses of Different Ages

Take no notice of the weight any horse receives from any other. Instead, consult the Age, Weight and Distance Tables on pages 4 and 5. Treat each horse separately, and compare the weight it has to carry with the weight prescribed for it in the tables, according to the age of the horse, the distance of the race and the month of the year. Then, add one point to the rating for each pound the horse has to carry less than the weight given in the tables: or, subtract one point from the rating for every pound it has to carry more than the weight prescribed by the tables. The highest resultant figure indicates the horse most favoured by the weights.

Example (1½ miles on June 30th)

(Table Weights: 5-y-o 10-0; 4-y-o 9-13; 3-y-o 9-1)

6 Nimitz (10-2)	. . . .	Rating 115	. . . .	subtract 2 . 113
4 Red Devil (9-9)	. . . .	Rating 114	. . . .	add 4 118
6 Sweet Cindy (9-5). . . .		Rating 115	. . . .	add 9 124
3 Jailhouse (9-2)	. . . .	Rating 120	. . . .	subtract 1 . 119
4 Haakon (8-11)	. . . .	Rating 101	. . . .	add 16 117
3 Fine Strike (8-7)	. . . .	Rating 108	. . . .	add 8 116

Sweet Cindy (124) has the best chance at the weights, with 5 lb in hand of Jailhouse.

TURF AND ALL-WEATHER RATINGS

When a horse has raced on turf and on all-weather and its form on one is significantly different from the other, the two ratings are given, the all-weather set out below the turf preceded by 'a'.

Thus with FREE FOR ALL 47
                              a55

the top figure, 47, is the rating to be used in turf races, and the one below, a55, is for use in all-weather races.

JOCKEYSHIP AND APPRENTICE ALLOWANCES

There is just one further point that arises in evaluating the chances of the horses on the basis of their ratings: the question of jockeyship in general, and apprentice allowances in particular. The allowance which may be claimed by an apprentice is given to enable apprentices to obtain race-riding experience against experienced jockeys. For the purposes of rating calculations it should, in general, be assumed that the allowance the apprentice is able to claim (3 lb, 5 lb, or 7 lb) is nullified by his or her inexperience. Therefore, the *weight adjustments to the ratings should be calculated on the weight allotted by the handicapper, or determined by the conditions of the race,* and no extra addition should be made to a rating because the horse's rider claims an apprentice allowance.

The above is the general routine procedure. But, of course, there is no reason why the quality of jockeyship should not be taken into account in assessing the chances of horses in a race. Quite the contrary. Nobody would question that the jockeyship of a first-class rider is worth a pound or two, and occasionally an apprentice comes along who is riding quite as well as the average jockey long before losing the right to claim. Once the age and weight adjustments have been made to the ratings, small additional allowances may, at the discretion of the reader, be made for these matters of jockeyship. Please note, though, that if a horse is regularly ridden by a claiming apprentice, the fact will have been taken account of when its previous performances have been assessed by our handicappers.

WEIGHING UP A RACE

The ratings tell you which horses in a particular race are most favoured by the weights; but complete analysis demands that the racing character of each horse, as set out in the commentary upon it, is also studied carefully to see if there is any reason why the horse might be expected not to run up to its rating. It counts for little that a horse is thrown in at the weights if it has no pretensions whatever to staying the distance, or is unable to act on the prevailing going.

These two matters, suitability of distance and going, are no doubt the most important points to be considered. But there are others. For example, the ability of a horse to accommodate itself to the conformation of the track. Then there is the matter of pace versus stamina: as between two stayers of equal merit, racing over a distance suitable to both, firm going, or a small field with the prospect of a slowly-run race, would favour the one with the better pace and acceleration; whereas dead or soft going, or a big field with the prospect of a strong gallop throughout the race, would favour the sounder stayer. There is also the matter of temperament and behaviour at the start: nobody would be in a hurry to take a short price about a horse with whom it is always an even chance whether it will give its running.

A few minutes spent checking up on these matters in the commentaries upon the horses concerned will sometimes put a very different complexion on a race from that which is put upon it by the ratings alone. We repeat, therefore, that the correct way to use Timeform, or this annual volume, in the analysis of individual races is, first to use the ratings to discover which horses are most favoured by the weights, and second, to check through the comments on the horse to discover what factors other than weight might also affect the outcome of the race.

Incidentally, in setting out the various characteristics, requirements and peculiarities of each horse in the commentary upon it, we have always expressed ourselves in as critical a manner as possible, endeavouring to say just as much, and no whit more than the facts seem to warrant. Where there are clear indications, and definite conclusions can be drawn with fair certainty, we have drawn them: if it is a matter of probability or possibility we have put it that way, being careful not to say the one when we mean the other; and where real conclusions are not to be drawn, we have been content to state the facts. Furthermore, when we say that a horse *may not* be suited by hard going, we do not expect the reader to treat it as though we had said that the horse *is not* suited by hard going. In short, both in our thinking and in the setting out of our views we have aimed at precision.

THE FORM SUMMARIES

The form summary enclosed in the brackets shows for each individual horse the distance, the state of the going and where the horse finished in each of its races on the flat during the last two seasons. Performances are in chronological sequence, the earliest being given first.

The distance of each race is given in furlongs, fractional distances being expressed in the decimal notation to the nearest tenth of a furlong. Races on an all-weather surface are prefixed by letter 'a'.

The going is symbolised as follows: h = hard or very firm; f = firm (turf) or fast (all-weather); m = on the firm side of good; g = good (turf) or standard (all-weather); d = dead, or on the soft side of good; s = soft, sticky or holding (turf) or slow (all-weather); v = heavy, very heavy or very holding.

Placings are indicated, up to sixth place, by the use of superior figures, an asterisk being used to denote a win.

Thus [1990 NR 1991 10s* 12f³ 11.7g a11g²] signifies that the horse was unraced in 1990. He ran four times in 1991, winning over 10 furlongs on soft going first time out, finishing third over twelve furlongs on firm going next time out, unplaced, not in the first six, over 11.7 furlongs on good going, and then second over eleven furlongs on standard going on an all-weather track.

Included in the pedigree details are the highest Timeform Annual ratings during their racing careers of the sires, dams and sires of dams of all horses, where the information is available.

Where sale prices are given F denotes the price in guineas sold as a foal, Y the price in guineas sold as a yearling. The prefix IR denotes Irish guineas.

THE RATING SYMBOLS

The following symbols, attached to the ratings, are to be interpreted as stated:-

p   the horse is likely to make more than normal progress and to improve on its rating.

P   there is convincing evidence, or, to say the least, a very strong presumption that the horse is capable of form much better than it has so far displayed.

+   the horse's form may be rather better than we have rated it.

d   the horse appears to have deteriorated, and might no longer be capable of running to the rating given.

§   a horse of somewhat unsatisfactory temperament; one who may give its running on occasions, but cannot be relied upon to do so.

§§   an arrant rogue or thorough jade; so temperamentally unsatisfactory as to be not worth a rating.

?   the use of a query without a rating implies that although the horse has form, its merit is impossible to assess with confidence. If used in conjunction with a rating this symbol implies that the rating is based upon inadequate or unsatisfactory data, or that the rating is suspect.

THE AGENCY
WITH A TRADITION
OF BUYING
GOOD HORSES

CURRAGH

BLOODSTOCK AGENCY

<table>
<tr><td>

ENGLAND
'CROSSWAYS'
23 THE AVENUE
NEWMARKET
SUFFOLK   CB8 9AA
Tel: 0638-662620 or 663791
Telex: 81426   Fax: 661658

</td><td>

IRELAND
MAIN STREET
NEWBRIDGE
CO. KILDARE
Tel: 045-31402
Telex: 60665   Fax: 32720

</td></tr>
</table>

RACEHORSES OF 1991

Horse	Commentary	Rating

A A BAMBA 2 b.f. (Feb 8) Slip Anchor 136 – Enchanting Dancer (FR) (Nijinsky (CAN) 138) [1991 7g⁶ 8.1g 8g⁴ 10m*] tall, angular, unfurnished filly: sixth foal: half-sister to 1½m winner Nahash and middle-distance stayer/successful jumper Folk Dance (both by Alias Smith) and winners abroad by Tap On Wood and Blakeney: dam never ran: quite modest performer: lowered in class, won 17-runner seller at Leicester (retained 3,800 gns) in October, staying on strongly: will be suited by 1½m + . *N. A. Callaghan.* **64**

AAHSAYLAD 5 b.h. Ardross 134 – Madam Slaney 92 (Prince Tenderfoot (USA) 126) [1990 12f⁵ 14g* 16g³ 17.6m⁴ 14g⁶ 13g* 13g³ 13f* 14.8m³ 14m³ 13d* 14d⁴ 15v³ 15d⁴ 1991 17.1m² 18f² 14g⁶ 16.5m* 16m⁴ 16.1m² 15g² 13g* 13.9g 13.9g 17.5m² 18m] big, good-topped horse: impresses good deal in appearance: improved handicapper: won at Doncaster and Ayr in summer: effective at 13f, and stays really well: acts on any going: ran well when visored once: refused to enter stalls once in late season: tough. *F. H. Lee.* **83**

AARON'S ROD 5 br.h. Mansingh (USA) 120 – Belinda Mede 86 (Runnymede 123) [1990 NR 1991 8m 6g 6.1m 5f 6m] leggy, quite good-topped horse: no worthwhile form. *F. J. Yardley.* **—**

AASFF (USA) 2 b.c. (Feb 26) Sovereign Dancer (USA) – Ecstatica (USA) 81 (Damascus (USA)) [1991 7m 7m⁶ 7f² 7f³ 8m* 7.6d] $160,000Y: well-made, lengthy colt: moderate walker: half-brother to 2 minor winners in North America by Grey Dawn: dam, 7.6f winner, is daughter of half-sister to King's Stand winner Flirting Around: modest performer: won maiden at Newcastle in October: last of 10 when favourite for Chester nursery final start: stays 1m: acts on firm going, possibly not on dead. *D. Morley.* **77**

ABBEY STRAND (USA) 2 b.f. (May 21) Shadeed (USA) 135 – Christchurch (FR) 88 (So Blessed 130) [1991 6s 7m³] quite good-topped filly: half-sister to several winners, including smart 6f to 10.5f winner Church Parade (by Queen's Hussar) and smart middle-distance stayer Castle Rising (by Blakeney): dam, 1½m winner, is half-sister to Highclere, grandam of Nashwan and Unfuwain: much better effort when 3 lengths third of 5, keeping on really well, to Snow Forest in minor event at York in October: will improve again, particularly at middle distances. *Lord Huntingdon.* **78 p**

ABBOTSHAM 6 b.g. Ardross 134 – Lucy Platter (FR) 74 (Record Token 128) [1990 NR 1991 22.2m 16.2g] big, lengthy gelding: lightly raced and little sign of ability on flat: winning hunter chaser. *W. R. Williams.* **—**

ABDICATE (IRE) 3 ch.f. Be My Guest (USA) 126 – Crown Godiva 83 (Godswalk (USA) 130) [1990 7g 1991 8m⁵ 7g* 7m⁶ 8m* 10f 8d⁵ 8m] good-topped filly: fair handicapper: won maiden at Goodwood in May and £18,000 event (on toes, gamely) at Newmarket in July: fair fifth of 10 in £11,400 event at Ascot final start, best effort after: stays 1m: sold 40,000 gns Newmarket December Sales. *L. M. Cumani.* **89**

ABELONI 2 ch.g. (Feb 23) Absalom 128 – Agreloui 59 (Tower Walk 130) [1991 5m⁶ 5m⁵ 5g] 13,000F, 21,000Y: leggy gelding: has scope: fourth reported living foal: brother to 1990 2-y-o 5f winner Absaloui: dam lightly-raced maiden from family of Sing Sing and Burglar: quite modest maiden: will be better suited by 6f. *A. A. Scott.* **66**

ABERFOYLE (IRE) 3 b.g. Vision (USA) – Princess John (Run The Gantlet (USA)) [1990 5m 6g 6m⁴ 7m 6m 7d a8g a6g a8g⁴ 1991 12d⁵ 11g² 15g* 14.1m² 14.1f⁵ **55**

12g 16.1g] leggy gelding: moderate walker: poor mover: plating-class performer: 13/8 on, won maiden claimer at Edinburgh in July: ran poorly last 3 starts: stays well: acts on good to firm ground and dead: twice blinkered at 2 yrs: winning hurdler. *M. H. Tompkins.*

ABIGAILS BOY (HOL) 2 gr.c. (Jun 4) Superlative 118 – Heartbreaker 71 (Steel Heart 128) [1991 6m 6m⁴ 6m 5.7g 5d⁵] 1,200Y: strong, close-coupled colt: half-brother to winners abroad: dam sprint maiden: plating-class performer, better at 6f than shorter: acts on good to firm and dead ground: bandaged off-hind second start. *Dr J. D. Scargill.*   55

ABIGAIL'S DREAM 4 gr.f. Kalaglow 132 – Moss Pink (USA) (Levmoss 133) [1990 a8g² a10g* a10g⁴ a7g⁴ 8m 9m² 10m⁶ 9f* 10m⁴ 10f⁵ 1991 a12g⁵ 11.8g⁶ a12g⁵] lightly-made mare: quite modest performer at best: claimed out of D. Burchell's stable £8,178 final start: stays 1¼m well: acts on firm going. *J. R. Jenkins.*   —

ABINGDON FLYER (IRE) 3 b.c. Pennine Walk 120 – Busca (USA) 49 (Mr Prospector (USA)) [1990 NR 1991 10f⁶ 10g 10d⁴ 8m 10g 10s 11.7f² 10m² 10f* 10.3m 10g] IR 52,000Y: lengthy, good sort: first living foal: dam (stayed 9.4f) is daughter of Kentucky Oaks winner and CCA Oaks second Bag of Tunes: quite modest performer: won ladies handicap at Brighton in September, leading over 1f out: stays 11.7f: seemingly needs top-of-the-ground: has joined M. Pipe. *R. Hannon.*   63

ABLAZE 3 ch.g. Absalom 128 – Great Lass (Vaigly Great 127) [1990 NR 1991 6f 8m a7g] 2,000Y: close-coupled, workmanlike gelding: third foal: dam never ran: no worthwhile form in claimers and seller: sold 1,100 gns Ascot July Sales: resold 1,100 gns Doncaster August Sales. *J. Wharton.*   —

ABLE JET (USA) 3 br.c. Northjet 136 – Princess Nicketti (USA) (Tom Rolfe) [1990 6g⁶ 6g⁵ 6m⁴ 5d² 5d⁴ 5f³ 5f* 5m⁵ 5.3h³ 7f 6m 5f⁴ 5f⁴ 5m³ 5m⁶ 5s* 5d 5g 1991 a5g* a5g² a5g³ a6g² a7g* a6g² 7d⁵ 6m³ 6g 8m⁵ 7m 10g⁵ 8m⁵ a7g² 7m a6g³ a6g⁴ 6m⁴ 6m³ 6f* 5m 5g⁶ 6d⁴ 6.1d 6m⁵ a7g] robust, attractive colt: poor mover: modest handicapper: won at Lingfield (claimers) in January and March and Yarmouth in September: stays 7f: acts on any going: effective with or without blinkers: has run well when sweating: game. *Mrs N. Macauley.*   74

ABLE LASSIE 3 gr.f. Grey Desire 115 – Clairwood (Final Straw 127) [1990 5f⁴ 6f⁵ 7g² 6g* 6m⁴ 6m⁴ 7m 7f² 8.2s² 1991 8m² 9.2d* 8.3d* 10.9g² 8g* 10.1m] smallish, angular filly: moderate mover: improved handicapper at 3 yrs: successful at Hamilton (apprentice event first occasion) twice in July and in claimer (below best, claimed £12,250) at Newmarket in August: well below form final start: will prove suited by 1¼m + : acts on any going: tough. *Mrs G. R. Reveley.*   74

ABLE MAC (USA) 3 ch.c. Red Ryder (USA) – Amber Amethyst (USA) (Staff Writer (USA)) [1990 5.8f³ 7f⁴ 5m 6m 5s a6g⁶ a5g⁶ 1991 a7g³ a7g a8g] lengthy colt: plating-class maiden: creditable third in handicap at Lingfield, easily best effort early in 1991: suited by 7f: twice blinkered at 2 yrs. *Mrs N. Macauley.*   44

ABLE PLAYER (USA) 4 b. or br.g. Solford (USA) 127 – Grecian Snow (CAN) (Snow Knight 125) [1990 a7g³ a8g² a8g 7m⁶ 9m 12.2m⁵ 8.5d 8g² 9m* 8h² 10f a8g 8m 1991 7h 7m 10f³ 11.9g* 12.3m 12m 12.1g] leggy, quite good-topped gelding: plating-class handicapper: gamely won at Haydock in August: stays 1½m: acts on hard ground: below form when blinkered once: none too consistent: winning hurdler. *C. W. Thornton.*   51

ABLE PRINCESS 3 ch.f. Music Boy 124 – Glamorous Girl (Caliban 123) [1990 NR 1991 5m⁴ 6s⁴ 5f 6m² 6m⁵ 5m² 5m 5m⁶ 6.1m a6g a5g a5g] workmanlike filly: moderate mover: sixth living foal: sister to fair 1988 2-y-o 5f and 6f winner Steele's and a winner in Hong Kong and half-sister to 1979 2-y-o 7f winner Georgina Park (by Silly Season): plating-class maiden: at least as effective at 5f as 6f: below form on very firm going: blinkered sixth to eleventh starts, 3 times sweating: usually wears bandages. *Mrs N. Macauley.*   53

ABLE QUEST (IRE) 2 ch.c. (Feb 28) Thatching 131 – Olinda 101 (Sassafras (FR) 135) [1991 7g³ 7g³ 6m*] 16,500F, 41,000Y: leggy, lengthy colt: has scope: has a roundish action: half-brother to several winners here and abroad, including 1990 2-y-o 6f winner Lominda (by Lomond): dam Irish 7.5f winner at 2 yrs: favourite, won 8-runner maiden at Newcastle in October by 3 lengths from Vying Victor: will stay 1m: acts on good to firm ground: may improve further. *R. W. Armstrong.*   79 p

ABLE SUSAN 3 b.f. Formidable (USA) 125 – Susanna (USA) 81§ (Nijinsky (CAN) 138) [1990 6m⁴ 7f⁴ 7d* 1991 8g⁵ 8.5f⁵ 8m* 7m² 8m² 8m* 8d* 8d 8g] angular filly: fairly useful handicapper: won at Doncaster (edged markedly under pressure) in June and at Kempton and Ascot (£11,400 event, quickened impressively final 1f) in   98

24

September: better at 1m than 7f: acts on good to firm ground and dead: sweating second and third starts. *G. Wragg.*

ABLE VALE 5 b.m. Formidable (USA) 125 – Valeur (Val de Loir 133) [1990 12.5f* 12f3 1991 10m 13.8f] close-coupled, deep-girthed mare: plating-class performer at 4 yrs: tailed off this summer: best form at 1½m: acts on firm ground. *J. D. Czerpak.*

ABOM SWIFT 3 gr.c. Absalom 128 – Swift Return 79 (Double Form 130) [1990 87 5g6 5f2 5m3 5.8h* 1991 5g 6.1d 6m a5g*] workmanlike, good-quartered colt: fractured off-hind at 2 yrs: has a quick action: fair form: blinkered, best effort to win 14-runner handicap at Southwell in November, racing virtually alone far rail: showed signs of retaining ability facing stiff tasks earlier in season: stays 6f. *A. Hide.*

ABOUT MIDNIGHT 2 b.f. (May 9) Jester 119 – Princess Andromeda 60 – (Corvaro (USA) 122) [1991 7.5f] second foal: dam, 9f seller winner, is out of half-sister to top-class jumper Night Nurse: slowly away and always behind in seller at Beverley in July. *R. Earnshaw.*

ABRIGO 4 b.g. Aragon 118 – Poshteen 86 (Royal Smoke 113) [1990 7m 6f3 a5g – 1991 6m 6g] sturdy gelding: poor sprint maiden: has been blinkered. *O. O'Neill.*

ABSALOUI 3 gr.f. Absalom 128 – Agreloui 59 (Tower Walk 130) [1990 5f3 6g 5f2 – 5.3h4 5m5 5v* 1991 5m 7d 8m 7.1g4 7.1m 9.7m6] leggy, workmanlike filly: quite modest winner at Chester as 2-y-o: no worthwhile form in 1991, including in sellers: should stay 6f, probably not 1m: looks ideally suited by plenty of give in the ground. *W. G. M. Turner.*

ABSCURE 2 b.f. (May 5) Absalom 128 – Villajoyosa (FR) (Satingo 129) [1991 5s – 6g 6d a6g4 7g 6g] 1,400F, 3,500Y: small, sparely-made filly: third foal: dam, plater, won at up to 1m in France: seems of little account: sold out of M. Fetherston-Godley's stable 1,050 gns Ascot September Sales after penultimate start. *B. R. Millman.*

ABSENT FOREVER 3 ro.g. Absalom 128 – Strawberry Fields 66 (Song 132) 58 [1990 5d5 5f5 1991 10f 7m 6.1d5 7g a7g] lengthy, good-topped gelding: plating-class maiden: form at 3 yrs only when fifth in ladies handicap at Chepstow: may well prove ideally suited by 7f/1m: acts on dead ground: blinkered final start: bolted and withdrawn intended fifth. *W. R. Muir.*

ABSENT LYRIC (IRE) 2 br.f. (Jan 3) Taufan (USA) 119 – Beyond Words 58 (Ballad Rock 122) [1991 6d4 6g5 6f6 8.3g3 8.9m 8.3s a8g6] 12,500Y: leggy, lengthy filly: good walker: first foal: dam unraced: plating-class maiden: gives impression will stay 1¼m: possibly suited by an easy surface: blinkered final start. *T. D. Barron.*

ABSENT MINDED 5 ch.m. Absalom 128 – Bourienne 58 (Bolkonski 134) [1990 – NR 1991 a8g] leggy, light-framed mare: very lightly raced and poor form. *J. Dooler.*

ABSENT RELATIVE 3 ch.f. Absalom 128 – Relatively Smart 76 (Great 60 Nephew 126) [1990 NR 1991 10d 10g 10.1m 11.4m5 a12g4 12d] 1,900F: workmanlike filly: second foal: dam, middle-distance maiden, is half-sister to Cesarewitch winner Sir Michael and very speedy 2-y-o Fats Waller: plating-class form: set strong pace in amateurs handicap final start: may be suited by return to shorter. *Miss B. Sanders.*

ABSO 3 b.g. Absalom 128 – Classical Vintage 80 (Stradavinsky 122) [1990 5f 5m6 72 § 6g a7g3 a7g 1991 8g6 8m 8f 7f6 7.1g 6g* 7m2 7m2 6m2 7f4 7g 6m 7g* 7d2] strong, lengthy gelding: modest handicapper: won at Brighton in July and improved efforts in large fields last 2 starts, winning at Salisbury in October: suited by 7f: acts on firm and dead ground: blinkered or visored seventh to thirteenth outings: usually hangs, and often looks irresolute. *R. Hannon.*

ABSOLUTE 2 gr.g. (May 4) Absalom 128 – All Risks 90 (Pitcairn 126) [1991 a7g] – sixth foal: half-brother to 3-y-o Orbost River (by King of Spain) and a winner in Austria by Star Appeal: dam 2-y-o 1m winner: soundly beaten in claimer at Southwell in July. *M. W. Ellerby.*

ABSOLUTELY NUTS 2 ro.f. (Jan 27) Absalom 128 – Double Stitch 74 (Wolver 69 Hollow 126) [1991 5d5 5m5 5m5 5.1g3 5m2 5d6] 5,000F: lengthy, workmanlike filly: has scope: fourth foal: dam 8.2f winner: quite modest maiden: should stay 6f: possibly unsuited by dead ground. *B. A. McMahon.*

ABSOLUTELY RIGHT 3 ch.c. Absalom 128 – Sun Worshipper (Sun Prince 56 128) [1990 5.8m 5f4 6m 8g3 9g3 7s 1991 10g 6f5 7g 8f 7m 7g 8.3m 9.7f2 10.8m 9s 10.8g3 11d2 10m 9.7s3 a12g2 a10g3] small, sturdy colt: has a quick action: fairly useful plater on his day: ran well in claimers at Lingfield last 2 starts: stays 1½m:

25

seems to act on any going: sometimes early to post: trained first 9 outings by S. Dow: inconsistent and has looked a difficult ride. *R. Akehurst.*

ABSOLUTE STEAL 5 ro.m. Absalom 128 – Thorganby Victory 82 (Burglar — 128) [1990 7.5m 8g 1991 8f 6f 6m] workmanlike mare: no form as 5-y-o: stayed 1m: acted on hard ground: dead. *B. Ellison.*

ABSOLUTION 7 gr.h. Absalom 128 – Great Grey Niece 74 (Great Nephew 126) 86 [1990 5m 5d 5g³ 5m 5m 5m⁵ 6m 5m* 5g² 6g 5g 5.6g 1991 a5g⁶ 5g5 5g5 5f 5d 5f 5d 5m³ 5g* 5m 5m* 5g 5f 5f 5m 5.2g² 5d] workmanlike, good-quartered horse: moderate walker and mover: fair front-running handicapper on his day: successful in July at Sandown and Newcastle: best at 5f: acts on any going: has won for apprentice: effective with or without blinkers: trained until after fifth start by D. Chapman, next 2 by K. McCauley. *M. P. Naughton.*

ABSOLUTLEY FOXED 2 gr.f. (Feb 27) Absalom 128 – May Fox 67 (Healaugh 45 Fox) [1991 5g 5g5 5m 6g a6g 7g⁴ 8m] 5,000Y: workmanlike filly: has a round action: half-sister to 10.6f winner Moorland Lady (by Swing Easy) and a winner in South Africa: dam 2-y-o 5f winner, is half-sister to Oaks second Mabel: poor maiden: suited by 7f. *B. A. McMahon.*

ABSONAL 4 gr.g. Absalom 128 – Aldbury Girl 79 (Galivanter 131) [1990 6g⁶ 6g* 83 6m⁴ 6m 7m² 7m* 8m* 8m⁶ 8g 8g 7m 8m 8g 1991 8d 8g⁵ 8d⁶ 8g] strong, good-topped gelding: fair handicapper: failed to confirm earlier promise in Royal Hunt Cup at Ascot (reportedly finished lame) final start: withdrawn once (again lame) afterwards: suited by 1m: acts on good to firm going. *R. Hannon.*

ABSURDE (FR) 2 b.f. (Feb 23) Green Desert (USA) 127 – Absolute (FR) 104 (Luthier 126) [1991 8g* 6.5g* 6m² 7v³] strong, close-coupled, rather plain filly: half-sister to 10.1f and 1½m winner Alphabel (by Bellypha) and French 12.5f winner Aetos (by General Assembly): dam French 6f and 1m winner: useful performer: successful in newcomers race at Deauville in August and listed race (by 6 lengths) at Evry in September: placed in Tattersalls Cheveley Park Stakes (finished strongly without troubling Marling) at Newmarket and in Criterium de Maisons-Laffitte won by Cardoun: will probably stay 1¼m: acts on good to firm and heavy ground. *F. Boutin, France.*

ABU HANIFAH 3 b.g. Ahonoora 122 – Nekhbet 74 (Artaius (USA) 129) [1990 75 NR 1991 a6g³ 6f³ 5g⁶ 5g 6h² 6g* 6m 5g* 5f³ 5d⁴ 5g 5g⁵ 5.1m] 24,000Y: lengthy gelding: has scope: third foal: half-brother to 1988 2-y-o 8.2f seller winner Hillside Rose (by Beldale Flutter): dam, in frame from 5f to 7f, is half-sister to Irish St Leger winner M-Lolshan and useful sprinter Chemin: modest handicapper: won at Nottingham (apprentice claimer) and Newmarket in June: no show from modest draw at Chester final start: stays 6f: acts on firm and dead going. *N. A. Callaghan.*

ABU NASSER (IRE) 3 b.c. Burslem 123 – Crimson Crest (Pampapaul 121) — [1990 NR 1991 8f 10d⁵ 9m 9.9m] 10,500F, IR 22,000Y: heavy-bodied colt: third reported foal: dam modest Irish sprint maiden best at 2 yrs out of fairly useful 5f performer Georgie Girl: well beaten in maidens then (blinkered) selling handicap. *J. D. Czerpak*

ACCESS CRUISE (USA) 4 ch.g. Wajima (USA) – Lady of Meadowlane (USA) 59 (Pancho Jay (USA)) [1990 10g⁶ 12m⁶ 14g 1991 10m⁵ 13d⁵ 10.2m⁶ 14.6m* 14.6m

Prix des Marettes, Deauville—Absurde makes a winning debut in this mile race

14.1m³ 16.1m] tall, sparely-made gelding: moderate walker and mover: plating-class handicapper: won at Wolverhampton in July: stays 1¾m: acts on good to firm ground: bolted and unseated rider to post once: keen sort, has worn crossed noseband and tongue strap: sold to join P. Blockley's stable 4,600 gns Newmarket September Sales. *R. Boss.*

ACCESS FLYER (IRE) 3 b.c. Reasonable (FR) 119 – Fenland Queen (King's Troop 118) [1990 7f⁴ 7g 10s a8g* 1991 a10g³ 10d 7m 5.3f* 6m⁴ 5g⁵ 6m⁴ 7f⁶ 7g⁵ 8.1m³ 7.9m⁵ 8m] good-bodied, workmanlike colt: poor mover: modest handicapper: won at Brighton in May: was suited by 1m: acted on firm going, possibly unsuited by a soft surface: blinkered final start: dead. *R. Boss.* **75**

ACCESS HOLIDAYS 3 ch.c. Faustus (USA) 118 – Lardana 65 (Burglar 128) [1990 6g² 5d* a6g* a6g² 1991 7g 7.5f 7m] leggy colt: modest winner at 2 yrs: chipped knee bone on reappearance, but good seventh of 9 in handicap at Beverley 5 months later: well beaten following week: should prove suited by 7f or stiff 6f: wore crossed noseband in 1991. *R. Boss.* **74**

ACCESS SKI 4 b.c. Bustino 136 – Crimson Lake (FR) 71 (Mill Reef (USA) 141) [1990 12.5f² 10m² 12d² 15.3m* 13.3m⁶ 18.4f² 16.2f² 18m* 15d⁴ 16m 18d 1991 16g⁶ 18.4d 18f*] close-coupled, robust colt: easy mover: fair handicapper at best: awarded race at Doncaster in May: suited by test of stamina and top-of-the-ground. *R. Boss.* **90**

ACCESS SPIRIT 2 b.c. (May 9) Hadeer 118 – Busted Love (Busted 134) [1991 5m] 4,700Y: rather unfurnished colt: third living foal: half-brother to 3-y-o Maggies Lad and 1¾m winner Johnsted (both by Red Johnnie): dam never ran: well beaten in maiden auction at Sandown in June: moved poorly to post. *R. Boss.* **—**

ACCESS SUN 4 b.g. Pharly (FR) 130 – Princesse du Seine (FR) (Val de Loir 133) [1990 11g⁶ 16m 8h⁶ 12g⁶ 1991 16g 14d 12g] leggy, quite attractive gelding: moderate mover: poor handicapper nowadays: should stay 1½m: acts on good to firm ground: winning hurdler. *J. S. King.* **—**

ACCESS SUPREME 3 b.c. Law Society (USA) 130 – Honeypot Lane 91 (Silly Season 127) [1990 10.2s⁴ 1991 14m⁴ 14g³ 14.1f⁶] tall, leggy, sparely-made colt: modest maiden: eased considerably when third at Nottingham in July: tailed-off last nearly 4 weeks later: bred to be suited by 1½m +: tended to hang on debut. *R. Boss.* **—**

ACCESS TRAVEL 5 b.h. Auction Ring (USA) 123 – Lady Tippins (USA) 83 (Star de Naskra (USA)) [1990 6f³ 5f 6f² 7m⁴ 5m 5m 5m 5g⁴ 1991 5d 5g⁵ 5m* 6g⁵ 6m 5.1g³ 5f³] small, sturdy horse: poor mover: fair handicapper: won £7,000 event at Sandown in April (bandaged off-hind): best form at 5f on a sound surface: ran very well in blinkers: carried head high: not the easiest of rides: stud. *R. Boss.* **88**

ACCESS VOYAGER 2 b.c. (Feb 7) Ballad Rock 122 – Marseillaise (Artaius (USA) 129) [1991 8.2m³] 6,800Y, 15,000Y: angular, lengthy colt: moderate mover: first foal: dam unraced half-sister to Irish 2000 Guineas winner Northern Treasure: 4/1, 6 lengths third of 4 to Alphard in minor event at Nottingham in October, headed over 2f out, eased once beaten: should improve. *R. Boss.* **67 p**

ACE GIRL 2 ch.f. (Apr 10) Stanford 121§ – Lucky Candy 61 (Lucky Wednesday 124) [1991 5m² 5d² 7.5f² 6.1m⁵ 5.1f a7g a5g⁵] sparely-made filly: second foal: dam, form only at 2 yrs, is out of half-sister to Gunner B: modest maiden: below form last 4 outings: better suited by 7.5f than shorter: blinkered final start. *S. R. Bowring.* **58**

ACHELOUS 4 b.c. Dominion 123 – Siren Sound (Manado 130) [1990 8.2m 9m 12.2d² a11g* 1991 a11g³ a12g³ a12g⁵ 13.8d³ 11s* 10d 12.3d] workmanlike colt: poor mover: modest handicapper at best: won apprentice event at Hamilton in April: best effort at 11f: acts on soft ground: blinkered fifth and sixth starts: goes very well with forcing tactics. *J. A. Glover.* **65**

ACKERS WOOD 3 b.g. Castle Keep 121 – Gloria Maremmana (King Emperor (USA)) [1990 8.2d⁴ 1991 10.2g⁶ 8.1s⁴ 7m⁴ 7.1g 7m] rangy gelding: quite modest performer: form only when narrowly-beaten fourth of 22 in amateurs handicap at Redcar third start: worth another try at 1¼m: formerly headstrong, carrying head high and finding little second start: sold to join K. Burke 5,800 gns Newmarket Autumn Sales. *R. F. Johnson Houghton.* **63**

ACQUA NOIR 4 ch.g. Kings Lake (USA) 133 – Late Sally 101 (Sallust 134) [1990 a8g a5g⁶ a6g 7.5d² 7g⁶ 8.3m* 8.3m⁴ 8m² 8m 10d 11.5g a12g a8g 1991 7m⁴ 8.3m 10g 10.8g] sparely-made gelding: moderate mover: poor handicapper: stays 1m: acts on good to firm ground and dead: below form when visored once: effective blinkered or not: sold 2,300 gns Doncaster October Sales. *R. J. R. Williams.* **43**

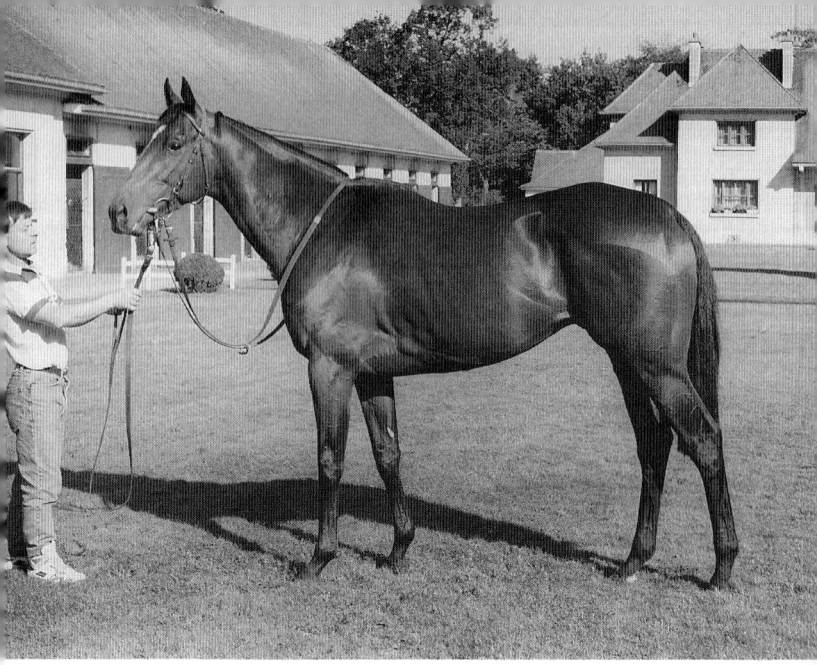

Paul de Moussac's "Acteur Francais"

ACQUISITION 4 b.c. Petorius 117 – Steady The Buffs 62 (Balidar 133) [1990 **51**
8.2g 8g2 1991 9s 8f2 8m 8h4 8s4 8g4 10.8m4 9m2 11.1f3 10.3m] quite good-topped
colt: plating-class performer: stays 10.8f: best efforts on sound surface (acts on hard
ground): has run well when blinkered: trained until after eighth outing by J. Berry. *J.
J. O'Neill.*

ACROBATE (USA) 2 ch.c. (Mar 17) Arctic Tern (USA) 126 – Musical Medicine   **— p**
(USA) (Margouillat (FR) 133) [1991 10g] $50,000F, 300,000 francs (approx £30,000)
Y: brother to a winner in USA and half-brother to another winner: dam, unraced,
from family of Horage and Snurge: 33/1 and very green, last of 9, slowly away, to
Bonny Scot in listed race at Newmarket in November. *P. A. Kelleway.*

ACROSS THE BAY 4 ch.g. Krayyan 117 – Siofra Beag (Steel Heart 128) [1990   **61 §**
6g 6f 5f3 6f2 6m5 7.6m 5m 5d 1991 5g4 5.3f 6g 6v6] close-coupled gelding: carries
condition: moderate walker and mover: quite modest performer at best nowadays:
hung left much of way third start: stays 6f: acts on firm going, ran poorly on heavy:
has taken little interest: not one to rely on. *S. Dow.*

ACROSS THE CARD 3 b.g. Lir 82 – Cornish Susie (Fair Season 120) [1990 NR   **56**
1991 10g 8.3m 10g4 9.7f] neat gelding: second foal: dam unraced: form (including in
seller) only when fourth of 9 to impressive Laburnum in maiden at Brighton, held up
and keeping on well: stays 1¼m. *A. Moore.*

ACROW LORD 4 b.g. Milford 119 – Miss Acrow (Comedy Star (USA) 121) [1990   **44**
12.5f4 11.7g 15.3m4 12.2g2 12m4 11.5f2 11m2 14m4 11m2 1991 12g 12.1d 10.2g4
10.1m4 10.8m3 14.1m5] close-coupled, good-bodied gelding: moderate mover: poor
performer nowadays: suited by 1½m: acts on firm ground: below form when
blinkered once: sold 1,550 gns Ascot July Sales after penultimate start: winning
hurdler afterwards. *M. C. Pipe.*

ACTEUR FRANCAIS (USA) 3 b.c. Al Nasr (FR) 126 – Kilmona (USA) 121 **118**
(Bold Bidder (USA)) [1990 7.5g* 6d3 8m3 1991 8g2 8d2 8g4 8g* 8g] rather

lightly-made colt: smart performer: evens, won Prix Messidor at Maisons-Laffitte in July narrowly from Boxing Day and Ganges, making most: headed post by Hector Protector in Dubai Poule d'Essai des Poulains at Longchamp and 3½ lengths fourth to Marju in St James's Palace Stakes (edgy) at Royal Ascot previous 2 starts: stays 1m: acts on good to firm ground and dead: raced freely (ran moderately) final start, in August. *A. Fabre, France.*

ACT OF UNION (IRE)   2 b.c. (Mar 28) Green Desert (USA) 127 – Carnival   **69** Dance 69 (Welsh Pageant 132) [1991 6f3 6f4 8.3g4 7g2] IR 26,000Y: rather leggy colt: has scope: seventh foal: half-brother to several winners, including smart 5f to 8.2f winner Sarab (by Prince Tenderfoot) and 12.2f winner Safe (by Kris): dam second over 1m and 1¼m: quite modest maiden: good second of 18 to Roar On Tour in nursery at Doncaster in October: should prove at least as effective at 1m as 7f: acts on firm ground: took strong hold first 3 starts. *W. J. Pearce.*

ACTRESS   5 b.m. Known Fact (USA) 135 – Tin Tessa 87 (Martinmas 128) [1990   **—** 7g 7g 5m5 6m 1991 a7g] good-bodied, angular mare: lightly raced and poor handicapper nowadays: stays 1m: acts on any going: has been tried blinkered: sold 1,700 gns Ascot May Sales. *D. C. Jermy.*

ADA CORR   2 b.f. (Mar 17) Adonijah 126 – Corr Lady (Lorenzaccio 130) [1991 6d]   **—** 500Y: half-sister to several winners here and abroad, including Irish 1¼m winner Tuff Stick (by Welsh Saint) and 1m and 9f winner Miami Star (by Miami Springs): dam never ran: 50/1 and backward, tailed off in 23-runner maiden at Haydock in October. *B. W. Lunness.*

ADAM SMITH   3 b.c. Sadler's Wells (USA) 132 – Krakow 85 (Malinowski (USA)   **103** 123) [1990 NR 1991 10g2 10g5] 300,000F, 680,000Y: strong, compact, good sort: fourth foal: brother to smart 10.1f to 15.5f winner Braashee and half-brother to Nell Gwyn winner/1000 Guineas fourth Ghariba (by Final Straw): dam, from good family, won at 7f: very promising neck second to Saddlers' Hall in £7,300 contest at Newmarket: co-second favourite, another useful effort when 5½ lengths fifth of 8 to Man From Eldorado in listed race (moved poorly down) at Goodwood later in May, never able to challenge: will be better suited by 1½m. *L. M. Cumani.*

ADDITIONAL RISK (IRE)   3 b. or br.c. Ahonoora 122 – Match Bend (USA)   **112** (Never Bend) [1990 NR 1991 8v 6d3 6g* 8m* 7m5 7m* 6.3g2 7m* 8g3 7m* 6d3 7g 7m*] half-brother to several winners, including fairly useful 1988 Irish 2-y-o 5f and 6f winner Comfort And Style (by Be My Guest) and Derby Italiano second My Franky (by Rheingold): dam ran twice in Ireland: very useful performer: successful in maiden at Gowran Park, handicaps at Gowran Park and Naas, listed races at Leopardstown and Hong Kong Invitation Bowl: ran moderately in Group 3 event at Goodwood penultimate start: best form at 7f and 1m: acts on good to firm ground. *D. K. Weld, Ireland.*

ADELBARAN (FR)   4 b.f. No Pass No Sale 120 – Airmail (FR) (Luthier 126)   **—** [1990 8s5 8f 8g6 8d4 8g3 1991 a8g 10.1s 8.3g 10g] leggy, angular, plain ex-French plater: awarded claimer at Saint-Cloud as 2-y-o and claimed out of T. Clout's stable 70,051 francs (approx £7,200) final 3-y-o start: little sign of ability here: stays 1m: acts on good to firm ground and soft: has been heavily bandaged: seemed effective with or without blinkers in France: sold 3,100 gns Ascot June Sales. *M. C. Pipe.*

ADELINE LYNN   5 ch.m. What A Guest 119 – Grande Promesse (FR) (Sea   **—** Hawk II 131) [1990 10g6 12f2 12.2m 1991 a11g a8g a12g 13.8f] sturdy ex-Irish mare: poor mover: little show since second in Irish maiden at 4 yrs: winning hurdler. *N. Tinkler.*

ADELPHI PRINCESS (IRE)   3 br.f. Anfield 117 – Princess Pageant 95   **67** d (Welsh Pageant 132) [1990 NR 1991 8m6 10d4 8.3d 8f4 8m5 8m3 7m 8m5 8.2m] leggy, shallow-girthed filly: fifth foal: half-sister to fair 4-y-o winning hurdler Kibreet (by Try My Best) and 2 useful winners in Italy: dam 7f to 1½m winner later placed in USA: plating class on most form: stays 1m: well below form on dead ground: has hung right: seems none too hearty: sold 1,800 gns Newmarket Autumn Sales. *J. W. Watts.*

ADENSO   2 gr.f. (May 4) Adonijah 126 – Zeddenosa (Zeddaan 130) [1991 5f]   **—** 2,400Y: tenth foal: closely related to 3-y-o 5f winner She's Smart (by Absalom), and half-sister to 2 winners in Belgium: dam French middle-distance winner: soon struggling in Beverley seller in May: dead. *M. H. Easterby.*

ADJACENT (IRE)   3 ch.f. Doulab (USA) 115 – Near The Door (USA) (Stage   **82** d Door Johnny) [1990 6m3 1991 10g5 8m6 10.2g* 9.9f2 10.5g4 12f2 10m3 10.5g6 9g a10g4 a12g* a12g] sturdy, lengthy filly: fair form at best: successful in maiden at Bath in June and in claimer (claimed out of B. Hills's stable £6,250) at Lingfield in

November: well beaten at Southwell in December: stays 1½m: acts on firm going. *M. Dixon.*

ADJARISTAN 4 b.c. Akarad (FR) 130 – Adjarida (Red God 128§) [1990 NR 1991 — 11.8g a14g² 12g 16.2d] small colt: half-brother to 4 winners, including fairly useful 10.1f winner Adjamoun (by Shirley Heights) and useful 7f winner Adjanada (by Nishapour): dam, useful winner over 1m and 1¼m in France, is half-sister to dam of Blushing Groom: very lightly raced: 10 lengths second in poor maiden at Southwell in June. *R. Simpson.*

ADJUSTING (IRE) 3 b.f. Busted 134 – Julip 99 (Track Spare 125) [1990 NR — 1991 8m] rangy, rather unfurnished filly: seventh foal: half-sister to disappointing Come And Stay (by Glenstal), useful miler Patriarch (by London Bells) and Irish 1½m winner Fiestal (by Last Fandango): dam 2-y-o 7f winner, stayed 1½m, from good family: slowly away and always behind in maiden at Doncaster in May. *J. W. Watts.*

ADMINISTER 3 b.f. Damister (USA) 123 – Apply 87 (Kings Lake (USA) 133) **74** [1990 7g 1991 10g 11m⁴ 12.1g*] lengthy, angular filly: moderate mover: won maiden at Chepstow in June by a neck, niggled along 1m out: stays 12.1f: sold L. Codd 3,100 gns Newmarket December Sales. *R. Charlton.*

ADMIRAL ALBERT (IRE) 2 gr.g. (Apr 11) Slip Anchor 136 – Magic Spell **65** (FR) (Dancer's Image (USA)) [1991 5m 7d⁴ 8m⁴ 6.9f⁵ 7d] 80,000F, 42,000Y: sturdy, quite attractive gelding: half-brother to very useful but untrustworthy 10.2f winner Marcinkus (by Tolomeo), very smart French 7.5f to 10.5f winner Metal Precieux (by High Line) and a winner over jumps in France by Crimson Beau: dam, second over 6f from 2 starts, is half-sister to very smart middle-distance performer Maitland: quite modest maiden: bought out of C. Brittain's stable 7,400 gns Newmarket Autumn Sales in between last 2 starts: may improve over 1¼m+: very free to post fourth start. *R. Akehurst.*

ADMIRAL BYNG (FR) 4 ch.c. Caerleon (USA) 132 – Pig Tail 98 (Habitat 134) — [1990 10f* 14m² 12f² 12m 1991 10g⁵ 11g⁵] workmanlike colt: moderate walker and mover: fairly useful performer at 3 yrs when trained by H. Cecil: soundly beaten in 1991: unlikely to stay beyond 1¾m: acts on firm going: usually makes the running. *M. J. Charles.*

ADMIRAL'S MISTRESS (IRE) 3 ch.f. Sexton Blake 126 – Little Cygnet (My **63** p Swanee 122) [1990 NR 1991 a12g*] IR 3,800Y: fifth foal: dam, placed in NH Flat race and over hurdles in Ireland, is half-sister to good jumpers Royal Dipper and Henry Mann: 12/1, won 11-runner claimer at Southwell in November by 1½ lengths from Tristiorum, green over 2f out, strong run to lead inside last: will improve. *P. J. Makin.*

ADMIRALS SEAT 3 ch.g. Ardross 134 – Sombreuil 95 (Bold Lad (IRE) 133) **58** [1990 NR 1991 8d⁴ 7.5g⁶ 8.5f 8m 8.2g⁴ 12d⁵] 4,800F, 21,000Y: big, strong, work-manlike gelding: half-brother to winners in France by Busted and Dance In Time: dam 1m winner: plating-class maiden, not seen out after June: should be suited by further than 1m. *Mrs J. R. Ramsden.*

ADMIRALS SECRET (USA) 2 ch.c. (May 19) Secreto (USA) 128 – Noble — Mistress (USA) (Vaguely Noble 140) [1991 7m 7.1s 7m] $31,000Y: good-quartered colt: has a round action: fifth reported foal: dam unraced: soundly beaten in maidens: bandaged off-hind second outing. *C. F. Wall.*

ADMIRALTY WAY 5 b.g. Petorius 117 – Captive Flower 99 (Manacle 123) **74** § [1990 8f⁴ 7.5m 10.4d* 10f 9m 12.3m⁵ 16f⁵ 10.6d 1991 10.4d* 10.8m⁵ 10.1f 10g⁴] leggy, quite attractive gelding: modest handicapper on his day: won at Chester (same race for second successive year) in May: stays 1¼m: acts on firm and dead going: has been tried in blinkers and visor: has pulled hard (bolted to post once): unreliable. *M. O'Neill.*

ADRASTE 2 ch.f. (Apr 22) Midyan (USA) 124 – Grand Opera 92 (Great Nephew — 126) [1991 6m 5f] 5,000F: sturdy filly: seventh foal: half-sister to several winners, including fair 1¼m performer/winning hurdler Operatic Score (by Kind of Hush): dam 7f winner at 2 yrs: soundly beaten in claimer at Haydock and maiden at Beverley. *J. A. Glover.*

ADVERSARY (USA) 3 b.c. Alleged (USA) 138 – Imperturbable Lady (CAN) **111** (Northern Dancer) [1990 NR 1991 10.1g* 10.1m² 12g 10.1m* 10g* 10.5g⁵ 10m⁶] strong, compact colt: half-brother to 5 winners, including Grade 2 winner Cool Northerner (by Dom Alaric) and graded-placed Dancing Minister (by Bold Agent): dam won 2 races at around 1m in Canada: successful in maiden (bandaged near-hind) at Windsor in May then minor event at Windsor and £7,500 contest at Newbury in

July: disappointing last in Group 3 events at Haydock and Goodwood (very much on toes) last 2 outings: stays 1¼m: held up, and has turn of foot: to race in USA. *G. Harwood.*

ADWICK PARK 3 b.c. Blazing Saddles (AUS) – Ana Gabriella (USA) (Master 90 Derby (USA)) [1990 5m⁴ 5g⁵ 6g⁵ 7m² 7d² 7.5f³ 7f* 7f* 7g 7f⁴ 7f* 6g* 6d 1991 7m⁴ 6g² 6g 6g] robust, good-quartered colt: impresses in appearance: fairly useful performer: good second to Sheikh Albadou in £25,000 handicap at York in June: not discredited in Stewards' Cup at Goodwood (soon driven along) final start: effective at 6f and 7f: seems unsuited by a soft surface: easily best form with strong handling: carries head rather high: suited by forcing tactics. *T. D. Barron.*

AEDEAN 2 ch.c. (Mar 5) Risk Me (FR) 127 – Finlandaise (FR) (Arctic Tern (USA) 71 126) [1991 6d 5g⁵ 6d⁴ 6.1s³ 6m* 6.1g³ 7m 6g³ 6g] 17,500F, 21,000Y: tall, leggy colt: moderate mover: fourth foal: half-brother to 3 winners by Seymour Hicks, including 1988 Irish 2-y-o 6f winner Ingmar: dam French 9f and 1m winner: modest performer: won 18-runner maiden at Windsor in August: better efforts subsequently when third in nurseries: best form at around 6f: acts on good to firm ground and soft: keen sort. *C. C. Elsey.*

AEGAEN LADY 2 b.f. (May 8) Lochnager 132 – Gamma (GER) (Zank) [1991 5m² 55 6f 5h⁵ 6.1m 5g a8g² a7g⁴ a7g⁵ a8g⁴] 2,000Y: sturdy filly: half-sister to numerous winners, including Royal Whip (by Pitskelly), winner at 8.5f at 2 yrs in Ireland and later successful in Norsk St Leger: dam placed over 1½m at 3 yrs in Ireland: plating-class maiden: seems suited by 1m: ran poorly when blinkered: has run well for 7-lb claimer. *J. Etherington.*

AEGINA (USA) 2 b.f. (Jan 23) Shahrastani (USA) 135 – Trojan Miss 104 (Troy 56 137) [1991 7g⁴ 8s⁴] leggy filly: first foal: dam 2-y-o 7f winner later stayed 1½m: plating-class form in autumn maidens at Redcar and Yarmouth: looks one paced, and will probably be well suited by middle distances. *M. R. Stoute.*

AELLOPOUS 3 b.f. Kris 135 – Graecia Magna (USA) 109 (Private Account 60 (USA)) [1990 6m⁴ 8g 1991 7m² 7.1d⁶ 7m⁵ 7m⁵ 6.9f 6.9f³ 7g] leggy, quite good-topped filly: moderate walker: quite modest maiden, seems unreliable: best 3-y-o effort when third at Folkestone, making most: should be suited by 1m +, though rather headstrong: acts on firm ground: sold 12,000 gns Newmarket Autumn Sales. *G. Harwood.*

AFFA 2 b.f. (Feb 23) Local Suitor (USA) 128 – Pine (Supreme Sovereign 119) [1991 58 6f 7.1d⁶ 6s a7g] leggy, unfurnished filly: fourth foal: half-sister to 1¼m winner Firgrove (by Relkino): dam ran twice: plating-class maiden: well below form on fibresand at Southwell: best run at 7f on good to soft ground. *T. Thomson Jones.*

AFFAIR OF HONOUR (IRE) 3 ch.c. Ahonoora 122 – Good Relations (Be My 68 Guest (USA) 126) [1990 5g³ 5m 5d⁵ 7h* 7m² 1991 8g⁶ 10m⁶ 12d 10.1g² 10d³ 10g⁵] strong colt: has a round action: quite modest handicapper: stays 1¼m: acts on hard and dead ground: sold to join J. J. O'Neill 4,500 gns Newmarket Autumn Sales. *P. F. I. Cole.*

AFFAIR OF STATE (IRE) 2 b.f. (Mar 8) Tate Gallery (USA) 117 – All Hat 99 (Double Form 130) [1991 5m³ 5d* 5m² 5g 6m* 6m] IR 11,000F, IR 6,400Y: neat filly: third foal: closely related to 2 maidens in Ireland: dam Irish 5f winner, is half-sister to Cherry Hinton and Musidora winner Everything Nice: fairly useful performer: off course 2 months, won IR £245,000 Tattersalls Breeders Stakes at the Curragh by ¾ length from Nifty Fifty, showing vastly improved form: previously successful in maiden auction event at Newbury: last of 9 in Tattersalls Cheveley Park Stakes at Newmarket final start: better suited by 6f than 5f: best form on good to firm ground, has won on dead. *M. R. Channon.*

AFFAIR TO REMEMBER 3 b.f. Persian Bold 123 – Princess Eboli 108 83 (Brigadier Gerard 144) [1990 NR 1991 7g⁵ 8.5m* 8m 10g⁴ 10f⁴ 10m⁵ 12m⁵ 11.7g² 12.1s⁵ 13.3g⁶] smallish, leggy filly: sixth foal: half-sister to ungenuine 11.5f winner Ebolito, untrustworthy 1¼m winner Babil (both by Welsh Pageant) and a winner in Italy: dam won Cheshire Oaks and Lancashire Oaks: fair handicapper: won maiden at Epsom in June: sweating and on toes, went rather in snatches but ran creditably last 2 starts: stays 13.3f: probably acts on any going. *P. T. Walwyn.*

AFFIDARE (IRE) 2 b.c. (Feb 4) The Noble Player (USA) 126 – Cala-Vadella 110 ? (Mummy's Pet 125) [1991 6g⁴ 5f³] 33,000F, 38,000Y: smallish, useful-looking colt: seventh foal: half-brother to 1987 2-y-o 6f winner Brilliant Bay (by Hello Gorgeous) and 6f winner Hokusan (by Reform): dam, sister to Runnett, won 4 times over 5f at 2 yrs: better effort when keeping-on fourth of 6 to Gold Desert in minor event at

31

Doncaster (slowly away) in June: odds on, third of 8 in maiden at Redcar following month: looked sort to do better. *M. H. Easterby.*

AFFIRMED'S DESTINY (USA)   2 b.g. (Apr 30) Affirmed (USA) – Grand   **62**
Destiny (USA) (Grand Central) [1991 7d5 7g2 8.1g 7.3m 7.6d6] $39,000Y: leggy, useful-looking gelding: has scope: half-brother to 6 winners in North America, 3 in minor stakes: dam won at up to 9f: quite modest form in maidens and a nursery: looked tricky ride second and third (sweating) outings: blinkered (fair effort, but found little) last time: should stay 1¼m: acts on dead ground: one to be wary of. *J. L. Dunlop.*

AFFORDABLE   3 b.g. Formidable (USA) 125 – Ophrys 90 (Nonoalco (USA) 131)   **75**
[1990 5f4 5m3 6m2 5m2 6g2 5g6 6m3 7m 1991 5m3 5m 5s5 7g4 7d3 7g8 8s 7g4 7g6 7.1m6 7m* 7m 7g4] strong, good-quartered gelding: has a quick action: modest handicapper: won at Leicester in July and Redcar in September: stays 7f: acts on good to firm ground and dead: ran badly when blinkered: used to look ungenuine (tended to hang and find nothing) but did nothing wrong in the autumn. *W. Carter.*

AFIF   2 b.c. (Mar 7) Midyan (USA) 124 – Alpine Sunset (Auction Ring (USA) 123)   **92**
[1991 5g3 6g5 5d* 5m* 5m3 5g6 6g6 6f* 6m* 6m 6.1s*] 22,000F, 22,000Y: neat, attractive colt: has a round action: first foal: dam unraced half-sister to Cyrano de Bergerac: fairly useful performer: won maiden at Ayr and nursery at Warwick in July, median auction event and 3-runner minor contest (by 5 lengths from Sylvan) at Folkestone in September and all-aged race (despite wandering) at Chepstow in October: ran moderately on several occasions: much better suited by 6f than 5f: probably acts on any going: effective with or without blinkers: goes well for claimer: usually looks very well. *Mrs J. Cecil.*

AFRICAN CHIMES   4 b.c. Kampala 120 – Rynville (Ballymore 123) [1990 8m   **61**
12.2m2 12f3 8g 10m6 8g 10m3 a8g a10g2 a10g* 1991 a8g2 a7g5 a7g* a7g a8g5 8m 6g   a **91**
7g6 7m* 7m3 7m3 a7g2 a7g* a6g2 a6g*] leggy, angular colt: has round action: fairly useful handicapper, much better on all-weather: won at Lingfield (2) and Southwell (2): effective at 6f and stays 1½m: acts on firm ground: effective blinkered or not: ran poorly when visored once: has wandered: has won for apprentice. *W. A. O'Gorman.*

AFRICAN GUEST   4 b.g. What A Guest 119 – Kalaya (Tanerko 134) [1990 8m 7d   —
a6g a11g a12g3 a14g 1991 a14g3 a14g 12.1m6] quite attractive gelding: plating-class maiden at best: stays 1½m: acts on soft ground: trained until after second start by J. Wilson. *L. Lungo.*

AFRICAN SPIRIT   7 b.g. African Sky 124 – Relic Spirit (Relic) [1990 a8g2 a8g4   —
8.2s4 10.4g 10.6d 8g 1991 a11g4 10.1g 9m5 12g4 12g6 a10g] good-topped gelding: carries condition: poor handicapper at best: stays 1½m: acts on any going: has been tried blinkered: has swished tail and looked none too keen: trained until after second start by R. Whitaker. *J. Pearce.*

AGAINST THE FLOW   4 ch.f. Salmon Leap (USA) 131 – Tricky Tracey   —
(Formidable (USA) 125) [1990 8m 1991 8.2f] lengthy filly: no sign of ability. *I. D. Czerpak.*

AGAINST YOU   4 b.f. Auction Ring (USA) 123 – Saranita 70 (Thatch (USA) 136)   —
[1990 8g5 8g 7g5 8d3 9.5m5 1991 10d6 8f6 14g4 10m 13.3d5 12v 11.7m] lengthy, workmanlike filly: poor mover: fourth foal: dam 1m winner in France: modest ex-Irish maiden: stays 13f: acts on good to firm and dead ground: ran well when blinkered once: trained at 3 yrs by J. Oxx. *R. Akehurst.*

AGAMA (USA)   2 ch.f. (May 19) Nureyev (USA) 131 – Agacerie (USA) (Exclusive   **44**
Native (USA)) [1991 7m 8.1s] $500,000Y: smallish, lengthy filly: third foal: half-sister to a winner in North America by Devil's Bag: dam won 9 races, including Grade 3 1½m event: poor form in autumn maidens at Redcar (better effort) and Edinburgh. *J. H. M. Gosden.*

A GENTLEMAN TWO   5 b.h. All Systems Go 119 – Solar Honey 77 (Roi Soleil   **47**
125) [1990 7m 9f 6m4 6g 7g* 8m2 8f5 8.5f3 7.5g4 1991 9s3 9m 8h6] lengthy horse: carries plenty of condition: moderate mover: poor performer: stays 9f: acts on good to firm and soft ground: winning hurdler. *G. M. Moore.*

AGE OF MIRACLES   4 b.g. Simply Great (FR) 122 – Single Gal 97 (Mansingh   **81**
(USA) 120) [1990 8.2f 7d 8m a8g 8m 9m3 12g6 10d* 10m* 10m 1991 a7g4 10m 12m 7g2 10d6 9s6 10g 7g4 11.9m5 8g 10g4 9m4 8m 12d a12g4] leggy, rather close-coupled gelding: moderate mover: fair handicapper: effective at 7f to 1½m: acts on good to firm ground and dead: ran poorly when blinkered once: difficult ride: inconsistent. *C. A. Cyzer.*

AGHAADIR (USA)   3 b.c. Private Account (USA) – Kris Kris (USA) (Hoist The   **99** p
Flag (USA)) [1990 7g* 1991 8d⁴ 7d 7m*] leggy, useful-looking colt: moderate
mover: promising second start (first for 3½ months) then put up much improved
performance to dead-heat with Go Executive for 19-runner £9,000 handicap at York
in October, rallying very gamely: should stay 1m: acts on good to firm ground and
probably on dead: may well improve again. *J. H. M. Gosden.*

AGHNIYAH (USA)   3 ch.f. Lyphard (USA) 132 – Goodbye Shelley (FR) 116   —
(Home Guard (USA) 129) [1990 6d 7g* 7m⁵ 8f⁴ 8d 1991 8g 8f 8m⁵ 8s⁵ 9m 8.9m⁶
10.2g 8m] small, workmanlike filly: modest winner at 2 yrs: below form in handicaps
in 1991: stays 1m: acts on firm and dead going. *P. T. Walwyn.*

AGINCOURT SONG (USA)   2 b.c. (Jan 16) Al Nasr (FR) 126 – La Francaise   **77**
(USA) (Jim French (USA)) [1991 7.1m² 7.1s4] lengthy, workmanlike colt: has scope:
closely related to French 1990 7f and 1m winner Laliffe (by Lypheor) and half-
brother to several winners in USA and France: dam, placed 4 times in France, is
half-sister to Alzao: green and on toes, better effort in maidens when keeping-on 7
lengths second of 11 to Zaahi at Sandown in September: raced keenly then found
little off bridle at Chepstow following month: may do better. *J. L. Dunlop.*

AGUNIJAH   2 ch.f. (Feb 2) Adonijah 126 – Gunnard 62 (Gunner B 126) [1991 5f 6g   **47**
6m⁵ 7.5f⁵ 8m] good-bodied filly: has no near-eye: moderate mover: fifth foal:
half-sister to 11f winner Foot Soldier (by Hotfoot) and 1½m seller winner Innovator
(by Relkino): dam won 1m and 1¼m sellers: poor form, in selling nursery (sweating)
final start: should be suited by further than 7.5f. *C. Tinkler.*

AHBAB (IRE)   2 b.f. (Jan 25) Ajdal (USA) 130 – Magic Slipper 97 (Habitat 134)   **66** p
[1991 7g⁵] big, heavy-topped filly: second foal: dam 1¼m and 11.5f winner, is
half-sister to Light Cavalry and Fairy Footsteps: 10/1 and backward, over 9 lengths
fifth of 15 finishers to Perfect Circle in minor event at Kempton in September, soon
prominent, leading briefly 2f out and not knocked about once headed: will do better.
P. T. Walwyn.

AHKAM (IRE)   2 ch.f. (Jan 22) Persian Bold 123 – Ghanayim (USA) 107 (Sharpen   **49**
Up 127) [1991 7g⁵ 7g 5m 6s⁶] good-bodied, quite attractive filly: moderate walker
and mover: first foal: dam 2-y-o 6f winner out of half-sister to Ribocco and Ribero:
poor maiden: gave impression something amiss on debut and subsequently off
course 3 months: hung left and carried head high next time. *H. Thomson Jones.*

AHURA (IRE)   2 b.c. (Feb 7) Kafu 120 – Gentle Heiress (Prince Tenderfoot   **50**
(USA) 126) [1991 5d⁵ 5g⁵ 5m⁴ 5g⁴ 5m³ 5d³ 5.2g³ 5s⁵ 5f³] IR 9,200Y: sturdy,
good-topped colt: poor mover: half-brother to several winners, including 1985 2-y-o
5f winner Queen of Sahara (by Royal Match) and 1½m winner Prince Newport (by
Prince Regent): dam placed at 2 yrs in Ireland: plating-class form in varied events,
including a seller: probably ideally suited by an easy surface: below best when
blinkered 3 times: not seen out after early-August. *N. Tinkler.*

AIDE MEMOIRE (IRE)   2 b.f. (Feb 12) Don't Forget Me 127 – Pharjoy (FR) 85   **41**
(Pharly (FR) 130) [1991 6g 7m 6d a8g] 11,000Y: leggy filly: second foal: half-sister to
1m winner El Volador (by Beldale Flutter): dam, best at 2 yrs when successful over
6f, is out of Prix Robert Papin second Promise of Joy: poor form in maidens: ran well
on fibresand at Southwell: will probably be better suited by 1¼m. *C. B. B. Booth.*

AIGUA BLAVA (USA)   3 b.f. Solford (USA) 127 – Watership (USA) (Foolish   —
Pleasure (USA)) [1990 NR 1991 9.9f⁵] good-topped, attractive filly: first reported
foal: dam maiden half-sister to Grade 1 13f (Turf) Canadian International Championship Stakes winner Great Neck: tailed-off last in maiden at Beverley in September.
G. Harwood.

AILEEN'S JOY   4 b. or br.c. Runnett 125 – Originality (Godswalk (USA) 130)   —
[1990 8g 8g 6m 8.2v 1991 8m⁵ 7g⁶ 9.2d] leggy colt: no worthwhile form. *R. F. Fisher.*

AILORT   4 b.f. Ardross 134 – Forres (Thatch (USA) 136) [1990 12m⁴ 12f⁴ 12.5m   —
12m⁵ 12.2d* 12.4s² a14g 1991 12s⁵ 16.2g 12.5g] smallish filly: moderate mover: quite
modest performer when trained by H. Cecil at 3 yrs: little worthwhile form in 1991:
stays 1½m: acts on good to firm and soft going: sold out of N. Tinkler's stable 2,000
gns Doncaster January Sales: resold to join G. Yardley's stable 1,400 gns Ascot
November Sales. *P. J. Jones.*

AIMAAM (USA)   3 b.c. Danzig (USA) – Lucky Lucky Lucky (USA) (Chieftain II)   **104**
[1990 6m* 7m* 8m⁴ 1991 10m³ 10g³ 10m² 12m⁵] well-made colt: fluent mover:
cracked knee bone at 2 yrs: useful form in £14,800 handicap at Newmarket and
3-runner minor event won by Opera House at Nottingham first and third starts:
checked 2f out in Newmarket listed race on final one: stays 1¼m well: yet to race on

33

a soft surface: reportedly returned lame second outing: to join T. Skiffington in USA. *J. L. Dunlop.*

AIN'TLIFELIKETHAT 4 gr.c. Godswalk (USA) 130 – Blue Alicia (Wolver **62** §
Hollow 126) [1990 a8g⁶ a8g⁶ a6g 6m 7m 8.2g 8.2m 7g 6g* 7g* 7m* 7f⁶ 8m 7m* 8h⁴ a57 §
6m 7m 7d 1991 7m³ 7g⁵ 7.6m⁶ 7d³ 6g⁵ 7g⁵ 7f² 7m* 7g⁶ 7m⁵ 6.9f⁵ 7f a7g³ 8g⁶ 7g
a8g⁴ a7g⁶] workmanlike, good-quartered colt: plating-class handicapper: won at
Brighton in August: stays 1m: acts on hard ground, possibly unsuited by dead:
visored (below form) once, usually blinkered nowadays: mostly slowly away:
untrustworthy. *T. J. Naughton.*

AIR DANCER 3 b.f. Teenoso (USA) 135 – Lasani (FR) (Appiani II 128) [1990 5m —
1991 10d 8v] sturdy, workmanlike filly: moderate walker: no worthwhile form in
maidens and minor event. *R. F. Johnson Houghton.*

AIREDALE (USA) 4 b.g. Dixieland Band (USA) – Good Hart (USA) (Creme **56**
Dela Creme) [1990 8f 10f* 10.6f³ 12.3g 12g 1991 a12g² 10.8g] good-topped, angular
gelding: plating-class handicapper: not seen out after April: effective at 1¼m and
1½m: acts on firm going: has worn tongue strap. *W. J. Haggas.*

AIRE VALLEY LAD 4 b.g. The Brianstan 128 – Rojael (Mansingh 120) [1990 6g —
6f 8g 8g 10m 9g 6f² 7.5g 1991 7f 8m 12.2g] lengthy, sparely-made gelding: has a quick
action: poor plater: stays 1m: acts on firm going. *R. Bastiman.*

AIR MUSIC (FR) 4 b.c. Fabulous Dancer (USA) 126 – Santa Musica (Luthier **91**
126) [1990 8f² 9g 12m³ 12g⁵ 10f³ 10d 1991 a10g* 12s⁵ 10d⁴ 10g⁶ 8d⁴ 10f⁴ 12g 12g⁶]
rather leggy, attractive colt: easily landed odds in apprentice maiden at Lingfield in
March: fairly useful form in the main after: below best when blinkered final 2 starts:
stays 1½m: acts on good to firm and dead (possibly unsuited by soft) ground:
sometimes wears eyeshield. *C. E. Brittain.*

AIR NYMPH 4 b.f. Elegant Air 119 – Elfinaria 79 (Song 132) [1990 6g⁵ 6f² 6g⁵ 6s⁶ **53**
a6g⁵ a8g a8g⁴ a7g³ 1991 a7g a7g² a7g⁵ a7g 6s³ 6g⁶ 6m³ 7g 6.1m 7g] strong, robust
filly: carries condition: moderate mover: quite modest maiden at best: lost her way
last 3 starts: effective at 6f to 1m: probably acts on any going: has been tried visored
and blinkered. *C. C. Elsey.*

AIR OF ELEGANCE 3 b.f. Elegant Air 119 – Mighty Fly 117 (Comedy Star —
(USA) 121) [1990 7m⁴ 7m⁴ 1991 10g 12m] leggy filly: moderate mover: modest form
in maidens at 2 yrs, none at 3: should stay at least 1¼m. *I. A. Balding.*

AIR SUPREMACY 2 b. or br.c. (Feb 19) Skyliner 117 – Runasca 49 (Runnymede —
123) [1991 5g³ 7m 8m 6s] neat colt: fourth foal: half-brother to a winner
abroad: dam plater, ran only at 2 yrs: well beaten in maidens: visored final start: off
course 6 months and sold out of T. Barron's stable 1,900 gns Doncaster July Sales
after debut. *D. Moffatt.*

AIR TIME 3 gr.g. Good Times (ITY) – Ville Air 85 (Town Crier 119) [1990 6f⁵ **64**
7m⁴ 7m³ 8d 7s⁶ 1991 8g 9d 11.7g⁴ 10g 11.7g 10m⁵ 15.4m⁵ 9.7g²] tall, leggy gelding:
quite modest maiden: effective at 1¼m and 11.7f: seemed unsuited by a soft surface:
often blinkered or visored: dead. *P. Mitchell.*

AITCH N'BEE 8 ch.g. Northfields (USA) – Hot Case 92 (Upper Case (USA)) **78**
[1990 a7g* a7g² a7g² a7g* a7g* 8.2d⁴ 7g 1991 a7g⁶ 8g* 7s⁶ 8g² 7m 8g³] small,
strong gelding: modest handicapper: won at Newmarket in August: stays 1m: acts
on any going: tried visored and blinkered early in career: goes very well on
fibresand, ran moderately once on equitrack: consistent. *Lady Herries.*

AJAAD (USA) 3 ch.c. Nureyev (USA) 131 – Execution (USA) (The Axe II 115) **110**
[1990 NR 1991 7g² 7f* 8m* 8m* 7f] $700,000Y: leggy, angular colt: moderate
walker: half-brother to 2 winners in USA, notably Grade 2 5-y-o 1¼m and 11f winner
on turf Possible Mate (by King's Bishop): dam never ran: won maiden at Redcar
in May, then Britannia Handicap (by 5 lengths, chasing leaders on bridle then
quickening in scintillating style) at Royal Ascot and £7,600 handicap (7/2 on) at
Newcastle week later: 6/4 on, moved moderately to post and never travelling
fluently when soundly-beaten last of 7 in Beeswing Stakes at Newcastle in July:
looked a most exciting prospect at Royal Ascot. *M. R. Stoute.*

AJANAC 7 br.g. Known Fact (USA) 135 – Majan 67 (Brigadier Gerard 144) [1990 —
6m 6m 6m⁶ 6m 6g 8m* 7m³ 8m³ 1991 6d] rather angular gelding: good mover:
useful performer at 6 yrs: tailed off in May handicap as 7-y-o: stays 1m: acts on any
going: below form in blinkers and visor: has run creditably when sweating. *R.
Charlton.*

Britannia Handicap, Ascot—Ajaad quickens clear

AJIB (USA)   2 ch.c. (Apr 12) Woodman (USA) 126 – Shelbiana (USA) (Chieftain II)   **84 p**
[1991 6m 7.9m*] $350,000Y: close-coupled, quite attractive colt: shade unfurnished: second foal: dam won at up to 9f at 2 yrs: 9/2, won 8-runner maiden at York in October, leading after 2f and running on really well last 150 yds to beat Beldi by a length: very green and slowly away in Doncaster minor event on debut: will stay 1¼m: will improve again. *J. H. M. Gosden.*

AJO (IRE)   2 b.c. (Mar 17) Ajdal (USA) 130 – Betty's Secret (USA) (Secretariat   **57 p**
(USA)) [1991 6d⁶ 7d] sturdy colt: closely related to several winners worldwide, notably Secreto (by Northern Dancer), and half-brother to a winner by Gregorian: dam unraced half-sister to French Derby winner Caracolero, from family of Crowned Prince and Majestic Prince: better effort in November maidens (burly on debut) when keeping-on eighth of 22 to For Reg at Doncaster: should stay at least 1¼m: should stay at least. *M. R. Stoute.*

AKAROA   4 ch.c. Kalaglow 132 – St Isadora (Lyphard (USA) 132) [1990 10g³ 12f⁶   **77**
10.5m² a12g² 10.6d⁴ a12g* 1991 10g 14m³] leggy, lengthy colt: modest handicapper: not seen out after May: stays 1¾m: acts on good to firm going: sold 2,200 gns Newmarket July Sales. *W. Jarvis.*

AKATOMBO   3 b.f. Ilium 121 – Miss Colleen (Joshua 129) [1990 NR 1991 8g 8g   **—**
11d] tall, leggy, quite attractive filly: third foal (previous 2 by Julio Mariner): dam unraced: behind in maidens and seller: trained first 2 starts by A. Turnell: sold 800 gns Ascot November Sales. *Mrs A. Knight.*

AKID (USA)   5 ch.h. Secreto (USA) 128 – Raise The Bridge (USA) (Raise A Cup   **—**
(USA)) [1990 6m 8g 1991 7g 6m 10.5g 7m 8.1s] sturdy, good-topped horse: has been tubed: useful as 2-y-o: lightly raced since and no worthwhile form for long time: stays 7f: acts on firm and dead ground: trained until after reappearance by D. Topley. *D. R. Franks.*

AKIMBO   4 ch.c. Bold Lad (IRE) 133 – Western Gem 86 (Sheshoon 132) [1990   **80**
8.5g* 8m* 10s³ 8v³ 8g 9f² 10m 8m 8g 1991 9g⁴ 8g 8d 8d³ 10.1d² 8.3m³ 10s 9g⁵] well-made colt: moderate mover: fair handicapper: ran poorly last 2 starts: stays 1¼m: acts on good to firm and heavy going: raced freely when visored once: sold to join W. Price's stable 13,000 gns Newmarket September Sales. *C. R. Nelson.*

AKKAZAO (IRE)   3 b. or br.f. Alzao (USA) 117 – Akka (Malacate (USA) 131)   **81**
[1990 5f² 6m² 6d⁴ 5d³ 6m⁴ 6m⁶ 1991 8s 7m² 7m² 9f² 7g 10.1g⁴ 10g 8m² 8.1g³ 8.3m² 8g] workmanlike filly: fair performer, though still a maiden: stays 9f: best efforts on a sound surface: blinkered twice: rather one paced: consistent. *W. Carter.*

AKURA (IRE)   2 b.f. (May 1) Vision (USA) – Bebe Altesse (GER) (Alpenkonig   **44**
(GER)) [1991 5m 7.5f 8.1m] quite good-topped filly: third known foal: half-sister to 3-y-o 7f winner Angelo's Double (by M Double M) and modest 1989 2-y-o 6f winner Saltessa (by Thatching): dam, winner in Germany, is out of good

German mare Bebe Girl: poor maiden: best effort in auction event at Beverley second start: bandaged near-hind final one. *M. Johnston.*

ALAMA MARIA 3 ro.f. Nishapour (FR) 125 – Carmen Maria (Bold Lad (IRE) — 133) [1990 NR 1991 8g] 4,600Y: angular filly: fifth foal: half-sister to Irish 5f and 6f winner My Precious Daisy (by Sharpo): dam ran once: moved badly down and showed nothing in July seller. *C. J. Hill.*

ALAMIRA (USA) 3 ch.f. Affirmed (USA) – Manchester Miss (USA) (Groton) — [1990 8m3 7.3s5 1991 7m 8g 12g6 10m] tall, sparely-made filly: modest form on her day: stays 1½m: takes keen hold: sold 3,500 gns Newmarket Autumn Sales. *P. F. I. Cole.*

ALAMIR (USA) 3 b.c. Shadeed (USA) 135 – Glamour Girl (FR) (Riverman — p (USA) 131) [1990 NR 1991 7g6] strong, good-topped colt: half-brother to smart middle-distance stayer Ilium (by Troy): dam, minor French 7f and 9.5f winner, is half-sister to dam of Gold River (by Riverman): weak favourite, well-beaten sixth of 12 in maiden at Lingfield in October: sold to join P. Hobbs 14,000 gns Newmarket Autumn Sales: should do better. *H. Thomson Jones.*

ALAMSHAH (IRE) 3 b.c. Lashkari 128 – Alannya (FR) (Relko 136) [1990 7m — 8.2s3 1991 15.3m5] compact colt: best effort (rated 49) in maidens final start at 2 yrs: should be well suited by 1¼m + . *Pat Mitchell.*

AL ANBA (USA) 4 b.f. Lear Fan (USA) 130 – Dacquoise (USA) (Lyphard (USA) 83 132) [1990 7m 10f 8f* 8m6 10m* 1991 11.5d 9m6 10.1m* 10m2 8.9g 10.5m6 12m6] sturdy filly: has a fluent action: fair handicapper: won at Yarmouth in July: best efforts at 1¼m: acts on firm ground: has found little and flashed tail under pressure: will prove ideally suited by extreme waiting tactics. *J. D. Czerpak.*

ALARM CALL (USA) 8 b.g. Alleged (USA) 138 – Sunelianne (USA) (Cyane) — [1990 NR 1991 a13g] tall, rangy gelding: poor mover: very lightly-raced and poor performer nowadays: stays 1¾m: best form on dead ground. *N. Kernick.*

AL BADETO 4 b.f. Hays 120 – Atedaun (Ahonoora 122) [1990 6m 6m3 7m2 8g6 — 8.2g 6h 7m6 6d2 6d 6s a6g 1991 a7g a11g 7d 7m 10d 12.3f 12m5] lengthy, rather sparely-made filly: plating-class maiden at 3 yrs: no form in 1991: stays 7f: acts on good to firm going and dead: has been tried visored and blinkered: has found little. *J. Norton.*

ALBANY SPARK 2 br.g. (Mar 22) Sparkling Boy 110 – Lauriston Cottage — (Welsh Saint 126) [1991 a7g] first reported foal: dam seemed of little account: 50/1, soundly beaten in 10-runner maiden at Lingfield. *G. H. Eden.*

AL BATAL (USA) 4 ch.c. Blushing Groom (FR) 131 – Salpinx (USA) 123 (North- — ern Dancer) [1990 10m 10g 10m 1991 10d6 10m 14m] close-coupled colt: poor maiden: took little interest final start: seems to stay 1¼m: sold 6,800 gns Newmarket December Sales. *J. L. Dunlop.*

ALBEMINE (USA) 2 b.g. (May 6) Al Nasr (FR) 126 – Lady Be Mine (USA) 76 — p (Sir Ivor 135) [1991 6m] good-topped gelding: fourth foal: half-brother to 2 winners, including leading 1989 2-y-o (unbeaten in 6 starts from 6f to 1m) Be My Chief (by Chief's Crown): dam, 1m winner, is daughter of half-sister to dam of Lord Seymour and Marwell: 4/1 and burly, well-beaten last of 7, prominent 4f, eased significantly when beaten, in maiden at Ascot in July: looked sure to improve but did not reappear. *H. R. A. Cecil.*

ALBERJAS (IRE) 2 b.f. (Mar 24) Sure Blade (USA) 130 – Street Light 120 (St — p Chad 120) [1991 6m] 32,000Y: leggy, workmanlike filly: half-sister to several winners here and abroad, including smart 1¼m and 11f winner Street Line (by High Line) and useful 5f and 6f winner Highland Light (by Home Guard): dam smart sprinter: 33/1 and backward, slowly away and always behind in maiden at New-market in October. *C. E. Brittain.*

ALBERT 4 b.c. Kings Lake (USA) 133 – Darine 114 (Nonoalco (USA) 131) [1990 58 10.6s 12g 12.3g5 13d 12v 15d 1991 8m 8.5f2 12g5 9d* 9.7s6 10g] good-bodied colt: shows a round action: plating-class handicapper: won amateurs event at Goodwood in June: stays 1½m: acts on any going, except perhaps heavy: inconsistent: sold 7,400 gns Doncaster November Sales. *C. W. Thornton.*

ALBERT THE BOLD 2 b.c. (Feb 17) Never So Bold 135 – Alcassa (FR) 56 (Satingo 129) [1991 5d5 5m5] 15,500F, 10,000Y: fourth foal: half-brother to 3-y-o Austrian winner So Persistent (by High Top): dam French 11f winner at 4 yrs: beaten around 10 lengths in mid-summer maidens at Newbury and Lingfield. *S. Dow.*

AL BILLAL 3 b.c. Enchantment 115 – Liana Louise (Silly Season 127) [1990 NR 1991 a14g] third foal: dam of little account: tailed off in Southwell claimer in November. *J. D. Czerpak.* —

ALBURY GREY 4 gr.f. Petong 126 – Infelice (Nishapour (FR) 125) [1990 NR 1991 9s 10.1m⁵ 11.9g⁶] workmanlike filly: second foal: half-sister to a poor animal: dam little form: behind in modest company in summer: winning selling hurdler in May: sold 2,600 gns Ascot November Sales. *R. Curtis.* —

ALCANDANCE 4 b.f. Alzao (USA) 117 – Dancing Sun (Will Somers 114§) [1990 5m³ 6m* 6m 5.8m³ 6h 6m⁴ 6s 1991 6g⁵ 7m 6m⁵ 6g a6g³ a5g] close-coupled, sturdy filly: plating-class handicapper: below form after reappearance: unlikely to stay beyond 6f: acts on good to firm ground and heavy: has been tried blinkered. *C. James.* **64 d**

ALCHEMIC (NZ) 7 br.g. Bold Venture (NZ) – Poldhullie 86 (Polyfoto 124) [1990 NR 1991 7g 8m 7.6d 12g] workmanlike New Zealand-bred gelding: has been tubed: always behind in varied company. *M. H. B. Robinson.* —

ALCOY (IRE) 2 b.c. (May 10) Glow (USA) – Organdy 84 (Blakeney 126) [1991 7m⁶ 7f⁶ 8m²] IR 12,000Y: good-topped colt: has plenty of scope: half-brother to fairly useful 7f winner View From Above and 1986 2-y-o 6f winner Sheer Royalty (both by Dara Monarch): dam, 1m winner at 3 yrs, is half-sister to useful 1983 2-y-o 7f and 1m winner Satinette: 5/1 from 10/1 and lowered in class, put up vastly improved effort when keeping-on second of 13 in maiden auction at Redcar in August: better suited by 1m than shorter: looks to have further improvement in him. *P. A. Kelleway.* **66 p**

ALDAHE 6 ch.g. Dalsaan 125 – Alanood 85 (Northfields (USA)) [1990 a8g² a7g* 8f³ 7m² 8.2s³ 8f⁵ 7m² 8h 6g a7g³ 8.2g⁵ 7g⁶ 6g 8m⁴ 6m⁶ 7.5m* 7m 8g 7d⁴ 1991 7f⁴ 7.5g⁵ 10.8m 8f⁵ 7.1m 7m* 7v⁴ 7.6g* 7f³ 7g 7g 7.6m³ 7.1g* 8m 7g 8m 7g] sparely-made gelding: has a round action: plating-class handicapper: won at Brighton, Chester and Chepstow in summer: stays 1m: acts on any going: best form without blinkers: often hangs, but goes very well for claimer: tough. *B. R. Millman.* **54**

AL-DAHLAWIA (IRE) 2 b.f. (Mar 23) Cyrano de Bergerac 120 – Dancing Sun (Will Somers 114§) [1991 6s 6d] IR 7,500F: smallish filly: half-sister to 3 winners, including 2-y-o sprint winners Dancing Fille (by Taufan) and Tricenco (by Kampala): dam never ran: backward, soundly beaten in late-season maidens at Yarmouth and Doncaster. *G. A. Pritchard-Gordon.* —

AL DAMOUR (USA) 4 b.c. Lypheor 118 – Visual Effects (USA) (Silent Screen (USA)) [1990 10.2f⁵ 11.7g 12f⁵ 1991 14.8g] sturdy colt: had a round action: modest maiden: probably stayed 1½m: dead. *C. D. Broad.* —

ALDBOURNE 5 b.m. Alzao (USA) 117 – Steady The Buffs 62 (Balidar 133) [1990 8m* 8m⁶ 7g² 8f⁵ 8.5f* 8.5s² 10s² 10g 1991 7d² 8g³ 8d²] tall, rather angular mare: moderate walker and mover: very useful performer: ran well in spring behind In The Groove in Trusthouse Forte Mile at Sandown and Colour Chart in 5-runner Group 3 event at Saint-Cloud final 2 starts: effective at 7f to 1¼m: acts on any going: sometimes on toes: game and consistent: sent to race in USA. *R. Guest.* **113**

ALESSANDRINA (USA) 2 b.f. (Jan 23) Alydar (USA) – Best Decision (USA) (Best Turn (USA)) [1991 7m] 150,000Y: leggy, lengthy, angular filly: third foal: half-sister to a winner in North America by Believe It: dam won 4 races at up to 1¼m: keeping-on over 7 lengths ninth of 20 to Modernise in maiden at Newmarket in October: will improve. *M. R. Stoute.* **59 p**

ALFAARES (USA) 3 b. or br.c. Danzig (USA) – Palm Reader (USA) (Sir Ivor 135) [1990 6m² 7m⁶ 1991 7m* 8g³ 6m⁴ 6g 6.1m⁶ 6g] strong, good-bodied colt: carries condition: powerful galloper, with a very round action: fairly useful performer: won maiden at Newmarket in April: below form last 4 starts, racing freely and prominent 4f in £12,400 handicap at York on final one: effective at 6f to 1m: blinkered last 3 starts: to join T. Skiffington in USA. *Major W. R. Hern.* **96**

ALFLORA (IRE) 2 b.c. (Jan 24) Niniski (USA) 125 – Adrana 86 (Bold Lad (IRE) 133) [1991 7g³ 7f⁴ 7m³ 6.1m* 7m 7m³] 25,000Y: big, rangy colt: has plenty of scope: third foal: half-brother to 3-y-o 6f winner Colossus (by Good Times): dam 2-y-o 5f winner on only start, is half-sister to Ardross: fairly useful performer: odds on, made all in maiden at Nottingham in September: ran well afterwards when eleventh of 30 to Young Senor in Tattersalls Tiffany Highflyer Stakes at Newmarket and third of 6 to Muhtarram in minor event at Leicester: will stay 1m: yet to race on soft surface: strong-galloping type. *C. E. Brittain.* **90**

AL FROLIC 4 b.g. Alzao (USA) 117 – Fun Frolic (Sexton Blake 126) [1990 10d 7.9m 8m⁶ 7m² 8.5m 8g 9g⁴ 8.2g 8d³ 9.1s 1991 12g⁶ 13d 12g 13m⁵ 13f³ 12.1d⁵ 15g⁶

10m 10m6] close-coupled, quite good-topped gelding: good mover: plating-class handicapper: stays 13f: acts on firm and dead going: has hung right and found little: has had tongue tied down: winning hurdler. *P. Monteith.*

ALFUJAIRAH   4 ch.c. Diesis 133 – Soluce 98 (Junius (USA) 124) [1990 8d* 7g   **89** 1991 8g 8d 7.3m3 8g] sturdy, lengthy colt: carries plenty of condition: shows knee action: lightly-raced but fairly useful handicapper: finished lame final start: acts on good to firm ground but goes particularly well on a soft surface: effective visored or not: sold 15,000 gns Newmarket Autumn Sales. *J. Gosden.*

ALGAIHABANE (USA)   5 b.g. Roberto (USA) 131 – Sassabunda 108 (Sassafras   **—** (FR) 135) [1990 a13g5 14.8m 14m 16.2g6 12m4 16m 16f4 16m 1991 12.3d] close-coupled, rather finely-made gelding: good mover: modest maiden at best: not seen out after June: stays 2m: acts on firm going: below form when blinkered once: has been bandaged off-fore. *Miss A. J. Whitfield.*

AL HAAL (USA)   2 b.c. (Feb 13) Northern Baby (CAN) 127 – Kit's Double (USA)   **61** p (Spring Double) [1991 7.1d 8d] lengthy, rather angular colt: has scope: brother to fairly useful 1m winner Sindeed and 1987 French 2-y-o 1m winner Double Wedge, later successful in USA, and half-brother to 2 winners: dam won from 6f to 9f in USA, including in minor stakes: quite modest form in mid-division of maiden at Chepstow (not knocked about) and minor event at Newmarket (swerved left stalls, never a factor) in autumn: may do better. *P. T. Walwyn.*

ALHAJRAS (USA)   4 b.c. Northern Dancer – Call Me Goddess (USA) (Prince   **—** John) [1990 10.5g 1991 10.8d5] attractive colt: twice behind in maidens. *J. L. Dunlop.*

ALHAMAD   2 b.c. (Mar 13) Slip Anchor 136 – Dafinah (USA) 89 (Graustark) [1991   **94** p 8m 8m2] rangy colt, rather unfurnished: first foal: dam 1¼m and 12.2f winner: favourite following highly promising debut, 1½ lengths second of 14 to Sonus, clear, in maiden at Leicester in October, leading after 2f until under 2f out, then rallying strongly until eased close home: will stay 1½m: will improve again and win a maiden at the least. *H. R. A. Cecil.*

ALHIJAZ   2 ch.c. (Mar 14) Midyan (USA) 124 – Nawara 75 (Welsh Pageant 132) **110** [1991 6g* 7m2 7m* 8m3 8v* 8s*] quite good-topped colt: fifth foal: half-brother to several winners, including 1¼m to 13f winner Usran (by Valiyar): dam 10.2f winner: very useful performer: successful in summer in maiden at Newmarket and minor event at Lingfield then good third to Seattle Rhyme in listed race at Goodwood: improved form in Italy in autumn, winning 11-runner listed event (by 6 lengths) then 13-runner Gran Criterium (by 2½ lengths from Governor's Imp) at Milan: suited by 1m: has form on good to firm ground, but seems well suited by plenty of give. *J. L. Dunlop.*

ALICANTE   4 b.c. Alzao (USA) 117 – Safe And Happy (Tudor Melody 129) [1990   **45** 8f5 12.3f 10g 7f 8g2 8m6 8f4 10.2f4 7.6g3 8.2g 8m2 7f4 8f2 9g6 a8g 1991 10.1m3 10.8m2] small colt: plating-class maiden: stays 10.8f: acts on firm going: ran moderately in blinkers: tends to edge left, and has looked none too keen. *P. A. Blockley.*

ALICE'S MIRROR   2 gr.f. (Mar 27) Magic Mirror 105 – Pousdale-Tachytees 60   **38** p (Tachypous 128) [1991 6s] third foal: dam maiden stayed 2m: 33/1, never dangerous in mid-division in maiden at Folkestone in November. *T. P. McGovern.*

ALIGHT (IRE)   2 b.f. (Mar 23) Alzao (USA) 117 – Pitaka (Pitskelly 122) [1991   **71** 6m6 7m5 8s*] 38,000Y: leggy, rather angular filly: sixth foal: half-sister to winning sprinters Friendly Claim (by Petorius) and Wanda (by Taufan): dam never ran: 20/1, much improved form when easy winner of maiden at Yarmouth in October, running on strongly: stays 1m: seems well suited by soft ground. *A. C. Stewart.*

A LITTLE HOT   4 gr.f. Petong 126 – Hot Money 50 (Mummy's Pet 125) [1990   **—** 5g4 5g4 6m 6d 6d 8d 1991 8m 8.3g 6f 8.3g] leggy filly: bad mover: poor performer nowadays: should stay at least 6f: has been blinkered. *E. A. Wheeler.*

A LITTLE PRECIOUS   5 b.g. Precocious 126 – The Silver Darling 75 (John   **68** Splendid 116) [1990 6m4 6m3 7m 7.6g 7m6 7g 8d 6g2 6m2 7g 1991 6g 6g6 8.3d 7m 7g3 6g2 6g* 6d5 7g4 7s4 7d] strong, close-coupled, attractive gelding: poor mover: quite modest handicapper: won at Hamilton in September: effective at 6f to 7f: yet to race on firm going, acts on any other. *J. R. Bostock.*

ALIVE AND KICKING   2 b.g. (Apr 30) Petong 126 – Hitopah (Bustino 136)   **70** [1991 6m 6m2 7s* a6g* 7f* 6m2 6m a7g* 7g6 7m 8m2 7.3m3 8g] 2,000Y, 3,600 2-y-o: neat gelding: moderate mover: fourth foal: half-brother to 7f winner Pimsboy (by Tender King): dam never ran: modest performer: successful in summer in sellers (no bid) at Lingfield and Catterick, and in claimer and apprentice nursery on

*Whatcombe Stakes, Newbury—Aljadeer looks a good prospect;
newcomer Top Register leads those strung out behind*

Lingfield equitrack: stays 1m: acts on any going: largely consistent: sent to Hong Kong. *S. Dow.*

ALJADEER (USA) 2 b. or br.c. (Apr 29) Alleged (USA) 138 – Return The Roses **106** p
(USA) (Carry Back) [1991 8m* 8g*] $50,000Y: rather leggy, unfurnished colt: fluent mover: half-brother to several winners, notably Grade 1 9f Florida Derby second No More Flowers (by My Gallant): dam won 2 races at up to 9f at 3 yrs: favourite, won maiden at Leicester in October by 4 lengths from Desert Force: heavily backed, followed up in 16-runner minor event at Newbury later in month, going on under 2f out and drawing 3½ lengths clear of Top Register with rest well strung out: will stay at least 1¼m: should make his mark in pattern company. *H. R. A. Cecil.*

ALJERNAAS 2 ch.c. (Apr 12) Rousillon (USA) 133 – Little White Star (Mill Reef **86** p
(USA) 141) [1991 7m 8m*] 82,000Y: lengthy, rather unfurnished colt: has scope: quite good mover: brother to a winner in Italy and half-brother to several winners, including very useful 7f and 1½m winner Beldale Star (by Beldale Flutter): dam poor daughter of half-sister to high-class miler Saintly Song: favourite, confirmed promise of debut at Newmarket, comfortably winning 15-runner maiden at Pontefract in October, chasing leader and pushed along to lead inside final 1f: will stay 1¼m: sure to improve again. *L. M. Cumani.*

ALKABAR 3 ch.g. Nordance (USA) – The Ice Maiden (Native Bazaar 122) [1990 **50**
NR 1991 8.2m 11.1d² 13g⁵ 12.3g 12m⁵ 12.3m⁴] 2,500Y: good-bodied gelding: third living foal: dam unraced daughter of sister to Green God: plating class at best: stays 11f well: acts on dead ground. *Miss L. C. Siddall.*

ALKARIF (USA) 2 ch.c. (Apr 13) Diesis 133 – Mystery Mood (USA) (Night **75** p
Invader (USA)) [1991 7m⁶ 8m⁶ 7.1s²] $300,000Y: lengthy, workmanlike colt: half-brother to several winners, including very useful miler Maximilian (by Mr Prospector) and smart 1981 American 2-y-o filly Mystical Mood (by Roberto): dam best at 2 yrs when smart stakes winner at up to 1m: improving form in maidens: always prominent in strongly-run race when second at Chepstow in October: stays 1m: races keenly: can win a modest race. *A. A. Scott.*

AL-KHAGOOLA (IRE) 3 b.f. Coquelin (USA) 121 – Demeter 83 (Silly Season **—**
127) [1990 5g⁶ 5f⁵ 6m⁵ 5f⁵ 7m 1991 8m] smallish, angular filly: keen walker: has a round action: poor maiden: should stay 7f. *J. L. Spearing.*

ALKIONIS 5 b.h. Dominion 123 – Norfolk Gal 100 (Blakeney 126) [1990 NR 1991 **35**
8f 8.1d 10.8g⁶ 11.5s³ 12m 14.6m] leggy horse: has a round action: worthwhile form only in handicap fourth start: stays 11.5f. *Mrs A. Knight.*

ALL'A BLAZE 2 b.f. (May 20) Blazing Saddles (AUS) – Bread 'n Honey 51 **—**
(Goldhills Pride 105) [1991 5v 5g 5g 6m] small, workmanlike filly: has a round action: second living foal: dam placed once from 4 races at 2 yrs, is half-sister to smart sprinter Prince Reymo: little worthwhile form, including in seller: not seen out after June. *C. Holmes.*

ALLARME SOCIALE (USA) 2 br.c. (Mar 17) Alleged (USA) 138 – Top **96**
Socialite (USA) 117 (Topsider (USA)) [1991 8f³ 8m 8.3g* 10v⁶] $50,000Y: first foal:

dam 5f (at 2 yrs) to 7.3f winner here later won 7 races in USA: well-backed 9/2-shot,
won maiden at Hamilton in September, travelling smoothly then running on well:
very good sixth of 18 to Jape, beaten around 5½ lengths, in Group 2 event at Rome 7
weeks later: stays 1¼m: acts on heavy ground. *B. Hanbury.*

ALL AT SEA (USA)   2 ch.f. (May 3) Riverman (USA) 131 – Lost Virtue (USA)   **82 p**
(Cloudy Dawn (USA)) [1991 8g*] tall, rangy, rather unfurnished filly: has scope:
half-sister to several winners here and abroad, notably smart 7f to 1¼m winner
Over The Ocean (by Super Concorde): dam unraced daughter of half-sister to
Damascus: 11/4-on shot, won 9-runner maiden at Wolverhampton in October by 3
lengths (value at least 6) from Arsaad, tracking leaders, leading on bridle 2f out,
eased last 50 yds: should stay 1¼m: useful filly in the making. *H. R. A. Cecil.*

ALL EARZ (IRE)   2 b.c. (May 14) Auction Ring (USA) 123 – Classic Choice   **58**
(Patch 129) [1991 5m 6.1m⁵ 6m⁶ 6g] 7,600Y: lengthy colt: moderate mover: fourth
foal: brother to 3-y-o Classic Ring, 7f winner at 2 yrs, and half-brother to 1989 2-y-o
7f winner Jones Beach (by Sandhurst Prince): dam unraced: plating-class maiden:
stays 6f: sold 2,200 gns Ascot November Sales. *M. Johnston.*

ALLEGRAMENTE   2 b.c. (Apr 7) Music Maestro 119 – Eastern Romance 73   **54**
(Sahib 114) [1991 5g⁶ 6g 6m 7f⁶ 7m 7f 6g] 6,800F, 9,400Y: rather lightly-made colt:
brother to 3-y-o Eastern Music, modest 6f winner at 2 yrs, and half-brother to
several winners, including fair miler Miss Cuddles (by Mummy's Pet): dam won 6f
seller at 2 yrs: plating-class maiden: swerved and unseated rider after 2f at
Yarmouth penultimate start: stays 7f: has run well for 7-lb claimer. *P. F. Tulk.*

ALLERFORD   3 b.c. Bay Express 132 – Ardverikie (Red Alert 127) [1990 NR   —
1991 7m⁶ 8.3m 7g] 3,800Y: neat colt: third foal: dam lightly raced and moderately:
plating-class maiden: blinkered, bolted before apprentice selling handicap and
withdrawn fourth intended start. *C. D. Broad.*

ALLE-ROY   3 b.g. Alleging (USA) 120 – Loyal And Regal 51 (Royal And Regal   **73 ?**
(USA)) [1990 NR 1991 8m⁵ 10.1g⁴ 10.1m² 12m³ 11.9m 15.9d 12.1s] leggy,
workmanlike gelding: fifth reported foal: half-brother to modest 1m and 1¼m
winner Cool Run (by Deep Run) and fair sprinter Tax Roy (by Dublin Taxi): dam
winning selling hurdler: modest maiden: well below form in handicaps last 3
outings, though showed retains some ability on final one: should stay 1½m: visored
fifth outing: possibly reluctant early on sixth. *M. H. Tompkins.*

ALLEZ-OOPS   4 ch.f. Moulin 103 – Ever So Cool (FR) (Never Say Die 137) [1990   **35**
12s³ 10.2m 13.8m 10.2m* 8m* 10.6s⁶ 10f⁴ 12m⁴ 10m 1991 8s 12f 16.5m 12g a14g⁴
10g⁶ 9.9m 7.5f⁵ 12f³ 13.8m a14g] smallish, sturdy filly: poor handicapper: best form
at up to 1½m: acts on firm ground, probably unsuited by soft: inconsistent. *A. Smith.*

ALL GREEK TO ME (IRE)   3 b.g. Trojan Fen 118 – Do We Know (Derrylin   **59**
115) [1990 7v⁴ 1991 7v⁴ 8s 9d* 12.3d 12g⁵ 9.2d² 10g 10.5g] leggy, rather good-topped
gelding: quite modest performer: won handicap at Hamilton in April: should stay
further than 9f: acts on dead ground: winning hurdler. *C. W. Thornton.*

ALLIED FORCE   9 b.g. High Line 125 – Summer Madness 88 (Silly Season 127)   —
[1990 NR 1991 a8g a12g⁶ 12f 12f] ex-Irish gelding: lightly-raced handicapper since
1989, tailed off as 9-y-o: stays 1½m: acts on any going. *A. W. Denson.*

ALLIMAC NOMIS   2 b.g. (Feb 12) Daring March 116 – Game For A Laugh 72   **50**
(Martinmas 128) [1991 7f 8m] 1,950Y: leggy, angular gelding: third foal: brother to
4-y-o winning hurdler Good For A Loan: dam 7f and 7.6f winner, is out of half-sister
to very smart sprinter Great Bear: always towards rear in maiden at Yarmouth
(slowly away) and 22-runner seller at Newmarket. *N. A. Callaghan.*

ALLINSON'S MATE (IRE)   3 b.c. Fayruz 116 – Piney Pass (Persian Bold 123)   **91**
[1990 5f² 5m² 5m* 5m* 6f² 6m² 6m 1991 6d² 6m 7m² 7m³ 8m 6d 6m 6.1m 6f
7m⁶ 6m] small, robust colt: carries condition: moderate mover: fairly useful
handicapper: below form last 7 starts but shaped promisingly on occasions, staying
on from rear when sixth of 19 in £9,000 event at York: probably needs further than 6f
nowadays, and should stay 1m: acts on firm and dead ground. *T. D. Barron.*

ALL IS REVEALED   9 b.g. Welsh Pageant 132 – Senorita Rugby (USA) 86   —
(Forward Pass) [1990 16g 16d 16m² 14g 16.2m* 18m⁶ 1991 14m 12m 14m 18m] big,
rangy gelding: modest handicapper at 8 yrs: always behind in autumn, off course 15
months before reappearance: suited by test of stamina and a sound surface: goes
well with forcing tactics: best visored: bandaged last 2 starts. *D. T. Thom.*

ALL PRESENT (IRE)   3 b.g. Reach 122 – Mar Del Plata 80 (Crowned Prince   **52**
(USA) 128) [1990 NR 1991 10m 10.1m 11.5m 12g 12.1d⁶ 9.2s*] 4,000Y: workmanlike,
rather angular gelding: moderate mover: fourth reported living foal: half-brother to
2 winners by Julio Mariner: dam 1m winner out of half-sister to Averof and Falkland:

co-favourite, won handicap at Hamilton in November, always in touch and leading on post: stays 9f well: best effort on soft ground. *R. Akehurst.*

ALL THE GIRLS (IRE)   2 b.f. (May 14) Alzao (USA) 117 – Second Service (Red   **49**
Regent 123) [1991 5m³ 6g³ 6g³ 6g 6f⁵ 5m 5m⁶ 7m] neat filly: moderate mover: third reported foal: dam behind in varied company: poor maiden: well beaten in selling nursery at Catterick final start: best form at 6f. *M. Johnston.*

ALL THE JOLLY   3 b.f. Bay Express 132 – Whisper Gently 91 (Pitskelly 122)   **44**
[1990 NR 1991 7g 7m⁵ 6.1m] rangy filly: fourth foal: half-sister to plating-class 1m winners Mascalls Lady (by Nicholas Bill) and Spanish Whisper (by Aragon): dam Irish 9.5f to 1½m winner: plating-class maiden: best effort second start: sold 760 gns Ascot November Sales. *P. J. Makin.*

ALL THE KING'S MEN (IRE)   3 b.c. Alzao (USA) 117 – Hill's Realm (USA)   **86 d**
(Key To The Kingdom (USA)) [1990 8s² 8v* 9v² 1991 10g⁵ 9m³ 11.7g 8.1s 8m⁵ a11g³] small, stocky colt: moderate mover: fairly useful at 2 yrs, winning listed race at Milan: easily best effort as 3-y-o (including in claimers) when third of 5 in apprentice contest at Lingfield in September: should stay 1¼m: acts on good to firm ground and heavy: blinkered fourth outing. *P. F. I. Cole.*

ALLTHRUTHENIGHT (IRE)   2 ch.c. (Feb 24) Precocious 126 – Time For   **82**
Pleasure (Tower Walk 130) [1991 5g 5g³ 5m³ 5g* 5m⁴ 5d] 5,000Y: good-quartered colt: fourth foal: half-brother to a winner in Austria: dam twice-raced daughter of half-sister to Blushing Groom: generally progressive form: won 13-runner maiden at Wolverhampton in August: sweating profusely and very much on toes, best effort when ninth of 11 to Magic Ring in Cornwallis Stakes at Ascot in October: likely to be as effective at 6f: active sort. *L. J. Holt.*

ALMAASEH (IRE)   3 b.f. Dancing Brave (USA) 140 – Al Bahathri (USA) 123   **—**
(Blushing Groom (FR) 131) [1990 6m⁵ 1991 5.9h³] leggy, sparely-made filly: quite modest form in maidens at Newmarket and Carlisle: may prove suited by further. *H. Thomson Jones.*

AL MANHAL (IRE)   3 ch.c. Glint of Gold 128 – Hossvend (Malinowski (USA)   **—**
123) [1990 6m 7f 8m 1991 12m 12m a12g a12g] little form. *R. Hollinshead.*

ALMASA   3 b.f. Faustus (USA) 118 – Superfrost 49 (Tickled Pink 114) [1990 5m⁴   **83 d**
5f⁴ 5m⁶ 6m² 6g* 5f 7g 6g⁵ 7m⁴ 6m² 7f³ 6f* 5g² 6m⁶ 6m³ 6d 1991 7g⁴ 6d⁴ 6g⁴ 6d⁴ 6d 5.2f 5m 8m 6m 7m 6m⁶] sparely-made filly: poor mover: fair form at her best: easily best effort for some time, still well below best, in handicap at Lingfield final outing: worth another try at 7f: best 3-y-o efforts on dead going, but has won on firm: tends to drift right: bandaged behind third start, off-hind only on fourth. *J. C. Fox.*

AL MAWOUD (USA)   2 b.c. (Mar 25) Doulab (USA) 115 – Last Request 92   **57 p**
(Dancer's Image (USA)) [1991 6.1g*] sixth foal: half-brother to 7f winner Mawsuff (by Known Fact), and 9f and 1¼m winner Wishiah (by Persian Bold): dam won over 1¼m at 2 yrs: long odds on but green and lethargic, won 6-runner maiden at Nottingham in August, soon ridden along and staying on to lead 1f out: seemed likely to improve but wasn't seen out again: sold 8,200 gns Newmarket Autumn Sales. *Major W. R. Hern.*

ALMOST A PRINCESS   3 b.f. Alleging (USA) 120 – Rabab (Thatching 131)   **63 d**
[1990 7m 8m⁴ 7g 8d 1991 8g 10g⁶ 8g³ 8d² 10g⁴ 8.1g 8.3m 8g 8.1s] leggy filly: quite modest maiden: easily best 3-y-o efforts in claimers fourth and fifth starts: stays 1¼m: acts on dead ground: blinkered third and seventh starts: trained until after seventh by R. Simpson. *J. Akehurst.*

ALMULABBI   2 b.c. (Mar 4) Wassl 125 – Labwa (USA) (Lyphard (USA) 132)   **—**
[1991 7g 7g] compact colt: second foal: half-brother to 3-y-o Lamseh (by Thatching), successful in Germany: dam unraced: bit backward at least, well beaten in maidens at Newmarket in August: sold 4,600 gns Newmarket Autumn Sales. *B. Hanbury.*

AL MUTAHM (USA)   3 b.c. Green Dancer (USA) 132 – Musical Medicine (FR)   **86**
(Margouillat (FR) 133) [1990 NR 1991 10m³ 12m* 16.2g 13.3g⁵ 11.9g³ 12g] $87,000F, 75,000Y: tall, rangy colt: fifth reported foal: half-brother to 2 winners in USA: dam unraced half-sister to Prix Jean Prat winner Master Guy and the dam of Snurge: won maiden at Haydock in May: easily best effort in handicaps last 3 starts when creditable third at Haydock: should stay beyond 1½m: hung persistently left fourth outing: worth a try in blinkers or visor: sold to join J. Old 30,000 gns Newmarket Autumn Sales. *A. C. Stewart.*

ALNAAB (USA)   3 b. or br.c. Mr Prospector (USA) – Hail Maggie (USA) (Hail To   **86**
Reason) [1990 7m 7m² 7f* 7m* 7g² 1991 8d⁶] quite attractive colt: very useful form at 2 yrs, in Solario Stakes at Sandown final start: well below best in £7,400 contest at

Thirsk in April, only outing in 1991: should stay 1m: possibly needs a sound surface. *J. L. Dunlop.*

ALNASR ALWASHEEK 2 b.c. (Mar 8) Sadler's Wells (USA) 132 – Someone **109** p
Special 105 (Habitat 134) [1991 7d² 7g* 7m³] 175,000Y: lengthy, unfurnished colt:
second foal: half-brother to 3-y-o Someone Brave (by Commanche Run): dam 7f
winner stayed 1m, is half-sister to top-class miler Milligram out of 1000 Guineas
winner One In A Million: progressive colt: comfortable winner of Kempton maiden
in September: excellent third of 30 to Young Senor in Tattersalls Tiffany Highflyer
Stakes at Newmarket following month, soon travelling smoothly after slow start,
leading 2f out and running on well: will improve again, particularly at 1m + . *M. R.
Stoute.*

ALNASRIC PETE (USA) 5 b.h. Al Nasr (FR) 126 – Stylish Pleasure (USA) **61**
(What A Pleasure (USA)) [1990 9g 10g 7.6m 6g⁶ 10m 12g⁶ 8g² 8m* 8g 7g⁴ a8g* a8g⁴
a8g a8g* 1991 6g 7d 7m 7m⁵ 7f 9d 8m⁴ 8.3m 7m* 8g 7f 8m 8m* 8m 8m³ 6.9s]
rather leggy, good-topped horse: carries condition: has a round action: quite modest
handicapper: won at Leicester (landed gamble) in July and Redcar (amateurs) in
September: suited by 7f/1m: acts on firm going: found nothing when blinkered once:
has been bandaged: takes keen hold, and best held up as long as possible:
inconsistent. *D. A. Wilson.*

ALNEZ (IRE) 3 b.c. Alzao (USA) 117 – Nesreen (The Parson 119) [1990 NR 1991 —
a7g] IR 9,500Y: fourth foal: dam 1¾m and 2m winner in Ireland, also successful over
hurdles: well beaten in maiden at Southwell in July. *R. W. Armstrong.*

ALONE CYGNET 8 ch.g. Swan's Rock – Anona-Anona (Alcide 136) [1990 NR —
1991 13.6m 12f] strong ex-Irish gelding: tailed off in autumn claimers. *J. P. Leigh.*

ALOSAILI 4 ch.c. Kris 135 – Vaison La Romaine 100 (Arctic Tern (USA) 126) —
[1990 12m 10.1m³ 10.4m³ 8m⁵ 1991 10.8m] lengthy, rather angular colt: has a round
action: modest maiden: well beaten only start on flat in 1991 (April): suited by 1¼m:
acts on good to firm ground: winning hurdler. *B. Stevens.*

ALPHA HELIX 8 b.g. Double Form 130 – Daidis 66 (Welsh Pageant 132) [1990 **36** §
12g⁵ 13g 13m⁴ 13f⁵ 1991 13.8d 12g 12m⁵ 13f 15g⁵ 13m] deep-girthed gelding: not a
good walker or mover: poor handicapper at best nowadays: pulled up lame final start
(June): stays 15f: yet to show his form on soft going, acts on any other: has worn
blinkers, visored nowadays: best held up: temperamentally unsatisfactory. *J. S.
Wilson.*

ALPHARD 2 gr.c. (Mar 29) Kalaglow 132 – Julia Flyte 91 (Drone) [1991 8.2m*] **81** p
14,000F: angular, useful-looking colt: fifth foal: half-brother to a winner in Italy and
winning 3-y-o hurdler Flighty Guest (by Be My Guest): dam 2-y-o 6f winner, is
half-sister to very useful Miss Petard, dam of Rejuvenate: 2/1, won 4-runner minor
event at Nottingham in October by short head from Rajai, leading 2½f out and
holding on really well: will be suited by 1¼m + : looks a good prospect. *H. R. A.
Cecil.*

ALPHONSO 2 b.c. (Mar 28) Forzando 122 – Alice Parry (Kampala 120) [1991 5m³ **67**
5.9h³ 5f² 5g⁴] sturdy, lengthy colt: has scope: second foal: dam poor daughter of a
1½m winner: quite modest maiden: stays 6f: acts on hard ground: ran creditably
(despite drifting slightly left) when very much on toes: tail flasher. *M. Johnston.*

ALQAIRAWAAN 2 b.c. (May 17) Ajdal (USA) 130 – Clare Island 108 (Connaught **81**
130) [1991 7m 8.1g⁴ 7.9m³ 8m³] lengthy, well-made colt: has scope: sixth foal:
half-brother to 3 winners, including 3-y-o 10.5f winner (stays 2m) Clare Heights (by
Shirley Heights): dam half-sister to very smart 1½m horse Caliban, won Princess
Elizabeth Stakes: fair maiden: will be very well suited by 1¼m + . *J. L. Dunlop.*

AL RAMIS (IRE) 2 b.c. (Feb 13) Crystal Glitters (USA) 127 – Diamond Spring **83**
(USA) (Vaguely Noble 140) [1991 7g 8s² 7m 7.6d*] 62,000Y: close-coupled, quite
good-topped colt: has a round action: half-brother to several winners in France,
including middle-distance performers Didwana (by Nijinsky) and Droiture (by Far
North): dam French 1m winner from family of Lyphard and Nobiliary: fair performer:
won 6-runner maiden at Chester in October, leading close home despite wandering:
ran creditably in Tattersalls Tiffany Highflyer Stakes at Newmarket (slowly away) 3
weeks earlier: will be suited by 1¼m + : acts on good to firm and soft ground. *C. E.
Brittain.*

ALRAYED (USA) 3 b.c. Alydar (USA) – Life's Magic (USA) (Cox's Ridge **86**
(USA)) [1990 8m 1991 12m³] big, strong, rangy colt: good mover, with a light action:
dam champion U.S. filly: 6½ lengths third of 9 to Young Buster in maiden at
Newmarket in April, disputing lead long way and looking one paced: withdrawn at
Bath (split a pastern on way to post) 2 weeks later. *Major W. R. Hern.*

ALREEF 5 b.g. Wassl 125 – Joey (FR) 110 (Salvo 129) [1990 10m² 10m⁵ 12m 11.5m **48**
10m⁵ 10m³ 10m 10.6d³ 10g³ 1991 10.8g⁵ 10g⁶ 9.7f] sparely-made, rather dipped-
backed gelding: plating-class handicapper: off course nearly 6 months after second
start: worth another try over 1½m: acts on good to firm and dead going (probably
unsuited by very soft): ran well when blinkered or visored: has won for amateur:
won over hurdles in February, 1991. *T. Thomson Jones.*

ALSAARIYAH (USA) 3 b.f. Diesis 133 – Welden (USA) (Danzig (USA)) [1990 **67**
NR 1991 8m³ 8.3f²] leggy, useful-looking filly: first foal: dam unraced daughter of
half-sister to Nureyev (by Northern Dancer): quite modest form in maidens at
Warwick and Hamilton: should stay further: sold 5,600 gns Newmarket December
Sales. *A. A. Scott.*

ALSAARM (USA) 2 b.c. (Jan 29) Danzig (USA) – Lucky Lucky Lucky (USA) **96**
(Chieftain II) [1991 7g* 8m³ 7m⁶ 6m³] lengthy, good-quartered colt: has scope:
usually looks extremely well: third foal: brother to 3-y-o Aimaam, 6f and 7f winner
at 2 yrs: dam, successful from 7f to 9f, won Kentucky Oaks: fairly useful performer:
won minor event at York (shade coltish) in September, off bridle 2f out then staying
on strongly: best effort about 4 lengths sixth of 8 in Somerville Tattersall Stakes
won by Tertian at Newmarket: likely to stay 1¼m. *J. L. Dunlop.*

ALSAAYBAH (USA) 3 b.f. Diesis 133 – Secretarial Queen (USA) (Secretariat —
(USA)) [1990 7m* 1991 8g] rangy filly: bandaged off-hind, promising winner of
Chepstow maiden at 2 yrs: co-favourite, bumped 3f out and quickly eased in
handicap at Newbury in April, 1991: should stay 1¼m: looked sure to do better. *J. L.
Dunlop.*

AL SABAK (IRE) 3 ch.c. Commanche Run 133 – Sea Swallow (FR) 90 (Dan **44**
Cupid 132) [1990 6f⁴ 7g 8m 7.6v⁴ a8g 1991 a8g⁴ 12.3s 12m 12m³ 15.3m 12.2m 12d
12.3m⁵ 12g⁶ 12f⁶ 14.6m⁶] sturdy colt: maiden plater: should be suited by test of
stamina: seemingly unsuited by firm going, acts on any other: suitable mount for
apprentice: visored last 3 starts, running fairly well on first occasion: sold 3,600 gns
Newmarket Autumn Sales: inconsistent. *R. Hollinshead.*

AL SADI 2 ch.c. (May 5) Sharpo 132 – Ibtisamm (USA) 71 (Caucasus (USA)) [1991 **79** p
6m⁶] rather leggy colt: fourth foal: half-brother to 3-y-o 6f winner Dosha (by
Touching Wood): dam 1m winner: 20/1, burly and green, around 3 lengths sixth of 14
to Yousefia in maiden at Newmarket in October, leading 4½f then weakening and
edging right under pressure: should improve. *C. E. Brittain.*

AL SAHIL (USA) 6 b.g. Riverman (USA) 131 – Tobira Celeste (USA) (Ribot 142) —
[1990 NR 1991 10v] smallish, sturdy gelding: bad mover: very lightly raced on flat
nowadays: blinkered, behind in claimer only start 1991 (March): seems to stay 1¼m.
J. White.

AL SHANY 5 ch.m. Burslem 123 – Paradise Regained 41 (North Stoke 130) [1990 **64**
a7g⁵ a7g⁴ 9f 10v 10f⁵ 8m 9f² 10m⁵ 10m 9m 10f² 10f⁶ 10m³ 10f² 9m⁴ a10g³ a12g² 1991
10v³ 10f² 12d* 10.8m⁴ 12m² 12g⁴ 10.8g* 11.7g 11.4m 12g⁶ 11.8g] close-coupled,
angular mare: usually looks very well: quite modest handicapper: won at Brighton in
April and Warwick in June: effective at 1¼m to 1½m: acts on firm and dead going:
best without blinkers or hood: sometimes wears tongue strap: has started slowly:
genuine and largely consistent. *W. Carter.*

AL SHAQRAH (USA) 3 ch.f. Sir Ivor 135 – Emmaline (USA) (Affirmed (USA)) **76**
[1990 NR 1991 12m² 14g² 15.8f² 14s 16m⁴ 14.6m⁶] $225,000Y: rather leggy,
workmanlike filly: moderate mover: second foal: sister to fairly useful 1¼m and
1½m winner My Ballerina: dam winner at up to 9f in USA, is closely related to smart
middle-distance horse Hatim and half-sister to Super Asset and Bates Motel:
narrowly beaten, showing modest form, in maidens and minor event: ran fairly well
in handicap (but tended to hang left) penultimate start, poorly (visored) on final one:
stays well: acts on firm going (burly when ran on soft): not an easy ride. *A. C.
Stewart.*

AL SHAREEF 6 b.g. Shareef Dancer (USA) 135 – Tarpoon (USA) (Vaguely **50**
Noble 140) [1990 a12g a10g⁵ 9s* 10v² 9s 1991 10s 9s² 10d² a7g⁴ a8g⁶ 10.3d⁶ a10g
a13g] quite attractive gelding: has a round action: modest handicapper: well beaten last
3 starts: needs further than 1m and stays 1¼m: ideally suited by plenty of give in the
ground: has run in snatches: ran well for apprentice: has worn bandage near-hind. *D.
Burchell.*

AL SKEET (USA) 5 b.g. L'Emigrant (USA) 129 – Processional (USA) (Re- — §
viewer (USA)) [1990 8m 11.7g 9g 1991 10g 12g a12g] lengthy, quite attractive
gelding: poor handicapper nowadays: stays 1½m: acts on any going: ran poorly in
blinkers: probably irresolute. *A. Moore.*

ALTAIA (FR) 4 gr.f. Sicyos (USA) 126 – Haloom (Artaius (USA) 129) [1990 7.6d² **90**
7m* 7.3m* 8g⁵ 7m 7g³ 7m 7.3g 6m 6d³ 1991 6.1m² 7f 6m³ 6m³ 7g 5m² 6f² 6g* 5m
6g²] leggy, workmanlike filly: fairly useful handicapper: had very good 1991,
winning at York in August: seems ideally suited by 6f: acts on firm and dead ground:
usually makes running: sometimes bandaged near-hind: consistent. *W. J. Haggas.*

ALTERMEERA 3 br.g. Noalto 120 – Mac's Melody (Wollow 132) [1990 7g³ 1991 **71**
8.2d² 10g⁶ 8g 9.7m⁴ 7m² 7f 7.1m²] tall, rangy gelding: shows knee action: modest
maiden: creditable second of 16 in handicap at Sandown final start, running on
strongly from rear: will prove ideally suited by 1m+: acts on good to firm and dead
ground: gets on toes, and has taken good hold. *Mrs Barbara Waring.*

ALTERNATION (FR) 2 ch.f. (Feb 21) Electric 126 – Alanood 85 (Northfields **50**
(USA)) [1991 a8g³ a8g] sixth live foal: half-sister to winning sprinter/miler Aldahe
(by Dalsaan) and 2 winners abroad, including Norsk Oaks winner Alhayat (by
Godswalk): dam 1½m winner: 4 lengths third of 13 to Grog in maiden at Southwell:
well beaten in similar event at Lingfield later in December. *P. F. I. Cole.*

AL THERAAB (USA) 3 ch.f. Roberto (USA) 131 – Golden Lamb (USA) **81**
(Graustark) [1990 NR 1991 10m⁵ 8m* 10f⁵ 11.9g² 12m⁵ 10.3d 12d] $560,000Y:
angular, useful-looking filly with scope: sixth foal: sister to a minor winner in North
America and half-sister to another by Raja Baba: dam minor winner at 3 yrs, is sister
to dam of Sunshine Forever: fair form: won maiden at Wolverhampton in July: better
at 1½m than shorter: below form on dead ground: sweating (ran well) fourth start.
A. C. Stewart.

ALTO 2 ch.g. (May 12) Superlative 118 – Rose Music 86 (Luthier 126) [1991 6g] —
14,000F, 4,500F, 8,300 2-y-o: well-made gelding: has scope: sixth foal: half-brother
to 3-y-o 9.9f winner Rose Alto (by Adonijah) and 3 other winners here and abroad,
including fairly useful winners at up to 9.2f Milligan (by Tap On Wood) and
Jalmusique (by Jalmood): dam won over 7f and 1m: backward, well beaten in maiden
at Ripon in July: moved well to post: looked sort to do better but wasn't seen out
again. *J. G. FitzGerald.*

ALTOBELLI 7 b.g. Northern Treat (USA) – Imagination (FR) (Dancer's Image —
(USA)) [1990 a13g² a12g⁵ a12g* a12g² a16g* a13g⁴ 12f⁶ 14f a12g a12g² a12g⁵ a12g³
a13g⁵ a13g* a12g a16g 1991 a12g a13g4] leggy, good-topped gelding: poor
handicapper: stayed 2m: acted on any going: dead. *P. Mitchell.*

ALTO DANCER 3 ch.f. Noalto 120 – Marching Dancer (Niniski (USA) 125) —
[1990 NR 1991 12m 15g³] 800F: leggy, light-framed filly: second foal: dam of no
account: well beaten in maiden and seller: sold 1,150 gns Doncaster October Sales.
W. J. Pearce.

ALTO JANE 2 ch.f. (Mar 3) The Minstrel (CAN) 135 – An Empress (USA) **89** p
(Affirmed USA) [1991 7f* 7m4] strong filly: has scope: first foal: dam, winner of
graded races at 8.5f at 3 yrs and second in 9f Hollywood Oaks, is out of outstanding
Venezuelan filly Blondy: won 13-runner maiden at Salisbury in September, niggled
along at halfway when running on well to lead line: over 4 lengths fourth of 8, pulled
hard, one pace, to Rose Indien in minor event at Newmarket following month: will
probably be better suited by 1m: likely to improve again. *G. Harwood.*

Princess Royal Stakes, Ascot—
Always Friendly wins from Finance Dancer (right) and Peplum

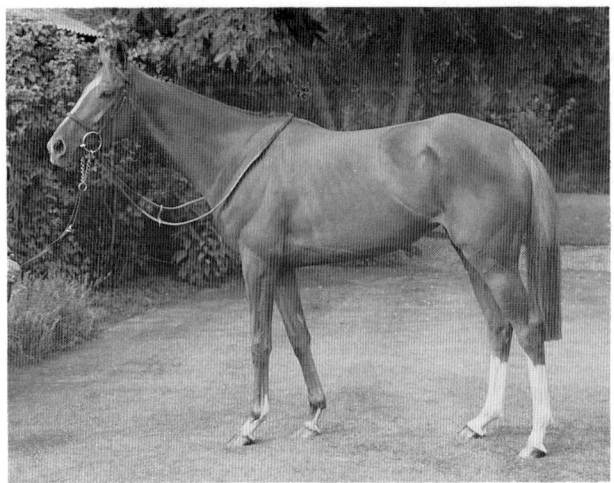

Mr Fahd Salman's "Always Friendly"

ALTON BAY 3 b.g. Al Nasr (FR) 126 – Dabbiana (CAN) (Fappiano (USA)) [1990 **75**
6m⁴ 6g⁵ 7f* 7m⁴ 7m 7m 1991 8.5g 10g 7g 7m⁴ 10g] leggy, close-coupled gelding:
modest performer: should stay 1m: acts on firm going: winning hurdler for Mrs D.
Haine: none too consistent. *A. A. Scott.*

ALTON BELLE 2 b.f. (May 1) Blakeney 126 – Oscilight 112 (Swing Easy (USA) **31**
126) [1991 7f 8.9m 8g] sturdy, angular filly: sister to modest 7f and 1m winner
Norfolk Breeze: dam sprinter: poor maiden. *Dr J. D. Scargill.*

AL-TORFANAN 7 b.g. Taufan (USA) 119 – Powder Box (Faberge II 121) [1990 —
a8g a8g* a7g 8f 8m 7.6m 7h² 8h⁴ 7g 7f* 8m⁵ 8f⁴ 8f 7.6m³ 8.3m² 7m⁶ 8f³ 7f⁵ 7f⁵ 7g
10f⁶ 1991 6m] leggy, good-topped gelding: carries plenty of condition: has a round
action: quite modest handicapper at 6 yrs: heavily bandaged and tailed off only start
1991 (April): suited by 7f to 1m: goes particularly well on top-of-the-ground: usually
visored: best racing up with pace: goes very well on switchback tracks. *M. C.
Chapman.*

ALWAYS ALEX 4 b.f. Final Straw 127 – Two High 89 (High Top 131) [1990 8m **45**
8g 8g 1991 10.1g 11.5g⁵ 11.8g⁶ 10.8m⁴ 12m³ 10.5g 12.5g 13.8m 11.5s²] smallish,
workmanlike filly: poor handicapper: stays 1½m: acts on good to firm and soft
ground: trained until after fourth start by Mrs B. Waring. *P. D. Evans.*

ALWAYS ALLIED (IRE) 3 b.g. Dalsaan 125 – Novesia (Sir Gaylord) [1990 **75**
a7g² 7m³ 7d² 8m⁴ 7s² 1991 10g³ 8m] modest maiden: creditable third in median
auction contest at Leicester: 50/1, never able to challenge in Britannia Handicap at
Royal Ascot: stays 1¼m: acts on good to firm ground and soft. *C. A. Horgan.*

ALWAYS A PRINCESS 2 br.f. (Apr 18) Prince Sabo 123 – Merchantmens Girl **43**
58 (Klairon 131) [1991 5m 5g⁵ 6g 5.7g 5d] tall, leggy filly: moderate walker and
mover: half-sister to several winning sprinters, including Lindsey (by Mummy's
Pet) and Barbezieux (by Petong): dam placed over 5f: poor form in maidens and
nurseries: sweating third start, mulish stalls final one: sold 2,000 gns Ascot
December Sales. *L. J. Holt.*

ALWAYS FRIENDLY 3 ch.f. High Line 125 – Wise Speculation (USA) (Mr **110**
Prospector (USA)) [1990 7m 1991 10s* 10f³ 11.9g² 14.6m⁴ 12d* 12g³] workmanlike

filly: has a markedly round action: very useful performer: successful in maiden at Sandown in July and Princess Royal Stakes (coming from rear to lead over 1f out and beat Finance Dancer 2½ lengths) at Ascot in October: fourth in Park Hill Stakes at Doncaster and third in St Simon Stakes at Newbury: stays 14.6f: probably acts on any going: consistent: reportedly remains in training. *H. Candy.*

ALWAYS READY 5 b.g. Tyrnavos 129 – Merchantmens Girl 58 (Klairon 131) 40 [1990 5g 5g 7m 5s 1991 5g 5d⁵ 5f² 5g⁵ 5m³ 5d* 5m⁵ 5g⁴ 5m³ 5f 5g⁶] strong, good-bodied gelding: poor handicapper nowadays: won at Lingfield in June: will stay 6f: acts on any going: usually visored or blinkered: sold 3,600 gns Ascot November Sales. *J. Balding.*

ALWAYS TREASURE 5 b.m. Lochnager 132 – Rosinka 62 (Raga Navarro — § (ITY) 119) [1990 a5g a5g⁴ a5g² a5g 5g 5g³ a5g 5m 1991 a5g³ a5g a6g a5g 5d a5g 8m 5g] lengthy, workmanlike mare: poor maiden: stays 6f: has been tried blinkered and visored: has hung left and looked unenthusiastic: one to treat with caution. *Miss G. M. Rees.*

AMAANI 3 ch.c. Kris 135 – Rowa 83§ (Great Nephew 126) [1990 NR 1991 10f⁶ 12f⁵ — 12m 9.7f 16m] sturdy colt: poor mover: has been tubed: third foal: half-brother to 1½m and 1¾m winner Barrish (by Wassl): dam best form at 1¼m but disappointing, is half-sister to Oh So Sharp (by Kris) and Roussalka: no worthwhile form, in sellers last 2 starts: broke out of stalls fourth intended outing: sold out of A. Stewart's stable 400 gns Newmarket July Sales after third start. *A. Moore.*

AMADEUS AES 2 b.c. (Jan 28) Dublin Lad 116 – Kind Lady 56 (Kind of Hush 77 118) [1991 5m⁶ 6g³ 6g² 6g 6f⁴ 7m² 7m⁶ 7m³ 7m² 7g² 7d a7g²] smallish, sturdy colt: has a roundish action: first foal: dam 2-y-o 6f seller winner probably stayed 1½m: modest maiden: very good second of 14 to Hadaad in nursery at Redcar on third-last outing: modest second on Lingfield equitrack in December: seems equally effective at 6f and 7f: visored last 6 starts: blinkered in Coventry Stakes fourth outing: usually looks well. *D. Morris.*

AMALFI 2 ch.f. (Feb 19) Sayf El Arab (USA) 127 – Good Natured § (Troy 137) 46 p [1991 7m 7m⁵] 1,000Y: workmanlike filly: first foal: dam temperamental maiden: poor form: better effort when staying-on fifth of 28 in seller at Redcar: will be better suited by 1m. *J. Pearce.*

AMARILLO 2 b.f. (May 1) Belfort (FR) 89 – Find The Sun 81 (Galivanter 131) 45 [1991 6d 5m 8.1s] unfurnished filly: fifth reported foal: half-sister to 11f winner Calton Colleen (by Sagaro): dam 2-y-o 7f winner stayed well and also won over hurdles: poor form in late-season maidens: best effort on good to firm ground. *M. W. Easterby.*

AMATORIAL 2 b.f. (Apr 11) Local Suitor (USA) 128 – Wolverene 114 (Relko 136) 67 [1991 7m² 7.5f⁵ 7m* 8m] big, leggy filly: has scope: has a markedly round action: half-sister to several winners, including useful middle-distance performers Shining Tor (by High Top) and Voracity (by Vitiges): dam game stayer: quite modest form: made most and ran on strongly to win maiden at Thirsk in August: should stay middle distances. *Sir Mark Prescott.*

William Hill Lincoln Handicap, Doncaster—Amenable's winning run continues; beyond him are St Ninian and Band On The Run

AMAZAKE 4 ch.g. Rousillon (USA) 133 – Kesarini (USA) 87 (Singh (USA)) [1990 —
8m 8.5g⁵ 10g 8m² 10.4g⁶ a8g⁵ 10m 10.6v⁶ a11g 1991 8m 8g 16.2d 10m 14.6m]
close-coupled, angular gelding: modest maiden at 2 yrs, on the downgrade
nowadays: should stay beyond 1m: acts on dead going: sometimes blinkered. *B. R.
Cambidge.*

AMAZE 2 b.g. (Apr 23) Natroun (FR) 128 – Entrancing 95 (Posse (USA) 130) [1991 **81** p
7g² 8.1g² 7m³] leggy gelding: second foal: dam 7f winner stayed 1m, is out of
half-sister to smart sprinter Laser Light: bandaged, placed in claimer at Leicester
and maidens at Chepstow and Lingfield: will probably stay 1¼m: may well prove
capable of better. *Lady Herries.*

AMAZING FEAT (IRE) 2 b.c. (Apr 26) Petorius 117 – Mountain Chase (Mount **62** p
Hagen (FR) 127) [1991 6m⁵ 6f⁴ 5m⁵] 6,200F, 8,000Y, resold 7,200Y: good-quartered
colt: easy mover: fourth foal: half-brother to 1½m winner Silk Dynasty (by Prince
Tenderfoot): dam never ran: caught eye in maiden at Haydock final start, travelling
comfortably in rear then keeping on well under considerate handling, despite
getting checked: should stay 1m: sure to do better. *Mrs G. R. Reveley.*

AMAZON EXPRESS 2 b.c. (Jan 30) Siberian Express (USA) 125 – Thalestria **53**
(FR) 91 (Mill Reef (USA) 141) [1991 a8g⁵ a7g⁵] leggy colt: second foal: half-brother
to 3-y-o School Teacher (by Never So Bold): dam won at 7f (at 2 yrs) and 11f (in
France at 4 yrs): plating-class form in late-year maidens at Lingfield: will stay 1¼m.
C. E. Brittain.

AMBASSADOR ROYALE (IRE) 3 gr.c. Pennine Walk 120 – Hayati 94 **84**
(Hotfoot 126) [1990 7g⁴ 7m 7f⁵ 8m⁵ 7.3g² 7m 1991 9g⁴ 10.2f* 10d⁴ 11.9m² 12d] big,
lengthy colt: fair performer: won maiden at Bath in September: very good second in
apprentice handicap at York, short of room final 1½f: stays 1½m: acts on firm going:
often wears dropped noseband nowadays, though didn't when running poorly final
start: blinkered twice at 2 yrs. *P. F. I. Cole.*

AMBER MILL 3 b.f. Doulab (USA) 115 – Millaine 69 (Formidable (USA) 125) **96**
[1990 5m² 5f² 5g² 5m* 6f* 5g⁶ 5m³ 6d 1991 5m* 6g⁵ 6m 5.1g² 5g 5m⁴ 5d 5d]
lengthy, quite good-topped filly: impresses in appearance: fairly useful performer:
won handicap at Sandown in April: ran very well in King George Stakes at
Goodwood and £10,700 handicap at Sandown fifth and sixth starts: should prove best
at 5f: acts on firm going, not on a soft surface. *J. Berry.*

AMBITIOUS VENTURE (IRE) 2 b.c. (Mar 23) Gorytus (USA) 132 – Aunty **75** ?
Eileen (Ahonoora 122) [1991 5g a6g⁴ 6d* 6m* 6d² 6d⁴ 8g⁶ 7.1m 7g] IR 8,000F: leggy
colt: has a round action: second foal: dam, unraced, from family of Mtoto: modest
performer: no bid after winning sellers at Thirsk and Doncaster in June: excellent
sixth in nursery at Goodwood after 2½ months absence: suited by 1m: acts on good
to firm and dead ground: edgy sort: sold 7,400 gns Newmarket Autumn Sales. *W. J.
Pearce.*

AMBUSCADE (USA) 5 ch.g. Roberto (USA) 131 – Gurkhas Band (USA) **58**
(Lurullah) [1990 8m⁵ 12m 16.2f² 14s⁴ 20m 16g⁶ 15g⁵ 16m² 18g⁵ 14m⁶ 1991 16.2g
16m⁴ 16.2f⁴ 17.6m 18f] lengthy gelding: fluent mover: plating-class handicapper,
still a maiden on flat: stays 2m: probably acts on any going: has found little off bridle:
has run well when blinkered: winning hurdler. *G. M. Moore.*

AMEERAT JUMAIRA (USA) 3 ch.f. Alydar (USA) – French Charmer (USA) **64**
(Le Fabuleux 133) [1990 NR 1991 8g 10g⁶ 10d⁵ 10.3g³] $575,000Y: sparely-made
filly: fifth foal: sister to Charmante, useful at up to 1m here later successful in
USA, and half-sister to 2 winners, notably top-class miler Zilzal (by Nureyev):
dam very smart stakes winner at up to 1¼m, is half-sister to dam of Polish Precedent:
quite modest maiden: best effort second start: tailed-off last of 3 at Chester in
July, apparently reluctant to race: stays 1¼m: wore dropped noseband. *M. R.
Stoute.*

AMEER DALHAM (IRE) 2 b.c. (Mar 18) Sure Blade (USA) 130 – Princess **76**
Nawaal (USA) 86 (Seattle Slew (USA)) [1991 7.1s² 7s³ 7m 8.2m² 8g] workmanlike
colt: first living foal: dam 8.5f and 9f winner: modest maiden: placed at Sandown,
Kempton and Nottingham (nursery, short-headed by Keep In Mind): will stay 1¼m:
acts on good to firm and soft ground: ran poorly at Chester and Goodwood: sold
22,000 gns Newmarket Autumn Sales. *Major W. R. Hern.*

AMENABLE 6 b.g. Kampala 120 – Kirin (Tyrant (USA)) [1990 a7g a8g³ a7g* **95**
1991 a8g a8g* a8g* a8g* a8g* 8d*] sturdy, compact gelding: fairly useful
handicapper: won at Southwell (2), Lingfield (2) and Doncaster (William Hill
Lincoln, impressively) early in 1991: suited by 1m: acts on any going: usually held

up: well ridden by A. Greaves: a credit to connections: looked certain to win more races but not seen out again. *T. D. Barron.*

AMERICAN EAGLE (IRE) 2 b.c. (Apr 27) Glenstal (USA) 118 – Prairie Saint 74 (Welsh Saint 126) [1991 6.1g³ 6m] 9,000F, 5,200Y: third living foal: dam, 2-y-o 5f winner: plating-class form in August maidens at Nottingham (very green) and Windsor: sold 2,200 gns Newmarket Autumn Sales. *B. A. McMahon.* **50**

AMERICAN HERO 3 ch.g. Persian Bold 123 – American Winter (USA) (Lyphard (USA) 132) [1990 7g⁶ 7m 1991 6g 10m² 8f* 10.2f⁵ 8.5m² 9.2d⁴ 8m 8.9m⁴ 8f* 8m² 8m] tall, quite good-topped gelding: modest handicapper: won at Carlisle in May and Newcastle in July: stays 8.5f: acts on firm going (ran fairly well on dead): usually front runner. *C. Tinkler.* **74**

AMETHYSTINE (USA) 5 ch.m. Barachois (CAN) – Amathus (Song 132) [1990 8m² 8m² 7f⁵ 7.6m³ 10m 9m 5.8f⁴ 7f* 8m* 8h³ 6h³ 7f 6m 1991 6g 7m 8f³ 7.1m* 8.5m 6.1d² 7v 7.1g* 8g 7.6m* 7g 5f 8g 6g 6.1d] sparely-made, angular mare: quite modest handicapper: won at Chepstow in May and July and Lingfield in August: lost her way after: needs further than 5f, and best at up to 1m: acts on firm and dead ground, well below form on heavy. *R. J. Hodges.* **69**

AMIDON REVE 3 ch.g. Starch Reduced 112 – Reno's Dream (Rupert Bear 105) [1990 7m 1991 7m 5.1d⁶ 6g] lengthy gelding: showed a little ability in claimer second start: beaten long way from poor draw in handicap 11 days later in June: should stay 6f. *B. Palling.* **—**

AMIGO MENOR 5 ch.h. Whistling Deer 117 – Chive (St Chad 120) [1990 6f 6m 6m* 6m⁵ 6d² 6m³ 6m² 6d 5m 6m² 6s* 6s⁵ 1991 6s 5g 6g* 6m* 6g 6m* 6f⁶ 6d⁴ 7g] leggy, lengthy horse: very useful performer: won handicaps at Lingfield in May and Royal Ascot (Wokingham Stakes, by 1½ lengths) in June and Group 3 event at Leopardstown in August: good fourth of 10 to Divine Danse in Group 3 event at Maisons-Laffitte: best racing up with pace over 6f: acts on any going: best blinkered: tough and genuine. *D. J. G. Murray-Smith.* **110**

AMIGOS 3 ch.g. Nordance (USA) – Hi Gorgeous (Hello Gorgeous (USA) 128) [1990 7m² 7d⁶ 1991 a7g³ 8g⁴ 7.6g 11.5s³ a10g* 9.7f² 9m⁶ 11.5g²] leggy gelding: modest handicapper: won at Lingfield in July, making most: stays 11.5f: acts on any going: refused to enter stalls third intended start: winning hurdler. *P. Mitchell.* **65**

AMOOD POINT 4 ch.g. Jalmood (USA) 126 – Nice Point (Sharpen Up 127) [1990 8.5g 9.1s⁵ 1991 10m 12f³ 12m⁵ 12h³ 13.6g 12.3f] lengthy, rather sparely-made **43**

Wokingham Handicap, Ascot—Amigo Menor goes one better than in 1990; Local Lass is a clear second ahead of Cantoris (one off rail)

gelding: poor handicapper: stays 1½m: acts on hard ground: effective visored or not. *J. Etherington.*

AMOUREUSE (IRE)   2 b.f. (Feb 27) Petorius 117 – Amorak 85 (Wolver Hollow   **53** § 126) [1991 5m 5d² 5m⁶ 5g* 6.1g² 6m⁵ 7g] IR 2,500F, 4,600Y: tall, leggy, plain filly: moderate mover: fourth foal: closely related to poor maiden Port Sharer (by Runnett) and half-sister to 1¼m winner Tap Dancing (by Sallust): dam won at 1m and stayed 1½m: plating-class form: won 10-runner maiden at Wolverhampton in June: ran badly final start: better suited by 6f than 5f: seems suited by some give in the ground: tends to sweat, and get on toes: twice very troublesome stalls and withdrawn: not to be trusted. *E. H. Owen jun.*

AMPHIGORY   3 b.g. Gorytus (USA) 132 – Peculiar One (USA) (Quack (USA))   **78** [1990 NR 1991 11.6m² 10.2f² 12m⁵] lengthy gelding: fluent mover: fourth foal: half-brother to useful 8.2f to 1½m winner Grand Tour (by Troy) and 1½m winner Hats High (by High Top): dam unraced out of sister to very smart 1977 American 2-y-o filly Stub: second in minor event at Windsor and maiden at Bath: visored, weakened quickly under pressure final start: courage under suspicion. *Lord Huntingdon.*

AMRON   4 b.g. Bold Owl 101 – Sweet Minuet (Setay 105) [1990 5s 5f 5g 6g a7g²   **71** 6m* 6g* 6g 6m⁵ 6f³ a6g⁴ a7g⁴ 6m 6g 6d 1991 5d* 5g 6d* 6m* 6g 6m 6m 6m³ 6m⁶ 6g⁴ 6d] sparely-made gelding: improved handicapper at 4 yrs: won at Doncaster, Ayr and Ripon in spring: best efforts at 6f: acts on any going: suitable mount for claimer. *J. Berry.*

AMTHAAL (USA)   2 b.c. (Feb 21) Mr Prospector (USA) – Maysoon 121 (Shergar   **75** 140) [1991 7d⁵ 7m⁴ 7m²] smallish, angular colt: has a smooth action: first foal: dam 6f and 7.3f winner third in Oaks, is daughter of Triple First, dam also of Oaks third Three Tails: modest maiden: best efforts when in frame at Leicester and Lingfield (made most) in October: will stay 1m. *M. R. Stoute.*

AMYNTAS (USA)   3 b.c. The Minstrel (CAN) 135 – Phaedra (USA) (Graustark)   **62** [1990 NR 1991 12m⁴ 8m³] big, unfurnished, angular colt: good mover, with a long stride: fourth foal: half-brother to winners in North America by Silver Buck and Irish Tower: dam won from 1m to 9f, including in California Oaks, and is half-sister to very smart American colt Barrera, successful at up to 9f: 7½ lengths third of 6 to 5/2-on shot Veriga in maiden at Newcastle in October, leading over 5f then hanging badly left: sold 5,800 gns Newmarket Autumn Sales. *M. R. Stoute.*

AMY'S STAR   5 b.m. Touch Boy 109 – Keep Believing (Sweet Revenge 129) [1990 8.5m 7d a8g 1991 10.2s 7.5f] lengthy, lightly-made mare: moderate mover: little sign of ability. *P. Wigham.*

ANAFI   3 b.f. Slip Anchor 136 – Linda's Fantasy 108 (Raga Navarro (ITY) 119)   **95** [1990 NR 1991 9.9f* 10.1f³ 14m* 13.3g4] 54,000F: leggy filly: third foal: half-sister to winning middle-distance stayer Lindross (by Ardross) and 9f and 10.8f winner Priceless Fantasy (by Dunbeath): dam won from 6f to 1m: won maiden at Beverley in August and moderately-run handicap at Newmarket in October: well-backed favourite, bit below Newmarket form and under pressure long way out when keeping-on fourth in handicap at Newbury 6 days later: will stay further. *H. R. A. Cecil.*

ANAGALL (USA)   2 ch.f. (May 24) Irish River (FR) 131 – Like A Charm (Pied   **81** d'Or) [1991 5g² 6g³ 5m² 5m4 5g³ 6m] $75,000Y: small, rather leggy filly: half-sister to numerous winners, including Herecomesthebride (by Al Hattab), stakes winner at up to 9f and later dam of very smart French miler Riverbride (by Riverman): dam minor winner at 2 yrs in USA: fair maiden: running-on fourth of 10 to Isdar in Windsor Castle Stakes at Royal Ascot: off course over 3 months, last (never a factor) in quite valuable nursery at Naas final start: should stay 1m. *J. S. Bolger, Ireland.*

ANAR (IRE)   2 ch.c. (Mar 28) Sharpo 132 – Only A Dream (FR) (Green Dancer   **62** (USA) 132) [1991 5m 5m⁵ 6g⁵ 7s⁵ 7m³ 7m 8g 7m] IR 42,000Y: leggy colt: poor mover: second foal: brother to fair 5f and 7f winner Shattered Dreams: dam, 11f winner at 4 yrs in France, is half-sister to 2 useful or better middle-distance performers in France and a daughter of a smart winner at up to 1½m in France: quite modest maiden: ran moderately in nurseries last 3 starts: should stay 1m: acts on good to firm and soft ground. *W. Carter.*

ANATROCCOLO   4 b.f. Ile de Bourbon (USA) 133 – Art Deco (Artaius (USA)   — 129) [1990 7f³ 10.2f⁶ 8g 10g 1991 7s 6.9f 7s] unfurnished filly: poor handicapper: stays 1m: acts on firm going. *C. A. Horgan.*

ANCHORAGE (IRE)   2 b.f. (Mar 15) Slip Anchor 136 – Cartridge (FR) 108 (Jim   — French (USA)) [1991 7g] 56,000F, IR 80,000Y: half-sister to 3 winners here and

Mr A. D. G. Oldrey's "Anchorite"

abroad, notably smart middle-distance stayer Brunico (by Bruni): dam 6f and 7f winner: 13/2, slowly away in 16-runner maiden at Kempton in September, and still behind when pulled up 3f out. *H. R. A. Cecil.*

ANCHOR INN 3 b.f. Be My Guest (USA) 126 – Quiet Harbour (Mill Reef (USA) 48 141) [1990 NR 1991 a10g a10g*] 40,000Y: half-sister to 3 winners, including quite useful Irish middle-distance performer Jazz Ballet (by Jaazeiro): dam lightly-raced half-sister to Coronation Cup winner Quiet Fling: 50/1, won claimer at Lingfield in January, staying on well to lead inside final 1f: tailed off in maiden there 2 weeks earlier: blinkered: sold in foal to Sharpo 10,500 gns Newmarket December Sales. *A. N. Lee.*

ANCHORITE 2 b.c. (Apr 28) Slip Anchor 136 – Elysian 94 (Northfields (USA)) 108 p [1991 6m³ 7f² 8.1f* 8g⁴] rather leggy, close-coupled colt: quite good mover: fourth foal: brother to 3-y-o Sea Goddess and half-brother to 1m winner Circe (by Main Reef) and winning hurdler Olympian (by High Line): dam 2-y-o 6f winner seemed to stay 1½m, is from excellent family: placed in listed race and a valuable maiden before winning 10-runner minor event at Haydock in September: very good 7 lengths fourth of 8, staying on never dangerous, to Seattle Rhyme in Racing Post Trophy at Doncaster 7 weeks later: will be well suited by 1¼m: useful already and likely to progress further. *P. T. Walwyn.*

ANDERSON ROSE 3 b.f. Kind of Hush 118 – Fille de Bourbon 71 (Ile de 35 Bourbon (USA) 133) [1990 7s a7g a8g a8g⁵ a7g a6g a8g 1991 a8g a8g⁶ 10d 12.3s 10m 15g* 15s 12g 13.8f³ a12g 11.9f⁵ 16m 12.3g 12m⁵ a14g] sturdy filly: has a round action: plater: won at Edinburgh (bought in 3,100 gns) in June: below form last 4 starts: stays 15f: acts on firm going: blinkered (pulled hard) penultimate outing: trained until after second by M. Chapman. *Capt. J. Wilson.*

50

ANDES 2 b.c. (Mar 3) Heights of Gold – Edna 92 (Shiny Tenth 120) [1991 6g⁶] big, **48** p
lengthy colt: has plenty of scope: fifth foal: half-brother to 6f and 7f winner Segovian
(by King of Spain) and a winner in Italy: dam soft-ground sprinter: 33/1 and green,
beaten around 10 lengths in 7-runner maiden at Goodwood in August: will improve.
W. G. R. Wightman.

AND ME 2 ch.f. (Mar 29) Don't Forget Me 127 – Nicola Wynn 83 (Nicholas Bill **36**
125) [1991 a6g a6g a6g⁵ 7g 7g a7g a8g] 2,400Y: leggy, rather sparely-made filly: first
foal: dam 1½m winner, is half-sister to dam of Brocade: bad maiden: best effort
(visored) in Newmarket seller fourth outing. *D. T. Thom.*

ANDRASSY (IRE) 3 ch.c. Ahonoora 122 – Anna Matrushka (Mill Reef (USA) **97**
141) [1990 6m* 1991 7m 8m² 7g³ 8.1g 9m² 8s²] small, sturdy colt: good mover: fairly
useful performer: placed in £11,200 handicap, minor events and apprentice race: ran
poorly in £9,000 handicap at Haydock fourth start, losing action and eased: will
prove suited by 1m +: acts on any going. *L. M. Cumani.*

ANDRATH (IRE) 3 b.c. Commanche Run 133 – Rathvindon 93 (Realm 129) **83**
[1990 7m⁵ 7f⁴ 7m 1991 8g⁵ 11.9g* 10m⁵ 14m] big, strong colt: easy mover: fair form:
made all in maiden at York in September: well below best in handicaps, tailed off
having set modest pace final start: will prove suited by further than 1¼m: acts on
firm going. *C. E. Brittain.*

ANDRELOT 4 b.c. Caerleon (USA) 132 – Seminar 113 (Don (ITY) 123) [1990 10g **—**
11.7m 14g² 14m 1991 12.3g 14.6g] leggy colt: poor handicapper: stays 1¾m: probably
best with give in the ground: has run creditably when blinkered. *K. White.*

ANDREW'S FIRST 4 br.g. Tender King 123 – Dame Kelly (Pitskelly 122) [1990 **64**
9f 10.2s⁴ a12g* a11g³ a12g² a11g* 1991 a11g² 10.8g] leggy, rather sparely-made
gelding: quite modest performer at 3 yrs: below best as 4-y-o (not seen out after
April), claimed out of T. Barron's stable £6,270 on reappearance: stays 1½m:
effective blinkered or not: claimer ridden: winning hurdler in January and February:
sold 7,600 gns Doncaster Spring Sales. *P. A. Blockley.*

ANDROBOTE (FR) 5 ch.g. The Wonder (FR) 129 – Andromeda (FR) (Dankaro **—**
(FR) 131) [1990 14g⁶ 16.2m³ 1991 16.5d] tall, leggy gelding: fair performer at best:
soundly beaten only start as 5-y-o (first run for around 17 months): well suited by
test of stamina: best efforts on an easy surface. *R. Curtis.*

ANDY JACK 2 ch.c. (Jan 24) Risk Me (FR) 127 – Gemma Kaye 91 (Cure The **70**
Blues (USA)) [1991 8.1g⁴ 7.1d⁴ 7d] 100,000Y: workmanlike colt: second foal: dam
maiden half-sister to Irish Oaks winner Olwyn: modest maiden: best effort at
Chepstow second start: will stay 1m +. *P. A. Kelleway.*

ANGEL BRIGHT 5 ch.m. Krayyan 117 – Godhood 86 (Green God 128) [1990 **47**
10.2f² 10m⁵ 10.2m 11m 9m 10f³ a8g² 10.6d 10g 1991 10m 10m 7m⁴] lengthy, angular
mare: poor handicapper, still a maiden: effective at 7f to 1¼m: acts on any going:
sometimes sweats: sold 1,000 gns Ascot May Sales. *D. A. Wilson.*

ANGEL FALLING 3 b.f. Scottish Reel 123 – Autumn Gift 65 (Martinmas 128) **—**
[1990 5m³ 6m 6s³ 6m⁴ 8d a8g⁶ a7g 1991 8m] leggy, angular filly: moderate mover:
poor maiden: should be suited by much further than 6f: acts well on soft ground (ran
moderately on all-weather). *E. H. Owen jun.*

ANGELICA PARK 5 b.m. Simply Great (FR) 122 – Rosana Park 83 (Music Boy **57**
124) [1990 8f 12.5g³ a12g⁶ 12m* 14m⁴ 12m 14g 17.6g* 14.6d⁶ 1991 a14g 14d 17m
14.6m³ 12g* 13.6m³ 12f3] stocky mare: plating-class performer: won claimer at
Newmarket in August: stays well: best form on a sound surface: winning hurdler
after. *J. Wharton.*

ANGEL LOVE (IRE) 3 b.f. Chief Singer 131 – Lumiere (USA) (Northjet 136) **70**
[1990 NR 1991 7d² 7.3g 7.6d³ 10g 10d 8g⁶ a12g⁴ a12g³ 14. 1f³ a12g² 18.2f⁴ 14.6m⁵] IR
26,000Y: big, lengthy, plain filly: first foal: dam French 9.5f winner at 4 yrs: modest
maiden: needs at least 1½m, but below form (in handicap, never able to challenge) at
2¼m: yet to race on soft ground, acts on any other: didn't handle track at Chester:
below form in blinkers: wore eyeshield on all-weather: sold 6,400 gns Newmarket
Autumn Sales. *P. A. Kelleway.*

ANGELO'S DOUBLE (IRE) 3 b.c. M Double M (USA) – Bebe Altesse (GER) **81**
(Alpenkonig (GER)) [1990 a7g² 7g 1991 8m³ 7.1g* a8g⁶] strong, workmanlike colt:
has plenty of scope: has a round action: won maiden at Haydock in October, always
in touch: favourite, prominent 6f in handicap at Lingfield month later: should stay
1m: bandaged in 1991. *J. H. M. Gosden.*

ANGELS ANSWER (IRE) 2 b.f. (May 12) Stalker 121 – Greek Music **66**
(Tachypous 128) [1991 5m 5m 6d³ 6m 5g² 5d² 5d* 5d² 5m³] IR 400Y, 5,200 2-y-o:

sparely-made filly: first foal: dam twice-raced close relative of smart 1¼m performer Galitzin: quite modest performer: won 5-runner maiden at Hamilton in July: off course 12 weeks, sweating and unimpressive in appearance, modest third of 5 in similar event at Pontefract (stiff task) final start: best efforts at 5f, but should prove as effective over 6f: easily best form with some give in the ground. *Mrs J. Jordan.*

ANGEL'S WING 2 ch.f. (Feb 19) Precocious 126 – Razor Blade 65 (Sharp Edge — 123) [1991 6f 7g 8m] 4,000Y: smallish, lengthy filly: moderate mover: seventh foal: half-sister to several winners here and abroad, including sprinter Keen Edge (by Good Times): dam 2-y-o 5f and 7f winner: well beaten in maidens, including auctions. *R. M. Whitaker.*

ANGEL TRAIN (IRE) 3 ch.f. Burslem 123 – Senama (FR) (Sanctus II 132) 40 [1990 5m⁴ 5m* 5g² 6g* 5m 7g⁴ 7g³ 6m 7d³ a8g² a7g³ a7g a7g⁴ a8g 1991 a8g⁶ 7d 8.2s 7.5g 8.2m⁴ 10f 7g² 8d 8f⁶] smallish, angular filly: very poor mover: plater: below best at 3 yrs: withdrawn lame once in mid-July and not seen out after August: suited by 1m: best efforts on a sound surface: blinkered fourth to sixth outings (better without): has been bandaged off-hind: inconsistent. *J. Parkes.*

ANGUISH (IRE) 2 b.f. (Apr 4) El Gran Senor (USA) 136 – Naval Light (USA) 42 (Majestic Light (USA)) [1991 6s⁵ 6f 8m 7g³ 7m] 72,000Y: leggy, angular filly: has a round action: second foal: dam, minor winner in USA, is half-sister to high-class American colt Polish Navy: poor maiden: should stay 1m: acts on good to firm ground. *N. A. Callaghan.*

ANJIZ (USA) 3 b.c. Nureyev (USA) 131 – Prayers'n Promises (USA) (Foolish 103 Pleasure (USA)) [1990 6m* 6m* 6m* 7d⁶ 1991 7m⁵ 5g 6m⁶ 6m 6m 5d] sturdy, good-quartered colt: carries condition: has a roundish action: useful on his day: easily best 3-y-o efforts when fifth in Free Handicap at Newmarket and sixth in listed race at Haydock: should have proved best at sprint distances: acted on good to firm ground: blinkered fourth and fifth outings: tended to hang second start: disappointing, and sent to join Brad Macdonald in California. *A. A. Scott.*

ANKARA'S PRINCESS (USA) 4 ch.f. Ankara (USA) 106 – Tales of Long Ago 64 (USA) (Raise A Cup (USA)) [1990 5d³ 6m 5m⁵ 6m³ 7g 6f⁶ 6d 7d 1991 5m⁵ 6m⁶ 5. 1d⁵ 6m⁶ 5.1m⁵ 5m⁶ 6.1d⁵] workmanlike filly: moderate walker and mover: quite modest handicapper: stays 6f: acts on good to firm ground and soft. *R. Hollinshead.*

ANLACE 2 b.f. (Apr 1) Sure Blade (USA) 130 – Ascot Strike (USA) 85 (Mr Pros- 81 P pector (USA)) [1991 7m*] rather leggy, useful-looking filly: third foal: half-sister to 3-y-o middle-distance stayer Strike Fire (by Touching Wood), 7.5f and 9f winner at 2 yrs: dam 1¼m winner: favourite, won 16-runner maiden at Leicester in October in very good style by 4 lengths from Silica, tracking leaders travelling strongly, leading under 2f out, soon clear: will stay at least 1m: sure to improve considerably and looks a most interesting prospect. *L. M. Cumani.*

ANNABELLE ROYALE 5 b.h. Anfield 117 – France (Milesian 125) [1990 10f³ 87 9g 8f⁵ 10.2m⁵ 7.6m* 8m⁵ 7m* 7g⁵ 7.6f⁴ 7.6m 7f* 7f* 7m* 10m² 8m 6m⁴ 7m 1991 8s 7g⁵ 8d⁵ 7m 7f* 8g⁵ 7m² 6m² 7f⁶ 6f* 7f* 7g 6f⁶] small, strong, lengthy horse: carries condition: moderate mover: fair handicapper: successful at Yarmouth (has won 5 times there) in June and August (2): effective at strongly-run 6f, and stays 1¼m: goes particularly well on top-of-the-ground: has worn bandages: has won when sweating: thrice successful at Lingfield (turf): tough and most genuine: a credit to his trainer. *Mrs N. Macauley.*

ANNACERAMIC 6 b.m. Horage 124 – Miss Redmarshall 80 (Most Secret 119) 67 [1990 NR 1991 6.9m* 8s³ 7f* 7.5f² 7.5f⁵ 7m 7.5f²] workmanlike mare: poor mover: quite modest handicapper nowadays: successful in June at Carlisle (claimer) and Redcar (seller, no bid): best form at up to 7.5f: probably acts on any going: effective visored or not. *R. M. Whitaker.*

ANNA MANANA 2 br.f. (Feb 28) Valiyar 129 – Blessit 79 (So Blessed 130) [1991 54 5m 5f³ 5g² 5m⁴ a5g⁵ 5s² 5g³ 6g² 6f³ 8.3g a6g³ a7g³] sturdy filly: second reported foal: half-sister to a poor maiden: dam sprinter: plating-class maiden: has run well in a selling nursery: stays 6f: probably acts on any going: blinkered fourth and final outings, visored eighth. *W. J. Pearce.*

ANNA PERENNA 2 b.f. (Feb 19) Alleging (USA) 120 – Anne de Guise (FR) 33 (Pharly (FR) 130) [1991 6m⁵ 7m⁶ 8.3g 8.1s] 1,100F: sturdy, rather angular filly: second foal: half-sister to a winner in Italy: dam unraced: poor maiden: blinkered final start: sold 700 gns Doncaster November Sales. *G. M. Moore.*

ANNA'S CAMEO 3 ch.f. Final Straw 127 – Traditional Miss 90 (Traditionalist — (USA)) [1990 NR 1991 8f 8.1s] leggy, sparely-made filly: fourth foal: half-sister to 6f seller winner First Tradition (by Sayyaf): dam, extremely tough and genuine, won 13 races over 7f to 1½m from 4 yrs to 7 yrs: slowly away, behind in median auction contest and claimer. *C. J. Hill.*

ANNAZIG (USA) 2 b.g. (Mar 7) Ziggy's Boy (USA) – Venielle (FR) (Arctic Tern (USA) 126) [1991 5g² 6g] $40,000Y: useful-looking gelding: not a good walker: has a long stride: third reported foal: half-brother to French middle-distance winner Folle d'Amour (by Foolish Pleasure): dam French maiden: good late headway in 4-runner minor event won by disqualified Magic Ring at Goodwood in May: last of 11 in maiden there following month: subsequently gelded: unruly stalls and withdrawn at Salisbury in August: sold 2,300 gns Newmarket Autumn Sales. *D. R. C. Elsworth.* **59**

ANNE BONNY 2 b.f. (Mar 28) Ajdal (USA) 130 – Sally Brown 120 (Posse (USA) 130) [1991 7m⁴] leggy, unfurnished filly: has scope: second living foal: dam won Ribblesdale Stakes and Yorkshire Oaks, and is half-sister to Untold: backed at long odds but green and troublesome at stalls, behind in 5-runner minor event at York (slowly away, soon pushed along, eased when beaten) in October: should stay 1¼m. *J. R. Fanshawe.* **— p**

ANNELI ROSE 4 gr.f. Superlative 118 – Red Rose Bowl (Dragonara Palace (USA) 115) [1990 6f a6g a8g⁴ a7g⁶ a6g² a6g* 1991 a6g⁴] poor handicapper: not seen out after February: best form at 6f: best form blinkered. *P. F. I. Cole.* **42 +**

ANNE'S BANK (IRE) 3 b.f. Burslem 123 – West Bank (Martinmas 128) [1990 7g* 6m³ 8.5g⁵ 7m⁴ 8g⁵ 6.3m⁵ 6d 1991 10d 7.8g 7m⁵ 7m 7.8g* 8.5g 7m³ 7m⁴ 6m 6g a6g] fourth foal: half-sister to 1987 2-y-o 7f winner Gunner's Hill (by Dara Monarch) and 1989 2-y-o 5f winner India's Twist (by Exhibitioner): dam winning Irish hurdler: modest maiden in Ireland: won maiden at Limerick at 2 yrs and handicap at Dundalk in July at 3 yrs: soundly beaten only outing here, first for over 3 months: stays 1m: acts on good to firm ground: sold out of J. Hayden's stable 2,300 gns Newmarket Autumn Sales after penultimate start. *A. Moore.* **77**

AN NOVA 7 ch.m. Anton Lad 103 – Bella Nova 58 (Right Boy 137) [1990 NR 1991 a8g] workmanlike mare: of no account. *A. P. Stringer.* **—**

ANOTHER BOB (USA) 3 b.c. Roberto (USA) 131 – Spicy Stuff (USA) 107 (Reviewer (USA)) [1990 8m² 8s* 1991 8s⁵ 10g⁴ 12g⁴ 11.9g² 13.3f³ 12m 12g⁶ 12.3d⁴ 14v] tall, close-coupled colt: moderate mover: useful performer: in frame as 3-y-o in listed Newmarket Stakes, Derby Italiano at Rome, listed race at Haydock and Ibn Bey Geoffrey Freer Stakes at Newbury: ran in Group 1 events on the Continent next 2 starts: well beaten in Chester minor event and Italian pattern contest last 2 starts: stays 13.3f: acts on any going: game. *M. A. Jarvis.* **107**

ANOTHER EPISODE (IRE) 2 b.g. (May 21) Drumalis 125 – Pasadena Lady 99 (Captain James 123) [1991 5s³ 5m⁵ 5m* 5m² 5m* 5d* 5g² 5g* 5g* 5m⁵] 3,600Y:

*Roses Stakes, York—the very speedy Another Episode
wins unchallenged from Fair Crack (right) and Regal Chimes*

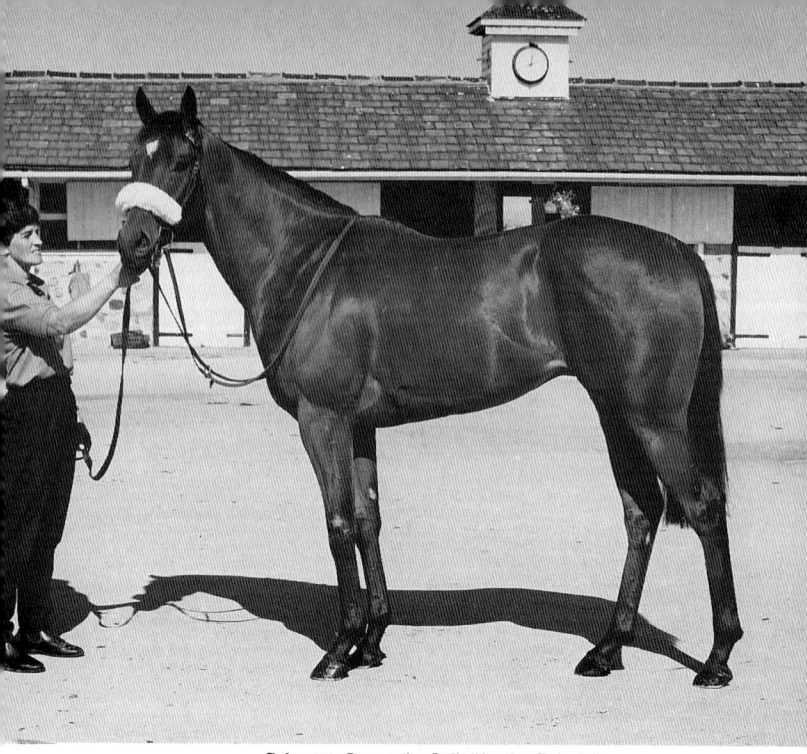

Palacegate Corporation Ltd's "Another Episode"

leggy, lengthy gelding: second foal: half-brother to 3-y-o 5f winner Sports Post Lady (by M Double M): dam never ran: useful sprinter: wide-margin winner in small fields for maiden at Catterick in May and minor events at Windsor in June: later successful at York in 6-runner listed race (by 2 lengths from Fair Crack) in August and 8-runner minor event (by ½ length from Miss Nosey Parker) following month: hung badly final start: very speedy: acts on good to firm and dead ground. *J. Berry.*

ANOTHER MARCH 5 b.g. Marching On 101 – River Sirene (Another River 89) **39** §
[1990 a8g 1991 6d 7m 6m 5g² 6m 5f 8g*] tall, leggy gelding: has a round action: poor handicapper: won at Edinburgh in June: effective at 5f to 1m: acts on firm and dead going: effective blinkered or not: has looked hard ride: not one to rely on: sold 3,100 gns Doncaster Summer Sales. *T. D. Barron.*

ANOTHER NICK 5 ch.g. Nicholas Bill 125 – Another Move 69 (Farm Walk 111) —
[1991 13v 1991 13d 10.5d] tall, lengthy, sparely-made gelding: very lightly raced and no worthwhile form. *J. M. Jefferson.*

ANOTHER NUT 2 b.f. (Mar 19) Blushing Scribe (USA) 107 – Manageress 74 **45** (Mandamus 120) [1991 5m 5f 5g⁴ 6m 7m a7g⁵ a6g a7g⁴] 1,600F: sparely-made filly: sister to 1988 2-y-o 6f seller winner Pacific Wave and half-sister to 7f and 1m winner Dealers Delight (by Ballacashtal): dam 6f winner at 2 yrs: poor maiden: has run in seller: possibly suited by 7f: has run well in a visor: has worn bandage near-hind. *P. D. Evans.*

ANOTHER RYTON 2 gr.g. (Apr 23) Another Realm 118 – Gemgem 54 **37**
(Lochnager 132) [1991 5f 5m 5f] 520Y: small, stocky gelding: third foal: brother to
3-y-o Indigo Jo: dam 7f seller winner: poor form in maiden auctions and a seller: not
seen out after July. *M. W. Ellerby.*

ANOTHER VINTAGE 2 ch.g. (May 19) Risk Me (FR) 127 – Meanieminymoe **47**
66 (Star Appeal 133) [1991 5f 6d 7.5f⁵ 7m⁵ a6g⁶] 23,000Y: quite attractive gelding:
first foal: dam ran 3 times at 2 yrs, third once over 7f: poor maiden: best effort when
sixth in claimer at Southwell in August final outing, despite slow start from poor
draw: blinkered previous 3 occasions: sold to join P. Cundell 820 gns Doncaster
October Sales. *M. H. Easterby.*

ANOTHER WARNING (IRE) 3 b.f. Horage 124 – Maggie Mine 85 (Native —
Prince) [1990 NR 1991 a8g] IR 8,000F: sister to fair 1988 2-y-o 5f winner Cherokee
Brave, closely related to smart 5f filly Storm Warning (by Tumble Wind) and fair 6f
and 1m winner Solway Winds (by Windjammer) and half-sister to 3 winners: dam
2-y-o 5f winner: weak 8/1, always behind in 14-runner maiden at Southwell in
November. *Lord Huntingdon.*

ANSWERSNOTPROBLEMS (IRE) 3 b.f. Runnett 125 – Gossip (Sharp —
Edge 123) [1990 NR 1991 7.1g 8m a6g] 7,000Y, 1,000 2-y-o: sturdy, lengthy filly:
seventh foal: sister to disappointing 1985 2-y-o 5f winner Running Edge and half-
sister to a winner abroad: dam showed no sign of ability: showed little in maidens
and (blinkered) Southwell claimer. *A. W. Denson.*

ANTAGONIST 4 b.g. Aragon 118 – Princess Story 64 (Prince de Galles 125) —
[1990 8g 7m⁶ 7m 10g² 8m⁶ 7f 1991 7g⁶ 10.8m 8g 7v 8.3g 10g] leggy, good-topped
gelding: poor handicapper nowadays, still a maiden: stays 1¼m: acts on good to firm
ground: has been tried blinkered and visored. *B. R. Millman.*

ANTEC EAGLE 3 ro.g. Music Boy 124 – Jenny Diver (USA) (Hatchet Man —
(USA)) [1990 NR 1991 10g] 13,000Y: fifth foal: half-brother to 1989 2-y-o 6f winner
Arbitrageur (by Ile de Bourbon), 8.5f seller winner Sukey Tawdry (by Wassl) and a
winner in Belgium: dam won twice in USA: visored, tailed off in claimer at
Nottingham in June: sold 820 gns Newmarket July Sales. *M. H. Tompkins.*

ANTE UP (IRE) 3 b.c. Sharpen Up 127 – Petillante (USA) (Riverman (USA) 131) **74**
[1990 7d⁶ 1991 8d⁶ 8m3 8m* 8m] tall, close-coupled colt: modest form: won 3-
runner maiden at Redcar in July: ran moderately in handicap following month: stays
1m: acts on good to firm ground: sold to join J. Akehurst 11,500 gns Newmarket
Autumn Sales. *L. M. Cumani.*

ANTICO NATIVO (IRE) 3 b.c. Be My Native (USA) 122 – David's Pleasure **67**
(Welsh Saint 126) [1990 NR 1991 8f 8g 7g 10g a12g3 14.1m a12g] IR 8,000F,
5,200Y: leggy colt: moderate walker: second foal: dam Irish middle-distance stayer:
worthwhile form only when third in maiden at Lingfield in September. *S.
Dow.*

ANTIGUAN FLYER 2 b.c. (Feb 22) Shirley Heights 130 – Fleet Girl **65** p
(Habitat 134) [1991 7g 7g⁶] lengthy, angular colt: brother to 7.6f and 9f winner
Darnelle and half-brother to several winners, including Oaks and Irish Oaks second
Bourbon Girl (by Ile de Bourbon) and Irish 4-y-o 1¾m listed winner Sleet Skier
(by Niniski): dam wide-margin winner of small races over 9f and 1½m in Ireland:
much better effort when sixth of 18 in maiden at Leicester in September, held up,
travelling keenly to halfway, not knocked about when beaten: sure to do better.
B. W. Hills.

ANTIL BOY (IRE) 2 b.g. (Apr 3) Salmon Leap (USA) 131 – Hollow Reef —
(Wollow 132) [1991 6f3 6g 7f 10m] 4,600F, 2,200Y: small, angular gelding: third foal:
half-brother to winning selling hurdler Reef Wind (by Tumble Wind): dam never
ran: no worthwhile form, including in sellers: trained first 2 starts by J. Norton: sold
1,000 gns Doncaster November Sales. *Mrs G. R. Reveley.*

ANTISAAR (USA) 4 b.c. Northern Dancer – Detroit (FR) 131 (Riverman (USA) **114**
131) [1990 10s3 10g* 10g* 10d* 12m2 12g 1991 10g2 12.5m 12m] close-coupled,
good-quartered colt: very smart performer at best: second as 4-y-o in listed event at
Saint-Cloud and Group 3 Prix Gontaut-Biron won by Muroto at Deauville: last of 7 in
Prix Foy at Longchamp final start: stayed 1½m: acted on good to firm ground and
dead: dead. *A. Fabre, France.*

ANXIOUS TIMES 3 b.f. Fast Topaze (USA) 128 – Maxencia (FR) **67**
(Tennyson (FR) 124) [1990 6f⁵ 7f* 6m⁶ 7m⁶ 6m 6m* 7m 1991 6m 5m3 6g 6g] rather
leggy, close-coupled filly: fluent mover: fair winner at 2 yrs: ran fairly well in April

handicap second start as 3-y-o: suited by 6f: sometimes edgy and sweating: sold 3,800 gns Newmarket July Sales. *N. A. Callaghan.*

A NYMPH TOO FAR (IRE)   2 b.f. (Mar 21) Precocious 126 – Faraway Places   **49** (Flair Path 122) [1991 5d 5.7f³ 6d 7g 7.1m a8g4] IR 13,000Y: angular, sparely-made filly: sixth foal: sister to useful 1988 Irish 2-y-o 6f and 7f winner Osmar and half-sister to 2 winners by Indian King, including sprinter Distant Ruler: dam French 7f winner out of sister to dam of good fillies Arctique Royale and Racquette: plating-class maiden: good fourth in Lingfield claimer final start: stays 1m: acts on firm ground, possibly unsuited by dead: sold 1,000 gns Doncaster November Sales. *Dr J. D. Scargill.*

ANYTIME ANYWHERE   4 b. or br.f. Daring March 116 – Martini Time 90   **61** (Ardoon 124) [1990 5f4 5d* 5m4 5g 5g 5d 5g 1991 5g² 5f 5m³ 5m] good-quartered filly: keen walker: has quick action: quite modest handicapper: best over sharp 5f: best efforts with give in the ground (acts on dead going). *M. R. Channon.*

APACHE CREEK (IRE)   3 ch.c. Rousillon (USA) 133 – Well Defined (Hello   — Gorgeous (USA) 128) [1990 NR 1991 10g] 18,500F: tall, lengthy colt: third foal: dam unraced daughter of Durtal, from excellent family: always behind in claimer at Newmarket in June: moved poorly down. *N. A. Callaghan.*

APACHE PRINCE   4 gr.g. Red Sunset 120 – Maxi Girl (My Swanee 122) [1990   **71** 12.2m6 14g 14m4 13m* 16m* 18g* 16.2m² 16f² 18g² 1991 17m4 18d 17.6m6 18g³ 16.5m 19m² 17.9f² 18.2f² 16.1m² 16m6 18.1m 13.6d6] rangy gelding: good walker and mover: modest handicapper: never placed to challenge final 2 starts: suited by thorough test of stamina: acts on firm ground, seems unsuited by dead: effective blinkered or not: tends to idle and looks a hard ride: has joined J. Ffitch-Heyes. *D. Morley.*

APOLLO KING   5 b.g. Indian King (USA) 128 – Mehudenna 77 (Ribero 126)   — [1990 a12g² 1991 14g] leggy, angular gelding: poor handicapper: stays 1½m: acts on firm and dead going: winning hurdler. *P. Mitchell.*

APPEALING TIMES (USA)   2 ch.c. (Feb 15) Timeless Moment (USA) –   **72** Appealing One (USA) (Valid Appeal (USA)) [1991 6m³ 5m² 5g4 6f² 6m5 7d a5g* a6g² a5g2] $22,000Y: smallish colt: first known foal: dam won 2 races at up to 7f at 2 yrs: sire smart sprinter: modest performer: successful (for claimer) at 2 yrs in late-year maiden at Lingfield: ran well afterwards: stays 6f: possibly unsuited by a soft surface: blinkered fourth and fifth outings. *W. A. O'Gorman.*

APPLE   2 b.g. (Mar 27) Balliol 125 – Crabtree (King of Spain 121) [1991 5s 5m6 5g   **55** 7m³ 6f6 8.2m] 1,500Y: lengthy, plain gelding: carries condition: shows knee action: first foal: dam unraced: plating-class maiden: best efforts fourth and fifth starts, latter occasion ridden by 7-lb claimer. *W. Holden.*

APPLEDORN   4 ch.f. Doulab (USA) 115 – Mythical Lady 86 (Track Spare 125)   **99** ? [1990 7m 7g 6g4 8m 8g 6m³ 7m² 7m³ 7m* 7g5 7g² 6g6 6m6 7v² 8g 1991 7g 7g³ 7.2g 7.3f 7g 7m5 7d] leggy, angular ex-Irish filly: has quick, moderate action: half-sister to 4 winners, including fairly useful performers Beeleigh (by Sallust), successful over 7f and 1m, and Petrillia (by Petorius), 5f winner at 2 yrs: dam won at 5f to 1¼m: fairly useful ex-Irish handicapper: won at Gowran Park as 3-y-o: appeared to show much improved form here when fifth to Bog Trotter in Group 3 event at Doncaster: failed to confirm that in £80,000 event later in September: stays 7f: acts on good to firm ground: often blinkered, not final 2 starts: virtually pulled up fifth one: trained at 3 yrs by D. K. Weld. *B. A. McMahon.*

APPLE PIP   5 ch.m. Takachiho 111 – Apple At Night (Carnival Night) [1990 NR   1991 a8g a6g 9s 7f] smallish mare: moderate mover: first foal: dam won over hurdles: well beaten in varied company: blinkered once. *B. Richmond.*

APPLIANCEOFSCIENCE   4 b.g. Bairn (USA) 126 – Moonlight Serenade 66   (Crooner 119) [1990 8d 7m 8f 10g² 10f6 10m4 10d 10g² 10.5g* 12m 1991 13.8f5 10g³ a12g] workmanlike gelding: moderate walker: plating-class handicapper: stays 1¼m: acts on good to firm ground: trained first 2 starts by G. Moore: blinkered last 2: inconsistent. *A. S. Reid.*

APPROACH THE BENCH (IRE)   3 b.c. Law Society (USA) 130 – Arguing 71   **116** (Pharly (FR) 130) [1990 7g³ 7g* 6.3g² 6d² 8d* 10s 1991 7g4 7g5 10g 8g 8g5 10m² 8m³ 7m² 7g 8d³ 9.7d5] second foal: dam, 13.8f winner later successful in Italy, is half-sister to Washington International winner Argument: successful in Juddmonte EBF Beresford Stakes at the Curragh as 2-y-o: ran well on several occasions in 1991, including when head second to George Augustus at Leopardstown, third at the Curragh to Star of Gdansk in Desmond Stakes and Julie La Rousse in listed race, and when fifth of 7 in Prix Dollar at Longchamp: stays 1¼m: acts on good to firm ground and dead. *J. E. Mulhern, Ireland.*

APRES HUIT 4 b.f. Day Is Done 115 – Ma Minti 62 (Mummy's Pet 125) [1990 — a6g² a5g* a5g² a6g² 5f² 5f 5f* 5.8f⁶ a5g 5.3h 5m³ a7g 5.8f 10.8f 6g a6g a5g 1991 a5g⁶ a 62 a7g⁶ a5g⁶ a7g a6g⁴ 5.1m a6g* 5.1m 6m] sparely-made filly: moderate mover: quite modest handicapper: form in 1991 only on all-weather: won apprentice event at Southwell in August: effective at 5f to 6f: best turf form on firm ground: below form when blinkered once: tends to hang. *Mrs N. Macauley.*

APRIL SHADOW 2 b.f. (Apr 8) Shardari 134 – X-Data 93 (On Your Mark 125) **40** [1991 6d 6m 5f] 5,400Y: leggy, angular filly: half-sister to several winners, including fair sprinter Dry Point (by Sharpo) and Irish 6f and 1m winner Omar Mukhtar (by Faraway Times): dam won over 5f and 6f: poor maiden: best effort at York second start: favourite, ran poorly at Beverley later in July: stays 6f. *C. W. Thornton.*

APSIMORE 4 ch.f. Touching Wood (USA) 127 – Balgreggan (Hallez (FR) 131) **67** [1990 12f³ 13.3m⁶ 10.1m 13.1m 14g 12f² 14m³ 1991 17.2g* 16.5d] sturdy filly: moderate mover: quite modest handicapper: won at Bath in October: stays 17f: form only on a sound surface: has run well when visored. *G. B. Balding.*

APTAKISIC (IRE) 3 b.c. Ahonoora 122 – African Doll (African Sky 124) [1990 **104** NR 1991 8f² 7.9g* 10m* 10d⁴] 320,000Y: quite good-topped colt: brother to 2000 Guineas winner Don't Forget Me and half-brother to a winning middle-distance plater: dam Irish 1½m winner: won maiden at York in September, unimpressively at 9/4 on, and £7,800 handicap at Newmarket in October, always front rank and keeping on gamely: good fourth of 5 to Mohican Girl in Newmarket listed race, leading 1m but hanging right and looking awkward ride: better at 1¼m than shorter: gave trouble at stalls third start. *L. M. Cumani.*

AQIQ 4 b.g. Shareef Dancer (USA) 135 – Miss Gris (USA) 120 (Hail The Pirates — (USA) 126) [1990 NR 1991 10.2m 11.5g⁶ 11.9g 11.8g 12m] big, workmanlike gelding: first foal: dam unbeaten in 10 starts in Italy, including 6 at 2 yrs and 11f Oaks d'Italia at 3 yrs, and close fifth in French Oaks: no worthwhile form. *J. R. Bostock.*

AQUAMARINE 2 ch.f. (May 14) Shardari 134 – Green Rock (FR) 86 (Mill Reef **51 p** (USA) 141) [1991 7m] big, rangy, unfurnished filly: has plenty of scope: third living foal: closely related to St Leger winner Toulon (by Top Ville) and half-sister to 1988 2-y-o 1m winner Greenovia (by Ahonoora): dam middle-distance winner, is sister to smart French middle-distance filly Green Reef and daughter of Prix Ganay winner Infra Green: backed at long odds though very green, not knocked about in mid-division of Newmarket maiden in October: will improve, particularly over middle distances. *B. W. Hills.*

ARABAT 4 b.c. Habitat 134 – Kalamac (FR) (Kalamoun 129) [1990 7g³ 7m² 8m* **59** 7.2d* 8g 1991 8d 7m 6g⁴ 8d 7m 7.1m⁶ 7g 5d] robust, attractive colt: quite modest handicapper: headstrong, and should prove best at 7f: acts on good to firm and dead ground: trained reappearance only by K. McCauley: inconsistent. *H. A. T. Whiting.*

ARABELLA JILL 2 b.f. (Apr 29) Aragon 118 – Crackerjill 37 (Sparkler 130) [1991 **83** 5m 5m³ 6.1d⁴ 6g⁴ 5m* 5m² 5.1m² 6.1m* 6m² 6g⁶] leggy filly: second reported foal: dam stayed 1m: fair performer: successful in nurseries at Folkestone in July and Nottingham (running on strongly) in September: ran really well in similar events at York and Newbury on last 2 starts: stays 6f: acts well on good to firm ground, not discredited on dead: has looked a difficult ride. *R. Hannon.*

ARABIAN BOLD (IRE) 3 br.g. Persian Bold 123 – Bodham 88 (Bustino 136) **90 p** [1990 7m³ 1991 10m² a12g* 11.7g*] leggy, quite attractive gelding: won maiden at Lingfield and handicap (comfortably made all) at Bath in September: should stay further: will progress again. *W. J. Haggas.*

ARABIAN KING 3 b.c. Sayf El Arab (USA) 127 – New Edition 72 (Great **74** Nephew 126) [1990 6d² 6g³ 1991 a8g² 6g⁴ 7.5g* 7m² 8m⁶ 7m³ 7f⁴ 7m³] work-manlike colt: modest handicapper, won best out after June: won maiden at Beverley in April: probably stays 1m: acts on firm going: bandaged behind sixth and seventh outings. *M. Brittain.*

ARABIAN SULTAN 4 b.g. Muscatite 122 – Church Bay 76 (Reliance II 137) **43** [1990 10.1m⁶ 10.1m⁵ 12.2f⁶ 10m 10g 1991 8.3g 10.1d 10.2g⁶ 10.1m 13d* 12.1m⁴] small, close-coupled gelding: poor handicapper: won (for first time) at Hamilton in July: stays 13f: acts on good to firm and dead ground: effective blinkered or not: prolific winning hurdler since joining M. Pipe. *J. White.*

ARAGONA 2 b.f. (Feb 14) Aragon 118 – Polly Worth 55 (Wolver Hollow 126) [1991 **41** 5.7m⁴ 5.7m 7g 7.1m] 4,200Y: leggy filly: second foal: dam, maiden, stayed 1m: poor maiden: well beaten in selling nursery at Sandown final start: sweating time before. *P. D. Cundell.*

ARAGON AYR   3 b. or br.g. Aragon 118 – Brig of Ayr 90 (Brigadier Gerard 144)   —
[1990 NR 1991 10g⁵ 9f⁴] compact gelding: poor mover: seventh foal: closely related to 1984 2-y-o 6f winner Ever So (by Mummy's Pet) and half-brother to 3 winners, including fair 5f to 7f winner Fag In Hand (by Music Boy): dam won from 1m to 11f at 4 yrs: plating-class form in claimers at Goodwood and Hamilton (claimed to join P. Monteith £12,505) in May. *J. M. P. Eustace.*

ARAGON COURT   3 b.g. Aragon 118 – Balatina 85 (Balidar 133) [1990 6m 7m   —
1991 10g 7m 8.2g a8g⁴ 7m⁶ 7m 7d⁶ 8m⁶] compact, good-topped gelding: has a very round action: no worthwhile form: blinkered sixth start. *J. Pearce.*

ARAK (USA)   3 b.c. Clever Trick (USA) – Twilight Flight (USA) (Quack (USA))   **83**
[1990 8.2d² 1991 10g⁵ 7g² 8m] rather leggy, quite attractive colt: has a long stride: fair form when second in minor event and (made most) Goodwood maiden: prominent early in Britannia Handicap at Royal Ascot: should prove best forcing pace at 7f or 1m. *R. W. Armstrong.*

ARALDO BLU (IRE)   3 b.g. Heraldiste (USA) 121 – Lisahunny (Pitskelly 122)   — §
[1990 5f 6d 5v² 5d² 1991 5s 6d 10m 5m⁶] neat, strong gelding: plater: no form in first half of 1991: should stay 6f: acts on heavy going: blinkered on reappearance: trained until after third start (virtually refused to race) by W. Pearce: unsatisfactory. *M. Johnston.*

ARANY   4 b.c. Precocious 126 – Bellagio 68 (Busted 134) [1990 6g⁴ 6m 7d⁵ 6m 7f **101**
8.5m² 8f⁵ 11s 8d* 9m 1991 8d 8g 8g⁵ 7.6d* 8.5f 7g² 7g 7m 8g 7g 7m 7d 8m 7.6d] lengthy, quite attractive colt: poor mover: useful performer at best: won £15,000 handicap at Chester (made all) in May and ran well in Group 3 events at Tipperary and Newmarket sixth and seventh starts: subsequently lost his form: stays 1m well: best on an easy surface: below form when visored and blinkered once. *M. H. Tompkins.*

ARATOS   3 ch.c. Night Shift (USA) – Sariza 79 (Posse (USA) 130) [1990 NR 1991   **83**
8.5f* 7g 7.6m⁴ 10g] strong, deep-girthed colt: impresses in appearance: good walker: has a fluent, long stride: first foal: dam, lightly raced at 3 yrs showing best form at 7f, is out of 1000 Guineas second Tolmi: fair form when impressive winner of Beverley maiden (hung left) in April and fourth in minor event (dropped away tamely) at Lingfield in June: last in £19,300 handicap at York and £7,000 handicap (took good hold in lead) at Newmarket: stays 8.5f: disappointing. *H. R. A. Cecil.*

ARAZI (USA)   2 ch.c. (Mar 4) Blushing Groom (FR) 131 – Danseur **135**
Fabuleux (USA) 106 (Northern Dancer) [1991 5m² 6g* 5g* 5.5g* 6g* 7m* 8d* a8.5f*]

Few horses achieve lasting fame through their performances as two-year-olds alone. To join the gallery of the famous they usually have to train on to win important races at three, no matter how good the form or impressive the victories at two. Whatever the future holds for Arazi, however, his name seems certain to be recalled as long as racing is talked about. His achievements as a two-year-old were exceptional and one striking victory in particular kindled the imagination of the racing public as much as any single performance by any horse of any age for a long time . . .

It's often said that moments of greatest sporting drama occur most frequently when they are expected least. In its short, nomadic history the Breeders' Cup had already provided some abiding memories: Piggott's dramatic victory on Royal Academy and Dayjur's cruel defeat at Belmont in 1990; Pebbles' superb win over a distance many thought she wouldn't stay at Aqueduct in 1985; Alysheba's unforgettable defeat of Seeking The Gold in the gathering gloom at Churchill Downs in 1988. And at Churchill Downs in November it provided perhaps the best of the the the lot. Arazi, Europe's champion two-year-old and the favourite at just over 2/1 but racing on dirt for the first time and seemingly uncomfortable from the kickback, set off down the back straight with only one of the thirteen other runners behind him and at least fifteen lengths to make up on his front-running market-rival Bertrando. But when Arazi found his stride he became proverbial poetry in motion, gliding past horse after horse with a surge of speed that was devastating in its execution. By the top of the turn Arazi had cruised through into second place; coming wide off the final bend he

58

Prix Morny Agence Francaise, Deauville—Arazi lands the odds

sailed past the vigorously-ridden Bertrando and into the lead; and in the four-hundred-and-eleven-yard stretch, where he drifted back to the inside rail, he was out on his own. His winning margin of six and a half lengths—it was officially returned as four and three quarters before being 'corrected' to five—was the longest in the eight-year history of the Juvenile: none of the previous winners had scored in such style, let alone from such an inauspicious position, or had to overcome the disadvantage of an unfamiliar surface and an outside draw on a track where the distance to the first tight bend is only seven hundred and fifty feet. As with all the other races on Breeders' Cup day the result of the Juvenile usually decides the destination of the divisional Eclipse Award: only Success Express in 1987 and Is It True (whose victim Easy Goer had already done enough to secure the title) in 1988 failed to end the year as recognized champions. Arazi's sparkling victory wasn't completely without disappointment, however. Some of its lustre was lost because the colt ran on the pain-killer bute which had been administered on the instructions of trainer Boutin (who also ran him bandaged behind), wary of exacerbating Arazi's knee problems. Arazi underwent surgery shortly after the Breeders' Cup to remove chip fractures from the top joint of both knees where bone spurs were forming and causing inflammation. The operation, a minor one by all accounts, was reported to be a complete success and after a month's recuperation Arazi was returned to France. Hopefully, his recovery will be a speedy and full one and won't prevent his showing his brilliance again in the forthcoming season.

Arazi's victory affected the Americans so profoundly that some commentators even predicted that he would become the first two-year-old since the legendary Secretariat in 1972 to be crowned 'Horse of the Year'. Since the American seasonal polls were inaugurated in 1936 only two other two-year-olds have achieved that distinction; Native Dancer in 1952 and Moccasin in 1965. The enormous kudos attached in the States to the title of 'Horse of the Year' isn't fully appreciated in Europe where an accolade of similar credibility doesn't exist. To earn the honour normally requires the building of a substantial record and a demonstrable superiority. Oddly enough Moccasin didn't even top the Experimental Free Handicap in her year—she was ranked fifth, 6 lb below Buckpasser—despite running up an eight-race unbeaten sequence. Native Dancer and Secretariat were widely recognized as outstanding two-year-olds, however, and headed their respective Free Handicaps by 7 lb and 4 lb after showing a dominance over their contemporaries that few two-year-olds have ever been able to match. Arazi is unequalled, however, in becoming the first two-year-old to head both the International Classification and the Experimental Free Handicap; and if the result of the Breeders' Cup Juvenile is an honest reflection of the merits of the American juveniles then his supremacy is more marked in the States than it is in Europe where he is clearly one of the best seen in the last twenty-five years. In the absence of any other collateral form it's very difficult to gauge exactly how good the American two-year-olds were. Widely-held opinion in the States had it that they weren't up to their usual standard, but Arazi's opponents included most of the protagonists from the best graded races. Second-placed Bertrando, who incidentally wasn't nominated to the Breeders' Cup and had to be supplemented at a cost of 120,000 dollars, was unbeaten in three starts and had annexed the Grade 1 Norfolk Stakes on his most recent outing by nine lengths; and three and a half lengths and more further back in the Breeders' Cup Juvenile came five other graded winners, one of whom, Tri To Watch, had won the Grade 1 Champagne Stakes last time up by seven and a half lengths, as well as three others who had finished placed in one or more such events. One of that trio, seventh-placed Pine Bluff, who was beaten around fifteen lengths by Arazi, reappeared at Aqueduct two weeks later and won the Grade 2 Remsen Stakes by five lengths from the Juvenile fourth Offbeat before going on to win yet another graded race; one of the previously-mentioned quintet, Dance Floor, came out and won a Grade 3 race over the Juvenile course and distance later in November by six lengths. The biggest drawback to Arazi's becoming 'Horse of the Year' was that he'd had just the one race in the States, but if dominance of an age group was the sole criterion then Arazi was a banker to emulate All Along and become only the second European-trained runner to achieve that accolade.

Had Boutin had his way Arazi might never have made it to the States. After the colt had lifted the Grand Criterium at Longchamp in October and consolidated his position as Europe's number-one two-year-old it was only at owner Paulson's insistence that Arazi ran in Kentucky, with a view to a tilt at the 1992 Kentucky Derby. Paulson, who had sold a half-share in the colt to Sheikh Mohammed prior to the Breeders' Cup for a sum reputed to be significantly more than the widely-reported five million dollars, clearly wasn't so far off the mark when after the Criterium, in answer to the question 'Is Arazi the best you've ever owned?,' he described him as 'the best *anyone* has ever owned'. Arazi certainly had a magnificent season in France. He won five pattern races, and became only the third two-year-old, following My Swallow in 1970 and Blushing Groom in 1976, to land the Prix Robert Papin, Prix Morny, Prix de la Salamandre and Grand Criterium in the same season. His form stood head and shoulders above that of any of his contemporaries and consistently had compliments paid to it from midsummer onwards: no fewer than *ten* horses whom he'd beaten handsomely at some stage or other in Europe went on to win pattern events. Arazi's sternest test in France appeared to lie, as a translation of the race title suggests it should, in the

Prix de la Salamandre, Longchamp—Arazi trounces Made of Gold

Ciga Grand Criterium, Longchamp—Arazi confirms himself Europe's best two-year-old, beating Rainbow Corner, Seattle Rhyme (rails) and St Jovite

Grand Criterium. The five opponents assembled against him had won eight of their fourteen races. The three-strong home challenge was spearheaded by the progressive Rainbow Quest colt Rainbow Corner who'd lost the Prix La Rochette and his unbeaten record on a stewards' ruling at Longchamp last time out; the overseas challenge consisted of the unbeaten Irish colt St Jovite, whose victories in the Anglesey Stakes and the Panasonic Smurfit Futurity Stakes entitled him to be considered as his country's leading staying two-year-old, and the British-trained Seattle Rhyme, an improving colt who'd won the listed Stardom Stakes comfortably after finishing second in the Solario Stakes and who was held in the highest regard by his astute trainer Elsworth. The quintet barely had Arazi ruffled. St Jovite was the first to try, setting a swinging gallop until, hard ridden, he was passed very easily by Arazi rounding the home turn; Seattle Rhyme, who'd been travelling smoothly on Arazi's heels, was the next to try, with a spirited challenge from the entrance to the final straight; but Arazi, who'd looked rather lethargic when he first came into the paddock but had bucked up considerably as the preliminaries progressed, was uncatchable. With his rider Mosse, who flew in from Hong Kong specifically to take the ride, needing only to shake the reins Arazi powered into an unassailable advantage with a furlong still to run; in the last two hundred yards horse and rider did no more than necessary to stroll home well ahead of Rainbow Corner whose late flourish deprived the subsequent comfortable Racing Post Trophy winner Seattle Rhyme of a hard-earned second place by a short head; St Jovite plugged on at the same pace to finish three quarters of a length behind in fourth followed by a gap of five lengths to the outsiders Code Breaker and Silver Kite. Arazi's three-and-a-half-length victory left no-one in any doubt whatsoever about the destination of the top spot in the International Classification. It was also the third successive year that Boutin had trained the official top two-year-old; he'd trained Machiavellian in 1989 and Hector Protector in 1990.

Arazi, coincidentally, undertook a very similar campaign to the one followed by Hector Protector in the previous season, its variants being that he contested the Prix du Bois and the Prix Robert Papin instead of the Prix de Cabourg. Unlike his stable companion, Arazi spoiled what would otherwise have been a flawless first-season record by losing his first race, the Prix d'Orgemont over five furlongs at Chantilly in May. Arazi gained swift revenge on the colt that beat him, Steinbeck, in the Prix du Bois at Longchamp five weeks later, having won the listed Prix La Fleche at Evry in between, turning the tables to the tune of over three lengths on top of a 4-lb penalty. Before July was out Arazi had beaten him again, and by further this time, in the Prix Robert Papin at Maisons-Laffitte where, despite losing ground at the start, he burst through with two furlongs to go, led shortly afterwards and sprinted home a length and a half clear with plenty in reserve from the July Stakes runner-up Showbrook. Arazi continued on the up in the Prix Morny Agence

61

Breeders' Cup Juvenile, Churchill Downs—a stunning performance on the dirt

Francaise at Deauville in August. None of the three opponents who took him on in what was a disappointing turn-out, considering the winning prize money exceeded £100,000, was able to match his acceleration from a furlong and a half out, and he passed the line with three lengths to spare over the Cabourg winner Kenbu and another three quarters of a length ahead of the subsequent Middle Park second Lion Cavern. At the finish of the Morny as well as the Robert Papin Arazi looked to have plenty of running left in him, and given the proximity of several quite stout elements in his pedigree it was no surprise to see him progress again when stepped up to seven furlongs in the Salamandre at Longchamp in September and then again when tried over a mile. Few could be found to oppose Arazi for the Salamandre—he started at 5/1 on—and he bolstered his growing reputation with a highly impressive victory over seven opponents some of whom, such as the Lanson Champagne runner-up Made of Gold, had useful and progressive form. Arazi travelled well within himself for the first five and a half furlongs behind the Cherry Hinton third Miss Bluebird and Made of Gold before unleashing a tremendous turn of foot that took him three lengths clear in a matter of strides and had increased to five at the line. In the weeks that followed, the merit of Arazi's performance was underlined time and time again: by the eve of the Grand Criterium the runner-up Made of Gold had won the Royal Lodge William Hill Stakes and sixth-placed Guislaine had taken the Prix d'Aumale; and not to be outdone fourth-placed Code Breaker went on to win the Prix Thomas Bryon and fifth-placed Cardoun took both the Prix Eclipse and the Criterium de Maisons-Laffitte.

Arazi (USA) (ch.c. Mar 4, 1989)	Blushing Groom (FR) (ch 1974)	Red God (ch 1954)	Nasrullah Spring Run
		Runaway Bride (b 1962)	Wild Risk Aimee
	Danseur Fabuleux (USA) (b 1982)	Northern Dancer (b 1961)	Nearctic Natalma
		Fabuleux Jane (ch 1974)	Le Fabuleux Native Partner

Arazi isn't an imposing colt to look at but is a more impressive mover, possessing a powerful, extravagant action. It was announced midway through the year that his sire Blushing Groom had been retired from stud duties on veterinary advice after failing to get any mares in foal in 1991; examinations

Mr A. E. Paulson's "Arazi"

revealed a growth in his abdominal cavity. Blushing Groom, who had been operating with only one testicle since 1988 after the other was removed because of a malignant seminoma tumour, possessed a record of the highest order both as a racehorse and as a stallion. He was champion two-year-old in Europe in 1976, and second only to Alleged in the International Classification the following season when he won two of his four races, including the Poule d'Essai des Poulains, and finished third to The Minstrel in the Derby. His lengthy list of top-class winners at stud includes Rainbow Quest, Nashwan, Blushing John and Al Bahathri; in all he's sired five classic winners and over seventy stakes winners from eleven crops of racing age. Arazi's dam Danseur Fabuleux comes from a first-rate family which invariably attracts the world's top buyers whenever any of its members come up for auction. Danseur Fabuleux was a useful if frustrating maiden who possessed the ability to finish second in the Group 3 Prix de Minerve over a mile and a half but also showed an inability to take full advantage of the easier opportunities that came her way. Arazi is her second winner from as many foals; her first River Sunset (by Irish River) won over six furlongs at Le Croise-Laroche as a two-year-old. Danseur Fabuleux was sold at the same Ralph C. Wilson Dispersal Sale at Keeneland in November 1989 that saw Arazi fetch 350,000 dollars as a foal (he was led out of the ring unsold at 300,000 dollars at Keeneland the following July, apparently rejected on account of a crooked off-fore knee) and her dam Fabuleux Jane fetch 800,000 dollars: in foal to Forty Niner, Danseur Fabuleux attracted the biggest bid of the trio, eventually falling for 1,400,000 dollars to Sheikh Mohammed who's put the resulting filly in training with Boutin for the coming year. Fabuleux Jane, a good middle-distance performer in France where she won the Group 3 Prix de Pomone and ran third in the Prix de Diane and Prix Vermeille, has produced six winners, most of them to Northern Dancer or one of his many sons, including Danseur Fabuleux's close relatives Fabuleux Dancer (by Nijinsky), a very useful winner at a mile and a half in France, and the minor two-year-old seven-furlong winner Jareer (by Northern Dancer) whose career on the racecourse never fulfilled the expectations that went with the 7,100,000 dollars he cost as a yearling. One well-known half-brother to Fabuleux Jane by Northern Dancer who did realize his exceptional early promise was Ajdal who achieved the status of champion sprinter in 1987 and into the bargain emulated his half-brother Formidable and half-sister Flying Partner, both Group 1 or Grade 1 winners.

Arazi's future remains unclear at the time of writing. The undisclosed terms of Sheikh Mohammed's half-share in the colt has led to uncertainty over where control of his racing future lies, but it seems probable that if he recovers speedily from his operation and comes through his prep races all right he'll bypass the Two Thousand Guineas and the Poule d'Essai des Poulains in favour of the Kentucky Derby which Paulson has a long-cherished ambition to win. Should Arazi win again at Churchill Downs then the most likely option would be not to travel to Epsom for the Derby but remain in the States and attempt to complete the triple crown (he may well stay a mile and a half round Belmont) which was last achieved in 1978 by Affirmed and which now carries the incentive of a five-million-dollar bonus. And if he fails . . . well, who knows? Exactly where he'll take his place among the gallery of stars will, hopefully, become much clearer in the next season. *F. Boutin, France.*

ARBORETUM (IRE) 2 b.f. (Jun 4) Green Desert (USA) 127 – Fear Naught 99 **82 p** (Connaught 130) [1991 6f⁵ 6.1f 7m] 48,000Y, resold 41,000Y: small filly: sister to very useful 3-y-o 7f winner Himiko and half-sister to 1½m winner Malipiero (by Persian Bold) and useful Irish winner (at up to 1m) Without Reserve (by Auction Ring): dam won Royal Hunt Cup: excellent fourteenth of 30, progress from 3f out until approaching last, to Young Senor in Tattersalls Tiffany Highflyer Stakes at Newmarket: ran moderately time before: better suited by 7f than 6f, and will stay 1m: will improve again. *R. Charlton.*

Tricity Bendix Series Six Chester Stakes, Chester—Arcadian Heights makes all

ARBUSHA (USA) 2 b.f. (Mar 31) Danzig (USA) – Lulu Mon Amour (USA) (Tom   **78** p
Rolfe) [1991 6m4] unfurnished filly: sister to very useful sprinter/7f performer
Nicholas, Irish 1m winner Danlu and a winner in North America, and closely related
to Irish 3-y-o 7f and 9f winner Gdansk Victory (by Danzig Connection): dam, winner
at around 1m, is half-sister to Nordance (by Danzig), smart stakes winner at up to
1m: 20/1 in appearance, 1½ lengths fourth of 14 to Yousefia in maiden at
Newmarket in October, soon behind and pushed along, then running on well up the
hill: will be suited by 7f: will improve. *Lord Huntingdon.*

ARCADIAN HEIGHTS 3 b.c. Shirley Heights 130 – Miss Longchamp 94 **111** p
(Northfields (USA)) [1990 NR 1991 12m 14.1f3 14.8g* 14g2 13.4m* 14.6m] lengthy,
good-topped colt with scope: did well physically: has a fluent round action: fifth foal:
half-brother to 1½m winner Jamin (by Teenoso) and 2 winners by Mummy's Pet,
including fair 1986 2-y-o 6f winner Le Favori: dam won at 7.2f and 1m at 3 yrs:
successful in smallish fields for maiden at Newmarket in June and listed race by 3
lengths from Secret Waters) at Chester in August, making virtually all: failed to
continue his progress in St Leger at Doncaster, but helped set probably too strong a
pace early on: stays 1¾m well: may prove capable of better. *G. Wragg.*

ARCADIAN PRINCESS 2 b.f. (Apr 2) Teenoso 135 – Top Shot 84   **—**
(Grundy 137) [1991 7.1m] 7,600Y: sturdy, lengthy filly: second foal: dam 1½m
winner, is daughter of Park Hill winner Reload, a half-sister to 1000 Guineas winner
Full Dress II: 33/1 and green, slowly away and always behind in 15-runner maiden
auction at Chepstow: likely to prove a middle-distance stayer. *Miss A. J. Whitfield.*

ARCANGUES (USA) 3 ch.c. Sagace (FR) 135 – Albertine 117 (Irish River (FR) **119**
131) [1990 10v 1991 9d* 10g* 10g2 12m3 12s3] third foal: brother to French
provincial 11.5f winner Afrique Bleu Azur: dam, French 1m and 9f winner also fourth
in 1¼m E. P. Taylor Stakes, is half-sister to Ashmore and Acoma: won maiden at
Longchamp in June and Prix Eugene Adam at Saint-Cloud in July: placed in Prix
Guillaume d'Ornano at Deauville and in Prix Niel Escada (¾ length behind Subotica,
having quickened clear early in straight) and Prix de Conseil de Paris at Longchamp:
stays 1½m. *A. Fabre, France.*

ARCHWAY (IRE) 3 ch.c. Thatching 131 – Rose of Jericho (USA) (Alleged (USA) **115**
138) [1990 6d4 1991 7g2 6g* 5m3 6g5 7g4 6d* 5d4 5d2] IR 50,000Y: well-made colt:
first foal: half-brother to leading 2-y-o Dr Devious (by Ahonoora): dam, unraced, is
out of half-sister to Critique: beat Mr Brooks in Greenlands Stakes in May and listed
race in September, both at the Curragh: placed in Dermot McCalmont Tetrarch
Stakes at the Curragh, King's Stand Stakes (visored, readily outpaced by Elbio) at
Royal Ascot and Prix du Petit-Couvert (favourite, promoted third) at Longchamp:

*Greenlands Stakes, the Curragh—Archway (right) gets up from Mr Brooks (blaze)
and Reference Light after missing the break*

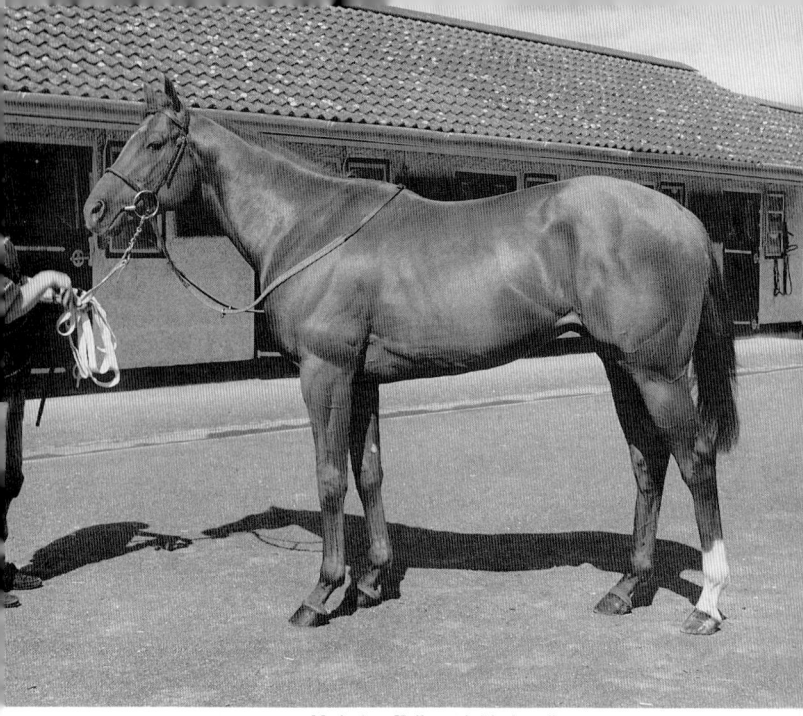

Mr Andrew Heffernan's "Archway"

very good strong-finishing fourth of 14 to Keen Hunter in Prix de l'Abbaye de Longchamp penultimate start: stayed 6f: went well on dead ground: retired to Castle Hyde Stud, Fermoy, fee reportedly IR 1,500 gns (Oct 1st, no foal no fee). *M. V. O'Brien, Ireland.*

ARC LAMP   5 b.g. Caerleon (USA) 132 – Dazzling Light 116 (Silly Season 127) **53** [1990 a6g a6g 5g 7m 1991 a6g² a6g a5g³ 6g 5m⁴ a5g² 5m a5g a6g 6g 5g⁴ 5g* 5m² 5s⁵ 5d a6g a6g⁵] workmanlike, angular gelding: plating-class handicapper nowadays: won at Catterick in October, making most: stays 6f: goes well on a sound surface: below form when blinkered once. *J. A. Glover.*

ARCTIC APPEAL (IRE)   2 b.f. (Mar 13) Ahonoora 122 – Arita (FR) **77** (Kronzeuge) [1991 5m* 5g 5f⁵ 6.1m² 6.1d³] rather sparely-made filly: third foal: half-sister to 1m and 9f winner Aribie (by Henbit): dam has been in Germany: fair perfomer: won maiden at Catterick in June: best effort when second of 12 in nursery at Nottingham: better at 6f than 5f: acts on good to firm and dead ground. *J. Berry.*

ARCTIC CIRCLE (IRE)   2 ch.c. (Apr 8) Northern Baby (CAN) 127 – High Quail **59** (USA) (Blushing Groom (FR) 131) [1991 7f 7m 8m 10m⁶] 24,000Y: leggy colt: second foal: dam, unraced, from family of Nishapour: progressive form in maidens: soon scrubbed along when sixth of 12 at Nottingham (stiff task, awkward stalls) in October: will probably stay 1½m. *Miss A. J. Whitfield.*

ARCTIC KEN   8 ch.g. Stanford 121§ – Peggy Dell (Sovereign Gleam 117) [1990 **—** NR 1991 a10g] sturdy gelding: carries plenty of condition: good mover: quite modest handicapper at 6 yrs: no subsequent form on flat: suited by 7f or 1m: unsuited by soft going, acts on any other. *B. Palling.*

ARCTIC OATS   6 ch.m. Oats 126 – Arctic Festival (Arctic Slave 116) [1990 NR   **60**
1991 16.2g⁴ 22.2m 11f] leggy, sparely-made mare: half-sister to 3 winning hurdlers,
including fairly useful stayer Singlecote (by Tycoon II): dam unraced: thrice-raced
mare: staying-on fourth in Beverley maiden in April: faced very stiff task next start:
likely to need test of stamina. *W. W. Haigh.*

ARCTIC SPLENDOUR (USA)   2 b.f. (Jan 25) Arctic Tern (USA) 126 – Field   **57**
Dancer 110 (Northfields (USA)) [1991 7g⁴ 8.1s⁴] rather sparely-made, quite attrac-
tive filly: second foal: half-sister to fairly useful, but inconsistent, 3-y-o Campestral
(by Alleged), 7f winner at 2 yrs: dam best around 1m, is out of Cheveley Park winner
Sookera: kept on when fourth in minor event at Warwick (green, slowly away) in
October and maiden at Edinburgh following month: will be well suited by 1¼m + . *P.
W. Chapple-Hyam.*

ARCTIC TEMPO (USA)   2 b. or br.c. (Feb 17) Arctic Tern (USA) 126 – Music   **57**
Lover (FR) (Luthier 126) [1991 8m 8m 8d] 5,000Y: unfurnished colt: half-brother to
3 winners in France, including 10.5f winner Loriquet (by Rheffic) and 1m winner
Love Music (by Margouillat): dam lightly-raced daughter of Prix Saint-Alary winner
Scala III: plating-class form in autumn: will be better suited by middle distances:
sold 4,400 gns Doncaster November Sales. *J. R. Fanshawe.*

ARDEN   7 b.g. Ardross 134 – Kereolle (Riverman (USA) 131) [1990 NR 1991 **100**
16.2m² 15.9m] close-coupled, good-topped gelding: usually looks very well: good
mover: one-time very useful performer: second in £7,100 event at Haydock: ran as if
something amiss in listed event final start (July): effective at 1½m and stays 2m:
acts on any going: inconsistent. *C. P. E. Brooks.*

ARDENT GROOM (IRE)   3 ch.g. Coquelin (USA) 121 – Arminiya (Roan   —
Rocket 128) [1990 a7g 7m⁵ 7d 7d a7g 1991 7s] dipped-backed gelding: poor maiden.
T. M. Jones.

ARDISIA (USA)   2 ch.f. (Jan 30) Affirmed (USA) – Princess of Man 104 (Green   **70** p
God 128) [1991 7.1m³ 8m 8.9d⁴] quite good-topped filly: easy mover: half-sister to
3-y-o Ausherra (by Diesis) 6f (at 2 yrs) to 11.5f winner, including Oaks Trial at
Lingfield, also to fairly useful 6f (at 2 yrs) to 1m winner Concorde Island (by Super
Concorde) and 2 winners in USA: dam won Musidora Stakes: best effort when
staying-on fourth of 19 in maiden at Wolverhampton: out of depth in May Hill Stakes
second outing: will stay 1¼m: likely to improve further. *P. F. I. Cole.*

AREMEF (USA)   2 b. or br.c. (Apr 16) Northern Baby (CAN) 127 – Bambina   **56** p
Linda (ARG) (Liloy (FR)) [1991 7m] $37,000Y: smallish, unfurnished colt: first
reported foal: dam Grade 1 winner in Argentina: green when in mid-division of
maiden at Leicester in October: will improve. *Mrs J. Cecil.*

ARE YOU SERIOUS   2 b.f. (May 15) Tinoco 80 – La Cazadora 51 (Faraway   **49**
Times (USA) 123) [1991 5s⁶ a5g⁵ 6g² 5.3m] small, angular filly: first foal: dam won
1¼m sellers: poor maiden: best effort second in claimer at Brighton: should prove
suited by further: sold 900 gns Ascot September Sales. *J. Ffitch-Heyes.*

ARFEY (IRE)   2 b.c. (Apr 10) Burslem 123 – Last Gunboat 50 (Dominion 123)   **61** p
[1991 8m] 20,000Y: workmanlike colt: fourth foal: half-brother to French 10.5f
winner James Star (by Star Appeal) and modest 1989 2-y-o 5.8f to 9f winner Bateau
Rouge (by Red Sunset), later successful over middle distances in listed company in
Italy: dam middle-distance maiden, is half-sister to Oaks placed Suni and Media
Luna: 16/1, staying on in mid-division of Leicester maiden in October: should stay
1¼m: should improve. *T. Thomson Jones.*

ARFUR'S TIPPLE   2 b.f. (Feb 12) Roaring Riva 103 – Jersey Maid 82 (On Your   —
Mark 125) [1991 5.7f 5m 8.1g 7m] 1,000F: sparely-made filly: second foal: half-sister
to 3-y-o 8.1f winner Mai Pen Rai (by All Systems Go): dam 2-y-o 5f winner stayed 7f:
seems of little account. *D. C. Tucker.*

ARGAKIOS   4 b.g. Busted 134 – Salamina 106 (Welsh Pageant 132) [1990 12m⁵   **73**
12m² 12m 12g⁴ 1991 12.1d⁶ 14.8d⁵ 18.5g⁴] leggy, lengthy, quite attractive gelding:
moderate mover: modest maiden: seems to stay well: acts on good to firm ground:
visored last 2 starts. *D. Burchell.*

ARIAL STAR   4 b.g. High Line 125 – Premiere Danseuse 72 (Saritamer (USA)
130) [1990 9m⁴ 10.6s⁵ 10.1m³ 11.7m* 12m² 14g⁶ 12.3g³ 12g⁴ 10m⁶ 1991 12.3s⁵]
good-topped gelding: moderate mover: modest handicapper: not seen out after
April: stays 1½m: acts on good to firm ground: winning hurdler in February and
April. *J. G. FitzGerald.*

ARIBIE   5 b. or br.m. Konigsstuhl (GER) – Arita (FR) (Kronzeuge) [1990 a11g
10.8m² 10f⁴ 9g* 10f⁶ 10.6s 8m 1991 10m 10d 12m 10.3d 8.2g 7.6g] plain mare: has

round action: poor handicapper, on the downgrade: stays 10.8f: acts on firm and dead going. *R. E. Peacock.*

ARINGAY (USA) 2 b.c. (Mar 6) Acaroid (USA) – Something Gay (USA) (Sir **44** Gaylord) [1991 7g 7m 6m] $10,000Y: sturdy, rather angular colt: half-brother to numerous winners, including minor sprint stakes winner Quiet Pansy (by High Steel): dam sprint winner: poor form, including in seller: wore severe noseband last 2 starts: bandaged near-hind on debut: sold 4,400 gns Newmarket Autumn Sales. *W. A. O'Gorman.*

ARISING (USA) 3 b.f. Secreto (USA) 128 – Assurgent (USA) (Damascus (USA)) **72** [1990 NR 1991 7g3 8m4 8g2] $120,000Y: rangy filly: half-sister to several winners, one in minor stakes: dam, minor winner at 2 yrs, is half-sister to Valdez, top class at around 1¼m: placed in maidens at Goodwood (hung left, best effort) in May and Ayr (beaten a neck) in July: didn't handle turn at Edinburgh: should be better suited by 1¼m. *J. H. M. Gosden.*

ARISTOCRATIC PETER (USA) 4 b.c. Sir Ivor 135 – Glimmer Glass (USA) — (The Axe II 115) [1990 10.1g 12g 17.1f 11.7h3 7f a7g2 1991 a8g a14g 10m 9m 9s] good-topped colt: has quick action: plating-class maiden at best as 3-y-o: no show at 4 yrs: stays 11.7f: has been blinkered: sold out of B. Preece's stable 1,750 gns Doncaster Spring Sales. *D. C. Jermy.*

ARIZAGA 2 ch.f. (Mar 9) Aragon 118 – Shooting Season 91 (Silly Season 127) **38** [1991 6g4 6g5] close-coupled, unfurnished filly: half-sister to several winners, including temperamental Out of Shot, winner at up to 1½m and disqualified third in Oaks, and stayer Full Choke (both by Shirley Heights): dam, placed at up to 1¾m, is sister to very useful stayers Shaft and Bunker: mulish leaving paddock, gave trouble at stalls and slowly away when keeping-on fourth of 9 in minor event at Windsor: favourite, below that form in maiden at Ayr later in July: probably needs further: sold 3,500 gns Newmarket Autumn Sales. *J. L. Dunlop.*

ARMAITI 3 b.f. Sayf El Arab (USA) 127 – Almitra (Targowice (USA) 130) [1990 6g **78** 7m 1991 6f2 7f2 7g* 7f* 7m2 7m 7g5 7m5 7.5f6 7d4 7d 7m3 7.1m5 7g2 7d] leggy, dipped-backed filly: modest handicapper: wandered when winning at Edinburgh (maiden) and Doncaster in May: very good second in £9,700 contest at Redcar in October: worth a try over further: acts on firm and dead going: game: joined C. Hill. *M. Johnston.*

ARMARAMA 2 ch.f. (Apr 9) Persian Bold 123 – Rossitor 78 (Pall Mall 132) [1991 **69** p 5m5 8s2] 54,000Y: good-topped filly: has scope: half-sister to several winners, including top-class middle-distance colt Kalaglow (by Kalamoun) and fairly useful 1m and 9f winner Gatchina (by Habitat): dam, winning stayer, raced and produced in error as Aglow: off course 5½ months, 1½ lengths second of 10 to Jasoorah in maiden at Yarmouth in October: will improve again, most probably over further. *C. E. Brittain.*

ARMED FORCE 4 b.g. Shernazar 131 – Skittish (USA) 73 (Far North (CAN) — 120) [1990 10m a12g5 10d 11.5g6 12m 16s 1991 12d a14g4 16.2g3 16.2d 16.4m6] tall, plain gelding: poor handicapper at best: seems to need good test of stamina: acts on good to firm ground. *C. A. Cyzer.*

ARMY OF STARS 6 b.h. Posse (USA) 130 – Starawak 68 (Star Appeal 133) **86** [1990 10f3 10f3 12f4 10m 10.5m 12m5 8g 10m6 10.4v4 12s2 1991 12.3s2 12g* 12s2 16g2 16.1m 16d 16.2g4 11.9g4] tall, useful-looking horse: impresses good deal in appearance: moderate mover: fair handicapper: won at Kempton in May: effective at 1½m, and stays 2m: acts on any going except seemingly heavy: blinkered once: has been bandaged behind: usually races up with pace: sold 8,000 gns Newmarket Autumn Sales. *C. E. Brittain.*

AROGOTO 3 b.g. Ahonoora 122 – Tikanova (USA) (Northern Dancer) [1990 6m6 **60** 1991 7v 8f2 7m3 a6g4] smallish, well-made gelding: has long stride: good walker: quite modest maiden: stays 1m: acts on firm going: blinkered last 2 outings, hanging and looking none too keen on final one: sold 4,600 gns Newmarket July Sales. *R. Charlton.*

AROKAT (USA) 3 gr.c. Caro 133 – Katsura (USA) (Northern Dancer) [1990 7g3 **95** 7g* 7g2 1991 9m5 10.4d3 8.2m3 12f] compact, workmanlike colt: has a fluent, round action: fairly useful performer: ran creditably first 3 starts in listed races at Newmarket and Chester (on toes) then 3-runner minor event at Haydock: in as pacemaker in Derby at Epsom: stays 1¼m: acts on good to firm ground and dead. *B. W. Hills.*

AROUND TOWN 10 br.g. Town And Country 124 – Scottish Circuit 87 (King's — Bench) [1990 NR 1991 12f 12d] rather leggy, workmanlike gelding: extremely lightly raced: bad maiden. *J. A. Bennett.*

ARRANVANNA 3 ch.f. Primo Dominie 121 – Smoke Creek 67 (Habitat 134) **113**
[1990 5g* 5m² 6g* 6g* 6s* 7.5g* 7v* 1991 8g² 8v* 8v³ 8g 8g⁶ 8g* 8v⁵ 8s 6v*]
7,000Y: big, lengthy filly: third foal: half-sister to untrustworthy 16.5f winner
Ardoran (by Little Wolf): dam maiden suited by 1¼m: won maiden at Phoenix Park
before transferred to Italy and unbeaten in 2 Group 3 events and 3 listed races as
2-y-o: victories in Premio Regina Elena and Premio Umbria and promoted third in
Premio Parioli, all at Rome, best efforts there in 1991: also won listed race at Milan
in September: fair 8 lengths sixth of 8 to Kooyonga in Coronation Stakes at Royal
Ascot, never able to challenge: stays 1m: acts on heavy going. *A. Renzoni, Italy.*

ARRASTRA 3 b.f. Bustino 136 – Island Mill 79 (Mill Reef (USA) 141) [1990 7m **79**
1991 10m² 10f4 11.7m4 13.1m² 14m* 14g³ 14m 14.6m] small, rather sparely-made
filly: modest form: favourite, won 5-runner maiden at Lingfield in August extremely
easily: good third at Kempton, easily best effort in handicaps subsequently: will stay
further: acts on firm going. *I. A. Balding.*

ARROW OF GOLD 2 gr.c. (Mar 9) Kalaglow 132 – Regal Decoy (Troy 137) — p
[1991 8.2m4] good-topped colt: second foal: half-brother to 3-y-o 1½m winner Sweet
Bubbles (by Dominion): dam Irish 1½m winner, is half-sister to Knockando (by
Kalaglow): 7/1 from 3/1 and edgy, soundly beaten when last in minor event at
Nottingham in October, never able to challenge, having been slowly away and
ducked right: went down well: should do better. *G. Harwood.*

ARSAAD (USA) 2 ch.f. (Apr 5) Topsider (USA) – Bar J Gal (USA) (Key To The **70**
Mint (USA)) [1991 6m 8g² 8.9d⁵] good-quartered, quite attractive filly: moderate
mover: fourth foal: sister to quite modest Sail and closely related to disappointing
3-y-o Balaat (by Northern Baby), fairly useful 1m winner at 2 yrs: dam second over
6f in USA, is half-sister to French 1m winner and very useful American middle-
distance stayer Properantes: modest form in Wolverhampton maidens won by All At
Sea and Taroob last 2 starts: stays 8.9f: acts on dead ground. *P. T. Walwyn.*

ART BLEU 4 ch.c. Legend of France (USA) 124 – Almyre (FR) (Wild Risk) [1990 **111**
12g4 11g6 11g² 12g* 12g* 1991 10.5g* 10g* 10g² 10.5g* 12m⁵ 12d] half-brother to
French 1m and 9f winner Albertine (by Irish River): dam won 3 times in France:
very useful French colt: successful in minor events at Saint-Cloud in April and
Longchamp in May and Group 3 La Coupe at Longchamp (beat Avec Les Bleus by
neck) in July: good fifth of 7 to Splash of Colour in Prix Foy at Longchamp: acted as
pacemaker (caused interference) in Ciga Prix de l'Arc de Triomphe there following
month: effective at 1¼m to 1½m: acts on good to firm ground. *E. Lellouche, France.*

ART CRITIC (IRE) 2 b.c. (Feb 7) Tate Gallery (USA) 117 – Point of View (FR) **46**
(Sharpman 124) [1991 6m 8.1m6] 6,000F, IR 20,000Y: smallish, good-bodied colt:
first foal: dam once-raced half-sister to dams of Lypharita (won Prix de Diane) and
Belmez: poor form: last in minor events at Windsor and Sandown (led 5f, tailed off)
week later in August: subsequently joined M. Heaton-Ellis. *R. Hannon.*

ART FORM (USA) 4 b.c. Little Current (USA) – Christi Dawn (USA) (Grey **77**
Dawn II 132) [1990 12m 10f 12m³ 14m 16.2d a14g* 18g² 17.4d 16m 16m⁶ 1991 a14g* a **84**
16g a12g* 12g* 14.1f* 16.5m⁵ 14.1g⁵ 18.8f* a16g* 20g⁵ 16m4 16.1m* 14m 17.2g
16m³ 18m a16g³ a12g a14g*] tall, angular horse: has a round action: fairly useful
handicapper: had fine season, winner 4 times on all-weather in 1991 (has won at
both Lingfield and Southwell), at Southwell final start: also successful on turf at
Leicester, Yarmouth and Warwick (2): effective at 1¾m, and stays 2½m: seems to
need a sound surface: tough. *C. A. Cyzer.*

ARTIC TRACKER (USA) 2 b.c. (Feb 8) Eskimo (USA) – Andy's Find (USA) **104**
(Buckfinder (USA)) [1991 7g* 7g* 7.1m³ 7m³] $39,000Y: smallish, sturdy colt: good
mover: first foal: dam unraced: sire (by Northern Dancer) won at up to 1m: useful
performer: well-backed favourite, impressive winner of maiden at Newmarket in
June and £9,600 event at Newbury in July: third in Group 3 Solario Stakes (beaten ½
length by Chicmond) at Sandown and Group 2 Laurent-Perrier Champagne Stakes
(looked very well, 6 lengths behind Rodrigo de Triano) at Doncaster: will stay 1m. *C. R. Nelson.*

ARTISTIC REEF 2 ch.c. (Apr 13) Claude Monet (USA) 121 – Kellys Reef 92 **92** p
(Pitskelly 122) [1991 5m 5g* 5g³] workmanlike colt: third foal: half-brother to quite
modest 7f winner Calypso Reef (by Cragador): dam sprinter: won 15-runner maiden
at Wolverhampton in September, making all and quickening on over 1f out: fine 3
lengths third of 6 to Tamim in listed race at Doncaster following month: may well
improve again. *G. H. Eden.*

ARTURIAN 3 b.c. Vaigly Great 127 – Aspark (Sparkler 130) [1990 5g³ 5d³ 5f4 6f³ **87** §
6f⁵ 5m² 5f² 5g4 5m* 5f³ 5g² 5m4 6s⁶ 5d4 1991 6g 6m³ 5m² 6m* 6m⁵ 6g 6m 6g⁵ 6g 8f
7g⁶ 7.6m 6m³ 6f 7d 6m 6m*] lengthy colt: keen walker, has a quick action: fair

handicapper on his day: won at Newmarket (£19,100 event) in May and Lingfield (by short head, raced virtually alone) in October: suited by 6f: acts on firm going: best in blinkers, and when held up: visored eighth to tenth starts: has given trouble at stalls: sometimes on toes: sold 28,000 gns Newmarket Autumn Sales: not one to rely on. *R. F. Johnson Houghton.*

ARVIDA (ITY)   2 br.f. (Jan 27) Big Reef 110 – Fuchsia Artaius (Artaius (USA) 129) [1991 7g³] small, rather sparely-made filly: first known foal: dam, listed winner in Italy, is daughter of half-sister to top 1960 2-y-o colt Typhoon: gave trouble at stalls when remote third of 5 in maiden at Yarmouth in June: moved moderately down. *B. Hanbury.*   —

ARYLH (USA)   3 b.f. Lyphard (USA) 132 – Riviere Enchantee (FR) (Riverman (USA) 131) [1990 6m² 6d* 1991 7g³ 6g* 8m 7m] lengthy, rather angular filly: third in handicap (best effort) at Newmarket then landed odds in minor event (edged left) at Leicester in May: ran moderately in quite valuable handicaps (had flu final start) and not seen out after July: should prove suited by further than 6f: possibly suited by an easy surface. *A. C. Stewart.*   **87**

ARZANNI   4 gr.c. Darshaan 133 – Astara 83 (Nishapour (FR) 125) [1990 10m⁴ 10m* 10.1m* 12g² 12m* 12m 16m* 1991 14g* 20g² 18m6]   **115**

On his final start as a three-year-old, Arzanni had shown himself to be a promising young stayer. The step up in trip from middle distances had seemed very much in his favour as he beat the Cesarewitch winner Trainglot convincingly by three lengths in the two-mile listed George Stubbs Stakes at Newmarket. He had progressed to such a degree since his debut in a Newbury claimer in mid-June that he went into winter quarters a possible successor to the Gold Cup winner Ashal. Sadly, in early-May Ashal died from a peritonitis-related illness, having suffered a torn intestine. At the time, he was being prepared for his reappearance in the Polo Mints Yorkshire Cup, and it was in this race that Arzanni stamped himself as one to beat at Royal Ascot in 1991. The field at York was up to standard, and included the first and second from the Insulpak Sagaro Stakes, Teamster and Shambo, the Ormonde Stakes winner Per Quod, and Great Marquess, who had won the Jockey Club Cup the previous autumn. Held up in a race run at a sound pace, Arzanni was still travelling strongly with half a mile to run and, after quickening to lead over a furlong from home, he forged clear to beat Shambo by three and a half lengths. It looked as if there was better still to come. The 13/8 favourite for the Gold Cup, Arzanni was somewhat fractious throughout the preliminaries, so much so that the trainer's assistant took over the job of leading him in the parade. But he ran very well. The key point in the race came just after the field had straightened up, where Trainglot was sent for home. A couple of lengths behind, Indian Queen went through a narrow gap between Retouch and Warm Feeling, whilst Arzanni, who was tracking Indian Queen, was switched round Warm Feeling, losing about a length in the process. Once back on an even keel, Arzanni quickened well to challenge Indian Queen, but could never quite

Polo Mints Yorkshire Cup, York—Arzanni wins impressively

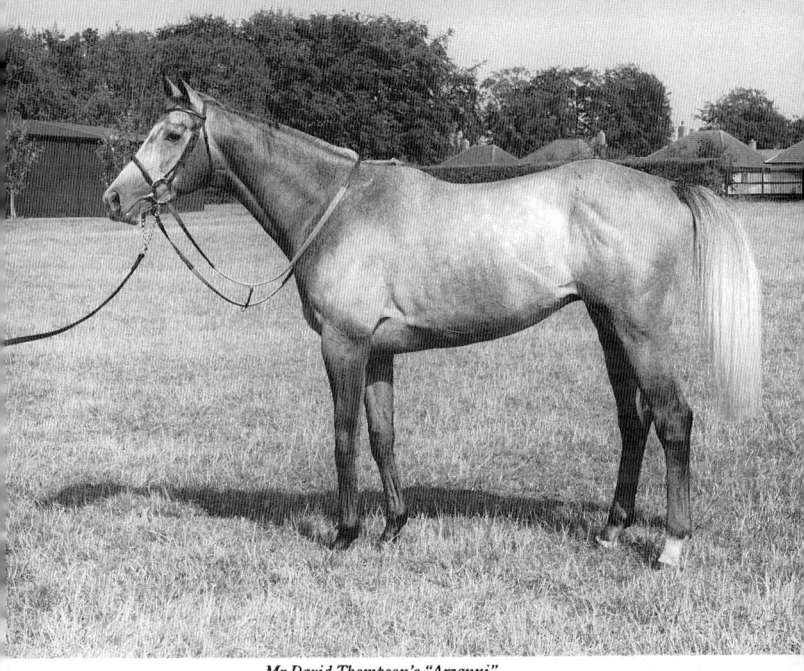

Mr David Thompson's "Arzanni"

get his head in front and the mare was always holding him in the last fifty yards. There is no doubt that Arzanni lost more ground two furlongs from home than the neck by which he was beaten, but we don't feel disposed to criticise Dettori. Not knowing for certain that Warm Feeling would weaken in time, and sitting on the favourite in the Gold Cup, he made sure his horse got a clear run. Besides, Indian Queen rallied very gamely when challenged and it is not certain that Arzanni would have won even with a trouble-free passage. Shortly after Ascot Arzanni was announced an intended runner for the Goodwood Cup, but Cumani subsequently stated that the horse's exertions in the Gold Cup had taken a lot out of him, and he wasn't seen out again until the Doncaster Cup in September. The 11/8 favourite, he couldn't get to grips with the eventual winner Great Marquess early in the straight, then faded in the final furlong and a half to finish sixth of eight. About a month later it was announced that Arzanni had injured a tendon and been retired.

Darshaan had a quieter year than in 1990, with Arzanni and Kotashaan, winner of the Group 3 Prix La Force over a mile and a quarter at Longchamp, his only pattern winners. Arzanni is the second and final foal of Astara, who died in 1987. She showed fair form, winning over seven furlongs as a juvenile and over eleven and a half furlongs the following year. Astara's half-sister Crepellana was top class: she won the Prix de Diane in 1969 on only her third start and also finished second, beaten a nose by Saraca, in the Prix Vermeille. The next dam Astana, winner of the Prix du Conseil Municipal by six lengths, was a half-sister to the Prix du Jockey-Club winner Philius. Further back in the pedigree, the fourth dam Souryva is a half-sister to the dual Arc winner Corrida and produced not only Theano (dam of six winners from seven foals, the non-winner throwing an Irish Oaks winner) but also Pharyva who herself

71

produced eight winners including the Derby winner Galcador and Poule d'Essai des Pouliches winner Galgala.

```
                    ┌Darshaan      ┌Shirley Heights   ┌Mill Reef
                    │ (br 1981)    │  (b 1975)        │Hardiemma
                    │              │Delsy             │Abdos
Arzanni             │              └ (b or br 1972)   └Kelty
(gr.c. 1987)        │              ┌Nishapour         ┌Zeddaan
                    │Astara        │  (gr 1975)       │Alama
                    └ (gr 1980)    │Astana            │Arbar
                                   └ (b 1956)         └Theano
```

Arzanni, a big, lengthy, quite attractive colt but a moderate mover, never raced on a surface softer than good. He showed equally good form at a mile and three quarters and two and a half miles and possessed a bright turn of foot for a stayer. He will stand for a fee of £800 (1st October terms) at the Cobhall Court Stud, Herefordshire, where for many years Celtic Cone, who also won the Yorkshire Cup and was second at Ascot, was the prime attraction. *L. M. Cumani.*

ASAASY (USA) 2 b. or br.c. (Feb 9) Danzig (USA) – Carduel (USA) **63** p (Buckpasser) [1991 7g⁶] sixth live foal: brother to smart 6f (at 2 yrs) to 1m winner Always Fair: dam, winner at up to 1m, is half-sister to smart Irish 1m/1¼m performer Punctilio and from family of Gay Fandango: carrying condition, beaten around 10 lengths in mid-division of minor event won by Badie at Kempton in September: moved moderately down: will stay 1m: will improve. *M. R. Stoute.*

AS ALWAYS (IRE) 3 ch.f. Hatim (USA) 121 – Red Magic (Red God 128§) [1990 **62** 6m 6f³ 6m 6d 8m 1991 10g 8f 10m 13.1f⁵ 14g² 16.2f* 18.5g² 16g³ 15.4f 16m⁶] good-topped filly: easy mover: quite modest handicapper: won at Beverley in July: never going well final start: stays well: acts on firm going: tried to make all last 4 starts. *G. Lewis.*

ASERBAIDSCHAN (GER) 6 ch.m. Dschingis Khan – Askania Nova (Sharpen — Up 127) [1990 NR 1991 8f] plain German-bred mare: burly and well beaten in Carlisle claimer in May, only run on flat here. *P. Monteith.*

AS GOOD AS GOLD 5 ch.g. Oats 126 – Goldyke 63 (Bustino 136) [1990 NR **35** 1991 12.1d⁴] robust, workmanlike gelding: very lightly raced: backward in handicap in October: should be suited by a test of stamina. *G. B. Balding.*

ASH AMOUR 4 gr.f. Hotfoot 126 – Loving Doll 72 (Godswalk (USA) 130) [1990 **35** 7g 8g⁵ 10f 10f³ 10f² 9g 10m³ 10d* 10g³ a12g⁶ a13g 1991 a12g 10.8m⁶ 10m 12g⁵ 14.1f⁴ 14d 11m 12f⁴ 12g a12g 10m⁵ 12.3g 10.1s⁶ 9.7s⁵] sparely-made filly: poor handicapper: stays 1½m: probably acts on any going: twice below form when blinkered: has carried head high and hung badly left. *R. J. R. Williams.*

ASHDREN 4 b.c. Lochnager 132 – Stellaris (Star Appeal 133) [1990 7g* 8.5m 7f² **85** 7g² 6m⁶ 7m⁵ 7d³ 7m 7d 100 1 6o⁷ 7m 7ᵢᵢ⁶ 0ᵦ⁶ 7ᵦ⁰ 3ᵢᵢᵢ 0ᵦ⁴ 6d³ 6ᵦ 6m 6t⁵ 6m⁶ 7m 8.1s²] angular colt: good walker: moderate mover: fair handicapper: won at Ripon in July: effective at 6f to 1m: probably acts on any going: effective visored or not: swishes tail: largely consistent. *A. Harrison.*

ASHGROVE CHERRY 3 b.f. Creetown 123 – Aldington Cherry (Legal Eagle **52** 126) [1990 6m 5f⁵ 5g⁴ 5m 1991 5g² 5m² a5g³ 6d⁵ 5m² 6m 6f 6f³ 6.1m 5g 5d] leggy, good-topped filly: has a quick action: plating-class maiden: stays 6f: best efforts on top-of-the-ground: hung left throughout on ninth outing: slowly away last 2: flashes tail. *B. A. McMahon.*

ASHKHER (IRE) 2 br.c. (Feb 6) Mister Majestic 122 – Sweet Princess (Prince **53** Regent (FR) 129) [1991 5d 6m⁶ 5d⁴ 5m⁵ 6g 7g] 17,000F, 22,000Y: strong, close-coupled colt: carries condition: half-brother to several winners, including 1½m winner Far Too Much (by Windjammer): dam unraced sister to useful filly Brightelmstone: plating-class maiden: best effort fourth of 13 at Windsor in June: showed nothing in nurseries last 2 outings: sold 4,000 gns Newmarket Autumn Sales. *C. J. Benstead.*

ASHTINA 6 b.g. Tina's Pet 121 – Mrewa (Runnymede 123) [1990 5m 5m 6d 5m **76** § 5g³ a6g* a7g⁵ a6g⁴ 1991 5f⁵ 5.8d 6v* 6g⁵ 5d⁵ 5d] leggy, good-topped gelding: modest handicapper: won at Kempton in June: best at sprint distances: acts on any going: untrustworthy. *J. Sutcliffe.*

ASIAN PUNTER (IRE) 2 ch.g. (Mar 4) M Double M (USA) – Centenary Year **56** (Malinowski (USA) 123) [1991 6f² 7m] IR 17,000F, IR 20,000Y: strong, sturdy gelding: second foal: dam ran twice at 3 yrs in Ireland: plating-class form in maiden auctions at Salisbury (favourite though carrying condition, kept on late) in August and Leicester following month: should stay 1m. *A. Hide.*

ASKELON 2 b.c. (Mar 18) Absalom 128 – Willowbed 66 (Wollow 132) [1991 5g² **56** 5m⁴ 6d² 7g⁶ 7f³ 8.2m⁵ 7m³] sturdy colt: has a round action: fifth foal: half-brother to 2m winner White Jasmin (by Jalmood) and 2 winners abroad, one also successful over 6f at 2 yrs here: dam won at 1¼m: plating-class form in varied events: ran well when blinkered and edgy in seller final start: bolted to post, unseated rider and withdrawn prior to next intended outing: should stay 1m: acts on firm and dead ground: sold 9,000 gns Newmarket Autumn Sales. *J. L. Dunlop.*

ASSESSOR (IRE) 2 b.c. (Mar 1) Niniski (USA) 125 – Dingle Bay (Petingo 135) **112** [1991 7s* 7f³ 8.1m² 7d* 8g³] useful-looking colt: fluent mover: brother to Irish 7f (at 2 yrs) to 1¼m winner Walliser: dam Irish 1m and 1¼m winner, is sister to high-class miler Pitcairn and very smart middle-distance stayer Valley Forge: progressive young stayer: very useful performer: successful in maiden at Kempton in August and minor event at Ascot in September, drawing clear close home both times: best effort keeping-on 5 lengths third of 8 to impressive Seattle Rhyme in Racing Post Trophy at Doncaster final outing: will be suited by middle distances: seems well suited by some give in the ground. *R. Hannon.*

ASSIGNMENT 5 b.h. Known Fact (USA) 135 – Sanctuary (Welsh Pageant 132) **79** [1990 8d 7g a7g³ a7g³ a6g* 1991 a7g² a5g* a7g³ a6g* 6s 6g 7.6m 6g 6f³ 6f³ 6m⁶ 8d a **82** 6m² a7g a6g³ a6g³] strong, deep-girthed horse: fair handicapper: won at Lingfield (2) early in season: suited by 6f: best form on turf on a sound surface: has worn severe noseband: sometimes bandaged behind: tough. *J. Ffitch-Heyes.*

ASTERIX 3 ch.c. Prince Sabo 123 – Gentle Gael 97 (Celtic Ash) [1990 6m³ 6m² **82** 5.8f* 6g⁵ 6g 1991 8s⁴ 8g 7d 8m 6g³ 8.3m 6f⁵ 7g* 7.6m 7.6g] smallish, lengthy colt: moderate mover: fair handicapper: made all at Kempton in September: below form at Lingfield afterwards: effective at 6f to 1m: has form on any going: visored last 6 starts: ran moderately at Chester: sold 7,500 gns Newmarket Autumn Sales. *C. C. Elsey.*

ASTRABEE 6 b.g. Show-A-Leg 107 – Manatay (Brilliant Blue) [1990 18f 1991 — a16g⁵ a14g⁶ 14.1f] leggy gelding: well beaten on flat: winning hurdler. *J. Wharton.*

ASTRAL FLYER (USA) 2 ch.c. (Apr 24) Assert 134 – Loa (USA) (Hawaii) **62** ? [1991 8m 8m⁴ 8.9m] $16,000F, $50,000Y: lengthy, unfurnished colt: first foal: dam won at up to 9f: quite modest form on debut: didn't confirm that, running poorly in claimer at York later in month: sold 6,200 gns Newmarket Autumn Sales. *Mrs J. R. Ramsden.*

ASTRAL'S DELIGHT 3 gr.f. Absalom 128 – Astral Suite 82 (On Your Mark — 125) [1990 5f* 5m 5.8h⁴ 6m 6d⁵ 8d 1991 6g⁴ 7.5g 7d 6d⁶ 5f 5.3f 6.9m] smallish, workmanlike filly: plating-class winner at 2 yrs: easily best 3-y-o effort on re-appearance: should stay 7f, very stiff task at 1m: yet to race on soft ground, acts on any other: sold out of J. Berry's stable 2,600 gns Doncaster July Sales after fourth start: joined J. Moore after final one. *J. White.*

ASTURIAS 8 b.g. Artaius (USA) 129 – Tanaka 106 (Tapalque 126) [1990 NR 1991 **41** a11g³ 12g² 13.8g 12g⁴ 12.3d 12g³] robust gelding: poor and lightly-raced handicapper on flat nowadays: effective at 1¼m to 1½m: acts on good to firm and soft going: raced too freely when blinkered once. *A. P. Stringer.*

ASWAMEDH 3 ro.c. Ore 116 – Asmalwi 61 (Averof 123) [1990 NR 1991 12m 16g⁴ **63** 16.2s³ 16.9g² 15.9d] big, good-bodied colt: second foal: half-brother to 4-y-o 10.1f seller winner Swift Silver (by Bairn): dam maiden, stayed 1¾m: quite modest maiden: sweating, soundly beaten at Chester final start: should be suited by thorough test of stamina: acts on soft going: joined P. Hobbs. *D. W. P. Arbuthnot.*

ATALL ATALL 8 b.h. Kampala 120 – Bint Africa 71 (African Sky 124) [1990 6v³ **74** 7.6d 6m³ 1991 6m* 6m² 7m⁵] rather leggy, attractive horse: not a good walker or mover: modest performer nowadays: won claimer at Haydock in May: would have won but for rider dropping reins next time: not seen out after June: best form at 6f: acts on any going: tailed off when blinkered. *G. M. Moore.*

ATATURK (USA) 3 ch.g. Ankara (USA) 106 – Wattle It Be (USA) (Bold **64** Commander (USA)) [1990 7f² 7m 8m³ 1991 7f² 8m³] close-coupled gelding: has a long stride: modest maiden at 2 yrs: not entirely discredited in small fields in July as 3-y-o: should stay 1¼m: sweating and on toes, wandered badly final start at 2 yrs: sold to join G. Barnett 6,000 gns Newmarket Autumn Sales. *J. Etherington.*

ATHAR (IRE) 2 b.f. (Mar 28) Master Willie 129 – Walladah (USA) 71 (Northern — Dancer) [1991 7m] workmanlike filly: fourth foal: dam, second 3 times at 1¼m, is

closely related to very smart performer at up to 7f Beaudelaire and a daughter of
very smart winner at up to 1m Bitty Girl: 20/1, backward and green, no real sign of
promise in 14-runner maiden at Leicester: moved poorly down. *P. T. Walwyn.*

ATHCLARE (IRE) 3 ch.c. Glow (USA) – Athry (Be Friendly 130) [1990 NR 1991 **76**
6v4 9v4 7d5 9d2 8.5g5 10g4 13m3 12m 10g6 a10g3] IR 38,000Y: ex-Irish colt: eighth
foal: closely related to Irish 1m and 9f winner Elke's Baby (by Northern Baby) and
half-brother to a NH Flat race winner and 2 winners abroad: dam maiden half-sister
to high-class French stayer Citoyen: modest form, trained until after penultimate
start (bought 9,000 gns Newmarket Autumn Sales) by J. Oxx: below form in claimer
(wandered under pressure) at Lingfield: probably stays 13f: acts on good to firm
ground and heavy: has worn blinkers. *J. Akehurst.*

ATHENE NOCTUA 6 b.m. Aragon 118 – Lady Lorelei 105 (Derring-Do 131) **—**
[1990 10.6s* 1991 10.2s] leggy, light-framed mare: poor mover: poor handicapper
nowadays: stays 10.6f: acts on any going: sold 975 gns Ascot May Sales. *B. A.
McMahon.*

ATHENIAN KING 3 b.c. Fairy King (USA) – To Oneiro 69 (Absalom 128) [1990 **79**
5f2 5f* 5d3 5f5 a6g* 5g5 5m5 1991 5g4 6m 6m5 6m2 6g6 5m* 5.1g4] smallish,
well-made colt: moderate mover: fair handicapper: won at Doncaster in June: ran
fairly well at Chester following month: effective at 5f and 6f: yet to race on soft
ground, has form on any other: has given trouble at stalls. *C. Tinkler.*

ATHENS BY NIGHT (USA) 5 ch.m. London Bells (CAN) 109 – Senorita **—**
Poquito 110 (Connaught 130) [1990 10.2f 12m5 14.8f 12h2 12f3 12f5 1991 10f 11.7g]
rather leggy, quite good-topped mare: moderate mover: quite modest maiden at 4
yrs: no show as 5-y-o: suited by 1½m: acts on hard ground. *Miss A. J. Whitfield.*

ATISAYIN (USA) 3 b.f. Al Nasr (FR) 126 – Savage Bunny (USA) (Never Bend) **—**
[1990 NR 1991 6d4 6s5 6g 8.2m 6.9f] $80,000Y: small, short-backed filly: half-sister
to several winners, including Irish 1m and 9f winner Alleged Savage (by Alleged):
dam minor stakes-winning sprinter: poor maiden: stiff tasks in handicaps: will be
suited by further than 6f: acts on soft ground. *A. Hide.*

ATLANTIC CLEAR 4 b.g. Starch Reduced 112 – Kathy King (Space King 115) **57 d**
[1990 6m 7f 7f3 a8g 8m 1991 7m4 a7g 7m 7f 7g 6.1m 8m] leggy, sparely-made
gelding: has free, rather round action: poor handicapper, still a maiden: stays 7f: acts
on firm going: below form when blinkered once. *J. E. Banks.*

ATLANTIC WAY 3 gr.f. Bold Owl 101 – Overseas 48 (Sea Hawk II 131) [1990 **—**
5m6 6m 6m5 a6g 1991 10.2d 8m 12.3m6 10.2g 10m] leggy filly: has a round action:
poor performer: probably stays 1½m: mounted on track and mulish to post fourth
start: very slowly away final one. *C. J. Hill.*

ATMOSPHERIC BLUES (IRE) 2 b.f. (Mar 3) Double Schwartz 128 – Saga's **91**
Humour 61 (Bustino 136) [1991 6d2 5m* 5g5 6m2 6g3 7m6 6g] IR 6,000F, 12,500Y:
close-coupled, quite attractive filly: has a roundish action: fifth foal: half-sister to 3
winners, including 1989 2-y-o 7f winner Woodside Heath (by King Persian) and
1¼m winner Haygate Park (by Final Straw): dam best at 6f: fairly useful performer:
won maiden at Sandown in May: best effort keeping on third of 9 to Mamma's Too in
listed race at Ayr in September, on first start for 3 months: probably stays 7f. *R. J. R.
Williams.*

A-TO-Z (IRE) 2 b.f. (Apr 9) Ahonoora 122 – Zenga (Try My Best (USA) 130) **87**
[1991 6m* 5g4 6m5 6g5 6.3s] IR 19,000Y: good-topped filly: has plenty of scope:
third foal: dam won in Italy: fair performer: won 6-runner maiden at Epsom in June,
not handling descent then quickening well: better form with some give in the
ground, notably when fourth of 14 to Marling in Queen Mary Stakes at Royal Ascot
(despite edging right) in June and fifth of 9 to Mamma's Too in listed race at Ayr in
September: will probably stay 7f. *M. Bell.*

AT PEACE 5 b.h. Habitat 134 – Peace 113 (Klairon 131) [1990 a8g* 8.3m 7.2g2 8d **57**
9m 10.2s6 1991 a7g a8g5 10.8m 8d 10g 9.2d2 8g2 8.3g] robust horse: carries plenty of
condition: plating-class handicapper nowadays: seems suited by 1m/9f: best on an
easy surface: below form when visored once: tried to bite a horse once as 5-y-o:
temperament under suspicion: winning hurdler. *J. White.*

ATTADALE 3 b.c. Ardross 134 – Marypark 93 (Charlottown 127) [1990 10s 1991 **69**
10g 12m5 14.1g6 16.1m* 16.1g5 17.9f4 16m3 16.1g3] rangy, good-topped colt: has a
round action: modest performer: won maiden at Newcastle in July: one paced, and
will prove suited by test of stamina: acts on firm going: sold to join L. Lungo 21,000
gns Newmarket Autumn Sales. *W. Jarvis.*

ATYAAF (USA) 2 ch.f. (Feb 22) Irish River (FR) 131 – Bank On Love (USA) **48**
(Gallant Romeo (USA)) [1991 5.2d5 7f5 a7g] $150,000Y: leggy, rather sparely-made

filly: half-sister to several winners, notably very useful 6f and 7.2f winner Weldnaas (by Diesis): dam unraced half-sister to Triumph Hurdle winner Solar Cloud: poor maiden: 3 months off between outings: sold out of D. Elsworth's stable 9,000 gns Newmarket Autumn Sales after second start. *M. J. Heaton-Ellis.*

AUCELOUN   3 ch.c. Rousillon (USA) 133 – Arderelle (FR) 80 (Pharly (FR) 130)   **58**
[1990 NR 1991 7m 10.2d² 12s³ 11.7m] 4,200Y: angular, lengthy colt: moderate mover: third foal: half-brother to French 10.5f winner Ellerton (by Sharpo) and 5f and 6f winner Premier Developer (by Precocious): dam 1¼m winner out of smart miler Arosa, also dam of Arokar: plating-class form placed in June claimers: stiff task in handicap: will prove suited by 1½m + : carried head awkwardly on debut. *R. F. Johnson Houghton.*

AUCTION KING (IRE)   2 b.c. (Mar 29) Auction Ring (USA) 123 – Brigadina   **61**
(Brigadier Gerard 144) [1991 5d³ 5g³ 5g² 5f² 5m⁶ 5f⁴ 5m⁵ 5f² 7g⁶ 5d 5m² 5g⁴ 5d] 5,000F, 1,500Y: workmanlike colt: has scope: first foal: dam ran twice in Ireland at 2 yrs: quite modest maiden: best form at 5f on a sound surface: ran moderately in blinkers fifth outing: sweating next 2 starts: ran well when edgy: has shown signs of temperament, and been reluctant at stalls. *A. Smith.*

AUCTION TIME   8 br.g. Auction Ring (USA) 123 – Autumn Flush 57 (Rustam   **55**
127) [1990 10.1g 1991 a10g⁶ 10v² a10g⁶ 10g] good-bodied gelding: lightly-raced handicapper nowadays: most unlucky second in claimer at Folkestone (badly impeded by loose horse near finish) in April: ran moderately after, off course 4½ months before final start: stays 1¼m: possibly needs the mud nowadays. *J. Akehurst.*

AUDE LA BELLE (FR)   3 ch.f. Ela-Mana-Mou 132 – Arjona (GER) (Caracol   **70** d
(FR)) [1990 NR 1991 10f³ 10f⁶ 8g⁵ 10g³ 10g 10m] 180,000 francs (approx £16,660) Y: small, light-framed filly: has a quick action: fourth foal: dam, winner in Germany, is half-sister to tough German middle-distance colt Acatenango out of Park Hill winner Aggravate: quite modest maiden: below form in handicaps last 2 outings: better at 1¼m than shorter: sweating final start, in August: sold 2,600 gns Doncaster November Sales. *A. A. Scott.*

AUGHFAD   5 b.h. Millfontaine 114 – Saulonika 94 (Saulingo 122) [1990 a5g⁴ a5g*   **89**
a6g³ a6g 6f² 6f 6m 6h⁴ 5f* 5g³ 5g² 6g² 6f 6m 6m⁵ 5m³ 5m* 5m⁴ 5g* 5s 1991 6s 5g 5m⁶ 5m 6d 5g* 6m* 5f⁴ 6d* 5d* 5m⁶ 5.2g 6g 6g³ 6m 5d 5d 5.2g 5g] strong, workmanlike horse: impresses in appearance: poor mover: fair handicapper: in good form in summer, successful at Goodwood (3) and Warwick: effective at 5f to 6f: acts on hard and dead going: effective with or without blinkers or visor: has won for apprentice. *T. Casey.*

AUGHTON RIDGE (IRE)   3 b.f. Hatim (USA) 121 – Vote Barolo (Nebbiolo   **34**
125) [1990 5s 7f⁶ 7g 8m 10.6s⁵ 1991 12m 8f⁵ a8g a12g a11g⁴ 12d a12g a12g a14g] smallish, angular filly: poor maiden: stays 11f: probably acts on any going: sold out of M. O'Neill's stable 1,100 gns Doncaster July Sales after sixth start. *M. C. Chapman.*

AUNTIE NELLIE   3 b.f. Uncle Pokey 116 – Set To Work (Workboy 123) [1990   —
NR 1991 8s 10m] 3,800Y: sixth living foal: sister to modest 1986 2-y-o 5f winner Upset and half-sister to 11.5f and 1½m winner Tour de Force (by Reliance II): dam never ran: behind in April maidens. *C. Tinkler.*

AUREOLE D'OR   2 b.c. (Feb 18) Cragador 110 – No Halo 74 (Aureole 132) [1991   —
5s² 6f 7g⁶ 6.9m] 6,000F, 3,000Y: close-coupled, quite attractive colt: eighth foal: half-brother to a winner in Italy: dam won over 1½m: probably of little account: not seen out after June. *R. Hollinshead.*

AUROREUM   4 ch.c. Glenstal (USA) 118 – Abelina (Thatch (USA) 136) [1990 6g   **61**
7d 6m³ 1991 6d 6m⁵ 5m⁵ 6g 5g 5g 5g³ 5.1s 5.1g] good-topped colt: poor mover: quite modest maiden: better at 6f than 5f: acted on good to firm ground: dead. *L. J. Holt.*

AUSHERRA (USA)   3 ch.f. Diesis 133 – Princess of Man 104 (Green God 128) **106**
[1990 6m* 7m² 8m 1991 8g⁴ 11.5g* 12m 11.9m³ 12g⁴ 14.6m 10s] tall, attractive filly: good walker: useful performer: won listed Marley Roof Tile Oaks Trial at Lingfield in May: best effort in pattern events subsequently when 3 lengths fourth to Lady Blessington in Prix Minerve (favourite) at Evry: should stay 1¾m. *P. F. I. Cole.*

AUSTRALART (USA)   2 b.g. (Feb 7) Surreal (USA) – Nabbo (USA) (Go Go   **61**
Roger (USA)) [1991 6g³ 5g 7g 5m⁶ 6m] $11,500Y: strong, close-coupled gelding: has scope: brother to a winner in USA at up to 1m and half-brother to another: dam won at up to 1¼m from 4 yrs to 6 yrs: sire half-brother to very useful 1985 Irish 1¼m and 11f winner Gold Meridian out of champion Canadian 2-y-o filly Queen Louie: quite modest form in varied events: may well be ideally suited by 6f: sold 9,000 gns Newmarket Autumn Sales and sent to Scandinavia. *W. A. O'Gorman.*

AUTHORSHIP (USA)   5 b. or br.g. Balzac (USA) – Piap (USA) (L'Aiglon   **53**
(USA)) [1990 a 13g³ 16m⁴ 14g 2 1.6m² 16.2g* 17.6m⁵ 14g 16m⁵ 1991 18g* 20g⁵] leggy
gelding: plating-class handicapper: won at Pontefract: put up improved performance
when staying-on fifth in Ascot Stakes later in June: stays extreme distances: acts on
good to firm ground. *W. J. Musson.*

AUTOCRACY (IRE)   2 b.c. (Apr 24) Alzao (USA) 117 – Addabub (Manado 130) **108**
[1991 6g⁶ 6m² 6d² 7g² 8.1f4 7g* 7s² 7.3g2] IR 35,000F, IR 62,000Y: angular,
useful-looking colt: has plenty of scope: has a quick action: first foal: dam Irish 1¼m
winner also successful over hurdles: useful performer: favourite, won maiden at
Salisbury in October: improved form when game second later in month in Goffs
Million at the Curragh (beaten short head by Fair Crack) and Horris Hill Stakes (2
lengths behind Lion Cavern) at Newbury: stays 1m: well suited by some give in the
ground, not discredited on firm: sold 230,000 gns Newmarket December Sales: to
race in Germany. *R. Hannon.*

AUTONOMOUS   6 b.g. Milford 119 – Mandrian 103 (Mandamus 120) [1990 a 14g³   **32** §
1991 a 14g 14m 16.4m⁵ a 18g² 18m] lengthy gelding: carries condition: poor and
unreliable handicapper: stays 19f: acts on firm and dead going: below form in
blinkers and visor: bandaged as 6-y-o: trained until after second start by W. Wilson:
winning hurdler. *C. N. Allen.*

AUVILLAR (USA)   3 br.c. Temperence Hill (USA) – Exquisita (USA) (Cougar   **58**
(CHI)) [1990 6m 6s 6f⁵ 1991 8.2d 8h⁵ 12g² a 11g* a 12g*] compact colt: moderate
walker: has a roundish action: made all in handicaps at Southwell in June (given very
hard race) and July: stays 1½m: visored or blinkered (third start) at 3 yrs: sold out of
J. W. Watts's stable 6,000 gns Doncaster July Sales before final start. *D. Burchell.*

AVISHAYES (USA)   4 b.c. Al Nasr (FR) 126 – Rose Goddess (Sassafras (FR)   **60**
135) [1990 10m⁴ 10g 10.1m 11.7m 11.7g 10m³ 12g 10g² 10.6s 10.2s 1991 10.2s 11s 8g⁵
7m³ 8h* 8g* 8m⁶ 8m³ 9m* 10m⁴ 10g³ 8.2f² 9.2f* 8m⁶] big, lengthy colt: usually
impresses in appearance: moderate mover: quite modest handicapper: won at
Carlisle (first success) and Pontefract (seller, bought in 6,000 gns) in June,
Newcastle in July and Hamilton in September: effective at 1m to 1¼m: acts on hard
ground: has been blinkered, not nowadays: best with waiting tactics: sold to join M.
Hammond's stable 10,500 gns Doncaster October Sales. *Mrs J. R. Ramsden.*

AVRO ANSON   3 b.g. Ardross 134 – Tremellick 87 (Mummy's Pet 125) [1990   —
8.2s 1991 8d 10f 10.2g] big, workmanlike gelding: plating-class maiden: best effort at
2 yrs: sweating and bit backward having been gelded, stiff task in July handicap as
3-y-o: should stay at least 1¼m. *M. J. Camacho.*

AWAY FROM REALITY   3 ch.f. Dreams To Reality (USA) 113 – Runaway Girl   **41**
(FR) (Homeric 133) [1990 7g 8m 1991 8m 11.7s 8.2m 10.1f⁶ 12g³ a 12g⁵] sturdy,
close-coupled filly: poor maiden: stays 1½m: acts on firm going, possibly unsuited
by soft: below form on all-weather: joined Mrs J. Pitman. *J. Banks.*

AWESOME POWER   5 b.g. Vision (USA) – Majestic Nurse 80 (On Your Mark   **58**
125) [1990 7g 7.9m 8s 7.9m⁵ 7d 7g* 7v 7d 7g⁴ a 8g² 1991 9m 7g 6m 8m 8.5g² 9m⁴ 7g⁴
9m⁵ 7.5g a 6g⁴ a 8g a 7g⁶] ex-Irish handicapper: ideally suited by 7f/1m: acts on firm
ground: has been tried in blinkers. *C. R. Nelson.*

AXE   3 ch.c. Kris 135 – Russian Ribbon (USA) 86 (Nijinsky (CAN) 138) [1990 NR   **91**
1991 8g 9m* 10.2m⁴ 8m] 520,000Y: lengthy, good-topped colt: has a quick action:
second foal: half-brother to smart 4-y-o 5f (at 2 yrs) to 1m winner Bold Russian (by
Persian Bold): dam 1m-winning daughter of half-sister to several smart performers:
won maiden at Kempton in May: looked very well but disappointed in minor event
(hung left, put head in air) and handicap (ran as if something amiss) in the summer.
H. R. A. Cecil.

AXIOPREPIS   3 ch.c. Formidable (USA) 125 – Nicholas Grey 100 (Track Spare   —
125) [1990 NR 1991 8.1m 11.1m³ a 12g 12.4m⁶ 9.9f 10.4m] 35,000Y: workmanlike
colt with scope: seventh foal: brother to quite useful but unreliable 6f winner
Butsova and half-brother to several winners, notably high-class middle-distance
colt Terimon (by Bustino): dam, winner from 5f to 7f here at 2 yrs, second in Oaks
d'Italia: disappointing maiden: worth another try at 1m: saddle slipped on
all-weather: sold 3,800 gns Newmarket Autumn Sales. *P. Calver.*

AYAH (USA)   3 b.f. Secreto (USA) 128 – Native Nurse (USA) (Graustark) [1990   —
7g⁵ 1991 9m 12.2f4] leggy, workmanlike filly: looked very well but edgy and taken
very steadily to post in maidens in summer as 3-y-o, pulling hard and finishing well
beaten. *M. R. Stoute.*

AY BEAT   2 ch.g. (May 6) Bairn (USA) 126 – Thorny Rose 81 (Tap On Wood 130)   — §
[1991 5g⁴ 7.1s 6.9f] compact gelding: second foal: brother to 3-y-o Bee Beat: dam

2-y-o 6f winner later suited by middle distances: no worthwhile form: blinkered after 3-month absence, reluctant to race at Folkestone last time: not one to trust. *E. A. Wheeler.*

AYODESSA 4 b.f. Lochnager 132 – Melody Song 74 (Saintly Song 128) [1990 5m 5f⁵ 6m 5g 5g 5m⁶ a5g 5m⁴ 5f³ 6m 6m³ 5f 6g 1991 a7g a6g 8d 6m 7d 8h³ 8m 6d⁴ a5g* a5g* 5m² a5g⁴ 5f⁵] good-topped filly: moderate mover: poor handicapper: won twice at Southwell in July: best at 5f or 6f: acts on firm and dead going: has been tried blinkered: in foal to Rambo Dancer. *Ronald Thompson.*   44

AYR CLASSIC 3 b.f. Local Suitor (USA) 128 – Iyamski (USA) 86 (Baldski (USA)) [1990 5v* 6g* 7f⁶ 6d 1991 7d⁴ 8.2m⁶] rather angular filly: moderate mover: mostly stiff tasks since modest winner in spring at 2 yrs: ran moderately in claimer final start at 3 yrs, in May: stays 7f: has form on any going. *J. S. Wilson.*   —

AYR HEAD 2 b.f. (Mar 26) Kind of Hush 118 – Basic Bliss 72 (Tumble Wind (USA)) [1991 5v³ 5m⁵ 5m⁶ 6d 5m³ 5g²] 1,200F: unfurnished filly: first foal: dam (maiden) stayed 7f: poor maiden: ran creditably in blinkers last 2 starts: should be better suited by 6f than 5f: hung left final outing. *M. W. Easterby.*   44

AYR RAIDER 4 ch.c. Claude Monet (USA) 121 – Thimothea (FR) (Timmy My Boy 125) [1990 8m⁶ 7.2g 6d 7m⁵ 7m⁵ 7g 1991 8m 8m⁶ 8s⁵ 5g* 6d 5d³ 5m³ 6f⁵ 5f 5g⁴ 5m⁵ 5m* 5m 5m] strong, workmanlike colt: modest handicapper: won at Edinburgh (amateurs) in July and Newcastle in October: effective at 5f to 7f: suited by a sound surface: effective with or without blinkers: below form when visored: trained by J. Wilson until after seventh start. *Miss L. A. Perratt.*   70

AZUBAH 4 b.f. Castle Keep 121 – Louisianalightning (Music Boy 124) [1990 7f⁶ 7g² 8m⁵ 7f* 8.5d⁵ 8f² 8f² 10m⁴ 10m³ 9g 1991 8f⁵ 12.3g⁴ 12h* 12m² 13d⁵ 9.9f* 10m⁶ 9.9f] lengthy, rather sparely-made filly: moderate mover: quite modest handicapper: won in July at Carlisle and Beverley (race void): stays 1½m: acts on hard ground, unsuited by dead: often makes running. *G. M. Moore.*   63

AZUREUS (IRE) 3 ch.g. Horage 124 – Effortless (Try My Best (USA) 130) [1990 6g² 7g⁵ 6m² 6s⁵ 6f* 7h² 7g⁵ 6d³ 6d 10.2s⁶ 1991 8d³ 7g⁴ 8m 11m² 7m⁵ 8m² 11s 11.9m⁶ 10g² 8m⁴ 11.9g 10.9m] strong, attractive gelding: modest handicapper: stays 1½m: acts on hard and dead ground: suitable mount for apprentice: trained by J. Wilson except last 2 starts: twice winning hurdler then refused to race third jumps outing. *Miss L. A. Perratt.*   74

AZZAAM (USA) 4 ro.c. Chief's Crown (USA) – Princess Oola (USA) (Al Hattab (USA)) [1990 9g 10.2g⁶ 10m* 12s* 1991 10s 12g 10v* 10.9m* 12g⁴ 12s⁴ 10v⁶] tall, close-coupled colt: has a sharp action: very useful performer: successful in listed races at Kempton in June and Ayr (made all and beat Spinning by 10 lengths) in   114

Doonside Cup, Ayr—Azzaam gains a runaway success, in record time

September: creditable fourth of 5 in Cumberland Lodge Stakes at Ascot (sweating and very edgy) next time: below best after in Group 2 Prix du Conseil de Paris at Longchamp and Group 1 Premio Roma: effective at 1¼m to 1½m: acts on good to firm and soft going: to join D. Hayes in Australia. *J. L. Dunlop.*

B

BAATISH (USA) 3 b.c. Slew O' Gold (USA) – Shukey (USA) (Key To The Mint **94** (USA)) [1990 5.1g3 7m5 8.2s2 8d* 1991 8g* 8d4] good-quartered colt: moderate mover: made all, putting up fairly useful effort, in handicap at Salisbury in June: below that form in £24,900 handicap following month: will stay 1¼m: acts on soft ground: sweating and edgy final start at 2 yrs: to join T. Skiffington in USA. *H. Thomson Jones.*

BABRAHAM (USA) 2 ch.c. (May 11) El Gran Senor (USA) 136 – Golden Screen **—** (USA) (Silent Screen (USA)) [1991 6g] $75,000Y: lengthy, good-topped colt: has scope: third reported foal: dam minor winner at up to 1¼m, is sister to a Norsk 1000 Guineas and Oaks winner: green and carrying condition, last in 12-runner maiden at Lingfield in October, slowly away and always behind: moved moderately to post. *A. A. Scott.*

BABY BOY 10 b.h. Mummy's Pet 125 – Lucent 117 (Irish Ball (FR) 127) [1990 NR **—** 1991 10f] strong, good-topped horse: bad handicapper: stays 11.7f: probably acts on any going. *C. Holmes.*

BABY CAMEO (USA) 2 ch.c. (Apr 15) Northern Baby (CAN) 127 – Cameo **51** p Native (USA) (Raise A Native) [1991 7g 7f] $500,000Y: good-bodied colt: has a round action: fifth foal: half-brother to a claimer winner at up to 1¼m in USA by Green Forest: dam minor winner at up to 1m: poor form in maidens at Newmarket (green) and Yarmouth (on toes) in August: looks sort to do better. *B. Hanbury.*

BACHELOR BOY 3 b.g. Ballacashtal (CAN) – Miss Solo (Runnymede 123) **—** [1990 6g 6d5 6g 6d 1991 7g 8.3g] compact gelding: has a round action: poor form at 2 yrs, none in May at 3 yrs. *W. G. R. Wightman.*

BADAWIAH 2 gr.f. (Apr 12) Siberian Express (USA) 125 – Jawhara 93 (Upper **67** ? Case (USA)) [1991 7m2 7m] 13,000Y: seventh foal: half-sister to several winners here and abroad, including fairly useful 1982 2-y-o 7f winner Jad (by Riboboy), and fair 1m to 10.6f winner Jadeite (by Crystal Glitters): dam won from 5f to 7f: 8/1 from 3/1, keeping-on head second of 13 in maiden auction at Southwell in August: bolted to start before running as if something amiss in maiden (heavily-backed second favourite) there following month. *W. A. O'Gorman.*

BADAWI (USA) 3 ch.f. Diesis 133 – Begum (USA) (Alydar (USA)) [1990 NR **82** + 1991 8.5m2 8g*] $170,000Y: lengthy, rather sparely-made filly: second known foal: sister to 1989 3-y-o 8.5f stakes winner Songlines: dam never ran: 6/4 on, easily won maiden at Redcar in June: stays 8.5f well. *J. H. M. Gosden.*

BADIE (USA) 2 gr.c. (Apr 16) Blushing Groom (FR) 131 – Desirable 119 (Lord **90** p Gayle (USA) 124) [1991 7g* 7d] close-coupled, good-topped colt: very good walker: has a quick, round action: second living foal: half-brother to Shadayid (by Shadeed): dam, 2-y-o 6f winner placed in 1000 Guineas and at 1¼m, is sister to Nashamaa and half-sister to Park Appeal and Alydaress: green, won 12-runner minor event at Kempton in September, pushed along vigorously 2f out then running on in excellent fashion last 150 yds: beaten soon after halfway in 9-runner similar event at Ascot later in month, giving impression unsuited by soft ground: will probably stay 1¼m: looked very interesting prospect at Kempton and is worth another chance. *J. L. Dunlop.*

BAHARLILYS 2 gr.f. (Mar 6) Green Dancer (USA) 132 – April Wind 91 **67** (Windjammer (USA)) [1991 7.1m5 8m 8d6 7m] 50,000Y: leggy, unfurnished filly: third foal: dam Irish 2-y-o 5f winner: quite modest form: highly tried (including in Brent Walker Fillies' Mile at Ascot, where badly hampered 2f out) and well beaten last 3 starts: very upset in preliminaries final outing: stays 1m: has joined N. C. Wright. *C. E. Brittain.*

BAHRAIN BRIDGE 6 b.g. Formidable (USA) 125 – Hide Out (Habitat 134) **—** [1990 NR 1991 7.6g] strong, good-topped gelding: quite modest handicapper at 4 yrs: no show only run in 1991 (May): stays 1m well: acts on firm going, possibly unsuited by soft: has been blinkered: none too reliable. *A. W. Denson.*

BAHRAIN QUEEN (IRE) 3 ch.f. Caerleon (USA) 132 – Bahrain Vee (CAN) —
(Blushing Groom (FR) 131) [1990 NR 1991 a8g⁵ a8g 10f 8.2m] light-framed filly:
second foal: sister to modest maiden Dancing Bride: dam twice-raced daughter of
close relation to top Canadian colt Giboulee: no worthwhile form in maidens and
handicap: wore eyeshield on all-weather: sold 640 gns Newmarket July Sales:
winning hurdler for C. Smith. *Mrs L. Piggott.*

BAILEYS BY NAME 2 b.f. (Feb 25) Nomination 125 – Water Pageant 58   **66**
(Welsh Pageant 132) [1991 6g 7m⁴ 6g* 6.1m* 6m* 6g⁶ 6f 6g 6m⁶ 6m⁵ 5d a6g²]
5,000F, 3,300Y: lengthy filly: half-sister to several winners, including middle-
distance stayer Sanchi Steeple (by Niniski): dam middle-distance maiden: quite
modest performer: successful in maiden auction at Doncaster and nurseries at
Nottingham and Ripon: creditable second to Dublin Indemnity in Southwell nursery
final outing: should stay 7f: acts on good to firm ground, and on fibresand: tends to
wander: has sweated: visored ninth to eleventh starts, tending to race freely:
changed hands 3,500 gns Doncaster October Sales. *M. Johnston.*

BAIRN FREE 3 gr.f. Bairn (USA) 126 – Rustling 68 (Rusticaro (FR) 124) [1990   —
NR 1991 8m⁴ 8m 7g 10m a12g] 5,400Y: leggy, sparely-made filly: second foal: sister
to modest 1¼m winner Neenawn: dam maiden best at 9f or 1¼m: showed signs of a
little ability in maidens: never dangerous in handicaps: should stay 1¼m: slowly
away last 3 outings: sold to join D. Wintle 3,100 gns Ascot November Sales. *D. W. P.
Arbuthnot.*

BAKHTARAN 4 b.c. Mouktar 129 – Badalushka 83 (Rex Magna (FR) 129) [1990   —
10m⁴ 10m⁶ 1991 16.9g 10.2m] first foal: dam 1½m winner: very lightly-raced ex-Irish
maiden (trained at 3 yrs by J. Oxx): tailed off in modest company at 4 yrs: stays 1¼m:
winning hurdler. *Mrs A. L. M. King.*

BALAAT (USA) 3 b.c. Northern Baby (CAN) 127 – Bar J Gal (USA) (Key To The   —
Mint (USA)) [1990 6f² 7g* 8m² 7m² 1991 7m 10g² 8m 9d 7.9m] leggy, rather angular
colt: moderate mover: fairly useful performer (rated 95) at 2 yrs: disappointing in
1991 (11/10 on in 3-runner minor event), including in handicaps: needs further than
7f nowadays, should stay 1¼m: gives impression ill at ease on top-of-the-ground:
sold to join M. Chapman 11,000 gns Newmarket Autumn Sales. *M. C. Chapman.*

BALADEE PET 2 gr.g. (Feb 3) Petong 126 – Baladee (Mummy's Pet 125) [1991   **54**
6f⁵ 5m 5f² 5f⁵ 5g³ 6f² 6f 5h] 10,000F, 6,400Y: leggy, close-coupled gelding: second
foal: half-brother to a winner in Macau: dam unraced: plating-class maiden: ran
poorly last 2 starts: stays 6f: acts on firm ground. *Mrs V. A. Aconley.*

BALASANI (FR) 5 b.h. Labus (FR) – Baykara (Direct Flight) [1990 10f 11.7g   **75**
11.7g 14m⁴ 12m³ 14g⁵ 12m 11.5g 1991 12v³ 11.8g* 12f* 14m* 13.3m³] sturdy horse:
vastly improved handicapper (untrustworthy at 4 yrs when trained by J. Jenkins):
won at Leicester in August and Salisbury and Sandown in September: heavily-
backed favourite, below-form third in Coral Autumn Cup at Newbury: better at 1¾m
than shorter: acts on any going: best held up: winning hurdler. *M. C. Pipe.*

BALDSKI BOY (USA) 3 b. or br.c. Baldski (USA) – Starlet Annie (USA)   —
(Silent Screen (USA)) [1990 8m⁶ a8g⁶ a8g 1991 10d 10.2g⁵ 8f 8.1s⁵] plain colt: plating
class, best effort on debut. *J. M. P. Eustace.*

BALIDARS BULLET 2 b.f. (Mar 4) Balidar 133 – Two Shots (Dom Racine (FR)   **32**
121) [1991 5g 6f⁵ 6.1m] 1,300F: small filly: poor mover: fifth foal: half-sister to
speedy 1989 2-y-o Two Toffs (by Another Realm): dam ran twice at 2 yrs: soundly
beaten in maidens. *I. Campbell.*

BALIDUCK 7 ch.m. Balidar 133 – Bombay Duck 65 (Ballyciptic 122) [1990 NR   —
1991 a7g] compact mare: lightly-raced plater: tailed off only start at 7 yrs (January):
stays 9f: yet to show her form on extremes of going. *R. G. Frost.*

BALIGAY 6 b.m. Balidar 133 – Gaygo Lady 113 (Gay Fandango (USA) 132) [1990   **84**
9f 8m 7f² 7f⁴ 7.6g⁵ 7m* 6f* 6h⁴ 7m* 7m 1991 7m 5.8f² 6.1m* 6m 6d² 6.1g 6.1m²
5f* 5m] lengthy, workmanlike mare: moderate mover: fair handicapper: won at
Chepstow (third win there) in May and Salisbury in August: effective at 5f to 7f: acts
on firm and dead ground: effective blinkered or not: good mount for claimer: none
too consistent. *R. J. Hodges.*

BALIGH 4 b.c. Sadler's Wells (USA) 132 – Santa's Sister (USA) 104 (Middle   **93**
Brother) [1990 12m 10m³ 10.2s² 1991 12m 14m⁴ 14m²] rangy, attractive colt:
moderate mover: lightly-raced handicapper, fairly useful nowadays: not seen out
after June: stays 2m: acts on good to firm and soft ground. *J. L. Dunlop.*

BALISHY 4 ch.f. Shy Groom (USA) – Bally 74 (Balidar 133) [1990 6f⁵ 7d² 8f 7f⁴   — §
6m² 5.8f² 6d 1991 5.8f 6.1m⁵ 7g 7.1g 6.1s 7f 7.1g 5.7f 7d] leggy, good-topped filly:

shows a round action: poor handicapper: stays 7f: probably acts on any going: has hung and looked irresolute: not one to trust. *R. J. Holder.*

BALI SUNSET   5 b.m. Balidar 133 – Orange Silk 68 (Moulton 128) [1990 5g² 5m²   **57** 6m² 6g* 5d⁴ 6m 6m 6m 5m⁵ 5g 5d 1991 6m³ 6m² 5m 6f 6f⁶] lengthy, workmanlike mare: poor mover: plating-class handicapper: effective at 5f and 6f: acts on firm and dead ground: ran well when blinkered final start. *G. M. Moore.*

BALLAD DANCER   6 ch.g. Ballad Rock 122 – Manx Image (Dancer's Image   **61** (USA)) [1990 10.8m 8m a7g⁴ a7g 1991 a6g⁶ 6s* 6d 6d⁵ 6m 5g* 5.1g 5s³ 5d² a5g² 6f 5m² 5m] angular, lengthy gelding: moderate mover: quite modest handicapper nowadays: won at Hamilton in April and Wolverhampton in June: effective at 5f to 7f: acts on good to firm ground but goes well on an easy surface: sometimes starts slowly. *E. J. Alston.*

BALLAD TUNE   6 b.g. Ballad Rock 122 – Haut Lafite (Tamerlane 128) [1990 6g   **34** 7f a6g a5g 1991 a6g⁴ a7g a6g a7g] poor performer: stays 6f: possibly temperamental. *S. R. Bowring.*

BALLA JIDAAL (USA)   2 b.c. (Feb 3) Shadeed (USA) 135 – Hiaam (USA) 110 **100** p (Alydar (USA)) [1991 5m⁴ 6m* 6m⁵] good-topped colt: has scope: has a quick action: first foal: dam very useful 6f (at 2 yrs) and 1m winner is half-sister to 1984 champion Canadian 3-y-o Key To The Moon and from very good family: well-backed favourite, gamely won 12-runner minor event at Doncaster in September by ½ length from Prince Ferdinand: 6 lengths fifth of 6, progress 2f out, unable to quicken thereafter, to Rodrigo de Triano in Newgate Stud Middle Park Stakes at Newmarket following month: will be better suited by 7f. *M. R. Stoute.*

BALLASECRET   3 ch.f. Ballacashtal (CAN) – Soft Secret (Most Secret 119)   **77** [1990 5m 6d a5g³ a5g³ 1991 a6g² a5g* a7g² 5d⁴ 6d⁴ 6m* 5m⁵ 5d⁵ 5m* 5m 5.1g 5.7m 7m 5.1s³ 5.2g⁴ 5d a5g] lengthy filly: modest handicapper: ridden by 7-lb claimer, won at Lingfield in January, Warwick in April and Catterick in May: best efforts in the autumn when in frame: will prove best at up to 6f: acts on good to firm ground and soft: best with forcing tactics. *R. Dickin.*

BALLASTRAND   3 b.f. Ballacashtal (CAN) – Tina's Magic (Carnival Night)   — [1990 5f³ᵈⁱˢ 5f⁴ 5.8f⁴ 5f 6s 6d 1991 5g] leggy filly: has a markedly round action: poor maiden: bit backward in April seller sole outing in 1991: stiff tasks over 6f. *J. C. Fox.*

BALLATER LASS (IRE)   3 ch.f. Burslem 123 – Courreges 75 (Manado 130)   **49** [1990 NR 1991 8.9g a7g³ a8g² a8g⁶ 8d a8g⁶ a12g] 1,800Y: leggy filly: turns near-fore out: fifth foal: dam placed at 5f and 6f at 2 yrs: second in maiden at Southwell in July: well below that form after, tailed off in claimer final start: stays 1m. *J. Wharton.*

BALLERINA BAY   3 ch.f. Myjinski (USA) – Lady Seville 64 (Orange Bay 131)   **68** [1990 NR 1991 a12g 10d 11.5g⁴ a12g³ 11.5m* 11.6m⁴ 8g⁵ 11.6m 9m⁴ 9m* 8.9m⁴ 10m a 54 8m 9g⁵ a10g a7g a8g²] lengthy, angular filly: has round action: modest handicapper, much better form on turf: second of 17 in amateurs handicap at Southwell in December: effective at 9f and stays 11.5f well: acts on good to firm ground: has won for apprentice: reared stalls and very slowly once. *D. T. Thom.*

BALLERINA ROSE   4 b.f. Dreams To Reality (USA) 113 – Ragtime Rose   — (Ragstone 128) [1990 7m 7m 8g 6g 1991 10f4] leggy filly: has a round action: no show on flat, including in handicap: winning hurdler. *O. O'Neill.*

BALLEROY (USA)   3 gr.c. Kaldoun (FR) 122 – Blanche Reine (FR) (Nureyev **115** (USA) 131) [1990 7g³ 7g⁶ 8m³ 9g² 1991 9v* 9.2g* 9.2m² 10d⁶ 9d 10g] 900,000 francs (approx £83,300) Y: second foal: half-brother to French 1½m winner Blanc Seing (by Shirley Heights): dam, French 1m winner, is close relation to Bellypha: won maiden at Maisons-Laffitte in March and Prix de Guiche (by a length from Tel Quel) at Longchamp in April: creditable second to Sillery in Prix Jean Prat at Longchamp: ran poorly last 2 starts, and not seen out after August: stays 9f: acts on good to firm and heavy. *J. de Roualle, France.*

BALLET CLASSIQUE (USA)   4 b.f. Sadler's Wells (USA) 132 – Estaciones   **70** (USA) (Sonny Fleet) [1990 10.5g² 11f² 11.5g² 12g² 12m⁴ 14m⁵] smallish, quite attractive filly: fifth foal: sister to Irish 9f winner Spanish Head, winner from 1¼m to 15f in Italy in 1990, and half-sister to useful 1m (at 2 yrs) and 1¼m winner Laxey Bay (by Caerleon) and a winner in Italy: dam, winner 3 times in Australia, is half-sister to No Lute and River Lady: 11/8 on, won maiden at Catterick in June: ran creditably in

Newmarket handicaps (moderately-run race over 1¾m) last 2 outings: stays 1¾m. *B. W. Hills.*

BALLY KNIGHT 5 b.g. Balidar 133 – Silk's Suggestion (Shantung 132) [1990 **63** a12g6 a8g3 a10g3 a10g6 a8g 13g2 16.5m* 16.5g* 16.5f4 16.1m2 1991 14d3 16.2g] smallish, workmanlike gelding: quite modest handicapper: not seen out after May: effective at 1¾m to 2m: acts on firm and dead ground: visored at 4 yrs on all-weather: won over hurdles in January for J. White. *D. Morris.*

BALLYMONEYBOY 2 ch.c. (Mar 7) Ballacashtal (CAN) – Honeybuzzard (FR) **56 p** (Sea Hawk II 131) [1991 6g] half-brother to several winners, including fairly useful 1m to 1½m winner Misaaff (by Mummy's Pet): dam Irish 1¼m winner: 25/1 and bandaged, 8 lengths seventh of 20 in claimer at Lingfield in October, hampered stalls and behind, then staying on well not knocked about: showed round action to post: likely to improve. *M. H. Tompkins.*

BALLYMORE PARK 6 b.g. Ballymore 123 – Tiltress (Tiepolo II 121) [1990 NR — 1991 17m] angular gelding: has a markedly round action: quite useful plater at 3 yrs: blinkered, tailed off only start at 6 yrs (April): should stay beyond 1½m: acts on heavy going, possibly unsuited by top-of-the-ground: won over hurdles in January. *M. D. Hammond.*

BALLYMUST (IRE) 2 ch.f. (Apr 28) Muscatite 122 – Bally 74 (Balidar 133) — [1991 6m 6m] 1,000Y: compact filly: poor mover: half-sister to sprint winner Balishy (by Shy Groom): dam best effort at 1m: soundly beaten in sellers at Windsor (hung markedly left throughout) in June and Leicester (blinkered) following month. *J. White.*

BALLYRANTER 2 ch.c. (Apr 13) Bold Owl 101 – Whipalash 73 (Stephen George **59** 102) [1991 7g 8m a7g2 a8g5 a8g3] 5,600F, 3,000Y, 4,600 2-y-o: strong colt: eighth foal: brother to a winner in Holland: dam placed at 7f: plating-class maiden: no form on turf: stays 1m. *H. J. Collingridge.*

BALLY SONG 3 b.g. Song 132 – Ballyreef (Ballymore 123) [1990 7m 7m 1991 — 12.5m6] compact, workmanlike gelding: little form in maidens. *J. S. King.*

BALLYSTATE 3 ch.f. Ballacashtal (CAN) – Brandenbourg 66 (Le Levanstell **69 d** 122) [1990 6m 7m 7m3 9m2 1991 10g3 10m5 12m3 12g 16g 11.6m 7f 11.5g] angular filly: modest maiden on flat: showed little in handicaps last 5 starts: stays 1½m: blinkered sixth and seventh starts: winning hurdler. *C. James.*

BALLYSTORM (IRE) 2 b.f. (Mar 14) Storm Bird (CAN) 134 – Raise Rain — p (USA) (Raise A Native) [1991 8m] leggy filly: third known foal: half-sister to 3-y-o Ballyrain (by Halo), 5f winner at 2 yrs: dam successful at up to 9f, is half-sister to top-class American filly Winning Colors: on toes, well-beaten ninth of 11 in maiden at Leicester in September: should do better. *P. F. I. Cole.*

BALSMO 3 ch.c. Absalom 128 – Nyeri 104 (Saint Crespin III 132) [1990 5g 6m3 6d **52** 6m2 6m a8g5 a6g* 1991 a6g a7g5 a8g 8.2d 5m 6g2 6g 6g a6g 6g5] sturdy, plain colt: fair plater: stiff tasks after good second at Leicester: suited by 6f: sometimes blinkered, including when successful: sold 1,400 gns Ascot November Sales. *D. Haydn Jones.*

BALTIC ICE (IRE) 2 gr.f. (Apr 18) Be My Guest (USA) 126 – Pastel Shade **50** (USA) (Affirmed (USA)) [1991 6g6 6m] 6,000Y: small, sparely-made filly: first foal: dam Irish 1½m and 2m winner, is daughter of very smart French middle-distance performer Paint The Town: plating-class form in claimer at Lingfield and large-field seller at Newmarket in October, staying on well both times: likely to stay 1¼m: sold 6,500 gns Newmarket Autumn Sales. *J. R. Fanshawe.*

BALTRA (USA) 2 br.f. (Mar 21) Known Fact (USA) 135 – Blue Grass Field 81 **84** (Top Ville 129) [1991 5g* 6g3 6g* 6m4] rather unfurnished filly: has scope: first foal: dam maiden stayed 8.5f: won 5-runner maiden at Sandown (held up) and 6-runner minor event at Lingfield (best effort, made all) in summer: ran moderately in minor event at Pontefract in September: should stay 1m. *B. W. Hills.*

BALUGA 2 ch.c. (Feb 12) Don't Forget Me 127 – Miss Zadig 102 (Thatch (USA) **69 p** 136) [1991 6g 7g5] lengthy, good-quartered colt: has scope: good mover: half-brother to 10.4f winner Timid Bride (by Blushing Groom), 1989 2-y-o 1¼m winner Adding (by Summing) and 2 winners in North America: dam 5f and 1m winner: modest form in maidens at Newmarket (backward, slowly away) in August and Leicester (looked very well, considerably handicapped when beaten) following month: will stay at least 1m: will improve further. *G. Harwood.*

BALWA (USA) 3 b.f. Danzig (USA) – Princess Oola (USA) (Al Hattab (USA)) **101 d** [1990 5g6 5m* 5m* 5f 5m4 5g 1991 7m* 8m5 7g 8g5 7m] small, quite attractive filly:

won £11,900 contest at Newmarket in May, strong run to lead close home: failed to reproduce that form in listed race and pattern events, pulling hard first 2 occasions: suited by 7f: easily best efforts on good to firm ground: edgy fourth start. *A. A. Scott.*

BALZAO (IRE)   2 b.g. (Apr 24) Alzao (USA) 117 – Balaine (GER) (Balidar 133)   **41** [1991 5g 6g 6d⁵ 7d 5g] IR 26,000F, 26,000Y: compact gelding: moderate mover: fifth foal: half-brother to 1989 Irish 2-y-o 6f winner Balage (by Horage) and Irish 9f winner Push Bike (by Ballad Rock): dam from family of Nanticious: poor maiden: best effort when considerably-handicapped fifth of 8 at Goodwood: should stay 1m: visored final start. *G. B. Balding.*

BALZAON KNIGHT   4 b.g. Alzao (USA) 117 – April Sal 65 (Sallust 134) [1990   **—** 7g 8m 8g 10d³ 1991 a11g] rather sparely-made, angular gelding: poor and lightly-raced maiden: stays 1m: acts on good to firm going: blinkered last 2 starts. *P. J. Makin.*

BANANA CUFFLINKS (USA)   5 b.h. Peterhof (USA) 116 – Heather Bee   **—** (USA) (Drone) [1990 7f 1991 18s 9g 7.6g 12m⁶ 10g] lengthy, attractive horse: has a round action: poor handicapper nowadays: may well prove ideally suited by 1m: acts on firm going: best form visored: sold 3,800 gns Doncaster November Sales. *J. R. Shaw.*

BANBURY FLYER   3 b.g. Mummy's Game 120 – Haddon Anna (Dragonara   **68** Palace (USA) 115) [1990 5m 6g 5g³ 5m* 5.8d⁴ 5d 1991 6g 6m⁵ 6g² 5d³ 5g 6m⁶ 5g⁵ 6m* 6f 6f 5d] smallish, rather leggy gelding: has a quick action: modest handicapper: below form after making all at Lingfield in July: stays 6f: acts on good to firm ground and dead. *Miss A. L. M. King.*

BANCROFT   4 b.f. Kabour 80 – Mrs Buzby 71 (Abwah 118) [1990 6d a6g a8g 1991   **—** a6g a6g 6f] sturdy filly: poor mover: no sign of ability. *D. W. Chapman.*

BANDMASTER (USA)   2 b.c. (May 21) Dixieland Band (USA) – Queen's Bid   **97** p (USA) (Hoist The Flag (USA)) [1991 7m⁴ 7f* 8g*] $250,000Y: well-made colt: closely related to a minor winner by Storm Bird and half-brother to several other minor winners: dam minor-winning half-sister to very useful 1985 Irish 1¼m and 11f winner Gold Meridian out of champion Canadian 2-y-o filly Queen Louie: progressive colt: successful in 9-runner maiden at Yarmouth and 8-runner minor event at Wolverhampton in September, staying on strongly both times: will stay 1¼m: sure to improve again. *Mrs J. Cecil.*

BAND OF HOPE (USA)   4 ch.f. Dixieland Band (USA) – Reflection 111 (Mill   **—** § Reef (USA) 141) [1990 8g⁵ 8g⁴ 8f 7.3m 1991 8m] workmanlike, rather plain filly: quite modest maiden at 3 yrs: tailed off only run at 4 yrs (April): best efforts over 1m with give in the ground: twice ran badly in visor: one to avoid. *W. Clay.*

BANDOLINE   2 br.f. (Jan 20) Top Ville 129 – Chic Belle (USA) (Mr Prospector   **56** p (USA)) [1991 7m 8.1s⁵] tall, lightly-made filly: moderate walker: fourth foal: half-sister to 3-y-o Lucy Moon (by Blushing Groom) and useful middle-distance performer Rudjig (by Secreto): dam winner of 4 stakes races at up to 7f in USA: plating-class form in autumn maidens at Leicester (green) and Edinburgh: should stay middle distances: likely to do better. *B. W. Hills.*

BANDOL (IRE)   3 gr.c. Blakeney 126 – Red Rose Bowl (Dragonara Palace   **85** (USA) 115) [1990 NR 1991 7d* 8m⁴ 8g] 35,000Y: smallish, quite attractive colt: reportedly split pastern at 2 yrs: good walker: fourth foal: half-brother to good-class sprinter Gallic League (by Welsh Saint) and 4-y-o 6f winner Anneli Rose (by Superlative): dam winner over 7f at 2 yrs in Ireland, is half-sister to Cesarewitch winner Private Audition: 11/10 on, won newcomers race at Doncaster in March: good fourth at Newmarket, easily better effort when favourite for handicaps in October: will prove suited by 1m+: sold 10,500 gns Newmarket Autumn Sales. *B. W. Hills.*

BAND ON THE RUN   4 ch.c. Song 132 – Sylvanecte (FR) 70 (Silver Shark 129)   **92** [1990 6m⁵ 6m* 7g* 7.6f² 8m² 8.2m³ 7.6g 1991 8d³ 7d² 8g⁴ 8g 8.1g² 7.9g 7.1f³] rather angular, good-topped colt: poor mover: improved handicapper at 4 yrs, placed in William Hill Lincoln and Insulpak Victoria Cup: effective at 7f to 1m: has form on firm ground, but best efforts on an easy surface: has hung left. *B. A. McMahon.*

BAND SARGEANT (IRE)   2 b.g. (May 7) Nashamaa 113 – Indian Honey   **55** (Indian King (USA) 128) [1991 5m⁵ 7d⁴ 5m⁶ 6m] IR 5,800F, IR 5,800Y: second foal: dam unraced: plating-class form at best: easily best effort in maidens when fourth of 8 at Ayr in July: not seen out after August: seems suited by a soft surface. *G. Richards.*

BANHAM COLLEGE   5 b.g. Tower Walk 130 – Baby Flo 67 (Porto Bello 118)   **56** [1990 5m² 7m 5d 1991 5d³ 5g⁵ 6g 5f² 6m 5g*] robust, rather dipped-backed gelding:

moderate mover: plating-class handicapper: won at Nottingham in June: should prove as effective at 6f + (mostly faced stiff tasks when tried): acts on firm and dead ground. *B. A. McMahon.*

BANISH 2 b.c. (Mar 15) Don't Forget Me 127 – Busca (USA) 49 (Mr Prospector (USA)) [1991 7.1d] IR 28,000Y: strong colt: second living foal: half-brother to 3-y-o 1¼m winner Abingdon Flyer (by Pennine Walk): dam (stayed 9.4f) is out of Kentucky Oaks winner and CCA Oaks second Bag of Tunes: burly and green, tailed off in large-field maiden at Chepstow in October, losing several lengths at start and not knocked about. *B. W. Hills.*   —

BANKER MASON (USA) 5 b.h. Sadler's Wells (USA) 132 – Alwah (USA) (Damascus (USA)) [1990 a12g 8.5f⁶ 10f 12f a7g 1991 9s 12d] smallish, sparely-made horse: has a rather round action: won maiden claimer at Lingfield late on as 3-y-o: no subsequent form: stays 1¼m: possibly unsuited by firm ground, acts on any other: blinkered last 2 starts: sold 920 gns Doncaster Summer Sales. *D. Yeoman.*   —

BANKROLL 4 b.g. Chief Singer 131 – Very Nice (FR) (Green Dancer (USA) 132) [1990 7m⁴ 12.3d 8g 10g⁴ 12m⁴ 12d 9m⁴ 1991 a12g³ a13g* a11g a10g⁵ a12g³ 12s a12g³ 12f* 10.1f⁵ a12g 17.2f 13.8f³ a16g³ 14.1f⁴ 11.9f⁵ 11.9g²] tall, workmanlike gelding: shows a round action: quite modest handicapper: won at Lingfield in January and Brighton in May: stays well: needs a sound surface: suited by forcing tactics. *C. A. Cyzer.*   **72 a 79**

BANTEL BAMBINA 3 gr.f. Bold Owl 101 – Bantel Baby (Warpath 113) [1990 5g 7f 5m² 6m 5g³ 5m³ 1991 5g 6d³ 8.1m 6f] plain filly: poor maiden: should stay beyond 6f: acts on dead ground: below best when blinkered final starts at 2 and 3 yrs: sold 1,700 gns Doncaster October Sales. *R. Allan.*   **43**

BANTEL BRIGADIER 2 ch.g. (Mar 21) Mandrake Major 122 – Bantel Baby (Warpath 113) [1991 5f 6d 5m⁵ 6f] good-bodied gelding: third foal: dam and grandam of no account: no worthwhile form in varied events. *R. Allan.*   —

BANTON LOCH 4 br.g. Lochnager 132 – Balgownie 43 (Prince Tenderfoot (USA) 126) [1990 8.2s 8v 8g 7g³ 7g 8.2d 1991 8.2s⁵ 16.2g] lengthy, good-topped gelding: poor maiden: no show at 4 yrs (visored): stays 1m: best efforts on good ground: sold 2,700 gns Ascot September Sales. *C. Tinkler.*   —

BARACHOIS PRINCESS (USA) 4 b.f. Barachois (CAN) – Egregious (USA) (Barbizon) [1990 8f³ 8.2m⁴ 10.4g 8g 1991 10.4d 10g 10.5m 10.3m 10.3m⁵ 14.1h⁵ 10.5g 7g⁵ a8g] workmanlike mare: moderate mover: poor handicapper: stays 1¼m: acts on firm going. *R. Hollinshead.*   **44**

BARBARA'S CUTIE 3 ch.f. Tina's Pet 121 – Eucharis 41 (Tickled Pink 114) [1990 5m 5f⁶ 6m 1991 5s² 5m⁵ 5g 5g⁶ 5m 5.1m 5g 5m³ 5d² a5g⁴ a5g⁴] small, sturdy filly: poor maiden: ran creditably in handicaps last 4 starts: should stay 6f: acts on good to firm ground and soft. *M. Blanshard.*   **46**

BARBARY REEF (IRE) 3 b.g. Sarab 123 – Brown's Cay 71 (Formidable (USA) 125) [1990 6f 7f⁵ 6d 1991 9d 14.1g 10g* 10.1m* 10.1m⁵ 8m 10m² 9g a12g⁶] strong gelding: moderate walker: quite modest handicapper: won at Nottingham and Yarmouth (made all) in July: well beaten at Lingfield final start: needs further than 1m, and may well prove ideally suited by 1½m: acts on good to firm ground: visored (ran poorly) eighth start. *G. H. Eden.*   **63**

BARBEZIEUX 4 b.c. Petong 126 – Merchantmens Girl 58 (Klairon 131) [1990 a7g 5f* 6g 5d⁴ 5m⁶ 5f 5m 5f 5f 5d 5g 5m 1991 5g 5m 5.1m 5g⁵ 5g³ 5d* 5d⁶ 5m² 5m* 5m 5m⁴ 6g⁴ 5f 7g 6m 5f 5.3g] strong, workmanlike colt: moderate mover: plating-class sprint handicapper at best: won at Goodwood (apprentices) and Leicester in summer: lost his way: acts on good to firm (possibly unsuited by very firm) and dead going: effective blinkered or not: hard ride: sold out of D. Wilson's stable 4,600 gns Newmarket July Sales after thirteenth start. *T. J. Naughton.*   **52**

BAR BILLIARDS 2 b.c. (Apr 22) Bold Arrangement 127 – Green Teable (FR) (Green Dancer (USA) 132) [1991 7m] fourth foal: dam placed over 11f from 3 starts in France: 50/1, soundly beaten in 9-runner maiden at Lingfield in October. *C. A. Austin.*   —

BARCHAM PRINCE 9 b.g. Balliol 125 – Barcham Bride 70 (Henry The Seventh 125) [1990 NR 1991 16.2g 16.2f] tall gelding: of no account. *T. Kersey.*   —

BARDOLPH (USA) 4 b.g. Golden Act (USA) – Love To Barbara (USA) (Stewvard) [1990 12m⁶ 11.7m 11.5g 8d 8m⁵ 10g⁴ 1991 9d⁶ 12d* 16.2d4 14s* 16.2g⁵ 18m² 16.5d⁵] compact gelding: moderate mover: modest handicapper: won at Salisbury (amateurs) in May and Sandown in July: second in moderately-run Tote Cesarewitch at Newmarket: seems ideally suited by test of stamina: acts on any   **78**

going: effective blinkered or not: has run well when sweating: usually bandaged off-hind: consistent: gelded after final start. *P. F. I. Cole.*

BARELY BLACK 3 br.g. Lidhame 109 – Louisa Anne 73 (Mummy's Pet 125) — [1990 6g 7f 5s 1991 8f⁴ 8.2m 6d 7f] big, leggy gelding: poor performer: form only at 1m on firm going: sometimes bandaged behind: sold to join N. Babbage 1,000 gns Doncaster August Sales. *J. S. Haldane.*

BARESI (IRE) 3 b.c. Alzao (USA) 117 – Hedwige (African Sky 124) [1990 6g 1991   **74** 8.5f² 8.5m³ 9.7m* 8m⁶] rather leggy colt: modest form in maidens: won at Folkestone, making virtually all and running on well: always pushed along in handicap later in July: better at 1¼m than shorter: sold to join J. O'Shea 5,500 gns Newmarket Autumn Sales. *H. R. A. Cecil.*

BARFORD LAD 4 b.g. Nicholas Bill 125 – Grace Poole (Sallust 134) [1990 8m   **78** 8.2s² 10g⁶ 8g 8m 7g⁴ 10f² 8v 8d* 1991 10.1g² 10m⁵ 8f³ 8.9g 8.1m⁴ 9m⁵ 8g³] good-topped gelding: modest handicapper: effective at 1m to 1¼m: acts on any going, with possible exception of heavy: pulled hard when visored: has run well when sweating: has looked none too easy a ride: consistent. *J. R. Fanshawe.*

BARGEE (USA) 2 b.c. (Feb 12) Riverman (USA) 131 – North Mist (USA) (Far North (CAN) 120) [1991 6d⁶] IR 57,000Y: good-topped colt: has plenty of scope: second foal: dam won at up to 9f in USA: 25/1 and green, around 13 lengths sixth of 19 to Dr Devious in maiden at Newbury (slowly away, soon niggled along, kept on steadily) in May: looked sure to improve, particularly over further, but wasn't seen again. *P. F. I. Cole.*

BARICHSTE 3 ch.g. Electric 126 – Be Sharp 85 (Sharpen Up 127) [1990 6s⁵ 6f   **39** a7g³ 8.2d 8d 1991 10f 12g 12.3g a12g 10.8m 12m 10m a12g³] tall, leggy gelding: plating-class maiden: little form as 3-y-o, third in claimer at Southwell in December: stays 1½m. *B. A. McMahon.*

BARJONAL 2 gr.f. (Mar 21) Absalom 128 – Hum 69 (Crooner 119) [1991 5d 6g 6g] — 5,000Y: lengthy, workmanlike filly: poor mover: sister to 3-y-o In Concert and 2-y-o sprint winners Absolutely Humming (stays 1m) and Skybolt, and half-sister to a 6f winner by Averof: dam stayed 1½m: well beaten in maidens and a minor event in mid-summer. *J. J. Bridger.*

BARKERVILLE (USA) 3 b.c. Mr Prospector (USA) – Euryanthe (USA) **104** p (Nijinsky (CAN) 138) [1990 7m³ 1991 10.4d² 9g² 8m 9g*] tall, leggy colt: 14/1 and bandaged near-fore, useful and improved effort to win 18-runner £30,800 People-Sporting Life Championship Handicap at Newbury in October by 3 lengths from Coltrane, making nearly all and running on very strongly: off course over 4 months after second start: probably stays 1¼m: sure to win more races. *M. R. Stoute.*

BARKSTON SINGER 4 b.f. Runnett 125 – Miss Flirt (Welsh Pageant 132)   **65** § [1990 8.5g 7m⁵ 8d² 7f³ 8f 8.2d⁵ 8g 1991 7f 7m 9m⁴ 10.5d 10m⁴ 8m² 9g a8g a10g] tall, leggy, lightly-made filly: poor walker: modest handicapper: stays 1¼m: acts on firm and dead going: ran poorly when blinkered once: trained reappearance by J. Harris: has proved very awkward stalls: has hung: difficult ride and has looked temperamental. *Mrs N. Macauley.*

BARLEY SPIRIT (IRE) 2 b.g. (Mar 9) Milk of The Barley 115 – Pink Stripes (Pyjama Hunt 126) [1991 5m 6d 6.9m] 4,000Y: smallish gelding: third foal: half-brother to poor maiden Roche (by Balliol): dam never ran: no worthwhile form in sellers, final one in June: slowly away first 2 starts: visored second. *Mrs G. R. Reveley.*

People-Sporting Life Championship 3-Y-O Handicap Final, Newbury—
Barkerville runs on very strongly ahead of Coltrane (visor), Mudaffar (left) and Daswaki

BARLOGAN 3 b.f. Dunbeath (USA) 127 – Corinthia (USA) (Empery (USA) 128) **70**
[1990 NR 1991 6m 7g³ 8g³ 7.6m³ 7g* 8m⁴ 8g] workmanlike filly: second foal:
half-sister to quite modest 1989 2-y-o 6f winner Rambadale (by Vaigly Great): dam,
lightly raced in France, is half-sister to smart miler Nino Bibbia: modest form:
sweating, won maiden at Lingfield in October: worth a try beyond 1m: acts on good
to firm ground. *C. F. Wall.*

BARMBRACK 2 ch.g. (Mar 15) Doulab (USA) 115 – Irish Cookie 80 (Try My **47**
Best (USA) 130) [1991 6.1m 6m 5g] useful-looking gelding: has a moderate action:
second foal: half-brother to 3-y-o Bold Cookie (by Never So Bold): dam 6f and 7f
winner, best at 4 yrs: poor form in maidens, best effort final start: gelded afterwards:
may do better. *R. M. Whitaker.*

BARNEYKIN 2 b.c. (Apr 16) Brotherly (USA) 80 – Make Amends 74 (Tutankhamen) [1991 5m] leggy, close-coupled colt: half-brother to 2 winners by Lochnager,
including useful 1977 2-y-o 6f winner Reparation: dam won over 5f at 2 yrs and
stayed well: backward and very green, very slowly away and soon tailed off in
10-runner seller at Bath in May: very troublesome at stalls. *D. J. Wintle.*

BARNSVIEW 2 ch.g. (Mar 2) Doulab (USA) 115 – Ridans Girl 89 (Ridan (USA)) **38**
[1991 5d 5g 5m⁴ 5h⁶ 5g] 1,800F, 1,500Y: leggy gelding: half-brother to a winner in
Belgium: dam 2-y-o 5f and 6f winner, is sister to good 1977 2-y-o Aythorpe and
half-sister to smart performer (at up to 7f) Royal Boy: poor maiden: best effort when
fourth in seller: sweating, and troublesome stalls, on debut: not seen out after June.
M. W. Ellerby.

BARON CORVO (USA) 7 ch.g. Sir Ivor 135 – A Medium Hello (USA) (Droll **—**
Role) [1990 17.4d 16.5d a14g 1991 12s 12d 12g] robust, round-barrelled gelding:
moderate mover: one-time useful winner: no form for long time: used to be suited
by a test of stamina. *K. B. McCauley.*

BAROQUE ANGEL (IRE) 3 b.f. Tate Gallery (USA) 117 – Blues In The Night **—**
(Cure The Blues (USA)) [1990 6d 1991 5f 6f] compact filly: well beaten in maidens:
dead. *D. A. Wilson.*

BARRIES PET 3 gr.f. Petong 126 – Second Event 86 (Fine Blade (USA) 121) **41**
[1990 a7g a7g a8g⁵ 1991 a8g² a8g³ a10g⁵] lengthy, sparely-made filly: plating-class
form: easily best effort when second in claimer at Southwell in February: suited by
1m: visored second start. *M. H. Tompkins.*

BARRISH 5 b.h. Wassl 125 – Rowa 83§ (Great Nephew 126) [1990 12f* 18f² 14m³ **78**
18.4d 16m³ 12d⁴ 12m* 12f² 14m* 12f⁴ 14g⁶ 12g² 13.3g⁶ 12m 12s 1991 12s 12m 12m²
12g 14g² 13.9g 14m* 14.6m⁴ 13.3m 12m⁶ 12g] angular horse: modest handicapper:
won at Sandown in August: best form at up to 1¾m: seems best on a sound surface:
often sweats: genuine. *R. Akehurst.*

BARRON'S BOY 3 b.g. Track Barron (USA) – Baltic Leap (USA) (Northern **—**
Dancer) [1990 6g a6g a7g 6d a5g 1991 10d 7g 5g 6f] rather angular gelding: poor form
at 2 yrs, none at 3 yrs: sold 675 gns Ascot July Sales. *W. Carter.*

BARRYBEN 2 b. or br.g. (Jun 16) Seymour Hicks (FR) 125 – Ensigns Kit (Saucy **—**
Kit 76) [1991 a7g a7g] first reported foal: dam winning jumper well beaten on flat:
tailed off in maiden and claimer at Southwell late in year. *W. M. Brisbourne.*

BARRYS GAMBLE 5 gr.h. Nishapour (FR) 125 – Scoby Lass (Prominer 125) **79**
[1990 5f* 5f² 5f 5f 6m 5.6g 5m³ 5m 5m 5s 1991 5g 5f 5m 5f4] robust, good-quartered
horse: carries plenty of condition: moderate mover, with a quick action: fair
handicapper: best at 5f on top-of-the-ground: occasionally blinkered: ridden by
claimer at 5 yrs. *T. Fairhurst.*

BARSAC 3 b.c. Sulaafah (USA) 119 – Counsel's Verdict (Firestreak 125) [1990 6g **66**
6g 6g 6m 6d⁶ 7d 6d 1991 7m 10.2d² 10.1d² 10.1m* 9.7f5 10m 12m³ 10g 10.5d*]
smallish, good-quartered colt: moderate mover: quite modest performer: won
sellers at Windsor (sweating, bought out of P. Makin's stable 6,600 gns) in July and
Haydock (gamely, no bid) in October: inconsistent in between: stays 1½m: acts on
good to firm ground and dead: blinkered twice at 2 yrs. *R. Akehurst.*

BARTOLINI (USA) 3 ch.c. Lyphard (USA) 132 – Jubilous (USA) (Sir Ivor 135) **—**
[1990 NR 1991 8d] 105,000Y: sturdy, rather angular colt: second foal: half-brother to
quite modest maiden Birthday Parade (by Chief's Crown): dam, graded stakes-
placed winner at up to 11f, is daughter of Grade 1 winner Bring Out The Band: no
promise in Pontefract maiden: dead. *M. W. Easterby.*

BARTOLOMEO (USA) 2 b.c. (Mar 18) Vaguely Noble 140 – Stonechurch **66**
(USA) (Naskra (USA)) [1991 7f 7g 8g4] 90,000Y: strong colt: first foal: dam sprint
winner in USA from family of Mt Livermore and Magical Wonder: quite modest

maiden: easily best effort when fourth of 11 at Bath in September, making most: will stay 1¼m: blinkered second start: sold to join Mrs J. Ramsden 12,000 gns Newmarket Autumn Sales: may improve further. *G. Harwood.*

BARTON PRIDE (IRE) 2 b.g. (Feb 13) Phardante (FR) 120 – Ginosa 62 **58** (Kalamoun 129) [1991 7m 7.6d⁵] close-coupled gelding: fifth foal: half-brother to 1988 2-y-o 5f winner Generousity Gem (by Burslem) and a winner in Scandinavia by Taufan: dam placed over 1½m: quite modest form in autumn maidens at Leicester and Chester (still bit backward, off bridle after 2f) week later: will be suited by 1m +. *R. Hollinshead.*

BARUD (IRE) 3 b.g. Persian Bold 123 – Pale Moon 58 (Jukebox 120) [1990 6g 6m — 6d 1991 7d 8.2d 6g 6.9s] leggy gelding: poor maiden: bred to stay 1m +: rather headstrong on occasions: sold to join C. Smith 2,600 gns Newmarket July Sales: subsequently gelded. *C. J. Benstead.*

BASHAMAH (IRE) 2 b. or br.f. (Mar 6) Nashamaa 113 – Raja Moulana 75 (Raja **50** Baba (USA)) [1991 7g 7m] rather unfurnished filly: moderate mover: first foal: dam 7f winner: bit backward, always towards rear in large fields of maidens at Newmarket. *C. E. Brittain.*

BASHOOFEK (IRE) 2 b.c. (Apr 9) Sadler's Wells (USA) 132 – Gracious Miss **63** (FR) (Gay Mecene (USA) 128) [1991 7g 7g⁴ 7f⁵ 8m] 78,000Y: good-quartered colt: second foal: half-brother to 3-y-o Merry Tinker (by Last Tycoon): dam French 9f winner, is half-sister to 2 smart winners in France, including miler Gay Minstrel: easily best effort when fourth of 14 in maiden at Newmarket in August, headed halfway, rallying final 1f: may well be unsuited by top-of-the-ground: sold 10,000 gns Newmarket Autumn Sales. *B. Hanbury.*

BASHOOSH (USA) 3 b.f. Danzig (USA) – Condessa 121 (Condorcet (FR)) — [1990 NR 1991 10g 12.2f³ 12.1g⁶ 11f] $700,000Y: smallish, leggy filly: fifth foal: closely related to 4-y-o 1m winner Valira (by Nijinsky) and to modest maiden Lydney (by Lyphard): dam won Yorkshire Oaks: about 13 lengths third of 6 at Catterick, best effort in maidens and apprentice handicap (sweating) in first half of season. *A. A. Scott.*

BASIC FUN 5 b.m. Teenoso (USA) 135 – Sirenivo (USA) 113 (Sir Ivor 135) [1990 — 11g 13g 12g 1991 a13g⁵] leggy, rather sparely-made mare: modest maiden at best: no form for long time: probably stays 1¾m: unsuited by top-of-the-ground. *J. L. Spearing.*

BASILICA 2 b.c. (Mar 11) Bold Arrangement 127 – Sunset Reef (Mill Reef (USA) **63** 141) [1991 8m⁶ 8m⁶ 6g] IR 30,000Y: workmanlike, sturdy colt: third foal: half-brother to disappointing 3-y-o Sunset Street (by Bellypha), fair 6f winner at 2 yrs, and a winner in France by Caerleon: dam, maiden, should have been suited by middle distances: quite modest form, staying on never dangerous, in northern maidens first 2 starts: soundly beaten in Racecall Gold Trophy at Redcar later in October: will stay 1¼m. *C. E. Brittain.*

BASMA (USA) 2 b.f. (Feb 24) Grey Dawn II 132 – Tilting (USA) (Seattle Slew **104** (USA)) [1991 6g* 6s⁴ 6f* 6m³] $375,000Y: big, close-coupled, attractive filly: has plenty of scope: fourth foal: sister to Dawn Quixote, graded-stakes winner in USA at up to 1m: dam ran once: useful filly: successful in maiden at Goodwood in August and 5-runner minor event at Salisbury (impressively) following month: best effort 1½ lengths third of 9, making most and keeping on, to Marling in Tattersalls Cheveley Park Stakes at Newmarket: will stay at least 1m: unsuited by soft ground. *Major W. R. Hern.*

BASSIO (BEL) 2 b.c. (Mar 26) Efisio 120 – Batalya (BEL) (Boulou (BEL)) [1991 **71** ? 5d⁴ 5s⁵ 5f⁴ 6m² 6g⁴ 6f* 6g* 7g⁶ 7.5f* 7f³ 8f⁶ a8g³] 500Y: neat colt: first reported foal: dam won 6 races in Belgium: successful in sellers at Yarmouth (no bid) and Nottingham (retained 5,500 gns) and nursery (by 10 lengths) at Beverley in summer: may stay 1¼m: acts very well on firm ground: blinkered third outing: suitable mount for a claimer: has given trouble stalls. *C. N. Allen.*

BATABANOO 2 ch.c. (May 24) Bairn (USA) 126 – For Instance (Busted 134) **71** [1991 5m² 6g³ 7f* 7m* 7m* 7m³ 8m* 8m³ 8g] 7,200Y: leggy, sparely-made colt: has a quick action: third foal: brother to 3-y-o Forbearance, 1m winner at 2 yrs: dam ran 3 times at 4 yrs: successful in July in claimer at Redcar and sellers (retained 12,500 gns second occasion) at Yarmouth and Redcar: showed improved form to win 14-runner nursery at Pontefract in September, staying on well: set plenty to do final start: will stay 1¼m: acts well on top-of-the-ground. *Mrs G. R. Reveley.*

BATON BOY 10 ch.g. Music Boy 124 – Lobela 77 (Lorenzaccio 130) [1990 7f³ 7m **32** 5d 6s a6g⁶ a8g⁴ a7g a7g 1991 7f³ 6g⁵ 7.6g³ 8f 6m 7m 8.3f⁵ 7m 10.5d] lengthy, rather sparely-made gelding: poor mover: poor handicapper nowadays: effective over stiff 6f and stays 1m: probably acts on any going: has run moderately in blinkers. *J. S. Wainwright.*

BATRA (USA)   3 b.f. Green Dancer (USA) 132 – Avatar's Court (USA) (Avatar (USA)) [1990 5f* 6m 1991 8g6] lengthy, unfurnished filly: backward on first run for nearly 10 months (broke blood vessel second start at 2 yrs) when good sixth of 19 in handicap at Kempton in April: should be suited by at least 1m: blinkered on debut. *P. F. I. Cole.*   **60**

BATTLE COLOURS (IRE)   2 b.c. (May 6) Petorius 117 – Streamertail 81 (Shirley Heights 130) [1991 5g6 6s2 a5g2 a6g*] IR 13,000Y: smallish, quite attractive colt: half-brother to fairly useful but reliable 6f (at 2 yrs) to 1¼m winner Jacamar (by Jalmood): dam 8.2f and 9f winner: modest performer: comfortable winner of 8-runner maiden at Lingfield late in year: better suited by 6f than 5f, and will stay 7f. *Sir Mark Prescott.*   **79**

BATTLE OF BRITAIN   2 b.c. (Mar 26) Beveled (USA) – Pink N' Perky (Tickled Pink 114) [1991 5m 5.1m4 a5g* 5g2 6.1g3 6m2 6g3 6g4 a6g*] 4,500Y: good-quartered colt: poor mover: second foal: dam poor maiden: sire (by Sharpen Up) won from 6f to 7f: modest performer: goes well on equitrack at Lingfield and won maiden there in June and claimer (claimed £6,200) in November: stays 6f: bandaged behind second outing: twice coltish: consistent. *J. Berry.*   **72**

BATTLE OF FLOWERS   4 b.f. Shernazar 131 – Valiant Cry (Town Crier 119) [1990 8m 10g4 7g3 8g6 7d4 7m3 1991 10.1g 10m4 8h4 8g] sparely-made filly: has quick, fluent action: plating-class maiden: stays 1¼m: acts on good to firm ground. *C. F. Wall.*   **53**

BATTLE ON   4 b.f. Blakeney 126 – Perfect Picture (FR) 78 (Hopeful Venture 125) [1990 11v4 11g3 10g* 12.4f5 16.2g4 12s 13v5 1991 16v 12d5 16m* 14m* 16m* 16g* 20g 16g2 14d* 14g3 16g* 16g5 16m4 16s] modest Irish handicapper nowadays: won at Wexford, Tralee, Clonmel, Roscommon, Killarney and Galway: well beaten, stiff task, in Ascot Stakes in June: brought down final start: stays 2m: acts on firm and dead ground: ran creditably when blinkered penultimate start. *J. S. Bolger, Ireland.*   **74**

BATTLERS GREEN (IRE)   3 b.g. Hard Fought 125 – Reparata (Jukebox 120) [1990 7g 8.2m6 8g4 8.2d 1991 10g 10g 10d 10g] rather angular gelding: quite modest maiden at 2 yrs: no worthwhile form in summer at 3 yrs, in amateurs handicap final start: stays 1m: best efforts on a sound surface. *G. B. Balding.*   **—**

BATTLING BELLA (USA)   2 b.f. (Feb 24) Fighting Fit (USA) – Belle Marina 82 (Lochnager 132) [1991 6g3 5g4 6.1m] sturdy, workmanlike filly: has a round action: second foal: dam 2-y-o 5f winner: quite modest maiden: in frame at Goodwood (best effort) and Lingfield within a week in August: sweating, below form at Nottingham (soon scrubbed along) 2½ months later: stays 6f. *Denys Smith.*   **59**

BATTUTA   2 ch.f. (Apr 3) Ballacashtal (CAN) – Valpolicella 63 (Lorenzaccio 130) [1991 5m3 6m4 6m3 6.1m4 7m6 6.1m 7m] 1,500Y: leggy, lightly-made filly: **53**

Timeform Nursery Handicap, Pontefract—Batabanoo, from Ribbonaire and Trial Times

half-sister to several poor animals: dam plater: plating-class maiden: below best, twice in nurseries, last 3 starts: stays 6f. *R. Earnshaw.*

BATZUSHKA (USA)   4 b.c. Danzig (USA) – Nicole Mon Amour (USA) (Bold **101** Bidder) [1990 5m⁵ 5m 6m 8.5m* 8m⁵ 8m* 8g³ 8g² 8g⁵ 7d⁴ 9g 1991 7g 8g 8m 8d⁵ 8g⁴ 8f⁴ 7g² 8g⁶ 7.3m] neat, strong, good-bodied colt: useful performer nowadays: best 4-y-o effort staying-on equal-second to Norton Challenger in listed event at York in August: stays 1m: acts on firm going: wears dropped noseband nowadays: effective blinkered or not: seems best with waiting tactics: bandaged first 4 starts. *Mrs L. Piggott.*

BAVARIA   2 b.f. (Apr 11) Top Ville 129 – Nuravia 91 (Nureyev (USA) 131) [1991   **83** p 6d*] second foal: half-sister to a winner in Austria by Kalaglow: dam, won twice at around 7f, is half-sister to Grand Prix de Paris second War Hero: 13/8 favourite, won minor event at Navan in October by 2 lengths: will stay 1m: should improve. *J. Oxx, Ireland.*

BAYADERE (USA)   2 b.f. (Jan 19) Green Dancer (USA) 132 – Azallya (FR)   — p (Habitat 134) [1991 7m] lengthy, sparely-made filly: first foal: dam French 8.3f winner, is half-sister to smart French 1¼m and 1½m winner Anitra's Dance (by Green Dancer) out of smart middle-distance performer Azurella: weak 20/1-shot and green, around 12 lengths eleventh of 17, never a threat, in maiden at Newmarket in October: will stay 1m: should improve. *M. R. Stoute.*

BAYAIREG (USA)   2 ch.c. (Apr 21) Diesis 133 – Cacti (USA) (Tom Rolfe) [1991   **72** 7g⁶ 8.1m³ 7g⁶] compact, useful-looking colt: brother to Oaks and Irish Oaks winner Diminuendo and half-brother to a winner in USA by Effervescing: dam minor winner at around 1m: modest maiden: 1¾ lengths third of 5 to King's Loch in minor event at Sandown in September: wearing crossed noseband, ran poorly at Warwick following month: stays 1m. *A. A. Scott.*

BAY BOB (IRE)   2 b.c. (Apr 14) Bob Back (USA) 124 – Princess Peppy (Pitskelly 122) [1991 5.3m⁶ 6m 6d] IR 3,300F, 2,600Y, 2,400 2-y-o: leggy colt: third foal: dam Irish maiden, placed at 1½m: well beaten, in June seller final start. *S. Dow.*

BAY CHIEFTAIN   2 ch.g. (May 11) Chief Singer 131 – Mischiefmaker 73   — (Calpurnius 122) [1991 a7g 8m a8g] 2,600Y: good-topped gelding: sixth living foal: half-brother to winners in Norway and Italy: dam 1m seller winner at 2 yrs stayed 1¼m: of little account: blinkered final start: sold 1,050 gns Ascot December Sales. *Mrs L. Stubbs.*

BAY CHIMES   4 b.f. Buzzards Bay 128§ – Wrekin Belle (Dance In Time (CAN))   — [1990 a5g 6s 1991 7f a7g] small filly: poor maiden: trained until after reappearance by D. Dutton. *J. Hetherton.*

BAYLORD PRINCE (IRE)   3 b.c. Horage 124 – Miss Moat (Dike (USA)) [1990   **48** 6m 7m 6f⁴ 8f⁵ 10s⁶ a8g² 1991 12m⁴ 8m⁴ 10f 10.1d] lengthy, good-topped colt: plater: ran creditably at Brighton (not handling track and carrying head awkwardly) second start, poorly afterwards: stays 1¼m (no chance at 1½m): acts on any going: joined J. Ffitch-Heyes. *W. Carter.*

BAY MEADOWS STAR   3 b.f. Sharpo 132 – Upper Caen (High Top 131) [1990   — 6m⁴ 6g 5f 7f 1991 6g] sparely-made filly: quite modest maiden: blinkered last 2 starts, running freely and tending to hang first occasion then looking none too keen when hooded as well on sole start in 1991: should stay 7f: one to be wary of: sold 750 gns Ascot 2nd July Sales. *I. A. Balding.*

BAYONNE   3 ch.f. Bay Express 132 – Lambay 88 (Lorenzaccio 130) [1990 NR   **72** 1991 6m² 6g² 7m² 7m 5.2f³ 5m* 5.1m* 5d] leggy, angular filly: fifth foal: sister to 7.6f winner Bay Bay and half-sister to 1¼m seller winner Toda (by Absalom) and useful 1m to 11f performer My Lamb (by Relkino): dam 2-y-o 7f winner: modest form: won maiden at Warwick in August and handicap at Chepstow in September: keen sort, speedy and suited by 5f: acts on firm (possibly unsuited by dead) ground: blinkered last 5 starts. *R. F. Johnson Houghton.*

BAYPHIA   3 ch.g. Bay Express 132 – Sophie Avenue (Guillaume Tell (USA) 121)   **53** [1990 6h⁶ 6m⁶ 5m 6g 6d⁶ 1991 6f 10.1s 10f 8d² 12g* 12m⁴ 14.1m 11.5m 10.8m] quite good-topped gelding: has a quick action: plater: won handicap (no bid) at Brighton in July: mostly ran moderately afterwards: stays 1½m well: best efforts with give in the ground: blinkered last 6 starts: sold to join J. Joseph 2,700 gns Ascot October Sales. *G. Lewis.*

BAYSHAM (USA)   5 b.g. Raise A Native – Sunny Bay (USA) (Northern Bay   **84** (USA)) [1990 10.8m 8m 6f² 6m² 5m⁶ 6d² 6m³ 7f² 6g 1991 6s 6g⁴ 6g* 6m* 6d³ 6g* 6g⁴ 6g 6m 5.6m² 7d⁵ 5d 5.2g] tall, close-coupled gelding: impresses in appearance: much improved handicapper at 5 yrs: successful at Salisbury in May and July: good second to Sarcita in Tote-Portland Handicap at Doncaster in September: effective at 5f to 7f: acts on firm and dead going: not discredited when visored, best form in blinkers: has run well when sweating: tough and consistent: a credit to his trainer. *B. R. Millman.*

BAYSH (USA) 5 gr.h. Silver Hawk (USA) 127 – Caterina 124 (Princely Gift 137) —
[1990 NR 1991 a6g] sturdy, good-topped horse: lightly-raced maiden: tailed off only run at 5 yrs. *J. D. Czerpak.*

BAY TERN (USA) 5 b.h. Arctic Tern (USA) 126 – Unbiased (USA) 81 (Foolish —
Pleasure (USA)) [1990 NR 1991 15m⁵ 14.1m⁴] rangy horse: fair form in 1989: well beaten at 5 yrs: should stay well: acts on soft ground. *M. H. Easterby.*

BAY TROUPER (IRE) 3 b.f. Bay Express 132 – Record Finish (Record Token —
128) [1990 5g 5m a6g⁴ a7g 1991 6g 8g 7g] sturdy filly: poor maiden: worthwhile form only on third start at 2 yrs. *M. Bell.*

BAZZROY (IRE) 2 ch.c. (Mar 28) King Persian 107 – Miss Noora (Ahonoora —
122) [1991 7f] IR 2,000Y: lengthy colt: second foal: dam Irish 1m and 1¼m winner: 33/1, burly and green, slowly away and always behind in claimer at Salisbury in September. *J. S. Moore.*

BDOORE (IRE) 3 b.f. Petoski 135 – Princess Biddy 86 (Sun Prince 128) [1990 —
7m⁶ 8m⁴ 1991 8m⁶ 10m] well-made filly: quite modest maiden at 2 yrs: mulish in preliminaries, pulled hard and tailed off in handicap in May, 1991: bred to stay 1¼m. *M. A. Jarvis.*

BEACHOLME BOY (IRE) 3 b.g. Dominion 123 – Bronte (USA) 88 (Bold —
Forbes (USA)) [1990 7m 7f 1991 10m] leggy, angular gelding: poor walker: soundly beaten in maiden auctions and claimer. *W. Wilson.*

BEACHY HEAD 3 gr.c. Damister (USA) 123 – No More Rosies 74 (Warpath 113) **66 +**
[1990 7v* 1991 8g⁴ 10d 15m⁵ 16.2d] leggy, sparely-made colt: shows knee action: 33/1 on first run for 5 months, appeared to run well when 8¾ lengths fifth of 6 to Romany Rye in minor event at Ayr in September: always behind in handicap 3 weeks later: stays 15f: acts on good to firm ground and heavy: coltish first 2 starts, looking unsatisfactory (soon well behind) on second of them. *C. W. Thornton.*

BE A HONEY 3 ch.f. Be My Guest (USA) 126 – Reltop 72 (High Top 131) [1990 **93**
6.5g⁶ 8.2v³ 1991 10d 12m 11.8m* 12f* 14.6m 12m] rangy filly: fairly useful performer: won maiden at Leicester and minor event at Newbury in summer: stiff tasks afterwards in Group 3 event (ran poorly nonetheless) at Doncaster and listed race (led 1¼m) at Newmarket: stays 1½m well: acts on firm ground. *N. A. Graham.*

BEAM ME UP SCOTTY (IRE) 2 br.c. (Apr 22) Orchestra 118 – Bright Path **62**
64 (He Loves Me 120) [1991 6g 5m⁵ 6f² 7m 6.1m 10m³ 8m] IR 2,200F, IR 3,500Y, 6,400 2-y-o: close-coupled, quite attractive colt: second foal: dam should have stayed 1m, is half-sister to Lucedeo: quite modest form: placed in maiden auction at Folkestone and seller at Leicester: suited by 1¼m. *P. Mitchell.*

BEAN BOY 13 ch.g. Some Hand 119 – Battling 75 (Pinza 137) [1990 12.8g 10.6s **36**
12.3g⁴ 12g³ 15.8d* 18g³ 12f 16.2m⁴ 15.8d⁶ 15d⁶ 16s⁴ 1991 a14g⁴ 17m² 21.6f⁶ 16.5m² 16m⁵ 16m³ 12.3d⁶ 16.5m⁴ 15.8g] sturdy, workmanlike gelding: carries plenty of condition: often dull in coat: grand old campaigner: stayed 2¼m: acted on any going: had worn blinkers: excellent mount for inexperienced rider: reportedly retired. *M. H. Easterby.*

BEAN KING 5 gr.g. Ardross 134 – Meanz Beanz (High Top 131) [1990 12m* **101**
12d* 12f 10m⁶ 12f 14g² 17.4d* 16d⁴ 1991 14.6d*] robust gelding: moderate mover: fairly useful handicapper: carrying plenty of condition on first run for over a year, won minor event at Doncaster in November by 2½ lengths from Jackson Flint: stays well: acts on good to firm and dead going: genuine. *R. W. Armstrong.*

BEAR WITH ME (IRE) 2 ch.f. (Apr 11) Ahonoora 122 – Bear's Affair (Gay —
Fandango (USA) 132) [1991 6s 7g] 28,000Y: workmanlike filly: fourth foal: half-sister to French 10.5f winner Chrysolite (by Crystal Glitters): dam unraced half-sister to French 1000 Guineas winner Ukraine Girl: well beaten in large-field autumn maidens at Kempton (burly, bandaged behind) and Newmarket. *M. Bell.*

BEATLE SONG 3 b.f. Song 132 – Betyle (FR) (Hardicanute 130) [1990 5m⁵ 5m² **70**
6m⁶ 5f² a7g a5g⁵ 1991 6f⁴ a8g² 8g a8g* a7g³ 5.7g* 5d⁶ 6g 5.1m 5.2f a6g⁴] good-quartered, workmanlike filly: won handicap at Southwell and claimer (led close home) at Bath in June: generally below form last 5 starts: best effort at 6f: acts on good to firm ground: sometimes pulls hard. *C. J. Hill.*

89

BEATT'YS LAD 7 gr.g. Cawston's Clown 113 – Donallan 42 (No Mercy 126) —
[1990 NR 1991 16.2g] lengthy, rather leggy gelding: of little account on flat. *R. Thompson.*

BEAU BENZ 7 b.g. Camden Town 125 – War Lass 100 (Whistler 129) [1990 13v 52
12m* 12d⁴ 10m⁵ 12g³ a11g 12s⁶ 10v² 11d³ 12s² a12g 1991 10.2s⁵ 10d 10g⁵ 12g 12.3d]
rather leggy, good-topped gelding: plating-class handicapper nowadays: effective at 1¼m to 1½m: acts on any going except possibly firm: effective with or without blinkers or visor: has started slowly: tends to carry head high: inconsistent. *M. H. Easterby.*

BEAUCHAMP EXPRESS 4 b.g. Castle Keep 121 – Jubilee 101 (Reform 132) 91 +
[1990 11d⁶ 12d³ 12m⁵ 15g⁴ 12f⁴ 15g⁵ 1991 15m²] rather angular gelding: useful performer at best as 3-y-o (reportedly finished lame final start): heavily bandaged, fairly useful effort in amateur riders event at Ayr only start in 1991: stays 15f: seems unsuited by very firm ground. *J. L. Dunlop.*

BEAUCHAMP FIZZ 3 ch.c. Jalmood (USA) 126 – Buss 102 (Busted 134) [1990 75
7m⁵ 7m² 8.2d 1991 9m 12g 12f⁵ 12f* 14g 14m⁴ 12g] small colt: favourite following several promising efforts, won handicap at Beverley in September, leading 3f out: creditable fourth in moderately-run race at Newmarket, easily best effort in similar events after: stays 1¾m: best efforts on top-of-the-ground: sold to join M. Pipe 21,000 gns Newmarket Autumn Sales. *J. L. Dunlop.*

BEAUCROFT 3 ch.c. Crofthall 110 – Patent Pending (Goldhill 125) [1990 8.2s —
1991 10m 10g] well-grown, close-coupled colt: no form in maidens and maiden auction: sold 2,000 gns Doncaster October Sales. *J. A. Glover.*

BEAU DADA (IRE) 3 b.f. Pine Circle (USA) – Beauvoir (Artaius (USA) 129) 61
[1990 5m⁶ 5g³ 5g² 5.8m⁶ 6f* 6m⁵ 6m⁵ 6m³ 1991 a6g³ 7f³ 8g 8.3g* 10g 8.3m⁶ 8.3m⁶
8s 9s] neat, quite attractive filly: quite modest handicapper: won claimer at Windsor in May: below form last 3 starts: suited by 1m: acts on firm going: tends to get on edge: visored final 2 starts in 1990. *J. White.*

BEAUJOLAIS NOUVEAU 4 ch.g. Aragon 118 – No Halo 74 (Aureole 132) §§
[1990 8f 7g² 8f⁴ 10g⁶ 8m 10g² 1991 a10g 10.8g 9s 10f] workmanlike gelding: moderate mover: quite modest maiden at best on flat: twice most reluctant to race at 4 yrs: stayed 1¼m: winning hurdler: dead. *M. R. Channon.*

BEAUMONT'S KEEP 5 b.h. Castle Keep 121 – Powderhall 81 (Murrayfield 43
119) [1990 5g⁴ 6m 6m 6g⁴ 6m² 5m⁵ 6m⁶ 5m² 5m 5m* 5m 5f⁶ 6f 5.8d⁶ 1991 8s 8.2s³
10m 7f⁶ 9m 5f* 6g 6g⁵ 6d⁶ 6f² 6m² 6m⁵ 6g 6g 6m 6s] good-topped horse: carries plenty of condition: moderate mover: plating-class handicapper at best: won at Doncaster (apprentices) in May: best at sprint distances: acts on firm and dead going: often slowly away: not one to trust implicitly: sold out of Mrs J. Ramsden's stable 1,500 gns Doncaster October Sales after penultimate start. *T. D. Barron.*

BEAUMOOD 5 b.g. Jalmood (USA) 126 – Falcon Berry (FR) (Bustino 136) [1990 52
12g⁵ 12m⁶ 12.2g* 12g 10m⁵ 12g² 12d⁵ 12m 12m⁶ 1991 12s 14d 12.3s 13.8m⁶ 12g²
11.9m 15g³ 12g* 12.1s⁵ 12.3m³ 12f 12.1g] neat gelding: poor mover: plating-class handicapper: won at Edinburgh in July: stays 13f: suited by an easy surface: goes very well with forcing tactics: effective visored or not. *C. Tinkler.*

BEAU NASH 7 b.g. Prince Tenderfoot (USA) 126 – Dominica (GER) (Zank) —
[1990 13.8m² 12.4f³ 13.8m 14g 12.4m⁶ 1991 a14g] compact gelding: carries plenty of condition: has a quick action: plating-class handicapper: no show only run on flat in 1991 (January): stays 1¾m: best form on a sound surface: won over hurdles in March: inconsistent. *A. P. Stringer.*

BEAU QUEST 4 b.c. Rainbow Quest (USA) 134 – Elegant Tern (USA) 102 (Sea 75
Bird II 145) [1990 12.3f* 12f² 12m⁵ 16.2s³ 12g⁴ 12.3g⁴ 12.5m⁵ 12h² 12f⁶ 14g 14d⁶ 16d
1991 a12g² a14g³ a14g² a14g² a14g² 14.8g² 14m² 16.2f² 16.5m⁵ 12.2d* 12.3g* 12.3f
13.9g 15.9m⁶ 11.9g 11.9m] small colt: has quick action: modest handicapper at best: won at Warwick and Chester in July: had badly scarred near-fore knee twelfth start: lost his way after: ideally suited by around 1½m: probably acts on any going: effective with or without blinkers or visor: tail flasher: has found little under pressure and suited by waiting tactics: trained first 8 starts by R. Hollinshead. *R. D. E. Woodhouse.*

BEAU SULTAN (USA) 3 ch.c. Bering 136 – Devalois (FR) 117 (Nureyev (USA) 118
131) [1990 7.5g* 8m* 8g³ 1991 10.5d² 12d³ 12g⁵ 10m* 11f³ 12f⁴] good-bodied French colt: powerful galloper: smart performer: won listed race at Longchamp in September: in frame in Prix Greffulhe and Prix Hocquart at Longchamp and in Man o' War Stakes and Rothmans International in North America: ran moderately in Derby Italiano: stays 1½m: acts on firm and dead going. *Mme C. Head, France.*

BEAU VENTURE (USA) 3 ch.c. Explodent (USA) – Old Westbury (USA) **84**
(Francis S) [1990 6s 6m³ 5m 5m* 5.8d³ 5g* 5d 1991 5m⁵ 5m² 6m² 5g 5g 6m⁵ 5g 5g*
5d] leggy, quite good-topped colt: poor walker: moderate mover: fair handicapper:
won at Goodwood in October, leading just inside final 1f: should prove best at 5f: acts
on good to firm ground: inconsistent. *F. H. Lee.*

BECKINGHAM BEN 7 gr.g. Workboy 123 – Pickwood Sue 74 (Right Boy 137) **50**
[1990 a6g⁶ a5g⁵ a5g² a5g* 5m⁴ a5g 5g 5m a5g² 5m³ 1991 a5g⁵ 5g⁶ 5d⁶ 5m⁵ 5g⁵ a **56**
a5g⁵ a6g a5g] tall gelding: quite modest handicapper: suited by 5f: acts on firm and
dead going: effective with or without visor or blinkers: has worn crossed noseband:
has looked none too keen: goes well with forcing tactics. *J. P. Leigh.*

BECKONING 3 b.g. Bellypha 130 – Courtesy Call (Northfields (USA)) [1990 —
7m 8.2d 1991 8g 12m 10d 12s⁶ 11.8m] sturdy, strong-quartered gelding: plating class
at best: well beaten in claimer and handicaps last 4 starts, twice edgy. *J. M. P.
Eustace.*

BE DEVIOUS 3 b.f. Bering 136 – Ulterior Motive 110 (Pyjama Hunt 126) [1990 **62**
NR 1991 12m⁵ 12m³ 9g 10.2s] 88,000Y: leggy filly: first foal: dam middle-distance
winner: easily best effort in maidens and handicap when third at Southwell: visored
(on toes, made most) third outing: carried head high on debut: wears bandages: sold
2,600 gns Newmarket Autumn Sales. *A. A. Scott.*

BEDOUIN PRINCE (USA) 4 b.c. Danzig (USA) – Regal Heiress 81 (English **53**
Prince 129) [1990 8m⁴ 8g 8.2m⁴ 10.1m 10g 8g 8m 1991 a8g a11g² a11g² a12g* a11g³
a12g³ a14g³ a12g 12s 12.3s 10f³ 11f² a11g² 16g⁶ 12g a12g 13.6g⁴ 16.1m a12g² a12g³
a12g] heavy-topped colt: carries condition: poor walker and mover: quite modest
handicapper at best: won at Southwell in January: first run for nearly 4 months,
tailed off there final start: stays 1¾m (stiff tasks over 2m): acts on firm going:
effective with or without visor, has been tried in blinkers: tough: trained until after
penultimate start by J. Harris. *C. R. Beever.*

BEDSWERVER (IRE) 3 gr.f. Doulab (USA) 115 – Aldern Stream 102 —
(Godswalk (USA) 130) [1990 NR 1991 8g⁵ 8m] 8,200Y: fourth foal: half-sister to
useful Irish 1988 2-y-o 7f winner Alpine Spring (by Head For Heights): dam won
over 5f and 7f: bandaged, no worthwhile form in maiden (some signs of ability) and
claimer in the spring. *T. Thomson Jones.*

BEE BEAT 3 ch.c. Bairn (USA) 126 – Thorny Rose 81 (Tap On Wood 130) [1990 **69** §
6d² 7m 7g 1991 a6g³ a8g⁴ 7s⁵ 10.2g³ 10m⁵ 11.5m 11.7g² 11.7m² 11.7m² 11.6m² 13.1f⁶
a12g⁶ 13.3m 12g⁴ 12.1d] leggy, lightly-made colt: quite modest maiden: second in
handicaps at Windsor: slowly away last 3 starts, reluctant to race in blinkers (also
troublesome beforehand) on final one: best at around 1½m: acts on good to firm
ground: also blinkered fourth to sixth starts: tends to wander, and has looked
reluctant: one to avoid. *E. A. Wheeler.*

BEEBOB 3 b.f. Norwick (USA) 120 – Anzeige (GER) (Soderini 123) [1990 7m⁵ **85**
7m⁴ 8.2v 1991 8g² 10g* 10g* 11.5g* 14g* 13.9g⁵ 14m² 14.6m² 16.2g] sparely-made
filly: progressed into a fair performer: successful in claimers at Sandown (twice) and
Newmarket (sweating) then £7,400 handicap at Goodwood in the summer: narrowly
beaten after in handicaps at Sandown and Doncaster: well below form (reportedly
finished lame) final start: should prove suited by 2m: acts on good to firm ground
(injured on heavy): claimed £6,311 then £15,127 out of B. Hanbury's stable first
start, Dr J. Scargill's on fourth: sometimes bandaged: taken down early last 4 starts:
joined M. Pipe. *G. Lewis.*

BEECHWOOD COTTAGE 8 ch.g. Malinowski (USA) 123 – Drora (Busted **63** d
134) [1990 a8g⁴ a7g⁴ a10g² a8g² a10g⁴ a10g² a8g* a10g⁴ a8g³ a8g⁶ a8g³ a8g 7g³ 8f
8.2f 7m 1991 a7g 7g⁵ a8g* a7g⁵ a8g⁶ a10g⁶ a8g a7g³ 7f 8g 7f 7m 5m 6m 8f 7g 6.9m
6f 7f³ 10f³ 10.5f 10m 8g] small, sturdy gelding: poor walker and mover: modest
handicapper on his day: won claimer at Lingfield in January: stays 1¼m: acts on any
going: effective with or without blinkers: visored once (below form): usually starts
slowly and gets behind: a difficult ride, and needs to be handled tenderly: thoroughly
unreliable. *A. Bailey.*

BEE DEE ELL (USA) 2 b.g. (Jan 20) Lemhi Gold (USA) 123 – Truth Above All **43**
(USA) (Far North (CAN) 120) [1991 6d⁶ 5s³ 7d⁶ 6g 5f⁶ 8.3g⁶ 8.1m 6s a6g] 24,000Y:
sturdy colt: first foal: dam won sprint claimer at 2 yrs: poor maiden: stays 8.5f: acts
on firm and soft ground: visored (well below form) fourth outing: has run creditably
for 7-lb claimer: trained first 4 starts by J. S. Wilson. *Miss L. A. Perratt.*

BEE HIVE HILL 3 ch.c. Aragon 118 – Sun Lamp 76 (Pall Mall 132) [1990 5f⁶ 5m —
5m* 5f⁵ 5m a5g 1991 5m 5m 6g] rangy colt: quite modest winner at 2 yrs: ran

moderately on all-weather, and in handicaps in first half of 1991: should stay 6f: very edgy first 2 outings, also sweating second of them: sold 1,200 gns Doncaster July Sales. *Ronald Thompson.*

BEEKMAN STREET   5 b.h. Jalmood (USA) 126 – Plato's Retreat 73 (Brigadier   **65** Gerard 144) [1990 17.1f³ 14g³ 14m 18.8f⁵ 1991 a14g 14m²] leggy horse: quite modest handicapper: not seen out after April: stays well: acts on any going: ran well when blinkered final start. *I. P. Wardle.*

BE FRESH   5 ch.h. Be My Guest (USA) 126 – Fresh (High Top 131) [1990 6d 6f²   **105** 6m* 5g 6m 1991 5g⁴ 5m 5g⁴ 5m 6m] good-topped, attractive horse: useful performer: very good fourth to Elbio in Palace House Stakes at Newmarket and Title Roll in King George Stakes at Goodwood: well beaten final 2 starts: effective at 5f and 6f: needs a sound surface: very slowly away final start: usually bandaged behind: sold 14,000 gns Newmarket December Sales. *L. M. Cumani.*

BEGUILED (IRE)   3 ch.f. Be My Guest (USA) 126 – Apple Peel 109 (Pall Mall   **34 §** 132) [1990 7g 1991 9m 11.8g 10g 8.1s⁴ 10g] leggy filly: disappointing maiden: should stay beyond 1m: visored final start: usually slowly away: has run in snatches: one to treat with caution. *Lord Huntingdon.*

BEIJA FLOR   4 gr.g. Busted 134 – Rusticello 94 (Rusticaro (FR) 124) [1990 NR   **79** 1991 8.5f⁴ 8.5f* 10.1f³ 10g²] lengthy, good-bodied gelding: poor mover: third foal: half-brother to 1989 U.S. 1m winner Cooter (by Night Shirt) and a winner in Italy: dam, half-sister to smart 1m to 1¼m performer Trucidator, won Virginia Water Stakes on debut but showed little on 2 other starts at 2 yrs: modest form when winning maiden at Beverley in May and one-paced third in handicap at Yarmouth: below-form second in claimer (claimed to join F. Jordan £10,252) at Newmarket in June: well worth a try over 1½m: acts on firm ground: usually swishes tail in paddock. *H. R. A. Cecil.*

BELAFONTE   4 b.g. Derrylin 115 – Ulla Laing 107 (Mummy's Pet 125) [1990 10g   **68** 10g³ 12.3g³ 10.5m³ 10m⁴ 12m 12.2d⁵ 9s 1991 10d³ 10m² 12m* 11.9m² 12g* 16.5g⁴ 11.9g 11.4m* 10m] compact gelding: quite modest handicapper: won at Doncaster in May, Salisbury in July and Sandown in September: seems to need further than 1¼m nowadays, and likely to prove ideally suited by short of 2m: acts on good to firm and dead ground: below best when blinkered or visored. *R. J. Holder.*

BELARIUS   3 b.g. Bellypha 130 – Celebrity 101 (Troy 137) [1990 8g 1991 10g 8.1s⁵   **46** 10.3g⁶] lengthy, workmanlike gelding: moderate mover: injured hock on debut: well backed, form only in claimer and seller last 2 starts: should prove better at 1¼m than shorter: best effort on soft ground: sold to join R. Barr 3,500 gns Newmarket Autumn Sales. *Lord Huntingdon.*

BEL BARAKA (IRE)   2 ch.g. (May 14) Bering 136 – Typhoon Polly 117 (Lord   **—** Gayle (USA) 124) [1991 7g] fourth known foal: dam 1m winner at 2 yrs in France, stayed 1¼m: weak 6/1-shot, ran green after slow start and well behind final 2f in maiden at Salisbury in October. *D. R. C. Elsworth.*

BELDALE STAR   8 b.g. Beldale Flutter (USA) 130 – Little White Star (Mill Reef   **74** (USA) 141) [1990 NR 1991 16.2g 16.2d 16m*] deep-girthed, quite attractive gelding: keen walker: good mover: very useful at best, lightly raced and not so good nowadays: form in 1991 only when winning at Lingfield in October: stays 2m: acts on any going: useful front-running hurdler at 7 yrs. *R. Akehurst.*

BELDINE   6 gr.g. Belfort (FR) 89 – Royal Celandine (Royal Palace 131) [1990   **55 +** 13g* 12g⁴ 12s 1991 12f*] lengthy, angular gelding: lightly-raced handicapper: easily won poor 4-runner race at Hamilton in May: stays 13f: acts on firm ground: winning hurdler/chaser. *P. Monteith.*

BELDI (USA)   2 ch.c. (Apr 18) Diesis 133 – Margie Belle (USA) (Vaguely Noble   **82** 140) [1991 7g³ 7g³ 8.1f 7.9m² 8g] sturdy colt: half-brother to French 1m winner Milde (by Desert Wine) and 2 winners in North America: dam French winner, is from family of Trillion, Triptych and Generous: fair maiden: best efforts when second of 8, raced keenly, kept on strongly, in maiden at York and last of 8 to Seattle Rhyme in Racing Post Trophy at Doncaster in October: will stay at least 1¼m: seems unsuited by very firm ground. *C. E. Brittain.*

BELFORT PRINCE   4 b.g. Belfort (FR) 89 – Turtle Dove (Gyr (USA) 131) [1990   **49** 8f⁶ 7g⁵ 8m³ 10g 13.8d² 11g 12g 1991 12.2f³ 8m] leggy, shallow-girthed gelding: plating-class handicapper, still a maiden: stays 1¾m: acts on firm and dead ground: sold 1,100 gns Doncaster October Sales. *G. M. Moore.*

BELFORT RULER   4 gr.g. Belfort (FR) 89 – Call Me Kate 72 (Firestreak 125)   **63 +** [1990 5g² 6m* 6d 6m 6g⁶ 8.3m 6g 6m 1991 6m⁵ 6m] close-coupled, workmanlike gelding: quite modest handicapper: not seen out after May: stays 6f: acts on good to firm ground. *B. Gubby.*

BELIEVE IN ME (IRE)   2 b.c. (Mar 30) Don't Forget Me 127 – Fast Bay (Bay   **79** p
Express 132) [1991 7g] 5,200Y: strong, useful-looking colt: has scope: good walker:
fourth foal: half-brother to Macau winner Do It My Way (by Bairn) and to modest
1990 2-y-o Hidden Bay, placed several times: dam lightly raced: 100/1 and burly,
over 11 lengths last of 7, slowly away, always behind, to Dr Devious in Lanson
Champagne Vintage Stakes at Goodwood in August: should stay 1m: seemed sure to
improve but wasn't seen again. *B. A. McMahon.*

BELIEVE IT   2 b.c. (Feb 23) Bellypha 130 – Hasty Key (USA) (Key To The Mint   **67** p
(USA)) [1991 8m4] quite attractive colt: fourth foal: half-brother to 3-y-o winning
selling hurdler Cixi (by Far Out East) and 2-y-o 7f winners Cutting Note (by Diesis)
and Hasty Vessel (by Raise A Cup): dam minor winner at up to 9f in USA: 33/1 and
bit backward, 5 lengths fourth to Pabouche in 15-runner maiden at Leicester in
October, keeping on steadily under hand riding last 2½f: should stay 1¼m: sure to
do better. *C. E. Brittain.*

BELJINSKI   3 b.f. Myjinski (USA) – Lady Bedale (Comedy Star (USA) 121) [1990   **27**
NR 1991 7g4 6s5 6g] leggy, lengthy filly: first reported foal: dam never ran: poor
form in seller, minor event and maiden in the summer. *B. J. McMath.*

BELLA BETTINA   2 ch.f. (Mar 22) Doulab (USA) 115 – Barbara Zapolia (ITY)   —
(Great Nephew 126) [1991 5d 6f 7g 7.6m] 5,400Y: leggy, rather sparely-made filly:
sister to a winner in Italy and half-sister to several winners, including useful 1987
2-y-o 5f winner Babita (by Habitat): dam won at 2 yrs in Italy: well beaten in varied
events. *R. Hannon.*

BELLAFONTE (USA)   2 b.f. (Jan 18) Lyphard's Wish (FR) 124 – Bucks Belle   —
(USA) (Buckpasser) [1991 7g] tall, leggy filly: seventh foal: half-sister to 1½m seller
winner Timbuck (by Verbatim): dam, placed once from 9 starts, is half-sister to
Targowice: 8/1, last of 10 in maiden at Goodwood in August, very slowly away then
ducking left 3f out and no progress: very upset in stalls: moved well to post: sold
2,000 gns Ascot November Sales. *B. W. Hills.*

BELLA RISK   2 b.f. (Feb 17) Risk Me (FR) 127 – Minabella (Dance In Time   —
(CAN)) [1991 5g 6m6 6f] 4,500Y: leggy filly: first foal: dam once-raced half-sister to
Miss Boniface out of half-sister to very smart English and German winner Whip It
Quick: poor plater: blinkered final outing: has twice carried head awkwardly:
refused to enter stalls once: one to be wary of: sold 580 gns Newmarket July Sales.
N. A. Callaghan.

BELLA RUN   2 ch.f. (Apr 13) Commanche Run 133 – Bonne de Berry (Habitat   —
134) [1991 8d 7g] 3,300Y: lengthy filly: third foal: half-sister to 1989 French 2-y-o
5.5f winner Sabaya (by Vayrann): dam French 1¼m winner: well beaten in median
auction at Wolverhampton (backward, green) and maiden at Salisbury in October. *R.
J. Hodges.*

BELLA SEVILLE   7 gr.m. King of Spain 121 – Tempered Wind (Fleece 114)   **71**
[1990 5m 5m 5d6 5g2 5g* 5m 5f2 5g* 5m4 5f3 1991 5m 5d 5d 5g5 5m 5d2 5.2g3 5m*
5g4] lengthy mare: modest handicapper: won at Edinburgh in August: best at 5f:
acts on any going: best in blinkers. *T. D. Barron.*

BELLA'S MATCH   2 b.f. (Feb 23) Royal Match 117 – Ty-With-Belle 62 (Pamroy   —
99) [1991 5m 6m 7g] sparely-made filly: has quick action: third foal: half-sister to
1989 2-y-o 5f seller winner Starchy Belle (by Starch Reduced): dam quite modest
maiden at 2 yrs, later placed over hurdles: seems of little account. *B. Palling.*

BELLATRIX   3 b.f. Persian Bold 123 – Sorebelle 95 (Prince Tenterfoot (USA)   — p
126) [1990 NR 1991 7g6] sixth foal: half-sister to 5f and 7f winner Abuzz (by
Absalom) and 7f winner Local Lass (by Local Suitor), both useful: dam best at up to
1m: 20/1, never-dangerous 17 lengths sixth of 13 to Navarra in maiden at Newmarket
in October, slowly away and green: should improve. *C. E. Brittain.*

BELLE DANSEUSE   3 b.f. Bellypha 130 – Rengaine (FR) (Music Boy 124)   —
[1990 6d6 6f 6f 6g 1991 a8g6] lengthy, good-quartered filly: poor maiden: sixth at
Lingfield in March, sole outing in 1991: better at 1m than 6f: sold 925 gns Ascot
September Sales. *M. Blanshard.*

BELLEFAN (IRE)   3 b.f. Taufan (USA) 119 – Bellinzona (Northfields (USA))   **93**
[1990 a6g5 7m5 6d4 6d 1991 10g* 10g4 10.2m2 8f* 8.5m2 8g3 8g*] workmanlike,
rather leggy filly: keen walker: fairly useful handicapper: successful at Kempton in
March, Brighton in May and in listed event at Bordeaux in July: effective at 1m and
1¼m: acts on firm going: suitable mount for claimer: game. *M. Bell.*

BELLE OF STEEL 3 ch.f. Official – Linpac Belle 70 (Steel Heart 128) [1990 a6g — 6g³ 7f⁶ 5g 5m 1991 6d 5g a7g 8g⁵ 10.2d 10.2g] workmanlike filly: poor plater: suited by 1m: blinkered 3 times. *D. Haydn Jones.*

BELLEZZA 4 b.g. Ardross 134 – Bobo Ema 81 (Auction Ring (USA) 123) [1990 — NR 1991 12g⁵] lengthy gelding: first foal: dam 2-y-o 6f winner well beaten at 3 yrs: well beaten in Edinburgh maiden in April, only start. *Denys Smith.*

BELLING BELLING (IRE) 3 b.f. Soughaan (USA) 111 – Dame Ross 85 (Raga 41 Navarro (ITY) 119) [1990 7g 7m 7m 10.6s 1991 9s 12f 16m⁴ 17.1m 11.8m²] leggy, sparely-made filly: poor maiden: best effort 33/1-second in selling handicap at Leicester in October, running on from towards rear: claimed to join M. Pipe £6,011: suited by 1½m. *Dr J. D. Scargill.*

BELL ONE (USA) 2 ch.g. (Mar 27) Lightning Leap (USA) – Ambrose Channel (USA) (Key To The Mint (USA)) rangy, rather unfurnished gelding: first foal: dam unraced daughter of sister to Diamond Shoal and Glint of Gold: green, withdrawn after refusing to enter stalls at Beverley in July: subsequently gelded: sold 3,200 gns Ascot November Sales. *I. A. Balding.*

BELLS OF LONGWICK 2 b.f. (Feb 23) Myjinski (USA) – Bells of St Martin 89 54 (Martinmas 128) [1991 6.1g 6g³ 7f 6g 6g⁴] leggy filly: moderate mover: fourth foal: half-sister to 1m and 8.3f seller winner My Diamond Ring (by Sparkling Boy) and 4-y-o 6f winner My Ruby Ring (by Blushing Scribe): dam 5f winner at 2 yrs: plating-class maiden: stays 6f. *D. R. Laing.*

BELLTINA 3 b.f. Belfort (FR) 89 – Bacchantina (Gulf Pearl 117) [1990 5m⁴ 5f⁶ 34 5f⁴ 5d⁴ a6g³ 7m³ 6g 6m⁵ 1991 7.5g 7.5f³ 7m 7g 6.9f] small, sparely-made filly: poor plater: below form as 3-y-o: stays 7f: visored final start (July): blinkered 5 times at 2 yrs, once looking reluctant to race. *B. W. Murray.*

BELLTON 3 gr.g. Bellypha 130 – Celestial Air 96 (Rheingold 137) [1990 NR 1991 79 p 10f⁶ 12.3f⁴ 12m* 11.9d] 8,000Y: workmanlike gelding: third foal: closely related to French 1m winner Sycophante (by Pharly): dam 1½m winner: won maiden at Southwell in September, held up travelling well, taken wide straight, running on to lead inside final 1f and holding on despite looking green: never placed to challenge or knocked about in handicap 3 weeks later: stays 1½m: one to keep an eye on in handicaps. *J. G. FitzGerald.*

BELL TURRET 4 b. or br.g. Beldale Flutter (USA) 130 – Base Camp 80 44 (Derring-Do 131) [1990 7g 8.2f 5g 6f 8g² 10.1m* 10m² 11.7g 8g 10g 1991 8g 9s⁶ 9m³ 10g 9.9m 9.2d 9m 9m⁴ 10.8m 10m 8m 10g 10.3g] good-topped gelding: poor performer: ran moderately last 5 starts: suited by around 1¼m: acts on good to firm and soft ground: below form when visored and blinkered once: has hung left. *A. W. Potts.*

BELMOREDEAN 6 ch.g. Be My Guest (USA) 126 – Hanna Alta (FR) (Busted 79 134) [1990 NR 1991 11.5m⁶ 10d⁵ a10g* 11.7m⁶ 12g⁵ a10g⁵ 11.5m* 11.4m a10g² a10g a10g³] angular, sparely-made gelding: fair handicapper: won at Lingfield in June and August: effective at 1¼m to 1½m: best turf form on top-of-the-ground: takes keen hold: forces pace. *R. J. O'Sullivan.*

BELSALAAMA (USA) 3 b.c. Alydar (USA) – Softly (USA) (Solo Landing 70 (USA)) [1990 7m⁵ 7s 7s³ 1991 11.1g 12d³ 15g 14m] leggy, unfurnished colt: modest maiden: stiff tasks in handicaps, well beaten after third at Newbury in June: stays 1½m: acts on soft ground: visored last 3 starts: sold to join G. Moore 3,800 gns Newmarket Autumn Sales. *M. R. Stoute.*

BELTHORN 2 ro.f. (Feb 18) Belfort (FR) 89 – Blowing Bubbles 72 (Native — Admiral (USA)) [1991 5g 7.1s 5g 5m⁴] tall, rather plain filly: second foal: dam won 5 times between 7f and 8.3f: poor maiden: has looked difficult ride. *J. J. Bridger.*

BE MY EVERYTHING (IRE) 2 b.f. (Mar 1) Be My Guest (USA) 126 — Everything Nice 107 (Sovereign Path 125) [1991 7m⁶] 28,000F, 26,000Y: small filly: half-sister to several winners abroad: dam won from 5f (at 2 yrs) to 10.5f: 100/1, green and woolly in appearance, around 20 lengths last of 6 in Rockfel Stakes at Newmarket in October: moved poorly to post. *R. Hollinshead.*

BE MY RUNNER 5 b.g. Runnett 125 – Ivorysguest (Be My Guest (USA) 126) — [1990 8g 8m³ 1991 9g 8g] leggy, quite attractive gelding: moderate mover: modest handicapper at best: stayed 1m: didn't race on firm going, acted on any other: dead. *J. Sutcliffe.*

BEN BLUFF 2 b.g. (Feb 2) Cyrano de Bergerac 120 – Makalu 79 (Godswalk 36 (USA) 130) [1991 6f⁴ 6d 7.1d] 14,000Y: strong gelding: has scope: first foal: dam stayed 1¼m: poor maiden: best effort at 6f on dead ground. *L. G. Cottrell.*

BENEFACT (USA) 2 b.c. (Feb 22) Known Fact (USA) 135 – Beneficence (USA) **59**
(Majestic Prince) [1991 6m² 6g 7m 8.2m 8m] $20,000Y: leggy, close-coupled colt:
third reported foal: dam won at up to 7f: plating-class maiden: best effort on debut:
well beaten in Newmarket seller final start: should stay at least 7f. *D. W. P.
Arbuthnot.*

BENGAL TIGER (IRE) 3 b. or br.g. Petoski 135 – Heart 'n' Soul 101 (Bold Lad **53**
(IRE) 133) [1990 NR 1991 10.1m⁴ 10.1m 12g 13.3g 10d* 10.3d a10g⁵ a12g⁶] 8,200F,
3,000Y, 1,100 2-y-o: lengthy gelding: bad mover: half-brother to modest 6f winner
Perpignan (by Rousillon) and a winner in Belgium by Final Straw: dam useful
sprinting 2-y-o in Ireland: blinkered first time, won claimer at Newmarket in
November, always close up: suited by 1¼m: acts on dead ground: bandaged
near-hind on debut: blinkered 3 of last 4 starts: trained first 2 outings by J. Sutcliffe.
J. Akehurst.

BENNO 3 ch.g. Chief Singer 131 – Swan Ann 84 (My Swanee 122) [1990 5m⁶ 6g²
6d² 6g 1991 8g a7g] stocky gelding: quite modest form at 2 yrs: stiff tasks, well
beaten in handicaps in summer as 3-y-o: should be suited by further than 6f: sold to
join A. Moore 3,100 gns Newmarket Autumn Sales. *J. A. R. Toller.*

BEN'S BOY (USA) 2 b.c. (Apr 13) Ziggy's Boy (USA) – Storyville (FR) (Dan- **59**
cer's Image (USA)) [1991 8m 8m] $35,000Y: big, rangy colt: powerful galloper with a
roundish action: half-brother to 3 winners in North America: dam granddaughter of
half-sister to French 1000 Guineas winner Mata Hari: quite modest maiden: much
better effort in mid-division at Newmarket (burly and green, never placed to
challenge) on debut in October: stays 1m. *B. Hanbury.*

BENTICO 2 b.c. (Apr 3) Nordico (USA) – Bentinck Hotel 74 (Red God 128§) [1991 **— p**
7d] 36,000F, IR 48,000Y: lengthy, well-made colt: brother to 1990 Irish 2-y-o 7f
winner Lucas Carton, closely related to 1989 sprinting 2-y-o Shamshoon (by Shareef
Dancer) and 2 other winners, and half-brother to several other winners, including
fairly useful 1¼m winner Benzina (by Jaazeiro): dam 2-y-o 5f winner: 25/1 and
carrying condition, never a factor in 18-runner maiden at Newmarket in August:
looks sort to do much better. *M. A. Jarvis.*

BE REASONABLE (IRE) 3 ch.c. Reasonable (FR) 119 – Dixie Girl (Realm **47**
129) [1990 NR 1991 10.1s 8m⁶ 6g 7g* 7d⁵ 6.9s* 7g⁵ 8.3m] IR 8,200F, IR 9,400Y:
strong, workmanlike colt: moderate mover: fourth foal: half-brother to Irish
1¾m and bumpers winner Sky Range (by Skyliner): dam ran twice: poor
handicapper: won at Salisbury and Folkestone in summer: should have stayed 1m:
acted on soft going: bandaged near-fore final start: had broken blood vessels: dead.
P. Mitchell.

BERKELEY HILL BOY 4 ch.g. Castle Keep 121 – Brown Velvet 68 (Mansingh **—**
(USA) 120) [1990 7m 8g 7g 7m 6f* 6f 6f 6g 6d 1991 6g 6f⁵ 7f⁴ 7m] rangy gelding: won
maiden at Brighton at 3 yrs when trained by R. Akehurst: no comparable form:
seems best at 6f: acts on firm going: has wandered under pressure: usually
blinkered. *Mrs J. R. Ramsden.*

BERLIN WALL (IRE) 3 b. or br.c. Thatching 131 – Friedrichsruh (FR) **86**
(Dschingis Khan) [1990 6m 1991 a8g* 7.1g 8m*] sturdy, good-bodied colt: won
maiden at Southwell (slowly away, making most) in August and 4-runner minor
event (easily best effort, still bit green then running on really well to beat 11/4-on
Cooley's Valve by ½ length) at Ayr in September: will stay 1¼m. *P. W.
Chapple-Hyam.*

BERNIE SILVERS 2 ch.g. (Apr 1) Risk Me (FR) 127 – Vacation 102 (Remainder **56**
106) [1991 6m⁵ 7.1d] 25,000Y: leggy, lengthy gelding: half-brother to 3 winners,
including 5f to 7f modern Witch's Point (by Lochnager): dam 2-y-o 5f winner:
wearing crossed noseband, in need of race, over 14 lengths fifth of 9 to Fair Cop in
Chesham Stakes at Royal Ascot: bolted to post when showing very little at
Chepstow in October: needs to settle: gelded after final start. *G. Lewis.*

BERNSTEIN BETTE 5 b.m. Petong 126 – Glenfield Portion 86 (Mummy's Pet **73**
125) [1990 6f 6m³ 6s 6m* 6m³ 6m 6m⁵ 6m⁶ 6m⁵ 6d 6f 1991 6d 6f 6g 6m⁴ 6f⁵
6g* 6m* 6m⁴ 6m 6f³ 7g 7s] good-quartered mare: carries condition: modest
handicapper: won at Leicester and Windsor in June: stays 6f well: probably acts on
any going: has given trouble at stalls: usually held up. *P. S. Felgate.*

BERSETO (USA) 2 b.c. (Mar 9) Secreto (USA) 128 – Bergid (USA) (Cool Moon **100 p**
(USA)) [1991 8m⁵ 7d*] $130,000Y: sturdy, good-bodied colt: third foal: half-brother
to a winner in North America by Alydar: dam won 22 races from 2 yrs to 7 yrs, best
at around 1m: 7/2, won 21-runner maiden at Newmarket in November by 3 lengths,

clear, from Kristianstad, making all, quickening 3f out and running on well: will stay beyond 1m: sure to improve again. *H. R. A. Cecil.*

BERTIE WOOSTER 8 ch.g. Homeboy 114 – Peace of Mind 81 (Midsummer 92 Night II 117) [1990 6f 6m³ 6m 7g 6d⁵ 7m 6m⁵ 6m 6g* 6m² 6d² 5m 6d² 6s⁵ 1991 5m³ 6g⁶ 6m 6g³ 6m 6g⁶ 6g 6g² 6g 6m 6m 6g] strong, compact gelding: moderate mover: fairly useful handicapper: suited by 6f: not at his best on soft going, acts on any other: has occasionally given trouble at start and sweated: effective with blinkers or without: usually gets behind: inconsistent. *R. J. Holder.*

BESCABY BOY 5 b.g. Red Sunset 120 – Charo (Mariacci (FR) 133) [1990 8.2m³ 66 10m 8g* 9f⁵ a8g⁵ 8m 8m⁶ 8m⁵ 8m⁶ 8d 1991 10s⁴ 8d* 8m² 10g 9m³ 10g 8m³ 8m⁴ 8g³ 10m³ 8.5f³ 10.5g 9g* a8g⁵ a12g³] strong, angular gelding: modest handicapper: won at Pontefract in spring and Newmarket in October: effective at 1m to 1½m: acts on any going: effective with or without blinkers: has worn bandages and given trouble at stalls. *J. Wharton.*

BESITO 4 b.f. Wassl 125 – Field Day 87 (Northfields (USA)) [1990 7.6d⁴ 12m 61 16m* 14g 16f⁴ 16m³ 16d* 1991 16g 16g 18.4d 20g 20g⁶ 16d² 18m] rather angular filly: good walker: moderate mover: quite modest handicapper: well suited by good test of stamina and a soft surface. *R. Simpson.*

BESSIE SURTEES 3 ch.f. Mansingh (USA) 120 – Stonebow Lady 52 51 (Windjammer (USA)) [1990 5m 6f² 1991 5s³ 5d² 6m 6g⁴ 6d⁵ 6s⁵ 6d 7g 6f³ 6m 6f] smallish, good-quartered filly: moderate mover: plating-class maiden: clearly best efforts when placed, sweating and edgy before handicap at Thirsk on last occasion: stays 6f: probably acts on any going: blinkered last 3 outings. *T. D. Barron.*

BEST EFFORT 5 ch.g. Try My Best (USA) 130 – Lunaria (USA) (Twist The Axe 53 (USA)) [1990 12g 10f⁴ 8m⁴ 9s³ a11g 1991 6s⁴ 8d 5m⁴ 5d⁵ 5s* 5g³ 5s⁴ 5f⁶ 6f* 6m⁴ 5g* 7g 5m] strong, workmanlike gelding: plating-class handicapper nowadays: won at Edinburgh in July and September, and Thirsk in August: seems best at sprint distances nowadays: acts on good to firm and soft going: usually soon ridden along: seems a hard ride, but has run creditably for amateur and claimer. *M. P. Naughton.*

BEST EMPEROR (USA) 5 gr.h. Secreto (USA) 128 – Port Aransas (USA) 80 — (Quack (USA)) [1990 11s³ 8v 12g 10g 12g 10m⁵ 1991 10.2s 13d 14d 12s⁶ 8g 11.1d⁴] workmanlike horse: carries plenty of condition: poor mover: poor maiden: best effort at 11f: usually slowly away. *K. A. Morgan.*

BEST FINISH 2 b.c. (Apr 25) Try My Best (USA) 130 – Bodham 88 (Bustino 74 136) [1991 6m 6g³ a5g* 7.5f³ 6m⁵ 6g² 7f⁵ 6g⁵] 10,500Y: leggy, close-coupled colt: sixth foal: closely related to fairly useful 1¼m winner Barcham (by Be My Guest) and half-brother to 3-y-o 1½m winner Arabian Bold (by Persian Bold) and a winner in France by Kalaglow: dam 1½m and 13.3f winner, is out of half-sister to Blakeney and Morston: modest performer: won 8-runner maiden at Southwell in July by 6 lengths going away: mostly ran creditably in nurseries last 4 starts: should stay beyond 1m: acts on firm ground: usually claimer ridden. *W. A. O'Gorman.*

BETALONGABILL 2 br.g. (Mar 28) Lir 82 – Cornish Susie (Fair Season 120) 56 [1991 6m² 6m⁶ 7m 6g 8g] leggy gelding: third foal: dam half-sister to 4 winners notably very smart middle-distance performer Karinga Bay: plating-class maiden: runner-up in seller at Windsor: no comparable form in better events: should stay beyond 6f. *M. Madgwick.*

BE THE BEST 3 b.g. Rousillon (USA) 133 – Shadywood 96 (Habitat 134) [1990 58 NR 1991 7g⁶ 7g³ 8m³] lengthy, attractive gelding: second foal: half-brother to very smart 9f to 14.6f winner Madame Dubois (by Legend of France): dam fairly useful middle-distance performer out of Cheshire Oaks winner Milly Moss: third in maiden (best effort) at Newmarket and claimer (moved moderately down) at Leicester: will be suited by further: sold to join H. Whiting 6,000 gns Newmarket Autumn Sales and gelded. *G. Harwood.*

BETTER BE BOLD 3 ch.f. Bold Owl 101 – Lake Superior 49 (Right Tack 131) — [1990 NR 1991 10m 12m 9m] 3,000F, 3,600Y: workmanlike filly: fourth living foal: half-sister to 1m to 10.7f winner Four For Uncle (by Uncle Pokey) and a winner abroad: dam, winning plater, stayed 11f: well beaten in seller and claimers. *M. Johnston.*

BETWEEN THE SHEETS 6 b.g. Crooner 119 – Miss Chianti (Royben 125) — [1990 16m a13g 1991 10f] rangy gelding: poor handicapper: tailed off since winning as 4-y-o: stays 2m: acts on firm going. *N. R. Mitchell.*

BETWEEN TWO FIRES 2 br.f. (Apr 12) Sulaafah (USA) 119 – Bluebell Time 59 (Good Times (ITY)) [1991 5d 6m⁴ 6g⁵ 7m³ 6.9m⁵ 7.5f* 7m⁵ a7g⁵ 8m⁵ 8m³ 7.5f² 8.3g 10.5d] 850Y: smallish, rather dipped-backed filly: moderate walker and poor mover: first foal: dam thrice-raced half-sister to fair sprinter Alpine Rocket: fairly useful plater: won 18-runner event (no bid) at Beverley in July: stays 1m: acts on firm going: twice blinkered, running well first occasion: has run well for 7-lb claimer, but has looked a tricky ride. *J. Berry.*

BEVELED EDGE 2 ch.f. (Apr 17) Beveled (USA) – Best Offer 96 (Crepello 136) — [1991 6.1d⁶] 800Y: leggy, sparely-made filly: sixth foal: half-sister to winners in Belgium and Italy: dam 7f and 1m winner: sire (by Sharpen Up) 6f to 7f winner: beaten about 8 lengths in 7-runner maiden at Chepstow in June: moved poorly to post. *B. Palling.*

BE VISIBLE (IRE) 3 b.g. Vision (USA) – Belitis 109 (Tudor Melody 129) [1990 69 NR 1991 8m³ 9g⁴ 8g³ 9m⁵ 9m 12.1g⁴ 13.8m* 15.1s*] IR 7,000Y: workmanlike gelding: moderate mover: half-brother to several winners, including Irish 7f and 1m winner Persian Potamania (by Persian Bold) and fairly useful 1980 Irish 2-y-o 6f winner Passion Wagon (by Bay Express): dam, winner from 5f to 1m, is daughter of Mesopotamia: successful in large-field handicaps at Catterick in October and Edinburgh in November: suited by test of stamina: acts on good to firm ground and soft. *M. Johnston.*

BEWARE OF AGENTS 2 b.c. (Mar 4) Tremblant 112 – Saltation 111 (Sallust 79 p 134) [1991 6m² 6d 6d² 6d*] big, strong, lengthy colt: has plenty of scope: half-brother to several winners here and abroad, including useful 7f and 1m winner Imperial Salute (by Imperial Fling): dam won 5 times over sprint distances: fair performer: rallied gamely to win 15-runner maiden at Doncaster in November by a head from Venture Capitalist: will stay 7f: acts on good to firm and dead ground: may well do better. *M. Johnston.*

BEY D'AO (FR) 3 b.g. Baillamont (USA) 124 – Ondoa (FR) (President (FR)) — [1990 NR 1991 10d 10m 15.3m⁴ 14g⁶ 12s] 65,000 francs (approx £6,010) Y: rather unfurnished gelding: third foal: half-brother to French provincial 7.7f and 10.5f winner Ken d'Ao (by Kenmare): dam French 1¼m (at 2 yrs) and 1½m winner: well beaten in maidens, handicap and claimer: sold 1,700 gns Newmarket Autumn Sales. *C. A. Cyzer.*

BEYNOUNAH (IRE) 3 b.f. Shareef Dancer (USA) 135 – Rare Roberta (USA) — 118 (Roberto (USA) 131) [1990 6m⁶ 5g* 7g⁵ 7m 1991 10d 7m 10g 7g] neat filly: has a round action: modest winner as 2-y-o: below form in handicap, claimers and seller in 1991: should stay beyond 7f: possibly suited by an easy surface: sold to Scandinavia 2,500 gns Newmarket July Sales. *B. Hanbury.*

BEYOND OUR REACH 3 br.c. Reach 122 – Over Beyond 78 (Bold Lad (IRE) 84 133) [1990 5f² 5s² 5f* 5f³ 5g5 5m⁴ 6f² 5g* a8g⁵ a6g 1991 6g 8m4 6.1m 8m* 7g 7f 8m³ 8d³ 7d 9g] small, sturdy colt: moderate mover: fair form: won claimer at Leicester in July: excellent third in handicap at Doncaster seventh start, not clear run then finishing well: never dangerous in £30,800 handicap final outing: better at 1m than shorter: acts on good to firm going: ran moderately on all-weather: sweated and hung badly seventh start. *C. J. Hill.*

BEYOND THE MOON (IRE) 2 b.f. (Apr 30) Ballad Rock 122 – Vivi (Welsh 58 Saint 126) [1991 6m⁴ 6m] IR 2,400Y: strong, good-bodied filly: has scope: sixth foal: half-sister to 3-y-o Scented Goddess (by Godswalk), 7f seller winner at 2 yrs, and a winner in Holland: dam unraced: backward, beaten over 7 lengths in 5-runner maiden at Ascot in June: last but one in 22-runner Tattersalls Breeders Stakes at the Curragh over 2 months later. *M. J. Fetherston-Godley.*

BEYTON (USA) 2 b.c. (Mar 18) Alleged (USA) 138 – Ann Stuart (USA) (Lyphard 96 (USA) 132) [1991 7g⁴ 7.1s⁴ 8.1g* 7.3m* 7m 10g³] 52,000Y: strong, well-made colt: brother to a graded stakes-placed winner in USA and half-brother to 2 winners, including 1¼m winner Secret Obsession (by Secretariat): dam unraced half-sister to outstanding filly Chris Evert: fairly useful performer: won maiden at Chepstow in August: showed improved form afterwards, including winning nursery at Newbury in September and coming creditable third to Bonny Scot in Newmarket listed race in November: will stay 1½m. *R. Hannon.*

BEZELLE 2 b.f. (Apr 16) Dominion 123 – Ideal Home 104 (Home Guard (USA) 103 p 129) [1991 6g⁵ 5d* 6m*] 16,000Y: leggy filly: fourth foal: half-sister to 3-y-o Shot Stopper (by Bellypha): dam 2-y-o 5f winner: successful in maiden at the Curragh (by 8 lengths) in June: won 10-runner Princess Margaret Stakes at Ascot following month (flashed tail repeatedly in paddock) by 1½ lengths from Twafeaj, soon travelling well close up, running on strongly: should stay 1m: looked sure to improve again, but reportedly suffered set-back in September and wasn't seen again. *C. Collins, Ireland.*

B GRADE   6 b.m. Lucky Wednesday 124 – Hitravelscene (Mansingh (USA) 120)   50
[1990 6g a7g 6d 6d⁶ a7g a8g 6m 6s² 6d 6s² 6s 6s 1991 6d 7m 6m² 6m 6g⁶ 6d 6s] leggy, plain mare: has a round action: poor handicapper: best at 6f/7f: acts on good to firm ground, and goes very well on an easy surface: often starts slowly. *J. Balding.*

B GREAT   3 ch.c. Vaigly Great 127 – Gunnard 62 (Gunner B 126) [1990 5g⁵ 5g   —
1991 8v⁴ 7.5g] angular, workmanlike colt: no form in maidens and handicap. *K. B. McCauley.*

BIDDERS LOVE LANE   3 b.f. Ring Bidder 88 – Bundling Bed 69 (Welsh   —
Pageant 132) [1990 5f⁶ 5f 5d* 6g 6m 5f⁶ 5g 5m⁶ 5g 1991 7m 6m 6d 8g 7g a5g] small filly: has a quick action: poor performer: soundly beaten as 3-y-o, including in sellers: should stay 6f: yet to race on soft going, acts on any other: visored thrice. *R. D. E. Woodhouse.*

BID FOR ELEGANCE   3 b.f. Nordance (USA) – Single Bid 68 (Auction Ring   66
(USA) 123) [1990 5m⁵ 6d² 5m² 7m⁴ 7m⁵ 1991 8d 7g² 8m* 10g² 12m² 12d³ 12s² 10g⁴ 10g* 11.9m 10d⁴] angular filly: poor mover: quite modest performer: won claimers at Salisbury in May and (always close up for 7-lb claimer) October: below form last 2 outings, very stiff task first time: stays 1½m: acts on good to firm ground and soft: sold 9,800 gns Newmarket December Sales. *R. Hannon.*

BID FOR SIX (USA)   2 br.c. (Feb 27) Saratoga Six (USA) – Savage Bunny   75 p
(USA) (Never Bend) [1991 6f⁴ 6g] $155,000Y: workmanlike colt: has scope: half-brother to several winners, including minor 6f and 8.5f (at 2 yrs) stakes winner Rascal Rascal (by Ack Ack): dam won at up to 7f: sire, half-brother to Dunbeath, unbeaten top-class 6f and 1m winner at 2 yrs, only season to race: considerately-handled fourth of 22 in maiden at Newbury in September: steadily to post, failed to confirm promise there following month: looks sort to do better. *R. Hannon.*

BID FOR STARDOM (IRE)   3 ch.c. Fayruz 116 – Windy Lady (Whistling Wind   —
123) [1990 7m 7g 6d 1991 7d] angular, good-topped colt: quite modest maiden: in need of race and blinkered by 7-lb claimer in April, 1991: better at 7f than 6f. *R. Hannon.*

BID ONLY   4 b.f. Creetown 123 – Cody (USA) (Giacometti 130) [1990 NR 1991 8m   —
10m 6g] dipped-backed filly: won 5f seller only start at 2 yrs: no form in 1991: visored second start, blinkered final one (hung badly left). *K. R. Burke.*

BIELEFELD   2 b.g. (Mar 15) Scottish Reel 123 – Transcendence (USA) 71 (Sham   —
(USA)) [1991 8m] 3,700F, 2,000Y: workmanlike gelding: first foal: dam 11f and 12.3f winner: 20/1 and backward, in mid-division of seller at Newmarket in October: moved moderately down. *E. Eldin.*

Princess Margaret Stakes, Ascot—Bezelle wins decisively for Ireland

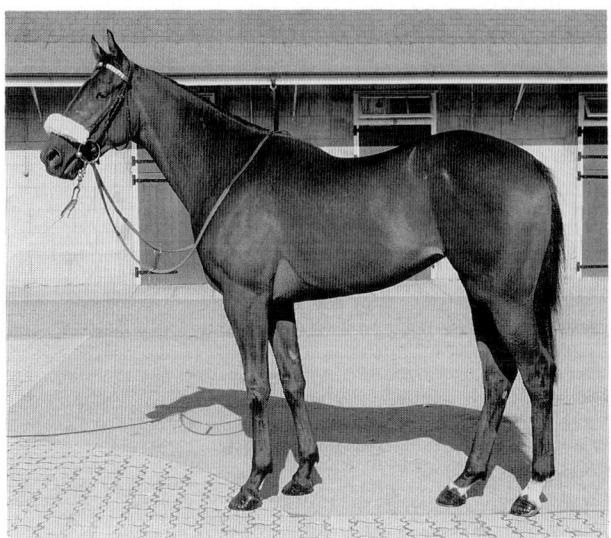

Mr James McNeil's "Bezelle"

BIENNIAL (USA) 5 b.h. Lear Fan (USA) 130 – Six Months Long (USA) —
(Northern Dancer) [1990 10g 11m³ 1991 10m 10.1s] good-topped horse: one-time
useful performer: tailed off as 5-y-o: stays 11f: acts on firm going, possibly unsuited
by a soft surface: usually taken down early: has worn net muzzle: winning hurdler
for M. Pipe in March: sold to join F. Watson 1,125 gns Ascot November Sales. *P. A. Kelleway.*

BIG BEAT (USA) 3 br.c. Super Concorde (USA) 128 – Embroglio (USA) **68**
(Empery (USA) 128) [1990 NR 1991 8m 10g⁶ 12m⁴ 10g³ 10g³ 10g] 16,000Y: rangy,
rather angular colt: brother to 1984 2-y-o 6f winner Durayd and half-brother to
winners in Brazil and North America: dam unraced close relative of Noble Decree:
modest maiden: well beaten and looked somewhat unsatisfactory, running wide
turn and drifting right, at Newbury final start: stays 1½m: wears dropped noseband:
rather headstrong. *D. R. C. Elsworth.*

BIG BLUE 2 b.c. (Mar 31) Bluebird (USA) 125 – Cassina 91 (Habitat 134) [1991 **78 p**
6f⁶ 7m²] 6,200F: good-topped colt: sixth foal: half-brother to very smart middle-
distance performer Top Class (by High Top) and 1986 2-y-o 7f and 1m winner State
Ballet (by Pas de Seul): dam 7f winner: keeping-on second to Pursuit of Love in
17-runner maiden at Newmarket in October: will stay 1m: will improve again, and is
sure to win a maiden. *C. E. Brittain.*

BIG BOAT 2 b.f. (Apr 21) Royal Vulcan 83 – Miss Felham 40 (Malinowski (USA) —
123) [1991 7.1d] strong, workmanlike filly: first reported foal: dam, plater, stayed 1m:
50/1 and better for race, tailed off in Chepstow maiden in October. *T. Casey.*

BIG EASY (IRE) 2 ch.c. (Mar 29) Ela-Mana-Mou 132 – Babilla (USA) (Raja Baba **70**
(USA)) [1991 8.1s a7g² a7g²] IR 32,000Y: fourth reported foal: dam unraced
daughter of very useful 1974 Irish 2-y-o 5f and 6f winner Tender Camilla: wore
eyeshield when second to Spanish Minor and Empeeka in maidens at Southwell in
November: will be better suited by 1m + . *Mrs J. Cecil.*

BIG ECK 4 b.g. Precocious 126 – Dora's Rocket 69 (Roan Rocket 128) [1990 a7g —
a5g 6m 5f 5s⁴ 5m⁴ 7m* 6g⁴ 8.2f³ 7f⁵ 7g² a8g 8.2g² 8.5d 9g 7g³ 8f⁵ 8.2m² 8f⁴ 9m³
8m 8.2s 1991 8f] close-coupled, good-quartered gelding: poor handicapper: soundly
beaten only start at 4 yrs, in April: best at 7f to 9f: acts on firm going (bit below best
on fibresand), possibly unsuited by dead: usually blinkered. *D. J. Wintle.*

BIG HAND (IRE) 2 b.g. (Mar 4) Tate Gallery (USA) 117 – Clonsella Lady (High **69**
Top 131) [1991 5f² 6f³ 6m² 6m³] IR 24,000Y: well-made gelding: half-brother to
fairly useful miler Chase The Door (by Red Sunset) and 2 other winners, including
Queen Alexandra winner Easy To Please (by What A Guest): dam 8.5f winner in
France: modest maiden: showed improved form at Pontefract third start, clear most
of last 3f but caught near line: will stay 7f: tends to carry head high. *J. W. Watts.*

BIGHAYIR 4 gr.g. Petong 126 – Nook (Julio Mariner 127) [1990 8.5g 10m 12m **63**
11.5f³ 10m* 11.7m 1991 10.1s 10.8m³ 8.5m* 10m² 8g⁴ 8g² 12g 10f³ 10.2m³ 8g 10.2s³
12.1d²] sturdy ex-Irish gelding: quite modest handicapper: won at Epsom in June:
effective at 1m to 1½m: probably acts on any going: effective blinkered or not:
consistent: sold to join M. Pipe's stable 13,000 gns Newmarket Autumn Sales. *B. R.
Millman.*

BIG LEAP (IRE) 2 b. or br.g. (May 11) Auction Ring (USA) 123 – Bristle 96 **72 p**
(Thatch (USA) 136) [1991 6m* 7m] IR 14,000Y: rather leggy, quite attractive
gelding: second foal: half-brother to 3-y-o Sweep Along (by Persian Bold): dam Irish
2-y-o 8.5f winner stayed 1½m, is out of half-sister to Old Country: weak favourite,
won 8-runner maiden at Pontefract in September, quickening well close home:
well-backed favourite but still green when unable to challenge in mid-division of
York nursery following month: should stay 1m: likely to do better. *M. Moubarak.*

BIG PAT 2 b.c. (Apr 19) Backchat (USA) 98 – Fallonetta 41 (Tachypous 128) [1991 —
7f 10m 8m] leggy colt: keen walker: second foal: dam, bad plater, stayed 1m: no form,
including in claimer. *J. Pearce.*

BIGWHEEL BILL (IRE) 2 br.g. (Mar 3) Last Tycoon 131 – Get Ahead 58 **83**
(Silly Season 127) [1991 7g² 7m⁴ 7m] 26,000Y: lengthy, angular gelding: half-
brother to several winners, including stayer Sugar Palm (by Gay Fandango) and
fairly useful middle-distance handicapper Main Reason (by Main Reef): dam
daughter of smart middle-distance stayer Guillotina: visored first time, slow-
starting nineteenth of 30, never a threat, to Young Senor in Tattersalls Tiffany
Highflyer Stakes at Newmarket, easily best effort: in frame previously in maidens
there and at Newcastle: will be better suited by 1m. *J. W. Watts.*

BIJOU PRINCESS 3 b.f. Glint of Gold 128 – Likeness 101 (Young Generation —
129) [1990 NR 1991 10.5g 12g 7g] 23,000F: rather leggy filly: first foal: dam maiden,
third in Rockfel Stakes at 2 yrs but disappointing and none too genuine at 3 yrs:
behind in autumn maidens: jinked, stumbled and rider unseated early on final start.
H. Candy.

BILATERAL (USA) 2 ch.c. (Feb 1) Blushing Groom (FR) 131 – Double Axle **97**
(USA) (The Axe II 115) [1991 7.1s³ 7g* 8g² 7m²] sturdy colt: has a quick action:
brother to 1990 2-y-o 6f winner Groombridge and half-brother to several winners,
including smart 1989 2-y-o 7f and 1m winner Digresssion (by Seattle Slew): dam
won 4 races at up to 1m: quite useful performer: looking extremely well and
favourite after promising debut, won 4-runner minor event at Goodwood in August,
despite running lazily: improved when runner-up in similar events in the Midlands:
likely to stay 1¼m. *H. R. A. Cecil.*

BILLION DOLLARBILL 3 ch.g. Nicholas Bill 125 – Rest Hill Dolly (Balinger —
116) [1990 8g 8.2s 7g 1991 12s 12f] workmanlike gelding: no sign of ability. *T. M.
Jones.*

BILL MOON 5 ch.g. Nicholas Bill 125 – Lunar Queen 96 (Queen's Hussar 124) **52**
[1990 11.5m 9g 7m⁴ 8m 7f* 7m 7m* 7g 6m³ 1991 7.6g 6f⁴ 7.1d⁴ a8g* 8.5f⁵ 7m 6m⁴
7m*dis 8m³ 6.1d² a7g] leggy, quite attractive gelding: quite modest handicapper:
first past post at Lingfield (amateurs) in June and Southwell (apprentices, demoted
for causing interference) in September: has form over stiff 6f and stays 1m: acts on
firm and dead ground: none too consistent. *P. J. Feilden.*

BILLOW 4 br.f. Nicholas Bill 125 – Time-Table 66 (Mansingh (USA) 120) [1990 —
10.2m 10g 15g 12m³ 1991 a12g] lengthy, sparely-made filly: no worthwhile form: sold
400 gns Newmarket July Sales. *W. Wilson.*

BILLSHA 5 b.m. Ahonoora 122 – Sanjana (GER) (Priamos (GER)) [1990 8m 10.6s —
10g 10.2f 9m 1991 10m 10g] rangy mare: little worthwhile form on flat: winning
hurdler. *B. R. Cambidge.*

BILLY BLAZER 2 ch.g. (Mar 9) Nicholas Bill 125 – Flaming Peace 104 (Queen's **79 p**
Hussar 124) [1991 6g⁴ 6f³ 6m* 8m²] 5,000Y: leggy gelding: moderate mover:
closely related to 2 winners by High Line, both successful over middle distances,
and half-brother to several winners, including 1980 2-y-o 6f winner Sovereign
Flame (by Supreme Sovereign): dam 2-y-o 7f winner: modest form: won maiden
auction at Pontefract in August, quickening well though carrying head bit high: well
backed, travelled strongly long way when good second to Nicely Thanks in
competitive nursery at Ayr following month: will be well suited by 1¼m + . *M. H.
Tompkins.*

BILLY LOMOND (IRE) 3 b.c. Lomond (USA) 128 – Relko's Belle (FR) (Relko **45**
136) [1990 6m⁵ 6d 7m⁴ 7m 7m 8m 1991 8m⁵ 9d 7m⁵ 8m⁶ a12g³ a12g⁵ a10g* 10.8m a **54**
a10g⁶ 16m a12g] smallish, strong-quartered colt: carries condition: has a quick
action: plater: won handicap (no bid) at Lingfield in August: well below form
afterwards: stays 1½m: acts on good to firm ground: blinkered seventh to ninth
starts. *C. A. Cyzer.*

BINDING CONTRACT (USA) 2 ch.f. (Jan 14) Bounding Basque (USA) – **69**
Gallant Nurse (USA) (Gallant Romeo (USA)) [1991 7m³ 7f⁵ 7m⁶ 8m⁵] $15,000F,
$26,000Y, $37,000 2-y-o: small, lightly-made filly: half-sister to winners in USA by
Far Out East and Traffic Breaker: dam minor winner at 6f: sire (by Grey Dawn)
Grade 1 winner from 1m to 1½m: quite modest maiden: well-backed favourite
(despite facing stiff task) following eye-catching run, creditable staying-on fifth of 14
in Doncaster nursery final start: will stay 1¼m. *P. W. Chapple-Hyam.*

BINGO BONGO 4 gr.f. Petong 126 – Daring Display 85§ (Daring March 116) **44 §**
[1990 6g³ 7f 10m⁴ 10m⁵ 7m 6m 8g 8m 1991 7d³ 6d 7d² 6m⁶ 7.1m 7g a8g] rangy filly:
plating-class maiden at best: likely to prove best short of 1¼m: acts on hard and
dead ground: ungenuine. *D. Burchell.*

BINKHALDOUN (USA) 2 ch.c. (Jan 2) Roberto (USA) 131 – Aviance 112 **92 p**
(Northfields (USA)) [1991 6f* 7m] 290,000Y: robust, good-bodied colt: third foal:
half-brother to 3-y-o 7f winner Imperfect Circle (by Riverman), very useful at 6f at 2
yrs, and smart miler Chimes of Freedom (by Private Account): dam 6f and 7f winner
from good family: heavily-backed favourite, won 22-runner maiden at Newbury in
September, always handy then quickening on over 1f out: carrying plenty of
condition still, around 6 lengths ninth of 30, front rank almost 6f, to Young Senor in
Tattersalls Tiffany Highflyer Stakes at Newmarket following month: bred to stay
1¼m: likely to improve further. *H. Thomson Jones.*

BIRCH BANKS (CAN) 2 b.c. (May 8) Bold Ruckus (USA) – My Anna Lee **74**
(USA) (J O Tobin (USA) 130) [1991 8m² 8m⁴ 8g³] $85,000Y: leggy colt: has scope:
fifth foal: half-brother to 2 winners, one in minor stakes: dam won at up to 6f at 2 yrs:
modest maiden: much improved effort when third of 14 to Sword Master at Bath in
October: looked a very difficult ride previously: will probably stay 1¼m: possibly
suited by some give in the ground. *G. Harwood.*

BIRD OF PEACE (USA) 3 ch.f. Sharpen Up 127 – Timotara (USA) (Secre- **—**
tariat (USA)) [1990 7m 7m 1991 8v 8g 8m 6g 12m 8m 8.2m 7g] close-coupled filly:
plating-class form at 2 yrs, little at 3 yrs: stays 7f. *D. R. Laing.*

BIRLING ASHES 3 gr.g. Magic Mirror 105 – Morning Miss 59 (Golden Dipper **38**
119) [1990 5f⁵ 5s 5g⁴ 6g 6g⁶ 7.5d 6m 5m 5m 5f 7f⁴ 8f 7g a8g a8g 1991 a8g⁴ 7d 8m 8f⁵
8g⁴ a12g⁶ 9.7m 12f] small, angular gelding: inconsistent plater: stays 1m: acts on
firm going: blinkered twice, hooded once: trained reappearance by R. Stubbs. *J. R.
Jenkins.*

BIRSTWITH (USA) 6 gr.g. Valdez (USA) – La Chaumiere (Thatch (USA) 136) **62**
[1990 10f* 10m 10.4d 8.2m 8m³ 8.2d⁴ 10.2m⁴ 10.6d 8d 9f⁶ 1991 8s⁶ 10s*] leggy,
close-coupled, angular gelding: quite modest handicapper: won at Leicester in
March, not seen out again: stays 1¼m: acts on any going: wore crossed noseband as
6-y-o: sold 4,000 gns Ascot April Sales, reportedly to race in Jersey. *C. W. C. Elsey.*

BIRTHDAYS' CHILD 3 b.f. Caerleon (USA) 132 – Shaara (FR) (Sanctus II 132) **75 d**
[1990 NR 1991 8g³ 10g 10m 11.5s] 31,000F, 480,000 francs (approx £44,400) Y:
leggy, unfurnished filly: half-sister to several winners, including smart 5f to 1m
winner Shasavaan (by Red God), useful 1m to 12.3f winner Secret Society (by Law
Society) and fairly useful 7f winner Shadiliya (by Red Alert): dam placed at up to 11f
in French Provinces: third in maiden at Yarmouth in June: well held in similar
events and handicap: should prove suited by further than 1m. *J. R. Fanshawe.*

BISHOPSTONE BILL 2 b.g. (Mar 24) Skyliner 117 – Sybilly (Nicholas Bill **—**
125) [1991 6.1g 5.7m 7g a7g] 1,700Y, 7,200 2-y-o: leggy, good-topped gelding: first

reported foal: dam strong-pulling maiden: no worthwhile form: not seen after July. *S. Mellor.*

BISTRO GARDEN (USA) 3 b.c. Green Dancer (USA) 132 – Noraa (USA) **116** (Maribeau) [1990 8g³ 8v³ 1991 8s* 9d³ 8g² 8d³ 8g* 9d² 8m³ 8d* 9f² 9g*] second foal: half-brother to minor sprint winner in USA by Spectacular Bid: dam ran twice, winning sprint maiden at 4 yrs: won maiden at Maisons-Laffitte in April, minor event at Longchamp in July and Prix du Rond-Point (wore tongue strap, led 2f out and held Goofalik by a nose) at Longchamp in October: second in Hollywood Derby and winner of Grade 3 Bay Meadows Derby in November: effective at 1m and 9f: smart and consistent. *P. Bary, France.*

BIT-A-MAGIC 2 b.c. (May 10) Beveled (USA) – Kissimmee (FR) (Petingo 135) **95** [1991 5g* 5f* 6f² 5g* 5m³ 5.2g 5m² 6m] 3,400F, 10,000Y: tall, leggy colt: half-brother to 3 winners here and abroad, including fair 1990 2-y-o 7f winner Recalde (by King of Spain): dam placed at 1½m in French Provinces: sire (by Sharpen Up) 6f to 7f winner: fairly useful performer: successful in maiden at Newmarket and minor event (after slow start) at Folkestone in May and 5-runner Premio Bimbi at Milan in June: dam 2-y-o 6f winner: broke leg in nursery at Doncaster, and was destroyed: best form at 5f. *J. Berry.*

BITIAH 2 ch.f. (Apr 6) Adonijah 126 – Ritsurin 79 (Mount Hagen (FR) 127) [1991 **59** 6g⁵ 6s³ 6m 8g] leggy filly: fifth foal: half-sister to several winners here and in Ireland, including 1987 2-y-o 6f winner Reformando (by Formidable) and 5.3f (at 2 yrs) to 1¼m winner Jagjet (by Vayraan): dam 2-y-o 6f winner: plating-class maiden: should stay 1m: seems suited by soft ground: trained first 3 starts by A. Lee: sold 1,500 gns Ascot November Sales. *I. A. Balding.*

BITMAC BOY 2 gr.c. (Jan 12) Another Realm 118 – Hedonist 74 (Mandamus 120) **—** [1991 6d 7f] 4,400F, 6,000Y: leggy, angular colt: half-brother to several winners here and abroad, including 1982 2-y-o 5f winner Flinders Range (by Native Bazaar): dam sprint plater: well beaten in maiden at Ripon (backward, slowly away) and claimer at Redcar (took keen hold) in mid-summer. *W. W. Haigh.*

BIT OF A LARK 3 b.g. Nomination 125 – Straffan Girl (Sallust 134) [1990 6d 6m **96** 5f* 5g³ 5m³ 5f* 5m* 5m 1991 6m⁴ 6m 6g 5g 5.6m 5.2m³] strong, sturdy gelding: fairly useful performer: easily best efforts as 3-y-o when in frame in £8,200 handicap at Newmarket and £6,800 minor event at Newbury: at least as effective at 6f as 5f: acts on firm going: suited by forcing tactics. *R. Hollinshead.*

BIT OF A LASS 5 br.m. Wassl 125 – Idiot's Delight (USA) (Bold Ruler) [1990 **—** a10g* a10g5 a10g 10m⁶ 10m 1991 a10g a10g a12g] angular, sparely-made mare: poor handicapper: no form since winning at Lingfield as 4-y-o: suited by 1¼m: acts on firm going: usually bandaged behind on all-weather. *D. W. P. Arbuthnot.*

BITOUT THE MIDDLE 2 b.g. (Mar 3) Jester 119 – Maleiha 78 (Martinmas **30** 128) [1991 5m⁶ a6g 7m a6g³ a7g] leggy, sparely-made, rather dipped-backed gelding: first foal: dam, headstrong maiden, stayed 7f: poor maiden: worthwhile form only when third in seller at Southwell: visored last 2 starts: gave trouble stalls second outing: not seen out after August. *J. L. Harris.*

BITSY CORRIGAN (IRE) 3 b.f. Lafontaine (USA) 117 – Jury Box (Jukebox **—** 120) [1990 NR 1991 12m 12m] IR 3,200Y: leggy filly: moderate mover: sister to Irish 7f winner Yasmin's Hope and half-sister to Irish 6f winner Glenhurst (by Tudor Music): dam Irish maiden: tailed off in maidens at Thirsk (saddle slipped) and Chepstow in May. *W. G. M. Turner.*

BLACK CORAL (IRE) 2 b.f. (May 1) Double Schwartz 128 – Countess Olivia **59** p 80 (Prince Tenderfoot (USA) 126) [1991 6m⁵] 4,600Y: lengthy, unfurnished filly: sixth foal: dam stayed 1¼m: 14/1 and green, in touch almost 5f after slow start in 6-runner minor event at Leicester in October: will improve. *C. F. Wall.*

BLACKDOWN 4 b.c. Rainbow Quest (USA) 134 – Cider Princess (Alcide 136) **64** [1990 9s⁵ᵈⁱˢ 9g⁴ 12s* 14d 12.3g² 12g² 12f* 12.7f 12d 1991 11.8g* 11.1s²a12g⁵] leggy ex-Irish colt: half-brother to very smart miler Tender King (by Prince Tenderfoot): dam 9f winner: won handicap at Sligo and minor event at Tramore at 3 yrs: wearing crossed noseband, won claimer at Leicester (drifted right) in September: stays 1½m: probably acts on any going: bought out of J. Oxx's stable 8,500 gns Newmarket Autumn (1990) Sales. *C. Weedon.*

BLACK JACK SILVER (CAN) 2 b.c. (Mar 10) Bold Ruckus (USA) – **73** Brunswick Dawn (USA) (Amber Morn (USA)) [1991 6m⁵ 7g⁶ 7.5f² 9m 8f³] $90,000 2-y-o: small, sturdy colt: half-brother to several winners in North America, including Let's Go Blue (by Bob's Dusty), champion older horse in Canada in 1986: dam 2-y-o 5f winner: sire smart 5f to 7f winner (stayed 9f), best at 2 yrs: modest maiden: blinkered, ran on gamely when good third in 6-runner nursery at Yarmouth in September: stays 1m: visored penultimate outing: tongue tied down last 3 starts: looks a very hard ride: sold 14,500 gns Newmarket Autumn Sales. *M. R. Stoute.*

BLACK MOSS   2 br.c. (Jan 27) Prince Sabo 123 – Pas de Chat (Relko 136) [1991 5f   **56** 6g 5m6 5m 5g 7.1s 7g] 3,200Y: lengthy colt: half-brother to 3 winners, all at up to 7f, including 3-y-o Katwil (by Gabitat) and thoroughly unreliable Jorvick (by Swing Easy): dam ran twice: plating-class maiden: tailed off final start: should be suited by further than 5f: has worn dropped noseband. *D. Haydn Jones.*

BLACKPATCH HILL   2 br.g. (Jun 3) Efisio 120 – Myrtlegrove (Scottish Rifle   **56** 127) [1991 6g 7f5 8g] lengthy gelding: fourth foal: half-brother to 3-y-o 9.7f and 1¼m winner Long Furlong (by Castle Keep): dam unraced daughter of half-sister to High Line: plating-class maiden: best effort second start: should prove suited by 1m + . *J. L. Dunlop.*

BLACKWATERFOOT   4 b.c. Kalaglow 132 – Twelve O'Clock (Hardicanute   **61** 130) [1990 10.6f3 11.7f5 10g5 a12g a10g 1991 7d2 8d* 8m3 7.6g2 7m2 7f 6f3] lengthy, angular colt: moderate mover: quite modest handicapper: won at Ayr in April: best at 7f to 1m: acts on firm and dead ground: has flashed tail and hung left under pressure: bandaged off-hind last 3 starts: largely consistent. *R. Boss.*

BLACKWATER PANTHER (IRE)   2 b.c. (Mar 27) Palace Panther 110 –   **54** Temple Goddess (USA) (Naskra (USA)) [1991 a7g a7g a8g6] third known foal: half-brother to a minor winner in North America: dam minor winner in North America: much improved effort in Southwell maiden (ridden by 7-lb claimer) final start, finishing around 8 lengths sixth of 13 to Citiqueen: may well be better suited by 1¼m. *C. N. Allen.*

BLACKWELL BAY   3 b.f. Bay Express 132 – Terex (Khalkis 127) [1990 NR   **—** 1991 10d] plain filly: sister to winner in Macau (as Home Master), and half-sister to several winners, including fairly useful stayer Ventrex (by Henry The Seventh): dam half-sister to very smart 1964 staying 2-y-o Brave Knight: very slowly away and always behind in maiden at Ripon in June. *P. Calver.*

BLACKWELLS GALLERY (IRE)   3 ch.f. Tate Gallery (USA) 117 – Caelidh   **47** 98 (Silly Season 127) [1990 6m 5m 8m6 8d 1991 6m 10.6m 7g 7g3 7g 6m] leggy, sparely-made filly: has a quick action: poor maiden: form as 3-y-o only when third in seller at Yarmouth: stays 1m: possibly unsuited by dead ground: headstrong second start: has looked difficult ride: sold 1,400 gns Newmarket September Sales: resold IR 3,000 gns Goffs November Sales. *R. Hannon.*

BLADE OF FORTUNE   3 b.g. Beldale Flutter (USA) 130 – Foil 'em (USA) 88   **—** (Blade (USA)) [1990 6g 5g5 7g5 7m 7g 1991 8.2f6 6m] leggy, rather unfurnished gelding: poor maiden: below form in spring as 3-y-o: has form at 7f, but is headstrong. *F. H. Lee.*

BLAKE END (USA)   2 b.c. (Apr 24) Valid Appeal (USA) – Fine Singing (USA)   **82** p (Diplomat Way) [1991 6m2 6m3] $57,000Y: strong, sturdy colt: has scope: half-brother to 2 winners in North America, one graded-stakes placed: dam minor winner at around 1m: sire smart winner from 6f to 9f: head second of 9 in maiden at Newmarket in August, losing far cry through inexperience: co-favourite, running-on third of 13 to Tamim in minor event at Pontefract (possibly set too much to do) following month: should stay 1m: looks very much type to train on and will win a maiden at the least. *W. A. O'Gorman.*

BLAKENEYS GIFT   5 gr.g. Blakeney 126 – Teleflora 89 (Princely Gift 137)   **—** [1990 8m* 11.5m 12g6 1991 10.8m] leggy gelding: poor handicapper: blinkered and tailed off only start in 1991 (April): stays 1½m: acts on good to firm and soft going. *B. Smart.*

BLAKE'S TREASURE   4 b.c. Mummy's Treasure 84 – Andamooka (Rarity   **48** 129) [1990 8m 8m3 8f2 8.3m5 8.2m2 a8g 1991 9s 10m 10g 10g 8.1g 8.3g 8.2f* 8.5f 8g] good-topped colt: moderate mover: poor handicapper nowadays: form as 4-y-o only when winning at Nottingham in September: suited by 1m: acts on firm ground: visored last 4 starts: has flashed tail. *T. Thomson Jones.*

BLARNEY STREET   3 ch.f. Smackover 107 – Stewart's Rise 52 (Good Bond   **—** 122) [1990 NR 1991 10.2g] 560Y: sparely-made filly: second foal: sister to bad plater Miss Mac: dam, plater, won from 1m to 1½m: 200/1, tailed off in amateurs event at Doncaster in July. *Mrs V. A. Aconley.*

BLASKET HERO   3 gr.g. Kalaglow 132 – Glory Isle 60 (Hittite Glory 125) [1990   **66** NR 1991 10v 12v 10d 12m 13m3 14g3 12m5 15.4m2 16d4 14.1m5] 4,600F, 4,800Y: rather sparely-made gelding: fourth foal: brother to Italian winner Grizzly and half-brother to 7f (at 2 yrs) to 1¼m winner Rio Pedras (by Kala Shikari): dam ran only at 3 yrs, when winner over 9f: modest maiden: off course nearly 4 months and gambled on, best effort beaten short head in amateur riders maiden at Folkestone: stays 2m, at least when conditions aren't testing: acts on good to firm ground: trained first 7 starts by L. Browne in Ireland, blinkered last 3 of them. *R. Akehurst.*

BLAZING BELLE 3 br.f. Belfort (FR) 89 – La Pepper 63 (Workboy 123) [1990 45 §
5f⁶ 5m⁶ 5.8h⁵ 7f⁴ 6g⁶ 6d⁵ a7g a6g² 1991 a6g* a8g a5g² 5d⁵ 5.7m 6m 6f 5g² 5d] a 60 §
smallish, good-quartered filly: plating-class performer: made all in maiden at
Lingfield in January: may prove ideally suited by 6f: best form on all-weather, with
give in the ground on turf: sometimes blinkered or visored: has worn bandages:
trained first 2 starts by M. Usher: inconsistent, has flashed tail and looked
ungenuine: sold 1,800 gns Ascot November Sales. *M. McCormack.*

BLAZING FEN 3 ch.c. Myjinski (USA) – Clipsall 57 (Petitioner 83) [1990 6m⁶ —
6g 5f 7f 7d a8g⁴ a7g a7g a7g 1991 a6g a7g⁶ a8g³ a10g³ a10g² a12g³ 8.5f a10g a12g] a 53
neat colt: poor mover: useful plater: best form on all-weather, though behind in
apprentice handicap (first run for 7 months) and maiden last 2 starts: probably stays
1½m: has run well for 7-lb claimer: carries head high, and has looked none too keen:
sometimes bandaged. *Mrs N. Macauley.*

BLAZING PEARL 3 b.f. Blazing Saddles (AUS) – Ring of Pearl (Auction Ring 38
(USA) 123) [1990 6f* 7f⁶ 6m 7g 6m 6m 1991 6f 5d 8m 7d 10m³ 11.8m⁴ a14g] small
filly: moderate mover: poor plater on most form: suited by middle distances:
blinkered second start: carried head high fifth outing: sometimes slowly away:
trained first 2 starts by R. King, next 2 by P. Feilden. *J. L. Harris.*

BLAZING SUNSET 4 ch.f. Blazing Saddles (AUS) – Krishnagar (Kris 135) —
[1990 a5g* a6g a6g⁴ 6d 5m 5g 6m⁵ 5m⁵ 6m 6m 5.3f 6m 5m a6g⁶ a5g a7g⁶ 1991 a7g]
workmanlike filly: has a round action: poor handicapper: stays 6f: acts on firm going:
sold 2,000 gns Ascot February Sales. *D. A. Wilson.*

BLAZON OF TROY 2 b.c. (May 1) Trojan Fen 118 – Mullet 75 (Star Appeal 133) —
[1991 6s] IR 8,000Y: fourth foal: half-brother to winning middle-distance performers
Cadency (by Teenoso) and Surcoat (by Bustino) and a winner over hurdles: dam
1¼m winner, is half-sister to very smart 7f to 13.3f winner Consol: 33/1, soundly
beaten in 20-runner maiden at Folkestone in November: bred to stay 1¼m. *T. Thomson Jones.*

BLENDERS CHOICE 9 b.g. Cavo Doro 124 – Harriny 94 (Floribunda 136) —
[1990 NR 1991 9g⁶] rangy, good-bodied gelding: one-time fair handicapper, but has
deteriorated considerably: faced stiff task only run as 9-y-o: stays 1½m: best on a
sound surface. *J. S. King.*

BLESSED HONOUR 2 b.f. (Jan 30) Ahonoora 122 – Blessed Event 117 (Kings 77 p
Lake (USA) 133) [1991 7m*] lengthy, angular, rather unfurnished filly: first foal:
dam 1¼m winner (stayed 1½m) out of German Oaks winner Friedrichsruh: 9/4, won
4-runner maiden at Yarmouth in July, making all and running on well: will stay at
least 1m: seemed likely to improve. *M. R. Stoute.*

BLETCHLEY PARK (IRE) 2 b.c. (Mar 21) Caerleon (USA) 132 – Enigma 87 104
(Ahonoora 122) [1991 6g⁸ 5m⁶ 6f⁰ 6m¹* 7m⁶] 50,000Y: close-coupled, attractive colt:
poor mover: second foal: half-brother to smart sprinting 3-y-o Shalford (by
Thatching): dam maiden sprinter, best at 2 yrs, is sister to very useful Irish sprinter
Princess Tracy: useful performer: put up much improved performance (reportedly
operated on for wind infirmity after previous start) to win BonusPrint Sirenia
Stakes at Kempton in September, held up (for first time) then showing fine turn of
foot: creditable fifth of 30 to Young Senor in Tattersalls Tiffany Highflyer Stakes at
Newmarket following month: may well stay 1m: wore crossed noseband and tongue
strap final 2 starts: sold 27,000 gns Goffs December Sales. *R. Hannon.*

BLIMPERS DISCO 2 gr.c. (May 16) Grey Desire 115 – In A Spin 74 (Wind- 52
jammer (USA)) [1991 5d 6m⁴ 7m 7.6d] 3,800Y: well-grown colt: moderate mover:
first foal: dam 1½m winner: plating-class maiden: best effort fourth of 7 in auction
event at Haydock (ridden by 7-lb claimer) in July: well beaten at Chester after,
seeming unsuited by track on first occasion. *E. H. Owen jun.*

BLINDING (IRE) 3 b.f. High Top 131 – Glinting 105 (Crepello 136) [1990 NR —
1991 7.6s 10.2s⁶] lengthy, unfurnished filly: sixth foal: half-sister to 4 winners,
including smart 7f and 1m performer Hadeer (by General Assembly) and fair 1¼m
winner Flaunting (by Kings Lake): dam best at up to 1m, from very successful
family: well beaten in maidens at Lingfield and Chepstow (pulled hard) in the
summer. *J. H. M. Gosden.*

BLOCKADE (USA) 2 b.g. (Mar 22) Imperial Falcon (CAN) – Stolen Date (USA) 83
(Sadair) [1991 7m 7g² 7f* 8f* 8g* 7d⁴ 8g⁴] IR 27,000Y: close-coupled, workmanlike

gelding: has been tubed: half-brother to 3 very useful winners, including 5f and 6f winner Taufan (by Stop The Music): dam minor winning sprinter, is half-sister to both dam of Malinowski and grandam of Try My Best and El Gran Senor: progressed into fair performer: successful in autumn claimer at Salisbury and nurseries at Yarmouth and Goodwood: very good fourth of 19 to Cumbrian Challenge in similar event at Redcar final start: better suited by 1m than 7f: acts on firm going, fair effort on dead. *M. Bell.*

BLOODLESS COUP 9 b.g. Free State 125 – Freely Given 69 (Petingo 135) — [1990 NR 1991 12s⁴ 14d 16.2g] lengthy gelding: poor mover: fair handicapper at one time: well beaten as 9-y-o, first runs on flat since 1986: stays well: best efforts on an easy surface. *C. C. Elsey.*

BLUE AEROPLANE 3 ch.c. Reach 122 – Shelton Song 60 (Song 132) [1990 95 5m³ 6h* 7f² 6g* 1991 7g⁵ 7g⁶ 7.1m³ 10g² 7g* 7g⁶ 9m] lengthy colt: fairly useful performer: blinkered, won handicap at Sandown in July, always close up and leading final strides: effective at 7f and probably stays 1¼m: best efforts on an easy surface: also blinkered final start: sold to join P. Nicholls 19,000 gns Newmarket Autumn Sales. *P. F. I. Cole.*

BLUE BIRDS FLY 3 ch.f. Rainbow Quest (USA) 134 – Pale Gold (FR) (New 78 Chapter 106) [1990 NR 1991 10.5g⁴ 10g* 12s] workmanlike filly: half-sister to several winners, including fairly useful 1¼m winner My Tony (by Be My Guest): dam minor French 6f and 11.5f winner: won maiden at Newbury in October by ¾ length from Majed: behind in listed race at Evry following month. *R. Charlton.*

BLUE CARNATION 3 gr.f. Carwhite 127 – Eyry 85 (Falcon 131) [1990 NR 1991 — 7g 7g 10m] smallish, sparely-made filly: half-sister to 7f winner Coraki (by Crofter), 1984 2-y-o 6f seller winner Jack's Lass (by Crimson Beau) and winners in Hong Kong and Belgium: dam 5f winner at 2 yrs: 33/1, well beaten in maiden and sellers. *J. M. P. Eustace.*

BLUE CENTURION 2 b.g. (Apr 8) Nishapour (FR) 125 – Lovers Light (Grundy — p 137) [1991 6m 7g] 9,600F, 1,500Y: rather unfurnished gelding: fourth foal: brother to 3-y-o 1½m winner Eliki and half-brother to a winner abroad by Mashhor Dancer: dam out of half-sister to Main Reef: better than twelfth-of-21 position suggests in Newmarket seller in August (well-backed favourite) second start, headway over 2f out, eased when held: likely to do better. *M. Bell.*

BLUE CROSS 2 b.f. (May 10) Mansingh (USA) 120 – Rosslayne Whisper 35 (Donibristle 96) [1991 6g 6m⁵ 6f⁵ 6f] small, sturdy filly: second reported foal: dam unraced: poor maiden. *P. S. Felgate.*

BLUE DAISY (USA) 3 gr.f. Shahrastani (USA) 135 – Blue Angel's Image (USA) 108 (Ruritania) [1990 8d* 1991 8m⁴ 10g³ 8g⁴ 8g² 8m² 7g* 8s* 7s²] leggy, sparely-made filly: useful performer: won listed race (15/8 on, made all) at Naas and Premio Bagutta-Memorial Sergio Cumani at Milan in October: also ran well behind Kooyonga at the Curragh in Goffs Irish 1000 Guineas (beaten 4½ lengths) and Matron Stakes (rec 12 lb and beaten length) first and fifth starts: should be suited by further than 1m: acts on good to firm ground and soft: edgy (below best) third start: reportedly to be trained by J. Hammond in France. *J. Oxx, Ireland.*

BLUE DISC 6 br.g. Disc Jockey 95 – Kaotesse (Djakao (FR) 124) [1990 a6g⁴ a7g³ — a8g⁴ 7f 1991 7.1m] workmanlike gelding: poor maiden: stays 1m: acts on any going: blinkered at 5 yrs: possibly ungenuine: winning hurdler. *C. R. Beever.*

BLUE DUN 2 b.g. (Jan 23) Petong 126 – Glyn Rhosyn (Welsh Saint 126) [1991 59 6.1m⁶ 6g] smallish, good-quartered gelding: fourth foal: brother to 3-y-o Blue Tail and half-brother to 1988 2-y-o 6f winner Ipo (by Mummy's Game): dam poor maiden: plating-class maiden: better effort when slowly away and never dangerous at Nottingham on debut: gave trouble stalls both starts: sold 720 gns Ascot November Sales. *P. J. Makin.*

BLUE GRIT 5 b.g. Thatching 131 – Northern Wisdom (Northfields (USA)) [1990 47 NR 1991 a12g a8g 10.2s 9s 8g² 9f* 8.5f* 8.2m² 9f⁴ 8m⁵ 8f⁴ 9f³ 8f² 8h⁴] leggy, quite attractive gelding: poor handicapper: won at Redcar (ladies) and Beverley (apprentices) in May: stays 9f: goes well on top-of-the-ground: visored first 3 starts, blinkered after: has run well when sweating: consistent. *M. Dods.*

BLUE INFANTA 3 br.f. Chief Singer 131 – Blue Queen 54 (Majority Blue 126) — [1990 NR 1991 10g⁶ 10m 7.6m] rather leggy, useful-looking filly: half-sister to several winners, including very useful middle-distance filly Reprocolor (by Jimmy Reppin), dam of Colorspin and Bella Colora: dam half-sister to Sandford Lad: plating-class form in maidens, best effort on debut: off course 5 months before final start: stays 1¼m: sold 8,500 gns Newmarket December Sales. *J. R. Fanshawe.*

BLUE IS TRUE (IRE) 2 b.f. (Apr 4) Bluebird (USA) 125 – Royal Wolff (Prince **43**
Tenderfoot (USA) 126) [1991 6f³] IR 28,000F, IR 18,000Y: good-quartered filly: third
foal: half-sister to a winner in Macau: dam Irish sprinter: green 3/1-shot, third in
6-runner maiden auction at Salisbury in August: sold 950 gns Newmarket Autumn
Sales. *A. C. Stewart.*

BLUE MARINE 2 b.f. (Mar 19) Bellypha 130 – Opale 117 (Busted 134) [1991 7d] **— p**
fourth foal: sister to modest 1990 2-y-o 7f winner Tenayestelign and half-sister to
fair 13.3f winner Pale Wine (by Rousillon): dam won Irish St Leger at 4 yrs: 16/1,
backward and green, signs of some ability when fourteenth of 21 in maiden at
Doncaster in November: should improve, especially over middle distances. *A. C.
Stewart.*

BLUE MISCHIEF 5 ch.m. Precocious 126 – Deep Blue Sea (Gulf Pearl 117) **43**
[1990 5f 5g 6m 5m⁵ 5d 7m⁵ 5d⁴ 7d⁶ 6s 1991 7g 6m³ 5f⁵] strong, lengthy mare:
carries plenty of condition: good walker: moderate mover: poor handicapper
nowadays: stays 7f: best on ground no softer than dead. *J. S. Haldane.*

BLUE ROOM 4 b.f. Gorytus (USA) 132 – Jokers High (USA) (Vaguely Noble 140) **65**
[1990 8f 8m 7m⁴ 7m 7m 7h* 7f* 7f² 7m 7g 1991 8f² 7g 7v a7g⁵] rather leggy,
lengthy filly: moderate mover: quite modest performer: well below form after
reappearance: effective at 7f and 1m: acts on hard going, seems unsuited by heavy
ground: bolted and withdrawn once at 4 yrs. *R. Akehurst.*

BLUE SAVANNAH (IRE) 3 ch.c. Ahonoora 122 – Infanta (USA) (Intrepid **—**
Hero (USA)) [1990 NR 1991 6f⁵ 6f 7m6 8.3g 7g 8f] IR 31,000Y: good-quartered colt:
fifth foal: half-brother to modest 1986 2-y-o 5f winner Take A Hint (by Pitskelly) and
1m winner Forty Or More (by Yashgan): dam twice-raced half-sister to dam of
Robellino: bad plater. *A. W. Denson.*

BLUES BALIDAR 3 ch.g. Balidar 133 – Kimble Blue 86 (Blue Refrain 121) **57**
[1990 6g 1991 7g 7m 7f³ 7g 8d⁴ 7.1g 8.2f a8g a7g] tall, workmanlike filly: quite
modest maiden: behind in handicaps last 4 starts: may prove best at up to 1m: acts
on firm and dead going: blinkered final start: headstrong, and wears crossed
noseband nowadays. *J. L. Spearing.*

BLUE TAIL 3 gr.f. Petong 126 – Glyn Rhosyn (Welsh Saint 126) [1990 5f² 5d⁴ 5f² **58**
a7g³ 1991 5g⁴ 7m⁴ 7d⁵] sparely-made filly: has a light action: quite modest maiden
at 2 yrs: well below form in claimer (ran on well) and seller (claimed to join P. Butler
£6,350) last 2 starts in 1991: should stay 7f: best form on a soft surface: sometimes
sweating and edgy. *P. J. Makin.*

BLUE TIGER (USA) 2 ch.g. (Mar 9) Storm Cat (USA) – Cecelia (USA) (Royal **100**
Levee (USA)) [1991 5m² 5m 5g 6g* 5g⁴ 6.1m⁶ 6f* 5m*] $160,000Y: workmanlike
gelding: good mover: half-brother to several winners, notably useful French miler
Absentia (by Raise A Cup), later stakes winner at 9f in USA and dam of Dancing
Dissident: dam unraced daughter of half-sister to top American colts Chieftain and
Tom Rolfe: sire leading American 2-y-o in 1985, has had excellent first season at
stud: progressive performer: won maiden at Yarmouth in July and nurseries at
Hamilton (comfortably) and Sandown (by a length from Miss Vaxette) in September:
stays 6f: acts on firm ground: reared and unseated rider stalls third outing: ran
poorly at Chester sixth start: sold 44,000 gns Newmarket Autumn Sales, reportedly
to go to California. *B. Hanbury.*

BLUE TOPAZE 3 ch.f. Fast Topaze (USA) 128 – Forever Mary 81 (Red Alert **—**
127) [1990 NR 1991 7d] 20,000Y: good-topped, close-coupled filly: third foal:
half-sister to fairly useful 6f (at 2 yrs) and 1m winner Silver Ore (by Silver Hawk):
dam, sprint maiden here later successful at up to 7f in USA, is out of half-sister to
very smart Greenland Park, dam of Fitnah: always behind after slow start in
newcomers race at Doncaster in March: joined M. Saunders. *D. R. C. Elsworth.*

BLUNHAM EXPRESS 2 b.f. (May 2) Never So Bold 135 – Park Parade 94 **52**
(Monsanto (FR) 121) [1991 5g 5m⁴ 6m² 6g² a6g⁵ 6m³ 8.1g⁴ 7m] 6,400Y: robust filly:
has a round action: fourth foal: half-sister to ungenuine plater Musical Ivy (by
Aragon): dam won 5 times at 1½m and is out of sister to Parthian Glance, best 3-y-o
staying filly of 1966: plating-class maiden: better suited by 1m than shorter. *T.
Fairhurst.*

BLUSHING BELLE 3 b.f. Local Suitor (USA) 128 – Shuteye 91 (Shirley **74**
Heights 130) [1990 7m 8m⁶ 7m 8f 10.6s* 1991 10g³ 12.2m³ 12m² a14g] rangy,
workmanlike filly: has a very round action: modest performer: ran well in handicaps
in the spring: tailed off in similar event at Southwell final start, first for 6 months:
should stay beyond 1½m: acts on good to firm ground and soft: sweating on
reappearance. *P. F. I. Cole.*

Rous Stakes, Newmarket—Blyton Lad (centre) takes the race for a second time; Notley (left) is second, Furajet (right) is third

BLUSHING OPAL 2 b.f. (Apr 29) Blushing Scribe (USA) 107 – Blesseen 71 (So —
Blessed 130) [1991 6m 7f 7m 6g 6g a7g] 820F: close-coupled, sparely-made filly:
sister to a winner in Sweden and half-sister to 1983 2-y-o 7f winner Quiet Solicitor
(by Roan Rocket) and a winner in Scandinavia: dam raced only at sprint distances:
seems of little account: blinkered fourth start. *B. Ellison.*

BLUSHING POPEYE 4 ch.g. Blushing Scribe (USA) 107 – Place In The Sun 48 —
(Sun Prince 128) [1990 8m 10f 7m 8h⁶ 6m 6g 1991 7.1d 8g] smallish gelding:
moderate mover: little worthwhile form. *M. P. Muggeridge.*

BLYOSTKA (USA) 2 ch.f. (Mar 16) Gone West (USA) – Calypsa (USA) 83 (The 54
Minstrel (CAN) 135) [1991 7m³ 7f⁴ 6f⁶ 7f] $40,000Y: leggy filly: third foal:
half-sister to 8.2f winner Nakora Bistraya (by Robellino): dam 2-y-o 7f winner from
3 starts: sire winner in USA at 1m and 9f, including Grade 1 Dwyer Stakes:
plating-class form in maidens first 3 starts: tailed off in Yarmouth nursery (stiff task)
in September: will stay 1m +. *G. A. Pritchard-Gordon.*

BLYTON LAD 5 b.g. Skyliner 117 – Ballinacurra (King's Troop 118) [1990 5f³ 115
5m⁴ 5m⁶ 5f² 5m 5m* 5d 1991 5m⁶ 5g 5g³ 5m³ 5m* 5m²] big, rangy gelding: smart
sprinter: won listed Rous Stakes at Newmarket by ¾ length from Notley: good
second to On Tiptoes in similar event there later in October: very good third to
Sheikh Albadou in Nunthorpe Stakes at York third start: best form at 5f: acts on firm
and dead going: often sweating and edgy: often unruly in preliminaries and taken
down early nowadays: twice withdrawn at start (refused to enter stalls once) at 4
yrs. *W. J. Pearce.*

BLYTON STAR (IRE) 3 b.g. Horage 124 – Saintly Angel 87 (So Blessed 130) —
[1990 5f 5m⁶ 1991 5g 5m⁶ 5m a7g] sturdy gelding: moderate walker: plating-class
maiden: little form in 1991: should stay 6f. *Miss G. M. Rees.*

BOADICEA'S CHARIOT 4 b.f. Commanche Run 133 – Indigine (USA) (Raise —
A Native) [1990 12d 12m 12g* 14m⁶ 12m 12g 10d 1991 12f 16m 14.6m 17.2g] lengthy,
workmanlike ex-Irish filly: fifth foal: half-sister to fair 7f to 1m and hurdles winner
Below Zero (by Northfields) and fair 1986 2-y-o winner In Glory (by Dalsaan): dam
lightly-raced 2-y-o 6f winner: won maiden at Galway at 3 yrs: no show on flat here at
4 yrs: stays 1½m: trained at 3 yrs by V. Rossiter: winning hurdler in April. *R. J.
Manning.*

BOARDING SCHOOL 4 b.g. Glenstal (USA) 118 – Amenity (FR) 76 (Luthier 92
126) [1990 8m* 8g² 10g² 10m 12g² 12.3g⁶ 10d⁴ 1991 16.5m²] good-topped ex-Irish
gelding: won maiden at Leopardstown when trained by M. O'Toole at 3 yrs: second,
including in listed event, at the Curragh after: fairly useful effort when 6 lengths
second to Spinning in minor event at Doncaster in October, 1991: stays 2m: acts on
good to firm and dead ground: useful hurdler. *C. Parker.*

107

BOBBIE BOLD 3 ch.g. Noalto 120 – Silk Imp 72 (Imperial Fling (USA) 116) —
[1990 NR 1991 10f a12g] 4,000Y: sturdy gelding: second foal: dam 1m winner stayed
1¼m: no worthwhile form in maidens at Ripon (signs of ability) and Southwell. *R.
O'Leary.*

BOBBY ON THE BANK 5 ch.g. Monsanto (FR) 121 – Dewberry 68 (Bay 30
Express 132) [1990 10.6f4 8m6 9g 10f2 10d6 9g5 8h 10.4g2 10m* 10.6s 1991 10d 10m3
8h6 a12g6 8.9m 10.5m] small, rather sparely-made gelding: moderate mover: poor
handicapper: stays 1¼m well: acts on any going: sold 1,100 gns Doncaster October
Sales. *M. J. O'Neill.*

BOB'S DAUGHTER (IRE) 2 ch.f. (May 2) Bob Back (USA) 124 – Tabriya 61 —
(Nishapour (FR) 125) [1991 a6g a6g 7m] IR 2,000Y: small filly: third foal: half-sister
to a winner in Italy by Tumble Wind: dam lightly raced: soundly beaten in sellers.
Ronald Thompson.

BOB'S GHAL (IRE) 2 gr.f. (Apr 16) Bob Back (USA) 124 – Alhargah (Be My 38
Guest (USA) 126) [1991 6g4 6m 6g6] IR 3,500Y: leggy, close-coupled filly: fourth
foal: half-sister to 3 winners, including 1990 2-y-o 6f winner Moy River (by
Dominion) and modest 1989 2-y-o 8.5f winner Toast The Host (by Elegant Air): dam
poor daughter of half-sister to high-class middle-distance colt Pelerin: poor form:
sweating, best effort in Lingfield seller on debut: twice slowly away: sold 1,200 gns
Doncaster July Sales. *J. Berry.*

BOBZAO (IRE) 2 b.c. (Feb 18) Alzao (USA) 117 – Brilleaux 73 (Manado 130) 98
[1991 6s* 7g4 8.1m3 7d2 7s] IR 32,000Y: useful-looking colt: has scope: third foal:
dam half-sister to useful miler Welsh Flame, herself grandam of Marju and Salsabil,
should have stayed 1¼m: fairly useful performer: won maiden at Folkestone in July:
excellent second of 9, making most, to Assessor in minor event at Ascot in
September: well below that form in Goffs Million at the Curragh 4 weeks later:
should stay 1¼m: acts on good to firm ground, but is well suited by a soft surface. *W.
Carter.*

BODARI 2 b.c. (Apr 22) Prince Sabo 123 – City Link Rose (Lochnager 132) [1991 68 p
5m6 5m4] good-quartered colt: third foal: half-brother to 5f sprinter City Link Pet
(by Tina's Pet): dam showed signs of ability on last of 3 starts: better effort in
September maidens when fourth of 11, leading briefly over 1f out, at Sandown: will
improve again. *D. A. Wilson.*

BODY COPY (IRE) 2 b.f. (Apr 28) Alzao (USA) 117 – Heather Hut (Shack — p
(USA) 118) [1991 6m] 6,600F, 6,000Y, 7,200 2-y-o: leggy filly: second foal: dam Irish
maiden, ran as 2-y-o and 5-y-o: 33/1 and very green, slowly away and always chased
along in rear in 11-runner maiden at Goodwood in September: should do better. *J. L.
Dunlop.*

BOGAZKOY 9 b.g. Hittite Glory 125 – Lady Captain (Never Say Die 137) [1990 —
NR 1991 20g] robust gelding: poor mover: poor handicapper: well beaten only run in
1991, first start on flat since 5-y-o: used to be suited by extreme test of stamina: acts
on firm going, appears unsuited by soft surface: has been blinkered. *C. Holmes.*

BOG TROTTER (USA) 3 ch.c. Irish River (FR) 131 – Chaleur (CAN) 119
(Rouge Sang (USA) 116) [1990 7g3 7g* 7m2 7d2 1991 7g* 8g 7m* 6s 7m5]
The racegoers' regard for a jockey tends to be rather fickle, but this
seems to be far less the case with the incomparable Piggott whose come-back,
after five years, is now in its second year, having yielded over a hundred
winners world wide and given the sport a precious extra flair. Piggott's
confidence and tactical audacity, in particular, provided some of the most
memorable finishes of the season, for instance on Golan Heights at
Newmarket and Rua d'Oro at Leopardstown in the spring. Waiting races seem
to figure most prominently in his repertoire nowadays, too prominently for
some, but on Bog Trotter Piggott produced two masterly rides to win the
Singer & Friedlander Greenham Stakes and Kiveton Park Stakes, making
almost every yard. It would be unfair, of course, to the other jockeys in those
races to conclude simply that they were outmanoeuvred—and to Bog Trotter.
He's a good horse on his day. That much had been established in Bog
Trotter's first season in which he'd won the Laurent-Perrier Champagne
Stakes and finished second in the Dewhurst, and the latter race had
demonstrated his particular effectiveness with forcing tactics. He's such a
keen sort that to bowl along in front had shown itself the best way to conserve
his energy. It was widely expected, however, that at Newbury in the

Singer & Friedlander Greenham Stakes, Newbury—
Bog Trotter (black cap) beats Mukaddamah (striped cap)

Greenham these tactics would merely see Bog Trotter give a nice lead to the well-touted Mukaddamah. Bog Trotter had also been the subject of favourable home reports, suggesting that he'd learnt to settle much better, but Mukaddamah was still made an even-money chance, with Bog Trotter sharing second favouritism with the Horris Hill winner Sapieha at 4/1. In the event, Sapieha forfeited all chance with a most awkward start and Mukaddamah only threatened briefly to live up to his home reputation. Piggott gave Bog Trotter a breather at halfway and took a long look round at his six opponents; then, really setting his mount alight at the distance, he found a most willing response and though Mukaddamah got to his quarters, Bog Trotter always had the edge. The Kiveton Park Stakes at Doncaster in September saw an even more impressive performance. On this occasion Norton Challenger tried to make sure that Bog Trotter and Piggott couldn't dictate matters entirely as they pleased, but the stronger pace had no debilitating effects on Bog Trotter at the finish. Far from it. At the three-furlong pole, Bog Trotter had a widening two-length advantage with his eleven pursuers well strung out, the vast majority of them most unlikely to get any closer. One still going reasonably well was the Jersey Stakes winner Satin Flower but she could close the gap only marginally in the final furlong and Bog Trotter had again tenaciously made all. Among those which never got in a blow were the pattern- or listed-race winners Only Yours, La Grange Music, Himiko, Sylva Honda and Rami.

With so much to like about those victories, how disappointing it is to relate the facts of Bog Trotter's three other races in 1991. Twelfth of fourteen in the Two Thousand Guineas; fourteenth of sixteen in the Diadem Stakes at Ascot and fifth of seven in the Challenge Stakes at Newmarket; Piggott's customary swift acceptance of defeat shouldn't mask the mediocrity of these performances. There were stamina doubts before Bog Trotter's attempt at a mile in the Guineas but he was headed well over two furlongs out in the main group before beating a swift retreat. His trainer was reportedly dissatisfied with Bog Trotter's condition for most of the four months that then went by before Doncaster. On his two outings after Doncaster, he could never comfortably keep up with the leader in the Diadem (for which he started 15/8 favourite) and was never asked to do so in the Challenge Stakes nineteen days later.

Bog Trotter (USA) (ch.c. 1988)	Irish River (FR) (ch 1976)	Riverman (b 1969)	Never Bend / River Lady
		Irish Star (b 1960)	Klairon / Botany Bay
	Chaleur (CAN) (b 1979)	Rouge Sang (b 1972)	Bold Bidder / Red Damask
		Brief Attire (b 1962)	Menetrier / Chorus Beauty

Bog Trotter is the fourth foal from his dam Chaleur, the previous three by Premier Account, Key To Content and Icecapade winning at least four races apiece, in minor stakes. Chaleur in her turn is one of four Canadian stakes winners out of her dam—taking the seven-furlong Glorious Song Stakes at two years—the others all sprinter-milers by Red God's lightly-raced half-brother Up Spirits, one of which has gone on to foal the very useful French sprinters Bold Apparel and Cedrico. Although Chaleur is by the Gran Premio di Milano winner and John Porter Stakes runner-up Rouge Sang and Bog Trotter by Irish River, it's not being especially controversial to suggest that Bog Trotter will prove best short of a mile, he's such a free-running individual capable of plenty of early speed. His best efforts remain at seven furlongs but his defeat in the Diadam can't be blamed solely on the trip. It's possible that the soft ground was against him (he has, incidentally, yet to be raced on firm). The theory that he goes well fresh is belied by the fact that his last three races as a two-year-old, all progressive efforts, came in a spell of little over a month. Bog Trotter, an angular, good-topped colt, invariably impresses with his well-being in the paddock. His in-and-out season undermines confidence in his prospects as a four-year-old; perhaps he needs things his own way up front. We'll have to wait and see. *W. J. Haggas.*

BO KNOWS BEST (IRE) 2 ch.g. (May 2) Burslem 123 – Do We Know 47 (Derrylin 115) [1991 5d 6g⁴ 7m³ 7g 7m] IR 3,000Y, 4,500 2-y-o: leggy gelding: fifth live foal: half-brother to 3-y-o 9f winner All Greek To Me (by Trojan Fen) and a winner in Spain by Pharly: dam thrice-raced half-sister to high-class 1¼m horse Rarity: modest plater: best effort battling-on third of 14 at Wolverhampton in July: should stay 1¼m. *J. Sutcliffe.*

BOLD AD 7 b.m. Bold Owl 101 – Norma's Way 70 (Great White Way (USA)) [1990 — NR 1991 13.8m⁴ 13.8f⁶] sparely-made mare: poor mover: poor plater: probably stays 13.8f: probably acts on any going. *J. L. A. Charlton.*

BOLD ANGEL 4 b.g. Lochnager 132 – Lobela 77 (Lorenzaccio 130) [1990 6f 7g 77 7m 6m 6d 1991 6m⁵ 6m² 7f³ 8d⁶ 7.1g 6g* 6.1m³ 7g 7.5f⁴ 6m² 6g⁵ 7g] strong, close-coupled gelding: carries condition: has a round action: modest handicapper: won at Pontefract in July: effective at 6f and 7f, and should stay 1m: acts on firm and dead ground: ran moderately when blinkered once. *M. H. Easterby.*

BOLD ANSWER 8 b.g. Bold Owl 101 – Subtle Answer (Stephen George 102) — [1990 12.3g 16.5g⁶ 12f 1991 a8g] poor handicapper: stays 1½m. *M. C. Chapman.*

BOLD ARABELLA 3 b.f. Never So Bold 135 – Nativity (USA) 71 (Native 67 Royalty (USA)) [1990 6f 6g 1991 7v³ 8d 7g³ 7g* 7d] big, workmanlike filly: best effort to win 4-runner maiden at Edinburgh in June, hanging left: last of 11 in Ayr handicap 3 months later: stays 7f. *J. Berry.*

BOLD BORIS 2 br.g. (Feb 14) Never So Bold 135 – Pride of Paris (Troy 137) 46 p [1991 a7g] 18,500F, 19,000Y: lengthy, quite attractive gelding: has scope: first foal: dam once-raced half-sister to smart miler Gwent: 20/1, over 10 lengths tenth of 12, always in rear, in late-year maiden at Lingfield: may do better. *R. W. Armstrong.*

BOLD BOSTONIAN (FR) 3 b.c. Never So Bold 135 – Miss Boston (FR) 88 (River River (FR) 111) [1990 6m* 6g³ 7m³ 7.3g⁵ 1991 8s 8g 12d 8d² 8g³ 8.9g⁶ 10m² 8.9m² 11g] quite good-topped colt: good mover: fair handicapper: creditable efforts when placed, soon niggled along in rear then staying on very strongly in £8,700 contest at York penultimate start: stays 1¼m: acts on good to firm ground and dead:

ridden by 7-lb claimer last 6 starts: sold to join P. Hobbs 28,000 gns Newmarket Autumn Sales. *H. Candy.*

BOLD CELT   8 b. or br.h. Brave Shot – Pearl Locket (Gulf Pearl 117) [1990 NR **35** 1991 6d4] leggy, quite good-topped horse: lightly raced and poor maiden: stays 7f: acts on dead ground. *C. B. B. Booth.*

BOLD COOKIE   3 b.f. Never So Bold 135 – Irish Cookie 80 (Try My Best (USA) **57** 130) [1990 5g2 1991 6m3 6m4 6m5] lengthy filly: didn't reproduce debut form, including in June handicap: most probably needs further, possibly an easy surface: tends to get on edge. *Miss S. E. Hall.*

BOLD ELECT   3 b.c. Electric 126 – Famous Band (USA) (Banderilla (USA)) **77** [1990 6m5 7.5m6 7m 8g 8g5 8g3 1991 9s 10f 13.9m5 10f4 9.9f2 12.3f* 12m 10.9m 13.9m4] sturdy, lengthy colt: carries penalty: modest performer: won maiden at Ripon in August very gamely: behind facing stiff tasks in handicaps (soon scrubbed along penultimate start) and minor event (wore severe noseband) afterwards: stays 1½m (stiff tasks over further): acts on firm going. *P. Wigham.*

BOLD FURY   8 ch.g. Bold Lad (IRE) 133 – Falassa (Relko 136) [1990 NR 1991   — 12g] workmanlike gelding: poor handicapper: should stay 1¼m: acts on good to firm ground: tried visored: sometimes bandaged: winning hurdler. *J. D. Roberts.*

BOLD HABIT   6 ch.g. Homing 130 – Our Mother 95 (Bold Lad (IRE) 133) [1990 **91** 7m4 8g5 7m 7f3 7g* 7f3 7f5 7.5g 8g2 7.3g5 7m3 6g3 a8g3 a7g5 a7g* 1991 7m 7.6g* a **99** 8g 5g* 7g* 6m6 5f* 6m 7m a7g3 a7g2] sturdy, strong-quartered gelding: moderate walker and mover: fairly useful handicapper, much improved at 6 yrs: successful at Lingfield in May, Sandown in July and Goodwood (apprentices) and Sandown in August: ran well at Lingfield last 2 starts: effective at up to 1m: acts on firm and dead going: goes very well for claimer G. Husband: has very good turn of foot, and best held up. *W. J. Pearce.*

BOLD ILLUSION   13 ch.g. Grey Mirage 128 – Savette (Frigid Aire) [1990 12d   — 1991 14d] close-coupled, sparely-made gelding: lightly raced and well below his best on flat nowadays: stays 1¾m well: used to go very well in the mud: best forcing pace: usually apprentice ridden: a grand old servant. *M. W. Eckley.*

BOLD LEZ   4 b.c. Never So Bold 135 – Classy Nancy (USA) (Cutlass (USA)) [1990 **102** 6g 6g2 5m* 6g 5m3 5m* 5g2 6m 5m3 5m 1991 6g 5g* 5m2 6g6 6m 5g4 5.6m5 6m 5d 5d3 5.2g] leggy colt: poor mover: useful handicapper: won at Newbury in April: best efforts after when running very well in Trafalgar House Sprint Stakes at Sandown and £16,700 event at Ascot sixth and penultimate starts: best form at 5f: acts on good to firm and dead ground (yet to race on extremes): has been bandaged. *M. J. Haynes.*

BOLD MELODY   2 b.f. (May 15) Never So Bold 135 – Broken Melody (Busted **42** 134) [1991 a6g a8g5] fifth foal: half-sister to a winner in Denmark by Valiyar: dam unraced half-sister to very useful middle-distance filly Sing Softly: plating-class form in late-year Southwell claimers. *P. C. Haslam.*

BOLD MEMORY   2 br.c. (Apr 22) Never So Bold 135 – Try To Remember **84** p (Music Boy 124) [1991 6m 6d*] rather unfurnished colt: third foal: dam, fairly useful hurdler, was maiden plater on flat: favourite, confirmed promise of debut when winning 7-runner maiden at Newmarket in November, again racing keenly then staying on strongly from 1½f out: may improve again. *D. R. C. Elsworth.*

BOLD MOOD   2 br.g. (May 17) Jalmood (USA) 126 – Boldie 81 (Bold Lad (IRE) **65** 133) [1991 8.3g 6d3 6.1d5 6s a7g] close-coupled, quite attractive gelding: fourth foal: half-brother to 3-y-o Bold Spark (by Electric), 7f winner at 2 yrs, and 7f winner Lord Patrick (by Formidable): dam won from 7f to 10.6f: quite modest maiden: best effort third of 23, staying on, to Prince Emilio at Haydock in autumn: no comparable form after. *J. Berry.*

BOLD NEPHEW   3 b.c. Never So Bold 135 – Cornelian 78 (Great Nephew 126)   — [1990 6m* 6m3 6f4 6f6 6m4 1991 7m 6m 7g5] useful-looking colt: has a quick action: quite useful performer at 2 yrs, fourth in Middle Park Stakes: ran poorly in 1991: should be suited by further than 6f: seems unsuited by firm ground: sweating final start: trained first 2 by R. Hannon: sold 13,500 gns Newmarket Autumn Sales. *J. R. Fanshawe.*

BOLD PERFORMER   4 b.c. Bold Lad (IRE) 133 – Miss St Cyr 86 (Brigadier **61** Gerard 144) [1990 10s6 10d3 9m5 10.2s4 1991 9s2] sturdy colt: modest performer: stayed 1¼m: acted on soft going: dead. *J. Wharton.*

BOLD PURSUIT (IRE)   2 b.c. (Mar 25) Thatching 131 – Pursue 78 (Auction **103** p Ring (USA) 123) [1991 7m3 8m*] 70,000Y: lengthy, useful-looking colt: second foal:

half-brother to 3-y-o Pay To Dream (by Runnett): dam 2-y-o 5f winner, is half-sister to smart miler Alert: won 22-runner maiden at Newmarket in October (bandaged behind) in excellent style by 3½ lengths from Delve: may prove best at around 1m: likely to progress further. *R. Hannon.*

BOLD RESOLUTION (IRE) 3 b.g. Shardari 134 – Valmarine (FR) (Val de **56** Loir 133) [1990 7m 8m 1991 10g⁶ 12f⁴ 11.7s 10g² 12f⁴ 12m 11.9g⁴ 11.9m⁶ 12fa 12g] big, close-coupled gelding: poor mover, with a round action: moderate walker: quite modest maiden: stays 1½m: acts on firm going (tailed off on all-weather): tailed off sixth start, subsequently gelded and ran poorly afterwards. *C. A. Cyzer.*

BOLD RUSSIAN 4 b.c. Persian Bold 123 – Russian Ribbon (USA) 86 (Nijinsky **117** (CAN) 138) [1990 7m* 8g* 7f² 7f³ 8g² 1991 8g* 8g⁴ 10m² 8g 8m² 7f* 8g* 8m] quite good-topped, attractive colt: smart performer: won Group 3 Beeswing Stakes at Newcastle (made all to beat Nicholas by 2½ lengths) in July and Group 2 Beefeater Gin Celebration Mile at Goodwood (noticeably edgy and sweating, gamely beat Flashfoot by neck) in August: below best in Prix du Moulin at Longchamp final start: effective at 7f, and stays 1¼m well: acts on firm going: tough and genuine. *B. W. Hills.*

BOLD SETKO (IRE) 2 b.c. (May 29) Bold Arrangement 127 – Ribamba 82 **43** (Ribocco 129) [1991 5h³ a6g 5.7m] IR 5,400Y: rather sparely-made colt: has a roundish action: eighth live foal: half-brother to very smart 1m and 1¼m winner Commodore Blake (by Blakeney) and fairly useful 5-y-o 7f performer La Bamba (by Laxton): dam, half-sister to Bruni, placed at 1m and 9f: poor maiden: not seen out after July: will be much better suited by 1m + . *J. M. P. Eustace.*

BOLD SPARK 3 br.g. Electric 126 – Boldie 81 (Bold Lad (IRE) 133) [1990 5m⁵ 6g — 7g³ 7m² a7g* 7f⁶ 7m⁵ a7g⁴ 7f² 8m 8m³ 8.2s⁴ 10.6s⁴ 7d² 1991 7d⁴ 8s 7g] sturdy gelding: good mover: fair plater at 2 yrs: easily best effort in 3-y-o handicaps on reappearance (awkward to post): may prove best around 1m: acts on any going: effective with or without blinkers or visor: has sweated up: game: sold to join M. Bradley 1,400 gns Ascot May Sales. *Mrs J. R. Ramsden.*

BOLD STROKE 2 br.c. (Feb 25) Persian Bold 123 – Fariha (Mummy's Pet 125) **88** [1991 7g² 8.2f² 8m* 8d⁶] 15,000F, 30,000Y: good-bodied colt: good walker: has a fluent action: third foal: half-brother to a winner in Brazil: dam twice-raced half-sister to smart miler Gwent: fair form: looking tremendously well, easily won 17-runner maiden at Ayr in September: tailed-off last of 6 in listed race at Ascot following month: will stay 1¼m: possibly unsuited by dead ground. *J. L. Dunlop.*

BOLD SURPRISE 2 b.c. (Mar 22) Ballad Rock 122 – Bombshell 76 (Le **63** p Levanstell 122) [1991 6f³ 6m⁶ 7m] 30,000Y: lengthy, quite attractive colt: has scope: half-brother to several winners, including 1988 2-y-o 1m winner Future Glory (by Ile de Bourbon) and 1¾m winner Orlandoland (by Reliance II): dam 8.5f winner: quite modest form in maidens: ran best race behind Modernise at Newmarket on final start, eased considerably from over 1f out into tenth of 20: will stay at least 1m: will improve further, and may be one to keep in mind in handicaps. *R. W. Armstrong.*

Beefeater Gin Celebration Mile, Goodwood—
a game performance from Bold Russian (left) to beat Flashfoot

Lord White of Hull's "Bold Russian"

BOLGHERI   3 b.g. Nicholas Bill 125 – Barrie Baby 86 (Import 127) [1990 8.2m 8d   —
8g 8v 1991 10g 14f 12f 12g 12.3g 11.1d 12.1d⁴ 13.8f⁵ 16m⁵ 11.1g 11m] workmanlike
gelding: poor maiden: joined N. Tinkler. *Don Enrico Incisa.*

BOLLIN MAGDALENE   3 b.f. Teenoso (USA) 135 – Klairlone 116 (Klairon   **48**
131) [1990 6s³ 6s⁴ 7f 8v 1991 12m 10g 12.3g⁴ 13d 12m⁴ a14g⁴ 17.9f 17.1m⁴ 15.8g³
15.1s] rather angular filly: moderate mover: plating-class maiden: stays well: acts on
good to firm ground and soft: blinkered last 3 starts, visored previous five. *M. H.
Easterby.*

BOLLIN PATRICK   6 b.g. Sagaro 133 – Bollin Charlotte 79 (Immortality) [1990   —
12m 14s³ 12m 12.2m⁴ 1991 10.5d 10m] strong, workmanlike horse: has a quick,
rather round action: fair handicapper at best as 5-y-o: burly and no promise in
October: stays 1¾m: possibly needs an easy surface nowadays: winning hurdler. *M.
H. Easterby.*

BOLLIN VICTORIA   2 b.f. (Jan 25) Jalmood (USA) 126 – Bollin Emily 82   **51**
(Lochnager 132) [1991 5m⁴ 6m⁴ 6m⁴ 7m³ 7f 7m] small, good-topped filly: good
walker: first foal: dam sprinter: poor form: best effort third of 7 in maiden at Ayr in
July: will probably stay 1m: steadily to post penultimate start, taken down early final
one. *M. H. Easterby.*

BOLLIN WILLIAM   3 b.c. Nicholas Bill 125 – Bollin Charlotte 79 (Immortality)   —
[1990 8g 1991 10.5g 10.4m] big, good-topped colt: behind in maidens, pulled up with
something amiss final start: winning hurdler. *M. H. Easterby.*

BOLT OF GOLD   3 b.f. Glint of Gold 128 – Habutai 70 (Habitat 134) [1990 NR   —
1991 10.1g⁵ 10g] close-coupled, quite attractive filly: second foal: half-sister to 1¼m
winner Tislam (by Formidable): dam maiden stayed 7f, is half-sister to Almaarad:
last in graduation event and claimer: sold to join L. Waring 3,100 gns Ascot October
Sales. *I. A. Balding.*

BOMBE SUPRISE (USA)   3 ch.f. Arctic Tern (USA) 126 – Dinner Surprise   —
(USA) (Lyphard (USA) 132) [1990 8m* 8d 1991 11.7g] lengthy, shallow-girthed filly:
dead-heated in maiden at Edinburgh at 2 yrs: not discredited in nursery next start:
always behind facing stiff task in Bath handicap nearly 12 months later: should stay
1¼m: has joined H. Cecil. *J. H. M. Gosden.*

BONANZA   4 ch.g. Glenstal (USA) 118 – Forliana 75 (Forli (ARG)) [1990 8v 8g6   —
7g 11m 13g 15g6 1991 12g5 16s4] lengthy, attractive gelding: no worthwhile form on
flat, soon ridden along in spring handicaps at 4 yrs: should prove suited by test of
stamina: winning hurdler. *Mrs G. R. Reveley.*

BONDAID   7 b.g. Main Reef 126 – Regency Gold (Prince Regent (FR) 129) [1990   **39**
NR 1991 a10g4 a10g a10g* a10g4 10g6] sturdy gelding: has been hobdayed: moderate
mover: lightly-raced handicapper: won at Lingfield in March: stays 1¼m: none too
consistent. *J. White.*

BONDSTONE   4 b.c. Miller's Mate 116 – Doumayna 79 (Kouban (FR)) [1990   **104**
10.1m2 10.8m2 12g* 1991 13.4d2 15.9m2 15.9g3 13.4m3 12m6] small, close-coupled
colt: carried plenty of condition: tended to look dull in coat: operated on for split
pastern at 3 yrs: improved performer in 1991: good third to Arcadian Heights in
listed event at Chester in August, fourth start: stayed well: acted on good to firm
and dead ground: dead (reportedly suffered heart attack on gallops). *H. R. A. Cecil.*

BONICA   2 b.f. (Mar 28) Rousillon (USA) 133 – Flaming Rose (USA) (Upper Nile   **56**
(USA)) [1991 5m5 6m4 6m6] leggy filly: second foal: half-sister to 3-y-o 6f (smart
form at 2 yrs) and 1m winner Chipaya (by Northern Prospect): dam, half-sister to
Gwydion, showed some ability in USA: plating-class form in maidens: off course
nearly 4 months after debut: sweating and unimpressive in appearance final start:
will be suited by 7f +. *J. R. Fanshawe.*

BONNIE KATE   3 br.f. Bold Owl 101 – Piccadilly Rose 63 (Reform 132) [1990 5g5   —
6g6 7m2 a7g3 7m5 1991 10d 11m 10g 12g 14.6m] neat filly: moderate plater: should
stay beyond 7f: tailed off on dead ground: best effort blinkered final start at 2 yrs. *D.
Haydn Jones.*

BONNY SCOT (IRE)   2 b.c. (Mar 9) Commanche Run 133 – Scots Lass 79   **113** p
(Shirley Heights 130) [1991 8m3 8.1d* 10g*]
   The St Leger winner Commanche Run has made a respectable start to
his career as a stallion, siring the winners of over a hundred races worldwide
from his first three crops, but his mostly late-developing stock have failed to
catch the eye of commercial breeders and it's no real surprise that he's
already been added to Coolmore's growing band of National Hunt stallions.
Probably the best horse he's sired is the promising Bonny Scot, who
progressed no end granted a test of stamina at two and will do so again over a
mile and a half plus in 1992. Bonny Scot made his debut in a maiden race at
Doncaster in September. Unfancied in the market and in need of the race, he
shaped like an assured future winner by keeping on strongly for third of

Sporting Life Zetland Stakes, Newmarket—Bonny Scot and Captain Horatius draw clear

nineteen behind Kingdom of Spain, and he duly landed the odds with plenty to spare in similar company at Haydock the following month. Stiffer opposition awaited Bonny Scot in the Sporting Life Zetland Stakes over an extra two furlongs at Newmarket in November: the impressive Haydock winner Captain Horatius and the nursery winners Beyton and Bundesbank all had fairly useful form to their credit. Nevertheless, Bonny Scot was a well-backed favourite and put up a smashing effort, drawing clear with Captain Horatius coming out of the Dip and gradually getting on top to win going away by a length and a half with Beyton eight lengths away in third and Bundesbank another five back in fourth. The victory took Bonny Scot's trainer Cumani beyond a million pounds in prize money for the second season in a row.

		Run The Gantlet	Tom Rolfe
	Commanche Run	(b 1968)	First Feather
	(b 1981)	Volley	Ratification
Bonny Scot (IRE)		(b 1965)	Mitrailleuse
(b.c. Mar 9, 1989)		Shirley Heights	Mill Reef
	Scots Lass	(b 1975)	Hardiemma
	(b 1982)	Edinburgh	Charlottown
		(b 1974)	Queen's Castle

Bonny Scot is out of Scots Lass, a modest and rather temperamental thirteen-furlong winner. He is his dam's second foal following the fairly useful mile-and-a-quarter winner Border Mate (by Be My Guest) while the third and fourth are a colt by Caerleon and a filly by Be My Guest. The second dam Edinburgh showed smart form over a mile in France at two and finished runner-up in a couple of minor pattern races at around a mile and a quarter the following year. She's produced several other winners at stud, including the very useful middle-distance stayer Queen Helen and the Prix de Lutece winner Sought Out; the third dam Queen's Castle is a half-sister to Reform. A sturdy, quite attractive colt, Bonny Scot hails from a family who clearly stay well and the true pace in the Zetland Stakes seemed to suit him ideally. His performance there was supported by a fast timefigure, and with determination to back up his obvious ability he looks a good young stayer in the making. *L. M. Cumani.*

BONNY'S GAME   3 b.f. Mummy's Game 120 – Ribonny (FR) 33 (Fast Hilarious   **31** (USA)) [1990 6g 1991 9.1s⁵ 12.2g 14f 15g³ 13.8f³ 16.2f³ 14m⁶ 13.8m⁵] workmanlike filly: poor maiden: stays 2m: acts on firm going: blinkered or visored (seventh start) last 4 outings. *C. W. C. Elsey.*

BONZER   2 br.g. (Mar 3) Electric 126 – Lady Doubloon (Pieces of Eight 128) [1991   **47** 8m 7m 8m] leggy, close-coupled gelding: fourth reported foal: brother to winning hurdler Bright-One and half-brother to 1986 2-y-o 5f winner Peter's Blue (by Riki Lash): dam unraced: poor form: well beaten in maidens (including maiden auction) in the North. *J. G. FitzGerald.*

BOOGIE BOPPER (IRE)   2 b. or br.g. (Apr 1) Taufan (USA) 119 – Mey 78   **65** (Canisbay 120) [1991 6m 7m² 6f⁵] IR 6,600Y: leggy, sparely-made gelding: half-brother to several winners, including smart 7f to 1½m winner Perchance (by Connaught) and 1990 2-y-o 5f and 6f winner May Reef (by Simply Great): dam, best at 1¼m, is half-sister to smart animals Albany and Magna Carta: quite modest form in maiden auctions, best effort second of 11 at Yarmouth in July: will stay at least 1m. *M. Bell.*

BOOGY LADY (IRE)   3 b.f. Glenstal (USA) 118 – Lady Regrets (FR) (Sir   **53** Gaylord) [1990 NR 1991 10m⁴ 11.5m⁵ 10m] 25,000Y: workmanlike filly: closely related to very useful stayer Daarkom and half-sister to 2 winners: dam unraced sister to good French 6.5f to 1m winner Delmora, herself dam of very smart 9f to 1¼m winner Corvaro: never placed to challenge or knocked about in claimer (claimed £8,001) at Newmarket, ladies event at Lingfield and maiden (first run for 5 months) at Leicester: best effort at 1¼m: trained first start by M. Jarvis, second by J. Pearce: may do better. *I. Campbell.*

BOOKCASE   4 b.g. Siberian Express (USA) 125 – Colourful (FR) 108 (Gay   **76** Mecene (USA) 128) [1990 8m⁴ 9m* 10.2m² 12g 12g⁵ 13.3m⁴ 14g 12.5g³ 13.3g 1991 12g* 12v 12g³ 11.7m³ 14f 12f⁴ 11.4m² 12g*] big, good-topped gelding: usually looks very well: modest handicapper: won at Kempton in June and Goodwood (sweating) in October: probably stays 13f: acts on firm ground: didn't find much in blinkers once: sometimes edgy: has hung left and shown signs of unsatisfactory temperament: suited by extreme waiting tactics: winning hurdler. *D. R. C. Elsworth.*

BOOMERANG (FR) 3 br.c. Sadler's Wells (USA) 132 – Millerette (Mill Reef **89** (USA) 141) [1990 NR 1991 10m³ 12m²] small, leggy, sparely-made colt: first foal: dam, second over 7f and 1¼m in Ireland on only 2 starts, is half-sister to very smart Irish 1¼m to 1¾m winner Dark Lomond: fair form in maidens at Newmarket (better effort) and Doncaster in the spring: sold 3,400 gns Newmarket Autumn Sales. *H. R. A. Cecil.*

BOON HILL 2 b.g. (May 6) Green Ruby (USA) 104 – Nyota 97 (Reform 132) **48** [1991 5m⁴ 6m⁶ 7g⁵ 7.5f 7.5f a6g⁴ 8m] 1,800Y: rangy gelding: moderate walker: half-brother to 1984 Irish 2-y-o 6f winner Formulator (by Double Form) and 1m winner Ny Over (by Smackover): dam won over 7f and 1½m: poor maiden: best effort at 7f: probably not suited by firm ground. *M. W. Ellerby.*

BOOZY 4 b.f. Absalom 128 – The High Dancer (High Line 125) [1990 5f² 5f³ 5f² 5d — 5m² 5f 5g* 5g⁵ 1991 5g 5m] deep-girthed, workmanlike filly: has a fluent action: very useful performer at 3 yrs: taken down very early, well below best in Group 3 event at Newmarket and King's Stand Stakes at Royal Ascot (last of 10) in 1991: suited by 5f: acts on firm going: makes the running: has run well sweating: game. *J. Berry.*

BORBOLETA (USA) 3 b.f. General Holme (USA) 128 – Naskrahoney (USA) **49** (Naskra (USA)) [1990 NR 1991 6m⁴ 8f³ 7m² 7.6g] $20,000Y: eighth foal: half-sister to 2 winners in North America: dam, 1m stakes winner, is half-sister to very useful American colt Honey Mark: plating-class maiden: well behind in handicap final start: should stay 1m (pulled hard second start): early to post last 2 outings: sold to join R. Frost 2,800 gns Newmarket Autumn Sales. *W. J. Haggas.*

BORDER MATE (IRE) 3 b.f. Be My Guest (USA) 126 – Scots Lass 79 (Shirley **90** Heights 130) [1990 7m³ 7g³ 1991 8d³ 10.3g* 10g²] leggy filly: progressive form: evens, easily won 3-runner maiden at Chester: set modest pace and headed close home in handicap at Newbury later in July: will stay 1½m: acts on dead going. *L. M. Cumani.*

BOREHILL BEAUTY 2 b.f. (Apr 26) Skyliner 117 – Sally Conkers (Roi Lear — (FR) 126) [1991 5g] 1,000Y: eighth foal: half-sister to 1982 2-y-o 6f winner Judy Conkers (by Swing Easy), 6f winner El Arab (by Sayf El Arab) and a winner over hurdles: dam well beaten: 20/1, tailed off in seller at Warwick in April. *W. G. M. Turner.*

BORN TO BE 2 b.f. (Mar 24) Never So Bold 135 – Beryl's Jewel 86 (Siliconn 121) **75 p** [1991 5m*] close-coupled filly: sixth foal: half-sister to several winners, including 5f winner Tylers Wood (by Homing) and 6f winner Murmuring (by Kind of Hush): dam best at 5f: 20/1 and green, won 15-runner maiden at Lingfield in September, slowly away and behind then leading 1f out: moved poorly to post: will improve and should win more races. *S. Dow.*

BORN TO FLY (IRE) 3 b.f. Last Tycoon 131 – Chilblains 83 (Hotfoot 126) [1990 **51** 0d⁰ 5m⁰ 5g 0.5g 1991 7.6d⁶ 6m 6g⁷ 6m 6m⁵ 7g 6.1m⁴ 6f⁵ 6g] close-coupled filly: plating-class maiden: suited by 6f: acts on firm ground: blinkered last 7 outings: sometimes sweating and edgy: hung right final start. *B. A. McMahon.*

BORRAM (IRE) 2 b.g. (May 20) Persian Bold 123 – Silken Topper (High Hat **45** 131) [1991 5m⁵ 6m 6d] IR 13,500Y: useful-looking gelding: brother to modest 1¼m winner Satin And Silk and half-brother to several winners, including fair middle-distance performer Grand Unit (by Home Guard): dam won over 1½m in Ireland: poor maiden: keen sort: sweating second start, on toes final one (June). *D. Nicholson.*

BOSAMBO (USA) 3 b.c. Our Native (USA) – Grey Dawn Girl (USA) (Grey **74 §** Dawn II 132) [1990 8g 8m⁴ 1991 8g⁶ 10f² 8m 11.9f³ 9d] tall, strong colt: easy mover: fair form at best: should stay 1½m: acts on firm going: blinkered final outing: sold to join C. Popham 1,400 gns Ascot October Sales: has flashed tail and carried head high: ungenuine and one to avoid. *G. Harwood.*

BOSCHERE 2 b.f. (Mar 15) Daring March 116 – Sussarando (Music Boy 124) — [1991 5m 6m 5m] workmanlike filly: first foal: dam, maiden, barely stayed 7f: well beaten in maidens and a seller (August) at Windsor: sold 600 gns Ascot November Sales. *M. R. Channon.*

BOTTLES (USA) 4 b.g. North Pole (CAN) 96 – Fooling Around (Jaazeiro (USA) **90 d** 127) [1990 8m³ 8.5m³ 8f* 10g² 8m⁵ 10g⁴ 8f⁴ 9m⁴ 8m³ 10m² 9m 12.2d² 10d* 1991 10g⁶ 11.5g² 12g 10g⁵ 10.5f⁶ 10.1f⁵ 12d] useful-looking gelding: fluent mover: fairly useful handicapper at best: below form after second start at 4 yrs: stays 1½m: has won on firm going but best efforts on easy surface (acts on dead ground): wore crossed noseband last 2 starts: has found little: winning hurdler. *J. E. Banks.*

BOULABAS (IRE) 2 ch.f. (Apr 22) Nashamaa 113 – Betty Bun (St Chad 120) **66** [1991 5m⁴ 5g* 5f² 5f² 5d 5d⁶] small, sturdy filly: half-sister to Irish 7f winner Coheal Lady (by Sweet Revenge) and modest 6f and 7f winner Nifty Griff (by Ardoon): dam unraced half-sister to smart sprinter Storm Warning: quite modest form: won 4-runner maiden at Ayr in June: off course 2 months after fourth start: improved effort when sixth of 20 in nursery at Wolverhampton (flashed tail under pressure) final start: will probably stay 6f: has form on firm and dead ground. *M. O'Neill.*

BOULEVARD GIRL 6 b.m. Nicholas Bill 125 – Gay Stampede (Lord Gayle **69** (USA) 124) [1990 14s⁵ 16.2d⁴ 15.3g⁶ a18g² 16g* 17.4d² 16g 18d 16.5d a16g⁵ a16g* 1991 a13g³ a16g* a14g⁴ 18s⁴] leggy mare: poor mover: quite modest handicapper: won at Lingfield in February: not seen out after March: suited by test of stamina: acts on any going: has won for apprentice. *C. B. B. Booth.*

BOUNDER ROWE 4 b.g. Henbit (USA) 130 – Arita (FR) (Kronzeuge) [1990 7g **—** 8f 8h² 8h 6f⁶ 16m³ 1991 10m 8g 14s⁶ 8g] rather leggy, quite attractive gelding: moderate mover: moderate plater at best: stays 1m: acts on hard ground. *J. Ffitch-Heyes.*

BOURBON ROSE 5 b.m. Ile de Bourbon (USA) 133 – Tantot 65 (Charlottown **—** 127) [1990 11.7m 10m⁶ 1991 10.8g] rangy, workmanlike mare: no worthwhile form. *P. Leach.*

BOURNVILLE 5 b.m. Lochnager 132 – Channing Girl 73 (Song 132) [1990 7m **76** 7g³ 7.6m* 8f 9m 7.6m 7g 8g 1991 9g⁶ 7.5f* 8d 7.6m² 8.9m⁵ 7.6m⁵ 7.3m 7d 8m³ 8g⁶] big, good-bodied mare: modest handicapper: won at Beverley in May: effective at around 7f, and shapes as if stays 9f: acts on firm going: has hung right: below best when visored once. *D. W. P. Arbuthnot.*

BOVVER BOY 3 b.c. Doc Marten 104 – Oh Well 61 (Sahib 114) [1990 6g a7g 7f **—** 1991 11f] smallish, sturdy colt: poor plater: pulled too hard over 11f: has had tongue tied down. *J. Mackie.*

BOWDEN BOY (IRE) 3 b.c. Never So Bold 135 – Glebehill 76 (Northfields **76** (USA)) [1990 6f 6m² 6d³ 1991 6d* 7m⁵ 8g⁵ 8g 8g 7g⁶ 8m] lengthy, rather angular colt: poor mover: modest handicapper: ridden by 7-lb claimer, won maiden at Nottingham in April: not seen out after July: stays 1m: acts on good to firm ground and dead: pulled hard fourth start: sometimes slowly away. *N. A. Callaghan.*

BOXING DAY (FR) 4 b.c. Deep Roots 124 – Flying Machine (Lightning 129) **115** [1990 8d² 8d⁶ 9g² 8d* 10d 9d⁴ 9g⁴ 8s⁶ 1991 8d² 8d³ 8d² 8g² 8m] very useful performer: contested pattern events in 1991, second to Goofalik in Prix du Chemin de Fer du Nord at Chantilly and Acteur Francais in Prix Messidor at Maisons-Laffitte final 2 placed occasions: stays 9f: acts on good to firm ground and dead: consistent. *E. Lellouche, France.*

BOX OFFICE 4 ch.g. Taufan (USA) 119 – Vera Van Fleet (Cracksman 111) [1990 **—** 10.6f 10m 12m 8m⁴ 8.3m 10m⁵ 8.2s 10g⁶ 1991 a12g⁵] tall gelding: moderate walker: fair plater: stiff task only start in 1991 (February): should prove better at 1¼m+ than shorter: acts on good to firm going: sold 4,800 gns Newmarket Autumn Sales. *J. H. Baker.*

BOY NEXT DOOR 3 b.c. Local Suitor (USA) 128 – Krishnagar (Kris 135) [1990 **—** NR 1991 10d 15.3m 7g] smallish, lengthy colt: shows high knee action: second foal: half-brother to winning sprint plater Blazing Sunset (by Blazing Saddles): dam never ran: looks of no account. *C. E. Brittain.*

BOYNTON 8 b.g. Riboboy (USA) 124 – Lingdale Lady 66 (Sandford Lad 133) **—** [1990 NR 1991 9f] sturdy, lengthy gelding: poor maiden: stayed 1½m: probably acted on any going: dead. *J. H. Johnson.*

BRACKEN BREEZE 6 ch.g. Kabour 80 – Lady Mede 74 (Runnymede 123) **—** [1990 NR 1991 a8g] leggy gelding: third foal: dam best at 5f: always behind in Southwell maiden in August, only start: in frame in NH Flat races. *M. W. Ellerby.*

BRADAWN BREEVER (IRE) 2 b.c. (Feb 25) Salmon Leap (USA) 131– **109** Ozone (Auction Ring (USA) 123) [1991 5v⁴ 5d² 6g*dis 6g* 6g² 6m³ 5m⁴ 6m* 5d³ 5d 6g]

Quite how the Heinz '57' Phoenix Stakes has maintained its spurious Group 1 status is one of racing's great mysteries. The Phoenix Stakes, a six-furlong event for two-year-olds run in the first half of August, a time when a sizeable proportion of the two-year-old population has still to be galloped seriously, has been won by a feeble succession of second- or third-rate animals continuing even since its elevation from Group 2 in 1979, among whom even the better ones, such as Minstrella, Superpower and Mac's Imp in recent years, have drifted into obscurity in their second seasons. Its latest winner, Bradawn Breever, a very useful young sprinter but hardly the best of his age, is very much a typical winner, and unless he makes significant improvement as a three-year-old (which seems unlikely, given that he's already had plenty of racing) he'll struggle in good sprint company. Bradawn Breever started at 14/1 for the Phoenix, which was switched to Leopardstown after the closure of Phoenix Park late in 1990. He was the most experienced member of the nine-runner field, having already run seven times, passing the post first in maidens at Leopardstown (his third start, after which he was disqualified for causing interference by swerving left two furlongs out) and the Curragh in May and then running good races in defeat behind Safety Tactic in a minor event at Naas and Fair Cop in the Chesham Stakes at Royal Ascot before finishing a fair fifth in the Group 3 Shernazar 2-Y-O EBF Curragh Stakes. Bradawn Breever wasn't the only runner at Leopardstown previously beaten in pattern company—Maledetto, Safety Tactic, and Storm Melody, one of the two British challengers, were others—but he at least left his previous form well behind with a much improved performance from a favourable far-rail draw. Wearing blinkers, as he did in all his races after getting disqualified, except his last, Bradawn Breever set a furious pace, entered the last two furlongs still three lengths up, then held on gamely by a head and the same from Maledetto and the Windsor Castle runner-up Festive Cheer. Given the tremendous early speed Bradawn Breever showed it wasn't a surprise to see him make further improvement back at five furlongs in the Meadow Meats EBF Flying Five at the same venue the following month. Once again Bradawn Breever made excellent use of his draw next to the far rail and scorching early pace, but he was pegged back inside the final furlong and went down by a length and a half and a head to the improving three-year-old Flowing and his contemporary Lute And Lyre. Bradawn Breever finished among the back-markers in his last two races. He was sent rather optimistically to Longchamp in October for the Ciga Prix de l'Abbaye in which he faded, after showing up well for three quarters of the contest, into a respectable ninth-of-fourteen position behind Keen Hunter; but in the Racecall Gold Trophy at Redcar later

Heinz 57 Phoenix Stakes, Leopardstown — Bradawn Breever just holds on from Maledetto, Festive Cheer and the almost-hidden Safety Tactic

Mr M. A. Murray's "Bradawn Breever"

in the month he raced with uncharacteristic lack of sparkle and was beaten before halfway.

Bradawn Breever (IRE) (b.c. Feb 25, 1989)	Salmon Leap (USA) (ch 1980)	Northern Dancer (b 1961)	Nearctic
			Natalma
		Fish-Bar (b 1967)	Baldric II
			Fisherman's Wharf
	Ozone (b or br 1977)	Auction Ring (b 1972)	Bold Bidder
			Hooplah
		Musical Watch (br 1964)	Tudor Melody
			Tikva

Buyers in search of a likely sprinting prospect at the autumn yearling sales wouldn't usually show much interest in the progeny of the Pacemaker International winner and Arc fifth Salmon Leap: he's an influence for stamina (the average winning distance of his progeny aged three or over to the end of 1990 was in excess of a mile and a quarter) and his four crops of racing age have so far produced just one older winner over five or six furlongs. It seems more likely that Bradawn Breever has inherited his speed from his dam Ozone. She wasn't a sprinter herself—three of her four wins in Ireland came at seven furlongs and the other came at nine—but she has produced the non-stayers Cronk's Quality and Great Ocean (who was successful over seven furlongs in Ireland as a two-year-old) to Main Reef and Simply Great

119

respectively and she is a granddaughter of the 1949 Cherry Hinton winner Tikva. This isn't a particularly distinguished family—Bradawn Breever cost only 10,000 guineas at the Irish National Yearling Sale—but it's thrown up plenty of minor winners under both codes in recent years, and some good ones, too, notably the Diadem winner Chummy's Favourite and the outstanding novice chaser Killiney. *K. Prendergast, Ireland.*

BRADBURY HALL 8 b.g. Comedy Star (USA) 121 – Grayshott Hall 70 (Compensation 127) [1990 NR 1991 8.2d] lightly-raced handicapper: tailed off only run at 8 yrs: stays 1½m: acts on any going: ran badly when visored once. *R. F. Marvin.* —

BRAEFORDIE 2 b.f. (Apr 27) Celestial Storm (USA) 132 – Ever So Cool (FR) (Never Say Die 137) [1991 8.9d 7.1d] workmanlike filly: half-sister to several winners here and abroad, including 10.2f winner Allez-Oops (by Moulin) and ex-French 15f winner Laxdaela (by Sagaro): dam French 11f winner: well beaten in large-field maidens at Wolverhampton (pulled hard) and Chepstow in October. *C. A. Austin.* 37

BRAMBLES WAY 2 ch.c. (Mar 4) Clantime 101 – Streets Ahead 67 (Ovid 95) [1991 5m⁴ 5f⁶ 6g 6f⁵ 5m] 5,600Y: compact colt: has a quick action: half-brother to 3 winners by Billion, including quite modest pair Bills Ahead (7f winner) and Running Money (11f to 17.1f winner): dam 6f to 1½m winner: poor form in varied events, including a York seller: better form at 6f than 5f: hung badly left second start. *Mrs G. R. Reveley.* 45

BRANDON PRINCE (IRE) 3 b.c. Shernazar 131 – Chanson de Paris (USA) (The Minstrel (CAN) 135) [1990 6g⁶ 7m 8g 1991 8g 11.7s⁶ 13.1f⁴ 11m* 16.2g² 16g* 16.5g* 14f⁵ 16.1m⁶ 16.2g* 18m] close-coupled colt: fairly useful handicapper: successful at Beverley in June, Newbury and Doncaster in July and in strongly-run £11,400 event (best effort) at Ascot in September: fourth favourite, always behind in Cesarewitch at Newmarket final start: better at 2m than shorter: best efforts on good ground: usually blinkered. *I. A. Balding.* 90

BRANSTON ABBY (IRE) 2 ch.f. (Apr 28) Risk Me (FR) 127 – Tuxford Hideaway 102 (Cawston's Clown 113) [1991 5g³ 5m* 5g² 6m⁶ 5f³ 8m 6.1m⁶] 6,000Y: tall, lengthy, light-bodied filly: second foal: half-sister to fairly useful 1990 2-y-o 6f and 7f winner Big Blow (by Last Tycoon): dam sprinter: modest performer: won maiden at Thirsk in April: much better efforts after when placed in auction event at Newmarket in May and minor event at Ripon in August: faced stiff tasks in nurseries last 2 starts: subsequently withdrawn at Pontefract (broke out of stalls) and Catterick (veterinary advice): stays 6f: active type, usually on toes: sweating fourth start. *M. W. Easterby.* 78

BRANTFELL 3 b.c.c. Say Primula 107 – Jendor 82 (Condorcet (FR)) [1990 5f 5f⁵ 5m⁵ 6v⁶ 1991 6.9f³ 13.6m² 13.8m⁵ 11m 12.1m⁶ 11d⁶ a12g⁶] compact colt: good walker: plater: ran moderately last 4 starts: should prove at least as effective at 1½m as 13.6f: acts on firm going (stiff task and hung left on heavy): has taken strong hold. *T. Fairhurst.* 52

BRASS MONKEY (USA) 3 ch.c. It's Freezing (USA) 122 – Josalee (USA) (Jolie Jo (USA)) [1990 7m 1991 8f* 8g⁵ 10.1g⁵ 10.1g³] rangy, angular colt: 9/4 on, won maiden at Carlisle in May: ran creditably in handicaps later in summer: should stay further: acts on firm going: blinkered and wore tongue strap (made most) final start. *W. J. Haggas.* 74

BRAVEBOY 3 b.c. Never So Bold 135 – Relkina (FR) 85 (Relkino 131) [1990 NR 1991 8g²] quite attractive colt: fourth foal: half-brother to maiden middle-distance stayer/winning hurdler Kino (by Niniski) and 2 poor maidens: dam 1m winner out of Queen Mary winner Grizel: 16/1, 1½ lengths second of 16 to Danube in maiden at Warwick in April, keeping on well. *C. E. Brittain.* 74

BRAVEFOOT 3 b.c. Dancing Brave (USA) 140 – Swiftfoot 119 (Run The Gantlet (USA)) [1990 7m* 7m* 7g⁵ 1991 10.5g 8g 8m] sturdy colt: good walker and mover: won maiden at Newmarket and listed race (running lazily in front) at Newbury in July at 2 yrs, before doped and running listless race in Laurent-Perrier Champagne Stakes at Doncaster: tailed off in varied company (blinkered in minor event final start) as 3-y-o: bred to stay middle distances: sold only 19,000 gns Newmarket Autumn Sales. *Major W. R. Hern.* —

BRAVE MELODY 5 b.h. Heroic Air 96 – Kaymay 76 (Maystreak 118) [1990 5m 5g 5d² 5m 5m³ a5g 5f⁶ 5m⁴ 5d* 1991 5g² 5f 5g³ 5.1m 5g³ 5g⁶ 5s⁴ 5g] compact horse: 47 d moderate mover: poor handicapper: best at 5f: acts on dead going, possibly unsuited by extremes of going nowadays: blinkered once. *Capt. J. Wilson.*

BRAVE MISSION 3 b.c. Dancing Brave (USA) 140 – Intermission 117 (Stage **77** Door Johnny) [1990 NR 1991 8m 10.4m⁴ 12.2m*] strong, angular colt: half-brother to several winners here and in France, notably good sprinter/miler Interval (by Habitat), and to dam of Invited Guest: dam, half-sister to Quiet Fling, Armistice Day and Peacetime, won Cambridgeshire: modest form in autumn maidens, winning at Catterick: stays 1½m: runs in snatches, and blinkered last 2 starts: sold 11,000 gns Newmarket Autumn Sales. *G. Harwood.*

BRAVE THE WIND 2 b.f. (Apr 16) Dancing Brave (USA) 140 – English Spring **67** (USA) 116 (Grey Dawn II 132) [1991 7.1m 7f⁵ 7g* 8.1d⁴] rather leggy, quite attractive filly: good walker: has a fluent action: half-sister to 3-y-o 1¼m winner Fragrant Hill (by Shirley Heights), also 7f winner at 2 yrs, and 1½m winner Spring To Glory (by Teenoso): dam stayed 1¼m: quite modest performer: won maiden at Redcar in September: creditable fourth of 7 in minor event at Haydock following month: will be suited by 1¼m +: acts on firm and dead ground. *I. A. Balding.*

BRAVURA 2 b.c. (Mar 4) Never So Bold 135 – Avahra 108 (Sahib 114) [1991 7g **72 p** 7m³] lengthy colt: has scope: half-brother to several winners here and abroad, including sprinters Cumbrian Melody (by Petong) and Mavahra and Pavahra (both by Mummy's Pet): dam stayed 6f: 50/1, vastly improved effort when 6 lengths third of 17 to Pursuit of Love in maiden at Newmarket, soon prominent then staying on steadily: will progress again and should win a similar event at 3 yrs. *W. J. Haggas.*

BREAK BREAD (USA) 2 b.c. (Mar 23) Bering 136 – Troyanna 109 (Troy 137) **108** [1991 8g* 8m³ 9d³] fourth foal: half-brother to quite useful 1989 2-y-o 7f winner Aquatic and 1¼m and 1¾m winner Trojan River (both by Riverman): dam 7f winner at 2 yrs and fourth in Irish Oaks is out of half-sister to very smart 1963 USA 2-y-o Traffic: successful in newcomers race at Deauville in August: better form when third at Longchamp in Prix La Rochette (beaten over 2 lengths by demoted Rainbow Corner) in September and Prix de Conde (3 lengths behind Cristofori) following month: will be suited by middle distances: acts on good to firm and dead ground. *D. Smaga, France.*

BREAKERS AHEAD (USA) 3 ch.g. Believe It (USA) – Emerald Reef 104 — (Mill Reef (USA) 141) [1990 8g 1991 8g⁴ 10g 8d 8m 8.9m 7.6m] workmanlike, rather angular gelding: disappointing maiden: stays 1m: wore net muzzle second outing: pulled up lame on fourth: sold to join R. Frost 5,000 gns Ascot October Sales. *I. A. Balding.*

BREAKFAST RIDE 3 ch.f. Formidable (USA) 125 – Beautiful Dawn (USA) — (Grey Dawn II 132) [1990 6m⁵ 6.5g 6d⁴ 6d 1991 a7g⁵ 8f 8m 6.1m] sturdy, good-bodied filly: fair form at best as 2-y-o, little as 3-y-o: bred to stay beyond 6f: blinkered twice at 2 yrs: bandaged behind on all-weather: sometimes pulls hard: bandaged, refused to go to post fifth intended start: sold 1,000 gns Newmarket December Sales. *D. R. Laing.*

BREAK LOOSE 5 ch.m. Krayyan 117 – Free Course 80 (Sandford Lad 133) — [1990 7m 6m* 6g² 6d³ 6g³ 7g 5m⁴ 6f* 6m 5f 6g 6d 1991 a5g⁶ a6g 6g 6f 6g 6f] lengthy mare: moderate mover: poor handicapper: no show at 5 yrs: best at sprint distances: acts on firm going, possibly unsuited by soft: usually blinkered or visored: sold 880 gns Doncaster August Sales. *D. W. Chapman.*

BRECKENBROUGH LAD 4 b.c. Uncle Pokey 116 – Fabulous Beauty 91 **64** (Royal Avenue 123) [1990 8g³ 8m⁵ 10.2g 12d 10.6v⁴ 10v* 10.4d 12s³ 1991 10.2s³ 10s³ 10s 10m⁵ 10.1m⁶ 12.1s 10.3d³ a12g⁶] leggy colt: moderate mover: quite modest handicapper: off course over 5 months after fifth start: suited by around 1¼m and plenty of give in the ground: has hung right and found little: has run well for inexperienced rider. *T. D. Barron.*

BRECON BEACONS (IRE) 2 b.f. (Feb 3) Shirley Heights 130 – Welsh **71** Daylight (Welsh Pageant 132) [1991 6m² 7g² 7f] leggy filly: half-sister to 3 winners abroad, including very useful French middle-distance performer Ordinance (by Henbit): dam won twice over 1¼m in Ireland: quite modest maiden: runner-up at Newmarket and Goodwood in July: ran badly at Salisbury 5 weeks later, finding little: should stay 1¼m. *R. Charlton.*

BREEZE AWAY 2 b.f. (Apr 1) Prince Sabo 123 – Ballad Island 83 (Ballad Rock **60** 122) [1991 6m⁶ 5g³ 5m³] 6,000Y: strong, lengthy filly: fourth foal: half-sister to winning sprinter Hong Kong Girl (by Petong): dam 7f and 1m performer: plating-class maiden: stays 6f. *R. M. Whitaker.*

BREEZED WELL 5 b.g. Wolverlife 115 – Precious Baby (African Sky 124) [1990 **80**
a 10g⁵ 8f 8g³ 7m 7.6d⁶ 8g³ 8m³ 7m³ 9m a7g⁶ a8g⁴ a10g³ 1991 a8g⁴ a8g⁵ a10g 8d 10g
9m 8f⁴ 8d³ 8d² 8g 8m³ 8m] smallish, sparely-made gelding: usually looks well: poor
mover: fair handicapper: stays 1¼m: acts on firm and dead going: tried blinkered
once: has won for 7-lb claimer: sold 4,400 gns Newmarket Autumn Sales. *C. N.
Allen.*

BREEZY DAY 5 ch.m. Day Is Done 115 – Bedouin Dancer 79 (Lorenzaccio 130) **82**
[1990 5d³ 5m 5s⁴ 5m 1991 5g 5d* 5m 6g² 6d³ 5.1d* 6.1g⁴ 5.2g² 5m⁵ 6f 5.6m 6m 5g
6.1d* 5d a6g a6g] compact mare: has round action: fair handicapper: won at Chester
in May, July and October (ridden by 7-lb claimer): below form after, pulled up
penultimate start, setting too strong pace final one: stays 6f: ideally suited by an
easy surface nowadays. *B. A. McMahon.*

BREGUET 8 b.m. Rouser 118 – Span (Pan II 130) [1990 14g 12g 12m² 12.3g⁶ 12g⁶ —
13m³ 12f 12m 17m⁵ 1991 12g 16.2g] small mare: poor mover: poor maiden: pulled up
halfway final start (June): probably didn't stay 2m: seemed to act on any going: dead.
Don Enrico Incisa.

BRENDA FROM HUBY 3 ch.f. Tina's Pet 121 – Dominion Blue 66 (Dominion **42**
123) [1990 5d⁶ 1991 7m 7m³ 8g 6m] good-topped filly: poor maiden: best effort at
7f on good to firm ground: wore tongue strap (soundly beaten) final start. *B. C.
Morgan.*

BRENDA HUNT (IRE) 2 gr.f. (Apr 7) Huntingdale 132 – Brenda (Sovereign —
Path 125) [1991 5d 5g 6g 7m] 2,000F, 3,000Y: leggy filly: half-sister to very useful 1m
to 11.7f winner Brady (by Pitcairn) and a winner in Belgium: dam unplaced 5 times in
Ireland: seems of little account. *J. S. Moore.*

BRERA (IRE) 3 b.f. Tate Gallery (USA) 117 – Anoint (Connaught 130) [1990 6g⁴ —
6g 7m⁶ 6m a7g 1991 a8g a5g⁴ a6g⁴ 6g⁵ 6m 7.6m] small, light-framed filly: shows
knee action: poor maiden: should stay 7f: twice hung badly left: wore eyeshield (3
times) then blinkers on all-weather: bandaged behind final start. *Mrs L. Piggott.*

BREYANI 4 b.f. Commanche Run 133 – Molokai 82 (Prince Tenderfoot (USA) **101**
126) [1990 14g⁴ 14g² 12d² 10g² 1991 11g* 14g³ 14g³ 12d³ 12d* 14d⁴ 16d* 12d* 11.9g⁴
16s] lengthy, rather angular filly: poor mover: third foal: dam 2-y-o 7f winner: useful
Irish filly: successful in minor event at Killarney in May, lady riders event there in
July and handicaps at Galway in July and Tipperary in August: ridden with little
enterprise when respectable fourth to Nibbs Point in Galtres Stakes at York
penultimate start: effective at 1½m to 2m: best efforts on dead ground. *T. Stack,
Ireland.*

BRICKHILLS 2 ch.g. (Mar 14) Say Primula 107 – Mandrake Madam 88 —
(Mandrake Major 122) [1991 6d a6g a6g 7m] 500F, 2,100Y, 2,000 2-y-o: small,
good-bodied gelding: first foal: dam barely stayed 6f: seems of little account. *D. W.
Chapman.*

BRIDAL DANCE (IRE) 3 ch.f. Coquelin (USA) 121 – Crosmieres (FR) —
(Lyphard (USA) 132) [1990 6m 7m⁶ 6g 7g 1991 8m 8f] neat, strong filly: poor maiden.
R. Hannon.

BRIDAL TRAIN (IRE) 3 b.f. Gorytus (USA) 132 – Last Clear Chance (USA) **90**
(Alleged (USA) 138) [1990 NR 1991 7g* 8g² 8m³ 10.5g⁶ 8.9g⁴ 10m] leggy filly: third
foal: half-sister to a winner in Italy by General Assembly: dam ran once: won maiden
at Kempton in April: ran well after when in frame, 6½ lengths fourth to Shaima in
listed race at York: broke pastern in valuable handicap at Newbury: stayed 9f: dead.
Lord Huntingdon.

BRIDGE PLAYER 4 ch.f. The Noble Player (USA) 126 – Auction Bridge 76 **53**
(Auction Ring (USA) 123) [1990 12.5g 10d 10m 1991 a8g⁵ 9s⁵ 13d⁶ 9.9m⁵ 12.3d³ 13d².
12.1f³ 12.2g³ 13.6d⁵ 15.1s² a16g² a14g*] class-coupled ex-Irish mare: plating-class
handicapper: won at Southwell in December: stays 15f: acts well on a soft surface:
good mount for 7-lb claimer. *D. Moffatt.*

BRIDLE TALK (IRE) 2 b.f. (Feb 10) Runnett 125 – Gossip (Sharp Edge 123) **51**
[1991 5m³ 5g⁶ 5d³ a5g³ a5g² 5.3f 5m] 4,000Y: rather lightly-made filly: has a round
action: sister to 1984 2-y-o 5f winner Running Edge, later successful in USA, and
half-sister to a winner in Malaysia: dam no sign of ability: plating-class maiden:
creditable second in seller on equitrack in July: ran moderately at Brighton
penultimate outing: has run creditably for 7-lb claimer. *M. McCormack.*

BRIEF TRUCE (USA) 2 b.c. (May 8) Irish River (FR) 131 – Falafel (CAN) **89** p
(Northern Dancer) [1991 6d*] tenth foal: half-brother to several winners, including
very useful Again Tomorrow (by Honest Pleasure), winner of Italian 2000 Guineas
and later successful in USA: dam sister to dam of Awaasif: 7/4 favourite, won

18-runner maiden at Fairyhouse in November by 2½ lengths from Polar Wind: will stay at least 1m: should improve. *D. K. Weld, Ireland.*

BRIER CREEK (USA) 2 b.c. (Mar 19) Blushing Groom (FR) 131 – Savannah   72 p
Dancer (USA) (Northern Dancer) [1991 7m⁵] leggy, unfurnished colt: third foal: half-brother to French 3-y-o 7.5f (at 2 yrs) to 9f winner Sha Tha (by Mr Prospector): dam won 6 races at up to 1¼m, including Grade 2 Del Mar Oaks, and is closely related to Geoffrey Freer winner Valinsky and half-sister to Oaks second Vals Girl, out of Oaks winner Valoris: weak 7/1-shot, running-on fifth of 16 in maiden at Leicester in October: will improve, particularly over further. *J. H. M. Gosden.*

BRIERY FILLE 6 b.m. Sayyaf 121 – Zeddera (FR) (Zeddaan 130) [1990 10.8m   56
10.1g 8.5g⁶ 10m² 10g 10m² 10f* 10g* 11.5g 1991 10.2s⁵ 10m⁵ a12g⁶ a12g] lengthy, angular mare: quite modest handicapper: stays 1½m: acts on firm going, probably unsuited by soft: good mount for 7-lb claimer: below form when blinkered and visored. *A. Hide.*

BRIGADIER BILL 6 ch.g. Nicholas Bill 125 – Sailing Brig (Brigadier Gerard   52
144) [1990 10m³ 11d² 9s⁴ a12g² a14g² 1991 a12g⁴ 12.4v⁶ 9m² 12.2g³ 11.1s⁵ 13d*
10.9g³ 12g⁵] big, angular gelding: moderate walker: plating-class performer: won (for first time) claimer at Ayr in July: effective at 9f, and stays 1¾m: acts on any going: sometimes finds little off bridle, and usually held up: winning hurdler: sold 950 gns Doncaster November Sales. *Mrs G. R. Reveley.*

BRIGADIERBROUGHTON 2 b.c. (Mar 3) Thatching 131 – Arctic Winter   87 p
(CAN) (Briartic (CAN)) [1991 6.1m² 7m] 40,000Y: smallish, strong, lengthy colt: third foal: brother to very useful sprinter Polar Bird: dam unraced sister to very smart Son of Briartic, successful in 1¼m Queen's Plate: second of 10 in maiden at Nottingham in September: still better for race, again stayed on not knocked about when very good fifteenth of 30 to Young Senor in Tattersalls Tiffany Highflyer Stakes at Newmarket following month: will improve again and win a maiden. *W. J. Musson.*

BRIGGS LAD (IRE) 2 ch.g. (Apr 17) Be My Native (USA) 122 – Zestino (Shack   65 p
(USA) 118) [1991 7m⁴ 8.3g⁵ 8m³] 8,000F, 4,300Y: second foal: half-brother to 3-y-o Wane's Secret (by Horage): dam unraced half-sister to Ginevra: quite modest form in maidens: has twice caught eye, notably when 2 lengths third of 11 to Redisham at Redcar in October, losing about 7 lengths when pace quickened at halfway, then running on strongly final 1f not knocked about: ran moderately second start: will stay 1¼m: will do better. *W. Jarvis.*

BRIGGSMAID 3 b.f. Elegant Air 119 – Merry Yarn 64 (Aggressor 130) [1990 7m   70
1991 10m² 12m³ 12f* 16.2g 13.1m³ 16m 14.1f³ 14m⁶ 12f⁵ 12g] lengthy, workmanlike filly: shows high knee action: modest performer: made all in maiden auction at Beverley in May: below form in handicaps last 3 starts: needs further than 1½m nowadays and may yet stay 2m: acts on firm ground. *J. M. P. Eustace.*

BRIGHTER LIGHT (USA) 2 b.f. (May 11) Bering 136 – Linklighter 89   —
(Busted 134) [1991 6.9f] leggy, angular filly: fifth foal: dam, 1¼m winner also successful at 6f at 2 yrs, is out of half-sister to Great Voltigeur winner Patch: 50/1 and better for race, beaten around 20 lengths in October maiden at Folkestone, prominent entering straight, running wide, eased once beaten: likely to need middle distances: sold 2,500 gns Newmarket Autumn Sales. *R. V. Smyth.*

BRIGHT FANTASTIC (IRE) 2 b.c. (Mar 14) Shareef Dancer (USA) 135 –   43
Bright Landing 78 (Sun Prince 128) [1991 5g 6g 6m 10.5d 8m a8g] 20,000Y: smallish, strong colt: half-brother to 3-y-o Elevated Landing and 2 winners, notably useful 9f (at 2 yrs) to 2m winner Upper Strata (also by Shirley Heights): dam, placed over 5f at 2 yrs, is granddaughter of very smart sprinter Lucasland: poor form in varied events, including a selling nursery: thrice blinkered: wore tongue strap final outing: sold 2,200 gns Doncaster November Sales. *R. F. Johnson Houghton.*

BRIGHT GLOW 3 b.c. Kalaglow 132 – Brighella (FR) (Baldric II 131) [1990 10g* 113
1991 12g² 10.5d⁴ 10.5d³ 12m⁵ 10g² 10g⁴ 8g² 10d⁵ 10d*] 520,000 francs (£48,100) Y: half-brother to several winners in France, including prolific middle-distance winner Dago (by Roi Dagobert) and 1m to 1¼m winner Bright Mecene (by Gay Mecene): dam French 2-y-o 1m winner: won minor event at Fontainebleau in October at 2 yrs and listed race at Deauville in October at 3 yrs: 7¼ lengths fifth of 7 to Suave Dancer in Prix du Jockey-Club at Chantilly: stays 1½m: very useful. *M. Zilber, France.*

BRIGHT RED 4 ch.c. Kris 135 – Chiltern Red (Red God 128§) [1990 7g³ 7m 1991   —
6g 6g 5m 5.3g 6g] short-backed colt: of little account nowadays: sold 675 gns Ascot November Sales. *H. Candy.*

BRIGHT SAPPHIRE 5 b.g. Mummy's Pet 125 – Bright Era 79 (Artaius (USA) —
129) [1990 a12g² a11g⁵ 1991 a16g⁶] small, lightly-made gelding: poor maiden
nowadays: not seen out after January: stays 1½m. *J. D. Thomas.*

BRIGHT SEA (USA) 3 b.g. Secreto (USA) 128 – Muriels Dream (USA) (Blue —
Prince II 123) [1990 NR 1991 6d 8g⁵ 11.5g 7g⁵ 7m⁴ 11.6m 7f 10g 5.1s 8.1d] $225,000Y:
small, sturdy gelding: has been tubed: half-brother to several winners here and
abroad, including smart 1980 Italian 2-y-o Panjandrum (by His Majesty): dam 5f and
6f winner, is half-sister to smart 6f and 9f winner Double Edge Sword: no worthwhile form, including in a claimer: blinkered ninth start: sold out of C. Brittain's
stable 5,200 gns Ascot 2nd July Sales after fourth. *W. R. Williams.*

BRIGINSKI 2 b.f. (Mar 19) Myjinski (USA) – Raunchy Rita (Brigadier Gerard 33
144) [1991 6g 6m⁴ a8g a7g] leggy filly: moderate mover: first foal: dam ran 3 times at
3 yrs: little worthwhile form in maidens and a seller: off course nearly 7 months
before third start. *J. W. Payne.*

BRIGTINA 3 b.g. Tina's Pet 121 – Bristle-Moss (Brigadier Gerard 144) [1990 55
7.5d 7d⁵ 8m⁵ 7.5m⁵ 8f 1991 14f⁵ 10d³ 10d] angular gelding: moderate mover:
plating-class maiden: third in handicap at Ripon, best effort in summer as 3-y-o:
stays 1¼m: acts on good to firm ground and dead: well below form when blinkered at
2 yrs: sold to join M. Bradley 2,400 gns Ascot November Sales. *B. W. Murray.*

BRILLIANT 3 ch.f. Never So Bold 135 – Diamond Hill 82 (High Top 131) [1990 62 d
NR 1991 7m 7g 7g² 7g⁶ 7g³ 8.9g 7m 9m 10.3g] rangy filly: fourth foal: half-sister to
fair 1988 2-y-o 5f winner Crag Hall (both by Sharpo): dam won over 7f and stayed
1½m: quite modest maiden: below form last 4 starts, in seller on final one: should
stay beyond 7f: visored fourth outing: sold out of J. W. Watts's stable 7,400 gns
Ascot 2nd July Sales after fifth. *J. Pearce.*

BRILLIANT DISGUISE 2 ch.f. (Jan 25) Ballacashtal (CAN) – Davemma 81 55
(Tachypous 128) [1991 5s³ 6m⁶ 6g 7f 8m 8.3g* 10.5d 7.1m⁶] rather sparely-made
filly: second foal: half-sister to 3-y-o Melting Tears (by Noalto), 7f winner at 2 yrs:
dam disappointing maiden, stayed 1½m: plating-class form: won 18-runner selling
nursery (no bid) at Hamilton in September: suited by 1m: acts on good to firm
ground: has run creditably when sweating and edgy: well beaten (over 10.5f) for 7-lb
claimer: blinkered fifth outing, visored after: trained first 3 starts by J. S. Wilson.
Miss L. A. Perratt.

BRIMPTON BERTIE 2 ch.g. (Apr 19) Music Boy 124 – Lady of Bath (Longleat 37
(USA) 109) [1991 8m⁶ 6f 7g] 6,000Y: workmanlike gelding: has a quick action: first
foal: dam of little account on flat showed a little ability over hurdles: well beaten in
autumn maidens. *C. A. Horgan.*

BRIPHILL 3 br.g. Martinmas 128 – Miss Shegas 65 (Rabdan 129) [1990 NR 1991 37
6g⁶ 6m 8.2f 5g 6m] 1,700Y: sturdy gelding: first foal: dam speedy 2-y-o winner: poor
form: should prove suited by further than 5f: form only on an easy surface: blinkered
(stiff task) final outing. *J. White.*

BRISAS 4 ch.g. Vaigly Great 127 – Legal Sound 85 (Legal Eagle 126) [1990 5d5 6f 74 d
5d 6f⁴ 6m⁵ 5m 6f⁶ 5g 5d⁰ 5d 5m 5d 5m 5m 1991 a6g* a5g² 5f⁴ 5m⁶ 5g 5m a5g⁶ 5m 5f
5m 5m 5h* 5g 5m a5g] strong-quartered, attractive gelding: has a quick action:
modest handicapper early in 1991, making virtually all at Southwell: below form
after, including when promoted winner at Carlisle in September: effective at 5f to 6f:
acts on hard going, possibly unsuited by heavy: blinkered: has looked none too
keen: untrustworthy. *T. Fairhurst.*

BRITAIN IS GREAT (IRE) 2 ch.g. (Mar 11) Mansooj 118 – Etrusca (Green 54
God 128) [1991 5m 6g⁶ 6m³ 5m⁶] 6,000Y: workmanlike filly: half-sister to 3 winners
in USA: dam French 2-y-o 4.5f and 5f winner: plating-class maiden: best effort third
of 7 in seller at Folkestone in July: better suited by 6f than 5f: seemed headstrong
first 2 starts, taken down early then unruly stalls final one: ridden by 7-lb claimer:
sold 420 gns Ascot October Sales. *G. Lewis.*

BROAD APPEAL 3 ch.f. Star Appeal 133 – Cinderwench 95 (Crooner 119) [1990 —
5m³ 5f* 7g³ 7m³ 1991 a7g⁵ a5g] angular filly: moderate mover: won seller at 2 yrs:
below form in January, 1991: will stay 1m. *M. Bell.*

BROAD STORY (NZ) 4 b.c. Diesis 133 – Broadway Hit (Hittite Glory 125) 76
[1990 5.5s* 8g⁴ 6g⁶ 6g³ 5g 8d a6g 1991 a7g² a8g³ 6m⁴ 6m 6d⁴ 6g 6g⁴] lengthy,
short-legged colt: ex-French handicapper: modest here: stays 1m: acts on good to
firm and soft ground. *P. Calver.*

BROADWAY RUCKUS (CAN) 2 br.f. (Feb 26) Bold Ruckus (USA) – —
Broadway Beauty (USA) (Chompion (USA)) [1991 6m⁶] $86,130Y: rangy filly: has
scope: half-sister to several winners, including stakes-winning dam of Irish Oaks

winner Knight's Baroness: dam minor winner at 2 yrs: sire, smart performer who stayed 9f, best at 2 yrs: 25/1 from 8/1 and bit backward, about 15 lengths last of 6 in minor event at Windsor in July. *D. R. Laing.*

BROCKETTE 3 ch.f. Bustino 136 – Explosiva (USA) 88§ (Explodent (USA)) **109**
[1990 7m 8m* 7.3s² 8v* 1991 10g² 12g3 10v² 10v 8s] lengthy, rather angular filly: useful effort, making most and rallying well having hung right, when beaten ½ length by Gussy Marlowe in listed race at Newmarket on reappearance: not discredited in Oaks d'Italia at Milan next start and beaten ½ length in listed race at Rome fourth start: well below form in Ribblesdale Stakes (sweating, checked early on and ran in snatches) at Royal Ascot and Italian pattern events: best form at 1¼m: acts on heavy ground. *J. L. Dunlop.*

BROCTUNE GREY 7 gr.m. Warpath 113 – Hitesca 110 (Tesco Boy 121) [1990 **61** +
12.3g 14m⁵ 15d³ 16g 16f³ 18d⁵ 1991 16.1m 16m] angular, sparely-made mare: quite modest handicapper: suited by extreme test of stamina: yet to race on soft going, acts on any other except possibly hard: visored (slowly away) once: has wandered, and is usually held up: irresolute hurdler. *Mrs G. R. Reveley.*

BRODESSA 5 gr.g. Scallywag 127 – Jeanne du Barry 74 (Dubassoff (USA)) [1990 **63**
NR 1991 12.1d² 12.4m⁵ 9m⁴ 12m⁶ 12m³ 12.4m⁴] big, workmanlike gelding: moderate walker: third foal: dam won 1m seller and also over hurdles: quite modest maiden: ran creditably in handicaps final 3 starts: acts on good to firm and dead ground: should prove capable of better when granted a stiffer test of stamina. *Mrs G. R. Reveley.*

BRONZE BLADE 4 ch.g. Sunley Builds 102 – Flyweight 69 (Salvo 129) [1990 —
12h⁵ 1991 8.3m] leggy, shallow-girthed gelding: twice raced and no sign of ability: sold 1,550 gns Ascot November Sales. *M. Madgwick.*

BRONZE RUNNER 7 ro.g. Gunner B 126 – Petingalyn (Petingo 135) [1990 10f⁶ **47**
10f⁵ 10.1g⁴ 10m* 10f⁴ 12h² 13.6g³ 10.2f² 10m² 12f³ 12m⁵ 10f⁴ 10.4g³ 10f⁴ 12f 10.2m² 1991 11.7g 11.5g⁴ 10.2f⁵ 11.7m⁵ 10.8m* 11m* 9.7f⁴ 10m⁶ 10.2g* 12g a12g a13g⁴ a12g⁴ a14g] leggy gelding: poor mover: plating-class handicapper: successful as 7-y-o at Warwick (selling event, no bid) in August and Southwell and Bath (apprentices): effective at 1¼m to 1½m: acts on any going: excellent mount for inexperienced rider: usually blinkered or visored: wore eyeshield final start: tough and consistent: a grand old campaigner. *E. A. Wheeler.*

BROOKLYN'S DANCE (FR) 3 b.f. Shirley Heights 130 – Vallee Dansante **119**
(USA) (Lyphard (USA) 132) [1990 8g* 8s* 1991 10.5d* 10.5d 12d⁶ 12.5d² 10.5v] lengthy, attractive filly: third foal: half-sister to 1m winner Diamond Valley and 1¼m claimer winner Vaillant Chevalier (both by Saint Cyrien): dam, 1m winner at 3 yrs, is closely related to Green Dancer: won newcomers race and minor event at Saint-Cloud at 2 yrs and Prix Cleopatre (comfortably) at Evry in May, 1991: ¾-length second to Saganeca in Ciga Prix de Royallieu at Longchamp, pulling hard but running on well: ran poorly final start: stays 12.5f: acts on soft ground: smart. *Mme C. Head, France.*

BROOKSIDE ROSE 3 b. or br.f. Beldale Flutter (USA) 130 – La Vie En Rose —
72 (Ile de Bourbon (USA) 133) [1990 NR 1991 8m 6.1m 14.6d] 900F: workmanlike filly: first foal: dam ran twice at 2 yrs, is out of half-sister to outstanding broodmare Peace: behind in claimer, maiden and competitive minor event in the autumn: sold 1,150 gns Ascot December Sales. *R. D. E. Woodhouse.*

BROOM ISLE 3 b.f. Damister (USA) 123 – Vynz Girl 82 (Tower Walk 130) [1990 **52**
7m³ 7m² 7f* 7f⁴ 1991 10g 12.3d 12g⁶ 12m⁴ 12.3m 10m⁴ 10.5g³ 12f⁶] lengthy, quite good-topped filly: carries condition: moderate mover: plating-class performer nowadays: ran creditably in amateur handicaps last 2 starts: should stay 1½m: acts on firm and dead going: bought out of J. W. Watts's stable 3,700 gns Doncaster July Sales before fifth start: winning hurdler. *Mrs A. Knight.*

BRORA ROSE (IRE) 3 b.f. Drumalis 125 – Run Swift (Run The Gantlet (USA)) **54**
[1990 7g 7g a8g⁴ 1991 8m⁴ 10f 10d⁶ 11.7d² 11.7m⁶ 12s³ 12d⁴ 12g 17.2g a14g a12g*] leggy, close-coupled filly: quite modest performer: won maiden at Lingfield in December: should stay 1¾m: best turf efforts on a soft surface: has run creditably in blinkers. *J. D. Bethell.*

BROTHERLY AFFECTION 2 ch.c. (Mar 16) Brotherly (USA) 80 – Lady **61**
Peggy (Young Nelson 106) [1991 8.2f 7.1s a8g³ a8g⁴] unfurnished colt: sixth foal: brother to poor sprint maiden My Lady Minstrel: dam unraced: quite modest maiden: easily best efforts on fibresand late in year: stays 1m. *R. Hollinshead.*

BROTHER RAY 4 b.c. Chief Singer 131 – Havara 82 (African Sky 124) [1990 **57**
a6g⁶ 6f 7f⁵ 7g* 7m* 7m 1991 7g 7m 8g³ 8g⁶ 8.1g 8.2m²dis 8f³ 8.2f 8m] leggy,

sparely-made colt: poor mover: plating-class handicapper nowadays: stays 1m: acts on firm ground: ran well when blinkered. *J. Sutcliffe.*

BROUGHPARK AZALEA 2 b.c. (Mar 1) Song 132 – Slip The Ferret 109 **45** (Klairon 131) [1991 6m5 6f4 7m 8m 8.3g] 5,000Y, 10,000 2-y-o: good-topped colt: has scope: good walker: has a round action: half-brother to Irish middle-distance winner Fly The Loop (by Kris) and a winner in Italy: dam very useful at up to 1m: poor maiden: stays 1m: acts on firm ground: unruly stalls penultimate outing. *J. J. O'Neill.*

BROUGHPARK JASMIN 2 b.c. (May 16) Northern Tempest (USA) 120 – **45** Arwa 69 (Hot Spark 126) [1991 8.3g6 8m] 3,200Y, 6,600 2-y-o: half-brother to fair 1984 2-y-o maiden Northern Treat (by Be My Guest), later successful in West Indies, and a winner in Macau: dam won over 1m: poor form: easily better effort when over 10 lengths sixth of 13, with leaders over 6f, in maiden at Hamilton in September. *J. J. O'Neill.*

BROUGHTON BLUES (IRE) 3 ch.g. Tender King 123 – Princess Galicia 82 **49** (Welsh Pageant 132) [1990 6g2 7g5 7m 6d6 a8g a8g 1991 a7g* a10g a8g4 8g 7.5g 9d 8d* 8m4 10g 10.9g4 a10g2 10.3m 9m 10m4 10g2 10m2] sparely-made gelding: fair plater: won handicaps at Lingfield (non-selling) in January and Ripon in June: stays 1¼m well: acts on good to firm ground and soft: sometimes on toes: blinkered 4 times, running well. *W. J. Musson.*

BROUGHTON'S GOLD (IRE) 3 b.f. Trojan Fen 118 – Smash Hit (Roan — Rocket 128) [1990 6d 6m 1991 a8g 7v 8.2d 12g 12m] lengthy, angular filly: moderate mover: poor form: probably stays 1½m: tended to hang final start. *W. J. Musson.*

BROUGHTON'S TANGO (IRE) 2 b.c. (May 8) Tender King 123 – Topless **48** Dancer (Northfields (USA)) [1991 5g 6g 6m 7m5 6g 6m 8m 6g5] IR 4,500F: leggy, lengthy colt: half-brother to 7f and 1m handicapper Well Rigged (by Windjammer) and a winner over jumps abroad: dam won over 1m in Ireland and also over hurdles in Ireland: poor maiden: good fifth in Newmarket nursery final start: should be well suited by further than 6f: ran creditably fourth start, but afterwards seemed suited by some given in the ground: usually bandaged. *W. J. Musson.*

BROWN AS A BERRY (IRE) 3 b.g. Glow (USA) – Sun Bed (Habitat 134) — [1990 6d a7g4 a7g a7g6 1991 a7g3 a7g5 a6g5 10f] robust gelding: poor maiden: best efforts when in frame: well beaten in selling handicap final start, in April: stays 7f: usually wears eyeshield on all-weather, also blinkers first and third outings: joined W. Storey. *Mrs L. Piggott.*

BROWN CARPET 4 b. or br.g. Never So Bold 135 – Geopelia 109 (Raffingora **40** d 130) [1990 5d 5m 7f 8m 11.5m 7g4 7m 1991 7g2 10m 8g 8.1g 8.3g] smallish, workmanlike gelding: has a quick action: poor handicapper nowadays: no form after reappearance: should stay beyond 7f: acts on firm ground: has been blinkered. *C. A. Horgan.*

BROWN FAIRY (USA) 3 b.f. Northern Baby (CAN) 127 – Chepstow Vale **73** (USA) 97 (Key To The Mint (USA)) [1990 5g2 6g2 6d 7f6 5g5 7g* 7f* 8m 8.2m 7g 1991 7.5g* 7.6g4 8g2 8.5m4 7.5f* 8m 7g 8g6 7d8* 7d a6g5 a7g3] leggy filly: modest handicapper: won at Beverley in April and in claimers at Beverley in July and Wolverhampton in October: needs strongly-run race at 7f, and is worth a try at 1¼m: acts on firm and dead going: on toes and sweating (ran poorly) sixth start. *Mrs N. Macauley.*

BRUMMEL (USA) 2 b.g. (Feb 5) Beaudelaire (USA) 125 – Palova (USA) (Iron **52** Ruler (USA)) [1991 6g3 5g6 a5g 7f6 5.1f 6f4] $5,300Y: sturdy gelding: half-brother to 2 minor winners in North America: dam ran once: plating-class maiden: possibly ideally suited by 6f: acts on firm ground: tends to hang: inconsistent: ridden by 5-lb claimer all starts: sold 825 gns Ascot October Sales. *W. A. O'Gorman.*

BRU-NA-BOINNE (IRE) 2 ch.f. (Apr 11) Huntingdale 132 – My Louise 54 — (Manado 130) [1991 7g] IR 4,800Y: tall, workmanlike filly: fifth living foal: half-sister to fairly useful handicapper (modest until 5 yrs) Just A Step (by Lochnager), best at 7f: dam seemed to stay 9f: 50/1, slowly away and always behind in 22-runner maiden at Newmarket in November. *R. Hollinshead.*

BRUNSWICK BLUE (IRE) 3 b.c. Sarab 123 – Lanata 64 (Charlottown 127) **47** [1990 7m 7g 8g 1991 a10g6 10g6 12m 10.2d4 12f2 11.8m 11.9g4 a12g] small colt: poor maiden: tailed off in Lingfield claimer final start: better at 1½m than shorter: acts on firm and dead going: blinkered last 5 starts: tends to race prominently. *J. Sutcliffe.*

BRUSQUE (USA) 7 b.g. Assert 134 – Cecelia (USA) (Royal Levee (USA)) [1990 **39** 12g 12g 13g5 14g 16g4 16.2s6 18d 16s 1991 13d2 16.5m 13d4 13.6g 12.1s* 13d5 12.1m2 12.1f4 12f4 15.1g2 16.1m] compact gelding: poor handicapper: made all at Hamilton (first win) in July: stays 2m: acts on any going: sometimes bandaged. *Don Enrico Incisa.*

BRYSON BOY (IRE) 2 b.c. (Mar 22) Horage 124 – Alitos Choice (Baptism 119) —
[1991 6d 6m] close-coupled, quite good-topped colt: third foal: dam never ran: no worthwhile form in sellers at Thirsk and Doncaster (coltish) in June: sold 1,100 gns Doncaster July Sales. *J. Berry.*

BUCARO BOY 3 br.g. Mummy's Game 120 – Izobia (Mansingh (USA) 120) [1990 **70**
7m 7.5m⁶ 10s⁴ 1991 10.8g⁶ 10g⁴ 11d⁴ 12.2m] strong, angular, plain gelding: good walker: modest maiden: wandered and carried head most awkwardly final start: stayed 1¼m: acted on soft going: dead. *W. G. M. Turner.*

BUCKINGHAM BAND (USA) 3 ch.c. Palace Music (USA) 129 – Intensive **58**
(USA) (Sir Wiggle (USA)) [1990 NR 1991 10m 10.5g⁵ 12.3d⁵ 12.1s⁶] IR 30,000Y: big, leggy colt: fifth foal: half-brother to 2 stakes winners in USA, including Grade 3 1¼m handicap winner Intensive Command (by Dust Commander), and to a minor winner in France: dam unraced daughter of Lowther and Molecomb winner Flying Legs: plating-class form: sixth of 17 in handicap at Hamilton, still in rear over 3f out: may need further: misbehaved first 2 starts: bandaged twice. *F. H. Lee.*

BUCKSWILL 7 b.g. Liboi (USA) – Berganza 83 (Grey Sovereign 128§) [1990 NR —
1991 a13g⁶ a7g⁶ a13g⁴ 14d] very lightly raced and no worthwhile form. *Mrs Barbara Waring.*

BUDDY (IRE) 2 b.c. (Feb 16) Double Schwartz 128 – Silk Trade (Auction Ring **63**
(USA) 123) [1991 5m 5m* 6g 6g] IR 5,000Y: workmanlike colt: half-brother to 2 winners, including 1985 2-y-o 6f winner Synthetic (by Reform): dam unraced daughter of half-sister to Troy: narrowly won 6-runner maiden auction at Hamilton in July: no comparable form: should stay 6f. *M. Bell.*

BUDDY'S FRIEND (IRE) 3 ch.c. Jester 119 – Hasta (Skymaster 126) [1990 — p
NR 1991 8m 7f⁶ 10g⁶ 8m 10d a10g⁵] smallish, workmanlike colt: poor mover: no worthwhile form, but showed signs of ability (prominent long way) when fifth of 14 in maiden claimer at Lingfield in December: retained by trainer 1,600 gns Doncaster November Sales. *R. J. R. Williams.*

BUDGET 3 ch.g. Bustino 136 – Australia Fair (AUS) (Without Fear (FR)) [1990 —
6m 1991 a12g] leggy, angular gelding: tailed off in maidens at Newbury and (in December) Lingfield. *A. J. Chamberlain.*

BUD'S BET (IRE) 3 b.g. Reasonable (FR) 119 – Pearl Creek (Gulf Pearl 117) **46** d
[1990 5f 6m² 6g⁴ 6m⁶ 6m 5m⁴ 5m⁵ 6m 6m 6d 1991 7d³ 6m⁵ 7g⁶ 7m 7m 8.3g 6m 6m 7g] compact gelding: carries condition: has a round action: plater: always behind last 4 starts: will prove better at 7f than shorter: acts on good to firm ground and dead: blinkered final start: sold to join J. McConnochie 2,100 gns Newmarket September Sales and gelded: winning hurdler. *L. J. Holt.*

BUFALINO (IRE) 3 b.c. Nomination 125 – Croglin Water (Monsanto (FR) 121) **112**
[1990 5g* 5g* 5m² 5m⁵ 5g* 6d⁴ 1991 6v* 7g*] very useful performer: successful at Leopardstown in the spring in smallish fields for minor event (by 2½ lengths from Mr Brooks) and listed 2000 Guineas Trial (by short head from Rinka Das): stays 7f: acts on good to firm ground and heavy: reportedly sent to USA. *J. S. Bolger, Ireland.*

BUILDMARK 5 ch.m. Longleat (USA) 109 – Crescentia (Crepello 136) [1990 —
a10g 1991 a8g a10g] workmanlike mare: quite modest maiden at best: no show at 5 yrs: suited by 1¼m: unruly at stalls once and withdrawn: dead. *W. G. M. Turner.*

BULLET PROOF (IRE) 3 ch.g. Mazaad 106 – Natija 70§ (Vitiges (FR) 132) **39**
[1990 6g 7s a6g⁶ a7g⁶ 1991 a8g a7g² a8g 8g 10d 8m 8.3m⁶ 8g] lengthy gelding: poor maiden: stays 1m: usually blinkered or visored: seems unreliable. *P. Howling.*

BUNDESBANK (USA) 2 b.c. (Feb 1) The Minstrel (CAN) 135 – Sassabunda **93**
108 (Sassafras (FR) 135) [1991 7d² 7m* 8.1g² 8g* 10g⁴] rangy colt: good walker and mover: half-brother to several winners, including useful 1m to 10.2f winner Habitassa (by Habitat) and quite useful 1m and 9f winner Sassagrass (by Thatch): dam short-head second in Irish Oaks: fairly useful performer: successful in maiden (wandered, below best) at Wolverhampton in July and 18-runner nursery (made all, battled on stoutly) at Warwick in October: respectable fourth of 9, racing keenly, gradually outpaced from over 2f out, to Bonny Scot in listed race at Newmarket: probably stays 1¼m: possibly suited by some give in the ground. *R. Charlton.*

BUNTY BOO 2 b.f. (Mar 6) Noalto 120 – Klairove 74 (Averof 123) [1991 6d⁴ **69**
6.1m² 6g²] 580Y: third foal: half-sister to poor maiden Klairover (by Smackover): dam, won 1m seller on flat also successful over hurdles, is daughter of half-sister to

high-class stayer Proverb: modest form in October maidens: second at Nottingham and Newmarket: should stay 1m. *B. A. McMahon.*

BUONARROTI 4 b.g. Ela-Mana-Mou 132 – Amiel (Nonoalco (USA) 131) [1990 10m 14g3 14g* 16.2d5 16g2 17.4d 1991 14s] big, strong gelding: moderate walker: fair performer at 3 yrs for H. Cecil: burly and tailed off only run in 1991: should stay beyond 2m: gave impression worth a try in blinkers or a visor at 3 yrs. *J. A. B. Old.* —

BURAIDA 3 ch.f. Balidar 133 – Really Sharp (Sharpen Up 127) [1990 NR 1991 7g 6s*] 18,000F, 44,000Y: lengthy, robust filly: moderate mover: fourth foal: sister to very useful sprinter Carol's Treasure and half-sister to Irish 7f winner Be Nimble (by Wattlefield): dam never ran: won maiden at Lingfield in June by 2 lengths from Glass Minnow, leading 2f out. *P. F. I. Cole.* **64**

BURDUR 3 b.c. Bering 136 – Mondialite (FR) (Habitat 134) [1990 8s 1991 8g 10g2 10.1m* 12g 8g* 10.5f 9m 8g] good-quartered, workmanlike colt: fairly useful performer: made most to win maiden at Epsom in June and £8,100 handicap at Goodwood in August: easily best effort in handicaps after when in mid-division, front rank long way and not at all discredited, in Cambridgeshire at Newmarket seventh start: stays 1¼m: acts on good to firm ground: trained first 6 starts by B. Hanbury. *D. R. Laing.* **95**

BURFORD (USA) 4 ch.g. Time For A Change (USA) – Windrush Lady (USA) (Unconscious (USA)) [1990 8m4 8g5 8f* 8.5m 1991 a8g 7.1m 10.6g 17.1d 16.2d 10m] leggy gelding: one-time modest performer: stays 1m: acts on any going: has looked reluctant: sold 1,900 gns Ascot October Sales. *D. R. Tucker.* — §

BURN BRIDGE (USA) 5 b.g. Linkage (USA) – Your Nuts (USA) (Creme Dela Creme) [1990 a12g6 10.6d 16.2s 1991 12m 12g3] small gelding: fair winner as 2-y-o: no worthwhile form for long time: likely to prove suited by shorter than 11f: acts on soft going: has been tried blinkered: winning hurdler. *M. D. Hammond.* —

BURNDITCH GIRL 5 ch.m. Raga Navarro (ITY) 119 – Queen of The Nile (Hittite Glory 125) [1990 9s 1991 10s] small, sparely-made mare: moderate mover: won amateurs handicap early as 3-y-o: lightly raced and no subsequent form: should stay further than 1m: best form on an easy surface. *M. W. Eckley.* —

BURNING POINT (IRE) 2 b.c. (Feb 22) Never So Bold 135 – Billante (USA) (Graustark) [1991 6g 7f2 7g3 6s3 a6g*] 21,000Y: leggy, quite attractive colt: moderate mover: half-brother to Irish 1¾m winner Youthful Miss (by Youth) and a winner in Italy (by Posse): dam unraced half-sister to 1000 Guineas winner Waterloo: quite modest performer: didn't need to run up to best when winning poor maiden at Lingfield in December: really needs further than 6f, and will be well suited by 1m. *Sir Mark Prescott.* **69**

BURNT FINGERS 7 ch.g. Busted 134 – Madame's Share 115 (Major Portion 129) [1990 NR 1991 18s] workmanlike gelding: moderate mover: quite modest handicapper in 1989: soundly beaten in March, only run on flat since: lacks pace, well suited by forcing tactics and a good test of stamina: best form on top of the-ground: often wears tongue strap: won over hurdles in May. *J. White.* —

BURNT SUGAR (USA) 3 b. or br.c. Raised Socially (USA) – Carmelize (USA) (Cornish Prince) [1990 NR 1991 a8g] $7,000Y, resold $25,000Y: ninth living foal: half-brother to a minor 9f winner in France by J O Tobin and 1989 Irish 2-y-o 6f winner Lochearnhead (by Lomond): dam, half-sister to top-class Chris Evert, was very useful winner at up to 9f: never a threat after slow start in claimer at Southwell in January: sold 1,200 gns Doncaster March Sales. *W. A. O'Gorman.* —

BURP (IRE) 3 ch.g. Tumble Wind (USA) – Devil's Drink (Red God 128§) [1990 NR 1991 10m] IR 7,000Y, resold IR 2,600Y: big, angular gelding: half-brother to several winners, including useful Irish sprinter Regaltess and useful Irish 1979 2-y-o Daness: dam showed ability at 2 yrs: burly and bandaged behind, tailed off in Leicester maiden in October. *D. Morley.* —

BURRACOPPIN 4 b.g. Niniski (USA) 125 – Favorite Prospect (USA) (Mr Prospector (USA)) [1990 8.2m 10g4 10.5g 1991 12m 8.2f 12m5 14.6g 12g] leggy, rather sparely-made gelding: poor maiden: visored once. *Mrs Barbara Waring.* —

BURSANA 5 b.m. Burslem 123 – Lady of Surana (Shirley Heights 130) [1990 10d 12g 12m2 10g5 12g 12.3g4 13.6g5 12.5g4 10.4g 14g 1991 a12g2 a16g2 a13g* 10.2s a12g] sparely-made mare: poor mover: poor handicapper nowadays: won at Lingfield (amateurs) in March: stays 2m: acts on good to firm and soft going: sold out of C. Booth's stable 2,200 gns Doncaster November Sales: winning hurdler. *J. L. Spearing.* **45**

BURSAR 4 b.f. Balliol 125 – Trading 74 (Forlorn River 124) [1990 a7g a7g 6g 1991 —
10.2s a5g] workmanlike filly: has a round action: no sign of ability. *W. Holden.*

BURSLEMS JOY (IRE) 3 b.f. Burslem 123 – Rathlin Sound (Margouillat (FR) **75**
133) [1990 NR 1991 7m⁴ 7m² 7m² 6s*] IR 2,000Y, 8,200Y: leggy, angular filly: fifth
foal: half-sister to winner in Belgium and to 1989 2-y-o 6f seller winner Tight Rein
(by Muscatite): dam ran 4 times in Ireland: won minor event at Folkestone in July:
would have stayed 1m: racing in Scandinavia. *C. N. Williams.*

BUSHFIRE MOON 3 ch.g. Julio Mariner 127 – Flea Pit (Sir Lark 101) [1990 NR —
1991 14. 1m 10m 12s⁴] leggy, lightly-made gelding: eighth foal: half-brother to Irish
1½m winner Mrs Peopleater (by Ancient Regime) and a winner in Belgium: dam
never ran: well beaten in autumn maidens. *C. N. Williams.*

BUSHY TAILED 3 b.c. Teenoso (USA) 135 – Bundu (FR) 88 (Habitat 134) [1990 **77**
8m³ 1991 12m⁵ 12m⁶ 10.1f* 10d⁶ 10m² 11.5f⁵ 10d 10m* 12g⁵] rather sparely-made
colt: modest handicapper: won at Yarmouth in June and Redcar in October: suited by
1¼m: acts on firm going, possibly unsuited by dead: put head in air sixth start: sold
21,000 gns Newmarket Autumn Sales, probably to Scandinavia. *G. Wragg.*

BUSINESS AS USUAL 3 b.g. Domynsky 110 – Pamora (Blast 125) [1990 5.8h⁵ —
6g 5.8m 7f 7m⁵ 6g* 6m 6d³ 6m⁶ 6d 1991 a6g a8g⁵ a7g⁶ 6v] small, rather
sparely-made gelding: moderate mover: winning plater at 2 yrs: below best in
claimers and handicap in 1991: suited by 6f: best efforts on an easy surface:
blinkered or visored last 9 starts: sold 725 gns Ascot April Sales. *Dr J. D. Scargill.*

BUSMAN (IRE) 2 ch.c. (Feb 27) Be My Guest (USA) 126 – Cistus 123 (Sun **66 p**
Prince 128) [1991 8g 7d⁵] workmanlike colt: sixth living foal: half-brother to French
10.5f winner All Found (by Alleged): dam good 1m to 1¼m performer, is half-sister
to high-class French middle-distance horse Lancastrian: quite modest form,
keeping on, in Newbury minor event in October and Doncaster maiden (won by For
Reg) 2 weeks later: will do better, particularly when given much stiffer test of
stamina. *Major W. R. Hern.*

BU-SOFYAN 7 b.g. Runnett 125 – London Spin 86 (Derring-Do 131) [1990 8f* —
8f² 7h⁴ 8.3m 8g 9g 1991 7m] tall, rather leggy gelding: modest handicapper at 6 yrs:
tailed off only run in 1991 (May): effective at 7f to 1m: acts on hard going, possibly
unsuited by soft: sold 1,500 gns Ascot July Sales. *M. Madgwick.*

BUSTAMENTE 8 b.g. Busted 134 – Blessed Damsel 99 (So Blessed 130) [1990 —
NR 1991 10g] strong, lengthy, dipped-backed gelding: poor walker and mover: quite
modest handicapper at 4 yrs: last in claimer as 8-y-o, only flat run since: best form at
2m: acts on good to firm ground, unsuited by heavy: winning chaser in April. *J.
White.*

BUSTED ROCK 6 b.h. Busted 134 – Mexican Two Step (Gay Fandango (USA) **88**
132) [1990 12f 12.2m³ 10f⁶ 10m 12g* 12.3g³ 12m* 12f² 12m 12m⁵ 13.3g 12d² 12v
1991 a11g³ a12g⁴ 10.8m² 10.8m* 10m* 10d² 10m² 10.1g* 10g 10m³ 10.4m³] rangy,
quite attractive horse: moderate mover: usually impresses in appearance: fair
handicapper: won at Warwick and Sandown in May and Yarmouth in July: effective at
1¼m to 1½m: acts on firm and dead going: has been bandaged: suited by waiting
tactics and firm handling: wore eyeshield first 2 starts, seemed unsuited by
Goodwood track ninth one: tough, genuine and consistent. *Mrs L. Piggott.*

BUSTER 3 br.g. Macmillion 110 – Valsette (Anfield 117) [1990 5g* 5d 5m³ 6f² **98 d**
6m* 6g⁶ 1991 7g* 6g⁶ 7m 8g⁶ 8g 6d] lengthy, sparely-made gelding: best effort to
win 4-runner minor event at Doncaster in July: fair at best otherwise, sixth of 9 in
£11,400 handicap at Ascot fourth outing: needs further than 6f, and should stay 1m:
acts on firm going: bandaged off-hind fourth start: tends to wander: usually taken
down early: game. *Mrs Barbara Waring.*

BUSTER'S PAL 3 ro.g. Scottish Reel 123 – Tula Singh 66 (Mansingh (USA) 120) —
[1990 7f 8d 8g 1991 10.2s 8.2s] heavy-bodied gelding: well beaten in maidens and
selling handicap: blinkered final start. *Denys Smith.*

BUSTINO BAY 3 b.c. Bustino 136 – Betsy Bay (FR) 107 (Bellypha 130) [1990 —
NR 1991 10.2s 10m 12g] 7,400F: sturdy colt: poor mover: third foal: dam, 6f to 7.3f
winner at 2 yrs, stayed 1m: behind in maidens, off course 5 months before final start.
M. R. Channon.

BUTLERS WHARF 6 b.g. Burslem 123 – Regal Promise (Pitskelly 122) [1990 — §
NR 1991 12f 12f⁵] big, lengthy gelding: one-time fair handicapper: no form at 6 yrs:
took no interest final start: stays 1½m well: acts on any going: has been tried in
blinkers and visor: thoroughly untrustworthy. *R. Hollinshead.*

Ascot Stakes, Ascot—Cabochon comes good; Haitham (rails) takes second, Good Hand (braces) third and Star Player fourth

BUZZARDS CREST 6 ch.g. Buzzards Bay 128§ – Diamond Talk (Counsel 118) **46** [1990 8.2f 12g a8g a14g 1991 10.2s* 10.2s* 12m³ 9d 11.9m 12d 10.5g⁵ a12g] lengthy gelding: plating-class handicapper: won at Doncaster (ladies) and Newcastle in spring: wearing eyeshield, tailed off at Southwell final start, first for almost 2 months: stays 1½m: acts on good to firm and soft going: usually bandaged on all-weather: trained until after reappearance by H. Collingridge. *R. W. Jones.*

BYARDS LEAP 3 b.g. Sulaafah (USA) 119 – Roncastella (Royal Palace 131) [1990 **—** 5f 5m 5m⁴ 5m⁶ 7m 8.2s 6g⁶ 1991 7f⁵ 7m 7m 6d] rather leggy, lengthy gelding: moderate mover: plating-class form at best, none in 1991: possibly best at around 6f: pulled hard when visored at 2 yrs. *Denys Smith.*

BY ARRANGEMENT (IRE) 2 b.f. (Mar 18) Bold Arrangement 127 – Eulalie **60** 85 (Queen's Hussar 124) [1991 6m³ 6g³ 7m⁴] 7,600Y: leggy, unfurnished filly: half-sister to several winners, including useful 7f and 1m winner Electric Lady (by Electric) and 9f and 1¼m winner Rattle Along (by Tap On Wood): dam, winner at up to 10.8f, is half-sister to very useful Suni and Honorius: quite modest maiden: best effort keeping-on fourth of 11 in auction event at Yarmouth in July: will probably stay 1¼m. *R. Guest.*

BYE BYE BABY (FR) 3 b.f. Baby Turk 120 – Bustelda (FR) (Busted 134) [1990 **58** 6d⁵ 6g⁵ 7f⁴ 7g 7m⁶ a8g 1991 a10g⁶ 12s³ 12f 11.7s² 11.7g 13.1f 14f² 11.7g 16m* 19m⁴ 16m⁴ 14.6g⁶] leggy, sparely-made filly: plating-class performer: favourite, won maiden claimer at Redcar in August, smooth headway to challenge over 2f out, edging left once in front: stays 19f: acts on any going. *S. Dow.*

BY FAR (USA) 5 b.m. Far North (CAN) 120 – Countess Babu (USA) (Bronze Babu) [1990 a12g a8g⁶ 10f 12.5m 12g⁶ 12d a12g 1991 a12g a16g⁶] smallish, close-coupled mare: one-time quite modest performer: no worthwhile form on flat as 5-y-o: seems to stay 1½m: winning hurdler. *O. O'Neill.*

BY HAND 2 ch.g. (Apr 8) Sayf El Arab (USA) 127 – Madame Laffitte 54 (Welsh **77** Pageant 132) [1991 6f a6g* 7m* 6m⁶ 7d] 4,000F, 4,000Y: well-made gelding: has scope: second foal: dam 7f winner at 2 yrs, only year to race: modest performer: successful in maiden auction at Southwell in mid-June and nursery (running on

130

strongly) at Chester 2½ months later: better suited by 7f than 6f: possibly unsuited by soft surface: ran respectably for 7-lb claimer penultimate outing. *W. J. Haggas.*

BYWELL LAD   6 ch.g. Mandrake Major 122 – Juliette (Julio Mariner 127) [1990   —
14g 16.2d 13.8d³ 16s⁴ 1991 a14g⁵] rangy, angular gelding: poor handicapper: not seen out after February: stays 2m well: acts on good to firm and soft going: tends to carry head high: moody: sold 2,800 gns Ascot April Sales then 825 gns there at July Sales. *R. Curtis.*

BYZANTINE   3 b.g. Damister (USA) 123 – Rustle of Silk 67 (General Assembly   **55**
(USA)) [1990 6m 7m 1991 10d 13.8g 12f³ 12.2m³ 12.3f³ 13.8m² 16.1m³ 16m 13.6d] leggy, quite good-topped gelding: has a round action: plating class on most form: well beaten in handicaps last 2 starts: should prove as effective at 1¾m as 2m: acts on firm going: visored last 5 starts: has run well when sweating and also when on toes. *Miss S. E. Hall.*

C

CABOCHON   4 b.g. Jalmood (USA) 126 – Lightning Legacy (USA) 78 (Super   **80**
Concorde (USA) 128) [1990 10m 12f 10.1g 10m⁵ 10g 14g* 16g³ 16.2s² 18d* 16s* 1991 16g⁶ 14.8m³ 18.4d 20g* 17.2g² 16.2d 18m⁶ 16.5d³] lengthy gelding: has a round action: fair handicapper: won Ascot Stakes at Royal Ascot: best efforts at 2m to 2½m with some give in the ground (acts on soft going). *M. F. D. Morley.*

CACHE   3 b.f. Bustino 136 – Lightning Legacy (USA) 78 (Super Concorde (USA))   —
[1990 NR 1991 12.3d 12g⁶ 12m⁵ 9.7f] smallish, rather sparely-made filly: third foal: closely related to useful 1¼m to 11f winner Black Monday (by Busted), subsequently good winner in USA, and half-sister to 4-y-o 1¾m to 2½m winner Cabochon (by Jalmood): dam, maiden, stayed 1m: well beaten in maidens and handicap. *L. M. Cumani.*

CADENCY   3 b.g. Teenoso (USA) 135 – Mullet 75 (Star Appeal 133) [1990 7dʷᵒ   **90** ?
8d⁴ 1991 10m 10.1g⁴ 11.6m* 12m⁵ 10d 12d 12g] small, sturdy gelding: moderate mover: fairly useful performer at his best: made all in minor event at Windsor in August: disappointing in handicaps last 3 starts: stays 11.6f: acts on good to firm ground: tended to hang on reappearance: has looked headstrong: sold to join M. Tompkins 8,000 gns Newmarket Autumn Sales and gelded. *P. T. Walwyn.*

CAERLINA (IRE)   3 b.f. Caerleon (USA) 132 – Dinalina (FR) (Top Ville **120**
129) [1990 5.5g* 6d³ 8g³ 8g² 1991 8d² 8d³ 10.5d* 10m* 12m]
     Caerlina, whose second place in the Prix Marcel Boussac established her as one of the leading two-year-old fillies of 1990, trained on well. The Boussac field turned out to be a distinguished one. There were future classic winners in it in Shadayid, Caerlina and Jet Ski Lady, plus a future Arc second in Magic Night. Caerlina's big moment came in the Prix de Diane Hermes, the French Oaks, at Chantilly in June where her closest pursuer was Magic Night. In the run-up to Chantilly, Caerlina had been in good form over a mile, finishing second to the subsequent One Thousand Guineas fourth Once In My Life in a listed race at Evry on her return in the spring and third to Danseuse du Soir in the Dubai Poule d'Essai des Pouliches at Longchamp. That third should have been another second. She was twice involved in scrimmaging caused by the

Prix de Diane Hermes, Chantilly—
Caerlina is pressed by Magic Night (right) and Louve Romaine

Prix de la Nonette, Longchamp—a blanket finish;
Caerlina and Magic Night are again involved,
with Pink Turtle (No. 3) and Polemic on their inside

subsequently-disqualified La Carene—early on, when almost brought down, then on the run round into the straight, where having to be switched outside cost her valuable momentum—yet she only just failed to catch Sha Tha, two lengths behind the winner.

Caerlina's dam won over a mile and a quarter as a two-year-old, so breeding as well as style of running gave plenty of encouragement for Caerlina's prospects of getting the extra two and a half furlongs of the Prix de Diane; indeed, for her prospects of improving. All the same, the race seemed wide-open, and there was more public confidence behind others in the field of thirteen, notably the stable-companions Treble and Brooklyn's Dance, who'd respectively won the Prix Saint-Alary and the Prix Cleopatre last time out and were proven over the trip, and Masslama, winner of the Prix Vanteaux from Treble in April but unraced since because of a set-back which had caused her to miss the Saint-Alary. Both Brooklyn's Dance and Masslama were unbeaten. The stable-companions had provided for them as a pacemaker the useful handicapper Ring Beaune who set what seemed just an ordinary gallop, attended by Brooklyn's Dance pulling for her head. A typically-French middle-distance contest ensued—most of the jockeys content to bide their time until well in line for home, congestion at around two furlongs out then a sprint finish. On this occasion nearly all the runners were in contention as they pulled back the pacemaker and Brooklyn's Dance in the straight, though Treble and another well-fancied filly Polemic had run into difficulties attempting to get through on the rails. Caerlina, tucked away early on, had improved by this stage to dispute the lead in the middle of a line of seven and she went on in the last half furlong, showing a good turn of foot, to win ridden out by three quarters of a length. Another four lengths covered the next six home behind the strong-finishing Magic Night, Polemic doing particularly well once she saw daylight to come through past the fading Sha Tha for fifth.

Caerlina wasn't seen out again until September when she took on Magic Night and Polemic in the Prix de la Nonette at Longchamp. In the meantime Magic Night had won the Prix de Malleret over a mile and a half while Polemic had run fifth in the Irish Oaks. Caerlina came out on top once more, in an unsatisfactory contest that ended in a blanket finish after an early crawl; Magic Night was touched off by a nose with the again-unlucky Polemic a head and a nose further back in fourth; a little over two lengths covered all seven runners. Another rematch, however, in the strongly-contested, strongly-run Prix Vermeille Escada at Longchamp later in the month, saw Magic Night decisively on top and on her way to the Prix de l'Arc de Triomphe. Caerlina, who reportedly returned with cuts, finished halfway down the field in seventh place, a little under six lengths behind the shorter-priced winner. She ran as though a mile and a half were beyond her best, weakening inside the last furlong after moving up two furlongs out. Further evidence of her stamina wasn't forthcoming unfortunately. She was announced as one of the nine European reserves for the Japan Cup but by then had been retired for the season because of a bad cough. However, she remains in training.

Caerlina (IRE) (b.f. 1988)	Caerleon (USA) (b 1980)	Nijinsky (b 1967)	Northern Dancer / Flaming Page
		Foreseer (b or br 1969)	Round Table / Regal Gleam
	Dinalina (FR) (b 1983)	Top Ville (b 1976)	High Top / Sega Ville
		Shahinaaz (b 1965)	Venture VII / Cherry

In her second season and a brief third, Caerlina's dam Dinalina was unable to add to her winnings; her form tailed off and in two attempts she failed to show she stayed further than a mile and a quarter. She was bred to stay further, by Top Ville out of Shahinaaz, the dam of several well-known animals by other sires including the Doncaster Cup and Jockey Club Cup winner of 1983 Karadar and the smart middle-distance performers Kalidar and Karamita (the last-named the dam of Kartajana). Shahinaaz, herself a winner at up to thirteen furlongs in France, was out of the Irish Oaks second Cherry. Caerlina is Dinalina's first foal and only runner to date; the second foal Maniana (a colt by Try My Best) is with Dinalina's former handler Collet.

The decision to keep Caerlina in training is a brave one. Her opportunities in Europe will be limited if it turns out that she doesn't stay; all the more so if she doesn't make the improvement necessary to put her up with the top colts at weight-for-sex, for there are few good races confined to fillies in which she can run, none in Group 1 at a mile to a mile and a quarter. Caerlina, on the small side, acts on good to firm ground and dead; she hasn't encountered anything more extreme so far. She is tough and consistent, and possesses a good turn of foot. *J. de Roualle, France.*

CAERULIA 3 gr.f. Absalom 128 – Liberation 63 (Native Breeder) [1990 5g⁵ 5m 5f 7m⁶ 6f 5m² 6m 5s⁴ 5d a5g 1991 a7g⁶ a7g a6g 7d] smallish, good-quartered filly: moderate mover: plating-class maiden: tailed off last 2 outings, in March: suited by 5f: acts on good to firm ground and soft. *W. J. Pearce.* —

CAESARS NIECE (IRE) 3 b.f. Rhoman Rule (USA) – Great Dora (Great Nephew 126) [1990 6h⁴ 6f 1991 8m 8g] good-topped, quite attractive filly: poor form: edgy, slowly away and ridden along from stalls in seller final start: sold 875 gns Ascot November Sales: may be unsatisfactory. *M. J. Fetherston-Godley.* —

CAETANI 7 b.g. Busted 134 – Spring In Rome (USA) (Forli (ARG)) [1990 NR 1991 12.2g 16.2f⁵ 16.5g² 20g⁴ 19m³] strong, lengthy gelding: has a quick action: modest handicapper, lightly raced: gives impression will prove best at up to around 2m: acts on good to firm ground, possibly unsuited by soft going. *M. W. Easterby.* **74**

CAHELIA (IRE) 3 b.g. Cataldi 123 – Helia 72 (Song 132) [1990 NR 1991 a7g 6f 10g 8m a12g] 7,000Y: leggy, close-coupled gelding: fifth foal: half-brother to Irish bumpers winner Slantz (by Castle Keep): dam best at 5f: seems of little account: trained first 2 starts by R. Guest, next 2 by M. Madgwick. *J. L. Harris.* —

Prix Saint-Roman, Evry—Calling Collect is well suited by the test of stamina

CAHEREA SCHOOL 2 ch.f. (May 16) Country Classic – Morse Princess 69 —
(Communication 119) [1991 a7g a8g] quite good-topped filly: second foal: sister to
3-y-o Mosswood Prince: dam, plater, stayed 1m: soundly beaten in seller and maiden
at Southwell. *J. P. Leigh.*

CAITHNESS CLOUD 3 ch.c. Lomond (USA) 128 – Moonscape 87 (Ribero 126) 88
[1990 8.2d 8m² 1991 12g4 12m* 16.2g6] angular colt, rather unfurnished: favourite,
easily won maiden at Newmarket: not discredited in Queen's Vase at Royal Ascot
month later, when held and restrained to rear, headway on outside until no extra in
straight: will stay beyond 1½m: looked capable of better. *M. A. Jarvis.*

CAITHNESS ROCK 2 ch.g. (Feb 3) Ballad Rock 122 – Thessaloniki 94 (Julio 69 p
Mariner 127) [1991 6d 6g6 7f3 8f4 7d] 43,000F, 52,000Y: close-coupled, stocky
gelding: fourth foal: closely related to 6f winner Tolo (by Bold Lad) and half-brother
to French 3-y-o Stolen Bride (by Siberian Express), 6f winner at 2 yrs: dam won 3
races at 1¼m and stayed 1½m: quite modest maiden: good staying-on fourth of 6 in
nursery at Yarmouth: slowly away and never placed to challenge, catching eye, in
22-runner nursery at Doncaster in November: will be better suited by 1¼m: likely
to do better. *M. A. Jarvis.*

CALACHUCHI 4 b.f. Martinmas 128 – Seleter (Hotfoot 126) [1990 7.5f* 8.5m* 74
8g² 8f 7.5f4 8h² 8.5f6 10.6g4 11s* 11d* 12.4s* 1991 12f² 9s* 12.3d5 10.6g* 10.3d²
12.2g* 10.5g* 10.5f] leggy filly: won claimers at Ripon in April and Haydock (2) and
Catterick in summer (making a career total of 8): stays 1½m: acts on any going:
keen sort, taken down early: genuine: credit to her trainer. *M. J. Camacho.*

CALAHONDA SCRIBE 3 ch.g. Blushing Scribe (USA) 107 – Smitten 72 (Run —
The Gantlet (USA)) [1990 6g 1991 12f5 10g] leggy, shallow-girthed gelding: showed
signs of ability in claimer on reappearance: dead. *Mrs I. R. Ramsden.*

CALAPAEZ 7 gr.g. Nishapour (FR) 125 – Charter Belle 60 (Runnymede 123) —
[1990 NR 1991 16d5] tall, leggy gelding: bad mover: plating-class maiden as 4-y-o:
faced very stiff task only run on flat since: stays 17f: acts on firm and dead going: fair
chaser. *Miss B. Sanders.*

CALEMAN 2 b.c. (Jun 1) Daring March 116 – Lillemor (Connaught 130) [1991 6g 86 p
6m3 7m* 7.6m*] leggy, narrow colt: poor mover: second foal: brother to 1990 2-y-o
6f winner Danneman: dam twice-raced half-sister to smart Italian winner Alpherat
out of half-sister to Steel Heart: fair performer: made most in 18-runner maiden
auction at York in October: followed up (when leniently handicapped) in Lingfield
nursery later in month, beating Mountain Ash 2½ lengths, pair clear: much better
suited by 7f + than 6f: raced with head high second start: likely to improve further.
R. Boss.

CALGARY REDEYE 4 gr.c. Kalaglow 132 – River Call (FR) 103 (Riverman 75 +
(USA) 131) [1990 12f² 12m* 11.7m4 12m3 13d 16d6 1991 a12g² 14.1f3 14.1g*
14.1m* 13.1f3 14g5] small, dipped-backed colt: moderate walker: modest handicapper: had good season as 4-y-o, winning Yarmouth claimers in July: got poor run
when very good fifth at Kempton: stays 14.1f: acts on firm and dead going: blinkered
nowadays: has hung left and looked none too keen: hard ride: has found little and
best with waiting tactics. *P. J. Makin.*

CALIBAIRN 3 ch.g. Bairn (USA) 126 – Calibina 101 (Caliban 123) [1990 6m 5f5 —
5f6 5.3f4 5m 6s a6g a5g4 a6g5 1991 5s 6g 7g 6.9s 6m] sparely-made gelding: plater:

134

well beaten as 3-y-o, edgy and very awkward to post on reappearance: best form at 5f: usually blinkered: has twice reared in stalls: takes keen hold. *E. A. Wheeler.*

CALL AT EIGHT (USA) 3 b.g. Barachois (CAN) – Same Thyme (USA) **59** (Delaware Chief (USA)) [1990 5m⁴ 5f⁴ 6g³ 6f⁴ 7h⁴ 7f 6g⁶ a6g² a6g² 1991 8g⁵ a8g⁵] strong gelding: good mover: quite modest maiden: seen out only in the spring as 3-y-o, giving impression would prove more effective back at 7f: acts on hard ground: often blinkered: sold 1,300 gns Doncaster November Sales. *J. Etherington.*

CALL FOR ROONEY 3 b.c. Music Maestro 119 – Sally Bowles 87 (Blakeney **63** 126) [1990 8f 1991 5f³ 7f³ 7f³ 8f⁴ 7f⁴ 10.3m 10.4m] lengthy, good-topped colt: quite modest maiden: well beaten in selling handicap final start: stays 1m: awkward on turn at Catterick. *A. Smith.*

CALLING COLLECT (USA) 2 ch.c. (Mar 22) Phone Trick (USA) – My **118** Little Guest (Be My Guest (USA) 126) [1991 7g* 8g³ 6g⁴ 9s* 10v²]
      Anyone familiar with only Calling Collect's breeding would be astonished to learn that his two best performances were not, as might be expected, in the Prix de Cabourg and the Prix Morny Agence Francaise over six furlongs but in the Prix Saint-Roman and the Criterium de Saint-Cloud over nine furlongs and a mile and a quarter. The first indications that Calling Collect, a son of the American sprinter Phone Trick out of a miler in France, might be regarded by his stable as a potential stayer came as early as the second week of July, when he made a winning debut by four lengths in a newcomers event over seven furlongs at Saint-Cloud. For his next two races, however, Calling Collect was brought back to six furlongs. Although he acquitted himself well to finish third, just over a length behind Kenbu in the five-runner Cabourg, and last of four, nearly six lengths down on Arazi, in the Morny, Calling Collect rarely held a winning chance in the former and just wasn't quick enough to improve his position in the latter. That Calling Collect had been running over a trip too sharp for him became evident in his next race, the Prix Saint-Roman, switched in the latest season from Longchamp to Evry, at the end of September: he put six lengths between himself and a field which contained the useful British challenger Tik Fa with a powerful finish from the distance. Five weeks later Calling Collect confirmed himself as one of the leading French staying two-year-olds with a performance of almost identical merit in the Criterium de Saint-Cloud. Starting even money Calling Collect looked set for his third win of the season when hitting the front from the Saint-Roman fourth Ca Alors two furlongs out but was short-headed in the final stride by his unbeaten stable-companion Glaieul after the pair had drawn five lengths clear. Without denying the possibility that the much softer ground that Calling Collect encountered in his last two races was responsible for his vast improvement—he'd raced only on good ground on his first three starts—we're satisfied, for the moment at least, that in spite of his pedigree the longer distances suiting best.

Calling Collect (USA) (ch.c. Mar 22, 1989)	Phone Trick (USA) (b 1982)	Clever Trick (b or br 1976)	Icecapade
			Kankakee Miss
		Over The Phone (ch 1965)	Finnegan
			Prattle
	My Little Guest (ch 1980)	Be My Guest (ch 1974)	Northern Dancer
			What A Treat
		Wind (ch 1974)	Tom Rolfe
			Whirled

      Calling Collect, a 25,000-dollar purchase from Fasig-Tipton's July Selected Yearling Sale, looks a snip in hindsight. His sire Phone Trick, whose second crop Calling Collect is from, is a son of the smart six-furlong to one-mile performer Clever Trick. Phone Trick won nine races (including three graded events) at up to seven furlongs from ten starts and 'may have been America's best sprinter of the decade' according to the authors of *Principal Racehorses of 1986* although they had cause to revise that controversial opinion the following season when his old rival Groovy hit such a rich seam of form. Phone Trick certainly hasn't made a bad start to his career as a stallion: he had the Norfolk Stakes winner Line Engaged in his first crop, and at the time of writing was lying second to Blushing Groom in the Juvenile Sire List with progeny earnings exceeding one million dollars and numerous other stakes winners to his name including the Grade 2 and 3 winner Caller I. D.. My Little Guest, Calling Collect's dam, was a racemare of more modest ability: she won a seven-furlong maiden at Le Touquet and minor events at a mile or thereabouts in France as a three-year-old and didn't improve upon transfer to the States as a four-year-old despite adding an allowance race at around six furlongs to her winning tally. Calling Collect is her fourth foal following minor sprint winners in North America by Mt Livermore and Highland Blade. Both the second dam, Wind, and the third dam, Whirled, had much better records on the track than at stud: Wind was a fairly useful filly who won five races from a mile to an extended ten furlongs, while Whirled was a smart miler who was placed in the Coronation Stakes and the Prix de la Foret besides winning four races here and in France. Quite how Calling Collect has come to need a test of stamina is not apparent from his pedigree, but stay he does and it's not beyond the realms of possibility that he'll get a mile and a half. As mentioned, he acts particularly well on very soft ground too. *E. Lellouche, France.*

CALLIPOLI (USA) 4 br.f. Green Dancer (USA) 132 – Minstrelete (USA) **72** (Round Table) [1990 8.5m5 8g6 8g* 9g3 8g* 8.5m3 8.2d 8m 10m2 10.6v 9g* 1991 10m 10g 10f2 12.3g6 10.1g3 10g3 9.9f3 8.9g5 10.1f3 10m2] close-coupled, rather sparely-made filly: modest handicapper: stays 1¼m well: seems to need a sound surface: has run well for apprentice: consistent. *Lord John FitzGerald.*

CALL ME A DREAMER 2 b.f. (Apr 12) Another Realm 118 – Bo' Babbity **—** (Strong Gale 116) [1991 5m 6f 7.6d6] fair sort: shows knee action: first foal: dam 2-y-o 5f winner, is half-sister to high-class sprinter Anita's Prince: well beaten in maidens: bandaged final start. *N. Bycroft.*

CALL RACECALL 4 b.g. Reasonable (FR) 119 – Miel (Pall Mall 132) [1990 a8g **—** 9s6 10.2f6 12g3 14f6 13.8m6 12g 12d2 1991 12.5g] smallish, sturdy gelding: has a quick action: poor maiden: no show only start at 4 yrs: should stay beyond 1½m: acts on dead going. *B. Palling.*

CALL THE BUREAU 2 ch.c. (May 6) Gorytus (USA) 132 – Mount of Light 61 **67** (Sparkler 130) [1991 5g 6m* 6.1s2] compact colt: good mover: sixth living foal: half-brother to 1987 2-y-o 5f and 6f seller winner Rustic Dawn (by Rusticaro): dam, half-sister to smart miler Richboy, stayed 1½m: won seller (retained 6,400 gns) at Warwick in May: much improved effort when second of 6 in nursery at Chepstow in July: will stay 1m: seemed likely to progress further, but wasn't seen out again: has joined M. Heaton-Ellis. *G. B. Balding.*

CALL THE GUV'NOR 2 b.c. (Mar 22) Saint Estephe (FR) 123 – Gay Charlotte **69** p 95 (Charlottown 127) [1991 8d5] 32,000Y: very tall colt, rather unfurnished: has plenty of scope: half-brother to several winners, including fairly useful middle-distance performer High Gait (by High Top), later dam of top-class stayer Royal Gait, and very smart middle-distance stayer Upend (by Main Reef): dam, winner over 7.5f at 2 yrs in Ireland and over 1m at 3 yrs in USA, is out of Irish Oaks winner Merry Mate: 20/1, kept on well from mid-division when fifth of 14 to Hill Glitter in minor event at Newmarket in November: will improve, particularly over further. *H. R. A. Cecil.*

CAL MAL 13 b.g. Charlie's Pal – Semona (Seminole II) [1990 NR 1991 11m] big, **—** angular gelding: one-time fair chaser (formerly trained by M. Pipe), lightly-raced nowadays: soon tailed off in Southwell claimer in August, only start on flat. *M. C. Chapman.*

CAL NORMA'S LADY (IRE) 3 ch.f. Lyphard's Special (USA) 122 – June **59** + Darling (Junius (USA) 124) [1990 6g* 6f* 7m* 7g4 8d 7s 1991 7m2 8.9m 8m 7.1g] lengthy, rather sparely-made filly: fair performer at 2 yrs: below form in 1991: should be suited by further than 7f: acts on firm going, not knocked about on a soft surface. *J. S. Wilson.*

CAL'S BOY 2 b.c. (Mar 29) Green Ruby (USA) 104 – Green Gypsy 83 (Creetown **31** 123) [1991 5d5 6m 5d4 5g 8d] leggy, rather close-coupled colt: has scope: third reported foal: dam sprinter: poor maiden: best efforts at 5f on dead ground. *J. P. Smith.*

CALVANNE MISS 5 b.m. Martinmas 128 – Blue Empress (Blue Cashmere 129) **—** [1990 5f* 6m2 7f2 6f5 5m* 5f3 5m 5f 5m4 5f 6g 5g2 6m* 5m* 1991 6g 5.8f 7.1m] leggy, sparely-made mare: quite modest handicapper at 4 yrs: no show in 1991, not seen out after May: effective at 5f to 7f: acts on firm going, possibly unsuited by a soft surface. *C. J. Hill.*

CAMARAT 3 ch.f. Ahonoora 122 – Nomadic Pleasure 91 (Habitat 134) [1990 NR **69**
1991 9m 10m 9f² 9.9f³ 9m* 10m] lengthy filly: moderate mover: fifth foal: half-sister
to Park Hill winner Trampship (by High Line), 11f to 14.6f winner Highflying and
very useful 10.6f and 12.2f winner Cruising Height (both by Shirley Heights): dam,
9f winner, is half-sister to Prix Vermeille winner Paulista: modest form in maidens,
winning at Redcar in August: stiffish task but ran poorly nonetheless in handicap
there 7 weeks later: stays 9f well: acts on firm going: bandaged behind first 2 and
last 2 starts: sold 31,000 gns Newmarket December Sales. *B. W. Hills.*

CAMBRIAN HILLS (IRE) 2 b.f. (Mar 18) Caerleon (USA) 132 – My Therape **95**
112 (Jimmy Reppin 131) [1991 6d* 6d* 6m⁴] 30,000Y: sturdy, good-quartered filly:
carries condition: half-sister to numerous winners, including very useful 1983 2-y-o
5f and 6f winner Domynsky (by Dominion), later middle-distance stakes winner in
USA, smart 1¼m and 1½m winner Petrullo (by Electric) and useful 6f winner
Anodyne (also by Dominion): dam won 7 times at up to 1¼m: progressive form:
successful in maiden at Goodwood and 4-runner Veuve Clicquot Champagne Stakes
at Salisbury in June, quickening well to beat Power Lake 3 lengths in latter event: 3
lengths fourth of 10, staying on well, to Bezelle in Princess Margaret Stakes at
Ascot following month: will be much better suited by further, and should stay 1¼m:
seemed sure to go on improving, but wasn't seen again. *P. W. Chapple-Hyam.*

CAMDEN KNIGHT 6 b.g. Camden Town 125 – Motionless 109 (Midsummer **55 d**
Night II 117) [1990 11s⁴ 13v³ 12g* 13g³ 12m⁶ 12g 10.6d 11d⁶ 15v 12s 1991 10.2s 12.4v⁴
11s⁴ 12d 13d³ 10.2m 11.9m 14g 10.3d] leggy, good-topped gelding: carries condition:
poor mover: quite modest handicapper at 5 yrs: below best in 1991: stays 13f: goes
particularly well with give in the ground: below best when blinkered: has been
bandaged: usually held up. *N. Bycroft.*

CAMDEN'S RANSOM (USA) 4 b.g. Hostage (USA) – Camden Court (USA) **78 ?**
(Inverness Drive (USA)) [1990 8m 10f³ 10m* 10m* 1991 a8g⁴ a10g* 10g 10g⁴ 10g³
10g⁴ 10.4m 10g] good-bodied gelding: has a long stride: modest handicapper: won at
Lingfield in March: best effort when fast-finishing fourth in strongly-run Royal
Hong Kong Jockey Club Trophy at Sandown sixth start: well worth a try over 1½m:
acts on good to firm ground: has run well when sweating: tends to edge under
pressure: wore dropped noseband final 4 starts. *M. J. Fetherston-Godley.*

CAMERON PRIDE 3 br.g. Kabour 80 – Sandra's Sovereign (Workboy 123) —
[1990 5s⁶ 5d 5m 7g 5m a8g 1991 12.2g] leggy, plain gelding: of little account. *J.
Dooler.*

CAMMY COME HOME 4 b.f. Camden Town 125 – Thank You Fans 67 (Be My —
Guest (USA) 126) [1990 NR 1991 a8g a8g 16.2g] leggy, rather narrow filly: poor
mover: well beaten in varied company. *Miss G. M. Rees.*

CAMOMILE 3 b.f. Bay Express 132 – Hot Spice (Hotfoot 126) [1990 NR 1991 10g] —
lengthy filly: fifth foal: half-sister to 3 winners, including smart 1m to 13.3f winner
Sesame (by Derrylin) and middle-distance stayer Turmeric (by Alias Smith): dam
never ran: moved poorly to post and showed little in maiden at Newbury in July. *D.
Morley.*

CAMPESTRAL (USA) 3 b.f. Alleged (USA) 138 – Field Dancer 110 **97**
(Northfields (USA)) [1990 7g* 1991 11.5g⁴ 11.9m⁶ 7.9g 10.3m² 10d 10m] leggy,
unfurnished, angular filly: fairly useful form in frame in listed race at Lingfield and
£7,600 handicap at Doncaster: suited by further than 1m: acts on good to firm
ground: has twice run moderately when sweating and edgy: hung left second outing:
inconsistent. *M. R. Stoute.*

CAMPSEA-ASH 7 gr.g. Rusticaro (FR) 124 – Lady d'Arbanville (FR) (Luthier —
126) [1990 NR 1991 12m⁴] half-brother to 2 winners, including French 8.5f winner
Clonsella Lady (by High Top): dam, minor 2-y-o winner, is granddaughter of
top-class La Sega: around 12 lengths fourth in celebrity event at Uttoxeter in
September, only run on Flat: fairly useful chaser. *F. Murphy.*

CANAAN VALLEY 3 ch.g. Absalom 128 – My Pink Parrot (Pirate King 129) **72**
[1990 6g 6g² 1991 6g³ 7m² 7m⁶ 7g* 7.9m³ 7f] lengthy, well-made gelding: has high
knee action: modest form: easily made all in lady riders maiden at Doncaster in
June: ran well in handicap next start, badly later in July: stays 1m: may be unsuited
by firm ground, also looked ill at ease second start: has pulled hard. *J. G. FitzGerald.*

CANADIAN CAPERS 2 ch.f. (Feb 10) Ballacashtal (CAN) – Carolynchris- **71**
tensen 58 (Sweet Revenge 129) [1991 6g⁴ 6m³ 6g² 5.7f* 6m⁶] big, angular filly:
moderate mover: third foal: half-sister to 3-y-o Rue de Remarque (by The Noble
Player) and modest sprint handicapper Maid Welcome (by Mummy's Pet): dam won
from 5f to 9.4f: modest performer: made all in median auction at Bath in August: had

stiff task in Kempton listed race on final start: will stay 7f: acts on firm ground: ran well when sweating and on toes third outing. *M. R. Channon.*

CANADIAN GOLD (IRE) 3 b.g. Coquelin (USA) 121 – Bold Design (Bold Lad (IRE) 133) [1990 a7g 8m³ 7.5m³ 7g 1991 12f⁵ 10g⁶] close-coupled gelding: quite modest form in auction events: stays 1½m: acts on firm going: sweated and edgy first start at 3 yrs and final one (blinkered, ran far too freely) at 2 yrs. *J. G. FitzGerald.* —

CANBRACK (IRE) 2 b.g. (Apr 24) Glenstal (USA) 118 – Cottage Style 65 (Thatch (USA) 136) [1991 6f⁶ 6m 6m³ 7m] rather unfurnished, angular gelding: fourth foal: dam, winner twice at 1½m, is daughter of half-sister to Lorenzaccio: plating-class maiden: best effort keeping-on third of 8 at Newcastle in October: ran badly final start: should be better suited by 7f than 6f. *W. A. Stephenson.* **59**

CANDESCO 5 b.m. Blushing Scribe (USA) 107 – Madame Mim 57 (Artaius (USA) 129) [1990 8v 8f a7g 8.2m a8g* 8m⁶ a8g a8g* 8.2v a7g² 1991 a7g a7g² a8g] a 65 strong, close-coupled mare: quite modest handicapper: easily best efforts at Southwell on all-weather: not seen again after running poorly there in June: stays 1m. *R. F. Marvin.* —

CANDLE KING (IRE) 3 b.g. Tender King 123 – Candelaria (FR) (Touch Paper 113) [1990 5g4 6m* 7g² 6m 7.3g⁵ 7m 1991 6g⁶ 6g 8d 8g⁶ 7m 7g* 7d* 8m³ 8m 7m] leggy, sparely-made gelding: moderate mover: modest performer: unimpressive in appearance, won sellers (bought in 6,200 gns, then 4,300 gns) at Leicester and Newmarket in August: stays 1m: acts on good to firm ground and dead: blinkered sixth to ninth starts: sometimes sweats: inconsistent. *M. J. Fetherston-Godley.* **71**

CANDY GLEN 4 b.c. Glenstal (USA) 118 – Maiden Concert (Condorcet (FR)) [1990 8g4 8g* 10d4 9d* 8g⁵ 8m2 8m 8v4 10s² 8v² 1991 8d³ 9m4 8g 10g³] strong, good-bodied colt: carries condition: good mover: very smart performer: very good fourth of 7 to Sanglamore in Prix d'Ispahan at Chantilly, beaten only about ¾ length: easily better subsequent effort when fair third of 6 to Muroto in Group 3 event at Deauville in August (co-favourite, well beaten in Queen Anne Stakes at Royal Ascot): stays 1¼m: acts on any going: tough and genuine. *C. F. Wall.* **121**

CANNONALE (IRE) 2 b.c. (May 21) Mummy's Treasure 84 – Sierra Princess (Vital Season 105) [1991 6f 7m] 3,100 2-y-o: lengthy colt: first foal: dam unraced: no worthwhile form: gave impression something amiss second start. *A. N. Lee.* —

CANNON'S VISION 3 ch.g. Fingora 85 – Ribble Reed 75 (Bullrush 106) [1990 NR 1991 8.5f 12m 8.5f⁵] 300F: short-backed gelding: half-brother to 1¼m and 1½m winner Wildrush (by Free State) and 7f to 2m winner Ribble Rouser (by Marcus Brutus): dam sprint plater: well beaten in maidens: hampered and unseated rider on debut. *M. Brittain.* —

CANNY BAIRN 2 ch.g. (May 15) Bairn (USA) 126 – Mint Julep (Mill Reef (USA) 141) [1991 a5g 6g a6g a7g⁶ 7m 7.5f] 3,000 2-y-o: plain, workmanlike gelding: moderate mover: sixth reported foal: dam unraced half-sister to Bedtime, high-class 1¼m to 1½m performer: of little account: has worn blinkers. *M. C. Chapman.* —

CANNY CHRONICLE 3 b. or br.g. Daring March 116 – Laisser Aller (Sagaro 133) [1990 7m² 6m* 7f 1991 8m4 8.2g³ 8m⁶ 12.4m* 12f4 13.9g 10.9m³ 12d* 12m 12d³] leggy gelding: moderate mover: fair handicapper: won at Newcastle in June and Ascot (apprentices) in September, both times quickening clear well over 1f out then idling: 8/1, very good third of 22 to Hieroglyphic in William Hill November Handicap at Doncaster final start: stays 1½m: acts on firm and dead going: winning hurdler. *M. H. Tompkins.* **85**

CANTICLE (USA) 3 ch.f. Stage Door Johnny – Melody Roulette (USA) 67 d (Northern Dancer) [1990 NR 1991 12m 12m² 12h² 13.6g 15.8f³ 15.1m4 12.2m] quite good-topped filly: sixth reported foal: sister or half-sister to 3 winners in North America, one stakes placed: dam, minor winner, is half-sister to Kentucky Derby second Woodchopper: modest maiden: ran fairly well in handicaps fifth (sweating and edgy) and sixth starts: best form short of 15f: acts on hard ground: blinkered (led over 9f) fourth start: visored (took strong hold) final one. *J. W. Watts.*

CANTORIS 5 b.m. Song 132 – Singing Witch 71 (Sing Sing 134) [1990 5m⁶ 5f* 95 5m³ 5f² 6m 5g² 5f* 5m² 6d⁶ 5m⁶ 5.8h 6m 5m 5g4 5m⁶ 5m³ 6m³ 5m* 5m³ 6d 5g² 5g4 5s³ 1991 5g⁵ 6m³ 5m⁵ 5g4 5m 5f* 6g 5g* 5g³ 5m² 5d4 5m⁶ 5d 6m 5d] leggy, close-coupled mare: has a quick action: fairly useful handicapper: won at Beverley in July and Haydock (£9,900 event) in August: ideally suited by stiff 5f or 6f: acts on any going: has run well for claimer: goes very well in strongly-run race: tremendously tough and consistent: a great credit to her trainer. *R. J. R. Williams.*

CANUTELL (FR) 3 b.f. Persepolis (FR) 127 – Dry Land 84 (Nonoalco (USA) —
131) [1990 6f 6f⁶ 5m 5m 1991 8m] small, stocky filly: no worthwhile form: blinkered
once at 2 yrs: sold 1,150 gns Newmarket Autumn Sales. *C. N. Williams.*

CAPA 11 ch.g. New Member 119 – Poshteen 86 (Royal Smoke 113) [1990 14.8m —
1991 15.8f] sturdy, plain gelding: poor handicapper: pulled up only start at 11 yrs:
stayed 2¼m: possibly needed a sound surface: one-time fairly useful hurdler: dead.
W. Storey.

CAP CAMARAT (CAN) 2 ch.f. (Apr 5) Miswaki (USA) 124 – Cap d'Antibes 52
(AUS) (Better Boy 91) [1991 5m⁶ 5m⁴ 5g⁶ 5g⁴ 8f⁵] IR 73,000Y: leggy, quite
close-coupled filly: half-sister to several winners, including smart French sprinter
Breath Taking (by Nureyev): dam won 2 of Australia's most important sprints after
finishing second in 12.5f VRC Oaks: plating-class maiden: blinkered, fifth of 12 in
nursery at Bath in September: better form at 1m than 5f, but may be worth a try at 7f.
P. F. I. Cole.

CAP DIAMANT (USA) 3 b.c. Secreto (USA) 128 – Baby Diamonds (Habitat —
134) [1990 NR 1991 10.2m] $425,000Y: sturdy, quite attractive colt: brother to useful
but disappointing maiden Benzine and half-brother to 3 winners in USA, notably
good-class miler Gem Master (by Green Dancer): dam 2-y-o 6f winner in USA, is
sister to smart 1982 2-y-o sprinter Tatibah: weak 7/1, saddle slipped in maiden at
Doncaster in June. *H. R. A. Cecil.*

CAPE PIGEON (USA) 6 ch.g. Storm Bird (CAN) 134 – Someway Somehow 74
(USA) (What Luck (USA)) [1990 7g 7m 7m 7g⁴ 8m⁴ 7m² 8g⁶ 8f³ 7m⁵ 8g⁶ 1991 7g⁶
7.6s* 7.1g² 7.6m* 7g 7g⁴ 7m² 7.6d⁶ a7g] big, strong, angular gelding: carries plenty
of condition: usually looks well: fair handicapper: twice successful at Lingfield in
1991: probably best at 7f to 1m: acts on any going: tried visored. *L. G. Cottrell.*

CAPITAL BOND (IRE) 3 b.c. Hegemony 112 – Have A Flutter (Auction Ring 72
(USA) 123) [1990 5f⁶ 6m⁵ 6g³ 7m² 7m⁶ 8g 8m 7g 1991 8g² 8d 8g⁶ 8g⁶ 8g⁴ 7m* 8.2f⁵
8m⁵ 10.2g² 8g* 9.7s⁴] smallish, compact colt: keen walker: has a quick action:
modest performer: successful at Salisbury in claimer in August and handicap in
October: effective at 1m and 1¼m: acts on good to firm ground and soft: well below
form when blinkered at 2 yrs. *R. J. Holder.*

CAPITAL IDEA (IRE) 2 b.c. (Apr 21) Mister Majestic 122 – Star Heading 74 61
(Upper Case (USA)) [1991 6g 6g⁵ 7m 5f* 5f³ 6m⁵ a7g] IR 2,500F, 2,600Y: strong,
compact colt: moderate mover: half-brother to poor 1986 2-y-o 5f winner Bingo
Queen (by Cajun): dam, best at 2 yrs, stayed 7f: quite modest performer: won
maiden auction at Beverley in July: ran quite well in face of stiff task penultimate
start, poorly on fibresand final outing: stays 6f: blinkered fourth and fifth starts:
claimed out of R. Boss's stable £5,526 fifth. *Ronald Thompson.*

CAPITAL LAD 2 ch.g. (Mar 23) Dublin Lad 116 – Wellington Bear (Dragonara —
Palace (USA) 115) [1991 5d 5g⁵ 7f4] big, workmanlike gelding: fifth foal: half-brother
to 1989 2-y-o 7f winner Freddie's Star (by Tina's Pet): dam never ran: no
worthwhile form, tailed-off last of 4 in minor event at Redcar (on toes) in July. *M.
Avison.*

CAPPAHOOSH (IRE) 2 ch.f. (Feb 19) Salmon Leap (USA) 131 – Tagik 56
(Targowice (USA) 130) [1991 7g 6f 8m³ 8.2m⁵] 8,200Y: good-topped filly: half-sister
to several winners, including Irish 1m and 8.5f winner Miss Retlaw (by Kampala):
dam, winner in Italy, is half-sister to high-class sprinter Green God: plating-class
maiden: better suited by 1m than shorter. *H. J. Collingridge.*

CAPRIATI (USA) 3 ch.f. Diesis 133 – Chateau Dancer (USA) 104 (Giacometti 83
130) [1990 NR 1991 8g² 10m³ 8.1m⁵ 9g³ 8m] $95,000Y: smallish, lengthy, rather
sparely-made filly: fifth foal: half-sister to 1990 3-y-o 1¼m winner Rejoneo (by El
Gran Senor) and modest maiden Officer Krupke (by Nureyev): dam won twice at 6f
and third in May Hill at 2 yrs then stakes placed in USA: fair maiden: best efforts
first 2 starts: stays 1¼m. *H. R. A. Cecil.*

CAPTAIN HORATIUS (IRE) 2 b.c. (Apr 22) Taufan (USA) 119 – One Last 113
Glimpse 73 (Relko 136) [1991 7.1s* 8.1f⁵ 8.1g* 10g²] 14,000F, 24,000Y: tall colt: has
scope: moderate mover: third foal: half-brother to 3-y-o sprint winner Running
Glimpse (by Runnett): dam second from 8.2f to 10.6f: successful in maiden at
Sandown in July and 4-runner minor event at Haydock in September: improved form
when 1½ lengths second of 9, well clear, to Bonny Scot in listed race at Newmarket
in November: a very useful young stayer: looked ill at ease on firm ground. *J. L.
Dunlop.*

CAPTAIN KEN (IRE) 2 b.c. (Mar 26) Vayrann 133 – Tableaux (FR) (Welsh 65
Pageant 132) [1991 6g a6g⁴ 6d³ 7m³ 7m² 8.1m 6m⁵ 7m²] 3,500Y: close-coupled,

rather leggy colt: half-brother to French 8.7f winner Living Image (by Kenmare): dam French maiden: useful plater: best effort when second at Redcar final start: should stay 1m: visored (last in non-selling nursery at Sandown) sixth outing: hung badly left on dead ground. *M. H. Tompkins.*

CAPTAIN MY CAPTAIN (IRE) 3 ch.c. Flash of Steel 120 – Amanzi 94 **66** (African Sky 124) [1990 7g 7g 7m⁴ 7m 1991 8d 8.2g 12g⁵ 10g 12f⁵ 10.2g⁶] lengthy colt: has plenty of scope: quite modest form: caught eye on several occasions before good fifth in King George V Handicap at Royal Ascot, no extra final 2f: well beaten in maiden and handicaps afterwards: should prove as effective at 1¼m as 1½m. *G. B. Balding.*

CAPTAIN'S BIDD 11 ch.g. Captain James 123 – Muffet 75 (Matador 131) [1990 — 6m 5m 5m⁶ 5m a5g a5g 1991 a6g] sturdy, workmanlike gelding: carries plenty of condition: moderate mover: quite modest handicapper at 9 yrs: no worthwhile form since: ideally suited by 5f: acts on any going: effective with or without blinkers or visor. *R. Thompson.*

CARABALI DANCER 3 ch.g. Ballacashtal (CAN) – Lillicara (FR) (Caracolero — (USA) 131) [1990 a7g 8.2d 8f 1991 a11g⁵ a12g⁶ 13g⁶ a12g⁴] lengthy gelding: plating-class maiden: edgy and well beaten final start, in July: stays 1½m. *D. T. Garraton.*

CARA MUFFIN 7 b.g. Dramatic Bid (USA) – Speedy Valley 92 (Wolver Hollow — 126) [1990 NR 1991 12m] third living foal: dam Irish 9f winner: well beaten in celebrity event at Uttoxeter in September, only flat run: poor novice hurdler/chaser. *J. Mackie.*

CARDEA CASTLE (IRE) 3 b.f. Fayruz 116 – Yamba (FR) (Amarko (FR)) [1990 — 7d 9g 1991 10m 10.3m 12m⁶] stocky filly: no worthwhile form: tongue tied down last 2 starts. *B. Ellison.*

CARDINAL POINT (USA) 3 ch.c. Sharpen Up 127 – Lavishly Bold (USA) **107** (Exuberant (USA)) [1990 NR 1991 7g* 9m* 8.1d* 8g²] IR 140,000Y: quite attractive colt: has a short, round action: first foal: dam, from family of Comtesse de Loir, won 6 times at up to 7f in USA: won maiden at York in May, then minor events at Newcastle (2 runners) and Chepstow (tremendously impressive in making all) in October: second favourite, 1½ lengths second of 7 to Hyabella in listed race at Newmarket, taking keen hold, always front rank and carrying head rather high over 1f out: useful form, and still looked inexperienced at Newmarket. *J. H. M. Gosden.*

CARDOUN (FR) 2 b.c. (Apr 25) Kaldoun – Cable Car (Fabulous Dancer) **122** [1991 6g² 6g* 7g* 7g² 7m⁵ 6.5d* 7v*]

One of the inevitable side effects of the continued success of the Breeders' Cup is that other significant races taking place at around the same time tend to be overlooked. In the latest season the two main trade papers

Criterium de Maisons-Laffitte—Cardoun beats the favourite Tertian

focussed their spotlight firmly on Churchill Downs for several days both before and after the Breeders' Cup took place, Arazi's scintillating display in the Breeders' Cup Juvenile providing the biggest talking point. And rightly so, but on the same day that Arazi demolished his rivals in Kentucky one of his earlier victims put up a performance to win the Criterium de Maisons-Laffitte which was worthy of better than the scant publicity it received. Cardoun was the horse in question, and the style of his victory suggests there's a good prize to be won with him in 1992 granted some give in the ground. Cardoun's promising debut at Saint-Cloud in June was followed by wins in a minor event at Evry and a listed race at Deauville, and after finishing a good second behind Marriage Secret in the valuable Challenge d'Or Piaget at Deauville again in August he was pitched in against Arazi in the Prix de la Salamandre at Longchamp. The task proved well beyond him at that point in his career. Prominent early, Cardoun couldn't respond as Arazi quickened early in the straight, and although he was staying on inside the final furlong he could manage only fifth of eight, close behind the placed horses yet some six lengths adrift of the highly impressive winner. With five outings behind him Cardoun seemed fairly well exposed; but much softer ground, as well as changed riding tactics, combined to allow him to show significant improvement on each of his last 2 outings. When waited with longer than previously in the Group 3 Prix Eclipse on dead ground at Saint-Cloud in October, Cardoun put up a smart performance to beat Pia Bride by three quarters of a length; and on ground that was very soft indeed at Maisons-Laffitte three weeks later he was seen in his most favourable light yet. Despite the fact that his Eclipse form gave him a leading chance, Cardoun started only third favourite in a field of eight behind the Somerville Tattersall Stakes winner Tertian (receiving 4 lb) and the Cheveley Park runner-up Absurde. Again he was ridden for a turn of foot, and the tactics paid a handsome dividend. Cardoun quickened smoothly in the testing conditions, drawing clear with Tertian in the final furlong and gradually getting the better of him to win by three quarters of a length with Absurde a further five lengths away in third. If Absurde ran up to the form she'd shown both at Newmarket and when winning a listed race at Evry by six lengths, Cardoun, and to a lesser extent Tertian, proved themselves potential classic contenders. Tertian may well have the greater scope for improvement, but Cardoun needs only to reproduce the best of his 1991 form to ensure that he won't be hard to place. A tilt at the Two Thousand Guineas in France or Britain will probably be his first main target.

		⎧Caro	⎧Fortino II
	⎧Kaldoun (FR)	⎨ (gr 1967)	⎩Chambord
	⎪ (gr 1975)	⎩Katana	⎧Le Haar
Cardoun (FR)	⎨	(b 1970)	⎩Embellie
(b.c. Apr 25, 1989)	⎪	⎧Fabulous Dancer	⎧Northern Dancer
	⎪Cable Car (FR)	⎨ (b 1976)	⎩Last of The Line
	⎩ (b 1984)	⎩Bay Area	⎧Youth
		(b 1979)	⎩Tyrant's Vale

Cardoun's sire Kaldoun is unlikely to be familiar to the majority of British racegoers. As a racehorse he was good without ever beating the best, winning five of his twenty starts at up to a mile between 1977 and 1980 and reaching the frame in a handful of pattern races. Now resident at the Haras d'Etreham, he's sired the winners of well over three hundred races including Balleroy, a smart colt at up to nine furlongs on his day, and the Prix du Cadran winner Mercalle. Cardoun is the first foal out of the Fabulous Dancer mare Cable Car and cost 320,000 francs (approximately £32,000) when sold as a yearling at Deauville in August. Cable Car won several times over middle distances at a modest level. Her dam Bay Area, successful at up to a mile and a quarter, has also produced winners by Bellman and Noblequest. At the moment Cardoun has shown clearly his best form over seven furlongs. He ought to have no problem staying a mile at three and may well prove effective over further. Whether he'll be so good a horse back on a fast surface is very much open to doubt. *E. Lellouche, France.*

CARD TRICK 3 ch.f. Good Times (ITY) – Double Shuffle 103 (Tachypous 128) — [1990 7m 1991 8g² 10.2d] sparely-made filly: no worthwhile form, in Newmarket

Challenge Whip (a match) and maiden claimer (bandaged off-hind) in summer at 3 yrs: should stay 1¼m. *G. A. Pritchard-Gordon.*

CAREFREE TIMES 4 b.g. Good Times (ITY) – Danaka (FR) (Val de Loir 133) [1990 9g6 8.5g3 8.2g2 11m* 12d 12g6 10d 1991 12d3 10.4d3 12g* 10.1m3 11.9m5 11s5 12g6 12f a11g5 10m5 11.8m 11.1s] big, strong gelding: poor mover: modest handicapper at 3 yrs: not so good nowadays: stays 1½m: acts on good to firm and dead ground: has found little: ran poorly when visored once: trained until after ninth start by M. Camacho: sold 4,500 gns Doncaster November Sales. *Miss S. E. Hall.*   **68** d

CAREFUL LAD 5 b.h. Precocious 126 – Arenetta (Bold Lad (IRE) 133) [1990 6m 7d 8m a8g 7g 1991 8m 8m 9m 8.2g 7m] sturdy, good-quartered horse: tubed: poor mover: bad handicapper nowadays: stays 7f: easily best effort on a soft surface: mostly blinkered at 5 yrs, visored once. *K. R. Burke.*   —

CARELESS LOVE 3 b.f. Top Ville 129 – La Carlotta (USA) (J O Tobin (USA) 130) [1990 7m 8g5 1991 10g 10.2m 8m2 7g5 8m4 8f 8m 8m] leggy filly: plating-class maiden: below form last 3 outings: likely to prove best at 1m: acts on good to firm ground: blinkered (stiff task, tailed off) final outing: has worn bandages: often slowly away: sold 1,400 gns Newmarket December Sales. *Mrs L. Piggott.*   **49**

CARESS 3 gr.f. Godswalk (USA) 130 – Skelton 70 (Derrylin 115) [1990 5f3 5f3 5g* 5m2 6f4 5g 7m 5v5 1991 a7g2 a7g4 a6g5 a8g3 8s5 6m3 6f*] leggy filly: poor walker and mover: plating-class performer: apprentice ridden, won claimer at Redcar in May: best form at 6f: seems unsuited by soft ground: usually bandaged. *Mrs N. Macauley.*   **51**

CARIBBEAN PRINCE 3 ch.c. Dara Monarch 128 – My Ginny 83 (Palestine 133) [1990 8g 7m 1991 7m 8.1s] strong, workmanlike colt: no worthwhile form in maidens and claimers: sold out of R. Hannon's stable 2,600 gns Newmarket September Sales after reappearance. *M. McCourt.*   —

CARISSIMA 3 b.f. Kind of Hush 118 – Divissima 62 (Music Boy 124) [1990 5g4 6m 6m 1991 a8g] strong, lengthy filly: poor maiden: tailed off in March claimer: seems unsuited by top-of-the-ground. *P. S. Felgate.*   —

CARLINGFORD (USA) 5 ch.h. Irish Castle (USA) – Delta Sal (USA) (Delta Judge) [1990 8m 12f 12g 12m4 1991 8g 8.2m4 12m 10.3m 8m4 10.5d5 13.8m3 13.6d3 15.1s4 a12g] rangy horse: lightly raced: quite modest handicapper nowadays: stays 13.8f: acts on firm and dead going: trained first 3 starts by K. McCauley. *H. A. T. Whiting.*   **60**

CARLTON APPOINTED (IRE) 2 b.f. (Mar 16) Auction Ring (USA) 123 – Overcall (Bustino 136) [1991 7m 7g3 7m6 8.1g] IR 7,000Y, 15,000 2-y-o: first foal: dam Irish middle-distance stayer: plating-class maiden: best effort third of 4 in auction at Edinburgh in July: should have stayed 1m: dead. *Denys Smith.*   **50**

CARLTON FLASH 3 b.f. Nishapour (FR) 125 – Photo Flash 119 (Match III 135) [1990 NR 1991 9g 10g 10m 8f] sturdy, plain filly: half-sister to several winners, including very useful stayer Golden Bowl (by Rheingold) and fairly useful 1985 2-y-o 7f winner High And Dry (by High Line): dam second in 1000 Guineas, is half-sister to Welsh Pageant: behind in maidens and median auction contest: sold 4,600 gns Newmarket December Sales. *K. O. Cunningham-Brown.*   —

CARLTON MOOR 4 gr.f. Mandrake Major 122 – Greyburn 85 (Saintly Song 128) [1990 8.2v6 8d 1991 8.2s] quite good-topped filly: no worthwhile form. *W. W. Haigh.*   —

CARLY-B (IRE) 3 b.f. Commanche Run 133 – Les Sylphides (FR) (Kashmir II 125) [1990 NR 1991 8g 11.5f 10g 10.1d3 13.8g6 11.8m 14.1m2 14.1f 12s a16g a12g] 8,200F, 15,500Y: good-topped filly: carries condition: moderate mover: half-sister to several winners, including 1m winner Na La Giri (by Nishapour) and useful 1986 2-y-o sprinter Quel Esprit (by What A Guest): dam, minor 1m winner in France, is sister to Moulines: worthwhile form only when second in seller at Nottingham: stays 1¾m: acts on good to firm ground: blinkered 4 times: trained first 8 starts by M. Ryan. *P. Howling.*   **42**

CARLYS GIRL 3 ch.f. Gabitat 119 – Adelong (Free State 125) [1990 NR 1991 8m 12m6 7g 10.2d 11m 8.9m] angular filly: second foal: dam little worthwhile form: no promise, including in sellers: unseated rider and bolted to post final start: joined M. Pipe. *J. M. Bradley.*   —

CARMELINA'S SHADOW 3 b.f. Shardari 134 – Carmelina 98 (Habitat 134) [1990 NR 1991 10m 10f 12f4 12.3f5 15.1g 15.1s] IR 9,400Y: leggy, unfurnished filly: has a round action: third foal: half-sister to 1m and 11f winner Copper River (by Glint of Gold) and Irish 1½m winner Corvallina (by Corvaro): dam, French 7.5f and 1m winner: plating-class maiden: should stay beyond 1½m: acts on firm going (tailed off on soft). *P. Calver.*

CARNBREA CUDDY (IRE) 3 ch.c. King of Clubs 124 – Mrs Tittlemouse 60 (Nonoalco (USA) 131) [1990 6g 6g⁴ 7m 7m* 8g 8m² 8.2s 1991 9s⁴ 10.2g 8g 7m³ 7m⁶ 7g 8m 12m 10.4m] leggy, workmanlike colt: has a round action: quite modest performer at best nowadays: ran in lack-lustre fashion last 2 starts: stays 1m: used to go well on good to firm ground: visored (below best) fifth start: sold 2,600 gns Newmarket Autumn Sales. *Dr J. D. Scargill.*

CARNEGIE DELI 4 b.f. Jester 119 – Lea Landing 81 (Meadow Court 129) [1990 47 d 9.5f 10g 8g 10m 10m 7d⁶ 5m 1991 a7g² a7g a7g⁵ 10v 10f 8m 6f 10.1d a7g⁶] sparely-made ex-Irish maiden: half-sister to several winners, including fairly useful 1979 Irish 2-y-o 7.5f winner Tilbury (by Realm): dam placed from 5f to 7f: poor form at best on Lingfield equitrack: no form on turf here: stays 7f: trained first 5 starts at 4 yrs by S. Dow. *J. J. Bridger.*

CARNFIELD 3 ch.f. Anfield 117 – Easterly Wind 94 (Windjammer (USA)) [1990 — NR 1991 10.6g 5f] 750F: lengthy, rather angular filly: moderate mover: sixth foal: half-sister to sprinter Northern Trust (by Music Boy) and 1m and 1¼m winner Shifting Breeze (by Night Shift): dam sprinter: behind in claimers, sweating profusely and on toes second start. *J. A. Glover.*

CARNIVAL BABY (USA) 3 ch.c. Northern Baby (CAN) 127 – Carnival 94 Princess (USA) (Prince John) [1990 7m⁶ 7s⁵ 1991 8m³ 8.5m* 8d* 10d* 10g 10.5f³ 10m 10d⁵] tall, good-topped colt: has scope: has a quick action: progressive form to win maiden at Beverley and handicaps at Ripon and Salisbury in June: inconsistent afterwards, good third to General Sikorski in £15,700 handicap at Haydock in September: will be much better suited by 1½m: acts on firm ground and dead. *M. R. Stoute.*

CARN MAIRE 3 b.f. Northern Prospect (USA) – Samsara (PER) (Golden Spur — (USA)) [1990 6g3 6g2 5m* 8f 6s2 5g6 1991 5d 8m 7m 8g 8.3m 6m] big, lengthy, angular filly: fair winner at 2 yrs: showed little in handicaps as 3-y-o: suited by 6f: easily best form on soft ground: sweating, on toes and took good hold penultimate start. *R. V. Smyth.*

CARNWATH 4 b.c. Auction Ring (USA) 123 – Carroldance (FR) (Lyphard (USA) 50 132) [1990 NR 1991 8.5f³] leggy, rather angular colt: closely related to Irish 1¼m winner Cold As Ice (by Bold Bidder) and half-brother to 1¼m seller winner Soft Shoe Shuffle (by Hard Fought) and fair 14.8f winner Freeby's Preacher (by Touching Wood): dam French 10.5f winner: 8 lengths third in maiden at Beverley in May: won 2 NH Flat races in January: dead. *C. E. Brittain.*

CAROLES CLOWN 5 gr.m. Another Realm 118 – Show Business 72 (Auction 33 § Ring (USA) 123) [1990 a6g a8g 12.5f 12m 12g5 1991 16.4m a16g6 15.4f³ 16m² 16m² 18.1m⁴ a16g a16g5] leggy, lightly-made mare: has a round action: poor handicapper nowadays: stays 2¼m: acts on firm ground: tried visored: has found little off bridle and looked a difficult ride. *M. J. Haynes.*

CAROLES EXPRESS 3 ch.f. Scottish Reel 123 – Peregrine Falcon (Saulingo 89 122) [1990 5d⁴ 6d² 6d³ 1991 7g³ 7.6d⁴ 7g² 7m* 7s* 7m 7g5 7.1m² 7.6m⁴ 8d² 6m 7m³] big, lengthy filly: moderate mover: fairly useful handicapper: won at Epsom (£7,100 event) and Lingfield in June: ran well most starts afterwards: best at 7f/1m: acts on good to firm ground and soft: usually makes running: tough and genuine. *R. Akehurst.*

CAROLE'S GUEST (IRE) 3 b.f. Be My Guest (USA) 126 – Mannevillette — (USA) (Foolish Pleasure (USA)) [1990 NR 1991 a8g 10g 10g 11.5m 16g 10.1m 10f a12g] 1,000 2-y-o: leggy, sparely-made filly: first living foal: dam unraced half-sister to very smart French 1m winner Nice Havrais: no sign of ability: blinkered final start. *C. Holmes.*

CAROLE'S KING (IRE) 3 b.g. Kings Lake (USA) 133 – Senane 86 (Vitiges 65 (FR) 132) [1990 6m* 7.5f6 6f5 7f4 8g3 8g5 8d3 1991 10g5 10g5 12g5 10m3 12d5 12g 10g 10m5 11.6m 8f5] good-bodied gelding: moderate walker and mover: modest handicapper: generally below form after fourth start: will prove better at 1½m than shorter: acts on firm and dead ground: effective with or without blinkers at 2 yrs: visored 4 times in 1991, running creditably on first occasion: not easiest of rides, and possibly unsatisfactory: winning hurdler. *W. Carter.*

CAROL'S PET (IRE) 3 b.f. Sadler's Wells (USA) 132 – Very Bissy (BRZ) — (Harken (URU)) [1990 NR 1991 8m³ 10.5g] 47,000Y: poor walker: third foal: half-sister to poor French maiden Circles of Dawn (by Blazing Saddles): dam Grade

1 winner in Brazil: no worthwhile form in maidens: mulish to post and looked reluctant to race after slow start final outing. *J. Banks.*

CAROLYN MAY 3 b.f. Gleaming Wave 103 – Smirloe VII (pedigree unknown) [1990 NR 1991 12d 10g 10.1m] sparely-made filly: has a round action: first foal: seems of little account. *R. J. R. Williams.* —

CAROMANDOO (IRE) 3 b.g. Simply Great (FR) 122 – Tanimara (Sassafras (FR) 135) [1990 6f⁴ a7g* 8g 7m* 7g³ 1991 a10g* a10g⁴ 10g² 12.3d 12g 10g* 10g 10m 10m] big, angular, unfurnished gelding: modest handicapper: won quite valuable events at Lingfield in March and July: stiffish tasks last 3 starts: best form at up to 1¼m: acts on good to firm ground: joined B. Murray. *M. Bell.* **75**

CAROMISH (USA) 4 br.f. Lyphard's Wish (FR) 124 – Carom (USA) (Caro 133) [1990 7.3m 6m 6m⁶ 6m 7g 6d 6m 7g³ 7.6v⁴ a8g 1991 6d⁶ 6m³ 6m 6v 6g⁶ 7f² 7f 7.6m 7m 7g 7d³ 6.1d] tall, rather leggy filly: fair handicapper at 3 yrs: mainly below form in 1991: stays 7f: probably acts on any going: inconsistent. *M. D. I. Usher.* **75 d**

CAROUSELLA 3 b.f. Rousillon (USA) 133 – Salchow 116 (Niniski (USA) 125) [1990 7m 8.2m 7m⁵ 1991 a8g a8g⁴ 8m 8.1m* 8d 7g 6.9s] rather leggy, close-coupled filly: has a quick action: quite modest form: won handicap at Sandown in September: should stay 1¼m: acts on good to firm ground: slowly away on all-weather: ran wide straight at Kempton (edgy, on toes) and Folkestone. *C. E. Brittain.* **62**

CAROUSEL MUSIC 4 b.f. On Your Mark 125 – Diana's Choice (Tudor Music 131) [1990 5m 9f 7m⁵ 8g² 9f⁵ 7d⁴ 8g 8m⁶ 10f⁴ 12f* 12m³ 12d⁴ 10m² 10m* 10g⁵ 10d⁵ 10s 1991 a13g a13g³ 9g 12m⁵] leggy filly: half-sister to Irish 9f and disqualified 1¼m winner Ramore Boy (by Corvaro): dam poor Irish maiden: won apprentice races at Ballinrobe and Limerick (handicap) as 3-y-o when trained by A. Hamill: no worthwhile form here, not seen out after June: stays 1½m: acts on firm and dead going. *J. Akehurst.* —

CAROUSEL ZINGIRA 2 b.f. (Mar 12) Reesh 117 – Lavenham Blue (Streetfighter 120) [1991 7m] 640f: good-topped filly: fourth foal: dam poor maiden: 100/1, burly and green, slowly away and always behind in 17-runner maiden at Ayr in September. *M. D. Hammond.* —

CARPANA 2 b.f. (Apr 7) Superlative 118 – Vestina 85 (Run The Gantlet (USA)) [1991 5.2d 5d² 5.1g* 6m⁵] quite good-topped filly: has scope: has a quick action: half-sister to fairly useful middle-distance winner Night-Shirt (by Night Shift), prolific Italian winner Mister Great (by Great Nephew) and a winner over hurdles: dam, 7f and 1¼m winner, is daughter of Irish 1000 Guineas winner Cloonagh: won maiden at Chester in July: ran moderately in nursery at Windsor following month: possibly unsuited by good to firm ground: sold 2,200 gns Newmarket Autumn Sales. *P. F. I. Cole.* **62**

CARPET CAPERS (USA) 7 b.g. Dance Bid (USA) 114 – Cofimvaba (FR) (Verrieres 131) [1990 NR 1991 10v 12f 16.4m] small, close-coupled gelding: poor handicapper at best: no form at 7 yrs: needs further than 7f and stays 1½m: acts on any going: seems best without blinkers or visor. *J. Ffitch-Heyes.* —

CARPET SLIPPERS 5 br.m. Daring March 116 – Mollified 67 (Lombard (GER) 126) [1990 14.8f⁵ 12g 11.7m³ 10m³ 10g* 10f* 12g 11.5g³ 12g 10d a10g⁶ 1991 12g⁴ 11.5m³ 10d 10g⁴ 10g 10g² 10f 11.4m 10g 10m a12g⁵ a10g⁶ a12g* a13g⁴] leggy, lengthy mare: quite modest handicapper: won at Lingfield in December: effective at 1½m to 1¾m: acts on firm going: has run creditably for lady: twice below form when blinkered: none too consistent. *J. D. Bethell.* **56**

CARRANTUOHILL (IRE) 2 b.f. (Mar 15) The Noble Player (USA) 126 – Translation (Fordham (USA) 117) [1991 7.1m 8m] IR 2,000Y, 6,800 2-y-o: unfurnished filly: second living foal: sister to a winner in Hong Kong: dam Irish maiden, is close relative of Sonnen Gold: bit backward, always behind in large-field maiden auctions. *A. Hide.* —

CARRIAGE BAY 2 br.c. (Apr 3) Carriage Way 107 – Central Carpets 70 (Garda's Revenge 119) [1991 5d] fourth foal: brother to poor 1988 2-y-o plater Valentine Lady, later successful abroad: dam sprinter: always well behind in seller at Doncaster in March: dead. *R. W. Stubbs.* **70**

CARRIG STAR (IRE) 2 b.c. (Apr 15) The Noble Player (USA) 126 – Tiefland (Right Tack 131) [1991 7.5d 7.5f 6d⁵] compact, sturdy colt: seventh foal: half-brother to Irish 5f winner Haulboulder (by He Loves Me): dam never ran: off course over 10 weeks and bit backward, kept on well when fifth of 23 in maiden at Haydock in October: will stay 7f: likely to improve again, and is one to bear in mind if dropped in class. *J. J. O'Neill.* **62 p**

CARROLLS MARC (IRE) 3 b.g. Horage 124 – Rare Find (Rarity 129) [1990 **65**
6m 6s³ a7g³ a7g³ a7g* 1991 a8g² a8g³] angular gelding: poor mover: modest winner
at 2 yrs: second at Lingfield, easily better effort in claimers early at 3 yrs: will stay
1¼m: joined P. Feilden. *M. Tompkins.*

CARRY ON CARY 5 b.g. Carriage Way 107 – Greenhill Lass (Upper Case **55**
(USA)) [1990 8m a10g a8g 1991 8f³ 10f² 8h 10.9g⁶ 9.7m⁴ 11.6m⁵ 14.6m] leggy,
sparely-made gelding: moderate walker and mover: quite modest handicapper at
best nowadays: pulled up lame final start: stays 1¼m: acts on any going: sometimes
bandaged. *R. W. Stubbs.*

CARTEL 4 b.g. Kris 135 – Meis El-Reem 124 (Auction Ring (USA) 123) [1990 6m³ **64**
8m³ 6f⁴ 1991 8d 8g 8.2f* 7m 8.2m 7m 8.2m* 8m a8g a7g] close-coupled gelding:
moderate handicapper: made all at Nottingham in September
(claimer, first win) and October: stays 1m: acts on firm ground: sold out of A. Scott's
stable 2,500 gns Newmarket July Sales after reappearance: none too consistent. *J.
L. Harris.*

CARVERALI (USA) 4 b.c. Roberto (USA) 131 – Far Beyond (USA) (Nijinsky **74**
(CAN) 138) [1990 10g 1991 10m⁵ 10f²] very big colt: lightly-raced maiden, not seen
out after second at Brighton in May: gave impression would be seen to better
advantage over 1½m on a flat, galloping track. *G. Harwood.*

CASA BELLA 4 b.f. Belfort (FR) 89 – Cassiar 84 (Connaught 130) [1990 8.5g **31**
8.2m 8g 8.2m⁶ 8.5f⁴ 10.6d 8m⁴ 9g 10m⁶ 8.2v 11m² 12d 1991 11g³ 12m⁶ 16m 11m⁴]
workmanlike filly: poor handicapper: stays 11f: acts on firm going: tried blinkered
once. *J. G. FitzGerald.*

CASANOVA (IRE) 2 b.c. (Feb 10) Petorius 117 – Silver Mantle 70 (Bustino 136) **51**
[1991 7m 7.1s 8m] IR 18,000Y: deep-girthed colt: keen walker: fifth foal: half-brother
to 3-y-o 1½m winner Master Foodbroker (by Simply Great) and minor French
middle-distance winner Pointe d'Argentee (by Pas de Seul): dam staying daughter
of Oaks third Moonlight Night, herself a half-sister to Main Reef: off course 3
months, worthwhile form only when eleventh of 15 in maiden at Leicester in
October: trained first 2 starts by R. Armstrong: sold 4,400 gns Newmarket Autumn
Sales. *R. Hannon.*

CASCADE 3 b.f. Shirley Heights 130 – Spin Turn (Homing 130) [1990 8.2m 8.2v **39** +
1991 12m 13.8m 14.1g 10g⁶] sturdy filly: poor on most form: stayed on well from rear
when sixth of 19 in seller (blinkered) at Ripon in July: will prove suited by more
enterprising tactics, and by return to 1½m: sweating penultimate start. *D. Morley.*

CASE LAW 4 ch.c. Ahonoora 122 – Travesty 63 (Reliance II 137) [1990 a6g* 6f* **113**
6g* 5d² 6g* 6f⁵ 6m⁶ a5g* 6g² 5.6g 6d 1991 6m* 6m 6g*] strong, good-bodied colt:
usually looks well: poor mover: very useful performer, improved as 4-y-o: won
listed race at Newmarket in April and Trafalgar House Sprint Stakes at Sandown
(gamely made all to beat Furajet by short head) in July: not seen out again,

Trafalgar House Sprint Stakes, Sandown—
Case Law (far side) and Furajet fight it out, with Montendre squeezed between them

reportedly had sinus operation: stays 6f: acts on good to firm ground: has won for apprentice: very tough and genuine: stays in training. *Sir Mark Prescott.*

CASEY OSCAR (USA)   2 b.c. (Apr 29) Known Fact (USA) 135 – Princess   **47**
Roberta (USA) (Roberto (USA) 131) [1991 8.1m⁵ 7m 10m] leggy, good-topped colt: third reported foal: half-brother to a winner in USA and France: dam stakes winner at up to 1m in USA: poor maiden: best effort on debut: sold 4,000 gns Newmarket Autumn Sales. *C. E. Brittain.*

CASH A MILLION (FR)   3 ch.g. Crofter (USA) 124 – Zertxuna (Averof 123)   **57**
[1990 NR 1991 6m* 7g a7g] 4,000Y: lengthy, good-quartered gelding: fifth foal: dam French 7.2f (at 2 yrs) and 11f winner out of Irish 1000 Guineas second Hannah Darling: 33/1, won maiden at Warwick in October, hanging left: always struggling in handicaps. *P. D. Cundell.*

CASHARII   4 ch.c. Ballacashtal (CAN) – Sister Rosarii (USA) (Properantes   —
(USA)) [1990 7f⁶ 1991 9s 7f⁶] workmanlike colt: poor mover: thrice raced and no worthwhile form in maidens. *W. G. M. Turner.*

CASHMIRIANA (IRE)   2 b.f. (Mar 2) Dominion 123 – Kashmiri Snow 83   **65**
(Shirley Heights 130) [1991 6s 5g⁴ 6g⁴] angular, useful-looking filly: has no near eye: third foal: half-sister to 3-y-o Pickles (by Petoski) and fairly useful 1m and 9f winner Gulmarg (by Gorytus): dam 1m winner: quite modest form when fourth in maidens at Folkestone (dwelt, stayed on well despite edging right) and Newbury (21 runners, keenly to post) in October: will be well suited by 7f +. *Miss H. C. Knight.*

CASHTAL DAZZLER   4 b.g. Ballacashtal (CAN) – Miss Meg 68 (John Splendid   **75**
116) [1990 8h⁵ 8m* 8.2f* 8g³ 8d 7.6f⁶ 8m² 8.2m 8m⁴ 10.6g 1991 8v⁵ 8m⁶ 8d⁴ 8m² 7m³ 8m⁶ 8d* 8.1g⁵ 8m⁶ 8d] leggy gelding: good walker: has a quick action: modest handicapper nowadays: won at Ayr in July: stays 1m: acts on any going: goes very well with forcing tactics: blinkered fourth to eighth starts, visored final one (ran moderately). *J. Berry.*

CASHTAL QUEEN   2 ch.f. (Mar 11) Ballacashtal (CAN) – Casbah Girl 79   **57**
(Native Bazaar 122) [1991 5g⁴ 5m³ 6f⁴ 6g² 6f* a6g* a6g⁶ 5m 6m⁵] rather leggy, sparely-made filly: first foal: dam 6f and 7f winner: quite modest form at best: easily made all in 4-runner selling nursery at Warwick (bought in 3,400 gns) and seller at Southwell (bought in 4,000 gns) later in July: stiff tasks after: stays 6f well: acts on firm going: gave trouble stalls first 2 outings. *J. Berry.*

CASHTAL RUNNER   2 ch.c. (Feb 3) Ballacashtal (CAN) – Woodrush 70   **51**
(Mummy's Pet 125) [1991 5m 5g 5f a6g 6d 5d⁴ 6d³ 5m⁴ 6g⁴ 5m 5.9h⁵ 8m] 500Y, 2,000 2-y-o: leggy, shallow-girthed colt: fifth foal: half-brother to 3-y-o C'Est Moi (by Kabour) and 1987 2-y-o 5f winner Quick Or Be Damned (by Mandrake Major): dam sprint plater: plating-class maiden: has run moderately in sellers: stays 6f: acts on hard and dead ground: effective with or without blinkers: has given trouble stalls: sometimes hangs, ran extremely wide bend at Ayr final start, and looks a difficult ride. *Mrs J. Jordan.*

CASIENNE (IRE)   3 ch.f. Doulab (USA) 115 – Borshch (Bonne Noel 115) [1990   **46**
5f⁵ 5.8h³ 8m 6m 8m 8.2d 1991 10.2g 9m 10.2d⁵ 8g⁵ 8f⁴ 8.9g³ 8f³ 8g⁶] sparely-made filly: poor maiden: stays 9f: acts on firm ground: blinkered fourth (below form) outing and final 3 at 2 yrs: winning hurdler. *R. J. Holder.*

CASILLA   3 b.f. Liboi (USA) 76 – Sdenka (FR) 79 (Habitat 134) [1990 NR 1991   —
10.2f⁴ 12m 10.2m 12g] smallish filly: tenth foal: sister to quite modest 1m winner Mansio and 1½m winner Incola: dam placed over 7f: well beaten in maidens and an apprentice event: bandaged behind and sweating final start. *H. Candy.*

CASNIKTONY   2 b.g. (Apr 26) Ilium 121 – Scottish Belle 78 (Scottish Rifle 127)   —
[1991 7.1s 7m] close-coupled gelding: fourth foal: dam placed 7 times from 6f to 7f at 2 yrs, stayed 2½m: soundly beaten at 100/1, latter occasion in minor event at Lingfield in August. *A. Moore.*

CASPIAN BELUGA   3 b.g. Persian Bold 123 – Miss Thames 105 (Tower Walk   **61**
130) [1990 6m² 7m² 7m 1991 8g 10.2g a12g] strong, close-coupled gelding: quite modest handicapper: 33/1 on first run for 6½ months, form as 3-y-o only when ninth of 16 at Lingfield final outing: evidently better suited by 1½m than shorter: sold out of M. Stoute's stable 7,000 gns Ascot June Sales after second start. *Mrs A. Knight.*

CASPIAN GATES   7 b.g. Persian Bold 123 – Galka 98 (Deep Diver 134) [1990   **47**
10.8m 11.7g 12f⁵ 13.8m³ 14m² 11.5g³ 16m 14m⁵ 12f² 14m⁶ a12g 1991 12m* 12g⁶ 11.5g 11f 12g] small, sturdy gelding: carries plenty of condition: has round action: quite modest handicapper at 6 yrs: well below form at 7 yrs after winning at Pontefract in May, not seen out after July: stays 1¾m: suited by a sound surface: ran badly on

Racecall Gold Trophy, Redcar—
Casteddu surges through to win from Prince Ferdinand,
Fair Crack (hooped sleeves), Herora (No. 25) and Diamond Mine

fibresand: has been tried in blinkers: often sweats: sold 1,000 gns Newmarket Autumn Sales. *A. N. Lee.*

CASPIAN GREY 3 gr.g. Absalom 128 – Sea Aura 89 (Roi Soleil 125) [1990 6m⁴ 6m* a7g⁶ 1991 6d 6g 6m 7m⁴ 8g] good-bodied gelding: modest winner at 2 yrs: showed he retains a little ability as 3-y-o penultimate start: should stay 1m: sold out of M. Tompkins' stable only 1,800 gns Doncaster January Sales. *D. A. Wilson.* **42 +**

CASPIAN MIST 6 b.m. Remainder Man 126§ – Bay Foulard (Shantung 132) [1990 14.8m² 16g⁵ 12f 12m⁴ 1991 16m⁵ 14.6m² 14.6g³ 16.2d] big, good-bodied mare: moderate mover: plating-class handicapper nowadays: stays 14.8f: acts on any going: sold 4,800 gns Doncaster October Sales. *R. Hollinshead.* **56**

CASTCAREAWAY (FR) 3 b.c. Caerleon (USA) 132 – Castaway (FR) (Filiberto (USA) 123) [1990 6d 7m⁵ 7m⁵ 6g² 7s 7d 6g⁴ 8g a7g² 1991 a6g⁶ a6g⁴ a10g⁶ 5d⁵ 7g 5m 5m 9.7m 11.5m²] angular colt: moderate walker and mover: plating-class maiden: better at 11.5f than shorter nowadays: acts on good to firm and dead ground: twice visored, often blinkered (wasn't final start): inconsistent. *C. A. Austin.* **53**

CASTEDDU 2 b.c. (Mar 25) Efisio 120 – Bias 108 (Royal Prerogative 119) [1991 5g⁴ 6g² 6g³ 7m* 7d* 6g*] 34,000Y, 60,000 2-y-o: smallish, sturdy colt: has a round action: half-brother to useful 3-y-o Vintage Only (by Sayf El Arab), 5f and 6f winner at 2 yrs: dam won from 7f to 10.4f: off course 2 months after finishing 4½ lengths third of 14 to Dilum in Coventry Stakes at Royal Ascot: well below best when winning maiden at Lingfield (met lot of trouble in running) in September: showed improved form final 2 starts, winning £10,100 graduation at Ascot shade comfortably by ¾ length from Secret Thing and £93,700 25-runner Racecall Gold Trophy at Redcar (looked in splendid shape) 17 days later, soon outpaced but staying on gamely to beat Prince Ferdinand by 1½ lengths: will probably stay 1m: acts on dead ground: often on toes in paddock, wasn't at Redcar: likely to make up into good-class performer at 3 yrs. *J. W. Payne.* **109 p**

CASTILIAN QUEEN (USA) 2 ch.f. (Feb 20) Diesis 133 – Royal Heroine 121 (Lypheor 118) [1991 6g* 6m⁶] sturdy filly: third reported foal: closely related to 3-y-o Regal Sabre (by Sharpen Up), useful 6f (at 2 yrs) and 7f winner who stays 1¼m: dam 6f to 9.2f winner later won Breeders' Cup Mile: impressive odds-on **71 +**

winner of 12-runner maiden at Leicester: well-beaten last of 6 when heavily backed in £9,300 event at Ascot later in June: will stay at least 1m. *J. H. M. Gosden.*

CASTILLET 2 b.c. (Apr 20) Rousillon (USA) 133 – Strident Note 89 (The **78** Minstrel (CAN) 135) [1991 7g 7m² 10m* 10g] rangy colt: third foal: dam, maiden best at 2 yrs, is half-sister to Teenoso and Topsy: modest performer: won maiden at Nottingham in October by ¾ unlucky Grand Master, taking keen hold then quickening to lead over 1f out: ran creditably behind Bonny Scot in listed race at Newmarket following month: stays 1¼m: acts on good to firm ground. *G. Harwood.*

CASTLEACRE 5 ch.g. Mr Fluorocarbon 126 – Misfired 101 (Blast 125) [1990 NR — 1991 8m 10.3d] small, angular, sparely-made gelding: quite modest maiden as 3-y-o: soundly beaten in handicaps in 1991: stays 11.5f: yet to race on very soft going, appears to act on any other. *C. A. Smith.*

CASTLE CARY 5 gr.m. Castle Keep 121 – Tibouchina 75 (Runnymede 123) **44** [1990 6m 5g⁴ 5f⁵ 5m⁵ 6m³ 5m 6m 5m⁴ 6g 5m² 5g a5g⁶ 1991 a5g 6v 5g 10m 5m* a5g 5m² 5f⁴ 5g 5.1s a6g] workmanlike mare: carries condition: has a quick action: poor handicapper: won (for first time) at Windsor in August: stays 6f: acts on any going: sometimes bandaged: blinkered on reappearance: has found little off bridle: sold out of M. Blanshard's stable 850 gns Ascot July Sales after fourth start, out of J. White's stable 2,600 gns Doncaster October Sales. *T. Craig.*

CASTLE CHANCEL 3 b.g. Castle Keep 121 – Peteona 97 (Welsh Saint 126) **100** [1990 NR 1991 10m² 11.7g² 12.2d² 14m* 12m* 16.2d] lengthy, workmanlike gelding: brother to 3 winners, including 1989 2-y-o 1m winner Castle Courageous, 13.3f and 14.8f winner in 1991: dam 5f to 1m winner: won maiden (6/4 on, easily) at Haydock in September and moderately-run £8,000 handicap at Newmarket in October: soundly beaten in £11,500 handicap at Ascot: effective at 1½m and 1¾m: acts on good to firm ground and dead: may prove capable of better. *Lady Herries.*

CASTLE CLOUD (USA) 2 ch.g. (Apr 3) Irish Castle (USA) – Tracy L (USA) **73** (Bold Favorite (USA)) [1991 5s* 5d* 5m⁴ 5m⁶ 6m 8g] leggy, close-coupled gelding: half-brother to a winner in USA by Cox's Ridge and quite modest Trace of Irony (by Cannonade): dam won at up to 9f: modest form: successful in maiden at Hamilton and 4-runner minor event at Ascot in spring: not discredited when last in listed race Group 3 event next 2 starts, soundly beaten in nurseries subsequently: should stay beyond 5f: acts on good to firm and soft ground: sold 13,500 gns Newmarket Autumn Sales. *J. Berry.*

CASTLE CLOWN 6 ch.g. Castle Keep 121 – Peteona 97 (Welsh Saint 126) [1990 **73** 10g² 11m⁵ 11.5m³ 1991 12m⁵ 10d⁵ 10m 9s 12s 11.4m²] tall, lengthy gelding: modest handicapper nowadays: stays 11.5f: yet to show his best form on extremes of going: best visored: has run well for amateur. *Lady Herries.*

CASTLE COURAGEOUS 4 b.g. Castle Keep 121 – Peteona 97 (Welsh Saint **94** 126) [1990 8m⁶ 12m³ 12m 12m 1991 12g⁶ 11d³ 13.3d* 14.8d* 14g⁴ 13.9g 14g 12d⁶] leggy, angular gelding: good walker: fairly useful handicapper: won at Newbury and Warwick in June: below form after next start: well worth a try over 2m: acts on good to firm and dead ground. *Lady Herries.*

CASTLE GALAH 4 b.f. Castle Keep 121 – My Pink Parrot (Pirate King 129) — [1990 8m 7d a8g 1991 10g] tall, leggy filly: half-sister to several winners here and abroad: always behind in maidens and claimers. *S. Woodman.*

CASTLE MAID 4 b.f. Castle Keep 121 – Village Lass (No Mercy 126) [1990 7m **45** 7m 6g 8m⁵ 1991 5g³ 5g⁴ 6g 6g⁶ 5m³ 5m⁶ 8.2f] rangy, workmanlike filly: poor handicapper: should stay beyond 5f: acts on good to firm ground. *R. J. Hodges.*

CASTLE MERLIN 3 ch.c. Scottish Reel 123 – Aunt Winnie (Wolver Hollow **50** 126) [1990 7m a8g a7g a8g⁵ 1991 a8g⁴ a10g a8g 12s² 12.3s⁶ 12m⁵ 15.9d⁵] leggy, close-coupled colt: plating-class maiden: well beaten in Chester handicap final start, first for 5½ months: shapes like a stayer: acts on soft going: trained first 2 starts by R. Muddle: sold out of R. Ingram's stable 3,200 gns Doncaster August Sales after sixth. *E. J. Alston.*

CASTLEREA LAD 2 b.c. (Mar 31) Efisio 120 – Halo 51 (Godswalk (USA) 130) **72** [1991 5d² 5d⁴ 5m³ 6g* 6f³ 6m³] 2,200F, IR 3,800Y: quite good-topped colt: third foal: dam poor daughter of sister to Thatching: modest performer: won maiden auction at Pontefract in June: good third in nurseries at Haydock (when bit backward) and Doncaster (sweating and edgy) within a week 3 months later: may not stay beyond 6f: acts on firm and good to soft ground: consistent. *R. Hollinshead.*

CASTLE SECRET 5 b.g. Castle Keep 121 – Baffle 87 (Petingo 135) [1990 14s **83** 16.2d* 16m 14m⁴ 16.2g³ 1991 17.6m² 22.2m⁵] quite attractive gelding: moderate mover with a quick action: fair handicapper: ungenuine at 4 yrs but gelded and did little wrong in 1991: fifth to Easy To Please in Queen Alexandra Stakes at Royal Ascot: stays very well: possibly unsuited by soft going nowadays, acts on any other: ran well when blinkered at 4 yrs. *D. Burchell.*

CASTORET 5 b.g. Jalmood (USA) 126 – Blaskette 99 (Blast 125) [1990 8g 8g⁶ **79** 10s* a10g⁵ 1991 12g⁴ 10.4d 11.1g* 12g 11.5d 14g* 13.3m² 16.2d⁵ 16.5d⁶ a14g] useful-looking gelding: fair handicapper: won at Kempton in May and September: good running-on second in Coral Autumn Cup at Newbury: below form after: seems suited by around 1¾m: acts on good to firm and soft going: suitable mount for an apprentice. *J. W. Hills.*

CASUAL FLING 2 b.f. (Jun 5) Sizzling Melody 117 – Melody Hour 105 (Sing **43** Sing 134) [1991 5g 6g 6g 6s 5g 6m] leggy filly: half-sister to several winners, including very useful middle-distance filly Sing Softly (by Luthier) and fairly useful stayer Military Band (by Sassafras): dam 5f winner at 2 yrs: form only in maiden at Kempton (flashed tail, looked irresolute) second start: visored in seller final outing: sold 880 gns Newmarket Autumn Sales. *D. R. Laing.*

CATALANI 6 ch.m. Music Boy 124 – Two Stroke (Malicious) [1990 NR 1991 a7g — a5g⁶ a6g⁵] workmanlike, angular mare: very lightly raced and fair performer at best as 4-y-o: behind in handicap and claimers at Lingfield in 1991: stays 6f: acts on good to firm ground, probably not at her best on heavy going. *T. J. Naughton.*

CATCHPENNY 2 b.f. (Mar 19) Petong 126 – Catechism (Mummy's Pet 125) — [1991 5d⁶ 5g] narrow, angular filly: poor walker: first foal: dam once-raced daughter of half-sister to high-class sprinter Caerphilly: soundly-beaten last in Pontefract maiden and claimer at Ayr in July: sold 600 gns Doncaster October Sales. *M. Brittain.*

CATEL RING (IRE) 2 b.c. (Mar 23) Auction Ring (USA) 123 – Dame Kelly **48** (Pitskelly 122) [1991 7m 8m 8m] 2,600Y: workmanlike colt: half-brother to 1m to 1½m winner Andrew's First (by Tender King) and a winner in Sweden: dam no worthwhile form in Ireland: poor maiden: well beaten in seller at Newmarket (bandaged behind) second outing: stays 1m. *I. Campbell.*

CATHERINE D'ORLEAC 2 b.f. (May 9) Mashhor Dancer (USA) – Tremellick — 87 (Mummy's Pet 125) [1991 5f 5m⁶] 2,400Y: sparely-made filly: sixth foal: half-sister to 1¼m seller winner Cadenette (by Brigadier Gerard) and useful hurdler Lanhydrock (by Tower Walk): dam won 3 times over 5f: well beaten in maiden auction at Pontefract (bandaged near-fore) and seller at Beverley in spring. *M. J. Camacho.*

CATHERINES WELL 8 ch.m. Junius (USA) 124 – Restless Lady (Sandford **68** Lad 133) [1990 NR 1991 6d 6m 6m 5m⁵ 5.9m⁶ 5f⁴ 5f* 6f³ 5.1m 5f⁴ 6f* 5m⁶ 6m 5m⁶ 5g⁴ 5s] lengthy mare: quite modest handicapper nowadays: went to stud in 1987, and has had 3 foals: successful in apprentice events at Catterick (landed gamble) in July and Ripon in August: effective at 5f and 6f: probably acts on any going. *M. W. Easterby.*

CATHOS (FR) 6 b.g. Bellman (FR) 123 – Charming Doll (Don (ITY) 123) [1990 **64** a14g³a12g⁴a16g²a16g²a13g* 12f 14g 14m 12g* 16m⁵ 16m⁵ 12f² 10m* 14m² 11.5m² 12f* 12.2f* 15.5f² 10.6d⁵ 11s 12s a16g a10g 1991 a14g³ a13g⁴ 12m 14m 10.6g 12.3d 12d⁶ 12m 12f* 10m 16.2f² 11.4m 10m 12.2m² 10.5g 12g 9.7f 10.3d] leggy gelding: has a rather round action: quite modest and inconsistent handicapper as 6-y-o: won amateurs event at Beverley in July: stays 2m: unsuited by very soft going, acts on any other: has worn blinkers: bandaged final start: often starts slowly: has looked unenthusiastic, and refused to race over hurdles once in 1991. *D. A. Wilson.*

CATUNDRA (IRE) 3 ch.f. Far North (CAN) 120 – 'tis A Kitten (USA) (Tisab **61** (USA)) [1990 a7g* 1991 9d 8m 7m² 6.9m 7d] leggy, angular filly: led post in maiden at Southwell at 2 yrs: contested handicaps then seller in 1991, showing she retains ability only when second at Wolverhampton: should stay beyond 7f: sweating, edgy and unruly at start final appearance: joined Mrs A. Knight. *W. Jarvis.*

CAUSLEY 6 br.g. Swing Easy (USA) 126 – Four Lawns 77 (Forlorn River 124) **75** [1990 a8g⁴ 9f² 8m⁶ 8.2f³ 10d⁴ 8f² 8.2s 8g* 8.2s* 8m² 8.2f² 8.2d² 8m 7g³ 7d³ 8d 1991 7.5g* 7.5f 8m² 7f⁶ 8.9m 8m⁵ 7.9m⁶ 8g³ 7.5f⁶ 8.3m³ 8f² 8.5f⁶ 8g 7.9m³ 7.6d⁴] good-topped, workmanlike gelding: has a round action: modest handicapper: won at Beverley in April: effective at 7f to 1m: possibly unsuited by extremes of going nowadays, acts on any other: good mount for inexperienced rider: well suited by forcing tactics: has been mulish at stalls: very tough and largely consistent. *B. A. McMahon.*

CAUTIONARY TALE 2 gr.c. (Mar 17) Sharrood (USA) 124 – Prudence 68 **74**
(Grundy 137) [1991 7m⁵ 8.2f⁴ 8.5f² 7m 8.1m*] 54,000F, 46,000Y: good-bodied colt:
has scope: third foal: half-brother to winners in Holland and Germany: dam, seemed
to stay middle distances, is half-sister to Ribblesdale winner Strigida: modest
performer: beaten at long odds on in 3-runner event at Beverley third outing: won
13-runner maiden at Edinburgh (awkward stalls) in October, making all and running
on well: will be suited by further than 1m: blinkered (ran well in valuable event)
penultimate start: sold 22,000 gns Newmarket Autumn Sales. *W. Jarvis.*

CAVEAT VENDOR 3 b.g. Auction Ring (USA) 123 – Star Court 102 (Aureole —
132) [1990 8f³ 8m³ 7d 7d 1991 8.3f⁶ 8m 12.1f⁶ 8m] workmanlike gelding: quite
modest maiden: best effort at 3 yrs, running fairly well, on reappearance: stays 1m
well: below form on dead ground: blinkered final start: has joined P. Haslam. *W. J.
Pearce.*

CAVE ROAD 2 b.c. (Jun 1) Crofthall 110 – Noor Jehan (Taj Dewan 128) [1991 5f⁴ **55**
5f⁶ 5m⁶ 8m 6m] rather leggy, unfurnished colt: looks weak: poor mover: fourth foal:
dam never ran: plating-class maiden: form only at 5f: sold 2,000 gns Newmarket
Autumn Sales. *J. G. FitzGerald.*

CAVIAR QUEEN (IRE) 3 ch.f. Kings Lake (USA) 133 – Syrian Sea (USA) —
(Bold Ruler) [1990 NR 1991 8g⁴ 10g 8d 9m⁴ 12m a8g³ a12g 10.1d a8g⁵ 10s] 24,000Y:
lengthy, angular filly: moderate walker: bad mover: half-sister to Alada (by Riva
Ridge), a good-class filly at around 1m in North America, and a winner in Argentina:
dam, one of leading 2-y-o fillies in USA in 1967, is sister to Secretariat: plating-class
maiden: may prove ideally suited by 1¼m: best efforts on a sound surface. *C. A.
Cyzer.*

CAVO GRECO (USA) 2 b.c. (Mar 31) Riverman (USA) 131 – Cypria Sacra — p
(USA) 103 (Sharpen Up 127) [1991 8.1d] smallish, lengthy colt: first foal: dam 11.7f
and 1½m winner: 14/1, slowly away and always behind in 10-runner maiden at
Haydock in October: wore small bandages behind: should do better. *P. F. I. Cole.*

CAWANAIGA (IRE) 3 b.g. Ballad Rock 122 – The Way She Moves (North —
Stoke 130) [1990 NR 1991 7m⁶ 8g] IR 3,000Y, 4,400Y: tall, rather sparely-made
gelding: fourth foal: half-brother to modest 1988 2-y-o 7f winner Welsh Governor
(by Welsh Term) and a winner in Scandinavia: dam, little worthwhile form, from
family of Master Willie: never dangerous in maiden and maiden claimer in the
spring. *E. H. Owen jun.*

CBS MERCHANT 2 b.c. (May 8) King of Spain 121 – Queens Welcome 60 —
(Northfields (USA)) [1991 6d 6g 6m 5d⁶ 7m] leggy colt: third foal: half-brother to
4-y-o 7f winner Susanna's Secret (by Superlative): dam, ran only at 2 yrs, is
half-sister to high-class 1973 2-y-o sprinter The Blues: seems of little account:
blinkered last 3 starts: has worn bandages. *M. Brittain.*

CBS RANDOLPH (IRE) 2 b.c. (Mar 28) Petorius 117 – Passage To India (FR) **44**
(Gay Mecene (USA) 128) [1991 a6g 5.1g 6m 7m 7m⁴ 7g 7g] IR 5,400Y, 12,500 2-y-o:
workmanlike colt: first foal: dam half-sister to useful stayer Angel City: worthwhile
form only when fourth of 8 in seller at Yarmouth in July: will stay 1m. *I. Campbell.*

CEATHARLACH 2 b.g. (Apr 7) Sayf El Arab (USA) 127 – Kilttaley 74 (Tower **44**
Walk 130) [1991 5d 6g 6.1g³] 750Y: leggy gelding: third foal: dam stayed 1m: poor
maiden: blinkered, best effort third of 6 in claimer at Chepstow. *R. J. Holder.*

CEE-EN-CEE 7 b.g. Junius (USA) 124 – Lady Red Rose 87 (Pitskelly 122) [1990 **66**
6f³ 6m² 6m 7g 6m⁵ 6m² 6g² 5m⁴ 6f⁵ 7f³ 5m 6m 7m⁶ 5.8f* 7g* 6g 5m 7g 1991 7m 6g⁶
6g 6g 7m³ 7g⁴ 7g⁵ 8.3m 6m⁵ 5.7f* 7s 5.1g⁴ a7g⁶ a7g² a7g a6g⁴] workmanlike
gelding: has a round action: quite modest handicapper: won Lyegrove Handicap (for
third time) at Bath in September: effective at 5f to 7f: goes particularly well on a
sound surface: has won for apprentice: best in blinkers or visor: inconsistent. *M.
McCourt.*

CEE-JAY-AY 4 gr.g. Free State 125 – Raffinrula 75 (Raffingora 130) [1990 9s 7m² **69**
7g 7f² 8m 7g² 7m* 7.6m* 8f* a7g* 7m³ 7.6g⁶ 7d 1991 a7g 7g² 7.6d⁵ 8m 7g⁵ 7m²
8.1m 7d⁶ 7m 8g² 7f⁴ 7.6m⁵ 7m⁶ 7.5f* 7g⁵ 7m⁴ 7.6d⁵ 12g⁴] smallish, workmanlike
gelding: easy mover: modest handicapper: effective at 7f and 1m: acts on firm and
dead going: below form when blinkered once: often slowly away. *J. Berry.*

CELERY SALT (USA) 3 ch.g. Miswaki (USA) 124 – Sea Flavour (Sea Bird II —
145) [1990 6f 6g 1991 6d 8m] compact, good-quartered gelding: no worthwhile form
in maidens and handicap: bandaged off-fore on reappearance: sweating and on toes
at 3 yrs: sold to join K. Morgan 3,600 gns Ascot June Sales and gelded. *J. L. Dunlop.*

CELESTIAL GUEST (USA) 4 b.c. Northjet 136 – Tobira Celeste (USA) **74**
(Ribot 142) [1990 10f³ 12f* 14m⁴ 12m 1991 13d 12m³ 12m 12m 10m³ 11.5d 10.1m²

10.1m² 10g³ 10g⁶ 12s] sturdy colt: has a fluent action: modest handicapper: should prove better suited by 1½m than shorter: suited by sound surface: has run well when sweating: has hung, and gives impression not easiest of rides: sold 26,000 gns Doncaster August Sales after penultimate start. *R. Guest.*

CELESTIAL SKY 3 ch.c. Bairn (USA) 126 – Angels Are Blue 73 (Stanford 121§) **58** [1990 5g⁶ 6m 5m⁵ 6g⁴ 7.3g⁴ 1991 8g⁵] sturdy, workmanlike colt: carries condition: progressive maiden at 2 yrs: ran creditably in April handicap, only outing in 1991: stays 1m. *P. W. Harris.*

CELESTINE 2 b.f. (May 1) Skyliner 117 – Stellaris (Star Appeal 133) [1991 5f 5f **52** 7m⁴ 7m 5g* 5m⁴ 5d] leggy, close-coupled filly: third living foal: half-sister to 6f and 7f winner Ashdren (by Lochnager): dam ran 4 times at 3 yrs: won claimer at Edinburgh in September: best form at 5f, but may prove ideally suited by further: acts on good to firm ground: blinkered fifth and sixth starts, visored (ran poorly) final one. *T. Fairhurst.*

CELIA BRADY 3 b.f. Last Tycoon 131 – Lucayan Princess 111 (High Line 125) **62** + [1990 NR 1991 8m* 8.1m] 35,000Y: leggy, sparely-made filly: first foal: dam 2-y-o 7f winner stayed 1½m: won maiden at Warwick in August by neck, very green: last of 10 facing extremely stiff task in handicap over 3 weeks later: may be capable of better. *H. Candy.*

CELLITO (IRE) 2 b.c. (Feb 18) Flash of Steel 120 – Apocalypse (Auction Ring **62** (USA) 123) [1991 a8g a7g² a8g] sixth foal: half-brother to 5f (at 2 yrs) and 8.2f winner Lars Porsena (by Trojan Fen): dam French 1m winner, is half-sister to King's Company and Deep Diver: quite modest form: second in late-year maiden at Southwell, easily best effort: should stay 1m. *W. A. O'Gorman.*

CELTIC BOB 11 ch.g. Celtic Cone 116 – Quaife Sport (Quayside 124) [1990 NR **53** 1991 a12g* a11g⁵ 12.1d³] small, sturdy gelding: only second run on flat, won maiden at Lingfield in January: stiff task final start, in July: will stay beyond 1½m: fairly useful hurdler. *O. O'Neill.*

CELTIC CHIMES 7 ch.m. Celtic Cone 116 – Dyna Bell 62 (Double Jump 131) — [1990 7m² 9m⁵ 1991 12f] stocky mare: moderate mover: little sign of ability on flat: has been tried blinkered and visored: sold 925 gns Ascot September Sales. *G. P. Enright.*

CENTENARY STAR 6 b.g. Broadsword (USA) 104 – Tina's Gold 66 (Goldhill — 125) [1990 a12g² 16m⁵ a14g⁶ 1991 16m] leggy gelding: trained by R. Hollinshead, form at 5 yrs only when second at Southwell: stiff task but showed signs of ability in Redcar handicap only start as 6-y-o (October): stays 1½m: usually apprentice ridden: fair hurdler: may do better. *Mrs G. R. Reveley.*

CENTERLAND (USA) 4 ch.c. Green Forest (USA) 134 – Pompoes (DEN) 117 **97** (Belmont (FR)) [1990 6m⁴ 6f* 7f* 6f* 6m* 6m⁴ 8g 5g³ 6m 1991 6g⁵ 6m 6f² 6m 8.5f] strong, lengthy colt: moderate walker: useful performer: best effort at 4 yrs when second of 5 in minor event at Folkestone in May: sweating, hampered start and always behind in claimer at Monmouth Park, USA, final one: stays 7f: acts on firm ground. *M. Moubarak.*

CENTRAL CITY 2 b.f. (Mar 22) Midyan (USA) 124 – Miss Silca Key 102 (Welsh **93** Saint 126) [1991 5g* 5m* 5g³] 26,000Y: well-grown filly, rather unfurnished: fourth foal: half-sister to 3-y-o 1m winner Consigliere (by Caerleon), useful 6f winner Silca Supreme (by Chief Singer) and useful but disappointing maiden Silca An' Key (by Commanche Run): dam won 7f Jersey Stakes: successful in 9-runner maiden at Kempton and 5-runner minor event (showed smart turn of foot) at Salisbury in spring: looking very well, showed improved form when over a length third of 14, leading over 4f, to Marling in Queen Mary Stakes at Royal Ascot: should stay 7f: seemed sure to win more races, but wasn't seen again. *R. Hannon.*

CERTAIN LADY 2 ch.f. (Mar 16) Absalom 128 – Bold Duchess 78 (Persian Bold **49** 123) [1991 5g 6g 5g³ 5.2g* 5s⁴ 6f 5.2f 5m 6.1m² a6g³ a6g] 1,000Y: lengthy, good-bodied filly: has a round action: first foal: dam 1m winner: no bid after winning Yarmouth seller in June: ran well when placed late in year: may well stay 7f: acts on good to firm ground and on equitrack: has run well for 7-lb claimer: inconsistent: retained by trainer 575 gns Ascot September Sales. *G. Blum.*

CERTAIN RISK 2 ch.f. (Apr 8) Risk Me (FR) 127 – Game Sovereign (Owen **77** Anthony 102) [1991 5d* 5d* 5s*] lengthy filly: has scope: third foal: dam unraced: successful in seller (retained 4,800 gns after winning by over 10 lengths) at Doncaster, and minor events at Ripon and Windsor in spring: acts well on soft ground: was progressing well: sold to race in Sweden. *R. Hannon.*

C'EST MOI 3 br.f. Kabour 80 – Woodrush 70 (Mummy's Pet 125) [1990 NR 1991 —
a7g a7g 8m⁵ 6g 5f 6f 6.1m 5g] sturdy filly: fourth reported foal: half-sister to quite
modest 1987 2-y-o 5f winner Quick Or Be Damned (by Mandrake Major): dam sprint
plater: no worthwhile form in maidens and handicaps: blinkered (swerved stalls)
final start: sold 700 gns Doncaster October Sales. *D. W. Chapman.*

CHADLEIGH HOUSE 2 gr.c. (Apr 28) Sharrood (USA) 124 – Hability (Habitat 77
134) [1991 5d* 5g³ 5d* 6g⁴ 5g³ 6g⁵ 6g³ 5v3] 6,800Y: sturdy colt: fifth living foal:
half-brother to 1989 2-y-o 7f winner Antoinette Jane (by Ile de Bourbon): dam
unraced daughter of July Cup winner Parsimony, from an excellent sprinting family:
modest performer: successful in minor events at Catterick in March and Chester in
May: left R. Hollinshead's stable after fourth outing: has since raced only in Italy,
including finishing third over 5f and 6f in 3 small-field listed races: stays 6f: goes
well with give in the ground. *R. Brogi, Italy.*

CHADWICK GREEN 3 b.f. Green Ruby (USA) 104 – Our Children 49 —
(Mandrake Major 122) [1990 NR 1991 7g⁴] lengthy filly: first foal: dam won 6f seller:
tailed-off last in useful company for minor event at Doncaster in July. *P. A. Blockley.*

CHADWICK'S GINGER 3 ch.f. Crofthall 110 – Knight Hunter (Skyliner 117) —
[1990 NR 1991 8m 11.8m³ 11.8g 11.8g] leggy, rather angular filly: first foal: dam
probably of little account: well beaten, but showed signs of ability: burly and
troublesome in preliminaries before handicap final start: likely to prove best short
of 1½m. *K. S. Bridgwater.*

CHAFF 4 b.g. Final Straw 127 – Silky (USA) 112 (Nijinsky (CAN) 138) [1990 7m 41
8m 8.2g 1991 a10g a7g 7f 7f 7g⁶ 7g 8.1g 9.7m 8m³ 9.7f 8m² 8m⁶] smallish, angular
gelding: shows a quick action: poor performer at best: worth another try beyond 1m:
acts on good to firm ground: inconsistent. *D. Morris.*

CHAIN SHOT 6 b.g. Pas de Seul 133 – Burnished (Formidable (USA) 125) [1990 —
NR 1991 a7g] sturdy, workmanlike gelding: moderate mover: quite modest
handicapper at best: no show only run at 6 yrs (January): effective at 5f and 6f: acts
on any going: sometimes blinkered or visored: not an easy ride. *J. H. Peacock.*

CHAKALAK 3 b.c. Damister (USA) 123 – Wig And Gown (Mandamus 120) [1990 62
8m 7s⁶ 1991 10d⁵ 10m 10g⁴ 12.2m* 12.5m* 12g⁴ 11.5g a12g* a12g² a14g*] a78
strong, compact colt: poor mover: fair handicapper: successful at Warwick and
Wolverhampton in May and at Southwell (soon got behind) in July and August:
better at 1¾m than shorter: best form on all-weather: worth a try in blinkers or a
visor: needs strong handling. *S. Dow.*

CHAMBROS 4 ch.g. Krayyan 117 – Chilcombe (Morston (FR) 125) [1990 11.7g* 77
11m³ 12m² 13.3m³ 1991 12s³] medium-sized gelding: moderate mover: modest
handicapper: ran very well at Doncaster in March, but not seen out again: suited by
1½m: acts on good to firm and soft going: tends to wander under pressure. *J.
Akehurst.*

CHAMPAGNE BREAK 2 ch.g. (Jun 14) Flying Tyke 90 – Horann (Horage 124) —
[1991 5g 5g] 700Y: close-coupled gelding: first foal: dam unraced: well behind in
sellers at Beverley and Leicester (virtually pulled up) in spring. *M. W. Ellerby.*

CHAMPAGNE DAISY 2 b.f. (Feb 18) Roaring Riva 103 – Lindrick Passion —
(Silly Season 127) [1991 5g 5g 5m a6g] sparely-made filly: second live foal: dam of
little account: seems of little account: sweating penultimate start, blinkered and
reluctant at stalls final one (July). *J. Balding.*

CHAMPAGNE SEASON (USA) 2 b.f. (Mar 18) Vaguely Noble 140 – Rheine 54
Falls (USA) (Rheingold 137) [1991 7.1d 7d] $55,000F, 80,000Y: lengthy filly:
half-sister to 3-y-o 7f (at 2 yrs) and 1¼m winner Grammos (by Bailjumper) and 2
winners in USA: dam minor winner in USA, is half-sister to dual Cambridgeshire
winner Baronet: plating-class form, never able to reach leaders, in late-season
maidens at Chepstow and Doncaster: will be suited by further. *A. A. Scott.*

CHAMPENOISE 3 b.f. Forzando 122 – Migoletty 59 (Oats 126) [1990 NR 1991 64
8g 10g⁴ 7.6s⁶ 8f² 8s² 8.3m⁵ 8g 8.1s 8.2m⁵ 9.2s] smallish, sturdy filly: fourth foal:
half-sister to winning hurdler Jabrut (by Young Generation): dam, 1½m winner,
is half-sister to useful Linda's Fantasy: quite modest form: creditable fifth at
Nottingham, easily best effort in handicaps and claimer last 4 starts: should prove
well suited by further than 1m (hampered at 9f): acts on any going: sold 6,200 gns
Newmarket December Sales. *P. J. Makin.*

CHANCE ALL (FR) 3 ch.f. Glenstal (USA) 118 – Auction Bridge 76 (Auction 76
Ring (USA) 123) [1990 5m² 5m* 5m* 5m⁵ 6d⁶ 1991 6g² 6g 7.1s⁴ 6s⁴ 6.5g⁵] lengthy
filly: modest performer: best effort in summer at 3 yrs when second in minor event

at Leicester, wandering under pressure: fifth of 10 in listed race at Munich: should stay 7f: acts on good to firm ground: fractious in stalls first 2 outings. *C. F. Wall.*

CHANCE REPORT 3 b.f. Beldale Flutter (USA) 130 – Report 'em (USA) 51 **47** (Staff Writer (USA)) [1990 a5g⁵ 5m⁴ 5f⁵ 5g 6m 5g 6v 1991 8m 7g⁴ 8.2d 7m* 8f 8.2m 8m⁴] rather leggy, sparely-made filly: moderate mover: poor performer: won seller (no bid) at Redcar in August: stays 7f: best form on a sound surface, though ran poorly on firm going: hung right final start: has worn bandages. *F. H. Lee.*

CHANCE TO DREAM 2 gr.f. (Apr 8) Petong 126 – Silken Purse (Posse (USA) **60** 130) [1991 5m² 5g 6d 5.7f³ 5.1g 6.9f⁶] leggy, unfurnished filly: has a quick action: first foal: dam once-raced granddaughter of sister to Dahlia: quite modest maiden: appeared not to stay 7f: acts on firm ground: off course around 4 months after third outing. *R. Hannon.*

CHANDANNE 4 ch.f. Ballad Rock 122 – Affirmation (FR) (Affirmed (USA)) **31** [1990 6f 7f 5g² 6g⁵ 5g⁵ 6m 8.2m 8.3m³ 9f⁵ 8.3g⁵ 10.8m a8g 7f 8.2s 1991 5m⁶ 7m⁴ 8.2m 8f] sturdy, compact filly: moderate mover: poor handicapper: stays 1m: acts on good to firm ground. *H. J. Collingridge.*

CHANDIGARH 3 br.c. High Top 131 – Lady Zi (Manado 130) [1990 NR 1991 **65 p** 6.1m⁴ 7.1g³] IR 100,000Y: good-topped, attractive colt: third foal: brother to Italian middle-distance winner Freeway of Love and half-brother to U.S. 4-y-o Grade 2 9f winner Anshan (by Persian Bold), a smart 7f and 1m winner here: dam, minor 1½m winner in France, is half-sister to dam of French 2000 Guineas winner No Pass No Sale: quite modest form in maidens at Chepstow and Haydock (wore net muzzle, taken last and steadily to post) in September: bred to stay further, but takes keen hold: can do better. *R. Charlton.*

CHANDLERY (USA) 3 b. or br.c. Woodman (USA) 126 – Sail Loft 74 (Shirley **96** Heights 130) [1990 7m³ 1991 10.1g³ 10f* 10g* 12m³] sturdy colt: has a quick action: fairly useful performer: easy winner in 3-runner races for maiden at Brighton in May and minor event at Pontefract in June, making all: 7½ lengths third of 4 to Luchiroverte in £11,200 contest at Ascot in June, taking keen hold and leading over 9f: should prove at least as effective back at 1¼m. *H. R. A. Cecil.*

CHANGE GUARD 5 b.m. Day Is Done 115 – Mittens (Run The Gantlet (USA)) **—** [1990 13.8m⁶ 8f 1991 7d 10.2s 7.5f] lengthy, angular mare: moderate mover: poor and lightly-raced maiden nowadays: stays 1m: acts on soft going. *Roy Robinson.*

CHANGING TIMES 2 b.c. (Mar 20) Last Tycoon 131 – Alata (Le Levanstell **95** 122) [1991 6g² 6d* 6m* 6m 6f⁵ 8g⁴ 7s 8g] 26,000F, IR 30,000Y: sturdy, lengthy colt: has scope: good mover: half-brother to several winners, notably 1983 Hoover Fillies' Mile winner Nepula (by Nebbiolo): dam Irish 9.5f winner: fairly useful performer: won maiden at Goodwood and minor event (showing good turn of foot) at York in mid-summer: very good fourth of 19, finishing strongly after having poor run virtually from stalls, in nursery at Goodwood: creditable seventh of 18 to Fair Crack in Goffs Million at the Curragh penultimate outing: suited by 1m: acts on good to firm and soft ground: blinkered (below best) fifth start: not particularly consistent. *W. Jarvis.*

CHANNON HILL (IRE) 3 b.f. Red Sunset 120 – Sabura (Busted 134) [1990 7s **58 d** 1991 8s⁴ 8m³ 8g⁴ 10g 8m 10.1d⁵ 8g⁶ 12.2f⁴ 8m 10g 11d³] leggy, rather unfurnished filly: inconsistent maiden: probably stays 1½m: tended to hang for 7-lb claimer final start: slowly away ninth and tenth, markedly so on first of them. *R. Hollinshead.*

CHANSEA MISS 2 ch.f. (Apr 21) Risk Me (FR) 127 – Bibelot (Blind Harbour 96) **—** [1991 5.1m] lengthy filly: first reported foal: dam unraced: 50/1 and bit backward, soon outpaced in claimer at Bath in July. *J. D. Czerpak.*

CHANTERESSE 4 b.f. Chantro 104 – Miss Friendly 72 (Status Seeker) [1990 **—** NR 1991 a8g] well beaten, including in seller. *W. J. Smith.*

CHANTRY BARTLE 5 ch.g. Say Primula 107 – Sallametti (USA) 69 **37** (Giacometti 130) [1990 12g³ 13.8m 12m⁶ 12g⁵ 12g⁶ 16f³ 15m* 16m³ 16m⁵ 15m³ 1991 12f⁴] sparely-made gelding: poor handicapper nowadays: creditable fourth at Beverley in May, not seen out again: stays 2m: acts on firm ground: good mount for claimer. *C. W. Thornton.*

CHANTRY BELLINI 2 ch.f. (Apr 24) Efisio 120 – Lifestyle 80 (Jimmy Reppin **— p** 131) [1991 5.1m] 900F: small, close-coupled filly: fourth living foal: half-sister to 1989 2-y-o 6f and 7.5f winner Merryfall (by Anfield): dam won twice at 2 yrs, and was also successful over hurdles: 50/1 and very green, around 8 lengths eighth of 10 in maiden at Catterick, having been virtually tailed off at halfway: should improve, granted stiffer test of stamina. *C. W. Thornton.*

CHAPELSTREET BLUES 4 b.f. Sagaro 133 – Warbury Dell 81 (Warpath 113) —
[1990 NR 1991 8.5f] close-coupled, sparely-made filly: first foal: dam, placed at 2 yrs,
failed to train on: showed nothing in Beverley maiden in May, only run on flat. *B. A. McMahon.*

CHAPLINS CLUB (USA) 11 ch.g. Parade of Stars (USA) – Nautical Rose **62**
(USA) (Henrijan) [1990 6f 6m⁵ 6g⁶ 6g 6g³ a6g 6m 6g 5d 7g 7d 8.2d 6s 1991 6s 6d 6g
5.9m 6d* 5g 6g 5m² 6d³ 7m³ 6g² 5m 6m 6m 6m 6m 6s] small, strong gelding: quite
modest handicapper at best nowadays: won at Pontefract in June: seems suited by 6f
or stiff 5f nowadays: acts on good to firm ground, but goes very well on an easy
surface: best with strong handling: has hung and is blinkered off-side only: usually
gets behind. *D. W. Chapman.*

CHARCOAL BURNER 6 br.g. Royal Match 117 – Resist 55 (Reliance II 137) **45**
[1990 10.8m 11.7f⁵ 11.7g⁶ 10m 8.2m⁴ 7m² 8m 7f 8h² 7m³ 9g² 7m 10.2m 1991 10.1s
10m⁵ 8.1g 8.3m² 8.3g⁴ 10s² 9.7f3] compact gelding: poor handicapper, has proved
untrustworthy: effective at 7f to 1¼m: acts on any going: seems best without visor:
often pulls hard: has gone freely to post and been taken down early. *B. R. Millman.*

CHARLAFRIVOLA 3 br.g. Persian Bold 123 – Tattle 61 (St Paddy 133) [1990 6g **67**
7f⁴ 6m² 6m⁵ 7f³ 8m 7m² 7m 7d⁴ 1991 7m⁵ 6m 8.5m³ 8.2d 8g³ 7g³ 7m* 7.5f⁵ 7m³ 7g
7.1m 7m⁶ 7m] rather leggy gelding: moderate walker: has a quick action: quite
modest handicapper: won at Ayr in July: ran well ninth outing, below form after:
should prove best at up to 1m: acts on firm going: blinkered or visored final 3 starts
at 2 yrs: sometimes on toes: sold to join T. Greathead 3,200 gns Newmarket
Autumn Sales. *F. H. Lee.*

CHARLES DEVON LAD 6 br.h. Fitzwilliam (USA) – Devon Maid (Meldrum **31**
112) [1990 NR 1991 5f⁵ 6m 6f⁶ 7m 6f] angular horse: moderate mover: lightly raced
and bad handicapper: should stay beyond 6f: has been tried blinkered. *Mrs P. A. Barker.*

CHARLIE'S DARLING 3 b.f. Homing 130 – Kip's Sister (Cawston's Clown **53**
113) [1990 5m 5m 6g* 6m a6g 7f 8m 1991 8.2d 12.2g³ 10d 12.2m* 12m⁵ 10g² 11.7d
10g 11.5m⁵ 13.8f² 10.3m⁴ 10g⁶ 13.8m⁶] angular filly: poor mover: plating-class
performer: won claimer at Catterick in May: will prove suited by further than 1¼m,
and stays 13.8f: acts on firm ground, seems unsuited by dead: put head in air and
found little sixth outing: joined J. White. *J. D. Czerpak.*

CHARLO 3 br.c. Chief Singer 131 – Dance Card 69 (Be My Guest (USA) 126) **94**
[1990 NR 1991 8d⁶ 9m² 10g* 8.9m²] IR 205,000Y: strong, workmanlike colt: has
scope: third foal: brother to Chief's Image, a fairly useful performer at up to 1m, and
half-brother to fairly useful 7f and 1m winner Home Truth (by Known Fact): dam
runner-up over 1m on second start, became disappointing: quite useful form: made
all in maiden at Leicester in May: favourite, moved poorly down but ran well in
£9,400 handicap at York following month: stays 1¼m: acts on good to firm going. *J. H. M. Gosden.*

CHARLYCIA 3 b.f. Good Times (ITY) Callie Law 01 (Galivanter 131) [1990 7m —
7f a7g³ 7m a8g 8.5m⁵ 1991 a11g 10g] leggy, rather angular filly: poor plater: stays
8.5f: edgy final start. *R. Earnshaw.*

CHARLY PHARLY (FR) 4 b.g. Pharly (FR) 130 – Burnished (Formidable **56**
(USA) 125) [1990 11f² a8g 11m⁵ 10.6d* 10.2m 15d 12s 10.5g⁵ 10.2s 1991 a7g* a7g a 71
7.6g⁵ a7g6 a8g* 10.5m* 8m* 8.9g 10.3m⁵ 10m 10.5d] good-topped, workmanlike
gelding: modest handicapper, best on all-weather: successful at Southwell in
January (claimer) and July (by 10 lengths) and in apprentice events at Haydock and
Newcastle in August: effective at 7f to 10.6f: acts on good to firm and dead ground:
has hung left: usually blinkered, once visored: keen sort, best when able to force
pace: inconsistent. *F. H. Lee.*

CHARMED KNAVE 6 b.g. Enchantment 115 – Peerless Princess (Averof 123) **56**
[1990 NR 1991 8m³ 7.1m² 8.1d* 8.1g² 8.3m⁴ 7.6m 7m 8f⁴ 7f* 7m⁴ 7.6m* 8g⁴ 6.9f]
lengthy gelding: poor mover: plating-class handicapper: won at Chepstow in June,
Brighton in August and Lingfield in September: stays 1m: acts on firm and dead
ground: sometimes blinkered, not when successful as 6-y-o. *D. R. Laing.*

CHARMING GIFT 4 b.f. Petorius 117 – Aubretia (USA) (Hatchet Man (USA)) **59**
[1990 7m 8g 8g² 8f⁴ 8s³ 7d a8g⁴ 1991 a8g² a8g⁶ 8m² 7m⁶ 8.5m 8m* 8m⁶ 10m² 10s²
8f⁵ 10s³ 10m⁴ 10.3g⁴ 10.1s 9.7s²] leggy filly: moderate mover: plating-class
handicapper: below best last 4 starts (blinkered last 2): sold 2,200 gns Doncaster
November Sales after penultimate one: effective at 1m to 1¼m: acts on any going. *R. J. R. Williams.*

CHARMING REPLY (IRE) 3 b.f. Prince Tenderfoot (USA) 126 – Breezy **32**
Answer (On Your Mark 125) [1990 5m 1991 8g⁶ 8m 8.2d 7m⁴ 8f 7m⁵ 7d⁶ 10.2f 10f⁵
15.4f 10m⁵] sturdy, workmanlike filly: poor maiden: stays 2m: acts on firm ground
and dead. *M. D. I. Usher.*

CHARMONIX 2 ch.f. (Feb 3) Scottish Reel 123 – Sand Valley (FR) 61 (Arabian) **48**
[1991 7g 7g 8s⁶ a8g] 1,800F: tall, leggy filly: half-sister to 1985 2-y-o 5f winner Alice
Hill (by Persian Bold) and a minor winner in USA: dam won 3 sellers at around 1¼m:
plating-class form in maidens and a minor event: well beaten on equitrack at
Lingfield: will be suited by middle distances: best effort on soft ground: slowly away
first 2 outings. *G. Wragg.*

CHAROLLES 2 b.f. (Apr 17) Ajdal (USA) 130 – Chalon 125 (Habitat 134) [1991 **82** p
6m³] sturdy, lengthy filly: has scope: fourth living foal: half-sister to high-class
French 7f (at 2 yrs) to 10.5f winner Creator (by Mill Reef): dam suited by 1m, out of
very speedy Areola: favourite but green, ½-length third of 14 to Yousefia in maiden
at Newmarket in October, slowly away, every chance down into Dip then keeping
on: moved moderately to post: will be well suited by 7f: should improve and win a
race. *H. R. A. Cecil.*

CHART CROSS 5 b.g. Millfontaine 114 – Whichcombe 79 (Huntercombe 133) **54** d
[1990 8.2m 10.8g² 10g 8.3m 9f⁴ 10.8m 8m 1991 8m 9.9m* 12m⁶ 10m 8.3m 8.2m²
7m 10.8m 9.9f⁴] rather leggy, angular gelding: not a good walker: plating-class
handicapper: won apprentice selling event (no bid) at Beverley in June by 8 lengths:
best at 1m to 1¼m: acts on firm and dead going: has broken blood vessel: inconsistent. *K. S. Bridgwater.*

CHARTER LIGHTS 4 gr.f. Kalaglow 132 – Charter Belle 60 (Runnymede 123) —
[1990 10.5g⁴ 10.5g 10.5d⁴ 12m 11g 12.5d 11g⁵ 15d 10.5v 1991 10v⁵ 16.2g 11f 10f] tall,
leggy filly: half-sister to 8.2f to 10.1f seller winner Allured (by Decoy Boy), later
successful over hurdles, and another 4 winning hurdlers: dam won 1¼m seller:
ex-French filly: fourth in maiden at Saint-Cloud and handicap at Evry in 1990: little
other worthwhile form on flat: stays 10.5f: has worn crossed noseband: has been
tried blinkered: trained at 3 yrs by F. Doumen. *J. R. Jenkins.*

CHART MOVES (IRE) 3 gr.c. Music Boy 124 – Morgiana (Godswalk (USA) —
130) [1990 NR 1991 5m 6m⁶] 6,000F, 13,000Y: lengthy, plain colt: poor mover: first
foal: dam lightly-raced half-sister to Cork And Orrery Stakes winner Kearney:
burly, tailed off in July maidens. *J. W. Payne.*

CHASMARELLA 6 b.m. Yukon Eric (CAN) – Miss Polly Peck (March Past 124) —
[1990 NR 1991 14g 12g] smallish, lengthy mare: poor and lightly-raced plater: stays
1½m: probably acts on any going: winning hurdler. *A. R. Davison.*

CHATAIN (USA) 3 ch.c. Sharpen Up 127 – Blushing Redhead (USA) (Blushing **84**
Groom (FR) 131) [1990 NR 1991 7m* 7.2m⁵ 7g] $190,000Y: leggy colt with scope:
has a fluent action: first foal: dam Irish-trained 7f (at 2 yrs) to 1¼m winner: won
maiden at Warwick in May: disappointing in summer handicaps: should be suited by
further: sold 3,200 gns Newmarket Autumn Sales, probably to Italy. *R. Charlton.*

CHATEAU NORD 2 ch.g. (Apr 8) Salmon Leap (USA) 131 – Touraine (FR) **78** d
(Luthier 126) [1991 5m* 6f² 6m 6d² 5d* 5f⁶ 5m³ 5g 5d] 9,400F, 5,000Y: lengthy,
rather leggy gelding: half-brother to 1¼m winner Where Is She (by Beldale Flutter)
and fair 1m and 1¼m winner Farm Club (by Kris): dam French 2-y-o 7f winner: fair
form at best: successful in auction events at Doncaster in May and Hamilton in July:
well below form subsequently, hampered by loose horse one occasion: stays 6f: has
won on good to firm ground but seems ideally suited by an easy surface: sweating
seventh start. *J. Berry.*

CHATHAM ISLAND 3 ch.g. Jupiter Island 126 – Floreal 68 (Formidable (USA) **77**
125) [1990 7m⁵ 7d 1991 a7g² 8g 8d 12g 10g² 10m⁵ 8f² 8m⁶ 10m* 10g* 10.4m²
10.3d⁶] rangy gelding: good walker: modest handicapper: neck winner at Sandown
in September, leading final 1f, and Lingfield in October, always prominent: ran
moderately at Chester final start: stays 1¼m well: acts on firm going, probably not
on a soft surface: changed hands 31,000 gns Newmarket Autumn Sales. *C. E.
Brittain.*

CHATINO 2 b.f. (May 28) Dancing Brave (USA) 140 – Nophe (USA) 95 (Super **67**
Concorde (USA) 128) [1991 7m⁵ 6.1d⁵] quite attractive filly: poor walker: third foal:
dam, 5f winner at 2 yrs who didn't turn on, is out of half-sister to dam of Lianga:
burly, keeping-on second of 14 at Leicester, better effort in October maidens: will be
suited by return to 7f+. *C. E. Brittain.*

CHATLEY HEIGHTS 2 b.f. (Mar 19) Absalom 128 – Temple Heights 72 **30**
(Shirley Heights 130) [1991 5g 6.1f 8.2m 6m] smallish, workmanlike filly: second

foal: half-sister to winning hurdler: dam 2m winner out of game stayer Hardirondo: poor maiden: off course 5 months, pulled much too hard when well beaten third start: sold 700 gns Ascot December Sales. *R. Hollinshead.*

CHECKPOINT CHARLIE   6 b.g. Artaius (USA) 129 – Clouded Issue (Manado   **61** 130) [1990 10m6 10g6 12f* 12m2 12g3 12s 1991 12d 12f2 12f6 12f3 11.9m3 12f* 14.1f4 11.5f6] useful-looking gelding: moderate mover: quite modest handicapper: won at Folkestone in August: stays 1¾m: needs a sound surface: good mount for inexperienced rider: none too consistent. *J. M. P. Eustace.*

CHEDZOY   3 ch.g. Niniski (USA) 125 – Pine (Supreme Sovereign 119) [1990 8m6   — 1991 11.7m6] leggy gelding: showed some ability in minor event and maiden: seemed likely do better over further: dead. *Major W. R. Hern.*

CHEEKY CHAPLIN   5 b.g. Anfield 117 – Saroan Meed (Midsummer Night II   **52** 117) [1990 NR 1991 10v 10.8d 8f4 6g 7m 8f] leggy gelding: second foal: dam, out of half-sister to high-class stayer Proverb, showed little on flat but won juvenile hurdle: form only when fourth in Brighton maiden. *D. R. Gandolfo.*

CHEEKY POT   3 b.c. Petoski 135 – Pato 90 (High Top 131) [1990 7g 7.5m4 6m   **69** 8m 8d* 8d5 8.2s 1991 10d3 12g4 12.3d 10.5g6 10.5d* 10.3d 11d5 12.1s2] compact colt: poor mover: modest handicapper: won apprentice contest at Haydock in October: ran poorly at Chester and Redcar (claimer) next 2 starts, well when blinkered on final one: stays 1½m: acts on soft going: usually visored: sold to join D. Smith 13,000 gns Doncaster November Sales. *M. J. Camacho.*

CHEERFUL CHARLIE   4 b.c. Roscoe Blake 120 – Cereum (USA) 84 (Tudor   — Grey 119) [1990 7.2d 7d a8g5 1991 8m 8h 8g] neat colt: no worthwhile form. *B. A. McMahon.*

CHEERFUL TIMES   8 b.g. Faraway Times (USA) 123 – Chevulgan (Cheval   **52** + 117) [1990 10g3 10.5m 10g 12.3g 12g 10.6d4 10.6v 8g5 1991 10d4] good-topped gelding: usually looks well: poor walker: quite modest handicapper nowadays: stays 1½m: acts on any going: has worn a visor, but better without: often apprentice ridden: occasionally reluctant at stalls: usually finds little off bridle, and well suited by extreme waiting tactics: winning hurdler. *B. A. McMahon.*

CHELSWORTH   3 b.f. Never So Bold 135 – Ash Ridge (USA) 93 (Bold Reason)   **56** [1990 6f5 6m2 7m3 1991 6m5 a7g2 8.9m 7m4 5.3g* 5g] plain, angular filly: good walker: quite modest form: won maiden at Brighton in October, leading final 1f: easily beat other 3-y-o effort on second start: should stay 1m: carried head high third start. *G. Wragg.*

CHEQUERS (IRE)   2 b. or br.g. (Mar 3) Red Sunset 120 – Mallabee 92 (Pall   **75** Mall 132) [1991 5m6 6m2 7.5f4 7.3m4 8g 7g3 8.3s] IR 8,200F, 26,000Y: tall, lengthy, workmanlike gelding: seventh foal: half-brother to 4 winners here and abroad, including useful Irish 1984 2-y-o 5f winner La Escala (by Brave Shot): dam, sprinter, best at 2 yrs: modest maiden: good third of 18 in nursery at Doncaster in October: probably stays 1m: acts on good to firm ground, ran respectably on soft; ran wide bend at Beverley. *R. J. R. Williams.*

CHERRO (USA)   2 b.c. (Apr 18) Acaroid (USA) – Cherished One (USA) (What A   **58** Pleasure (USA)) [1991 7g 8m 6.9f6 8m] $11,000Y: rangy, workmanlike colt: sort to carry condition: has a round action: half-brother to winners in North America by Court Trial and Valid Appeal: dam unraced: sire Grade 1 9.5f winner: quite modest maiden: showed improvement last 2 starts: may do better in handicaps in due course: sold 8,500 gns Newmarket Autumn Sales. *W. A. O'Gorman.*

CHERRY BOB   2 ch.f. (Mar 3) Adonijah 126 – Cherry Picking 85 (Queen's   — Hussar 124) [1991 6m6 8g] 900F, 1,000Y: leggy, rather angular filly: eighth reported foal: half-sister to 3-y-o Cherry Dance (by Nordance), 6f seller winner at 2 yrs: dam middle-distance winner: bit backward, never a threat in claimer at Haydock or seller at York in summer. *C. W. Thornton.*

CHERRY DANCE   3 ch.f. Nordance (USA) – Cherry Picking 85 (Queen's   **37** Hussar 124) [1990 5s2 5g3 6g* 6v 1991 6m 7g6 6g5 6d6 7m 6d4 a5g] workmanlike filly: moderate mover and walker: quite modest winner at 2 yrs: only poor form since: probably stays 7f: hung left fourth start: changed hands 2,100 gns Doncaster August Sales. *D. W. Chapman.*

CHERRYGROVE   5 ch.g. Roman Warrior 132 – Soldiers Dream (Spartan   — General 109) [1990 NR 1991 14.1m4] workmanlike gelding: first foal: dam winning chaser: won a point-to-point in Ireland at 4 yrs: tailed off in 4-runner maiden at Yarmouth in July: behind in NH Flat race earlier in 1991. *R. Curtis.*

CHESHIRE ANNIE (IRE)   2 br.f. (Feb 20) Double Schwartz 128 – So Valiant   ?
80 (So Blessed 130) [1991 5g 5m 5g⁵ 6f² 6g 6g] 6,400Y: unfurnished filly: half-sister
to several winners, including useful but temperamental sprinters Our Freddie (by
Cajun) and Heroic Air (by Song): dam 2-y-o 5f winner: quite modest maiden: easily
best effort when second of 8 in maiden at Brighton in September: well beaten in
nurseries: better suited by 6f than 5f. *W. Carter.*

CHESHIRE NELL   3 b.f. Absalom 128 – Quenlyn (Welsh Pageant 132) [1990   40
5g⁴ 5g² 6d 5m 5f³ 6m³ 6g 6m⁵ 1991 6f 7f 7g 6.9s 7m⁴ 7g 8g] close-coupled, leggy
filly: poor performer: form as 3-y-o only when staying-on fourth of 17 in handicap at
Leicester: stays 7f: taken down alone at 3 yrs: has worn crossed noseband:
headstrong, and one to be wary of. *W. Carter.*

CHESNUT TREE (USA)   3 b.f. Shadeed (USA) 135 – Expansive 111 (Exbury   97
138) [1990 7g⁵ 1991 12g 12m* 12m⁴ 12d] tall, leggy, unfurnished filly: fairly useful
performer: won maiden at Salisbury in August: good fourth of 6 to Surrealist in
listed race at Doncaster, one pace over 2f out then staying on again inside last: last
of 8 in Princess Royal Stakes at Ascot month later, pulling too hard: stays 1½m:
possibly unsuited by dead ground. *Lord Huntingdon.*

CHESTER BELLE   2 b.f. (Apr 4) Ballacashtal (CAN) – Cascabel 82 (Matahawk   42
127) [1991 5f 6g⁶ 5g 6f 5m] 2,500Y: sturdy filly: second foal: dam 7f and 1m winner:
poor maiden: no show in face of stiff tasks in nurseries last 2 starts: should stay 7f.
P. C. Haslam.

CHESTER TERRACE   7 ch.g. Crofter (USA) 124 – Persian Mourne (Mourne   41
126) [1990 12.2m³ 12m 1991 10.8m³ 9.9g] compact gelding: moderate mover: poor
handicapper: stays 1½m: probably acts on any going. *K. S. Bridgwater.*

CHESWOLD   7 ch.g. Dominion 123 – Soft Voice 66 (Simbir 130) [1990 NR 1991   44
12.2g⁶ 12.1s4] sturdy, close-coupled gelding: first foal: dam, 1½m winner, stayed
well: lightly-raced ex-Irish gelding: poor form here in summer: stayed very well:
acted on good to firm ground and soft going: winning hurdler: dead. *J. H. Johnson.*

CHEVELEY CHIEF   3 ch.g. Chief Singer 131 – Hawks Nest 66 (Moulton 128)   —
[1990 6m⁵ 6f* 6m³ 6m⁵ 7m 7m 1991 7m 8m 10.4m 12.4m] big, strong gelding: quite
modest winner at 2 yrs: well beaten in autumn at 3 yrs, including in selling handicap:
stays 6f: blinkered (virtually bolted) final start: sold 1,150 gns Newmarket Autumn
Sales. *T. Fairhurst.*

CHEVEUX MITCHELL   4 ch.c. Dunbeath (USA) 127 – Hide Out (Habitat 134)   83
[1990 7f⁵ 6g* 7m 7f⁵ 7m⁴ 7f* 7m 7m 6m⁴ 7m* 6m 7.6m* 7g⁴ 8m 8m 1991 7m 8g⁵
7m* 7.6m* 7f 7d* 7.6s⁵ 7m 8m⁴ 7f⁴ 7g 7.6m 7.6m] sturdy colt: fair handicapper:
won at Kempton in May and Lingfield (2) in June: seems ideally suited by around 7f:
acts on firm and dead ground: visored nowadays: sometimes bandaged behind: goes
very well with forcing tactics: inconsistent. *M. R. Channon.*

CHEW IT OVER (IRE)   3 b.g. Taufan (USA) 119 – Stop The Cavalry (Relko   62
136) [1990 7m 8.2s 7g⁶ 1991 8f⁴ 7m 10g a8g 10g³ 10m² 10m 8m³ 9s 8.2m⁶ 8m] sturdy
gelding: has a round action: quite modest maiden: placed in claimers: suited by
1¼m: acts on good to firm ground: claimed out of M. Jarvis' stable £8,011 sixth start.
C. A. Smith.

CHIANINA   3 b.f. Forzando 122 – Cow Pastures (Homing 130) [1990 5m⁶ 1991   —
6d⁶ 5m 5g 5m] good-topped filly: poor form, mostly finding little and eased: sprint
bred: blinkered last 2 starts: sold 600 gns Ascot 2nd July Sales. *A. A. Scott.*

CHIARINA   3 b.f. Chief Singer 131 – Karine (Habitat 134) [1990 NR 1991 10d 10g   56
10d 12m² 11.8m 12m 13.8m] 14,500Y: sturdy filly: half-sister to Irish 1m winner
Uptothehilt (by Kris), subsequently successful in USA, and a winner in Malaysia:
dam lightly-raced half-sister to 9f Earl of Sefton Stakes winner Heaven Knows: sign
of ability only when second of 5 in slowly-run maiden auction race at Hamilton in
May. *J. M. P. Eustace.*

CHICAGO'S BEST   4 br.g. Try My Best (USA) 130 – Maryville Bick (Malacate   — §
(USA) 131) [1990 10m 8d⁵ 12m 10g 10g 12g 1991 12.5d 10m 11.5g 10g 14.6g⁵ 14g 12g]
workmanlike gelding: second reported foal: dam Irish 11f winner: poor ex-Irish
maiden (trained by V. Rossiter): wears blinkers: very reluctant to race once:
winning hurdler. *P. Burgoyne.*

CHICARD   2 b.f. (Apr 5) Mashhor Dancer (USA) – Two Stroke (Malicious) [1991   48
6m² 6m⁵ 5m] 2,300Y: smallish filly: fifth foal: half-sister to 5f winners Vivaldi (at 2
yrs) and Catalani (both by Music Boy): dam poor half-sister to very useful French
1¼m winner Aberdeen Park: poor maiden: well beaten after debut: should stay 1m.
W. Jarvis.

CHICARICA (USA) 3 b.f. The Minstrel (CAN) 135 – Little Lady Luck (USA) **112**
(Jacinto) [1990 6d* 6d* 6m* 1991 7.3g³ 6m² 6m⁵] big, strong, attractive filly: placed
in Fred Darling Stakes at Newbury and Cork And Orrery Stakes (improved form,
always front rank and rallying gamely, short head behind Polish Patriot) at Royal
Ascot: co-third favourite but sweating, creditable 5½ lengths fifth of 8 to Polish
Patriot in July Cup at Newmarket, readily outpaced over 1f out: very useful at 6f,
though bred to stay further. *J. H. M. Gosden.*

CHIC CAROLE 5 ch.m. Dalsaan 125 – Valley of Diamonds 74 (Florescence 120) —
[1990 a12g 1991 a12g⁶ a12g³] leggy mare: bad maiden. *Mrs P. A. Barker.*

CHICMOND (IRE) 2 b.c. (Feb 12) Lomond (USA) 128 – Chicobin (USA) (J **106** p
O Tobin (USA) 130) [1991 6d⁴ 6g* 6d* 6f* a7g* 7.1m*]

Few pattern-race winners get taken to Southwell's fibresand track
en-route, but that happened in the latest season to the Henry II Stakes
winner Top of The World and then to the Solario Stakes winner Chicmond.
'All-weather' racing, as it's popularly but erroneously known, wasn't designed
for the benefit of horses as useful as Chicmond and Top of The World: its
primary functions are to provide extra opportunities for low-grade horses and
to bolster the betting levy on winter days when racing on turf is abandoned,
though it also proved popular when firm ground was prevalent in the summer.
Its progression from the inaugural twelve-race meeting at Lingfield's
equitrack surface in October 1989 to a position now where a new fibresand
circuit is planned at Wolverhampton's existing venue hasn't been without its
problems: several early meetings fell foul of frost, and attendances at some
afternoon fixtures, particularly during the winter, are still on the low side.
1991 saw the forward-looking executive at Southwell take steps to upgrade
some of its races. One step, which met with enough success to be worth
repeating, was the re-introduction of two old-style maidens-at-closing races
at its three-day summer meeting; both races were framed for horses who
hadn't run before July 1st. Not surprisingly for a horse who'd already shown
fairly useful form in defeating the subsequent Ascot winner Red Slippers in a
maiden at Nottingham before winning small-field minor events at Ayr and
Catterick, Chicmond didn't have to run anywhere near his best to come home
unchallenged in one of those races, the Timeform Race Card Opportunity
Stakes, in August. Even though his trainer seldom runs his horses out of their
class it was still somewhat unexpected to see Chicmond declared for the

Solario Stakes, Sandown—Chicmond has to battle to hold off
Seattle Rhyme (extreme right), Artic Tracker (noseband) and Mack The Knife

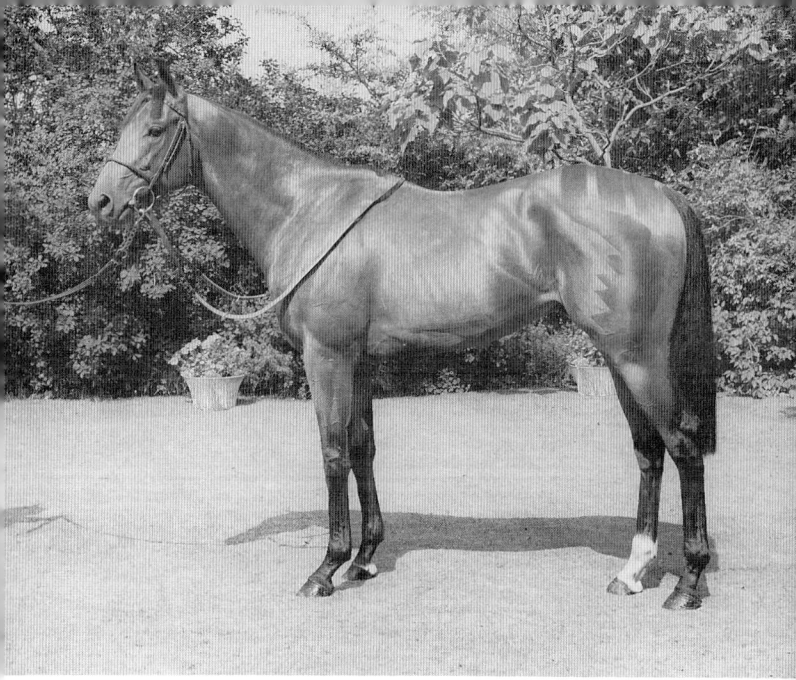

Mr P. G. Goulandris' "Chicmond"

Group 3 Solario Stakes at Sandown later in the month. The trainer's judgement was vindicated, however, when Chicmond made all the running from a field which included the much-vaunted Artic Tracker, Mack The Knife, Seattle Rhyme and the Gimcrack second Taylor Quigley. Chicmond's finishing effort, giving no quarter to take the spoils in a multiple photo from Seattle Rhyme and Mack The Knife, was very much in keeping with his first three victories; at Nottingham he'd knuckled down gamely after looking likely to come off second best for much of the way and at Catterick (where he'd looked in splendid condition, despite having won at Ayr three days earlier) he'd again run very lazily and needed rousting on a track that probably didn't suit him ideally. Chicmond wasn't seen out again. He would most likely have improved a little further granted an extra furlong, as did both Seattle Rhyme and Mack The Knife, but there was no real indication in his trainer's candid post-race comments that significant improvement could be expected.

Chicmond (IRE) (b.c. Feb 12, 1989)	Lomond (USA) (b 1980)	Northern Dancer (b 1961)	Nearctic
			Natalma
		My Charmer (b 1969)	Poker
			Fair Charmer
	Chicobin (USA) (b 1984)	J O Tobin (br 1974)	Never Bend
			Hill Shade
		Chic Chick (b 1979)	Bold Forbes
			Trick Chick

Unusually, none of the first three dams in the bottom line of Chicmond's pedigree ever ran. It's a well-known family, though, and several descendants of Chicmond's fourth dam Fast Line have won notable races over the last thirty years. Fast Line produced the excellent American racemare and broodmare Fairway Fun (whose offspring include the smart sprinter Torsion and the good 1973 American two-year-old Fairway Fable), the 1972 Prix Morny winner Filiberto and the Grade 1 Alabama Stakes, Kentucky Oaks and the Delaware Oaks winner White Star Line. Trick Chick is also a broodmare of some note, having produced numerous winners including the high-class American middle-distance performer On The Sly (a fairly strong influence for stamina as a stallion) and the top-notch French filly Northern Trick, successful in the French Oaks and Prix Vermeille among other races and an excellent second in the Arc. Trick Chick's daughter Chic Chick has had only a few foals at stud while her granddaughter Chicobin, whose first foal Chicmond is, has since produced a colt by Ballad Rock. *Sir Mark Prescott.* –

CHIEF CELEBRITY (USA) 3 b.f. Chief's Crown (USA) – My Nord (USA) **85 +** (Vent du Nord) [1990 8d² 1991 12m*] half-sister to numerous winners, including smart stayer At Talaq (by Roberto) and Grade 1 8.5f and 9f winner Annoconnor (by Nureyev): dam won 2 sprint claiming races: won maiden at Doncaster in May easing down by 5 lengths (value 10) from Boomerang, leading over 2f out. *M. R. Stoute.*

CHIEF MINISTER (IRE) 2 br.c. (Apr 25) Rainbow Quest (USA) 134 – **— p** Riverlily (FR) (Green Dancer (USA) 132) [1991 8d] 110,000Y: rather leggy, quite attractive colt: sixth foal: half-brother to several winners here and abroad, including 1¼m winner Steel Spark (by Persepolis): dam, placed over middle distances in France, is half-sister to high-class French 1972 2-y-o Robertino: 9/1, always towards rear in 14-runner minor event at Newmarket in November: rather mulish beforehand: looks sort to do better. *L. M. Cumani.*

CHIEF OF STAFF 2 ch.c. (Mar 25) Caerleon (USA) 132 – Fanny's Cove 89 **84 p** (Mill Reef (USA) 141) [1991 7m⁴ 7.1m²] 74,000Y: lengthy colt: sixth foal: halfbrother to very useful 3-y-o 1¼m and 11.9f winner Nibbs Point (by Sure Blade) and 3 other winners, including useful 1988 2-y-o 7f and 1m winner Prince Ibrahim (by Be My Guest): dam won over 1¼m on only start: favourite though bit green, demoted after winning maiden at Chester in August, full of running turn, squeezing through then quickening well not unduly knocked about: keeping-on second of 10 at Sandown following month: will stay middle distances: likely to do better. *P. F. I. Cole.*

CHIEF ORNAMENT (USA) 3 b.f. Chief's Crown (USA) – Embellished (USA) **88** (Seattle Slew (USA)) [1990 6g⁴ 1991 7f² 7m 8.5m* 8g 9.9f*] leggy, rather sparely-made filly: has a quick action: successful in handicaps at Beverley in June and (leading over 1f out and staying on strongly) July: better at 1¼m than shorter: acts on firm going. *H. R. A. Cecil.*

CHIEFS BABU 3 ch.g. Chief Singer 131 – Nullah 71 (Riverman (USA) 131) [1990 **81** 6g 6g 1991 8d⁶ 6m 12d* 11m* 11.5m* 12g² 10m⁴ 10m 11.9g] good-topped gelding: poor mover: capable of fair form: successful in May in claimer at Kempton and handicaps, making all for best efforts, at Hamilton (very easily) and Sandown: tailed off final start: needs further than 1¼m, and should stay 1¾m: yet to race on extremes of going: retained by trainer 15,000 gns Newmarket Autumn Sales and gelded. *B. Hanbury.*

CHILD'S PLAY (USA) 2 ch.f. (Mar 4) Sharpen Up 127 – Picnicing 104 (Good **54** Times (ITY)) [1991 6m 6.1m] leggy, sparely-made filly: first foal: dam sprinting half-sister to Precocious, Jupiter Island and Pushy (by Sharpen Up): plating-class form in maidens at Newmarket (considerably handled) and Nottingham in October. *Mrs J. Cecil.*

CHILD STAR (FR) 2 gr.f. (Mar 16) Bellypha 130 – Miss Shirley (FR) 76 **40** (Shirley Heights 130) [1991 a7g a7g⁶] 8,000F: angular, light-framed filly: second foal: half-sister to 3-y-o Marameb (by Formidable): dam 1½m winner, is half-sister to high-class French miler Mendez (by Bellypha): well beaten in late-year maidens at Lingfield. *D. Marks.*

CHILIBOY 4 gr.c. Precocious 126 – Chili Girl 112 (Skymaster 126) [1990 6m* **72** 6m³ 6m³ 6m 6m⁴ 6m² 6d 6f² 5m* 5s 1991 5g 5m⁴ 5m 5m 5g 5f 5.1m⁴ 5.2m⁵ 6m³ 5m² 5m²] stocky colt: carries condition: chipped knee bone at 2 yrs: fairly useful handicapper at 3 yrs, only modest nowadays: best form at 5f on a sound surface: blinkered nowadays: sold 11,500 gns Newmarket Autumn Sales. *J. L. Dunlop.*

CHILL WIND 2 gr.c. (Apr 22) Siberian Express (USA) 125 – Springwell 73 **48** (Miami Springs 121) [1991 5g 5m⁶ 5m 6m³ 5m 7m] 1,600Y: tall colt: has scope: second foal: half-brother to a winner in Sweden by Primo Dominie: dam 10.2f winner: poor maiden: well beaten last 2 starts, final one (burly) first for almost 4 months: better suited by 6f than 5f. *N. Bycroft.*

CHIMAYO (IRE)   3 b.g. Sure Blade (USA) 130 – Seattle Siren (USA) 101 (Seattle Slew (USA)) [1990 6g* 1991 7m 10.1g] quite attractive gelding: won maiden at Newmarket at 2 yrs: last in handicaps at same course (£8,000 event) and Windsor: should be suited by 7f+: sold 4,300 gns Newmarket July Sales and gelded: winning hurdler for P. Hedger. *B. W. Hills.* —

CHIMES OF THE DAWN   7 ch.g. Tower Walk 130 – Neptia's Word (Great Nephew 126) [1990 NR 1991 11s a10g 9m 12.1d 7f 7d] workmanlike gelding: shows plenty of knee action: no form on flat since modest winner at 4 yrs: suited by 1m: acts on firm and dead going: winning hurdler. *D. Burchell.* —

CHINA BEACH   3 ch.f. Superlative 118 – Alanood 85 (Northfields (USA)) [1990 NR 1991 a8g[2] a8g* a10g[6] 10m a8g] workmanlike filly: fifth living foal: half-sister to 6f to 7.5f winner Aldahe (by Dalsaan) and to 2 winners abroad, including Norsk Oaks winner Alhayat (by Godswalk): dam 1½m winner: won maiden at Southwell in March: well beaten in handicaps and (in between, raced alone) claimer: stays 1m: blinkered: reluctant to go to post third start, reluctant to race on final one: sold 1,000 gns Newmarket July Sales: one to treat with caution. *W. A. O'Gorman.* 55 §

CHINAMAN   2 b.c. (Feb 23) Noalto 120 – Diorina 91 (Manacle 123) [1991 5d 5d 5d 7g 6f[4] 6f[3] 7f[2] 7g 7.1s 6g] 1,900Y: well-made colt: has a round action: half-brother to 3-y-o Mardior (by Martinmas), winning sprinters by Swing Easy and Air Trooper and a winning hurdler: dam best at 2 yrs, when 5.3f winner: plating-class maiden: suited by 6f or 7f: best efforts on firm ground, seems unsuited by dead: very stiff task when visored final start, blinkered previous five. *W. G. R. Wightman.* 59

CHINA SKY   3 b.g. Tina's Pet 121 – Buy G's 60 (Blakeney 126) [1990 8.2s 8m a8g 1991 a10g a8g a10g[6] 8.2s[2] 8s[6] 9d 12.5m 12g a8g[2] a8g a8g[2] a8g[3] a7g[4] 8.3m[2] 8f* 8f* 8f[6] 8m] rather sparely-made gelding: successful in seller (bought in 6,200 gns) and handicap at Yarmouth in August: below best after: probably stays 1¼m: acts on any going: has raced freely, in visor second start. *C. N. Allen.* 53

CHINA'S WAY (USA)   5 b. or br.m. Native Uproar (USA) – China Tea (USA) 95 (Round Table) [1990 12f[5] 1991 14.1f 12f 11m[5]] leggy, angular mare: keen walker: plating-class maiden at best: well beaten at 5 yrs: suited by 1½m: possibly unsuited by extremes of going: temperamental over hurdles in 1991 when trained by M. Pipe. *J. Mackie.* —

CHIPAYA   3 b.f. Northern Prospect (USA) – Flaming Rose (USA) (Upper Nile (USA)) [1990 5m[3] 5m[5] 6d 6m* 6d* 6d* 1991 6d[5] 7g 6s[6] 8d* 8s[3]] small, workmanlike filly: moderate mover: reportedly suffered arthritic knee after 2-y-o season: returned to near 2-y-o form when winning listed race at Ascot in October by 2 lengths from Umniyatee, staying on from rear to lead 1f out: easily best other 108

Moss Bros October Stakes, Ascot—Chipaya returns to form and beats Umniyatee

efforts in 1991 when sixth in Diadem Stakes (having got behind) at Ascot and third in Group 3 contest at Milan: much better at 1m than shorter nowadays: goes well on a soft surface: edgy first 3 starts, sweating second. *J. R. Fanshawe.*

CHIPPER 2 b.c. (Apr 8) Risk Me (FR) 127 – Dunphate (Dunphy 124) [1991 8.1s⁶] **62** p 5,200Y: first foal: dam unraced half-sister to Princes Gate: 25/1, over 5 lengths sixth of 13, slowly away, good progress from 2f out, to Valseur in maiden at Edinburgh in November: will improve. *R. Boss.*

CHLOES DIAMOND (IRE) 3 ch.f. Heraldiste (USA) 121 – Salique (Sallust **64** 134) [1990 6f4 6m³ 7s⁴ 1991 8m³ 9m 8.1g 8m 7.9g² 9d 9m* 9m² a10g² a10g] unfurnished filly: quite modest performer: won 2-runner auction event at Redcar in September: good second of 14, easily better effort in handicaps on Lingfield equitrack in November: stays 1¼m: below best on soft going: often sweats: sold out of C. Booth's stable 3,000 gns Doncaster October Sales after eighth start. *J. L. Spearing.*

CHOICEINMUSIC 2 ch.f. (Apr 27) Music Boy 124 – Orien (Goldhill 125) [1991 **60** 6d³ 5f* 5.1m⁶ 5m⁵] 5,800Y: lengthy filly: sixth foal: sister to 3-y-o 5f winner Oriental Music: dam never ran: quite modest form: won maiden at Ripon in August: below that form after: will stay 6f: bandaged behind all starts: sold 1,500 gns Doncaster November Sales. *J. Berry.*

CHOIR LEADER 4 b. or br.f. Chief Singer 131 – View 88 (Shirley Heights 130) — [1990 7g⁴ 10.5g⁵ 8m⁴ 7m⁵ 8m² 8g³ 8g³ 9m² a8g³ 1991 7.1g 7m] tall, leggy filly: modest maiden at 3 yrs: no form in 1991: should have stayed 1¼m: acted on good to firm ground: dead. *M. C. Pipe.*

CHOIR MASTER (CAN) 4 b.c. Assert 134 – Choral Group (CAN) (Lord **85** Durham (CAN)) [1990 10.1g 10g³ 10.1m* 10f 1991 12g² 12.3d 12g] tall, useful colt: fair handicapper: not seen out after June: should prove better suited by 1½m than 1¼m: acts on firm ground, possibly unsuited by dead: sold to join A. Moore's stable 19,000 gns Newmarket Autumn Sales. *Major W. R. Hern.*

CHOIR PRACTICE 4 ch.g. Chief Singer 131 – Good Try 92 (Good Bond 122) **93** [1990 8m 8f⁵ 7g⁴ 5m* 5m² 5m² 6d 1991 5g* 5g³ 5g 6g² 6m 5.2g⁶] big, workmanlike gelding: fairly useful handicapper: won at Kempton in April: not seen out after July: stays 6f: best form on a sound surface: sold 10,500 gns Newmarket Autumn Sales and gelded. *H. Candy.*

CHOPPY CHOPPY (USA) 2 gr.f. (Feb 25) Woodman (USA) 126 – Bien Sur **70** (USA) (Storm Bird (CAN) 134) [1991 6g 6f² 7d⁵ 8g²] $55,000Y: small, stocky filly: second reported foal: dam minor winner at 1m: modest maiden: over 7 lengths last of 5 to Musicale in Prestige Stakes at Goodwood in August: stays 1m: acts on firm and dead ground. *B. W. Hills.*

CHORAL SUNDOWN 5 b.m. Night Shift (USA) – Choir (High Top 131) [1990 **64** 8.5f² 8f 10.4d 10f⁶ 10.2m² 8m³ 10.5m 8g 9m 12g⁴ 10.4d 12s 1991 8m³ 7m⁴ 9m* 10g² 8.9m 8d 9.9f 11m³ 10.1m 8f 10.3m 11.9m³] stocky mare: carries condition: moderate mover: quite modest handicapper nowadays: won at Redcar in June: effective at 1m to 1½m: yet to show her form on very soft going, acts on any other. *B. W. Murray.*

CHORUS BOY 6 br.g. Sonnen Gold 121 – Toccata (Kythnos 126) [1990 8.2s⁵ 8f **33** 10.6s⁶ 8g³ 8g⁴ 10f⁴ 10.6s 11d 9s⁶ 1991 12f³ 14m⁶ 12m 10m] tall, useful-looking gelding: shows traces of stringhalt: has a rather round action: poor handicapper, still a maiden: stays 1½m: acts on any going: seems a difficult ride, ideally needs strong handling. *E. Weymes.*

CHOUGH 3 br.g. Green Ruby (USA) 104 – Lochmar (Lochnager 132) [1990 5f 6f² — 5.3h 6g⁵ 6m⁴ 6d⁵ 1991 6.1d 7.1g 7.6m 7.1m] smallish, lengthy gelding: plating-class maiden: below form in handicaps and seller in 1991: should be suited by further than 6f: acts on firm and dead going: visored third start. *C. R. Barwell.*

CHRIS HUGHTON (IRE) 2 b.c. (May 5) The Noble Player (USA) 126 – **69** Crimson Crown (Lord Gayle (USA) 124) [1991 6g⁵ 6f 6g* 6g a7g] 4,600Y: neat colt: has a round action: half-brother to Irish 7f and 9f winner Crimson Glen (by Glenstal) and Irish 1½m winner Crimson Kiss (by Hello Gorgeous): dam, runner-up twice at 2 yrs in USA and once at 3 yrs in Ireland, is half-sister to smart 1982 staying 2-y-o Polished Silver: much improved effort to win Folkestone maiden: fair fourth of 18 to Don't Smile in nursery at Newbury (pulled hard to post) later in October, much better subsequent effort: should stay 7f: possibly unsuited by fibresand. *J. Akehurst.*

CHRISTIAN LAD 3 gr.g. Belfort (FR) 89 – California Split (Sweet Revenge — 129) [1990 5m⁴ 5f* 5d³ 6m³ 6m² 6m² 6m⁵ 6d⁴ 5m⁴ 1991 6s 5f 6m 7m⁴ 5.9m 5m 6f 5f] leggy, rather angular gelding: good walker: quite modest performer: ran respectably second start, poorly afterwards: stays 6f: acts well on firm ground: blinkered once at 2 yrs: tends to wander, and is a difficult ride. *J. Berry.*

CHRISTIAN WARRIOR 2 gr.c. (Mar 3) Primo Dominie 121 – Rashah 67 **78** (Blakeney 126) [1991 5g³ 6f⁵ 6d 6m² 5.1g³ 5.1m² 6g⁵ 6g³ 7.1m² 8f³ 7g² 7m 7d⁶] 5,600F, 8,600Y: neat, quite attractive colt: second foal: half-brother to 3-y-o Daragency (by Dara Monarch): dam probably stayed 1½m: progressed, and ran really well when placed in nurseries in autumn at Bath (1m) and Brighton: below form subsequently: probably ideally suited by 1m: seems suited by a sound surface: hung left (ran moderately) sixth start. *R. Hannon.*

CHRONOLOGICAL 5 b.g. Henbit (USA) 130 – Forward Princess (USA) **63** (Forward Pass) [1990 13.8m⁵ 16.5m⁴ 17.6m 14g⁵ 15.8g⁴ 16.5g⁵ 13m⁵ a12g a14g* a14g² a16g³ a14g³ 1991 a14g a13g* a12g⁴ a12g⁴ a14g⁶ a16g⁶ a14g* a14g²] sparely-made, angular gelding: moderate walker and mover: modest performer: won at Lingfield (claimer) in February and Southwell in December: stays well: visored first 3 and last 2 outings: pulled hard when blinkered once. *M. H. Tompkins.*

CHUCKLESTONE 8 b.g. Chukaroo 103 – Czar's Diamond 66 (Queen's Hussar — 124) [1990 18f 16g⁶ 16d⁴ 18f⁵ 17.1f* 17.1f² 16m³ 17.6f² 17.6f³ 16m 17.1m* 17.1d 1991 16g 17.1m] neat gelding: has a free, rather round action: modest handicapper at 7 yrs: well beaten in 1991, not seen out after May: suited by good test of stamina: particularly well suited by top-of-the-ground: races up with pace: tailed off when visored: genuine. *J. S. King.*

CHUMMY'S DILEMMA 2 b.c. (Mar 12) Reesh 117 – Hodsock Venture (Major **60** Portion 129) [1991 6g⁶ a6g⁵ 7g⁴ 6g⁴ 7.1m⁶ 8m 6m 6g⁶] 5,500F, 6,000Y: leggy, good-topped colt: has a round action: has scope: half-brother to 2 winners, including sprinter Chummy's Pet (by Song): dam no worthwhile form: useful plater: best effort sixth of 18 for 7-lb claimer in non-selling nursery at Newmarket final start: stays 7f: bandaged off-hind on debut: sold 3,200 gns Doncaster November Sales. *N. A. Callaghan.*

CHURCHILL EXPRESS 4 b.c. Full of Hope 125 – Nello (USA) 85 (Charles **46** Elliott (USA)) [1990 7m⁶ 7m⁶ 10m 10g⁴ 12.2d⁶ 10g a10g 1991 12f³ 17.1d⁴ 14.6m 14.6m² 14.9m⁵] leggy colt: poor handicapper: may prove best at up to 2m: acts on firm and dead ground: sold 780 gns Newmarket Autumn Sales. *R. Akehurst.*

CHURCH MISSIONARY (USA) 4 b.f. Miswaki (USA) 124 – Christchurch **76** (FR) 88 (So Blessed 130) [1990 7g 10g² 1991 12s⁴ 12g⁴ 10s³ 10d² 12s* 12.3d 10m 11g⁵ 12d⁶] lengthy, good-quartered filly: modest handicapper: won apprentice event at Ascot in May: good sixth in November Handicap at Doncaster: stays 1½m: acts on soft ground: ran as if something amiss sixth start: covered by Teenoso (not in foal): sold 42,000 gns Newmarket December Sales. *Lord Huntingdon.*

CHURCH STAR 7 b.m. Cajun 120 – Lady of Rathleek (Furry Glen 121) [1990 — § 10m 7m 1991 9g 9v⁶ 9.7s] compact, good-bodied mare: ungenuine maiden: stays 1½m: wears bandages. *J. J. Bridger.*

CIBOURE 3 ch.f. Norwick (USA) 120 – Brandon Creek 79 (Be My Guest (USA) **65** 126) [1990 5m 6m⁴ 5g⁶ 5f⁴ 6m⁶ 6h* 7h⁶ 6m⁴ 5.8h³ 6m 6m* 6g⁵ 7m³ 7f⁵ 6m 1991 8g 6f 7m⁶ 6g⁶ 7m⁴ 8g* 8d⁶ 7.5f² 8m³ 10m⁴ 8s 9d² 7.1m³ 8m 8m 8.1g⁶ 8d⁶] leggy, lengthy filly: quite modest performer: won claimer at Goodwood in June: stays 9f: acts on hard and dead ground: has hung right: visored twice at 2 yrs: got loose from stalls and withdrawn final intended outing: tough. *M. D. I. Usher.*

CINDEROSA (IRE) 3 b.f. Kings Lake (USA) 133 – Rosalita (USA) (Key To The — Kingdom (USA)) [1990 6m³ 6m⁴ 8m 8f⁵ 7g 1991 8.2d 11m 10.9g 13d 14.1f⁶] rather sparely-made filly: has a long stride: poor maiden: stiff tasks, well beaten in handicaps and claimer (blinkered, sweating) in summer as 3-y-o: stays 1m: visored final start (ran creditably) at 2 yrs and first 3 at 3 yrs. *T. Thomson Jones.*

CINDORA (IRE) 2 b.f. (May 15) Fairy King (USA) – West of Eden (Crofter **84** (USA) 124) [1991 6m² 5m* 5g* 6m⁴ 5m* 6f⁴ 5m³ 6g 5d 5g⁴] 4,500Y: leggy, sparely-made filly: moderate mover: first foal: dam unraced: fair performer: successful in summer in maiden auction at Windsor, 4-runner minor event at Pontefract and 4-runner nursery at Thirsk: mostly ran well subsequently, including in listed race at Ayr and Cornwallis Stakes (won by Magic Ring) at Ascot: stays 6f: acts on good to firm and dead ground. *M. H. Tompkins.*

CINDY'S BABY 2 ch.f. (Apr 20) Bairn (USA) 126 – Miss Cindy 95 (Mansingh **36** (USA) 120) [1991 6.1m 6s a8g a7g⁶] 31,000Y: sparely-made filly: sister to 3-y-o Gipsy Fiddler, useful sprinter at 2 yrs, and half-sister to several winners here and abroad, including 1986 2-y-o 5f and 6f seller winner Miss Drummond (by The Brianstan): dam 5f to 7f performer, is sister to Petong: poor maiden. *J. J. O'Neill.*

CINNAMON FERN (IRE) 3 b.f. Sadler's Wells (USA) 132 – Osmunda (Mill —
Reef (USA) 141) [1990 NR 1991 12.2m 10m] IR 180,000Y: small filly: fourth foal:
half-sister to fairly useful 1½m and 16.5f winner Icecapped (by Caerleon): dam, Irish
1¼m winner, is half-sister to smart middle-distance performers Snow and Icelandic:
well beaten in maidens at Catterick and Leicester in October. *L. M. Cumani.*

CINQ CENT ROUGE 2 ch.f. (Apr 22) Rabdan 129 – Dame du Moulin 81 (Shiny —
Tenth 120) [1991 5g 5g 5m] 500Y: plain filly: third foal: half-sister to 3-y-o De Valera
(by Faustus): dam, 2-y-o 7f winner, is half-sister to useful middle-distance fillies
Rollrights and Rollfast: no worthwhile form in sellers in spring. *W. J. Musson.*

CIRCUIT RING 5 b.g. Electric 126 – Brookfield Miss 73 (Welsh Pageant 132) **63**
[1990 12f⁴ 12.3d 12m⁶ 13.8m⁴ 16.2d* 16.5m² 16.5f² 19f* 16m⁴ 16.2m³ 16f⁶ 1991
16.2g³ 16m⁴ 20g 16.2f² 20g 16.5m] leggy, workmanlike gelding: quite modest
handicapper: suited by 2m+: acts on firm and dead going: below form when
blinkered once, has worn visored: sometimes taken down early: trained until
after fifth start by P. Calver. *T. H. Caldwell.*

CIRCUS LIGHT 3 gr.c. Kalaglow 132 – Circus Plume 124 (High Top 131) [1990 **98**
7m⁶ 8.2m* 8m² 1991 12g² 11.5g⁶ 10.1g* 10.8d* 10m] rangy colt: good mover, with
long stride: useful on his day: made all in median auction contest at Windsor and
3-runner minor event (bandaged off-hind) at Warwick in June: well beaten,
weakening tamely and hanging left, in listed race in August: stays 1¼m: acts on
good to firm ground and dead: gets on toes: has found little and wandered under
pressure: tends to carry head awkwardly: not one to trust, and seems best when
able to dominate early on. *J. L. Dunlop.*

CISEAUX (USA) 2 ch.c. (Apr 20) Nureyev (USA) 131 – Sharp Ascent (USA) 97 **84 p**
(Sharpen Up 127) [1991 7d⁴ 6.3m³ 6m* 6g*] third foal: sister to 1989 2-y-o 5f winner
Ascending Dream: dam 2-y-o 5f performer here later Grade 3 8.5f winner in USA, is
daughter of Rivermande, a very useful winner at around 1m in France: successful in
maiden at the Curragh and minor event at Naas (by neck from Persian Creek, pair 10
lengths clear) in autumn: will stay 7f. *D. K. Weld, Ireland.*

CITIQUEEN (IRE) 2 ch.f. (Mar 12) Lomond (USA) 128 – Supremely Royal **71 p**
(Crowned Prince (USA) 128) [1991 a8g*] closely related to 6f and 10.2f winner Royal
Invitation (by Be My Guest) and half-sister to several winners, including stayer
Elegant Monarch (by Ardross) and very smart Capricorn Belle (by Nonoalco),
successful from 6f to 1m: dam poor maiden from top American family: co-favourite
and ridden by 7-lb claimer, won late-year maiden at Southwell by 2 lengths from Sir
Pageant: should improve. *H. R. A. Cecil.*

CITRUS KING 4 ch.g. Tender King 123 – Lucy Limelight 98 (Hot Spark 126) —
[1990 NR 1991 a8g⁵ 10m a8g a8g⁵ 10m] leggy, workmanlike gelding: half-brother to
fairly useful sprint handicapper Lucedeo (by Godswalk) and a winner in France: dam
2-y-o 5f winner: poor and lightly-raced maiden: trained debut by G. Huffer. *J. Banks.*

CITY BOUQUET 3 b.f. Top Ville 129 – Roses To Rachel (Artaius (USA) 129) —
[1990 NR 1991 8m] big, workmanlike filly: second foal: half-sister to modest
middle-distance maiden Deadlock (by The Minstrel): dam placed twice in USA, is
half-sister to top-class 1985 2-y-o Huntingdale: carrying plenty of condition, tailed
off in maiden at Warwick in August: walked very poorly in paddock but moved freely
to post. *B. Smart.*

CITY INDEX (USA) 5 b.g. J O Tobin (USA) 130 – Fannie Annie (USA) —
(L'Enjoleur (CAN)) [1990 NR 1991 a11g] sturdy ex-Irish gelding: third foal: dam
never ran: form as 3-y-o only when second in maiden at Fairyhouse: well beaten in
Southwell maiden in February: stays 7f: has worn blinkers. *N. A. Smith.*

CITY LINE 2 b.g. (Feb 9) Capricorn Line 111 – Racine City 71 (Dom Racine (FR) **52**
121) [1991 7g 7d] leggy gelding: second reported foal: dam, best at 2 yrs over 5f, is
out of half-sister to Irish Oaks second Tuscarora: plating-class form in autumn
maidens at Salisbury and Doncaster. *R. Hannon.*

CITY LINK PET 5 b.m. Tina's Pet 121 – City Link Rose (Lochnager 132) [1990 **72**
6g 5g 5g* 5m* 5m* 5m⁶ 5m⁶ 5m 5m* 6m⁵ 5m 5.6g 5d 5g 5s 1991 5g 6m 5g² 5g* 5m
5d³ 5m⁵ 5g 5g* 5m 5.1m 5.2f 5g 5.1s 5.2g 5g] strong mare: carries plenty of
condition: moderate mover: modest handicapper: won at Salisbury in June and
Goodwood (apprentices) in August: suited by 5f: acts on good to firm and dead
ground: has won for apprentice: inconsistent. *D. A. Wilson.*

CITYPLUMBJO 3 b.g. Hotfoot 126 – Vaula 49 (Henbit (USA) 130) [1990 6g 7m —
7f 7g 7g 1991 10.8g] leggy, lengthy gelding: poor maiden: always behind at Warwick
in April: should be suited by middle-distances: sold 780 gns Doncaster July Sales. *M.
R. Channon.*

CITY SOLACE 3 b.c. Last Tycoon 131 – Sheeog 80 (Reform 132) [1990 5f* 5f* **84**
5m⁶ 6m³ 6f 7g 7g 6m 1991 8g 6m⁵ 7g 9m³ 12g³ 10g² 10d² 10g 12f³ 12f* 11.9g⁴
10.3m⁶] leggy colt: moderate mover: fair handicapper: mostly in good form, winning
£7,600 contest at Newbury in August: stays 1½m: acts on firm and dead going: ran
moderately when blinkered at 2 yrs: has looked moody and difficult ride: sold 5,200
gns Newmarket Autumn Sales, probably to Italy. *R. Hannon.*

CIXI 3 b.f. Far Out East (USA) – Hasty Key (USA) (Key To The Mint (USA)) [1990 **46**
7m⁵ 7m 7m⁵ 9g² 1991 12d 8g⁴ 10g³ 8g⁴ 8m] sparely-made filly: shows knee action:
poor maiden on most form: should stay beyond 9f: best form on a sound surface:
usually sweats, edgy third start: bandaged on reappearance: sold 3,400 gns
Newmarket July Sales: winning selling hurdler for M. Pipe. *A. N. Lee.*

CLARE HEIGHTS 3 b.f. Shirley Heights 130 – Clare Island 108 (Connaught **99**
130) [1990 8g* 1991 10.5g* 12g 12m⁴ 16g⁴] workmanlike, angular filly: useful, but
lightly raced: won £7,400 contest at York in May, edging left: ran as if something
amiss in Ribblesdale Stakes at Royal Ascot: good fourth in autumn listed races at
Newmarket won by Surrealist and Hawait Al Barr: stays 2m: changed hands before
final start. *J. R. Fanshawe.*

CLARE KERRY LASS 2 b.f. (Apr 21) Alleging (USA) 120 – Gay Hostess (FR) **70**
(Direct Flight) [1991 5s³ 6g* 6f³ 6m* a6g² 6m 5m³ 6m 7g⁴ 7.6m⁵ a6g⁴ a8g² a8g³]
leggy filly: sixth foal: half-sister to 3-y-o Merciful Lad (by Beldale Flutter) and 2
winners in France, including 9f winner Rasi Brasak (by Kenmare): dam French 7f
(at 2 yrs) and 1¼m winner: modest performer: successful in seller (retained 7,200
gns) at Lingfield in May and claimer at Brighton in June: ran creditably in nurseries
and claimers last 5 starts: stays 1m: acts on good to firm ground, and on equitrack at
Lingfield: has worn bandages: consistent. *T. J. Naughton.*

CLAREMONT BOY 3 b.c. Another Realm 118 – Lady Eton 106 (Le Dieu d'Or **65**
119) [1990 6g⁴ 1991 8g 7g⁵ 8m³ 8d 10g⁵ 11.8g³] strong colt: quite modest maiden:
stays 1½m: acts on good to firm ground, possibly unsuited by a soft surface: sold to
join J. Jenkins stable 5,400 gns Newmarket Autumn Sales. *M. A. Jarvis.*

CLARET (IRE) 3 b.c. Rousillon (USA) 133 – Consolation 95 (Troy 137) [1990 **109**
7m³ 8g² 1991 8g³ 7g² 8m* 8.2m² 10.4g⁴ 8f* 8m³ 8m⁵ 10m* 9f] rangy, good sort:

Lord Rotherwick's "Claret"

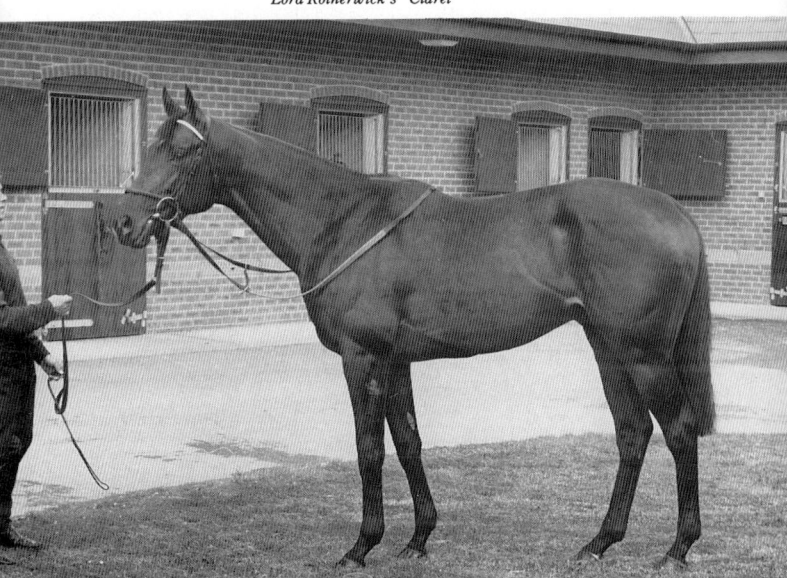

impressive in appearance: good walker and mover: useful performer: won maiden at Newmarket in May, £8,300 handicap at Newbury in August and minor event at Leicester in October, making virtually all last 2 occasions but at slow early pace on last of them: behind in Hollywood Derby final start: best effort at 1m: acts on firm ground: wears tongue strap nowadays: has tended to wander and carry head high. *Major W. R. Hern.*

CLASS ACT 5 b.g. Shirley Heights 130 – Thespian 76 (Ile de Bourbon (USA) 133) — [1990 12h* 14g4 16m2 16.2f2 13.8m* 16f2 a14g 1991 12g] sturdy gelding: moderate mover: quite modest handicapper at 4 yrs (resolution under suspicion): virtually pulled up lame only start as 5-y-o (June): stays 2m: acts on hard going: blinkered on all-weather: sold 1,200 gns Ascot July Sales. *J. W. Hills.*

CLASSIC ACCOUNT 3 ch.g. Pharly (FR) 130 – Money Supply (Brigadier 50 Gerard 144) [1990 7m 7s a8g 1991 a10g2 a10g* a10g5 a10g4 10g 9d 10g 11.5s* 14.1g4 a 55 11.5m5 12s2] workmanlike gelding: moderate mover: successful at Lingfield in maiden in January and handicap (made all) in June: good second in apprentice handicap at Kempton in August: should stay 1¾m: goes well on soft ground: trained until after seventh start by C. Wildman: gelded after final one. *J. Akehurst.*

CLASSICAL CHARMER 2 ch.f. (May 6) Ardross 134 – Very Nice (FR) (Green 55 Dancer (USA) 132) [1991 6f 7g 8s] 7,400F: workmanlike filly: fifth foal: half-sister to fair middle-distance handicapper Bank Roll (by Chief Singer): dam, winner from 9f to 11f in France, is out of sister to Dahlia: plating-class maiden: best effort at York second start: very much on toes next time: should stay well. *B. R. Millman.*

CLASSIC COURT 3 b.g. Lidhame 109 – Cocoban (Targowice (USA) 130) [1990 — 6f 8g 7f6 7d6 6s 1991 a8g 8d 10g 9.9f 10g 8m] rather sparely-made gelding: plater: below form in 1991: doesn't stay 1¼m: acts on firm and dead ground: often races freely: blinkered final start: sold 800 gns Doncaster August Sales. *M. Brittain.*

CLASSIC EXHIBIT 2 b.g. (Mar 23) Tate Gallery (USA) 117 – See The Tops 59 (Cure The Blues (USA)) [1991 6m 7m a6g6] 12,000F, 9,400Y: unfurnished, leggy gelding: first foal: dam never ran: plating-class maiden: well-supported second favourite on Lingfield equitrack final start, but ran moderately. *A. Hide.*

CLASSIC RING (IRE) 3 b.f. Auction Ring (USA) 123 – Classic Choice (Patch 38 129) [1990 5g 5m5 6g3 6g3 6d5 7g5 7m* 7f 6m 7m4 7m3 a8g 8.5m2 8.2g3 10.6s 7d 1991 8d 7m 6f 8f 8g3 7g2 10m 8.1m 8m] leggy filly: has a roundish action: winning plater at 2 yrs: ran creditably in 1991 only when placed in non-selling handicaps at Edinburgh: stays 1m: seems unsuited by a soft surface: sometimes taken down early. *J. I. A. Charlton.*

CLASSICS PEARL (IRE) 3 gr.f. Reasonable (FR) 119 – Zanskar (Godswalk 49 (USA) 130) [1990 6m 6g5 6m6 6m6 7f6 6d 10.6s 1991 7m3 8.3m 9d 8f 10m] strong, stocky filly: moderate walker: third in Newmarket claimer in August, staying on strongly: didn't reproduce that: should be suited by further than 7f: acts on firm ground: blinkered (headstrong) penultimate start. *N. A. Twiston-Davies.*

CLASSIC STATEMENT 5 ch.h. Mill Reef (USA) 141 – Lady Graustark (USA) — (Graustark) [1990 14g6 14g 16.2m5 18g5 1991 14g] leggy, quite attractive horse: modest handicapper at 4 yrs: in need of run, well beaten only start as 5-y-o: needs extreme test of stamina: acts on good to firm and dead ground: winning hurdler in October. *R. Lee.*

CLASSIC SUITE 5 b.g. Ya Zaman (USA) 122 – Lady Bidder (Auction Ring (USA) 48 123) [1990 8f 10v 8f5 7.5d a8g a8g 10d6 1991 10.2s5 8g 8d3 8d3 8.5f5 8m5 8.3d2 10d 8m 8g3 8g] lengthy, sparely-made gelding: moderate walker: poor mover: poor handicapper nowadays: best form at about 1m: acts on any going: has worn dropped noseband: none too consistent. *R. D. E. Woodhouse.*

CLAUDETTE 3 b.f. Claude Monet (USA) 121 – Miss Twights (Hopeful Venture — 125) [1990 6f 6f 6g 8.2g 1991 10.2f5 10g 13.8f6 a12g] lengthy filly: has round action: of little account: blinkered twice. *F. J. Yardley.*

CLAUDIA MISS 4 b.f. Claude Monet (USA) 121 – Palace Travel (High Top 131) 63 [1990 8g6 10.6s 8m2 8.2s4 7g 7g5 7f4 7v* 1991 7.5g3 7m4 8m6 8m2 8g5] workmanlike filly: poor mover: quite modest handicapper: not seen out after July: stays 1m: acts on any going, with possible exception of very firm: often wears crossed noseband. *W. W. Haigh.*

CLAYBANK (USA) 2 ch.c. (Mar 4) Vice Regent (CAN) – Captain's Mate (USA) 73 (Turn-To) [1991 5m2 5m3] quite good-topped colt: half-brother to several winners, including very smart Irish 6f (at 2 yrs) to 9f winner Hugenot (by Forli) and Irish 5f and 7f winner Summer Fantasy (by Never Bend): dam unraced sister to Captains Gig, a very smart winner at up to 1m in USA: modest maiden: kept on well at Haydock and Sandown in September: will be suited by 6f + . *B. W. Hills.*

CLEAN SINGER 2 b.f. (May 5) Chief Singer 131 – Rosalka (ITY) (Relko 136) **42** [1991 8.1g 8m 8m] 3,000F, 4,100Y: half-sister to several winners, including fair 5f performer Bella Rossi (by Mummy's Pet) and French 7f and 1m winner John Hawkwood (by Irish River): dam won 4 times in Italy: poor maiden: best effort at Pontefract final start. *N. Bycroft.*

CLEAR COMEDY (IRE) 3 br.f. Jester 119 – Clear Belle (Klairon 131) [1990 7m **53** 7g 6d⁶ a6g* 1991 7s 6g 6.1d⁶] workmanlike filly, rather unfurnished: quite modest winner at 2 yrs: not seen out again until late-September and faced stiff tasks in handicaps, sixth of 20 in ladies event at Chepstow: stays 6f: acts on dead going. *R. Hannon.*

CLEAR IDEA (IRE) 3 ch.g. Try My Best (USA) 130 – Sloane Ranger 84 **—** (Sharpen Up 127) [1990 8g⁴ 8g 1991 a8g⁵ 10.2g⁶ 11.7g 10g 7g] tall, quite attractive gelding: fluent mover: plating class on most form: best at 1m: visored (raced too freely) third start. *C. R. Nelson.*

CLEAR LIGHT 4 ch.c. Exhibitioner 111 – Beach Light 89 (Bustino 136) [1990 **70** 7m 8g 8d⁴ 10m 9m 10v⁵ 10g* 1991 a12g* 12.2d* 14.8m² 12.3d³ 17.6m⁴ 14.8d⁴ 14.6m⁶] angular colt: modest handicapper: won at Southwell and Warwick in spring: not seen out after July: stays 14.8f: acts on good to firm and dead ground: sometimes blinkered, including when visored (sweating) once at 3 yrs: good mount for claimer: lazy, suited by forcing tactics. *M. C. Pipe.*

CLEAR SOUND 2 b.f. (Feb 25) Bellypha 130 – Cecilia Bianchi (FR) (Petingo **— p** 135) [1991 7m⁵ 8m⁵] neat filly: half-sister to several winners, including very useful 3-y-o 1¼m to 1½m winner Torchon (by High Top) and 1m and 1¼m winner White-Wash (by Final Straw): dam, winner in Italy, is half-sister to very smart 1m to 1½m filly Calderina: favourite though green, swerved violently left at start when tailed-off last of 5 finishers in Yarmouth maiden in July: moderate late headway in 11-runner similar event at Leicester 8 weeks later: likely to do better. *G. Wragg.*

CLEFTI'S SLIPPER 3 b.f. Skyliner 117 – Glenn's Slipper (Furry Glen 121) **—** [1990 NR 1991 a6g] first foal: dam 2-y-o 7f winner: 33/1, behind in Southwell claimer in December. *J. Hill.*

CLEO MODENA (IRE) 3 b.f. Dalsaan 125 – Modena 66 (Sassafras (FR) 135) **—** [1990 NR 1991 a6g] IR 5,200Y, resold IR 6,000Y, 16,000 2-y-o: sixth foal: closely related to useful 1986 2-y-o sprinter Crofter's Cline, nowadays a modest winner at up to 1m, and 6f and 1m seller winner Mine's A Double (both by Crofter): dam of no account: 33/1, always behind after slow start in Southwell claimer in December. *M. O'Neill.*

CLEVER CLAUDE 5 b.g. Cragador 110 – La Mirabelle 92 (Princely Gift 137) **—** [1990 8.3m⁵ 1991 10.1s] leggy, shallow-girthed gelding: poor form at best nowadays: seems to stay 1m: has been tried blinkered. *K. S. Bridgwater.*

CLIFTON CHARLIE (USA) 3 b.c. Crafty Prospector (USA) – Illustrious **—** Joanne (USA) (Illustrious) [1990 6g⁶ 5d* 5g³ 5m* 6m* 5m² 1991 6m 6g] lengthy colt: progressed into useful sprinter at 2 yrs: well beaten in listed race (second favourite) at Newmarket and Group 3 contest at York in spring as 3-y-o: acts on good to firm ground, and has won on dead: sometimes sweats. *C. R. Nelson.*

CLIFTON CHASE 2 ch.c. (May 22) Try My Best (USA) 130 – Mrs Cullumbine **60 p** 60 (Silly Season 127) [1991 6m 6d] angular, workmanlike colt: fourth foal: half-brother to 3-y-o 13.8f to 2m winner Our Aisling (by Blakeney) and fairly useful 7f and 1½m winner Rakes Lane (by Pitskelly): dam, stayed 1½m, is half-sister to useful 6f winner Chantry Bridge: backward, never placed to challenge or knocked about in autumn maidens at Newmarket and Doncaster: will stay at least 1m: probably capable of better. *M. A. Jarvis.*

CLIFTON CRUISER (USA) 2 ch.c. (May 8) Miswaki (USA) 124 – Atomic **63** Juice (USA) (Sauce Boat (USA)) [1991 7g⁵ 7m 7g] $42,000Y: rather leggy, useful-looking colt: second foal: dam minor sprint winner at 3 yrs: quite modest maiden: best effort at Newmarket (bit backward) on debut: ran moderately at Brighton final outing: may do better in handicaps. *C. R. Nelson.*

CLIFTON GIRL 5 b.m. Van Der Linden (FR) – Wrekin Belle (Dance In Time **—** (CAN)) [1990 NR 1991 6.1s 5.1m⁵ 7.5f] angular mare: poor at best: has hung: keen sort. *K. White.*

CLIFTON HAMPDEN 3 b.g. Blakeney 126 – Red Ruby 113 (Tudor Melody **74**
129) [1990 8d⁴ 1991 10g 12m⁴ 11.5m 12m 17.2g² 18m] compact, rather sparely-made
gelding: modest form: best effort strong-finishing second in handicap at Bath,
pushed along with plenty to do 5f out: stays well: possibly needs give in the ground:
blinkered fourth and final (pulled hard) starts: has looked a difficult ride: not one to
trust implicitly. *Lady Herries.*

CLIPPERINA (USA) 3 b.f. L'Emigrant (USA) 129 – Wield (USA) (Judger **71**
(USA)) [1990 7g⁴ 1991 8g⁵ 7.1d⁴ 7m³ 8g 8m] tall, lengthy filly: modest maiden: ran
poorly in handicaps last 2 starts, well backed on first occasion (visored) then
disputing lead 6f on second: should be suited by further than 1m: acts on good to firm
ground and dead: sold 22,000 gns Newmarket December Sales. *M. R. Stoute.*

CLIPPER ONE 3 b.f. Dreams To Reality (USA) 113 – Sleekit 78 (Blakeney 126) **71**
[1990 NR 1991 7d⁴ 8f* 8m 10g a8g] leggy, close-coupled filly: fifth foal: half-sister to
1¼m winner Kitty Clare (by Milford): dam winner at 1½m: won median auction
contest at Brighton in September: failed to reproduce that form in handicaps and
claimer: stays 1m well: sold out of I. Balding's stable 4,000 gns Newmarket Autumn
Sales after fourth start. *K. O. Cunningham-Brown.*

CLIPPING 3 b.f. Kris 135 – Valkyrie 87 (Bold Lad (IRE) 133) [1990 6g³ 6m³ 1991 **56** +
8m* 9d] rather unfurnished filly: has a quick action: evens, won slowly-run maiden
at Warwick in April in workmanlike style: looking really well, well beaten in minor
event at Wolverhampton 16 days later: should stay beyond 1m: possibly unsuited by
a soft surface: sold 8,200 gns Newmarket December Sales. *H. R. A. Cecil.*

CLIVOLI (IRE) 3 b.c. Muscatite 122 – Miss Annie 73 (Scottish Rifle 127) [1990 **—**
6g⁵ 1991 11m⁶ 8.3d] sparely-made colt: last in maiden events: sold 980 gns Doncaster July Sales. *J. S. Wilson.*

CLOCHE D'OR 3 b.f. Good Times (ITY) – Chrysicabana 88 (Home Guard (USA) **102**
129) [1990 6m² 6g³ 7m³ 6m* 6m³ 6.5g⁵ 1991 7m⁴ 8g 6m² 6m 7m 8g 6d] big, lengthy,
angular filly: useful performer: in frame for Nell Gwyn Stakes at Newmarket and
listed race (awkward leaving stalls, hung left final 1f) at Haydock: ran poorly in
£13,500 handicap and listed races last 3 starts, off course over 3½ months after first
of them: stays 7f: best form on good to firm ground: sold 37,000 gns Newmarket
December Sales. *C. E. Brittain.*

CLOGGETTE 2 ch.f. (Apr 14) Risk Me (FR) 127 – Golden Guilder 69 (Sonnen
Gold 121) [1991 5f 5m 6.1f] leggy filly: first foal: dam sprinting daughter of smart
sprinter Dutch Gold: no worthwhile form, including in a seller. *M. W. Easterby.*

CLOS DU BOIS (FR) 5 b.g. High Top 131 – Our Shirley 84 (Shirley Heights **45**
130) [1990 11.5g 10d³ a11g 1991 a16g⁴ a14g a16g² 12m⁶] small, sparely-made gelding:
poor maiden: stays 2m: acts on good to firm and dead going: bandaged nowadays: ran
as if something amiss second start. *Mrs N. Macauley.*

CLOSE FRIEND (IRE) 3 gr.c. Law Society (USA) 130 – Bellifontaine (FR) **93**
(Bellypha 130) [1990 7g 1991 8g² 10.5g³ 10.1m³ 12g* 14.8m⁴] deep-girthed colt: has
a round action: quite useful form: easily won 3-runner minor event at Doncaster in
June: moved poorly down and driven along some way out when 7½ lengths fourth of
5 to Jendali in listed race at Newmarket following month: should stay beyond 1½m:
likely to prove best on an easy surface. *B. W. Hills.*

CLOUD OF DUST 2 b.f. (Mar 30) Aragon 118 – Lady Bequick 81 (Sharpen Up **80** p
127) [1991 6d² 6m*] leggy, quite attractive filly: half-sister to 3 sprint winners,
notably useful Joytotheworld (by Young Generation), and modest 1¼m performer
Every One A Gem (by Nicholas Bill): dam ran only at 2 yrs, winning at 5f: favourite
after promising debut at Ascot, beat Western Approach by a length going away in
8-runner maiden at Leicester in October: will stay 7f: will do better. *J. L. Dunlop.*

CLOUD PEAK (USA) 3 b.f. Storm Bird (CAN) 134 – Good Lassie 86 (Moulton **60**
128) [1990 NR 1991 9.7m⁶ 10g³ 12m⁶ 12s] $800,000Y: lengthy, rather unfurnished
filly: fifth foal: closely related to Marcel Boussac winner Ashayer (by Lomond), also
winner over 1¼m as 3-y-o: dam, from excellent family, won over 6f at 2 yrs and bred
to stay 1½m: quite modest maiden: stays 1¼m: well beaten on soft ground: on toes
first 2 starts. *L. M. Cumani.*

CLOUDY AXE 2 gr.f. (Mar 29) Petong 126 – Immodest Miss 73 (Daring Display **—**
(USA)) [1991 5f] 4,000Y: leggy filly: eighth foal: half-sister to several winners,
including 3-y-o Itsagame (by Mummy's Game), successful at up to 7f, and useful
1985 2-y-o 5f and 6f winner Prince Peccadillo (by Dragonara Palace): dam won 1¼m
seller: 11/1 from 4/1 and bit backward, slowly away, green and always behind in
maiden auction at Bath in May. *R. J. Hodges.*

CLOVERMILL 3 b.f. Sayf El Arab (USA) 127 – Opinion 71 (Great Nephew 126)   —
[1990 6m³ 1991 7g 8.5m 8f⁵ 7m 6g 7g 10m] leggy, lengthy filly: has a quick action: disappointing maiden: well beaten in claimers, handicap and seller: should be suited by at least 1m: blinkered third and fourth outings: sold to join W. Bentley 2,800 gns Newmarket Autumn Sales. *H. Candy.*

CLURICAN (IRE) 2 ch.c. (Apr 10) Dara Monarch 128 – Jane Bond 59 (Good   **62**
Bond 122) [1991 6d 7g⁴ 7m 7.1s] IR 7,400F, 9,500Y: close-coupled colt: half-brother to several winners, including listed Italian winner Ettore Gatti (by Bustomi) and useful Irish hurdler Jennycomequick (by Furry Glen): dam 2-y-o 5.1f winner: quite modest maiden: best effort second start: stays 7f: usually sweating and on toes. *D. Nicholson.*

CLYRO 3 b.f. Kind of Hush 118 – Clear As Crystal 80 (Whitstead 125) [1990 6m⁴   **55**
6m* 6f⁴ 8d⁶ 8m² 1991 10m 10.8m 12.1d⁶ 10.2d 10.2g 8.2m⁵ 8f] angular filly: modest winner at 2 yrs: generally well below form in handicaps as 3-y-o: best form at 1m: acts on firm and dead ground: sometimes on toes: once had tongue tied down. *R. J. Holder.*

CLYTIE (USA) 2 br.f. (Jan 24) El Gran Senor (USA) 136 – Counting Rainbows   **73** p
(USA) (Halo (USA)) [1991 7g³] $175,000Y: workmanlike filly: has scope: first foal: dam unraced daughter of outstanding racemare Shuvee: 11/1 from 20/1 but better for race, about 3 lengths third of 9 to Mystery Play in maiden at Newmarket in July, off bridle 3f out then keeping on well: should stay 1¼m: seemed sure to improve, but wasn't seen out again. *H. Candy.*

COASTAL EXPRESS 2 ch.g. (Feb 27) Viking (USA) – Hold Me Fast (USA)   **65**
(Angle Light (USA)) [1991 5m 5m a7g³ 7s³ 7.5f² 7g* 8m 7g 7m⁵ a7g] 6,600F, 5,200Y: strong, lengthy gelding: shows knee action: half-brother to winners in USA and Denmark: dam won 4 times in USA: quite modest form: sweating and on toes, gamely won maiden auction at Doncaster in July: below best after: should stay 1m: probably acts on any going: didn't handle bend at Southwell third outing: pulled much too hard seventh. *E. Weymes.*

COAT OF DREAMS 2 b.g. (Mar 29) Ballacashtal (CAN) – Montelimar 108   **56**
(Wolver Hollow 126) [1991 5f⁴ 5g⁶ 6d⁵ 6m* 7m 5m] 2,500F: leggy gelding: seventh living foal: brother to 5-y-o 7f winner Morcinda and half-brother to 1m seller winner Saffron Poser (by Sagaro) and a winner abroad: dam 2-y-o 5f and 6f winner didn't train on: plating-class form: led close home in 4-runner nursery at Yarmouth in July on first run for 6 weeks: ran moderately in similar events afterwards: best form at 6f: acts on good to firm ground: wore crossed noseband last 3 starts, early to post first 2 of them. *R. Bastiman.*

COBB GATE 3 b.c. Creetown 123 – Glazepta Final (Final Straw 127) [1990 6m   —
6g⁵ 7m 1991 10d⁶ 9m] bog, good-topped colt: seems of little account. *B. Stevens.*

COBBLERS HILL 2 gr.c. (May 19) Another Realm 118 – Morning Miss 59   **53**
(Golden Dipper 119) [1991 5m* 5m³ 6f³] 2,100F, 1,800Y: plain, workmanlike colt: seventh foal: half-brother to 3-y-o Birling Ashes and 1989 2-y-o 5.8f and 1m winner Conjurer (both by Magic Mirror): dam lightly raced: fairly useful plater: won at Bath (retained 3,900 gns) in May: not seen out after third in nursery at Warwick in July: stays 6f. *J. White.*

COCHABAMBA (IRE) 2 br.f. (May 16) Thatching 131 – Bolivia (GER)   **94** p
(Windwurf (GER)) [1991 6.1g² 7m* 7g⁵ 6m* 7d³ 7.3g³] quite attractive filly: has a quick action: third foal: half-sister to 3-y-o Mystic Crystal (by Caerleon), fair 7f winner at 2 yrs, and a winner in Italy: dam useful winner at 2 yrs in Germany: successful at Ayr in maiden in July and nursery (despite hanging throughout and giving impression ill at ease on ground) in September: third in nursery at Ascot and listed race at Newbury (behind Soiree) afterwards: will stay 1m: improving. *P. W. Chapple-Hyam.*

COCHINEAL (USA) 3 br.f. Vaguely Noble 140 – Crimson Queen (USA)   **52**
(Crimson Satan) [1990 NR 1991 10m 10.2g 11.7m⁵ 11.8m 16m⁵] $375,000Y: lengthy, unfurnished filly: has a markedly round action: half-sister to at least 6 winners in North America, including 2 stakes winners: dam, minor sprint winner at 2 yrs and 3 yrs in USA, is half-sister to good American colts Barbizon and Hillsborough: plating-class maiden: moderate fifth of 13 in Nottingham handicap, headway travelling well straight then fading (not striding out at all well) closing stages: stays at least 11.7f: may do better on a softer surface. *B. W. Hills.*

CO-CHIN (IRE) 2 gr.c. (Mar 15) Coquelin (USA) 121 – Whiffswatching (USA)   **79**
(Sassafras (FR) 135) [1991 5d² 5d² 5m³ 7m* 7g³ 7m 7.6d⁴ 8g] IR 4,600F, 3,000Y: leggy, sparely-made colt: first foal: dam sister to smart French middle-distance colt

Prix Thomas Bryon, Saint-Cloud—
Code Breaker holds the persistent challenge of Tabac by three quarters of a length

Gap of Dunloe: modest performer: won minor contest at Ayr in June: should stay 1¼m: acts on good to firm and dead ground. *D. Moffatt.*

COCKED HAT GIRL   4 ch.f. Ballacashtal (CAN) – Screen Goddess 65 (Caliban —
123) [1990 8g a12g 10g 10m⁵ 10m⁵ 10.6v³ 12.5m² 18d 12d a11g⁵ 1991 a11g⁶ 14d] big, workmanlike filly: poor plater: stays 1½m: acts on any going: below form when blinkered. *S. R. Bowring.*

COCO QUEEN   2 b.f. (Feb 26) Today And Tomorrow 78 – Zarnina 56 (The   **46**
Brianston 128) [1991 5.1g⁵ 5m⁴ 5.3f² 5.2f 5f] 620Y: leggy filly: moderate mover: fourth foal: half-sister to poor sprint maiden Russian Express (by Bay Express): dam 2-y-o 5f seller winner: ran poorly in sellers last 2 starts. *J. Berry.*

COCOS ISLAND (USA)   2 b.g. (Mar 19) Proud Birdie (USA) – Devious Dancer   **60 p**
(USA) (Raise A Bid (USA)) [1991 7g⁵ 6g⁵ 6f⁶] $65,000 2-y-o: tall, good-topped gelding: has scope: second known foal: half-brother to a minor winner in North America: dam 7f winner: sire best at 1¼m: quite modest form at Newbury (minor event) and York (quite valuable maiden won by Great Palm) first 2 starts: evens, below best in Folkestone maiden (better for race) 2 months later in October: gelded after final start: possibly suited by some give: likely to make up into better 3-y-o. *P. W. Chapple-Hyam.*

CODE BREAKER (FR)   2 b.c. (Feb 27) Cariellor (FR) 125 – Tinderella (Hot   **111**
Spark 126) [1991 7.5g² 7g* 7m⁴ 8d⁵ 8s*] 300,000 francs (approx £30,000) Y: strong, good sort: sixth foal: half-brother to 2 winners in France, including 5f (at 2 yrs) to 1m winner Never Late (by Mendez): dam poor maiden: successful in listed race (by a head from Silver Kite) at Deauville in August and 4-runner Prix Thomas Bryon (by ¾ length from Tabac) in October: ran behind Arazi in Prix de la Salamandre (better effort) and Ciga Grand Criterium (never a factor) at Longchamp in between: suited by 1m: acts on good to firm and soft ground: very useful. *P. Bary, France.*

COFFEE ICE   2 b.f. (May 3) Primo Dominie 121 – Cafe Noir 74 (Comedy Star   **101 d**
(USA) 121) [1991 5.2d* 6g² 6m² 6m⁶ 6g 6g] leggy, lightly-made filly: has a smooth action: first foal: dam 2-y-o 6f winner stayed 1m: won maiden at Newbury in June: narrowly beaten runner-up at Newmarket in Ewar Stud Farm Stakes and Hillsdown Cherry Hinton Stakes, finishing strongly behind Musicale latter occasion having been short of room 1f out: subsequently ran moderately in Princess Margaret Stakes at Ascot (said to have suffered from an infection), listed contest at Ayr and Racecall Gold Trophy at Redcar: useful on her day: sold 44,000 gns Newmarket December Sales. *R. Hannon.*

COINAGE   8 gr.g. Owen Dudley 121 – Grisbi 96 (Grey Sovereign 128§) [1990 12h⁵   —
16.2m 11.5m⁶ 12m 16m 1991 11.5m⁶ 12d 16.2d] big, rangy gelding: poor performer nowadays: blinkered and no show at 8 yrs: used to be suited by a test of stamina and top-of-the-ground: has run tubed: winning chaser in May. *R. F. Johnson Houghton.*

COINCIDENTAL   9 b.g. Persian Bold 123 – Gentle Mulla (Sun Prince 128) [1990   **48**
a7g² a7g⁵ a8g 7g 8m a7g 8.3f³ 8.3m⁵ 8g 8f⁴ 7.5m a8g⁶ a7g 1991 8f] close-coupled, workmanlike gelding: poor mover: poor handicapper: not seen out after June:

effective at 7f to 9f: acts very well on top-of-the-ground, unsuited by heavy: keen sort. *D. Morris.*

COIR 'A' GHAILL 3 b.f. Jalmood (USA) 126 – Karsavina 89 (Silly Season 127) **27** [1990 6m 6f² 6g 7m 1991 10d 14f 15g² 15g⁶ 15s 15g⁴ 13d] leggy, close-coupled filly: plater: stays 15f: below form on soft going: blinkered 4 times, including last 2 starts: sold to join P. Hobbs 1,500 gns Ascot July Sales. *C. B. B. Booth.*

COLD MARBLE (USA) 6 b.g. Told (USA) – Coney Dell 77 (Ercolano (USA) — 118) [1990 12g⁴ 16m⁶ 14s 15m² 14.6d⁴ 1991 11.8g 12f] rather leggy, workmanlike gelding: poor mover: modest handicapper at 5 yrs when mostly trained by W. Haggas: tailed off in 1991: stays 2m: acts on firm and dead going. *D. R. Tucker.*

COLD SHOWER (IRE) 2 b.g. (Apr 4) Kings Lake (USA) 133 – Arctic Ford **52** (FR) 85 (Arctic Tern (USA) 126) [1991 a8g⁴ a7g³] 6,000Y, 4,000 2-y-o: second living foal: dam 7f winner: plating-class form for 7-lb claimer in late-year maidens at Southwell: will stay 1¼m. *J. A. Glover.*

COLERIDGE 3 gr.c. Bellypha 130 – Quay Line 117 (High Line 125) [1990 NR **78** § 1991 11g 11.7g⁴ 15.3m* 11.5m⁴ 16.2g³ 16.2g 14s⁴ 20g 16.1m] 5,800 2-y-o: tall, leggy colt: moderate mover: sixth living foal by thoroughbred stallion: half-brother to 3 winners, including middle-distance stayer Mill Line (by Mill Reef) and useful 1986 2-y-o 1m winner Known Line (by Known Fact): dam won Park Hill Stakes: modest performer: won maiden at Wolverhampton in May, making most: swishing tail in paddock and on toes, ran badly final start: suited by test of stamina: acts on good to firm ground, probably not on soft: blinkered first 3 starts, visored afterwards: not one to trust implicitly. *M. R. Channon.*

COLIN SELLER 4 ch.g. Noalto 120 – Mallow 70 (Le Dieu d'Or 119) [1990 12f³ — 12.3f 10.2m a12g 5m² 6f* a5g⁵ 6m 6g⁶ 5f² 5.1m⁶ 6g 1991 5g 6d 8m 6m 6f 8.2d 7m 5.9m] good-topped, workmanlike gelding: has a quick action: quite modest handicapper at best, on the downgrade nowadays: stays 6f: goes well on firm going: effective with or without blinkers: tried visored once: trained first 4 starts by P. Blockley. *R. W. Stubbs.*

COLLABORATE (IRE) 2 b.c. (Mar 7) Shareef Dancer (USA) 135 – Royal Saint — p (USA) (Crimson Satan) [1991 8g] good-bodied colt: has scope: sixth foal: half-brother to French 3-y-o 1½m to 13.5f winner Elevated (by Shirley Heights): dam, winner from 1m to 1¼m in USA, is half-sister to dam of Mt Livermore and Magical Wonder: 20/1, green and very much in need of race, one of first off bridle in 16-runner minor event at Newbury in October: looks sort to do much better: retained 8,800 gns Ascot November Sales. *G. Harwood.*

COLLIDE 3 ch.f. High Line 125 – Collapse 107 (Busted 134) [1990 NR 1991 8v* **102** 7.1s² 8m* 8d] rather unfurnished filly: has a quick action: sister to winning Irish stayer Carricero and half-sister to several winners, including fair 6f winner Lapse (by Bold Lad): dam won from 5f to 1m: won minor events at Kempton in June and Newbury (easily best effort, quickened well to lead 1f out and beat Heart of Darkness 3½ lengths) in September: co-favourite in Ascot listed race final start: uncertain to stay much beyond 1m, though bred to do so: probably acts on any going: tends to get on toes. *H. Candy.*

COLLINA DEL FONTE 3 b.f. Reesh 117 – Bellina Benedetta (Pablond 93) — [1990 NR 1991 a8g a6g] fourth living foal: dam lightly-raced maiden on flat and over hurdles: well beaten in maiden and claimer at Southwell late on. *J. Balding.*

COLLINS AVENUE (USA) 3 b.c. Linkage (USA) – Trolling (USA) (Sir **106** Gaylord) [1990 6d² 1991 8d* 8d* a12g² 12g⁶ 11.9g³ 10g⁴ 12m² 11.9g³] lengthy, unfurnished colt: impresses in appearance: has a markedly round action: useful performer: won maiden at Doncaster and minor event at Ayr in spring: excellent 8 lengths third of 7 to Corrupt in Great Voltigeur Stakes at York final start, never able to challenge: stays 1½m: acts on good to firm ground and dead. *B. W. Hills.*

COLONEL FAIRFAX 3 gr.g. Alias Smith (USA) – Mistress Meryll 61 (Tower **50** Walk 130) [1990 NR 1991 6g 6s⁶ 5m 10.2f 11g⁶ 10m³ 8m²] workmanlike gelding: seventh foal: half-brother to 7f to 8.3f winner Sergeant Meryll (by Marching On) and a winner abroad: dam sprinter: plating-class form: worthwhile form only when placed, running on really strongly from rear in apprentice handicap at Newcastle final start, in August: stays 1¼m: acts on good to firm ground: mulish to post fourth start. *J. W. Watts.*

COLONEL POPSKI 9 ch.g. Niniski (USA) 125 – Miss Jessica 90 (Milesian 125) — [1990 NR 1991 16.2g 17m] very lightly raced and little form on flat. *Miss G. M. Rees.*

Mr K. Abdulla's "Colorific"

COLONIAL OFFICE (USA) 5 ch.g. Assert 134 – Belles Oreilles (CAN) —
(Nentego 119) [1990 NR 1991 17.2g] workmanlike gelding: one-time quite modest
maiden: tailed off only start at 5 yrs: suited by 2m: acts on firm going. *P. J. Hobbs.*

COLORADO INSIGHT 3 b.f. Green Ruby (USA) 104 – Holly Burton 73 (King —
Emperor (USA)) [1990 NR 1991 12.3d 12f³ 15.8f⁵ 12.1f⁵ 12.2g] 1,000Y: small, angular
filly: moderate walker and mover: sixth foal: half-sister to a winner in Hong Kong by
Skyliner: dam, half-sister to smart sprinter Tackerton, placed over 5f at 2 yrs and
unraced at 3 yrs: plating-class maiden on flat: flattered in slowly-run 3-runner race
at Beverley: winning hurdler. *Mrs V. A. Aconley.*

COLORADO ROCKY 3 gr.g. Belfort (FR) 89 – Continental Divide 50 (Sharp —
Edge 123) [1990 NR 1991 10g 8f a7g 15g] workmanlike gelding: has very round
action: eighth foal: half-brother to 5f (at 2 yrs) to 8.5f winner Honey Boy Simba (by
Mansingh): dam poor plater: little sign of ability in maidens and sellers: appeared
not to stay 15f. *P. S. Felgate.*

COLORFAYRE 3 ch.f. Tate Gallery (USA) 117 – Independentia 68 (Home Guard —
(USA) 129) [1990 7m⁴ 7f³ 7m a6g³ 1991 8g 5g 10g 7g⁴ a7g 7m] lengthy, sparely-
made filly: plating-class form as 2-y-o, none in 1991: stays 7f: blinkered fourth start.
L. J. Codd.

COLORIFIC 2 b.c. (Apr 26) Rainbow Quest (USA) 134 – Miss Petard 113 **109**
(Petingo 135) [1991 7m 7f* 7m 8s²] workmanlike colt: tenth living foal: half-brother
to several winners, including Musidora and Park Hill winner Rejuvenate (by Ile de
Bourbon) and useful miler Cracking Form (by Habitat): dam won at up to 1½m:
favourite following promising debut, won 18-runner maiden at Newbury in August:

172

useful form after in Prix de la Salamandre (beaten around 7 lengths by Arazi) at Longchamp and Juddmonte EBF Beresford Stakes (beaten 2½ lengths by El Prado) at the Curragh: will stay middle distances: acts on any going: likely to win more races. *B. W. Hills.*

COLOSSUS 3 ch.c. Good Times (ITY) – Adrana 86 (Bold Lad (IRE) 133) [1990 8s 1991 10g³ 10m 8g⁴ 8g³ 11.5m 10.1g 5s⁴ 7g 6m⁴ 7m 6f⁴ 7d 6d*] robust, lengthy colt: moderate mover: quite modest on most form, racing far rail when making all in 20-runner handicap at Haydock in October: best later efforts at 6f: may well be suited by an easy surface: blinkered 3 times. *C. E. Brittain.* **66**

COLOUR CHART (USA) 4 b.f. Mr Prospector (USA) – Rainbow Connection (CAN) (Halo (USA)) [1990 9d⁶ 10.5d³ 10.5d⁴ 10d⁵ 10g* 9.2g* 1991 8d* 9m 8g⁴ 9.5f² 9d² 10f⁶ 9f⁵] smart performer: won Group 3 Prix du Muguet (beat Aldbourne by short head) at Saint-Cloud in May: ran well last 4 starts in Grade 1 Beverly D Stakes at Arlington (1¾ lengths second to Fire The Groom), Ciga Prix de l'Opera at Longchamp (beaten ¾ length by Martessa), Grade 1 Yellow Ribbon Stakes at Santa Anita and Grade 1 The Matriarch Stakes at Hollywood Park: stays 10.5f: acts on firm and dead ground. *A. Fabre, France.* **117**

COLOURING BOOK (IRE) 2 ch.f. (Apr 9) Krayyan 117 – Her Name Was Lola (Pitskelly 122) [1991 5g 6.9f] 1,800Y: sturdy filly: half-sister to a winner in Holland by Sallust: dam ran 3 times at 2 yrs in Ireland: no worthwhile form in southern maidens: moved poorly down on debut. *M. J. Haynes.* **—**

COLOUR QUEST 3 ch.f. Rainbow Quest (USA) 134 – Formulate 119 (Reform 132) [1990 7g⁶ 1991 10.3m⁵ 10m] compact, rather angular filly: seventh live foal: half-sister to several winners, including 1¼m winner/Oaks second Game Plan (by Darshaan) and 15.8f winner Almarreekh (by Glint of Gold): dam top staying 2-y-o filly of 1978, ran only twice afterwards: no worthwhile form in maidens: sold 8,200 gns Newmarket December Sales. *C. E. Brittain.* **—**

COLOUR SERGEANT 3 br.g. Green Desert (USA) 127 – Tartan Pimpernel 109 (Blakeney 126) [1990 6g⁴ 6g 1991 6f³ 8.2m⁵ 8m⁵ a8g* 8m³ 9g 8g] strong, close-coupled gelding: fair form: 9/4 on, won maiden at Southwell in August: easily best effort in handicaps after when very good third at Newmarket, outpaced 2f out then running on strongly: should stay beyond 1m: acts on good to firm ground: gelded after final start. *Lord Huntingdon.* **82**

COLTRANE 3 b. or br.c. Dominion 123 – Rainbow's End 83 (My Swallow 134) [1990 NR 1991 7m a8g* 9m 9g²] 40,000Y: leggy, quite attractive colt with scope: sixth foal: half-brother to several winners, including fairly useful stayer Cap Del Mond (by Troy) and Varnish (by Final Straw), fair 7f winner at 2 yrs: dam 2-y-o 6f winner: 9/4 on, won maiden at Southwell in July: 25/1 and visored, very good second of 18 to Barkerville in £30,800 handicap at Newbury, always prominent: stays 9f: wore crossed noseband last 2 outings. *Lord Huntingdon.* **77**

Prix du Muguet, Saint-Cloud—Colour Chart (No. 3) just gets the better of Aldbourne;
Boxing Day (No. 2) beats Zille in another close finish for third

COLWAY ANN 3 b.f. Nomination 125 – Sharp Run (Sharpen Up 127) [1990 5f6 **51** 6d3 5f4 7f 6m 6v3 5s3 1991 5m6 5g a5g* a5g6 5g] close-coupled, unfurnished filly: poor performer: well below form after making all in seller (bought in 3,800 gns) at Southwell in May: stays 6f: acts on any going: carries head high: rather temperamental: sold 1,650 gns Ascot July Sales. *A. P. Stringer.*

COLWAY BOLD 2 br.c. (Apr 6) Never So Bold 135 – Jhansi Ki Rani (USA) 94 **103** (Far North (CAN) 120) [1991 6g* 6m* 6f* 5m3 6.3s* 6g] IR 21,000Y: good-topped, useful-looking colt: fourth foal: half-brother to 3-y-o 1m winner Jamestown Boy (by King of Clubs), fair 7f and 1m winner Kikala (by Kalaglow) and 11f winner Kings Rank (by Tender King): dam 7f and 1m winner: useful performer: won maiden at Ripon and 4-runner minor event at Redcar on first 2 starts: best efforts when successful in 3-runner BonusPrint Champion Two-Year-Old Trophy at Ripon (by 1½ lengths from Harvest Girl in August) and 21-runner Goffs Premier Challenge Race at the Curragh (by short head from Lucky Lindy in October): subsequently unable to dominate (ran moderately) in Racecall Gold Trophy at Redcar: needs further than 5f and will stay 7f: acts on any going: races keenly. *J. W. Watts.*

COLWAY CROWN (IRE) 3 b.c. Wassl 125 – Dignified Air (FR) 70 (Wolver — Hollow 126) [1990 8.2s 8m 1991 8s 6g 11g 8m] workmanlike colt: moderate mover: behind in maidens and handicaps: dead. *A. P. Stringer.*

COLWAY DOMINION 3 ch.c. Dominion 123 – My Therape 112 (Jimmy Reppin **69** 131) [1990 5m* 6f5 1991 8g 8m4 7.2m4 8.2g6 6d 6m 8m2 7m 7.6d] useful-looking colt: modest handicapper: ran moderately, making most, at Chester final start: stays 1m: acts on good to firm ground and dead: visored and early to post last 3 outings: sold 11,000 gns Newmarket Autumn Sales: may be of unsatisfactory temperament. *J. W. Watts.*

COLWAY GIRL 2 ch.f. (Mar 30) Celestial Storm (USA) 132 – Petsy 84 — (Mummy's Pet 125) [1991 7m 7f 10m] 920Y: leggy, angular filly: third foal: half-sister to a winner in Spain: dam 2-y-o 6f winner: no worthwhile form, including in claimer: sweating and edgy final start. *B. Hanbury.*

COLWAY PRINCE (IRE) 3 b.g. Prince Tenderfoot (USA) 126 – El Cerrito — (Tribal Chief 125) [1990 6f5 7v 7d 1991 7.5g 5g a7g] workmanlike gelding: well beaten in maidens and handicap: sold 2,600 gns Ascot July Sales: resold out of Miss K. George's stable 2,700 gns Ascot November Sales having run once over hurdles. *A. P. Stringer.*

COMANECI (IRE) 3 b.f. Ahonoora 122 – Church Mountain 83 (Furry Glen 121) **68** [1990 NR 1991 8m 10m4 10.2g 7g 10d] 24,000F, 16,000Y: lengthy, good-topped filly:

Goffs Premier Challenge, the Curragh—
Colway Bold, Lucky Lindy and Taylor Quigley (left to right) head a strong British challenge

has a round action: half-sister to fair 1985 2-y-o 6f winner Mac's Flyer (by Godswalk): dam won over 6f at 2 yrs, but failed to train on: modest maiden at best, form only on second start: soundly beaten in claimer on final one: should stay further: trained first 3 starts by H. Cecil. *J. Akehurst.*

COMBINATION 2 b.c. (Apr 11) Primo Dominie 121 – Port Na Blath (On Your **91** Mark 125) [1991 5m 6m* 6g* 6g 7m⁵ 6m³ 6m⁶] 17,500F, 30,000Y: sturdy, lengthy colt: second foal: half-brother to 3-y-o Recording Contract (by Song): dam Irish 6f winner: quite useful performer: successful in good style in maiden at Nottingham in May and minor event at Pontefract following month: suited by 6f: pulled much too hard fifth outing: sold 30,000 gns Newmarket Autumn Sales. *Mrs J. R. Ramsden.*

COMEDIE FLEUR 3 b.f. Martinmas 128 – Welsh Flower (Welsh Saint 126) — [1990 6f⁶ 5f 5m 5v 199 1 6m 6f 5f] unfurnished filly: no worthwhile form, including in sellers: blinkered once: trained until after reappearance by J. Balding. *J. Berry.*

COMEDY FUN 7 b.g. Comedy Star (USA) 121 – Get Involved 79 (Shiny Tenth — 120) [1990 NR 1991 10f 7.5m 10.5m 10.2g a8g] big, good-topped gelding: has a round action: no worthwhile form. *B. Ellison.*

COMEDY RIVER 4 br.c. Comedy Star (USA) 121 – Hopeful Waters 66 (Forlorn — River 124) [1990 6f⁵ 6f³ 5.8h⁴ 6f³ 5m³ 6f⁶ 7f³ 8m⁶ 6m⁴ 7d³ 6d⁵ a10g² 1991 a10g a11g⁶] leggy, rather sparely-made colt: moderate walker: has a roundish action: plating-class maiden: may well prove best at up to 1¼m: acts on firm and dead going. *J. L. Spearing.*

COME HOME ALONE 3 ch.g. Sayf El Arab (USA) 127 – Apprila (Bustino 136) **54** [1990 6m⁵ 6m⁴ 7f⁵ a8g⁴ a8g² a7g⁴ a7g³ 1991 10.1d 10m 10g⁶ 10g⁴ 8.2f a8g] angular gelding: plating-class maiden: below form after fourth in claimer at Windsor in July: stays 1¼m: best efforts at 2 yrs on all-weather: bolted to post on reappearance: joined N. Gaselee. *R. Hannon.*

COME ON CHASE ME 7 ch.h. Sharpo 132 – Dragonist 82 (Dragonara Palace — (USA) 115) [1990 NR 1991 5f] rather leggy, good-quartered horse: poor mover: fair form at best as 5-y-o: tailed off in July claimer, only run on flat since: best form at 5f: acts on any going: wears crossed noseband. *J. Etherington.*

COME ON DANCER (IRE) 3 ch.c. Ahonoora 122 – Crimson Royale 84 (High — Line 125) [1990 NR 1991 a8g⁴ 10.5g] IR 62,000Y: good-topped colt: fourth foal: half-brother to Irish juvenile hurdle winner Loose Ends (by Persian Bold): dam, 1¼m to 11.7f winner, is sister to very smart 1¾m horse Crimson Beau: no worthwhile form in maidens, off course over 3 months in between: sold to join J. White 5,000 gns Newmarket Autumn Sales. *D. R. C. Elsworth.*

COME ON MY GIRL (IRE) 3 gr.f. To-Agori-Mou 133 – Travelin' Joan (USA) **64** (Al Hattab (USA)) [1990 7g³ 8g³ 1991 8g³ 6f* 6d 6g⁵ 7m a6g⁴ 5g 5.2f 5m³ 6.1m 6.1m⁴] lengthy filly: quite modest handicapper on her day: won maiden at Brighton in April: ran creditably in claimers ninth and final starts: seems best at 6f: acts on firm going: ran fairly well on all-weather: blinkered fourth and fifth starts: sold to join S. Chadwick 3,200 gns Doncaster October Sales: temperament under suspicion. *R. Boss.*

COME TO GOOD 4 br.f. Swing Easy (USA) 126 – Demta (Astec 128) [1990 8m⁵ — a12g 1991 10v 8f] plain filly: seems of little account. *M. P. Muggeridge.*

COME TO TERMS 5 gr.g. Welsh Term 126 – Sparkling Time (USA) (Olden **70** Times) [1990 a12g* a14g² 1991 13.8d² 12.3s⁴ 12m² 12f 12f⁴ 15.8f³ 15g⁴] tall, leggy gelding: moderate mover: modest handicapper: stays 15.8f: acts on any going: usually held up and set quite a bit to do: has run well for amateur: bandaged: largely consistent. *T. D. Barron.*

COMIC RELIEF 4 br.f. Comedy Star (USA) 121 – Moberry 54 (Mossberry 97) — [1990 7g 6m 6d 6g 8.2s 6d 1991 5f 6m 10.2f 8.9m] sturdy filly: moderate mover: poor maiden. *B. C. Morgan.*

COMINO GIRL 5 b.m. Indian King (USA) 128 – Arab Art (Artaius (USA) 129) — [1990 a11g³ a10g⁴ a11g* a13g⁴ 11.7m 1991 a12g] small, sturdy mare: poor performer: stays 11f: usually blinkered: sold 1,200 gns Ascot Summer Sales. *A. S. Reid.*

COMMANCHE DANCER (IRE) 2 b.c. (Jan 27) Commanche Run 133 – Final **89 p** Act 64 (Decoy Boy 129) [1991 6g 6f² 6m² 6.1m*] 13,000F, 10,000Y: strong, sturdy colt: has scope: moderate mover: half-brother to 2 winners, including very useful 1984 2-y-o sprinter Vaigly Oh (by Vaigly Great): dam won three 1m sellers: made all in 6-runner minor event at Chester in August, running on well despite drifting right: virtually refused to race on debut: will stay 1m+: progressing well. *W. A. O'Gorman.*

COMMANCHE GUEST (IRE) 3 b.g. Commanche Run 133 – Canadian Guest **70**
74 (Be My Guest (USA) 126) [1990 8m^6 7m^3 7s 1991 11.7s^3 12d 12m* 12h^2 12g]
lengthy, angular gelding: modest handicapper: well backed despite poor previous
effort when winning at Edinburgh in June: second of 4 at Carlisle and behind at
Royal Ascot (chased leaders 1m) after: stays 1½m: probably acts on any going:
joined Mrs L. Piggott. *R. Guest.*

COMMANCHE LAD (IRE) 3 b.g. Commanche Run 133 – Miss Upward 77 **— p**
(Alcide 136) [1990 NR 1991 12.1d^6 16m^4] 7,400Y: good-bodied gelding: half-brother
to several winners, including very useful middle-distance filly Miss Petard (by
Petingo), the dam of Musidora and Park Hill winner Rejuvenate: dam won at 1¼m:
bit backward, 10 lengths fourth of 7 in maiden claimer at Redcar in August: shapes
like a stayer: can improve again. *Miss L. C. Siddall.*

COMMANCHE SIOUX (IRE) 3 b.f. Commanche Run 133 – Papsie's Pet **58**
(Busted 134) [1990 NR 1991 12.2m^3 12m* 13.8g] 3,000Y: small, lengthy
filly: half-sister to fair 1m winner Acestes (by Gorytus) and a winner in USA by
Kings Lake: dam, Irish 9f winner, is daughter of very smart sprinter Merry Madcap:
always close up when winning claimer at Doncaster in June: favourite, lost position
very quickly 2½f out in handicap at Catterick: worth another chance at beyond
1½m: sold to join K. Morgan 8,600 gns Newmarket July Sales. *A. C. Stewart.*

COMMANDING OFFICER 4 b.g. Be My Guest (USA) 126 – Honeypot Lane **46**
91 (Silly Season 127) [1990 10.1m 10f 10m 1991 12f 10d 12.5d 10f^4 8f^4 8g^2 7.6d 7g]
lengthy gelding: poor performer at best: evidently suited by 1m: possibly unsuited
by dead ground: reluctant in blinkers once: sold 850 gns Newmarket Autumn Sales.
C. A. Cyzer.

COMMENDABLE (IRE) 3 b.c. Baillamont (USA) 124 – Praise (FR) 116 (Hard **102**
To Beat 132) [1990 8g* 1991 10.5g^4 12m 11g^6] lengthy, good-bodied colt: promising
efforts when winning 2-y-o maiden and 12 lengths fourth of 8 to Environment Friend
in Dante Stakes in May, both at York: easily better effort in October handicaps when
blinkered 9 lengths sixth of 14 to Halkopous at Newbury, front rank 9f: probably
stays 11f. *G. Harwood.*

COMMON COUNCIL 2 br.g. (May 2) Siberian Express (USA) 125 – Old **73**
Domesday Book 93 (High Top 131) [1991 5g a7g^3 7m^3 8g^6 7m* a8g*] compact
gelding: second foal: half-brother to 3-y-o Survey (by Glint of Gold): dam 10.4f
winner better at 1½m: modest form: made most in late-year maiden at Lingfield,
beating Paper Clip ½ length: won 2-runner Newmarket Challenge Cup on previous
start: stays 1m: has run well for 7-lb claimer. *G. A. Pritchard-Gordon.*

COMPUTER KID 2 b.c. (Mar 10) Alleging (USA) 120 – Melanoura (Imperial **90**
Fling (USA) 116) [1991 5g^4 5f* 5m^2 5g^3 6g^4 6m^4 7.5g* 8v^3 9v^2] 900F: workmanlike,
good-quartered colt: poor walker and mover: first foal: dam ran twice at 2 yrs: fair
performer on English form: won maiden at Redcar in May: 8 lengths fourth of 14 to
Dilum in Coventry Stakes at Royal Ascot and (blinkered) over 7 lengths last of 4 to
Showbrook in Anglia Television July Stakes at Newmarket: subsequently left G.
Moore's stable, winning listed event at Firenze: stays 1m: probably acts on any
going. *A. Renzoni, Italy.*

COMSTOCK 4 ch.g. Coquelin (USA) 121 – Maura Paul (Bonne Noel 115) [1990 **87**
10.6s^6 10g* 10m^3 12m* 12m 1991 12g^3 12.3g 11.9m^3 12g 13.9g 12m^2 10m 12d]
lengthy gelding: good mover: fairly useful handicapper at best: none too consistent
in 1991: should stay beyond 1½m: acts on good to firm ground. *J. G. FitzGerald.*

COMTEC FLYER 3 ch.f. Valiyar 129 – Comtec Princess 73 (Gulf Pearl 117) **46**
[1990 a7g a8g 1991 a8g^6 a8g^5 a8g^2 a8g* a10g a8g 9d^6 10m a8g] compact filly:
plating-class performer: made all in handicap (apprentice ridden) at Southwell in
February: should stay further than 1m: hung badly left on good to firm ground: often
blinkered: visored final start (May). *J. F. Bottomley.*

CONCERT PITCH 12 ch.g. Royal Match 117 – Ballychord (DEN) (Ballymoss **45 d**
136) [1990 a8g^5 a11g^3 a8g^2 a8g^5 a8g* a8g^5 8.2f^4 8f^3 8m^6 7f^3 7m^2 7.6g 8g 7m 7g^5 6m
1991 a8g a8g^3 a8g^2 a8g^6 a7g^4 8m 8m 7.1d a8g] strong, dipped-backed, lengthy
gelding: has a round action: poor handicapper: best at 7f to 1m: acts on any going:
has won in blinkers: good mount for inexperienced rider. *B. Palling.*

CONE LANE 5 ch.g. On Your Mark 125 – Cee Beauty 74 (Ribero 126) [1990 7h* **35**
7f 1991 a7g^6 7g 7m^5] workmanlike gelding: poor handicapper: suited by 6f or easy
7f: acts on hard going: ran poorly in blinkers: tends to pull hard. *B. Gubby.*

CONFOUND (IRE) 2 b.g. (Feb 9) Wolverlife 115 – Arachosia (Persian Bold 123) **—**
[1991 6d 6g 5d] IR 7,800F, 8,400Y: lengthy, rather unfurnished gelding: moderate

mover: second foal: dam ran once at 3 yrs in Ireland: well beaten in varied events, final one in June. *J. Akehurst.*

CONFRONTER 2 ch.c. (Feb 19) Bluebird (USA) 125 – Grace Darling (USA) **82** (Vaguely Noble 140) [1991 7d 7.1m³ 7g² 6m⁵ 6.1d² 6s*] strong, workmanlike colt: second foal: half-brother to 3-y-o 1m winner Sixofus (by Glenstal), also fair 6f winner at 2 yrs: dam twice-raced daughter of half-sister to Sussex Stakes winner Ace of Aces: fair performer: favourite, comfortably won 20-runner maiden at Folkestone in November: will stay 1m: has form on good to firm ground but seems well suited by soft. *P. F. I. Cole.*

CONGRESS (IRE) 2 b.f. (Mar 12) Dancing Brave (USA) 140 – Celtic Assembly **86 p** (USA) 95 (Secretariat (USA)) [1991 7g 7f³ 8m* 7m²] good-bodied filly: moderate mover: fourth foal: closely related to 1m winner In Vision (by Bellypha) and half-sister to 2 winners, including 3-y-o Volksraad (by Green Desert), successful at 6f (at 2 yrs) and 7f: dam 10.6f winner, is daughter of Welsh Garden, top 2-y-o filly in Ireland in 1975: made all, showing much improved form, in maiden at Leicester in September, quickening over 1f out to win by 6 lengths: creditable second in nursery at Newmarket following month: strong-running type, likely to prove suited by at least 1¼m. *M. R. Stoute.*

CONISTON LAKE (IRE) 2 ch.g. (Mar 16) Coquelin (USA) 121 – High Lake **62** (Quisling 117) [1991 6g⁴ 6g⁴ 8m] IR 3,400Y, 17,000 2-y-o: neat gelding: half-brother to several winners, including useful 1983 2-y-o 6f winner Ziggurat (by Pitskelly): dam won from 9f to 13.5f in Ireland: quite modest maiden: stays 1m: joined G. Lewis. *Denys Smith.*

CONJURING (USA) 3 b.c. Devil's Bag (USA) – Hint (USA) (Nijinsky (CAN) **65** 138) [1990 NR 1991 8m² 10g] $250,000Y: tall, leggy colt: has been hobdayed: has a round action: second foal: half-brother to useful 1989 French 2-y-o Sentimental Side (by Diesis), a 1m winner at 3 yrs: dam, 3-y-o maiden winner at about 1m in USA, is closely related to Glow: easily beaten 6 lengths by 5/2-on shot Veriga in maiden at Newcastle, staying on: again with tongue tied down, well beaten in similar event at Newbury later in October. *J. H. M. Gosden.*

CONNED AGAIN 2 b.g. (Apr 23) Prince Sabo 123 – Baby's Smile 68 (Shirley **65** Heights 130) [1991 5d 5f⁶ 5g* 5f⁴ 5m⁴ 6g* 6d 7m* 6m² 6m² 6.1m* 7g 5m⁶ 7.9g⁶ 6g⁴ 6m⁴] 8,800F, 5,200Y: plain, leggy, close-coupled gelding: moderate mover: fourth foal: half-brother to 3-y-o 1½m winner Smiles Ahead (by Primo Dominie) and staying plater For A While (by Pharly): dam suited by a good test of stamina: quite modest performer: successful in median auction maiden at Thirsk in May, then seller (no bid) at Redcar and claimers at Leicester and Nottingham in mid-summer: stays 7f: best form on a sound surface: effective with or without blinkers: bandaged near-hind fourth outing: has sweated: often on toes: inconsistent. *M. W. Easterby.*

CONOR LILY (USA) 3 b.f. Darby Creek Road (USA) – Lilting Lily (King **99** Emperor (USA)) [1990 7d³ 6s⁶ 1991 8v² 8d² 8g² 11.3d² 11g³ 11m⁴ 10m² 10g⁵ 10s² 12d* 10s²] seventh foal: half-sister to fairly useful 6f winner Key To The Music (by Key To The Kingdom) and 2 winners in USA: dam once-raced half-sister to Irish St Leger winner Conor Pass: useful Irish performer: second to Peplum and fifth to Ruby Tiger in 6-runner races for Cheshire Oaks at Chester and Pretty Polly Stakes at the Curragh fourth and eighth starts: often narrowly beaten in Ireland, but justified favouritism in maiden at the Curragh in November: stays 1½m: possibly needs an easy surface. *K. Prendergast, Ireland.*

CONQUETE (IRE) 3 gr.f. Godswalk (USA) 130 – Day Dress (Ashmore (FR) **64** 125) [1990 7s a8g⁶ a7g 1991 a8g³ 8g 10m⁵ 8g] sparely-made filly: has a quick action: quite modest performer: stays 1m well: 3 times a winner in Scandinavia. *C. C. Elsey.*

CONQUISTA 3 ch.f. Aragon 118 – Divine Fling (Imperial Fling (USA) 116) [1990 **87** 7m⁴ 7f 6g⁴ 7m⁵ 7g⁶ 8d⁴ 1991 7m² 7m 8s³ 7g⁴ 7f² 7.1g³ 8m⁵ 8g* 8m⁴] leggy, workmanlike filly: progressive form: won handicap at Brighton in September, leading near finish: fourth of 17 in similar event at Doncaster month later, coming from towards rear: stays 1m: easily best efforts on a sound surface: blinkered last 6 starts: headstrong, taken down early nowadays: sometimes mounted on track: retained 7,400 gns Ascot October Sales. *Lady Herries.*

CONSIGLIERE 3 ch.c. Caerleon (USA) 132 – Miss Silca Key 102 (Welsh Saint **84** 126) [1990 NR 1991 7d² 8m* 7g] 36,000Y: quite attractive colt: third foal: half-brother to useful but disappointing 1990 3-y-o Silca An' Key (by Commanche Run) and useful 6f winner Silca Supreme (by Chief Singer): dam won 7f Jersey Stakes: fair form in Goodwood maidens first 2 starts, successful in September: second favourite, soundly beaten in apprentice event at Ascot 12 days later, dropping tamely away having led 3½f: should stay beyond 1m. *R. Charlton.*

CONSTRUCTIVE (IRE) 3 ch.c. Gorytus (USA) 132 – Shirley's Joy (Shirley   —
Heights 130) [1990 5m 8m⁵ 6m a7g a7g³ a8g 1991 10d] lengthy colt: plating-class
maiden: driven along early when in mid-division in April handicap as 3-y-o: best
effort over 7f on all-weather: blinkered last 2 starts at 2 yrs: has been bandaged
near-hind. *B. W. Hills.*

CONSTRUCTIVIST (IRE) 2 b.c. (Feb 26) Fools Holme (USA) – Spire 75   **69**
(Shirley Heights 130) [1991 6m 7g² a7g²] IR 40,000F, 54,000Y: quite attractive colt:
first foal: dam maiden stayed 1¾m: second to Well Saddled at Salisbury and Liability
Order at Southwell late in year: will be suited by 1m +. *B. W. Hills.*

CONSULATE 5 gr.g. Absalom 128 – Maiden Pool 85 (Sharpen Up 127) [1990 NR   **67**
1991 6m 7m 5g² 5g⁵ 5d* 6g 5d² 5m³ 5g⁴ 5m] stocky gelding: quite modest
handicapper: won at Ayr in July: effective at sprint distances, and has raced over 1m:
acts on good to firm and dead ground: successful twice on equitrack at 3 yrs. *J.
Balding.*

CONTACT KELVIN 9 br.g. Workboy 123 – Take My Hand 49 (Precipice Wood   —
123) [1990 12g 13g 12m 12d 1991 12m] big, strong gelding: no form on flat for long
time: winner over fences in October. *N. Bycroft.*

CONTESSA (USA) 3 b.f. Blushing Groom (FR) 131 – Last Feather (USA) 120   **92**
(Vaguely Noble 140) [1990 NR 1991 8s⁴ 8m* 9m⁶ 10d⁵] deep-girthed filly: moderate
mover: half-sister to French 9f winner Phar Feather (by Lyphard) and Irish 1¼m
winner Limber Dancer (by Nijinsky): dam 7.3f and 10.5f winner third in Oaks: won
maiden at Pontefract in October: ran well facing stiff task in Newmarket listed races
won by Susurration and (last of 5) Mohican Girl: stays 1¼m. *G. Harwood.*

CONTESTED BID (USA) 2 b. or br.c. (May 17) Alleged (USA) 138 – Queens **111**
Only (USA) (Marshua's Dancer (USA)) [1991 8g⁴ 8d* 10v³ 8f*] eighth foal:
half-brother to 4 winners, including smart 1982 American 2-y-o 1m and 9f winner
Only Queens (by Transworld) and quite useful 1988 2-y-o 6f winner Roback (by
Roberto): dam, 6f to 1m winner in USA, is closely related to Native Royalty, smart at
about 9f: won 9-runner Hoist The Flag Stakes (Div.2) at Hollywood Park in
December by 1¾ lengths: previously successful in maiden at Saint-Cloud and 5
lengths third of 9 to Glaieul in Criterium de Saint-Cloud: stays 1¼m: acts on any
going. *M. Zilber, France.*

CONTINENTAL CARL (IRE) 3 b.c. Two Punch (USA) – Lady Roberta   —
(USA) (Roberto (USA) 131) [1990 6g⁶ 5f* 6f 5f 5m 6d 6m a7g a6g³ a6g² a6g³ 1991 a 66
a6g⁴ a6g* 6g 6g 6g 6g 7g] good-topped colt: put up clearly best effort when making
all in claimer at Southwell in March: better at 6f than 5f: acts on firm and dead
ground: wears blinkers or visor. *J. R. Jenkins.*

CONTRACTORS DREAM 3 b.g. Librate 91 – Opal Lady 64 (Averof 123) [1990   —
a6g 8m 1991 7m 6m⁶ 5.1d] workmanlike gelding: bad plater. *J. M. Bradley.*

CONVIVIAL 3 b.f. Nordance (USA) – Rensaler (USA) (Stop The Music (USA))   **75**
[1990 6m³ 6g² 1991 8d* 7g 7m⁶ 8.2g⁵ 7v] rather leggy, quite attractive filly: modest
walker: modest performer: won median auction maiden at Thirsk in April: fair sixth
of 8 at Thirsk, best effort in handicaps: stayed 1m: acted on dead ground: in foal to
Never So Bold. *A. A. Scott.*

CONYGAR PARK 4 b.c. Mummy's Treasure 84 – Whistling Girl 68 (Whistling   —
Wind 123) [1990 10s 10g 12d 1991 10f⁵ 9f 6g 5m] tall, leggy colt: little worthwhile
form: probably stays 1¼m: tried blinkered once: sold 2,000 gns Ascot November
Sales. *R. Guest.*

COOCHIE 2 b.f. (May 16) King of Spain 121 – York Street (USA) (Diamond Shoal   **36**
130) [1991 5f 6g 5.7m 6m 7f⁵ 10.5d] 1,500Y: small, rather leggy filly: first foal: dam
ran twice at 2 yrs: poor maiden: has run in sellers: may well prove suited by 1m:
blinkered second start: sold 1,300 gns Newmarket Autumn Sales. *I. A. Balding.*

COOLABA PRINCE (IRE) 2 b.c. (Feb 18) Red Sunset 120 – Acquire 105   **52**
(Burglar 128) [1991 5g⁵ 5g⁶ 5m⁴ 5f⁴ 5g⁵ 5d⁴] 16,000Y: sturdy, rather angular colt:
half-brother to several winners, including smart 5f performer Chellaston Park (by
Record Token): dam won twice over 5f at 2 yrs: plating-class maiden: visored,
creditable fourth in Doncaster nursery final outing: acts on firm and dead ground:
has run creditably in blinkers. *F. H. Lee.*

COOL COQUELIN (IRE) 3 ch.f. Coquelin (USA) 121 – Cool Gales 85 (Lord   —
Gayle (USA) 124) [1990 5m⁵ 6m⁶ 5f⁵ 5.3h³ 5f³ 5.1m⁶ 5f³ 5g a6g⁴ a6g 1991 8f] small,
plain filly: moderate plater: shaped quite well at Brighton in May but not seen out
again: likely to stay 1m: acts on firm going: ran respectably on equitrack: tail flasher:
inconsistent at 2 yrs. *J. R. Jenkins.*

COOL ENOUGH 10 ch.g. Welsh Captain 113 – Sundrive (Status Seeker) [1990 **48**
7m³ 7.5m* 8f² 8f² 7.5m⁴ 7m² 7m 7g 8.2m⁵ 7g³ 8.5g 7m* 7m⁴ 7f⁴ 8m 6m³ 7f⁴ 7m
6s⁶ 1991 7d⁴ 8d 7.5f 6g⁴ 7m⁴ 7h* 7f 8d 8m 8g⁴ 7f 7f⁵] small, sturdy gelding:
plating-class handicapper: won at Carlisle in May: ideally suited by 7f to 1m: acts on
any going: often apprentice ridden, not at Carlisle: usually taken quietly to post:
tough. *Mrs J. R. Ramsden.*

COOLEY'S VALVE (IRE) 3 b.c. Pennine Walk 120 – First Blush (Ela-Mana- **98**
Mou 132) [1990 NR 1991 8g 8d* 10.4g² 7d² 11.9g⁶ 8m²] 150,000Y: rangy,
good-topped colt: impresses in appearance: good walker: moderate mover: first foal:
dam half-sister to Chief Singer: fairly useful form: won maiden at Kempton in May:
½-length second in slowly-run listed race at York then minor events at Salisbury
and (11/4 on, below form) Ayr: will prove suited by further than 7f, and should be
suited by stronger pace at 1¼m: acts on dead ground. *B. W. Hills.*

COOLINSKY 3 b.f. Domynsky 110 – Cooling 89 (Tycoon II) [1990 NR 1991 8g⁶ **— p**
10d⁵ 12.2g] lengthy, angular filly: fifth foal: half-sister to 1983 2-y-o 5f winner
Airling (by Import) and quite modest 6f winner Lucky Blue (by Blue Cashmere):
dam won at 1¼m and 13f: well beaten but some promise in summer maidens,
keeping on not knocked about first 2 starts and chasing leaders 9f (took keen hold)
on third: may well prove capable of better, particularly short of 1½m. *M. H. Easterby.*

COOLNESS (USA) 3 b.f. Cool (USA) – Allegedly Flashing (USA) (Alleged **—**
(USA) 138) [1990 NR 1991 8m 10m⁵ 12s⁶ a13g] smallish, lengthy filly: second foal:
dam unraced half-sister to Laugh And Be Merry, winner of Grade 1 1¼m Flower
Bowl Handicap at 5 yrs: sire 1m winner in France at 3 yrs later graded 1m and 1¼m
winner in USA: 50/1, best effort when 11¾ lengths fifth of 16 to Missed Again in
maiden at Leicester, taking keen hold and never nearer: possibly unsuited by soft
going. *J. H. M. Gosden.*

COOL PARADE (USA) 3 ch.g. Listcapade (USA) – Yours Trudy (USA) (Star **55**
Envoy (USA)) [1990 8g 7s⁴ 1991 7s⁴ 10m⁵ 8.2d 8m 8.5f* 9.2d⁶ 9m⁴ 9.9f 8h 10.5d
12.2g⁴ 8m*] leggy, quite good-topped gelding: quite modest performer: won minor
event at Beverley in July and handicap (ridden by 7-lb claimer) at Leicester in
October: should prove best at up to 1¼m: acts on any going, except seemingly on
hard: visored (ran creditably) eighth outing: inconsistent: sold to join G. Moore
10,000 gns Newmarket Autumn Sales. *S. G. Norton.*

COOL RUN 6 b.m. Deep Run 119 – Loyal And Regal 51 (Royal And Regal (USA)) **72**
[1990 12f⁴ 11m⁴ 10.6s 10g* 10m² 10f⁶ 12g² 12m 10.6g² 13.3g 10.5g² 10d⁵ 1991 9.9f⁶
10g² 10.5m 10m 10.5d] leggy, quite good-topped mare: carries plenty of condition:
moderate mover: modest handicapper: ran moderately last 3 starts: best at 1¼m to
1½m: probably acts on any going: tough. *B. A. McMahon.*

COOL SOCIETY (USA) 2 ch.c. (Apr 26) Imp Society (USA) – Icy Friend (USA) **66 ?**
(It's Freezing (USA)) [1991 6g⁶ 6g 6.1g⁶ a7g⁴ 8m* 8.1m 8.2m] $58,000Y:
good-quartered colt: has a quick action: fourth reported foal: brother to a winner in
USA at up to 1m: dam minor sprint winner in USA: sire best at 8.5f to 1¼m: easily
best effort when winning nursery, apprentice ridden, at Warwick in August, running
on well to lead post: stays 1m: inconsistent. *C. R. Nelson.*

COOLULAH 4 b.g. Dominion 123 – Phoebe Ann 76 (Absalom 128) [1990 6m⁶ 5g*
6m² 6g 6m 5m⁴ 1991 a7g 8.3g 8m] sparely-made gelding: quite modest handicapper
at 3 yrs: no form in 1991: stayed 6f: acted on good to firm ground: sold out of M.
Pipe's stable 1,550 gns Ascot June Sales: dead. *M. C. Chapman.*

COPPER BURN 3 ch.f. Electric 126 – Divetta 72 (Ribero 126) [1990 7m* 7g **68**
8.2d5 1991 10.1f 11m² 10g² 11.5g] smallish, angular filly: fluent mover: quite modest
performer: strong-finishing second in handicap at Southwell, second and best effort
at 3 yrs: should stay 1½m: tends to sweat in preliminaries. *J. R. Fanshawe.*

COPPER BUTTERFLY (USA) 2 ch.f. (Apr 24) Blushing Groom (FR) 131 – **64**
Copernica (USA) (Nijinsky (CAN) 138) [1991 7m⁵ 8s³] half-sister to several
winners, including good-class 1987 2-y-o Crusader Sword (by Damascus), Grade 1
winner at 6.5f: dam won 5 races, showing smart form at 2 yrs when successful at up
to 6f: quite modest form in October maidens: will stay 1¼m. *J. H. M. Gosden.*

COPPERMILL LAD 8 ch.g. Ardoon 124 – Felin Geri (Silly Season 127) [1990 **61 d**
5m 6d 6m 6m 6m 6m* 6m 6d 6s³ 6s⁵ 1991 6v² 6d⁴ 6g⁶ 7g⁶ 6m 6d⁵ 6v³ 5d⁴ 6g⁵ 5g⁵
7g] compact gelding: carries plenty of condition: has a round action: modest
handicapper at best, not so good nowadays: suited by 6f: acts any going, but seems
ideally suited by plenty of give in the ground: usually gets behind. *L. J. Holt.*

COPPER PLATING 3 b.c. Rousillon (USA) 133 – Etching 109 (Auction Ring **64**
(USA) 123) [1990 7m² 7m³ 1991 7g⁴] big, strong colt: modest form in maidens:

sweating and in need of race, good fourth of 7 at Sandown in June: will stay 1m. *P. W. Harris.*

COPPER RIVER 4 b.g. Glint of Gold 128 – Carmelina 98 (Habitat 134) [1990 8g* **60** 12f² 12f³ 1991 a11g* a11g⁶ 12.5d 12g³ 13.8f² 12m² 13.6g⁶ 12.2g⁴ 13.8f⁴ 16.5g a12g⁵ 14.6m] lengthy, quite attractive gelding: plating-class performer: stayed 13.8f: acted on firm ground: dead. *R. Hollinshead.*

COPPER TOP 4 b.f. Longleat (USA) 109 – Quorn Rocket (Roan Rocket 128) — [1990 5m 8f 6g 8g 7.5f 1991 6g 5f 5g 6m 5g 10.1s] small filly: of little account nowadays: sold 900 gns Ascot November Sales. *H. J. Collingridge.*

COPPER TRADER 2 gr.f. (Apr 23) Faustus (USA) 118 – Alicia Markova 64 **53** (Habat 127) [1991 5m⁶ 8m 6s⁵] 2,000F: leggy filly: half-sister to several winners, including 1987 2-y-o 6f winner Markstyle (by Morestyle) and 3-y-o 8.3f winner Internal Affair (by Aragon): dam, half-sister to Music Maestro, Saulingo and Outer Circle, ran 3 times at 2 yrs: plating-class form in Yarmouth maiden final start: beaten in seller on debut: seems well suited by soft ground. *K. S. Bridgwater.*

COPY LANE (IRE) 2 br.c. (Apr 30) Runnett 125 – Airy Queen (USA) (Sadair) **55** [1991 6m 7d 5.7f⁴ 5.7m 6m⁴ 8.2m⁵ 8g 7.6m] 8,400Y: leggy colt: half-brother to several winners, including fairly useful 1981 Irish 2-y-o 6f winner Okanango (by Homeric): dam won at 2 yrs and 3 yrs in Italy: inconsistent maiden: seems suited by 1m: best form on top-of-the-ground. *M. R. Channon.*

CORAL FLUTTER 4 b.f. Beldale Flutter (USA) 130 – Countess Olivia 80 **46** (Prince Tenderfoot (USA) 126) [1990 10g³ 8f² 8.2m⁵ a8g 1991 a7g⁶ a10g 7d⁴ 9s 7m² 7d 8.3g⁴ 7m³ 7m 7g⁵ 6.9f⁶ 8f⁶ 7m² 8g⁵] lengthy, good-quartered filly: has a quick action: poor maiden: effective at 7f and stays 1¼m: acts on firm going: keen sort: has run creditably when blinkered or visored. *J. W. Payne.*

CORALS DREAM (IRE) 2 b.c. (Jan 18) Petorius 117 – Walkyria (Lord Gayle **101** (USA) 124) [1991 5d* 6g² 5m 6m² 7m⁴ 8g³ 7.6d* 8g³] IR 32,000F, 21,000Y: lengthy, useful-looking colt: has scope: has a fluent, round action: fourth foal: dam Irish middle-distance winner from family of Slip Anchor: useful performer: won maiden at Pontefract in April and nursery (impressively) at Chester in October: ran several other good races, notably when fourth of 5 to Rodrigo de Triano in Laurent-Perrier Champagne Stakes at Doncaster and when third of 19 to Cumbrian Challenge in Redcar nursery final start: stays 1m: has form on good to firm ground but gives impression will prove best suited by some give: usually on toes: taken down early second start. *J. J. O'Neill.*

CORCINA 3 gr.f. Kalaglow 132 – Feather Flower 74 (Relkino 131) [1990 6m⁴ **86** a7g* 7g* 8g² 7.3g 1991 8s⁴ 8g⁵ 10f 10.6g* 12g⁴] leggy filly: fair performer: made all in £11,900 handicap at Haydock in June: again 20/1, set strong pace and clear 2f out when fair fourth of 19 in King George V Handicap at Royal Ascot 12 days later: contested Italian listed races first 2 starts: may prove best at 1¼m: takes keen hold, too headstrong and reportedly swallowed tongue third outing: wore tongue strap afterwards. *M. Bell.*

CORDILLERO 5 b.g. Head For Heights 125 – Petipa (FR) 115 (Habitat 134) — [1990 8f 7m 11.5m 10m* 12g* 10d 1991 9.7m] angular ex-Irish gelding: poor mover: quite modest performer at 4 yrs: ran badly only start in 1991 (July): stays 13.6f: acts on good to firm going: has been blinkered: sometimes bandaged. *A. Moore.*

CORINTHIAN GOD (IRE) 2 b.c. (Apr 12) Red Sunset 120 – Rathcoffey — Duchy (Faberge II 121) [1991 5.7f⁶ 7m] IR 10,000F, 17,500Y: half-brother to several winners, including useful 1977 Irish 2-y-o 5f and 6f winner Rathcoffey Dodo (by Jukebox) and 1½m winner Rathage (by Horage): dam won from 7f to 11f in Ireland: well beaten in maidens at Bath and Wolverhampton in July. *P. W. Harris.*

CORLEY BOY 3 b.g. Elegant Air 119 – Corley Moor 97 (Habitat 134) [1990 7g 7m **63** 8d 1991 8g 10g 8s 8.2d* 10g 8m² 8.1g 10g] quite good-topped gelding: moderate mover: quite modest form on his day: ridden by 7-lb claimer and sweating, first form when winning claimer at Nottingham in April: should stay 1¼m: acts on good to firm ground and dead: visored fourth to sixth outings: trained until after sixth by Lord Huntingdon. *D. R. Gandolfo.*

CORLEY FLOWER 2 b.f. (Apr 28) Sizzling Melody 117 – Dame Corley **42** (L'Enjoleur (CAN)) [1991 5.1m 6f 6m 8m] 6,200Y: sparely-made filly: first foal: dam unraced daughter of fairly useful 2-y-o 5f winner Corley Moor: quite modest plater: races keenly, and probably doesn't stay 1m. *P. D. Cundell.*

CORLY SPECIAL 4 b.g. Lyphard's Special (USA) 122 – Courreges 75 (Manado — 130) [1990 NR 1991 14.6s] workmanlike gelding: fourth foal: half-brother to 2 poor animals: dam placed over 5f and 6f at 2 yrs: third in NH Flat race at Lingfield in February: backward in Doncaster maiden on debut in March. *L. J. Codd.*

CORN FUTURES 3 b.f. Nomination 125 – Hay Reef 72 (Mill Reef (USA) 141) 77 [1990 6g⁵ 6g² 6d* 5d 1991 6d² 6m² 5g² 6d⁵ 7g 7f 8d⁴ 8d 7.6d² 7g] compact filly: has a quick action: modest handicapper: good second at Kempton, Epsom, Sandown and Chester: ran poorly final start: may prove ideally suited by 7f: acts on good to firm ground and dead: often takes keen hold: sweating at Chester: has joined J. Leigh. *R. F. Johnson Houghton.*

CORNHILL MELODY 3 ch.f. The Minstrel (CAN) 135 – French Cutie (USA) — (Vaguely Noble 140) [1990 NR 1991 12h³ 14.8f⁵ 16m³ 11.5f 10g] 30,000Y: stocky filly: eighth foal: half-sister to 3 winners (at up to 9f) by Northern Prospect, including 5-y-o 7f and 1m winner Threshfield, and to 2 winners by Distinctive Pro: dam unraced: well beaten in 3 small-field maidens then handicaps: blinkered fourth start. *J. L. Spearing.*

CORNISA 3 gr.f. Dawn Johnny (USA) 90 – Lallax 109 (Laxton 105) [1990 8.2m — 1991 10g³ a7g] tall, leggy, sparely-made filly: always behind in minor events (behind fairly useful pair on reappearance) then maiden. *M. R. Leach.*

CORN LILY 5 ch.m. Aragon 118 – Ixia 91 (I Say 125) [1990 12m 12.8g⁶ 13m⁵ 78 12.2d² 11g² 11m⁵ 12f² 12f* 10m* 12.3m² 12m⁶ 12g 12m³ 12m 1991 11f² 13d² 12.3f³ 12.3f* 12m* 12f⁵ 12f* 13.8m*] tall, leggy mare: modest handicapper: better than ever at 5 yrs (trained as 4-y-o by N. Tinkler): successful at Ripon and Southwell in August and Thirsk and Catterick (ridden by 7-lb claimer) in September: stays 1¾m: acts on firm and dead going: well suited by forcing tactics: genuine and consistent: credit to her trainer: winning hurdler. *Mrs G. R. Reveley.*

CORPORATE TYPE (IRE) 3 b.g. Last Tycoon 131 – Sherkraine 98 (Shergar — 140) [1990 5m 6m⁵ 7m 7h⁶ 8g⁴ 8.2g⁴ 8m 7m² a7g a7g⁵ a7g a8g 1991 a10g a10g 12.2g 12m 9.9f 10m⁵ 10f 10m a11g a12g⁵ a12g] medium-sized gelding: quite modest maiden at best, but lost his way: probably stays 1¼m: has carried head high. *D. W. Chapman.*

CORRESPONDENT 2 b.f. (Apr 8) Double Schwartz 128 – Kala's Image 55 — (Kala Shikari 125) [1991 6.1m] 1,600F, IR 3,000Y: small filly: first foal: dam sprinter: 33/1 and burly, tailed-off last of 18 in Nottingham maiden in October. *C. B. B. Booth.*

CORREZE 3 b.f. Stanford 121§ – Our Mandy (Mansingh (USA) 120) [1990 7m a7g — a6g 1991 10g 12s 8.3m 12g] leggy filly: soundly beaten in maidens, handicaps and sellers. *P. Howling.*

CORRIENDO LIBRE 7 b.g. Tumble Wind (USA) – Bouganville (Gulf Pearl — 117) [1990 11g 8m 1991 6m 7.1m] sturdy ex-Irish gelding: won maiden at Mallow as 3-y-o: little subsequent form: stays 7f. *J. Parkes.*

CORRIN HILL 4 b.g. Petorius 117 – Pete's Money (USA) (Caucasus (USA)) 74 [1990 a7g³ 6m 6m 7m 6m 6m 6f* 7m 6f⁶ 6m⁶ 6m 1991 6f³ 5.8f 7g* 7m 7g* 7g 7f 7g] useful-looking gelding: modest handicapper: won at Brighton (2) in summer: stays 7f: acts on firm going: effective with or without blinkers: sometimes hangs, and flashes tail: often comes from well behind: inconsistent. *B. W. Hills.*

CORRUPT (USA) 3 b.c. Lear Fan (USA) 130 – Nirvanita (FR) (Right 121 Royal V 135) [1990 7g* 7m⁴ 7m² 7f⁵ 1991 8g* 11.5g* 12f⁶ 12g⁵ 10d² 11.9g* 14.6m⁶]

Corrupt forced himself into Derby calculations with an impressive win in the Maxims Club Trial at Lingfield in May, his second win from as many starts as a three-year-old following a much-improved display in the BonusPrint Easter Stakes at Kempton where Selkirk and Environment Friend chased him home. Corrupt seemed well suited by the extra three and a half furlongs at Lingfield, coped well with the undulations and sharp downhill turn, and showed a good turn of speed to finish well on top. Unsurprisingly the 20/1 offered about his chance at Epsom quickly disappeared. The Lingfield race has a good reputation as a classic trial. In the run-up to the Derby Corrupt's form began to look as sound as any in a wide-open contest—he'd won by four lengths and a length from Young Buster and Selkirk; the next two, Walim and Marcus Thorpe, had since done well in the Derby Italiano—and on the day he started co-favourite with Toulon at 4/1.

However, not one of those who'd played a significant part in the middle-distance trials made the frame in the Derby. Corrupt finished a disappointing, remote sixth, ridden from behind with a confidence that proved misplaced when, asked to close the big gap between himself and Generous from inside the three-furlong marker, he just kept on steadily past weakening rivals. Corrupt's subsequent performances, which ended with a big defeat in the St Leger, were also disappointing to some degree, apart from a spreadeagling win in the Great Voltigeur Stakes at York in August which thrust him once again into the classic spotlight. He was soundly beaten into fifth place behind Saddlers' Hall in the King Edward VII Stakes at Royal Ascot, and though his three-length second to Zoman in the Scottish Classic at Ayr in July was an improvement on that (particularly as he was carried wide and gave the impression he wasn't quite three lengths inferior on the day) it scarcely advertised the fact that he was about to fulfil his Lingfield promise. Corrupt went on from Ayr to win the Voltigeur by six lengths from Saddlers' Hall with one of those highly effective front-running displays which were a feature at the August meeting. He was travelling clearly the best of the field of seven from early in the straight and when pushed along two furlongs out he was able gradually to increase his advantage to around six lengths in the space of a furlong, then maintain it convincingly. Corrupt was immediately promoted to ante-post favourite for the St Leger, drifting as the race drew closer because of doubts about the Voltigeur form as well as Corrupt's stamina and effectiveness on firmish ground. He finished over twenty-five lengths behind Toulon in sixth place. It became clear soon after he began to be chased along to hold onto a good position early in the straight that he wasn't going to play any significant part in the rest of proceedings; he just kept on at the same pace.

Great Voltigeur Stakes, York —
Corrupt keeps up the gallop and wins by six lengths from Saddlers' Hall

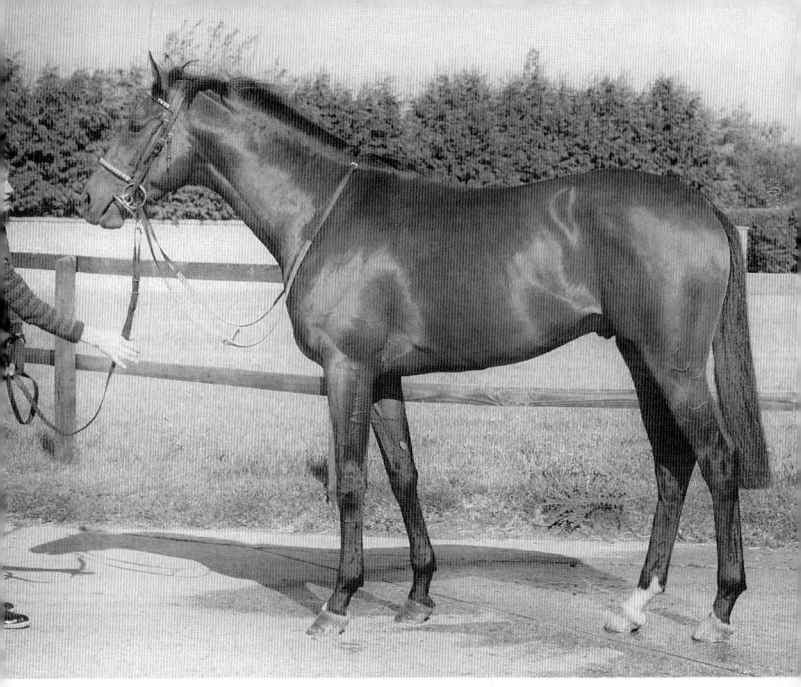

Mr F. M. Kalla's "Corrupt"

		Roberto (b 1969)	Hail To Reason Bramalea
	Lear Fan (USA) (b 1981)		
		Wac (b 1969)	Lt Stevens Belthazar
Corrupt (USA) (b.c. 1988)			
		Right Royal V (br 1958)	Owen Tudor Bastia
	Nirvanita (FR) (b 1971)		
		Nuclea (bl 1961)	Orsini Nixe

There must now be the strongest of suspicions that a firm surface is against Corrupt. He had three successive runs on good to firm or firmer as a two-year-old, showing improved form on the second occasion then disappointing on the third; the Derby and Leger are his two races on a firm surface since. Corrupt was beaten too far out at Doncaster to say he didn't stay but whether he will stay further than a mile and a half is open to question. The unraced dam produced two previous runners successful beyond a mile and a half in France by other stallions, including No Ballet (by Green Dancer) who won at very nearly a mile and three quarters; three of her five other winning produce won at around a mile and a quarter in France. The next dam Nuclea, the second-highest rated two-year-old filly in Germany in 1963, spent much of her time in France and won there at up to nine furlongs. Among her foals to reach the track was the top-class Nadjar, winner of the Prix Jacques le Marois in 1980 from Final Straw. Nuclea is one of twelve winners out of Nixe; best-known of the others are Neckar (Deutsches Derby) and Naxos (Preis der Diana). Corrupt is a tall, leggy colt; he shows some knee action. He is to be kept in training as a four-year-old and has reasonable prospects of winning another good race or two over a mile and a half if he comes back to his best. *N. A. Callaghan.*

CORYPHEE 3 b.f. Touching Wood (USA) 127 – Dance In Rome 79 (Dance In — Time (CAN)) [1990 8d a8g a8g 1991 a8g] sturdy filly: soundly beaten in handicap in January: blinkered last 2 starts: thrice slowly away: sold 1,150 gns Ascot February Sales. *Sir Mark Prescott.*

COSIMO (USA) 4 b.c. Lyphard's Wish (FR) 124 – Vashti (USA) (Iron Ruler 57 (USA)) [1990 7d* 8m a8g³ 10.6d² 8.2v² 10.4v a12g² a12g* a12g⁵ 1991 a11g² a12g a12g 13.8d 12g] sturdy colt: moderate performer at 3 yrs: lost his form: should stay beyond 1½m: probably acts on heavy going: has been tried blinkered. *P. A. Blockley.*

COSMIC DANCER 4 ch.g. Horage 124 – Royal Cloak (Hardicanute 130) [1990 52 12f³ 12.5g* 12m³ 15.3g³ 13m² 16f* 14m 1991 a14g² 17m⁶ 14.6g] small, good-quartered gelding: moderate walker and mover: plating-class handicapper: stays 2m: acts on firm going: winning hurdler. *A. Hide.*

COSMIC FUTURE 2 gr.c. (Feb 26) Siberian Express (USA) 125 – Bourgeon- 75 p ette 81 (Mummy's Pet 125) [1991 7g 7m*] 8,400Y: lengthy, angular colt: fifth foal: half-brother to 5f to 7f winner Wantage Park (by Pas de Seul), 1½m to 13f winner Silks Domino (by Dominion) and to a winner in Italy: dam 1m and 1¼m winner: won 19-runner maiden auction at Leicester in September, drawing away close home: will improve again, particularly at 1m + . *A. Hide.*

COSMIC RAY 6 b.g. Comedy Star (USA) 121 – Hey Skip (USA) (Bold Skipper 29 (USA)) [1990 NR 1991 13.8d⁶ 16s² 17m 16.5m⁴ 16m⁵ 16.5m 14.1f 14.1h⁴] leggy, workmanlike gelding: has a round action: poor performer nowadays: suited by good test of stamina: acts on good to firm and heavy going: has been blinkered and visored. *Mrs V. A. Aconley.*

COSSACK NOIR 3 b.g. Lidhame 109 – Almeda 54 (Martinmas 128) [1990 6g 6g — § 5v 7d⁶ 7d 1991 11g 7m 11g⁵ a6g] neat gelding: poor maiden: seems not to stay middle distances: seems unsuited by heavy ground: blinkered once at 2 yrs: trained until after third start by J. S. Wilson: subsequently gelded and off course 5 months: one to be wary of. *M. P. Naughton.*

COSSACK STRIKE (IRE) 3 b.c. Siberian Express (USA) 125 – My Destiny — (USA) 97 (L'Enjoleur (CAN)) [1990 NR 1991 10g 11.7g 10m 12d 10g⁶ 11.9f⁶ 11.5g] rangy colt: third foal: half-brother to French 1m and 1¼m winner Golden Mountains (by In Fijar): dam 2-y-o 7f winner, once-raced at 3 yrs: no worthwhile form: may prove better at 1m: acts on good to firm ground: sold out of D. Elsworth's stable 4,000 gns Ascot 2nd July Sales after fifth start: resold 975 gns Ascot November Sales. *W. R. Muir.*

COST EFFECTIVE 4 ch.g. Burslem 123 – Perle's Fashion (Sallust 134) [1990 35 8f 10g 8g⁵ 12m⁵ 12.3g⁵ 12f⁴ 12g⁶ 11m³ 14g 12.5m⁵ 1991 14d⁵ 16s³ 13.8g 16.5m* 16.2f¹ 16m 16m 11d 16.6m 16m 17.1m⁶ 13.1m⁷ 16.1s⁶] narrow, angular gelding: poor handicapper: won at Doncaster in May: stays very well: probably acts on any going: below form when visored. *M. Brittain.*

COT LANE 6 ch.g. Remainder Man 126§ – Smokey Princess 83 (My Smokey 125) — [1990 NR 1991 16.5m] strong, workmanlike gelding: has a round action: plating-class maiden as 3-y-o: tailed off in minor event, only flat run since: stays 10.8f: acts on good to firm and soft ground. *F. J. Yardley.*

COTTAGE GALLERY (IRE) 3 b.f. Tate Gallery (USA) 117 – Cottage Style 65 29 (Thatch (USA) 136) [1990 NR 1991 7f⁶ 6m 8f² 6f⁴ 5m 6m 5m] small, sturdy filly: third foal: closely related to plating-class maiden Canbrack Style (by Glenstal): dam, winner twice at 1½m, is out of half-sister to Lorenzaccio: poor maiden: well beaten in handicaps last 3 starts, hanging right first occasion: bred to stay at least 1m: blinkered final outing. *W. A. Stephenson.*

COTTON BANK (IRE) 3 ch.g. Sandhurst Prince 128 – Cotton Town — (Takawalk II 125) [1990 NR 1991 7g 8m 7m⁴ 6d a6g] 3,000Y: workmanlike gelding: half-brother to several winners here and abroad, notably fairly useful 1987 2-y-o 5f and 6f winner Cotton Auction (by Auction Ring): dam unraced half-sister to dams of Mr Fluorocarbon and Ksar: well beaten, including in seller. *P. Butler.*

COTTON BLOSSOM (IRE) 3 ch.f. On Your Mark 125 – Valbona (FR) (Abdos — 134) [1990 5g 5d 5g 5m² 5f⁶ 1991 7g] rather leggy filly: poor maiden at 2 yrs: didn't settle in rear and ran wide final turn in Edinburgh handicap in June, 1991: should be suited by 6f + : best effort on good to firm ground. *P. Monteith.*

COTTONWOOD 2 b.f. (Mar 13) Teenoso (USA) 135 – Smoke Creek 67 (Habitat **68** p
134) [1991 8m] leggy, unfurnished filly: fourth foal: half-sister to Irish 3-y-o
Arranvanna (by Primo Dominie), successful in Italian 1000 Guineas, and
untrustworthy 16.5f winner Ardoran (by Little Wolf): dam maiden suited by 1¼m:
33/1, slow-starting seventh of 22, staying on well, to Bold Pusuit in maiden at
Newmarket in October: showed a quick action: will do better, particularly over
further. *Lord Huntingdon.*

COUGAR 5 ch.g. Song 132 – Flying Milly (Mill Reef (USA) 141) [1990 NR 1991 8g] —
workmanlike gelding: fair plater at 3 yrs: no show only run in 1991 (May): should
stay 11f. *Mrs S. M. Austin.*

COUNT BARACHOIS (USA) 3 b.g. Barachois (CAN) – Seattle Queen (USA) **71**
(Seattle Slew (USA)) [1990 NR 1991 10g 9f⁶ 10m² 12.4m³ 10.4g⁵ 10.3m] robust
gelding: second foal: dam minor winner in USA: modest maiden: ran badly in
handicap final start: should prove effective at 1½m: best effort on good ground: sold
10,500 gns Newmarket Autumn Sales. *M. A. Jarvis.*

COUNT BERTRAND 10 b.h. Brigadier Gerard 144 – Gingerale (Golden Horus **35**
123) [1990 7.5m 8.2m² 8g⁶ 8f² 8.5f³ 8m⁴ a8g⁵ a10g⁴ 1991 a10g 8.5f⁶ 8f⁶] lengthy
horse: poor handicapper: suited by 1m and top-of-the-ground: bandaged on
all-weather: often starts slowly and gets behind: inconsistent. *W. Holden.*

COUNTER BLAST 2 b.f. (May 6) Valiyar 129 – Trading 74 (Forlorn River 124) —
[1991 a7g a7g] fourth live foal: dam won 7 races from 1m to 1¾m: soundly beaten in
maiden and a claimer at Southwell late in year. *W. Holden.*

COUNTERCHECK (IRE) 2 b.c. (Apr 13) Try My Best (USA) 130 – Swift **58**
Reply (He Loves Me 120) [1991 6g 6m 7.1s⁶ 6s] IR £27,000Y: quite lengthy colt: has
scope: third foal: brother to 3-y-o Italian 7.5f winner Gortlemon Star, also 1m winner
in Ireland at 2 yrs: dam 1½m winner: plating-class maiden: best effort when sixth in
strongly-run event at Chepstow: should stay at least 1m. *C. F. Wall.*

COUNTESS OF POLAND (USA) 3 b.f. Danzig Connection (USA) – **71**
Priceless Countess (USA) (Vaguely Noble 140) [1990 7f⁴ a6g⁴ 1991 a8g³ a6g² 5f²
6g* 5.8m² 6g* 5m 6m² 6m⁴ 6f 6m] tall, workmanlike filly: quite modest
handicapper: won at Kempton in April and Ripon in May: below form last 3 starts, in
apprentice event second occasion, after bolting to post on third: suited by 6f: acts on
firm going: wears bandages, eyeshield on all-weather: game. *Mrs L. Piggott.*

COUNT ME OUT 6 ch.g. Vaigly Great 127 – Balatina 85 (Balidar 133) [1990 a6g **41** §
a7g* a6g a7g a7g⁶ a7g³ a7g³ 5f³ 6g 7.6m 7h a8g a6g a7g a5g⁴ a6g³ 1991 a6g² a7g⁵ a 51 §
a6g⁶ a7g⁶ a7g³ a6g 6v⁴ 7d 6d³ 6f 6.1m a6g³ a7g a6g³ a7g⁵ a7g] lengthy, plain
gelding: poor mover: plating-class handicapper: trained until after tenth start by R.
Hoad, off course over 6 months subsequently: stays 7f: acts on any going: used to
wear blinkers, not last 8 starts: often finds little: unreliable. *J. Pearce.*

COURAGE-MON-BRAVE 3 gr.g. Bold Owl 101 – Bri-Ette (Brittany) [1990 —
7m 8g⁶ 1991 10.8g 11.7s 12f a12g] compact gelding: has a round action: plating-class
maiden: never dangerous in handicaps last 3 starts: sprint bred, but seems to stay
10.8f: winning hurdler in August: sold to join J. Roberts 1,500 gns Ascot October
Sales. *G. A. Pritchard-Gordon.*

COURAGEOUS KNIGHT 2 gr.c. (May 7) Midyan (USA) 124 – Little Mercy 90 **67**
(No Mercy 126) [1991 7g 6f 7m⁶] 15,500Y: lengthy colt: has scope: fifth foal:
half-brother to very tough and useful 6f to 7.3f winner Knight of Mercy (by Aragon)
and modest 1987 2-y-o 6f winner Silent Sister (by Hind of Hush): dam, 7f and 1m
winner, best at 5 yrs: quite modest form in autumn maidens at Newbury and
Leicester last 2 starts: may well stay 1m. *R. Hannon.*

COURT CIRCULAR 2 b.c. (Apr 10) Miswaki (USA) 124 – Round Tower 93 **77**
(High Top 131) [1990 6d 8.1g⁵ 8m² 8g] strong, lengthy colt: has scope: has a long,
round action: sixth foal: half-brother to 3-y-o 11.7f and 13.1f winner Moat Garden (by
Sportin' Life) and 3 other winners, including useful 1986 2-y-o 7f winner Roundlet
(by Roberto): dam 10.1f and 10.6f winner, is out of half-sister to Highclere: modest
maiden: best effort game second of 17 at Ayr in September: seemed to be
progressing well, but never landed a blow in 19-runner nursery at Redcar month
later: will be well suited by 1¼m + . *Lord Huntingdon.*

COURTENAY BEE 2 b.c. (Mar 26) Absalom 128 – Broken Accent (Busted 134) **70**
[1991 6g 7m⁶ 7m³ a7g⁴ a8g*] 7,600F, 11,500Y: good-bodied colt: fourth foal:
half-brother to 3-y-o Nip (by Bay Express): dam ran twice: won 9-runner maiden at
Lingfield late in year: suited by 1m. *W. Jarvis.*

COURTING NEWMARKET 3 b.g. Final Straw 127 – Warm Wind 84 (Tumble **46**
Wind (USA)) [1990 6m a6g a6g 6m³ 1991 9d³ 8s 8m] leggy, good-topped gelding:

moderate mover: quite modest at best, poor at 3 yrs: form only when third in handicaps: stays 9f: acts on good to firm ground and dead: blinkered twice: wore eyeshield on all-weather: sold to join Mrs A. Knight 5,800 gns Doncaster August Sales. *Sir Mark Prescott.*

COURTING NIECE 2 br.f. (Mar 8) Local Suitor (USA) 128 – Captain's Niece 84 **66** (Vitiges (FR) 132) [1991 6g a6g⁶ 7f 7g² 7m⁴ 8m] sparely-made filly: first foal: dam 1m to 1¼m winner: quite modest maiden: on toes, best effort when fourth of 20, beaten 3 short heads, in selling nursery at Catterick in October: weakened final 1f when below form in similar event at Doncaster 6 days later: stays 7f: best efforts when making running: edged left under pressure last 2 starts: flashed tail closing stages time before: sold 6,400 gns Newmarket Autumn Sales. *Lord Huntingdon.*

COURTLINE JESTER 2 ch.c. (Mar 3) Caerleon (USA) 132 – Bottom Line 90 **63** p (Double Jump 131) [1991 8m 8m] good-bodied colt: has plenty of scope: eighth foal: brother to useful 1½m winner Knight Line Dancer, later better in Italy, and half-brother to 3 winners, including fairly useful 1983 2-y-o 5f winner Red Line Fever (by Bay Express): dam won from 1m to 1½m: shaped promisingly when backward and green in large-field maidens at Newmarket and Leicester (stayed on well under considerate ride) in October: will improve further, particularly over 1¼m +. *M. A. Jarvis.*

COURT MINSTREL 2 br.g. (May 7) Hadeer 118 – Sheer Bliss 76 (St Paddy **51** 133) [1991 5m 5m 6m 6f 6s⁴] 16,500Y: strong gelding - good walker: half-brother to several winners, including useful Irish middle-distance winner Sheringham (by Blakeney): dam maiden, best at 2 yrs: plating-class maiden: off course 2½ months, improved efforts last 2 starts: will be well suited by 7f: acts on any going. *L. J. Holt.*

COURT ROOM 2 b.g. (Feb 15) Aragon 118 – Ladysave (Stanford 121§) [1991 5d⁴ **42** 5m 5g 7m 7g⁵ 5m 8m] smallish gelding: third foal: half-brother to 3-y-o Manaolana (by Castle Keep) and quite modest 2m winner Powersurge (by Electric): dam ran twice: poor maiden: well beaten in Doncaster selling nursery (pulled hard) final outing: stays 7f: visored last 3 starts. *Denys Smith.*

COURT TOWN 8 gr.m. Camden Town 125 – Luciennes 108 (Grey Sovereign —
128§) [1990 NR 1991 a8g] leggy, close-coupled mare: has a round action: quite modest handicapper at 6 yrs: well beaten only run in 1991 (February): suited by 1m: acts on any going: excellent mount for inexperienced rider. *D. R. Gandolfo.*

COUSIN ELLY 3 ch.f. Claude Monet (USA) 121 – Arbor Lane 70 (Wolverlife 115) **62** [1990 NR 1991 12g² 12f4 11.3d⁶ 10.6m⁴ 16.2g 10.5g 10.5d 12s*]6,000F: big, angular, plain filly: second foal: dam 1¼m to 2¼m winner: returned to form to win maiden at Folkestone in November easing down by 10 lengths from Statia, making all: stays 1½m well: goes well on soft ground (ran in snatches on firm): bandaged third and fourth starts. *P. D. Evans.*

COUTURE INNOVATORS 4 b.c. Music Boy 124 – Miss Couture 59 **57** (Tamerlane 128) [1990 10m 13.8m³ a14g* 16f² 14f6 1991 14d 14m 18d⁴ a14g² 16.2g² 14g] sturdy, lengthy colt: carries condition: has a round action: plating-class handicapper: stays 2m: acts on firm going. *P. J. Makin.*

COV TEL LADY 2 ch.f. (Feb 6) Celestial Storm (USA) 132 – Silette 84 (Siliconn **55** 121) [1991 5d³ 6m⁵ 5m³ 8g] unfurnished filly: looks weak: moderate mover: eighth foal: half-sister to several winners here and abroad, including 1983 2-y-o 7f winner Anything Else (by Absalom): dam top-of-the-ground 1¼m performer: plating-class maiden: beaten at odds on penultimate start in July, running creditably but finding 5f on sharp side: bit backward, well beaten in 18-runner nursery at Warwick over 2 months later: should be suited by around 1m. *M. H. Tompkins.*

COWORTH PARK 6 gr.g. Wolver Hollow 126 – Sparkling Time (USA) (Olden —
Times) [1990 16.2d⁶ 1991 13.3d] big, good-topped gelding: thrice raced on flat, and no worthwhile form: very stiff task in listed event in May: useful hurdler. *P. Mitchell.*

COX CREEK 4 ch.g. Coquelin (USA) 121 – Grande Maison (Crepello 136) [1990 **56** 7g⁴ 7m⁵ 7m⁵ 7m 7g 7m⁵ 7.6g 7m³ 7m 7.6m² 7.6d 1991 a7g³ a8g³ a7g a7g* a7g⁵ 7g 7.6g⁶ a7g⁴ a7g³ a8g⁶ a8g] rangy gelding: poor performer: won maiden at Lingfield in February: stays 1m: probably best on top-of-the-ground on turf: ran respectably when blinkered once: sold out of P. Mitchell's stable 5,200 gns Ascot February Sales after fourth start. *W. A. O'Gorman.*

CRABBY BILL 4 br.g. Blakeney 126 – Dancing Kathleen 53 (Green God 128) **59** [1990 10.1g 10m 10.1m a12g⁵ a13g⁵ 1991 12m⁴ 16.2g⁴ 14m 14m⁵ 11.4m⁵ 14m 17.2g⁵] leggy, lengthy gelding: quite modest handicapper at best: stays 2m: acts on good to firm ground: looked none too keen fourth outing: below form when blinkered final one. *Miss B. Sanders.*

CRACK 4 ch.c. High Line 125 – Kiss 88 (Habitat 134) [1990 12g* 12m* 12m3 14m3 **101** 14g2 16.5d2 1991 14g* 16m2 20g 15.9m4 13.4m4] rangy, well-made colt: has a powerful, markedly round action: useful performer: easily landed odds in Salisbury minor event in May: length second to Top of The World in Cementone Beaver Henry II Stakes at Sandown later in month: returned to best when fourth of 6 to Arcadian Heights in listed event at Chester final start: stays 2m: acts on good to firm ground: one paced: sent to Italy. *L. M. Cumani.*

CRACKLING 2 gr.f. (Apr 23) Electric 126 – Birch Creek (Carwhite 127) [1991 **56** 5s3 5m5 6.1d3 6.1g 7g4 7m3 a7g4 9m5 7g 8g] 8,000Y: angular filly: has a round action: third foal: half-sister to 3-y-o Final Deed (by Final Straw), successful at 7f (at 2 yrs) and 1¼m: dam maiden placed in pattern company in Italy: plating-class maiden: below best in nurseries last 3 starts: should stay well beyond 7f: acts on good to firm and soft ground, and on equitrack: suitable mount for a 7-lb claimer. *D. Marks.*

CRADLE DAYS 2 b.c. (Apr 2) Dance of Life (USA) – Dream Chaser 92 (Record **67** Token 128) [1991 5g2 6m3 6m6 5.1d2 5m5] lengthy colt, shade unfurnished: second foal: half-brother to 3-y-o Dream For Two (by Reach): dam suited by 6f: quite modest maiden: out of depth in Chesham Stakes at Royal Ascot third outing, never able to go pace in Windsor nursery (stiff task) final one: likely to be suited by at least 7f: best form with some give in ground. *R. Hannon.*

CRADLE OF LOVE (USA) 3 b.f. Roberto (USA) 131 – Kadesh (USA) (Lucky **87** Mel) [1990 NR 1991 7g 8m2 9g* 9m 10m4] $175,000Y: leggy, light-framed filly: sister to 3 winners, notably smart 1m (at 2 yrs) and 1¼m winner Mamaluna, and half-sister to several winners: dam 2-y-o 5f stakes winner: won maiden at Redcar in September, leading 3f out: tailed off in listed race and minor event following month: should stay beyond 9f. *J. W. Hills.*

CRAFT EXPRESS 5 b.g. Bay Express 132 – Lydia Rose 68 (Mummy's Pet 125) **77 d** [1990 6v 5m 5m2 5g4 6d 6g3 6m6 6m 5.6g 6d 5d2 6d 5m 6d 1991 a6g3 a7g2 a7g2 6m5 6g 7.6d 6d4 6m3 6d 6d6 6g 6g 6f 7m 6d] compact gelding: poor mover: modest handicapper: needs stiff 5f, and stays 7f: acts on good to firm ground and heavy: effective with or without blinkers or visor: often hangs: inconsistent, and hard to win with. *M. Johnston.*

CRAGSIDE 9 b.h. Hot Spark 126 – Amerella (Welsh Pageant 132) [1990 NR 1991 **—** 5.1s 5.2g] sturdy horse: one-time smart performer: damaged tendon as 7-y-o: last in October handicaps, first runs since: stays 6f: acts on any going: tried in blinkers: has been to stud: sold 600 gns Ascot December Sales. *G. Lewis.*

CRAIL HARBOUR 5 b.g. Don 128 – Broccoli (Welsh Saint 126) [1990 a7g a6g2 **63** a6g* a5g5 a6g6 a6g 6s2 6v 5g* 5g* 5g a5g5 a6g6 6s6 5d 1991 6d3 5f3 5f4 5m4 6m 5f2] angular, sparely-made gelding: quite modest handicapper: suited by 6f or stiff 5f: probably acts on any going: has been bandaged near-hind: ran creditably when visored once. *P. C. Haslam.*

CRAKAFU 5 b.g. Kafu 120 – Gayles Bambina 75 (Lord Gayle (USA) 124) [1990 **56** 6m2 5m* 6f 5m2 a5g2 5g5 5d* 5m3 6f5 1991 5g 5d 5g4 5f6 5m 5m 5g] rather unfurnished gelding: has been tubed: plating-class handicapper nowadays: best at 5f: acts on firm and dead going: ran well when blinkered once: often hangs. *M. H. Easterby.*

CRANFIELD COMET 2 b.g. (Mar 21) Beveled (USA) – Return To Tara (Hom- **76** ing 130) [1991 5v5 5s 5m3 6m5 a5g* 5m* 5g* 5m* 5m3] tall, leggy, close-coupled gelding: second foal: dam well beaten: sire (by Sharpen Up) 6f to 7f winner: made all in mid-summer in sellers (no bid) at Southwell and Wolverhampton, and claimers at Ayr and Edinburgh: below form at 6f: probably ideally suited by a sound surface: blinkered or visored last 7 starts: has tended to wander. *J. Berry.*

CRASH BANG WALLOP (IRE) 3 b.c. Le Johnstan 123 – Attendre Moi **—** (Saulingo 122) [1990 6g 6m 6m 8d 1991 8m 11.5m5] rather leggy, unfurnished colt: well-beaten fifth in ladies event at Lingfield (bandaged) in June, only form. *R. A. Bennett.*

CRAWICK GLEN 3 b.g. Bay Express 132 – Buttermilk Sky (Midsummer Night **—** II 117) [1990 NR 1991 9s 12.1d 8g] good-topped gelding: half-brother to several winners, including 5-y-o 5f winner Spanish Sky (by King of Spain) and Glideaway (by Gay Fandango), successful at up to 1¾m in Ireland: dam ran twice: well behind in maiden claimer, amateurs event and seller. *J. S. Wilson.*

CRAZY HORSE DANCER (USA) 3 b.g. Barachois (CAN) – Why Pass (USA) **70**
(Pass (USA)) [1990 5m⁵ 5f³ 5m⁴ 6g⁶ 1991 8.5m⁵ 7.5f⁶ 6.9f⁴ 10m* 10f* 10.3m 10.5g²]
good-quartered, workmanlike gelding: has plenty of scope: modest performer: won
sellers at Ripon (no bid, then bought in 9,200 gns) in August: another improved
effort when second in claimer (claimed to join F. Jordan £12,200) at Haydock: worth
a try at 1½m: acts on firm going: wore crossed noseband last 2 outings: game. *J.
Etherington.*

CREAKE'S PET 6 b. or br.h. Mummy's Pet 125 – Creake 80 (Derring-Do 131) —
[1990 NR 1991 a8g] leggy horse: won handicap at Phoenix Park as 3-y-o: behind in
varied events since: stays 7f: acts on any going: has been tried blinkered: sold 950
gns Doncaster March Sales. *K. White.*

CREAM AND GREEN 7 b.g. Welsh Chanter 124 – Jumana (Windjammer **36** §
(USA)) [1990 a7g 6g 6d 6d 1991 6d 8m a7g 10.3d⁴ 7.1g⁴ 7.6g 6.1s⁶] leggy,
close-coupled, sparely-made gelding: poor handicapper: best at 6f to 1m: suited by
plenty of give in the ground: below form when visored: headstrong, often wears
severe bridle: often slowly away: not to be trusted. *K. White.*

CREAM SILK LADY (FR) 3 b.f. Dancing Brave (USA) 140 – Loveshine (USA) —
(Gallant Romeo (USA)) [1990 6f⁴ 1991 7m] leggy, angular filly: quite modest form in
Newmarket maidens: should stay 1m. *A. A. Scott.*

CRECHE 2 b.c. (Mar 25) Bairn (USA) 126 – Melody Park 104 (Music Boy 124) **74**
[1991 5s⁴ 5g 5f⁴ 5d 6g 5m⁴ 5.1f⁴ 5m⁴ 5m² 5m² 5g² 5m⁵ 5m⁵ a5g*] 8,200F, 900Y:
leggy colt: moderate mover: second foal: brother to 3-y-o Qualitair Melody: dam
sprinter: quite modest performer: has run in sellers: made all in late-year nursery at
Southwell, beating Appealing Times by 5 lengths: will prove best at 5f: best form on
turf on a sound surface, but clearly goes well on fibresand: effective with or without
blinkers: has run creditably for 7-lb claimer. *Mrs N. Macauley.*

CREEAGER 9 b.g. Creetown 123 – Teenager 71 (Never Say Die 137) [1990 —
12.3d⁶ 12m* 12m³ 14g* a12g⁴ 15.3g³ 15g 16.5d⁵ 1991 16.5d] lengthy, good-bodied
gelding: carries plenty of condition: poor mover: modest handicapper at 8 yrs: off
course almost a year, always behind only outing in 1991: stays 2m: unsuited by soft
going, acts on any other: has worn blinkers: best held up. *J. Wharton.*

CREEFLEUR 5 b.m. Creetown 123 – Florence Mary 51 (Mandamus 120) [1990 —
6g 6g 8m 10.8g⁶ 8m⁴ 8.2m 1991 9s] workmanlike non-thoroughbred mare: poor
handicapper: stays 1m: effective on good to firm and soft going. *W. R. Muir.*

CREEGO 2 b.c. (Apr 26) Creetown 123 – Go Flamingo (Relkino 131) [1991 5g 6d **47**
6m⁴ 7m⁴ a6g⁴ 7f³] 1,200F: tall, lengthy colt: second foal: dam probably of little
account: fair plater: effective at 6f and 7f: acts on firm ground. *W. J. Pearce.*

CREE LEADER 6 b.g. Creetown 123 – Figurehead (Seaepic (USA) 100) [1990 —
NR 1991 12g 16s 12.3d] rangy, workmanlike gelding: little sign of ability. *N. Bycroft.*

CREPT OUT (IRE) 2 ch.c. (Apr 24) On Your Mark 125 – Valbona (FR) (Abdos **63**
134) [1991 6g 6f³ 5h 6m 5s⁴] 7,000Y: sturdy colt: eighth living foal: brother to 3-y-o
Cotton Blossom and half-brother to several winners in France, including useful
middle-distance performer Vanann (by Kouban): dam never ran: quite modest
maiden: will probably stay 7f: acts on any going. *Miss S. E. Hall.*

CRESELLY 4 b.f. Superlative 118 – Gwiffina 87 (Welsh Saint 126) [1990 7f* 7g **69**
7f⁵ 10f⁵ 7m⁶ 7m⁶ 6s⁵ 7d 1991 7f* 7m 7m² 7m 7d* 7.5f 8f 8.1g⁵] compact,
workmanlike filly: modest handicapper: won at Redcar in May and Ayr in July:
suited by 7f: probably acts on any going: tried visored: inconsistent. *J. G. FitzGerald.*

CRESTHILL 2 b.g. (Feb 21) Jester 119 – Rainbow Vision 73 (Prince Tenderfoot —
(USA) 126) [1991 5s] third foal: dam 2-y-o 7f winner: tailed off in 8-runner maiden at
Hamilton in April: sweating and very fractious in stalls. *N. Tinkler.*

CRESTWOOD LAD (USA) 2 ch.c. (Apr 3) Palace Music 129 – Sweet **56**
Ellen (USA) (Vitriolic) [1991 6m³ 6g³ 6g 6m⁶ 7g] $40,000Y: rather leggy,
workmanlike colt: moderate walker: has a round action: fifth reported foal:
half-brother to several winners, notably very useful sprinter Shuttlecock Corner
(by Cresta Rider): dam successful at around 6f: plating-class form in maidens,
showing speed long way first 4 starts: worth a try at 5f. *J. Berry.*

CRETOES DANCER (USA) 2 br.g. (Apr 18) Secreto (USA) 128 – Mary Read **65**
(USA) (Graustark) [1991 6f 7m 6f 6g² 5d⁵ 6g] $20,000Y: good-bodied gelding:
moderate mover: eighth reported foal: half-brother to smart 1984 2-y-o Stone White
(by Broadway Forli), successful at up to 1¼m: dam unraced: quite modest maiden:
worth another try at 7f: acts on dead ground: has run well in blinkers. *W. R. Muir.*

CRIBELLA (USA) 4 b.f. Robellino (USA) 127 – Crinoline 72 (Blakeney 126) **71 d**
[1990 11.5g⁶ 10.1m⁵ 8f 17.6m 1991 a12g* a12g* a14g 12.4v⁵ 12g] strong,
workmanlike filly: quite modest handicapper: won early-season events at Southwell
(made all): well below best subsequently, not seen out after April: should stay
beyond 1½m: possibly unsuited by heavy ground. *P. Calver.*

CRIMINAL LAW 4 b.c. Law Society (USA) 130 – Indian Maid 117 (Astec 128) **100**
[1990 12.5f* 14m* 16.2f⁵ 14.8m² 1991 13.4d⁵ 16g 13.3f] big, lengthy colt: has a long,
rather round action: useful performer: first run for almost 3 months, not at all
discredited when around 10 lengths eighth of 10 to Further Flight in Goodwood Cup:
faced stiff task in Geoffrey Freer Stakes at Newbury later in August: stays 2m: acts
on firm going, probably on dead: game. *R. Hollinshead.*

CRIMSON BLADE 2 ch.c. (May 17) Crever 94 – Red Velvet 114 (Red God 128§) **41**
[1991 5g 6g 6m] workmanlike colt: closely related to 2 winners by Crepello,
including very useful 1974 2-y-o sprinter Red Cross, and half-brother to several
winners, including useful 7f to 9f winner Scarlet Blade (by Kris): dam at best at 2 yrs
when winner over 5f and 6f: poor maiden: off course 3½ months, weakened quickly
final 1f as lack of condition told at Southwell final start. *P. W. Harris.*

CRIMSON CLOUD (IRE) 3 ch.g. Red Sunset 120 – Shangara (Credo 123) **70 d**
[1990 5f 5g 5g⁶ 6g⁴ 6g⁴ 7g⁴ 7g² 7g 8m³ 8.2s² 8m³ 7v² 7d⁴ 8.2s³ 7s⁴ 1991 10.2s⁴
12.2d² 10d 12m* 12f² 11m 12d⁴ 13.8g 12f⁶ 10.9g⁵ 12.3f 12f³ 12.4m⁶ 13.6d²]
close-coupled gelding: moderate mover: modest handicapper at best, winner at
Carlisle in April: mostly well below form afterwards: suited by 1½m: acts on good to
firm ground and heavy: has sweated: gives trouble at stalls: often makes the
running: winning hurdler. *N. Tinkler.*

CRIMSON CONQUEST (USA) 3 ch.f. Diesis 133 – Sweet Ramblin Rose **85**
(USA) (Turn-To) [1990 6f* 7g² 7m⁶ 1991 8g 10m² 9m⁴] lengthy, sparely-made filly:
fluent mover: fair performer: off course nearly 4 months, good second in minor
event at Windsor, keeping on well: disputed lead until ran wide turn in Lingfield
apprentice race final start: stays 1¼m. *H. R. A. Cecil.*

CRIMSON CONSORT (IRE) 2 b.g. (Feb 19) Red Sunset 120 – Purple **39**
Princess 93 (Right Tack 131) [1991 5d⁵ 5g 6m 7m 7.5f 8.9m] 15,000F, 13,500Y:
sturdy gelding: moderate mover: brother to winning sprinter Shades of Night and
half-brother to 3 winners, including quite modest 1989 2-y-o 5f winner Amber
Lightning (by On Your Mark): dam won 3 times at around 7f: poor form in varied
events, including a selling nursery. *N. Tinkler.*

CRISTOFORI (USA) 2 b. or br.c. (May 22) Fappiano (USA) – Somfas (USA) **110**
(What A Pleasure (USA)) [1991 7g* 7d² 7g⁴ 8m⁴ 9d*] seventh foal: closely related
to a winner by Conquistador Cielo and half-brother to 3 winners, including very
useful 1988 2-y-o 6f winner Russian Bond (by Danzig) and useful 7f winner Adbass
(by Northern Dancer): dam, from excellent family, won at up to 6f: successful in
maiden at Compeigne in July and 6-runner Prix de Conde (best effort, by 1½ lengths
from Sharp Counsel) at Longchamp in October: in frame in minor event at Évry
(behind Guislane), listed contest at Deauville (behind Code Breaker) and Prix La
Rochette at Longchamp (beaten about 2½ lengths by demoted Rainbow Corner) in
between: will stay 1¼m: acts on good to firm and dead ground. *A. Fabre, France.*

CRNAGORA (FR) 3 b.f. Esprit du Nord (USA) 126 – Dame Modeste (FR) (Iron **117**
Duke (FR) 122) [1990 8d⁶ 9d² 8v 1991 10v* 10.5s³ 10.5g³ 12d² 12d³ 12g² 12.5d*
12.5m² 12m³ 12f] leggy filly: first foal: dam placed at 1¼m at 2 and 3 yrs in France:
won maiden at Saint-Cloud in March and listed race at Deauville: ran well, always
close up, behind Snurge in Grand Prix de Deauville Lancel and Magic Night in Prix
Vermeille Escada at Longchamp eighth and ninth outings: eighth of 9 in Oak Tree
Invitational at Santa Anita, USA, on final one: stays 1½m: acts on good to firm
ground and heavy. *F. Boutin, France.*

CROAKER (IRE) 2 b.f. (Jan 10) Taufan (USA) 119 – Say Something 51 (Reform **32**
132) [1991 5f 6.1f 6d] IR 4,400F, 6,800Y: workmanlike, good-bodied filly: has a round
action: second foal: half-sister to 3-y-o Drawl (by Alzao): dam middle-distance
maiden: little worthwhile form, best effort on dead ground. *M. W. Easterby.*

CROESO 3 b.g. Sayf El Arab (USA) 127 – Coral Princess (Imperial Fling (USA) **46**
116) [1990 6m 6g⁵ 7d 6d 8d 1991 11.7s 12.2m 9d 8d⁵ 10g 10.8g⁴] lengthy,
good-quartered gelding: poor maiden: blinkered, fourth in selling handicap at
Warwick, driven along over 5f out: mostly well beaten in handicaps otherwise, twice
in amateur events: should stay 1½m: acts on dead ground. *C. A. Horgan.*

CROFTER'S CLINE 7 b. or br.g. Crofter (USA) 124 – Modena (Sassafras (FR) **50**
135) [1990 6m⁴ 6f² 5g 6g 10g 6g 6f 6f 1991 6m 9m⁴ 8h² 8h³ a8g* a7g* 8.1m⁶ 7m⁵ a8g a 67

189

a8g] strong gelding: modest handicapper: won at Southwell (2) in July: stays 1m: acts on any going: usually blinkered or visored: goes very well with forcing tactics: best form in 1991 on fibresand. *M. O'Neill.*

CROFT IMPERIAL   4 ch.c. Crofthall 110 – Farinara (Dragonara Palace (USA)   **76** 115) [1990 5f 5f⁵ 5m³ 6m 5g 6s 5s 1991 5f 5m 5g⁵ 5m 5g² 5.2f 5.1m³ 5g⁵ 5g] workmanlike, good-quartered colt: keen walker: has a quick action: one-time fairly useful handicapper, modest nowadays: best at 5f: seems to act on any going: effective with or without blinkers or visor: tends to idle: trained first 2 starts by J. Balding, next one by K. McCauley: inconsistent. *M. Johnston.*

CROFT VALLEY   4 ch.c. Crofthall 110 – Sannavally (Sagaro 133) [1990 6m³ 6g²   **78** 6d³ 6m 6m⁶ 6f² 6m* 6f⁶ 7m 6g⁴ 6f a7g⁵ a6g⁴ a6g a8g³ a10g 1991 8.5f² 8.5f* 8f³ 7g 8m² 8f⁴ 8m 8.5f* 8m⁵ 9m 8m* 7g⁶ 8g a8g] workmanlike colt: modest handicapper: won at Beverley in July (amateurs) and September and Newmarket in October: stays 9f: acts on firm and dead going: sometimes visored (ran well) at 3 yrs. *R. M. Whitaker.*

CROMER'S EXPRESS   2 ch.c. (Apr 15) Mansingh (USA) 120 – Sallusteno 80   **60** (Sallust 134) [1991 5g⁴ 5m⁴ 6d 5.2g² 6m³ 6m⁶ 7m 6g⁴ 5d²] leggy, close-coupled colt: good mover: sixth live foal: dam stayed 1m: useful plater: ran well when visored in non-selling nurseries last 2 starts, but spoilt finishing effort by ducking right both times: blinkered previous 4 starts: stays 6f: acts on firm and dead ground: twice mulish stalls: trained first 4 outings by Dr J. Scargill. *Miss L. C. Siddall.*

CRONK'S COURAGE   5 ch.g. Krayyan 117 – Iresine (GER) (Frontal 122) [1990   **67** 6m 6m 5m 6d 6m² 6g³ 6d* 6f⁴ 5m 6m² 6g² 6m 5d 6g 6m 6d* 5.8d 1991 6d² 6s² 6g* a 75 6g⁶ 6g 6m⁶ 6d⁴ 6.1s 6g² 6f⁵ 6m 6m 6m 6.1m⁶ a6g² a6g² a6g⁴ a6g* a5g a8g* a6g] big, strong, lengthy gelding: has a quick action: fair handicapper won at Kempton (gamely) in May and Southwell in November and December (amateurs): claimed out of G. Lewis' stable £4,447 after sixteenth start: effective at 6f to 1m: has won on firm going, but goes particularly well with give in the ground nowadays: visored or blinkered: often makes running. *E. J. Alston.*

CRONK'S DOMINION   3 ch.f. Dominion 123 – Zanubia 81 (Nonoalco (USA)   **47** 131) [1990 6m 7m 7m 7s 1991 8m 10m 10f 12m 10.2d⁵ a10g⁴ a10g* 8f] angular filly: won seller (no bid) at Lingfield in September, held up and leading post: behind in selling handicap 6 days later: may prove best at 1¼m: acts on good to firm ground and dead, but clearly best effort on equitrack: blinkered last 5 starts, twice making most. *G. Lewis.*

CRONK'S QUALITY   8 b.g. Main Reef 126 – Ozone (Auction Ring (USA) 123)   **56** [1990 6m 6m 6m 6d³ 6s a6g a8g 1991 6v⁶ 6d² 6f⁵ 7f 6g³ 6m 5.1m 6f* 6m⁵ 7.1g⁶ 7m⁵ 6.1m³ 7f* 7m 7.6m⁵ 7.1g 7.1m 6m⁴ 7g³ 7d 6.9f³ 7s 6.9s] small, good-quartered gelding: moderate mover: plating-class handicapper nowadays: won at Folkestone (seller) in June and Yarmouth in August: effective at 6f to 7f: acts on any going: ran poorly when blinkered: often bandaged: has bolted to post: inconsistent: sold 700 gns Ascot November Sales. *G. Lewis.*

CROSBY   5 b.h. Music Boy 124 – Yelney 65 (Blakeney 126) [1990 6f³ 7.6m a5g⁴   **65** a7g² 1991 a8g a7g⁴ a7g* a7g a7g⁵ a7g* 6d 7g² 7m⁶ 7.6g 5m 7g⁵ a6g* a7g³ a6g² a6g³ a 76 a7g⁶ a8g* a8g² a7g] good-bodied horse: fair handicapper, best on all-weather: successful in 1991 at Southwell and Lingfield (3, twice in claimers): effective at 6f to 1m: seems to act on any going: often sweats: has worn eyeshield, including when successful: effective blinkered or not: inconsistent on turf. *P. A. Kelleway.*

CROSBY PLACE   5 gr.m. Crooner 119 – Royal Bat 69 (Crowned Prince (USA)   **55** 128) [1990 a7g⁵ a10g⁴ a10g* a10g⁶ a10g² a10g² 10.2f* 10.8m a10g² 10m a12g 10g a10g 1991 a10g a10g² 10.2s³ 12m 12g a12g⁵ 9.7s* 10g⁵ 10m* 11.5f 10m 12g 12f* 10.3d] workmanlike, close-coupled mare: carries condition: plating-class handicapper: won at Folkestone in July (amateurs) and October and Pontefract in August: effective at around 1¼m to 1½m: probably acts on any going: effective with or without blinkers: none too consistent. *M. J. Haynes.*

CROSSILLION   3 b.c. Rousillon (USA) 133 – Croda Rossa (ITY) (Grey   **93** Sovereign 128§) [1990 6m⁴ 7m² 1991 8d² 7m 8f* 7g³ 8m a10g* a10g*] lengthy, quite attractive colt: good walker: easy mover: fairly useful performer: made most to win apprentice maiden at Yarmouth in September: improved form on Lingfield equitrack, winning 10-runner handicaps in November (made most, battled on well) and December (held up behind strong pace): stays 1¼m: acts on firm and dead ground, and on equitrack: goes well for claimer F. Norton. *G. Wragg.*

CROSS MAGS   4 ch.f. Hasty Word 84 – Red Squaw 61 (Tribal Chief 125) [1990 8m   **57** 7f 12.5g 1991 5m* 5f² 5f⁶ 6m 5f⁶ 6m⁵ a7g 5.1g a6g] small, stocky, plain filly: quite modest handicapper: soon outpaced when winning claimer at Warwick in spring: ran well in seller (claimed out of D. Burchell's stable £6.300) next time: below form last 6 starts: should stay 7f +: easily best efforts on top-of-the-ground: trained third to eighth starts by T. Barron. *D. Burchell.*

CROUPIER 4 b.c. Night Shift (USA) – Countess Walewski 85 (Brigadier Gerard **107** d 144) [1990 8g 8f6 8f* 8m4 1991 9m 10m3 10g6 10m5 7g 8g 10.1f 8m] rather leggy, attractive colt: useful performer at best: ran well in Brigadier Gerard Stakes at Sandown and Prince of Wales's Stakes at Royal Ascot second and third starts: way below best in varied company after: stays 1¼m: acts on firm going: found to have wrong blood count after fourth start, sweating and swishing tail before following one: blinkered final start. *C. E. Brittain.*

CROWN ANGEL (USA) 3 ch.f. The Minstrel (CAN) 135 – State Treasure — (USA) (Secretariat (USA)) [1990 5m5 6g 8m5 1991 7m 10.1g] leggy, angular filly: plating-class maiden: stiff task in handicap final start, in May: stays 1m. *R. Hannon.*

CROWN BALADEE (USA) 4 b. or br.g. Chief's Crown (USA) – Naseem **66** Baladee 82 (Kris 135) [1990 10g 8m 1991 11.5g2 10f5] strong, close-coupled gelding: has round action: quite modest and lightly-raced maiden: better at 11.5f than shorter: ran fairly well when blinkered final start: sold to join M. Usher's stable 8,000 gns Newmarket July Sales. *A. A. Scott.*

CROWN RESERVE 3 br.c. Another Realm 118 – Stardyn (Star Appeal 133) — [1990 6f2 6m2 7g3 a6g 1991 a7g5 8m a10g a12g4 a12g] sturdy colt: quite modest maiden at 2 yrs: below-form fourth of 12 in claimer at Lingfield: well beaten in handicaps (stiff tasks at first) otherwise in 1991: stays 7f. *M. J. Ryan.*

CROWPOST 3 gr.c. Lucky Wednesday 124 – Alpha Centauri 56 (Grey Mirage — 128) [1990 5m 5m 8m 1991 a8g] smallish, leggy colt: of no account. *S. R. Bowring.*

CROWTHERS 5 gr.g. Mandrake Major 122 – Milnsbridge (Dragonara Palace **43** (USA) 115) [1990 NR 1991 7f 8g5 a7g6] leggy, plain gelding: moderate walker: has a quick action: quite modest handicapper at 3 yrs: no show in 1991: stays 1m well: acts on any going. *E. Weymes.*

CRUACHAN (USA) 3 b.c. Lear Fan (USA) 130 – Sugar Hollow (USA) (Val **124** de L'Orne (FR) 133) [1990 7g2 1991 10g* 10.5g* 8m2 10m2]

Cruachan was a significant absentee from the Derby field. He was looking very promising when he chipped a bone on his off-fore just days before Epsom, and when able to return briefly in the autumn he went on to show form of a high order. At the time he got injured Cruachan stood as short as 10/1 in the ante-post market for the Derby as a result of a six-length defeat of Saddlers' Hall in a graduation race at York in May preceded by a decisive win in a maiden at Leicester. He produced an impressive burst of acceleration approaching two furlongs out at York, and went eight or nine lengths clear before being eased. October had arrived before Cruachan was seen out again in the Main Reef Stakes at Newmarket, and while he appeared fit enough in the paddock he ran as though he needed the race, tiring on the hill and going under by two lengths to Rudimentary after holding the upper hand two furlongs from home. He stepped up considerably on that form against stronger opposition in the Dubai Champion Stakes at the same venue a fortnight later when, at 8/1, he finished a half-length second of twelve to the French three-year-old Tel Quel. He was assisted by a fine ride. Kept nicely in touch in a race run for the first half mile or more at an ordinary pace, he was dashed into the lead with under half a mile to go, quickened two or three lengths clear chased by the eventual winner and Young Buster, and he held on gamely under pressure on the far rail until near the finish. There might be a doubt about Cruachan's being second-best in the Champion Stakes field, given that the fast-finishing In The Groove and Ristna were ridden less enterprisingly. But he's very much open to improvement over the winter and could be set for a good season in the top middle-distance races as a four-year-old. He shouldn't be too difficult to place early on, for he'll get into pattern races without a penalty. Something like the Brigadier Gerard Stakes at Sandown should be right up his street provided the going is suitable.

A strong, lengthy, impressive individual, Cruachan has been so lightly raced that we know little about his ground requirements; he's been seen out only on good and good to firm, clearly acting on both. The trainer, in a *Timeform Interview* given after Leicester, seemed to imply that he regarded

Mrs Michael Ennever's "Cruachan"

Cruachan (USA) (b.c. 1988)	Lear Fan (USA) (b 1981)	Roberto (b 1969)	Hail To Reason
			Bramalea
		Wac (b 1969)	Lt Stevens
			Belthazar
	Sugar Hollow (USA) (b 1980)	Val de L'Orne (b 1972)	Val de Loir
			Aglae
		Sporty Bird (b 1959)	Double Jay
			Good Sport

Cruachan as being suited by—needing even—a sound surface, commenting that if it was really fast at York he might let him run in the Dante Stakes. Describing Cruachan as a typical Lear Fan—'a big, galloping horse with a good cruising speed'—Harwood went on to reveal that the work riders felt the colt would get a mile and a half while the stable jockey felt a mile and a quarter was his trip. On racecourse evidence Cruachan is better suited by a mile and a quarter than a mile, and on breeding and temperament would seem to have a fair chance of getting a mile and a half. Lear Fan, who had a good season with his runners in 1991, has sired plenty of horses that stay better than he apparently did, including Corrupt, Run Don't Fly and Fly Away Soon. Bred in the United States—he was bought at the Keeneland Sales for only 12,000 dollars—Cruachan is out of an unraced mare by the French Derby winner Val de l'Orne. Sugar Hollow's only previous foal was placed as a two-year-old in the States. The family is respectably workaday. The second dam Sporty Bird and third dam Good Sport were minor winners who at stud produced eleven winners between them. Sporty Bird was clearly the better broodmare; among her five successful produce was a stakes-winning sprinter called Little Big Chief. *G. Harwood.*

192

CRU EXCEPTIONNEL 3 b.c. Scottish Reel 123 – Elton Abbess 86 (Tamer- **82** lane 128) [1990 6m⁶ 1991 8d 7g⁵ 9s² 8m⁵ 8.5f*] strong, good-bodied colt: fair performer: won maiden auction contest (unruly stalls) at Beverley in August, leading final 1f: may prove as effective at 1m as 9f when conditions are testing: acts on any going: wore tongue strap last 2 starts. *P. J. Makin.*

CRUISE PARTY (IRE) 3 b.c. Slip Anchor 136 – Cider Princess (Alcide 136) **93** [1990 7m⁵ 8g⁴ 1991 10g³ 11d² 13m* 12m* 16.1m⁴ 14g⁵ 11.7g 13.3g] big, lengthy colt: has a high knee action: fairly useful handicapper: won at Hamilton and Chepstow (sweating) in May: ran fine race (best of those up with pace early) when fourth in Northumberland Plate at Newcastle: well below form afterwards: probably needs further than 1½m nowadays, and stays 2m: best form on good to firm ground: takes keen hold and carries head high. *W. Jarvis.*

CRYSTADO (FR) 2 ch.c. (May 3) Crystal Glitters (USA) 127 – Kantado 93 **64 p** (Saulingo 122) [1991 7g⁶] rangy colt: half-brother to several winners, including useful 6f and 7f winner In Excess (by Siberian Express), later top-notch 4-y-o in USA, possibly best at around 9f, also to fair 1990 sprinting 2-y-o Kandara (by Dalsaan): dam raced mainly at 5f: 14/1 from 8/1, carrying condition and very green, over 9 lengths sixth of 11, lost position home turn then kept on steadily, to Alnasr Alwasheek in minor event at Kempton in September: will stay 1m: will improve. *W. A. O'Gorman.*

CRYSTAL BEAM 4 b.g. Crystal Glitters (USA) 127 – Jem Jen 85 (Great Nephew **—** 126) [1990 9g⁵ 8.5g⁶ 10.4d⁴ 12d 8m⁵ 8m⁴ 10.8m⁴ 8m⁵ 8d⁶ 1991 16.5m⁴] leggy gelding: fair performer: ran well in minor event at Doncaster in October: probably stays 2m: acts on good to firm ground: sold 9,000 gns Newmarket Autumn Sales. *P. A. Kelleway.*

CRYSTAL CROSS (USA) 2 b.f. (Feb 27) Roberto (USA) 131 – Crystal Cup **71 p** (USA) (Nijinsky (CAN) 138) [1991 7g 7f 8.2m³ 8.9d³] leggy, close-coupled, rather sparely-made filly: looks weak: third reported foal: dam twice-raced half-sister to very useful 1980 2-y-o 7f winner Golden Bowl (later won Lupe Stakes), out of top-class racemare Rose Bowl: staying maiden: progressing well, and might have won at Wolverhampton final start (behind Taroob) had she not been hampered early on: will improve further over 1¼m +. *I. A. Balding.*

CRYSTAL GAZING (USA) 3 b.f. El Gran Senor (USA) 136 – Crystal Bright 75 **114** (Bold Lad (IRE) 133) [1990 6m² 6m* 7d* 1991 7m* 8g³ 8g⁵] sturdy, compact filly: very useful performer: favourite, won Shadwell Stud Nell Gwyn Stakes at Newmarket in April: ran well when 3 lengths third of 14 to Shadayid in General Accident 1000 Guineas at same course and 4½ lengths fifth of 8, never able to challenge, to Kooyonga in Coronation Stakes at Royal Ascot: stayed 1m: reportedly retired. *L. M. Cumani.*

CRYSTAL GEM 2 b.f. (Apr 14) Crystal Glitters (USA) 127 – Josephine Gibney **—** (High Top 131) [1991 5g] neat filly: third foal: half-sister to 5f (at 2 yrs) to 1m winner

Shadwell Stud Nell Gwyn Stakes, Newmarket —
the favourite Crystal Gazing is pushed out to win from Tetradonna and Lilian Bayliss

Super One (by Superlative) and 3-y-o Sabo's Girl (by Prince Sabo): dam winner in Italy from family of high-class sprinter Green God: 20/1 from 8/1 and bit backward, well beaten in 11-runner seller at Pontefract in June. *P. C. Haslam.*

CRYSTAL HEIGHTS (FR)   3 ch.c. Crystal Glitters (USA) 127 – Fahrenheit 69   **81** (Mount Hagen (FR) 127) [1990 7m 6g³ 1991 a8g* a7g² a6g³ 7g* 8m4] big, strong, lengthy colt: has plenty of scope: fair performer: won maiden at Southwell in January and 4-runner minor event at Brighton in July: below form in £18,000 handicap at Newmarket in July: should prove suited by further than 6f: hung left second start, blinkered third. *W. A. O'Gorman.*

CRYSTAL JACK (FR)   3 b.g. Crystal Glitters (USA) 127 – Cackle (USA) (Crow   **81** (FR) 134) [1990 5f4 5f4 5d* 5f4 5g³ 6f* 7s 6g 6g³ 7d 1991 7m 6g 7m 6m³ 5.1g* 6.1g⁵ 6m³ 5m 5.1m⁶ 5.1m 6m4 5g 6m 6.1d⁶ 5d] leggy, quite good-topped gelding: has a quick action: fair handicapper: won at Chester in July: led 2f out then found little thirteenth and fourteenth outings: acts on firm and dead ground: visored ninth to thirteenth outings: tends to get on edge, and often sweats: takes keen hold: inconsistent. *F. H. Lee.*

CRYSTAL PATH (FR)   3 ch.f. Crystal Glitters (USA) 127 – Flower Parade **111** (Mill Reef (USA) 141) [1990 7m² 6m* 7d³ 1991 7d² 8d* 8m² 10v² 8m6 8g² 8g³ 8m⁵] workmanlike filly: useful performer: won 3-runner minor event at Sandown in May: placed afterwards in listed races at Sandown and Kempton, Prix d'Astarte at Deauville and Beefeater Gin Celebration Mile (3¾ lengths behind Bold Russian, making most) at Goodwood: ran moderately final start: stays 1¼m: acts on good to firm ground and heavy: blinkered (raced too freely) fifth start. *M. Moubarak.*

CRYSTAL RING (IRE)   3 b.f. Kris 135 – Crown Treasure (USA) (Graustark)   **81** § [1990 7m² 7g² 1991 8.5m⁶ 10.2g 8.1g* 10g4 8m 8d] rangy filly: fair form: won handicap at Haydock in August, smooth headway from rear to join issue 2f out: should stay 1¼m: found nil last 2 outings, and is not to be trusted. *I. A. Balding.*

CUBAN SWINGER   3 b.f. Swing Easy (USA) 126 – Cuba Libre (Rum (USA))   **50** [1990 NR 1991 8g⁵ 6.9f⁶ 7m³ 7m 8m⁵ 10m⁶ 8.2m⁶] angular filly: poor mover: eighth

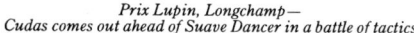

Prix Lupin, Longchamp—
Cudas comes out ahead of Suave Dancer in a battle of tactics

Mr A. E. Paulson's "Cudas"

living foal: half-sister to 7f and 1m winner Grey Rum (by Absalom), 6f and 1m winner Hudsons Mews (by Young Generation) and a winner in Norway: dam ran 3 times in Ireland: fair plater: probably stays 1¼m: acts on good to firm ground: sold 920 gns Doncaster October Sales, to Scandinavia. *W. J. Pearce.*

C U CORAL   2 ch.f. (Feb 27) Hard Fought 125 – Sweet And Sour 96 (Sharpen Up   **45** 127) [1991 6g 6g⁶ 7m] 1,700F: sturdy filly: has scope: fifth foal: sister to 3-y-o Heartburn and 7f to 1m winner Hackforth and half-sister to quite modest 12.2f winner Buy G's (by Blakeney): dam 2-y-o 5f winner: poor maiden: should be better suited by 7f than 6f. *M. C. Pipe.*

CUDAS (USA)   3 b. or br.c. Seattle Song (USA) 130 – Aspern (FR) (Riverman **120** (USA) 131) [1990 8s⁵ 9d² 9s* 1991 10g* 10.5d* 12m³ 10d⁴ 10d⁵ 9.7d⁶ a10f] big, rather leggy, quite attractive colt: third reported foal: half-brother to French 1¼m winner River Mike (by Icecapade) and a winner in North America by Cresta Rider: dam twice raced: successful in maiden at Maisons-Laffitte in December at 2 yrs, then in listed race and Prix Lupin (enterprisingly ridden to beat Suave Dancer in slowly-run race) at Longchamp in spring at 3 yrs: bit below best afterwards, in Prix du Jockey-Club Lancia at Chantilly and Grand Prix de Paris at Longchamp first 2 occasions: no show in Breeders' Cup Classic on final one: stays 10.5f: may prove suited by give in the ground: often mulish at stalls: ridden by lad in paddock, on toes and sweated at Chantilly. *F. Boutin, France.*

CUE DIRECTORS (IRE)   2 b.f. (Apr 19) Parliament 117 – Syllabub (Silly   **42** Season 127) [1991 6.9m⁶ 6m⁴ a7g 6g 8m] workmanlike filly: has scope: has quick action: half-sister to one-time fairly useful sprinter Judgement Call (by Alzao) and a winner in Spain: dam never ran: poor maiden: best effort fourth of 15 in seller at Windsor: ran moderately afterwards: should stay 7f. *W. J. Pearce.*

CULTURED   2 b.c. (Mar 19) Saint Cyrien (FR) 128 – Made of Pearl (USA)   **72** (Nureyev (USA) 131) [1991 8m 8m] useful-looking colt: shade unfurnished: first known foal: dam French 7f and 1m winner: modest form in October maidens at Newmarket, behind Wesaam (better effort) former occasion, never placed to challenge latter one: may do better. *M. R. Stoute.*

Lowther Stakes, York—progressive Culture Vulture readily accounts for three opponents

CULTURE VULTURE (USA)   2 ch.f. (Apr 23) Timeless Moment (USA) **110**
– Perfect Example (USA) (Far North (CAN) 120) [1991 6d* 5g² 6g* 8d* 8d*
a8.5f]

Paul Cole's Whatcombe stable housed a varied collection of two-year-olds in 1991 among whom a select quintet showed themselves capable of very useful form in pattern races over distances from five furlongs to a mile and a quarter. Magic Ring and Dilum, two of those five, joined forces with the subsequently unraced Fair Cop to provide Cole with a rarely-achieved Royal Ascot treble; Culture Vulture, Great Palm and Magic Ring kept the flag flying from midsummer onwards; and Grand Master rounded off the best season so far for the stable with an excellent but scarcely-noticed performance in France on Breeders' Cup weekend. It's a paradoxical fact of pattern-race life that the level of form required to succeed at what is supposed to be its highest level isn't necessarily sufficient to win at its supposed lowest, as Culture Vulture and Magic Ring's respective seasons finely illustrates. Culture Vulture 'won' two Group 1 races (she was awarded the Brent Walker Mile at Ascot on the disqualification of Midnight Air) and one Group 2 but her form still fell short of Magic Ring's in two successes at Group 3 level. Nonetheless Culture Vulture was just about the best of the British two-year-old fillies in what was a relatively weak year within the division; she'll need to make significant improvement to stay top of the tree at three.

Culture Vulture went to Ascot in September having won two races, notably the Pacemaker Update Lowther Stakes, and finished second in the other, the Queen Mary at Royal Ascot. It wasn't the marginal interference which occurred inside the final two furlongs that allowed Marling to beat her by a length in the Queen Mary, as her rider Quinn claimed at a subsequent stewards inquiry and her trainer still asserted was the case after the Lowther, but her lack of early pace; for having broken smartly she dropped to the back of the field before staying on strongly on the climb to the line. That Culture Vulture found the five furlongs at Ascot on the sharp side wasn't altogether surprising considering that she'd run on in excellent fashion through the final furlong and a half when winning a maiden over six furlongs on good to soft ground at Newbury in May; and she confirmed that six furlongs suited her much better than five with a convincing victory in the Lowther at York in August. Culture Vulture didn't look especially well in herself at York and had

196

a small bandage on her near-hind, apparently covering a small cut she'd sustained at Ascot, but she'd have been hard pressed to win in better style. Joining the front-running Miss Bluebird at halfway, Culture Vulture went to the front in the face of strong challenges from the Molecomb winner Sahara Star and the impressive York winner Poolesta inside the two-furlong marker, then galloped on in formidable style as her rivals tired to win by four lengths. Culture Vulture looked considerably better in her coat before the Brent Walker Mile at Ascot five weeks later. She went down by a length and a half to the wide-margin May Hill winner Midnight Air but was awarded the race as the winner was adjudged to have initiated the bump which threw Culture Vulture violently to her left when Culture Vulture was making smooth headway with about a furlong and a half to run. Our view of the race is that Midnight Air was idling close home and probably won on merit, but the decision to award Culture Vulture the prize was the correct one as the rules stand. The step up to a mile caused Culture Vulture no problems; indeed the manner in which she renewed her effort in the dying stages of what was a strongly-run race on rain-softened ground, showing improved form in the process, suggested it suited her ideally.

The Prix Marcel Boussac at Longchamp on Arc day has always been an important pointer to the classics and, if anything, has had its reputation fortified in recent years—it was won by five subsequent classic winners between 1984 and 1990—but it was difficult to work up much enthusiasm beforehand for the classic prospects of any of the fourteen fillies that went to post for the latest renewal and the result, which saw around four lengths cover the first seven home, did little significantly to alter that. Culture Vulture, who started fourth favourite behind the supplemented impressive Ascot winner Red Slippers, the Prix du Calvados winner Verveine and the Prix de Cabourg winner Kenbu in an open-looking affair which also featured the Prix d'Aumale first and second Guislaine and Hatoof as well as the Calvados second and d'Aumale third Lady Normandy, landed her second Group 1 race in the space of eight days, but this time was definitely fortunate to do so, benefiting handsomely from the trouble in running that affected the runner-up Hatoof. While Culture Vulture was given a canny ride, being kept handy in a race run at a fair gallop until quickening into a decisive advantage with a furlong and a half to go, Hatoof wasn't able to obtain a clear run until later. A stride past the post, after a tremendous spurt, Hatoof was in front but at the line Culture Vulture held the lead by a short head, with a length back to Verveine in third and half that back to Guislaine in fourth. Culture Vulture should be forgiven her moderate display on dirt in the Breeders' Cup Juvenile Fillies' at Churchill Downs in November. Although she looked well and was generally on good terms with herself beforehand, things didn't go her way in the race, and after getting hampered soon after missing the break she made

Brent Walker Fillies' Mile, Ascot—
Culture Vulture renews her challenge after being bumped by Midnight Air;
the others in the picture are Mystery Play (rails) and Party Cited

Ciga Prix Marcel Boussac, Longchamp—Hatoof (No. 1) almost catches Culture Vulture; Verveine and Guislane come next

her ground too quickly down the back-stretch before fading from the home turn into ninth place. She didn't run on bute or lasix, incidentally, and for the first time since York wasn't equipped with bandages behind.

Culture Vulture (USA) (ch.f. Apr 23, 1989)	Timeless Moment (USA) (ch 1970)	Damascus (b 1964)	Sword Dancer
			Kerala
		Hour of Parting (ch 1963)	Native Dancer
			Sweet Sorrow
	Perfect Example (USA) (b 1982)	Far North (b 1973)	Northern Dancer
			Fleur
		Bold Example (b 1969)	Bold Lad
			Lady Be Good

The compact, quite attractive Culture Vulture fetched 120,000 dollars at Keeneland's September Yearling Sale. In a long career at stud—he was retired in the mid-'seventies after winning ten of his twenty-seven races, including Grade 3 events over six and seven furlongs—her sire Timeless Moment has yet to sire anything out of the top drawer, including in Europe where his best representatives have been the prolific winner Timeless Times, the Derby Italiano third Half A Tick and the useful staying two-year-old Tik Fa. Culture Vulture's dam Perfect Example never made the racetrack but has certainly lived up to her name as a broodmare. Culture Vulture is her fourth winner from four foals following a minor winner in North America by Super Concorde and the useful brother and sister Perfay and Perfolia (by Nodouble) who between them have won five races at seven furlongs or a mile in the last two seasons. Perfect Example is extremely well related. Two of her half-sisters, the Del Mar Oaks winner French Charmer and the unraced Past Example, are the dams of Zilzal and Polish Precedent, who mopped up virtually all the top mile races in Europe between them in 1989; while another, the stakes winner Highest Regard, is the dam of the Kentucky Derby third Awe Inspiring. What's more, Perfect Example's dam Bold Example, a stakes-placed winner of three races over short distances, is a half-sister to In Hot Pursuit, the dam of Posse. Culture Vulture is likely to prove best at around a mile too. She has a long way to go before she matches the achievements of some of her illustrious relatives but she's made a good start and there seems no reason why she shouldn't add to her winning total in the coming season; she may even run into a place in the One Thousand Guineas. Culture Vulture acts well on good to soft ground; she has yet to race on a firm surface on turf. *P. F. I. Cole.*

CUMBRIAN CAVALIER 2 b.g. (Mar 5) Mansingh (USA) 120 – Lilac Star 75 **50** §
(Hard Man 102) [1991 5g 5f⁶ 5d⁶ 5g² 6.1m⁴ 6m⁶] 4,800Y: lengthy gelding: has scope:

fourth foal: brother to modest 5f to 7f winner Ebony Queste: dam won 6 races over 5f at 2 yrs and 4 yrs: plating-class maiden on his day: better form at 5f than 6f: blinkered last 4 starts: slowly away (in seller) final one: a difficult ride, and seems of dubious temperament: sold 775 gns Ascot September Sales. *M. H. Easterby.*

CUMBRIAN CEILIDH   4 ch.g. Simply Great (FR) 122 – Elm 88 (Realm 129)   — [1990 9. 1m³ 8g² 8g⁶ 8.2m⁵ a8g 10m* 10g⁵ 1991 12g⁶] angular, workmanlike gelding: good walker and mover: plating-class performer: stayed 1¼m: acted on good to firm ground: winning hurdler: dead. *L. Lungo.*

CUMBRIAN CHALLENGE (IRE)   2 ch.g. (Apr 7) Be My Native (USA) 122 –   **90** p Sixpenny (English Prince 129) [1991 5g⁴ 6f³ 7m 7m² 8m* 8m³ 8g*] 13,000Y: leggy gelding: has a round action: sixth foal: half-brother to 1988 Irish 2-y-o winner Hit For Six (by Tap On Wood): dam unraced daughter of Mesopotamia, best 2-y-o filly of 1963 and third in Irish 1000 Guineas: very much on the upgrade: successful at Redcar in maiden auction in August and 18-runner nursery (gamely by ½ length from Wesaam) in October: will be well suited by 1¼m: acts on good to firm ground. *M. H. Easterby.*

CUMBRIAN CLASSIC   2 b.g. (Apr 24) Glint of Gold 128 – Blubella 86 (Balidar   — 133) [1991 6g 8f] 6,500F, 15,000Y: second living foal: half-brother to 3-y-o Sovereign Heights (by Elegant Air): dam sprinter: well beaten in maidens at Haydock (slowly away) and Thirsk in late-summer: sold 1,250 gns Ascot October Sales. *M. H. Easterby.*

CUMBRIAN WALTZER   6 ch.g. Stanford 121§ – Mephisto Waltz 98 (Dancer's   **106** Image (USA)) [1990 5m² 5g³ 5m² 6m 5m³ 6m² 6m⁵ 5.6g⁵ 6d⁴ 5m 6s⁴ 1991 6d³ 5m⁵ 6m* 6m* 5m² 6g 6g 6g 6m 6m* 7g⁵] leggy gelding: often dull in coat: good mover: useful handicapper: won at York in May, June and October (£12,300 event): ideally suited by 6f or stiff 5f: acts on any going: has sweated: tough, genuine and largely consistent: a great credit to his trainer. *M. H. Easterby.*

CUNNING PLAN   3 gr.g. Belfort (FR) 89 – Chinese Princess (Sunny Way 120)   **58** [1990 6f² 5f⁶ a7g⁴ 7g⁵ 8.5m⁶ 6g⁴ a6g a6g³ a7g⁵ 1991 a6g³ a7g* a8g³ a7g³ a8g4] leggy, rather unfurnished gelding: good walker: won claimer at Southwell in January: suited by 7f: not an easy ride, but won for apprentice: blinkered last 5 starts: dead. *T. D. Barron.*

CURIOUS FEELING   5 gr.m. Nishapour (FR) 125 – Noirima 110 (Right Tack   — 131) [1990 NR 1991 a10g⁵ a12g] leggy, angular mare: poor and lightly-raced maiden on flat: stays 1¼m: winning hurdler. *J. R. Bosley.*

CURLILOCKS   3 ch.f. Glenstal (USA) 118 – Merry Sharp (Sharpen Up 127) [1990   **40** 5d 1991 8m⁴ 8m 8.3m³ 8m 9.7g⁴ 10m] small, light-framed filly: plater: form only when in frame at Windsor and Folkestone: better at 9.7f than 1m: acts on good to firm ground: sweating final start: sold 440 gns Ascot December Sales. *Mrs Barbara Waring.*

CURRENT EDITION (IRE)   3 ch.c. Deep Run 119 – Paperchain (Articulate   — 121) [1990 NR 1991 16.2s⁴] well-made colt: fourth foal: half-brother to winning hurdlers Robin Goodfellow and The Decent Thing (both by Decent Fellow): dam once-raced half-sister to useful hurdler Sheer Silk: 14/1, bit backward and very green, showed signs of ability when last of 4 to 12/1-on shot Shahi in minor event at Chepstow in July: moved moderately down. *G. B. Balding.*

CURTAIN UP (FR)   4 ch.g. Sicyos (USA) 126 – Angelina d'Or (Sun Prince 128)   **44** [1990 7g 8g 7m 1991 8d 10m 8f³ 8g² 8.3g 8m⁴ 8f] big, angular, rather dipped-back gelding: poor mover: poor handicapper: stays 1m: acts on firm ground: inconsistent: sold 2,600 gns Ascot September Sales. *R. Guest.*

CUSHTY   2 b.f. (Feb 9) Aragon 118 – Cricklewood Green (Welsh Saint 126) [1991   — 5g 6m 6m] 5,200F, 5,200Y: unfurnished filly: first foal: dam once-raced sister to very speedy Brondesbury: behind all races, final one in Lingfield seller (missed break, not at all knocked about again) in September. *J. Sutcliffe.*

CUT A CAPER   9 b.g. Gay Fandango (USA) 132 – Brilliant Gem 83 (Charlottown   **38** 127) [1990 a10g⁶ 1991 a12g² a13g² a12g² a13g⁶ a12g³ a13g 12d] small gelding: poor mover: poor handicapper: stays 13f: probably acts on any going: ran freely in blinkers: none too consistent. *R. J. O'Sullivan.*

CUT CLEAR   2 b.f. (Jan 29) Kris 135 – Shoot Clear 111 (Bay Express 132) [1991   **82** p 6g²] lengthy, rather unfurnished filly: fourth foal: half-sister to 1990 2-y-o 7f winner Dance Ahead (by Shareef Dancer) and 2 middle-distance winners, including useful Shoot Ahead (by Shirley Heights): dam 5f to 7f winner at 2 yrs and fourth in 1000 Guineas, is half-sister to Sally Brown and Untold: favourite, 2½ lengths second of 21 to Katakana in maiden at Newbury in October, tracking leaders and keeping on strongly to draw clear of remainder: sure to improve, particularly at 7f +, and win a maiden at the least. *J. H. M. Gosden.*

CUT THE LINE 2 ch.f. (Apr 19) Sharpo 132 – Tap The Line (Tap On Wood 130) **53** [1991 6g 6g* 7g 6m 6.1m] 1,050Y: leggy, close-coupled filly: second foal: dam French middle-distance winner: plating-class form: won maiden auction at Nottingham in June: didn't run to that form in nurseries: stays 6f: blinkered final start: sold 3,200 gns Newmarket Autumn Sales. *M. Bell.*

CUT THE MUSIC (IRE) 3 b.g. Sure Blade (USA) 128 – Monaco Melody 103 — (Tudor Melody 129) [1990 6f5 7g2 8f 7g 7.6v5 1991 12.3s 12g 10.2f 10g] big, lengthy gelding: moderate mover: hasn't reproduced second 2-y-o effort: soundly beaten in handicaps in first half of 1991: should stay at least 1m: possibly unsuited by extremes of going: blinkered and reared stalls penultimate start. *M. Bell.*

CUT THE MUSTARD (IRE) 3 b.c. Niniski (USA) 125 – Cutlers Corner 111 — (Sharpen Up 127) [1990 8m 8s 1991 12m 12m] strong colt: no worthwhile form in maidens and minor event: sold 8,200 gns Newmarket Autumn Sales. *J. L. Dunlop.*

CUTTING REEF (IRE) 2 b.f. (Apr 12) Kris 135 – Quiet Harbour (Mill Reef **66** (USA) 141) [1991 7d5 8.5f3 8g3] 74,000Y: leggy filly: half-sister to 4 winners, including 3-y-o 1¼m winner Anchor Inn (by Be My Guest) and quite useful 1985 Irish 3-y-o middle-distance performer Jazz Ballet (by Jaazeiro): dam lightly-raced half-sister to Coronation Cup winner Quiet Fling: quite modest maiden: third at Beverley (drifted markedly right) and Wolverhampton (outpaced from 2f out) in autumn: will stay well. *A. N. Lee.*

CYRILL HENRY (IRE) 2 b.g. (May 3) Mister Majestic 122 – Stamina 78 (Star **54** Appeal 133) [1991 a6g a7g6 7m4 7.5f5 8.3g] 6,800Y: sturdy, good-topped gelding: third foal: dam won over 1¼m and is sister to Star, 1981 champion 2-y-o filly in Hungary: fair plater: stays 7.5f: possibly suited by firm ground: has run well for 7-lb claimer. *T. D. Barron.*

D

DAARIS (USA) 2 ch.c. (Jan 28) Diesis 133 – Que Sympatica 108 (Young **75** Generation 129) [1991 6g3 7g2 7m5] 92,000Y: small, sturdy colt: first foal: dam 6f to 1m winner also successful in Italy, is out of sister to Park Hill winner Quay Line: modest maiden: bit backward (first run for 3 months), easily best effort when second of 7, making most, at Warwick in October: pulled hard, carried head awkwardly and beaten 2f out at Newcastle 6 days later: will stay 1m. *D. Morley.*

DAAZAM (IRE) 3 b.f. Mazaad 106 – Jamie's Girl (Captain James 123) [1990 5g **41** 5d4 6m4 7g4 5d2 6g* 6f4 8.5m 6d 1991 7d 8m 7m2 6f 6g5 6g 6.9m 6m4 6f a5g 6f] lengthy filly: has a round action: plater: best 3-y-o efforts in frame: probably ideally suited by 6f: best form on an easy surface: often blinkered or visored: won when sweating and edgy: ran poorly in ladies contest. *Ronald Thompson.*

DADDY'S DARLING 6 b.m. Mummy's Pet 125 – Annie Get Your Gun 69 **50** (Blakeney 126) [1990 a12g* a10g a12g5 a16g3 12f* 12f* 12g6 12m2 12g2 12m 1991 12g2 12g 11.9f4 15.4f a13g a16g4] small, rather sparely-made mare: moderate mover: poor handicapper nowadays: best short of 2m: acts on hard and dead going: effective with or without blinkers or visor: sold 2,500 gns Ascot December Sales. *J. T. Gifford.*

DAFRAH (USA) 3 b.f. Danzig (USA) – Capo di Monte 118 (Final Straw 127) **78** [1990 NR 1991 7g 8g* 8m 7g3 7f5 7.1g] good-bodied filly: poor mover: first foal: dam winner from 6f (at 2 yrs) to 11f (in USA), is granddaughter of Highclere, also grandam of Nashwan and Unfuwain: won maiden at Kempton in July: ran well in handicaps at Newmarket and Newbury (£8,100 event) fourth and fifth starts: should be suited by return to 1m: acts on firm going: pulled hard for lady third start. *M. R. Stoute.*

DAGGER POINT 3 b.c. Kris 135 – Twixt (Kings Lake (USA) 133) [1990 NR 1991 **80** 10.1m3 10m* 9m6 7.6g] lengthy, angular colt: poor mover: first foal: dam French 6.5f and 7f winner, is daughter of Cambridgeshire winner Intermission, also dam of Interval: 50/1, dead-heated with Nibbs Point in maiden at Windsor in August, having quickened on over 3f out: needs further than 7.6f, and stays 1¼m: sold 12,000 gns Newmarket Autumn Sales. *R. V. Smyth.*

DAGON (IRE) 3 br.c. Damister (USA) 123 – Full of Reason (USA) 105 (Bold **87** Reason) [1990 NR 1991 8g2 8.2d* 8m5 10.5m* 8.9m* 12g5 10m3 10.4m4 8g]

35,000Y: robust colt: carries condition: moderate mover: half-brother to 2 winners, including fair middle-distance performer Magnus Pym (by Al Nasr): dam 1½m performer: won 2-runner minor event at Nottingham in June and handicaps at Haydock and York (£7,800 contest) in July: ran creditably in frame in handicaps at Redcar and York: best from 9f to 10.5f: acts on good to firm ground: sold 25,000 gns Newmarket Autumn Sales. *F. H. Lee.*

DAHLAWISE (IRE) 3 b.f. Caerleon (USA) 132 – Cornish Heroine (USA) 101   **75** §
(Cornish Prince) [1990 a6g* 6m2 7m6 1991 a8g4 8g 7.5f5 9d3 10m] small, sparely-made filly: modest form: good third in handicap at Kempton in May, staying on well: mulish to post then refused to race in similar event at Leicester 2 months later: should stay 1¼m: acts on firm and dead going. *W. J. Haggas.*

DAILY SPORT AUGUST 2 gr.f. (May 18) Risk Me (FR) 127 – Susie Hall (Gold   **52** d
Rod 129) [1991 5g6 a6g2 a6g3 a5g6 a6g* 6m 6m 6g a7g a6g a6g a5g] compact filly: moderate performer: made all in summer seller (sold out of J. Berry's stable 5,800 gns) at Southwell: no form after: stays 6f: visored third start, blinkered fourth. *M. C. Chapman.*

DAILY SPORT GIRL 2 b.f. (Apr 29) Risk Me (FR) 127 – Net Call 108 (Song   **51**
132) [1991 5m5 5d3 5f a5g3 7s3 a7g* a7g5 a7g5] lengthy, unfurnished filly: tenth foal: half-sister to fair 1m winner Dayajeer and fairly useful 6f and 7f winner Raabihah (both by Shirley Heights): dam seemed best at 6f: won claimer at Southwell in July: will stay 1m: ran creditably for apprentice final start: subsequently sold 1,200 gns Doncaster August Sales: consistent. *N. A. Callaghan.*

DAILY SPORT NOW 2 b.c. (Mar 25) Risk Me (FR) 127 – Julia Mawe   —
(Dominion 123) [1991 a5g 5d 5g] sturdy colt: first foal: dam unraced half-sister to useful sprinter Our Dynasty: no worthwhile form, in seller in April final start. *J. Berry.*

DAISY GIRL 5 b.m. Main Reef 126 – Mellow Girl 88 (Mountain Call 125) [1990   **62**
12.3d 9s 12m 10g* 10m* 10.4d6 11s 1991 12.4m2 11.9m 10f4 9.9f2 10.1m 10.2m] sturdy, workmanlike mare: quite modest handicapper: second at Beverley (race void) fourth start: below best after: effective at 1¼m to 1½m: suited by a sound surface: has had tongue tied down: withdrawn (reared stalls) intended reappearance: winning hurdler. *J. Mackie.*

DAISY GREY 3 ro.f. Nordance (USA) – Great Grey Niece 74 (Great Nephew   **36**
126) [1990 9g 1991 12d 9m 8f 7g3 8m4 6.9m 10.8g 8m a8g] leggy filly: poor performer: suited by 1m: acts on good to firm ground: blinkered as 3-y-o: claimed out of A. Hide's stable £3,001 fifth start, trained next one by Dr J. Scargill. *A. S. Reid.*

DAJA 2 b.c. (Mar 26) Doulab (USA) 115 – Awatef (Ela-Mana-Mou 132) [1991 6d5   **86**
6.1g3 7f* 7m* 8f5 8g 7m4 7g] 37,000Y: strong, useful-looking colt: second foal: dam poor French maiden from good family: fair performer: won maiden at Yarmouth and median auction at Wolverhampton in late-summer: may prove ideally suited by 7f: acts on firm ground: visored final 2 starts: sold 25,000 gns Newmarket Autumn Sales. *A. A. Scott.*

DAKI (USA) 3 ch.f. Miswaki (USA) 124 – Devon Diva (USA) (The Minstrel   **90**
(CAN) 135) [1990 6g3 6d* 6g2 1991 7g* 7.3d] workmanlike filly: comfortably won 4-runner minor event at Leicester, quickening to lead over 1f out: odds-on favourite, found little over 2f out and well beaten in handicap later in June: stud. *J. H. M. Gosden.*

DALBY DANCER 7 b.m. Bustiki – Wensum Girl (Ballymoss 136) [1990 13.3m   **63**
14g2 14s 16m 15.3m2 14m2 14.8f* 14f4 17.6f3 16m5 17.6f4 13.3g 15.3g4 18d 1991 14.9m4 14.6m4 16.1m2 13.9g3 14.6m 14.6g 16.2d3 13.8m2 16.5d a14g6 a14g4] workmanlike mare: moderate mover: modest handicapper: stays well: acts on any going: has won for apprentice: tough. *B. A. McMahon.*

DALE HILL DAISY 3 b.f. Mummy's Game 120 – Just Irene 50 (Sagaro 133)   **84**
[1990 5m2 5m* 5m 5f* 5g6 5m6 5d3 5m5 5m 5.1m] small, good-topped filly: poor mover: fair performer: ran creditably in minor event at Newbury and £7,100 Epsom handicap second and third starts: may well be suited by 5f: yet to race on soft ground, probably acts on any other: sold only 1,000 gns Doncaster November Sales. *B. A. McMahon.*

DALE HILL IDEA 3 b.c. Alleging (USA) 120 – Late Idea 78 (Tumble Wind   **85**
(USA)) [1990 NR 1991 11g 10g* 10.1d* 10g 11.9g 10.2m] 11,000Y: big, good-topped colt: moderate mover: sixth foal: half-brother to useful middle-distance plater by Radetzky (by Cawston's Clown) and a winning middle-distance plater by Radetzky: dam 1m winner: easy winner of auction event at Nottingham and minor contest at Windsor in

June: below form afterwards: stayed 1¼m: went well on dead ground: broke leg at Chepstow in September. *M. A. Jarvis.*

DALE PARK   5 b.h. Kampala 120 – Coshlea 63 (Red Alert 127) [1990 12d 12g 12d   47
15v 14.6d³ 15d⁵ 16.5d 1991 12g³ 12d 13d⁶ 12f³ 13f⁵] leggy, sparely-made horse: has a round action: poor handicapper at best nowadays: should stay 1¾m: acts on any going, with exception of firm. *N. Tinkler.*

DALESIDE   3 gr.g. Full Out (USA) – All Regal (Run The Gantlet (USA)) [1990   68
5m⁵ 6g⁴ 6d² 7.5f 1991 10f² 11.9g 12m⁴ a14g a14g a12g] good-topped, rather leggy   a —
gelding: 33/1, put up easily best efforts in frame in autumn maidens at Ripon and (made most) Pontefract: stays 1½m. *T. Fairhurst.*

DALESIDE LADYBIRD   5 b.m. Tolomeo 127 – Dawn Redwood 63 (Mummy's   45
Pet 125) [1990 6m 6f² 7g 6g² 6f² 6m 6d⁴ 5f³ 6f⁶ 6f³ 7m⁶ 6f⁴ 6m⁵ 6g 5f 6g 6g 10m 8g 1991 5f* 5g 6f⁴ 5h⁴ 6g⁴ 6d² 5.9m] rather leggy, good-topped mare: carries condition: usually looks really well: has a round action: poor handicapper: won at Carlisle in May: stays 6f: acts on firm and dead ground: has run creditably when visored: sometimes slowly away. *T. Fairhurst.*

DALEY BRIOCHE   3 b.c. Pharly (FR) 130 – Flaretown 63 (Town Crier 119)   53
[1990 5m⁶ 7d* 7.5f² 8d 7g⁴ a7g⁴ 1991 7g 11.5m 8g⁶ 7g⁴ 9f 8m 7g 6f⁵ 6g³ 7m⁶ 7g 6s] sparely-made colt: has a round action: plating-class handicapper nowadays: has form at 6f and 1m: acts on firm and dead ground, ran well on fibresand: blinkered final start: trained until after fourth by M. Tompkins. *P. C. Haslam.*

DAL MISS   4 b.f. Dalsaan 125 – Loyal And Regal 51 (Royal And Regal (USA))   —
[1990 6s 8g 5m 6g 7d 1991 6m 8.2g a7g] workmanlike filly: has round action: no worthwhile form. *R. E. Peacock.*

DALMORE   5 b.g. Runnett 125 – Fade To Grey (Gay Fandango (USA) 132) [1990   — §
12m 12g 1991 12g] leggy, sparely-made gelding: plater: carried head high and hung badly only run in 1991: sold 2,900 gns Doncaster September Sales: one to avoid. *F. Watson.*

DAMAAZ (IRE)   3 ch.g. Mazaad 106 – Sharpwinds (Tumble Wind (USA)) [1990   59
5g 7m 6f⁶ 7f a7g² a6g⁴ a6g⁶ 7g 7d 6s a6g³ a6g⁶ 1991 a7g² a7g⁴ a7g³ a7g⁶ a6g* a7g 6f⁵ a7g] quite good-topped gelding: has a round action: won apprentice maiden at Southwell in March by short head: stiff tasks after, off course 5 months before final start: stays 7f: usually blinkered or visored: races keenly: inconsistent. *J. S. Wainwright.*

DAMASKEEN (USA)   5 b.g. Caveat (USA) – Double Damask (USA) (Damascus   59
(USA)) [1990 5m 6m 5m a5g² 5m⁴ 5m⁴ 5m⁴ 5m⁴ 6m 5m⁶ 5.3f* 5m² 5m5 1991 a5g*   a 68
a5g³ a6g* 5g⁶ 5.3f 5m³ 6g 5d 5d] compact gelding: has a quick, fluent action: plating-class handicapper: won at Lingfield in January and March: stays 6f: acts on firm going: effective with or without blinkers: has won for apprentice: sometimes sweats: has broken blood vessel, including when collapsing final start. *Mrs S. Armytage.*

DAME HELENE (USA)   2 b.f. (Mar 25) Sir Ivor 135 – Rep's Retton (USA) (J O   —
Tobin (USA) 130) [1991 7m] 8,200Y: sturdy, rather dipped-backed filly: first foal: dam, winner in USA, is daughter of Repetitious, dam of high-class French middle-distance colt Sarhoob and sister to Nanticious: 25/1, backward and green, slowly away and always behind in 19-runner maiden auction at Leicester in September: moved poorly down. *P. C. Haslam.*

DAMES RUBY   3 b.f. Green Ruby (USA) 104 – Dame Caroline 50 (Wollow 132)   —
[1990 NR 1991 7g 8m 6f] workmanlike, rather leggy filly: first foal: dam plater suited by 1m: tailed off in claimer and maidens. *D. J. Wintle.*

DAMISTERS PET (IRE)   2 b.c. (Jun 6) Damister (USA) 123 – Jemarjo Pet   71
(USA) (Peter Peter) [1991 7m⁶ 7g 7.5f² 7m 7m] IR 1,400Y: leggy, close-coupled colt: half-brother to several winners, notably good-class sprinter Orojoya (by Gold Stage) and very smart American colt Bywayofchicago (by Well Mannered), successful at up to 9f: dam won at up to 1m: modest maiden: strong-finishing second in Beverley auction in September: not discredited when last of 8 in Somerville Tattersall Stakes at Newmarket next start, ran moderately in nursery there final one: will be well suited by 1m + . *C. N. Allen.*

DANCE ON SIXPENCE   3 b.c. Lidhame 109 – Burning Ambition (Troy 137)   72
[1990 7f⁴ 6m² 5m* 5m² 6d⁵ 1991 6g 8g 7m⁵ 6g³ 6f 7.1m* 7m 7.1m a8g³ a8g] rangy colt: modest handicapper: won at Sandown in September: visored at Lingfield on equitrack late in year, easily better effort when creditable third of 12: stays 1m: acts on good to firm ground and dead. *H. J. Collingridge.*

DANCE PARTOUT (IRE) 3 ch.c. Glow (USA) – Coven (Sassafras (FR) 135) **86**
[1990 7d³ a7g² 7m⁶ 8g 8f² 8m⁶ 10s² 1991 10d⁵ 12g³ 15.3m³ 12h* 11.7g* 11.7d*
11.7g* 16.1m⁵ 12g⁶ 15.9m⁵] good-topped colt: fair performer: completed 4-timer in
maiden at Carlisle and 3 handicaps (in space of 2 weeks, all out, none by more than
½ length) at Windsor in the summer: below form last 2 starts: best form at around
1½m: acts on any going: goes well with forcing tactics: most game. *N. A. Callaghan.*

DANCE SCENE (IRE) 2 b.c. (Mar 18) Dance of Life (USA) – Citissima 96 **88**
(Simbir 130) [1991 5m 7g 7.1d³ 7g*] smallish, lengthy colt: has scope: half-brother
to 2 winners by General Assembly, including Irish 1m to 11f winner City Council,
later successful in USA: dam Irish 9f and 1¼m winner: easily best form in maidens
when winning at Salisbury in October, making all and quickening clear 2f out: will be
at least as effective at 1m + . *D. R. C. Elsworth.*

DANCE WITH A DEVIL 3 br.c. Superlative 118 – Crystallize (Reliance II 137) —
[1990 NR 1991 8g 10.4d] 16,500F, 5,200Y: good-topped colt: half-brother to fairly
useful 1986 2-y-o 6f and 7f winner Authentic and smart 1982 2-y-o 6f to 1m winner
Johnny Nobody (both by Derrylin): dam unraced half-sister to very smart miler
Greengage: behind in maidens at Newbury and (green, moved poorly down)
Chester: sold 700 gns Ascot July Sales. *R. Simpson.*

DANCING BEAU (IRE) 2 b.c. (Jan 12) Dance of Life (USA) – Kentucky Belle **78**
80 (Glint of Gold 128) [1991 6f⁴ 7g* 7g⁴ 6.1g⁵ 7f³ 8g] IR 7,000Y: smallish, sturdy,
good-quartered colt: first foal: dam twice-raced daughter of half-sister to Wollow:
modest performer: won maiden auction at Doncaster in June: should be suited by
1m: acts on firm ground. *Mrs L. Piggott.*

DANCING BLUES 2 b.f. (Mar 8) Bluebird (USA) 125 – Karonga (Main Reef **50**
126) [1991 5m⁴] 6,400Y: leggy, lightly-made filly: first foal: dam, French 9f winner,
is daughter of half-sister to Karamita (dam of Kartajana) and Karadar: 12/1, bit
backward and green, staying-on fourth of 13 in maiden auction at Doncaster in May:
seemed sure to improve, but wasn't seen out again. *M. H. Easterby.*

DANCING BOY (USA) 2 ch.c. (Mar 23) Seattle Dancer (USA) 119 – Clef En Or **97**
(USA) (Alydar (USA)) [1991 6f* 6m 6.1m* 6m] $75,000Y: sturdy, quite attractive
colt: has an easy action: second foal: dam showed a little ability in France: fairly
useful performer at best: won maiden at Thirsk in August and minor event at
Nottingham following month: unable to dominate other starts, and well below form:
should stay 1m. *Mrs J. Cecil.*

DANCING BREEZE 4 ch.f. Horage 124 – Lady's Guest (Be My Guest (USA) **54**
126) [1990 5f 5s⁵ 6g a8g³ 8m² 8.5g 8d 8g⁶ 8f³ 8.3m⁶ 10f 10m a8g² 7.6d 10g a8g⁶ 1991
a10g⁶ a8g² a7g a8g⁵ a10g³ a8g⁶ 9s] lengthy, workmanlike filly: plating-class
maiden: effective at 7f to 1¼m: acts on firm going, probably unsuited by soft. *Pat
Mitchell.*

DANCING BRIDE 4 ch.f. Caerleon (USA) 132 – Bahrain Vee (CAN) (Blushing **43**
Groom (FR) 131) [1990 8f² 8m 10.2f⁵ 13.1h⁵ 12m 1991 10.8m 10g 12m 16g⁶ 16m⁴
a16g⁴ 16m² 11.8g 14g³ 15.8g 15.1s] tall, leggy filly: poor handicapper: stays 2m: acts
on good to firm ground: effective blinkered or not: none too consistent: sold 6,000
gns Newmarket December Sales. *J. D. Bethell.*

DANCING CHIEF 3 br.g. Lidhame 109 – Darlinga 98 (Derring-Do 131) [1990 —
6m 6m 1991 7m 8.3d⁶] leggy, unfurnished gelding: no worthwhile form in maiden
contests: sold to join T. Carr 1,650 gns Doncaster November Sales. *Denys Smith.*

DANCING DANCER 2 b.f. (May 17) Niniski (USA) 125 – Verchinina 99 (Star — p
Appeal 133) [1991 7d] unfurnished filly: fourth foal: dam 1m winner: 20/1 and
backward, always mid-division in 22-runner maiden at Doncaster in November: will
improve, particularly over further: has joined N. C. Wright. *C. E. Brittain.*

DANCING DAYS 5 ch.h. Glenstal (USA) 118 – Royal Agnes 71 (Royal Palace **40**
131) [1990 12.4f⁶ 11f³ a12g² 12m 12d 11d³ a12g a12g² 10d a12g⁴ a12g⁶ 1991 a12g 13.8d
12.3d 12f 10m³ 12m² 10.8m 12f 12m⁴ 15.8g⁵ a16g] smallish, workmanlike horse: poor
mover: poor handicapper nowadays: suited by 1½m: acts on firm and dead ground:
effective with or without blinkers or visor: sometimes wanders under pressure:
none too consistent. *J. Parkes.*

DANCING LEGEND (IRE) 3 b.g. Lyphard's Special (USA) 122 – Princess — §
Nabila (USA) (King Pellinore (USA) 127) [1990 8m 7m 6g 8.2s⁵ 1991 12.1s⁶ 10.8m
12.1m] big, lengthy gelding: plating-class form at 2 yrs: none at 3 yrs, looking
reluctant and eventually pulled up in seller second start: should be suited by
1¼m + : acts on soft ground: trained until after second start by M. O'Neill: one to
avoid. *J. Parkes.*

DANCING MONARCH 6 ch.h. Dara Monarch 128 – Maiden's Dance 65 **66**
(Hotfoot 126) [1990 8f³ 8h³ 8g 8.2m 9f* 9m 8f 1991 8m 8m 8.2m⁵ 10.6g 9m² 9m*
7.5f²] strong, lengthy, quite attractive horse: moderate walker and mover: quite
modest performer nowadays: won seller (straightforward task, no bid) at Redcar in
August: needs further than 7f and stays 9f: best on a sound surface: has won when
visored: held up and ideally suited by strong gallop: has hung. *R. Hollinshead.*

DANCING NORTH 6 b. or br.g. Shareef Dancer (USA) 135 – Icena 117 (Jimmy —
Reppin 131) [1990 6m⁵ 10.1m 8m⁶ 1991 12g 12.1f] big, heavy-topped gelding: carries
plenty of condition: bad mover: no worthwhile form on flat: winning hurdler. *R.
Allan.*

DANCING PADDY 3 b.c. Nordance (USA) – Ninotchka 72 (Niniski (USA) 125) **59**
[1990 6g 1991 10.1m⁶ 10g⁵ 16.1g⁴ 12.1d a16g] leggy, quite attractive colt: 33/1,
worthwhile form only when fourth of 19 in handicap at Warwick in October, good
headway to lead 4f out but weakening inside last: may prove ideally suited by 1¾m.
K. O. Cunningham-Brown.

DANCING PET 2 b.f. (May 27) Dance of Life (USA) – Mummy's Whistler **34**
(Mummy's Pet 125) [1991 6m 6.1m 5g] workmanlike filly: fifth reported foal:
half-sister to 3-y-o Derring Pet (by Daring March) and 7f seller winner Pokey's Pet
(by Uncle Pokey): dam poor plater: poor form in October maidens: will be better off
in sellers. *W. W. Haigh.*

DANCING SENSATION (USA) 4 b.f. Faliraki 125 – Sweet Satina (USA) **55**
(Crimson Satan) [1990 6m⁴ 6g⁵ 7f³ 7f⁶ 8m⁵ 7m² 7f* 7m⁴ 7m 7.6m³ a8g⁵ a11g 1991
8g 8m 10m⁶ 8.5m³ 8g⁵ 8.1g² 8.3g² 12m 12g 10.2s] big, good-topped filly: fluent
mover: plating-class handicapper nowadays: stays 1m: acts on firm going. *A. W.
Denson.*

DANCING STREET 3 ch.f. Scottish Reel 123 – Florence Street (Final Straw **62**
127) [1990 6m 6f 7g 1991 7f³ 7f⁴ 9f² 9.2d 9g³ 12f⁵ 10m² 10.5m² 10f⁴ 9d⁴ 10g⁴]
tall, leggy, workmanlike filly: carries condition: quite modest maiden, placed in
handicaps: worth another try beyond 1¼m: acts on firm ground (ran fairly well on
dead): has run well for apprentice: visored fifth start. *R. M. Whitaker.*

DANCING TUDOR 3 b.g. Absalom 128 – String of Beads 63 (Ile de Bourbon **54**
(USA) 133) [1990 6f⁵ 7f² 7.5f² 7g 7g 8d a7g⁶ 1991 7v⁶ 10.2f⁶ 10g 14.1f 12f² 11.7f⁵
13.8m] lengthy gelding: good walker: plating-class maiden: beaten neck in claimer
at Thirsk, disputing lead virtually throughout: ran poorly afterwards: stays 1½m:
best efforts on firm going: joined G. Barnett. *J. Etherington.*

DANCING WILD 2 ch.f. (Feb 22) Battle Hymn 103 – Peking Dancer 38 (Orbit **33**
Dancer (USA)) [1991 6m 7m] good-topped, close-coupled filly: fourth foal (previous
3 by Ivotino): dam bad plater: poor form in large-field sellers at Redcar in autumn.
Mrs G. R. Reveley.

DANCING YEARS (USA) 2 b.f. (Feb 28) Fred Astaire (USA) – Resembling **44**
(USA) (Nasty And Bold (USA)) [1991 6f⁵ 7m⁴ 7m] $32,000Y: lengthy filly: has
scope: second foal: half-sister to a winner in North America at up to 7f: dam minor
sprint winner at 2 yrs: sire (by Nijinsky) third in Breeders' Cup Mile: poor form in
maidens: made late progress first 2 starts, none final one when edgy and on toes:
will probably stay 1m. *Denys Smith.*

DANDOON 4 b.c. Rainbow Quest (USA) 134 – Good Lass (FR) (Reform 132) **59**
[1990 10m⁶ 12m² 1991 8.5f 10.8m 12m⁵ 14m a14g] close-coupled colt: poor mover:
plating-class handicapper: below form last 2 starts, off course 5½ months before
final one: stays 1½m: acts on good to firm ground. *J. D. Czerpak.*

DANDY DESIRE 2 ch.c. (May 14) Grey Desire 115 – Karsavina 89 (Silly Season —
127) [1991 6d] 8,000Y: workmanlike colt: half-brother to 3-y-o Coir 'a' Ghaill (by
Jalmood) and 3 winners, including fairly useful 1m and 9f winner The Shrew (by
Relko): dam, runner up in Cherry Hinton, is half-sister to very useful miler
Boswelia and Triumph Hurdle winner Peterhof: 33/1, backward and green, tailed off
in 10-runner maiden at Doncaster in November. *B. C. Morgan.*

DANGINA 2 b.c. (Apr 13) Song 132 – Shere Beauty 83 (Mummy's Pet 125) [1991 —
6g 7m a8g] 4,100 2-y-o: leggy, workmanlike colt: seventh foal: closely inbred:
half-brother to 3-y-o Sans Frais (by Forzando) and untrustworthy 1m winner
Colombiere (by Sallust): dam 2-y-o 5f winner became very temperamental: soundly
beaten in claimers and a maiden at Lingfield: trained by Dr J. Scargill on debut:
bandaged all round final outing. *A. S. Reid.*

DANGORA (USA) 3 b.f. Sovereign Dancer (USA) – Mofida 115 (Right Tack 131) —
[1990 6m* 6f* 6m² 1991 7m⁵] strong-quartered, attractive filly: has a quick action:
useful form at 2 yrs, second in Lowther Stakes at York: 4/1 and looking really well,

lost action over 1f out and carried head high when last of 5 in Nell Gwyn Stakes at Newmarket in April: stud. *B. W. Hills.*

DANIEL CHALLENGER 3 ch.g. Creetown 123 – Sally Young (Hasty Word 84) [1990 NR 1991 a6g] first foal: dam never ran: 50/1, always behind in Southwell claimer in December. *J. P. Smith.* —

DANNY BLANCHFLOWER 4 ch.g. Rabdan 129 – Caffre Lily (Hittite Glory 125) [1990 10f 8g 12m⁵ 12f a12g³ a11g⁴ 10d 10d⁶ 1991 7g* a8g³ a7g a8g a7g⁶ 7.5g 7m⁵] workmanlike gelding: moderate walker: has a round action: poor handicapper: won claimer (claimed out of P. Felgate's stable £4,005) at Southwell in January: not seen out after April: seems best short of 1¼m: acts on good to firm ground: ran poorly when visored once: inconsistent. *M. C. Chapman.* **49**

DANNY KANE 2 b.g. (Apr 6) Faustus (USA) 118 – Haywain 58 (Thatching 131) [1991 5g⁴ 5f² 6m⁴ 7g 7f²] 13,000F, 5,500Y: sturdy, good-bodied gelding: second foal: dam 7f winner: plating-class form: in frame in maiden auctions (rider dropped hands when race appeared won at Carlisle second outing) and when visored in Redcar claimer final start: stayed 7f well: dead. *C. Tinkler.* **58**

DANRAB 5 b.g. Rabdan 129 – Friendly Pet (Be Friendly 130) [1990 7.5d a7g² a7g³ 1991 8m 8m a7g² a7g⁴ a7g⁴ a7g 8m] compact, good-bodied gelding: moderate a 35 mover: poor maiden: form at 4 yrs and 5 yrs only on all-weather: stays 7f: tried visored: sold 2,000 gns Doncaster Summer Sales. *M. J. O'Neill.* —

DANS DANCER 2 b.c. (May 10) Ballacashtal (CAN) – Domino Rose 67 (Dominion 123) [1991 5m] 1,600Y: sparely-made colt: first foal: dam 6f winner: coltish and green, little promise in seller at Bath in May. *J. D. Czerpak.* —

DANSE D'ESPRIT 3 b.f. Lidhame 109 – Bel Esprit (Sagaro 133) [1990 6g 6d⁴ 7g* 7m 8d 8d 1991 7g 7g 7g⁵ a6g 7m⁵ 7f] rather sparely-made filly: poor handicapper: mainly stiff tasks at 3 yrs: may need return to further: acts on dead going: has worn blinkers and visor: ran poorly for 7-lb claimer final 2-y-o start. *G. H. Eden.* **42**

DANSEUSE DU SOIR (IRE) 3 b.f. Thatching 131 – Dance By Night 84 (Northfields (USA)) [1990 5g* 5.5g² 5.5g* 1991 8d* 8d* 8g⁴ 8g³ 8m⁵ 7d* 8g⁴] **121**

Danseuse du Soir's quick step was as telling in the autumn as it had been in the spring. Clearly the best three-year-old filly over a mile in her own country, as Kooyonga and Shadayid were in theirs, Danseuse du Soir wasn't quite so good as either of those fillies but proved just as tough and beat them both in the Breeders' Cup Mile at Churchill Downs in November. All three won their respective One Thousand Guineas, Danseuse du Soir establishing her pre-eminence in almost as good a style in the Dubai Poule d'Essai des Pouliches as she had in her trial, also at Longchamp, the Prix de la Grotte. Neither field lacked credible opposition. The Grotte runners included some of the previous season's leading two-year-olds in Magic Night, Sha Tha and Polemic along with the recent Maisons-Laffitte winner La Carene and when the eventual principals from that contest were put together with the first three in the Prix Imprudence, The Perfect Life, Divine Danse and Zanadiyka, there wasn't much missing in the Pouliches. There was only one foreign-trained challenger, Only Yours, but this looked a stronger race in depth than its British counterpart ten days earlier. Sha Tha quickened clear entering the straight at which point Danseuse du Soir, who'd been slowly into her stride from the stalls and held up on the outside, had about four lengths to make up—but she was in front herself a furlong and a half out and soon went clear.

Dubai Poule d'Essai des Pouliches, Longchamp—
Danseuse du Soir is chased home by Sha Tha then the unlucky Caerlina (noseband)

Her winning margin was two lengths as she changed her legs and tired in the last half furlong. Caerlina, who'd suffered most in early scrimmaging, was a short head behind Sha Tha, a result which corresponded almost identically to what Shadayid had achieved against the same placed horses in the Prix Marcel Boussac. A clash between Danseuse du Soir and Shadayid was what everyone wanted and, for once, it took place, with the Irish and Italian Guineas winners thrown in for good measure in the Coronation Stakes at Royal Ascot. Although running creditably, Danseuse du Soir was unable to produce the same turn of foot that characterised her wins at home and was beaten about two and a half lengths into fourth behind Kooyonga.

Having her limitations exposed there, however, didn't dissuade Danseuse du Soir's connections from pursuing an ambitious programme, beginning with the two top mile races in France. Of the seven other Pouliches winners that contested both the Prix Jacques le Marois and Prix du Moulin de Longchamp since 1945, only Miesque won both races and Ginetta (the 1959 Moulin winner) one of them. Eleven Pouliches winners ran in one of those races in the same season, with Pola Bella triumphing in the 1968 Moulin. Danseuse du Soir didn't win either of them but had victory in the Marois snatched from her only in the dying strides, chasing the pacemaker on the bridle when most of the jockeys had been pushing at their mounts long before, then quickening a length and a half clear as the leader folded, only to have Hector Protector and Lycius battle back. Four weeks later Danseuse du Soir wasn't nearly so well positioned when the race for the Moulin began in earnest, not settling so well in mid-division and getting checked entering the straight; and she can be forgiven a slightly below-par effort on the form-book. And that was her only run that does have to be forgiven. Lycius' modest showing left little by way of opposition in the seven-furlong Prix de la Foret at Longchamp—it was, in fact, left to the Swedish-trained Itsabrahma to chase her home—but Danseuse du Soir could do little more than win comfortably. In the Breeders' Cup Mile she was allowed to go off at 41/1, the longest priced of Europe's six challengers. Numerically this was Europe's strongest challenge for the race and Danseuse du Soir proved the strongest challenger of the six, finishing about three and a half lengths behind the winner Opening Verse and just in front of Priolo. In truth, Shadayid would probably have beaten her narrowly but for being badly hampered close home but who's to say that Danseuse du Soir's mastery of the new conditions, breaking well and able to travel easily close to the pace, hugging the rail and avoiding all the trouble in running, didn't deserve the greater reward?

One has to go a fair way back in the dam's family to find a racehorse of similar class to Danseuse du Soir; the third dam Relicia was a half-sister to the redoubtable Ardneasken, dam of Warpath and Dakota. Relicia herself won

Prix de la Foret, Longchamp—Danseuse du Soir repels the foreign challenge; Itsabrahma takes second for Sweden, Osario (chevrons) third for Britain

M D. Wildenstein's "Danseuse du Soir"

		Thatch	Forli
	Thatching	(b 1970)	Thong
	(b 1975)	Abella	Abernant
Danseuse du Soir (IRE)		(ch 1968)	Darrica
(b.f. 1988)		Northfields	Northern Dancer
	Dance By Night	(ch 1968)	Little Hut
	(ch 1982)	Elvina	Dancer's Image
		(gr 1975)	Relicia

over a mile and a quarter for Jim Bolger late on as a three-year-old. Relicia built a very respectable breeding record from unspectacular opportunities, her best offspring being the useful two-year-old Delicia and Stewards' Cup winner Rotherfield Greys. Danseuse du Soir's dam Dance By Night, a daughter of the Irish three-year-old six-furlong and mile-and-a-quarter winner Elvina, was a genuine and consistent individual like her daughter, although she only had one season to show it before injury intervened, winning seven-furlong nurseries at Brighton and Epsom when trained by Lewis. At stud she has a hundred per cent record for throwing fillies—and winners, Danseuse du Soir being preceded by the early-season two-year-old scorer Sarah Georgina (by Persian Bold) and followed by Reveuse du Soir (by Vision) who won a seven-furlong newcomers race at Evry in September then failed to reach the frame in a listed and Group 3 contest, also trained by Lellouche. Dance By Night's 1990 and 1991 foals are by Aragon and Kahyasi respectively. Danseuse du Soir fetched 40,000 guineas when sent to the Highflyer Sales, about 7,200 guineas more than the average price of a Thatching yearling in 1989. Danseuse du Soir obviously kept Thatching in the public eye in France and, with such as the smart sprinters Archway and Shalford to represent him, he had his best season's prize money total in Great Britain and Ireland with over half a million pounds and at the end of the turf season he shared first position in the sires' tables for number of winners and number of races won.

Danseuse du Soir has been retired and will visit Lear Fan, sire of M Wildenstein's 1991 Criterium de Saint-Cloud winner Glaieul and Marcel Boussac third Verveine, in 1992. Verveine will do very well to fill the shoes of Danseuse du Soir. The leggy Danseuse du Soir came to hand soon enough to win two races, including the Prix Robert Papin, early on as a two-year-old and kept her form remarkably well during a tough second season. She was effective at seven furlongs and a mile and never raced on extremes of going. A fine turn of foot was as much a feature of Danseuse du Soir's performances as her consistency. *E. Lellouche, France.*

DANUBE 3 b.g. Kings Lake (USA) 133 – Alpine Niece 87 (Great Nephew 126) **77 §**
[1990 NR 1991 8g* 8d 7.6g6 8s6 10.3m] 32,000Y: quite attractive gelding: has a quick action: half-brother to dual 2000 Guineas winner Tirol (by Thatching), 5f performer Relatively Sharp (by Sharpen Up) and quite useful 1984 2-y-o 5f winner Lady Donna (by Dominion): dam placed at up to 1½m: fair form: gambled-on winner of maiden at Warwick in April: got well behind penultimate start and refused to race (blinkered) on final one: should stay 1¼m: one to avoid. *C. N. Williams.*

DANZA HEIGHTS 5 br.h. Head For Heights 125 – Dankalia (Le Levanstell **43**
122) [1990 12d6 8f6 8.2m 10m 18d 16s 1991 12g* 15.1m* 11.8g5 12.3f4] tall, quite good-topped horse: has a round action: first form at 5 yrs (trained as 4-y-o by P. Felgate), winning handicaps at Doncaster in July and Ayr in August: wandered under pressure final start: stays 15f: acts on good to firm ground but may do better granted testing conditions: winning hurdler. *Mrs G. R. Reveley.*

DANZARIN (IRE) 3 b.g. Kings Lake (USA) 133 – Sodium's Niece (Northfields **87**
(USA)) [1990 6m3 6m 6g6 6m* 1991 8g 8d3 10.1m 9m* 10m4 10m4 10g 8.9g] leggy, quite good-topped gelding: fair handicapper: won at Sandown in June: ran well next 3 starts: moved moderately down, never dangerous in £13,400 event at York on final one: should stay beyond 1¼m: acts on good to firm ground and dead: gelded after final start. *R. Hannon.*

DANZIG LAD (USA) 3 b.g. Ziggy's Boy (USA) – Sexy Ways (USA) (Our Native **45**
(USA)) [1990 5m3 6g5 a6g3 7g 8d 7g3 1991 a7g4 a7g6 a8g4 12g6 a7g a10g] smallish gelding: has a long stride: poor maiden nowadays: best effort in 1991 on reappearance: off course nearly 8 months before penultimate start: probably stays 1m (little chance at 1½m): effective with or without visor: gelded after final start. *M. P. Naughton.*

DARAGENCY 3 b.f. Dara Monarch 128 – Rashah 67 (Blakeney 126) [1990 5g 7g **—**
8.2s 10.6s 1991 9.1s4] leggy filly: poor plater. *J. S. Wilson.*

DARAKAH 4 ch.f. Doulab (USA) 115 – Ladytown (English Prince 129) [1990 6m **67**
5m5 6m6 6m3 7f* 7g 7g3 7g5 7.6d 7g2 a7g 1991 6g 8g 10.1g 6g* 8f6 5.8d5 7g 6m6 6m2 8m 7g3] leggy filly: quite modest handicapper: moderate mover: won at Kempton in May: effective at 6f and stays 1m: acts on firm and dead going (ran badly on all-weather at Southwell as 3 y o)r none too consistent. *C. J. Hill.*

DARA LOCH (IRE) 3 b.c. Dara Monarch 128 – Kumari (FR) 78 (Luthier 126) **—**
[1990 7d6 8d 8.2s6 8v 8d 1991 7g 8d] leggy, close-coupled colt: has a very round action: poor maiden: showed little in autumn at 3 yrs: bred to be suited by 1m+: sweating last 3 starts. *M. P. Naughton.*

DARA MELODY (IRE) 2 b.g. (Jan 21) Dara Monarch 128 – Ascensiontide **61**
(Ela-Mana-Mou 132) [1991 7.5f5 6g5 7m6 8m4 8.2m4] 15,000Y, 16,500Y: leggy, rather sparely-made gelding: first foal: dam Irish 1½m winner, is daughter of Child Stakes winner Rose Above: quite modest maiden: blinkered, ran respectably in sellers final 2 starts: stays 1m. *J. G. FitzGerald.*

DARAVI 2 ch.c. (Feb 16) Dara Monarch 128 – Vitry 48 (Vitiges (FR) 132) [1991 6f **41**
5m 5m 6g 8m 5s] 9,200F, 6,200Y, 5,000 2-y-o: strong, compact colt: second foal: half-brother to 3-y-o Up That Drive (by Kalaglow): dam, stayed 1½m, is half-sister to very useful 6f and 1¼m winner Homeboy: poor maiden: has run in a seller: should stay 1m: blinkered final 3 starts, running badly first 2 occasions: sold 500 gns Doncaster November Sales. *J. W. Payne.*

D'ARCYS GOLD 2 b.f. (Mar 28) Jalmood (USA) 126 – Primrose Way 59 (Young **—**
Generation 129) [1991 5f 7g 8d 7g] 1,000 (privately) Y: lengthy filly: moderate walker: second foal: dam middle-distance maiden: soundly beaten, including in sellers. *R. J. Hodges.*

DARCY'S THATCHER 7 b. or br.h. Thatching 131 – Lancette (Double Jump **88**
131) [1990 8g* 10d* 12d4 1991 a7g4 a8g 10g* 12g* 8m3 10g2] leggy, attractive

horse: fair Irish performer nowadays: ran on all-weather here in January: won claimers at the Curragh in June and Tramore in August: probably needs further than 1m nowadays, and stays 1½m: acts on good to firm ground and soft going: tried blinkered: winning hurdler. *M. Browne, Ireland.*

DARE TO DREAM (IRE) 2 b.g. (May 11) Baillamont (USA) 124 – Tears of **44** Allah (FR) (Troy 137) [1991 7g 6.9f 6s] 6,000F: tall, rather leggy gelding: first foal: dam French maiden from family of Comtesse de Loir: poor form in autumn maidens at Salisbury and Folkestone: looks a long-term prospect and will be suited by 1¼m +: gelded at end of year. *G. Lewis.*

DARIKA LAD 3 gr.g. Belfort (FR) 89 – Lindrake's Pride (Mandrake Major 122) **70 d** [1990 7m⁵ 6g⁵ 7.5m* 7g 1991 7v⁵ 5f⁶ 6m 6m² 6d⁴ 7m⁴ 7f 8f⁶ 6f⁶ 9m 8m] workmanlike gelding: quite modest handicapper: ran moderately last 5 starts, very strong hold to post before final one: stays 7.5f: best efforts on good to firm ground: visored ninth start: unsatisfactory. *A. Harrison.*

DARING JOY 4 b.f. Daring March 116 – African Berry 84 (African Sky 124) [1990 — 9g 12f⁶ 14g² 18d⁶ 14.6d⁵ 1991 14.6g] big, workmanlike filly: plating-class handicapper: soundly beaten only run in 1991 (needed race): should prove best short of 2¼m: acts on dead going. *B. A. McMahon.*

DARINGLY 2 b.c. (Mar 31) Daring March 116 – Leylandia 69 (Wolver Hollow — 126) [1991 8m] 4,000Y: leggy, unfurnished colt: eighth reported foal: half-brother to 3 winners, notably very useful Irish 7f (at 2 yrs) to 1¾m winner Thetford Forest (by Blakeney): dam won over 2m at 4 yrs: 66/1, tailed off in 15-runner maiden at Leicester in October. *R. Curtis.*

DARI SOUND (IRE) 3 b.g. Shardari 134 – Bugle Sound 96 (Bustino 136) [1990 **46** 8.5m² 8g 1991 8.5f 12.3d 10d 9.9f⁶ 8m 10m 11m3] strong gelding: moderate mover: only occasional signs of ability, best effort staying-on third of 17 in selling handicap at Redcar: stays 11f: acts on good to firm ground: blinkered final start at 2 yrs: winning hurdler. *J. G. FitzGerald.*

DARK HERITAGE 8 b.g. Scorpio (FR) 127 – Mother of The Wind 82 (Tumble **53** Wind (USA)) [1990 a12g 1991 a10g⁶ a13g⁴ a12g* a12g] big, strong, good-bodied gelding: quite modest handicapper at best: won at Lingfield in January: effective from 1¼m to 1½m: acted on firm going: ran moderately in blinkers: dead. *D. J. G. Murray-Smith.*

DARK ISLE 3 b.g. Mashhor Dancer (USA) – Dark Amber 68 (Formidable (USA) — 125) [1990 7g 7d⁵ 1991 11g 10.1m 8d 10.1d] leggy, sparely-made gelding: quite modest form second start at 2 yrs: none in 1991: should stay 1m: on toes last 2 starts, sweating when blinkered final one. *M. McCourt.*

DARK KRISTAL (IRE) 3 b.f. Gorytus (USA) 132 – Kristallina 84 (Homeric **66** 133) [1990 5m⁵ 5f⁶ 5m⁵ 6d³ 1991 5m⁵ 6g* 6m 6f⁶ 7.1m⁴ 7m] small filly: quite modest handicapper: won at Brighton in July: stumbled turn and eased at Warwick final outing: stays 7f: acts on good to firm ground and dead. *R. Hannon.*

DARK MIDNIGHT (IRE) 2 br.g. (May 5) Petorius 117 – Gaelic Jewel 89 **60** (Scottish Rifle 127) [1991 5m⁵ 5f² 6f 6f⁶ a8g] 11,000Y: leggy gelding: fourth foal: half-brother to 3-y-o Emerald Gulf (by Wassl) and 5f (at 2 yrs) and 10.6f winner Irish Emerald (by Taufan): dam 1¼m winner, is daughter of very useful miler Red Ruby, a half-sister to Laser Light: easily best effort second in claimer at Beverley: showed nothing in nurseries. *P. C. Haslam.*

DARK ROOTS 3 b.f. Tina's Pet 121 – Tinted Blonde (USA) (Charles Elliott — (USA)) [1990 NR 1991 7s 6m] leggy, lengthy, rather shallow-girthed filly: second foal: dam lightly raced: tailed-off last in maiden and claimer. *J. Ringer.*

DARK VISION 2 br.f. (Apr 27) Noalto 120 – Valeur (Val de Loir 133) [1991 5m **38** 5.1m 6g 7m 5.7m] 3,000Y: workmanlike filly: half-sister to several winners, including stayer Vision of Wonder (by Tyrnavos) and 1m and 9f winner Make Your Bid (by Auction Ring): dam second over 10.5f in France: little worthwhile form in varied events: blinkered final start (July): pulls hard: tends to sweat. *J. S. King.*

DARLING DIANNE (IRE) 3 ch.f. Burslem 123 – Escalado (Homing 130) — [1990 5f 6m* 6m 6d a7g 1991 6g 7g 7g 6f 7m 10g] compact filly: has a quick action: won seller at 2 yrs: well beaten in handicaps and ladies seller since: stays 6f: twice blinkered, including when successful: sometimes visored: sold 1,250 gns Doncaster November Sales. *M. P. Naughton.*

DARLING MISS DAISY 2 ch.f. (Apr 8) Tina's Pet 121 – Kakisa 81 (Forlorn **77** River 124) [1991 6.1f 5m* 6m³ 6.1d²] lengthy filly: has scope: third foal: sister to 3-y-o 6f winner Fenton Lake, also winner over hurdles (has looked ungenuine), and fair sprinter Lake Mistassiu: dam 5f and 6f winner: won maiden at Wolverhampton in September: placed subsequently in minor events at Ayr and (very stiff task) Chester: may prove best at sprint distances: acts on good to firm and dead ground: progressive. *G. A. Pritchard-Gordon.*

DARTING MOTH 4 br.f. Mansingh (USA) 120 – Crescent Dart 103 (Sing Sing 134) [1990 7.6d 6d⁶ a6g² a6g⁶ 1991 6d a5g⁴ 6.9m 7g] lengthy, slightly dipped-backed a 52 filly: poor maiden: clearly best efforts on all-weather at Southwell: stays 6f: sold 840 gns Newmarket September Sales. *G. A. Pritchard-Gordon.*

DARTREY (IRE) 3 b.f. Darshaan 133 – Secala (USA) (Secretariat (USA)) [1990 111 7m* 1991 8g⁶ 10.5m² 12m⁶ 10m² 10.5v] leggy, sparely-made filly: beaten head by Gussy Marlowe in Tattersalls Musidora Stakes at York and 4 lengths by Ristna in moderately-run Cheveley Park Stud Sun Chariot Stakes (always prominent, readily outpaced final 1f) at Newmarket: looking very well, below that form in Gold Seal Oaks at Epsom in between, chasing leader 1¼m: prominent 9f in Group 3 event at Saint-Cloud in November: stays 10.5f well: very useful. *M. R. Stoute.*

DARUSSALAM 4 ch.f. Tina's Pet 121 – Chinese Falcon 81 (Skymaster 126) 69 [1990 8f⁶ 7m⁶ 7h 8g 6g⁵ 6f² 6m* 6m⁴ 6g 6f⁴ 5m 6m⁴ 5m 5f 5g 5d 1991 a6g 6s 7g 6m 6m* 6f² 6f³ 6d² 6m⁵ 6.9m⁶ 6d² 5.9f² 6f⁴ 7.1g⁶ 6g* 6g 5.1d* 6s⁶ 5d⁴] sparely-made filly: has a round action: much improved and a reformed handicapper in 1991: won at Hamilton in May, Leicester in September and Chepstow in October: best at 5f to 6f: has form on firm ground but best effort with give (acts on soft going): best without blinkers: sold out of T. Craig's stable 4,400 gns Doncaster August Sales after thirteenth start. *R. Lee.*

DASHING APRIL 3 b.f. Daring March 116 – Ritruda (USA) 95 (Roi Dagobert 64 128) [1990 NR 1991 8g⁶ 7.1d³ a7g⁴ 8s⁴ 8g⁶ 10.5g] 4,400Y: moderate mover: half-sister to 4 winners, including 5f and 1¼m winner Sidab (by Lochnager): dam stayed 7f: quite modest maiden: stays 1m: acts on dead going: well beaten on fibresand: sweating (ran creditably) fifth start: retained by trainer 5,800 gns Newmarket Autumn Sales. *D. T. Thom.*

DASHING FELLOW (IRE) 3 b.g. Sure Blade (USA) 128 – Belle Viking (FR) 57 (Riverman (USA) 131) [1990 7g 7g 7m 6d 1991 10f² 10.2d³ 12.3m*] rather angular gelding: has a round action: plating-class form: won handicap at Wolverhampton in July, leading 3f out and holding on by a short head: better at 1½m than 1¼m: sold to join Mrs A. Knight 3,200 gns Doncaster November Sales. *P. F. I. Cole.*

DASHING STYLE (IRE) 3 b.g. Red Sunset 120 – Rare Sound 69 (Rarity 129) — [1990 6d 7m⁶ 7d⁶ 6d a7g* a7g 1991 a6g⁶ 12v] small, sturdy gelding: poor mover: easily best effort to win maiden at Lingfield late on at 2 yrs: stays 7f: seems not to act on heavy ground: trained until after reappearance by R. Guest: subsequently gelded. *A. Hide.*

DASHING TYKE 3 gr.g. Flying Tyke 90 – Habatashie 62 (Habat 127) [1990 5m — 1991 7m] last in maiden auction and claimer: sold 1,000 gns Doncaster November Sales. *A. Smith.*

DASWAKI (CAN) 3 b.g. Miswaki (USA) 124 – Nice Manners (CAN) (Barachois 91 (CAN)) [1990 7m⁶ 7m⁴ 7m³ 6m³ 5m⁵ 6d* 6m* 1991 6g 8m 7g 10.1m 8m² 8m* 8s* 9m³ 8m* 8m* 9g4] sturdy, rather angular gelding: moderate walker: fairly useful handicapper: gelded after fourth start and in fine form afterwards: successful at Goodwood (£7,800 event, made all) in July, Kempton in August, Doncaster in September and Newmarket (quickening on in good style 2f out) in October: good fourth of 18 to Barkerville in £30,800 contest at Newbury: probably stays 9f: acts on good to firm ground and soft: sweating seventh and eighth starts: looked very well in the autumn. *R. Hannon.*

DAUNTESS 4 ch.f. Formidable (USA) 125 – Cantico 58 (Green Dancer (USA) — 132) [1990 7g* 8g 6g³ 8m⁵ 8m 1991 7f 7v] lengthy, sparely-made, angular filly: fair performer at 3 yrs: well beaten at Epsom (looked ill at ease on turn) and Kempton (sweating) in summer: stays 1m: tends to be a handful at the start, and once refused to enter stalls at 3 yrs: has been bandaged behind. *D. R. C. Elsworth.*

DAUNTING PROSPECT 7 b.g. Formidable (USA) 125 – Acquire 105 (Burglar — 128) [1990 NR 1991 a14g a16g] small, strong gelding: poor mover: seems of little account nowadays. *M. C. Chapman.*

DAUNTLESS KNIGHT (USA) 3 ch.c. Sir Ivor 135 – Colinear (USA) — (Cohoes) [1990 7g 8.2d⁴ 1991 10g 15.3m⁴ 17.2g 16.1g 18.1m] good-topped, lengthy colt: easy mover: quite modest maiden at best: no worthwhile form in 1991: had given impression would prove suited by extreme test of stamina: pulled very hard in blinkers final start: visored time before: sold 6,500 gns Newmarket Autumn Sales. *G. Harwood.*

DAUNT NOT 3 gr.f. Kalaglow 132 – Dare Me 101 (Derring-Do 131) [1990 NR 1991 **65** 8g² 8m] leggy, workmanlike filly: seventh foal: half-sister to several winners, including good sprinter Fortysecond Street (by Sharpen Up) and 2m winner Scolt Head (by Troy): dam won three 5f races from 5 starts: second of 10, making most and easily better effort in maidens at Warwick in the spring. *G. Wragg.*

DAVAMAL 2 ch.f. (Feb 11) Little Wolf 127 – Princess Glory 58 (Prince de Galles — 125) [1991 6g 7m] plain filly: fourth known foal: dam poor plater: no worthwhile form in sellers in mid-summer. *J. M. Bradley.*

DAVID'S OWN 2 b.g. (May 15) Petong 126 – Carvery 71 (Milford 119) [1991 5d **53** a6g⁴ 6.1g² 8m 8.1g 7.1m] 7,000Y, 8,000 2-y-o: good-bodied gelding: has a quick action: second foal: dam middle-distance maiden: plating-class maiden: best effort when second at Nottingham (led 5f) in August: stays 6f: ran creditably on fibresand. *S. Mellor.*

DAWADAR (USA) 4 b.g. Exceller (USA) 129 – Damana (FR) (Crystal Palace — (FR) 132) [1990 10m² 12.3m* 12d* 12v 1991 11.9d] lengthy, rather sparely-made gelding: fairly useful handicapper at best: burly only run on flat in 1991: will stay beyond 1½m: acts on good to firm ground, seems unsuited by heavy: winning hurdler. *N. Tinkler.*

DAWES OF NELSON 6 b. or br.g. Krayyan 117 – Killyhevlin (Green God 128) **41** [1990 6f 6f 6m⁴ 6g⁵ 6g² 5g* 6m⁵ 6m³ 6d⁴ 5.8d⁴ 1991 6m⁶ 6m 5d² 6g 6d² 5s* 5m⁵ 6g⁶ 5.1s⁶ 6.9f 6s⁵] workmanlike gelding: has long stride: poor handicapper: won at Hamilton in July: probably stays 7f: acts on good to firm and soft going: has hung left. *M. J. Bolton.*

DAWN BELL 6 b.m. Belfort (FR) 89 – Dobrina (FR) (Our Mirage 123) [1990 a6g — a5g 5f² 5m 6m* 6m 5m 1991 5m 5.1m 6.1d 6.9m 5m 6.1m] good-bodied mare: carries plenty of condition: moderate mover: poor performer at best nowadays: best at 6f: acts on firm going: has worn blinkers. *J. M. Bradley.*

DAWN GREY 3 gr.c. Nishapour (FR) 125 – Geoffrey's Sister 102 (Sparkler 130) **67** [1990 6g² 8d 8d³ 1991 6g 8s³ 10g⁶ 9.2d* 8.9m⁵ 9.2m* 11.1g* 11d⁴] small, leggy, sparely-made colt: quite modest handicapper: successful at Hamilton in June, July and (claimer) September: ran moderately final outing: stays 11f well: acts on good to firm ground and soft: sold W. Muir 10,000 gns Doncaster November Sales. *C. W. Thornton.*

DAWN'S DELIGHT 13 b.g. Dawn Review 105 – Bird of Passage (Falcon 131) **51** [1990 6f 6m 6s 6m 6d⁵ 6m a7g 6m 1991 6v 6m 6g 6g 6m 6g⁶ 7g* 7g 6g 7m 7g 7s⁵] leggy, workmanlike gelding: moderate mover: has won 20 races in his career: plating-class handicapper nowadays: won seller (no bid) at Ayr in July: stays 7f: suited by some give in the ground (acts on heavy going): has worn blinkers and visor: often on toes: usually gets behind (didn't at Ayr): suited by strong gallop. *K. T. Ivory.*

DAWN SUCCESS 5 br.h. Caerleon (USA) 132 – Dawn Echo (Don (ITY) 123) **84** [1990 7.5v⁶ 8g 7g⁶ 8f 8f⁶ 9g⁵ 7.6g 7m 9m 6s 1991 a8g³ a8g 8d 8d³ 8g 8.9g² 10.5f 9m 10d 10m a6g a6g a8g] leggy, close-coupled horse: fairly useful handicapper on his day, on the downgrade nowadays: effective at 6f to 9f: acts on any going: has worn eyeshield on all-weather: sold out of C. Brittain's stable 7,000 gns Newmarket Autumn Sales after tenth start. *D. W. Chapman.*

DAWSON CITY 4 ch.g. Glint of Gold 128 – Lola Sharp (Sharpen Up 127) [1990 — 9f² 10v* 10.6s² 11.5f⁴ 8m 11d* 10.4v⁵ 1991 11.9m] sturdy gelding: fairly useful handicapper at 3 yrs: very much in need of run only start at 4 yrs, first for almost 10 months: stays 11.5f: best efforts with plenty of give in the ground (acts on heavy): winning hurdler. *M. H. Easterby.*

DAWSON PLACE (USA) 3 b.c. Green Desert (USA) 127 – Casual (USA) **103** (Caro 133) [1990 NR 1991 7g³ 7g² 7m* 8g² 8g²] $110,000Y: good-topped colt: has scope: has a round action: fourth foal: half-brother to 10.5f and 11f winner Ostura (by Sir Ivor) and 2 winners in USA: dam winner at up to 9f from family of top Canadian performer Giboulee: won maiden at Kempton in July: second in Jersey Stakes (beaten 6 lengths by Satin Flower) at Royal Ascot and in 3-runner minor events at Newmarket and Goodwood: stays 1m: sold 42,000 gns Newmarket Autumn Sales, reportedly to race in Germany. *G. Harwood.*

DAYDAYSI 3 b.f. Dawn Johnny (USA) 90 – Mayab 100 (Maystreak 118) [1990 6m — 8.2g 1991 6g 6.1m] small, sparely-made filly: well beaten in maidens, seller and claimer. *M. R. Leach.*

Henri Chalhoub's "Dear Doctor"

DAYS OF THUNDER 3 ch.c. Vaigly Great 127 – Silent Prayer 58 (Queen's Hussar 124) [1990 7m⁴ 1991 7g 10m⁶ 12m] sturdy colt: easily best effort in maiden events on debut: gave impression failed to stay 1¼m: edgy second outing: sold J. White 3,400 gns Newmarket Autumn Sales. *M. E. D. Francis.* —

DAZLA 4 b.f. Dublin Taxi – Shahrazad (Young Emperor 133) [1990 8g 8g 7s* 8g 7m 8d 1991 a7g 8m a12g 10g] close-coupled ex-Irish filly: second living foal: dam poor Irish maiden: won maiden at Sligo in 1990: no form here in 1991: stays 7f: ran badly when tried blinkered. *P. Burgoyne.* —

DAZ ZAD 3 ch.f. Bladon 85 – Sardine 74 (Saritamer (USA) 130) [1990 NR] light-framed filly: third foal: dam probably stayed 6f: 33/1, unruly and withdrawn before 4-runner Brighton maiden in May. *T. J. Naughton.*

DAZZLE THE CROWD (IRE) 3 b.g. Simply Great (FR) 122 – Katie Roche (Sallust 134) [1990 6g 1991 7g⁵ 6.1m 10d a12g⁶] sturdy, angular gelding: no worthwhile form in maidens and claimers: bred to stay at least 1m. *C. A. Cyzer.* —

DAZZLING DISPLAY (IRE) 2 b.c. (Apr 16) Mazaad 106 – Standing Ovation (Godswalk (USA) 130) [1991 7d 7f 7.1d] 19,000Y: compact colt: fifth foal: brother to Irish 3-y-o 1¼m winner Crowded House and half-brother to 1989 2-y-o 7f winer Go Holimarine (by Taufan): dam Irish 1½m winner: poor form in maidens: blinkered (slowly away) second outing: sold 4,500 gns Newmarket Autumn Sales. *G. Harwood.* **46**

DAZZLING FIRE (IRE) 2 b.f. (Mar 21) Bluebird (USA) 125 – Fire Flash 74 (Bustino 136) [1991 7g³ 7g³ 8m⁴] IR 36,000Y: smallish filly: good mover: third foal: **78**

half-sister to 2 winners in Austria: dam, never tried beyond 1¼m, is out of smart 7f and 1m performer Dazzling Light, a half-sister to Welsh Pageant: modest maiden: third at Goodwood in August, behind Bilateral in 4-runner minor event second occasion: ran moderately at Leicester following month: should stay 1m: possibly unsuited by good to firm ground. *B. W. Hills.*

DAZZLINGLY RADIANT 4 gr.f. Try My Best (USA) 130 – Elvina (FR) 81
(Dancer's Image (USA)) [1990 8.2g 8f² 7f⁶ 7f² 7g³ 6g* 5.8m² 6m* 6g³ 6m⁴ 6m⁵ 6d
1991 6g 6d* 6g 6.1g] leggy, quite good-topped filly: moderate walker and mover: fair handicapper: form at 4 yrs only when winning at Salisbury in June: suited by 6f: acted on firm and dead ground: in foal to Thatching. *R. Hannon.*

DAZZLING MAID (IRE) 2 b.f. (Feb 8) Tate Gallery (USA) 117 – Lautreamont 64
(Auction Ring (USA) 123) [1991 6m⁴ 6m⁶ 6f² 5f³ 6g 7g⁶] 62,000F: quite attractive filly: first foal: dam French 9f and 10.5f winner: quite modest maiden: ran moderately second (gave trouble stalls) and final 2 outings: should stay 1m: acts on firm ground: blinkered last 4 starts. *M. H. Easterby.*

DEADLOCK 4 ch.g. The Minstrel (CAN) 135 – Roses To Rachel (Artaius (USA) —
129) [1990 11d 12f 10m⁴ 10m⁶ 10g⁶ 12m 12g⁶ 12m³ 11.7m⁴ 1991 a10g4] well-made gelding: moderate walker and mover: quite modest maiden at best: not seen out after March: stays 1½m: acts on good to firm ground: often makes the running. *D. R. C. Elsworth.*

DEADLY TOUCH 3 b.c. Touching Wood (USA) 127 – Katharina 105 (Frankin- —
cense 120) [1990 6g a7g 7f 8g 1991 11.7g 12g] neat, good-bodied colt: behind, blinkered in selling handicap final start. *P. Howling.*

DEAR DOCTOR (FR) 4 b.c. Crystal Glitters (USA) 127 – Adele Toumignon 120
(Zeddaan 130) [1990 10s² 10.5g* 10g⁴ 10g⁶ 10g³ 10d* 9.7g⁶ 10s² 10v* 1991 10s² 10g³
10.5g³ 12d* 12m⁵ 11f² 12g² 12g] tall, leggy attractive colt: third reported foal: half-brother to Genereux Genie (by General Assembly), middle-distance winner in France, including in listed company: dam French 9f winner: good-class French colt: won Group 2 Prix Jean de Chaudenay at Saint-Cloud (beat Passing Sale by 1½ lengths) in May: bit below best when fifth in Hardwicke Stakes at Royal Ascot but ran well in Grade 1 Man o' War Stakes and Turf Classic, both at Belmont Park: in rear in Breeders' Cup Turf at Churchill Downs final start: worth a try beyond 1½m: acts on any going: reportedly stays in training. *J. E. Hammond, France.*

DEAREST 4 b.f. Alzao (USA) 117 – Lover's Rose (King Emperor (USA)) [1990 52
7m² 7g⁵ a12g⁶ 1991 a8g* a10g⁶] rangy, rather unfurnished filly: plating-class handicapper: won at Southwell in January: not seen again after running at Lingfield following month: best form at 1m. *P. F. I. Cole.*

DEBACLE (USA) 2 b.c. (Mar 9) Raft (USA) 125 – Kuala (USA) (Hawaii) [1991 — p
7m] sturdy, attractive colt: good walker: half-brother to 7f seller winner Fruity O'Rooney (by Accipiter): dam 2-y-o 7f winner: 16/1, burly and green, soon off bridle and never on terms in Doncaster maiden in October: will stay 1m +: looks capable of better: retained by trained 8,400 gns Ascot November Sales. *G. Harwood.*

DEBJANJO 3 b.g. Critique (USA) 126 – Miss White (FR) (Carwhite 127) [1990 56
6m⁴ 5m² 6g⁴ 6f³ 6m 6g 1991 6f⁶ 6m 8m* 8g 11.7g 8m⁵ 8.2f 9.7m] tall, leggy gelding: moderate mover: fair plater: hung left then ran on strongly to lead post at Brighton (bought in 11,500 gns) in May: stays 1m well: acts on firm going: blinkered (ran poorly) once at 2 yrs: sometimes sweating and edgy: has found little, and is one to have reservations about. *J. R. Jenkins.*

DEBORAH SHELLEY 2 b.f. (Apr 2) Sweet Monday 122 – Avenmore Star 47 —
(Comedy Star (USA) 121) [1991 6m 8m] smallish, leggy filly: first foal: dam poor sprint maiden: no promise in minor event at Windsor in July and maiden at Warwick in October: broke out of stalls and withdrawn at Leicester later in month. *E. A. Wheeler.*

DEB'S BALL 5 b.m. Glenstal (USA) 118 – De'b Old Fruit (Levmoss 133) [1990 7f 62 +
7f 8g 9.1m³ 8m 12f 1991 12d* 13d* 12f² 13.1m² 12.4m*] quite good-topped mare: quite modest handicapper: in cracking form as 5-y-o, successful at Pontefract in April, Ayr in July and Newcastle in October: should stay beyond 13f: acts on firm and dead ground: ran well when visored once: has idled, and best with extreme waiting tactics: has flashed tail: quite useful hurdler. *D. Moffatt.*

DEB'S HONDA 2 b.f. (Apr 1) Thatching 131 – Verette (Posse (USA) 130) [1991 —
7m 8s] 3,500Y: second foal: dam modest daughter of Criterium des Pouliches winner Vela: soundly beaten in median auction at Wolverhampton and maiden (prominent to 2f out) at Yarmouth in autumn. *C. E. Brittain.*

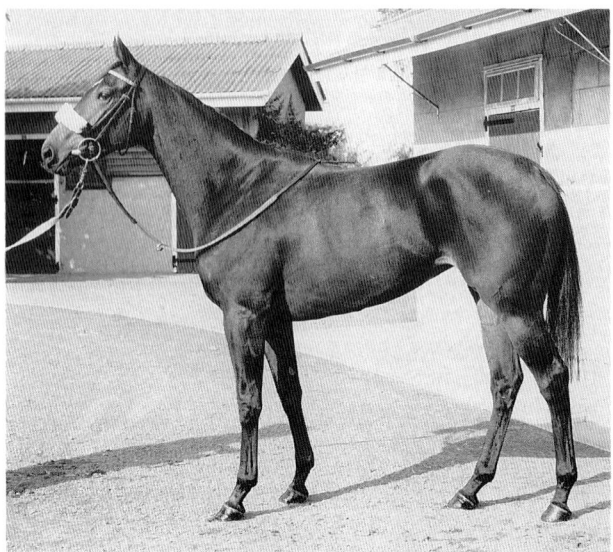

Mrs C. Collins' "Dedicated Lady"

DEBSY DO (USA) 2 b.f. (Feb 22) Dance Bid (USA) 114 – Diablesse (USA) **64**
(Dewan (USA)) [1991 6m³ 5.1d² a7g⁶ 7m⁵ 8m a7g³ a7g*] good-bodied filly: third
foal: closely related to a winner in North America by One For All: dam ran 4 times:
quite modest performer: showed much improved form on Southwell fibresand last 2
starts, winning nursery by a length from Talented Ting: suited by 7f: has run
respectably on good to firm ground. *S. G. Norton.*

DECIDED (CAN) 8 b.g. Affirmed (USA) – Expediency (USA) (Vaguely Noble —
140) [1990 16.2s 1991 10.3d] big, strong, good-topped gelding: moderate walker and
mover: fair winner as 4-y-o when trained by H. Cecil: needed last 2 starts, only
subsequent ones on flat: stays 1½m well: fairly useful hurdler/chaser at best. *R. Lee.*

DECKERWAY LADY 2 br.f. (Mar 13) Today And Tomorrow 78 – Runager 74 **47**
(Lochnager 132) [1991 5m a6g⁵] leggy filly: second foal: sister to poor 1990 2-y-o
Grey Earl: dam 2-y-o 5f winner: around 5 lengths fifth of 14 to Battle of Britain in
claimer at Lingfield in November, much better effort. *R. Akehurst.*

DEDICATED LADY (IRE) 2 b.f. (Feb 15) Pennine Walk 120 – Salabella 64 **101**
(Sallust 134) [1991 5d⁶ 5v³ 5g* 5g³ 6g* 7g⁵ 6.3s*] IR 6,500Y: fourth foal: half-sister
to useful 1986 2-y-o 6f winner Rockfella (by Ballad Rock) and useful 7f and 1m
winner Silk Petal (by Petorius): dam, half-sister to Irish St Leger winner
M-Lolshan, stayed 11f: useful performer: successful in maiden at Down Royal in
May and IR £6,900 event at Leopardstown following month: off course 2½ months,
won very valuable Goffs 2-y-o Fillies Challenge Race at the Curragh by 2½ lengths
from Cardinal Press, always prominent keeping on well and showing much improved form: may well stay 1m: acts well on soft going, yet to race on top-of-
the-ground. *C. Collins, Ireland.*

DEE AND EM 6 ch.g. Crofter (USA) 124 – Cousin Clare (Pontifex (USA)) [1990 —
5f 6g 8f⁵ 7h 5m³ 5m* 5m⁶ 5m 5m 7m 7m 5m 1991 a6g³ a7g a5g a6g⁶ 7.5g a5g]

compact, workmanlike gelding: poor mover: poor handicapper: ideally suited by sprint distances: acts on firm and dead going: effective with or without blinkers: has carried head high: inconsistent. *M. C. Chapman.*

DEEP REEF 5 ch.g. Main Reef 126 – Kareela (FR) (Deep Diver 134) [1990 6f 7g 7m 6m 8m 11.7m 1991 a5g a7g 5m 7g 5f] lengthy, rather angular gelding: fair handicapper at one time: has lost his form: stays 6f: acts on firm and dead going: sometimes blinkered. *J. H. Baker.* —

DEERHOUND (USA) 3 b.c. Danzig (USA) – Lassie Dear (USA) (Buckpasser) **64** p [1990 NR 1991 6m4] $1,750,000Y: strong, good-topped colt: closely related to a winner in North America by Nijinsky and half-brother to several winners, including useful 1987 2-y-o 6f winner Al Mufti (by Roberto), later stayed 1½m, and good American 2-y-o Weekend Surprise (by Spectacular Bid): dam very useful stakes winner at 2 yrs from fine family: 5/1 on, keeping-on 6 lengths fourth of 7 to Lochsong in maiden at Redcar in October, very slowly into stride then beaten over 2f out: looks sort to do better. *J. H. M. Gosden.*

DEER HUNT 2 b.c. (Apr 4) Hadeer 118 – Celestial Air 96 (Rheingold 137) [1991 **61** p 7d] 10,000Y: fourth foal: half-brother to 3-y-o 1½m winner Bellton (by Bellypha) and French 1m winner Sycophante (by Pharly): dam 1½m winner: 50/1, burly and green, keeping-on eighth of 21 to Berseto in maiden at Doncaster in November: will improve, most likely over further. *P. J. Makin.*

DEEVEE 2 b.c. (May 3) Hallgate 127 – Lady Woodpecker 61 (Tap On Wood 130) **47** [1991 5d 5m 5m 6g] 11,500Y: close-coupled colt: second foal: dam, maiden, stayed 15f: poor form in varied events, usually slowly away: off course 4½ months before final start. *C. J. Benstead.*

DEIGHTON LASS 2 b.f. (Jan 31) Dreams To Reality (USA) 113 – Jolliffe's — Treble (Lochnager 132) [1991 5f 5m 6m 7f 6m] 3,000Y: sparely-made filly: fourth foal: half-sister to 1987 2-y-o Barnby Moor (by Raga Navarro), disqualified 6f winner: dam never ran: of little account: blinkered final start: sold 490 gns Doncaster October Sales. *M. Dods.*

DEJA (USA) 3 ch.c. Bering 136 – Doha (FR) (New Chapter 106) [1990 NR 1991 **115** 10g* 10d* 9g6 10d* 12s2] seventh reported foal: half-brother to French 1m winner Feu de Dieu (by Sharpen Up) and to 2 winners in North America: dam quite useful French maiden: successful in newcomers race at Longchamp in April and listed races at Chantilly in June and Longchamp in October: best effort ½-length second to Sleeping Car in Prix du Conseil de Paris at Longchamp: suited by 1½m: possibly best on a soft surface. *Mme C. Head, France.*

DE LA BILLIERE (IRE) 3 b.c. King of Clubs 124 – Crazyfoot 76 (Luthier 126) **60** d [1990 NR 1991 8d6 8g 9s 8f2 8m4 8m 11m 8d 8f4 7m 9m 9m 8g6 8m] IR 15,500Y: tall, leggy colt: fourth reported foal: half-brother to a winner in Italy: dam, 4-y-o 11.7f winner, is half-sister to Home On The Range, dam of Reference Point: plating-class maiden: worth a try at 1¼m: acts on firm going, unsuited by a soft surface: blinkered eleventh start: twice bandaged late on: has run creditably when sweating. *J. D. Czerpak.*

DEL'S FARGO 2 ch.c. (May 7) Scottish Reel 123 – Aunt Winnie (Wolver Hollow — 126) [1991 7f6 a7g 7m] 4,400F, 3,000Y: rather leggy, close-coupled colt: moderate walker: has a roundish action: brother to 3-y-o Castle Merlin and half-brother to 6f seller winner Sing Galvo Sing (by Music Boy) and a winner in Belgium: dam poor maiden: soundly beaten in maidens (including auctions) in summer. *J. L. Harris.*

DELTA FOXTROT (USA) 2 b.c. (Mar 27) Seattle Dancer (USA) 119 – Dame **61** du Nil (FR) (Targowice (USA) 130) [1991 7g 7.1m 10m5] 16,000Y: lengthy, well-made colt: good walker: fourth reported foal: dam French 1¼m and 11f winner is half-sister to Phardante: quite modest maiden: easily best effort when fifth of 12, rallying final 1f, at Nottingham in October: suited by 1¼m: bandaged near-hind on debut. *D. W. P. Arbuthnot.*

DELVE (IRE) 2 ch.f. (May 15) Shernazar 131 – Safe Haven (Blakeney 126) [1991 **89** p 7d5 8m2] 38,000F: close-coupled, unfurnished filly: half-sister to smart sprinter Lugana Beach (by Tumble Wind) and Irish 7f and 1¼m winner Madame Eileen (by Stradavinsky): dam, French plater, is half-sister to Mtoto: 3½ lengths second behind Bold Pursuit, running on really well from 2f out, in 22-runner maiden at Newmarket in October: will develop into a useful middle-distance performer. *J. L. Dunlop.*

DEMOCRATIC (USA) 3 ch.c. Miswaki (USA) 124 – Allegra (USA) (Alleged **92** (USA) 138) [1990 5g2 5m3 6.5g4 7m* 8g2 7m3 8v3 1991 8m3 9m2 8g* 9m 10d5] sturdy colt: carries condition: fairly useful performer: won minor event at Leicester in September, setting modest early pace: in mid-division for Cambridgeshire Handicap at Newmarket (co-second favourite) and listed event at Longchamp afterwards: probably stays 9f: acts on good to firm ground and heavy. *M. Bell.*

DEMOKOS (FR) 6 ch.g. Dom Racine (FR) 121 – Eagletown (FR) (Dictus (FR) 126) [1990 NR 1991 13.8d 14m⁴ 16.5m⁵ 13m a14g 14.1f 12.2m* 12.3f² 12.3f² 12f4 13.8m⁶ a14g] lengthy gelding: has long stride: plating-class handicapper: won at Catterick in August: needs strong pace at 1½m, and stays 2m: acts on firm ground, has seemed unsuited by soft going: has won when sweating: good mount for claimer. *A. P. Stringer.*   **51**

DENCAST 4 b.c. Battle Hymn 103 – Ishiyama 62 (Owen Anthony 102) [1990 8g a7g 1991 6m⁶] rather sparely-made colt: seems of little account. *M. C. Chapman.*   **—**

DENIM BLUE 2 ch.c. (Apr 27) Mandrake Major 122 – Delphinium 93 (Tin King 126) [1991 6m 7m 6s5] quite attractive colt: moderate mover: half-brother to several winners, including middle-distance winner Gunmetal Blue (by Warpath): dam stayed 6f: quite modest form: best effort staying-on fifth of 15 in maiden at Hamilton in November: will improve further, particularly back at 7f+. *C. W. Thornton.*   **61**

DENITZ (FR) 9 ch.g. Sharpman 124 – Djerba (My Swallow 134) [1990 a10g² a10g a12g² a10g a12g³ a12g² 10.8m 10m⁶ 11.5m a7g5 10g a10g 1991 10m a11g⁶ 12m² 14g 12g] good-bodied gelding: has been hobdayed: poor handicapper: stays 1½m: acts on good to firm ground and heavy going: tried visored once: inconsistent. *H. J. Collingridge.*   **37**

DENSBEN 7 b.g. Silly Prices 110 – Eliza de Rich 57 (Spanish Gold 101) [1990 5f 6m⁴ 6v5 6f* 6m 6d4 6m 6g4 7m 6d 6g 6s 7d 7d 1991 6d 6s4 6d 7m 6m4 6f3 6g 6g* 7m5 6m 6m4 6g4 6.1m⁵ 6f 6g 7g] smallish, sparely-made gelding: quite modest handicapper: won at Pontefract in June: ideally suited by 6f: acts on any going: below form when visored: good mount for inexperienced rider: has started slowly: inconsistent. *Denys Smith.*   **62**

DEPOSKI 3 ch.c. Niniski (USA) 125 – Deposit 73 (Thatch (USA) 136) [1990 8g5 8g 1991 10m 11.7s* 11.7g* 12g* 13.4d* 16d4 13.9g* 12s4] sparely-made, angular colt: progressed into useful handicapper: apprentice ridden, made virtually all to

Tote Ebor (Handicap), York—Deposki makes virtually all; Tidemark (rails) is second and Roll A Dollar (left) third but the placings are later reversed

win Tote Ebor at York in August penultimate start by 5 lengths from demoted Tidemark: creditable fourth to Tidemark in £70,900 event at Ascot over 5 weeks later: earlier won at Windsor (twice, idled and wandered under pressure once in front on first occasion), Goodwood and Chester: seems best at up to 1¾m: acts on soft ground: visored last 7 starts. *M. R. Stoute.*

DEPRECATOR (USA) 3 ch.c. Topsider (USA) – Deposit (USA) (Mr Prospector (USA)) [1990 NR 1991 7.6d⁴ 7d* 7.1g* 6.9m*] $90,000Y: big, lengthy colt: first foal: dam minor winner at 3 yrs: made all in maiden at Warwick, handicap at Sandown and 3-runner minor event (9/1 on) at Folkestone, all in July: well beaten at Chester and seems to have some difficulty with turns: will stay 1m: bandaged behind last 2 starts: looked capable of better. *J. H. M. Gosden.* **91**

DEPUTY TIM 8 ch.g. Crofter (USA) 124 – Kindle (Firestreak 125) [1990 a7g 8f 8m² 8.2f 9g 10f⁵ 10m⁴ 11m⁴ 8.2g* 8.2g* 8f a7g² a8g 10.4g⁵ 8.2m 8m* 8.2d* a8g⁵ a7g⁶ 1991 7m] neat gelding: carries plenty of condition: moderate mover: quite modest handicapper: never placed to challenge only run in 1991, first for almost a year: best form at around 1m: acts on any going: best without blinkers: best ridden up with pace: has hung left. *R. Bastiman.* —

DERAB (USA) 5 b.h. Alleged (USA) 138 – Island Charm (USA) (Hawaii) [1990 12s⁵ 12.3g² 12g² 15.5g⁶ 12g² 12d 12.5d 12.5g² 12.5d 14g* 14g* 12s* 1991 16.2d] workmanlike, angular horse: has a sharp, rather round action: fairly useful performer at 3 yrs here: trained at 4 yrs in France by A. Fabre and successful 3 times, including in handicap at Maisons-Laffitte: blinkered and in need of run, showed clear signs that retains ability in October handicap only start on flat in 1991: stays 1¾m: probably acts on any going: winning hurdler. *S. E. Sherwood.* —

DERAILED 4 ch.g. Siberian Express (USA) 125 – Lasani (FR) (Appiani II 128) [1990 a8g 10m 12.5f 8f 8.3g 7m 17.6m² a12g⁵ 12.5m 12d 1991 10v 16.2g a12g a8g] lengthy, angular gelding: easy mover: poor form: blinkered in 1991: sold 1,350 gns Ascot Summer Sales. *C. A. Austin.* —

DERRING PET (IRE) 3 br.g. Daring March 116 – Mummy's Whistler (Mummy's Pet 125) [1990 5m 1991 12.2d⁵ 12.2g⁶ 10m 12m 10g 7.5f 12g] tall, leggy, close-coupled gelding: has a round action: few signs of ability, including in sellers: blinkered last 3 starts, edgy and sweating first occasion. *J. Parkes.* —

DERRY HEIRESS 3 ch.f. Scorpio (FR) 127 – Kefhalik (Precipice Wood 123) [1990 NR 1991 12f⁶ 10g 12d³ 16.2m] 2,600Y: tall, close-coupled filly: moderate mover: half-sister to a winning hurdler: dam, winning hurdler, lightly raced on flat: 50/1, 2¼ lengths last of 3 to 7/1-on shot Stylish Senor in auction contest at Thirsk in June, always last but staying on: well behind in handicap 17 days later: stays 1½m: fell second start. *J. A. Glover.* **49**

DERRY LOVE 4 gr.f. Derrylin 115 – Rough Love 105 (Abwah 118) [1990 8f 7.2d 7m 1991 7d 10.6g a7g⁵] workmanlike filly: no worthwhile form. *L. J. Barratt.* —

DERRY REEF 4 b.f. Derrylin 115 – Ballyreef (Ballymore 123) [1990 8m 8.2f 10.6f⁶ 12m² 12m³ 16m 14g³ 1991 14.6m³ 14.1f⁵ 14.1f² 16m⁴ 12.1g⁵ 12g²] good-topped filly: moderate mover: poor handicapper: best form at 1½m to 1¾m: acts on firm ground: has wandered under pressure: still a maiden. *Mrs J. R. Ramsden.* **43**

DESERT DIRHAM (USA) 3 ch.c. Blushing Groom (FR) 131 – Capricorn Belle 115 (Nonoalco (USA) 131) [1990 7m* 9m* 8g] tall colt, rather unfurnished: has scope: good mover: first run for over 10 months, won 4-runner minor event at Yarmouth in July by 1½ lengths from Desert Sun, making all and running on strongly: short-priced favourite, well below that form in Schweppes Golden Mile at Goodwood (misbehaved down at start) 4 weeks later, rearing as stalls opened, staying on but no chance of winning when badly hampered inside final 1f: will stay 1m: looked very useful prospect at Yarmouth. *M. R. Stoute.* **108**

DESERT DITTY 3 b.f. Green Desert (USA) 127 – Royal Loft 105 (Homing 130) [1990 NR 1991 6f 6d⁵ 6m 5f 6.1m² 6.1m* 6m 6.1m] smallish, lengthy filly: first foal: dam 6f and 7f winner stayed 1m: won maiden at Nottingham in September: ran fairly well in handicap at Newmarket next outing: best form to stay beyond 6f: acts on good to firm ground: trained first 3 starts by W. Jarvis. *R. Hannon.* **67**

DESERT FORCE (IRE) 2 b.c. (Mar 25) Lomond (USA) 128 – St Padina 91 (St Paddy 133) [1991 7m⁶ 8m²] 24,000F, IR 26,000Y: sturdy, quite attractive colt: has a quick action: half-brother to several winners, including useful 1¼m winner Double Lock (by Home Guard), later dam of Sure Blade, and 2m winner Invasion (by Kings Lake): dam 1m winner, is half-sister to Irish Oaks winner Celina: weak 3/1-shot following promising debut, 4 lengths second of 15, staying on, to Aljadeer in maiden **81** p at Leicester in October: will be better suited by 1¼m: will improve again. *M. Moubarak.*

DESERT GEM 3 b.f. Green Desert (USA) 127 – Jem Jen 85 (Great Nephew 126) — [1990 6m³ 6.5g 8m 1991 10g⁵ 14m⁵ 12.3g 8m] big, good-bodied filly: fair form at 2 yrs: well beaten in listed race, maiden and handicaps in 1991: stays 1m: bandaged behind final start: trained until after second by P. Kelleway: sold 25,000 gns Newmarket December Sales. *G. Lewis.*

DESERT MIST 2 gr.f. (Apr 4) Sharrood (USA) 124 – Misty Halo 93 (High Top **31** p 131) [1991 7m 8.9d 8s a8g] big, strong filly: third foal: half-sister to 3-y-o Jahzeelan (by Never So Bold) and 1¼m winner Rock Face (by Ballad Rock): dam prolific winner at 1m to 2¼m: well beaten in maidens: backward first 2 starts. *Sir Mark Prescott.*

DESERT SPLENDOUR 3 b.c. Green Desert (USA) 127 – Lost Splendour **97** d (USA) (Vaguely Noble 140) [1990 5g³ 5m⁴ 7g³ 7m 7g² 7m* 7m* 6d 8v 1991 9m³ 8.9g 7d 9m 8.9m 6m 10.3d] robust, useful-looking colt: impresses in appearance: has a round action: fairly useful performer at best: good third of 5 in listed race at Newmarket (made most) on reappearance: off course 4½ months then well beaten afterwards: stays 9f: acts on good to firm and dead going. *C. E. Brittain.*

DESERT SPORT (FR) 3 b.c. Green Desert (USA) 127 – Majestic Kahala **79** (USA) (Majestic Prince) [1990 NR 1991 6m⁶ 7.9m⁵ 5g* 6m 8d] sturdy, quite attractive colt: poor walker and mover: half-brother to several winners, including very useful 6f (at 2 yrs) and 12.3f winner Malaak (by The Minstrel): dam good winner at up to 1¼m in Canada: quite modest form: beaten about length in moderately-run £7,300 maiden at York and easily landed odds in Edinburgh maiden, both in June, second and third starts: behind in handicaps, off course 3 months in between: stays 1m: possibly unsuited by a soft surface: sold 10,000 gns Newmarket Autumn Sales. *M. R. Stoute.*

DESERT SUN 3 b.c. Green Desert (USA) 127 – Solar 120 (Hotfoot 126) **120** [1990 7s* 1991 8m² 8g⁶ 7g³ 7g² 8m*]

'Suffice to say that he's a most interesting prospect, almost certainly capable of a good deal better than his one appearance at two permits us to rate him.' A year on and 27 lb improvement in Desert Sun appears to be a realisation of that statement in *Racehorses of 1990* but one win in a minor event at Doncaster still leaves a feeling of unfulfilled potential. He won't improve another 27 lb, but after his final performance at three he strikes us as one who should make his mark in pattern company.

At one point in the spring Desert Sun was the ante-post favourite for the General Accident Two Thousand Guineas. A six-length winner of a Doncaster maiden when ridden by Cauthen at two, he had been impressing on the gallops, prompting the normally-reticent Cecil to enthuse about his colt's chances. Despite looking as if the race would just put him right, Desert Sun started a warm favourite for the Craven over the Rowley Mile. Held up initially by Eddery, Desert Sun quickened to lead two furlongs from home, but couldn't match Marju's turn of foot on meeting the rising ground, and was beaten a length and a half. As a result it was Marju that lined up favourite for the Guineas while Desert Sun started third favourite in a field of fourteen but both failed to run to the form of the Craven, let alone improve on it. Off the bridle some way from home, Desert Sun eventually finished about ten lengths behind Mystiko in sixth, a bumping match with Hokusai as they ran down into the Dip not helping, but barely affecting, his chance. It must have been disappointing to connections that he didn't fare better, but worse was to come. Further encouragement at home ensured he was sent off the 11/10 favourite for the fourteen-runner Jersey Stakes at Royal Ascot. Always prominent on this occasion, he began to drift right and was unable to quicken from the two-furlong marker, eventually finishing ten lengths behind the impressive Satin Flower in third. Cecil stated that, according to Pat Eddery, Desert Sun wasn't concentrating, and that he would be tried in blinkers. However, they were left off as Desert Sun's fortunes reached their nadir in a minor event at Yarmouth fifteen days later. The 11/8-on favourite for what seemed a simple task in a field of four, he was held up behind the front-running Desert Dirham then brought to challenge two furlongs out, but tended to swish his tail under pressure and was unable to get on terms. There ensued a ten-week break and

Sun Princess Graduation Guaranteed Sweepstakes, Doncaster—
Desert Sun is very impressive

when Desert Sun returned in a six-runner graduation event at the St Leger meeting he looked in magnificent shape. Only third favourite behind Ristna and Claret, the real Desert Sun showed up, ridden for the first time by Ryan. Waited with as Claret set a good pace, he didn't get the best of runs initially, but, eased to the outside and making his challenge at the same time as Ristna over a furlong from home, he quickened clear most impressively, winning by a long-looking five lengths and going on well at the finish. Notwithstanding Ristna's improvement over a mile and a quarter later in the autumn, it was still a very smart performance from the winner to beat her and Claret in such a fashion. Unfortunately Desert Sun did not run again— he was withdrawn shortly before the Champion Stakes, for which he was disputing favouritism, after a viral disorder left him with a high count of white blood cells.

		Danzig		Northern Dancer
	Green Desert (USA)	(b 1977)		Pas de Nom
	(b 1983)	Foreign Courier		Sir Ivor
Desert Sun		(b 1979)		Courtly Dee
(b.c. 1988)		Hotfoot		Firestreak
	Solar	(br 1966)		Pitter Patter
	(ch 1973)	L'Anguissola		Soderini
		(b 1967)		Posh

We thought Desert Sun would stay a mile at three. That issue is now settled, but the question left unanswered by his withdrawal at Newmarket is whether he'll stay a mile and a quarter. While the average winning distance for Green Desert's first crop of three-year-olds is below a mile, he has sired the two-mile winner Hawait Al Barr, the useful mile-and-a-quarter performer Elfaslah and Umniyatee who also stays a mile and a quarter, all out of stoutly-bred dams. Solar did not stay so well as any of their dams but she was effective at a mile and a quarter. Her offspring have stayed a variety of distances. They include sprinters by Great Nephew and Sharpen Up, middle-distance performers by Blakeney and Shirley Heights and a stayer by High Line. On pedigree then, Desert Sun is not certain to stay a mile and a quarter, but neither is he certain not to, and is therefore well worth a try at the trip, at which his turn of foot would be even more of an asset than it is at a mile.

Desert Sun is a strong, lengthy colt who carries condition and usually impresses a good deal in appearance. A good mover with a long, fluent action, he is always likely to be seen to best advantage on galloping tracks. He'd probably be all at sea on the tight turns of Gulfstream Park if he ever improved enough to get in the Breeders' Cup Mile, but we'd be disappointed if he didn't make it tempting for connections to send him by winning at least one good race in 1992. *H. R. A. Cecil.*

DESERT VICTRESS (USA) 3 ch.f. Desert Wine (USA) – Elegant Victress (CAN) (Sir Ivor 135) [1990 5m 6g4 8g 1991 7m 8m4 9.2d] lengthy filly: modest fourth at Goodwood, best effort in handicaps in first half of 1991: will prove suited by at least 1m: seems unsuited by a soft surface: blinkered final start. *C. F. Wall.* —

DESERVE 2 b.c. (Mar 11) Green Desert (USA) 127 – Scimitarra 115 (Kris 135) [1991 7m*] first foal: dam won from 6f (at 2 yrs) to 1¼m, and is half-sister to Double Form: well-backed favourite, comfortably won 15-runner maiden at Lingfield in October, tracking leaders then shaken up inside final furlong: showed a roundish action: will improve. *H. R. A. Cecil.* 77 p

DESIGNATE (USA) 3 b.f. Nureyev (USA) 131 – Elect (USA) 113 (Vaguely Noble 140) [1990 NR 1991 10m4 10m5 10.2g2 10g* 10g 10m2 10.5f 8g2 8g3] strong, lengthy, good-bodied filly: third foal: sister to 1988 2-y-o 6f winner Mythyaar and half-sister to a graded stakes-placed winner by Damascus: dam 1¼m to 12.3f winner from excellent family: fair form: won maiden at Newbury in July: ran well in handicaps at Brighton and Salisbury last 2 starts: effective at 1m, and has given impression may stay beyond 10.5f: possibly unsuited by firm ground: usually races prominently. *L. M. Cumani.* 82

DESIGNER STUBBLE 3 ch.g. Final Straw 127 – Miami Melody (Miami Springs 121) [1990 7f6 6g2 6f2 7m5 7g6 1991 6m 7g 6g 8g5 7.1g 6g] good-quartered gelding: quite modest maiden: will be suited by return to 1m: below form on firm ground: visored (ran creditably) fourth start. *G. B. Balding.* 61

DESIGN WISE 7 b.g. Prince Bee 128 – Wollow Princess (Wollow 132) [1990 NR 1991 8f8.3f 12f5 11.1s a12g] compact gelding: poor handicapper: stays 1½m: probably acts on any going: tried blinkered. *D. Moffatt.* —

DESIRED GUEST 2 gr.g. (Mar 7) Be My Guest (USA) 126 – As You Desire Me 112 (Kalamoun 129) [1991 7m5] 26,000Y: sixth foal: brother to useful but untrustworthy 6f to 1m winner Intimate Guest and half-brother to 4 winners, including fairly useful 7f and 1m winner Prince Lyph (by Bellypha): dam, from very good family, won 3 times at around 1m in France: 10/1, kept on steadily when fifth of 11 to Alhijaz in minor event at Lingfield in August: wasn't unduly knocked about, and looked likely to improve, but didn't run again (gelded after final start). *M. R. Stoute.* 69 p

DESIRE'S DOUBLE 3 gr.c. Grey Desire 115 – Strip Fast 71 (Virginia Boy 106) [1990 5f4 6g4 6g3 6g4 5m4 5g4 7f 6g 6g 8f 1991 8g 9d 8m 10m 10g] leggy colt: has a round action: plating class maiden: no worthwhile form in 1991: stays 1m: possibly needs a sound surface: blinkered last 3 outings: sold 2,600 gns Doncaster October Sales. *M. Brittain.* —

DESPERATE MAN 2 b.g. (Feb 21) Ballacashtal (CAN) – Priors Dean 61 (Monsanto (FR) 121) [1991 6.1m 6f 5f 5g] 4,000F, 4,000Y: big, rangy gelding: fourth foal: half-brother to a winner in Macau: dam ran only at 2 yrs, when best at 6f: plating-class maiden: best effort in auction event at Redcar final start: sprint bred. *R. Thompson.* 50

DETOUR (IRE) 3 br.f. Soughaan (USA) 110 – Lost Path (Sovereign Path 125) [1990 a7g5 6f4 a6g* 7m* 7g a6g 1991 a8g4 a8g4] smallish, angular filly: quite modest winner at 2 yrs: below form afterwards: probably better at 7f than 6f: bandaged near-hind hock final start: sold 1,300 gns Ascot February Sales to race in Scandinavia. *W. J. Haggas.* 39

DE VALERA 3 b.f. Faustus (USA) 118 – Dame du Moulin 81 (Shiny Tenth 120) [1990 6s3 6m 6s 6g 8d 7s 1991 7f4 9m 8g 8m 8f 13.8f] workmanlike filly: poor mover: poor maiden, form only on debut: often sweating and edgy in 1991. *W. Bentley.* —

DEVA'S GEM 3 b.f. Green Ruby (USA) 104 – Deva Rose 80 (Chestergate 111) [1990 5f 5g 1991 5f 5m 5f 5m 6.1m] workmanlike filly: of little account: sold 640 gns Doncaster October Sales. *R. Hollinshead.* —

DEVIL'S SOUL 3 b.g. Faustus (USA) 118 – Ragged Moon 72 (Raga Navarro (ITY) 119) [1990 6m 1991 6m 7g 8g4 8s* 8g5 8.3m6 8m6 8m* 7.6g6 10m] neat gelding: quite modest handicapper: won at Goodwood in June and (leading just 65

inside final 1f) September: never dangerous in apprentice contest at Newmarket final start: should stay beyond 1m: acts on good to firm and soft going. *R. Akehurst.*

DEVIOSITY (USA) 4 b.c. Spectacular Bid (USA) – Reinvestment (USA) (Key 70 To The Mint (USA)) [1990 10m 7m 9g3 1991 10g 12m2 12g* 15g2] lengthy, good sort: lightly-raced colt: modest handicapper: won at Edinburgh in June despite looking most ill at ease on bends: effective at 1½m to 15f: acts on good to firm ground: has wandered under pressure. *B. W. Hills.*

DEVON DANCER 2 b.f. (Feb 3) Shareef Dancer (USA) 135 – Devon Defender 73 90 (Home Guard (USA) 129) [1991 6m2 7g* 7g 8.1f] 11,500Y: workmanlike filly: good mover: second foal: dam 2-y-o 5f winner probably stayed 1m, is granddaughter of smart stayer Seascape: quite modest form: sweating slightly, won 5-runner maiden at Chester in July, leading 1f out and battling on well: didn't progress as anticipated, running moderately in Haydock minor event final outing: should be well suited by 1m. *M. H. Easterby.*

DIACO 6 b.g. Indian King (USA) 128 – Coral Cave 79 (Ashmore (FR) 125) [1990 6g 74 7f 7m5 7g 7.6g5 7m3 6f6 8f* 8f* 7m 8.2d2 1991 8.2g5 8m3 8.1g 7.6m* 8f5 8.2f5 8m* 8m 8g* 9.7s] leggy, quite attractive gelding: usually looks very well: modest handicapper: won at Lingfield in July and at Pontefract and Bath in October: best at around 1m nowadays: acts on hard and dead going: below best when blinkered: goes well with waiting tactics, particularly on switchback track. *M. A. Jarvis.*

DIAMOND BLUE 4 b.g. Dunphy 124 – Tumble And Toss (USA) (Rough'n — Tumble) [1990 9f6 10.6s 8m6 1991 10g 11.5m a12g 16.5m] leggy gelding: well beaten in varied company. *R. W. Jones.*

DIAMOND CITY (USA) 3 b.f. Mr Prospector (USA) – Honey's Flag (USA) 104 (Hoist The Flag (USA)) [1990 7f* 7m2 1991 7g3 8g* 10m*] leggy, rather angular filly: has a roundish action: bandaged near-fore, won moderately-run 3-runner minor events at Newmarket and Lingfield (odds on, by length from Jimlil) in July: stays 1¼m: acts on good to firm ground: useful. *H. R. A. Cecil.*

DIAMOND CUT (FR) 3 b.c. Fast Topaze (USA) 128 – Sasetto (FR) (St Paddy 72 133) [1990 7f3 7m6 8m5 1991 8g 10m 10.2m3 10.1f4 8.9g3 11.7m5] good-topped colt: modest maiden: creditable fifth of 13 in handicap at Windsor in July final start, having set strong pace: needs further than 9f, and stays 11.7f: acts on firm going: joined M. Pipe. *M. Moubarak.*

DIAMOND INTHE DARK (USA) 3 b.c. Diamond Prospect (USA) – Implicit 67 (Grundy 137) [1990 a6g6 a6g6 5m3 6g a6g2 a5g5 1991 6m6 8g5 7g2 7.1m* a8g a8g] angular, rather dipped-backed colt: quite modest handicapper: won at Edinburgh in October, leading 1½f out: well beaten at Southwell in December: suited by 7f: acts on good to firm ground: ran poorly when blinkered at 2 yrs. *C. Tinkler.*

DIAMOND JILL 3 ch.f. Bay Express 132 – Crackerjill 37 (Sparkler 130) [1990 — NR 1991 8m 8.9m 8.3m] leggy, light-framed filly: first reported foal: dam poor maiden, stayed 1m: showed signs of ability, never nearer, in mid-division for apprentice claimer second start: should prove suited by 1¼m +: unseated rider in preliminaries on debut. *T. B. Hallett.*

DIAMOND MINE (IRE) 2 ch.c. (Mar 18) M Double M (USA) – Light Diamond 96 (Florescence 120) [1991 5g* 5g* 5g* 5m* 6f2 5m3 5.2g 5mʷᵒ 6g3 5m4 5m4 6m6 6g5] 17,500Y: quite attractive colt: half-brother to several winners, including fairly useful miler Paterno (by Young Emperor): dam won over 5f at 4 yrs in Ireland: sire won from 6f to 9f: fairly useful performer: successful in maiden and minor events in the North: mostly ran in useful company afterwards, usually running with credit: very good fifth to Casteddu in Racecall Gold Trophy at Redcar on final outing: stays 6f: acts on good to firm ground: has run well when sweating: looked ill at ease on turn and descent at Epsom: flashed tail third start: sometimes on toes: sold 41,000 gns Newmarket Autumn Sales. *J. Berry.*

DIAMOND PATH 5 ch.g. Morston (FR) 125 – Glide Path 91 (Sovereign Path 64 125) [1990 16.2f5 14f5 9m 1991 9s* 9s3 10.1s 12g* 9m3 10.3d3 11.1s*] strong gelding: has a quick action: quite modest performer nowadays: won claimers at Hamilton (2) and seller at Thirsk in first half of 1991: stays 1½m: acts on good to firm ground and soft going: ran badly when visored: finds little off bridle. *N. Tinkler.*

DIAMOND SINGH 4 b.c. Mansingh (USA) 120 – Prime Thought 69 (Primera 23 131) [1990 8v 11g 10g 14g 15.3g 1991 a7g a11g a7g 8h a7g 8m 8m2] rather unfurnished colt: poor mover: form only when second in Thirsk seller in August: has been tried blinkered and visored. *J. S. Wainwright.*

DIAMOND WEDDING (USA) 2 b.f. (Mar 23) Diamond Shoal 130 – Wedding — p (USA) (Noholme II) [1991 8.1g] lengthy, workmanlike filly: half-sister to several winners in France, including 10.5f and 1½m winner White King (by Vaguely Noble): dam French 1¼m winner, is half-sister to Dahlia: 20/1, backward and green, not knocked about towards rear in maiden at Haydock in September: will improve. *N. A. Graham.*

DIBLOOM 3 b.g. Nomination 125 – Tosara 84 (Main Reef 126) [1990 7m 1991 8g3 8d2 8.1s* 8g] tall, leggy, lengthy gelding: fair form in maidens: made all in 5-runner race at Sandown in July: ran as if something amiss in £8,100 handicap at Goodwood following month: should be suited by further than 1m: acts on soft ground. *H. Candy.* **77**

DICEBIRD 3 b.f. Marching On 101 – Gambling Wren 53 (Knave To Play 79) [1990 NR 1991 a7g 9m 5f] angular, quite good-topped filly: has a quick action: first reported living foal: dam 4-y-o 1½m winner who stayed well and also won over hurdles: no worthwhile form, in claimers last 2 starts: has pulled hard. *Mrs V. A. Aconley.* **—**

DICIEMBRE 2 ch.g. (Feb 17) Dominion 123 – Until June (USA) (Be My Guest (USA) 126) [1991 7g4] first foal: dam French 9f winner: weak 6/1-shot, staying-on fourth of 11 in maiden at Salisbury in October having been pushed along in rear 3f out: will improve, particularly over 1m + . *I. A. Balding.* **54 p**

DICKENS LANE 4 b.g. Caerleon (USA) 132 – Easy Landing 110 (Swing Easy 126) [1990 8g4 7s3 8m5 6m2 8m 6d5 6m4 6s6 1991 8f3 7g 6f4 6d 6.1g 7g 7.1m* 8.2m 5g] lengthy, leggy ex-Irish gelding: poor mover: closely related to a poor maiden and half-brother to a winner in France and useful 1m and 9f winner Airfield (by Northfields), later successful in USA: dam sprinting 2-y-o: won seller (sold out of R. Hannon's stable 8,200 gns) at Chepstow in September: little form otherwise in 1991: stays 1m: probably acts on any going: tried blinkered. *R. J. Hodges.* **68**

DICK'S THE BOY 3 br.g. King of Spain 121 – Green Diamond (Green God 128) [1990 NR 1991 8g 7d6 a6g4] good-bodied gelding: moderate mover: half-brother to 4-y-o 1¼m and 13f winner Russian Red (by Kind of Hush), 1986 2-y-o 8.2f seller winner Ribogirl (by Riboboy) and a winner in Italy by Windjammer: dam placed over hurdles: tailed off in Salisbury maiden: showed signs of ability, probably having no chance, in minor events afterwards: will be well suited by return to further: may well prove capable of better. *W. G. R. Wightman.* **— p**

DICK WHITTINGTON 2 br.c. (May 8) King of Spain 121 – Miss Dicky (Lepanto (GER)) [1991 5m 7m6 8.3g 7g] 3,800Y: tall, lengthy colt: first known foal: dam won 6 races in Belgium: poor maiden: best effort sixth of 10 in minor event at Ayr in June: soundly beaten in autumn, very stiff task in nursery final start: stays 7f: sold 1,200 gns Doncaster November Sales. *C. Tinkler.* **48**

DIDDLEY (IRE) 3 ch.c. Sandhurst Prince 128 – Regal Rhapsody (Owen Dudley 121) [1990 5f5 1991 8m 5.3g6 8g] leggy, angular colt: well beaten in maidens and handicap. *J. J. Bridger.* **—**

DIET 5 b.g. Starch Reduced 112 – Highland Rossie 67 (Pablond 93) [1990 6m6 6v2 5m4 6f5 6m2 6m6 5g 6m4 6m4 6g 5m* 6d 7d 6s3 1991 6s 6d5 5f 5f3 6m 6f5 6m* 6d* 6d 6m3 6.1m 5m 6m 6m 5m 6s] angular gelding: carries condition: modest handicapper on his day: won at Ayr (apprentices) and Hamilton in summer: best form over 6f or stiff 5f: acts on any going: usually visored: has hung under pressure: suited by forcing tactics: inconsistent. *Miss L. A. Perratt.* **75**

DIGGER DOYLE 2 b.c. (Apr 7) Cragador 110 – Chaconia Girl (Bay Express 132) [1991 7d 7m5 6.1m 7m] 5,600Y: good-bodied colt: first foal: dam of little account: plating-class maiden: best effort on second outing when ridden by 7-lb claimer: no form subsequently. *C. N. Allen.* **60**

DIGS 3 b.g. Doulab (USA) 115 – Helcia 86 (Habitat 134) [1990 7m3 6m* 6g2 6g3 7.3g 8d 1991 8d 9m 8g* 8m* 8g4 8f] sturdy gelding: has a quick action: modest performer: led well inside final 1f to win claimers at Newmarket in June and Leicester (claimed out of F. J. Houghton's stable £11,100) in July: ran poorly last 2 starts: stays 1m well: acts on good to firm ground: blinkered once at 2 yrs. *C. A. Smith.* **63**

DIKAY (IRE) 2 b.f. (Apr 21) Anita's Prince 126 – Clodianus (Bay Express 132) [1991 a5g a6g a5g4 5m4] IR 500F, 660Y: sparely-made, quite attractive filly: fourth foal: sister to tough and useful 3-y-o handicapper Terrhars, best at around 5f: dam never ran: plater: not seen out after July: only form at 5f: acts on good to firm ground and fibresand: bandaged final start. *P. S. Felgate.* **44**

DILUM (USA) 2 br.c. (Apr 8) Tasso (USA) – Yanuka 111 (Pitcairn 126) [1991 6d2 6g* 6g* 6g* 6g4 6f3] **115**

'He's not our best two-year-old—and he never has been!' At the height of the summer Dilum, despite his trainer's subsequent declaration, had staked a very solid claim to being the best two-year-old seen out from his or

Coventry Stakes, Ascot—
Dilum leads from halfway to win from Dr Devious and Casteddu (right)

any other trainer's stable in Britain. Not only did he look the part, being strong and good-bodied, a fine walker and mover, he had markedly superior form to any of his counterparts and, what's more, seemed to possess the scope to go on and consolidate his position at the head of the betting for the Two Thousand Guineas. By the middle of autumn, however, Dilum had flopped twice and had all but been removed from the Guineas betting. The form that he showed in mid-summer still entitles him to a place among the top dozen or so home-trained two-year-olds, and if he recaptures that sparkle he could yet make it to Newmarket in May.

Dilum held centre stage in British two-year-old racing until a set-back in the Scottish Equitable Gimcrack Stakes at York in August. He reeled off three victories after a defeat at the hands of Dr Devious in a maiden at Newbury, following up a twelve-length drubbing of ten opponents in a Goodwood maiden in June with emphatic successes in the Coventry Stakes at Royal Ascot and the Scottish Equitable Richmond Stakes at Goodwood. After his highly impressive maiden success, which he achieved easing up from a field comprised mostly of well-regarded newcomers, Dilum was the heaviest-backed horse on the opening day of the Royal meeting. His three-length victory over Dr Devious, with the eleven other runners behind third-placed Casteddu well strung out, landed over £300,000 in recorded bets; and from the moment he began to draw clear steadily under firm riding from the two-furlong pole his supporters never had cause to worry. The following month only three runners, one of them the no-hoper Silvio Alfredo, opposed Dilum in the Richmond at Goodwood. Once again Dilum won as his form entitled him to while leaving the impression, as he had at Ascot, that while he was a particularly smart colt for the time of the year he wasn't the horse of outstanding merit that some observers were making him out to be; if anything, his three-and-a-half-length winning margin over the useful colt Showbrook was slightly disappointing given the ease with which he was travelling when he hit the front two furlongs out.

Dilum's eagerly-awaited next appearance on the racecourse became the subject of daily updates in the Press as York's Ebor meeting approached. At first it seemed as if he might take on Arazi in the Prix Morny at Deauville, but even after that option was waived, apparently because his trainer was wary of repeating the upsetting experience the same journey had had upon Generous

223

Scottish Equitable Richmond Stakes, Goodwood—Dilum is always travelling best, and wins from Showbrook (right) and Diamond Mine (left)

the year before, it seemed he'd miss the Gimcrack, too, leaving the Ladbroke Sprint Cup as a possible target, until a late change of plan saw his lining up at York with a third successive pattern victory well within his sights. Only five went to post, with only River Falls, second to Rodrigo de Triano in the Manton Rose Bowl Stakes at Newbury on his previous outing, the other runner to start at odds of less than 20/1. For the first three and a half furlongs all seemed well as Dilum, travelling smoothly, tracked the front-running River Falls down the centre of the track; but when asked for his effort he was beaten in a matter of strides, and by the time he reached the post, nearly nine lengths behind River Falls, he'd ended up on the far rail. We shouldn't be sure that the heavily-watered ground, which was the subject of much adverse comment during the meeting, was the sole reason for his defeat as his trainer and rider suggested at a subsequent stewards inquiry. A month later Dilum ran an almost identical race on firm ground in the Rokeby Farms Mill Reef Stakes at Newbury. There was nothing in his demeanour beforehand (he'd sweated up at York and, getting on edge, had needed two handlers to lead him round the paddock) to suggest another below-par performance was imminent; indeed he couldn't have looked in better condition, but after racing upsides the eventual winner Showbrook, whom he was meeting on the same terms as in the Richmond, for nearly four furlongs, he was unable to quicken and wandered both ways before coming in third, four lengths down. Dilum's loss of form was in some ways reminiscent of that of another recent Coventry winner of similar size and scope, Chief Singer, who went to pieces as a two-year-old after looking a tremendous prospect when winning the Coventry on his first appearance in public. Happily Chief Singer recovered his form in no uncertain manner as a three-year-old; Dilum may well do the same but until he has given solid proof that his problems are behind him he should be treated with caution.

Dilum (USA) (br.c. Apr 8, 1989)	Tasso (USA) (b 1983)	Fappiano (b 1977)	Mr Prospector
			Killaloe
		Ecstacism (b 1977)	What A Pleasure
			Toute Belle
	Yanuka (b 1976)	Pitcairn (b 1971)	Petingo
			Border Bounty
		Strong Light (b 1967)	Fortino II
			Flare

Dilum was acquired for 75,000 guineas at the Irish National Yearling Sale having already passed through the ring as a foal for 24,000 dollars at Keeneland's November Breeding Stock Sale. He's from the first crop of the

224

leading 1985 American two-year-old Tasso whose slender defeat of Storm Cat in the second running of the Breeders' Cup Juvenile earned himself a share of the juvenile championship. Tasso never managed another graded victory in sixteen starts and two further seasons on the racetrack (the authors of *Principal Racehorses of 1986* called him 'the worst two-year-old to win the Eclipse Award until Capote came along'), but he made the frame on several occasions and ran one of his better races when second to Ferdinand in the Hollywood Gold Cup Handicap over a mile and a quarter as a four-year-old. Dilum is easily his best representative so far; indeed, to the start of December he'd had only two other winners in Europe or North America from around a dozen runners. Dilum's dam Yanuka was a pretty useful filly herself; she won two races, both over six furlongs, as a two-year-old, finished third in the One Thousand Guineas (at odds of 33/1) and Coronation Stakes the following season then went to the States after her purchase by Robert Sangster before being retired to stud after just one race there. Dilum is her fourth living foal and second winner following the modest American sprinter By Consensus (by Lydian). Yanuka is a daughter of the genuine and consistent miler Strong Light whose several other winners as a broodmare include the two-year-old seven-furlong winner Norfolk Light, better known as the dam of the Derby Italiano winner Welnor. The third dam Flare was a minor winner at a mile and a half. *P. F. I. Cole.*

DIME BAG 2 ch.f. (May 16) High Line 125 – Blue Guitar 88 (Cure The Blues   **60** p
(USA)) [1991 7m⁵] lengthy filly: has scope: second foal: half-sister to 1990 2-y-o 7f winner Cajun Cure (by Glint of Gold): dam suited by 1m, is half-sister to Polished Silver, a smart winner over 7f and 1m at 2 yrs: weak 5/1-chance and very green, one-paced fifth of 16 to Anlace in maiden at Leicester in October: will improve, particularly over further. *B. W. Hills.*

DIRCE (USA) 2 b.f. (Jan 12) Mogambo (USA) – Dormir (USA) (Halo (USA)) [1991   **82**
5v* 5g* 5g] $17,000Y: tall, rangy, unfurnished filly: third foal: dam won at up to 9f: sire (by Mr Prospector) won at up to 8.5f, including in Grade 1 event as 2-y-o: successful in maiden (by 9 lengths) and listed event (That'll Be The Day beaten 2¾ lengths in third) at Rome in May: swishing tail repeatedly and on toes, well beaten in Queen Mary Stakes at Royal Ascot: should stay 1m. *L. Brogi, Italy.*

DIRECT SOURCE 3 b.f. Noalto 120 – Love Unspoken 54 (No Mercy 126) [1990   —
6f 5m 5.3h 5f 7m 6g a6g⁶ a5g 1991 a7g] plain filly: has a round action: poor maiden: once blinkered. *A. Moore.*

DISCORD 5 b.g. Niniski (USA) 125 – Apple Peel 109 (Pall Mall 132) [1990 8.3m⁶   **68**
14g 1991 12.1d 12d a14g⁴] tall gelding: reportedly injured near-fore after final start at 4 yrs: modest handicapper: best effort in 1991 when seventh in November Handicap at Doncaster second start: stays 13.3f well: acts on good to firm and dead ground: visored last 2 starts. *Lord Huntingdon.*

DISSIMULATEUR (FR) 2 b.c. (Mar 2) Legend of France (USA) 124 – Dartana **100** p
(FR) (Roi Dagobert (FR) 128) [1991 8v² 10s*] second foal: dam ran twice: runner-up in newcomers race at Saint-Cloud in November before winning 6-runner listed event there in December by 1½ lengths from Mon Domino: will be suited by 1½m: yet to race on a sound surface. *F. Boutin, France.*

DISSONANT (USA) 5 ch.g. Diesis 133 – Nashualee (USA) (Nashua) [1990 10m   **88**
10m² 10m² 10f³ 10m⁶ 1991 10m⁵ 8m⁵ 9g³ 8g 8g³ 8m⁶ 10g 10m³ 9m* 9m] rather leggy, useful-looking gelding: good mover: fair handicapper: won at Goodwood in September: ran moderately in Cambridgeshire at Newmarket following month: stays 1¼m: acts on any going: has edged left: sold 16,500 gns Newmarket Autumn Sales. *Mrs J. Cecil.*

DISTANT HOME 3 b.c. Homeboy 114 – Distant Sound (Faraway Times (USA)   —
123) [1990 NR 1991 7m 7.6m⁴ 7g⁶ 8m] smallish, workmanlike colt: first foal: dam of little account: showed signs of ability in maiden second start: joined C. Jones. *R. Hannon.*

DISTANT MEMORY 2 gr.g. (Apr 16) Don't Forget Me 127 – Canton Silk 108   **66**
(Runnymede 123) [1991 6d⁶ 7m⁴ 6f³ 7m] 26,000Y: neat gelding: half-brother to several winners, including very smart 7f and 1m filly Brocade (by Habitat) and useful 1¼m winner Organza (by High Top): dam 5f performer: quite modest maiden: staying-on third of 6 in median auction at Folkestone in September: stiff task in

Tattersalls Tiffany Highflyer Stakes at Newmarket 3 weeks later: should be better suited by 7f than 6f. *J. W. Hills.*

DI STEFANO 3 b.g. Chief Singer 131 – Doree Moisson (FR) 84 (Connaught 130) **59** [1990 NR 1991 7d 10m⁴ 9s] close-coupled gelding: fourth foal: half-brother to a winner in Italy by Rousillon: dam 11f winner, is half-sister to Bruni and smart middle-distance winner Royal Blend: in need of race, 6¾ lengths fourth of 12 in claimer at Goodwood (moved short to post) in September, fading after headway over 2f out: possibly best on sound surface: retained 4,600 gns Ascot October Sales. *G. Harwood.*

DISTINCT THATCHER (USA) 2 b.c. (Mar 1) Stifelius – Clearly Early (USA) **97** p (Distinctive (USA)) [1991 6f* 6m*] $12,000F, 11,000Y: rangy, useful-looking colt: has plenty of scope: brother to useful 1987 American 2-y-o Defined, successful at up to 1m, and half-brother to another winner: dam winner of 3 races: sire (by Thatch) Italian 6f to 1m winner, including Group 1 Premio Emilio Turati: made all in 6-runner maiden auction at Salisbury in August: followed up in minor event at Leicester 2 months later, quickening really well to win in good style by 3½ lengths from Tate Dancer: should stay 1m: will continue progressing. *R. Hannon.*

DIVE FOR COVER (USA) 2 b.c. (Jan 31) Lear Fan (USA) 130 – Wistoral **69** p (USA) (Exceller (USA) 129) [1991 7g*] $40,000Y: sturdy, close-coupled colt: second foal: half-brother to Crafty's Wish (by Crafty Prospector), winner of 3 races at up to 1¼m: dam sprint winner at 4 yrs: well-backed favourite, created very favourable impression when winning 8-runner maiden at Ayr in July by 6 lengths from O'Donnell's Folly: showed roundish action to post: looked sure to improve, but not seen out again: sold 70,000 gns Newmarket Autumn Sales. *Mrs J. R. Ramsden.*

DIVINE CALL 3 b.g. Aragon 118 – Sweet Louise 67 (Sweet Revenge 129) [1990 — NR 1991 10m 8g⁶ 9g 12g 10.1m 7g] 5, 100Y, 1,900 2-y-o: leggy gelding: half-brother to a winner over hurdles: dam placed over 5f at 2 yrs: poor form: best effort at 1m: bandaged behind: blinkered fourth and fifth starts: sold 1,650 gns Ascot November Sales. *P. J. Feilden.*

DIVINE DANSE (FR) 3 ch.f. Kris 135 – Dance Quest (FR) 117 (Green **118** Dancer (USA) 132) [1990 6g* 5g² 5.5g² 6d² 5g* 6m³ 7s³ 1991 7g² 8d⁴ 5m* 6g* 5g⁴ 6d* 5d⁶]

So many French races end up testing the judge's skills, let alone those of a race-reader. A case in point was the seven-furlong Prix Imprudence at Maisons-Laffitte in April, arguably the best known of France's Guineas trials for fillies, which resulted in finishing distances of a short head, nose, nose, neck, a dead-heat, three quarters of a length and a short head separating the entire field! Luckily for them, those looking for a Pouliches winner were able to ignore this confusing result and latch on to the Prix de la Grotte winner Danseuse du Soir. What turned out to be the two best fillies in the Imprudence, Divine Danse (second) and Magic Night (joint-fifth) weren't milers anyway. The modest early pace which leads to so many bunched finishes in France was in evidence in the Imprudence, but Divine Danse and Magic Night's racing character (if not the level of their ability) was still pretty clear. Divine Danse was held up racing keenly and must have been six lengths off the leader at halfway before quickening to such good effect that she'd hit

Prix de Ris-Orangis, Evry—Divine Danse beats Roman Prose in this Group 3 event

the front herself approximately one hundred yards out, only to weaken and be headed on the post by The Perfect Life. Sprinting looked her game and so it proved after her bid for the Pouliches had resulted in a fourth place, pulling much too hard early on. Three of France's eight pattern sprints open to three-year-olds fell to Divine Danse. She wasn't hard pressed to register any of those victories, worth more than the two and a half lengths she beat Touch And Love in the Prix du Gros-Chene at Chantilly and the length she had to spare over both Roman Prose in the Prix de Ris-Orangis at Evry and Danzante in the Prix de Seine-et-Oise at Maisons-Laffitte. Held up on each occasion, Divine Danse led at, or inside, the distance and had only to be pushed out to justify favouritism. When most British eyes were on her, however, Divine Danse didn't shine. In the Nunthorpe Stakes at York, starting 2/1 favourite, she was steadied as the stalls opened then ridden along with a sizeable deficit to make up from an early stage, making an impression only in the final furlong. The Prix de l'Abbaye de Longchamp, in which she was beaten just over two lengths behind Keen Hunter, seemed to confirm that five furlongs was too short a distance to find Divine Danse at her best.

Divine Danse (FR) (ch.f. 1988)	Kris (ch 1976)	Sharpen Up (ch 1969)	Atan
			Rocchetta
		Doubly Sure (b 1971)	Reliance II
			Soft Angels
	Dance Quest (FR) (b 1981)	Green Dancer (b 1972)	Nijinsky
			Green Valley
		Polyponder (ch 1974)	Barbizon
			Second Thought

In being a smart sprinter, the big, lengthy Divine Danse is following in the footsteps of both her dam and grandam. Dance Quest was best at two years, winning twice before failing by a short head in the Prix de la Vallee d'Auge at Deauville, and having to make do with a minor event at Vichy for success as a three-year-old. Her dam Polyponder reached her best at four years, winning the Prix de Saint-Georges, the Gros-Chene and the Prix du Petit Couvert, though she had also gained victories at seven furlongs and a mile the previous season. She came fourth in the Abbaye. Divine Danse is Dance Quest's third foal. The second, Derniere Danse (by Gay Mecene), managed a place in the French Provinces and the fourth is the Henry Cecil-trained Pursuit of Love (by Groom Dancer). An impressive winner of a Newmarket maiden and fourth in the Dewhurst, Pursuit of Love looks sure to keep this family in the spotlight in 1992. *Mme C. Head, France.*

DIVINE PET 6 br.g. Tina's Pet 121 – Davinia 92 (Gold Form 108) [1990 6f 6f 5m⁴ **69** 6d 6f² 6h⁶ 5g³ 5m³ 5d 6s⁴ 5.8d³ 1991 5g 6g 6d 6g² 5.8d⁴ 6d 7g⁶ 6f* 5.2f* 6g 5.2f³ 6g 5d 5.2g⁶] strong, good-topped gelding: carries plenty of condition: has been hobdayed: has a quick action: modest handicapper: won at Brighton (£7,900 event) and Newbury in August: should stay 7f: acts on dead ground (yet to show his form on soft) but seems ideally suited by top-of-the-ground: usually gets behind: none too consistent. *W. G. R. Wightman.*

DIVING (USA) 3 b.c. Silver Hawk (USA) 123 – Challenging Stage (USA) (Gold — Stage (USA)) [1990 8g 7g⁵ 7m 1991 8g 10.8m 9m] lengthy colt: poor walker: quite modest maiden: behind as 3-y-o, in apprentice handicap final start: should stay 1m: possibly needs an easy surface: sold to join Mrs V. Aconley 9,200 gns Newmarket Autumn Sales. *R. Charlton.*

DIXEY KING (IRE) 2 ch.g. (May 9) King of Clubs 124 – Yellow Plume (Home — Guard (USA) 129) [1991 5.7m 7.1s 5m] compact gelding: eighth foal: brother to a winner in Norway: dam, daughter of Prix de Diane winner Sweet Mimosa, won over 7.9f at 2 yrs in Ireland: no worthwhile form in summer maidens. *C. L. Popham.*

DIZZY (USA) 3 gr.f. Golden Act (USA) – Bergluft (GER) (Literat) [1990 6g 6m **80** 7m³ 1991 8m² 8.5m³ 10.1g² 9.7m* 8g³ 13.8m² 8.1d³ 11.1s*] rangy, workmanlike filly: modest performer: short-priced favourite, won maiden at Folkestone in July and claimer (didn't have to be at best, claimed to join P. Monteith £8,050) at Edinburgh in November: suited by 1¼m: acts on good to firm ground and soft: usually makes running. *B. W. Hills.*

DJEBEL PRINCE 4 b.g. Ile de Bourbon (USA) 133 – Noirmont Girl 95 (Skymaster 126) [1990 NR 1991 9g⁵ 10.2m 10m a7g 9m] sturdy gelding: brother to a poor animal and half-brother to several winners, including smart and very speedy 1977 2-y-o Noiritza (by Young Emperor), the dam of Al Sylah: dam ran only at 5f: well beaten after showing modest form on debut in June. *J. W. Hills.*

DOCTOR ROY 3 ch.c. Electric 126 – Pushkar (Northfields (USA)) [1990 6d 8f **65** 8m 8d⁴ 1991 8d⁵ 8m* 7g⁶ 7f⁵ 5d⁵ 7m 8.9m⁶ 10f] strong, angular colt: quite modest handicapper: won at Doncaster in May: generally disappointing afterwards, sweating badly and hanging left final start: should be suited by further than 1m (pulled hard at 8.9f): acts on good to firm ground and dead: tends to get on edge. *N. Bycroft.*

DOCTOR'S REMEDY 5 br.g. Doc Marten 104 – Champagne Party (Amber **42** Rama (USA) 133) [1990 8m a12g 1991 12f³ 12f⁴ 12.2f* 11f* 12f⁴ 12f⁴ 12.3f⁶ 12.2m⁴ 12.3f 12.2m 12m] sturdy, rather dipped-backed gelding: carries condition: has a round action: poor handicapper: won in July at Catterick and Redcar: lost his form: stays 1½m: acts well on firm ground: often soon off bridle. *Mrs J. Jordan.*

DODGER DICKINS 4 gr.g. Godswalk (USA) 130 – Sronica (Midsummer Night **49** § II 117) [1990 10.6f 8.2g 6m⁶ 8g* 8m⁴ 8.2m* 8m⁴ 8f⁶ 8f³ 10m 8.2m 12m 9f 1991 10m* 10d 10m 14m* 18g 14g 14.6m⁴ 14.1f 14.9m⁶ 12.3f 14.1f 11.8m 14.1m⁴ 17.1m² 18m³ a14g] workmanlike gelding: poor handicapper nowadays: twice successful at Nottingham in spring: stays 18f: acts well on good to firm ground: apprentice ridden when successful: has carried head high: thoroughly unreliable: winning hurdler. *R. Hollinshead.*

DODGY 4 b.c. Homing 130 – Beryl's Jewel 86 (Siliconn 121) [1990 8m⁶ 7.6g* 8m⁵ **62** 8f* 7f² 8g 7.6d 7g 1991 7g⁶ 7g 7.6m 8.2f 7.1m³ 8g* 7d a8g] workmanlike colt: poor mover: quite modest handicapper: won at Salisbury in October, making most: below form after: stays 1m: acts on firm ground: usually bandaged: effective blinkered or not: tail swisher: game. *W. J. Haggas.*

DOESYOUDOES 2 b.f. (Mar 5) Bay Express 132 – Captain Bonnie 60 (Captain **59** James 123) [1991 a6g⁶ 5m² 5g 5.2f³ 5m 5m⁶ 5d³ 6m a6g⁴ a5g³ a6g³ a5g⁶] lengthy, rather plain filly: plating-class maiden: better at 5f than 6f: acts on firm and dead ground, and on equitrack and fibresand: has run creditably in a visor. *D. T. Thom.*

DOIRE 3 gr.g. Belfort (FR) 89 – Derrygold (Derrylin 115) [1990 7m³ 7g⁴ a6g⁵ 8.2g **52** § 8m 6g 7d a8g³ 1991 7m 10f² 9.9m 9m⁵ 10g 7.5f⁵ 6.9f³ 8.1g] leggy gelding: fair plater: effective at 7f and 1¼m: goes well on firm ground: blinkered and visored (ran well) once: carries head high and has found little: virtually refused to race twice at 2 yrs: inconsistent, and one to be very wary of. *T. Fairhurst.*

DOKKHA OYSTON (IRE) 3 b.g. Prince Sabo 123 – I Don't Mind 97 (Swing **82** Easy (USA) 126) [1990 5m⁴ 6g* 6d² 6m³ 6m³ 6g 6d 1991 6d⁶ 5g 6g² 6g³ 5g* 5.9m⁴ 5.1g⁴ 5f³] lengthy gelding: fair performer: contested claimers last 6 starts, well below best after overcoming slow start to justify favouritism at Edinburgh in June: stays 6f: acts on good to firm ground and dead: blinkered fifth to seventh outings: gelded after final start. *J. Berry.*

DOLLAR WINE (IRE) 2 b.c. (Mar 27) Alzao (USA) 117 – Captain's Covey **66** (Captain James 123) [1991 5m⁴ 5.3m* 6d³ 6m 6.1m⁶ 6g⁵ 6g 6g 6m 8.3s³] 30,000F, IR 39,000Y: sturdy colt: usually takes eye in appearance: third foal: dam Irish maiden: quite modest performer: won maiden at Brighton in May: will stay 1¼m: acts on good to firm and soft ground: blinkered in Newmarket seller penultimate outing. *R. Hannon.*

DOLLY MADISON (IRE) 2 b.f. (May 31) Shirley Heights 130 – Shellshock 110 **49** p (Salvo 129) [1991 7m] half-sister to numerous winners, including good middle-distance stayer Seismic Wave (by Youth) and very smart 1m (at 2 yrs) to 10.2f winner Missionary Ridge (by Caerleon): dam 1000 Guineas third who stayed 13f, is half-sister to top-class Dibidale and to dam of Tony Bin: 16/1 and backward, slowly away, held up and not at all knocked about towards rear in 17-runner maiden at Newmarket in October: will stay middle distances: will improve. *B. W. Hills.*

DOLPOUR 5 b.h. Sadler's Wells (USA) 132 – Dumka (FR) 117 (Kashmir II 125) **113** [1990 10m* 10m⁵ 10.5g⁵ 12s 12d⁴ 1991 8.5f 8g⁶ 12m 11.3m³ 9.7d 10m 8v²] leggy, attractive horse: has quick action: very useful performer at best nowadays: easily best efforts in 1991 when placed in September Stakes at Kempton and Group 3 event (beaten 5 lengths by Susurration) at Saint-Cloud: should stay 1½m: acts on good to firm and heavy going: heavily bandaged on reappearance. *D. R. C. Elsworth.*

DOMAIN 3 b.c. Dominion 123 – Prelude 85 (Troy 137) [1990 7g 1991 8g⁶ 10g 10f⁴ **57** 11.7g 12v 14m] neat, good-bodied colt: has a round action: moderate walker: quite modest maiden on flat: should stay beyond 1¼m: acts on firm going: blinkered third start: trained first 3 by I. Balding: sold to join R. Weaver 8,400 gns when blinkered winner of selling hurdle. *J. Akehurst.*

DOME LAWEL (USA)　3 b.f. Blushing Groom (FR) 131 – Par Excellance (CAN)　—
(L'Enjoleur (CAN)) [1990 6m² 5m* 1991 6m 5g 5f] small, quite attractive filly: good walker: impressively landed odds in maiden at Sandown at 2 yrs: stiff tasks on that form but disappointing nonetheless in handicaps: bred to stay further. *M. R. Stoute.*

DOMIANA　3 br.f. Primo Dominie 121 – Tatiana 59 (Habitat 134) [1990 6g 6d⁴　**43**
1991 6g⁵ 5f⁶ 7m 7d 5m 5m 6.1m⁴ 5g 6g 6.1m³ 6m⁵] leggy filly: poor maiden: suited by 6f: acts on firm and dead ground. *M. Blanshard.*

DOMICKSKY　3 b.g. Dominion 123 – Mumruffin 101 (Mummy's Pet 125) [1990　**93** ?
6d⁵ 7f* 1991 7d* 7m³ 8g6 8g* 7.6g* 8m 8g 8.1m 7.9m a7g⁵ a6g] good-topped gelding: has scope: carries condition: fair handicapper: successful at Brighton in April and Newmarket (£7,500 event, edged right) and Lingfield (flashed tail) in May: disappointing afterwards, but showed retains some ability on all-weather at Lingfield and Southwell (front rank 5f) late on: stays 1m well: acts on firm and dead going: takes good hold: gelded after final start. *M. J. Ryan.*

DOMINANT SERENADE　2 b.c. (Feb 2) Dominion 123 – Sing Softly 112　**64**
(Luthier 126) [1991 6g 7.5f³ 7m³ 7f⁵ 7.1d] smallish, good-bodied colt: fourth live foal: dam 6f winner at 2 yrs later very useful over middle distances: quite modest maiden: should stay 1m: best efforts on firm ground. *P. W. Harris.*

DOMINIE STAR　3 b.f. Primo Dominie 121 – Starlust 79 (Sallust 134) [1990 6g　**64**
6g⁴ 1991 6m 6m 6g³ 5.9h² 6m* 5f⁴ 6f⁵ 5f* 6.1m] smallish, sturdy filly: quite modest performer: won sellers (bought in 3,800 gns, then no bid) at Ripon in July and Beverley (in good style, best effort) in September: effective over stiff 5f and 6f: acts on hard going: has wandered under pressure: has looked lazy in front, probably best with waiting tactics: sold 3,400 gns Newmarket Autumn Sales. *R. M. Whitaker.*

DOMINIO (IRE)　3 b.f. Dominion 123 – La Tuerta 96 (Hot Spark 126) [1990 5m⁴　**99**
5f² 5m* 6m³ 5g* 5g⁵ 1991 5g 5m² 6m 5g⁵ 5g⁵ 5g⁶ 5m⁶ 5.2m⁴] leggy, workmanlike filly: has a quick action: quite useful performer: best efforts in Temple Stakes at Sandown, King George Stakes at Goodwood and Newbury minor event second, fifth and final starts: suited by 5f: acts on good to firm ground. *P. T. Walwyn.*

DOMINION GOLD　3 b.c. Domynsky 110 – Lush Gold 91 (Goldhill 125) [1990　**115**
6g* 6d² 6s* 6m* 6d⁶ 6m³ 6g⁴ 6d⁶ 1991 8d 7g³ 8.5m*] rangy, unfurnished colt: has a round action: useful colt here: gamely made all in £14,200 handicap at Epsom in June: will prove better suited by 1m than shorter: acts on good to firm and soft ground: sold to race in USA, putting up very useful effort when about 3 lengths fifth of 11 to Eternity Star in Hollywood Derby (Nov 17). *M. H. Easterby.*

DOMINIS　2 b.f. (Jan 30) Dominion 123 – Lagta 75 (Kris 135) [1991 6f⁶] leggy filly:　—
first foal: dam 1½m and 1¾m winner: 12/1, soundly beaten in 6-runner maiden at Yarmouth in September, pulling hard and hanging left: sold 1,550 gns Newmarket Autumn Sales. *C. E. Brittain.*

DOMINO DANCING　3 br.g. Lidhame 109 – Atlantic Air (Air Trooper 115)　**55**
[1990 5m⁴ 5f⁴ 5f* 5.3f 1991 6g 5.1g 5g⁶ 5s⁶ a5g 6m⁴ 7m] workmanlike gelding: plating-class performer: should stay 7f: acts on firm going: visored third (raced very freely) and fourth starts: led to post on fifth: sold 1,500 gns Ascot November Sales. *C. R. Nelson.*

DOMINORA　3 b.f. Dominion 123 – True Nora 99 (Ahonoora 122) [1990 6g⁵ 6d³　**63**
1991 a8g² a8g* 8g² 8m² 7m] lengthy, rather angular filly: quite modest form: made all in claimer at Southwell in March: ran badly final start, in May: unlikely to stay much beyond 1m: may be ideally suited by an easy surface. *C. R. Nelson.*

DOMINO TRICK　3 b.f. Primo Dominie 121 – Tricky Tracey (Formidable (USA)　**48**
125) [1990 5m² 5m² 5g* 5g* 5g³ 5d⁴ 5f⁶ 5f 5m 1991 a5g⁴ a5g⁵ a6g a6g a5g a6g⁶] small, sturdy filly: quite modest winner at 2 yrs: well below form in 1991: formerly speedy: easily best form on an easy surface: trained until after third start by S. Dow: blinkered final one. *A. Moore.*

DOMINUET　6 b.m. Dominion 123 – Stepping Gaily 79 (Gay Fandango (USA)　**87** §
132) [1990 5m⁵ 5g⁴ 5m⁴ 5f⁵ 6g⁴ 5d* 5g² 5g* 5g² 6m⁴ 5m³ 5f 5m 5g⁶ 6s 5d 1991 5g⁴ 5f 6g² 6m 5m* 6g² 5m⁴ 6d 5.1g* 5g⁴ 5g² 6g⁶ 6m³ 5d 6m] lengthy, quite attractive mare: fair handicapper: won at Haydock in May and Bath in June: effective at 5f and 6f: acts on good to firm and dead going: has often given trouble in preliminaries and taken down early nowadays: thoroughly inconsistent. *J. L. Spearing.*

DOM WAC　3 b.c. Dominion 123 – Noble Wac (USA) (Vaguely Noble 140) [1990　**83**
8.2d a7g⁴ 1991 a8g* a8g⁶ 8g⁴ 8g⁴ 8g 10.1m⁶ 12d² 16.2m* 18.5g³ 14g⁴ 11.4m* 11.9g

229

12d4] robust colt: carries condition: shows knee action: won maiden at Lingfield in March and handicaps at Haydock in July and Sandown (£7,900 amateurs event) in August: effective at 1½m, and stays well: acts on good to firm ground and dead: game and consistent. *M. Bell.*

DONEGAL DANDY (IRE) 2 b.c. (May 12) Runnett 125 – Winsong Melody **64 p** (Music Maestro 119) [1991 5d² a7g*] 8,400Y: sturdy, quite attractive colt: second foal: half-brother to 3-y-o 5f winner El Yasaf (by Sayf El Arab): dam never ran beyond 7f: well-backed co-favourite on first run since mid-April (trained then by P. Haslam), won late-year maiden at Southwell by a length from Cellito: will improve again. *J. A. R. Toller.*

DONNA ELVIRA 5 b.m. Chief Singer 131 – Countess Olivia (Prince Tenderfoot — (USA) 126) [1990 7f 6s 7.6m⁴ 7m⁶ 8d 7d⁶ 8v 1991 7m] quite attractive mare: has a quick action: modest maiden nowadays: well beaten only start in 1991 (April): best efforts at 7f: acts on good to firm going. *C. F. Wall.*

DONS-BEST-BOY 3 ch.g. Tickled Pink 114 – Lamdant (Redundant 120) [1990 **46** NR 1991 8g 10g 10g 8g⁶ 8m⁶ 8.2f] light-framed, plain gelding: third foal: dam never ran: plater: form only at 1m: acts on good to firm ground: visored fifth start. *J. Pearce.*

DONT BEAT THE BABY 3 br.f. Sulaafah (USA) 119 – Molucella (Connaught **41** 130) [1990 6m⁵ 6g 6m 7g 8d⁶ 1991 11.7s⁴ 12.2m 11.8m] small, good-bodied filly: poor performer: raced freely and tailed off in selling handicap final start, first for 5½ months: stays 1½m: yet to race on firm ground, has form on any other: has got on edge. *J. D. Roberts.*

DON'T BE SHY (IRE) 3 b.f. Kafu 120 – Cat O'Mountaine (Ragusa 137) [1990 — NR 1991 7m a7g 10d] IR 55,000Y: rather leggy filly: has a round action: half-sister to several winners, notably 2000 Guineas winner Tap On Wood (by Sallust): dam winner at 1¼m in Ireland and 1½m in France, is half-sister to high-class stayer Bounteous: no sign of ability in maidens. *J. R. Fanshawe.*

DON'T BLUSH 3 b.g. Jalmood (USA) 126 – Caribbean Blue (Blue Cashmere — 129) [1990 NR 1991 8m] 10,000F, 4,000Y: lengthy, workmanlike gelding: fourth reported foal: dam poor maiden: tailed off in Newmarket claimer in July. *C. J. Hill.*

DON'T CRY 3 b.f. Dominion 123 – Black Veil 53 (Blakeney 126) [1990 NR 1991 **66 d** 8s² 8m 10d⁶ a11g 11.9d 9.7s a10g] small, lengthy filly: third reported foal: half-sister to 1987 2-y-o 5.3f winner Enchanted Seal (by Enchantment): dam 1½m seller winner out of sister to high-class 5f to 7f performer Blue Cashmere: quite modest maiden: off course over 4 months, then showed little in handicaps and apprentice claimer last 3 starts: stays 1¼m: best efforts on a soft surface. *J. D. Bethell.*

DON'T DROP BOMBS (USA) 2 ch.c. (May 2) Fighting Fit (USA) – Promised **64** Star (USA) (Star de Naskra (USA)) [1991 6d⁵ a7g] $40,000Y: fourth reported foal: half-brother to 2 winners in North America: dam won at up to 9f: sire won from 6f to 9f: 16/1 and backward, missed break and soon behind then stayed on well from halfway into fifth-of-10 behind Shujan in maiden at Doncaster: well beaten in similar event at Southwell later in November. *A. A. Scott.*

DON'T FORSAKE ME 2 ch.f. (Mar 15) Don't Forget Me 127 – Pirate Lass **59 p** (USA) 90 (Cutlass (USA)) [1991 7m 8m 8m] 7,400F, 9,800Y: big, strong, lengthy filly: has plenty of scope: third foal: half-sister to 1989 2-y-o 1¼m seller winner Fyfield House (by Gorytus) and 3-y-o Khojohn (by Chief Singer): dam 6f and 7f winner at 2 yrs, is out of half-sister to smart Father Hogan: quite modest form in large-field maidens in the autumn: given very tender ride by apprentice at Leicester final start: looks sort to do better. *D. Morley.*

DON'T GIVE UP 3 b.c. Nomination 125 – Tug Along (Posse (USA) 130) [1990 — 5f⁴ 5.3f* 5m⁶ 6m⁶ 6g 5.8f² 6m 7m 7m² 6m 6m 1991 8f⁴ 6g 7d⁶ 7f 5m⁵ 7s 6g 12g 11.8g] workmanlike colt: has a quick action: modest form at 2 yrs, little in 1991: stays 7f: acts on firm going: usually blinkered or visored. *R. A. Bennett.*

DON'T LEAVE ME (FR) 2 b.c. (Jan 10) Tate Gallery (USA) 117 – Sans **84** Condition (USA) (Sir Ivor 135) [1991 5g* 5d⁴ 6g⁵ 7f⁵ 7m⁵ 8.2m³ 7g* 8m⁴ 7m* 7.6m³] 72,000Y: sturdy colt: has a quick action: first foal: dam once-raced half-sister to dam of L'Emigrant: fair performer: won 3-runner maiden at Kempton in March and nurseries at Brighton and Newmarket (finishing strongly) in autumn: very good third of 15 in similar event at Lingfield final outing: may stay 1¼m: acts on good to firm and dead ground: suitable mount for a 7-lb claimer. *G. Lewis.*

DON'T MOVE (IRE) 2 ch.f. (Jun 11) Soughaan (USA) 111 – Adamantos 92 — (Yellow God 129) [1991 a6g 6m a7g a8g] IR 1,500F: small, close-coupled filly: half-sister to several winners here and abroad, including fair 1m and 1¼m winner Sergeant Smoke (by Known Fact) and 1¼m and 12.2f winner Arkan (by Prince

Tenderfoot): dam 2-y-o 7f winner, is half-sister to top 1960 2-y-o colt Typhoon: apparently of little account. *M. H. Tompkins.*

DON'T PRESUME   3 b.f. Pharly (FR) 130 – Roxy Hart (High Top 131) [1990 7f³   **91**
6m* 7d 7d⁶ 1991 8g³ 9d⁴ 8g* 8.5m 8m⁴] strong, quite attractive filly: progressed into fairly useful handicapper: won £7,400 event at Leicester in May: contested quite valuable events afterwards, running creditably final start (June): will be better suited by 1¼m: acts on good to firm ground and dead. *M. H. Tompkins.*

DON'T RUN ME OVER   2 b.c. (Mar 26) Kafu 120 – Singalong Lass 63 (Bold   **38**
Lad (IRE) 133) [1991 5g 6d 6d] 4,000F, 5,700Y: neat colt: fourth foal: dam placed at 1m and 9.4f at 3 yrs: poor maiden: off course 6 months after debut. *B. C. Morgan.*

DON'T SMILE   2 b.f. (Apr 11) Sizzling Melody 117 – Swift To Conquer 87   **77**
(Solinus 130) [1991 6g 6g 6f 6f² 6g* 6m 6m³ 6g*] 2,600F, 7,000Y: leggy, close-coupled filly: has a round action: half-sister to 1987 2-y-o 5f winner Kinloch (by Tachypous), 5f winner Jive Music (by Music Boy) and a winner in Belgium: dam 2-y-o 6f winner: modest performer: showed improved form winning large-field nurseries at Haydock and Newbury in the autumn: may stay 7f. *M. H. Tompkins.*

DON'T WORRY (IRE)   2 ch.f. (May 21) Hatim (USA) 121 – Nadja 77 (Dancer's   **57**
Image (USA)) [1991 5g⁶ 6m 6g⁴ 7m³ 7g 7.1m] IR 2,800Y: workmanlike filly: seventh foal: half-sister to 3 winners here and abroad, including 1990 2-y-o 7f seller winner Too Much Champagne (by Kafu): dam won over 1m at 2 yrs: plating-class maiden: well backed after near 2-month absence, third of 12 in nursery at Goodwood in September: ran poorly afterwards: will stay 1m: best form on good to firm ground. *M. H. Tompkins.*

DORADUS   3 br.g. Shirley Heights 130 – Sextant 98 (Star Appeal 133) [1990 NR   **71**
1991 10m⁵ 10g⁵ 11.8g 9.7m⁵] good-topped gelding: has scope: sixth foal: half-brother to 7f winner Pilot (by Kris) and a winner in Italy by Brigadier Gerard: dam won twice at around 1¼m, and is out of smart half-sister to Bireme and Buoy: modest maiden: best effort second start: should stay 1½m+: joined J. FitzGerald. *D. Morley.*

DORDOGNE   2 ch.c. (Feb 26) Rousillon (USA) 133 – Home Fire 99 (Firestreak   **64**
125) [1991 6d 7.1s 7m⁴ 8g⁵ 7.6m⁴] 46,000Y: sturdy, close-coupled colt: good walker: half-brother to several winners, including fair middle-distance stayer By The Fireside (by Ardross) and useful 7f (at 2 yrs) and 1¼m winner Spitfire (by Shirley Heights): dam sprinter: quite modest performer: blinkered and best efforts last 3 starts, finishing strongly: will be suited by further than 1m. *J. L. Dunlop.*

DORIMAR   4 b.g. Wolverlife 115 – Ahoy Dolly (Windjammer (USA)) [1990 9m 8g⁴   **—**
7m⁵ 1991 10.2s 8m a8g 16.2d] leggy, rather unfurnished gelding: plater: no show in 1991: stays 1m. *B. R. Cambidge.*

DORKING LAD   9 b.g. Cawston's Clown 113 – High Voltage 82 (Electrify) [1990   **64**
6f 6f⁶ 6m 6m 6m⁶ 6d⁵ 6s⁶ 6s⁴ 6d 6s³ a7g 1991 6g⁵ 6m² 6g³ 7g⁴ 6m⁴ 6g⁶ 6m⁴ 6g² 6m⁴ 7g 6s a6g] lengthy, dipped-backed gelding: has a round action: modest handicapper nowadays: suited by 6f: not at his best on firm going, acts on any other: often gets behind and suited by strongly-run race: hard to win with. *M. H. Tompkins.*

DORMERS DELIGHT (IRE)   3 ch.g. Hatim (USA) 121 – Tuna 63 (Silver   **63**
Shark 129) [1990 7g⁴ 7g⁵ 1991 11.5m³ 13.1m 10m 14m⁴ 10m⁶] compact gelding: has a quick action: quite modest maiden: in frame twice at Lingfield: stays 1¾m: blinkered fourth start: gelded after final outing. *D. R. C. Elsworth.*

DOROTHEUM (IRE)   3 b.f. Glenstal (USA) 118 – Mrs Simpson (USA) (Windsor   **62**
Ruler (USA)) [1990 6g 8d 1991 a8g* a7g³ 10g 8m a7g a8g³ a7g] IR 5,000F: unfurnished filly: moderate mover: fourth reported foal: sister to 4-y-o 7f winner Windsor Highness and half-sister to 2 minor winners, including Irish 1m winner Bent To Rule (by Bold Reason): dam never ran: 33/1, won claimer at Lingfield in March: broke leg at same course in July: best form at 1m: blinkered last 2 starts: trained at 2 yrs by Mrs P. Doyle in Ireland: dead. *M. P. Muggeridge.*

DORSET DUKE   4 b.g. Beldale Flutter (USA) 130 – Youthful (FR) (Green   **90**
Dancer (USA) 132) [1990 10m² 10.5g6 12m 12g 9m 10m⁴ 10.5g⁵ 1991 a7g* 7m* 7.6d³ 8m⁶ 8d⁴ 7m a7g² a7g] rather leggy, attractive gelding: good mover: fairly useful handicapper: won in April at Lingfield (slowly away) and Thirsk: most reluctant to race and always tailed off sixth start (edgy): also very slowly away final one: seems best at up to 1m nowadays: acts on good to firm and dead ground: blinkered third start at 3 yrs, wore severe noseband subsequently: mostly bandaged. *G. Wragg.*

DORSEY   4 ch.g. Music Boy 124 – Miss Trilli 89 (Ardoon 124) [1990 6f 6m 6m³ 6d⁶   **45**
6d a5g⁶ 1991 a7g⁴ a6g a8g 6d a11g a10g] small gelding: poor maiden: stays 7f: usually blinkered or visored nowadays: has worn eyeshield. *P. J. Feilden.*

DOSHA 3 ch.f. Touching Wood (USA) 127 – Ibtisamm (USA) 71 (Caucasus (USA) **47** 127) [1990 NR 1991 6f³ 5g 8m a7g⁶ 6g* 7m 8.3g 13f] smallish, workmanlike filly: good mover: third foal: dam 1m winner: won handicap at Brighton in June: well beaten in apprentice handicap at Tralee final start: best form at 6f: trained first 7 starts by R. O'Sullivan. *V. T. O'Brien, Ireland.*

DOSSERI 3 b.g. Bellypha 130 – Hants 111 (Exbury 138) [1990 NR 1991 a10g **58** 10.1m² 10g⁶] sturdy gelding: half-brother to several winners, including 6f to 1m winner Potemkin (by Sir Gaylord) and 7f and 1½m winner Tants (by Vitiges), both very useful: dam won 4 times at about 1¼m: second in seller at Yarmouth in July, leading over 1m: ran creditably in Newmarket maiden 15 days later: should stay 1½m: sold out of W. Jarvis' stable 1,300 gns Doncaster March Sales after debut: joined R. O'Sullivan. *R. W. Jones.*

DO THE BUSINESS (IRE) 2 b.c. (Apr 2) Important Business (USA) – **42** Ehricka Jean (USA) (T V Colony (USA)) [1991 6m⁴ 7m5 6m 5.3f⁵ 6m 7f 7f⁵ a8g] lengthy colt: moderate mover: poor plater: should stay 1m: showed little when visored third start. *C. N. Allen.*

DO THE RIGHT THING 3 ch.f. Busted 134 – Taniokey (Grundy 137) [1990 **71** NR 1991 12m⁶ 10m⁴ 12m* 13.8m] tall, sparely-made filly: second foal: dam Irish 1m winner, is half-sister to Kittyhawk (by Bustino): easily best effort to win 5-runner maiden at Folkestone in September, leading 2½f out: disputed lead 1¼m when tailed off in claimer 4 weeks later: should stay beyond 1½m: sold to join J. Old 9,000 gns Newmarket Autumn Sales. *A. C. Stewart.*

DOTS DEE 2 ch.f. (Apr 20) Librate 91 – Dejote 60 (Bay Express 132) [1991 6g — 7m] lengthy, rather close-coupled filly: first foal: dam sprint maiden: soundly beaten in sellers in mid-summer. *J. M. Bradley.*

DOT'S JESTER 2 b.c. (Apr 3) Jester 119 – Taylors Renovation 58 (Frimley Park — 109) [1991 5d⁶ 5g 7g 6m 6d a7g] 1,600Y: tall, leggy colt: second foal: half-brother to 3-y-o Frimley Dancer (by Northern Tempest): dam 2-y-o 6f and 7f winner appeared to stay 1¼m: seems of little account: visored in seller fourth start. *E. J. Alston.*

DOUBLE DECREE 3 b.f. Sayf El Arab (USA) 127 – Sterlonia 96 (Sterling Bay **69** (SWE)) [1990 NR 1991 7f⁶ 6g* 6d⁴ 7g 8m 8m] 1,800F: close-coupled filly: moderate mover: seventh foal: sister to 6f winner Magic Flame and half-sister to several winners, including useful 1986 2-y-o 5f winner Nutwood Lil (by Vaigly Great): dam 7f and 1m winner: won maiden at Pontefract (apprentices) in June: ran poorly after finishing fourth in £7,700 handicap at same course: should stay 7f: best effort on dead ground: blinkered and swished tail on debut: usually bandaged. *B. Ellison.*

DOUBLE DUTCH 7 b.m. Nicholas Bill 125 – Dutch Princess 70 (Royalty 130) **100** [1990 18f⁴ 16g² 16m⁴ 14m² 18g⁶ 1991 16g² 16.2s³ 16m⁵ 20g 16d³] lengthy, workmanlike mare: turns fore feet out: usually unimpressive in appearance: useful performer: in very good form in first half of 1991: third in Insulpak Sagaro Stakes and never-dangerous seventh of 12 to Indian Queen in Gold Cup second and fourth starts, both at Ascot: suited by testing conditions at 1¾m and stayed 2½m: acted on any going: often sweated: had a turn of foot and boot in strongly run race: splendidly tough, genuine and consistent: a credit to her trainer: in foal to Midyan. *Miss B. Sanders.*

DOUBLE ECHO (IRE) 3 br.c. Glow (USA) – Piculet 69 (Morston (FR) 125) **73** [1990 6g 7g⁴ 7m⁵ 1991 8g⁶ 9d⁴ 8g 8m 8m² 8m⁵ 8g a10g⁴ a10g a10g* a10g*] compact colt: modest handicapper: won maiden claimer and handicap at Lingfield in December: should stay 1½m: acts on good to firm ground: blinkered (made most) ninth start. *J. D. Bethell.*

DOUBLE ENTENDRE 5 br.m. Dominion 123 – Triumphant 90 (Track Spare **74** 125) [1990 10g 8g* 9m³ 8m⁶ 8g* 8g a10g 1991 a10g* a8g² 9g* 10m³ 8d 8g⁶ 8f 8.9g³ 8d* 7.9m* 8g] leggy mare: moderate mover: modest handicapper: successful at Lingfield (apprentices) and Kempton in spring and Ayr and York in autumn: effective at 1m to 1¼m: acts on good to firm and soft going: genuine. *J. Akehurst.*

DOUBLE FEATURE (IRE) 2 ch.g. (Feb 23) Exhibitioner 111 – Elmar 87 **63** (Lord Gayle (USA) 124) [1991 5f³ 5d* 6m⁶ 6m 6m 6g³] IR 4,100F, 9,200Y: leggy gelding: first reported live foal: dam 7f and 1m winner stayed 1¼m: quite modest performer: won median auction maiden at Thirsk in June: ran creditably in nursery at Newmarket final start: stays 6f: suited by an easy surface: changed hands 4,000 gns Newmarket Autumn Sales. *Mrs J. R. Ramsden.*

DOUBLE FLUTTER 2 b.f. (Apr 16) Beldale Flutter (USA) 130 – Perfect **72** p Double 43 (Double Form 130) [1991 8.1d² 7.1d⁵] lengthy, unfurnished filly: first foal: dam winning stayer/jumper: length second of 7 to Lobinda in minor event at

Haydock in October, running on well, though green: respectable fifth in 18-runner Chepstow maiden 12 days later, racing too freely early on: bred to stay middle distances: should do better, but needs to settle. *M. R. Channon.*

DOUBLE LARK 2 b.c. (Mar 28) Bairn (USA) 126 – Straffan Girl (Sallust 134) [1991 7m 6.1m⁵ 8g] 30,000Y: well-made colt: good walker: third foal: half-brother to 3-y-o Bit of A Lark (by Nomination), fair 5f winner at 2 yrs, and 1988 2-y-o 6f winner My Audrees (by Auction Ring): dam never ran: again looking very well, best effort fifth of 10 in maiden at Nottingham in September: well beaten other starts, final one after travelling smoothly 5f: seems not to stay 1m: looks sort to do better in time. *R. Hollinshead.* **73 p**

DOUBLE MERIT (IRE) 3 ch.f. Doulab (USA) 115 – Borehard (Bonne Noel 115) [1990 NR 1991 8.2m⁵ a7g⁵ 6g⁴ a6g 8.2f 7m 7.1m 10m 8g] IR 9,500Y: leggy, workmanlike filly: moderate mover: fourth foal: half-sister to 1m winner On My Merit (by Bold Lad (IRE)) and 1¼m winner Caribean Conexion (by Indian King): dam placed over middle distances in Ireland: poor maiden: should be suited by 7f+: acts on good to firm ground: blinkered first 3 starts: visored (ran well) on seventh. *F. H. Lee.* **45**

DOUBLES 3 b.f. Damister (USA) 123 – Obertura (USA) 100 (Roberto (USA) 131) [1990 NR 1991 10.4g² 10.1f² 12g⁴ 14.1m*] tall, unfurnished filly: second foal: half-sister to 1990 3-y-o 1¼m winner Berillon (by Rousillon), later winner in USA: dam stayer: fair form: favourite, won maiden at Nottingham in October, leading over 2f out and staying on strongly: will stay 2m: to race in France. *J. H. M. Gosden.* **85**

DOUBLE SIX (IRE) 2 b.c. (Feb 13) Don't Forget Me 127 – Sharp Ego (USA) (Sharpen Up 127) [1991 6f] IR 26,000F: leggy colt: first foal: dam Irish 5f winner: backed at long odds, faded final furlong when seventh of 18 in seller at Yarmouth in September: will improve. *N. A. Graham.* **44 p**

DOUBLE STRAND 4 ch.f. Crofthall 110 – Excavator Lady 65 (Most Secret 119) [1990 8f 8f 6s 6f 8f 1991 12d 9.9m] angular filly: poor mover: no worthwhile form. *R. M. Whitaker.* **—**

DOUBLE THE STAKES (USA) 2 b.c. (Mar 8) Raise A Man (USA) – Je'da Qua (USA) (Fleet Nasrullah) [1991 5m⁵ 5g⁵ 6g 7.5f 7g⁴ 7m] $28,000Y: good-topped colt: has scope: half-brother to a winner in USA by Relaunch: dam winner at up to 9f: poor maiden: swerved left 3f out and unseated rider fourth start: will stay 1m: not seen after July. *F. H. Lee.* **50**

DOUBLOVA (IRE) 3 ch.f. M Double M (USA) – Danova (FR) (Dan Cupid 132) [1990 5f* 5f* 6m² 5f³ 5m* 6d* 1991 6m* 6m* 6m 6g⁵ 6f* 5d² 6f* 5f* 5m* 5m³ **98**

Queensberry Fillies Stakes, Newmarket —
one of six victories in 1991 for the admirable Doublova (right, just holding Futuh)

5.1g⁶] smallish, rather dipped-backed filly: carries condition: useful performer: won claimer at Nottingham, £6,900 contest at Newmarket then claimers (odds on) at Catterick, Hamilton and (twice) Sandown: suited by 6f: best on a sound surface: game and genuine: sold 24,000 gns Newmarket Autumn Sales to race in Italy. *J. Berry.*

DOUCEUR (USA) 4 b.f. Shadeed (USA) 135 – Jamila (Sir Gaylord) [1990 9g³ — 11.5g⁴ 8.2g³ 10.5g 9g³ 10d 10g⁵ 9.5g* 10.6g⁴ 12.5g 12.5g 1991 10v 12f] lengthy ex-French filly: half-sister to unreliable 1½m winner Non Constat (by Vaguely Noble) and to 3 winners abroad: dam, half-sister to French 1000 Guineas winner River Lady and high-class middle-distance performer No Lute, placed in France: raced mainly in Provinces as 3-y-o, winning minor event in October: behind in March claimers here: stays 10.6f: usually blinkered, not in 1991. *R. V. Smyth.*

DOUGHMAN 2 b.g. (Mar 17) Runnett 125 – Trila Love (Lomond (USA) 128) **50 p** [1991 6g⁶ 6f] smallish, lengthy gelding: first foal: dam unraced half-sister to Doncaster Cup second Bourbon Boy: poor maiden: better effort at Thirsk (moved moderately to post) in August, second start: seemed likely to improve again. *J. Etherington.*

DOULAB'S IMAGE 4 ch.c. Doulab (USA) 115 – Haneena 118 (Habitat 134) **69** [1990 6g 6m⁵ 6m 5g² 4g⁷ 5g a7g a7g* 1991 a8g* a8g⁶ a8g⁴ a7g⁵ a7g* a6g⁵ 7d⁵ 8d² 10g 8m 8.2m³ 8m³ 10g⁶ 7d a8g a8g] smallish, good-bodied colt: good mover: modest handicapper, won at Southwell (2) early in 1991: off course over 5 months after thirteenth start and not at all knocked about subsequently: seems to need further than 6f, and stays 1m: acts on good to firm and heavy going: best blinkered: good mount for apprentice: best held up and suited by strongly-run race. *J. A. Glover.*

DOULALLY 4 ch.f. Doulab (USA) 115 – June Maid 56 (Junius (USA) 124) [1990 6g — 6d 5f³ 5m⁶ 6m⁶ 6g⁵ 5m 5g 1991 5s⁶ 5m] small, lengthy filly: poor handicapper at 3 yrs: suited by 6f: acts on firm going: sometimes blinkered, not in 1991. *R. Allan.*

DOURAJ (IRE) 2 b.c. (Apr 29) Doulab (USA) 115 – Serraj (USA) 57 (Seattle **67** Slew (USA)) [1991 6m 7m⁴ 7f³ 6m 8g] neat, quite attractive colt: fourth foal: half-brother to 3-y-o 11f winner Rabsha (by Taufan): dam third over 1m from 3 starts at 2 yrs: quite modest maiden: may stay 1¼m. *C. E. Brittain.*

DOVALE 3 ch.f. Superlative 118 – Astonishing (Jolly Good 122) [1990 5g³ 5m* 6g **73** 7m⁴ 6m 1991 8g³ 8g³ 9.9m² 10.1g] sturdy, lengthy filly: good mover: modest handicapper: placed at York, Leicester and Beverley: stays 1¼m: blinkered (ran moderately) final start, in July. *W. Jarvis.*

DOVENBY (USA) 5 b.h. Fit To Fight (USA) – Dovie Lee (USA) (Drone) [1990 — NR 1991 8.2s 8.5f 5f] leggy, angular, lightly-made horse: has round action: quite modest as 2-y-o: well beaten since: has been tried visored and blinkered: sold 1,100 gns Doncaster Summer Sales. *Ronald Thompson.*

DOVESGATE 3 b.g. Superlative 118 – Venetian Sky 85 (Touch Paper 113) [1990 — 5m 6f 7m 8.2s 8m 5s* 6d 6d a5g 1991 a8g 6d a12g] angular, workmanlike gelding: little worthwhile form other than when winning claimer at 2 yrs: bred to stay at least 7f: acts well on soft ground: blinkered 5 times, including when successful: one to be wary of. *D. W. Chapman.*

DOWN MARLEY 2 b.g. (Apr 10) Auction Ring (USA) 123 – Chrism (Baptism **57** 119) [1991 6g 6d 6d³ 6g 7g⁵ 8.9m⁴] IR 18,500Y: good-topped gelding: moderate mover: third foal: dam Irish maiden half-sister to Shining Finish and Bright Finish: quite modest maiden: ran well when claimer ridden in Redcar nursery and York claimer last 2 starts: stays 9f. *C. Tinkler.*

DOWNSHIRE (IRE) 3 b.f. Darshaan 133 – Swift And Sure (USA) 98 (Valdez — (USA)) [1990 NR 1991 12.2m] second foal: closely related to modest 1990 3-y-o maiden Reliant (by Shirley Heights), placed at up to 1¾m: dam 5f and 10.5f winner: 16/1, always behind in 8-runner maiden at Catterick in October. *J. H. M. Gosden.*

DOWN THE FLAG (USA) 4 ch.c. Stalwart (USA) – Hunt's Lark (CAN) **110** (Knightly Dawn (USA)) [1990 12m* 12d² 12s 12f4 10m³ 12m* 12s* 1991 12g 16m² 12m] rangy colt: smart performer, gained last success at 3 yrs in St Simon Stakes at Newbury: easily best effort in 1991 when second to 1990 Deutsches St Leger winner Elsurimo in Group 3 Oleander-Rennen at Baden-Baden in May: well beaten in Hardwicke Stakes at Royal Ascot following month (broke down): best form at 1½m under testing conditions (went very well on soft ground), and stayed 2m: has been retired. *B. Hanbury.*

DOWN THE MIDDLE 3 b.g. Swing Easy (USA) 126 – Into The Fire 74 **60** (Dominion 123) [1990 5m 5g* 5g⁴ a6g* 6m² 7m⁴ 6m* a6g⁶ a6g³ 6m 1991 6d⁵ 6f* 6d* 6g 6s³] leggy, workmanlike gelding: smart plater: no bid when winning at

Carlisle in May and Hamilton in June: below form twice in July: suited by 6f: acts on firm and dead going: below best for 7-lb claimer: usually slowly away: joined K. Oliver. *J. Berry.*

DOYCE 2 b.f. (Feb 26) Formidable (USA) 125 – Current Raiser 108 (Filiberto 71 (USA) 123) [1991 8f⁵ 7m⁶ 8.1g 7g⁴ 6m 8.1s*] workmanlike filly: third foal: dam won Lupe Stakes: modest performer: 25/1-winner of 12-runner maiden at Edinburgh in November, showing much improved form: will stay 1¼m: evidently suited by soft ground. *J. Etherington.*

DRAGON SPIRIT 2 gr.g. (Feb 18) Absalom 128 – Fair Eleanor (Saritamer 72 (USA) 130) [1991 6g 5d⁶ 5f⁴ 6g⁴ 7g⁴ 7m a8g] 17,000Y: lengthy, rather unfurnished gelding: second foal: half-brother to 1989 2-y-o 7f winner Ardelle Grey: dam poor plater (stayed 1m) from family of Swiss Maid: modest performer: much improved when fourth in nurseries at Windsor and Leicester in late-summer: better suited by 6f and 7f than 5f. *A. Hide.*

DRAMATIC EVENT 6 b.g. Kind of Hush 118 – Welsh Jane 71 (Bold Lad (IRE) 58 133) [1990 NR 1991 8g 8.3m 10g²] strong, close-coupled gelding: has a round action: plating-class handicapper nowadays: not seen out after July: effective at 1m to 1¼m: acts on good to firm ground: often on toes: winning hurdler early in 1991. *J. S. Moore.*

DRAMATIC PASS (IRE) 2 ch.c. (Feb 17) Coquelin (USA) 121 – Miss Flirt 48 (Welsh Pageant 132) [1991 8m⁶ 7m 8m] 6,600Y: leggy, rather angular colt: looks weak: half-brother to 3 winners, including ungenuine 1989 2-y-o 1m winner Barkston Singer (by Runnett) and 1½m and 2m winner Russian Affair (by Red Sunset): dam lightly raced: green, poor form in maiden auctions first 2 starts: nearly fell 3f out in similar event at Redcar final outing: will stay middle distances. *Mrs G. R. Reveley.*

DRAWL (IRE) 3 b.c. Alzao (USA) 117 – Say Something 51 (Reform 132) [1990 — NR 1991 8d] 28,000F, 33,000Y: robust, deep-girthed colt: first foal: dam middle-distance maiden: carrying plenty of condition and very green, tailed-off last of 12 in claimer at Newbury in June: moved moderately to post. *L. M. Cumani.*

DR BILL 3 ch.g. Domynsky 110 – Miss Barnaby 75 (Sun Prince 128) [1990 6f³ 60 § 7m⁵ 6g 6m³ 6g⁵ 6g 1991 8d 8.5f⁴ 10.2f² 13.8m² 12.4m⁴ 9.9f⁴ 10.9g 10f³] sturdy, close-coupled gelding: carries condition: has a round action: quite modest maiden: in frame in handicaps: blinkered fourth (hung badly left and looked reluctant) and fifth (made most, found little) occasions: stays 1½m: acts on firm going: visored once at 2 yrs: one to treat with caution. *M. H. Easterby.*

DR BULASCO 7 b.g. Sexton Blake 126 – Bodnant (Welsh Pageant 132) [1990 NR 68 1991 a10g³ 9s4 10.4d a8g³ a8g² a7g] strong, sturdy gelding: good mover: quite modest handicapper nowadays (has been at stud in Belgium): stays 1¼m: ideally requires plenty of give in the ground on turf: has worn tongue strap, and crossed noseband: keen sort: winning hurdler. *D. J. G. Murray-Smith.*

DR DEVIOUS (IRE) 2 ch.c. (Mar 10) Ahonoora 122 – Rose of Jericho 117 (USA) (Alleged (USA) 138) [1991 6d* 6g² 7m* 7g* 7m² 7m*]

'Where we went wrong then wasn't in predicting great things, but sending Michael late-developing horses. We didn't have a single winner before September, had only four in the entire season and it all ended unhappily.' In direct contrast to Michael Dickinson's first and only season as private trainer to Robert Sangster at Manton, Peter Chapple-Hyam's first year there in the same capacity had a greatly more satisfactory outcome. The stable annexed some important two-year-old events, including the Three Chimneys Dewhurst Stakes with Dr Devious and the Newgate Stud Middle Park Stakes with Rodrigo de Triano; Chapple-Hyam sent out the winners of twenty-seven races and earned almost £450,000 in win and place monies; while Sangster, who with the help of his other trainers accumulated fifty-four victories, including two pattern wins from his promising filly Musicale, finished the season in sixth place in the owners' table. Since he was leading owner five times between 1977 and 1984 Sangster has been forced to give way to the Al-Maktoum family and, although he has continued to enjoy great success elsewhere, notably in Australia, his best finishing position in the seven years since came in 1987 when Barry Hills succeeded Dickinson at Manton and helped to hoist Sangster into third spot. Ironically though, Sangster no longer had ownership of Dr Devious when the colt crowned Chapple-Hyam's first season by winning the Dewhurst at Newmarket in

Lanson Champagne Vintage Stakes, Goodwood—
Dr Devious is switched outside and quickens past Made of Gold and Governor's Imp

October. By that race, the contest with which Sangster's name was almost synonomous in the late-'seventies and early-'eighties, when he won it five times, including with such top-class colts as El Gran Senor and Storm Bird, ownership had passed to Italian-based Luciano Gaucci who now has his soundest chance yet of winning an English classic.

The nine-runner field for the latest Dewhurst, sponsored for the fourth time by Three Chimneys Farm, contained no animal of the calibre of El Gran Senor or Storm Bird and was generally short on the quality that one has come to expect in a race which for most of the last twenty years has been Europe's premier test for two-year-olds: not even Dr Devious had a smart performance to his name, and he was the clear choice on form which included second place in the Coventry Stakes and a comfortable victory over the subsequent Royal Lodge winner Made of Gold in the Lanson Champagne Vintage Stakes at Goodwood. If any of the other runners were to prevent Dr Devious from justifying favouritism then one of the lightly-raced trio of Great Palm (representing the connections of the 1990 winner Generous), Pursuit of Love and Zaahi appeared the most likely; all were expected to leave their winning form in maiden company last time out well behind; the only other candidate seriously considered in the betting and possessing the form to match was the improving El Gran Senor colt Young Senor, whose latest victory had been at the expense of a race-rusty Dr Devious in the Tattersalls Tiffany Highflyer Stakes over the Dewhurst course and distance two weeks previously. This time a sharper Dr Devious very decisively turned the tables on Young Senor and simultaneously thwarted his up-and-coming rivals with a performance of considerable merit. Apart from surrendering the lead to Thourios for a furlong or so from the three-furlong marker, Dr Devious was in front all the way; and once he regained the advantage a furlong and a half from home he needed only to be administered two reminders to keep the lead, which crossing the line he'd extended to two and a half lengths over Great Palm, who'd been close up all the way but had encountered problems handling the undulations. Next came the Lanson Champagne disappointment Thourios with Pursuit of Love and Zaahi back in fourth and fifth. At the time of writing, Dr Devious stands at around 20/1 for both the 1992 Two Thousand Guineas and Derby. His price for the Derby in particular seems to have been overly influenced by the subsequent exploits of the 1990 Dewhurst winner Generous, for he's not certain to stay a mile and a half let alone to make the considerable improvement necessary to win the race; his chances would appear to be rosier in the Guineas where the mile will suit him well.

*Three Chimneys Dewhurst Stakes, Newmarket—Dr Devious fights back;
the inexperienced Great Palm (half hidden) is second
ahead of Thourios (left) and Pursuit of Love (right)*

Dr Devious, a 52,000-guinea foal resold for 56,000 guineas as a yearling, had looked a colt of above-average merit when he made his initial appearance on the racecourse in the May Stakes over six furlongs at Newbury. One of fourteen newcomers in a field of nineteen, Dr Devious defied his slightly burly appearance with a hard-fought three-quarter-length victory over the long-time leader Dilum in what was a quite useful early-season maiden. When the first two met again in the Coventry Stakes at Royal Ascot the following month Dilum had run away with a similar event at Goodwood by twelve lengths; and on ground faster than that at Newbury Dr Devious was unable to peg him back and went down by three lengths, a length and a half ahead of Casteddu, after looking likely to finish out of the frame when scrubbed along vigorously in mid-field at halfway. In both races, but particularly at Ascot, Dr Devious had left the impression that a seventh furlong would be to his advantage, and he confirmed that, firstly in the listed Krug Superlative Stakes at Newmarket and then three weeks later in the Lanson Champagne in July. At Newmarket Dr Devious was soon travelling strongly on the heels of the leaders before running on strongly from two furlongs out to beat Young Senor, who was conceding 3 lb, by three quarters of a length; and at Goodwood, where his seven rivals included the eight-length Salisbury winner and well-backed favourite Thourios, the July Stakes runner-up Made of Gold, and the unbeaten northern challenger Ernestan, he unleashed an impressive turn of speed after being held up and twice denied a run to win by a length and a half. Dr Devious carried Sangster's colours for the last time—he'd actually sold him before the Champagne at Goodwood but had leased him back for his next two runs—in the Tattersalls Tiffany Highflyer Stakes, where he was one of three of Sangster's in a field of thirty. Looking tremendously well after his two-month break, Dr Devious failed by a head to land first prize and the bonus of half a million pounds. Had he been taken to race on the far side from his middle draw instead of being covered up towards the stand side he might well have won; as it was he had to settle for second (and a bonus of just £200,000) after putting in a spirited late rattle which would have taken him to the front in a few more strides.

Dr Devious comes from a family which has thrown up many useful or better winners in the last twenty years. Four of them—the smart French one-mile to mile-and-a-quarter performer Pluralisme, the useful six-furlong and one-mile winner Only, the Virginia Stakes winner Singletta and the Chester Vase third Classic Tale—descend from the Irish nine-furlong winner

237

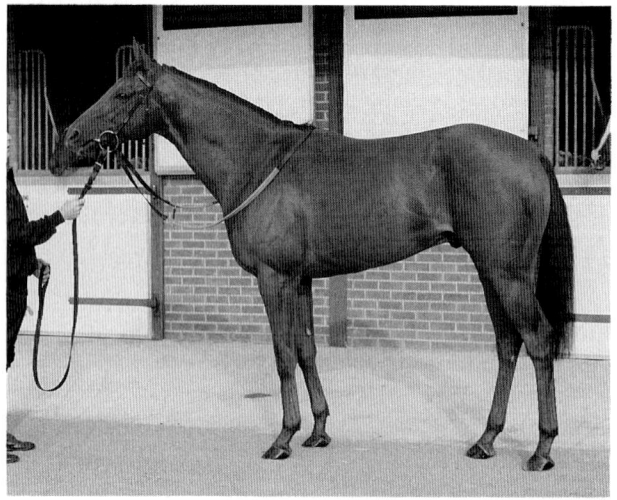

Luciano Gaucci's "Dr Devious"

		Lorenzaccio	Klairon
	Ahonoora	(ch 1965)	Phoenissa
	(ch 1975)	Helen Nichols	Martial
Dr Devious (IRE)		(ch 1966)	Quaker Girl
(ch.c. Mar 10, 1989)		Alleged	Hoist The Flag
	Rose of Jericho (USA)	(b 1974)	Princess Pout
	(b 1984)	Rose Red	Northern Dancer
		(ch 1979)	Cambrienne

Cambretta, a half-sister to Dr Devious' grandam Rose Red; while another, the rattling good miler Markofdistinction, is out of Cambretta's daughter Ghislaine. Cambretta is a full sister to the high-class middle-distance performer Critique, whose tally of six wins in three seasons at the top level includes the Cumberland Lodge Stakes and the September Stakes. Their dam Cambrienne, a one-time record-priced yearling who could win only a minor race at around seven furlongs as a two-year-old, is a daughter of the French-trained filly Torbella III, who was as useful a proposition on the racecourse—she won the Dewhurst in 1957 and the mile-and-a-quarter Prix de Malleret the following year—as she was in the paddocks where she produced ten winners including the Sussex Stakes winner Carlemont, the good-class French stayer Tourangeau and the very smart French eight- to ten-furlong performer Avaray as well as the dam of the high-class 1974 two-year-old Princesse Lee (herself the dam of the Prix Morny and Prix de la Salamandre winner Princesse Lida) and the French One Thousand Guineas runner-up Boreale. Rose Red, a minor winner over six furlongs as a two-year-old in Ireland, hasn't proved so valuable at stud as most of those but her unraced daughter Rose of Jericho, whose second foal Dr Devious is, has maintained the family's fine traditions: her first foal is the Irish sprinter Archway (by Thatching) who finished an excellent fourth to Keen Hunter in the Prix de l'Abbaye at Longchamp.

The quite attractive, medium-sized Dr Devious was better as a two-year-old at seven furlongs than at six, and although his sire Ahonoora was first and foremost a sprinter there's little doubt that Dr Devious will be suited by a mile to a mile and a quarter at three. A fluent mover with a quick action, he won on dead going on his debut, then raced only on good or good to firm; the going was good to firm for the Dewhurst. *P. W. Chapple-Hyam.*

DREAM CARRIER (IRE) 3 b.c. Doulab (USA) 115 – Dream Trader (Auction **76** Ring (USA) 123) [1990 6g 5m⁵ 6f⁵ 6m 6g 6m⁴ 6g⁴ 7s 6d 1991 7d² 7d² 8m⁶ 7m 7m* 8m² 7f* 7g⁵ 7g² 7.6g* 7g³ 8f 8m 8g⁵ 7m] strong, close-coupled colt: carries condition: moderate walker: has a round action: modest handicapper: won at Sandown in May, Folkestone in June and Chester in July: below best last 4 starts: stays 1m: acts on good to firm ground and dead: has run well for 7-lb claimer. *R. Hannon.*

DREAM FOR TWO 3 ch.f. Reach 122 – Dream Chaser 92 (Record Token 128) **57** [1990 6g 7m⁴ 1991 7g⁴ 10f³ 11.7f⁶ 10.2s] leggy, shallow-girthed filly: quite modest maiden: ran creditably in 4-runner races at Newmarket and Brighton: seems to stay 1¼m (took strong hold at 11.7f): stiff task on soft ground. *R. Hannon.*

DREAM ISLAND (IRE) 2 b.f. (May 22) Ela-Mana-Mou 132 – Starlite Night **40** (USA) 105 (Star de Naskra (USA)) [1991 a7g³ 7f 8.2m] rather angular filly: third foal: half-sister to 3-y-o Fast Run (by Commanche Run) and poor maiden Ardnamurchan (by Ardross): dam 7f winner: modest plater: best effort (always prominent) on fibresand: sweating, well below that form subsequently: should stay 1m: sold 4,000 gns Newmarket Autumn Sales. *Sir Mark Prescott.*

DREAM OF TOMORROW 3 b.g. Today And Tomorrow 78 – Targow Girl **58** (Targowice (USA) 130) [1990 5f² a5g² 6h⁴ a6g* 6f* 6m² 6m 6m² 6g a6g* 1991 5d⁴ 5s⁴ 5.8m⁶ 5.3f³ 6m 6d⁶ 6g a6g] leggy gelding: plating-class handicapper as 3-y-o, best efforts third and fourth starts: better at 6f than 5f: acts on firm going: blinkered final outing: takes keen hold. *J. Berry.*

DREAM ON 3 ch.f. Absalom 128 – Great Exception 84 (Grundy 137) [1990 5f⁶ 5g **42** 5d 5d 5d⁵ a6g³ a7g 1991 7.5f⁵ 8h 7g 8.3d³ 8.3d⁴ 9.2m⁶ 10g⁵ 11.1g⁶] small filly: plater: stays 1¼m: acts on dead ground: visored sixth start. *M. Johnston.*

DREAMS END 3 ch.c. Rainbow Quest (USA) 134 – Be Easy 110 (Be Friendly **93** 130) [1990 7m NR 1991 10.2s* 10g 10g* 11.9g⁵ 10.1f⁴ 12s⁶] sparely-made, quite attractive colt: half-brother to 5 middle-distance winners, notably very useful Glowing With Pride (by Ile de Bourbon) and Whipp's Cross (by Kris): dam best at up to 7f: won maiden at Newcastle in April and handicap at Newmarket in August: ran well, set plenty to do, in £8,900 handicap at Yarmouth and £70,900 handicap at Ascot last 2 starts: stays 1½m: acts on any going: struck into second start, bandaged next two. *G. Wragg.*

DREAMS EYES 3 b.c. Dreams To Reality (USA) 113 – Hairbrush (USA) (Sir — Gaylord) [1990 5f 7m³ 8.2m 7m 6m² 8f⁶ 8d 6s a7g 1991 6g 7.5g 7g 6m a5g 7m⁵ 8m 6m 6.1m 6m 6m] leggy, angular colt: has a moderate action: quite modest maiden at 2 yrs: has lost his way: should stay 1m: acts on good to firm ground: visored final start: bandaged as 3-y-o. *R. Bastiman.*

DREAM TALK 4 b.c. Dreams To Reality (USA) 113 – Lala 91 (Welsh Saint 126) **115** [1990 5m⁴ 5d 5f³ 5m* 5d² 5m⁶ 1991 6.5g² 6.5g* 6s⁴ 6d* 5m⁴ 6d* 6g 5d³ 6v²] leggy colt: fair handicapper here at 3 yrs for J. Berry: developed into smart performer in 1991: won minor event at Cagnes-sur-Mer in March, handicap in May and listed race in June, both at Evry, and Group 3 De Kuyper-Preis at Hamburg (beat Feenpark and Nicholas by nose and 1¾ lengths) in July: ran well after when placed in Group 3 event at Longchamp and Group 2 race at Rome: effective at 5f and 6f: acts on any going: ran well when blinkered here: tough and consistent. *N. Clement, France.*

DREAMTIME DANCER 5 b.m. Town And Country 124 – Aleda Rose 56 — (Charlottown 127) [1990 NR 1991 12m 8.1d 14.6m] lengthy mare: has a round action: no worthwhile form: should stay middle distances. *A. Barrow.*

DREAMTIME ECHO 3 b.f. Green Ruby (USA) 104 – Aleda Rose 56 — (Charlottown 127) [1990 NR 1991 5g 6m 6m⁶ 5s⁵] lengthy filly: fourth living foal: half-sister to a winner abroad: dam, plater, won from 7f to 1¼m: poor form in claimer, maidens and seller: may need further. *J. Balding.*

DREAMTIME QUEST 3 b.f. Blakeney 126 – Rotisserie 106 (Tesco Boy 121) — [1990 NR 1991 10s⁵ 11.4m 8m 10g 8.1d 9.2s] strong, good-bodied filly: shows knee action: sister to useful 1½m and 1¾m winner Rowlandson and half-sister to 3 winners: dam won Fred Darling Stakes: no worthwhile form, hinting at a little ability never dangerous in mid-division for handicaps last 2 starts: needs further than 1m. *R. Hannon.*

DRINKS PARTY (IRE) 3 b.f. Camden Town 125 – Holy Water (Monseigneur (USA) 127) [1990 a6g 6g⁴ 6g a8g 6m⁶ 8m* 10m³ 7d⁵ a7g⁴ 1991 10d² 12.3s* 8m 10m⁶ 10.6m³ a11g⁶ 12s³ 11.1d 10.5d 11.8m⁵ 10d³ a11g] compact filly: poor moderate: plating-class handicapper: won at Ripon in April: best effort for some time, running fairly well, on final start: suited by 1½m: acts on good to firm ground and soft. *J. Wharton.* **51** d

DRIVING FORCE 5 ch.g. Be My Native (USA) 122 – Frederika (USA) (The Minstrel (CAN) 135) [1990 7g² 7d 8g 1991 10d⁵ 12.1d⁵] first foal: dam, Irish maiden, stayed 11f: ex-Irish gelding: won 1m maiden at Tralee at 3 yrs: never dangerous in apprentice events here: stays 1m: acts on dead ground: trained as 4-y-o by J. Canty: winning hurdler. *M. McCourt.* —

DR MACCARTER (USA) 4 gr.c. Dr Carter (USA) – Now Voyager (USA) (Naskra (USA)) [1990 a7g⁴ a8g² a10g³ a10g* a12g⁶ a10g² 1991 a12g* a10g² a12g⁴ a10g² a12g² a12g³ 11.1g a10g³ a10g² 10.3m a10g² a12g⁴ a10g] sturdy colt: carries condition: fairly useful handicapper at best on equitrack at Lingfield, won claimer in January: below best there late in 1991, claimed out of W. O'Gorman's stable £6,375 eleventh start, virtually refusing to race and always tailed off final one: below form on turf as 4-y-o: effective at 1¼m to 1½m: blinkered or visored: usually claimer ridden: sold 2,500 gns Ascot December Sales. *C. C. Elsey.* a83 d

DROPS 2 b.f. (Jan 31) Nordance (USA) – Lucky Love 65 (Mummy's Pet 125) [1991 a5g⁶ a6g⁵ a6g] leggy filly: sixth foal: half-sister to a winner in West Indies: dam won 6f seller at 3 yrs: no worthwhile form, twice slowly away, in sellers at Lingfield and Southwell in summer. *D. R. Laing.* —

DR SOCK IT TO ME 6 b.g. Stanford 121§ – Dr Shadad (Reform 132) [1990 NR 1991 7.6d 7.1g³ 6g 7m⁴ 7m 8.3m] leggy, lengthy gelding: poor maiden: stays 7f: acts on any going: has been tried blinkered and visored: has worn dropped noseband. *J. Sutcliffe.* **37**

DRUMHEAD 5 ch.g. High Line 125 – Wig And Gown (Mandamus 120) [1990 16g* 18.4d⁵ 16m 16m⁴ 15g² 17.4d⁴ 18d 19m1 16g 16.1m 16d 12.3g⁴ 12m] workmanlike gelding: moderate walker: fairly useful handicapper at 4 yrs: lost his form: blinkered and heavily bandaged in Newmarket claimer (reportedly finished lame) final start: suited by test of stamina: probably unsuited by firm going, acts on any other: sometimes visored: sometimes sweats: sold out of P. Walwyn's stable 10,000 gns Doncaster Spring Sales: one to treat with caution. *Mrs L. Stubbs.* **?**

DRUMMER HICKS 2 b. or br.c. (Apr 12) Seymour Hicks (FR) 125 – Musical Princess 66 (Cavo Doro 124) [1991 8m⁶ 7m 8.1s³] workmanlike colt: third foal: half-brother to 1m to 1½m winner Oh Danny Boy (by Rabdan): dam won 4 times at 1½m and 1m at 5 yrs: quite modest maiden: best effort at Edinburgh in November final start: will be well suited by 1¼m. *E. Weymes.* **65**

DRUMMER'S DREAM (IRE) 3 b.f. Drumalis 125 – Peaches And Cream (FR) (Rusticaro (FR) 124) [1990 6g⁴ 5f² 5f 1991 6f⁴ 5m 6m 8g 6m a5g 6f 6.1m⁴ 5.3g⁵ a6g⁴ a5g³ a5g³] small filly: poor performer: in frame in claimer and handicaps at Southwell last 3 starts: should be suited by return to 6f: usually mounted on track: trained until after sixth outing by J. Mackie. *Mrs N. Macauley.* **47**

DRUM SERGEANT 4 b.g. Elegant Air 119 – Cala-Vadella 110 (Mummy's Pet 125) [1990 6m² 6m² 6s a6g³ a6g 1991 8m 6m 6g 7.5g⁴ 7.5m² 8d 6g³ 6m 5f⁴ 5f⁶ 5f³ 7g 5m² 5g² 5m³ 5s²] strong, sturdy gelding: moderate mover: plating-class handicapper: effective at 5f to 7.5f: acts on any going: goes well visored, below best when blinkered once. *J. Parkes.* **56**

DRUM TAPS (USA) 5 b.h. Dixieland Band (USA) – Lavendula Rose 108 (Le Levanstell 122) [1990 12f* 12g 12s* 13f⁶ 11f⁵ 12d* 9f⁴ 1991 11f 12g² 12f³ 12f* 13.3f* 12g* 12s² 12f] **124**

Horses for courses is a well-known racing adage. Nowadays owners are realising that not only should they run their horses on suitable tracks but also, ideally, in the countries whose racing structure suits them. A smart European animal whose optimum trip lies between a mile and a mile and a quarter, and who acts on a sound surface, is especially worth trying in the States if recent results are anything to go by. Three startling examples of what can be achieved there are provided by In Excess, Opening Verse and Twilight Agenda. In Excess earned only £14,679 as a three-year-old when

Hoover Cumberland Lodge Stakes, Ascot—
Drum Taps rallies splendidly against Rock Hopper (right), Young Buster and Azzaam (grey)

rated 116 in *Racehorses of 1990*, yet won seven pattern races in America in the year from October 1990, the last four Grade 1, and around a million dollars in prize money. Opening Verse achieved a rating of 122 in *Racehorses of 1989*, winning only once yet earning £76,334 in the process; however, in the past two seasons he earned about 1.5 million dollars, whilst picking up five stakes races, including the Breeders' Cup Mile. Twilight Agenda was rated 102 in *Racehorses of 1990*, winning only a minor event at Phoenix Park whilst earning a scant IR £7,112; in eleven races as a five-year-old in America, he won six times, ran second in the Breeders' Cup Classic and earned over 1.5 million dollars in the process. While these examples may seem to be the stuff which dreams are made of, there are others. Take Eton Lad: unable to win a pattern race in 1991, and running well without success under big weights in handicaps, he won his first start at Santa Anita, breaking the world nine-furlong record in the process; given normal luck there he'll far out-earn the paltry £4,303 he won in Britain in 1991. And then there's Drum Taps, who stays further and whose search for the best opportunities has led to his crossing the Atlantic twice. By the autumn of his three-year-old career Drum Taps had already shown himself to be smart. In his final win for Hern's stable, the Doncaster EBF Handicap at Newcastle, he gave weight and a beating to the subsequent November Handicap winner Firelight Fiesta. With the horse in form, the season drawing to its close, and the prospect of high weights in handicaps the next spring, the decision was taken to send him to Neil Howard in Florida. During his eighteen months in the United States Drum Taps raced twelve times, scoring five wins and three minor placings and earning 188,360 dollars in the process. His most important successes as a four-year-old were in the Grade 2 W. L. McKnight Invitational at Calder, Florida in January and, after a five-month break, the Grade 3 Laurence Armour Handicap at Arlington in July. It was clear that a mile and a half was practically a minimum for Drum Taps by this stage and, with breeder-appeal also very much in mind, he was sent back to England in May to join Lord Huntingdon having already had four runs (the final one a win in an allowance race) at Gulfstream Park and Keeneland in the spring.

The Ibn Bey Geoffrey Freer Stakes at Newbury in August marked Drum Taps' reappearance in Britain and he looked extremely well in the paddock. Held up behind the strong pace set by Spinning, he closed on the leader from three furlongs out, led at the distance and ran on well to draw two and a half lengths clear. The time was a course record and the five other runners were strung out behind. Nearly six weeks later Drum Taps lined up as a 13/2-shot in

Lord Carnarvon's "Drum Taps"

a select field for the Hoover Cumberland Lodge Stakes at Ascot. Opposing him were Rock Hopper, who had been third in the King George, Young Buster, fresh from a win over Quest For Fame in the September Stakes at Kempton, Azzaam who had raced away with the Doonside Cup at Ayr, and Hateel, the disappointing favourite at Newbury. It turned out to be one of the most exciting races of the year. Although there was a sound gallop initially, Carson on Azzaam steadied it on the run up from Swinley Bottom and the race became more of a test of speed. Drum Taps quickened well to lead under two furlongs out, was challenged on his inside by Young Buster, and no sooner had he beaten off the three-year-old with a hundred yards to run, than Rock Hopper was produced on his outside. Responding gamely for Dettori, Drum Taps held on all the way to the line to win by a head, putting up probably his best effort to date. Not entered for the Ciga Prix de l'Arc de Triomphe, Drum Taps came very close to Group 1 success in the Gran Premio del Jockey Club run on soft ground in Milan. Leading around three furlongs out, he pulled three and a half lengths clear of Snurge, but was unable to hold Passing Sale in the last hundred and fifty yards, going down by a neck. Second prize of more than £115,000 was more than double his previous highest earnings in a single race. Drum Taps faced very different conditions for his final start, the Japan Cup, and never got into the race, his trainer stating that he came back with pulled muscles in his off quarters. The good news is that he will stay in training as a six-year-old. Whilst clearly not a tip-top performer, he is certainly a very smart and genuine one. His best trip nowadays will most likely prove to be from a mile and a half to a mile and three quarters; he acts on any going. He goes well fresh, looks sure to win more races outside the very best company and the John Porter Stakes and the Yorkshire Cup look suitable early-season targets for him.

Drum Taps (USA) (b.h. 1986)	Dixieland Band (USA) (b 1980)	Northern Dancer (b 1961)	Nearctic / Natalma
		Mississippi Mud (b 1973)	Delta Judge / Sand Buggy
	Lavendula Rose (b 1968)	Le Levanstell (b 1957)	Le Lavandou / Stella's Sister
		Inquisitive Rose (b 1952)	Grand Inquisitor / Rosemary's Queen

Lavendula Rose won only a mile-and-a-half maiden at Clonmel, though she did achieve useful form when third to Altesse Royale in the 1971 Irish Guineas Oaks. She had a remarkable career at stud, producing eleven foals, all of which won. Her tenth produce, Drum Taps, is clearly the best of them, but she also threw useful performers in Miss Mars (by Red God) who won a Grade 3 event in America, Torenaga (by Bold Lad (Ire)) whose best form was as a juvenile hurdler, and Stats Emmar (by Steel Heart), winner of the listed St Catherine's Stakes as a two-year-old. Lavendula Rose is herself half-sister to six winners including Goodwood Cup winner Wrekin Rambler, who was later a fairly successful National Hunt stallion. Further back in the pedigree, both Inquisitive Rose and Rosemary's Queen were unraced. Dixieland Band, out of a Grade 1-winning mare, was a smart performer in America, winning from five and a half furlongs as a two-year-old to nine furlongs at three and four, including the Pennsylvania Derby and the Massachusetts Handicap, both Grade 2 events. He has four crops of racing age and has made a fair start. Drum Taps is his best performer, but Box Office Gold and Dixieland Brass are others to have made their mark in Grade 2 company. *Lord Huntingdon.*

DRY POINT 5 ch.g. Sharpo 132 – X-Data 93 (On Your Mark 125) [1990 6s 6g* 6f* **80** 6m² 6m 5m⁵ 6m³ 6d 6d 6s 1991 7m 6g* 6g⁶ 6f⁶ 6g 6f² 7g 6m³ 6m⁵ 6g] strong, angular, workmanlike gelding: has a round action: fair handicapper: won at Newmarket in May: best form at 6f: seems to need a sound surface: occasionally bandaged: wears crossed noseband: none too consistent. *J. A. R. Toller.*

DR ZEVA 5 b.h. Busted 134 – Dance In Rome 79 (Dance In Time (CAN)) [1990 **53 d** 10f* 10m² 10m 8m 10g* 10m 10m 10f⁵ 10f 8.2v 10s⁶ 1991 a10g* 10d² a12g 10m 10g 10.8m 10m 10.2g] big, deep-girthed horse: poor mover: plating-class handicapper at best: won selling event (no bid) at Lingfield in May: mainly disappointing after: suited by 1¼m: acts on firm and dead going: below form once when blinkered. *J. R. Jenkins.*

DUBITABLE 2 b.f. (May 8) Formidable (USA) 125 – Duboff 120 (So Blessed 130) **59** [1991 6m⁶ 6g⁴ 8m⁵ 7g³] 21,000Y: unfurnished filly: sister to 5f and 6f winner Elegant Rainbow and half-sister to several winners, including fair middle-distance winner Durun (by Run The Gantlet): dam won 11 races, including Sun Chariot Stakes and Child Stakes: plating-class maiden: better suited by 1m than 6f. *H. Candy.*

DUBLIN BREEZE 4 b.g. Dublin Taxi – Dusty Foot (Simbir 130) [1990 12.5g **46 d** 12m⁴ 12m 12f⁶ 12m 10d³ 1991 10m⁴ 11f⁶ 10m 12.3g 10.3g] leggy, rather sparely-made gelding: poor mover: plating-class handicapper: ran poorly after reappearance: stays 1½m: acts on firm ground and dead: sold out of M. Tompkins's stable 3,000 gns Doncaster January Sales. *J. L. Harris.*

DUBLIN DREAM 2 b.f. (Apr 26) Dublin Lad 116 – Warthill Lady 60 (Hittite **39** Glory 125) [1991 6m 5m⁵] leggy filly: second foal: dam 5f and 6f winner: fifth of 9 in seller at Haydock in July: ridden by 7-lb claimer on debut. *M. Brittain.*

DUBLIN INDEMNITY (USA) 2 b.c. (Feb 12) Alphabatim (USA) 126 – **62** Sailongal (USA) (Sail On-Sail On) [1991 5g 6m 8d a6g* a7g⁴ a7g²] rangy, good-topped colt: poor mover: won nursery at Southwell in November: excellent second to Quiet Miss in similar event at Lingfield: should stay 1m: blinkered last 3 starts. *N. A. Callaghan.*

DUBLIN LASS 2 ch.f. (Apr 5) Dublin Lad 116 – Sharphaven 63 (Sharpo 132) **—** [1991 5m 6m 5g] small filly: first foal: dam 2-y-o 6f winner: no worthwhile form, including in sellers. *M. Brittain.*

DUBLIN RAINBOW 2 b.c. (Feb 22) Dublin Lad 116 – Running Rainbow 56 **—** (Runnett 125) [1991 5f⁴ a5g⁵ 5m 5m 5m 5d a6g⁶] 500Y: leggy, sparely-made colt:

second foal: half-brother to 3-y-o Running Grey (by Grey Desire): dam, maiden, placed over 5f at 2 yrs: well beaten in varied events, including a seller. *M. Brittain.*

DUBLIN STAR 2 b.c. (Apr 4) Dublin Lad 116 – Riverstyle (River Knight (FR) **44** 118) [1991 5m 5g⁵ 5f⁵ 5m 6g 6m a7g⁶] leggy, close-coupled, sparely-made colt: moderate mover: first foal: dam 6f winner: poor maiden: ran badly last 4 starts, last 2 in sellers: not seen out after July: sold 690 gns Doncaster October Sales. *M. Brittain.*

DUC DE BERRY (USA) 3 ch.c. Chief's Crown (USA) – L'Extravagante (USA) **97** (Le Fabuleux 133) [1990 7d² 1991 10f* 12.3g* 11.9m²] tall, good-topped colt: won minor events at Nottingham (led close home having been hard ridden after only 4f) in September and Wolverhampton (5/1 on, hung left, took plenty of time to get on top) in October: 3 lengths second of 3 to Kansk in similar contest at York, putting head in air and hanging fire early in straight: stays 1½m: yet to race on soft ground, probably acts on any other: probably worth a try in blinkers or a visor, as he's a difficult ride. *G. Harwood.*

DUCKEY FUZZ 3 b.c. Ardross 134 – Twine (Thatching 131) [1990 NR 1991 10g **71** + 7g⁴ 7m*] 19,000Y: lengthy colt: has scope: third foal: half-brother to very useful 6f (at 2 yrs) to 1¼m winner Native Twine (by Be My Native) and a winner in Spain: dam unraced granddaughter of high-class Mesopotamia: progressive form: led 2f out to win 20-runner claimer at Goodwood in May: should stay beyond 7f. *J. Sutcliffe.*

DUCKINGTON 7 b.h. Bustino 136 – Cribyn 96 (Brigadier Gerard 144) [1990 6f **83** 6m⁴ 6m 6g 6f⁴ a7g³ 6g⁴ 7m 7g 1991 7.5g⁶ 6m³ 7m³ 7.5f* 7m² 7.6m⁴ 7g⁴ 7m⁴ 7.1m⁴ 6m 6m] leggy, close-coupled horse: has had soft palate operation: fair handicapper: won at Beverley in May: ideally suited by strong gallop at 6f and has won over 1m: particularly well suited by top-of-the-ground: probably unsuited by track at Epsom: twice bandaged in 1991: best covered up: consistent. *M. H. Easterby.*

DUCKITE 3 b.g. Vin St Benet 109 – Sandy Keerie (Sandy Creek 123) [1990 NR — 1991 10.2g] 2,500Y: strong, workmanlike gelding: third foal: dam unraced: always behind in maiden at Chepstow in July. *K. O. Cunningham-Brown.*

DUGGAN 4 b.c. Dunbeath (USA) 127 – Silka (ITY) (Lypheor 118) [1990 10g⁶ 10f* **69** 10.6f* 10m² 12.2g* 12m³ 12m³ 12.3g* 14m⁶ 12m 12m⁶ 13.3g 12s 1991 10g 12f 11.5g⁶ 12f* 11f⁶ 12.3f² 12f* 12.3f⁴ 12m 14.1f⁵ 12.3f 9.7s a12g* a13g⁵] lengthy, rather sparely-made colt: modest handicapper won at Beverley and Carlisle in July and Southwell (returned to form) in November: stays 1½m: goes well on firm ground: quite often apprentice ridden, not when successful as 4-y-o: usually looks very well. *R. J. R. Williams.*

DUKE OF EUROLINK 2 b.c. (Feb 12) Jupiter Island 126 – Lady Eurolink 55 **67** P (Kala Shikari 125) [1991 8m 8m] rangy, rather unfurnished colt: first foal: dam 1m winner: only modest form in maidens won by Wesaam and Bold Pursuit at Newmarket but caught eye being given very considerate ride each time: gives impression capable of significantly better, probably over middle distances. *L. M. Cumani.*

DUKE OF MONMOUTH (USA) 3 b.g. Secreto (USA) 128 – Queen For The **81** Day (USA) (King Emperor (USA)) [1990 NR 1991 10g 11f* 11.6m* 12f⁴ 11.6m⁴] 80,000Y: well-made gelding: impressive in appearance: third foal (all by Secreto): brother to a winner in USA: fair form: short-priced favourite, won maiden at Redcar in July and handicap at Windsor in August: creditable fourth in handicaps: lacks turn of foot, and is worth a try over further: gelded and joined S. Sherwood: winning hurdler. *G. Harwood.*

DUKE OF PADUCAH (USA) 4 gr.c. Green Dancer (USA) 132 – Flordelisada **110** (USA) (Drone) [1990 9g² 11.5m* 12g⁶ 12m⁴ 1991 9m⁴ 12g 12m⁴ 12g⁴ 15g] tall, attractive colt: good walker: very useful performer: ran well in 1991 when fourth in Earl of Sefton Stakes at Newmarket, Hardwicke Stakes at Royal Ascot and Group 1 event won by Lomitas at Dusseldorf: well beaten in Prix Kergorlay at Deauville final start: stays 1½m well: acts on good to firm ground, yet to race on a soft surface. *G. Harwood.*

DULCEATA (IRE) 3 b.f. Rousillon (USA) 133 – Snowtop (Thatching 131) [1990 — NR 1991 8g] IR 140,000Y: sturdy filly: first foal: dam Irish sprinting half-sister to Al Hareb and Ulster Harp Derby winner Rising: always behind in maiden at Newmarket in August. *Lord John FitzGerald.*

DULCIMAL (IRE) 3 b.f. Heraldiste (USA) 121 – Ultimate 77 (Galivanter 131) — [1990 5g 6m⁶ a6g 5m 1991 6f a5g a12g 5m a6g⁶ 5m 6m a10g⁶ 9.7f 16m] small, angular filly: poor plater: blinkered once: trained first 7 starts by M. Chapman. *K. T. Ivory.*

DULVERTON 4 ch.c. Ela-Mana-Mou 132 – Parsimony 121 (Parthia 132) [1990 —
8m 10s 1991 12g] neat colt: no worthwhile form, including in seller (blinkered) in
May: sold 3,200 gns Newmarket Autumn Sales. *J. Parkes.*

DULZURA 3 b.f. Daring March 116 – Comedy Lady 46 (Comedy Star (USA) 121) —
[1990 6g 6g 5m 1991 a8g⁶ a6g] leggy filly: no form in maiden contests and handicap
on flat. *A. P. Jarvis.*

DUMBRECK 4 b.f. Another Realm 118 – Eagle's Quest 62 (Legal Eagle 126) **64 d**
[1990 6m 6g⁵ 7g⁴ 7.6g 7m 8d⁵ 6s 6s 1991 6d 7m⁵ 8.2m* 8.2f⁵ 7g² 8.3d⁵ 8.1m⁴ 8.3s*
7d² 7.6m⁶ 7.1f 10.6g 6g 7d⁶ 7g a7g] workmanlike, good-quartered filly: moderate
mover: modest handicapper at best: won at Hamilton in May and July: below form
last 6 starts: best form at 7f and 1m: acts on good to firm and soft ground: heavily
bandaged nowadays: trained by J. S. Wilson first 9 starts, next 4 by Miss L. Perratt.
A. Bailey.

DUNE RIVER 2 b.c. (Feb 8) Green Desert (USA) 127 – River Spey 96 (Mill Reef **78 p**
(USA) 141) [1991 7m⁴ 7m] 30,000Y: robust, good-topped colt with plenty of scope:
good walker: third foal: half-brother to very useful 3-y-o 1¾m winner Jahafil (by
Rainbow Quest) and plating-class maiden Loch Spey (by Formidable): dam 2-y-o
7.3f winner later stayed middle distances, is out of sister to very smart Joking Apart:
created favourable impression when staying-on fourth of 11 in Lingfield maiden
(very green) in September, then when twenty-third of 30 in Tattersalls Tiffany
Highflyer Stakes at Newmarket (still carrying plenty of condition) 2 weeks later:
looks sort to do good deal better as a 3-y-o and will win races. *Sir Mark Prescott.*

DUNSTABLE (IRE) 3 b.c. Formidable (USA) 125 – Dunoof 92 (Shirley Heights —
130) [1990 NR 1991 8f 7g 10.1d⁶] strong colt: first foal: dam 2-y-o 7f winner, is sister
to high-class middle-distance stayer High Hawk, the dam of In The Wings: behind in
maidens and celebrity sweepstakes: wore net muzzle final start: sold to join B.
Rothwell 4,100 gns Newmarket July Sales. *I. A. Balding.*

DUPLICITY (IRE) 3 b.c. Double Schwartz 128 – Goirtin (Levmoss 133) [1990 **101**
6g 1991 6m³ 6m² 6f* 6m 5g⁶ 5.2m² 6s 5d*] leggy, good-topped colt: has scope: has a
markedly round action: useful sprinter, highly tried on occasions: won maiden at
Yarmouth in June and minor event (by ¾ length from Mathkurh, making most) at
Haydock in October: good second to On Tiptoes in £6,800 minor event at Newbury
sixth start: at least as effective at 5f as 6f: acts on firm ground (stiff task on soft):
sweating second start: has hung right. *L. J. Holt.*

DURNELTOR 3 br.g. Hard Fought 125 – Pounelta 91 (Tachypous 128) [1990 **73 d**
6m³ 6m⁵ 6g 6m* 6s 1991 6g 7m⁴ 8g 9g⁵ 8.5m 8g 7d* 7.1g⁵ 8.1s 7.1g⁵ 8m 9s] leggy,
good-topped gelding: quite modest handicapper: won at Salisbury in June, making
most and rallying well: suited by 7f: acts on good to firm ground and dead: edgy
penultimate start: gelded after final one: mostly disappointing, and is not one to
trust. *R. Hannon.*

DURUNROO 2 gr.f. (Mar 6) Sharrood (USA) 124 – Durun 89 (Run The Gantlet **70**
(USA)) [1991 5g⁴ 6g⁴ a6g² 5m⁴ 5m4] compact filly: half-sister to several winners,
including fair middle-distance stayer Dwadme (by High Top) and 1¾m to 2m winner
Durbo (by Bustino): dam, 1¼m to 1½m winner, is daughter of Duboff: modest
performer: successful in 3-runner maiden (from 2 poor opponents) at Edinburgh in
June and 16-runner seller (retained 7,200 gns) at Newcastle in August: bred to stay
well, but better form at 5f than 6f: ran moderately on fibresand, respectably when
sweating final start: sold 14,500 gns Newmarket Autumn Sales. *Sir Mark Prescott.*

DUST D'THRONE (USA) 3 b.c. Bob's Dusty (USA) – Dethroned (USA) **41**
(Grenfall (USA)) [1990 7v 8d a7g 10.2s 1991 8.2m² 8.2m⁴ 10g 8.1g³ 8m⁶] quite
attractive colt: has a round action: poor maiden: stays 1m: best form on good to firm
ground. *Miss L. C. Siddall.*

DUTCH BLUES 4 b.g. Dutch Treat 112 – My Polyanna 81 (Polyfoto 124) [1990 —
10g⁵ 13m⁵ 1991 16.2g 12f] leggy, plain gelding: plating-class form at 3 yrs: no show in
1991: may prove best short of 13f. *Mrs S. M. Austin.*

DUTCH CZARINA 3 b.f. Prince Sabo 123 – Dutch Princess 70 (Royalty 130) **53**
[1990 7m⁵ 8g⁵ 1991 10v³ 10g 11.7d⁵ 8s⁶ 8f] lengthy filly: poor maiden: faced stiff
tasks in handicaps, running creditably third and fourth starts: possibly doesn't stay
11.7f: acts on heavy going: visored final outing: races keenly. *Miss B. Sanders.*

DUTYFUL 5 b.m. Bold Owl 101 – My Duty 70 (Sea Hawk II 131) [1990 12f 11.7g **53**
11.5m⁴ 12g² 12m⁵ 14m⁶ 14g⁶ 14g⁵ 16f³ 16.2d⁴ 16s² a16g⁴ 1991 14d 16m 16.2d⁵ 16m⁵
16m* 16d³ 17.2g²] workmanlike mare: plating-class handicapper: won at Lingfield
in September: stays 17f: acts on any going. *M. J. Haynes.*

DUTY SERGEANT (IRE) 2 b.g. (Mar 13) Pennine Walk 120 – Plainsong (FR) **73**
(Amen (FR)) [1991 5g² 5f* 6m³ 6d⁴ 6g⁴ 6d⁶ 5m⁶ 7d 6g 5.7g] 3,000F, 2,900Y:
smallish, sturdy gelding: moderate mover: half-brother to 1990 2-y-o 8.2f winner
Sandicliffe Way (by Doulab) and a winner in Italy: dam French 1½m winner from
family of Grey Dawn II: made all in maiden auction at Bath in May: well below form
in nurseries in October: should be suited by 7f: acts on firm and dead ground: once
refused to enter stalls in spring. *M. P. Muggeridge.*

DUXFORD LODGE 4 b.f. Dara Monarch 128 – Simmay (Simbir 130) [1990 8f —
7m 11m 12m⁴ 12f⁶ a14g 11s 10d 12s 1991 13d 12f] close-coupled, sparely-made filly:
poor plater: should stay 1¾m: acts on firm and dead going: tried blinkered. *J. F.
Bottomley.*

DYD 3 b.f. Sulaafah (USA) 119 – Wrekin Belle (Dance In Time (CAN)) [1990 NR **75**
1991 8g 9d* 10.5g] rangy filly: third foal: dam ran twice: 25/1 and carrying plenty of
condition, won claimer at Goodwood in August by 6 lengths, plenty to do 4f out:
favourite though edgy, well beaten in similar event at Haydock (claimed £12,000 to
join F. Jordan) 5 weeks later, stumbling turn, improving on unfavoured centre of
track over 2f out, no extra and eased: stays 9f. *P. J. Makin.*

DYNASTY (IRE) 2 b.c. (Feb 10) Last Tycoon 131 – Lady Chesterfield (USA) (In —
Reality) [1991 5g] 30,000F, IR 20,000Y: lengthy colt: second foal: dam unraced: 12/1
and backward, held up and not knocked about in maiden at Leicester in May. *W. J.
Haggas.*

E

EAGER DEVA 4 b.c. Lochnager 132 – Deva Rose 80 (Chestergate 111) [1990 **95**
a6g⁶ 5f* 6f⁴ 6m 5.8f² 5g 5m³ 6m 5f⁵ 5g 6g⁴ 5d 5.6g 5d 5m⁶ 5m³ 5g⁴ 5g³ 1991 5d²
5g³ 5g* 5f* 5.1g⁶ 5.1g* 5.6m 5f* 5g³ 5.1g³] robust, good-quartered colt: usually
impresses in appearance: good walker and easy mover: fairly useful handicapper:
successful at Beverley (2) in April, Chester (claimer) in July and Beverley in
September: best form at 5f: acts on dead ground, and goes very well on firm: tough:
goes well with forcing tactics. *R. Hollinshead.*

EAGLE BID (IRE) 3 b.g. Auction Ring (USA) 123 – Gay Folly (Wolver Hollow —
126) [1990 7m 1991 10d 10.1s 10g 12m 11.8g] good-quartered gelding: no worthwhile
form, including in claimer. *S. Dow.*

EAGLE FEATHER (IRE) 3 b.g. Commanche Run 133 – Peacefully (Nonoalco **82**
(USA) 131) [1990 NR 1991 8g⁵ 10g 8g³] IR 18,000Y: lengthy gelding: second foal
(both by Commanche Run): dam, lightly raced, modest Irish maiden out of good
broodmare Fighting: fair form in maidens at Newbury in April and Salisbury (moved
moderately down) in June: favourite, found little at Leicester in between: should
stay 1¼m: gelded after final start. *J. L. Dunlop.*

EAGLES LAIR 5 b.h. Head For Heights 125 – Just A Shadow (Laser Light 118) —
[1990 NR 1991 a7g a7g a10g⁵ 10.8m⁶ 10g 10m] rather sparely-made, attractive horse:
poor handicapper at best nowadays: well worth a try over 1½m: acts on good to firm
ground. *D. Marks.*

EARLY BLOOM 2 b.f. (Feb 19) Superlative 118 – Rheinbloom 66 (Rheingold **45**
137) [1991 6g⁶ 6.1m⁶ 8m] sturdy, good-topped filly: half-sister to fairly useful
middle-distance stayer Rhusted (by Busted) and a winner in USA: dam 1½m winner,
is half-sister to high-class Gold Rod: poor maiden: best effort, though hung badly
right, on debut: sold 900 gns Doncaster October Sales. *R. Boss.*

EARLY BREEZE 5 b.g. Tumble Wind (USA) – Dawn Hail 74 (Derring-Do 131) —
[1990 a7g 6m 8m⁶ 10.8g³ 10g⁶ 6d⁵ 7g 1991 a12g⁶ 8.3m] compact gelding: poor
handicapper nowadays: seems to stay 1½m: suited by give in the ground on turf:
below form when visored: winning hurdler. *M. McCourt.*

EARLY MORNING LADY (IRE) 2 ch.f. (Feb 6) The Noble Player (USA) 126 **51**
– Cree's Figurine 61 (Creetown 123) [1991 5f 6m 5d⁴ 5s* 5m³ 6g 5g 5m 5d] IR
3,000Y: leggy, lengthy filly: moderate mover: first foal: dam 2-y-o 5f winner:
dropped in grade, won 8-runner seller (retained 3,800 gns) at Folkestone in July:
didn't reproduce that (mostly in nurseries): blinkered and on toes penultimate start:
clearly suited by soft ground: sold 4,000 gns Newmarket Autumn Sales. *M. J.
Fetherston-Godley.*

EARLY STAR 2 b.c. (May 10) Precocious 126 – Staritsa (USA) (Alleged (USA) **75**
138) [1991 7m⁵ 6m] IR 14,000Y: rather leggy, quite good-topped colt: fifth foal:
half-brother to fairly useful 3-y-o 6f (at 2 yrs) and 7f winner Go Executive (by
Sharpo) and temperamental 1987 2-y-o 5f winner Miss Caro Star (by Rusticaro):
dam unraced daughter of very smart Roussalka, sister to Our Home and half-sister
to Oh So Sharp: easily better effort when fourteenth of 22 in Tattersalls Breeders
Stakes at the Curragh in August: raced keenly on debut in maiden at Leicester:
should stay 7f: sold 6,600 gns Newmarket Autumn Sales. *C. E. Brittain.*

EARTHLY PLEASURE 5 b.m. Music Boy 124 – May Fox 67 (Healaugh Fox) —
[1990 12g a8g 8f⁵ 1991 8m 10.3m⁶ 9.7f⁶ 9.7m] good-topped mare: poor handicapper:
stays 1½m: acts on firm going: has been tried blinkered. *W. M. Brisbourne.*

EARY ALICE 3 br.f. Lidhame 109 – Fayette 80 (Dom Racine (FR) 121) [1990 NR —
1991 7g 10g 6m 8.9m] leggy, close-coupled filly: moderate walker: dam third foal:
dam 1¼m winner: behind, in seller and handicap last 2 starts. *R. J. Holder.*

EASILY LED 2 b.f. (Feb 14) Beveled (USA) – Dame Scarlet (Blakeney 126) [1991 **60**
5m 5m 6.1m 5g 6f⁵] 800Y: rather sparely-made filly: third foal: dam unraced: quite
modest maiden: easily best effort when keeping-on fifth of 8 at Folkestone in
October: will stay further: sweating last 2 starts: sold 1,000 gns Newmarket Autumn
Sales. *H. Candy.*

EAST BARNS (IRE) 3 gr.c. Godswalk (USA) 130 – Rocket Lass (Touch Paper **58**
113) [1990 5f⁶ 5m⁴ 5g⁶ 5f³ 6g³ 6g 7m* 7g 7m 6d 9g 7d 1991 7.5g⁵ 8.5f 8.2f* 7d⁶ 8m⁶
8.5m⁴ 9m 11s 8.2f⁵ 8f⁶ 8m 8.3f a8g⁵] close-coupled colt: has a quick action: quite
modest handicapper at his best: successful at Hamilton in May: showed retains
some ability in amateurs race at Southwell final start: stays 8.5f well: acts on firm
going: often blinkered or visored, but has run creditably without them: sold out of J.
Wainwright's stable 5,400 gns Doncaster October Sales before final start. *T. D.
Barron.*

EASTER BABY 5 ch.m. Derrylin 115 – Saintly Miss 63 (St Paddy 133) [1990 —
a6g⁴ a12g⁴ a16g⁴ 10.1g 12.5g 1991 a13g] lengthy mare: little sign of ability. *P. D.
Cundell.*

EASTERN AURA (IRE) 3 ch.f. Ahonoora 122 – Sybaris 91 (Crowned Prince —
(USA) 128) [1990 5m 6m 7d⁶ 1991 8m 10.2m 7f 7g] workmanlike filly: poor form at 2
yrs, none at 3: blinkered third start. *B. W. Hills.*

EASTERN MAGIC 3 b.c. Faustus (USA) 118 – Hithermoor Lass 75 (Red Alert **72**
127) [1990 7g³ 7g* 1991 10g 10m⁵ 10.3m 10.5g 10.3d4] rather leggy colt: modest
performer: ran creditably in handicaps at Doncaster (£7,600 event) and Chester
(visored) third and final starts: stays 10.3f: acts on good to firm ground and dead:
sold to join J. Akehurst 10,000 gns Newmarket Autumn Sales. *J. W. Hills.*

EASTERN MUSIC 3 b.g. Music Maestro 119 – Eastern Romance 73 (Sahib 114) **62**
[1990 5f³ 5f³ 5m⁴ 6g³ 6g³ 6g 6d⁴ 7s⁶ 1991 8.2d⁶ 6g 6.9f 6f⁴ 6f⁴ 6s³ 5g] lengthy,
rather sparely-made gelding: quite modest performer: clearly best efforts as 3-y-o
when fourth in handicap at Ripon and claimer at Hamilton: suited by 6f: acts on firm
and dead going: visored last 3 starts: usually on toes: very slowly away on second
start. *R. Hollinshead.*

EASTERN SUNSET 4 b.c. Scott Joplyn 108 – Victory Corner 68 (Sit In The **37**
Corner (USA)) [1990 7m 7.6g 10d 1991 a8g⁵ a8g a12g] workmanlike colt: has round
action: poor maiden: stays 1m. *H. Collingridge.*

EASTERN WHISPER (USA) 4 gr.c. Arctic Tern (USA) 126 – Mazyoun **64**
(USA) 57 (Blushing Groom (FR) 131) [1990 10g 12f* 12d⁵ 12m 10d 10.6v 9.1s³
1991 15.8f² 15g³] compact, rather angular colt: moderate mover: quite modest
handicapper: not seen out after June: suited by test of stamina nowadays: acts on
any going: somewhat temperamental as 3-y-o (visored once). *Denys Smith.*

EASTER TERM 3 b.f. Welsh Term 126 – Silly Woman (Silly Season 127) [1990 —
5f 1991 12m 8g] lengthy, good-topped filly: showed nothing in maidens then listed
race. *B. R. Millman.*

EASTLEIGH 2 b.c. (Feb 12) Efisio 120 – Blue Jane 81 (Blue Cashmere 129) [1991 **68**
5d² 5m⁴ 6m⁵ 5m⁶ 5g⁵ 6g⁴ 6m⁴ 6m 5d 6m² 5d⁴] 12,000Y: lengthy, workmanlike colt:
half-brother to one-time smart sprinter Ever Sharp (by Sharpo): dam 6f winner:
quite modest maiden: ran well for 7-lb claimer in nurseries at Pontefract and
Newmarket last 2 starts: stays 6f: acts on good to firm and dead ground. *R.
Hollinshead.*

*Queen Alexandra Stakes, Ascot—Easy To Please is well suited by the extreme distance;
Nomadic Way runs well in defeat*

EAST SUNRISE   3 ch.g. Gabitat 119 – Rueful Lady (Streetfighter 120) [1990 6m   —
6m⁵ 1991 8f 8.3m] narrow, angular gelding: poor maiden: should stay beyond 6f:
tried visored and blinkered: sold 1,150 gns Ascot November Sales. *B. Gubby.*

EASY DELTA   2 ch.f. (Apr 17) Swing Easy (USA) 126 – Songless (Song 132) [1991   —
6m 5m 7m] 825F: small filly: moderate walker: third foal: dam unraced: no worthwhile form. *C. Holmes.*

EASY DOES IT   2 b.f. (Mar 4) Swing Easy (USA) 126 – Pearl Pet 56 (Mummy's   **50**
Pet 125) [1991 5m 5g 6m a6g a8g³ a7g] workmanlike filly: second foal: dam, maiden,
stayed 10.8f: plating-class maiden: seventh of 27 in Newmarket seller third start:
respectable third to Kingchip Boy in Southwell nursery penultimate outing: stays
1m: visored last 3 starts. *C. C. Elsey.*

EASY LINE   8 ch.g. Swing Easy (USA) 126 – Impromptu 88 (My Swanee 122)   **96**
[1990 6m 6m 6m⁴ 6m⁴ 6g³ 6m* 6f³ 6m* 6m 6m 5m⁴ 5m² 6m 5m* 6d⁶ 7d 1991 6g 5m
6g³ 6g⁶ 7m⁵ 7g 8m 7g⁵ 6g* 6m 6f* 5m*] tall, lengthy gelding: moderate mover:
fairly useful handicapper: won at Newmarket and Yarmouth in August and Sandown
(claimer) in September: ideally suited by 6f: probably not at his best on soft going,
acts on any other: tried visored once: often hangs, and best covered up. *P. J. Feilden.*

EASY MATCH   5 b.m. Royal Match 117 – Flying Easy (Swing Easy (USA) 126)   **50**
[1990 NR 1991 6f² 7.1m⁶ 7.1m⁵] big, workmanlike mare: progressive form: dropped
in class, under 6 lengths fifth of 20 to Dickens Lane in seller at Chepstow in
September, always prominent in strongly-run race: slowly away first 2 starts: stays
7f. *C. J. Hill.*

EASY OVER (USA)   5 ch.g. Transworld (USA) 121 – Love Bunny (USA)   **59**
(Exclusive Native (USA)) [1990 10f⁶ 1991 13.8d⁵ 12.3s³ 13m³ 11.9d 12.1d⁵ 12.1s⁴]
big, workmanlike gelding: quite modest handicapper at best: well worth another try
beyond 1½m: acts on good to firm and heavy going: winning hurdler. *G. M. Moore.*

EASY PURCHASE   4 br.c. Swing Easy (USA) 126 – Dauphiness 76 (Supreme   **54**
Sovereign 119) [1990 10m a8g 9m⁵ 10.2f² 12.5g² a12g⁵ 10g² 12m a11g³ a12g* 1991
a11g⁴ a12g⁴ 12s 12.5g⁶ 11.8m⁶] big, angular colt: has a quick action: plating-class

248

handicapper: stays 1½m: acts on good to firm ground: tends to carry head high. *R. J. Holder.*

EASY TOOMEY 3 br.g. Swing Easy (USA) 126 – Miss Twomey (Will Somers 114§) [1990 6m⁶ 5m⁶ a7g⁶ 6m 1991 10g 10.1f] lengthy gelding: poor maiden: carries head high and may be unsatisfactory. *J. R. Jenkins.* —

EASY TO PLEASE 4 ch.f. What A Guest 119 – Clonsella Lady (High Top 131) [1990 10g 12m* 12g* 12d 14d² 12d² 12g 12d⁶ 16d⁵ 12g² 16d 1991 12g* 14g³ 13g³ 14g² 22.2m*] good-topped Irish filly: very useful performer: third foal: half-sister to Irish 1989 1¼m and 1½m winner Eliakim (by Nishapour) and 1m to 9f winner Chase The Door (by Red Sunset): dam French 8.5f winner: improved form when winning Queen Alexandra Stakes at Royal Ascot by 7 lengths from Nomadic Way: earlier awarded handicap at Leopardstown in April: suited by extreme test of stamina: acts on good to firm and dead ground. *J. S. Bolger, Ireland.* **102**

EAU D'ESPOIR 2 b.f. (Feb 9) Monsanto (FR) 121 – Hopeful Waters 66 (Forlorn River 124) [1991 5g 5f 6.9m 7m⁶ 7m⁴ 7.1m⁶ 8m 8m⁶ 10m⁵] smallish filly: keen walker: third foal: half-sister to winning hurdler Comedy River (by Comedy Star): dam 6f and 7f winner: poor form: suited by 1¼m: acts on good to firm ground: consistent. *J. L. Spearing.* **45**

EBAZIYA (IRE) 2 b.f. (Mar 18) Darshaan 133 – Ezana (Ela-Mana-Mou 132) [1991 7g³ 7g* 8d²] second foal: dam, French 11.5f winner, is half-sister to French Group 3 10.5f winner Demia: favourite, won maiden at Fairyhouse in August by 3 lengths from Misako Togo: 2 lengths second of 10 to same horse in Group 3 event at Leopardstown over 5 weeks later: likely to prove suited by middle distances. *J. Oxx, Ireland.* **97**

EBONY ENTERTAINER (IRE) 3 br.g. Kafu 120 – Naval Artiste (Captain's Gig (USA)) [1990 6m⁵ 5m⁶ 6g 1991 6g 6m] good-topped gelding: poor mover: plating-class maiden: tailed off in handicaps as 3-y-o, changing hands 700 gns Ascot May Sales in between: sprint bred. *S. Dow.* —

EBRAAZ 2 b. or br.c. (Feb 9) Green Desert (USA) 127 – Littlefield 100 (Bay Express 132) [1991 6m⁶ 5g* 6m⁵ 6f 7g⁵] close-coupled, quite attractive colt: first foal: dam won from 5.8f (at 2 yrs) to 1m: quite modest performer: won maiden at Windsor in July, always front rank: good fifth of 13 in Brighton nursery final outing: stays 7f: blinkered last 2 starts: sold 15,000 gns Newmarket Autumn Sales. *Major W. R. Hern.* **69**

ECHO DOMINO 2 b.c. (Mar 6) Dominion 123 – Defy Me 75 (Bustino 136) [1991 6d⁵ 5f 7m 7.1m] 10,000Y: smallish, angular colt: second foal: dam 2-y-o 5f winner: quite modest plater: should be suited by 7f: sold 550 gns Doncaster November Sales. *J. Berry.* **44**

ECHOES (FR) 4 b.f. Niniski (USA) 125 – Equal Honor (USA) (Round Table) [1990 9.5g³ 12g² 11.5g³ 12g² 12g² 12.5g³ 12g4 10.5v4 12g 1991 12g⁵ 10.5g* 12s⁵ 12m⁶ 12g³ 12.5m⁵ 12m³ 12.5d⁶ 12g4 12g⁵] closely related to French 9f and 1¼m winner Tarascan (by Kings Lake) and French 7f and 1m winner Equinol (by Nijinsky) and half-sister to another winner there by High Top: dam unraced: very useful French filly: won Group 3 Prix Corrida at Saint-Cloud (by 1½ lengths from La Tritona) in April: ran well most starts after, third to Splash of Colour in Prix Foy at Longchamp seventh one: stays 12.5f: acts on good to firm and soft ground. *D. Sepulchre, France.* **112**

ECHO LADY (IRE) 3 b.f. Vaigly Great 127 – Final Act 64 (Decoy Boy 129) [1990 5m 5f4 6g 6m 6d 6d 1991 6g 7g 7m 8g² 8d⁵ 8.3g⁵ 8g 8.1s³] leggy filly: plater: sweating, ran well in handicap at Windsor sixth start: better at 1m than shorter: below form on a soft surface: on toes last 2 outings. *G. B. Balding.* **53**

ECHO-LOGICAL 2 gr.c. (Mar 17) Belfort (FR) 89 – North Pine (Import 127) [1991 5d* 6f³ 5.1d* 5m⁴ 5d² 5g²] 8,200 (privately) Y: tall, rather unfurnished colt: third foal: half-brother to useful 3-y-o 5f sprinter Heaven-Liegh-Grey (by Grey Desire) and 1988 2-y-o 5f seller winner Springlake's Lady (by Music Boy): dam poor half-sister to top-class sprinter Lochnager: fairly useful performer: successful in maiden at Chester in May and minor event at Chepstow in July: showed improved form in nursery at Haydock, then listed race (held up, ran Tamim to 2 lengths) at Doncaster last 2 starts: should stay 6f: acts on good to firm and dead ground: sold 10,000 gns Doncaster November Sales. *J. Berry.* **95**

ECLIPSING (IRE) 3 b.f. Baillamont (USA) 124 – Exgravity (USA) (Explodent (USA)) [1990 NR 1991 10m 8g² 8g* 8m 8.1m⁵ 8m²] tall, leggy, lengthy filly: good mover, with a long stride: first foal: dam French 6f (at 2 yrs) to 9.2f winner out of half-sister to excellent broodmare Miss Manon: won maiden at Yarmouth in June: **83**

sweating, creditable second of 15 in handicap at Kempton in September: worth another try beyond 1m: sold 23,000 gns Newmarket December Sales. *R. Charlton.*

ECLIPTIC (IRE) 2 b.c. (Mar 11) Lomond (USA) 128 – Circulate (High Top 131) **65** [1991 7m³ 7.5m 7m⁵ 8m] 32,000Y: tall, leggy, lengthy colt: has scope: first foal: dam Irish 1¼m winner, is from family of Nashwan: quite modest maiden: stays 1m: trained until after final start by J. Berry. *P. W. Chapple-Hyam.*

ECOLOGIST 3 b.c. Rainbow Quest (USA) 134 – Infra Green 121 (Laser Light **109** 118) [1990 NR 1991 12g 15m* 15g* 15g⁶ 15d⁶] half-brother to several winners, including useful 1m to 2m (in USA) winner Verdance (by Green Dancer), smart 7f and 1m performer Greensmith (by Known Fact) and to dam of Toulon: dam won from 6f to 1½m, including Prix Ganay: won maiden at Chantilly in May and Prix Berteux at Longchamp in June: below-form sixth in pattern events at Longchamp, off course 3 months in between: stays 15f: useful. *A. Fabre, France.*

ECONOMY EXPRESS 3 b.f. Bay Express 132 – Massawa (FR) (Tennyson **—** (FR) 124) [1990 6g 6g 7g 6d a7g⁴ 1991 a8g⁶ 12v 10m 12g] sparely-made filly: poor maiden: stays 1¼m: sold 1,250 gns Ascot October Sales. *W. J. Musson.*

ECOSSAIS DANSEUR (USA) 5 ch.h. Arctic Tern (USA) 126 – Northern **—** Blossom (CAN) (Snow Knight 125) [1990 a12g⁴ 12g⁵ 12f³ 10m 1991 12f] lengthy, rather angular horse: moderate mover: fair handicapper at 3 yrs: always behind only run on flat in 1991: best at around 1¼m: has won on firm going, and goes well on a soft surface: winning hurdler. *J. L. Spearing.*

EDEN'S CLOSE 2 ch.c. (Feb 12) Green Dancer (USA) 132 – Royal Agreement **90 p** (USA) (Vaguely Noble 140) [1991 8m⁴ 6m⁶] good-topped colt: has scope: fifth foal: dam won at up to 9f in North America: easily better effort when around 8 lengths last of 6, outpaced from 2f out, to Rodrigo de Triano in Newgate Stud Middle Park Stakes at Newmarket in October: will improve again, particularly back over further, and looks a sure-fire winner of a maiden at the least. *M. H. Tompkins.*

EDEN'S DAWN 4 ch.g. Godswalk (USA) 130 – Fresh As A Daisy (Stanford 121§) **—** [1990 NR 1991 6f 8m 5.8f 7.1d 14.1f] leggy, quite good-topped gelding: good walker and mover: poor maiden: no form in 1991, unseated rider and bolted once: best form at 6f: tried blinkered: sold out of B. Millman's stable 1,500 gns Ascot July Sales after penultimate start. *D. J. G. Murray-Smith.*

EDGEAWAY 2 b.f. (Feb 12) Ajdal (USA) 130 – Kaweah Maid (General Assembly **70 p** (USA)) [1991 6m 6.9f²] 29,000Y: workmanlike filly: second foal: dam, maiden, best run at 1¼m, is half-sister to top 1979 2-y-o Monteverdi: easily better effort in maidens when ½-length second of 12 to Vying Victor at Folkestone in October, slowly away then staying on really strongly final 1f: will improve again and should stay 1m. *J. W. Hills.*

EDIMBOURG 5 b.h. Top Ville 129 – Miss Brodie (FR) (Margouillat (FR) 133) **—** [1990 NR 1991 13.3d 16.2m⁶] tall, lengthy, lightly-made horse: second foal: dam unplaced once here and 5 times in French Provinces: very lightly-raced ex-French performer: won 1m minor event at Maisons-Laffitte at 2 yrs: close fifth in 10.5f listed race at Maisons-Laffitte and well beaten in Prix du Jockey-Club at Chantilly at 3 yrs: bandaged, tailed off at 5 yrs in listed event at Newbury and minor event at Haydock (not seen out after May): stays 10.5f: formerly trained by A. Fabre. *C. E. Brittain.*

EDIREPUS 3 b.g. Lightning Dealer 103 – Pentland Beauty 49 (Remainder Man **—** 126§) [1990 NR 1991 10g] big, angular gelding: first reported foal: dam, poor maiden, stayed 1m: behind in maiden at Leicester in May. *J. Pearce.*

EDUCATED PET 2 gr.g. (Feb 1) Petong 126 – School Road 88 (Great Nephew **54** 126) [1991 5d⁵ 5f⁴ 5f 6f² 6f³ 7g 7m 6g 5d] 7,600F: strong, sturdy gelding: carries condition: seventh living foal: half-brother to several winners, including 1990 2-y-o 6f winner Penny Mint (by Mummy's Game): dam sister to smart miler Saher, ran only at 4 yrs when 6f and 7f winner: plating-class maiden: better suited by 6f and 7f than 5f: acts on firm ground: blinkered penultimate start, visored final one: gelded at end of year. *M. Johnston.*

EDWARD LEAR (USA) 5 b.g. Lear Fan (USA) 130 – Coed (USA) (Ribot 142) **49** [1990 10.6s 10g a8g³ 8.2m² a12g 10m⁵ 11m⁴ 10.4d 8d⁶ 1991 11s 7m³] workmanlike horse: moderate mover: plating-class handicapper nowadays: blinkered, staying-on third in seller at Thirsk in April: stays 11f: suited by top-of-the-ground: has twice run as if something amiss. *J. G. FitzGerald.*

EDWARD SEYMOUR (USA) 4 b.c. Northern Baby (CAN) 127 – Regal **—** Leader (USA) (Mr Leader (USA)) [1990 8g 9g² 1991 10m 11.1s⁵ a12g] lengthy colt: trained by L. Cumani, fair form as 3-y-o: easily best effort in 1991 in Edinburgh claimer second start: seems to stay 11f: sold out of S. Mellor's stable 5,800 gns Doncaster Spring Sales, resold 4,100 gns Doncaster November Sales. *P. Calver.*

EFHARISTO 2 b.c. (Mar 13) Dominion 123 – Excellent Alibi (USA) (Exceller (USA) 129) [1991 7g 7.1m⁴ 6s⁶] 25,000F, 48,000Y: workmanlike colt: has scope: second reported foal: half-brother to 4-y-o fairly useful 1¼m (at 3 yrs) to 16.2f winner Witness Box (by Lyphard): dam, French 1¼m and 1½m winner, is closely related to Dahlia: modest maiden: keeping-on fourth of 10 at Sandown in September: ran moderately at Yarmouth 6 weeks later: will probably be better suited by 1¼m. *C. E. Brittain.* **78**

EFRA 2 b.c. (Jan 22) Efisio 120 – Ra Ra (Lord Gayle (USA) 124) [1991 5d 5g⁶] 7,800F, 12,500Y: good-topped colt: second foal: half-brother to a winner in Macau: dam never ran: no worthwhile form in minor events at Doncaster in March and Sandown (green, 6 ran) in July. *S. Dow.* **—**

EIDOLON 4 b.f. Rousillon (USA) 133 – Eider 80 (Niniski (USA) 125) [1990 14d 1991 5m 8f⁵ 8m 6.1d 10.2g] leggy, angular filly: has quick action: behind in varied company. *R. J. Holder.* **—**

EID (USA) 2 b.c. (Mar 26) Northern Baby (CAN) 127 – Millracer (USA) 79 (Le Fabuleux 133) [1991 8f⁸ 8g⁴ 8g] $45,000F, $335,000Y: good-topped colt: second foal: dam 7.2f winner later successful in USA, is out of half-sister to smart 1981 2-y-o sprinter Peterhof: impressive winner of 9-runner maiden at Yarmouth in September: didn't confirm that in minor event at Wolverhampton (not knocked about after poor run) and nursery at Redcar: will stay 1¼m: unruly stalls first 2 starts. *D. Morley.* **73**

EIGHTANDAHALF (IRE) 2 b.c. (Mar 10) Be My Guest (USA) 126 – Nancy Chere (USA) (Gallant Man) [1991 8m 7m] good-topped, attractive colt: has scope: sort to carry condition: sixth reported foal: brother to useful 1¼m and 1½m winner Cameo Performance: dam, stakes-placed winner at up to 1m, is half-sister to some smart animals: quite modest form in autumn maidens at Doncaster (carrying condition and green, smooth progress soon after halfway, faded into seventh of 19) and Newmarket (ridden along firmly from some way out) 3 weeks later: likely to do better over middle distances. *P. W. Chapple-Hyam.* **66 p**

EIGHTEENTHIRTYFOUR 3 b.c. Ballad Rock 122 – Weavers' Tack (Weavers' Hall 122) [1990 7g 7s 1991 8f 10d 10m] leggy, good-topped colt: behind in maidens: bandaged final start (May). *A. Moore.* **—**

EILEEN JENNY (IRE) 3 ch.f. Kris 135 – Sorbus 121 (Busted 134) [1990 8d² 1991 9g² 12g* 12m³ 12m³ 14d⁵ 11g³ 12s*] strong, lengthy filly: sixth living foal: half-sister to very useful 1½m winner Bahamian (by Mill Reef) and 3 other winners in Ireland, including smart miler Captivator (by Artaius): dam disqualified winner of Irish Oaks: won maiden at the Curragh in June and listed race at Milan in November: ran well on former course when 3½ lengths third of 10 to Possessive Dancer in Kildangan Stud Irish Oaks and when ½-length third to Sardaniya in Meld Stakes: below form in Irish St Leger at the Curragh and listed race (6/4 on) at Naas fifth and sixth outings: stays 1½m: acts on good to firm ground and soft. *J. Oxx, Ireland.* **112**

EIRE LEATH-SCEAL 4 b.c. Legend of France (USA) 124 – Killarney Belle (USA) (Irish Castle (USA)) [1990 9.1m⁴ 8.2f* 8f³ 8m 9m⁴ 10.6s⁵ 9g 8m² 9m 10.2g 8d⁶ 8g⁴ 9g 10.2s⁵ 7d 1991 8d⁵ 10g⁶ 10s⁵ 10g 12m⁴ 12f* 12m 12.3g⁵ 11.9m⁴ 12g³ 11.9m² 12f⁴ 12.3f⁵ 11.9g 13.9g 13.1m* 11.9g 11.9d⁵ 12m⁵ 12g⁶ 16.5d] small, attractive colt: usually looks well: poor mover: modest handicapper: won at Beverley in May and Ayr in September: effective at 1¼m to 13f: acts on firm and dead going: goes well with forcing tactics: tough and genuine. *M. Brittain.* **75**

ELADHAM 5 b. or br.g. Lyphard's Special (USA) 122 – Derrede (Derring-Do 131) [1990 8.5g² 8m⁴ 10g⁴ 10d 8.2m³ 10.2m* 11f³ 1991 10m 13.8g 13.8m⁵ 10g 10m 8.3f 9.9f 8m] angular, sparely-made gelding: has been tubed: quite modest handicapper as 4-y-o: below best in 1991, tried blinkered: best form at up to 1¼m: acts on good to firm going. *M. D. Hammond.* **—**

ELAINE TULLY (IRE) 3 b.f. Persian Bold 123 – Hanna Alta (FR) (Busted 134) [1990 NR 1991 8m⁴ 8g* 8m⁵ 10g³ 10g⁶ 12m⁴ 12d³] 11,000Y: sturdy filly: half-sister to fairly useful 1¼m to 1½m winner Belmoredean (by Be My Guest) and a winner in Italy: dam French 1½m winner out of smart French 7f winner Hamada: won maiden at Kempton in May: ran well in handicaps last 4 starts: seems suited by 1½m: acts on good to firm and dead ground. *I. A. Balding.* **76**

ELANMATINA 2 ch.f. (May 7) Burslem 123 – Sally St Clair (Sallust 134) [1991 6f⁸ 6f² 6.1m⁵ 6m] 2,800Y: workmanlike filly: fourth foal: half-sister to 6f and 7f winner Just Jennings and 1990 2-y-o 7f winner Makemeastar (both by Horage): **77**

dam, winner in Canada, is half-sister to Superlative: modest performer: won maiden auction at Ripon in August: ran moderately in nurseries last 2 starts: will stay 7f: yet to race on a soft surface. *C. F. Wall.*

EL ARAB 4 ch.g. Sayf El Arab (USA) 127 – Sally Conkers (Roi Lear (FR) 126) **67**
[1990 6m³ 6g 6m* 6g⁵ 6m⁶ 6g⁴ 7g³ 6m⁶ 6d 6m² 6f⁵ 7.2g³ 7d⁵ 6s a7g² a6g* 1991 a7g⁴ 6s⁵ 6m 7.6d 7m] leggy, good-topped gelding: moderate mover: fair handicapper: stayed 7f: acted on any going: often visored, including when successful: dead. *E. J. Alston.*

ELATHIR (USA) 3 ch.g. Alydar (USA) – Mohair (FR) (Blue Tom 127) [1990 NR **84** 1991 7g⁶ 10.1m²] $850,000Y: useful-looking gelding: good mover, with a quick action: half-brother to very smart French middle-distance filly Marie de Litz (by Dictus) and useful French 1¼m and American winner Marie d'Argonne (by Jefferson), latter dam of Polar Falcon: dam unraced daughter of smart Imberline: 2 lengths second of 13 to Burdur in maiden at Epsom in June, always in touch and keeping on well: sold 14,000 gns Newmarket Autumn Sales and gelded afterwards. *A. C. Stewart.*

ELBIO 4 b.c. Precocious 126 – Maganyos (HUN) 112 (Pioneer (USA)) [1990 **125** 6m⁴ 6s* 5m* 5m* 6m 1991 6m² 5g* 5m* 5m* 6m³ 5g⁵]

After missing the entire second half of the 1990 season through injury, Elbio had a remarkable rise from relative obscurity to the top of the sprinting division in early-summer. He had been unraced at two years but had looked a good prospect before his injury, a hair-line fracture of his off-hind cannon bone, reeling off wins in a maiden and two handicaps. A belated confirmation of Elbio's potential came in Newmarket's Abernant Stakes, a listed event over six furlongs at the Craven meeting. On his first run for over nine months he finished a most promising second to Case Law, promise that was realised with a neck defeat of Sir Harry Hardman in the Palace House Stakes at the same track the following month. Our enthusiasm for his prospects was tempered somewhat by the fact that he'd found less off the bridle than had seemed likely in the Palace House. But there was no faulting the style of his next two wins, at Sandown and Ascot; having been held up, he readily forged clear when asked for his effort entering the final furlong. He put two and a half lengths between himself and nearest pursuer Dominio in the UB Group Temple Stakes, and it was three lengths back to Irish Shoal in the King's Stand with Archway another half a length behind in third. For all that the King's Stand had attracted runners from France, Ireland and Italy in Irish Shoal, Archway and Rufina respectively, it was far from a vintage edition, however. The Carroll Foundation July Cup provided a sterner test. Amongst the opposition in an eight-strong field at Newmarket were the French-trained pair Lycius (Two Thousand Guineas runner-up) and Polar Falcon (subsequent Ladbroke Sprint winner), both reverting to sprint distances, along with the Cork And Orrery first and second Polish Patriot and Chicarica. Elbio, having to carry 3 lb more than weight-for-age on our scale, ran up to his best in finishing third, beaten two lengths and half a length, to the year-younger pair Polish Patriot

Palace House Stakes, Newmarket—
Elbio (second right) holds on from Sir Harry Hardman (stars) and Furajet (second left)

King's Stand Stakes, Ascot—Elbio quickens clear of Irish Shoal and Archway

and Lycius, but in a race that wasn't strongly run by any means he gave the impression that he might prove ideally suited by a return to five furlongs; still full of running at the two-furlong pole, Elbio couldn't find any extra inside the last and merely kept on at one pace. Connections brought him back to the minimum trip for the Keeneland Nunthorpe Stakes but Elbio failed to give his best running. He was never in contention and finished around four lengths fifth of nine to Sheikh Albadou. Sadly, that was the last we saw of Elbio; a pricked foot forced him out of the Ladbroke Sprint whilst muscle trouble denied him a run in the Abbaye.

		Precocious	Mummy's Pet	Sing Sing
Elbio		(b 1981)	(b 1968)	Money For Nothing
(b.c. 1987)			Mrs Moss	Reform
			(ch 1969)	Golden Plate
		Maganyos (HUN)	Pioneer	Pieces of Eight
		(br 1980)	(b 1971)	Irish Rule
			Marimba	Indikator
			(b 1973)	Marshgate Lass

Except for Elbio the nearest Precocious has got to siring a pattern winner is with Arany, second in a Group 3 race at Tipperary in June, and Sheer Precocity, third in the Beeswing Stakes at Newcastle in July. Precocious has also sired the two-year-old listed winners Osmar (in Ireland) and Golden Precocious (in Italy). Elbio was bought for 29,000 guineas as a yearling at the Newmarket October Sales. The distaff side of his pedigree makes for most interesting reading. Maganyos was first seen by racegoers here in 1985 when as a five-year-old she showed fairly useful form over hurdles for Henderson, winning three times at two miles and showing form at twenty-one furlongs. England marked the last stop on an extensive tour of Europe. Hungarian bred, she started her career in her native land and was successful over five furlongs as a juvenile. Bought by Pat Samuel she continued her career in the hands of French trainer Yann Porzier for whom she gained six wins in her next two seasons, in France (listed races over a mile and a half at Chantilly and Nantes), Switzerland (the Swiss Derby at Frauenfeld), Italy and Germany. Maganyos continued on her travels after having Elbio, her first foal, and is now in New Zealand. Elbio's grandam Marimba didn't see the racecourse. Interestingly, Marimba is by German-born sire Indikator who's bred on the same lines as Slip Anchor's dam Sayonara. Elbio's third and fourth dams gained solitary wins here in five-furlong sellers. A good-topped, attractive colt, Elbio tends to get on edge in the preliminaries. Although successful on a soft surface as a three-year-old, easily his best form is on good to firm ground. He remains in training. *P. J. Makin.*

EL CASTANO 2 ch.g. (Apr 12) Ballacashtal (CAN) – La Perricholi (FR) 80 **39** (Targowice (USA) 130) [1991 7m 7g] 1,800Y: third foal: brother to 1990 2-y-o 7f winner La Mariquita: dam 6f winner: poor form in big fields in seller (backed at long odds) at Redcar and maiden auction at Doncaster 6 days later in June: should stay 1m. *J. Hetherton.*

EL CORTES (USA) 2 b.c. (May 18) El Gran Senor (USA) 136 – Millingdale **89** p Lillie 119 (Tumble Wind (USA)) [1991 6m*] attractive colt: fourth known foal: brother to 1¼m seller winner Sao Paulo and closely related to 1¼m winner Festival City (by The Minstrel): dam, second in Cheveley Park Stakes and Irish 1000 Guineas, won 8.5f stakes race on only start in USA: weak 4/1-shot but looking very well, won 14-runner minor event at Ayr in September by 2 lengths from Isaiah, quickening well to lead final furlong: should stay 1¼m: sure to improve, and is said to be highly regarded. *P. W. Chapple-Hyam.*

EL DINERO (IRE) 3 b.c. Last Tycoon 131 – Eltisley (USA) 82 (Grey Sovereign **105** 128§) [1990 5.1g* 6f³ 7d⁶ 7.3g⁶ 1991 8g⁵ 8v 8g³ 8g⁴ 8m² 8v 8v⁶] rather leggy, attractive colt: useful performer: ran creditably in listed race at Kempton on reappearance: ran in Italy afterwards, in frame in listed races: stays 1m: possibly unsuited by heavy going. *W. Jarvis.*

EL DOMINIO 3 b.c. King of Spain 121 – Domicile (Dominion 123) [1990 6g⁵ 5g² **67** § 6m 6m² 6f³ 7m⁴ 7g⁵ 8m 8d* 1991 8s³ 8g 9d 11.7g⁶ 10d 8g 8g* 8g⁶ 8s 8g 8g a10g] close-coupled colt: quite modest handicapper on most form (appeared to run far better on reappearance): behind after winning handicap at Salisbury in July: should stay middle distances: acts on soft going: inconsistent and not one to rely on. *K. O. Cunningham-Brown.*

ELECKYDO 2 ch.f. (May 17) Electric 126 – Deed 86 (Derring-Do 131) [1991 8d — 7g] workmanlike filly: closely related to fair 1978 2-y-o 6f winner Super Jack (by Blakeney) and half-sister to 4 winners, including smart 7f and 1¼m winner Busaco (by Bustino): dam 2-y-o 5f winner: soundly beaten in median auction at Wolverhampton (backward, sweating) and maiden at Salisbury in October. *R. J. Hodges.*

ELECTRIC DANCER 5 br.g. Electric 126 – Chicory (Vaigly Great 127) [1990 — a12g 16g 17.6g² 17m* 17.1d 1991 a16g 21.6f] rather leggy gelding: has been tubed: poor handicapper: well beaten in first half of 1991: dyed-in-the-wool stayer: acts on good to firm ground. *C. A. Horgan.*

ELECTRIC QUEEN 2 b.f. (Apr 1) Electric 126 – Consistent Queen 55 (Queen's **35** Hussar 124) [1991 6g⁶ a6g⁶ 6m] 700Y: small, sturdy filly: half-sister to 3 winning platers, including (over 11.8f) 3-y-o Lifetimes Ambition (by Hotfoot): dam 1m seller winner: poor plater: should stay middle distances. *J. Berry.*

ELECTROJET 3 b.f. Electric 126 – Shy Talk 93 (Sharpen Up 127) [1990 5s 5g⁶ — 6m⁴ 6f* 6m 6d 1991 7g 7m 8.9m] angular filly: moderate mover: poor performer: should stay 7f. *B. A. McMahon.*

ELEGANT APPROACH 3 b.f. Prince Ragusa 96 – Honest Opinion 68 (Free **48** State 125) [1990 7g 8.2g³ 8g 1991 8g 9m 12d³ 12g² 13.8f⁴ a12g] sparely-made filly: plater: below form last 2 starts, off course almost 5 months in between: may prove best at around 1½m: sometimes pulls hard. *W. W. Haigh.*

ELEGANT FRIEND 3 ch.g. Music Boy 124 – Cardinal Palace 85 (Royal Palace **78** 131) [1990 NR 1991 8m 6m⁶ 5.9h* 5g³ 5g³ 6m⁵ 6m 8d⁵ 8.1d] leggy, angular gelding: fourth live foal: half-brother to middle-distance winners by Sharpo, Thatching and Never So Bold: dam won from 9.4f to 1½m: won maiden at Carlisle in June: ran creditably in handicaps at Ayr (£17,500 event) and Chepstow last 2 starts: stays 1m: has form on hard and dead ground: usually apprentice ridden. *M. H. Tompkins.*

ELEGANT ROSE 5 ch.m. Noalto 120 – Shapina 105 (Sharp Edge 123) [1990 **62** a8g² a6g* a7g a7g² a7g³ a6g³ 6m² 6f 7g³ 6m* 6m a7g a5g⁵ a6g 1991 a6g a7g³ a8g a **55** a8g⁵ a8g⁴ a8g a6g² 6d⁵] sturdy mare: quite modest handicapper: not seen out after March: best form at 6f or 7f: acts on good to firm ground and dead: effective with or without blinkers: good mount for apprentice. *O. O'Neill.*

ELEGANT SOLUTION 2 b.f. (Mar 5) Elegant Air 119 – Persevering 95 **73** (Blakeney 126) [1991 7.1m* 8m 7g²] 10,500F, 180,000 francs (approx £18,000) Y: close-coupled filly: eighth living foal: half-sister to several winners, including 3-y-o 1¼m winner Winoski (by Petoski) and fairly useful sprinter Fair Test (by Fair Season): dam winner 4 times at up to 2m, is out of half-sister to very smart middle-distance stayer Petty Officer: 33/1-winner of 9-runner maiden at Sandown in August, leading well inside final furlong: creditable second in minor event at Warwick in October: outclassed in between: should stay 1m: reportedly fractured off-fore going to post at Deauville final appearance. *J. W. Hills.*

ELEGANT STRANGER   6 b.g. Krayyan 117 – Tumvella (Tumble Wind (USA))   —
[1990 8m 1991 a11g⁵ 10m 10g] good-quartered, attractive gelding: very lightly raced and poor form on flat nowadays: suited by 1m: acts on any going: fair hurdler. *M. H. Tompkins.*

ELEGANT TOUCH   2 b. or br.f. (Mar 9) Elegant Air 119 – Teye (Mummy's Pet   **78**
125) [1991 5m² 6d⁴ 6f⁵ 7m² 7f² 8m* 8d⁴] 4,000Y: leggy, lengthy filly: sister to poor middle-distance maiden Hazel Mill and half-sister to modest 6f winner Hazel Bee (by Starch Reduced) and a winning hurdler: dam showed little ability: modest performer: won nursery at Pontefract in October, staying on well: modest fourth in Wolverhampton maiden auction later in month: best effort at 1m on good to firm ground: wore tongue strap last 2 outings. *M. Moubarak.*

ELEGANZA (IRE)   2 b.f. (Mar 30) Kings Lake (USA) 133 – Belmont Blue 75   **62**
(Kashmir II 125) [1991 7g 7.5f³ 7g³] 7,600Y: leggy, close-coupled filly: sixth foal: half-sister to 7f winner Blue Brilliant (by Thatching) and a winner in Italy by Rusticaro: dam won over 1¼m: quite modest form: will stay 1m. *M. H. Easterby.*

ELEMENTARY   8 b.g. Busted 134 – Santa Vittoria 100 (Ragusa 137) [1990 8g²   **106**
10g* 8g⁴ 9m³ 12.3d* 1991 12d³ 12g 10g] strong, quite attractive gelding: very useful performer at 7 yrs: below best in 1991, including in 2 big handicaps in Britain: effective from 1m to 1½m: acts on any going: has been blinkered, but not since 4 yrs: high-class hurdler at best: now with M. Pipe. *J. S. Bolger, Ireland.*

ELEMENT OFSURPRISE   2 ch.f. (May 22) Ballacashtal (CAN) – Moonsail   **32**
(Windjammer (USA)) [1991 7g 8m a8g a6g] 1,100F, 2,200Y: leggy filly: half-sister to 12.3f winner Mazeltov Linda (by Remainder Man) and a winner abroad: dam never ran: seems of little account. *Capt. J. Wilson.*

ELEPHANT POINT (IRE)   2 br.c. (Mar 12) Groom Dancer (USA) 128 –   **48**
Hamada (FR) 116 (Habitat 134) [1991 6f⁵ 6g 7f] 56,000F, 30,000Y: sturdy colt: half-brother to several winners in France, notably useful sprinter Harifa (by Green Dancer): dam (raced only at 2 yrs when successful at 5f and 6.5f in France) later won Group 3 events at 7f and 1m: poor form in varied company, including selling. *M. H. Tompkins.*

ELEVEN LIGHTS (USA)   7 ch.g. Lyphard (USA) 132 – Eleven Pelicans (USA)   **41**
(Grey Dawn II 132) [1990 12h* a12g⁴ 15m* 15.8d⁴ 15d 1991 13.6g³ 12m* 15.8g³ 16.2f²] small gelding: moderate walker and mover: poor handicapper: won at Carlisle (amateurs) in June: stays 2m: acts well on top-of-the-ground: has found little off bridle: sold 4,100 gns Doncaster October Sales. *Mrs G. R. Reveley.*

ELFASLAH (IRE)   3 b.f. Green Desert (USA) 127 – Fair of The Furze 112   **107**
(Ela-Mana-Mou 132) [1990 6g⁶ 7f³ 7m 1991 8g² 8g 7m³ 8m² 8.9m³ 10f² 10.4g* 10.1f* 10s* 10.5v⁵] sturdy, workmanlike filly: useful performer: in excellent heart in the autumn, winning maiden at York, minor event at Yarmouth and listed event (by 3 lengths from Zivania) at the Curragh: will stay 1½m: acts on any going. *H. Thomson Jones.*

ELGIN   2 b.g. (Mar 10) Lochnager 132 – Targos Delight (Targowice (USA) 130)   **43**
[1991 6g 5d 7g 7.5f a7g⁵ 7.1m⁴ 6f 8.3g] 3,000Y: plain, workmanlike gelding: has a round action: ninth foal: half-brother to 3 minor winners: dam unraced half-sister to top 1974 Irish 2-y-o Sea Break: poor maiden: claimed out of M. W. Easterby's stable £6,090 sixth outing: suited by 7f: acts on top-of-the-ground and fibresand: blinkered (in selling nursery) final start. *Miss L. A. Perratt.*

ELHUDHUD   4 ch.c. Habitat 134 – Green Lucia 116 (Green Dancer (USA) 132)   **49**
[1990 6s² 8g⁴ 7g² 6f² 9m 7d⁶ 8g 7d a6g a8g³ a10g² 1991 a10g⁴ a12g³ a11g⁶ a10g 10v* 9g⁵ 10.2s⁶ 10f] leggy, quite good-topped colt: moderate walker and mover: plating-class performer: won (for first time) claimer at Folkestone in March: not seen out after April: stays 1¼m: acts on heavy ground: often blinkered or visored nowadays (hooded once): sold 900 gns Newmarket July Sales. *R. W. Stubbs.*

ELIKI   3 b.f. Nishapour (FR) 125 – Lovers Light (Grundy 137) [1990 NR 1991 a10g²   **74**
12f* 14.6m⁴] 14,000Y: lengthy, workmanlike filly: third foal: half-sister to a winner in Austria by Mashhor Dancer: dam out of half-sister to Main Reef: set slow early pace and held on by a neck in maiden (moved moderately down) at Thirsk in August, ducking left 2f out: fair fourth in handicap at Doncaster over 2½ months later, making most: should stay 1¾m. *H. R. A. Cecil.*

ELIOT 3 b.f. Silly Prices 110 – Elitist 72 (Keren 100) [1990 NR 1991 9f] good- —
bodied, angular filly: second foal: sister to an animal of little account: dam promised
to stay 1¼m: very slowly away when tailed off in maiden at Newcastle in July. *N.
Chamberlain.*

ELITE REG 2 b.c. (May 11) Electric 126 – Coppice (Pardao 120) [1991 7g 8.1g 34
a8g] 11,000Y: good-bodied colt: half-brother to 3-y-o Parbold Hill (by Carwhite) and
several winners, including fair 1m to 10.2f winner Madame Bovary (by Ile de
Bourbon) and 1986 2-y-o 5.1f winner Nightdress (by Pyjama Hunt): dam second in
small 9f race in France: soundly beaten in maidens, final one on fibresand. *P. F. I.
Cole.*

ELIZABETHAN AIR 2 b.f. (Mar 4) Elegant Air 119 – Lizabeth Chudleigh 40
(Imperial Fling (USA) 116) [1991 7m 8m 7m] 9,800Y: angular filly: fourth foal:
half-sister to modest but later unreliable 1988 2-y-o 6f winner Syrus P Turntable (by
King of Spain) and very useful Irish 8.5f to 1¼m winner Jonjas Chudleigh (by
Aragon): dam never ran: beaten long way in large-field maidens. *A. N. Lee.*

ELIZA WOODING 3 b.f. Faustus (USA) 118 – Red Gloves 83 (Red God 128§) 44 +
[1990 6g4 7f* 7m4 7m 8g 8m6 8m 8m5 8d4 1991 8m 6m 10g 10.2d6 10.1d 8m4] tall,
leggy filly: modest plater nowadays: best 3-y-o effort at Pontefract final start: worth
another try at 1¼m: yet to race on very soft going, acts on any other. *C. J. Hill.*

ELLAFITZETTY (IRE) 2 b.f. (Mar 16) Ela-Mana-Mou 132 – Etty 81 (Relko 60
136) [1991 6f4 7d 7m 10m5] 22,000F, IR 19,000Y: neat filly: has a quick action: sister
to a winner in Belgium and half-sister to very useful middle-distance filly Miss
Boniface (by Tap On Wood) and a winner over hurdles: dam 1¼m winner, is
half-sister to Whip It Quick, a very smart colt in Britain and Germany: quite modest
maiden: stays 1¼m: blinkered final start. *R. F. Johnson Houghton.*

ELLA STREET 4 b.f. King of Spain 121 – More Fun (Malicious) [1990 8v 8g —
10.2m 8.2g 1991 10m 12f 10g6] workmanlike filly: no worthwhile form: trained until
after reappearance by N. Tinkler. *M. O'Neill.*

ELLEBANNA 3 b.f. Tina's Pet 121 – Mainly Dry (The Brianstan 128) [1990 5g* 69
5g5 5f 5m4 5s4 5s5 1991 5g* 5m4 5m* 5m6 5m 5.2m 5d6] leggy, quite attractive
filly: has rather round action: modest handicapper on her day: made all at Edinburgh
(apprentices) in May and Wolverhampton in July: speedy: needs a sound surface:
occasionally sweating and on toes: has reportedly broken blood vessels: sold 5,200
gns Newmarket Autumn Sales: seems best when fresh, but isn't one to trust. *J.
Berry.*

EL NIDO 3 ch.g. Adonijah 126 – Seleter (Hotfoot 126) [1990 5g 5d5 6g 6m 7f 7d 48
1991 8s 8f3 11g* 9m* 12.2m6] leggy, workmanlike gelding: has a round action: took
keen hold and set pace when winning handicaps at Edinburgh in June and Redcar
(rallied really well, awarded race) in July: sweating, edgy and wearing crossed
noseband, set too strong a pace in similar event final start: should prove suited by
further than 9f: acts on firm going. *M. J. Camacho.*

EL PERSA (USA) 3 gr.c. Persepolis 110 – A Realgirl (USA) (In Reality) [1990 —
NR 1991 10g4 12.1g 11.5g 8.1g 8s 8f] big, workmanlike colt: sixth foal: half-brother to
several winners, including useful 1986 2-y-o 6.3f and 7f winner Snow Finch (by
Storm Bird) and Sicuterat (by Commanche Run), a winner in Italy who stays middle
distances: dam minor stakes winner at up to 9f in USA: no worthwhile form:
troublesome in preliminaries fourth start, wore crossed noseband and early to post
final one: sold 2,200 gns Ascot October Sales. *G. Harwood.*

EL PRADO (IRE) 2 gr.c. (Feb 3) Sadler's Wells (USA) 132 – Lady Capulet 119
(USA) 116 (Sir Ivor 135) [1991 6g* 6g* 6.5m2 7m* 7m 8s*]

The combination of very soft ground and a step up to a mile paved the
way for El Prado's very smart and much improved performance in the
Juddmonte Beresford EBF Stakes at the Curragh in October on his final
outing. Until then El Prado had raced only at six to seven furlongs on either
good or good to firm ground and had looked no more than a useful colt,
apparently flattered by his standing as a Group 1 winner but nonetheless
considerably better than his twelfth-of-thirty placing behind Young Senor in
the Tattersalls Tiffany Highflyer Stakes at Newmarket on his only run away
from the Curragh would suggest. Back on home soil four weeks after his
journey to Newmarket, El Prado gave weight and a handsome beating to nine
rivals including four—Political Fact, Governor's Imp, the eventual runner-up
Colorific, and Mekong—with useful form, being waited with nearer to the
leaders than usual before challenging between Governor's Imp and Sylvan

National Stakes, the Curragh—
a workmanlike win for El Prado over Nordic Brave (blinkers),
Mekong and Safety Tactic (noseband)

Sabre two furlongs out (causing the stewards to hold an inquiry) and coming clear from the furlong-pole to win by two and a half lengths.

El Prado travelled to Newmarket having won three of his four races. He'd run out a comfortable winner of an ordinary maiden on his debut back in June and then reappeared quickly to take the John J. Long Memorial Stakes over the same course and distance by a length and a half from Leading Time. El Prado, who still looked short of peak fitness, almost forfeited the race through inexperience, losing his position after joining the leaders at halfway before running on gamely despite looking around and drifting markedly right to lead close home. All things considered El Prado seemed certain to progress again but he didn't make the anticipated significant improvement in either of

Juddmonte EBF Beresford Stakes, the Curragh—
El Prado stays on too strongly for the British challengers Colorific and Governor's Imp

Mr R. E. Sangster's "El Prado"

his next two races, the EBF Anglesey Stakes or the seven-furlong National Stakes, most likely on account of the good to firm ground in both instances. His half-length victory over Nordic Brief and three others in a particularly substandard running of the National Stakes, in which he came from last to first with a sustained run, took his earnings beyond IR £120,000, a figure which was increased by £10,000 (as a consequence of the bonus scheme operated by Tattersalls) despite his finishing out of the prize money at Newmarket. El Prado's running there can be ignored; wearing a tongue strap, he was soon niggled along in the main bunch of runners on the stand side but met trouble when trying to improve his position two furlongs out and was unable to put in a challenge. Not for the first time El Prado raced with his head slightly high. His finishing efforts are genuine enough though, and it seems he's no more than a difficult ride who was handled capably by Piggott in all his races in Ireland.

El Prado (IRE) (gr.c. Feb 3, 1989)	Sadler's Wells (USA) (b 1981)	Northern Dancer (b 1961)	Nearctic Natalma
		Fairy Bridge (b 1975)	Bold Reason Special
	Lady Capulet (USA) (ro 1974)	Sir Ivor (b 1965)	Sir Gaylord Attica
		Cap And Bells (gr 1958)	Tom Fool Ghazni

At 330,000 guineas, the strong, lengthy El Prado was one of ten by Sadler's Wells sold for 300,000 guineas or more at the European yearling sales in 1990. His dam Lady Capulet achieved the extremely rare feat of winning a classic (the Irish One Thousand Guineas) on her debut. She never realized the promise of that performance, getting touched off by Orchestration in the Coronation Stakes before ending her brief career on the racecourse well beaten in the ten-furlong Pretty Polly Stakes on possibly unsuitably firm ground. Lady Capulet should have stayed a mile and a quarter; her sire Sir Ivor won the Derby and ran second in the Arc and is a well-established influence for stamina, while her dam Cap And Bells, a minor winner who finished second in the six-furlong Arlington Lassie Stakes (now a Grade 3 event) as a two-year-old, is a full sister to the Preakness third Dunce. Cap And Bells is also closely related to the unbeaten six- to eight-and-a-half-furlong winner Drone, who gained recognition here in the 'eighties as the sire of the King's Stand winner Sayf El Arab. Cap And Bells has produced four winners besides Lady Capulet, notably her full brother Sir Wimborne, who 'won' all three races as a two-year-old (he was awarded the Royal Lodge Stakes on a disqualification), and the minor six-furlong winner Turban, better known as the dam of the Cherry Hinton winner Turkish Treasure (by Sir Ivor) and the grandam of the useful sprinter Magic Mirror. Lady Capulet has bred only one other winner from six foals of racing age, namely the high-class mile to mile-and-a-quarter performer Entitled; her seventh foal, a full brother to El Prado, was sold for 190,000 guineas at the Highflyer Sale. *M. V. O'Brien, Ireland.*

EL RABAB (USA) 2 br.f. (Feb 6) Roberto (USA) 131 – Brave Raj (USA) (Rajab (USA)) [1991 6m⁵ 8.1g* 8.1d³] $375,000Y: sturdy, attractive filly: good walker and mover: first foal: dam won Breeders' Cup Juvenile Fillies: modest form: virtually pulled up after being struck into behind on debut in June: weak 5/1-shot, won 15-runner maiden at Haydock in September, quickening clear in very good style: looking really well, respectable third of 7 to Lobinda in minor event there following month: may stay 1¼m. *H. Thomson Jones.*   **70**

ELSA 2 gr.f. (Apr 6) Green Ruby (USA) 104 – Classey (Dubassoff (USA)) [1991 6.1g 6.1m 7m 8f] leggy, sparely-made filly: first reported foal: dam ran once on flat and showed a little ability over hurdles: poor maiden: has run in seller: stays 1m. *R. J. Holder.*   **31**

EL SHADDAI 3 br.c. Green Ruby (USA) 104 – Miss Serlby 65 (Runnett 125) [1990 5g 6m⁶ 5f 5m 1991 8m 8m] neat colt: has a quick action: poor maiden: well beaten in claiming handicap in October: looked difficult ride when visored. *M. O'Neill.*   **—**

ELSHARH (IRE) 2 br.c. (Mar 12) Sure Blade (USA) 130 – Urjwan (USA) 98 (Seattle Slew (USA)) [1991 7.5f 7f⁶ 8f 8.2m 8m] smallish, close-coupled colt: first foal: dam 1m winner from 2 starts, is out of Kentucky Oaks winner White Star Line: plating-class maiden: one paced, and will be suited by a thorough test of stamina: sold 2,300 gns Doncaster November Sales. *H. Thomson Jones.*   **54**

EL TARANDA 2 ch.f. (Mar 31) Ela-Mana-Mou 132 – Bustara 92 (Busted 134) [1991 8s⁵] second foal: half-sister to 3-y-o Young Buster (by Teenoso), very smart 11.1f and 1½m winner: dam 2-y-o 6f winner stayed 10.2f, is daughter of Romara: 11/1, over 8 lengths fifth of 10 to Jasoorah in maiden at Yarmouth in October, one pace final 2f: should improve, particularly over middle distances. *G. Wragg.*   **— p**

ELTON LEDGER (IRE) 2 b.c. (Apr 8) Cyrano de Bergerac 120 – Princess of Nashua (Crowned Prince (USA) 128) [1991 5m³ 5m² 6g² 5g⁴ 6g 6f² 6g* 6m² 6m 6g] 40,000Y: useful-looking colt: has scope: fifth living foal: half-brother to 1990 2-y-o It's All Academic (by Mazaad) and 2 other winners: dam unraced granddaughter of high-class filly Victoria Cross: fair performer: made all in maiden at Haydock in August: looked really well when very good ninth of 25 to Casteddu in Racecall Gold Trophy at Redcar final start: stays 6f: yet to race on a soft surface: tends to hang: sold 14,500 gns Ascot November Sales. *J. Berry.*   **83**

ELUSIVE SPIRIT 3 ch.f. Absalom 128 – Sister Jinks 88 (Irish Love 117) [1990 5s³ 6g 7.5d 8m⁴ 8.2m 1991 12s⁶ a12g⁵ 15g⁴] leggy, light-framed filly: has a roundish action: plater: gives impression stays 15f: acts on good to firm ground: sold 1,500 gns Newmarket July Sales. *Dr J. D. Scargill.*   **27**

ELVETT BRIDGE (IRE) 3 b.g. Sallust 134 – Mamie's Joy (Prince Tenderfoot (USA) 126) [1990 NR 1991 8f⁵ 9m 8f³ 8.3f 8m⁴ 8m] IR 3,400Y: workmanlike gelding: first foal: dam lightly raced in Ireland: easily best efforts when in frame in maidens: **— §**

stays 1m: very reluctant to enter stalls first start, to come out of them on second: trained until after then by D. Topley. *D. R. Franks.*

EL VOLADOR   4 br.c. Beldale Flutter (USA) 130 – Pharjoy (FR) 85 (Pharly (FR)   **61**
130) [1990 10g 8f* 8f³ 10d⁴ 8m⁵ 10g 10f 1991 a10g 8s 9m⁵ 10g 10g² 10.1d a10g a7g*]
medium-sized colt: poor mover: quite modest handicapper: off course 4½ months
after selling event (claimed out of M. Channon's stable £6,311) sixth start: returned
to form when winning at Lingfield in December: effective at 7f to 1¼m: acts on firm
and dead ground: sold 2,400 gns Ascot October Sales. *R. J. O'Sullivan.*

ELWAZIR (USA)   2 b. or br.c. (Apr 6) The Minstrel (CAN) 135 – Romeo's Coqu-   **— p**
ette (USA) (Gallant Romeo (USA)) [1991 6g] $115,000Y: compact colt: half-brother
to several winners, including 1989 2-y-o 5f winner Green's Sisley (by Dr Carter) and
Billy Sue's Rib (by Al Hattab), stakes winner at up to 9f: dam, winner at up to 7f, is
half-sister to My Bupers, dam of champion sprinter My Juliet (dam of Stella Madrid)
and Lyphard's Special: 25/1 from 12/1, very green and better for race, slowly away
when towards rear in large-field Newbury maiden in October, not knocked about
once held: should improve. *P. T. Walwyn.*

EL YASAF (IRE)   3 b.c. Sayf El Arab (USA) 127 – Winsong Melody (Music   **89**
Maestro 119) [1990 5g⁵ 5g* 5m 1991 5m⁴ 5d* 5m 5d* 5d 5g 6f 5m⁶ 5m⁵ 5.2g]
sturdy, good-quartered colt: fairly useful handicapper: often stiff tasks after winning
at Ayr in April and Kempton in May: ran fairly well penultimate start, moderately on
final one: behind in Swedish Group 3 event when tried over 6f: goes well on a soft
surface. *Mrs L. Stubbs.*

ELYSIAN SPRITE   2 b.c. (Apr 4) Petorius 117 – Pleasure Island 57 (Dalsaan   **45**
125) [1991 5g 5g 6.1m³ a6g³ a7g 6.1g⁴ 7f 6m] 9,200F, 10,000Y: sturdy colt: second
foal: dam 7.5f winner: poor maiden: best form at 6f: often visored: sold 2,000 gns
Newmarket Autumn Sales. *N. A. Graham.*

EMALLEN (IRE)   3 b.g. Prince Regent (FR) 129 – Peperonia (Prince Taj 123)   **33**
[1990 7m⁶ 7m 6g 8.2g 8m 1991 12.5m 13.1f² 14f⁶ 16.2g 11.5m a14g 17.2g] robust
gelding: good walker: staying-on second in handicap at Bath, only form: should stay
further than 13f (no chance at 2m+): acts on firm going. *D. A. Wilson.*

EMAURA   2 ch.f. (Apr 29) Dominion 123 – Klaire 85 (Klairon 131) [1991 5m 5g]   **—**
9,200Y: leggy filly: half-sister to several winners, including smart sprinter Young
Hal (by Young Generation) and 1989 2-y-o 5f winner Norton Challenger (by
Absalom), now useful at up to 7f: dam 2-y-o 7f winner, is half-sister to high-class
stayer Proverb: soundly beaten in autumn maidens at Lingfield (swerved left out of
stalls) and Folkestone. *Miss B. Sanders.*

EMBLAZONRY   2 br.c. (Apr 4) Shareef Dancer (USA) 135 – Embla 121   **—**
(Dominion 123) [1991 6f] compact colt: second foal: brother to French 3-y-o 9f (stays
12.5f) winner Nordic Myth: dam 6f (at 2 yrs) and 1m winner is out of sister to Blue
Cashmere: weak 16/1-shot and blinkered, well beaten in maiden at Carlisle in May:
sold 1,000 gns Newmarket July Sales. *J. W. Watts.*

EMBLEY PARK (IRE)   2 b.g. (May 5) Fools Holme (USA) – Floating Petal 90   **—**
(Wollow 132) [1991 7f 7g] 7,200Y: leggy, unfurnished gelding: moderate mover: fifth
foal: half-brother to 7f winner Sockem (by Nordico): dam won over 1m at 4 yrs in
Ireland: well beaten in claimer and maiden at Salisbury in autumn. *R. Hannon.*

EMDEO   3 b.c. Starch Reduced 112 – Lana's Secret 79 (Most Secret 119) [1990 6m   **—**
6d 1991 8.5f 8.5f⁵ 7f⁵ a8g] strong, good-topped colt: no worthwhile form in maidens:
sweating third start. *R. Hollinshead.*

EMERALD EARS   2 ch.f. (Apr 5) Dublin Lad 116 – Impish Ears 65 (Import 127)   **59**
[1991 7.5f 8.3g² 7m⁶ 7m] 620Y: small, rather sparely-made filly: sixth foal: half-
sister to several poor animals, one a temperamental sprint plater: dam stayed 7f:
plating-class maiden: runner-up, making most, at Hamilton: below form afterwards:
better suited by 1m than 7f: may prove best with some give in ground. *R. M. Whitaker.*

EMERALD RULER   4 b.g. Tender King 123 – Blue Gulf 68 (Gay Fandango   **—**
(USA) 132) [1990 7m⁵ 7g 7d⁴ 7g³ 7f 7s³ 8.5d³ 1991 12m⁶ 10.8m⁴] workmanlike
ex-Irish gelding: half-brother to useful sprinter Ginny Binny (by Ahonoora): dam,
10.2f winner, is half-sister to very useful 5f performer Blue Persian: quite modest
maiden: well beaten in 1991: stays 8.5f: seems best with some give in ground. *F. Jordan.*

EMERALD VENTURE   4 b.g. Seclude (USA) – No Time For Tears (Grange   **—**
Melody) [1990 NR 1991 16.2g] leggy gelding: first foal: dam poor Irish maiden
jumper: won NH Flat race at Southwell in February: soundly beaten in Beverley
maiden in April, only run on flat. *T. H. Caldwell.*

EMERITUS 4 b.g. Niniski (USA) 125 – Her Grace 101 (Great Nephew 126) [1990 —
15.3m² 16.2d* 1991 18s 17m 16m 16m⁵ 17.9f] workmanlike gelding: quite modest
performer at 3 yrs (trained by P. Cole): little form in 1991 (tried blinkered): looked
out-and-out stayer: acted on good to firm ground and dead: winning hurdler: dead.
W. Bentley.

EMILIA ROMAGNA (USA) 3 b.f. Forli (ARG) – Pailleron (USA) (Majestic 93
Light (USA)) [1990 7m² 6g* 1991 8g* 8m⁶ 8m⁴ 8g 10s⁵] rather leggy, close-coupled
filly: moderate mover: won handicap at York in May, quickening in good style from
towards rear: returned to form when fifth to Elfaslah in listed event at the Curragh:
stays 1¼m: seems best with give in the ground: sweating penultimate start. *B. W.
Hills.*

EMMA VICTORIA 3 b.f. Dominion 123 – Gwiffina 87 (Welsh Saint 126) [1990 —
NR 1991 10m 7g 10.2g 8.2g³ 10.5m⁵ 10f 10.5d 11d] leggy filly: has a round action:
second foal: half-sister to 4-y-o 7f winner Creselly (by Superlative): dam 2-y-o 6f
winner stayed 7f, didn't train on: tailed off, including in amateur events and sellers:
wears bandages. *T. Kersey.*

EMPEEKA (USA) 2 b.c. (May 1) At The Threshold (USA) – Laughing Ruler 76
(USA) (Iron Ruler (USA)) [1991 a6g a6g 7g 7f³ 6g a7g² a7g* a7g²] $14,000Y: sturdy
colt: half-brother to several winners, one placed in minor stakes: dam won once
from 9 starts, at 5f at 2 yrs: sire, Grade 1 winner, stayed 1¼m: former plater: well
backed when winning late-year maiden at Southwell: blocked in for much of straight
when creditable second to Stylish Gentleman in nursery there final outing: will
probably be better suited by 1m: hooded last 4 starts: usually claimer ridden:
retained 2,000 gns Newmarket Autumn Sales. *W. A. O'Gorman.*

EMPEROR ALEXANDER (IRE) 3 b.c. Tender King 123 – Persian Apple 69
(USA) (No Robbery) [1990 NR 1991 10.1m³ 10.2g⁵ a12g⁵ 10g* 11d²] IR 32,000Y:
lengthy, rather unfurnished colt: good walker: half-brother to several winners here
and abroad, including smart 6f and 1¼m winner Sarania (by Sassafras) and dam of
Pennine Walk: dam sprint winner in USA, is out of sister to Arc winner Migoli: first
form leading post in claimer at Goodwood in October: good second in similar event
(claimed to join J. Hellens' stable £12,300) at Redcar: should stay 1½m. *Lord
Huntingdon.*

EMPEROR CHANG (USA) 4 b.g. Wavering Monarch (USA) – Movin Mitzi 57
(USA) (L'Heureux (USA)) [1990 10g 10m⁵ 8d 9f³ 12g* 12m² 12g 12.3g⁴ 12f 12g 12m
1991 12.3d 12f 10.6g 8.3m 10m 10.5g⁴ 10.5d] compact ex-Irish gelding: plating-class
performer at best nowadays: best form at 1½m: acts on good to firm ground: below
form when blinkered. *B. A. McMahon.*

EMPEROR FOUNTAIN 4 b.c. Chief Singer 131 – Set Sail 64 (Alpenkonig 112
(GER)) [1990 10m³ 10m⁴ 10m* 10.5m* 10m 11d⁴ 12m 1991 9m² 12g⁵ 10m⁵ 10d³]
workmanlike colt: moderate mover: very useful performer: best efforts at 4 yrs
when placed at Newmarket in Earl of Sefton Stakes in April and listed event in
November (carrying plenty of condition on first run for over 5 months, creditable
never-nearer third of 5 to Mohican Girl): effective at 9f to 11f: yet to race on
extremes of going: effective held up or ridden from front: has joined Mrs F. Walwyn.
J. A. R. Toller.

EMSBOY 3 b.g. Lidhame 109 – Fille de Phaeton (Sun Prince 128) [1990 6g 6d 5v⁵ —
6d a7g 1991 8.1s] small, sparely-made gelding: poor maiden: little chance in October
claimer, only start in 1991: bred to stay 1m: blinkered fourth start. *P. D. Cundell.*

EN ATTENDANT (FR) 3 ch.g. Bairn (USA) 126 – Vizenia (Vitiges (FR) 132) 82
[1990 NR 1991 7m⁵ 10.1s³ 10.1g³ 8g* 6g⁴ 7.6m 7d⁶ 10g⁵ 7m³ 7m* 7d⁵] 180,000
francs (approx £16,666) Y: useful-looking gelding: second foal: dam, lightly-raced
French maiden, is granddaughter of Bella Paola: won maiden (swishing tail) at
Edinburgh in June and moderately-run minor event at Leicester in October: best at
7f/1m: acts on good to firm and soft ground: tends to hang, and is a difficult ride:
gelded after final start. *B. Hanbury.*

ENAYA 2 br.f. (Mar 22) Caerleon (USA) 132 – Ardassine (Ahonoora 122) [1991 99 p
6s* 7m²] lengthy, useful-looking filly: has scope: third foal: dam 1½m winner in
Ireland from family of Slip Anchor: won 17-runner maiden at Kempton in September
in good style, making all and clear from 2f out: stayed on well when length second of
8 to Rose Indien in minor event at Newmarket 11 days later: likely to stay middle
distances: will improve again, and win another race or two. *R. W. Armstrong.*

ENCHANTED FLYER 4 b.c. Doulab (USA) 115 – Enchanted 116 (Song 132) —
[1990 8.5g⁵ 7m 10m⁵ 5m 10f⁵ 1991 9m 10g 12.2g] angular, close-coupled colt:
moderate walker: half-brother to several winners, notably smart miler Lofty (by

The Queen's "Enharmonic"

High Top) and quite useful middle-distance performer Woodpecker (by Touching Wood): dam sprinter at 2 yrs: poor ex-Irish maiden: little worthwhile form here: may prove ideally suited by 1¼m: often blinkered: trained at 3 yrs by D. Weld. *T. W. Donnelly.*

ENCHANTING HABIT   4 b.g. Enchantment 115 – Miss Worth 73 (Streak 119)   — [1990 8f 8g⁴ 8.2g 8g³ 7g² a8g 7m⁵ 7g 8g 1991 8m 10m 10m⁵ 12g] medium-sized gelding: poor maiden: stays 1¼m: acts on any going: has been tried blinkered: has run well when visored. *C. A. Horgan.*

ENCORE UNE FOIS (IRE)   2 b.f. (Jan 26) Shirley Heights 130 – Guest   **63** Performer 117 (Be My Guest (USA) 126) [1991 8.1g³ 8g³] lengthy filly: first foal: dam 7f winner, is out of half-sister to smart 1982 2-y-o Polished Silver: quite modest maiden: sweating and slowly away when third at Chepstow and Bath: will be suited by 1¼m: may do better. *P. W. Chapple-Hyam.*

ENDOLI (USA)   4 b.c. Assert 134 – Grabelst (USA) (Graustark) [1990 NR 1991 **101** 14.6s 10d* 14g* 14m⁵ 12m³ 12g 12g² 13.9g⁵ 12s⁵ 12m³ 16g²] strong, lengthy colt: good mover: useful handicapper: 8-length winner at Brighton (minor apprentice race) and Sandown (drifted right) in April: good second to Hawait Al Barr in listed event at Newmarket in the autumn final start: effective at 1½m and sure to stay further than 2m: acts on good to firm and soft ground: consistent: should do well at 5 yrs. *C. E. Brittain.*

ENDURING   3 b.f. Sadler's Wells (USA) 132 – Arrangement 72 (Floribunda 136)   — [1990 NR 1991 10m 10.5g] 110,000Y: smallish, leggy, lightly-made filly: closely related to 1990 3-y-o Flower Arrangement (by Lomond) and half-sister to 4 winners, notably Bold Arrangement (by Persian Bold), high class at up to 1¼m: dam stayed 7f: well beaten in maidens at Sandown and Haydock in the summer. *M. R. Stoute.*

ENERGIC (IRE) 2 b.g. (Apr 3) Burslem 123 – Advocada (FR) (Advocator) [1991 **51**
5s⁵ 5g 6f 5m 7.5f³ 7m 8m⁶] IR 6,400F, 5,500Y: sparely-made gelding: moderate
mover: brother to fair 1987 2-y-o 5f winner Bajan Bess and half-brother to a winner
in Holland: dam ran once at 3 yrs in Ireland: plating-class maiden: will be suited by
1m +: acts on firm ground: blinkered fourth outing: joined C. Allen. *Lord John
FitzGerald.*

ENFANT DU PARADIS (IRE) 3 b.f. Shernazar 131 – Fille de L'Orne (FR) **52**
(Jim French (USA)) [1990 NR 1991 11m 9m⁵ 10m⁶ 14.6g⁴ 15s* 13d 15.8f⁶ 14.6m²
14.6m³ 16.1m 16.9m⁴ 15.1g 13.8m² 13.6d] IR 28,000F, 2,100Y: small, angular,
sparely-made filly: half-sister to 4 minor winners abroad: dam unraced half-sister to
Val de L'Orne: won selling handicap (no bid) at Edinburgh in July: ran poorly in
handicap (sweating) final start: stays well: acts on good to firm and soft going. *P. D.
Evans.*

ENGLISH RAJ (USA) 3 ch.g. Raja Baba (USA) – Salem Ho (USA) (Salem —
(USA)) [1990 7g 7g 1991 11.5g] angular, deep-girthed gelding: always behind in a
minor event, maiden and claimer. *D. R. C. Elsworth.*

ENHARMONIC (USA) 4 ch.c. Diesis 133 – Contralto 100 (Busted 134) [1990 **111**
7m* 7.6f⁵ 7m* 7d³ 1991 8.5f⁴ 7g 8g* 8g* 8g⁴] angular, good-topped colt: very
useful performer: successful in Group 3 events in August at Cologne and Baden-
Baden (beat Message Pad comfortably by ¾ length): below form in Group 2 event at
Cologne final start: stays 8.5f: yet to race on soft going, acts on any other:
headstrong, best held up. *Lord Huntingdon.*

ENKINDLE 4 b.f. Relkino 131 – Nelion 102 (Grey Sovereign 128§) [1990 NR 1991 **39**
12.2m⁵ 10.2m 11f⁵ a12g 17.9f⁵ 16.2f³ 16m 18.1m³] leggy, close-coupled filly:
half-sister to several winners here and abroad, notably high-class stayer Recupere
(by Reliance II): dam won over 6f and 1m at 2 yrs: poor handicapper: stays very well:
acts on firm ground. *C. W. C. Elsey.*

ENQELAAB (USA) 3 b.c. Chief's Crown (USA) – Affirmatively (USA) —
(Affirmed (USA)) [1990 7m⁴ 7m³ 8g³ 1991 11.5m⁵] strong, close-coupled colt:
modest maiden: moderate fifth in handicap at Sandown in May: should stay further:
sold 22,000 gns Newmarket Autumn Sales. *M. R. Stoute.*

ENSHARP (USA) 5 b.g. Sharpen Up 127 – Lulworth Cove 114 (Averof 123) **60**
[1990 7f⁶ 7f³ 8h 6f³ 6f⁶ 6f² a7g* 6g a8g⁵ 1991 a7g⁶ a6g³ a7g* a6g⁴ a7g³ 7d a7g 7m
7.5f a6g a8g a7g] sturdy, good-bodied, attractive gelding: carries plenty of condition:
has long stride: modest performer at best: won handicap at Southwell in February:
lost his form after: stays 7f: acts on any going: tried blinkered. *J. P. Leigh.*

ENTERPRISE LADY (FR) 4 ch.f. Gorytus (USA) 132 – Calder Hall (Grundy **45**
137) [1990 8g⁴ 10m⁶ 8.3m* 8.3g* 8m² 8g 8.2s² 10d² 1991 11.7g 7g³ 10.1d 8.3g 8f
8.3m] leggy, lengthy filly: poor performer: effective at 7f to 1¼m: acts on any going:
below form when blinkered penultimate start: unreliable. *R. J. Hodges.*

ENTHRAL (IRE) 2 ch.f. (Apr 8) Ahonoora 122 – Captive Island 116 (Northfields **49**
(USA)) [1991 5f² 6.1m⁴ 5m] sparely-made filly: good mover: second foal: half-sister
to French 3-y-o 11f winner Kernia (by Raise A Cup): dam French 6f and 1m winner:
plating-class maiden: in frame at Doncaster (on toes, very green) in May and
Nottingham (kept on) in August: ran poorly at Wolverhampton later in month: will
stay 7f. *B. W. Hills.*

ENTITLEMENT (IRE) 2 gr.c. (Apr 26) Dara Monarch 128 – Danielle Delight —
(Song 132) [1991 5m 6m 6m 6.1m 6.1m] IR 3,700F, 1,700Y: small, sparely-made colt:
fifth foal: half-brother to 1990 2-y-o 5f seller winner Travelling Blues (by Ballad
Rock), Irish 1½m winner Vision's Pride (by Vision), a winner in USA and one over
hurdles: dam (showed some ability in USA) is sister to dam of Prince Sabo: little
promise in varied company, including selling: sold 1,600 gns Doncaster November
Sales. *R. Hollinshead.*

ENVIRONMENT FRIEND 3 gr.c. Cozzene (USA) – Water Woo (USA) **128**
102 (Tom Rolfe) [1990 7g⁶ 7m* 1991 8g³ 8m⁵ 10.5g* 12f 10d* 10.4g⁵ 10d² 10m]
This indisputably high-class colt won two of the most prestigious races
in the Calendar yet barely figured amongst the also rans in another three.
Environment Friend, but no friend to most students of the form-book. His
wins were surprises if the starting prices are anything to go by; 20/1 in the
William Hill Dante Stakes at York and 28/1 in the Coral-Eclipse Stakes at
Sandown. The Dante Stakes, the most valuable Derby trial, was a fascinating
renewal with no great stretch of the imagination required to see most of the
eight runners as legitimate Derby contenders, if not winners. Environment

Friend, however, didn't really come into either category. His win in a New-market maiden race the previous October had marked him out as a useful prospect at least but his first two runs in 1991, in the Easter Stakes at Kempton and the Craven at Newmarket, hadn't suggested much better than that, although he'd looked likely to be well suited by a step up in distance. Contrastingly, 1990's unbeaten staying two-year-old Peter Davies (favourite on his reappearance), the Thresher Classic Trial winner Hailsham, and runaway White Rose Stakes winner Perpendicular had all shown pattern-class form already. Environment Friend's pedigree was unfamiliar, certainly when compared to the regally-bred Habaayib and Bravefoot, and what was known about it didn't shout middle distances. And those unimpressed by Environment Friend's credentials on paper were most unlikely to be won over by a sight of him in the flesh; a close-coupled individual, he looked up to nearly all his rivals in the preliminaries. None of which prevented Environment Friend from brushing them all aside with ease in the race. Held up last of eight as Peter Davies set a strong pace, Environment Friend made smooth headway on the outside over three furlongs out, was shaken up to lead approaching the final furlong and, given a couple of cracks, forged clear. The final winning margin of five lengths (over Hailsham and Perpendicular) was the greatest for fourteen years.

Coincidentally, the 1977 Dante winner Lucky Sovereign was also the last 20/1 winner of the race and his progress through the season after York turned out to be similar to that of Environment Friend's—distinctly chequered. Both went to the Derby with place prospects at least, Lucky Sovereign to be beaten twenty-six lengths and Environment Friend over forty. Environment Friend had worked disappointingly on reportedly firm ground a week before Epsom and on similar going in the race itself he was soon struggling in arrears. However, as with Lucky Sovereign (a length-and-a-half second to The Minstrel in the Irish Derby), Environment Friend rebutted his Derby showing in astounding fashion on his next start. The field for the Eclipse looked a particularly strong one at the time. Impressive Brigadier Gerard Stakes and Prince of Wales's Stakes winner Stagecraft headed the betting, followed by the Derby runner-up Marju, who'd won the St James's Palace in the interim; Trusthouse Forte Mile and Hanson Coronation Cup winner In The Groove; the d'Ispahan winner Sanglamore, who had a pacemaker in Green's Ferneley; and that pattern-race journeyman Terimon. Imagine the surprise therefore when, Stagecraft having easily taken up the

William Hill Dante Stakes, York—
outsider Environment Friend beats Hailsham (right) and Perpendicular

Coral-Eclipse Stakes, Sandown—Environment Friend belies his odds again; a 28/1-shot, he has a head to spare over the favourite Stagecraft

running two furlongs out, Environment Friend came through on the outside, first of all looking the one most likely to get second then, Stagecraft quickening approaching the furlong marker, Environment Friend not only stayed with him but got to the front himself about seventy-five yards from home and held on by a head as Stagecraft rallied. The pair drew seven lengths clear of Sanglamore. Back in 1977, we suggested that Lucky Sovereign's inconsistency might well have been rooted in an unsatisfactory temperament but we would not ascribe the same failing to Environment Friend. His was certainly a tremendously resolute display in the Eclipse. How then are we to explain Environment Friend's subsequent poor efforts in the Juddmonte International at York and Champion Stakes at Newmarket? He was one of many which disappointed on the heavily watered and much criticised ground at York but, given his victories held up in two strongly-run races, it's likely that the very different tactical contest at York was not at all in his favour. His trainer reported that, having been 'on the go throughout the season' (he never had a break of more than seven weeks between races), Environment Friend returned 'with a mucky throat' after the Champion Stakes. He isn't, of course, the only horse to have flopped on his final start. Plausible individual explanations, then, amounting to a disconcerting whole. But before getting bogged down in complicated post-mortems, let's not forget Environment Friend's second in the Meadow Mints Irish Champion Stakes at Leopardstown in September. In celebrating Suave Dancer's consummate performance, it is easy to overlook the credit due to those behind him, and this was a good effort by Environment Friend. He beat Stagecraft two lengths on terms 2 lb worse than in the Eclipse, pushed along over three furlongs out then taken to the centre of the course off the turn into the straight (as a result of connections' inspection of the track beforehand) and staying on well, beaten four lengths.

Environment Friend (GB) (gr.c. 1988)	Cozzene (USA) (gr 1980)	Caro (gr 1967)	Fortino II
			Chambord
		Ride The Trails (b 1971)	Prince John
			Wildwook
	Water Woo (USA) (ch 1976)	Tom Rolfe (b 1962)	Ribot
			Pocahontas II
		Waterloo (ch 1969)	Bold Lad
			Lakewoods

Environment Friend's sire Cozzene retired at the peak of his racing career, the last of his twenty-four starts being his triumph over a Breeders'

Cup Mile field that included European challengers Palace Music, Shadeed, Rousillon, Never So Bold and Chapel Cottage. That five-year-old season also included wins under top weight in a six-furlong allowance race and graded handicaps over nine furlongs and eight and a half. Unraced at two and successful only in maiden and allowance company as a three-year-old, Cozzene finished third in the inaugural Breeders' Cup Mile but had still not won a graded race by the end of his four-year-old season. Although Cozzene's sire Caro was a particularly successful stallion himself, the same is far from true of his sons. Cozzene's early runners did not suggest that he'd be up-setting the trend and his 1990 yearlings sold for an average of 24,640 dollars which barely outstripped his covering fee. How little appeal he had is further illustrated by Water Woo's sale carrying Environment Friend for 45,000 dollars at the Keeneland November Sales and by Environment Friend's having to be bought back for 23,000 guineas at the Highflyer. And there's plenty to like about the dam's side of this pedigree, most notably her dam the Cheveley Park and One Thousand Guineas winner Waterloo. Waterloo was sold for reportedly well over £100,000 at the end of her three-year-old career to go to the United States where she foaled the good 1985 J O Tobin two-year-old Water Cay and several others capable of at least fairly useful form, including Water Woo. Trained by Boutin, Water Woo won her only race at two years, a valuable six-furlong newcomers' race at Chantilly, but failed to live up to that considerable promise by a long chalk in three runs the following year when she wasn't seen out until mid-September. Water Woo's early years at stud didn't promise a great deal; they produced two minor winners, by Buckfinder (in North America) and Coastal (in Italy). Water Woo was barren to Chief Singer in 1989 and threw a colt by Bustino in 1990.

Environment Friend remains in training and will doubtless be campaigned in similarly fighting fashion. It was at the owner's insistence that Environment Friend lined up in the Dante Stakes and not the Glasgow Graduation Stakes the following day. Another attempt at a mile and a half is, we're told, very much on the agenda for 1992 and, despite his pedigree, Environment Friend's style of running suggests that that is an option worth pursuing. We know that he is game in the finish and best held up (he helped make the running in the Craven) but such a see-saw season as that of 1991 obviously doesn't help us, or the racing public, towards a complete understanding of the horse. His best efforts are all on an easy surface but, as we've intimated already, the reasons behind his inconsistency may well be more complicated. *J. R. Fanshawe.*

EPERVIER BLEU 4 b.c. Saint Cyrien (FR) 128 – Equadif (FR) (Abdos **129** 134) [1990 10s* 10f* 10.5s* 10.5g* 12m² 12m* 12g² 1991 12s? 12m*]
Epervier Bleu's season was over by the end of June, just when it seemed to be gathering pace with his victory in the Grand Prix de Saint-Cloud. Ambitious objectives had been announced for the 1990 Ciga Prix de l'Arc de Triomphe runner-up earlier in the year, including the King George VI and Queen Elizabeth Diamond Stakes, the Arc and the Breeders' Cup. But Ascot went by without him and in September, in the same week that the Arc trials were due to be run at Longchamp, at a time when the horse was generally ante-post second favourite to Generous, the owner's son announced crypti-

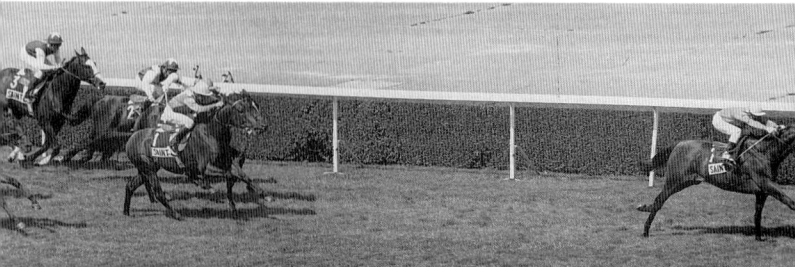

Grand Prix de Saint-Cloud—a convincing performance from Epervier Bleu, but he's not seen out again

M D. Wildenstein's "Epervier Bleu" (D. Boeuf)

cally: 'Now we know that Pistolet Bleu is coming back to his best, we have no need to run Epervier Bleu in the Arc. He has done all that we wanted of him this season and we won't need his presence as Pistolet Bleu will be backed up by Arcangues. He will soon be off to the fields of Normandy for a break but will be back in training next year.' Let's hope that he will.

Arguably, a fully-fit Epervier Bleu would have been a stronger card to play than Pistolet Bleu, well though the latter acquitted himself on the day. On his strong-finishing three-quarter-length second to Saumarez in the Arc, Epervier Bleu was the best of his generation still in training at the start of 1991. The Grand Prix de Saint-Cloud went just about as far as it could go to confirming his standing. A larger-than-average field of twelve turned out for the race, made up of older horses plus the Derby fifth Hundra. The field had fair strength in depth—the rank outsider Echoes is more than useful, and one of the pacemakers Wayfaring had won a listed race last time—but Epervier Bleu, a promising second to Wajd in the Grand Prix d'Evry earlier in the month on his seasonal reappearance, looked a cut above most of the opposition and started at odds on coupled with his pacemaker Franc Bleu Argent, ahead of Rock Hopper (3/1). Wajd started at 5/1 coupled with the Prix d'Harcourt winner Panoramic and Wayfaring. Epervier Bleu won convincingly, value for slightly more than the official three-length margin. He had little trouble lying up in the race, turned for home in fourth place behind the two pacemakers and Wajd, quickened on a furlong and a half out and was soon well on top. Rock Hopper came through to give chase but found Passing Sale a tough nut to crack for second place and could make no impression on the winner.

Epervier Bleu's win took his total to six from nine starts; his others include those in the Prix Greffulhe, Prix Lupin and Prix Niel as a three-year-old; he has yet to come worse than second, the only other horse to have beaten him being Sanglamore who caught him late on in the Prix du Jockey-Club Lancia. Nothing anywhere near so good as Epervier Bleu has been seen so far in the rest of the Grand Criterium winner Saint Cyrien's stock. The mare who produced him, Equadif, is a minor French middle-distance winner from a well-known, inbred French family. Her only previous foal to race, La Potita (by Dom Pasquini), was placed in the Spanish Oaks and won there. The tabulated pedigree needs extending another generation to reveal the inbreeding—Altagracia is by Djebel (sire of Arbar) out of Pretty Lady, the dam of other good horses besides Abdos, notably the Champion Stakes winner and Arc third Dynamiter.

Epervier Bleu (b.c. 1987)	Saint Cyrien (FR) (b 1980)	Luthier (b or br 1965)	Klairon
			Flute Enchantee
		Sevres (b 1974)	Riverman
			Saratoga
	Equadif (FR) (b 1976)	Abdos (b or br 1959)	Arbar
			Pretty Lady
		Gracilla (b 1963)	Prince Bio
			Altagracia

The strong, deep-bodied Epervier Bleu has had plenty of experience of a wide range of ground conditions in a relatively short career and he seems to act on any. As to his distance, although he possesses a turn of foot he is much better suited by a mile and a half than a mile and a quarter. He is a genuine and most consistent colt. *E. Lellouche, France.*

EQUINOR 4 b.c. Norwick (USA) 120 – Cithern 91 (Canisbay 120) [1990 a10g⁴ a10g² a10g³ a10g⁵ 12f² 12f³ 14g 10m 13.8m* 16.2f 1991 15.8g] workmanlike colt: moderate walker: plating-class handicapper at 3 yrs: burly and tailed off only run on flat in 1991, first for over a year: stays 1¾m: acts on firm going. *R. A. Bennett.* —

EQUITY CARD (IRE) 3 b.g. King of Clubs 124 – Carntino (Bustino 136) [1990 NR 1991 10g 12.3g²] 4,200Y: close-coupled gelding: fourth foal: dam once-raced in Ireland: 50/1 and backward on first run for 5 months, 1½ lengths second of 8, clear, to 5/1-on Duc de Berry in minor event at Wolverhampton in October, held up pulling hard then keeping on no progress with winner: should stay further: should improve again. *G. A. Pritchard-Gordon.* **83 p**

ERDELISTAN (FR) 4 br.c. Lashkari 128 – Eunomia (FR) (Abdos (FR) 134) [1990 10.5d* 12g³ 12m³ 11s* 12g 12v* 1991 10d* 11g* 12g² 10g² 11g5] very smart Italian performer: successful at Milan in listed races in March and May: ran well when beaten ¾ length by Snurge in Group 1 Gran Premio di Milano next start: below form after, in Group 3 contest at Milan final outing: stays 1½m well: acts on any going: trained at 3 yrs mostly by A. de Royer-Dupre. *L. d'Auria, Italy.* **117**

EREVNON 4 b.c. Rainbow Quest (USA) 134 – Embryo (Busted 134) [1990 10m 12.3v³ 14.6d a12g³ a14g* 1991 12s 12.2d6 14.1f² 20g 12g6 a12g] rather unfurnished colt: quite modest handicapper: well beaten final start, first for 5 months: may prove best at 1¾m: acts on firm ground, seems unsuited by soft going: has won for claimer: sold out of C. Brittain's stable 2,600 gns Newmarket Autumn Sales after penultimate start. *J. L. Harris.* **62**

ERGANA 4 b.f. The Wonder (FR) 129 – Eloura (FR) (Top Ville 129) [1990 10s² 12d² 10.5m 1991 10f 10f² 8g5 14.1g 8f 9.7f² 9.7m5] leggy filly: second foal: half-sister to fairly useful French maiden Ersari (by Nishapour), stayed 10.5f: dam 10.5f and 11.5f winner in France: ex-French filly: trained by A. de Royer-Dupre, placed in maidens at Saint-Cloud as 3-y-o: poor handicapper here: stays 1¼m: acts on firm ground. *W. Holden.* **35**

ERGON 2 ch.f. (Mar 5) Stanford 121§ – Heavenly Harmony 47 (Music Boy 124) [1991 a7g] 5,600F, 8,200Y, 3,000 2-y-o: first foal: dam maiden seemed suited by 1m, is daughter of Lingfield Oaks Trial winner Heaven Knows: 33/1, around 18 lengths tenth of 13 in late-year maiden at Southwell. *P. J. Feilden.* —

ERIC'S PET 4 gr.g. Petong 126 – When I Dream (Sparkler 130) [1990 6g 8.2f 7f 8h 6f5 7d 7m 10m³ 8m³ 12h6 10m 8f* 8f5 1991 8f] rangy gelding: plater: stays 1m: best efforts on firm going: below form when blinkered. *M. D. I. Usher.* —

ERIK ODIN 4 b.g. Nordico (USA) – Assurance (FR) (Timmy Lad 130) [1990 a7g² 5f 6f 6g a8g 6d a6g³ a7g a6g² 1991 a6g a6g a6g³ a6g³ a7g a6g* a6g a6g a6g] sturdy, lengthy gelding: poor walker and mover: quite modest handicapper at best: won at Lingfield (first run for over 4 months, bandaged behind) in August: stays 7f and needs further than 5f: inconsistent. *Mrs L. Piggott.* **51**

ERINY (USA) 2 br.g. (Apr 22) Erins Isle 121 – Memorable Girl (USA) (Iron Ruler (USA)) [1991 7g³ 7.5f 7m³ 8m 8.2m 7m] $8,000Y: leggy, close-coupled gelding: **60**

moderate mover: half-brother to 2 minor winners in North America: dam placed 6 times from 18 starts: quite modest maiden: best effort third outing: should stay 1m: gives impression will prove suited by easy ground: blinkered final start. *S. G. Norton.*

ERLEMO 2 b.c. (Apr 16) Mummy's Game 120 – Empress Catherine 73 (Welsh **67** Pageant 132) [1991 7.1s 7d 7m 8s³ 8g 7.6m] 9,200F, 15,000Y: leggy, good-topped colt: fourth foal: brother to 3-y-o 7f and 1½m winner Kirby Opportunity and closely related to 2 winners by Mummy's Pet, including fair 7f and 1m winner Green's Seascape: dam 1½m winner out of sister to Connaught: quite modest form when third of 14 in maiden at Kempton in September: no comparable form, in nurseries subsequently: possibly requires plenty of give in the ground. *C. J. Benstead.*

ERNESTAN 2 ch.c. (Apr 10) Stanford 121§ – Lobela 77 (Lorenzaccio 130) [1991 **96** 5d* 5m* 5m* 6m* 7g⁴] tall, leggy colt: fifth reported foal: half-brother to 3 winners, all at up to 7f, including fair Baton Boy (by Music Boy): dam won at 1m and 1¼m: fairly useful performer: finished strongly after getting outpaced when successful in maiden at Nottingham in April and minor events at Doncaster and Ayr in June: looking very well, won 5-runner Cock of The North Stakes at Haydock in July, despite drifting left: best effort never-nearer fourth of 7 to Dr Devious in Lanson Champagne Vintage Stakes at Goodwood following month: may well stay 1m. *M. H. Easterby.*

ERNIE 3 b.c. Miller's Mate 116 – Bempton 57 (Blakeney 126) [1990 8g 1991 **71** 11.8m⁶ 10m 14.1f² 14.1h* 13.8m³ 17.1m⁵] leggy colt: modest performer: won maiden at Carlisle in September: ran creditably after in claimer at Catterick and handicap (bandaged off-hind) at Pontefract: takes keen hold, but stays 17f: yet to race on soft surface: visored last 4 starts: sold 9,000 gns Newmarket Autumn Sales. *D. Morley.*

ERRIS EXPRESS 6 b.g. Bay Express 132 – Royal Home 69 (Royal Palace 131) **79** d [1990 5f 5g 6f 5m 5g 5m³ 5m³ 6g* 5m* 5m* 6m 5m 6g³ 5m 5d⁶ 6d 1991 a6g³ a5g* a7g⁴ a7g* a6g* a6g² 5m⁵ 6m⁶ 6d 5m⁵ 5m 5m 5.2f⁶] good-bodied, attractive gelding: carries condition: poor mover: fair performer on his day: won claimers at Southwell in February and Lingfield (2) in March: below best after, mulish to post final 2 starts: has won over 7f, but best form at shorter: not at best on very soft going, acts on any other: wears bandages: usually races up with pace: tough: trained first 8 starts by F. Durr. *K. T. Ivory.*

ESBOOAIN (FR) 2 b.c. (Apr 16) Rainbow Quest (USA) 134 – Wind Spring (FR) **76** (Baldric II 131) [1991 7g⁵ 8m⁵] 50,000Y: rather leggy, good-topped colt: half-brother to 5 winners in France, 4 of them in listed company, including 1¼m winner Wind Jet (by Tennyson) and 1m to 1¼m winner Classical Way (by Bellypha), former later successful in USA: dam, 5f winner at 2 yrs, ran 4 times: modest form in minor events at York (well backed, stayed on strongly) and Newbury (favourite, not knocked about when beaten) in September: should stay middle distances. *L. M. Cumani.*

ESCADARO (USA) 2 b.g. (Feb 1) Liloy (FR) 124 – Mlle Chanteuse (USA) (The **—** Minstrel (CAN) 135) [1991 7m] $26,000Y, resold $10,500Y: tall, useful-looking gelding: second foal: half-brother to 1989 French 2-y-o 7f and 9f winner Crinkov (by Procida): dam apparently never ran: ridden by 7-lb claimer, slowly away and soon well behind in maiden at September. *S. G. Norton.*

ESCAPE TALK 4 gr.f. Gabitat 119 – Getaway Girl 63 (Capistrano 120) [1990 7m **29** 7.5f⁴ 9f 8.5d⁴ 8m⁴ 8f⁶ 10.2m⁵ 9m⁶ 9g 7m 9f⁶ 10f³ 12m⁴ 13.8m³ 12g 12f 10m⁴ 10m 10d 1991 8g⁴ 8h³ 9.9m³ 10g³ 14.6g 12.2g 11f³ 8f⁶ 12g 12f] smallish, close-coupled filly: moderate mover: poor handicapper nowadays: effective at 1m, and stays 13.8f: goes well on firm ground, and acts on dead: tried blinkered once: often edgy: has looked a hard ride: trained first 4 starts by Mrs J. Ramsden. *J. Dooler.*

ESPRIT FORT (USA) 2 b.f. (Jun 5) Last Tycoon 131 – Spirit of The Wind (USA) **60** (Little Current (USA)) [1991 6m 6.1d³ a8g² a7g a7g⁴] leggy, quite attractive, rather sparely-made filly: second foal: half-sister to 3-y-o 11f winner North Wind (by Lomond): dam unraced half-sister to Grade 1 1¼m winner Dawn's Curtsey: quite modest form when placed in maidens won by Major's Law at Chester and Sybaritic Sam at Lingfield: ran poorly last 2 starts: suited by 1m. *B. W. Hills.*

ESSAYEFFSEE 2 b.g. (Mar 3) Precocious 126 – Floreal 68 (Formidable (USA) **59** 125) [1991 6g 5g³ 6m⁶ 6m³ 7m³ 7.9g⁵ 7m⁴ 6m 5d] 8,200F, 10,000Y: workmanlike gelding: second foal: closely related to 3-y-o 1¼m winner Chatham Island (by Jupiter Island): dam ran twice at 2 yrs: plating-class maiden: has run well in a seller: stays 1m: acts on good to firm ground: blinkered last 3 starts: usually bandaged behind. *M. H. Easterby.*

ESTRELLE 3 b.f. Claude Monet (USA) 121 – Queensbury Star 76 (Wishing Star — 117) [1990 NR 1991 6.9f 7f 10m] leggy filly: has a round action: fourth foal: half-sister to 1989 2-y-o 6f and 7f winner Beehive Boy and to 7f winner Vuchterbacher (both by Longleat): dam won over 6f at 2 yrs but no form after: tailed off in maiden and sellers in autumn: sold 810 gns Doncaster October Sales. *P. F. Tulk.*

ETERNAL FLAME 3 br.f. Primo Dominie 121 – Cameroun 106 (African Sky **64** 124) [1990 5m⁴ 6d³ 6m³ 1991 7m* 8.5m* a8g⁴ 8.1m² 7.1m 8g] lengthy filly: quite modest form: favourite, successful in claimers at Warwick in May and Epsom in June: well below form in handicaps last 2 starts: stays 8.5f: acts on good to firm ground and dead: sold 2,600 gns Newmarket Autumn Sales. *J. W. Hills.*

ETERNITY STAR (USA) 3 br.c. Majestic Light (USA) – Northern Eternity **121** (USA) 108 (Northern Dancer) [1990 6d* 7d⁴ 8m² 7.5d⁴ a8.5f 6d* 7d⁴ 8m² 7.5d⁴ a8.5f 1991 8s³ 8d* 9d⁵ 9f* 9g³ 9f* 12g⁴] first foal: dam 2-y-o 6f winner also second in Lowther Stakes, is half-sister to good 1980 French 2-y-o 5f and 7f winner Miswaki: useful form in France, trained by F. Boutin at 2 yrs and A. Falourd at 3 yrs: won listed race at Longchamp in June and about 4 lengths fifth of 8 to Tel Quel in Prix Daphnis at Evry in July: much better in USA in second half of season, winning Del Mar Invitational Derby in August and Hollywood Derby in November: narrowly beaten after apparently poor run in Volante Handicap at Santa Anita and good fourth to Miss Alleged in Hollywood Turf Cup (set slow pace): effective at 9f and in slowly-run 1½m: has won on dead ground, and clearly goes well on firm: changed hands after reappearance. *R. Frankel, USA.*

ETHAN FROME (FR) 4 ch.c. Pharly 130 – Festive Lady (Margouillat 133) **104** [1990 9g³ 12g* 12g⁵ 15m² 15g⁵ 15g² 15g² 15g 1991 12g⁶ 14.5s 15.5m⁶ 20g 12g² 12.5g 15g] tall, lengthy colt: useful French performer: ran respectably third and fourth starts in Group 2 event at Longchamp and Gold Cup (bandaged behind, eighth of 12 to Indian Queen, beaten over 10 lengths) at Royal Ascot: below best after, in Prix Kergorlay at Deauville final start: stays 2½m: acts on good to firm ground: effective with or without blinkers. *D. Smaga, France.*

ETINCELLE 2 b.f. (Feb 23) Pharly (FR) 130 – Eastern Command (USA) (Far — Out East (USA)) [1991 7g⁶] small, workmanlike filly: second foal: dam, maiden, should have stayed 1m: 33/1 and bit green, beaten over 8 lengths in 9-runner minor event at Warwick in October, slowly away then keeping on steadily: sold 675 gns Ascot November Sales. *I. A. Balding.*

ETON LAD 4 b.c. Never So Bold 135 – Carolside 108 (Music Maestro 119) [1990 **109** 7m³ 8.2g² 8.5g* 8g⁴ 8.5g* 8m 8g⁵ 9g 1991 10d³ 9m 10g⁴ 8.5f⁵ 10v⁵ 10.4m 8.9g³] sparely-made colt: fluent mover, with a long stride: very useful performer: ran well in Group 3 events second to fourth starts and at York final 2 outings here in John Smith's Magnet Cup (would have finished second to Halkopous but for saddle slipping and unseating rider) and Andy Capp Handicap: effective at 1m to around 1¼m: acts on firm and dead (possibly unsuited by heavy) ground: raced too freely when blinkered once: keen sort, goes very well with forcing tactics: sent to USA and won 9f allowance race at Santa Anita final start. *N. A. Callaghan.*

EUROBLAKE 4 b.g. Roscoe Blake 120 – Pie Eye 88 (Exbury 138) [1990 8f 8.5m⁴ — 8.2f² 8g² 10.6f⁵ 8f⁵ 8g 8g⁶ a8g² 8f² 8f* 8h⁶ 7.5g* 8m 7.5m 8m⁶ 7d² a7g* a7g a83 1991 a7g³ a7g* a8g² a7g² 8f 7m⁶ 8m 8f 8d⁶ a6g³ a6g* a8g* a7g⁶] compact, good-quartered gelding: turns off-fore in: fair handicapper, best form on all-weather nowadays: won at Southwell in February and December: effective at 6f to 1m: has form on firm and dead ground: sometimes takes keen hold: tends to be on toes: has sometimes hung markedly. *T. D. Barron.*

EURO FESTIVAL 2 ch.c. (May 5) Precocious 126 – Quisissanno 76 (Be My **77** Guest (USA) 126) [1991 5m⁴ 6f* 6m⁵ 6f 7g⁶ 7m] 10,500Y: workmanlike colt: fourth foal: half-brother to 1990 2-y-o 7f winner Mulciber (by Head For Heights), Irish 1½m to 1¾m winner Montezuma (by Commanche Run) and a winner in Austria: dam 1½m winner: won maiden at Hamilton in August: didn't progress as anticipated, and looked ungenuine penultimate outing: should stay 7f: blinkered last 2 starts: one to be wary of. *Miss L. C. Siddall.*

EUROFLIGHT 2 b.f. (Feb 20) Natroun (FR) 128 – Bustling Nelly 94 (Bustino **61** 136) [1991 6g⁴ 7m² 7g⁵] small, leggy, plain filly: fourth foal: half-sister to 15f and 2m winner Silk Degrees (by Dunbeath) and 1½m winner Passion And Mirth (by Known Fact): dam middle-distance winner, is out of Cambridgeshire winner Flying Nelly (dam of Further Flight): plating-class maiden: off course 2 months, respectable staying-on fifth of 14 at Redcar in September: will stay well. *B. W. Hills.*

EURO GALAXY 4 ch.g. Crofthall 110 – Patent Pending (Goldhill 125) [1990 7h³ — 7g* 7f² 7m³ 1991 7g] leggy, lengthy, sparely-made gelding: turns fore-feet out:

*Royal Hunt Cup, Ascot—Eurolink The Lad shows a good turn of foot;
second place goes to Operation Wolf (right),
third to Pontenuovo and fourth to Mellottie (spotted cap, behind winner)*

modest handicapper at 3 yrs: bandaged off-hind, well beaten only start in 1991 (June): should prove best at 6f or 7f: acts on hard ground: refused to enter stalls intended reappearance at 3 and 4 yrs. *R. M. Whitaker.*

EUROLINK THE LAD   4 b.g. Burslem 123 – Shoshoni Princess (Prince **97** Tenderfoot (USA) 126) [1990 6m 7f² 7f³ 7g* 7.6m⁴ 7.3g* 7m⁵ 8g 1991 8m⁵ 8g* 7m] rather unfurnished gelding: fairly useful handicapper: improved form to win Royal Hunt Cup at Ascot in June by neck from Operation Wolf: looked very well but ran way below best in Bunbury Cup at Newmarket following month: stays 1m: has won on firm going, but best efforts with give in the ground: winning hurdler for M. Pipe in April. *J. L. Dunlop.*

EURO MARK (IRE)   3 ch.g. On Your Mark 125 – Old Acquaintance (Virginia   **—** Boy 106) [1990 5.8m 5m 6m⁶ 5.3h² 5m⁵ 7m 5f⁴ 1991 8m 6g 6g⁵ 8d 6m⁶ 7g 10m 7m⁶] sturdy gelding: fair plater at 2 yrs: showed little at 3 yrs: should stay beyond 5f: acts on hard ground: has hung left: blinkered and visored once. *M. Madgwick.*

EUROTWIST   2 b.c. (Mar 1) Viking (USA) – Orange Bowl (General Assembly   **53** (USA)) [1991 5f 6m⁵ 5m⁵ a7g⁵ 7f³ 7m⁶ 7m 7m 7m] 3,400Y, 6,200 2-y-o: small, close-coupled colt: third foal: half-brother to a winner in Scandinavia: dam unraced daughter of Lupe Stakes winner Golden Bowl: fair plater: best effort when third: never near to challenge last 3 starts: stays 7f: acts on firm ground, soundly beaten on fibresand. *T. D. Barron.*

EVADING   3 br.f. Petoski 135 – Hiding 84 (So Blessed 130) [1990 7f 8m⁵ 9g a7g*   **54** 1991 8.2d² 8m 8g³ 8d 10.2g* 10m⁵ 12.3g] sparely-made filly: fair plater: on toes and starey in coat, won at Chepstow (sold out of Lord Huntingdon's stable 7,500 gns) in July: ran well in claimer next time: should stay beyond 1¼m: acts on good to firm and dead ground: visored twice: bandaged penultimate start. *Miss S. J. Wilton.*

EVASIVE PRINCE (USA)   3 b.c. Secreto (USA) 128 – Overstate (USA)   **95** (Speak John) [1990 7m² 7s* 1991 10g⁴ 10.4d 7g* 8d 8d] leggy, quite attractive colt: good mover: fairly useful performer: won minor event at Newmarket in June, running on strongly to lead close home: easily best other effort at 3 yrs (off course 3 months before final outing) in Thresher Classic Trial at Sandown on reappearance: will prove best at up to 1m: acts on soft going: takes keen hold: edgy second start: sold 15,000 gns Newmarket Autumn Sales. *M. R. Stoute.*

EVENING AFFAIR   5 b.m. Red Sunset 120 – Miss Flirt (Welsh Pageant 132)   **—** [1990 10f² 10.2m⁶ 9g⁴ 10g⁵ 10h* 10h⁶ 9f² 1991 7d 7g 9s 10g 11.8g 10.3d] lengthy, sparely-made mare: moderate mover: modest handicapper at 4 yrs: always behind in 1991: stays 1¼m: acts well on very firm going: usually blinkered, was 5-y-o. *W. Holden.*

EVENING DRESS   2 ch.f. (Mar 25) Night Shift (USA) – Maple Rock (Music Boy   **49** 124) [1991 6f 6.1f 7.1m⁴ 7g 8m a7g] compact filly: plating-class maiden: strong-finishing fourth to Sterling Prospect in auction event at Chepstow: no form after: should stay 1m. *T. Thomson Jones.*

EVENING SESSION (IRE)   2 ch.g. (May 24) Burslem 123 – Icefield   **—** (Northfields (USA)) [1991 6m] 2,100 2-y-o: small, sturdy gelding: seventh foal:

half-brother to 1984 2-y-o 6f winner Harvester King (by Pitskelly): dam unraced daughter of Portland Handicap winner Gold Pollen: 33/1, backward and ridden by 7-lb claimer, last of 14 in maiden auction at Pontefract in July. *J. Norton.*

EVENING STAR   5 b.m. Red Sunset 120 – Avereen (Averof 123) [1990 a8g* – a8g⁴ a8g² a8g³ a8g⁵ a8g² 8f 9f 8m 8m 8.2m a8g⁴ 8g* 8g a8g* a8g* a8g a8g⁴ 1991 a a8g⁶ a8g³ a8g 8s 8d a8g³ 8m a8g a8g a8g³ a8g] leggy mare: modest handicapper: easily best form on all-weather: form on turf since 3 yrs only when winning at Salisbury as 4-y-o: stays 1m: seems to need give in the ground: has won for apprentice: tried visored. *A. Hide.*   63

EVERGLADES (IRE)   3 b.c. Green Desert (USA) 127 – Glowing With Pride   **76** 114 (Ile de Bourbon (USA) 133) [1990 7m⁴ 7m 1991 8s⁴ 7g2] sturdy colt: carries condition: modest maiden: made most when second at Catterick in April: found little off bridle on reappearance: bred to stay 1m. *G. Wragg.*

EVER RECKLESS   5 ch.m. Crever 94 – Gold Spangle 97 (Klondyke Bill 125)   — § [1990 5m 8m 5d⁶ a5g² a7g 6f⁶ 5f⁴ 5m⁴ 7m² 7d a5g⁴ 6m⁵ 5m* 5f⁵ a5g* 5m 5m³ 5m a6g a5g³ a5g² a6g 1991 a5g⁶] leggy, lengthy, unfurnished mare: poor walker: quite modest handicapper at 4 yrs: below form only run in 1991 (February): best at 5f: acts well on top-of-the-ground: usually wears blinkers or visor: wears bandages behind on all-weather: often sweats: has looked unenthusiastic and goes well for tender handling: inconsistent: sold 1,050 gns Ascot September Sales. *D. T. Thom.*

EVERSET (FR)   3 b.c. Green Desert (USA) 127 – Eversince (USA) (Foolish   **79** Pleasure (USA)) [1990 NR 1991 7g⁵ 6g² 6g* 7g 6f² 6s 6f 6.1m² 5d a6g*] close-coupled colt: moderate mover: first foal: dam 1m winner at 2 yrs in France: fair form: won 3-runner maiden at Catterick (12/1 on) in July and claimer at Southwell in November: should be as effective at 7f as 6f: acts on firm ground: has run creditably for 7-lb claimer: sold out of L. Cumani's stable 5,200 gns Newmarket Autumn Sales after eighth start. *W. J. Musson.*

EVER SO ARTISTIC   4 ch.g. Claude Monet (USA) 121 – Ever So 78 (Mummy's   **59** Pet 125) [1990 7f 7f a7g 6m⁵ 6m⁶ 5m 5m 6f⁵ 5.1m 5.3f 6g a5g* 1991 a5g* a5g³ a5g⁶ a5g² a5g* a6g⁶ 5.3f 5m* 5g 5m 5.8d 5.2m a5g a5g a5g4] sparely-made gelding: quite modest handicapper: made virtually all at Lingfield (2) and Newmarket early in 1991: below form after: best at 5f: acts on good to firm ground: usually visored or blinkered: has been bandaged behind: has won for apprentice: inconsistent on turf. *P. Howling.*

EVERSO IRISH   2 b.c. (Apr 30) Hatim (USA) 121 – Ever So 78 (Mummy's Pet   **58** 125) [1991 7g 7d 7m⁶ 8m³ a7g⁶] leggy colt: has a round action: third foal: half-brother to 5f winner Ever So Artistic (by Claude Monet) and 3-y-o Coney Island (by Flash of Steel): dam 2-y-o 6f winner: 4 lengths third of 22, staying on well, to Mister Bandit in seller at Newmarket: never able to challenge in Southwell nursery final outing: will be suited by 1¼m. *M. H. Tompkins.*

EVER SO LONELY   2 br.f. (Mar 16) Headin' Up – Lonely Dawn (USA) 63   **72** (Plenty Old (USA)) [1991 5m* 5m² 6g 5g⁶ 5d] rather unfurnished filly: moderate mover: fourth foal: sister to 6f winner Lonsom Lass: dam won sellers at 7f and 1m: sweating, won maiden at Warwick in July: easily best effort in nurseries when second at Wolverhampton: should stay 6f. *A. Bailey.*

EVER SO SHARP   8 br.h. Caruso 112 – Sealed Contract 76 (Runnymede 123)   — [1990 a11g a11g a8g a6g 5m⁴ 5m 5g⁶ 5.8h³ 5.8f 5f 5f 6m 5m 5m 8.2v 1991 5m 8f 8m 8h 8.1g 6m 12f 7.5f 12.3g] small, workmanlike horse: bad mover: poor handicapper at best nowadays: seems to stay 1m: acts on hard going: usually blinkered: has carried head high and wandered under pressure. *J. P. Smith.*

EVERY ONE A GEM   4 ch.g. Nicholas Bill 125 – Lady Bequick 81 (Sharpen Up   **70** 127) [1990 10f 10m 8m⁵ 9f³ 11.5g² 1991 10f* 10m 10g4 10m* 10m* 10.1m* 10.1f⁴ 10d² 10.1m⁶] big, good-bodied gelding: improved handicapper in first half of 1991: won at Brighton (2), Pontefract (sweating) and Newcastle in spring: will prove at least as effective at 1½m: acts on firm and dead ground: not discredited when blinkered: sold to join M. Dixon's stable only 3,200 gns Newmarket Autumn Sales. *M. J. Ryan.*

EWALD (IRE)   3 b.c. Green Desert (USA) 127 – Popular Win 103 (Lorenzaccio   — 130) [1990 NR 1991 7v⁵ 8.2m³] IR 24,000Y, 52,000 2-y-o: leggy, quite attractive colt: half-brother to 5 winners here and abroad, including 1988 2-y-o 6f winner Coq du Nord (by Coquelin) and Irish 7f to 9.5f winner Popular Glen (by Glenstal): dam 5f and 7f winner out of Musidora winner Jakomima: well beaten in maiden at Newcastle and minor event at Nottingham in April: joined M. Naughton. *J. S. Wilson.*

EXCELLED (IRE)   2 gr.f. (Apr 11) Treasure Kay 114 – Excelling Miss (USA)   — (Exceller (USA) 129) [1991 5v 6m] IR 2,200Y: leggy, sparely-made filly: first foal:

dam Irish maiden half-sister to Shy Groom: backward, well beaten in southern maidens in spring. *B. Gubby.*

EXCELSIS 5 b.h. Shirley Heights 130 – Sacred Ibis (Red God 128§) [1990 a12g **56** 10m 10.1m⁵ 11.5f² 11.7f² 12f⁵ 12m⁶ 1991 12f 10f* 12m* 11.7m 10g 11.9f] neat horse: plating-class handicapper: below form after winning at Brighton in June (apprentices) and July: stays 1½m: acts on firm going: below form when visored once. *J. R. Jenkins.*

EXCLUSION 2 ch.c. (Mar 17) Ballad Rock 122 – Great Exception 84 (Grundy **66** p 137) [1991 6g] strong, rather angular colt: second foal: half-brother to 3-y-o Dream On (by Absalom): dam won over 12.2f and 14.7f: 50/1, green and better for race, around 10 lengths seventh of 21 to Katakana in maiden at Newbury in October, staying on strongly under tender handling for 7-lb claimer: will be suited by 1m+: sure to improve a fair bit. *H. Candy.*

EXCLUSIVE VIRTUE (USA) 3 b.f. Shadeed (USA) 135 – Exclusive Order **94** (USA) (Exclusive Native (USA)) [1990 7g² 7m* 1991 8g 9m⁴ 10.6g² 10g 9m² 12m⁵ 12d] lengthy, good-bodied filly: has a powerful, round action: fairly useful hand-icapper: good second at Haydock and Sandown: raced too keenly in apprentice race final start: stays 1½m: very edgy (not discredited) fourth outing: acts on good to firm ground: raced too freely for an apprentice final start: lacks turn of foot. *M. R. Stoute.*

EXECUTION ONLY (IRE) 3 b.c. Sure Blade (USA) 130 – Headin' Home 105 **62** (Habitat 134) [1990 6m⁴ a6g a6g 1991 10d 8m³ a8g⁵ 8m⁴ 8d* 10m³ 10g⁴ 9d⁵ 7.6d] heavy-topped colt: quite modest handicapper: won at Warwick in June: needs further than 7.6f, and stays 1¼m: acts on good to firm ground and dead: visored last 5 outings, blinkered previous 3: has hung right: joined J. J. O'Neill. *J. W. Watts.*

EXHAUST MAN 7 b.g. Crooner 119 – Silk Fashion 61 (Breeders Dream 116) — [1990 15.5f* 14.8m³ 8m 1991 a16g a16g 15.5f⁶] small gelding: plating-class handicapper at 6 yrs: no worthwhile form in 1991: stays 2m: acts on any going, but well suited by top-of-the-ground: has hung right: ran moderately in blinkers. *Miss B. Sanders.*

EXHELLA (IRE) 3 ch.f. Exhibitioner 111 – Junella 95 (Midsummer Night II 117) **23** [1990 5m 7.5d³ 7d 6f⁴ 7.5f 7f 7d 8.2s 1991 10m 8.2f 6f³ 8g 8m] close-coupled, workmanlike filly: poor maiden: stays 1m: has form on any going: visored once and blinkered 3 times, running moderately: trained first 4 starts by K. McCauley. *H. A. T. Whiting.*

EXIT TO NOWHERE (USA) 3 b.c. Irish River (FR) 131 – Coup de Folie **112** (USA) 112 (Halo (USA)) [1990 8g² 8m² 7.5d* 1991 9d² 9.2m⁵ 6m⁶ 6.5g³ 8m⁶ 7d⁵ 8d⁵] tall, good sort: has a markedly round action: smart performer: won Prix Thomas Bryon at Saint-Cloud as 2-y-o: ran creditably in listed race at Evry, July Cup (looking tremendously well, ran on again from well behind when pace quickened) at Newmarket and Prix Maurice de Gheest at Deauville first, third and fourth starts in 1991: below form last 2 starts: stays 9f: probably best on an easy surface. *F. Boutin, France.*

EXPANSIONIST 2 b.c. (May 11) Midyan (USA) 124 – Dastina 80 (Derring-Do **49** 131) [1991 8m 8m a8g] 12,000F, 4,000Y: small, close-coupled colt: has a quick action: half-brother to 1¼m winner Mashhor John (by Mashhor Dancer) and several more winners here and abroad: dam second over 7f at 2 yrs, is sister to smart 7f performer Tudor Mill: well beaten in late-season maidens, final one on fibresand. *A. Hide.*

EXPECT ANYTHING (IRE) 3 b.c. Anita's Prince 126 – Summer Serenade — (FR) 96 (Petingo 135) [1990 NR 1991 8.2d] IR 2,000F, 3,000 2-y-o: close-coupled colt: half-brother to several winners, including 2m winner Jamaica George (by Sexton Blake) and Scoutsmistake (by Prince Tenderfoot), modest handicapper at up to 1¼m: dam stayed at least 9f: very green, led over 5f then eased in claimer at Nottingham in April. *Dr J. D. Scargill.*

EXPLOSIVE SPEED (USA) 3 b.c. Exceller (USA) 129 – Strait Lane (USA) **52** (Chieftain II) [1990 7m⁵ 1991 10g 10m 10.8m 10f⁵ 12.3g] leggy, workmanlike colt: plating-class maiden: soundly beaten facing stiff task in handicap final start, in May: bred to stay 1½m: best 3-y-o effort on firm going: sold to join M. Hammond 2,800 gns Newmarket September Sales. *M. Moubarak.*

EXPRESS ACCOUNT 4 b.f. Carr de Naskra (USA) – Miss Audimar (USA) (Mr **78** Leader (USA)) [1990 8g 8m* 8m 8d 10f⁵ 8h⁴ a8g 9m⁶ 8g* 8g⁴ 10m* 9m³ 10d a10g⁵ a12g⁴ a11g 1991 a12g⁵ 10g⁵ 10f 10m⁵ 10.1f² 11.9m* 12.4m* 10.4m 12f* 12f⁶ 11.9m⁴ 11.4m 12f 12d 10m] leggy, rather dipped-backed filly: modest handicapper: won at York (apprentices, gamely), Newcastle and Thirsk in summer: below best last 5

273

starts, tailed off final one: effective at 1¼m to 1½m: goes well on top-of-the-ground, unsuited by dead: has run creditably when blinkered, moderately when sweating and edgy: goes well for claimer: inconsistent. *R. J. R. Williams.*

EXPRESS GIFT 2 br.g. (May 8) Bay Express 132 – Annes Gift (Ballymoss 136)   **45** p
[1991 6m⁴ 6m] smallish, plain gelding: half-brother to 1982 2-y-o 5f seller winner Leandros (by Lepanto) and 2 winners abroad: dam of no account: poor form in maidens at Pontefract (soon disputed lead after slow start, faded 2f out) and Redcar (eased) in autumn: may well do better. *Mrs G. R. Reveley.*

EXPRESS SERVICE 2 b.c. (Feb 10) Hotfoot 126 – Avon Belle 75 (Balidar 133)   **72** p
[1991 6f 6d²] good-bodied colt: fourth foal: half-brother to useful 3-y-o 5f and 6f winner Spaniards Close (by King of Spain): dam best at sprint distances: better effort in autumn maidens when keeping-on second of 23 to Prince Emilio at Haydock: will probably improve again, particularly at 7f. *P. J. Makin.*

EXPRESS SIGNMAKER (IRE) 2 b.f. (May 28) Paean 123 – Moment of   **46**
Weakness 76 (Pieces of Eight 128) [1991 6g³ 7m 6m 7g³ 8m] 500F: angular filly: fifth reported foal: half-sister to modest 9f and 1¼m winner African Affair (by Be My Native) and 5f (at 2 yrs) to 1m winner Give In (by Harlow): dam won from 6f to 10.2f: quite moderate plater: finds 6f too sharp, and should be well suited by 1m +: best form on good ground. *J. White.*

EXTRA HIGH (USA) 3 ch.g. Nepal (USA) – Evening Scarlet (USA) (Bold   —
Commander (USA)) [1990 NR 1991 10g 10g] $23,000Y, resold $50,000Y: rangy gelding: half-brother to minor winners in North America: dam minor winner at around 1m (by Raja Baba) best at around 9f: behind in maiden at Kempton and claimer (blinkered) at Newmarket: joined V. Thompson. *B. Hanbury.*

EXXO (USA) 2 b.g. (Apr 10) Exuberant (USA) – Dip's Joy (USA) (Sr Diplomat   **54**
(USA)) [1991 7m⁴] $6,700Y: strong, workmanlike gelding: fifth reported living foal: half-brother to 3 minor winners in USA: dam placed twice from 13 starts in North America: 6/1 and bit backward, staying-on fourth of 10 in maiden at Southwell (slowly away) in September: sold 3,800 gns Newmarket Autumn Sales: exported to Scandinavia. *W. A. O'Gorman.*

EYECRAFT (USA) 2 ch.c. (May 17) Our Native (USA) – Ornamental (USA)   **49** p
(Triple Crown (USA)) [1991 6s] $25,000Y: brother to winning selling hurdler Orsett and half-brother to 3 winners here and in USA, including 3-y-o 7f and 1m winner Green's Seago (by Fighting Fit): 16/1, showed up to 2f out in 13-runner maiden at Yarmouth in October: should improve. *Mrs J. Cecil.*

EZIO DE CESARI (ITY) 2 br.c. (Feb 25) Big Reef 110 – Strong On The Sly   **84**
(USA) (On The Sly (USA)) [1991 6d 8g* 8v* 8v4] fair sort: looks weak: first known foal: dam, American bred, went to Italy at 2 yrs: off course over 3 months after Newbury maiden on debut, for C. Brittain: successful in maiden at Milan in August and minor race at Rome in September: over 7 lengths fourth to Alhijaz in listed race at Rome 2 weeks later: should stay middle distances. *L. Camici, Italy.*

EZZOUD (IRE) 2 b.c. (May 6) Last Tycoon 131 – Royal Sister II (Claude) [1991   **87** p
7m* 7m] 360,000Y: sturdy, quite attractive colt: fifth foal: half-brother to high-class miler Distant Relative (by Habitat) and 1¼m seller winner Lightning Thunder (by Dara Monarch): dam, from good family, won over 1¼m at 4 yrs in Ireland, and also won in Italy: second favourite but better for race, won minor event at Doncaster in September, green early then running on strongly final 1½f: didn't make anticipated improvement in 30-runner Tattersalls Tiffany Highflyer Stakes at Newmarket following month, chasing leaders 5f then fading and not knocked about: looked a fine prospect at Doncaster, and is worth another chance. *M. R. Stoute.*

F

FAAZ (USA) 2 b.c. (Feb 10) Fappiano (USA) – Charmie Carmie (USA) (Lyphard   **53** p
(USA) 132) [1991 8f 8f 7m³] $650,000Y: fifth foal: half-brother to Himmah (by Habitat), fair 6f and 7f winner: dam, placed in USA is half-sister to Chris Evert and All Rainbows (dam of Winning Colors): bit backward still, best effort when staying-on third of 8, not knocked about, in maiden at Newcastle in October: should stay beyond 1m: slowly away all starts: has scope, and will probably do better. *A. A. Scott.*

FABIUS CUNCTATOR (IRE)   2 b.c. (Mar 23) Cyrano de Bergerac 120 –   —
Flower Centre (USA) (Jaipur) [1991 6g 7m 6f] IR 4,600Y, 8,000 2-y-o: good-bodied
colt: half-brother to several winners here and abroad, including 5f (at 2 yrs) and 8.3f
winner Stamen (by Ballymore) and Irish Cesarewitch winner The Neurologist (by
Ragstone): dam won twice over 1m at 2 yrs: well beaten in maidens then a seller. *B.
J. McMath.*

FABULOUS QUEEN (FR)   8 b.m. Fabulous Dancer (USA) 124 – Moquerie   —
(FR) 120 (Beaugency (FR) 126) [1990 11.5m4 1991 a7g a12g] lengthy ex-French
mare: successful over 1m at 2 yrs to 4 yrs, including in listed event at Evry: thrice
raced and no worthwhile form here. *R. V. King.*

FACE NORTH (IRE)   3 b.g. Fayruz 116 – Pink Fondant (Northfields (USA))   —
[1990 5f* 5f* 5g2 6m4 1991 5g 6g 7m 5m 5g 7.6m 5g 6.9s] small, sturdy gelding:
moderate mover: winner of 2 sellers at 2 yrs: mostly stiff tasks in handicaps in 1991,
well beaten last 4 starts: stays 6f: acts on firm going. *A. R. Davison.*

FACE UP   4 br.c. Top Ville 129 – Pomade 79 (Luthier 126) [1990 8m5 7g2 8g* 8m   —
1991 11.5g] smallish, angular colt: moderate walker and mover: fair form when
winning claimer (claimed out of H. Cecil's stable) at Newmarket last June: below
that form since, well beaten only run in 1991 (May): bred to stay beyond 1m, but
seems keen sort. *J. Wharton.*

FACILITY LETTER   4 gr.g. Superlative 118 – Facetious 88 (Malicious) [1990   ?
a6g3 7m5 7d5 7m 8.5g2 7d 1991 9s 8m5 12.3m5] sturdy gelding: good walker:
plating-class handicapper: well below form in 1991, but was off course 4 months
after second start: stays 8.5f: best efforts with some give: has been tried in blinkers,
better form without: winning hurdler. *G. M. Moore.*

FACT OR FICTION   5 br.g. Known Fact (USA) 135 – Noble Wac (USA)   **64** d
(Vaguely Noble 140) [1990 9f2 10.6f 10.1g6 9g2 8.2m 8m5 9f* 8f2 10f3 10f 8m5 a10g*
a10g2 a10g5 1991 a12g* a13g2 a12g 8m 12s 12m a12g] strong, angular gelding:
modest handicapper: won at Lingfield (claimer) in February, making all: stays 13f:
acts on firm going: mostly blinkered or visored nowadays: has won for apprentice.
Miss B. Sanders.

FACTUALLY   2 gr.f. (Feb 16) Known Fact (USA) 135 – Alydear (USA) (Alydar   **58**
(USA)) [1991 5m5 6.1d2 6m6 6m4] leggy, close-coupled filly: has a quick action: third
reported foal: dam won at around 1m: quite modest maiden here: stays 1m: easily
best form here on dead ground: blinkered final start: difficult stalls third outing: sold
3,000 gns Newmarket July Sales, sent to Scandinavia and won over 1m in Sweden in
September. *B. Hanbury.*

FACTUELLE   4 ch.f. Known Fact (USA) 135 – Cayla (Tumble Wind (USA)) [1990   **60**
5d 5m 5g 5m2 5g3 5f4 5m 5m 5g 1991 5.3f4 5g2 5m2 5g3 5d2 5m2 5.2m* 5d 5f3
5.2f* 5g3 5m] small, stocky filly: quite modest handicapper: won at Yarmouth in July
and September: effective at 5f to 6f: acts on any going: largely consistent: sold 5,000
gns Newmarket December Sales. *M. J. Fetherston-Godley.*

FAILAND   4 b.f. Kala Shikari 125 – What A Mint (Meadow Mint (USA) 120) [1990   —
8m 8f 7f4 7f2 7m* 7.6g3 8f5 7m 7m 8g 7g 1991 a8g a7g] smallish, angular filly: poor
walker: has a quick action: poor handicapper: visored no worthwhile form in early
1991: best at around 7f: acts on firm going: sold to join R. Brotherton's stable 1,900
gns Ascot February Sales: winning hurdler. *R. Holder.*

FAIR AMERICAN (USA)   2 ch.c. (Mar 20) Mr Prospector (USA) – Win Nona   **79** p
(USA) (Jacinto) [1991 6m5 7m*] $800,000F: angular, useful-looking colt: moderate
mover: seventh reported foal: half-brother to several winners in North America,
notably Grade 1 1½m winner Little Missouri (by Cox's Ridge): dam minor winner in
North America: confirmed promise of debut (bandaged) when making all in 9-runner
event at Lingfield later in October: will do better, most probably over 1m. *M. R.
Stoute.*

FAIR AVERAGE   3 ch.c. Ahonoora 122 – Fair Head 87 (High Line 125) [1990   **104**
6g 7g4 8d* 1991 8g* 10.4d5 8.5f2 8g3] workmanlike colt: useful performer: won
4-runner £6,900 contest at Kempton in April: ran very well behind Sylva Honda in
Diomed Stakes at Epsom and Sikeston in Queen Anne Stakes at Royal Ascot last 2
starts, running on strongly from towards rear: stays 1m (ran in snatches over 10.4f
at Chester): acts on firm and dead ground. *H. Candy.*

FAIR COP (USA)   2 b.c. (Feb 12) Al Nasr (FR) 126 – Exclusive Life (USA)   **97**
(Exclusive Native (USA)) [1991 6g* 6f* 6m*] compact, good-quartered colt: first
foal: dam sprint winner in USA: progressive form: successful in maiden at
Goodwood and minor event at Catterick (despite appearing not to handle bend at all
well) on first 2 starts: looked in excellent shape when winning 9-runner Chesham

Chesham Stakes, Ascot—Fair Cop (right) runs on strongly;
Governor's Imp beats Bradawn Breever (blinkers) for second

Stakes at Royal Ascot, staying on strongly to beat Governor's Imp by 3½ lengths:
should stay 1m: looked sure to improve further. *P. F. I. Cole.*

FAIR CRACK (IRE)   2 b.c. (Feb 18) Fairy King (USA) – Have A Flutter **109**
(Auction Ring (USA) 123) [1991 5d⁶ 5d³ 5g* 6m⁴ 5.2g⁵ 6m* 5g² 7s* 6g³ 8f]
     When the Cartier Million was inaugurated four seasons ago its critics
gave dire warnings of all manner of calamities about to befall racing as a result.
Tattersalls were prevented from running a copycat event in this country as
the Jockey Club stood resolute in fear of corrupted stallion statistics and the
prospect of two-year-olds running for the higher prize money rather than for
pattern prestige. In practice the Million never threatened to disturb the
two-year-old pattern. The fourth and final running—under Goffs' name after
the original backers withdrew—didn't even include a pattern-race winner
among its eighteen-strong field, and we are unable to rate the winner Fair
Crack among the top thirty of his generation. No matter. Enterprise of the
type shown by Goffs ought to be applauded in a sport where novelty is all too
often treated with suspicion rather than enthusiasm.
     Previously the Irish had managed to keep the Million's massive prize at
home, very much against the trend in the big races in recent years, and
the Vincent O'Brien-trained Fairy Fable, fourth in the Moyglare Stud Stakes
on her previous start, was sent off the favourite at 7/2 to complete the home
defence. Most fancied among the eleven British challengers was Bobzao at
5/1, with Irish Memory at 11/2 also preferred in the market to Fair Crack—a
13/2 shot, the winner of a maiden at Newbury in April, a minor event at
Windsor in July and second in the Roses Stakes at York on his previous
outing. In the event it was stable-companion Autocracy that gave the winner
most to do, going on around a furlong and a half out and rallying gamely after
being passed by Fair Crack just inside the last. Only a short head separated
them in a driving finish, the pair drawing five lengths clear of Fairy Fable in
third. It was a superb training achievement by Hannon, one of many in a
season when he sent out over a hundred winners for the first time, and his
final total of one hundred and twenty-six winners was beaten only by Berry.
Both trainers have shown that large-scale Arab backing and horses with
fashionable pedigrees aren't prerequisites for success on the flat today. Fair
Crack cost only IR 19,000 guineas as a yearling, cheap enough to qualify for
lowish weights in two other valuable sales-based races in which he came close
to landing another massive prize for connections. In the Newbury Sales Super
Sprint Trophy in July he was beaten under a length in fifth behind Paris House
(trained by Berry), pushed along throughout racing over a trip that was
already on the sharp side for him. In the Racecall Gold Trophy at Redcar in
October—in which the weights are allocated in relation to the median sale
price of the sire's progeny—Fair Crack came around two lengths third of
twenty-five to Casteddu, finishing well having been checked slightly entering
the final furlong.
     Fair Crack, a smallish, good-topped colt with a quick action, is the third
foal and winner out of Have A Flutter, after the modest 1988 two-year-old
five-furlong winner Done Better (by Dunphy), later successful in Sweden, and
the three-year-old Capital Bond (by Hegemony), a winner over seven furlongs
and a mile in the latest season. Have A Flutter, who also has a foal by Jareer,
was placed at seven furlongs in Ireland, while the grandam Another Flutter

276

Goffs Million, the Curragh—
a short head separates the stable-companions Fair Crack (far side) and Autocracy

Fair Crack (IRE) (b.c. Feb 18, 1989)	Fairy King (USA) (b 1982)	Northern Dancer (b 1961)	Nearctic / Natalma
		Fairy Bridge (b 1975)	Bold Reason / Special
	Have A Flutter (b 1981)	Auction Ring (b 1972)	Bold Bidder / Hooplah
		Another Flutter (ch 1966)	Credo / Flutter-By

was a modest handicapper, winning over an extended mile as a four-year-old. The stud career thus far of his sire Fairy King, also the sire of Fairy Fable, makes an interesting study. When this full brother to Sadler's Wells was first retired to the Ballysheehan Stud his fee was set at IR 6,000 guineas, but it was half that amount by the time his first crop saw the racecourse in 1989. That first crop contained eight individual winners, including the useful filly Pharaoh's Delight, and resulted in Fairy King's fee for 1990 being pushed up to IR 20,000 guineas. For 1992 his fee has been set at IR 12,500 guineas, and this after the £449,541 won by Fair Crack and £82,563 won by Fairy Fable in the Million placed Fairy King among the season's leading sires. Given the tremendous progress Fair Crack made throughout the season there's no reason why he shouldn't train on. Fair Crack stays seven furlongs well, and should get a mile. He ran disappointingly when tried over that trip in a Grade 3 race at Hollywood Park on his final outing but the firm ground was almost certainly against him there; easily his best efforts have been on an easy surface. *R. Hannon.*

FAIR DARE 3 b. or br.f. Daring March 116 – Fair Madame 88 (Monseigneur **46** (USA) 127) [1990 6m⁴ 6d⁴ 1991 8s⁴ 6g 8g 7f 11g⁴ 10g⁴ 8g* 8f 8m⁴ 10.4m 8.2m] leggy filly: moderate mover: plating-class performer: won maiden at Ayr in July: mostly below form afterwards: suited by 1m: acts on good to firm ground. *C. B. B. Booth.*

FAIR ENCHANTRESS 3 b.f. Enchantment 115 – Pts Fairway (Runnymede **64** 123) [1990 6g 6m² 7f 6m 1991 6f 7m 5m³ 5m* 5m⁴ 5m 6m⁵ 5.1d 7m⁴] workmanlike, good-quartered filly: keen walker: quite modest performer: made all in maiden at Doncaster in June: showed little last 2 starts: stays 6f: acts on good to firm ground: blinkered second to sixth outings: visored on eighth. *J. A. Bennett.*

FAIR FLYER (IRE) 2 b.c. (Apr 6) Tilt Up (USA) – Fair Siobahn (Petingo 135) **58** [1991 5m 6d 6m⁴ 7g 8m 7f⁶ 6f³ 6m 6g 7.1m*] 22,000Y: lengthy, sparely-made colt: closely related to a winner in USA by Full Pocket and half-brother to 4 winners, all minor: dam won at up to 9f in USA: plating-class performer: won claimer (claimed £2,200 to join P. Monteith) at Edinburgh in October: really needs further than 6f, and stays 1m: acts on firm ground: has run creditably (including when successful) in blinkers. *G. Lewis.*

FAIRFORD 2 br.g. (Apr 8) Forzando 122 – Fuddled 74 (Malacate (USA) 131) — [1991 6g] 14,000F, 16,000Y: fourth foal: half-brother to 3-y-o Lauravale (by Kind of Hush) and a winner in Norway: dam 1½m winner: 20/1, towards rear in median auction at Nottingham in June. *J. G. FitzGerald.*

FAIRGROUNDPRINCESS 3 ch.f. Kalaglow 132 – Hide Out (Habitat 134) **46** [1990 NR 1991 12m⁶ 10.1m 10d 10.9g 16m⁴ 14.6m 12.3g4 12f* 11.8m 11.4m] close-coupled filly: half-sister to several winners, including 1984 2-y-o 5f winner Fair Charter (by Be My Guest) and 4-y-o Cheveux Mitchell (by Dunbeath), winner from 6f to 7.6f: dam ran once: won handicap at Thirsk in August despite iron breaking 1f out: well beaten in similar events following month: stays 1½m: acts on firm going: bandaged behind. *F. H. Lee.*

FAIR PROSPECT 5 b.g. Shirley Heights 130 – Sans Blague (USA) 108 (The **67** + Minstrel (CAN) 135) [1990 NR 1991 14g2] tall, good sort: trained by R. Hern, fairly useful form at 3 yrs: first run on flat since, way below that form in Salisbury minor event in May: shapes as if will prove best at 1½m+: acts on soft ground: winning hurdler in September. *P. J. Hobbs.*

FAIR SHARE 2 b. or br.f. (Jan 15) Sharpo 132 – Sea Fairy 64 (Wollow 132) [1991 **47** 5v⁴ 5g 5d* 5g⁵ 5m² 5.3f⁵ a5g 5.2g⁴ 5f] 5,200Y: smallish, sparely-made filly: moderate mover: first foal: dam 2-y-o 6f winner, later won in Spain: poor form: won claimer at Hamilton in April: good second in seller at Bath following month: below form afterwards: may do better at 6f: acts on good to firm and dead ground: soundly beaten on fibresand: flashes tail, and is probably none too genuine: sold 580 gns Doncaster October Sales. *R. W. Stubbs.*

FAIRSPEAR 2 b.c. (Apr 9) Faustus (USA) 118 – Emma's Star (Comedy Star **64** (USA) 121) [1991 7g 8.1g 8g 7.1s⁵ 7g⁴ 6s3] rather unfurnished colt: first reported foal: dam of little account: generally progressive form: possibly not ideally drawn when in frame in maidens at Salisbury (visored) and Folkestone in autumn: should stay 1m: may prove best suited by an easy surface. *L. G. Cottrell.*

FAIRWAY ROYALE 6 b.g. Runnett 125 – Lady Salinia (Sovereign Path 125) — [1990 NR 1991 10s 10g] lengthy, quite attractive gelding: has a quick action: modest maiden at 4 yrs: twice raced and no form since: stays 1¼m: acts on firm going: sold 950 gns Ascot April Sales. *R. Curtis.*

FAIRY FABLE (IRE) 2 b.f. (Mar 15) Fairy King (USA) – Gentle Freedom **95** (Wolver Hollow 126) [1991 6m⁴ 7m* 6m⁴ 7s3] 15,000F, IR 47,000Y: second foal: sister to Italian 3-y-o Tampopo: dam unraced: won maiden at Tipperary in August: much better form in Moyglare Stud Stakes (under 2 lengths fourth of 8 to Twafeaj) 17 days later and Goffs Million (5 lengths third to Fair Crack) at the Curragh in October: stays 7f: acts on good to firm and soft ground. *M. V. O'Brien, Ireland.*

FAIRY FLAX (IRE) 3 b.f. Dancing Brave (USA) 140 – Fairy Tern 109 (Mill Reef **97** (USA) 141) [1990 6g⁶ 6m² 1991 6.1m* 7g² 8d⁶ 8s] sturdy, angular filly: fluent mover: won maiden at Chepstow in September: much better efforts behind Volksraad in minor event and Chipaya in listed race (on toes, pulled hard), both at Ascot, next 2 starts: well beaten in Group 3 contest at Milan: should prove better at 1m than shorter: possibly unsuited by soft ground: sold 42,000 gns Newmarket December Sales. *I. A. Balding.*

FAIT ACCOMPLI (FR) 2 ch.c. (Mar 10) Fayruz 116 – Artipiar 106 (Tyrant **56** (USA)) [1991 5f⁶ 5m⁶ 7m 5g 5g² 5d] 18,000Y: neat colt: fifth foal: half-brother to 3-y-o Interrogate (by In Fijar), 1985 2-y-o 6f winner Faye (by Monsanto) and a winner in Norway: dam sprinter: plating-class maiden: good second in claimer at Edinburgh in September: should stay 6f: below best when blinkered fourth and final (on toes, tailed off) starts. *J. J. O'Neill.*

FALCON FLIGHT 5 ch.g. Tampero (FR) 115 – Kemoening 78 (Falcon 131) [1990 a7g⁶ 1991 8m 7m 7m⁴ 8.2d² 8m³ 8.1m 8.2m] smallish, rather sparely-made gelding: quite modest handicapper: stays 1m well: acts on firm and dead ground: bandaged nowadays: winning hurdler. *J. Mackie.* **62**

FALCONS DAWN 4 b.c. Exhibitioner 111 – African Bloom (African Sky 124) [1990 7f 5g⁴ 6m⁵ 6m⁵ 8.2m² 8g³ 8d³ 8g⁶ 8m⁴ 1991 8s 7.5f³ 8.2m⁶ 8.2g² 8m⁴ 7.6m³ 8d 7m 10.3d a8g] leggy, quite good-topped colt: has a round action: quite modest handicapper: best form at around 1m: acts on any going: usually visored: has proved awkward at stalls: goes well with forcing tactics. *M. O'Neill.* **67**

FALCON'S DOMAIN (IRE) 3 b. or br.c. Hegemony 112 – Cova Kestrel (Ovac (ITY) 120) [1990 5m² 5f* 5d⁵ 6f⁴ 6g³ 6m 7s 1991 6d 6m 7f 7g 8m⁵ 7.1m] compact colt: fair winner at 2 yrs: well below form in 1991, blinkered and finding little in claimer (hung right) and handicap last 2 starts: better at 6f than 5f: seems best on a sound surface: sold 1,800 gns Newmarket Autumn Sales: unsatisfactory. *J. M. P. Eustace.* — §

FALDO (USA) 3 gr.g. Caro 133 – Binky (FR) 113 (Faraway Son (USA) 130) [1990 7s 7m 7f 1991 a7g³ a10g⁵ 12m* 12.5m 12.3d 10g⁶ 9d] leggy gelding: plating-class performer: won ladies handicap at Thirsk in May: stays 1½m: acts on good to firm ground: blinkered once in 1990: sold 6,500 gns Newmarket Autumn Sales. *P. A. Kelleway.* **55**

FALLING REIGN 2 ch.c. (Feb 22) Dara Monarch 128 – Fall To Pieces (USA) 101 (Forli (ARG)) [1991 7g⁶ 7g⁴ 8d] workmanlike colt: ninth living foal: closely related to 1980 2-y-o 6f winner Piece of The Realm (by Realm) and half-brother to several winners, including useful 1989 sprinter Splintering (by Sharpo) and fair 7f and 1m winner Makeshift (by Night Shift): dam won over 7f and 1m: poor maiden: stays 1m: sold 2,000 gns Doncaster November Sales. *P. T. Walwyn.* **43**

FALLOW DEER 4 ch.f. Jalmood (USA) 126 – Regent's Fawn (CAN) 72 (Vice Regent (CAN)) [1990 a8g³ a8g² 8m⁵ 7g⁵ 9f³ 8m² 7g⁶ 10m⁴ 10m² 10m³ 10m* a12g 1991 10.1d 10.2g 10.1m⁶ a10g] small, lengthy filly: poor mover: little form since winning seller at Lingfield (sold out of B. Hills's stable) as 3-y-o: stays 1¼m: acts on good to firm ground: not an easy ride: sold 860 gns Ascot November Sales. *D. J. Wintle.* —

FALLOWFIELD GIRL 2 b.f. (Apr 19) Lochnager 132 – Ensign Steel 57 (Majority Blue 126) [1991 5g³ 5g 5m 5s³ 6m⁶ 6m⁶ 6f⁵ 5m] angular, close-coupled filly: sister to several winners, including fair sprinter and useful hurdler Benfen, and half-sister to winning jumper Samfen (by Sonnen Gold): dam, placed over 6f, is half-sister to 3 very useful sprinters: poor sprint maiden: ideally suited by very soft ground. *M. H. Easterby.* **46**

FALSE PASSPORT 4 ch.g. Alias Smith (USA) – Hussy 82 (Queen's Hussar 124) [1990 a10g 12d 1991 12f 10f] robust gelding: well beaten, including in selling handicap (blinkered). *M. J. Bolton.* —

FAMILY AT WAR (USA) 3 b.f. Explodent (USA) – Sometimes Perfect (USA) (Bold Bidder) [1990 5f² 5m* 5g⁵ 5s² 1991 6g 5f⁶ 5g⁶ 8m 6g] attractive filly: quite modest performer: best efforts at 5f on top-of-the-ground, though should stay 6f. *J. Etherington.* —

FAMILY LINE 3 b.g. High Line 125 – Princess Dina 87 (Huntercombe 133) [1990 8g 1991 10g 11d* 16.2g] smallish, workmanlike gelding: shows knee action: 20/1, won handicap at Hamilton in May, leading inside final 1f: beaten before final turn in handicap at Haydock following month: should stay 1½m: sold 5,000 gns Doncaster November Sales. *M. J. Camacho.* **81**

FAMILY PRIDE 6 b.g. Shareef Dancer (USA) 135 – Our Home 115 (Habitat 134) [1990 NR 1991 14.6m⁵] big, lengthy, quite attractive gelding: lightly raced and modest maiden at best: stayed 1½m well: didn't race on soft going, acted on any other: dead. *P. J. Bevan.* —

FAMILY ROSE 2 gr.c. (Jun 5) Absalom 128 – Greenhill Lass (Upper Case (USA)) [1991 5m] 16,500F, 15,000Y: close-coupled colt: brother to speedy 2-y-o's Faraway Grey (later stayed 1m) and Absaloute Service and half-brother to 2 winners, including 1988 2-y-o 5f winner Carry On Cary (by Carriage Way), later stayed 1½m: dam unraced daughter of half-sister to Sing Sing: slowly away and well behind final 2f in maiden at Carlisle in April: showed a quick action. *R. W. Stubbs.* —

Mr K. Abdulla's "Fanmore"

FAMOUS BEAUTY 4 br.f. Vision (USA) – Relfo 124 (Relko 136) [1990 10.6f² **54**
10.2m 10g⁵ 12h² 12.3g 12m⁵ 12d⁶ 12m⁵ 12m* 13.6d⁶ 16s 1991 12d 16m⁶ 13.8m
12.3g 12.1d³ 12.3d⁴ 12m⁴ 16.2f⁵ 12.3g⁴ 14.1f³ 12f⁵ 14m⁴ 14.6m² 12.1g* 11.9m³
13.8m⁴ 14g⁴ 16m 12.1d³ 13.6d 12.1s] sparely-made filly: plating-class handicapper:
won apprentice event at Chepstow (goes very well there) in August by 12 lengths:
stays 2m: acts on hard and dead ground: usually claimer ridden. *R. Hollinshead.*

FAMOUS DANCER 3 b.c. Top Ville 129 – Dancing Place (FR) (Green Dancer **74** ?
(USA) 132) [1990 8g 1991 10g⁴ 10.2g³ 13.3g 10g 10g] tall, lengthy, attractive colt:
modest maiden: well beaten last 3 starts, bandaged in handicap on first occasion:
may prove best at around 1¼m: edgy in stalls second start: sold 10,000 gns Newmarket Autumn Sales. *D. R. C. Elsworth.*

FAMOUS LAST WORDS (IRE) 2 br.c. (May 17) Lead On Time (USA) 123 – **73**
Miss Boston (FR) (River River (FR) 111) [1991 6m³ 6f³] 4,700Y, 26,000 2-y-o: leggy,
workmanlike colt: second foal: half-brother to fairly useful 3-y-o handicapper Bold
Bostonian (by Never So Bold), 6f winner (at 2 yrs) who stays 1¼m: dam French 5f
winner at 2 yrs, stayed 1¼m: under 2 lengths third of 9 in minor event at Windsor
and maiden auction at Yarmouth in summer: will stay 7f. *Dr J. D. Scargill.*

FANATICAL (USA) 5 b.h. Lear Fan (USA) 130 – Gal A Tic (USA) (Assagai) **64**
[1990 12.8g* 12.3g 1991 12m⁶ 12m 12f² 12.1d 12d³ 12g⁵ 13.1m* 14.6m³ 12.1g 12g³
12d⁴] rather good-topped horse: moderate mover: quite modest handicapper: won at
Bath in July: suited by 1½m + : acts on firm and dead ground: has run creditably in
blinkers. *J. H. Baker.*

FANCY ME 3 b.f. Dunbeath (USA) 127 – Friendly Thoughts (USA) (Al Hattab **71**
(USA)) [1990 7g 6m 6g* 7m 1991 7d⁵ 8.2m 8.3d³ 7d 10g* 10s⁶ 10.1f² 11.5f* 11m*
12m³ 11.5f³ 11.9m⁴] angular filly: modest performer: won claimer (sweating) at
Newmarket in July and handicaps at Yarmouth and Redcar (apprentices) in August:

280

stays 1½m: acts on any going, except soft: edgy fourth (blinkered) and fifth starts: appeared to find little off bridle on eleventh: consistent: sold 16,500 gns Newmarket Autumn Sales. *W. Jarvis.*

FANLIGHT 3 b.c. Beldale Flutter (USA) 130 – Carib Flash (Mill Reef (USA) 141) **45** [1990 6s 6m⁴ 1991 8d 10g 14g⁴ 12m⁵] neat, quite attractive colt: poor form: may prove better at 1¾m than shorter: joined R. Akehurst. *C. F. Wall.*

FANMORE (USA) 3 b.c. Lear Fan (USA) 130 – Lady Blackfoot 108 (Prince **108** Tenderfoot (USA) 126) [1990 NR 1991 8m* 8d² 8m*] $62,000Y: big, strong, rangy colt: half-brother to 1988 Irish 2-y-o 5f winner Monasteroris (by Northern Jove) and a winner in North America by J O Tobin: dam speedy Irish filly: favourite, won £7,800 newcomers race at Newmarket in April and £17,600 Kingfisher Lager Whitsun Cup Handicap (impressively, quickening on final 1f) at Sandown in May: 13/8 on, had to set pace when second of 3 to Crystal Path in minor event at Sandown: headstrong, and likely to prove suited by a strong pace: should have improved again. *G. Harwood.*

FAR APART 3 ro.f. Bellypha 130 – Joking Apart 120 (Jimmy Reppin 131) [1990 — NR 1991 8d 11m] workmanlike filly: eleventh foal: half-sister to several winners, including very useful 1983 2-y-o 5f and 7f winner Reflection (by Mill Reef) and Galtres Stakes winners Deadly Serious (by Queen's Hussar) and Sans Blague (by The Minstrel): dam very smart at up to 1m: no worthwhile form in claimers: dead. *I. A. Balding.*

FARAT (USA) 3 ch.c. Woodman (USA) 126 – Solac (FR) (Gay Lussac (ITY) 116) **86** [1990 6g⁴ 1991 8.2g² 10m³ 12m³ 14s²] good-bodied colt: progressive form: second of 14 in handicap at Kempton final start, held up, improved to lead over 1f out (despite edging left), caught last strides: stays 1¾m: acts on good to firm and soft ground. *J. L. Dunlop.*

FAR BUT NEAR (USA) 2 b.f. (Mar 11) Far North (CAN) 120 – Kesar Queen **88 p** (USA) 117 (Nashua) [1991 6f*] leggy filly: has scope: half-sister to 3-y-o Wish of Luck (by Diesis), and to fair 1m winner Majestic Ace (by Majestic Light) and 1981 2-y-o 5f winner Kesarini (by Singh): dam won Coronation Stakes: 7/2, won 6-runner maiden at Yarmouth in September by 1½ lengths from Swellegant, travelling well, leading 2f out and running on well: will stay 1m: sure to improve. *H. Thomson Jones.*

FARFELU 4 b.c. Lyphard's Special (USA) 122 – Spring Azure 98 (Mountain Call **100** 125) [1990 6m⁵ 5g² 6m³ 5.8h* 6m 5g⁴ 7.6d 6m³ 6s 1991 6g² 6m 6m 5m* 6g⁶ 5m* 5.6m 6m 5d⁶ 6.1s] robust, good-quartered colt: improved handicapper in 1991: won quite valuable events at York (easily) in July and Sandown (drifted right last 1f) in August: still going strongly when unseating rider 2f out in Tote-Portland Handicap at Doncaster on seventh start: easily best form at 5f: acts on hard and dead ground, unsuited by soft going: blinkered nowadays. *W. R. Muir.*

FAR GLOW 5 gr.g. Kalaglow 132 – Faridetta 107 (Good Bond 122) [1990 NR 1991 12.4m 18.5g] big, strong, close-coupled gelding: moderate walker: fair maiden at 3 yrs: seemed to stay 19f: acts on firm ground: bandaged: dead. *A. P. Stringer.*

FARHOLME LADS 2 b.g. (Mar 27) Balidar 133 – Rose of Shenfield 86 (Upper **61** Case (USA)) [1991 5g 5f² 5m* 6m² 5m* 6m³ 5g* 5g³ 5m³] 2,600F, 4,000Y: tall, leggy gelding: quite good mover: half-brother to 1988 2-y-o 7f winner Fit For Counsel (by Hotfoot), also successful over hurdles: dam, suited by 6f, is out of half-sister to Vilgora: quite modest performer: successful in summer in sellers (no bid) at Beverley and Redcar and in 4-runner claimer at Edinburgh: better form at 5f: acts on good to firm ground: withdrawn once after twice unseating rider stalls. *C. Tinkler.*

FARMER JOCK 9 ch.h. Crofter (USA) 124 – Some Dame 72 (Will Somers 114§) **67** [1990 a5g² a5g³ a7g⁴ a5g² a6g³ a6g⁵ a6g⁵ 5f 5m 5.8h² 5g⁵ 6d 5m 5g⁴ 6g 5f⁴ 5.8h³ 6h* 6m⁴ 6h⁴ 1991 7f 6s* 5g 6g 6g 6f⁴ 5f 6g⁶ 5m³ 5d⁶ 6.1m] strong, good-bodied horse: carries condition: quite modest handicapper: won at Kempton in April: best at 5f or 6f: acts on any going: effective with or without blinkers or visor: has worn bandages: tends to hang: needs strong handling and best held up. *Mrs N. Macauley.*

FARMER'S FIRE (IRE) 2 ch.c. (May 29) Ahonoora 122 – Forlene 108 (Forli **62 p** (ARG)) [1991 7g 7g] 30,000Y: strong, lengthy colt: has scope: seventh foal: half-brother to 5 winners here and abroad, including untrustworthy 3-y-o 10.1f winner Jungle Dancer (by Sadler's Wells) and 10.8f winner Mesleh (by Alleged): dam Irish 2-y-o 7f and 1m winner out of very smart Arkadina: much better effort (though very green) when around 6 lengths ninth of 13 to Alsaarm in minor event at York in September, held up after slow start then staying on: will stay 1m: sort to do better at 3 yrs. *C. F. Wall.*

FARMER'S PET 2 ch.f. (May 27) Sharrood (USA) 124 – Rectitude 99 (Runny- 55
mede 123) [1991 7m 7d] 14,500F, 7,000Y: rather plain, sparely-made filly: half-sister
to several winners, including useful 1985 2-y-o 7f winner Normanby Lass (by
Bustino) and 1¼m winner Rectillon (by Rousillon): dam winner at up to 8.5f, is out
of smart Altitude: never better than mid-division in late-season maidens at Doncaster, better effort (though backward) on debut: will stay 1m. *G. A. Pritchard-
Gordon.*

FAR MORE 5 ch.g. Gorytus (USA) 132 – Demare (Pardao 120) [1990 14g 18f 10.6s —
11.5m 12m⁴ 1991 a14g⁶] workmanlike gelding: moderate mover: quite modest
maiden at best: no form since 3-y-o: stays 1½m: acts on hard ground, probably
unsuited by a soft surface: below form in blinkers: often bandaged: has worn crossed
noseband: not the easiest of rides: has joined Ronald Thompson. *J. H. Johnson.*

FARM STREET 4 b.g. Henbit (USA) 130 – Mill Hill (USA) (Riva Ridge (USA)) 81
[1990 10m⁴ 12f⁴ 8.5d* 8d 8.5m 8m 10m 8d 1991 8d 7g* 7.6d 7f⁴ 8d 8g 7g]
workmanlike, good-quartered gelding: moderate mover: fair handicapper at best:
won very strongly-run event at Kempton in April despite drifting right: best at 7f to
1m: best efforts with give in the ground: has edged left and raced too freely:
inconsistent. *P. T. Walwyn.*

FAROOTS (FR) 2 b.g. (Feb 9) Deep Roots 124 – Farahdyne (FR) (Bolkonski 65
134) [1991 5d 5f³ 5d³ 5f³ 5m² 5m³ 5f* 5.2f* 5h³ 5m] 11,000 francs (approx £1,100) Y,
4,000 2-y-o: strong, deep-girthed gelding: has plenty of scope: moderate mover:
dam French maiden: quite modest performer: won 12-runner claimer at Beverley
and seller at Yarmouth (no bid) in August: moderately drawn (not discredited) in
Redcar nursery final start: best efforts over stiff 5f and will stay 6f: visored last 4
outings: largely consistent. *C. Tinkler.*

FAR PAVILION (IRE) 3 b.f. Pennine Walk 120 – Fair Abode (Habitat 134) 81
[1990 6g* 6g4 1991 7m 7g 7m² 8m 7.1g 7g 7.1m] lengthy, workmanlike filly: fair
performer: staying-on second in handicap at Sandown: failed to confirm that
improvement in similar events: suited by 7f: sweating and on toes last 2 starts:
blinkered (free to post, made most) final one. *R. Charlton.*

FARSI 3 gr.c. Nishapour (FR) 125 – Pot Pourri 97 (Busted 134) [1990 NR 1991 84
15.3m* 16.2g 16.2f3 13.9g6 18m* 16.2f4 16m³ 18m³] close-coupled, good-bodied
colt: carries condition: has a quick action: half-brother to 3 winners, including
one-time fair stayer Podrida (by Persepolis): dam staying half-sister to very smart

Phil Bull Trophy, Pontefract—a close race between Farsi and Jackson Flint

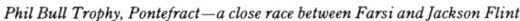

Almiranta: successful in maiden at Wolverhampton in May and minor event at Pontefract in September: good third in handicaps at Newmarket, behind Go South in Tote Cesarewitch final start: suited by thorough test of stamina: acts on good to firm ground: tends to carry head awkwardly. *R. Hollinshead.*

FARYAL 2 gr.f. (Feb 7) Bellypha 130 – French Cutie (USA) (Vaguely Noble 140) **56** [1991 6.1f 7g 8.1s] 3,600Y: close-coupled, good-bodied filly: half-sister to 3-y-o Cornhill Melody (by The Minstrel) and several winners here and abroad, including 7f/1m performer Threshfield (by Northern Prospect): dam unraced: plating-class maiden: should stay 1¼m: seems well suited by soft ground. *J. L. Spearing.*

FASCINATION WALTZ 4 b.f. Shy Groom (USA) – Cuckoo Weir (Double **80** Jump 131) [1990 7m 6m* 6m* 6m 1991 6g4 6g 6m 5.1m5 6g] angular, sparely-made filly: fair handicapper: stays 6f: acts on good to firm ground: wore crossed noseband last 4 starts: none too consistent. *J. Mackie.*

FASHION PRINCESS 5 gr.m. Van Der Linden (FR) – Pendle's Secret 73 (Le — Johnstan 123) [1990 NR 1991 16m] small mare: lightly raced and no worthwhile form on flat: winning hurdler. *Mrs A. Knight.*

FASHION SCENE (USA) 5 ch.m. London Bells (CAN) 109 – Yes Please 108 — (Mount Hagen (FR) 127) [1990 8v 8m5 11g6 1991 a8g] rangy, sparely-made mare: poor maiden: stays 1m: acts on good to firm ground: visored (below form) on reappearance. *W. Storey.*

FASSFERN (USA) 2 b.c. (Jun 5) Alleged (USA) 138 – Comtesse de Loir (FR) **77** p 131 (Val de Loir 133) [1991 7g4 8m3] workmanlike colt: half-brother to several winners in France and North America, including French 9f and 1½m winner Heron Cove (by Bold Bidder) and French 3-y-o 1¼m winner Yggdrasil (by Riverman): dam top-class French middle-distance filly: easily better effort in October maidens when 3½ lengths third of 15 to Aljernaas at Pontefract, running on really well: will improve again over middle distances. *Mrs J. Cecil.*

FASTBIT 4 ch.c. Henbit (USA) 130 – Fastilious (Guillaume Tell (USA) 121) [1990 **49** 11m5 14m6 1991 12.5d3] second foal: dam never ran: won 1m maiden at Tralee, only start at 2 yrs and behind in minor events in 1990: poor form when third in claimer at Wolverhampton in April: formerly trained by L. Browne. *C. F. C. Jackson.*

FAST MANOUVRE (FR) 2 b.c. (Apr 28) Fast Topaze (USA) 128 – Cephira **85** (FR) (Abdos 134) [1991 8m4 8m3] leggy, angular colt: has a quick action: half-brother to several winners, notably useful 1987 French 2-y-o 5f winner Shaindy (by American Stress), later successful at up to 7f: dam fourth over 6f at 2 yrs: fair form in October maidens won by Wesaam and Bold Pursuit at Newmarket, latter occasion favourite and soon pushed along: will stay 1¼m. *M. Moubarak.*

FASTO 2 b.f. (Apr 14) Faustus (USA) 118 – Bounding (Forlorn River 124) [1991 5m — 5s 6g] leggy, sparely-made filly: has a round action: half-sister to 3-y-o Yeoman Bound (by Norwick) and several winners, including sprinter Pendor Dancer (by Piaffer): dam never ran: seems of little account. *K. T. Ivory.*

FAST RUN (IRE) 3 ch.g. Commanche Run 133 – Starlite Night (USA) 105 (Star — de Naskra (USA)) [1990 6m 7f4 7f2 7f 9g a8g 1991 12d6 15.3m 16g 12g 12m 9.7m 11.8m 10d] leggy gelding: little form since third 2-y-o start: should be suited by a test of stamina: blinkered once at 2 yrs: bandaged behind last 5 outings at 3 yrs, off-hind only last 3: joined J. Elliott. *Pat Mitchell.*

FAST-TALKIN TINKER (IRE) 3 b.g. Bold Owl 101 – Our Ena (Tower Walk **57** 130) [1990 7f2 8.2g6 8.2s5 1991 8.2m 11.1d5 12.4m5 12.3g 10.5d] workmanlike gelding: best efforts as 3-y-o (still below best) in handicaps third and final starts: should prove suited by return to 1½m: best form on top-of-the-ground: sold 7,200 gns Doncaster October Sales. *G. Richards.*

FATACK 2 b.c. (Feb 13) Kris 135 – Ma Petite Cherie (USA) 93 (Caro 133) [1991 8d **66** 7d] finely-made, quite attractive colt: second foal: half-brother to 3-y-o 1¼m winner Flaming Arrow (by Dancing Brave): dam French 1m (at 2 yrs) to 1¼m winner: seventh of 14, taking keen hold over 5f, fading gradually, in minor event at Newmarket (ridden by 7-lb claimer) in November: never placed to challenge in maiden at Doncaster later in month: should stay 1¼m: may do better. *M. R. Stoute.*

FATEFUL (USA) 3 b.f. Topsider (USA) – Fate's Reward (USA) (Key To The **86** Mint (USA)) [1990 6d* 1991 7m* 8g4 7d 6m] useful-looking filly: moderate mover: good walker: fair form: 9/4 on, won minor event at Wolverhampton in May: never able to challenge in moderately-run listed race and £80,000 handicap (stiff task) next 2 starts: tongue tied down, not entirely discredited in mid-division for £8,400 handicap on final one: stays 7f. *J. H. M. Gosden.*

283

FATHER FIGURE 3 ch.g. Crofthall 110 – Farinara (Dragonara Palace (USA) — 115) [1990 6m⁶ 7f³ 8m⁶ 7m 8m⁵ 10s 1991 10.8d 10f] sturdy gelding: modest maiden: ran moderately in spring at 3 yrs, in selling handicap final start: seems to stay 1m: blinkered twice: sold 1,400 gns Doncaster October Sales. *R. Hannon.*

FAUSTUS LAD 3 gr.c. Faustus (USA) 118 – Rich Lass (Broxted 120) [1990 7m — 7.5m a7g 8m 8.2s 1991 14g] close-coupled colt: poor maiden at best: should stay 1m: sold 1,050 gns Doncaster July Sales. *M. Brittain.*

FAVOURED NATIONS (IRE) 3 b. or br.c. Law Society (USA) 130 – Lady **114** Lavery (USA) (Northern Dancer) [1990 7d* 9d² 1991 11g* 12s³ 12s] first foal: dam thrice-raced half-sister to Irish St Leger winner Leading Counsel, Princess Royal winner Sylph and very useful American winner (at up to 11f) Present The Colors: didn't reappear until October as 3-y-o but won listed race at Naas and ran very well when ½-length third to Topanoora in Blandford Stakes at the Curragh: odds on, well below form on final outing: stays 1½m: acts on soft going. *M. V. O'Brien, Ireland.*

FAWAAYID (USA) 2 b.f. (Mar 1) Vaguely Noble 140 – Clara Bow (USA) **92 p** (Coastal (USA)) [1991 7.8g² 10d* 7s* 9d*] $57,000Y, resold $85,000Y: second foal: dam won 3 times from 6 starts at up to 9f in USA: progressive form: successful in autumn in 16-runner maiden at Listowel (odds on) and listed events at Leopardstown (by ¾ length from Miznah) and the Curragh (by length from Arrikala) 11 days later: will stay 1½m: acts well on a soft surface, yet to race on top-of-the-ground. *J. S. Bolger, Ireland.*

FAY EDEN (IRE) 3 ch.f. Fayruz 116 – Dainty Eden 53 (Orbit 106) [1990 6m 6m **60** 5m 5g 5.8d 1991 7g⁴ 8s 5g⁵ 6g* 5.1d⁴ 5.7g 6.9m] small, workmanlike filly: moderate mover: 10/1 from 33/1, won 20-runner seller (no bid) at Leicester in May: appeared to put up easily best effort in claimer at Chepstow next start, staying on well: should prove suited by 6f or 7f: possibly unsuited by very soft ground. *R. J. Hodges.*

FAYNAZ 5 ch.h. Tumble Wind (USA) – Ceduna (FR) (Right Tack 131) [1990 7g **58** 7.6m⁶ 6m⁴ 6f* 6m 8.2m⁴ 7m* 8g⁴ 8g 1991 7g 6m³ 5.8f 7m⁵ 6m⁶ 7m⁴ 6f 10g] well-made horse: quite modest handicapper: stays 7f: acts on firm going, yet to race on soft: effective with or without blinkers: has been bandaged behind: inconsistent. *W. R. Muir.*

FAY'S SONG (IRE) 3 ch.f. Fayruz 116 – Harp (Ennis 128) [1990 5.8m⁵ 5f* 5g⁵ **76** 5m² 1991 5m⁶ 6d⁴ 6g² 5g 6g³ 5f⁴ 6m 5m² 5g⁴ 5.2g] compact filly: moderate mover: modest performer: stays 6f: acts on firm ground, seems unsuited by a soft surface: sweating (ran creditably) penultimate start. *R. Akehurst.*

FAZAAZ (IRE) 2 b.c. (May 27) Caerleon (USA) 132 – Steel Habit (Habitat 134) **55** [1991 7m 8m] 160,000Y: compact colt: moderate mover: fifth foal: half-brother to 3 winners, including very smart 7f to 10.5f winner Batshoof and useful 1¼m winner Dress Parade (both by Sadler's Wells): dam, winner twice in Italy, closely related to high-class sprinter Steel Heart: plating-class form, beaten long way, in maidens at Newmarket and Leicester in October: likely to stay 1¼m. *A. A. Scott.*

FEARLESS NATIVE 6 br.g. Final Straw 127 – Nativity (USA) 91 (Native — Royalty (USA)) [1990 10g 1991 10f] leggy, close-coupled gelding: plating-class winner as 3-y-o: lost his form: suited by 1¼m: acted on firm ground: dead. *R. J. Manning.*

FEELING FOOLISH (IRE) 2 ch.g. (Apr 29) Fools Holme (USA) – Felin Geri **65** (Silly Season 127) [1991 6d² 6m³ 8.1g² 8m² 7m⁵ 8.1s⁵ a7g a8g*] IR 1,000Y, 10,000 2-y-o: useful-looking gelding: half-brother to several winners, including Akrotiri Bay (by Ya Zaman), 1m and 8.2f winner at 2 yrs, and 5f and 6f winner Coppermill Lad (by Ardoon): dam unraced half-sister to Kalaglow: quite modest performer: apprentice ridden and visored, won late-year claimer at Southwell by 2½ lengths: will be suited by 1¼m: acts on good to firm and soft ground: appeared to run ungenerously when blinkered fifth outing: joined T. Fairhurst. *S. G. Norton.*

FEENPARK (GER) 6 ch.h. Park Romeo – Feenlied (Literat) [1990 6.5g* 6g² **115** 6d* 6d 8g³ 6g 5d* 5g* 5v³ 1991 6g⁴ 6.5d² 6g² 6d² 6g* 6g⁵] German-bred horse: smart performer: successful as 5-y-o in listed events at Hanover, Bremen and Cologne and in Dortmunder Fleigerpreis at Dortmund: won Group 3 Prix de Meautry at Deauville in August by 2 lengths from Ganges: in frame in Germany earlier as 6-y-o: effective at 5f and 6f: acts on a soft surface. *H. Cohn, Germany.*

FELICIDAD 2 ch.c. (Feb 15) Be My Guest (USA) 126 – Fresh (High Top 131) — p [1991 6g⁶ 7g] good-bodied colt: fluent mover: fourth foal: brother to useful sprinter Be Fresh and half-brother to modest 11f winner Dr Robert (by Commanche Run): dam, good middle-distance performer in Italy, is half-sister to Free Guest, dam of 3-y-o Shamshir: well beaten in maidens at Yarmouth in July and Brighton (still green, eased considerably) in September: looks sort to do much better. *L. M. Cumani.*

FELIM BLWM 3 b.g. Sayf El Arab (USA) 127 – Dawn Loch (USA) (Grey Dawn II 132) [1990 NR 1991 8m 7d 10g] stocky gelding: first foal: dam lightly raced, fourth once at 1¾m: showed nothing in claimer and sellers: blinkered final start: sold 880 gns Newmarket Autumn Sales.*J. A. R. Toller.* —

FELSEN (IRE) 2 b.f. (Jan 30) Ballad Rock 122 – Alaria (GER) (Kaiseradler) [1991 6.1m3 6f] rather leggy filly: eighth foal: half-sister to several winners worldwide, including useful 1986 Irish 2-y-o 7f winner Antic Boy (by Nebos): dam best 2-y-o filly in Germany in 1978, also won German Oaks: never-nearer third of 12 in maiden at Nottingham (started slowly) in August: comfortably held at Newbury later in month: likely to stay 1m. *B. Hanbury.* 54

FEMININE WILES (IRE) 2 b.f. (Apr 29) Ahonoora 122 – Instinctive Move (USA) (Nijinsky (CAN) 138) [1991 8.1m5 8m2 8m*] 14,000Y: lengthy, quite attractive filly: has scope: good mover with rather a round action: fourth foal: dam, minor winner in USA, is half-sister to Legal Bid, Law Society and Strike Your Colors: easily best effort when 5 lengths third of 14 (promoted) to Midnight Air in May Hill Stakes at Doncaster in September, hampered twice before staying on strongly from 2f out: 7/4 on, needed to be driven out to win 19-runner maiden at Warwick by ½ length from Morsun following month: will be well suited by 1¼m: sort to make a better 3-y-o. *P. W. Chapple-Hyam.* 88 p

FEN DANCE (IRE) 2 b.f. (Mar 16) Trojan Fen 118 – Madame Nureyev (USA) (Nureyev (USA) 131) [1991 6f4 6.1m2] 15,000Y: leggy filly: first foal: dam French 2-y-o 6f winner: better effort in maiden auctions when neck second of 23 to Room With A View at Nottingham in September, quickening to lead 2f out, caught close home: may prove best from 6f to 7f: sure to improve again. *P. J. Makin.* 74 p

FENGARI 2 ch.c. (Apr 14) Formidable (USA) 125 – Foreseen (Reform 132) [1991 a7g3] good-quartered colt: second foal: dam unraced half-sister to Derby Italiano winner My Top: 14/1, 4 lengths third of 12, always thereabouts, to Liability Order in November maiden at Lingfield: sold 8,400 gns Doncaster Sales later in month. *P. T. Walwyn.* 58 p

FENNEL 3 b.f. Slew O' Gold (USA) – Fenney Mill 99 (Levmoss 133) [1990 6m* 6.5g3 1991 10d6 12g] leggy, sparely-made filly: good mover: capable of fairly useful form: favourite, set modest pace when sixth to Magnificent Star in listed race at Newbury in May: 20/1, never able to challenge and soundly beaten in Ribblesdale Stakes at Royal Ascot: bred to be suited by middle distances: reportedly to join G. Jones in USA. *M. R. Stoute.* 93 +

FEN PRINCESS (IRE) 3 b.f. Trojan Fen 118 – Cenerentola (FR) (Caro 133) [1990 NR 1991 8g 10g3 10g2 8.3f6 12.1g 10.4m 12.2g5] neat filly: fifth foal: half-sister to French provincial 9f winner Town Centre (by Top Ville) and a winner in Norway: dam very useful 1m winner in France: modest maiden at best: should stay beyond 1¼m: visored sixth start: trained first 3 starts by Lord Huntingdon. *P. C. Haslam.* 72 d

FENTON LAKE 3 b.g. Tina's Pet 121 – Kakisa 81 (Forlorn River 124) [1990 6f3 5d2 5m3 5g2 6m2 1991 6g* 6d2 7g4 7g3 6g4 6f6 6m3 7d] good-topped gelding: won maiden at Lingfield in May: probably stays 7f: acts on good to firm ground and dead: has carried head high: winning hurdler: sold 7,200 gns Ascot November Sales. *G. A. Pritchard-Gordon.* 78

FERDIA (IRE) 2 b.c. (Mar 19) Petorius 117 – Kilvarnet 78 (Furry Glen 121) [1991 6g 6g6 6m 6m6 8.1d 7m a7g* a7g5] tall, rather leggy colt: has scope: first foal: dam 5f (at 2 yrs) and 7.6f winner: quite modest performer: won late-year nursery at Southwell by a length from Empeeka: never-dangerous fifth in similar event there final start: stays 1m: sometimes races keenly. *R. Hollinshead.* 65

FERMOY (USA) 2 b.f. (Mar 5) Irish River (FR) 131 – Victoress (USA) (Conquistador Cielo (USA)) [1991 6m2 6m3] leggy, close-coupled filly: first foal: dam lightly-raced French 11f winner, is half-sister to Awaasif (dam of Snow Bride) and several other good winners: modest form in maidens at Newmarket (well backed) and Redcar (favourite) in October: bred to stay middle distances: should win a race. *L. M. Cumani.* 76

FERN 2 b.f. (Feb 11) Shirley Heights 130 – Free Guest 125 (Be My Guest (USA) 126) [1991 7d3 8m2dis 8d4] rather unfurnished, quite attractive filly: second live foal: half-sister to 3-y-o Shamshir (by Kris), very useful 7f and 1m winner at 2 yrs and runner-up in Oaks: dam high-class 7f (at 2 yrs) to 1½m winner, won 9 of 15 starts: fairly useful maiden: caused interference when extricated from poor position 2f out and subsequently disqualified when strong-finishing 1½ lengths second of 13 behind 97 idling Midnight Air in May Hill Stakes at Doncaster in September: disappointing fifth (promoted) behind demoted Midnight Air in Brent Walker Fillies' Mile at Ascot later in month: will stay middle distances: certainly capable of winning races, and is worth another chance to confirm favourable impression from Doncaster. *L. M. Cumani.*

FEROX 5 b.g. Formidable (USA) 125 – La Grange 79 (Habitat 134) [1990 6f⁴ 5g 5m⁶ 8.3m 6d 5g* a6g a5g² 1991 a5g a6g⁶] strong, good-bodied gelding: has a quick action: modest handicapper at 4 yrs: no form in January, 1991: best form at 5f: may prove useful by given in the ground: usually bandaged: wore blinkers and eyeshield final start. *Mrs J. Cecil.*

FERROVIA 2 b.f. (Mar 20) Never So Bold 135 – Ouija 104 (Silly Season 127) [1991 6m 7m⁶] half-sister to several winners, notably useful 4-y-o 7f (at 2 yrs) to 8.2f winner Message Pad (by Rousillon) and high-class 1m to 1¼m performer Teleprompter (by Welsh Pageant): dam best at 1m: plating-class form in minor event at Ayr and maiden at Redcar in autumn: should stay at least 7f. *J. W. Watts.*　**55**

FERRYCROSTHEMERSEY (IRE) 2 b.f. (Feb 8) Red Sunset 120 – Glomach (USA) 73 (Majestic Light (USA)) [1991 5g 6m 7.5f 5.1g 6m 5m] IR 6,000F: neat filly: has a round action: fifth living foal: dam 7f winner, is out of half-sister to top-class American horses Fort Marcy and Key To The Mint: seems of little account. *A. Smith.*　**—**

FESTIVE CHEER (IRE) 2 b.c. (Feb 21) Fayruz 116 – Granny Bunn (Wolver Hollow 126) [1991 6g 5g² 5f* 5m² 6m³] 6,800Y: strong-quartered, quite attractive colt: third foal: dam never ran: fairly useful performer: odds-on 5-length winner of 7-runner maiden at Tralee: beaten a neck behind Isdar in Windsor Castle Stakes at Royal Ascot later in June, and when strong-finishing third to Bradawn Breever and Maledetto in Heinz '57' Phoenix Stakes at Leopardstown in August: better suited by 6f than 5f: acts on firm going. *T. Stack, Ireland.*　**98**

FESTIVE FALCON 5 ch.g. Sandhurst Prince 128 – Caelidh 98 (Silly Season 127) [1990 11g* 10m* a12g² a12g a8g a12g 1991 a10g 14m a12g] tall, close-coupled gelding: quite modest performer at 3 yrs: lost his form: stays 1½m: acts on good to firm going: blinkered final start: sold 1,050 gns Ascot July Sales. *R. T. Juckes.*　**—**

FETISH 2 b.f. (Mar 12) Dancing Brave (USA) 140 – Bold Fantasy 115 (Bold Lad (IRE) 133) [1991 6g⁵] sister to French 3-y-o 1½m winner Famosa and half-sister to several winners, including Lowther winner Kingscote (by Kings Lake) and French 9f winner Esna (by Troy): dam Irish 7f winner second in Irish 1000 Guineas: beaten around 7 lengths in 7-runner maiden won by She's Pleased at Newmarket in October: will improve over further. *H. R. A. Cecil.*　**62 p**

FETTLE UP 3 ch.g. Lyphard's Special (USA) 122 – Fire Risk (Thatch (USA) 136) [1990 8f 10s a8g 1991 10m 12m] neat gelding: no worthwhile form in maidens and claimers. *J. Wharton.*　**—**

FEZZAN 2 b.c. (Feb 21) Green Desert (USA) 127 – Little Loch Broom 60 (Reform 132) [1991 6m 6g] 240,000Y. strong, useful-looking colt: good walker: half-brother to 3-y-o 8.2f (at 2 yrs) and 1¼m winner Paris of Troy (by Trojan Fen), and 4 other winners, including very useful 1983 2-y-o 6f winner Fawzi (by Young Generation) and fairly useful 11f and 13.3f winner Musaahim (by Pharly): dam placed over 1m and 1¼m, is out of very useful Sleat, grandam of Reprimand: travelled comfortably to 2f out then eased considerably when beaten, in autumn maidens in the South: will improve. *J. H. M. Gosden.*　**53 p**

FIALA (IRE) 3 b.f. Persian Bold 123 – Goody Blake 103 (Blakeney 126) [1990 NR 1991 8f⁴ 10g 12s² a12g² a13g*] 33,000Y: workmanlike filly: has a round action: second foal: dam 1¼m winner would have been suited by 1¾m: much improved effort when winning 7-runner handicap at Lingfield in December by 8 lengths: will stay further: acts on soft going: bandaged off-hind on debut. *J. H. M. Gosden.*　**88**

FICTION 2 br.f. (Mar 17) Dominion 123 – Sans Blague (USA) 108 (The Minstrel (CAN) 135) [1991 5.2g³ 5f* 6g 7m] leggy filly: sixth foal: half-sister to 3-y-o Motley (by Rainbow Quest), very useful 1986 2-y-o 6f and 7.3f winner Nettle (by Kris) and middle-distance winner Quip (by High Line): dam suited by 1½m, is half-sister to very useful middle-distance filly Deadly Serious: odds on, won 4-runner maiden at Beverley in August: ran respectably next start, moderately final one: should stay 7f: sold 5,200 gns Ascot November Sales. *I. A. Balding.*　**60**

FIDDLING 4 ch.f. Music Boy 124 – Penny Pincher 95 (Constable 119) [1990 5m* 5d² 5g 1991 5g 5f 5m 5m² 5f⁶ 5g³ 5g 5m³ 5m²ᵈⁱˢ 5f³] workmanlike, good-quartered filly: good walker: moderate mover: fair handicapper: well worth a try over 6f: acts on good to firm ground: usually slowly away. *Mrs J. R. Ramsden.*　**82**

FIELD OF DREAMS   2 b.f. (Mar 24) Celestial Storm (USA) 132 – Silka (ITY)   —
(Lypheor 118) [1991 7g] fourth reported foal: half-sister to 3-y-o 1¼m (at 2 yrs) and
1½m winner Merchant of Venice (by Precocious), 1¼m and 1½m winner Duggan
(by Dunbeath) and 6f and 7.5f winner Cluzo (by Sharpo): dam won in Italy:
soundly-beaten eighth in 11-runner maiden at Salisbury in October. *C. F. Wall.*

FIELD OF HONOUR   3 b.c. Ahonoora 122 – Brickfield Queen (High Top 131)   90
[1990 NR 1991 7m⁴ 8.5m² 8m* 8g² 8.9m² 7g] 140,000Y: angular, quite attractive
colt: good walker: third foal: half-brother to fairly useful 11.5f winner Limeburn (by
Young Generation): dam French provincial 10.8f winner from family of Lord Gayle:
won maiden at Brighton in June: second in handicaps at Yarmouth and (looked sure
to win when challenging over 1f out, edged left) York: bit backward final start: stays
9f: acts on good to firm ground. *L. M. Cumani.*

FIELDRIDGE   2 ch.c. (Feb 1) Rousillon (USA) 133 – Final Thought (Final Straw   79
127) [1991 8m² 8.1g³] 47,000Y: tall, lengthy colt: second foal: dam unraced
half-sister to Middle Park winner Creag-An-Sgor: fair form in maiden at Doncaster
(ran on well) and 4-runner minor event at Haydock (soon niggled along, kept on
steadily) in September. *C. R. Nelson.*

FIELD RUNNER   4 ch.g. Precocious 126 – Orange Squash 78 (Red God 128§)   —
[1990 10.1m⁴ 1991 11.8g a14g 11m⁵ 11.6m] tall gelding: lightly raced and no
worthwhile form: blinkered final start: sold 950 gns Ascot September Sales. *G. A.
Pritchard-Gordon.*

FIERCE   3 ch.g. Carwhite 127 – Nosey 96 (Nebbiolo 125) [1990 7m⁵ 7f⁴ 8m⁴   62 p
8m 1991 10g⁶ 11.5g⁴] tall, close-coupled gelding: quite modest form: tenderly
handled both starts in summer as 3-y-o, catching eye when running-on fourth in
claimer at Sandown: stays 11.5f: winning hurdler: probably capable of better. *J. R.
Jenkins.*

FIESOLE   5 ch.m. Sharpo 132 – Flaming Peace 104 (Queen's Hussar 124) [1990   —
8m 8.2s 8f³ 8m 8f 8m* 8f³ 8.2m⁵ 8f 1991 8.2s⁴ 16.2g] leggy mare: poor plater: stayed
1m: acted on firm ground: dead. *G. M. Moore.*

FIFE (IRE)   3 b.f. Lomond (USA) 128 – Fiddle-Faddle 85 (Silly Season 127) [1990   95
8m³ 1991 8g* 10g³ 12g⁵ 11.9g⁶ 13.9m³] lengthy filly: fairly useful performer: 25/1,
won 5-runner £6,800 contest at Sandown in April: good efforts in listed race at
Goodwood and Ribblesdale Stakes at Royal Ascot next 2 starts and when 7½ lengths
third to Hawait Al Barr in moderately-run minor event at York on final one: should
be better at 1¾m than 1½m. *B. W. Hills.*

FIFTH OF APRIL (IRE)   3 b.c. Jester 119 – Polisteppin 92 (Jimmy Reppin 131)   —
[1990 NR 1991 6m] 7,000 2-y-o: workmanlike colt: second foal: dam Irish 1m and
1½m winner: well beaten in maiden at Newmarket in April, very slowly away. *S.
Dow.*

FIGARO   6 b.h. Comedy Star (USA) 121 – Jolly Bay 108 (Mill Reef (USA) 141)   —
[1990 NR 1991 10v] very lightly-raced maiden: heavily bandaged on first run since 2
yrs, no promise in Folkestone claimer. *J. E. Long.*

FIGHTER SQUADRON   2 ch.g. (Feb 12) Primo Dominie 121 – Formidable   47
Dancer 70 (Formidable (USA) 125) [1991 6g a7g 5f⁶] 9,000F, 9,400Y, 11,000 2-y-o:
second foal: dam modest, stayed 1½m: poor form in summer, including in claimers:
ridden by 7-lb claimer first 2 starts: should stay 7f. *J. A. Glover.*

FIGHTING CHRISTINE (USA)   4 ch.f. Fighting Fit (USA) – Born Anew   39
(USA) (Avatar (USA)) [1990 a8g⁴ a8g⁴ a7g* 8g⁵ a8g 8m 7m² 8.2v² 7g 1991 a7g 7d
7.5g 9m⁶ 8h⁵ 6.9m⁴ 7f⁴ 8m⁵ 10m] rangy filly: has a quick action: poor performer
nowadays: best form at 7f/1m: acts on any going: sometimes hangs left: has run
fairly well when blinkered or visored: bandaged at 4 yrs: winning hurdler in August:
has joined Mrs L. Stubbs. *P. C. Haslam.*

FIGHTING TEMERAIRE (IRE)   2 b.c. (Mar 31) Tate Gallery (USA) 117 –   84
Maid of Erin (USA) (Irish River (FR) 131) [1991 5m² 5m³ 5d³ 5.7f² 6g² 6d⁵ 6m⁶] IR
17,500Y: rangy, good-topped colt: has scope: third foal: half-brother to 3-y-o Mizyan
(by Melyno) and quite modest 1989 2-y-o My Mavournin (by L'Emigrant): dam, ran
once in France, is sister to good-class River Dancer, from family of Sun Princess:
fair form: very good second of 9, drifting right close home, in nursery at Ascot fifth
outing: probably better suited by 6f than 5f: seems unsuited by a soft surface: races
keenly: has run creditably for 7-lb claimer: sold 21,000 gns Newmarket Autumn
Sales. *P. F. I. Cole.*

FIGHT TO WIN (USA)   3 b.g. Fit To Fight (USA) – Spark of Life (USA) (Key   65
To The Mint (USA)) [1990 8m 1991 10m⁴ 12m 12m⁵ 14g 17.2f³ 16m² 16m³ 16.9g⁴
15.4m³] sturdy gelding: shows knee action: quite modest maiden: mostly ran

creditably in second half of season, in amateurs event at Folkestone final outing: stays well: acts on firm going: blinkered seventh start: one paced. *I. A. Balding.*

FIGMENT 4 b.f. Posse (USA) 130 – Honey Thief 77 (Burglar 128) [1990 5m⁵ 5g⁶ **63** 5m³ 5f² 5m* 6f³ a5g 5m² 5g* 6m* 5m 5m 7m 5g 1991 a6g 5m³ 5d 6m 6g 5d⁴ 5m 5g 5m 7g 5f] strong, good-topped filly: quite modest handicapper: stays 6f: probably acts on any going: has won with or without blinkers: once wore eyeshield: somewhat temperamental, and seems to go well with tender handling: inconsistent. *D. W. Chapman.*

FILET MIGNON (USA) 2 ch.f. (Apr 19) Topsider (USA) – Passerine (USA) — (Dr Fager) [1991 5m] $23,000Y: workmanlike filly: sister to very useful sprinter Doulab, closely related to 2 winners, including 3-y-o 5f winner Rawaabe (by Nureyev), and half-sister to another: dam, 6f winner, is half-sister to high-class performer Properantes: 20/1 and green, slowly away and always behind in 11-runner maiden at Sandown: bandaged all round. *W. J. Haggas.*

FILIA ARDROSS 5 b.m. Ardross 134 – Sari Habit (Saritamer (USA) 130) [1990 **114** 10m⁶ 8.5g³ 7m² 7.3g⁵ 10m² 10m³ 10d⁵ 1991 10m⁴ 10g⁵ 10m* 10m* 10m⁴ 12g² 10.5v] strong, good-topped mare: very useful performer: won listed event at Windsor (gamely) in August then moderately-run Group 3 event at Goodwood (well ridden) in September: ran well after when in frame in moderately-run Sun Chariot Stakes at Newmarket and St Simon Stakes at Newbury (caught close home by Further Flight): stays 1½m, and effective at much shorter: acts on good to firm and soft going: visored third to fifth starts, blinkered last 2: game and largely consistent. *A. C. Stewart.*

FILICAIA 5 ro.m. Sallust 134 – Fine Flame (Le Prince 98) [1990 6f 7f 7m 7f³ a7g **59** 7m⁴ 6g 7m³ 6f³ 6m 6m³ 6m* 5f⁴ 6g 6s 1991 6m 6g 6m² 6f² 5h* 5d 6g⁶ 6m* 6f 6m 6f² 5h³ 5f⁵ 5m⁴ 6m² 6g] compact mare: plating-class handicapper: won at Carlisle and Ripon in summer: seems ideally suited by 6f or 7f: acts on hard and dead going: best visored: often slowly away: has got on edge: tough. *Don Enrico Incisa.*

FINAL ACE 4 ch.c. Sharpo 132 – Palmella (USA) 89 (Grundy 137) [1990 5f* 6g **56** 6m 5m³ 6s 8d 1991 6m 7m 6m⁵ 8d 8g⁵ 8.2m 8.9m³ 10.8m³ 10.2m⁶ 9s 10.8g] robust type: plating-class performer nowadays: claimed out of J. Etherington's stable £6,711 seventh start: stays 10.8f: acts on firm going, seems unsuited by soft: often wears crossed noseband nowadays: inconsistent. *Miss S. J. Wilton.*

FINAL ALI 4 ch.g. Final Straw 127 – Bargouzine 67 (Hotfoot 126) [1990 8.2d — 10.4m⁶ 10.2f⁵ 7m³ 8m⁴ 7f 11d a8g 1991 8m 8m 10.5m 10.3g 8m] big, plain gelding: shows traces of stringhalt: poor maiden: no form in 1991: stays 1m: form only on good to firm ground: sold 4,000 gns Doncaster November Sales. *Capt. J. Wilson.*

FINAL BOUT 3 br.f. Final Straw 127 – Bourton Downs 74 (Philip of Spain 126) — [1990 NR 1991 6g 6d 8f⁵ 6f 6m] 900 2-y-o: small, stocky filly: poor mover: eighth foal: half-sister to 11f winner Just Great (by Simply Great), a winner in Italy by Blakeney and 8.2f winner Neverdown (by Never So Bold): dam 2-y-o 5f winner didn't train on: no form in maidens and handicaps: blinkered final start: has swished tail. *R. D. E. Woodhouse.*

Abtrust Select Stakes, Goodwood—
Filia Ardross (visored) gradually takes the measure of Gai Bulga;
In The Groove (right) has too much to do

FINAL DEED 3 gr.g. Final Straw 127 – Birch Creek (Carwhite 127) [1990 6g³ **72**
7g* 7m² 6m⁴ 7g 8m 8v 7s 1991 10d 12g 11m⁵ 12g 10g* 9.9f⁶ 10g*dis 10g³ 10.5f⁵ 9d³
10.5g] big, good-bodied gelding: has a round action: modest performer: first past
post in handicaps at Nottingham in June and Ayr (edging left and disqualified for
interference) in July: stays 1¼m: below form on extremes of going: usually on toes:
blinkered last 8 starts: tends to hang, and has carried head high: sold 12,000 gns
Newmarket Autumn Sales: inconsistent and not one to trust implicitly. *F. H. Lee.*

FINAL FAREWELL (USA) 2 ch.f. (Apr 10) Proud Truth (USA) – Spring — p
Adieu (CAN) (Buckpasser) [1991 6g] $100,000Y: leggy, lengthy filly: half-sister to 2
winners and to dam of Danehill: dam sprinting half-sister to Northern Dancer: sire
won Breeders' Cup Classic: 8/1, well beaten in 21-runner maiden at Newbury in
October, fading final 2f and eased: may prove suited by further: should do better. *P.
W. Chapple-Hyam.*

FINAL OFFER (USA) 3 gr.f. Spectacular Bid (USA) – Geiger Countess (USA) **34** §
(Mr Prospector (USA)) [1990 6m⁴ 6g a6g 1991 8m 7g⁴ 10g⁵ 8.2f 8g⁵ 8f 10m]
close-coupled filly: poor performer: should prove best at up to 1m: blinkered once at
2 yrs: often sweating: has worn bandages: twice withdrawn after trouble at stalls:
pulls hard: trained first 5 starts by E. Eldin: temperamental. *M. Bell.*

FINAL SHOT 4 br.f. Dalsaan 125 – Isadora Duncan (Primera 131) [1990 5f⁵ 5d **83**
6m 7m² 7g² 6m* 7f³ 6m⁶ 6m³ 6d* 6g 7.6v 1991 7.6d 7m 6m 6g 6d⁴ 6m² 6d⁶ 6m 6g
6m 6g 7g] small, workmanlike filly: fairly useful handicapper at best: well beaten
last 3 starts (visored once): effective at 6f and 7f: acts on firm but very best efforts
on dead ground: game. *M. H. Easterby.*

FINANCE DANCER (IRE) 3 b.f. Shareef Dancer (USA) 135 – Mahabba (USA) **106**
74 (Electionist (USA)) [1990 NR 1991 10d² 11.5f* 12g² 12g³ 12d² 12g] IR 32,000Y:
angular filly: has scope: half-sister to 1986 Irish 2-y-o 7.9f winner Abbaham (by
Kris) and a winner in Italy: dam 1½m winner out of Lancashire Oaks winner
Amphora: won maiden at Yarmouth in June: placed afterwards in Ribblesdale Stakes
at Royal Ascot, listed race at Goodwood (unimpressive in appearance, edged right
and found little) and Princess Royal Stakes (best effort, running on behind Always
Friendly) at Ascot: ran poorly facing stiff task in St Simon Stakes at Newbury: stays
at least 1½m: has won on firm ground but best efforts with some give: sold 74,000
gns Newmarket December Sales. *A. C. Stewart.*

FINDLAYS CHOICE 2 b.f. (May 9) Jupiter Island 126 – Truly Blest 75 (So **53**
Blessed 130) [1991 6g⁵ 6.1d 7m² 6m⁶ 7m⁵ 8d⁵] 2,000Y: leggy, angular filly:
half-sister to winners abroad by Pas de Seul and General Holme: dam 9f winner in
Ireland at 4 yrs, is half-sister to Cry of Truth: plating-class maiden: burst through
stalls and withdrawn under orders at Chepstow second outing: likely to stay 1¼m:
acts on good to firm and dead ground. *M. J. Ryan.*

FINE AS FIVEPENCE 2 b.f. (Feb 8) Sulaafah (USA) 119 – Shes Broke (Busted **40**
134) [1991 8g 8d 8g] rather sparely-made filly: second living foal: dam once-raced
half-sister to useful middle-distance performer Ravel: poor maiden: should stay
1¼m. *Mrs A. Knight.*

FINELY BALANCED (USA) 4 b.c. Topsider (USA) – Your Nuts (USA) —
(Creme Dela Creme) [1990 NR 1991 14.6s 8d 14g 16m 14.6d⁶] tall, lengthy colt:
brother to very useful 1983 2-y-o Maajid and 9f winer Sohail and half-brother to 2
winners: dam 2-y-o 6f winner: no form in varied company: tried blinkered: winning
hurdler. *R. Curtis.*

FINGERS CROSSED 7 b.m. Touching Wood (USA) 127 – La Pythie (FR) 89 —
(Filiberto (USA) 123) [1990 NR 1991 14m] neat, strong mare: lightly raced and poor
maiden, not seen on flat after April: winning hurdler in September. *K. A. Morgan.*

FINJAN 4 b.c. Thatching 131 – Capriconia (Try My Best (USA) 130) [1990 7m* **85**
7m 6m² 6g* 6m² 6d² 1991 6g 6g² 6d 6m 6m* 6m⁶ 6g 6g⁶ 6g³ 6m 6d² 6m] strong,
sturdy colt: keen walker: fair handicapper at best: won at Haydock in July: virtually
pulled up as if something amiss final start: suited by 6f: acts on good to firm and dead
ground: visored last 5 starts: reportedly broke blood vessel third start: sold to join
H. Whiting's stable 4,500 gns Newmarket Autumn Sales. *P. T. Walwyn.*

FIORINI 3 br.f. Formidable (USA) 125 – Egnoussa 76 (Swing Easy (USA) 126) **54**
[1990 5g⁴ 6d 1991 5s⁵ 5d a7g⁶ 6s* 5g 6g] small filly: 25/1, apparently much improved
to win 5-runner seller (no bid) at Hamilton in July, making virtually all: well beaten
facing stiffish tasks in handicaps afterwards: will prove suited by further than 5f:
acts on soft ground: blinkered last 3 starts. *C. B. B. Booth.*

FIREFIGHTER 2 ch.c. (Jun 4) Sharpo 132 – Courtesy Call (Northfields (USA)) —
[1991 6f⁵] 7,200Y: compact colt: fifth foal: half-brother to 3-y-o Beckoning (by

Bellypha), 10.2f winner Royal Passion (by Ahonoora), 6f winner Courtoisie (by Thatching) and a winner over hurdles in Ireland: dam thrice-raced half-sister to smart 1976 2-y-o 5f performer Piney Ridge: better for race, well-beaten fifth of 6 in maiden auction at Salisbury in August: moved poorly down. *J. Sutcliffe.*

FIREGLOW 3 b.f. Mummy's Game 120 – Burnt Amber (Balidar 133) [1990 7m **34** 8m 6m⁵ 6d 1991 10m⁴ 8m 8f 11g⁵ 10.1m 11m] angular, plain filly: poor mover: modest plater: stays 1¼m: blinkered (slowly away) final start: usually bandaged. *J. A. R. Toller.*

FIRE (IRE) 2 b.c. (May 10) Legend of France (USA) 124 – Fandangerina (USA) **73** (Grey Dawn II 132) [1991 5d 7g³ a7g* 8m] lengthy, useful-looking colt: has scope: has a quick action: closely related to very useful 1987 2-y-o 6f and 7f winner Western Gun (by Lypheor) and half-brother to useful 3-y-o 1¼m and 12.2f winner Ocean Air (by Elegant Air), also 7f and 8.2f winner at 2 yrs: dam won at up to 1m: modest form: won maiden at Southwell in July: looked to be progressing well, but ran moderately in Doncaster nursery nearly 2 months later: bred to stay 1¼m. *R. W. Armstrong.*

FIRE LADY 5 ch.m. Hotfoot 126 – Hindu Flame 83 (Shiny Tenth 120) [1990 8.3g **—** 8f 10.1m² 11.7m 1991 a11g a8g a13g] big, lengthy mare: poor plater: stays 1¼m: acts on firm going: sold 950 gns Ascot April Sales. *J. D. Thomas.*

FIRE TOP 6 br.h. Hotfoot 126 – Sirnelta (FR) (Sir Tor) [1990 10g 10g⁴ 10.4d 10g* **100** 10m³ 10.5m 10m 10f² 10m² 10.6g³ 10g 10.2s² 10g 1991 10g 12g 10.1f* 10g² 10g⁵ 10m³ 10.5f² 10m 10d⁴] sparely-made horse: usually looks really well: useful handicapper: won £17,400 event at Epsom in June: suited by around 1¼m: acts on any going: races up with pace: tremendously tough and genuine: largely consistent: credit to his trainer. *R. Akehurst.*

FIRM PRICE 10 b.g. Our Mirage 123 – Strip Poker 70 (Raise You Ten 125) [1990 **48** NR 1991 16.1m⁴ 17.1m] big, workmanlike gelding: quite modest handicapper at 7 yrs: better for outing both starts in 1991, only runs on flat since: needs at least 1½m, and stays well: acts on good to firm ground: fair hurdler/chaser for J. Edwards in 1990. *Mrs G. R. Reveley.*

FIRST AVENUE 7 b.g. Tina's Pet 121 – Olympus Girl 65 (Zeus Boy 121) [1990 **55** 11.5m⁵ 10g⁵ 11.7m⁶ 10h⁶ 10f² 10f* 10f⁵ 12m⁴ 1991 10s 10m* 9.7f* 9.7f³ 9.7m³ 10g] compact gelding: plating-class handicapper: won at Pontefract (apprentices) and Folkestone in August: stays 1½m: acts very well on firm going: has worn blinkers and visor: goes very well at Folkestone: tough and consistent. *Andrew Turnell.*

FIRST BID 4 ch.g. Crofthall 110 – Redgrave Design 77 (Nebbiolo 125) [1990 10g **52** 10d 12.2d⁴ 10d³ 9s 10.2s 1991 12.3s 11f 9.9g² 9.9f⁵ 11f⁵ 10m² 9.9f² 10.1m 10.5d³ 10m a14g] workmanlike gelding: plating-class handicapper: stays 1½m: acts on firm and dead ground: effective with or without visor or blinkers: goes well with forcing tactics. *R. M. Whitaker.*

FIRST CENTURY (IRE) 2 b.c. (Mar 14) Petorius 117 – Parima 72 (Pardao 120) **91** [1991 7d* 6.3s⁴ 8s] IR 34,000Y: neat, good-quartered colt: half-brother to 3 winners here and abroad, including smart 7f to 1¼m performer Trucidator (by Auction Ring) and fairly useful 1983 2-y-o 6f winner Rusticello (by Rusticaro): dam won over 9f and 1¼m in Norway: fairly useful performer: won maiden at Newmarket in August: good fourth of 21 in Goffs Premier Challenge Race at the Curragh in October: not discredited when tenth of 13 in Gran Criterium at Milan later same month: probably stays 1m: yet to race on a sound surface. *P. F. I. Cole.*

FIRST EMERALD 3 b.f. Sulaafah (USA) 119 – Mavela (USA) (Empery (USA) **—** 128) [1990 7.5g⁵ 7m 8m² a8g 1991 a8g] sparely-made filly: second in apprentice seller at 2 yrs: has run moderately at Southwell since: should stay 1¼m. *N. A. Graham.*

FIRST FLUSH 5 b.g. Precocious 126 – Rosananti 107 (Blushing Groom (FR) **33** 131) [1990 6f a5g 7g* 7f a7g⁵ a6g* 5m a6g 5m 1991 5m 6m 6m a7g 7m 6f 8.3m 6.9f⁴ 6m⁵ 7.1m 6g 6.1m 7s³] sturdy gelding: carries condition: poor walker: poor handicapper: stays 7f: acts on any going: below form when blinkered: wears bandages: inconsistent. *K. T. Ivory.*

FIRST FOR APRIL 3 b.f. Welsh Captain 113 – Glorious Spring 41 (Hittite Glory **—** 125) [1990 6m 5f 1991 5g 7m 10.2d] bad plater. *J. M. Bradley.*

FIRST GOLD 2 gr.c. (Mar 1) Absalom 128 – Cindys Gold 69 (Sonnen Gold 121) **—** [1991 5m] 31,000Y: second reported foal: dam plater stayed 7f, is daughter of sister to good sprinter Petong: weak 12/1-shot, burly and green, never better than mid-division from halfway in maiden at Sandown in April. *J. Wharton.*

FIRST HEIRESS (IRE)   2 b.f. (Apr 11) Last Tycoon 131 – Age of Elegance   **63** p
(Troy 137) [1991 7m] lengthy, lightly-made filly: third foal: half-sister to fair 1990
2-y-o 6f winner Accolade (by Auction Ring) and to smart 6f (at 2 yrs) and 7.6f winner
Sheer Precocity (by Precocious): dam French 11f and 1½m winner, is half-sister to
Elegant Air: 15/2, beaten around 8 lengths in mid-division for large-field maiden at
Doncaster in October: may improve. *M. R. Stoute.*

FIRST HOME   4 b.g. Homing 130 – Mill Wind 68 (Blakeney 126) [1990 a8g⁴ a11g⁶   —
11.5g⁴ 10f 11.5f⁶ 8f a10g⁶ 1991 a10g] rather leggy gelding: has a quick action:
inconsistent plater: stays 7f. *Pat Mitchell.*

FIRST RIGHT   2 b.f. (Apr 12) Primo Dominie 121 – Right Mall (Pall Mall 132)   **62**
[1991 6g 6g 5g³ 7g 6m 8m² 8.9m*] 6,000F, 9,200Y: workmanlike filly: half-sister to
several winners, including 1½m winner Regal Castle (by Tachypous) and useful
1982 2-y-o 5f and 6f winner Right Dancer (by Dance In Time): dam, closely related
to Sallust, won 3 times at 3 yrs in Italy: quite modest performer: runner-up in
Newmarket seller before winning 19-runner claimer at York in October: will stay
1¼m: ran poorly in visor fifth outing. *R. J. R. Williams.*

FIRST SAPPHIRE   4 b.f. Simply Great (FR) 122 – Yelney 65 (Blakeney 126)   —
[1990 NR 1991 a8g] sixth living foal: closely related to middle-distance stayer
Golden Heights (by Shirley Heights) and half-brother to 2 winners, including fair
5-y-o 6f to 1m winner Crosby (by Music Boy) and useful 6f performer Darley Knight
(by Formidable): dam, 1½m winner, is out of Cheshire Oaks winner Yelda: around
18 lengths ninth of 14 in maiden at Southwell in November, always behind. *W. Jarvis.*

FIRST STAGE   4 b.c. Shareef Dancer (USA) 135 – Bright Landing 78 (Sun Prince   **58**
128) [1990 9g* 14m⁵ 9.5f⁵ 12f⁵ 12m⁵ 1991 a13g² a12g³ a13g* 12g⁴ 15.5f⁴ 12.5d²
a12g³ 12m³ a12g⁶] small, sturdy ex-Irish colt: fifth foal: half-brother to fairly useful
1987 2-y-o 9f and 1¼m winner Upper Strata (by Shirley Heights), later winner at
2m: dam, placed over 5f at 2 yrs, is granddaughter of very smart sprinter Lucasland:
plating-class performer: won claimer at Lingfield in March: claimed out of Dr J.
Scargill's stable £7,600 penultimate start: stays 1¾m: acts on good to firm and dead
ground: has edged left: trained first 3 starts by I. Campbell: winning hurdler. *J. G. M.
O'Shea.*

FIRST SUCCESS (IRE)   3 gr.g. Wassl 125 – Ardmay 57 (Roan Rocket 128)   **64**
[1990 6m 8.2d⁵ 7m⁶ 7.3g 6m³ 5d 1991 6g⁴ 6m⁶ 6m³ 5m 7m⁴ 9m] good-quartered
gelding: quite modest maiden: ran creditably at Pontefract third start: stays 7f: acts
on good to firm ground: often blinkered: also wore eyeshield third and fourth
outings: has flashed tail: trained first 5 starts by R. Boss. *J. D. Czerpak.*

FIRST VICTORY   5 gr.h. Concorde Hero (USA) 101 – Cestrefeld 94 (Capistrano **100**
120) [1990 11m² 14m* 13.3m⁴ 12f² 16m⁵ 14g⁴ 13.3g* 12m⁴ 12s 1991 14m² 12g³
16.1m³ 16g⁶ 13.9g⁶ 14.6m³ 12s 16.2d⁶ 12g⁴ 12d] tall, angular horse: useful
handicapper: ran well in varied events, including Goodwood Cup (sweating), Tote
Ebor at York (set too much to do) and £15,100 event at Doncaster (apprentice
ridden, tended to edge left) fourth to sixth starts: effective at 1½m to 2m: needs
a sound surface: usually comes from behind, and is suited by strong gallop:
consistent. *R. Hannon.*

FISHIN' TACKLE (USA)   3 b.g. Sportin' Life (USA) – Perilune (USA) (Soy   **97**
Numero Uno (USA)) [1990 7m 1991 8d 8g* 11.5m⁶ 12m* 12g 10.5m*] tall,
useful-looking gelding: good walker: won maiden at Thirsk in May, handicap at
Epsom in June and claimer (best effort) at Haydock in July: soundly beaten in
handicap at Royal Ascot: stays 1½m: acts on good to firm ground: claimed to join L.
Lungo £26,090 final outing and gelded. *A. A. Scott.*

FISHKI   5 b.m. Niniski (USA) 125 – Ladyfish 79 (Pampapaul 121) [1990 a8g a12g⁶   —
11.5f* 12f³ 9g 12s* 15v* 1991 18.4d 12.1g 16.2d 15.1s] workmanlike, angular mare:
quite modest handicapper at 4 yrs: well below best in 1991: stays 15f: has won on
firm going, but goes particularly well in the mud: occasionally bandaged behind:
winning hurdler. *M. D. Hammond.*

FITAHL (USA)   3 br.c. Chief's Crown (USA) – Love's Dream (FR) (Rheingold   **98**
137) [1990 5m* 6m 5m³ 1991 5m⁴ 7g⁵ 8g 8m*] tall, well-made colt: has a round
action: fairly useful at best: won 3-runner minor event at Brighton in August by ½
length from Shaima, no room before quickening well to lead close home: better at
1m than shorter: rather headstrong and has been taken early to post: sold BBA
(Italia) 5,200 gns Newmarket Autumn Sales. *H. Thomson Jones.*

FIT FOR LIFE (IRE)   3 b.g. Local Suitor (USA) 128 – Strike It Rich (FR)   —
(Rheingold 137) [1990 NR 1991 a14g] IR 80,000Y: third foal: half-brother to 2
winners, including useful 1m to 1½m winner Lady Bentley (by Bellypha): dam Irish

9f and 1¼m winner, is half-sister to smart stayer Yawa: blinkered, tailed off in Southwell claimer in November. *Mrs L. Stubbs.*

FITNESS FANATIC   3 b.g. Nishapour (FR) 125 – Bustling Nelly 94 (Bustino   **45**
136) [1990 7g 8g 6d 1991 10g 10g⁵ 11.9m² 12d⁶] rangy gelding: poor performer: second in handicap at Brighton, always close up: better at 1½m than shorter: acts on good to firm ground. *D. A. Wilson.*

FIT ON TIME (USA)   2 ch.c. (Apr 28) Lead On Time (USA) 123 – Fitnah 125   **72**
(Kris 135) [1991 6.1m⁴ 6.9f⁵ 6s⁴] leggy, rather finely-made colt: shows knee action: second foal: half-brother to 1990 2-y-o 5f winner Mayaasa (by Green Desert): dam French 9.5f and 1¼m winner, second in French Oaks, is out of good sprinter Greenland Park: modest performer: easily best effort (despite slow start) in Nottingham minor event on debut: should stay 7f. *M. R. Stoute.*

FIT THE BILL   3 b.g. Nicholas Bill 125 – Golden Windlass 79 (Princely Gift 137)   **67 d**
[1990 6m³ 6m 5d 8d⁴ 8.2g² 1991 6g² 8d³ 6s² 7d* 9.2d* 7g² 10f 8m 10g 8m 9g] lengthy gelding: poor mover: modest form at best: ran 4 times in July, narrow winner of claimer at Ayr and seller (bought in 15,000 gns) at Hamilton: well below best after claimed out of Mrs G. Reveley's stable £11,888 sixth outing but showed signs of return to form in £30,800 Newbury handicap final start: effective at 7f and 9f: acts on soft ground: winning hurdler. *J. S. Wainwright.*

FIVE CASTLES   3 b.g. Castle Keep 121 – Teftu 85 (Double Jump 131) [1990 8g 7s   —
6d 1991 10m 11.5g 11.5m] angular gelding: behind, in seller final start: bandaged second start. *G. P. Enright.*

FIVESEVENFIVEO   3 ch.f. Enchantment 115 – Miss Times 78 (Major Portion   **67**
129) [1990 5g 5g* 6f² 5m² 6m⁴ 5m³ 6m 1991 5m² 5g* 5f² 5.1d* 5.7g⁴ 5f⁴ 6f* 6m* 6m⁶ 6f² 5m⁶ 6g] close-coupled, good-quartered filly: tends to look dull in coat: has a quick action: smart plater: favourite, successful at Bath in April, Chepstow (claimer) in June and at Thirsk (ladies event) and Windsor in August: retained 5,200 gns, no bid and 7,400 gns afterwards: stays 6f: acts on firm and dead going: ran very well for claimer tenth start: has hung left: sold 5,000 gns Doncaster October Sales. *J. Berry.*

FIVE TO SEVEN (USA)   2 br.c. (Jun 2) Little Missouri (USA) – French Galaxy   **82 ?**
(USA) (Majestic Light (USA)) [1991 7.6d² 8.1s²] $13,000Y: rather leggy, useful-looking colt: first foal: dam (ran once) from family of Midway Lady): sire Grade 1 1½m winner: runner-up in late-season maidens at Chester (better effort, beaten head by Al Ramis) and Edinburgh: will stay 1¼m: yet to race on sound surface. *S. G. Norton.*

FIZZ TIME   3 b.c. Good Times (ITY) – More Fizz (Morston (FR) 125) [1990 5d 5d   **74**
6d 1991 8.2d² 6d* 7m* 6m² 7m* 8d] leggy, rather angular colt: usually looks well: modest form: won seller at Ayr, claimer at Doncaster and handicap at Newmarket in the spring: should stay 1m: best efforts on good to firm ground: blinkered on reappearance: sold 18,000 gns Newmarket Autumn Sales. *Mrs J. R. Ramsden.*

FLAMING ARROW   3 br.c. Dancing Brave (USA) 140 – Ma Petite Cherie   **95**
(USA) (Caro 133) [1990 NR 1991 10.2m³ 10f* 10g 10m²] compact colt: first foal: dam French 1m (at 2 yrs) to 1¼m winner: 11/8 on, won maiden at Ripon in July: ran moderately in £30,600 handicap next start, very well when 1½ lengths second of 4 to Nucleus in minor event (made most) at Leicester nearly 3 months later: will stay 1½m. *H. R. A. Cecil.*

FLAMING GLORY   4 b.g. Alzao (USA) 117 – Engage (Whistling Wind 123) [1990   — §
12.3d⁶ 12d³ 12g 16.2f⁴ 16f⁶ 16.2g² 18g 1991 14.8g 16.2g 21.6f] stocky gelding: modest handicapper at 3 yrs: tailed off in first half of 1991, seeming reluctant to race second start: stays 2m: acts on firm ground and dead: wore hood last 2 starts, blinkered previous 6: trained reappearance by P. Blockley: sold 1,900 gns Doncaster Spring Sales. *R. W. Stubbs.*

FLAMINGO ROSE (IRE)   2 ch.f. (Mar 7) Antheus (USA) 122 – Tigresse   **39 p**
d'Amour (USA) (Stage Door Johnny) [1991 a7g⁴] 350,000 francs (approx £35,000) Y: third foal: closely related to useful 1¼m winter Tiger Flower (by Sadler's Wells): dam, French 2-y-o 7f winner, is sister to high-class American middle-distance stayer One On The Aisle: weak 9/2-shot, over 12 lengths fourth of 16, keeping on from rear, to Empeeka in late-year maiden at Southwell: will improve. *H. R. A. Cecil.*

FLAMING RED   3 b.g. Remezzo 111 – Sohara (pedigree unknown) [1990 NR   —
1991 8g 8m] first reported foal: tailed off in maidens. *J. P. Smith.*

FLASH BID (IRE)   2 b.g. (Jan 9) Runnett 125 – Lone Bidder 97 (Auction Ring   **36**
(USA) 123) [1991 5f 6f 7m⁶ 8.2m] 8,200Y: workmanlike, good-bodied gelding: half-

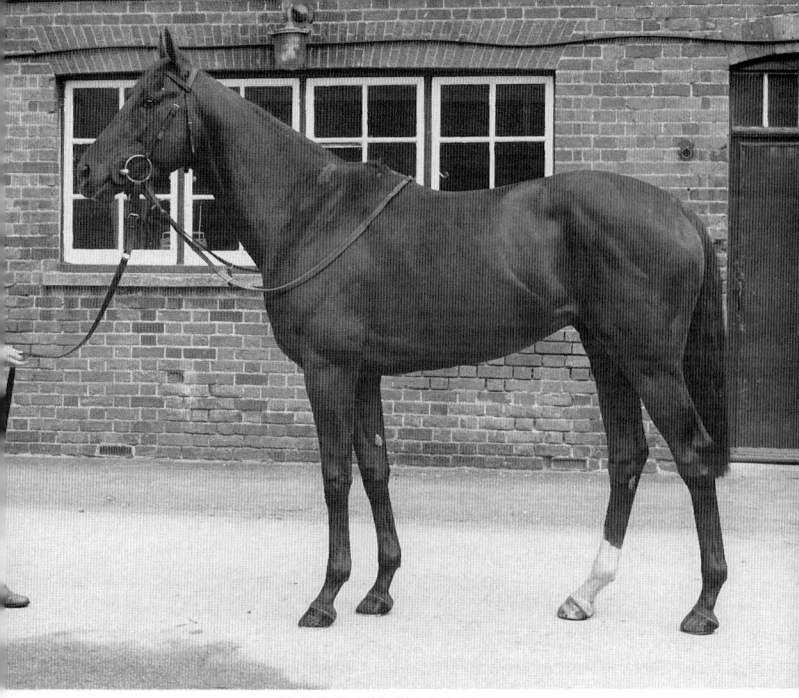

Mr J. C. Smith's "Flashfoot"

brother to middle-distance winners in Ireland by Habitat and Henbit: dam Irish 2-y-o 6f and 7f winner: poor plater: trained by M. W. Easterby on debut. *J. Berry.*

FLASH BULB 4 b.g. Electric 126 – Saffron Ring (Auction Ring (USA) 123) [1990   **53**
NR 1991 11g² 8m 10.6g⁵ 13.6g 11f* 10s 9m⁵ 11m⁴ 11m³ 10g 12.1m a12g³ a12g⁶]
lengthy, heavy-topped gelding: carries plenty of condition: poor walker and mover:
quite modest handicapper at best, won at Redcar (apprentices) in July: suited by
middle distances: best effort on firm ground, seems unsuited by soft. *J. Hetherton.*

FLASHFOOT 3 ch.c. Rousillon (USA) 133 – Miellita 98 (King Emperor (USA))   **115**
[1990 8g⁵ 8m 1991 8g⁴ 9g* 10.4g³ 10g² 8g* 8g² 8d] big, lengthy colt: very useful
performer: successful at Goodwood in maiden in May and 3-runner minor event in
August: best effort but tended to hang when neck second of 5 to Bold Russian in
Beefeater Gin Celebration Mile at same course penultimate start: never going well
in Group 2 event at Longchamp 6 weeks later: best form at 1m: possibly needs a
sound surface: carries head high, and not an easy ride. *I. A. Balding.*

FLASHY'S SON 3 b. or br.c. Balidar 133 – Flashy Looker 92 (Good Bond 122)   **53**
[1990 NR 1991 6f⁵ 5.9m⁵ 6m 7f⁵] sturdy, angular colt: first live foal: dam sprinter:
plating-class form in first half of season: claimed out of Ronald Thompson's stable
£7,100 on promising debut: tended to carry head bit high final start. *A. Harrison.*

FLASS VALE 3 b.g. Final Straw 127 – Emblazon 91 (Wolver Hollow 126) [1990 5f   **50**
5m 6g³ 7m⁴ 7d³ 7.5f⁴ 7f⁴ 7f⁶ 1991 7g⁵ 8f 8g 12f³ 11f⁴ 13.8f² 16m³ 16.2f⁵ 11m 14.1h³]
good-topped gelding: carries condition: has a round action: plating-class maiden:
needs further than 11f, and stays 2m: acts on hard and dead ground: blinkered once,
visored (ran well final start) twice: suitable mount for claimer. *T. Fairhurst.*

FLAT RATE 2 b.f. (Mar 18) Prince Sabo 123 – Hellene (Dominion 123) [1991 **47** 5.1g⁶ 5m⁵ 6f⁵ 5.2f⁵ 5f 6m a6g⁴ a7g] 3,800Y: workmanlike filly: third live foal: half-sister to 6f winner Sideloader Special (by Song): dam unraced: plater: ran moderately on equitrack late in year: seems best at 6f: blinkered fifth outing: sold out of G. Lewis' stable 625 gns Ascot October Sales before seventh outing. *J. White.*

FLEETING RAINBOW 2 b.f. (Apr 28) Rainbow Quest (USA) 134 – Taplow — **p** (Tap On Wood 130) [1991 7g] 26,000Y: quite attractive filly: second foal: half-sister to 3-y-o 6f winner Olifantsfontein (by Thatching): dam unraced from family of Bassenthwaite and Hadeer: 20/1, never a factor in 22-runner maiden won by stable-companion Oumaldaaya at Newmarket in November. *J. L. Dunlop.*

FLETCHINNI (IRE) 2 ch.c. (May 17) Exhibitioner 111 – All The Same (Cajun — 120) [1991 5m⁵ 7m 7m] IR 2,600F, 4,800Y: leggy colt: poor mover: second reported foal: half-brother to a winner abroad by Dublin Taxi: dam unraced: no worthwhile form, in Catterick seller in August on final start. *M. O'Neill.*

FLEUR D'ETE (IRE) 3 gr.f. Miller's Mate 116 – Lily of The Valley (GER) — (Pentathlon) [1990 NR 1991 10f 10d⁶ 10.2m 12.3g] leggy filly: first living foal: dam winner at around 1m to 1¼m in Germany: no worthwhile form in maidens and handicap: pulls hard, and wears crossed noseband: sold 1,350 gns Newmarket December Sales. *J. W. Watts.*

FLIGHT LIEUTENANT (USA) 2 b.c. (Apr 7) Marfa (USA) – Lt Golden Girl **75 p** (USA) (Lt Stevens) [1991 6d 7s²] $11,000Y, resold $36,000Y: tall, lengthy colt: has scope: fifth foal: half-brother to winners in USA by Hawkin's Special and Explodent: dam minor winner at 3 yrs at up to 9f: sire won 9f Santa Anita Derby: 25/1 and off course over 2 months, much better effort when staying-on second of 14 to Assessor in maiden at Kempton (slowly away, brought wide straight) in August: staying type: likely to improve again. *P. Mitchell.*

FLIGHT OF PLEASURE (USA) 3 b.f. Roberto (USA) 131 – Journey (USA) **53** (What A Pleasure (USA)) [1990 a5g 6g* 7g* 7m⁶ 7h³ 8m 1991 8g 10.2m⁶ 8.2m⁵ 11.6m⁵ 14.1f³ 11.5f 9.2f] leggy filly: good mover: modest winner at 2 yrs: plating-class form third to fifth (made most, flashed tail) starts in 1991: stays 1¾m: acts on hard ground: blinkered last 5 starts. *B. Hanbury.*

FLIGHTY GUEST 3 gr.f. Be My Guest (USA) 126 – Julia Flyte 91 (Drone) [1990 — 7m 7g⁶ 8m 1991 11.1d 10.9g 16m⁶] lengthy filly: poor form: should stay beyond 1m: winning hurdler. *Mrs G. R. Reveley.*

FLIM FLAM ALY (USA) 2 br.c. (Apr 2) Tim Tam Aly (USA) – Okala Lass **58** (USA) (Florida State) [1991 a6g 6.1m² 6m⁵ 7g² 7f² 7m³ 8f⁶ 7m a8g a6g⁵ a7g] $5,500Y: leggy colt: fifth reported foal: brother to minor winner and half-brother to minor winner by British Tar in USA: dam claimer winner at up to 7f: sire unraced half-brother to champion 3-y-o filly Davona Dale: useful plater on his day: demoted after winning at Thirsk in August: below best last 5 starts: suited by 7f: blinkered nowadays: gave trouble stalls second outing. *Mrs N. Macauley.*

FLIRTING 7 b.m. Free State 125 – Mrs Palmer 88 (Martinmas 128) [1990 — NR 1991 9m 12.2g 12m] rather plain mare: seems of little account nowadays. *J. Mulhall.*

FLIRTING A LITTLE (USA) 4 gr.f. Little Current (USA) – On My Knee **71** (USA) (Secretariat (USA)) [1990 8g⁶ 10g³ 1991 8d⁴ 10m⁴] sturdy filly: has scope: modest and lightly-raced maiden: one-paced fourth to Surrealist in Windsor minor event in August: never placed to challenge 4 months earlier: should prove much better suited by 1¼m+ than 1m. *J. H. M. Gosden.*

FLITCHAM 4 b.f. Lyphard (USA) 119 – Elegant Air 119 – Seldom (Rarity 129) [1990 8.2g³ 8m 10g 10g **43** 10g a13g a13g a16g⁵ 1991 10.2s 12.4v² 12d⁵ 13d* 14m⁶ 14d⁴ 15s³] small, close-coupled, angular filly: poor handicapper: won at Hamilton in April: stays 15f: acts on good to firm and heavy ground: sold to join J. Bostock's stable 3,900 gns Ascot November Sales: consistent. *W. J. Musson.*

FLIT (USA) 3 b.f. Lyphard (USA) 132 – Nimble Folly (USA) (Cyane) [1990 NR **72** 1991 7g³ 7.9m⁶ 10.5g 12.3f² 9.9f* 10g] strong, deep-girthed filly: has a quick action: closely related to 4 winners, including useful 2-y-o 5f winner Old Alliance and good 1984 American 2-y-o Contredance (both by Danzig), latter successful at up to 9f, and fairly useful 1¼m winner Shotiche (by Northern Dancer): dam unraced sister to useful American filly Misgivings: won maiden at Beverley in September, leading 3f out: well below form in handicap 15 days later: may prove best at up to 1¼m: acts on firm going. *B. W. Hills.*

294

FLOATING LINE 3 ch.c. Bairn (USA) 126 – County Line 75 (High Line 125) **58**
[1990 6m* 7m 1991 8m 9.9m5 9.9f6 8m] sparely-made colt: has a round action:
modest winner at 2 yrs: best effort in handicap company when sixth of 10 at
Beverley, prominent 1m: bred to stay at least 1m. *P. Wigham.*

FLOATING NOTE 6 ch.m. Music Boy 124 – Red Crest 64 (Red God 128§) [1990 — §
a5g a7g 6g 7m 7f 8m a8g 7m 1991 7f] leggy, close-coupled mare: no longer of much
account. *J. S. Wainwright.*

FLOATING RATE 2 gr.f. (Feb 20) Absalom 128 – Dortia (Martinmas 128) [1991 **52**
6f a5g6 5m3 5m4 5g3 5m 6s] 7,500Y: rather leggy filly: fourth foal: half-sister to
quite modest 1988 2-y-o Miss Mischievous (by Star Appeal): dam, half-sister to very
smart 1979 2-y-o Sonnen Gold, unplaced at 2 yrs on only outing: plating-class
maiden: should stay 6f: seems unsuited by soft ground. *J. White.*

FLORADO 3 b.f. Faustus (USA) 118 – Fuchsia 66 (Hot Spark 126) [1990 5f 6m5 —
7m3 8.2g 8m 1991 8m 7m 10.2d 10g] small, close-coupled filly: plating-class maiden:
probably stays 1¼m: reluctant to race once at 2 yrs: sold 725 gns Ascot 2nd July
Sales. *M. Blanshard.*

FLORAL BOUQUET 2 ch.f. (Feb 16) Never So Bold 135 – My Fair Orchid 71 **43**
(Roan Rocket 128) [1991 6g5 7g6 6m] 8,200Y: angular, sparely-made filly: fourth
foal: half-sister to 3-y-o Orchanda (by Pennine Walk) and fair 7f winner Oriental
Splendour (by Runnett): dam plater, showed form only at 5f: poor form in Yorkshire
maiden auctions in summer: seems to stay 7f. *J. Etherington.*

FLORALIA 3 b.f. Auction Ring (USA) 123 – Norpella 95 (Northfields (USA)) **81**
[1990 NR 1991 5f6 6f6 7m* 7m2 8.9g* 7g5 8m 9m2 10.2g5 10f 7m] good-topped filly:
first foal: dam 1¼m and 1½m winner out of half-sister to Teenoso: fair performer at
best: won maiden at Catterick (on toes) in May and median auction contest at
Wolverhampton in June: easily best effort in handicaps last 5 starts when second at
Redcar: stays 9f: acts on good to firm ground: reluctant to post ninth outing: has
taken good hold: swishes tail in paddock: sold 7,400 gns Newmarket December
Sales. *G. Wragg.*

FLORET (USA) 4 b.g. Roberto (USA) 131 – Florera (USA) (Bold Bidder) [1990 —
6f5 a8g 9m 11v6 12d4 a12g4 1991 a 16g] leggy, good-topped gelding: poor performer at
best: worth a try at 1¼m: acts on dead ground: has run well when blinkered: visored
on only start in 1991 (January). *M. C. Pipe.*

FLORIDA GOLD 4 b.g. Hard Fought 125 – Klairelle (Klairon 131) [1990 7g 8.3g —
10f 7m5 8f6 8.3m 10f* 8h 12m6 10m 1991 a13g 10.2g 12g] compact gelding: moderate
mover: plater: no form in 1991: stays 1¼m: acts on firm ground: tried blinkered at 3
yrs: sold out of D. Wilson's stable 1,750 gns Ascot April Sales: resold 900 gns Ascot
September Sales. *R. Lee.*

FLOURISHING (IRE) 2 b.f. (Apr 6) Trojan Fen 118 – Well Off (Welsh Pageant **85**
132) [1991 7m* 7.1s2 7g4 8m4 7m5] 13,000Y: sparely-made filly: lacks scope:
half-sister to several winners, including useful 6f and 7f winner Royal Loft (by
Homing) and fairly useful 9f winner Jiggery Pokery (by Final Straw): dam, of little
account, is half-sister to useful sprinter Doc Marten: fair performer: won 9-runner
maiden at Wolverhampton in July: best efforts in May Hill Stakes at Doncaster in
September and minor event at Newmarket (behind Rose Indien) following month:
will stay 1¼m. *G. Wragg.*

FLOWER DANCER 3 b.g. Mashhor Dancer (USA) – Raina Perera 71 —
(Tyrnavos 129) [1990 7f 7m 1991 10d 10f 7d 8m] sparely-made gelding: poor plater:
should be suited by further than 7f: edgy then mulish stalls second start: sweating
third: sold 620 gns Newmarket July Sales. *Miss A. J. Whitfield.*

FLOWER MELODY 3 b.f. Liboi (USA) 76 – Milford Moss (Record Token 128) —
[1990 a8g6 1991 6d 7.6s 10.2f 8m] sparely-made filly: moderate mover: poor form at
best in maidens and apprentice handicap. *H. Candy.*

FLOWER OF SCOTLAND 3 b.f. Hotfoot 126 – La Piccolina 85 (Tudor **50** d
Rhythm 112) [1990 6g 6m5 7m 7f 10s4 1991 8d6 12f6 12m4 12.4m 10g 13.6m5 14.6m
10m 10g] leggy, angular filly: plating-class maiden: out of form most of 1991: needs at
least 1½m: acts on good to firm and soft ground: has worn severe noseband and been
taken last and steadily to post: sold 880 gns Doncaster November Sales. *P. Calver.*

FLOWER REEF 3 b.f. Cragador 110 – Kellys Reef 92 (Pitskelly 122) [1990 NR **53**
1991 5f5 6f3 5m3 5f4 5f 5d5] workmanlike filly: second foal: sister to quite modest 7f
winner Calypso Reef: dam sprinter: plating-class maiden: bandaged off-hind, fair
fifth at Wolverhampton, easily better effort in handicaps last 2 starts: stays 6f: acts
on firm going. *G. H. Eden.*

Mr P. J. Baer's "Flowing"

FLOWING (USA) 3 gr.f. El Gran Senor (USA) – Flo Russell (USA) (Round **111** Table) [1990 6m* 5g² 6d 1991 7g³ 7g³ 6m* 5d* 6g² 5d* 5d⁵] IR 75,000Y: neat filly: sixth foal: closely related to useful Irish 1m winner who stayed 1½m Crockadore (by Nijinsky) and half-sister to useful 8.2f winner Double Encore (by Nodouble) and 2 winners in USA: dam placed in USA: successful at 3 yrs in minor event at Naas, listed race at Tipperary and Meadow Meats EBF Flying Five at Leopardstown: excellent fifth of 14 to Keen Hunter in Prix de l'Abbaye de Longchamp, running on well: best form at 5f: acts on good to firm ground and dead: sold 280,000 gns Newmarket December Sales but reportedly remains with same trainer. *D. K. Weld, Ireland.*

FLOWN 4 b.c. Hotfoot 126 – My Own II 96 (El Relicario 124) [1990 10.1m⁴ 10f* **90** 12m³ 12g 12g 1991 12m 11.1g 11.7g 11.7m* 12g* 13.1f* 11.4m⁶ 13.3m⁴ 12g²]lengthy, attractive colt: fair handicapper: won at Windsor in July and Goodwood and Bath (idled) in August: ran very well final start: stays 13f: acts on firm ground, yet to race on soft: usually on toes: blinkered last 6 starts: well below best for amateur seventh start: has won when held up and from the front: has joined N. Henderson. *R. Hannon.*

FLUIDITY (USA) 3 b.c. Robellino (USA) 127 – Maple River (USA) (Clandes- **66** tine) [1990 7m⁴ 7m⁵ 7m a7g* a7g* 1991 8g 8.1s 10s⁴ 9s⁴ 10g² 12g 10m² 12.1m³ 10.1s] neat colt: moderate mover: modest form when winner twice at Lingfield as 2-y-o: not so good in 1991, eventually staying on well when third in seller at Edinburgh: stays 1½m: acts on good to firm ground and soft: blinkered (ran poorly) final start: may prove best with waiting tactics: has wandered under pressure: trained first 4 starts by J. Gosden: joined J. O'Shea. *G. Lewis.*

FLUORESCENT FLO 4 ch.f. Ballad Rock 122 – Ridans Girl 89 (Ridan (USA)) — [1990 8m 8g 5g³ 6g 6m 7f 7f 1991 a8g 5g] ex-Irish filly: third in maiden at Mallow in 1990, virtually only show: well beaten in modest company here as 4-y-o. *D. Moffatt.*

FLUTE (USA) 2 b. or br.f. (May 3) Woodman (USA) 126 – Popular By Far (USA) **53** p
(Far North (CAN) 120) [1991 6g⁴] well-made filly: fourth foal: half-sister to a minor
winner in North America: dam won at around 9f: bit backward when 8 lengths fourth
of 5 to Misterioso in Blue Seal Stakes at Ascot in September, effort 2f out, soon
beaten: should stay 1m: will improve. *C. E. Brittain.*

FLY AWAY SOON (USA) 3 b.c. Lear Fan (USA) 130 – Awenita (Rarity 129) **115**
[1990 7f² 1991 10g* 12g⁴ a12g* 12g* 14.6m⁵] workmanlike, good-bodied colt: smart
performer: won maiden at Kempton in April, 4-runner minor contest (making all) at
Lingfield in May and 5-runner listed event (coming from rear in moderately-run
race, beat Magnificent Star ¾ length) at Goodwood in August: well-beaten fifth of 10
in St Leger at Doncaster, every chance 4f out: stays 1½m: hung badly on second
start. *P. F. I. Cole.*

FLY FOR GOLD (IRE) 2 b.f. (Jan 25) Simply Great (FR) 122 – Golden —
Pheasant (Henbit (USA) 130) [1991 8g] IR 3,200Y: third foal: half-sister to Irish 1¼m
winner Rion River (by Taufan): dam unraced: 50/1, well beaten in 14-runner maiden
at Bath in October. *D. W. P. Arbuthnot.*

FLYING BECKEE (IRE) 3 gr.f. Godswalk (USA) 130 – Late Swallow (My **60**
Swallow 134) [1990 NR 1991 7d⁵ 7.1d 7m] 15,000Y: leggy, close-coupled filly: poor
mover: sister to very useful sprinter A Prayer For Wings and half-sister to 2
winners, including fair 1m winner March Bird (by Dalsaan): dam never ran:
bandaged off-hind, 6½ lengths fifth of 8 to easy winner Imperfect Circle in minor
event at Salisbury: well below that form in maidens in July. *W. Carter.*

FLYING BRAVE 3 b.c. Persian Bold 123 – Flying Sauce 107 (Sauce Boat (USA)) **109**
[1990 6g* 6d³ 7f² 7m* 8g⁴ 1991 7m⁴ 8g 8g* 8g² 8g* 8f⁴ 8s⁶] compact, attractive
colt: has a quick action: useful performer: ran well in Free Handicap and 2000
Guineas (seventh) at Newmarket first 2 starts: campaigned abroad afterwards, won
Mehl-Muhlens-Rennen (German 2000 Guineas) at Cologne in May and Group 3
Mercedes Benz-Preis at Hoppegarten in July: in frame in Group 2 event at Milan
(apparently unlucky) and valuable contest in Turkey: should stay at least 1¼m: acts
well on top-of-the-ground: gets on toes. *J. L. Dunlop.*

FLYING CONNECTION 3 b.g. Never So Bold 135 – Gunner's Belle 69 —
(Gunner B 126) [1990 NR 1991 10.1g⁶ a11g 12.2m³ 10.1m] IR 50,000Y: rangy gelding:
third foal: half-brother to 1988 2-y-o 5f winner Gunmaster (by Precocious): dam won
from 7f to 1¼m: no worthwhile form in maidens and handicap: sold 2,100 gns
Newmarket September Sales. *M. R. Stoute.*

FLYING DOWN TO RIO (IRE) 3 b.c. Try My Best (USA) 130 – Gay France **59**
(FR) 91 (Sir Gaylord) [1990 7g⁶ 7m⁴ 7g⁴ 1991 10g 10.1s 8d 7m⁶ 7.6g 10m] work-
manlike colt: fair 2-y-o: form as 3-y-o only when sixth of 9 in claimer at Epsom in
June: should stay 1¼m: blinkered third start: sold to join M. Naughton 6,200 gns
Newmarket Autumn Sales. *R. Hannon.*

Schroders Glorious Stakes, Goodwood—
Fly Away Soon strikes the front having come from the rear;
Magnificent Star takes second ahead of Finance Dancer (rails) and Stapleford Manor

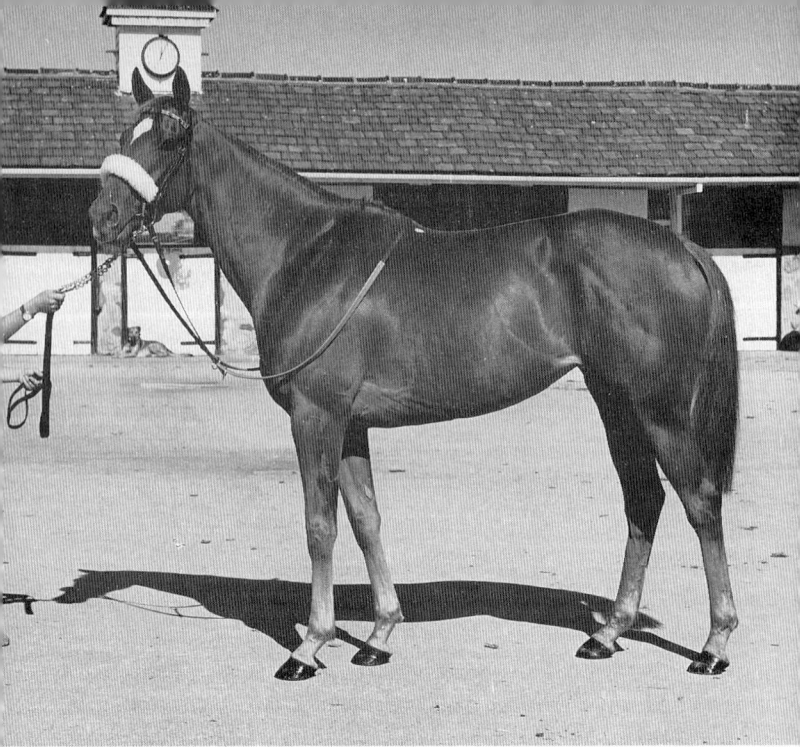

Mr J. David Abell's "Food of Love"

FLYING PHAROAH   2 b.c. (Apr 23) Flying Tyke 90 – Hatshepsut (Ardross —
134) [1991 5g 5f 7m] sturdy, good-bodied colt: first foal: dam of little account: seems
of little account. *A. Smith.*

FLYING PROMISE   3 ch.c. Stanford 121§ – Impailand (Imperial Fling (USA)   **58**
116) [1990 5f 5g4 5m4 5g6 5d a5g2 a5g2 1991 a6g5 a5g6 5m3 5.3f 5s 5m6 5g4 5g2 5g
5m 6g4 6m 7g a6g4] strong, lengthy colt: quite modest maiden: ran well at Southwell
in December: tailed off in apprentice event 3 months earlier: probably stays 6f: acts
on good to firm ground: tried blinkered once: below best when sweating twice. *R. A.
Bennett.*

FLYING QUEST   2 b.g. (Jan 18) Salmon Leap (USA) 131 – Aspatia (Henbit (USA)   **58**
130) [1991 5g6 5d5 6m4 7g4 7m 8m 7.5f4 10m] 2,200F, 2,000Y: lengthy, angular
gelding: first living foal: dam twice-raced daughter of very useful Rose Bed, herself
sister to Rose Bowl and half-sister to Ile de Bourbon: plating-class maiden: ran
below best in sellers on several occasions, including when weakening quickly 2f out
at Leicester (blinkered) final start: should stay beyond 7.5f: acts on firm ground. *R.
Boss.*

FLYING SPEED (USA)   3 b.g. Far North (CAN) 120 – Diatoma (FR) (Diatome   —
132) [1990 NR 1991 8g 10.4m6] good-bodied gelding: seventh reported living foal:
closely related to minor French winner at around 1m Divinia (by Northern Treat)
and half-brother to 4 winners abroad, including French 1m (at 2 yrs) to 1¾m winner
Diatomica (by Homing): dam French 1m winner: chased leaders until about 3f out in
maidens at Newbury in April and York in October: joined M. Pipe. *M. Moubarak.*

FLY TO THE MOON (USA) 3 ch.f. Blushing Groom (FR) 131 – Disconiz **90**
(USA) (Northern Dancer) [1990 6m² 7m² 1991 8m* 10.5g³ 10m³] neat, quite
attractive filly: fairly useful form: won maiden at Warwick in March in £7,400
contest at York and minor event (favourite on first run for over 5 months, moved
moderately down) won by Nucleus at Leicester: should stay 1½m. *H. R. A. Cecil.*

FOLIA 2 b.f. (Mar 19) Sadler's Wells (USA) 132 – Dunoof 92 (Shirley Heights 130) **— P**
[1991 7m⁶] good-topped filly: has plenty of scope: second foal: half-sister to 3-y-o
Dunstable (by Formidable): dam, 2-y-o 7f winner, is sister to high-class middle-
distance stayer High Hawk, later dam of In The Wings (by Sadler's Wells): weak
9/2-chance, burly and green, around 10 lengths sixth of 16 to Anlace in maiden at
Leicester in October, outpaced 3f out then keeping on under considerate ride: a
most likeable sort, probably capable of considerably better. *H. R. A. Cecil.*

FOLK DANCE 9 b.g. Alias Smith (USA) – Enchanting Dancer (FR) (Nijinsky **—**
(CAN) 138) [1990 14m⁴ 16m³ 16m 14m⁵ 14.8m* 16m³ 14m³ 14g 1991 14m 14s] big,
strong gelding: modest handicapper at 8 yrs: no show on flat in 1991: stays well: acts
on any going: usually visored: has won for apprentice: none too enthusiastic and
best covered up. *G. B. Balding.*

FOLLOW THE SEA 5 b.h. Tumble Wind (USA) – Seapoint (Major Point) [1990 **—**
8.3m 9m² 9g 10g⁵ 1991 a8g 9s] sturdy, lengthy horse: quite modest maiden at 4 yrs:
below form in 1991: stays 9f: acts on good to firm and heavy going: sold to join D.
Turner's stable 1,700 gns Ascot September Sales. *R. Akehurst.*

FONTAINE LADY 4 b.f. Millfontaine 114 – Lady Begorra (Roi Soleil 125) [1990 **49**
10.1g 8g 10.1m 10m 6m* 7g 6m 6f 8f 5m³ 5m 6d 1991 6.1d³ 5d⁴ 5m* 5.2f² 5g⁴ 5f]
leggy filly: good walker: poor handicapper: won at Lingfield in July: effective at 5f to
6f: acts on firm and dead going: has won when blinkered. *T. Thomson Jones.*

FOOD OF LOVE 3 ch.f. Music Boy 124 – Shortbread 104 (Crisp And Even 116) **109**
[1990 5g³ 5m* 5m² 5f 5f² 5g⁴ 5m* 5m² 5d³ 1991 5m² 5m* 5m⁵ 5d⁵ 5g² 5g⁵ 5m]
close-coupled filly: moderate mover: useful handicapper: successful in quite
valuable events at Newcastle in May, Ascot in June and York (by 1½ lengths from
Sarcita, making all for best effort) in August: ran well in King George Stakes at
Goodwood fifth start, poorly in Doncaster listed race (favourite) on final one:
speedy: possibly best on a sound surface: tends to hang left: bandaged behind as
3-y-o: splendidly game and consistent. *J. Berry.*

FOO FOO (IRE) 3 ch.f. The Noble Player (USA) 126 – Unmistakable 83 (Hello **39**
Gorgeous (USA) 128) [1990 6g 5m 7m⁴ 7g 5m⁴ 6d³ a7g 1991 6g 8d 6m³ 6m⁵ 8.3m
6.9m² 7m⁶ 6m⁶] workmanlike filly: poor mover, has markedly round action: poor
maiden: second in apprentice handicap at Folkestone: may prove best at 7f: acts on
good to firm ground and dead. *D. Marks.*

FOOLISH DANCER 2 b.f. (Mar 31) Mashhor Dancer (USA) – Blakesware Gift **63**
74 (Dominion 123) [1991 5g³ 5g⁵ 5g 5.7f⁴ 7f² 8f 7g³ 6g] workmanlike filly: second
live foal: dam 1½m seller winner, is out of half-sister to Gimcrack winner Wishing
Star: quite modest maiden: should stay 1m: acts on firm ground: best held up:
inconsistent: sold 700 gns Ascot November Sales. *B. R. Millman.*

FOOLISH MASQUERADE (USA) 3 gr.f. Silver Buck (USA) – Flip For Luck **41 §**
(USA) (Flip Sal (USA)) [1990 NR 1991 9m 8f⁴ 12f² 12m⁴ 12f] $30,000Y: leggy filly:
first known foal: dam won 11 races at up to 1m: plater: showed little interest (before
finishing well) penultimate start, none on final one: stays 1½m: blinkered fourth
start: subsequently sold out of J. Etherington's stable 3,800 gns Doncaster August
Sales: one to avoid. *R. J. Hodges.*

FOOLISH TOUCH 9 b.g. Hot Spark 126 – Nushka (Tom Fool) [1990 6s 6v* 6m **67**
6m 6d⁶ 6g 7g 6m² 6f* 6m 7m³ 7g 7g 7m 7g² 8d 7d⁵ a8g⁵ a8g⁶ 1991 a8g⁴ a8g³ a8g 8s
7g 8.2d⁴ 7.6g⁵ 7m³ 7f² 8d* 8d⁵ 8.3m 8g² 7g⁴ 8d 7m 8m 7g² 7d] lengthy gelding:
poor walker and moderate mover: quite modest handicapper nowadays: won at
Newbury (apprentice) in June: effective at 6f to 1m: acts on any going: has worn
blinkers, often visored: usually bandaged: usually starts slowly and gets behind: has
won 5 times at Newmarket. *W. J. Musson.*

FOR ALL TIME 2 ch.f. (Mar 22) Forzando 122 – Altana 71 (Grundy 137) [1991 **— p**
a7g] third foal: half-sister to maidens Well And Truly (by Rousillon) and Spitfire
Jubilee (by Chief Singer): dam 1½m and 1¾m winner: very weak in market, around
10 lengths seventh of 13 to Donegal Dandy in late year at Southwell: sold 1,300 gns
Ascot December Sales. *Lord Huntingdon.*

FORBEARANCE 3 ch.f. Bairn (USA) 126 – For Instance (Busted 134) [1990 **—**
8g* 1991 8g 10g 11.9g⁵] big, rangy filly: modest winner as 2-y-o: easily best effort in
handicaps in summer as 3-y-o when fifth of 7 at Haydock, travelling well long way

but weakening and wandering under pressure over 1f out: may prove best short of 1½m: twice refused to enter stalls in 1991: winning hurdler for Mrs G. Reveley. *M. Johnston.*

FORBOURNE 2 b.f. (Feb 1) Forzando 122 – Texita 65 (Young Generation 129) — [1991 5m 5g] 800Y: smallish filly: first foal: dam ran 3 times here at 2 yrs, later winner in Norway: no form in Midlands sellers in spring: sold 520 gns Doncaster October Sales. *R. Guest.*

FORD KING 4 b.f. Sandhurst Prince 128 – Douala (GER) (Pentathlon) [1990 7f **49** d 7f* 7m 7d 1991 7d 8.5f³ 10m a8g 7.6g 7f] sparely-made, leggy filly: poor handicapper: stays 1m: acts on firm going, probably unsuited by dead: ran poorly when visored and sweating badly final start: inconsistent. *M. O'Neill.*

FOREIGN ASSIGNMENT (IRE) 3 b.g. Reasonable (FR) 119 – Lady Pitt **52** (Pitskelly 122) [1990 6g 6m 6g 1991 8d 7g 7d 8.3g³ 8f* 10g⁵ 9.7m⁵ 8m] rangy gelding: moderate walker and mover: plating-class form: won handicap at Bath in July, leading final 1f: ran fairly well in claimer and seller (claimed out of G. Lewis' stable £6,011) next 2 starts: stays 1m: acts on firm going. *J. White.*

FORELINO (USA) 2 b.f. (Feb 3) Trempolino (USA) 135 – Forelie 88 **56** (Formidable (USA) 125) [1991 7g 8.1g] well-made filly: third foal: half-sister to untrustworthy 3-y-o Paper Dart (by Lear Fan) and fair middle-distance maiden Cavalcanti (by Sir Ivor): dam, 6f winner who raced only at 2 yrs, is half-sister to Derby Italiano winner My Top: plating-class form in minor event at Kempton and maiden at Haydock in September: should stay middle distances. *J. L. Dunlop.*

FOREST FAIRY 2 b.f. (Feb 3) Faustus (USA) 118 – Faridetta 107 (Good Bond **66** 122) [1991 5f² 6f³ 5g⁶ 7m⁴] 6,000Y: leggy, close-coupled, angular filly: moderate mover: half-sister to several winners, including 19f winner Far Glow and modest 1¾m and 2m winner Mighty Glow (both by Kalaglow) and 1983 2-y-o 5f winner Dramatic (by Dragonara Palace): dam won four 5f races at 2 yrs: quite modest maiden: best efforts when third of 6 to Showbrook in £10,400 event at Epsom and sixth of 14 to Marling in Queen Mary Stakes at Royal Ascot in June: favourite, appeared not to stay at Wolverhampton following month. *R. Boss.*

FOREST LAW (USA) 2 ch.g. (Jan 30) Green Forest (USA) 134 – Sierva (ARG) **61** (Super Cavalier 112) [1991 5g³] IR 92,000Y: leggy gelding: brother to a winner in USA: dam won 5 races in USA, including in stakes, at up to 1¼m: 10/3 and green, always-prominent third of 7 in maiden at Newbury in April: seemed sure to improve. *P. F. I. Cole.*

FOREVER DIAMONDS 4 ch.g. Good Times (ITY) – Mel Mira 68 (Roi Soleil **65** 125) [1990 6s 5v³ 8.2g² 6g⁵ 6m 6d³ 6d⁶ 6s 1991 6d² 8f* 6m³ 6m³ 6g 7.1m³ 11.1s] leggy, rather sparely-made gelding: quite modest handicapper: won claimer at Carlisle in spring: stays 1m: acts on any going: has twice run moderately in blinkers: game: largely consistent: trained until after first start by J. S. Wilson. *Miss L. A. Perratt.*

FORGE BAY 4 b.c. Buzzards Bay 128§ – Korresia (Derring-Do 131) [1990 7.2d⁵ **46** 9m⁵ 7d a10g 1991 a7g a12g² a12g 10.8g 8d² 8m⁵ 7.5m 8.3m 10g*] leggy, good-topped colt: poor handicapper: won at Goodwood (apprentices) in October: effective at 1m to 1½m: acts on good to firm and dead ground: inconsistent. *H. J. Collingridge.*

FORGETFUL 2 br.f. (Feb 21) Don't Forget Me 127 – Peak Squaw (USA) **65** p (Icecapade (USA)) [1991 5.7f⁵ 7.1m⁶] first foal: dam Irish 2-y-o 6f winner: better effort when around 5 lengths sixth of 9 in Sandown maiden in August: claimer ridden: may stay 1m: may well improve again. *R. Hannon.*

FOR HEAVEN'S SAKE (FR) 6 br.g. Be My Guest (USA) 126 – Woolf (FR) — (Roi Dagobert 128) [1990 NR 1991 10.6g 12.3d⁶ 10.3d 16.2d] workmanlike gelding: second foal: dam 10.2f winner, stayed well: no worthwhile form on flat: wears bandages: blinkered first 2 starts: winning hurdler in August. *C. D. Broad.*

FORLORN DIVER 3 ch.g. Ballacashtal (CAN) – Four Lawns 77 (Forlorn River — p 124) [1990 NR 1991 6g 6g 5f] 5,000Y: lengthy gelding: sixth live foal: half-brother to quite modest 6f winner Swing Dancer and modest miler Causley (both by Swing Easy): dam 5f winner: showed signs of ability, travelling comfortably 3f and eased when held, in maiden at Windsor (bandaged) and well-contested claimer at Sandown last 2 starts: probably capable of better. *B. Gubby.*

FORMAL INVITATION (IRE) 2 ch.c. (Apr 27) Be My Guest (USA) 126 – — Clarista (USA) 67 (Riva Ridge (USA)) [1991 6d 7m] fifth foal: half-brother to winning German 3-y-o Maitre (by Law Society): dam one-paced maiden stayed 1¼m, is half-sister to Topsy and Teenoso: soundly beaten in October maidens at Goodwood and Lingfield: likely to stay 1¼m. *G. Lewis.*

FORMAL OCCASION (IRE)   3 b.f. Shirley Heights 130 – Princess Tiara 111   **61**
(Crowned Prince (USA) 128) [1990 NR 1991 10m 11.7g⁵ a11g⁴ 12g* 13m⁶ a14g⁵
17.2g⁵ 16.1g 15.1s⁵] tall, angular filly: half-sister to several winners, including smart
French 7f to 1¼m winner What A Guest (by Be My Guest), very smart 10.4f winner
Infantry (by Northfields) and 1½m to 2m winner Royal Standard (by Sadler's Wells):
dam 2-y-o 7f winner appeared to stay 1¼m at 3 yrs: quite modest handicapper: won
at Pontefract in June: inconsistent after: stays 17f: best efforts on good ground: sold
18,500 gns Newmarket December Sales. *P. W. Chapple-Hyam.*

FORM MISTRESS   2 b.f. (Jun 5) Formidable (USA) 125 – Proud Miss (USA)   **52**
(Semi-Pro) [1991 5g⁶ 5.1g 5.7f² 6m] small, angular filly: half-sister to 3-y-o Transatlanticdream (by Fast Gold) and 3 winners in USA: dam unraced: plating-class
maiden: best effort neck second of 7, always front rank, at Bath: not seen out after
August. *I. A. Balding.*

FOR MOG (USA)   2 ch.c. (Feb 16) Mogambo (USA) – Forever Command (USA)   **— p**
(Top Command (USA)) [1991 7m] $90,000Y: second reported foal: brother to fairly
useful 3-y-o 1¼m to 14.1f winner Masai Mara: dam won at up to 11f, including in
stakes: sire best at around 1m: 50/1 and backward, slowly away and never a factor in
16-runner maiden at Leicester in October. *C. E. Brittain.*

FOR NOTHING   6 gr.h. Bay Express 132 – Flitterdale 81 (Abwah 118) [1990   **a 43**
a7g* a7g² a7g* a8g a7g a7g 8.2m a7g⁶ a8g 1991 a7g³ 8m a11g a7g] good-bodied
horse: poor handicapper: no form after reappearance: best form at up to 1m: seems
best on all-weather nowadays. *J. A. Glover.*

FOR REAL   4 ch.f. Tina's Pet 121 – Golden Decoy 73 (Decoy Boy 129) [1990 5f 6f³   **48**
5f⁶ a5g 6m* 6f* 6g³ 6g² 6g⁴ 6m³ 6f* 6m⁵ 6g⁵ 5f⁵ 6m⁴ 6g a6g² a7g³ 1991 a7g² 7f⁴
7f⁶ 5.9f5] small, good-quartered filly: plating-class handicapper: not seen out after
July: stays 7f: acts on firm going: usually wanders. *J. Etherington.*

FOR REG (IRE)   2 b.c. (May 9) Theatrical 128 – Swalthee (FR) (Sword Dancer   **89 p**
(USA)) [1991 7d*] short-backed, quite attractive colt: half-brother to several
winners, including Tralthee (by Tromos), useful winner at 7f (at 2 yrs) and 1¼m:
dam, winner over extended 1¼m in France, is half-sister to dam of Galant Vert: 14/1,
bit backward and green, won 22-runner maiden at Doncaster in November by a
neck, clear, from Mimique, never far away then staying on well: will stay 1¼m at
least: will improve. *A. C. Stewart.*

FORT-GALAS PRIDE   3 br.f. Belfort (FR) 89 – Lingala (Pinturischio 116)   **—**
[1990 NR 1991 8d 7.5m⁵ 8g] rather sparely-made filly: half-sister to a winner abroad:
dam lightly raced on flat and over hurdles: no worthwhile form in maidens: sold
1,000 gns Doncaster August Sales. *B. W. Murray.*

FORT HOPE   2 gr.g. (Mar 6) Belfort (FR) 89 – Hopeful Katie 67 (Full of Hope   **§§**
125) [1991 5s* 5m⁴ 6g³ 6m a5g* a6g* a7g 5m a6g a5g⁴] leggy, lengthy gelding:
modest performer on his day: gained last 2 wins in sellers at Lingfield, second
occasion sold out of J. Berry's stable 9,200 gns after winning very easily: has looked
thoroughly ungenuine several other starts: stays 6f: wears eyeshield or blinkers on
fibresand or equitrack: has worn bandages: one to avoid. *T. J. Naughton.*

FORTINA   2 ro.f. (Feb 26) Belfort (FR) 89 – Nicolini 56 (Nicholas Bill 125) [1991   **45**
5d⁶ 7m 8.1g 5m] 1,000Y: leggy filly: first foal: dam middle-distance winner: poor
maiden: off course 6 months after debut: best effort final start: sold 580 gns
Doncaster October Sales. *D. Moffatt.*

FORTUNE'S WHEEL (IRE)   3 b.c. Law Society (USA) 130 – North Forland   **113**
(FR) 99 (Northfields (USA)) [1990 5g³ 6d⁴ 7.5g⁵ 7.5g⁶ 8g* 9g³ 10s³ 10v* 8v⁶ 1991
8v² 8v⁴ 12g 10g² 10s² 10s 10v] smart French colt: first past post in Premio Parioli at
Rome in April on second start but hung left and demoted for interference: second,
beaten ¾ length by Arcangues then 3 lengths by Kartajana, in Prix Eugene Adam at
Saint-Cloud and Grosser Mercedes-Benz Preis Bayerisches Zuchtrennen at
Dusseldorf: should stay beyond 1¼m: acts on heavy going: blinkered first 2 starts at
2 yrs. *R. Collet, France.*

FORTY NINER DAYS (USA)   4 gr.g. Conquistador Cielo (USA) – Party   **121**
Bonnet (USA) (The Axe II 115) [1990 8f* 8f* 9f 6g 7f⁴ 1991 8f² 8.5f⁵ 8d* 8f 8.5f* 9f²
11f* 9.5f² 10f⁴ 11f² 8d⁵ 12f 9f²] $80,000Y, $150,000 2-y-o: tall, workmanlike gelding:
second foal: dam, minor stakes winner at around 1m at 5 yrs, is daughter of unraced
half-sister to multiple graded-stakes winners Late Bloomer and Late Act: good-
class American gelding: raced on dirt at 2 and 3 yrs (off course April-December in
1990), only on turf in 1991: successful in Grade 3 events at Golden Gate Fields in
March and April and Grade 2 contest there in June: 20/1 and tongue tied down, not at
all discredited when fifth of 9 to Selkirk in Queen Elizabeth II Stakes at Ascot

eleventh start: good second in Grade 2 Bay Meadows Handicap in December, easily better subsequent effort: effective at 1m and stays 11f: acts on firm and dead ground. *Roger Stein, USA.*

FORTY OR MORE 4 ch.g. Yashgan 126 – Infanta (USA) (Intrepid Hero (USA)) — [1990 8m 8m² 8d* 10d 1991 10.2s] lengthy gelding: modest winner at 3 yrs: behind in handicaps since, backward only run at 4 yrs (March): stays 1m: best effort on dead going. *C. F. Wall.*

FORZA AZZURRI (IRE) 2 ch.c. (Apr 3) On Your Mark 125 – Miss Legend — (USA) (Bold Legend) [1991 7m a6g a6g] IR 1,600Y, 3,300 2-y-o: angular, close-coupled colt: moderate mover: half-brother to useful 1978 Irish 2-y-o 5f winner Devilish (by Red God) and several winners abroad: dam won twice over 6f in USA: no worthwhile form, including in sellers: unruly stalls first 2 starts. *R. W. Stubbs.*

FORZINA 3 b.f. Forzando 122 – Tibouchina 75 (Runnymede 123) [1990 NR 1991 — 8s⁶ 8g 10m 8m] good-quartered filly: moderate mover: fourth foal: half-sister to sprint winner Castle Cary (by Castle Keep): dam lightly raced over sprint distances: tailed off 3 of 4 starts, in May claimer on final one. *M. Blanshard.*

FOUNTAIN LOCH 4 b.f. Lochnager 132 – Fountain 90 (Reform 132) [1990 6f* **52** 6s⁵ 6m 7m 6s² 6g⁶ 6f4 6m² 7g* 6d5 6m 6g 7d 5s 1991 7d 7m 7m 8m 7m⁶ 6m 7m 7m] small, good-quartered filly: has quick action: quite modest handicapper at 3 yrs: below form in 1991: should stay 1m: acts on any going. *R. J. Holder.*

FOUNTAIN PLAZA (IRE) 2 b.f. (May 16) Red Sunset 120 – June Darling — (Junius (USA) 124) [1991 7m 8.3g 8.9d] IR 8,500Y: lengthy, angular filly: third foal: half-sister to 1990 2-y-o 6f winner and 7f winner Cal Norma's Lady (by Lyphard's Special): dam never ran: no worthwhile form in maidens: sold 780 gns Doncaster November Sales. *J. A. C. Edwards.*

FOURHEARTSDOUBLED 3 b.g. Mashhor Dancer (USA) – Sunset Ray 74 — (Hotfoot 126) [1990 a8g a8g a8g⁶ 1991 a12g⁵ 14.1m³ 13.8f⁶ 15.1g] smallish, lengthy gelding: shows knee action: poor maiden: apparently best effort third in moderately-run claimer at Yarmouth: stays 1¾m. *Dr J. D. Scargill.*

FOUROFUS 2 b.c. (Apr 27) Wassl 125 – Que Sera 91 (Music Boy 124) [1991 5m **57** 5g⁵ 5s] 8,000Y: strong colt: has scope: second foal: half-brother to fair 5f winner Rancho Mirage (by Superlative): dam 2-y-o 5f winner out of half-sister to Chapel Cottage: plating-class form in maidens, including auctions: failed to make anticipated progress at Edinburgh final start: worth another chance. *R. Boss.*

FOURSINGH 3 b.rg. Mansingh (USA) 120 – Maycrest (Imperial Fling (USA) **56** § 116) [1990 5f* 6g² 6g 6m 6m³ 6f³ 7f 8.2g 1991 12m 7.5f⁶ a7g² 8g 7d 7g5] smallish, lengthy gelding: moderate walker: has quick action: modest performer at 2 yrs: best form for long time when beaten head, running on well for 7-lb claimer, in seller at Southwell in May: best form at up to 7f: blinkered last 5 starts: carries head high, and probably irresolute: joined C. Booth. *C. B. B. Booth.*

FOURSTARS ALLSTAR (USA) 3 b.c. Compliance (USA) – Broadway **122** Joan (USA) (Bold Arian (USA)) [1990 a5.5f² a6f³ a5d³ a6s* a6f a8s 8.5f* 8.5f² 9f* 8f* a8f 1991 8.5g² 8.5f* 8g* 8.5f4 10f² 9g³ 8.5f4 8.5s² 10s 9f³]
There was an American challenge for both Irish Guineas in the latest season; a challenge for either race would have been enough to disprove the theory that there's nothing new under the sun. The two challengers, stable companions, had differing fortunes, Fourstars Allstar putting up a remarkable performance to win the colts' race, Irish Linnet coming eighth in the fillies'. Fourstars Allstar arrived at the Curragh a veteran of thirteen races, eleven of them at two years. He started off on dirt, but took four attempts to get off the mark (in a maiden at Saratoga in August) and he improved dramatically on turf in the autumn, picking up an allowance race at Belmont, running a neck second to River Traffic in the Laurel Futurity, then winning the Grade 3 Pilgrim Stakes and the restricted Damon Runyon Stakes at Aqueduct. It was reportedly at this stage that the Airlie/Coolmore Irish Two Thousand Guineas came under consideration, and after the horse ran no sort of race back on dirt in December it was decided he would travel to Ireland. Fresh from winning an allowance race at Belmont the week before—where in receipt of 7 lb he had beaten Solar Splendor by a length and a quarter—Fourstars Allstar lined up the 9/1 third favourite behind Lycius at evens and Ganges at 6/1, both of whom had been in the frame for the General Accident Two Thousand Guineas.

Airlie/Coolmore Irish Two Thousand Guineas, the Curragh—one for the record books; New York-based Fourstars Allstar (visor) pips Star of Gdansk

Drawn against the inside rail, Fourstars Allstar broke quickly and, not unduly challenged, was able to relax in the lead and set just a steady pace. Just before the intersection of the courses he drifted slightly left allowing Star of Gdansk through. The Irish colt took the lead over two furlongs from home but never went more than a length up as the pair drew clear of the field. Mike Smith, riding Fourstars Allstar, remained very low in the saddle and, without great force from the whip, drove his mount back up to catch Star of Gdansk twenty yards from the post and win by a head, with Lycius, who didn't have the best of runs, six lengths back in third.

European-based horses have been contesting valuable races in North America for many years, and their successes are still headline news. American challengers in Europe have been very much a trickle against the tide, and in terms of important victories you would have to go back to the 1928 Kentucky Derby winner Reigh Count's win in the following year's Coronation Cup to find something at all comparable to Fourstars Allstar's feat. However, as the latter came on the same day as Hansel won the Preakness Stakes at Pimlico by seven lengths, the achievement did not receive the acclaim in his native land that it might have. This is a pity because a golden chance to advertise the opportunities available in Europe and thereby help create a truly international arena for racing was lost. Whilst it's true there are a great number of valuable races in the USA, not one of them is a mile event for three-year-olds of greater importance than the Irish Guineas. The classic did not take an immense amount of winning and subsequent events suggest that Fourstars Allstar is not a top-class horse; hopefully this will encourage more American owners and trainers to come and compete in Europe. Although

303

Fourstars Allstar finished in the frame in all but one of his subsequent races, including five Grade 3 events, he never won again, nor, in all probability, did he quite recapture the form he showed at the Curragh. The two runs which probably carry most meaning to European racegoers were his fourth of seven, beaten three lengths at level weights, to subsequent Man o' War and Turf Classic winner Solar Splendor in the Saratoga Budweiser Breeders' Cup in August and his three-length second to Star of Cozzene (later third in the Breeders' Cup Mile) in the Nureyev Stakes at Belmont five weeks later. They were over eight and a half furlongs. He was twice tried over a mile and a quarter. The first time he seemed to run respectably in a Grade 3 contested by a small field, but the next time he finished a long way behind in the Grade 1 Budweiser International won by Leariva at Laurel. The evidence suggests he acts on any going.

Fourstars Allstar (USA) (b.c. 1988)	Compliance (USA) (b 1978)	Northern Dancer (b 1961)	Nearctic Natalma
		Sex Appeal (ch 1970)	Buckpasser Best In Show
	Broadway Joan (USA) (ch 1979)	Bold Arian (b 1970)	Noble Jay Riverval
		Courtneys Doll (b 1971)	Wakefield Tower Rapport

Compliance owes his position at stud not to his merit as a racehorse—the best he managed in three starts was a third in a poorly-contested listed event at Leopardstown—but to the fact that he has two illustrious brothers. He is three years younger than Try My Best and three years older than El Gran Senor and stands at The Stallion Park, Millbrook, New York for a fee of 7,500 dollars. From his six crops there have been around eighty winners from one hundred and forty foals, but only a handful of them in stakes races. Broadway Joan was unraced, having bowed a tendon whilst in training. Her sire was a modest performer whose stakes success came as a five-year-old in a race restricted to New Jersey-breds, whilst her dam, Courtneys Doll, won five minor events from fifty-two starts and produced a total of three unraced foals and one maiden. Courtneys Doll's parents were of a similar status, so the prospects for Broadway Joan's progeny can hardly have looked great when she set out at stud. However, all of her four foals of racing age, all by Compliance, have won races, and besides Fourstars Allstar there's the six-year-old Fourstardave, a very useful performer. To date he has won ten stakes races worth more than 1,200,000 dollars and has become a standing dish at the five-week-long meeting at Saratoga, where he has won at least one stakes race in each of the last five years. Broadway Joan slipped in 1989, but the following year produced a colt by Secreto (called Similar Star and already entered for the 1993 Derby). *L. O'Brien, USA.*

FOURTIMELUCKY   2 b.f. (Mar 3) Alleging (USA) 120 – Yavarro 44 (Raga   —
Navarro (ITY) 119) [1991 5m 5g 6d a6g] 640F, 1,500Y: close-coupled filly: first foal:
dam plater stayed 1¼m: seems of little account. *J. Balding.*

FOURWALK   7 br.h. Godswalk (USA) 130 – Vaunt (USA) (Hill Rise 127) [1990   67
a5g a7g5 a6g 6f3 6m 1991 6m 5.8f* 5m6 7m] strong, close-coupled, plain horse: poor
walker and bad mover: quite modest handicapper: won at Bath in May: well below
form after: stays 6f: acts on any going: has been tried visored: has worn tongue
strap. *Mrs N. Macauley.*

FOX CHAPEL   4 b.g. Formidable (USA) 125 – Hollow Heart 89 (Wolver Hollow   78 d
126) [1990 7m 10.1m5 8d* 8m 8f 7d 8g 8m 1991 8d 10g 10s2 10.2m4 11d 10.1f 12d 11.5d
10.3d] good-bodied gelding: quite modest handicapper nowadays: effective at 1m to
1¼m: acts on good to firm and soft ground: twice below form when visored: trained
first 8 starts by R. Hannon: thoroughly unreliable: winner over hurdles. *J. G.
FitzGerald.*

FOXES DIAMOND   3 b.f. Sallust 134 – Rahesh 111 (Raffingora 130) [1990 6g3   47
5m2 6f6 6g 5d 5m 8f 7d 1991 8d 7.5f 10f6 8m5 7g6 5m 6m2 7f2 6f3 7m3 7m4 6f4 6f6 5f2
6.1m 6g 6m] leggy, angular filly: plater: effective over stiff 5f, and stays 7f: acts on
firm going: sometimes blinkered: has been mounted on track: has been bandaged
off-hind: trained first 3 starts by D. Dutton. *J. Hetherton.*

FOXTROT PIE   3 ch.f. Shernazar 131 – Round Dance 73 (Auction Ring (USA)   52
123) [1990 7m 7m 10s2 1991 11d2 12.3d 15.3m3 a12g3 16g5 12.1s3 13d4 12m5] sturdy

filly: plating class on most form: should prove suited by 1½m + : acts on soft ground: ran creditably on Southwell all-weather: blinkered penultimate outing: ran creditably for amateur on final one. *G. A. Pritchard-Gordon.*

FRAAR (USA) 3 b.c. Topsider (USA) – Alchaasibiyeh (USA) 85 (Seattle Slew **96** (USA)) [1990 6d* 7m³ 8m* 1991 8g² 9m 8.5m³ 8m⁶ 8g⁴ 10m⁶ 7m² 8.1d3] rather leggy, good-topped colt: moderate mover: fairly useful performer: in frame in handicaps, listed race and minor events: stays 1m well: acts on good to firm ground and dead: blinkered (ran well) last 2 starts: to join D. Hayes in Australia. *H. Thomson Jones.*

FRAGILE EARTH 3 ch.g. Known Fact (USA) 135 – Cresta (FR) 84 (Ribero 126) **—** [1990 NR 1991 a7g a10g a10g] 4,000Y: rather sparely-made gelding: half-brother to 3 minor winners: dam, half-sister to high-class middle-distance winner Electric, won over 7f at 2 yrs on only start: soundly beaten in claimers and maiden in January. *C. N. Allen.*

FRAGONARD (IRE) 2 b.c. (Mar 5) Pharly (FR) 130 – Girl On A Swing 79 (High **64** Top 131) [1991 5d 6g² 7d*] 15,000Y: workmanlike colt: has scope: fifth living foal: half-brother to several winners, including 1¾m winner Dame Elusive (by Blakeney): dam, placed twice at around 7f from 4 starts at 3 yrs, is out of half-sister to Irish Oaks winner Pampalina, dam of Pampapaul: progressive form: odds on, won 8-runner maiden at Ayr in July: started slowly time before: will stay 1¼m: acts on dead ground. *G. A. Pritchard-Gordon.*

FRAGRANT HACKETTE 2 ch.f. (Mar 1) Simply Great (FR) 122 – Martin- **32** Lavell News 90 (Song 132) [1991 5m⁴ 5s] 4,300Y: good-topped filly: third foal: half-sister to 5f winner Musical Flash (by Music Boy): dam won twice over 5f from 4 starts at 2 yrs: poor form in maiden auctions at Salisbury in May and Edinburgh (better for race) in November. *A. Hide.*

FRAGRANT HILL 3 b.f. Shirley Heights 130 – English Spring (USA) 116 (Grey **101** Dawn II 132) [1990 8m³ 7g* 7d⁶ 1991 10g* 12m 11.9m] lengthy, workmanlike filly: moderate walker: 33/1, much improved form to win listed Lupe Stakes at Goodwood in May by neck from Sipsi Fach: well behind in Oaks (finished distressed, reportedly struck into) at Epsom and Lancashire Oaks at Haydock: should stay 1½m: well beaten on dead ground: has swished tail: useful. *I. A. Balding.*

FRANCIS ANN 3 br.f. Balidar 133 – Supper Party (He Loves Me 120) [1990 NR **42** 1991 a7g a7g⁶ a7g² a8g⁵] 1,500F, 3,400Y: leggy, rather dipped-backed filly: moderate mover: third foal: sister to a winner abroad: dam never ran: 50/1, 10 lengths second of 10 in maiden at Southwell, first form: well beaten in handicap there later in July: wears crossed noseband. *J. F. Bottomley.*

FRANCISCAN 4 b.g. Godswalk (USA) 130 – Athenian Primrose (Tower Walk **—** 130) [1990 8.2s 8f 10.6f4 10s⁵ 10f 8.2g* 8m² 11m³ 10g a8g⁶ 8.2d a8g 1991 14m 13d] well-made gelding: plating-class handicapper: not seen out after April: seems to stay 1¾m: acts on good to firm and dead ground: has wandered under pressure: winning hurdler in February. *B. Preece.*

FRANKUS 2 b.g. (May 31) Nicholas Bill 125 – Sigh 75 (Highland Melody 112) **50** [1991 6m 6f⁵ 7.1s 5.7g] 1,000Y, 6,800 2-y-o: leggy gelding: fourth foal (all by Nicholas Bill): brother to a winner in Hong Kong: dam won at 1m: plating-class maiden: should stay 1m at least: best efforts on top-of-the-ground. *S. Mellor.*

FRANSYLCO 3 b.c. Bold Owl 101 – Sodina 75 (Saulingo 122) [1990 7.5d⁶ 7g⁵ 7f⁵ **46** a7g⁵ 8d 8d⁵ 1991 8f⁴ a11g 12m⁵ 10.3d 10g³ 10.8m] sturdy colt: plater: form as 3-y-o only when third of 19 at Ripon in July, making most: stays 1¼m: acts on firm and dead going: ran well when blinkered once at 2 yrs: visored once. *J. Etherington.*

FRAULEIN EQUILIA (IRE) 2 b.f. (Mar 22) Glow (USA) – Astania (GER) **66** (Arratos (FR)) [1991 7m 8.1g⁵ 8.1d³ 8.3s] IR 19,500Y: leggy, workmanlike filly: has a round action: sister to 1990 2-y-o 9f winner Glowlamp, closely related to 2 winners by Northern Baby, including temperamental 10.2f and 1½m winner Northants, and half-sister to winners by Naskra and Sham: dam Irish 13f winner, is half-sister to dam of leading German middle-distance colt Alpenkonig: quite modest maiden: best effort once-paced third to easy winner Bonny Scot at Haydock: will stay 1¼m: acts on dead ground. *J. M. P. Eustace.*

FREAK TOSS (ARG) 4 ch.c. Egg Toss (USA) – Frau Lamanche (ARG) (Frari **82** (ARG)) [1990 6g⁴ 10g³ 10m⁵ 7g⁶ a6g⁵ a8g² a8g 1991 8d² 9g 10.1f*] lengthy colt: successful over 6f in Argentina in March at 3 yrs: fair handicapper here: won at Yarmouth in June, making all: stays 1¼m: acts on firm and dead ground: ran well when visored at 3 yrs. *J. M. P. Eustace.*

FREDDIE LLOYD (USA) 2 ch.c. (Jan 24) Barrera (USA) – Shredaline (USA) **87**
(Shredder (USA)) [1991 6m³ 5m 5m* 6m³ 5m² 6g⁶ 5d²] robust, good-quartered
colt: carries condition: has a roundish action: second known foal: half-brother to a
minor winner in North America: dam won at up to 7f: sire smart winner at up to 7f:
fair performer: favourite, won maiden at Folkestone in July: ran really well last 3
starts, including when sixth to Casteddu in 25-runner Racecall Gold Trophy at
Redcar in October, then second to Isaiah in nursery at Newmarket (mulish stalls) 3
days later: stays 6f: trained first 4 starts by A. Lee: has run well for 7-lb claimer. *N.
A. Callaghan.*

FRED FOR FUN 5 b.g. Crofthall 110 – Jolly Sweet (Entanglement 118) [1990 NR —
1991 7g 8g 5m a12g 7m] workmanlike gelding: third foal: dam winning hurdler/
chaser: seems of little account. *R. Thompson.*

FREEDOM WEEKEND (USA) 3 ch.f. Shahrastani (USA) 135 – Glorious —
Quest (USA) (Hawaii) [1990 6m 1991 10m 12.2f⁶] quite good-topped, attractive filly:
behind in maidens, weakening quickly and hanging right 2f out at Brighton on
reappearance. *J. R. Fanshawe.*

FREE FLYER (IRE) 2 b.c. (Feb 15) Bluebird (USA) 125 – Lassalia (Sallust 134) **103** p
[1991 7g⁴ 7.1m* 7m⁵ 7m⁶] well-made colt: good mover: fifth foal: half-brother to 6f
winner Pilgrim's Path (by Godswalk) and 3 other winners, including Irish 1½m
winner Snowy Lane (by Commanche Run): dam placed from 6f to 9.5f in Ireland:
progressive form: won maiden at Sandown in September, quickening impressively
2f out: best effort under 6 lengths sixth of 9 to Dr Devious in Dewhurst Stakes at
Newmarket following month, outpaced 2½f out then running on again final 1f: will
probably improve further over 1m. *M. Moubarak.*

FREE FOR ALL 3 ch.c. Mummy's Game 120 – Free On Board 73 (Free State **47**
125) [1990 6m 6m 6m 5g⁵ 6g 1991 8f⁶ 7m 8g a8g³ a8g⁵ 8.3m 9.7f⁵] lengthy colt: has a a 55
round action: plating-class maiden: best effort at 1m on Lingfield equitrack: mulish
in paddock second and third starts: visored last 4: sold 2,700 gns Newmarket
September Sales. *L. J. Holt.*

FREE FORM 6 b.m. Glenstal (USA) 118 – Free Wheeler (Prince Tenderfoot —
(USA) 126) [1990 12d 1991 10g 14.1g] sturdy mare: fifth foal: half-sister to a winner in
Italy by Tap On Wood: dam never ran: poor ex-Irish maiden: behind in claimers as
6-y-o: stays 1½m: winning hurdler in September: joined A. Forbes. *C. Weedon.*

FREE MINX 5 b.g. Free State 125 – Musical Minx 75 (Jukebox 120) [1990 10.2f **57**
11s² 10v4 12g 1991 15.8f⁴ 16.5g⁶ 12.1f* 13.8m³ 12.1g³ a12g a14g⁴] sturdy gelding:
quite modest handicapper: won (for first time) at Hamilton in August: stays 15.8f:
acts on any going: tried blinkered and visored once: has been reluctant at stalls. *Mrs
V. A. Aconley.*

FREEPHONE (CAN) 2 b.c. (Mar 6) Phone Trick (USA) – Flying Aristocrat **41**
(USA) (Prince John) [1991 6f 5m 6m] $45,000Y: good-bodied colt: half-brother to
several winners, including 1½m winner Royal Suitor (by Blushing Groom): dam
never ran: poor maiden: reared stalls final start: may be worth a try at 7f. *J. W. Hills.*

FREE SKIP 7 b.m. Free State 125 – Economy Pep 69 (Jimmy Reppin 131) [1990 —
NR 1991 14d] leggy mare: plating-class handicapper at 5 yrs: first run since, never
placed to challenge at Nottingham in April: suited by a thorough test of stamina:
unsuited by firm going, acts on any other. *P. S. Felgate.*

FREE TRANSFER (IRE) 2 b.c. (Apr 1) Dara Monarch 128 – Free Reserve **58**
(USA) (Tom Rolfe) [1991 6g a7g 8.5f³ 8.9m⁶ a8g a8g⁶ a8g⁶] 5,400F, 6,000Y:
workmanlike colt: has scope: moderate mover: third foal: half-brother to 3-y-o
Metal Oiseau (by Ela-Mana-Mou) and a winner in Switzerland: dam placed from 8.5f
to 1¾m in Ireland: plating-class maiden: ran moderately last 2 starts: has been
coltish, and given trouble at stalls: seems suited by a test of stamina. *P. F. Tulk.*

FREEWHEEL (USA) 2 ch.f. (Feb 17) Arctic Tern (USA) 126 – Dinner Surprise **85** p
(USA) (Lyphard (USA) 132) [1991 6.1f* 7m*] fourth foal: sister to 1990 2-y-o 1m
winner Bombe Suprise and half-sister to 2 winners in North America by Overskate:
dam from family of Legal Case and good French sprinter Gem Diamond: won
24-runner maiden at Nottingham (hardly came off bridle) by 6 lengths from Rose
Indien: heavily-backed favourite, followed up in 8-runner minor event at Newbury
later in September by 1½ lengths from Guilty Secret, quickening over 1f out and
keeping on under vigorous hand riding: should stay 1¼m: likely to continue
progressing, and win more races. *L. M. Cumani.*

FREEZING (IRE) 3 gr.f. Siberian Express (USA) 125 – Field Day 87 (North- **56**
fields (USA)) [1990 7m⁶ 1991 12s 10g⁴ 12.1d] workmanlike filly: best effort at 1¼m:

sold out of W. Muir's stable 1,900 gns Ascot 2nd July Sales after reappearance: winner of selling hurdle. *R. Simpson.*

FREIGHT CAR (USA) 3 ch.c. Tank's Prospect (USA) – Chalk Face (USA) (Neartic) [1990 NR 1991 12d] $38,000Y: ninth foal: half-brother to 2 winners: dam won 6 times and second as 2-y-o in Grade 2 8.5f Oak Leaf Stakes: well beaten in claimer at Kempton in May: sold 725 gns Ascot October Sales. *C. A. Austin.* —

FRENCH FLAIR (USA) 2 ch.f. (May 16) Bering 136 – Princess Cariole 103 (Jaazeiro 127) [1991 7s*] 20,000Y: first foal: dam, half-sister to 6 winners, useful 6f (at 2 yrs) and 1m winner later successful twice in USA: 14/1, won 13-runner maiden at the Curragh in October by 2½ lengths from Treasure Hope: will stay at least 1m: should improve. *T. Stack, Ireland.* **85 p**

FRENCH IVY (USA) 4 ch.g. Nodouble (USA) – Lierre (USA) (Gummo (USA) 117) [1990 10.6d⁵ 13.6m² 12g² 12d⁶ 1991 14d 17.6m* 18f⁵ 15.9m*] leggy gelding: fairly useful handicapper: won at Wolverhampton in May and Chester (first run for over 3 months) in August: should prove as effective at 1¾m as 2m+: probably needs a sound surface: ran well when visored at 3 yrs. *Mrs A. L. M. King.* **90**

FRENCH LEGIONNAIRE 4 b.g. Legend of France (USA) 124 – Angail 89 (Northfields (USA)) [1990 7m 9f⁴ 12m 10d 10f* 1991 a7g⁶ a12g a7g⁵ 10.8g 8.1d] good-bodied ex-Irish gelding: fifth foal: half-brother to useful 1985 2-y-o 5f and 6f winner Homing Angel (by Homing): dam fair 5f performer at 2 yrs: won maiden at Clonmel at 3 yrs: plating-class form in first half of 1991: faced very stiff tasks last 2 starts: should prove suited by return to around 1¼m: acts on firm ground: sold 1,600 gns Ascot July Sales. *Mrs S. Armytage.* **48**

FRENCH REVOLUTION (FR) 2 ch.f. (Apr 13) Midyan (USA) 124 – French Beauty (FR) (Jim French (USA)) [1991 a8g5] 180,000 francs (approx £18,000) Y: half-sister to a winner in North America: dam half-sister to Allez France: weak 8/1-shot, over 5 lengths fifth of 13, slowly away, kept on, to Grog in late-year maiden at Southwell: should improve. *Michael Cunningham.* **48 p**

FRENI 2 b.f. (Apr 30) Primo Dominie 121 – F Sharp 83 (Formidable (USA) 125) [1991 5f 5m 5.2g 6m 6m⁴ 5m⁵ 8m⁵] 1,550Y: lengthy filly: moderate mover: third foal: half-sister to poor maiden Ragtime Cowboy (by Indian King): dam, 1¼m winner stayed 1½m, is out of sister to Lancashire Oaks winner Rhein Bridge and half-sister to very smart Connaught Bridge: quite modest plater: has form from 5f to 1m: acts on good to firm ground. *M. D. I. Usher.* **42**

FRESCOBALDO (USA) 5 b.h. Master Willie – Voice of The River (USA) (Speak John) [1990 11s 12.3f² 12g² 16f 12m 12m* 12.4m² 13f⁶ 12.3m⁵ 1991 13.8d 13.8g² 12g 13.8m² 15.8f⁴ 12.4m⁵ 12m 12.3m* 12.3f⁵ 12.3f⁵ 12f* 10.9m* 10m⁶ 12m a12g a12g4] leggy, rather sparely-made horse: has a rather round action: quite modest handicapper: won at Ripon in August and Thirsk (claimer) and Ayr in September: stays 15.8f: acts on firm going, unsuited by soft: pulled hard when visored: lacks turn of foot, and goes very well with forcing tactics: has won when sweating and for apprentice: game. *M. P. Naughton.* **64**

FRESH FROM VICTORY 7 b.g. Hotfoot 126 – Triumphant 90 (Track Spare 125) [1990 a12g 1991 a10g³ a10g 10.1s 11.5g] workmanlike, angular gelding: poor and very lightly-raced performer nowadays: stays 1¼m: possibly needs an easy surface. *A. Moore.* **35**

FRIDAYATPISSARRO'S 3 b.f. Prince Sabo 123 – Contadina (Memling) [1990 5m 6g² 6m³ 7m 8.2v 1991 7f 8m 8g] leggy filly: quite modest maiden at 2 yrs: well beaten at 3 yrs, in seller final start: best form at 6f: possibly unsuited by heavy ground: sold 1,500 gns Doncaster July Sales. *M. R. Channon.* —

FRIDAY FOURBALL 3 ch.g. Monsanto (FR) 121 – Sparkling Ears 61 (Sparkler 130) [1990 6g 6g 7m⁴ 7m 7g² a8g⁴ 7f⁵ 10.6s 7d 7d² a8g 1991 8s 10m 11m 8d 9.9f 10g 8.3d⁴] workmanlike gelding: poor mover: fairly useful plater at best: little worthwhile form in 1991: best form at 7f: acts on dead ground: visored fifth start: sweating previous 2: joined R. O'Leary: inconsistent. *E. Weymes.* —

FRIDAY NIGHT GIRL 3 b.f. Good Times (ITY) – Final Call 79 (Town Crier 119) [1990 NR 1991 7m 8m 6.9f] 8,600Y: lengthy, angular filly: half-sister to 3 winners, including quite useful 1985 2-y-o 7f winner Stage Hand (by Sagaro), later successful in France: dam, 5f winner who ran only at 2 yrs, is half-sister to good sprinter On Stage: well beaten in maidens: wore tongue strap final start: sold 725 gns Ascot November Sales. *W. Carter.* —

FRIEDLAND (USA) 3 b.c. Nijinsky (CAN) 138 – Fenella 92 (Thatch (USA) 136) [1990 7d 1991 10.2s³ 10d* 10.1m⁴ 10m² 10.2g* 10m⁶ 10.2m* 10m⁶] lengthy, good-topped colt: moderate mover: fair performer: successful in maiden at **89**

Nottingham in April, amateurs event at Doncaster in July and handicap at Chepstow in September: will stay 1½m: yet to race on firm ground, probably acts on any other: sold 56,000 gns Newmarket Autumn Sales, reportedly to race in Germany. *H. R. A. Cecil.*

FRIENDLY CLAIM (IRE)   3 b.g. Petorius 117 – Pitaka (Pitskelly 122) [1990   **72** 5m⁶ 5f 5g* 5g* 6f a6g* a5g* 1991 a6g³ a6g 6g* 6m 7m² 7m 5g⁴ 6m a6g² a6g* a6g²] a 83 compact gelding: good walker: modest performer: won claimers at Carlisle in March and Southwell in December: should prove as effective at 7f as 6f: acts on good to firm ground: suitable mount for a claimer: often set fair bit to do. *T. D. Barron.*

FRIENDLY FARMER   3 ch.g. Final Straw 127 – Ragirl (Ragusa 137) [1990 NR   **—** 1991 10g] angular gelding: half-brother to several winners, including very speedy 1974 2-y-o Fats Waller (by Sing Sing) and middle-distance stayer The Prudent Prince (by Grundy): dam never ran: behind in maiden at Salisbury: dead. *J. R. Fanshawe.*

FRIENDLYPERSUASION (IRE)   3 b.g. Legend of France (USA) 124 –   **49** Waladah (Thatch (USA) 136) [1990 NR 1991 10.5m⁵ 10g⁶ 7m 10.5f 10.5d³ 11d* 10.3g 9.7s a11g⁶] IR 4,000Y, 2,500 2-y-o: lengthy, angular gelding: half-brother to 1½m winner Dream Merchant (by Welsh Pageant): dam ran twice: plater: below form after winning at Wolverhampton (no bid) in October by a short head, leading final 1f: should stay 1½m: acts on dead going. *R. Hollinshead.*

FRIENDLY SONG   3 ch.f. Song 132 – Friendly Jester 90 (Be Friendly 130) [1990   **48** NR 1991 5f 5m⁶ 5g² 5f⁵ 5f 5g] smallish, lengthy filly: sister to smart sprinter Fayruz, closely related to 1983 2-y-o 5f winner Haiffan (by Mummy's Pet) and half-sister to 3 sprint winners: dam 5f winner, is half-sister to dam of Jester: plating class on most form: no show in handicaps last 2 starts: hung right on debut. *T. Fairhurst.*

FRIEND OF A FRIEND   3 b.f. Nishapour (FR) 125 – Marista (Mansingh (USA)   **49** 120) [1990 7m 1991 7v³ a7g⁶ 8m⁵ 9m 9.7f] tall filly: plating-class maiden: stiff tasks in handicaps, showing nothing final start: should be better at 1m than shorter: acts on heavy going. *Dr J. D. Scargill.*

FRIMLEY DANCER   3 b.f. Northern Tempest (USA) 120 – Taylors Renovation   **54** 58 (Frimley Park 109) [1990 5f⁶ 6m 6g 5f⁴ 5g⁴ 6m⁴ 1991 5.7g 5.1f² 5m² 5d 5m⁵ 6f* 5.7f⁶] leggy, plain filly: poor mover: plating-class performer: ridden by 7-lb claimer, did nothing wrong when winning handicap at Brighton in September, leading final ½f: stays 6f: acts on firm going, possibly unsuited by a soft surface: has wandered under pressure, and looked reluctant third start. *C. J. Hill.*

FRIMLEY PARKSON   7 br.g. Frimley Park 109 – Frimley Grove (Tower Walk   **62** d 130) [1990 5m² 5g* 6m 6m 5m⁵ 5m² 5f⁶ 5m⁶ 5m 5m⁵ 5d⁶ 5d³ 1991 5g 5g⁵ 5m 5m⁶ 5m² 6g⁶ 5m⁴ 5m⁴ 5g⁶ 5m³ 5.1d³ 5g² 5g² 5g 5m³ 5m 6f 5f 5m⁶ 5.3g 5g 5m 5.1d] sturdy, compact gelding: carries plenty of condition: bad mover: quite modest handicapper: lost his form: effective at 5f and 6f: acts on any going: effective with or without blinkers or visor: not easiest of rides: hard to win with. *P. Howling.*

FROINECH   2 ch.f. (Mar 31) Prince Sabo 123 – Valentine Song 63 (Pas de Seul   **45** 133) [1991 5d³ 5m⁴ 6s a6g] 800F: first foal: dam 1m winner: poor maiden. *T. D. Barron.*

FRONT PAGE   4 ch.g. Adonijah 126 – Recent Events (Stanford 121§) [1990 8g   **60** 6m³ 7d 6g² 6m⁶ 6m* 7g 6f⁴ 6m a8g 1991 8s* 9s² 8.5g³ 8g 8.2m 9g] workmanlike gelding: carries condition: quite modest handicapper: won at Doncaster and most unlucky second at Kempton (apprentices, clear when eased inside last 1f) in spring: stays 9f: acts on any going: below form when blinkered once: winning hurdler in November. *J. Akehurst.*

FROSCH (USA)   3 b.c. Irish River (FR) 131 – Valderna (FR) (Val de Loir 133)   **94** [1990 NR 1991 11.7g* 11.5g] big, strong colt: closely related to quite modest maiden Riva and a 9f winner in USA (both by Riverman) and half-brother to 3 winners abroad, including 1m winner here Alderney (by Great Nephew), successful over 7f and 1m in Italy in 1990: dam useful 10.5f winner in France, is half-sister to Durtal and Detroit: 13/8 on, won 15-runner maiden at Bath in April in good style, making most: virtually bolted to post when last of 8 in Group 3 event at Lingfield 11 days later: wore severe noseband: dead. *G. Harwood.*

FROZEN FOREST   3 ch.g. Touching Wood (USA) 127 – Ever So Cool (FR)   **—** (Never Say Die 137) [1990 8m 8d 7s 10.2s a8g 1991 a10g] strong, compact gelding: carries condition: plating-class maiden: ran poorly on all weather: stays 1¼m: acts on soft going: sold to join S. Kettlewell 1,600 gns Doncaster January Sales. *S. E. Kettlewell.*

FRUITFUL AFFAIR (IRE)   2 b.f. (Mar 8) Taufan (USA) 119 – Lucky Engage-   **68** p
ment (USA) 75 (What Luck (USA)) [1991 6f*] 5,300Y: lengthy filly: fourth foal: half-
sister to 3-y-o Harry's Lady (by Alleging): dam, maiden, stayed 7f: 12/1, won
8-runner maiden at Folkestone in October, tracking leaders, green when asked to
quicken, then galloping on strongly closing stages: moved moderately to post:
should improve, particularly over 7f. *T. Thomson Jones.*

FULL CRY (USA)   3 ch.c. The Minstrel (CAN) 135 – Raise 'n Dance (USA)   **74**
(Raise A Native) [1990 NR 1991 8f* 7.6g⁴ 8m] $370,000Y: lengthy, rather sparely-
made colt: half-brother to winners in North America and Alleged: dam 6f
stakes winner: off course 6 months after winning maiden (wore crossed noseband)
at Brighton in March: good staying-on fourth of 20 in handicap at Lingfield, always
close up: favourite, always behind in Newmarket handicap 16 days later: stays 1m
well. *J. H. M. Gosden.*

FULL FLIGHT   2 b.f. (Mar 29) Full Extent (USA) 113 – Strata VII (pedigree   —
unknown) [1991 a7g] first reported foal: dam non-thoroughbred: 25/1, slowly away
and always behind in late-year claimer at Southwell. *R. Bastiman.*

FULL HEARTED (USA)   7 b.g. Full Out (USA) – Heladi (Traffic Judge) [1990   —
8.2s⁶ 8v 12g 1991 a12g] rather leggy, good-topped gelding: modest winner as 3-y-o:
very lightly raced and no worthwhile form since: should stay 1½m: acts on any
going: has worn blinkers and visor: sold 950 gns Doncaster March Sales. *W. J.
Musson.*

FULL OF PLUCK (IRE)   3 b.c. Try My Best (USA) 130 – Tomona (Linacre   —
133) [1990 8m² 8g⁴ 7g* 8v⁵ 1991 7m 8v] tall, useful-looking colt: good mover: useful
at 2 yrs, winner at York and fifth in Gran Criterium at Milan: in need of race in
£8,000 handicap on reappearance: well beaten in Premio Parioli at Rome later in
April: will stay 1¼m: acts on heavy going. *B. Hanbury.*

FULL OF TRICKS   3 ch.c. Mossberry 97 – Duchess of Hayling VII (pedigree   —
unknown) [1990 NR 1991 10g 8g] tall colt: first reported foal: dam non-thoroughbred: tailed off in maidens. *R. J. O'Sullivan.*

FULL QUIVER   6 br.g. Gorytus (USA) 132 – Much Pleasure (Morston (FR) 125)   **66**
[1990 11.7g* 10m 11.7m* 10m⁴ 12g³ 12s 10.2s⁵ 1991 a8g 10.8m 10g³] leggy gelding:
fair handicapper at 5 yrs: not seen out in 1991 after April: stays 1½m: acts on any
going: tried blinkered once, effective with visor or without: sometimes sweats: has
worn tongue strap: often finds little, best held up. *Mrs Barbara Waring.*

FULL SIGHT (IRE)   2 b.c. (Apr 9) Vision (USA) – Peaches And Cream (FR)   **50**
(Rusticaro (FR) 124) [1991 6m 7m 7m 8m 10.5d³] IR 6,500F, IR 9,700Y:
close-coupled colt: moderate mover: second foal: half-brother to 3-y-o Drummer's
Dream (by Drumalis): dam placed at 9f and 9.5f in Ireland: poor maiden: third of 20 in
selling nursery at Haydock: will stay well: acts on dead ground. *M. H. Tompkins.*

FULL STEAM   2 b.g. (Feb 26) All Systems Go 119 – Mature (Welsh Pageant 132)   **60**
[1991 5g 5m⁵ 7s⁶ 5g³ 6.1m² 7g³ 7f⁶ 8m] 7,400Y: workmanlike gelding: fifth living
foal: brother to 1990 2-y-o 6f winner Steam Ahead and a winner abroad, and
half-brother to 1¼m seller winner Carbo Booster (by Good Times): dam, maiden,
ran best race at 7f: quite modest maiden: ran moderately in nurseries last 2 starts:
should stay 1¼m: has run well in blinkers and visor: acts on good to firm ground:
bandaged behind final outing: sold 7,000 gns Newmarket Autumn Sales. *J. W. Watts.*

FULLY STRETCHED   3 ch.g. Reach 122 – Errol Emerald 60 (Dom Racine (FR)   —
121) [1990 NR 1991 8g 7f⁶ 6m 7m⁵ 11.5m] rather leggy, angular gelding: second foal:
dam rather temperamental 1¼m to 1½m winner: bandaged and backward, well
beaten in maidens, median auction contest and ladies event in first half of 1991. *G.
Lewis.*

FUNOON (IRE)   2 ch.f. (Jun 3) Kris 135 – Golden Oriole (USA) (Northern   **68** p
Dancer) [1991 7d⁴] 290,000Y: well-grown, attractive filly: third foal: half-sister to
1m (at 2 yrs) and 1¼m winner Gold Law (by Law Society): dam Irish 6f winner, is
sister to El Gran Senor and Try My Best: very weak 10/1-shot though looking very
well, well-beaten fourth of 7, held up, never able to challenge, in minor event at
Ascot in September: will stay 1m: looks sure to improve. *M. R. Stoute.*

FURAJET (USA)   3 ch.f. The Minstrel (CAN) 135 – Zummerudd (Habitat 134) **101**
[1990 5m* 5d* 5f³ 6m⁵ 1991 5g³ 6m⁵ 5m⁴ 5g² 6m⁵ 5m³ 5m³ 5.5f] small, sturdy,
attractive filly: has a quick action: useful form in listed races and pattern events as
3-y-o: beaten short head by Case Law in listed race at Sandown: good third in similar
events won by Blyton Lad and On Tiptoes at Newmarket: last of 9 in handicap at
Hollywood Park final outing: best at 5f: game and consistent. *A. A. Scott.*

FURIELLA   3 ch.f. Formidable (USA) 125 – Palmella (USA) 89 (Grundy 137)   **56**
[1990 5f 6g⁶ 6g 5f⁴ 5.1m² 5m⁶ 6d 1991 7f⁵ a8g⁴ 7h⁶ 6m⁶ 6f² 5m³ 6f*] stocky filly:
poor mover: plating-class performer: favourite, easily won handicap at Hamilton in
September, making virtually all: effective at 5f to 7f: acts on firm going: blinkered
twice: sweating and edgy penultimate start: sold out of P. Feilden's stable 4,300 gns
Doncaster January Sales. *P. C. Haslam.*

FURRY DANCE (USA)   3 ch.f. Nureyev (USA) 131 – Kenanga 105 (Kris 135)   —
[1990 NR 1991 8m] leggy, rather sparely-made filly: first foal: dam 11.5f and 1½m
winner, is half-sister to Ribblesdale winner Strigida out of Ribblesdale winner
Catalpa: 16/1 and ridden by 7-lb claimer, took keen hold and showed signs of only a
little ability in maiden at Warwick in May: sold 3,100 gns Newmarket December
Sales. *H. R. A. Cecil.*

FURTHER FLIGHT   5 gr.g. Pharly (FR) 130 – Flying Nelly 107 (Nelcius **118**
133) [1990 11.7f* 12.3d* 12f 12d² 15g* 14g* 18d² 1991 12m* 12g 15g* 16g*
15g² 15.5m 16m* 12g*]
   When Gildoran gained his second Ascot Gold Cup win in 1985, it
prompted us to say that 'no horse could better deserve the epithet battler'.
There's one who comes close in the same stable's Further Flight who ended a
fine season in 1991 with victory in the St Simon Stakes, after which it was
announced that he would bid to emulate Gildoran in the next edition of
staying's show-piece event. We look forward to seeing him there. Few better
candidates for long-distance honours of 1992 emerged during the season.
He'll stay the two and a half miles all right, the one slight doubt about him
being that he's performed moderately on the only occasions he's run at Ascot,
in the hurly-burly of the last two Bessborough Handicaps.
   Further Flight ended the latest campaign better than ever at the age of
five. He'd won the Ebor and been second in the Cesarewitch in 1990 then
picked up in the same form as he'd left off on his reappearance, with a facile
victory under 10-0 in a handicap at York in May. After another handicap win (at
Ayr in July) Further Flight graduated to pattern events and was first past the
post in four of them with performances that emphasised his thoroughly
genuine character as well as his ability. In the Dickins & Jones Goodwood
Cup (now over two miles) Further Flight quickened to lead one furlong out
and, idling somewhat, had a length to spare at the line over Great Marquess,
Shambo and Silver Rainbow who had to be separated by a photo finish. The
camera was used for Further Flight himself when Turgeon gave him 2 lb and a
rare duel in the Prix Kergorlay at Deauville but it took the French stewards to
thwart Further Flight's hat-trick bid, reversing the placings for interference
after he'd won by a head. His seventh of nine in the Prix Gladiateur at
Longchamp was a moderate effort but he bounced back in typical fashion,
demonstrating in doing so that versatility was another of his attributes. Few
proven stayers are able to revert successfully to a mile and a half. Further

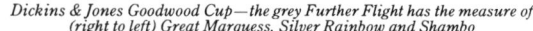

Dickins & Jones Goodwood Cup—the grey Further Flight has the measure of
(right to left) Great Marquess, Silver Rainbow and Shambo

Flight proved that he was up to it, however, by winning the St Simon Stakes at
Newbury just three weeks after winning the Jockey Club Cup at Newmarket.
The 7/4 favourite in a field of six at Newmarket, he came with his customary
late surge to take it up at the furlong pole and, under firm driving, held
stable-companion Supreme Choice by one and a half lengths with Shambo a
further three lengths back. Many doubted Further Flight's ability to overcome the drop in distance in the St Simon and he was sent off 6/1 in a
competitive eleven-strong field behind three-year-olds Red Bishop (favourite
following his most impressive Ascot handicap win), Always Friendly (the
Princess Royal winner) and Opera House. In the event it was left to a fellow
five-year-old, the revitalised Filia Ardross, to throw down the most serious
challenge. In a race run at a searching gallop, Opera House went on early in
the straight but had no more to give two furlongs from home. Filia Ardross
looked to have the race in safe keeping when quickening almost two lengths
clear entering the last furlong but Further Flight, who'd made headway from
mid-division having been pushed along quite vigorously from the home turn,
responded magnificently to the strongest of pressure and cut down Filia
Ardross inside the final twenty yards or so, passing the post a neck to the
good. The pair pulled two and a half lengths clear of Always Friendly who kept
on to finish a half length ahead of a tired Opera House.

		Lyphard	Northern Dancer
	Pharly (FR)	(b 1969)	Goofed
	(ch 1974)	Comely	Boran
Further Flight		(ch 1966)	Princesse Comnene
(gr.g. 1986)		Nelcius	Tenareze
	Flying Nelly	(br 1963)	Namagua
	(gr 1970)	Flying By	Bleep-Bleep
		(gr 1964)	Japhette

Owned and bred by Mr Wingfield Digby, Further Flight is the eighth foal
of Flying Nelly, who carried his colours to some success in the early-
'seventies. Like her son, Flying Nelly was genuine, consistent and improved
with age. Successful three times at around a mile and a quarter at three,
she developed into a useful handicapper at four, her two wins including the
Cambridgeshire. At five she won once and was in the frame in four good-
class handicaps, twice unlucky, and a good fifth in the Sun Chariot Stakes.
She's a half-sister to several winners in Australia, notably the Grade 2 winner
Outpace. Further Flight was her final foal for after producing him she was
twice barren to Touching Wood and then died in September 1988. She
managed to produce five winners prior to Further Flight though, including the
mile-and-a-quarter performer Neltino (by Bustino) and the stayer Morning
After (by Busted), both quite useful. In contrast to Flying Nelly who stayed

Mr S. Wingfield Digby's "Further Flight"

thirteen furlongs well, her dam Flying By was a five-furlong performer. Flying By won five times through two and three years and also finished third in the Nunthorpe Stakes. A daughter of champion sprinter Bleep-Bleep, she too was a game and genuine sort—as was Further Flight's sire the ultra-consistent Pharly. Gameness and consistency seem to be watchwords in Further Flight's pedigree. Pharly, at his best at up to a mile and a quarter, has shown himself to be quite an influence for stamina. His numerous winners include Harly, successful in the Henry II Stakes, and Phardante, dual winner of the Jockey Club Stakes. A leggy, angular gelding, the round-actioned Further Flight is often bandaged behind. He acts on good to firm and dead ground. He has improved every year since being gelded at two and is a great credit to his trainer. Let's hope he enjoys yet another successful year. *B. W. Hills.*

FUSION 7 b.g. Mill Reef (USA) 141 – Gift Wrapped 116 (Wolver Hollow 126) [1990 — NR 1991 10g] rangy gelding: landed gamble in selling handicap at 5 yrs: lightly raced and little form since: should stay 1½m: acts on firm going: usually bandaged: has been taken down early: blinkered on reappearance. *R. Earnshaw.*

FUTUH (USA) 3 gr.f. Diesis 133 – Hardship (USA) (Drone) [1990 6d² 6f* 6m² 88 6d⁵ 5d² 1991 6m² 5m⁶ 5.1g³] small, quite good-topped filly: has a long, roundish stride: fairly useful performer: placed in £6,900 contest at Newmarket in May and handicap at Chester in July: worth a try at 7f: yet to race on very soft going, acts on any other. *H. Thomson Jones.*

FUTURES GIFT (IRE) 2 b.c. (May 6) Try My Best (USA) 130 – Plum Cordial 56 (USA) (Proudest Roman (USA)) [1991 5m⁵ 6d⁶ 5f⁶ 6g⁵ 6f³ 7m 7.5f⁶ 7m 8m³] 5,200F: smallish, quite attractive colt: has a roundish action: second living foal: dam unraced: fairly useful plater: stays 1m: acts on firm ground: has run creditably for 7-lb claimer: fairly consistent. *A. W. Potts.*

FYLDE FLYER   2 ch.c. (Apr 30) Music Boy 124 – Djimbaran Bay (Le Levanstell   **92** 122) [1991 5g⁶ 6m* 7m⁶ 6m³ 6d* 6m* 6m² 6m² 6g² 6m⁴ 6g³ 6m* 6g⁵] 8,800Y: sturdy, lengthy colt: progressing well physically: moderate walker: half-brother to numerous winners here and abroad, including useful 1¼m winner Bettyknowes (by Satingo) and fair 6f winner Portvasco (by Sharpo): dam won at up to 1¼m in France: fairly useful performer: successful in maiden auction, claimer and nursery at Hamilton in summer: ran creditably in varied events before winning nursery at York in October: stays 7f: acts on good to firm and dead ground: game, and most consistent. *J. Berry.*

G

GABBIADINI   4 b.g. Taufan (USA) 119 – Galerida (Silver Shark 129) [1990 6g 7g⁶   **82** 7h* 8.5d² 7m² 7m 8d 7.5f 8f² a8g* 8g⁶ 7.6m³ 7m 1991 8m⁵ 7d⁵ 7.5f⁵ 7m 8g 7m³ 7.9m 7.1s² 7.1m* 7.6m³ 8d⁴ 8m⁶ a7g a8g²] close-coupled, angular gelding: fair handicapper: won at Haydock in August: stays 8.5f: probably acts on any going: visored last 7 starts: ran poorly for 7-lb claimer. *M. H. Tompkins.*

GABBY HAYES   3 ch.g. Gabitat 119 – Night Cap (SWE) (Hornbeam 130) [1990   **54** 6g 7m a8g 1991 a10g a10g² a10g⁶ a10g⁶ 12v⁵ 11.7s 7m a8g⁶] lengthy, angular gelding: had a round action: plating class at best: stayed 1¼m: visored final start, blinkered previous 2: dead. *P. Mitchell.*

GABES   2 b.c. (Feb 6) Aragon 118 – First Time Over (Derrylin 115) [1991 5d 5g 5f   **74** 6m³ 6f* 6d] 2,900F, 1,000Y: workmanlike colt: first foal: dam maiden placed at 1m, is half-sister to temperamental Out of Shot, winner at up to 1½m and disqualified third in Oaks: much improved over 6f, winning maiden auction event at Yarmouth in June: suffered fracture of off-hind pastern when pulled up in £6,000 event at Newbury 9 days later: dead. *J. W. Payne.*

GABIBTI (IRE)   3 ch.f. Dara Monarch 128 – Torriglia (USA) (Nijinsky (CAN)   **74 d** 138) [1990 5f 5g* 5d* 6m³ 6f⁴ 6f³ 6d 6m* 7.3g 1991 6f⁴ 6d³ 7g⁵ 6m 6d 5s³ 6g 6f 5g 6.1m 6m] small, good-quartered filly: has a quick action: modest performer: out of form in handicaps last 5 starts: stays 7f: acts on any going: sweats and gets on edge. *B. Gubby.*

GABISH   6 b.g. Try My Best (USA) 130 – Crannog (Habitat 134) [1990 a12g⁴ 1991   **—** a16g] compact gelding: modest winner early as 3-y-o, but has deteriorated considerably: stays 1m: acts on firm and dead going: has been tried blinkered. *J. Ffitch-Heyes.*

GABY   3 b. or br.g. Sure Blade (USA) 130 – Mpani 97 (Habitat 134) [1990 NR 1991   **—** 11.7f 12.3g] workmanlike gelding: second foal: dam 1¼m winner out of Cheshire Oaks and Park Hill winner African Dancer: no sign of ability in maiden claimer and seller: bought out of G. Wragg's stable 1,450 gns Newmarket October (1990) Sales. *A. P. James.*

GACHETTE   2 b.c. (Mar 16) Lidhame 109 – Renira 60 (Relkino 131) [1991 7g⁶   **51** 7m⁶ 6g] 6,600Y: workmanlike colt: third foal: half-brother to 1990 2-y-o 5f winner Summer Sands (by Mummy's Game): dam poor maiden: best effort when sixth of 12 at Lingfield, not clear run and keeping on not knocked about: wore dropped noseband final start: better suited by 7f than 6f. *J. Sutcliffe.*

GAELIC CHIEF   3 b.g. Lidhame 109 – Celtic Sonata (Music Boy 124) [1990 6f*   **—** 6g 7f⁶ 1991 8.5f 8m 6d] smallish, rather leggy gelding: modest winner at 2 yrs: showed nothing in handicaps and seller (visored) in first half of 1991, and gelded: stays 6f: one to be wary of. *C. Tinkler.*

GAELIC DANCER   4 ch.c. Town And Country 124 – Verily Jane 53 (Royben   **47** 125) [1990 10m a8g³ 10g⁶ a8g⁴ 16m 1991 10d 12g a8g 8.3g⁶ 8.3m] rather sparelymade colt: poor mover: poor handicapper: stays 1m: ran too freely in blinkers: often bandaged. *L. J. Codd.*

GAELIC HOPE   4 ch.g. Horage 124 – Amiga Mia 71 (Be Friendly 130) [1990 8s   **—** 8m 5g a8g 1991 5.1d] lengthy, rather unfurnished gelding: poor mover: no worthwhile form. *B. R. Millman.*

GAELIC ROOTS (IRE)   2 b.f. (Mar 3) Pennine Walk 120 – Spring Life   **—** (Wolverlife 115) [1991 5m] IR 8,200F, 3,000Y: workmanlike filly: first foal: dam never ran: green and in need of race, never a threat in 13-runner seller at Windsor in August. *J. S. Moore.*

GAI BULGA 3 b.f. Kris 135 – Dancing Rocks 118 (Green Dancer (USA) 132) **110** [1990 NR 1991 10m* 12g² 11.5g² 12g⁴ 10f* 10.1m* 10m²] big, lengthy, angular filly: fifth foal: sister to 10.4f winner Kirpan and half-sister to fairly useful 1m winner Gayle Yaka (by Habitat): dam won Nassau Stakes: won maiden at Pontefract in April then minor event at Salisbury and 3-runner listed race at Newcastle in August: good efforts in listed race (ran wide turn and hung left) at Lingfield, Ribblesdale Stakes at Royal Ascot and Abtrust Select Stakes at Goodwood third, fourth and final outings: stays 1½m well, and should prove suited by forcing tactics and strong pace: progressive. *G. Wragg.*

GAILY DANCE 3 b.f. Monsanto (FR) 121 – Step You Gaily 71 (King's Company — 124) [1990 NR 1991 8.3m 6m 7m 10m] 1,000Y: sturdy filly: half-sister to several winners here and abroad, including 6f to 1½m winner Vague Dancer (by Vaigly Great): dam best at 2 yrs when placed at 8.2f: poor plater: sweating and edgy final start: joined N. Ayliffe. *C. J. Hill.*

GALAGAMES (USA) 4 ch.g. Lyphard (USA) 132 – Morning Games (USA) — (Grey Dawn II 132) [1990 10f² 12h² 11.5m³ 14m³ 14f⁴ 14d a13g 1991 10.8g⁶] round-barrelled gelding: carries condition: modest maiden at best: well below form only run as 4-y-o (April): should stay 1¾m: acts on hard ground: lacks turn of foot. *R. J. Hodges.*

GALAXY EXPRESS 3 ch.g. Bay Express 132 – Heaven And Earth (Mid- **45** summer Night II 117) [1990 5f 5f 1991 6g⁶ 8g 5g 6f 5m⁶ 6m⁵ 6m³] workmanlike gelding: has a quick, fluent action: poor maiden: stays 6f: acts on good to firm ground: bandaged third and fourth (also visored) starts. *G. H. Eden.*

GALAXY GLOW 3 b.f. Kalaglow 132 – Lone Galaxie (USA) 69 (Nodouble — (USA)) [1990 7.5f⁶ 7m 7f 1991 8m 11.1g] small filly: poor maiden. *P. Beaumont.*

GALLANT EFFORT (IRE) 3 b.c. Thatching 131 – Meeting Adjourned 94 **48** (General Assembly 130) [1990 NR 1991 a8g⁵ a8g⁵ a7g 8.5m a7g 11.9f⁶ 11.8g 10m³ a10g] IR 14,000Y: tall colt: has a round action: second foal: dam Irish 1m and 11f winner: plating-class form at best: seems to stay 1½m: wore eyeshield first 3 starts: subsequently sold out of Mrs L. Piggott's stable 5,000 gns Ascot May Sales: trained following 2 outings by K. Wingrove. *S. Dow.*

GALLANT HOPE 9 ch.g. Ahonoora 122 – Amiga Mia 71 (Be Friendly 130) [1990 **61** 5g 6d 5m³ 5m 6m 6m 5m⁶ 6m 5.8f 6g³ 5m⁶ 6s a6g 1991 6g 6g 5.8f⁴ 6.1m 5f³ 6m² 5.8d⁶ 5d⁵ 5g³ 5g 6g 6f 5f⁶ 5f³ 5.7f 5.3g⁶ 5.1s 5g] small, stocky gelding: carries plenty of condition: has been hobdayed: quite modest sprinter nowadays: unsuited by soft ground, acts on any other: best blinkered: used to be best with strong handling: sometimes gets behind. *B. R. Millman.*

GALLANT JACK (IRE) 2 b.g. (Feb 23) Flash of Steel 120 – Milveagh 92 **66** (Milesian 125) [1991 7g³ 6g³ 7.1s 7.1m² 8.1g⁶] 10,500Y: tall, leggy gelding: has scope: half-brother to numerous winners here and abroad, including useful 1987 2-y-o 6f winner Madam de Seul (by Pas de Seul) and 5f winner Coming About (by Right Tack): dam won at up to 1m: quite modest maiden: off course 8 weeks, best effort when second of 15 in auction event (sweating) at Chepstow in September: should stay 1m. *D. Haydn Jones.*

GALLATEEN 3 gr.g. Touching Wood (USA) 127 – Lune de Minuit (USA) (Caro **60** 133) [1990 NR 1991 10.1s 12m 12g³] good-bodied gelding: has a markedly round action: second foal: dam lightly raced: first sign of ability when third in claimer at Goodwood: will be well suited by 1¾m: refused to enter stalls fourth intended start: sold 21,000 gns Newmarket July Sales and gelded: winning hurdler for G. Richards. *B. Hanbury.*

GALLERY ARTIST (IRE) 3 ch.c. Tate Gallery (USA) 117 – Avec L'Amour 75 **59** (Realm 129) [1990 5g 6g² 6f 6d² 6v³ 6g³ 6d⁵ a7g⁶ 1991 a7g³ a6g* 5.1f⁶ 6m⁴ 6f a6g 6g⁵ 5g⁶] small colt: poor mover: quite modest performer: won maiden at Lingfield in February: best form at 6f: acts on any going: has run well for claimer: blinkered twice at 2 yrs. *R. Guest.*

GALLERY NOTE (IRE) 2 b.f. (May 3) Tate Gallery (USA) 117 – Thank You — Note 73 (What A Guest 119) [1991 6.1m 6m⁶] IR 30,000F, 16,000Y: smallish, quite attractive filly: has a quick action: first foal: dam 1m and 11f winner: well beaten in Midlands maidens: will stay 1m. *B. W. Hills.*

GALLEY GOSSIP 2 b.g. (Mar 16) Dunbeath (USA) 127 – Mother Brown 103 **59** (Candy Cane 125) [1991 6g² 6f³ 6m⁴] half-brother to several winners, including 1m winner Macarthurs Head (by Dom Racine): dam genuine handicapper at up to 1¼m:

quite modest maiden: best effort when keeping-on fourth of 20 in claimer at Leicester in October: will be well suited by 1m+: takes keen hold, has worn a crossed noseband, and been taken quietly to post: can win a seller at least. *Mrs J. R. Ramsden.*

GALLIVANTING 2 b.c. (Apr 5) Formidable (USA) 125 – Travel On 111 — (Tachypous 128) [1991 5m] 29,000F, 45,000Y: sturdy colt: fourth live foal: dam won Cherry Hinton Stakes: 14/1, never dangerous in maiden at Newmarket in April: looked sure to improve. *P. W. Chapple-Hyam.*

GALLOWAY RAIDER 7 br.g. Skyliner 117 – Whispering Breeze (Caliban 123) — [1990 a13g 13v 12g² 14g⁵ 13g⁵ 18m² 16.2d⁴ 16m* 16.5g² 16.2g⁵ 16m 15m⁵ 16m⁶ 16f⁴ 18g⁶ 1991 16m⁶ 16.2g 12g⁶] tall, leggy gelding: has a round action: poor handicapper: stays 2¼m: acts on hard going: raced freely in visor: winning hurdler. *Denys Smith.*

GALWAY PRINCE (IRE) 2 ch.c. (May 17) Sandhurst Prince 128 – Pall Nan 86 — (Pall Mall 132) [1991 a5g 7m 8.9m] IR 3,400F, 3,200Y, 1,500 2-y-o: good-bodied colt: half-brother to numerous winners here and abroad, including useful Irish 7f and 1¼m winner Domino's Nurse (by Dom Racine) and fairly useful 1979 2-y-o 7f winner Appleby Park (by Bay Express): dam best at 5f: tailed off, in York claimer final start. *M. C. Chapman.*

GAMELAN 2 b.c. (Apr 30) Music Boy 124 – Cymbal 80 (Ribero 126) [1991 5m 6g³ **51** 7f* 7g 6m] 2,500Y: leggy, workmanlike colt: has a quick action: half-brother to 1¼m winner Beau Mirage (by Homing) and a winner abroad by Moulton: dam, half-sister to smart performers Band and Zimbalon, won 3 times over middle distances from only 5 starts: gamely won 6-runner maiden auction at Catterick in July: no comparable form afterwards: will stay 1m: visored final start. *M. H. Tompkins.*

GAME PLAN 4 b.f. Darshaan 133 – Formulate 119 (Reform 132) [1990 10g³ 10m² **103** 12d² 10g* 12g⁶ 12m 1991 10g³ 10m⁶ 12m] close-coupled filly: smart performer at best, second in Epsom Oaks and successful in Pretty Polly Stakes (edged right) at the Curragh at 3 yrs: below best in 1991, 7½ lengths third to Spritsail in listed race at Goodwood in May: suited by 1½m: acted on good to firm ground and dead: thrice below form when sweating: reportedly in foal. *C. E. Brittain.*

GANESHAYA 2 gr.c. (Mar 21) Formidable (USA) 125 – Lammastide 93 (Martin- **57** mas 128) [1991 6g⁵ 6m* 7m 7m² 6.1g] sturdy colt: moderate mover: second foal: half-brother to 1990 2-y-o 6f winner Musabiq (by Superlative): dam 2-y-o 5f winner: fairly useful plater: heavily-backed favourite, won 20-runner contest (bought in 7,200 gns) at Windsor in June: good second of 13 at Wolverhampton (claimed out of J. Akehurst's stable 4,800 gns) in August: stays 7f. *M. F. Barraclough.*

GANGES (USA) 3 gr.c. Riverman (USA) 131 – Paloma Blanca (USA) (Blushing **115** Groom (FR) 131) [1990 7.5g⁶ 7.5g³ 8s* 9g⁴ 7s* 1991 7g* 8g³ 8g⁴ 8g³ 8g 6g² 10d⁴ 7d] tall, useful-looking colt: shows plenty of knee action: smart performer: sweating, won Prix Djebel at Maisons-Laffitte in April: bit below best in respective 2000 Guineas at Newmarket and the Curragh next 2 starts: 2 lengths second to Feenpark in Prix de Meautry at Deauville: stays 1m: yet to race on top-of-the-ground, and goes well on soft. *F. Boutin, France.*

GANT BLEU (FR) 4 ch.g. Crystal Glitters (USA) 127 – Gold Honey (Artaius **61** § (USA) 129) [1990 7f 6f³ 6m 8f⁶ 7d 9f⁶ 7.5g 8m³ 7m² 8d a8g 1991 8d 7g³ 8f² 8g* 7.5g⁵ 8g² 8f⁵ 7f³ 9m 8f 7m 7f³ 8m 7m 8m³ 8m] leggy, rather sparely-made gelding: moderate mover: plating-class handicapper: won claimer at Ripon in May: ideally suited by 1m: best form on a sound surface: well below form in visor once: often wears crossed noseband: inconsistent, and one to treat with caution. *R. M. Whitaker.*

GAPTON PREY (IRE) 3 b.g. Auction Ring (USA) 123 – Double Eagle 71 — (Goldhill 125) [1990 NR 1991 7g 8m 6.1m 9.2s] IR 20,500Y: leggy, close-coupled gelding: half-brother to several winners here and abroad, including useful Irish sprinters Flaming Eagle (by Green God) and Do The Hustle (by Sun Prince): dam 5f seller winner at 2 yrs: behind in maidens, claimer and handicap. *M. H. Tompkins.*

GARDA'S GOLD 8 b.g. Garda's Revenge (USA) 119 – Mielee (Le Levanstell — 122) [1990 11s⁶ 12m 11.5m* 10g 10m⁴ 10m 1991 10s] leggy, narrow gelding: moderate mover: poor handicapper: stays 1½m: acts on good to firm and soft going: effective with or without visor: tried blinkered, including on reappearance (below form): has worn crossed noseband: inconsistent. *R. Dickin.*

GARDENBLAKE 2 b.g. (Mar 20) Viking (USA) – Barely Hot (Bold Lad (IRE) — 133) [1991 5g 5f 5f 7.5f] 5,800F, 5,700Y: smallish, sturdy gelding: fifth foal: half-brother to 1989 2-y-o 5f seller winner Or Nor (by Cure The Blues) and a winner in Italy: dam, half-sister to Trojan Fen and Kashi Lagoon, placed over 5f in Ireland:

seems of little account: pulled hard, and ran wide into straight, in blinkers final start: sold 700 gns Ascot July Sales. *J. G. FitzGerald.*

GARTH 3 gr.g. Petong 126 – Doppio 62 (Dublin Taxi) [1990 5d 5g* 5m 1991 6m 5d 6m² 6m⁶ 6m] sturdy, rather dipped-backed gelding: fair performer on his day: very good second of 16 in handicap at Haydock, always front rank: below form in similar events at Epsom and York (blinkered, disputed lead over 3f and wandered under pressure) later in summer: stays 6f: acts on good to firm ground. *P. J. Makin.* **78**

GASCOIGNE WOOD 3 b.c. Petoski 135 – Be My Queen 84 (Be My Guest (USA) 126) [1990 NR 1991 10m 9g 7f⁴ 10m] 7,200Y: leggy, unfurnished colt: third foal: half-brother to 4-y-o middle-distance maiden Elmdon Prince (by Ela-Mana-Mou): dam 1m winner out of half-sister to Derby second Cavo Doro: little sign of ability in maidens and seller: should be suited by further than 7f. *Miss S. E. Hall.* **—**

GAVELKIND (IRE) 2 ch.c. (Feb 27) Mazaad 106 – Eirene Oge (Green God 128) [1991 6m 6g 6m² 7f 6g⁴ 7.6m] IR 9,800Y: good-quartered colt: half-brother to a winner in Belgium by Touch Paper: dam Irish maiden: inconsistent maiden: blinkered, best effort when fourth in Goodwood claimer in October: seems suited by 6f: possibly unsuited by firm going: visored (ran poorly) final start: has raced with head high: bandaged on debut. *M. Bell.* **60**

GAVIN ALLEN 3 ch.g. Heraldiste (USA) 121 – Vernair (USA) 73 (Super Concorde (USA) 128) [1990 a6g⁶ 6f³ a6g³ 7m⁵ 7g³ 7d³ 7m⁴ 1991 a8g² a7g* a8g⁴ 8m] small, sparely-made gelding: quite modest performer: odds on, won maiden at Southwell in February: bandaged all round on first run for 8 months, showed little in claimer final start: stays 1m: acts on firm and dead ground: suitable mount for a claimer. *C. N. Allen.* **64**

GAY GLINT 4 b.g. Glint of Gold 128 – Gay Hellene 111 (Ela-Mana-Mou 132) [1990 10m* 12g⁶ 11.5m⁴ 11.7m³ 14m* 14g⁵ 16m² 16.2m² 1991 14m* 16g⁵ 16g 11.9m 14g³ 16.1g* 18m 16.2d² 18m] unfurnished gelding: good mover: fairly useful handicapper: won at Newmarket in April and August: ran moderately in Cesarewitch at Newmarket final start: not discredited in Doncaster Cup seventh one: ideally suited by 2m +: acts on good to firm and dead ground. *N. A. Graham.* **95**

GAY MING 2 b.f. (Feb 26) Gay Meadow 52 – Miss Admington 71 (Double Jump 131) [1991 6m 7.6d⁵ a7g] leggy, lightly-made filly: fifth reported live foal: dam probably stayed 1½m: little worthwhile form in maidens and a claimer. *R. Hollinshead.* **35**

GAY REVENGE 3 b.g. Sweet Monday 122 – Mummys Colleen 75 (Mummy's Pet 125) [1990 6g a6g 1991 a8g] quite attractive gelding: no sign of ability in maidens. *D. Burchell.* **—**

GAY RUFFIAN 5 b.g. Welsh Term 126 – Alcinea (FR) 93 (Sweet Revenge 129) [1990 13s* a12g 1991 a12g 17m⁵] lengthy, sparely-made gelding: has a round action: plating-class handicapper: below form as 5-y-o, not seen out after April: stays 17f: acts on top-of-the-ground, but ideally suited by soft: useful hurdler, winner in March. *D. Burchell.* **37**

GDANSK'S HONOUR (USA) 2 b.f. (May 11) Danzig (USA) – Royal Honoree (USA) (Round Table) [1991 7g³ 7g*] sister to useful 1988 2-y-o 5f and 6f winner Honoria and half-sister to several winners, including Irish St Leger runner-up Father Rooney (by Val de L'Orne): dam, winner 3 times at up to 6f, is sister to top 1972 French 2-y-o Targowice and half-sister to dam of Manila and Stately Don: joint favourite, made all in 14-runner maiden at the Curragh in September, winning by 8 lengths: will stay 1m. *J. S. Bolger, Ireland.* **91 p**

GEE DOUBLE YOU 5 ch.g. Tap On Wood 130 – Repicado Rose (USA) (Repicado (CHI)) [1990 NR 1991 10.2s] rangy, angular gelding: quite modest handicapper as 3-y-o: backward and bandaged only run in 1991: should stay 1½m: acts on good to firm ground. *D. Haydn Jones.* **—**

GEMINI BAY 2 b.c. (Mar 27) Petong 126 – Deux Etoiles 86 (Bay Express 132) [1991 5s 5g 6s 6m* 6g* 6m* 6g] 5,200Y: close-coupled colt: half-brother to 1¼m seller winner Five Star Affair (by Mummy's Game), a winner abroad and a winner over hurdles: dam 2-y-o 5f winner: fair performer: started slowly and showed nil first 3 starts: successful in summer in seller (no bid) at Folkestone and nurseries at Windsor, best effort third occasion when held up in strongly-run race then forging well clear: sweating, well beaten in Newmarket nursery later in August: will stay 7f: acts on good to firm ground: blinkered final 5 starts: tends to wander. *R. Voorspuy.* **84 ?**

GEMINI FIRE 7 br.g. Mansingh (USA) 120 – Sealady (Seaepic (USA) 100) [1990 5g 5g 5d 5s* 5m³ 5m 5g⁶ 5d 5d 6g 6s 1991 5d³ 5g² 5g* 5f 5g* 5m 5d] sparely-made gelding: fair handicapper: won at York (£11,650 event) in May and Haydock in July: **83**

stays 6f: acts on any going except probably heavy: has worn visor: often edgy: wore net muzzle to post on reappearance: sometimes taken down early. *M. P. Naughton.*

GENAIR (FR)   6 ch.g. General Assembly (USA) – Metair 118 (Laser Light 118)   **58**
[1990 8.2s⁵ 8g⁴ 8m⁶ 8.2s⁶ 8m* 8m³ 8.5f* 10.2m⁴ 10f⁶ 8f* 8.2d 8m 8g⁶ 8m⁴ 8g 9m 8d 1991 8.5g 7.5f⁴ 8m 7.5f 8m⁶ 9m³ 8h* 8d 8m⁴ 7.9m⁴ 9f 9m³ 8m⁵] big, rather dipped-backed gelding: has had soft palate operation: plating-class handicapper nowadays: won at Carlisle in June, ridden halfway: often gets behind, and ideally suited by strongly-run race at 1m/9f: best efforts on top-of-the-ground: effective blinkered or not. *G. M. Moore.*

GENERAL ALCAZAR (IRE)   2 b.g. (Apr 17) Alzao (USA) 117 – Cape of   —
Storms (Fordham (USA) 117) [1991 5d] 19,000Y: leggy gelding: third foal: dam (well beaten at 2 yrs) out of staying half-sister to top-class sprinter Sandford Lad: green, prominent 3f in 9-runner maiden at Pontefract in April. *J. Berry.*

GENERAL JO   3 b.g. Cree Song 99 – My Marie (Sovereign Bill 105) [1990 NR   **43**
1991 5m⁶ 7m 5g⁵ 5f 7m 6d³ 6m 6g³ 6d] leggy gelding: third reported foal: half-brother to a winning hurdler: dam poor sprint plater: poor maiden: tailed off in handicap final start, in July: should stay 7f (stiff task at trip): best effort with give in the ground: sweating last 2 outings: visored (tailed off) seventh. *Mrs J. Jordan.*

GENERAL JOHN (IRE)   2 br.c. (Mar 8) Cyrano de Bergerac 120 – Hill's   — p
Realm (USA) 68 (Key To The Kingdom (USA)) [1991 a7g] 18,000F, 25,000Y: fifth foal: half-brother to 3-y-o All The Kings Men (by Alzao), 9f winner at 2 yrs, and 2 other winners: dam stayed 6f: around 16 lengths ninth of 16, slowly away, to Empeeka in late-year maiden at Southwell. *P. C. Haslam.*

GENERAL SIKORSKI   3 b.c. Petoski 135 – Cristalga 90 (High Top 131) [1990   **99** p
NR 1991 10m⁵ 10.1g² 10.1m* 12g² 10g² 10.5f*] 30,000F, 36,000Y: strong colt: good mover: fourth foal: half-brother to 1¼-mile seller winner/successful hurdler Au Bon (by Song): dam won at 1¼m and stayed 1½m: won 3-runner median auction race at Windsor in July and £15,700 handicap at Haydock in September: favourite, extremely impressive in winning at Haydock by 3 lengths from Fire Top, travelling strongly to challenge over 2f out and only nudged out to quicken clear: effective at 1¼m and 1½m: progressive form, has physical scope to improve again, and is sure to win more good handicaps. *P. J. Makin.*

GENEROUS (IRE)   3 ch.c. Caerleon (USA) 132 – Doff The Derby (USA)   **139**
(Master Derby (USA)) [1990 5m* 6m² 7f³ 6d 8g* 7d* 1991 8g⁴ 12f* 12g* 12m* 12d]

In the space of fifty-three days and three races Generous raised his status to that of a sporting wonder. 'Generous first, daylight second' was the story of Britain's two biggest middle-distance events, the Ever Ready Derby and the King George VI and Queen Elizabeth Diamond Stakes; and in between Generous beat the Prix du Jockey-Club winner Suave Dancer by three lengths in the Budweiser Irish Derby. The feat of winning the Derby at both Epsom and the Curragh has now been achieved on ten occasions since prize money for the Irish Derby was boosted in 1962 to make it a race of international importance, and Generous became the sixth of the dual Derby winners to go on to success in the King George, following Nijinsky, Grundy, The Minstrel, Troy and Shergar. Mill Reef and Nashwan completed a similar treble, contesting the Eclipse instead of the Irish Derby between Epsom and Ascot. Generous' three successes were all gained most emphatically and his official margin of victory in the King George—seven lengths—was the greatest in the history of the race.

Generous' credentials now speak for themselves but before he ran at Epsom few could have envisaged that he would develop into one of the finest middle-distance horses seen in Europe in the past forty years or so. His two-year-old career, which began with a win over five furlongs as early as May and a second in the Coventry Stakes at Royal Ascot, eventually yielded three wins from six starts and culminated in a 50/1 success in the Three Chimneys Dewhurst Stakes at Newmarket. Generous won the Dewhurst by three quarters of a length from the Laurent Perrier Champagne Stakes winner Bog Trotter, in a field which had seemed dominated beforehand by the unbeaten Mujtahid who had looked a potential champion during the summer. Generous' performances earned him 119 in the International Classification for two-year-olds, placing him joint-ninth behind French-trained Hector Protector who

*Ever Ready Derby, Epsom—Generous routs the opposition;
Marju is seven lengths clear of the rest*

headed the weights on 126. Success in the Dewhurst—still widely accepted as
Britain's premier championship event for staying two-year-olds—would have
made its winner the leading candidate for the classics in some years. But the
race has lost ground recently and hadn't been won by a horse who'd gone on to
classic success since El Gran Senor in 1983; El Gran Senor had been preceded
in a fifteen-year period by The Minstrel, Wollow, Grundy, Mill Reef and
Nijinsky. The 1989 Dewhurst winner Dashing Blade had been well beaten in
the Two Thousand Guineas and managed only fourth in the St James's Palace
Stakes before having his sights lowered, and Generous too looked likely to
find it tough going in top company in Britain as a three-year-old. Readers of
Racehorses of 1990 won't need reminding (neither do we!) of our view that
'enterprising placement might be necessary if he's to win more good races'.

On form, Generous had 10 lb or more to find to win an average Two
Thousand Guineas, which was his first target as a three-year-old. He was one
of three in a field of fourteen to tackle the Guineas without a preparatory race,
having had his training interrupted by a foot injury. Generous was in the front
rank until after halfway at Newmarket but when the race began in earnest he
was found wanting; after struggling to keep up and then losing ground, he kept
on gamely up the hill for fourth, about eight and a half lengths behind the
winner Mystiko. The recent record of Two Thousand Guineas runners in the
Derby isn't so good as the longer-term record. Until Nashwan, no Derby
winner had run in the Two Thousand Guineas since The Minstrel in 1977; but
in the forty-year period before 1991 twelve Derby winners had contested the
Guineas, three of them coming second at Newmarket, one (The Minstrel)
finishing third and three unplaced. Five of the thirteen runners in the latest
Derby had been in the Guineas field: Mystiko, Generous, Hokusai (eighth at
Newmarket), Marju (eleventh) and Mujaazif (thirteenth). Mystiko, seeking to
complete the Two Thousand Guineas-Derby double achieved by Crepello,
Royal Palace, Sir Ivor, Nijinsky and Nashwan in the previous forty years,
started at 5/1; Generous, looking to have every chance on pedigree of being
suited by the extra half mile, was a 9/1-chance; Marju, who reportedly injured
himself when a hot favourite for the Guineas, started at 14/1; with Hokusai
(the mount of Piggott) and Mujaazif at 25/1 and 33/1 respectively. The
recognised Derby trials with the best recent records are the Dante Stakes at
York and the Lingfield Derby Trial. The Dante, which had been used as a
stepping-stone by three of the previous thirteen Derby winners (Shirley
Heights, Shahrastani and Reference Point), produced a five-length winner in

318

Environment Friend whose form looked even better when the runner-up Hailsham, also in the Derby field, went on to success in the Derby Italiano. The Lingfield Derby Trial winners in the 'eighties included Teenoso, Slip Anchor and Kahyasi, and the latest race provided another prominent Derby candidate in Corrupt whose four-length victory over Young Buster looked just about the best form of any, especially after the well-beaten fourth and fifth, Walim and Marcus Thorpe, ran well in the Derby Italiano. Corrupt started 4/1 joint favourite at Epsom with the impressive Chester Vase winner Toulon. Toulon was joined in the French-trained challenge by 6/1-chance Hector Protector, who had extended his unbeaten sequence to eight in the Poule d'Essai des Poulains; Hector Protector was the outstanding individual on looks in the Derby field. There was one Irish-trained challenger Star of Gdansk who had been beaten a head in the Irish Two Thousand Guineas in which the running of the Guineas second and third, Lycius and Ganges, hadn't done a great deal for the Newmarket form. All in all, the Derby field was thoroughly representative, though some of the leading candidates looked far from certain to possess Derby-winning stamina, even though the prevailing going was as firm as it ever is for a modern-day Derby.

The story of the Derby is soon told. Only two horses showed in front, the Guineas winner Mystiko and Generous. The free-running Mystiko set a cracking gallop (Toulon's pacemaker Arokat couldn't pass him) until Generous, always travelling comfortably in the front rank and full of running at Tattenham Corner, swept past about two and a half furlongs out. Generous soon opened up a decisive lead and kept up the gallop (under the whip in the final furlong) to win by five lengths from Marju who went a long way to redeeming his reputation, staying on strongly in the last two furlongs to finish seven lengths ahead of third-placed Star of Gdansk, with Hector Protector, the 66/1-shot Hundra and Corrupt close behind. Neither Toulon (ninth) nor Environment Friend (eleventh) produced anything like his true running. Generous' official Derby-winning margin equalled that of Nashwan and the 1958 winner Hard Ridden, and had been bettered on only five occasions in the previous forty years—by Arctic Prince and Relko, both of whom won by six, by the seven-length winners Troy and Slip Anchor, and by Shergar whose ten-length win was the most prodigious in the long history of the race. The twelve lengths which separated Generous from Star of Gdansk was, incidentally, the second-greatest recorded margin between winner and third in a Derby (the distance was thirteen in Slip Anchor's year).

Generous' performance at Epsom was outstanding even by classic standards and we rated it superior to that of the Prix du Jockey-Club Lancia winner Suave Dancer who had created a great impression when routing his field, showing a top-class turn of foot, at Chantilly four days earlier. Arguments about whether Generous' performance at Epsom or Suave Dancer's at Chantilly was the best of the season by a three-year-old were thankfully put to one side when the two Derby winners clashed in the Budweiser Irish Derby at the end of June, the highlight of the European season up to that time. Generous and Suave Dancer dominated a six-horse turn-out—the smallest field for the Irish Derby for fifty-four years—coming well clear of Star of Gdansk and the unbeaten O'Brien-trained Sportsworld in the straight. With no strong-galloping front-runner in the field, Generous was sent on after about half a mile, and when he stretched out in earnest soon after rounding the home turn only Suave Dancer, ridden by Swinburn in place of the injured Asmussen, could stay with him. Suave Dancer threw down his challenge at the two-furlong marker, drawing almost alongside, but Generous proved the stronger and ran on stoutly to win most decisively. Suave Dancer began hanging towards the rail when he had no more to give and was beaten three lengths (officially that is; it looked slightly less); third-placed Star of Gdansk finished eight lengths behind Suave Dancer, virtually reproducing his Epsom running with Generous.

Generous was now firmly established as the outstanding three-year-old in Europe and he was put to the test against his elders for the first time in the King George VI and Queen Elizabeth Diamond Stakes at Ascot in July. He'd have faced a stronger test had the Grand Prix de Saint-Cloud winner Epervier Bleu, who'd apparently had the King George as a major target all season, not

Budweiser Irish Derby, the Curragh—Generous proves stronger than Suave Dancer as the pair leave Star of Gdansk and Sportsworld behind

defected. With the likes of the Coronation Cup winner In The Groove and the 1990 St Leger winner Snurge (a stable-companion of Generous) also absent, the older horses were headed by the 1990 Prix du Jockey-Club winner Sanglamore, third in the Coral-Eclipse on his latest outing and back at a mile and a half for the first time since winning from Epervier Bleu at Chantilly. Rock Hopper, winner of four of his six races in 1991 and beaten three lengths by Epervier Bleu in the Grand Prix de Saint-Cloud, was also in a nine-horse line-up that looked weak overall for a King George. Second favourite to the odds-on Generous was, in fact, another three-year-old, the runaway King Edward VII Stakes winner Saddlers' Hall. Generous outclassed them all. After settling well in a very strongly-run race, he surged into a decisive lead soon after the home turn providing a spectacular display to win, eased before the line, by seven lengths, surpassing the six-length winning margins in the race of Dahlia and Mill Reef. Sanglamore won the battle for second place, finishing a length ahead of Rock Hopper who was slightly hampered by the runner-up. Terimon came fourth, the 40/1-shot Sapience fifth and Saddlers' Hall sixth.

Generous' performances at Epsom, the Curragh and Ascot virtually assured him of Horse of the Year honours. The panel of journalists which decides the official award at the end of each season—for which only horses that ran in Britain are eligible—voted him a landslide victory: he polled all twenty-eight votes, becoming only the third unanimous choice, following Brigadier Gerard in 1972 and Dancing Brave in 1986, since the award was established in 1965. The owner-trainer-jockey team of Fahd Salman, Paul Cole and Alan Munro enjoyed a season they will never forget, highlighted by the successes of Generous and by the achievement of having three Royal Ascot two-year-old winners Dilum, Magic Ring and Fair Cop. Mr Salman led the owners' table for much of the season before being over-hauled by the big battalions of Sheikh Mohammed and Hamdan Al-Maktoum. Generous' victories in the Derby and King George helped Cole to the trainers' championship which went to a stable outside Newmarket for the first time since 1983. Second place, incidentally, went to another 'outsider', Marlborough-based Richard Hannon, whilst reigning champion Henry Cecil dropped to seventh overall. Jockey Alan Munro's association with Generous shot him to prominence. He took over as first jockey to Mr Salman—a surprise move at the time—shortly before the Derby (Quinn rode Generous in the Guineas) and his low, crouching American style, which makes him easily distinguishable, soon became familiar to the racing public at large, as well as to the professionals who'd seen him develop into one of the most promising young jockeys for some time. Munro's handling of the Press after his Derby victory, however, didn't please some. One writer described him as 'self confident to the point of arrogance', another as 'the new Piggott' (an eighteen-year-old Piggott dismissed his first Derby victory, on Never Say Die, with the remark: 'Excited—not particularly. Why should I be? It's just another race'). Any rift between Munro and certain sections of the Press seemed, thankfully, to have been healed by the end of the season which Munro ended in fourth place in the jockeys' table, notching his first century, and, ironically, being voted Jockey of the Year by the Horserace Writers' Association.

The boxing adage 'No fight is better than the wrong fight' might equally be applied to racing—'No race is better than the wrong race'. The history of France's great show-piece event the Prix de l'Arc de Triomphe, run at Longchamp in October, is littered with failures by British-trained champions. ome of them have borne out Noel Murless' saying that the Arc is 'just three weeks too late for a horse which has undergone a proper classic preparation, working up to the Guineas in the spring, followed by Epsom and Ascot'. Mill Reef and Dancing Brave established themselves as truly exceptional three-year-olds, setting the seal on their greatness with magnificent victories in the Prix de l'Arc after all-encompassing spring and summer campaigns in Britain. But defeat in the Arc has damaged a number of reputations over the years and Generous' flop in the latest edition may lead more connections of future champions to decline the challenge presented by the Arc. Generous, who started odds on, was one of the most distinguished horses ever beaten in an Arc and to see him fade so tamely, faltering like a once-great actor who can no longer remember his lines, was both pathetic and puzzling. Generous seemed poised for victory approaching the home turn, perfectly placed travelling smoothly in the leading group, but he went out like a light early in the straight. Munro confirmed afterwards that Generous 'was going as well as he has ever been in any of his races . . . then the next second he was as weak as a kitten'. The reason for Generous' poor showing—he faded into eighth, around nine lengths behind the winner Suave Dancer—is difficult to fathom. He went into the Arc without the benefit of a preparatory race after his connections opted for giving him a break after Ascot, when he reportedly spent three weeks out in a paddock followed by a week's roadwork before resuming full training. But he completed a trouble-free preparation for Longchamp, which included a public gallop before racing at Newbury in September, and his trainer reported on the eve of the Arc that Generous was 'firing on all cylinders . . . and anyone who bets against him is either brave or foolish'. Confidence in the Generous camp couldn't have been higher, the only signs of concern showing in apparent indecision over whether or not to delay transporting Generous to Longchamp until the morning of the race. Generous had run poorly in the Prix Morny at Deauville as a two-year-old after becoming upset overnight, supposedly by the noise of the yearling sales. He had been sent over for the Irish Derby on the day of the race. In the end, however, it was decided not to risk delaying Generous' journey to Longchamp and he was flown over the day before. The fact that Generous ran so far below form in the Arc inevitably took some of the shine off his glittering record, as did an ensuing series of stories about a possible retrieval mission in the Dubai

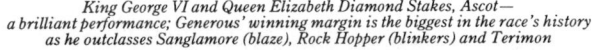

*King George VI and Queen Elizabeth Diamond Stakes, Ascot—
a brilliant performance; Generous' winning margin is the biggest in the race's history
as he outclasses Sanglamore (blaze), Rock Hopper (blinkers) and Terimon*

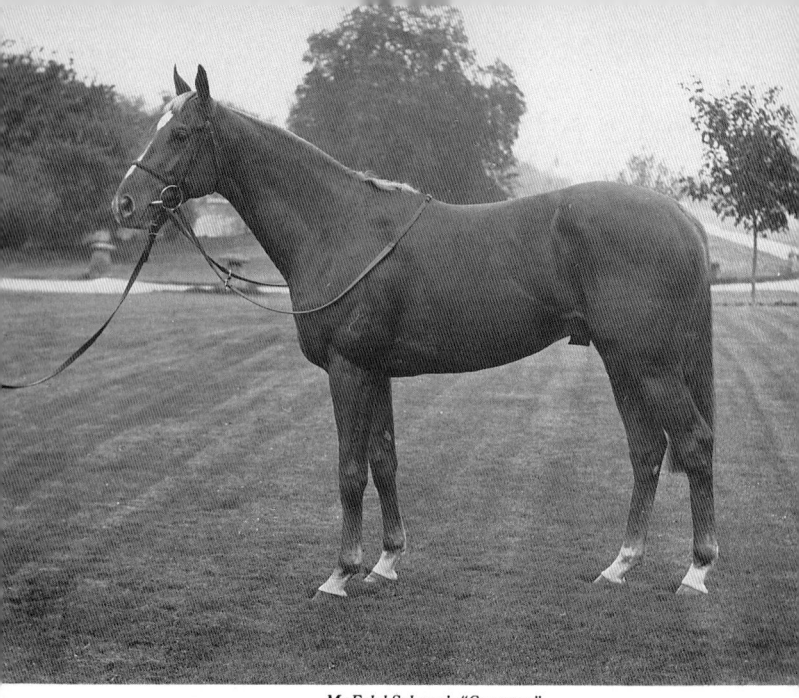

Mr Fahd Salman's "Generous"

Champion Stakes. It had been announced in August that the Arc would almost
certainly be Generous' final race before retirement to the Banstead Manor
Stud at Newmarket, Juddmonte Farms having purchased a major shareholding
in Generous at a sum which reportedly placed a value on the horse of
£7,875,000 (forty-five shares at £175,000). Defeat at Longchamp, however,
was followed by an announcement the following week that connections were
'thinking about the possibility of Generous running again', veterinary tests
reportedly having revealed no explanation for Generous' Arc running. 'If he is
a hundred per cent, he will run somewhere, either the Champion Stakes or the
Breeders' Cup', said his owner five days after the Arc. 'Generous doubtful'
was the front-page headline in *The Sporting Life* on Monday October 14th,
amid reports of further 'exhaustive' veterinary tests on the horse. Two days
later the *Racing Post* carried a front page story under the banner 'We're ready
to run', quoting Generous' owner as saying 'I'm very pleased to say the horse
is one hundred per cent. The blood tests came out well, and I will go to
Whatcombe tomorrow morning to see him work. If he goes well he will
definitely run on Saturday (in the Champion Stakes)'. With the ink barely dry
on this particular story came the announcement of Generous' retirement, a
statement from Mr Salman's racing manager explaining that Generous had
not been working 'with his usual sparkle' and revealing that a 'high fibrinogen
level' had come to light in one of the tests taken after the Arc 'indicating the
presence of a viral infection'. 'It is clear,' the statement went on, 'that the
exertions of running in the Arc de Triomphe whilst not one hundred per cent
have taken their toll. Prince Fahd . . . is most disappointed.' It was sad to see

322

the career of an outstanding racehorse end in anti-climax, but Generous wasn't the first horse to which it has happened, nor will he be the last. Truth to tell, the prospects of Generous' bouncing back so soon after such a clear-cut defeat in the Arc always seemed poor and it's unfortunate that the 'will he run again, or won't he' saga took place.

Generous (IRE) (ch.c. 1988)	Caerleon (USA) (b 1980)	Nijinsky (b 1967)	Northern Dancer
			Flaming Page
		Foreseer (b or br 1969)	Round Table
			Regal Gleam
	Doff The Derby (USA) (b 1981)	Master Derby (ch 1972)	Dust Commander
			Madam Jerry
		Margarethen (b 1962)	Tulyar
			Russ-Marie

Generous isn't an imposing individual but he filled out over the winter and carried more condition as a three-year-old than he had at two when we'd described him as angular. He looked well before all his races, though he was beginning to go in his coat at Longchamp (his posed portrait was taken after he'd finished racing). Generous went through the sale-ring as a foal (fetching IR 80,000 guineas at the Goffs December Sales) and as a yearling when he was bought on Mr Salman's behalf for IR 200,000 guineas at the Goffs Cartier Million Sales. Generous was bred at the Barronstown Stud in Ireland which has close links with the Coolmore operation. Generous' dam Doff The Derby, an unraced half-sister to that tremendously tough and genuine racemare Trillion, was first covered as a two-year-old, producing a minor stakes winner over seven furlongs in the States called Windy Triple K (by Jaklin Klugman). Since arriving in Ireland in 1985 Doff The Derby has visited six different Coolmore stallions, all of them sons or grandsons of Northern Dancer: to Kings Lake, she produced the useful ex-Irish filly Wedding Bouquet who added the Grade 3 Monrovia Handicap at Santa Anita to her record in the latest season; then came Generous; followed by a colt by Sadler's Wells who died; then a colt by Lomond (now named The King, and a 1993 Derby entry in training with Cole) who made 180,000 guineas as a foal at the 1990 December Sales; a colt by Last Tycoon who fetched 440,000 guineas (the third-highest price for a foal in Britain) at the 1991 December Sales; and in 1991 Doff The Derby was in foal to Royal Academy. Doff The Derby's sire Master Derby won the Preakness Stakes but hasn't set the world alight as a stallion; Doff The Derby's dam, however, the very tough stakes-winning Margarethen has made a name for herself as a broodmare, breeding four other winners apart from Trillion, who herself became the dam of Triptych and another pattern-race winner, the French middle-distance filly Barger. Another of Trillion's daughters, the unraced Trevilla, is the dam of the 1991 Prix Saint-Alary winner Treble. Generous' sire the Prix du Jockey-Club winner Caerleon has produced good horses over a variety of distances, though the average distance of races won at three and upwards by his progeny is around ten and a half furlongs, the distance of the Prix de Diane (French Oaks) the latest edition of which was won by Caerleon's daughter Caerlina. The aptly-named Generous —he was very game and genuine—stayed a mile and a half thoroughly and acted well on firm going (he never ran on anything softer than dead). He was, in our view, without question the best racehorse in Europe in 1991. *P. F. I. Cole.*

GENOTIN 8 b.g. Pitskelly 122 – Bazaar Goddess (USA) (Bazaar) [1990 8m 10m **37** 9m 8m 7m 8m⁴ 10f 12d 10m 10.2s 1991 a8g⁵ 8.9g² 12f] leggy, good-topped gelding: poor handicapper nowadays: stays 1½m: acts on any going: sometimes bandaged: has often hung. *C. Weedon.*

GENTLE ARIA 3 b.f. Elegant Air 119 – Lady Capilano 87 (Nebbiolo 125) [1990 **91** d 7m* 8.2v* 1991 7.3g⁶ 8g 10.6g 7g⁶ 11.9g⁶] tall, lengthy filly: useful winner at 2 yrs: took strong hold and hung left when creditable sixth of 7 in moderately-run Fred Darling Stakes at Newbury: below form afterwards, edgy when well behind in handicaps third and final starts: stays 1m: acts very well on heavy ground. *Miss A. J. Whitfield.*

GENTLE HERO (USA) 5 ch.g. Hero's Honor (USA) – Tender Camilla 115 **97** (Prince Tenderfoot (USA) 126) [1990 6v 6m⁵ 6m 7m⁵ 6m 6m⁵ 6m³ 7m 6d 1991 5g⁵ 6d⁶ 6g⁴ 7m 6m³ 7g* 5g* 6d³ 7m³ 6d* 6s² 6m 7m⁶ 6m] sturdy gelding: blind in right

Crawley Warren Handicap, York—
a desperate finish between Gentle Hero (right) and Nordic Brave

eye: often dull in coat: moderate mover: improved handicapper in 1991, successful in summer at York and Ayr (2, including £11,800 event): very good second to Montendre in listed event at Newmarket in August: effective at 5f to 7f: acts on good to firm ground, but best effort on soft going: has hung under pressure: effective with or without visor. *M. P. Naughton.*

GENTLY GENTLY   4 b.c. Prince Tenderfoot (USA) 126 – Domani 106 (Mourne   —
126) [1990 6m⁶ 6m 6m 8m 1991 a7g] lengthy colt: has quick action: little sign of ability: blinkered once. *R. Hannon.*

GENUINE LADY   3 b.f. Lidhame 109 – Responder 70 (Vitiges (FR) 132) [1990   53
NR 1991 8m² 10d] leggy filly: first foal: dam, maiden who stayed 1¼m, out of fairly useful 2-y-o 7f winner Clean Canasta: ridden by 7-lb claimer and 33/1 on first run on flat, second of 19 in claimer at Leicester in October, leading briefly 2f out: second favourite and wearing tongue strap, well beaten in similar event at Newmarket 3 days later. *A. P. Jarvis.*

GEORGE AUGUSTUS (USA)   3 b.c. El Gran Senor (USA) 136 – Surely **115**
Georgies (USA) (Alleged (USA) 138) [1990 8m³ 9d* 1991 7g³ 10g² 12g 9g* 10m* 12m* 12m⁴ 10g* 12f] rather leggy, quite good-topped colt: third foal: half-brother to a winner in USA by Conquistador Cielo: dam Grade 3 1m winner at 2 yrs, placed in Grade 3 11f contest at 3 yrs: won listed races at Leopardstown, Royal Whip (9/4 on) at the Curragh and listed race at Hoppegarten: good fourth of 8 to Subotica in Prix Niel at Longchamp, last entering straight: in mid-division in Rothmans International, Woodbine, final start: stays 1½m well: acts on good to firm ground and dead: blinkered last 8 starts: reported by jockey to have banged head in stalls when refusing to race in King Edward VII Stakes at Royal Ascot: reportedly to be trained by F. Brothers in USA. *J. Oxx, Ireland.*

GERALIA   3 b.f. Last Tycoon 131 – Gerania (FR) (Arctic Tern (USA) 126) [1990   42
7m 7g 6d 1991 7g⁵ a8g⁵] compact filly: plating-class maiden: should be suited by 1m+: sent to Scandinavia. *C. C. Elsey.*

GERICAULT (USA)   2 b. or br.c. (Feb 11) Greinton 119 – Lovelier (USA)   44
(Affirmed (USA)) [1991 6d 7m⁶ 7.1m 8m] $100,000Y: lengthy colt: has a quick action: first foal: dam, winner at up to 1¼m at 2 yrs, including in Grade 3 event, is closely related to high-class 1984 American 2-y-o filly Outstanding: poor maiden: blinkered, well beaten in seller final start: stays 7f: sold 2,700 gns Newmarket Autumn Sales. *G. Harwood.*

GHALYOON (USA) 2 b.c. (Feb 17) Deputy Minister (CAN) – Foot Stone (USA)   **70** p
(Cyane) [1991 7g 6m* 6m] sturdy, lengthy colt: has scope: first reported foal: dam
8.5f stakes winner at 3 yrs: modest form: won maiden at Southwell in September,
running on well: better than eleventh-of-18 position suggests (squeezed 2f out, not
knocked about) in Newmarket nursery 15 days later: will stay 1m: likely to do better.
P. T. Walwyn.

GHOSTED HASSLE 2 ch.f. (Apr 4) Jester 119 – Little Revenge (Runnymede   —
123) [1991 a6g 5d 5m] 620F, 600Y: leggy, close-coupled filly: fourth foal: dam
unraced: soundly beaten in summer, including in seller. *P. Burgoyne.*

GHOSTLY GLOW 2 gr.g. (Jun 6) Kalaglow 132 – Amerella (Welsh Pageant 132)   —
[1991 7.1m 7g 6.9f] 11,000Y: lengthy, unfurnished gelding: ninth foal: half-brother to
several winners, including one-time smart sprinter Cragside (by Hot Spark) and fair
6f and 1m winner Mudrik (by Sparkler): dam Irish 1¼m winner, is out of Molecomb
winner Lowna: soundly beaten in maidens. *C. C. Elsey.*

GHURRAH (IRE) 2 ch.f. (Mar 2) Sharpo 132 – Buthayna 85 (Habitat 134) [1991   **53**
6s 6m 6.1m] tall, good-topped filly: second foal: half-sister to 3-y-o Alkuwah (by
Sure Blade): dam placed at 6f, is half-sister to Reach out of Lingfield Oaks winner
Gift Wrapped: plating-class maiden: below best when sweating final start: stays 6f:
acts on good to firm ground. *C. J. Benstead.*

GHYLLDALE 3 b.f. Sweet Monday 122 – Dreamy Desire 50 (Palm Track 122)   **43** §
[1990 a6g a7g 7f 1991 8s 10d³ 10f* 10g 11m⁵ 8f 10g⁴ 11m² 11.8m³] leggy, angular filly:
plater: won handicap (no bid) at Redcar in May: ran up to form last 2 starts, but hung
right and no extra once in front on final one: stays 11f: acts on firm and dead ground:
visored last 3 starts: sometimes sweating: carries head high: probably ungenuine.
R. Bastiman.

GIBBOT 6 b.g. Taufan (USA) 119 – Gaychimes (Steel Heart 128) [1990 a10g²   **45** §
a10g⁵ a10g³ a10g² a10g² 10.2f⁶ 9f* a10g⁶ 8m² 10m⁵ 9m⁶ 8m⁶ 10m⁶ 9g⁵ 10d 10s a10g

Sheikh Mohammed's "George Augustus"

a13g 1991 10f⁶ 9s³ 8m⁶ 8m⁴ 9g 9d 9.7s 9m 8.3m* 7.6m 8.2f 10g 8g a13g] close-coupled, workmanlike gelding: carries plenty of condition: has a round action: poor handicapper: won at Windsor in August: effective at 1m to 1¼m: acts on any going: occasionally slowly away (including when blinkered): has worn tongue strap and bandages: successful for apprentice: reluctant to race once: untrustworthy. *P. Howling.*

GILBERT'S GIRL 4 b.f. Castle Keep 121 – Traditional Miss 90 (Traditionalist (USA) [1990 10m 10.1m 8f 10m² 12d³ 1991 12g 11.9f⁴ 9.7m⁶ 10.2g] leggy, sparely-made filly: poor handicapper: stays 1½m: acts on firm and dead ground: tends to wander under pressure. *C. J. Hill.*   **30**

GILDED OMEN 3 b.f. Faustus (USA) 118 – Fine Asset (Hot Spark 126) [1990 a5g⁵ 6g⁴ a6g⁵ a7g a7g 1991 a7g 8f a12g⁶] close-coupled, deep-girthed filly: poor plater: wore eyeshield final 2 starts at 2 yrs: sold 800 gns Ascot May Sales. *J. J. Bridger.*   **—**

GILDED PAST 4 ch.g. Glint of Gold 128 – Historia 71 (Northfields (USA)) [1990 8f 10f⁴ 12g 10m⁴ 10g⁵ 10f 10m 10m 1991 a8g] one-time quite modest maiden: ran poorly in seller only run at 4 yrs (February): should have stayed 1½m: acted on firm ground: dead. *M. C. Chapman.*   **—**

GILDERDALE 9 ch.g. Gunner B 126 – Mertola (Tribal Chief 125) [1990 8f 7m 9m* 8f4 8m² 8f 9m* 10g* 9m⁵ 9m 8m⁵ 1991 8g* 8m* 10.1f⁶ 10g 8f* 9g² 10m*] close-coupled gelding: has quick action: fairly useful handicapper: had good season in 1991, successful at Salisbury and Warwick (amateurs) in May and Bath and Sandown (amateurs) in August: effective at 1m to 1¼m: goes particularly well on a sound surface: usually held up: tough: a credit to his trainer. *J. W. Hills.*   **91**

GILT THRONE 4 b.c. Thatching 131 – Nikara (FR) (Emerson) [1990 6d*dis 7g² 8g 5g4 1991 7f⁵ 5m* 6m 6d 6m⁴ 5d* 5d* 6g* 6d²] leggy, workmanlike colt: has round action: third foal: half-brother to quite modest 1987 2-y-o 7f winner Nilgai (by Valiyar), later successful in Italy: dam won over 6f and 7.5f at 2 yrs in France: ex-Irish colt: developed into useful performer here in 1991: won claimer at Sandown (very slowly away) in May, handicaps at Ascot in September and October (very strongly-run Bovis Handicap) and Doncaster (very gamely) in October: good second of 12 to Snaadee in listed race at Doncaster: effective at 5f and 6f: has won on good to firm ground but best form with some give. *M. H. Tompkins.*   **105**

GIN AND ORANGE 5 b.g. Mummy's Pet 125 – Amberetta 72 (Supreme Sovereign 119) [1990 10.6f⁵ 8f⁶ 9g³ 10m² 11.7m 1991 a10g a13g 10.2s 10d 7m 8f 7.6d a12g a14g] rangy, quite attractive gelding: moderate mover: quite modest handicapper at best: below form in 1991: needs further than 7f, and stays 1¼m: acts on firm and dead going: has hung left: sold out of C. Nelson's stable 8,000 gns Newmarket Autumn Sales. *J. R. Jenkins.*   **—**

GINA'S CHOICE 5 b.m. Ile de Bourbon (USA) 133 – Modern Romance (Dance In Time (CAN)) [1990 10g 8f4 1991 8.9m⁴ 8.2m] big, rather plain mare: has a round action: poor performer: stays 1m: acts on good to firm ground: sometimes bandaged: has worn net muzzle and had tongue tied down: winning hurdler. *P. A. Pritchard.*   **28**

GINA'S DELIGHT 3 ch.f. Valiyar 129 – City Swinger (Derrylin 115) [1990 5g 6d a6g 1991 7.5f⁶ 10.5d a6g] leggy, good-topped filly: has a quick action: poor plater: should stay 1m. *J. Wharton.*   **—**

Bovis Handicap, Ascot—Gilt Throne (noseband) produces a storming late run to pip Spaniards Close and Bold Lez (far side)

GIPPESWYCK LADY 4 b.f. Pas de Seul 133 – Estivalia (Persian Bold 123) 70
[1990 10f 10g² 12m² 14m³ 14d* 16m² 15.3g² 14d⁴ 16s* 1991 14.8m⁵ 15.8f⁶ 14.8s⁶
17.5m* 14g²] leggy, workmanlike filly: moderate mover: modest handicapper:
gamely won at Ayr in September: stays 2m well: acts on good to firm ground and
soft: often ridden by claimer, not last 2 starts. *M. H. Tompkins.*

GIPSY FIDDLER 3 b.c. Bairn (USA) 126 – Miss Cindy 95 (Mansingh (USA) 104
120) [1990 5g* 5f* 5d* 5m⁵ 6m³ 1991 7m⁵ 7f⁶ 7.1f] close-coupled colt: moderate
mover: useful colt as 2-y-o, successful in Windsor Castle Stakes at Royal Ascot:
creditable fifth of 14 in £7,600 handicap at Newcastle in June, easily best effort in
1991: stays 7f: best efforts on good to firm ground. *J. J. O'Neill.*

GIPSY KING 3 gr.g. Magic Mirror 105 – Sarah Gillian (USA) (Zen (USA)) [1990 58
6g⁵ 6g² 7m 7.5g⁴ 8m⁶ 7g a7g⁵ 1991 a8g² a8g³ a10g a11g² a10g⁶ a12g⁴] leggy,
rather sparely-made gelding: has round action: plating-class maiden: stays 11f: wore
eyeshield early start: blinkered since: has been bandaged off-hind: carries head
awkwardly, and gives impression may be ungenuine. *P. A. Kelleway.*

GIROLAMO 2 b.c. (Feb 12) Shareef Dancer (USA) 135 – Lucent 117 (Irish Ball 71 §
(FR) 127) [1991 7m 7s 8.1g⁴ 7.6m] strong colt: half-brother to unreliable 1¼m
winner Sonic Lord (by Final Straw) and winning hurdler Taxodium (by Sharpen Up):
dam, daughter of good sprinter Lucasland, smart winner at 1m to 1½m from 2 yrs to
4 yrs: modest form: fourth of 16, making most, in maiden at Chepstow (unruly going
out on to track) in August: took keen hold first 3 starts: edgy and excitable sort, not
one to rely on: sold 14,000 gns Newmarket Autumn Sales. *G. Harwood.*

GIRTON DEGREE 2 b.f. (Apr 6) Balliol 125 – Cheb's Honour 70 (Chebs Lad 39
120) [1991 5d 5.7m 7g⁵] 5,000Y: leggy, rather angular filly: sister to 3 winners,
notably smart sprinter Singing Steven, and half-sister to 3 winners by Firestreak:
dam placed over 5f at 2 yrs: poor form in summer: fifth of 21 in Newmarket seller
final start: may stay 1m. *R. Hannon.*

GIVE IN 4 gr.c. Harlow (USA) 111 – Moment of Weakness 76 (Pieces of Eight 128) —
[1990 a7g² a8g* a8g⁵ a8g⁵ 9m 8.2f 6m 8g 7.5f⁶ a7g a7g 1991 a8g a11g 14m 10m 11m⁶
a12g⁵] leggy, narrow colt: plating-class handicapper: little form since landing odds
at Southwell in January, 1990: stays 1m: has been tried blinkered and visored: sold
1,300 gns Ascot July Sales, resold 800 gns Ascot December Sales. *Mrs N. Macauley.*

GIVEMEACALL 3 b.c. Kind of Hush 118 – Darymoss 79 (Ballymoss 136) [1990 —
5m⁵ 6s 6g 6g 7.5g⁶ 7.5m 8.2s 10.6s³ a8g 10.2s 1991 12.3s 12.2g 10d⁵ 11f⁶ 12.2m⁶ 10f
10.8m 14.1m] workmanlike colt: poor mover: poor plater: stays 1½m (very stiff task
at 1¾m): acts on good to firm and soft ground: blinkered once at 2 yrs: often wears
severe noseband: has carried head awkwardly and may be unsatisfactory temperamentally: successful in selling hurdles. *N. Tinkler.*

GIVE ME HOPE (IRE) 3 b.f. Be My Native (USA) 122 – Diamond Gig (Pit- —
skelly 122) [1990 6g 7s⁴ 1991 10g 12.3d⁴ a12g a8g⁶ 10.1f] leggy, light-framed filly:
quite modest form at 2 yrs: ran poorly last 3 starts in 1991, blinkered (sweating and
pulled hard) and never dangerous in handicap on final one: stays 1½m: best effort
on soft going: sold to join R. Brazington 1,700 gns Ascot October Sales. *R. G.
Brazington.*

GIVENTIME 3 ch.g. Bustino 136 – Duck Soup 55 (Decoy Boy 129) [1990 a7g 77
a8g³ 1991 7s³ a11g⁵ 10.1m⁴ 10m* 11.6m⁴] sturdy gelding: has a markedly round
action: 20/1-winner of maiden at Pontefract: creditable fourth of 7 to Cadency in
minor event at Windsor later in August: stays 1½m: acts on good to firm ground.
Andrew Turnell.

GIVE US A TREAT 3 b.f. Cree Song 99 – Another Treat 82 (Derring-Do 131) — p
[1990 NR 1991 6g 6f⁴ 5f 7g 6f 8f] workmanlike filly: seventh foal: half-sister to
several winners, including 5f (at 2 yrs) to 1¼m winner Stride Home (by Absalom)
and 1½m winner Another Thrill (by Morston): dam 1¼m and 1½m winner: showed a
little ability, never placed to challenge, in seller, claimer and handicap last 3 starts:
should stay 1m: may do better. *M. W. Easterby.*

GIZLAAN (USA) 2 ch.f. (Feb 13) Alydar (USA) – Kamikaze Rick (USA) (Hasty — p
Flyer (USA)) [1991 7f] $200,000Y: second foal: dam won 7 races, notably Grade 1 9f
Gazelle Handicap: 25/1 and bit backward, slowly away, held up in rear and not
knocked about in 14-runner maiden at Yarmouth in August: moved moderately to
post: should do better. *B. Hanbury.*

GLACIAL MOON (USA) 2 b.f. (Apr 3) Arctic Tern (USA) 126 – Hortensia 86 p
(FR) 119 (Luthier 126) [1991 7d²] rather sparely-made filly: seventh foal: sister to
Derby second Glacial Storm, later 15.5f winner in France, and modest maiden
Helen's Song, closely related to 3-y-o 11f winner Kiska (by Bering) and half-sister to

2 middle-distance winners: dam smart at around 1¼m in France: 12/1 and green, 6 lengths second of 7, staying on no chance with winner, to most impressive Red Slippers in minor event at Ascot in September: sure to improve, particularly over further, and win a race. *B. W. Hills.*

GLADEER (IRE)   2 ch.f. (Mar 11) Hadeer 118 – Really Sharp (Sharpen Up 127)   **59** [1991 6g⁵ 6.1m⁴] 14,000F, 37,000Y: sparely-made filly: fifth foal: half-sister to smart sprinter Carol's Treasure and 6f winner Buraida (both by Balidar) and Irish 7f winner Be Nimble (by Wattlefield): dam never ran: easily better effort in maidens when always-prominent fourth of 18 at Nottingham in October: stays 6.1f: may improve further. *W. Carter.*

GLADONIA   4 gr.f. Godswalk (USA) 130 – Aingeal (Fordham (USA) 117) [1990   **62** NR 1991 14d³ 14g a 12g] sparely-made filly: first foal: dam 2m winner in Ireland: very lightly-raced ex-Irish filly: won 2m NH Flat race at Clonmel in June: third in minor event at Tipperary in July: tailed off in Southwell seller only run here: formerly trained by Miss A. Crowley. *J. Parkes.*

GLAD TO BE GREY   3 ch.c. Song 132 – Faraway Grey 99 (Absalom 128) [1990   — 5f 6d a5g⁶ 1991 10m 6g 8m] angular, sparely-made colt: bad mover: poor maiden: trained reappearance by R. J. R. Williams: sold 1,100 gns Newmarket September Sales. *Dr J. D. Scargill.*

GLAIEUL (USA)   2 b. or br.c. (Jan 25) Lear Fan (USA) 130 – Gracious   **118** p Lassie (Kalamoun 129) [1991 9d* 10v*]

Following Epervier Bleu's narrow defeat by Sanglamore in the Prix du Jockey-Club in 1990 and Pistolet Bleu's late, injury-enforced withdrawal from the same event in 1991, the trainer-owner combination of Ellie Lellouche and Daniel Wildenstein will no doubt be hoping for better luck in 1992 with their promising colt Glaieul, who won the usually-informative Criterium de Saint-Cloud on only his second appearance in public. That the Criterium is run over a mile and a quarter in November, almost invariably in bottomless ground, hasn't affected its value as a classic pointer; and even if Glaieul doesn't follow the example set by such as Darshaan, Escaline, Mouktar and Fast Topaze, all of whom won the event prior to its elevation to Group 1 status in 1988, and Snurge, who won the race in 1989 only to be disqualified, and go on to classic success, he'll make a better three-year-old than two-year-old. Glaieul, who was supplemented for the Criterium after justifying favouritism, easily by all accounts, by three lengths in a nine-furlong newcomers event at Evry in

*Criterium de Saint-Cloud—
nothing between two of the top French staying two-year-olds,
Glaieul and Calling Collect (No. 2)*

October, won with much less in hand than did Pistolet Bleu the previous year, making progress from the rear of the nine-runner field rounding the turn into the short home straight, getting within hailing distance of his stable-companion Calling Collect approaching the final furlong then battling on willingly, despite showing clear signs of inexperience, to secure the verdict in the very last stride. The proximity, over five lengths back in fourth place, of the British challenger Grand Master, who'd been beaten in a run-of-the-mill maiden at Nottingham last time out, might appear at first glance to cast doubts over the strength of the form but it's probably no coincidence that easily his best previous effort, when fifth to Made of Gold in the Royal Lodge William Hill Stakes at Ascot, had been on the only other occasion on which he'd encountered soft ground. And there's no disputing the credentials of Calling Collect, who'd shown smart form when cruising home five lengths clear in the nine-furlong Prix Saint-Roman under similarly testing conditions at Longchamp in September, and assuming he gave his running then Glaieul recorded a very smart performance. Third-placed Contested Bid certainly didn't let the form down when he appeared in Division 2 of the Hoist The Flag Stakes at Hollywood Park in December and beat the seven other runners, including the Goffs Million winner Fair Crack, by upwards of a length and three quarters. So Glaieul ended his first season the only French-trained two-year-old colt apart from Arazi to have won a Group 1 race. He's held in high regard by his trainer, who also has care of the Criterium de Maisons-Laffitte winner Cardoun, and if he trains on satisfactorily he'll probably improve past his more experienced stable-companion as a three-year-old.

	Lear Fan (USA) (b 1981)	Roberto (b 1969)	Hail To Reason Bramalea
		Wac (b 1969)	Lt Stevens Belthazar
Glaieul (USA) (b. or br.c. Jan 25, 1989)			
	Gracious Lassie (br 1977)	Kalamoun (gr 1970)	Zeddaan Khairunissa
		Gracious (b 1972)	Habitat Glaneuse

Glaieul was one of five individual winners of nine pattern races sired by the top-class miler Lear Fan in a year which represented a considerable upturn in his fortunes as a stallion: prior to 1991 his only successful runner in pattern company was the much-travelled Sikeston whose victories had come in Italy. Being a son of the Derby winner Roberto, Lear Fan was bred to stay beyond a mile but was never given the opportunity to do so, probably on account of his free-running style. Most of his best offspring, who include Corrupt, Run Don't Fly and the Champion Stakes runner-up Cruachan, have stayed middle distances, and Glaieul will most probably be suited by a mile and a half. He's the sixth foal and second Group 1 winner from his dam Gracious Lassie: her other winner at that level, Oczy Czarnie (by Lomond), won a weakly-contested Prix de la Salamandre as a two-year-old in 1988 but never won in pattern company in France again, although she did manage a victory in the Grade 3 Pucker Up Handicap at Aqueduct as a three-year-old. Gracious Lassie, whose two other winning foals are the French six-and-a-half-furlong winner Factual Grace (by Known Fact) and Glaieul's full brother Learycal, a useful maiden in France and a winner subsequently at up to a mile and a quarter in the States, ran just three times, all at two years when she was kept to five furlongs, winning a newcomers event at Chantilly before being placed in small-field minor events at Vichy. She's one of numerous foals produced by her dam Gracious, whose other winners include the fast French two-year-old Greenway and the smart French miler Gay Minstrel. This is a family full of good winners. In the same year (1980) that Greenway won the Prix d'Arenberg and the all-aged Prix du Petit Couvert, his dam's half-sister Gold River won the Prix Royal-Oak; she continued in the same vein the following year, winning the Arc, and at stud has produced the Prix Saint-Alary and Prix Vanteaux winner Riviere d'Or as well as the Poule d'Essai des Pouliches runner-up Goldneyev. Gold River is a daughter of the very smart filly Glaneuse, a half-sister to the One Thousand Guineas runner-up Gleam and successful in the Prix Chloe, Prix de Malleret and Gran Premio del Jockey Club as well as finishing third in the Prix de Diane. *E. Lellouche, France.*

GLAISDALE (IRE)   2 b.c. (Mar 28) Lomond (USA) 128 – Glass Slipper 100   **66 p**
(Relko 136) [1991 7.9m 8m⁵] good-quartered, useful-looking colt: has scope: closely
related to 3-y-o 1¼m winner Mafatin (by Sadler's Wells) and half-brother to several
winners, including 1000 Guineas winner Fairy Footsteps (by Mill Reef) and St Leger
winner Light Cavalry (by Brigadier Gerard): dam staying half-sister to Royal Palace:
bit backward and green still, better effort in October maidens when fifth of 14 at
Leicester, given reminder after sluggish start, well outpaced over 2f out then
keeping on steadily: very much a staying type, sort to do much better at 3 yrs. *H. R.
A. Cecil.*

GLANCE OF GOLD (USA)   3 ch.c. Mr Prospector (USA) – Over Your   **71 d**
Shoulder (USA) 77 (Graustark) [1990 6m³ 1991 10m³ 8d 11.8g 12s 9.7m⁵] strong
colt: regressive maiden: probably stays 1¼m: blinkered, carried head awkwardly
final start: not one to trust. *G. Harwood.*

GLASGOW   2 b.c. (Apr 27) Top Ville 129 – Glasson Lady (GER) 108 (Priamos   **75 p**
(GER) 123) [1991 6f³] close-coupled, quite good-topped colt: half-brother to modest
1¼m winner Glassblower (by Shareef Dancer) and a winner in Italy by Formidable:
dam useful Irish 7f winner: 33/1 and bit backward, shaped most promisingly under
considerable ride in 22-runner maiden won by Binkhaldoun at Newbury in September, travelling comfortably in rear most of way then finishing strongly: will stay
at least 1m: sure to win races. *B. W. Hills.*

GLASSBLOWER   4 b.g. Shareef Dancer (USA) 135 – Glasson Lady (GER) 108   **78**
(Priamos (GER) 123) [1990 8g² 10g⁵ 12m³ 10m⁴ 10m* 10m 1991 8f² 10.1s 10f* 8.5m
8.3m² 7.6m² 10f* 8.9g] lengthy gelding: second foal: half-brother to a minor winner
in Italy by Formidable: dam useful Irish 7f winner: ex-Irish performer: modest
handicapper: won at Folkestone (claimer, idled) in May and Brighton (led close
home) in August: better suited by 1¼m than 1m: best efforts on top-of-the-ground:
has won for apprentice: trained at 3 yrs by J. Oxx. *R. Akehurst.*

GLASS MINNOW (IRE)   3 b.f. Alzao (USA) 117 – Abertywi 87 (Bounteous   **59**
125) [1990 NR 1991 6s² 5m² 6m⁴] 25,000F: small filly: poor mover: half-sister to
several winners here and abroad, including 1988 2-y-o 7f winner Down The Valley
(by Kampala) and 1m and 10.2f winner Meziara (by Dominion): dam 7f and 1m
winner, is sister to high-class sprinter Abergwaun: quite modest form in summer
maidens, below-form favourite at Redcar final start: will be suited by 1m. *P. J.
Makin.*

GLASTONDALE   5 b.g. Beldale Flutter (USA) 130 – Glastonbury 73 (Grundy   **50**
137) [1990 a12g4 a11g a14g4 10.2f³ 10m² 12f⁵ 12.4f² 12f 12m² 12g⁶ 10m 11m⁶ 11d²
12g* 12f² 12f² 12.3g³ 1991 11s⁵ 12g⁵ 12d* 11f³ 12g² 12g 12g⁴ 12d 15.8g 12g² 13d³ 12g]
compact gelding: moderate mover: carries condition: poor maiden handicapper nowadays:
won at Thirsk in April: inconsistent after: stays 1½m: acts on firm and dead going:
visored early in career: has won for apprentice: lacks turn of foot, and goes well
forcing pace. *T. D. Barron.*

GLENAIRLIE (IRE)   3 b.f. Glow (USA) – Celtic Symphony (Orchestra 118)   **—**
[1990 6m 6m4 8m⁴ 8m 1991 9s 8g] smallish, good-topped filly: plating-class
performer: below form in spring as 3-y-o: probably better at 1m than 6f: visored on
reappearance. *J. S. Wilson.*

GLENCROFT   7 b.g. Crofter (USA) 124 – Native Fleet (FR) (Fleet Nasrullah)   **83 d**
[1990 a5g⁶ a5g³ 5f* 5f* 5m* 5m a5g 5m 5g 5m⁵ 5m⁶ 5g 5d* 5g² a6g* 6s 5s² a5g*
a6g⁴ a5g⁴ a6g³ 1991 a5g* a6g³ a5g² 5m 5g³ 5.9m 5m⁵ 6m 5h² 5g 5g³ 5m⁶ 5.1s 5m 5s
a5g] big, strong gelding: has been hobdayed and tubed: prolific winner: won
handicap at Southwell in February: ran poorly last 4 starts: none too consistent on
turf in 1991: better suited by 5f than 6f (looked unsuited by 6f track at Lingfield):
seems to act on any going: blinkered nowadays: tough. *D. W. Chapman.*

GLENELIANE (IRE)   3 b.f. Glenstal (USA) 118 – Sweet Eliane (Birdbrook 110)   **48**
[1990 6g 5f³ 5d⁶ 5f² 5m³ 6f⁴ 5f² a6g² 5m⁶ 6d⁶ 5m⁵ 7g⁴ 8m 1991 9.9g⁶ 9.2d⁶ 11g⁴
8.2f³ 8f⁵ 7m⁶] lengthy, good-quartered filly: plating-class handicapper, still a
maiden: claimer-ridden third at Nottingham, best effort at 3 yrs: stays 1m: acts on
firm going: tail flasher. *Denys Smith.*

GLENFIELD GRETA   3 ch.f. Gabitat 119 – Glenfield Portion 86 (Mummy's Pet   **72**
125) [1990 5g² 5f⁵ 6g 5f³ 5f* 5m⁴ 6m 6d⁵ 1991 6g 6f* 6m⁴ 5f² 5m⁴ 6f³ 6s² 6f⁵ 6m]
small, sturdy filly: modest handicapper: quite consistent after winning at Carlisle
(favourite and ridden by 7-lb claimer) in May: stays 6f: acts on any going: carries
head high. *P. S. Felgate.*

GLEN FINNAN   3 ch.f. Ballacashtal (CAN) – Glen Kella Manx 97 (Tickled Pink   **—**
114) [1990 5.8f⁶ 6m 6m 5.8f⁶ 5m 1991 6g 8d 8d⁶ 7.1m] compact filly: has a round
action: no worthwhile form, including in sellers. *J. C. Fox.*

GLEN MADDIE   4 b.f. Reasonable (FR) 119 – Iresine (GER) (Frontal 122) [1990   —
8.2g 6g 8.2v 5s a6g a6g* 1991 a8g a7g⁵ 6s⁶ 6d 5m 6m 6d] strong, dipped-backed filly:
carries condition: poor mover: poor handicapper: may be worth another try beyond
6f: acts on soft ground: trained first 2 starts in 1991 by J. Mackie. *J. S. Wilson.*

GLENMERE PRINCE   5 b.g. Prince Tenderfoot (USA) 126 – Ashbourne Lass   —
(Ashmore (FR) 125) [1990 8.2f 1991 8f⁶ 10m a8g a8g] leggy gelding: poor form: stays
7f: acts on firm going: has been tried blinkered: seems headstrong. *P. S. Felgate.*

GLENSCAR   5 gr.g. Glenstal (USA) 118 – Caranina (USA) (Caro 133) [1990 5m 5f   42
6m 7m 6g⁵ a8g 6m² 6g 7m 5d⁶ 6d 6m⁶ 8g² 1991 10.8g² 10f⁶ 10.8m² 10m 10.8m 9d⁴
8m³ 8.1g³ 9.7s³ 8f² 10g 8.2m⁴ 7m⁵ 8.3m⁴ 7.1g] angular, sparely-made gelding: poor
walker and mover: poor handicapper nowadays: effective at 7f to 1¼m: acts on any
going: often slowly away. *J. L. Spearing.*

GLENSTAL ABBEY (USA)   5 ch.g. Gregorian (USA) 115 – Full Delivery   —
(USA) (Irish Ruler (USA)) [1990 a12g³ 12.5f a12g 1991 a13g] lengthy, workmanlike
ex-Irish gelding: moderate mover: poor maiden: soundly beaten only run on flat in
1991 (January): stays 1½m: often blinkered: sold 1,500 gns Ascot November Sales.
R. Akehurst.

GLENSTAL PRINCESS   4 ch.f. Glenstal (USA) 118 – Jessamy Hall 77   71
(Crowned Prince (USA) 128) [1990 7d 6m 5.8m⁶ 7.6f³ 7f 7.6g 6m⁴ 6m 6s 1991 5d⁶
6g* 6d² 6g 6g 6m⁶ 7m] lengthy filly: modest handicapper: won at Haydock in June:
should stay 7f: acts on firm and dead ground: ran creditably when visored once: none
too consistent. *R. Hollinshead.*

GLENSTAL PRIORY   4 b.f. Glenstal (USA) 118 – Jumbolia (Wolver Hollow   48
126) [1990 7m 8g³ 10m² 10.2f⁶ 12m⁵ 9m⁵ 1991 a10g 10f 12f 14m² 12m⁴ 16.4m* 16m²
16.9m 17.2g a16g⁵ a14g²] small, sparely-made filly: has a quick action: poor
handicapper: won (for first time) at Folkestone in July: stays 2m: acts on good to
firm going. *P. F. I. Cole.*

GLIDE PATH (USA)   2 ch.c. (May 29) Stalwart (USA) – Jolly Polka (USA) (Nice   66
Dancer (CAN)) [1991 7f 7m⁶ 7m³ 7m⁶ 8.3s²] $35,000Y: close-coupled, rather
unfurnished colt: has a round action: closely related to winning American sprinter
Tolly Mariner (by Fifth Marine) and half-brother to 2 winners: dam, unraced, from
family of top Canadian horse Dauphin Fabuleux: quite modest maiden: good
staying-on second of 18 in nursery at Hamilton in November: may well stay 1¼m:
possibly suited by soft ground. *J. W. Hills.*

GLITY (USA)   3 ch.c. Crystal Glitters (USA) 127 – Green City (FR) (Green   117
Dancer (USA) 132) [1990 9g⁵ 10v* 10v⁵ 1991 10g³ 12g² 12d⁴ 10g³ 10g* 10d³ 10m]
strong, close-coupled colt: third foal: half-brother to French 11f winner Green Moon
(by Shirley Heights) and French provincial 7f (at 2 yrs) and 1¼m winner Golden Sea
(by Saint Cyrien): dam useful French 1¼m and 10.5f winner: won maiden at
Saint-Cloud in November at 2 yrs and Prix Guillaume d'Ornano (narrowly from
Arcangues and Kotashaan, quickening on early in straight) at Deauville in 1991:
good third of 5 to Passing Sale in Prix du Prince d'Orange at Longchamp: 50/1,
beaten when badly bumped over 2f out in Champion Stakes at Newmarket 4 weeks
later: seems ideally suited by 1¼m: acts on heavy going, possibly not on good to
firm. *J. M. Beguigne, France.*

GLORIFY (USA)   4 b.c. Nijinsky (CAN) 138 – Autumn Glory (Graustark) [1990   114
10.5g⁶ 12g* 12.5g⁴ 15g³ 15.5v 1991 12g³ 12g* 12d⁴] fourth foal: half-brother to
French 1½m winner Autumn Tint (by Roberto): dam winner in USA at up to 1¼m
and placed in Grade 1 event: very useful French colt: won Group 3 Prix d'Hedouville
at Longchamp in April by ½ length from Luthier Enchanteur: ran well when fourth
of 6 to Dear Doctor in Group 2 Prix Jean de Chaudenay at Saint-Cloud in May: sent
to USA, and fair fifth to Filago in Grade 1 Oak Tree Invitational at Santa Anita in
October: probably stays 15f: acts on good to firm and dead ground. *A. Fabre, France.*

GLOWING ARDOUR   3 b.f. Dancing Brave (USA) 140 – Cocotte 111 (Troy 137)   98
[1990 7m² 7m² 8m* 8m* 8m 1991 10d 8m⁵ 7m* 7g⁴] strong, lengthy filly: fairly
useful performer: won £13,500 handicap at Newmarket in July, quickening on over 1f
out: good fourth to Himiko in listed event at Goodwood later, running on after being
squeezed out over 1f out: stays 1m: almost certainly unsuited by dead ground:
tended to hang second start. *M. R. Stoute.*

GLOWING DEVIL   2 ro.c. (May 29) Kalaglow 132 – Romantiki (USA) (Giboulee   46
(CAN)) [1991 7m⁵ 8m] 2,500Y: tall, leggy, unfurnished colt: fourth foal: brother to a
winner over hurdles: dam, half-sister to high-class filly at up to 1m Barely Even,
showed a little ability: form only when fifth of 15 in maiden auction at Redcar in
August: sold to join D. Barron 3,800 gns Doncaster November Sales. *P. Calver.*

GLOWING MANTLE (IRE) 3 ch.f. Glow (USA) – Dismantle 75 (Aureole 132) —
[1990 6.3g 7g 7g6 1991 a8g 7g6 12f6] sparely-made filly: half-sister to 5 winners, including quite useful 1984 sprint 2-y-o Detached (by Thatching): dam won over 7f at 2 yrs: plating-class ex-Irish maiden: 50/1-sixth of 7 at Beverley final start, making most and best effort here in the spring: should be suited by at least 1m, possibly doesn't stay 1½m: trained at 2 yrs by M. O'Toole: joined R. Peacock. *N. A. Smith.*

GLOWLAMP (IRE) 3 b.f. Glow (USA) – Astania (GER) (Arratos (FR)) [1990 **78**
7f4 7m2 7f2 9m* 7.3s3 8v 1991 8g4 10f6] big filly: quite good mover: fairly useful filly at 2 yrs: sweating, below form in minor events in August, 1991: should stay 1¼m: well beaten on heavy going (in Italy), seems to act on any other. *B. Hanbury.*

GLOW OF SUMMER 3 b.f. Glow (USA) – Summer Madness 88 (Silly Season **66**
127) [1990 7f 7d 1991 a10g4 12f2 12m3 14f2 14f* 13.1m2 16.4m 13.8f* a14g5 16m6] a 46
leggy filly: quite modest handicapper: won at Redcar in May (made most) and Catterick in July: stays 13.8f, set too strong a pace over 16.4f: goes well on top-of-the-ground: sold 7,200 gns Newmarket Autumn Sales. *M. Bell.*

GLOW OF THE GLEN 2 b.f. (May 5) Lochnager 132 – Glow Again (The **48**
Brianstan 128) [1991 5d4 5g5 6d5 5f2 7m3 7.1m2 7m3 7f 6m] 8,000Y: neat filly: has a round action: first foal: dam 2-y-o 5f and 6f winner: moderate plater: below form in visor last start: stays 7f: later sold 3,200 gns Newmarket Autumn Sales. *M. H. Easterby.*

GOD BLESS YOU 4 b.g. Vision (USA) – Maestrette 77 (Manado 130) [1990 — §
8.2s* 10v3 9m5 10.6s 10d* 10.6g 10.2g 10m 10.6v3 10d 1991 10g 9f] lengthy, sparely-made gelding: modest handicapper at 3 yrs: reluctant to race in 1991, tailed off final start: stays 1¼m: yet to race on firm going, acts on any other: has twice refused to race: one to avoid. *W. Carter.*

GODSALL 4 gr.f. Godswalk (USA) 130 – Sallail (Sallust 134) [1990 6g 7v 1991 a6g
a8g] leggy, sparely-made filly: poor form at 2 yrs, none since: has ducked markedly under pressure and seems a bit temperamental. *Mrs N. Macauley.*

GODSCHARM (IRE) 3 b.f. Godswalk (USA) 130 – Polynesian Charm (USA) **49**
(What A Pleasure (USA)) [1990 5f3 5m2 5f* 5f 5d2 6m4 5d5 5m3 6f2 7h 6m3 6m 6m 1991 8g 8g 7g 6g4 6m5 7m 6m] leggy filly: poor walker: moderate mover: plating-class handicapper: should stay 7f: acts on firm and dead going: sweating and edgy penultimate outing: tends to wander: inconsistent. *M. Brittain.*

GODS GIFT 3 b.f. Godswalk (USA) 130 – Asturiana (Julio Mariner 127) [1990 **35**
a5g6 5s a5g 1991 6m 7m4 8m5 a7g 7g 7g 10.1m 8.3m 7m2 7m 6m] light-framed filly: poor plater: stays 1m: acts on good to firm ground. *K. T. Ivory.*

GODSMINT 3 b.c. Godswalk (USA) 130 – What A Mint (Meadow Mint (USA) —
120) [1990 7m 7g 1991 7m 12g 16.2d 16m] workmanlike colt: no sign of ability: blinkered in handicap final start. *R. J. Holder.*

GODS SOLUTION 10 gr.h. Godswalk (USA) 130 – Campitello (Hornbeam 130) **68**
[1990 6m3 a6g 6m* 7m 6m2 6m 6g4 6f 6d6 1991 6d*] rangy horse: poor mover: modest handicapper: won at Catterick (same race for sixth time and eighth win there) in March: stayed 7f: not at his best in very soft going, acted on any other: had worn blinkers, but not for long time: went very well with forcing tactics on a turning track: has been retired. *T. D. Barron.*

GOEWIN 2 b.f. (Feb 21) Stanford 121§ – Mistress Bowen (Owen Anthony 102) **31**
[1991 5m 5. 1g a6g3 6g 5.3m6 5.3f 7m 7g6 7f 5f 7m] 600F, 1,700Y: lengthy filly: eighth foal: half-sister to 3-y-o Mr Mad (by Good Times) and a winner in Holland by Sagaro: dam ran 3 times: poor maiden: visored or blinkered of late: sold 500 gns Ascot October Sales. *M. D. I. Usher.*

GO EXECUTIVE 3 b.g. Sharpo 132 – Staritsa (USA) (Alleged (USA) 138) [1990 **93**
5d 6g2 6m* 1991 a6g3 6m 5m 7.6g3 7m2 8m 6m 7.9g 7g2 7d3 7m* 8g] leggy, close-coupled gelding: keen walker: moderate mover: fairly useful handicapper: in good form ninth to eleventh starts, dead-heating for 19-runner £9,000 event at York in October: stays 1m: acts on good to firm ground and dead: sometimes sweating: wore eyeshield on reappearance: bandaged next 4 outings: tends to race up with pace. *C. E. Brittain.*

GO FORUM 6 ch.g. Tumble Wind (USA) – Devine Lady (The Parson 119) [1990 **47**
11.1m 14m 11.7m 14g 14g 14g5 1991 12s2 12f a10g] sturdy, good-bodied gelding: poor handicapper nowadays: off course over 7 months before final start: stays 1¾m: probably acts on any going: tried blinkered once. *J. Sutcliffe.*

GOGOLETTE 2 ch.f. (Feb 26) All Systems Go 119 – Sarphele Larches (Gay **43**
Fandango (USA) 132) [1991 5m 6f 6m 7g⁶] 1,200Y: workmanlike filly: second foal:
dam never ran: poor form, including in seller: worth a try at 1m. *M. O'Neill.*

GO GOTT 3 b.g. All Systems Go 119 – La Bird 61 (Le Johnstan 123) [1990 6g 1991 —
10g 11.1g] workmanlike gelding: behind in maiden, seller and claimer. *R. Bastiman.*

GOIN AND GROWIN (USA) 3 b.c. Roberto (USA) 131 – Nile Empress (USA) **87**
98 (Upper Nile (USA)) [1990 NR 1991 10m⁵ 12m³ 12.2m* 11.9m 12m⁶ 14s⁴ 16.2d*
16.5d] $185,000Y: strong, quite attractive colt: second foal: dam 6f (at 2 yrs) and
1¼m winner later successful in USA, is out of sister to dam of Sookera: won maiden
(9/2 on) at Catterick in June and handicap (led 2f out) at Haydock in October:
possibly in need of race, never going well final outing: better at 2m than shorter:
acts on good to firm ground and dead: swerved left fourth start. *L. M. Cumani.*

GOLAN HEIGHTS 4 b.g. Shirley Heights 130 – Grimpola (GER) (Windwurf **94**
(GER)) [1990 9g³ 10.1g* 12s² 12m 14g³ 12g⁵ 1991 10g 12m* 14g] good-bodied
gelding: carries condition: has a rather round action: fairly useful handicapper: won
£7,300 event at Newmarket in April: not seen again after finishing last at Haydock in
June (said to have been retired): stayed 1½m: acted on good to firm and soft going:
genuine. *Mrs J. Cecil.*

GOLD AISLING 3 gr.f. Sonnen Gold 121 – My Aisling 72 (John de Coombe 122) —
[1990 8m 5f⁶ 5m 1991 10m] lengthy filly: poor maiden. *P. D. Evans.*

GOLD BELT (IRE) 2 gr.f. (Apr 29) Bellypha 130 – Golden Braid 109 (Glint of **61**
Gold 128) [1991 6g⁴ 7f 6m² 6m 7.1m⁴] leggy, lightly-made filly: lacks scope: first
foal: dam 7f (at 2 yrs) and 1¼m winner: quite modest maiden: will stay at least 1m:
sold 3,100 gns Ascot November Sales. *Lord Huntingdon.*

GOLD BLADE 2 ch.c. (Apr 23) Rousillon (USA) 133 – Sharp Girl (FR) — p
(Sharpman 124) [1991 7g] good-topped colt: has scope: second foal: brother to
French 3-y-o 1m and 10.6f winner Razor's Edge: dam French 1¼m winner stayed
1½m from good family: 25/1 from 10/1, backward and very green, last of 14 in maiden
at Salisbury in October: moved poorly to post: looks sort to do better at 3 yrs. *N. A.
Graham.*

GOLD CIRCLE (IRE) 2 b.f. (Mar 11) Auction Ring (USA) 123 – Golden **42**
Sunlight (Ile de Bourbon (USA) 133) [1991 5d⁴ 5f⁴ 6g⁵ 5.1g⁴ 5m³ 5.9h 6g] 6,000Y:
leggy, sparely-made, angular filly: first foal: dam unraced: poor maiden: stays 6f:
acts on hard and dead ground: ran moderately in blinkers final start: wandered
second outing: sold 780 gns Doncaster November Sales. *J. A. C. Edwards.*

GOLD DESERT (IRE) 2 b.c. (Feb 8) Green Desert (USA) 127 – Fine Honey **100**
(USA) 90 (Drone) [1991 6g⁴ 5d* 6g* 6m² 6m³ 8f⁴] sturdy, quite attractive colt:
sixth foal: half-brother to fairly useful 1986 2-y-o 7f winner Pollenate (by High
Line), later successful in USA, and a winner in Belgium: dam lightly-raced 2-y-o 5f
winner from family of Bates Motel, Super Asset and Hatim: generally progressive
form: successful in maiden at Nottingham and minor event at Doncaster in June:
around 1½ lengths fourth in Hoist The Flag Stakes (Div.1) at Hollywood Park in
December: stays 1m: has sweated and got on edge: races prominently: to remain in
USA. *R. Charlton.*

GOLD EMBLEM 3 b.f. Tina's Pet 121 – Bar Gold 80 (Lucky Brief 128) [1990 —
6m³ 6m³ 7m³ 8m 6m a7g 1991 6f 7.5m⁶ 8d] small, angular filly: quite modest plater:
below best last 6 starts, though showed a little in handicap penultimate one: should
stay 1m. *Miss S. E. Hall.*

GOLDEN 4 ch.f. Don 128 – Roll Up (Roll of Honour 130) [1990 10.6f⁴ 12m³ 12m —
12.4f* 16f³ 16m⁶ 15d⁵ 16g² 1991 16m 16.2f⁶] angular, workmanlike filly: good
walker: quite modest handicapper: not seen out after May: stays 2m: seems to act
on firm and dead going. *C. W. C. Elsey.*

GOLDEN ANCONA 8 ch.g. London Bells (CAN) 109 – Golden Darling 86 **56**
(Darling Boy 124) [1990 7f⁵ 6v⁴ 8g 8.2s 8f 7m⁵ 7m a7g 8m 8m⁵ 8d 7m 7m 8g⁴ 7.6v⁵
a8g⁵ 1991 8v² 8d 7.5g 8m⁵ 10.4d 8.5m a8g⁵ 8d² 8g⁶] close-coupled, lightly-made
gelding: poor mover: plating-class handicapper nowadays: not seen out after July:
stays 1m: particularly well suited by give in the ground: has worn blinkers and a
visor, but better without: usually gets behind: inconsistent, and hard to win with. *M.
Brittain.*

GOLDEN BEAU 9 b.g. Crimson Beau 124 – Kantado 93 (Saulingo 122) [1990 **44** d
a8g 8f⁶ 8.2s 8m⁴ 8f4 9f⁵ 9g⁶ 8m² 8g² 8m 8.2s⁴ 8m* 8m² 8.2d 8g³ 8d 8m 8v³ 8d⁵ 8m
1991 8s 10d⁵ 9f⁶ 9.9g⁵ 10g⁴ 10g⁵ 10d⁶ 8g 8.3s⁴ 8.3d⁵ 7f³ 8.1m⁶ 8.3f* 8f 8h 10g]
sparely-made, rather hollow-backed gelding: good mover: poor handicapper: on
downgrade, but won at Hamilton in August: suited by 1m: acts on any going, except

possibly hard: below form when blinkered: effective with or without visor: often gets on edge: hung badly right eighth start, looked none too keen next one. *A. Harrison.*

GOLDEN BIRCH 3 gr.c. Heights of Gold – Silver Birch 122 (Silver Shark 129) **89** [1990 5f³ 7g 6m³ 6m² 6g* 7g* 1991 7m⁶ 7g 6d 8m 8f 7.6m] big, lengthy colt: fairly useful winner at 2 yrs: ran well facing stiff tasks in competitive Newmarket handicaps first 2 starts as 3-y-o: sweating, well beaten in lady riders event and handicaps after: best form at 7f: acts on good to firm ground: sold 2,200 gns Newmarket December Sales. *W. G. R. Wightman.*

GOLDEN CAP (USA) 3 ch.f. Hagley (USA) – Mrs Hat (Sharpen Up 127) [1990 **76** 5f* 1991 6m 6g³ 5g 5g⁴ 5f 8m² 8m⁴ 7g 6.1m* 6m] lengthy, good-quartered filly: modest handicapper: best effort when easily winning at Nottingham in September, leading over 1f out: ran poorly in another large field, at Newmarket, 10 days later: stays 1m: acts on good to firm ground: blinkered fourth and fifth starts: sold 11,000 gns Newmarket Autumn Sales. *P. F. I. Cole.*

GOLDEN CHIP (IRE) 3 ch.g. M Double M (USA) – Kimangao (Garda's **67** Revenge (USA) 119) [1990 NR 1991 7.5g⁵ 10m³ 8.5f³ 10m* 10m 10.5g 10m⁴ 8m² 8f² 8m⁶ 8m² 8m³ 8m⁴ 10.3g³ a8g⁵ a8g*] IR 2,300F: strong gelding: moderate walker: second foal: half-brother to Irish 12.5f winner Jane Doe (by The Noble Player): dam 3-y-o winner in Belgium: won maiden claimer at Ayr in June: mostly in good form in the autumn, leading close home in handicap at Southwell in December: suited by 1m: acts on firm going: unseated rider to post third start, and mostly taken down alone since. *A. P. Stringer.*

GOLDEN DELLA 4 b.f. Glint of Gold 128 – Shindella 104 (Furry Glen 121) [1990 — 12m⁶ 12f⁶ 12m³ 14m 10m 9m⁴ 8.2g* 9s 8.2v⁵ 8v 1991 a6g⁴ a8g⁴ 8d 8.2m 6m 6d 8f 8m 6f 8.3f] leggy, workmanlike filly: poor performer nowadays: no form in 1991: best effort at 1m: acts on good to firm ground, not soft: visored last 3 starts. *D. Moffatt.*

GOLDEN DISPLAY 7 b.g. Golden Fleece (USA) 133 – Minnie Hauk (USA) 100 — (Sir Ivor 135) [1990 NR 1991 14.1f] big, rangy ex-Irish gelding: very lightly raced: runner-up in minor race at Tralee (blinkered) at 3 yrs: first run on flat since 4-y-o, tailed off in handicap: stays 1½m. *J. Mackie.*

GOLDEN DIVOT 4 b.g. Chief Singer 131 – Action Belle (Auction Ring (USA) — 123) [1990 10m 10m 10.2m² 12.4f 16f² 1991 16.2g a12g] sturdy, attractive gelding: moderate mover: plating-class performer at 3 yrs: soundly beaten in spring of 1991: seems to stay 2m: acts on firm ground. *D. Morrill.*

GOLDEN GENERAL 3 ch.g. Blushing Scribe (USA) 107 – Broken Paws — (Busted 134) [1990 5f⁵ 6m⁴ 7f³ 7f 7f 7f⁵ 8f 1991 12m⁵ 12.2g 10m 9.9f] big, strong gelding: plating-class maiden at best: no promise as 3-y-o: should stay beyond 7f: blinkered last 3 outings: sweating and on toes final one: sold 1,750 gns Ascot September Sales. *M. Avison.*

GOLDEN GLORIOUS 3 ch.c. Tremblant 112 – Sweet Jane 59 (Furry Glen 121) — [1990 NR 1991 8.2f⁵] strong, good-topped colt: seventh foal: half-brother to 3 middle-distance winners by Daring March, including fairly useful Our Jock: dam best at 5f: very burly and green, slowly away and always tailed off in 5-runner maiden at Nottingham in July. *J. D. Czerpak.*

GOLDEN GUNNER (IRE) 3 ch.g. Mazaad 106 – Sun Gift (Guillaume Tell **64** (USA) 121) [1990 7d⁵ a6g 1991 10m⁶ 12f* 11m 16.2g⁵ 11.7d⁶] workmanlike gelding: favourite, easily best form when winning handicap at Carlisle in May: changed hands 1,050 gns Doncaster January Sales: winning hurdler: sold to join M. McCourt 10,000 gns Newmarket Autumn Sales. *M. H. Tompkins.*

GOLDEN ORCHY 3 b.g. Uncle Pokey 116 – Strath of Orchy 96 (Lochnager 132) — [1990 7.5d 6d⁴ 6g 7f 1991 8.5f 8d 6g 6d] leggy, workmanlike gelding: poor maiden: behind in selling handicap final start, in July: headstrong, and seems best short of 1m: acts on dead going. *C. Tinkler.*

GOLDEN PROPOSAL 2 gr.f. (May 11) Nomination 125 – Jellygold 95 (Jellaby **42** 124) [1991 5f 6g² 5m 6m⁴ 7.1m⁵ 7g] 3,000Y: leggy, lengthy filly: third foal: half-sister to French 3-y-o 1m winner Misterric (by Damister): dam 6f winner at 2 yrs: poor maiden: ran creditably in nurseries fourth and fifth (seller) starts, badly when blinkered in similar event final one: stays 7f: acts on good to firm ground. *M. Bell.*

GOLDEN REVERIE (USA) 3 b.g. Golden Act (USA) – Our Reverie (USA) (J — O Tobin (USA) 130) [1990 5m 6g 8.2s 1991 12h⁵ 11.1d⁵ 13d] sparely-made gelding: poor maiden: no worthwhile form in maiden and handicaps (blinkered) as 3-y-o: should prove suited by 1m +. *M. D. Hammond.*

GOLDEN SICKLE (USA) 2 b.g. (Feb 11) Amazing Prospect (USA) – — p
Marisickle (USA) (Maris) [1991 a7g⁵] $3,200Y: sixth reported foal (4 unraced):
half-brother to minor sprint winner Solid Mahogany (by Bluewood): dam ran once:
showed signs of ability in late-year maiden at Southwell: will improve. *W. A.
O'Gorman.*

GOLDEN STRIDES 5 ch.h. Northern Tempest (USA) 120 – Deux Mille Plus —
(Communication 119) [1990 NR 1991 a8g 8.3m] sparely-made horse: thrice raced and
no worthwhile form: sold 1,650 gns Ascot October Sales. *R. J. Hodges.*

GOLDEN TORQUE 4 br.g. Taufan (USA) 119 – Brightelmstone 105 (Prince 72
Regent (FR) 129) [1990 9.1m* 9m 8f 9m² 9m 11m 10m 1991 10.2s 8d 8m 8.2d* 8.2g⁵
8.3d³ 10.1m⁴ 10m 10.1m⁵ 10.5m³ 11.9g* 10.5d* 12d a12g⁴] strong, close-coupled
gelding: good walker: modest handicapper: won at Nottingham in June and Haydock
(2) in autumn: effective at 1m to 1½m: acts on good to firm ground and soft: effective
with or without a visor: has won for 7-lb claimer: best held up. *R. Bastiman.*

GOLDEN VINTAGE 5 ch.g. Glint of Gold 128 – Boissiere (High Top 131) [1990 43
a11g 1991 a16g 12s⁵] poor handicapper nowadays: not seen out after March: stays
11.7f: acts on good to firm ground: tailed off on all-weather: visored on reappearance: winning hurdler in January. *S. Dow.*

GOLD GLEN (IRE) 3 ch.c. Red Sunset 120 – Park Lady 82 (Tap On Wood 130) —
[1990 NR 1991 8g 16g³] 23,000Y: sturdy colt: third foal: brother to fairly useful 5f and
6f winner Lady Tap: dam 2-y-o 6f winner out of half-sister to smart American horse
Point du Jour: 25/1, 25 lengths third of 14 to odds-on Shahi in maiden at Nottingham
in June, staying on from rear. *P. J. Makin.*

GOLD HILT 2 b.g. (Mar 31) Sure Blade (USA) 130 – Fleur de Lyphard (USA) 73§ —
(Lyphard (USA) 132) [1991 7.1m] sturdy, quite attractive gelding: second living foal:
dam 5f winner, is half-sister to smart 1979 Irish 2-y-o Thousandfold and very smart
sprinter Faliraki, later successful over 9f in USA: eased considerably when beaten
in 10-runner maiden at Sandown in September: sold 4,200 gns Newmarket Autumn
Sales: sent to Scandinavia. *I. A. Balding.*

GOLD JUBILEE 2 b.f. (Feb 27) Damister (USA) 123 – Tiny Jubilee 59 (Hard 55
Fought 125) [1991 5g⁵ 5.2g⁴ 6s⁵ 8d] 21,000Y: useful-looking filly: has a quick action:
first foal: dam 6f winner at 2 yrs later sent to Norway, is half-sister to Enstone
Spark: plating-class form: should stay 1m: acts on soft going. *P. J. Makin.*

GOLD LAW (IRE) 3 b.c. Law Society (USA) 130 – Golden Oriole (USA) 83
(Northern Dancer) [1990 8m² 8f* 1991 10g*] lengthy colt: won handicap at Sandown
in April: should have stayed further: dead. *P. F. I. Cole.*

GOLDLINE SEEKER 3 b.c. Damister (USA) 123 – Bottom Line 90 (Double 94
Jump 131) [1990 8.2d 10.2s³ 1991 12m* 14m⁶ 12m³ 16.1m⁴ 16.2g² 16g³ 15m³ 14v⁶]
rangy colt: fairly useful performer: won minor event at Thirsk in April: in frame in
handicaps, German listed race then minor event: well beaten in good-class company
in Italy final start: shapes like an out-and-out stayer: blinkered third start. *M. A.
Jarvis.*

GOLDSMITHS' HALL 2 b.c. (Mar 6) Glint of Gold 128 – Pipina (USA) 81 (Sir 76 p
Gaylord) [1991 8.2f⁵ 8m²] tall, workmanlike colt: has plenty of scope: half-brother to
winning stayer Pipitina (by Bustino), very useful 1¼m and 1½m winner Pipsted (by
Busted) and useful 7f to 1m winner Night Out Perhaps (by Cure The Blues): dam,
10.5f winner, is half-sister to smart 5f performer Amaranda and 1000 Guineas
runner-up Favoridge: well-backed favourite after encouraging debut, neck second
of 10, staying on relentlessly, to Aasff in maiden at Newcastle in October: will
improve again, particularly over 1¼m + , and win a modest race. *G. Wragg.*

GOLD TRUST 4 b.c. Bellypha 130 – Abbey (FR) (Jim French (USA)) [1990 10.2s 47
1991 a10g⁴ a12g⁵ 10m 9m⁶] good-bodied colt: poor maiden: stays 1¼m: acts on good
to firm ground. *P. J. Makin.*

GOLDVEIN (SWE) 3 b.g. Superlative 118 – Follow Me Follow 92 (Wollow 132) 64
[1990 6g 1991 6.1m² 6m³ 6m³ a6g⁶ a5g] neat, good-quartered gelding: quite modest
maiden: blinkered all starts: has found little, and may be faint-hearted. *W. A.
O'Gorman.*

GOLD WING 2 b.c. (Feb 4) Bluebird (USA) 125 – High Matinee (Shirley Heights 66 ?
130) [1991 6m 6d 5.1g² 7d⁴ 7f] smallish, well-made colt: good walker: has a moderate
action: fourth foal: half-brother to winners in Belgium and Scandinavia: dam
unraced daughter of Portland Handicap winner Matinee: quite modest maiden:
finished strongly in frame at Bath and Sandown, having looked extremely difficult
ride: ran moderately in Salisbury claimer 2 months later: will probably stay 1m:

possibly unsuited by firm ground: blinkered last 3 starts: sold 4,400 gns Newmarket Autumn Sales. *D. R. C. Elsworth.*

GOMARLOW 4 gr.c. Belfort (FR) 89 – Tringa (GER) (Kaiseradler) [1990 7m 54 6m⁴ 7m⁴ 8g⁴ 10s 10g 7d 1991 10.1g⁵ 8m² a8g⁴ 8f4] big, lengthy colt: plating-class performer: stays 1m: acts on firm ground: visored (carried head high) once: not one to trust implicitly. *D. Morley.*

GONDO 4 br.g. Mansingh (USA) 120 – Secret Valentine 71 (Wollow 132) [1990 7d 76 a7g⁴ 7m 6d 7v³ 6d 6d³ a6g a6g* a7g a6g⁵ 1991 a7g 6d³ 6d⁴ 6m* 6m⁴ 6g 6m⁴ 5.1d² 6.1g⁶ 6m⁴ 5m⁶ 6m 6m⁵ 5.1m 5m⁴ 5g* 6g² 5.2g] compact gelding: has a quick action: modest sprint handicapper: won at Carlisle in April and Haydock in September: acts on good to firm and soft going: effective with or without visor: tough and consistent. *E. J. Alston.*

GONDOLIER 3 b.g. Slip Anchor 136 – Grimpola (GER) (Windwurf (GER)) [1990 82 NR 1991 12g⁵ 12m⁴ 14m*] rangy gelding: second foal: closely related to useful 4-y-o Golan Heights (by Shirley Heights), winner at 8.2f (at 2 yrs) and 1½m: dam won at 6f and 1m in Germany and stayed 1½m: made all in maiden at Redcar in June: will be better suited by 2m: acts on good to firm ground: moved moderately down penultimate start: gelded after final one. *H. R. A. Cecil.*

GONE BROKE 2 b.g. (Apr 3) Aragon 118 – Bad Payer 72 (Tanfirion 110) [1991 5d — a6g 5m] 7,200Y: rather leggy, close-coupled gelding: second foal: dam 2-y-o 5f winner: seems of little account. *M. W. Easterby.*

GONE BUST (IRE) 2 gr.g. (Jan 8) Aragon 118 – Ludovica (Bustino 136) 61 [1991 5g⁴ 5d² 5m 7m a7g] IR 8,000Y: sparely-made gelding: second foal: half-brother to 3-y-o Where's Carol (by Anfield), 6f winner at 2 yrs: dam unraced daughter of Ebor second Lorelene: quite modest maiden: ran poorly in Newmarket seller fourth outing: not discredited in Southwell nursery 5 months later: should be suited by further than 5f: blinkered third outing: sweating fourth. *R. F. Johnson Houghton.*

GONE SAVAGE 3 b.c. Nomination 125 – Trwyn Cilan 89 (Import 127) [1990 78 5g² 5d² 5m* 5g 1991 6g⁶ 5.8m⁴ 5m 5.1g 8g] strong, good-bodied colt: carries condition: good walker: capable of fair form: fourth in handicap at Bath, easily best effort as 3-y-o when not seen out after August: stays 5.8f: acts on good to firm ground and dead: blinkered fourth start: sold 5,500 gns Newmarket Autumn Sales. *P. F. I. Cole.*

GOOD AS GOLD (IRE) 2 ch.f. (Mar 27) Glint of Gold 128 – Salote (USA) 109 50 p (Forli (ARG)) [1991 a8g4] 13,000F, 8,000Y: closely related to fairly useful 1½m winner Mountain Isle (by Shirley Heights) and half-sister to several winners abroad: dam suited by 1½m: 20/1, over 5 lengths fourth of 9 to Paper Clip in December maiden at Lingfield: will improve, particularly over further. *J. L. Spearing.*

GOODBYE MAGGIE (IRE) 3 b.f. Thatching 131 – Glorious Fate (Northfields 37 (USA)) [1990 NR 1991 a6g 7d? 8m⁶ 8.3g⁵ 0g 7.1d 7d⁴ 6m³ 7g⁶ 7m 6m 6m⁴ a8g] 10,500Y: compact filly: moderate mover: second foal: dam, from good family, never ran: poor maiden: best efforts at 7f: acts on dead going: ran moderately for amateur: blinkered last 6 starts: tends to hang. *M. J. Fetherston-Godley.*

GOODBYE MR MARKS (IRE) 3 b.c. On Your Mark 125 – Ciao (Mandamus 65 120) [1990 6m⁵ 7g a6g² 1991 a5g³ 5s²] big, workmanlike colt: best efforts, showing quite modest form, on fibresand: favourite but still bit backward, made most when beaten head in maiden auction at Hamilton in April: at least as effective at 5f as 6f. *N. Bycroft.*

GOOD FOR A LOAN 4 b.g. Daring March 116 – Game For A Laugh 72 — (Martinmas 128) [1990 10.1g 8g⁵ 9g 8.2g⁵ 7f 11.5m² 12g⁵ 10d 1991 10g 10m] well-made gelding: moderate walker and mover: modest handicapper at 3 yrs: no form in 1991: stays 11.5f: acts on good to firm ground, possibly not on dead: keen sort: sold to join R. Lee's stable 16,000 gns Newmarket Autumn Sales: winning hurdler in October. *A. C. Stewart.*

GOOD FOR THE ROSES 5 b.g. Kampala 120 – Alleyn (Alcide 136) [1990 8g 50 8m⁶ 10g⁴ a8g⁵ a8g³ 1991 8.2d* 8m] leggy gelding: has a round action: plating-class handicapper: made all at Hamilton in April: well below form at Kempton following month: suited by 1m: acts on firm and dead ground. *M. McCormack.*

GOOD HAND (USA) 5 ch.g. Northjet 136 – Ribonette (USA) (Ribot 142) [1990 86 16f* 18.4d⁴ 18m⁴* 20m⁴ 20.4m** 17.4d⁶ 16.2s 18d 1991 16m⁵ 18.4d 18f4 20g³ 16.1m 20g³ 16.2f³ 17.5m⁵ 18m] close-coupled, sparely-made gelding: fair handicapper:

first past post at Doncaster in May (relegated for interference) third start: largely consistent after: an out-and-out stayer: acts on firm and dead going (unsuited by soft): has been tried blinkered: probably best on a galloping track: usually soon off bridle, and not easiest of rides. *J. W. Watts.*

GOOD IMPRESSION (IRE) 3 b.c. Blushing Scribe (USA) 107 – Derring Venture — (Camden Town 125) [1990 7m 6m 8.2g a7g 1991 a7g] neat colt: soundly beaten, including in sellers and handicap. *R. Champion.*

GOODISON GIRL 2 ch.f. (Mar 31) Creetown 123 – Mrs Hubbard 73 (Silly Season 127) [1991 8m 6s] third reported foal: dam stayed 1½m: well beaten in late-season maidens at Redcar (bit backward, showed up well to halfway) and Hamilton. *M. J. Camacho.*

GOODNITEOUT (IRE) 2 b.f. (Feb 16) Dance of Life (USA) – Schweppes **87** p Forever 112 (Lord Gayle (USA) 124) [1991 6f 7g³ 7d⁴] workmanlike filly: half-sister to Irish 9f winner Joviality (by Cure The Blues) and 2 winners abroad: dam very useful 6f and 7f winner at 2 yrs: sweating, around 4 lengths fourth of 7 to Casteddu in minor event at Ascot in October: will do better, particularly over further: can win an ordinary maiden. *D. R. C. Elsworth.*

GOOD OLD GEORGE (IRE) 2 ch.c. (Mar 12) Muscatite 122 – Tolaytala (Be **37** My Guest (USA) 126) [1991 5s² 5g 7g 6d⁵ 8m] IR 1,700Y, resold 3,100Y: workmanlike colt: fourth foal: half-brother to 1¼m seller winner/successful hurdler Champagne Run (by Runnett): dam once-raced daughter of half-sister to Take A Reef: quite modest plater: best effort (in non-selling maiden) on debut: should stay 7f. *M. D. I. Usher.*

GOOD POLICY (IRE) 3 b.f. Thatching 131 – Good To Follow 82 (Wollow 132) **80** [1990 6m⁵ 6g⁶ 8m² 7m² 8.2m* 1991 9d⁶ 8g 7.1g³ 8.1g 8m a10g⁵] leggy, good-quartered filly: fair performer at her best: disappointing in handicaps last 3 starts, prominent 6f: stays 1m: acts on good to firm ground. *P. T. Walwyn.*

GOOD PROFILE (USA) 3 b.c. Liloy (FR) 124 – I Sparkle (USA) (Gleaming **92** (USA)) [1990 6d⁵ 7d² 1991 8d² 7m* 8.5f* 8m² 7m* 7f⁴ 8.9g 9d² 10m² 10.3d³] tall, angular colt: quite useful performer: won maiden at Carlisle in April, handicap at Beverley in May and minor event at Catterick in June: ran creditably last 2 starts in handicaps at Newmarket and Chester: effective at 7f and stays 1¼m: acts on firm and dead ground: sold to join G. Moore 60,000 gns Newmarket Autumn Sales: winning hurdler. *S. G. Norton.*

GOOD REFERENCE (IRE) 2 br.f. (Apr 9) Reference Point 139 – Impudent **75** Miss 105 (Persian Bold 123) [1991 7g³ 7f* 7m 7m] 72,000Y: lengthy, quite attractive filly: good walker: fourth foal: half-sister to 3-y-o Sword's Point (by Sure Blade) and 6f and 7.6f winner King Al (by Indian King): dam, 5f to 1m winner at 2 yrs in Ireland, is half-sister to very smart sprinter Sayyaf: favourite, won 4-runner minor event at Redcar in July, off bridle at halfway then staying on determinedly: off course 2 months (reportedly injured herself at Leopardstown in early-August), last of 30 in Tattersalls Tiffany Highflyer Stakes at Newmarket: will be suited by 1m. *M. Bell.*

GOOD TIME BOY 3 b.g. Good Times (ITY) – Galetzky 86 (Radetzky 123) **64** [1990 5m³ 5s* 5m 5m⁴ 6g⁵ 1991 8g 7m⁵ a8g 8g 8.1s a8g] lengthy, rather angular gelding: plating-class performer: soundly beaten in handicaps last 3 starts, off course over 6 months after first of them: stays 7f: acts on good to firm ground and soft. *M. Brittain.*

GOOD TO DANCE (IRE) 2 b.f. (Feb 7) Groom Dancer (USA) 128 – Good To **?** Beat 114 (Hard To Beat 132) [1991 8g⁵ 8d⁵ 10s*] fifth foal: half-sister to French 7f (at 2 yrs) and 11f winner Grand Fleuve (by Irish River): dam French 1m (at 2 yrs) to 10.5f winner: fifth in maidens at Deauville in August and Maisons-Laffitte following month before winning similar event at former course by 8 lengths in October: should stay 1½m: may improve further. *A. Fabre, France.*

GOODY FOUR SHOES 3 gr.f. Blazing Saddles (AUS) – Bronzamer 86 **60** (Saritamer (USA) 132) [1990 5m⁵ 5m* 5m 6d⁶ 5s⁶ 1991 5.1g⁶ 5d⁴ 5.2f⁵ 5m] leggy, close-coupled filly: has a round action: quite modest performer: should stay 6f: acts on firm ground and dead: mulish to post first 2 starts. *C. J. Hill.*

GOOFALIK (USA) 4 b.c. Lyphard (USA) 132 – Alik 113 (Targowice (USA) 130) **118** [1990 8g* 10g² 10d⁵ 10g² 10g* 8v⁶ 1991 10g² 8d* 7g³ 9.5f³ 10g* 8d² 10s³] leggy colt: has round action: smart French performer: won Group 3 Prix du Chemin de Fer du Nord at Chantilly (beat Boxing Day by 1½ lengths) in June and Group 2 contest at Frankfurt (by neck) in September: third in Criterion Stakes at Newmarket in June: ran well last 2 starts behind Bistro Garden in Ciga Prix du Rond-Point at Longchamp

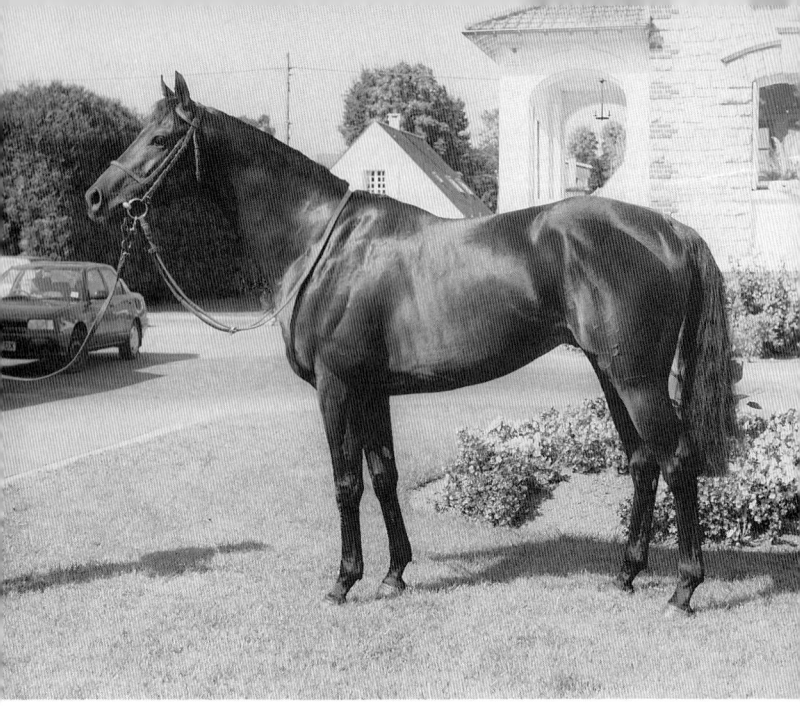

Mr David Thompson's "Goofalik"

and Leariva in Grade 1 Budweiser International Sweepstakes at Laurel, USA: effective at 7f to 1¼m: probably acts on any going: tough and consistent: a credit to his trainer. *J. E. Hammond, France.*

GOOGLY 2 ch.f. (Mar 24) Sunley Builds 102 – Cheri Berry 87 (Air Trooper 115) **52**
[1991 5d 5.7m⁴ 7f 6g 7.1d 6g 6s a6g] 2,200Y: leggy, rather unfurnished filly: half-sister to 3-y-o Madagans Grey (by Carwhite), 6f (at 2 yrs) to 2m winner, and to 6f winner Inswinger (by Swing Easy): dam sprinter: plating-class maiden: seems best at 6f. *W. G. R. Wightman.*

GORDANO 4 ch.g. Muscatite 122 – Coral Star (Tarboosh (USA)) [1990 7m⁴ 5f —
10.2f⁶ 10.1m 12f⁶ 1991 9v 11.5m] neat gelding: poor plater: stays 7f: sold out of R. Holder's stable 950 gns Ascot May Sales. *D. C. Jermy.*

GORINSKY (IRE) 3 ch.g. Gorytus (USA) 132 – Grapette (Nebbiolo 125) [1990 **85**
5f⁵ 6m* 5d² 6m* 5m² 5f³ 5g² 5d² 6v* 5g 1991 6m⁴ 6g² 6g 5g a6g² 6g⁴ 6m 6g⁵ 6m²
6.1d a6g²] sturdy gelding: has a quick action: fair but somewhat inconsistent handicapper: second in quite valuable event at York and claimer at Lingfield 2 of last 3 starts: stays 6f: acts on turf going, and on equitrack: races prominently. *J. Berry.*

GO SOUTH 7 b.g. Thatching 131 – Run To The Sun (Run The Gantlet (USA)) **76**
[1990 a 13g⁴ 18f 15.5f⁴ 14m² 14g⁶ 14.8m⁵ 14.8m³ 16m 16.5f³ 16.2s* 18d⁵ 16s⁶ a14g⁴
a 16g* a16g³ 1991 14m 18d³ 18.4d⁴ 14m 20g⁶ 17.2g⁵ 16d² 18.5g* 16.2g⁶ 16.2g⁴ 18m*
16.5d4] sturdy gelding: moderate mover: modest handicapper: won at Chester in July and moderately-run Tote Cesarewitch at Newmarket (33/1, by 2½ lengths from Bardolph) in October: fourth to Royal Standard at Doncaster final start: needs good test of stamina: probably acts on any going: blinkered: has dropped himself out and taken little interest. *J. R. Jenkins.*

GO TALLY-HO 3 b.f. Gorytus (USA) 132 – Brush Away (Ahonoora 122) [1990 **57** d
5m* 5m* 1991 6f5 6m 12f 6f 8m 8h 7m] sparely-made filly: winner twice in summer
as 2-y-o: showed retains some ability in handicaps first and fourth starts: should
stay 7f: soundly beaten in blinkers: visored (outpaced and never dangerous) final
start: trained until after second by J. Berry: winning hurdler. *J. J. O'Neill.*

GOTCHA (BAR) 2 br.c. (Jan 26) Bentom (USA) 98 – Hotcha 70 (Hotfoot 126) **79** p
[1991 7g5 7.1s*] sturdy, good-quartered colt: dam 6f and 7f winner, went to
Barbados in 1979: sire 7f and 1m winner: weak 9/1-shot, won 13-runner maiden at
Chepstow in October, leading line: will be suited by 1m: will improve again. *R.
Hannon.*

GOTHIC FORD 7 b.g. Stanford 121§ – Gothic Lady (Godswalk (USA) 130) [1990 —
a8g8* a7g4 a7g2 a7g3 a7g* a7g3 a8g2 a8g3 a7g2 a7g3 a8g 8f 7.5m a8g a8g6 a8g a8g6
a11g 1991 a11g] short-legged, rather dipped-backed gelding: moderate mover: below
best since quite modest form on all-weather early at 6 yrs: in rear only outing in 1991
(January): ideally suited by 7f or 1m: acts on any going: has been tried in visor and
severe bridle: below form when tried in eyeshield and blinkers: sold 1,200 gns
Doncaster January Sales. *C. Tinkler.*

GOTTA BE JOKING 3 ch.g. Funny Man 107 – Palimony (Communication 119) —
[1990 NR 1991 12m5 14.1f5] workmanlike gelding: fourth reported living foal:
half-brother to 5f winner Double Gift (by Cragador): dam never ran: bit backward,
well beaten in maidens at Chepstow and Yarmouth (bandaged behind, ran in
snatches) 4 months later. *T. M. Jones.*

GOTT-LE-GEAR 2 b.g. (Apr 16) Doc Marten 104 – La Bird 61 (Le Johnstan 123) —
[1991 6g] leggy, unfurnished gelding: fourth foal: half-brother to 3-y-o Go Gott (by
All Systems Go): dam won at 1m and 1¼m: last of 9 in maiden at Haydock in July. *G.
Richards.*

GOTT'S DESIRE 5 ch.g. Sweet Monday 122 – Steel Lady 60 (Continuation 120) **51**
[1990 a8g4 a7g 7.6m 7m5 7f* 7f4 7g2 7m4 7m* 7m 7.6m* 7m 8m 8.2d 7d 1991 7f 7m
9.9f 7m 7.6m2 7.5f3 7m* 7g 7m 7s6] angular gelding: quite modest handicapper at
best: won at Catterick in September, gamely making all: keen sort, suited by about
7f: probably acts on any going: has won for claimer: none too consistent. *R.
Bastiman.*

GOVERNORSHIP 7 ch.g. Dominion 123 – Angel Beam (SWE) 115 (Hornbeam **49** §
130) [1990 7m 9f 7.6m* 6f 8.3m 8.5f 8f 6g 7d 11d 1991 8m a8g5 8.3s3 9f4 8.1m 8.3f 8f3
8h 7m 9m 10.5d] lengthy, good-topped gelding: poor walker: has a quick action: poor
handicapper nowadays: stays 9f: probably acts on any going: best in blinkers:
thoroughly unreliable: sold 2,000 gns Doncaster October Sales. *D. W. Chapman.*

GOVERNOR'S IMP (USA) 2 b.c. (Jan 9) Imp Society (USA) – Lady Limbo **105**
(USA) (Dance Spell (USA)) [1991 5g3 5m3 6g* 6m2 7g2 7g3 8s4 8s2 10v] lengthy,
good-quartered colt: fifth foal: half-brother to winners in USA by Doonesbury and
Rich Cream: dam minor winner at 6f: sire best from 8.5f to 1¼m: useful performer:
won 14-runner maiden at Haydock in June: ran well in pattern events last 3 placed

Tote Cesarewitch, Newmarket—
a surprise result as 33/1-shots Go South and Bardolph (centre) finish first and second

outings, including when over 3 lengths third of 7 to Dr Devious in Lanson
Champagne Vintage Stakes at Goodwood and 2½ lengths second of 13 to Alhijaz in
Gran Criterium at Milan: well beaten in Premio Guido Berardelli at Rome in
November: suited by 1m: acts on good to firm, but best form on soft: sometimes bit
edgy: sweating seventh outing. *M. Bell.*

GOZONE 4 ro.g. Carwhite 127 – Perlesse 88 (Bold Lad (USA)) [1990 10.1m 7m **50 d**
6d³ 6s⁵ 5g a6g⁶ a7g a8g² 1991 a10g a7g² a7g⁵ 6v 7f 6f 7.6g] leggy gelding:
plating-class maiden: no form in first half of 1991 after second start: stays 1m: acts
on dead going: sold 2,000 gns Ascot October Sales. *P. Mitchell.*

GRACE CARD 5 b.g. Ela-Mana-Mou 132 – Val de Grace (FR) (Val de Loir 133) —
[1990 16.2m² 16.2f⁶ 17.6m⁶ 16m 17m² 18g a16g a14g 1991 14.6s 16.2g 21.6f] lengthy,
workmanlike gelding: plating-class maiden at 4 yrs: ran poorly in spring of 1991:
suited by test of stamina: acts on good to firm ground. *R. Hollinshead.*

GRACELAND LADY (IRE) 3 b.f. Kafu 120 – Theda 61 (Mummy's Pet 125) —
[1990 5f 5m³ 5g* 5m⁶ 5g⁶ 5g⁴ 6d 1991 5m 7g 6m 5d 6f⁵ 5g] tall, leggy filly: poor
mover: plating-class performer at 2 yrs: should stay beyond 5f: sold out of M. H.
Easterby's stable 1,800 gns Doncaster July Sales after fourth start. *J. K. Kinane.*

GRACIOUS BEAUTY (USA) 3 b.f. Nijinsky (CAN) 138 – Gold Beauty (USA) **67**
(Mr Prospector (USA)) [1990 NR 1991 8.1d² 10g³ 10m⁶ 7d⁶ 6m³ 7.1g² 7m 8.2m]
$1,600,000Y: big, strong, deep-bodied filly: third foal: sister to American Grade 1 9f
and 1¼m winner Maplejinsky and closely related to outstanding sprinter Dayjur (by
Danzig): dam champion sprinter in USA: quite modest maiden: below form in
handicaps last 2 starts: will prove suited by 1m + : acts on good to firm ground and
dead: blinkered/visored last 4 starts. *Major W. R. Hern.*

GRAF (USA) 4 b.c. Danzig (USA) – Michelle Mon Amour (USA) (Best Turn —
(USA)) [1991 10m 8g 10.9m⁵ 7.9m a7g] small, sturdy, close-coupled ex-American
colt: second foal: brother to Posen, multiple graded-stakes winner in USA from 1m
to 11f: dam won 5 races at up to 1m: won 2 races at 3 yrs at around 1m: clear signs of
ability when close eighth of 16 in Lingfield handicap final start: stiff tasks, including
in 3 listed events, previously here: stays 1m. *Mrs L. Piggott.*

GRAMMOS (USA) 3 b.c. Bailjumper (USA) – Rheine Falls (USA) (Rheingold **96**
137) [1990 7m* 10g⁶ 1991 10g* 9v² 8m 10.2m² 10.8m²] big, workmanlike colt: fairly
useful performer: won median auction contest at Leicester in June: good second in
apprentice race at Chepstow and minor event at Warwick last 2 outings: stays 11f:
acts on good to firm ground: has looked headstrong. *H. R. A. Cecil.*

GRAN ALBA (USA) 5 gr.h. El Gran Senor (USA) 136 – Morning Games (USA) —
(Grey Dawn II 132) [1990 8f⁶ 10f⁵ 10g² 10m 9g 10.6g⁴ 9m 10.4v² 1991 11g]
heavy-topped horse: carries condition: moderate walker: has a roundish action:
useful at best at 4 yrs: better for race, well beaten in Newbury handicap only run on
flat in 1991 (October): needs further than 1m and stays 1½m: needs an easy surface:
sometimes blinkered or visored: high-class hurdler. *R. Hannon.*

GRANBERA (USA) 3 b.f. El Gran Senor (USA) 136 – Satin Ribera (USA) **54**
(Mickey McGuire (USA)) [1990 7s² 1991 6.1m³ 8m⁶] light-framed filly: moderate
mover: quite modest form placed in maidens, staying on strongly at Nottingham in
September: well-beaten second favourite in similar event at Newcastle 3 weeks
later: should stay at least 1m: sold 2,000 gns Newmarket December Sales. *B. W.
Hills.*

GRAND FELLOW (IRE) 2 br.g. (May 21) Thatching 131 – Concave —
(Connaught 130) [1991 6.1m] IR 3,000Y: angular, close-coupled gelding: third foal:
half-brother to 1987 Irish 2-y-o 7f winner Impressive Lady (by Mr Fluorocarbon):
dam lightly-raced maiden: backward, no promise in maiden auction at Nottingham in
September. *J. D. Bethell.*

GRAND GUIGNOL 3 ch.g. Superlative 118 – Boule de Suif 88 (Major Portion **74**
129) [1990 NR 1991 6f a7g² a7g* 7m⁵ 6f 7.6m a7g 7m⁵ 7m* 8g a7g] workmanlike
gelding: half-brother to several winners here and abroad, including 1m to 1½m
winner Dumplino (by Bustino): dam, who stayed 1m, is half-sister to 3 good
performers: modest form: made all in maiden at Southwell in July: easily best
subsequent effort when winning handicap at Catterick in October in good style,
quickening on over 2f out: stays 7f: acts on good to firm ground, and fibresand:
blinkered fifth start. *G. Wragg.*

GRAND HAWK (USA) 3 b.g. Silver Hawk (USA) 123 – Ginger Lass (USA) 114 **81**
(Elocutionist (USA)) [1990 NR 1991 8m 8f⁴ 7.9m²] well-made gelding: second foal:
half-brother to French 6.5f and 6f (at 3 yrs) winner Ginger Candy (by Hilal): dam,
French 9f winner, is half-sister to Lyphard's Special and champion sprinter My

Juliet: progressive maiden: in frame, staying on well, at Yarmouth and York in June: will be suited by further. *M. Moubarak.*

GRAND MASTER (IRE) 2 b.c. (Jan 1) Sadler's Wells (USA) 132 – Lady's **109** Bridge (USA) 81 (Sir Ivor 135) [1991 7f³ 8m² 8d⁵ 10m² 10v4] 180,000Y: big, strong, lengthy colt: has plenty of scope: moderate mover: second foal: dam, won over 11f and 14.7f,is daughter of half-sister to very smart Pass The Glass, a winner 6 times at up to 9f: very useful staying maiden: much improved effort in 9-runner Criterium de Saint-Cloud final start, finishing over 5 lengths fourth of 9 to Glaieul: best previous form when around 12 lengths fifth of 8 to Made of Gold in Royal Lodge William Hill Stakes at Ascot: will stay 1½m: well suited by heavy ground: sure to win a maiden at the very least. *P. F. I. Cole.*

GRAND PRIX 6 b.h. Formidable (USA) 125 – Mumruffin 101 (Mummy's Pet 125) **91** [1990 5g 5.8h 5m⁴ 5m* 5m⁵ 5m 6m* 5m 5m⁵ 5g⁶ 1991 6g* 6m⁵ 6m 5g⁶ 6g 6f² 6g 6m] neat, good-bodied horse: moderate mover: fairly useful handicapper: won £12,200 event at Goodwood in May: ran poorly there last 2 starts (hung right first occasion): best at 6f or stiff 5f: goes well on top-of-the-ground: often sweating and on edge: sometimes starts slowly. *D. R. C. Elsworth.*

GRAND TIME 2 ch.c. (Mar 23) Clantime 101 – Panay 77 (Arch Sculptor 123) **58** [1991 5d* 5d³ 5f* 5g² 5.7g 5d a7g] 7,800Y: neat colt: half-brother to 1987 2-y-o 5f winner Hatay (by Alias Smith): dam 2-y-o 5f winner: made all or most when winning maiden at Catterick and claimer at Beverley: well beaten in autumn nurseries (faced stiff tasks) and a Southwell claimer: trained until after penultimate start by J. Berry. *C. J. Hill.*

GRAND VITESSE (IRE) 2 br.c. (Apr 16) Alzao (USA) 117 – Au Revoir 79 **77** p (Ballymoss 136) [1991 7d⁶ 6f⁴ 7f*] 30,000F: quite attractive colt: half-brother to 2 winners, including 1m winner Abide (by Habitat): dam, 1½m winner, is from good staying family: made most in maiden at Brighton in September, forging clear from 1f out: will stay 1m: likely to improve further. *R. Hannon.*

GRANITE BOY 2 b.c. (Apr 11) Music Boy 124 – Jouvencelle 68 (Rusticaro (FR) **68** 124) [1991 6g 5m 6m⁴ 7g 6m a8g a7g³ a8g³] 28,000Y: strong, attractive colt: third foal: half-brother to 3-y-o 1½m winner Valiant Warrior (by Valiyar) and fair 9f winner Land Afar (by Dominion): dam, maiden at up to 14.7f: quite modest maiden: best effort final start, on equitrack: suited by 1m: blinkered fifth outing: bought out of B. Hanbury's stable afterwards 10,500 gns Newmarket Autumn Sales. *P. J. Feilden.*

GRANITTON BAY 4 b.c. Prince Tenderfoot (USA) 126 – Miss Redmarshall 80 **76** (Most Secret 119) [1990 5f 5v 7h² 5d⁵ 7m³ 8m* 7m* 7g* 7m⁵ 7.6g⁵ 8.5m⁴ 9m 8m 8g 8m* 9m 8d 1991 9f5 8f* 8g⁴ 8.1m² 8.9g] lengthy, rather dipped-backed colt: moderate walker: poor mover: modest handicapper: won at Thirsk in August: effective from 7f to 9f: acts on hard and dead going: usually visored nowadays: has run well for amateur. *R. M. Whitaker.*

GRANITTON PRINCE 2 b.c. (Mar 23) Clantime 101 – Chevet Lady 65 (John **—** de Coombe 122) [1991 5f] 2,100Y: sparely-made colt: first reported foal: dam 8.5f (at 2 yrs) and 1¼m winner: 33/1, always behind in 16-runner maiden auction at Pontefract in April: pulled hard to post. *R. M. Whitaker.*

GRANNY MC 4 br.f. Sparkling Boy 110 – Marcus Miss (Marcus Superbus 100) **52** [1990 NR 1991 7m⁴ 12.3d 10.3d a6g 6f⁴ 7.1m⁵ 6g 6g² 6d 7.1m] big, plain, workmanlike filly: third living foal: dam tailed off in NH Flat race on only start: plating-class handicapper: seems to stay 7f: acts on good to firm ground, possibly unsuited by dead. *E. J. Alston.*

GRANNY'S GIRL 3 b.f. Mummy's Game 120 – Michaelmas 72 (Silly Season **44** 127) [1990 5m 6g a8g⁵ 1991 7g 7.3d⁶ 7g 8g⁴ a8g 8.3m 8.1g 10m] close-coupled filly: plating-class form at best: should stay 1m: visored (tailed off) fifth outing: blinkered third (ran creditably) and sixth: sold out of I. Balding's stable 1,700 gns Doncaster July Sales after third outing. *J. L. Harris.*

GRAVETTE 3 ch.f. Kris 135 – Highland Light 105 (Home Guard (USA) 129) **76** [1990 7m 6m 7g² 1991 10d³ 10f³ 8g⁴ 8m* 8m 8d* 8.1d*] angular, workmanlike filly: has a roundish action: moderate walker: modest form: won maiden at Wolver-hampton in July and handicaps at Goodwood (ridden by 7-lb claimer) and Chepstow (gamely) in October, twice making virtually all: effective at 1m and 1¼m: acts on firm and dead going: takes keen hold: sold 40,000 gns Newmarket December Sales. *H. R. A. Cecil.*

GREAT ABSALOM 2 gr.c. (May 13) Absalom 128 – Sallytude (Tudor Music **—** 131) [1991 5f⁵ 5h 7.5f] 7,600F, 2,000Y, 8,000 2-y-o: leggy, unfurnished colt: fifth live foal: half-brother to a winner abroad and to a winner over hurdles: dam, winner at up to 1m in Ireland, is granddaughter of dual German classic winner Santa Cruz III: no worthwhile form: off course nearly 4 months before final outing. *J. S. Wainwright.*

GREATEST OF ALL (IRE) 3 ch.f. Ela-Mana-Mou 132 – Red Jade 82 (Red **40** God 128§) [1990 6m⁶ 6.5g 7m 1991 8.3m 7m³ 6.9m⁴ 8.9g 8.9m 6m] tall, leggy, plain filly: poor performer: suited by 7f: acts on good to firm ground: edgy and pulled hard penultimate start: sold 8,400 gns Newmarket December Sales. *R. Hannon.*

GREAT FRIENDSHIP 4 b.g. Bairn (USA) 126 – Badwell Ash (Morston (FR) — 125) [1990 8.2g⁶ 10g⁵ 10g 10d 8m³ 8m 1991 8m] leggy, angular gelding: plating-class maiden: should have stayed 1¼m: acted on good to firm ground: dead. *C. W. Thornton.*

GREAT FUN 3 b.f. Bustino 136 – Its A Romp (Hotfoot 126) [1990 NR 1991 8g⁴ **63** 10.2g⁵ 10g³ 13.3g 10.3d] lengthy filly: has a round action: first live foal: dam, half-sister to Whitstead, won sprint claimer in North America: quite modest maiden: didn't get best of runs in handicap then never placed to challenge in ladies contest last 2 starts: should stay beyond 1¼m: sweating third and fourth starts: trained first 4 by D. Elsworth. *Mrs J. R. Ramsden.*

GREAT GUSTO 5 b.g. Windjammer (USA) – My Music 68 (Sole Mio (USA)) **43** [1990 16.5g 10.4g a11g 8m a12g a7g 1991 a10g a11g 10.1s 8.1d² 8.1g 8f³ 10g⁵ 10.5g 10.3m²] leggy, good-topped gelding: poor handicapper nowadays: stays 1¼m: acts on firm and good ground: has won for amateur: carried head awkwardly final start: sold 1,650 gns Ascot November Sales. *R. J. Holder.*

GREAT HALL 2 gr.c. (Mar 30) Hallgate 127 – Lily of France 81 (Monsanto (FR) **50** 121) [1991 5.7m⁶ 5.3m² 5m 6f⁵ 5m 7g 7g 5.7g a6g⁶ 6s a8g⁵ a7g⁵] 2,300Y, resold 2,900Y: compact colt: moderate mover: third foal: half-brother to plating-class 3-y-o Marwell Bianca (by Carwhite): dam sprinter: plating-class maiden on balance of form: best run at 5f on good to firm ground: twice blinkered, once visored: sweating third outing: has been bandaged behind. *W. G. R. Wightman.*

GREAT HAND 5 b.h. Tumble Wind (USA) – Great Aunt 74 (Great Nephew 126) **54** [1990 a10g a8g 9f⁶ 8f⁶ 8m³ 10f* 8.2f² 8g² 10m 10.6d 10m 10s 1991 a10g a8g a12g 10v⁶ 10.8g⁴ 10d³ 10m² 9f⁶ 12g⁶ 10m 10g 9.9f 8.2m* 8.3m³ 8f* 9.7f⁶ 8.2f 7m⁵ 8.2m] leggy horse: plating-class handicapper: won at Nottingham and Salisbury in August: effective at 1m to 1¼m: acts on firm and dead going: has run well when sweating: possibly best on galloping track: none too consistent: sold out of D. Wilson's stable 7,000 gns Newmarket September Sales after seventh start. *R. Guest.*

GREAT HEIGHTS 4 b.g. Shirley Heights 130 – As You Desire Me 112 **104** (Kalamoun 129) [1990 10m* 11.5m³ 1991 13.3d⁴ 11g⁴] big, good-topped gelding: has a quick action: lightly-raced but useful performer: first run for a year, 5 lengths fourth of 8 to Snurge in listed event at Newbury in May: favourite, never able to challenge in moderately-run 5-runner minor event at Beverley following month: will be well suited by 1¾m + : looked worth another chance, but not seen out again. *Mrs J. Cecil.*

GREAT IMPOSTOR 3 ch.g. Valgly Great 127 – Lady Waverton (Huntercombe **56** § 133) [1990 NR 1991 7f 8m³ a10g⁶] 7,800Y: close-coupled gelding: fifth live foal: half-brother to a winner in Norway by Ile de Bourbon: dam unraced half-sister to One In A Million: third of 14 in claimer at Salisbury, carrying head high and not going through with effort: below that form in similar event at Lingfield 7 months later: sold 1,700 gns Ascot December Sales. *P. T. Walwyn.*

GREAT LORD (IRE) 2 b.g. (Feb 23) Last Tycoon 131 – Mummy's Favourite **66** 104 (Mummy's Pet 125) [1991 6g⁵ 6g⁴ 7m⁵ 7m⁴ 7g⁶] 72,000F: tall, leggy, close-coupled gelding: first foal: dam 6f and 7f winner: quite modest maiden: visored, pulled hard when well beaten in nursery at York (August) final start: should stay 7f: swished tail repeatedly before running moderately third outing. *J. W. Watts.*

GREAT MARQUESS 4 b.c. Touching Wood (USA) 127 – Fruition 89 **115** (Rheingold 137) [1990 10m* 14g² 14.6g5 16m* 1991 14g⁶ 16m 15.9m* 16g² 15g 18m* 14d⁶]

As the 1990 season drew to a close, trainer Henry Cecil could have been forgiven for entertaining hopes of sweeping the board in the next year's Cup races with the three-year-old pair River God and Great Marquess. Both colts seemed sure to make up into good Cup horses. However, River God was a bitter disappointment, tailed off in the Sagaro Stakes at Ascot on his re-appearance and not seen again after being withdrawn lame at the start in the Ormonde Stakes at Chester in May. Great Marquess did much better without fully living up to expectations. Although he won the Doncaster Cup, he failed to improve on the form he showed at three, and furthermore he proved none too consistent. There were three high points in Great Marquess' season: his win in the listed Foster's Silver Cup Stakes at York in June (a substandard contest in which, Great Marquess aside, only runner-up and stable-companion Bondstone, beaten two and a half lengths in a field of seven, gave his true running); a good length second to Further Flight in the Goodwood Cup; and the win in the Doncaster Cup. Eight went to post at Doncaster; they included Arzanni, having his first run since the Gold Cup and sent off 7/4 favourite, the progressive three-year-old Supreme Choice, Mountain Kingdom, Trainglot and Champion Hurdler Morley Street. The handicappers Gay Glint and Haitham led the field at a modest pace until early in the straight whereupon the always-prominent Great Marquess stole a march on the other principals when sent on approaching the three-furlong pole. Having beaten off the challenge of Arzanni with a furlong and a half to run, Great Marquess looked an assured winner when holding a two-length lead at the distance. But Morley Street, who'd been held up in rear—hardly the ideal tactics the way the race developed—had started to find his stride and while being handled considerately, with an eye to the future no doubt, he finished with a flourish to go down by the narrowest of margins to an all-out Great Marquess, the pair four lengths clear. The remainder of Great Marquess' season amounted to little. He was well beaten on his first two starts in the Yorkshire Cup and Henry II Stakes (last of seven) when not looking fully wound up—Cecil reported that he was a very lazy worker—and he fared little better on his fifth and his final outings behind Turgeon in both the Prix Kergorlay at Deauville and Irish St Leger at the Curragh.

Great Marquess' pedigree details were noted in *Racehorses of 1990*, in particular that he is a half-brother to the good stayer Kneller (by Lomond) and that his dam is a half-sister to Flame of Tara, the dam of Salsabil and now Marju. Since producing Great Marquess, Fruition was barren to Mummy's Game in 1988 and her 1989 foal, a colt called McCoist (by Dunbeath), has yet to see the racecourse. A close-coupled colt who carries plenty of condition, Great Marquess usually impresses in appearance. He has a quick action. Yet

Doncaster Cup—the Champion Hurdler Morley Street (left)
gives Great Marquess a good race

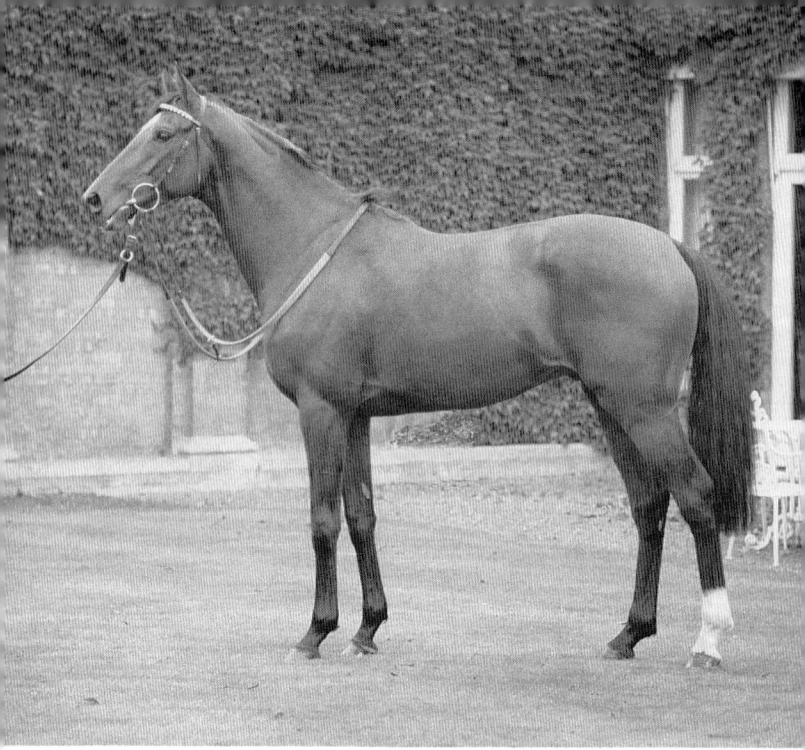

Mr C. A. B. St George's "Great Marquess"

		Roberto	Hail To Reason
	Touching Wood (USA)	(b 1969)	Bramalea
	(b 1979)	Mandera	Vaguely Noble
Great Marquess		(b 1970)	Foolish One
(b.c. 1987)		Rheingold	Faberge II
	Fruition	(br 1969)	Athene
	(b 1978)	Welsh Flame	Welsh Pageant
		(b 1973)	Electric Flash

to race on extremes of going, he acts on good to firm and disappointed in his only race on dead. Reportedly he has been bought by Sheikh Mohammed to race in Saudi Arabia. *H. R. A. Cecil.*

GREAT MAX (IRE) 2 b. or br.g. (May 15) Simply Great (FR) 122 – Lockwood **48** Girl 81 (Prince Tenderfoot (USA) 126) [1991 a7g⁶ 8f 8f⁵] IR 26,000Y: leggy, lengthy gelding: sixth living foal: half-brother to fairly useful 11.7f winner Dunphy's Special and a winner in Italy (both by Dunphy) and to Irish 1½m winner Sligunda (by Shardari): dam winning sprinter: poor maiden: best effort when fifth of 9 at Yarmouth in September: gives impression will stay quite well. *Sir Mark Prescott.*

GREAT MUSIC 3 ch.g. Music Boy 124 – Amadina 96 (Great Nephew 126) [1990 — 5f 5g² 5g⁶ 5m 1991 6d 5m 6f 8m 7g 7m 7.5f 6g] robust gelding: has a round action: quite modest form at 2 yrs, none at 3: bandaged behind final start: sold 1,400 gns Doncaster October Sales. *J. S. Wainwright.*

GREAT ORATION (IRE) 2 b. or br.c. (Apr 16) Simply Great (FR) 122 – Spun **61**
Gold 106 (Thatch (USA) 136) [1991 8m⁶ 8m] IR 19,000Y: rather leggy colt: has a
round action: first foal: dam 7f (at 2 yrs) and 12.2f winner, is daughter of useful 1¼m
to 1¾m winner Colourful, a close relative of smart staying filly Pink Gem: better for
race, keeping-on sixth of 19 in maiden at Doncaster in September, better effort:
heavily-backed favourite for large-field seller at Newmarket following month: will
stay middle distances: sold 1,600 gns Doncaster October Sales. *M. Bell.*

GREAT PALM (USA) 2 gr.c. (Apr 8) Manila (USA) – Hat Tab Girl (USA) **111** p
(Al Hattab (USA)) [1991 6g* 7m²]
The Three Chimneys Dewhurst runner-up Great Palm is just the type to
improve, possibly into a classic contender, in his second season. A leggy,
angular, unfurnished colt, by no means a precocious type, and bred to shine
over middle distances, Great Palm was restricted to just two races, over six
and seven furlongs, as a two-year-old, and it augurs well that he was able to
show such a useful level of form. York in August was the venue for his first
racecourse appearance. He lined up as second favourite of eleven for the
usually-informative Moorestyle Convivial Maiden Stakes, which has fallen to
such as In The Groove, Danehill and Local Suitor in recent years. Great Palm
won in good style, recording a particularly significant rating and timefigure
(102) for a newcomer, travelling comfortably tracking the heavily-backed
favourite Wesaam, quickening to challenge two furlongs out, taking Wesaam's
measure passing the furlong pole then forging two and a half lengths clear
under firm hands-and-heels riding. A most promising debut, and Great Palm
confirmed it with an excellent two-and-a-half-length second to the vastly
more experienced Dr Devious in the Dewhurst at Newmarket nearly two
months later, despite encountering problems handling the gradients on the
Rowley Mile. Entering the final quarter-mile Great Palm, who'd started to be
pushed along a furlong earlier, held every chance but he was never able to
utilize his long, smooth stride to full advantage on the falling ground in the
Dip, having to change his stride pattern several times, and really began to get
going only approaching the winning post. Not surprisingly, Great Palm was
immediately introduced prominently into the betting for the 1992 Derby, but
whether connections can follow up their victory with Generous must be open
to some doubt; Great Palm will have no difficulty staying a mile and a half but

Moorestyle Convivial Maiden Stakes, York—pleasing debuts by Great Palm and Wesaam

whether Epsom will suit him is another matter, and it may well be that a more level track such as the Curragh will turn out more in his favour.

Great Palm (USA) (gr.c. Apr 8, 1989)	Manila (USA) (b 1983)	Lyphard (b 1969)	Northern Dancer
			Goofed
		Dona Ysidra (b 1975)	Le Fabuleux
			Matriarch
	Hat Tab Girl (USA) (b 1979)	Al Hattab (ro 1966)	The Axe II
			Abyssinia
		Desperate Action (b 1971)	Bold Commander
			Crafty Alice

Great Palm is from the first crop of the top-class North American middle-distance turf performer Manila who built a formidable record on the racetrack before injury forced his retirement after eighteen races, twelve of which he won. Manila wasn't a precocious type either; he lost all his three starts at two but improved out of all recognition at three when he landed six graded events, including a defeat of Theatrical and Dancing Brave in the Breeders' Cup Turf, to earn himself an Eclipse Award. Manila had five races in his injury-curtailed third year, ending it with victory in the mile-and-a-quarter Arlington International. His first yearlings sold well at the American Sales in 1990; at 200,000 dollars, Great Palm fetched nearly 80,000 dollars more than the average. Great Palm's dam Hat Tab Girl was a useful performer who won six of her twenty-four races, including a minor stakes over an extended mile. Easily the best of her three other winning foals is the Miswaki horse Black Tie Affair, a grand performer who's won one or more graded stakes in each of the last four years and proved himself better than ever during the latest season when he put together a sequence of six wins in graded events which culminated in victory in the Breeders' Cup Classic. Neither the second dam Desperate Action nor third Crafty Alice won in other than minor company and the only other significant winner from the family in recent years is the Kentucky Derby third Reinvested. *P. F. I. Cole.*

GREAT PRECOCITY   4 b.c. Precocious 126 – Rip Roaring (Royal And Regal (USA)) [1990 NR 1991 a8g 7m 12m 7.1m] angular, close-coupled colt: second foal: half-brother to a winner in Italy by Wassl: dam unraced daughter of Arctic Melody, from family of Ardross: no form in varied company: blinkered: sold 1,500 gns Doncaster October Sales. *F. H. Lee.*   —

GREAT SERVICE   4 ch.c. Vaigly Great 127 – Janlarmar 69 (Habat 127) [1990 a8g4 a7g3 a8g4 a8g* a8g5 9s4 11v2 12d 12d 12.3g 16.2d a11g a14g 9f 8v5 8g* 8d3 1991 10.2s 10f 10.5d2] angular colt: has a rather round action: quite modest handicapper on his day: stays 11f: acts on heavy ground, seems unsuited by firm: tried blinkered once: has been bandaged near-hind: looks a hard ride: not one to trust implicitly. *G. M. Moore.*   55

GREAT SHOW   2 b.f. (Apr 16) Superlative 118 – Ex Dancer (USA) (Executioner (USA)) [1991 7.1m6 6m 7g3 8d5] 1,700F, 3,100Y: close-coupled filly: sister to plating-class maiden Panico and half-sister to several winners here and abroad, including 1½m winner Disciple (by Hello Gorgeous): dam Irish 6f winner at 4 yrs: plating-class maiden: raced keenly in median auction event at Wolverhampton final start, and appeared not to stay 1m: sold 4,000 gns Newmarket Autumn Sales. *H. Candy.*   54

GREAT STAR   3 ch.f. Vaigly Great 127 – Cracked Up (Busted 134) [1990 6f3 8f5 7d4 9m3 1991 10f3 8m 10.5d 10m] leggy, lengthy filly: moderate mover: quite modest maiden at 2 yrs: well beaten as 3-y-o, in sellers last 2 starts: stays 9f: acts on good to firm and dead ground: visored (edgy) final start. *E. Weymes.*   —

GREAT UNCLE   3 b.g. Uncle Pokey 116 – Petrinella 79 (Mummy's Pet 125) [1990 NR 1991 10g 12g] 1,700F, 5,000Y: leggy gelding: has high knee action: brother to 1987 2-y-o 5f and 6f winner Cousin Keeling and half-brother to 1986 2-y-o 5f winner The Granitton (by Free State): dam 2-y-o 6f winner: last in claimers. *C. J. Hill.*   —

GRECIAN BELLE   2 b.f. (Jan 14) Ilium 121 – Bourbon Queen 77 (Ile de Bourbon (USA) 133) [1991 5.1g 7m 7m] robust filly: first foal: dam, maiden, should have stayed 1¼m: 66/1, bit backward and green, only worthwhile form when around 8 lengths seventh of 8 in minor event at Bath in September, slowly away, pushed along halfway, late progress: never a factor in minor event (best effort) then maidens in autumn: bred to stay middle distances. *D. A. Wilson.*   53

GRECIAN REBEL   3 b.g. Absalom 128 – Navarino Bay 102 (Averof 123) [1990   **56** d
a7g⁵ 5m 7m⁵ 1991 a8g³ a10g⁴ a8g⁴ a8g⁶ 12s 10d a7g⁵ 8g] plain gelding: has a round
action: plating-class form in frame in varied company at Southwell in January:
should stay 1¼m: sold out of M. Bell's stable 2,000 gns Ascot May Sales after sixth
start: joined Grenville Richards. *D. J. Wintle.*

GREEK AIR (IRE)   2 b.f. (Mar 1) Ela-Mana-Mou 132 – Sea Singer (USA) 104   **107**
(Sea Bird II 145) [1991 8d 7v* 8v²] seventh live foal: sister to smart 1986 French
2-y-o 6.5f and 7f (awarded Criterium de Maisons-Laffitte) winner Grecian Urn, later
very smart 1m/1¼m performer: dam won over 1¼m: successful in maiden at
Saint-Cloud in October: improved again when 2½ lengths second of 7 to Litron in
Group 3 event at Evry following month: will stay 1¼m: yet to race on a sound
surface. *D. Smaga, France.*

GREEK CHIME (IRE)   2 gr.c. (May 4) Bellypha 130 – Corinth Canal 77 (Troy   **69** p
137) [1991 8d6] angular, workmanlike colt: rather unfurnished: third foal: half-
brother to 3-y-o 12.5f winner Sea War (by Gorytus): dam once-raced sister to Helen
Street: weak 10/1-shot, keeping-on sixth of 14 in minor event at Newmarket in
November: showed a moderate action: will stay 1¼m: sure to improve. *Lord
Huntingdon.*

GREEK TYCOON (IRE)   2 b.c. (May 8) Last Tycoon 116 – Praise (FR) 116   **87** p
(Hard To Beat 132) [1991 7f²] IR 40,000Y: good-topped colt: half-brother to many
winners, including one-time smart French middle-distance winner Extol (by Green
Dancer) and 3-y-o Commendable (by Baillamont), 1m winner at 2 yrs: dam smart
1¼m winner, is sister to good French middle-distance stayer Hard To Sing: 12/1, bit
backward and slowly away when keeping-on 1½ lengths second of 18 to Colorific in
maiden at Newbury in September: will stay 1m: sure to improve. *P. F. I. Cole.*

GREEN CHANNEL   2 b.c. (Apr 12) Import 127 – Greenhill's Girl 44 (Radetzky   —
123) [1991 5.9h⁵ 5m 6d 7m 7f] compact colt: first foal: dam 2-y-o 5f winner stayed 11f:
seems of little account. *D. Moffatt.*

GREENDALE (FR)   3 b.g. Green Desert (USA) 127 – Lastcomer (USA) 100   **80**
(Kris 135) [1990 6d4 1991 7g⁶ 9m 7.6m² 7.9m⁴ 8m³ 8.1d] quite attractive gelding: in
frame in minor event at Lingfield, £7,300 maiden at York and £11,200 handicap at
Newmarket: in need of race final start: stays 1m: takes good hold, and may do better
allowed to stride on: tends to sweat and get on edge. *C. E. Brittain.*

GREEN DANUBE (USA)   3 ch.f. Irish River (FR) 131 – Chere Amie (FR) (Gay   **92**
Mecene (USA) 128) [1990 7m 1991 7.6s* 10g* 10v 12d] neat filly: progressed well to
win maiden at Lingfield in June and £30,600 Leslie And Godwin Spitfire Handicap
(going away by 3½ lengths from Run Rings, leading 1½f out) at Goodwood in
August: behind in Group/Grade 2 events at Rome and Belmont Park last 2 starts:
stays 1¼m well. *Lord Huntingdon.*

GREEN DOLLAR   8 b.g. Tickled Pink 114 – Burglars Girl 63 (Burglar 128) [1990   **89**
6g 5m⁵ 6f⁵ 6m⁵ 6m* 6f⁵ 7g 6d 6m* 6f* 5m 6f⁴ 6m 6m 6m⁶ 6f³ 6h* 6m 5m⁵ 6m⁶ 6m⁶
6d 1991 6d 6.1m 6f* 6m* 6d² 6m 6d⁶ 6m² 6g 6f⁴ 6m⁴ 6g 5f⁴ 6g* 6m⁴] smallish
gelding: fair handicapper: won at Brighton (fifth win there) in May, Epsom (£8,560)
in June and York (£16,700 event) in September: best at 6f: acts on firm ground and
dead: has worn blinkers and visor, but not for some time: has run well when
sweating: tough and genuine. *E. A. Wheeler.*

*Leslie And Godwin Spitfire Handicap, Goodwood—
Green Danube draws away from Run Rings and the rest*

GREEN GLOW 3 b.g. Green Ruby (USA) 104 – Jonesee 64 (Dublin Taxi) [1990   **71**
6m⁴ 5d³ 5m* 5m³ 6d 8.2s⁴ 1991 6g³ 6g⁵ 7f³ 6g³ 6d⁴ 6m⁵ 7g 7.6g] sturdy gelding:
carries condition: poor mover: modest handicapper: below form last 3 outings,
struck into on penultimate one: seems best at 6f: acts on good to firm ground and
soft: visored fourth to sixth starts. *M. H. Tompkins.*

GREENHILLS JEWEL 5 gr.m. Mourtazam 120 – Antique Seeker 66 (Status   —
Seeker) [1990 NR 1991 5m 8f⁶ 10m 6f] leggy, sparely-made mare: poor mover:
second reported foal: half-sister to 1985 2-y-o 5f winner Greenhills Girl (by
Radetsky) also placed over 11f: dam 1¼m winner: well beaten in first half of 1991,
including in seller: hung left and put head in air second start. *J. R. Jenkins.*

GREENHILLS LAD (IRE) 3 b.c. Mazaad 106 – Kimstar 61 (Aureole 132)   **53**
[1990 5m 6m⁴ 7f³ 7f⁶ 7g⁶ 8g 7g 7d 1991 10g 8f² 8.5m² 10.2d* 10g⁴ 10g³ 10m⁶ 8.2f⁶
10m] small colt: keen walker: plating-class performer: won maiden claimer at Bath
in June: well below form final start: suited by 1¼m: acts on firm and dead going:
blinkered last 8 starts: has run creditably sweating and edgy: has looked a hard ride:
claimed out of R. Akehurst's stable £7,211 sixth outing. *A. S. Reid.*

GREENHILLS PRIDE 7 b.g. Sparkling Boy 110 – Soheir 74 (Track Spare 125)   —
[1990 11s9s⁶ 12m⁴ 11.5m³ 11g² 11g³ 13f³ 1991 10.8m 10d 12f⁴ 12g] tall, close-coupled
gelding: poor handicapper: stays 1½m: possibly unsuited by firm going, acts on any
other: has been tried in blinkers and visor. *J. R. Jenkins.*

GREENHILLS WARRIOR 5 ch.g. Tina's Pet 121 – Soheir 74 (Track Spare   —
125) [1990 NR 1991 10.1s] fourth living foal: half-brother to 2 middle-distance
winners: dam won over 10.2f: tailed off in Yarmouth claimer on debut on flat: won 13f
NH Flat race at Lingfield in March, 1990. *M. J. Ryan.*

GREEN LANE (IRE) 2 b.c. (Apr 25) Green Desert (USA) 127 – Road To The   **82** p
Top 84 (Shirley Heights 130) [1991 7g²] lengthy, rather unfurnished colt: fourth
foal: half-brother to fairly useful 1988 2-y-o 6f winner Road To Reason (by Known
Fact), later stayed 1½m: dam 1¼m winner, from good family: 8/1 and very green,
beaten a neck in a maiden at Warwick in October, chased along in touch then staying
on very well final 2f: will stay 1m: sure to improve and should win a maiden. *R.
Charlton.*

GREEN LANE (USA) 3 ch.g. Greinton 119 – Memory Lane (USA) 100 (Never   **84**
Bend) [1990 6m 8m* 8.2g 7g 8m⁶ 1991 10g 12g 11.7g³ 12m⁴ 12m⁴ 17.2g* 16.2m³
16.2f³ 16f³ 16.2f* 15.9m²] leggy, close-coupled gelding: good mover: fair handicapper: won at Bath in June and Beverley (more enterprisingly ridden than is often
the case, leading over 3f out) in August: finished strongly and beaten short head in
£7,100 event at Chester final start: consistent after given test of stamina: acts on
firm ground: gelded after final start. *I. A. Balding.*

GREEN LINE EXPRESS (USA) 5 ch.h. Green Forest (USA) 134 – Laylitna   **117**
(USA) (Key To The Mint (USA)) [1990 8m⁶ 7.6f* 8f² 8g 7g* 8m³ 9f³ 1991 6g* 6m
7.6g* 8g 9f] good-quartered, quite attractive horse: high-class performer at best:
not quite so good at 5 yrs: won Duke of York Stakes at York in May and listed event
at Lingfield (comfortably made all, beating Lee Artiste by 1½ lengths) in July:
behind in Cork And Orrery Stakes at Royal Ascot, Sussex Stakes at Goodwood and
Grade 1 Handicap at Monmouth Park, USA, other starts: effective at 6f to 9f: acts on
firm going: has run very well when sweating: used to wear tongue strap: genuine.
M. Moubarak.

GREEN MEDINA (IRE) 3 gr.f. Seattle Song (USA) 130 – Bernica (FR) 114   **84**
(Caro 133) [1990 NR 1991 10d⁵ 10f² 10.1m* 11.9mʷᵒ] well-made filly: has a quick
action: moderate walker: sixth foal: half-sister to several winners, including smart
1985 French 2-y-o 6f winner Excalibur's Lake (by Nureyev): dam, from very good
family, won 3 times at around 1m in France: fair form second start: landed odds in
maiden (again set pace) at Windsor by 2½ lengths from Sword's Point and walked
over in minor event at Haydock later in summer: sold 7,000 gns Newmarket
December Sales. *H. R. A. Cecil.*

GREENORE ROSE 5 b.m. Main Reef 126 – Sarah Purser (Upper Case (USA))   —
[1990 NR 1991 a8g a12g 9s 13d⁵ 12m] lengthy, workmanlike ex-Irish mare: no form
in 1991: trained first 4 starts by K. McCauley. *H. A. T. Whiting.*

GREEN'S BONHEUR 3 gr.f. Never So Bold 135 – Rectitude 99 (Runnymede   **53** d
123) [1990 NR 1991 a6g² a6g³ 8g 8m⁶ 7m a8g a5g] 22,000F, 31,000Y: angular, leggy
filly: sixth foal: half-sister to 4 winners, including useful 1985 2-y-o 7f winner
Normanby Lass (by Bustino): dam, daughter of smart Attitude, won at up to 8.5f:
plating-class form in maidens first 2 starts: should stay beyond 6f: blinkered fifth
start: trained first 5 by P. Cole. *M. P. Naughton.*

GREEN'S CASSATT (USA) 3 ch.f. Apalachee (USA) 137 – Royally Rewarded **63**
(USA) (Bold Forbes (USA)) [1990 5f² 5m² 6f* 7g² 1991 8s³ 7m⁴ 7.6d 7f⁴] leggy,
angular filly: moderate walker: quite modest form: well below form in summer
claimers last 2 starts: stays 1m: has form on any going: joined Mrs J. Evans. *P. F. I.
Cole.*

GREEN'S COLOURIST (USA) 2 b.c. (Mar 24) Lear Fan (USA) 130 – Anna **77**
Geranios (USA) (Raja Baba (USA)) [1991 6m² 7m² 7f² 8.2f³ 7m² 7m³ 7g³] $15,000F,
$52,000Y: good-bodied colt: has a round action: first foal: dam won 3 races in North
America and stakes placed at around 1m: modest maiden: consistent until below
best last 2 outings: stays 1m: has raced only on a sound surface: swished tail on
debut: sold 26,000 gns Newmarket Autumn Sales. *P. F. I. Cole.*

GREEN'S EXHIBIT 2 b.c. (Feb 22) Song 132 – Scotch Thistle 73 (Sassafras **52**
(FR) 135) [1991 6m⁵ 7.1s 6m³ 7g 7f³ 9m 8m a8g] 10,000F, 8,000Y: leggy, close-
coupled colt: moderate mover: half-brother to several winners, including modest 1m
to 10.4f winner Flying Scotsman (by Tower Walk) and 7f winner Scotch Rocket (by
Roan Rocket): dam placed at up to 1½m: plating-class maiden: well beaten last 3
starts, on equitrack final one: stays 7f: best form on firm ground: sold 700 gns Ascot
November Sales. *R. Akehurst.*

GREEN'S FERNELEY (IRE) 3 gr.c. Taufan (USA) 119 – Rossaldene 79 **99**
(Mummy's Pet 125) [1990 7m³ 7m* 8.2d³ 8m³ 8v 1991 8.2d* 10g⁵ 10.4d⁴ 10d 8m⁴
8.3m* 11.1m⁴ 8m³] leggy colt: quite useful performer: made most to win minor
events at Nottingham in April and Windsor (rallied well) in August: acted as
pacemaker (as on fourth outing) when creditable fourth of 5 in September Stakes at
Kempton: effective at 1m, seemingly at 11f: yet to race on very firm ground, acts on
any other: blinkered last 2 starts at 2 yrs: trained first 3 at 3 yrs by W. Haggas: game.
R. Charlton.

GREENSIDE 3 b.f. Hotfoot 126 – Akola (Hard Tack 111§) [1990 a5g⁴ a6g² a7g² **—**
7.5f 7f³ 7h a6g a7g a8g 1991 a7g⁵ a7g 11.8m] angular, sparely-made filly: poor
maiden: showed nothing final start, first on flat for 7½ months: stays 7f: best efforts
on all-weather: joined N. Smith. *R. Thompson.*

GREEN SIDE (USA) 4 b.f. Green Dancer (USA) 132 – Belka (FR) 115 **37**
(Riverman (USA) 131) [1990 11g⁵ 10.3d³ 11.5d 11g 10.7g* 11g⁴ 1991 10.1s 8.3g 8m
a12g 10s⁵ 8.1g⁴ 10m⁵ 10g 10.8g⁵ 8m 9.7s] tall, lengthy ex-French filly: second foal:
dam won over 1m, including in Group 3 event, in France: won maiden at Le
Croise-Laroche in 1990: poor handicapper here: blinkered and tailed off in seller
final start: should stay 1½m: acts on good to firm ground and dead: trained at 3 yrs
by Mme C. Head. *T. Casey.*

*Duke of York Stakes, York—Green Line Express drops down to six furlongs
and wins from Nicholas (almost hidden) and La Grange Music*

GREEN'S LE SIDANER (USA) 3 b.g. Ziggy's Boy (USA) – Matriarchal **70** (USA) (Pronto) [1990 NR 1991 7f² 6d² 6s² 6f* 7m⁴ 6f⁶ 5f] $25,000Y: smallish, workmanlike gelding: has a round action: half-brother to several winners in USA, one in minor stakes: dam ran 4 times: sire won at up to 1m: modest handicapper: won 4-runner maiden at Thirsk in July, making most but hanging left final 1½f: below form last 2 starts: stays 7f: acts on any going: refused to enter stalls on intended debut: sold 7,400 gns Newmarket Autumn Sales. *P. F. I. Cole.*

GREEN SLIPPERS 2 br.f. (Mar 4) Green Dancer (USA) 132 – Our Reverie **— p** (USA) (J O Tobin (USA) 130) [1991 8.9d] leggy, close-coupled filly: first known foal: dam winner at up to 11f, is half-sister to good-class Sharrood: 10/1 and green, slowly away, brief headway early in straight then eased right down when beaten in 19-runner maiden at Wolverhampton in October: should improve. *G. Harwood.*

GREEN'S MOILLON (USA) 3 b.f. Hagley (USA) – My Mademoiselle (USA) **31** (Buckaroo (USA)) [1990 5g⁶ 5f⁵ 6m a6g 5.1m⁵ 8m⁶ 8.2g 7f 1991 6m 10d a7g³ 6m a7g 7m 8m] close-coupled filly: poor walker: has a round action: poor plater: stays 7f: best 3-y-o effort on fibresand: visored fifth outing: trained until after then by J. Harris. *C. R. Beever.*

GREEN'S SEAGO (USA) 3 ch.g. Fighting Fit (USA) – Ornamental (USA) **62** (Triple Crown (USA)) [1990 a5g⁵ 5m⁴ 6m⁶ 6m³ 5m⁴ 8m⁴ 7m⁴ 8.2d a8g a8g* a7g² a8g 1991 a7g* a8g a7g² a8g 7d 8m] rather sparely-made gelding: easy mover: quite modest performer: made all in claimer at Southwell in January: off course 9 months, then showed signs of retaining ability last 2 outings: effective at 7f to 1m: acts well on all-weather surfaces, best turf form on top-of-the-ground: has tended to hang: none too consistent: retained 2,700 gns Doncaster March Sales. *J. L. Harris.*

GREEN'S STUBBS 4 b.g. Ballad Rock 122 – Aventina 83 (Averof 123) [1990 6m **43** 6m 6m 1991 7g 5m 6m 5.8f 5.1m⁴ 6.1d⁵ 5d 6g 6g² 5m⁵ 8f 5.1m 5.7f³ 5.1s 5.1d a6g] close-coupled gelding: has a sharp action: poor handicapper nowadays: stays 6f: acts on firm and dead ground: tried blinkered once: inconsistent. *A. Barrow.*

GREEN'S THORBURN (USA) 3 b. or br.g. Vaguely Noble 140 – Halo Again **—** (USA) (Halo (USA)) [1990 NR 1991 10.1g 11.1d⁶ 10g 9.7f 16m] $75,000Y: unfurnished gelding: half-brother to a 2-y-o winner in North America by Vice Regent: dam won at up to 9f in North America: no sign of ability in maidens and (sweating) sellers: has sweated: sold out of W. Jarvis' stable 2,600 gns Newmarket July Sales after third start. *A. Moore.*

GREEN'S VAN GOYEN (IRE) 3 b.g. Lyphard's Special (USA) 122 – Maiden **65** Concert (Condorcet (FR)) [1990 6m 7g 7g 1991 8m⁵ 12g⁵ 12m* 12g 11.5g⁶] workmanlike, lengthy gelding: has a quick action: quite modest performer: below form after winning claimer at Goodwood in May, making virtually all: one paced, and worth a try over further: sold 6,500 gns Newmarket July Sales: genuine: winning hurdler. *R. Akehurst.*

GREEN TURBAN 3 b.c. Shareef Dancer (USA) 135 – Miss Petard 113 (Petingo **93** 135) [1990 7g⁵ 8m 1991 12g 8g* 8m 8m* 8m⁴ 10m* 10m⁵ 10.3d] small, sturdy colt: fairly useful performer: won maiden at Pontefract (made all) in June, handicap at Newcastle in July and claimer at Ayr in September: effective at 1m and 1¼m: acts on good to firm ground: takes keen hold: game: sold 45,000 gns Newmarket Autumn Sales, to Scandinavia. *B. W. Hills.*

GREENWICH BAMBI 3 b.f. Music Boy 124 – Coca (Levmoss 133) [1990 5m⁴ **62** 5f⁴ 6d⁵ 7d⁴ 1991 8g 8d 10m⁶ 12.3m a10g³ 9.7f⁴ 11.9f² 10g* 11.9g* 12g³] rather unfurnished filly: quite modest performer: easily best 3-y-o efforts last 3 starts, winning seller (bought in 3,800 gns) at Leicester and handicap at Brighton in September: best at middle distances: has form on firm ground, best efforts on good. *W. Carter.*

GREENWINE (USA) 5 br.g. Green Dancer (USA) 132 – Princesse Margo **—** (Targowice (USA)) [1990 NR 1991 10g] workmanlike gelding: fifth foal: half-brother to French 1¼m winner Queen Margaret (by Val de L'Orne): dam unraced: trained by Mme C. Head, quite useful maiden in France: never placed to challenge or knocked about in claimer at Goodwood in June, first run on flat here: won over hurdles in April: sold to join Mrs L. Clay's stable 7,400 gns Ascot Summer Sales. *J. Akehurst.*

GREETLAND FOLLY 2 ch.f. (Apr 22) Crofthall 110 – Bit of A State 68 (Free **82** State 125) [1991 5m 5f⁵ 6m* 6f² 6d* 6m⁵ 7m 7g 7m³ 6m³ 6m] neat filly: second reported foal: dam, a plater, ideally suited by 1m: fair performer: won maiden at Hamilton in May and minor event at Pontefract in July: ran well in nurseries last 3 starts: stays 7f: acts on firm and dead ground: ran poorly in visor eighth outing. *R. M. Whitaker.*

GREETLAND ROCK   3 ch.g. Ballacashtal (CAN) – Zamindara (Crofter (USA)   **57**
124) [1990 a5g a6g⁴ 5m² 5m⁴ 5f* 5m³ 5v⁶ a5g⁴ 1991 5m⁴ 5f³ 5g a5g³ a5g* 5d³ a 71
5m³ 5m⁵ 5.1f⁴ 5g⁵ 5.3f³ a5g* 5f³ 5g² 5m⁴ 5m 5g³ 5m⁵ a5g] neat gelding: quite
modest sprint handicapper: won at Southwell in June and August: acts on firm
ground, seems unsuited by heavy: blinkered after tenth start, except when below
form on sixteenth: sometimes bandaged near-fore late on: consistent: sold P.
Howling 6,200 gns Doncaster November Sales. *J. Berry.*

GREY AREA   4 gr.c. Petong 126 – Little Mercy 90 (No Mercy 126) [1990 7m² 7f⁶   **47**
1991 7f⁴ 7.6g 7m 7m³ a7g 11m 6d³ 6.1m⁵ 7m 6.9m⁶] good-topped colt: plating-class
handicapper nowadays: stays 7f: acts on firm and dead ground: mostly blinkered in
1991: bandaged: inconsistent. *Mrs N. Macauley.*

GREY BUT ROSY (IRE)   2 gr.f. (Apr 28) Kafu 120 – Rossaldene 79 (Mummy's   **45**
Pet 125) [1991 5m 5.1m⁴ 6g⁶ 7g⁶ 6m] IR 12,000Y: leggy filly: half-sister to several
winners, including fairly useful 1985 2-y-o 5f winner Lammastide (by Martinmas)
and 3-y-o Green's Ferneley (by Taufan), 7f (at 2 yrs) to 8.3f winner: dam 2-y-o 5f
winner: poor form in varied events, including seller: stays 6f: acts on good to firm
ground: wears bandages: has run well for 7-lb claimer. *D. R. C. Elsworth.*

GREY CHARMER (IRE)   2 gr.c. (Apr 2) Alzao (USA) 117 – Sashi Woo   **66**
(Rusticaro (FR) 124) [1991 5g⁵ 5m 6d⁵ 5m³ 6f* 5m 6g 6g 6m] 11,000Y: close-coupled
colt: moderate mover: fourth foal: dam lightly-raced Irish maiden: quite modest
performer: won maiden auction at Brighton in August: will probably stay 7f: acts on
firm and dead ground: hung badly left fourth outing and appeared not to go through
with effort. *C. James.*

GREY COMMANDER   3 gr.c. Grey Desire 115 – Melowen 75 (Owen Dudley   **45**
121) [1990 5m⁵ 6g⁵ a5g³ 6g 8d 1991 10d 8s⁵ 10d⁵ 12.5m⁵ a12g 12d* 13.8g³ 11. 1d³ a14g⁶
15.1s a14g⁵ a12g² a12g] leggy, sparely-made colt: moderate mover: won selling
handicap (bought in 4,200 gns) at Pontefract in July: good second in claimer at
Southwell, easily best effort last 5 outings: stays 13.8f: goes well on a soft surface:
usually bandaged behind. *M. Brittain.*

GREY DANCER   3 gr.c. Petong 126 – Infelice (Nishapour (FR) 125) [1990 8g 7g   **46**
10.2s 1991 8g⁵ 10g a12g⁴] compact colt: poor form: good fourth in maiden at Lingfield
in December, first run for 5 months: stays 1½m: possibly unsuited by soft going:
trained first 2 starts by C. Allen. *J. White.*

GREY DECISION   2 gr.c. (Mar 3) Grey Desire 115 – Miss Realm 86 (Realm 129)   **—**
[1991 6m] leggy, close-coupled colt: fourth foal: half-brother to quite modest 1989
2-y-o 5f winner Spanish Realm (by King of Spain), multiple winner in Scandinavia in
1991: dam 2-y-o 5f winner: 50/1, last of 12 in maiden at Redcar in October. *M. Brittain.*

GREY ILLUSIONS   3 gr.g. Nishapour (FR) 125 – Morica 88 (Moorestyle 137)   **59**
[1990 6g 6d⁶ 6g² 1991 7m 7d⁵ 7.6s⁵ 8.1d⁶ 7m⁶ 7f] strong gelding: moderate walker:
quite modest maiden: stays 1m: acts on good to firm ground and soft: sweating and
edgy last few starts. *L. J. Holt.*

GREY MERLIN   4 gr.g. Derrylin 115 – Sea Kestrel 82 (Sea Hawk II 131) [1990 8g   **32**
8m⁶ 8.2d² 10.4g⁵ 9g 8.2v⁶ 1991 8.2s 12g 12m 8h 9m 15s⁶] sturdy gelding: has a
markedly round action: plating-class maiden at 3 yrs: well below form in 1991:
visored (seemed to take little interest) on reappearance, blinkered next 2 starts:
stays 1¼m: acts on dead going: temperament under suspicion: sold 3,000 gns
Doncaster Summer Sales. *A. Harrison.*

GREY POWER   4 gr.f. Wolf Power (SAF) – Periquito (USA) (Olden Times) [1990   **76**
8f² 10.2m² 11m 12m⁶ 12m³ 13.3g³ 1991 11.5d² 12g³ 14.8s³ 14m 12m 12.1s*]
good-topped filly: modest handicapper: won at Hamilton in November: claimed out
of Lord Huntingdon's stable £9,475 time before: stays 14.8f: acts on good to firm and
soft ground. *Miss L. A. Perratt.*

GREY RECORD   3 gr.c. Grey Desire 115 – Record Lady (Record Token 128)   **55**
[1990 6g 6d³ 5v³ a7g⁶ 1991 7d³ 7v³ 7.5g⁴ 10g 9d 8m 9.2s 11.1s⁶] rather angular colt:
shows knee action: plating-class maiden: fair sixth in claimer at Edinburgh, best
effort for some time: may well stay 11f: acts on heavy going: ran moderately on
fibresand. *M. Brittain.*

GREY RUM   6 gr.g. Absalom 128 – Cuba Libre (Rum (USA)) [1990 a7g a6g⁵ a7g³   **—**
7m⁵ 7.5m³ 8f 7g 8.2m 6f⁵ 8f³ 7.6m² 7f³ 7m⁵ 7f* 7f² 6m² 7m 7m 1991 8m]
workmanlike gelding: plating-class handicapper: heavily bandaged, no show in
Redcar amateurs event in September: effective over stiff 6f to 1m: acts on any going:

effective with or without blinkers: good mount for inexperienced rider: winning hurdler. *R. Lee.*

GREY SONATA 4 gr.f. Horage 124 – The Grey (GER) (Pentathlon) [1990 11.7f — 8f⁶ 6m 7m 1991 8.9m] leggy filly: poor walker and mover: quite modest maiden at best: well beaten only run in 1991: stays 1m: acts on firm going: tried blinkered once: has looked unsatisfactory. *C. L. Popham.*

GREY STARLING 3 b.f. Pharly (FR) 130 – Jolly Bay 108 (Mill Reef (USA) 141) **70 ?** [1990 8g 7m⁶ 1991 10m⁶ 8d 7f⁵ 8.9m 7m⁴ 7g a7g⁶] rather leggy, quite attractive filly: quite modest handicapper: below form last 2 outings, blinkered first of them: best form at 7f: acts on firm going: sold 3,400 gns Newmarket December Sales. *R. Charlton.*

GREY TUDOR 4 gr.g. Import 127 – Grey Morley 78 (Pongee 106) [1990 a6g⁶ 5f **34** 5s² 7g 5g a7g 7m 10f³ 10f 10m 6m⁶ 6g 6d* 5s⁴ a6g a6g⁴ a7g 1991 6v 6s a5g⁵ 6d⁵ 6d 6.1d a6g] leggy, workmanlike gelding: plating-class handicapper at best: should prove suited by at least 6f: probably acts on any going: tried blinkered once. *C. N. Allen.*

GREY WOLF 4 gr.g. Bellypha 130 – Matinee 119 (Zeddaan 130) [1990 6f⁴ 6m² — a7g 5.8h³ 6m 8f a8g⁶ a8g a6g⁵ 1991 a6g⁶] tall gelding: poor mover: modest maiden at best: should have stayed beyond 6f: dead. *K. O. Cunningham-Brown.*

GRIS ET VIOLET (FR) 4 ch.g. Iron Duke (FR) 122 – Darkeuse (FR) (Dark — Tiger) [1990 12m 1991 16.2g] workmanlike gelding: moderate mover: twice raced on flat and well beaten in modest company: winning hurdler as 3-y-o. *J. G. FitzGerald.*

GROG (IRE) 2 b.c. (Apr 25) Auction Ring (USA) 123 – Any Price (Gunner B 126) **66** [1991 5g 5m 7g⁵ 7g 7f 7g³ 7g 8m 10m⁶ a8g⁴ a8g* a7g⁶] IR 9,000F, 9,400Y: strong, compact colt: carries condition: has a round action: fourth foal: dam once-raced half-sister to smart 1982 2-y-o 6f and 7f winner All Systems Go: 16/1, made all in late-year Southwell maiden, beating Receptionist 2 lengths: inconsistent otherwise, and twice well beaten in sellers: stays 1m: best form on easy ground and fibresand: raced freely in visor fifth outing. *M. R. Channon.*

GRONDOLA 4 b.f. Indian King (USA) 128 – Trysting Place (He Loves Me 120) — [1990 a8g* a10g⁶ a10g³ 8.5m⁵ 10f³ 8g⁶ 8m 1991 8f] leggy, close-coupled filly: plating-class performer at best: tailed off only start in 1991: keen sort, seems best at 1m. *D. Burchell.*

GROUSE-N-HEATHER 2 gr.f. (May 18) Grey Desire 115 – Heldigvis 63 (Hot — Grove 128) [1991 7m⁶ 7s] third foal: dam 2-y-o 7f and 1m winner: no worthwhile form, including in seller. *Mrs G. R. Reveley.*

GROVE SERENDIPITY (IRE) 3 b.g. Glenstal (USA) 118 – Huppel 83 **71** (Huntercombe 133) [1990 6m 7g⁶ 7f² 7m 7.6v⁶ 1991 12m a12g* 14g 16m⁵ 12g² a **76** 11.5s⁵] close-coupled, workmanlike gelding: modest performer: won maiden at Southwell in August: easily best effort in handicaps afterwards when beaten neck at Goodwood: should stay 1¾m: acts on firm going: visored last 3 starts. *A. Hide.*

GROWING POWER 7 b.g. Red Sunset 120 – Margaree (Energist) [1990 NR — 1991 15g] close-coupled gelding: second foal: half-brother to Gods Lane (by Godswalk), Irish 5f and 6f winner: dam bad Irish maiden: ex-Irish gelding: won 1½m handicap at Clonmel as 3-y-o: first run on flat since, soon tailed off in Edinburgh seller in June: stays 1½m. *P. Liddle.*

GROWN AT ROWAN 4 b.f. Gabitat 119 – Hallo Rosie 67 (Swing Easy (USA) **66** 126) [1990 6h⁶ 5.3h³ 5g² 6f³ 5m² 5m² 7m* 8g 6m⁶ 1991 6g 7m⁶ 8f 7.6d 7m³ 6m² 6m 6g² 6g⁴ 7g] rather leggy filly: moderate mover: quite modest handicapper: probably best at 6f or 7f: acts on hard ground: inconsistent. *M. Madgwick.*

GRUBBY 2 b.f. (Apr 9) Green Ruby (USA) 104 – Via Vitae 67 (Palm Track 122) **44** [1991 5m⁶ 5m 6.1m 5g a6g] workmanlike filly: first reported foal: dam 6f winner: poor sprint maiden. *R. Hollinshead.*

GRUNDONIAN 3 b.g. Tina's Pet 121 – Sound Type 92 (Upper Case (USA)) **54** [1990 NR 1991 10.1d⁴ 10.1m⁵ 10m 16.1g] 14,000Y: small, lengthy gelding: good walker: sixth foal: half-brother to 9f and 1¼m seller winner Final Sound (by Final Straw) and a winner in Belgium by Busted: dam 7f and 1¼m winner: plating-class maiden: showed little in handicap final start: stays 1¼m. *C. A. Horgan.*

GUADALCANAL (IRE) 3 b.c. Sadler's Wells (USA) 132 – Red Coral (AUS) — (Red God 128§) [1990 NR 1991 11.7m] 200,000Y, 5,200 2-y-o: brother to French 11.5f winner Rayonne and half-brother to 2 winners, notably useful 5f and 6f winner Tarib (by Habitat): dam graded winner in Australia: extremely green and moved very poorly to post, soon tailed off in maiden at Bath: sold 1,000 gns Newmarket July Sales. *P. W. Chapple-Hyam.*

GUAPA 3 b.f. Shareef Dancer (USA) 135 – Sauceboat 120 (Connaught 130) [1990 8g 1991 8.2d* 8.5f⁴ 8m* 8f² 8m² 8g⁵ 7g] lengthy, leggy filly: fair performer: won maiden at Hamilton in April and handicap at Wolverhampton in August: may prove best at 1m: best efforts on top-of-the-ground, though won on dead: takes keen hold. *M. R. Stoute.* **80**

GUECA SOLO 3 ch.f. Pharly (FR) 130 – Atitlan (Relko 136) [1990 6m⁶ 1991 8g* 10m² 9m³ 7g⁵] small, sparely-made filly: has a round action: fairly useful at best: won maiden at Yarmouth in July by 8 lengths: ran moderately in apprentice race and minor event (first run for 2½ months, soon ridden along) last 2 outings: effective at 1m and 1¼m. *H. R. A. Cecil.* **93**

GUEST PLAYER 4 ch.f. Horage 124 – Guestaway (Be My Guest (USA) 126) [1990 8g 7g² 7d⁴ 8g⁵ 7m 8g⁶ 7g³ 7d⁴ 7m* 7.5d 6s 8g⁴ 1991 5m 8f⁵ 10.1s 8g 8m 10.1m 13.1m³] sparely-made filly: first foal: has round action: dam placed from 6f to 7.9f in Ireland: ex-Irish filly: won maiden at Down Royal in 1990 when trained by J. Hayden: quite modest handicapper at best here: stays 13f: acts on good to firm ground and dead: sometimes blinkered (including when successful), not in 1991. *D. J. Wintle.* **60**

GUEST RIGHT 4 b.c. Be My Guest (USA) 126 – Miss Allowed (USA) (Alleged (USA) 138) [1990 8.2s 8v 8.2g² 11g 12d⁶ 10g 9m 10.5g⁶ 10d 1991 a12g⁴ 10.8g 12d³ 12g* 12d² 12.4m 11s³] lengthy, angular colt: plating-class handicapper: won at Edinburgh in April: not seen out after July: stays 1½m well: best efforts with some give in the ground (acts on soft ground): tough and genuine. *M. Brittain.* **53**

GUIDO DA SPOLETO (IRE) 3 b.g. Hatim (USA) 121 – Divine Fleece (Status Seeker) [1990 NR 1991 5m 5g³ 6s⁴ 6m 8f] IR 14,000F, IR 6,500Y: sturdy gelding: eighth foal: half-brother to 4 winners, including fairly useful 1988 2-y-o 7f winner Divine Guest (by What A Guest): dam second over 7f and 7.9f in Ireland: well beaten, in handicap penultimate start: blinkered on debut: refused to race final appearance: sold 520 gns Doncaster October Sales. *Dr J. D. Scargill.* **— §**

GUILTY SECRET (IRE) 2 ch.f. (Jun 14) Kris 135 – Miss Toshiba (USA) 113 (Sir Ivor 135) [1991 7m² 7m⁶] rangy, rather unfurnished filly: fluent mover: sister to fairly useful 7f and 1m winner Oriental Mystique and half-sister to several winners: dam won from 7f to 1½m, including in USA where very smart: 1½ lengths second of 8 to Freewheel in minor event at Newbury in September, green when pushed along 3f out, running on strongly closing stages: never travelling well when well-backed favourite for maiden at Newmarket 2 weeks later: will be suited by 1m+: worth another chance to confirm promise of debut. *P. W. Chapple-Hyam.* **74 p**

GUISLAINE (FR) 2 br.f. (Apr 1) Tropular – Clodette (FR) (Ben Trovato (FR)) [1991 6d³ 6g 6g* 7d* 7m³ 7m⁶ 8g* 8d⁴] second foal: half-sister to French 8.5f winner Claus (by Sky Lawyer): dam French 7f and 1m winner also successful over jumps: sire (by Troy) French 1m and 9.2f winner: successful in minor events at Evry in July and Prix d'Aumale (by a nose from Hatoof) at Longchamp in September: creditable 1½ lengths fourth of 13 finishers, staying on well, to Culture Vulture in Prix Marcel Boussac at Longchamp: will be suited by 1¼m: blinkered first 6 outings: trained first 5 by B. Vanheeghe. *P. Bary, France.* **107**

GULFLAND 10 ch.g. Gulf Pearl 117 – Sunland Park (Baragoi 115) [1990 a12g³ 12g² 12m² 12.4m⁵ 12g* a12g⁵ 12d⁶ 12m* 12.2m 12g 1991 12g 12g² 12m³ 13d⁶ 12m⁵ 11.5s] workmanlike, good-bodied gelding: carries condition: moderate mover: poor handicapper nowadays: suited by 1½m: acts on any going: held up: has won for amateur. *G. A. Pritchard-Gordon.* **45 d**

GULF PALACE (USA) 6 ch.h. Green Dancer (USA) 132 – Sanctum Sanctorum (USA) (Secretariat (USA) [1990 12m² 12d⁵ 10m² 10m 12f² 12f³ 12s³ 1991 12g 12g³ 11.9g* 12m 11.9d² 11g 12d] rangy, well-made horse: moderate mover, with a quick action: fairly useful handicapper: won strongly-run £11,800 event at York in August: well beaten in November Handicap at Doncaster final start: stays 1½m well: acts on any going: usually held up: largely consistent. *R. Akehurst.* **92**

GULF SAILOR (IRE) 3 b.c. Darshaan 133 – Grecian Sea (FR) (Homeric 133) [1990 NR 1991 10m⁵ 10s⁴] quite attractive colt, shade unfurnished: fine mover: sixth foal: brother to Yorkshire Oaks winner and St Leger second Hellenic and half-brother to 3 winners, including useful 6f to 1½m winner Golden Wave (by Glint of Gold): dam won over 6f at 2 yrs in France: second favourite, fair form in maiden (edging right) at Newmarket and 5-runner £10,700 event at Ascot in the spring: should be better suited by 1½m. *M. R. Stoute.* **83**

GULMARG 4 b.c. Gorytus (USA) 132 – Kashmiri Snow 83 (Shirley Heights 130) **81**
[1990 7g⁵ 7f⁴ 8d² 8m⁴ 8f* 9m* 9m 1991 8d 7g 7d 7.6d 7m] rangy, attractive colt: moderate mover: fairly useful handicapper at best: wearing dropped noseband, ran moderately after second start: off course over 5 months before final one: stays 9f: acts on firm and dead going: sold 14,000 gns Newmarket Autumn Sales: to be trained by M. Tompkins. *H. Candy.*

GUNNER STREAM 7 ch.g. Gunner B 126 – Golfers Dream 70 (Carnoustie 132) **—**
[1990 NR 1991 17.2g] big, angular, workmanlike gelding: quite modest handicapper as 3-y-o: brought down at Bath in October, first start on flat since: stays 9f well: acts on any going. *R. J. Holder.*

GUN RULE 7 ch.g. Posse (USA) 130 – Brave Lass 114 (Ridan (USA)) [1990 NR **57**
1991 a7g a7g⁵] big, workmanlike gelding: carries plenty of condition: has scar on near quarter: bad mover: quite modest handicapper nowadays: should stay 1m: acts on firm ground, possibly unsuited by soft. *D. R. Laing.*

GUNRUNNER GIRL 4 ch.f. Longleat (USA) 109 – Witchingham Lass 83 **—**
(Sweet Revenge 129) [1990 7m 7f 5m 1991 12f] rangy, rather unfurnished filly: seems of little account. *R. Voorspuy.*

GURTEEN BOY 9 ch.g. Tickled Pink 114 – Joie d'Or (FR) (Kashmir II 125) [1990 **—**
13s³ 12s 1991 13d] strong, sturdy, plain gelding: had a round action: showed signs of stringhalt: poor handicapper: stayed 13f: went particularly well with plenty of give in the ground: was tried in blinkers, visor and hood: dead. *J. J. O'Neill.*

GUSHY 5 ch.g. Hard Fought 125 – Be Gustful (Ballymore 123) [1990 8.2s 8v 8m³ **—**
8m* 8.2s³ 8f⁵ 8m* 8m⁵ 8g⁵ 8d³ 8m⁶ 8f³ 1991 a8g a10g a11g] smallish, workmanlike gelding: moderate walker and mover: fairly useful plater at 4 yrs: tailed off in 1991: best form at 1m: acts on any going: usually blinkered or visored. *C. R. Beever.*

GUSSY MARLOWE 3 b.f. Final Straw 127 – Lady Lorelei 105 (Derring-Do 131) **118**
[1990 NR 1991 8m³ 10g* 10.5m* 8g³ 10g⁴ 11.9g] strong, close-coupled filly: did well physically: third foal: half-sister to 10.6f winner Athene Noctua (by Aragon): dam 5f to 1m winner: successful in smallish fields for Pretty Polly Stakes at Newmarket and Tattersalls Musidora Stakes (by head from Dartrey) at York in May: 2¼ lengths third of 8 to Kooyonga in Coronation Stakes at Royal Ascot: ran moderately in Nassau Stakes at Goodwood and Yorkshire Oaks at York last 2 starts: should stay 1½m: goes well with forcing tactics: very game. *C. E. Brittain.*

GYMCRAK CYRANO (IRE) 2 b.f. (Mar 24) Cyrano de Bergerac 120 – Sun **61**
Gift (Guillaume Tell (USA) 121) [1991 6d⁶ 6.9m³ 7m² 7.1m* a7g 7.1m³ 9m² 8m⁶ 7.6d⁵ 8.3s] IR 3,000F, 7,200Y: small, leggy filly: fourth foal: half-sister to 3-y-o 1½m winner Golden Gunner (by Mazaad) and 1989 2-y-o 6f winner Times Gift (by Burslem): dam unraced: quite modest performer: retained 6,200 gns after winning seller at Edinburgh in August: stays 9f: consistent on good to firm ground: ran moderately only on a soft surface and on fibresand. *M. H. Easterby.*

Tattersalls Musidora Stakes, York —
Gussy Marlowe (rails) responds most genuinely to beat off Dartrey, Shamshir and Ristna

Mrs John Van Geest's "Gussy Marlowe"

GYMCRAK DANCER 2 b.f. (Apr 30) Pennine Walk 120 – Silent Sun 90   **45**
(Blakeney 126) [1991 5d⁵ 6g 7f⁵ 6g 5f⁵ 7m³ 7g⁴ 8m] 4,000Y: leggy, rather
sparely-made filly: has quick action: third foal: half-sister to 3-y-o Lady of Light (by
Glow) and 1989 2-y-o 6f to 1m winner Closed Shop (by Auction Ring): dam won over
1¼m here and 1m in France: quite modest plater: should prove suited by further
than 7f: acts on firm and dead ground: largely consistent. *M. H. Easterby.*

GYMCRAK MAJESTIC (IRE) 2 b.f. (Mar 4) Mister Majestic 122 –   —
Whichcombe 79 (Huntercombe 133) [1991 7m 6m 8m] IR 1,800F, 2,100Y: lengthy,
plain filly: half-sister to 9f seller winner Chart Cross (by Milfontaine), 2 winners
abroad and a winner over hurdles: dam second over 6f at 2 yrs on only start: well
beaten in maidens, including auctions. *M. H. Easterby.*

GYMCRAK PREMIERE 3 ch.g. Primo Dominie 121 – Oraston 115 (Morston   **98**
(FR) 125) [1990 5f² 1991 6g* 7m³ 8m* 9m* 8.2m³ 8m³ 8m² 10g 8m² 8.1m²]
lengthy, workmanlike gelding: fairly useful performer: successful in maiden and
handicap at Carlisle then £6,500 handicap (tending to idle) at York in the spring: ran
well afterwards when placed, including in Britannia Stakes at Royal Ascot: stays 9f:
acts on good to firm ground: genuine. *M. H. Easterby.*

GYMCRAK SOVEREIGN 3 b.g. Ballacashtal (CAN) – Get Involved 79 (Shiny   —
Tenth 120) [1990 6g 7.5g² 5f 7f 8d 8v 1991 11.8m 8m] leggy, quite good-topped
gelding: has a round action: poor performer: sweating, tailed off facing stiff tasks in
autumn handicaps: stays 1m: below form on extremes of ground. *M. H. Easterby.*

GYMCRAK TYCOON 2 b.c. (Apr 19) Last Tycoon 131 – Brazen Faced 84 (Bold   **74**
And Free 118) [1991 5m* 5.1f² 6g* 6m⁵] 6,000Y: leggy, close-coupled, quite
attractive colt: half-brother to several winners, including useful 7f and 1m winner
Sheer Cliff (by Shirley Heights) and useful sprinter Wanton (by Kris): dam 2-y-o 5f
winner: modest performer: successful in maiden at Wolverhampton and nursery

355

(impressively) at Leicester in late-summer: slowly away (ran moderately) final start: may stay 7f. *M. H. Easterby.*

GYPSY TRAIL (USA) 3 b.g. Darby Creek Road (USA) – Majestic Native (USA) **59** (Majestic Prince (USA)) [1990 8g* 8m 1991 8g⁵ 8s 10.1s 10.2m⁵ 12g⁴ 11.7g 11.4m 11.7g 16.1g⁶] sturdy, close-coupled gelding: moderate walker: second foal (both by Darby Creek Road): dam, lightly-raced winner at around 7f in USA, is sister to smart American 1979 2-y-o Royal Suite: trained by A. Fabre until after reappearance, winning newcomers race at Deauville as 2-y-o: quite modest form here, running fairly well in handicap final start: best form here at 1½m: sold to join J. Joseph 4,200 gns Newmarket Autumn Sales. *M. E. D. Francis.*

H

HABAAYIB 3 ch.c. Blushing Groom (FR) 131 – Awaasif (CAN) 130 (Snow Knight **105** 125) [1990 7g² 1991 10g* 10.5g⁵ 12.3g* 11.9m² 12m² 12.1d⁵] leggy, good-topped colt: has a fluent, quick action: won maiden at Leicester in April and minor event at Ripon in May: second in £10,000 ladies race at York (below form, spoilt chance by hanging left) and 4-runner £11,200 event at Ascot (carried head rather high) in June: suited by 1½m: acts on good to firm ground, well below form on dead: tongue tied down second start: useful. *M. R. Stoute.*

HABETA (USA) 5 ch.h. Habitat 134 – Prise (Busted 134) [1990 10.2m* 8.2s⁴ **70** 8g⁶ 8m⁶ 8.2m⁶ 8g* 8g⁵ 8g⁴ a8g⁵ a10g⁴ 1991 8m* 8m 8m⁴ 8.2d³ 8m² 9m² 9f⁴ 8.9g 8m⁶ 8m 9g⁴ a8g⁶] quite good-topped horse: carries plenty of condition: modest handicapper: won at Ripon in April: also ran well on fifth to seventh outings: effective at 1m to 1¼m: acts on any going. *J. W. Watts.*

HACIENDA 4 b.g. Habitat 134 – Bare Minimum (Bustino 136) [1990 7f⁶ 10f⁶ 8g **72** a8g* a8g* 9m 8d a8g 1991 10.8m 8d 5m* 7.1d⁶ 5.9m* 6g³ 6d 5.9f³ 6g² 6g 6f 6m⁶ 6g⁶] well-made gelding: quite modest performer: won amateurs handicap at Hamilton in May and claimer (claimed out of D. Burchell's stable £7,022) at Carlisle in June: effective at 5f, and stays 1m: acts on good to firm and dead ground: inconsistent. *Mrs L. Stubbs.*

HACKFORTH 5 ch.h. Hard Fought 125 – Sweet And Sour 96 (Sharpen Up 127) **69** [1990 a8g³ a8g³ a7g³ a7g a7g⁵ 7m* 7f* 7.6d* a7g² 7.6g* 7.2g 7m 7g⁵ 7.6v 1991 8s 7g 8m 8m a7g* a7g 7m 7.6g] neat horse: has done well physically: quite modest handicapper: blinkered and wearing eyeshield, easily best effort at 5 yrs when winning at Southwell in May (made all): best at 7f to 1m: acts on firm and dead going (unsuited by heavy): used to be held up: visored penultimate start. *C. Tinkler.*

HADAAD (USA) 2 ch.c. (Feb 17) Mr Prospector (USA) – Etoile d'Amore (USA) **79** 81 (The Minstrel (CAN) 135) [1991 7g⁶ 6g⁴ 5.9h² 7g*] good-topped colt: has plenty of scope: third foal: half-brother to modest 1989 2-y-o maiden Loving Omen (by Touching Wood): dam twice-raced 7f winner, is out of high-class sprinter Gurkhas Band: progressive form: won nursery at Redcar in September, despite hanging left and needing plenty of driving: better suited by 7f than 6f. *A. A. Scott.*

HAFHAFAH 4 b.f. Shirley Heights 130 – Shurooq (USA) 94 (Affirmed (USA)) **53** [1990 8g 10.2f² 10g 10m⁵ 10f³ 10m 10m³ 9m³ 10m 1991 a10g 16.2g 10g 8.9g 8.3f* 8m] leggy, shallow-girthed filly: plating-class handicapper nowadays: form at 4 yrs only when 25/1-winner of claimer (claimed out of P. Haslam's stable £2,500) at Hamilton in September: stays 1¼m: needs top-of-the-ground. *Miss L. C. Siddall.*

HAIL AND BLEST (IRE) 3 b.c. Alzao (USA) 117 – Sarong 97 (Taj Dewan 128) **93** [1990 NR 1991 7m⁴ 7g* 7.6m* 8m 8m⁴ 7.9g 8m] 36,000Y: good-topped colt with scope: has fluent, round action: half-brother to several winners, including useful 5f and 1m winner Hindi and quite useful 1985 2-y-o 7f winner Illumineux (both by Mummy's Pet): dam 1m winner: won maiden at Goodwood in May and minor event (idling) at Lingfield in June: never dangerous in valuable handicaps last 2 starts: should stay beyond 1m: sold to Scandinavia 44,000 gns Newmarket Autumn Sales. *L. M. Cumani.*

HAILSHAM (CAN) 3 b.c. Riverman (USA) 131 – Halo's Princess (CAN) (Halo **113** (USA)) [1990 6g* 6m 7g 8m⁴ 1991 8m⁴ 10g* 10.5g² 12g* 12f 10d⁴ 12m] strong, lengthy colt: has a powerful, round action: very useful performer: contested only pattern events as 3-y-o, winning Thresher Classic Trial at Sandown in April and Derby Italiano at Rome in May: creditable fourth of 5 to Zoman in Scottish Classic at Ayr: set strong pace in King George VI and Queen Elizabeth Diamond Stakes at Ascot 2 weeks later: stays 1½m: best efforts with give in the ground. *C. E. Brittain.*

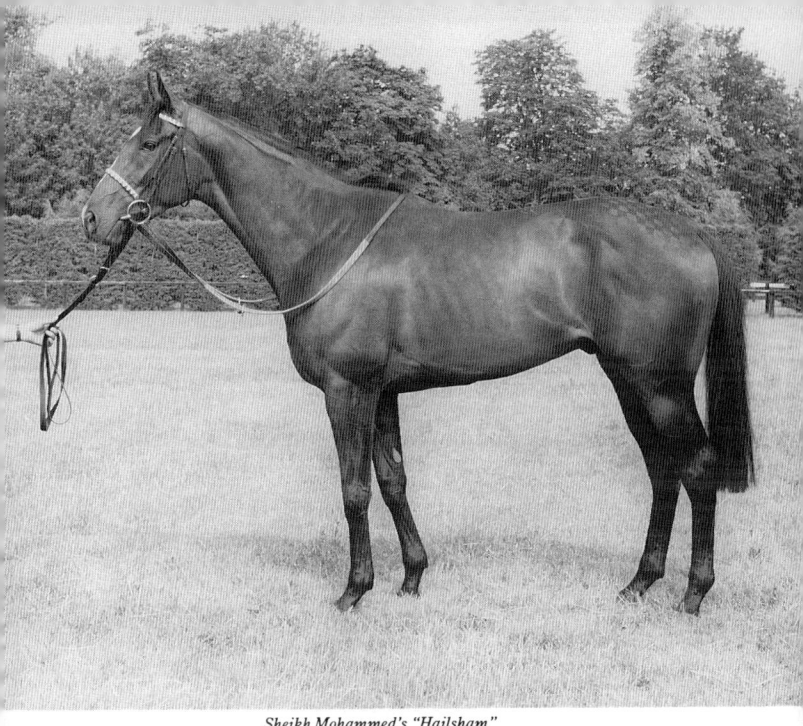

Sheikh Mohammed's "Hailsham"

HAITHAM 4 b.c. Wassl 125 – Balqis (USA) 93 (Advocator) [1990 10m⁴ 11f⁴ 14g* **95**
16.2d⁶ 12m³ 1991 14g⁵ 20g² 16d⁵ 16.1m³ 20g* 18m³ 16m⁶ 18m] rather leggy colt:
moderate mover: much improved for new stable in 1991: won £10,600 handicap at
Goodwood in July: appeared to put up easily best effort in moderately-run Doncaster
Cup sixth start: well beaten after at Newmarket in Jockey Club Cup and Tote
Cesarewitch: stays 2½m: acts on firm and dead ground: has been awkward at stalls,
broke out of them and withdrawn once. *R. Akehurst.*

HAJAIM (IRE) 3 ch.c. Doulab (USA) 115 – Sharrara (CAN) 61 (Blushing Groom **90**
(FR) 131) [1990 7m⁴ 7f* 7m 1991 7d⁴ 8.2m⁶ 7.6d* 10m⁵ 8m⁵ 10g* 11.9g* 10d] rather
leggy, attractive colt: has a quick action: fairly useful performer: won handicaps
at Chester in June, Newmarket in August and York (£14,900 event, quickened
impressively) in September: never travelling well final start: stays 1½m well: has
won on firm going, but best form with some give: sometimes sweating and on toes:
has hung left, badly so for apprentice. *C. E. Brittain.*

HAKY (FR) 3 ch.c. Miswaki (USA) 124 – Honey Stage (USA) (Stage Door **99**
Johnny) [1990 6f⁴ 7m 7g² a8g* 1991 a6g* a7g² 6g* 8d⁵ 6m 5m² 6s 6m 5.5f] useful
handicapper: won at Southwell in February and awarded £7,300 contest (hampered
early) at Kempton in April: 25/1, creditable seventh of 16 to Cumbrian Waltzer in
£12,300 Coral Sprint Trophy at York last run here, running on well: ran in handicap
at Hollywood Park final start: best form at sprint distances: acts on good to firm
going: blinkered once: taken last and quietly to post at York. *W. A. O'Gorman.*

HALBERT 2 b.c. (Jan 31) Song 132 – Stoneydale 83 (Tickled Pink 114) [1991 6m³ **72**
6g⁴ 5.1m² 5m²] 15,500F: sturdy colt: has scope: first foal: dam sprinter: modest
maiden: placed at Newmarket, Chester and in minor event at Goodwood: will prove

best at sprint distances: acts well on top-of-the-ground, ran badly (raced too keenly) second start. *R. Hannon.*

HALEIM 4 ch.c. Formidable (USA) 125 – Miss Reasoning (USA) (Bold Reasoning (USA)) [1990 6m² 6f² 7f 1991 8d 6g 7f 6g] sturdy colt: moderate mover: fair performer at 3 yrs: no show, including in seller, in 1991: should stay 7f: acts on firm ground: blinkered final start. *Dr J. D. Scargill.* —

HALF A BILLION 3 b.g. Nicholas Bill 125 – Half Asleep 64 (Quiet Fling (USA) 124) [1990 NR 1991 12g³] first foal: dam 14.7f winner: 33/1, comprehensively outpaced final 4f when last of 3 in minor event at Doncaster in June: subsequently gelded. *J. Hetherton.* —

HALF A TICK (USA) 3 b.g. Timeless Moment (USA) – Moon Star Miss (USA) (Star Envoy (USA)) [1990 5f* 6m² 6g⁴ 7g* 7f² 7f⁶ 7f³ 8.5f⁵ 1991 9m* 10.4d² 12g³ 11g⁵] neat, quite attractive gelding: moderate walker: has a roundish action: won listed race at Newmarket in April: ran well placed in similar event at Chester and Derby Italiano at Rome: fifth of 9 in Group 2 event at Cologne: stays 1½m: acts on firm and dead going: gelded after final start: useful. *P. F. I. Cole.* **107**

HALKOPOUS 5 b.g. Beldale Flutter (USA) 130 – Salamina 106 (Welsh Pageant 132) [1990 10g 12g³ 10m⁴ 10m⁴ 10.5m² 12f 12.3g² 12g⁵ 13d 12m⁴ 9m 12m 11s* 12s 1991 10m³ 10.1f⁴ 10g² 11.5d⁴ 10.4m* 10.5f⁴ 12s 9m⁶ 10m⁶ 11g*] good-bodied, workmanlike gelding: carries plenty of condition: moderate mover: fairly useful handicapper: wide-margin winner at York (John Smith's Magnet Cup, gambled on) in July and Newbury in October: suited by 1¼m: acts on any going: best visored: tough, genuine and consistent. *M. H. Tompkins.* **93**

HALLOWED GROUND (IRE) 3 b.f. Godswalk (USA) 130 – Stony Ground (Relko 136) [1990 5f⁵ 5m⁵ 5m 5m³ 1991 6g 5.1f³ 6f 6.1m 5m 6.1m³] leggy filly: moderate walker: quite modest maiden at best: has at least 4 times given impression something amiss: stays 6f: tends to sweat: sometimes edgy: sold 1,300 gns Doncaster November Sales: can't be trusted. *C. F. Wall.* **57 §**

HALLOW FAIR 6 b.h. Wolver Hollow 126 – Fingers 124 (Lord Gayle (USA) 124) [1990 NR 1991 11.7g 12m 14m 10.2g 11.8g* 12g⁵] leggy, attractive horse: poor handicapper: won at Leicester in July: effective at 1¼m to 1½m: acts on firm going: winning hurdler in August. *C. A. Horgan.* **44**

HALL PORTER 2 ch.c. (May 24) Crofthall 110 – Portvally (Import 127) [1991 7m 7m 7m a8g] 2,300Y: good-topped colt: fifth foal: brother to 1989 2-y-o 6f seller winner Stop High: dam never ran: no form in maidens and a seller. *R. M. Whitaker.* —

HALOOB (USA) 3 ch.f. Sharpen Up 127 – Clear Ridge (USA) (Cox's Ridge (USA)) [1990 NR 1991 8g 10.4g] angular, sparely-made filly: second foal: closely related to U.S. winner Arno (by Diesis): dam minor winner at up to 7f: no worthwhile form in maidens at Newmarket and York (mulish in preliminaries) in late-summer: sold 1,000 gns Newmarket December Sales. *R. W. Armstrong.* —

HALSTON PRINCE 4 b.c. Petorius 117 – Repicado Rose (USA) (Repicado (CHI)) [1990 8g* 7f* 8m² 8f³ 8d² 10m* 10g⁵ 1991 10g 8g 8g] compact, robust colt: moderate walker and mover: useful performer at 3 yrs: well below form in handicaps in first half of 1991: stays 1¼m: best efforts on top-of-the-ground. *H. R. A. Cecil.* —

HALVOYA 6 gr.m. Bay Express 132 – Porsanger (USA) (Zeddaan 130) [1990 5g² 5m³ 5m⁴ 5m 5g* 5g⁴ 5m* 5m 5m⁶ 5m 6g 5m 5d 5m³ 5.8d a6g⁵ a6g a5g² a5g* a5g⁶ a5g³ 1991 a5g⁴ a5g⁶ a5g a6g³ a5g⁴ a5g⁵ a6g⁵ 5g³] leggy, rather angular mare: poor handicapper: not seen out after April: better suited by 5f than 6f: possibly needs sound surface nowadays: blinkered 5 times: has run well for amateur: best with forcing tactics and tender handling. *J. L. Spearing.* **47**

HAMADRYAD (IRE) 3 b.c. Fairy King (USA) – Clifden Bottoms (Wolver Hollow 126) [1990 7m⁵ 7g³ 7m² 7d 1991 6d⁴ 8m² 8.2f³ 8m³ 6f 7m* 7m⁵ 7s] leggy, quite attractive colt: has a quick action: modest performer: odds on, won maiden at Catterick in September: needs further than 6f, and stays 1m: acts on good to firm ground. *W. Carter.* **76 d**

HAMANAKA (USA) 2 b.f. (Apr 30) Conquistador Cielo (USA) – Tastefully (USA) (Hail To Reason) [1991 7.1m⁵ 7m 7m⁴] $40,000Y: tall, leggy, angular filly: half-sister to 2 winners in North America, including Bon Gout (by Dewan), successful at up to 1¼m and third in Grade 3 Arlington Oaks: dam minor winner at 3 yrs: well-backed favourite following promising debut, saddle slipped and rider unseated just before line when about to win maiden at Redcar in October: quickly beaten over 2f out in 5-runner Houghton Stakes at Newmarket (dull in coat, on toes) 11 days later: will stay 1m. *J. R. Fanshawe.* **70**

HAMILTON LADY (IRE) 3 b.f. Zino 127 – Villasanta (Corvaro (USA) 122) —
[1990 6m 5d 8.2d 8.2v 1991 8.1m⁶ 9.2d 16.1m⁶] lengthy, rather angular filly: little
worthwhile form. *D. Moffatt.*

HAMLET CROFT 3 b.f. Manor Farm Boy 114 – Haverhill Lass 67 (Music Boy **34**
124) [1990 6m a6g² a8g⁴ 1991 a5g a7g a6g⁶ a6g³ 5g] lengthy filly, rather unfurnished: plating-class maiden: below form early on as 3-y-o: stays 1m: blinkered
last 2 outings. *A. Bailey.*

HAMMY'S LASS 2 b.f. (Mar 25) Wassl 125 – Antilla 87 (Averof 123) [1991 5g —
6.9m 7m] lengthy, dipped-backed filly: poor mover: sixth foal: half-sister to 3-y-o
Statia (by Slip Anchor), 7f winner Sympathy (by Precocious) and 1986 2-y-o 6f
winner Uniformity (by Formidable): dam 2-y-o 5f winner, is half-sister to very smart
John French and daughter of half-sister to Derrylin: no worthwhile form in sellers:
dead. *P. C. Haslam.*

HAMOUDI 3 b.g. Miller's Mate 116 – Wanton 106 (Kris 135) [1990 6m 8.2d 6d —
1991 6m 6f] compact gelding: moderate walker: poor maiden: best form at 6f: below
form on firm going: changed hands 2,500 gns Doncaster January Sales. *D. Morley.*

HAND PAINTED 7 br.g. Rabdan 129 – Morkulla (SWE) 49 (Royal Park 114) **56**
[1990 10m⁶ 10f 11.5f⁴ 12m⁶ 10.8m² 10m⁴ 10g⁵ 1991 a8g² a8g⁴ a11g³ a8g³ a10g⁴ a10g
a12g³ 9f⁴ a10g² 10f² 8f² a8g 9m³ a8g⁶ 11.5m³ 11.5m³ 11.6m² 10.8m² a10g⁵ 10g²
10.1s³ a11g* a12g*] leggy gelding: has a round action: in excellent form late in 1991,
winning claimers at Southwell in November (first win) and December: should stay
1¾m: suited by sound surface on turf: sometimes wears crossed noseband: often
wears bandages: has put head in air. *C. R. Beever.*

HANDY LASS 2 b.f. (May 11) Nicholas Bill 125 – Mandrian 103 (Mandamus 120) —
[1991 5g 6m] leggy, sparely-made filly: sixth foal: half-sister to 1m to 19f winner
Autonomous (by Milford): dam won over 8.2f and 12.2f: no worthwhile form in
Midlands sellers in spring. *J. Wharton.*

HANIM (IRE) 3 gr.f. Hatim (USA) 121 – Silk Empress (Young Emperor 133) —
[1990 NR 1991 10m] half-sister to 12.2f winner Desert Emperor (by Ahonoora): dam,
unplaced in 4 races, is closely related to disqualified 1978 Italian 1000 Guineas
winner Romantic Love: well beaten in maiden at Newmarket in April: gave trouble
at start: sold 3,200 gns Doncaster July Sales. *F. Durr.*

HANJESSDAN 3 b.g. Reesh 117 – Palace Travel (High Top 131) [1990 NR 1991 —
10m] robust gelding: fifth foal: half-brother to 7f winner Claudia Miss (by Claude
Monet), fair 1988 2-y-o 6f winner Miss Bentley (by Simply Great) and a winner in
Spain: dam lightly-raced daughter of half-sister to very smart performers Command
Freddy and Ridaness: gave trouble at stalls before tailed off in maiden at Leicester
in October. *D. Haydn Jones.*

HANNAH BROWN (IRE) 3 ch.f. Carlingford Castle 126 – Liebeslied 91 (Dike —
(USA)) [1990 a6g 1991 8g 8m 8.5f] close-coupled, sparely-made filly: headstrong,
tailed off in maidens: wore hood final start: joined B. McMahon. *B. A. McMahon.*

HANNAH'S BOY 5 ch.g. Smackover 107 – Saint Motunde 84 (Tyrant (USA)) —
[1990 6m 5d³ 6m 6d 6g⁶ 6m 5f a5g⁴ a6g⁶ 6m⁴ a6g⁴ 5g³ 6m⁴ 5f⁵ 5d⁵ 6d³ 1991 8h 6m]
big, lengthy, sparely-made gelding: poor mover: plating-class handicapper at 4 yrs:
no form in 1991: stays 6f: best on an easy surface: sometimes blinkered: has started
slowly. *W. Storey.*

HANSOM LAD 8 b.g. Dublin Taxi – Trackalady 96 (Track Spare 125) [1990 a6g⁴ **48**
a6g² a6g 5m 5g a5g a7g 6s a6g a6g² a5g* a6g³ 1991 a6g² a6g a6g⁴ a5g 6m 5f² 5f 5m a **65**
5m 6.1m a6g*] big, good-topped gelding: carries plenty of condition: quite modest
handicapper on all-weather: won claimer at Southwell in November (last 3 wins all
on fibresand): plating class at best on turf: suited by sprint distances: acts on firm
ground: none too genuine. *W. W. Haigh.*

HAPPY CAVALIER 6 b.g. King of Spain 121 – Happy Donna 106 (Huntercombe **34** §
133) [1990 NR 1991 6f⁵ 7m 9g⁵] compact gelding: has a round action: poor maiden:
seems to stay 9f: probably acts on any going: often blinkered as 4-y-o, not in 1991. *R.
E. Barr.*

HARBOUR KNIGHT (IRE) 3 b.g. Caerleon (USA) 132 – So Directed 98 **65**
(Homing 130) [1990 5g³ 6g 6m 8.2d 1991 10g³ 10m² 10g 10g* 13.3g⁶ 11.9m] lengthy,
unfurnished gelding: poor walker: quite modest handicapper: won at Brighton in
July: ran moderately previous start and both afterwards: should stay 1½m: possibly
unsuited by dead ground. *J. M. P. Eustace.*

HARDIHEROINE 4 b.f. Sandhurst Prince 128 – Hardirondo 93 (Hardicanute —
130) [1990 10f⁴ 12d⁶ 12.3g 17.1f⁵ 8.2m⁴ 7f 1991 12d 10g] smallish, sparely-made filly:

good walker: has a quick, moderate action: one-time modest performer: on the downgrade: should stay beyond 1m: acts on hard ground: blinkered final start (April). *M. C. Pipe.*

HARDLINER   2 b. or br.c. (Jun 6) Sizzling Melody 117 – Miss Trilli 89 (Ardoon 124) [1991 6f 6m⁵ 6m 6g] 6,200Y: quite good-topped colt: sixth foal: half-brother to 7f winner Twiller (by Noalcoholic), 12.2f winner Princegate (by Absalom) and 5f winner Time Lord (by Good Times): dam 5f handicapper: modest form in maidens first 3 starts: well beaten in Racecall Gold Trophy at Redcar (wore dropped noseband) final one: stays 6f. *J. R. Shaw.*   **74**

HARD SELL   4 ch.g. Hard Fought 125 – Misoptimist 111 (Blakeney 126) [1990 7f* 8f² 8m⁶ 7f³ 6f⁴ 7m 6g 8m a7g* a7g² 1991 a8g⁵ a7g² a7g² a7g a7g³] leggy gelding: quite modest handicapper: not seen out after March: stays 1m: acts on firm going: wears eyeshield nowadays: often hangs, but has won for apprentice. *J. G. FitzGerald.*   **65**

HARD TO FIGURE   5 gr.h. Telsmoss 91 – Count On Me 77 (No Mercy 126) [1990 5f⁶ 6f³ 7g* 7m 7.6d 7g⁴ 6d 5f² 5m* 6g³ 6m⁶ 5m 6d 10.6v 1991 6g 6g³ 7f 5.8d* 6d 5.1g⁴ 5g⁵ 6g⁵ 8f⁵ 6g² 6g 6m² 6g³ 6m³ 6m* 6d⁶] rather leggy, workmanlike horse: fairly useful handicapper: won at Bath in June and Newmarket in October: never dangerous in listed race at Doncaster final start: effective from stiff 5f, to 1m: acts on firm and dead ground: held up: tough and consistent. *R. J. Hodges.*   **98**

HARD TO GET   4 b.g. Rousillon (USA) 133 – Elusive 94 (Little Current (USA)) [1990 10f⁵ 12g 10m 10m 12.5g 1991 12f⁶] close-coupled, angular gelding: good walker: quite modest form at 2 yrs, none since: stays 9f: best efforts on an easy surface: tends to carry head high and looks a difficult ride. *A. W. Jones.*   **—**

HARD TO SNUB   3 b.c. Shardari 134 – Snub (Steel Heart 128) [1990 8s 1991 12g 10m] rangy colt: backward, well beaten in maiden and minor events, showing signs of ability final start. *M. Madgwick.*   **—**

HAREDEN (USA)   3 b.c. Cougar (CHI) – Chippewa (USA) (Jacinto) [1990 6g³ 6d⁶ 7f² 7f* 8g⁵ 1991 10g 10g⁶ 14m] close-coupled, good-topped colt: poor walker: fair performer as 2-y-o: below form in handicaps and claimer in 1991: should stay middle distances: sold 6,200 gns Newmarket Autumn Sales. *G. Harwood.*   **—**

HARKEN PREMIER   6 gr.g. Hard Fought 125 – Maraquiba (FR) (Kenmare (FR) 125) [1990 12f⁴ 11.7g 10h² 12h³ 10m⁶ a12g 10g 1991 10v] strong, lengthy gelding: ungenuine handicapper: stays 1½m: acts on hard going: often blinkered: sold 1,400 gns Doncaster Spring Sales, resold 2,300 gns Ascot July Sales. *J. R. Jenkins.*   **— §**

HARLEQUIN GIRL   3 ch.f. Primo Dominie 121 – Song of Gold 85 (Song 132) [1990 5m 7f 1991 7g 8d⁶ 7g 8.3m 5.3f⁶ 7m⁴ 6f⁴ 6m⁴ 6m² 6m a6g a8g] leggy filly: poor maiden: stays 6f well: acts on firm ground: bandaged behind first 4 starts: sold out of J. White's stable 775 gns Ascot April Sales before reappearance: visored ninth start: refused to wear blinkers and withdrawn intended eighth. *K. T. Ivory.*   **43**

HARMER (IRE)   3 b.f. Alzao (USA) 117 – Native Flower (Tumble Wind (USA)) [1990 6f² 6g 1991 7g² 7.5f 7f⁶ 8.1m³] leggy, rather angular filly: quite modest form at best: below form in claimers last 3 starts, though saddle slipped (was running fair race) on first of them: stays 7f: hocks bandaged: sold 2,400 gns Newmarket Autumn Sales. *Lord John FitzGerald.*   **61**

HARMONIOUS   2 b.f. (Feb 24) Sharrood (USA) 124 – Harp Strings (FR) 109 (Luthier 126) [1991 6g⁵ 6m* 7g⁴ 6f 7g] compact, attractive filly: fifth living foal: half-sister to 3 winners here and abroad, including fairly useful 1986 2-y-o 6f winner Gentle Persuasion (by Bustino) and fair 10.1f winner Full Orchestra (by Shirley Heights): dam useful at up to 9f: quite modest performer: made all in Pontefract maiden in August: well beaten afterwards: bred to stay at least 7f: races keenly: tail swisher: sold 3,100 gns Ascot November Sales. *I. A. Balding.*   **69**

HAROLDON (IRE)   2 ch.c. (Apr 29) Heraldiste (USA) 121 – Cordon 89 (Morston (FR) 125) [1991 6d³ 6m² 6m⁴] IR 13,000F: leggy, close-coupled colt: half-brother to several winners here and abroad, including fair 1¼m winner Fayette (by Dom Racine): dam won over 7f and 1½m: fair maiden: placed at Newbury (behind Dr Devious) in May and Epsom (beaten short head by A-To-Z) in June: sweating, ran moderately in £9,300 event at Ascot later in summer: should stay 1¼m. *B. Palling.*   **82**

HARPLEY   4 gr.g. Beldale Flutter (USA) 130 – Jellygold 95 (Jellaby 124) [1990 8m 8g 1991 12g 13.8f⁴ 12.2m 13.6m⁴] sturdy gelding: poor handicapper: well worth another try over 1¾m+: acts on firm ground: winning hurdler in October: has joined S. Kettlewell. *S. E. Kettlewell.*   **—**

HARREEK   6 ch.g. Tap On Wood 130 – Footway 97 (Sovereign Path 125) [1990   **57**
NR 1991 12g 12m 16.2g⁶ 14m³ 12g] useful-looking gelding: carried plenty of
condition: moderate mover: quite modest handicapper: broke hind leg final start:
stayed very well: acted on good to firm ground and dead (unsuited by very soft): has
been visored: bandaged as 6-y-o: dead. *M. Madgwick.*

HARRY'S COMING   7 b.g. Marching On 101 – Elegant Star 86 (Star Moss 122)   **69**
[1990 5f* 5m* 5g⁴ 6f 5g³ 5g⁵ 5m* 6d⁵ 5.8m² 5m 5m⁵ 5f⁴ 6f⁵ 5g 1991 5g* 5g 5m
6g³ 5m³ 6m 6g* 5d³ 6v⁵ a6g* 5.7m⁵ 6.1m a6g⁵ 5f⁶ 5.1m] leggy, good-topped
gelding: quite modest handicapper: won at Warwick, Kempton and Lingfield in first
half of 1991: effective at 5f to 6f: acts on firm and dead going, unsuited by heavy: tried
in blinkers and visor at 3 yrs: good mount for apprentice. *R. J. Hodges.*

HARRY'S GEM (IRE)   3 br.g. Green Ruby (USA) 104 – Miami Blues 54 (Palm   **33**
Track 122) [1990 7g 1991 8f 10g 7g⁶] tall, unfurnished gelding: plating-class maiden:
best effort at 7f: bandaged behind second start. *M. E. D. Francis.*

HARRY'S GOING   3 b.c. Marching On 101 – Elegant Star 86 (Star Moss 122)   —
[1990 NR 1991 6m 8m 6f] leggy, lengthy colt: brother to sprint winners Harry's
Coming and Marching Star and half-brother to 9f and 9.4f winner Elegant Bill (by
Nicholas Bill): dam middle-distance winner: signs of a little ability, never able to
challenge, in claimer and seller first 2 starts: sweating, round action to post final
one, in June: will probably be suited by further than 6f. *R. J. Hodges.*

HARRY'S JOY   3 b.f. Aragon 118 – Happy Donna 106 (Huntercombe 133) [1990   —
a7g 1991 5d 7.1m 6m 5d 6m] leggy, plain filly: 50/1 and ridden by 7-lb claimer, signs
of ability when staying-on seventh of 17 in handicap at Wolverhampton penultimate
start: hampered final one: should stay 6f: once refused to enter stalls: bandaged
behind third start. *C. J. Hill.*

HARRY'S LADY (IRE)   3 b.f. Alleging (USA) 120 – Lucky Engagement (USA)   —
75 (What Luck (USA)) [1990 6m³ 1991 8m 10g⁵ 10m 8.2f⁶ 9.2s a8g] small, leggy filly:
quite modest maiden: running-on fifth in median auction contest at Leicester in
June: failed to confirm that promise in handicaps: stays 1¼m: usually bandaged. *T.
Thomson Jones.*

HARTLEY   4 gr.g. Final Straw 127 – She Who Dares (Bellypha 130) [1990 6s 6m 8f   **42**
8f⁴ 8.2d³ 8m 6d⁴ 6g² 6s 7d a7g 1991 a7g 6d⁵ 8g 6g] angular, rather leggy gelding:
poor mover: poor handicapper nowadays: off course over 5 months before final
start: should stay 7f: probably unsuited by top-of-the-ground, acts on soft: none too
consistent. *T. Fairhurst.*

HARVEST GIRL (IRE)   2 b.f. (Apr 11) Thatching 131 – June Maid 56 (Junius   **100**
(USA) 124) [1991 5d² 6m* 5.2g² 5.2f² 6f² 6g² 5d² 7.3g⁴] 7,000Y: leggy,
workmanlike filly: third foal: half-sister to 1990 2-y-o 6f winner Bold Heart (by
Pennine Walk) and 1989 2-y-o 5f seller winner Doulally (by Doulab): dam second
over 7f at 3 yrs, is half-sister to very useful 6f and 1m winner Magnetic Field: useful
performer: won maiden at Newmarket in July: much improved form after, beaten
2½ lengths in listed race at Ayr (by Mamma's Too) and in Cornwallis Stakes at
Ascot (by Magic Ring) in autumn: ran moderately final outing: stays 6f: acts on firm
and dead ground: has drifted left. *G. A. Pritchard-Gordon.*

HARVEST SPLENDOUR (USA)   4 b.f. Solford (USA) 127 – Autumn Splen-   —
dour (AUS) (Luskin Star (AUS)) [1990 8f 6m 7m 8g³ a8g⁶ 7v 7d a11g 1991 10.1d]
leggy filly: moderate mover: plating-class handicapper at best: never placed to challenge in Windsor selling handicap in June: may prove best at 7f. *M. H. Tompkins.*

HASTY AMY   2 b.f. (Mar 18) Daring March 116 – Babe In The Wood (Athens   —
Wood 126) [1991 6m a6g a7g] 1,750F, 1,500Y: lengthy, workmanlike filly: half-sister
to 5 winners, including Western Moxy (by Connaught), successful at up to 1½m:
dam ran 3 times: no worthwhile form in summer sellers. *M. W. Ellerby.*

HASTY RESPONSE (IRE)   2 gr.c. (Apr 17) Auction Ring (USA) 123 –   —
Kashapour 81 (Nishapour (FR) 125) [1991 5d² 6,200F, 3,400Y: neat colt: first foal:
dam placed at 6f and 7f at 2 yrs, is half-sister to 2000 Guineas winner Roland
Gardens and to dam of Kooyonga: 25/1, bit backward and green, behind in 16-runner
seller at Folkestone in September: moved moderately down: sold to Scandinavia
680 gns Newmarket Autumn Sales. *B. A. McMahon.*

HASTY SHUFFLE (USA)   2 ch.f. (Apr 30) Arctic Tern (USA) 126 – Fast   **62**
Shuffle (USA) (Northfields (USA)) [1991 5m⁵ 6g⁶ a6g⁵ a7g⁶ 7g⁶ 7f* 7f² 8.2m]
compact filly: third foal: half-sister to a winner in North America: dam placed 5 times
from 19 starts: quite modest performer: sweating, won claimer at Salisbury in
September: ran poorly in seller (taken very steadily down) final start: best form at 7f

on firm ground: signs of temperament third outing, visored (ran poorly) fourth: twice slowly away. *C. R. Nelson.*

HASTY SPARK 3 b.g. Shardari 134 – Fire And Ice (FR) (Reliance II 137) — [1990 NR 1991 10m a12g 12.3g] close-coupled gelding: half-brother to quite modest 1½m winner Shenestone (by Sharpen Up) and a winner in Italy by Cure The Blues: dam, little sign of ability in 4 races in France, is out of sister to St Leger winner Boucher: no worthwhile form: bandaged on debut: gelded after final start. *C. F. Wall.*

HATAAL (IRE) 2 ch.f. (Mar 6) Hatim (USA) 121 – Tenoria 82 (Mansingh (USA) 36 120) [1991 5f⁶ 5g 6d³ 6m 7m⁶ 7f⁶ 7.5f 7m] IR 2,200F, resold IR 1,200Y: unfurnished filly: has a round action: half-sister to 2 winners, including Irish 1½m winner Welsh Tenor (by Welsh Saint): dam 7f (at 2 yrs) and 10.6f winner: poor, inconsistent plater: stays 7f. *J. Balding.*

HATEEL 5 b.h. Kalaglow 132 – Oatfield 69 (Great Nephew 126) [1990 12f* 10g² **112** 11m* 12d³ 12f* 12s* 12f³ 13.4g 12m 1991 10g³ 10d* 10g 13.3d³ 12m* 12g⁴ 14g* 12g² 13.3f⁶ 12g⁵ 12s⁶] strong, well-made horse: carries condition: moderate mover: smart performer at best: successful in Pontefract minor event in April and £17,250 handicap at Epsom and listed event at the Curragh in June: well below best in pattern company after finishing creditable second to Lomitas in Group 1 event at Dusseldorf: effective from 1¼m to 14f: acts on any going: tough and genuine: remains in training. *P. T. Walwyn.*

HATMI 2 b.c. (Mar 24) Wassl 125 – Nouvelle Star (AUS) (Luskin Star (AUS)) — p [1991 6g] smallish, well-made colt: third foal: half-brother to 3-y-o 7f winner Sariah (by Kris): dam won from 5f to 8.2f in Australia and was champion older filly at 4 yrs: 17/2, well beaten in maiden at Lingfield in October, slowly away and not knocked about once held: likely to stay 1m: will do better. *C. J. Benstead.*

Hamdan Al-Maktoum's "Hateel"

HATOOF (USA)   2 ch.f. (Jan 26) Irish River (FR) 131 – Cadeaux d'Amie **110** p (USA) 115 (Lyphard (USA) 132) [1991 8g* 8g² 8d²]
   Culture Vulture may have taken the spoils by a short head but the *meilleure impression*, to borrow a well-known phrase from *Paris-Turf*, in the Prix Marcel Boussac at Longchamp on Arc day was made by the runner-up Hatoof who finished fast from a near-impossible position on the home turn. Relegated to the back of the fourteen-runner field by a stumble after a furlong or so, Hatoof was kept to the inside rail until two furlongs out, where, in ninth position and hemmed in behind a wall of horses, she was switched belatedly to the outside. Hatoof didn't make much headway initially—she was in seventh place still, and probably five lengths down, with little more than a furlong to go—but then she fairly flew, leaving the impression that she was more than a mite unfortunate not to have given her trainer her first victory in the race. The Boussac wasn't the first race that Hatoof had lost in a photo-finish; two weeks previously, in the Prix d'Aumale over the same course and distance, she'd also found the post coming a stride too soon and was beaten a nose by Guislaine who, incidentally, finished two places and a length and a half behind her in the Boussac. Longchamp's Grande Piste had also been the venue of Hatoof's only previous run; then, in the Prix de Toutevoie, she'd made most of the running to account for five other newcomers by a length and more.

Hatoof (USA) (ch.f. Jan 26, 1989)	Irish River (FR) (ch 1976)	Riverman (b 1969)	Never Bend
			River Lady
		Irish Star (b 1960)	Klairon
			Botany Bay
	Cadeaux d'Amie (USA) (ch 1984)	Lyphard (b 1969)	Northern Dancer
			Goofed
		Tananarive (b 1970)	Le Fabuleux
			Ten Double

   Hatoof is by the Poule d'Essai des Poulains winner Irish River out of a Lyphard half-sister to the Prix de Diane winner Mrs Penny. Her dam, Cadeaux d'Amie, who fetched 925,000 dollars as a yearling, was at her best as a two-year-old when she had a similar campaign to Hatoof, winning a newcomers event over a mile at Deauville before finishing a close third in the Prix d'Aumale and running a moderate race in the Boussac; she showed useful form the following season when she tried her luck without success in minor pattern events on three occasions and managed only a victory in a minor contest at Evry over a mile and a quarter. In contrast, Mrs Penny improved upon her smart two-year-old form (she won the Cherry Hinton, Lowther, and Cheveley Park Stakes) at three to beat a representative field at Chantilly and a very strong one in the mile-and-a-half Prix Vermeille. Mrs Penny wasn't so good at four in the States, although she still managed to take the Grade 3 eleven-furlong Queen Charlotte Handicap and run second in the Grade 2 mile-and-a-quarter Manhattan Handicap. Her dam Tananarive was bred by M Wildenstein and won three races, from six furlongs to a mile and three quarters, for him in France before her export several years later to America. Tananarive is a half-sister to the good European and American performer Tahitian King as well as the good French staying two-year-old Tuxpan, out of a daughter of a half-sister to the Belmont Stakes winner One Count.
   Hatoof is reportedly to be sent over for the One Thousand Guineas but her optimum distance as a three-year-old is more likely to be a mile and a quarter (or thereabouts) than a mile; and if she does make the journey, conditions at Newmarket are likely to be much faster than they were in the Boussac when the ground was on the soft side and stamina was brought into play. On the positive side, Hatoof should have few difficulties boosting her winning tally and her prospects of going one better in pattern company seem good, especially as she won't carry any penalties, initially at least. She strikes us a likely candidate for the Prix de Diane. *Mme C. Head, France.*

HATTA'S MILL   2 b.c. (Mar 31) Green Desert (USA) 127 – Mill On The Floss 117 **81** p (Mill Reef (USA) 141) [1991 7g²] good-topped, attractive colt: second foal: half-brother to 3-y-o 10.2f and 1½m winner Top Mill (by High Top): dam 7f (at 2 yrs) and 1½m winner from very good family: joint favourite but burly and very green, 1½ lengths second of 6 to Torrey Canyon in £10,400 maiden at Ascot in July, outpaced 3f out then finishing very strongly final furlong: looked certain to improve considerably and win races, but didn't reappear. *H. R. A. Cecil.*

HAUNTING OBSESSION (USA) 3 ch.f. Barachois (CAN) – Vitale (Vitiges 72 (FR) 132) [1990 5f² 5m* 1991 6m² 6f] tall, rather angular filly: modest form: bit backward and on toes, easily beaten 4 lengths by Sharpthorne in minor event at Kempton, running on well: failed to confirm that promise in handicap later in September: stays 6f: wore crossed noseband in 1991. *J. Etherington.*

HAUT-BRION (IRE) 2 br.g. (May 21) Alzao (USA) 117 – Romanee Conti (Will 52 Somers 114§) [1991 7d 7g 8.1g] 32,000Y: strong, good-topped gelding: brother to 3-y-o Sauvignon and half-brother to several winners, including useful 1979 2-y-o 7f and 1m winner Schwepperusschian (by Take A Reef) and fair 1m winner Taken For Granted (by Martinmas): dam placed at up to 1¼m in Ireland: plating-class maiden: sweating, well beaten final start (stumbled early on). *P. W. Chapple-Hyam.*

HAVE A CARE 3 b.f. Rainbow Quest (USA) 134 – Danger Ahead (Mill Reef — (USA) 141) [1990 NR 1991 12m⁵ 10.3m⁴ 10g⁶ a12g⁶] 66,000Y: lengthy, workmanlike filly: moderate mover: second foal: dam unraced half-sister to very useful 1976 2-y-o 5f winner Easy Landing: no form in maidens and claimers. *R. Charlton.*

HAVE A NIGHTCAP 2 ch.g. (May 2) Night Shift (USA) – Final Orders (USA) 56 (Prince John) [1991 7.1m 7g⁶ 8.1m⁶] 10,500Y: robust gelding: brother to 3-y-o 6f (at 2 yrs) and 7.1f winner Time Gentleman and half-brother to several winners, notably very useful stayer Hans Brinker (by Dike) and useful middle-distance performer Yard Bird (by Busted): dam ran twice: plating-class maiden: should stay 1m: best effort (still bit backward) on good ground. *M. A. Jarvis.*

HAVEYOUALLDONE (IRE) 3 b.c. Auction Ring (USA) 123 – Elated 80 53 (Sparkler 130) [1990 7g 7m 1991 10g 8m 11m² 12g 12.3g 11d⁶] angular, unfurnished colt: poor mover: form only when short-head second in seller at Wolverhampton, staying on well: off course 4 months before fifth start: suited by 11f: acts on good to firm ground. *S. Dow.*

HAVON AIRCO 5 b.g. Lafontaine (USA) 117 – Sunland Park (Baragoi 115) [1990 — NR 1991 15s 14.1g⁶] robust, deep-girthed gelding: carries condition: fair winner as 2-y-o: lightly raced since, no show in summer: should stay beyond 7f: best efforts on good ground (probably unsuited by top-of-the-ground): well beaten when blinkered. *C. R. Beever.*

HAWAIIAN ROMANCE (USA) 5 ch.m. Hawaii – Chateau Princess (USA) — (Majestic Prince) [1990 10s* 12g⁶ 12g 10d 1991 16.2g 12.3g] big, lengthy mare: has a rather round action: won handicap at Nottingham (sweating) in early 1990: no form since: stays 1¼m: seems to need soft ground. *R. Curtis.*

HAWAII STORM (FR) 3 b.g. Plugged Nickle (USA) – Slewvindaloo (USA) — (Seattle Slew (USA)) [1990 6m 8.2d⁶ 7g⁶ 8d 1991 8.2g 6d 7m 7m 8m] leggy gelding: plating-class form at 2 yrs, none (stiff tasks in handicaps) as 3-y-o: best effort over 7f: bandaged near-hind fourth start: retained by trainer 740 gns Newmarket Autumn Sales. *Miss A. J. Whitfield.*

HAWAII AL BARR 3 b.f. Green Desert (USA) 127 – Allegedly Blue (USA) 106 99 (Alleged (USA) 138) [1990 7m³ 7f⁵ 1991 10g² 12f* 11.9m² 12g 14.6m⁵ 13.9m* 16g*] tall, leggy filly: good mover: successful in maiden at Brighton in May then 4-runner minor event (set modest pace, held Romany Rye by 1½ lengths) at York and listed race at Newmarket in October, making all first 2 occasions: led 5f out and kept on gamely to beat Endoli 1½ lengths at Newmarket: stays 2m: useful. *M. R. Stoute.*

HAWA LAYAAM (IRE) 2 ch.g. (Feb 11) Kris 135 – Palais Rose (USA) 77 (Northern Dancer) [1991 7g 7f⁵ 7m⁶ 8m³ 7m³ 6g] 290,000Y: tall gelding: second foal: half-brother to Irish 3-y-o 6f (at 2 yrs) and 1m winner Legal Profession (by Law Society): dam Irish 1m winner, is granddaughter of Coronation Stakes winner Lisadell: modest maiden: ran creditably last 3 outings: probably needs further than 6f, and stays 1m: blinkered (made most) final 2 starts. *A. A. Scott.*

HAWKISH (USA) 2 b.c. (Mar 29) Silver Hawk (USA) 123 – Dive Royal (USA) 35 p (Inverness Drive (USA)) [1991 a8g⁵] $25,000Y, 5,400 2-y-o: half-brother to several minor winners: dam minor winner at up to 7f: 20/1, slow-starting 12 lengths fifth of 9 to Paper Clip in late-year maiden at Lingfield: should improve. *P. Mitchell.*

HAWWAM 5 b.h. Glenstal (USA) 118 – Hone 79 (Sharpen Up 127) [1990 8g 8g 8f — 9m 8g⁶ 10m⁶ 8d 10m⁴ 9m 8d³ 10.2s³ 1991 10.4d] good-topped, quite attractive horse: usually takes the eye: one-time useful handicapper: has become disappointing: stays 1¼m: acts on any going, except perhaps firm: has worn severe bridle: has wandered and idled, and best with waiting tactics and strong handling. *S. Mellor.*

HAXBY LASS 2 b.f. (Apr 26) Sizzling Melody 117 – Gold Market (Hotfoot 126) **46** [1991 5d 5g⁴ 5f 5m² 6m⁵ 6d⁴ 6g 6.1m 5m⁴ 5g⁴ 6m⁶ 5d] leggy, sparely-made filly: moderate mover: sixth foal: half-sister to 1989 2-y-o 7f winner Fosse Gill (by Night Shift) and a winner in Sweden: dam ran once: quite modest plater: likely to prove best at 5f: acts on good to firm and dead ground: usually bandaged nowadays: inconsistent: sold 550 gns Doncaster October Sales. *M. Brittain.*

HAYBURY 2 b.c. (Apr 2) Song 132 – Mrs Kaydagawn (Final Straw 127) [1991 5g⁵ **53** 5g 6f 7m] leggy, unfurnished colt: first foal: dam poor half-sister to very useful 1976 2-y-o 5f to 7f winner Sky Ship and smart 1¼m filly Upper Deck, also family of Cut Above: plating-class maiden: looked unsatisfactory in Yarmouth seller third start: trained until after then by B. Hanbury: ran creditably at Doncaster nearly 3 months later: sold 2,400 gns Newmarket Autumn Sales. *Sir Mark Prescott.*

HAYMARKET 2 b.c. (Mar 13) Danzig (USA) – Glorious Song (CAN) (Halo **80** p (USA)) [1991 6m⁴ 7m² 7g*] good-topped, attractive colt: has scope: fluent mover: closely related to useful 9f and 10.2f winner Rakeen (by Northern Dancer) and half-brother to 3 winners, including 3-y-o 7.6f winner Morn of Song and very useful 6f (at 2 yrs) and 1m winner Rahy (both by Blushing Groom): dam top class at around 9f, is sister to champion 2-y-o colt Devil's Bag: fair form: 5/2 on, comfortably won 7-runner maiden at Warwick in October: may prove best at up to 1m: likely to improve further: to join N. Drysdale in USA. *M. R. Stoute.*

HAY YUEN 2 b.f. (Feb 22) Primo Dominie 121 – June Fayre (Sagaro 133) [1991 **71** 5m³ 5m³ 5d* 5m³ 5g 7.5g 7.5g⁵ 7.5v 5v⁴] 5,000 (privately) Y: leggy, unfurnished filly: fifth foal: half-sister to 3 winners here and abroad, including plating-class 6f to 9f winner Express Edition (by Comedy Star): dam twice-raced daughter of Pasty, best British 2-y-o filly of 1975: quite modest form: successful at Chester in May: ran in Italian listed races last 5 starts, 5 lengths fourth of 8 to Whittingham in September: may prove best at sprint distances: acts on good to firm and heavy ground: tail flasher. *P. A. Kelleway.*

HAZARADJAT (IRE) 2 b.f. (May 10) Darshaan 133 – Hazy Idea 118 (Hether- **82** p sett 134) [1991 7g*] sister to Irish 3-y-o 1¼m winner Hashar and half-sister to numerous other winners, including very smart 1975 2-y-o Hittite Glory (by Hab- itat): dam won from 6f to 1¾m: 11/4 joint favourite, won 17-runner maiden at Fairyhouse in October by 2 lengths from Gorgeous Dancer: bred to be suited by middle distances: should improve. *J. Oxx, Ireland.*

HAZARA (FR) 4 b. or br.f. Vayrann 133 – Hecalene (FR) (Sir Gaylord) [1990 8g — 10g³ 1991 10v] ex-French filly: half-sister to 2 minor winners abroad: dam French 1m winner: third in minor event in Provinces in 1990: bandaged and better for run, soundly beaten in Folkestone claimer 10 months later: stays 1¼m. *J. Ffitch-Heyes.*

HAZAR (IRE) 3 b.f. Thatching 131 – Etoile des Galles (Busted 134) [1990 NR **75** 1991 a7g* 7g⁴ a8g³ a8g* 8.9m* 8.1m²] lengthy, angular filly: moderate mover with a round action: fourth live foal: half-sister to smart 7f and 1m winner Llyn Gwynant (by Persian Bold) and a winner in Malaysia: dam lightly-raced half-sister to dam of Gay Lemur: successful in maiden and handicap at Southwell (driven along virtually throughout) in the summer and in handicap at Wolverhampton in September: will be better suited by 1¼m: game. *Sir Mark Prescott.*

HAZM (USA) 2 b. or br.c. (Mar 5) Danzig (USA) – Cold Hearted (USA) (The Axe **91** p II 115) [1991 5m* 6m²] $350,000Y: sturdy, quite attractive colt: second foal: half-brother to a winner in North America by Damascus: dam graded stakes-placed winner at up to 1¼m, is half-sister to Belmont Stakes winner Caveat: won maiden at Sandown in September: much improved form when 1½ lengths second of 6 to impressive Wolfhound in minor event at Doncaster following month, keeping on well to draw clear of remainder: likely to stay 1m: will improve again. *H. Thomson Jones.*

HAZY SHADES 2 gr.f. (May 8) General Wade 93 – Gellifawr 80 (Saulingo 122) — [1991 7.1m] tall, lengthy filly: fifth foal: sister to 3-y-o Shades of Jade and half-sister to 8.3f seller winner Singing Gold (by Gold Claim): dam best at 5f: green, tailed off in maiden at Sandown in September: got loose at start and withdrawn from similar event at Lingfield 8 days earlier. *J. J. Bridger.*

HEAD TURNER 3 b.f. My Dad Tom (USA) 109 – Top Tina (High Top 131) [1990 **51** 6g⁴ 6d 1991 8g² 8m⁶ 8.2f⁴ 10m 7.6g] rather sparely-made filly: plating-class form at best: should prove suited by beyond 1m: best efforts on good ground. *M. R. Channon.*

HEAR A NIGHTINGALE 4 br.g. Pitskelly 122 – Calarette 85 (Caliban 123) — [1990 10g 12m⁶ 11g³ 14.8m² 16.2s⁶ 17.1f* 15.3g⁴ 16.1m³ a18g⁶ 16g³ 18.1m⁴ 16.2s³

18d 1991 14.8g 21.6f³] small gelding: has a rather round action: modest handicapper at 3 yrs: bandaged, well below best in spring of 1991: stays 17f: acts on any going: effective with or without visor: tried blinkered once. *T. Thomson Jones.*

HEARD A WHISPER   3 b.c. Bellypha 130 – Breadcrumb 111 (Final Straw 127)   **97** [1990 5m⁵ 6d* 6m* 6m² 6f 5d* 1991 6d⁴ 6m 7g 6g 5g 6m⁵ 6g] strong, lengthy colt: has a quick action: fairly useful performer: good fifth of 28 to Sarcita in Ladbrokes (Ayr) Gold Cup, easily best of last 5 efforts: well worth another try at 7f: acts on good to firm and dead ground: sweating second and third starts: sold 15,500 gns Newmarket Autumn Sales. *G. Lewis.*

HEARTBURN   3 ch.f. Hard Fought 125 – Sweet And Sour 96 (Sharpen Up 127)   **36** [1990 5m 5f 5m 1991 7g⁴ 7g 8g 10m a6g a8g] leggy, sparely-made filly: plater: fourth at Brighton in July: didn't reproduce that: bred to stay 1m: blinkered (stiff task) final start: sometimes sweating: retained 1,050 gns Ascot September Sales. *J. D. Bethell.*

HEART FLUTTER   2 gr.c. (May 24) Beldale Flutter (USA) 130 – Courting Day   **49** 90 (Right Boy 137) [1991 6m 6g 7m 8m a7g] workmanlike colt: eighth living foal: half-brother to several winners, including 1988 2-y-o 5f winner Lockhart (by Loch-nager) and useful 7f and 1m winner Courting Season (by Silly Season): dam 1m winner: plating-class maiden: ran creditably in Doncaster selling nursery penul-timate outing: blinkered, ran badly on fibresand final start: will stay 1¼m: twice slowly away. *J. Hetherton.*

HEART OF DARKNESS   3 br.c. Glint of Gold 128 – Land of Ivory (USA) 109 **108** (The Minstrel (CAN) 135) [1990 6f⁴ 7g* 7m* 1991 8m² 8m⁶ 9m² 10d²] strong, good-bodied colt: useful performer, not seen out until late-September as 3-y-o: second in minor event at Newbury and Newmarket listed races won by Susurration and Mohican Girl: should prove best at up to 1¼m: acts on good to firm ground and dead: sweating and edgy second start: headstrong, usually held up in rear. *I. A. Balding.*

HEART'S LEGEND (IRE)   2 b.g. (May 28) Legend of France (USA) 124 –   **34** Queen of Hearts 97 (Thatching 131) [1991 5.9f² 5m] IR 1,300F, IR 900Y: sturdy, lengthy gelding: first foal: dam unraced: eighth of 16 in seller at Newcastle in August, easily better effort: wears severe bridle: sold 900 gns Doncaster November Sales. *J. H. Johnson.*

HEATHER BANK   2 b.c. (May 9) Nordance (USA) – Miss Rossi (Artaius (USA)   **82** 129) [1991 6f² 5g³ 5m⁴ 5d⁴ 6g* 6g* 6m² 6g³ 6m⁴ 5m⁵ 5d⁵] strong, lengthy, workmanlike colt: carries condition: third foal: half-brother to useful 5f winner Dancing Music (by Music Boy) and 3-y-o 5f winner Lyndon's Linnet (by Prince Sabo): dam unraced: fair performer: made all in maiden at Ayr and nursery at Goodwood (gave trouble stalls) in summer: subsequently ran well in similar events: equally effective at 5f and 6f: acts on good to firm and dead ground: runs well with blinkers or without: bandaged near-fore eighth start: consistent. *J. Berry.*

HEAVEN-LIEGH-GREY   3 gr.f. Grey Desire 115 – North Pine (Import 127)   **90** [1990 5m* 5g4 5m² 5f² 5.3h* 5m* 5f³ 5g⁵ 1991 6m 5d 5m 5m² 5m* 5.1d⁴ 5g² 5g⁵ 5g 5.6m 5m³] workmanlike filly: fairly useful handicapper: won at York in June: early to post, back to form when third of 12 at same course: suited by 5f: best efforts on a sound surface: visored once: often bandaged behind late on as 3-y-o: has carried head awkwardly, but game. *J. Berry.*

HEAVENLY HOOFER   8 b.g. Dance In Time (CAN) – Heavenly Chord 89   **25** (Hittite Glory 125) [1990 8g 12g⁵ 12g⁴ 11m³ 12h³ 1991 12m⁴ 15s² 15.8f 12.1f 12.2m⁶] lengthy gelding: poor handicapper: stays 15f: acts on any going: well beaten when blinkered: inconsistent. *W. Storey.*

HEAVENLY QUEEN   3 b.f. Scottish Reel 123 – Celeste 83 (Sing Sing 134)   **—** [1990 5f 5m 6g 1991 7d⁶ 6g 6.9m 8g] small, sturdy filly: moderate mover: little form, including in seller: sweating final start: sold 740 gns Newmarket September Sales. *G. Blum.*

HEAVENLY WATERS   2 b.f. (Feb 2) Celestial Storm (USA) 132 – Idle Waters   **51** 116 (Mill Reef (USA) 141) [1991 7g 7m 8g] workmanlike filly: moderate mover: half-sister to several winners, including very useful stayers Shining Water (by Kalaglow) and Secret Waters (by Pharly): dam smart 1½m to 14.6f winner: poor form in minor event and maidens: likely to stay well. *R. F. Johnson Houghton.*

HEAVY METAL   2 ch.c. (Mar 24) Beveled (USA) – Lara's Song (USA) 69   **—** (Russian Bank (USA) 110) [1991 5m 5d⁶ 6d] tall, leggy colt: has a round action: fifth foal: half-brother to 13.1f winner/successful hurdler Russian Lullaby (by Sparkler) and 3-y-o Italian Group 2 1¼m winner Lara's Idea (by Primo Dominie): dam winning stayer: sire (by Sharpen Up) 6f and 7f winner: no worthwhile form, including in sellers: sold 600 gns Newmarket July Sales. *N. Tinkler.*

HEAVYWEIGHT (IRE) 2 gr.c. (Mar 23) Bellypha 130 – Pennyweight (Troy — p 137) [1991 a7g] 76,000Y: fourth foal: half-brother to fairly useful 5f winner On Tiptoes (by Shareef Dancer) and 2 other winners, including useful 6f and 7f winner Penny Candle (by Be My Guest): dam poor half-sister to Wassl: weak in market, around 18 lengths ninth of 13 to Donegal Dandy in late-year maiden at Southwell: should do better. *Sir Mark Prescott.*

HECTOR PROTECTOR (USA) 3 ch.c. Woodman (USA) 126 – Korveya **124** (USA) 116 (Riverman (USA) 131) [1990 5g* 6d* 6g* 6d* 7g* 8g* 1991 8g* 8d* 12f⁴ 8g* 8m 8d⁶]

In answer to someone who complained that a particular rating was 'an insult' to a certain horse, Phil Bull once said: 'You can't insult a racehorse, brother'. True enough when you think about it, but you can offend his connections as, for instance, the Breeders' Cup selection committee did by rating five-time Group 1 winner Hector Protector not good enough to get in the fourteen—the limit on the size of the field—for the Breeders' Cup Mile at Churchill Downs in November. While Polar Falcon, Priolo, Second Set and the fillies Danseuse du Soir, Kooyonga and Shadayid represented Europe, he made only first reserve. How much of an insult this really was is debatable. The committee made a point of taking current form into account. Hector Protector had finished out of the money in the Prix du Moulin and the Queen Elizabeth II Stakes in his most recent races, beaten in one or other by five of the six Europeans who ran in the Mile. And in any case, although the best of his form was as good as, or slightly superior to, that of some in the field, it fell well short of making him an outstanding miler the race could ill-afford to lose; he'd amassed his victories in workmanlike fashion and was by no means a Miesque or a Last Tycoon, both winners of the race for France.

Much less contentious than Hector Protector's precise merit is his racing record: little doubt that it's outstanding. He ran undefeated through eight races up to the Derby, six of them, including the Prix Morny, the Prix de la Salamandre and the Grand Criterium, as a two-year-old, and after Epsom he took the Prix Jacques le Marois before his first reverse at up to a mile in the Moulin. That run of success as a two-year-old, rounded off with a clear-cut win in the Grand Criterium, led to Hector Protector's topping the International Classification. He deserved to, but there was a feeling that he would need to improve to stay on top at three. As in his first season Hector Protector was ready early in 1991. He was trained for the Dubai Poule d'Essai des Poulains at Longchamp in May, and, having made a satisfactory reappearance in the Prix de Fontainebleau on the course, he seemed to have been handed the classic on a plate when only five accepted against him—his pacemaker Mousquetaire, Acteur Francais and Crack Regiment who'd finished second and third respectively in the Fontainebleau, Orage Noir who'd possibly been flattered by his third to Ganges in a slowly-run Prix Djebel, and the Greenham Stakes fourth Sapieha. However, there was very nearly an upset. Mousquetaire set a furious pace which soon had the 10/1-on shot Hector Protector off the bridle, and Hector Protector came under the whip almost as soon as they'd turned for home, where Acteur Francais, having travelled easily in second place, slipped into the lead. Halfway up the straight Acteur Francais looked sure to hold on; but inch by inch Hector Protector wore him down, went a head up about a hundred yards out then held on well, the pair of them four lengths clear of Sapieha.

The Ever Ready Derby came next on the agenda. Hector Protector's presence added spice to the contest, making a fascinating puzzle all the harder to solve. On looks he was the outstanding individual in the field; but would he stay, would he act on the firm ground or on the undulating track? His style of running and his pedigree, particularly the former, suggested a mile wouldn't be his limit. However, he found the extra half mile too much. Fourth favourite at 6/1, he lay handy despite seeming slightly ill at ease on the hill, quickened with Marju to chase after Generous three furlongs out and for a while promised to finish a clear third. Inside the distance his stamina began to run out, Star of Gdansk lasting the better to relegate him to fourth by half a length.

Dubai Poule d'Essai des Poulains, Longchamp—a close shave for Hector Protector (No. 4)

After this there were no half-measures like running Hector Protector in the Eclipse. He was returned to a mile in the Prix du Haras de Fresnay-le-Buffard Jacques le Marois at Deauville in August, when he had his first opportunity to tackle his elders. Defeat in the Derby had done little harm, understandably, to his reputation and along with Mousquetaire he started a shade of odds on against most of the best over the trip in France, including the previous year's winner Priolo, the Pouliches winner Danseuse du Soir and the second and third in the Two Thousand Guineas, Lycius and Ganges. The race could have been billed as the French mile championship, but the outcome wasn't decisive. Hector Protector prevailed under firm pressure in a blanket finish, by a nose and a short head from Lycius who was in front just after the line, and

Prix du Haras de Fresnay-le-Buffard Jacques le Marois, Deauville—
close again, between Hector Protector, Lycius (almost hidden) and Danseuse du Soir (rails)

Zenya Yoshida's "Hector Protector"

Hector Protector (USA) (ch.c. 1988)	Woodman (USA) (ch 1983)	Mr Prospector (b 1970)	Raise A Native Gold Digger
		Playmate (ch 1975)	Buckpasser Intriguing
	Korveya (USA) (ch 1982)	Riverman (b 1969)	Never Bend River Lady
		Konafa (b 1973)	Damascus Royal Statute

Danseuse du Soir who was in front just before it. Half a length further back Polar Falcon kept fourth by a short head from the strong-finishing Priolo who found himself short of room to make his effort as Mousquetaire weakened. Hector Protector, prominent throughout, did well to pull the race out of the fire after Danseuse du Soir quickened a furlong from home and he deserved full marks for preserving his record at up to a mile. However, it is impossible to look at the result and concur with his rider Freddie Head's opinion on dismounting that the horse must be one of the best post-war milers. Having been praised to the skies, Hector Protector turned in his first moderate performance four weeks later in finishing eighth of twelve to Priolo in the Moulin, a race in which his trainer apparently never wanted to run him. He dropped to the rear in some scrimmaging before halfway, was soon under pressure and, unlike in the Poulains, couldn't get into contention. A less moderate, though in some ways similar, performance followed in the Queen Elizabeth II Stakes, when Hector Protector, still looking tremendously well, finished sixth of nine to Selkirk; off the bridle a long way out, he was slightly hampered on the home turn, couldn't quicken with Shadayid but ran on steadily.

Hector Protector was sold by his owner-breeder Mr Niarchos for a reported 9,000,000 dollars in the summer and raced in the colours of Zenya Yoshida at Ascot. He is to stand at the latter's Shadai Farms in Japan alongside twenty or more stallions, including the Arc winners Tony Bin and Carroll House and the Kentucky Derby winner Sunday Silence. Hector Protector's sire Woodman, incidentally, was represented in the latest Kentucky Derby by the unplaced Hansel who later played his part in keeping Woodman's first crop in the public eye through classic wins in the Preakness Stakes and the Belmont Stakes. Hector Protector's family details were set out in *Racehorses of 1990*. Korveya, the dam, was a smart performer in her own right at up to nine furlongs in France and is out of the 1976 One Thousand Guineas second Konafa, a half-sister to the good American colt Akureyri (misspelt in *Racehorses*) and the top-class middle-distance filly Awaasif. Korveya's producing record needs updating—her third foal Shanghai (by Procida) won a six-furlong maiden race at Chantilly in June before running unplaced in the Prix de Cabourg at Deauville.

As we said, Hector Protector was the best-looking in the Derby field, a strong, good-bodied colt turned out in a condition which, like his racing record, was a tribute to his trainer. Whether the firm going as well as the distance was against him at Epsom can only be guessed at, though in that context his run in the Moulin on the other occasion he encountered top of the ground might be significant, as might his markedly round action. *F. Boutin, France.*

HEIR OF EXCITEMENT   6 b.g. Krayyan 117 – Merry Choice (Yankee Gold   —
115) [1990 a 12g⁴ 10.2m* 11f⁶ 10s 11m³ 10.2m⁶ 1991 12d⁵ 11f 12g 11m 10.3m] lengthy gelding: carries plenty of condition: usually looks well: poor handicapper: has looked irresolute: stays 11f: acts on any going: often visored at 4 yrs, blinkered first 4 starts as 6-y-o: has worn tongue strap. *A. P. Stringer.*

HELAWE   8 ch.g. Last Fandango 125 – Pigmy (Assagai) [1990 6g⁴ 7m* 7h* 7h³   **73**
8m 7h² 7f³ 7f* 7f* 7f² 7m⁴ 7g a7g* a7g⁴ 1991 a7g* 7f² 7g⁵ a7g* 7m* 7m a7g⁴ 7m⁴   a 87
a7g* a7g⁵ a8g a7g⁶] big, lengthy, angular gelding: good walker: fair handicapper on equiturack, successful at Lingfield in January, July and November: not so effective on turf but won at Warwick in July: stays 7f: best on sound surface: lazy sort, who needs blinkers: goes extremely well on switchback track (has won 5 times at Brighton): ran as if something amiss (reportedly broke blood vessel) sixth start: tough and largely consistent. *Sir Mark Prescott.*

HELEN'S BOWER (IRE)   3 gr.f. Bellypha 130 – Queen Helen 112 (Troy 137)   **78**
[1990 7g⁵ 1991 10d² 11.8g³ 10d³ 11.1m* 11.9g 10m] strong, lengthy filly: moderate mover with high knee action: fair performer: 9/4 on, easily won 4-runner maiden at Edinburgh in August: well beaten in listed race (stiff task) and handicap after: will prove better at 1½m than shorter: acts on good to firm ground and dead: sold 15,000 gns Newmarket December Sales. *N. A. Graham.*

HELIOS   3 br.c. Blazing Saddles (AUS) – Mary Sunley 62 (Known Fact (USA) 135)   **72**
[1990 5g⁵ 6d⁶ 7v³ 1991 10g 8g 7.6d² 7f* 7m⁴ 7d 7g⁴ 7g 7m⁵ 6f 7g a10g] leggy, angular colt: moderate mover and walker: quite modest form: made all in maiden at Brighton in May: below form in handicaps last 3 starts, off course 3½ months before final one: stays 7f: acts on firm and dead going (first run for 4 months on heavy): bandaged second start. *R. Simpson.*

HELLEBORUS   3 b.f. King of Spain 121 – Budget Queen 101 (Good Bond 122)   —
[1990 NR 1991 8g] leggy filly: fourth foal: dam 7f and 1¼m winner: showed signs of a little ability, never able to challenge, in maiden at Kempton in July, hanging right: moved moderately down. *P. Mitchell.*

HELLESPONT (IRE)   3 b.c. Beldale Flutter (USA) 130 – Thalassa (IRE) 94   **75** d
(Appiani II 128) [1990 6d⁴ 7m⁵ 6f³ 8m 7m 10s³ 1991 a10g⁵ 10g³ 12g⁵ 16.2g⁴ 12g²
13.3g 10m 12.3g⁴ 9.7g⁶ 11.8m 12s⁵ a14g] leggy colt: has a quick action: modest form on his day: has run in selling handicaps: suited by 1½m, possibly by an easy surface: tends to hang, and has carried head high: trained until after fifth start by C. Brittain: sold 5,200 gns Ascot November Sales, to Italy: has far from ideal attitude. *C. A. Austin.*

HELL OF A GUY   4 b.c. Absalom 128 – Outward's Gal 78 (Ashmore (FR) 125)   —
[1990 NR 1991 12g] first foal: dam should have stayed 1m: won NH Flat race in January, 1991, when trained by C. Thornton: ran out early in celebrity race at Hexham in November on debut. *Denys Smith.*

HELLO MY DARLING (IRE)   3 b.c. Law Society (USA) 130 – Helaplane   **73**
(USA) 68 (Super Concorde (USA) 128) [1990 7.6s⁵ 1991 10m 11.9g⁵ 14s² 16m*]
good-bodied colt: modest form: 12 lengths second of 4 to Moving Out in handicap
(showed quick action) at Sandown in July: 6/4 on, struggled to win 3-runner maiden
at Nottingham following month: shapes like a stayer: acts on soft going. *W. R. Muir.*

HELMSLEY PALACE   2 b.f. (May 3) Dominion 123 – Queen Midas 119 (Glint   **45 p**
of Gold 128) [1991 7g⁵] workmanlike, rather angular filly: first foal: dam 1½m winner
out of half-sister to Abwah and Owen Dudley: 14/1 and green, slow-starting fifth of 9
in minor event at Warwick in October: will stay at least 1m: wasn't knocked about,
and will improve. *Mrs J. Cecil.*

HEMINGBY   4 ch.f. Seclude (USA) – Capsville (USA) (Cyane) [1990 8g 8g⁵ 7g 7d   **61**
7m 7g³ 7f⁴ 6.3m 1991 7g³ 8g⁴ 11f⁴ 11.1m⁴] quite attractive filly: half-sister to several
winners, including fair stayer Harlyn Bay (by Wolver Hollow) and useful 1¼m
winner Shyouskha (by Shy Groom): dam, placed in USA, is sister to smart stakes
winner Pinch Pie: ex-Irish maiden: quite modest form here: should prove at least as
effective at middle distances as 7f: below form when blinkered once. *J. J. O'Neill.*

HEMMERLY   2 ch.f. (Mar 28) Dublin Lad 116 – Minizen Melody (Hello Gorgeous   **—**
(USA) 128) [1991 6g] plain filly: first foal: dam, ran 3 times at 2 yrs, is daughter of
half-sister to Pas de Seul: 33/1 and backward, always behind in maiden at Haydock in
August: dead. *K. R. Burke.*

HEMSWORTH LAD (IRE)   2 gr.g. (Apr 2) Standaan (FR) 118 – Majestic's   **61**
Gold (Rheingold 137) [1991 6f 6.1m 5s⁶] IR 4,600Y: leggy, shallow-girthed gelding:
half-brother to fair 7f winner Muhim (by Pas de Seul), fair 1984 2-y-o 1m winner
Aristocrat Velvet (by Bold Lad) and a winner in Brazil: dam unraced: quite modest
maiden: best effort in Edinburgh claimer final start: seems well suited by soft
ground. *P. Calver.*

HENBURY HALL (IRE)   3 gr.g. Bellypha 130 – Rustic Stile (Rusticaro (FR)   **83**
124) [1990 NR 1991 8g 7.9m* 10m⁶] 35,000Y: angular, good-topped gelding: first
foal: dam unraced half-sister to King's Island and Bengal Fire: well backed, won
£7,400 maiden at York in June, outpaced 3f out then rallying gamely: bit slipped
when tailed off in minor event at Newmarket following month: should be better at
1¼m than shorter: carried head high: sold to join M. Hammond 8,200 gns
Newmarket September Sales. *J. L. Dunlop.*

Cadogan Stakes, York—Henbury Hall rallies to win from Grand Hawk (blinkers)

HENLEY REGATTA   3 br.g. Gorytus (USA) 132 – Straw Boater 89 (Thatch   **66**
(USA) 136) [1990 6m 7m 7m³ 7g 7f⁶ 7s 1991 8g 10m 10.2s² 11.9m³ 11.4m⁶ 11.7g⁵]
tall, leggy gelding: quite modest maiden: better at around 1½m than shorter: acts on
any going. *G. B. Balding.*

HENRI LE COMTE   4 gr.g. Sunley Builds 102 – Countess Mariga (Amboise   –
113) [1990 8f 8g 12m 11.5f 10f a8g 1991 a10g a12g 12f⁶ 14g 12f⁶] leggy gelding: has a
round action: no worthwhile form: visored once. *M. McCormack.*

HENRY LODGE (USA)   3 b.c. Dixieland Band (USA) – Lodging (USA) (King   –
Pellinore (USA) 127) [1990 6m 1991 10g 10.1m 9v 11.5g] smallish colt: behind, in
handicap final start: sold 400 gns Ascot November Sales. *G. P. Enright.*

HENRY WILL   7 b.g. Nicholas Bill 125 – Silver Cygnet 71 (My Swanee 122) [1990   **46**
6f³ 6g* 6f⁴ 7.6d 7m³ 6g 6g* 6g² 6g* 6m 6g² 6m² 6f⁶ 7m 7f 7m 6g 1991 5g⁶ 6m 6g 6m
7m⁵ 7g³ 7f 6d² 7m 7f 7m⁶ 6f⁴ 6m 7m 7.1m 7s 8.1s⁴ a6g] workmanlike, angular
gelding: poor mover: poor handicapper nowadays: effective at 6f to 1m: acts on any
going: has been blinkered. *T. Fairhurst.*

HENRY WILLIAM   6 b.g. Known Fact (USA) 135 – Kesarini (USA) 87 (Singh   **34**
(USA)) [1990 5m 5g 5m² 5.1f³ 5m a5g⁵ 6f⁴ 5f 5m 5g a5g⁴ 1991 a5g⁵ a6g 5m 5m⁵ a5g
5.2f⁴] small, short-backed gelding: poor mover: poor maiden: stays 6f: acts on firm
going. *Pat Mitchell.*

HEPBURN (IRE)   3 b.f. Pitskelly 122 – Bradden 77 (King Emperor (USA))   **51**
[1990 NR 1991 7g 8d⁶ 10d 10.1g 10g 8.1s a8g⁵ a10g² a12g²] 4,000Y: compact filly:
half-sister to 2 winners abroad: dam 10.1f and 2m winner: poor performer: second in
maiden events at Lingfield (claimer first occasion) in December: better at 1½m than
shorter: retained 2,800 gns Ascot December Sales before final start. *M. J.
Fetherston-Godley.*

HERALDINA (IRE)   3 b.f. Heraldiste (USA) 121 – Fotostar (Polyfoto 124) [1990   –
NR 1991 7d] IR 3,200Y: leggy filly: half-sister to useful sprinter Wolverstar (by
Wolverlife) and a winner in Hong Kong: dam Irish 4-y-o 5f winner: second favourite
but bit backward, took keen hold and well beaten in Warwick claimer: mounted on
track: sold 1,000 gns Ascot 2nd July Sales. *M. Bell.*

HERE COMES A STAR   3 b.g. Night Shift (USA) – Rapidus (Sharpen Up 127)   **59**
[1990 6d a7g 1991 6m 6d 5m³ 5m* 5f 5f⁶ 5m] sturdy, lengthy gelding: quite modest
performer: favourite, won 5-runner maiden at Catterick in August: should stay 6f:
acts on good to firm ground: blinkered (well below form) final start: edgy (always
struggling) on fifth: sold 1,700 gns Doncaster November Sales. *J. Etherington.*

HERE HE COMES   5 b.g. Alzao (USA) 117 – Nanette 100 (Worden II 129) [1990   **58**
10.2f 8f a10g 6f 7g 7m⁶ 7m 9g 10m⁵ 10f 10d* 10g⁴ 10d 1991 8m⁴ 10g² 10.8m 10d 10m
10.2g 10m⁴ 10g 9.7f⁴ 10m² 9.7m 10g⁵] angular gelding: has round action: poor
handicapper nowadays: should stay 1½m: acts on firm and dead going: has been
blinkered: has worn crossed noseband: inconsistent. *W. Carter.*

HEROES SASH (USA)   6 b.h. Lypheor 118 – Salish (USA) (Olden Times) [1990   **64**
7m⁵ 8f⁵ 7m 8f 7g³ 8g 1991 8g 10.1g 8g 9d⁶ 7f⁵ 7g⁶ 7g 7g] useful-looking horse: poor
mover: quite modest handicapper at best nowadays: stays 9f: acts on firm and dead
going: has run well when blinkered. *A. Moore.*

HERORA (IRE)   2 b.f. (May 3) Heraldiste (USA) 121 – Kilfenora (Tribal Chief   **98**
125) [1991 5g 6g* 5m* 6g⁴ 6g⁴] sparely-made filly: half-sister to fair 1989 2-y-o 6f
winner African Chief (by Kafu) and winners in USA and Macau: dam Irish 2-y-o 5f
winner: successful in claimer at Leicester (in good style) and £7,800 event at
Beverley in summer: off course over 3 months afterwards: excellent battling-on
fourth of 25 (for 5-lb apprentice unable to claim) to Casteddu in Racecall Gold
Trophy at Redcar final start: will stay 7f: genuine. *N. A. Graham.*

HERO'S LIGHT (USA)   2 ch.c. (Feb 14) Hero's Honor (USA) – I Love You   **81**
Baby (USA) (Damascus (USA)) [1991 6m⁵ 7m² 7m* 7d 8d⁴ᵈⁱˢ 9s²] strong, lengthy,
good-quartered colt: second foal: half-brother to a winner in North America by Lear
Fan: dam sprint winner: sire by Northern Dancer, was easily best at 4 yrs when
stakes winner from 8.5f to 11f: fair performer: won median auction at Wolverhampton in September: good second to Sarasota Bay in listed race at Milan final
start: stays 9f: acts on good to firm and soft ground. *P. F. I. Cole.*

HERRIDGE   3 b.c. Forzando 122 – Eaves (Thatching 131) [1990 NR 1991 7d 8m⁵   **79**
5.7g² 5.7m 6g³ 5.1m* 7g⁴ 6f⁴ 7f] 1,300F, 4,000Y: lengthy, good-topped colt: third
foal: half-brother to a winner in Austria by Elegant Air: dam never ran: modest
performer: won maiden at Bath in July: effective from 5f to 7f: acts on firm ground:
sold 3,000 gns Doncaster October Sales, probably to Scandinavia. *R. Hannon.*

HESTER STANHOPE 2 b.f. (Jan 19) Lomond (USA) 128 – Martha Stevens **56** p
(USA) 102 (Super Concorde (USA) 128) [1991 6g 7g] strong, sturdy filly: first foal:
dam 6f and 7f winner out of CCA Oaks winner Magazine: plating-class form in
maiden at York (green, took keen hold, not knocked about behind Great Palm) and
minor event at Kempton (still bit backward) in late-summer: will stay 1m: should do
better. *P. W. Harris.*

HEY BABA RIBA 2 b.g. (Mar 19) Formidable (USA) 125 – Geopelia 109 **76**
(Raffingora 130) [1991 5m5 6g4 5m* 5.2f4] 38,000Y: sturdy gelding: has a quick
action: brother to a bad maiden and half-brother to several winners, including
ungenuine 1m winner Flitterkiss Park (by Beldale Flutter): dam sprinter: modest
performer: off course 10 weeks, won maiden at Haydock: looking really well, fair
fourth of 8 in nursery at Newbury later in September: likely to prove best at sprint
distances. *M. A. Jarvis.*

HIBISCUS IVY (AUS) 3 b.f. Rancher (AUS) – Melodia (AUS) (Sir Tristram —
115) [1990 NR 1991 a7g 6m] leggy, unfurnished filly: first reported foal: dam
unraced: tailed off in maidens: bandaged near-hind on debut. *I. Campbell.*

HICKORY WIND 4 ch.g. Dalsaan 125 – Derrain (Prince Tenderfoot (USA) 126) **54**
[1990 10v 9m 7m2 7m 7g 8f3 7m 7d 1991 10.2s 8v3 8d 8.2m4 8h* 9m4 8.3d 8g4 11s
a8g] big, angular gelding: turns off-fore in: plating-class handicapper: won at
Carlisle (apprentices) in May: suited by 1m/9f: acts on any going: effective visored
or not: inconsistent: sold 7,200 gns Doncaster August Sales. *Denys Smith.*

HIDDEN COVE (IRE) 3 b.g. Slip Anchor 136 – Glancing 113 (Grundy 137) **94**
[1990 8s5 1991 10m* 10m* 10g4 12f3 10.5f5 10d3] lengthy gelding: has a rather round
action: fairly useful form: won maiden at Pontefract in April and £10,400 handicap at
Ascot in June: good third in £9,600 handicap at Ascot final start: suited by 1¼m: acts
on firm and dead ground: tends to carry head high: winning hurdler. *I. A. Balding.*

HIDDEN FLOWER 2 b.f. (Apr 1) Blakeney 126 – Molucella (Connaught 130) **49**
[1991 6g 7g3 6g 7g 6m] compact filly: second foal: half-sister to 3-y-o Don't Beat The
Baby (by Sulaafah): dam poor half-sister to smart miler Fair Season: poor maiden:
should stay 1¼m: not seen out after July. *J. D. Roberts.*

HIDDEN LAUGHTER (USA) 2 b.f. (Mar 12) Kris S (USA) – More Hilarious **71**
(USA) (Fast Hilarious (USA)) [1991 7g2 7g* 8m] $80,000Y: rangy, rather unfurn-
ished filly: half-sister to winners in North America by Mr Justice and Unpredictable:
dam won at up to 7f: sire won from 5f to 9f: modest form: won maiden at Goodwood
in July, rallying well to lead again line: well beaten in May Hill Stakes at Doncaster 6
weeks later: should be better suited by 1m than 7f. *B. W. Hills.*

HIDDEN LIGHT (IRE) 2 ch.c. (Mar 25) High Line 125 – Beach Light 89 **74** p
(Bustino 136) [1991 8m6] tall, leggy colt: first foal: half-brother to 3 winners,
including 1987 2-y-o 7f winner Mayohora (by Final Straw) and fair 1m to 12.2f winner
Clear Light (by Exhibitioner): dam 1¼m winner, is daughter of smart sprinter
Street Light: 33/1, over 11 lengths sixth of 22, racing keenly then one pace, to Bold
Pursuit in maiden at Newmarket in October: will improve, particularly over further.
M. A. Jarvis.

HIDDEN QUEST (IRE) 3 b.c. Rainbow Quest (USA) 134 – Salidar (Sallust **93**
134) [1990 NR 1991 8g 12f* 12g4 11.9m2 14g4 16.2g3] 190,000Y: good-topped colt:
has quick action: fourth reported foal: half-brother to 6f and 7f winner Budapest (by
Diesis): dam winner over 9.5f in Ireland, is half-sister to Park Appeal and Desirable
(dam of Shadayid): fairly useful form: won maiden at Folkestone in May: in frame in
handicaps, good third of 14 in £11,400 event at Ascot: stays 2m: yet to race on soft
surface. *G. Harwood.*

HIDDEN QUIVER (USA) 5 b.g. Secreto (USA) 128 – Feather Bow (USA) —
(Gun Bow) [1990 12d 12.3g 11.7m 14m 1991 8m] heavy-topped gelding: no worthwhile form on flat: in need of run, first for 7 months, always behind in amateurs
handicap in September: winning hurdler in October. *Mrs G. R. Reveley.*

HIDDEN (USA) 4 ch.f. Secreto (USA) 128 – Shark Song 103 (Song 132) [1990 **71**
10g 11.7g4 14f* 14g5 14m 13.6d a14g* a14g* 1991 a14g2 14m] deep-girthed filly: has a
quick action: quite modest handicapper: not seen out after May: will prove best at up
to 1¾m: acts on firm going: usually blinkered: headstrong. *H. Thomson Jones.*

HI DOL (IRE) 2 b.c. (Apr 27) Drumalis 125 – Abbe's Realm (Realm 129) [1991 **65**
5m 6g6 6f3 7.5f2 7g3 6g6 7m* 7.5f5 8.1m4 7f4 7g3 7m] IR 7,000Y: tall, lengthy colt:
has scope: ninth reported foal: brother to 3-y-o Qualitair Rhythm and half-brother to
4 winners, including useful 1m to 10.6f winner Monarch O Th Glen (by Glenstal):
dam won over 7f in Ireland: quite modest performer: stayed on strongly to win
maiden auction at Redcar in August: ran creditably in Wolverhampton seller

penultimate outing: worth another try at 1m: acts on firm ground: blinkered fifth outing onwards: sold 2,100 gns Doncaster November Sales. *G. Lewis.*

HIEROGLYPHIC (IRE)   3 b.c. Darshaan 133 – Sphinx (GER) (Alpen- **120** ? konig (GER)) [1990 NR 1991 10d³ 12g* 12g* 12.3d* 12m³ 18m⁴ 12d* 14v²]

Hieroglyphic has an impressive record, one of almost constant improvement. He's won four of his eight starts and never been out of the frame. A maiden at Edinburgh and handicaps at Leicester and Chester fell to Hieroglyphic in the space of twenty-three days in the spring before injury, reportedly a cracked knee bone, intervened and forced him off the track for nearly five months. When it was confirmed—after a creditable third in a Newmarket handicap on his return—that he would be contesting the Tote Cesarewitch, Hieroglyphic became the ante-post favourite despite never having had a race over much more than two thirds of the Cesarewitch distance. There was little doubt that he would stay further than a mile and a half but on the day he never looked like winning. Held up towards the rear early on, Hieroglyphic was pushed along vigorously by Carson throughout the final three quarters of a mile and, having hung and carried his head awkwardly approaching the Dip, he could only stay on to justify each-way support, snatching fourth by a short head from the eased Postage Stamp, who was carrying the owner's second colours. Hieroglyphic ran as if he stayed but wasn't at ease on the good-to-firm ground. With very different conditions underfoot he was able to make a successful return to a mile and a half in the last big race of the domestic season then graduate from the handicap ranks with the performance of his life in Italy. John Gosden's father trained the winner of the November Handicap four times between 1956 and 1965, on three occasions when it was run at Manchester followed by its first running, when known as the Manchester Ovaltine Handicap, at Doncaster. 'My father used to lay one out specially each year' reflected Gosden junior after his latest win in the latest edition, a late decision to run being rewarded after a dour struggle. Under a vintage ride from Carson, Hieroglyphic was taken wide initially then disputed second behind Al Therab on rejoining the rest on the turn. Western Dynasty, Linpac West and Canny Chronicle all overtook him at various stages up the straight but Hieroglyphic, roused along from well before the three-furlong marker, was a length in front at the post and going away. The Premio UNIRE Consiglio Europeo-Roma Vecchia, billed as the world's richest Group 3 race with very nearly £100,000 first prize

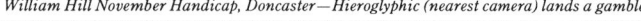

William Hill November Handicap, Doncaster—Hieroglyphic (nearest camera) lands a gamble

money, saw him produce something of an altogether different order. Over a mile and three quarters on heavy ground—'the swamp-like conditions were some of the worst seen at the Rome course' according to one report— Hieroglyphic was able to run Snurge to two lengths and beat another classic winner Turgeon four lengths into third. Although there was no surprise in these conditions suiting Hieroglyphic admirably, there have to be doubts about the value of the form. It was first reported that Hieroglyphic would not have an opportunity to confirm it, to us at least, as he'd be sent to Australia and trained for the Melbourne Cup, but we now understand that he'll be with Gosden again at the start of the 1992 season.

Hieroglyphic (IRE) (b.c. 1988)	Darshaan (br 1981)	Shirley Heights (b 1975)	Mill Reef / Hardiemma
		Delsy (b or br 1972)	Abdos / Kelty
	Sphinx (GER) (b 1978)	Alpenkonig (b 1967)	Tamerlane / Alpenlerche
		Senitza (b 1963)	Waldcanter / Suleika

Hieroglyphic is from the family of Slip Anchor, his dam Sphinx being a granddaughter of Suleika, as is the Derby winner. The import of Slip Anchor's dam Sayonara in the late-'seventies has resulted in plenty of other winners, notably her daughter Sandy Island and descendants Sardegna, Spritsail and Emperor Fountain to add to a host of good winners for the family in their native Germany. The year 1976 was a particularly fruitful one for them with descendants of Suleika annexing three German classics via Stuyvesant (Derby and St Leger) and Swazi (Two Thousand Guineas). Hieroglyphic's branch of the family entered the British Isles when his dam Sphinx was purchased privately from France in 1985. Her three foals prior to Hieroglyphic included a nine-furlong winner in Denmark, Sunniva (by Pas de Seul), and Saint Georges (by Peloponnes) who is still running in the French Provinces at the age of six having won four races from nine and a half furlongs to a mile and a half. Hieroglyphic is followed by the twice-raced Suez Canal (by Commanche Run), another colt by Darshaan and Sphinx is now in foal to Alzao. Sphinx was successful at both three and four years in Germany, five times in all, at around a mile. Her dam Senitza was a winning two-year-old.

Heiroglyphic is an unfurnished colt with a round action. His prospects in 1992 seem to rest largely with the state of the going; he probably needs conditions relatively testing to be effective at a mile and a half, and top-of-the-ground may be against him, anyway. If the ground does come up soft then the John Porter Stakes would be a likely target though races over further will suit him better. It could well be that, Australia or not, Hieroglyphic still ends up challenging for prizes overseas. *J. H. M. Gosden.*

HIGH BACCARAT 2 ch.g. (Apr 10) Formidable (USA) 125 – By Surprise 68 **49** (Young Generation 129) [1991 5g⁵ 6m⁶ 7g 7m] 9,000Y: rather leggy gelding: third foal: half-brother to 7f and 1½m winner Sapphirine (by Trojan Fen): dam 1m winner from family of Little Wolf: poor maiden: will stay 1m. *R. Akehurst.*

HIGH BEACON 4 ch.g. High Line 125 – Flaming Peace 104 (Queen's Hussar **95** d 124) [1990 10g* 12g³ 12m⁵ 16.2f⁶ 16m⁴ 16m³ 1991 14.8m⁵ 14m³ 16g⁵ 10d³ 12. 1d³ 12g 13.9g⁶ 14s 11g] sturdy, workmanlike gelding: keen walker: easy mover: useful handicapper at best: below form last 4 starts: stays 2m: acts on good to firm and dead ground: sold 26,000 gns Newmarket Autumn Sales. *H. Candy.*

HIGHBROOK (USA) 3 b.f. Alphabatim (USA) 126 – Tellspot (USA) (Tell **76** p (USA)) [1990 8g⁶ 1991 10g* 11.9g⁶] lengthy filly: won maiden at Newmarket by 5 lengths from Rudimentary, smooth headway over 2f out and quickening clear entering last: 9/2, 18 lengths sixth of 9 to Nibbs Point in listed race at York later in August, never able to challenge: should stay 1½m: sold N. Tinkler 5,800 gns Newmarket December Sales: has scope, and should do better. *J. H. M. Gosden.*

HIGH CASTE 4 ch.g. Carwhite 127 – Brazen 83 (Cash And Courage 116) [1990 **—** 12.5f 12.3d 12m⁴ 16g 16f* 15.3f³ 17.6f⁶ 1991 17.1m 16.9m] angular gelding: plating-class handicapper at 3 yrs: no form in 1991: stays 2m: acts on firm going: visored final start. *B. C. Morgan.*

HIGH COST 2 b.g. (May 8) Nicholas Bill 125 – Hi-Hunsley 82 (Swing Easy (USA) **69** §
126) [1991 5d 5m³ 5g 6.1g² 6g 5m⁴ 6g⁵ 6m 6.9f⁴] close-coupled gelding: third foal
(all by Nicholas Bill): dam sprinting sister to very useful sprinter Swinging Sam:
quite modest form on his day: suited by 7f: acts on firm ground: ran creditably in
blinkers: has looked irresolute: not one to rely on: sold 5,000 gns Newmarket
Autumn Sales. *H. Candy.*

HIGH DEGREE 3 b. or br.c. Superlative 118 – St Colette (So Blessed 130) [1990 **41**
NR 1991 8s 12g 7f⁵ 10m 8m 7f⁵ 8.2f] IR 48,000Y: lengthy, good-bodied colt: seventh
foal: half-brother to 1½m winners General Pershing (by Persian Bold) and Dudley's
Impact (by Owen Dudley): dam unraced half-sister to Busted: poor maiden: best
efforts at 7f on firm ground: sold to join R. Brotherton 2,100 gns Newmarket
Autumn Sales. *C. E. Brittain.*

HIGHEST ODY (FR) 2 b.c. (Apr 5) Highest Honor (FR) 124 – Odyssee (FR) **?**
110 (Frere Basile (FR) 129) [1991 8v*] 300,000 francs (approx £30,000) Y: fourth
foal: half-brother to winners in France by The Wonder and Kenmare: dam French
10.5f winner, successful in Prix de Royaumont: won 9-runner newcomers event at
Saint-Cloud in November, beating Dissimulateur by 2 lengths: will stay 1¼m:
should improve. *P. Bary, France.*

HIGHEST PRAISE (USA) 8 ch.g. Topsider (USA) – Prides Promise (USA) **68**
(Crozier (USA)) [1990 7f* 7m 7m 7g 7m⁶ 7.6g² 7m 7.6m⁶ a7g 1991 7.6g 7m 7.6d²
7v⁵ 7d³ 7.6m² 7g² 7g* 7g² 7g⁵ 7.6m 7g⁴] strong, good-bodied gelding: moderate
mover: quite modest handicapper: won at Lingfield in August: stays 7.6f: acts on any
going: good mount for apprentice: has found little: best with waiting tactics. *D.
Morris.*

HIGHFLYING 5 br.g. Shirley Heights 130 – Nomadic Pleasure 91 (Habitat 134) **88**
[1990 8.5g³ 8.5g 11m* 12.4m* 12g⁴ 12m* 10.6m² 12.3g* 14m* 14.6g² 12m³ 14.6d*
12s 1991 14g⁵ 16.2g³ 13.9g 13.9g] strong, good-bodied gelding: carries plenty of
condition: usually impresses in appearance: poor mover: fair handicapper: good
third in £10,900 event at Ascot: twice last at York afterwards, including when
favourite for Tote Ebor, giving impression something amiss each time: effective at
1½m to 2m: acts on good to firm and dead going (unsuited by very soft): has worn
bandages: genuine. *A. Harrison.*

HIGH GRADE 3 b.g. High Top 131 – Bright Sun (Mill Reef (USA) 141) [1990 **49** §
10.2s³ a8g 1991 11.7g 11.7m⁵ 13.1f⁶ 16m] sturdy, lengthy gelding: good walker:
poor maiden: seems to stay 13f: gelded after giving moody performance visored
penultimate outing: swished tail throughout on return: sold to join S. Dow 4,000 gns
Newmarket Autumn Sales: one to avoid: winning hurdler. *P. F. I. Cole.*

HIGH HABIT 3 b.f. Slip Anchor 136 – Manx Millenium 66 (Habitat 134) [1990 **79** d
NR 1991 10d 11.5f² 11.5m⁶ 10.5g⁴ 10g] lengthy filly: fluent mover: sixth foal:
half-sister to 5-y-o 9f winner Northern Habit (by Salmon Leap): dam placed at 1m at
3 yrs: modest maiden: easily best efforts when in frame: should prove better at 1½m
than shorter. *I. A. Balding.*

HIGH KICKING 3 b.f. Kalaglow 132 – Can Can Girl 69 (Gay Fandango (USA) **52**
132) [1990 7m 8g 1991 6g⁵ 7.5g⁶ 10g 9g⁵] lengthy, quite attractive filly: plating-class
maiden: blinkered, ran creditably in June handicap final start, making most: stays 9f:
joined D. Burchell. *J. W. Watts.*

HIGHLAND BATTLE (USA) 2 ch.g. (Feb 13) The Minstrel (CAN) 135 – **55**
Battle Drum (USA) (Alydar (USA)) [1991 7g 7g 8m] close-coupled, rather
sparely-made gelding: first known foal: dam won maiden at 3 yrs at around 1m:
plating-class form, well beaten, in maidens and minor event: may stay 1¼m: may do
better in handicaps. *I. A. Balding.*

HIGHLAND CEILIDH (IRE) 3 b.f. Scottish Reel 123 – Savage Love 78 **100**
(Wolver Hollow 126) [1990 7g 7m² 8f* 1991 8g⁴ 10.2m* 12d² 10.7g³ 13.5g 12m 12s³
12s⁶] workmanlike filly: has a round action: good walker: won handicap at Bath in
May: placed at Newbury and in 2 Group 3 events in Germany: stiffish task, soundly
beaten at Newmarket and in Milan listed race sixth and final starts: stays 1½m: acts
on good to firm and soft going. *J. L. Dunlop.*

HIGHLAND HERO 4 b.g. Doc Marten 104 – Lush Secret 50 (Most Secret 119) **—**
[1990 8.2g 6s* 6s 1991 6g 7m 6g] big, lengthy gelding: won minor event at Hamilton
at 3 yrs: below form since but gave impression retains ability in September handicaps: stays 6f: clearly goes well on soft ground: twice reared stalls at 4 yrs. *M. H.
Easterby.*

HIGHLAND MAGIC (IRE) 3 b.g. Stalker 121 – Magic Picture (Deep Diver **71**
134) [1990 5g⁶ 5g⁶ 5g⁴ 6m² 6d a6g⁴ a7g* 1991 7g² 7d³ 6d 7d⁶ 6g² 6m³ 6g 6g³ 5m 7d

7m⁴ 7g] compact gelding: moderate mover: fair handicapper: best efforts in 1991 when in frame: effective at 6f and 7f: acts on good to firm ground and dead: sometimes bandaged off-hind: sold 2,300 gns Newmarket Autumn Sales and gelded. *M. J. Fetherston-Godley.*

HIGHLAND PARK 5 ch.g. Simply Great (FR) 122 – Perchance 77 (Connaught 130) [1990 12f 12.5f⁴ 14g⁶ 13.8m 15m 15d⁴ 1991 13f* 13d² 16m² 12.1s² 13d⁶ 12m* 12.1f] deep-girthed, workmanlike gelding: usually impresses in appearance: plating-class handicapper: won at Hamilton in May and Pontefract in August: effective at 1½m, and probably stays 2m: probably acts on any going: ran poorly when blinkered once: tried visored: not easiest of rides, best held up. *Mrs G. R. Reveley.* **50**

HIGHLAND RUBY 3 b.f. Green Ruby (USA) 104 – Highland Rossie 67 (Pablond 93) [1990 5f⁴ 6m⁶ 1991 6g³ 6g² 7g 6g⁵ 6.9f⁵ 8g] workmanlike filly: moderate mover: quite modest maiden: should stay 7f: best efforts with give in the ground: didn't handle turn (but ran fairly well) at Folkestone penultimate start. *B. A. McMahon.* **59**

HIGHLAND SPIRIT 3 ch.f. Scottish Reel 123 – Salacious (Sallust 134) [1990 5g 5g⁵ 6g⁴ 5g 6f* 6f⁴ 7g³ 7m* 7f² 7g⁵ 6d 1991 8g 8m 7m⁶ 8g 8.5f⁵ 8m⁶ 8d 8m 8m] small, angular filly: has a round action: modest handicapper: stays 1m: acts on firm going: sometimes slowly away: has joined M. Pipe: inconsistent and not one to rely on. *R. M. Whitaker.* **65**

HIGH LOW (USA) 3 b.g. Clever Trick (USA) – En Tiempo (USA) (Bold Hour) [1990 NR 1991 7g³ 8m 7f* a8g²] $105,000Y: sturdy, quite attractive gelding: good mover: fifth reported foal: half-brother to French 1¼m and 10.5f winner After Party (by Tom Rolfe), later Grade 3-placed in USA, and to 2 winners in North America: dam minor winner at 3 yrs in USA: best effort on debut: easily won maiden at Thirsk and fair second of 3 to State Governor in minor event at Southwell in August: should stay 1m: acts on firm ground: gelded after first start. *W. J. Haggas.* **70 +**

HIGHLY PRAISED 3 b.c. Shirley Heights 130 – Ever Genial 117 (Brigadier Gerard 144) [1990 NR 1991 10d 10.1m⁶ 10d³ 12m² 11.8m² 10f* 8v] close-coupled, good-topped colt: first foal: dam 7f to 1m winner: fair form in maidens: 7/1 on, easy task to win at Ripon in August: well beaten in Group 2 event at Rome in November: better at 1½m than 1¼m: possibly needs a sound surface: ridden in paddock and got upset in stalls before pulling hard on debut: is taken down early. *H. R. A. Cecil.* **85**

HIGHLY SECURE 4 b.c. Shirley Heights 130 – Caring (Crowned Prince (USA) 128) [1990 8.5m² 10m⁴ 8g² 8d 8d 8m 1991 8d⁵ 9g 8.1d 9m] compact, quite attractive colt: good walker: modest handicapper: no form after reappearance: best effort at 1m: acts on good to firm and dead ground: keen sort: sold to join R. Callow's stable only 4,200 gns Ascot July Sales. *J. L. Dunlop.* **72 d**

HIGH POST 2 b.g. (May 21) Lidhame 109 – Touch of Class (FR) 47 (Luthier 126) [1991 6m 5.7m 6m 6d³ 5.7g 6g a8g] 3,200Y: smallish gelding: poor mover: half-brother to several winners here and abroad, including useful 1986 2-y-o 7f winner Rhondaling (by Welsh Pageant): dam, winning plater, stayed 1½m: poor maiden: ran creditably on equitrack: stays 1m. *D. Marks.* **46**

HIGH PREMIUM 3 b.c. Forzando 122 – High Halo 64 (High Top 131) [1990 6g 5d 5d 1991 5g² 7g² 7.6d⁵ 6g* 7f* 8.9g⁴ 8m* 8m 9m²] sturdy, good-topped colt: progressive handicapper: successful at Ayr and Newcastle in July then in £7,400 event at Newcastle in August: 14/1, excellent head second of 29 to Mellottie in William Hill Cambridgeshire at Newmarket final start, always prominent, leading 2f out until close home: stays 9f: acts on firm going: sweating and misbehaving beforehand when well beaten at Chester third start: changed hands 72,000 gns Newmarket Autumn Sales: useful performer in the making, sure to win more races. *Mrs J. R. Ramsden.* **92 p**

HIGH PRESSURE 4 ch.f. Kings Lake (USA) 133 – Celestial Storm (Relko 136) [1990 7g³ 8m² 9f* 8m³ 6.3g 8m³ 9m² 8.5m 8d² 8.5g* 7d² 8d* 1991 8d² 9m² 10g² 10g² 12g⁵] second foal: half-sister to Irish 1988 2-y-o 7f winner Glenstorm (by Glenstal): dam once-raced sister to high-class Irish middle-distance filly Give Thanks: useful Irish filly: good second to Prudent Manner in listed event at Leopardstown and Ruby Tiger in Group 2 Sea World Pretty Polly Stakes at the Curragh second and third starts: ran well when under 3 lengths fifth to Sardaniya in Group 3 Meld Stakes at the Curragh final one: stays 1½m: acts on good to firm and dead ground: effective blinkered or not. *J. S. Bolger, Ireland.* **105**

HIGH PRINCIPLES 2 br.g. (Mar 18) Risk Me (FR) 127 – The High Dancer (High Line 125) [1991 5g² 5d² 5d⁴ 6f⁶] 62,000Y: leggy, close-coupled gelding, shade unfurnished: good mover: fourth foal: half-brother to very useful 5f performer **56**

Boozy (by Absalom): dam poor maiden: plating-class maiden: gave trouble stalls when runner-up in small fields in the spring: ran moderately in summer: should be better suited by 6f than 5f. *J. Berry.*

HIGH SAVANNAH 3 ch.f. Rousillon (USA) 133 – Stinging Nettle 90 (Sharpen Up 127) [1990 7m4 8g2 1991 12g3 12m3] rangy filly: modest form: third in maiden at Kempton and amateurs race at Newmarket in the summer: stays 1½m. *M. A. Jarvis.* **72**

HIGH SEVENS 2 ch.f. (Mar 2) Master Willie 129 – Oatfield 69 (Great Nephew 126) [1991 6f* 6f2 6g] 20,000Y: light-framed filly: closely related to 3 winners, including 2m winner High Plains (by High Line) and very useful (at around 1m) Barley Bill (by Nicholas Bill), and half-sister to very useful middle-distance stayer Hateel (by Kalaglow): dam, out of half-sister to High Line, ran 3 times: fair form: won maiden at Newbury in August, soon handy, leading 1f out, running on well: ran well behind Basma in 5-runner minor event at Salisbury in September: never travelling well in listed race at Ayr later same month: should stay 1¼m. *H. Candy.* **86**

HIGH STEPPE 3 b.f. Petoski 135 – High Gait 90 (High Top 131) [1990 NR 1991 10m* 11.5m 13.3g3] 2,800Y: quite attractive, rather unfurnished filly: fifth foal: half-sister to top-class stayer Royal Gait (by Gunner B) and ungenuine Miller's Gait (by Mill Reef): dam middle-distance winner: won median auction contest at Salisbury in May, carrying head high: not given hard race in handicap next start: 20/1, 8½ lengths third of 10 to Supreme Choice in similar event at Newbury, staying on steadily from mid-division: should prove suited by further, possibly by more forcing tactics: sold 8,000 gns Newmarket December Sales. *J. R. Fanshawe.* **82**

HIGH TIME GIRL (IRE) 3 b.f. Nicholas Bill 125 – Carnival Fugue 58 (High Top 131) [1990 6g 7m 1991 10g] lengthy filly: well beaten in maidens then (in need of race, never placed to challenge) claimer. *C. J. Hill.* **–**

HIGHTOWN EXECUTIVE (IRE) 3 b.f. Reasonable (FR) 119 – Tintale (Tin Whistle 128) [1990 5f6 7f3 a5g a8g 1991 a5g6] bad maiden: stays 7f: blinkered only start in 1991 (January). *J. S. Moore.* **–**

HIGHTOWN-PRINCESS (IRE) 3 gr.f. King Persian 107 – Ambient 68 (Amber Rama (USA) 133) [1990 6d 1991 7v 6g 8m 6.9m] leggy, workmanlike filly: no worthwhile form, in July handicap (first run for 3 months) final start. *R. J. Hodges.* **–**

HIGH WATER 4 ch.g. High Line 125 – Sextant 98 (Star Appeal 133) [1990 9s 10.2f2 12g 11m5 10g 11m2 10f 8h 10.2m 10m2 12d 10d6 10m 1991 9s 8m 11m 11s 11f] strong, round-barrelled gelding: has a round action: quite modest handicapper at 3 yrs: no form in 1991: should stay 1½m: acts on any going: has reportedly broken blood vessel. *T. Fairhurst.* **–**

HILL GLITTER 2 b.c. (Feb 7) High Top 131 – La Galette 76 (Double Form 130) [1991 8d*] 35,000Y: rather leggy, unfurnished colt: third foal: closely related to fair 4-y-o 6f and 1m winner La Domaine (by Dominion) and half-brother to fair 6f winner Quiche (by Formidable): dam, lightly-raced maiden, is daughter of Cambridgeshire and Irish 1000 Guineas winner Lacquer and half-sister to good middle-distance colt Shining Finish and very smart stayer Bright Finish: 9/1, won 14-runner minor event at Newmarket in November by a length from Young Freeman, travelling strongly in rear, looking likely to win well when leading 1½f out, then running green: will stay 1¼m: sure to improve. *Mrs J. Cecil.* **81 p**

HILLS OF HOY 5 b.g. Teenoso (USA) 135 – Fairy Tern 109 (Mill Reef (USA) 141) [1990 8.5g 7m 8.5d 7.6g 8.5g2 7g3 8f9g 12m5 1991 9m a12g 10.2f* 10s 9.7f* 10m 10g] compact, quite attractive gelding: has been hobdayed: moderate mover: quite modest handicapper: won apprentice events at Bath in July and Folkestone in September: seems suited by 1¼m: best efforts on a sound surface: inconsistent. *K. C. Bailey.* **64**

HILLTOWN BLUES 2 gr.g. (Mar 28) Le Solaret (FR) – Herminda 80 (King of Spain 121) [1991 5f3 7g5 7f 7m 7f 6m3 5d] 3,300Y, 6,800 2-y-o: leggy gelding: has a quick action: second foal: half-brother to 1990 2-y-o 5.8f winner Lucky Manley (by Ballacashtal): dam disappointing maiden, form only at 5f at 2 yrs: sire (by Le Marmot) won from 1m to 11f in France and USA: plating-class maiden: seems suited by 6f: blinkered last 3 starts. *M. H. Easterby.* **57**

HILLZAH (USA) 3 ch.c. Blushing Groom (FR) 131 – Glamour Girl (ARG) (Mysolo 120) [1990 7m* 7g3 7g 8m 1991 8g 10f* 11g2 12g 11.9m 12m 11g4] workmanlike colt: moderate walker: fairly useful performer at his best: won £7,400 handicap at Newbury in May: ran fairly well in handicap at same course final start: stays 1½m well: acts on dead going: usually held up, and has pulled hard: ran moderately when sweating: sometimes on toes: wore pricker off-side sixth intended start (withdrawn **94**

lame): has hung markedly and looks a hard ride: sold 15,000 gns Newmarket Autumn Sales. *P. T. Walwyn.*

HILTI'S HUT (USA) 3 b.c. Blushing Groom (FR) 131 – Northernette (CAN) **91** (Northern Dancer) [1990 6m⁶ 8m* 8m⁶ 1991 12.3d⁵ 10.2m² 10g⁵ 10m] good-topped, attractive colt: moderate mover: fairly useful performer: 25/1, on toes on first run for 9 weeks, very good staying-on fifth of 16 in £30,600 handicap at Goodwood, not getting best of runs: well beaten in Sandown handicap later in August: should stay 1½m (stiff task at trip): has given trouble at stalls: sold 21,000 gns Newmarket Autumn Sales. *R. Charlton.*

HIMIKO (IRE) 3 b.f. Green Desert (USA) 127 – Fear Naught 99 (Connaught **109** 130) [1990 6m² 6m* 6m⁴ 6.5g⁴ 6d² 6m 1991 8g² 8m 8.2d² 7m⁴ 7.1s* 7g* 7m⁶ 7g 7m⁴] sturdy filly: has a quick action: useful performer: won minor event at Chepstow and listed event (much improved to beat Satin Flower 1½ lengths) at Goodwood in July: failed by some way to reproduce form of latter in pattern events at Doncaster, Goodwood and (5 lengths behind Mystiko) Newmarket: stays 1m: possibly needs easy ground. *B. W. Hills.*

HINARI HI FI 6 b.m. Song 132 – Sarah Siddons (Reform 132) [1990 a6g a6g 6f² **46** 5f⁵ 7f 6f³ 6m⁶ 6g* 6d² 6m³ 6m 6g 6m³ 6g³ 1991 6d 6m 6m 6m⁶ 5h² 5.9m⁵ 7g⁶ 5m⁵ 6g⁴ 5m⁴ 6m³] sparely-made mare: poor mover: poor handicapper: stays 6f: acts on hard and dead going: good mount for apprentice: sometimes wears crossed noseband: has joined P. D. Evans. *W. Haigh.*

HINARI SUNRISE 5 ch.g. Tap On Wood 130 – Miss Markey 98 (Gay Fandango **—** (USA) 132) [1990 12f 12f 12g 1991 12f 12f⁴ 12.3d] leggy, sparely-made gelding: modest winner as 3-y-o: not nearly so good nowadays: stays 1½m: acts on firm going. *S. E. Kettlewell.*

HINARI TELEVIDEO 5 b.m. Caerleon (USA) 132 – Red Jade 82 (Red God **93** 128§) [1990 5m 5d 5g⁵ 5m 5m 5m² 5m a5g 6m* 6m 5.6g 6d 5m 5g³ 5m 6s 5s a7g 1991 6g³ 6g 6.1m⁴ 6m² 6g⁵ 5f 5.6m 6m 5m* 5m] lengthy, good-quartered mare: has a quick, moderate action: fairly useful handicapper: won at York in October: stiffish task on listed event at Newmarket later in month: effective at 5f to 6f: best form on a sound surface: sometimes gave trouble at stalls: best held up and had turn of foot: sold 17,500 gns Newmarket December Sales, in foal to Sharpo. *M. Johnston.*

HINARI VIDEO 6 b.g. Sallust 134 – Little Cynthia 76 (Wolver Hollow 126) **68** d [1990 a5g* a5g a5g* a5g a5g⁵ a5g² 5g⁶ 5g 5d² 5g⁴ 5g⁴ a5g² 5g 5g² 5m³ a5g a5g 6m* 6m 6m 5d* 6d 6s a6g⁵ 1991 a6g³ a6g⁵ a5g⁴ a5g* a5g* 5g² 6m 6g 6d 6d a5g³ 5m⁴ 6g⁴ 6f⁶ 6m⁴ 5m⁵ 5m⁶ 5m 5g⁶ 5s] smallish, workmanlike gelding: moderate mover: quite modest handicapper: won at Lingfield and Southwell in early part of 1991: ideally suited by 5f or easy 6f nowadays: possibly not at best on extremes of going: has worn blinkers. *M. S. Johnston.*

HINARI VISION 4 b.f. Kings Lake (USA) 133 – Get Ahead 58 (Silly Season 127) **—** [1990 8f⁵ 9m 8.2g⁶ 12s 1991 10g a14g 12.1m⁵ 15.1s] sparely-made filly: poor handicapper at best: stays 1m: trained first 2 starts by B. McMath. *P. Monteith.*

HIP TO TIME (USA) 3 b.c. Roberto (USA) 131 – Luv Luvin' (USA) **96** Native) [1990 8.2d* 1991 11g² 10g⁵] rangy, good sort: won minor event at Nottingham as 2-y-o: useful effort when 3 lengths second of 5 to Widyan in moderately-run minor event (11/8 on) at Newbury in April, 1991, leading 3f out until last: blinkered, ran badly in listed Newmarket Stakes 2 weeks later: should stay at least 1½m. *H. R. A. Cecil.*

HIRAM B BIRDBATH 5 b.g. Ragapan 118 – At The King's Side (USA) (Kauai **—** King) [1990 NR 1991 11.5g] sturdy, workmanlike gelding: brother to Irish 1½m winner King Ragapan and plating-class 1¾m and 2¼m winner The Irish Rhine: dam won claiming races at up to 1¼m in USA: tailed off in amateurs maiden at Yarmouth in July, only run on flat: winning hurdler after. *J. A. Glover.*

HISSMA 2 ch.f. (May 18) Midyan (USA) 124 – Double Celt 93 (Owen Dudley 121) **60** p [1991 6m*] medium-sized, quite attractive filly: fourth foal: half-sister to fairly useful 1990 2-y-o 6f and 7f winner Sedair (by Green Desert) and winners in Sweden and Yugoslavia: dam, from good family, suited by 1¼m: 6/4 and ridden by 7-lb claimer, won 6-runner maiden at Ripon in August, soon disputing lead, running on well final 1½f: will stay 1m: seemed sure to improve. *H. R. A. Cecil.*

HITCHENSTOWN 8 b.g. Town And Country 124 – Veinarde (Derring-Do 131) **—** [1990 10.6f 8f 5s 12f* 13g a12g 7.6m⁵ 8f⁴ 8h⁵ 12m 10.4g⁶ 1991 10.3d 11.1s] strong, lengthy gelding: carries plenty of condition: poor handicapper: well beaten in summer: effective at 1m and stays 1½m: acts on any going: occasionally blinkered. *M. O'Neill.*

HIZEEM 5 b.g. Alzao (USA) 117 – Good Member (Mansingh (USA) 120) [1990 **32** §
8f⁵ 8f 7f 10m 8f 7g* 8m⁵ 8m 7f⁵ 8m³ 8.2m 9g 1991 8g⁵] small gelding: poor handicapper: effective at 7f to 1¼m: acts on firm going: often blinkered: one to avoid. *K.
B. McCauley.*

HOB GREEN 2 ch.g. (Apr 8) Move Off 112 – Prejudice 83 (Young Generation **54** p
129) [1991 6m 8m 6g⁵] sturdy gelding: has a quick action: first foal: dam maiden
suited by 1m: drifted left off bridle in seller at Newmarket: best effort when fifth of 11
in very strongly-run claimer at Catterick later in October, tenderly ridden and soon
with great deal to do then catching eye staying on very strongly: may well prove
capable of better, particularly back over further. *Mrs J. R. Ramsden.*

HOKUSAI (USA) 3 b.c. Fighting Fit (USA) – Angling (USA) (Angle Light **119**
(USA)) [1990 6g* 7m* 1991 8m³ 8g 9.2m⁴ 12f 8g³] compact, attractive colt: smart
performer: in frame in Craven Stakes at Newmarket, Prix Jean Prat (staying on from
rear behind Sillery) at Longchamp and St James's Palace Stakes (best effort, 2
lengths behind Marju, making most) at Royal Ascot: close up long way in Derby at
Epsom: may prove suited by 1¼m: has sweated and got on edge, particularly so at
Ascot: sold to race in USA, sixth in 9f Hollywood Derby (Nov 17). *H. R. A. Cecil.*

HOLD COURT (IRE) 3 ch.c. The Noble Player (USA) 126 – Sindos 89 (Busted **54**
134) [1990 7g 8.2s 6d* 1991 10g⁶ 10g 9d⁶ 10.1g 10g³ 11.5m⁵ 10m 11.7m 10g] rather
leggy, lengthy colt: moderate mover: plating-class form in first half of 1991 season:
has raced keenly, and may prove best at up to 1¼m: may well need an easy surface:
blinkered fourth and final starts. *N. A. Callaghan.*

HOLD FAST (IRE) 3 b.g. Dara Monarch 128 – No Flight (Nonoalco (USA) 131) —
[1990 a7g a8g⁴ 1991 7d⁵ 6g 7m 8.1s a10g] good-topped gelding: good walker: poor
maiden: should stay 1m: retained by trainer 740 gns Newmarket July Sales. *H.
Candy.*

HOLETOWN 2 b.c. (Mar 6) Prince Sabo 123 – Cubby Hole (Town And Country **80**
124) [1990 6d 6s² 6m³ 6f* 6m* 5.2f³] neat colt: has a quick action: first foal: dam
poor half-sister to Gold Cup winner Little Wolf: fair performer: made most to win
maiden at Brighton and virtually all in nursery at Doncaster in September: stays 6f:
may prove best on a sound surface. *R. Hannon.*

HOLIDAY ISLAND 2 ch.c. (May 5) Good Times (ITY) – Green Island 89 (St **71**
Paddy 133) [1991 5d³ 7d⁵ 6m 9m⁴ 8g² 7g⁵] good-topped colt: half-brother to winners
abroad by Final Straw and Welsh Pageant: dam won over 1¼m: modest maiden:
best efforts in nurseries last 2 starts: may well stay 1¼m: retained 13,000 gns
Newmarket Autumn Sales. *C. E. Brittain.*

HOLLYWOOD HARRY 2 ch.c. (May 20) Miswaki (USA) 124 – Bonnie Hope **77**
(USA) (Nijinsky (CAN) 138) [1991 7g⁵ 6m⁵ 7d 6f² 7m 6g³] 18,000Y: angular,
workmanlike colt: half-brother to 1½m and 1¾m winner Raahin (by Super
Concorde) and 2 winners abroad: dam ran only at 2 yrs, when successful at around
1m: modest maiden: ran well (though well beaten) in Tattersalls Tiffany Highflyer
Stakes at Newmarket penultimate outing: will stay 1m: ran creditably in blinkers
final outing, and when sweating: sold 19,000 gns Newmarket Autumn Sales. *C. E.
Brittain.*

HOLY WANDERER (USA) 2 b.c. (Apr 8) Vaguely Noble 140 – Bronzed **53**
Goddess (USA) (Raise A Native) [1991 6m 7f 6g] $25,000Y, resold $28,000Y:
compact colt: half-brother to numerous winners in North America, 2 in minor
stakes: dam minor winner: poor maiden: best effort at 7f: bandaged near-hind final
start. *D. W. P. Arbuthnot.*

HOME JANE 3 b.f. Homeboy 114 – Rhythm 64 (Bleep-Bleep 134) [1990 6m 7g —
5m 1991 7m 8g 11.7g] compact filly: poor form: well beaten in claimers and handicap
in summer as 3-y-o. *R. J. Holder.*

HOME LOAN 4 b.f. Homing 130 – Rambert (Mandamus 120) [1990 8.2m 8d⁶ 12d —
1991 10g] leggy filly: poor maiden at best: seems to stay 1m. *M. McCourt.*

HOME RULE (FR) 8 b. or br.g. Home Guard (USA) 129 – Sierra (March Past —
124) [1990 6d 1991 10.2s⁶ 7d] useful performer at 3 yrs here: sent to Ireland, won 6f
apprentice handicap at the Curragh as 5-y-o: only poor nowadays: not seen out after
April: has won on firm going, but much better suited by plenty of give in the ground.
J. S. Moore.

HOMESTEAD LAD 3 b.g. Homing 130 – Greenstead Lady 67 (Great Nephew **26**
126) [1990 7.5m 7f a8g 1991 10f 11g 9.9f 10g³ 8m⁶ 12.1f 8.1g 11m] leggy gelding: bad
maiden: worthwhile form only at 1¼m. *D. W. Chapman.*

380

HOMILE   3 b.c. Homing 130 – Rocas 48 (Ile de Bourbon (USA) 133) [1990 7m⁵ 7m   **50**
7g⁶ a6g⁵ a7g³ 1991 8f 8m 10d 8f 9.2m² 8.3m* 7m] leggy, lengthy colt: poor performer: sweating, won seller (sold out of R. Hannon's stable 4,800 gns) at Windsor
in August: slowly away and tailed off much of way at Southwell (apprentices) 7
weeks later: stays 9f: acts on good to firm ground: blinkered last 3 outings: carried
head rather high time before. *P. A. Blockley.*

HONEY BOY SIMBA   5 ch.g. Mansingh (USA) 120 – Continental Divide 50   **50**
(Sharp Edge 123) [1990 7m⁴ 8m³ 8m 8.5g* 9s 10f a8g² 8g 8f* 8m³ 8m⁵ 8.5m⁵ 8.2d
8g³ 1991 8g* 8d⁵ 8m 8m] smallish, lengthy gelding: carries condition: poor mover:
plating-class handicapper: won at Carlisle (apprentices) in March: off course over 6
months before well beaten last 2 starts, running moody race final one: best form at
7f to 1m: below form on hard ground, probably acts on any other: usually visored. *M.
J. O'Neill.*

HONEYCHURCH (USA)   3 b.f. Bering 136 – Countess Tully (Hotfoot) [1990   **93**
NR 1991 10.5g* 10m³ 11.4m³] 36,000Y: tall, useful-looking filly: fourth foal:
half-sister to useful 1988 French 2-y-o 1m winner Russian Countess (by Nureyev):
dam useful winner at 8.5f and 1¼m in Ireland: later successful in USA: won maiden
at Haydock in July, making virtually all: beaten 3 lengths behind Lord Charmer then
4½ lengths behind Mohican Girl in minor events at Newmarket and Sandown: stays
1½m: moved moderately to post at Sandown: sold 9,000 gns Newmarket December
Sales. *L. M. Cumani.*

HONEY DANCER   7 b.g. Tyrnavos 129 – Hello Honey 105 (Crepello 136) [1990   **74**
NR 1991 14m⁴ 18m] well-made gelding: moderate mover: modest handicapper: first
start since 5 yrs, ran well when fourth at Sandown in September: well beaten in
Cesarewitch at Newmarket month later: needs further than 1½m and stays 2¼m:
acts on any going: pulled too hard in blinkers. *Miss A. J. Whitfield.*

HONEY DAY   2 ch.f. (Mar 25) Lucky Wednesday 124 – Honeydant (Ascendant   —
96) [1991 5f 6m a7g] leggy, lightly-made filly: first reported foal: dam ran once over
hurdles: no form in claimer at Beverley or maidens at Southwell. *S. R. Bowring.*

HONEY HEATHER (IRE)   2 ch.f. (Feb 14) Kris 135 – Heatherfields (North-   **52**
fields (USA)) [1991 5m³ 6.1d⁴ 6s] 700,000 francs (approx £70,000) Y: small, lengthy
filly: first foal: dam Irish middle-distance winner, is half-sister to Flash of Steel (by
Kris): plating-class maiden: will stay 1m: ran moderately on soft ground. *C. F. Wall.*

HONEY MILL   5 b.m. Milford 119 – Sharp Venita 84 (Sharp Edge 123) [1990 a6g   **41**
a8g⁴ a8g 7g a5g a6g 1991 a6g a7g a6g 7d 7m⁶ 7f 7f⁵ 7m⁵ 6.1d 8g] rangy mare: poor
handicapper, still a maiden: should stay at least 1m: acts on firm going, seems
unsuited by dead: often blinkered, has worn hood. *O. O'Neill.*

HONEY SNUGFIT   2 ch.f. (May 8) Music Boy 124 – Buy G's 60 (Blakeney 126)   **44**
[1991 5m⁶ a5g³ 5g⁴ a7g⁴ a7g³ 7.1m³ 7m⁶] 7,200Y: lengthy filly: has scope: moderate
mover: third foal: half-sister to 3-y-o 1m winner China Sky (by Tina's Pet) and 1989
2-y-o 6f winner Scorpio Lady (by Vaigly Great): dam 12.2f winner: modest plater:
stays 7f: acts on firm ground, and on fibresand: blinkered and on toes final outing. *J.
Berry.*

HONEY VISION   2 b.f. (Feb 4) Vision (USA) – Straw Bonnet (Thatch (USA) 136)   **57**
[1991 5f 7m 6f 8m⁴ 9m 8.2m 8m⁵ 7m⁶ a8g³ a7g²] 4,000F, 4,000Y: lengthy filly:
half-sister to 5f performer Panama Princess (by Indian King): dam unraced daughter
of very useful Irish 7f and 1m winner and Irish Oaks fourth I've A Bee, half-sister to
2 good stayers: blinkered when placed in claimer and maiden (went clear then
caught close home) on equitrack at Lingfield: fifth in Newmarket seller previously:
visored seventh and eighth starts: hung left second outing: inconsistent. *G. H.
Eden.*

HONING STONE (IRE)   3 b.c. Flash of Steel 120 – Prestigious (Cure The   **68**
Blues (USA)) [1990 7g⁴ 7m³ 7m² 7g⁶ 8m⁵ 8d 8g³ 8m a7g⁵ a7g² a8g* 1991 a8g* a8g²
a10g a8g² 10g] compact, good-quartered colt: moderate mover: quite modest
performer: won handicap at Southwell in January: ran poorly in handicap at
Kempton in March: seems unsuited by a soft surface: has had tongue tied down: has
won for apprentice. *C. N. Allen.*

HOON KING   2 ch.c. (Feb 16) Midyan (USA) 124 – Capel Curig 74 (Welsh   **95**
Pageant 132) [1991 6g³ 6g² 6g* 7g 7f* 7f² 8g⁵ 6m³] 25,000F, 29,000Y: smallish,
good-quartered colt: fluent mover: second foal: half-brother to 3-y-o 7f winner
Volcalmeh (by Lidhame): dam 2-y-o 1¼m winner: fairly useful performer: easily
won maiden at Pontefract in July and nursery at Thirsk in September: ran well
subsequently: will stay 1¼m: acts well on firm ground. *Mrs J. Cecil.*

HOOTING DON 3 gr.g. Bold Owl 101 – Donna Pavlova (Don (ITY) 123) [1990 **75** 6g³ 6f³ 6g³ 7g² a7g³ a7g⁴ 7.5g* 8g⁶ 8d³ 9g 1991 8g³ 9.1s² 8.5f⁶ 9m⁶] close-coupled gelding: modest performer: headed post in claimer at Newcastle in April, edging left: stays 9f well: best on easy ground: sold 1,600 gns Doncaster October Sales. *J. Berry.*

HOPEFUL BID (IRE) 2 b.g. (Mar 30) Auction Ring (USA) 123 – Irish Kick **64** p (Windjammer (USA)) [1991 6m 6g⁶ 6f] 23,000F, 25,000Y: leggy, close-coupled, unfurnished gelding: half-brother to several winners, including very useful 6f winner Sharp N' Early (by Runnett) and fair 1985 2-y-o 5f winner St Croins Castle (by Godswalk): dam never ran: best effort when fourteenth of 22, beaten only around 6 lengths having been close up almost 5f, in maiden at Newbury (backed at long odds, awkward stalls) in September: may prove best at sprint distances: likely to improve further. *R. Hannon.*

HOPSCOTCH 4 b.f. Dominion 123 – Tartan Pimpernel 109 (Blakeney 126) [1990 — a10g⁶ 1991 11.7g 17.1m] lightly-made filly: moderate mover: quite modest maiden at best on flat: wearing crossed noseband, ran poorly in handicaps in spring: should stay middle distances: useful and prolific front-running winning hurdler: sold 30,000 gns Ascot June Sales. *M. C. Pipe.*

HORIZON (IRE) 3 b.g. Red Sunset 120 – Vahila (Relko 136) [1990 NR 1991 10g⁵ **75** 12d 12s⁴ 10g* 10g* 16.2f⁴ 10.2g* 10.5m* 10.2m 12d⁶] IR 11,800F, 40,000Y: rangy gelding: third foal: dam lightly-raced Irish maiden, is half-sister to Park Hill winner Borushka: made all in amateurs handicap at Salisbury and claimer (claimed out of G. Harwood's stable £13,000) at Sandown in July and in handicaps at Chepstow (by 10 lengths and best effort, unchallenged) in August and Haydock in September: well below form last 2 starts: best efforts with forcing tactics at around 1¼m: acts on good to firm ground: soon off bridle third start, blinkered afterwards. *T. Thomson Jones.*

HORIZONTALE 2 b.f. (Apr 27) Night Shift (USA) – Jenny Mere (Brigadier **45** Gerard 144) [1991 6g 7g 6f⁶ 6m 7m] close-coupled filly: first foal: dam unraced: poor maiden: should stay 7f. *C. E. Brittain.*

HORN PLAYER (USA) 4 ch.c. The Minstrel (CAN) 135 – Qualique (USA) — (Hawaii) [1990 8m⁵ 8m 8.5d² 12.3g³ 12g 1991 14.8g] big, lengthy colt: poor mover: modest maiden at 3 yrs for B. Hills: bandaged and tailed off only run in 1991 (April): stays 12.3f: acts on good to firm ground and dead. *F. Jordan.*

HOSTESS QUICKLY 4 b.f. Hotfoot 126 – Linda Dudley 81 (Owen Dudley 121) — [1990 12f5 a12g² 12m* a11g² 12g a11g⁴ 12m 13v² 1991 a14g a12g] leggy filly: poor handicapper on most form at 3 yrs: well beaten in claimers in November: should stay 1¾m: has won on good to firm ground, but goes well on heavy going: ungenuine hurdler. *M. R. Channon.*

HOTFOOT HANNAH (IRE) 3 b.f. Anita's Prince 126 – Serendip (Sing Sing — 134) [1990 NR 1991 6m 6m⁵ 6.1m] 600 2-y-o: good-topped filly: moderate mover: half-sister to several winners, including very useful miler Serencia (by Great Heron) and fair 1984 2-y-o 5f winner Master Crofter (by Crofter), subsequently successful in USA: dam never ran: bit backward, no worthwhile form in maidens and claimer. *P. S. Felgate.*

HOT HOPE 4 b.f. Blazing Saddles (AUS) – Return Home (Nonoalco (USA) 131) — [1990 a6g⁴ a6g⁵ a5g* 5f⁴ 5m⁴ 6f 5m⁵ 5g 5g 5m a5g a7g 1991 a10g a5g⁵ a6g⁶ a6g a5g⁶] plain filly: poor handicapper: no form for long time: best at 5f: acts on firm going: sold 1,200 gns Ascot May Sales. *J. J. Bridger.*

HOT LAVENDER (CAN) 2 b.f. (Jan 27) Shadeed (USA) 135 – Wind Spray 69 **56** (Mill Reef (USA) 141) [1991 5g⁴ 5m³] $28,000Y: lengthy filly: sister to fair 1989 2-y-o 5f winner Megyaas, closely related to a fair maiden by Czaravich and half-sister to a winner by Coastal: dam, second over 1½m at 3 yrs in Ireland, is half-sister to Shining Finish and Bright Finish and from family of Teenoso: sweating, plating-class form in minor event at Sandown (moved poorly down) and maiden at Folkestone (led under 2f out, headed below distance) in July: bred to stay at least 1m: seemed likely to improve further. *C. F. Wall.*

HOT PERFORMER 4 ch.f. Hotfoot 126 – Show Business 72 (Auction Ring — (USA) 123) [1990 8f⁶ 7m 8.2f⁵ 7h⁶ 8.2g 7g 8d 10g⁵ 12f* 10g 13.8f 10m² 11v 1991 7g 10.5d] tall, lengthy filly: has round action: poor handicapper: no show in 1991: stays 1½m: acts on firm going, tailed off on heavy: somewhat temperamental. *T. Fairhurst.*

HOT PUNCH 2 ch.g. (May 8) Dara Monarch 128 – Glebehill 76 (Northfields **50** (USA)) [1991 5m 5m² 6d 6m⁶ 7.5f 8m] 3,000Y: sparely-made gelding: half-brother to several winners, including 5f winner Java Jive (by Hotfoot), 1m and 1¼m winner Alkinor Rex (by Welsh Pageant) and 3-y-o 6f winner Bowden Boy (by Never So Bold): dam 2-y-o 6f winner, is out of smart sprinter Pendlehill: plating-class maiden: should stay beyond 6f: looked difficult ride third outing. *P. Calver.*

HOT ROCK   2 b.c. (Mar 18) Sizzling Melody 117 – Arch Sculptress 85 (Arch   — Sculptor 123) [1991 6f 7g] 9,200Y: good-topped colt: fifth foal: closely related to 5f and 6f winner Psalm (by Song) and half-brother to 1m to 1¼m performer San Roque (by Aragon) and a winner in Italy: dam, soft-ground sprinter, is half-sister to smart French middle-distance colt El Famoso: no form, in Yarmouth seller on debut: sold to Scandinavia 1,100 gns Newmarket Autumn Sales. *Lord John FitzGerald.*

HOT SEAT   2 b.c. (Apr 2) Blazing Saddles (AUS) – Vent du Soir (Main Reef 126)   **33** [1991 5m 6m 7m⁴ 7.5f 7m⁵ a7g 8.3g 7m] 2,500Y: leggy, rather sparely-made colt: first foal: dam never ran: poor plater: stays 7f: sold 1,150 gns Doncaster October Sales. *J. F. Bottomley.*

HOT SUNDAY SPORT   3 b.f. Star Appeal 133 – Alpine Alice 94 (Abwah 118)   **42** [1990 6g 7f³ 8m 1991 a12g² 12f 12.2g⁴ 11f⁵ 11m] leggy filly: poor mover: plater: form in spring as 3-y-o only when in frame: stays 1½m: seems best with give in the ground: blinkered last 3 outings. *P. A. Kelleway.*

HOT TIP   2 b.f. (Mar 28) Beldale Flutter (USA) 130 – Summer's Darling 63 (Final   **48** Straw 127) [1991 7m 8.9m 8.1s] 1,000F: workmanlike filly: second foal: dam, maiden best at 1m, is daughter of sister to Rheingold: best effort seventh of 19 in claimer at York (late headway never dangerous) second start: will stay 1¼m: well beaten on soft ground. *B. Ellison.*

HOT TOOTSIE   4 b.f. Hotfoot 126 – Lady of The Isle 72 (Pitskelly 122) [1990 6g   — 6m 1991 6d 6m 6f 6m⁵ 6m 6m a6g] small, good-bodied filly: has been hobdayed: useful plater at 2 yrs: no worthwhile form in 1991: suited by 6f: seems to act on any going: difficult ride: sold 820 gns Doncaster November Sales. *J. Balding.*

HOULSTON'S WILL   2 ch.f. (May 16) Nicholas Bill 125 – Falcrello 51 (Falcon   **76** p 131) [1991 7m³] close-coupled, workmanlike filly: sister to 7f (at 2 yrs) to 11f winner Own Free Will and half-sister to Wiki Wiki Wheels (by Import), useful winner at up to 1m: dam won 11f seller: 50/1 and better for race, 2 lengths third of 18 to Mahool in maiden at Doncaster in October, plenty to do at halfway, ran on well not knocked about: will improve, particularly over middle distances. *Mrs J. R. Ramsden.*

HOUSE OF FRUIT   4 b.g. Munsingh (USA) 120 – Rheinbloom 66 (Rheingold   — 137) [1990 a10g 1991 14d 10g 10m 16.5m] tall, rather unfurnished gelding: no form since quite modest at 2 yrs: stays 7f: blinkered final start. *C. N. Allen.*

HOWJAL (USA)   6 b.g. Conquistador Cielo (USA) – Taylor Park (USA) (Sir   **44** Gaylord) [1990 12g 1991 15.8f 14d⁶ 12m³ 16.2d] angular, well-made gelding: poor handicapper nowadays: tailed off when pulled up lame final start (July): should stay 2m: acts on good to firm and dead ground. *J. R. Bostock.*

HOW'S YER FATHER   5 b.g. Daring March 116 – Dawn Ditty 100 (Song 132)   **74** [1990 a6g² a6g 6g⁶ 6f 6d 5m⁴ 5f⁴ 5.3f⁶ 5g³ 5m⁶ 1991 5m⁶ 5.3f* 6m* 5g 6f² 6d³ 5.1g² 6g² 6.1s* 7g² 6f⁶ 7f³ 7f⁴ 7m 6g 5.1s* 6.1d⁴ 5g² 7d 5d] leggy gelding: improved handicapper in 1991: won at Brighton (2) in spring and Chepstow in July and October: effective at 5f to 7f: acts on any going: sometimes blinkered: has run creditably when sweating and edgy: tough. *R. J. Hodges.*

HTHAAL (USA)   3 b. or br.c. Caro 133 – Endurable Heights (USA) (Graustark)   **77** [1990 6d⁵ 1991 7f³ 7.5m² 11.9m²] big, leggy, close-coupled colt: moderate walker: modest maiden: second of 5 in handicap at Haydock in July, making most: stays 1½m well: acts on firm going: sold to join L. Lungo 21,000 gns Newmarket Autumn Sales. *H. Thomson Jones.*

HUBBERS FAVOURITE   3 ch.f. Anfield 117 – Printafoil (Habat 127) [1990 NR   — 1991 7g 10m 12m 10g a12g⁴ 12m⁶ 8.3m 10m 17.1m a12g] sturdy filly: moderate mover: third living foal: half-sister to 8.5f (at 2 yrs) and 11f winner Hard To Name (by Connaught): dam poor half-sister to smart middle-distance stayer Major Green and Irish Guineas fourth Miss Connaught: form only when fourth of 12 in handicap at Southwell: stays 1½m: looks one paced: trained first 9 starts by E. Eldin. *M. J. Heaton-Ellis.*

HUCKLEBERRY WIN (USA)   4 ch.c. Riverman (USA) 131 – Waterloo 120   — (Bold Lad (IRE) 133) [1990 7f³ 10g 8d⁴ 7.2d³ 8v* 7.6v 1991 8.2g] compact colt: modest handicapper at best: should have stayed 1¼m: best efforts with plenty of give in the ground: dead. *M. D. Hammond.*

HUD HUD (USA) 3 b.f. Alydar (USA) – Tax Dodge (USA) (Seattle Slew (USA)) — [1990 7g 1991 12m6 12f6] unfurnished filly: no worthwhile form in maidens: takes good hold: not seen out after May. *A. A. Scott.*

HUDSON BAY TRADER (USA) 4 b.g. Sir Ivor 135 – Yukon Baby (USA) — (Northern Dancer) [1990 8f 10g3 10.6f* 11.7g5 11m 12g 10g4 1991 12.2g] strong, attractive gelding: trained by C. Wall, modest handicapper at 3 yrs: in need of run, first for 7 months, well beaten only flat run in 1991: should be suited by 1½m + : acts on firm ground: quite modest hurdler for N. Henderson. *M. Avison.*

HUGGING 2 b.f. (May 24) Beveled (USA) – Pillowing 69 (Good Times (ITY)) **59** [1991 6f4 5g5 6.1m6] tall filly: good mover: first live foal: dam sprinting daughter of half-sister to Blushing Groom: quite modest maiden: on toes last 2 starts: will prove better suited by 6f than shorter. *M. McCormack.*

HUMOUR (IRE) 2 b.f. (Apr 21) Sadler's Wells (USA) 132 – Princess Tracy 111 **59** p (Ahonoora 122) [1991 7m] 46,000Y: leggy filly: closely related to 3-y-o Tracy's Prince (by Be My Guest) and half-sister to 1m and 9f winner Topasannah (by Commanche Run): dam Irish sprinter, sister to dam of Shalford: 20/1, one-paced seventh of 14 in maiden at Leicester in October: should stay 1m: will improve. *C. F. Wall.*

HUMSTER 3 ch.g. Song 132 – Primrolla 64 (Relko 136) [1990 NR 1991 7g 8d2 **62** 7m3 7g2 8m6 8g] leggy gelding: fourth foal: closely related to 5f and 1m winner Primulette (by Mummy's Pet): dam 1¼m winner, also useful young hurdler: quite modest maiden: placed at Warwick (apprentices), Lingfield and Newmarket: below best last 2 starts: should prove suited by 1m + : third third outing: sold to join J. J. O'Neill 10,500 gns Newmarket Autumn Sales. *H. Candy.*

HUNDRA (USA) 3 ch.g. Arctic Tern (USA) 126 – Nur Jahan (USA) (Raja Baba **114** (USA)) [1990 8s4 1991 10g5 12m4 10.4d* 12f5 12m 12g 10f] angular, close-coupled gelding: improved form when winning listed Dee Stakes at Chester and when 12½ lengths fifth of 13 to Generous in Ever Ready Derby (plenty to do entering straight, staying on well but checked 1f out) at Epsom 4 weeks later: well beaten in 2 Group 1 events on Continent and Arlington Million, Chicago, last 3 starts: better at 1½m than shorter: acts on firm and dead going: blinkered second 3-y-o outing: gelded after final one. *P. A. Kelleway.*

HUNDRED ISLANDS 4 br.f. Hotfoot 126 – Bally Tudor 75 (Henry The — Seventh 125) [1990 7.5d 8m 15g5 10m3 13.8m3 1991 12d6 12f] lengthy, good-topped filly: has a long stride: poor maiden: worth another try at beyond 1½m: acts on firm and dead ground. *M. J. Camacho.*

HUNTED 4 ch.g. Busted 134 – Madam Cody (Hot Spark 126) [1990 10.5m4 14m5 — 12m3 1991 16d] sturdy gelding: has a quick action: fair maiden at 3 yrs: bandaged on first run for nearly 9 months, tailed off in handicap at Sandown in July: should stay beyond 1½m: acts on good to firm ground: well beaten over hurdles (tried to run out once). *A. R. Davison.*

HUNTING GROUND 3 b.c. Dancing Brave (USA) 140 – Ack's Secret (USA) **84** p (Ack Ack (USA)) [1990 NR 1991 10m2] good-bodied colt: fifth foal: half-brother to 3 winners in USA: dam high-class winner at up to 11f: weak 8/1, 2½ lengths second of 16 to Missed Again in maiden at Leicester in October, keeping on strongly: should stay 1½m: sure to improve. *G. Harwood.*

HUNT THE SLIPPER (IRE) 2 b.c. (Apr 28) Fools Holme (USA) – Silver — Glimpse 108 (Petingo 135) [1991 7g 7m6] IR 28,000Y: sturdy colt: half-brother to several winners here and in France, including 1¼m and 11.7f winner Hintlesham Harry (by Pas de Seul): dam 7f winner at 2 yrs in France: well beaten in maidens at Brighton (slowly away) and Newcastle: sold 3,200 gns Newmarket Autumn Sales. *W. Jarvis.*

HURRICANE POWER 4 br.c. Wolverlife 115 – Libby Jayne 67 (Tumble Wind **64** (USA)) [1990 6m2 6m* 5d 6m4 6s a7g3 1991 a8g a7g a7g4 7d 7d4 10m 8.3m* 8.1g 7g6 8m 8.1m 6g3 6m5 6.1m] rangy, quite attractive colt: moderate mover: quite modest handicapper: won at Windsor in July, making all: best at 6f to 1m: acts on good to firm going, possibly unsuited by dead: has found little: blinkered seventh and last 6 starts: none too consistent: sold 9,800 gns Newmarket Autumn Sales. *J. D. Bethell.*

HURRY TO GLORY (USA) 2 b.f. (Apr 22) On To Glory (USA) – Hurry Marie **42** (USA) (Hurry To Market) [1991 6m 5g 6s] sturdy, close-coupled filly: quite good mover: half-sister to 1990 2-y-o 6f winner In A Whirl (by Island Whirl), and several other winners, one in minor stakes in North America: dam won 9 races at up to 1¼m: poor maiden: best effort at 5f. *M. A. Jarvis.*

HUSH KATIE 3 b.f. Kind of Hush 88 – Perlesse 88 (Bold Lad (USA)) [1990 NR 1991 a8g a8g a10g 12f 12.3d 12d] 3,000Y: sturdy filly: sixth foal: sister to ungenuine sprinter Samleon and half-sister to 6f winner Flighting Moon (by Moorestyle) and 4-y-o Gozone (by Carwhite): dam 2-y-o 6f winner: behind, in selling handicap (sweating) final start: unlikely to stay middle distances: joined I. Campbell. *J. Pearce.* —

HUSO 3 ch.g. Sharpo 132 – Husnah (USA) 85 (Caro 133) [1990 6m⁶ 6m 6m 6m⁵ 6g⁴ 1991 6d 8s⁵ 8.5f³ 8.2m* 8.9g* 8g² 8m 8m 9m⁴ 8m⁶ 8.1s a8g] good-quartered gelding: modest handicapper: won at Nottingham in May and Wolverhampton (made all) in June: best effort when unlucky second at Newmarket, but mostly well below form on flat afterwards: visored (made most) on good to firm ground: stays 9f: acts on good to firm ground: visored (made most) final start: winning hurdler. *P. C. Haslam.* 77

HUSTHWAITE HILLS 2 b.c. (May 23) Efisio 120 – Malise (Royal Palace 131) [1991 6m 6g 7s⁶] angular colt: moderate walker: half-brother to 1984 2-y-o 5f winner Esilam (by Frimley Park): dam ran twice: no worthwhile form in summer sellers: sold 640 gns Ascot July Sales. *M. H. Tompkins.* —

HUTNER 6 b.g. Henbit (USA) 130 – Fountain 90 (Reform 132) [1990 NR 1991 16.2g⁵ 15.8f] rangy, angular gelding: has round action: quite modest form at 3 yrs: behind in 1991, only runs on flat since: may prove ideally suited by 1¾m: has run well when visored: winning hurdler in May. *M. Dods.* —

HYABELLA 3 b.f. Shirley Heights 130 – Bella Colora 119 (Bellypha 130) [1990 NR 1991 10m⁴ 10.2m² 10m⁴ 8.1m* 8m 7d 8g*] leggy, sparely-made filly: second foal: half-sister to high-class 4-y-o 1¼m and 10.5f winner Stagecraft (by Sadler's Wells): dam 6f to 1¼m winner, is half-sister to Irish Oaks winner Colorspin: successful in second half of season in minor event at Newmarket and listed races at Sandown (led over 1f out and ran on strongly to beat Cardinal Point 1½ lengths) Newmarket: well beaten in between: best effort at 1m: possibly unsuited by a soft surface: last and quietly to post seventh outing: tail swisher: very useful. *M. R. Stoute.* 111

HYDEONIUS 6 b.g. Crystal Palace (FR) 132 – Razannda (FR) (Labus (FR)) [1990 12.3g 10m² 11m* 14m* 12f* 12f⁴ 12g* 12f* 15d⁴ 12.2f² 15.5f 12m⁶ 13.8d 13.6d 16d* a14g⁶ a16g 1991 12d 12m 13f 12g] workmanlike gelding: keen walker: moderate mover, with quick action: quite modest handicapper at 5 yrs: well beaten in 1991: stays 2m: acts on firm and dead going. *C. Tinkler.* —

HYMN BOOK (IRE) 2 b.f. (Apr 18) Darshaan 133 – Divina (GER) (Alpenkonig (GER)) [1991 8.1m⁴ 8.1g] 40,000Y: lengthy, quite attractive filly: has scope: half-sister to 3 winners abroad: dam winner in Germany: fourth of 6 in minor event at Sandown (swishing tail in paddock) in August, held up then staying on really well: favourite but better for race still, checked 2f out and little impression thereafter in maiden at Haydock following month: should stay 1¼m. *M. R. Stoute.* 64

HYMNE D'AMOUR (USA) 3 b.f. Dixieland Band (USA) – La Francaise (USA) (Jim French (USA)) [1990 NR 1991 11.6m⁶ 8s 10m] smallish, lengthy filly: half-sister to several winners in France and USA, including French 1990 7f and 1m winner Laliffe (by Lypheor): dam, placed 4 times in USA, is half-sister to Alzao: no worthwhile form in minor event and maidens. *Miss H. C. Knight.* —

HYMN OF HARLECH 8 b.g. Welsh Chanter 124 – Church Bay 76 (Reliance II 137) [1990 7.6m² 8m* 9m⁴ 8.3m 7m a8g 1991 9g] smallish gelding: has a quick action: fair handicapper: below form only run in 1991 (April): stays 9f: ideally suited by top-of-the-ground: wears blinkers: races up with pace: has looked none too enthusiastic and best handled tenderly. *D. R. C. Elsworth.* —

HYPNOTIST 4 b.g. High Top 131 – Tamilian 89 (Tamerlane 128) [1990 10f³ 10f⁴ 10f² 10m 8m* 1991 9m a8g 8.2m] lengthy, workmanlike gelding: has a round action: quite modest handicapper: backward and no form in 1991, off course over 4 months before final start: possibly suited by 1m: acts on firm ground: sold to join W. Bentley's stable 2,300 gns Newmarket Autumn Sales. *C. A. Cyzer.* —

HYPOLIXO (FR) 2 b.c. (Apr 24) Antheus (USA) 122 – Quemora (FR) 114 (Riverman (USA) 131) [1991 8s* 8s*] third foal: brother to French 3-y-o 1½m winner Anthequo and half-brother to French 1989 3-y-o 1¼m winner Ramonda (by Fabulous Dancer): dam won at 1½m and 1¾m in France: successful in 14-runner newcomers event at Saint-Cloud in September and 5-runner minor event at Longchamp month later: bred to be suited by 1½m: yet to race on a sound surface: may improve further. *Mme C. Head, France.* 104 p

HYSSOP 3 ch.g. Absalom 128 – Willow Herb 68 (Habat 127) [1990 5g⁶ 6d 7f* 7f³ 7g 7g⁶ 8.5m 1991 8s 7g] rangy gelding: chiefly below form since winning seller at 2 —

yrs: seems suited by 7f: acts on firm ground, possibly unsuited by dead: joined J. J. O'Neill. *J. Berry*.

I

IBN MAJED 9 gr.g. Godswalk (USA) 130 – La Meme 90 (Pall Mall 132) [1990 NR 1991 a14g⁶] big, lengthy gelding: plating-class handicapper: wearing blinkers and eyeshield on first run since 1988, never dangerous at Southwell in March: stays very well: acts on good to firm and soft going: winning jumper, but thoroughly unreliable. *J. G. FitzGerald*. —

IBN NAAS (USA) 5 ch.g. Diesis 133 – La Vie (USA) (Le Fabuleux 133) [1990 a8g 1991 a11g⁵ a8g³ a12g⁶] sparely-made gelding: poor and lightly-raced performer nowadays: should be suited by middle distances: of doubtful temperament. *B. J. McMath*. 38

IBN SINA (USA) 4 b.c. Dr Blum (USA) – Two On One (CAN) (Lord Durham (CAN)) [1990 7h³ 10m 11.5m³ 12.3f² 12m⁶ 1991 10f] lengthy, well-made colt: has a round action: fair form at 2 yrs: below best since, not seen out in 1991 after March: should stay well: acts on good to firm ground: has pulled hard. *M. H. B. Robinson*. —

I BROKE THE RULES (IRE) 2 b.f. (Apr 25) Montekin 125 – Dar-A-Meter (Dara Monarch 128) [1991 6d⁴ 5m⁴ 6m⁶ 6g 7.1d] 2,800 2-y-o: smallish, rather sparely-made filly: second foal: half-sister to 3-y-o 5f winner Misdemeanours Girl (by Fairy King): dam Irish maiden: poor maiden: possibly requires a soft surface: sold out of M. Channon's stable 900 gns Ascot September Sales after fourth start. *A. J. Chamberlain*. 42

IBSEN 3 b.c. Gorytus (USA) 132 – State of Mind (Mill Reef (USA) 141) [1990 NR 1991 a10g²] 13,000Y: fourth foal: half-brother to a winner in Italy by Glenstal: dam unraced daughter of useful 1976 French 2-y-o Miss Reasoning and granddaughter of French 1000 Guineas winner Pampered Miss: 14/1, length second of 14 to Double Echo in maiden claimer at Lingfield in December, held up and running on well: should improve. *P. J. Makin*. 63 p

ICANSEEFORMILES (IRE) 3 gr.c. Godswalk (USA) 130 – Saintly Tune (Welsh Saint 126) [1990 6g 1991 8f 10d⁶ 10.1g 10d² 11.7g 10s* 10g² 9m⁵ 9.7f] close-coupled, workmanlike colt: quite modest handicapper: won apprentice event at Lingfield in June, leading close home: suited by 1¼m: acts on soft going: hung left and looked reluctant fourth and seventh starts. *R. Hannon*. 60 §

ICARUS (USA) 5 b.g. Wind And Wuthering (USA) 132 – Cedar Waxwing (USA) (Tom Fool) [1990 NR 1991 10.2s] sturdy gelding: quite modest performer at 3 yrs: well beaten in ladies handicap at Doncaster in March, only run on flat since: stays 10.6f: acts on dead going: lacks a turn of foot: winning hurdler/chaser. *M. H. Easterby*. —

ICEHAND 2 ch.g. (Mar 16) King of Clubs 124 – Ice Galaxie (USA) (Icecapade (USA)) [1991 7f⁶ 7g² 7m 7.1m] tall, lightly-made gelding: has a round action: third foal: half-brother to 1987 2-y-o 5f and 6f winner Icefern (by Moorestyle): dam showed only a little ability: plating-class here, but winner in Sweden: should be better suited by 1m: sold 6,400 gns Newmarket Autumn Sales. *Sir Mark Prescott*. 57

ICE ICE BABY (IRE) 3 b.f. Tate Gallery (USA) 117 – Arctic Winter (CAN) (Briartic (CAN)) [1990 NR 1991 8f 8d 12g 12m a10g 15.4f] 10,000Y: angular filly: second foal: half-sister to very useful 5f (at 2 yrs) and 6f winner Polar Bird (by Thatching), subsequently successful in USA: dam unraced sister to very smart Son of Briartic successful in Canadian 1¼m Queen's Plate: sign of ability only in mid-division for claimer third start, every chance 3f out: blinkered second and fifth (also wore eyeshield) outings: bandaged 3 times. *T. J. Naughton*. —

ICE MAGIC 4 ch.c. Red Sunset 120 – Free Rein (Sagaro 133) [1990 6g 8f³ 10g* 11m³ 13.8m² 12g⁶ 12f³ 13.8f² 1991 12g 14m 15.8f 13.6g 12m³ 12.2d⁵ 12.2f⁵ 12.2m² 12f 13.8m⁵] sparely-made colt: quite modest handicapper: stays 1¾m: acts on firm going: tailed off when blinkered penultimate start: has carried head awkwardly: none too consistent: sold 5,000 gns Newmarket Autumn Sales. *P. Calver*. 65

ICE WALK 2 gr.f. (Feb 25) Kalaglow 132 – Krishnagar (Kris 135) [1991 7d] leggy, lengthy, lightly-made filly: third foal: half-sister to plating-class 5f and 6f winner Blazing Sunset (by Blazing Saddles): dam never ran: 20/1, always towards rear in 21-runner maiden at Doncaster in November. *W. Jarvis*. —

ICHI BAN SON 7 b.h. Hotfoot 126 – My Bushbaby 100 (Hul A Hul 124) [1990 NR 1991 16.2g] big horse: poor handicapper: blinkered and bandaged on first run on flat since 4 yrs, behind in seller in April: best form at 1¼m: suited by a sound surface (yet to show his form on very firm going): won over hurdles in March. *A. Smith.* —

ICY KNIGHT (USA) 2 b.c. (Feb 12) Lear Fan (USA) 130 – Ice House 89 (Northfields (USA)) [1991 5g² 5d² 6g³ a7g⁵ 7s⁴] sturdy colt: first foal: dam 2-y-o 1m winner, is sister to very useful middle-distance winner Open Day out of very useful sister to Reform: quite modest maiden: sweating and edgy, ran poorly on fibresand: will stay 1m: acts on soft ground: not seen out after August. *C. R. Nelson.* **66**

IDEAL CANDIDATE 2 b.f. (Feb 6) Celestial Storm (USA) 132 – Rising Star (St Paddy 133) [1991 6g⁵ 8.9d 7m] 4,000F, 7,200Y: leggy, plain filly: half-sister to several winners abroad: dam temperamental half-sister to very useful animals Riot Act and Laurentian Hills: plating-class maiden: probably finds 7f too sharp, and will stay 1¼m: acts on dead ground. *C. A. Cyzer.* **57**

IDIR LINN (IRE) 3 b.g. Camden Town 125 – Dippy Girl 104 (Sandford Lad 133) [1990 7m 7g⁶ 6s 1991 6v 7g 7g 6m 10g a7g] stocky, good-quartered gelding: fourth foal: dam placed in Ireland at 6f and 7f: plating-class form at best in Ireland when trained by K. Connolly, finishing lame second 3-y-o start: no worthwhile form in 3 maidens then (on equitrack) handicap here: should stay at least 7f. *D. J. G. Murray-Smith.* —

IDOL MIO (USA) 3 ch.f. Shadeed (USA) 135 – Ionian Idol (USA) (Prince John) [1990 NR 1991 8g 6d] 68,000Y: leggy, quite attractive filly: half-sister to several winners in USA: dam minor winner in USA: last in listed race and minor event at Kempton: sold 8,000 gns Newmarket July Sales. *C. E. Brittain.* —

IHSAAS 4 b.c. Niniski (USA) 125 – Justicia 87 (Nonoalco (USA) 131) [1990 NR 1991 12.1m a12g a14g a16g] leggy, angular colt: fourth foal: half-brother to fair 1m winner Justaglow (by Kalaglow) and 6f and 1m winner Crown Justice (by High Top): dam won twice over 5f at 2 yrs and is half-sister to very useful 5f to 8.5f winner Royal Pinnacle: lightly raced and no sign of ability. *M. P. Naughton.* —

IJTIHAAD (USA) 4 b.c. Arctic Tern (USA) 126 – Corita (Satingo 129) [1990 10f* 10m³ 13.3g⁵ 10.2g⁵ 12m 10m* 1991 10g 10g 10m* 10g* 10m⁶ 10.5f] well-made, attractive colt: has a fluent, round action: useful handicapper: always prominent when winning £11,500 event at Ascot in July and Racal Chesterfield Cup at Goodwood in August: below that form in listed event at Windsor and £15,700 contest at Haydock after: worth another try at 1½m: acts on firm going: bandaged behind at 4 yrs: to join T. Skiffington in USA. *Major W. R. Hern.* **99**

IKEBANA (IRE) 3 b.f. Sadler's Wells (USA) 132 – Miss Toshiba (USA) 113 (Sir Ivor 135) [1990 NR 1991 10g* 11.9m³ 12.3d²] big, lengthy, deep-girthed filly: good **93**

Sandringham Handicap, Ascot—a tight finish to a slowly-run race, between (left to right) Ijtihaad, Stop Press and Lucky Guest

mover: ninth foal: closely related to Irish 9f winner Tobolsk (by Storm Bird) and Irish 7f winner North Eastern (by Northern Dancer), and half-sister to 1¼m winner Horseshoe Reef (by Mill Reef) and fairly useful 7f to 1m winner Oriental Mystique (by Kris): dam won from 7f to 1½m, including in USA where showed very smart form: most impressive winner of maiden at Sandown in April: easily better effort in October minor events when creditable 8 lengths second of 5 to Uluru at Chester: stays 1½m. *H. R. A. Cecil.*

IKSAB 4 b.g. Lyphard's Special (USA) 122 – Some Dame 72 (Will Somers 114§) [1990 7f* 8.2g⁶ 7m³ 6m* 7d 6m 6s* 6m 6f³ a7g 1991 6s 6g² 6g 6m 5m³ 5.9m² 6g² 5m² 6g 5g 6m] rangy gelding: moderate mover: modest performer: best at 5f or 6f: acts on any going: keen sort, usually wears crossed noseband: has worn tongue strap: blinkered final start: inconsistent: sold to Scandinavia 2,800 gns Doncaster October Sales. *R. Boss.*   **76**

IKTESHAF 3 b.c. Green Desert (USA) 127 – Colourful (FR) 97 (Gay Mecene (USA) 128) [1990 6g³ 5f² 6g³ 6m* 1991 7g 5d⁴ 6.1m 5m³ 6f² 6m 6g* 5d⁵ 6.1d³] compact, attractive colt: moderate mover: fair handicapper: won claimer at Hamilton in September: good third of 16 at Chester final start, staying on strongly from towards rear: stays 6f: acts on firm and dead ground: blinkered fourth start: sweating third and sixth: changed hands 19,500 gns Newmarket Autumn Sales. *B. Hanbury.*   **76**

IL BAMBINO 3 ch.g. Bairn (USA) 126 – Trapani (Ragusa 137) [1990 6m 7m² 7f³ 7s a7g 1991 8m 8.2m 8g* 8g³ 10g³ 9.7f] leggy, lightly-made gelding: won seller (bought in 4,400 gns) at Brighton in June, despite drifting right: well below form in handicap final start: stays 1¼m: possibly unsuited by soft ground: joined M. Pipe. *P. F. I. Cole.*   **47**

ILDERTON ROAD 4 br.f. Noalto 120 – Mac's Melody (Wollow 132) [1990 10m⁴ 10m³ 7g⁵ 7f³ 8.2m⁵ 8m⁵ 10g³ 8m² 8g⁴ 1991 8g⁵ 10m⁵ 7.1m⁴ 11.8g 8g 9.7s] big, rangy filly: quite modest handicapper, still a maiden: stays 1¼m: acts on firm going. *Mrs Barbara Waring.*   **62 d**

ILEWIN 4 br.c. Ile de Bourbon (USA) 133 – City Swinger (Derrylin 115) [1990 NR 1991 a14g 9.7m 8f] sturdy colt: no form, including in selling handicap: trained on reappearance by J. Wharton. *J. R. Jenkins.*   **—**

I'LL SOON KNOW 4 ch.f. Known Fact (USA) 135 – Soolyn (Dominion 123) [1990 6m 6m⁴ 6g² 6f* 7f 7m⁶ 1991 a8g a8g] smallish, angular mare: plating-class handicapper at 3 yrs: not seen out until late-November and well below form: should stay 1m: acts on firm going: has flashed tail. *B. Palling.*   **—**

ILLUMINATING 2 ch.f. (Apr 14) Electric 126 – Jarama (Amber Rama (USA) 133) [1991 7m² 8.1g²] 6,000Y: leggy filly, rather unfurnished: sister to Irish middle-distance winner Red Rose Garden and half-sister to French 9f winner Kenoba (by Young Generation): dam unraced half-sister to top-class 1972 2-y-o Jacinth: second in maidens at Leicester and Haydock (auction, staying on) in September: should stay middle-distances: will improve again. *Mrs J. R. Ramsden.*   **61 p**

IMAGINARY PLANE 3 b.g. Petoski 135 – Dalmally 89 (Sharpen Up 127) [1990 8m 8f 8.2g 1991 13.8m] rather angular gelding: no worthwhile form. *M. H. Easterby.*   **—**

IMAGINING 4 b.c. Fairy King (USA) – Shancarnan (AUS) (Galway Bay (FR)) [1990 7g⁵ 8m* 8m 8.2m³ 9m 8d 1991 8m⁶ 8d⁶ 10g 8m 8f 8m² 8m⁴ 7g] sturdy colt: quite modest handicapper nowadays: stays 1m: acts on good to firm ground: twice below form when blinkered at 4 yrs. *J. W. Hills.*   **61**

I'M ALERT 6 b.h. Kampala 120 – Last Trip (Sun Prince 128) [1990 NR 1991 8g] tall, workmanlike horse: lightly raced and little sign of ability. *J. K. Kinane.*   **—**

IMCO CHAMP (IRE) 2 b.c. (Mar 29) Grey Dawn II 132 – Vaguely Modest (CAN) (Vaguely Noble 140) [1991 8m 8m⁴ 7m³ 10v] 53,000F, 46,000Y: rather unfurnished colt: half-brother to fairly useful 1m winner Modesty On Ice (by Overskate): dam, half-sister to Danzatore, won 1m stakes race: modest maiden: unplaced in Premio Guido Berardelli at Rome in November: should stay 1¼m. *M. A. Jarvis.*   **70**

IMCO CLASSIC (IRE) 2 br.c. (Mar 1) Bob Back (USA) 124 – Special Thanks (Kampala 120) [1991 7.1s 8.2f⁶ 7m⁴ 7m⁵] IR 32,000Y: close-coupled, angular colt: has plenty of scope: second foal: half-brother to 3-y-o Red Poppy (by Coquelin): dam Irish 7f winner: modest maiden: will stay 1¼m. *M. A. Jarvis.*   **76**

IMCO DOUBLE (IRE) 3 ch.c. Double Schwartz 128 – Cupids Hill (Sallust 134) [1990 NR 1991 7g 6d 6s 5m⁶ a6g³ a6g² 6m a5g² a5g* a5g⁵] IR 48,000Y, 960 2-y-o: close-coupled colt: half-brother to several winners abroad, including French sprinter County Camden (by Camden Town): dam unraced half-sister to Ardoon: quite modest form: comfortably won 18-runner handicap at Southwell in December: ran moderately in similar event there 5 days later: likely to prove best at sprint distances: trained first 8 starts by E. Eldin. *C. N. Allen.*

IMCO LISI (ITY) 3 ch.f. Ahonoora 122 – Lisistrata (ITY) (Pareo (FR)) [1990 6g³ **110** 7.5d* 7.5d* 7.5d² 8g* 8v³ 8v² 8v 1991 8s³ 8v² 10f² 12g² 10g² 11g² 9s* 10v⁶ 14v] 78,000,000 lire (approx £35,300) Y: first foal: dam successful 4 times in Italy, including in Group 2 1m race at 2 yrs and 1m listed race at 3 yrs: very useful Italian filly: successful in minor event and 2 listed races at 2 yrs and in minor event at Milan in September at 3 yrs: beaten 1¾ lengths by Arranvanna in Premio Regina Elena at Rome, 2 lengths by Possessive Dancer in Oaks d'Italia at Milan and short neck by Lara's Idea in Group 3 event (made most) at Milan second, fourth and fifth starts: stays 1½m: acts on heavy going. *A. Renzoni, Italy.*

IMITATE (IRE) 3 b.f. Tate Gallery (USA) 117 – Exemplary 106 (Sovereign Lord **37** 120) [1990 5f⁴ 5g² 6s* 5d⁴ 6m⁵ 1991 a8g a7g⁶ a6g 7m a5g² a5g 6d 5m⁵ 5g a5g 5m 7m 5g⁴ 6g 5d 5g] compact filly: moderate mover: almost only form at 3 yrs when in frame in handicaps at Southwell (unruly in paddock) and Wolverhampton: best form at 5f: seemed suited by an easy surface: often blinkered: ran moderately when sweating: tends to hang. *D. W. Chapman.*

IMMORTAL IRISH 6 b.g. Lord Gayle (USA) 124 – Royal Meath 83 (Realm 129) **35** [1990 NR 1991 a10g² a10g³ 9.9g⁴ 11.5g³ a12g] rather sparely-made gelding: poor handicapper: not seen out after June: stays 11.5f: keen sort: sold 2,000 gns Ascot October Sales. *D. R. Gandolfo.*

IMPACT (IRE) 3 b.f. Green Desert (USA) 127 – Fair Salinia 125 (Petingo 135) **81** [1990 NR 1991 7g³ 7.6s² 6g* 6g 7.1m⁵] workmanlike filly: fifth reported foal: half-sister to 1988 2-y-o 1m winner Horn Dance (by Green Dancer), who stayed 1¾m but probably of unsatisfactory temperament, and fairly useful 1983 2-y-o maiden Fair Habit (by Habitat): dam won Oaks and awarded Irish Oaks: fair form: landed odds in maiden at Lingfield in July: visored, fair fifth in handicap at Sandown following month: better at around 1m than shorter: acts on good to firm ground and soft. *M. R. Stoute.*

IMPERFECT CIRCLE (USA) 3 b.f. Riverman (USA) 131 – Aviance 112 **94 +** (Northfields (USA)) [1990 6f² 6d* 6m² 1991 7d* 6g] lengthy, sparely-made filly: has a quick action: very useful form at 2 yrs, winning listed race at Ayr and second in Cheveley Park Stakes at Newmarket: hardly came off bridle in winning minor event at Salisbury in June as 3-y-o by ½ length from Cooley's Valve: favourite, ran moderately in listed race at Newbury 3 weeks later, one pace 2f out: bred to stay 1m. *R. Charlton.*

IMPERIAL BALLET (IRE) 2 b.c. (Apr 3) Sadler's Wells (USA) 132 – **— P** Amaranda (USA) 115 (Bold Lad (IRE) 133) [1991 7d] angular, quite attractive colt: eighth living foal: closely related to 9f winner Town Square (by The Minstrel) and half-brother to 3 winners, including very useful 6f (at 2 yrs) and 7f winner Bold Citadel (by Caerleon): dam, smart sprinter who stayed 7f, is daughter of Irish 1000 Guineas winner Favoletta: 7/1, backward and green, much better than nineteenth of 22 to For Reg in November maiden at Doncaster suggests, recovering quickly from very slow start and soon travelling smoothly, then eased considerably once fading from 2f out: likely to do considerably better. *H. R. A. Cecil.*

IMPERIAL GLORY 6 b.g. Ahonoora 122 – Sovereign Bloom (Florescence 120) **—** [1990 a6g 1991 a8g] rather leggy gelding: extremely lightly raced but has shown a little ability. *S. Mellor.*

IMPERIAL SOVEREIGN 3 b.c. Fairy King (USA) – Next-of-Kin (Great **—** Nephew 126) [1990 NR 1991 7m] good-topped colt: seventh foal: half-brother to 2-y-o sprint winners Next Witness and Penang Beauty (both by Garda's Revenge): dam never ran: close up 4f then hung left and weakened quickly in maiden (showed quick action to post) at Lingfield in July. *P. Howling.*

IMPETULENCE 5 ch.m. Kind of Hush 118 – Longgoe 70 (Lorenzaccio 130) **—** [1990 NR 1991 8.3f a6g] rather sparely-made mare: has a slightly round action: lightly raced and no worthwhile form: has appeared somewhat temperamental. *W. Storey.*

IMPORTANT RISK 2 ch.g. (Feb 19) Risk Me (FR) 127 – Miss Import 101 **—** (Import 127) [1991 a6g a7g] lengthy, angular gelding: moderate walker: third foal: dam, useful sprinter, won 10 races all at 5f: no worthwhile form in sellers at Southwell in summer: sold 760 gns Doncaster August Sales. *P. A. Kelleway.*

I'M SPECIAL (IRE)   3 ch.f. Lyphard's Special (USA) 122 – Doon Belle (Ardoon   **68** d
124) [1990 NR 1991 8g² 8.5f⁵ 13d⁴ 8.3f 9.2f 10g⁵ 9.2s⁴] 7,800Y: rather leggy filly:
fourth live foal: half-sister to 6f winner Go With The Flo (by Indian King) and 1985
Irish 2-y-o 7f winner La Belle Princesse (by Royal Match): dam Irish 5f and 7f
winner, is half-sister to smart 7f to 1¾m performer Rocamadour: didn't reproduce
debut form, staying-on fourth of 16 in handicap at Hamilton final start: should stay
1¼m: visored last 2 outings: trained first 3 by M. H. Easterby. *A. Harrison.*

IM TELLING YOU MR   2 b.f. (Feb 7) Monsanto (FR) 121 – Hopeful Way 72   —
(Hopeful Venture 125) [1991 5.3m⁵ 5.3f⁶ 6g a6g⁵ 7m 7m] plain, sparely-made filly:
has a round action: half-sister to 6f and 7f winner Hopeful Waters (by Forlorn
River): dam won 1½m seller: poor maiden: tailed off on equitrack: sold 700 gns
Ascot December Sales. *J. Ffitch-Heyes.*

I'M UNFORGETTABLE   7 b.m. Dublin Taxi – Pink Streamer (Birdbrook 110)   —
[1990 NR 1991 10.6g 12.3d] rather leggy mare: very lightly raced and no worthwhile
form. *C. D. Broad.*

INAN (USA)   2 b.c. (Mar 18) El Gran Senor (USA) 136 – Assez Cuite (USA) 114   **48** p
(Graustark) [1991 8.1g 8m] good-topped, attractive colt: has plenty of scope: good
walker: has a quick action: half-brother to several winners, including Prix Royal-
Oak winner El Cuite (by Vaguely Noble) and dam of Michelozzo and Micheletti: dam
smart French 2-y-o: well beaten after racing keenly in maidens at Haydock and
Leicester: bred to stay middle distances: looks capable of better. *J. L. Dunlop.*

IN A WHIRL (USA)   3 br.f. Island Whirl (USA) – Hurry Marie (USA) (Hurry To   **63**
Market) [1990 6m* 5d⁵ 6d 1991 7m 8g 5m 5g⁶ 5m³ 6m⁵ a6g 7s 5m 6.1m a6g² a5g⁴
a7g³] tall, close-coupled filly: quite modest handicapper: ran well at Southwell late
in year: needs further than 5f, and stays 7f: effective blinkered or not: has given
trouble at stalls: trained until after eleventh start by N. Callaghan. *D. W. Chapman.*

INBIHAR   4 br.f. Doulab (USA) 115 – Silojoka 95 (Home Guard (USA) 129) [1990   —
5f 6f 6g 7g⁵ 7m 9f⁵ 10.2m 1991 8f 10g 7g 8.2g 7.6m] sparely-made filly: poor maiden:
will stay 1m: has been mulish at stalls: blinkered last 2 starts. *C. J. Benstead.*

INCHCAILLOCH (IRE)   2 b.c. (Feb 15) Lomond (USA) 128 – Glowing With   **83** p
Pride 114 (Ile de Bourbon (USA) 133) [1991 7m⁴ 8g³] big, strong, lengthy colt: fourth
foal: half-brother to 3-y-o Everglades (by Green Desert): dam 7f and 10.5f winner:
better effort when over 7 lengths third of 16 to Aljadeer in minor event at Newbury
(still green) in October, one pace from 2f out: should stay 1¼m: has plenty of scope,
will improve further and seems sure to win a maiden. *R. Charlton.*

INCOLA   5 b.g. Liboi (USA) 76 – Sdenka (FR) 79 (Habitat 134) [1990 a11g a10g   **49**
a12g4 12f 10s⁴ 12f4 11.5g* 12f² 12f* 12f4 1991 11.7g 12f* 12f 12.2d³ 12g6 12m6 11.6m²
11.8m²] small, angular gelding: plating-class handicapper: won at Folkestone in
May: better suited by 1½m than shorter: acts on firm and dead ground: below form
when blinkered once: goes very well with forcing tactics: largely consistent. *H.
Candy.*

IN CONCERT   3 ch.f. Absalom 128 – Hum 69 (Crooner 119) [1990 6g⁵ 6g4 6m⁶   —
a7g⁶ 1991 10d 9s 10g 10m] lengthy, rather angular filly: has a round action: poor
maiden: probably stays 7f: sold 1,050 gns Doncaster November Sales. *M. Brittain.*

INDELIBLE MARK   5 b.g. Bustino 136 – Current Pattie (USA) 102 (Little   —
Current (USA)) [1990 8m 10h⁵ a14g4 10.4g 8g 1991 13.8m 8.2g 8.9g 11.9f] lengthy,
attractive gelding: no worthwhile form: has been tried visored. *Mrs A. L. M. King.*

INDEPENDENT AIR   3 gr.g. Elegant Air 119 – Tranquility Base 112 (Roan   —
Rocket 128) [1990 6g 6f 7m 7f 5f 6h² 5f⁶ 6g 7f⁵ 6m 8f4 1991 10m 10m a11g6 11.7g a11g
a12g 6m] smallish, good-quartered gelding: poor maiden: stays 7f: acts on hard
ground: sometimes visored: sold 1,500 gns Newmarket Autumn Sales. *D. T. Thom.*

INDIAN DECISION   2 b.c. (Feb 26) Wassl 125 – It's Terrific (Vaguely Noble   **69** p
140) [1991 6f 7g] leggy colt: half-brother to several winners, including useful 7f and
1m winner Model Village (by Habitat): dam won from 1¼m to 13f in Ireland: 25/1,
eye-catching ninth of 22, beaten around 4 lengths, in maiden at Newbury in
September, held up and behind after slow start then finishing strongly: below that
form at Salisbury (dropped out in rear, not knocked about) 11 days later: likely to
stay 1¼m: will prove capable of better. *J. L. Dunlop.*

INDIAN ENDEAVOUR   2 b.f. (Feb 1) Green Desert (USA) 127 – Swanilda   **73**
(FR) (Habitat 134) [1991 5m⁴ 5m³ 5g* 5d²] 33,000Y: sturdy filly: half-sister to
several winners, including useful stayer Arizelos (by Shirley Heights), 1988 2-y-o 6f
winner Plumbe Tempest (by Lyphard) and 1¼m winner Ephemeral (by Shernazar):
dam won over 1m in France, and is half-sister to Super Dan, a very useful winner at
up to 9f: modest performer: made all in maiden at Pontefract in June: hung

persistently left in minor event at Windsor later in month: bred to stay 1m: possibly unsuited by dead ground. *R. Guest.*

INDIAN FLUTE 4 b.f. Indian King (USA) 128 – Corista (Tudor Music 131) [1990   —
11g⁴ 8.2g⁴ 11s³ 12m 11.5g⁵ 1991 a16g a13g⁵ a12g⁵ 10d] rangy filly: poor maiden: should stay at least 1½m: possibly needs an easy surface: sold 1,800 gns Ascot May Sales. *W. J. Musson.*

INDIAN GUEST 2 b.f. (Apr 17) Precocious 126 – Indian Love Song 68 (Be My   —
Guest (USA) 126) [1991 5f 5f⁵ 6d] neat filly: first foal: dam middle-distance maiden granddaughter of Oaks runner-up Maina: no worthwhile form in maidens. *F. H. Lee.*

INDIAN MOHAWK (IRE) 3 ch.c. Ahonoora 122 – Joshua's Daughter 61   —
(Joshua 129) [1990 NR 1991 7g 6d 7d 7m 7g 7.1m 6m] tall, leggy, rather shallow-girthed colt: has a round action: brother to a winner in Italy and half-brother to several winners, including very useful 6f to 7.6f winner On Tap (by Tap On Wood) and fairly useful sprinter Glen Kella Manx (by Tickled Pink): dam stayed 1½m: little form (in handicaps last 4 starts) but did hint at some ability: bandaged off-hind sixth start. *J. C. Fox.*

INDIAN OCEAN (IRE) 3 b.f. Commanche Run 133 – Inland Sea (Kings Lake   —
(USA) 133) [1990 NR 1991 12m] 16,500F: lengthy, plain filly: first foal: dam unraced: well beaten in claimer (moved moderately down) at Doncaster: sold 1,050 gns Newmarket July Sales. *M. H. Tompkins.*

INDIAN PLUME 4 b.g. Commanche Run 133 – Fettle (Relkino 131) [1990 8.5g⁴   —
8g² a8g* 12.3g 12d 9g a14g a11g* 1991 a8g] compact gelding: moderate mover: modest performer: stayed 11f: blinkered twice, including when successful: dead. *D. Burchell.*

INDIAN QUEEN 6 ch.m. Electric 126 – Taj Princess 88 (Taj Dewan 128) **111**
[1990 12g 13.5d³ 11.1g⁶ 15.5v* 1991 10s² 16.2s⁵ 13.4d³ 20g*]

    Six-year-old Indian Queen became the first mare to win the Gold Cup since Gladness in 1958. Good-class fillies aren't generally kept in training beyond the age of three and only two others had been placed in the Gold Cup in the interim, both of them as four-year-olds, Royal Hive in 1978 and Shoot A Line in 1981. Unlike Royal Hive and Shoot A Line—both of whom were top staying fillies at three—Indian Queen was no better than useful as a three-year-old when her five victories included one in the listed Grand Prix de Bordeaux and another in the nine-furlong 'Mail On Sunday' Handicap Final at

Gold Cup, Ascot—Indian Queen and Arzanni give their all

Sir Gordon Brunton's "Indian Queen"

Newmarket. Indian Queen was improving significantly at the end of her three-year-old days and the decision to keep her in training paid dividends when she won pattern races at Milan and the Curragh (Blandford Stakes) as a four-year-old. At five she showed further improvement, dead-heating at 25/1 with Braashee, the pair clear, in the Prix Royal-Oak at Longchamp on the last of four outings. The Prix Royal-Oak trip was the longest Indian Queen had tackled and she proved well suited by it, keeping on well in extremely testing conditions after making the running.

Laudable as Indian Queen's achievements were, they had been largely forgotten by the time the Gold Cup came round. She was beaten in all three of her races as a six-year-old before Royal Ascot, finishing well behind three Gold Cup runners—Teamster, Shambo and Double Dutch—when fifth in the Insulpak Sagaro Stakes at Ascot, and a creditable third behind two others —Per Quod and Warm Feeling—in the Ormonde EBF Stakes at Chester. Hot favourite for the Gold Cup was the four-year-old Arzanni who had run the best trial, winning the Polo Mints Yorkshire Cup at York decisively—running on strongly—from Shambo, Teamster and Per Quod. Teamster had also contested the Cementone Beaver Henry II Stakes at Sandown, another of the traditionally important Gold Cup trials, and had come third to Top of The World and Crack, both of whom were also in the twelve-strong Gold Cup field. Arzanni started at 13/8, with the Tote Cesarewitch winner Trainglot second favourite at 5/1 and Teamster (7/1) and Warm Feeling (8/1) the only others at shorter than 12/1; Indian Queen was among the 25/1 shots. Indian Queen was kept handy from the start as usual and, unlike Arzanni who had to be extricated from the pack to make his run, she had a clear one to chase Trainglot when he opened up a lead turning into the home straight. Indian

Queen kept on gamely, driven along, and gradually wore down Trainglot to lead inside the final two furlongs and then rallied strongly to resist the last-furlong challenge of Arzanni, the pair coming close together as Indian Queen drifted off a true line. It was a tremendous finish with the issue in doubt right to the line where Indian Queen was a neck up; Warm Feeling finished third, beaten a further three and a half lengths, with Trainglot fourth and the unlucky-in-running Teamster fifth. The Ascot Trustees, incidentally, have yet to agree to the reduction of the distance of the Gold Cup from two and a half miles to two; the Goodwood executive acceded to the wishes of the Stewards of the Jockey Club and reduced the distance of the Goodwood Cup to two miles in 1991. Whether Ascot will eventually follow suit isn't clear, and so far the Jockey Club hasn't repeated its threat that the Gold Cup's Group 1 status might have to be reviewed if Ascot don't fall into line. Watch this space . . .

		Blakeney	Hethersett
	Electric	(b 1966)	Windmill Girl
	(b 1979)	Christiana	Double Jump
Indian Queen		(ch 1967)	Mount Rosa
(ch.m. 1985)		Taj Dewan	Prince Taj
	Taj Princess	(br 1964)	Devinette
	(b 1974)	Pink Velvet	Petingo
		(ch 1970)	Fleeting Moon

The good-topped Indian Queen, who has always carried plenty of condition, was already in foal to In The Groove's sire Night Shift when she ran in the Gold Cup. The original plan was that Indian Queen would keep on racing, possibly contesting the Irish St Leger and the Prix Royal-Oak. But she wasn't seen out again. Her sire the good middle-distance performer Electric, who began as a stallion at the Whitsbury Manor Stud, is now standing in Ireland covering mostly jumping mares. Indian Queen's dam Taj Princess, who was out of an unraced mare who bred numerous winners, was just a fair performer, successful in a maiden auction race over five furlongs at Wolverhampton as a two-year-old and in handicaps over a mile at Windsor and Bath as a four-year-old. Taj Princess is now dead but all her six living foals have won, the best of them apart from Indian Queen being the useful sprinter Far Too Young (by Young Generation). Taj Princess's three other winners in Britain, Sivaji (by Connaught), Tajika (by Rusticaro) and Taj Victory (by Final Straw) have all proved suited by a mile and a half. Indian Queen is a thorough stayer, best with some give in the ground. She usually wore blinkers or a visor and sometimes sweated and got on edge before her races, but she was notably tough and genuine. *Lord Huntingdon.*

INDIAN SLAVE (IRE)　3 ch.c. Commanche Run 133 – Commanche Belle 74　**64**
(Shirley Heights 130) [1990 7m 7m4 7s5 1991 7m3 8f2 10f3 11.1d2 11.5s6 10f3 12.3g 8h 11.8g] leggy colt: quite modest maiden: in need of race in handicap final start: needs further than 9f, and stays 11f: acts on firm and dead going. *R. Guest.*

INDIAN STAR　4 b.f. Indian King (USA) 128 – Salique (Sallust 134) [1990 5f 6m3　**53**
6g* 6m3 7m 7g 6g3 6m3 7f4 6g 7g 7d 1991 5.9m3 6.9m3 6g2 6d 7d5 6f 7m 6g 7m] leggy, light-framed filly: moderate walker: has round action: plating-class handicapper nowadays: lost his form: effective at 6f and 7f: acts on firm ground, seems unsuited by soft surface: ran fairly well when visored once. *M. Brittain.*

INDIAN STYLE (IRE)　2 b.f. (May 10) Ahonoora 122 – Spirit In The Sky 106　**58 p**
(Tudor Melody 129) [1991 6f4] IR 52,000F, £22,000Y: workmanlike filly: half-sister to several winners, including very useful 7f to 1¼m winner Pixie Erin (by Golden Fleece) and high-class performer at up to 1¼m in Britain and USA Star Pastures (by Northfields): dam won from 6f to 1½m: 50/1 and backward, 3½ lengths fourth of 9 to Jigsaw Boy in maiden at Folkestone in October, outpaced 2f out then keeping on: showed round action: will improve over 7f. *R. Guest.*

INDIAN TERRITORY　2 ch.g. (Mar 6) Dominion 123 – Lady Capilano 87　**54**
(Nebbiolo 125) [1991 7m 7g 6d] stocky gelding: fourth foal: half-brother to useful 1990 2-y-o 7f and 1m winner Gentle Aria (by Elegant Air): dam 1½m winner: plating-class maiden: best effort keeping on seventh of 23 at Haydock final start: should be better suited by 7f+ than 6f. *D. Haydn Jones.*

INDIGO　3 ch.f. Primo Dominie 121 – Blueit (FR) 101 (Bold Lad (IRE) 133) [1990　**86**
5m* 5d 5f3 5f4 5f* 5f4 5m 1991 5d 5g2 5m 5m 5m 5m] close-coupled filly: moderate

walker: fairly useful efforts in handicap at Thirsk and Temple Stakes at Sandown second and third starts: tailed off in handicaps at Newcastle last 2 outings: speedy: acted on firm ground: in foal to Clantime. *R. M. Whitaker.*

INDIGO BLUE (IRE)   2 ch.f. (Feb 3) Bluebird (USA) 125 – Decadence (Vaigly   **56** Great 127) [1991 6g 6g] IR 21,000Y: first foal: dam is sister to Hallgate: better effort in October maidens when around 9 lengths last of 7 to She's Pleased at Newmarket second start: sprint bred. *N. A. Callaghan.*

INDIVISIBLE   5 ch.m. Remainder Man 126§ – Red Ragusa 62 (Homeric 133)   **31** [1990 a11g² a12g a11g³ 10.2f 10.6f 8f⁶ 8f² 8m⁴ a8g⁶ 8g 8f 8.2m 10.4g 1991 10m 12.3f 12f⁶ 10m³ 12.1f⁵ 10.3m⁴ 10m 8.1g] leggy mare: poor handicapper, still a maiden: stays 1¼m: acts on firm going: inconsistent. *R. Hollinshead.*

INDUBITABLE   6 ch.m. Sharpo 132 – Veracious 86 (Astec 128) [1990 12d 12.3g²   **70** 1991 12s 13d⁵ 14d⁵ 12.1d] workmanlike mare: modest and lightly-raced handicapper nowadays: off course 5½ months before final start (never placed to challenge): stays 1¾m: acts on good to firm and dead going. *G. B. Balding.*

INDY EXPRESS   3 b.f. Bay Express 132 – Indy 77 (Indigenous 121) [1990 NR   **41** 1991 a5g 5m⁴ 5m⁴ 5.7g] sturdy filly: second foal: dam 5f winner at 2 yrs who promised to stay further: poor form in maiden and claimers: sold 800 gns Ascot July Sales: resold 800 gns Ascot September Sales. *T. P. McGovern.*

IN EXCESS (FR)   3 b.g. Dunphy 124 – Electric Song (FR) (African Song 121)   **63** [1990 NR 1991 8v⁵ 10g 7g 9g² 8.5g² 11g 6m] first foal: dam French 1¼m winner on only start: second in minor event and maiden in French Provinces: 66/1, last of 7 in maiden at Redcar in October on first run for 4 months: stays 9f: blinkered third start: trained first 3 outings by Mme C. Head, remaining 3 in France by D. Boulard. *N. Tinkler.*

INFEB   4 gr.f. Another Realm 118 – Sweet Rosina 61 (Sweet Revenge 129) [1990   **46** 8.2g 10g⁶ 12.5g 8g 10m 9f³ 12m² 10f³ 12m 10g 1991 12f 14.8m⁶ 16.2g⁵ 14.6g* 15s 16.2f* 14.1f] rather leggy, workmanlike filly: poor handicapper: won at Wolverhampton (seller, no bid) and Beverley in summer: ran badly in ladies event final start: suited by test of stamina: suited by a sound surface: has won for claimer: sold to join Granville Richards' stable 3,800 gns Doncaster October Sales. *J. L. Spearing.*

INFERRING   3 b.g. Alleging (USA) 120 – Be My Darling 82 (Windjammer (USA))   **53** [1990 10s 10.2s⁴ 1991 a10g³ a10g² a10g³ a11g 10g⁶ 12.1g] good-topped, angular gelding: shows knee action: plating-class maiden: off course over 11 weeks and below form after third start: stays 1¼m: blinkered on debut: wore eyeshield first 3 starts at 3 yrs: trained until after penultimate start by Mrs L. Piggott: subsequently gelded. *P. A. Blockley.*

INHERENT MAGIC (IRE)   2 ch.f. (May 24) Magical Wonder (USA) 125 – Flo   **65** Kelly (Florescence 120) [1991 6s⁶ a5g* a6g³] IR 1,000Y: half-sister to several winners, including useful 5f and 7f winner Kellord (by Lord Gayle): dam fairly useful Irish sprinter: won late-year maiden at Lingfield by neck from Myasha: creditable third in Southwell nursery final start: stays 6f. *M. McCormack.*

INISHDALLA (IRE)   3 b.f. Green Desert (USA) 127 – Costly Wave (FR) 117 **103** (Caro 133) [1990 6m² 5g² 6m* 6m⁵ 6g² 6m² 5g² 1991 7g* 8m⁶ 6m 6m²] angular filly: useful Irish performer: won listed race at the Curragh in April: ran well (going smoothly 2 out) in Irish 1000 Guineas at same course next start: below that form in Cork and Orrery Stakes at Royal Ascot and Waterford Foods Phoenix Sprint Stakes (2½ lengths behind Amigo Menor) at Leopardstown: stays 1m. *D. K. Weld, Ireland.*

INJAKA BOY   2 gr.c. (May 9) General Wade 93 – Injaka 102 (Right Boy 137) [1991   **45** 6g 7m 6.1m⁵ 6m] leggy, sparely-made colt: eighth reported living foal: dam won at up to 7f: poor maiden: blinkered in Folkestone seller last start. *R. Hannon.*

INKALA   3 b.f. Kalaglow 132 – Intoxication 73 (Great Nephew 126) [1990 NR 1991   **71** 11.8m⁴ 12m⁴ 14.6m 15.4m⁴] 10,000F, 10,500Y: leggy filly: second foal: sister to 14.6f winner Innerglow: dam stayed 1½m, is daughter of Princess Royal winner Shebeen: modest form first 2 starts in maidens at Leicester and Salisbury: found little in amateurs contest at Folkestone final outing: should stay beyond 1½m. *J. M. P. Eustace.*

INKOSI (USA)   2 b.c. (Mar 6) Our Native (USA) – Glitter Ice (USA) (Icecapade   **83** (USA)) [1991 5m² 5d⁶ 6f* 6f⁶ 7m² 7m⁵ 7f* 7.9g³ 7.3m⁶ 7g⁴ 7m³] $35,000Y: rather unfurnished, quite attractive colt: has a roundish action: keen walker: fourth foal: half-brother to a 2-y-o winner in USA: dam won 4 races at up to 9f at 4 yrs: fair performer: won minor event at Doncaster in May and nursery at Thirsk in August: stays 1m: acts on firm ground: consistent: sold 25,000 gns Newmarket Autumn Sales. *F. H. Lee.*

INNERGLOW 4 gr.f. Kalaglow 132 – Intoxication 73 (Great Nephew 126) [1990 **63**
12.2g⁴ 11.5m⁶ 10m⁴ 15.3m³ 15.5f⁴ 13.8d² 1991 10g 12m² 14.1g 14.6m*] leggy,
angular filly: quite modest handicapper: allowed to dictate pace when winning at
Bath in July by 5 lengths: stayed 15.3f: acted on good to firm ground and dead: lacked
turn of foot: sold 2,000 gns Newmarket December Sales, in foal to Statoblest. *A. C.
Stewart.*

INNOCENT GEORGE 2 b.g. (Apr 30) Hallgate 127 – Are You Guilty 83§ **47**
(Runnett 125) [1991 5d⁶ 5v⁴ 5m 5d 6d² 5m⁶ 6m 5f⁶ a6g 6m] 5,200Y: small gelding:
has a round action: second foal: dam unreliable 7.6f winner: only worthwhile form
(raced on heavily-favoured stand rail) when second in seller at Thirsk: stays 6f:
blinkered fourth start: sold 800 gns Doncaster November Sales. *M. Brittain.*

IN NO DOUBT 2 b.c. (Mar 3) Precocious 126 – Global Lady 94 (Balliol 125) [1991 **46**
7g⁴ 7.5f 6g⁶] 19,000Y: good-topped colt: has scope: first foal: dam won from 6f (at 2
yrs) to 7.6f: poor maiden: not given hard race at Haydock (August) last time out:
looks sort to need time. *J. J. O'Neill.*

IN ORBIT 6 b.g. Habitat 134 – Aryenne (FR) 125 (Green Dancer (USA) 132) [1990 —
9g 10g⁶ 10m* 1991 9m⁴ 9.9f a12g] good-bodied gelding: has a rather round action:
poor handicapper: best at up to 1¼m: ran poorly on extremes of going: sold to join J.
P. Leigh's stable 1,550 gns Doncaster October Sales. *A. P. Stringer.*

IN PLACE (USA) 3 b.c. Roberto (USA) 131 – Placer Queen (Habitat 134) [1990 —
8g 8.2d 1991 10.5g] big, strong colt: has plenty of scope: has a markedly round
action: plating-class form in maidens: bit backward, never dangerous at Haydock in
September, 1991: may do better over further. *P. W. Harris.*

IN PURSUIT 4 ch.g. Rainbow Quest (USA) 134 – Silk Stocking 109 (Pardao 120) **81**
[1990 10.8m⁵ 10.1g⁵ 13.3m³ 12.3g² 14m² 14m* 12m* 12s 1991 11d² 16.1m 11.4m⁴
13.3m⁵ 12m⁴] leggy, rather unfurnished gelding: has long, rather round stride: fair
handicapper: good fourth to Kiveton Kabooz at Newmarket final start: subsequently
sold 34,000 gns Newmarket Autumn Sales: suited by forcing tactics at around 1½m,
and stays 1¾m: acts on good to firm and dead going: consistent. *Lord Huntingdon.*

IN QUARTO 2 ch.c. (Jan 14) Shahrastani (USA) 135 – Imperial Dancer 103 **?**
(Tudor Music 131) [1991 9v*] 900,000 francs (approx £90,000) Y: half-brother to
smart French middle-distance 4-y-o Top Waltz (by Top Ville) and 2 winners in
France by Crystal Palace: dam Irish 9.5f winner at 2 yrs and French 9.2f and 1¼m
winner at 3 yrs: successful in 12-runner newcomers event at Maisons-Laffitte in
November by ½ length: will stay 1¼m: should improve. *E. Lellouche, France.*

INQUIRENDO (USA) 3 ch.f. Roberto (USA) 131 – Quest (USA) 90§ (The **81 p**
Minstrel (CAN) 135) [1990 NR 1991 11.5f³ 12.2g*] smallish, workmanlike filly:
fourth foal: half-sister to 12.5f winner Rozinante (by Sir Ivor) and useful 6f winner
Bequest (by Sharpen Up): dam, 9f and 1¼m winner, is sister to high-class 1983
French 2-y-o Treizieme and half-sister to Gold Cup second Eastern Mystic: 11/8 on,
won maiden at Catterick in July in fine style: will stay 1¾m: sold 37,000 gns Newmarket December Sales. *L. M. Cumani.*

INSCONCE (USA) 3 b.f. Alleged (USA) 138 – Sconce (USA) (Majestic Light **87**
(USA)) [1990 NR 1991 10g 12g* 13.3g 15m⁴ 16.2d² 15.9d³ 16.5d] $110,000Y: lengthy,
angular, unfurnished filly: third reported foal: dam, maiden winner at around 1m at 3
yrs in USA, is sister to Grade 2 1¼m and 11f turf winner Lucence: fair performer:
won apprentice maiden at Newmarket in June: placed in handicaps at Haydock and
Chester (sweating) in October: better at 2m than shorter: acts on dead going:
bandaged, all round on second to fourth starts. *J. H. M. Gosden.*

INSEYAB 3 b.f. Persian Bold 123 – Strike Home 82 (Be My Guest (USA) 126) **70**
[1990 5d 6d⁵ 7d 1991 8s 7f⁶ 8h² 8g⁶ 7g* 7g³ 8f* 8m* 7f 8f* 8m⁴ 9.2f³] leggy, close-
coupled filly: moderate walker and mover: modest handicapper: won at Edinburgh
in June then at Thirsk (apprentices, awarded race), Redcar and Ripon in August:
stays 9.2f: acts on hard ground: sometimes bandaged behind: on toes seventh (also
sweating) and eighth starts: unseated rider and bolted before last intended outing.
P. C. Haslam.

INSWINGER 5 br.g. Swing Easy (USA) 126 – Cheri Berry 87 (Air Trooper 115) —
[1990 a8g⁶ a6g⁵ a5g⁴ a6g² 5f 7f 5m 6m a6g⁴ 1991 a8g² a8g³ a8g² a6g* a10g a 47
a5g⁴ a6g² 6f 7m a5g³ a8g a6g a6g5] small, lengthy, slightly dipped-backed gelding:
carries condition: poor handicapper on all-weather: won (for first time) at Lingfield
(amateurs) in February: no form on turf for long time: stays 1m: acts on firm going:
tried blinkered and visored. *W. G. R. Wightman.*

INTENT 2 ch.c. (Mar 22) Kris 135 – Interval 122 (Habitat 134) [1991 7m⁴] compact **50 p**
colt: first foal: dam, winner from 5f (at 2 yrs) to 1m and third in 1000 Guineas, is out

of Cambridgeshire winner Intermission: 13/2 on, 9 lengths fourth of 7 in maiden at Thirsk in August, one pace final 2f: showed a quick, roundish action. *H. R. A. Cecil.*

INTENTIONS 3 ch.f. Local Suitor (USA) 128 – Alpine Damsel 46 (Mountain Call **65** d
125) [1990 NR 1991 a8g² a8g 8m⁵ 8g 12.2m 10.2g 8m] plain, leggy filly: moderate mover: half-sister to several winners, including fairly useful 1984 2-y-o 6f winner Hilly (by Town Crier): dam bad plater: poor form after debut, in seller (blinkered) and handicap (as if something amiss) last 2 starts: should stay 1¼m. *D. J. G. Murray-Smith.*

INTERLOPER 3 b.c. Robellino (USA) 127 – Blushing Cousin (Great Nephew **62**
126) [1990 6f 7m³ 7d⁶ 1991 8f³ a7g³] sturdy colt: quite modest maiden: third at Brighton and (in median auction contest) Lingfield in the spring: will be suited by return to 1m: possibly unsuited by dead ground. *J. H. M. Gosden.*

INTERNAL AFFAIR 3 gr.f. Aragon 118 – Alicia Markova 64 (Habat 127) [1990 **49**
5m⁶ 5m⁵ 1991 8.9g³ 8.3d* 8m⁵ 8.9m 7g⁵ 8.2m³ a10g] leggy, rather close-coupled filly: plating class on most form: won median auction maiden contest at Hamilton in July: hampered final start: stays 9f: best efforts on an easy surface: sold out of A. Stewart's stable 5,200 gns Newmarket Autumn Sales after penultimate start. *J. Pearce.*

INTERROGATE 3 b.f. In Fijar (USA) 121 – Artipiar 106 (Tyrant (USA)) [1990 **54**
6d⁵ 1991 8m² 11d⁵ 7.6g 8m] big, lengthy, rather plain filly: quite modest maiden: disputed lead over 5f (went too fast) in July claimer final start: should prove best short of 11f: sold 1,800 gns Ascot November Sales. *R. Boss.*

IN THE FRAME 3 br.g. Claude Monet (USA) 121 – Venetian Joy 80§ (Wind- **—**
jammer (USA)) [1990 7f 7g 8m 1991 8s 11.7s 11.5m 11.5m 8f⁶ 11.8m 14.1m] rangy gelding: moderate mover: poor maiden: seems to stay 1½m: acts on firm going: tried in blinkers and visor: often wears bandages. *G. H. Eden.*

IN THE GAME (IRE) 2 b.f. (Jan 26) Mummy's Game 120 – Carado 82 (Manado **53**
130) [1991 6f⁵ 6g 7m³ 7m⁵ 7g⁶ 8m 6.1m 6d a7g⁴] 16,000Y: tall, leggy filly: second foal: half-sister to 3-y-o Windmill Girl (by Blakeney): dam 8.2f winner later successful over hurdles: plating-class maiden: ran well on equitrack final outing: looked temperamental on several occasions: stays 7f: sometimes sweats: gave trouble stalls second outing: one to be wary of. *Miss A. J. Whitfield.*

IN THE GROOVE 4 b.f. Night Shift (USA) – Pine Ridge 80 (High Top 131) **123**
[1990 7m² 8m 10.5m* 8g* 12d⁴ 10.5g* 12m³ 12g 10d* 1991 8g* 8d² 12m* 10d⁴ 10m³ 12d⁶ 10m³ 12g]

In The Groove, whose reputation reached its height with a victory in the 1990 Dubai Champion Stakes at Newmarket, returned there in October needing a repeat success to live up, at least in part, to the prediction that she might become the 'Triptych of the 'nineties'. The tough and versatile In The Groove had added the Trusthouse Forte Mile at Sandown and the Hanson Coronation Cup at Epsom to her splendid record but she'd run some way below her best in the Coral-Eclipse and, returning after a two-month lay-off, had been beaten in a warm-up race before finishing sixth in the Ciga Prix de l'Arc de Triomphe. Defeat in the Arc had been no bar to success in the Champion for In The Groove the previous year—when she came ninth at Longchamp—nor, incidentally, had it been for Triptych who came third in the Arc in the two years that she won the Champion Stakes. In The Groove should have won the latest Champion. The old racing saying that 'you can give weight but you can't give distance' may not stand up to argument, but anyone seeking to demonstrate its validity need look no further for ammunition than Asmussen's riding of In The Groove at Newmarket. Acceleration has always been In The Groove's greatest weapon and she is usually brought late, but it was perplexing to see her set so much to do (she was ten lengths behind the leaders with about three furlongs to run) especially as the pace in the first part of the race hadn't been so strong as usual. In The Groove made up most of the leeway, despite encountering trouble and having to be switched when making her run, and was gaining hand-over-fist on the leaders as the post was reached. She finished half a length and the same behind Tel Quel and Cruachan and was a desperately unlucky loser. In The Groove looked in tremendous shape at Newmarket and was sent to Churchill Downs for the Breeders' Cup Turf a fortnight later when, after coming seventh to Miss Alleged, Sheikh Mohammed purchased her for stud (reportedly paying £750,000) and she was retired.

In The Groove's overall record as a four-year-old didn't match that of the previous season but her victories in the Group 2 Trusthouse Forte Mile and the Group 1 Coronation Cup provided ample justification of her owners' decision to keep her in training. She won a shade comfortably from Zoman at Sandown, confidently ridden by Cauthen who has been her most regular jockey and knows her well. Cauthen also got her home in a tremendous finish with Terimon and Rock Hopper at Epsom, driving her along firmly as she seemed to idle after showing an impressive burst of speed to lead over a furlong out. In The Groove followed Time Charter (1984) and Triptych (1987 and 1988) as the latest of her sex to win the Coronation Cup which has only a small band of fillies and mares on its winning roll. In The Groove's Coronation Cup win was her fourth in a Group 1 race, following her successes as a three-year-old in the Irish One Thousand Guineas, the Juddmonte International and the Champion. In The Groove was very versatile so far as distance was concerned, effective at a mile to a mile and a half, and although she never encountered extremes of going she was effective on good to firm and dead.

		Northern Dancer	Nearctic
	Night Shift (USA)	(b 1961)	Natalma
	(b 1980)	Ciboulette	Chop Chop
In The Groove		(b 1961)	Windy Answer
(b.f. 1987)		High Top	Derring-Do
	Pine Ridge	(b 1969)	Camenae
	(b 1980)	Wounded Knee	Busted
		(ch 1973)	La Lidia

The very robust In The Groove carried plenty of condition even when racing fit. She usually took the eye in the paddock and on the way to post—she was a good mover with a powerful action—and was a credit to her stable. In The Groove was also a fine advertisement for the young Northern Dancer stallion Night Shift who was repatriated to North America after the latest covering season; Night Shift won only a six-furlong minor event from seven attempts in the States but has been a success as a stallion, his fee rising from

Trusthouse Forte Mile, Sandown—right to left, In The Groove, Zoman and Aldbourne

Hanson Coronation Cup, Epsom—
In The Groove beats Terimon, Rock Hopper and Quest For Fame

£2,500 in 1988, the year his first runners reached the racecourse, to £20,000 in 1991. In The Groove, from Night Shift's second crop, was only a 20,000-guinea yearling. Her dam Pine Ridge was a moderate racehorse, a winner twice at a mile and a half, but her first four foals have all won, namely the fairly useful miler Spanish Pine (by King of Spain), the minor American winner Stripped Pine (by Sharpo), In The Groove and the three-year-old Pineapple (by Superlative), winner of a mile-and-a-half maiden race at Beverley in July. The grandam Wounded Knee was a minor winner over a mile and a half and a mile and three quarters and is a half-sister to Sinzinbra, the dam of a number of horses who have made their mark over jumps including the Grand National runner-up Mr Snugfit and the good class two-mile chaser Young Snugfit. Wounded Knee and Sinzinbra are out of a half-sister to both the Irish Derby winner Your Highness and to Phyllis Court, grandam of the 1970 Oaks and 1971 Coronation Cup winner Lupe. In The Groove reportedly starts her career at stud with a visit to Mr Prospector. *D. R. C. Elsworth.*

IN THE MARINES (USA) 2 b.g. (Apr 26) Ack Ack (USA) – Strait Lake   **45**
(Sallust 134) [1991 5d 5d⁵ 5g 5m⁴ 6m³ 6g 7f 7m] $25,000Y: strong, workmanlike gelding: moderate walker: has a round action: half-brother to 2 winners in North America, one in stakes: dam ran 3 times at 2 yrs: poor maiden: should prove suited by 7f: tongue tied down last 2 starts: sold 2,000 gns Newmarket Autumn Sales. *M. W. Easterby.*

IN THE MONEY (IRE) 2 b.c. (Apr 11) Top Ville 129 – Rensaler (USA) (Stop   **69** p
The Music (USA)) [1991 8.1f 7m] 50,000Y: workmanlike colt: fifth foal: half-brother to several winners, including 3-y-o 1m winner Convivial (by Nordance) and 1989 2-y-o 6f winner Jovial (by Northern Jove), later successful in graded stakes in USA: dam, winner at around 1m in USA, is half-sister to smart 1982 American 3-y-o Rose Bouquet: quite modest form in minor event at Haydock in September and maiden at Doncaster (still bit better for race) 7 weeks later. *R. Hollinshead.*

IN THE MOOD 3 b.f. Lidhame 109 – Siliferous (Sandy Creek 123) [1990 6m⁵   **49**
7m³ 6m³ 1991 8m 10g³ 10g⁵ 8f 8.3m* 8f² 8g 8.2m] sparely-made filly: has free, rather round action: plater: ridden by 7-lb claimer, made all at Windsor (bought in

4,200 gns) in August: stays 1¼m: likely to prove best on a sound surface: seems to go well with forcing tactics: sold 1,100 gns Ascot November Sales. *M. J. Fetherston-Godley.*

IN THE PAPERS 4 b.f. Aragon 118 – Mistress Gay 76 (Lord Gayle (USA) 124) — [1990 5d 5g⁶ 6d³ 1991 6g] strong, compact filly: fair handicapper at best: bit backward, soundly beaten only run in 1991 (May): stays 6f: acts on good to firm ground and dead. *J. Sutcliffe.*

IN THE PICTURE (IRE) 2 ch.c. (May 7) Tate Gallery (USA) 117 – Mille **70** p Fleurs (USA) 100 (Jacinto) [1991 6g⁴ 7f 8.2f] 50,000F, 32,000Y: small, unfurnished colt: closely related to useful stayer Crusader Castle (by The Minstrel) and half-brother to several winners: dam, successful over 7.6f, is half-sister to Mill Reef: quite modest form in maidens at Goodwood (eased close home) and Newbury in August: never placed to challenge at Nottingham following month: may well do better in handicaps. *R. Hannon.*

IN THE PRINT 3 b.g. Night Shift (USA) – Filwah (High Top 131) [1990 7d 1991 8.2f] sturdy gelding: behind in maiden auction and (wore tongue strap) claimer 11 months later. *Mrs Barbara Waring.*

IN THE SPOTLIGHT (IRE) 3 b.c. The Noble Player (USA) 126 – On Her — Own 80 (Busted 134) [1990 NR 1991 8s 8g] 8,600F, 12,500Y: good-topped colt: sixth reported foal: brother to 4-y-o Showman and half-brother to 1988 Irish 2-y-o 6f winner Out On Her Own (by Superlative) and a winner in USA: dam winning stayer: burly, showed little in minor event and maiden in the spring: sold to join R. Curtis 1,600 gns Ascot July Sales. *J. Sutcliffe.*

INTO THE FUTURE 4 b.g. Mummy's Game 120 – Valley Farm 88 (Red God **30** 128§) [1990 6m 7g 8m 10m 8g 8f³ 9.1m⁴ 10m⁵ 10m⁴ 10.8m⁴ 11m a 12g⁶ a 14g 1991 8.2d 10.5m⁶ 10m 8m⁴ 10.3m³ 9.2f⁴ 9.9f 12m] smallish, good-quartered gelding: poor handicapper: stays 1¼m: acts on firm ground: winning hurdler. *A. P. Stringer.*

INTREPID FORT 2 gr.c. (Jan 24) Belfort (FR) 89 – Dauntless Flight (Golden **59** Mallard 103) [1991 5g⁶ 5m² 5m³ 6m 6f⁵ 5m⁵ 7g 8m 6m] workmanlike colt: first reported foal: dam unraced: plating-class maiden: ran too freely over 1m: mostly below form in blinkers. *B. W. Murray.*

INTRICACY 3 b.f. Formidable (USA) 125 – Baffle 87 (Petingo 135) [1990 6g 7m **61** 1991 8d 10g² 11.7g⁴ 11.5s² 12.3m⁴ 11.7g⁶ 11.5g⁶ a 12g* a 14g* a 14g² a 16g² a 14g³] a **72** sturdy, quite attractive filly: has a quick action: quite modest handicapper: in good form on equitrack and fibresand late on, easily winning 2 November claimers at Southwell: claimed out of Lady Herries' stable £16,270 after second win: stays 2m: also acts on good to firm ground and soft: blinkered (soon under pressure, below form) sixth start: has edged left and run in snatches. *C. C. Elsey.*

IN TRUTH 3 ch.c. Dreams To Reality (USA) 113 – Persian Express (Persian Bold **59** 123) [1990 8d 8g 10s 8.2s* 1991 10d⁴ 12.3s⁵ 12g* 11.5m 12g 12.3g 10g⁵ 12.4f⁵ 12.1g a 12g] rangy colt: moderate mover: plating-class handicapper: won at Thirsk in May: stays 1½m: acts on soft going, seems unsuited by top-of-the-ground: suited by forcing tactics: trained first 6 starts by R. Earnshaw. *D. W. Chapman.*

INTUITIVE JOE 4 b.g. Petorius 117 – Super Girl (Super Sam 124) [1990 8f³ 8g **57** d 8m⁵ 8g³ 8.2m⁶ 7.6g 8m* 8.3m 7f a 8g a 7g² 10f² 10f 1991 7d 10f² 10g a 10g 10f³ 8m 10m 9.7s 10.1m] smallish, attractive gelding: poor handicapper: well below best after second start: stays 1¼m: acts on firm going: often taken down early: has looked a hard ride: blinkered final start. *G. Lewis.*

INUGO 2 b.f. (Feb 21) In Fijar (USA) 121 – Garnet 95 (Thatch (USA) 136) [1991 5m **34** 6g] leggy, rather sparely-made filly: first foal: dam 2-y-o 5f winner: poor form in southern maidens in July, second one a claimer. *C. N. Allen.*

INVERTIEL 7 b.g. Sparkling Boy 110 – Phyl's Pet (Aberdeen 109) [1990 7.5d³ 8f **63** 8g 8m⁴ 7m 7g⁴ 8d 1991 8s 12g³ 11f* 12g 9f* 9m⁵ 8m] quite good-topped gelding: easy mover: quite modest handicapper: won at Redcar (twice) in May: off course 4 months before final start: effective at 7f, and probably stays 1½m: well suited by firm going: has good turn of foot, tends to idle in front and best held up: has won for apprentice: trained until after penultimate start by Mrs G. Reveley: winning hurdler. *P. Monteith.*

INVIGILATE 2 ch.c. (Mar 28) Viking (USA) – Maria da Gloria (St Chad 120) **56** [1991 5g⁶ 5d⁵ 8.1g⁵ 8.3g 8m a 7g a 7g⁴] 2,600F, 9,000Y: workmanlike colt: half-brother to several winners here and abroad, including 5f performer Mummy's Glory (by Mummy's Pet): dam never ran: plating-class maiden: stays 1m: has run respectably for apprentice: trained by K. McCauley first 2 starts. *H. A. T. Whiting.*

INVINCIBLE ARMADA 2 b.c. (Mar 14) King of Spain 121 – Sailing Brig **70**
(Brigadier Gerard 144) [1991 6m⁶ 7m* 6m⁶ 6m] 5,600F, 10,000Y: quite well-made,
attractive colt: has scope: good walker: third reported live foal: half-brother to 13f
winner Brigadier Bill (by Nicholas Bill): dam never ran: won maiden auction at
Southwell in August: below that form in October nurseries at York (stiff task, not
entirely discredited) and Newmarket (checked and eased) 8 days later: will be
suited by 1m: sold 13,000 gns Newmarket Autumn Sales. *P. W. Chapple-Hyam.*

INVISIBLE ARMOUR 2 gr.g. (May 11) Precocious 126 – Haunting 79 (Lord —
Gayle (USA) 124) [1991 6m¹ 6m] 7,400Y, 7,000 2-y-o: half-brother to numerous winners,
including 3-y-o 6f to 7.2f winner Panikin (by Red Sunset) and useful 1986 2-y-o 5f
and 6f winner Amigo Sucio (by Stanford): dam stayed 1m: 33/1, slowly away and
always behind in 8-runner maiden auction at Hamilton in May. *J. S. Wilson.*

INVISIBLE HALO (USA) 4 b.f. Halo (USA) – Placer Queen (Habitat 134) —
[1990 8m 1991 9g 12g 9.7s] leggy filly: no form since modest at 2 yrs: best form at 7f:
sold 4,800 gns Ascot November Sales. *P. W. Harris.*

INVOCATION 4 ch.c. Kris 135 – Royal Saint (USA) (Crimson Satan) [1990 10m —
10f⁵ 12g⁵ 12m 16s 12d⁶ 1991 10g] big, strong colt: carries condition: moderate
walker: bad mover: little worthwhile form: tried blinkered once. *A. Moore.*

IOTA 2 b. or br.f. (Jan 22) Niniski (USA) 125 – Iosifa 108 (Top Ville 129) [1991 7m⁴] **66** p
smallish, leggy, sparely-made filly: first foal: dam 2-y-o 7f winner stayed 1½m,
seemed to become temperamental: weak 14/1-chance and green, under 2 lengths
fourth of 14, staying on well, in maiden at Leicester in October: showed a fluent
action: will stay middle distances: will improve. *Mrs J. Cecil.*

I PERCEIVE 4 b.g. Vision (USA) – Wavetree (Realm 129) [1990 10.6f² 8.2m⁵ **58**
8.2d⁶ 10.6d 10.6v 1991 10.2s 8d 10g 8m³ 7g 10.3d*] tall, good-bodied gelding:
plating-class handicapper nowadays: wearing tongue strap, won at Doncaster
(ladies) in November: stays 10.6f: acts on firm and dead ground: below form when
blinkered penultimate start: none too consistent. *F. H. Lee.*

I RAN LOVELY 2 b.f. (May 21) Persian Bold 123 – Sweet And Lovely 111 (Prince —
Tenderfoot (USA) 126) [1991 5m] 1,100F: close-coupled filly: sixth foal: half-sister to
3 winners, including fair 1¼m winner Cane Mill (by Mill Reef) and 1½m seller
winner Lily of Laguna (by Warpath): dam ran only at 2 yrs, winning 3 sprint races
from 6 starts: 66/1 and very green, slowly away and always outpaced in maiden at
Wolverhampton in September. *J. L. Spearing.*

IRISH FLASHER 4 b.g. Exhibitioner 111 – Miss Portal (St Paddy 133) [1990 6f —
5m 9f 1991 17.9f] tall, rather plain gelding: no form for long time, including in sellers:
acts on heavy going: carries head high. *J. M. Jefferson.*

IRISH GROOM 4 b.g. Shy Groom (USA) – Romany Pageant (Welsh Pageant **34**
132) [1990 6m 10.2f 8g² 8.2m 8.2m⁵ a8g⁶ 8m⁶ 8m³ 8d⁶ 1991 10g⁵ 10.2g 10m⁶ 8g⁵
9.9f⁶ 12m 10.8g 8m] angular gelding: moderate mover: poor handicapper: seems to
stay 1¼m: acts on good to firm ground and dead: effective blinkered or not: has
looked none too keen: none too consistent. *I. P. Smith.*

IRISH HONEY (IRE) 2 b.f. (May 28) Last Tycoon 131 – Great Guns 109 —
(Busted 134) [1991 7.1m 8.1g] 105,000Y: quite attractive filly: half-sister to several
winners, notably good 1¼m and 12.2f winner Home On The Range (by Habitat),
later dam of Reference Point: dam prolific winner from 1¼m to 2m: no significant
promise in maidens at Sandown in August and Haydock month later. *B. Hanbury.*

IRISH IMPULSE (USA) 3 b.f. Irish River (FR) 131 – Exclusively Raised —
(USA) 116 (Exclusive Native (USA)) [1990 6m⁶ 6.5g 1991 8d 11.7g⁶ 11.8m]
sparely-made filly: poor form: moved poorly down before tailed off in handicap final
start, first for 3 months: stays 11.7f. *R. J. R. Williams.*

IRISH MEMORY 2 b.c. (Apr 26) Don't Forget Me 127 – Irish Isle 67 (Realm **100**
129) [1991 6g* 6g³ 7d* 7m* 7s⁵ 7s²] 28,000 (privately) F: half-brother to several
winners, including useful 6f and 7f winner Benz (by Free State): dam won over 1m:
won maiden at Leopardstown in May, then 3-runner minor event at Galway and
6-runner listed Reference Point EBF Tyros Stakes (by short head, with Spanish
Storm 1½ lengths back in third) at the Curragh in August: around 6 lengths fifth of
18 to Fair Crack in Goffs Million at the Curragh and 2 lengths second of 7 to Swing
Low in Group 3 EBF Leopardstown Stakes in October: will stay 1m: acts on good to
firm and soft ground: useful. *J. S. Bolger, Ireland.*

IRISH NATIVE (IRE) 3 b.g. Be My Native (USA) 122 – Irish Bride (Track **73**
Spare 125) [1990 7s 1991 8g⁶ 10g² 8.9m⁶ 11d* 12g³ a12g³ a14g³ a11g² a12g² a8g a14g⁵]
angular gelding: modest form: won claimer at Redcar in October: ran creditably

after when placed: stays 1½m: possibly unsuited by good to firm ground: blinkered last 6 outings: trained until after third start by H. Candy. *C. A. Smith.*

IRISH PASSAGE 8 gr.g. Welsh Captain 113 – Honey's Queen (Pals Passage **67** 115) [1990 a8g3 a8g* a8g* a8g* a8g* a8g* a8g3 a8g 8.5f* 8f4 8.5f2 8m2 a8g4 8g5 8f* 8.5m3 8g a8g 1991 8d4 a8g 8m6 8f3 8m3 8f5 8f3 8h] workmanlike gelding: carries plenty of condition: good mover: quite modest handicapper nowadays: inconsistent in 1991 (has had heart problems): stays 9f: possibly unsuited by soft going, acts on any other: tried blinkered once: has hung left under pressure: best covered up. *T. D. Barron.*

IRISH SHOAL (USA) 3 b.c. Diamond Shoal 130 – Irish Wave (USA) (Raise A **112** Native (USA)) [1990 8g4 8m5 7v* 1991 7g5 6d5 6g* 6s* 5m2 6g 6g 5m6] $21,000Y: good-topped, angular colt: fourth foal: half-brother to smart 1m and 1¼m winner Hibernian Gold (by Golden Act) and a winner in USA: dam minor winner: won 2-y-o maiden at Saint-Cloud then handicap at Maisons-Laffitte and listed race at Baden-Baden in May as 3-y-o: 16/1, very good 3 lengths second of 10 to Elbio in King's Stand Stakes at Royal Ascot, keeping on despite flashing tail: below form in Group 3 contests and listed race in France afterwards: best form at sprint distances: acts on good to firm ground and heavy. *J. E. Hammond, France.*

IRON BARON (IRE) 2 b.c. (Mar 29) Sure Blade (USA) 130 – Riverine (FR) **55** p (Riverman (USA) 131) [1991 6g 7f6] 48,000F, 22,000Y: compact colt: sixth foal: half-brother to 3-y-o 1m winner Perjury (by Try My Best) and 3 other winners here and abroad, including quite useful 1986 2-y-o 6f winner Lucayan Knight (by Dominion): dam French 1¼m winner: sixth in maiden at Brighton in September, disputing second entering final furlong, eased when beaten: hung left on debut: should stay 1m: will improve again. *J. R. Fanshawe.*

IRON KING 5 gr.h. Tender King 123 – Zanskar (Godswalk (USA) 130) [1990 5f2 **65** 6f 6f4 5.8h 5m2 5f3 6m 6m 5f4 5m 6f3 6m 5m 6f3 6m 1991 6f4 5.3f5 5g4 6m2 6f6 6.1d* 6m 5d3 6g 5m3 6g 5f 6f 6g3 6g6 5g* 5m* 5.1s 6.1d 5s4] sturdy horse: poor mover: quite modest handicapper: has proved inconsistent: won at Chepstow in June, Wolverhampton in September and Warwick in October: effective from 5f to 7f: acts on firm and dead ground, possibly not soft: has run creditably visored, moderately when blinkered once. *J. L. Spearing.*

IRON RED 3 b.f. Never So Bold 135 – Rosie Pug (Mummy's Pet 125) [1990 6m 5d **50** 6g a5g4 a6g3 1991 a6g5 a5g5 a5g2 a5g2 a5g4 5m5 5.2m6 8m 6m2 5m4 6f] lengthy filly: sprint maiden: acts on good to firm ground, and all-weather: blinkered fourth, fifth and last 3 outings: sold 2,600 gns Newmarket September Sales. *M. A. Jarvis.*

ISABEAU 4 b.f. Law Society (USA) 130 – Elodie (USA) (Shecky Greene (USA)) — [1990 9g 10.6s 10.1m4 a12g 10m6 1991 14m] rather sparely-made filly: little worthwhile form on flat: should stay 1½m: winning hurdler. *K. A. Morgan.*

ISAIAH 2 gr.c. (Feb 27) Bellypha 130 – Judeah 69 (Great Nephew 126) [1991 6f5 **94** p 6m2 7m4 6m* 6m* 5d*] strong, good-topped colt: has plenty of scope: moderate mover: half-brother to 1½m winner Failsafe (by No Lute) and 6f to 1m winner Solomon's Song (by Night Shift): dam, 6f winner, is half-sister to very useful middle-distance winner Cesarea: successful in maiden at York and nurseries at Pontefract and Newmarket (soon chased along, lost action running into Dip then ran on well to catch Freddie Lloyd) in autumn: should stay 7f: likely to keep progressing and will win more races. *M. Johnston.*

ISAMBARD 4 b.c. Star Appeal 133 – Mertola (Tribal Chief 125) [1990 10m3 — 11.5m4 9m3 12d a12g 1991 10.8m 8m 12g 8.1g] close-coupled colt: fair maiden at best at 3 yrs: no form in first half of 1991, tailed off when blinkered once: sold out to join Mrs P. Sly's stable 2,700 gns Ascot September Sales. *P. F. I. Cole.*

ISCA'S SON (IRE) 3 ch.g. Caerleon (USA) 132 – Mingoon Bell 75 (Ragusa 137) **45** [1990 NR 1991 12m 11.8m 12.2m2 12f 8.1g2 8m2 9.2s3] IR 8,000Y, 10,000 2-y-o: lengthy gelding: moderate mover: half-brother to several winners in Europe, including French 1¼m to 1½m winner Lagnard (by Lord Gayle): dam Irish 9f winner, is half-sister to Irish Derby second Exdirectory and smart French middle-distance stayer Royal Land: plating-class form: placed in maiden and handicaps: probably best short of 1½m: acts on good to firm ground and soft: ran in snatches sixth start: winning hurdler. *J. G. FitzGerald.*

ISDAR (USA) 2 b. or br.c. (Jan 22) Known Fact (USA) 135 – Reyah 83 (Young **92** Generation 129) [1991 5m* 6.1m3 5d6] smallish, strong, deep-girthed colt: carries condition: second foal: half-brother to useful 7f (at 2 yrs) and 1m winner Abs (by Nureyev): dam 6f and 8.2f winner: fairly useful form: 8/1, won 10-runner Windsor Castle Stakes at Royal Ascot by a neck from Festive Cheer, leading over 1f out and running on well though drifting right: didn't confirm form, but wasn't discredited behind Isaiah in 9-runner nursery at Newmarket final start, first for 2 months: bred to stay 1m: may do better. *H. Thomson Jones.*

I SEE ICE 4 b.f. High Top 131 – Climb The Heights (USA) (Majestic Light (USA)) **73** [1990 a8g² a8g³ 10f a 11g² 12f* 13.8m² 12g³ 10.2f 1991 11.5m³ 12f* 12.4m 12m 12f² 11.9f 12f* 12g² 12f²] lengthy, rather leggy filly: modest handicapper, somewhat inconsistent: won at Folkestone in June and claimer at Beverley (straightforward task) in September: suited by 1½m: acts on firm going: tries to dominate: sold 14,000 gns Newmarket Autumn Sales. *W. J. Haggas.*

ISLAND BLADE (IRE) 2 b.c. (May 14) Sure Blade (USA) 130 – Queen's Eyot **56** 79 (Grundy 137) [1991 7m⁴ 8.2f 10m] 9,400Y: sturdy, angular colt: third foal: half-brother to 9f and 11f winner Persuasive (by Sharpo): dam suited by 1¼m: plating-class maiden: stays 1¼m: sold 5,600 gns Newmarket Autumn Sales. *P. T. Walwyn.*

ISLAND DESERT (IRE) 3 b.f. Green Desert (USA) 127 – Salote (USA) 109 **55** (Forli (ARG)) [1990 NR 1991 9s⁵ a12g⁵ 12m³ 11d³ 12.1m²] smallish filly: ninth foal: half-sister to fairly useful 1½m winner Mountain Isle (by Shirley Heights) and several winners abroad, including 3 at 10.5f+ in France: dam suited by 1½m: quite modest maiden: fair second in seller at Edinburgh in October, always front rank, going on 3f out and looking winner long way: well worth another try at 1¼m or 11f: acts on good to firm ground: sold to join J. Moore 7,000 gns Newmarket Autumn Sales. *Lord Huntingdon.*

ISLAND JETSETTER 5 ch.g. Tolomeo 127 – Baridi 82 (Ribero 126) [1990 **51** 10.6s³ 12.3g 8g⁴ 8.5g³ 10f³ 12f⁵ 8.5g² 10m 9s 1991 a8g⁵ 9s⁵ 8.3d 8g³] workmanlike, angular gelding: has a rather round action: plating-class maiden on flat nowadays: stays 1¼m: acts on any going: sometimes bandaged behind: winning hurdler/chaser: often finds little off bridle: has joined J. FitzGerald. *N. Tinkler.*

ISLAND LILY 3 b.f. Jupiter Island 126 – Caffre Lily § (Hittite Glory 125) [1990 **—** NR 1991 11.7f 10g] 2,300Y: stocky filly: second foal: half-sister to 4-y-o 7f winner Danny Blanchflower (by Rabdan): dam poor maiden: bit backward, well beaten in autumn claimers. *C. J. Hill.*

ISLAND UNIVERSE (USA) 3 b.c. Lyphard (USA) 132 – Carefully Hidden **100** (USA) (Caro 133) [1990 6m* 1991 8m 6m⁴ 7g] rangy colt: most impressive winner of maiden at Ascot as 2-y-o: easily best effort in 1991 (pulled hard in Craven, tailed off in Jersey Stakes) when creditable running-on fourth of 9 to Lee Artiste in listed race (looked very well, but carrying condition) at Haydock: outpaced early: should be suited by further than 6f: seemed unsatisfactory: sent to USA. *L. M. Cumani.*

ISOBAR 5 b.g. Another Realm 118 – Lady Eton 106 (Le Dieu d'Or 119) [1990 NR **—** 1991 a14g⁴ a14g a14g] close-coupled, leggy gelding: moderate mover: won sellers as 2-y-o: lightly raced and below form since: best efforts at 7f: blinkered or visored: winning chaser. *M. C. Chapman.*

ISTANBULLU 2 b. or br.c. (Feb 28) Jalmood (USA) 126 – Windy Sea 105 (Sea **—** Hawk II 131) [1991 7d] 1,200F: lengthy colt: half-brother to 3-y-o Pavers Good Shoes (by Good Times), fairly useful 6f and 8.2f winner Sharp Sea (by Sharpen Up) and a winner in Holland: dam won over 7f and 1¼m: 25/1 and carrying condition, slowly into stride and never better than mid-division in 15-runner maiden at Salisbury in June: looked sort to do better, but didn't run again. *M. Bell.*

ITHKURNI (USA) 2 b.f. (Feb 14) Green Forest (USA) 134 – Queen's Visit (Top **59** Command (USA)) [1991 6m² 7g⁴] sturdy filly: has scope: second foal: dam maiden suited by 1¼m, is half-sister to very smart 1984 2-y-o 6f and 7f winner Khozaam: plating-class form in mid-summer maidens at Doncaster (led over 4f) and Sandown (still bit backward, faded final 2f) 6 days later: will stay at least 1m. *B. Hanbury.*

ITHMID 3 b.c. Elegant Air 119 – Via Tritus 103 (Sovereign Path 125) [1990 NR **— §** 1991 10.1g 10.1m] 29,000Y: strong colt: half-brother to 5 winners, including 1m winner In The House (by Sharpen Up) and Irish middle-distance stayer Shocking Speed (by Electric): dam won twice at around 1m: tailed off in maidens, taking little interest when blinkered final start: one to treat with caution: sold 950 gns Ascot 2nd July Sales. *C. J. Benstead.*

ITQAN (IRE) 3 b.f. Sadler's Wells (USA) 132 – Photo 83 (Blakeney 126) [1990 7g **92 p** 7f 1991 12.2m² 12.2f² 11.9f* 14.8s* 14.6m* 16m²] sturdy, good-bodied filly: very good walker: successful in 3-runner maiden at Brighton (made all but awkward on descent) and handicaps at Newmarket (easily) and Doncaster (£15,100 event by a head, tending to idle) in late-summer: beaten short head in handicap at Newmarket in October: stays 2m: acts on any going: has turn of foot, and probably best with waiting tactics: progressive, and remains in training. *B. W. Hills.*

ITSABRAHMA 5 ch.h. Kind of Hush 118 – My Habibi 102 (Habitat 134) [1990 **113** 6.7g* 6d 6d* 6s⁴ 5g* 6g 8g⁴ 6v² 8g* 1991 6g² 6f* 6g* 6d⁵ 8d* 5.5g* 8g* 6f* 8g* 8.5s³ 7d²] fourth living foal: half-brother to modest 1½m winner Brianchon (by Mill Reef): dam 2-y-o 5f winner: very useful Swedish horse, topped Svensk Generalhandikap in 1990: seemed even better at 5 yrs, successful 3 times at Taby in mid-summer (including Swedish Open Mile), at Jagesro in August, then twice more at Taby (including Plaza Open Championship) and at Cologne (Group 2 event) in autumn: 2 lengths second of 7 to Danseuse du Soir in Prix de la Foret at Longchamp final start: effective from 5f to 8.5f: seems to act on any going. *Mme E. Nordling, Sweden.*

ITSAGAME 3 br.c. Mummy's Game 120 – Immodest Miss 73 (Daring Display **92** (USA) 129) [1990 5f* 5f* 5f² 5m 1991 7d 6g² 7m 6m² 6d 6m 6f³ 6g 7g* 7.9g 8m 7.3m 7m] close-coupled, sturdy colt: fairly useful handicapper: best effort to win £8,200 event at Goodwood in August, detached last long way: never dangerous afterwards, showing little final start: stays 7f: acts on firm going: sold 9,500 gns Newmarket Autumn Sales. *S. Dow.*

IT'S NOT MY FAULT (IRE) 3 b.g. Red Sunset 120 – Glas Y Dorlan 80 (Sexton Blake 126) [1990 6f a7g 8m 10s 1991 13.8m⁶ 14.1g⁵ 13d] sturdy, workmanlike colt: poor maiden: probably stays 1¾m: blinkered last 2 starts, running moderately on second of them. *Dr J. D. Scargill.*

IT'S ONLY MONEY 2 b.c. (Feb 1) Prince Sabo 123 – Marimba 82 (Music Boy **62** 124) [1991 6m 5h² 5d* 5m² 5.1f⁶ 5d] 6,000Y: strong, good-topped colt: grand walker: usually looks well: first foal: dam 2-y-o 5f winner, is half-sister to smart 6f to 1m winner Larionov: quite modest performer: won maiden auction at Ripon in June, making all: speedy, and likely to prove best at 5f: acts on hard and dead ground: sold 4,100 gns Doncaster November Sales. *J. Berry.*

IVANOV (USA) 3 b.c. Nijinsky (CAN) 138 – Fine Spirit (USA) (Secretariat — (USA)) [1990 NR 1991 12.3d⁵ 11.8g⁴ 10.5g 16.1g] $700,000Y: lengthy colt: first foal: dam third in Breeders' Cup Juvenile Fillies and 7f stakes winner at 3 yrs: well beaten in maidens and (very stiff task, headway 5f out and eased right down once beaten) handicap: joined P. Mitchell. *M. R. Stoute.*

IVAN THE TERRIBLE (IRE) 3 ch.g. Siberian Express (USA) 125 – **61** Chrisanthy 81 (So Blessed 130) [1990 6m⁶ 6d⁶ a6g⁴ 7d 8.2d a8g⁶ a7g* 1991 8d 7f⁶ 7m 11.5g⁵ 10m* 12g³ 9d 11.1g⁵ a11g] lengthy, workmanlike gelding: quite modest performer: edgy, won claimer (claimed out of P. Cole's stable £8,011) at Leicester in July: sweating, third in similar event at Newcastle 10 days later, easily best other effort at 3 yrs: stays 1½m: seems unsuited by a soft surface: blinkered once at 2 yrs: takes strong hold. *Miss S. J. Wilton.*

IVATO (IRE) 3 ch.c. Diesis 133 – Ivory Smooth (USA) (Sir Ivor 135) [1990 NR **56** 1991 12.5m⁵ 10m⁵ 7.6m⁶] IR 35,000Y: smallish colt: seventh foal: half-brother to 1m and 1½m winner North Pacific (by Hawaii), 1987 2-y-o 6f winner Foujita (by Tap Shoes) and a winner in USA: dam 1m winner at 4 yrs and 6 yrs in USA: plating-class form: best effort 11 lengths sixth of 10 to Pride of Storm in maiden at Lingfield: should prove suited by further than 7.6f: claimed out of R. Charlton's stable £6,750 after Sandown claimer second start. *P. Mitchell.*

I'VE GOTTA TELL YA 5 b.g. Petong 126 – Super Jennie 80 (Stephen George — 102) [1990 10.6f 12m* 14g² 12m⁴ 16.2d⁵ 15m* 12g³ 13m⁶ 16f 15.8d a14g 1991 12m⁶ 12.3f] big, rather leggy gelding: moderate mover: poor handicapper: no form in 1991: stays 2m: acts on firm and dead going. *Capt. J. Wilson.*

IVINGHOE 3 b.c. Taufan (USA) 119 – Upper Sister (Upper Case (USA)) [1990 — NR 1991 7g⁴ 8m⁴] half-brother to several winners in Italy, including 1990 7f winners Satrico (by Homing) and Silcone (by Pas de Seul): dam won in Italy: bandaged, fourth of 13 in ladies maiden at Lingfield in June: well beaten in Wolverhampton maiden 17 days later. *M. McCormack.*

IVOR'S FLUTTER 2 b.g. (May 10) Beldale Flutter (USA) 130 – Rich Line (High **40** p Line 125) [1991 7.1d] workmanlike gelding: sixth foal: half-brother to winning plater Lucky Jo (by Martinmas) and a winner abroad: dam never ran: 20/1 and better for race, well beaten in large-field maiden at Chepstow in October, slowly away and well behind, some late progress: bred to stay 1¼m: should improve. *D. R. C. Elsworth.*

IVORS PRINCESS 2 b.f. (Apr 16) Mandrake Major 122 – Double Birthday **39** (Cavo Doro 124) [1991 6g⁵ 6f] 750Y: leggy filly: fourth reported foal: sister to 5f (at 2 yrs) and 1m winner Major Ivor: dam ran once: 20/1 and very green, keeping-on fifth of 11 at Catterick in July, better effort in maiden auctions. *Mrs G. R. Reveley.*

IVORY BRIDE   3 b.f. Domynsky 110 – Ivoronica 89 (Targowice (USA) 130) [1990   **86**
5m³ 6g² 5d³ 6s* 6m* 6m 6d⁴ 6m 1991 6d⁶ 7d⁴ 8m⁵ 8m⁶] leggy, unfurnished filly: fair performer: 33/1, returned to form when fifth in £11,200 handicap at Newmarket, running on from rear: ran poorly in £18,000 handicap at same course 9 days later: stays 1m: yet to race on very firm ground, acts on any other: visored final 2 starts at 2 yrs: sold 12,500 gns Newmarket December Sales. *M. H. Tompkins.*

IVYANNA (IRE)   2 b.f. (Mar 11) Reference Point 139 – Ivy (USA) (Sir Ivor 135)   **87** p
[1991 8s* 8d*] 220,000Y: fourth foal: half-sister to 1989 2-y-o 7f winner Ivrea (by Sadler's Wells), useful over middle distances at 3 yrs, and Irish 7f (at 2 yrs) and 13f winner Royal Climber (by Kings Lake): dam, placed twice at 2 yrs in USA, is half-sister to Santa Anita Derby winner An Act: odds on, successful in 12-runner maiden at the Curragh then 9-runner minor event at Navan (made all, by 4 lengths from Bally Pourri) 10 days later in October: will be suited by middle distances: likely to improve further. *J. S. Bolger, Ireland.*

IVY COTTAGE   3 br.f. Damister (USA) 123 – Debutina Park 87 (Averof 123)   **56**
[1990 5f² 5m³ 5d⁴ 6d 1991 6f⁴ 8g 8g 7.5m⁴ 7g 6m³] lengthy, good-quartered filly: plating-class maiden: should stay 1m: probably acts on firm and dead going: visored fourth start: has wandered and found little. *J. Etherington.*

IWAN   3 b.g. Elegant Air 119 – Clouded Vision 74 (So Blessed 130) [1990 NR 1991   — §
10g 10g⁴ 12.3d 10g 10.1m⁵] 35,000Y: strong, deep-girthed gelding: fourth living foal: half-brother to 1½m winner Voltage (by Electric) and a winner in Italy: dam 6f winner at 3 yrs: no worthwhile form, including in handicaps last 2 starts, finding little first occasion and taking no interest on second: best effort at 1¼m: sometimes bit coltish: blinkered last 4 starts: sold 3,200 gns Doncaster August Sales and gelded: one to avoid. *D. Morley.*

IYWAAN (IRE)   2 b.c. (Jan 17) Sadler's Wells (USA) 132 – Maria Roberta (USA)   **70**
(Roberto (USA) 131) [1991 7d 8m⁴ 7.9m⁶] 300,000Y: rangy, useful-looking colt: has scope: second foal: half-brother to a winner in Italy: dam won in Italy and came fourth in Italian Oaks: modest maiden: carrying condition and green still, best effort when under 5 lengths fourth of 19, staying on, not knocked about, at Doncaster in September: looks sort to do better. *P. T. Walwyn.*

IZIOFF   5 ch.g. Sayyaf 121 – Maroua (FR) (The Marshal 118) [1990 a6g³ a6g² a10g⁶   —
a8g 10s 1991 8g] smallish ex-Irish gelding: moderate mover: plating-class maiden: probably stayed 1m: dead. *R. Akehurst.*

J

JACK BOY   6 b.g. Sparkling Boy 110 – Miss Deed 83 (David Jack 125) [1990 5f⁴   **44**
5g⁶ 5g* 5m⁶ 5d² 5d⁴ 5g³ 5f 5d 5g⁵ 5d 1991 5m 5g⁵ 5f⁴ 5m⁵ 5g⁴ 5d² 5.2f⁵ 5m 5m⁴ 5s] small, sturdy gelding: carries condition: has a round action: poor 5f handicapper: goes particularly well with give in the ground (yet to race on heavy): tried blinkered once: none too consistent: sold 1,700 gns Doncaster November Sales and joined J. J. O'Neill. *J. Balding.*

JACK BUTTON (IRE)   2 b.g. (Mar 9) Kings Lake (USA) 133 – Tallantire (USA)   **65**
(Icecapade (USA)) [1991 7m 7.5f⁶ 8m 10m⁴] 4,000Y, 3,300 2-y-o: good-topped gelding: third foal: dam ran once: 33/1 and visored, easily best effort when staying-on fourth of 12 in maiden at Nottingham: better suited by 1¼m than shorter. *Bob Jones.*

JACK HILL   2 br.c. (Jan 30) Lidhame 109 – Alice Hill 78 (Persian Bold 123) [1991   **49**
5m⁵ 5m⁶ 5m 5.3f³ 5m 6m⁶ 5f⁶ 5m 6g] sparely-made colt: first foal: dam 2-y-o 5f and 5.3f winner failed to train on: inconsistent plater: suited by 5f and firm ground: sold 500 gns Ascot November Sales. *W. Carter.*

JACK LANG   3 b.c. Damister (USA) 123 – Jilt (ITY) (Bolkonski 134) [1990 NR   **103**
1991 8m⁶ 10.1m⁵ 12m* 11.9g⁵ 12g⁵ 11v* 14v] 10,000F: tall, leggy, rather shallow-girthed colt: half-brother to 4 winners in Italy, notably Premio Roma and St Leger Italiano runner-up Jung (by Sexton Blake): dam won 5 races in Italy: 6/5, led final strides in maiden at Pontefract in July: won minor event at Rome in October: quite stiff tasks in between: should stay beyond 1½m: coltish first 2 starts, edgy second: trained first 5 starts by L. Camici, Italy. *L. Cumani, Italy.*

JACK'S CROFT   3 b.g. Damister (USA) 123 – Smagiada (Young Generation 129)   —
[1990 NR 1991 10m 10d⁴ 14g⁴ 16.1g 18.1m] 72,000Y: leggy gelding: third foal:

half-brother to modest 1988 2-y-o 5f winner Sweet 'N' Sharp (by Sharpo): dam, winner in Italy, is half-sister to leading 1982 Italian 2-y-o filly Stemegna: showed signs of a little ability and unsatisfactory temperament: may prove best short of 2m: visored second and last 2 starts: sweating final one. *Lord Huntingdon.*

JACKSON FLINT 3 b.c. Nishapour (FR) 125 – Scamperdale 61 (French Beige **99** 127) [1990 NR 1991 8g* 12m 13g* 14.1f* 13.9g4 18m2 13.3g* 14.6d2] 17,500Y: strong, lengthy colt with scope: shows knee action: half-brother to several winners, including useful stayer Stavordale (by Dance In Time) and very smart French middle-distance performer Alfred's Choice (by So Blessed): dam stayed well: won Newmarket Challenge Whip in May, maiden auction contest (wandered badly under pressure) at Ayr in June and handicaps at Redcar in July and Newbury (challenged on bridle 2f out, idled in front) in October: below-form second to Bean King in Doncaster minor event final start: below best over 2¼m: acts on firm ground: will prove best with waiting tactics. *H. Thomson Jones.*

JADA (IRE) 3 ch.g. Shy Groom (USA) – La Loie Fuller (FR) (Rheffic (FR) 129) **81** [1990 6m6 7g 7d4 8m4 7.9m* 1991 7v2 9d6 10g2 13.5g4 10m 9.5m2 11g5 13.5m5 8.5g4 9m4 10d4] IR 45,000Y: angular, workmanlike gelding: half-brother to 2 winners, including 1984 2-y-o 6f and 7f winner Rusty Law (by Rusticaro): dam of little account in France, is half-sister to smart 1973 French 2-y-o Banjer: modest performer: won maiden at Dundalk at 2 yrs: ran respectably in celebrity event at Ascot final start in 1991: effective from 8.5f to 13.5f: acts on good to firm and heavy ground: sold 8,800 gns Newmarket Autumn Sales. *K. Prendergast, Ireland.*

JADE GREEN 2 b.f. (Apr 23) Midyan (USA) 124 – Pilley Green 100 (Porto Bello **50 p** 118) [1991 a7g3] 6,400Y: half-sister to several winners, including 7.2f and 1m winner Bold Pillager (by Formidable): dam best at 6f: weak 12/1-shot, remote third of 11, late progress after slow start, to Spanish Miner in late-year maiden at Southwell. *P. J. Makin.*

JADIDH 3 b.f. Touching Wood (USA) 127 – Petrol 73 (Troy 137) [1990 NR 1991 **64** 14.1m2] leggy, plain filly: third foal: sister to 2m winner Dhakrah and half-sister to 1m and 9f Zammah (by Jalmood), later successful in USA: dam won at 1m and stayed 1¼m: second of 4 to impressive 15/8-on shot Marie de France in maiden at Yarmouth in July: sold to join Miss J. Thorne 2,800 gns Newmarket Autumn Sales. *A. C. Stewart.*

JAEGER (USA) 4 ch.c. Storm Bird (CAN) 134 – Asoka (USA) (Youth (USA) 135) **69** [1990 NR 1991 8d6 8.5f2 10m6 10m6 10d5 8m6] tall colt: third foal: brother to 1m winner Scarron: dam unraced half-sister to champion American filly Gallant Bloom: quite modest maiden: ran moderately (blinkered, drifted right) final start: stays 1m: acts on good to firm ground: sold to join J. Jenkins' stable 5,000 gns Newmarket Autumn Sales. *J. H. M. Gosden.*

JAFFA LINE 3 b.f. High Line 125 – Jacquinta 95 (Habitat 134) [1990 6d4 7m3 **105** 7m* 7m* 8m4 7d4 1991 10g2 10.5m5 12m4 12g 12m 14.6m6] sturdy, angular filly: keen walker: has powerful, round action: useful performer: short-head second to Hailsham in Thresher Classic Trial at Sandown: ran creditably in Gold Seal Oaks at Epsom and Park Hill Stakes at Doncaster third and final starts, poorly in Ribblesdale Stakes at Royal Ascot and Irish Oaks at the Curragh in between: probably stays 1¾m: yet to race on extremes of going. *D. R. C. Elsworth.*

JAGGED EDGE 4 ch.c. Sharpo 132 – Tura (Northfields (USA)) [1990 6g 6m 6m **59 d** 7m 7d 6s 8g 1991 7d2 6d4 6g 7.1m 7.1d 6g3 6g5 6m 7g 7g3] sturdy colt: plating-class handicapper at best: stays 7f: seems suited by some give in the ground: has flashed tail: twice below form when blinkered: inconsistent. *R. J. Holder.*

JAGJET 4 ch.c. Vayrann 133 – Ritsurin 79 (Mount Hagen (FR) 127) [1990 10v 8f6 **—** 6m 7m 10g 10m4 10m5 9f* 10f* 12f4 1991 12g] smallish, good-topped colt: poor mover: poor performer: bandaged, finished badly lame only run in 1991 (July): stays 1¼m: acts on firm ground: below form when visored once, hung right for 7-lb claimer once: sold 5,000 gns Newmarket September Sales. *J. S. Wilson.*

JAHAFIL 3 b.c. Rainbow Quest (USA) 134 – River Spey 96 (Mill Reef (USA) 141) **108** [1990 7g4 8g* 7g* 8m2 1991 10g3 10g4 12g 11.9g6 12f2 14g* 14.6m] big, rangy, attractive colt: good walker and mover: useful performer: won 5-runner listed race at Goodwood in August by 1½ lengths from Arcadian Heights, making virtually all and running on strongly: ran as if something amiss 3 times as 3-y-o, having set very strong early pace in St Leger at Doncaster final start: stays 1¾m: acts on firm ground: blinkered (very edgy and pulled hard) third outing: usually wears tongue strap and crossed noseband nowadays: sometimes sweating: remains in training. *Major W. R. Hern.*

JAHIZ 3 br.c. Damister (USA) 123 – Tribal Feast 100 (Tribal Chief 125) [1990 NR 1991 7m 10g5 10m5 10.2f 10m] IR 160,000Y: workmanlike colt: hobdayed at 2 yrs: half-brother to smart 1984 2-y-o Brave Bambino (by Jaazeiro), 11f winner Tribal Pageant (by Welsh Pageant) and 5f and 6f winner Superbrave (by Superlative): dam speedy half-sister to high-class sprinter Runnett: disappointing maiden: easily best effort apparently on second start: visored fourth start: sold 2,100 gns Newmarket Autumn Sales. *P. T. Walwyn.*   —

JAHZEELAN 3 b.c. Never So Bold 135 – Misty Halo 93 (High Top 131) [1990 a7g4 7.5f4 7h2 8d 1991 11m3 11s2] tall, lengthy colt: has plenty of scope: has a round action: improved performer in summer at 3 yrs: placed in handicaps at Redcar (on toes) and Edinburgh: will stay 1½m: acts on any going. *Sir Mark Prescott.*   **76**

JAILBREAKER 4 ch.g. Prince of Peace 109 – Last Farewell (Palm Track 122) [1990 12d 1991 7f 17.1m4 14m4 20g 11.8g6 17.2g] tall, close-coupled gelding: poor mover: poor handicapper: suited by test of stamina: acts on good to firm ground. *B. R. Millman.*   **47**

JAIRZINHO (USA) 2 b.c. (Apr 2) Robellino (USA) 127 – B F's Sailingal (USA) 103 (Sail On-Sail On) [1991 6g5 6m3 7f* 7m2 8d* 10v2] $38,000Y: angular, useful-looking colt: has scope: brother to smart 6f to 1m winner Faustus and fairly useful 1987 2-y-o 7f winner Yachtsman: dam won at up to 1m and is sister to very smart Sailingon: progressive form: comfortable winner of maiden at Brighton in August and median auction at Wolverhampton in October: 1½ lengths second of 18 to Jape in Premio Guido Berardelli at Rome in November: suited by 1¼m: acts on any going. *R. Hannon.*   **103**

JALDI (IRE) 3 b.f. Nordico (USA) – Havara 82 (African Sky 124) [1990 6g 1991 5f 5g 5.8f] sturdy, angular filly: bit backward, showed signs of ability in maidens and handicap in the spring: will prove suited by 6f + . *J. Sutcliffe.*   —

JALLAD 3 b.c. Blushing Groom (FR) 131 – Petrava (NZ) (Imposing 80 (AUS)) [1990 6m* 7g 1991 8.9g 7g4 6m6] heavy-topped colt: carries condition: has been hobdayed, and not seen out until September in 1991: capable of fair form: easily best effort since debut when creditable fourth of 6 in minor event at Ascot: should prove suited by further than 7f: sold 6,600 gns Newmarket Autumn Sales: can't be backed with confidence. *P. T. Walwyn.*   **80**

JALMUSIQUE 5 ch.g. Jalmood (USA) 126 – Rose Music 86 (Luthier 126) [1990 100 8f2 8f* 8g 10f 8g 8m6 10m2 9f3 8.2d 8m5 1991 8m* 10.2m3 8m4 8.1m* 8m* 10f2 8.1g4 8f* 8m] strong, good-bodied gelding: carries condition: has a long stride: improved handicapper: had fine season in 1991, successful at Thirsk in May, Haydock (apprentices) and Pontefract in July and Ripon in August: best at 1m to 1¼m: well suited by top-of-the-ground: below form when visored once: has been bandaged near-hind: usually races up with pace: very tough and genuine: a great credit to his connections. *M. H. Easterby.*   **100**

JAMAICA GEORGE 6 gr.g. Sexton Blake 126 – Summer Serenade (FR) 96 (Petingo 135) [1990 a16g3 a16g4 1991 a16g] sparely-made gelding: moderate mover: quite modest handicapper: soundly beaten only start at 6 yrs (January): stays well: effective visored or not: joined R. Spicer. *T. Thomson Jones.*   —

JAMAICA JOE 3 b.c. Music Boy 124 – Pasha's Dream (Tarboosh (USA)) [1990 5m 5f4 6m 6f 6g5 7g 6m6 6d a6g 1991 a7g] leggy, good-quartered colt: fair plater at 2 yrs: tailed off in handicap in January, 1991: better at 6f than 5f: possibly ideally suited by an easy surface: blinkered last 6 outings: has sweated: sometimes races too freely. *R. Hannon.*   —

JAMAICAN PUNCH (IRE) 3 b.f. Shareef Dancer (USA) 135 – House Tie (Be Friendly 130) [1990 NR 1991 16.9g 12.3g] 38,000Y: compact filly: eighth foal: closely related to fairly useful sprinter Bag O'Rhythm (by Be My Guest), half-sister to 4 other winners, including French 1m and 1¼m winner Academic (by Mill Reef): dam Irish 1m winner out of high-class 2-y-o Mesopotamia: always behind in maiden and seller. *D. Morley.*   —

JAMAIS BLEU 2 ch.c. (Apr 26) Never So Bold 135 – Ahnoora Blue (Ahonoora 42 122) [1991 6m 6g 7m 6s] 4,600Y: smallish colt: first foal: dam, maiden, stayed 1¼m: poor maiden: off course 4 months, best effort in claimer second start. *T. J. Naughton.*   **42**

JAMEELATY (USA) 3 ch.f. Nureyev (USA) 131 – Bright Omen (USA) (Grey 96 Dawn II 132) [1990 5g5 6g* 6m* 7m2 7f2 6m 1991 7g4 8m3 8g 7.1g3] leggy, sparely-made filly: has a smooth, quick action: fairly useful performer: ran well in smallish fields for minor event at Yarmouth and listed race at the Curragh first 2 starts: well below form in Chepstow minor event on final one: stays 1m: acts on firm going: sometimes sweating and edgy. *A. A. Scott.*   **96**

JAMES IS SPECIAL (IRE) 3 b.c. Lyphard's Special (USA) 122 – High Explo- **66**
sive (Mount Hagen (FR) 127) [1990 7f 7s 1991 10g 12.5m² 12g* 12d³ 14s³ 12d* 12g³
12.1s³ 13.3g5] tall, leggy colt: carries condition: poor mover: moderate walker: quite
modest handicapper: successful at Goodwood in June and August: ran creditably last
3 starts: stays 1¾m: acts on soft ground. *H. J. Collingridge.*

JAMES RIVER 5 ch.h. Star Appeal 133 – Yorktown (Charlottown 127) [1990 —
a11g6 1991 11.7g 16.2g 14.6g] leggy, light-framed horse: plating-class handicapper at
best: tailed off in first half of 1991: stays 1½m: headstrong: twice blinkered (very
fractious in preliminaries second occasion): looks one to avoid. *Mrs A. Knight.*

JAMESTOWN BOY 3 b.g. King of Clubs 124 – Jhansi Ki Rani (USA) 94 (Far **51**
North (CAN) 120) [1990 7f 7f6 7f 1991 10f³ 8f*] leggy gelding: has a markedly round
action: fair plater: won handicap (no bid) at Yarmouth in June, making virtually all:
stays 1¼m: acts on firm going: winning hurdler for G. Pritchard-Gordon: sold 1,300
gns Ascot December Sales. *Sir Mark Prescott.*

JAMMAAYIL (IRE) 2 ch.f. (Apr 8) Lomond (USA) 128 – Loveliest (USA) **80**
(Tibaldo) [1991 5m4 7m* 7m³ 7.1s* 8d 7m] 175,000Y: leggy, unfurnished filly: good
walker and mover: half-sister to several winners here and in USA, including smart
6f (at 2 yrs) to 10.5f winner Optimistic Lass (by Mr Prospector), also fourth in Oaks
and dam of Golden Opinion: dam was very useful at up to 10.5f in France and won at
up to 9f in USA: fair performer: won minor event (ran lazily) at Newcastle in June
and 3-runner £7,400 event (sweating, made all) at Sandown in July: ran creditably
(better than twenty-second position implies) in Tattersalls Tiffany Highflyer Stakes
there on final start: will stay 1m: may prove best on a sound surface. *M. R. Stoute.*

JANBIYA (IRE) 3 ch.f. Kris 135 – Spark of Fire (Run The Gantlet (USA)) [1990 **86**
6d6 7g* 7.6s6 1991 8g4 7.3d4 10.1g6 10m* 10f³ 11.9g5 10d4] quite attractive filly,
rather unfurnished: fluent mover: fair performer: ran well in handicaps fourth to
sixth starts, winning at Salisbury in August: stays 1½m: acts on firm ground: sometimes sweating: has run well when edgy and on toes: tends to race prominently. *H.
Thomson Jones.*

JANE'S BRAVE BOY 9 b.g. Brave Shot – Jane Merryn (Above Suspicion 127) —
[1990 a6g 7m 8g6 8.5g 6g a7g 8m4 8m 7f 1991 7f 6f 6g] workmanlike gelding: carries
plenty of condition: poor handicapper: no form in 1991: suited by 7f and a turning
track: possibly unsuited by soft going, acts on any other. *J. K. Kinane.*

JANE'S FANTASY 3 ro.f. Enchantment 115 – Sea Farer Lake 74 (Gairloch 122) —
[1990 7g 6h6 1991 10g 10s 7m5 16m4 14.6m] workmanlike filly: no worthwhile form,
in claimers and sellers in 1991: blinkered/visored last 3 starts. *M. D. I. Usher.*

JANESWOOD (IRE) 3 b.f. Henbit (USA) 130 – Stipa (Silver Shark 129) [1990 —
NR 1991 12.3f6 12f6 12f4] sparely-made, angular filly: half-sister to many winners,
mostly in Belgium, including listed winner there Ile de Rhodes (by Welsh Saint):
dam won at up to 6.5f in France: well beaten in maiden and claimers: blinkered final
start. *J. Parkes.*

JANISKI 8 b.g. Niniski (USA) 125 – Seasurf 106 (Seaepic (USA) 100) [1990 14.8m² **70**
16m² 16.2m 14g 17.1m4 16.2d 14.6d5 1991 14.8d² 16.4m4 14.9m³ 14m* 16.1m³ 14m]
strong gelding: has a quick action: quite modest handicapper: won at Haydock in
August: has won only on top-of-the-ground, but seems also to act on dead:
has run well in blinkers, usually visored: a difficult ride: largely consistent. *Mrs
Barbara Waring.*

JAN STEDMAN 3 b.g. Legend of France (USA) 124 – Young May Moon —
(Hopeful Venture 125) [1990 NR 1991 10d 11.7m 12s] 4,800F: strong gelding: fourth
living foal: half-brother to 8.3f seller winner Sea Crossing (by Kala Shikari): dam
unraced half-sister to 1000 Guineas second Abbeydale: no worthwhile form in
maidens: trained first 2 starts by T. Thomson Jones. *J. White.*

JAPE (USA) 2 b.c. (May 22) Alleged (USA) 138 – Northern Blossom (CAN) **106**
(Snow Knight 125) [1991 7g² 8g² 10v*] 130,000Y: lengthy, good-quartered colt:
good walker: fourth foal: half-brother to fair 9f winner Ecossais Danseur (by Arctic
Tern) and a winner in North America: dam champion 3-y-o filly in Canada: vastly
improved form to win 18-runner Premio Guido Berardelli at Rome in November by
1½ lengths from Jairzinho: will stay 1½m: acts well on heavy ground. *P. F. I. Cole.*

JAPONSKI (USA) 3 ch.c. Blushing Groom (FR) 131 – Kiliniski 119 (Niniski **71**
(USA) 125) [1990 NR 1991 10g4 12m4] neat colt: first foal: dam 1½m winner fourth in
Oaks, is out of half-sister to Nureyev: modest form in maidens at Salisbury (coltish,
better effort) and Newmarket in May: should stay 1½m: bandaged. *J. H. M. Gosden.*

JAROMIC 2 b.c. (Apr 28) Tina's Pet 121 – Jose Collins 91 (Singing Bede 122) **55**
[1991 5m 5m 6m a5g³ a6g² a5g] 4,400Y: good-bodied colt: moderate mover: fifth live

foal: half-brother to a winner in Italy: dam best at 5f: placed in small-field maidens at Lingfield late in year: last of 13 in Southwell nursery final start: stays 6f. *P. F. Tulk.*

JARRWAH 3 ch.f. Niniski (USA) 125 – Valiancy 87 (Grundy 137) [1990 7s 1991 **43** § 8.9g⁴ 10.2g 10g] unfurnished filly: plater: ran badly after fourth in median auction contest at Wolverhampton: should stay middle distances: sold 3,500 gns Newmarket July Sales to join J. Spearing: found little final start, and probably unsatisfactory. *B. Hanbury.*

JARZON DANCER 3 br.g. Lidhame 109 – Long Valley 71 (Ribero 126) [1990 6g⁴ **49** 7f⁵ 6m⁵ 1991 7g 8m 10g⁴ 10g 8.1s] leggy, rather sparely-made gelding: plating-class performer: form in handicaps in first half of season only when staying-on fourth of 22 at Nottingham: moved poorly down next start: stays 1¼m: gave impression ill at ease (hung badly) on firm ground: gelded after final start. *C. F. Wall.*

JASOORAH (IRE) 2 b.f. (Mar 7) Sadler's Wells (USA) 132 – Fenney Mill 99 **72** p (Levmoss 133) [1991 8s*] 135,000F, 370,000Y: closely related to useful 7f and 14.7f winner Red Guitars (by Nijinsky) and half-sister to 1990 2-y-o 6f winner Fennel (by Slew O' Gold) and modest 1¼m and 1½m winner Dual Capacity (by Coastal): dam Irish 1¼m winner stayed 1½m, is out of Irish 1000 Guineas and St Leger winner Pidget: odds on, comfortably won 10-runner maiden at Yarmouth in October, challenging 2f out and running on well, though rather green: will stay 1¼m: will improve. *A. C. Stewart.*

JAWAB (CAN) 4 ch.c. Vice Regent (CAN) – Rare Secretary (USA) (Secretariat **93** (USA)) [1990 7m* 7h² 8.2m² 7f* 1991 7f 8f⁶ 7.6m* 8g 7m] well-made colt: fairly useful handicapper: confirmed earlier promise when winning at Lingfield in September: stays 1m: yet to race on a soft surface: ran poorly when sweating badly penultimate start: sold 30,000 gns Newmarket Autumn Sales. *A. C. Stewart.*

JAWANI (IRE) 3 b.c. Last Tycoon 131 – Fabled Lady (Bold Lad (IRE) 133) [1990 **51** 6m 7m⁶ 8m 1991 8.2d⁶ 10g 10m 12.3m a16g⁴ a12g3] big, rather leggy colt: plating-class handicapper: easily best efforts when in frame at Southwell and Lingfield: stays 2m: retained by trainer 10,000 gns Newmarket Autumn Sales after fourth start: sold 3,000 gns Ascot December Sales after final one. *Dr J. D. Scargill.*

JAYLEE 2 b.f. (May 17) Aragon 118 – Laser Beam (High Top 131) [1991 6g 6g a6g⁶ — 7g] 640F: small filly: first foal: dam unraced daughter of Lucent and granddaughter of Lucasland: poor maiden: pulled up lame final outing: dead. *T. J. Naughton.*

JAZILAH (FR) 3 br.c. Persian Bold 123 – Muznah 92 (Royal And Regal (USA)) **79** d [1990 NR 1991 8m* 8.9g 9d 7m 7.1m] rather leggy, good-topped colt: fourth foal: half-brother to Irish 1¾m winner Fayafi (by Top Ville): dam 7f and 1m winner seemed to stay 1½m: won 4-runner maiden at Thirsk in August: didn't reproduce that form in handicaps, stiff tasks initially: blinkered, edgy, sweating and pulled hard final start: needs further than 7f and should stay 1¼m: acts on good to firm ground: sold to join M. Naughton 15,000 gns Newmarket Autumn Sales. *H. Thomson Jones.*

JAZZ 2 gr.f. (May 21) Sharrood (USA) 124 – Rainbow's End 83 (My Swallow 134) **76** [1991 7m² 7f² 7m²] sturdy, quite good-topped filly: has scope: half-sister to several winners, including fairly useful stayer Cap Del Mond (by Troy) and fairly useful 1986 2-y-o 5f winner Chasing Moonbeams (by Final Straw): dam 2-y-o 5f winner: modest maiden: travelled well, then ran on strongly under pressure when beaten a length by Daja in Wolverhampton median auction in September, final start: will stay 1¼m: may well do better. *L. M. Cumani.*

J BRAND 4 b.g. Persian Bold 123 – Napa Valley 89 (Wolver Hollow 126) [1990 **62** 12f* 12m* 12.3d 11f⁶ 11.7m* a12g 1991 12s 11.7g 12m 11.6m* 11.4m 11.8m 11.9g⁶] workmanlike gelding: has a short, sharp action: quite modest handicapper: returned to form (had soft palate operation) when gamely winning at Windsor in August: well beaten after: stays 1½m: acts on firm going, possibly unsuited by soft: sold to join J. Moore's stable 4,200 gns Newmarket Autumn Sales. *P. F. I. Cole.*

J CHEEVER LOOPHOLE 6 gr.g. King of Spain 121 – Sally's Silver 62 (No **69** Mercy 126) [1990 a5g³ a6g² a6g* 5f² 5g 6m⁶ 5m 5m⁵ 5g⁵ 5m a6g² a5g⁴ a6g 1991 6m 5f³ 5m 6f 5h³ 5d a6g 6f] lengthy gelding: modest handicapper: went well over 6f on all-weather, better suited by 5f on turf: probably acted on any going: sometimes blinkered or visored: went well with forcing tactics: dead. *C. Tinkler.*

JEAN LUC (USA) 3 b.c. Alleged (USA) 138 – Don't Joke (USA) (Shecky Greene **61** (USA)) [1990 NR 1991 a7g⁴ 9s² 10m⁵] 41,000Y: smallish colt: moderate mover: first reported foal: dam best at 2 yrs, winning stakes events at 6f and 8.5f: quite modest form in maidens: should prove suited by greater test of stamina. *B. Hanbury.*

JEANS VALENTINE 3 gr.f. Green Ruby (USA) 104 – Roanette (Roan Rocket **50** d 128) [1990 5f³ 6g* 6g² 6m⁴ 6g⁴ 6m* 6f³ 6f* 6m⁶ 1991 6f³ 6f 6g 6d⁴ 6m 6d⁶ 8m] leggy, workmanlike filly: moderate mover: consistent plater at 2 yrs: best 3-y-o effort on reappearance: stays 6f: acts on firm going: usually bandaged behind: sold 2,100 gns Doncaster August Sales. *J. Berry.*

JEETHGAYA (USA) 3 ch.f. Critique (USA) 126 – Born Anew (USA) (Avatar **61** (USA)) [1990 7m 8f³ 1991 12m⁵ 10d a11g 10m³ 9.7f² a12g⁴] workmanlike filly: quite modest performer: in frame in minor event, handicap and (favourite, travelling strongly 1m then finding little) claimer: may well prove suited by 1¼m: acts on firm going. *A. Hide.*

JEFFERSON DAVIS (IRE) 2 b.c. (May 22) The Noble Player (USA) 126 – **71** Bay Supreme (Martinmas 128) [1991 6m 5m⁵ 6s* a7g³] IR 5,200F, 6,400Y: close-coupled, quite good-topped colt: fourth foal: half-brother to 3-y-o Pesidanamich (by Mummy's Treasure), successful at 6f and 7f, and 2 winners in Scandinavia: dam unraced: won maiden at Hamilton in November: good third, apprentice ridden, in Lingfield nursery following month: stays 7f: acts on soft ground, and on equitrack. *W. J. Pearce.*

JEHOL 5 b.g. Teenoso (USA) 135 – Buz Kashi 123 (Bold Lad (IRE) 133) [1990 10f³ — 12g 11g 10m 10m 10m* 10f⁵ 12.3g* 11d⁴ 12m 1991 10d⁶ 10g 12m] lengthy, attractive gelding: fairly useful handicapper at 4 yrs: well below best in 1991: stays 1½m: acts on firm going: takes keen hold, and usually held up: has been taken down early: sold only 5,000 gns Newmarket Autumn Sales. *G. Wragg.*

JELLYROLL BLUES 2 b.f. (Apr 6) Tremblant 112 – Daring Ditty (Daring — March 116) [1991 5m⁶ 6f 8m] sturdy, close-raced daughter of useful sprinter Dawn Ditty: poor form in maidens. *Mrs G. R. Reveley.*

JENDALI (USA) 3 b.c. Nijinsky (CAN) 138 – Jellatina (Fortino II 120) [1990 8g⁴ **111** 1991 14.1f² 16.2g* 14.8m* 14.6m] strong, good-topped colt: successful in Queen's Vase at Royal Ascot, pushed along some way out before leading final strides, and 5-runner listed race at Newmarket in July, making all to beat Krius 3½ lengths: subsequently suffered tendon injury, lethargic in preliminaries and well beaten in St Leger at Doncaster on return: stays well: very useful. *H. R. A. Cecil.*

JENDEE (IRE) 3 b.c. Dara Monarch 128 – Bunch of Blue (Martinmas 128) [1990 **69** NR 1991 a8g* 10.1m² 8.9m⁵ 12g⁶] IR 16,000F, IR 67,000Y: rather leggy colt: half-brother to 2 winners in Ireland, one of them useful jumper The Musical Priest (by Baptism), and a winner in South Africa: dam winner at up to 13f in France, is half-sister to Man o' War Stakes winner Czar Alexander: modest form, winning maiden at Southwell in February and second in minor event at Windsor in July: soundly beaten in claimer (claimed to join J. Hellens £10,025) final start: stays 1¼m. *P. F. I. Cole.*

Queen's Vase, Ascot—Jendali (right) gets up close home from Silver Rainbow;
Le Corsaire is third

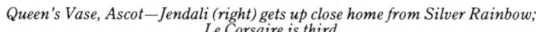

JENPAT 3 b.f. Mashhor Dancer (USA) – Russeting 76 (Mummy's Pet 125) [1990 **33**
6f 1991 7m 7m 8.2m 11.1d⁶ 12.2g 10g 9.2d³ 9.2m⁵ 10m] leggy filly: plater: stays 9f:
acts on dead ground (has run fairly well on good to firm): subsequently won 2 selling
hurdles for N. Tinkler then bolted to post and withdrawn on another intended outing
on flat: sold 3,500 gns Newmarket Autumn Sales. *Don Enrico Incisa.*

JENUFA (IRE) 3 br.f. Last Tycoon 131 – Love Lost (Home Guard (USA) 129) **82**
[1990 6g* 6g*ᵈⁱˢ 7m 1991 7m³ 7g⁴ 7d³] lengthy, unfurnished filly: fair performer:
ran well in minor events first 2 starts as 3-y-o: will stay 1m: seems unsuited by a soft
surface: not seen out after June. *J. W. Hills.*

JESS REBEC 3 br.f. Kala Shikari 125 – Laleston 73 (Junius (USA) 124) [1990 5f⁶ **54**
6d⁴ 6d⁵ a5g⁴ a5g² a5g⁴ 1991 5m⁴ 5g⁵ 5d 5f⁴ 6.1s 5.7m 5.3f² a5g⁶ 6f⁴ 5.3g³ 5m² 5d
5.1d 6m] smallish, workmanlike filly: has a quick action: plating-class maiden:
effective at 5f and 6f: acts on firm ground, seemingly not on a soft surface: blinkered
(ran poorly) final start: wore tongue strap on fourth. *R. Dickin.*

JESTERS FAREWELL (USA) 3 ch.f. The Minstrel (CAN) 135 – Forever **61**
Waving (USA) (Hoist The Flag (USA)) [1990 6m 6d 1991 10g 9m 11m² 11m² 11.8g⁴
10.1f* 11.5f³ 8.9m 10.5d] rangy filly: has a fluent, round action: moderate walker:
quite modest performer: won claimer at Yarmouth in August, staying on very
strongly and late: stays 11.5f: acts on firm ground: sweating final start: usually set
fair bit to do: sold 7,800 gns Newmarket Autumn Sales. *P. W. Harris.*

JESTER'S GEM 2 ch.f. (May 8) Jester 119 – Tresanna (Treboro (USA) 114) **40**
[1991 5g 6m 7m 7m 8.9m 7m 8m] 1,000Y: quite good-topped filly: dam
unraced: modest plater: stays 9f well: blinkered last 3 outings. *B. W. Murray.*

JET PET 3 b.g. Tina's Pet 121 – Spinnaker Lady 70 (Windjammer (USA)) [1990 **43**
5m⁴ a5g² 6m 6m a6g⁵ a7g⁶ 6m³ 8.2s³ 6m⁵ 8d 6s* a8g³ 1991 a7g 7d 6d⁶ 8g⁴ a8g 8d
a8g 8g a8g² a10g a8g² 8f] small, angular gelding: moderate mover: plating-class
handicapper: form as 3-y-o only when in frame: stays 1m: acts well on soft ground:
visored 6 times: has been bandaged: joined R. Brotherton: not one to rely on. *D. T.
Thom.*

JET SKI LADY (USA) 3 ch.f. Vaguely Noble 140 – Bemissed (USA) **122**
(Nijinsky (CAN) 138) [1990 6m* 6m³ 7g* 8g 1991 10g* 10g⁴ 12m* 12m²
11.9g² 12d]
The Gold Seal Oaks fell sensationally to Jet Ski Lady: on merit by ten
lengths at 50/1. Since the first running in 1779 only Sun Princess in 1983 had
won the Oaks by further and none of its winners had started at longer odds;
Formosa in 1868 and Noblesse in 1963 both won by ten lengths, Vespa started
at 50/1 in 1833. Jet Ski Lady was actually the rank outsider in a field of only
nine. Apart from the probability that she would be better suited by the step
up to a mile and a half than the hot favourite Shadayid, there seemed little to
be said for her chance. Her form, current or past, did not match up to the
favourite's. Shadayid's two runs as a three-year-old in the Fred Darling
Stakes and the One Thousand Guineas had extended her unbeaten sequence
to five, whereas Jet Ski Lady's two had resulted in a length-and-a-half win
from Classic Minstrel in a listed race at the Curragh followed by a staying-on
fourth, hampered early in the straight, behind Runyon and two other Irish
colts in the Derrinstown Stud Derby Trial at Leopardstown. The previous
season Jet Ski Lady had finished around five lengths seventh of nine to
Shadayid after leading for six furlongs in the Prix Marcel Boussac on her final
outing; before that she'd won two out of three in Ireland, including a
Leopardstown nursery under 9-7.
     Jet Ski Lady made virtually all at Epsom but there's no suspicion that she
caught the opposition unawares. The early pace wasn't a strong one and they
kept very close order to halfway. At the top of the hill Jet Ski Lady held a
narrow advantage and at one point on the descent she seemed briefly to be
niggled along. Once in line for home though, she began to open out in grand
style. She soon had the others stretched, and when she'd established a two-
length advantage over clear second Shadayid approaching the two-furlong
pole, Shadayid beginning to labour, it became obvious that Jet Ski Lady would
take a great deal of catching. Kept up to her work until eased slightly near the
end, she galloped on relentlessly, covering the ground with a raking stride.
While Shadayid faded quickly Shamshir came through under strong pressure
to take the runner-up spot by three quarters of a length, the hot favourite

Gold Seal Oaks, Epsom—a memorable sight as Jet Ski Lady strides away;
Shadayid is still second at this point, ahead of Shamshir and Jaffa Line (rails)

having built up just enough of an advantage to ensure third ahead of Jaffa Line and Magnificent Star. There had to be reservations about the value of the form. Shadayid palpably failed to get the trip; Shamshir, who took the preliminaries badly, seemed for most of the way unlikely to feature in the finish, being one of the first off the bridle down the hill, bumping with Shadayid and forced to race wide; and Magnificent Star looked all at sea on the track.

The nine Oaks runners won only one race between them afterwards, yet most of them, including Jet Ski Lady, succeeded in doing themselves justice. Plans to take on the colts with Jet Ski Lady were shelved for the time being, and she was sent for the Kildangan Stud Irish Oaks then on to the Aston Upthorpe Yorkshire Oaks. She lost the first by half a length to the unbeaten Italian Oaks winner Possessive Dancer, the second by the narrowest of margins to Magnificent Star, giving a stout staying display on each occasion. She showed the better form at York. At the Curragh, where connections thought the ground a little too lively for her (it seemed just as lively at Epsom), Jet Ski Lady could never get away from the field. She led by a length from the eventual third Eileen Jenny into the straight and hung on gamely, coming under the whip two furlongs out, until Possessive Dancer edged ahead over the final hundred and fifty yards. At York Jet Ski Lady was sent on over three furlongs out after racing close up, and she gradually increased the pressure on the others. Approaching the last furlong she'd gone a length up and was running on strongly, but Magnificent Star on the rails steadily closed the gap, getting her nose in front right on the line. The pair of them pulled five lengths clear of Shamshir. Jet Ski Lady was shaping very much like a St Leger type. However, she was sent straight for the Prix de l'Arc de Triomphe, bypassing both Doncaster (she would have had to have been supplemented) and the Curragh (the Irish Leger took place only fifteen days before the Arc). She ran moderately at Longchamp, finishing tailed off, having had trouble keeping prominent to halfway, and has now been retired. It was her first race on ground softer than good.

Jet Ski Lady at Epsom evoked memories of her sire Vaguely Noble—he gave the impression he could gallop for ever. Vaguely Noble died in 1989 having stood at Gainesway Farm in Kentucky since his retirement from racing after winning the Arc twenty-one years earlier. As a sire he was an influence for stamina. While Jet Ski Lady was his first Oaks winner he got other good, and in some cases superior, fillies, including Dahlia, the Derby runner-up Nobiliary and the Budweiser-Arlington Million winner Estrapade.

411

The American champion older horse Lemhi Gold, Exceller and Empery were among his many pattern-winning or graded stakes-winning colts. Jet Ski Lady's dam and maternal grandam both won graded stakes, Bemissed the Grade 1 Selima Stakes over eight and a half furlongs and the Grade 3 Miss Grillo Stakes over nine as a two-year-old. Bemissed was rated in the top five of her age and sex in the States that season; she went on to take her total of victories to five and finish third in the Kentucky Oaks the next. Jet Ski Lady is the second above-average runner she's produced from three foals, following Lady Bemissed (by Sir Ivor), a stakes-placed miler. Few of the family have been seen out in Europe in recent times, and it's doubtful whether Jet Ski Lady would have been but for the dispersal of her breeder, Ryehill Farm, in 1988; she fetched 335,000 dollars at the sale. However, as the extensive entry in the catalogue showed, there is at least one significant European member. The Irish Guinness Oaks and Park Hill Stakes second of 1975, Tuscarora, is out of a half-sister to the third dam Orissa.

		Vienna (ch 1957)	Aureole
Jet Ski Lady (USA) (ch.f. 1988)	Vaguely Noble (b 1965)		Turkish Blood
		Noble Lassie (b 1956)	Nearco
			Belle Sauvage
	Bemissed (USA) (b 1980)	Nijinsky (b 1967)	Northern Dancer
			Flaming Page
		Bemis Heights (b 1975)	Herbager
			Orissa

The pedigree is just about as stout as there is to be found in North American catalogues nowadays. Jet Ski Lady would surely have shown that she stayed further had she been given the chance, and she might well have shown that further suited her better. At a mile and a half she was clearly well suited by having plenty of use made of her. A lengthy, good-quartered filly, she acted on good to firm ground. As to her merit: while a plan to miss the

Maktoum Al-Maktoum's "Jet Ski Lady"

Irish Oaks in favour of the Irish Derby seemed not in the least over-ambitious immediately after Epsom, events ultimately showed Jet Ski Lady some way behind the best of the colts and, in all probability, no better than an average Oaks winner, though winning a classic by ten lengths was still an extraordinary feat and the way in which she achieved it is certain to be long remembered. *J. S. Bolger, Ireland.*

JEUNE 2 ch.c. (Mar 29) Kalaglow 132 – Youthful (FR) (Green Dancer (USA) 132) **101** [1991 6m* 6f² 7d³ 7.3g⁴] tall, leggy, quite attractive colt: third foal: half-brother to 4-y-o fairly useful 7f/1m handicapper Dorset Duke (by Beldale Flutter): dam, French 1½m winner, is out of high-class French staying 2-y-o First Bloom: useful performer: very easy winner of 3-runner maiden at Yarmouth in July: ran well in Mill Reef Stakes (freely to post, behind Showbrook) and Horris Hill Stakes (taken very steadily down, pulled hard early, kept on behind Lion Cavern), both at Newbury: third at Ascot in between: will prove suited by 7f+ : needs to settle better. *G. Wragg.*

JEWELLERY QUARTER (IRE) 2 b.c. (Feb 17) Bluebird (USA) 125 – No **85** Jargon (Nonoalco (USA) 131) [1991 5m⁶ 6g⁴ 6m* 6g³ 7m³ 7f² 7m² 7f⁴] 20,000Y: good-bodied colt: progressing well physically: good walker: fourth foal: half-brother to 1990 2-y-o 1m winner Toshiba Comet Too (by Gorytus) and a winner in Belgium by Ela-Mana-Mou: dam won twice at both 6f and 7f in Ireland: fair performer: won maiden at Redcar in June: ran well afterwards: better suited by 7f than 6f: acts on firm ground: consistent. *W. Jarvis.*

JEWEL OF THE EAST (IRE) 3 b.f. Pennine Walk 120 – Smash (Busted 134) **65** [1990 NR 1991 12.2d* 10.2s³ a16g⁵ 12d] angular, long-backed filly: half-sister to good-class 1m and 1¼m winner Broken Hearted (by Dara Monarch) and 1¼m winner Smashing Millie (by Mill Reef): dam once-raced daughter of sister to Selhurst and half-sister to Royal Palace: modest form first 2 starts, winning maiden at Catterick in March: soundly beaten in handicaps, off course over 3 months before each of them: should prove suited by test of stamina. *M. Bell.*

JEWEL OF THE NILE 3 b.f. Glenstal (USA) 118 – Miller's Daughter (Mill **45** d Reef (USA) 141) [1990 NR 1991 6s² 6m 9m 11m 8g⁴ 9.9f⁴ 10.1m⁴ 14.1m⁶ 11.9f 10m⁶] leggy, sparely-made filly: second foal: dam poor half-sister to Goodwood Cup winner Tug of War: plater: stays 1¼m and acts on any going: visored last 5 starts: sold 440 gns Ascot December Sales. *D. Morley.*

JEZEBEL MONROE (USA) 2 b.f. (Feb 11) Lyphard (USA) 132 – Alliance **65** p (USA) (Alleged (USA) 138) [1991 6g⁵] angular, unfurnished filly: fifth foal: sister to 3-y-o Loure: closely related to quite useful 1½m and 13.3f (stays 2m) winner Matador and French provincial 11.5f and 1½m winner Beaute Dangereuse (both by Nureyev): dam French 10.5f winner who stayed 1½m is half-sister to numerous winners, including Blushing Groom: 33/1 and very green, around 9 lengths fifth of 21 to Katakana in maiden at Newbury in October, pushed along firmly at halfway then keeping on: will stay 1m+ : sure to improve. *R. Charlton.*

JIGGERAK 2 b.f. (Apr 29) Belfort (FR) 89 – Errol Emerald 60 (Dom Racine (FR) **61** 121) [1991 5s* 6m⁴ 6.1d⁶ 8.3s a6g] leggy, workmanlike filly: third foal: dam 1¼m to 1½m winner often gave trouble at start: won maiden at Edinburgh in July: ran moderately in nurseries last 2 starts, final one in November: stays 6f: went freely to post second start, taken steadily down third. *S. G. Norton.*

JIGGING 3 ch.g. Scottish Reel 123 – Kesarini (USA) 87 (Singh (USA)) [1990 8d⁵ **—** 1991 10.2s⁵] strong, heavy-bodied gelding: easily better effort in maidens on debut: gave trouble stalls both starts. *Miss S. E. Hall.*

JIGSAW BOY 2 ch.c. (May 19) Homeboy 114 – Chiparia 82 (Song 132) [1991 6g⁶ **72** p 6f*] quite good-topped colt: brother to quite modest 1989 2-y-o Run Home and half-brother to several winners, including 1985 2-y-o 6f winner Our Tilly (by Grundy): dam best at 5f: 10/1 from 6/1, won 9-runner maiden at Folkestone in October, again bit slowly away, running on really strongly to lead close home: should stay 7f: may well improve again. *R. J. Holder.*

JIMLIL 3 b.f. Nicholas Bill 125 – Ozra 63 (Red Alert 127) [1990 5f⁴ 5f² 6d³ 6m² 7f **99** 6g⁴ 7m 6d* 7s 1991 8g 9d² 9m 10d⁴ 10v³ 10m² 12f³ 8m⁴ 10g⁴ 10m⁴ 11g] workmanlike filly: has a round action: fairly useful performer: in frame in listed races and minor events, creditable fourth to Desert Sun at Doncaster on eighth start: soundly beaten in handicap final one: suited by 1¼m: acts on good to firm and heavy going: sometimes gives trouble at stalls. *B. Palling.*

413

Duchess of Kent Stakes, York —
the well-backed Jode beats Changing Times on her only outing at two years

JIMMY BARNIE   3 ch.c. Local Suitor (USA) 128 – Sharper Still (Sharpen Up **114**
127) [1990 6m² 6m* 6m* 5f*dis 6d* 5m 1991 5m³ 6m² 6m⁴ 6d 6.5g⁴ 7.3f² 7g]
lengthy colt: very useful performer: fourth in Cork And Orrery Stakes at Royal
Ascot (2 lengths behind Polish Patriot giving him 8 lb) and Prix Maurice de Gheest
at Deauville: good ¾-length second to Only Yours in Hungerford Stakes at
Newbury penultimate start: worth a try at 1m: acts on firm and dead going. *J. L.*
Dunlop.

JIMMY MAC JIMMY   4 b.g. Carriage Way 107 – Tuthill Bello 64 (Porto Bello   —
118) [1990 NR 1991 9f] lengthy gelding: second foal: dam poor sprint maiden:
sweating and bit backward, behind in maiden at Newcastle in July on debut on flat:
fifth in NH Flat race at 3 yrs. *J. S. Wilson.*

JIMMY PIP   4 b.g. Creetown 123 – Beth of Houndhill (Filiberto (USA) 123) [1990   —
NR 1991 a8g 7.1m 7m 5s] leggy gelding: first reported foal: dam poor maiden: seems
temperamental and of little account. *B. A. McMahon.*

JIM'S WISH (IRE)   3 b.c. Heraldiste (USA) 121 – Fete Champetre 80 (Welsh   —
Pageant 132) [1990 6m* 6m³ 6m⁶ 6m³ 7m⁴ 7f⁵ 8g⁴ 8m 7v⁴ 8d 1991 8.1s 8.1d]
workmanlike colt: fair winner at 2 yrs: no worthwhile form in October, 1991: suited
by 1m: best form on a sound surface: sold to join G. Moore 6,000 gns Newmarket
Autumn Sales. *M. D. I. Usher.*

JINGA   6 b.h. Castle Keep 121 – Eldoret 100 (High Top 131) [1990 14m⁶ 12m 12g⁶   **75**
13.1h⁴ 1991 15.5f⁵ 14d* 16.2g⁵ 14m⁴ 12d⁴ 16.2d* 14s² 14m⁵ 14s³ 16m⁶] lengthy,
quite attractive horse: modest handicapper: won at Sandown in May and Chepstow
(amateurs) in July: stays well: acts on good to firm and heavy going: raced too freely
when blinkered on reappearance: has run in snatches: winning hurdler. *Lady*
Herries.

JINSKY'S JEWEL   3 b.g. Myjinski (USA) – Song of Pride (Goldhills Pride 105)   —
[1990 NR 1991 a11g 7m 6.1m] small, sparely-made gelding: third foal: half-brother to
2 poor maidens: dam never ran: tailed-off last in maiden, claimer and seller. *R.*
Thompson.

JITTERBUGGING   2 b.c. (Mar 4) Try My Best (USA) 130 – Dancing Sally 100   **93**
(Sallust 134) [1991 6d* 7s⁶ 7.3g⁶] compact colt: half-brother to several winners,

414

including Irish middle-distance winner Tikhomirov (by Star Appeal) and 1¼m winner Joruri (by High Line): dam useful at up to 1m, is half-sister to good miler Scottish Reel: fairly useful performer: won maiden at Newbury in June, despite wandering when clear: best effort around 6 lengths sixth of 18 to Fair Crack in Goffs Million at the Curragh: failed to confirm that in 7-runner Group 3 event at Newbury later in October, tending to carry head bit awkwardly: should stay 1m: acts on soft ground. *B. W. Hills.*

JIVE MUSIC 5 b.m. Music Boy 124 – Swift To Conquer 87 (Solinus 130) [1990 6m⁴ 6f 5f 5m³ 5f⁵ 5d 5m 5m⁵ 5m 5f 5g a5g 8.5f 5m² 5m⁵ 5m⁴ 5f³ 5.3f 5d 1991 a5g⁴ a6g 6d⁶ 5d* 5g³ 5f² 5f² 5m² 5h 5s⁵ 5g² 5g⁴ 5f 5m⁶ 5m 5f 5g⁶ 5m 5g 5m⁶ 5s] smallish, good-quartered mare: bad mover: poor handicapper: won at Thirsk in April: best at 5f: acts on firm and dead going: often blinkered or visored. *N. Bycroft.* **41**

JOB LOT 3 ch.g. Precocious 126 – Do Your Best 89 (Try My Best (USA) 130) [1990 NR 1991 7v⁶ 5m 7f⁶ 7f⁶ 8d 8m] good-topped, workmanlike gelding: third foal: dam 1m winner: well beaten in varied company, including selling: sometimes bandaged: sold 850 gns Ascot 2nd July Sales. *M. H. Easterby.* **—**

JODE (USA) 2 b.f. (Apr 11) Danzig (USA) – Belle de Jour (USA) (Speak John) [1991 6g*] smallish, leggy, close-coupled filly: closely related to a winner by One For All and half-sister to several winners, notably Kentucky Derby winner Spend A Buck (by Buckaroo): dam won 6f claiming race: well-backed favourite, won 9-runner maiden at York in June by 2½ lengths from Changing Times, travelling strongly and leading 2f out: should stay 1m: looked a useful prospect. *A. A. Scott.* **72 p**

JODIE BOBS 2 ch.f. (Feb 9) Adonijah 126 – Lunaria (USA) (Twist The Axe (USA)) [1991 6g 6d 6m 7.5f 5f] plain, sparely-made filly: fifth live foal: half-sister to 1½m winner Super Gunner (by Homing) and 5f and 6f winner Best Effort (by Try My Best): dam thrice-raced half-sister to smart sprinter Abeer: seems of little account. *R. D. E. Woodhouse.* **—**

JOE BLOW 3 b.c. Today And Tomorrow 78 – Baby Bunting (Pyjama Hunt 126) [1990 5g² 6m³ 5d⁵ 7g 7.5g a6g 6m 5v⁵ 1991 6g 7g 8.9g 6m] rather sparely-made colt: modest plater: soundly beaten in 1991: should stay beyond 5f: best effort on heavy going: blinkered/visored 4 of last 5 starts. *P. Burgoyne.* **—**

JOE FROM MONACO (IRE) 2 b. or br.c. (May 5) Treasure Kay 114 – Chiarella (Relkino 131) [1991 5s⁶ 5g 5d 6f⁶ 8m] 4,000Y: well-made colt: second reported foal: dam won in Italy: well beaten, including in sellers: has hung left: bolted to start and withdrawn second intended start: headstrong. *G. Lewis.* **—**

JOE SUGDEN 7 b.g. Music Boy 124 – Sum Star 67 (Comedy Star (USA) 121) [1990 5f³ 5g³ 5m³ 5d² 5g² 6d* 6d 5f⁶ a5g⁴ 5m³ 5g³ 5.6g³ 6m² 5m 6d⁴ 6d² 5s⁵ 1991 5d⁵ 5m 6g 5f 6m 5g⁶ 5.7m 6g 5d⁴ 5.2f 5m 5.1m³ 5.2f⁴ 5d³ 5g⁴ 5d 6.1d 5d² a5g⁴] tall gelding: moderate mover: quite modest handicapper nowadays: effective at 5f to 6f: acts on any going: has been tried in visor: ran well when blinkered last 2 starts: has won for apprentice: tough. *P. Howling.* **68**

JOHANNA THYME 4 b.f. Reesh 117 – Sea Thyme (Persian Bold 123) [1990 5s⁶ 6g a7g 1991 a7g a6g⁶ 7f 5f 5m* 5d⁴ 5.9m* 6g 5.9f 6f 6m² 6s a5g] leggy, lengthy mare: poor mover: poor handicapper: won at Beverley (gamely, first worthwhile form) and Carlisle in June: in-and-out form after: stays 6f: acts on good to firm and dead ground: has started slowly for apprentice. *R. Bastiman.* **49**

JOHNNY COME LATELY (IRE) 3 b.c. Le Johnstan 123 – Invisible (King Emperor (USA)) [1990 6g 7g 1991 8s 8.5f⁶ a11g 10g] tall, lengthy, angular colt: well beaten, in handicap last time. *J. S. Wainwright.* **—**

JOHNNY ROSE 7 b.g. Le Johnstan 123 – The Rose Royale (Takawalk II 125) [1990 NR 1991 12f 11.7g⁴ 10.1g² 11.5m] leggy, close-coupled gelding: moderate mover: poor performer nowadays: stays 1¼m well: acts on firm ground. *R. Akehurst.* **40**

JOHN O'DREAMS 6 b.g. Indian King (USA) 128 – Mississipi Shuffle 78 (Steel Heart 128) [1990 10m 5m⁵ 7m 5m⁶ 6d² 5.8d² 5s⁵ 1991 6f 6g 6m 6m] sturdy ex-Irish gelding: poor walker: moderate mover: plating-class handicapper: not seen out after May: gives impression will be better suited by further than 6f, and has form over 1½m in Ireland: best efforts here on soft going: blinkered twice at 3 yrs: effective with or without visor. *Miss J. Thorne.* **—**

JOHN ROSE 2 b.c. (Apr 5) Tina's Pet 121 – City Link Lass 92 (Double Jump 131) [1991 5d⁴ 5m* 6g⁶ 5m 7g² 8.1f³ 8d⁴] 13,500Y: tall, useful-looking colt: half-brother to 6.5f winner Vague Lass and 6f and 7f winner Sporting Simon (both by Vaigly Great): dam 2-y-o 5f and 6f winner: fairly useful performer: won maiden at Newmarket in April: much better form last 3 starts, behind Ninja Dancer in listed race at Ascot final one: stays 1m: acts on firm and dead ground. *P. A. Kelleway.* **91**

JOHNS GAMBLE 3 b.c. Alleging (USA) 120 – Fair Filly (Silver Shark 129) [1990 **52** §
5f⁵ 6d³ 7m a6g 5d⁶ 6d⁵ 1991 8g² 8.2d 10m 8f² 8h 8m] good-quartered colt: moderate
mover: poor maiden: stayed 1m: acted on firm and dead going: usually visored or
blinkered: sometimes sweating and edgy: inconsistent: dead. *T. Fairhurst.*

JOHN SHAW (USA) 3 b.c. L'Emigrant (USA) 129 – Ivory Wings (USA) (Sir **85**
Ivor 135) [1990 NR 1991 10m a 11g* 10g² 11.9g 13.8m* 15.9d a 12g] 56,000Y: compact
colt: third reported foal: half-brother to French 1¼m to 11f winner Wings of Wishes
(by Alydar): dam French 1¼m and 1½m winner later successful in USA, is out of
high-class mare Kittiwake: made all in maiden at Southwell in May and claimer at
Catterick in September: ran badly in Chester handicap and Southwell claimer last 2
outings: stays 13.8f: acts on good to firm ground: sweating fourth and sixth (early to
post) starts. *W. J. Haggas.*

JOHNS JOY 6 b.g. Martin John – Saybya (Sallust 134) [1990 8m 9m 10m³ 8f⁴ 9m² **77**
1991 10g⁴ 10.8m5 10g 10.1s* 8m* 9g⁶ 10g² 8d⁴ 10g⁶ 8g 10m] angular gelding: has a
round action: modest handicapper: won at Windsor (claimer) in April and Salisbury
in May: not seen out after July: effective at 1m to 1¼m: probably acts on any going.
D. R. C. Elsworth.

JOIE DE ROSE 6 b.m. Tickled Pink 114 – Joie d'Or (FR) (Kashmir II 125) [1990 **43**
7.5m⁴ 7.5m⁶ 7f 7m* 7g 7m 7.6m⁵ 7f³ 8.2m* 8.3f* 8.3m² 8m³ 8g 8m⁴ 8m 8m³ 1991
a8g⁶ 8d 8g 8.1g 8.3g 8.3m⁵] plain mare: has a round action: poor handicapper:
withdrawn (refused to enter stalls) final intended outing: best at 7f or 1m: acts on
any going: tried blinkered once: usually races up with pace: has won for apprentice.
M. Blanshard.

JOIE DE SOIR 3 b.f. Caerleon (USA) 132 – Late Evening (USA) (Riverman **97**
(USA) 131) [1990 a7g² a7g* 1991 8g³ 8g 8g* 7g 10g 8g 8.9g] leggy, unfurnished filly:
improved effort to win 5-runner listed race at Kempton in May: mostly well beaten
in good company afterwards: suited by 1m: sold 30,000 gns Newmarket December
Sales. *R. F. Johnson Houghton.*

JOKER IN THE PACK (IRE) 3 b.g. Alzao (USA) 117 – Balela (African Sky —
124) [1990 5d⁵ 6g 7d 1991 a8g 10.8d] IR 86,000Y: second foal: half-brother to 4-y-o
Taulela (by Taufan): dam unraced half-sister to dam of Geoffrey Freer winner Top
Class: poor ex-Irish maiden: sold out of M. O'Toole's stable 750 gns Goffs November (1990) Sales: well beaten in the spring at 3 yrs. *N. A. Smith.*

JOKERS PATCH 4 ch.g. Hotfoot 126 – Rhythmical 69 (Swing Easy (USA) 126) **65**
[1990 8f² 8m³ 10m* 10d 1991 12f* 10.8m 12.5d* 16.9m⁵ 14.6g4 12m⁶ 12f]
workmanlike gelding: has a quick action: quite modest handicapper: won claimers at
Brighton and Wolverhampton in spring: should stay 2m: has won on dead, but best
efforts on top-of-the-ground: has carried head high: takes keen hold, sometimes
goes in snatches and not easiest of rides: below form for amateur once: winning
hurdler. *R. J. Holder.*

JOKIST 8 ro.g. Orchestra 118 – What A Picture 80 (My Swanee 122) [1990 5f 6f* **71**
6m 6m 6m 5m 6f* 7f⁶ 7m⁵ 6m 7g³ 7d 1991 6g 7m³ 7g* 7m³ 7v 7m* 7f² 7f 7.3m 7g⁶
7.1m² 7g] workmanlike gelding: modest but thoroughly inconsistent handicapper:
won at Edinburgh and Yarmouth in summer: didn't find as much as seemed likely
penultimate start: effective at 6f and 7f: seems suited by a sound surface nowadays:
has been tried blinkered. *W. Jarvis.*

JOLI'S GREAT 3 ch.f. Vaigly Great 127 – Jolimo 92 (Fortissimo 111) [1990 7d² **73** d
7m 7f 1991 10d4 7.5g³ 9d² 8g4 8.2m4 9m 10.1f⁶ 8m⁵ 8d 10m] small filly: modest
handicapper: disappointing last 5 starts though showed signs of return to form when
staying-on fifth of 15 at Kempton: will prove suited by further than 1m: acts on good
to firm ground and dead: blinkered final start. *M. J. Ryan.*

JOLI'S PRINCESS 3 br.f. Prince Sabo 123 – Joli's Girl 79 (Mansingh 120) [1990 **103**
6f* 6m* 6f 7g² 7m4 7m 6g² 1991 8g* 8g*] close-coupled filly: useful form: led
inside final 1f when successful at Kempton in £9,000 contest in March and listed
race (last of 12 on entering straight, beat Himiko a neck) in April: may well have
stayed beyond 1m: best efforts with give in the ground: game: sent to USA. *M. J.
Ryan.*

JOLIZAL 3 ch.f. Good Times (ITY) – New Central 74 (Remainder Man 126§) **48**
[1990 7f 7g³ 8.2g5 a8g⁵ a8g³ 1991 a7g⁵ a7g⁶ 8.2d 8m4 8g 9d 7g³ 8g* 8f² 10m 8f³
8.2m] lengthy filly: poor performer: won seller (bought in 3,200 gns) at Leicester in
July: should stay beyond 1m: acts on firm going: blinkered second start: ran
moderately in ladies race: ran well on equitrack at 2 yrs. *D. Morris.*

JOLLY FISHERMAN (IRE) 3 ch.g. Montekin 125 – Ruby Relic (Monseig- **54** d
neur (USA) 127) [1990 a7g 5f a7g² a7g 6g 8.5m a6g a5g² a6g⁶ 7s a7g* a5g a7g a6g⁶

a7g a8g⁴ 1991 a6g⁵ a7g⁴ a7g* a5g⁵ a7g⁶ 7d 7m⁴ a7g a8g a7g a7g 12d a7g⁵ 8f 7m a8g 5g 10.3g a6g] neat gelding: poor mover: won handicap at Southwell in February: only poor form afterwards and was gelded: effective at 7f and 1m: best form on all-weather: has been tried in blinkers: sold 850 gns Doncaster November Sales. *M. C. Chapman.*

JOLLY FLIER 3 br.g. Prince of Peace 109 – Ceile (Galivanter 131) [1990 7m 1991 — 10.2m 10g 17.2g] plain, close-coupled gelding: no sign of ability. *N. Kernick.*

JOLLY JESTER 2 b.g. (May 10) Jester 119 – Casbar Lady 79 (Native Bazaar 122) [1991 a8g] 1,600Y: half-brother to 3 sprint winners, one also successful over hurdles: dam won 5 times over 5f: well beaten in December maiden at Lingfield. *T. J. Naughton.*

JOLTO 2 b.c. (Apr 5) Noalto 120 – Joytime (John de Coombe 122) [1991 5g 5m 6m — 6f] leggy colt: third foal (second to a thoroughbred stallion): dam ran once: of little account. *J. D. Czerpak.*

JOMANA 5 ch.m. Roman Warrior 132 – Tina's Magic (Carnival Night) [1990 7f 7f⁶ — 5.8f 8m⁶ 10f⁶ 8.3m² 9f² 10m⁵ 8f 1991 10g 12.1d⁴ 12m 10.2g] tall mare: poor handicapper: hasn't won since 2 yrs: seems to stay 1½m: acts on firm and dead ground: blinkered once: trained at 4 yrs by J. Fox. *J. M. Bradley.*

JOMOVE 2 ch.c. (Apr 18) Move Off 112 – Windlestrae (Bilsborrow 85) [1991 6.9h³ **46** 7m 8.1m] good-quartered colt: has a quick action: third live foal: dam tailed-off last in 2 outings over hurdles: poor maiden: tailed off in seller second start: stays 7f. *J. J. O'Neill.*

JONJAS CHUDLEIGH 4 ch.g. Aragon 118 – Lizabeth Chudleigh (Imperial **107** Fling 116) [1990 8g² 11g² 12f² 9m⁵ 8.5m² 8m* 10g* 8m* 8g* 1991 10g⁶ 8g⁴ 9m⁴ 8g⁶ 9m 8.5g² 8m 8m⁶ 8m⁶ 8s 10d] angular gelding: useful Irish handicapper: ran creditably most outings in 1991, including when sixth in Royal Hunt Cup at Royal Ascot on fourth start: stays 1¼m: probably acts on firm going, possibly unsuited by soft: has run creditably when blinkered: game: winning hurdler. *E. P. Harty, Ireland.*

JOOD (USA) 2 b.f. (Apr 17) Nijinsky (CAN) 138 – Kamar (USA) (Key To The **66 p** Mint (USA)) [1991 7g³] $2,000,000Y: tall, unfurnished filly: has scope: closely related to 3-y-o 7f winner Wilayif (by Danzig), also half-sister to several other winners, including very useful 6f to 1m winner Hiaam (by Alydar), 1984 champion Canadian 3-y-o Key To The Moon (by Wajima) and 1990 Kentucky Oaks winner Seaside Attraction (by Seattle Slew): dam and grandam champions in Canada: heavily-backed favourite but very green beforehand, over a length third of 10 to Hidden Laughter in maiden at Goodwood in July, outpaced 3f out then staying on well close home: will stay 1m: looked sure to improve. *M. R. Stoute.*

JORURI 6 ch.g. High Line 125 – Dancing Sally 100 (Sallust 134) [1990 12f⁵ 12.3g — 10m⁶ 10.6d a12g 1991 16.5m] good-topped gelding: carries plenty of condition: useful winner as 3-y-o when best on sound surface (stayed 1½m): seems of little account nowadays. *F. J. Yardley.*

JOSEPH'S WINE (IRE) 2 b.g. (Mar 24) Smile (USA) – Femme Gendarme **36** (USA) (Policeman (FR) 124) [1991 8m 7m 6f] IR 14,000Y: lengthy gelding: first foal: dam won at up to 9f in USA: sire won Breeders' Cup Sprint: little worthwhile form, including in seller. *M. Johnston.*

JOUD 3 b.f. Dancing Brave (USA) 140 – Rapide Pied (USA) 117 (Raise A Native) — [1990 6m* 8g⁵ 7d⁵ 1991 8g 8.2m 6g] leggy filly: impressively made all at Newmarket as 2-y-o: very disappointing in May Hill Stakes (pulled very hard) at Doncaster next start and in handicaps as 3-y-o: bred to stay 1m. *M. R. Stoute.*

JOVEWORTH 8 gr.g. Monsanto (FR) 121 – Flitterdale 81 (Abwah 118) [1990 NR — 1991 6m] robust, stocky gelding: carries condition: poor mover: useful handicapper at 6 yrs: behind but gave impression retains plenty of ability at York in May, first run since: effective at 6f to 1m: acts on any going: good mount for apprentice: joined B. Richmond. *M. O'Neill.*

JOVIAL KATE (USA) 4 gr.f. Northern Jove (CAN) – Flashy Feet (USA) (Pre- — tense) [1990 a6g² a6g² a5g³ a6g³ a6g² a6g⁴ 5m 5f 5.8f⁵ 6f 6m 6m 5.3h³ 7f⁶ 5m⁵ 6g a 55 1991 a6g³ a6g² a5g* a6g⁶ a6g⁴ a7g 5m a6g a6g⁴] lengthy, workmanlike filly: quite modest handicapper on all-weather surfaces, won at Lingfield in January: hasn't shown much on turf: stays 6f: tried blinkered once: usually wears bandages behind: has carried head awkwardly: has run moderately when sweating: not one to trust implicitly. *M. D. I. Usher.*

JOYFUL THOUGHT 2 b.f. (Jan 11) Green Desert (USA) 127 – Happy Thought **51** (FR) 57 (Kauai King) [1991 6m⁴ 6m⁴ 6g] rather sparely-made, quite attractive filly:

417

half-sister to 2 winners, including very smart 1983 2-y-o Creag-An-Sgor (by Captain James): dam slow half-sister to smart stayer Stetchworth: plating-class maiden: blinkered final start: trained until before then by Mrs J. Cecil. *D. R. C. Elsworth.*

J P MORGAN 3 b. or br.g. Law Society (USA) 130 – Queen of The Brush (Averof **62** 123) [1990 8m⁴ 1991 10m⁵ 11m⁴ 11g² 12.4m² 12.3g⁶ 16m² 16.2f⁶ 8.1g⁴ 13.8m⁴ 10.4m] leggy, shallow-girthed, angular gelding: quite modest maiden: stays 2m: acts on good to firm ground: blinkered on debut: visored (ran poorly) twice: runs in snatches, and is a difficult ride. *M. P. Naughton.*

J-TEC BOY 5 gr.g. Orange Reef 90 – Fotostar (Polyfoto 124) [1990 a7g⁵ 1991 13d **—** 12g⁵] leggy, sparely-made gelding: little worthwhile form on flat in varied company: won selling hurdle in May. *J. K. Kinane.*

JUBAL EARLY (IRE) 2 b.g. (Mar 10) The Noble Player (USA) 126 – Miss **63** Galwegian (Sandford Lad 133) [1991 5m³ 6f4 6g⁴ 7s a7g* 7m² 6m² 7g a8g a7g⁶] IR 4,200F, 5,000Y: useful-looking gelding: fourth foal: half-brother to 3-y-o Rutherglen (by Pitskelly): dam placed over 6f at 2 yrs in Ireland: quite modest performer: won summer seller (claimed out of W. Pearce's stable £6,000) at Southwell: ran poorly last 3 starts: stays 7f: acts on good to firm ground and fibresand: blinkered or visored nowadays: has worn a tongue strap. *C. N. Allen.*

JUBILATA (USA) 3 ch.f. The Minstrel (CAN) 135 – All Gladness (USA) (Alydar **54** (USA)) [1990 7f⁵ 7f³ 1991 a8g⁶ a7g 6s⁵ 7.5g 7d 7f 8.1g 6g 10.4m² 11m* 10m] leggy filly: has a round action: plater: form as 3-y-o only in 2 handicaps in October, bought in 4,400 gns after winning at Redcar: should stay 1½m: acts on firm going: visored seventh start: bolted before eighth and reluctant to go down at Redcar: trained first 6 by K. McCauley. *H. A. T. Whiting.*

JUBRAN (USA) 5 b.g. Vaguely Noble 140 – La Vue (Reviewer (USA)) **66** [1990 12f 13s 12m⁴ 12g⁶ a11g 1991 9s⁴ 9s⁴ 8.2d 8g* 8m³ 8d³ 7.1g* 7.9m* 7g⁴ 10g² 10g] quite attractive, close-coupled gelding: has round action: quite modest handicapper: won at Edinburgh (seller, bought in 5,600 gns) in May and strongly-run races at Haydock and York in July: ran rare poor race (as if something amiss) final start: effective at 7f to 1¼m: acts on good to firm and soft ground. *M. P. Naughton.*

JUCEA 2 b.f. (Apr 19) Bluebird (USA) 125 – Appleby Park 98 (Bay Express 132) **57** [1991 5m 6s 5g⁶] sturdy, rather angular filly: fifth living foal: half-sister to useful 7f and 1m winner Cromwell Park (by Moorestyle): dam lightly-raced 2-y-o 7f winner: blinkered, first form when sixth of 13 in maiden at Folkestone in October: should prove more effective back at 6f. *D. W. P. Arbuthnot.*

JUDGE AND JURY 2 br.c. (Apr 13) Law Society (USA) 130 – Full of Reason **72** (USA) (Bold Reason) [1991 7f 7.1m 7g³ 7g⁵ a8g*] 6,800Y, 26,000 2-y-o: compact colt: half-brother to 3-y-o 8.2f to 10.5f winner Dagon (by Damister) and 2 more winners, notably fair middle-distance performer Magnus Pym (by Al Nasr): dam 1½m performer: blinkered first time when winning late-year maiden at Lingfield by ¾ length: gives impression will stay well. *M. J. Fetherston-Godley.*

JUDGED LUCKY (FR) 4 br.g. Vayrann 133 – Friluck (USA) (Judger (USA)) **—** [1990 NR 1991 10.3d] big, leggy gelding: twice raced on flat and no form. *B. W. Lunness.*

JUDGEMENT CALL 4 b.c. Alzao (USA) 117 – Syllabub (Silly Season 127) [1990 **73** 6f³ 6f⁴ 7d 7m 6m⁴ 5d 6m* 6f* 7m⁴ 5m³ 7.6m⁶ 6g³ 1991 5g 6g 6m⁶ 6g 6m 5m 6m³ 6g 7f⁴ 7g 7f² 7g 8f⁶ 6f] close-coupled, good-quartered colt: sort to carry condition: has a quick action: modest handicapper nowadays: last at Yarmouth final 2 starts: stays 7f: goes well on top-of-the-ground, possibly unsuited by dead: below form when blinkered once: sometimes bandaged: inconsistent. *P. Howling.*

JUDYS GIRL (IRE) 2 b.f. (Mar 5) Simply Great (FR) 122 – Sistina 76 (Charlot- **—** town 127) [1991 6d 7m 7m 6m 7.1m] 3,200Y: close-coupled, leggy, sparely-made filly: half-sister to several winners, including useful French middle-distance stayer Wolverist (by Wolver Hollow) and 1987 2-y-o 6f winner Cool Combination (by Indian King): dam staying half-sister to 3 very speedy fillies: of little account: blinkered final start. *T. Fairhurst.*

JUKARI 2 ch.f. (Mar 17) Bay Express 132 – Hotazur 52 (Hotfoot 126) [1991 a5g⁵ **37** 6m a6g 7.5f] ninth foal: half-sister to 1982 2-y-o 5f winner Palace Beau (by Dragonara Palace) and Lord Ludo (by Owen Anthony), successful at around 9f: dam plater from good family: poor form in sellers. *J. A. Glover.*

JULDEE 2 br.f. (Feb 18) Cragador 110 – Westminster Waltz (Dance In Time **63** (CAN)) [1991 7m* 7m 8d] 500Y: leggy filly: first foal: dam twice-raced daughter of half-sister to Busted: quite modest performer: won 8-runner seller (bought in 6,500 gns) at Yarmouth in July: well beaten afterwards in better company: should stay 1m. *R. Guest.*

JULFAAR (USA) 4 b.c. Arctic Tern (USA) 126 – Nijit (USA) (Nijinsky (CAN) 138) [1990 10m6 12m* 14g4 1991 10g5 10m5 11.5f4 11.9m6] rather leggy colt: moderate walker: has a rather round action: modest handicapper, but clearly difficult to train: stays 1½m well: acts on good to firm ground: sweating at 4 yrs: sold 15,500 gns Newmarket Autumn Sales. *A. C. Stewart.*　**79**

JULIA SABINA 2 b.f. (Jun 16) Prince Sabo 123 – Bernice Clare 68 (Skymaster 126) [1991 6m 5d6 6m 6.1m] 2,000Y: small, sturdy filly: half-sister to 3-y-o Lime St Nightmair (by Elegant Air) and several winners here and abroad, including quite modest 8.2f winner Question of Degree (by Known Fact): dam won over 1m at 4 yrs: poor maiden: stays 6f. *C. C. Elsey.*　**37**

JULIE LA ROUSSE (IRE) 3 ch.f. Lomond (USA) 128 – Gold And Purple 114 (Golden Fleece (USA) 133) [1990 7g* 1991 8m2 10g3 12m5 8d* 9s2] 58,000F: strong filly: first foal: dam unraced daughter of Arkadina, dam also of Irish St Leger winner Dark Lomond (by Lomond): won listed race at the Curragh in September: also ran well when second in Goffs Irish 1000 Guineas at the Curragh (beaten 3 lengths by Kooyonga) and All Along Stakes at Laurel (½ length to Sha Tha): 5¾ lengths fifth of 10, having got well behind, to Possessive Dancer in Kildangan Stud Irish Oaks, also at the Curragh: effective at 1m, and seems to stay 1½m: blinkered third start: reportedly to be trained by A. Penna in USA. *J. Oxx, Ireland.*

JULIE'S STAR (IRE) 3 ch.f. Thatching 131 – Red Roman 87 (Solinus 130) [1990 6g 7m 1991 8m2 8m3 10g 8m6 8.3m 6m] strong, lengthy filly: poor maiden: below form last 4 starts: worth another try at 1¼m: visored fourth and fifth starts: sold 1,200 gns Ascot November Sales. *C. James.*　**45**

JULIETSKI 3 gr.f. Niniski (USA) 125 – Plum Blossom (USA) (Gallant Romeo (USA)) [1990 10s 1991 a10g5 12f3 12.2m6 15.8f4 12g2 11.7f3 12f4] small, angular filly: quite modest maiden: below form in claimers and handicap last 3 starts: one paced, and should stay beyond 1½m: acts on firm going: wore eyeshield on reappearance: trained first 6 starts by Mrs L. Piggott. *M. D. Hammond.*　**63 d**

JUMBY BAY 5 b.g. Thatching 131 – Ridge The Times (USA) 78 (Riva Ridge (USA)) [1990 8g 8m 8f 6g4 8d a7g3 a6g3 a6g2 1991 a6g4 a7g a7g] big, rangy gelding: modest handicapper on his day: off course 10 months after reappearance: effective at 6f and stays 1m: acts on firm going: twice below form when blinkered: takes strong hold: has hung markedly left: not one to trust. *M. Johnston.*　**— §**

JUNGLE DANCER (IRE) 3 b.g. Sadler's Wells (USA) 132 – Forlene 108 (Forli (ARG)) [1990 8g5 8.2d3 1991 10.1m* 12g3 11.9g2 11.9g] good-quartered, attractive gelding: fairly useful form: won 5-runner maiden at Yarmouth in July: best effort when second in £11,800 handicap at York, always in touch, leading over 2f out then carrying head bit awkwardly and hanging left: stays 1½m: blinkered (irresolute) final start and subsequently gelded: one to treat with caution. *M. R. Stoute.*　**91 §**

JUNGLE KNIFE 5 b.g. Kris 135 – Jungle Queen (Twilight Alley 133) [1990 8v4 9s* 10d* 1991 8v* 8d4 10.3d5] tall, workmanlike gelding: moderate walker and mover: modest handicapper: won at Newcastle in April: first run for 5½ months, creditable fifth at Chester in October: stays 1¼m: probably needs an easy surface, and acts on firm going: useful hurdler. *M. H. Tompkins.*　**72**

JUNIPER BERRY (IRE) 2 b.f. (Feb 3) Last Tycoon 131 – Jackie Berry 97 (Connaught 130) [1991 6d5] lengthy filly: third foal: dam fair 8.5f winner at 2 yrs (and 7f at 3 yrs) in Ireland, is out of sister to good middle-distance filly Cranberry Sauce: bit backward when never-dangerous fifth of 7 in maiden at Ascot in October: taken very steadily to post: likely to stay 1m: will do better. *P. W. Chapple-Hyam.*　**67 p**

JUNK BOND 3 b.c. Last Tycoon 131 – What A Pity 97 (Blakeney 126) [1990 6g* 7d* 1991 7m3 8g 8g6 7s] small, leggy colt: useful winner at 2 yrs: good third in Ladbroke European Free Handicap at Newmarket on reappearance: tailed off in 2000 Guineas there 17 days later: about 3½ lengths sixth of 8 to Enharmonic in Group 3 event at Baden-Baden better effort after: probably stays 1m: trained until after second start by R. Charlton. *A. Renzoni, Italy.*　**98**

JUPITER MOON 2 b.c. (Feb 3) Jupiter Island 126 – Troy Moon (Troy 137) [1991 7.1s* 8g] stocky colt: third foal: closely related to 3-y-o 7f winner The Cuckoo's Nest (by Precocious): dam maiden stayed 1½m, is out of half-sister to Sharpen Up: 16/1, backward and green, won maiden at Chepstow in September, soon well behind, then staying on strongly: never on terms in minor event at Newbury following month: will stay 1¼m: possibly needs soft ground. *C. E. Brittain.*　**79**

JUPITER SPARKLE 3 b.f. Northern Tempest (USA) 120 – Star Alert (Red — Alert 127) [1990 NR 1991 8m 12s] big, workmanlike filly: fifth foal: dam ran 4 times: no promise in claimer (sweating and edgy) and maiden: joined P. Hedger. *D. A. Wilson.*

JUPITER STAR 2 b.c. (May 16) Jupiter Island 126 – Carribean Sound 76 (Good — Times (ITY)) [1991 6.9f] good-topped colt with scope: second foal: dam 7f winner: slowly away and never placed to challenge in maiden at Folkestone in October: moved moderately to post: sold 5,400 gns Newmarket Autumn Sales. *C. E. Brittain.*

JURA 3 ch.c. Rousillon (USA) 133 – Reuval 102 (Sharpen Up 127) [1990 7g² 1991 **105** p 8.2m² 10g* 10.1f* 10m*] leggy, rather angular colt: useful form: won maiden at Lingfield in May, £8,900 handicap at Yarmouth in September and 3-runner minor event (5/4 on, by short head from Nucleus) at Nottingham in October, getting up close home on last 2 occasions: will be better suited by 1½m: acts on good to firm going: may improve again. *H. R. A. Cecil.*

JURIS PRUDENCE (IRE) 3 b. or br.f. Law Society (USA) 130 – Virginia Sham — (USA) (Sham (USA)) [1990 NR 1991 10.4d⁵ 10d 12m⁶ 10.5g 14m⁴ 15m⁶ 14g 14.1m 10.3d] IR 17,500F, 16,000Y: rather leggy, lengthy filly: second foal: half-sister to 4-y-o La Gran Senora (by El Gran Senor): dam winner at up to 9f in USA, is half-sister to Niniski: well beaten, including in handicap: blinkered eighth start. *B. A. McMahon.*

JURRAN 6 ro.g. Formidable (USA) 125 – Queen's Counsellor 92 (Kalamoun 129) — § [1990 10m 16m 1991 10.1d³ 10d³] strong, lengthy gelding: has a free action: quite modest performer nowadays: stays 1¼m: acts on firm and dead going: ran moderately in blinkers: ungenuine. *H. Thomson Jones.*

JURZ (IRE) 3 b.c. Pennine Walk 120 – Kawkeb (USA) 72 (Vaguely Noble 140) **81** [1990 8.2s 7m² 1991 8d³ 8.2m 10.6g⁵ 8m 9g* 8m 8m 8d⁴] strong, workmanlike colt: fair performer: made all in amateurs handicap at Goodwood in August: well beaten in handicap (found very little) and apprentice race (very stiff task, headstrong) last 2 starts: stays 9f: possibly best on an easy surface: blinkered last 2 starts: sold 22,000 gns Newmarket Autumn Sales: winning hurdler for J. Baker. *H. Thomson Jones.*

JUST A LOOK 3 ch.c. Doulab (USA) 115 – Gentle Look (Tower Walk 130) [1990 **57** § 5f a6g a6g³ a8g⁶ 1991 a7g* a8g⁶ a7g 7d a7g] sparely-made colt: plating-class handicapper: below form after winning at Southwell in January: seems best at 7f: visored final start: blinkered previous 6: virtually refused to race fourth start, and clearly not one to trust. *D. J. G. Murray-Smith.*

JUSTAMANDA 2 b.f. (Mar 19) Prince Sabo 123 – Auntie Cyclone (USA) 52 **62** (Dust Commander (USA)) [1991 5g 5g 5d⁴ 6m³ 5g*] 900Y: leggy, sparely-made filly: poor mover: first foal: dam, plater, suited by 1m: progressive form: off course 12 weeks and ridden by 7-lb claimer, won maiden at Redcar in September. *W. Holden.*

JUST A MEMORY 5 b.g. Kafu 120 – Souveniers (Relko 136) [1990 6g* 7g 6.3g — 8g³ 1991 10f⁵ 8.1d⁶ 14.6d] lengthy, good-bodied gelding: first foal: dam third over 1m at 2 yrs: ex-Irish handicapper: won at the Curragh in 1990: subsequent form only when third at Laytown: well beaten in minor events in autumn: stays 1m: trained at 4 yrs by P. Prendergast: winning selling hurdler in April. *R. J. Manning.*

JUST A MIRAGE 2 b.f. (Mar 1) Green Desert (USA) 127 – Just You Wait **65** p (Nonoalco (USA) 131) [1991 6m³] big filly: has scope: fifth foal: half-sister to 3 winners, notably good-class 6f to 9f winner Reprimand (by Mummy's Pet) and progressive 3-y-o 1m to 1¼m Wiorno (by Wassl), winner of Prix Dollar: dam unraced daughter of very useful 1¼m winner Sleat, herself half-sister to St Leger winner Athens Wood: 9/4 but green and in need of race, 5 lengths third of 8 to Cloud of Dust in maiden at Leicester in October, leading over 2f out, not knocked about when beaten: moved well to post: should stay 1m: seems sure to do better. *A. A. Scott.*

JUST A STEP 5 br.h. Lochnager 132 – My Louise 54 (Manado 130) [1990 a7g 7g **92** 7m⁴ 7m² 7m⁵ 7m² 7.6m⁴ a6g⁴ a6g 7m 7g⁵ a7g 7d 1991 7g* 7g⁴ 7m² 7m² 7m⁵ 7d* 7.1g⁵ 7g 8g 7d] small, sturdy horse: moderate mover: much improved handicapper in 1991: won at Warwick in April and Goodwood (minor event) in June: excellent fifth at Chepstow, easily best effort after: suited by 7f: acts on firm going, and goes very well with some give in the ground: has sweated: goes well with forcing tactics. *M. McCormack.*

JUSTASUNDAYSPORT 3 ch.f. Star Appeal 133 – Justine (GER) (Luciano) — [1990 7g 1991 10.2d 12.2g a10g⁴] angular, rather sparely-made filly: no worthwhile form in maidens: blinkered then wore eyeshield last 2 starts. *P. A. Kelleway.*

JUST BELIEVE 3 gr.f. Nishapour (FR) 125 – Gallant Believer (USA) (Gallant —
Romeo (USA)) [1990 NR 1991 a8g] 5,400Y: sixth foal: sister to 1¼m and 1½m
winner Bold Republic and half-sister to fairly useful sprinters Norgabie (by
Northfields) and Olympic Hero (by Dreams To Reality): dam never ran: tailed off in
maiden at Southwell in February: joined L. Barratt. *C. N. Williams.*

JUST BOB 2 b.c. (Apr 26) Alleging (USA) 120 – Diami 81 (Swing Easy (USA) 126) 71
[1991 5g2 5m* 5m2 5f3 6m3 5m2] 4,300F, 1,000Y: smallish, rather angular colt:
moderate mover: second foal: dam 2-y-o 5f winner stayed 7f: modest performer:
won maiden auction at Redcar in June: best subsequent efforts when second in
nurseries: races keenly. *S. E. Kettlewell.*

JUST FOR KICKS 5 br.g. Saher 115 – Kix 71 (King Emperor (USA)) [1990 9d4 —
7d 7.9g 1991 9s 8f 8m 12.1d 10.9g5 10m 10.5g] rather leggy, sparely-made ex-Irish
gelding: half-brother to 2 winners, including fair 7f winner Glen Na Smole (by
Ballymore): dam in frame in early-season maidens at 2 yrs: won apprentice nursery
at the Curragh: behind in varied company since: stays 1m: acts on soft going: tried
blinkered. *J. J. O'Neill.*

JUST-GO-AGAIN 2 ch.g. (Apr 10) All Systems Go 119 – Argostone (Rockavon 47
120) [1991 5m 6.9h6 5f 6m a7g] leggy gelding: brother to 1989 2-y-o 6f seller winner
Just Go and half-brother to 1m winner/successful hurdler Little Miss Horner (by Sit
In The Corner): dam poor: poor maiden: twice well beaten in sellers: possibly suited
by 5f and very firm ground. *J. M. Jefferson.*

JUSTICE (FR) 3 b.c. Saint Estephe (FR) 123 – Jastarnia (Junius (USA) 124) 108
[1990 8d2 8g2 9d3 1991 10.5v3 12g* 12g4 12m 15g*] first foal: dam, French 8.5f to 11f
winner, is half-sister to smart French stayer Mardonius: won maiden at Saint-Cloud
in April and Prix Hubert de Chaudenay at Longchamp in July: beaten narrowly in
listed race at Longchamp and about 10 lengths when last of 7 in Prix du Jockey-Club
(set pace) at Chantilly in between: suited by further than 1½m. *A. Fabre, France.*

JUST IMPOSSIBLE 2 ch.c. (Apr 27) Superlative 118 – Okavamba 82 (Wollow 59
132) [1991 6d2 6g2] strong, close-coupled colt: seventh foal: dam 2-y-o 6f winner:
kept on strongly in seller at Ripon (backward, green) then maiden at Ayr in summer:
should stay 7f. *E. Weymes.*

JUST JEAN 4 b.f. Kala Shikari 125 – Curzon House 73 (Green God 128) [1990 a8g —
12m 1991 7g 7d6 8.5f 7m 7.1g] workmanlike, good-quartered filly: plating-class
maiden at 2 yrs: behind, mostly facing stiff tasks, in handicaps since: appears to stay
1m: tried blinkered: has been bandaged: joined M. Pipe. *H. A. T. Whiting.*

JUST MY BILL 5 ch.g. Nicholas Bill 125 – Misnomer 85 (Milesian 125) [1990 78
13v2 12.3d3 12m5 14s 12g2 12m5 1991 12.3s* 13d2 12.3d6 11.9g] leggy, rather
sparely-made gelding: modest handicapper: won at Ripon in April: always behind
final start, first for 3½ months: suited by about 1½m and give in the ground: visored
first 3 starts, blinkered final one. *J. Hetherton.*

JUST ONE (IRE) 3 b.g. Stalker 121 – Angelica (SWE) (Hornbeam 130) [1990 6g 49
7d 7m a6g5 a7g a8g2 a8g4 1991 a7g a10g4 a8g4 8g a10g a10g] good-quartered
gelding: moderate mover: plating-class maiden: gelded and off course 7 months
after third start, then behind in handicaps and claimer: effective at 1m to 1¼m:
usually blinkered or visored. *M. McCormack.*

JUST READY (IRE) 3 b.g. Petorius 117 – Lacey Brief (USA) (Roi Dagobert 51
128) [1990 7m 7m 7g 8v 1991 a10g3 a10g a8g5 8g 11.7g 11m6 8f* 7m 8g] leggy,
workmanlike gelding: has a quick action: fair plater: made all in handicap at Brighton
(bought in 4,200 gns) in May: below form following month: probably stays 1¼m: acts
on firm going: blinkered fourth start: often pulls hard: sold out of Sir Mark
Prescott's stable 3,600 gns Ascot April Sales after fourth start. *G. A. Ham.*

JUST RUN (IRE) 3 b.f. Runnett 125 – Wild Justice 76 (Sweet Revenge 129) 45
[1990 5m 1991 5m5] leggy, lengthy filly: showed a little ability in maiden at
Folkestone in July: bred to prove best at up to 1m. *W. G. M. Turner.*

JUST THREE 5 b.h. Tina's Pet 121 – Mio Mementa 61 (Streak 119) [1990 8f 8f3 —
7.2f2 8g* 8m 7.2s5 8g* 7m3 8g5 8g4 8m 8g 1991 8d5 10s6 7g 8.5f] lengthy,
useful-looking horse: usually impresses in appearance: very useful performer at 4
yrs: below form in first half of 1991, set too strong pace when blinkered in Group 3
event final start: suited by 7f/1m: acts on any going: suited by forcing tactics:
genuine. *G. Lewis.*

JUVENARA 5 b.g. Young Generation 129 – Sharrara (CAN) 61 (Blushing Groom 62
(FR) 131) [1990 6s3 5m 6f* 8g4 6f6 6f2 6d 8f6 6f6 8f4 8.3m* 6m 6h 8h 8.3g 8f3 8f2
10f3 1991 6v 7d6 8f* 8d 8f 7m 7g3 7d2 7.6s3 6g 8m3 8f6 7m5 8.2f 9m 7g] small,
workmanlike gelding: poor walker: quite modest handicapper: won at Brighton in

April: needs further than 6f nowadays and stays 1¼m: goes very well on top-of-the-ground: often claimer ridden, wasn't at Brighton: none too consistent. *R. J. Hodges.*

K

KABCAST 6 b.g. Kabour 80 – Final Cast 50 (Saulingo 122) [1990 a6g⁵ a5g³ 5f 5m **65** 5m 5m 5f 5d 5g³ 5f⁴ 5f 5m² 5m 5f 5m* 5.3f 1991 5g 5f⁵ 5f⁵ 5g 5g⁶ 5d⁶ 5s² 5g⁵ 5f³ 5.2m³ 5f² 5.1m* 5f 5f 5f* 5m 5.2f 5g 5m* 5s⁶] good-bodied gelding: quite modest handicapper nowadays: won at Nottingham, Thirsk and Edinburgh in autumn: best at 5f: acts on any going, but goes particularly well on a sound surface: best blinkered: often sweats: suited by forcing tactics: none too consistent. *D. W. Chapman.*

KABERA 3 b.g. Kabour 80 – Boldera 69 (Persian Bold 123) [1990 6d 1991 a7g⁶ — 8.3f 5g 6s a6g⁶ a6g⁵] workmanlike gelding: no worthwhile form, including in handicaps. *D. W. Chapman.*

KACHINA MAID 6 b.m. Anfield 117 – Grey Twig 68 (Godswalk (USA) 130) **30** [1990 6f 7h⁵ 7m 8m 7f⁴ 7m⁵ 8m 8h⁵ 8f² 8f 8f 1991 a8g a10g³ a13g⁵ 10d 10.1s] sturdy, workmanlike mare: poor handicapper: stays 1¼m: acts on hard and dead ground: tried blinkered once: wore net muzzle final start (April). *Mrs A. Knight.*

KADAN (GER) 7 b.g. Horst-Herbert – Ling Lady (GER) (Marduk (GER)) [1990 — 7f³ 1991 8m] rather sparely-made gelding: moderate mover: quite modest handicapper at 6 yrs: unseated rider only start as 7-y-o (carried wide bend when trying to jump prostrate horse) in April: probably best around 1m: possibly unsuited by soft going, acts on any other. *M. H. Tompkins.*

KADARI 2 b.f. (Feb 11) Commanche Run 133 – Thoughtful 86 (Northfields (USA)) **55** ? [1991 5g 6f⁶ 7s² 7g² 7f³ 7.5f³ 8.1g* 8m] 3,000Y: workmanlike filly: fourth foal: half-sister to fair middle-distance stayer Muse (by High Line) and another winner over hurdles: dam, 1¼m winner, is half-sister to Princess Royal winner Heavenly Thought, dam of Homing and Water Mill: plating-class performer: stayed on well to win maiden auction at Edinburgh in September: looked none too keen (flashed tail) in Pontefract nursery 3 weeks later: will be suited by 1¼m: best form on an easy surface: one to be wary of. *A. Harrison.*

KADRA 7 b. or br.m. High Top 131 – Sunset Ray 74 (Hotfoot 126) [1990 NR 1991 — 12.1d] lengthy, workmanlike mare: tailed off in Chepstow apprentice event in July, first run since 3 yrs. *R. J. Weaver.*

KAGRAM QUEEN 3 b.f. Prince Ragusa 96 – Arodstown Alice (Sahib 114) [1990 **54** 5g 7g⁵ 6g⁵ 7f* 7f² 7m⁵ 7f 7f² 1991 7g 7f⁵ 10m² 10f 10f² 8.3f³ 10g⁴ 8m] lengthy, dipped-backed filly: fair plater: largely consistent, but below form last 2 starts: should stay 1½m: acts on firm going: looked none too keen fifth outing: winning hurdler. *Mrs G. R. Reveley.*

KAHER (USA) 4 b.g. Our Native (USA) – June Bride (USA) (Riverman (USA) **97** d 131) [1990 10g² 11.5g* 12g² 12m⁴ 12.5f* 12m 1991 12g³ 12m³ 10.1f⁵ 11.9m⁵ 11.9m 10.2g² 12m⁴] compact gelding: fair handicapper: below best after third start: effective at 1¼m to 1½m: acts on firm going: takes keen hold: trained first 2 outings by A. Stewart: winning hurdler. *N. A. Callaghan.*

KAHHAL (IRE) 3 gr.f. Doulab (USA) 115 – Queen's Counsellor 92 (Kalamoun — 129) [1990 6d 1991 7g⁵ 8m⁵ 11.7f] compact filly: poor maiden: apparently best effort over 7f on easy ground: sold out of H. Thomson Jones's stable 1,900 gns Newmarket July Sales after second start. *Mrs A. Knight.*

KAIKOURA 3 br.f. Full On Aces (AUS) – Jandell (NZ) (Shifnal) [1990 7s⁶ 1991 — 11.5f 10.2g 8.1g] rangy filly: half-sister to 3 winners at up to 11f: dam top-rated filly in 1973/4 in New Zealand, successful at 3 yrs to 5 yrs and over 6f to 13f: well beaten in maidens and claimer: sold 3,000 gns Newmarket Autumn Sales. *W. Jarvis.*

KAILUA 4 b.f. Kafu 120 – Gilana (Averof 123) [1990 5m 8m⁴ 8.2g 6m 1991 a5g 6d] — tall filly: no form. *P. Monteith.*

KAIPHAS 4 b.g. Pharly (FR) 130 – Kaiserstadt (GER) (Dschingis Khan) [1990 **61** 7m⁴ 8m 1991 9s⁶ 8.1d⁴ 7m⁶ 7m³ 7.1g⁴ 7f³ 7m⁶ 8m] sturdy, attractive gelding: quite modest handicapper, still a maiden: may prove ideally suited by 1m: acts on firm and dead ground: wore net muzzle fourth start. *I. A. Balding.*

KAJAANI (IRE) 2 b.c. (Mar 19) Simply Great (FR) 122 – Finlandia (FR) (Far- **76** p away Son (USA)) [1991 8.1g³ 10m²] IR 150,000Y: good-bodied colt: has scope: half-brother to several winners, including 1990 2-y-o 7f winner Suomi (by Tate Gallery) and St Leger winner Snurge (by Ela-Mana-Mou): dam modest half-sister to some good winners: favourite though better for race, placed in maidens at Chepstow in August and Nottingham (beaten head by National Emblem) in October: stays 1¼m: can improve, but gives impression is lazy and possibly worth a try in blinkers. *P. F. I. Cole.*

KALABRIDGE   3 gr.f. Kalaglow 132 – Tickton Bridge (Grundy 137) [1990 6m 6g   **29** 8f 6d 6d² 6d² 1991 9d a8g 8f 7g³ 8d 8g] leggy, unfurnished filly: poor mover: poor maiden: form as 3-y-o only when third in seller at Leicester: should be suited by 7f + : acts on dead ground. *M. J. Ryan.*

KALAKATE   6 gr.g. Kalaglow 132 – Old Kate 110 (Busted 134) [1990 NR 1991   **—** 13.3d⁶ 16.2m] big, lengthy gelding: has a sharpish action: useful handicapper at 3 yrs: bandaged, well beaten at Newbury (listed race) and Ascot in first half of 1991: stays 1½m well: best form on top-of-the-ground. *R. Simpson.*

KALAMIS   3 gr.f. Kalaglow 132 – Buz Kashi 123 (Bold Lad (IRE) 133) [1990 NR   **—** 1991 8s] quite attractive filly: sixth live foal: half-sister to 1¼m and 1½m winner Jehol (by Teenoso) and seemingly ungenuine 1m winner Kash Juwain (by Habitat): dam disqualified winner of Coronation Stakes: burly and green, tailed off in maiden at Kempton in September. *G. Wragg.*

KALAMOSS   2 ch.f. (Apr 11) Kalaglow 132 – Moss Pink (USA) (Levmoss 133)   **—** [1991 5g 6m 7g 7m] 600F: smallish filly: sister to 9f and 1¼m winner Abigail's Dream and half-sister to 2 winners, including 7f and 1¾m winner Ben's Surprise (by Lucky Wednesday): dam placed over 5f at 3 yrs in Ireland: no worthwhile form in summer. *N. R. Mitchell.*

KALAR   2 b.g. (Apr 8) Kabour 80 – Wind And Reign 55 (Tumble Wind (USA)) [1991   **—** a5g a6g a6g] strong, good-bodied gelding: third foal: dam, plater, seemed to stay 1m: of no account. *D. W. Chapman.*

KALMADENE   4 gr.c. Kalaglow 132 – Almadena 73 (Dairialatan 111) [1990 12.5f³   **100** 12f* 12g 11.5f² 12m* 12g* 1991 12g 16.1m² 16.2g 12f*] leggy, quite attractive colt: useful handicapper: did well to win 5-runner event at Salisbury in August, held up long way in moderately-run race: seems to stay 2m: acts on firm going: sold 36,000 gns Newmarket Autumn Sales. *P. F. I. Cole.*

KALOKAGATHOS   2 b.c. (Feb 22) King of Spain 121 – Kip's Sister (Cawston's   **—** Clown 113) [1991 7g] 7,400Y: workmanlike colt: third foal: half-brother to 3-y-o 12.2f winner Charlie's Darling (by Homing): dam unraced: 16/1 and backward, nearly always in rear in 15-runner maiden at Salisbury in October: has joined C. Cox. *M. McCormack.*

KALOOKI QUEEN   3 ch.f. Joshua 129 – Hill of Fare (Brigadier Gerard 144)   **—** [1990 6g⁶ 5m 6m 6d 6g⁶ 1991 12g 14g] leggy, angular filly: poor plater: sold 1,100 gns Doncaster July Sales: resold 550 gns Doncaster August Sales. *M. R. Channon.*

KAMART   3 gr.f. Belfort (FR) 89 – Practicality (Weavers' Hall 122) [1990 5m³   **—** 6m* 6g 6m⁶ 1991 8s 8m 8.5m 8d 8s] rather unfurnished filly: moderate mover: little form on flat since quite modest winner at 2 yrs: stays 6f: acts on good to firm ground: claimed to join M. Barnes £3,500 after claiming hurdle in September. *Denys Smith.*

KANANGA   3 b.f. Local Suitor (USA) 128 – Kandia (GER) (Luciano) [1990 NR   **—** 1991 10f⁵ 12.2g⁶ 10f 12.3m⁶] tall, leggy filly: has high knee action: half-sister to French 10.5f winner Kalmia (by Miller's Mate) and 4 winners in Germany, including St Leger winner Kamiros (by Star Appeal): dam won from 9f to 1½m in Germany, and champion older mare at 4 yrs: well beaten in maidens and handicap after debut, twice failing to handle bends: visored final start: sold 1,800 gns Newmarket December Sales: one to treat with caution. *J. W. Watts.*

KANDARA (FR)   3 b.f. Dalsaan 125 – Kantado 93 (Saulingo 122) [1990 5g⁴ 5g*   **63** 5d² 5f 6m a6g³ 6m* 6g 6d⁴ 1991 6d 7m 6f³ 8m 7m] lengthy, dipped-backed, strong-quartered filly: moderate mover: quite modest performer: best efforts at up to 6f: acts on firm going: inconsistent. *P. C. Haslam.*

KANDY SECRET (USA)   2 b.g. (Mar 4) Secretariat (USA) – Marshua's Rose   **71** (USA) (Marshua's Dancer (USA)) [1991 7g 7.1m 8m] $95,000Y: quite attractive gelding: has scope: has a quick action: fourth known foal: brother to minor winner in USA at up to 7f and half-brother to a winner: dam won 6 of 11 races at 3 yrs, including minor stakes race: modest maiden: best effort at Sandown second start: subsequently moved badly down at Newmarket (possibly still in need of race, well beaten) in October: may do better. *R. Hannon.*

KANNDABIL   4 gr.c. Nishapour (FR) 125 – Katana (FR) (Le Haar 126) [1990   **—** 9.1g⁵ 9g³ 9.5g³ 9g 10g³ 1991 10m] compact ex-Irish colt: dam French 10.5f winner:

trained by A. de Royer-Dupre, placed in minor events in French Provinces at 3 yrs: tongue tied down and bit backward on first run for 6 months, no show in Redcar maiden in October: stays 1¼m: fair winning hurdler. *N. Tinkler.*

KANOOZ (IRE) 3 br.g. Wassl 125 – Countess Candy 106 (Great Nephew 126) **62** [1990 8d a8g4 1991 a8g2 a10g2 a10g* 10d 10.2s] workmanlike gelding: quite modest performer: won maiden at Lingfield in March, leading 1f out: well behind in handicaps after: blinkered first, third and fourth outings: sold out of Sir Mark Prescott's stable 6,000 gns Ascot April Sales after fourth. *S. Mellor.*

KANSK 3 b.c. Top Ville 129 – Kanz (USA) 115 (The Minstrel (CAN) 135) [1990 NR **100** 1991 11g3 10.5g* 11.9m* 12.3d3] good-bodied colt: has a powerful round action: second living foal: half-brother to 1989 2-y-o 6f winner Peterhouse (by Habitat): dam winner at about 1m who stayed 1½m, is half-sister to dam of Glint of Gold and Diamond Shoal: won maiden at Haydock in September, quickening on over 3f out, and 3-runner minor contest at York, making all and comfortably holding Duc de Berry by 3 lengths: ran poorly in Chester minor event final start: stays 1½m: seems to need a sound surface. *J. H. M. Gosden.*

KARA 2 gr.f. (May 20) K-Battery 108 – Nicara (Rusticaro (FR) 124) [1991 5m6 7m **—** 7m] small, sparely-made filly: second foal: dam Irish 2-y-o 6f winner: no worthwhile form in summer: sweated up in seller final start. *C. W. C. Elsey.*

KARAZAN 4 gr.g. Nishapour (FR) 125 – Celestial Path 101 (Godswalk (USA) 130) **92 d** [1990 9f5 8g 10.2m3 10.5m4 9g 7d3 9m 1991 8d6 8.5g* 10f5 8g 12f2 11.9g 10.4m6 12d] big, strong gelding: has quick action: fairly useful handicapper: won at Beverley in April: seems best at up to 1¼m: acts on firm and dead ground: has run moderately when blinkered: tends to carry head high. *J. G. FitzGerald.*

KAREN LOUISE 2 ch.f. (Mar 13) Risk Me (FR) 127 – Whose Lady (USA) **75** (Master Willie 129) [1991 7g6 7m2 7.1d3 6g4] lengthy, angular filly: first foal: dam unraced sister to useful 1987 2-y-o 5f and 7f winner William's Bird: modest maiden: placed at Newmarket (best effort) and Chepstow: better suited by 7f than shorter: acts on good to firm and dead ground: races keenly. *Miss H. C. Knight.*

KARINGA BAY 4 ch.c. Ardross 134 – Handy Dancer 87 (Green God 128) [1990 **114** 10m3 10.5g2 12g5 12m* 12g3 14.6g6 1991 10g3 12g3 12m5 10g4 10d3 10g3 9m] big, strong, close-coupled colt: fluent mover: smart performer: mostly ran well in pattern company in 1991, creditable third to Turfkonig in Group 3 event at Baden-Baden penultimate start: last of 14 in Hong Kong Invitation Cup at Sha Tin final one: effective at 1¼m, but worth another try over 1¾m: acts on good to firm ground: seemed ill at ease on descent at Epsom: difficult ride, but game. *Denys Smith.*

KARTAJANA 4 b.f. Shernazar 131 – Karamita 119 (Shantung 132) [1990 10m* **120** 10m* 12d 10f* 12g2 10m* 10d6 1991 10g4 10.5g* 9m5 10s* 10f3 12f3 12g] close-coupled, angular filly: moderate mover: high-class filly, trained here at 3 yrs by M. Stoute: trained in France by A. de Royer-Dupre first 5 starts at 4 yrs: successful in Prix Ganay at Longchamp (beat Passing Sale by neck) in May and Group 1 Grosser Mercedes-Benz Preis Bayerisches Zuchtrennen at Munich (beat Fortune's Wheel by 3 lengths) in August: best effort after when very good third of 10 to Tight Spot in Arlington Million next start: best form at 1¼m: probably acts on any going: has tended to sweat. *N. Drysdale, USA.*

Prix Ganay, Longchamp—Kartajana and Passing Sale (No. 2) stretch out for the line; almost hidden behind the winner is third-placed Dear Doctor

KASAYID 4 br.c. Niniski (USA) 125 – Raabihah 98 (Shirley Heights 130) [1990 **91**
8m* 10.5g³ 12f* 16.2f³ 14.8m³ 20f³ 16g³ 1991 15m³ 16d⁶ 16.5m³] lengthy, lightly-
made colt: moderate mover: fairly useful performer: stays 2½m: acts on firm
ground, not dead: has run well for amateur: sold to join L. Codd's stable 11,000 gns
Newmarket Autumn Sales. *H. Thomson Jones.*

KASHMIRI WIND 5 b.m. Tumble Wind (USA) – Lady Cromer (Blakeney 126) —
[1990 NR 1991 a8g] big, strong, workmanlike mare: lightly raced: first run on flat
since 2 yrs, behind in maiden at Southwell: dead. *J. R. Bosley.*

KASHMIR ROSE 2 b.f. (Mar 22) Local Suitor (USA) 128 – New Central 74 **33**
(Remainder Man 126§) [1991 5m 6g 7.5f 7f⁵ 7m 7m] 820F: sparely-made filly:
second foal: half-sister to 3-y-o 1m winner Jolizal (by Good Times): dam 6f to 1m
winner: worthwhile form only when fifth of 8 in seller at Catterick: sold 520 gns
Doncaster October Sales. *M. Brittain.*

KASIKCI 2 b.f. (Jan 27) Petoski 135 – Top Call 89 (High Top 131) [1991 6m 6g* **81**
7g³ 8m⁵ 10g] 5,200Y: rather unfurnished filly: seventh foal: closely related to
middle-distance winner in Italy by Niniski and half-sister to several winners,
including 1990 2-y-o 7f winner Soft Call (by Ardross), a winner 5 times in Austria at
3 yrs: dam 2-y-o 7f and 1m winner, is half-sister to Final Straw and Achieved: fair
performer: apprentice-ridden winner of Goodwood claimer in May: ran creditably in
May Hill Stakes at Doncaster, respectably in listed race at Newmarket last 2 starts:
should be suited by 1¼m. *N. A. Callaghan.*

KASISI (IRE) 2 b.f. (May 3) Bluebird (USA) 125 – Inchmarlo (USA) (Nashua) —
[1991 7g] IR 20,000Y: sturdy, useful-looking filly: good walker: half-sister to several
winners, including useful 1¼m to 1½m winner Governor's Harbour (by Lomond)
and very useful Australian winner Joy (by Habitat): dam won over 6f at 2 yrs: 12/1
and backward, no sign of promise in 22-runner maiden at Newmarket in November.
A. C. Stewart.

KASMAYO 2 b.c. (Apr 16) Slip Anchor 136 – Sorbus 121 (Busted 134) [1991 7g²] **78 p**
140,000Y: seventh living foal: half-brother to 4 winners, including very useful 1½m
winner Bahamian (by Mill Reef) and smart Irish miler Captivator (by Artaius): dam
disqualified winner of Irish Oaks: weak 3/1-shot, one-paced second of 11 in maiden at
Salisbury in October, always close up: will improve, particularly over middle
distances. *J. H. M. Gosden.*

KATAKANA (USA) 2 b.f. (Jan 28) Diesis 133 – Winds Aloft (USA) (Hoist **93 P**
The Flag (USA)) [1991 6g*]
There's been an air of predictability to the theme of Michael Stoute-
trained fillies and the One Thousand Guineas over the last few years. The
reaction gets under way a long time before the big race takes place. As a rule
the first development is the leaking of reports of sparkling gallops from the
Newmarket work watchers, usually during the summer or autumn of the
filly's two-year-old season. Then the one in question makes her debut; more
often than not she wins against ordinary opposition, and the next step is for
the bookmakers promptly to promote her to a position close to, or at the top
of, their betting on a race still several months away. So far this jigsaw has been
completed only once, by virtue of Musical Bliss in 1989, but on the whole it's
fair to say that the bookmakers' tendency to err on the side of caution has
proved well founded. Since 1985 the Stoute stable has saddled thirteen
runners in the One Thousand Guineas, of whom Musical Bliss won and seven
others reached a place, including fine animals like Sonic Lady, Bella Colora

EBF Theale Maiden Stakes, Newbury—
Katakana raises classic hopes with this impressive win

and Milligram. The latest Stoute-trained fancy for the race is Katakana, who's as low as 8/1 in the ante-post lists following an impressive performance in a maiden event at Newbury in October. The EBF Theale Maiden Stakes was the same race in which Stoute sent out the subsequent Guineas runner-up Heart of Joy to make a successful debut two years previously. Like that filly, Katakana attracted plenty of interest in the market and ran out a clear-cut winner. Always travelling comfortably showing a fluent action, she ranged upsides the leaders with over a furlong to run then showed a useful turn of foot, striding away smoothly in the closing stages to beat another well-regarded newcomer Cut Clear by two and a half lengths with the rest of a twenty-one-runner field well back.

Katakana (USA) (b.f. Jan 28, 1989)	Diesis (ch 1980)	Sharpen Up (ch 1969)	Atan
			Rocchetta
		Doubly Sure (b 1971)	Reliance II
			Soft Angels
	Winds Aloft (USA) (br 1980)	Hoist The Flag (b 1968)	Tom Rolfe
			Wavy Navy
		Pressing Date (b or br 1974)	Never Bend
			Monade

Katakana, a rangy, unfurnished, quite attractive filly, is the first of her dam's foals to run following a filly by Blushing Groom and a colt by Storm Bird, the latter having died. Her pedigree is that of a horse who will have no difficulty in staying at least a mile in her second season. Her sire Diesis has got good horses at a variety of distances, while her twice-raced dam Winds Aloft hails from an excellent family. Winds Aloft's dam Pressing Date was a good-class filly at up to a mile and a quarter in the States. Her dam Monade was one of the best Oaks winners of the last fifty years and proved herself almost as good over a mile by finishing second in the Prix Jacques le Marois. Several of Monade's daughters have gone on to succeed as broodmares and it's interesting to note that one of them, the very useful Elect, produced Mythyaar, yet another Stoute-trained filly who attracted support for the One Thousand Guineas after winning her only start at two. Mythyaar didn't progress from two to three, failing to win in three attempts and becoming rather headstrong, but given the promise she showed at Newbury it'll be most surprising if Katakana doesn't win more races. Whether she'll be up to winning the Guineas is another matter. Suffice it to say that she's a first-rate prospect, almost certainly a good deal better than her Newbury form allows us to rate her, but to go beyond that is impossible on the evidence that's currently available. In short, only her performance in one of the established trials will reveal whether she's truly made of the stuff required to lift one of the top prizes. *M. R. Stoute.*

KATANGO BEAT 4 b.f. Dunbeath (USA) 127 – Kittycatoo Katango (USA) (Verbatim (USA)) [1990 a10g6 10f3 8h a11g 12m6 10f6 1991 a14g6] angular filly: moderate walker: poor plater: stays 1¼m: acts on firm ground: tried blinkered. *B. S. Rothwell.* —

KATE ROYALE 2 b.f. (Apr 17) Beveled (USA) – Silk Lady 97 (Tribal Chief 125) [1991 5m6 5g5 5m2 6m5 6m3 6d2 5f3 5m] leggy, sparely-made filly: eighth living foal: half-sister to 7 winners, including sprinter Mzeff (by Ahonoora), 5f to 7f winner Mister Colin (by Lord Gayle) and 1990 2-y-o 5f and 5.8f winner Toledo Bay (by Flash of Steel): dam won three 5f races at 2 yrs: sire 6f to 7f winner: fair plater: blinkered and on toes, below form at Warwick (nursery) final start: stays 6f: acts on firm and dead ground: has tended to hang. *C. James.* 53

KATHS CHOICE 3 b.f. Dunbeath (USA) 127 – Beaufort Star 95 (Great Nephew 126) [1990 7m 6g 6d 1991 5g 6g2 7m 6.9m* 7g4 6.9m 6g 7s 8m a8g] lengthy filly: plating-class performer: ridden by 7-lb claimer, easily best effort to win 16-runner handicap at Folkestone in July, leading final 1f: well beaten facing very stiff tasks last 2 starts: better at 7f than shorter: acts on good to firm ground: sometimes sweating: inconsistent. *H. J. Collingridge.* 49

KATHTEEN 5 b.m. Teenoso (USA) 135 – Kath (Thatch (USA) 136) [1990 a8g 7m 6v 7m 1991 8f] lengthy mare: little worthwhile form: tailed off in claimer only run in 1991: tried visored once. *D. H. Topley.* —

KATHY COOK 6 b.m. Glenstal (USA) 118 – Belmont Blue 75 (Kashmir II 125) [1990 18f 1991 18s5 16m 18.1m] good-topped mare: moderate mover: unreliable — §

maiden: stays 17f: acts on firm going: not genuine: sold 3,500 gns Ascot November Sales. *R. Hollinshead.*

KATHY FAIR (IRE) 2 b.f. (Mar 24) Nicholas Bill 125 – Fair Flutter (Beldale **34** Flutter (USA) 130) [1991 5.7m⁵ 8.1g 7.1m] 5,400Y: tall filly: second foal: dam unraced daughter of sister to Master Willie (by High Line): poor maiden: sweating profusely, and on toes, last 2 starts. *J. H. Baker.*

KATIE-A (IRE) 2 b.f. (Feb 20) Cyrano de Bergerac 120 – Que Tranquila 65 — (Dominion 123) [1991 5f⁴] 7,200F, 7,600Y: plain, leggy filly: second foal: dam twice-raced daughter of half-sister to dam of Pebbles: backward, fourth of 8, ducking left stalls, smooth headway halfway, one pace, in maiden at Redcar in July. *R. M. Whitaker.*

KATIE JO 5 b.m. Taufan (USA) 119 – Wyn Mipet (Welsh Saint 126) [1990 10.2f⁶ **57** 10f²9g* 10f 10g⁵ 10m 10g⁴ 10m³ 12m² 12m² 10.6d⁵ 12m³ 12g 10g² 10d* a12g* a12g⁴ 1991 a12g⁴ 9.9m² 10s 9.7m] stocky, quite attractive mare: quite modest handicapper at best nowadays: not seen out after July: best efforts at around 1¼m: acts on good to firm ground: good mount for apprentice: bandaged last 2 starts. *J. Akehurst.*

KATIE SCARLETT 5 b.m. Lochnager 132 – Final Request 63 (Sharp Edge 123) **32** [1990 a10g* a16g⁴ 10f 12g 10g a10g 1991 a8g⁵ a10g a13g³] big, short-backed mare: good mover: past performer: stays 13f: best efforts on equitrack. *J. J. Bridger.*

KATIE'S DREAM (IRE) 2 b.f. (Apr 7) Welsh Term 126 – Miss Slip (USA) 107 **44** (Coursing) [1991 6g⁴ 6g 6g⁶ 7m⁴ 7m] IR 1,100F: leggy filly: good mover: half-sister to several winners abroad: dam won Molecomb Stakes: poor maiden: will stay 1m. *P. S. Felgate.*

KATIES FIRST (USA) 4 b.f. Kris 135 – Katies 125 (Nonoalco (USA) 131) [1990 **110** 7f⁵ 6f² 5h* 6d⁴ 5m 5m* 6m 5g 5g⁴ 5.6g² 5m 6m² 6s* 1991 6d 6g⁶ 5m* 5d⁶ 5d 5s⁶] sparely-made filly: fairly useful here at 3 yrs when trained by G. Lewis: very useful performer in 1991: won listed event in August by 4 lengths: best effort after when fair seventh of 14 to Keen Hunter in Ciga Prix de l'Abbaye de Long-champ: stays 6f: acts on any going: visits Zilzal. *J. Hammond, France.*

KATIESIMP 2 gr.f. (May 19) Import 127 – Katie Grey 60 (Pongee 106) [1991 8m] — smallish, angular filly: fourth foal: half-sister to quite modest 1½m winner/success-ful hurdler Mils Mij (by Slim Jim): dam won novice hurdle: 50/1 and green, no show in maiden at Newcastle in October. *S. G. Payne.*

KATIE'S SUNSET (IRE) 2 b.f. (May 20) Red Sunset 120 – Little Spinner 57 **48** (Tachypous 128) [1991 6.1f 6f] leggy, angular filly: third foal: half-sister to 3-y-o Lord Future (by The Noble Player): dam 1¼m winner: poor form in large fields at Nottingham (better effort) and Yarmouth (seller) in September: will stay 1m + : sold 4,600 gns Newmarket Autumn Sales. *C. F. Wall.*

KATIE VALENTINE 3 gr.f. Belfort (FR) 89 – Call Me Kate 72 (Firestreak 125) — [1990 5m 5m⁴ 5g² 5g⁴ 6d 6m 6m³ 7g⁶ 7m 6d² 6v⁶ 6d 6s⁶ 1991 6f 7m] rather sparely-made filly: poor maiden: suited by 6f: best form in visor: has worn bandages: sold 875 gns Ascot July Sales. *Dr J. D. Scargill.*

KATUSHA-MAY 3 gr.f. Skyliner 117 – Gem-May 71 (Mansingh (USA) 120) — [1990 NR 1991 6f⁶ 8f⁴] leggy, workmanlike filly: third foal: half-sister to plating-class 1989 2-y-o 5f winner Susha (by Bay Express): dam, maiden plater, stayed 1½m: no promise in claimer and maiden. *T. Fairhurst.*

KATY ANN BEE (USA) 3 ch.f. Banner Bob (USA) – A Bit O' The Mick (USA) **89** (Barrera (USA)) [1990 NR 1991 7m² 7g² 7g⁴ 7f* 7g² 7g³ 7m²] good-topped filly: poor mover: second foal: dam unraced: sire won from 6f to 8.5f: fairly useful form: won maiden at Yarmouth in June: ran well afterwards in minor events at Newmarket, Yarmouth and Ayr: should stay 1m: acts on firm going: sold 11,000 gns Newmarket Autumn Sales. *M. J. Ryan.*

KATY'S LAD 4 b.c. Camden Town 125 – Cathryn's Song (Prince Tenderfoot **62** (USA) 126) [1990 7m⁵ 9m² 8m* 10.6f³ 8.5d³ 8f 7.6g⁶ 8.5m 8f⁶ a8g 9m⁵ 8m 10.8m⁴ 10.4d⁵ 1991 8s 7g³ 10m⁴ 10f 10.8m 10g* 10.8g² 10d* 10.2d⁴ 10.3d⁴ 10.3d] leggy colt: has a quick action: quite modest handicapper: won at Pontefract (2) in summer: stays 11f: acts on any going: best without blinkers. *B. A. McMahon.*

KATY'S PET 3 b.f. Tina's Pet 121 – Our Katy 68 (Dragonara Palace (USA) 115) **58** d [1990 6g³ 6m⁵ 6g³ 6g⁵ 6d² 1991 6f⁶ 7g⁶ 6g⁴ 6g⁵ 7m² 6.9s⁵ 7g² 7f⁶ 8m 8f 9.7m a6g] smallish, sparely-made filly: quite modest form at best: should stay 1m: acts on good to firm ground and dead: tried blinkered: claimed out of D. Morley's stable £5,800 after seventh start, trained next 4 by A. Denson: refused to race last 4 starts and must be avoided. *R. P. C. Hoad.*

KATZAKEENA 4 b.f. Gorytus (USA) 132 – Current Bay (Tyrant (USA)) [1990 **88** 6g* 6f³ 5m* 6m* 5m³ 6m⁵ 6m⁴ 6g⁶ 1991 6g 6m 6m 6s³ 6m 8g 6d] close-coupled, good-quartered filly: fair performer: good third in listed event at Newmarket: effective at 5f, and seems to stay 1m: probably acts on any going: ran moderately when edgy and blinkered once. *P. J. Makin.*

KAUSAR (USA) 4 b.c. Vaguely Noble 140 – Kozana 127 (Kris 135) [1990 10g **88** d 12g⁵ 14g* 12g 1991 16g* 9v³ 15.9m⁵ 12m⁶ 17.5m⁴ 14g⁶] sturdy, lengthy colt: has round action: first reported foal: dam, 1m and 1¼m winner and third in Prix de l'Arc de Triomphe, is half-sister to several winners, notably Prix du Cadran winner Karkour: fair ex-Irish handicapper at best: won minor events at Gowran Park in 1990 and the Curragh in March (trained by J. Oxx): best effort here when fourth at Ayr in September: stays well: acts on good to firm and heavy ground. *G. M. Moore.*

KAWARAU QUEEN 4 b.f. Taufan (USA) 119 – Hasty Goddess 72 (Nebbiolo — 125) [1990 8.2g³ 8g³ 7.5g³ 8.2m* 8g³ 9m 8m 6g⁴ 6d 8m 6d 1991 10.9g⁶ 8.1m 7m 8.3f] workmanlike, deep-girthed filly: has markedly round action: quite modest handicapper at best at 3 yrs: well beaten in 1991: stays 1m: acts on good to firm ground. *C. Parker.*

KAWWAS 6 b.h. Persian Bold 123 – Tifrums 77 (Thatch (USA) 136) [1990 7g 7g² **36** 7g² 7f* 8h⁶ 7m 7f² 8m 7m 8d 8m 1991 7f 8m 8.1d 8g⁵ 7f⁵ 7m* 7f 7m³ 7s] smallish, attractive horse: poor mover: poor handicapper at best: stays 7f: seems to need a sound surface: tried blinkered once: has been bandaged: has given trouble at stalls and tended to hang: inconsistent. *W. Holden.*

KAYARTIS 2 b.f. (Feb 23) Kaytu 112 – Polyartis 78 (Artaius (USA) 129) [1991 7f⁴ **35** 7m⁶ 8m] 760Y: sparely-made filly: second foal, placed over 6f at 2 yrs, is daughter of half-sister to very smart stayer Noble Saint: fourth of 8 in seller at Catterick in summer, only form: will stay 1m. *Mrs G. R. Reveley.*

KAY BEEYOU (IRE) 2 b.f. (Apr 7) Petorius 117 – Damaslin (Camden Town **65** 125) [1991 6m³ 5.7f³ 6f 6g⁶ 6f³ 6s⁴ a8g⁶] 3,000Y: leggy filly: second foal: dam Irish 2-y-o 7f winner: quite modest maiden: worth a try at 7f: acts on any going. *T. Thomson Jones.*

KAYFAAT (USA) 3 b.c. Spend A Buck (USA) – Duped (USA) (On The Sly **74** (USA)) [1990 NR 1991 8m 10g⁵ 14m⁴ 14.1f⁴ 12g 14.6m* 14.6g* 15.9d²] $55,000Y: leggy, quite attractive colt: moderate mover: first foal: dam won at up to 9f: modest performer: successful in seller (well below best, sold out of B. Hanbury's stable 11,500 gns) and handicap at Wolverhampton in September: good second in handicap at Chester: stays 2m: best effort on an easy surface: winning hurdler. *M. C. Pipe.*

KAY LARGO (IRE) 2 b.f. (Feb 23) Treasure Kay 114 – Seven Hills (FR) — (Reform 132) [1991 6d] IR 2,700Y, resold 2,000Y: first foal: dam 13.8f and 1¾m winner stayed 2¼m: 33/1, no show in 10-runner maiden at Doncaster in November. *E. H. Owen jun.*

KAYS BROWN SUGAR (IRE) 2 b.f. (Apr 9) Slew Machine (USA) – Miss **31** Woodlawn (USA) (Soy Numero Uno (USA)) [1991 5f⁵ 6m 8m] IR 700Y: lengthy, angular filly: first foal: dam won 3 races at up to 9f in USA: was unraced: well beaten in maiden auctions: pulled hard second outing: sold 700 gns Doncaster October Sales. *R. M. Whitaker.*

KAY'S DILEMMA (IRE) 3 b.f. Ya Zaman (USA) – Brook's Dilemma 80 — (Known Fact (USA) 135) [1990 NR 1991 8g 6.5s 7d a8g a10g] first foal: dam 3-y-o 6f winner out of half-sister to dam of Irish 1000 Guineas winner More So: well beaten in Irish maidens (first 3 starts), Southwell maiden then Lingfield claimer: wore eyeshield final start: trained first 4 starts by Michael Cunningham. *P. A. Kelleway.*

KAYTAK (FR) 4 b.g. Mouktar 129 – Kaythama (Run The Gantlet (USA)) [1990 **75** 12v* 12g⁵ 12d⁶ 1991 14g⁶ 11.5g⁴ 7.6m⁵ 11.5g* 12v⁵ 12m 12d] leggy, sparely-made gelding: third reported foal: dam French 1¼m winner, stayed 1½m: ex-French gelding: won maiden at Maisons-Laffitte and close sixth in Group 3 event at Chantilly at 3 yrs: modest handicapper at best here: won at Sandown in June: should stay beyond 1½m: acts on heavy ground: trained at 3 yrs by A. de Royer-Dupre. *J. R. Jenkins.*

KAYVEE 2 gr.g. (Feb 7) Kaldoun (FR) 122 – Secret Life (USA) (Elocutionist **86** (USA)) [1991 5g² 6g² 6m² 7g² 6.9f* 7m⁵] 5,000Y: big gelding, with scope: second foal: dam French 1m winner: fair performer: won maiden at Folkestone in October, making all, quickening clear straight, eased: stays 7f: wore crossed noseband third and fourth starts: consistent. *G. Harwood.*

KAZOO 3 gr.f. Shareef Dancer (USA) 135 – Kallista (Zeddaan 130) [1990 NR 1991 **108** 8s² 8m* 8g* 10.5d 7m] good-topped, workmanlike filly: fourth foal: half-sister to a winner in Germany by King of Clubs: dam won from 7f to 9f in Germany, and is daughter of champion older German mare Kandia: won 3-runner Carlisle maiden in April and Arag-Preis Deutsches 1000 Guineas at Dusseldorf in May: beaten about 8 lengths in Prix de Diane Hermes at Chantilly, long way in Group 2 contest at Newmarket over 4 months later: stays 1m: visits Diesis. *J. W. Watts.*

K-BRIGADE 6 b.h. Brigadier Gerard 144 – Kajetana (FR) (Caro 133) [1990 13v⁴ **55**
1991 10.1m⁴ 12.4m⁴ 12g⁴ 10.1m² 10.9m⁵] big, lengthy horse: plating-class handicapper nowadays: stays 2m: possibly not at his best on firm going, acts on any other: lacks turn of foot and normally ridden up with pace: game. *C. W. C. Elsey.*

K C RAPIDE 4 b.c. Rapid River 127 – Duty Watch 40 (Import 127) [1990 6m² 5d **— §**
5m⁵ 6d a7g 1991 5f⁵ 5h 6d 5g 5s⁶] smallish, sturdy colt: has markedly round action: plating-class handicapper at best: tailed off final start (July): refused to race second one (tongue tied down): stays 6f: acts on firm going: tried blinkered: temperamental, and one to avoid. *R. W. Stubbs.*

KEEN HUNTER (USA) 4 ch.c. Diesis 133 – Love's Reward (Nonoalco **122** p
(USA) 131) [1990 6m* 6m* 6m⁵ 1991 6g* 5d*]
 Prior to the Prix de l'Abbaye de Longchamp, Keen Hunter had been limited to just one racecourse appearance in fifteen months. Two impressive wins in minor company at three years had marked him out as a sprinter of considerable promise but in finishing fifth in the 1990 July Cup, an excellent effort for one so inexperienced, Keen Hunter sustained a joint injury. Just over a year had passed before Keen Hunter reappeared with a comfortable success from Sizzling Saga and Montendre in the listed Hackwood Stakes at Newbury but, just when his well-being had finally been confirmed, a virus reportedly laid low the majority of Gosden's Stanley House stables, and Keen Hunter with it. Gosden's achievement in bringing Keen Hunter back to land the Abbaye after such a preparation was one of the training performances of the season. He was sent off at 115/10 at Longchamp, coupled with the now French-trained Katies First, bettered in the market by the principal French hope Divine Danse and the English-trained trio comprising Sheikh Albadou and the two-year-olds Magic Ring (favourite) and Paris House. None of the others in the fourteen-runner field made much appeal. Paris House soon led at a blistering early pace, closely followed by Irish juvenile Bradawn Breever and Sheikh Albadou. The Nunthorpe winner went to the front two furlongs from home but no sooner had he done so than Keen Hunter, who'd tracked him closely throughout, quickened in fine style when rousted along by Cauthen to go a length or so to the good. Having got to the front Keen Hunter then showed signs of inexperience, carrying his head a shade awkwardly, but he still held a length advantage over Sheikh Albadou at the finish. Magic Ring

Hackwood Stakes, Newbury—Keen Hunter makes a successful return

Ciga Prix de l'Abbaye de Longchamp—Keen Hunter holds on firmly to his lead; behind in line abreast are (from rails) Sheikh Albadou, Magic Ring, Flowing and Archway, then Divine Danse

kept on well to take third, a further head behind, himself a short head and neck in front of the strong-finishing Irish pair Archway and Flowing. Although Sheikh Albadou and Magic Ring went on to success in the Breeders' Cup Sprint and Cornwallis Stakes respectively, the Abbaye was a far from vintage edition. That said, however, Keen Hunter deserves extra credit for, in a race where the leaders probably went too fast for their own good, he was able to keep up with the pace and show a turn of foot.

Incidentally, Keen Hunter was Sheikh Mohammed's first Group 1 winner of the season in France, Britain or Ireland and victory also gave Keen Hunter's sire, Diesis, the notable record of Group 1 winners over five furlongs and a mile and a half. Keen Hunter was primed to give them further successes but the season wasn't long enough; Gosden's reaction to Keen Hunter's surprisingly being given no place in either the six original places decided by the international handicappers, or the first three reserves, for the Breeders' Cup Mile, the inaugural running of which he'd won with Royal Heroine, was an understandably frustrated: 'We're all dressed up with nowhere to go'. Still, there's always 1992 when Keen Hunter will surely have a say in the top sprints if all remains well with him. He's still inexperienced and is capable of better yet.

	Diesis (ch 1980)	Sharpen Up (ch 1969)	Atan Rocchetta
Keen Hunter (USA) (ch.c. 1987)		Doubly Sure (b 1971)	Reliance II Soft Angels
	Love's Reward (ch 1981)	Nonoalco (b 1971)	Nearctic Seximee
		Splashing (b 1971)	Petingo Pelting

Keen Hunter was purchased privately by Sheikh Mohammed as a yearling. His dam Love's Reward raced only as a three-year-old when from three starts the best she could manage was a fifth place in a Yarmouth maiden. This poor record didn't stop her being sold to the BBA for 130,000 guineas at the Newmarket December Sales later in the year as she comes from a most successful family. Her dam Splashing was very smart, putting up her best display when winning the Cornwallis Stakes. Besides Love's Reward, she's produced the Middle Park and Prix d'Arenberg winners Bassenthwaite and Glancing. Love's Reward's grandam, the five-furlong sprinter Pelting (none over further than a mile) besides Splashing, is the dam of eleven winners, most of them useful. They include the miler Fighting (dam of Krakow, herself the dam of Ghariba and Braashee) and Nell Gwyn third Glinting (dam of Hadeer). Keen Hunter is the second foal of Love's Reward following the fair handicapper Amoodi (by Forli) who was successful at a mile and three quarters and stayed nineteen furlongs. The third foal, the three-year-old Shedad, is a brother to Keen Hunter, but has proved headstrong and a major disappointment; he was sold for only 3,000 guineas at the latest Newmarket July Sales. A tall, quite attractive colt, Keen Hunter is effective at five and six furlongs. Although successful on good to firm ground, his best form is with some give; having been badly jarred up in the July Cup he sported a bandage on his near-fore in 1991. *J. Gosden.*

KEEN MELODY (USA) 4 b.f. Sharpen Up 127 – Sweet Abandon (USA) — (Lyphard (USA) 132) [1990 8m⁶ 8g⁶ 7m² 8g 7m 7g a10g a7g⁶ 1991 7g] small, sparely-made filly: one-time quite modest maiden: below form last 6 starts: stays 1m: acts on good to firm ground: tried blinkered once. *R. Hannon.*

KEEN VISION (IRE) 3 b.g. Vision (USA) – Calvino (Relkino 131) [1990 7m 7g 53 7g 1991 9d 8.2m² 10d³ 9m 8.2f² 10g² 7m⁵ 8.2f 10m] workmanlike gelding: plating-class and rather unsatisfactory maiden on Flat: stays 1¼m: acts on firm ground: bandaged third and fourth starts: has put head in air, and tends to find little: winning hurdler. *D. W. P. Arbuthnot.*

KEEP IN MIND (IRE) 2 b.c. (Jan 30) Don't Forget Me 127 – Astra Adastra 81 (Mount Hagen (FR) 127) [1991 6m² 6m³ 7f² 8.2m* 7m] IR 25,000Y: leggy, rather angular colt: half-brother to 3 winners, including fairly useful 1½m winner Baraz (by Busted) and 3-y-o 5f (at 2 yrs) and 7f winner Precious Air (by Precocious): dam Irish 2-y-o 5f winner, is half-sister to Ballad Rock: fair performer: led post in nursery at Nottingham, showing improved form: much better suited by 8.2f than less, and will stay well: refused to enter stalls fourth intended outing: sold 28,000 gns Newmarket Autumn Sales. *J. L. Dunlop.*

KEEP IN TRIM 3 ch.f. Pharly (FR) 130 – Silverhall (Sparkler 130) [1990 6g 1991 — a8g a8g 8m 10.2d 10.8m] workmanlike filly: poor plater: sold to join R. Lee 700 gns Ascot 2nd July Sales. *D. Marks.*

KEEP YOUR WORD 5 ch.m. Castle Keep 121 – So True 116 (So Blessed 130) 69 [1990 10g 8m 8g* 8f 9g* 9s² 10.6v⁵ 10d⁵ 1991 9s⁵ 10d⁶ 8g³ 10.1g 9d 8d³ 8g* 8g⁴ 7g 8.1m 10g 10.2s] tall, sparely-made mare: poor walker: quite modest mover: quite modest handicapper: won at Kempton in July: well below form last 4 starts: suited by 1m/9f: goes well with some give in the ground, probably not at best on firm: has won for apprentice. *G. B. Balding.*

KELIMUTU 2 br.f. (Feb 11) Top Ville 129 – Soemba 86 (General Assembly — p (USA)) [1991 7g] narrow leggy filly: second foal: half-sister to useful but possibly unsatisfactory 3-y-o Sumonda (by Lomond), successful at 7f and 1m: dam 9f winner: 50/1, around 17 lengths tenth of 22, held up, ran on in quite good style under considerate ride, to Oumaldaaya in maiden at Newmarket in November: may well stay 1¼m: will improve. *C. F. Wall.*

KELLY COLLEEN 2 ch.f. (Apr 30) Myjinski (USA) – Easter Hope (The — Go-Between 129) [1991 7m a7g 6m] 380F: smallish, rather angular filly: first foal: dam unraced: no worthwhile form in sellers: sold 460 gns Doncaster November Sales. *A. Harrison.*

KELLYS KINGDOM (IRE) 3 b.c. King Persian 107 – Kellys Risc (Pitskelly — 122) [1990 5m 5f⁴ 5m² 5m* 6m⁴ 6m² 6f⁴ 6m 6m⁴ a8g 1991 6m 8m 7g] compact colt: moderate walker and mover: quite modest handicapper: ran creditably at Warwick, first start in first half of 1991: suited by 6f: acts on firm going. *R. A. Bennett.*

KELLY'S KITE 3 br.f. Buzzards Bay 128§ – Bold Kelly 83 (Pitskelly 122) [1990 — 5g 6g 1991 10m 8f 6m 6.1m] compact filly: poor plater. *H. J. Collingridge.*

KELTIE (USA) 3 ch.c. Storm Bird (CAN) 134 – Classy Twist (USA) (Twist The 71 § Axe (USA)) [1990 8m³ 8d³ 10.2s² 1991 12d 12d⁵ 13.1m⁴ 14s 12f³ 13.6d] long-backed colt: modest maiden: third in amateurs handicap at Folkestone: probably stays 13f (burly over 1¾m): acts on good to firm ground and soft: blinkered last 3 outings: tongue tied down on third, wore dropped noseband fourth: sold 10,500 gns Newmarket Autumn Sales: none too keen final start and one to leave alone. *G. Harwood.*

KEMPINSKI (IRE) 3 b.c. Valiyar 129 – Kalista 109 (Bellypha 130) [1990 NR 80 1991 6m⁵ 8f* 8m² 8.1m⁵ 8g] well-made colt: carries condition: first foal: dam French 1m winner: won 3-runner median auction contest at Brighton in May: made virtually all in handicap there next start: ran poorly afterwards: stays 1m: carried head high and looked none too keen fourth outing: sold 15,500 gns Newmarket September Sales, reportedly for stud in Germany. *L. M. Cumani.*

KENBU (FR) 2 gr.f. (Feb 28) Kenmare (FR) 125 – Tarlace (FR) (Targowice **106** (USA) 130) [1991 6d² 6g* 6g* 6g² 8d⁵] half-sister to 3 winners by Fabulous Dancer in France, all at 1m or thereabouts: dam French maiden: useful performer: won minor event at Saint-Cloud in June, then 5-runner Prix de Cabourg at Deauville by ½ length from Lion Cavern: ran creditably in 4-runner Prix Morny Agence Francaise at Deauville (beaten 3 lengths by Arazi) later in August and 14-runner Prix Marcel Boussac at Longchamp behind Culture Vulture in October: stays 1m: yet to race on top-of-the-ground. *F. Boutin, France.*

KENNINGTON SAMARA 3 ch.f. Afzal 83 – Rayne Park (Julio Mariner 127) — [1990 NR 1991 8m a12g] leggy filly: first foal: dam once-raced on flat and of little account: showed nothing in claimers. *R. T. Juckes.*

KENT HOUSE 2 b.c. (Apr 20) Kings Lake (USA) 133 – When The Saints (Bay — Express 132) [1991 7m] 1,500Y: half-brother to fair 7f to 9f performer Sno Serenade (by Song): dam won over 6f at 3 yrs in Ireland: 33/1, backward and green, tailed off in 20-runner maiden at Newmarket in October.*J. D. Czerpak.*

KENTUCKY CHICKEN (USA) 2 b.f. (Jan 4) Secreto (USA) 128 – Stark Ice — (USA) (Icecapade (USA)) [1991 7g] $60,000Y: lengthy filly: first foal: dam unraced: 50/1, always towards rear in 22-runner maiden at Newmarket in October: moved poorly down. *N. A. Graham.*

KENTUCKY RAIN 2 b.g. (Apr 5) Green Ruby (USA) 104 – French Touch 57 **67** (Dieu Soleil 111) [1991 5f⁵ 5f⁵ 5f² 7m⁶ 6f* 7.5f* 7m] 6,000Y, 6,800 2-y-o: fair sort: first reported foal: dam sprinter: quite modest form: successful in selling nurseries at Ripon (no bid) in August and Beverley (retained 4,400 gns after making all) in September: stays 7.5f: acts on firm ground.*J. G. FitzGerald.*

KENTUCKY STARLET (USA) 2 b.f. (Mar 1) Cox's Ridge (USA) – Empress **69** of Canada (CAN) (Accomplish) [1991 6d 7g² 7g 7g² 7g² 8m²] $85,000F: leggy, good-bodied filly: sister to very useful 1987 2-y-o Grade 3 7f runner-up Accomplish Ridge and half-sister to several winners, including 1983 2-y-o 1m winner Maricourt (by One For All) and 3-y-o 8.5f winner Private Access (by Private Account): dam won 6 races at up to 1m: sire top-class maiden: quite modest maiden: much improved when runner-up in nurseries last 3 starts, just caught at Warwick last time: stays 1m: acts on good to firm ground. *R. Hannon.*

KENYATTA (USA) 2 b.c. (Mar 20) Mogambo (USA) – Caranga (USA) (Caro **60** 133) [1991 5g⁴ 5g⁵ 6m⁴ 7d² 7g 7m⁶ 7m] $20,000Y: leggy, quite attractive colt: moderate walker: has a round action: third foal: half-brother to a minor winner by Cutlass: dam minor winner at 6f: sire best from 1m to 1¼m: quite modest maiden: never-nearer second of 8 in maiden at Ayr, pulling very hard, snatched up after 2f then staying on well final 1f: showed little afterwards: should stay 1m: possibly suited by give in the ground: has run well in visor. *Denys Smith.*

KERRY BOY 4 ch.g. Sallust 134 – Silk Imp 72 (Imperial Fling (USA) 116) [1990 — a7g⁶ a7g³ a6g⁶ 6m 7g⁵ 12.5g 7d 1991 a6g a7g] small, sturdy gelding: plating-class maiden at best: tailed off in early part of 1991: should be suited by 1m + .*P. J. Feilden.*

KERTALE (IRE) 2 b.g. (Feb 15) Soughaan (USA) 111 – Shapely 84 (Parthia 132) **54** [1991 6m⁴ 5m⁵ 5.3f⁴ 5m 5.2f 6m⁵ 7.1m 6m] IR 4,200F, 4,000Y: smallish, leggy gelding: poor mover: half-brother to 3 winners, notably useful Irish 5f (at 2 yrs) and 7f winner Red Emerald (by Red God): dam stayed 1¾m: fair but inconsistent plater: stays 7f: has sweated. *R. Boss.*

KESTREL FORBOXES (IRE) 3 b.g. Seymour Hicks (FR) 125 – Dance **74** Mistress (Javelot 124) [1990 5m⁶ 5f² 5g³ 5.8m* 6m* 6f⁶ 6f* 6m³ 6g⁵ 1991 6d⁵ 6m³ 6m³ 5.7m 6.9f* 7f* 8m⁴ 8.1m* 7m⁴ 8.3f⁴ 7f⁶ 7d⁴] close-coupled gelding: moderate mover: modest performer: favourite, made all in summer claimers at Carlisle, Catterick and Haydock: ran moderately after: stays 1m: acts on firm going: claimed £5,250 final start.*J. Berry.*

KEVINSBELLE 3 b.f. Belfort (FR) 89 – Manna Green (Bustino 136) [1990 5m⁶ **48** 5m² 5f⁵ 7f² 7f* 7m 7f 6m 7d 1991 7g 6m 7m 9.7m 8.3m³ 8f 8.3m⁴ 8g³ 8.2m 8m⁶ a8g⁶] light-framed filly: poor walker: fair plater nowadays: stays 8.3f: acts on firm going: somewhat headstrong and highly strung: inconsistent: trained until after third start by E. Eldin, next 4 by J. Pearce.*I. Campbell.*

KEVINSLINE (IRE) 3 b.g. Montelimar (USA) 122 – Priceless Pin (Saint Cres- — pin III 132) [1990 5f 5m 5g 7f 7g 1991 10d 8m 10f⁴ 14.1g³ a12g] leggy, sparely-made gelding: poor maiden: stays 1¾m: acts on firm ground: sweating and edgy fourth outing: blinkered last 2 starts: trained until after fourth by E. Eldin: sold 1,300 gns Doncaster November Sales. *I. Campbell.*

KHALLOOF (IRE) 2 b.c. (Feb 4) Ballad Rock 122 – Tapiola 71 (Tap On Wood **78**
130) [1991 7g* 7f³ 6m] IR 52,000Y: sturdy, heavy-topped colt: has scope: good
walker: third foal: brother to quite modest 1988 2-y-o maiden Miss Rossetti and
half-brother to 3-y-o Lara's Baby (by Valiyar): dam 2-y-o 6f winner: favourite, won
maiden at Yarmouth: good third of 4 in minor event at Redcar later in July: never
travelling well in Newmarket nursery in August: better suited by 7f than 6f: acts on
firm ground. *M. A. Jarvis.*

KHAZAR (USA) 2 b.c. (Mar 26) Nureyev (USA) 131 – Kathleen's Girl (USA) **76**
(Native Charger) [1991 7.1s⁶ 7.1d 7g*] $975,000F: leggy, good-topped colt: has
scope: half-brother to several winners, including very smart (at up to 9f) Fifth
Division (by Fifth Marine) and 9f Santa Anita Derby winner Mighty Adversary (by
Mr Reddy): dam minor sprint winner at 3 yrs: weak 6/1-chance, won 11-runner
maiden at Salisbury in October, soon prominent and battling on well: in need of race
previously: will stay 1m. *Sir Mark Prescott.*

KHIOS (USA) 4 b.g. Lord Gaylord (USA) – Monelia (USA) (Mongo) [1990 8f
12.5g 16.2d 10f 10m 1991 a12g] compact gelding: no worthwhile form on flat, blinkered only run in 1991: has been heavily bandaged: sold 1,550 gns Doncaster Summer
Sales. *K. T. Ivory.*

KHOJOHN 3 ch.g. Chief Singer 131 – Pirate Lass (USA) 90 (Cutlass (USA)) [1990 **52**
5g 6s 6g⁶ 6g 8d 1991 a8g² a8g³ a8g⁴ 10.2s² 10f 12.3d 10.6m a11g³ 10m⁶ 7.1g⁶ 10.4m⁴]
plain gelding: plating-class maiden: stays 11f: probably best on an easy surface:
visored third to ninth starts: trained until after ninth by C. W. C. Elsey. *R. D. E.
Woodhouse.*

KHOREVO 6 b.g. Tyrnavos 129 – Amina 80 (Brigadier Gerard 144) [1990 10f* — §
10.8m 10.1g 8g 10f 12f³ 12f² 1991 a14g⁵] sturdy gelding: moderate mover: poor
handicapper: not seen out after January: probably stays 1¾m: acts on firm going,
possibly unsuited by soft: apprentice ridden: goes well visored: reluctant to race
once at 4 yrs. *I. Campbell.*

KHULM 4 b.c. Kafu 120 – Little Wild Duck 78 (Great Heron (USA) 127) [1990 6m⁶ —
5m 6f* 6m⁴ 6m 5m 7m³ 8m⁵ 7g 8m 1991 7m] leggy, close-coupled colt: moderate
mover: quite modest handicapper: tailed off only run in 1991 (May): well worth a try
at beyond 1m: acts on firm going: hung right for 7-lb claimer: has won when sweating. *M. Madgwick.*

KIANGSU (IRE) 3 b. or br.f. Double Schwartz 128 – Silk Trade (Auction Ring —
(USA) 123) [1990 NR 1991 8d 8m] IR 7,800Y: sturdy filly: sixth living foal: half-sister
to 1985 2-y-o 6f winner Synthetic (by Reform) and a winner in France by Niniski:
dam unraced daughter of half-sister to Troy: never dangerous in median auction
maiden and claimer: sold 540 gns Doncaster October Sales. *R. Guest.*

KICKED OUT 3 br.c. Undulate (USA) – Midsummer Girl (Midsummer Night II —
117) [1990 6m 6f 7m 1991 12d] angular colt: no form, including in seller: visored on
reappearance: dead. *B. Stevens.*

KICK ON MAJESTIC (IRE) 2 b.g. (Apr 26) Mister Majestic 122 – Avebury **50**
Ring (Auction Ring (USA) 123) [1991 5g⁴ 5.9h³ 5g³ 7f⁶ 7m² 7g 7m 7f* 7f⁵ 6.9h² 7.5f]
IR 9,000F, 11,500Y: neat gelding: moderate mover: half-brother to fair miler
Twotime Bid (by Taufan) and 15f seller winner Barricade (by Viking): dam Irish 5f
winner: fair plater: promoted winner of seller at Thirsk (no bid) in August: stays 7f:
acts on firm ground: ran poorly in blinkers third outing: trained first 3 starts by J.
Berry. *N. Bycroft.*

KID LEWIS 4 b.g. Thatching 131 – Mirkan Honey 83 (Ballymore 123) [1990 8.2s⁶ — §
7g 7d² 8m 8d 1991 10f 12.5d] leggy gelding: has been tubed: quite modest maiden at
best: ran poorly in spring of 1991: should stay 1m: easily best effort on dead going:
probably ungenuine. *Mrs A. Knight.*

KIEGY 3 b.f. Mansingh (USA) 120 – Blickling 64 (Blakeney 126) [1990 5g 6g 1991 **43**
7d 5s⁴ 6d³ 6m⁴] small, sparely-made filly: poor maiden: should be suited by further
than 6f: form only on a soft surface. *J. Berry.*

KIJAFA (USA) 3 b.f. Chief's Crown (USA) – Herb Wine (USA) (Full Pocket **65**
(USA)) [1990 NR 1991 11.9g² 11.9g 12m² 14.1m* 14.6m²] strong, lengthy filly: third
foal: half-sister to 1989 8.2f winner Almuinjjid (by Blushing Groom) and U.S. winner
Plentyofit (by Mr Prospector): dam, half-sister to good 1979 2-y-o Romeo Romani,
won at up to 9f in USA: quite modest performer: won 5-runner maiden at Redcar in
October: fair second in handicap at Doncaster: will stay 2m: sold 16,500 gns Newmarket December Sales. *L. M. Cumani.*

KIKAM 3 b. or br.f. Ardross 134 – Ruda (FR) (Free Round (USA)) [1990 NR 1991 **79**
10g 12m² 14.8g⁴ 15.8f³ 14.1f* 14f³ 14.1f* 14.6m⁶ 16m*] leggy filly: first reported

foal: dam unraced: modest form: successful in 2 claimers at Yarmouth in August and in handicap at Newmarket in October: suited by test of stamina: acts on firm ground: lacks turn of foot: game. *Lord John FitzGerald.*

KILDONAN 4 b.g. Welsh Captain 113 – Madam Import 63 (Import 127) [1990 a8g⁵ a7g² a8g⁴ a10g² a10g 12f 1991 12g] big, good-topped gelding: carries condition: quite modest handicapper at best: no form for a long time: stays 1¼m: acts on firm going. *N. A. Twiston-Davies.* —

KILLICK 3 b.f. Slip Anchor 136 – Enthralment (USA) 78 (Sir Ivor 135) [1990 NR 1991 7g⁶ 11.5g⁵ 8g 10s⁶ 8g⁶] leggy, workmanlike filly: fifth foal: half-sister to a winner in Belgium by Kings Lake: dam winner over 6f on 2-y-o debut but well beaten after, is out of sister to Forli: fair form in newcomers race at Newbury and listed race at Lingfield first 2 starts: didn't come near to reproducing that in maidens and claimer: sold 800 gns Newmarket December Sales. *R. V. Smyth.* 69

KILLINGHALL (IRE) 3 b.g. Glow (USA) – Joma Kaanem (Double Form 130) [1990 5d 5f³ 6g 1991 7m 7g³ 7f³ 8m⁴ 8h² 7f⁵ 6m² 7f² 8.1g* 9m 7.1m] lengthy, good-quartered gelding: powerful mover: modest handicapper: well beaten after making most to win at Edinburgh in September: stays 1m: acts on hard going: blinkered fourth and fifth starts: visored (awkward on turn) on eighth: has taken strong hold: sold 20,000 gns Newmarket Autumn Sales and gelded. *J. W. Watts.* 72

KILLY 2 ch.c. (Feb 3) Dominion 123 – Figini 74 (Glint of Gold 128) [1991 6m* 6.1m⁴ 7m⁴ 7s] 13,000Y: lengthy, rather angular colt: moderate mover: first foal: dam lightly-raced half-sister to high-class middle-distance colt Electric out of half-sister to very smart Calpurnius: fair performer: won auction event at Haydock in August: best effort when fourth in Doncaster minor event penultimate start: last of 18 in Goffs Million at the Curragh: will be suited by 1m: seems unsuited by soft ground: blinkered on debut and on final start. *F. H. Lee.* 81

KILMARNOCK (USA) 3 b.c. Sagace (FR) 135 – Killapata (USA) (L'Enjoleur (CAN)) [1990 NR 1991 11.8m³ 12f² 10.5g² 10m*] compact colt: has round action: first reported foal: dam minor winner at about 1m in USA: fairly useful form: favourite, won maiden at Redcar in October, running on well having led over 1½f out: will prove at least as effective back over 1½m: sold 34,000 gns Newmarket Autumn Sales. *G. Harwood.* 90

KILMELFORD 2 b.c. (Mar 11) Beldale Flutter (USA) 130 – River Aire 82 (Klairon 131) [1991 6f a6g² a7g² 7m⁴ 7.3m 7m] 3,600Y: compact colt: half-brother to 3-y-o None Go By (by Daring March) and 3 winners, including sprinter Mizuwari (by Blazing Saddles) and Irish middle-distance stayer Boggy Peak (by Shirley Heights): dam placed over 7f and 1m: quite modest maiden: ran moderately in nurseries at Newbury and Newmarket last 2 starts: will be suited by 1m + . *J. A. R. Toller.* 68

KILTROUM (FR) 2 gr.g. (Mar 6) Courtroom (FR) 113 – Kiltie (Habat 127) [1991 5g⁵ 5d 5f 6g 7.5f] 70,000 francs (approx £7,100) Y: sturdy, close-coupled gelding: half-brother to 3 winners in France by R B Chesne, 2 over 1¼m + : dam never ran: sire French 1m and 1¼m winner: poor maiden: easily best effort on debut: visored third start, blinkered final one. *C. Tinkler.* 44

KIMBA 3 ch.f. Noalto 120 – Princess Tavi (Sea Hawk II 131) [1990 NR 1991 10m 10.5d] lengthy, good-topped filly: has a markedly round action: sixth live foal: half-sister to 1981 2-y-o 6f and 7f winner Straeker (by Sharpen Up), 1½m to 18.4f winner Tilly Tavi (by Welsh Pageant) and 7f and 1m winner Vanroy (by Formidable): dam well behind in autumn maiden and seller. *G. M. Moore.* —

KIMBERLEY PARK 3 b.f. Try My Best (USA) 130 – Georgina Park 88 (Silly Season 127) [1990 a6g⁶ 5m⁴ 5d 1991 a8g 7m³ 7g* 7g³ 8m 8.1m⁵ 7s 7m⁴ 7g³ 6.9s²] compact filly: progressive handicapper: won at Doncaster in June: stays 1m: acts on good to firm and soft ground: consistent: bandaged behind first 2 starts: usually held up. *D. W. P. Arbuthnot.* 69

KIMBERS (IRE) 3 b.c. Lomond (USA) 128 – Take Your Mark (USA) (Round Table) [1990 8g 7m* 7.6s4 1991 12.1d* 12g⁵ 14g⁵] lengthy, useful-looking colt: good mover: much improved to win £14,600 event at Chepstow in July by 1½ lengths from Maraakiz, coming from rear to lead final ½f: last of 5 in Goodwood listed races, not discredited when 8 lengths behind Fly Away Soon in moderately-run race on first occasion, some late headway having become detached: stays 1½m. *C. R. Nelson.* 104

KIMTECH 3 ch.c. Pharly (FR) 130 – Kissin' Cousin (Be Friendly 130) [1990 NR 1991 a7g⁵ 8g³ a8g⁶] 9,200F, 31,000GS: compact colt: half-brother to 2 winners by Owen Dudley, including very useful sprinter Coquito's Friend, and a winner in Italy: dam twice-raced sister to very useful sprinter As Friendly: no worthwhile form in summer maidens. *Lord John FitzGerald.* —

KINCHERINCHEE 3 b.f. Dunbeath (USA) 127 – Kaisersage (FR) (Exbury 138)   **47** d
[1990 NR 1991 7g 9.7m 9.7s] 4,000Y: lengthy filly: poor mover: second live foal: dam
won in Germany: no form in maiden (trained by J. Sutcliffe) and sellers. *R. P. C.
Hoad.*

KINDLY LADY 3 b.f. Kind of Hush 118 – Welcome Honey 70 (Be Friendly 130)   —
[1990 5.3f⁶ 5m 5f⁴ 5g a6g a8g 1991 8.3m a10g 10.3m 11.9g] leggy, rather sparely-
made filly: has a round action: of little account: sold 1,000 gns Ascot November
Sales. *C. J. Hill.*

KIND OF LUCK 2 gr.c. (Jan 27) Kind of Hush 118 – Fille de Bourbon 71 (Ile de   —
Bourbon (USA) 133) [1991 a7g] plain, good-topped colt: fourth foal: brother to
3-y-o 15f seller winner Anderson Rose and half-brother to a winner in Italy by
Carwhite: dam placed over 7f and 1m: slow-starting eighth of 10 in maiden at
Southwell in July: hurt himself in stalls there following month and was later
destroyed. *G. A. Pritchard-Gordon.*

KIND OF MAGIC 6 b.g. Record Token 128 – Gay Twenties 70 (Lord Gayle   —
(USA) 124) [1990 NR 1991 a13g] leggy, sparely-made gelding: lightly raced and poor
maiden: visored and tailed off only run in 1991: sold 2,000 gns Ascot July Sales. *A. P.
Jones.*

KIND OF USEFUL 5 b.g. Kind of Hush 118 – Klaire 85 (Klairon 131) [1990 NR   —
1991 10.6g 7.1d] workmanlike gelding: lightly-raced plater: tailed off in 1991, first
runs on flat since 2 yrs: should stay 1m: visored final start. *P. D. Evans.*

KINDRED CAMEO 2 ch.f. (Feb 28) Risk Me (FR) 127 – First Experience 58   —
(Le Johnstan 123) [1991 5d] 25,000Y: compact filly: second foal: dam 5f winner, is
sister to smart 1982 2-y-o 5f winner Cat O'Nine Tails: in need of race, not knocked
about in maiden at Salisbury in June: seemed sure to improve. *G. Lewis.*

KIND STYLE (IRE) 3 ch.c. Doulab (USA) 115 – Dankalia (Le Levanstell 122)   —
[1990 5f³ 5m 5g 6g 6g³ 6g 8f² 8m 8d a8g a8g⁵ a8g³ 1991 a8g² a8g³ 8m 9m 8d 10g
10.8m 11.7f⁴] compact colt: moderate walker and mover: plating-class maiden:
generally disappointing after reappearance: stays 1m: acts on firm going: withdrawn
lame final appearance: difficult ride and not one to be interested in. *R. Hollinshead.*

KINEMATIC (USA) 3 b.c. Sovereign Dancer (USA) – Kinema (USA)   **91** +
(Graustark) [1990 NR 1991 8.1m*] good-topped, rather angular colt: has a long,
rather round stride: first foal: dam winner at 1m in USA, is half-sister to dam of
Shareef Dancer: won 7-runner maiden at Haydock in July by 3 lengths from Rahif,
leading inside final 1f and running on well: should stay 1¼m. *J. H. M. Gosden.*

KING ATHELSTAN (USA) 3 b.c. Sovereign Dancer (USA) – Wimbledon Star **101** p
(USA) (Hoist The Flag (USA)) [1990 NR 1991 8m⁴ 10.4m* 9g²] $250,000Y: lengthy,
good-topped colt with scope: fourth reported foal: closely related to French 1m
winner Line Call (by The Minstrel): dam minor winner in USA, is daughter of Chris
Evert, grandam of Chief's Crown: favourite, won maiden at York by 5 lengths,
making most: evens, ½-length second of 4 to Lilian Bayliss (rec 13 lb) in £7,000
contest at Newmarket later in October: will stay 1½m: may well prove capable of
better. *J. H. M. Gosden.*

KINGCHIP BOY 2 b.g. (Mar 14) Petong 126 – Silk St James (Pas de Seul 133)   **59**
[1991 5.3m 6s 6m a6g a7g a8g*] compact gelding: first reported foal: dam unraced:
20/1-winner (by a head) of late-year claimer at Lingfield: evidently suited by 1m:
blinkered third outing, visored fourth. *M. J. Ryan.*

KING CRACKER 4 ch.c. King of Clubs 124 – Brenda (Sovereign Path 125) [1990   —
9m⁴ 8m⁶ 10f⁵ 10f 15m³ 19m 8g 8g] leggy, close-coupled colt: has quick action: poor
maiden: soundly beaten in first half of 1991: probably stays 15f: didn't look keen once
(sweating) at 3 yrs: sold 1,600 gns Doncaster Spring Sales. *M. D. Hammond.*

KINGDOM OF SPAIN (USA) 2 b.c. (Apr 28) El Gran Senor (USA) 136 –   **85** p
Mystical River (USA) (Riverman (USA) 131) [1991 8m* 8d⁵] IR 180,000Y: strong,
good-bodied colt: first foal: dam ran twice: won 19-runner maiden at Doncaster, slow
start, leading after 2f, quickening 2f out and running on strongly: heavily backed
again, but very much on toes, soundly-beaten fifth of 6 in listed race at Ascot later in
autumn, losing position home bend and dropping away quickly: may be unsuited by
dead ground: may well stay 1¼m: worth another chance. *H. R. A. Cecil.*

KING DUNCAN 4 b.g. Claude Monet (USA) 121 – Gipsy Scott 87 (Sky Gipsy   **54** d
117) [1990 NR 1991 a6g² a6g 6d⁶ a5g 5m 8.9m 8f⁵] tall, workmanlike gelding: sixth
foal: half-brother to a winner in Scandinavia: dam 2-y-o 5f winner: poor maiden:
gives impression will prove ideally suited by 7f: acts on firm ground: twice below
form when blinkered, once when visored (wandered noticeably). *Mrs N. Macauley.*

KING FERDINAND 4 b.c. King of Spain 121 – Gundi 57 (Mummy's Pet 125)   **68**
[1990 7g 1991 a8g² 8d 7m* a7g³] workmanlike colt: moderate mover: very lightly-raced handicapper: won at Salisbury in May: best efforts at 7f: acts on good to firm ground: sold to join D. R. Tucker's stable 2,000 gns Newmarket Autumn Sales. *D. R. Tucker.*

KINGLOW (USA) 2 b.c. (Mar 9) Sovereign Dancer (USA) – Sconce (USA)   **78 p**
(Majestic Light (USA)) [1991 7m⁵ 7m*] $100,000Y: quite attractive colt: fourth reported foal: half-brother to 3-y-o 1½m winner Insconce (by Alleged): dam maiden winner at around 1m at 3 yrs in USA is sister to Grade 2 middle-distance turf performer Lucence: favourite following highly promising debut, won 8-runner maiden at Newcastle in October, leading at halfway and staying on well: will be suited by middle distances: will improve again. *Mrs J. Cecil.*

KING MARCOS (USA) 4 b.c. His Majesty (USA) – Spanish Fake (USA) (Sham   **—**
(USA)) [1990 11.5m² 1991 11.8g⁶ 12.3d 10m] quite modest form at best: looked sort to prove best short of 1½m when conditions were testing: wore tongue strap on debut: dead. *K. A. Morgan.*

KING OF CHANCE (IRE) 3 b.g. Indian King (USA) 128 – Midnight Chance   **74**
(Run The Gantlet (USA)) [1990 NR 1991 6g 7.5g 7g⁶ 8m⁶ 10.1m³ 10.3m⁶ 8m* 8m² 8m² 8m²] IR 3,600Y, resold 15,000Y: angular, good-topped gelding: tends to be unimpressive in coat: third foal: dam lightly raced: modest handicapper: won at Pontefract in September: ran very well afterwards: should be suited by return to 1¼m: acts on good to firm ground: sold 27,000 gns Newmarket Autumn Sales. *Mrs J. R. Ramsden.*

KING OF NORMANDY (IRE) 2 ch.c. (Apr 30) King of Clubs 124 – Miss   **57**
Deauville (Sovereign Path 125) [1991 5g 6d² 7d 8.1m⁵ 8m 6g 7.1s] leggy, workmanlike colt: half-brother to a winner in Italy by Mummy's Pet: dam twice-raced sister to very useful 6f to 1m winner Miss Paris: plating-class maiden: ran moderately last 2 outings: should stay 1m: acts on dead ground. *R. Hannon.*

KING OF REDS 2 b.c. (May 1) Another Realm 118 – Red Sanders 71 (Red Alert   **—**
127) [1991 6m] sturdy colt: fifth reported foal: half-brother to a winner in Austria by Carwhite: dam raced only at 2 yrs, placed over 5f: 33/1, last of 27 in seller at Newmarket in October. *B. J. McMath.*

KING OF SHANNON 2 br.c. (Apr 26) Town And Country 124 – Bonny Music   **—**
(Music Boy 124) [1991 7.1m 6m] 2,100Y: workmanlike colt: second reported foal: half-brother to 1988 2-y-o 5f winner Merry Mannequin (by Latest Model): dam ran 3 times on flat and of little account over hurdles: well beaten in maiden auction (ridden by 7-lb claimer) at Chepstow and seller at Newmarket in autumn. *C. A. Horgan.*

KING OLAF (IRE) 2 b.g. (Feb 15) Thatching 131 – Regiura (High Top 131) [1991   **89 p**
6m²] good-topped gelding: has scope: first foal: dam never ran: 11/1 from 6/1 and green, short-head second of 14 to Yousefia in maiden at Newmarket in October, rallying gamely: moved poorly to post: will stay 7f: sure to improve and win a similar event at least. *P. W. Chapple-Hyam.*

KING OPTIMIST 2 ch.c. (Apr 27) King Persian 107 – Misoptimist 111   **45**
(Blakeney 126) [1991 5d⁵ 5g⁵ 6m⁴ 6m⁶ a6g⁶ 7m⁵ 7.5f 7f 7.5f 6m 10m] tall colt: half-brother to 4-y-o 7f winner Hard Sell (by Hard Fought) and to 3 winners abroad: dam won over 6f and 1¼m: modest plater: seems to stay 1¼m: has run creditably in blinkers: ran very wide bend at Southwell: has twice given trouble stalls. *A. Smith.*

KING PHILIP 4 b.c. King of Spain 121 – Midnight Music (Midsummer Night II   **—**
117) [1990 6g 5g⁵ 5g a6g a8g 6g 6g 5m 1991 7m 9m4] stocky colt: good walker: moderate mover: poor maiden at best: stays 6f: acts on soft going: has been tried blinkered. *Denys Smith.*

KINGSDOWN EVENT 2 b.g. (Apr 27) Superlative 118 – Loma Breeze 64   **—**
(Cure The Blues (USA)) [1991 6f⁶ 7.1s 6g 6g] 7,000F, 4,500Y: strong gelding: has scope: first foal: dam, maiden, stayed 1m, also showed ability over jumps: seems of little account. *R. Hannon.*

KING'S GUEST (IRE) 2 b.g. (Apr 7) Tender King 123 – Saintly Guest (What A   **44**
Guest 119) [1991 6d a6g 7m⁵ 7m 7d] 5,000Y: good-bodied gelding: first foal: dam lightly raced in France from family of Sandford Lad: poor maiden: will stay 1m: has form on firm and dead ground. *G. A. Pritchard-Gordon.*

KINGSLEY 4 b.f. Kings Lake (USA) 133 – Bushti Music 63 (Bustino 136) [1990 8f   **60**
12s² 12f² 12g² 13g² 12.4f⁶ a14g⁵ 12g 10d⁵ 12.5g² 12m* 1991 12.3f 12g³ 13.8f* 14.1m* 16.2f* 16.9m] leggy, sparely-made filly: quite modest performer: wide-margin winner in sellers at Catterick (no bid) in July and Nottingham (sold out of M.

Johnston's stable 7,200 gns) in August and claimer at Beverley in August: ran lack-lustre race final start: suited by 1¾m to 2m: probably acts on any going: goes well with forcing tactics: good mount for inexperienced rider. *Miss S. J. Wilton.*

KING'S LOCH (IRE) 2 b.c. (Mar 7) Salmon Leap (USA) 131 – Regal Beauty **104** p (USA) (Princely Native (USA)) [1991 8.2f* 8.1m* 8d² 8g⁶] 52,000F, 780,000 francs (approx £78,000) Y: big, good-bodied, attractive colt: has plenty of scope: moderate walker and mover: second foal: half-brother to high-class 1988 2-y-o 6f to 1m winner High Estate (by Shirley Heights): dam ran twice: progressed into useful performer: made all in large-field maiden at Nottingham and moderately-run minor event at Sandown in September: staying-on runner-up in listed race at Ascot then one-paced sixth of 8 to Seattle Rhyme in Racing Post Trophy at Doncaster in October: will be well suited by 1¼m+. *H. R. A. Cecil.*

KING'S MOVE 2 b.c. (Apr 10) King of Clubs 124 – Naturally Fresh 91 (Thatching **62** p 131) [1991 7m⁵] second foal: half-brother to a winner in Sweden: dam 2-y-o 5f winner out of half-sister to smart Romper: 16/1, faded final furlong in 9-runner maiden at Lingfield in October: should improve. *J. M. P. Eustace.*

KING'S SHILLING (USA) 4 b.g. Fit To Fight (USA) – Pride's Crossing (USA) — (Riva Ridge (USA)) [1990 8.5m* 10g 10.2f² 10d 9g⁵ 9m 8h⁵ 8m 7m 7.6d⁵ 8m 1991 a10g⁶] leggy, sparely-made gelding: modest handicapper at 3 yrs: ran moderately only start in 1991 (January): stays 1¼m: acts on any going: seems suited by forcing tactics: inconsistent. *Mrs S. Oliver.*

KING'S TREASURE (USA) 2 b.c. (Feb 21) King of Clubs 124 – Crown **55** p Treasure (USA) (Graustark) [1991 8g⁶] closely related to several winners, including Diamond Shoal and Glint of Gold (both by Mill Reef) and half-brother to useful stayer Crystal Spirit and 3-y-o 8.1f winner Crystal Ring (both by Kris): dam very useful at 2 yrs in USA when winner at 5f: backed at long odds, 9 lengths sixth of 14 to Sword Master in maiden at Bath in October: should improve, particularly over middle distances. *I. A. Balding.*

KING TREVISIO 5 b.g. King of Spain 121 – Gundi 57 (Mummy's Pet 125) [1990 6g 6g⁶ 8.2g⁴ 6m³ a8g² 8.2m 6d 1991 a12g] workmanlike gelding: poor mover: bad maiden: stays 1m. *J. L. Harris.*

KING VICTOR (IRE) 3 br.g. Tender King 123 – Wyn Mipet (Welsh Saint 126) **46** [1990 5d 6m 8.2g 6m 1991 7m⁶ 6f 5m 5m a6g² 5m² 5g 5f 5.1g a5g⁵ 5.1m³ a5g⁴ 6f 5h⁴] leggy, sparely-made gelding: has a round action: plating-class maiden: stays 6f: acts on firm ground, and Southwell fibresand: blinkered fifth to tenth starts. *R. O'Leary.*

KING WILLIAM 6 b.g. Dara Monarch 128 – Norman Delight (USA) (Val de **34** + L'Orne (FR) 130) [1990 12m⁴ 12f* 12f³ 12.2m 12g 12m³ 12g⁴ 12m 12f³ 12g⁵ a12g 1991 12g 12f 12m 16.2d³ 16.2f*] robust gelding: moderate mover: carries condition: poor handicapper nowadays: won at Beverley (amateurs) in August: stays 2m: acts on firm and dead ground (ran badly on soft): inconsistent. *J. L. Spearing.*

KINLACEY 4 b.f. Aragon 118 – Mimika 85 (Lorenzaccio 130) [1990 7g 6f² 7m* **66** 8f⁵ 8f⁴ 7d³ 1991 8.5g 9m 8m⁴ 7.5g² 8d 8.2g² 7.1s 6f³ 7m 10.5g 8m 9g 7d a7g² a8g a7g] lengthy, workmanlike filly: good walker: has a long stride: quite modest handicapper: ideally suited by 7f/1m: needs a sound surface: has run well for apprentice. *B. A. McMahon.*

KINLET VISION (IRE) 3 b.f. Vision (USA) – Verandah (Jaazeiro (USA) 127) **41** [1990 5m³ 5m² 5.3h* 6m⁶ 6g⁴ 6m* 6g⁵ 6d 1991 5s⁴ 6m 6d⁴ 7m 6f a6g] leggy filly: plating-class performer: should stay 7f (race needed when tried over trip): best on top-of-the-ground: visored final start: winning hurdler for K. Oliver. *J. Berry.*

KINO 4 b.g. Niniski (USA) 125 – Relkina (FR) 85 (Relkino 131) [1990 10g 12d 12m⁴ — 14m³ 16.2f 16.1m⁶ 1991 12.5g] leggy, unfurnished gelding: quite modest maiden at 3 yrs: little show only run on flat in 1991: seems suited by 1¾m: best efforts on good to firm ground: has run well when sweating: winning hurdler. *S. E. Sherwood.*

KINOKO 3 ch.g. Bairn (USA) 126 – Octavia (Sallust 134) [1990 5m² 6g² 6m² 6s⁴ **52** § 7m 6d⁴ a7g⁴ 1991 a8g³ a8g a8g² a8g² 8d³ 10d² 11m³ a11g 10.2g²] lengthy gelding: fair plater: stays 11f: acts on good to firm and dead going: usually troublesome in preliminaries: has seemed reluctant and temperamental, one to treat with caution. *R. Hollinshead.*

KINTARO 3 b.c. Glint of Gold 128 – Tzarina (USA) (Gallant Romeo (USA)) [1990 **65** § 7d 1991 12f² 10g 14f⁶] leggy, angular colt: quite modest form: reluctant second in maiden auction at Beverley in May: stays 1½m: acts on firm going: blinkered (sweating) first and third starts: unruly in preliminaries and virtually refused to race on second: winning hurdler in August: sold 1,700 gns Ascot November Sales: must be avoided. *D. J. G. Murray-Smith.*

KIPINI 2 b.f. (Apr 9) Roaring Riva 103 – Kivulini (Hotfoot 126) [1991 5g⁴ 6m a5g⁴ **43**
6g 6g] 640Y: unfurnished filly: fourth reported foal: dam unraced: poor maiden:
stays 6f. *W. J. Musson.*

KIRBY OPPORTUNITY 3 ch.f. Mummy's Game 120 – Empress Catherine 73 **57**
(Welsh Pageant 132) [1990 5m 5g⁴ 6g⁴ 6g³ 6g 7f 6m 5m 6m 1991 6g³ 6f⁵ 7g⁶ 7g* 7g³
7d 8m² 7f² 8g² 10.8g 8.2m 7s a8g³ a12g* a12g²] leggy filly: has a high knee action:
plater: successful at Brighton (no bid) in July and in claimer at Southwell in
December: stays 1½m: best turf efforts on a sound surface, and acts on firm going:
blinkered twice: sometimes sweating, and on toes. *J. Pearce.*

KIRBY'S BEST 4 ch.f. Sayf El Arab (USA) 127 – Betty's Bid (Auction Ring **—**
(USA) 123) [1990 6m 6g 5g 6g³ 7f 7m 7m 7f 6d a7g 1991 7m 7m 8m 8f] small filly: has
a markedly round action: plater: probably stays 7f: has been tried blinkered: sold
1,000 gns Newmarket September Sales. *G. Blum.*

KIR (IRE) 3 ch.g. M Double M (USA) – Wolver Rose (Wolver Hollow 126) [1990 **64**
7m 8m 1991 a8g² 9m⁵ a10g a12g] workmanlike gelding: modest maiden: best effort
second of 10 at Southwell in August, losing prominent position on home turn then
running on strongly: stays 1m well: blinkered final start: winning hurdler. *M.
McCormack.*

KIRKBY BELLE 2 b.f. (May 4) Bay Express 132 – Kirkby 85 (Midsummer **46**
Night II 117) [1991 5m 5g³ 6g² 7m] 6,800Y: leggy, rather angular filly: moderate
walker: sister to 7f winner Train of Thought and half-sister to several other
winners, including 6f to 10.6f winner Majority Holding (by Mandrake Major): dam
won twice over 1¼m: plating-class maiden: staying-on second of 11 in auction event
at Catterick: better suited by 6f than 5f: not seen out after July. *E. Weymes.*

KIRRIEMUIR 3 b.f. Lochnager 132 – Maxine's Here 52 (Copte (FR)) [1990 5m*
5f³ 6m³ 6f⁴ 6m a8g 1991 7d] strong, close-coupled, workmanlike filly: soundly
beaten in varied events since debut, in need of race in seller only start in 1991:
should stay beyond 5f. *R. J. Hodges.*

KIRSTEN 2 b.f. (May 1) Kris 135 – Sushila (Petingo 135) [1991 7m³] compact filly: **77** p
eighth foal: half-sister to several winners, including top-class middle-distance
performer Petoski (by Niniski) and 1990 2-y-o 5f and 7f winner Shimmering Sea (by
Slip Anchor): dam, winner twice at around 1m in France, is out of sister to Val de
Loir: 8/1, backward and green, 6½ lengths third of 5 to Shuailaan in Houghton
Stakes at Newmarket in October, outpaced running down into Dip then staying on
again: went keenly to post showing round action: sure to improve, particularly over
1m +. *W. Jarvis.*

KISKA (USA) 3 ch.f. Bering 136 – Hortensia (FR) 119 (Luthier 126) [1990 8g² **78**
1991 11.7m³ 11m* 12f² 12.3f³ 14f² 13.9g² 17.5m⁶ a12g] big, leggy, sparely-made filly:
fair handicapper: won at Edinburgh (maiden) in June: one paced, and should stay
beyond 1¾m: acts on firm going (ran fairly well on equitrack): bandaged behind first
3 starts. *B. W. Hills.*

KISSAVOS 5 ch.h. Cure The Blues (USA) – Hairbrush (USA) (Sir Gaylord) [1990 **61**
6g 5m 5m 6f a6g² a7g³ a8g⁴ 6m⁵ 6m² a6g a7g⁴ a6g⁶ 1991 8d 6m 5.1m* 7m³ 6.1d⁴
7.6d⁴ 7d⁵ 5.1d² a6g⁵ a7g* a7g²] small, angular horse: quite modest handicapper:
won at Chepstow (selling event, bought in 4,000 gns) in May and at Lingfield in
December: effective at 5f to 1m: acts on good to firm and heavy going: blinkered or
visored: sold out of M. Pipe's stable 1,800 gns Newmarket Autumn Sales after
eighth start. *C. C. Elsey.*

KISS ME LAUREL (IRE) 2 b.f. (Mar 31) Heraldiste (USA) 121 – Fizzy (Gala **35**
Performance (USA)) [1991 6g 5d⁵ 5g⁴ 6f 5g⁵ 6m] 9,000F, 3,000Y: angular, rather
leggy filly: half-sister to 3 winners, including 1977 2-y-o 5f winner Beloved Mistress
(by Rarity), later the dam of Hallgate, and useful sprinter Petrovich (by Malin-
oski): dam unraced daughter of very speedy Thyra Lee: poor maiden: better form at
5f than 6f: sold 650 gns Doncaster October Sales. *Mrs G. R. Reveley.*

KISS THE DEALER 2 b.f. (Feb 9) Midyan (USA) 124 – Double Shuffle 103 **34**
(Tachypous 128) [1991 5g 6d 6g 7f⁶ a6g⁶ a7g] 6,200F, 11,000Y: fourth
foal: half-sister to 3-y-o Card Trick (by Good Times): dam 1½m winner: poor plater:
best effort at 7f on firm ground: sweating profusely (showed little) penultimate
outing. *M. W. Easterby.*

KISU KALI 4 ch.g. Kris 135 – Evita 111 (Reform 132) [1990 10.2f² 10f³ 10d⁴ 9m² **—**
12m⁴ 1991 11.5g 7m 7f] big, angular gelding: has a markedly round action: trained by
H. Cecil, modest maiden at 3 yrs: little sign of ability over hurdles or in handicaps on
flat in 1991: stays 1½m: acts on firm ground, seems unsuited by dead: has hung:

trained by C. Brooks, twice pulled up over hurdles: sold 3,600 gns Ascot Summer Sales. *J. Ffitch-Heyes.*

KITWOOD (USA) 2 b.c. (May 12) Nureyev (USA) 131 – Kittywake (USA) (Sea Bird II 145) [1991 7.5d*] half-brother to several winners, including top-class filly Miss Oceana (by Alydar), successful in 6 Grade 1 events, and Larida (by Northern Dancer), good-class winner at up to 9f and later dam of Coronation Stakes winner Magic of Life: dam, high-class winner of 18 races at up to 9f, from very good family: successful in newcomers event at Saint-Cloud in October: will stay 1m: should improve. *A. Fabre, France.*   **?**

KIVETON KABOOZ 3 b.c. Rousillon (USA) 133 – Sea Chant (Julio Mariner 127) [1990 NR 1991 8m⁴ 10g* 12d⁴ 10.6g³ 11.9g³ 12s 12m* 12d²] 18,000F, 52,000Y: good-topped, useful-looking colt: fourth foal: half-brother to 1988 2-y-o 7.5f and 8.5f seller winner Pansong (by Absalom): dam unraced daughter of half-sister to dam of Pitcairn: fairly useful form: won maiden at Salisbury in May and handicap (led final strides) at Newmarket in October: good second in Newmarket handicap final start despite hanging badly left: stays 1½m: acts on good to firm ground and dead: pulled hard sixth start: soon comes off bridle, and not an easy ride. *L. M. Cumani.*   **90**

KIVETON KOMET 4 ch.f. Precocious 126 – Beaufort Star 95 (Great Nephew 126) [1990 NR 1991 5f* 5g⁵ 6f² 6g 5m 5.9f* 6m² 5f⁶ 6f 5m⁴ 5m 6m 6g a6g] leggy filly: quite modest handicapper: won at Beverley (maiden) in May and Carlisle in July: stays 6f: best efforts on top-of-the-ground: sometimes bandaged. *M. Johnston.*   **66**

KIYONAGA 3 gr.g. Kalaglow 132 – Creake 80 (Derring-Do 131) [1990 NR 1991 10g² 14m*] 13,000Y: lengthy, unfurnished gelding: half-brother to 1m winner Affaire de Coeur (by Imperial Fling) and 2 winners in Ireland, including 6f and 7f winner Creake's Pet (by Mummy's Pet): dam 1½m winner from 3 starts, out of half-sister to Blakeney and Morston: 7/2 on, won 5-runner maiden at Newmarket in May in workmanlike style: second to Cruachan in similar event at Leicester: stays 1¾m: gelded after final start. *H. R. A. Cecil.*   **99 +**

KLAIROVER 4 b.f. Smackover 107 – Klairove 74 (Averof 123) [1990 8m 5.8f 5.8m⁵ 1991 5.1m² 6g 5.1g⁵ 6.1s 5f⁴ 6m] big, workmanlike filly: poor mover: plating-class handicapper: will stay at least 6f: seems suited by top-of-the-ground. *C. J. Hill.*   **49**

KLASSY BRIEFCASE (USA) 6 ch.m. Medieval Man (USA) – Leather Gallery (USA) (The Pruner (USA)) [1990 5f⁴ 5f* 5f² 6f 5f* 5d* 5f* 5f* 6f⁵ 8f² 1991 5f* 5f⁵ 5h* 5f* 5f* 5g] strong, robust, lengthy mare: fourth foal: half-sister to a couple of minor winners in USA: dam minor winner at up to 7f: a leading U.S. sprinter on turf, winner of 18 of her races there and over $360,000: gained last 3 successes in allowance races at Monmouth Park in summer, reportedly recording American track record for 5f on turf when winning by 7½ lengths third start: 9/1 and bandaged, last of 9 in Keeneland Nunthorpe Stakes at York, wandering under pressure after leading for 2f: goes very well on top-of-the-ground: reportedly tore tendon in near fore and retired. *Philip M. Serpe, USA.*   **?**

KNIFEBOARD 5 b.h. Kris 135 – Catalpa 115 (Reform 132) [1990 NR 1991 14g 16.2g] big, round-barrelled horse: has a round action: trained by H. Cecil, useful performer at 3 yrs: tailed off in handicaps in 1991, first runs on flat since: stays 15f, and should stay very well: acts on firm ground. *T. B. Hallett.*   **—**

KNIFEBOX (USA) 3 b.c. Diesis 133 – Matoki (USA) (Hail To Reason) [1990 6g² 7m⁴ 7s* 10.2s* 8v 1991 10.4d⁶ 10g 8.9g 10.3m³ 10d 10.3d* 10.3d* 10s* 10.5v⁵] sparely-made colt: has a powerful, round action: useful performer: inconsistent in handicaps, winning in good style at Chester in October: made most to win minor event at Doncaster and listed race at Marseilles (by 3½ lengths from Muroto) following month: stays 1¼m well: goes very well on a soft surface: wore crossed noseband and tongue tied down second outing: sweating fourth and fifth starts. *J. H. M. Gosden.*   **106**

KNIGHT OF HONOUR 3 ch.g. Touching Wood (USA) 127 – Nobly Born (USA) (The Minstrel (CAN) 135) [1990 NR 1991 14g³ 16g⁴ᵈⁱˢ 14.8f⁴ 16.1m² 19m⁶] sturdy, quite attractive gelding: has rather round action: second foal: dam once-raced sister to Free Handicap winner and French 2000 Guineas second Noble Minstrel: quite modest maiden: blinkered, ran poorly in handicap final start: stays 2m: sold to join M. Dods 5,400 gns Newmarket Autumn Sales and gelded. *I. A. Balding.*   **61**

KNIGHT OF MERCY 5 b.g. Aragon 118 – Little Mercy 90 (No Mercy 126) [1990 8g 6m⁴ 6m³ 7g⁴ 7m* 6d* 6m* 6d 7m⁶ 6d⁵ 6s³ 1991 6m 6g⁴ 6g⁴ 6g 6g 7.3m* 7d 7m⁴] strong, good-bodied gelding: carries condition: useful handicapper: won at   **103**

Newbury in September: ran well when fourth in Group 3 Prix de Meautry at Deauville third start: stays 7.3f: acts on any going except possibly heavy: slowly away in blinkers: tough. *R. Hannon.*

KNIGHT'S SPUR (USA)   4 b.g. Diesis 133 – Avoid (USA) (Buckpasser) [1990   **63** d
NR 1991 a8g³ 7f⁵ 7f² 10.1g 8.5m 8m] tall, lengthy, quite attractive gelding: half-brother to Irish 1m winner Avoid The Step (by Go Step) and 2 winners in USA: dam unraced half-sister to graded winner Doodle: lightly-raced plating-class maiden at best: stays 1m: acts on firm ground. *J. Webber.*

KNOCK KNOCK   6 ch.g. Tap On Wood 130 – Ruby River (Red God 128§) [1990   **89**
10.2f9g 10.8f² 8h⁶ 9g³ 8g* 10f* 8m³ 10h⁴ 10g³ 9m⁴ 10.6d 10m³ 1991 10g 10g 10.1g* 8m² 11.9m⁴ 9v⁴ 9m* 8.5f² 10m² 10f* 9m] good-quartered gelding: fair handicapper: won at Windsor in May, Kempton in July and Salisbury in September: effective at 1m to 1½m: suited by a sound surface: best without blinkers or visor: has found little, and ideally suited by good gallop, waiting tactics and tender handling: good mount for inexperienced rider: winning hurdler. *I. A. Balding.*

KOLINSKY   5 ch.g. Dunbeath (USA) 127 – Kolomelskoy Palace 77 (Royal Palace   —
131) [1990 10m 12g³ 12g⁵ 12f² 12m 12g² 11f²a12g²a12g²a11g⁶a12g³ 10.2m 10.6sa11g a12g⁴ a14g³ a14g⁴ 1991 a14g⁶] tall, leggy, good-topped gelding: carries condition: moderate mover: poor handicapper: not seen out after February: stays 1½m: acts on firm going: tried blinkered and visored: goes well with forcing tactics: none too keen. *M. C. Chapman.*

KOMOMBO (IRE)   3 b.c. Sadler's Wells (USA) 132 – Gertrude Lawrence   **97**
(Ballymore 123) [1990 6m 1991 10f² 10.2f* 10.6g² 10g] sturdy, close-coupled colt: won maiden at Bath in May: beaten head in amateurs handicap next start, long way in £53,300 handicap at Sandown in July: will stay 1½m: sold only 5,400 gns Newmarket Autumn Sales. *G. Harwood.*

KONIG   5 ch.h. Jalmood (USA) 126 – Spring Lane 85 (Forlorn River 124) [1990 NR   —
1991 11.5g] leggy, rather angular horse: blind in off-side eye: moderate mover: rated 81 when winning claimers at 3 yrs: always behind in handicap in July, only run on flat since: stays 1½m: acts on any going: sometimes hangs left: has worn eyeshield: sold 560 gns Ascot October Sales. *Dr J. D. Scargill.*

KOOYONGA (IRE)   3 ch.f. Persian Bold 123 – Anjuli (Northfields (USA))   **123**
[1990 7m* 7g* 7d² 7d* 1991 7g* 8g² 8m* 8g* 8m* 8d² 8g]
The Coronation Stakes was one of the highlights of Royal Ascot. Nothing less had been anticipated once it became known that the winners of the One Thousand Guineas and its equivalents in Ireland, France and Italy would be in opposition; and the race developed into a tremendous battle between two of them, Kooyonga and Shadayid, once the Musidora winner Gussy Marlowe's attempt to shake off the field going into the home turn had failed. Always handy, Kooyonga was driven ahead two furlongs out. She went a length up on Shadayid and, though pressed hard all the way to the line, she kept on finding more and more under very strong handling to stay in front by three quarters of a length. Close enough if good enough on the turn, the Pouliches winner Danseuse du Soir finished fourth, pipped by Gussy Marlowe, while the Italian filly Arranvanna finished a respectable sixth of eight.

Goffs Irish One Thousand Guineas, the Curragh—Kooyonga has the race sewn up, having found a run on the rails as Umniyatee (striped cap) tired

Kooyonga, of course, was representing the Goffs Irish One Thousand Guineas form in the Coronation Stakes, having been beaten two lengths by Shadayid at Newmarket. The pair met again in the Queen Elizabeth II Stakes at Ascot in September where both ran very well to be placed, Kooyonga just in front, and again in the Breeders' Cup Mile at Churchill Downs in November where Kooyonga ran the first moderate race of her life. But more of that later. Let's begin at the beginning of this outstandingly game and consistent filly's career. She made her first appearance as a two-year-old in a maiden race at Gowran Park in August, won it, and by the time she was retired to winter quarters had also won a listed race at Phoenix Park and the Group 3 Leopardstown Stakes. She had four lengths to spare in the last-named and was obviously useful, an assessment backed up by her only defeat, her length-and-a-half second to Rinka Das in the Cartier Million. At that stage she was owned by M. C. Throsby who'd bought her for IR 82,000 guineas as a yearling at the Million Sale, and she remained in his ownership until she'd caught Japanese attention by running second in the General Accident One Thousand Guineas. Kooyonga lined up at Newmarket as something of a dark horse with the attraction of being in form and ridden by Piggott, having added the Leopardstown One Thousand Guineas Trial to her tally twelve days previously, and she was backed down from 25/1 to 14/1. In the race she was ridden to cover Shadayid's every move and was upsides going into the Dip, but she had to be pushed along from that point and couldn't hold the winner in the closing stages.

Piggott's post-race opinion that '. . . nine times out of ten she would have won the Guineas . . .', meaning, presumably, that she would have won nine out of ten Guineas, was greeted with some scepticism and would be very difficult to justify now. However, Kooyonga lost no time in consolidating her position among the leading fillies of her own generation in the Irish One Thousand at the Curragh. Piggott switched to the unbeaten Rua d'Oro, his place taken by the previous year's champion Irish apprentice Warren O'Connor who kept the job on merit for the rest of the season. Compared with later races, particularly the two at Ascot, O'Connor enjoyed a fairly undemanding ride. He might have been a shade fortunate to get a clear passage up the rail inside the final quarter of a mile, but once that came the result was not in doubt. Having jumped smartly out of the stalls Kooyonga was able comfortably to track the front-running Umniyatee, and as the latter began to tire and drift left Kooyonga quickened through to lead at the distance and put three lengths between herself and the chasing Julie La Rousse before the post. Rua d'Oro finished fifth of twelve, the American challenger Irish Linnet eighth. Surprisingly, in view of her outstanding claims on form, Kooyonga started only second favourite to Rua d'Oro.

Mitsuo Haga's "Kooyonga"

With Royal Ascot behind her, Kooyonga had a well-earned break until early-September when she warmed up for the Queen Elizabeth II Stakes giving weight away in the Group 3 Matron Stakes at the Curragh. In the circumstances, her length defeat of the Irish One Thousand Guineas fourth Blue Daisy and Rua d'Oro at a 12-lb disadvantage was very encouraging, and she started the 7/2 second favourite behind Second Set at Ascot with Shadayid on 9/1 in the field of nine. Things went differently in the fillies' second meeting over the course, inasmuch as this time Shadayid had the advantage two furlongs out, having been allowed to bowl along with the leaders and sent ahead on the turn. The always-prominent Kooyonga chased Shadayid into the straight, seemingly in vain, but wore her down near the end after Selkirk had come past them both with a wet sail. Kooyonga finished a length and a half second, a neck up on Shadayid who beat the favourite by three lengths for third place. Thus far, Kooyonga had been beaten by only three horses in her life, and had never finished worse than second. A marvellous record that didn't survive beyond the Breeders' Cup Mile, for she beat only one home. She'd probably had enough for the year. Her young rider gave her every assistance, making sure she had a good position in the first six to halfway, but she came under pressure rounding the home turn and, just for once, was unable to find anything more in the straight. Danseuse du Soir, by the way, did best of the European-trained runners; she finished fourth.

Kooyonga is going to be kept in training, it's said, with the Japan Cup as a long-term objective. But she's most unlikely to stay a mile and a half: on breeding and style of racing a mile and a quarter may well be her limit. Three

```
                              ┌Bold Lad        ┌Bold Ruler
               ┌Persian Bold  │(b 1964)        ┤Barn Pride
               │(br 1975)     ┤Relkarunner     ┌Relko
Kooyonga (IRE) │              │(b or br 1968)  ┤Running Blue
   (ch.f. 1988)│              ┌Northfields     ┌Northern Dancer
               │Anjuli        │(ch 1968)       ┤Little Hut
               └(ch 1978)     ┤Katricia        ┌Skymaster
                              │(ch 1968)       ┤Anxious Call
```

of the unraced dam's four previous runners, including the two that won, the useful fillies Hatton Gardens (by Auction Ring) and Jaljuli (by Jalmood), had definite stamina limitations; however, a modest gelding by Tap On Wood out of the mare called Tap Duet stayed a mile and a half. The grandam Katricia was a sprinter, so was her grandam Julie, and Julie's daughter Anxious Call, although she showed nothing on the racecourse, evidently gave the impression to her trainer that she was a sprinter too. Katricia produced the 1978 Two Thousand Guineas winner Roland Gardens to Derring-Do. Another of her foals Nonno, by Wollow, won over a mile and a quarter in Ireland and later at up to a mile and a half in the USA. Kooyonga is a good-topped filly. She's a particularly good walker but shows a markedly round action when galloping. A winner on good to firm going and good to soft, she has yet to encounter extremes. *M. Kauntze, Ireland.*

KORACLE BAY   4 b.f. Kind of Hush 118 – Sea Aura 89 (Roi Soleil 125) [1990 6g   65
6m 7.3m⁵ 7.6g 7f⁵ a8g⁶ a8g 10.6d⁶ 1991 6m⁴ 7m 9m 9m³ 9s³ 10g⁶ 8m³] big, lengthy
filly: moderate mover: quite modest handicapper: will prove better suited by around
1¼m than shorter: acts on good to firm and soft ground: has run poorly when
visored, and at Chester: sold 9,500 gns Newmarket Autumn Sales. *C. F. Wall.*

KORYPHEOS   12 b.g. He Loves Me 120 – Silly Song (Silly Season 127) [1990 NR   59
1991 a7g a7g⁶ 7d² 7g 7m* 7f] leggy, lightly-made gelding: quite modest handicapper: won at Brighton in May: ideally suited by further than 6f and stayed 1m:
acted on any going: bandaged: dead. *S. Dow.*

KOTASHAAN   (FR)   3 b.c. Darshaan 133 – Haute Autorite (USA) 111 116
(Elocutionist (USA)) [1990 8v² 9v* 1991 11g⁵ 10.5d* 10g* 10d³ 10g³ 10d²] first foal:
dam French 7f (at 2 yrs) and 1m winner: smart performer: won maiden at
Maisons-Laffitte in November at 2 yrs then listed race and Prix La Force (by short
neck from Funny Baby) at Longchamp in spring at 3 yrs: placed in Grand Prix de
Paris Louis Vuitton at Longchamp, Prix Guillaume d'Ornano at Deauville and La
Coupe de Maisons-Laffitte (1½ lengths second to Tel Quel): should be better suited
by 1½m: acts on heavy going. *Mme C. Head, France.*

KOVALEVSKIA   6 ch.m. Ardross 134 – Fiordiligi 109 (Tudor Melody 129) [1990   44
a10g⁴ 12f⁵ 12.5m 11.5m 15.5f⁶ 12g 12m 12g* 12d a12g⁴ a10g a10g 1991 a13g⁶ a13g³
a12g⁶ 12g 12g 12f 11.8m] small, sparely-made mare: unreliable handicapper: stays
13f: possibly unsuited by firm going, acts on any other: best ridden up with pace: has
gone well for amateur. *D. A. Wilson.*

KREISCHIM (IRE)   3 b.g. Kreisler – Chimela (Ela-Mana-Mou 132) [1990 5g⁴
6g 6m 6d 6m⁵ 7m⁴ 7g a6g⁴ 7m⁴ 6g⁴ 6d⁵ 6d a7g a5g³ 1991 7d⁴ 7g 8m⁶ 8g 8.3g 6m 5m
5.3f 6m a10g 8g] angular, workmanlike gelding: has a round action: quite modest
maiden at 2 yrs: below best in 1991: will prove suited by sprint distances: apparently
best effort on Southwell fibresand: blinkered once at 2 yrs: carries head high: has
sweated. *M. Madgwick.*

KRISFIELD   6 b. or br.g. Anfield 117 – Kristallina 84 (Homeric 133) [1990 6g⁵ 7m   53
6m 6m⁶ 6s 6s 6d 7d 1991 a7g a7g² 7f² 7.1d² 6g 8g³ 8.3m⁴ 8.3m⁴ a8g a7g] lengthy
gelding: poor mover: plating-class handicapper: off course over 4 months after
eighth outing, and little show on return: stays 1m: acts on any going. *T. P.
McGovern.*

KRISTIANSTAD   2 b.c. (Apr 20) Kris 135 – Our Home 115 (Habitat 134) [1991   93 p
7d²] quite attractive colt: sixth foal: half-brother to French 1m winner Giant's
Castle (by Great Nephew): dam second in 1000 Guineas, is sister to Roussalka and
half-sister to Oh So Sharp: odds on but green, 3 lengths second of 21, clear, to
impressive Berseto in maiden at Doncaster in November, staying on in excellent
fashion from 2f out: will stay 1m: sure to improve, and win races. *Mrs J. Cecil.*

KRISTIS GIRL   4 ch.f. Ballacashtal (CAN) – Fleur d'Amour 85 (Murrayfield 119)   63
[1990 a7g 6m² 5v* 7d² 6m² 7.2s⁶ 5d 5m⁴ 6f⁶ 7.6g 7m 6d 1991 5d 6d 6.1d 6v 6g⁴ a6g²
a6g 7.6m a7g⁵ 6g 6g³ 6.1d 7g⁵ a8g* a7g⁴ a8g⁴] plain, angular filly: moderate mover:

quite modest handicapper nowadays: won at Southwell in November: needs testing conditions at 5f, and stays 1m: has form on good to firm ground, but probably best with give. *D. Haydn Jones.*

KRITSO (USA) 2 b.c. (Feb 3) Dixieland Band (USA) – Overnight (USA) (Mr **100** Leader (USA)) [1991 8v* 8v⁵ 9v²] $40,000Y: first foal: dam won at around 1m at 3 yrs: successful in newcomers race at Saint-Cloud in November: better form same month in Group 3 event (behind Litron) and listed contest at Evry: will stay 1¼m: yet to race on sound surface. *F. Boutin, France.*

KRIUS 3 b.c. Shirley Heights 130 – Meliora 73 (Crowned Prince (USA) 128) [1990 **97** 7s 1991 10m⁶ 14m* 16.2g 14.8m²] tall, good-topped colt: has a fluent, round action: impressively won minor contest at York in May: better subsequent effort (favourite, travelled strongly long way in Queen's Vase at Royal Ascot) when 3½ lengths second of 5 to Jendali in listed race at Newmarket in July, sweating and edgy beforehand then wandering and swishing tail under pressure in race: stays 1¾m well: sold only 7,000 gns Newmarket Autumn Sales, resold 6,400 gns Doncaster November Sales. *W. Jarvis.*

KRONPRINZ (IRE) 3 b.g. Local Suitor (USA) 128 – Kaiserchronik (GER) — (Cortez (GER)) [1990 7g³ 8.2s⁵ a8g 1991 a8g 10g 12.2g⁵] leggy gelding: has a round action: quite modest maiden at 2 yrs: fair fifth of 20 in 3-y-o seller, weakening final 2f: should stay 1¼m: blinkered on reappearance: sold to join C. Trietline 2,900 gns Doncaster May Sales: winning hurdler. *A. P. Stringer.*

KRUSAVITCH 5 ch.m. Sunley Builds 102 – Dipsicato (Music Maestro 119) [1990 — § NR 1991 12.2m] sparely-made, plain mare: plating class at best at 3 yrs (looked temperamental): no show only run in 1991: one to leave alone. *J. L. Spearing.*

KTOLO 5 b.m. Tolomeo 127 – Miss Kate (FR) (Nonoalco (USA) 131) [1990 10m **55** 11.5m 11.7m² 11.7m⁴ 12m⁵ 12d 1991 10g³ 11.8g 11.6m⁶ 10f] leggy mare: has a round action: plating-class handicapper nowadays: stays 1½m: acts on any going: takes keen hold. *R. Akehurst.*

KUMMEL KING 3 b.g. Absalom 128 – Louise 71 (Royal Palace 131) [1990 5f 5g² **57** 5g⁵ 5m⁵ 5f⁴ 5f⁵ 5m⁴ 5m⁶ 7s 1991 6f² 7m³ 6m⁴ 7g⁵ 6g⁴ 7m⁵ 5h⁵ 6m⁶ 8m] compact gelding: plating-class handicapper: stays 7f: acts on firm going: blinkered once at 2 yrs. *Capt. J. Wilson.*

KUWAIT SUNSET (IRE) 3 ch.f. Exhibitioner 111 – Kuwait Night 67 (Morston — (FR) 125) [1990 6g 1991 8f 8.3m 6f 15.4f] leggy filly: tailed off in sellers and handicaps. *M. J. Bolton.*

KWACHA 5 b.h. Reesh 117 – Madame Quickly 80 (Saint Crespin III 132) [1990 — a14g 13g 1991 a14g] rather leggy, workmanlike horse: little sign of ability: tried blinkered once. *T. Craig.*

L

LA BALLERINE 5 b.m. Lafontaine (USA) 117 – Kirsova (Absalom 128) [1990 **39** 8m⁴ 10f 14.8f* 12m³ 10g³ 11.5g⁵ 13g 12m 14f² 14m 13.8d a12g4 1991 a14g 11.5f⁵ 15.4f] good-topped mare: moderate walker: poor handicapper: finds 1¼m on short side and stays 15f: acts on firm going: occasionally sweats: has put head in air: best with strong handling and exaggerated waiting tactics. *C. E. Brittain.*

LA BAMBA 5 br.g. Laxton 105 – Ribamba 82 (Ribocco 129) [1990 7m³ 7m⁴ 8g⁶ **88** 7f² 7m⁶ 7m 7m* 7m⁵ 7g* 7d* 1991 7m 7f⁴ 7m* 7g³ 7g⁶ 7f² 7m* 7m² 7g² 7m 7g³ 7d*] leggy gelding: fair handicapper: won at Redcar in June and August and Doncaster in November: should stay 1m: acts on firm and dead going: usually slowly away: has wandered: has turn of foot, and best held up. *G. A. Pritchard-Gordon.*

LABAS (IRE) 2 b.f. (Apr 8) Dominion 123 – Petrol 73 (Troy 137) [1991 5m 6m² **65** 6g 7m 6g] sturdy filly: has a quick action: fourth foal: half-sister to 3-y-o Jadidh, to 2m winner Dhakrah (both by Touching Wood) and to modest 1m and 9f winner Zammah (by Jalmood), later successful in USA: dam won at 1m and stayed 1¼m: quite modest maiden: ran poorly last 3 starts: should stay 7f: on toes in visor penultimate outing: sold 2,300 gns Doncaster November Sales. *P. T. Walwyn.*

LABEEBA (IRE) 3 ch.f. Thatching 131 – Badiya (USA) (Sir Ivor 135) [1990 6m — 6m³ 8m 1991 7.5f 7g 6d 5m 6.1m] sturdy filly: disappointing plater: should stay beyond 6f. *H. A. T. Whiting.*

LA BELLE VIE 5 b.m. Indian King (USA) 128 – Engage (Whistling Wind 123) **68** [1990 7m⁵ 7f² 6g³ 6m² 7m* 6g 7f⁶ 6m⁴ 6m 6m² 7m³ 6m² 6m⁵ 6m 7g⁵ 8g 7g² 7d

1991 7f² 6d⁵ 8g⁴ 7m³ 7f⁶ 7.1g 8m³ 7m 7s 6.1d* a7g] workmanlike, good-quartered mare: moderate mover: quite modest handicapper: won ladies event at Chepstow in October despite hanging left: effective at 6f to 1m: acts on firm and dead ground: suitable mount for apprentice: goes extremely well at Yarmouth: tough. *J. H. Baker.*

LA BUCA   3 b.f. Giacometti 130 – Sarah Louise 66 (Double-U-Jay 120) [1990 a7g   —
1991 a8g 12.2d 8s] leggy, sparely-made filly: has a round action: looks of little account: blinkered final start: sold 800 gns Doncaster May Sales. *D. Yeoman.*

LABURNUM   3 gr.c. Glint of Gold 128 – Lorelene (FR) 97 (Lorenzaccio 130)   **76** p
[1990 NR 1991 10.4g⁶ 10g* 10d³] big, lengthy, angular colt: has plenty of scope: eighth foal: half-brother to fairly useful 1m winner Ladrone (by High Top), 1½m winner Latvian (by Rousillon) and 1½m winner and hurdler Leon (by Niniski): dam 1¼m to 1½m winner and second in Ebor: not seen out until September: very promising debut at York and easily made all in maiden at Brighton: 7/4 on, disappointing third of 5 in handicap at Redcar: seems to need a 1½m +: seems to need a sound surface: may well be capable of better. *L. M. Cumani.*

LABYRINTH   2 b.f. (Apr 29) Belfort (FR) 89 – La Bleu 67 (Blue Cashmere 129)   **34**
[1991 6m⁶ 6m 7m 7m⁵] lengthy, sparely-made filly: second foal: sister to 3-y-o The Five Sisters: dam won 9f and 1¼m sellers: poor plater: stays 7f: ran creditably for 7-lb claimer final outing: looked ungenuine second start. *J. G. FitzGerald.*

LA CARENE (FR)   3 gr.f. Kenmare (FR) 125 – La Passionaria (Reform 132) **111**
[1990 8v³ 1991 9v* 8d² 8d⁵dis 9g* 8g⁵ 10g*] 410,000 francs (approx £38,000) Y: second foal: sister to useful French 1¼m winner Kenaria: dam unraced: won maiden at Maisons-Laffitte in March, Prix Chloe (by 1½ lengths from Sha Tha) at Evry in July and valuable listed Piaget d'Or at Deauville: behind Danseuse du Soir in Prix de la Grotte and Poule d'Essai des Pouliches (disqualified for interference) at Long-champ second and third starts: stays 1¼m: acts on heavy going. *P. Bary, France.*

LA CASSONADE   3 b.f. Sulaafah 119 – My Sweet Melody 62 (Music Boy   —
124) [1990 6g 6m a6g 1991 5g 5g a5g⁵ 5m 6g] smallish, good-quartered filly: plating-class form at 2 yrs: never dangerous in 1991: will prove suited by at least 6f: sometimes sweating: sold 775 gns Ascot November Sales. *M. D. I. Usher.*

LACE PAROSOL   5 ro.m. Neltino 97 – Anglophil 61 (Philemon 119) [1990 8m 9g   —
7f⁴ a6g 1991 a13g⁶ 10v 10d] close-coupled mare: well beaten in varied events: dead. *C. Holmes.*

LACK OF EVIDENCE (IRE)   3 ch.c. Heraldiste (USA) 121 – Naglaa (USA)   —
(State Dinner (USA)) [1990 NR 1991 a7g 7f 7g] IR 7,500Y, resold 33,000Y, 7,000 2-y-o: first foal: dam unraced: no promise in spring maidens, first an auction race. *D. A. Wilson.*

LACONIC   3 ch.g. Nicholas Bill 125 – Hi-Conkers 86 (Sica Boy 132) [1990 6g 6d 8d   —
1991 7m⁶] sparely-made gelding: poor maiden: likely to have proved suited by further than 6f: dead. *J. M. Jefferson.*

LA COUSINE   2 b.f. (Apr 20) R B Chesne 123 – Princess Lieven (Royal Palace   —
131) [1991 7g] leggy, unfurnished filly: fourth living foal: closely related to fair 11.5f winner Beau Ideal (by Brigadier Gerard) and 3-y-o 9.7f winner St Patrick's Day (by Night Shift): dam unraced daughter of sister to Brigadier Gerard: unruly stalls and withdrawn at Yarmouth in September: 50/1, showed up to 2f out in 22-runner maiden at Newmarket in November. *C. E. Brittain.*

L'ACQUESIANA   3 ch.f. Crofthall 110 – Well Connected (Bold And Free 118)   —
[1990 NR 1991 10g 10.2m a12g³ a8g⁵ a12g 8.5f⁶ 8.2m] 4,200Y, 960 2-y-o: lengthy filly: poor mover: fifth foal: sister to 7f to 1m winner Serlby Connection and half-sister to 5f and 6f seller winner My Topic (by Mansingh): dam poor maiden: poor maiden: best effort over 1m on fibresand. *S. R. Bowring.*

LA DAMA BONITA (USA)   2 ch.f. (Jan 5) El Gran Senor (USA) 136 – Marie   **76**
d'Argonne (FR) (Jefferson 129) [1991 6.1f⁴ 6f² 5.1g* 7.3g⁶] $52,000Y: rather leggy filly: second foal: closely related to high-class French 6f to 1m performer Polar Falcon (by Nureyev): dam French 1¼m winner successful also at 8.5f and 9f in USA, is half-sister to very smart French middle-distance filly Marie de Litz: modest performer: won minor event at Bath in September: stiff task, not discredited behind Soiree in listed race at Newbury following month: really needs further than 5f and should stay 1m. *D. W. P. Arbuthnot.*

LA DOMAINE   4 b.f. Dominion 123 – La Galette 76 (Double Form 130) [1990   **65**
6.5g³ 8d* 7m 7m 8g 8g⁵ 8f³ 8.3m a8g 8d* 8g 1991 8d⁵ 10g 10g 8.3d 8g⁴ 8g 8g 8d] lengthy, good-quartered filly: good walker: has a fluent, roundish action: quite modest handicapper: stays 1m: acts on any going: inconsistent. *C. R. Nelson.*

LADY BARAKA (IRE)   3 b.f. Shernazar 131 – Lady Wise (Lord Gayle (USA)   52
124) [1990 6f⁴ 7m² 5m 7d 1991 10g⁴ 10g² 10.1m* 10m⁶ 11.5f 10m³ a11g] small filly:
moderate mover: plating-class performer: won seller (no bid) at Yarmouth in July:
should stay beyond 1¼m: acts on good to firm ground: sweating (ran well) second
start: trained first 6 by J. Pearce. *I. Campbell.*

LADY BLESSINGTON (FR)   3 ch.f. Baillamont (USA) 124 – Lady Sharp (FR) 112
(Sharpman 124) [1990 NR 1991 10.7g* 9s* 10g 12g* 10g⁶ 12m 10f] 280,000 francs
(approx £25,900) Y: third foal: half-sister to French provincial 9.5f winner El
Labrador and French 7.5f (at 2 yrs) to 11f winner Lowell (both by General Holme):
dam, French 1¼m winner, is half-sister to smart French 6.5f to 1m winner Prospero:
won maiden at Le Croise-Laroche in May, minor event at Evry in June and 7-runner
Prix Minerve (easily best effort, held up when beating Crnagora 1½ lengths) at Evry
in July: in mid-division in Yellow Ribbon Stakes at Santa Anita final start, running
creditably: stays 1½m: acts on any going. *J. M. Choubersky, France.*

LADY BLUES SINGER   5 ch.m. Chief Singer 131 – Moaning Low 85 (Burglar   —
128) [1990 a7g⁴ 1991 8d6 17.2g] close-coupled mare: poor form at best: seems to stay
7f: acts on any going. *A. J. Chamberlain.*

LADY BUNTING   4 b.f. Well Decorated (USA) – Lady's Flag (USA) (Fifth   48
Marine 133) [1990 8f³ 8m 7m 7m³ 8m 8m 7m 8m³ 1991 6s 7d 7g 8m³ 8f² 8f
8f* 9.7f 9.7s] leggy filly: poor handicapper: won seller (bought in 4,800 gns) at Bath
in September: best form at 7f or 1m: best efforts on top-of-the-ground: tried
blinkered once: inconsistent: sold 2,600 gns Ascot December Sales. *L. G. Cottrell.*

LADY DOOLEY (IRE)   2 b.f. (Feb 8) Dominion 123 – Alhaan 71 (Tap On Wood   —
130) [1991 5s³ 5g a6g] rather leggy, plain filly: second foal: dam Irish 1½m
winner, from good family: no worthwhile form, including in sellers. *J. Wharton.*

LADY DUNDEE (USA)   2 b.f. (Feb 18) Northern Baby (CAN) 127 – Add Mint   — p
(USA) (Vigors (USA)) [1991 a8g] $50,000Y: second foal: dam graded stakes-placed
winner at up to 1¼m: slow-starting eleventh of 13 to Citiqueen in late-year maiden
at Southwell: will improve. *Mrs J. Cecil.*

LADY GRENVILLE   4 b.f. Aragon 118 – Tri'as (Tyrant (USA)) [1990 a8g⁶ a7g³   —
a8g⁶ 6f⁴ 7f 1991 7g 7d 12f] medium-sized filly: quite modest maiden at 2 yrs: below
form since: best form at 6f: acts on firm going: has been slowly away. *P. Leach.*

LADY GWENMORE   3 b.f. Town And Country 124 – Ment More 62 (Sahib 114)   55
[1990 8m 8.2m 7m 1991 12.3g 15.4f⁶ 17.2g* 17.1m³ 18.1m] workmanlike filly:
plating-class handicapper: won at Bath in September, leading over 1f out, edging left
and holding on by ½ length: stays 17f: may be ideally suited by some give in the
ground. *R. Akehurst.*

LADY IN RED (FR)   3 b.f. Shareef Dancer (USA) 135 – Dressed In Red (Red   68
Alert 127) [1990 6g 6m⁵ 6.5g 1991 8g 8g³ 10g⁵] leggy, attractive filly: quite modest
form: ran creditably in summer handicaps at Kempton and Newbury (on toes,
moderately-run race) last 2 starts: stays 1¼m: sold 5,400 gns Newmarket December Sales. *R. Charlton.*

LADY KALLISTE   3 gr.f. Another Realm 118 – Lady Killane 62 (Reform 132)   —
[1990 5m 7s 1991 8d 9d 7s⁵] workmanlike filly: poor mover: no worthwhile form in
maidens and handicaps. *P. Mitchell.*

LADY LACEY   4 b.f. Kampala 120 – Cecily (Prince Regent (FR) 129) [1990 8.3f²   59
7f* 8g⁴ 8m³ 8.2v² 8m² 8g³ 1991 7g 8g 8m 8d⁴ 9s³ 8m 8g² 10g 9s 8g 10.5d 8d*]
rather lightly-made, quite attractive filly: moderate mover: plating-class handicapper nowadays: won selling event (no bid) at Doncaster in November: stays 9f:
acts on any going: usually held up: none too consistent. *G. B. Balding.*

LADY LAX   7 ch.m. Henbit (USA) 130 – Spoilt Miss (USA) 96 (Riva Ridge (USA))   —
[1990 NR 1991 10m] lengthy, workmanlike mare: of no account. *J. White.*

LADY LINNET   2 b.f. (Mar 10) Nomination 125 – Shiny Kay 65 (Star Appeal 133)   64
[1991 5g 5g 5d⁵ 6d⁵ 6m* 7.1m 6m² 6g² 6m a8g* a8g] 3,500Y: small, sparely-made
filly: moderate mover: first foal: dam 1½m winner, is half-sister to K-Battery:
successful in seller (retained 3,800 gns) at Folkestone and claimer at Lingfield: ran
moderately on fibresand final start: stays 1m: acts on good to firm ground, and on
equitrack: blinkered third outing: sweating eighth. *P. F. I. Cole.*

LADY LYDIA   2 b. or br.f. (May 23) Ela-Mana-Mou 132 – Sumaya (USA) §§   66
(Seattle Slew (USA)) [1991 8.9d⁶ 8s] 1,700F: workmanlike, rather unfurnished filly:
fourth foal: half-sister to a winner in Norway by Dominion: dam well bred, became
very disappointing: 50/1 and bit backward, form in October maidens only when
staying-on sixth of 19 at Wolverhampton: should stay 1¼m. *M. A. Jarvis.*

LADY MACBETH 2 b.f. (Apr 10) Dublin Lad 116 – Act of Treason 80 (Absalom —
128) [1991 5g 5m 5g a5g 7m] smallish, leggy, workmanlike filly: first foal: dam best at
2 yrs later stayed 1¼m: of little account. *J. Balding.*

LADY MARRIOTT 3 b.f. Niniski (USA) 125 – Braconda 86 (So Blessed 130) 63 +
[1990 NR 1991 10m4] lengthy filly: fifth foal: half-sister to a winner in Malaysia by
Cut Above: dam 2-y-o 5f and 6f winner: in need of race, 7½ lengths fourth of 12 in
median auction contest at Salisbury in May, never able to challenge. *L. M. Cumani.*

LADY NORMANDY (FR) 2 b.f. (Apr 1) Saint Estephe (FR) 123 – Landlady 106
(FR) (Arctic Tern (USA) 126) [1991 6d* 5.5g* 7m5 8g3 8d] 130,000 francs (approx
£13,000) Y: second foal: half-sister to French 1990 2-y-o 6.3f winner Artic Lady (by
No Pass No Sale): dam 1¼m and 10.5f winner: useful performer: successful in
newcomers race at Chantilly and minor event at Maisons-Laffitte in June: ran in
pattern races afterwards, beaten around 3 lengths by Verveine in Prix du Calvados
at Deauville and a length by Guislaine in Prix d'Aumale at Longchamp: broke leg in
Prix Marcel Boussac at Longchamp: stayed 1m: dead. *A. Fabre, France.*

LADY NORWICK 2 b.f. (Jan 29) Norwick (USA) 120 – Superb Lady 106 (Marcus —
Superbus 100) [1991 a7g] 500Y: sparely-made filly: sister to a winner in Macau and
half-sister to 2 winners, including 5f winner Jacqui Joy (by Music Boy): dam best at
5f: well beaten in seller at Southwell in July. *C. N. Allen.*

LADY OF LETTERS 2 ro.f. (Feb 8) Primo Dominie 121 – Teacher's Game 64 44
(Mummy's Game 120) [1991 5g4 5g3 5d 6.1s5 6m4 7m5 6m 6m a7g] workmanlike
filly: has a quick action: poor maiden: visored (showed nothing) penultimate outing. *T. Thomson Jones.*

LADY OF LIGHT (IRE) 3 b.f. Glow (USA) – Silent Sun 90 (Blakeney 126) —
[1990 6g 7s a7g 1991 12g 11.5s 12.3m 9.7m] quite attractive filly: poor maiden:
showed nothing in seller final start: likely to prove suited by middle distances:
blinkered last 2 outings: saddle slipped on third: sold 950 gns Ascot September
Sales. *D. J. G. Murray-Smith.*

LADY OF MANN (USA) 2 ch.f. (May 11) Great Above (USA) – Dessi O'Day 73
(USA) (Cutlass (USA)) [1991 a5g* 5m3 5m3] $12,000Y, $47,000 2-y-o:
leggy filly: second foal: dam won 10 races at up to 1m: sire smart sprinter: well-
backed favourite, won maiden at Southwell in May: best effort in £7,800 event at
Beverley on final start, in June: will be better suited by 6f. *P. W. Chapple-Hyam.*

LADY OF SARDINIA (BEL) 2 b.f. (Jan 27) Efisio 120 – Lady Of The Manor 74 p
78 (Astec 128) [1991 7m4 7f 8.2m* 8g3] leggy, close-coupled filly: fourth reported
foal: half-sister to Tirso (by Niniski), winner at middle distances in Belgium: dam,
half-sister to very smart stayer Ragstone, placed at 1¼m: gambled-on 8/1-shot (well
beaten in Yarmouth maidens previously), won 19-runner seller (retained 7,500 gns)
at Nottingham in September by 6 lengths: best effort in nursery at Warwick 2 weeks
later, running on well having been set a lot to do: better suited by 1m than 7f and may
stay 1¼m: may well be capable of better still. *J. W. Payne.*

LADY OF THE FEN 3 b.f. Myjinski (USA) – Flying Glory (Flying Mercury) 41
[1990 5g5 5g 6f5 5m5 5f5 5f3 5f* 6m5 5f6 5m4 5m2 5f6 5f5 6m5 7g 7f4 6m 8d 1991 7m a 71
5m5 a5g* 6m 7g 5.1f a5g2 a5g2 5f a5g6 a5g a5g a5g2] leggy filly: has a quick action:
quite modest handicapper: won at Southwell in May: suited by 5f: best form on
all-weather: visored twice, blinkered (ran badly) twice: flashes tail and carries head
high. *Mrs N. Macauley.*

LADY OF THE TURF 3 b.f. Nordance (USA) – Town Lady 93 (Town Crier 119) —
[1990 NR 1991 6g a7g4] 6,600Y: leggy, lightly-made filly: moderate mover: half-
sister to several winners, including 1¼m and 1½m winner The Freshes (by Good
Times): dam 2-y-o 5f winner: showed signs of a little ability in summer maidens. *P.
T. Walwyn.*

LADY PHILIPPA (IRE) 3 b.f. Taufan (USA) 119 – Katie Koo 82 (Persian Bold 70
123) [1990 a6g3 a8g2 1991 a8g* a8g* a10g* a10g2 8.1g5 7f 8m 10.2s4 10m4 a10g] a 77
neat filly: moderate mover: progressive form pre-turf season, winning maiden and
handicaps at Lingfield: best effort in handicaps on turf when leading 9f at Chepstow
eighth start: better at 1¼m than 1m: seems to act on soft going. *B. W. Hills.*

LADY POLY 3 b.f. Dunbeath (USA) 127 – First Temptation (USA) (Mr Leader 43
(USA)) [1990 6m 6m 7f 1991 a7g4 10f 11.5m 8.5m3 10m6 11.5s4 10g5 a10g] small,
leggy filly: poor maiden: stays 1¼m: acts on good to firm ground. *Miss B. Sanders.*

LADY RANDOLPH 2 b.f. (Apr 18) Elegant Air 119 – Cara Rose (Rheingold 137) 49
[1991 6g 7g4 7f5 7f 8.2m 8.3g5 10.5d] sturdy, compact filly: half-sister to several
winners, including Irish 9f winner Dominion Dancer (by Dominion) and 1987 2-y-o
6f seller winner Madam Cyn (by Hello Gorgeous): dam unraced from family of

Greenland Park and Red Sunset: poor maiden: seems suited by 1m: tends to sweat: tail flasher: sold 1,000 gns Doncaster November Sales. *I. Campbell.*

LADY RISK ME   2 gr.f. (Apr 8) Risk Me (FR) 127 – Donrae 106 (Don (ITY) 123)   —
[1991 a7g 7m] leggy, shallow-girthed filly: eighth foal: half-sister to moderate 6f winner Brampton Grace (by Tachypous) and 7.2f and 12.2f winner Lyn Rae (by Derrylin): dam best at 2 yrs, winning over 5f: no form, including in seller. *P. A. Kelleway.*

LADY ROXANNE   2 br.f. (Feb 13) Cyrano de Bergerac 120 – Red Lory 87 (Bay   — p
Express 132) [1991 5m] leggy filly: third foal: half-sister to winner in Holland: dam 2-y-o 5f winner: 33/1, bit backward and on toes, eased by 7-lb claimer when held in 11-runner maiden at Sandown in September: sure to improve. *Lord Huntingdon.*

LADY RUNFAST   2 ch.f. (Feb 12) Montekin 125 – Tarte Aux Pommes 75 (Song   30
132) [1991 5d 5g⁵ 5f a6g a5g⁶ 6d 6g] 1,250F, 460Y: compact filly: moderate mover: seventh foal: half-sister to 2 winning sprint platers by Record Token: dam sprinter: of little account: blinkered second start. *T. Fairhurst.*

LADY SABO   2 br.f. (Jan 25) Prince Sabo 123 – Nice Lady 65 (Connaught 130)   65
[1991 5m³ 5d⁴ 5f* 6m 6g 6m³ 6.1m⁵] 2,500F, 7,000Y: neat filly: second foal: half-sister to a winner in Italy by Nordance: dam lightly-raced maiden, second over 9.4f: quite modest form: won maiden auction at Warwick in July: ran creditably next 3 starts: well worth a try over 7f: often bandaged behind: slowly away and edged left final start (only 4 days after previous one). *G. Lewis.*

LADY'S MANTLE (USA)   7 ch.m. Sunny Clime (USA) – Alchemilla (USA)   53
(Quadrangle) [1990 5m 5f 5m 5m 5m⁵ 5f² 5g⁴ a5g⁵ 5m⁴ 5m⁶ 5f⁴ 5m² 5m³ 5m 5f* 5.1m³ 5.3f⁴ 5d⁵ 5d⁶ 1991 5d 5g 5g 5f⁴ 5f* 5g 5g⁶ 5f* 5.2m² 5f⁴ 5m* 5f⁶ 5f² 5.2f⁴ 5m] compact, good-bodied mare: usually dull in coat: moderate mover: plating-class handicapper: won at Folkestone in June, Catterick in July and Windsor in August: suited by 5f: acts on dead going, and goes particularly well on top-of-the-ground: has been tried in blinkers and visor: often wears crossed noseband: has won for apprentice and when sweating. *R. Bastiman.*

LADY ST LAWRENCE (USA)   2 ch.f. (Apr 15) Bering 136 – Lady Norcliffe   65
(USA) (Norcliffe (CAN)) [1991 8.2m²⁶ 8.9d 8.1s³ a8g] workmanlike filly: fourth foal: half-sister to 1989 Irish 2-y-o 5f and 7f winner Shagudine (by Shadeed): dam good winner at up to 11f: quite modest maiden: should stay beyond 1m: acts on soft ground. *Sir Mark Prescott.*

LADY VIOLET   4 gr.f. Superlative 118 – Declamation 93 (Town Crier 119) [1990   28
8m 8s⁴ 1991 8d 7f³ 8.2m 7h 7m⁵ 8m 7f 7g⁴ a8g 8.1g 8m] leggy filly: has round action: poor handicapper at best: stays 7f: acts on firm ground: joined G. Moore. *Don Enrico Incisa.*

LADY WESTGATE   7 b.m. Welsh Chanter 124 – Church Bay 76 (Reliance II   38
137) [1990 12f 12m 16g* 16m² 16.5f* 16f⁵ 14m⁶ 1991 17.1m 16.2g 14.8m⁴ 12.1d 16.2g⁶ 16.2d² 16.4m 14.6m⁶⁵] leggy, rather plain mare: poor handicapper at best nowadays: stays 2m: acts on firm and dead going: tried visored once. *G. B. Balding.*

LADY WINIFRED (IRE)   3 ch.f. The Noble Player (USA) 126 – Pollymere   —
(Scorpio (FR) 127) [1990 7m 7g 6g 1991 8m 8f 12s] workmanlike filly: plating-class form at 2 yrs, none in first half of 1991: should stay 1m. *J. D. Czerpak.*

LAFKADIO   4 b.g. Gay Mecene (USA) 128 – Lakonia (Kris 135) [1990 8g⁴ 8g a8g   55
a11g a12g a14g⁴ 1991 a14g* a14g* a12g⁵ a14g² a14g³ 13.8d⁴ 17m³ 21.6f* 16.2f* 18g⁴ 20g 16.5m* 16.5g³ 16f⁴] smallish, good-bodied gelding: poor mover: improved handicapper and had fine season, successful at Southwell (2, one amateurs) in January, Pontefract and Beverley in spring and Doncaster (by 6 lengths) in June: not at all discredited after: well suited by really good test of stamina: acts on firm and dead ground and fibresand: winning hurdler, but refused to race once in autumn: game, genuine and most consistent on flat. *M. C. Chapman.*

LAGGARD'S QUEST   2 br.c. (Apr 21) Daring March 116 – Doubtful Request   —
(Cheveley Lad 105) [1991 7.1s] sturdy colt: half-brother to several minor winners, including 1985 2-y-o 5f winner Cabask (by Dublin Taxi): dam never ran: 33/1, backward and coltish, took very strong hold then weakened quickly from halfway in maiden at Chepstow in October. *C. D. Broad.*

LA GRANGE MUSIC   4 ch.c. Music Boy 124 – Great Care 66 (Home Guard   111
(USA) 129) [1990 6m* 6m* 6g³ 6m* 6m² 7g⁵ 6g* 1991 6g³ 6m 7g* 7m⁴ 8d 7m⁶] leggy, good-topped colt: very useful performer: won Van Geest Criterion Stakes at Newmarket in June: creditable fourth (got poor run) to Bog Trotter in Group 3 event at Doncaster in September: ran poorly in Group 2 event at Newmarket final start: effective at 6f to 7f (faced very stiff task over 1m): acted on good to firm ground:

Van Geest Criterion Stakes, Newmarket—
La Grange Music has a length to spare over Local Lass and almost-hidden Goofalik

sometimes sweating and slowly away: retired to Benson Stud, Colchester, £800 (Oct 1 terms). *J. R. Fanshawe.*

LAHARNA GIRL 7 b.m. Star Appeal 133 – Avise La Fin 83 (Scottish Rifle 127) [1990 NR 1991 18g⁶ 16.5m 15s⁵ 16.2f] small, sparely-made mare: lightly raced and poor handicapper nowadays: stays 15f: best form on soft going: visored in 1991: winning hurdler in August. *G. R. Oldroyd.* **23**

LAHIB (USA) 3 b.c. Riverman (USA) 131 – Lady Cutlass (USA) (Cutlass (USA)) [1990 NR 1991 8g² 8g*] rangy, useful-looking colt: good mover: fifth living foal: half-brother to fairly useful 7f and 1m winner Sajjaya (by Blushing Groom), and to 3 other winners, including Irish 1985 2-y-o 1m winner Lady of The North (by Northern Baby), subsequently successful in USA: dam, 5f to 7f winner in North America, is half-sister to high-class middle-distance performer General Holme: 11/10 but green, won 10-runner maiden at Newmarket in May by neck from Close Friend, quickening well to lead 1f out then idling: beaten short head by Ristna in big field at Newbury previous month: had plenty of scope, and looked sure to improve again: remains in training. *J. L. Dunlop.* **102**

LAHIN 3 b.f. Rainbow Quest (USA) 134 – Rivers Maid 83 (Rarity 129) [1990 NR 1991 12f⁵] tall, angular, unfurnished filly: sister to twice-raced Mahat and half-sister to 1985 2-y-o Nomination (by Dominion), very smart at up to 7f, and several maidens: dam won over 7f at 2 yrs and is sister to very useful middle-distance performer and good hurdler Decent Fellow: last of 5 in slowly-run maiden at Thirsk in August: sold 980 gns Newmarket December Sales. *D. Morley.* **—**

LAIRD OF BALMORAL 4 b.c. Lochnager 132 – Baggin Time 91 (Pinsun 108) [1990 8d⁵ 9m 8m² 1991 a6g⁵ 8d 8v⁴ 8.5g 12m 8m 10g³ 10d⁵ 8g 7m⁵] compact, good-quartered colt: good walker: has round action: quite modest handicapper nowadays: not seen out after July: stays 1¼m: acts on good to firm ground and heavy: twice below form when blinkered at 4 yrs: none too consistent: sold 1,200 gns Doncaster November Sales. *M. H. Easterby.* **72**

LAKE DOMINION 2 b.c. (Mar 16) Primo Dominie 121 – Piney Lake 54 (Sassafras (FR) 135) [1991 6d 6d³ 6m³ 7g⁴] 17,500F, 26,000Y: close-coupled, quite good-topped colt: half-brother to several winners, including 1985 2-y-o 6f winner Cafe Noir (by Comedy Star): dam placed at 1m and 1¼m: modest maiden: in frame on Group 1 tracks: most probably better suited by 7f than 6f: gave impression ill at ease on good to firm ground. *P. W. Harris.* **76**

LAKE MISTASSIU 4 b.f. Tina's Pet 121 – Kakisa 81 (Forlorn River 124) [1990 5f² 5g⁵ 5g³ 5m⁶ 5d 5g⁴ 5s³ 5g 1991 5g 5m⁶ a5g³ 5m² 5m* 5g² 5d⁶ 5.2f 5g⁴] smallish, strong filly: fair handicapper: won at Lingfield in June: races only at 5f: best form on a sound surface: effective with or without blinkers. *G. A. Pritchard-Gordon.* **85**

LA LA NOO 2 b.f. (Apr 29) Lidhame 109 – Janlarmar 69 (Habat 127) [1991 7f 6m] —
2,500F, 2,400Y: leggy filly: half-sister to 5f (at 2 yrs) and 1m winner Great Service
and 6f seller winner Crimpsall (both by Vaigly Great): dam won 6f seller: signs of
ability, in seller second start: bandaged behind: sold 950 gns Newmarket Autumn
Sales. *M. D. I. Usher.*

LALLAPALOOSA 3 b.f. Superlative 118 – Tsar's Bride (Song 132) [1990 6m⁵ **88**
6m⁴ 6f⁵ 6g* 6m⁶ 6m⁵ 1991 6g 6d⁶ 6d* 7g 6g³ 6m 6m] workmanlike filly: has a quick
action: quite useful but inconsistent performer: won handicap at Windsor in June:
should stay 7f: acts on good to firm and dead ground: best form in blinkers:
sometimes edgy, and has sweated: sold 9,200 gns Newmarket Autumn Sales. *J. L.
Dunlop.*

LAMARSH (IRE) 3 ch.c. Be My Guest (USA) 126 – Annabella 88 (Habitat 134) **86**
[1990 7m 7g 7s³ 1991 7d² 8f* 8g⁵ 8g* 7g 8m] stocky colt: successful, making
virtually all, in maiden (straightforward task) at Brighton in April and handicap
(gamely) at Goodwood in May: in need of race in £23,300 handicap final start, first
for 3 months: stays 1m: acts on firm and dead ground: wears severe bridle. *J. H. M.
Gosden.*

LA MASAAS (USA) 3 b.g. Miswaki (USA) 124 – Skeeb (USA) 94 (Topsider **74**
(USA)) [1990 5g 5m* 5f³ 5d² 6d 5g⁵ 5d 1991 a6g* a6g⁴ a5g* 5d] neat gelding: poor
mover: modest performer, not seen out after April: successful in claimers at
Lingfield: stays 6f: best turf effort on dead ground: blinkered final outing at 2 yrs,
very upset in preliminaries: has worn tongue strap. *P. C. Haslam.*

LAMASTRE 2 b.f. (Mar 5) Jalmood (USA) 126 – Daring Lass 87 (Bold Lad (IRE) **61**
133) [1991 5g* 5f⁴ 5.8d³ 6g] 2,800Y: smallish filly: has a quick action: half-sister to
fairly useful 1988 2-y-o 6f and 7f winner Fly By Knife (by Kris) and a winner abroad
by Henbit: dam, half-sister to top-class middle-distance stayer Homeric, was
second over 5f and 7f at 2 yrs: quite modest performer: well-backed favourite, won
13-runner seller (retained 4,800 gns) at Wolverhampton in April despite very slow
start: seems rather headstrong, but bred to stay 1¼m: easily best effort on dead
ground: bandaged near-fore debut: tends to hang. *R. J. Hodges.*

LAMBADA GIRL (IRE) 3 b.f. Petorius 117 – Spear Dance (Gay Fandango **57**
(USA) 132) [1990 5.8m 5.8h³ 6m 6g 6m 5.8d 1991 5.7g 6.9m 6m² 6m* 6m⁴dis 6f³ 7m
6.1m 6g³ 6m] small, workmanlike filly: poor mover: plating-class performer: won
handicap at Folkestone in August, always front rank: should stay 7f: acts on good to
firm ground: blinkered final start and last 3 at 2 yrs: no show in amateurs handicap:
sometimes bandaged behind: sold 3,000 gns Newmarket Autumn Sales. *D. W. P.
Arbuthnot.*

LAMBADA STYLE (IRE) 3 b.f. Dancing Brave (USA) 140 – Santa's Sister **81**
(USA) 104 (Middle Brother) [1990 NR 1991 8g* 8g 10.6g 11.9m² 11.7f² 12g 14.6m]
94,000Y, resold 90,000Y: leggy, close-coupled filly: half-sister to numerous
winners, including A-y-o Baligh (by Sadler's Wells), very useful 1m winner at 2 yrs,
and 7f winner and Irish Oaks fourth My Sister (by Nonoalco): dam winner at up to
1m, is half-sister to Yorkshire Cup winner Noble Saint: won maiden at Warwick in
April: good second in handicaps at Haydock and Bath: much better at 1½m than
shorter: acts on firm going. *R. Hannon.*

LAMBOURN RAJA 5 b.g. Indian King (USA) 128 – Take A Chance (FR) **68 +**
(Baldric II 131) [1990 8f³ 8m² 8.2v* 8.2d⁴ 7g* 7g* a7g* 1991 a7g 8g 7m⁶] lengthy,
rather angular gelding: fair handicapper at 4 yrs: below best in first half of 1991:
better at 7f than 1m: has form on any going, but goes very well with some give: tried
visored once: has won for apprentice: sold only 3,800 gns Ascot June Sales. *M. C.
Pipe.*

LAMBSON 4 b.g. Petorius 117 – Julie Be Quick (USA) (Selari) [1990 8m 9f⁵ 8g⁶ —
9g⁴ 10m 8.2m 10m 11d 1991 10f 10f 8m⁴ 10m 10.2g 12g] leggy gelding: moderate
walker and mover: poor performer nowadays: seems to stay 1¼m: acts on firm
ground. *R. M. Whitaker.*

LA MEZERAY 3 b.f. Nishapour (FR) 125 – La Pythie (FR) 89 (Filiberto (USA) —
123) [1990 5f 1991 10f6] tall, close-coupled filly: has a round action: no sign of ability
in seller and well-contested minor event. *B. Palling.*

LA MONALISA (FR) 3 ch.f. Gorytus 132 – Lady Jeff (Jefferson 129) [1990 8g² **113**
8d² 8g* 1991 10.5s* 10.5g* 10g⁵ 10.5d 12d² 10m] 16,000 francs (approx £14,800) Y:
half-sister to French 9f winners Artistic Dancer (by Arctic Tern) and, at 2 yrs,
Chalabiah (by Akarad), and to 1987 French 2-y-o 1¼m winner Fabulous Partner (by
Fabulous Dancer): dam, winner 5 times in Austria, is half-sister to good French colt
Bon Sang: won maiden at Longchamp at 2 yrs then listed race and Prix Penelope at

Saint-Cloud in spring at 3 yrs: best effort in pattern events subsequently when 2 lengths second to Magic Night in Prix de Malleret at Longchamp: stays 1½m. *E. Lellouche, France.*

LAMORE RITORNA 2 br.f. (Feb 12) Lidhame 109 – Arbor Lane 70 (Wolverine 115) [1991 7.1m⁵ 7g] 2,500Y: smallish, rather leggy filly: third foal: half-sister to 3-y-o 1½m winner Cousin Elly (by Claude Monet): dam 1¼m to 2¼m winner: poor form in maiden auctions at Chepstow and Goodwood (raced prominently, no extra from distance) in autumn: will probably stay 1¼m. *I. A. Balding.*   **43**

L'AMOUR PRECIEUX 2 b.g. (Mar 8) Precocious 126 – La Mortola (Bold Lad (IRE) 133) [1991 5m 5m4] 6,200Y: workmanlike gelding: has scope: third foal: brother to 1990 Irish 2-y-o 6f winner Luttrellstown: dam unraced half-sister to Katies and Millfontaine: lowered in class, fourth of 16, keeping on unable to challenge, in seller at Newcastle in August: will be suited by 6f+: gives impression likely to do better. *M. W. Easterby.*   **49 p**

LANCEVAL (FR) 5 gr.h. Kenmare (FR) 125 – Right River (FR) (Riverman (USA) 131) [1990 8g⁵ 7g⁵ 1991 8.1d 7m⁵ a11g] leggy horse: fourth foal: half-brother to 2 winners, including partly useful middle-distance filly Calorge (by Nebos): dam placed over 13f in French Provinces at 3 yrs: ex-French horse: successful as 3-y-o in 1m maiden at Saint-Cloud: fifth in minor events when trained by A. Fabre at 4 yrs: tailed off in modest company here: stays 1m: acts on good to firm ground: blinkered penultimate start. *C. A. Austin.*   **—**

LANDED GENTRY (USA) 2 b.c. (May 14) Vaguely Noble 140 – Phydilla (FR) 126 (Lyphard (USA) 132) [1991 7g 8g] good-bodied colt: has scope: has a long stride: fifth foal: half-brother to useful maiden Mysteries (by Seattle Slew): dam won from 6f to 1m in France: beaten 18 lengths or so when not fully wound up in maiden at Salisbury and minor event (won by Aljadeer) at Newbury in October: will stay 1¼m: will improve again. *P. W. Chapple-Hyam.*   **59 p**

LANDOWNER (IRE) 2 b.c. (Jan 25) Kris 135 – Laluche (USA) 100 (Alleged (USA) 138) [1991 7m4] first foal: dam won from 6f to 1m at 2 yrs, from excellent family: weak 12/1-shot, over 4 lengths fourth of 15, slowly away, steady progress from 2f out, to Deserve in maiden at Lingfield in October: will stay 1m: should improve. *J. H. M. Gosden.*   **66 p**

LANDSTAR 2 b.c. (May 8) Heights of Gold – Ribogirl 64 (Riboboy (USA) 124) [1991 7.1s 6f 7g] sturdy colt: first foal: dam 2-y-o 8.2f seller winner: poor maiden: sweating last 2 starts. *W. G. R. Wightman.*   **—**

LAND SUN (IRE) 3 b.c. Red Sunset 120 – Great Land (USA) (Friend's Choice (USA)) [1990 5g 5g 5f⁵ 5g4 5g* 6m4 6g⁶ 6m4 5m* 6f 5m⁶ 5.8h 6m 5m* 6g 5f² 5m 5m 5m 5v* 5m 6s 5g 1991 a5g³ 5m 5.3f 5.1d] small, sturdy colt: moderate mover: quite modest performer on his day: below form after reappearance: suited by 5f: acts on any going: effective with or without blinkers or visor: sold 1,200 gns Doncaster July Sales: thoroughly unreliable. *M. R. Channon.*   **58 §**

LANDYAP (USA) 7 b.h. Fappiano (USA) – My Candidate (USA) (Prince John) [1990 13.3m³ 10m⁶ 8.5g² 10g³ 10.1g² 10m³ 12s⁵ 9g4 1991 8d4 10s³ 9m⁵] rangy horse: good mover: very useful ex-U.S. performer: 16/1, easily best effort in spring of 1991 when close-up fifth of 11 to Terimon in strongly-run Group 3 event at Newmarket: best at 1m to 1¼m: suited by a sound surface: has edged left: blinkered last 4 starts: joined R. Frost: placed over hurdles. *D. R. C. Elsworth.*   **111**

LANGTONIAN 2 br.g. (Feb 7) Primo Dominie 121 – Yankee Special 60 (Bold Lad (IRE) 133) [1991 6f³ 6d* 6m² 6m² 6d4 6m] 7,500Y: strong, sturdy gelding: carries condition: good walker: third foal: brother to 3-y-o Primera Ballerina: dam plating-class maiden: fair performer: won maiden at Hamilton: good second in £9,300 event at Ascot and Group 3 event at Milan later in summer: ran poorly afterwards: stays 6f: best efforts on top-of-the-ground. *J. Berry.*   **82**

LANGTRY LADY 5 b.m. Pas de Seul 133 – Arianna Aldini (Habitat 134) [1990 a8g* a8g² a7g4 8f* 8g 8m 8m 7f a7g⁶ 8m² 8g² 8s³ 8g³ 1991 a8g² 8d 7m 7.6d² 7m 8f4 8m* 7s² 8.5f³ 7.6m⁵ 7.6m⁵ 8m² 8d² 8d³ 7.6d³ 8g] leggy, sparely-made mare: fairly useful handicapper: won at Brighton in June: effective at 7f to 1m: acts on any going: often ridden by claimer, below form for amateur once: has carried head high and worn dropped noseband: most consistent. *M. J. Ryan.*   **90**

LANGUEDOC 4 b.c. Rousillon (USA) 133 – Can Can Girl 69 (Gay Fandango (USA) 132) [1990 7m³ 6m 5m4 5m 1991 a6g4 a5g* a5g² a6g4 5d 5m4 5m³ 5f 5g 5f 7g³ 7m² 7m 6g³ 7g 8.1s* a6g² a8g* a8g4] tall, attractive colt: modest handicapper: successful at Southwell in February and Edinburgh and Lingfield in November: effective at up to 1m: acts on good to firm and soft ground, and on all-weather   **76 a82**

surfaces: ran moderately when blinkered once: has carried head high: trained until after eighth start at 4 yrs by K. McCauley. *H. A. T. Whiting.*

LANNER (USA) 3 ch.c. Diesis 133 – Syndaar (FR) (Lyphard (USA) 132) [1990 **96** NR 1991 8g 7f² 7g* a7g* a6g* 6g 7f*] big, lengthy, good-topped colt: sixth foal: closely related to a winner in Italy and half-brother to a winner in USA: dam 6f winner in USA: odds on, comfortably made all in maiden at Catterick, apprentice race at Lingfield and minor events at Lingfield and Thirsk in the summer: stays 7f: to race in USA. *B. W. Hills.*

LA PEREET (IRE) 3 b.f. Vision (USA) – Great Alexandra (Runnett 125) [1990 — 5m⁶ 6g 5f⁵ 7m⁴ 7f⁴ 7g 7.5g³ 1991 12.2g 9d 8m⁵ 8.2f 6g] leggy, sparely-made filly: has a round action: plating-class maiden: ran poorly in 1991: best form at 7f: acts on firm going: blinkered or visored last 6 outings: trained first 3 in 1991 by M. Bell: sold 800 gns Ascot October Sales: winning hurdler for K. Morgan. *C. N. Allen.*

LAPIAFFE 7 b.g. Piaffer (USA) 113 – Laval (Cheval 117) [1990 NR 1991 16m² **41** 17.1d* 17.2g⁴ 17.2f] rather sparely-made gelding: moderate mover: lightly raced on flat: won handicap at Bath in June: stays 17f: acts on good to firm and dead ground: often edgy. *R. J. Hodges.*

LAPLAND LIGHTS (USA) 3 b.f. Northern Prospect (USA) – Blushing Emy **83** (USA) (Blushing Groom (FR) 131) [1990 6m² 5d 1991 6m* 7.3d² 7m 6f⁵] leggy, lengthy filly: favourite and on toes, won maiden at Salisbury in May, rallying well: looked very well but ran moderately in handicaps last 2 outings: will prove better at 7f than shorter: acts on good to firm ground and dead. *A. C. Stewart.*

LA RAPTOTTE 4 b.f. Alzao (USA) 117 – Maypole Hie (Bold Lad (IRE) 133) [1990 — 7m* 8m² 7f 7g⁶ 7g 8.2m 10m 8g 8m⁴ 8.2s⁶ 1991 7g⁴ a8g³ 10.8g 10.8g 12.2d⁶ 12s 8.9g] angular filly: plating-class handicapper, none too consistent: best form at around 1m: acts on good to firm going: tried blinkered and visored: winning hurdler. *M. J. Charles.*

LARA'S BABY (IRE) 3 ch.f. Valiyar 129 – Tapiola 71 (Tap On Wood 130) [1990 **68** 6m 7m 7g 7m² 7s³ 1991 10g 8m³ 8g⁴ 8.5m 11.7m 12.1s⁵ a12g*] sturdy filly: moderate mover: quite modest form: favourite, won claimer at Southwell in December: much better at 1½m than shorter distances, and will stay further: acts on soft ground and good to firm: ran poorly at Epsom. *R. Akehurst.*

LARA'S IDEA 3 b.f. Primo Dominie 121 – Lara's Song (USA) 69 (Russian Bank **118** (USA) 110) [1990 7g⁶ 8g* 8d³ 7.5d⁴ 8.5g³ 8s² 8s* 10v⁵ 9d* 1991 8g* 8s* 8v³ 12g⁴ 10g* 11g* 10g⁵ 10s* 10v* 10v²] 3,100F: fourth foal: half-sister to 13.1f winner and successful hurdler Russian Lullaby (by Sparkler): dam winning stayer: leading Italian filly: won maiden and 2 minor events at 2 yrs: successful as 3-y-o in minor event and listed race at Rome in the spring, Group 3 contest at Milan and listed race at Merano in the summer, and in minor event at Milan and Premio Lydia Tesio (by 2¼ lengths from Ocean Air) at Rome in September: beaten 2 lengths by Sikeston in Premio Roma final start: seems best at 1¼m: acts on heavy going. *L. Camici, Italy.*

LA REINE ROUGE (IRE) 3 ch.f. Red Sunset 120 – Free Rein (Sagaro 133) — [1990 NR 1991 a12g] 18,000Y: third reported foal: sister to quite modest middle-distance performers Ice Magic and Sunset Reins Free: dam unraced from family of Troy: 25/1, tailed off in claimer at Southwell in December. *P. J. Makin.*

LARK RISE (USA) 3 ch.g. The Minstrel (CAN) 135 – Glowing Prospect (USA) **68** (Mr Prospector (USA)) [1990 NR 1991 9g⁵ 8g 8d³ 10.2s*] angular gelding: has a long, round stride: first reported living foal: dam, successful 3 times in North America, is half-sister to 3 graded winners in USA, notably Grade 1 9.5f and 11f turf winner Hero's Honor (by Northern Dancer): quite modest form in maidens: made all in 6-runner contest at Chepstow in July: stays 1¼m: acts on soft going: sold to join C. Weedon 15,000 gns Newmarket Autumn Sales. *I. A. Balding.*

LARS PORSENA 4 b. or br.g. Trojan Fen 118 – Apocalypse (Auction Ring — § (USA) 123) [1990 6f² 6g⁵ 6m³ 5m 7m² 7g 7m⁶ 6m⁶ 8m⁴ 8m² 8f² 8h² 8f⁴ 7.6m² 7g³ 8.2m* 8d⁵ 1991 8.2m 8m 7m] close-coupled, good-quartered gelding: carries condition: fair handicapper at 3 yrs: no form in 1991, tailed off final start: effective over 7f and 1m: acts on hard going: irresolute and best covered up: has joined M. W. Easterby. *R. M. Whitaker.*

LASERPRINT (USA) 2 ch.f. (Jan 24) Secretariat (USA) – Meteoric 102 (High **42** Line 125) [1991 6g 6s] sparely-made filly: second foal: dam sprinting daughter of game sprinter Metair: poor form in maidens at Haydock (slowly away, June) and Yarmouth nearly 5 months later: should stay 1m. *J. H. M. Gosden.*

LA SKY (IRE) 3 b.f. Law Society 130 – Maryinsky (USA) (Northern **107** Dancer) [1990 NR 1991 10d* 10m* 11.9m² 14g³] 260,000Y: lengthy, good sort with scope: has a long stride: closely related to Legal Case (by Alleged), winner of Champion Stakes, and half-sister to a winner in USA: dam winner twice at up to 9f in USA from family of smart French sprinter Gem Diamond: won maiden at Newbury and minor event at Nottingham in May: looking extremely well, beaten 1½ lengths by Patricia in Lancashire Oaks at Haydock (best effort) and 1¾ lengths behind Jahafil in listed race at Goodwood: probably stays 1¾m. *H. R. A. Cecil.*

LASSOO 3 ch.f. Caerleon (USA) 132 – Siouan 78 (So Blessed 130) [1990 7d² 8.2v² 1991 11d³ 12.3d] tall, unfurnished filly: maiden, clearly best effort second start at 2 yrs: well backed at Hamilton and Ripon (apprentices, ran badly) in first half of 1991: should be well suited by middle distances: seems to need very testing conditions. *C. W. Thornton.* —

LAST APPEARANCE 2 b.f. (Mar 22) Slip Anchor 136 – Thespian 76 (Ile de Bourbon (USA) 133) [1991 7g] close-coupled filly: third foal: closely related to 1½m and 13.8f winner Class Act (by Shirley Heights): dam 7f winner: 10/1, around 14 lengths tenth of 16, running as if in need of race, to Perfect Circle in minor event at Kempton in September: will improve over middle distances. *M. Bell.* 55 p

LA ST CLAIR 3 ch.f. Music Boy 124 – Soosjoy 89 (Sexton Blake 126) [1990 5m a6g 1991 10d 6g 6g 8.3d⁶] smallish, angular, sparely-made filly: no worthwhile form, including in seller. *J. White.* —

LAST CONQUEST (IRE) 2 b.g. (Apr 11) Slip Anchor 136 – Migiyas 87 (Kings Lake (USA) 133) [1991 8s 8.1d⁵ 10m⁶ 8.1s] good-topped gelding: second foal: dam 5f (at 2 yrs) and 7f winner: quite modest maiden: should stay 1¼m: acts on dead ground. *P. F. I. Cole.* 62

LAST CRUSADE (IRE) 3 b.g. Last Tycoon 131 – Berengaria (ITY) (Teodoro Trivulzio) [1990 6g 6d 8d a7g a7g 1991 10g 12d 11.6m 16m] leggy gelding: poor maiden: showed little as 3-y-o, wearing net muzzle on third start: sold 850 gns Ascot October Sales: one to be wary of. *H. Candy.* — §

LAST DATE 2 ch.g. (Apr 15) Bold Owl 101 – Marwick (Roan Rocket 128) [1991 6g] 4,000Y, resold 3,700Y, 400 2-y-o: close-coupled gelding: third foal (all by Bold Owl): dam ran once: 33/1, slow-starting last of 15 in seller at Nottingham in June. *N. Tinkler.* —

LAST EXIT 2 b.f. (Apr 29) Dominion 123 – Nepula 105 (Nebbiolo 125) [1991 6g* 6d* 6f³ 6g⁶ 6.3s⁴] 16,500F, IR 20,000Y: workmanlike filly: thriving physically: fourth foal: half-sister to 3-y-o Flower Princess (by Slip Anchor): dam 7f and 1m winner at 2 yrs lost form as 3-y-o: fairly useful performer: won maiden at Leicester and minor event at Newbury in early-summer: off course 2½ months and looking very well, much-improved second (demoted) to Colway Bold in BonusPrint Champion Two-year-old Trophy at Ripon in August: confirmed form when fourth of 15 to Dedicated Lady in Goffs Fillies Challenge at the Curragh: ran poorly in listed event at Ayr in between: will be better suited by 7f and 1m: acts on any going. *W. Jarvis.* 93

LAST LION (USA) 3 b.c. Skywalker (USA) – Satan's Pride (USA) (Crimson Satan) [1990 NR 1991 a8g³ 8g* 9g* 8.5f² 8m 8.1s] angular colt: has a round action: moderate walker: half-brother to several winners in North America, including Grade 3 7f winner Devil's Bride (by Caro): dam successful in 8 stakes races from 2 yrs to 4 yrs: odds on, comfortable winner of maiden at Edinburgh and handicap at Redcar in June: off course 3½ months after fourth start, tenderly handled at Doncaster then getting poor run (eased late 1f) at Edinburgh on return: stays 9f: ran creditably but looked ill at ease on firm ground: may prove capable of better. *J. H. M. Gosden.* 91 +

LAST MATCH 3 b.g. Final Straw 127 – Light Duty 113 (Queen's Hussar 124) [1990 NR 1991 10g 11.8m] big, rangy gelding: half-brother to 5 winners, including useful 1985 2-y-o Laughter (by Shirley Heights) and Paradise Bay (by Mill Reef), very useful at up to 1½m: dam middle-distance performer, is sister to Highclere: little sign of ability in maidens at Newbury (pulled hard) and Leicester: sold to join B. Preece 2,400 gns Newmarket Autumn Sales. *Lord Huntingdon.* —

LAST ORDERS (USA) 2 b. or br.f. (Mar 4) Temperence Hill (USA) – Tyrants Escape (Tyrant (USA)) [1991 6m 8.1g 6.1f 6d] $18,000Y: leggy, sparely-made filly: half-sister to several winners, including useful 7f (at 2 yrs) and 1¼m winner Dalgan (by Diamond Shoal): dam, 2-y-o 5f winner in Ireland later successful in USA: poor maiden: should stay beyond 6f. *R. Hannon.* 37

LA STRAVAGANZA 3 b.f. Slip Anchor 136 – St Isadora (Lyphard (USA) 132) [1990 7m⁵ 1991 8d⁴ 10f⁴ 11.5f] leggy, unfurnished filly: modest form in maidens: 74

failed to confirm earlier promise when last of 12 at Yarmouth (held up taking keen hold) in June: stays 1¼m. *W. Jarvis.*

LAST STRAW 3 b.g. Blushing Scribe (USA) 107 – Straw Reef 64 (Final Straw 127) [1990 5f 6d 6s 1991 7g 7g6 7m] sturdy gelding: showed ability only on debut: has wandered under pressure. *A. W. Jones.* —

LATBALLY 2 b.f. (Feb 21) Touching Wood (USA) 127 – Baddaweeya (Formidable (USA) 125) [1991 6.1m 7f 7f 8.2m] sparely-made filly: third foal: dam once-raced daughter of fairly useful sprinter Elegida: no worthwhile form, including in seller: twice slowly away: sold 2,000 gns Newmarket Autumn Sales. *B. Hanbury.* —

LATE LADY 3 br.f. Latest Model 115 – Landed Lady 89 (Realm 129) [1990 NR 1991 8m 9d 8m] workmanlike filly: has a round action: fourth reported living foal: dam, sister to Greenham winner Another Realm, won over 5f at 2 yrs: no sign of ability, in claimer last time. *R. J. Holder.* —

LATIN LEEP 4 b.c. Castle Keep 121 – Balatina 85 (Balidar 133) [1990 a7g2 a8g* a8g6 a10g* a8g6 8h3 11.5m4 12m5 10g3 10.1m3 10f* 10.2f4 10f4 1991 10m5 10.1m3 a10g3] sturdy colt: quite modest performer: best efforts at 1¼m: acts on firm going: has run creditably for lady rider: effective blinkered or not: consistent. *J. Pearce.* 67

LATIN LIMBO (IRE) 2 br.g. (Apr 16) Rhoman Rule (USA) – Fire Dance (FR) (Habitat 134) [1991 6g 8m] 8,000Y: good-bodied, quite attractive gelding: half-brother to several winners, including fair 1¼m winner Staravia (by Star Appeal) and 1980 2-y-o 5f winner Disco Dancer (by Record Token): dam never ran: backward, tailed off in maidens in Yorkshire: off course 3½ months in between: sold 850 gns Doncaster November Sales. *M. J. Camacho.* —

LATIN MASS 3 ch.f. Music Boy 124 – Omnia 80 (Hill Clown (USA)) [1990 5f2 5m3 5m2 5m3 5g3 5m4 a6g5 5m 1991 5g 5f a5g5 6f5 7g6 7m3 7.1d 7g 6m 7m 8f 6m] workmanlike filly: has quick action: poor maiden: showed little (including in sellers) last 5 starts: stays 7f: acts on firm going: sometimes bandaged behind: sold out of J. Berry's stable 4,000 gns Doncaster July Sales after sixth start. *A. Barrow.* 43 d

LATIN QUARTET 3 b.g. Chief Singer 131 – Pampas Miss (USA) (Pronto) [1990 7m 7m 8.2d 1991 8v* 9d4 10m* a11g2] strong, attractive gelding: poor mover: set pace when winning apprentice race (hung right) at Newcastle in April and handicap at Salisbury in May: creditable second in handicap at Southwell in June, pushed along before halfway: should stay 1½m: acts on good to firm ground and heavy: game: sold to join L. Codd 13,500 gns Newmarket Autumn Sales. *W. J. Haggas.* 58

LATOSKY 3 br.g. Teenoso (USA) 135 – Patosky 94 (Skymaster 126) [1990 7s 1991 8v3 8d4 8f3 10m] good-topped gelding: quite modest maiden: easily best effort when fourth in median auction contest at Thirsk: off course 5 months before final start: stays 1m: acts on dead ground: hung right on reappearance: sold to join J. Norton 5,000 gns Doncaster November Sales. *M. J. Camacho.* —

LATOUR 3 b.c. Lafontaine (USA) 117 – Lucky Omen 99 (Queen's Hussar 124) [1990 7g5 7m 7m 1991 10v* 12d2 12g2 14g6 13.9g 10m] rather leggy, quite attractive colt: fair performer: 6/5 on, won maiden at Folkestone in March: improved second in £7,400 handicap (edging left and swishing tail) at Newbury and King George V Stakes at Royal Ascot (3 lengths second to Torchon): below form after, particularly so last 2 starts: should stay 1¾m: acts on heavy going: edgy and ran in snatches fourth start. *C. E. Brittain.* 79

LATVIAN 4 gr.c. Rousillon (USA) 133 – Lorelene (FR) 97 (Lorenzaccio 130) [1990 NR 1991 11f3 12.2f8 12f2 11.9g3 13.1m3 16.1m] lengthy colt: moderate walker: modest handicapper: won at Catterick (maiden) in July: ran well after when placed: will stay 1¾m: has raced only on a sound surface: carries head high and doesn't look easiest of rides. *R. Allan.* 76

LAUGHING FALCON 2 b.f. (Apr 1) Bellypha 130 – Falcon Berry (FR) (Bustino 136) [1991 7m 6s] 33,000Y: fourth foal: half-sister to quite modest middle-distance winner Beaumood (by Jalmood) and fair miler Top Berry (by High Top): dam lightly-raced daughter of Cheveley Park runner-up Red Berry: better effort in maidens when seventh of 20, running on late, at Folkestone in November: should stay 1¼m. *J. L. Dunlop.* 46 p

LAUGHTON LADY 2 ch.f. (Apr 15) Crofthall 110 – No Illusion 48 (Grey Mirage 128) [1991 6g a5g 7.5f] compact filly: second reported living foal: dam won 1¼m seller: probably of little account. *Mrs N. Macauley.* —

LAUNDE ABBEY 3 ch.f. Absalom 128 – More Fun (Malicious) [1990 6g2 5m* 6f 1991 5m6 6g 5g 5m6] lengthy, good-topped filly: modest form at best: disappoint- 70

ing after shaping well in handicap on reappearance: should prove suited by further than 5f. *C. E. Brittain.*

LAUNDRY MAID 2 b. or br.f. (Feb 10) Forzando 122 – Spin Dry (High Top 131) **65**
[1991 5g 7f⁶ 6s³] useful-looking filly: has a quick action: half-sister to several winners, including 1½m winner In A Spin (by Windjammer) and 1983 2-y-o 5f winner Oystons Propweekly (by Swing Easy): dam little form in France: easily best effort when staying-on third of 17 in maiden at Kempton in September: should stay 7f: seems suited by soft ground. *H. Candy.*

LAURAVALE 3 b.f. Kind of Hush 118 – Fuddled 74 (Malacate (USA) 131) [1990 —
8m 7f 1991 12.2m³ 8m] angular filly: has a round action: poor form at 2 yrs: last in maiden and selling handicap (sweating) in 1991. *D. R. Franks.*

LAUREL CONNECTION 2 b.c. (Mar 3) Precocious 126 – Becky Sharp 66 —
(Sharpen Up 127) [1991 5f 6m 8.1g 8m] 3,500Y: good-topped colt: third living foal: half-brother to 3-y-o Danish winner Milly Sharp (by Nishapour): dam 1m winner: well beaten in maiden auctions: sold 1,200 gns Doncaster November Sales. *J. Berry.*

LAUREL QUEEN (IRE) 3 ch.f. Viking (USA) – Prima Bella 76 (High Hat 131) **66**
[1990 5m⁴ 6f³ 7f* 7f 7g* 7f⁴ 7m* 7g⁵ a8g 1991 7g* 7m⁴ 7m* 7m³ 8.2m* 8h² 6.9m⁵ a8g 8m⁵ 8.1g* 7m* 8.2m 7d² 8m* 8.1s] neat filly: quite modest form: successful in claimers at Warwick, Carlisle and Hamilton in the spring and at Edinburgh, Southwell and Leicester in the autumn: stays 1m: acts on good to firm ground and dead, below form on fibresand: has looked awkward ride, very slowly away and seeming reluctant to race twelfth outing: great credit to trainer. *J. Berry.*

LAW CHAMBERS 4 b.c. Law Society (USA) 130 – Amata (USA) (Nodouble —
(USA)) [1990 10s 12g* 1991 10f⁴ 15m] rangy colt: good mover: half-brother to several winners abroad, including useful French 1m and 9.5f winner Grammene (by Grey Dawn II): dam French middle-distance winner later successful in USA: very lightly-raced ex-Irish colt: fair form when winning maiden at the Curragh at 3 yrs (trained by M. V. O'Brien): sold 3,800 gns Doncaster March Sales: well beaten in Nottingham minor event and amateur riders event at Ayr in September: suited by 1½m. *M. P. Naughton.*

LAWNSWOOD GOLD (IRE) 3 b.g. Godswalk (USA) 130 – Octet (Octavo **59 p**
(USA) 115) [1990 NR 1991 12.5m 8m³ 12m] 1,000 2-y-o: sturdy gelding: good mover: fourth foal: half-brother to 13.8f winner Far Too Loud (by Taufan): dam daughter of Lancashire Oaks winner Red Chorus: 50/1 but backward, easily best effort in maidens when 12 lengths third of 12 to Contessa at Pontefract in October, keeping on from towards rear: never placed to challenge 17 days later: should prove capable of better. *R. Hollinshead.*

LAWNSWOOD JUNIOR 4 gr.g. Bairn (USA) 126 – Easymede 85 (Runnymede **51**
123) [1990 8.2f⁴ 12.3d⁴ 9m 10g⁴ 9m⁵ 8g 8d 9g⁵ 8m⁵ 11d² 12.4s³ 1991 a10g³ a10g³ 10.8g 12.2m a12g 10.3d⁶] workmanlike gelding: moderate mover: modest handicapper at best: below form in 1991, last 3 starts after 5½-month absence: should prove ideally suited by 1¼m: possibly best on a sound surface: below form when blinkered once: has run well when visored. *J. L. Spearing.*

LAWNSWOOD PRINCE (IRE) 2 b.g. (Apr 20) Anita's Prince 126 – La **63**
Croisette (Nishapour (FR) 125) [1991 5d 5d 5m 5m 5g² 5m 5m³ 5m⁴ 5.7g] sturdy, lengthy gelding: fifth foal: half-brother to 1989 2-y-o 5f seller Ivory's of Radlett (by Alzao): dam ran once at 2 yrs in Ireland: quite modest maiden: ran moderately last 2 starts: blinkered (ran poorly in seller) third outing: inconsistent: sold 3,600 gns Doncaster November Sales. *R. Hollinshead.*

LAXMI (USA) 3 b.c. Lyphard's Wish (FR) 124 – Camarina (USA) (Vaguely Noble **80**
140) [1990 7g⁵ 8d⁵ 1991 8f³ 8g² 10m 8f*] rather leggy colt: shows high knee action: fair performer: won apprentice maiden at Yarmouth in August, always prominent: last of 10 after some headway over 2f out in £14,800 handicap at Newmarket: stays 1m well: acts on firm going: has worn severe noseband. *M. R. Stoute.*

LAZY HILL 4 b.f. Kabour 80 – Hilly's Daughter (Hillandale 125) [1990 NR 1991 —
a6g a8g 6f 8m 5m 6g 6m a5g] strong, close-coupled filly: third foal: dam bad maiden: no worthwhile form, including in handicaps: blinkered last 3 starts on turf. *D. W. Chapman.*

LAZY RHYTHM (USA) 5 gr.g. Drone – Ritual Dance 84 (Godswalk (USA) 130) —
[1990 NR 1991 7.1g 6g 8.3m 7m 5.1d 5s⁶] lengthy gelding: carries condition: has been pin-fired: trained by J. Dunlop, modest handicapper at 3 yrs: behind in 1991, including in seller: best form at around 1m: acts on soft going, possibly unsuited by firm: often bandaged. *D. C. Jermy.*

LEABRANNAGH LASS 3 ch.f. Ballad Rock 122 – Kenton's Girl 86 (Record —
Token 128) [1990 5g 5f⁶ 6d 1991 10m 8m] sturdy filly: poor form at 2 yrs: behind in
seller and claimer in autumn as 3-y-o. *M. C. Pipe.*

LEADING TIME (FR) 2 b.c. (Feb 24) Lead On Time (USA) 124 – Copy Cat **92**
(FR) (King of Macedon 126) [1991 6g² 5d* 5m* 5g6] 200,000 francs (approx
£20,000) Y: sturdy, lengthy colt: good walker: second foal: dam sprint winner in
France from 2 to 5 yrs: fairly useful performer: won maiden at Tipperary in June and
Group 3 Shernazar Curragh Stakes (by a head from Safety Tactic) in July: always
outpaced in Philip Cornes Molecomb Stakes at Goodwood 3 weeks later: best form
at 5f: acts on good to firm and dead ground. *J. S. Bolger, Ireland.*

LEAD THE DANCE 2 b.c. (Apr 9) Lead On Time (USA) 124 – Maiyaasah 75 **95**
(Kris 135) [1991 6m² 6f* 6s² 7m² 7m4] tall, quite attractive colt: second foal:
half-brother to 3-y-o Perfidy (by Persian Bold): dam lightly-raced maiden, ran only
at 1m: fairly useful performer: 5/1 on, won 5-runner maiden event at Yarmouth in
August without coming off bridle: runner-up in minor events at Newmarket and
Doncaster: creditable fourth of 8 to Tertian in slowly-run Somerville Tattersall
Stakes at Newmarket: should stay 1m: acts on any going. *H. R. A. Cecil.*

LEANARDO BLU (USA) 2 b.g. (Apr 24) Magesterial (USA) 116 – Birch Bark —
(USA) (Apalachee (USA) 137) [1991 7m 8m] 10,000Y: strong gelding: has plenty of
scope: third foal, first 2 (including a full brother) successful in USA: dam won 2 races
at up to 9f: bit backward, well beaten in large-field maidens at Redcar in autumn,
latter an auction: has joined M. Johnston. *W. J. Pearce.*

LEAN'N MEAN (IRE) 3 b.g. Heraldiste (USA) 121 – Pyjama Game 56 (Cavo **43**
Doro 124) [1990 8m⁴ 7d³ a8g a8g⁴ 1991 12v⁴ 10f⁶ 11f 11.5s5] leggy, sparely-made
gelding: has a quick action: fair plater: visored, best effort as 3-y-o in non-selling
handicap on reappearance: stays 1½m: acts on heavy going: blinkered last 3 starts:
sold 2,200 gns Newmarket Autumn Sales. *M. Bell.*

LEAP IN THE DARK (IRE) 2 br.c. (Jan 15) Shadeed (USA) 135 – Star Guide **71** p
(FR) (Targowice (USA) 130) [1991 8.1m² 8m*] 7,500Y: big, lengthy, unfurnished
colt: has scope: half-brother to French 3-y-o River Gleam (by Riverman): dam
French 2-y-o 7.5f winner, is half-sister to Irish River: odds on following promising
effort behind King's Loch in Sandown minor event, won 28-runner maiden auction
at Redcar in October, travelling smoothly 5f then staying on well: will stay 1¼m:
likely to do better. *J. L. Dunlop.*

LEARIVA (USA) 4 ch.f. Irish River (FR) 131 – Leandra (FR) 125 (Luthier 126) **119**
[1990 10.5d² 8g 8d³ 8g² 9d* 10g⁴ 10g² 10s* 10.5v² 1991 10v* 10g⁶ 10.5g 8g* 8m⁶ 9d
10s* 10f] smart French filly: fourth foal: half-sister to good-class French horse
Alesso (by Alleged), successful at 10.5f and 12.5f but suited by test of stamina: dam
won 1¼m Prix de Malleret and Prix de la Nonette and second in Prix Vermeille: won
Group 3 Prix Exbury at Saint-Cloud in March, Group 2 Prix d'Astarte at Deauville in
August and Grade 1 Budweiser International Stakes at Laurel (beat Sillery by 1¾
lengths) in October: effective at 1m to 1¼m: best efforts with give in the ground
(acts on heavy going). *D. Smaga, France.*

LEAVE IT TO LIB 4 b.f. Tender King 123 – Nuit de Vin (Nebbiolo 125) [1990 6f **60**
6g 7m* 7d 1991 7g⁴ 8m⁴ 7m⁵ 7h⁴ 8g³ a7g⁵ 7.6g² 8f* 8.1m* 7m⁵ 8f* 8d 8m] small,
sparely-made filly: quite modest handicapper: won at Thirsk (apprentices) in July
and Edinburgh and Thirsk in August: suited by around 1m: goes very well on
top-of-the-ground: suited by forcing tactics, particularly on turning track. *P. Calver.*

LE BARON PERCHE (FR) 2 b.c. (Mar 5) Vayrann 133 – Dayira (Sparkler **72**
130) [1991 6m 7f⁴ 7f* 8g] sturdy colt: third foal: half-brother to French 1¼m winner
Dayoula (by Mouktar): dam unraced half-sister to Dazari and Dihistan: modest
form: won 16-runner claimer at Yarmouth in September, quickening into lead 2f out
and keeping on well: ran respectably in nursery at Goodwood following month:
stays 1m: acts on firm ground. *C. James.*

LE CHIC 5 b.g. Kabour 80 – Boom Shanty 66 (Dragonara Palace (USA) 115) [1990 **63**
5m² 5m* 5f⁴ 5g⁵ 5d³ 5g 5g² 5m² 6f² 5m³ 5m 5d 5g 5m³ 5m² 5d 6d a6g a5g³ 1991 5f
5d² 5d² 5m* 5d 5m² 5m⁴ 5g 5m 5.2f 5g 5g] strong, workmanlike gelding: quite
modest handicapper: has proved untrustworthy: won at Wolverhampton in July: ran
moderately last 4 starts: stays 6f: acts on firm and dead going: tried blinkered once:
sometimes doesn't find much, and best with extreme waiting tactics. *D. W.
Chapman.*

LE CORSAIRE (USA) 3 br.c. Nureyev (USA) 131 – Little Bonny 126 (Bonne **104**
Noel 115) [1990 7m⁶ 7m⁴ 1991 10m² 12g** 12.3g² 16.2g³ 12g* 12g3] strong,
deep-girthed colt: won minor events at Newmarket in May and July: 5/2 on,

reportedly had flu virus when 2 lengths last of 3 to Stylish Senor in Gordon Stakes at Goodwood 11 days after latter, leading travelling well 2f out then coming under strong pressure and (as at Ascot in Queen's Vase fourth start) not finding as much as seemed likely: should prove suited by further than 1½m: has got on toes, including when successful: courage under suspicion. *L. M. Cumani.*

LEE ARTISTE 3 b.f. Tate Gallery (USA) 117 – Mirkan Honey 83 (Ballymore **104** 123) [1990 5m3 6m2 5m* 6m* 7d2 8v6 1991 7.3g4 8g 6m* 7.6g2 7g5 6s] smallish, compact filly: shows knee action: moderate walker: useful performer: on toes, won listed race at Haydock in May, pushed along some way off pace early on: very good second of 5 to Green Line Express at Lingfield, best effort in similar events afterwards: stays 7.6f: unsuited by soft ground. *P. F. I. Cole.*

LEGAL CASE 5 b.h. Alleged (USA) 138 – Maryinsky (USA) (Northern Dancer) **108** + [1990 10m4 12m5 12m 12g6 10d3 10s* 1991 12g* 10v5] lengthy, attractive horse: high-class performer at best, winner of Champion Stakes in 1989: very lightly raced in 1991: won minor event at Salisbury (simple task on first run for nearly a year) in October: below form in Premio Roma following month: stays 1½m: best form with give in the ground: has run well when sweating. *L. M. Cumani.*

LEGAL EMBRACE (CAN) 2 ch.f. (Apr 16) Legal Bid (USA) 120 – Tina Rosa **61** p (CAN) (Hans I) [1991 6.9f3] leggy, quite attractive, rather unfurnished filly: fifth reported foal: half-sister to a minor winner in North America: dam minor winner there: 14/1 and green, 7½ lengths third of 12 to Kayvee in maiden at Folkestone in October, soon chasing pace and keeping on: will improve, particularly over further. *J. R. Fanshawe.*

LEGAL LEGACY 3 b.f. Norwick (USA) 120 – Jambalaya (Amboise 113) [1990 — NR 1991 a12g 11d 12f] 1,700F: lengthy, angular filly: third foal: dam staying maiden: showed little in maiden, seller and claimer: sold 1,400 gns Newmarket Autumn Sales. *C. A. Cyzer.*

LEGAL VIEW (USA) 3 b.c. Riverman (USA) 131 – Dictina (FR) (Dictus (FR) **93** 126) [1990 7d 1991 10d2 9g* 11g] close-coupled, rather leggy colt: has a quick action: good walker: favourite, won maiden at Ripon in July by short head from Oh Mercy: below form in handicap 3½ months later, after headway from rear 2f out: may well prove best at up to 1¼m: acts on dead ground. *L. M. Cumani.*

LEGAL WIN (USA) 3 ch.c. Arctic Tern (USA) 126 – Banker's Favorite (USA) **55** (Lyphard (USA) 132) [1990 7s6 1991 10.2s5 10.8d 11.7s5 13.1f* 16m 14.1g2 14.1g] sturdy, quite attractive colt: plating-class handicapper: won at Bath in May: worth another try at 2m: acts on firm going: blinkered third start, visored afterwards: sold to join F. Jordan 10,500 gns Newmarket July Sales. *M. Bell.*

LEGENDARY (IRE) 2 b.c. (Apr 11) Sadler's Wells (USA) 132 – Godzilla 106 **52** p (Gyr (USA) 131) [1991 7g3] leggy, close-coupled colt: brother to 3-y-o 7f (at 2 yrs) and 9f winner Lilian Bayliss, and very useful French sprinter/miler Ernani, closely related to high-class French miler Phydilla (by Lyphard) and half-brother to several winners, notably Observation Post (by Shirley Heights): dam won at up to 7.5f in Italy and showed form at 6f here: weak 5/1-shot and green, 11½ lengths third of 7, slowly away, soon chased along, no progress final 2f, to Haymarket in maiden at Warwick in October: will stay at least 1m: will improve. *P. W. Chapple-Hyam.*

LEGEND DULAC (IRE) 2 b.c. (Feb 9) Legend of France (USA) 124 – Westerlake (Blakeney 126) [1991 6g] 3,100 2-y-o: second foal: half-brother to 1¼m winner Western Loch (by Reesh): dam twice-raced half-sister to good 1975 2-y-o 5f performer Western Jewel and Queen Anne winner Mr Fluorocarbon: 40/1, bit backward and green, slow-starting last of 12 maiden at Lingfield in October. *J. L. Harris.*

LEGEND OF SCOTLAND 3 b.c. Scottish Reel 123 – Visitation 84 (Tarqogan — 125) [1990 5m 6g a7g 1991 8.2d 8s] leggy colt: of little account: blinkered final start. *J. D. Czerpak.*

LEGION OF HONOUR 3 b.c. Ahonoora 122 – Shehana (USA) 86 (The **79** Minstrel (USA) 135) [1990 6m3 1991 8m3 10.5g3 12g3 12m*] lengthy colt: has round action: fair form in maidens: won at Pontefract in October, leading well over 1f out: stays 1½m: lacks turn of foot. *W. Jarvis.*

LEGITIM 2 br.g. (May 30) Move Off 112 – Eliza de Rich 57 (Spanish Gold 101) **48** [1991 5f 6m4 7m] 8,000Y: leggy, rather angular gelding: has a quick action: third reported foal: half-brother to winning sprinter Densben (by Silly Prices): dam winning miler: poor maiden: best form over 13 lengths last of 4 in minor event at Redcar in August: should stay 7f. *J. M. Jefferson.*

LEGUARD EXPRESS (IRE) 3 b.c. Double Schwartz 128 – All Moss 66   **63** d
(Prince Tenderfoot (USA) 126) [1990 NR 1991 7g³ 8f⁶ 8g³ 7g 8d⁵ 8.2g 8g 8m 8d]
12,000F, 18,000Y: good-topped colt: half-brother to 1½m winner Crystal Moss (by
Kris) and a winner in Belgium: dam stayed 1½m, is from good family: quite modest
maiden: off course nearly 3 months, then well beaten in handicaps (seller last time)
last 3 starts: should stay beyond 1m: seems unsuited by firm going: blinkered,
sweating and edgy final start. *W. Carter.*

LEIF THE LUCKY (USA) 2 ch.c. (Mar 1) Lemhi Gold (USA) 123 – Corvine   **83** p
(USA) (Crow (FR) 134) [1991 8g⁴] 32,000Y: half-brother to 2 winners in USA: dam
unraced half-sister to champion American sprinter Star de Naskra: 50/1 and on toes,
around 8 lengths fourth of 16, soon prominent racing keenly, no headway from 2f
out, to Aljadeer in minor event at Newbury in October: will improve. *W. Jarvis.*

LEIGH CROFTER 2 ch.c. (Feb 24) Son of Shaka 119 – Ganadora (Good Times   **69**
(ITY)) [1991 5g⁶ 5m⁶ 6d⁴ 6g² 7g 6g 7m* 7m⁶] 1,000Y: workmanlike colt: second
foal: half-brother to 3-y-o Vittoria Glenn (by Town And Country): dam unraced:
quite modest form: won 20-runner selling nursery at Catterick in October, soon far
away and staying on gamely: better suited by 7f than 6f: inconsistent. *R. J. Holder.*

LE JOUEUR (USA) 4 ch.g. Riverman (USA) 131 – Happy Bride 116 (Royal   —
Match 117) [1990 10m⁵ 14f 1991 16.2g] medium-sized gelding: thrice raced and no
worthwhile form in maidens: refused to enter stalls (wore crossed noseband)
intended debut. *Mrs P. A. Barker.*

LENNOX AVENUE (USA) 3 b.c. Topsider (USA) – Party Bonnet (USA) (The   **88**
Axe II 115) [1990 NR 1991 8g⁵ 10.2m 8m⁶ 10m² 10g] angular, workmanlike colt: has a
roundish action: third living foal: half-brother to good-class American winner Forty
Niner Days (by Conquistador Cielo): effective from 1m to 11f: dam won 3 races,
including minor 8.5f stakes at 5 yrs, and is from good family: fair maiden: 20/1, easily
best effort when second of 11 at Redcar, staying on well: worth a try over 1½m: sold
A. Falourd 16,000 gns Newmarket Autumn Sales. *J. H. M. Gosden.*

LEOLENE POKEY 2 b.c. (May 13) Uncle Pokey 116 – Gamuza VII (pedigree   —
unknown) [1991 6f 5f 7m] leggy colt: first foal: dam non-thoroughbred mare: soundly
beaten in northern maidens. *W. W. Haigh.*

LEONADIS POLK 2 ch.g. (Mar 21) Hadeer 118 – Brokelsby Anne 69 (Dunphy   **64**
124) [1991 5f* 5m⁶ 6d³ 6m³ 6g 6m⁴ 6m⁴ 8.3s⁴] 4,200Y: tall, workmanlike gelding:
moderate mover: first foal: dam, maiden, ran only at 2 yrs, is out of half-sister to
King's Company and Deep Diver: quite modest performer: won maiden auction at
Redcar in May: ran well (including in sellers) when in frame: stays 8.3f: acts on any
going: visored fifth outing (raced freely), blinkered penultimate one. *W. J. Pearce.*

LEPOUSHKA 5 b.m. Salmon Leap (USA) 131 – Polifontaine (FR) (Bold Lad   **91**
(USA)) [1990 8g 8g* 7m⁵ 9g 7g 8m³ 8g* 7s² 1991 8d 7d⁶ 8m³ 7m³ 8m⁵ 8d] lengthy,
workmanlike mare: fairly useful Irish performer: eleventh of 25 behind Amenable in
William Hill Lincoln at Doncaster: best effort creditable third to Additional Risk in
listed event at Leopardstown: stiff tasks last 2 starts: effective at 7f and 1m: acts on
good to firm and soft going. *P. Hill, Ireland.*

LER CRU (IRE) 2 b.c. (Jan 30) Lafontaine (USA) 117 – Kirsova (Absalom 128)   **63** p
[1991 7m⁵ 8d] 7,800F, 16,000Y: strong-quartered, sturdy colt: brother to 9f and 14.8f
winner La Ballerine: dam lightly raced: 20/1, better effort in maiden at Newmarket
in July: backward, tailed-off last of 8, dropping away quickly from over 2f out, in
Royal Lodge William Hill Stakes at Ascot nearly 3 months later: likely to do better,
particularly over middle distances. *C. E. Brittain.*

LE SAINT GERAN (FR) 5 b.g. Margouillat (FR) 133 – Rain Later (USA)   —
(Rainy Lake) [1990 NR 1991 10f⁵ 12.3d 11.6m 16m] leggy gelding: poor walker and
mover: very lightly raced on flat and no worthwhile form, including in handicaps:
sold 1,000 gns Ascot November Sales. *H. J. Collingridge.*

LES AMIS 4 b.f. Alzao (USA) 117 – Les Sylphides (FR) (Kashmir II 125) [1990   **52**
6m⁴ 6g 9m 8g 8m 6d⁴ 7g⁵ a7g⁴ 7d a10g² a10g⁶ a8g³ᵈⁱˢ a8g 1991 10d⁵ 8m³ 8m*
9m⁴ 8g 8.1g 8m⁵ 8.2m⁴ 8g⁵ 8d a8g³] sturdy, workmanlike filly: plating-class
handicapper: won at Kempton (apprentices) in May: stays 1¼m: acts on good to firm
and dead ground, and all-weather surfaces: has run well when blinkered: has worn
dropped noseband: largely consistent. *M. J. Ryan.*

LE SAULE D'OR 4 br.f. Sonnen Gold 121 – Richesse (FR) (Faraway Son (USA)   **38**
130) [1990 8.2f 8m⁴ 10.2m⁴ 8f 10m⁶ 8g⁴ 8.5m 9m⁵ 8.2d 1991 10.8m 10d a7g 8m⁵ 8.2g
10g 8.1g 9.7m⁴ 9.7g] leggy, sparely-made filly: poor handicapper nowadays: stays
1¼m: acts on firm ground and dead: often blinkered and slowly away: inconsistent.
B. J. McMath.

LES JAZZ HOT 2 b.f. (Jan 1) Sizzling Melody 117 – La Reine de France (Queen's 37
Hussar 124) [1991 6m 5.2g 5h 7m] 9,400Y: workmanlike filly: has round action: fifth
foal: half-sister to 3 winners (all at sprint distances), including Nailem (by Absalom):
dam never ran: poor maiden: sold 1,100 gns Newmarket Autumn Sales. *M. A. Jarvis.*

L'ETE (IRE) 3 b.f. Kafu 120 – Miss Merryweather (Sexton Blake 126) [1990 5g2 55
5m6 5m2 5m2 5m 5g* 1991 6v6 5d 5g 6d 5g 5m 5m6 5d] good-quartered,
workmanlike filly: fair winner at 2 yrs: showed little at 3 yrs except in 18-runner
handicap (bandaged behind, moved poorly to post) penultimate outing: best form
over sharp 5f: sometimes sweating. *P. Mitchell.*

LET'S BE ON 3 b.f. State Diplomacy (USA) – Wings At Night (Decoy Boy 129) —
[1990 6f 1991 10f 8g 10d 8.5f6] leggy, lengthy, sparely-made filly: behind in maidens
and handicaps: doesn't stay 1¼m: unruly and sweating second start. *P. Beaumont.*

LETSBEONESTABOUTIT 5 b.g. Petong 126 – My Bushbaby 100 (Hul A Hul 96
124) [1990 6f4 6f5 6f* 7f3 6m 6f2 6m* 6d3 6m2 6d 6g 6f3 6m4 6m 7f4 6g6 6m* 5.6g 6d
1991 6d4 6g 6s 6m3 6m 5.8d2 6m5 6d 6d 6f 7m 6m3 6g* 6m4 6m3 6g 6d] tall, strong
gelding: poor mover: fairly useful handicapper: a reformed character: had another
very busy season: won at Haydock in September: best at 6f: acts on firm and dead
(unsuited by very soft) ground: has been tried in visor, usually blinkered: races up
with pace. *Mrs N. Macauley.*

LET'S GET LOST 2 ch.c. (Feb 8) Chief Singer 131 – Lost In France 80 88 p
(Northfields (USA)) [1991 7.1m3 8m2] lengthy, quite good-topped colt: has scope:
first foal: dam (showed ability only on debut) is half-sister to top-class French and
American middle-distance performer Perrault: much better effort when always-
prominent 2 lengths second of 18 to Wesaam in maiden at Newmarket in October,
leading briefly 3f out and staying on really well: likely to stay 1¼m: will improve
again and win a maiden. *W. J. Haggas.*

LET'S GO LOCHY 5 b.m. Lochnager 132 – Happy Donna 106 (Huntercombe —
133) [1990 5m 10m 1991 5.1g] good-bodied mare: poor walker: thrice raced and no
worthwhile form. *C. J. Hill.*

LETTEREWE 5 b.m. Alias Smith (USA) – Princess Nefertiti (Tutankhamen) —
[1990 NR 1991 14.6s6] leggy, sparely-made mare: very lightly raced on flat and no
worthwhile form: blinkered only run in 1991: won over hurdles at 4 yrs (has also
refused to race). *G. A. Pritchard-Gordon.*

LETTS GREEN (IRE) 3 ch.c. Exhibitioner 111 – Cress (Crepello 136) [1990 46
NR 1991 10v4 10.8g 10g 12.2m 11.5m4 11.5d3 14g 9.7s2 10g 9m] 6,000Y: strong,
compact colt: has a markedly round action: half-brother to several winners,
including speedy 1976 2-y-o Self Portrait (by Jukebox) and 1¼m winner Dhofar (by
Octavo): dam ran 3 times: poor maiden: 33/1-second in amateurs handicap at
Folkestone: tailed off in handicaps afterwards: keen sort, possibly best at up to
1¼m: acts on soft going. *J. D. Czerpak.*

LEVEL UP 2 ch.f. (Feb 1) Beveled (USA) – Haiti Mill 68 (Free State 125) [1991 59
5d6 5d5 a8g3 a8g4] 12,000Y: second foal: half-sister to 3-y-o Nigel's Lucky Girl (by
Belfort), modest 7f winner at 2 yrs: dam maiden suited by 1m, is out of sister to
high-class Petong: first run since mid-July, third of 9, finishing well, to Paper Clip in
late-year maiden at Lingfield, easily best effort. *R. Guest.*

LEVEL XING 3 ro.g. Stanford 121§ – Lucky Song 91 (Lucky Wednesday 124) —
[1990 5f2 5g* 5m 6m* 6g2 6m2 6m4 6m2 6m5 6g5 6m 7m 1991 6g 8m 7m 6g] strong
gelding: good walker: moderate mover: fair winner at 2 yrs: well below form in 1991:
best form at 6f: visored and tongue tied down penultimate start: subsequently
gelded, and blinkered 10 weeks later: sold to Scandinavia 2,100 gns Newmarket
Autumn Sales. *C. N. Allen.*

LEXUS (IRE) 3 b.g. Gorytus (USA) 132 – Pepi Image (USA) 111 (National) [1990 59 d
NR 1991 8f5 10.4g 10.2m4 10g3 11.5s a16g] IR 24,000Y: good-bodied gelding:
half-brother to several winners, including 7f to 9f winner National Form (by Gay
Fandango): dam third in Irish 1000 Guineas: disappointing maiden: apparently
suited by 1m: acts on firm going: sold 2,600 gns Doncaster November Sales and
gelded. *R. J. R. Williams.*

L'HERMINE 2 b.c. (Mar 28) Slip Anchor 136 – Mondialite (FR) (Habitat 134) 91 p
[1991 7f 7m 7m*] leggy, workmanlike colt: second foal: half-brother to 3-y-o 1m and
10.1f winner Burdur (by Bering): dam French 6.5f winner, is half-sister to smart
French 1m to 1¼m performer Malaspina: 33/1 and blinkered, showed much
improved form when winning 11-runner maiden at Lingfield in September by 8
lengths from Castillet, chasing leader, going on 3f out and galloping on really
strongly: will probably stay 1¼m: has joined H. Candy. *B. Hanbury.*

459

LIABILITY ORDER 2 b.c. (Feb 16) Norwick (USA) 120 – Starky's Pet **68** (Mummy's Pet 125) [1991 7g 7m 8m⁶ 8d³ a7g* a8g⁵] 3,500Y: lengthy, angular colt: moderate mover: fourth foal: brother to lightly-raced maiden Sunset And Vine and half-brother to 7f winner Southern Sky (by Comedy Star): dam behind in 4 starts on flat and over hurdles: quite modest form: has run in a seller: won late-year maiden at Lingfield in quite good style: ran creditably in nursery there final start: stays 1m: active sort: wore crossed noseband first 2 outings, blinkered third. *R. Boss.*

LIANNE RISE 3 b.f. Scorpio (FR) 127 – Top Secret 90 (Manacle 123) [1990 NR — 1991 a8g⁴ 8m] close-coupled, rather sparely-made filly: half-sister to 1m seller winner Star Issue (by Comedy Star): dam won over 5f and 1m: little form in maidens in the summer. *Miss H. C. Knight.*

LIBK 3 b.c. Kalaglow 132 – Balqis (USA) 93 (Advocator) [1990 7m 8m* 8g* 8m **105** 1991 12d 11.5m* 11.9m* 11.9m* 14g⁴ 14.6m 12m³] strong, well-made colt: impresses in appearance: has a quick action: successful in ladies events at Lingfield and York (£10,000 event) then £23,900 Old Newton Cup Handicap at Haydock in the summer: in frame, running creditably, in listed races won by Jahafil at Goodwood and Surrealist at Newmarket: soundly beaten in St Leger at Doncaster penultimate start: well worth a try at 2m: acts on good to firm ground: useful: remains in training. *H. Thomson Jones.*

LIBRA LEGEND (USA) 2 ch.c. (Mar 24) Believe It (USA) – Posslq (USA) **63** (Cyane) [1991 7m 7f⁴ 7m 6g] $37,000F, 20,000Y: lengthy, good-topped colt: has plenty of scope: half-brother to winners in North America by Well Decorated and Devil's Bag: dam, winner of 2 races at up to 9f at 4 yrs, is sister to dam of Rockfel winner At Risk: quite modest maiden: ran creditably in face of very stiff task in Tattersalls Tiffany Highflyer Stakes at Newmarket penultimate start: will be better suited by 1m. *C. E. Brittain.*

LIDANZIA 3 br.f. Lidhame 109 – Lady Antonia 66 (Owen Anthony 102) [1990 5f⁵ **44** 6d 1991 8m 8.2m 10g 8m⁶ 8.1s² 10g⁴ 12.1g⁵] leggy, sparely-made filly: moderate mover: poor performer: stays 1¼m: best 3-y-o form with give in the ground: sweating final start. *R. J. Holder.*

LIFETIME FAME 2 b.c. (Jan 23) Sayf El Arab (USA) 127 – Hot Momma 81 **72** (Free State 125) [1991 6g⁶ 6d 7m] 9,600F, 18,000Y: leggy, quite attractive colt: second foal: dam 1¼m winner but better at 2 yrs: blinkered, best effort when seventh of 18 to Mahool at Doncaster in October, final start, showing very good speed 5f, weakening closing stages: may prove best at around 6f. *J. W. Payne.*

Queen Mother's Cup, York—
Europe's richest race for lady riders is won by Libk (noseband) from Habaayib

LIFETIME FORTUNE (IRE)   2 ch.c. (Apr 30) Be My Native (USA) 122 – Flat   —
Refusal (USA) (Ribero 126) [1991 6f 6m 6g a7g] IR 5,200F, 14,000Y: leggy colt:
half-brother to several winners, including modest sprinter Tread Lika Prince (by
Prince Tenderfoot): dam won twice over 6f in North America: seems of little
account. *J. W. Payne.*

LIFETIMES AMBITION   3 br.c. Hotfoot 126 – Consistent Queen 55 (Queen's   52
Hussar 124) [1990 5m 5g 6f 5m³ 5d 8m 8g 10.2s 1991 8s 10g 9.2d⁵ 9.2m⁴ a8g⁵ 12m³
10.6g 11.1g³ 12d³ 11.8m*] compact colt: has a quick action: fair plater: won handicap
(sold 5,200 gns to join T. Casey) at Leicester in October, leading 1f out: will stay
beyond 1½m: acts on good to firm ground and soft: looked temperamental when
blinkered at 2 yrs. *T. Casey.*

LIFEWATCH VISION   4 b.c. Vision (USA) – Maellen (River Beauty 105) [1990 **108**
8f* 8.5g² 8g² 10f⁵ 8m 10.1g 8m² 9g 1991 8d⁶ 8f* 8f² 8g⁵ 8d* 12f* 8m⁴ 10m⁵ 8.9g³
12s 8m³ 8d² 9m] angular, workmanlike colt: has a round action: useful performer:
successful in minor events at Brighton in April and Newbury in June and in auction
event at Beverley in July: ran well in varied company after: effective at 1m, and stays
1½m: acts on firm and dead ground: pulled too hard when blinkered: largely
consistent. *M. Johnston.*

LIFFEY RIVER (USA)   3 ch.c. Irish River (FR) 131 – Close Comfort (USA)   67
(Far North (CAN) 120) [1990 NR 1991 7g⁶ 6f⁶ 5m² 6g 5m* 5f⁵ 5m 6.1m] compact
colt: poor mover: moderate walker: fourth foal: brother to 1987 2-y-o 7f winner
Gazayil and half-brother 1¼m to 1½m winner Husyan (by Alleged): dam unraced
half-sister to leading French performers Cricket Ball and Ancient Regime: won
maiden at Folkestone in July, hanging right and leading inside final 1f: easily best
effort in handicaps subsequently when good fifth at Salisbury: stays 6f: acts on firm
ground: wore tongue strap last 4 starts: bandaged last time. *Mrs L. Piggott.*

LIFT AND LOAD (USA)   4 b.c. Lyphard's Wish (FR) 124 – Dorit (USA)   99
(Damascus (USA)) [1990 8d 8m⁴ 10d* 12g* 12s⁵ 12g* 12m⁶ 12s⁴ 1991 12s⁴ 10s 12g⁵
12s³ 12g* 12m 12g⁶ 11.9m³ 12g⁵ 13.9g 12m* 13.3m 12s³ 12m 12d⁵] lengthy,
good-quartered colt: shows knee action: fairly useful handicapper: won at
Goodwood in May and Doncaster (claimer ridden) in September: ran well after when
third in £70,000 Krug Trophy at Ascot and fifth in November Handicap at
Doncaster: should prove at least as effective over 1¾m as 1½m: acts on good to firm
ground, and goes very well with some give (yet to race on heavy): occasionally on
toes and sweating: sometimes wanders: lazy, but game: tough: winning hurdler. *R.
Hannon.*

LIFT BOY (USA)   2 b.c. (Feb 27) Fighting Fit (USA) – Pressure Seat (USA)   51
(Ginistrelli (USA) 117) [1991 5d 5m⁵ 6d 6m 6g 6m 6.1d⁶] $18,000Y: sturdy colt: first
foal: dam won at up to 7f: sire won from 6f to 9f: plating-class maiden: will stay 7f:
twice visored, running creditably first occasion: sweating, on toes and steadily to
post final one. *Denys Smith.*

LIGHT DANCER   5 ch.g. Niniski (USA) 125 – Foudre 76 (Petingo 135) [1990   52
15m 1991 14.8g⁵ 14.6m⁵ 16m⁶ 16.2d⁶ 18.1m⁵] compact, sparely-made gelding:
plating-class handicapper: stays 2¼m: acts on good to firm and dead ground:
winning hurdler. *L. J. Codd.*

LIGHT HAND   5 br.m. Star Appeal 133 – No Cards 109 (No Mercy 126) [1990   80
10g* 10m³ 10f² 9m³ 10d* 10.6d* 1991 a12g⁴ 10.6g³ 10g* 10.2g³ 10.5m³ 10.9m²]
leggy, workmanlike mare: moderate mover: fair handicapper: won at Pontefract in
June: not seen out after July: suited by around 1¼m: acts on firm ground but ideally
suited by some give: raced freely when blinkered: consistent. *M. H. Tompkins.*

LIGHT-HEARTED LADY   3 gr.f. Norwick (USA) 120 – Lady Andrea (Andrea   61
Mantegna) [1990 NR 1991 10.2f⁴ 8.9g⁶ 8m³ 8m⁶ 7.1g 8.9m 11.7f² 12m 12f] 1,700Y:
sparely-made filly: fourth foal: half-sister to 6f and 10.2f winner Logical Lady (by
Tina's Pet) and 9f and 11f winner Likeable Lady (by Piaffer): dam never ran: quite
modest maiden: good running-on second in claiming event at Bath: stays 11.7f: acts
on firm going: has pulled hard. *R. J. Holder.*

LIGHTNAGER   2 br.g. (Mar 31) Lochnager 132 – Light The Way 72 (Nicholas   —
Bill 125) [1991 6m] 1,000Y: first foal: dam won 8.2f seller: 20/1, tailed off in 9-runner
maiden at Redcar in June: has joined Mrs V. Aconley. *C. Tinkler.*

LIGHTNING TRACK (USA)   2 ch.g. (Apr 2) Fulmar (USA) – Waki Miss   44
(USA) (Miswaki (USA) 124) [1991 8.2f 8f 6.9f] $11,000Y: sturdy gelding: third foal:
dam unraced: sire (by Northern Dancer) French 1m and 1¼m winner: poor maiden:
gave trouble stalls on debut: sold 3,500 gns Newmarket Autumn Sales. *W. A.
O'Gorman.*

LIGHT-OF-THE-LOCH   3 b.f. Lightning Dealer 103 – Balmenoch (Queen's   —
Hussar 124) [1990 5m⁴ 5d⁶ 5d 5v⁴ 6s² 1991 6g⁶ 7m 7g 6d a8g 10.5d⁶] leggy, rather
narrow filly: has a round action: poor plater: stays 1¼m: acts on soft ground: wore
severe bridle and very slowly away fifth start. *A. W. Potts.*

LIGHT ON HER TOES   4 b.f. Cragador 110 – Oscilight 112 (Swing Easy (USA)   —
126) [1990 7m 8.2s 1991 10v 7d 7g] lengthy, angular filly: seems of little account. *M.
J. Bolton.*

LIKE A PRAYER   4 b.g. Carwhite 127 – Dark Amber 68 (Formidable (USA) 125)   —
[1990 10m 10f 8.5m 1991 a12g 9s 8m] smallish ex-Irish gelding: first foal: dam 1m
winner, half-sister to Rakaposhi King: poor maiden: no form here, including in
seller, in spring of 1991: sold 1,100 gns Doncaster Spring Sales. *J. Parkes.*

LILIAN BAYLISS (IRE)   3 b.f. Sadler's Wells (USA) 132 – Godzilla 106 (Gyr **100**
(USA) 132) [1990 6g² 7d* 1991 7m³ 10g⁶ 9g*] rather finely-made, attractive filly:
has a fluent, roundish action: useful form: won 4-runner £7,000 event at Newmarket
in October by ½ length from King Athelstan, keeping on steadily to lead inside final
1f: off course over 3½ months after third in Nell Gwyn Stakes at same course:
should stay 1¼m: yet to race on extremes of going: sent to USA. *M. R. Stoute.*

LILLI REACH   2 ch.f. (Mar 10) Reach 122 – Lilli Parkin 90 (Crowned Prince   —
(USA) 128) [1991 6s] fourth foal: half-sister to 1984 2-y-o 6f winner Classic
Capistrano (by Song): dam won over 1m at 2 yrs: 33/1, slow-starting eleventh of 13 in
maiden at Yarmouth in October. *C. F. Wall.*

LILLY CAMILLY   4 ch.f. Electric 126 – Be Sharp 85 (Sharpen Up 127) [1990 8m   —
8f* 8m 1991 8h⁶ 9m 10m 9.2d 7f 8m 8.1g] lengthy, sturdy filly: selling handicapper:
lost her form: stays 1m: acts on firm ground: tried blinkered once. *Miss L. C. Siddall.*

LILY'S LOVER (USA)   5 b.g. Sensitive Prince (USA) – Rushing Stream (USA)   **55**
(Delta Judge) [1990 10.4d 12m 12f 10m 1991 7m² 10.3m³ 8g³] tall, sparely-made
gelding: moderate walker and mover: plating-class handicapper nowadays: effective
at 7f to 1½m: best form on sound surface. *D. Burchell.*

LILY'S SUN   4 gr.g. Kala Shikari 125 – Lily of France 81 (Monsanto (FR) 121)   —
[1990 6f² 6g 5g³ 5h⁶ 5g⁶ 6h 7g 5.3f⁵ 7g a5g 1991 8f 7m 6.1d 6g] leggy, lengthy
gelding: moderate mover: quite modest maiden at best: no show in first half of 1991:
stays 6f: acts on firm going: sometimes bandaged behind. *W. G. R. Wightman.*

LILY SUGARS   3 ch.f. Ardross 134 – Bobo Ema 81 (Auction Ring (USA) 123)   —
[1990 a7g a8g 1991 8g 10.2d] sturdy filly: has a round action: well beaten in maidens
and seller: bred to stay further: claimed £4,051 to join R. Juckes when successful in
claiming hurdle. *J. S. Moore.*

LIMBALI   3 b.c. Touching Wood (USA) 127 – Sizzler 67 (Blakeney 126) [1990 NR   —
1991 12m 12m 12d] 8,200Y: smallish, workmanlike colt: half-brother to Irish 11f
winner Down The Line (by Brigadier Gerard) and a listed winner in Italy: dam, 11f
winner, is closely related to More Light and half-sister to Shoot A Line: well beaten
in maiden (trained by F. Durr) then claimers: sold 1,150 gns Doncaster July Sales. *K.
T. Ivory.*

LIME ST NIGHTMAIR   3 b.g. Elegant Air 119 – Bernice Clare 68 (Skymaster   —
126) [1990 8g 1991 12d⁵ 12g 14m⁶ 11.1d 16g] rather sparely-made gelding: no
worthwhile form: left A. Stewart's stable £10,001 after claimer second start: may
prove best short of 1½m: sold to join D. Bell 700 gns Ascot 2nd July Sales. *N.
Tinkler.*

LIME STREET LIL   3 br.f. Precocious 126 – Merchantmens Girl (Klairon 131)   —
[1990 NR 1991 6d 7g 6.1m 6m 7g] lengthy filly: moderate mover: closely related to
winning sprinter Lindsey (by Mummy's Pet) and half-sister to several winning
sprinters, including fairly useful 1983 2-y-o Netsuke (by Tachypous): dam placed
over 5f: no worthwhile form in maidens: visored last 3 starts: sold 1,600 gns Ascot
November Sales. *J. Balding.*

LIMPOPO   2 gr.f. (Apr 16) Green Desert (USA) 127 – Grey Goddess 117   **49**
(Godswalk (USA) 130) [1991 5g⁴ a5g² 5d³ 5m 7m] small, rather leggy filly: moderate
mover: first foal: dam Irish 7f to 8.5f winner: poor maiden: faced stiff tasks when
well beaten in August nurseries at Windsor and Chester last 2 starts: bred to stay
1m: sold 5,400 gns Newmarket Autumn Sales. *Sir Mark Prescott.*

LINAVOS   8 b.h. Tyrnavos 129 – Linmill 74 (Amber Rama (USA) 133) [1990 a6g   —
1991 a5g] compact horse: poor performer: not seen out after January: stays 6f: acts
on firm and dead going. *P. Howling.*

LINCHMERE LAD (IRE)   3 b.g. Petorius 117 – Adamantos 92 (Yellow God   **60**
129) [1990 7g⁵ 7g⁴ 1991 7g 9d 12g⁶ 10f⁶ 10g] good-topped, quite attractive gelding:

quite modest maiden: worth another try at 1½m: acts on firm ground: sometimes edgy and sweating: sold to join T. Greathead 4,000 gns Ascot November Sales. *Lady Herries.*

LINCSTONE BOY (IRE)   3 b.g. Kafu 120 – Babylon (Hello Gorgeous (USA)   **48** §
128) [1990 6g 6g 5m* 5m 1991 6m⁵ 5m 5f 8f a5g 6f 5g 5g 5s⁴ 5s³ a5g] tall, plain gelding: poor sprinter: acts on good to firm ground and soft: often blinkered: carries head high: hard ride, inconsistent and not one to rely on. *A. Smith.*

LINDEMAN   2 b.g. (Feb 22) Reach 122 – Montana Moss (Levmoss 133) [1991   **54**
7m⁶ a8g³ a7g a8g] 2,000Y, 5,600 2-y-o: good-bodied gelding: half-brother to several winners, including 13.8f winner Joe Bumpas (by Noalto): dam won from 1m to 1¼m in Ireland at 3 yrs and 4 yrs and also won over hurdles: plating-class maiden: best effort when third on equitrack: will be suited by 1¼m + . *S. Dow.*

LINDFIELD BELLE (IRE)   3 b.f. Fairy King (USA) – Tecmessa (Home   —
Guard (USA) 129) [1990 6m⁵ 5m⁴ 5f* 5g⁴ 6m⁵ 6d 5m⁶ 6s 7s 1991 5m 5d] lengthy filly: carries condition: has a quick action: modest winner at 2 yrs: wintry in appearance, ran poorly in handicaps in spring as 3-y-o: stays 6f: acts on firm and dead ground, but seems unsuited by soft. *D. A. Wilson.*

LINE DRUMMER (USA)   3 ch.c. Topsider (USA) – Samarta Dancer (USA)   —
(Marshua's Dancer (USA)) [1990 NR 1991 7m a12g⁶ a12g] close-coupled colt: closely related to fair 1m and 10.1f winner Knighted Dancer (by The Minstrel) and a winner in USA, and half-brother to a winner in France: dam, best at 4 yrs, won 9 races at up to 1m, including stakes: well beaten in maiden (bandaged, very slowly away) at Kempton in July and claimers at Lingfield in December: sold out of J. Gosden's stable 3,500 gns Newmarket Autumn Sales after debut. *P. A. Kelleway.*

LINE ENGAGED (USA)   3 b.c. Phone Trick (USA) – Quick Nurse (USA) (Dr   —
Fager) [1990 5m³ 5g* 6m* 6d 5g⁴ 6g⁵ 1991 5m⁶ 5m] lengthy, angular colt: has a quick action: useful as 2-y-o, successful in Norfolk Stakes at Royal Ascot: led 3f and not entirely discredited in Group 2 contest at Sandown on reappearance: behind in King's Stand Stakes at Royal Ascot 4 weeks later: seems equally effective at 5f and 6f: acts on good to firm ground and dead: joined P. Walwyn. *D. R. C. Elsworth.*

LINGDALE LASS   2 gr.f. (Apr 24) Petong 126 – Our Mother 95 (Bold Lad (IRE)   **60** ?
133) [1991 5g⁶ 5f 5f³ 5m 5d² 6.9m 6d* 6d⁶] 10,000Y: small, leggy filly: half-sister to several winners here and abroad, including fairly useful 5f to 7.6f handicapper Bold Habit (by Homing): dam ran only at 2 yrs, winning at 5f: quite modest form: fortunate winner of claimer at Hamilton in July, rider dropping hands on leader close home: stays 6f: seems best on a soft surface: visored third start, ran badly in blinkers fourth: takes a lot of driving: inconsistent, and has looked ungenuine. *Mrs G. R. Reveley.*

LINK MARKET (USA)   5 b.m. Linkage (USA) – Motor Mouse (USA) (Outing   **52**
Class) [1990 14g² 14g* 14m³ 14d⁴ a14g² a12g* a12g* 14m⁵ a16g* a13g² a14g a62   a62
a16g² 1991 a13g a14g⁵ 14m 14.1g³ 16m³ 19m⁵ a18g⁴ 14.1m² 12.5g³ a16g²] rangy mare: poor mover: quite modest handicapper: best at up to 2m: acts on good to firm ground: has run creditably for apprentice: best form on all-weather surfaces: retained 10,500 gns Newmarket Autumn Sales after penultimate start. *M. J. Ryan.*

LINPAC LIGHT   4 gr.f. Kalaglow 132 – North Page (FR) 81 (Northfields (USA))   **68**
[1990 10m 12m⁶ 12d³ 12v a12g⁴ 1991 10g⁴ 10.5m² 10g² 10m* 11.9g 10.5m⁴] unfurnished filly: quite modest handicapper: gamely won at Newmarket in August: effective at 1¼m to 1½m: acts on good to firm and dead ground: consistent: sold 6,000 gns Newmarket December Sales. *C. W. C. Elsey.*

LINPAC WEST   5 b.h. Posse (USA) 130 – North Page (FR) 81 (Northfields   **101**
(USA)) [1990 10g 12m² 12s⁴ 10g⁴ 14g 13.4g⁴ 13d⁴ 12m⁶ 12s 1991 8d⁴ 10.4d² 11d* 10g 12d²] lengthy, angular horse: poor mover: useful handicapper: won £7,040 event at Newbury in May: off course 4 months before good second of 22 to Hieroglyphic in November Handicap at Doncaster: stays 13f, and effective at shorter: best on an easy surface, and acts well in the mud: has edged under pressure. *C. W. C. Elsey.*

LION CAVERN (USA)   2 ch.c. (Feb 13) Mr Prospector (USA) – Secret- **114** p
tame (USA) (Secretariat (USA)) [1991 6g* 6g² 6g³ 6m² 7.3g*]

By and large British two-year-old races hold little appeal for French trainers, with the exception of those at Royal Ascot and the autumn Group 1 events at Newmarket and Doncaster, so the presence of Lion Cavern and Tertian, two challengers from Andre Fabre's stable, at Newbury and Newmarket for the Vodafone Horris Hill Stakes and the Somerville Tattersall Stakes respectively was a considerable tip in itself. Both were impressive winners in their different ways: Tertian did extremely well to come from last to first in a slowly-run and trouble-fraught affair; while Lion Cavern, who had the easier task, had a clear run throughout and was seldom in any danger. If the truth be told, Lion Cavern, who was the clear pick on his placed efforts behind Arazi and Rodrigo de Triano on his last two outings, had only the Goffs Million runner-up Autocracy and the Rokeby Farms Mill Reef second Jeune, who'd since disappointed at Ascot, to fear among his six rivals. The extra furlong which Lion Cavern was attempting for the first time, having been confined to six in all his previous races, seemed sure to suit him well too, and so it seemed to prove, although Lion Cavern didn't actually need to improve on his earlier form. Taking a keen hold, initially at least, in a race run at a moderate gallop, Lion Cavern swung into the straight in fourth place, made smooth headway to lead just inside the two-furlong pole and drew clear without needing to be shown the whip to win comfortably by two lengths from Autocracy, with the subsequent Newmarket winner Muharib three and a half lengths back in third. Lion Cavern's post-race quote of 25/1 for the Two Thousand Guineas seems a fair one; the manner in which he saw the final furlong out suggests he'll have no trouble staying a mile.

Lion Cavern's visit to Newbury was his second to Britain: three weeks previously he'd accompanied Tertian to Newmarket and run in the Newgate Stud Middle Park Stakes. His form in France, where he'd won a minor event at Maisons-Laffitte by four lengths before finishing second to Kenbu in the Prix de Cabourg and nearly four lengths third to Arazi in the Prix Morny Agence Francaise, suggested third place was the best he would manage in a field which also contained the unbeaten Laurent Perrier Champagne winner Rodrigo de Triano and the Scottish Equitable Gimcrack winner River Falls, but despite some trouble in running he recorded a much improved effort, possibly on account of the good to firm ground, to split that pair and go down by a length. Oddly enough Lion Cavern, who was the pick of the paddock, found himself in much the same predicament during the race that befell Tertian the following day. Stuck on the rail with two furlongs to go and with little prospect of an opening there, he had to be pulled round to begin his challenge again, but finished with a tremendous flourish from that point and was gaining quickly at the line. Lion Cavern wasn't an unlucky loser, however; Rodrigo de Triano was almost certainly idling in front and won with something in hand.

Lion Cavern (USA) (ch.c. Feb 13, 1989)	Mr Prospector (USA) (b 1970)	Raise A Native (ch 1961)	Native Dancer
			Raise You
		Gold Digger (b 1962)	Nashua
			Sequence
	Secrettame (USA) (ch 1978)	Secretariat (ch 1970)	Bold Ruler
			Somethingroyal
		Tamerett (b or br 1962)	Tim Tam
			Mixed Marriage

At 950,000 dollars, the angular, good-topped Lion Cavern was the ninth highest-priced colt sold at public auction in North America in 1990. It hardly

Vodafone Horris Hill Stakes, Newbury—
French colt Lion Cavern lands the odds decisively from Autocracy

Sheikh Mohammed's "Lion Cavern"

needs saying that he's superbly bred. His sire Mr Prospector, who finished the year second to Danzig in the General Sire List, remains one of the world's most sought-after stallions—those of his yearlings sold at the most recent American Sales once again averaged over 500,000 dollars—while his dam Secrettame, whose fifth foal and fifth winner he is, has a good race-record as well as a fine pedigree. Easily the best of her previous foals, four of whom were sired by Mr Prospector, is Lion Cavern's very smart full brother Gone West, who was widely considered to be best at a mile, over which distance he won two Grade 2 events, the Gotham Stakes and the Withers Stakes, even though he managed to win the Grade 1 Dwyer Stakes over nine furlongs. Secrettame won six races, at up to a mile and a quarter, from ten starts and finished second in the Grade 2 nine-furlong Gazelle Handicap. Her dam Tamerett is a top-class broodmare. Besides Secrettame she's produced the Two Thousand Guineas winner Known Fact, the high-class six-furlong to nine-and-a-half-furlong winner Tentam, the leading 1970 American two-year-old Tamtent and the very good grass horse Terete; and if that wasn't enough she's also the grandam of Tappiano, one of the leading two-year-old fillies in the States in 1986 and the winner of three Grade 1 events and nearly 1,400,000 dollars. The next of Secrettame's foals, a full brother to Lion Cavern, may well be racing here in the coming season; he was purchased by the Curragh Bloodstock Agency for 475,000 dollars at Keeneland's Selected Yearling Sale in July. *A. Fabre, France.*

LISALEE (IRE) 3 b.f. Montekin 125 – Ivy Holme (Silly Season 127) [1990 6s⁴ — 5d⁶ 6f 1991 8m 8m 9.9f 12.1m] workmanlike filly: moderate mover: poor plater: best effort on dead ground. *J. Parkes.*

LISA ROSA 4 b.f. Ardross 134 – Macaw 85 (Narrator 127) [1990 10m 10f 1991 a12g⁵ a16g a16g⁵ 16s⁶] big, lengthy filly: no worthwhile form, including in handicaps: joined Miss S. Wilton. *W. J. Musson.*

LISBON LASS 3 b.f. Roman Glory § – Solar Temptress 58 (Status Seeker) [1990 NR 1991 7m a12g] workmanlike filly: first reported foal: dam maiden who stayed 1½m: tailed off in claimer (very edgy) at Salisbury and maiden at Lingfield 4 months later. *P. Howling.*

LITERARY SPARK 3 ch.c. Kalaglow 132 – My Lady Muriel (USA) (Visible 81 (USA)) [1990 NR 1991 10.1g⁶ 12m² 14m³] 10,000F, 10,500Y: lengthy, good-bodied colt: moderate mover: fourth foal: dam lightly raced: won claimer at Newmarket in October, leading over 1½f out: creditable third of 9 in moderately-run handicap there 2 weeks later: will prove suited by greater test of stamina: sold 17,000 gns Newmarket Autumn Sales. *W. Jarvis.*

LITHO BOLD FLASHER 2 b.g. (Mar 4) Bold Owl 101 – Flash O' Night 52 (Patch 129) [1991 6m 8.1m a8g⁶ a8g⁵] 4,500F: sturdy gelding: half-brother to a winner in Denmark: dam unraced: plating-class maiden: best effort on debut. *W. J. Pearce.*

LITMORE DANCER 3 br.f. Mashhor Dancer (USA) – Daring Charm (Daring 60 March 116) [1990 7g 1991 7g² 6s⁶ 7.1d⁵ 7g 7f 6.1m 8m⁵ 6.9f a8g* a7g²] lengthy, angular filly: has a round action: quite modest performer: made all in maiden at Southwell in November: held up when good second at Lingfield following month: stays 1m: well below form on soft ground, acts on any other. *J. D. Bethell.*

LITRON (GER) 2 gr.c. (Apr 3) Grauer Wicht (GER) – Livre (GER) (Lombard 116 (GER) 126) [1991 6.5g 7g* 7g* 8g* 8v*] German-bred colt: successful in 3 races in Germany, including valuable Dortmunder Auktionsrennen in September, then made all in 8-runner Prix des Chenes at Evry (by 2½ lengths from Greek Air) in November: stays 1m: acts on heavy ground. *T. Grieper, Germany.*

LITTLE BANG 3 ch.f. Bustino 136 – Live Ammo 94 (Home Guard (USA) 129) 46 [1990 NR 1991 7g² 8f³ 8.3m 7d⁴ 7f⁵ 9.7g] lengthy, sparely-made filly: fifth foal: half-sister to 3 winners here and abroad, including smart sprinter Powder Keg (by Tap On Wood): dam 2-y-o 6f winner: plater: good hold to post, never dangerous facing stiff task final start: should prove better at 1m than 7f: acts on firm and dead going. *Lord John FitzGerald.*

LITTLE BIG 4 b.c. Indian King (USA) 128 – Route Royale (Roi Soleil 125) [1990 a8g* 7f² 8.2f³ 8.5d* 10.6s 8d 7.6f⁴ a8g 10d³ 10d 8d 8m a10g6 1991 8.3g 8m 10.2s 9.7s] well-made colt: one-time fair handicapper: below form since ninth start (blinkered) at 3 yrs: suited by 1¼m: acts on any going. *B. J. Curley.*

LITTLE CONKER 3 ch.c. All Systems Go 119 – L'Irondelle (On Your Mark 125) — [1990 6m 7g 5d 6f⁶ 8.5m 6m a7g 1991 10g 15.3m a11g] workmanlike, close-coupled colt: has a round action: bad plater: no chance in spring as 3-y-o: best form at 5f and 6f. *A. Smith.*

LITTLE IVOR 2 b.g. (Apr 29) Kings Lake (USA) 133 – Ange Gris (USA) (Grey 51 Dawn II 132) [1991 7s 7f² 7f⁵ 7m 8m 7m] 7,000F, 3,000Y: rather unfurnished gelding: has a round action: half-brother to 3 winners abroad: dam from family of Sir Ivor: plating-class maiden: ran moderately last 3 starts, visored and on toes final one: should stay 1m. *Denys Smith.*

LITTLE KRAKER 4 b.f. Godswalk (USA) 130 – Wyn Mipet (Welsh Saint 126) 57 [1990 7m⁴ 8h⁴ 7d* 8m 8f⁶ 8.3f² 7m⁶ 10.6d 10m⁴ 10g⁵ 1991 8m 8f 7m³ 7g 7.1g 10.2d⁵ 10.2g³ 11.5m⁵ 12f] lengthy filly: moderate mover: plating-class handicapper: best at up to 1¼m: acts on firm and dead going, seems unsuited by hard: inconsistent. *P. J. Jones.*

LITTLE NOD 2 ch.c. (Apr 9) Domynsky 110 – Vikris (Viking (USA)) [1991 7m 62 8m⁵ 8.1s⁴ a7g⁶ a8g⁴] quite good-topped colt: second foal: dam thrice-raced half-sister to useful sprinter Westacombe: quite modest maiden: not sure to stay beyond 1m. *M. J. Camacho.*

LITTLE PARK 2 b.f. (Apr 22) Cragador 110 – Liberated Girl (Free State 125) — [1991 7m 8s] smallish filly: first reported foal: dam no sign of ability: 50/1, always behind in October maidens at Leicester and Yarmouth. *J. Pearce.*

LITTLE PRESTON (IRE) 3 b.f. Pennine Walk 120 – Blessingtonia 79 (So 47 Blessed 130) [1990 5f 6m a7g² a7g⁵ 1991 10.2d 10.1m⁵ 9.7m³ a12g⁶] leggy, lengthy filly: moderate mover: plater: never dangerous at Southwell final start: stays 1¼m: acts on good to firm ground: bandaged in 1991. *N. A. Callaghan.*

LITTLE ROUSILLON   3 b.c. Rousillon (USA) 133 – Carolside 108 (Music   **67**
Maestro 119) [1990 NR 1991 7m 8f³ 7g⁵ 7g⁵ 9.2s²] 27,000F, 72,000Y: sturdy, lengthy, attractive colt: good mover: fourth foal: half-brother to useful 4-y-o 8.5f and 9f winner Eton Lad (by Never So Bold) and unsatisfactory 6f winner Sure Gold (by Glint of Gold): dam 2-y-o 5f winner didn't progress: quite modest maiden: co-favourite, caught post in 16-runner handicap at Hamilton in November, having quickened on over 2f out: stays 9f: acts on any going. *A. C. Stewart.*

LITTLE SABOTEUR   2 ch.f. (Feb 16) Prince Sabo 123 – Shoot To Win (FR)   **72**
(Rabdan 129) [1991 5m⁴ 6m² 6g³ 6.1m⁴ 5d⁴ 5s* a6g⁴] 1,200F, 2,800Y, 5,800 2-y-o: useful-looking filly: has scope: second foal: dam French 7.5f winner: modest performer: won claimer at Edinburgh in November: ran moderately on fibresand final outing: easily best form at 5f on soft surface: blinkered last 2 starts. *P. J. Makin.*

LITTLE SPUD   2 b.c. (Jun 10) Battle Hymn 103 – Ball And Chain 73 (Manacle   **—**
123) [1991 5f] 800Y: small, light-framed colt: second reported living foal: dam 1m winner: 100/1, always behind in maiden auction at Pontefract in April. *E. H. Owen jun.*

LIU LIU SAN (IRE)   3 ch.f. Bairn (USA) 126 – The Saltings (FR) (Morston (FR)   **—**
125) [1990 6m 7m 1991 7g a10g a13g] good-topped filly: poor maiden: stiff tasks in handicaps. *P. Butler.*

LIVE ACTION   4 b.c. Alzao (USA) 117 – Brig O'Doon (Shantung 132) [1990 8.5d³   **99**
8.5g² 8m* 12m 10.2s* 9.1s* 1991 8g⁴ 8d 8g 10.3d⁴] good-bodied colt: has powerful action: quite useful handicapper: excellent staying-on fourth in Newbury Spring Cup: burly on first run for nearly 5 months (ran as if something amiss in between), showed he retains ability when fourth in Doncaster minor event in November: stays 1¼m well: goes very well with some give in the ground: has joined Miss H. Knight, but is to return to former trainer for the Lincoln. *L. M. Cumani.*

LIVE FOR TODAY   2 b.c. (Mar 31) Today And Tomorrow 78 – Rhythm Maker   **—**
(Song 132) [1991 7m] 1,000Y: leggy colt: second foal: dam (ran once) from family of high-class sprinter Swing Easy: 33/1, bandaged behind and better for race, tailed-off last of 18 in Lingfield maiden in September. *P. Burgoyne.*

LIVELY LUKE (IRE)   3 b.g. Rule of Clubs 124 – Waitotara (Habitat 134) [1990   **—**
NR 1991 8f 8g] 4,800F: rather leggy, lengthy gelding: moderate mover: half-brother to a winner in Germany by Ela-Mana-Mou: dam lightly-raced Irish 1¾m winner: about 4½ lengths eighth of 11 in maiden at Yarmouth, slowly away: showed nothing in Newmarket claimer later in June: sold 650 gns Ascot 2nd July Sales. *M. H. Tompkins.*

LIVING IMAGE   3 b.c. Taufan (USA) 119 – Visible Form 99 (Formidable (USA)   **98**
125) [1990 7g² 8.2d* 1991 9m⁴ 7m⁵ 10m⁴ 10m* 10g³] leggy, attractive colt: good mover: fairly useful performer: won 4-runner handicap at Redcar in August: again given hard ride when creditable third in £15,300 handicap at Newmarket 2 weeks later: stays 1¼m: acts on good to firm ground and dead: joined A. Turnell. *W. Jarvis.*

LIZZIE DRIPPIN (CAN)   2 b.f. (Apr 27) Artichoke (USA) – Adieu (FR)   **—**
(Tompion (USA)) [1991 6m 6g 6m a7g a8g⁶] $10,000Y: half-sister to several minor winners abroad: dam French 1¼m winner: little worthwhile form: blinkered (in seller) third start. *M. D. I. Usher.*

LLANGOLLEN (IRE)   3 b.f. Caerleon (USA) 132 – Keep The Thought (USA)   **87**
84 (Valdez (USA)) [1990 NR 1991 7g⁴ 10.4d* 10m 11.9g 10m⁴ 12m² 12d* a16g⁴] good-topped filly: second foal: closely related to winning selling hurdler Kings Alderman (by Kings Lake): dam 1m winner out of sister to dam of Seattle Slew and Lomond: won £7,300 maiden at Chester in May and handicap (edging right when in front final 1f) at Newmarket in November: creditable fourth in Lingfield handicap final start, having got behind: stays 2m: acts on good to firm ground and dead: blinkered last 2 outings. *B. W. Hills.*

LLANTHONY   2 b.c. (May 19) Dancing Brave (USA) 140 – Welsh Note (USA) 111   **54**
(Sharpen Up 127) [1991 5m 5m⁴ 5m] smallish, sturdy colt: has quick action: second foal: dam 5f performer, is out of half-sister to French 2000 Guineas winner Recitation: plating-class maiden: easily best effort when fourth of 7 at Folkestone in August after 3 months absence: well beaten in minor event at Warwick 12 days later: visored last 2 starts: sold 4,200 gns Newmarket Autumn Sales. *D. W. P. Arbuthnot.*

LOADER   3 b.c. Jester 119 – Savahra 82 (Free State 125) [1990 NR 1991 a7g⁴]   **—**
strong colt: fifth foal: closely related to very useful winner at up to 7f Savahra Sound and a winner in Belgium (both by Song) and half-brother to 1½m winner Tesora (by

Busted), later successful in USA: dam 11f and 13f winner: favourite and bandaged off-fore, fourth of 9 in maiden at Southwell in June: moved poorly down: dead. *W. J. Haggas.*

LOBILIO (USA) 2 b.c. (Apr 26) Robellino (USA) 127 – Nabila (USA) 58 (Foolish Pleasure (USA)) [1991 8d] 100,000Y: well-made colt: has scope: fourth reported foal: closely related to useful Italian 8.5f (at 2 yrs) to 1½m winner Nydrion (by Critique): dam, 8.2f winner at 3 yrs, is out of very useful winner at up to 1m Opec: 13/2 and green, 8 lengths eighth of 14 to Hill Glitter in minor event at Newmarket in November, not knocked about when held: should stay 1¼m: will improve. *C. E. Brittain.* **63** p

LOBINDA 2 b.f. (Feb 26) Shareef Dancer (USA) 135 – Lobbino 72 (Bustino 136) [1991 7g 8.5f* 8.1d* 9s5] stocky filly: second foal: dam, maiden should have stayed middle distances, is out of sister to 1000 Guineas and Prix de Diane winner Highclere: modest performer: successful in maiden at Beverley and minor event at Haydock (best effort, despite tending to idle) in autumn: modest fifth of 10 to Sarasota Bay in listed race at Milan: will stay 1¼m + . *J. L. Dunlop.* **78**

LOCAL DEALER 3 ch.g. Scottish Reel 123 – Green Pool 39 (Whistlefield 118) [1990 7.5g2 8f 1991 6g 7.5g 8f a7g] smallish, workmanlike gelding: didn't reproduced debut form, in maidens and handicaps: not bred to stay much beyond 1m: blinkered (headstrong and edged right) second start: trained until after third by A. Stringer. *R. O'Leary.* —

LOCAL DERBY 4 ch.c. Local Suitor (USA) 128 – Honey Match 98 (Match III 135) [1990 10.2f* 12.3d 12f* 12g 12m 12m* 14g 14m2 12m 1991 12m2 14g6 12g2] big, strong colt: carries condition: fairly useful handicapper: easily best efforts in 1991 when good second, in Bessborough Stakes (sweating, beaten neck by Rinja) at Royal Ascot third start: withdrawn (bolted and unseated rider to post) in July, not seen out again: stays 1¾m: acts on firm going: has edged right under pressure: sometimes led round by 2 handlers in paddock. *J. W. Watts.* **94**

LOCAL GRIFFIN 2 b.f. (Mar 22) Local Suitor (USA) 128 – Sheeog 80 (Reform 132) [1991 6g 6m6 7s 5.1m a6g2 a6g4 a6g a6g6] 2,000F: tall, leggy filly: fourth foal: half-sister to 3-y-o 5f (at 2 yrs) and 1½m winner City Solace (by Last Tycoon) and a winner in Belgium by Wassl: dam 5f and 6f winner: of little account. *C. A. Cyzer.* —

LOCAL LASS 4 b.f. Local Suitor (USA) 128 – Sorebelle 95 (Prince Tenderfoot (USA) 126) [1990 7g 7m 6g2 7g* 7f 8m4 7g 6d3 6m 1991 8d 7m2 7d 6m2 7g2] lengthy, good-quartered filly: 33/1, showed improved form when length second of 12 to La Grange Music in Van Geest Criterion Stakes at Newmarket final start (June): fairly useful handicapper on previous form, second in Wokingham Stakes at Royal Ascot: best effort at 7f: acts on good to firm ground (faced very stiff task on firm) and dead going: has run well when edgy. *C. E. Brittain.* **106**

LOCH CLAIR (IRE) 2 b.f. (May 25) Lomond (USA) 128 – Burghclere 86 (Busted 134) [1991 7m5 8s4] 120,000Y: lengthy filly: closely related to 2m winner Invite (by Be My Guest) and half-sister to smart 6f and 1¼m winner Capo di Monte (by Final Straw) and 1¾m winner Kingsmill (by Kings Lake): dam, 1¾m winner, is daughter of Highclere: better effort around 8 lengths fourth of 10, fading from over 1f out, in maiden at Yarmouth in October: likely to stay 1¼m. *Mrs J. Cecil.* **53** p

LOCH DERG LASS 3 ch.f. Night Shift (USA) – Chance Match 73 (Royal Match 117) [1990 NR 1991 11g 12m 12g6 16g] workmanlike filly: sixth foal: half-sister to a winner abroad by Belfort: dam Irish 1½m winner: well beaten in maidens and claimer. *R. Simpson.* —

LOCH DUICH 5 ch.h. Kris 135 – Sleat 112 (Santa Claus 133) [1990 10m5 12.5f* 10m* 10m6 8d 1991 10.8m 8.1d] leggy horse: modest handicapper at 4 yrs: no form in first half of 1991: needs at least 1¼m and stays 1½m: acts on firm ground: has run well when sweating: takes keen hold: bandaged off-fore final start. *J. H. Baker.* —

LOCH GARANNE 3 br.f. Lochnager 132 – Raperon 81 (Rapid River 127) [1990 NR 1991 8s 12m6] lengthy, angular filly: third reported living foal: dam won selling hurdle: sixth of 13 in claimer at Thirsk in May, prominent long way: should be suited by return to shorter. *M. J. Camacho.* —

LOCH NIAL (IRE) 2 b.f. (Mar 6) Mansooj 118 – Theda 61 (Mummy's Pet 125) [1991 5g4 5g2 5g 5m 5g6 5m 6g 5s] 2,000Y: smallish, sparely-made filly: has a quick action: third foal: half-sister to 1990 2-y-o 5f winner Graceland Lady (by Kafu): dam stayed 7f: poor sprint maiden: sold 650 gns Ascot November Sales. *J. L. Spearing.* **47**

LOCH SHIN 4 b.g. Lochnager 132 – Nellie Bly 80 (Dragonara Palace (USA) 115) [1990 NR 1991 a5g] first foal: dam non-thoroughbred 5f winner was best at 2 yrs: well beaten in maiden at Southwell: dead. *M. H. Easterby.* —

468

LOCHSONG 3 b.f. Song 132 – Peckitts Well 96 (Lochnager 132) [1990 NR 1991 **74** p
7f² 6m* 7g*] lengthy, angular filly: first foal: dam sprinter: wintry in coat, won
maiden at Redcar and 19-runner apprentice handicap at Newbury (by short head,
quickening clear over 3f out and tiring inside last) in October: will prove best at up
to 7f: may well be capable of better. *I. A. Balding.*

LOCK KEEPER (USA) 5 b.g. Riverman (USA) 131 – Jamila (Sir Gaylord) [1990 **62** d
11g³ 12g 12d⁵ 1991 10.8m a7g* a8g* a7g² 8m³ 8.3s a8g 7m 8.2m a8g] stocky,
attractive gelding: moderate walker: quite modest handicapper: twice made
virtually all at Southwell in summer: lost his form: stays 1m well: acts on good to
firm ground, possibly not soft. *J. Mackie.*

LOCK LANE (IRE) 2 b.g. (Feb 11) Blakeney 126 – Travel Free (Be My Guest **32**
(USA) 126) [1991 5g⁵ 5m 6f a8g] IR 5,000F, 3,400Y: small, stocky gelding: has a
round action: third foal: half-brother to 3-y-o Beltane Boy (by Forzando): dam ran 3
times at 2 yrs: bit backward, soundly beaten, including in Yarmouth seller: sold 900
gns Doncaster October Sales. *P. F. Tulk.*

LODESTAR (IRE) 3 b.c. Rainbow Quest (USA) 134 – Air Distingue (USA) 120 **81**
(Sir Ivor 135) [1990 7g² 1991 10d³ 10m* 12g] big, good-topped colt: has a markedly
round action: 6/5 on, won 16-runner maiden at Sandown in May, always close up and
running on strongly: 11/1, looking really well and on toes, ran wide home turn, no
extra and eased, in Bessborough Handicap at Royal Ascot: should be much better at
1½m than 1¼m: sold to join N. Tinkler 11,000 gns Newmarket Autumn Sales. *G.
Harwood.*

LODGING 4 ch.g. Longleat (USA) 109 – Mollified 67 (Lombard (GER) 126) [1990 **46**
8g 8f⁵ 10g 8m⁴ 8h⁶ a8g⁴ 8m³ 7g 8m⁴ 9g³ 8m 1991 10f 10f a12g⁵ 10g 12.3d 11s 12f⁵
12.3f* 12g³ 12f 12m⁵ 14.1f 12f] smallish, workmanlike gelding: poor handicapper
nowadays: sold out of J. Bethell's stable 5,400 gns Doncaster Spring Sales: won at
Ripon in July: below form last 4 starts, tailed off final one: stays 1½m: suited by
sound surface (below form on hard ground): visored or blinkered nowadays: has
hung left. *G. R. Oldroyd.*

LOFT BOY 8 b.g. Cawston's Clown 113 – Burglar Tip 73 (Burglar 128) [1990 **79**
5.8h* 5m⁵ 5.8f² 5f⁶ 5m³ 5f* 5.8h² 5m² 5.8f⁴ 5m 6g³ 6s 1991 6g³ 5m³ 6g 5.1g⁴ 5g³
5g⁴ 6g 6f 5.2f² 5m 6m 5g] sturdy gelding: moderate mover: modest handicapper: ran
poorly last 2 starts: effective at 5f to 6f: acts on any going: usually blinkered or
visored: occasionally badgered off-hind: tough. *J. D. Bethell.*

LOFTY LADY (IRE) 3 b.f. Head For Heights 125 – Octavia Girl 104 (Octavo **94**
(USA) 115) [1990 8m* 8m 1991 10d³ 11.7g² 12g⁶ 11.8g² 12.2g² 11.8m² 15m* 18m]
sturdy, attractive filly: moderate mover: fairly useful performer: won amateurs race
at Ayr in September, leading 2f out and keeping on really well: every chance 3f out
but weakened last when tenth of 22 in Cesarewitch Handicap at Newmarket month
later: best form at 15f: possibly unsuited by a soft surface. *B. W. Hills.*

LOGARITHM 3 b.f. King of Spain 121 – Hearten (Hittite Glory 125) [1990 NR **—**
1991 8g 8g 8m 8g 7g a11g] rangy, useful-looking filly: fourth foal: sister to 1988
2-y-o 5f winner Spanish Oak and 7f and 1m winner Spanish Heart, and half-sister to
useful sprinter Northern Goddess (by Night Shift): dam unraced daughter of smart
middle-distance stayer Nortia: no worthwhile form in maidens, handicaps and
claimer. *P. J. Makin.*

LOGWOOD BLACK 3 b.c. Aragon 118 – Little Egret 74 (Carwhite 127) [1990 **—**
6m a7g 1991 a7g 7m 9.9f 15.8f⁶] neat colt: no form in claimers, selling handicap and
maiden. *R. Hollinshead.*

LOKI (IRE) 3 ch.g. Thatching 131 – Sigym (Lord Gayle (USA) 124) [1990 6m 6d **78**
7m* 1991 8g³ 9m 11.5m 8.5m⁴ᵈⁱˢ 8m 8g² 7.1g² 8m⁶ 8s³ 8m² 10.2g³ 8g 10g² 12.1s²
10.3d² 10d*] strong gelding: sometimes unimpressive in coat: fluent mover: modest
handicapper: won at Redcar in October: stays 1½m: acts on good to firm ground and
soft: has run well in blinkers: usually prominent from the off, but wasn't last 3
starts: consistent: gelded after final start. *G. Lewis.*

LOMBARD OCEAN 2 ch.g. (May 5) Ballacashtal (CAN) – Realm Gift 75 (Realm **66**
129) [1991 5f 5g* 6m⁵ 5m⁴ 6m* 7g 6g² 5d] 3,700F, 1,000Y: tall, workmanlike
gelding: has scope: moderate mover: half-brother to 2 winners abroad: dam, maiden
ran only at 2 yrs, is half-sister to dam of Roland Gardens: quite modest performer:
successful in maiden auction at Haydock in June and 4-runner nursery at Catterick
in August: easily best effort when second of 17 in nursery at Haydock in October:
suited by 6f: possibly unsuited by dead ground. *M. O'Neill.*

LOMBARD SHIPS 4 ch.f. Orchestra 118 – Tina's Star (Simbir 130) [1990 8f⁵ **63**
8.2f² 8.2m⁴ 8g⁵ 8.2g³ 7f 7g² 7f² 7.2d² 8.2v* 8m⁴ 7d 1991 7.5f 8f* 8m 8.1m³ 8f² 8g]

sparely-made filly: has a quick action: quite modest performer: won claimer at Carlisle in May: not seen out after July: stays 1m: acts on any going: has got on toes: none too consistent. *M. O'Neill.*

LOMBOK 4 ch.c. Lomond (USA) 128 – Enthralment (USA) 78 (Sir Ivor 135) [1990 — 10g 10g 8g⁶ 8g 1991 8g] small, angular colt: moderate mover: no worthwhile form, in selling handicap only run in 1991: should stay 1¼m. *K. R. Burke.*

LOMINDA (IRE) 3 b.f. Lomond (USA) 128 – Olinda 101 (Sassafras (FR) 135) **73** [1990 6g 6m* 6d³ 1991 8g⁵ 7.3d⁵ 10g] lengthy filly: has a rather round action: modest performer: disappointing in handicaps after reappearance, tailed off final start: should stay beyond 1m: acts on good to firm ground, unsuited by a soft surface. *J. W. Hills.*

LOMITAS 3 ch.c. Niniski (USA) 125 – La Colorada (GER) (Surumu (GER)) **129** [1990 8g* 8g* 1991 8.5f* 11g* 12g² 12g* 12m* 12g*]

Germany picked up three pattern races outside its own borders in 1991 thanks to Feenpark in the Prix de Meautry, Martessa in the Ciga Prix de l'Opera and Litron in the Prix des Chenes, and in Lomitas it has a horse capable of winning far more important prizes than that. He's probably not in the same class as Generous or Suave Dancer but Lomitas would have given a good race to any other middle-distance horse in Europe. On eight starts in Germany, he's been beaten only once. That was in the BMW Deutsches Derby at Hamburg in July when he had every chance but was beaten half a length in a field of nineteen by the Lanfranco Dettori-ridden Temporal, a 37/1-shot who was apparently the least fancied of four runners saddled by Bruno Schutz. On the strength of four victories, three in listed races, Lomitas had been made a short-priced favourite for the Deutsches Derby. Three outings later, his supporters that day had the rather scant consolation of knowing that they were on easily the best horse in the race. In the Grosser Preis der Berliner Bank at Dusseldorf, Lomitas beat Hateel two lengths with those further behind including the 1989 Polish triple crown winner Krezus in third, Hundra and Duke of Paducah, the very useful German four-year-olds Indica and Mandelbaum, and the French-trained Steamer Duck. A rematch with Temporal in the Grosser Preis von Baden proved to be no match at all, Lomitas bolting home by seven lengths. This time Spinning and Another Bob were challengers from Britain, Top Waltz and Wajd from France. Wajd, the Grand Prix d'Evry winner, was beaten no less than eleven lengths behind Lomitas into third. The foreign challenge dried up somewhat for Lomitas' final start, the Geno-Europa-Preis at Cologne two weeks before the Arc, the only one to take the field from Britain or France being the very useful French filly Spendomania. She was beaten fourteen and a half lengths into fourth, with another half length back to the subsequent Group 3 winner Highness Lady; up front it was Lomitas in glorious isolation, eight lengths clear of runner-up Indica. Lomitas had won three Group 1 contests in a row, the last two by an aggregate of fifteen lengths. Those sort of winning margins have to raise eyebrows whatever the conditions. They're more common when the ground is soft, of course, but at Cologne the going was returned as good, at Baden-Baden good to firm.

		Niniski (USA)		Nijinsky		Northern Dancer
Lomitas (ch.c. 1988)		(b 1976)		(b 1967)		Flaming Page
				Virginia Hills		Tom Rolfe
				(b 1971)		Ridin' Easy
		La Colorada (GER)		Surumu		Literat
		(ch 1981)		(ch 1974)		Surama
				La Dorada		Kronzeuge
				(b 1974)		Love In

Lomitas is owned and bred by the Gestut Fahrhof but he's by Niniski who stands at Newmarket. Among Niniski's other runners in 1991 were Sapience, the French four-year-old Echoes, and Louis Cyphre, who seems finally to have found his stride in the United States. Lomitas is the third foal out of La Colorada following Los Rinos (by Beldale Flutter), who won quite valuable events over eleven furlongs and a mile and a half in Germany in the latest season, and the listed-placed two-year-old winner La Florida (by Ile de Bourbon). Her next three foals are a filly by Rousillon and a filly then colt by

Konigsstuhl. La Colorada won a Group 3 contest over ten and a half furlongs and her dam La Dorada was the top German two-year-old of her sex in 1976, winning all three of her starts that year but being unable to add to that tally the following season. La Dorada's half-sister Liranga has had a considerable impact as a broodmare, producing the 1984 Deutsches Derby winner Lagunas and the 1986 Jacques le Marois winner Lirung.

Surely we'll be seeing Lomitas in some of the top middle-distance races in 1992. It's to be hoped he fares better than Mondrian who had a wretched season trained in Britain in 1991 which ended for him when he trailed in last behind Lomitas in his bid for a third successive Grosser Preis von Baden. It was reported that Mondrian suffered from a bronchial problem, seemingly exacerbated by the strain of travel. Lomitas embarks on his four-year-old season without quite the prolific winning record that Mondrian had, but with better form. His trainer, for whom Lomitas was reportedly the three-hundredth winner when winning at Baden-Baden, is one of those to have already tasted success outside Germany, with Martessa at Longchamp on Arc day. *A. Wohler, Germany.*

LONDON STANDARD 6 b.g. Shack (USA) 118 – Red Realm (Realm 129) [1990 a6g3 a8g* a7g2 8m a10g4 a7g3 a8g3 11.7m a7g5 a8g3 a6g3 a6g a7g a10g a8g 1991 a10g6 a8g a10g5] workmanlike gelding: quite modest handicapper at 5 yrs: below form in 1991: ideally suited by further than 6f, and stayed 1m: often used to wear blinkers, but didn't last 2 seasons: visored final start: dead. *P. Mitchell.* —

LONELY LASS 5 b.m. Headin' Up – Lonely Dawn (USA) 63 (Plenty Old (USA)) [1990 a6g 5g a7g5 1991 a5g2 5g 5d5 5.1g5 a5g4 5m] lengthy, rather sparely-made mare: poor handicapper: stays 6f: acts on good to firm ground: has edged left: ran as if something amiss second start: has run well on fibresand. *L. J. Barratt.* **44**

LONESOME TRAIN (USA) 2 ch.c. (Mar 7) Crafty Prospector (USA) – Alaki Miss (USA) (Olden Times) [1991 6m2 7f 7f 7m] $75,000Y: sturdy colt: has a round action: half-brother to several winners in North America: dam placed at 2 yrs: sire (by Mr Prospector) stakes-placed winner from 6f to 8.5f: plating-class form in maidens: will stay 1m: may do better in handicaps. *J. H. M. Gosden.* **57**

LONG BAY 9 b.h. Song 132 – Sundream (Petingo 135) [1990 a10g4 a8g5 a10g4 10f 8.2f 10m 8m 8m 7f 1991 8m] sturdy, workmanlike horse: carries condition: moderate mover: bad performer: stays 1¼m: acts on firm going: has worn blinkers. *H. J. Collingridge.* —

LONGDRUM 4 ch.g. Sayf El Arab (USA) 127 – Geppina Umbra (Sheshoon 132) [1990 8g 12.5g2 12m4 10d4 12d 1991 11.7g] tall, strong, rangy gelding: poor maiden: well beaten only run in 1991 (April): stays 1½m well: best efforts on an easy surface. *M. J. Fetherston-Godley.* **49**

LONG FURLONG 3 b.g. Castle Keep 121 – Myrtlegrove (Scottish Rifle 127) [1990 6m5 6m 8.2g2 10m* 1991 12s 7g 8m 12.2g 10d 12f5 a10g 10m* 10g* 9.7f* 10m 9.7s2] leggy gelding: revitalised after joining R. Akehurst, winning autumn handicaps at Nottingham (seller, bought in 4,000 gns), Brighton and Folkestone: should stay 1½m: acts on any going: blinkered and bandaged first 7 starts: carries head high, and not easiest of rides: trained first 5 starts by D. Jermy, next 2 by B. Millman, then rejoined D. Jermy after final one. *R. Akehurst.* **65**

LONG KNIVES 3 b.c. Known Fact (USA) 135 – Ides of March 87 (Mummy's Pet 125) [1990 5f2 6g4 1991 6f2 7.1m* 7.6m4 7m] good-bodied colt: fair form: promising winner of maiden at Haydock in September: improved only a little on that in handicap next start and well beaten on final one: should stay 1m: taken early to post: sold A. Falourd 17,000 gns Newmarket Autumn Sales. *G. Harwood.* **85**

LONG LANE LADY 5 ch.m. Longleat (USA) 109 – Teresa Way 66 (Great White Way (USA)) [1990 6m a7g3 a7g5 6d a7g 1991 a5g6 6g4 6d* 6g 6g5 6.1m2 6d a6g] lengthy, good-quartered mare: plating-class handicapper: won at Thirsk in June: suited by 6f: acts on good to firm and dead ground: often has tongue tied down: inconsistent. *J. Mackie.* **50**

LONGSHOREMAN 4 gr.g. Longleat (USA) 109 – Cabotage 54 (Sea Hawk II 131) [1990 a11g2 a12g2 13.3m 11.7m* 14m5 12d3 a12g3 1991 16.2g 12m 11.5m4 12.3d 10g 10g* 10m 11.5m* 14.1f4 10f] sturdy gelding: poor handicapper nowadays: won at Brighton in July (drifted left) and Lingfield (made all) in August: below form in ladies events last 2 starts: stays 1½m: acts on good to firm and dead going: tailed off when wearing tongue strap once: claimed out of N. Tinkler's stable £6,310 on **54**

reappearance: sold 6,800 gns Newmarket Autumn Sales: none too consistent. *M. Bell.*

LONGWOOD LEGEND   3 b.c. Legend of France (USA) 124 – Phlox 101   **32**
(Floriana 106) [1990 a6g 8m a8g a6g a6g 1991 7g 6m⁵ 5m⁴ a5g⁵ a6g³ 6f⁶ 6m 6g]
leggy, rather sparely-made colt: poor mover: poor plater: stays 6f: acts on firm
going: blinkered third outing: visored last 3: bandaged and wore tongue strap
penultimate start: sold 500 gns Doncaster October Sales. *Pat Mitchell.*

LONSOM LASS   3 ch.f. Headin' Up – Lonely Dawn (USA) 63 (Plenty Old (USA))   **73**
[1990 NR 1991 5f 6f* 5.2m⁶ 5.1s] shallow-girthed filly: third foal: sister to plating-
class sprinter Lonely Lass: dam won sellers at 7f and 1m: made all in maiden at
Thirsk in September, carrying head high: good 8 lengths sixth of 10 to On Tiptoes in
£6,800 minor event at Newbury: prominent 3f facing stiff task in handicap following
month: possibly unsuited by soft going: wanders under pressure. *L. J. Barratt.*

LOOKINGFORARAINBOW (IRE)   3 ch.g. Godswalk (USA) 130 – Bridget   **69**
Folly (Crofter (USA) 124) [1990 5m 5m⁵ 5m² 5g³ 6m⁵ 5g 1991 6f 6m 5m³ 5m⁵ 5d²
9.7m² 9f* 8m 9m⁵ 10.5d⁶ 9g] close-coupled gelding: modest performer: won
maiden at Newcastle in August, leading close home: took good hold and well beaten
in £30,800 handicap final start: suited by 9f: acts on firm ground, ran creditably on
dead as sprinter. *R. W. Jones.*

LOON   3 ch.g. Bairn (USA) 126 – Patois (I Say 125) [1990 NR 1991 9g 10.2d 12s⁵ 10s]   **—**
4,800F: workmanlike gelding: half-brother to several winners, including middle-
distance fillies Louise (by Royal Palace) and La Bandera (by Morston): dam twice-
raced half-sister to smart stayer Petty Officer: fifth of 11 in claimer at Goodwood,
headway from rear then weakening final 1f: sweating and very stiff task, well behind
in apprentice handicap: sold to join J. Joseph 4,200 gns Ascot July Sales. *J. L. Dunlop.*

LOOSE SPIRIT   2 b.f. (Feb 26) Mummy's Game 120 – Maycrest (Imperial Fling   **44**
(USA) 116) [1991 7m a6g 7m 7.5f 6m⁵ 7m] angular, rather sparely-made filly: poor
mover: second foal: half-sister to 3-y-o Foursingh (by Mansingh), 5f winner at 2 yrs:
dam ran once: modest plater: seems better suited by 6f than 7f: blinkered last 3
starts: ran well when fifth for claimer: often slowly away: sold 570 gns Doncaster
October Sales. *P. C. Haslam.*

LOOSE ZEUS (USA)   2 b.c. (Feb 11) Double Zeus (USA) – Dareing Driver (USA)   **38**
(Sadair) [1991 7.5f 8.1g 8m] 625Y: good-topped colt: moderate mover: brother to
minor sprint winner in USA: dam unraced: sire stakes winning sprinter: poor maiden: not bred to stay beyond 1m: ridden by lad in paddock first 2 starts. *C. F. Wall.*

LOOTING (USA)   5 b. or br.g. Pirate's Bounty (USA) – Bank Examiner (USA)   **56**
(Buckfinder (USA)) [1990 a6g³ a6g³ a6g² a7g² a6g⁴ a7g* a6g⁶ 7f 7m 6d* 6m* 6m³
6g 6f 6h 1991 6g 6d⁶ 6g 6g 6.1s 6g⁶ 6m⁴ 7s 6g 6g] strong, good-bodied gelding:
modest handicapper: below best in 1991, pulling up injured final start: worth another
try over 7f: acts on good to firm going, possibly unsuited by soft. *M. D. I. Usher.*

LORD ADVOCATE   3 br.c. Law Society (USA) 130 – Kereolle (Riverman (USA)   **51**
131) [1990 5g 5m 6m 8m 1991 9f⁵ 11.1d³ 13.8g a12g a12g³ a13g a10g*] workmanlike
colt: moderate mover: 20/1, won maiden claimer at Lingfield in December, always
prominent: seems suited by 1½m: acts on firm and dead ground: visored last 3
starts. *M. P. Naughton.*

LORD ALFIE   2 ch.c. Beveled (USA) – Fair Nic (Romancero 100) [1991 7g 6f]   **58**
tall, leggy colt: half-brother to 3-y-o Stock Hill Lady (by Tina's Pet) and fair
sprinter/miler Stock Hill Lass (by Air Trooper): dam runner-up in 3-runner 1½m
maiden at 4 yrs on only outing on flat: last in maidens at Warwick and Folkestone
(again bit slowly away) in October: looks weak. *R. J. Hodges.*

LORD BELMONTE (IRE)   2 b.g. (Feb 26) Cyrano de Bergerac 120 – Noble   **—**
Nancy (Royal And Regal (USA)) [1991 7f 7m 8d] 7,200Y: leggy, angular gelding: fifth
foal: half-brother to 3-y-o Vague Nancy (by Mazaad) and 1m seller winner Dusky
Nancy and a winner in Norway (both by Red Sunset): dam Irish 1¾m winner: no
worthwhile form: sold 4,000 gns Newmarket Autumn Sales. *C. A. Cyzer.*

LORD CHARMER (USA)   4 b.c. Our Native (USA) – Embellished (USA)   **109**
(Seattle Slew (USA)) [1990 8m* 8f⁶ 7m 1991 10g² 10g² 8g 10m* 10.5g³ 10m² 8.9g⁶
9f⁵] strong, round-barrelled colt: usually impresses in appearance: has a powerful,
round action: useful performer on his day: made all in minor event at Newmarket
(goes very well there) in July: good second of 8 to Filia Ardross in listed event at
Windsor: fair fifth of 8 to Fly Til Dawn in Grade 2 handicap at Hollywood Park:
better suited by 1¼m than shorter: acts on good to firm ground: often swishes tail
under pressure: found very little third (blinkered) and penultimate starts. *J. Gosden.*

LORD FUTURE (IRE)   3 ch.g. The Noble Player (USA) 126 – Little Spinner 57   **47**
(Tachypous 128) [1990 a8g⁶ a7g 1991 a8g³ a10g a8g⁴ 10g⁵ 11.1s² 13d³ 12m 17.1m

13.8m] leggy gelding: has a round action: plating-class maiden: placed in claiming events at Hamilton and Ayr: stays 13f: acts on soft, seemingly not on top-of-the-ground: trained first 6 starts by G. Pritchard-Gordon: joined A. Potts. *A. Harrison.*

LORD HASTIE (USA) 3 b.c. Affirmed (USA) – Sheika (USA) (Minnesota Mac (USA)) [1990 NR 1991 10.2s* 10d⁶ 11.9g 11.9d*] $42,000Y: tall, rather leggy colt: half-brother to 3 winners in North America: dam minor winner at 3 yrs: impressive winner of maiden at Doncaster in March: easily best other effort (off course nearly 6 months after second start) when gamely winning 14-runner handicap at Haydock in October, leading 1½f out: stays 1½m: goes well on soft ground: may be capable of better. *S. G. Norton.* **76**

LORD HIGH ADMIRAL (CAN) 3 b.c. Bering 136 – Baltic Sea (CAN) (Dang (USA)) [1990 NR 1991 8s 7g⁴ 7f4] 46,000Y: leggy colt: second foal: dam never ran: modest form in minor event and maidens: prominent long way first 2 starts, slowly away and got well behind on final (first for 4 months) one: may well be suited by return to 1m: sold 8,200 gns Newmarket December Sales. *Lord Huntingdon.* **67**

LORD LEITRIM (IRE) 2 b.c. (Feb 12) Nordico (USA) – Brave Louise 76 (Brave Shot) [1991 7m a7g a8g³] IR 6,200F, IR 20,000Y: leggy, lightly-made colt: second foal: half-brother to 9f winner Torghia (by Taufan): dam, 6f to 1½m winner, is out of half-sister to Irish Oaks winner Aurabella: around 6 lengths third of 9 to Judge And Jury in late-year maiden at Lingfield, easily best effort: will be suited by 1¼m + . *N. A. Callaghan.* **57**

LORD MAGESTER (FR) 4 ch.g. Magesterial (USA) 116 – Lady Zia (FR) (Sir Tor (FR)) [1990 7g 7f⁴ 7m 6s 6f³ 5.3f² 6m⁵ 1991 a6g] lengthy, good-quartered gelding: quite modest maiden at 3 yrs for L. Cumani: not seen out in 1991 after March: may prove best at 6f, though bred to stay at least 1m: acts on firm going, seems unsuited by soft. *J. H. Johnson.* **—**

LORD NEPTUNE 2 gr.c. (Feb 4) Petong 126 – Odile (Green Dancer (USA) 132) [1991 6.1m⁶ 6g³] 16,000Y: sturdy, angular colt: third foal: half-brother to fair 6f winner Odilesa and 1m (seller) and 8.5f winner Odilex (both by Mummy's Pet): dam once-raced granddaughter of 1000 Guineas winner Waterloo: joint favourite, third of 12 in maiden at Lingfield in October, no extra final 2f: likely to stay 1m: may be capable of bit better. *M. A. Jarvis.* **58**

LORD OBERON (IRE) 3 b.g. Fairy King (USA) – Vaguely Jade (Corvaro (USA) 122) [1990 7f⁴ 6m⁴ 8d⁴ 7m 1991 7.6g 10g 8.2g* 9m⁵ 8g² 8f 10m² 8.2m* 8m* 7.9m⁴ 8g] angular, lengthy gelding: has a round action: fair handicapper: won at Haydock in June, Nottingham (claimer) in September and Newcastle in October: stays 1¼m: acts on good to firm (possibly unsuited by firm) ground: often wears severe noseband: blinkered final start at 2 yrs: sold to join R. O'Sullivan 27,000 gns Newmarket Autumn Sales. *B. Hanbury.* **81**

LORD OF TUSMORE 4 b.c. Al Nasr (FR) 126 – Princess Toy (Prince Tenderfoot (USA) 126) [1990 8f* 8.2m² 9m² 10f 9g² 10g* 9m 1991 8d 10g² 10g³ 8g² 8g 11.9m⁴ 10g⁴ 10.5g* 11.1m⁵ 10m*] good-topped, attractive colt with plenty of scope: impresses a good deal in appearance: has a quick, rather round action: useful per- **104**

*Burtonwood Brewery Rose of Lancaster Stakes, Haydock —
the entire field in shot for this Group 3 event; Lord of Tusmore wins from
Song of Sixpence (left), Lord Charmer (rails), Nayland (blaze) and Adversary*

former: won Group 3 Burtonwood Brewery Rose of Lancaster Stakes at Haydock (by 1½ lengths from Song of Sixpence) in August and apprentice handicap at Newmarket (by 2½ lengths) in November: effective at 1m, and probably stays 1½m: acts on good to firm ground. *B. W. Hills.*

LORD PATRICK   7 b.g. Formidable (USA) 125 – Boldie 81 (Bold Lad (IRE) 133)   — [1990 NR 1991 7s] good-bodied gelding: keen walker: modest handicapper at 4 yrs: lightly raced and below form since: effective at 7f and 1m: acts on any going: has bolted, and usually taken quietly to post. *J. A. R. Toller.*

LORD RANDOLPH   3 b.c. Norwick (USA) 120 – Inca Girl (Tribal Chief 125)   — [1990 7m 7d a8g 1991 10v⁶ 10d] leggy colt: poor form in maidens and claimer. *J. E. Long.*

LORD'S FINAL   4 ch.c. Royal Match 117 – White Cone (Celtic Cone 116) [1990   — 8m 1991 10.8g] close-coupled colt: twice raced and no show in modest company (finished lame in April, 1991). *C. R. Barwell.*

LORD VIVIENNE (IRE)   2 b.g. (Mar 26) Don't Forget Me 127 – Lady Vivi-   **79** p enne (Golden Fleece (USA) 133) [1991 a8g* a8g*] first foal: dam Irish 1½m winner, is half-sister to smart Erin's Hope, successful at up to 1¼m, and good middle-distance performer Erin's Isle: favourite, won maiden at Southwell and nursery at Lingfield (by 1½ lengths from Paper Clip, despite hanging left) late in year: may well stay 1¼m: likely to improve again. *P. F. I. Cole.*

LORELEI   2 ch.f. (Feb 7) Domynsky 110 – Naufrage (Main Reef 126) [1991 5m 5g²   **51** 7s 7f 7f² 7.5f⁶ 7f] 2,600Y: small, sparely-made filly: first foal: dam unraced: plating-class maiden: has run moderately in sellers: stays 7f: acts on firm ground: blinkered (ran well first occasion) last 3 starts. *M. H. Easterby.*

LORETTO (USA)   4 b.c. Danzatore (CAN) 127 – Desirable (AUS) (Without Fear   — (FR) 128) [1990 a12g 1991 10g] close-coupled, sparely-made colt: twice raced and no show in modest company: sold 750 gns Ascot July Sales. *R. F. Johnson Houghton.*

LORYMAYA (FR)   3 b.f. River River 117 – Luna Blue (Cure The Blues (USA))   **111** [1990 7d² 10g² 1991 10m* 10g* 12m 9d] first foal: dam 11f winner, is half-sister to Linamix: successful in maiden at Chantilly in June and Prix de Psyche (by 1½ lengths from Pink Turtle) at Deauville over 2 months later: towards rear after in Prix Vermeille Escada and Ciga Prix de l'Opera, both at Longchamp: stays 1¼m: yet to race on extremes of going. *F. Boutin, France.*

LOTS OF LUCK   8 gr.m. Neltino 97 – Safe Passage (Charlottown 127) [1990 8m   **73** d 8m³ 8m⁴ 10g* 10m 10.5m 10f² 10f 10g⁶ 10m³ 10g 10.6d* 10.6v 10.4d 1991 a11g* a12g* 10g 11.8g 9g 10.3d] smallish, workmanlike mare: moderate mover: modest handicapper: won at Southwell and Lingfield (subsequently off course over 6 months): last in ladies event (lame) final start: acts on any going: has run creditably when blinkered: good mount for inexperienced rider. *J. Pearce.*

LOUDEST WHISPER   3 b.g. Reach 122 – Dancela 74 (Ela-Mana-Mou 132)   **69** [1990 6g a8g³ 1991 8d 10.1f³ 8m] tall, close-coupled, angular gelding: modest form: staying-on third of 9 in moderately-run handicap at Yarmouth: on toes, soundly beaten in handicap at Newmarket 4 months later: will benefit from more strongly-run race at 1¼m: sold to join K. Bridgwater 6,000 gns Newmarket Autumn Sales. *C. E. Brittain.*

LOUISA SCARLETT (IRE)   2 b. or br.f. (Apr 14) Cyrano de Bergerac 120 –   **82** Salacia 93 (Seaepic (USA)) [1991 5g⁶ 6m 6m 5d 6m* 6m* 6d² 5m* 5m⁶ 6m* 7m 7d* 7g] IR 3,000F, IR 3,200Y: smallish filly: moderate mover: sixth reported foal: half-sister to 1¼m winner Red Hill Girl (by Riboboy) and a winner in Malaysia: dam disqualified 7f winner at 2 yrs: fair performer: had a fine season: successful in sellers at Windsor (no bid) and Leicester (retained 6,250 gns) in July, nursery at Windsor in August, claimer at Haydock in September then 16-runner nursery at Ascot (best effort) by ½ length, clear, from Prince Secreto: better suited by 7f than 6f: acts on good to firm and dead ground: sold 23,000 gns Newmarket Autumn Sales. *G. Lewis.*

LOUISVILLE BELLE (IRE)   2 ch.f. (Apr 9) Ahonoora 122 – Lomond Fairy   **43** p (Lomond (USA) 128) [1991 7d] IR 1,700F: sturdy filly: first foal: dam unraced: 66/1, backward and green, well beaten in 22-runner maiden at Doncaster in November: should improve. *M. D. I. Usher.*

LOUKARA GOLD   4 b.g. Taufan (USA) 119 – Blue Parrot (FR) (Lyphard (USA)   — 132) [1990 10f 7m 10m 7g 15.5f² 16m⁴ 13.8d 1991 16m⁶ 12f⁶] neat gelding: quite modest handicapper at 3 yrs: no form in 1991: may prove ideally suited by around 1¾m: acts on firm ground. *R. Akehurst.*

LOURE (USA) 3 b.f. Lyphard (USA) 132 – Alliance (USA) (Alleged (USA) 138) **66**
[1990 NR 1991 8f 10.1f² 12g] $575,000Y: leggy filly: has a round action: fourth foal:
closely related to quite useful 1½m and 13.3f winner Matador and French provincial
11.5f and 1½m winner Beaute Dangereuse (both by Nureyev): dam, French 10.5f
winner who stayed 1½m, is half-sister to numerous winners including Blushing
Groom: 15 lengths second of 5 to odds-on Rudimentary in maiden at Yarmouth: well
beaten in similar event at Folkestone 6 weeks later. *L. M. Cumani.*

LOUVE ROMAINE (USA) 3 b.f. Alydar (USA) – Lupe 123 (Primera (USA) **117**
131) [1990 NR 1991 10g* 9.2g⁵ 10g³ 10.5d³ 10d⁵ 8d³] eighth reported foal: half-sister
to several winners, including very smart 1m and 9f winners Legend of France (by
Lyphard) and Louveterie (by Nureyev), and very useful 1990 French 1¼m winner
Louve Bleue (by Irish River): dam won Oaks and Coronation Cup: won maiden at
Longchamp in April: beaten 2¾ lengths behind Treble then about a length behind
Caerlina in Prix Saint-Alary at Longchamp and Prix de Diane Hermes at Chantilly
third and fourth starts: best effort at 10.5f. *A. Fabre, France.*

LOVEALOCH (IRE) 3 b.f. Lomond (USA) 128 – Civility 108 (Shirley Heights **108**
130) [1990 6m 7m* 1991 8g* 12m² 8g² 8.2m 9m* 10v³ 8d⁵] good-topped filly: won
handicaps at Kempton in April and Sandown (impressively and much improved
form) in August: ran creditably in Group 2 event at Rome penultimate start, fairly
well in Ascot listed race 12 days later: stays 1¼m (soundly beaten at 11/10 on over
1½m): acts on good to firm ground and heavy: tongue tied down last 2 starts here:
useful. *M. Bell.*

LOVE AND LEGEND (USA) 3 ch.f. Lyphard's Wish (FR) 124 – Lore 'n **72**
Legend (USA) (Bold Forbes (USA)) [1990 8g4 1991 11.5f⁵ 8.9g²] tall filly: modest
form and some promise in maidens at Yarmouth and median auction contest
(making most and rallying well, in June) at Wolverhampton: should have been suited
by return to further. *H. R. A. Cecil.*

LOVE JAZZ (USA) 2 b.c. (Mar 14) State Dinner (USA) – Snow Lover (USA) **92**
(Knightly Sport (USA)) [1991 5m 6f* 7.5f⁵ 7m* 7m* 7g 7m³ 7f⁶ 7m] $20,000F,
$32,000Y: leggy, short-backed colt: fourth foal: half-brother to a minor winner by
Wavering Monarch: dam won 3 races at up to 7f, including in minor stakes: sire (by
Buckpasser) late-developing good-class 1m to 1½m performer: fairly useful
performer: won maiden at Hamilton and nurseries at Ayr and Redcar in summer: ran
moderately at York sixth and final outings: well worth a try at 1m: acts on firm
ground: sometimes sweats: largely consistent. *T. D. Barron.*

LOVE LEGEND 6 ch.h. Glint of Gold 128 – Sweet Emma 108 (Welsh Saint 126) **92**
[1990 a5g* a6g⁴ a6g⁴ 5g* 5m 5m² 5g 5m* 6m 5m 6m 5g* 5.6g* 5m 1991 a5g³
a6g⁴ 5d⁶ 5g 5d² 5g⁴ 6m² 5m 5m⁴ 6g 6g 5.6m 6m 6g⁵ 5m² 6m 5.2g 5d⁵] smallish,
sparely-made horse: poor walker: has a quick action: fairly useful handicapper:
mostly ran well in 1991: runs as though needs further than 5f nowadays: acts on firm
and dead ground: effective with blinkers or without: often bandaged behind: has won
for apprentice. *D. W. P. Arbuthnot.*

LOVE OF THE ARTS (IRE) 3 b.f. Tate Gallery (USA) 117 – Royal Daughter **91**
(High Top 131) [1990 5m 6m* 6s² 6m⁴ 1991 8g⁵ 8g⁶] sturdy, workmanlike filly: has a
round action: keen walker: quite useful form in listed race at Kempton and handicap
at York in the spring: worth a try over further: acts on soft ground: reportedly to be
trained by R. Frankel in USA. *M. A. Jarvis.*

LOVE PRINCE 5 b.g. Indian King (USA) 128 – Chanrossa (High Top 131) [1990 **—**
5m 6m 8f 7f⁵ 8f⁶ 8m 7m 7f² 1991 7g 7m] leggy, quite good-topped gelding:
plating-class handicapper: behind in April of 1991: stays 7f: acts on firm going: tried
blinkered once: often starts slowly: inconsistent. *W. Carter.*

LOVE RETURNED 4 b.f. Taufan (USA) 119 – Miss Loving 89 (Northfields **88**
(USA)) [1990 5s* 5v⁵ 5m² 5.8h⁶ 6g² 5g* 5g² 5g 6g³ 5.6g 5m⁴ 5d 1991 5g* 6d 5f
5.1d⁶ 5.1g 5.1g² 6m* 5m 6f⁶ 5.6m³ 6m 6g³ 5.1g*] lengthy, unfurnished filly:
moderate mover: fair performer: won minor event at Carlisle in March and claimers
at Ayr in July and Bath in October: best at 5f: acts on any going, with possible
exception of heavy: has sometimes found little off bridle: inconsistent. *W. Jarvis.*

LOVE SCENE 3 b.f. Carwhite 127 – Mrs Waddilove 79 (Bustino 136) [1990 NR **—**
1991 6f] sparely-made filly: first foal: dam maiden stayed 7f, is out of sister to
Runnett: 25/1, green and always behind in maiden at Brighton in April. *R. Hannon.*

LOVES REVENGE 3 ch.f. Mansingh (USA) 120 – Malicious Love 79 (Mal- **—**
icious) [1990 NR 1991 7m⁶ 10m 6g 10g 8f] sparely-made filly: fifth foal: half-sister to
staying maiden Lovenko (by Relkino): dam stayer: no worthwhile form in sellers
and apprentice claimer: visored final start. *R. M. Whitaker.*

The Dowager Lady Beaverbrook's "Luchiroverte"

LOVE TALK   3 br.f. Hotfoot 126 – Sirnelta (FR) (Sir Tor) [1990 8s⁶ 1991 10g² 11g   **62**
10g⁶] lengthy, sparely-made filly: quite modest form in maidens, set plenty to do
first 2 outings: stiff task in listed race final one, in May: stays 1¼m. *D. R. C.*
Elsworth.

LOVE TO RUN   2 b.f. (Mar 14) Taufan (USA) 119 – Mzuri Sana (Hello Gorgeous   **—**
(USA) 128) [1991 7.5f 8m] 3,000Y: leggy filly: first foal: dam poor half-sister to good
Irish maiden Celestial Bounty out of useful Irish middle-distance stayer Heavenly
Bounty: well beaten in maiden auctions in the North: sold 900 gns Doncaster
November Sales. *J. Etherington.*

LOVING OMEN   4 ch.c. Touching Wood (USA) 127 – Etoile d'Amore (USA) 81   **43**
(The Minstrel (CAN) 135) [1990 NR 1991 12s 12.3d 12g 12g 12.3d 16.5m⁶ 12f⁶ a14g⁴
15.8f² 12g² 16f 12.3g² 12.1f² 15.1g⁵ 11.9g] big colt: poor handicapper nowadays:
effective at 1½m, and stays 15.8f: acts on firm ground: often sweating: has hung and
looked difficult ride: sold to join Miss Z. Green's stable 920 gns Doncaster October
Sales. *R. Hollinshead.*

LOVISTE BAY   2 b.f. (Mar 28) Mummy's Game 120 – Miss Maina (Thatching   **—**
131) [1991 5g 6m a8g] neat filly: first foal: dam twice-raced granddaughter of Oaks
second Maina: well beaten in maidens at Lingfield: tailed off on equitrack: gave
trouble stalls debut: sweating second start. *J. Ffitch-Heyes.*

LOWAWATHA   3 b.c. Dancing Brave (USA) 140 – Shorthouse 102 (Habitat 134)   **61**
[1990 NR 1991 11.8g⁶ 12.5m³ 10.3d] good-topped colt with scope: has high knee
action: sixth living foal: half-brother to smart miler Ever Genial (by Brigadier
Gerard): dam 2-y-o 7f winner out of smart middle-distance stayer Guillotina:
staying-on third in maiden at Warwick: tailed off in minor event over 3 months later:

476

will be suited by further than 1½m: sold out of H. Cecil's stable 11,500 gns Newmarket Autumn Sales after second start. *D. Morris.*

LOWLANDS BOY 2 b.c. (Apr 15) Claude Monet (USA) 121 – Aquarian Star **63** (Cavo Doro 124) [1991 5m 6d 7.5f* 7m⁵ 6m 7g] workmanlike colt: has scope: has a round action: third living foal: brother to Margs Girl, a modest performer at 1m/1¼m: dam temperamental half-sister to smart 1¼m performer The Dunce: quite modest performer: won claimer at Beverley in July: ran badly last 2 starts: will stay 1¼m. *T. Fairhurst.*

LOXLEY RANGE (IRE) 3 ch.g. Hatim (USA) 121 – Chantal 74 (Charlottesville — 135) [1990 5g 7m 1991 7m⁴ 6h⁶ 10d 11.1s 12m] leggy gelding: no worthwhile form: ran in claimers last 2 starts: bred to stay 1½m: best effort on good to firm ground: takes keen hold. *O. Brennan.*

LUCAYA 3 br.g. Gabitat 119 – Queen's Bidder 84 (Auction Ring (USA) 123) [1990 **36** 5m 6m 6g 5m 1991 a6g⁵ 5d 6m 6m 6m 5f] lengthy gelding: has a long stride: poor maiden: stays 6f: best effort on equitrack: has been visored and blinkered: sometimes sweating and edgy: sold 900 gns Ascot November Sales. *B. Gubby.*

LUCEDEO 7 ro.g. Godswalk (USA) 130 – Lucy Limelight 98 (Hot Spark 126) **93** [1990 5m⁴ 5f* 5m* 5m* 6f* 6f⁴ 5m³ 5g* 5g³ 5m³ 6d⁶ 6m⁵ 5m³ 5m 5m* 5m 5d 5.6g 5m⁶ 5m 5g⁶ 5m 1991 5g 5g 5m 5g² 6g⁵ 5m² 5g⁴ 6m 5m* 5m⁶ 6g 6m² 5.6m 6m 5f 5m 5.2g 5d⁶] sturdy, compact gelding: carries condition: fairly useful handicapper: won £11,800 Gosforth Park Cup at Newcastle in June: in-and-out form after: effective at 5f and 6f: best form on sound surface: below form when blinkered once: excellent mount for inexperienced rider: claimed £11,856 sixth start: splendidly tough: usually away. *J. L. Spearing.*

LUCHIROVERTE (IRE) 3 b.c. Slip Anchor 136 – Green Lucia 116 (Green **115** Dancer (USA) 132) [1990 NR 1991 11g⁶ 12.3d² 10g² 12m⁴ 12m* 12m 14.6m⁴] 250,000Y: lengthy, useful-looking colt: has scope: good walker: good mover with a long stride: fourth foal: closely related to Irish 1¾m winner Euromill (by Shirley Heights) and half-brother to 1988 2-y-o 7f winner Muthaiga (by Kalaglow) and 4-y-o 1¼m winner Elhudhud (by Habitat): dam placed in Irish Oaks and Yorkshire Oaks: won £11,200 event at Ascot in June: in frame in Chester Vase (beaten 1½ lengths by impressive Toulon), Predominate Stakes at Goodwood, Prix du Jockey-Club at Chantilly (over 6 lengths fourth to Suave Dancer) and Coalite St Leger (on toes, lost position early in straight then stayed on, well beaten behind Toulon) at Doncaster: resolute galloper, very much a staying type: acts on good to firm ground and dead: smart. *C. E. Brittain.*

LUCID (IRE) 2 ch.f. (Apr 8) Nashamaa 113 – Fleur-de-Luce (Tumble Wind **71** (USA)) [1991 5g* 6m 5d] IR 8,800Y: sparely-made filly: third foal: half-sister to 3-y-o Twilight Flame (by Red Sunset) and Irish 2-y-o 6f winner Lady Be Magic (by Burslem): dam Irish 9.5f winner: won 16-runner maiden auction at Sandown in May: creditable fifteenth of 22 in Tattersalls Breeders Stakes at the Curragh in late-August: well beaten in nursery at Haydock in October: bred to stay 1m +: sold 7,600 gns Newmarket Autumn Sales. *Lord Huntingdon.*

LUCKNAM DREAMER 3 b.g. Macmillion 110 – River Damsel (Forlorn River **79** 124) [1990 6m³ 6m 6m² 6m² 1991 7f³ 8d⁵ 8d 7d² 7m* 7g² 7.6g] tall, leggy gelding: modest performer: won maiden at Lingfield in July, making virtually all: ran well in handicap there next start, poorly (bandaged off-hind) 8 weeks later: stays 1m: acts on good to firm ground and dead: usually on toes: sweating (well beaten) third start. *Mrs Barbara Waring.*

LUCKNAM STYLE 3 b.g. Macmillion 110 – Mrs Currie 74 (He Loves Me 120) — [1990 6g⁶ 7m* 6g³ 1991 6f⁶] leggy, sparely-made gelding: modest winner at 2 yrs: stiff task, sixth of 7 in minor event at Folkestone in April, only start in 1991: stays 7f: wears a tongue strap: tends to get on toes. *Mrs Barbara Waring.*

LUCK OF EDEN HALL (IRE) 2 b.f. (Feb 9) Taufan (USA) 119 – Silvera 73 **36** (Ribero 126) [1991 5d⁵ 5m 7m] 14,500Y: big, good-topped filly: has scope: moderate mover: half-sister to fair 6f and 8.5f winner Pontevecchio Due (by Welsh Pageant) and 2 winners abroad: dam won over 1m: poor maiden: should stay 1m. *Dr J. D. Scargill.*

LUCKY AGAIN 4 br.g. Ile de Bourbon (USA) 133 – Soft Pedal 92 (Hotfoot 126) — [1990 8m⁴ 7m 10.1m³ 1991 12f⁵ 9f] stocky colt: fair maiden as 3-y-o for P. Cole: behind in summer, first runs for a year: acts on good to firm ground. *W. A. Stephenson.*

LUCKY ASSET 3 b.f. Nomination 125 – Wild Asset (Welsh Pageant 132) [1990 — 6d a8g a7g⁵ 1991 10g⁶ 10m 11d] workmanlike filly: poor form at 2 yrs, none in autumn at 3 yrs: stays 1m. *G. A. Pritchard-Gordon.*

LUCKY BLUE 4 b.g. Blue Cashmere 129 – Cooling 89 (Tycoon II) [1990 6m 6g* — 6f* 6m* 6g5 6m3 6m6 6f2 6m 5m5 6m 1991 6g] workmanlike gelding: quite modest performer: stiff task only run in 1991 (May): better at 6f than 5f: acts on firm going: visored once (ran poorly), blinkered once: sold 1,450 gns Ascot November Sales: inconsistent. *J. C. Fox.*

LUCKY CRYSTAL 5 ch.m. Main Reef 126 – Please Oblige (Le Levanstell 122) **36** [1990 7.6m 9m 1991 a7g5 a12g a7g 7f 7d] lengthy mare: poor maiden: stays 7f: acts on good to firm and dead going: has worn crossed noseband. *A. Moore.*

LUCKY GUEST 4 bl.c. Be My Guest (USA) 126 – Gay Fantasy (Troy 137) [1990 **109** 10g2 12m2 10g* 12d3 10f 10d* 9g* 9g2 1991 8g 8d 8g 8d 10m3 10.8m* 9.5g* 10v] tall, attractive colt: has done well physically: impresses good deal in appearance: has quick action: useful performer: returned to form late in 1991, winning minor event at Warwick (easily landed odds) and Group 2 event in Turkey: creditable eighth of 20 to Tashkourgan in Group 3 event at Milan final start: best short of 1½m: acts on good to firm ground, and goes very well on an easy surface. *J. L. Dunlop.*

LUCKY LINDY (IRE) 2 b.c. (Mar 11) Trojan Fen 118 – Excruciating (CAN) **103** p (Bold Forbes (USA)) [1991 7f4 7g2 6.3s2] IR 21,000Y: sturdy, quite attractive colt: fifth foal: half-brother to Irish 3-y-o Bold Princess (by M Double M) and useful 7f winner Hard Act (by Hard Fought): dam unraced daughter of half-sister to Riboboy: looking really well, ½-length second of 12 to Badie in minor event at Kempton in September, always prominent: improved again when head second of 21 to Colway Bold in Goffs Premier Challenge Race at the Curragh following month: will stay 1m: sure to win a race. *R. Hannon.*

LUCKY LOGAN (IRE) 2 ch.g. (Jan 30) Hatim (USA) 121 – Lucky Pick 69 — (Auction Ring (USA) 123) [1991 5d4 5g] IR 7,500Y: small, strong gelding: has a quick action: first foal: dam maiden best at 1¼m: carrying condition, well beaten in 4-runner minor event at Thirsk and maiden at Leicester in spring: sold 680 gns Newmarket July Sales. *M. H. Tompkins.*

LUCKY MOON 4 b.c. Touching Wood (USA) 127 – Castle Moon 79 (Kalamoun — 129) [1990 10f6 10.2h5 14g* 12f* 12.3g* 16.1f* 20f* 18g 1991 16.2s6] lengthy, quite attractive colt: moderate mover: useful performer at 3 yrs, gained final win in Goodwood Cup (suffered joint injury) in August: below best since in Doncaster Cup and 7-runner Insulpak Sagaro Stakes (stiff task) at Ascot, latter only race in 1991: stays well: acts on firm going: sold only 5,000 gns Newmarket December Sales. *J. L. Dunlop.*

LUCKY NOIRE 3 b.f. Aragon 118 – Noire Small (USA) (Elocutionist (USA)) **73** [1990 6g 7m6 7m3 7m2 8m 1991 8m3 10.1g 10m5 8g4 7.6d3 9.7s 8f* 8.3m3 8.3g* 7m 8.3m* 8m3 8.1m 8g] good-topped filly: modest performer: successful in apprentice claimer at Warwick and handicaps at Windsor in the summer: suited by 1m: acts on firm and dead going: mostly ridden by 7-lb claimer and has won only for J. Smith: has worn net muzzle, including when successful: sometimes bandaged: rather headstrong. *G. Harwood.*

LUCKY VERDICT 5 b.g. Touching Wood (USA) 127 – Noor 76 (Mill Reef (USA) **88** 141) [1990 18f* 16g3 18.4d 20m2 1991 17.6m3 20g] smallish, sturdy gelding: has rather round action: fair handicapper: eighth of 20 in Ascot Stakes in June: not seen out again: suited by good test of stamina and top-of-the-ground: best in blinkers: best held up on a galloping track. *M. C. Pipe.*

LUCY DANCER (IRE) 3 ch.f. No Pass No Sale 120 – Daoulas (Thatching 131) **67** d [1990 5m5 6m 5m2 5f 5g* 5m 1991 6g3 6m6 5s3 5g 5.1g 5f5 a5g a7g a8g] compact filly: moderate mover: quite modest performer: ran creditably in minor event and handicaps first 3 starts: effective at 5f and 6f: acts on good to firm ground and soft. *M. McCormack.*

LUCY MOON 3 b.f. Blushing Groom (FR) 131 – Chic Belle (USA) (Mr Prospector **73** (USA)) [1990 NR 1991 10g 10m4 10m4 12m5] leggy, lengthy filly: third foal: sister to lightly-raced 1990 Irish 3-y-o Society Pride and half-sister to useful 5-y-o middle-distance stayer Rudjig (by Secreto): dam winner of 4 stakes races at up to 7f in USA: modest maiden: best effort in minor event at Sandown second start: seems suited by 1¼m: wore bandages behind first and last 2 outings. *J. H. M. Gosden.*

LUKE'S BRAVE BOY 3 ch.c. Prince Ragusa 96 – Golden Baby 52 (Sharpen Up **61** 127) [1990 7m 9g 1991 7m 10.2f 8g 10g 10.1m5 10m2 10.5d2 10m* 11.1s3] workmanlike colt: has a fluent, round action: useful plater: looking extremely well, won 15-runner handicap (bought in 9,500 gns) at Nottingham in October, always close up: will be better suited by 1½m: acts on good to firm ground and soft: blinkered second and third outings. *A. Hide.*

478

LUKS AKURA 3 b.c. Dominion 123 – Pacificus (USA) 65 (Northern Dancer) 47 [1990 6d⁴ 5s⁴ a7g⁵ a7g⁶ 1991 a8g³ a10g⁵ 12.3s 8.2f⁴ 8f⁴ 8g* 7g 8m² 7g³ 8d⁶ 8g 8f 8m³] small, sturdy colt: poor handicapper, won at Ripon in May: should stay 1¼m: probably acts on any going: blinkered fourth start, visored afterwards. *M. Johnston.*

LUNA BID 8 b.g. Auction Ring (USA) 123 – Moonscape 87 (Ribero 126) [1990 6f 71 6m 6m⁶ 6m⁶ 6s 6m⁴ 6m³ 6g 6m² 6m³ 6m 6g 7m 6d 6s 6s 1991 6m 6g⁵ 6g³ 6g⁴ 6d* 6.1m³ 6g⁴ 6m 6d⁴ 6m 6g 6g 6m 6g 6d³ 6m⁶ 7g 7g⁴ 7d] good-topped gelding: carries plenty of condition: turns fore-feet in markedly: modest mover: poor handicapper: won at Newbury in May: best form at 6f: acts on any going: usually gets behind and is hard to win with: has hung right: has reportedly broken blood vessels. *M. Blanshard.*

LUNAR LUNACY (IRE) 3 b.f. Ahonoora 122 – Flinging Star (USA) (Northern — Fling 126) [1990 NR 1991 7g 8m] leggy filly: fourth live foal: moderate mover: half-sister to 5-y-o 7f and 1m winner You Are A Star (by Persian Bold) and 1m winner Bronze Buck (by Silver Buck): dam, from family of Thatch and Nureyev, won at 6f at 2 yrs in USA: tailed off in maiden and claimer: sold 1,050 gns Newmarket July Sales. *J. W. Hills.*

L'UOMO CLASSICS 4 b.g. Indian King (USA) 128 – Sperrin Mist 83 (Camden 71 + Town 125) [1990 7m⁵ 7m* 8d⁵ 8m⁴ 7g 9m² 9m 8m 1991 8.2m³ 8d⁵] good-quartered gelding: keen walker: moderate mover: modest handicapper: not seen out after June: stays 9f: acts on good to firm ground and dead: will prove best with strong handling, and worth a try in blinkers or a visor. *Mrs J. Pitman.*

LUPESCU 3 ch.f. Dixieland Band (USA) – Keep Me Posted (USA) (Stage Door 98 Johnny) [1990 7m² 7.3s⁴ 1991 10m*] lengthy, good-topped filly: has plenty of scope: has a fluent, rather round action: good walker: favourite and looking really well, most impressive in winning 13-runner maiden at Sandown in June eased by 12 lengths from Mubin, always prominent travelling comfortably: will stay 1½m: looked certain to improve again and win more races. *H. R. A. Cecil.*

LUST OF LOVE 5 b.m. Sallust 134 – Aridje 79 (Mummy's Pet 125) [1990 7f 7f² 66 7m⁵ 7m² 7g 7f⁵ 6m 7m 1991 7m* 7f* 7m 7m⁴ 7g 7m] leggy, rather sparely-made mare: poor walker and mover: quite modest handicapper: won at Doncaster (apprentices) in May and Redcar in July: stays 7f: acts well on top-of-the-ground: bandaged last 3 starts: ran moderately when blinkered once. *J. G. FitzGerald.*

LUSTREMAN 4 ch.g. Sallust 134 – Miss Speak Easy (USA) (Sea Bird II 145) 40 [1990 10.1g 10m 10g 10f² 11m* 10f⁶ 12h⁴ 1991 12g 10g 12s⁵ 11.5m⁴] workmanlike, close-coupled gelding: poor handicapper: stays 1½m: probably acts on any going: has won when sweating: winning hurdler. *M. R. Channon.*

LUTE AND LYRE (IRE) 2 b.f. (Feb 2) The Noble Player (USA) 126 – Kool For 96 Kats (Malinowski (USA) 123) [1991 6m 6m 5g* 6d² 5m* 5.2f⁵ 5d²] IR 3,000F, IR 1,800Y: neat filly: good mover: second foal: dam Irish 7f and 9f winner: fairly useful performer: successful in maiden at Bellewstown and nursery at Mallow in summer: fair fifth of 7, bit slowly away, outpaced over 1f out, to Mamma's Too in listed race at Newbury: showed much improved form when 1½ lengths second of 9 to Flowing in Meadow Meats EBF Flying Five at Leopardstown in September: should stay 6f. *E. J. O'Grady, Ireland.*

LUTHIOR (FR) 5 gr.g. Carwhite 127 – Luthiana (FR) (Luthier 126) [1990 12m⁴ — 12f⁵ 8h³ 1991 12g 9m] leggy ex-French gelding: moderate walker: has a rather round action: fair performer at 3 yrs: little show in handicaps in 1991, off course over 5 months after reappearance: stays 1½m: acts on good to firm and dead ground. *R. Simpson.*

LUVLY JUBLY 2 gr.c. (Mar 19) Belfort (FR) 89 – Manna Green (Bustino 136) 71 [1991 5d⁴ 6g a5g* 5g² 5f* 5.3m³ 6g⁶ 5.7g] 3,500F, 8,000Y: leggy colt: brother to 1990 2-y-o 7f winner Kevinsbelle and half-brother to 3 winners here and abroad, including 9f claimer winner Taxi Man (by Dublin Taxi): dam ran twice: modest form: successful in claimers at Ayr in the spring, and at Southwell (after slow start) and Beverley in mid-summer: off course 10 weeks before penultimate start, and didn't recapture best form: should be at least as effective at 6f as 5f: acts on firm and dead ground: sold 7,000 gns Newmarket Autumn Sales. *J. Berry.*

LUZUM 7 ch.h. Touching Wood (USA) 127 – Velvet Habit 89 (Habitat 134) [1990 77 d 8.5g 7g⁴ 7m 7.3g³ 7m³ 7.6v 1991 a8g⁴ a8g 9s 8f⁴ 7m] small, sturdy horse: moderate mover: one-time very useful performer, only quite modest nowadays: not seen out in 1991 after May: suited by 7f to 1m: acts on any going except seemingly heavy: usually wears blinkers, didn't on reappearance. *J. A. Glover.*

LYCIUS (USA) 3 ch.c. Mr Prospector (USA) – Lypatia (FR) (Lyphard **124** (USA) 132) [1990 6d⁴ 7d⁸ 7g² 6m* 1991 7g² 8g² 8g³ 6m² 8g² 8m³ 7d5]

'Defeated the winners of 15 Group One races' states the advertisement for Lycius, now retired to the Dalham Hall Stud. As a three-year-old, of course, he couldn't win one himself but racing frequently assails the soundness of such statements as 'winning is everything' and 'you get nothing for coming second', coaching cliches best left unquestioned in the dressing room. Most obviously in Lycius' case, not winning didn't prevent his collecting about £165,000 in prize money for his connections. In a total of eleven starts, seven as a three-year-old, Lycius reached the frame on all but one occasion. In doing so he showed very smart form, established himself as a leading colt at both two and three years, and demonstrated a level of consistency which was conspicuously lacking in some of his contemporaries. Conversely, in racing as in many other sports, a record such as his tends to provoke questions of temperament as well as comments of admiration. A bout of 'seconditis' can be damaging to reputation, and a want of evidence beyond the form figures does not necessarily scotch the popular suspicions.

Lycius' reputation entering the latest season was that of a bona-fide classic contender following his victory, coming with a rare late rattle, over Distinctly North in the Newgate Stud Middle Park Stakes. The context to the series of placed efforts that followed was not that of a desperate search for the easiest opportunity like some of the other 'seconditis' sufferers described in these pages. Indeed, few horses were given a more challenging programme than Lycius in 1991, trying as he did for a second Group 1 triumph in six of his seven races. The exception was his reappearance, a rather disappointing show when looking fit and well in the moderately-run Prix Djebel at Maisons-Laffitte, but Lycius lined up for the General Accident Two Thousand Guineas and bounced back in very nearly the best possible manner. Sent off at 16/1, Lycius was soon at the back of a group of eleven runners towards the centre of the track but made smooth progress to head that group one and a half furlongs out and had left them behind by the furlong pole in pursuit of Mystiko who was

Sheikh Mohammed's "Lycius" (S. Cauthen)

racing against the rails. The pair drew six lengths clear, with little to choose between them, but Mystiko was a head in front at the post. The eventual third was Ganges who had beaten Lycius at Maisons-Laffitte. In both those races and for the rest of the season, Lycius was equipped with a sheepskin noseband, not something his trainer normally uses nor used on Lycius in the Middle Park. Two weeks later Lycius was an even-money shot in the Airlie/ Coolmore Irish Two Thousand Guineas at the Curragh but he never got remotely close to justifying favouritism, having a considerable deficit to make up when extricated from the pack two furlongs out, though he seemed not to be travelling with the same fluency as at Newmarket, anyway. This time he beat Ganges by only three quarters of a length.

A large number of horses trained for the spring classics have gone on to run well in the top sprints and it was no surprise to see Lycius sent to try and do likewise. Soviet Star had performed the feat for Fabre in the 1988 July Cup, Golden Opinion went close the following year, and Lycius made his third trip to Newmarket for the latest running. He also responded well to the change in discipline. A modest pace helped him early on, as he'd been slow emerging from the stalls (having had to be dragged into them), and it didn't prevent him from eventually showing the way home to the likes of Elbio, Polar Falcon and Chicarica, too late however to catch Polish Patriot. There followed two more attempts to win a top mile race and Lycius came within inches of doing so when he lost out only to Hector Protector in a massed sprint at the close of the Prix du Haras de Fresnay-le-Buffard Jacques le Marois at Deauville. Lycius was in front just after the line. The Moulin four weeks later also saw him produce a powerful finishing burst but this was another of those races in which Lycius never got in a blow and on this occasion he hindered his cause by hanging right when asked for his effort. Lycius had shown his form at six furlongs and a mile, and he should have been able to show it at the inter- mediate distance, but when put back to seven furlongs for the Prix de la Foret at Longchamp in October he disappointed at odds on, failing to reach the frame for the first time, after which connections decided to call it a day. Perhaps the soft surface was against him, for although he'd won a listed race on dead ground as a two-year-old, his best efforts came when conditions were less testing. To watch Lycius in, for instance, the Jacques le Marois, it is difficult to believe he didn't win a race in 1991, but in criticism of his temperament let's just say that he wasn't the easiest of rides. That was certainly the case in the Moulin, and the tactics used to get the best out of him, usually settling him towards the rear for a late run, carry an extra risk of bad luck in running.

		Raise A Native (ch 1961)	Native Dancer
Lycius (USA) (ch.c. 1988)	Mr Prospector (USA) (b 1970)		Raise You
		Gold Digger (b 1962)	Nashua
			Sequence
	Lypatia (FR) (b 1975)	Lyphard (b 1969)	Northern Dancer
			Goofed
		Hypatia (ro 1968)	High Hat
			Purple Queen

Dalham Hall now has the two most significant sons of Mr Prospector standing in Europe, with Lycius and Machiavellian. The tall, close-coupled Lycius, not the best of walkers, will cover at a fee of £12,000, October 1st. Sheikh Mohammed has a sister to Lycius purchased for 950,000 dollars at the Keeneland July Selected Yearling Sale in 1991, one of fifteen yearlings by the world's leading active sire (by progeny earnings) which were sold there for an average of about 650,000 dollars, nine of them to Darley Stud Management. Lycius himself made half a million dollars at Keeneland. He's the seventh foal, sixth winner and third stakes winner out of Lypatia, the rest including the French winner Akabir (by Riverman) who went on to win two graded contests, over nine and a half furlongs and one and a half miles, on turf in the USA as a six-year-old before being sent to Japan. Lypatia was a minor winner over six and a half furlongs at three years in France and a mile at four years in the USA. Her dam Hypatia and grandam Purple Queen both showed fair form in winning over a mile and over five furlongs respectively as two-year-olds, but managed just one run between them as three-year-olds. The fourth dam, incidentally, is the high-class sprinting two-year-old of 1953 Crimson. *A. Fabre, France.*

LYDIA MARIA   3 b.f. Dancing Brave (USA) 140 – Connaught Bridge 124   **47**
(Connaught 130) [1990 8g⁶ 8g⁶ 1991 8m³ 10g⁵ 10g 10.2f³ 10m 11.8g 10g] strong,
deep-girthed filly: poor maiden: showed retains some ability in apprentice handicap
final start: worth another try over 1½m: best effort with give in the ground. *P. W.
Harris.*

LYDIA'S WALTZ   2 b.f. (Apr 5) Lidhame 109 – Fille de Phaeton (Sun Prince 128)   –
[1991 5s] leggy filly: sister to 3-y-o Emsboy and half-sister to 2 winners in Belgium:
dam never ran: 20/1 and backward, slowly away and always behind in 8-runner seller
at Folkestone. *R. V. Smyth.*

LYNAM PRINCE (IRE)   3 br.c. Fairy King (USA) – Come True (FR) (Nasram   **87**
II 125) [1990 7m 1991 8g² 8.2g* 8m⁵ 9g] angular, workmanlike colt: fair form in
maidens first two 3-y-o starts, easily landing odds in 4-runner race at Nottingham in
August: below form in October handicaps, virtually tailed off in £30,800 contest at
Newbury: should stay beyond 1m: sold 9,600 gns Newmarket Autumn Sales. *A. C.
Stewart.*

LYNDISCHARM   6 b.m. Enchantment 115 – Belinda Mede 86 (Runnymede 123)   –
[1990 NR 1991 7f 5g] workmanlike mare: poor walker and mover: lightly raced and
bad maiden: stays 6f: acts on good to firm ground. *E. J. Alston.*

LYNDON'S LINNET   3 b.g. Prince Sabo 123 – Miss Rossi (Artaius (USA) 129)   **67**
[1990 NR 1991 10.8g 6f² 6g² 5m* 6m³ 5m⁵ 6g⁴ 6g⁶ 6m a6g] 4,500F, 7,200Y: lengthy,
plain, rather dipped-backed gelding: second foal: half-brother to useful 5f winner
Dancing Music (by Music Boy): dam unraced: modest performer: won maiden
auction at Warwick in May: below form in handicaps last 3 outings: will prove better
at 6f than 5f: sold out of R. Ingram's stable 8,000 gns Doncaster August Sales after
eighth start: joined M. O'Neill. *K. R. Burke.*

LYN'S RETURN (IRE)   2 b.c. (Mar 24) Nordico (USA) – Salmas (FR) (Right   **59**
Royal V 135) [1991 7d³ 7g 8m³ 9m 8.9m 8m] IR 2,300Y, 3,200 2-y-o: smallish colt:
half-brother to Irish middle-distance winner Kamsala (by Kampala): dam French
9.5f winner: plating-class maiden: stays 1m: acts on good to firm and dead ground:
sold 575 gns Ascot December Sales. *R. Simpson.*

LYPHAR DANCER   3 b.g. Bellypha 130 – Western Gem 86 (Sheshoon 132)   –
[1990 6m 7g⁶ 8m 1991 a10g⁴] attractive gelding: plating-class maiden: moderate
fourth in handicap at Lingfield in February: stays 1¼m: winning hurdler. *P. C.
Haslam.*

LYPHARD'S SONG (IRE)   3 b.f. Lyphard's Special (USA) 122 – Supreme Song   –
(Supreme Sovereign 119) [1990 NR 1991 12m⁴ 12g⁴ 10m 15.8g 15.1s] IR 9,600F, IR
12,000Y: long-backed filly: half-sister to several winners, including very useful 1981
Irish 2-y-o Philip Martin (by Tumble Wind): dam ran once: well beaten in maidens
then handicaps: hampered home turn at Catterick then front rank 11f at Edinburgh
last 2 outings. *N. A. Graham.*

LYSIRRA (USA)   2 ch.f. (Jan 23) Lyphard (USA) 132 – Hopespringsforever (USA)   **49** p
82 (Mr Prospector (USA)) [1991 7g] lengthy, good-topped filly: has plenty of scope:
first foal: dam, placed at 1m at 3 yrs but somewhat temperamental, is sister to
Miswaki: 16/1, chased leaders to 2f out, eased when beaten, in 16-runner minor
event at Kempton in September: showed a quick action: will stay 1m: will do better.
B. W. Hills.

M

MAAMUR (USA)   3 gr.c. Robellino (USA) 127 – Tiger Trap (USA) 80 (Al Hattab   **86**
(USA)) [1990 NR 1991 10.2s² 11g² 12g] big, good-bodied colt: fluent mover: fifth foal:
brother to 9f and 1¼m winner False Start and highly-strung maiden Hungry Griebel
and half-brother to very useful 1m and 9f winner Wood Dancer (by Malinowski): dam
2-y-o 6f winner: second in maidens at Newcastle and (best effort) Newbury: ran
moderately in minor event at Newmarket in May: should be suited by 1½m + : sold
8,500 gns Newmarket Autumn Sales. *D. Morley.*

MABEL BROWN   3 b.f. Enchantment 115 – Charlotte Daughter (Brigadier   –
Gerard 144) [1990 NR 1991 11.7g 11.7m 10.2d 8d 10m] leggy, sparely-made filly: has a
round action: first foal: dam unraced half-sister to fair 1¼m to 1¾m winner Chiclet:
well beaten, in claiming events last 3 outings: blinkered twice: trained first 4 starts
by J. Roberts. *J. R. Jenkins.*

MA BELLA LUNA   2 b.f. (Apr 27) Jalmood (USA) 126 – Macarte (FR) (Gift Card   **65** p
(FR) 124) [1991 7g⁵ 8.1g⁴] sturdy filly: sixth foal: sister to 3-y-o Matamata and
half-sister to 6f winner Mariano (by Aragon) and 1m (at 2 yrs) and 9f winner Marasol
(by Siberian Express): dam minor French 1m and 9f winner: quite modest form in
maidens at Newmarket in July and Chepstow (still better for race) in August: should
stay 1¼m: likely to improve again. *J. L. Dunlop.*

MABONNE   2 b.f. (May 24) King of Spain 121 – Monsarah 63 (Monsanto (FR) 121)   **63**
[1991 6s 6d⁴ 6f³] quite good-topped filly: good walker: second foal: dam 2-y-o 5f
seller winner: progressive form in maidens: keeping-on third of 8 at Folkestone in
October, having been pushed along in last at halfway: should be better suited by 7f.
J. L. Dunlop.

MABTHUL (USA)   3 b.c. Northern Baby (USA) 127 – Persuadable (USA) (What   **—** §
A Pleasure (USA)) [1990 8g⁶ 8.2s³ 10s 1991 7g 10f 10.6m] big, rangy colt: moderate
mover: modest form at 2 yrs but looked ungenuine in handicaps in 1991: stays 1m:
acts on soft going: blinkered final start: sold to join M. Heaton-Ellis 5,200 gns
Newmarket July Sales: not one to trust. *D. Morley.*

MACCONACHIE   4 b.c. Good Times (ITY) – High Point Lady (CAN) (Knightly   **43**
Dawn (USA)) [1990 8.2s 8f 8f⁵ 11g⁶ 12d⁵ 12m⁵ 10m³ 10f³ 10m 11d⁶ a7g⁴ 1991 a11g⁴
a10g³ a12g² a12g³ 12m⁴ 13.6g 10m 12.3f⁴ 12f³ 12m⁵] leggy, angular colt: poor
walker: poor handicapper, stays 1½m: acts on firm going: blinkered last 4 starts: has
looked a tricky ride, and is still a maiden: trained until after penultimate start by T.
Barron. *M. Dods.*

MACEDONAS   3 b.c. Niniski (USA) 125 – Miss Saint-Cloud 102 (Nonoalco (USA)   **72** d
131) [1990 7g⁵ 7m 1991 10.6g⁴ 12d² 12.2d⁵ 11.7m 11.5m⁶ 10.3m 9m] tall, leggy
colt: disappointing maiden: will prove better at 1½m than shorter: best on an easy
surface: sold 11,000 gns Newmarket Autumn Sales. *Miss A. J. Whitfield.*

MACFARLANE   3 br.c. Kala Shikari 125 – Tarvie 101 (Swing Easy (USA) 126)   **81**
[1990 5m⁵ 5m² 5f³ 6s³ 5d* 1991 6m³ 6m 5d* 6g 5.1d 5g⁴ 6m 5d 6.1d² 5.2g⁵ 5g⁴] stocky,
lengthy colt: poor mover: fair handicapper: won at Chester in May: back to form
when second at same course in October: probably suited by 6f nowadays: best
efforts on dead ground: has worn tongue strap. *M. J. Fetherston-Godley.*

MAC KELTY   4 b.c. Wattlefield 117 – Thevetia 65 (Mummy's Pet 125) [1990 5s⁶   **49**
7f 6g 8.2g² 11m 9g⁶ 7g 8g⁴ 6m⁴ 6g 9s⁶ 10.5g 8d⁴ 8d a5g a6g a11g 1991 8h 8.2f* 8g]
stocky colt: carries condition: poor handicapper: won at Hamilton in May: seems
best at 1m/9f: acts on good to firm going and heavy: effective blinkered or not: sold
out of N. Bycroft's stable 1,850 gns Doncaster January Sales. *T. D. Barron.*

MACK THE KNIFE   2 b.c. (Feb 25) Kris 135 – The Dancer (FR) 122 **116**
(Green Dancer (USA) 132) [1991 6m² 7g* 7.1m⁴ 8d² 8g²]
   Here's a colt who in all probability will fall short of what's required to
make an impact in championship company. However, Mack The Knife
deserves far more than a passing mention in these pages after a first season
during which he improved each time he set foot on a racecourse and finished
runner-up in two of Britain's best staying races for two-year-olds. It became
clear from an early stage that staying was Mack The Knife's game. It's almost
certain that a slowly-run race over six furlongs on firmish ground wasn't ideal
for him when he made his debut behind Phyliel in a five-runner maiden race at
Newmarket in July. He made no mistake in similar company over an extra
furlong on the same course the following month and from that point on he
contested solely pattern events. Firstly there was the Solario Stakes at
Sandown where he finished a close fourth of seven behind Chicmond. The way
he stuck to his task that day indicated he'd be an even better proposition over
a mile. Prior to the Royal Lodge William Hill Stakes at Ascot in late-September Mack The Knife very much took the eye in the paddock. His performance
in the race confirmed he was strongly on the upgrade, as having taken up the
running on the home turn he battled on splendidly under pressure to go down
by only three quarters of a length to the Prix de la Salamandre runner-up
Made of Gold. Mack The Knife was the only runner from the Royal Lodge to
go on and contest the Racing Post Trophy at Doncaster. As at Ascot he
seemed to have something to find on form, but, despite the fact that his lack of
finishing speed was exposed again, he ran a cracking race, improving on the
outside to have every chance two out and running on strongly to finish a clear
second, three and a half lengths behind Seattle Rhyme.

Mack The Knife comes from a successful and well-known family. His dam The Dancer was one of the best of her sex in 1979 and 1980. Defective vision troubled The Dancer as a two-year-old when she ran out a convincing winner of the May Hill Stakes. She was completely blind in her left eye by the time she reappeared as a three-year-old, yet from only three outings she recorded a couple of fine front-running performances to win the Sir Charles Clore Memorial Stakes at Newbury and to finish third behind her stable-companion Bireme in the Oaks. Mack The Knife is his dam's seventh foal. He's clearly the best she's produced so far, although Pilot Bird (by Blakeney) over a mile and a quarter and Pretty Lady (by High Top) over sprint distances at two years, both showed fair winning form. The Dancer's dam Khazaeen, who never ran, has proved an exceptional bargain. Sold for a mere 1,250 guineas in Ireland in 1975, she's produced several other winners besides The Dancer. Moreover, Khazaeen's half-sisters Runaway Bride and Zannira respectively produced Blushing Groom and the Italian Oaks winner Zabarella; and her close relative Flaming Heart showed smart form and produced Maroun, a very good winner at up to nine furlongs.

	Kris (ch 1976)	Sharpen Up (ch 1969)	Atan / Rocchetta
		Doubly Sure (b 1971)	Reliance II / Soft Angels
Mack The Knife (b.c. Feb 25, 1989)			
	The Dancer (FR) (b 1977)	Green Dancer (b 1972)	Nijinsky / Green Valley
		Khazaeen (b 1968)	Charlottesville / Aimee

Like his dam, and his sire for that matter, Mack The Knife is a horse with plenty of substance, strong and with the scope to train on. He has his dam's

Sir John Astor's "Mack The Knife"

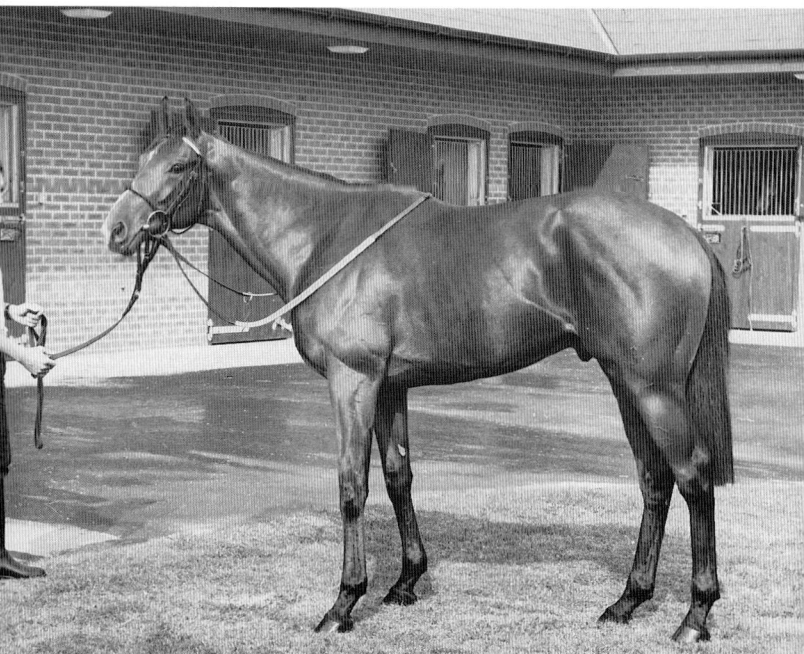

tendency towards a slightly nervous disposition. The Dancer didn't always look at ease in the paddock, and Mack The Knife was very much on his toes at Ascot and somewhat mulish before going down at Doncaster. However, he is as genuine as they come once racing. He'll be well served by a mile and a quarter plus at three and should win another race or two if not too highly tried. A round-actioned colt, he seems to act on a firm and a soft surface; it may be worth noting that The Dancer ran poorly the only time she encountered very soft ground. *Major W. R. Hern.*

MACLAINES PRIDE (USA) 2 b.g. (Mar 5) Proud Birdie (USA) – Little Romp **62** (USA) (Nashua) [1991 7g a7g² 7d] $10,000Y, resold $11,000Y: good-bodied gelding: has scope: half-brother to several minor winners in North America: dam placed 6 times from 22 starts: sire best at around 1¼m: quite modest maiden: keeping-on second of 6 to easy winner Chicmond in Timeform Race Card Opportunities Stakes at Southwell: sweating, last of 18 at Newmarket (went keenly down) later in August: subsequently gelded: sold 6,600 gns Newmarket Autumn Sales. *W. A. O'Gorman.*

MACQUARIE RIDGE (USA) 3 ch.f. Cox's Ridge (USA) – Ocean's Answer **48** (USA) (Northern Answer (USA)) [1990 NR 1991 7g 10d 12m 12d 8.2m a8g³] $120,000Y: big, lengthy filly: seventh foal: half-sister to 5 winners, notably smart sprinter Al Zawbaah (by Mr Prospector), and to promising 1989 2-y-o Soy Roberto (by Roberto): dam, 2-y-o 1m stakes winner, is closely related to Storm Bird: third of 14 in maiden at Southwell in November, first form: sweating, on toes and pulled hard fifth start. *B. Hanbury.*

MAC RAMBLER 4 b.g. Hotfoot 126 – Arkengarthdale (Sweet Story 122) [1990 **34** 8v⁵ 8.2g 10g 12g 1991 8g⁴ 10.2s 10d a11g⁶ 10.5d 13.8m] poor handicapper: stays 10.5f: acts on dead ground: looks headstrong, and probably not one to rely on. *N. Bycroft.*

MACROBIAN 7 b.g. Bay Express 132 – White Domino 67 (Sharpen Up 127) **94** [1990 6m 6m⁵ 6m⁴ 6m⁶ 5m 6m* 6m 6m⁵ 6m 6d 5g 1991 5m 5g 6f⁶ 6d⁵ 6.1g³ 6m² 6g* 6g²] good-bodied gelding: has had operation for soft palate: fairly useful handicapper: won at Doncaster (by 5 lengths, making all) and second of 29 (first home on near side) to Notley in William Hill Stewards' Cup at Goodwood later in July: not seen again after being withdrawn start (broke blood vessel to post) in August: suited by 6f: best on a sound surface: suited by forcing tactics: visored twice, blinkered twice. *M. H. Easterby.*

MACS BID (CAN) 2 b.c. (Apr 18) Summing (USA) – Hope She Does (USA) (Mr **71 p** Leader (USA)) [1991 a7g*] $4,700F, $3,200 2-y-o: half-brother to numerous minor winners in North America: dam won 9 races in USA: sire won Belmont Stakes: weak 9/1-shot and ridden by claimer, won 13-runner maiden at Southwell easily by 6 lengths from poor field: showed a fluent action: sure to improve. *W. A. O'Gorman.*

MACS BUCKAROO (USA) 2 b.g. (Mar 11) Buckaroo (USA) – Tonka (USA) **72** (Prince John) [1991 5d⁵ 5g a5g* 5d³ a6g³ 7m 6g⁴ 6m] $12,000F, $16,000Y: sturdy, good-quartered gelding: impresses in appearance: half-brother to 2 minor winners in USA: dam, minor winner at around 6f, is half-sister to very smart (at up to 7f) Barrera and 2 other good winners: sire high class, best at 1m/9f: modest performer: made all in 7-runner maiden at Lingfield in April: excellent fourth of 12, making most, in nursery at Leicester in September: suited by 6f: best efforts on good ground and on all-weather surfaces: blinkered third and fourth starts: subsequently off course 4 months: inconsistent: sold 9,000 gns Newmarket Autumn Sales. *W. A. O'Gorman.*

MAC'S FIGHTER 6 ch.h. Hard Fought 125 – Geoffrey's Sister 102 (Sparkler **107 d** 130) [1990 6f* 6m⁴ 5f⁶ 7g⁶ 6s 1991 6g⁵ 7m 6g 6g 7m 7m 6m 8g a7g⁴ a8g⁴ a6g*] compact horse: moderate mover: smart performer at best, fairly useful handicapper nowadays: won claimer at Lingfield in December: effective at 6f to 1m: possibly unsuited by soft going, acts on any other: often blinkered or visored: held up, and suited by strong gallop. *W. A. O'Gorman.*

MAC'S IMP (USA) 3 b.c. Imp Society (USA) – Flaming Reason (USA) (Limit To — Reason (USA)) [1990 5f² 5f* 6m* 6m* 6m* 6f² 6f* 6m* 1991 6d 5m⁶] lengthy, robust, good-quartered colt: smart and game sprinter as 2-y-o, gaining last 3 successes in Coventry Stakes at Royal Ascot, Scottish Equitable Richmond Stakes at Goodwood and Heinz '57' Phoenix Stakes at Phoenix Park: favourite, ran poorly in £7,400 contest and minor event in spring at 3 yrs: acted on firm ground: twice hung left: usually taken early and very quietly to post: suited by forcing tactics: to stand at Tally Ho Stud, Ireland, IR £3,000 (Oct 1st). *W. A. O'Gorman.*

MACS MAHARANEE   4 b.f. Indian King (USA) 128 – High State 72 (Free State   **78**
125) [1990 6f 6m⁶ 5m⁴ 5g* 6m² 5m² 5f⁴ 5g 6m* 6f⁵ 1991 6g 6m 5f⁶ 6g² 6f² 6g 6f³ 6f⁴
6m* 6f³ 6m⁵ 6g⁶ 5d] leggy, lengthy filly: moderate mover: modest handicapper:
won at Redcar in August: seems ideally suited by 6f: acts on firm ground: has edged
right. *P. S. Felgate.*

MAC'S MUSIC   5 ch.g. Music Boy 124 – Annathena 83 (Homeric 133) [1990 6g 5g   —
1991 5m a6g] sturdy, lengthy gelding: no worthwhile form, including in seller. *L. J.
Barratt.*

MAC'S PRINCESS (USA)   3 b.f. Sovereign Dancer (USA) – Jungle Princess   **66**
(USA) (Jungle Road) [1990 8.2m² a7g⁵ 7s 1991 a7g² a8g³ 7m 8g² 8m 9g a8g³ a8g²
a7g a8g³] smallish, workmanlike filly: quite modest handicapper, still a maiden:
seems better at 1m than shorter: goes well on fibresand: has looked an awkward
ride: changed hands 14,500 gns Newmarket December Sales after ninth start. *W. A.
O'Gorman.*

MADAGANS GREY   3 gr.g. Carwhite 127 – Cheri Berry 87 (Air Trooper 115)   **93** §
[1990 5f² 6g* 6g 6d⁵ 6m⁴ 5m 7g 8g* 8g 8m 10g⁴ 1991 8d⁵ a12g³ 16g 16.2g⁴ 14.8m⁵
13.9g 16d* 16.5m⁵] leggy gelding: moderate walker and mover: fairly useful at best:
fourth in Queen's Vase at Royal Ascot, soon having a lot to do then staying on
strongly: made all in Goodwood minor event in October: suited by test of stamina:
acts on good to firm and dead ground: blinkered twice at 2 yrs: has worn crossed
noseband: found little final start: inconsistent and not one to trust. *R. Boss.*

MADAME SOURIRE   2 ch.f. (Feb 14) Master Willie 129 – Princesse Smile 99   **37**
(Balidar 133) [1991 7f⁶ 8.3g] small filly: half-sister to several winners in France,
including 1983 2-y-o 7f winner Island Smile (by Ile de Bourbon) and 7f (at 2 yrs) and
1½m winner Shy Gremlin (by Home Guard): dam 7f to 9f winner in Italy, is sister to
Bolkonski: better effort when sixth in claimer at Yarmouth in September, late
headway after slow start: should be suited by middle distances: apprentice ridden:
sold 3,000 gns Newmarket Autumn Sales. *W. Jarvis.*

MADAME SULAAFAH   3 b.f. Sulaafah (USA) 119 – Madame Rochas 72   —
(Midsummer Night II 117) [1990 NR 1991 5g 6g 10.2d] plain filly: seventh reported
foal (5 by Golden Shields): dam 11f winner: behind in sellers, very mulish in stalls
second start. *Miss J. Thorne.*

MADAM JAC   5 b.m. Anfield 117 – Lucky Petina 88 (Mummy's Pet 125) [1990 a7g   **46**
6f³ 7f³ 7f 7f 7.6m⁴ 7.6g a10g³ 1991 a10g a10g a12g 7m⁶ 8.3m 10g* 10s⁵ 9d a10g⁴]
rather leggy mare: plating-class performer: won (for first time) claimer at Windsor
in July: stays 1¼m: probably acts on any going. *R. Akehurst.*

MADAM PETOSKI   2 b.f. (Feb 4) Petoski 135 – Proper Madam 93 (Mummy's   **61**
Pet 125) [1991 5.1g² 6g 5g² 5.2f 6.1m 5.1g⁵] leggy, close-coupled filly: fifth living
foal: half-sister to 3 winners, all at sprint distances, including Madam Millie and
Naive Charm (both by Milford): dam sprinter: quite modest maiden: easily best form
at around 5f on good ground: should stay 6f: usually on toes: wore blinkers and
eyeshield final start. *R. Boss.*

MADAM TAYLOR   6 b.m. Free State 125 – Hourglass (Mansingh (USA) 120)   —
[1990 a12g 10.6d 10.4g 10m 10.2s² 12s 1991 a11ga14g³ 10fa11ga12g³ 12m 10.2ga11g*   a 49
a12g*] dipped-backed mare: moderate mover: plating-class handicapper: twice
successful at Southwell in July: stayed 1½m: won on firm going, but suited by an
easier surface on turf: sometimes blinkered: has worn bandages behind and tongue
strap: in foal to Hubbly Bubbly. *R. E. Peacock.*

MADELEY'S PET   4 ch.f. Tina's Pet 121 – Thornaby 75 (Decoy Boy 129) [1990   —
5v⁶ 1991 8d 6m 6m 6h⁵ a7g 5d 6m] sturdy, good-quartered filly: moderate mover:
poor maiden: soundly beaten in 1991: form only at 5f. *Denys Smith.*

MADE OF GOLD (USA)   2 ch.c. (Apr 19) Green Forest (USA) 134 – **117**
Vindaria (USA) (Roi Dagobert 128) [1991 6d* 6m² 7g² 7m² 8d*]
   Made of Gold hasn't yet fulfilled the expectations that came with his
name but he's already a marketable asset, being an established pattern-race
performer still progressing. Made of Gold's season culminated in success
in the Royal Lodge William Hill Stakes at Ascot in September in which his
seven opponents included the Solario fourth Mack The Knife, the improving
Twist And Turn, favourite at 7/4 after victories at Yarmouth and Sandown, and
the unbeaten Torrey Canyon, already a winner over the course and successful
in the Acomb Stakes at York last time out. In a race run at a fair gallop in
driving rain, Made of Gold soon held a prominent position and turned into the
straight travelling best of all in fourth spot as Mack The Knife went to the

Royal Lodge William Hill Stakes, Ascot—two lengths cover the first four,
as Made of Gold wins from Mack The Knife, Twist And Turn and Torrey Canyon

front pursued by the fairly useful maiden Grand Master and Twist And Turn.
Switched to the outside of the leading trio early in the straight, Made of Gold
was waited with until taken to the front passing the furlong pole but instead of
drawing clear, as his smooth progress had suggested he would, he edged right
and had to be hard driven; far from winning comfortably he won with little in
hand by three quarters of a length from Mack The Knife, who battled on
resolutely as did Twist And Turn and Torrey Canyon close behind in third and
fourth. Most of the recent Royal Lodge winners haven't achieved a great deal
in their second seasons but there's little logic in assessing Made of Gold's
prospects on the records of his predecessors and, anyway, Mack The Knife,
who finished a clear-cut second to Seattle Rhyme in the Racing Post Trophy at
Doncaster the following month, and fifth-placed Grand Master, an excellent
fourth when getting easy ground again in the Criterium de Saint-Cloud in
November, certainly did nothing to devalue the form. And Made of Gold, a
quite good-topped colt with plenty of scope, looks just the type to maintain his
improvement in the coming season. He shouldn't be difficult to place.

Made of Gold will, after all, be seen in Britain again as his owner Mah-
moud Fustok revised plans to take his entire string as well as his private
trainer Moubarak back to the stables at Chantilly which he vacated three
years ago. Made of Gold may well do some of his racing in France, however,
and is already acquainted with Longchamp where he ran an excellent race to
finish second to Arazi in the Prix de la Salamandre in September. Had Arazi
not been in the field then Made of Gold would have made virtually all the
running; although he had no answer as Arazi swept past on his way to a five-
length victory he kept on to hold off Silver Kite and Code Breaker narrowly for
second place. The Salamandre was the third time in succession that Made of
Gold had filled the runner-up spot in a pattern race since his impressive
seven-length winning debut in a twenty-one-runner maiden at Ripon in June;

Ecurie Fustok's "Made of Gold"

he'd found Showbrook three and a half lengths too good in the four-runner Anglia Television July Stakes at Newmarket on ground that placed the emphasis firmly on speed, and Dr Devious a length and a half too good in the Lanson Champagne Vintage Stakes over seven furlongs at Goodwood in August. Made of Gold needed a mile to show to best advantage at two years, however, and further improvement will probably be forthcoming at a mile and a quarter; and although he acts on good to firm ground he seems ideally suited by an easy surface.

Made of Gold (USA) (ch.c. Apr 19, 1989)	Green Forest (USA) (ch 1979)	Shecky Greene (b 1970)	Noholme II
			Lester's Pride
		Tell Meno Lies (gr 1971)	The Axe II
			Filatonga
	Vindaria (USA) (b 1974)	Roi Dagobert (b 1964)	Sicambre
			Dame d'Atour II
		Heavenly Body (b 1957)	Dark Star
			Dangerous Dame

Made of Gold is one of the best sons of the exported French miler Green Forest, a top-class racehorse in his day and one of a select octet to have won the Prix Morny, Prix de la Salamandre and Grand Criterium in the post-war period. His other leading progeny include the Irish One Thousand Guineas winner Forest Flower, the high-class five-year-old Green Line Express and the very useful 1989 two-year-old sprinters Somethingdifferent and Ozone Friendly. Made of Gold's dam Vindaria has had a very chequered career as a broodmare: her first foal was the smart French ten-and-a-half-furlong winner Snow Day (by Reliance II), since the dam of the Derby runner-up Blue Stag, but in the period before Made of Gold came along she produced five non-winners, was barren on three occasions and aborted once. Vindaria is an unraced mare by the Arc fourth Roi Dagobert out of the high-class American two-year-old filly Heavenly Body, rated the second-best of her age and sex in 1959 after winning three stakes races including the Matron Stakes. Heavenly Body, a sister to the Kentucky Oaks winner Hidden Talent, turned out to be a fine broodmare. One of her foals, A Thousand Stars, was a smart racemare who was effective at a mile, as she showed when winning the Prix Perth and finishing third in the Poule d'Essai des Pouliches, and stayed a mile and a half; and another was the Prix de Minerve third Tobira Celeste, the dam of the top-class middle-distance stayer Celestial Storm. Tobira Celeste is also the grandam of the good French fillies River Memories, who also won the Grade 1 Rothmans International and finished second in the Grade 1 Turf Classic. *M. Moubarak.*

MAD MILITANT (IRE) 2 b.c. (Mar 10) Vision (USA) – Ullapool (Dominion 123) [1991 7f 7m* 8.1f 6.3s 7.6d³ 8.3s] IR 12,000F, IR 12,000Y: compact colt: third foal: half-brother to Irish 1m (at 2 yrs) and 1¼m winner Lively Mite (by Elegant Air): dam unraced: sire, brother to Caerleon, won from 8.5f to 1½m, including Grade 1 Secretariat Stakes: fair performer: promoted winner of maiden at Chester in August, leading 1f out then swishing tail and unable to quicken: ran poorly in Hamilton nursery final start: will probably stay beyond 1m: acts on good to firm and dead ground. *R. Hollinshead.* **81**

MADONETTA 3 ch.f. Sharpo 132 – Woodwind (FR) 103 (Whistling Wind 123) [1990 6g 7d⁴ 1991 6d* 7g² 7g 8d⁶ 7m 7g⁶] leggy, rather close-coupled filly: moderate mover: won minor event at Kempton in May and short-head second in handicap at Leicester: well below form afterwards: should stay 1m: acts on dead ground: sold 7,000 gns Newmarket Autumn Sales. *R. Charlton.* **77**

MADRAJ (IRE) 3 b. or br.c. Double Schwartz 128 – Poka Poka (FR) (King of Macedon 126) [1990 NR 1991 8m² 9m² 10.2f³ 8m 8.1m²] 25,000F, 24,000Y: good-topped colt: has a fluent, round action: first foal: dam won from 5f to 9.2f in France, from family of Stanerra: modest maiden on flat: second at Redcar (twice) and Edinburgh: stays 9f: sold to join J. Baker 17,000 gns Newmarket Autumn Sales: winning hurdler. *H. Thomson Jones.* **73**

MAESTROSO (IRE) 2 b.c. (May 9) Mister Majestic 122 – That's Easy (Swing Easy (USA) 126) [1991 6m* 6g⁶ 6g⁶ 6m⁶ 6m] IR 13,000Y: strong, sturdy colt: fifth foal: half-brother to fair Irish 1990 2-y-o winner On Display (by Exhibitioner) and 1988 Irish 2-y-o 6f winner Flaming Sunset (by Hays): dam Irish 9f winner: won 9-runner minor event at Windsor in July: ran well (including in listed race) next 2 outings, poorly final start: may be better suited by 7f. *R. F. Johnson Houghton.* **78**

MAFATIN (IRE) 3 b.f. Sadler's Wells (USA) 132 – Glass Slipper 100 (Relko 136) [1990 NR 1991 10g 10d 14.6f³ 10g* 10g 10m] leggy, rather close-coupled filly: sister to 11f-placed Fairy Feet and half-sister to several winners, including 1000 Guineas winner Fairy Footsteps (by Mill Reef) and St Leger winner Light Cavalry (by Brigadier Gerard): dam staying half-sister to Royal Palace: won handicap at Kempton in July: form otherwise only on third start: probably stays 14.6f: visits Woodman. *P. T. Walwyn.* **74**

MAGADEER (USA) 2 b.f. (May 10) Mogambo (USA) – Star Silhouette (USA) (Dancer's Profile (USA)) [1991 6m³ 7m⁴ 6.9f²] $7,500Y: useful-looking filly: has scope: sixth foal: half-sister to 3 minor winners in North America: dam never ran: sire Grade 1 2-y-o winner, seemed best at around 1m: progressive form: off course 6 weeks, keeping-on second of 12 in maiden at Folkestone in October, having been niggled along at halfway: should improve over 1m+. *J. L. Dunlop.* **70 p**

MAGDALENE HEIGHTS 3 ch.c. All Systems Go 119 – Carreg-Wennol (Dublin Taxi) [1990 7m 8g 1991 8h 11m 12.2m⁵ 17.9f] lightly-made colt: soundly beaten, including in handicaps: takes good hold, and wore severe bridle final (saddle slipped) start: trained first 2 by D. Topley. *D. R. Franks.* —

MAGDALENE (IRE) 3 b.f. Runnett 125 – Grattan Princess (Tumble Wind (USA)) [1990 6f 6d⁴ 5s 1991 5m a8g] plain, angular filly: no sign of ability, in handicap last time. *T. Fairhurst.* —

MAGGIE SIDDONS 3 b.f. Night Shift (USA) – Sarah Siddons (Reform 132) [1990 6m 5.8m 5m 7g³ 6m 7g* 7m² 5.8d* 7s³ 1991 8g 8g 9d 7d² 5.7m* 5.7m* 6g* 8f² 6m 7d⁴ 6m 8g] good-topped filly: carries condition: has a round action: fairly useful handicapper: successful at Bath twice in July then at Newmarket in August: **92**

below form after good fourth of 29 in £80,000 event (staying on late) at Ascot: may prove ideally suited by 7f/1m: probably acts on any going. *C. J. Hill.*

MAGGIES LAD   3 b.g. Red Johnnie 100 – Busted Love (Busted 134) [1990 5f 5m 5m3 5f3 6g3 5g4 5g3 7.5d5 7f4 5f4 8f5 8v6 7d a7g3 1991 a7g a7g 6g6 8s3 11f3 11g 8g* 8s5 12.1d2] workmanlike gelding: poor mover: plating-class performer: made all in seller (no bid) at Ayr in June: second of 7 in claimer at Hamilton following month: effective at 1m and stays 1½m: acts on any going: effective with or without blinkers or visor: good mount for a claimer: winning hurdler. *T. Fairhurst.*   **58**

MAGGIE'S SONG   2 b.f. (Apr 9) Sizzling Melody 117 – Izobia (Mansingh (USA) 120) [1991 5g 5m 5d6 6g 5m6 5g3 6m] 3,600Y: workmanlike filly: has a round action: fifth live foal: half-sister to 3-y-o Bucaro Boy (by Mummy's Game) and winning (but unreliable) sprint plater Firmly Attached (by Tina's Pet): dam ran 4 times: poor plater: blinkered final outing. *M. W. Easterby.*   **—**

MAGICAL DREAM (USA)   3 ch.f. Lyphard's Wish (FR) 124 – Green Lass 98 (Green God 128) [1990 5f 5g3 5g3 6g* 6g2 6g2 7.5g* 7m3 7.5f3 8.2g* 8m3 8v5 1991 10m4 9m 10g 8g] neat filly: modest winner as 2-y-o: easily best effort in claimers in 1991 on reappearance: should prove as effective at 1m as 1¼m: best on a sound surface: sometimes sweating and edgy. *J. Etherington.*   **60** d

MAGICAL VEIL   3 ch.f. Majestic Light (USA) – Jameelapi (USA) 94 (Blushing Groom (FR) 131) [1990 8m4 1991 10d 12.2g2 12.5m2 11.6m* 11.5m4 11.7f4 10g] smallish, rather sparely-made filly: has a free, rather round action: modest handicapper: won at Windsor in August: better at around 1½m than shorter: acts on good to firm ground: visored last 5 starts: makes the running. *M. R. Stoute.*   **73**

MAGIC AT DAWN (USA)   6 ch.g. Diamond Prospect (USA) 126 – Implicit (Grundy 137) [1990 9f5 8m 11m 12.2m5 9f 1991 11f4 11f3] sturdy, deep-girthed gelding: has been operated on for a soft palate: plating-class handicapper: not seen out after July: stays 11f: acts on firm going: below form when blinkered once: winning hurdler in August. *G. M. Moore.*   **50**

MAGIC EXPRESS (USA)   4 ch.c. Green Forest (USA) 134 – Secretariat Flag (USA) (Secretariat (USA)) [1990 8f4 8.5g4 8.2g*dis 8m5 10f2 10f2 9m2 9m* 9m 9f* 10d 1991 8f3 8d6 8m 8.5m4 10g6 10m 9f] stocky colt: moderate walker: has quick action: quite useful handicapper at 3 yrs: not so good at 4 yrs: unplaced in Grade 3 race in USA in August: best efforts at around 9f: acts on firm going, possibly unsuited by dead: used to wear tongue strap: goes well with forcing tactics: none too consistent. *M. Moubarak.*   **81**

MAGIC NIGHT (FR)   3 b.f. Le Nain Jaune (FR) 121 – Pin Up Babe (Prominer 125) [1990 6g* 7g2 7g2 8g* 8g6 1991 7g5 8d4 10g4 10.5d2 12d* 10m2 12m* 12d2 12f2]   **128**

Fillies haven't shown up so prominently in recent Prix de l'Arc de Triomphe results as they did in the 'seventies and early-'eighties, and none has won the race since All Along became the fifth in a row in 1983. With the

Prix Vermeille Escada, Longchamp—
Magic Night stays on strongly ahead of Pink Turtle and Crnagora

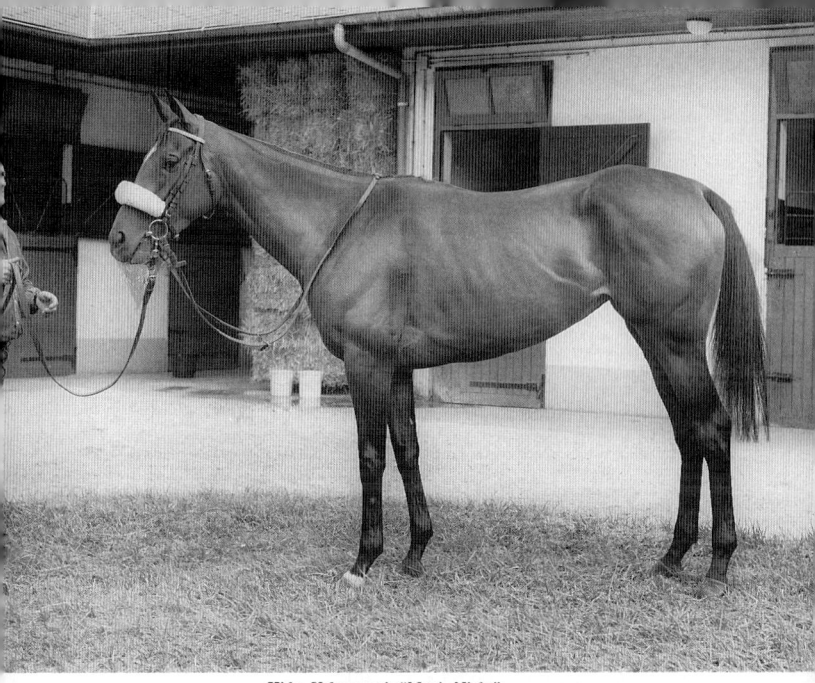

Hideo Yokoyama's "Magic Night"

latest Arc billed as the showdown between the Derby winners Generous and Suave Dancer there seemed little chance of the trend being reversed. But ignore improving French three-year-old fillies at your peril in the Arc. The slight and unfashionably-bred Prix Vermeille winner Magic Night produced a high-class performance to account for all except Suave Dancer. Held up on the inside, she tracked Pistolet Bleu round the final turn, and made her effort between him and Quest For Fame at the same time as Suave Dancer made his on the outside; and though unable to match the winner's acceleration at that point she stayed on well to beat Pistolet Bleu by a length for second place, two lengths down on Suave Dancer. Magic Night ran in a change of colours in the Arc, having carried those of her trainer's wife previously. Her new owner had the opportunity of seeing her on his native soil eight weeks later in the Japan Cup in Tokyo. On her Arc form she held clearly the best chance of the European-trained contestants—Rock Hopper, Drum Taps, Terimon, Wajd and Splash of Colour were the others—and she didn't leave her form on the aeroplane. Another game, high-class performance saw her stay on to divide the colts Golden Pheasant and Shaftesbury Avenue, the distances being a length and a half and the same. These last two runs confirmed the evidence of the Prix Vermeille Escada that Magic Night was the leading European middle-distance filly of her age, while they also showed her to be an even better one than that result. Like most of the season's top fillies' races the Vermeille was quite closely contested, with little more than three lengths covering the first six home (Shamshir sixth, a place behind the favourite Magnificent Star) and little more than seven lengths covering the first ten (Possessive Dancer tenth) in a very strongly-run affair. Magic Night travelled

491

well and prominently from the start, made her effort from fifth or sixth place and looked in no real danger once she struck the front over a furlong out. Pink Turtle, beaten by Caerlina and Magic Night in a blanket finish to the Prix de la Nonette at Longchamp earlier in the month on their previous meeting, took second; Crnagora, runner-up to Snurge in the Grand Prix de Deauville on her most recent outing, took third.

Thus the season ended on a very high note for Magic Night. Yet at its beginning, serious doubts existed whether she had the scope to improve on her two-year-old form which included a win in the Prix d'Aumale and a staying-on sixth to Shadayid in the Prix Marcel Boussac; and they weren't entirely put to rest until her fourth start, when she went close to winning the Prix de Diane Hermes. The point is there wasn't, and still isn't, much of Magic Night: she's a sparely-made, unprepossessing little thing. She spent the spring in classic trials, giving no hint whatsoever that she would be up to running second in the Diane though she wasn't disgraced when fourth in the Prix de la Grotte and the Prix Saint-Alary. Starting at odds of 45/1 in the Diane, she turned the Saint-Alary form on its head by putting Louve Romaine, Polemic and Treble behind her with the now-familiar strong finish. She went down by three quarters of a length to the Pouliches second Caerlina. Magic Night confirmed her improvement with a workmanlike victory over La Mona-lisa and Crnagora in the Group 2 Prix de Malleret at Longchamp later in June; then, after a break, she did very well considering the two-furlong drop-back in distance, to run Caerlina to a nose in the mile-and-a-quarter Nonette at the same track.

		Pharly	Lyphard
	Le Nain Jaune (FR)	(ch 1974)	Comely
	(ch 1979)	Lady Berry	Violon d'Ingres
Magic Night (FR)		(ch 1970)	Moss Rose II
(b.f. 1988)		Prominer	Beau Sabreur
	Pin Up Babe	(ch 1962)	Snob Hill
	(b 1972)	Mini Skirt	Kythnos
		(br 1967)	Modern Lady

Magic Night's success calls into question some of the accepted wisdom about thoroughbred conformation and breeding. Apparently she was so small that several trainers turned her down before the Demercastels agreed to take her. Since then she's run fourteen times and proved toughness exemplified; she'd had the busiest season of any in the Arc field, incidentally. Her breeding is not so ordinary as some have made out, since she's by a Grand Prix de Paris winner out of a mare who won three races, but it's not the height of fashion, either. Le Nain Jaune, himself out of the Prix Royal-Oak winner Lady Berry, hasn't been well patronized at the French National Stud and hasn't sired another high-class performer. The dam Pin Up Babe, who raced until the age of seven and won three times at around eleven furlongs in France, produced two previous foals, neither of whom made the track. She was knocked down at auction carrying Magic Night for the paltry sum of 2,500 francs, approximately £250, and is reportedly in foal again to Le Nain Jaune. The second dam Mini Skirt won over a mile and a half at Roscommon and Listowel. In a long career at stud in France she has produced many and varied winners besides Pin Up Babe, including the useful flat performers Bleu Nuit and Musimara and a useful chaser called Kawan. The third dam Modern Lady was an unraced sister to the 1965 Musidora Stakes winner Arctic Melody, herself a grandam of Ardross. Whatever else, this is a staying pedigree—the Grand Prix de Paris was still run over fifteen furlongs in Le Nain Jaune's day—and there is no doubt whatsoever that Magic Night will stay further than a mile and a half, given the opportunity. At a mile and a half or less she is extremely well suited by a strong pace; the stiffer the test of stamina the better. She acts on firm going and on dead, the latter the easiest she has so far encountered. *P. Demercastel, France.*

MAGIC POTION 3 gr.g. Sayf El Arab (USA) 127 – Mercy Cure 81 (No Mercy **57** d 126) [1990 7g 6g6 1991 6f4 6d4 8.2d 7g5 6.9s6 6.1m 7g 7m 7.1m 6g6] lengthy gelding: plating-class maiden: below form last 5 outings: best form at 6f: acts on firm going: blinkered seventh to ninth starts: sold 1,200 gns Ascot November Sales. *M. E. D. Francis.*

MAGIC RING (IRE)   2 b.c. (Feb 11) Green Desert (USA) 127 – Emaline **115** p
(FR) 105 (Empery (USA) 128) [1991 5g* 5g*dis 5m* 5d³ 5d*]

'Since resuming, Magic Ring's work has been of the highest order and
already he is being mentioned by his stable in the same breath as the brilliant
Mumtaz Mahal'. Neil Morrice's inside news from Paul Cole's Whatcombe
yard, published in the *Racing Post* on the eve of the Prix de l'Abbaye at Longchamp in October, could almost have been lifted from the script of BBC's im-
plausible horse-racing drama 'Trainer'. 'The Flying Filly', as Mumtaz Mahal
was popularly known, was trained at Whatcombe in the early-'twenties. She
topped the Free Handicap as a two-year-old, having won the Queen Mary
Stakes, the Molecomb Stakes, the National Breeders' Produce Stakes and the
Champagne Stakes, all very easily, by an aggregate of twenty-seven lengths,
went on to win the King George Stakes and the Nunthorpe the following
season and generally had a reputation so high that her appearance on a
racecourse was said to frighten away the opposition. The same could hardly
be said of Magic Ring as a two-year-old, although he showed form of a good
standard over five furlongs. He won three of his five races, including the
Norfolk Stakes and the Cornwallis Stakes, passed the post first well clear in
another only to be disqualified, and returned from a three-and-a-half-month
absence to finish a close third in the Abbaye. He's a long way to go, though,
before he's earned himself a place in the history books!

The optimism surrounding Magic Ring's work on the gallops at Whatcombe must have contributed to his starting a very short-priced favourite in a
non-vintage field at Longchamp. Considering that he had something to find on
the book with almost all of his thirteen rivals (and plenty with such as Sheikh
Albadou and Divine Danse) and that he was race-rusty after being side-lined
with sore shins and a recurrent fetlock injury, Magic Ring ran a sterling race
to fill third spot, little over a length behind Keen Hunter and just a head
behind Sheikh Albadou. Magic Ring, who was invariably turned out looking a
picture, looked better than ever at Longchamp. In the race he was never
travelling so comfortably as his supporters might have expected, as his fellow

Norfolk Stakes, Ascot—
Magic Ring beats Paris House and lowers the track record for two-year-olds

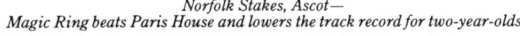

Cornwallis Stakes, Ascot—Magic Ring is in command;
Harvest Girl (right) and Power Lake run well again to be placed

two-year-olds Bradawn Breever and Paris House set a blistering gallop, but
he kept on strongly in the run to the line to achieve the best placing in the
Abbaye by one of his age since Sicyos filled the same position behind Habibti
in 1983. Magic Ring took his race in France extremely well and the following
Saturday he ran in the Cornwallis at Ascot, having been supplemented in the
meantime, wastefully as it turned out, for the forthcoming Three Chimneys
Dewhurst Stakes. Magic Ring reproduced his Longchamp form almost to the
pound and ran out an emphatic winner, taking command approaching the last
half-furlong and coming home two and a half lengths clear of the consistent
filly Harvest Girl.

Magic Ring had earmarked himself as a likely candidate for higher
honours when slamming thirteen other finishers on his debut in a minor event
at Windsor in May. The mishap to the favourite Blue Tiger, who reared in the
stalls and lost his rider, most probably didn't make any significant difference
to the result for Magic Ring came back with six lengths to spare. Ten days
later Magic Ring passed the post first, five lengths clear this time, in a similar
event at Goodwood but he was disqualified and placed last of the four runners
on account of an act of indiscretion by his regular rider Munro, who pushed
him through a narrow gap at the furlong-marker when he had enough time and
room to switch his mount round the pair blocking his way. Magic Ring's
performance served to confirm that the Norfolk Stakes was the right target
for him at Royal Ascot, and a month later he lined up there as the 7/4 favourite
in a stronger-than-usual nine-runner field, all of whom were previous winners
and seven of whom had won last time out. Magic Ring was ridden for a late

494

burst of speed and produced just that, launching his challenge entering the final furlong, where the eventual runner-up Paris House was coming to the end of his tether, and being driven a length and a half clear. His winning time shaved 0.04 seconds off the two-year-old course record set by Mujadil in the Cornwallis Stakes the previous autumn.

			Danzig	Northern Dancer
Magic Ring (IRE) (b.c. Feb 11, 1989)	Green Desert (USA) (b 1983)		(b 1977)	Pas de Nom
		Foreign Courier (b 1979)	Sir Ivor
			Courtly Dee
	Emaline (FR) (ch 1981)	Empery (b 1973)	Vaguely Noble
			Pamplona II
		Chere Alise (ch 1975)	Caro
			Kalise

The powerful-quartered Magic Ring, altogether a well-made colt, is a son of the high-class sprinter Green Desert who built on the excellent start he made to his stallion career in 1990 (when he was leading first-season sire) by finishing among the top five stallions of 1991 ranked by total money won, by number of races won and by number of winners. Magic Ring's dam Emaline looked set for a blossoming career when she won a seven-furlong newcomers race, but she didn't fulfil the promise of that or her other outing at two (when she was a close fourth in the Group 3 Prix Thomas Bryon); the following season her only placing from seven attempts came in an event of no importance over nine furlongs at Maisons-Laffitte. Magic Ring is her fourth foal; her first, Oasis (by Valiyar), won a small race over hurdles after two runs on the flat; her second, Monarda (by Pharly) has proved himself a reliable handicapper over middle distances in the past two seasons; and her third, Rainstone (by Rainbow Quest), hasn't been seen on the racecourse since two promising efforts on the all-weather as a two-year-old. Emaline is one of several winners from her dam Chere Alise, a very useful winner from a mile to a mile and a quarter in France and a full sister to the very useful miler Cenerentola and the useful staying two-year-old Bold Raider. Although Magic Ring's third dam Kalise won over six furlongs as a two-year-old before her export to France (where she showed useful form at up to nine furlongs) and fourth dam Claironette finished third in the Prix du Bois, very few members of this family have turned out to be sprinters. Magic Ring is reportedly to be given the opportunity to tackle seven furlongs in the Greenham Stakes at Newbury in April with a tilt at the Two Thousand Guineas a possibility afterwards if his stamina is not in doubt. He'll certainly be better suited by six furlongs than five in the coming season, and from what we know of him he should settle well enough to give himself every chance of staying further, maybe even a mile. Whatever his optimum distance turns out to be, Magic Ring, who acts on good to firm and good to soft ground, has the look of a better three-year-old than two-year-old and we expect him to pick up another pattern race or two. *P. F. I. Cole.*

MAGIC SECRET 3 b.c. Local Suitor (USA) 128 – Meissarah (USA) (Silver Hawk (USA) 123) [1990 6m⁴ 7g³ 7f² 7.5f³ 7.5g² 8f² 8.2s* 1991 10g² 10g⁶ 10g³ 10.1g³ 8.9g 10.3m 10d² 8d 10.3d a12g² a12g*] rangy colt: has a round action: modest handicapper: won claimer at Southwell in December: stays 1½m: best turf form with give in the ground: has run well when blinkered: sold out of B. Hanbury's stable 17,000 gns Newmarket Autumn Sales after ninth start. *P. C. Haslam.* **79**

MAGIC STEPS 2 b.f. (Feb 10) Nomination 125 – Magic Tower 76 (Tower Walk 130) [1991 5.1m* 5.2f*] sturdy filly: first reported foal: dam 1½m winner: narrowly won maiden at Chester in August: followed up in nursery at Newbury following month, soon niggled along then running on well to beat Tino Tere by ¾ length: will be at least as effective at 6f+: likely to improve again. *C. E. Brittain.* **74 p**

MAGNATE'S CROWN (IRE) 3 b.c. Last Tycoon 131 – Chapelet 71 (Habitat 134) [1990 6g⁴ 6m² 6m² 7m 1991 6d² 8g² 8g 10m⁶] strong, compact colt: poor mover: modest maiden, not seen out after July: stays 1¼m: acts on good to firm ground: visored (didn't settle) third start: sold 13,500 gns Newmarket Autumn Sales. *P. W. Harris.* **78**

MAGNETIC POINT (USA) 2 ch.f. (Jan 31) Bering 136 – Nonoalca (FR) 120 (Nonoalco (USA) 131) [1991 7d] $100,000Y: half-sister to several winners, including **— p**

French 7.5f (at 2 yrs) to 1½m winner Narghile (by Foolish Pleasure), later successful in USA, and fairly useful 6f winner Nucleon (by Mr Prospector): dam second in French 1000 Guineas: 14/1 and bandaged, faded into mid-division behind Berseto in 21-runner maiden at Doncaster in November: will improve. *A. A. Scott.*

MAGNETIC PRINCE 2 b.g. (May 26) Tina's Pet 121 – Miss Magnetism **43** (Baptism 119) [1991 6f⁶ 6m 6g³ 6m 7g 8.2m 10.5d] sparely-made gelding: first foal: dam poor plater on flat won over hurdles: quite modest plater: ran well for 7-lb claimer penultimate start: tailed off final one: stays 8.2f. *G. Blum.*

MAGNIFICENT 2 b.c. (Jan 29) Damister (USA) 123 – Tantalizing Song (CAN) **66** p (The Minstrel (CAN) 135) [1991 7g 6m*] leggy colt: moderate mover: third foal: dam ran 5 times in North America: 10/1, won 10-runner maiden at Southwell in September, soon handy, quickening over 1f out: will stay 1m: likely to improve again. *M. A. Jarvis.*

MAGNIFICENT STAR (USA) 3 b.f. Silver Hawk (USA) 123 – Gulanar **122** (Val de Loir 133) [1990 NR 1991 7g⁵ 8m³ 10d* 12m⁵ 12g² 11.9g* 12m⁵]

There was so little between the top three-year-old middle-distance fillies in Britain and Ireland that the casting of lots might have produced a similar result in the season's distribution of pattern victories. That hardly looked likely after Jet Ski Lady had spreadeagled her field in the Oaks, even less so that Magnificent Star, about eleven lengths back in fifth on Oaks day, would partake in the shareout and emerge as as strong a candidate as any for top filly in the division. But it was Magnificent Star's day at York in August. Conditions for the Oaks and Yorkshire Oaks were, of course, very different. At Epsom, Magnificent Star had been found out by the descent to Tattenham Corner, going into it with a prominent position before emerging with none behind her, but York's galloping track posed no such problems. Underfoot conditions had also turned in her favour, give in the ground bringing this most powerful, round-actioned individual into her element just as it had done when

Aston Upthorpe Yorkshire Oaks, York—
Magnificent Star (right) gets up by a short head from the equally-game Jet Ski Lady

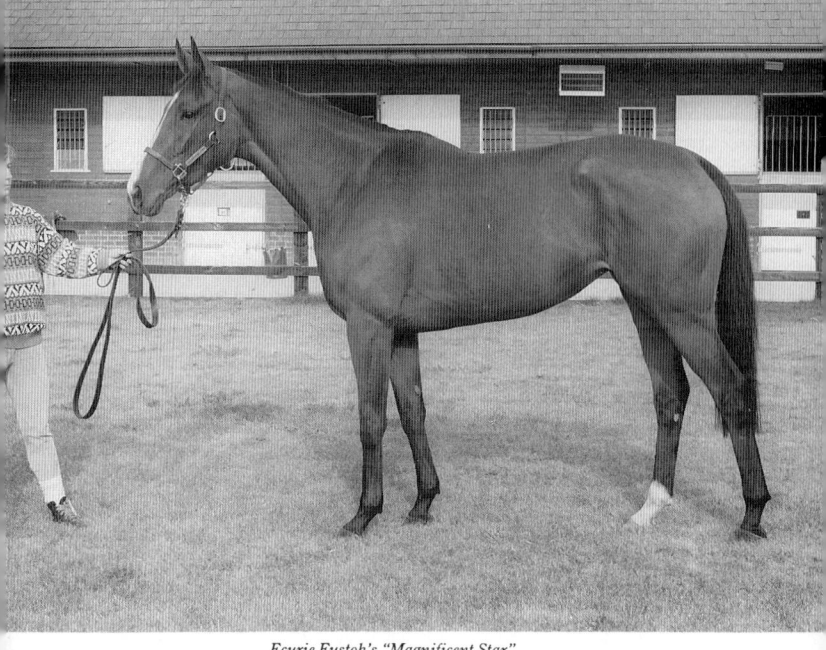

Ecurie Fustok's "Magnificent Star"

she'd stormed home in the Racal Telecom Fillies Trial at Newbury in May. A good pace at a mile and a half—which she'd failed to get over Goodwood's pronounced gradients in lesser company on her fifth start—and the benefit of experience were the final ingredients which brought Magnificent Star into her own. It all seems so straightforward now. At the time, however, Magnificent Star was a 16/1-chance in a field of seven with only Fife at longer odds. She looked in need of at least a dozen pounds improvement to stand a chance of winning. Against her were Jet Ski Lady; Possessive Dancer who'd beaten Jet Ski Lady in the Irish Oaks; the Epsom runner-up Shamshir; and the winners of the Musidora Stakes and Ribblesdale Stakes in Gussy Marlowe and Third Watch. Magnificent Star needed everything in her favour as her superiority over this most representative field, was far from obvious both during the race and for several minutes afterwards. The contest developed into a test of stamina; Gussy Marlowe and Third Watch never threatened to get into it, and with the pace-setting Fife, Possessive Dancer then Shamshir dropping away successively, Jet Ski Lady and Magnificent Star had it between them going into the final furlong and a half. The Oaks winner had a clear advantage through most of the desperate struggle which followed but in the last hundred yards, having changed her legs several times, Magnificent Star was galvanised to challenge again on the far rail. A photograph was needed to show that Magnificent Star had won by the narrowest of margins, and a stewards inquiry to confirm that she'd not hampered Jet Ski Lady (the pair came very close) in doing so. It was afterwards reported that Magnificent Star would shortly be operated on for an injury sustained as a yearling to her off-fore suspensory, but the operation was deferred until after the Prix Vermeille in which she ran creditably for fifth place behind Magic Night, given that conditions provided for a rather different test from that she'd received at York.

Magnificent Star (USA) (b.f. 1988)	Silver Hawk (USA) (b 1979)	Roberto (b 1969)	Hail To Reason
			Bramalea
		Gris Vitesse (gr 1966)	Amerigo
			Matchiche II
	Gulanar (b 1974)	Val de Loir (b 1959)	Vieux Manoir
			Vali II
		Gulab (b 1966)	Prince Bio
			Esmeralda II

Magnificent Star's sire, the Solario and Craven Stakes winner Silver Hawk, also had a somewhat unhappy time of it at Epsom, getting a particularly poor run before staying on strongly for third in Golden Fleece's Derby. A cracked cannon bone led to his retirement after he'd been a distant second to Assert in the Irish equivalent. With the 1989 Prix de Diane winner Lady In Silver and other Grade 1 successes in North America with Hawkster and Silver Ending, Silver Hawk has risen above the apparent lack of interest in him during his early days at stud. His Average-Earnings Index of over 3.00—only the top five per cent of stallions have a lifetime progeny AEI of 2.00 or higher—further helps to explain why Silver Hawk has spectacularly bucked the trend in stallion fees, standing in 1991 at a reported 40,000 dollars and in 1987 (the year Magnificent Star was conceived) at 2,500 dollars. *Racing Update*'s analysis of 756 stallions between 1985 and 1990 showed a decline in fees of 46%. Silver Hawk has already rewarded M. Fustok's patronage of stallions which raced for him by producing Lady In Silver and the Irish Oaks third Silver Lane. Neither is Magnificent Star the first runner of note for him out of the dam Gulanar. Her first foal was Mysterieuse Etoile (by Northern Dancer), winner of the Prix de la Grotte and runner-up in both the Marcel Boussac and Poule d'Essai des Pouliches. From her five foals between Magnificent Star and Mysterieuse Etoile, Gulanar had two winners, including the Prix de l'Avre second Bilal (by Green Forest). Her 1989 offspring by Blushing Groom fetched 100,000 dollars, then called Blushing Nar, at the Keeneland Select Sale in 1990 and was in training with Clive Brittain. Gulanar visited Silver Hawk again in 1991. On the racecourse she gained five successes from fifteen starts in Italy, including in two listed races at about a mile and a quarter. She's a daughter of Gulab, a fairly useful handicapper at up to a mile and a quarter in France whose grandam was a half-sister to Petite Etoile. We haven't seen a great deal of this family in Britain and it seemed that we'd be seeing a great deal less of Magnificent Star in her four-year-old season after her owner's apparent rapprochement with the French racing authorities led to Mohammed Moubarak's departure from Newmarket to Chantilly. However, it's now reported that following a delay in obtaining his licence in France, Moubarak is now on his way back to Britain; Magnificent Star and all. Magnificent Star could reappear in the Yorkshire Oaks in 1992, the race being opened to older horses for the first time in 1991, though none actually took part. We are confident that she'll prove at least as good as she was at three, probably better, but, as we've stressed already, Magnificent Star is not a horse to back regardless of the conditions. Those who availed themselves of odds of 6/4 on for a Warwick maiden race over seven furlongs on top-of-the-ground back in May will remember him. *M. Moubarak.*

MAGNIFIED (USA) 2 br.c. (Apr 12) Known Fact (USA) 135 – Mofida 115 (Right **66** p Tack 131) [1991 6g³ 6m* 5g⁵] rather leggy, quite attractive colt: good walker: modest mover: ninth foal: half-brother to fairly useful 1990 2-y-o 6f winner Dangora (by Sovereign Dancer) and smart miler Zaizafon (by The Minstrel): dam, very tough winner of 6 races at up to 7f, is grandam of Elmaamul: long odds on following promising debut, won maiden at Doncaster in May: looking very well, over 8 lengths fifth of 8, never able to challenge, to Another Episode in minor event at York over 3 months later: will be better suited by 7f/1m: likely to do better. *B. W. Hills.*

MAGNUM STAR (IRE) 2 b.c. (Feb 23) Damister (USA) 123 – North Telstar **62** 104 (Sallust 134) [1991 6m 6g 6m⁴ 7m⁶ 7g 8s] 26,000F, IR 38,000Y: tall, leggy, short-backed colt: first foal: dam Irish 6f (at 2 yrs) and 9f winner: quite modest form when staying-on fourth of 9 to Fair Cop in Chesham Stakes at Royal Ascot: well beaten in listed event and maidens in Ireland otherwise: should stay at least 1¼m. *J. E. Mulhern, Ireland.*

MAGSOOD 6 ch.g. Mill Reef (USA) 141 – Shark Song 103 (Song 132) [1990 NR 1991 12f] lengthy, good-looking gelding: moderate mover: fair winner as 3-y-o: lightly raced since and has lost his form: stays 1½m: acts on firm going, probably unsuited by soft: has won when blinkered. *S. Mellor.* —

MAHAASIN 3 b.f. Bellypha 130 – Dame Ashfield 90 (Grundy 137) [1990 NR 1991 10m⁵ 10m⁵ 12s] 100,000Y: leggy, quite attractive filly: third foal: half-sister to Dame Rousara (by Rousillon), fair 6f and 7f winner at 2 yrs, and winning hurdler Valiant Dash (by Valiyar): dam 1½m winner, is out of Cheshire Oaks and Park Hill winner African Dancer: modest form when fifth in minor event and (reluctant stalls) maiden: blinkered, bumped several times but ran poorly nonetheless at Folkestone in November: should stay 1½m: seems not to act on soft going: sold L. Codd 2,000 gns Newmarket December Sales. *A. C. Stewart.* 70

MAHAIRY (USA) 2 b.c. (May 12) Theatrical 128 – Papamiento (USA) (Blade (USA)) [1991 7d] $235,000Y: tall, close-coupled, attractive colt: ninth foal: half-brother to smart sprinter Gwydion (by Raise A Cup) and to 2 other winners: dam placed at 2 yrs and 3 yrs in USA: 8/1 from 5/1, held up after slowish start and never reached leaders in 22-runner maiden at Doncaster in November: will stay 1m: looks capable of better. *A. A. Scott.* — p

MAHASIN (USA) 2 b.f. (Mar 28) Danzig (USA) – Icing 112 (Prince Tenderfoot (USA) 126) [1991 6g²] big, good-topped filly: has plenty of scope: closely related to William Hill Futurity winner Al Hareb (by El Gran Senor) and smart French 9f to 1¼m winner Dr Somerville (by Chief's Crown) and half-sister to several winners, including Ulster Harp Derby winner Rising (by Relkino): dam won from 5f to 1m at 2 yrs, including Argos Star Fillies Mile: well-backed favourite though green and gave trouble stalls, 1½ lengths second of 8 to Sun And Shade in £9,500 maiden at Ascot in July, pulling very hard early on, quickening to lead 1½f out but drifting right, soon headed and no extra: bred to stay 1m: should improve. *J. L. Dunlop.* 84 p

MAHFIL 3 b.g. Head For Heights 125 – Polavera (FR) (Versailles II) [1990 7m⁴ 8.2s⁴ 1991 10.1s⁵ 12m² 12g⁴ 11.9g* 11.8g⁴ 10m² 10.5d] lengthy gelding: fair performer: won apprentice maiden at Brighton in July, leading over 1f out: ran creditably in handicaps next 2 starts: should prove better at 1½m than shorter: acts on good to firm ground: early to post, pulled hard fifth start: sold 12,000 gns Newmarket Autumn Sales and gelded. *A. C. Stewart.* 74

MAHONG 3 gr.g. Petong 126 – Balearica 90 (Bustino 136) [1990 6g⁵ 7s² 1991 a7g* 7.6g 8g 8m⁶ 9s⁶ 8.1s*] leggy gelding: modest form: won median auction contest at Lingfield in May and 22-runner claimer (set fair bit to do, claimed to join Mrs H. Parrott £8,500) at Chepstow in October: stays 9f: acts on soft ground. *J. W. Hills.* 72

MAHOOL (USA) 2 b.c. (Mar 31) Alydar (USA) – Tax Dodge (USA) (Seattle Slew (USA)) [1991 8m⁵ 7m*] $1,200,000Y: angular, unfurnished colt: has scope: second foal: brother to 3-y-o Hud Hud: dam won at up to 9f, including in stakes: 10/1, confirmed promise of debut when winning 18-runner maiden at Doncaster in October by head from Wainwright, again making most, then rallying bravely to lead close home: should stay 1¼m: may well improve further. *A. A. Scott.* 87 p

MAHRAJAN 7 b.h. Dominion 123 – Dame Julian 84 (Blakeney 126) [1990 9g 10m⁵ 11.5m⁵ 11.7m* 11.7g* 12g 12g 1991 12g 12m 11.7g⁴ 11.7m* 11.7m 11.6m³ 14g 12g* 11.8g⁴ 12d⁵] rangy horse: moderate mover: quite modest handicapper: won at Windsor (third win there) in July and Salisbury in October: stays 1½m: acts on any going: flashed tail and looked none too keen once: usually held up: none too consistent. *C. J. Benstead.* 68

MAHSUL (IRE) 3 br.c. Ela-Mana-Mou 132 – Afrah (USA) 85 (Our Native (USA)) [1990 NR 1991 6m⁴ 6d⁵ 6g⁶ 6g 7m* 7g² 8m⁶] good-bodied colt: bad mover: second foal: dam, 2-y-o 5f winner who lost her form at 3 yrs, is out of a smart stakes winner at up to 1¼m: won maiden at Lingfield in August, coming from towards rear to lead close home: unlucky second at Kempton, easily better effort when favourite for handicaps following month: better at 7f than 6f, and should stay further: best form on top-of-the-ground. *C. J. Benstead.* 67

MAHZOOZ 2 ch.c. (May 19) Crystal Glitters (USA) 127 – Gandoorah 90 (Record Token 128) [1991 6m⁵ 7g⁵ 7m 6s⁶] 4,000Y: lengthy, good-topped colt: good mover: fourth foal: half-brother to quite modest 1987 2-y-o 6f and 7f winner Axia (by Comedy Star) and a winner in Scandinavia: dam 2-y-o 5f winner out of half-sister to top-class sprinter Roman Warrior: quite modest maiden: should stay 1m: possibly 64 unsuited by soft ground: very edgy and swishing tail (ran moderately) penultimate start. *M. Moubarak.*

MAID MARINER 9 br.m. Julio Mariner 127 – Molly Polly (Molvedo 137) [1990 — 14g 1991 16.2g] lengthy mare: extremely lightly raced and no worthwhile form. *Miss G. M. Rees.*

MAID OF ESSEX 5 b.m. Bustino 136 – Magelka 77 (Relkino 131) [1990 10.2f³ **61** 10.2f³ 14m 12m⁴ 8m⁵ 10m⁵ 10.2g 7g⁶ 8g³ 8.2d 1991 a10g² a8g* a8g²] attractive mare: quite modest handicapper: won at Lingfield: not seen out after failing to land odds there later in February: best at 1¼m: acts on firm going: wore eyeshield last 3 outings: often sweats: races keenly. *C. E. Brittain.*

MAID OF ICE 2 b.f. (Feb 21) Siberian Express (USA) 125 – Kalorama (FR) 102 — (Bold Lad (IRE) 133) [1991 7m 8s] 27,000Y: sturdy, good-bodied filly: first foal: dam Irish 2-y-o 6f winner: soundly beaten in maidens at Leicester and Yarmouth (front rank to halfway) in October. *Dr J. D. Scargill.*

MAID WELCOME 4 br.f. Mummy's Pet 125 – Carolynchristensen 58 (Sweet **74** Revenge 129) [1990 a6g⁴ 6f⁴ 5g 5f⁴ 6m 5g 5m⁶ 5.8h² 5f 5.1f⁵ 5.3h* 6f² 6m⁴ 6m 6f⁴ 5f 5.3f 6d 5g* a5g² a6g⁶ a5g⁵ 1991 a5g⁵ a6g³ a5g³ a5g⁵ a5g² 5.3f² 5f* 5g 5f 5m a5g* 5m³ 6m² 5m 5m⁴ 5m 5.1g² 5d a5g a6g³] sturdy filly: has a round action: modest handicapper: made all at Redcar in May and Southwell in August: effective at 5f and 6f: easily best form on top-of-the-ground (acts on hard) and fibresand: blinkered nowadays: suitable mount for apprentice. *Mrs N. Macauley.*

MAIN BID (IRE) 2 b.c. (Mar 17) Auction Ring (USA) 123 – Annabella 88 **87 p** (Habitat 134) [1991 7m⁵ 7g*] 17,000F, 68,000Y: strong, workmanlike colt: has scope: sixth living foal: half-brother to 3-y-o 1m winner Lamarsh (by Be My Guest): dam 2-y-o 5f winner stayed 1m, is out of high-class 5f and 1m winner Sovereign and half-sister to Irish Derby second Lucky Sovereign: confirmed promise of debut when winning maiden at Salisbury in October, rallying well: likely to stay 1m: will improve again. *M. Moubarak.*

MAINLY ME 2 b.f. (Jan 31) Huntingdale 132 – Mainmast 63 (Bustino 136) [1991 **76** 6m² 6g³ 7m⁵ 6s⁶ 6m³ 6m²] workmanlike filly: first foal: dam twice-raced granddaughter of half-sister to high-class Buoy and Oaks winner Bireme: modest maiden: stays 7f: acts on top-of-the-ground, possibly unsuited by soft: largely consistent. *Mrs J. Cecil.*

MAIORO (CAN) 5 b.m. Bates Motel (USA) – Toys Are Fun (USA) (Go Marching — (USA)) [1990 9g 12g 1991 12g 13.8f] leggy mare: no sign of ability. *M. W. Ellerby.*

MAI PEN RAI 3 ch.g. All Systems Go 119 – Jersey Maid 82 (On Your Mark 125) **57** [1990 6g 6g 6m² 6m² 6m³ 6m³ 7f 7f³ 8m* 8.2d 1991 9d 11.7g 10g 7g 10.1d 8m² 7g 8.1s* 9.9f⁴ 8s 6f 10.5m² 10m⁵ 8g 8.2m 8d a7g] sparely-made, angular gelding: plating-class performer: won apprentice handicap at Sandown in July, wandering in front: ran very well in handicap at Haydock twelfth start: better at around 1¼m than shorter: acts on any going. *C. J. Hill.*

MAJAL (IRE) 2 b.g. (Feb 14) Caerleon (USA) 132 – Park Special (Relkino 131) **88** [1991 6g⁵ 7m² 7.5f* 7g³ 7m] 60,000Y: good-bodied gelding: first foal: dam Irish 1¼m winner, is half-sister to useful 1987 Irish 2-y-o 7f winner Careafolie (by Caerleon), Horris Hill winner Gouriev and smart French 1985 2-y-o 7f winner Pantile: progressed into fair performer: easily won maiden at Beverley in July: very good third of 5, leading around 5f, to Torrey Canyon in Deploy Acomb Stakes at York in August: ran moderately in Chester nursery (keen, on toes, poorly drawn) 11 days later: will stay 1m+: sold 23,000 gns Newmarket Autumn Sales and gelded. *B. Hanbury.*

MAJAZ (USA) 3 b.g. Elocutionist (USA) – Googolmiss (USA) (Iron Ruler (USA)) — [1990 NR 1991 10g 11d⁶ 12.2d⁴ 16.1g] lengthy gelding: has a round action: fifth foal: half-brother to 2 winners in USA, including useful Galba (by Best Turn): dam showed a little ability: no worthwhile form in maidens and handicap: sold out of R. Armstrong's stable 2,300 gns Newmarket July Sales after third start. *J. A. Glover.*

MAJBOOR (IRE) 2 b.c. (May 12) Wassl 125 – Mashteen (USA) (Majestic Prince) — **p** [1991 6g] rangy, good sort: has scope: brother to 3-y-o Mubin and half-brother to 4 winners, including very useful 1984 2-y-o 6f winner Foulaad (by Raja Baba) and very useful 1983 French 2-y-o 1m winner Cedilla (by Caro): dam, smart stakes winner at 6f and 7f, from excellent family: 8/1, ninth of 16 in maiden at Newmarket in August, effort at halfway, green then not knocked about: sure to do better. *P. T. Walwyn.*

MAJED (IRE) 3 b.c. Wolverlife 115 – Martin Place (Martinmas 128) [1990 7m **77** 8d² 7g³ 1991 11.1d³ 11.5m⁴ 11.7m a12g² 12m⁵ 10g² 11.5s* a12g²] useful-looking colt: good walker: fair handicapper: well-backed favourite, won at Yarmouth in October, driven out after smooth headway to challenge over 2f out: creditable second at Lingfield 8 days later: stays 1½m: best turf efforts with give in the ground: blinkered fifth start. *N. A. Callaghan.*

MAJENICA (USA) 3 b.f. Majestic Light (USA) – Hope For All (USA) (Secretariat (USA)) [1990 NR 1991 10m 10m⁶] leggy, workmanlike filly: sixth foal: sister to French Oaks winner Lacovia and half-sister to a minor winner in USA: dam, placed from 6f to 8.3f in USA, is half-sister to Miswaki: 12/1 and in need of first run in 3 months, 7¾ lengths sixth of 7 to Percy's Girl in minor event at Sandown in September: bandaged behind on debut: visits Shaadi. *J. H. M. Gosden.* — p

MAJESTIC IMAGE 5 ch.m. Niniski (USA) 125 – Regal Twin (USA) 77 (Majestic Prince) [1990 NR 1991 a11g² a14g* 14d* 14m* 16d* 13.9g] workmanlike, rather angular mare: has a rather round action: off course since 3 yrs: returned in cracking form in 1991, successful in handicaps at Southwell and Nottingham in spring and Sandown (2, ran on strongly despite edging right in £7,000 event for final win): held up and never able to challenge in Tote Ebor at York, first run for 1½ months: will be suited by further than 2m: acts on good to firm ground, but goes very well on dead: well ridden by 5-lb claimer D. Harrison. *Lord Huntingdon.* 75

MAJESTIC MAYBE (IRE) 2 b.f. (May 14) Mister Majestic 122 – Lady Wise 41 (Lord Gayle (USA) 124) [1991 5m 6.1m⁵ 7m 6m a8g] IR 2,100F: small, leggy filly: half-sister to Irish 2-y-o 5f winner Before The Storm (by Thatching) and 3-y-o 10.1f winner Lady Baraka (by Shernazar): dam, placed over 8.2f at 2 yrs in Ireland, is half-sister to Middle Park winner Spanish Express: poor maiden: worth another try at 7f: usually on toes. *T. H. Caldwell.*

MAJESTIC MELODY 3 ch.f. Crooner 119 – Royal Birthday (St Paddy 133) 52 [1990 NR 1991 7g⁴ 7.6s 8g 7g] fifth live foal: half-sister to 8.3f seller winner and good hurdler Royal Derbi (by Derrylin): dam lightly raced: plating-class maiden: easily best effort on debut. *W. Carter.*

MAJESTIC SINCLAIR (IRE) 2 b.c. (Apr 29) Mister Majestic 122 – Katie's 50 p Delight (Relko 136) [1991 6d] 6,400Y: big, useful-looking colt: half-brother to several winners abroad: dam unraced daughter of useful 1m to 1¼m filly Catherine's Plea: 33/1, backward and green, around 10 lengths ninth of 23, late headway, to Prince Emilio in maiden at Haydock in October: will improve, particularly over further. *R. Hollinshead.*

MAJI 2 b.f. (Mar 25) Shareef Dancer (USA) 135 – Majoritat (GER) (Konigsstuhl — p (GER)) [1991 7g] compact filly: first known foal: dam German bred: 50/1 and burly, ninth of 22 to Oumaldaaya in maiden at Newmarket in November, slowly away and behind, late progress: should stay 1¼m: will improve. *D. Morley.*

MAJLOOD (USA) 3 b.c. Danzig (USA) – Qui Royalty (USA) (Native Royalty 110 (USA)) [1990 6f³ 6g* 6m³ 1991 8g⁶ 6m 7g² 5g] rather lightly-made, attractive colt: impresses in appearance: very useful efforts in Group 1 events at Royal Ascot (no extra over 1f out) and Newmarket first 2 starts: headed post in 4-runner minor event at Doncaster in July, quickening clear over 2f out but idling and no extra inside last: favourite, well beaten in King George Stakes at Goodwood (missed break, soon scrubbed along) week later: may well have proved best short of 1m: took keen hold: dead. *M. R. Stoute.*

MAJMU (USA) 3 b.f. Al Nasr (FR) 126 – Affirmative Fable (USA) (Affirmed 105 (USA)) [1990 7f³ 7m² 8g* 8m⁶ 1991 10d³ 12g] tall, leggy filly: has a round action: useful filly: game winner of May Hill Stakes at Doncaster at 2 yrs: good third in moderately-run listed race (pulled hard) at Newbury on reappearance: unimpressive in coat, tailed off in Ribblesdale Stakes at Royal Ascot: stays 1¼m: possibly needs an easy surface: visits Machiavellian. *J. H. M. Gosden.*

MAJOR BOLD (IRE) 3 b.g. Glenstal (USA) 118 – Misty Hill (Hill Clown (USA)) — [1990 NR 1991 10g] IR 6,400F, 16,000Y: workmanlike gelding: half-brother to 3 winners here and abroad, including very useful 5f (at 2 yrs) and 1m winner Mary Mitsu (by Tarboosh): dam won over 13f and 1¾m in France: never dangerous in maiden at Beverley in April: sold 1,300 gns Newmarket Autumn Sales. *C. A. Cyzer.*

MAJOR BUGLER (IRE) 2 b.c. (Apr 1) Thatching 131 – Bugle Sound 96 76 (Bustino 136) [1991 7g⁶ 7g³ 7d³] 16,000Y: big, workmanlike colt: has plenty of scope: brother to Irish 6f winner Sound of Victory and half-brother to 1984 Irish 2-y-o 1¼m winner Over The Waves (by Main Reef) and a disqualified 1¾m winner by Beldale Flutter: dam stayed 1¾m, is out of Melodina, dam also of Dubian and See You Then: modest maiden: stayed on into third in late-season events at Salisbury and (tenderly handled behind Berseto) Doncaster: will be well suited by 1m + . *G. B. Balding.*

MAJOR INQUIRY (USA) 5 b.g. The Minstrel (CAN) 135 – Hire A Brain (USA) —
92 (Seattle Slew (USA)) [1990 14f³ 18.4d 20m³ 1991 14g] sturdy gelding: fairly useful
performer at 4 yrs: gelded after and seemed to take little interest when tailed off in
Sandown handicap in April, 1991: stays extreme distances: acts well on top-of-
the-ground: useful hurdler (has broken blood vessel). *D. R. C. Elsworth.*

MAJORITY HOLDING 6 b.h. Mandrake Major 122 – Kirkby 85 (Midsummer —
Night II 117) [1990 10.1g 1991 12.5g] lengthy, rather dipped-backed horse:
plating-class handicapper as 4-y-o: off course 18 months, showed little on
reappearance: sold 1,500 gns Newmarket Autumn Sales: stays 10.6f: acts on good to
firm and heavy going: usually bandaged. *K. T. Ivory.*

MAJOR IVOR 6 ch.g. Mandrake Major 122 – Double Birthday (Cavo Doro 124) 63 +
[1990 8g 7m 8m 1991 8m 9m⁶ 10m] big, workmanlike horse: carries condition: quite
modest handicapper: creditable staying-on sixth at Redcar: raced wide home turn
and not knocked about there later in October: stays 9f: acts on firm and dead going:
well suited by strong handling. *Mrs G. R. Reveley.*

MAJOR JACKO 8 b.h. Mandrake Major 122 – Toreadora 103 (Matador 131) [1990 35
a7g 6f 8m 6f³ 7h4 6m⁶ 7f⁵ 7m 7f³ 6m⁶ 6f* 6g 6m 6m a6g⁴ a7g 1991 6v 6f 7m²
7.1m 7m⁶ 7f 7m⁴ 6m⁵] big, lengthy horse: moderate mover: poor handicapper:
effective at 6f to 7f: acts on any going: effective with or without visor or blinkers:
often apprentice ridden. *R. Hannon.*

MAJOR MOUSE 3 ch.g. All Systems Go 119 – Tzu-Hsi 66 (Songedor 116) [1990 67
NR 1991 5m² 5g4 5f³ 6m⁶ 6m³ 7f² 6.9f* 7.5f⁶ 8m² 7m³] strong, compact gelding:
half-brother to several winners here and abroad, including sprinter Dragonist (by
Dragonara Palace), herself dam of useful Come On Chase Me: dam 6f winner: quite
modest form: won 3-runner maiden at Carlisle in July: ran well in handicaps last 2
starts: stays 1m: acts on firm going: ducked out of stalls and withdrawn final
appearance. *W. W. Haigh.*

MAJOR RISK 2 ch.g. (Mar 23) Risk Me (FR) 127 – Brampton Grace 80 (Tachy- —
us 128) [1991 6g⁶ a8g] tall, leggy gelding: first foal: dam rather highly-strung
sprinter: beaten around 14 lengths in late-season maidens at Lingfield: wore
eyeshield final start. *P. A. Kelleway.*

MAJOR ROGERS (USA) 3 ch.c. Sauce Boat (USA) – European Passer (USA) 69
(Caucasus (USA)) [1990 7g 7g³ 6g a7g³ a7g* a8g⁵ 1991 6f⁵ 7g* 7d 8d⁵ 7g 7f 7g⁶ 7g
7m 7.6g² 7m] stocky colt: modest handicapper: won apprentice race at Salisbury in
May: ran badly final start: should prove better at around 1m than shorter: acts on
firm and dead going: blinkered fifth (checked early) and seventh (below form)
outings: sold 8,000 gns Newmarket Autumn Sales. *D. J. G. Murray-Smith.*

MAJOR'S LAW (IRE) 2 b.c. (Mar 29) Law Society (USA) 130 – Maryinsky 78
(USA) (Northern Dancer) [1991 7m² 7m 7m 8m 6.1d*] 42,000Y: compact,
good-bodied colt: brother to 3-y-o 1¼m winner La Sky, closely related to high-class
middle-distance performer Legal Case (by Alleged) and a winner in USA by To The
Quick: dam won at up to 9f in USA: fair performer: made all in maiden at Chester in
October: may prove best at up to 1m: acts on good to firm and dead ground: pulled
too hard penultimate start. *C. E. Brittain.*

MAKBUL 4 b.c. Fairy King (USA) – Royaltess (Royal And Regal (USA)) [1990 —
9.1s² 1991 10d 8m] compact, good-quartered colt: easy mover: useful at best, lightly
raced: well beaten in well-contested minor event at Pontefract and £11,550 handicap
at Thirsk (stiff task) in spring of 1991: will prove suited by further than 6f: acts on
firm ground. *D. Morley.*

MAKEMEASTAR (IRE) 3 ch.f. Horage 124 – Sally St Clair (Sallust 134) [1990 —
6m⁵ a7g* 1991 8g] compact filly: won maiden at Southwell in July at 2 yrs: mulish to
post, always behind in claimer in June, 1991. *W. A. O'Gorman.*

MAKE ME PROUD (IRE) 2 b.f. (Feb 28) Be My Native (USA) 122 – Miami 54
Life (Miami Springs 121) [1991 6f 7g 7g] tall, unfurnished filly: second foal: sister to
1½m winner Distinct Native: dam daughter of half-sister to Wolverlife: plating-class
maiden: may be better suited by middle distances. *R. W. Armstrong.*

MAKEMINEMUSIC 2 ch.g. (May 22) Music Boy 124 – Ultra Vires 87 (High 56
Line 125) [1991 5d⁶ 6d 5f² 6g 5m³ 7m] 5,400P, 7,400Y: leggy gelding: eighth foal:
half-brother to 3-y-o Shareef Star (by Shareef Dancer) and several winners,
including stayer Prince Sobur (by Jalmood) and Galtres Stakes winner Ulterior
Motive (by Pyjama Hunt): dam winning stayer: plating-class maiden: free-running
sort, probably best at up to 6f: has run creditably when sweating: bolted to post
second start and sixth intended outing: withdrawn after rider unseated and injured
latter occasion: trained first 5 starts by J. Berry: has been gelded. *Mrs G. R. Reveley.*

Mr D. H. W. Dobson's "Maledetto"

MAKE MUSIC 2 ch.c. (May 9) Music Boy 124 – Ewe Lamb 86 (Free State 125) **70**
[1991 5m² 5f⁶ 5f³ 5m⁴ 5.1m³ 5m 5g 5m] 9,400Y: good-quartered colt: first foal: dam
2-y-o 5f winner later successful over hurdles, is out of very useful 5f performer
Mummy's Darling: modest maiden: ran badly final 2 starts: will be better suited by
6f: ran creditably in blinkers fourth start: inconsistent: sold 1,400 gns Doncaster
October Sales. *J. Berry.*

MAKESHIFT 4 b.f. Night Shift (USA) – Fall To Pieces (USA) 101 (Forli (ARG)) **69**
[1990 5f 7g a7g⁴ 7f² 7f* 8m* 8f* 7g 1991 8g 8f⁵ 10.1f 7.6m⁶] smallish filly: modest a 79
handicapper nowadays: not seen out after July: stays 1m: acts on firm going: wears
tongue strap. *A. N. Lee.*

MALAMUTE SALOON (USA) 5 ch.g. Arctic Tern (USA) 126 – Square **68**
Generation (USA) (Olden Times) [1990 NR 1991 15.8f a14g* 18.8f³ a18g* 16.1m⁵]
leggy, sparely-made gelding: fair performer, very lightly raced on flat nowadays:
10-length winner in June maiden and August handicap at Southwell: seems to stay
18.8f and act on firm ground. *M. C. Pipe.*

MALANINKSHEA (IRE) 2 b.f. (Mar 28) Mister Majestic 122 – Northern **—**
Amber (Shack (USA) 118) [1991 5g⁶ 5m 5d] 3,500Y: small, leggy filly: third foal:
half-sister to 3-y-o 5f winner Minizen Music (by Anita's Prince): dam ran several
times: no worthwhile form, not fully wound up: not seen out after June. *B. Palling.*

MALEDETTO (IRE) 2 b.c. (Feb 19) Double Schwartz 128 – Croglin Water **98**
(Monsanto (FR) 121) [1991 5v* 5v* 5g* 5m⁶ 6g³ 6m²] IR 32,000Y: close-coupled,
quite attractive colt: has a quick action: second foal: half-brother to Irish 3-y-o
Bufalino (by Nomination), very useful winner at up to 7f: dam lightly raced: fairly

503

useful performer: successful in maiden at Leopardstown, minor event at Navan and 8-runner Oral B Marble Hill Stakes at the Curragh in the spring: narrowly-beaten second to Bradawn Breever in Heinz '57' Phoenix Stakes at Leopardstown in August final start, running on well from 2f out: better suited by 6f than 5f, and may well stay 7f: acts on good to firm and heavy ground. *J. S. Bolger, Ireland.*

MALENOIR (USA)   3 b.g. Solford (USA) 127 – Viewed (USA) (Alydar (USA))   **68 d**
[1990 10s 10.2s 1991 a11g² a12g² 12d⁶ 11.6m⁶ a12g 16m 12.1s a13g a12g] leggy, quite attractive gelding: second in Southwell maidens: plating-class form at best afterwards: should be well suited by 1¾m+: blinkered sixth, seventh and final outings: trained until after seventh by M. Bell. *W. J. Pearce.*

MALIBU MAGIC (IRE)   3 b.g. Be My Native (USA) 122 – Nishapours Baby   **87**
(Nishapour (FR) 125) [1990 6m⁵ 8.2d² 8d⁵ 1991 10.2s³ 9s* 8d² 10.4d] lengthy, unfurnished gelding: good walker: won auction contest at Ripon in April, setting pace: had stiff task in listed race at Chester final start, in May: gives impression stays 10.2f: acts on soft going. *J. M. P. Eustace.*

MALINDI BAY   3 gr.c. Grey Desire 115 – Malindi (Mansingh (USA) 120) [1990   **52**
5m⁶ 6g 6g a6g 7g 6m⁵ 8.2g 6d 1991 a7g 8g² 8m 12g 10m² 10g³ 9.7m] angular, close-coupled colt: plater: tailed off final outing: better at 1¼m than shorter: acts on good to firm ground: edgy (ran creditably) penultimate start: blinkered final one at 2 yrs. *B. J. McMath.*

MALLAU   5 b.h. Runnett 125 – Brierley Lodge 67 (Lorenzaccio 130) [1990 6f 8f   **41**
6m 6m 6g 7m 6g 7g a6g* a7g a6g a7g 1991 7f⁴ 7g 7m 6.1m⁶ 6.9m 6m 5f] good-topped horse: poor handicapper: effective at 6f and easy 7f: acts on firm ground: below form when visored and blinkered: inconsistent. *L. J. Holt.*

Mr J. K. Brown's "Mamma's Too"

MALMESBURY 4 ch.g. Burslem 123 – Malmsey (Jukebox 120) [1990 7g 9f⁴ 10g — 1991 8m 10g 10f⁵] workmanlike gelding: has a long stride: well beaten since quite modest form at 2 yrs: should stay 1¼m. *G. B. Balding.*

MALMSEY (USA) 3 b.c. Topsider (USA) – Rebut (USA) (Graustark) [1990 NR **110** 1991 10s* 10.5d³ 11s* 12g⁴] good-topped colt: carries condition: second foal: dam minor stakes-placed winner: won maiden at Maisons-Laffitte in March and Group 2 Grosser Hertie Preis von Deutschland at Munich in May: 7/1, below-form fourth of 9 to Saddlers' Hall in King Edward VII Stakes at Royal Ascot: stays 11f. *A. Fabre, France.*

MALSMAN 3 br.c. Mansingh (USA) 120 – Montana (Mossborough 126) [1990 5m — 5.3f 7s 1991 6m] leggy colt: soundly beaten, in seller (sweating) in July, 1991. *P. Butler.*

MALTBY HYUNDAI (IRE) 3 b.c. Tumble Wind (USA) – Beltichbourne 73 — (Targowice (USA) 130) [1990 7f 1991 a7g a8g a8g 8s] sparely-made colt: of little account. *R. V. King.*

MALTHOUSE MAESTRO (IRE) 3 b.c. Kafu 120 – Taotl (Yellow God 129) — [1990 5m⁶ 5m⁶ 1991 6f 5.1m] good-topped colt: moderate mover: poor maiden: retained 1,500 gns Doncaster November Sales. *W. R. Muir.*

MALUNAR 6 gr.g. Mummy's Pet 125 – Tranquility Base 112 (Roan Rocket 128) **71** [1990 5g⁶ 6g² 6m⁴ 6g⁴ 6m⁵ 6g 6m⁴ 6m⁶ 7m⁴ 6d⁴ 6s⁴ 6g² 6d 5s² a6g³ a7g² 1991 5m 6f⁶ 6f* 7g⁵ 7m² 7.1g⁴ 6.1g²] close-coupled gelding: modest handicapper: won at Yarmouth (apprentices) in June: stays 7f: probably acts on any going: blinkered 3 times: effective with or without visor: hung right and looked none too easy ride fourth start: suited by strongly-run race. *M. H. Tompkins.*

MALVERNICO (IRE) 3 b.c. Nordico (USA) – Malvern Beauty 100 (Shirley **97** Heights 130) [1990 5m* 5g* 6g² 5m* 6.3g* 7m² 1991 8g 8g] leggy Irish colt: successful 3 times and head second, caught near line, in GPA National Stakes at the Curragh (final start) at 2 yrs: not discredited towards rear in 2000 Guineas at Newmarket and Irish 2000 Guineas at the Curragh in 1991: probably stays 1m. *J. S. Bolger, Ireland.*

MAMALAMA 3 ch.f. Nishapour (FR) 125 – Gauloise 93 (Welsh Pageant **48** 132) [1990 5f 6m³ 6f3 7f 7g 8m 1991 7g 8m³ 10g³ 12d⁴ 11.7m 10g⁵ 14.1f³ 12f³ 16m³ 15.4f⁴ 17.2g] leggy, angular filly: plating-class maiden: contests mostly claimers, running well when in frame: stays 2m: acts on firm ground and dead. *L. J. Holt.*

MAMMA'S TOO 2 b.f. (Feb 28) Skyliner 117 – Maple Syrup 89 (Charlottown **104** 127) [1991 5f* 5m² 5m⁴ 5.1m* 5g* 5m² 5.2f* 5f² 6g* 5d⁴] 4,400Y: compact filly: half-sister to 3 winners, including Irish 9f and 11f winner Fish Merchant (by Blue Cashmere): dam, placed over 6f and 1¼m, is daughter of Sweet Solera: successful in maiden auction at Pontefract in spring, claimer at Bath, nursery at Leicester and St Hugh's Stakes at Newbury in summer, then Shadwell Estate Firth of Clyde Stakes (best effort, by ½ length from Harvest Girl) at Ayr in autumn: respectable fourth of 11 to Magic Ring in Cornwallis Stakes at Ascot final start: stays 6f well: acts on firm ground, probably on dead: usually makes running: game. *J. Berry.*

MANAOLANA 3 b.f. Castle Keep 121 – Ladysave (Stanford 121§) [1990 7d 1991 **45** 10.2s⁶ 11f⁴ 10m² 13d] big, heavy-bodied filly: second of 8 in maiden claimer at Ayr in June, always prominent: should stay 1½m: possibly needs a sound surface. *Denys Smith.*

MANBAA (IRE) 2 ch.f. (Feb 11) Doulab (USA) 115 – Dayajeer 85 (Shirley **70** Heights 130) [1991 7m* 8.3s] sturdy, lengthy filly: first foal: dam 1m winner: bit backward when fortunate winner of maiden at Redcar in October, left clear when saddle slipped on Hamanaka and rider unseated near line: well beaten in Hamilton nursery (stiff task) following month: should stay 1m. *H. Thomson Jones.*

MANDALAY PRINCE 7 b.g. Nishapour (FR) 125 – Ops (Welsh Saint 126) — § [1990 NR 1991 16s⁵ 18d⁵ 18f] lengthy, well-made gelding: has a round action: poor handicapper: out-and-out stayer: acts on firm going, unsuited by soft surface: has been tried in blinkers and visor: sometimes bandaged: ran out once at 4 yrs. *T. Kersey.*

MANDIKA 3 b.c. Flash of Steel 120 – Bushti Music 63 (Bustino 136) [1990 NR **62** 1991 10g 12m 14g⁴ 16.9g³ 14.6g] 32,000F, 44,000Y: strong colt: fourth foal: half-brother to 1½m to 2m winner Kingsley (by Kings Lake): dam, who stayed 9f, is half-sister to very useful sprinters Hanu and Sanu: third of 10 at Wolverhampton, first worthwhile form in maidens: well beaten in handicap 5 weeks later: evidently suited by test of stamina. *M. A. Jarvis.*

MANDRITA 2 b.f. (Apr 25) Dance of Life (USA) – Petillante (USA) (Riverman — (USA) 131) [1991 6g] leggy filly: second foal: half-sister to 3-y-o 1m winner Ante Up (by Sharpen Up): dam won at up to 9f: 25/1 and green, modest late progress in 21-runner seller at York in August, having been slowly away and well behind. *M. W. Easterby.*

MAN FROM ELDORADO (USA) 3 b.c. Mr Prospector (USA) – Promising **115** Girl (USA) (Youth (USA) 135) [1990 7g4 7s2 1991 10g2 10g*] big, lengthy colt: has plenty of scope: 10/1 from 16/1 and sweating, much improved form to win A R Dennis Bookmakers Predominate Stakes at Goodwood in May by neck and 3/4 length from Luchiroverte and Selkirk, quickening from rear over 2f out and staying on well to lead close home: took good hold to post: gives impression will stay 1½m: looked as if would improve again. *G. Harwood.*

MANGO MANILA 6 b.h. Martinmas 128 – Trigamy 112 (Tribal Chief 125) [1990 **84** 7g8 6m 6m2 7m 8m 1991 7g3 6g 7v2 7g5 7.1s* 6g2 7g2 8m6 7d 6m 7d4] robust horse: bad mover: improved handicapper in 1991: won at Sandown (landed gamble) in July: good fourth of 22 to La Bamba at Doncaster in November: effective over stiff 6f, to 1m: acts on good to firm and heavy going: usually wears crossed noseband nowadays: has been bandaged. *C. A. Horgan.*

MANGROVE MIST (IRE) 3 b.f. Nishapour (FR) 125 – Antiguan Cove (Mill **46** Reef (USA) 141) [1990 8g a8g a7g6 1991 13.8m 15g2 12.1d3 16.1m5] leggy, lightly-made filly: better at 2m than shorter: acts on good to firm and dead ground: trained first 3 starts by Sir Mark Prescott. *P. Monteith.*

MAN OF GOLD (USA) 3 b.c. Chief's Crown (USA) – Trove (USA) (Key To **82** The Mint (USA)) [1990 NR 1991 8.2d3 10m* 12d 8g 10m* 10m5 8.9m 10d5] $450,000Y: small, good-topped colt: has a quick action: third foal: half-brother to quite useful 1986 2-y-o 7f winner Simple Taste (by Sharpen Up): dam stakes winner at up to 9f out of half-sister to top-class U.S. performer/broodmare Nataschka: won maiden at Ripon in April and handicap (made all) at Leicester in September: below form in handicaps afterwards: stays 1¼m well: best form on top-of-the-ground: has carried head high, and looked none too keen when visored fourth start. *J. H. M. Gosden.*

MAN OF MAUM 6 ch.h. Stanford 121§ – Kitty Ellis (Le Levanstell 122) [1990 **32** NR 1991 9s a8g4 a11g] angular horse: poor maiden: stays 1m. *R. Earnshaw.*

MAN OF THE MOMENT (USA) 2 b.c. (May 3) Moment of Hope (USA) – **90** Daddy's Dish (USA) (Marshua's Dancer (USA)) [1991 5f2 5m* 5g2 6g2 6g2 6m*] $13,000Y: strong, compact colt: second foal: dam won at up to 9f: sire smart 6f to 9f performer: fairly useful performer: successful in median auction maiden at Beverley in May and claimer at Newcastle (second race in 2 days, made all, easily) in June: was better suited by 6f than shorter: blinkered last 2 starts, pulling hard first occasion: dead. *S. G. Norton.*

MAN OF THE SEASON (USA) 2 ch.c. (Apr 11) Naked Sky (USA) – Kizzie **62** (USA) (Naskra (USA)) [1991 6m3 5m4 5f 6g a6g a5g5 a5g] $4,000Y: compact colt: moderate mover: fifth reported foal: half-brother to Molded Class (by Strike The Anvil) a winner of 12 races: dam sprint winner: quite modest sprint maiden: ran creditably on equitrack, moderately on fibresand: blinkered fourth, fifth and final starts. *Mrs N. Macauley.*

MANOUSHKA 6 b.m. Ile de Bourbon (USA) 133 – Gilwanigan (Captain's Gig **42** (USA)) [1990 NR 1991 10v4 15.5f] close-coupled mare: poor mover: poor and lightly-raced maiden: tailed off final start (April): stays 1¼m: acts on good to firm and heavy ground: tried blinkered and visored: unreliable. *P. Butler.*

MANSBER (IRE) 2 b.g. (May 16) Mansooj 118 – Our Bernie (Continuation 120) **49** [1991 5d 6m5 5m6 5m 5g 6m5 6g] IR 1,650F, IR 7,200Y: rather leggy gelding: has a round action: seventh living foal: half-brother to several winners, including fairly useful sprint winner Tauber (by Taufan): dam second 3 times at up to 1m in Ireland: poor maiden: stays 6f: acts on good to firm ground. *Pat Mitchell.*

MANSE KEY GOLD 4 ch.f. Vaigly Great 127 – Carafran (Stanford 121§) [1990 **39** 6f3 6g3 7g* 7.5g4 7f 7g2 8g4 7m 7g2 7m 7m 7d4 a8g 1991 8g 7.5g 8.2d 8.2d 8m 10d 8m* 8.2m 8m5 8m 10.8g] compact filly: poor nowadays: backed at long odds, first form as 4-y-o when winning selling event (no bid) at Yarmouth in July, despite drifting markedly right: may prove best at around 1m: acts on good to firm ground, but goes very well with some give: tailed off on fibresand at Southwell: none too consistent. *R. Bastiman.*

MANSOOB 2 b.c. (Mar 15) Wassl 125 – Yaqut (USA) 77 (Northern Dancer) [1991 **40**
7g 7m 7m] small, sturdy colt: first foal: dam 2-y-o 7f winner from family of Alydar:
poor maiden: should stay 1m: sold 2,200 gns Newmarket Autumn Sales. *J. L. Dunlop.*

MANTRAKI 4 ch.c. Good Times (ITY) – Tota Tora (Home Guard (USA) 129) —
[1990 8f⁴ 12m 9f² 10g 8f 8m* 9g 1991 a11g a13g⁵] leggy, workmanlike colt: has a
quick action: modest handicapper at 3 yrs: way below form in early 1991: should stay
1¼m: acts on firm going: has run as if something amiss: sold only 3,100 gns
Doncaster March Sales. *N. Tinkler.*

MANULEADER 2 b.g. (Feb 28) King of Spain 121 – Balnerino 68 (Rolfe (USA) **59**
77) [1991 5g 5g³ 5d² a5g² 6m² 7f⁴ 6m] 13,000F, 7,000Y: strong gelding: has scope:
first foal: dam 5f (at 2 yrs) and 1m winner: quite modest maiden: stays 7f: acts on
firm and dead ground: bandaged behind on equitrack. *W. J. Pearce.*

MANULIFE 2 b.g. (Apr 3) King of Spain 121 – Try G's (Hotfoot 126) [1991 6m³ 6g **62**
5f³ 6m² 6f⁵ 7m] 5,200Y: quite good-topped gelding: has scope: has a quick action:
second foal: half-brother to a winner in Italy: dam unraced: quite modest maiden:
suited by 6f: acts on top-of-the-ground: inconsistent. *W. J. Pearce.*

MANWAH (USA) 3 ch.f. Lyphard (USA) 132 – Height of Fashion (FR) 124 **72**
(Bustino 136) [1990 NR 1991 10d 10s³ 11.9m² 11.9g⁴ 12m²] sturdy filly: fifth foal:
closely related to Alwasmi (John Porter winner), Unfuwain (both by Northern
Dancer) and 4-y-o 1½m winner Mukddaam (by Danzig), and half-sister to Nashwan
(by Blushing Groom): dam 7f to 1½m winner from very good family: modest maiden:
in frame at Sandown, Haydock, York (sweating) and Pontefract: looks one paced and
well worth a chance over further: visits Riverman. *Major W. R. Hern.*

MANZOOR SAYADAN (USA) 3 b.g. Shahrastani (USA) 135 – Icing 112 **73**
(Prince Tenderfoot (USA) 126) [1990 NR 1991 10.4m² 10g⁴ 14.6d⁴] $300,000Y:
good-bodied gelding: half-brother to several winners, notably smart 1988 2-y-o 7f
and 1m winner Al Hareb (by El Gran Senor) and smart French 9f and 1¼m winner Dr
Somerville (by Chief's Crown): dam 2-y-o 5f to 1m winner: modest form in maidens
at York and Newbury then minor event at Doncaster: stays 1¾m: sold out of A.
Stewart's stable 25,000 gns Newmarket Autumn Sales after second start, gelded
after final one. *R. Simpson.*

MAPATO (IRE) 3 ch.c. Dara Monarch 128 – Edansa (Majority Blue 126) [1990 **46**
NR 1991 7d 7.5g 5g⁴ 6g 6g³ 6g 6.9s a6g 7g⁵] IR 8,600F, IR 12,500Y: quite
good-topped colt: closely related to a winner in Italy by Realm and half-brother to
French 1m winner November Rose (by Huntercombe): dam, French 8.5f winner, is
sister to very smart French 5.5f (at 2 yrs) to 10.5f winner Odisea: poor performer:
stays 7f: visored 4 times: wears bandages: has had tongue tied down: looked
reluctant final start, and is not one to trust. *N. A. Graham.*

MA PETITE CHOU 4 gr.f. Known Fact (USA) 135 – Boule de Suif 88 (Major —
Portion 129) [1990 8m⁴ 8g 8g 8f⁶ 10m 1991 8.3g a10g⁴ a10g] smallish, sturdy filly:
poor maiden: probably stays 1¼m: acts on firm ground: has found little. *P. Hayward.*

MAPLE BAY (IRE) 2 b.c. (Mar 31) Bold Arrangement 127 – Cannon Boy (USA) — p
(Canonero II (USA)) [1991 7g] IR 27,000Y: fifth foal: dam won 9 races in USA,
including Grade 3 9f event: 16/1, better than last-of-11 position suggests in Salisbury
maiden won by Dance Scene in October, prominent 5f then eased: will improve. *P. J. Makin.*

MARAAKIZ (USA) 3 ch.c. Roberto (USA) 131 – River of Stars (USA) (Riverman **102**
(USA) 131) [1990 7m* 7f² 8.2g³ 7m³ 7v² 1991 8s² 10f* 11.7g* 10g⁶ 11.5d* 12.1d²
12f* 12s³ 12g²] strong colt: useful performer: successful in 3-runner minor events
at Brighton, Bath and Lingfield then in Group 2 Bosphorus Trophy (easily, in July)
in Turkey: placed last 2 starts in Group 1 contest in Spain and minor event
(appearing to run very well behind Legal Case) at Salisbury: stays 1½m: acts on any
going: usually makes running: to join D. Hayes in Australia. *J. L. Dunlop.*

MARAASID (IRE) 3 b.f. High Top 131 – Welwyn 92 (Welsh Saint 126) [1990 NR —
1991 9.7m⁶] lengthy filly: third foal: half-sister to poor 7f winner Bashaq (by
Jalmood): dam, suited by 6f, is half-sister to very useful sprinter Welshwyn: moved
badly down and showed nothing in maiden at Folkestone in August: sold 620 gns
Newmarket September Sales. *C. J. Benstead.*

MARA ASKARI (IRE) 3 b.c. Night Shift (USA) – Madam Cody (Hot Spark 126) [1990 **76**
7m² 8g⁴ 1991 9g³ 12g a10g⁴ 12g 15.4f* 16m a12g a14g] good-bodied colt: won
handicap at Folkestone in September: well beaten in similar event previous start
and all afterwards: suited by test of stamina: acts on firm going: sold out of G.
Harwood's stable 4,000 gns Newmarket Autumn Sales after sixth start. *J. L. Harris.*

MARAATIB (IRE) 3 b.f. Green Desert (USA) 127 – Shurooq (USA) 94 **93**
(Affirmed (USA)) [1990 5f² 5m* 5f⁵ 6m³ 5m* 6d² 1991 8g 6m 6m* 5m* 6g 6m]
small filly: has a quick action: fair performer: neck winner of 6-runner handicaps at
Epsom in June and Redcar (sweating and unimpressive in appearance) in August,
making virtually all: effective at 5f and 6f: acts on good to firm ground and dead:
visits Lycius. *H. Thomson Jones.*

MARABELLA STAR (USA) 2 b.c. (May 4) Imp Society (USA) – Percentage **100** p
(USA) (Vaguely Noble 140) [1991 6.1m* 6g³ 7m*] $50,000Y: unfurnished colt: has
some scope: seventh foal: half-brother to Percentile (by Silver Hawk), champion
3-y-o filly in Panama, and 2 winners in North America: dam unraced half-sister to 2
stakes winners: sire, best at 4 yrs, smart 8.5f to 1¼m winner: easy winner of maiden
at Nottingham in July and nursery at York (from Well Appointed, making most) in
October: something probably amiss in between, subsequently off course 2 months:
will stay 1m: useful already, and likely to improve again. *H. R. A. Cecil.*

MARANDISA 4 ch.f. Pharly (FR) 130 – Marissiya (Nishapour (FR) 125) [1990 **59**
12.8m² 10m³ 12.8m* 12g² 10m* 1991 a11g a12g a12g 8m 12d⁵ 15.1g³ 12.2m³ 12.1g]
leggy, close-coupled ex-Irish filly: first foal: dam unraced half-sister to several good
winners, including Prix de Diane Hermes third Masmouda: winning ex-Irish
handicapper: worthwhile form in 1991 only when third: stays 15f: acts on good to
firm ground: sold out of J. Oxx's stable 8,000 gns Newmarket December (1990)
Sales: trained first 5 starts at 4 yrs by K. McCauley. *H. A. T. Whiting.*

MARCHAM (IRE) 3 b.c. Sadler's Wells (USA) 132 – Dazzling Light 116 (Silly **100**
Season 127) [1990 7m* 8s³ 1991 8g⁴ 8m⁵] won maiden at Goodwood and third of 4 in
Racing Post Trophy at Doncaster at 2 yrs: 7½ lengths fourth of 10 to Corrupt in
listed race at Kempton, pulling hard and leading briefly over 2f out: well beaten in
competitive Doncaster minor event 5½ months later: should stay at least 1¼m: *B.
W. Hills.*

MARCH GENERATION 5 b.h. Young Generation 129 – Walk By 113 (Tower —
Walk 130) [1990 8g 1991 10d⁶ 12g 8f] leggy horse: half-brother to fair sprinter
Scintillio (by Hot Spark) and a winner in Belgium: dam sprinting half-sister to smart
fillies Smarten Up (dam of Cadeaux Genereux) and Solar: very lightly raced, and no
worthwhile form. *R. Voorspuy.*

MARCHING PAST 3 br.c. Daring March 116 – Storm Crest 80 (Lord Gayle **67** §
(USA) 124) [1990 6g³ 7f² 5m² 6g² 6d² 1991 7f³ 6g 8f² 7m* 7m 7.1g 6.9s] well-made
colt: modest performer on his day: won handicap at Doncaster in June: refused to go
through with effort next start, tailed off afterwards: stays 7f: acts on good to firm
ground and dead: visored final start, blinkered previous 3: below form when
sweating: trained first 6 starts by A. Stewart: not one to trust. *H. J. Collingridge.*

MARCHING STAR 5 ch.m. Marching On 101 – Elegant Star 86 (Star Moss 122) **31** §
[1990 a8g 8m 8f⁵ 5m 7g⁵ 8g 12g 5g 7f² 7f 9g 7f 7d⁵ 6s 1991 8.2d 7f³ 8g⁶ 5m 7h⁵ 7m²
7g⁶ 7g 7f⁶ 7m 7m⁵ 8.3f] neat mare: moderate mover: unreliable plater: probably
stays 1m: acts on any going: used to wear blinkers or visor: sometimes bandaged. *J.
S. Haldane*

MARCHMAN 6 b.g. Daring March 116 – Saltation 111 (Sallust 134) [1990 NR 1991 **51**
11.7g⁶ 10m⁴ 12g³ 10.2g] big, strong, good-topped gelding: carries condition: plating-
class handicapper: needs a strongly-run 1¼m and stays 1¾m: acts on firm going:
needs strong handling. *J. S. King.*

MARCROFT 5 ch.m. Crofthall 110 – Squires Girl (Spanish Gold 101) [1990 8f 7f **62**
7.6d⁴ 7g 7g 6m⁶ 7.6m³ 7m² 7f⁵ 7m* 8m⁴ 8m 7.6g⁵ 7m 7d 7f 7m 6s 7d³ 7d⁵ 7d 1991
6m⁵ 7m⁵ 7m* 7.5g³ 6.1d⁶ 7.1g³ 7.6g⁴ 7f⁶ 7.5f² 7.6m 7m 7m⁶ 7m] sparely-made,
close-coupled mare: quite modest handicapper: well backed, won at Catterick
(second win there) in May: best at 7f to 1m: acts on any going: ran poorly when
visored once: tends to carry head high: best held up, and suited by strong gallop. *R.
Hollinshead.*

MARCUS JACK 2 b.g. (Mar 21) Sparkling Boy 110 – Gresham Girl 99 (Right —
Tack 131) [1991 6.1m 5g 6.1d] smallish, angular, sturdy gelding: eighth foal:
half-brother to several winners, including fair 1983 2-y-o 5f winner Lady Pretender
(by Dragonara Palace): dam 6f winner, out of very speedy Granville Greta: no
worthwhile form in maidens. *Mrs A. L. M. King.*

MARCUS THORPE (USA) 3 ch.c. Palace Music (USA) 129 – Guilty Miss **109**
(USA) (Mr Redoy (USA)) [1990 8g² 10g³ 1991 10g² 11.5g⁵ 12g² 12g³ 12.5g⁶ 12s⁴ 12g⁴
12s⁶] lengthy, quite good-topped colt: has a quick action: very useful maiden: best
efforts behind Hailsham in Derby Italiano at Rome and Saddlers' Hall in King
Edward VII Stakes at Royal Ascot third and fourth outings: ran in pattern races

abroad afterwards, just over 5 lengths fourth of 11 to Pigeon Voyageur in Gran Premio d'Italia at Milan on penultimate outing: suited by 1½m: sold out of H. Cecil's stable after reappearance. *P. A. Kelleway.*

MARDESSA   3 b.f. Ardross 134 – Marquessa d'Howfen 93 (Pitcairn 126) [1990   **74** 6s⁶ 7f² 7.5f⁵ 8g 7g 8d⁵ 1991 10d* 10d² 12m⁵ 10.2m³ 10.6m* 11m* 11.9m 10.2g⁴ 10.9g³ 10.1m² 11.9g³ 10.3m² 10.9m 11.9g 10.3d] workmanlike filly: modest handicapper: successful at Nottingham, Haydock and Redcar in first half of season: below form last 4 starts: travels long way on bridle, giving impression may prove ideally suited by strongly-run race at around 1¼m: acts on firm and dead ground: tough. *F. H. Lee.*

MARDIOR   3 b.f. Martinmas 128 – Diorina 91 (Manacle 123) [1990 5m 6g 7m 6g   — a6g 1991 7m 8d 12f⁵ 10f] leggy filly: poor maiden. *W. G. R. Wightman.*

MARDONIUS   5 b.h. Persian Bold 123 – Dominica (GER) (Zank) [1990 15.5d² **113** 15g* 1991 12g² 14.5s* 16m⁴] very useful French horse: won 9-runner Group 3 Prix de Barbeville at Saint-Cloud by length from Turgeon: well below form when fourth to Top of The World in moderately-run Cementone Beaver Henry II Stakes at Sandown later in May, running on strongly from poor position 2f out: stays very well: acts on good on firm and soft going: wears blinkers. *A. Fabre, France.*

MARDOOD   6 b.h. Ela-Mana-Mou 132 – Tigeen (Habitat 134) [1990 NR 1991 8g   — 8m 10g 12.3d 12g⁵ 11.9m⁴ 11f⁵ 9g 10.3d] strong, lengthy horse: poor mover: fair performer at best: not nearly so good nowadays: stays 12.2f: best form on soft going: has been tried blinkered and visored: trained first 3 starts by N. Graham. *T. Kersey.*

MARGS GIRL   4 b.f. Claude Monet (USA) 121 – Aquarian Star (Cavo Doro 124)   **69** [1990 6m⁵ 6f 7g* 7g⁵ 6g⁶ 7g⁴ 7d³ 7g² 7.5f* 8h* 7.5g⁵ 8g a8g* 7d 8v² 8d⁴ a8g⁴ 1991 a11g 10.2s* 10s* 10f 10.4d 12.3g² 12g⁶ 12d² 12m⁵ 12.2f² 12f³ 12f² 11.9g⁶ 12.3f 12g] leggy filly: poor mover: quite modest handicapper: won at Doncaster (apprentices) and Ripon in spring: ran poorly last 2 starts: stays 1½m: acts on any going: genuine and largely consistent. *T. Fairhurst.*

MARIA CAPPUCCINI   3 ch.f. Siberian Express (USA) 125 – Mary Martin (Be   **60** My Guest (USA) 126) [1990 5m* 5g² 5f 5m 1991 5d 6g 7.3d 6s⁵ 7m³ 6.9f 7g⁴ 5.7f 8g] rather sparely-made filly: good mover: modest winner at 2 yrs: form in handicaps in 1991 only when in frame at Brighton and Kempton (blinkered): stays 7f: acts on good to firm ground: sweating second start, edgy on sixth. *I. A. Balding.*

MARIA DONIA   3 ch.f. Siberian Express (USA) 125 – Nafla (FR) (Arctic Tern   — (USA) 126) [1990 5g⁵ 1991 7g 5.7g] small filly: off course over 12 months after debut: behind in maiden and claimer (edgy) in 1991: sold 1,150 gns Ascot July Sales. *I. A. Balding.*

MARIA MEDICI   3 b.f. Never So Bold 135 – Lady Regent (Wolver Hollow 126)   **55** [1990 NR 1991 6m⁵ 7f 10.2m a8g] 2,400Y: leggy, plain filly: fourth foal: half-sister to 6f and 7f winner Trojan General (by Trojan Fen) and moderate plater Foot Perfect (by Pas de Seul): dam won over 7f at 3 yrs in Ireland: apparently best effort in maidens on debut: wore eyeshield final start, first for 5 months: bandaged. *Mrs L. Piggott.*

MARIAN EVANS   4 b.f. Dominion 123 – Kindjal 84 (Kris 135) [1990 7m⁴ 7f³ 6g   — a6g 1991 8.2m] sturdy filly: quite modest maiden at 3 yrs: below form only start in 1991 (May): best form at 7f: acts on firm ground: sold out of P. Harris's stable 680 gns Doncaster January Sales. *T. Craig.*

MARIECURIE EXPRESS   2 b.f. (Mar 9) Sizzling Melody 117 – K-Sera 95   **51** (Lord Gayle (USA) 124) [1991 5m⁴ 5g 5.7m* 5m⁴ 6m³ 5h⁶ 6m] 7,400Y: leggy, good-quartered filly: moderate mover: half-sister to 3 winners here and abroad, including quite modest sprinter Yukosan (by Absalom): dam 2-y-o 7f winner: plating-class form: made all for claimer in maiden auction at Bath in July: sold 850 gns Doncaster October Sales: stays 6f: bandaged behind penultimate outing. *J. Berry.*

MARIE DE FRANCE (USA)   3 ch.f. Diesis 133 – Fabled Land (USA) (Grau-   **72** stark) [1990 NR 1991 10.2m⁵ 11f² 14.1m* 16.1g⁴ 16.1m⁵ 16.2f⁴] rather leggy filly: fourth reported foal: half-brother to winning hurdler Rastannora (by Al Nasr) and a winner in USA by Irish River: dam, from excellent family, won at around 1m: modest performer: landed odds in 4-runner maiden at Yarmouth in July: stays 2m: acts on firm ground: visits Most Welcome. *H. R. A. Cecil.*

MARIETTE   2 ch.f. (Apr 21) Blushing Scribe (USA) 107 – Targuette (Targowice   **35** (USA) 130) [1991 6f 7m 6.9f] 500F, 1,250Y: workmanlike filly: half-sister to 1984 2-y-o 5f winner Rocket Royale (by Roan Rocket) and 2 winners in Italy: dam poor plater: poor plater: sold 580 gns Ascot December Sales. *J. Pearce.*

MARIETTE LARKIN 2 b.f. (Feb 1) Elegant Air 119 – Straw Boater 89 (Thatch —
(USA) 136) [1991 7.1d] 3,500F: workmanlike, good-quartered filly: second foal:
half-sister to 3-y-o Henley Regatta (by Gorytus): dam 9.4f winner: 20/1, well beaten
in maiden at Chepstow in October. *G. B. Balding.*

MARINE DIVER 5 b.g. Pas de Seul 133 – Marine Life (Deep Diver 134) [1990 72 §
10f² 10g 11m⁶ 10h² 9g² 10g² 10m 1991 10g⁴ 8.2g 8d² a10g⁵ 9m⁴ 12m⁴ 8g* 7g³ 8m⁶
8g³ 8d 8g²] quite attractive gelding: carries condition: good walker: has a slightly
round action: modest handicapper: won claimer (trained until after then by P. Cole)
at Goodwood in August: probably best at up to 1¼m nowadays: acts on firm and dead
going: sometimes wears severe bridle: tailed off on equitrack and penultimate start
(pulled extremely hard): has drifted badly left and failed to go through with effort:
difficult ride. *B. R. Millman.*

MARINE SOCIETY 3 b.c. Petoski 135 – Miranda Julia 73 (Julio Mariner 127) 80
[1990 7g⁶ 8g 8m⁵ 7m 1991 12d 12.1g⁵ 12g² 12s⁵ a14g] well-made colt: grand walker:
fair maiden: good second at Folkestone: tailed off in handicap at Southwell final
start: should be suited by further than 1½m: well beaten on a soft surface: trained
first 3 starts by D. Elsworth. *P. T. Walwyn.*

MARINSKY (USA) 2 ch.f. (Apr 13) Diesis 133 – Indoor (FR) 113 (Caracolero 63
(USA) 131) [1991 7m³ 7g⁶] rangy, unfurnished filly: has a powerful action: sister to
3-y-o Wayzgoose and half-sister to 2 winners in USA: dam won 10.5f Prix de Flore:
better effort in maidens when third of 13 finishers at Redcar in October, slowly
away, kept on never dangerous: looked rather headstrong at Newmarket following
month: bred to stay 1¼m. *Mrs J. Cecil.*

MARIOLINO 4 b.g. Buzzards Bay 128§ – Banking Coyne 76 (Deep Diver 134) 56 d
[1990 8m 7m 5m 6m 8d 10d 1991 8.3g² 8f 7g a6g4] workmanlike gelding: has round
action: easily best effort when second in claimer (pulled hard) at Windsor in May:
remote last in Lingfield handicap final start (July): stays 1m: below form when
blinkered: sold 1,650 gns Ascot July Sales. *T. M. Jones.*

MARION'S WAY 2 b.f. (May 13) Dunbeath (USA) 127 – Naturally Bold (Bold —
Lad (IRE) 133) [1991 8.3g] 2,200Y, 2,200 2-y-o: first foal: dam unraced: 33/1, over 16
lengths ninth of 13, very slowly away, nearest finish, to Mr Ziegfeld in maiden at
Hamilton in September: sold 660 gns Doncaster October Sales. *Miss L. A. Perratt.*

MARITIME LADY (USA) 2 b.f. (Mar 27) Polish Navy (USA) – Quixotic Lady 61 p
(USA) (Quadratic (USA)) [1991 6g⁶] $300,000Y: fourth foal: half-sister to winners in
North America by Cox's Ridge and Grey Dawn: dam, from good family, won several
graded races, including 9f Monmouth Oaks: sire (by Danzig) won from 5.5f (at 2 yrs)
to 9f, including 3 Grade 1 events: favourite, around 7 lengths sixth of 7, tracking
leaders, eased when beaten, to She's Pleased in maiden at Newmarket in October:
will stay 1m: will improve. *M. R. Stoute.*

MARJONS BOY 4 ch.c. Enchantment 115 – Nevilles Cross (USA) 67 (Nodouble 52 d
(USA)) [1990 a10g* a10g² 12f4 13.1h 12m 11.5g⁶ 10g 10m⁶ 10m² 10d 8m⁴ 8g* 1991 8g
8v 8f³ 8m² 8m⁶ 8m 8d⁶ 8g 8m³ 10.1f4 9m a10g⁶ a10g] big, angular colt: moderate
mover: poor handicapper: below form last 4 starts: effective at 1m to 1¼m: best
efforts on a sound surface: often blinkered or visored: good mount for claimer:
trained until after eleventh start by M. Bell: inconsistent. *C. D. Broad.*

MARJORIE WOOD (IRE) 3 ch.f. Dreams To Reality (USA) 113 – Beechwood 33
(USA) (Blushing Groom (FR) 131) [1990 5m⁴ 5g 6d 8m 7d 1991 8s 12.2g 12f⁶ 13m
15g⁵ 15s 12g 13.8f4] small, sparely-made filly: has round action: probably
stays 15f: acts on firm going: sometimes on toes. *S. G. Norton.*

MARJU (IRE) 3 br.c. Last Tycoon 131 – Flame of Tara 124 (Artaius (USA) 127
129) [1990 7m* 1991 8m* 8g 12f² 8g* 10d⁶ 10m]

Rest failed to cure Marju's stifle problem which first affected his
performance in the General Accident Two Thousand Guineas, and after
consecutive disappointing runs in the Coral-Eclipse and the Dubai Champion
Stakes he was retired. A pity, for at his best he would have gone close in all
three. The very easy winner of a York minor event on his only appearance as a
two-year-old, Marju came into the season with a sky-high reputation plus
something else to live up to in that he was a half-brother to Salsabil. Despite
none-too-encouraging reports from the gallops he made the best possible
start by winning what's been the most significant Guineas trial in recent
years, the Charles Heidsieck Champagne Craven Stakes at Newmarket. His
length-and-a-half and head defeat of Desert Sun and Hokusai was sufficiently
impressive to put him back at the head of the Guineas market, and on the day

Charles Heidsieck Champagne Craven Stakes, Newmarket—
Marju lives up to his reputation; it is close for second
between the stable-companions Desert Sun and Hokusai (almost hidden)

he started the 6/4 favourite. For once the Craven proved no help in finding the classic winner. Marju himself was never going well, and failed to respond when asked for his effort after being switched outside approaching the last quarter of a mile, dropping right out in fact. He was soon reported lame, as a result of an injury to his near-hind stifle that could have been inflicted when he was leaving the stalls.

Marju's future on the track was in doubt at this point but fortunately it was possible to run him in the Ever Ready Derby and the St James's Palace Stakes. Fortunate because he was able to take the chance to show himself a high-class, versatile colt. Marju got the trip very well at Epsom, something by no means assured beforehand with Last Tycoon as his sire, and came a clear second to Generous. The first half of the race went none too smoothly for him. He was bumped by Corrupt in the early jostling for position, then became slightly boxed in in seventh or eighth place down the hill. But driven along as they straightened up, he obtained a clear passage up the rail and began to run on strongly from over two furlongs out without ever threatening to get to Generous who beat him five lengths; there was a further seven back to third-placed Star of Gdansk. Two weeks later Marju proved versatile enough to win a St James's Palace Stakes which developed into a three-furlong sprint. The turnout for the race, below standard, consisted of two from the Guineas field (Marju and Hokusai), two from its French equivalent (the second Acteur Francais and third Sapieha), the Middle Park Stakes third Majlood making his seasonal reappearance, the Thirsk Classic Trial winner Soleil Dancer and, last but by no means least, though lacking in experience and stepped up in class, the unbeaten Second Set. Marju, his Guineas running forgiven in the light of Epsom, started a 7/4 favourite, ahead of Acteur Francais (3/1) and Second Set (4/1). Marju's acceleration impressed enormously. He was asked to produce it on the outside round the home turn after the bunched field had been taken along by Hokusai, Marju tucked away at the back with Soleil Dancer. Marju

St James's Palace Stakes, Ascot—Marju is pushed out to win from Second Set;
Hokusai finished third again, Acteur Francais fourth

seemed to take no time at all to get to the front, but he was soon being driven along, apparently idling, and through the final half furlong he was made to work really hard to keep the rallying Second Set at bay by a head. There Marju's racing career effectively came to an end. For the record, he started joint-second favourite with In The Groove for the Eclipse and with Ristna for the Champion Stakes; on both occasions he was eased right up when unable to make any impression, patently having lost his action at Newmarket. He is now standing at the Derrinstown Stud in Ireland, at the reasonable fee of IR 7,000 guineas.

Marju (IRE) (br.c. 1988)	Last Tycoon (b 1983)	Try My Best (b 1975)	Northern Dancer Sex Appeal
		Mill Princess (b 1977)	Mill Reef Irish Lass II
	Flame of Tara (b 1980)	Artaius (b 1974)	Round Table Stylish Pattern
		Welsh Flame (b 1973)	Welsh Pageant Electric Flash

There are some notably versatile animals on both sides of Marju's pedigree. Last Tycoon, of course, was top class at five furlongs and a mile (he inspired the advertising slogan 'the fastest horse in Europe and the most versatile in the world' when he was retired). Both Salsabil and her dam Flame of Tara won at six furlongs—as two-year-olds—to a mile and a half. Flame of Tara ran for three seasons. She was at her best as a three-year-old when she won four races, including the Coronation Stakes, and was involved in a very close finish with Cormorant Wood and the disqualified Tolomeo in the Dubai Champion Stakes. All her foals of racing age have reached the track; to the latest, Rajai, falls the task of adding to the achievements of his brother Marju, Salsabil (by Sadler's Wells) and the 1989 Ribblesdale Stakes third Nearctic Flame (also by Sadler's Wells). Rajai failed by the narrowest of margins to get off the mark first time of asking in a mile maiden at Nottingham in the autumn. Flame of Tara foaled a filly by Caerleon in 1990 and a colt by Sadler's Wells in 1991, so hasn't been barren once yet. Reportedly she tends to foal early, something which may have been inherited by Salsabil whose first foal nearly caught connections out by arriving on January 1st. The second dam Welsh Flame, a miler out of a half-sister to the Derby winner Parthia, is also the second dam of the Doncaster Cup and Jockey Club Cup winners Kneller and Great Marquess. *J. L. Dunlop.*

512

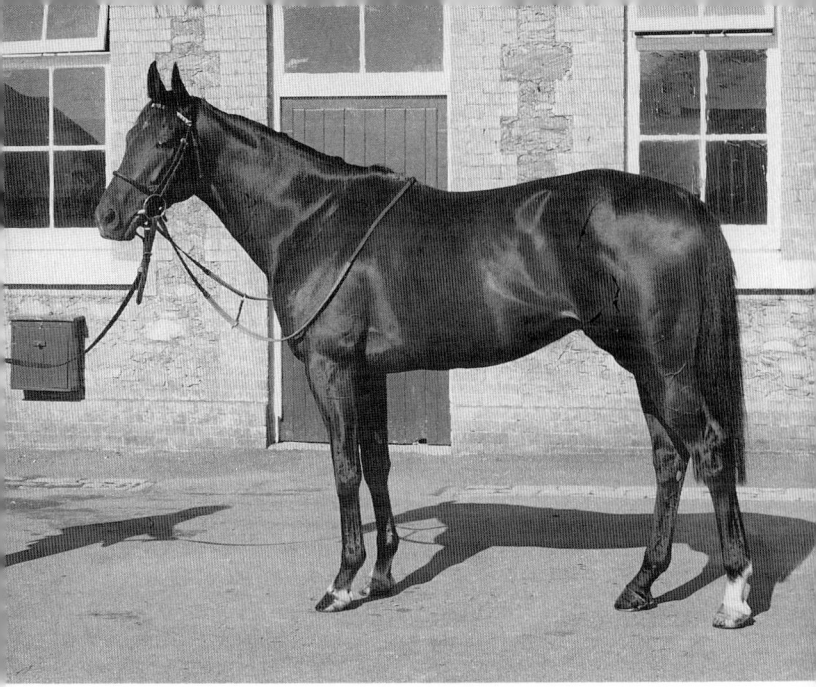

Hamdan Al-Maktoum's "Marju"

MARKED CARD 3 b.g. Busted 134 – Winter Queen 60 (Welsh Pageant 132)   **78**
[1990 NR 1991 12m⁵ 15.3m² 12g² 12.1g² 12f² 12g⁶] 28,000Y: angular, unfurnished
gelding: fourth living foal: brother to poor 1990 3-y-o Winterhalter and half-brother
to very useful 1m and 1¼m winner Main Objective (by Main Reef): dam won over 13f
at 4 yrs in Ireland: modest maiden: second at Wolverhampton, Brighton, Chepstow
and Thirsk: will prove best at up to 1½m: visored (took good hold, below form) final
start: joined O. Sherwood: game. *A. C. Stewart.*

MARKET TRADER 2 ch.f. (Mar 1) Viking (USA) – Magelka 77 (Relkino 131)   —
[1991 a6g] 680F: fifth foal: half-sister to 1m winner Maid of Essex and a
winner in Denmark (both by Bustino): dam, half-sister to very smart Easter Sun,
best effort at 1m: 33/1 and backward, always behind in 16-runner seller at Southwell
in July. *M. F. Barraclough.*

MARK OF SILVER (IRE) 2 b.c. (Apr 30) On Your Mark 125 – Silver Shoals   **52**
(USA) 98 (Mill Reef (USA) 141) [1991 5d 5g³ 5g 5g⁴ 5m 5m⁶ 5g 6m⁶ 5g³] IR 2,500Y:
lengthy colt: poor walker: moderate mover: half-brother to a winner in Malaysia:
dam won over 5f and 6f at 2 yrs: plating-class maiden: usually makes running: stays
6f: ran creditably in blinkers then visor last 2 outings: sold 1,300 gns Doncaster
October Sales. *R. Hollinshead.*

MA'R LARKIN 2 b.f. (Mar 1) Cragador 110 – Sancilia (Dalsaan 125) [1991 5m²   **50**
5m⁶ 6g⁶] 3,000Y: neat filly: first foal: dam sprint maiden: plating-class maiden:
strong-finishing second of 10 at Warwick in May: subsequently last at York and
Edinburgh (July): should stay 6f. *J. Berry.*

MARLEE LOCH 3 b.f. Rolfe (USA) 77 – Cadenette 76 (Brigadier Gerard 144)   —
[1990 5m⁶ 1991 8m⁴ 10.5d] leggy filly: no form, in seller final start. *G. M. Moore.*

513

MARLINGFORD 4 ch.g. Be My Guest (USA) 126 – Inchmarlo (USA) (Nashua) **50**
[1990 13.6m 1991 14.6s 12f² 16.2f⁵ 15.8f 16.5m 22.2m 16.2f⁶ 11.9g² 12.3f 13.1m]
good-topped gelding: plating-class handicapper: stays well: acts on firm ground:
below form when sweating once: none too consistent: winning hurdler. *Mrs J.
Jordan.*

MARLING (IRE) 2 b.f. (Mar 17) Lomond (USA) 128 – Marwell 133 (Habi- **109** p
tat 134) [1991 5g* 5m* 5g* 6m*]
  Comparisons are odious, they say, but in racing they're also as inevitable
as night follows day, particularly when the two-year-old careers of a broodmare and her daughter mirror each other in the way that those of Marwell and
Marling did. Back in 1980 Marwell signed off for the season unbeaten with a
decisive victory in the Cheveley Park Stakes, a race which at the time was
Britain's only Group 1 race for two-year-old fillies. Eleven years on her fifth
foal and first daughter Marling did the same, and the similarities don't end
there. Like her dam at the same stage of her career Marling, a good-looking
filly, has a sharp turn of acceleration which marks her as out of the ordinary,
though her form is nowhere near so good as that her dam showed at two.
Marwell was put away for the winter with a doubt in the minds of many as to
whether she'd stay well enough for the One Thousand Guineas. Similar
doubts are now being voiced about Marling, who's bound to be trained with
the Guineas as her first major objective. One person who put his cards on
the table early was Ladbrokes' representitive Mike Dillon. After Marling's
victory in the Cheveley Park, Dillon quoted her at 25/1 for the Guineas,
arguing 'I don't think she'll get the mile. Her half-brother Caerwent failed to
stay in Nashwan's Guineas and went back to sprinting, and the dam line leads
me to believe she'll always be a speed filly'. Only time will tell, but it wasn't at
all surprising that backers were keen to take up the offer. Even allowing for
the doubts about her stamina, 25/1 seemed big odds for one with Marling's
credentials, especially in a year in which fillies with genuine classic potential
were thin on the ground.
  Marling was in action unusually early for a Wragg-trained juvenile. It was
May 3rd on a cold afternoon at Newmarket where she justified hefty support
in a maiden event, despite seeming green showing a turn of foot. She used
that asset to good effect again in the Charles Heidsieck National Stakes at
Sandown later in the month to beat the newcomer Miss Bluebird by a neck,
the pair twelve lengths clear in a useful time, and on lining up for the Queen
Mary Stakes at Royal Ascot she was the clear form choice and went off the
11/4 favourite. The Queen Mary looked a strong contest. Thirteen of the
fourteen runners had won eighteen races between them. Eight, including the
highly-regarded Central City, were unbeaten, and Marling didn't have things
all her own way. Held up travelling well within herself, she was switched
slightly left to challenge passing halfway and looked sure to win when joining
the front-running Central City entering the final furlong. Her followers
had an anxious moment or two as she flashed her tail soon after, but once
Carter put his whip down Marling quickened and ran on very strongly up the
hill to beat the fast-finishing Culture Vulture by a length with Central City a

*Queen Mary Stakes, Ascot—Marwell's daughter Marling shows a sharp turn of foot
against Culture Vulture (left) and Central City*

Tattersalls Cheveley Park Stakes, Newmarket — Marling remains unbeaten; Absurde just beats Basma (rails) for second place, Twafeaj is fourth

neck away in third. In post-race interviews Marling's trainer expressed the opinion that she needed a break prior to contesting races like the Heinz '57' Phoenix Stakes and possibly the Moyglare Stud Stakes. In the event both contests went by without her. A combination of a cough and sore shins kept Marling inactive for most of the summer, and the next and final chance to see her in action came in the Tattersalls Cheveley Park Stakes at Newmarket in October.

The standard of performance required to win the Cheveley Park has fallen in the last few years and the latest renewal confirmed the trend. The nine who faced the starter had shown a range of ability. Despite her lengthy lay-off Marling was the 15/8 favourite ahead of the unbeaten French filly Absurde, a six-length winner of a listed race at Evry on her latest start, with the Moyglare Stud Stakes winner Twafeaj and the progressive Basma both on 5/1; Affair of State, who'd shown vastly improved form to win the richly-endowed Tattersalls Breeders Stakes at the Curragh, was a 12/1 chance with the remainder, including three maidens, ranging from 20/1 to 100/1. With the free-running Basma setting a strong gallop, Marling was settled travelling with her usual fluency just off the pace. She led in the Dip and when shaken up quickened to go two lengths clear, but she seemed to decide she'd done enough soon after and had to be kept up to her work nearly all the way to the line to hold off Absurde by a length and a half with Basma a head away in third. Absurde was turned out again in November for the Criterium de Maisons-Laffitte. She didn't boost the Cheveley Park form in finishing a well-beaten third behind Cardoun and Tertian. On reflection, there's a possibility that Marling was asked to go about her business a little earlier than was ideal in the Cheveley Park. She certainly appeared to be idling once she got clear of her rivals and we'd expect her to show further improvement ridden a shade less aggressively.

Now back to the burning question of whether Marling will stay a mile. Marwell didn't quite last home in the Guineas, narrowly holding on to fourth place about a length behind Fairy Footsteps, prior to proving herself exceptional back at sprint distances with wins in the King's Stand Stakes, the July Cup and the Prix de l'Abbaye. However, we think that, all things considered, Marling has good prospects of staying seven furlongs and a better-than-even chance of staying a mile. Marwell's sire Habitat was an influence for speed with the average distance of races won by his stock aged three and upwards being fractionally less than a mile. Marling's sire, the 1983 Two Thousand Guineas winner Lomond, was bred to stay at least a mile and a quarter. The average winning distance of his three-year-olds and upwards is a mile and a quarter. They include good stayers such as Kneller and Dark

Lomond (both out of staying mares), and in addition to Marling in the latest season he was also represented by the Solario Stakes winner Chicmond and the smart French filly Once In My Life. Marwell has produced a couple of other winners. Her Rainbow Quest colt Selaah is capable of useful form at up to a mile, and her Caerleon colt Caerwent saw that trip out well enough to finish second in the Irish Two Thousand Guineas and third, running on, in the St James's Palace Stakes. Marwell has so far done well mated with stallions from the Northern Dancer line, so it'll be interesting to see how her 1992 two-year-old colt by Sadler's Wells turns out. The history of Marwell's family has been well chronicled in previous editions of *Racehorses*. Her unbeaten dam Lady Seymour foaled the Mill Reef Stakes winner Lord Seymour to a previous covering by Habitat and subsequent to Marwell she produced the very useful middle-distance colt Lord Grundy. Lady Seymour's dam My Game is a half-sister to the Eclipse winner Arctic Explorer, and figures not only as the third dam of the Oaks winner Unite but also of three recent Cecil-trained Royal Ascot winners, namely Shavian, Be My Chief and the Gold Cup winner Paean.

		Northern Dancer (b 1961)	Nearctic
			Natalma
	Lomond (USA) (b 1980)	My Charmer (b 1969)	Poker
Marling (IRE) (b.f. Mar 17, 1989)			Fair Charmer
		Habitat (b 1966)	Sir Gaylord
			Little Hut
	Marwell (b 1978)	Lady Seymour (b 1972)	Tudor Melody
			My Game

A lengthy filly, Marling is a good walker and shows a quick action in her faster paces. Her dam had an unusually placid temperament for a filly. Marling doesn't seem quite so relaxed, but we've seen nothing to suggest she'll ever beat herself by boiling over. At the time of writing, she's on offer at around 16/1 for the Guineas and along with Cecil's pair Musicale and Midnight Air she looks a live contender for that race. If events show she doesn't stay a mile there'll doubtless be plenty of opportunities for her back at shorter distances. She's done all her racing so far on a sound surface. *G. Wragg.*

MAROWINS 2 ch.c. (Apr 7) Sweet Monday 122 – Top Cover (High Top 131) [1991 **46** 5f⁶ 6m⁴ a7g³ a7g⁴ 7m 8m 8.1g 10.5d] 1,700F, 2,750 (privately) Y: robust colt: has a quick action: first foal: dam ran twice at 2 yrs: modest plater: probably stays 1m: visored last 4 starts. *M. O'Neill.*

MARSH HARRIER (USA) 10 b.g. Raise A Cup (USA) – Belle de Jour (USA) — 74 (Speak John) [1990 a10g a13g 1991 a12g] big, strong, rangy gelding: no form since 8 yrs: stays 1¼m: used to be suited by a sound surface: has run creditably when blinkered and sweating: best with strong handling: has worn a tongue strap. *A. Moore.*

MARSH'S LAW 4 br.g. Kala Shikari 125 – My Music 68 (Sole Mio (USA)) [1990 — 6m a8g⁵ a7g a11g⁵ 7m 10.2s⁵ 10g³ 8d² 1991 a7g⁶] sturdy gelding: plater: not seen out after January: better at 1¼m than shorter: acts on good to firm going and soft: often bandaged: sold 3,100 gns Doncaster January Sales. *O. Brennan.*

MARSH WARBLER 3 b.g. Wattlefield 117 – Be Lyrical 95 (Song 132) [1990 7m — 7m 1991 8g 7g] lengthy, good-bodied gelding: good walker: behind in maidens then handicap: sold to join R. Frost 1,550 gns Ascot June Sales. *G. A. Pritchard-Gordon.*

MARTANDA LIGHT 2 gr.c. (Mar 10) Nishapour (FR) 125 – Nice Point **70** (Sharpen Up 127) [1991 7g² 7m⁴ 6f* 6g 6g⁴ 7m 6m⁵] 54,000Y: leggy colt: moderate mover: third foal: half-brother to fair 1988 2-y-o 5f and 6f winner Northern Alert (by Northern Tempest), later successful in Italy: dam never ran: modest form: favourite, won maiden at Newcastle in July running on well: should prove better at 7f than shorter: sometimes slowly away: saddle slipped sixth start: has run well in blinkers (though not successful): sold 14,000 gns Newmarket Autumn Sales to go to Italy. *B. Hanbury.*

MARTESSA (GER) 3 b.f. Solarstern (FR) – Manege (GER) (Neckar (GER)) **120** [1990 8g* 7g* 8g* 1991 8g² 11s* 11v⁴ 10.5g³ 12g* 9d*] half-sister to several winners in Germany, 2 placed in listed races: dam fairly useful 5f (at 2 yrs) and 11f winner in Germany: unbeaten at 2 yrs, including in 2 listed races: second to Kazoo in Arag-Preis Deutsches 1000 Guineas at Dusseldorf: successful at 3 yrs in Preis der Diana at Mulheim, Group 3 contest at Hanover and Ciga Prix de l'Opera (led well inside final 1f to beat Colour Chart ¾ length, 66/1) at Longchamp: effective at 9f and 1½m: reportedly sold for about £300,000 to join R. McAnally in USA. *A. Wohler, Germany.*

MARTINA 3 b.f. Tina's Pet 121 – Tin Tessa 87 (Martinmas 128) [1990 a7g a7g⁶ **59** 1991 a6g⁴ 6g³ 6m 6d² 6d 6g² 7m⁵ 7g] workmanlike filly: quite modest handicapper: best at up to 6f: seems to need an easy surface: swished tail final start. *J. Wharton.*

MARTINI EXECUTIVE 3 b.c. King of Spain 121 – Wigeon 80 (Divine Gift 127) **70** d [1990 a6g* 6f³ 7f⁵ 6m* 6m² 7.3g⁶ 1991 a6g⁴ a8g³ a8g⁴ 9m 8m 9m 9m a8g a10g] lengthy, workmanlike colt: moderate mover: modest performer: off course 4 months and well beaten after fifth start: stays 1m: possibly unsuited by very firm ground: often slowly away. *W. J. Pearce.*

MARTINI'S COURIER 4 br.g. Lucky Wednesday 124 – Be My Sweet 78 **41** § (Galivanter 131) [1990 7.5f⁵ 6v a7g 10.2m 8m⁴ 7.5f 8f⁴ 10m 1991 12f 8.1g⁵ 10g³ 8m] leggy gelding: turns off-fore in: poor performer: looked ungenuine final start: stays 1¼m: acts on firm ground: has been tried blinkered: carries head awkwardly: one to leave alone. *R. E. Barr.*

MARTINOSKY 5 b.g. Martinmas 128 – Bewitched 63 (African Sky 124) [1990 **57** 6m 6f⁴ 6f* 5f² 6m 8h⁶ 6m³ 6m³ 6g⁶ 6m 1991 6m 6g³ 6g⁶ 6g³ 5f² 7m 5.3g⁵ 5g⁶ 5.1s 6.1d³ 7g 7g] big gelding: good walker: plating-class handicapper: best at 6f or stiff 5f: acts on any going: effective with or without blinkers: none too consistent. *W. G. R. Wightman.*

MARTINSTAR 4 b.f. Norwick (USA) 120 – Martin Place (Martinmas 128) [1990 — 7m³ 8f⁵ 8f⁵ 8h 7g 1991 9.9m] leggy, sparely-made filly: poor handicapper: tailed off only run in 1991 (June): should be better suited by 1¼m than shorter: acts on firm going: ran poorly when edgy. *Mrs A. Knight.*

MARTIYA 3 b.f. Martinmas 128 – Tia Song (Acrania 110) [1990 NR 1991 12m⁶] — smallish filly: fourth foal (others by Vital Season): dam winning hurdler: 33/1, slowly away, pushed along over 5f out but some late headway in maiden at Salisbury in August. *G. B. Balding.*

MART LAGACHE (FR) 3 b.g. Crofter (USA) 124 – Match Point (Hotfoot 126) — [1990 NR 1991 a7g 8m a7g⁶ a8g a12g] 3,100 2-y-o: big, workmanlike gelding: moderate mover: half-brother to French 4-y-o Boustros (by Solicitor), successful in Provinces from 9f (at 2 yrs) to 11f: dam unraced daughter of Carrot Top, dam also of good Canadian filly Carotene: no worthwhile form, in handicap (sweating) final start: sold 1,100 gns Doncaster August Sales. *D. W. Chapman.*

MARVELOUS MOLLY 2 b.f. (Apr 5) Shardari 134 – Dunninald 93 (Mill Reef **77** ? (USA) 141) [1991 6f 7g⁴ 8.1g] leggy filly: first foal: dam 2-y-o 6f winner later stayed 8.5f, is out of sister to very smart Joking Apart: best effort keeping-on fourth of 16 to Perfect Circle in minor event at Kempton: ran poorly at Haydock later in September: should stay 1m. *I. A. Balding.*

MARWELL BIANCA 3 b.f. Carwhite 127 – Lily of France 81 (Monsanto (FR) — 121) [1990 5g 5f⁶ 5.3h⁴ 5.8h² 5m⁶ 6d a5g³ a7g² a7g 1991 6f 6g 7g 6m 9m] neat filly: plater: no form in 1991: stays 7f: sometimes bandaged behind: blinkered fourth start. *W. G. R. Wightman.*

MARY FROM DUNLOW 3 ch.f. Nicholas Bill 125 – Abrasive 53 (Absalom 128) **37** [1990 a5g² 5.1m* 5d² 5f 5.3h* 5f 5m 1991 5m⁶ 5.1m 8d³ 8g 7f 7m² 6f 8h⁵ 7m 8m] narrow, plain filly: inconsistent plater: best form as 3-y-o at 7f and 1m: acts on any going: blinkered sixth and seventh outings. *J. Berry.*

MARY MACBLAIN 2 b.f. (Feb 3) Damister (USA) 123 – Tzarina (USA) (Gallant **49** Romeo (USA)) [1991 5m⁵ 5g a6g 7g 7m 8.1s] plain, rather sparely-made filly: sixth reported foal: half-sister to 3-y-o winning hurdler Kintaro (by Glint of Gold) and fairly useful sprinter Mandub (by Topsider): dam placed 3 times in USA: poor maiden: seems suited by 7f: well below best on soft ground: has raced freely: refused to enter stalls third intended outing. *J. L. Harris.*

MARY'S SPECIAL 2 b.f. (Apr 8) Dublin Lad 116 – My-Elane (Welsh Saint 126) **37** [1991 5m 5m⁶ 5m⁵ 5.3f² 6g a7g a6g a5g] 1,500Y: small, sparely-made filly: first foal: dam, maiden, stayed 1m: runner-up in poor seller at Brighton: soundly beaten in face of stiff tasks on fibresand last 3 starts: tends to be on toes: trained first 5 outings by M. Channon. *C. N. Allen.*

MARZOCCO 3 ch.g. Formidable (USA) 125 – Top Heights (High Top 131) [1990 **54** NR 1991 7g 10g 10g 7m* 8.2g⁶ 8g 10g 6.9f⁶ 8m] 13,000Y: good-topped gelding: moderate mover: first foal: dam unraced sister to useful 2-y-o 7f winner, later middle-distance filly, Top Hope: plating-class performer: won handicap at

Brighton in June: stays 1m: acts on good to firm ground: trained first 5 outings by R. Hannon. *J. Ffitch-Heyes.*

MASAAWM 3 ch.c. Kris 135 – Tarib 108 (Habitat 134) [1990 NR 1991 6m 5f²] **64** strong, good-quartered colt: first foal: dam sprinter: running-on second of 7 in maiden at Bath in May: will stay 6f: remains in training. *H. Thomson Jones.*

MASAD (IRE) 2 b.c. (May 7) Sadler's Wells (USA) 135 – Marmolada (Sassafras **98** p (FR) 135) [1991 7d⁶ 7m²] 210,000Y: strong, good-topped colt: has plenty of scope: has fluent action: fifth foal: dam won 13 races in Italy, including Italian Oaks: still green, confirmed favourable impression of debut, showing vastly improved form, when 1½ lengths second of 5 to Shuailaan in Houghton Stakes at Newmarket, headed over 1f out then keeping on well: will improve again, particularly over further, and is certain to win races. *L. M. Cumani.*

MASAI MARA (USA) 3 ch.c. Mogambo (USA) – Forever Command (USA) **89** (Top Command (USA)) [1990 8m 1991 7m 10g⁵ 9m² 10m* 10.6g² 10g* 10m 14.1m* 13.9g 12.3f* 12m 16m⁵ 12m² 12m] tall, useful-looking colt: carries condition: fairly useful performer: won claimers at Nottingham (2, claimed out of L. Cumani's stable £19,156 on second occasion) then handicaps at Yarmouth and Ripon in the summer: ran well at Newmarket twice in 3 days twelfth and thirteenth starts: should prove ideally suited by 1¾m+: acts on firm ground: became mulish at stalls: soon off bridle, and edges right, worth a try in blinkers: will prove best with strong handling: winning hurdler. *P. C. Haslam.*

MASAKEN 3 ch.f. Doulab (USA) 115 – Amalee 57 (Troy 137) [1990 6m 7m 6g³ — 1991 7g] workmanlike filly: quite modest form in 2-y-o maidens: sweating, tailed off in seller as 3-y-o: stays 1m: sold to join T. Kersey 680 gns Newmarket July Sales. *B. Hanbury.*

MASELLA 4 ch.f. Aragon 118 – Winter Resort (Miami Springs 121) [1990 a7g⁶ 6m³ **36** 6g* 6m 7g 7d a6g 1991 7d⁴ 7m 6g⁶ 6g a6g 8f⁶ 10.8m 8m³] leggy, close-coupled filly: has round action: poor handicapper: stays 1m: acts on firm and dead ground: twice below form when blinkered: inconsistent: sold 950 gns Ascot October Sales. *J. W. Hills.*

MASHAAER (USA) 2 b.f. (Feb 24) Shadeed (USA) 135 – Princess Sucree **75** p (USA) (Roberto (USA) 131) [1991 6g³] useful-looking filly: has scope: fourth foal: half-sister to useful 1988 2-y-o 6f and 7f winner Rasheek (by Topsider) and 1986 2-y-o 7f winner Tipatina (by Northern Baby): dam, placed over 6f and 8.5f at 4 yrs in USA, is half-sister to Kentucky Derby winner Cannonade: 16/1 and bit backward, tenderly handled when staying-on over 2 lengths third of 16 to Storm Dove in maiden at Newmarket in August: sure to improve, and win races. *R. W. Armstrong.*

MASHAALLAH (USA) 3 b.c. Nijinsky (CAN) 138 – Homespun (USA) (Round **99** p Table) [1990 NR 1991 10m⁶ 10.2m* 11.9m*] $525,000Y: good-bodied colt: brother to 4 winners in North America, including graded-stakes performers Folk Art and Sportin' Life, and half-brother to several winners: dam minor winner: favourite, won 20-runner maiden at Doncaster and 8-runner £7,600 handicap (easily) at York in the summer: better at 1½m than 1¼m: looked sure to win more races. *J. H. M. Gosden.*

MASHHOR JOHN 3 b. or br.g. Mashhor Dancer (USA) – Dastina 80 **58** (Derring-Do 131) [1990 7m⁶ 7f⁶ 8.5m³ 7f² 8m⁵ 7d⁴ 8.2s 1991 10d⁴ 10m* 10g⁴] sturdy gelding: good walker: quite modest form: well-backed favourite, easily won seller (retained 13,500 gns) at Ripon in April: ran very wide turn then edged left under pressure in handicap following month: stays 1¼m: best form on top-of-the-ground: blinkered last 3 outings at 2 yrs: sold 4,000 gns Newmarket Autumn Sales. *D. Morley.*

MASKED BALL 11 b.h. Thatch (USA) 136 – Miss Mahal (Taj Dewan 128) [1990 **70** a11g³ a11g* a11g² a12g³ 10.2f* 10.2m³ 10.6f² 12f* 12m² 10.6s² 10.6s* 12f* 10m⁶ 10.6g 1991 11.9m⁴ 12f³] lengthy, good-topped horse: modest performer: off course almost 10 months and ran fairly well in July as 11-y-o: best at 1¼m to 1½m: acts on any going: wears bandages: excellent mount for apprentice: held up: a grand old servant. *P. Calver.*

MASKOONA 6 b.m. Electric 126 – Hound Song 84 (Jukebox 120) [1990 a12g a14g — 1991 a14g] of little account. *D. W. Chapman.*

MASNUN (USA) 6 gr.g. Nureyev (USA) 131 – Careless Kitten (USA) (Caro 133) **97** [1990 5g 6f⁶ 6m 6d 6m⁵ 7m 6m⁴ 6m³ 6m* 6m 6g⁶ 6s⁶ 1991 6s 7g 6g 6m 7g³ 7.6m⁵ 6m 5g³ 6f⁵ 6g* 6g 6m* 7g 6m 6m³] strong, sturdy gelding: fairly useful handicapper: twice successful at Goodwood in quite valuable events in autumn: third in Stewards' Cup there earlier: stays 7f: seems to act on any going, but particularly effective on a sound surface: often on toes: has hung right: reluctant to post once. *R. J. O'Sullivan.*

MASONS EXPRESS (IRE) 2 b.f. (Feb 6) Kings Lake (USA) 133 – Sheer Auda- —
city (Troy 137) [1991 5g 7s 6m] 5,400Y: small, sparely-made filly: first foal: dam, placed in Italy, is closely related to very useful middle-distance filly Miss Petard: no form, including in a seller: sold 850 gns Ascot November Sales. *Miss B. Sanders.*

MASSLAMA (FR) 3 ch.f. No Pass No Sale 120 – Marmana (USA) (Blushing **114**
Groom (FR) 131) [1990 8g* 8g* 1991 9.2g* 10.5d⁴ 10d] very useful form: won Prix Vanteaux at Longchamp in April by 1½ lengths from Treble: about 2½ lengths fourth of 13 to Caerlina in Prix de Diane Hermes at Chantilly, given a lot to do and staying on well: stiff task but ran respectably nonetheless in Grand Prix de Paris at Longchamp later in June: stays 10.5f well. *A. de Royer-Dupre, France.*

MASTER CHINNERY (IRE) 2 b.g. (May 17) Mister Majestic 122 – Ciarain's —
Choice (Young Emperor 133) [1991 6g⁶] IR 4,000F, IR 6,000Y: angular, unfurnished gelding: third reported foal: half-brother to a winner abroad: dam Irish 5f winner: well beaten in maiden at Goodwood in June: dead. *J. M. P. Eustace.*

MASTERCLASS (USA) 3 ch.c. The Minstrel (CAN) 135 – Monroe (USA) 102 **112**
(Sir Ivor (USA) 135) [1990 8m* 8g² 7s⁴ 1991 8g² 6.5g² 8m* 8d⁴ 9f] strong, compact, attractive French colt: good walker: won Prix Quincey at Deauville in tight finish with Safawan and Bistro Garden: in frame in listed race at Longchamp, Prix Maurice de Gheest at Deauville and Ciga Prix du Rond-Point at Longchamp: stays 1m: possibly unsuited by soft ground: very useful: sent to USA, and finished unplaced in Hollywood Derby in November. *A. Fabre, France.*

MASTER COPY (IRE) 2 b.c. (Apr 25) Bluebird (USA) 125 – Music of The —
Night (Blushing Groom (FR) 131) [1991 7g 7.5f⁶] IR 9,500Y: compact colt: first foal: dam unraced half-sister to Champion Stakes runner-up Prima Voce: always behind in maiden at Doncaster and minor event (blinkered) at Beverley in mid-summer. *C. B. B. Booth.*

MASTER DANCER 4 b.g. Mashhor Dancer (USA) – Silent Dancer 76 (Quiet —
Fling (USA) 124) [1990 12d 14f 15.8d 1991 18s⁶] leggy gelding: has a round action: no form since quite modest at 2 yrs: winning hurdler in January: sold 6,000 gns Doncaster Spring Sales. *Miss L. C. Siddall.*

MASTER EUROLINK 2 b.c. (Apr 23) Dominion 123 – Late Evening (USA) **67**
(Riverman (USA) 131) [1991 5g⁵ 6g⁵ 5g³] 26,000Y: workmanlike colt: has a round action: third foal: half-brother to 3-y-o 7f (at 2 yrs) and 1m winner Joie de Soir (by Caerleon) and a winner in Italy: dam French maiden: quite modest form in maidens: ran moderately at Folkestone second start: should stay 6f +. *J. Berry.*

MASTER FOODBROKER (IRE) 3 br.g. Simply Great (FR) 122 – Silver **84**
Mantle 70 (Bustino 136) [1990 NR 1991 12g* 12m⁴ 14s] 11,000Y: workmanlike gelding: fourth foal: closely related to lightly-raced Irish filly Silver Cloak (by Wassl) and minor French 1½m winner Pointe d'Argentee (by Pas de Seul): dam staying daughter of Oaks third Moonlight Night, herself a half-sister to Main Reef: won maiden at Kempton in July: never placed to challenge in handicap final start: stays 1½m: may be capable of better: winning hurdler. *D. R. C. Elsworth.*

MASTER GLEN 3 ch.g. Rabdan 129 – Rage Glen 67 (Grey Mirage 128) [1990 6m **63**
8g 8d 1991 8s 10d* 10m 10g 10g⁶ 10.9g* 10g* 8.9g] smallish gelding: moderate mover: quite modest performer: won seller (bought in 8,000 gns) at Nottingham in April and 2 handicaps in as many days at Ayr (awarded race second occasion) in July: stays 1¼m: unsuited by top-of-the-ground: winning hurdler. *G. R. Oldroyd.*

MASTER HYDE (USA) 2 gr.c. (Mar 9) Trempolino (USA) 135 – Sandspur **62**
(USA) (Al Hattab (USA)) [1991 6s⁶ 7.1s⁶ 6m⁶ 6g⁵] leggy, workmanlike colt: half-brother to several winners in North America, 2 in minor stakes: dam unraced: quite modest maiden: below form last 2 starts: best effort (when sweating) at 7f on soft ground: should stay further. *P. Mitchell.*

MASTER LEASE (USA) 3 ch.c. Master Willie 129 – Travertine (Habitat 134) **79**
[1990 NR 1991 7f* 10.1s² 10m 10.1m⁵] angular, unfurnished colt: ninth reported foal: half-brother to 3 minor winners in USA and closely related to 1½m winner It's High Time (by High Line): dam Irish 3-y-o 6f winner: won maiden at Folkestone in April: much better efforts when second in median auction contest at Windsor and fifth (set plenty to do, staying on despite carrying head high) in £7,200 handicap at Epsom: stays 1¼m: not seen out after June. *J. Akehurst.*

MASTER LINE 10 ch.h. High Line 125 – Fair Winter 111 (Set Fair 129) [1990 **53** d
12.2m⁶ 11.7g* 11.7m⁵ 12g⁶ 12g a12g⁴ 12g⁶ 1991 10.8m⁵ 12g² a12g a14g] small,

sparely-made horse: has a sharp action: plating-class handicapper nowadays: tailed off last 2 starts after returning from 5½-month lay-off: stays 13f: probably not at best on extremes of going: has been bandaged. *H. Candy.*

MASTER OF PASSION 2 b.c. (Feb 9) Primo Dominie 121 – Crime of Passion **101** 115 (Dragonara Palace (USA) 115) [1991 5g* 5m 6m* 6m³] 45,000Y: lengthy, rather angular colt: has a quick action: fourth foal: half-brother to fair 1988 2-y-o 5f winner Cardinal Sin (by Pharly) and a winner in Belgium: dam smart sprinting 2-y-o didn't train on: useful performer: favourite, won maiden at Leicester in May and 3-runner minor event at Lingfield in July: improved form when third of 8, staying on well, to Misterioso in Rockingham Stakes at York 7 weeks later: better at 6f than 5f. *J. M. P. Eustace.*

MASTER OFTHE HOUSE 5 b.g. Kind of Hush 118 – Miss Racine (Dom **50** Racine (FR) 121) [1990 6m⁶ 8f 5g 6m 7g³ 8m⁴ 7g³ 7m² 7f² 7m³ 6m⁶ a7g³ 7m³ 7d 7d⁴ 1991 7d 9f²] sturdy gelding: poor mover: plating-class handicapper: seems to stay 9f: acts on any going: has been tried in blinkers and visor: winning hurdler. *M. D. Hammond.*

MASTER OF THE HUNT (IRE) 2 b.c. (Mar 30) Huntingdale 132 – Lady **40** Juliet (USA) (Gallant Man) [1991 6d 6m 5m 5.2f⁶ 5f 6g 10m 8g a8g⁶] IR 6,800F: leggy colt: poor mover: half-brother to several winners abroad, including stakes winner Lord de L'Orne (by Val de L'Orne): dam, 6f winner, is sister to top-class Gallant Romeo: poor plater: ran creditably in maidens at Bath (for inexperienced apprentice) and Lingfield (equitrack) last 2 starts: stays 1m: twice blinkered: has been bandaged behind. *R. A. Bennett.*

MASTER OF TROY 3 b.g. Trojan Fen 118 – Gohar (USA) (Barachois (CAN)) **74** [1990 8.2d 1991 11g 10.1g⁵] close-coupled gelding: modest form: should stay 1½m: joined N. Twiston-Davies. *B. Hanbury.*

MASTER PIERRE 4 b. or br.g. Gabitat 119 – Emerglen (Furry Glen 121) [1990 — 6m 7g⁶ 7m⁵ 8.3m 8m⁵ 8f⁴ 8m⁵ 10g 8m³ 8g a10g⁶ a12g³ a12g³ 1991 10f 12f] lengthy, good-topped gelding: has a round action: poor maiden: well beaten in handicaps in spring of 1991: stays 1½m: acts on firm ground: sometimes sweats: sold to join A. Batey's stable 2,600 gns Ascot Summer Sales. *L. J. Holt.*

MASTER PLAN (FR) 5 b.g. Carwhite 127 – Manene (Francia (FR) 123) — [1990 a8g⁵ a12g 10.2f⁶ 10.6f 10m 8h⁴ 9g 9s 8g⁴ 10.6s 12g⁴ 12.3g⁵ 8.5g⁵ 9g* 8m⁵ 10f⁶ 8m* 8.2m 10.6g 8m⁶ 8g² 8m 1991 10.2s 8g 8.5f⁶ 8.3s 8f 10.5g] compact gelding: moderate mover: quite modest handicapper on his day at 4 yrs: little since, tailed off final start: stays 1¼m: probably acts on any going. *J. S. Wilson.*

MASTER PLANNER 2 b.g. (Apr 14) Night Shift (USA) – Shaky Puddin **81** (Ragstone 128) [1991 6g* 6d³ 6g 6m² 6f² 6m 5g⁵] leggy, close-coupled, angular gelding: seventh foal: half-brother to modest 1987 2-y-o plater Hidden Flame (by Longleat): dam poor maiden: fair performer: won maiden at Brighton in June: creditable fifth of 7, never able to challenge, to Sahara Star in Philip Cornes Molecomb Stakes at Goodwood in August: will stay 7f: not easiest of rides. *C. A. Cyzer.*

MASTER POKEY 7 br.g. Uncle Pokey 116 – September Fire (Firestreak 125) **85** [1990 6m 6m* 6m 6g* 6m* 5.6g 6d⁵ 6g 1991 5d 6s 6d 7m 6m⁴ 7g⁶ 6m⁵ 6d² 6g 7g 5.6m 6m] sturdy, good-quartered gelding: carries plenty of condition: fair handicapper: ideally suited by 6f: probably not at his best on very soft going, acts on any other: often heavily bandaged in front: tends to give trouble at stalls nowadays. *M. W. Easterby.*

MASTER REACH 2 br.c. (Jun 3) Reach 122 – Lady Donaro 76 (Ardoon 124) **39** [1991 7f 7.9m] tall, workmanlike colt: third foal: half-brother to a winner in Belgium and 1988 2-y-o 5f winner Night Lady (both by Night Shift): dam 1m winner: well beaten in claimer at Salisbury and 7-runner maiden (slowly away, soon behind, not knocked about) at York in autumn: will stay 1m. *R. Hannon.*

MASTER SHIKARI 2 b.g. (Feb 16) Kala Shikari 125 – La Bambola 95 (Be **44** Friendly 130) [1991 5v³ 5m 7d a7g] lengthy gelding: dam won from 7f to 14.7f: poor maiden: probably best effort (very much on toes) on third start: should stay at least 1m: not seen out after July. *S. Dow.*

MASTER TYKE 6 gr.g. Flying Tyke 90 – Habatashie 62 (Habat 127) [1990 a6g⁴ — a8g⁵ a8g⁵ a7g* a7g² 10f a6g 7.6m 7.6m a8g a10g a8g 1991 a8g a10g 10v] sturdy gelding: poor mover: poor form when winning claimer at Lingfield in March, 1990: no form since next outing: stays 1m: acts on good to firm and dead going: effective with or without blinkers. *R. P. C. Hoad.*

MATA CARA 3 b. or br.f. Storm Bird (CAN) 134 – Fatah Flare (USA) 121 (Alydar **98**
(USA)) [1990 6m⁴ 6m⁴ 1991 7m 7m 7m* 8m³ 7g* 7.1g* 7d] compact, deep-girthed
filly: progressive efforts in the summer to win handicaps at Wolverhampton and
Doncaster then 4-runner minor event (ran on well to beat Pipsqueak a length) at
Chepstow: never dangerous in £80,000 Ascot handicap in September: best form at
7f: acts on good to firm ground. *L. M. Cumani.*

MATADOR (USA) 4 ch.c. Nureyev (USA) 131 – Allicance (USA) 113 (Alleged **94**
(USA) 138) [1990 11.7f² 12m* 14f 11.7m²? 12g³¹³ 3g* 1991 16g⁴ 16g⁵ 14g² 16.2m³
12s] leggy colt: has a long stride: fairly useful handicapper: in good heart in summer,
making most when third to Straldi in £10,260 event at Ascot: first run for over 3
months, never dangerous in £70,000 event at Ascot in September: effective at 1¾m
to 2m, and will stay further: acts on good to firm ground: genuine. *R. Charlton.*

MATAHIF (IRE) 3 b. or br.c. Wassl 125 – Reves Celestes (USA) 82 (Lyphard **—**
(USA) 132) [1990 6d² 7m² 8.2m² 8d² 7m³ 10s* 10g* 1991 12g⁵ 12g 16d 14g]
leggy, sparely-made colt: easy mover: progressive 2-y-o, winning listed race at
Newmarket final start: well beaten in listed race and handicaps in 1991: should stay
1½m+: acts on good to firm ground and soft: bandaged final start: sold 4,600 gns
Newmarket Autumn Sales. *R. W. Armstrong.*

MATAMATA 3 br.g. Jalmood (USA) 126 – Macarte (FR) (Gift Card (FR) 124) **66**
[1990 6m 6m 6g 8f³ 1991 10.2m 11.7g 12g⁴ 10g⁶] round-barrelled gelding: quite
modest maiden: good sixth of 19 in handicap at Brighton in July, never nearer:
should be suited by return to 1½m: acts on firm going: looked reluctant to race at
halfway on reappearance: not one to trust implicitly. *J. L. Dunlop.*

MATCHING GREEN 2 b.f. (Jan 25) Green Ruby (USA) 104 – Accuracy 83 **47** p
(Gunner B 126) [1991 7g⁶ 7d] first foal: dam suited by a test of stamina: backward
still, caught eye staying on under considerate handling into mid-division in 22-
runner maiden at Doncaster in November: sure to do better. *G. B. Balding.*

MATHAAYL (USA) 2 br.f. (Apr 18) Shadeed (USA) 135 – Manal (FR) 74 **79** p
(Luthier 126) [1991 6g² 7m⁵] big, well-made filly: has plenty of scope: good walker:
sixth foal: half-sister to Princess Margaret winner Muhbubh (by Blushing Groom),
sprint winner Mathkurh (by Riverman) and 1986 2-y-o 7f winner Mubdi (by Star de
Naskra): dam thrice-raced sister to French Derby second Twig Moss: heavily-
backed favourite, ½-length second of 5 to Misterioso in Blue Seal Stakes at Ascot in
September, looking likely winner until weakening closing stages: well held in
6-runner Rockfel Stakes at Newmarket 3 weeks later, losing her action when asked
to quicken: should stay 1m: looks capable of better. *H. Thomson Jones.*

MATHAL (USA) 2 b.c. (Apr 8) Storm Bird (CAN) 134 – Bare Essence (USA) **59** p
(Youth (USA) 135) [1991 8d] $450,000Y: lengthy colt: third foal: half-brother to a
minor winner by Clever Trick: dam, minor winner at up to 11f, is half-sister to dams
of Zilzal and Polish Precedent: 10/1 from 4/1 and burly, held up and never placed to
challenge or knocked about in 14-runner minor event at Newmarket in November:
moved poorly down: may well stay 1¼m: will improve. *M. R. Stoute.*

MATHKOOR 3 ch.c. Be My Guest (USA) 126 – Smarten Up 119 (Sharpen Up **73**
127) [1990 NR 1991 7g⁴ 7f⁴ 8g² 9s³ 11.9m³ 10m³ 8m² 8f 8.1g] 200,000Y: rather leggy
colt: half-brother to top-class 5f to 7f winner Cadeaux Genereux (by Young
Generation) and 4 other winners, including useful 1m and 9f winner Military
Fashion (by Mill Reef): dam sprinting half-sister to smart fillies Walk By and Solar:
modest maiden: ran poorly last 2 starts: seems suited by 1m: possibly doesn't act on
soft ground: visored final start, blinkered previous 3: sold 10,500 gns Newmarket
Autumn Sales. *A. A. Scott.*

MATHKURH (USA) 3 b.f. Riverman (USA) 131 – Manal (FR) 74 (Luthier 126) **97**
[1990 5d* 1991 6g* 6s⁶ 5d² 5m⁵] neat, quite attractive filly: won 4-runner minor
event at Lingfield in July: best efforts in minor event at Haydock and listed race
(looking very well and on toes) won by On Tiptoes at Newmarket last 2 starts:
effective at 5f and 6f: acts on good to firm and dead going: visits Caerleon. *H.
Thomson Jones.*

MATOMANI 4 b.f. Beldale Flutter (USA) 130 – Bundu (FR) 88 (Habitat 134) **50**
[1990 8g 8g⁴ 8m⁵ 10.6s 9m 1991 a10g⁵ a10g a10g² 10.8g a12g⁶] leggy filly: quite
modest maiden at best: ran poorly last 2 starts, visored first one: stays 1¼m: seems
unsuited by soft ground. *D. J. G. Murray-Smith.*

MATTER OF LAW 4 b.g. Blakeney 126 – Opera Star (FR) 70 (Appiani II 128) **44**
[1990 a12g⁵ 12f 15.3m 16.2d 15.3g 10g 12f³ 14f² 13.8m² 14m³ 15.3f⁴ 1991 a14g 14m³
14g 14.1g⁴] stocky gelding: has a rather round action: turns fore-feet in:

plating-class handicapper: one-paced stayer, well worth another try at 2m + : best efforts on top-of-the-ground: below form when blinkered once. *C. A. Cyzer.*

MATTS BOY 3 b.g. Runnett 125 – Thatchville 65 (Thatch (USA) 136) [1990 6m   **77**
1991 7v* 7m 7g⁵ 8m* 8.9m 8f] good-topped, attractive gelding: reportedly fractured hind joint after debut: modest form: won maiden at Newcastle in April and moderately-run handicap at Pontefract in May: well behind in handicap final start: better at 1m on shorter: acts on good to firm ground and heavy: bandaged off-fore third start: sold 5,000 gns Doncaster November Sales. *Miss S. E. Hall.*

MATUSADONA 4 b.f. Tumble Wind (USA) – Ceiling (Thatch (USA) 136) [1990   **—**
6g 7d a8g⁶ a8g⁵ 1991 14.6g 11.8g] workmanlike filly: bought for 3,000 gns Doncaster March Sales: little worthwhile form, tailed off in autumn: winning hurdler. *J. L. Harris.*

MAYAASA (FR) 3 b.f. Green Desert (USA) 127 – Fitnah 125 (Kris 135) [1990   **82**
5m* 6g 1991 6m³ 6m³ 6f 6g] strong-quartered, compact filly: chipped near-fore knee at 2 yrs: fair handicapper: ridden by 7-lb claimer, third at Newmarket and York (4 days later) in July: below form following month: worth a try over further: bandaged. *A. A. Scott.*

MAY BE BOLD 4 b.f. Never So Bold 135 – Plum Run (USA) 87 (Run The Gantlet   **—**
(USA)) [1990 8m⁶ 8m 7d⁴ 8m 10g 1991 a12g 12d 10f 12f a11g] small, leggy filly: poor maiden: should stay 1¼m: probably needs easy surface: edgy and tailed off when blinkered once: has been bandaged. *K. A. Morgan.*

MAYBE LUCKY 4 b. or br.f. Monsanto (FR) 121 – Eddie Brooks (Palm Track   **—**
122) [1990 10f 10f 10.1m 1991 a12g] smallish, leggy filly: lightly raced and well beaten, including in handicap. *A. Moore.*

MAY HILLS LEGACY (IRE) 2 b.f. (Apr 3) Be My Guest (USA) 126 – May Hill   **64**
124 (Hill Clown (USA)) [1991 6g* 8g] small, angular filly: sixth living foal: closely related to 3-y-o 7f and 1m winner Rising Tempo (by Lomond) and half-sister to fairly useful 1½m and 13f winner Picea (by Mummy's Pet): dam won Yorkshire Oaks and Park Hill Stakes: 14/1 from 7/1 and green, won 12-runner maiden at Lingfield in October, running on strongly to lead post: well beaten in minor event at Newbury later in month: should stay beyond 6f. *D. W. P. Arbuthnot.*

MAYLES LASS 2 b.f. (Feb 13) Absalom 128 – Gosforth Lady 73 (Linacre 133)   **—**
[1991 5d 5.7m 6g 6m 6f] 3,000Y: close-coupled filly: moderate mover: half-sister to several winners, including Norsk St Leger winner Statecraft (by Sheshoon) and fair 7f and 1m winner Madam Mo (by Star Appeal): dam, half-sister to Champion Stakes winner Giacometti, won at up to 9f: seems of little account. *J. J. Bridger.*

MAYO MAN (IRE) 2 ch.c. (Feb 18) Master Willie 129 – Kuwaiti 77 (Home   **—**
Guard (USA) 129) [1991 6g 7g 6m] 9,000F, 7,200Y: angular colt: half-brother to fairly useful 7f to 1½m winner Santoline (by Connaught) and 2 winners abroad: dam, from excellent family, won over 5f at 2 yrs: no form, including in a seller. *Mrs G. R. Reveley.*

MAY QUEEN 4 b.f. Dara Monarch 128 – Markon (Un Your Mark 125) [1990   **—**
12.2m² 7g 1991 10d] leggy, angular filly: moderate mover: lightly raced and soundly beaten. *S. E. Kettlewell.*

MAY REEF (IRE) 3 b.f. Simply Great (FR) 122 – Mey 78 (Canisbay 120) [1990   **—**
6f* 5m* 6m 6s 1991 7.5f 7m⁶ 9.7f] sparely-made filly: good mover: modest winner at 2 yrs: has run poorly since: bred to stay at least 1¼m, but may well not do so: bandaged and sweating last 2 starts: joined R. Frost. *A. N. Lee.*

MAYSPARK LAD 3 b.c. Miramar Reef 100§ – Norman Native (FR) (Bourbon   **—**
(FR) 129) [1990 NR 1991 12m] 540Y: sturdy colt: brother to poor maiden Reef Native and closely related to 3 winners in France by Moulin, including 1¼m winner Mill of The North: dam once raced at 2 yrs in France: gave trouble at stalls, slowly away and always behind in maiden at Salisbury in May. *A. R. Davison.*

MAY SQUARE (IRE) 3 ch.g. Nicholas Bill 125 – Casa Rosada (Known Fact   **59**
(USA) 135) [1990 8g 8g 1991 10.2m 8.2g* 8.2f 8.2f³ 9.7m²] angular, workmanlike gelding: has been operated on for soft palate: won handicap at Nottingham in July: ran well last 2 starts: stays 1¼m: acts on firm ground, yet to race on dead: sold to join K. Bailey 11,000 gns Newmarket Autumn Sales. *D. Morley.*

MAZARINE BLUE 3 b.f. Bellypha 130 – Maiden Pool 85 (Sharpen Up 127)   **65**
[1990 5m⁶ 1991 5f⁴ 5g² 5f* 5m⁴ 5g³ 5m⁵ 5g⁶ 5f⁵] close-coupled, workmanlike filly: has a round action: quite modest performer: won maiden at Bath in May: should stay 6f: acts on firm going. *M. A. Jarvis.*

MAZATLAN 3 b.g. Mazaad 106 – Ashbocking 55 (Dragonara Palace (USA) 115) —
[1990 7g⁶ 6d 7g 1991 6f 7.5f] workmanlike, good-quartered gelding: easy mover:
quite modest maiden at best: well beaten in seller final start: probably stays 7f: sold
1,100 gns Newmarket July Sales. *J. G. FitzGerald.*

MAZIN 3 b.c. Faustus (USA) 118 – Polly Oligant (Prince Tenderfoot (USA) 126) —
[1990 5d 5f⁵ 5f⁶ 7g 6m⁶ a7g⁵ 1991 6.9s 10m 8.3m] sturdy colt: poor maiden: behind
in July handicaps: should prove better at 7f than 6f: acts on firm going. *C. J. Benstead.*

MAZWOOD (IRE) 3 b.c. Mazaad 106 – Putt Wood 62 (Record Token 128) [1990 —
5g 7m 1991 7d] close-coupled colt: showed little in maidens and minor event:
blinkered final start at 2 yrs: sold 800 gns Ascot November Sales. *M. McCourt.*

MCA BELOW THE LINE 3 ch.g. Lucky Wednesday 124 – Delayed Action 113 **69**
(Jolly Jet 111) [1990 5g⁶ 5m² 5f* 5d⁴ 7f* 7.5f⁵ 7g² 7m³ 7f⁶ 1991 7g* 8.5f² 8.3m
7f* 7m⁵ 8d 7m³ a8g⁴] dipped-backed gelding: moderate mover: quite modest
handicapper: led inside final 1f to win at Catterick in July and Yarmouth (seller, no
bid) in September: ran creditably last 2 outings: stays 8.5f: acts on firm going:
usually blinkered, though not on reappearance. *W. J. Pearce.*

MEADOW CHANT 3 b.g. Meadowbrook 83 – Princess Davinia (Saintly Song —
128) [1990 NR 1991 15g⁶ 16.1m 12m] leggy, rather lengthy filly: fifth reported foal:
dam bad 2-y-o plater out of smart Sylphide: last in maidens and claimer. *M. Avison.*

MEADOW GAME (IRE) 2 ch.f. (May 16) Stanford 121§ – Rose Meadow —
(Mummy's Game 120) [1991 6m a8g] 580Y: workmanlike filly: first foal: dam won
1¼m seller: bit backward, slowly away and always behind in claimers at Leicester
and Lingfield. *W. G. M. Turner.*

MEADS BROW 5 b.h. Petong 126 – Pams Gleam 89 (Sovereign Gleam 117) **33**
[1990 6f 7.6m 7f 9m 7.6m 10.1m 8.3m³ 8f³ 7f a6g 1991 a7g⁴ a8g a8g* a8g⁵ 7m 9m
a7g] compact horse: carries plenty of condition: has a quick action: poor handicapper: won at Lingfield in January: below form after: suited by 1m: best turf form
on top-of-the-ground: blinkered nowadays: sold 600 gns Ascot July Sales. *R.
Voorspuy.*

MEALLWASHA (IRE) 3 b.f. Wassl 125 – Nathacha (Thatch (USA) 136) [1990 **56** §
6g 7d 1991 8m³ 10m³ 10.2g 10g] shallow-girthed, light-framed filly: third in claimers
at Salisbury and Nottingham: as good as refused to race in sellers last 2 starts:
should stay further: blinkered final start: sometimes sweating: joined N. Henderson: one to avoid. *J. R. Fanshawe.*

MECADO 4 b.g. Ballacashtal (CAN) – Parma Nova 58 (Dominion 123) [1990 7m —
8g 10.2m 10m 9f 12.5g 12.5m 1991 12f] compact gelding: no worthwhile form,
including in sellers: tried blinkered and visored. *F. J. Yardley.*

MEDAILLE D'OR 3 ch.c. Primo Dominie 121 – Alezan Dore 82 (Mountain Call **99**
125) [1990 5m³ 5m⁶ 5f* 5m⁵ 1991 6g³ 6m² 5s* 5d⁶ 5m* 5.1g* 5g⁶ 5g 5m] quite
good-topped, lengthy colt: good walker: fairly useful performer: won handicap at
Windsor in April then small-field minor events at Kempton in May and Chepstow in
June: ran creditably in smart company next 2 starts: moved moderately down and
showed little in listed race on final one, first for 2½ months: may well prove best at
5f: probably acts on any going: visored last 5 starts: takes keen hold: sometimes on
edge. *J. W. Payne.*

MEDBOURNE (IRE) 2 b.f. (Apr 20) Alzao (USA) 117 – Dress In Spring 63 **39**
(Northfields (USA)) [1991 6g 6m⁵ a6g 7g a7g a8g a8g] 9,200Y: smallish, good-topped
filly: second foal: dam 6f and 7f winner: poor maiden: seems to stay 1m: has run
creditably on fibresand: has twice hung right: trained first 4 outings by Pat Mitchell.
J. L. Harris.

MEDIA MESSENGER 2 b.c. (Jun 5) Hadeer 118 – Willow Court (USA) (Little **72**
Current (USA)) [1991 6g⁵ 8m 8.1d³] close-coupled colt: half-brother to several
winners in USA: dam unplaced from 11 starts: modest maiden: off course 4 months
after debut: better suited by 1m than 6f: acts on dead ground: sold 16,000 gns
Newmarket Autumn Sales. *C. E. Brittain.*

MEDIA STAR 6 ch.m. Star Appeal 133 – Linduna (Derring-Do 131) [1990 a11g **38**
a16g⁶ 10.2f 14m⁴ 18f 15.3g⁴ 15.8d³ 15.8m⁶ 13.8d 1991 12g⁴ 13.8f 13.6g* 16.5m
14.6m* 14.1f⁴ 16m 14.6m 14.1m 13.8m 13.6d] leggy, angular mare: has a round
action: poor handicapper: won at Redcar and Wolverhampton in summer: stays 2m:
acts on firm and dead going: usually bandaged: none too consistent. *T. Kersey.*

MEDIATOR 2 b.c. (Apr 2) Valiyar 129 – Blushing Cousin (Great Nephew 126) **48**
[1991 a7g⁵ a8g⁴] second foal: half-brother to 3-y-o Interloper (by Robellino): dam

(showed a little ability in USA) is out of half-sister to Blushing Groom: plating-class form, soon ridden along, in late-year maidens at Lingfield. *P. F. I. Cole.*

MEDOSO 2 ch.c. (May 1) Never So Bold 135 – Formido 61 (Formidable (USA) 125) [1991 6g6 5f* 5m6 6m6] close-coupled, sparely-made colt: third foal: half-brother to modest 1989 2-y-o 7f winner Tasarly (by Miller's Mate): dam, 7f winner, is granddaughter of 1000 Guineas winner Fleet: plating-class form: won maiden at Beverley in July, soon pushed along, strong late run: no comparable form in nurseries, second one in August. *A. A. Scott.* **55**

MEESON GOLD 3 b.c. Sonnen Gold 121 – Meeson Secret (Most Secret 119) [1990 5m 5m4 5g2 5m6 5f4 5f 6s 1991 a8g 6g] close-coupled colt: moderate mover: fair plater: didn't handle turn at Carlisle final start: best form at 5f on a sound surface: ran poorly when blinkered: sold 675 gns Ascot May Sales. *B. A. McMahon.* **—**

MEESON KAMP 5 b.g. Kampala 120 – Turin Rose (Martinmas 128) [1990 5g2 5g2 5m4 5g 5g5 5f* a5g 5g 5m 1991 5g 6m 5g 5g 5d] modest handicapper at best: no show in 1991: best at 5f: acted on any going: trained first 2 starts by R. Holder: blinkered last 2: dead. *J. Berry.* **—**

MEESON TIMES 3 b.f. Enchantment 115 – National Time (USA) (Lord Avie (USA)) [1990 6m 6m* 6m 6d 6d 8d a5g 1991 6f6 7m 7m6 7g4 7g 6.9f2 8.2m 7m 6g5 6m 6m5 6m6 5s* a6g6 a5g2 a5g*] sturdy, compact filly: has round action: plating-class handicapper: won at Hamilton (seller, no bid) and Southwell late in 1991: effective at 5f and 7f: acts on any going: twice below form when visored at 2 yrs. *B. Ellison.* **56**

MEET MY GUEST (IRE) 2 ch.c. (Jan 31) Be My Guest (USA) 126 – Ringtail 102 (Auction Ring (USA) 123) [1991 a5g5 5s] sturdy colt: second foal: half-brother to fairly useful 1990 2-y-o 6f winner Mohawk Chief (by Ahonoora): dam 2-y-o 5f winner: well beaten in maiden (favourite) at Lingfield in April and seller at Folkestone in July: sold 680 gns Ascot September Sales. *P. F. I. Cole.* **—**

MEGA STEP 2 b.c. (Apr 25) Beveled (USA) – Lonely Shore (Blakeney 126) [1991 5d3] 4,300Y: small colt: first foal: dam won in Italy: 12/1 from 6/1 and green, third of 5 in maiden at Nottingham in June, pushed along at halfway, wandering badly inside final furlong: seemed likely to improve. *C. F. Wall.* **54**

MEKLUP 3 b.f. Dunbeath (USA) 127 – Little Fire 69 (Bold Lad (IRE) 133) [1990 NR 1991 7g 10m 10m 8d 12d 14.1m] 3,100Y: workmanlike filly: moderate mover: first foal: dam lightly raced from good family: well beaten, including in selling handicaps: blinkered last 3 starts. *E. Eldin.* **—**

MEKONG (USA) 2 b.c. (Feb 12) Riverman (USA) 131 – Thunderdome (USA) 80 (Lyphard (USA) 132) [1991 6m* 6g4 7g* 7m3 8g3 8s5 7s6] first reported foal: dam 1¼m winner, later successful in minor stakes in USA at around 1m: fairly useful performer: won maiden at the Curragh in May and 6-runner listed event at Leopardstown (by 4 lengths from Nordic Brief) in July: competed in pattern races otherwise, behind El Prado in National Stakes (beaten 1¼ lengths) and Juddmonte EBF Beresford Stakes (beaten around 7 lengths) fourth and sixth starts: below best final outing: should stay 1¼m: acts on good to firm and soft ground. *J. Oxx, Ireland.* **99**

MELANCOLIA 5 b.m. Legend of France (USA) 124 – Fardella (ITY) (Molvedo 137) [1990 8m 9m4 9g 1991 10.1g 11.5m 10.6g4 12d 10.1g4 10.9g2 10g4 10.5g4 10.5d] rather leggy mare: moderate mover: quite modest handicapper nowadays: should stay 1½m: acts on firm ground, possibly unsuited by soft. *J. Pearce.* **63**

MELARINOS (USA) 3 b.c. Greinton 119 – Gay Current (USA) (Little Current (USA)) [1990 7g 1991 9m4 9f3 9.7m3 11.9g5 11.8g 8m4 8g a12g] close-coupled, rather plain colt: has a long, round stride: fair form in maidens first 2 starts: ran moderately after: should prove much better at 1¼m than 1m: acts on firm ground: visored (tailed off) final start: sold out of G. Harwood's stable 7,600 gns Newmarket Autumn Sales after seventh. *M. McCourt.* **80** d

MELDON SONG 3 b.f. Pitskelly 122 – Daughter of Song 73 (Song 132) [1990 6m3 7f5 1991 6m 6g 7f 6d 6.9m] leggy filly: poor mover: poor maiden: blinkered last 2 starts: sold 950 gns Doncaster August Sales. *W. Bentley.* **—**

MELFA 6 b.m. Auction Ring (USA) 123 – Nejwah (Morston (FR) 125) [1990 a10g a8g2 a8g5 7.6g 10m 10g 1991 a8g a12g] sparely-made ex-Irish mare: no form (stiff tasks this year) since second in claimer at Lingfield in January at 5 yrs: stays 9f: acts on firm going: has worn blinkers. *A. W. Denson.* **—**

MELFORD 3 b.f. Petoski 135 – Coral Fury (Mill Reef (USA) 141) [1990 NR 1991 10m] tall, leggy, shallow-girthed filly: first foal: dam unraced half-sister to Teenoso: 20/1 and ridden by 7-lb claimer, 16 lengths seventh of 16 in Leicester maiden in

October, pulling hard then wandering under pressure: taken last and very steadily to post: sold K. Morgan 1,900 gns Newmarket December Sales. *H. R. A. Cecil.*

MELLABY (USA)   3 ch.c. Nureyev (USA) 131 – Hitting Irish (USA) (Irish Ruler **102** (USA)) [1990 NR 1991 8s* 8g2 8g6 10.1m* 10g5 10.3d5] $425,000F, 700,000Y: rangy, quite attractive colt: closely related to a minor winner in USA by Shareef Dancer and half-brother to a minor winner there by Arctic Tern: dam graded stakes-placed winner of 9 races: won maiden at Ripon in April and minor event (7/1 on) at Newcastle in June: about 10 lengths sixth to Fourstars Allstar in Irish 2000 Guineas at the Curragh: ran moderately in £7,500 event and minor contest last 2 starts, off course 3½ months in between: should prove better at 1¼m than 1m. *M. R. Stoute.*

MELLOTTIE   6 b. or br.g. Meldrum 112 – Lottie Lehmann 69 (Goldhill 125) [1990 **100** 10.2f 9f6 12g5 10m3 9f* 9f4 8g 10m3 9f* 11f2 9g3 9m* 10m* 9m2 1991 10.2m* 8g* 10f2 8g4 8.9g 8.9g4 8m2 9m*] good-topped gelding: carries plenty of condition: useful handicapper, much improved in 1991: won 29-runner William Hill Cambridge-shire at Newmarket in October by head from High Premium: earlier successful in good style at Doncaster and York (£15,800 event) in May: effective at 1m to 1¼m: goes well on top-of-the-ground, yet to race on a soft surface: held up, and has good turn of foot: genuine and most consistent: a great credit to his trainer. *Mrs G. R. Reveley.*

MELODIC HABIT   4 b.f. Muscatite 122 – Magyar Melody (Prince Tenderfoot   — (USA) 126) [1990 8m2 10d3 7g 7g4 6d 7g 7m* 8.5m5 10g 1991 a8g 7.1s5 8f] leggy, sparely-made filly: half-sister to fairly useful miler Hungarian Prince (by Monseigneur): dam won over 5f and 1m at 2 yrs in Ireland: ex-Irish filly: won handicap at Tipperary in 1990: well beaten, including in seller, in summer of 1991: stays 1m: acts on good to firm ground: below form when blinkered: formerly trained by K. Connolly. *Mrs A. Knight.*

MELODY ANNE   2 ch.f. (Apr 5) Clantime 101 – Louisa Anne 73 (Mummy's Pet   — 125) [1991 5m6 5s4 5g6 5m] leggy, unfurnished filly: fifth foal: half-sister to 3-y-o Barely Black (by Lidhame), 1988 2-y-o 5f and 7f winner Nite Nite Louisa (by Night Shift) and a winner in Belgium: dam sprinter: poor sprint maiden: has been bandaged behind. *J. S. Haldane.*

MELODY'S HONOUR   7 b. or br.m. Unknown Melody 70 – Honour Girl   — (Honour Bound 109) [1990 NR 1991 8g] smallish, angular non-thoroughbred mare: dam unraced: tailed off in Pontefract claimer in July, only run. *J. Dooler.*

MELPOMENE (USA)   3 b.f. Lear Fan (USA) 130 – Melodrama 102 (Busted 134) **102** [1990 8g* 7d2 1991 7.3d4* 7.3f5 8.1m4 8d3 8d6] lengthy, good-topped filly: has a round action: won handicap at Newbury in June: ran well in Hungerford Stakes at same course and listed race (checked over 1f out, running on strongly) at Ascot second and fourth starts: sixth of 11 in Longchamp listed race on final one: well worth a try at 1¼m: acts on firm and dead ground: useful. *Lord Huntingdon.*

MEL'S ROSE   6 ch.g. Anfield 117 – Ragtime Rose (Ragstone 128) [1990 7f3 7m*   **75** 7f3 a7g 8m3 7m 8m2 7d a10g3 a8g 1991 7g2 7.1g6 7g 8m 8f2 7m4 8m3 7g] tall gelding: has a quick action: modest handicapper: suited by 7f to 1m: acts on firm and dead going: tried blinkered once: good mount for apprentice. *Dr J. D. Scargill.*

MELTING TEARS   3 b.f. Noalto 120 – Davemma 81 (Tachypous 128) [1990 6g6   — 5d6 7g* 7.5f 7m2 7m5 7m 8.2s 1991 8.2s 8g] leggy filly: poor performer: showed nothing in selling handicaps in the spring: should be well suited by 1m: unsuited by a soft surface. *J. S. Wilson.*

MELTONBY 2 ch.f. (Mar 10) Sayf El Arab (USA) 127 – Superlife (USA) 64 (Super **65**
Concorde (USA) 128) [1991 5m⁶ a6g³ 6d* 6.9m* 7g² 7.5f³ 7m 6m 7g 7m⁴ 7.1m⁵
a6g* a7g² a8g*] 1,400Y: leggy, close-coupled filly: first foal: dam maiden suited by
7f: moderate mover: quite modest performer: won sellers (no bid) at Ripon and
Carlisle and nurseries at Southwell: suited by 1m: acts on dead ground and good to
firm, and on fibresand: good mount for 7-lb claimer: genuine. *J. Hetherton.*

MEMORIVE (USA) 3 b.f. Riverman (USA) 131 – Le Vague A L'Ame (USA) **81**
(Vaguely Noble 140) [1990 7f² 1991 8m* 10.6g⁶ 10m 10.2m⁵ 9m2] rangy filly: fair
form: promising winner of maiden at Bath in May: disappointing in handicaps next 2
starts: edgy, good staying-on second of 15 in similar event at Redcar: should prove
suited by 1¼m + . *G. Harwood.*

MEMSAHB 2 b.f. (Feb 15) Prince Sabo 123 – Hyatti 74 (Habitat 134) [1991 5m³ **67**
5g* 5m* 5m* 5g] leggy, good-topped filly: moderate walker: first foal: dam, maiden,
form only at 9f: modest performer: won maiden at Lingfield, minor event at
Newmarket and £8,000 event at Epsom (drifted left then quickened well): below
form in Queen Mary Stakes at Royal Ascot on only subsequent start: quite speedy. *J.
Berry.*

MEMU (USA) 2 b. or br.f. (Jan 22) Tsunami Slew (USA) – Ahrex (USA) (Dr **78**
Fager) [1991 5g* 6f⁴ 5.2f⁶ 6.1m* 7d] $180,000F: leggy, lengthy filly: sister to a
winner in North America at up to 9f and half-sister to several other winners,
including useful 1988 2-y-o Grade 2 6f winner Pat Copelan (by Copelan): dam
unraced: sire best at 9f/1¼m: won maiden at Salisbury in June and nursery at
Nottingham (best effort, made all in good style) in October: should be suited by 7f:
acts on top-of-the-ground, possibly not on dead: tends to sweat and/or get on toes.
D. R. C. Elsworth.

MENDIP MENTOR 2 b.g. (Apr 15) Dunbeath (USA) 127 – Tantot 65 **53**
(Charlottown 127) [1991 5m³ 7f 5.7f] good-bodied gelding: sixth foal: half-brother to
1984 2-y-o 6f winner Kentucky Quest (by Darby Creek Road): dam, stayed 1½m, is
half-sister to 2000 Guineas winner Mon Fils: plating-class form in maidens and a
claimer: off course 4 months after debut: will stay 1m. *M. C. Pipe.*

MENDIP MIST 3 ch.f. Known Fact (USA) 135 – Silver Surprise 78 (Son of Silver **—**
123) [1990 6m 7g³ 5m⁵ 6m⁵ 5.8h⁶ 7m 6m 1991 8m 8f 8g] leggy filly: poor maiden: no
form in 1991: bred to stay 1m + : blinkered final start. *M. C. Pipe.*

MENDOCINO (USA) 2 b. or br.c. (Apr 7) Theatrical 128 – Brorita (USA) (Caro **108**
133) [1991 6g* 5.5g⁶ 8d*] fourth foal: half-brother to French 1990 3-y-o 10.5f
winner Turgut (by Nijinsky): dam minor stakes winner at up to 1¼m in USA: won
newcomers race at Saint-Cloud in June and 9-runner listed event at Evry (easily
best effort) in September: soundly-beaten last of 6 in Prix Robert-Papin at
Maisons-Laffitte in between: will stay 1¼m: yet to race on top-of-the-ground. *F.
Boutin, France.*

MENNOCK GLEN (IRE) 2 b.g. (Apr 8) The Noble Player (USA) 126 – **—**
Teletype (Guillaume Tell (USA) 121) [1991 5s] IR 7,800F, IR 5,000Y: neat gelding:
half-brother to Irish 2m winner Deliffin (by Wolverlife): dam Irish maiden, ran only
at 2 yrs: 33/1, in need of race and on toes, slow-starting seventh of 8 in maiden at
Hamilton in April. *J. S. Wilson.*

MENTALASANYTHIN 2 b.g. (Feb 20) Ballacashtal (CAN) – Lafrowda 71 **85**
(Crimson Beau 124) [1991 7m 7s⁵ 6d* 7g 7m 6f 8m⁶ 6g² 8.3s* 6s*] 2,600F, 2,800Y:
sturdy gelding: second foal: dam 6f and 7.6f winner: fair performer: successful in
maiden auction at Hamilton in July: much improved form for new trainer in
November, second of 18 to Night Asset in nursery at Newmarket before winning
similar events at Hamilton (easily) and Folkestone all within 9 days: effective at 6f
and stays 1m: acts well on soft going: trained first 3 outings by J. S. Wilson, next 4 by
Miss L. Perratt. *A. Bailey.*

MERCERS MAGIC (IRE) 3 ch.g. Dalsaan 125 – Rixensart 77 (Credo 123) **50**
[1990 7f⁶ 8m 8.2d 1991 10d⁵ 10d 12g 10.6g a11g a14g 12m² 10g 13.8m] workmanlike
gelding: very little form apart from when strong-finishing head second of 11 in
claimer at Southwell in September: suited by 1½m: acts on good to firm ground:
blinkered last 3 starts: bandaged final one: sold 1,100 gns Ascot December Sales. *D.
Haydn Jones.*

MERCHANT HOUSE (IRE) 3 ch.c. Salmon Leap (USA) 131 – Persian Polly **—**
99 (Persian Bold 123) [1990 5m 1991 8d 7m] no worthwhile form in maiden contests:
bandaged behind in 1991: should be suited by further: joined W. Holden. *R. W.
Stubbs.*

MERCHANT OF VENICE 3 b.c. Precocious 126 – Silka (ITY) (Lypheor 118) **53** [1990 7g 10.2s a8g⁶ 1991 a8g² a10g* 10d 12m⁶ 13m² 13f² 13d³ a12g* 12.4f³ 16.1g⁵ a 67 13.8m] good-topped colt: quite modest handicapper: won at Lingfield in February and Southwell in July: stays 13f: acts on firm ground and all-weather surfaces: mostly blinkered in 1991, sometimes on toes: hung persistently right seventh start: sold 12,500 gns Newmarket Autumn Sales. *W. J. Pearce.*

MERE CHANTS 2 b.f. (Feb 16) Kings Lake (USA) 133 – Rengaine (FR) (Music **57** Boy 124) [1991 5d⁵ 5.7m⁶ 7g² 7g⁵] 1,500Y: good-topped filly: has scope: moderate mover: second foal: half-sister to 3-y-o Belle Danseuse (by Dellypha): dam French 8.5f and 11f winner: plating-class maiden: best efforts in large fields at Goodwood (auction, beaten neck) and Newmarket last 2 starts: should stay 1m. *D. R. C. Elsworth.*

MERITSU (IRE) 3 ch.f. Lyphard's Special (USA) 122 – Ferry Lane (Dom Racine **54** (FR) 121) [1990 5m⁴ 5f⁵ 6g 6m 7g a7g⁴ 1991 a5g² a10g² a8g² a7g⁴] small, angular filly: good walker: plating-class maiden, not seen out after March: best form at 1m to 1¼m: wore eyeshield last 2 starts: blinkered fourth at 2 yrs. *D. R. C. Elsworth.*

MERLINS WISH (USA) 2 ch.c. (Feb 16) Yukon (USA) – Dear Guinevere **96** (USA) (Fearless Knight) [1991 6g 6g⁶ 6m 6m* 7d⁴] $75,000Y: quite attractive colt: has scope: good mover: eighth foal: half-brother to several winners in USA, including stakes-placed Alberta Clipper (by It's Freezing): dam unraced: fairly useful performer: backed at long odds and looking fully fit for first time, won 18-runner nursery at Newmarket (led final strides) in October: creditable fifth of 7, making most, to Casteddu in minor event at Ascot week later: suited by 7f: acts on good to firm and dead ground. *R. Hannon.*

MERLS PEARL 2 b.f. (May 3) Aragon 118 – Thrice Nightly (Gallant Romeo **45** (USA)) [1991 7m 8m 7g a6g] 720F: leggy filly: third reported live foal: half-sister to fair 1¼m winner Lisianthus (by Dalsaan): dam poor half-sister to Oaks winner Ginevra: well beaten: blinkered in Southwell nursery final start. *J. A. Glover.*

MERRY DEVIL (IRE) 2 b.f. (Mar 13) Sadler's Wells (USA) 132 – Stylish Genie **—** (USA) (Bagdad) [1991 7m] smallish filly: closely related to 2 winners abroad, notably very useful French 9f to 11f winner Lichine (by Lyphard), and half-sister to another: dam, stakes winner, won at up to 9f and is half-sister to top-class 1m to 1½m colt Artaius: 7/1, soon left behind 2f out when ninth of 12 to Casteddu in maiden at Lingfield in September: lacks scope: sold 12,000 gns Newmarket December Sales. *M. R. Stoute.*

MERRYHILL MADAM 2 b.f. (Apr 9) Prince Sabo 123 – Western Line (High **64** Line 125) [1991 6g 6.1m² 6.1f³ 7g] tall, leggy filly: third foal: dam unraced half-sister to Queen Anne winner Mr Fluorocarbon: progressive form in seller then maidens first 3 starts: ran respectably in Wolverhampton nursery final start: should be suited by further than 6f. *J. L. Harris.*

MERRYHILL MAID (IRE) 3 ch.f. M Double M (USA) – Piazza Navona **71** (Upper Case (USA)) [1990 a6g 6f⁴ 6g³ 5m* 6g 5g 6m 6d* 6d³ 1991 6g⁵ 6g* 6m⁴ 6g 6d 5m² 6m⁶ 6s⁵ 8m 6f 6.1m 6m* 6m 6g 7g] leggy, angular filly: poor walker: moderate mover: modest handicapper: won at Newmarket in May: not so good in second half of season, clearly best effort to win seller (bought in 5,600 gns) at York in October: should stay 7f (never dangerous at 1m): acts on good to firm ground and dead: visored (soundly beaten) eleventh start. *J. L. Harris.*

MERRY MARIGOLD 5 b.m. Sonnen Gold 121 – Manna Green (Bustino 136) **57** [1990 NR 1991 10d⁴ 10.8m 8f⁵ 10.1s⁶ 12g a12g* 10.2g² 12g 12.1d² 10g²] lengthy, workmanlike mare: has a rather round action: plating-class handicapper nowadays: won at Lingfield in June: stays 1½m: acts on any going: none too consistent. *J. D. Roberts.*

MERSEY RACING 4 br.g. Roscoe Blake 120 – Kelton Lass (Lord Nelson (FR) **—** 107) [1990 NR 1991 a7g] tall gelding: third foal: dam ran once: soon struggling in claimer at Southwell in January, only run: sold 2,100 gns Doncaster July Sales. *T. H. Caldwell.*

MERSEYSIDE MAN 5 b.g. My Dad Tom (USA) 109 – Chanita (Averof 123) **—** [1990 a8g* a8g* a7g* a8g* a8g³ a7g 8f 8f 8h⁴ 9m⁴ a8g³ 1991 a8g⁴ a8g a10g 7m] lengthy, workmanlike gelding: poor mover: modest form when successful in 4 handicaps at Lingfield early in 1990: lost his form: stays 1m: acts on firm going: blinkered penultimate start: usually wears visor and ridden by 7-lb claimer: often slowly away. *Dr J. D. Scargill.*

MERTOLA'S PET 5 b.m. Tickled Pink 114 – Mertola (Tribal Chief 125) [1990 **81** 5.8h⁴ 5m* 5g 5f* 5m² 5.8h 5m 5m 5f⁶ 5.3f⁵ 5d 1991 5.8f⁵ 5f* 5g² 5g⁵ 5.2g

5.1m* 5.6m] small, quite good-quartered mare: modest handicapper: won at Epsom (£14,200 event) in June and Chester (improved form, impressively by 3½ lengths) in August: best at 5f: acts well on top-of-the-ground: very speedy, and best forcing pace. *L. G. Cottrell.*

MERTON MILL 4 b.f. Dominion 123 – Brookfield Miss 73 (Welsh Pageant 132) **68** [1990 10.1g⁵ 10g 11.7m⁶ 10m* 10.6s³ 10.4d² 11.5g³ 12s⁶ 1991 12g 10g 10g 10m 10d 12f5 12g³ 14g⁵ 14.1g* 14.1f* 16m* 14.1f² 14.1m 17.2g³ 16.5d] workmanlike filly: usually looks very well: moderate mover: quite modest handicapper: won in summer at Yarmouth and Nottingham (2): stays very well: probably acts on any going. *D. Morley.*

MESAAFI (IRE) 2 b.f. (Feb 22) Slip Anchor 136 – Nijinsky Sentiment (USA) 86 **85** (Nijinsky (CAN) 138) [1991 6g* 7d² 8m] IR 28,000Y: quite attractive filly: has a round action: third foal: half-sister to a winner in Italy by Kris: dam, 7f winner stayed 1m, is daughter of smart sister to Steel Heart: fair performer: won maiden at Goodwood in July: length second of 5 to Musicale in Prestige Stakes there following month, headed 2f out but keeping on really well: eased considerably when headed over 2f out in May Hill Stakes at Doncaster in September: should stay 1m: possibly unsuited by top-of-the-ground: races keenly. *Major W. R. Hern.*

MESLEH 4 b.c. Alleged (USA) 138 – Forlene 108 (Forli (ARG)) [1990 8m⁵ 10f² **84 +** 1991 10.8g*] strong, lengthy colt with scope: moderate mover: lightly raced and fair performer: favourite, impressive 7-length winner of maiden at Warwick in April: will be suited by 1½m: gives strong impression will prove best with give in the ground. *J. H. M. Gosden.*

MESSAGE PAD 4 ch.c. Rousillon (USA) 133 – Ouija 104 (Silly Season 127) [1990 **104** 7m⁶ 7g⁴ 8d 8m⁵ 8.2f* 8m* 9m² 7m 1991 8f* 8.5f 8m⁴ 8g²] rangy colt: good walker: has a long stride: useful performer: evens, won moderately-run minor event at Pontefract in May, hanging right: good second of 8 to Enharmonic in Group 3 event at Baden-Baden in August: stays 9f: acts on firm ground, seems unsuited by dead: headstrong, and often taken down early: has been equipped with special noseband and severe bridle, not for some time: should prove best with extreme waiting tactics. *J. W. Watts.*

METAL BOYS 4 b.g. Krayyan 117 – Idle Gossip (Runnett 125) [1990 5f* 5f⁵ 5d³ **88** 6g 1991 5g⁶ 5g 6g 5g³ 5m⁵ 5m⁴ 5.9m⁶ 5m⁴ 5.2g⁵ 5f* 5m* 5.2f 5m* 5g 5m⁴ 5m*] good-bodied gelding: poor mover: fair handicapper: won claimers at Beverley in July and Pontefract (2) and Haydock in autumn: best at 5f: acts on hard and dead ground: speedy, usually races up with pace. *R. Hollinshead.*

METAL OISEAU (IRE) 3 ch.g. Ela-Mana-Mou 132 – Free Reserve (USA) **—** (Tom Rolfe) [1990 NR 1991 10g 12d a8g⁵ 12d 12m 15.4m] IR 12,000F, 11,000Y: workmanlike gelding: moderate mover: second foal: half-brother to a winner in Switzerland: dam placed from 8.5f to 1¾m in Ireland: well beaten, including in selling handicap: blinkered fourth start: got loose and withdrawn intended second one: won selling hurdle (blinkered) for J. Moore. *K. T. Ivory.*

METAL STORM (FR) 3 b.c. Kenmare (FR) 125 – Porphyrine (Habitat 134) **112** [1990 NR 1991 8g* 8s² 7d⁶ 8g*] 380,000 francs (approx £35,200) Y: fifth foal: half-brother to French provincial 9.5f and 11f winner Pink Horizon (by Fabulous Dancer) and to Pale Rider (by Crystal Palace), 3 times successful over 1m in France: dam unraced half-sister to Grise Mine and Kostroma: won minor event at Evry in April and Prix de la Jonchere (by short head from Bistro Garden, coming from rear to lead close home) at Chantilly in June: stays 1m: possibly best on a sound surface. *A. Fabre, France.*

METRO LINER 5 br.g. Zino 127 – Bellinzona (Northfields (USA)) [1990 8f 1991 **—** 5m 1½g] rather sparely-made gelding: showed ability when trained in Ireland at 3 yrs: well beaten here: stays 1m: sold 900 gns Ascot July Sales. *R. Akehurst.*

METTERNICH 6 b.g. Habitat 134 – Sarah Siddons (FR) (Le Levanstell 122) **—** [1990 8g 1991 9v⁵] heavy-topped gelding: seventh foal: half-brother to 1m winner Saratino (by Bustino) and 1986 2-y-o 6f seller winner Sands of Time (by Dance In Time): dam, French 8.5f winner, is sister to top 1982 Italian 2-y-o Anguillo: twice raced on flat and well beaten in maiden at Gowran Park and ladies event at Kempton: won 2m NH Flat race at Down Royal early at 5 yrs: formerly trained by J. Gorman. *M. H. Tompkins.*

MEXICAN DANCER 2 b.f. (Feb 14) Dance of Life (USA) – Mexican Two Step **68 ?** (Gay Fandango (USA) 132) [1991 5d³ 6m⁶ 6g⁴ 6f⁶ 6m] 14,000Y, 5,200 2-y-o: unfurnished filly: seventh foal: closely related to 7f seller winner Mexican Vision (by Vision) and half-sister to several winners, including useful 1¼m to 1½m winner

Busted Rock (by Busted): dam fairly useful Irish 2-y-o 6f winner: quite modest maiden: ran poorly in Newmarket nursery final outing, first for nearly 2 months: will be much better suited by 7f + . *R. J. Holder.*

MEXICAN VISION   4 b.g. Vision (USA) – Mexican Two Step (Gay Fandango (USA) 132) [1990 8m 8f⁴ 6g 7m 7f⁵ 7g* 7m 8.2m 9m 8.2v⁴ 1991 10.8g 8d 8m] strong, lengthy gelding: had a round action: plating class as 3-y-o: no worthwhile form in spring of 1991, fell final start: stayed 7f: probably best with give in the ground: mostly blinkered: winning hurdler: dead. *I. Campbell.* —

MEZAAJ (USA)   3 br.g. Shadeed (USA) 135 – Honor To Her (USA) (Sir Ivor 135) [1990 6g 1991 12m⁵ 10.2s⁴ 10g⁶ 12.3g] sturdy, compact gelding: moderate mover: little signs of ability, including in handicaps: seemingly best effort at 1¼m on soft ground: blinkered final outing: sold to join B. Preece 2,300 gns Newmarket Autumn Sales. *M. A. Jarvis.* —

MEZIARA   10 b.g. Dominion 123 – Abertywi 87 (Bounteous 125) [1990 NR 1991 10m 10.5g] good-bodied gelding: poor performer: no form in 1991: suited by testing conditions at 1¼m and stays 1½m: yet to show his form on firm going, acts on any other: effective with or without blinkers or visor: has hung badly right. *D. R. Tucker.* —

MIA FILLIA   4 b.f. Formidable (USA) 125 – As Blessed 101 (So Blessed 130) [1990 8m 7f 8g⁵ 8.2s 7m 8g⁴ 10f⁶ 10g² 11.5m⁴ 8m 1991 a7g³ a7g a8g a8g⁶ a11g⁴ a8g³ 7d 8.2s] strong, compact filly: has a quick action: poor maiden: not seen out after April: suited by 1¼m: possibly best with give in the ground, though seems unsuited by soft: sold 2,000 gns Ascot May Sales. *N. Tinkler.*   **40**

MIAMI BANKER   5 ch.g. Miami Springs 121 – Banking Coyne 76 (Deep Diver 134) [1990 6m⁶ 5m⁶ 6m⁶ 5g* 6d 5d² 5.6g 5m 5d 5s⁶ 1991 6g 5s⁴ 5.1d 5g 5m 5d 5g] strong, lengthy gelding: moderate mover: fair handicapper: appeared to run extremely well when fourth in Longchamp Group 3 event in May: well below form after final outing: best at 5f: acts on any going: blinkered nowadays: tends to idle and is suited by strong handling and waiting tactics: trained first 3 starts by P. Howling. *R. Akehurst.*   **87**

MIAMI BEAR   5 b.g. Miami Springs 121 – Belinda Bear (Ragstone 128) [1990 12m⁵ 1991 12s 12m 12m] strong, good-bodied gelding: has a round action: plating-class maiden at 3 yrs: ran moderately in 1991: probably stays 1½m: best effort on soft ground: keen sort: winning hurdler. *J. Berry.* —

MICHELETTI (USA)   3 b.c. Critique (USA) 126 – Tres Agreable (FR) (Luthier 126) [1990 NR 1991 11.8g* 12g* 13.9g* 14.6m³ 16m⁴ 12g] leggy, lightly-made colt: has a fluent, round action: third foal: half-brother to St Leger winner Michelozzo (by Northern Baby): dam, half-sister to Prix Royal-Oak winner El Cuite, won over 10½f in France at 4 yrs: won maiden at Leicester in July, minor event at Newmarket and £16,600 handicap at York in August: 16½ lengths third of 10 to Toulon in Coalite St Leger at Doncaster, held up in rear and checked 3f out: better effort in Group 3 contests won by Further Flight following month when creditable fourth of 6 in Jockey Club Cup at Newmarket, having quickened easily to front 3f out: effective at 1¾m and 2m: very useful. *H. R. A. Cecil.*   **109**

MICHIKA (IRE)   3 b.f. Runnett 125 – Soudchika (GER) (Dschingis Khan) [1990 5m 6d⁶ 5d 1991 8g 6.1d 5.7g] lengthy filly: has a round action: poor maiden: well beaten at 3 yrs. *O. O'Neill.* —

MICRONOVA   5 ch.g. Homing 130 – Tula Music 62 (Patch 129) [1990 NR 1991 12f 17.1d 16.2g 10g 11.9f] leggy, sparely-made gelding: little sign of ability. *E. A. Wheeler.* —

MIDAS BLUE (IRE)   3 ch.f. Burslem 123 – Lady's Guest (Be My Guest (USA) 126) [1990 6f 7f³ 7d a7g a7g² a7g 1991 a8g⁵ a7g⁶ a7g 6f⁶ 8m 8m] leggy filly: plating-class maiden: virtually refused to race 4 times in 1991: has been blinkered and visored: joined L. Barratt: one to avoid. *A. Bailey.*   **§§**

MIDAS WELL   2 b.g. (May 8) Midyan (USA) 124 – Sobriquet (Roan Rocket 128) [1991 5d 6.1g 7m 7m] 4,000Y, 7,200 2-y-o: workmanlike gelding: third foal: half-brother to 3-y-o Tender Music (by Music Boy): dam poor half-sister to very useful 1976 2-y-o 5f performer The Andrestan: seems of little account. *G. A. Ham.* —

MIDDAY SHOW (USA)   4 b.c. Roberto (USA) 131 – Worlds Fair (USA) (Our Hero (USA)) [1990 8g 12g⁶ 12f² 14d³ 1991 14.6s 12.5d⁵ 10f* 10. 1f 11.7m] well-made ex-Irish colt: fifth reported foal: half-brother to 2 minor winners in USA: dam once-raced half-sister to Super Asset, Bates Motel and Hatim: modest ex-Irish performer: won claimer at Folkestone in May by 6 lengths: tailed off in handicaps after: stays 1¾m: acts on firm and dead going: bandaged behind fourth start: trained at 3 yrs by M. V. O'Brien. *J. R. Jenkins.*   **71**

MIDIFINA   3 b.f. Green Desert (USA) 127 – Vielle 123 (Ribero 126) [1990 NR   **84**
1991 10m² 10g³ 8m³ 8.3f* 8.1m⁶ 8m²] 90,000Y: lengthy filly: sixth foal: half-sister
to fair 12.2f winner Chevrefeuille (by Ile de Bourbon) and a winner in Belgium by
Mill Reef: dam very smart middle-distance filly: fair performer: won maiden at
Hamilton in September: stays 1¼m: bandaged off-hind final start: sold 11,500 gns
Newmarket Autumn Sales. *B. Hanbury.*

MIDNIGHT AIR (USA)   2 br.f. (Feb 20) Green Dancer (USA) 132 – **111** p
Evening Air (USA) (J O Tobin (USA) 130) [1991 7g² 7f* 8m* 8d*dis]
     A browse through any dictionary of quotations reveals numerous and
varied observations on the subject of statistics, none of them particularly
complimentary. By some way the best known is Disraeli's reference to 'lies,
damned lies and statistics', but there are plenty of other interesting ones. One
commentator likened the use of statistics to a bikini in that 'what they reveal
is suggestive, but what they conceal is vital', while the British poet and critic
Andrew Lang argued that proponents of statistics use them 'as a drunken man
uses lamp-posts—for support rather than illumination'. Racing enthusiasts
have at their disposal more and more statistical information, and it's true to
say that not all the material that's published is useful. However, backers
who've played their part in making lightly-raced fillies like Katakana,
Mahasin, Sun And Shade and Freewheel prominent in the ante-post market
for the One Thousand Guineas might be a little concerned if they examined
recent trends in that race. Much has been written in the last few years about
the tendency of top trainers to bring their best horses along slowly, missing
pattern races at two in order to concentrate on what they consider more
significant objectives the following year, but the evidence suggests that in the
One Thousand Guineas at least, pattern-race form at two still remains highly
significant. During the 'eighties eleven horses who hadn't contested a pattern
race at two reached a place in the Two Thousand Guineas, among them
Shadeed, Dancing Brave, Doyoun and Nashwan, but the situation among the
fillies was very different. True, a handful of fillies who didn't contest a pattern
race in their first season did go on to reach a place in the One Thousand, and of
those the likes of Sonic Lady and Time Charter went on to win races at the
highest level. But the fact remains that of the last dozen One Thousand
Guineas winners only Pebbles and On The House (who both finished runner-
up in the Cheveley Park Stakes) failed to win a pattern race at two, and
although the top fillies in the latest season weren't by any means an exceptional bunch it's hard to escape the conclusion that a couple have been under-
estimated in the Guineas market. Midnight Air is one of them.
     Midnight Air's progress through 1991 wasn't attended by the publicity
that's usually associated with up-and-coming two-year-olds from the Cecil
stable. Her debut came in a seven-furlong maiden event at Newmarket in July.
She shaped with plenty of promise despite finding Mystery Play too strong,
and after a decisive win in similar company at Yarmouth the following month
she was stepped up in class for the Group 3 May Hill Stakes at Doncaster, a
race her trainer has dominated in the past decade. The field of thirteen wasn't

*May Hill Stakes, Doncaster—Midnight Air improves Cecil's outstanding record in the race,
at the expense of subsequently-disqualified Fern*

especially strong—seven were maidens—and Midnight Air started 3/1 second favourite behind the well-regarded Fern, a half-sister to the previous year's runner-up Shamshir and a most encouraging third in a maiden at Newmarket on her debut. Midnight Air, ridden close to the pace, quickened in eye-catching fashion over two furlongs out, opening up a gap of six lengths in a very short space of time as Fern struggled to find room, then ran on strongly despite drifting left to beat the favourite by a length and a half with the rest well back. Fern hampered several rivals as she squeezed through, earning herself disqualification and her rider Dettori a four-day ban, and afterwards opinions were divided as to which would have come out on top in a trouble-free race. Our race-reader's view was that Midnight Air would have found extra had it been required. Little over two weeks later the pair renewed rivalry in the Group 1 Brent Walker Fillies' Mile at Ascot. Once again the race ended in controversy and this time the outcome wasn't favourable to Midnight Air's followers. In a field of seven, the Lowther winner Culture Vulture was the 5/2 favourite with Midnight Air at 11/4; Fern was 3/1 and Mystery Play, having only her second race, the only other to attract support, at 4/1. As at Doncaster, Midnight Air was tucked away just off the pace early on and the race turned on what happened approaching the two-furlong pole. In easing his mount left to challenge, Eddery on Midnight Air gave a hefty bump to Culture Vulture who in turn caused interference to Super Sarena and Baharlilys. None of the four was done any favours by the scrimmaging, but after taking up the running just over a furlong out Midnight Air always had the edge and despite idling again she beat Culture Vulture by three quarters of a length with Mystery Play two lengths away in third and Fern disappointing in fifth. Midnight Air was almost certainly the best horse on the day, but after a stewards inquiry and an objection by the connections of Culture Vulture she was predictably disqualified, her rider being given an eight-day suspension for careless riding.

	Green Dancer (USA) (b 1972)	Nijinsky (b 1967)	Northern Dancer
Midnight Air (USA) (br.f. Feb 20, 1989)			Flaming Page
		Green Valley (b or br 1967)	Val de Loir
			Sly Pola
	Evening Air (USA) (br 1982)	J O Tobin (br 1974)	Never Bend
			Hill Shade
		Nellie Forbes (b 1977)	Secretariat
			Comely Nell

Midnight Air has proved an excellent buy, having cost only 46,000 guineas as a yearling at the Highflyer Sale, and although her pedigree isn't out of the top drawer it's hardly bargain basement, either. Like Midnight Air, Green Dancer gained the first big success of his career over a mile at Doncaster when he won the Observer Gold Cup in 1974. He went on to win the Poule d'Essai des Poulains and the Prix Lupin the following year, and after producing a steady stream of good horses at stud he came to the fore in the latest season through Suave Dancer. Midnight Air's dam Evening Air was brought to be trained in Europe but never ran. Covered by Caerleon as a three-year-old, she produced a colt who died as a foal. The following year she foaled a filly by High Top who didn't run, and Midnight Air was her first American foal following her return there in 1988. Midnight Air's second dam Nellie Forbes won over a mile in Ireland on her only start at two. She's responsible for a couple of useful winners at up to eleven furlongs, namely Ancient Times and Nucleus, and her unraced dam Comely Nell made a lasting name for herself at stud as dam of the Kentucky Derby and Belmont Stakes winner Bold Forbes and grandam of the William Hill Futurity winner Dunbeath and the unbeaten American colt Saratoga Six.

Midnight Air should stay middle distances as a three-year-old yet she's by no means short of pace; the turn of foot she displayed in the May Hill was impressive. Furthermore, the odds are she's capable of better than she's shown so far. Physically she wasn't quite the finished article at two, being somewhat unfurnished. Rangy, she has plenty of scope, and could well develop into an imposing filly over the winter. As we've said, 1991 was some way removed from being a vintage year for two-year-old fillies. Midnight Air was patently one of the best of the bunch, however, and in what's presently a wide-open ante-post market on the One Thousand Guineas she certainly merits each-way consideration at the 25/1 or thereabouts on offer at the time of writing. *H. R. A. Cecil.*

MIDNIGHT BANKER 3 b.c. Today And Tomorrow 78 – Banking Coyne 76 **60** (Deep Diver 134) [1990 NR 1991 6m 6g⁴ 6d 7g] sturdy colt: fifth foal: half-brother to 5f performer Miami Banker (by Miami Springs) and 1m seller winner Greek Banker (by Avgerinos): dam best at 5f: fourth in maiden at Lingfield, easily best effort: chased leaders 5f in seller final start: stays 6f. *R. Akehurst.*

MIDNIGHT GALAXY 2 b.g. (Apr 9) Natroun (FR) 128 – Sister Jinks 88 (Irish **46** Love 117) [1991 8m 7d] leggy, workmanlike gelding: eighth foal: half-brother to 3-y-o Elusive Spirit (by Absalom) and 2 winners by Horage, including 1988 2-y-o 5f and 7f winner James Payne: dam Irish 2-y-o 9f winner: soundly beaten in late-season maidens at Leicester (slowly away) and Doncaster. *A. N. Lee.*

MIDNIGHT JESTOR (IRE) 3 b.f. Jester 119 – Midnight Patrol (Ashmore **—** (FR) 125) [1990 6m 7f 7m 8m 6d 1991 7g 7g 10.2f] leggy filly: no form, in handicaps as 3-y-o: has been bandaged: tried in visor and blinkers at 2 yrs: sold 1,500 gns Ascot November Sales. *R. J. Holder.*

MIDNIGHT LASS 3 b.f. Today And Tomorrow 78 – Capel Lass (The Brianstan **49** 128) [1990 5m² 5f⁴ 5m² a6g⁶ 5f* 5.1m* 1991 6v⁵ 5g 5.1f 5m³ 5d⁵ a5g 5m] leggy filly: moderate mover: plating-class handicapper: should prove best at 5f: acts on firm going (stiff task on dead): trained until after second start (ran as if something amiss) by J. Berry. *P. Howling.*

MIDNIGHT LEISURE 2 br.f. (Mar 30) Sula Bula 109 – Golden Bunting **—** (Golden Dipper 119) [1991 6m 7f] smallish, rather sparely-made filly: first reported foal: dam showed no form over hurdles: tailed off, including in seller. *R. Voorspuy.*

MIDNIGHT SAGA 3 b.c. Mashhor Dancer (USA) – Honey Pot 111 (Hotfoot 126) **64** [1990 a7g 1991 a6g⁶ a6g⁶ 7.5g 7f* a8g³ 9.2d⁵ 8m 8.2f⁴ 9.7f 10m 8.1s² 8m] good-topped, lengthy colt: 33/1, much improved when second of 22 in claimer at Chepstow: only plating-class handicapper otherwise, gambled-on winner at Carlisle in May: best form at 1m: has won on firm ground, but clearly best on soft: blinkered seventh start: bandaged last 2: trained first 8 by Sir Mark Prescott, then joined B. Curley after final one. *Mrs L. Piggott.*

MIDNIGHT VIOLET 2 b.f. (Apr 6) Sulaafah (USA) 119 – Nocturnal Bliss **54** (Pyjama Hunt 126) [1991 5g⁵ 5g 5g³ 5m⁴ 5m⁴ 5d 6g*] 1,500Y: lengthy, rather dipped-backed filly: moderate mover: third foal: half-sister to 1989 winning 2-y-o sprint plater Ballet Bliss (by Balidar): dam ran twice: won seller (no bid) at Warwick in June: was better suited by 6f than 5f: ran moderately on dead ground: carried head high third start: dead. *W. G. M. Turner.*

MIDSUMMER BREEZE 4 b.f. Tumble Wind (USA) – Pam Story (Sallust 134) **54** [1990 5m 5m⁶ 1991 a6g⁴ 5m 6g] sparely-made filly: lightly-raced and plating-class performer nowadays: stays 6f: acts on firm ground. *J. H. Baker.*

MIDSUMMER COMMON 3 b.f. Hotfoot 126 – Summer Fayre 64 (Reform **—** 132) [1990 5m 5g³ 6m⁶ 6g⁵ 7g 7m³ 7.5g⁵ 8m 1991 a6g⁴ a8g⁵ a7g⁵] small, sparely-made filly: has a round action: moderate plater: stays 1m: sold out of D. Morley's stable 850 gns Newmarket Autumn Sales. *A. Moore.*

MIDSUMMER DREAM 2 ch.c. (Mar 26) Midyan (USA) 124 – Saniette **63** (Crystal Palace (FR) 132) [1991 6m⁵ 6g³ 6f⁵] leggy, rather unfurnished colt: moderate mover: fourth foal: half-brother to 13.1f winner Shoe Tapper (by Song) and a winner in Switzerland by Crystal Palace: dam ran once in France: quite modest maiden: third of 23 in claimer at Goodwood: will be better suited by 7f: acts on firm ground: sold 8,200 gns Newmarket Autumn Sales. *I. A. Balding.*

MIDWEEK STORM 2 b.c. (Apr 10) Northern Tempest (USA) 120 – Lucky **51** Saran 72 (Lucky Wednesday 124) [1991 5g²] useful-looking colt: second foal: dam plater suited by 1m, is half-sister to useful sprinter Cyril's Choice: 25/1, staying-on second of 15 in seller at Beverley (claimed £6,405) in April: may stay 1m: seemed likely to improve. *W. J. Pearce.*

MIGHTY GLOW 7 gr.g. Kalaglow 132 – Faridetta 107 (Good Bond 122) [1990 **45 §** a13g 16m⁶ 14m* 12.5m 12f⁴ 14g* 12h 12m 10.6s 12g 14d 16m 16.2f³ 16m 10g 12m 1991 a14g a14g a16g² a14g a13g 14m 12m 12.1d 12.3d] leggy, workmanlike gelding: moderate mover: thoroughly unreliable handicapper: tailed off in amateur events final 2 starts: stays 2m: acts on firm going: often visored: has looked ungenuine: sold 7,400 gns Doncaster October Sales. *C. Tinkler.*

MIGHTY LADY (IRE) 2 b.f. (Feb 13) Petorius 117 – Great Land (USA) **57** (Friend's Choice (USA)) [1991 5g⁴ 5g² 6m⁵ 5.1m³ 5m³ 6m⁴ a6g⁶ a5g⁶ a6g a7g] 8,000Y: close-coupled filly: moderate mover: fourth foal: half-sister to 3-y-o Land Sun (by Red Sunset), unreliable sprint plater at 2 yrs: dam won 9 races at up to 9f in North America: plating-class maiden: ran badly (on equitrack and fibresand) last 3 outings: stays 6f: inconsistent. *M. R. Channon.*

MIGHTY-Q (IRE) 2 ch.c. (Mar 20) Red Sunset 120 – Kilpeacon (Florescence **49** 120) [1991 5g* 5d⁴ 5m⁵ 6m³ 5g 6d a7g³] IR 4,800F, 4,800Y: light-bodied colt: brother to Irish 1½m winner Tracy's Sundown and half-brother to 3 other winners, including 1987 2-y-o 5f seller winner Peaconpala (by Kampala): dam won from 5f to 7f in Ireland: plating-class form: won seller (retained 4,200 gns) at Warwick in April: good third of 10 in apprentice nursery on equitrack in August: stays 7f. *M. R. Channon.*

MIGHTY WIND 3 ch.c. Kris 135 – Storm Warning 117 (Tumble Wind (USA)) **50** [1990 NR 1991 7f⁵ 8g 6m⁶] rangy colt: first foal: dam sprinter: plating-class maiden: best effort over 1m: coltish first 2 starts: sold 6,400 gns Newmarket Autumn Sales, probably to Italy. *Lord Huntingdon.*

MILAGRO 2 br.f. (Mar 11) King of Spain 121 – Milva 56 (Jellaby 124) [1991 5g 6g² **78** 7g⁵ 6f³ 6m* 6m⁵ 6.1m³] robust filly: third foal: half-sister to modest 1989 2-y-o 7f winner Miltiades (by Magic Mirror) and 3-y-o Serious Time (by Good Times): dam 6f winner: modest form in varied events: won nursery at Windsor in August: seems suited by 6f: acts on firm ground: consistent. *R. Hannon.*

MILANESE 2 b.f. (Apr 13) Elegant Air 119 – Embroideress 80 (Stanford 121§) **60** p [1991 7g⁴] leggy filly: sister to 3-y-o 5f (at 2 yrs) and 6f winner Sacque and half-sister to 1m and 1¼m seller winner Tom Clapton (by Daring March): dam 5f to 7f winner: 50/1 and ridden by 7-lb claimer, promising 10 lengths fourth of 22 to Oumaldaaya in maiden at Newmarket in November, catching eye running on well final 1½f: will stay 1m +: sure to improve, and win a race. *D. Morley.*

MILITARY EXPERT 2 ch.c. (Jun 9) Superlative 118 – Times 55 (Junius (USA) **73** 124) [1991 6.9m 6g 7m a6g 7m³ 7.5f 7g* 7m* 7.6d²] 2,000Y, 2,500 2-y-o: workmanlike colt: poor mover: second reported foal: dam disappointing maiden: modest performer: made all in large-field sellers at Wolverhampton (no bid) and Redcar (retained 8,000 gns) in autumn: below best in Chester nursery final start: suited by 7f: below form on very firm ground: suited by forcing tactics. *Capt. J. Wilson.*

MILITARY FASHION 5 ch.h. Mill Reef (USA) 141 – Smarten Up 119 (Sharpen **107** Up 127) [1990 10m² 9m* 12s 1991 9m³ 8g⁶] tall, good-topped horse: moderate walker: poor mover: useful performer: suffered hairline fracture of cannon bone in 1990: first run for 11 months, very good third to Susurration in listed event at Newmarket in October: ran moderately in similar event there following month: stays 1¼m: acts on good to firm going. *L. M. Cumani.*

MILITARY HONOUR 6 b.g. Shirley Heights 130 – Princess Tiara 111 **47** (Crowned Prince (USA) 128) [1990 NR 1991 16s 16.2g²] lengthy, attractive gelding: poor mover: very lightly raced on flat, plating-class performer nowadays: stays 2m: acts on soft going: blinkered (ran well) final start: bandaged. *M. W. Easterby.*

MILIYEL 2 ch.f. (Feb 26) Rousillon (USA) 133 – Amalee 57 (Troy 137) [1991 6m⁶] — good-bodied filly: fourth foal: half-sister to 3-y-o Masaken (by Doulab) and 1988 2-y-o 6f winner Musil (by Mummy's Pet): dam maiden stayed 14.6f, may have been temperamental: 16/1 from 8/1, burly and green, running-on sixth of 16 in maiden at Lingfield (slowly away) in May: seemed sure to improve. *B. Hanbury.*

MILLADOR 2 b.f. (Apr 17) Glint of Gold 128 – Tsar's Bride (Song 132) [1991 6m **44** 7.5f⁵ 6.1f 7m] 3,300Y: big, good-topped filly: has scope: seventh foal: half-sister to 3-y-o 6f winner Lallapaloosa (by Superlative) and 2 other winners, including 1½m winner Winter Palace (by Persian Bold): dam lightly raced: poor maiden: sweating (stiff task, ran poorly) in York nursery final outing: will be suited by 1m +. *M. H. Tompkins.*

MILL BURN 2 ch.c. (Mar 17) Precocious 126 – Northern Ballerina 52 (Dance In — Time (CAN)) [1991 7m 8m] 4,200Y, 6,500Y, 13,000 2-y-o: lengthy colt: third foal: brother to 3-y-o 6f winner Pretonic: dam won sellers at 7f and 8.2f: poor form in late-season Leicester maidens. *I. Campbell.*

MILL DE LEASE 6 b.g. Milford 119 – Melting Snows 88 (High Top 131) [1990 — a14g 11g a11g 14d⁶ 17m] leggy, workmanlike, angular gelding: poor performer at 4 yrs: no worthwhile form since: probably needs further than 1m and stays 1½m: probably acts on any going: has been bandaged. *J. Dooler.*

MILLERS TALE (USA) 3 bl.c. Nureyev (USA) 131 – Mill Queen 86 (Mill Reef **84**
(USA) 141) [1990 NR 1991 7d⁴ 7f*] good-topped, attractive colt: fifth foal:
half-brother to 1½m winner Golden Mill (by Mr Prospector): dam won at 7f and 9f:
improved considerably to win 7-runner maiden at Salisbury in August by 3 lengths
from Lochsong, leading 3f out: sold to join M. Brittain 10,500 gns Newmarket
Autumn Sales. *G. Harwood.*

MILLFIT (USA) 2 b.f. (Mar 24) Blushing Groom (FR) 131 – Musique Royale **62**
(USA) (Northern Dancer) [1991 6f⁴ 8f⁶ 7g³] $235,000Y: leggy filly: has scope: third
foal: half-sister to 1990 French 3-y-o Sombre Lady (by Sharpen Up), successful
twice at around 9f, and middle-distance maiden Out On Allege (by Alleged): dam,
Irish 7f winner at 3 yrs, is half-sister to Gay Fandango: quite modest maiden: easily
best effort at Catterick (on toes, always prominent) final start: likely to stay 1m+.
B. Hanbury.

MILL FLIGHT (IRE) 3 b.f. Millfontaine 114 – Diyala (FR) (Direct Flight) [1990 **—**
5m 5g⁶ 6d³ 6g a7g 7d 1991 7d 7m⁶ 8g] leggy filly: poor on most form, including in
sellers: should be suited by further than 6f. *Mrs P. A. Barker.*

MILLIE (USA) 3 ch.f. Master Willie 129 – La Zonga (USA) (Run The Gantlet **64**
(USA) [1990 7g 1991 10.1g 10f⁵ 11.7g 10m* 10m³ 12g³ 10.5g³ 12f³] sparely-made
filly: moderate mover: quite modest performer: won apprentice handicap at
Kempton in July: sweating, fair third in claimer (claimed to join J. Jenkins £5,689) at
Folkestone final start: worth a try at 1¾m: acts on firm going. *H. Candy.*

MILLION MILES (USA) 3 b.c. Dixieland Band (USA) – Highly Noble (USA) **102**
(Vaguely Noble 140) [1990 6m⁵ 8d⁶ 7m³ 1991 10.8g³ 12m⁵ 14.6f* 16.2g* 16.1m*]
attractive colt, rather dipped backed: has a round action: developed into a useful
performer in the summer, winning maiden (on toes, edged left) at Doncaster and
handicaps at Haydock and Newmarket: stays 2m: acts on firm going: reportedly
fractured off-fore cannon bone just before Cesarewitch. *B. W. Hills.*

MILLPOND BOY 7 ch.g. Connaught 130 – Nonsensical 99 (Silly Season 127)
[1990 11.7g² 10m 14g 1991 12.3g] workmanlike gelding: has quick action: plating-
class winner as 4-y-o: little form since: stays 13f: acts on any going: has hung left.
R. J. Hodges.

MILLROUS 3 b.f. Rousillon (USA) 133 – Brookfield Miss 73 (Welsh Pageant 132) **44**
[1990 NR 1991 12.2g⁴ 14.1m³ 12m 9.7g 8.2m⁴] 8,000Y: tall, leggy, angular filly:
seventh foal: half-sister to several winners, including 1¼m to 2m winner Merton
Mill (by Dominion) and useful 7f and 1m filly Littlefield (by Bay Express): dam
showed a little ability at 2 yrs: running-on fourth of 18 in apprentice selling handicap
at Nottingham, first worthwhile form since debut: may be suited by return to
further: carried head high second and third starts: retained by trainer 1,100 gns
Newmarket Autumn Sales. *R. Guest.*

MILLSOLIN (IRE) 3 b.c. Millfontaine 114 – Isolin (Saulingo 122) [1990 6m 7m **61**
6d 1991 8.2d⁵ 8m⁶ 10g 8d 7m⁴] leggy, workmanlike colt: has a round action: quite
modest maiden: stays 1m: easily best efforts on good to firm ground: has wandered
under pressure: sometimes sweating. *A. R. Davison.*

MILLY BLACK (IRE) 3 b.f. Double Schwartz 128 – Milly Lass (FR) 85 (Bold **56**
Lad (USA)) [1990 5m² 6m 1991 7g³ 10.1d² 10m 10g 9s 10.8g² 11m⁵ 11.8m 8d]
close-coupled filly: plating-class performer: stays 11f: acts on dead ground and good
to firm: blinkered last 4 starts: ridden by 7-lb claimer, hung badly left final start:
inconsistent: sold 2,600 gns Newmarket December Sales. *I. A. Balding.*

MILLY-MANDY 3 b.f. Dominion 123 – Ulla Laing 107 (Mummy's Pet 125) [1990 **—**
6d 1991 5m 6.9f] leggy, light-framed filly: signs of a little ability on debut, none as
3-y-o: sold 540 gns Ascot November Sales. *R. Akehurst.*

MILNE'S WAY 4 ch.f. The Noble Player (USA) 126 – Daring Way (USA) 78 **68**
(Alydar (USA)) [1990 6g 6g⁶ 6m 8.5d⁵ 8m 8h* 8f³ 8.3m 7m⁵ 10d 8g⁴ 8m 1991
8m⁴ 8f* 8f³ 8.5m⁶ 10m³] workmanlike filly: has a round action: quite modest
handicapper: won at Bath in May: set too much to do when good equal-third at
Newmarket final start: should prove better at around 1¼m than shorter: acts on
hard going: often edgy. *G. Lewis.*

MILTON BURN 10 b.h. Sexton Blake 126 – Neasden Belle 66 (Sovereign Path **40**
125) [1990 16.2m 16s 1991 16g 12s* 12g 12f 12g 20g 12v 16.2g] leggy, angular horse:
poor walker: has rather a round action: quite modest handicapper on his day: usually
at his best in spring, and 33/1-winner at Kempton (fourth win there) in April: well
below that form after: effective at 1½m and stays very well: ideally suited by an easy
surface: has worn blinkers and a visor. *C. A. Austin.*

MILTON ROOMS (IRE)   2 ch.c. (Mar 21) Where To Dance (USA) – Raga Rine   —
(Raga Navarro (ITY) 119) [1991 6g6] 5,000F: first reported foal: dam won over 6f in
Ireland: 33/1, well beaten in maiden at Ayr (slowly away) in July. *C. B. B. Booth.*

MILZIG (USA)   2 b.c. (Feb 9) Ziggy's Boy (USA) – Legume (USA) (Northern   **84**
Baby (CAN) 127) [1991 7g5 7.1m5 8.1g2 8m3 8m4] $20,000Y: strong, lengthy colt:
has a quick action: first foal: dam unraced: sire stakes-winning sprinter/miler: fair
maiden: in frame, staying on, at Newmarket behind Wesaam and Bold Pursuit last 2
starts: suited by 1m: bandaged first 2 starts. *D. R. C. Elsworth.*

MIMINING   5 ch.m. Tower Walk 130 – Louisianalightning (Music Boy 124) [1990   **53**
6m 5m5 5g3 6g a7g5 a5g 6g* 5d3 a6g* 6g 1991 6g 6m 6.1m6 6g 6d 6m4 5.1d 6s3 a5g
a7g] lengthy, good-quartered mare: turns near-fore in: moderate mover: plating-
class handicapper: below form last 2 starts: ideally suited by 6f: acts on good to firm
and goes well on an easy surface (acts on heavy): none too consistent. *G. M. Moore.*

MIMIQUE   2 b.c. (May 30) Sadler's Wells (USA) 132 – Millieme 107 (Mill Reef   **88** p
(USA) 141) [1991 8d4 7d2] IR 200,000Y: quite good-topped colt: good walker:
brother to smart French middle-distance performer Myth To Reality and
half-brother to several winners, including useful 1987 2-y-o 1m winner Titus Groan
(by Gorytus): dam, fourth in 1m Prix des Reservoirs at 2 yrs in France, is sister to
Shirley Heights: in frame in minor event at Newmarket (burly) and 22-runner
maiden at Doncaster (favourite, carried head high after quickening 2f out and caught
post by For Reg) in autumn: races keenly: will stay 1¼m, further if settling better.
H. R. A. Cecil.

MINARET   3 b.f. Jalmood (USA) 126 – Montania 68 (Mourne 126) [1990 NR 1991   **42**
10g 12g5 14.1m4 14.1f4] smallish, workmanlike filly: has a round action: sister to
modest maiden Indian Hill and half-sister to several winners, including middle-
distance performers High Tension (by Vitiges) and Base Camp (by Derring-Do):
dam 7f winner: fourth, showing poor form, in summer claimers. *G. A. Pritchard-
Gordon.*

MINDOMICA   2 b.f. (Apr 8) Dominion 123 – Nordica 99 (Northfields (USA))   **63**
[1991 6f2 7g2 7g*] 5,000Y: sparely-made filly: second foal: dam winner at 6f (in
Ireland) and 1m, is out of half-sister to Oaks winner Fair Salinia: quite modest form
in maiden auctions: made all at Edinburgh (15/8) in July: will stay 1m +. *M. Bell.*

MIND THE STEP   4 b.c. Shareef Dancer (USA) 135 – Mytinia 94 (Bustino 136)   **84**
[1990 10.6s6 10d* 10.2s 1991 11.7g2 10g* 11.6m3 11.9m4 10m] lengthy, quite
attractive colt: has a quick action: fair handicapper: won at Windsor in July despite
wandering: soon off bridle final start: effective at 1¼m to 11.7f: often on edge or
coltish: temperament under suspicion. *G. Harwood.*

MINDY (IRE)   3 b.g. Salmon Leap (USA) 131 – Malija (FR) (Malicious) [1990 6f   **42**
7m 8d 7g 8m 6d 1991 11.7g a11g 6m a8g* a8g4 a8g2 7m3] workmanlike gelding: made
all in handicap at Southwell in July: suited by 1m on fibresand: blinkered last 6
outings: winner over hurdles. *N. A. Callaghan.*

MINERS LAW (IRE)   3 b.c.c. Law Society (USA) 130 – Lighted Lamp (USA) (Sir   **58** §
Gaylord) [1990 7m 7g 7m 1991 10.8d 12f3 12.2m2 12.5m 12g3 12d6 11.5g2 11.7m 12m2
12m2 16.2f2 14.1f4 14.6m2 10m] rather leggy colt: has a round action: in frame,
showing quite modest form, in handicaps, claimers then seller: probably stays 2m:
acts on firm going: often blinkered, once visored: trained until after eleventh start
by G. Lewis: has run in snatches and looked untrustworthy. *B. Preece.*

MING BLUE   2 ch.f. (Mar 23) Primo Dominie 121 – Burnt Amber (Balidar 133)   **52**
[1991 6m4 7g 7.6d4] 23,000Y: strong filly: second foal: half-sister to 3-y-o Fireglow
(by Mummy's Game): dam unraced half-sister to Lockton: plating-class maiden:
best efforts when in frame, at Chester (sweating) in October: should stay 1m: acts
on good to firm and dead ground. *P. J. Makin.*

MING COURT   3 br.f. Daring March 116 – Slick Chick 89 (Shiny Tenth 120) [1990   **37**
5m5 6g 6m 6d 8m a7g 1991 a8g2 a10g3 a7g4 8.2d6 6m 7g] good-topped filly: poor
maiden: stays 1¼m: seems unsuited by a soft surface: visored penultimate start: not
best of rides for an apprentice: sold 750 gns Ascot May Sales. *S. Dow.*

MINGUS (USA)   4 b.c. The Minstrel (CAN) 135 – Sylph (USA) 110 (Alleged   **76**
(USA) 138) [1990 10g2 12g3 12d* 1991 11.9g4 12m 12g 12.1d] compact, heavy-topped
colt: has long stride: modest handicapper: ran moderately after reappearance:
better at 1½m than shorter: best efforts with give in the ground (acts on dead):
tends to hang: blinkered penultimate start: sold to join Mrs J. Ramsden's stable
17,000 gns Newmarket Autumn Sales. *G. Harwood.*

MINIMIZE   4 b.c. Alzao (USA) 117 – Timinala 58 (Mansingh (USA) 120) [1990 8f2   **97**
8.5g2 10d6 10f* 10f4 10m2 9m 10s2 12s 1991 10g2 10.1f2] strong, close-coupled colt:

fairly useful handicapper: ran well in quite valuable events at Kempton and Epsom in first half of 1991: worth another try over 1½m: acts on any going. *L. M. Cumani.*

MINIZEN MUSIC (IRE)   3 b.g. Anita's Prince 126 – Northern Amber (Shack (USA) 118) [1990 5g* 5m* 5m 6g 6g 5m⁶ 5m 5v² 5m a5g 5d 1991 5s⁵ 6d⁵ 5f 6m 6g⁶ 5m 5m* 5m 5s² 6d⁵ 6g³ 5m² 6m³ 6f³ 5f 5m 6f⁶ 5m 6m 6g 5d] leggy, sparely-made gelding: poor mover: plating-class handicapper: won at Carlisle in June: below form last 7 starts: effective at 5f and 6f: acts on any going: blinkered (ran creditably) once at 2 yrs: changed hands 1,550 gns Doncaster May Sales after third start. *M. Brittain.*   **52** d

MINKES BOY (IRE)   3 ch.g. Krayyan 117 – Willow Bird 74 (Weepers Boy 124) [1990 7f⁴ a7g 8m 1991 a11g 10g 10m⁶ 12.3f 11.9g 9.9f] strong, lengthy gelding: good walker: poor maiden: blinkered last 7 outings: sold 800 gns Doncaster October Sales. *J. S. Wainwright.*   —

MINOAN LIGHT (IRE)   2 b.c. (May 23) Trojan Fen 118 – Ashton Amber (On Your Mark 125) [1991 a6g⁵ a8g] IR 4,300F, 13,000Y: half-brother to several winners, including 6f winner Saffron Light (by Hard Fought) and 6f to 1m winner and Irish 2000 Guineas second Mr John (by Northfields): dam once-raced half-sister to Red Alert: beaten long way in December maidens at Lingfield. *R. Hannon.*   —

MINSK   5 ch.m. Kabour 80 – Wedded Bliss 76 (Relko 136) [1990 a7g a5g 8m⁵ 7m 7g 6g 7f 8f⁶ 12m 8f 10m 1991 5f 5g⁶ 5g⁶ 5h 5g] workmanlike mare: bad plater: unseated rider to post on reappearance. *J. K. Kinane.*   —

MINSKIP (USA)   3 ch.f. The Minstrel (CAN) 135 – Fabulous Native (USA) (Le Fabuleux 133) [1990 5m⁴ 5m* 5m⁶ 6m 1991 7m⁴ 8m⁴] neat filly: moderate walker: modest performer: fourth of 5 in handicaps in the summer: should have been suited by further: sweating and bandaged near-hind final start: stud. *B. W. Hills.*   **64**

MINSTREL MAGIC (IRE)   2 gr.f. (May 2) Double Schwartz 128 – Margaree (Energist) [1991 5g² 6m 5f² 5f] IR 6,500F: leggy, close-coupled, sparely-made filly: half-sister to several winners in Ireland, including middle-distance winner Growing Power (by Red Sunset): dam Irish maiden: poor maiden: dead. *J. Berry.*   **46**

MINSTREL'S AGE (USA)   2 b.c. (Feb 22) The Minstrel (CAN) 135 – Wayage (USA) (Mr Prospector (USA)) [1991 5g⁵ 7m 7m⁴ 6m⁶ 7.9g² 7f* 8s] leggy, close-coupled colt: first foal: dam French maiden daughter of smart French mare Waya, later top class at up to 1½m in USA: fairly useful performer: made all, racing wide, in nursery at Yarmouth in September: looked to be progressing well, but ran moderately in Gran Criterium at Milan 6 weeks later: stays 1m: possibly unsuited by soft ground: active type, usually edgy and on toes, and sometimes sweats. *C. E. Brittain.*   **90**

MINT ADDITION   2 b.f. (Jan 31) Tate Gallery (USA) 117 – Nana's Girl 109 (Tin Whistle 128) [1991 5m 5m⁴ 6g² 5.3m⁴] rather sparely-made filly: has a quick action: sister to 3-y-o Port Sunlight, successful at 8.2f (at 2 yrs) and 9f, and half-sister to numerous winners, including good 1977 2-y-o Aythorpe (by Ridan) and Royal Boy (by Realm), smart at up to 7f: dam, useful at up to 1m, is sister to very smart Tin King: plating-class maiden: bred to stay 1m+: not seen out after August. *R. Hannon.*   **50**

MIRAMEDE   3 b.f. Norwick (USA) 120 – Mrewa (Runnymede 123) [1990 NR 1991 6.9f 5.3g⁴ 5.1g] lengthy filly: has scope: seventh foal: half-sister to one-time useful but unreliable sprinter Ashtina (by Tina's Pet): dam twice-raced maiden: ridden by 7-lb claimer, 6½ lengths fourth of 6 to Chelsworth in maiden at Brighton in October: tailed off in claimer 4 weeks later. *R. J. Hodges.*   —

MIRA MONTE   2 b.f. (Apr 15) Baillamont (USA) 124 – Mirea (USA) 104 (The Minstrel (CAN) 135) [1991 8v*] half-sister to French 10.5f to 11f winner Minime (by Glint of Gold) and French 8.3f (at 2 yrs) and 1m winner Magical Mystery (by Procida): dam French 2-y-o 7f winner: successful in maiden at Deauville in October by 4 lengths: should improve. *F. Boutin, France.*   ?

MIRANDA JAY   3 b. or br.f. Night Shift (USA) – Assisi (Habitat 134) [1990 7g³ 7m* 1991 8d² 8g 8m⁵ 7.1s⁶ 6g² 7m³ 7.6d] strong, deep-bodied filly: moderate mover: fairly useful at best: second in £7,400 contest at Thirsk and (first form after) minor event at Leicester: tailed off in handicap final start: should prove ideally suited by further than 6f, and stays 1m: acts on good to firm ground and dead. *M. A. Jarvis.*   **90** d

MIRANDINHA   7 ch.g. Nicholas Bill 125 – Matsui 61 (Falcon 131) [1990 NR 1991 16.2g] big, heavy-bodied gelding: fifth foal: dam stayer: well beaten in maiden at Beverley in April, only run on flat: winner over fences in January. *B. Ellison.*   —

MIRROR'S IMAGE 3 ch.f. Never So Bold 135 – Mirabiliary (USA) 74 (Crow **44** (FR) 134) [1990 6f⁶ 1991 8d⁴ 8g 8.3d³ 8g 6m] lengthy filly: plating-class maiden: best effort on reappearance: stays 1m: form only on dead going: blinkered and mulish at stalls third and fourth starts: sold 2,500 gns Newmarket December Sales. *G. A. Pritchard-Gordon.*

MIRUJON 3 br.c. Prince Sabo 123 – Quick Kick (Saritamer (USA)) [1990 NR 1991 — 6s] 4,400Y: workmanlike colt: fourth foal: dam ran twice: last of 8 in maiden at Newcastle: dead. *R. Guest.*

MISAKA TOGO (USA) 2 b.f. (Mar 8) Theatrical 128 – Eastland (USA) 110 **101** (Exceller (USA) 129) [1991 7g² 7m³ 7g³ 7m* 8d* 8.5s] second foal: half-sister to French 3-y-o 1½m winner Joshua (by Riverman): dam won 10.5f Prix Cleopatre, later also Grade 3 winner in USA at 1½m: successful in maiden at Limerick (by 4 lengths) and Group 3 event at Leopardstown (by 2 lengths from Ebaziya) within 4 days in September: well beaten in Selima Stakes at Laurel Park 5 weeks later: bred to be suited by middle distances: acts on good to firm and dead ground. *D. K. Weld, Ireland.*

MISCHAK (USA) 4 b.g. Miswaki (USA) 124 – Chuckles (USA) (Riverman **40** (USA) 131) [1990 8m 8g⁵ 8g 10m⁴ 8g a8g⁴ a12g² a14g a10g³ a11g 1991 8.2d⁵ 10d 12m⁵ a18g 14.6m] workmanlike gelding: moderate walker: poor handicapper: soundly beaten last 2 starts, visored final one: stays 1½m: best efforts on all-weather surfaces: very slowly away and looked to take little interest once at 3 yrs. *D. T. Thom.*

MISCHIEVOUS TYKE 5 ch.m. Flying Tyke 90 – Habatashie 62 (Habat 127) **42** [1990 8.2f a7g³ 1991 7.5g 6m 7m a5g⁴] leggy, good-topped mare: carries condition: poor handicapper: stays 7.5f: acts on firm and dead going. *A. Smith.*

MISDEMEANOURS GIRL (IRE) 3 b.f. Fairy King (USA) – Dar-A-Meter **64** (Dara Monarch 128) [1990 5m 5.3h⁶ 5f³ 6m 1991 a7g⁶ a7g⁵ a6g⁵ a6g³ a5g² 5f⁵ 5g³ 5.8m⁵ 5m³ 5m² 5m² 5.1d³ 6d² a6g³ 5g* 5f³ 5f 5.1m 5m⁴ 6.1m] small, lengthy, sparely-made filly: quite modest handicapper: won at Sandown in July: stays 6f: acts on firm and dead going: largely consistent. *M. R. Channon.*

MISIL (USA) 3 ro.c. Miswaki (USA) 124 – April Edge (The Axe 115) [1990 6s* **120** 6g² 6g² 7s² 8v³ 1991 8s* 8v* 8g* 8d* 8v² 8v*] $40,000F, 21,000Y: sixth foal: half-brother to 3 winners in USA: dam, minor winner at around 1m in USA, is sister to smart American colt April Axe and daughter of useful Irish filly (in frame at up to 1m) April Bloom: won maiden at Milan at 2 yrs: developed into a very smart performer in 1991, successful in minor event at Milan and Premio Parioli (on demotion of Fortune's Wheel) at Rome in April, Premio Emilio Turati (by 2 lengths from Flying Brave) at Milan in June, minor event at Milan in September, and Group 2 Premio Ribot at Rome in November (by 3½ lengths from Sikeston): beaten length by Sikeston in Premio Vittorio di Capua at Milan: stays 1m: acts on heavy going. *V. Caruso, Italy.*

MISSAL (IRE) 2 b.f. (May 20) Alzao (USA) 117 – Priors Mistress 71 (Sallust 134) **46** [1991 5g⁵ 6g 6f 9m 6g 6m 6.9f 7.6m] 3,500Y: compact filly: fourth reported foal: half-sister to 1m winner Prior Charge (by Tender King) and 1¼m seller winner Super Idea (by Red Sunset): dam disappointing: poor maiden: sometimes blinkered: sold 2,900 gns Newmarket Autumn Sales. *Pat Mitchell.*

MISS ALLEGED (USA) 4 b.f. Alleged (USA) 138 – Miss Tusculum **125** (USA) (Boldnesian (USA)) [1990 11g* 10.5g* 12d* 12m² 1991 12d³ 12s³ 12m⁴ 10d² 12d 10s⁵ 12g* 12g*]

In one of the season's most extraordinary results, the rank outsider Miss Alleged provided Europe with its fourth winner in eight runnings of the Breeders' Cup Turf, which was run at Churchill Downs in early-November. Few of those familiar with Miss Alleged's performances in Europe in 1991 would have given her a prayer. Returning to the track after cracking a pedal bone when dividing Salsabil and In The Groove in the Prix Vermeille as a three-year-old, Miss Alleged failed to win in six starts as a four-year-old before the Breeders' Cup Turf—her record included fourth in the Grand Prix de Saint-Cloud and eleventh in the Arc (in which she met with interference)—and she was the last to gain entry to the field, as a reserve. Eight of the twenty-one European-trained runners in the Breeders' Cup races ran in the Breeders' Cup Turf, won previously for Europe by Lashkari (1984), Pebbles (1985) and In The Wings (1990). The Prix de l'Arc de Triomphe third Pistolet Bleu, who started favourite, and the tough and genuine filly In The Groove, an

unlucky loser in the Champion Stakes on her latest outing, looked the pick of
the European challenge which also included Quest For Fame and Saddlers'
Hall from Britain. Miss Alleged was in the leading group from the start and
fought out the finish with North America's 1990 champion turf colt Itsallgreektome. Itsallgreektome had the misfortune the previous year to be run
out of it close home in the Mile by Royal Academy and a similar fate befell him
in his chosen race in 1991. He looked to have the Breeders' Cup Turf in his
grasp when taking over from the front-running Canadian challenger Sky
Classic (winner of his previous six races) early in the straight, but Miss
Alleged produced a storming finish under hard riding to win by half a length,
with Quest For Fame two lengths further back in third, ahead of Sky Classic
and Pistolet Bleu, who had every chance; In The Groove came seventh and
Saddlers' Hall tenth.

That Miss Alleged should recover her best form in the Breeders' Cup
Turf was timely for her connections, but her success raised a few eyebrows.
She ran on bute and lasix, two proprietary preparations which are permitted in
Kentucky. Such medication is prohibited in Europe and there have been
persistent calls from European interests for the Breeders' Cup organisers to
ban medication in the seven Breeders' Cup races. Both bute and lasix are
considered by many to assist horses on whom they are used, though neither is
a performance-enhancing drug in its own right. Bute is used to relieve pain
associated with inflammation of joints and muscles; lasix is a diuretic drug,
often used in the States on horses that tend to break blood vessels, 'bleeders'
as they are known. Miss Alleged reportedly burst a blood vessel in the Prix de
l'Arc. Scientific evidence that lasix decreases the incidence of broken blood
vessels is tenuous but some American trainers swear by it, claiming a horse's
performance is usually improved the first time on lasix. European-trained
Breeders' Cup runners have been treated with permitted medication before
—Miesque for example, who ran without medication in 1987, was on bute
when gaining her second successive Breeders' Cup Mile victory in 1988. It's
perhaps unfortunate, however, that more European owners and trainers are
nowadays following a 'when in Rome . . .' policy. No fewer than ten of the
twenty-one European challengers in the latest Breeders' Cup races were
listed on the official programme to run on medication in their respective
races: Quest For Fame, Pistolet Bleu and Dear Doctor were also treated with
bute in the Turf; as was the Breeders' Cup Juvenile winner Arazi and the
Breeders' Cup Classic runner Cudas; Danseuse du Soir was down to run on
bute and lasix in the Breeders' Cup Mile, in which Polar Falcon, Priolo and
Second Set were listed as having bute. Had European owners and trainers
maintained a united front it would surely have made it more likely that the
Breeders' Cup organisers would eventually have offered some sort of com-
promise solution on the burning issue of the use of medication. A ban on
preparations such as bute and lasix might at least have been achieved in the
two grass races on the programme which draw the strongest numerical

538

European challenge each year (there were three runners from France, two from Britain and one from Ireland in the latest Mile). Whether or not the use of bute and lasix made any difference to Miss Alleged's performance it is difficult to say, but there will always be those who firmly believe it did. For the record, she ran on lasix when a fair fifth in the Budweiser International at Laurel a fortnight before the Breeders' Cup.

Miss Alleged (USA) (b.f. 1987)	Alleged (USA) (b 1974)	Hoist The Flag (b 1968)	Tom Rolfe
			Wavy Navy
		Princess Pout (b 1966)	Prince John
			Determined Lady
	Miss Tusculum (USA) (b 1970)	Boldnesian (b 1963)	Bold Ruler
			Alanesian
		Sailor Town (b 1965)	Sailor
			Dashing

Like her sire, Miss Alleged was a late-developer. She didn't see a racecourse at two and had only four races at three, remaining unbeaten, stepped up in class on each outing, until the Prix Vermeille. Miss Alleged is typical of many of Alleged's best progeny which tend to take time and need ten furlongs plus. The European classic winners Law Society (Irish Derby), Leading Counsel (Irish St Leger), Midway Lady (One Thousand Guineas and Oaks), Sir Harry Lewis (Irish Derby) and Hours After (Prix du Jockey-Club) are among Alleged's best-known offspring. Alleged's name as a sire is also likely to become firmly established through the achievements of his daughters as broodmares. Suave Dancer's dam is by Alleged, as is the dam of the 1990 Belmont Stakes winner Go And Go; both Suave Dancer and Go And Go are by Northern Dancer stallions (there's no Northern Dancer influence in Alleged's pedigree). Miss Alleged's dam never ran but she has produced two other noteworthy winners in North America in Bold Josh (by Tentam) and Nancy's Champion (by Northern Jove); Bold Josh won several stakes races at around a mile and stayed at least a mile and a quarter, and Nancy's Champion won stakes races at up to nine furlongs. Miss Alleged stays a mile and a half well and acts on any going from good to firm to soft (she has never encountered more extreme conditions). She remained in the States after the Breeders' Cup and went into training with Charlie Whittingham who saddled her to win the slowly-run Hollywood Turf Cup in mid-December when she confirmed Breeders' Cup form with Itsallgreektome and Quest For Fame who again filled the minor places: she won by a head and a length and a quarter. *P. Bary, France.*

MISS ARAGON 3 b.f. Aragon 118 – Lavenham Blue (Streetfighter 120) [1990 6d **42** 5v³ 5s 1991 6d 6m⁶ 6f 10g 6m⁴ 6s⁴ a6g³] rangy filly: good mover: poor maiden: ran well last 3 starts: doesn't stay 1¼m, should stay beyond 6f: has form on good to firm ground and heavy. *Miss L. C. Siddall.*

MISS BELL RINGER 3 b.f. Belfort (FR) 89 – Immatation (FR) 67 (Polyfoto **49** 124) [1990 5.8f⁵ 5f⁶ 6d5 a6g⁶ a7g 1991 5f⁶ 6g 5m 6m*] workmanlike, good-quartered filly: best effort to win 17-runner apprentice selling handicap (no bid) at Leicester in October: suited by 6f: acts on good to firm ground. *C. J. Hill.*

MISS BLUEBIRD (IRE) 2 b.f. (Feb 14) Bluebird (USA) 125 – Welsh Dancer **98** 94 (Welsh Saint 126) [1991 5m² 6m³ 6g⁴ 7m 7s] IR 21,000Y: tall, lengthy filly: has plenty of scope: second living foal: half-sister to Irish 3-y-o 7f winner Sparkling Solo (by Glow): dam Irish 2-y-o 5f winner: fairly useful form in listed or pattern races on all 5 starts, running Marling to a neck in Charles Heidsieck National Stakes at Sandown and Musicale to around a length in Hillsdown Cherry Hinton Stakes at Newmarket: ran well when around 7 lengths last of 8 to Arazi in Prix de la Salamandre at Longchamp in September, poorly in Goffs Million at the Curragh 5 weeks later: probably better suited by 7f than less: possibly unsuited by soft ground. *P. A. Kelleway.*

MISS BOBBY BENNETT 4 b.f. Kings Lake (USA) 133 – Karen Lee M (USA) **71** § (Roman Line) [1990 8g 8m⁴ 10g5 12.4m⁵ 13.1m² 13.1m⁷m* 11.7m* 12g⁶ 11.7g 11.5m⁵ 1991 12g⁴ 13.3m] quite good-topped filly: modest handicapper: tailed off (soon off bridle) in Newbury Autumn Cup final start: should stay further than 13f: acts on good to firm ground: below form when visored once: has twice hung badly left, has run in snatches: winning hurdler: one to leave alone. *M. C. Pipe.*

MISS BRAFIELD 3 ch.f. Ballacashtal (CAN) – Ardtully Lass 64 (Cavo Doro —
124) [1990 NR 1991 7m 9m⁵] smallish filly: sixth foal: dam 1m and 1¼m winner:
always behind in maiden and apprentice race at Lingfield: sold 775 gns Ascot
November Sales. *R. Simpson.*

MISS BRIGHTSIDE 3 ch.f. Crofthall 110 – Fidget (Workboy 123) [1990 5d 1991 46
5m³ 6d⁴ 6g² 6f³ 7f⁵ 6f 6.1m⁵ 6m 6m⁵] leggy filly: plating-class maiden: worth
another try beyond 6f: acts on firm and dead going: has run creditably when
sweating. *A. Smith.*

MISS BROUGHTON 3 b.f. Never So Bold 135 – Yelney 65 (Blakeney 126) 60
[1990 NR 1991 a7g⁵ a6g⁶ 6s⁴ 6d* 7g 6g 7g⁶ 9d 8d 8d a8g] 12,000Y: workmanlike
filly: half-sister to 5-y-o 6f to 1m winner Crosby (by Music Boy), and 2 other
winners, including middle-distance stayer Golden Heights (by Shirley Heights):
dam 1½m winner out of Cheshire Oaks winner Yelda: quite modest form at best:
won handicap at Hamilton in April: best effort at 6f on dead ground: usually soon
behind: seems unreliable. *W. J. Musson.*

MISS BURFIELD 3 ch.f. Faustus (USA) 118 – Lady Acquiesce 67 (Galivanter 41
131) [1990 5m 7g 6d a6g a7g⁴ 1991 a10g⁶ a7g 8g 8g⁵ 10.2d 8d³ 6m⁶ 8.3m² 8.3m² 8f]
plater: stays 8.3f: acts on good to firm ground: blinkered (sweating, ran fairly well)
sixth start. *R. Hannon.*

MISS CALCULATE 3 ch.f. Mummy's Game 120 – Antique Bloom 101 (Sterling —
Bay (SWE)) [1990 5m 5f 5m³ 5f⁶ 6g 6g 5g² a6g* 6f² a7g* a6g* 7g 7d⁵ a8g⁴ 1991 7m]
lengthy, angular filly: has a moderate action: successful in sellers and a claimer at
Southwell at 2 yrs: in need of race only start in 1991, in May: best form at 6f and 7f,
and when blinkered. *Capt. J. Wilson.*

MISS CARANGE (IRE) 3 ch.f. Henbit (USA) 130 – Carange (Known Fact —
(USA) 135) [1990 5m 7m 1991 6m 10g] workmanlike filly: no show in sellers and
claimers: bred to stay at least 1m. *C. J. Hill.*

MISS COOKIE 3 ch.f. Nicholas Bill 125 – Maryland Cookie (USA) 101 (Bold 75
Hour) [1990 6g⁴ 1991 7f² 7m³ 8g² 7d⁵ 6.9f⁴ 7g³ 5d] sturdy filly: modest maiden:
below form last 4 starts: needs further than 5f, and stays 1m: acts on firm ground:
has looked difficult ride: sold 4,200 gns Newmarket Autumn Sales. *H. Candy.*

MISS CRESTA 2 b.f. (Apr 13) Master Willie 129 – Sweet Snow (USA) (Lyphard 67 p
(USA) 132) [1991 7f⁴ 7m⁵] 6,400Y: sturdy, lengthy, quite attractive filly: second
living foal: dam 10.5f winner in France, is out of Kentucky Oaks winner Sun And
Snow: quite modest form in maiden at Salisbury and minor event at Newbury
(headed under 2f out, one pace behind Freewheel) in September: will stay at least
1m: will do better given stiffer test of stamina. *H. Candy.*

MISS CRUSTY 3 gr.f. Belfort (FR) 89 – Blue Empress (Blue Cashmere 129) 36
[1990 5f³ 6g⁵ 7m a6g 1991 6.1s 5f 5m 5.1s 5.1d] sparely-made filly: has a round
action: poor maiden: stiff tasks as 3-y-o, running creditably in handicap penultimate
start: should be suited by return to further, and stays 7f: acts on good to firm ground
and soft: well beaten on fibresand. *O. O'Neill.*

MISS DEBONAIR 2 gr.f. (Mar 28) Elegant Air 119 – Normanby Lass 100 60 p
(Bustino 136) [1991 7m 6m⁴] 6,200Y: leggy, quite good-topped filly: second foal:
half-sister to 3-y-o Vaigly Maid (by Vaigly Great): dam 2-y-o 7f winner: not fully
wound up when beaten 7 lengths in October maidens at Leicester won by Sea
Clover and Cloud of Dust: will do better, particularly back at 7f+. *D. Morley.*

MISS DOODY 2 b.f. (Mar 12) Gorytus (USA) 132 – Kittycatoo Katango (USA) 63
(Verbatim (USA)) [1991 6d⁶ 6m 6g 6d⁶ 6m* 6m⁴ 6g³ 7g 6g² 6m* 6g 7m] 9,000Y:
smallish, sturdy filly: moderate mover: second foal: half-sister to poor plater
Katango Beat (by Dunbeath): dam winner in Italy: quite modest form: won seller at
Leicester (no bid) in July and nursery at Lingfield (ran on strongly to lead final ½f) in
August: should stay 7f: acts well on good to firm ground: visored last 3 starts:
sometimes slowly away: often on toes. *M. R. Channon.*

MISS ECHO 3 ch.f. Chief Singer 131 – Uranus (Manacle 123) [1990 6f³ 7d³ 7m⁴ — §
8d⁴ 1991 10g 8.9g 7g⁵ a11g⁵ 11d] rather leggy, close-coupled filly: fair maiden at 2
yrs: well below form in 1991: should stay 1¼m: trained first 4 starts by M.
Tompkins: has started slowly, refusing to race early on final start. *Mrs G. R. Reveley.*

MISSED AGAIN 3 b.f. High Top 131 – Out of Shot 116§ (Shirley Heights 130) 84
[1990 7m² 7m³ 1991 8g4 10g⁴ 10m* 10.3d³] rangy filly: fair performer: on toes, made
all in maiden at Leicester in October: good third in minor event at Doncaster: stays
1¼m: acts on good to firm ground and dead. *J. L. Dunlop.*

MISS EL ARAB (IRE) 3 ch.f. Sayf El Arab (USA) 127 – Shining Bright (USA) **67**
(Bold Bidder) [1990 5m* 5f⁴ 5d⁶ 5d³ 5g* 6s⁴ 5m 5g⁶ 5d⁵ 5m 1991 5m⁴ 5m⁴ 5m⁶
5m³ 5f⁵ 6m 5m 5m 5g 5d] workmanlike filly: has a quick action: quite modest
performer: below form last 5 starts: suited by 5f: acts on firm and dead ground: has
sweated: takes keen hold. *E. J. Alston.*

MISS EMMAJANE 4 b.f. Dublin Taxi – Linanbless (So Blessed 130) [1990 8m —
7.5d 8g 8d 1991 a7g a11g] big, lengthy, rather sparely-made filly: poor plater: tried
blinkered. *J. G. M. O'Shea.*

MISS FORMIDARE 3 b.f. Formidable (USA) 125 – Relatively Sharp **86**
(Sharpen Up 127) [1990 6g² 5m² 6f³ 6f⁴ 5m 7m 6d 1991 a5g a6g 7g 7f] leggy filly: has
round action: poor maiden: well beaten in handicaps (on toes) and sellers in 1991:
stays 6f: possibly unsuited by dead ground: hung left when blinkered: bandaged
near-hind third start: has carried head awkwardly. *R. F. Marvin.*

MISS FOXTROT 3 b.f. Bustino 136 – Java Jive 63 (Hotfoot 126) [1990 7m 7g⁵ **71**
1991 8m² 10m³ 12m*] compact, quite attractive filly: modest form: favourite, won
maiden at Chepstow in May, setting modest early pace and rallying well: should
prove better at 1½m than shorter: may prove suited by forcing tactics. *J. L. Dunlop.*

MISS GROSSE NEZ (IRE) 2 b.f. (Mar 12) Cyrano de Bergerac 120 – Fait **50**
Dodo (On Your Mark 125) [1991 5m 6d 5m⁴ 5f³ 5m³ 6f 5m] IR 4,200F, 4,800Y:
lengthy, rather sparely-made filly: moderate mover: first foal: dam Irish 2-y-o sprint
winner: plating-class maiden: better form at 5f than 6f: has worn bandages behind:
bought out of J. Berry's stable 1,900 gns Doncaster July Sales after third start. *C. W.
Thornton.*

MISS HOCROFT 3 ch.f. Dominion 123 – As Blessed 101 (So Blessed 130) [1990 —
NR 1991 10.1m⁵] leggy, lengthy filly: half-sister to 3 winners, including 1984 2-y-o 5f
and 6f winner Glory of Hera (by Formidable) and to 1¼m and 2m winner Have
Blessed (by Averof): dam 2-y-o 5f winner, stayed 1m: 6/1, tailed-off last in Yarmouth
maiden in July: sold 2,700 gns Newmarket Autumn Sales. *C. E. Brittain.*

MISS HOSTESS 4 gr.f. Petong 126 – Rosalina 71 (Porto Bello 118) [1990 11g 11m —
8g⁶ 7m⁶ 8g⁵ 8d 7g 8m⁶ 8.2m 12g 1991 11m⁵ 13d 8g⁶ 7g 7f] leggy, quite good-topped
filly: poor maiden at best: stays 1m: acts on good to firm ground: below form when
blinkered: often takes keen hold. *J. K. Kinane.*

MISS HYDE (USA) 2 br.f. (Mar 15) Procida (USA) 129 – Little Niece 79 (Great **66**
Nephew 126) [1991 6g² 6m⁶ 8m] well-grown filly: third foal: half-sister to quite
modest 10.6f winner Straw Blade (by Final Straw): dam 1¼m winner: quite modest
maiden: best effort on debut: likely to stay 1¼m. *J. A. Glover.*

MISSILE MAGIC (IRE) 2 b.c. (Apr 17) Magical Wonder (USA) 125 – Ardmay **70**
57 (Roan Rocket 128) [1991 6d⁴ 6m 7g 8g 8d³ 8.1m³] 36,000Y: useful-looking colt:
sixth foal: half-brother to 3-y-o First Success (by Wassl) and 4 winners, including
fair 6f and 1m winner Irgaim (by Valiyar), later Group 3 winner in Italy: dam sister to
Gairloch and Whistlefield: modest maiden: will probably stay 1¼m: acts on good to
firm and dead ground: ran well in blinkers last 2 starts: sold to Scandinavia 23,000
gns Newmarket Autumn Sales. *J. L. Dunlop.*

MISSISSIPPI BEAT (USA) 4 b.g. Dixieland Band (USA) – Jungle Dance **41**
(USA) (Graustark) [1990 8.2s 9f⁴ 12h⁵ 12g² 13.8m⁴ 12m⁴ 15g⁴ 13m⁶ 11m⁴ a12g²
12g⁵ a11g⁵ 16m 12d³ a14g a16g⁴ a14g² 1991 a14g⁴ 14.6s 15g 14.6g a14g³ a14g a16g⁵
a16g⁶] lengthy, dipped-backed gelding: moderate mover: poor staying handicapper:
acts on firm and dead going: swishes tail: often visored. *M. P. Naughton.*

MISSISSIPPI QUEEN 2 b.f. (Jun 7) Nishapour (FR) 125 – Honey Pot 111 —
(Hotfoot 126) [1991 a8g a8g] half-sister to several winners, including useful 1987
2-y-o 5f winner Ship of Fools (by Windjammer) and quite useful 6f to 1m winner
Great Northern (by Dom Racine): dam sprinting 2-y-o: well beaten in maiden at
Lingfield and claimer at Southwell late in year. *R. J. R. Williams.*

MISS JULIEANN 2 ch.f. (Feb 17) Noalto 120 – Ann Wilson (Tumble Wind —
(USA)) [1991 7s 8.1g 7f 7m 7g] workmanlike filly: sixth foal: sister to 2 poor animals:
dam never ran: of little account. *D. R. Laing.*

MISS KATANGA 3 b.f. Lochnager 132 – Moment To Remember (USA) (Assa- —
gai) [1990 5f³ 7g 1991 a5g a7g⁵ 10.2s⁶] sturdy filly: poor form, including in seller. *J.
A. B. Old.*

MISS KINGFISHER (USA) 2 b.f. (Apr 14) Temperence Hill (USA) – Glory **55**
Street (USA) (The Pruner (USA)) [1991 6f⁶ 6m⁵ 7g 6d] $13,500Y, resold $40,000Y:
leggy filly: moderate mover: half-sister to several minor winners in North America:
dam, minor winner at around 6f at 2 yrs, is half-sister to dam of French 2000 Guineas

third Glory Forever: plating-class maiden: ran moderately final start: stays 7f. *S. G. Norton.*

MISS KIVE   5 b.m. Kabour 80 – Final Cast 50 (Saulingo 122) [1990 a5g 5m 5.1m⁵   **30**
a5g 1991 a6g 5g 5f 6m a5g 7f 7f 6f*] leggy, rather angular mare: poor handicapper nowadays: form in 1991 only when winning (for first time) at Thirsk in August: stays 6f: acts on firm ground: has been visored, and blinkered (including final start): has looked irresolute. *D. W. Chapman.*

MISS KNIGHT   4 ch.f. Longleat (USA) 109 – Ethel Knight (Thatch (USA) 136)   **50**
[1990 a6g² a7g* a5g* a6g⁴ a5g³ 5f⁵ 5s³ 6f 6g 7m 7m 6g³ 6m* 7m 5m a6g a5g 6g a6g 1991 a7g⁶ a7g² a7g³ a7g 7d 6d² a7g 6g 8g 7m 6d* 7g³ 6.1m⁵ 6g 8.2m] smallish, compact filly: carries condition: moderate walker: poor handicapper nowadays: won selling event (bought in 6,000 gns) at Ayr in July: below form last 3 starts: effective at 6f and 7f: acts on firm and dead going: has hung left: sometimes sweating and unruly in preliminaries: has run well for 7-lb claimer: often slowly away: inconsistent. *R. Bastiman.*

MISS MAGENTA (IRE)   3 b.f. Tate Gallery (USA) 117 – Crimson Crown (Lord   —
Gayle (USA) 124) [1990 NR 1991 a8g⁵ a7g a6g⁵ 6m 5f 7g 7d⁵ 6f 6g 6m 7s] IR 5,500F: leggy, sparely-made filly: poor mover: fifth foal: dam, runner-up twice at 2 yrs in USA and once at 3 yrs in Ireland, is half-sister to smart 1982 staying 2-y-o Polished Silver: poor maiden: very slowly away fourth start. *R. Thompson.*

MISS MICROCHIP   4 b.f. Dreams To Reality (USA) 113 – Strawberry Ice   —
(Arctic Storm 134) [1990 a7g a8g a12g⁶ 12m⁴ 15.3f 12d⁵ 1991 11f] small, rather leggy filly: poor plater: may prove ideally suited by 1¼m: acts on good to firm ground and dead. *J. Wharton.*

MISS MIRROR   3 gr.f. Magic Mirror 105 – Rhein Symphony 74 (Rheingold 137)   **64**
[1990 7m⁵ 1991 10g⁵ 9.9f⁴ 8m⁴ 8.1m⁴ 8g* 8.1d³ 9.7s⁶ a10g³ a8g] tall, rather sparely-made filly: quite modest handicapper: won at Wolverhampton in October: ran creditably at Lingfield penultimate start, moderately at Southwell on final one: stays 1¼m: best efforts on an easy surface: best racing prominently. *W. J. Haggas.*

MISS MITCHELL   6 gr.m. Sexton Blake 126 – Knapping (Busted 134) [1990   **96**
14g² 16m⁴ 20m⁵ 14m 16g 1991 14g* 14g* 14d 15.9g] workmanlike, angular mare: won minor events at Tipperary in May and Leopardstown in June: well beaten in listed events at Tipperary and York (gave impression something amiss) final 2 starts: stays extremely well: acts on firm and dead going. *R. Lister, Ireland.*

MISS MOODY   5 ch.m. Jalmood (USA) 126 – Ice Galaxie (USA) (Icecapade   **35**
(USA)) [1990 5f 7m 5f 1991 6v 7m 7.1g 6.1m⁴] workmanlike, good-quartered mare: poor plater: should stay beyond 6f: acts on good to firm and soft going: winning hurdler. *J. M. Bradley.*

MISS MOVIE WORLD   2 b.f. (Mar 16) Slim Jim 112 – Regal Artist 72 (Break-   **39**
spear II) [1991 6m 7.5f 7.1m 5f⁶ 5m⁵ 5g] sturdy, angular filly: half-sister to winners by Prince de Galles and Dragonara Palace: dam stayed 7f: poor plater: saddle slipped and rider unseated in Edinburgh claimer final outing: possibly best at 5f though not entirely discredited at 7.5f: hung markedly left 2f out on fourth outing: trained on debut by D. Topley. *N. Bycroft.*

MISS NARNIA   2 b.f. (Feb 18) Viking (USA) – Nagalia 80 (Lochnager 132) [1991   **48**
6g⁵ 5f⁵ 5g⁴ 7m 8m 6g a6g a6g⁴] 1,100F: sparely-made filly: third reported foal: dam 5f and 6f winner at 2 yrs: poor maiden: stays 7f: sometimes gets very edgy: trained first 2 starts by Bob Jones, next 4 by B. Ellison. *A. P. Jarvis.*

MISS NOSEY PARKER (IRE)   2 b. or br.f. (Mar 5) Cyrano de Bergerac 120 –   **97**
Renzola (Dragonara Palace (USA) 115) [1991 5v 5s* 5.2g³ 5g² 5.2f³ 5m* 5g² 5m*] 5,400Y: small, sturdy filly: good walker: poor mover: second foal: half-sister to Irish 3-y-o Quiet Dream (by Mazaad): dam never ran: fairly useful performer: won maiden auction at Kempton in April, 4-runner minor event at Salisbury in August and 6-runner Harry Rosebery Challenge Trophy (gamely from Regal Chimes) at Ayr following month: will stay 6f: acts on any going: most consistent. *R. Hannon.*

MISS OASIS   2 b.f. (Mar 6) Green Desert (USA) 127 – Mrs Bacon 82 (Balliol 125)   **54** p
[1991 6m6] rather sparely-made filly: sixth reported live foal: sister to 3-y-o Tharif and half-sister to smart sprinter Sizzling Melody (by Song) and 2 winning hurdlers, including Beat The Retreat (by Town And Country): dam 2-y-o 5f winner didn't train on: 9/2 and carrying condition, around 8 lengths sixth of 9, held up, outpaced 2f out, kept on, to Sunday's Hill in maiden at Newmarket in August: will stay 1m: sure to improve. *P. J. Makin.*

MISS PARKES   2 ch.f. (Jan 10) Mummy's Game 120 – Bonne Baiser 88 (Most   **56**
Secret 119) [1991 7m⁴ 6m² 7m] leggy, rather lengthy filly: fourth foal: half-sister to

1989 2-y-o 6f and 7f winner J R Jones (by Blakeney): dam sprinter: plating-class maiden: best effort strong-finishing neck second of 21 in seller at Redcar in September: ran moderately in similar event at same course 11 days later: should stay 7f. *J. Berry.*

MISS PINOCCHIO 4 b.f. Noalto 120 – Floral 82 (Floribunda 136) [1990 7m⁴ 6f — 5m⁵ 5g 6m³ 6m 5f⁴ 6m* 6m³ a5g 5m 7m⁵ 1991 7g 8g] angular filly: fair plater: plating-class performer at 3 yrs: no show in first half of 1991: best at 6f or 7f: best form on top-of-the-ground. *T. Fairhurst.*

MISS PIN UP 2 gr.f. (Apr 29) Kalaglow 132 – Allander Girl (Miralgo 130) [1991 5g **53** 6g⁵ 6g⁶ 6d 7m² 7m 7g 7f 6m⁵ 8m] 5,200F, 2,100Y: leggy, sparely-made filly: half-sister to several winners, including fairly useful miler Saynete (by Night Shift) and fair sprinter Gaelic Affair (by Irish Love): dam unplaced 5 times in Ireland: plating-class maiden: should stay 1m: possibly unsuited by dead ground: blinkered (below best) eighth and ninth starts: sometimes (twice very) slowly away: possibly of dubious temperament. *Pat Mitchell.*

MISS PLUM 2 b.f. (Mar 12) Ardross 134 – Heaven High (High Line 125) [1991 **77** p 7g³] tall, rather leggy filly: third foal: dam lightly raced, probably stayed 1½m, is granddaughter of smart 5f to 1¼m filly Pugnacity: 10/1, 3 lengths third of 22, staying on very well, to Oumaldaaya in maiden at Newmarket in November: moved very well to post: sure to improve, particularly over further, and win a race. *H. R. A. Cecil.*

MISS POKEY 5 b.m. Uncle Pokey 116 – Silken Swift 83 (Saulingo 122) [1990 12m — 17.1d* 16.5d⁶ 1991 17.1m⁶ 17.2g 17.2g] leggy mare: poor mover: plating-class handicapper: little promise final 2 starts: stays well: best effort on dead going: tried blinkered. *R. J. Holder.*

MISS PORTIA 4 ch.f. Import 127 – Mistress Meryll 61 (Tower Walk 130) [1990 — 7g 8g 7g 6m⁶ a6g 6g² 5s a5g⁵ 1991 7.1d 6.1s 7m] good-topped filly: has quick action: poor handicapper at best: no form in summer of 1991: best effort at 6f: possibly unsuited by soft going: has wandered under pressure. *D. R. Tucker.*

MISS PRASLIN 3 ch.f. Nordance (USA) – Carrivos (Tyrnavos 129) [1990 6m 6f⁵ — 6f 7.5m 7f 1991 6g 10m] sparely-made filly: poor maiden: no form in sellers at 3 yrs: stays 7.5f. *M. P. Muggeridge.*

MISS PRECOCIOUS 3 b.f. Precocious 126 – Hissy Missy 70 (Bold Lad (IRE) — 133) [1990 6d⁵ a7g a7g 1991 10d] plating-class maiden, form only on debut. *F. J. O'Mahony.*

MISS RELSUN 7 ch.m. Le Soleil 96 – Relax 73 (Seminole II) [1990 10d³ 10f **45** 10.2m³ 10d⁴ 11m 10f⁶ 10.2m² 10f³ 10g³ 10.2m² 10m⁵ 9m² 12g² 10m⁶ 1991 10f⁵ 12f⁶ 12f⁶] big, workmanlike mare: carried condition: quite modest handicapper at best: stayed 1½m: acted on firm and dead going: dead. *C. W. Thornton.*

MISS RITA 2 ch.f. (Apr 22) Master Willie 129 – Florita 86 (Lord Gayle (USA) 124) **46** p [1991 6g³] sparely-made filly: fourth foal: half-sister to a winner in Jersey: dam 1¼m winner: green and better for race, third of 11 in maiden at Lingfield in October, carrying head high halfway then staying on well final 1f: bandaged behind: will probably stay middle distances: should do better. *C. F. Wall.*

MISS SARAHSUE 5 br.m. Van Der Linden (FR) – Blakesware Dancer 68 — (Dance In Time (CAN)) [1990 10.1g 6f⁵ 7.6m 12f⁶ 11.5f⁵ 10h² 10m⁵ 10f a12g 1991 9.7s 10m] poor maiden: faced very stiff task in amateurs event final start: stays 1¼m: acts on hard going: ran poorly when blinkered once: has broken blood vessel. *J. E. Long.*

MISS SARAJANE 7 b.m. Skyliner 117 – Taffeta 72 (Shantung 132) [1990 a8g 8f **58** 8m* 8f 8m 9g 8m 8g⁴ 8.2s 8f² 8m 9s 8.2v 8g 8m⁶ 1991 a8g* a8g 8s 8g³ 8d⁶ 8.2d 9m² 8m³ 8m* 8.1m⁶ 8f² 9f 8.2m⁴ 9m 8m⁵ 9g a8g] leggy, workmanlike mare: good mover: plating-class handicapper: won at Southwell (claimer) in February and Carlisle in June: stays 1¼m: probably unsuited by softish surface nowadays, acts on any other: good mount for claimer: usually races up with pace. *R. Hollinshead.*

MISS SCHWARTZKOPF 2 ch.f. (Apr 23) War Hero 116 – Miss Metro 65 **40** (Upper Case (USA)) [1991 5d 6.1g 6m⁵] workmanlike filly: second foal: dam poor maiden on flat (should have stayed 1¼m) won over hurdles: poor form, in 6-runner minor event at Windsor (still carrying condition) in July final start. *C. L. Popham.*

MISS SCHWEPPES 3 b.f. Slip Anchor 136 – Alteza Real 84 (Mansingh (USA) — 120) [1990 NR 1991 8s⁵ 11.5m 7.1d 7m⁴ 7g] leggy, lengthy filly: fifth foal: half-sister to useful 1987 2-y-o sprinter Infanta Real (by Formidable) and 8.5f winner Maksoud (by High Top): dam 5f winner, is half-sister to Forzando: no worthwhile form in maidens: takes keen hold: trained first 2 starts by H. Cecil: sold 3,200 gns New-market December Sales. *L. J. Holt.*

MISS SHADOWFAX   2 ch.f. (Jan 25) Absalom 128 – Ring of Pearl (Auction Ring   **62** (USA) 123) [1991 5g⁶ 5m 6g⁶ a5g⁵ 5m* 5m² 5m³ 5g* 5.1f 5.7g 6g] 4,400F: compact filly: second foal: half-sister to 1990 2-y-o 6f seller winner Blazing Pearl (by Blazing Saddles): dam ran 3 times at 2 yrs: quite modest performer: narrowly won seller (retained 2,700 gns) and nursery at Wolverhampton in summer: ran moderately subsequently: suited by 5f: acts on good to firm ground: has run well when sweating: suitable ride for 7-lb claimer. *C. N. Allen.*

MISS SHARPO   3 b.f. Sharpo 132 – Taiga 69 (Northfields (USA)) [1990 6m 6m⁵   **72** 6f⁴ 7m² 7d³ 1991 8d 7m* 8g² 7m⁵ 8g⁶ 7m³ 8.2f² 8.1m⁵ 8g* 8g⁴] small, sparely-made filly: modest handicapper: won at Sandown in June and Bath in September: best efforts at 1m, and may stay further: acts on good to firm ground and dead: visored last 5 starts: sweating, edgy and refused to settle on reappearance: sold 10,500 gns Newmarket Autumn Sales. *R. Hannon.*

MISS SIHAM (IRE)   2 ch.f. (Jan 23) Green Forest (USA) 134 – Miss Derby   **59** (USA) (Master Derby (USA)) [1991 5m⁶ 5m⁵ 5g* 5m⁵ 5m³ 6g⁶ 5.1f⁵ 6m⁴ 5m² 5d] IR 11,000Y: sturdy filly: moderate mover: half-sister to 3-y-o 7f winner Orba Gold (by Gold Crest) and 1985 French 2-y-o 6f winner Madame Nureyev (by Nureyev): dam, minor winner in USA, from family of Diamond Shoal and Glint of Gold: plating-class form: won maiden at Ripon in May: should stay 6f: possibly unsuited by dead ground: largely consistent: sold 2,800 gns Doncaster October Sales. *M. Moubarak.*

MISS SIMONE   5 b.m. Ile de Bourbon (USA) 133 – Nanga Parbat (Mill Reef (USA)   **—** 141) [1990 a12g 1991 a12g] small, leggy mare: moderate mover: modest maiden at 2 yrs: lightly raced and no promise since: stays 1m: acts on firm ground: tried blinkered. *N. A. Twiston-Davies.*

MISS SIMPLICITY (IRE)   3 b.f. Simply Great (FR) 122 – Mexican Two Step   **—** (Gay Fandango (USA) 132) [1990 7m 8g* 7.3s⁶ 1991 10m 11.5m] close-coupled filly: good mover: won maiden at Kempton at 2 yrs: behind since in listed race, median auction contest and handicap: should stay 1¼m: sold 2,000 gns Newmarket December Sales, probably to Italy. *D. R. C. Elsworth.*

MISS SOUTER   2 b.f. (Mar 24) Sulaafah (USA) 119 – Glenn's Slipper 62 (Furry   **49** Glen 121) [1991 5m² 5m 5.1g 5g⁵ 6m⁶ 5.7f⁶ 5f] lengthy filly: second foal: dam 2-y-o 7f winner: poor maiden: will be suited by 7f: blinkered, unruly in paddock before fourth start. *J. D. Roberts.*

MISS TALECA   3 ch.f. Pharly (FR) 130 – Sweet Emma 108 (Welsh Saint 126)   **—** [1990 NR 1991 8.3d 8m] 7,600Y: rather leggy filly: fourth foal: half-sister to fairly useful sprinter Love Legend (by Glint of Gold) and a winner in Denmark by Formidable: dam best at 2 yrs, winning 3 times over 5f in Ireland including Heinz '57' Phoenix Stakes: no worthwhile form in median auction event and maiden (sustained injury) in July. *M. O'Neill.*

MISS TEALEAF (USA)   3 br.f. Lear Fan (USA) 130 – Samata (FR) (Rheffic   **— p** (FR) 129) [1990 NR 1991 11.9m³] leggy, quite good-topped filly: sixth foal: half-sister to several winners, including useful but inconsistent 6f to 1¼m winner Samarid (by Blushing Groom) and 1¾m winner Samatrana (by Alleged): dam very useful middle-distance performer: 7/1 and green, 13 lengths last of 3 to impressive Scimitarlu in maiden at Haydock in August, taking keen hold and leading 1m: should improve. *M. Johnston.*

MISS U LIKE CRAZY (USA)   3 ch.f. Miswaki (USA) 124 – Summersault   **63** (USA) (Vaguely Noble 140) [1990 6m⁶ 6g* 1991 8g 7m⁵ 8f⁶ 8.1g³ 8g] sturdy filly: quite modest performer: ridden by 7-lb claimer, third of 14 in Edinburgh claimer, best effort as 3-y-o: should stay beyond 1m: possibly unsuited by firm ground: sold 1,500 gns Newmarket Autumn Sales. *J. W. Hills.*

MISS UPSHIRE   4 b.f. Norwick (USA) 120 – Longgoe 70 (Lorenzaccio 130)   **—** [1990 10.6s 16g 1991 a12g a16g] sparely-made filly: no sign of ability: sold 750 gns Ascot April Sales. *D. R. Laing.*

MISS VAXETTE   2 b.f. (Feb 6) Norwick (USA) 120 – Langton Herring (Nearly A   **72** Hand 115) [1991 6d⁴ 5d⁴ 5f³ 5.3m* 5m⁴ 5m* 5g 5m² 6g⁶ 5m] 7,000Y: compact filly: sister to 1m (at 2 yrs) and 9f winner San Pier Niceto and half-sister to useful but untrustworthy 3-y-o Sylvan Breeze (by Sulaafah) and quite moderate 1987 2-y-o 5f winner Sleep Easy (by Ballacashtal): dam unraced half-sister to very smart Sylvan Barbarosa: won maiden at Brighton and minor event (showing much improved form) at Warwick in August: better form at 5f than 6f: acts on good to firm ground: inconsistent: retained by trainer 3,800 gns Doncaster November Sales. *J. L. Spearing.*

MISS WAGER 4 ch.f. Crested Lark 78 – Mrs Love It 70 (Rapid River 127) [1990 — 7d 1991 a7g] small filly: second reported foal: dam sprinter: twice raced and no worthwhile form in modest company. *Miss G. M. Rees.*

MISS WITCH 3 gr.f. High Line 125 – Magic Spell (FR) (Dancer's Image (USA)) **59** [1990 NR 1991 8.9g^5 11.7m^6 12.5m^4 12.3g^3 12g^2] leggy filly: has round action: sister to very smart French 7.5f to 10.5f winner Metal Precieux and half-sister to smart but ungenuine 10.2f winner Marcinkus (by Tolomeo) and a jumps winner in France: dam second over 6f from 2 starts, is half sister to very smart middle-distance performer Maitland: quite modest maiden: placed in handicaps at Wolverhampton and (ridden by 7-lb claimer) Salisbury: will stay further: sometimes sweating, including at Salisbury. *H. Candy.*

MISSY-S (IRE) 2 b.f. (Mar 19) Sarab 123 – Monaco Lady 83 (Manado 130) [1991 **54** 6g 5m^6 6m^4 6f^4 7g 7m] 4,000Y: leggy, rather sparely-made filly: third foal: half-sister to 1¼m seller winner Uniroyal Windway (by Runnett), also successful in France, and a winner in Macau by The Noble Player: dam, second twice over 1m, is granddaughter of smart middle-distance filly Pretty Puffin: plating-class maiden: should stay 7f. *G. A. Pritchard-Gordon.*

MISTER BANDIT (FR) 2 b.c. (Jan 30) Sicyos (USA) 126 – Balsamique (FR) **72** (Tourangeau (FR)) [1991 5m 5d^2 5.3m^4 6m 5m* 5m^3 5g^5 5.3m^2 6g 5.1m^4 5.2f^5 5m 8m* 7d^6] 480,000 francs (approx £48,000) Y: leggy, workmanlike colt: good mover: half-brother to several winners in France, including very useful 1987 2-y-o 5f to 7f winner Blue Note (by Habitat): dam won from 5.5f to 11.5f in France: modest performer: won nursery at Folkestone in July and 22-runner seller (no bid, shade comfortably) at Newmarket in October: suited by 1m: acts on good to firm ground, possibly unsuited by dead: blinkered twelfth outing: has run respectably for 7-lb claimer: sold 13,000 gns Newmarket Autumn Sales. *N. A. Callaghan.*

MISTER CASUAL 2 br.g. (Apr 21) Damister (USA) 123 – Something Casual 87 **40** (Good Times (ITY)) [1991 7g 7m^5 7g 8m] 5,000Y: angular gelding: moderate mover: second foal: dam 2-y-o 7f winner: poor plater: blinkered, not entirely discredited in 1m nursery at Leicester: bandaged second start. *G. A. Pritchard-Gordon.*

MISTER GOFF 3 b.c. Taufan (USA) 119 – Spring Bride 57 (Auction Ring (USA)) **50** d 123) [1990 6m 8g 6d 1991 10g^2 9d^5 10f 10.6m^6 9f^5 12.4m 11f 8f] leggy, lengthy colt: poor handicapper: easily best effort on reappearance: stays 1¼m: possibly needs an easy surface: blinkered twice (keen hold then wandered badly first occasion), visored twice. *S. G. Norton.*

MISTERIOSO 2 b.f. (Jan 24) Forzando 122 – Ragged Moon 72 (Raga Navarro **98** p (ITY) 119) [1991 5m^3 6g* 6m*] 7,600F: rather leggy filly: third foal: half-sister to 3-y-o 1m winner Devil's Soul (by Faustus): dam won 1m sellers: confirmed promise

*Rockingham Stakes, York—Misterioso (No. 8) looks a useful prospect;
she battles on to beat Prince Ferdinand (centre) and Master of Passion (left)*

of debut when winning Blue Seal Stakes at Ascot by ½ length from Mathaayl, always close up and running on resolutely: sweating and edgy, followed up, by ¾ length from Prince Ferdinand, in Rockingham Stakes at York in October, staying on from 2f out and battling on gamely: will stay 1m: fairly useful already, and likely to keep improving. *D. R. C. Elsworth.*

MISTER JOLSON   2 br.g. (Apr 5) Latest Model 115 – Impromptu 88 (My   **45** Swanee 122) [1991 6f 5g] sturdy gelding: half-brother to several winners, including sprinter Easy Line (by Swing Easy): dam won over 7f and 1¼m: poor form in maidens: should stay 7f. *R. J. Hodges.*

MISTER MAJOR   3 ch.g. Absalom 128 – Gay Tamarind (Tamerlane 128) [1990   — 5m 6m 6m⁴ 7f⁵ 6m 8.2d 1991 6v⁴ 7g⁵ 6m 6g 10d 9.7s⁶ a12g a16g] strong, workmanlike gelding: has a round action: poor maiden: should stay beyond 7f: joined G. Balding. *L. J. Holt.*

MISTER POLLY   2 ch.c. (Feb 10) All Systems Go 119 – Bold Event (Persian   — Bold 123) [1991 5m] sturdy colt: first foal: dam poor maiden: 25/1, soon outpaced in seller at Nottingham in April. *C. W. Thornton.*

MISTER SAYERS   3 b.g. Balliol 125 – Deer Forest (Huntercombe 133) [1990   — 6m a7g² 7m 1991 a8g 7d 7g 10.2d] leggy, light-framed gelding: poor form: easily best effort in seller at Southwell at 2 yrs: stays 7f. *P. Mitchell.*

MISTFLOWER (USA)   3 b.f. Alleged (USA) 138 – Swoonmist (USA) (Never   — Bend) [1990 NR 1991 10.2f⁶ 15.4m 11d] $75,000Y: workmanlike filly: seventh foal: sister to 4-y-o 1½m winner Straight Laced and half-sister to 2 winners in North America by Far North: dam unraced daughter of sister to Swoons Son: bought 1,150 gns Newmarket July (1991) Sales: no promise in maidens and seller. *D. R. Tucker.*

MISTITLED (USA)   3 b.f. Miswaki (USA) 124 – Untitled 98 (Vaguely Noble   — 140) [1990 5g* 6m 5m 5m 1991 6f] leggy, shallow-girthed filly: plating-class winner at 2 yrs: showed nothing in handicap in March, 1991: should be suited by further than 5f: blinkered (ran creditably) final start at 2 yrs. *R. Hannon.*

MISTRAL GIRL (IRE)   3 b.f. Tumble Wind (USA) – Arthashat (Petingo 135)   **39** [1990 5m 7f a7g 1991 7d 10f⁶ 10.2d 10.2f 10.1m² 10m 10.8m] workmanlike, close-coupled filly: poor performer: second in seller at Windsor, best effort: should stay 1½m: acts on firm going: sold to join R. Frost 3,200 gns Newmarket September Sales. *R. Hannon.*

MISTRAL'S DANCER   4 br.f. Shareef Dancer (USA) 135 – Mythical Assembly   — (General Assembly (USA)) [1990 8g 8.2g⁵ 8f 10m 12m 10g 12.2m⁵ a8g⁵ a8g 1991 a12g a7g] smallish, workmanlike filly: moderate walker: plating-class maiden at best: soundly beaten last 6 starts: best effort over 7f on top-of-the-ground. *R. Hollinshead.*

MISTRESS CARROLL   4 ch.f. Simply Great (FR) 122 – Cariole 84 (Pardao 120)   — [1990 7g⁵ 8m³ 7d⁵ 7d* a8g 7g 6g 1991 7d a7g⁵ a7g a6g] leggy filly: plating-class performer at 3 yrs: below form in 1991: stays 7f: acts on good to firm ground and dead: vigored final start. *J. G. M. O'Shea.*

MISTY GLOW   4 gr.f. Kalaglow 132 – Six Ashes (Bruni 132) [1990 10f⁴ 12m 10g²   — 12.2g² 1991 12g6 a14g 12.1m] tall, leggy filly: plating-class handicapper at 3 yrs: well below form in 1991, off course almost 5 months before final start: stays 1½m: acts on firm ground: trained first 2 outings by J. Etherington. *W. W. Haigh.*

MISTY GODDESS (IRE)   3 gr.f. Godswalk (USA) 130 – Silent Sail (Aglojo 119)   **58** [1990 6g 7f³ 8m⁵ 7m 7f* 8d² 1991 7g 8.2m 8f³ 8m⁴ a10g] sturdy filly: plating-class performer: creditable fourth in claimer at Newcastle, not clear run final 1f: never dangerous in apprentice handicap at Lingfield 3 months later: should stay 1¼m: acts on firm and dead going. *M. A. Jarvis.*

MISTY NIGHT   3 gr.f. Grey Desire 115 – Maha (Northfields (USA)) [1990 5g⁵ 6g   — 5m³ 6m 8f 8.2s⁶ 10.6s 8d 1991 12f³ 15g⁶ 11.1d 15s 15g⁵ 12.1d] small, workmanlike filly: plating-class performer: well beaten in varied events after reappearance: stays 1½m: acts on any going. *P. Monteith.*

MISTY VALLEY (USA)   3 ch.c. Majestic Light (USA) – Orchid Vale (USA)   **116** (Gallant Man) [1990 7g² 7g* 8g* 1991 10g⁴ 10g⁵ 8m⁶ 8g² 8m² 7g² 8d²] half-brother to several winners in Australia, including graded-stakes winner Lady's Slipper (by Dancer's Image): dam unraced sister to champion American filly Gallant Bloom: won Panasonic Smurfit EBF Futurity Stakes at the Curragh in 1990: runner-up at 3 yrs in listed races at Fairyhouse, Tralee then the Curragh (twice), running particularly well behind Julie La Rousse final occasion: best at 1m: possibly needs an easy surface. *M. Kauntze, Ireland.*

MISTY VIEW   2 gr.f. (Feb 12) Absalom 128 – Long View 68 (Persian Bold 123)   **73**
[1991 6m³ 6g⁶ a7g² a7g³ 7g* 8m⁴ 7g³ 7m⁵ 7.6m] 5,200F: sturdy filly: first foal: dam
9f winner: modest performer: won Leicester nursery in August: ran creditably in
nurseries next 3 starts, moderately drawn final one: stays 1m: acts on good to firm
ground: has run well for 7-lb claimer. *M. A. Jarvis.*

MISUNDERSTANDING (IRE)   2 b.g. (Mar 15) Wolverlife 115 – Wallpark   **88**
Princess (Balidar 133) [1991 5m³ 6g 6m³ 7m* 7g* 7m⁵ 8m* 7d] IR 7,400F, 14,000Y,
24,000 2-y-o: strong, lengthy gelding: has a roundish action: fourth reported foal:
half-brother to 1988 2-y-o 5f winner Tee Wall (by Tampero): dam Irish middle-
distance maiden: fair performer: won seller (by 7 lengths, retained 20,000 gns) at
Newmarket in July and large-field nurseries at York in August and Doncaster
(ridden by 7-lb claimer) in September: ran poorly sixth outing (4 days after York
win) and moderately final one: stays 1m: acts on top-of-the-ground, possibly
unsuited by dead: retained 43,000 gns Newmarket Autumn Sales and gelded. *Mrs J.
R. Ramsden.*

MIZAAYA   2 ch.c. (Mar 16) Riverman (USA) 131 – Exclusive Order (USA)   **60 p**
(Exclusive Native (USA)) [1991 7.1d] 140,000Y: useful-looking colt: fifth foal:
brother to French 6.5f and 1m winner Maitre A Bord, closely related to useful 1988
French 2-y-o 5.5f and 7f winner Irish Order (by Irish River) and half-brother to 1990
2-y-o 7f winner (stays 1½m) Exclusive Virtue (by Shadeed): dam French 6f to 7f
winner stayed 1m: 13/2 from 7/2, around 8 lengths eighth of 20 to Sharp Prince in
maiden at Chepstow in October, racing keenly then wandering closing stages: will
stay 1m: will improve. *M. R. Stoute.*

MIZNAH (IRE)   2 b.f. (Apr 5) Sadler's Wells (USA) 132 – La Dame du Lac (USA)   **93**
(Round Table 81) [1991 6.3m² 6m* 7m 7s²] 400,000Y: smallish, quite attractive
filly: closely related to 5 winners, notably useful 1990 Irish 2-y-o 6f to 7f winner
Nazoo (by Nijinsky) and half-sister to a stakes-placed winner by Exceller: dam
unraced, from very good family: fairly useful performer: made all in listed event at
the Curragh in August: creditable seventh of 30, staying on well unable to challenge,
to Young Senor in Tattersalls Tiffany Highflyer Stakes at Newmarket: ¾-length
second to Fawaayid in listed race at Leopardstown later in October: will stay 1m:
acts on good to firm and soft ground. *J. S. Bolger, Ireland.*

MIZYAN (IRE)   3 b.c. Melyno 130 – Maid of Erin (USA) (Irish River (FR) 131)   **63**
[1990 6m 1991 8d⁵ 8g 8m⁶ 10m² 10g³ 12.4m⁶ 10g³ 10g⁴ 12m 12.1s 10.3d⁴] tall, leggy
colt: has a round action: quite modest maiden: creditable fourth in ladies handicap at
Doncaster final start: suited by 1¼m: acts on good to firm ground and dead: trained
first 10 starts by J. Czerpak. *J. E. Banks.*

MOAT GARDEN (USA)   3 b.g. Sportin' Life (USA) – Round Tower 93 (High   **93 p**
Top 131) [1990 8g⁴ 8g⁶ 1991 11g 11.7g³ 11.7m* 12g 13.1m*] rather leggy,
good-topped gelding: has plenty of scope: easy mover: favourite, successful in good
style in maiden in May (made most) and handicap (bandaged, particularly easily) in
July, both at Bath: reportedly found to be suffering from colic when well behind in
handicap at Royal Ascot: stays 13f: acts on good to firm going: on toes at 2 yrs:
gelded after final start: useful stayer in the making. *I. A. Balding.*

MODEL NURSE   4 b.f. Exhibitioner 111 – Majestic Nurse 80 (On Your Mark   **45**
125) [1990 7d 8m 7h² 7h 8.3g² a8g³ a8g* 8g⁵ a8g 1991 a10g⁴ a8g a8g 7d⁵ a10g]
close-coupled filly: has a quick action: poor performer: stays 1¼m: acts on hard and
dead ground: visored third start (below form): none too consistent: sold 900 gns
Ascot November Sales. *Mrs A. Knight.*

MODEL RISK   2 ch.c. (Apr 9) Risk Me (FR) 127 – Maria Whittaker (Cure The   **—**
Blues (USA)) [1991 a7g] first foal: dam ran 3 times: never dangerous in seller at
Southwell in August: sold 3,700 gns Newmarket Autumn Sales. *R. Hannon.*

MODERN BALLET   2 b.c. (Mar 30) Alzao (USA) 117 – Ziobia 78 (Tribal Chief   **—**
125) [1991 7d⁶ 7g] 45,000Y: strong colt: had scope: sixth foal: half-brother to several
winners here and abroad, including fairly useful performers Greens Masterpiece (by
Taufan), successful at 2 yrs over 5f, and Qualitair Flyer (by Kampala), unreliable 6f
and 8.2f winner: dam placed at up to 7f: sixth of 15 in maiden at Salisbury in June:
brought down in similar event at Ayr 24 days later: dead. *P. W. Chapple-Hyam.*

MODERN BRITISH   4 b.g. Elegant Air 119 – Song of Gold 85 (Song 132) [1990   **61**
7f⁶ 7f⁶ 10m 8f⁶ 7d 5m⁵ 6g³ 6m 6m² 7f² a7g⁶ 7m 7m⁵ 6d 6d⁴ a8g² a10g* 1991
a10g³ a12g³ a8g* a8g⁶ a10g] lengthy, workmanlike gelding: moderate mover: quite
modest performer: won claimer at Lingfield in January: stayed 1¼m: acted on firm
and dead going: dead. *C. A. Cyzer.*

MODERNISE (USA) 2 ch.c. (Jan 26) Known Fact (USA) 135 – Modena (USA) **83** p
(Roberto (USA) 131) [1991 7g² 7m*] rather finely-made, useful-looking colt: good
walker: third foal: half-brother to 3-y-o 7f and 1¼m winner Modesto (by Al Nasr)
and high-class middle-distance colt Elmaamul (by Diesis): dam unraced half-sister
to smart miler Zaizafon and daughter of Mofida, very tough winner of 8 races at up to
7f: well-backed second favourite, won 20-runner maiden at Newmarket in October,
headway over 2f out, drifting right, then staying on really well: will be much better
suited by 1m: will improve again. *R. Charlton.*

MODERN JAZZ 4 b.g. Swing Easy (USA) 126 – Abstract 73 (French Beige 127) —
[1990 11.5g 10m⁴ 1991 a12g] rather leggy gelding: scratchy mover: lightly raced and
well beaten in modest company. *C. C. Elsey.*

MODEST HOPE (USA) 4 b.c. Blushing Groom (FR) 131 – Key Dancer (USA) **56**
(Nijinsky (CAN) 138) [1990 10m 10m3 11.7g² 12f³ 1991 14.6s 9s 9g 8.2d⁵ 9s 8.2g
10.2g 8.2m 10g⁶ 10.3g²] big, rather angular colt: poor walker and mover: plating-
class handicapper nowadays: stays 1½m: acts on firm going: usually bandaged
behind: unseated rider at start once in 1991. *G. H. Eden.*

MODESTO (USA) 3 b.c. Al Nasr (FR) 126 – Modena (USA) (Roberto (USA) 131) **85** d
[1990 7m⁴ 1991 7g* 10.5m 10.1m⁴ 10s* 10m⁶ 10m 9m 10.2s⁶ 8.1d a10g]
useful-looking colt, rather unfurnished: fair performer at his best: won maiden at
Sandown and claimer at Kempton (trained until after then by B. Hills) in summer:
well below form in handicaps after: worth a try at 1½m: best effort on good to firm
ground: blinkered fourth to sixth starts: sometimes bandaged: inconsistent and not
one to trust. *K. O. Cunningham-Brown.*

MOD SQUAD 5 ch.m. Montekin 125 – Fauchee (Busted 134) [1990 8v 1991 7m 8f **31**
12.3d⁵] lengthy mare: poor handicapper at best nowadays: stays 12.3f: acts on dead
ground: tried in blinkers and visor. *W. Storey.*

MOFADOR (GER) 7 br.h. Esclavo (FR) – Mantilla (GER) (Frontal 122) [1990 **71**
7m 8.2f 8f a7g* a7g* a8g² 7g² a7g* a8g⁴ 8.2m* 9s 8.2d³ 8v a8g² 7d 1991 7g 8d⁴ 8d
7.5f⁴ 8m² 8m² 8.3d* 8d* 8d 7.9m 7.5f 8.2m 8.1s] lengthy, round-barrelled horse:
impresses in appearance: modest handicapper: won at Hamilton and Thirsk (made
all) in June: lost his form: acts on firm and goes very well on dead ground and
fibresand (unsuited by very soft going): good mount for apprentice: has won
when sweating. *F. H. Lee.*

MOGWAI (IRE) 2 b.c. (May 6) Alzao (USA) 117 – Maltese Pet 74 (Dragonara **68**
Palace (USA) 115) [1991 5d 7m⁴ 7m 6g* 6m⁴ 6g 6s] IR 11,000Y: smallish, strong colt:
fourth live foal: dam 7f winner: quite modest performer: narrowly won 23-runner
claimer at Goodwood in October: ran moderately last 2 outings: seems suited by 6f:
possibly unsuited by a soft surface. *R. F. Johnson Houghton.*

MOHANA 2 b.f. (Apr 8) Mashhor Dancer (USA) – The Ranee (Royal Palace 131) **65**
[1991 7f 7m 8.9d] rather plain filly: fourth foal: half-sister to 7f and 1m winner
Alipura (by Anfield): dam behind in modest company: quite modest maiden: will stay
well. *J. L. Dunlop.*

MOHAWK CHIEF (IRE) 3 b.c. Ahonoora 122 – Ringtail 102 (Auction Ring **101**
(USA) 123) [1990 6d* 6m² 6g⁵ 6g⁶ 1991 6d* 7g⁵ 6g 7f⁵ 6s] small, quite attractive
colt: moderate mover: won 2-runner minor event at Nottingham in June: best effort
running-up fifth of 12 to La Grange Music in Group 3 contest at Newmarket second
outing, again held up: best form at 7f: seems not to act on very soft ground: visored
(keen hold, ran fairly well) fourth start. *G. Wragg.*

MOHICAN GIRL 3 b.f. Dancing Brave (USA) 140 – Unsuspected 95 (Above **106**
Suspicion 127) [1990 NR 1991 10d* 10d² 11.9m⁴ 11.4m* 12d 10d*] lengthy,
workmanlike filly: seventh foal: half-sister to several winners, notably Yorkshire
Oaks winners Sally Brown (by Posse) and Untold (by Final Straw) and very useful
performer at up to 1m Shoot Clear (by Bay Express): dam won 8 times from 1m to
1¾m: successful in maiden at Sandown in May, minor event at Sandown in August
and 5-runner listed race (led 2f out, beat Heart of Darkness 2 lengths) at
Newmarket in November: below form in Lancashire Oaks at Haydock and Princess
Royal Stakes at Ascot: should stay 1½m: acts on good to firm ground and dead. *J. R.
Fanshawe.*

MO ICHI DO 5 b.g. Lomond (USA) 128 – Engageante (FR) (Beaugency (FR) 126) —
[1990 12.3f 1991 16.5g 16.2f⁶] angular gelding: has a rather round action: modest
maiden at best: little promise in handicaps in summer: stays 1¼m: possibly
unsuited by top-of-the-ground: winning but unreliable hurdler. *Miss S. J. Wilton.*

MOJAVE 2 b.c. (Apr 8) Green Desert (USA) 127 – Out of Shot 116§ (Shirley **107**
Heights 130) [1991 6s* 7g³ 7m²] 72,000Y: compact, rather angular colt: lacks scope:

third foal: half-brother to 3-y-o 1¼m winner Missed Again (by High Top): dam temperamental 1½m winner: progressive form: won 5-runner minor event at Newmarket in August: neck second of 8 to Tertian in Somerville Tattersall Stakes at Newmarket, quickening to lead 2f out, headed well inside final 1f: will probably stay 1m. *M. R. Stoute.*

MOLLY MALONESKI 2 b.f. (Apr 25) Dublin Lad 116 – Mazurkanova (Song 132) [1991 5m] leggy, sparely-made filly: first foal: dam 2-y-o 6f winner stayed 7.5f: soundly beaten in seller at Nottingham in May: dead. *M. Brittain.*   —

MOLLY'S DAUGHTER 2 gr.f. (Jan 22) Sulaafah (USA) 119 – Miss Melmore (Nishapour (FR) 125) [1991 7g 6f] leggy, close-coupled filly: poor walker: second living foal: dam placed over 6f in Ireland: green, tailed off in minor event at Warwick and (gave trouble stalls) maiden at Folkestone in October. *R. J. Hodges.*   —

MOLLY SPLASH 4 b.f. Dunbeath (USA) 127 – Nelly Do Da 78 (Derring-Do 131) [1990 a8g6 8m 10f4 8m2 8g 9f4 8g2 9m 8m 1991 8f 10d 10s3 10m6 10s3 10g 10s 7.6m6 12.3g5 9.7g5] small, compact filly: has round action: plating-class handicapper nowadays, still a maiden: stays 1½m: acts on any going. *C. A. Cyzer.*   **49**

MOLO 4 b.g. Castle Keep 121 – Eldoret 100 (High Top 131) [1990 7f 1991 a8g] leggy gelding: no worthwhile form, including in handicap: bred to stay middle distances. *Lady Herries.*   —

MOLTEN COPPER (IRE) 2 ch.g. (May 9) Pennine Walk 120 – Danger Signal 106 (Red God 128§) [1991 5g5 5m2 a7g 5f a6g* 7g4 7.9g* 8m 7m] 20,000F, 12,000Y: sturdy gelding: good walker and mover: half-brother to several winners, including 1982 2-y-o 5f winner Red Roman (by Solinus) and Irish middle-distance performer Sonic Signal (by Trojan Fen): dam, speedy 2-y-o, is half-sister to dam of Roland Gardens: quite modest performer: successful in nurseries at Southwell and York (much better effort, by 4 lengths) in late-summer: ran moderately subsequently, very backward final start: suited by 1m and an easy surface: blinkered fifth and sixth starts: quite active type. *M. W. Easterby.*   **70**

MOMENTITO (USA) 2 ch.c. (Mar 20) Timeless Moment (USA) – Winell (USA) (Rising Market (USA)) [1991 7g 5m 5m 7.5f] $35,000F, $50,000Y: small, sturdy colt: half-brother to several winners including Nizhanee (by Pago Pago), minor stakes winner at up to 1m: dam unraced: little worthwhile form, in selling nursery final start: blinkered or visored last 3 outings: twice slowly away. *A. A. Scott.*   **31**

MOMENT OF TRUTH 7 b.g. Known Fact (USA) 135 – Chieftain Girl (USA) (Chieftain II) [1990 16m2 12m 1991 15.1m5] close-coupled, good-topped gelding: good mover: very lightly raced on flat: sweating and in need of run, ran respectably in handicap at Edinburgh in August: may prove best slightly short of 2m: acts on good to firm ground: wore crossed noseband last 3 starts: useful chaser. *P. Monteith.*   **37 +**

MOMSER 5 ch.g. Mr Fluorocarbon 126 – Jolimo 92 (Fortissimo 111) [1990 a13g 12f6 11f 12f2 12g5 1991 a12g5 16.2g3 14.1g2 12m3 14.1m2 14.1f3 14.6m6 12m] leggy gelding: often dull in coat: quite modest handicapper, still a maiden on flat: seems to stay 2m: acts on firm and dead going: often claimer ridden: has failed to go through with effort: winning hurdler: temperament under suspicion. *M. J. Ryan.*   **66**

MONAAFIS 2 b.c. (Mar 28) Kris 135 – Mangayah (USA) 115 (Spectacular Bid (USA)) [1991 8g] second foal: brother to 3-y-o Trahin: dam, smart French 9f to 1½m winner is out of half-sister to dam of Shareef Dancer: 33/1, tailed-off last of 16 in minor event at Newbury in October. *A. A. Scott.*   —

MONA CHIC 4 ch.g. Noalto 120 – Lady Justice 90 (Status Seeker) [1990 NR 1991 16.2g] half-brother to useful 5f and 6f winner Sharp Justice (by Sharpo): dam won 4 times at 1¼m at 4 yrs: tailed off in seller at Beverley in April, first run on flat: second in NH Flat race in March. *M. J. Ryan.*   —

MONARCH EXPRESS (USA) 3 b.g. Key To The Kingdom (USA) – Pleasingly Quick (USA) (To The Quick (USA)) [1990 8.2d 8d3 1991 10g 12g 8f3 8.2m 7m] big, leggy gelding: has round action: only poor form as 3-y-o: best at 1m: acts on dead ground: bandaged in 1991: blinkered final start: sold 3,000 gns Newmarket Autumn Sales. *N. A. Graham.*   **41**

MONARCH'S GAMBLE (IRE) 3 b.g. Kings Lake (USA) 133 – Risk All 90 (Run The Gantlet (USA)) [1990 NR 1991 10d 12m5] 8,200Y: big gelding: third foal: dam 7.6f and 1¼m winner out of half-sister to Castle Keep, Ragstone and Castle Moon: bit backward on first run for 4 months, around 8 lengths fifth of 10 to Bellton at Southwell (soon pushed along in mid-division) in September, better effort in maidens. *J. L. Dunlop.*   —

MONARDA 4 ch.g. Pharly (FR) 130 – Emaline (FR) 105 (Empery (USA) 128) **69**
[1990 a7g⁵ 6f 12.5g* 13.1h² 12d* 13.3m⁵ 12m⁴ 1991 12d 14g 12m* 11.5m* 11.5m⁴
12.2d⁴ 12m 11.7f*] leggy, close-coupled gelding: has a round action: modest
handicapper: won at Kempton in May and Bath in September: effective at 11.5f and
will stay 1¾m + : yet to race on very soft going, acts on any other: has run well for
7-lb claimer. *P. F. I. Cole.*

MONARU 5 b.g. Montekin 125 – Raubritter (Levmoss 133) [1990 NR 1991 12.3m —
16.1m⁴ 15.1g 16.1m] smallish, lengthy gelding: plating-class handicapper at best:
little form in 1991: best effort at 2m on firm ground: often bandaged behind: has run
well visored: winning hurdler. *Mrs G. R. Reveley.*

MONASTERY 5 b.g. General Assembly (USA) – Sweet Habit (Habitat 134) **82**
[1990 10m 12d⁴ 10m⁶ 10.5m 10f 10g 9m 10.6v 1991 a10g*] leggy gelding: smart
performer as 3-y-o: lost his way in 1990 before winning handicap at Lingfield (wore
eyeshield) in March: suited by 1¼m: acts on firm going: has run creditably when
sweating. *Mrs L. Piggott.*

MONBODDO 2 b.c. (Mar 19) King of Spain 121 – Diamante 83 (Sparkler 130) **53**
[1991 7g 6m⁴ 6m 6g] 6,800Y: rangy, workmanlike colt: has a round action: sixth foal:
half-brother to 3-y-o Tequila Gold (by Green Ruby) and a winner abroad: dam 2-y-o
7f winner: plating-class maiden: worth another try at 7f: slowly away final start. *J. J.
O'Neill.*

MONDRIAN (GER) 5 ch.h. Surumu (GER) – Mole (GER) (Espresso 122) [1990 —
12g* 12g 12g⁶ 12g² 12g* 12s* 12s* 12s 1991 12g 13.3f⁵ 12m] good-topped horse:
carries plenty of condition: moderate mover: good-class performer at best: winner
of 11 of his 15 races in Germany since 2 yrs, notably 7 Group 1 contests: below form
in 1991, twice running as if something amiss: stayed 1½m: acted on soft going:
trained at 4 yrs by U. Stoltefuss: has been retired to stud in Germany. *P. F. I. Cole.*

MONETARY FUND 7 br.g. Red Sunset 120 – Msida (Majority Blue 126) [1990 —
13v⁶ 14m 1991 14.8g⁴] tall, close-coupled gelding: quite modest handicapper at best:
lightly raced and not so good nowadays: stays 2m: acts on any going: ran poorly in
blinkers: has run in snatches: fairly useful hurdler at best: sold to join Mrs P. Joynes
only 2,100 gns Ascot May Sales. *R. Akehurst.*

MONEY SPIDER 3 b.c. Domynsky 110 – Carribean Tyme 85 (Tyrnavos 129) —
[1990 NR 1991 a8g³] 7,000Y: first foal: dam 2-y-o 6f winner: tailed-off last of 3 in
minor event at Southwell in August. *C. B. B. Booth.*

MONEY SPINNER (USA) 2 b.f. (Mar 1) Teenoso (USA) 135 – Silver Dollar —
106 (Shirley Heights 130) [1991 7m] sturdy filly: second foal: dam 2-y-o 6f winner
below best over 1½m at 3 yrs, is daughter of half-sister to Highclere: 20/1 and green,
always behind in maiden at Leicester in October. *Lord Huntingdon.*

MONKEY LOVE 4 gr.c. Carwhite 127 – Minne Love 67 (Homeric 133) [1990 7g —
7f³ 7f 8m 1991 8m 6g 6.1m] good-topped, workmanlike colt: plating-class maiden at 3
yrs: no form in 1991, twice visored: stays 7f: acts on firm going: sold 1,200 gns Ascot
October Sales. *A. P. Jones.*

MONOROSE 2 b.f. (Mar 24) Nomination 125 – Phoenix Rose 85 (Frankincense **56**
120) [1991 6g 6g 5.7f² 6m³ 7m⁴ 7g] 5,000Y: lengthy filly: half-sister to several
winners, including 7f to 10.9f winner Rose Glen (by Lochnager) and 9f winner
Arcville Fred (by Miami Springs): dam won sellers over 9f and 10.6f: plating-class
maiden: stays 7f: usually on toes: reluctant to go down (ran respectably) final
outing. *D. Haydn Jones.*

MONSCOMA (IRE) 3 b.c. Montelimar (USA) 122 – Scoma (Lord Gayle (USA) —
124) [1990 7d 6g⁶ 6d 1991 7m 7.6d] sturdy colt: poor form: should prove suited by
further than 6f. *A. R. Davison.*

MONTBARD (USA) 3 b.g. Medieval Man (USA) – Allouette (USA) (Proud —
Birdie (USA)) [1990 NR 1991 a8g⁴ a8g a8g 10d 12.3s a12g⁶] leggy gelding:
half-brother to Nannerl (by Valid Appeal), stakes-placed 2-y-o winner in 1989: dam
won 3 times at up to 1m, and is half-sister to very smart North American
middle-distance stayer Fact Finder: no worthwhile form. *J. Wharton.*

MONTE BRE 5 ch.h. Henbit (USA) 130 – Madame du Barry (FR) (Wollow 132) —
[1990 NR 1991 9s 8.1d] lengthy, workmanlike horse: moderate walker and mover:
won apprentice maiden at the Curragh (for J. Oxx) as 3-y-o: very lightly raced and
well beaten since: stays 11f: acts on heavy going. *R. Akehurst.*

MONTENDRE 4 b.c. Longleat (USA) 109 – La Lutine 95 (My Swallow 134) [1990 **111**
7g² 6g 6m⁴ 7f⁵ 7g 6s 1991 6d² 6g 6m³ 5g³ 6g³ 6s* 5m⁴ 6s² 6d⁴] leggy, rather
angular colt: fluent mover: very useful performer: narrowly won listed event

at Newmarket in August: third to Polish Patriot in Cork And Orrery Stakes and second to Shalford in Diadem Stakes, both at Ascot, third and penultimate starts: effective at 5f to 7f: acts on good to firm and soft ground: tough and consistent. *M. McCormack.*

MONTEROS BOY 6 ch.g. Crofter (USA) 124 – Prima Bella 76 (High Hat 131) **58** §
[1990 9f 9g 8m* 10f⁶ 8m³ 8f* 8f² 8m² 7f² 10.2g⁶ 8m⁴ 1991 8d 8f² 8.5m⁵ 8m⁴ 7m 8f⁵ 8g 7.1m] good-topped gelding: modest mover: plating-class handicapper: ran moody race final start: finds fast 7f on sharp side and stays 1¼m: probably acts on any going: effective with blinkers or without: good mount for apprentice: seems unreliable nowadays: sold 3,600 gns Newmarket Autumn Sales. *B. W. Hills.*

MONTI BEPPO 2 ch.f. (Feb 24) Flying Tyke 90 – Habatashie 62 (Habat 127) **47**
[1991 5g⁶ 5m² 5.3f* 5m⁶ 5.2g⁶ 5m 7m] 2,500Y, resold 2,400Y: good-bodied filly: fourth foal: sister to 3-y-o Dashing Tyke and 2 winners at up to 7f, including in sellers: dam plating-class maiden: poor form: retained 6,400 gns after winning seller at Brighton in May: below that form afterwards: has been bandaged off-hind: has joined L. Barratt.*J. Berry.*

MONTPELIER BOY 3 b.g. Bustino 136 – Leg Glance 87 (Home Guard (USA) **89** p
129) [1990 NR 1991 8d* 8.9m* 11g³] tall, leggy gelding: fourth foal: half-brother to 7f winner/leading juvenile hurdler Montpelier Lad (by Elegant Air): dam 2-y-o 7f winner: won claimer at Newbury in June and £8,700 handicap at York in October: favourite, good third of 14 in handicap at Newbury, travelling really strongly long way but checked 2f out: stays 11f: sold 46,000 gns Newmarket Autumn Sales, reportedly to join N. Henderson: capable of better. *Lord Huntingdon.*

MONTROSE LAD 2 b.g. (Apr 12) Kabour 80 – Tolly's Best 58 (Hittite Glory —
125) [1991 a6g a5g 7m 7m] small, sturdy gelding: third foal: dam poor sprint maiden: probably of little account: sold 1,550 gns Doncaster November Sales. *D. W. Chapman.*

MOONA (USA) 3 b.f. Lear Fan (USA) 130 – Dance Empress (USA) (Empery **73**
(USA) 128) [1990 a5g⁶ 7f 6d⁴ 1991 7m 7.1d² 6.9m⁶ a7g* 7.1m] leggy, close-coupled filly: modest form: 6/5 on, easily made all in 5-runner maiden at Lingfield in August: stays 7f: seems to need an easy surface: has been led very early to post: sold to join G. Moore 4,700 gns Newmarket Autumn Sales. *P. F. I. Cole.*

MOON FESTIVAL 3 gr.f. Be My Guest (USA) 126 – Castle Moon 79 (Kalamoun **74**
129) [1990 7m⁵ 7g⁶ 1991 10m³ 12d 10g⁵ 10g⁵ 12d³] leggy, sparely-made filly: has a round action: modest maiden: good fifth in handicaps at Kempton and Windsor: stays 1¼m: acts on good to firm ground: takes keen hold: has swished tail, and found little. *Lady Herries.*

MOONJID 3 b.c. Shirley Heights 130 – Psylla 96 (Beldale Flutter (USA) 130) **61**
[1990 8g 7m 8d 1991 10g 8m 7m 10s² 10m* 10m] compact colt: moderate walker and mover: quite modest handicapper: won at Leicester in July, not clear run 2f out: disappointing favourite (reportedly cracked knee bone) at Ayr 2 weeks later: should be better suited by 1½m: acts on good to firm and soft ground: visored (edgy) third start: sold out of P. Walwyn's stable 11,500 gns Newmarket July Sales after fifth start. *N. Tinkler.*

MOONLIGHT IMAGE 2 b.f. (Apr 29) Magic Mirror 105 – Serenata (Larrinaga **49**
97) [1991 6g⁴ 7f² 6.1m³ 7m⁵] 4,200Y: leggy, sparely-made filly: third foal: half-sister to 1¼m winner Seremo (by Morston) and a winner in Germany: dam ran twice: modest plater: probably better suited by 7f than 6f: acts on firm ground: on toes (ran moderately) final start, in August. *T. D. Barron.*

MOONLIGHT QUEST 3 gr.c. Nishapour (FR) 125 – Arabian Rose (USA) **86**
(Lyphard (USA) 132) [1990 NR 1991 8m⁵ 10.1g⁵ 10.5g² 12g* 13.3g 12d⁶] 5,800Y: close-coupled, workmanlike colt: carries condition: first foal: dam ran once in France: fair form: won maiden at Folkestone in September by 4 lengths, always close up: ran moderately in handicaps after: stays 1½m well. *B. Hanbury.*

MOONLIGHT SAIL 4 ch.f. Main Reef 126 – Moonlight Sonata 78 (So Blessed —
130) [1990 7m 6m 7s 7.9m 10f a8g* 8g² 10m⁶ a8g a8g a8g⁵ a11g 1991 a10g 12f 11g 12g 8h 12g] sparely-made filly: blinkered, won handicap at Laytown at 3 yrs: no worthwhile form here in 1991, including in selling handicaps: stays 1m: tried visored once: sold 940 gns Newmarket July Sales. *R. W. Stubbs.*

MOON REEF 5 ch.m. Main Reef 126 – Malmsey (Jukebox 120) [1990 11.7g 12m⁵ —
14g⁵ 14m 12m a11g 1991 12d 14m a12g] big, rangy mare: modest handicapper as 3-y-o when best at up to 1½m: has lost her form: acts on any going: ran poorly in visor once. *C. D. Broad.*

MOON RISK 2 ch.f. (Apr 19) Risk Me (FR) 127 – Squires Girl (Spanish Gold 101) **53** p
[1991 8g] 3,100Y: workmanlike filly: has scope: sixth reported foal: half-sister to 5f
to 7f winner Marcroft (by Crofter) and smart sprinter Jonacris (by Broxted): dam
never ran: 33/1 and better for race, never dangerous in maiden at Wolverhampton in
October: should improve. *R. Hollinshead.*

MOON SPIN 2 b.f. (May 13) Night Shift (USA) – Hors Serie (USA) 103 (Vaguely **68**
Noble 140) [1991 6g 8m⁶ 7.1d 7g²] quite good-topped filly: half-sister to several
winners, including fairly useful 1½m and 1¾m winner/successful hurdler Bespoke
(by Relkino): dam signed 1½m: quite modest maiden: showed much improved form
(for 7-lb claimer) final start, staying on well at Salisbury in October: should be suited
by 1m. *Major W. R. Hern.*

MOOR FROLICKING 5 ch.m. Morston (FR) 125 – Woodland Frolic (Hittite —
Glory 125) [1990 a8g* a7g a7g 8m* 8m⁶ 8m 8m 1991 a7g a10g] small mare: keen
walker: has a round action: poor handicapper: stays 1m: acts on good to firm and
heavy going: has been bandaged: inconsistent. *T. M. Jones.*

MOOR LODGE (USA) 2 b.c. (Feb 13) Hero's Honor (USA) – Prospector's Star **65**
(USA) (Mr Prospector (USA)) [1991 5g 6g 7m⁵ 7m 8m² 8.3s] $14,000F: leggy colt:
first foal: dam Irish 7.9f winner: sire good 7f to 11f winner: quite modest maiden:
vastly improved performance when neck second of 20 in selling nursery at
Doncaster in October: ran fairly well in nursery at Hamilton following month: stays
1m: best form on good to firm ground. *M. H. Tompkins.*

MOOTAWEL (USA) 2 b.c. (Feb 1) Northern Baby (CAN) 127 – Elk's Ellie **58** p
(USA) (Vaguely Noble 140) [1991 7g⁴] $210,000Y: brother to a minor winner in
North America and half-brother to French 1m winner Ombrageux (by Super Con-
corde): dam minor winner in North America from good family: favourite, 7 lengths
fourth of 9, leading 4f, short of room 1f out, one pace, to Well Saddled in maiden at
Salisbury in October: will stay 1m: will improve. *H. Thomson Jones.*

MOOT POINT (USA) 3 b.c. Sharpen Up 127 – Gaelic Logic (USA) (Bold **66** p
Reason) [1990 NR 1991 8.3m⁵ 15.4m*] $200,000Y: lengthy colt with scope:
eighth foal: brother to very useful and very speedy filly Welsh Note, and half-
brother to 3 winners in North America: dam, 3-y-o 6f winner, is half-sister to Grand
Criterium and French 2000 Guineas winner Recitation: looking very well, won
amateur riders maiden at Folkestone in September, staying on well to lead close
home: sold to join J. Jenkins 19,500 gns Newmarket Autumn Sales: may improve
again. *G. Harwood.*

MORAL TALES (IRE) 3 b.g. The Noble Player (USA) 126 – Bellinote (FR) 71 —
(Noir Et Or 125) [1990 7v 1991 6m⁶ 10m⁵ 11.1d 9.2m a12g⁶] leggy, close-coupled
gelding: no worthwhile form, including in handicap and claimer. *D. Moffatt.*

MORCINDA 5 ch.g. Ballacashtal (CAN) – Montelimar 108 (Wolver Hollow 126) **51**
[1990 5g³ 7m⁵ 5g² 6g 6g 5m⁵ 8.2m⁶ 7d⁵ 8g 6s⁶ 1991 6f 5d 5g⁵ 8s⁶ 7g* 7m² 8.1m⁵]
strong, lengthy gelding: poor mover: plating-class performer: won (for first time)
seller (no bid) at Edinburgh in July: seems suited by 7f: acts on good to firm and dead
going: has been bandaged: tends to get on edge: has started slowly: ran fairly well
when visored once. *P. Monteith.*

MORE DOMINION 3 b.f. Domynsky 110 – More Rheola (Morston (FR) 125) **43**
[1990 NR 1991 8g⁶ 8m² 8f 8m 6f⁶] small, good-topped filly: fourth foal: dam behind in
NH Flat race and novice hurdle: best effort in claimers and seller when second at
Leicester: stays 1m well: blinkered (headstrong) final start: bandaged all starts:
flashes tail: sold 1,100 gns Newmarket September Sales. *A. A. Scott.*

MORE GLITTERS (USA) 3 ch.f. Silver Hawk (USA) 123 – Pompoes (DEN) **75**
117 (Belmont (FR)) [1990 NR 1991 9g³ 8.2f² 8m⁶ 10.3d] long-backed, rather
unfurnished filly: seventh foal: half-sister to several winners, including useful 6f
and 7f winner Centerland (by Green Forest) and Three Generations (by Alydar), 7f
and 1m winner in France later graded-stakes placed at up to 8.5f: dam outstanding
5.5f to 7f winner in Denmark and Sweden later placed in good company in France,
stayed 9f well: modest maiden: soundly beaten in minor event final start, first for
over 3 months: should stay 1¼m: sold out of M. Moubarak's stable 3,000 gns
Newmarket September Sales after third start. *T. Fairhurst.*

MOREIRWEN 4 b. or br.f. Bold Owl 101 – Neophyte II (Never Say Die 137) [1990 **33** §
a8g³ a8g 1991 a10g 9s 11.5m a12g 12g⁵ 11.5m 11.6m⁴ 11.9f*] plater: won (for first
time) apprentice event at Brighton (no bid) in September: reluctant to race time
before: stays 1½m: acts on firm ground. *J. O'Donoghue.*

MORE LARKS (IRE) 3 b. or br.c. Godswalk (USA) 130 – Charmeuse (Cut **47**
Above 130) [1990 5v 1991 8g 5g⁵ 7m⁶ a5g⁴ a7g³ 5.1d a5g a5g] strong, compact colt:

plating-class maiden: best effort at Southwell fifth start: stays 7f: wore net muzzle to post twice: blinkered last 6 starts: has pulled hard: gave trouble in stalls final one. *M. B. James.*

MORGANNWG (IRE)   3 br.f. Simply Great (FR) 122 – Kitty's Sister (Bustino   **86** 136) [1990 7g 1991 7.9m³ 8.1m³ 7.1d* 8m 7f* 7.1f⁶ 8d 6.1s⁶] strong, angular filly: fair performer: won maiden at Chepstow in July and 21-runner £8,100 handicap (impressively, coming from rear) at Newbury in August: below form afterwards: best form at 7f: acts on firm and dead ground: somewhat headstrong: taken early to post. *R. Dickin.*

MORLEY STREET   7 ch.g. Deep Run 119 – High Board (High Line 125) [1990   **111 +** 16.2d* 1991 15.9g⁴ 18m²] big, angular, good-topped gelding: fluent mover: top-class hurdler, won 1991 Champion Hurdle: 33/1 and still carrying condition, easily best performance on flat when short-head second of 8 to Great Marquess in moderately-run Doncaster Cup, fair bit to do over 2f out then running on really strongly under hand riding (would have won ridden with more enterprise): stays 2¼m: clearly capable of winning good races on flat. *G. B. Balding.*

MORNING JOY   4 b.f. Mummy's Pet 125 – Satellite (Busted 134) [1990 6m 7f   **—** 1991 12d] workmanlike filly: moderate mover: poor maiden: likely to prove best at up to 1m: sold 1,300 gns Doncaster Spring Sales. *W. Wilson.*

MORN OF SONG (USA)   3 b. or br.f. Blushing Groom (FR) 131 – Glorious   **80** Song (CAN) (Halo (USA)) [1990 NR 1991 7g³ 7.6d* 8.5m⁵ 8.9m] lengthy, leggy, unfurnished filly: fluent mover: sister to very useful 6f (at 2 yrs) and 1m winner Rahy and half-sister to useful 9f and 10.2f winner Rakeen (by Northern Dancer): dam top class at around 9f, is sister to champion 2-y-o colt Devil's Bag: 7/4 on, led close home in 5-runner maiden at Chester in May: below form in quite valuable summer handicaps at Epsom and (visored, very edgy) York: should stay 1m: to join N. Drysdale in USA. *M. R. Stoute.*

MOROCCO (IRE)   2 b.g. (Apr 11) Cyrano de Bergerac 120 – Lightning Laser 68   **74** (Monseigneur (USA) 127) [1991 5g 5d⁵ 5.7m* 6g 6s] IR 15,000F, 18,000Y: small, workmanlike gelding: first foal: dam, raced only at 2 yrs winning over 7f, is out of sister to very useful 1979 2-y-o Highest Bidder: modest performer: comfortably won maiden auction at Bath in July: blinkered, well beaten in nursery at Newbury (seemed unfavoured by draw) 3 months later: ran moderately final start: should stay 6f: seems unsuited by soft ground. *R. Charlton.*

MORPICK   4 ro.g. Morston (FR) 125 – Pickwood Sue 74 (Right Boy 137) [1990 6m   **58** 5d 5g⁵ 5m⁵ 5m⁶ a6g⁶ 5d a6g⁴ a6g⁴ a5g² a6g² 1991 a5g⁵ a6g* a6g⁶ a5g⁶ a6g*] plain, close-coupled gelding: poor walker: plating-class performer: won claimers at Southwell in January and March: effective at 5f and 6f: acts on good to firm going and dead: has run creditably when sweating and for apprentice: goes well with forcing tactics. *J. P. Leigh.*

MORSKI   2 ch.c. (Mar 30) Morston (FR) 125 – Lady Gainsborough (Sky Gipsy 117)   **45** [1991 7m 8m] leggy colt: fifth reported foal: dam unraced: slowly away and always behind in maidens at Redcar and Pontefract (moved badly to post) in autumn. *M. J. Camacho.*

MORSUN   2 b.g. (Jan 13) Aragon 118 – Sunley Sinner 93 (Try My Best (USA) 130)   **73** [1991 7f 8m² 10m⁴] 11,500F: close-coupled, rather angular gelding: first foal: dam 2-y-o 7f winner, is out of very useful filly (at around 1¼m) Sirenivo: modest maiden: stays 1¼m: should win a modest event in due course. *D. Morley.*

MORY KANTE (USA)   4 b.f. Icecapade (USA) – Mousseline de Soie (FR) (River-man (USA) 131) [1991 6g 6m 7g 9g 7g 8f] leggy, sparely-made ex-German filly: poor mover: fifth foal: half-sister to 2 winners in USA, one at up to 1¼m in stakes company, and Silk Stage (by Stage Door Johnny), 9.5f winner and Group placed in Germany: dam winner at up to 9f in USA is daughter of Oaks placed La Manille: won twice in Germany at 3 yrs from 7f to 1m: no worthwhile form in listed and handicap company here in first half of 1991. *Lord John FitzGerald.*

MOSCOW DYNAMO   4 br.c. Siberian Express (USA) 125 – County Line 75   **—** (High Line 125) [1990 7.6d⁴ 7m* 8.5d⁴ 1991 8f 7g] lengthy, attractive colt: fair performer at 3 yrs, lightly raced: stiff tasks in handicaps in 1991: stays 8.5f: acts on good to firm ground and dead: usually taken down early: has worn severe noseband: sold to join Mrs A. Knight's stable 3,000 gns Newmarket September Sales. *M. R. Stoute.*

MOSSWOOD PRINCE   3 ch.g. Country Classic – Morse Princess 69 (Com-   **—** munication 119) [1990 6f a6g 6m 1991 7.5f a5g a5g] leggy, workmanlike gelding:

headstrong plater: has sweated: has worn blinkers and crossed noseband. *J. P. Leigh.*

MOSSY ROSE 5 b.m. King of Spain 121 – Mosso 81 (Ercolano (USA) 118) [1990 **56**
a6g³ 6s 7.6m 6m 6d 7m a6g* a6g² 6m 7g⁴ a7g a7g 1991 a7g⁴ a6g³ 6v* 6g 6.1m
6.1d] strong, good-bodied mare: poor mover: plating-class performer: won minor
event at Folkestone in May: didn't confirm that form: stays 7f: acts on any going:
inconsistent. *Lord Huntingdon.*

MOSTIMUS 3 ch.f. Doulab (USA) 115 – Jennyjo 64 (Martinmas 128) [1990 5m* —
6m⁵ 6g a6g a7g a7g 1991 5m 7m 10.2f 11m⁵ a11g 7g 7m 10.4m⁶] good-quartered filly:
quite modest at best: ran badly last 4 starts: probably stays 1¼m: sometimes
bandaged behind: sometimes on toes, also sweating final start. *G. R. Oldroyd.*

MOST OF ALL 5 gr.m. Absalom 128 – Beech Tree 67 (Fighting Ship 121) [1990 —
8f 10f 1991 10.2s 7.5g 5f 8m 5f 7f 8m 7f 9m 10.5m 11m⁶] angular mare: poor mover:
seems of little account. *T. Kersey.*

MOST SURPRISING (IRE) 2 b.c. (Feb 7) Runnett 125 – Blue Elver (Kings **57**
Lake (USA) 133) [1991 5m³ 5f* 5g 6m⁴] 10,000F, 8,000Y: lengthy, quite attractive
colt: first foal: dam maiden daughter of half-sister to top 1960 2-y-o colt Typhoon:
plating-class form: well-backed 7/2-shot, narrowly won 6-runner maiden at Carlisle
in May, leading halfway then veering markedly left and changing legs: out of depth
third outing, modest last of 4 in Catterick nursery (looked really well) in August:
should stay 6f. *R. M. Whitaker.*

MOTCOMBS 4 gr.f. Glenstal (USA) 118 – Roof (Thatch (USA) 136) [1990 6f* 6f —
6m⁵ 8.2s 8m 7f 8m⁴ 1991 8.3g] workmanlike, good-quartered filly: quite modest
performer at 3 yrs: always behind only run in 1991 (May): probably stays 1m: acts on
firm going: tried blinkered and visored once: sold out of M. McCormack's stable
2,100 gns Ascot April Sales: inconsistent. *J. White.*

MOTHER HEN 6 b.m. Ardross 134 – Lucayan Lady 81 (Swing Easy (USA) 126) **38**
[1990 12m 12.3g 9s 1991 9m⁵ 13f⁶ 10g] strong, lengthy mare: quite modest
handicapper at 3 yrs, not so good nowadays: stays 1¼m: acts on good to firm ground:
often on edge. *K. B. McCauley.*

MOTHERS DAY MAGIC 5 ch.m. Kabour 80 – Gay Walk 67 (Farm Walk 111) —
[1990 NR 1991 13.8f6 18m⁵] sparely-made, angular mare: first foal: dam middle-
distance maiden and seller winner over hurdles: twice raced and tailed off in modest
company in 1991: also tailed off in 2 NH Flat races. *J. Dooler.*

MOTLEY 3 br.f. Rainbow Quest (USA) 134 – Sans Blague (USA) 108 (The —
Minstrel (CAN) 135) [1990 NR 1991 10g⁶] fifth foal: half-sister to very useful 1986
2-y-o 6f and 7.3f winner Nettle (by Kris) and 12.2f winner Quip (by High Line): dam
suited by 1½m, is half-sister to very useful middle-distance filly Deadly Serious:
10½ lengths sixth of 9 in maiden at Brighton in October, held up, weakening and
hanging left over 2f out: sold 4,600 gns Ascot November Sales. *Lord Huntingdon.*

MOTOVSKI 2 b.g. (May 21) Nomination 125 – Murmansk 73 (Red God 128§) **72**
[1991 5f5 5.1m* 6m⁵ 5m² 6g⁵ 6m⁵ 5h² 5m⁶ 5m³ 5m 5d] 6,000Y: stocky gelding:
fluent mover: half-brother to 3 winners in Italy and a winner over hurdles: dam
stayed 1¼m: won maiden auction at Chepstow in May: ran creditably on occasions
afterwards, moderately in nurseries last 2 starts: will prove better suited by 6f than
5f: acts on hard ground: has run respectably in blinkers: sold 10,500 gns Newmarket
Autumn Sales. *R. F. Johnson Houghton.*

MOTTRAM'S GOLD 6 ch.g. Good Times (ITY) – Speed The Plough (Grundy —
137) [1990 NR 1991 13d] leggy, sparely-made gelding: moderate mover: poor
handicapper, very lightly raced nowadays: stays 9f: acts on any going: tried visored
and blinkered: a difficult ride. *R. Dickin.*

MOUFAJAH (IRE) 3 b.c. Touching Wood (USA) 127 – Nuit d'Ete (USA) 90 **83**
(Super Concorde (USA) 128) [1990 6m 7g⁵ 1991 8g³ 10.4g 10m² 12m⁴] workmanlike
colt: fair form: second in claimer at Ayr, outpaced over 3f out then staying on
strongly despite hanging left: claimed to join J. O'Shea £12,580 in similar event 13
days later: stays 1¼m: acts on good to firm ground: has taken strong hold and
carried head awkwardly. *B. Hanbury.*

MOUGINS (IRE) 2 ch.c. (Mar 4) Ela-Mana-Mou 132 – Western Goddess 95 **104**
(Red God 128§) [1991 7.1s² 7g* 8v⁴] IR 20,000F, IR 15,000Y: good walker: moderate
mover: half-brother to 3 winners, including useful miler Hollywood Party (by Be My
Guest) and hurdler Go West (by Akarad): dam Irish sprinting half-sister to very
smart 1975 2-y-o Western Jewel and Mr Fluorocarbon: excellent fourth to Litron in
Prix des Chenes at Evry in November: earlier won Goodwood maiden (bandaged,

hung) going away by ¾ length: will be well suited by 1¼m: acts well on heavy going. *D. R. C. Elsworth.*

MOUKTARPOUR (IRE) 3 br.c. Mouktar 129 – Jam Treacle (USA) (Jaipur) — [1990 8d 1991 10m 10g 15.3m⁶ 13f⁴] lengthy, good-bodied colt: has shown a quick action: plating-class form in the spring: stays 13f: acts on firm going. *C. F. Wall.*

MOULAAF 2 ch.c. (Feb 25) Kris 135 – Basoof (USA) 83 (Believe It (USA)) [1991 **64 p** 6d⁵] quite attractive colt: second foal: dam 1m winner, is half-sister to Shadeed: 10/1 from 4/1, over 7 lengths fifth of 7, racing keenly, fading from over 1f out, to Bold Memory in maiden at Newmarket in November: showed a quick action: likely to stay 1m: sure to improve. *A. A. Scott.*

MOUNTAIN ASH 2 b.f. (Mar 18) Dominion 123 – Red Berry 115 (Great Nephew **84** 126) [1991 6m³ 6g² 7g* 7.6m² 7d*] 32,000Y: good-topped, workmanlike filly: has plenty of scope: half-sister to several winners, including 3-y-o 8.2f (at 2 yrs) winner Red Rainbow (by Rainbow Quest) and very useful 1m to 10.5 winner New Berry (by Sir Gaylord) and useful 7f winner Lidhame (by Nureyev): dam second in Cheveley Park Stakes: fair performer: won maiden at Catterick (easily) and 22-runner nursery at Doncaster (by ½ length from Sovereign Rock) in autumn: will stay 1m: acts on good to firm and dead ground: sold 27,000 gns Newmarket December Sales. *W. J. Haggas.*

MOUNTAIN BLOOM (IRE) 3 b.f. Shirley Heights 130 – Sally Rose 92 **83** (Sallust 134) [1990 NR 1991 10g⁶ 10.5g⁵ 10f² 12m² 14.1f* 16m] big, good-topped, attractive filly: fifth foal: closely related to maiden Ship of Gold (by Glint of Gold) and half-sister to French 1m and 10.5f winner Prairie (by Posse) and 1986 2-y-o 7f winner Trojan Miss (by Troy), later useful over middle distances: dam won 3 times from 1m to 10.2f: fair form: favourite, hacked up in 6-runner maiden at Yarmouth in September: taken down early, ran as if something amiss in Newmarket handicap 15 days later: better at 1¾m than shorter. *L. M. Cumani.*

MOUNTAIN GLOW 4 gr.g. Siberian Express (USA) 125 – Bombshell 76 (Le — Levanstell 122) [1990 9g⁵ 10.2g 11m² 10f⁴ 10g³ 10m 10g³ 1991 a11g 10.2s a7g] compact, rather angular gelding: modest maiden at 3 yrs: soundly beaten in handicaps in 1991: may prove ideally suited by 1¼m: probably unsuited by firm going. *J. L. Harris.*

MOUNTAIN HARVEST (FR) 3 b. or br.f. Shirley Heights 135 – Bitter Rice **64 §** (Sassafras (FR) 135) [1990 NR 1991 10d 12m⁵ 14.1f⁴ 12.3g⁵] good-bodied filly: half-sister to 2 winners in USA by Ya Zaman, one also successful at 1¼m in France: dam French 1½m winner: quite modest maiden: late headway, having got behind, last 2 starts: probably stays 1¾m: tail flasher: hung badly left second start: sold 2,000 gns Newmarket September Sales: resold 2,000 gns Doncaster November Sales: looks ungenuine. *M. Moubarak.*

MOUNTAIN KINGDOM (USA) 7 b.h. Exceller (USA) 129 – Star In The **113** North (USA) 94 (Northern Dancer) [1990 9.5v³ 12v⁴ 16m² 20d 13.3g³ 12.5g 12m 1991 12s² 12g⁴ 12g² 14g⁵ 12m⁵ 12m⁵ 16g⁵ 15g⁶ 18m] lengthy, quite attractive horse: one-time good-class performer, hasn't won since 5 yrs: best efforts in 1991 neck second to idling Rock Hopper in slowly-run Jockey Club Stakes at Newmarket and fifth of 10 to Further Flight in Goodwood Cup third and sixth starts: effective at 1½m to 2m: has won on heavy going, but best form on a sound surface: tailed off when blinkered: bandaged behind of late: trained in 1990 by C. Brittain: winning hurdler. *D. R. C. Elsworth.*

MOUNTAIN WIND 4 b.g. Tumble Wind (USA) – Bustina (FR) (Busted 134) — [1990 8f 10.1g 7m⁵ 10.8g 10h 1991 10f] sturdy gelding: poor form at best. *J. Sutcliffe.*

MOUNT HELENA 2 b.f. (Feb 16) Danzig (USA) – Helen Street 123 (Troy 137) **82 P** [1991 6.1m*] strong, compact filly: has badly scarred fore-joints: third foal: sister to Irish 3-y-o Helenus: dam won from 6f (at 2 yrs) to 1½m (Irish Oaks): favourite, won 18-runner maiden at Nottingham in really good style by 3½ lengths from Bunty Boo, held up with fair bit to do at halfway, quickening well under 2f out: moved poorly to post: will stay 1m: sure to improve considerably. *H. R. A. Cecil.*

MOVEABLE FEAST 3 b. or br.f. Primo Dominie 121 – Cottage Pie 106 — (Kalamoun 129) [1990 5m 1991 6m 6m] lengthy, good-bodied filly: in need of race, always behind in maiden events then seller: off course long time between outings: sold 620 gns Doncaster November Sales. *R. J. R. Williams.*

MOVING FORCE 4 b.g. Muscatite 122 – Saint Simbir 82 (Simbir 130) [1990 7h⁶ **50** 5.8f* 5f⁵ 5f⁵ 7f⁴ 7f⁴ 5m⁶ 7.6d* 8g 1991 7m 5.8f 7g 6d 6g 5.7m 7g 7.6m⁵ 8g⁴ 6.9f 8g] leggy gelding: plating-class handicapper nowadays: stays 1m: acts on firm and dead ground: none too consistent. *L. J. Holt.*

MOVING OUT 3 b.c. Slip Anchor 136 – New Generation 91 (Young Generation **83**
129) [1990 8d a8g* 1991 14f³ 16.2g² 14s* a14g³ 16.5d a16g8*] sturdy colt: has knee
action: easily best effort, showing fair form, to win 4-runner handicap at Sandown in
July by 12 lengths: favourite, comfortably made all in handicap at Southwell in
December: will prove suited by thorough test of stamina: goes well on soft ground.
Sir Mark Prescott.

MOVINO 2 gr.f. (Jan 19) Move Off 112 – Vinovia (Ribston 104) [1991 7m 7m 6m —
7.5f] sparely-made filly: half-sister to moderate jumpers: dam novice selling
hurdler: seems of little account. *N. Chamberlain.*

MR BEAUJOLAIS (IRE) 2 b.g. (Mar 13) Mister Majestic 122 – Bonvin —
(Taufan (USA) 119) [1991 5m 5m 5m] IR 5,000Y: leggy gelding: first foal: dam Irish 5f
(at 2 yrs) and 1m winner: well beaten, last time in seller at Haydock in July. *C.
Tinkler.*

MR BROOKS 4 b.c. Blazing Saddles (AUS) – Double Finesse 97 (Double Jump **114**
131) [1990 7g² 8m⁵ 12g 5g² 6m³ 1991 6v² 7d⁴ 6g² 5m* 7g* 8g⁶ 6d²] strong,
close-coupled colt: very useful Irish performer: won Gladness Stakes at the
Curragh in April and Group 3 events in June at Leopardstown and Tipperary (by 2½
lengths from Arany): first run for 3 months, good second to Archway in listed race at
the Curragh final outing: seems best at up to 7f nowadays: acts on good to firm
ground and dead going (below form on heavy): effective blinkered or not: raced
freely when visored (also edgy) once: trained until after penultimate outing by K.
Connolly: consistent. *J. S. Bolger, Ireland.*

MR CHEEKYCHOPS 4 ch.g. Blue Cashmere 129 – Tzu-Hsi 66 (Songedor 116) **40** d
[1990 a10g 7.5f² 8.2s⁴ 9f² 7m⁵ 7.5d* 11m 8m 8g 1991 a11g⁶ a8g³ a8g³ a7g 8.2s 8g⁶
8.5f 9m 7m 9.9m] leggy, angular gelding: poor performer: stays 9f: acts on firm and
dead going: often sets pace: has been bandaged: sold 1,250 gns Doncaster
November Sales. *M. Brittain.*

MR CHRIS CAKEMAKER 7 ch.m. Hotfoot 126 – Polonaise (Takawalk II 125) —
[1990 8.2s² 8v* 12g 9s³ 10d 8g 8.2s² 10.6d 10d 9s 1991 10m 10.8m 10g 10.5d 13.8m]
lengthy mare: poor mover: plating-class handicapper at 6 yrs: well beaten in 1991:
effective at 1m to 11f: acts very well in the mud: has been to stud. *M. P. Naughton.*

MR COMFYSEAT 3 b.g. Layal 94 – Pink Princess (Tickled Pink 114) [1990 NR —
1991 a8g] sparely-made gelding: second living foal: dam unraced: bandaged off-hind,
moved badly down and looked of little account in maiden at Southwell in February.
R. A. Bennett.

MR CONFUSION (IRE) 3 b.c. Kafu 120 – Mrs Foodbroker (Home Guard **73**
(USA) 129) [1990 NR 1991 8d² 8m⁵ 7.6m⁴ 8d³ 8.1m⁴] IR 24,000Y: workmanlike colt:
has a long stride: good walker: closely related to 2 winners in Italy by African Sky
and half-brother to 2 other winners: dam poor maiden: modest maiden: 11/10 on,
found little at Edinburgh final start: stays 1m well: best form on dead ground. *Sir
Mark Prescott.*

MR DORMOUSE 5 b.g. Comedy Star (USA) 121 – Tea-Pot 77 (Ragstone 128) —
[1990 16g⁶ 1991 17.2g] close-coupled gelding: moderate mover: poor handicapper:
tailed off only run in 1991 (October): shapes like out-and-out stayer: best run on
top-of-the-ground: tried blinkered and visored. *I. A. Balding.*

MR ELK 2 gr.c. (May 12) Bellypha 130 – Shuteye 91 (Shirley Heights 130) [1991 **42**
7m 7.1m⁵ 7m] 4,200Y: angular colt: fourth foal: closely related to modest maiden
Soporific (by Pharly) and half-brother to 1990 2-y-o 10.6f winner Blushing Belle (by
Local Suitor): dam 1m and 11.7f winner, is half-sister to Bedtime: quite modest
plater: needs a much stiffer test of stamina. *Mrs G. R. Reveley.*

MR FLOOD (USA) 2 gr.c. (Mar 22) Al Nasr (FR) 126 – Flood (USA) (Riverman **78** p
(USA) 131) [1991 6d⁴] $50,000Y, resold $75,000Y: close-coupled, deep-girthed colt:
first foal: dam, minor winner at 6f at 4 yrs, is from family of Triptych and Generous:
4/1 from 6/1 but burly and green, over 2 lengths fourth of 7 to Bold Memory in
maiden at Newmarket in November, taking keen hold after slowish start then
keeping on well: likely to stay 1m: should improve. *Mrs J. Cecil.*

MR MAD 3 b.g. Good Times (ITY) – Mistress Bowen (Owen Anthony 102) [1990 —
5m 5f⁴ 5g 7f 1991 5s 8.3d 8m] close-coupled gelding: well beaten, including in a
seller: has worn bandages: sold 2,000 gns Doncaster August Sales. *J. S. Haldane.*

MR MOCCASIN 4 b.g. Doc Marten 104 – Some Cherry 41 (Some Hand 119) —
[1990 8.2s⁵ 8v³ 8.2g⁴ a8g a8g a11g 1991 a11g 8g 10d 16.5m 5m] workmanlike gelding:
has deteriorated: modest form early at 3 yrs: stays 1m: possibly needs the mud:
tried blinkered. *J. A. Glover.*

556

MR NEWS (IRE) 2 b.c. (Mar 13) Trojan Fen 118 – Princess Biddy 86 (Sun **59** Prince 128) [1991 a6g 7g⁶ a7g⁶ 8m⁵ 8.1g³ 8m] IR 8,400Y: close-coupled colt: half-brother to several winners, including 1986 2-y-o 6f winner Hydraulic Power (by Northfields) and 6f winner Fawley's Girl (by He Loves Me): dam stayed 7f, is half-sister to Royalty, Double Jump and Sunyboy: plating-class maiden: best efforts in auction events: ran poorly final outing: will stay 1¼m: no form on fibresand. *W. J. Pearce.*

MR REINER (IRE) 3 br.g Vision (USA) – Yvonne's Choice (Octavo (USA) 115) — [1990 5f 6m³ 8f 7m 1991 8d 9.1s³ 8g 9m 12m 13g 15s] leggy gelding: poor walker: plater: ran poorly last 5 starts: should be suited by further than 6f: acts on good to firm ground: blinkered once, visored twice: joined J. Wade. *Denys Smith.*

MR RISK 2 ch.c. (Apr 30) Risk Me (FR) 127 – Gold Ribbon 106 (Blast 125) [1991 — 5m 6g a5g a7g⁶] 7,000Y: half-brother to several minor winners, including 2-y-o 5f winners Silver Ribbon (by Legal Eagle) and Super Bee Jay (by Mummy's Pet): dam 7f and 1m winner at 2 yrs: seems of little account: sold 700 gns Ascot July Sales. *J. L. Harris.*

MRS BARTON (IRE) 3 gr.f. Faustus (USA) 118 – Phar Lapa 59 (Grundy 137) **76** [1990 5g 6g 6m² 7g 1991 10g* 12d* 16.2m⁴ 13.8f* 14.1f² 13.1f² 16.1m* 16.2f² 15.9d4] small filly: good mover: modest performer: won selling handicap at Leicester (no bid), claimers at Goodwood and Catterick (apprentices) and handicap at Newcastle, all in the summer: suited by test of stamina: acts on firm and dead going: consistent. *B. W. Hills.*

MRS BUN 3 b.f. Miller's Mate 116 – Clarandal 80 (Young Generation 129) [1990 — NR 1991 8v4] leggy filly: first foal: dam 1m winner: edgy, showed signs of ability in fairly useful company for minor event at Kempton in June: dead. *Lord Huntingdon.*

MRS CLAYPOOL 3 br.f. Petong 126 – Rare Legend 69 (Rarity 129) [1990 7m — 6m⁶ 7d4 a8g³ 1991 8.2m a12g 8.1s 12g⁶] smallish, sparely-made filly: plating-class maiden: no form in 1991: better at 1m than shorter: ran well on Southwell all-weather. *M. A. Jarvis.*

MR SEELEY 2 ch.c. (Mar 10) Bay Express 132 – Ro (Absalom 128) [1991 5.2f] — 8,000Y: neat colt: third foal: half-brother to 1988 2-y-o 5f seller winner No More Mas (by Reesh): dam (unraced) from family of Dominion: 12/1 and better for race, slow-starting eighth of 11 in seller at Yarmouth in August. *P. F. Tulk.*

MRS FISHER (IRE) 2 b.f. (Feb 19) Salmon Leap (USA) 131 – Amboselli 73 **88** (Raga Navarro (ITY) 119) [1991 a7g² 7m⁴ 7m² 7g* 7m* 8.1m²] angular filly: fourth reported foal: sister to 1m winner River Chase and half-sister to 7f winner Yankee Trader (by Stanford) and modest sprinter Nikki Dow (by Tanfirion): dam placed over 5f at 2 yrs: fair performer: won claimers (made all) at Newcastle and Leicester and nursery at Newcastle in summer: creditable 1½ lengths second of 8 to White Blade in Sandown nursery 4 days later: stays 1m: acts on good to firm ground: looked ill at ease on track at Brighton on third outing. *Sir Mark Prescott.*

MR SMILEY 4 b.g. Pharly (FR) 130 – Yelming 76 (Thatch (USA) 136) [1990 7m — 7m 7m⁵ 7m 8m 7m 10f a10g 1991 7f 6d 6f⁵] small, deep-girthed gelding: quite modest form at best: well beaten in first half of 1991: should stay beyond 7f: acts on firm ground: tried blinkered once. *J. H. Baker.*

MR SNAIL 3 b.g. Petorius 117 – Spring Lane 85 (Forlorn River 124) [1990 NR **72** p 1991 7m*] 14,000Y: good-bodied gelding: third living foal: half-brother to 1m (at 2 yrs) to 11.5f winner Konig (by Jalmood): dam 7f and 1m winner at 2 yrs: weak 10/1, won 9-runner claimer (claimed £7,444) at Carlisle in April, making virtually all: should stay further. *Sir Mark Prescott.*

MRS NORMAN 2 b.f. (Mar 26) Lochnager 132 – Economy Pep 69 (Jimmy — Reppin 131) [1991 5g 6m a5g 7m] unfurnished filly: third reported foal: half-sister to winning stayer Free Skip (by Free State): dam won over 1½m and stayed well: seems of little account. *P. S. Felgate.*

MRS SKINNER 4 ch.f. Electric 126 – Equal Chance 95 (Hitting Away) [1990 8g⁵ — 8g⁶ 8g 10f⁶ 10m 10m 1991 a7g⁶ 8g a11g 7f 13.8f⁵ a8g 10m⁵] leggy, close-coupled filly: seems of little account nowadays. *Mrs P. A. Barker.*

MR TAYLOR 6 b.g. Martinmas 128 – Miss Reliant 65 (Reliance II 137) [1990 — 12m⁶ 12.5m 18f³ 16.2g 18m³ 16m 10.6s 16.5d a16g 1991 16m 16.5m⁶] leggy, angular gelding: poor mover: poor handicapper: stays 2¼m: yet to race on soft going, acts on any other: none too reliable. *H. J. Collingridge.*

MR WISHING WELL 5 ch.g. Dunbeath (USA) 127 – Little Change 70 (Grundy **56** 137) [1990 8.2s 10.5m⁵ 10m 1991 10m 10.1g 9d a8g4 10s a8g 12s* 11.8g a11g* a63

12.3g6 12m 12d 11.5s a12g* a12g* a12g5] good-quartered gelding: quite modest handicapper: had good season, winning at Kempton (apprentices) and Southwell in August, then Lingfield (2) in November: will stay beyond 1½m: acts on good to firm ground, goes very well on soft and all-weather surfaces: thrice below form when visored, twice for amateur. *R. J. R. Williams.*

MR ZIEGFELD (USA) 2 b.c. (May 4) Fred Astaire (USA) – I Assume (USA) **80 p**
(Young Emperor 133) [1991 7m4 7g 8.3g* 8d2] $39,000Y: strong, lengthy colt: has scope: half-brother to several winners, including fairly useful 6f (at 2 yrs) to 1¼m winner Nile Empress (by Upper Nile), later minor stakes winner in USA: dam, second once from 12 starts, is sister to dam of Cheveley Park winner Sookera: sire (by Nijinsky) stayed 11f: won maiden at Hamilton in September, staying on strongly: good second of 13 to Jairzinho in median auction event at Wolverhampton following month: will stay 1¼m: on the upgrade. *Sir Mark Prescott.*

MU-ARRIK 3 b. or br.c. Aragon 118 – Maravilla 73 (Mandrake Major 122) [1990 **60**
5f4 6d6 1991 7m 8g6 7.5m 7f3 7m 7m 6f4 6f4 7m 6.9f] unfurnished colt: has a quick action: quite modest maiden: in frame in handicaps: showed little final start: may prove ideally suited by 7f: acts on firm going: blinkered seventh to ninth outings: sold out of H. Thomson Jones's stable 5,200 gns after seventh start. *D. A. Wilson.*

MUBAARIS 8 ch.g. Hello Gorgeous (USA) 128 – Aloft 118 (High Top 131) [1990 **—**
NR 1991 a18g5 16m a14g] robust gelding: carries condition: winning, temperamental hurdler: has also won on flat, but best ignored in that sphere nowadays: bandaged. *B. Richmond.*

MUBIN (IRE) 3 b.c. Wassl 125 – Mashteen (USA) (Majestic Prince) [1990 NR **77**
1991 7g 10g3 10m2 12.1g 11.6m6 11.9g2 10m3 12g 10m3] strong, angular colt: has a round action: half-brother to 4 winners, including very useful 1984 2-y-o 6f winner Foulaad (by Raja Baba) and very useful 1983 French 2-y-o 1m winner Cedilla (by Caro): dam smart stakes winner at 6f and 7f from excellent family: modest maiden: suited by 1½m: sometimes takes strong hold: sold to join C. C. Elsey 27,000 gns Newmarket Autumn Sales. *P. T. Walwyn.*

MUCH SOUGHT AFTER 2 b.g. (Apr 26) Adonijah 126 – Lady Clementine 68 **69 p**
(He Loves Me 120) [1991 7g 7m 8m6 8m4] close-coupled gelding: third foal: dam 5f winner: quite modest form in maidens: caught eye behind Sonus at Leicester final start, staying on strongly having been held up then found trouble in running: looks sort to do better in handicaps, possibly over further. *D. Morley.*

MUDAFFAR (IRE) 3 b.c. Simply Great (FR) 122 – Baleen (Lochnager 132) **90**
[1990 7s4 7s 1991 7s2 8s* 10g 8.1m3 10m 8m* 8m3 8m2 9g3] small colt: moderate mover: fair handicapper: won at Ripon in April and Doncaster (led post) in September: also came from rear, running well, at Newmarket and Newbury (£30,600 contest) last 2 starts: suited by strongly-run race at 1m, and should stay 1¼m: acts on good to firm and soft ground. *R. W. Armstrong.*

MUDDY LANE 3 b.g. Ilium 121 – Monstrosa 70 (Monsanto (FR) 121) [1990 5m2 **48**
6g3 5f5 8f6 1991 12f7g 10.2d* 8g 10g 10g] leggy gelding: held up when winning seller (no bid) at Bath in June: well beaten in handicaps and claimer later in summer: suited by 1¼m: acts on dead going: blinkered second start: sometimes troublesome at stalls. *B. R. Millman.*

MUD WRESTLING (USA) 2 ch.f. (Apr 2) Irish River (FR) 131 – Luv Luvin' **84**
(USA) (Raise A Native) [1991 6s4 6m* 6.1g* 7f4 6m2 5g6] $210,000Y: rather leggy, sparely-made filly: good walker and mover: sister to useful French 5.5f (at 2 yrs) and 7f winner Or Vision and half-sister to 3 other winners, including 1990 2-y-o 8.2f winner Hip To Time (by Roberto): dam stakes-placed winner at up to 7f: fair performer: won maiden at Ripon and nursery at Chepstow in summer: never able to challenge in listed event at Doncaster (taken down early) final start: seems suited by 6f: acts on good to firm ground. *L. M. Cumani.*

MUHARIB (USA) 2 b. or br.c. (Apr 8) Far North (CAN) 120 – Rachael Ten- **97 p**
nessee (USA) (Matsadoon (USA)) [1991 6d3 7.3g3 7g*] 76,000Y: useful-looking colt: has scope: moderate mover: third foal: dam, placed in USA, is half-sister to Pirate Army and Lear Fan: best effort staying-on third to Lion Cavern in Horris Hill Stakes at Newbury in October: well-backed favourite, won 7-runner mixed-aged event at Newmarket 9 days later, always prominent and keeping on well: will be well suited by 1m+. *N. A. Callaghan.*

MUHIT (USA) 2 b.f. (Apr 30) El Gran Senor (USA) 136 – Petrava (NZ) (Imposing **53 p**
(AUS)) [1991 6m5] lengthy filly: third foal: half-sister to 1990 2-y-o 6f winner Jallad (by Blushing Groom): dam won from 6.5f to 9f in South Africa where champion filly at 3 yrs: 12/1, green and better for race, 9 lengths fifth of 8, prominent over 4f, to

Cloud of Dust in maiden at Leicester in October: went freely down: will probably stay 1m: will improve. *P. T. Walwyn.*

MUHTARRAM (USA) 2 b.c. (Feb 22) Alleged (USA) 138 – Ballet de France (USA) 101 (Northern Dancer) [1991 7m* 7m*] angular, good-bodied colt: third foal: dam Irish 2-y-o 6f and 7f winner, is half-sister to St Hilarion: favourite, won maiden at Leicester in July, coming clear in good style from over 1f out: heavily-backed odds-on shot but better for race, followed up in minor event there in late-October quite impressively by a length from Bilateral, striding out well in final furlong: will be well suited by 1m +: sure to improve further, and looks an interesting prospect. *J. H. M. Gosden.* **97 p**

MUIRFIELD VILLAGE 5 b.g. Lomond (USA) 128 – Ukelele (USA) (Riva Ridge (USA)) [1990 10.1g 6f2 10m* 10m 10g 10m 10s5 1991 9s6 10m 10.1s4 10m 11.5g2 14m5 11.5g 12g3 12.1d 11.5m4 12s 10m6] good-bodied gelding: split a pastern at 2 yrs: plating-class performer nowadays: inconsistent in 1991: seems to stay 1¾m: acts on good to firm ground and soft going: not genuine. *S. Dow.* **53 §**

MUIR STATION (USA) 3 b.c. Darby Creek Road (USA) – Donna Inez (USA) (Herbager 136) [1990 8m2 10d* 1991 14g5 14g* 14m3 12m3 14d4 16d4 16s4 12s5 12.3g* 16s] seventh foal: half-brother to useful 1m (at 2 yrs) and 1¼m winner Topsider Man (by Riverman) and 3 winners in North America: dam, half-sister to Kentucky Derby and Breeders' Cup Classic winner Ferdinand, won 4 races at up to 9f and placed in Del Mar Oaks: won maiden at Listowel at 2 yrs and minor events at Galway and Down Royal at 3 yrs: flattered when 6¾ lengths fourth to Turgeon in Jefferson Smurfit Memorial Irish St Leger at the Curragh fifth outing: stays 2m: possibly suited by give in the ground: blinkered fifth, sixth and last 3 starts. *J. S. Bolger, Ireland.* **98**

MUIZENBERG 4 b.g. Mashhor Dancer (USA) – Allotria 86 (Red God 128§) [1990 8g a7g* 7m 7.6m4 1991 10.4d5 11.5m2 10d 13.4d3 12.3g2] useful-looking gelding: good walker: reportedly cracked a sesamoid as 2-y-o: quite modest handicapper: stays 11.5f: acts on good to firm ground: has wandered, swished tail and pulled hard: has found little. *J. A. C. Edwards.* **67**

MUJAAZIF (USA) 3 b.c. Alydar (USA) – Miss Snowflake (USA) (Snow Sporting (ARG)) [1990 6m2 6f3 8f* 8m* 8s4 1991 8g 12f] lengthy, quite attractive, rather finely-made colt: has a fluent, light action: rated 116 after winning Royal Lodge William Hill Stakes at Ascot at 2 yrs: looked very well but ran poorly last 3 starts here, tailed off in 2000 Guineas (reportedly suffered back injury) at Newmarket and Derby at Epsom: should be suited by middle distances: gets on toes: reportedly sent to N. Drysdale in USA. *M. R. Stoute.* **— §**

MUJADIL (USA) 3 b.c. Storm Bird (CAN) 134 – Vallee Secrete (USA) (Secretariat (USA)) [1990 6g5 5m* 5m2 6f5 5g2 5m* 1991 6s 5m 6s5 5m] quite attractive colt: poor walker: moderate mover: smart performer at 2 yrs, winning Cornwallis Stakes at Ascot final start: not seen out until late-August in 1991, useful efforts behind Notley in listed race at Doncaster and Shalford in Diadem Stakes at Ascot second and third starts: may prove suited by return to 6f: below form on firm ground: remains in training. *R. W. Armstrong.* **105**

MUJID (IRE) 2 gr.c. (Feb 28) Kalaglow 132 – Ibtidaar (USA) 90 (Danzig (USA)) [1991 8f3 8.1s6] sturdy colt: first foal: dam 7f winner, is out of half-sister to very smart It's Freezing: quite modest form in maidens at Yarmouth (backward, stayed on) and Edinburgh in autumn: may stay 1¼m. *H. Thomson Jones.* **59**

MUKADDAMAH (USA) 3 b.c. Storm Bird (CAN) 134 – Tash (USA) (Never Bend) [1990 6g* 7f* 8s2 1991 7g2 8g5 7g4 8g* 10.4g6 8m2 8d] **125 ?**

Overcoming any linguistic difficulty, Mukaddamah seemed to be the name on everyone's lips in the run-up to the classic trials. For most of Craven week he was favourite for the General Accident Two Thousand Guineas, at about 7/2. However, having been reported 'catching pigeons' in the spring, the clear highlight of Mukaddamah's racecourse achievements came when he caught almost everyone by surprise in coming within a short head of winning the Emirates Prix du Moulin de Longchamp in September at 33/1. Mukaddamah wasn't just a talking horse entering his second season—he had form to match his good looks having won the Lanson Champagne Vintage Stakes and been short-headed in the Racing Post Trophy, but by the end of Craven week the bubble had burst. Mukaddamah's Guineas trial was the Singer & Friedlander Greenham Stakes at Newbury on the Saturday and, starting at evens, he was beaten fair and square by Bog Trotter. Piggott gave Bog Trotter a fine ride to make all but if Mukaddamah were a Guineas winner, he certainly began his challenge in plenty of time in the Greenham. Incidentally, the same connections had suffered a very similar disappointment with Rami in the 1990 Greenham Stakes. Ante-post vouchers on Mukaddamah weren't completely useless, just unattractive, when Guineas day came round with Mukaddamah still in the field; having had every chance at the two-furlong pole he eventually finished fifth of fourteen, eight and three quarter lengths behind Mystiko and Lycius. In the paddock beforehand Mukaddamah seemed not to have really filled his imposing frame yet, and we were somewhat put off by his noticeably nervous disposition.

The tendency to sweat and get on edge in the preliminaries became a regular feature of his racecourse appearances and over the next couple of months the level of Mukaddamah's ability seemed to have been pretty well established as well, some way off the top rank. What he had achieved in the Racing Post Trophy looked much less impressive, none of the three other runners that day cutting much ice as a three-year-old. Mukaddamah got going much too late in the Jersey Stakes at Royal Ascot, under an 8-lb penalty for his Group 3 success in 1990, then brought up the rear having pulled hard in the moderately-run Juddmonte International at York. He did register an impressive victory in a strongly-run race for the John Roarty Memorial International at the Curragh, challenging two and a half furlongs out and storming clear from Prudent Manner, but only in the context of a pretty weak field by Group 2 standards. The Moulin could hardly have looked more contrasting: Hector Protector was unbeaten in France and was joined by other Group 1 winners Priolo, Lycius, Danseuse du Soir, Sillery and Sikeston and the Group 2 winners Bold Russian and Leariva. Even the Spanish challenger Primer Amor was preferred in the betting to Mukaddamah. Carson soon had Mukaddamah ideally positioned just behind the two pacemakers, who set a good gallop, and was able to quicken a length and a half clear when they dropped out halfway up the straight. Priolo was the only one who proved up to the challenge, Mukaddamah running on gamely but being caught close home. We're somewhat reluctant to award Mukaddamah full credit for that effort on the bare result as he very much got the run of the race and had not shown comparable form previously. Neither did he show it afterwards, hampered early on before trailing in some forty lengths behind Selkirk in the Queen Elizabeth II Stakes at Ascot.

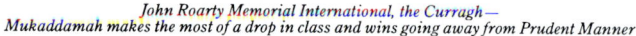

John Roarty Memorial International, the Curragh—
Mukaddamah makes the most of a drop in class and wins going away from Prudent Manner

Hamdan Al-Maktoum's "Mukaddamah"

Mukaddamah (USA) (b.c. 1988)	Storm Bird (CAN) (b 1978)	Northern Dancer (b 1961)	Nearctic
			Natalma
		South Ocean (b 1967)	New Providence
			Shining Sun
	Tash (USA) (b or br 1977)	Never Bend (b 1960)	Nasrullah
			Lalun
		Natashka (b 1963)	Dedicate
			Natasha

Mukaddamah's sire Storm Bird had a quiet season in 1991 although his 1990 Preakness Stakes winner Summer Squall won the Grade 2 Fayette Stakes and another of his sons Storm Cat featured prominently in the first season sires' list. One notable disappointment was Mujadil who missed most of the season and failed to recapture his two-year-old form. Mukaddamah's maternal grandam is Natashka, an excellent individual both on the racecourse and in the paddocks. She was joint top-rated filly in the United States as a three-year-old, winning three of her five starts (from six to nine furlongs) and gaining another (the mile-and-a-quarter Alabama Stakes) on a disqualification. Her offspring include the top-class American filly Truly Bound; the Eclipse and King George third Gregorian; the triple classic-placed filly Arkadina and the high-class stayer Blood Royal; and her daughters' offspring include Irish St Leger winner Dark Lomond and high-class middle-distance stayer Gold And Ivory. Tash hadn't done a great deal to further the family name before Mukaddamah came along although she was a winner herself (twice over six furlongs at two years in North America) and four of her previous six foals were winners. One was Mukaddamah's brother Contempt, a minor two-year-old stakes winner. Tash's 1990 foal is a close relation to them, a colt by Secreto which fetched 210,000 dollars at Keeneland in July. On pedigree alone Mukaddamah would have good prospects of staying a mile and a quarter, but he's probably too highly strung. He didn't race on extremes of going in 1991 (though it was pretty testing at Ascot) but had form on firm and soft as a two-year-old. A tall, rather leggy colt, with a long stride, Mukaddamah remains in training in 1992 when, for us, he'll have something to prove. *P. T. Walwyn.*

MUKDDAAM (USA) 4 b.c. Danzig (USA) – Height of Fashion (FR) 124 **116** (Bustino 136) [1990 8f* 8g4 12m2 1991 12g6 14g 12g* 12m2] big, strong, rangy colt: carries plenty of condition: has a powerful, round action: smart performer: swishing tail in paddock and mulish stalls, won moderately-run listed event at Newmarket in June by short head from Tiger Flower: ran very well when head second of 6 to Rock Hopper in Princess of Wales's Stakes there following month, running on strongly to lead inside last 1f but caught post: stays 1½m: acts on firm going, yet to race on a soft surface: ducked right stalls first 2 outings at 3 yrs: to join T. Skiffington in USA. *Major W. R. Hern.*

MULCIBER 3 b.g. Head For Heights 125 – Quisissanno 76 (Be My Guest (USA) **83** 126) [1990 7m2 7f2 7m2 7g* 1991 9s5 7m2 7g2 8g3 8g5] unfurnished gelding: fair performer: pulled hard in lead over 5f and below form in apprentice handicap in July final start: stays 1m: acts on firm ground, possibly not on soft: has carried head awkwardly: blinkered last 2 starts. *G. Harwood.*

MULL HOUSE 4 b.g. Local Suitor (USA) 128 – Foudre 76 (Petingo 135) [1990 **68** 8m 11.7g 11m* 13.3m* 13.3m5 16.1m* 12m 18d 1991 13.3d6 12g 14g6 12f5 13.9g 16m3 16.2g] strong, rangy gelding: has a markedly round action: modest handicapper: disapointing in 1991: suited by 2m: acts on good to firm ground: sometimes sweating: tried blinkered once: sold to join F. O'Mahony's stable 7,800 gns Newmarket Autumn Sales. *J. Sutcliffe.*

MULOOF 3 ch.c. Rousillon (USA) 133 – Troyenne 81 (Troy 137) [1990 7f4 7h4 6g **61** 1991 a10g* 12d6 13.1m 11.6m] lengthy colt: landed odds in maiden at Lingfield in January: below form in handicaps: suited by 1¼m: broke pelvis and destroyed at Windsor in August. *P. F. I. Cole.*

MUMMY 5 b.m. Mummy's Game 120 – Rotondo (Royal Buck) [1990 NR 1991 a8g — a12g6] useful-looking mare: quite modest maiden here at 2 yrs: since winner twice in Jersey: behind in claimers in early part of 1991: sold 975 gns Ascot September Sales. *D. R. Gandolfo.*

MUMMY'S EMERALD 3 ch.f. Mummy's Game 120 – Emerald Eagle 78 **76** (Sandy Creek 123) [1990 5m6 6m4 6m* 6m 6g 1991 7m 7m5 7d3 7g* 7m 7d3 7m 7d] leggy filly: has free, rather round action: modest handicapper: won at Ayr on second run in 3 days in July, leading 2½f out: behind last 2 outings: stays 7f: acts on good to firm ground and dead: sold N. Tinkler 5,000 gns Doncaster November Sales. *C. B. B. Booth.*

MUMMY'S FOX 4 b.g. Mummy's Game 120 – May Fox 67 (Healaugh Fox) [1990 — 10f 10g 7m 8f 8g 1991 a7g] small, close-coupled gelding: poor performer: well beaten last 4 starts: should stay 1m (stiff task and pulled hard over 1¼m): acts on firm ground: inconsistent. *W. G. M. Turner.*

MUMMYS ROCKET 2 ch.f. (Apr 28) Mummy's Game 120 – Rockery (FR) 101 **41** (Roan Rocket 128) [1991 6g 5f 7m5 8m] 1,200F, 2,300Y: sturdy, lengthy filly: half-sister to 2 winners by Blakeney, including fair 1½m and 2m winner Rough Stones: dam 6f winner at 2 yrs: quite modest plater: sweating (well beaten) final start: should stay 1m. *M. O'Neill.*

MUMMYS VALENTINE 2 b.g. (Feb 14) Mummy's Game 120 – Miss Henry 78 **61** (Blue Cashmere 129) [1991 5f3 5d 5f5 5m* 6m 5m 6m2] 7,000Y: small gelding: fourth foal: half-brother to winners abroad by Homing and Blue Cashmere: dam, 7f winner, is half-sister to very useful Rhodomantade: quite modest performer: sweating and edgy, won seller (retained 5,000 gns) at Windsor in August: very good second in Leicester claimer final outing: better suited by 6f than 5f: acts well on good to firm ground, possibly unsuited by dead: sold 4,800 gns Newmarket Autumn Sales. *P. J. Makin.*

MUNDAY DEAN 3 ch.g. Kind of Hush 118 – Nancy Brig 63 (Brigadier Gerard **72** 144) [1990 6g* 1991 a8g3 a7g4 8g6 10m4 10.9g 12.1g6 12g* 12.1d] good-quartered gelding: has a markedly round action: modest performer: best effort to win strongly-run handicap at Folkestone in October, always prominent: under pressure long way out in similar event 16 days later: better at 1½m than shorter: sold to join D. Arbuthnot 14,000 gns Newmarket Autumn Sales. *Sir Mark Prescott.*

MUNTGIAK (IRE) 3 b.c. Ela-Mana-Mou 132 – Les Saintes (Kris 135) [1990 NR **67** 1991 a10g* 10s⁵ 10.5g⁵] IR 30,000F: good-topped colt with scope: has a rather round action: second foal: half-brother to Irish 1990 sprint maiden Quiet Victory (by Never So Bold): dam French 1¼m and 11f winner from family of Sassafras and Criterium des Pouliches winner Oak Hill: wearing eyeshield, won maiden at Lingfield in March by 8 lengths: well beaten in useful company in May: gave trouble at stalls second start. *C. E. Brittain.*

MURASIL (USA) 2 b.c. (Apr 12) Diesis 133 – Minstinguette (USA) (Boldnesian) **66** p [1991 7g 7g⁶ 7g⁴] $200,000Y: well-made colt: good walker and mover: half-brother to 3-y-o Sweet Soul Dream (by Conquistador Cielo) and several winners, including top-class sprinter Committed (by Hagley): dam ran once: quite modest form in maidens: better than fourth-of-10 position behind Native Chieftain at Brighton in September suggests, hampered 2f out then eased when beaten: not certain to stay beyond 1m: gives impression likely to do better, particularly in handicaps. *Major W. R. Hern.*

MURMURING 5 b.m. Kind of Hush 118 – Beryl's Jewel 86 (Siliconn 121) [1990 **41** a6g⁴dis a6g⁵ a6g* a6g 5g 6m 5m⁶ 5m 6h² 6f 6h 5m 7f a5g³ a6g⁴ 1991 a6g³ a5g⁴ a6g² a 61 a6g² a7g³ a6g³ a7g⁴ a7g³ 7m 7g⁴ 6g⁴ a6g² 5m a5g⁵ a6g* a6g²].angular mare: good walker: has a quick action: quite modest handicapper: usually gives a fair account of herself on all-weather, winning at Lingfield in December: below form last 3 starts on turf: stays 7f: acts on hard ground: good mount for apprentice. *S. Dow.*

MUROTO 5 b.h. Busted 134 – Maresca (Mill Reef (USA) 141) [1990 10.5g 10.5g⁴ **123** 11d³ 12d 10g* 10g⁴ 10g⁶ 10v⁴ 1991 10.5g 10.5m* 10g³ 10g* 9.7d² 10v 10s²] good-topped horse: fourth foal: brother to very useful French 4-y-o 9f and 1¼m winner Vanya: dam once-raced half-sister to high-class French middle-distance colts Romildo and Pevero: very smart French horse: won listed event at Longchamp in July and Group 3 Prix Gontaut-Biron at Deauville (beat Antisaar and Candy Glen by 3 lengths and 2 lengths) in August: very good second of 7 to Wiorno in Prix Dollar at Longchamp (led until near finish) in October: well below form final 2 starts in Group 1 Premio Roma and listed event won by Knifebox at Marseilles: effective at around 9f, and stays 11f: acts on good to firm ground and dead. *F. Boutin, France.*

MURRAY'S MAZDA (IRE) 2 ch.c. (Apr 13) M Double M (USA) – Lamya 73 **53** (Hittite Glory 125) [1991 5f³ 6g² 5d⁵ 6d⁶ 5f⁵] IR 6,400F, 4,800Y: leggy colt: sixth foal: half-brother to a winner in Belgium: dam won 3 races in Sweden: plating-class maiden: below best in claimers last 3 starts, particularly so on dead ground: stays 6f. *J. Berry.*

MURRAY WALKER (USA) 2 b.g. (Mar 7) Track Barron (USA) – Mink Hat **53** (USA) (Northern Prospect (USA)) [1991 7g⁵ 7f 7m⁵ 8m 8m] $32,000Y: compact gelding: fifth foal: half-brother to minor winners by Lear Fan and Greinton: dam minor winner at up to 7f: sire won 4 Grade 1 events and stayed 9f: plating-class maiden: ran poorly in selling events last 2 starts: should be better suited by 1m than 7f: inconsistent. *G. A. Pritchard-Gordon.*

MUSE 4 ch.g. High Line 125 – Thoughtful 86 (Northfields (USA)) [1990 10g³ 10g⁶ **80** 10.1m 13.1m⁵ 12.2f* 12m* 13.1h² 14g⁵ 14g⁴ 1991 12s* 16g³ 12m 16.2g² 16.2d⁴ 18m⁶] leggy gelding: has a rather round action: fair handicapper: won at Doncaster in March: off course over 5 months after second start and returned in good form, staying-on sixth of 22 to Go South in moderately-run Tote Cesarewitch at Newmarket: well suited by test of stamina: probably acts on any going: suited by forcing tactics: winning hurdler. *D. R. C. Elsworth.*

MUSHY BOFF 3 ch.f. Tina's Pet 121 – Rely On Guy 73 (Reliance II 137) [1990 **56** 5m⁴ 5m³ 5s* 5g⁶ 5d³ 5v³ 5.8d⁵ 5d 1991 5d 6m 7g 5. 1d² 5g⁶ 7d² 8f 6.1s⁵ 7f 6g 6.1d 8d] sturdy filly: plating-class performer: below form in handicaps last 4 starts: stays 7f (never placed to challenge at 1m): goes well on a soft surface. *C. J. Hill.*

MUSICAL CASCADE (IRE) 2 ch.f. (Mar 14) Fayruz 116 – Isa (Dance In Time **68** (CAN)) [1991 5f⁵ 5g³ 5m⁴ 5m² 5m a5g⁴ 5f* 5m 5m² 5m* 6m] IR 5,000F, 10,000Y: sturdy, rather close-coupled filly: fourth foal: half-sister to prolific 1988 2-y-o sprint winner Time To Go Home (by Day Is Done), listed winner in Germany at 3 yrs: dam never ran: modest sprinter: successful in nurseries at Thirsk in August and Wolverhampton in September: will stay 6f: acts on firm going: blinkered last 8 starts: rather inconsistent: sold 7,400 gns Newmarket Autumn Sales. *T. D. Barron.*

MUSICALE (USA)   2 ch.f. (Apr 27) The Minstrel (CAN) 135 – Gossiping **109** p (USA) (Chati (USA)) [1991 6m* 7g* 6m* 7d* 7m*]

After seeing Musicale trot up in the Rockfel Stakes at Newmarket on Dewhurst day it was hard to believe newspaper reports that two months earlier the filly had been close to death. Apparently Musicale had suffered a serious attack of colic immediately after extending her unbeaten record to four in the Prestige Stakes at Goodwood; although she didn't require corrective surgery she wasn't considered well enough to travel back to her Newmarket stable for another two days. Once home, Musicale was given three weeks recuperation before starting steady work again, but if she was still suffering any effects from her traumatic experience they weren't apparent on her return to the racecourse in the Rockfel in which her impressive and confidence-boosting pillar-to-post victory, highlighted by a most effective turn of speed, belatedly thrust her forward as a first-rate each-way prospect for the One Thousand Guineas. Musicale's five opponents at Newmarket were, in betting order, the Brent Walker Mile runner-up Mystery Play, who had the best form of all the runners, the Blue Seal runner-up Mathaayl, the unbeaten Lingfield and York winner Snow Forest, the Sweet Solera winner Pearl Angel and the newcomer Be My Everything. None of them ever threatened to stretch Musicale; she was always travelling best, quickened immediately when shaken up with under two furlongs to run and easily went at least three lengths clear as her vigorously-ridden rivals were left to fight for second. At the line Musicale, eased right down, had a length and a half to spare over Mystery Play who rallied strongly to wrench second spot from Snow Forest by three parts of a length with a gap of six lengths back to the remainder. It was always on the cards that Musicale, who possessed useful form over six furlongs, having won the Cherry Hinton Stakes back in the summer on the adjoining July Course, would have too much speed over seven furlongs on top-of-the-ground for Mystery Play, coming back in distance after a fine effort over a mile; but her victory couldn't have been more emphatic. In a year in which there's little between the top fillies that we know about, the progressive Musicale looks at this stage to have her stable-companion Midnight Air and the unbeaten Marling to overcome if she's to provide her owner Mr Sangster with his first winner of the One Thousand Guineas.

In hindsight it's perhaps unwise to attach too much significance to Musicale's hard-fought win in the Prestige Stakes at Goodwood in August. At the time, though, we thought it a resolute effort from a filly who'd been well placed to build an unbeaten sequence but whose hard-earned length victory

Hillsdown Cherry Hinton Stakes, Newmarket—
Musicale (centre) is strongly pressed by Coffee Ice (left) and Miss Bluebird

Rockfel Stakes, Newmarket—much easier this time for progressive Musicale;
she's value for much more than the winning margin over Mystery Play and Snow Forest

over Mesaafi and Super Sarena showed no improvement on her previous form and wasn't evidence enough to suggest she was a filly of classic potential. It's difficult to know if Musicale's troubles affected her before and during the race. She was certainly unusually mulish beforehand, rearing up in the paddock and having to be taken onto the track to be mounted; but equally, in the race she may not have been ideally suited by the softish ground—she's a fluent mover and strode out particularly well on the good to firm ground in the Rockfel. Whatever, the evidence of her narrow win in the Cherry Hinton the previous month had intimated that Musicale would improve significantly when asked to tackle seven furlongs again. Then, Musicale had required a forceful ride to land the spoils in a race which wasn't run at an end-to-end gallop; never worse than second as Miss Bluebird forced the pace, she quickened to lead with over a furlong to run and, although pressed strongly by the runner-up Coffee Ice, kept pulling out extra to emerge the better by a head. Rather surprisingly for an unbeaten filly trained by Cecil, Musicale had started fourth favourite of six for the Cherry Hinton. Her facile victory over two vastly inferior opponents in an extremely slowly-run seven-furlong minor event at Warwick in June hadn't revealed any more about her prospects in the Cherry Hinton than had her four-length beating of fifteen modest opponents in a six-furlong maiden at Lingfield in May, which was that she needed to find significant improvement; she did so though, and those qualities, which she revealed again later in the year, will serve her well at Newmarket in May.

		The Minstrel (CAN) (ch 1974)	Northern Dancer (b 1961)	Nearctic Natalma
Musicale (USA) (ch.f. Apr 27, 1989)			Fleur (b 1964)	Victoria Park Flaming Page
		Gossiping (USA) (ch 1981)	Chati (b 1973)	Terrible Tiger Sun Lover
			Minstinguette (b 1975)	Boldnesian Royal Warrant

The home-bred Musicale, a sturdy, useful-looking filly, is easily the best of her dam Gossiping's first four foals. Only the second of the previous three, Idle Chat (by Assert), managed to win, showing fairly useful form in a career spanning just four races, winning over an extended mile as a two-year-old and finishing placed on both her starts at three, including in the Marley Roof Tile Oaks Trial over a mile and a half; the first, Jennifer's Diary (by London Bells) died after a couple of races in Ireland and the third, Bird's Eve (by Storm Bird) was listed in the 1990 American Produce Records as having been sent to France. Gossiping, a minor winner at around six furlongs in North America as a three-year-old, is by the little-known stallion Chati, a smart winner of eighteen of his seventy-one races over five seasons including two graded events and best at around a mile, out of the Boldnesian mare Minstinguette whose several other winners at stud include the top-class sprinter Committed. Committed was the best Irish-trained sprinter of her sex since Abergwaun in the early-'seventies but strangely enough wasn't raced at her best distance, five furlongs, until late on as a four-year-old when she won both the William Hill Sprint Championship and the Prix de l'Abbaye in 1984: she's now at stud and her first foal Committed Dancer won three times at around a mile in Ireland in the latest season. The once-raced Minstinguette is a half-sister, out of the lightly-raced Royal Warrant, to Miss Toshiba who won the mile-and-a-quarter Pretty Polly Stakes in Ireland as a three-year-old before winning four of her five races, including the nine-furlong Grade 1 Vanity Handicap, the following year in the States where she showed high-class form. Mr Sangster has reason to know both sides of Musicale's pedigree inside out: not only did Committed and Miss Toshiba carry his colours but the Derby winner The Minstrel did as well. The average winning distance of the The Minstrel's progeny lies between nine furlongs and a mile and a quarter but he's proved equally capable of siring good-class sprinters such as Silver Fling and middle-distance performers such as Treizieme and Bakharoff. Musicale will probably be very well suited by a mile as a three-year-old; she may even stay a mile and a quarter. She acts on dead ground but has shown her best form on good to firm. *H. R. A. Cecil.*

MUSICAL LYRICS 3 b.f. Song 132 – Spanish Ribbon (Pieces of Eight 128) [1990 **52** ?
5f² 5f² 5f 5d⁴ 5m 1991 8g 5f⁶ 7g 6g² 6g 6m 5d] small, sparely-made filly: second in maiden at Windsor, keeping on well: only poor plating form otherwise: stays 6f. *M. McCourt.*

MUSICAL NOTE 4 ch.f. Sharpo 132 – Fair And Wise 75 (High Line 125) [1990 **41**
12m 14g 10f 10m 10.6v² 1991 10v⁶ 10f* 10.1g⁴ 11.5g 10g³ 12.1d² 10.2g⁴ 10g 12s 11.8g³ 12f⁵ 11.8m³ 10.5g 10g³ 11.8m] leggy filly: poor mover: poor handicapper: won selling event (no bid) at Folkestone in April: effective at 1¼m to 1½m: acts on any going. *M. Blanshard.*

MUSIC DANCER 2 b.g. (May 1) Music Boy 124 – Stepping Gaily 79 (Gay **60**
Fandango (USA) 132) [1991 6g⁶ 5g³] rather leggy, close-coupled gelding: sixth foal: brother to 1990 2-y-o 5f winner Rhythmic Dancer and a winner in Belgium and half-brother to 2 winning sprinters: dam winning sprinter: quite modest form in maidens at Haydock (behind Rodrigo de Triano) and Wolverhampton (favourite, kept on) 7 weeks later in summer: seemed likely to do better. *J. Berry.*

MUSIC IN MY LIFE (IRE) 2 b.f. (Apr 9) Law Society (USA) 130 – Music And **49**
Dance (USA) (Northern Dancer) [1991 7.1d 6s⁵] 100,000Y: compact, good-quartered filly: first foal: dam Irish sprinter, is daughter of top-class French 7f/1¼m performer Producer: around 10 lengths fifth of 20 to Confronter at Folkestone, better effort in late-season maidens: should stay 7f. *W. Jarvis.*

MUSKET SHOT 3 br.g. Zambrano – Now You Know (Scottish Rifle 127) [1990 **—**
NR 1991 7m 8.3m⁴ 10m 8g 8.2m] leggy gelding: first living foal: dam behind in NH Flat races and novice hurdle. some signs of ability against fair opposition first 3 starts, little in handicaps afterwards: sweating final start. *T. Thomson Jones.*

MUSKET SUCCESS (IRE) 2 b.c. (Apr 28) Muscatite 122 – Caroline's Mark **59**
(On Your Mark 125) [1991 6m 5m⁵ 5g⁵ 6g 8m] IR 900F, IR 1,350Y, 2,300 2-y-o: leggy colt: half-brother to a winner in Belgium: dam Irish 2-y-o 5f winner: quite modest maiden: ran poorly in nurseries (final one a seller) last 2 starts: will stay beyond 5f. *E. Eldin.*

MUSTAHIL (IRE) 2 gr.g. (May 18) Sure Blade (USA) 130 – Zumurrudah (USA) **74**
82 (Spectacular Bid (USA)) [1991 7f 8.2f 8.5f* 8g 7d] small, good-topped gelding: carries condition: second foal: dam, 1m winner, half-sister to top-class middle-distance filly Awaasif, top-class American colt Akureyri and 1000 Guineas second Konafa: modest performer: narrowly won 3-runner maiden at Beverley in September, pushed along 5f out, staying on well straight: subsequently ran moderately in nurseries, blinkered former occasion: will be suited by 1¼m: sold out of H. Thomson Jones's stable 15,000 gns Newmarket Autumn Sales before final start. *R. J. Hodges.*

MUSVAL 2 ch.f. (Apr 4) Music Boy 124 – Marie's Valentine (Piaffer (USA) 113) **51**
[1991 5g⁴ 5.2g] lengthy, unfurnished filly: second foal: dam maiden stayed 1m: plating-class form in summer maidens, better effort at Sandown on debut: will stay at least 6f. *R. Hannon.*

MUTABAHI (CAN) 2 b. or br.c. (Mar 8) Woodman (USA) 126 – Vallee Secrete **87**
(USA) (Secretariat (USA)) [1991 6d⁴ 6g* 7.1m⁶] small, sturdy colt: carries

condition: half-brother to several winners, including useful 1985 2-y-o 5f winner Kombus (by Known Fact) and smart 1990 2-y-o sprinter Mujadil (by Storm Bird): dam French 1m winner from excellent family: fair form: weak 7/2-chance but looking really well after 2½-month absence, won 4-runner maiden at Goodwood in August, getting behind then running on well: below best in Solario Stakes at Sandown (off bridle halfway) 4 weeks later: bred to stay 1m. *R. W. Armstrong.*

MUTAMARRID 3 br.c. Sure Blade (USA) 130 – Raabihah 130 (Shirley Heights   **86**
130) [1990 7m* 1991 10.5g4 12.3g3 12.1d3 13.1m6 10.1f* 10m* 10m4] leggy, attractive colt: fair performer: won August handicaps at Yarmouth, setting modest early pace, and Sandown, leading inside final 1f: probably best efforts at 1¼m, but should stay further: acts on firm going: edged left and didn't find as much as seemed likely final start. *H. Thomson Jones.*

MUTARJJAM (USA) 3 b. or br.c. Stop The Music (USA) – So Smooth (USA)   **74**
(Third Martini) [1990 NR 1991 6v6 8d4 9g6 8m3 8g* 8.5g6 10g 9m3 10m3 10m3 10d6] $80,000Y: seventh foal: half-brother to several winners including graded stakes-placed Double Smooth (by Overskate), best at around 1m: dam unraced, from good family: sire stakes winner at 2 and 3 yrs, won at up to 1¼m: modest performer: won maiden at Bellewstown in July: soundly beaten in celebrity event at Ascot final start: effective at 1m to 1¼m: acts on good to firm ground (below form on a soft surface): sold 8,500 gns Newmarket Autumn Sales. *K. Prendergast, Ireland.*

MUTHAIGA 5 gr.h. Kalaglow 132 – Green Lucia 116 (Green Dancer (USA) 132)   **37**
[1990 13.3m5 12f 8m 8g 8g6 a11g3 a12g a11g 1991 a11g3 a8g a12g 8s 9m 8d 8m 8g 8g 9m4 8f 7m5 7g 10g6] big, leggy, lengthy horse: poor handicapper nowadays: suited by middle distances: acts on good to firm ground: often bandaged: often has tongue tied down: has worn eyeshield: sold 2,000 gns Newmarket Autumn Sales. *N. Tinkler.*

MUWAZI 3 b. or br.c. Lear Fan (USA) 130 – Sentimental Roses 74 (High Top 131)   **64**
[1990 NR 1991 8.5f2 10g4 10.5m4] 520,000 francs (approx £48,150) Y: rather sparely-made colt: first reported foal: dam 1m winner: modest maiden: probably stayed 10.5f: carried head high on debut: dead. *R. W. Armstrong.*

MUZO (USA) 4 b.c. Irish River (FR) 131 – Dance Flower (CAN) (Northern   **—**
Dancer) [1990 10m5 12.3m3 12m3 10.6d* 1991 10s] strong, well-made colt: fairly useful performer at 3 yrs for H. Cecil: ran poorly in Ripon handicap only start in 1991 (April): stays 1½m: acts on good to firm and dead ground: sold only 2,500 gns Ascot July Sales. *Mrs J. Cecil.*

MY ABBEY 2 b.f. (Feb 9) Hadeer 118 – Rose Barton (Pas de Seul 133) [1991 5s2   **77 ?**
5m* 5d3 5m5 5g 5d2 5d3 5.1m* 5g] 1,800Y: leggy, rather close-coupled filly: first foal: dam unraced daughter of sister to Blue Cashmere: modest performer: successful in maiden at Ripon in April and 6-runner nursery at Chester (first run for 6 weeks, easily best effort) in August: gave impression something amiss in Ayr nursery afterwards: speedy: ran poorly when sweating third outing: has run creditably when visored. *E. J. Alston.*

MY ALIBI (IRE) 3 ch.c. Hatim (USA) 121 – Serriyya 53 (Tap On Wood 130)   **49**
[1990 6f4 6f* 6f2 6m4 7g5 7.3g 1991 10d 8m4 8.3m 8f 8m4 10g 8m] workmanlike colt: plating-class performer: soundly beaten in handicaps last 2 starts: stays 1m: acts on firm going: usually blinkered: has carried head high. *W. Carter.*

MY ALMA (IRE) 3 b.f. Reasonable (FR) 119 – Lady Bidder (Auction Ring (USA)   **42**
123) [1990 5f3 5d3 5m* 5f2 6g 5f3 6g2 5m 1991 5.8m 8m 7d 7g 6m 6m 7.1m 6g] small filly: has a quick action: modest winner but inconsistent at 2 yrs: ran poorly in handicaps and sellers in 1991: probably stays 6f: acts well on firm ground: blinkered 3 times: sometimes sweating. *R. J. Holder.*

MYASHA (USA) 2 b.c. (May 16) Imp Society (USA) – Mauna Loa (USA)   **68**
(Hawaii) [1991 5g4 5d5 5g6 5g3 5m4 5.2f a5g2 a5g3] 70,000Y: neat colt: half-brother to 1m winner Pontchartrain (by Lyphard) and a winner in North America: dam, half-sister to Exceller and top 2-y-o Capote, won 7f claiming race at 2 yrs: quite modest maiden: ran creditably on equitrack at Lingfield penultimate start: ran moderately on fibresand final outing: will be suited by 6f: wore eyeshield last 2 outings. *Mrs L. Piggott.*

MY BED TIME 3 b.f. Blakeney 126 – Noddy Time 97 (Gratitude 130) [1990 6g4   **—**
1991 10f5 12m4] smallish, workmanlike filly: turned fore feet in: quite modest form in maidens: better at 1½m than shorter: dead. *M. H. Tompkins.*

MYBELLA ANN 4 br.f. Anfield 117 – Sandra Bella 70 (Crooner 119) [1990 NR   **—**
1991 a12g6 8.3g 10f] lengthy, rather sparely-made filly: third foal: dam stayed 1½m

on flat and won over hurdles: no promise in claimers in May: trained by B. Morgan, behind in 3 NH Flat races earlier in year. *J. Akehurst.*

MY BOY BUSTER 2 b.c. (Jan 29) Kind of Hush 118 – Happy Donna 106 (Huntercombe 133) [1991 6m] close-coupled colt: eighth reported foal: half-brother to 6f to 1m winner Imperial Friend (by Imperial Fling): dam won 3 times over 5f at 2 yrs: 12/1 and green, very slowly away, swerved left and always behind in 18-runner claimer at Haydock in September. *C. J. Hill.* —

MY BROWN EYED GIRL 2 b.f. (Apr 10) Sizzling Melody 117 – High Halo 64 (High Top 131) [1991 5g 6g] 2,600Y: tall, leggy filly: second foal: half-sister to fairly useful 3-y-o 6f to 1m winner High Premium (by Forzando): dam thrice-raced 1m winner, would have stayed further: tailed-off last in maidens at Sandown and Brighton: sold 750 gns Ascot September Sales. *G. Lewis.* —

MY CHIARA 5 b.m. Ardross 134 – My Tootsie 98 (Tap On Wood 130) [1990 10g⁵ 10m 12g 12f 11.7m⁴ 11.7m⁵ 11.7m 12m* 16.2m 11s 1991 10g 15.5f³ 12g 12m* 12g⁶ 12f² 12m³ 12d² 11.5d 12f³ 12f⁴ 12m³ 13.9g 12f 12.2m⁴ 12.1g 12f⁵] leggy, quite good-topped mare: keen walker: modest handicapper: won at Hamilton (ladies) in May: below form last 5 starts: subsequently sold to join P. Bevan's stable 10,000 gns Newmarket Autumn Sales: finds 1¼m on sharp side, and worth another try over 1¾m: acts on firm and dead ground: goes well with forcing tactics: tough and genuine. *M. D. I. Usher.* 74

MY CONCORDIA 5 b.m. Belfort (FR) 89 – Princess Sharpenup 63 (Lochnager 132) [1990 NR 1991 a8g* 8d a7g] leggy, lengthy mare: first run on flat since 3 yrs, won maiden at Southwell in March: no form after: suited by 1m: acts on firm and dead going. *C. D. Broad.* 43

MY COQUETTE 4 ch.f. Coquelin (USA) 121 – River Lane (Riverman (USA) 131) [1990 8m 10.6s⁴ 8f² 10.4g 8m 8.2v 7d⁶ 1991 a10g] tall, leggy filly: modest form at best: tailed off only run in 1991 (January): may prove best over 1m: acts on any going, except possibly heavy. *C. E. Brittain.* —

MY CZECH MATE 2 ch.g. (Apr 19) Risk Me (FR) 127 – Legal Sound 85 (Legal Eagle 126) [1991 5g⁶ 5g⁴ 8m 6g⁶ 5m] 47,000Y: good-bodied gelding: fourth foal: half-brother to 3-y-o Special Request (by Jalmood) and winning sprinter Brisas (by Vaigly Great): dam 6f winner: poor maiden: stays 1m: off course almost 5 months before third outing. *R. Hannon.* 47

MY DESIRE 3 ch.f. Grey Desire 115 – Another Move 69 (Farm Walk 111) [1990 7g 8g a7g 1991 13.8g² 12.3g³ 12.4f* 16.2f² 17.9f* 16.2f* 16m⁶] leggy, shallow-girthed filly: quite modest handicapper: favourite, won at Newcastle in July, Ripon (hung right) in August and Beverley in September: stays well: acts on firm ground: usually held up, and not easiest of rides. *Mrs G. R. Reveley.* 65

MY DUCATS (IRE) 3 b.f. Red Sunset 120 – Saulonika 94 (Saulingo 122) [1990 NR 1991 8.2g⁴ 6m 5.2m 6m 6.1d] sturdy, workmanlike filly: sixth reported foal: half-sister to fairly useful sprinter Aughfad and to sprint winner Rushanes (both by Millfontaine): dam 5f winner: no worthwhile form: bandaged on debut: blinkered third outing. *T. Casey.* —

MYFONTAINE 4 b.c. Persepolis (FR) 127 – Mortefontaine (FR) (Polic 126) [1990 8f a11g⁶ 14g 11.7m* 11.5m⁵ 11.7m⁶ a14g 10m 11.5g a12g⁴ a11g⁵ 1991 10.8g* 10.8m* 11.7g² 11.5d⁵ 10s 11.6m⁵ 11.5g⁴ 10.5d 9.7f 11.5m⁶] leggy colt: quite modest handicapper: won at Warwick (2) in April: mostly below form after: stays 1½m: easily best form on good and good to firm ground. *K. T. Ivory.* 66

MY GIRL FRIDAY 2 b.f. (Mar 19) Scorpio (FR) 127 – Nikancy 76 (Castlenik 107) [1991 a6g] lengthy, workmanlike filly: seventh foal: half-sister to a winning hurdler by Tycoon II: dam modest hurdler: carrying condition, soon well behind in maiden at Southwell in July. *D. W. Chapman.* —

MY GRAIN 2 ch.f. (Apr 7) Ballacashtal (CAN) – Sequoia 87 (Sassafras (FR) 135) [1991 6d 8m] unfurnished filly: half-sister to several winners, including useful 7f and 1m handicapper Travelguard (by Nishapour): dam 2-y-o 6f winner: backward, poor form in late-season maidens at Haydock and Leicester. *R. Hollinshead.* 37

MYHAMET 4 b.c. Gorytus (USA) 132 – Honey Bridge 99 (Crepello 136) [1990 13.3m 12m⁵ 14g 13.3g 1991 16g] rangy colt: good mover: fair handicapper at best: blinkered, well beaten only run in 1991 (March): should stay 1¾m +: acts on firm ground. *P. J. Hobbs.* —

MY HELENE 3 b.f. Mummy's Game 120 – Il Regalo (Meadow Mint (USA) 120) [1990 7m 1991 8m 10.2d 5.7g] sparely-made, leggy filly: seems of little account. *D. R. Tucker.* —

MY JERSEY PEARL (IRE) 2 b.f. (May 12) Cyrano de Bergerac 120 – Bles- **61**
singtonia 79 (So Blessed 130) [1991 5g* 6m3 6g6 6f3 6f4 6m 6.1m 7d] IR 2,000Y:
close-coupled filly: half-sister to 3-y-o Little Preston (by Pennine Walk) and 2-y-o 5f
winners Dunloring (by Dunphy) and Tennis Penny (by Auction Ring): dam raced
only at 5f, winning once at 2 yrs: quite modest performer: made all in maiden at
Salisbury in May: ran poorly last 3 starts, since leaving J. Berry's stable: stays 6f.
Don Enrico Incisa.

MY KIA 4 ch.f. Good Times (ITY) – Troy Moon (Troy 137) [1990 7g5 1991 10d 8f5 —
16m 17.1d6] tall, good-topped filly: no worthwhile form: very reluctant to go down
second start, also refused to enter stalls once at 3 yrs. *R. P. C. Hoad.*

MYKINDOFMUSIC 2 b.f. (Mar 17) Petong 126 – Harmonious Sound (Auction **55**
Ring (USA) 123) [1991 a5g6 5g* 5g* 5f6 a6g4 5m3 5.3m4 a5g] 2,000Y: smallish,
lengthy filly: half-sister to 3-y-o Powerful Pierre (by Mummy's Game) and 1½m to
2m winner Puff Puff (by All Systems Go): dam unraced: plating-class performer:
won maiden auction at Kempton in April: may be worth another try at 6f: twice
unruly in preliminaries, and was mounted outside paddock and taken down early last
2 outings on turf. *M. J. Haynes.*

MY LIFE'S AMBITION (IRE) 3 b. or br.g. Wolverlife 115 – Carnation For —
Me (Kala Shikari 125) [1990 8m 1991 a5g5 a8g] workmanlike gelding: no worthwhile
form. *P. C. Haslam.*

MY MEMOIRS 2 b.c. (Apr 26) Don't Forget Me 127 – Julip 99 (Track Spare 125) **91**
[1991 6.1g* 7m* 7g6 7m2 7m] 31,000F, 17,000Y: leggy, quite good-topped colt: has
scope: moderate walker: half-brother to 3-y-o Adjusting (by Busted), useful miler
Patriach (by London Bells) and Irish 1½m winner Fiestal (by Last Fandango): dam
2-y-o 7f winner, stayed 1½m, from good family: fairly useful performer: won maiden
at Chepstow and minor event at York in mid-summer: ran respectably afterwards,
including in Group 3 event won by Dr Devious at Goodwood (sweating) and Tattersalls Tiffany Highflyer Stakes (led stand side nearly 5f) at Newmarket: stays 7f:
sweating third outing. *R. Hannon.*

MY MOODY GIRL (IRE) 2 b.f. (Mar 24) Alzao (USA) 117 – Young Grace —
(Young Emperor 133) [1991 6.1d 6.1g 7f] IR 8,800Y: compact, good-bodied filly:
fourth reported foal: half-sister to 1m to 1¼m winner Young George (by Camden
Town): dam placed at 1½m in Ireland: soundly beaten, in Redcar claimer in July last
time. *J. Berry.*

MY MUSZKA 7 ch.m. Viking (USA) – Honey To Spare 63 (Track Spare 125) **50**
[1990 NR 1991 a14g 18f6 16.2g3 16.5m] sparely-made mare: has a quick action:
lightly raced and plating-class handicapper nowadays: stays 2m: has form on hard
going, but probably needs an easy surface nowadays: winning hurdler in March. *S.
G. Norton.*

MY NOMINEE 3 b.c. Nomination 125 – Salala 83 (Connaught 130) [1990 NR 1991 **68**
8g 8g4 7f5 7f* 7g] 3,100 2-y-o: workmanlike, angular colt: second foal: half-brother
to quite modest maiden Sashtal (by Ballacashtal) who stayed at least 1m: dam, won
once at 7f, is half-sister to Beau Sher: modest form in maidens: awarded 5-runner
race at Thirsk in July: below form, again making most, in handicap 7 weeks later:
probably stays 1m: hung left second and third starts, and wore pricker near side on
final one. *S. E. Kettlewell.*

MY OPINION 5 b.m. Beldale Flutter (USA) 130 – Opinion 71 (Great Nephew —
126) [1990 11f5 8.5g 8g 11.5m 12f a14g 10v3 a16g5 1991 a14g] compact mare: poor
handicapper at best: should stay 2m: possibly needs plenty of give in the ground. *E.
Eldin.*

MY POLISHED CORNER (IRE) 3 ch.f. Tate Gallery (USA) 117 – Mettle **53**
(USA) 107 (Pretendre 126) [1990 NR 1991 8m 10g 10.5g6 a10g3 11.1m2 16.9g 12m
12m4 12.4m5 a12g] IR 40,000Y: rather unfurnished filly: has a quick action: closely
related to a winner in USA by One For All and smart 1982 2-y-o 7f and 1m winner
Polished Silver (by Try My Best) and half-sister to several winners: dam 2-y-o 5f
winner stayed 1¼m: plating-class maiden: stays 11f: raced freely and set pace when
visored (ran fairly well) then blinkered last 2 outings. *J. W. Hills.*

MY RUBY RING 4 b.f. Blushing Scribe (USA) 107 – Bells of St Martin 89 **46**
(Martinmas 128) [1990 8m 8m 8.2f 6g4 6m5 6d 6m 6m 8.3m 7f 1991 8f4 8f 7f 7.1g 8m
6.1s2 7m4 6m4 6f* 6m 6g 6m2 6g2 5.1d] leggy, angular filly: moderate mover: poor
handicapper: won at Brighton (maiden) in August: ideally suited by 6f: probably acts
on any going: often bandaged: has proved awkward at stalls. *D. R. Laing.*

MY SCENE (FR) 5 b.m. Gay Mecene (USA) 128 – My Hawk (FR) (Sea Hawk II **70** d
131) [1990 11.2g* 10g2 10g 8g5 7m5 8g 8g 7d5 a8g a6g6 1991 a5g3 a6g* a5g2 a6g4

Sheikh Mohammed's "Mystery Play"

7f 7d 5g a6g⁵ 5m] leggy ex-French mare: fair handicapper at best here: won at Lingfield in February: below best last 6 starts: worth another try beyond 6f: acts on dead ground. *C. A. Austin.*

MY SENOR 2 b.g. (May 10) Jalmood (USA) 126 – San Marguerite 80 (Blakeney 126) [1991 5m 7m 7m 7g 8m] 1,500Y: neat gelding: half-brother to useful 1985 2-y-o 5f and 7f winner Andartis (by Final Straw), later disappointing, to 5-y-o 6.9f winner Spanish Love (by Precocious) and to a winner in USA: dam 1¼m winner, is half-sister to St Leger second Zilos: seems of little account. *L. J. Holt.*

MY SHOUSHOU 3 b.f. Shirley Heights 130 – Crystal Fountain (Great Nephew 126) [1990 7g⁶ 1991 10.2g² 11.7m* 10m] leggy, workmanlike filly: modest form: 2/1 on, made most and rallied gamely to beat sole opponent Northern Trial a head in minor event at Bath in July: ran as if something amiss in handicap 2 months later: will prove better at 1½m than shorter. *B. W. Hills.* **78**

MY SOVEREIGN (USA) 2 b.f. (Jan 26) Sovereign Dancer (USA) – Copper Creek 78 (Habitat 134) [1991 5.2g⁶ 6m⁴] $120,000Y: good-bodied filly: has scope: moderate mover: first foal: dam 6f winner from good family: off course 3 months, better effort in maidens when around 5 lengths fourth of 12 to Wolfhound at Redcar in October, keeping on not knocked about: may well stay 1m: will improve again. *J. R. Fanshawe.* **62 p**

MYSTERIOUS MAID (USA) 4 ch.f. L'Emigrant (USA) 129 – Body Heat (USA) (Sir Ivor 135) [1990 10f⁴ 8m³ 8g³ 10.2f* 10m 1991 10.1g 11.5m⁶ 10g³ 12.3d* 11.5g⁵ 11.8g* 12g⁴ a12g² a14g⁶] lengthy, rather angular filly: modest handicapper: won at Ripon (ladies) in June and Leicester in October: stays 1½m: acts on firm and dead ground: ran well on equitrack, moderately on fibresand (1¾m) late in year. *J. Pearce.* **76**

MYSTERY BAND (USA) 5 b.h. Dixieland Band (USA) – Lindaria (USA) (Sea 57 d
Bird II 145) [1990 10m⁶ 8f⁶ 8g³ 12.3g 9m⁴ 8m⁶ 10.8f* 12f⁴ 10m³ 11m² 10.8m⁵ 10m
10m⁵ 12m⁴ a11g² 10m⁴ 12m⁶ 1991 a11g⁴ a11g* a12g³ a12g² a14g⁶ a12g² a12g² a14g⁴
10d a12g⁴ a12g] big, angular horse: poor mover: plating-class handicapper
nowadays: won at Southwell in February: ran as if something amiss final start (July):
best form at 1½m: acts on firm ground: has run moderately for amateur, well for
apprentice: lost near-eye after third start as 3-y-o, has worn eyecover since: sold
420 gns Ascot November Sales. *C. R. Beever.*

MYSTERY CARGO (USA) 3 b.c. Storm Bird (CAN) 134 – Verset Holiday 55
(USA) (Ribots Holiday (USA)) [1990 6m⁴ 6m 1991 8g 7m 5d⁴ 6m⁵ 5g* 5m⁵ 6g 5d 7d]
rather leggy, quite good-topped colt: plating-class handicapper: won handicap at
Lingfield in May, quickening well from some way behind: below form afterwards:
stays 6f: acts on good to firm ground and dead: wears dropped noseband or citation
bridle: took charge of apprentice rider and withdrawn before third intended start:
taken down alone afterwards: not one to trust implicitly. *N. A. Callaghan.*

MYSTERY LAD (IRE) 2 b.c. (Feb 7) Ela-Mana-Mou 132 – Bold Miss (Bold Lad 65
(IRE) 133) [1991 8s 8m 8m 8.3s a8g a8g²] IR 30,000Y, 16,000 2-y-o: workmanlike
colt: third foal: half-brother to Irish 1¾m winner Tellyrand (by Cut Above): dam
unraced daughter of Park Hill Stakes winner Mulvilla: blinkered first time,
¾-length second of 9, making most, to Paper Clip in maiden at Lingfield, easily best
effort: will probably stay 1¼m. *N. A. Callaghan.*

MYSTERY PLAY (IRE) 2 b.f. (Mar 10) Sadler's Wells (USA) 132 – Kereolle 104 p
(Riverman (USA) 131) [1991 7g* 8d² 7m²] 120,000F: leggy filly: eighth foal:
half-sister to 3-y-o Lord Advocate (by Law Society), very useful stayer Arden (by
Ardross) and fair 1m winner Knyf (by Kris): dam second over 6f at 2 yrs in France
but mainly disappointing, is half-sister to very good broodmare Miss Manon: useful
performer: won 9-runner maiden at Newmarket in July: best effort under 3 lengths
third (promoted) to disqualified Midnight Air in 7-runner Brent Walker Fillies' Mile
at Ascot in September: creditable 1½ lengths second of 6 to Musicale in Rockfel
Stakes at former course 3 weeks later, rallying well having been outpaced: likely to
develop into a very useful middle-distance filly. *B. W. Hills.*

MYSTICAL DANCER (IRE) 2 b.g. (Apr 16) Soughaan (USA) 111 – Dancing 76
Lass (King Emperor (USA)) [1991 5f 5m 6d³ 5.7m² 7m*] IR 8,800F, 7,700Y: leggy
gelding: half-brother to very useful 1987 2-y-o 5f and 6f winner Crafty Chris (by Kafu) and 3
winners in Italy, one over jumps: dam won in Italy: won nursery at Brighton in
August, soon close up and running on well: better suited by 7f than shorter: was
progressing well, but wasn't seen out again. *R. Hannon.*

MYSTICAL GUEST 5 b.g. Be My Guest (USA) 126 – Saygood (USA) (Royal 66
Ascot) [1990 NR 1991 10.2d⁶ 14s⁵ 10.3m 12.1g² 12.5g* 10.2s* 12.1d 10.3d]
lengthy, angular gelding: quite modest handicapper: won at Warwick (apprentices)
and Chepstow in October: suited by middle distances: acts on soft going, seems
unsuited to top-of-the-ground: well beaten when blinkered once: has hung left:
none too consistent. *J. R. Bostock.*

MYSTICAL LADY 4 ch.f. Sagaro 133 – L'Angelo di Carlo 46 (Record Token —
128) [1990 10.1m 1991 8.3g] small filly: little worthwhile form, including in sellers.
M. P. Muggeridge.

MYSTIC CRYSTAL (IRE) 3 b.f. Caerleon (USA) 132 – Bolivia (GER) 83
(Windwurf (GER)) [1990 8m⁵ 7m⁶ 6m 6d⁴ 8d a8g² a7g* a7g* 1991 8g² a12g⁴ 8g 7s⁴
8m⁶ 8g a7g⁵ a7g³] leggy, rather sparely-made filly: fair at best: blinkered and back
to form last 2 starts, soon behind when third of 12 in handicap at Lingfield: effective
at 7f, and should stay 1¼m: acts on dead ground: has won for apprentice: may be
untrustworthy. *W. A. O'Gorman.*

MYSTIC MEMORY 2 b.f. (Jun 2) Ela-Mana-Mou 132 – Mountain Memory 109 63 p
(High Top 131) [1991 7f] quite good-topped filly: first foal: dam 6f (at 2 yrs) and 8.2f
winner suited by 1¼m, is sister to Derby Italiano winner My Top: 20/1 from 5/1 and
in need of run, around 3 lengths seventh of 13 to Alto Jane in maiden at Salisbury in
September, running on well not knocked about: will improve, particularly when
granted middle distances. *P. T. Walwyn.*

MYSTIC PANTHER 3 b.g. Sulaafah (USA) 119 – Aljaw 66 (Touching Wood 49
(USA) 127) [1990 NR 1991 7d³ 7g⁶ 8.3m⁴ 9.7f 10g 5.1g⁵] smallish gelding: first foal:
dam ran 3 times at 3 yrs, seeming to stay 1¼m: plater: blinkered, appeared to run
creditably facing very stiff task in claimer final start: stays 9.7f: acts on firm ground
and dead: hung badly left on debut: wore near-side pricker fourth start. *R. J. Holder.*

MYSTIC PARK   2 ch.c. (Feb 27) Rainbow Quest (USA) 134 – Nuryana 107   **86** p
(Nureyev (USA) 131) [1991 7g² 8.1g*] leggy, rather unfurnished colt: first foal: dam
1m winner, is out of half-sister to 1000 Guineas winner On The House: runner-up
in minor event at Kempton before staying on well to win Haydock maiden in
September by 2 lengths from Milzig: will probably stay 1¼m: will improve again. *R. Charlton.*

MYSTIKO (USA)   3 gr.c. Secreto (USA) 128 – Caracciola (FR) (Zeddaan **124**
130) [1990 6m² 6f* 6g³ 1991 7m* 8g* 12f 8g 6f⁴ 7m*]
A coiled spring. Each turn of the pre-race formalities brought an
additional tension, from entering the parade ring to the jockey mounting and
then the pair of them getting to post, before the moment came when Mystiko
could expend all that energy as the stalls opened. He's a natural front runner,
at his best allowed to stride on, attempting to make every yard. In the General
Accident Two Thousand Guineas none could overhaul him. Mystiko raced
against the stand rail, virtually alone for most of the race as Bog Trotter had
the overall lead in a much larger group in the centre. The 6/4 favourite Marju
was one of the first under pressure (and finished lame) and Bog Trotter had
given way by the two-furlong marker but at that stage most of the others in a
fourteen-runner field were still in contention, spread across the track, in
pursuit of Mystiko who had a lead of about a length. Lycius, who'd been held
up in rear, and Shalford looked to be travelling best of the pursuers, and it was
Lycius who provided the challenge, a severe one. Mystiko and Lycius drew
six lengths clear before Mystiko's unflinching efforts saw him pass the post a
head in front. Hector Protector remained in France for the Poulains and
Mujtahid was injured but, their absence aside, the Guineas field looked a very
strong one at the time. The first three in the Craven Stakes (Marju, Desert
Sun and Hokusai), the Greenham (Bog Trotter, Mukaddamah and Shalford), three of the first four in the Free Handicap (Mystiko, Junk Bond and
Flying Brave) and the first two in the Prix Djebel (Ganges and Lycius) were all
there plus the winners of two of the most important two-year-old races, the
Dewhurst (Generous) and Royal Lodge (Mujaazif). The line-up was completed by the National Stakes runner-up Malvernico. Mystiko started 13/2
second favourite following his three-and-a-half-length victory at 11/1 in a
field of eleven for the Ladbroke European Free Handicap at the same course
sixteen days earlier, his win that day representing a marked improvement on
his efforts as a two-year-old which included an all-the-way success in a
Newmarket maiden and third in the Gimcrack Stakes.

The test of a champion, some tell us, is versatility, and the experience of
1991's two Guineas winners, Mystiko and Shadayid, will reinforce that view; it
was the source of some fascinating speculation beforehand but neither proved
nearly so effective at a mile and a half or six furlongs. Mystiko disputed
favouritism for the Derby from Guineas day onwards, even after he'd had an
injury scare (a corn on his off-fore) on the weekend before the race. In the
event, he finished sound but soundly beaten at Epsom, failing to stay.
Together with the pacemaker Arokat, Mystiko had a lead of several lengths
after only a couple of furlongs but the pack, headed by Generous, had closed
right up on him by the three-furlong marker and left him behind by the
two-furlong pole. After he'd failed to please his trainer in the run-up to the
July Cup, the first suitable opportunity to test Mystiko at six furlongs again,

Ladbroke European Free Handicap, Newmarket—Mystiko is well on top

General Accident Two Thousand Guineas, Newmarket—Mystiko has the rail all the way;
he and Lycius come right away from the rest, led by Ganges;
Generous (extreme left) finishes fourth while the favourite Marju (striped cap)
beats only three home

with the sprint championship wide open, was the Ladbroke Sprint Cup at Haydock. This time the writing was on the wall for Mystiko even sooner than in the Derby; he managed a share of the lead but not for long, and had dropped out of contention at halfway, eventually finishing six and a half lengths fourth of six, which was much better than had seemed likely entering the final furlong. That was, in fact, Mystiko's third comprehensive defeat in a row. Between the Derby and the Ladbroke Sprint he'd gone to Goodwood for the Sussex Stakes and turned in easily his worst performance of the year, keeping close tabs on the leader before weakening rapidly entering the straight. The experimentation over distance could explain two of those failures and Brittain's stable was generally out of form when it came round to Goodwood but it may not be purely coincidence that Mystiko's three best efforts have all come at Newmarket, on the Rowley Mile. Returned there in October, he showed that nothing too serious could have been wrong with him in the summer by winning the seven-furlong Challenge Stakes. Selkirk's late withdrawal drastically weakened the opposition which eventually comprised Bog Trotter; the recently-returned Volksraad; the Child and Hungerford Stakes winner Only Yours; the Van Geest Criterium winner La Grange Music and the listed winner Himiko; and Kazoo who hadn't raced since the Prix de Diane. Mystiko, drawn near to the stand rail again, immediately stepped into the lead and produced a performance of very nearly the same order that won him the Guineas. Bog Trotter didn't take him on this time, Mystiko stretched the field approaching the Dip and was ridden out firmly to beat Only Yours two lengths. That Mystiko's good days to date have all come at

Challenge Stakes, Newmarket—another win on the track;
Mystiko draws away from Only Yours and Volksraad, having made all

Newmarket *might* be relevant to his future prospects; it would not be too surprising if a highly-strung type such as him reacted badly to travelling. If that is an important factor then his prospects in 1992 look none too bright. Brittain has stated that all the top mile races are on the agenda, beginning with the Trusthouse Forte Mile at Sandown and the Queen Anne Stakes at Royal Ascot, ending with the Breeders' Cup Mile in Florida. The Van Geest Criterion Stakes and Challenge Stakes are the only pattern events over seven furlongs for older colts at Newmarket. There aren't any over a mile. Brittain, however, believes that Mystiko is maturing mentally and has compared him to Pebbles: 'difficult at three but a piece of cake at four'. Mystiko was noticeably less edgy on his last two appearances, with no parade in either, coming into the paddock very late at Haydock, then on his toes but not sweating up—on a very cold day—at Newmarket. One thing we know for certain: seven furlongs or a mile is his distance, and allowed to concentrate at that he may prove more consistent in 1992.

Mystiko failed to stay in the Derby but he's by a Derby winner, one whose ability to see out the trip thoroughly denied El Gran Senor by a short head in 1984. Secreto was not seen out again and a half-share in him was reportedly purchased by Calumet Farm for 20,000,000 dollars. Calumet's star and that of Secreto have fallen somewhat since those days. Calumet is currently involved in bankruptcy proceedings with alleged debts, according to the *Thoroughbred Times*, estimated at 127,000,000 dollars at the time of the dispersal of most of their racing and breeding stock in November. Covering a large number of mares—he had 161 foals in his first three crops—couldn't guarantee Secreto success as a stallion. Mystiko fetched 150,000 dollars at the Keeneland Selected Yearling Sale, about 25,000 dollars above the average for Secreto's yearlings in 1989, but the average has dropped to about 35,000 dollars in each of the last two years. He's had Grade 2 winners in the USA in Lea Lucinda and Group 2 in Italy with Rufina and Miss Secreto and several useful performers in Britain, including Palace Street and Rudjig, but Mystiko must be the best of his offspring. Mystiko is also much the best produced by his dam Caracciola. Her five previous foals included two minor winners in North America by Far North and Topsider, the pattern-placed French seven-and-a-half-furlong winner Mer Belle (by Far North) and Lyphinale (by Lypheor) who was placed in a French listed race at two years. Caracciola's 1989 foal was a sister to Mystiko. Caracciola had nine starts in France as a three-year-old, between seven and eight and a half furlongs, but could not win one despite being sent to the Provinces. Mystiko's breeder purchased her for 170,000 dollars in 1983. A look at her dam Cendres Bleues' producing record explains why she was worth so much and why she's spent so much of her time at stud visiting sons of Northern Dancer. To Lyphard Cendres Bleues threw Calderina, one of the best middle-distance fillies in France in 1978, and to Lyphard she had the Grand Criterium, Prix Lupin and Grand Prix de Paris runner-up Pasakos. Cendres Bleues was herself a useful middle-distance performer in Italy and is a half-sister to the good Italian colts Claude and

The Dowager Lady Beaverbrook's "Mystiko"

Crivelli. Their dam Aigue-Vive, who produced another seven winners, was successful over jumps in France as a three-year-old.

		Northern Dancer (b 1961)	Nearctic
	Secreto (USA) (b 1981)		Natalma
		Betty's Secret (ch 1977)	Secretariat
Mystiko (USA) (gr.c. 1988)			Betty Loraine
		Zeddaan (gr 1965)	Grey Sovereign
	Caracciola (FR) (gr 1978)		Vareta
		Cendres Bleues (b 1968)	Charlottesville
			Aigue-Vive

The sturdy Mystiko has already had more than twice as many races as his sire and, as we stated, is due to race again as a four-year-old. His owner's policy is one the racegoers can be thankful for. Mystiko has yet to race on a soft surface. He has a quick action but don't expect to see much of it on the way to post as Roberts takes him down as steadily as possible nowadays. *C. E. Brittain.*

MY SWAN SONG   6 b.g. Soul Singer 97 – Palmaria (Be Friendly 130) [1990 a11g a12g⁴ a14g a11g⁴ a14g a12g 1991 12.3g] close-coupled gelding: poor in all his paces: stays 12.5f: seems to act on any going: has been tried blinkered: winning hurdler. *J. P. Smith.*   —

MYTASKI   5 b.h. Niniski (USA) 125 – Mytinia 94 (Bustino 136) [1990 16g 11.7f³ 12m 1991 a13g³] lengthy horse: fair maiden at 4 yrs: well below form only run in 1991: stayed 1¾m: acted on firm going: a difficult ride: dead. *A. Moore.*   **47**

575

MY THREE GIRLS (IRE) 3 b.f. Tumble Wind (USA) – Winter Harvest — (Grundy 137) [1990 NR 1991 8m 8g 7m 8.2m] IR 3,100F, 2,600Y: angular, leggy, sparely-made filly: fourth foal: sister to modest Irish maiden Reuben James, placed at 7f, and half-sister to 1987 2-y-o 6f seller winner L'Ancressan (by Dalsaan): dam second over 1½m in Ireland: no form, in selling handicap final start. *H. J. Collingridge.*

MY TURN NEXT 3 b.f. King of Spain 121 – Its My Turn 80 (Palm Track 122) — [1990 6s 6m 6f⁵ 8.2v 6d 1991 8g 9d 6m 8g 10g 8g] big, lengthy filly: plating-class maiden: ran moderately last 5 starts: stays 1m: best 2-y-o efforts on top-of-the-ground: headstrong. *R. Hollinshead.*

N

NAAFIR (USA) 3 ch.c. Lyphard (USA) 132 – Miss Summer (Luthier 126) [1990 **70** NR 1991 8g 10.4g 10g² 12.2m³] 380,000Y: angular, unfurnished colt: brother to French 1m winner Ofanto and closely related to smart French 1987 2-y-o Most Precious (by Nureyev): dam French 1m winner, is half-sister to Lydian (by Lyphard), Sharpman and Ballinderry (dam of Sanglamore): placed in maidens at Brighton and (making most) Catterick: stays 1½m: sold 9,800 gns Newmarket Autumn Sales. *A. C. Stewart.*

NACONA 5 b.g. Noalto 120 – Party Girl 96 (Pardao 120) [1990 NR 1991 10.8g] big, — rather leggy gelding: has a round action: bad maiden on flat: winning hurdler in March. *J. S. King.*

NADIAD 5 b.g. Darshaan 133 – Naveen (Sir Gaylord) [1990 NR 1991 10.5g] big, — workmanlike gelding: fairly useful form at best at 3 yrs for L. Cumani: soundly beaten in amateur riders event at Haydock, only run in 1991: should stay 1½m: acts on good to firm ground: winning hurdler. *D. McCain.*

NAEL (IRE) 2 b.c. (May 25) Never So Bold 135 – Night Encounter (Right Tack — 131) [1991 6f] 30,000F, IR 38,000Y: half-brother to 3 winners, including French 9f (at 2 yrs) to 15f winner North Col (by Head For Heights): dam, sister to Take A Reef, won at up to 12.5f in France: 16/1, backward and green, always behind in 22-runner maiden at Newbury in September. *C. J. Benstead.*

NAFPLION 6 b.m. Young Generation 129 – Time For Thought 75 (Crooner 119) — [1990 a8g a8g 10.6f 5s⁶ 6f 7m 1991 7g 8f 10.6g 7.1d 7.6g 8.9m a11g 10.3m a11g] rather leggy, workmanlike mare: of little account nowadays. *R. E. Peacock.*

NAGEM 8 b.m. Headin' Up – Eleonora 70 (Falcon 131) [1990 a6g a6g 6m 6g a5g⁵ **39** 5g³ 5g² 6d⁴ 6f⁵ 1991 5d 6m 5.1m⁶ 6g 6.1d 5.1d 7.6g 6m] strong, lengthy mare: has run tubed: poor mover: one-time modest front-running sprint handicapper: acts on any going: has run respectably in blinkers: usually on edge. *L. J. Barratt.*

NAI HARN 3 b.c. Petong 126 – Pacific Polly (Mount Hagen (FR) 127) [1990 6g **67** 6f* 6f⁵ 6g³ 7f 7m 1991 7g⁵ 8.5f²] leggy colt: quite modest performer. *C. F. Wall.*

NAIL DON 6 b.g. Don 128 – Vivungi (USA) (Exbury 138) [1990 NR 1991 10.1s³ **47** 10g] compact gelding: fairly useful performer as 4-y-o: poor nowadays: pulled up feelingly final start: best form at 1m: acts on good to firm and soft going. *R. Hannon.*

NAILEM 4 b.c. Absalom 128 – La Reine de France (Queen's Hussar 124) [1990 — a8g 1991 10f a7g 9.7m a12g] sturdy colt: has a round action: carries condition: modest winner at 2 yrs: soundly beaten since, including in seller: best form at 5f: acts on firm going. *R. P. C. Hoad.*

NAJAAH 3 b.f. Green Desert (USA) 127 – Sarajill (High Line 125) [1990 7s 1991 — 7m 7g 7f⁵ 8d 7g] workmanlike filly: plating-class maiden: bred to stay beyond 7f: form only on firm ground. *R. W. Armstrong.*

NAJEB (USA) 2 b.c. (Mar 9) Chief's Crown (USA) – Modiste (USA) (Sir Ivor **80** 135) [1991 8m³ 6m* 7m] $200,000Y: smallish, well-made colt: good walker: brother to 3-y-o French 1¼m winner Taffeta Pipkin and half-brother to several winners: dam unraced: fair form: well-backed 11/8-shot, won maiden at Newcastle by ½ length from Beware of Agents, soon prominent and staying on well: soundly beaten in nursery at Newmarket later in October: bred to stay 1¼m. *B. Hanbury.*

NAKED TRUTH 2 b.f. (Apr 9) Natroun (FR) 128 – Much Too Risky 87 (Bustino **63** 136) [1991 7f 8f² 8.3g²] leggy, close-coupled, unfurnished filly: third foal: half-sister to 1990 2-y-o 5f and 6f winner Seductress (by Known Fact) and 13f winner Boy Emperor (by Precocious): dam 2-y-o 7.2f and 1m winner, is out of half-sister to very smart animals He Loves Me and Wattlefield: quite modest form in maidens: will stay at least 1¼m: acts on firm ground. *M. R. Stoute.*

NAKORA BISTRAYA (USA)   4 b.f. Robellino (USA) 127 – Calypsa (USA) 83   **73**
(The Minstrel (CAN) 135) [1990 8m³ 8.2s* 10m⁵ 8.2s* 8m⁴ 9m 1991 8v⁶ 9s⁵ 10.3d
10d² a10g] close-coupled filly: has a markedly round action: modest handicapper:
sold 6,000 gns Newmarket Autumn Sales after penultimate start: stays 1¼m: goes
very well with plenty of give in the ground: off course nearly 4 months before (below
form) third outing. *G. A. Pritchard-Gordon.*

NAMASTE   3 b.c. Petoski 135 – View 88 (Shirley Heights 130) [1990 NR 1991 8m   **74**
14m⁴ 11.9g⁶ 12m⁴ 10g⁴ 8.1m* 8.1c³] lengthy, workmanlike colt: moderate mover:
third foal: dam 6f and 1m winner: 20/1, won maiden at Edinburgh in October:
possibly best at 1m: acts on good to firm ground. *B. Hanbury.*

NAN A BUCK (USA)   2 b.c. (Feb 16) Spend A Buck (USA) – Nosey Nan (USA)   **84**
(Nantallah) [1991 7f⁶ 7g* 8d 8s] $27,000F: good-topped colt: half-brother to
numerous winners, including Table The Rumor (by Round Table), stakes winner at
up to 1¼m: dam, unraced, from family of champion 3-y-o filly Gamely: sire won
Kentucky Derby: fair performer: backed at long odds, won 18-runner maiden at
Leicester in September, quickening to lead 2f out and running on very well: out of
depth in Royal Lodge William Hill Stakes at Ascot and Gran Criterium at Milan (not
discredited) afterwards: may stay 1¼m: acts on soft ground. *B. Hanbury.*

NAN'S BOY   3 b.c. Blakeney 126 – Classy Nancy (USA) (Cutlass (USA)) [1990   **35**
5.8m 7m 7d 7g 1991 12v³ 12.3s 9g 12g 12.1g³ 14.1m] workmanlike colt: poor maiden:
probably suited by test of stamina: acts on heavy going: headstrong in blinkers third
start: trained until after fourth by J. Ffitch-Heyes. *R. J. Holder.*

NAO FAZ MAL   3 b. or br.f. Chief Singer 131 – Pine Away 74 (Shirley Heights   **56**
130) [1990 6m 7m⁵ 7m 7m 1991 8h² 9m⁴ 8m³ 8m 8f⁴ 8.9m² 8g⁴ 10.4m³ 8.2m² 10m]
leggy, sparely-made filly: plating-class form: stays 1¼m: acts on hard going: may
need exaggerated waiting tactics: ran poorly for 7-lb claimer fourth start: sold 7,200
gns Newmarket Autumn Sales. *Lord John FitzGerald.*

NAOMI'S KEEPSAKE   3 b.f. Nomination 125 – Rebecca (Quorum 126) [1990   —
7d 7d a6g 1991 8s 12.2g 12f] poor plater. *C. W. Thornton.*

NASAB   3 ch.g. Nordance (USA) – Piccadilly Etta 76 (Floribunda 136) [1990 7m   **86**
8.2m³ 8g* 1991 10g 10g 8f⁴ 10.1f² 11.9g 9m* 10g 8m] lengthy, rather angular
gelding: fair performer: favourite, won handicap at Redcar in September, leading
over 2f out: below that form in similar events afterwards: stays 1¼m: acts on firm
going: sold 16,000 gns Newmarket Autumn Sales. *D. Morley.*

NASEBY (IRE)   3 b.f. Kafu 120 – First Contact 79 (Simbir 130) [1990 5m 5v³ 5d   —
6g⁶ 5m 1991 6d 6m 8.2d 8f 8.1s] leggy filly: moderate mover: poor maiden: stays 6f:
acts on good to firm ground and heavy: sweating final outing. *D. Haydn Jones.*

NASEER (USA)   2 b.c. (May 12) Hero's Honor (USA) – Sweet Delilah (USA)   **54** p
(Super Concorde (USA)) [1991 7m 8.2f 8m] $12,000Y, resold 370,000 francs (approx
£37,000) Y: lengthy colt: has scope: third foal: half-brother to Super Fan (by Lear
Fan), useful winner at up to 1¼m in USA, including in Grade 3 event: dam winner at
1m: sire won from 7f to 11f: around 17 lengths twelfth of 18, catching eye, not at all
knocked about, to Wesaam at Newmarket, final and easily best effort (bit backward
at least previously) in maidens: will improve again, and may well do better in handicaps. *N. A. Callaghan.*

NASHAAT (USA)   3 b.c. El Gran Senor (USA) 136 – Absentia (USA) 108 (Raise   **90**
A Cup (USA)) [1990 6m 1991 7g⁴ 7g⁶ 6g² 6f* 6m² 6f⁶] stocky, good-topped colt: fair
performer: best efforts fourth and fifth starts, making all in 5-runner maiden at
Folkestone in August: gave temperamental display before and during (ridden along
throughout) final start: stays 6f well: acts on firm ground: gives trouble at stalls,
refusing to enter them fourth intended outing: sold 27,000 gns Newmarket Autumn
Sales: clearly not one to trust implicitly. *Major W. R. Hern.*

NASHOON (IRE)   2 b.c. (Apr 28) Nashamaa 113 – Nistona (Will Somers 114§)   **65**
[1991 6g⁵ 7f 6m] IR 5,200F, 4,000Y, 6,700 2-y-o: leggy colt: moderate walker: sixth
foal: half-brother to several winners, including 13f to 2m winner Panama Jack and
1987 2-y-o 1m seller winner Lover's Secret (both by Skyliner): dam unraced
half-sister to very smart miler Cyrus: quite modest form in maidens and a claimer:
will stay 1m: races with head high: has joined N. Graham. *R. F. Johnson Houghton.*

NASHVILLE BLUES (IRE)   2 ch.f. (Apr 11) Try My Best (USA) 130 – Re-   **60**
quena (Dom Racine (FR) 121) [1991 6g³ 7g³] 12,000Y: angular, rather unfurnished
filly: has scope: moderate mover: third foal: half-sister to a winner in USA: dam,
Irish maiden, stayed 1¼m: easily better effort in midsummer maidens when third of
18 at Salisbury in July second start: bred to stay at least 1m: seemed likely to
improve again. *J. W. Hills.*

NASSEER 2 br.c. (Mar 4) Top Ville 129 – Ibtihaj (USA) 97 (Raja Baba (USA)) — p
[1991 8s] sturdy colt: fourth foal: half-brother to quite useful 1986 2-y-o 5f winner
Abhaaj (by Kris) and 1989 2-y-o 5f winner Al Mujil (by Shareef Dancer): dam, 2-y-o
5f winner, is half-sister to Danzig: 8/1 and very backward, behind in maiden at
Kempton in September, leading almost 5f, weakening quickly and eased: should do
better. *A. C. Stewart.*

NASTY BOSS 3 b.g. Nicholas Bill 125 – Dark Finale (Javelot 124) [1990 NR 1991 —
14.1f5 16g 14.1m5 16m] tall gelding: poor mover: closely related to several winners
by High Line, including Oaks fourth Shore Line and Park Hill winner Quay Line, and
half-brother to a winner: dam won at up to 1½m in Ireland: poor form in maidens,
claimer and seller: sold 2,000 gns Newmarket Autumn Sales. *C. A. Cyzer.*

NASWARA (USA) 3 br.f. Al Nasr (FR) 126 – Sound Of Summer (USA) (Drone) 88
[1990 7m 1991 11.5f4 12.3d* 12.1d* 12f2 14.6m 12.1s4] strong, rangy filly: fair
performer: won apprentice contests at Ripon in June and Chepstow in July: suited
by 1½m: acts on any going: ridden from the front. *H. R. A. Cecil.*

NATASHA NADINE 4 b.f. Bay Express 132 – Sweet Candice 71 (African Sky —
124) [1990 NR 1991 9s 8.5f] leggy, close-coupled filly: no form. *R. M. Whitaker.*

NATIONAL EMBLEM (FR) 2 b.c. (Mar 30) Sadler's Wells (USA) 132 – 77 p
Kaliopa (FR) (Zeddaan 130) [1991 10m*] IR 200,000Y: sturdy, workmanlike colt:
half-brother to several winners here and in France, including smart 1m to 1¼m
performer Katowice (by Targowice): dam won twice at up to 1¼m: 12/1 from 5/1,
backward and green, won 9-runner maiden at Nottingham in October by a head from
Kajaani, slowly away, then staying on well despite carrying head high: will improve,
and stay further. *P. F. I. Cole.*

NATIONAL MIST 2 gr.f. (Apr 8) Northern Tempest (USA) 120 – Slap Bang 62 —
(Pitskelly 122) [1991 5m] small, stocky filly: second foal: dam ungenuine 1½m
winner: 33/1 and bandaged near-hind, swerved leaving stalls and always behind in
maiden at Ripon in April. *C. W. Thornton.*

NATIVE CHIEFTAN 2 b.c. (May 2) Trojan Fen 118 – Habituee (Habitat 134) 84
[1991 5m 6g 7m4 7m2 7g* 7d] 27,000Y: close-coupled colt: half-brother to several
winners here and abroad, including smart 7f and 1m winner Dabaweyaa (by Shareef
Dancer) and Oaks second Acclimatise (by Shirley Heights): dam French 1½m
winner: fair form: comfortably won maiden at Brighton in September: seemed to
be progressing well, but ran moderately in Ascot nursery final outing: will stay
1m: possibly unsuited by dead ground. *R. Hannon.*

NATIVE CROWN (IRE) 3 b.g. Be My Native (USA) 122 – Crystal Halo 78 (St —
Chad 120) [1990 NR 1991 9m6] 2,800Y: leggy, rather sparely-made gelding: sixth
foal: half-brother to 13f to 2m winner Holy Zeal (by Alzao) and Irish 5f and 6f winner
Playing Safe (by Reasonable): dam stayed 1½m: showed a little ability when never-
dangerous sixth of 13 in claimer (moved moderately down) at Redcar in June: not
given hard race: joined Miss L. Perratt. *B. Hanbury.*

NATIVE LASS (IRE) 2 ch.f. (Mar 21) Be My Native (USA) 122 – Fun Frolic —
(Sexton Blake 126) [1991 5g 5m5 6g 5m] IR 2,000Y, resold 2,300Y: workmanlike
filly: third foal: half-sister to 4-y-o Al Frolic (by Alzao): dam placed mostly over
middle distances in Ireland: seems of little account. *J. Balding.*

NATIVE MAGIC 5 ch.m. Be My Native (USA) 122 – Tuyenu 77 (Welsh Pageant 75
132) [1990 13.3m2 12f6 12s 14d3 12g3 12s a14g 1991 12d6 13.9g4 14.6m 14s 15.8g*
13.6d4 16.5d a14g] sparely-made, angular mare: modest handicapper: won moderately-run contest at Catterick in October: good fourth at Redcar, best subsequent
effort: stays 2m: unsuited by soft going: usually held up. *R. W. Armstrong.*

NATIVE MISSION 4 ch.g. Be My Native (USA) 122 – Sister Ida (Bustino 136) 80
[1990 14f3 13.6m5 1991 14.6s*] unfurnished gelding: comfortably won maiden at
Doncaster in March by 3½ lengths, edging left and carrying head high last 1f: will
stay 2m: best effort on soft ground: fairly useful hurdler. *J. G. FitzGerald.*

NATIVE STREAM 3 ch.f. Deep River 103 – Native Love 77 (Native Prince) —
[1990 5m6 6d 1991 8.9m] sparely-made filly: no sign of ability. *E. H. Owen jun.*

NATIVE SUITOR 4 b.g. Local Suitor (USA) 128 – Bronte (USA) 88 (Bold 44
Forbes (USA)) [1990 8f 8.5g a7g 8m4 1991 a7g2 a8g4 a8g 7m a8g] lengthy, good-
quartered gelding: moderate mover: poor maiden: stays 1m: acts on good to firm
ground: twice pulled hard in blinkers. *P. A. Blockley.*

NATRAL EXCHANGE (IRE) 2 b.c. (Apr 23) Natroun (FR) 128 – Aladja (Mill 74
Reef (USA) 141) [1991 7f 7g6 10m3] IR 70,000F: smallish, rather unfurnished colt:
half-brother to 1986 French 2-y-o 7f winner Aleyda (by Sharpman): dam winner at 9f

in France, is half-sister to Aliysa: modest maiden: best effort always-prominent third of 9 at Nottingham in October: stays 1¼m. *J. W. Hills.*

NAUGHTY NORA 3 b.f. Lir 82 – Amberush 41 (No Rush) [1990 a7g 1991 10d 12f 12f 12g] sparely-made filly: poor maiden. *A. Moore.* —

NAUGHTY NORMAN 2 b.c. (Mar 22) Sulaafah (USA) 119 – Play For Time (Comedy Star (USA) 121) [1991 5g 6d³ 5d³ 5g³ 5g 6m 6m 6s] 7,800Y: leggy colt: has a quick action: first foal: dam never ran: poor maiden: well beaten last 4 starts, blinkered in seller penultimate one: stays 6f: acts on dead ground: sold 2,600 gns Doncaster November Sales. *P. Mitchell.* **47**

NAUTAE SILVAE 3 b.f. Sweet Monday 122 – Moonlight Bay 53 (Palm Track 122) [1990 NR 1991 8d 8.5f 8g 7m⁴ a8g 8f] lengthy, angular filly: shows traces of stringhalt: third foal (all by Sweet Monday): dam won 1m seller: poor maiden: seems better at 7f than 1m: edgy last 2 starts. *R. Earnshaw.* **34**

NAVARESQUE 6 b.m. Raga Navarro (ITY) 119 – Esquinade 84 (Silly Season 127) [1990 7h 8h 7m³ 7f* 8g⁵ 8f² 8m* 10h 8f⁵ 8.2m³ 6g* 6g 6d⁶ 7d³ 1991 7g 7.1d 7.1g⁵ 8g* 8.1g⁶ 8.3g 7g 6.9f* 7f 8g 6g⁶ 6.9f² 7g] leggy, angular mare: has a round action: plating-class handicapper: won at Brighton in July and Folkestone in August: effective at 6f to 9f: acts on firm and dead going: none too consistent. *R. J. Hodges.* **54**

NAVARRA (USA) 3 b.f. El Gran Senor (USA) 136 – Image of Reality (USA) (In Reality) [1990 NR 1991 7g*] fifth reported living foal: half-sister to 4 winners in North America, including Canadian 4-y-o Grade 3 7f winner Image of Class (by Codex): dam smart 4-y-o in USA, successful in Graded 8.5f races: weak 10/1, won 14-runner maiden at Newmarket in October by 2½ lengths from Sauvignon, leading 2f out: should improve. *J. H. M. Gosden.* **68** p

NAWASSI (USA) 4 b.f. Shadeed (USA) 135 – Scintillate 119 (Sparkler 130) [1990 6g³ 6g² 7m⁴ 7m² 7.5d 6s 1991 a6g 7f 6g 6.1s 7g² 5m 6m] moderate mover: quite modest maiden at 3 yrs: no form in 1991: bred to stay further than 7f: acts on good to firm ground. *K. O. Cunningham-Brown.* —

NAWWAR 7 ch.h. Thatching 131 – Priceless Pin (Saint Crespin III 132) [1990 7g 6m 7m⁵ 6m 7m² 7m² 7m 7m³ 7g 7m a7g 1991 6s⁴ 7m 6g 6g⁴ 7m³ 7g4] strong, close-coupled horse: plating-class handicapper: good running-on third of 20 at Leicester: best at 6f or 7f: acts on good to firm and dead going: often gets behind. *C. J. Benstead.* **59**

NAYLAND 5 ch.h. Be My Guest (USA) 126 – Troytops 66 (Troy 137) [1990 8g² 7.6d⁵ 8g² 8f 8m* 7m² 8f⁵ 8g³ 7m² 1991 8d³ 7g⁵ 8g⁵ 10f* 8g⁴ 10v⁴ 10.5g4 10m⁴ 8.9g⁵ **102**

Zetland Gold Cup, Redcar—Nayland gets the trip and holds off the favourite Mellottie

8g²] lengthy, angular horse: moderate mover: useful performer: won Zetland Gold Cup (Handicap) at Redcar in May: mostly ran well after, at Ascot in Queen Anne Stakes and £11,350 handicap next and final starts: stays 1¼m: best efforts on a sound surface: has wandered under pressure, and ideally suited by waiting tactics: ran creditably when visored once: consistent: sent to Dubai. *G. Wragg.*

NAZARE BLUE   4 b.g. Absalom 128 – Top Stream 87 (Highland Melody 112)   **45**
[1990 7f 6f 6m² 5g 6m³ 6f 6g 7m 6g 6d 1991 7.6g 6g 7.1g 5m⁵ 6.1s³ 6m* 6g 6g³ 6.1m⁵] big, rather angular gelding: quite good mover: poor handicapper: won (for first time) at Lingfield in August: stays 6f: acts on any going: sometimes wears dropped noseband. *Mrs Barbara Waring.*

NAZMIAH   5 b.m. Free State 125 – Irish Ballad 65 (Irish Ball (FR) 127) [1990 10f   **49**
11m 10m 10m 10g² 10f³ 10g* 10m 10.2g 12m 1991 10m⁶ 10.2m⁵a 11g⁵ 10g 10.2g⁴ 11m* 12m* 11.8m⁴ 10g] leggy mare: plating-class handicapper nowadays: won at Redcar and Southwell (gamely) in August: stays 1½m: acts on firm and dead going: has worn dropped noseband of late. *A. Hide.*

NDITA   5 b.m. Be My Native (USA) 122 – Orangery (Realm 129) [1990 9g 10m⁴   **49**
10.6s⁴ 11m 11v³ a8g 1991 10v³ 10m 8g⁶ 9m] tall, leggy mare: moderate walker and poor mover: poor performer nowadays: not seen out after May: stays 10.6f: acts on good to firm and soft going: sold 2,400 gns Ascot September Sales. *R. J. Hodges.*

NEARLY HONEST   3 ch.f. Nearly A Hand 115 – Miss Saddler (St Paddy 133)   **—**
[1990 NR 1991 7.1m³ 6.9f 10g] workmanlike filly: fourth living foal: sister to 1¼m winner/useful jumper Teletrader: dam won over hurdles: always behind in maidens: needs further. *R. J. Hodges.*

NEARLY MARCH   2 ch.c. (Feb 28) Stanford 121§ – Simmies Love 48 (Record   **—**
Token 128) [1991 5g 7m] plain colt: third foal: dam winning 1m plater: sweating, well beaten in maidens at Wolverhampton (visored, on toes) and Doncaster (blinkered) in autumn: sold 820 gns Doncaster November Sales. *J. Balding.*

NECTAR COLLECTOR   2 b.c. (May 13) Natroun (FR) 128 – Mirkan Honey 83   **67** p
(Ballymore 123) [1991 6f⁴ 8m²] 24,000Y: close-coupled colt: half-brother to 3-y-o Lee Artiste (by Tate Gallery), successful at 5f and 6f, and useful Scandinavian colt Tiger Bill (by General Assembly): dam Irish 4-y-o 2m winner: in frame in maidens at Yarmouth (weak odds-on shot, green) and Redcar (well backed, looked likely winner 2f out then one pace) in autumn: will be well suited by 1¼m + : likely to improve further. *L. M. Cumani.*

NED'S BONANZA   2 b.c. (Feb 2) Green Ruby (USA) 104 – Miss Display 47   **69**
(Touch Paper 113) [1991 5d² 5m² 5m* 5m* 5f² 5g³ 5m³ 6g] 6,200Y: first foal: dam, maiden, best form at 5f: modest performer: won maiden at Edinburgh in June: good keeping-on third of 9 in nursery at Newmarket penultimate start: had stiff task in Racecall Gold Trophy at Redcar final one: worth another try at 6f. *R. M. Whitaker.*

NEDTEX   2 b.c. (Apr 27) Dreams To Reality (USA) 113 – Sleekit 78 (Blakeney   **68**
126) [1991 5m⁶ 5f a5g⁴ 6g* a7g²] 3,000Y: close-coupled, leggy colt: has a roundish action: brother to 3-y-o 1m winner Clipper One and half-brother to 1¼m winner Kitty Clare (by Milford) and a winner over hurdles: dam 1½m winner: very useful plater: won at Yarmouth (no bid) in July: improved form when narrowly beaten at Southwell 9 days later: likely to stay 1m. *M. H. Tompkins.*

NEEDHAM LAD (IRE)   3 b.g. Wassl 125 – Blue Shark (Silver Shark 129) [1990   **49**
7m⁶ 8.2m 10s 1991 a10g² a10g] close-coupled gelding: poor maiden: keeping-on second in claimer at Southwell: ran badly in Lingfield maiden 4 weeks later: better suited by 1¼m than shorter: sold 2,500 gns Doncaster March Sales. *P. A. Kelleway.*

NEEDWOOD MUPPET   4 b.g. Rolfe (USA) 77 – Sea Dart 55 (Air Trooper 115)   **49**
[1990 8.2d⁴ 8g³ 8.2g⁶ 8.2d 10.6v⁶ 10.4d 9s 1991 12g 12m²] angular gelding: has a round action: poor maiden: yet to show he stays 1½m. *B. C. Morgan.*

NEEDWOOD POPPY   3 b.f. Rolfe (USA) 77 – Needwood Nap (Some Hand 119)   **—**
[1990 6f 7g 6d 1991 10.5d 10m 11.1s] compact filly: has a quick action: poor plater. *B. C. Morgan.*

NEEDWOOD SPRITE   5 ch.m. Joshua 129 – Sea Dart 55 (Air Trooper 115)   **45**
[1990 9g 9s⁴ 10g 8.2s³ 11g⁴ 10.4g³ 10.6g 12s² 13.8d⁴ 13.6d 12s⁴ 1991 12g² 13d³ 12g 13.8m] plain mare: poor handicapper: stays 13.8f: acts on good to firm and soft going: visored in 1991: winning hurdler. *B. C. Morgan.*

NEGATORY (USA) 4 ch.g. Secreto (USA) 128 – Negation (USA) (Mongo) [1990 **66**
NR 1991 a14g8g5 15.9g5 11m 12m* 11m 16.5m6 10.3d a14g] big, workmanlike
gelding: carries condition: bad mover: eighth foal: half-brother to 4 winners in USA,
notably graded-stakes winner Lord Lister (by Sir Lister): dam won 11 times in minor
company in USA: 66/1, worthwhile form only when winning maiden at Pontefract in
September, tailed off at halfway: stays 1½m: acts on good to firm ground: winning
hurdler. *M. C. Chapman.*

NEGEEN (USA) 3 b.f. Danzig (USA) – Sunny Smile (USA) (Boldnesian) [1990 **78**
5g6 5f2 5g* 6d2 1991 5s 7m* 7g* 8m] good-bodied filly: progressive form when
successful in handicaps at Epsom and Yarmouth in June, tracking leaders and
keeping on well to lead close home: raced too freely, close up 6f, in £11,200 handicap
at Newmarket in July: should stay 1m: acts on good to firm ground and dead (in need
of race on soft): visits Cadeaux Genereux. *A. C. Stewart.*

NEIEB (USA) 2 b.f. (Apr 28) Alleged (USA) 138 – Victoria Star (CAN) (Northern **63**
Dancer) [1991 8g5 8.1d5] $100,000Y: leggy, good-topped filly: has a quick action:
half-sister to numerous winners here and abroad, including fairly useful 1988
2-y-o 5f and 6f winner Stellaria (by Roberto): dam, minor winner at 2 yrs, is out of
Canadian Oaks winner Solometeor: much better effort in October maiden at
Wolverhampton (slowly away, soon prominent, no extra 2f out) on debut. *B.
Hanbury.*

NEITHER NOR 2 ch.f. (Mar 3) Norwick (USA) 120 – Leap In Time (Dance In **63**
Time (CAN)) [1991 5.7f6 6d2 6f6] quite good-topped filly: has knee action: first foal:
dam ran twice at 2 yrs: quite modest maiden: best effort when caught post at
Goodwood: not discredited at Folkestone later in October: bred to stay 1¼m. *R. J.
Holder.*

NELLIE DEAN 2 ch.f. (Apr 1) Song 132 – Pubby 73 (Doctor Wall 107) [1991 5m2 **59**
5s4 5m3] close-coupled, sparely-made filly: first foal: dam middle-distance performer, is out of half-sister to 1000 Guineas and Oaks second Spree and top-class
broodmare Set Free: quite modest form in maidens and a minor event in the spring:
ridden by 7-lb claimer on debut.*J. A. R. Toller.*

NELSON'S LASS (IRE) 3 b. or br.f. Carwhite 127 – Praise The Lord (Lord **—**
Gayle (USA) 124) [1990 5f 5m5 6f4 7f 6m5 6g 1991 8d 7m 8f5 9f 8m6 12f5 10f 11m]
small, good-topped filly: has a round action: poor performer at best: should stay
beyond 6f. *Mrs S. M. Austin.*

NELTEGRITY 2 b.c. (Mar 29) Neltino 97 – Integrity 108 (Reform 132) [1991 6f **?**
7m 8.1g 10.5d5 7.6d2 7m 7d] 6,600F, 6,000Y: close-coupled, quite good-topped colt:
moderate walker and mover: half-brother to several winners, notably 3-y-o Radwell
(by Dunbeath), very useful at up to 1m: dam, ideally suited by 6f, is daughter of Cry
of Truth: poor maiden on most form: almost certainly flattered when 2½ lengths
second of 7 to Rully in slowly-run maiden at Chester, beaten inside final 1f: probably
stays 10.5f: best efforts with some give in the ground. *T. H. Caldwell.*

NEO-CLASSICAL 2 b.f. (Mar 21) Primo Dominie 121 – Musical Sally (USA) **72**
(The Minstrel (CAN) 135) [1991 6d3 6g2 6m2 7g*] 17,000Y: rangy, unfurnished filly:
has scope: powerful mover: fifth foal: half-sister to 2 winners in USA by Summing:
dam never ran: easily made all in 5-runner maiden at Yarmouth in June: better form
at 7f than 6f. *B. W. Hills.*

NEPTUNE'S PET 3 b.c. Tina's Pet 121 – Abalone (Abwah 118) [1990 5m3 6g6 5f **76**
5f5 6m 1991 8g 7m 7.1g4 8m3 9.7m* 9m4 10g3 9g] tall, workmanlike colt: has a long
stride: modest performer: won maiden at Folkestone in August: ran creditably in
frame in handicaps, making most penultimate start: stays 1¼m: acts on good to firm
ground. *W. Carter.*

NEROLI 3 b.f. Nishapour (FR) 125 – Norska 67 (Northfields (USA)) [1990 6d 7m* **78 §**
7m 6f 1991 9g 8f 7.1s3 7f3 7.1m6 10f 7.6g5 10f 6g5] lengthy, angular filly: modest
performer on her day: stays 7.6f: acts on any going: carries head high: joined A. P.
Jones: not one to trust. *A. P. Jones.*

NESSFIELD 5 b.m. Tumble Wind (USA) – Ceiling (Thatch (USA) 136) [1990 NR **—**
1991 11.8g] useful-looking mare: second in 1¼m claimer at Nottingham as 3-y-o,
only worthwhile form on flat: tailed off in handicap in October: fair winning hurdler.
K. A. Morgan.

NEST 2 ch.f. (Apr 21) Sharpo 132 – Sanctuary (Welsh Pageant 132) [1991 6f **59 p**
5m6] leggy filly: fifth living foal: half-sister to Sheikh Albadou (by Green Desert)
and 1987 Irish 2-y-o 5f winner Sawlah and 5f to 7f winner Assignment (both by
Known Fact): dam unraced half-sister to Little Wolf and Smuggler: better effort in

maidens when around 5 lengths sixth of 11 to Hazm at Sandown in September, slowly into stride, green, finished well: will improve again, particularly back at 6f. *Lord Huntingdon.*

NETTINA (IRE) 3 b.f. Runnett 125 – Inner Pearl (Gulf Pearl 117) [1990 6m⁶ 6g² 6m 6f 5m⁴ 8.2g 1991 8m] good-bodied filly: plating-class maiden: no promise in handicap in June: doesn't stay 1m: blinkered penultimate outing at 2 yrs: active sort. *P. Calver.* —

NEVADA MIX 7 gr.h. Alias Smith (USA) – Northern Empress 80 (Northfields (USA)) [1990 6f 6f 7f² 1991 6g 6m a7g 7m 6.1d 6g 6f* 6f 6m² 8d 6g] strong, stocky horse: poor mover: inconsistent and plating-class handicapper nowadays: won at Hamilton in August: effective over stiff 6f and stays 7f: acts on any going: below form in blinkers: trained first 6 starts by N. Gaselee. *Miss L. A. Perratt.* **55**

NEVER A CARE (USA) 2 b.f. (May 18) Roberto (USA) 131 – Imperturbable Lady (CAN) (Northern Dancer) [1991 7.1d*] workmanlike filly: half-sister to several winners, including useful 3-y-o 1¼m winner Adversary (by Alleged) and Grade 2 Canadian winner Cool Northerner (by Dom Alaric): dam won 2 races in Canada at 8.5f: 33/1 and better for race, won 18-runner maiden at Chepstow in October in good style by 6 lengths from Sharriba, but slowly away and held up, improving smoothly from halfway and leading inside final 1f: sure to improve fair bit and looks useful middle-distance filly in the making. *B. W. Hills.* **88** p

NEVER CRY WOLF 3 b.c. Little Wolf 127 – Ma Belle Amie (Never Say Die 137) [1990 NR 1991 12.2d⁶ 14.8f⁶ 12.5m 12m 16.9g 8m a14g] leggy, rather close-coupled colt: moderate mover: half-brother to modest 7f and 1m winner Lavender Gray (by Bay Express): dam well beaten in 5 starts: tailed off in maidens and handicaps: blinkered penultimate start. *L. J. Codd.* —

NEVER DOUBT 2 ch.f. (Apr 27) Believe It (USA) – Ruler's Dancer (USA) (Irish Ruler (USA)) [1991 6s 5g] 7,400 2-y-o: smallish, quite good-bodied filly: half-sister to a winner in North America by Caro: dam won 8 races and placed in Grade 3 6f event, is half-sister to Breeders' Cup Sprint winner Eillo: bit backward, poor form in maidens at Kempton (on toes) and Folkestone in autumn. *R. Hannon.* **43**

NEVER GIVE UP 4 b.g. Law Society (USA) 130 – Hardiemma 81 (Hardicanute 130) [1990 11.5g 1991 11m 14.1f⁵ 16m] lengthy gelding: poor mover: lightly raced and no sign of ability. *Mrs Barbara Waring.* —

NEVER IN 5 b.g. Aragon 118 – Recent Events (Stanford 121§) [1990 6m 7m⁶ 8f⁶ 8d 1991 a8g⁵ a7g⁶] big, angular gelding: poor performer: stays 1m: acts on firm going: keen sort: usually blinkered or visored nowadays: sold 875 gns Ascot April Sales. *K. R. Burke.* —

NEVER IN THE RED 3 b.g. Wattlefield 117 – Swing Gently 78 (Swing Easy (USA) 126) [1990 5f² 5s⁵ 5m* 5f* 5f* 5m³ 5g² 5m⁵ 1991 5s³ 5m³ 5m 5m² 5g³ 5m³] leggy, lengthy gelding: fairly useful handicapper: ran well at Newcastle, Goodwood and the Curragh (favourite, headed close home in 19-runner £9,700 event) last 3 starts: very speedy: acts on any going: blinkered or visored last 3 outings. *J. Berry.* **98**

NEVER LATE 2 b.f. (Mar 20) Never So Bold 135 – New Edition 72 (Great Nephew 126) [1991 5d⁴ 5m⁶ 5m³ 5g² 5.1g³ 6m 5f² 5m³] 9,500Y: rather leggy, quite attractive filly: good walker: second foal: half-sister to 3-y-o 7.5f winner Arabian King (by Sayf El Arab): dam, 5f winner at 2 yrs, appeared to stay 7f: plating-class maiden: ran creditably in blinkers final 2 outings: better form at 5f than 6f: fairly consistent: not seen out after August. *M. H. Easterby.* **57**

NEVER SO HIGH 4 b.g. Never So Bold 135 – High Gait 90 (High Top 131) [1990 7g a8g² 8d⁶ a10g² 1991 12s] leggy, quite attractive gelding: fair handicapper at best at 3 yrs: well beaten only run in 1991 (April): well worth another try over 1½m: possibly unsuited by soft ground. *R. W. Armstrong.* —

NEVER SO SURE 3 br.g. Never So Bold 135 – Amerella (Welsh Pageant 132) [1990 5g⁵ 6g² 6s* 7g 8d 1991 6g* 6g² 6m² 6g⁶ 6d] workmanlike gelding: moderate mover: won claimer at Haydock in July: progressed into fair handicapper, though well beaten final start: stays 6f: acts on good to firm ground and soft: found less than seemed likely third start: sold 10,500 gns Newmarket Autumn Sales. *Mrs J. R. Ramsden.* **83**

NEVER TOUCHED ME 4 b. or br.f. Belfort (FR) 89 – Realm Gift 75 (Realm 129) [1990 NR 1991 6d] angular filly: sixth foal: sister to a winner in Denmark and half-sister to a winner in Belgium by Hill's Forecast: dam, placed at 5f at 2 yrs, is —

half-sister to dam of Roland Gardens: bandaged, tailed off in Ripon maiden in June, only run. *J. L. Spearing.*

NEWARK ANTIQUEFAIR   3 b.c. Rolfe (USA) 77 – Sea Dart 55 (Air Trooper   **41** 115) [1990 8d 10.2s 1991 12g 13.8m³ 11.8m⁶ 15.1s] small, angular colt: poor performer: easily best effort at 13.8f: acts on good to firm ground. *B. C. Morgan.*

NEW ARRANGEMENT   5 b.g. Trojan Fen 118 – Cariole 84 (Pardao 120)   — [1990 12f 14.8m⁵ 16g 1991 a12g⁵] workmanlike gelding: fair performer at 3 yrs: way below form since: stays 1½m: acts on good to firm ground: winning hurdler. *J. R. Jenkins.*

NEW BEGINNING   8 b. or br.h. Persian Bold 123 – Bumble-Bee (High Line   **49** 125) [1990 NR 1991 12.1d 5g 6f 6m 6f 8.3f⁵ 8m 12.1s 8.1s] leggy, lengthy ex-Irish horse: poor handicapper at best nowadays: stays 1m: acts on firm going: wears bandages. *J. S. Haldane.*

NEW IDENTITY (USA)   3 gr.c. Runaway Groom (CAN) – Foreign Store (USA)   **75** + (Distant Land (USA)) [1990 NR 1991 9m⁵] leggy, good-topped colt: second reported living foal: half-brother to a winner in North America: dam lightly-raced half-sister to good U.S. colt Double Discount: sire champion colt in Canada: bit backward, never-nearer fifth of 19, going on really well under hands and heels, in maiden at Kempton in May: looked sure to improve. *J. H. M. Gosden.*

NEWMARKETING   3 b.f. Balliol 125 – Glebe 83 (Tacitus 124) [1990 NR 1991   — 10d] 6,400Y: lengthy filly: half-sister to several winners, including 7f winner Cannon Hall (by Singing Bede): dam, 2m winner, is half-sister to good staying filly Bringley: blinkered, moved poorly down and well beaten in April seller. *G. A. Pritchard-Gordon.*

NEWRY   2 br.f. (Mar 29) Rousillon (USA) 133 – Newquay 79 (Great Nephew 126)   **54** p [1991 5.7f⁵] rather leggy, quite attractive filly: second foal: dam 1½m winner out of Park Hill winner Quay Line: 9/1 from 5/1, soon pushed along in maiden at Bath in September: will improve, particularly over further, and is bred to stay 1¼m: sold 5,200 gns Newmarket Autumn Sales. *R. Charlton.*

NEWTON POINT   2 b.g. (Feb 26) Blakeney 126 – Assertive (USA) (Assert 134)   **51** [1991 a7g⁵ 7m⁶ 8.2f] 6,800F: workmanlike, good-bodied gelding: second foal: dam unraced: plating-class maiden: gives impression will stay well. *G. A. Pritchard-Gordon.*

NIANI (IRE)   3 ch.f. Niniski (USA) 125 – Royal Nugget (USA) 104 (Mr Pros-   **92** pector (USA)) [1990 NR 1991 10g⁴ 12m* 10m²] lengthy filly: first foal: dam placed from 6f to 1m and very disappointing at 3 yrs, is out of Regal Gal, smart at up to 1¼m: 2/1 on, won Thirsk maiden in May: good second of 4 in minor event at Nottingham 2 weeks later, making most: should prove as effective at 1½m as 1¼m. *J. L. Dunlop.*

NIBBS POINT (IRE)   3 ch.f. Sure Blade (USA) 130 – Fanny's Cove 89 (Mill   **107** Reef (USA) 141) [1990 NR 1991 10m² 10m* 11.9g* 14.6m² 12s² 12d⁶] smallish, lengthy, sparely-made filly: fifth foal: half-sister to 11f winner Dancing Cove (by Shareef Dancer), useful 1988 2-y-o 7f and 1m winner Prince Ibrahim (by Be My

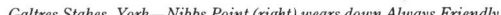

Galtres Stakes, York—Nibbs Point (right) wears down Always Friendly

Lady Halifax's "Nibbs Point"

Guest) and a winner in Italy: dam won over 1¼m on only start: won maiden at Newmarket (demoted for slight interference) in July then similar event (dead-heated) at Windsor and listed race at York in August: second to Patricia in A F Budge Park Hill Stakes at Doncaster and Tidemark in £70,900 Krug Trophy (Handicap) at Ascot: favourite, though sweating and light in condition, ran moderately in Princess Royal Stakes at Ascot: effective at 1½m and will probably stay 2m: acts on good to firm ground and soft: reportedly stays in training. *L. M. Cumani.*

NICE DICE 3 b.c. Double Schwartz 128 – Danaka (FR) (Val de Loir 133) [1990 7s 1991 8d 8.2d⁶ 10f⁵ 14f] close-coupled colt: well beaten in maidens and handicaps. *M. J. Camacho.*   —

NICELY THANKS (USA) 2 b.c. (Mar 17) Great Charmer (USA) – Laque de Chine (USA) (Lord Avie (USA)) [1991 5g² 6m 6m 8m 8m⁴ 8m* 8m²] $6,200F, 21,000Y: strong, good-quartered colt: first foal: dam unraced granddaughter of Lupe: sire (by The Minstrel) closely related to Lomond and half-brother to Seattle Slew: well-backed favourite, gamely won 15-runner nursery at Ayr in September: improved form when strong-finishing second of 19 to Elegant Touch in similar event at Pontefract following month: will be very well suited by 1¼m + , and is likely to make up into fair handicapper. *T. D. Barron.*   **73** p

NICE PICTURE (IRE) 3 b.c. Kings Lake (USA) 133 – Nana Mana Mou (Ela-Mana-Mou 132) [1990 7m 8g 7g 8d a8g 1991 a10g a10g 12m] sturdy, dipped-backed colt: poor mover: poor maiden. *R. Champion.*   —

NICHOLAS (USA) 5 b.h. Danzig (USA) – Lulu Mon Amour (USA) (Tom Rolfe) [1990 10.2m² 10m⁶ 7f² 7m⁶ 7g⁶ 7m³ 6m* 5d⁵ 6s² 1991 6m³ 7m* 7d³ 6g² 6m 6m 6d³ 7f² 7.3f 6g* 6v] big, good-topped, sprint type: usually impresses in appearance: ex-American horse: very useful performer, improved in 1991: won handicap at Newmarket (impressively under 10-0) in April and Group 2 event (by ½ length) at Baden-Baden in August: ran creditably, mostly in pattern company, when placed in   **111**

H. de Kwiatkowski's "Nicholas"

between: below form in Group 3 event at Rome final start, first for 2½ months: best at 6f or 7f: acted on firm and soft ground: below form when blinkered once: retired to Aston Park Stud, fee £2,500 (Oct 1). *Mrs L. Piggott.*

NICHOLESS   3 ch.f. Nicholas Bill 125 – Lunar Queen 96 (Queen's Hussar 124)   —
[1990 a7g 1991 a8g³ 8m⁶] smallish, sturdy filly: sixth of 15 in maiden at Warwick in April, taking keen hold, running on not knocked about: stays 1m: blinkered on reappearance. *H. Candy.*

NICKEL SILVER (FR)   7 ch.g. Son of Silver 123 – Dana's Return (USA) 87   —
(Turn-to) [1990 12d 12s 1991 12.1m] strong gelding: winner in France early as 3-y-o: no form in handicaps last 3 starts: stays 10.7f. *G. Richards.*

NICQUITA   4 ch.f. Nicholas Bill 125 – Jacquinta 95 (Habitat 134) [1990 7m 6m 7m   **46**
6f⁶ 6f³ 7m⁵ 7m* 7f 7g² 7g 8g 7m² a7g a10g 1991 7g 7m 9m 10g 6.9m³ 6.9f³ 7.1g 9m⁶
7m³ 8g⁴] leggy, quite good-topped filly: has round action: poor handicapper now-adays: stays 1m: acts on any going: sometimes visored. *C. C. Elsey.*

NIDOMI   4 ch.c. Dominion 123 – Nicholas Grey 100 (Track Spare 125) [1990 7f 7f⁵   —
7g⁴ 7.5g 9g 7m 1991 12f] leggy, good-topped colt: moderate mover: plating-class maiden at 3 yrs: tailed off only run in 1991: should stay middle distances: acts on firm ground. *G. P. Enright.*

NIFTY FIFTY (IRE)   2 b.f. (Mar 30) Runnett 125 – Swift Verdict 89 (My   **97**
Swallow 134) [1991 5g² 5g* 5s⁵ 5m* 5f* 5g⁴ 6m² 6f⁵] IR 3,200Y: leggy, quite good-topped filly: ninth foal: half-sister to a minor winner in Europe by Red Sunset: dam Irish 1¼m winner: successful in maiden auction at Edinburgh in spring and

585

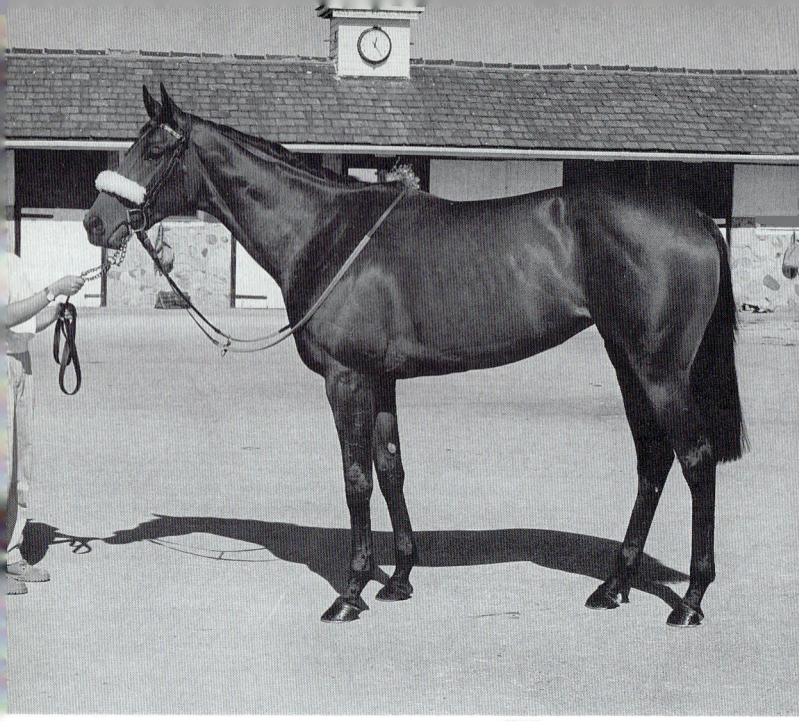

Mrs Norma Peebles' "Nifty Fifty"

minor events there and at Thirsk (most impressive in very fast time) in mid-summer: good ¾-length second of 22 to Affair of State in Tattersalls Breeders Stakes at the Curragh in August: stays 6f: easily best form on firm ground, unsuited by soft: has run well when sweating: often on toes: makes running. *J. Berry*.

NIGALS FRIEND 2 ch.g. (May 28) Sharpo 132 – No Cards 109 (No Mercy 126) **72**
[1991 6.1g⁵ 5.7m² 6m³ 6g 5d⁶ 5.7g⁶] 3,800Y, 5,300 2-y-o: tall gelding: moderate mover: half-brother to several winners, including 8.9f and 10.1f winner Tell No Lies (by High Line) and fairly useful 7f and 1m winner Daboub (by Habat): dam won at up to 1m: modest maiden: below form in nurseries last 2 starts: will probably be suited by 7f. *D. Haydn Jones*.

NIGEL LANE 4 b.g. Class Distinction – Autumn Harvest (Martinmas 128) [1990 **—**
NR 1991 8g a8g⁶] strong gelding: fourth reported foal: half-brother to Just Moving (by Swing Easy) and Jackie Blair (by Rupert Bear), modest 2-y-o 6f and 5f winners respectively: dam of no account: twice raced and never dangerous in Brighton seller and Lingfield claimer in June. *J. J. Bridger*.

NIGEL'S LUCKY GIRL 3 gr.f. Belfort (FR) 89 – Haiti Mill 68 (Free State 125) **66**
[1990 7f⁵ 6f² 6g* 6m² 6m⁶ 7d 1991 5m⁵ 6m 8g 7m a6g⁴ a7g] leggy, quite good-topped filly: has fluent action: quite modest handicapper: easily best effort in 1991 when staying-on fourth at Lingfield in November: should prove suited by further than 6f: possibly needs a sound surface on turf. *R. Guest*.

NIGHT ASSET 2 b.g. (Feb 14) Night Shift (USA) – Fine Asset (Hot Spark 126) **63**
[1991 5g⁵ 5g⁴ 6g 5g⁶ 5m 5.7g⁵ 6g*] 22,000Y: strong, sprint type: carries condition: moderate mover: fourth living foal: half-brother to 3-y-o Gilded Omen (by Faustus)

and 6f winner Faultless Speech (by Good Times): dam poor half-sister to smart 7f performer Tudor Mill: showed much improved form to win 18-runner nursery at Newmarket in November by ½ length from Mentalasanythin: better suited by 6f than 5f, and may stay 7f: possibly suited by some give in the ground: blinkered last 2 starts: appeared not to handle track at Goodwood third outing. *G. Lewis.*

NIGHT CLUB (GER) 7 ch.g. Esclavo (FR) – Nightlife (GER) (Priamos (GER) 123) [1990 a11g⁶ a11g a8g a8g a7g³ a8g⁵ a7g² a7g a8g 8f⁵ 1991 a7g 7.5f⁴] tall, lengthy, sparely-made gelding: poor performer: stays 7f: acts on firm ground: ran respectably when blinkered. *J. P. Smith.* —

NIGHT DUTY (IRE) 2 b.c. (Apr 24) Night Shift (USA) – Sarah Siddons (Reform 132) [1991 6m² 5g* 5m⁶ 5m* 5.5g⁴ 5m 6g² 5d] 14,500Y: useful-looking colt: has a fluent action: brother to 3-y-o 5.7f to 7f winner Maggie Siddons, closely related to 1986 2-y-o 6f seller winner Sands of Time (by Dance In Time) and half-brother to 2 winners: dam French 8.5f winner: fairly useful performer: successful in maiden at Leicester and 3-runner Fairview New Homes Chesterfield Stakes at Newmarket in mid-summer: ran creditably in Prix Robert Papin at Maisons-Laffitte won by Arazi and listed races at Doncaster (slowly away, behind Notley) and the Curragh (second to Safety Tactic): below best in Cornwallis Stakes at Ascot final start: stays 6f: possibly unsuited by dead ground: wore a tongue strap first 3 outings: sold to South Africa. *P. W. Chapple-Hyam.* 94

NIGHT FANCY 3 ch.g. Night Shift (USA) – Smooth Siren (USA) (Sea Bird II 145) [1990 NR 1991 10d 10.2m 12f² 16.1m³ 12.3f³ 10.9m] 12,000Y: strong, good-bodied gelding: half-brother to several winners here and abroad, including fairly useful 1985 2-y-o Thalassino Asteri (by Formidable) and very useful 1¼m winner Serenivo (by Sir Ivor): dam 6f winner in USA: modest maiden: placed at Beverley, Newcastle and (wandering under pressure) Ripon: stays 2m: ran badly in visor final start: sold to join Mrs A. Woodrow 2,700 gns Ascot November Sales. *M. H. Easterby.* 71

NIGHT JAR 4 b.f. Night Shift (USA) – Fodens Eve 80 (Dike (USA)) [1990 6f⁵ 5g* 6g² 7m³ 6m 1991 6g⁴ 6.1m⁴ 7.1g* 7g 7d*] lengthy filly: useful handicapper: 33/1, rallied gamely when winning 29-runner £80,000 Tap And Spile (Handicap) at Ascot in September by 2 lengths from Sky Cloud: earlier successful at Chepstow: suited by 7f: best efforts with some give in the ground (yet to race on very soft). *Lord Huntingdon.* 98

NIGHT MANOEUVRES 2 b.c. (Mar 13) Night Shift (USA) – Rattle Along 80 (Tap On Wood 130) [1991 6d² 6g*] 41,000Y: sturdy, round-barrelled colt: first foal: dam 9f and 1¼m winner, is out of half-sister to very useful animals Honorius and Suni: 9/4 and carrying condition, confirmed promise of debut when winning 13-runner maiden at Newbury in July by neck from Sunday's Hill, travelling well, leading inside final 1f and running on well: will stay 1m: seemed likely to improve again. *H. Candy.* 75 +

NIGHTSLIP 2 b.f. (May 16) Night Shift (USA) – Elevena (AUS) (Just Great 127) [1991 6m⁵ 7g⁵ 6g 6d⁶ 7f 7g⁴] compact filly: half-sister to Australian middle-distance stayer Chiamare (by Claude): dam, winner 4 times in Australia, is sister to leading 1972/3 Australian 2-y-o filly Just Topic: little worthwhile form, including in seller: should stay middle distances: sold 2,300 gns Newmarket Autumn Sales. *R. V. Smyth.* 33

Tap And Spile Handicap, Ascot—Night Jar picks up over £80,000;
Go Executive (rails) finished third and Maggie Siddons (left) fourth,
with runner-up Sky Cloud off picture

Bovis Autumn Stakes, Ascot—Ninja Dancer (right) holds King's Loch up the straight

NIGHT TRADER (USA)   5 br.m. Melyno 130 – Disco Girl (FR) (Green Dancer   —
(USA) 132) [1990 a8g a12g 1991 16.2g] big, workmanlike mare: no form, including in
handicap. *H. A. T. Whiting.*

NIGHT TRANSACTION   4 ch.f. Tina's Pet 121 – Beech Tree 67 (Fighting Ship   **52**
121) [1990 8m 10m 8g 10g 8m⁵ 9f² 9m² 9m 8d 1991 7.6g 9g⁶ 8m* 8.1g 10g⁴ 7m 9s
8.2m² 8d⁵ a8g³ a7g⁵] stocky filly: plating-class handicapper: won ladies event at
Redcar (by 8 lengths) in June: stays 9f: acts on firm and dead ground, and on
fibresand: usually blinkered, not last 4 starts. *A. Hide.*

NIKITAS   6 b.g. Touching Wood (USA) 127 – Hi There 89 (High Top 131) [1990   **64**
14f² 14m⁴ 14s² 14m⁴ 12m 14f³ 14f* 16g² 14g⁴ 16f⁶ 14d 1991 16g 14.8m⁴ 14g 14m⁵
14g* 13.4d⁵ 14m³ 14.6m] good-topped gelding: quite modest handicapper: made all
at Haydock in June: stays 2m: acts on any going: best when allowed to dominate:
bandaged near-fore nowadays: winning hurdler. *Miss A. J. Whitfield.*

NIKKI DOW   5 b.g. Tanfirion 110 – Amboselli 73 (Raga Navarro (ITY) 119) [1990   —
5f 6f 5m⁶ 5m a6g 6g 5g⁶ a6g 1991 6v 6g 5m⁶ 7.1g 6g 5.1g] small, angular gelding: poor
walker and mover: very little form since: suited by 6f or stiff
5f: acts on hard and dead going. *P. Howling.*

NIKLAS ANGEL   5 b.g. Petorius 117 – The Woodbird (Tudor Melody 129) [1990   **60**
8m 9g 6d 7f 8f 10.2m 8m* 8g⁶ a8g⁴ 8d a7g 1991 8g* 8f³ a7g⁶ 8h* 7.6d⁶ 8s² 7g³ 8m*
8m³ 8f] leggy, lightly-made gelding: poor mover: quite modest handicapper: won
at Edinburgh and Carlisle in spring and Brighton (claimer) in August: effective at 7f
to 1m: acts on any going: best blinkered or visored: has run well for apprentice:
genuine. *M. H. Tompkins.*

NIKOZETTE (IRE)   3 b.f. Auction Ring (USA) 123 – Tondbad (Furry Glen 121)   **47** §
[1990 5m⁶ 7g 1991 a10g a10g⁴ 12.3s] big, good-topped filly: poor form at best: stays
1¼m: bandaged final outing: unseated rider soon after start second outing at 2 yrs,
and has shown other signs of unsatisfactory temperament: sold 2,800 gns Ascot
May Sales. *R. W. Armstrong.*

NIL NISI NIXU (USA)   2 b.c. (May 18) Cutlass (USA) – Free Saint (USA)   **65**
(Freepet (USA)) [1991 5d 5d* 7g⁵ 7m 6m³ 6m 8.3s] $77,000 2-y-o: sturdy, quite
good-topped colt: carries condition: third foal: dam won 14 races, at up to 1¼m, from

102 starts: sire won from 6f to 8.5f: quite modest performer: visored, won 3-runner minor event at Hamilton in July: below form after good running-on third in nursery at Ayr: bred to stay beyond 6f: acts on good to firm and dead ground: blinkered fourth to sixth starts, running much too freely first occasion: sold 2,800 gns Doncaster November Sales. *J. Berry.*

NIMBLE DEER 2 ch.f. (Mar 16) Hadeer 118 – Nibelunga (Miami Springs 121) **85** [1991 7m² 6.1m 6m⁶] 2,500Y: big, lengthy filly: has scope: half-sister to 6f winner African Dash (by African Sky): dam, winner at around 1m, is half-sister to smart French 6f to 8.5f winner African Joy, and Kilijaro: 100/1, over 8 lengths sixth of 9 to Marling in Tattersalls Cheveley Park Stakes at Newmarket in October, outpaced, stumbling 2f out, then running on: no comparable form in maiden auction events: likely to win a modest race at up to 1m. *B. W. Hills.*

NIMIEZA (USA) 3 b.f. Nijinsky (CAN) 138 – Classy Cathy (USA) (Private **70** Account (USA)) [1990 NR 1991 10g⁵ 11.5f⁶ 12.4m² 14m² 14g] leggy filly: first reported foal: dam successful in 3 Grade 1 races (at 8.5f to 1¼m) at 3 yrs: modest maiden: second at Newcastle and Haydock: ran as if something amiss in handicap final start: probably stays 1¾m: visits Anshan. *M. R. Stoute.*

NINE CARAT (USA) 3 b.c. Slew O'Gold (USA) – Fortune's Folly (USA) **112** (Graustark (USA)) [1990 NR 1991 8v* 8s* 10.5d⁴ 9.2m³] $80,000Y, $120,000Y: second foal: dam unraced half-sister to dam of Suave Dancer: won newcomers race at Saint-Cloud in March and listed race at Maisons-Laffitte in April: in frame in Prix Lupin and Prix Jean Prat (3½ lengths behind Sillery) at Longchamp in May: stays 9f. *A. Fabre, France.*

NINETY-NINE (IRE) 3 b.c. Pitskelly 122 – Nighty Night (Sassafras (FR) 135) **49** [1990 7m 8g a7g⁵ 1991 10g⁵ 10d⁶] sturdy colt: has a round action: poor form: favourite, failed to confirm promise of reappearance in handicap at Ripon in June: stays 1¼m: possibly needs a sound surface: sold 650 gns Doncaster October Sales. *R. W. Armstrong.*

NINJA DANCER (USA) 2 b.c. (May 23) Miswaki (USA) 124 – Professional **110** Dance (USA) (Nijinsky (CAN) 138) [1991 6g⁴ 7.1s* 7m 8d* 8g⁵] 85,000Y: rangy, angular colt: has some scope: sixth foal: half-brother to several winners, including fair stayer Tartique Twist (by Arctic Tern): dam unraced half-sister to dam of good French performers L'Emigrant and Salpinx: very useful performer: successful in maiden at Sandown in July and 6-runner Bovis Autumn Stakes at Ascot (best effort) in October when soon prominent, leading 2f out and running on strongly to beat King's Loch by 3 lengths: fair fifth of 8 to Seattle Rhyme in Racing Post Trophy at Doncaster: will stay 1¼m: acts very well on a soft surface, ran poorly on good to firm: looked extremely well last 2 starts. *Mrs J. Cecil.*

NIODINI (USA) 2 b.f. (Apr 16) Nijinsky (CAN) 138 – Home Thoughts (USA) **95** (Tom Rolfe) [1991 6g³ 7g² 7f* 8v⁵] well-made, attractive filly: good mover: half-sister to several winners, including Super Cook (by Best Turn), graded-stakes winner at up to 9f in USA: dam unraced: fairly useful form when neck second of 5 to Torrey Canyon in Deploy Acomb Stakes at York in August and over length fifth of 13 to Lasting Lass in Group 3 event at Milan (best effort) in October: 9/4 on, didn't have to be near best to win maiden at Salisbury in between: should stay 1¼m: acts on heavy ground, and has won on firm. *M. R. Stoute.*

NIP 3 br.f. Bay Express 132 – Broken Accent (Busted 134) [1990 NR 1991 11g⁶ — 10.1s] 5,800Y: third foal: half-sister to quite modest maiden Taskforce Fixed It (by Aragon): dam ran twice: behind in maiden auction race (badly hampered when headed 3f out, trained by Dr J. Scargill) and claimer 4 months later. *A. S. Reid.*

NIPOTINA 5 b.m. Simply Great (FR) 122 – Mothers Girl (Huntercombe 133) **42** [1990 a11g² a11g⁴ a14g⁴ a11g⁴ a8g⁶ 12.5f² 12.5g³ 12m⁶ a12g⁵ 10.2f⁴ 12.2m³ 13.1h² 12f4 13.1h³ 11m* a12g⁶ 12.2m⁶ 1991 a12g³ a12g³ 12d³ 12f 12f 12f⁵ 12g 16.2g⁶ 12m⁵ 10.1d⁴ 15.8g² 17.2f⁴ 16m² a12g⁵ 16m³ 11m³ 16.9m²] small mare: moderate mover: poor handicapper nowadays: stays 17.2f: acts on hard and dead going: has run well when sweating: often claimer ridden: consistent. *R. Hollinshead.*

NISHA 3 gr.f. Nishapour (FR) 125 – Eary Glas (Reform 132) [1990 7g 7g 1991 — 10.5g] leggy, workmanlike filly: quite modest form in autumn at 2 yrs: led over 6f when tailed-off last of 7 in £7,400 contest at York in May, 1991: has twice given trouble at stalls. *W. J. Haggas.*

NISHCOR 3 gr.c. Nishapour (FR) 125 – Corsage (FR) (Nureyev (USA) 131) [1990 **49** 6g⁴ 7m 6f⁴ 6v⁴ 7d⁶ 8.2s⁶ 1991 8s 7m³ a7g* a8g⁶ 9g⁶ 8f 6f² 6f 6f] rather sparely-made colt: fair plater on his day: won at Southwell (bought in 4,000 gns) in

May: stays 1m: acts on any going: sweating (ran well in ladies event) seventh start: visored/blinkered last 4 starts: has carried head high. *Miss S. E. Hall.*

NISHKINA   3 b.g. Nishapour (FR) 125 – Varishkina 103 (Derring-Do 131) [1990   **45**
6f³ 6f² 7g 7f 1991 10f⁵ 11m 11g³ 8.3d⁵] leggy, lengthy gelding: plater: stays 11f: acts on firm going: blinkered once at 2 yrs: carried head high and found little final start at 3 yrs: winning hurdler. *M. H. Easterby.*

NOBBY   5 b.g. Dalsaan 125 – Parkeen Princess (He Loves Me 120) [1990 NR 1991   —
8.2m] workmanlike gelding: has a round action: modest handicapper as 3-y-o: first run on flat since, behind in October: likely to prove suited by return to 1¼m: acts on any going. *M. H. Tompkins.*

NOBBY BARNES   2 b.c. (May 24) Nordance (USA) – Loving Doll 72 (Godswalk   **62**
(USA) 130) [1991 6f 5g⁶ 7m⁴ 6.1m] 4,600Y: neat colt: half-brother to poor 1¼m winner Ash Amour (by Hotfoot): dam stayed 7f and would have been suited by further: quite modest maiden: ran poorly final start: will stay 1m: acts on good to firm ground. *R. W. Armstrong.*

NOBBY CLARK   5 b.g. Posse (USA) 130 – Jennyjo 64 (Martinmas 128) [1990 NR   —
1991 a14g 8.5f⁶ 9g 7g⁶ 7g] workmanlike, plain gelding: no worthwhile form: tried visored once. *G. R. Oldroyd.*

NO BIG DEAL   3 b.c. Kris 135 – Sophisticated Lady (FR) (Habitat 134) [1990 NR   —
1991 8s 8m⁶ 5m⁵ 5g 5d a5g a6g] close-coupled colt: poor mover: second foal: dam sister to Sigy and Sonoma: plating-class form, best effort third start. *M. D. I. Usher.*

NOBLE BID   7 b.h. Kings Lake (USA) 133 – First Round 97 (Primera 131) [1990   —
NR 1991 14.1f] lengthy horse: poor mover: fairly useful handicapper at 4 yrs: twice raced on flat since and well beaten: suited by 1¼m: acts on any going: winning hurdler in September. *Miss S. J. Wilton.*

NOBLE CAUSE (IRE)   2 b.c. (Apr 24) Reasonable (FR) 119 – Luan Causca 70   **62**
(Pampapaul 121) [1991 5g 5m³ 6g⁶ a6g³ a7g³ 7g⁵ 6g 6g⁵ 8m⁵] IR 5,800F, 5,000Y: leggy, sparely-made colt: fifth reported foal: half-brother to plating-class 6f and 7f winner Tite Spot (by Muscatite) and a winner in Norway: dam 2-y-o 5f winner: quite modest maiden: stays 1m: acts on good to firm ground and fibresand: very free to post and in race (below best) sixth outing: usually on toes. *R. Earnshaw.*

NOBLE DESTINY   3 b.f. Dancing Brave (USA) 140 – Tender Loving Care 105   —
(Final Straw 127) [1990 7m* 1991 10g 10m] lengthy, angular filly: has a long stride: won maiden at Leicester in October at 2 yrs: disappointed in 1991, 9 lengths eighth of 9 to Fragrant Hill in listed race at Goodwood in May, chasing leader 1m and eased: ran moderately in minor event 5 months later: should stay at least 1m. *M. R. Stoute.*

NOBLE FLUTTER (IRE)   3 ch.f. The Noble Player (USA) 126 – Night of Wind   **84**
101 (Tumble Wind (USA)) [1990 5m² 6m² 6m³ 6m⁴ 6g² 5d² 1991 6g* 6m 6g* 5.8d³ 6g 6f] rather leggy, unfurnished filly: has a quick action: fair performer: successful in minor event at Warwick and median auction contest at Thirsk in the spring: below form in Stewards' Cup at Goodwood and handicap at Ripon last 2 starts: suited by further: acts on good to firm and dead ground: carried head awkwardly early on second start. *P. W. Chapple-Hyam.*

NOBLE KARA (FR)   4 b.f. Noblequest (FR) 124 – Karabice (Karabas 132) [1990   **101**
8f 8s 7g² 7g³ 8g* 7m⁵ 8g 6d² 5v⁶ 1991 6d⁵ 7d⁶ 5m³ 6g⁴ 5g⁶ 5m³ 5d] good-topped, quite attractive filly: sixth foal: half-sister to several winners, including useful hurdler Maelkar (by Maelstrom Lake): dam 1½m winner: useful French filly: ran well when third to Divine Danse in Group 2 Prix du Gros Chene at Chantilly in May and staying-on sixth to Title Roll in King George Stakes at Goodwood in August: below best in listed race at Deauville and Ciga Prix de l'Abbaye de Longchamp final 2 starts: best at up to 1m: acts on good to firm and dead ground. *A. Spanu, France.*

NOBLE PARTNER   4 b.g. Blushing Scribe (USA) 107 – Super Fortune (USA)   —
(Super Concorde (USA) 128) [1990 a12g³ a12g 12m 1991 10g] angular gelding: third in Southwell maiden: tailed off, including in handicaps, after: probably stays 1½m: sold 900 gns Ascot July Sales. *D. J. G. Murray-Smith.*

NOBLE PATRIARCH   4 b.c. Alzao (USA) 117 – Pampala (Bold Lad (IRE) 133)   **115**
[1990 8g⁶ 8g⁴ 8m 8.5g 10m⁴ 10d* 9g 10s⁶ 1991 10s* 9m 10g* 10v³ 12g²] stocky, quite attractive colt: usually looks well: smart performer: held up when winning listed event at Kempton (by 5 lengths) and CCH Gordon Richards Stakes at Sandown (beat Stapleford Manor 3 lengths) in April: stays 1½m: easily best efforts with give in the ground: often bandaged near-fore: sent to Germany, placed in pattern events. *J. L. Dunlop.*

NOBLE PET   2 gr.c. (Mar 21) Petong 126 – Barbary Court (Grundy 137) [1991 5m   **69**
6g² 6f² 6g] sturdy, angular colt: first foal: dam poor maiden: quite modest maiden:
second at Lingfield and Folkestone in October: raced freely in blinkers in Newmarket nursery final start, running well below form: stays 6f. *P. J. Makin.*

NOBLE POWER (IRE)   2 ch.c. (Apr 20) The Noble Player (USA) 126 – Power   **72**
Girl 77 (Tyrant (USA)) [1991 5m² 5g* 5m³ 6d5] IR 9,500F: leggy, sparely-made
colt: half-brother to 1987 2-y-o 5f winner Powerful (by Tumble Wind) and winners in
Hong Kong and Canada: dam won over 5f and 6f: modest performer: won maiden at
Leicester in April: not raced after June: will stay 7f: acts on good to firm ground. *B.
Palling.*

NOBLE SINGER   2 ch.f. (Apr 17) Vaguely Noble 140 – Shark Song 103 (Song   **63**
132) [1991 7m² 8s6 a8g4 a8g² a8g2] fifth foal: half-sister to 4-y-o Hidden (by
Secreto), modest 14f winner, and 3 other winners here and abroad, including fair but
later disappointing 1½m winner Magsood (by Mill Reef) and 5f winner Bundukeya
(by Beldale Flutter): dam, winner from 5f to 9f including in USA, is sister to very
smart sprinter Prince Sabo: quite modest maiden: ran well on Lingfield equitrack
last 2 starts: will stay 1¼m. *H. Thomson Jones.*

NOBLE SOCIETY   3 b.g. Law Society (USA) 130 – Be Noble (Vaguely Noble   **62**
140) [1990 8g5 8d² 1991 10m6 12.5m 11m6 11g 11.1d3] angular gelding: poor walker
and mover: disappointing maiden: should stay 1½m: sold 680 gns Doncaster November Sales. *E. Weymes.*

NOBLE SON   5 b.g. Thatching 131 – Eden Quay (King's Bench 132) [1990 a11g   **—**
a7g4 a8g 7m 9s 12.5f4 12.5f 11m³ 15g4 15m4 12g 15m4 11m 11m* 12.2f5 11v5 a12g
a12g 1991 11.7g] workmanlike gelding: inconsistent plater: blinkered, tailed off only
run in 1991: stays 15f, at least in slowly-run race: acts on firm going: visored first 5
starts at 4 yrs. *Mrs N. S. Sharpe.*

NOBLE TENOR (IRE)   2 b.c. (Apr 21) The Noble Player (USA) 126 – Flower   **41**
Dell 72 (Wolver Hollow 126) [1991 5v4 5g 6g² 5d 6m 5m 5.3f6 5m 7g] IR 2,600Y:
small, leggy colt: ex-Irish: poor walker and mover: third reported foal: dam maiden
daughter of half-sister to Italian Oaks winner Claire Valentine: poor plater: may be
suited by easy surface: blinkered (well beaten) sixth outing: trained first 3 starts by
N. Chance: sold 650 gns Newmarket Autumn Sales. *R. W. Stubbs.*

NOBLE VIENNA (USA)   2 ch.c. (Mar 28) Vaguely Noble 140 – Native Lovin   **57**
(USA) (Exclusive Native (USA)) [1991 10m 8d a7g] $30,000Y: sturdy colt: half-
brother to 2 winners in USA, one in minor stakes company: dam won 6 races at up to
7f: ridden by 7-lb claimer, and still burly, around 11 lengths eleventh of 14 to Hill
Glitter in minor event at Newmarket, second and easily best effort. *R. Hollinshead.*

NO CANDLES TONIGHT   3 b.f. Star Appeal 133 – Kochia 54 (Firestreak 125)   **71**
[1990 8d3 1991 8m5 12h4 11.1d* 11.1d* 12.1m3 10g* 12.3f4 10.5d² 10.3d5 12.1s3]

CCH Gordon Richards EBF Stakes, Sandown—
Noble Patriarch wins running on from Stapleford Manor and Karinga Bay

close-coupled, sparely-made filly: fluent mover: modest handicapper: won at Hamilton (twice) then Nottingham in the summer: ran creditably final start: stays 1½m: seems suited by some give in the ground: pulled hard and wandered under pressure second start: usually makes the running. *M. Johnston.*

NOCATCHIM   2 b.c. (Mar 31) Shardari 134 – Solar 120 (Hotfoot 126) [1991 7m 6f]   **67** p
smallish, sturdy colt: half-brother to several winners, including useful sprinter Cutler's Corner (by Sharpen Up), stayer Solamente (by High Line) and very smart 3-y-o 1m winner Desert Sun (by Green Desert): dam third in 1975 Cheveley Park Stakes: better for race still, around 5 lengths twelfth of 22 to Binkhaldoun in maiden at Newbury in September, pushed along at halfway then keeping on despite impeded run: will improve again over 1m. *B. W. Hills.*

NO COMEBACKS   3 b.f. Last Tycoon 131 – Dead End (Bold Lad (IRE) 133)   **55**
[1990 6m2 1991 7g3 6f2 6m4 a8g6 7.1m 11m 9s 10.4m 8.2m* 6m2 8d] leggy filly: plating-class handicapper on her day: won apprentice selling event (no bid) at Nottingham in October: appears to stay 9f: has form on any going: blinkered third start: has carried head high and looked none too keen: sold 2,600 gns Doncaster November Sales. *R. J. R. Williams.*

NOCTURNAL REVERIE (USA)   4 b.f. Assert 134 – Grey Dream 101   **45**
(Auction Ring (USA) 123) [1990 12g 14m4 9m 12.5m4 12d a14g2 1991 a12g6 a14g a12g5 a12g* a13g6 a12g4 16.2g 12f 10.1d6 12g a16g] leggy filly: moderate mover: poor handicapper: won at Lingfield in March: soundly beaten last 2 starts (in summer): stays 1¾m: acts on good to firm and dead ground: effective blinkered or not: inconsistent. *T. J. Naughton.*

NODDLE (USA)   3 ch.c. Sagace (FR) 135 – Formartin (USA) (Forli (ARG)) [1990   **68**
NR 1991 11f* 13m4 12m6 11.1d* 10.9g6 12f5] $60,000Y: good-topped, rather angular colt: fourth foal: half-brother to 2 winners in USA: dam, unraced half-sister to a graded-stakes winner at up to 9f, is daughter of sister to Damascus: successful in maiden claimer (claimed out of W. Haggas' stable £16,860) in May and handicap in June: stays 13f: acts on firm and dead going. *L. Lungo.*

NODOLYA   4 b.f. Niniski (USA) 125 – Press Corps 93 (Realm 129) [1990 7g 6g a8g   **57**
10m3 10g* 10.5g2 10g 1991 a13g2 a12g a13g 12s 10m] leggy, lengthy filly: quite modest performer on her day: not seen out after running poorly at Brighton in May: stays 13f: acts on good to firm ground: has hung. *J. Ffitch-Heyes.*

NOEL (IRE)   2 b.g. (Feb 23) Fairy King (USA) – Glenardina (Furry Glen 121)   **77** p
[1991 7m 7.6d3] 12,500Y: unfurnished gelding: half-brother to two 2-y-o winners in Ireland: dam Irish 7f winner: 2 lengths third of 6 to Al Ramis at Chester in October (not clear run over 1f out), easily better effort in maidens: capable of better still and will stay 1m. *G. A. Pritchard-Gordon.*

NOELREAC JULIAN   3 b. or br.g. Caerleon (USA) 132 – Interviewme (USA)   **71**
(Olden Times) [1990 6g2 1991 a7g* 8g 10.4d 8m] strong, lengthy gelding: moderate walker: won maiden at Lingfield in January: out of depth in listed races in the spring: prominent 5f and well beaten in handicap final start, first for 5½ months: should be better at 1m than shorter: sold 4,500 gns Newmarket Autumn Sales. *C. E. Brittain.*

NOGGINGS (IRE)   2 b.c. (Feb 22) Cyrano de Bergerac 120 – Coshlea 63 (Red   **59**
Alert 127) [1991 5d 5g 5d3 6m 7f6 7m2 7f3 7.9g] 14,000Y: compact colt: fourth foal: half-brother to 3 winners, including 5f (at 2 yrs) to 13f winner Dale Park (by Kampala) and 3-y-o No Hard Feelings (by Alzao), successful from 5f (at 2 yrs) to 1½m: dam placed from 11f to 15f: quite modest maiden: finished strongly from rear when placed in nurseries at Ayr and Thirsk (set plenty to do): ran poorly final outing: should be suited by 1m: acts on firm ground: blinkered (best effort to that point) third start. *N. Tinkler.*

NO HARD FEELINGS (IRE)   3 b. or br.f. Alzao (USA) 117 – Coshlea 63 (Red   **61**
Alert 127) [1990 5m* 5m2 6m2 6m3 6g* 6m3 6d5 7f* 7g4 8v* 8d3 1991 7d6 8g5 12g 8.2g 8d 12.4m 10g2 11.1d4 10.1m3 12f* 12m* 11.1f* 11.8g 11.1g4] strong, sturdy filly: carries condition: bad mover: quite modest performer: favourite, won seller (no bid) at Thirsk, claimer at Pontefract and 3-runner seller (bought in 5,400 gns) at Hamilton in August: disappointing last 2 starts: will prove suited by 1½m +: acts on any going: sometimes visored, including for first two 3-y-o successes. *N. Tinkler.*

NOMADIC ROSE   2 b.f. (Feb 8) Nomination 125 – Tina Rosa (Bustino 136) [1991   **45** p
5.2g 6f5 7f] lengthy filly: second foal: dam poor half-sister to very smart 7f to 1½m winner Saros: poor form: below form final start: should be better suited by 7f than 6f: likely to do better in handicaps. *B. W. Hills.*

NOMADIC WAY (USA)   6 b.h. Assert 134 – Kittyhawk 113 (Bustino 136) [1990   **103**
NR 1991 16g4 18.4d2 22.2m2] small, lengthy horse: usually looks well: moderate

mover: useful performer: good second to Star Player in Ladbroke Chester Cup and Easy To Please in Queen Alexandra Stakes at Royal Ascot: stays extreme distances: acts on any going: lazy, and usually blinkered: suited by strong handling: tough and consistent: high-class hurdler. *B. W. Hills.*

NOMICA 3 b.f. Nomination 125 – Majica 73 (Morston (FR) 125) [1990 NR 1991 10g 8m 10m] 8,000Y: lengthy, sparely-made filly: second foal: dam minor winner at 11f in France as 4-y-o, is closely related to Princess Royal winner Believer: well beaten in maidens and median auction contest: bandaged behind second start. *W. R. Muir.* —

NOMINEE PRINCE 2 b.g. (May 10) Nomination 125 – Be Royal 97 (Royal Palm 131) [1991 6s 6s] sixth reported foal: brother to 3-y-o Regal Value and half-brother to useful 6f and 7f winner Native Oak (by Tower Walk): dam, 2-y-o 5f winner, is half-sister to dam of Pas de Seul: 50/1, never-dangerous tenth of 13 at Yarmouth on debut, better effort in late-season maidens. *R. Guest.* **43**

NO MORE THE FOOL 5 ch.g. Jester 119 – Prima Bella 76 (High Hat 131) [1990 12f⁶ 12.5m⁵ 10.4d⁶ a12g* a12g* 11m* a11g* a12g⁵ a14g 1991 a12g³ 11f² 12g 12m³ 11.4m 12g] tall, leggy, lengthy gelding: has a long stride: quite modest handicapper: stays 1½m: acts on firm going: usually blinkered or visored nowadays: good mount for claimer: inconsistent. *J. Berry.* **68**

NONANNO 2 b.g. (May 7) Noalto 120 – Fortune's Fancy (Workboy 123) [1991 6m⁶ 6g] big, plain gelding: fifth foal: half-brother to quite modest 6f winner Ballafort (by Ballacashtal): dam daughter of very smart sprinter Polly Peachum: better for race, soundly beaten in minor event at Leicester and maiden at Newbury (again slowly away) in October. *A. J. Chamberlain.* **35**

NONCOMMITAL 4 b.c. Mummy's Pet 125 – Shadow Play (Busted 134) [1990 NR 1991 8g⁶ 10.2m 8g⁵ 7m 8.2m 8m 9.2s] good-topped colt: fourth living foal: closely related to fair 7f and 1m winner My Buddy (by Mummy's Game): dam unraced daughter of half-sister to very smart sprinter Honeyblest: no worthwhile form, including in handicaps: keen sort. *J. Mackie.* —

NON CONSTAT (USA) 7 b.g. Vaguely Noble 140 – Jamila (Sir Gaylord) [1990 a12g⁴ a14g 12g a12g³ 13.6g⁴ 14.8m⁴ a12g³ a8g⁵ 1991 a11g⁴ 10s⁶ 12.2d³ 14.8m* 14g 18.4d 12g⁵ 14.8m] tall, attractive gelding: none too trustworthy handicapper: won at Warwick in April: stayed 2m: acted on hard and dead going: tried blinkered and visored: dead. *R. Ingram.* **63** §

NONE GO BY 3 br.f. Daring March 116 – River Aire 82 (Klairon 131) [1990 7g 1991 7g 6d 6g 6g⁶ 6g 8g 10.2d³ 10.1d 10.2g] sturdy, lengthy filly: plater: below form last 2 starts: better at 1¼m than shorter: acts on dead ground: visored sixth start. *G. B. Balding.* **44**

NONE SO BRAVE 3 b.c. Dancing Brave (USA) 140 – So Fine 113 (Thatching 131) [1990 NR 1991 12g³ 14d² 13g* 14.6d⁵] angular, useful-looking colt: second living foal: dam Irish 6f to 1¼m winner, is half-sister to very useful Irish 2-y-o sprinter Takachiho II, later successful at up to 1½m: 7/4 on, won maiden at Dundalk in October: 10/1, chased leaders long way then eased in 10-runner Doncaster minor event 25 days later: stays 1¾m: sold out of J. Oxx's stable 8,000 gns Newmarket Autumn Sales after third start: winning hurdler. *R. Akehurst.* **85**

NON PARTISAN (USA) 2 b.c. (Jan 16) Alleged (USA) 138 – Sunny Bay (USA) (Northern Bay (USA)) [1991 9d*] seventh foal: brother to Jalaajel, successful from 9f to 12.5f in France, including in listed events, and half-brother to several winners here and abroad, including very useful 1987 2-y-o 6f and 7f winner Suntrap (by Roberto): narrowly won 8-runner newcomers event at Longchamp in October: should be suited by middle distances: should improve. *A. Fabre, France.* **?**

NO QUARTER GIVEN 6 b.g. Don 128 – Maggie Mine 85 (Native Prince) [1990 6s⁶ 5g⁵ 7f³ 7.6m 6m³ 6g³ 6d³ 5g³ 6g³ 5g* 6f² 5m* 5m 5d⁴ 5d⁴ 5g² 5s 1991 6s 5g 5f³ 5m⁴ 6g 6d 6g³ 5.1g³ 5g³ 5m⁴ a5g² a5g⁴ 5.2f* 5.1m 5m⁵ 6m] rangy, well-made gelding: carries plenty of condition: modest handicapper: won at Yarmouth in August, making all: probably best at sprint distances: acts on any going: good mount for apprentice: largely consistent. *P. S. Felgate.* **72**

NORDAN RAIDER 3 ch.f. Domynsky 110 – Vikris (Viking (USA)) [1990 NR 1991 9g 8m⁶ 10.5d 8m] compact filly: first foal: dam thrice-raced half-sister to useful sprinter Westacombe: showed a little ability in seller and handicap last 2 starts: takes good hold, and may prove suited by 7f/1m: retained by trainer 1,200 gns Doncaster November Sales. *M. J. Camacho.* —

NORDANSK 2 ch.c. (May 13) Nordance (USA) – Free On Board 73 (Free State 125) [1991 6m⁶ 6g⁴ 5m 7m] workmanlike colt: has scope: second foal: half-brother to **47**

Mr D. H. W. Dobson's "Nordic Brief"

3-y-o Free For All (by Mummy's Game): dam stayed 1¼m: poor maiden: backward and well beaten in nursery: should stay 1m. *J. Balding.*

NORDIC BRAVE 5 b.h. Indian King (USA) 128 – Belle Viking (FR) (Riverman **76** (USA) 131) [1990 6m3 6s 6m* 6f3 6m 5m 6g 6m4 7m2 7g 7d 6d 7g 1991 6s5 6s 6d* 6m 7g 6m 6m 7m4 6m 7g2 6d* 7m 6d 6d 6m 6g 6m 7g 7m* 8d 7m 7m5 7d] leggy, lightly-made, angular horse: moderate mover: modest handicapper: won at Ripon in April and June and Ayr in September: effective at 6f to 7f: acts on good to firm and soft ground: has won for apprentice, and when sweating: suited by forcing tactics. goes well at York: inconsistent. *M. Brittain.*

NORDIC BRIEF (IRE) 2 b.c. (Feb 25) Nordico (USA) – Bold And Brief (Bold **101** Lad (IRE) 133) [1991 5g* 7m2 7g2 6m6 6m6 7m2] fourth live foal: half-brother to a winner in Czechoslovakia by Touching Wood: dam Irish 1¼m winner at 3 yrs: narrow winner of Leopardstown maiden in April: sixth in Heinz '57' Phoenix Stakes there (around 2 lengths behind Bradawn Breever) and Tattersalls Breeders Stakes at the Curragh (won by Affair of State) in August: 20/1, best effort when ½-length second of 5 to El Prado in National Stakes at latter course in September, running on when headed inside final 1f: will stay 1m: acts on good to firm ground: blinkered last 3 starts: useful. *J. S. Bolger, Ireland.*

NORDIC FLASH 4 b.g. Nordico (USA) – Rosemore (Ashmore (FR) 125) [1990 **72** 12m6 12m3 1991 10s2 11g*] first foal: dam Irish 1½m winner: ex-Irish gelding, lightly raced on flat: favourite on first run here, won claimer at Edinburgh in May: stays 1½m: probably acts on good to firm and soft ground: trained until after first start by J. Bolger. *D. J. Wintle.*

NORDIC ROMANCE (IRE) 3 b.c. Nordico (USA) – Romantic Air 62 (He — Loves Me 120) [1990 NR 1991 8.2d] IR 5,000Y: second foal: half-brother to poor 4-y-o Hunza's Choice (by Thatching): dam ran 3 times at 2 yrs, showing better form at 1m than 5f: moved badly down and showed nothing in April claimer. *C. N. Allen.*

NORFOLKIEV (FR) 5 b.h. In Fijar (USA) 121 – Touraille (FR) (Jim French **71** d (USA)) [1990 6m6 6h2 7g* 6g 7m6 6m 6m2 6m2 6g* 6s 1991 6m3 6m4 6v 6g5 7f3

7.6m 6g] good-bodied horse: moderate mover: modest handicapper: below form after reappearance, blinkered final start: probably better suited by 6f than 7f: acts on hard going, seems unsuited by heavy ground: used to have tongue tied down. *M. Moubarak.*

NORFOLK LADY 3 br.f. Norwick (USA) 120 – Belle (DEN) (Comedy Star (USA) 121) [1990 8g 6d 1991 8g 9g 8m 7g] compact filly: no worthwhile form, including in ladies races: sweating and edgy final start: usually mounted on track: sold 680 gns Newmarket July Sales. *D. T. Thom.* —

NORFOLK LASS 3 b.f. Blakeney 126 – Balgreggan (Hallez (FR) 131) [1990 7g 1991 12m6 11.8m 14.1f5 14.1f5 16m] angular, plain filly: has a round action: little form: stays 1¾m. *M. A. Jarvis.* —

NORFOLK THATCH 5 b.g. Thatching 131 – Pellarosa (Crepello 136) [1990 NR 1991 8.9g 8g4] lightly raced and poor handicapper nowadays: gambled-on favourite, hung persistently left at Brighton final start: should stay beyond 1m. *K. S. Bridgwater.* 40 +

NORMA JEAN 5 ch.m. Horage 124 – Goccia d'Oro (ITY) (Bolkonski 134) [1990 8.5m6 7m 8m 10f2 8g2 11d 9d 1991 8g2 9g 9m 8g3 8g2 8.5g 8.5g a11g a8g] second foal: half-sister to Irish 7f winner Silver Patrol (by Rusticaro): dam lightly-raced Irish maiden, stayed 1m: ex-Irish handicapper: twice raced here and behind in all-weather claimers: stays 1¼m: acts on firm ground: trained until after seventh outing by P. Flynn. *M. H. Tompkins.* 73

NORMAN WARRIOR 2 gr.g. (May 11) Petong 126 – Petulengra 98 (Mummy's Pet 125) [1991 7m 7d] 2,000Y: seventh foal: dam 5f and 6f winner at 2 yrs: well beaten in late-season Doncaster maidens. *D. Morris.* 41

NORMEAD LASS 3 b.f. Norwick (USA) 120 – Meads Lass (Saritamer (USA) 130) [1990 6g 1991 7.1d 10.2s5 10m5 9.7f] leggy filly: poor form in sellers last 2 starts: may well stay 1½m: acts on firm ground: joined Miss P. Hall. *G. B. Balding.* 36

NORQUAY (USA) 6 ch.g. Arctic Tern (USA) 126 – Godetia (USA) 119 (Sir Ivor 135) [1990 a8g4 8.2s2 8f 8f* 8.2g3 8g2 8.2s3 8.2g5 8.5f2 8f 8v6 8d a8g a11g 1991 10.8g 8.5g 8.2d6 9f3 8f4 9m4 8m6 8h5 8.3s2 8.3d6 8m5 8.1m4 8.3f3 8.5f5 9m 13.8m 8.2m3] close-coupled, workmanlike gelding: moderate mover: poor handicapper: effective at 1m, and seemed to stay 13.8f: acted on any going: won for amateur: usually got behind: winning hurdler: dead. *N. Tinkler.* 48

NORTHENDERLEY 4 b.f. Northern Tempest (USA) 120 – Darkness Visible 68 (Decoy Boy 129) [1990 NR 1991 a6g a5g6 a7g 8.5f6 a5g a12g] sturdy, workmanlike filly: no sign of ability: dead. *J. P. Leigh.*

NORTHERN ASCENT 3 ch.c. Northern Tempest (USA) 120 – Rose Rocket (Roan Rocket 128) [1990 NR 1991 8m 10g] leggy, close-coupled colt: first foal: dam lightly-raced plater: bandaged, behind in claimers. *K. O. Cunningham-Brown.* —

NORTHERN BLADE (IRE) 2 b.c. (May 7) Sure Blade (USA) 130 – Secala (USA) (Secretariat (USA)) [1991 7d6 8.1g5 8m 7g6] IR 16,000Y: leggy, workmanlike colt: has a round action: ninth foal: half-brother to several winners, including useful Irish middle-distance winner Sir Simon (by Sir Ivor) and very useful 3-y-o Dartrey (by Darshaan), 7f winner at 2 yrs and stays 10.5f well: dam won at up to 1m in USA: plating-class form in fair-quality maidens then a mixed-aged event at Newmarket (7 ran) final start: not certain to stay 1¼m: below form on good to firm ground. *R. Hollinshead.* 54

NORTHERN BLUEBIRD (IRE) 2 b.c. (Apr 25) Bluebird (USA) 125 – Bean Siamsa (Solinus 130) [1991 6g3 6m4 5g* 6m5 6.3m4] IR 85,000Y: half-brother to 3 winners here and in Ireland, including 9f and 1¼m winner Gorytus Star (by Caerleon) and 1988 2-y-o 5f winner Gorytus Star (by Gorytus): dam never ran: fairly useful performer: successful in maiden at Tipperary in August: easily better subsequent effort when over 2 lengths fifth to Bradawn Breever in Heinz '57' Phoenix Stakes at Leopardstown: suited by 6f: blinkered last 3 starts: not seen out after August. *D. K. Weld, Ireland.* 92

NORTHERN CONQUEROR (IRE) 3 ch.c. Mazaad 106 – Gaylom (Lord Gayle (USA) 124) [1990 5m3 5m2 5m3 a5g* 6g2 5m4 6m5 6f5 7g2 7g2 8m5 9g4 7m 1991 a5g5 a7g4 10.1s4 10g* 8.5m4 10g* 10m6 a10g6 7.6m6 10.1f 10g a10g] small, lightly-made colt: easy mover: fair performer at best: won claimer at Goodwood in May and £7,200 handicap (plenty to do 3f out) at Sandown in June: ran poorly then never dangerous (wearing eyeshield) last 2 starts: better at 1¼m than shorter: acts on good to firm ground and soft: visored once at 2 yrs: sometimes edgy: suitable mount for 7-lb claimer. *T. J. Naughton.* 83 a 63

NORTHERN EMPEROR (IRE)   2 b.g. (Mar 13) The Noble Player (USA) 126   —
– Staderas (Windjammer (USA)) [1991 6m 7m 8m 7m] IR 6,200F, 5,000Y: leggy
gelding: half-brother to modest sprinter My Pal Popeye (by Runnett) and a winner
in Hong Kong: dam never ran: well beaten in maidens and a median auction. *M.
Brittain.*

NORTHERN FLYER   3 ch.c. Bairn (USA) 126 – Fly The World (USA) 74   **74** d
(Empery (USA) 128) [1990 6m 6g 7m 1991 7g⁴ 7m 10d* a10g² 10g⁶ 10m³ 12g⁵ 11g
a12g a10g⁶ a12g⁵] rather sparely-made colt: modest handicapper: made all at Goodwood in June: ran moderately last 4 starts: should stay 1½m: acts on good to firm
ground and dead: has got on edge and worn net muzzle: pulled hard for apprentice:
sold out of P. Walwyn's stable 5,000 gns Ascot December Sales before final start. *M.
C. Chapman.*

NORTHERN GALLERY (IRE)   3 ch.c. Tate Gallery (USA) 117 – Cliona (FR)   —
(Ballymore 123) [1990 6m a8g 1991 8m 6g 8f 6m] leggy, good-topped colt: poor
plater: bred to stay beyond 6f: sometimes bandaged behind: blinkered 3 times, wore
eyeshield on all-weather. *Mrs L. Piggott.*

NORTHERN GODDESS   4 b.f. Night Shift (USA) – Hearten (Hittite Glory **107**
125) [1990 6g 5.8f* 6g⁶ 6m² 5d 5g* 6m* 6m² 1991 6d³ 6g 5m² 6s] compact,
attractive filly: useful performer: first run for nearly 4 months, easily best effort in
1991 when second to Notley in Scarborough Stakes at Doncaster: unsuited by ground
in Diadem Stakes at Ascot later in September: stays 6f: goes very well on top-
of-the-ground: tends to get on toes: has swerved left, and swished tail: best held up:
sold 96,000 gns Newmarket December Sales. *I. A. Balding.*

NORTHERN GRADUATE (USA)   2 b.g. (Apr 19) Northrop (USA) – Lady   **60**
Blackfoot 108 (Prince Tenderfoot (USA) 126) [1991 6m 6m⁶ 6.1d] 2,500F:
useful-looking gelding: has scope: closely related to 1988 Irish 2-y-o 5f winner
Monasteroris (by Northern Jove) and half-brother to fairly useful 3-y-o 1m winner
Fanmore (by Lear Fan) and a winner in North America by J O Tobin: dam speedy
Irish filly: sire, minor stakes-winning son of Northern Dancer, successful at up to
1¼m: quite modest form in minor event on debut: gave impression something amiss
at Pontefract second start: visored and on toes, well beaten at Chester final one. *S.
G. Norton.*

NORTHERN HABIT   5 ch.g. Salmon Leap (USA) 131 – Manx Millenium 66   **90**
(Habitat 134) [1990 6f 8m³ 7f³ 7.5f³ 8m² 7.6g⁴ 8g 8m 8g² 1991 9g* 8.9m³ 8m⁵]
leggy, quite good-topped gelding: fairly useful handicapper: won at Goodwood in
May: ran really well after, set far too much to do when running-on fifth to Susurration in ladies event at Ascot in July: will stay 1¼m: has raced only on sound
surface: wears net muzzle nowadays: often slowly away, and goes well with waiting
tactics. *I. A. Balding.*

NORTHERN HAL   4 b.c. Sadler's Wells (USA) 132 – Northern Script (USA) 95 **101**
(Arts And Letters) [1990 8.2m* 11g⁴ 10.1m² 12m⁵ 10m* 8g² 8m 1991 9m 8.5f⁶ 9g*
10v 10.4m? 9g³ 10m*] lengthy, good-topped colt: has a quick action: useful
performer: won ladies event at Kempton in June and listed race at Baden-Baden
(beat Averax by 1¾ lengths) in August: effective at 1m to 1¼m: goes well on a sound
surface, unsuited by heavy going (yet to race on soft): may well prove best held up.
P. T. Walwyn.

NORTHERN HALO   10 ch.g. Northfields (USA) – Halomata 68 (Hallez (FR)   —
131) [1990 NR 1991 a12g] close-coupled gelding: poor maiden: tailed off in Lingfield
claimer, first run on flat since 1985: poor hurdler. *G. A. Ham.*

NORTHERN LIMIT   2 ch.f. (May 6) Scottish Reel 123 – Patience Unlimited   —
(Sweet Revenge 129) [1991 5m] 700Y: lengthy filly: fifth foal: dam unraced: 33/1 and
better for race, soon outpaced in maiden auction at Salisbury in May: moved poorly
down. *B. R. Millman.*

NORTHERN LION   8 br.g. Northfields (USA) – Pride of Kilcarn 74 (Klairon   —
131) [1990 16g 1991 a12g 10.6g 12m] ex-Irish gelding: won over 1½m at Tipperary in
1987: well beaten in claimers and amateurs event (out of depth) this year: winning
hurdler. *R. Thompson.*

NORTHERN NATION   3 b.g. Nomination 125 – Ballagarrow Girl 66 (North   **48**
Stoke 130) [1990 5f 5m⁵ 5f⁵ 5m⁵ 5m* 5g² 5m⁵ 5g⁶ 5v 1991 5m 5g 7m 8g 8.9g 7g⁵
6.9s⁴ a6g 7m⁵ 6m⁵] workmanlike, good-quartered gelding: plating class at 3 yrs:
best form at sprint distances: acts on good to firm ground and soft: visored fourth
outing: carries head high: a difficult ride: sold 4,200 gns Ascot October Sales: won
selling hurdle for W. Clay. *S. Mellor.*

NORTHERN OPTIMIST   3 b.f. Northern Tempest (USA) 120 – On A Bit 66   **34**
(Mummy's Pet 125) [1990 5g³ 6g⁵ 6f* 7m 7g 1991 7.5f 8g 7.5f³ 6f 8.1g 8.2m] close-coupled, angular filly: fluent mover: modest winner at 2 yrs: form as 3-y-o only in seller third start: needs further than 6f, and should stay 1m: acts on firm going: blinkered third and fourth starts: sold to join B. Llewellyn 2,100 gns Newmarket Autumn Sales. *J. G. FitzGerald.*

NORTHERN RAINBOW   3 b.g. Rainbow Quest (USA) 134 – Safe House 81§   **69**
(Lyphard (USA) 132) [1990 6m² 8d³ 1991 8s 12g⁶ 10.4d⁴ 8g⁵] lengthy gelding: modest maiden: may prove best at 1¼m: acts on any other: blinkered (ran creditably) final start, in May. *P. F. I. Cole.*

NORTHERN RISING   3 ch.g. Bairn (USA) 126 – Lucky Petina 88 (Mummy's   **65**
Pet 125) [1990 6m⁶ 6s⁴ 1991 6m² 7m² 8.5m 8s* 8.9m⁵ 7d² 8m] leggy, close-coupled gelding: quite modest form: won claimer at Edinburgh in July: stayed 1m: acted on good to firm ground and soft: dead. *A. N. Lee.*

NORTHERN ROCKET   4 b.g. Northern Tempest (USA) 120 – Scotch Rocket   —
60 (Roan Rocket 128) [1990 a7g 7.5d 6m² 6g 5g⁶ 6m⁵ 7m⁶ a6g⁶ a6g⁵ a6g 6d a6g 1991 a7g] leggy gelding: quite modest performer at 3 yrs, below that form (stiff task) in Southwell handicap in December: suited by 6f: acts on fibresand: effective with or without blinkers: has been visored: has run creditably for 7-lb claimer and when sweating: races freely. *J. P. Leigh.*

NORTHERN SPARK   3 b.g. Trojan Fen 118 – Heavenly Spark (Habitat 134)   **75**
[1990 5g* 6m⁴ 6g 6d 8v 1991 9m 6m⁶ 6m* 7m* 6m² 7f⁶ 6m⁵ 7d 7m] leggy gelding: has a round action: modest handicapper: progressive form to win at Redcar and York in June: best subsequent effort when beaten a head at York, making most: stays 7f: acts on good to firm going, hampered on heavy: bandaged off-hind seventh start. *C. W. Thornton.*

NORTHERN TRIAL (USA)   3 b.g. Far North (CAN) 120 – Make An Attempt   **86** d
(USA) (Nashua) [1990 NR 1991 8g⁴ 10s³ 10.2f³ 10g 11.7m² 10g⁶ 10f² 10g²] $68,000Y: sturdy gelding: half-brother to several winners in North America: dam minor winner in North America: fair form at best in varied events: looked sure to beat sole opponent until final ½f in minor event at Bath fifth start: probably stays 1½m: possibly unsuited by firm going: blinkered (found little) sixth start: not one to trust: gelded after final start. *C. R. Nelson.*

NORTH ESK (USA)   2 ch.g. (Apr 1) Apalachee (USA) 137 – Six Dozen (USA)   **80**
(What A Pleasure (USA)) [1991 6m* 6m⁴ 6g] $47,000Y: good-topped, quite attractive gelding: fourth foal: half-brother to a minor winner of 19 races by Believe It: dam minor winner from family of top-class Gallant Romeo: very green favourite, won moderately-run maiden at Newcastle in June: subsequently ran in nurseries at Doncaster (good fourth to Holetown, still looked inexperienced) and Ascot (poor effort) in September: will be suited by 7f+: acts on good to firm ground: wore crossed noseband last 2 starts. *J. W. Watts.*

NORTH FLYER   2 b.c. (Jan 25) Norwick (USA) 120 – Minuetto 59 (Roan Rocket   **55**
128) [1991 5f 5m² 5m 5h⁴ 8g 7m] 1,700Y: smallish, rather leggy colt: sixth foal: dam placed at 5f at 2 yrs, only season to race: plating-class maiden: races keenly, and has no form beyond 5f: acts on hard ground: sometimes claimer ridden, best efforts when not. *B. A. McMahon.*

NORTHGATE GIRL (IRE)   3 ch.f. Gorytus (USA) 132 – Red Line Fever 94   —
(Bay Express 132) [1990 5f 5m⁴ 5f³ 5m³ 5m² 5d⁴ 5g 5d⁶ a5g 1991 5g 5m a5g 5m] neat, good-quartered, sprint type: plating-class maiden: below form in handicaps as 3-y-o: acts on good to firm ground: has worn bandages: sold 920 gns Doncaster July Sales. *M. Brittain.*

NORTHGATE KING   4 b.c. Fairy King (USA) – Dollyful (Track Spare 125)   **47**
[1990 7.5g 7.5d* 8g⁶ a8g 9g² 8.2g² 8.2m⁴ 11m² 10g⁴ 10m 10.2m⁶ 9g 1991 8s³ 8g 8.5g⁴ 8.2d³ 10f 12m² 10.1m⁵ 11.5g⁵ 12.3d⁶ 11.8g] neat colt: bad mover: plating-class handicapper: bandaged, ran poorly last 2 starts: effective under testing conditions at 1m and stays 1½m: acts on good to firm (possibly unsuited by very firm) and soft going: sold 1,150 gns Doncaster November Sales. *M. Brittain.*

NORTH LODGE   3 b.g. Norwick (USA) 120 – Horns Lodge (High Line 125)   —
[1990 NR 1991 10g 10g 10.5d 11d] sturdy gelding: first foal: dam ran twice: bandaged, well beaten in claimers and sellers. *P. J. Makin.*

NORTH OF WATFORD   6 ch.h. Jasmine Star 113 – Wallie Girl (Right Tack   **55**
131) [1990 5m³ 5g³ 5g* 5g 6g* 5d* 6g* 6m 5g⁴ 5f 5m⁵ 5g⁴ 6g 6s 5s a5g² a6g⁵ 1991 a5g⁴ a5g⁵ 5f⁶ 5f 5g⁶ 6f 5d³] lengthy, good-quartered horse: moderate walker and mover: plating-class handicapper nowadays: best at 5f or 6f: acts on good to firm and

dead ground: has won when sweating: probably unsuited by track at Chester: none too consistent: joined H. Whiting. *K. B. McCauley.*

NORTHUMBRIAN LADY 2 b.f. (Apr 29) Full Extent (USA) 113 – Emerin 85 — (King Emperor (USA)) [1991 5g 6d 6m 5f 5m⁶] 2,000Y: smallish, good-topped filly: half-sister to 3 winners on flat and over hurdles, including 1988 2-y-o 5f winner Katherines Emerald (by Aragon): dam won twice over 6f: seems of little account: blinkered last 2 starts: sold 950 gns Doncaster August Sales. *C. W. Thornton.*

NORTH-WEST ONE (IRE) 3 b.g. Camden Town 125 – Shahrazad (Young — Emperor 133) [1990 NR 1991 7.6m 7g a12g] 6,000Y: workmanlike gelding: moderate mover: third reported foal: half-brother to Irish 7f winner Dazla (by Dublin Taxi): dam Irish maiden: well beaten in autumn maidens and claimer at Lingfield. *H. J. Collingridge.*

NORTH WIND (IRE) 3 b.f. Lomond (USA) 128 – Spirit of The Wind (USA) **101** (Little Current (USA)) [1990 7g 8g³ 1991 11g* 11.3d³ 10g³ 11.9g] strong, lengthy filly: useful form: won maiden at Newbury in April: third, progressing again, to Peplum in Cheshire Oaks and Ruby Tiger in Nassau Stakes at Goodwood 3 months later: second favourite, led 9f before weakening tamely in listed race at York final start: stays 1½m. *B. W. Hills.*

NORTHWOLD STAR (USA) 5 br.m. Monteverdi 129 – Its A Romp (Hotfoot **67** d 126) [1990 16g 14m 18.4d a14g² 14g³ 15.3g² 16m 18.8f* 16.5f⁵ a14g⁴ 18d 18g* a16g² a16g² a16g⁴ a16g⁶ 1991 16.1g³ 14.8s² 15.9m 18.2f⁵ 18m 18m⁵] smallish, close-coupled mare: turns off-fore in: quite modest handicapper: ran moderately last 4 starts: stays really well: unsuited by firm going, acts on any other: tried blinkered once, often visored. *D. T. Thom.*

NORTINO 3 ch.g. Norwick (USA) 120 – Soft Chinook (USA) (Hitting Away) [1990 — NR 1991 8s⁶ 7d⁵ 9.2d⁶ 10f 12m⁶ 11m] leggy, shallow-girthed gelding: half-brother to several winners, including 9f winner Tarlogie (by Touching Wood) and 1m winner Si Sawat (by Superlative): dam French plater: no worthwhile form, in selling handicap final start: retained 860 gns Newmarket Autumn Sales. *Mrs G. R. Reveley.*

NORTON CHALLENGER 4 gr.c. Absalom 128 – Klaire 85 (Klairon 131) [1990 **111** 5v⁴ 7g² 6m² 6m² 8m⁵ 1991 6d* 7g² 6g 7.2g² 6m 7g* 7m 7g³ 6d³] rangy, good-topped colt: good walker and mover: very useful performer: won £7,400 event at Thirsk in April and listed event at York (made virtually all) in August: good third to Osario in Group 3 event at Goodwood and Snaadee in listed event at Doncaster (visored): stays 7f: best efforts with some give in the ground (acts on heavy going): sometimes bandaged. *M. H. Easterby.*

NORTON'S COIN 10 ch.g. Mount Cassino 92 – Grove Chance (St Columbus 98) — [1990 NR 1991 22.2m] lengthy, angular gelding: first foal: dam unraced: high-class chaser, won Cheltenham Gold Cup in 1990: never-nearer eighth in Queen Alexandra Stakes at Royal Ascot. *M. McCourt.*

NORWICK STAR 3 b.f. Norwick (USA) 120 – Gentle Star 77 (Comedy Star — (USA) 121) [1990 a7g 1991 9f 12.2g 13d⁵ 8f⁵ 16m a12g 10m] rather angular filly: good mover: poor performer: bandaged, no show in seller final start: may prove best short of 1½m: acts on firm going: visored (found little), blinkered or wore eyeshield last 4 outings: trained until after fifth by W. Pearce: sold 2,000 gns Ascot November Sales. *T. M. Jones.*

NOSEEIM (IRE) 2 b.c. (Feb 11) Dance of Life (USA) – Shabby Doll 69 **59** (Northfields (USA)) [1991 5d⁵ 5f³ 6d⁴ 6g² 7m⁴ 6m⁵ a7g⁴ 10.5d⁴] leggy colt: first foal: dam 1¼m and 11f winner, is out of half-sister to very useful middle-distance colt Beauvallon: fairly useful plater: tired noticeably closing stages final start, though ran creditably: has form at 10.5f, but gives impression may prove ideally suited by 1m/9f: races keenly: sold 8,000 gns Newmarket Autumn Sales. *N. A. Callaghan.*

NO SID NO STARS (USA) 3 ch.g. Diamond Shoal 130 – Side Saddle (USA) **79** (Codex (USA)) [1990 8.2m 1991 8d³ 8.5f* 9d 10f* 10.1f² 10d⁴ 10.1g 10.3m 10m⁴ 9m⁵] sturdy gelding: good walker and mover: fair handicapper: won at Beverley in April (claimer) and May, making all on second occasion: best efforts after, running fairly well, last 2 starts: stays 1¼m well: acts on firm going: sold to join G. Moore 14,500 gns Newmarket Autumn Sales. *D. Morley.*

NO SUBMISSION (USA) 5 b.h. Melyno 130 – Creeping Kate (USA) (Stop The **87** Music (USA)) [1990 8g 8f 8.2s³ 8f 8.3m² 8m⁵ 8d 10m⁴ 1991 10g* 10g* 10f³ 10g 10d⁶] tall, leggy, quite attractive horse: poor mover: fair handicapper: won valuable events at Kempton in April, dictating at modest gallop: first run for over 3 months, set strong pace when below-form sixth in £12,100 event at Ascot in October: stays

1¼m: acts on any going: once spoilt chance by hanging left: sometimes on edge: best dominating: goes well for D. Holland. *C. R. Nelson.*

NOTABLE EXCEPTION 2 b.g. (May 5) Top Ville 129 – Shorthouse 102 **50** (Habitat 134) [1991 7g 8m 8m] 29,000Y: lengthy gelding: seventh living foal: half-brother to 3-y-o Lowawatha (by Dancing Brave) and smart miler Ever Genial (by Brigadier Gerard): dam, daughter of smart middle-distance stayer Guillotina and sister to Princess Royal winner One Way Street, won twice over 7f at 2 yrs: poor maiden: best effort second start: gives impression will do better over further. *J. W. Hills*

NOTANOTHERONE (IRE) 3 b.g. Mazaad 106 – Maltese Pet 74 (Dragonara **49** Palace (USA) 115) [1990 5m4 5.3h3 6m 7g 6d a6g5 a7g5 1991 a7g a7g4 a6g 6f5 6d5 7m] leggy, close-coupled gelding: poor maiden: stays 7f: acts on hard ground, ran fairly well on dead penultimate start: often visored in 1991: none too consistent. *J. E. Long.*

NOTED STRAIN (IRE) 3 b.c. Gorytus (USA) 132 – Almuadiyeh 69 (Thatching **62** 131) [1990 NR 1991 10g4 10g4 10m4 10m5 10m3 10.4m5 10d5 a14g5 a11g4 a10g5] a49 22,000F, 16,000Y: good-topped colt: second foal: dam, out of half-sister to smart stayers Frascati and The Admiral, raced only at 2 yrs when placed over 7f: quite modest maiden: below form in selling handicap and claimers last 5 starts: should stay 1½m: has had tongue tied down: retained by trainer 1,750 gns Ascot December Sales. *P. J. Makin.*

NOT GORDONS 2 b.c. (Mar 18) All Systems Go 119 – Lady Abernant 90 (Abwah — 118) [1991 7m 7m 8.3g] 1,200Y, 3,500Y, IR 8,200Y, 7,600 2-y-o: angular, quite good-topped colt: fourth foal: dam fairly useful 2-y-o 7f winner won over 1½m at 4 yrs: well beaten in maidens and a claimer. *J. H. Johnson.*

NOTHING COMPARES 2 b.f. (Mar 27) Pharly (FR) 130 – Foiled Again 110 **39** (Bold Lad (IRE) 133) [1991 a7g6 a7g5 a8g5] half-sister to 3-y-o Tip of My Tongue (by Beldale Flutter) and several winners, including 1m to 1½m winner Scales of Justice (by Final Straw) and 7f winner Cut No Ice (by Great Nephew): dam won from 6f to 1¼m: poor form in late-year maidens at Southwell and Lingfield. *J. W. Hills.*

NOTHING'S FREE 4 b.f. Free State 125 – Wayward Polly 63 (Lochnager 132) **32** [1990 7.5f3 8f2 7f4 6f2 6m 8m 1991 7.5g 7m 8m a7g 7.5m3 6d4 6g] rather leggy filly: moderate mover: poor handicapper nowadays: probably stays 1m: seems to act on any going: usually blinkered or visored, not final start (well beaten): tends to get on toes: has had tongue tied down: sold 1,150 gns Newmarket Autumn Sales. *M. W. Easterby.*

NOT IN DOUBT (USA) 2 b.c. (Feb 15) Tom Rolfe – Trillionaire (USA) 111 — (Vaguely Noble 140) [1991 7m] 34,000Y: close-coupled, unfurnished colt: half-brother to 2 winners abroad, one graded-stakes placed: dam middle-distance performer: 50/1 and backward, always behind in maiden at Newmarket in October. *H. Candy.*

NOTLEY 4 b.g. Formidable (USA) 125 – Riviere Bleue (Riverman (USA) 131) **110** [1990 6m5 1991 5g 6m4 6m4 5.1g* 6g* 5m* 5m2 6d5] strong, sturdy gelding: lightly

William Hill Stewards' Cup, Goodwood—
Notley turns this big handicap into a one-horse race;
the second, Macrobian, is on the stand rail attended by Farfelu;
the grey on the far side is third-placed Masnun along with the fading Aughfad

Mr D. F. Cock's "Notley"

raced before developing into very useful performer in 1991, successful in handicaps at Chepstow and Goodwood (William Hill Stewards' Cup, impressively) in July and listed Scarbrough Stakes at Doncaster (by head from Northern Goddess) in September: good second to Blyton Lad in listed event at Newmarket: respectable fifth to Snaadee in similar event at Doncaster: effective at 5f and 6f: acts on good to firm and dead ground: has edged left: often ridden by 5-lb claimer. *R. Hannon.*

NOT MISTAKEN 2 b.g. (Apr 6) Sulaafah (USA) 119 – Before Long (Longleat (USA) 109) [1991 5g⁵ 6m 6f⁵ 5.7f 7g] leggy, quite good-topped gelding: moderate walker: second foal: brother to 3-y-o hurdle winner Our Martha: dam never ran: plating-class form in varied events: best efforts last 2 starts: stays 7f: acts on firm ground. *J. D. Roberts.* **52**

NOT SO PLEASING 2 ch.f. (Mar 4) Domynsky 110 – Pleasing Prospect 74 (Imperial Fling (USA) 116) [1991 5g] 4,000Y: smallish, workmanlike filly: second foal: dam maiden best at 1¼m, is half-sister to smart 5f to 1m winner Lady Mere: bit backward, always behind, not knocked about, in median auction maiden at Thirsk in May. *M. H. Easterby.* **—**

NOT SO SIMPLE (IRE) 3 b.f. Simply Great (FR) 122 – Drifting Shadow (Welsh Saint 126) [1990 NR 1991 a7g 11.7g] IR 750Y: sparely-made filly: third foal: dam behind all 3 starts (at 2 yrs) in Ireland: tailed off in early-season maidens at Southwell and (edgy, sweating and pulled hard) Bath. *A. J. Chamberlain.* **—**

NOT YET 7 b.g. Connaught 130 – Ritratto (Pinturischio 116) [1990 8f 8.5g⁵ 9f⁵ 10d* 10g² 10m⁵ 8.5f⁵ 10.6d³ 8m* 8.5m 8.2d 8m 1991 9m 10g⁵ 10d 9.9f 9m 10m⁴ 10.5m⁵ 8m⁴ 8h³ 9.9f⁵ 10g* 8.2m 8m] small, compact gelding: carries plenty of **44**

600

condition: bad mover: poor handicapper nowadays: won selling event at Redcar (no bid) in September: suited by 1¼m nowadays: appears to act on any going: excellent mount for apprentice: usually held up. *E. Weymes.*

NOUSHY 3 ch.f. Ahonoora 122 – Bolkonskina (Balidar 133) [1990 5m 6m⁴ 5m⁵ 6.5g 7m⁶ 8g 1991 7m 6m 10g⁶ 8m⁵] small, workmanlike filly: modest maiden at 2 yrs: well beaten in 1991: stays 7f: sold to join K. Bridgwater 1,000 gns Newmarket Autumn Sales. *C. E. Brittain.*

NOVA DANCER (IRE) 2 ch.f. (Feb 24) Glad Dancer – Novapour (Nishapour (FR) 125) [1991 a6g a7g] tall, workmanlike filly: first foal: dam unraced: visored, tailed off in sellers at Southwell in July: unruly stalls and withdrawn from maiden at same course in June. *P. J. Bevan.*

NOVA SPIRIT 3 b.f. Electric 126 – Miss Casanova 84 (Galivanter 131) [1990 NR 1991 10m] sparely-made filly: half-sister to several winners, mostly over middle distances, including Morality Stone (also successful at 1m at 6 yrs) and good hurdler Ra Nova (both by Ragstone): dam 2-y-o 6f winner: tailed off in median auction contest at Salisbury in May: joined M. Saunders. *R. J. Holder.*

NOW BOARDING 4 b.f. Blazing Saddles (AUS) – Strictly Swing 89 (Swing Easy (USA) 126) [1990 6m⁶ 7d² 6m² 8h⁴ 1991 7.1d 8m 7m] lengthy filly: plating-class performer at 3 yrs: well beaten in first half of 1991: stays 1m: acts on hard and dead going. *R. J. Hodges.*

NOWHISKI 3 b.c. Petoski 135 – Be Faithful 93 (Val de Loir 133) [1990 7m 6d 1991 10.8g 12.2m 8.2m 14.1g 10f⁵] rangy colt: no worthwhile form: unimpressive in appearance last 2 starts: should be suited by middle distances: visored final start. *H. J. Collingridge.*

NUCLEAR EXPRESS 4 b.g. Martinmas 128 – Halka (Daring March 116) [1990 6s⁵ 5m* 5m² 5g² 5.8f³ 5m⁶ 5g⁵ 5f* 5m⁶ 5g 5d 1991 5f 5f⁵ 6m⁴ 5g a8g] leggy, workmanlike gelding: turns fore-feet in: modest handicapper at 3 yrs: no form at 4 yrs: stays 5.8f: acts on firm and dead going: ran moderately when blinkered: tends to hang and carry head high: sold out of D. Chapman's stable 1,400 gns Doncaster August Sales after penultimate start. *D. J. Wintle.*

NUCLEUS (USA) 3 b.c. Nureyev (USA) 131 – Nellie Forbes (USA) 80 **102** (Secretariat (USA)) [1990 NR 1991 8g* 8m³ 10.4m⁶ 8g² 8d² 10m² 10m* 9f] tall, well-made colt: fifth reported living foal: closely related to fairly useful Irish 1m to 11f winner Ancient Times (by Nijinsky): dam, Irish 2-y-o 1m winner, is half-sister to Kentucky Derby and Belmont winner Bold Forbes: useful performer: won maiden at Salisbury in June and 4-runner minor event at Leicester in October: stays 1¼m: acts on good to firm ground and dead: visored last 3 starts, hanging badly right in apprentice race on first occasion: bandaged near-fore first 3 starts: should prove best with strong handling: ran in USA final start, and has joined D. Wayne Lukas. *J. H. M. Gosden.*

NUDGE THE FUDGE 2 b.f. (Apr 21) Ballacashtal (CAN) – Into The Fire 74 **32** (Dominion 123) [1991 5f 6d⁶ a6g⁵] 4,400Y, 4,000 2-y-o: sparely-made filly: second foal: half-sister to smart 3-y-o sprint plater Down The Middle (by Swing Easy): dam, stayed 1¼m here, won in Guernsey: poor form, including in sellers: blinkered on equitrack in July. *D. J. G. Murray-Smith.*

NUNIVAK (USA) 3 ch.f. Bering 136 – Snow The Judge (USA) (Court Recess **79** (USA)) [1990 7f³ 7f* 1991 10g 10.2m⁴ 8m⁴ 10g⁴] workmanlike filly: modest handicapper: unimpressive in appearance, creditable fourth at Newmarket final start, in July: better at 1¼m than shorter: acts on firm going: takes keen hold. *A. C. Stewart.*

NUN THE WISER (IRE) 2 b.f. (Feb 8) Commanche Run 133 – Welsh Abbey **39** (Caerleon (USA) 132) [1991 7f 7.5f 7m 8.9d] sturdy, close-coupled filly: moderate mover: first foal: dam unraced half-sister to Derby third Shearwalk and very useful middle-distance filly Santiki: poor maiden: bred to be suited by a good test of stamina: sold 900 gns Doncaster November Sales. *J. Berry.*

NUR (USA) 2 ch.f. (Mar 14) Diesis 133 – Shicklah (USA) 106 (The Minstrel **74** (CAN) 135) [1991 5m* 5m 5.1m³ 6g* 6.1m] sturdy, lengthy filly: moderate mover: fifth foal: sister to useful sprinter Ra'a: dam useful 5f and 6f winner at 2 yrs, from family of Habitat: modest performer: made virtually all to win maiden at Haydock in May (swished tail) and 19-runner nursery at Folkestone in October, running on strongly: gave impression something amiss (off course nearly 3 months subsequently) second start, ran poorly final one: should prove best at up to 6f: yet to race on soft surface. *H. Thomson Jones.*

O

OAK APPLE (USA) 2 ch.f. (Apr 27) Theatrical 128 – Virginia Hills (USA) (Tom **67**
Rolfe) [1991 7m⁵ 6.1m² 8.1g⁵ 7m 7g⁵] $155,000Y: leggy, close-coupled filly:
half-sister to Niniski (by Nijinsky) and 3 winners in North America: dam 9f winner:
quite modest maiden: ran poorly last 2 outings: stays 1m: acts on good to firm
ground: sweating (ran creditably) third start: has looked none too easy a ride. *B.*
Hanbury.

OAKBOURNE 3 b.c. Daring March 116 – Jacoletta 74 (Artaius (USA) 129) [1990 **52 d**
6d 6g 8d⁶ 1991 8g⁵ 8m 10f 8f 9m 9.7m] leggy, workmanlike colt: poor maiden:
bandaged, best effort in handicaps on reappearance: stays 1m: acts on dead going,
showed little on firm. *T. Thomson Jones.*

OAKHURST 3 b.f. Mandrake Major 122 – Rock Psalm (Saintly Song 128) [1990 **— §**
6m⁵ 6f³ 6m 1991 8d 6d 8g] leggy filly: moderate walker and mover: plating-class
maiden at best: has looked thoroughly temperamental. *Ronald Thompson.*

OAK PARK (IRE) 3 br.g. Prince Tenderfoot (USA) 126 – Louisa Stuart (FR) **65**
(Ruysdael II 122) [1990 7d 5.8m 6f⁵ 6g⁶ 6d a6g² a5g² a6g⁵ 1991 a5g⁵ a7g³ a8g² a6g²
a7g* 7d⁴ a7g 10.2g² 9d 10g] quite modest performer: won maiden at Lingfield in
March: tongue tied down, ran poorly last 2 outings: better at 1¼m than shorter: acts
well on equitrack, and seems suited by an easy surface on turf: winning hurdler for J.
Pickering. *R. W. Stubbs.*

OBELISKI 5 b.g. Aragon 118 – Pasha's Dream (Tarboosh (USA)) [1990 12v 12s* **53 +**
1991 10d⁴ a11g a14g] leggy, angular gelding: has a round action: plating-class
handicapper: better at 1½m and 1¾m than shorter: goes very well on soft going:
won over hurdles in March: trained until after second start by M. Tompkins. *P. C.*
Haslam.

O'BERON'S DAUGHTER 4 b.f. Fairy King (USA) – Precocious Angel **— §**
(Persian Bold 123) [1990 6m a8g⁵ a7g³ a7g⁵ 9g a8g⁵ 9f4 8d a7g a8g 1991 a8g⁵ a10g
12m] tall, leggy, narrow filly: poor maiden: stays 9f: acts on firm going: has been
mulish in preliminaries-temperamental. *R. Thompson.*

OBSIDIAN GREY 4 gr.c. Lyphard's Special (USA) 122 – Marcrest (On Your **61 +**
Mark 125) [1990 NR 1991 a5g² a7g*] sixth foal: half-brother to 2 winners, including
fairly useful Nadasdy (by Queens Hussar), a winner at up to 9f in Ireland later
successful in USA: dam won 5 races in Italy: twice raced: evens, won maiden at
Southwell in March by 8 lengths: looked sure to improve. *B. A. McMahon.*

OBSIDIAN KNIGHT 2 gr.g. (Feb 14) Belfort (FR) 89 – Haida (Astec 128) [1991 **—**
7m] 8,400F, 17,000Y: half-brother to several minor winners here and abroad: dam
poor half-sister to Lorenzaccio: soundly beaten in maiden auction at Leicester in
September: sold 1,000 gns Doncaster October Sales. *M. Bell.*

OCEAN AIR 3 b.f. Elegant Air 119 – Fandangerina (USA) (Grey Dawn II 132) **108**
[1990 7m* 8.2g* 8.2d² 1991 10d* 12.2g* 10m⁶ 12m² 10v²] good-topped filly: has a
quiet action: successful in listed race at Newbury and 2-runner minor event (9/4 on)
at Warwick in June: beaten little more than a length in slowly-run Prix de la Nonette
at Longchamp third start, about 2 lengths afterwards in Doncaster listed race
(behind Surrealist) and Group 2 event at Rome (behind Lara's Idea): effective at
1¼m and 1½m: acts on good to firm ground, probably on heavy: useful. *H. R. A.*
Cecil.

OCO ROYAL 2 b.c. (May 7) Tinoco 80 – Queen's Royale 80 (Tobrouk (FR)) [1991 **63**
6g 6g 7g³ 7g 8m 10m² 8m] leggy, quite attractive colt: third reported foal: half-
brother to 4-y-o Rocquaine Bay (by Morston): dam won from 6f to 1m: quite modest
maiden: second in Leicester seller (drifted right) penultimate start: will stay 1½m:
usually blinkered: sold 600 gns Ascot December Sales. *J. Ffitch-Heyes.*

ODILEX 4 b.g. Mummy's Pet 125 – Odile (Green Dancer (USA) 132) [1990 7m⁵ **66 d**
6f⁵ 8h* 8.5g* 8f² 1991 7f⁶ 7g⁶ 8m 7f 8g 11.7m⁶] sturdy gelding: modest handicapper
at best: below form last 4 starts: stays 8.5f well: yet to race on heavy going, acts on
any other. *N. A. Gaselee.*

ODOEN (USA) 2 b.c. (Mar 25) Capitol South (USA) – Charbon Risque (USA) **—**
(Bold Reason) [1991 6m] $3,000Y: fifth foal: half-brother to Coax Chad (by Coax Me
Chad), minor stakes winner at up to 9f: dam unraced: sire (by Roberto), Grade 1 6f
winner at 2 yrs, best at sprint distances: 50/1 and backward, slow-starting last of 14
in minor event at Ayr in September. *Denys Smith.*

O'DONNELL'S FOLLY 2 b.g. (Mar 9) Beveled (USA) – Silk Imp 72 (Imperial **57**
Fling (USA) 116) [1991 6m 7m⁴ 7s 7d⁵ 7g² 7m] 4,100Y, 9,500 2-y-o: leggy, quite

good-topped gelding: third foal: dam 1m winner stayed 1¼m: sire (by Sharpen Up) 7f to 9f winner: plating-class maiden: stays 7f: acts on good to firm and dead ground. *J. S. Wilson.*

OFFICER CADET 4 b.g. Shernazar 131 – Selection Board 75 (Welsh Pageant 57 132) [1990 10.6f 11f⁵ 8g* 10g* 11m⁵ 10.6d⁴ 9s 11d* a12g³ 1991 10g 10.4d 10g² 10g² 10d 10.2g² 11.8g² 14m⁴ 14m] close-coupled gelding: moderate mover: plating-class handicapper: effective at 1¼m to 1¾m: acts on good to firm ground, but ideally suited by some give: wandered markedly when blinkered: has hung left: sold out of J. W. Watts's stable 13,500 gns Ascot July Sales after sixth start: winning hurdler in November. *R. Curtis.*

OFFSHORE TRYST (IRE) 3 b.f. Try My Best (USA) 130 – Crestia (Prince 46 Tenderfoot (USA) 126) [1990 7m 7g 1991 8d 12m⁶ 7.6s⁴ 8.1g 8.3m 7g² 6g⁵ 6.9f] rather leggy, angular filly: poor maiden: needs further than 6f, and stays 7.6f: acts on soft ground: blinkered last 3 starts, running creditably first occasion: sold 2,500 gns Goffs November Sales. *R. Hannon.*

OFFSPRING 2 ch.f. (Apr 12) Move Off 112 – Spring Garden 54 (Silly Prices 110) — [1991 5g 6d⁵ 6m 8.2m] sparely-made, dipped-backed filly: first foal: dam poor maiden: seems of little account: blinkered third outing: once refused to enter stalls. *N. Chamberlain.*

OFTEN AHEAD (IRE) 3 b.f. Head For Heights 125 – Often (Ballymore 125) 108 [1990 7d 1991 11m² 12g² 12m⁴ 12m] IR 24,000Y: third foal: half-sister to Irish 7f winner Outeniqua (by Bold Lad) and quite modest 1990 3-y-o maiden Golden Loft (by Thatching): dam unraced half-sister to very useful Foiled Again: second in maidens at Naas and the Curragh: 150/1, improved effort when 5½ lengths fourth of 10 to Possessive Dancer in Kildangan Stud Irish Oaks at the Curragh, always close up: didn't reproduce that in Meld Stakes at same course in August: stays 1½m. *J. M. Canty, Ireland.*

OH DANNY BOY 7 br.g. Rabdan 129 – Musical Princess 66 (Cavo Doro 124) 50 [1990 10f 10m 10d 12m 12.8g² 10m 12g² 10m² 12.3m³ 12.3m 12.3g 10m³ 1991 12f² 12.3f 9.9f⁵ 12f 10m 13.8m] lengthy gelding: moderate mover: poor handicapper: effective at 1¼m to 1½m: probably needs a sound surface nowadays: goes very well with forcing tactics and at Beverley: none too consistent. *E. Weymes.*

OH MERCY (FR) 3 ch.f. Be My Guest (USA) 126 – Grammene (Grey Dawn II 88 132) [1990 6m⁵ 1991 7f² 8.5m⁵ 9g² 8.2f* 8g² 8.3m² 8f² 8d³ 8m*] well-made filly: has a quick action: fair performer: won maiden at Nottingham in July and minor event at Leicester in October: well worth a try at 1¼m: acts on firm and dead going: consistent. *H. R. A. Cecil.*

OH SO CHEEKY (IRE) 2 br.f. (May 15) On Your Mark 125 – Settled 61 (Blue 46 Cashmere 129) [1991 5f³ 6m⁶ 5m⁵ 5m⁵] small, close-coupled filly: sixth foal: dam won 3 races over 5f at 2 yrs: poor maiden: not seen out after August. *T. H. Caldwell.*

OH SO FINE 4 b.g. Welsh Term 126 – Miss Ultra Sound (USA) (Groshawk — (USA)) [1990 11.5m 10.1m 11.5g 1991 8.1d 12.1d] leggy, plain gelding: no sign of ability. *G. B. Balding.*

OH SO RISKY 4 b.c. Kris 135 – Expediency (USA) (Vaguely Noble 140) [1990 90 8m³ 11.5m* 12g 10f 1991 10g³ 12g] tall, useful-looking colt: fairly useful handicapper: wearing dropped noseband, good staying-on third in £11,160 event at Newmarket in May: better for race and stiff task in St Simon Stakes at Newbury 5½ months later: should stay 1½m: acts on good to firm ground: smart hurdler: goes well fresh. *D. R. C. Elsworth.*

OH SO ROSY 2 gr.f. (May 7) Lomond (USA) 128 – Red Rose Bowl (Dragonara 55 p Palace (USA) 115) [1991 6.1m] fifth foal: half-sister to several winners, including good sprinter Gallic League (by Welsh Saint) and 3-y-o 7f winner Bandol (by Blakeney): dam Irish 2-y-o 7f winner, is half-sister to Cesarewitch winner Private Audition: 5/1 and green, around 8 lengths seventh of 18 to Mount Helena in maiden at Nottingham in October, soon chased along then staying on closing stages: moved moderately to post: will stay 7f: should improve. *P. F. I. Cole.*

OKA FLOW 3 b.c. Vaigly Great 127 – Atoka 97 (March Past 124) [1990 7m 7s² 49 1991 9g⁶ 10d 10g⁶ a8g³ a11g4] leggy, angular colt: has a quick action: plating-class maiden: third of 6 at Southwell, soon behind and ridden along looking none too keen, then keeping on from over 1f out: stays 1m: blinkered last 3 starts: sold to join P. Blockley 3,100 gns Newmarket September Sales: not one to trust implicitly. *J. R. Fanshawe.*

OKAKU 4 b.g. Be My Guest (USA) 126 – Be My Darling 82 (Windjammer (USA)) — [1990 8m a8g a7g 8m 1991 a8g 7g] strong, good-topped gelding: seems of little account. *K. G. Wingrove.*

O K NURSE 7 gr.m. Mandrake Major 122 – Grisma (Grisaille 115) [1990 9m⁴ — 8.5m 1991 7m⁶ 7.5m⁶ 7g⁵ 8.5f] lengthy mare: behind in varied events. *J. Mulhall.*

OLD COMRADES 4 ch.g. Music Boy 124 – Miss Candine 66 (King Emperor **61** (USA)) [1990 5g 5m 5g⁵ 1991 5g 5m 6g 5.8f 5.1m 8.1d 8.1g 8m⁴ 8f⁶ 8f² 8f⁵ 8g* 7g⁴ 6.9f* 6.9s⁴] workmanlike, good-quartered gelding: poor mover: quite modest handicapper: won at Brighton (seller, no bid) and Folkestone in autumn: effective at 7f to 1m: acts on any going. *L. G. Cottrell.*

OLD DEFENSIBLE 3 b.g. Sulaafah (USA) 119 – Impregnable 66 (Never Say **56** Die 137) [1990 a7g a7g a7g⁶ a8g 1991 a8g⁴] narrow, very leggy gelding: plating-class performer: fourth in claimer at Southwell in January: will be very well suited by 1¼m + : sold to join S. Payne 1,950 gns Doncaster August Sales. *R. J. Muddle.*

OLD EROS 7 ch.g. Bold Owl 101 – Piccadilly Rose 63 (Reform 132) [1990 NR 1991 — a11g 14.1f⁶] workmanlike gelding: modest handicapper in 1988: behind only outings on flat since: stays 1¼m: best form on a sound surface: used to go well with forcing tactics: winning hurdler in March. *M. J. Ryan.*

OLD GLORY 3 ch.c. Valiyar 129 – Old Kate 110 (Busted 134) [1990 NR 1991 10d **67 p** 8.5f⁴ 7.1m² 7g*] fifth foal: half-brother to 4 winners, including very useful 11f and 1½m winner Kalakate (by Kalaglow) and 1¾m winner Take One (by Teenoso): dam 9f and 10.2f winner, is sister to very smart soft-ground stayer Old Bill: won maiden at Catterick in October, battling on well: will improve when returned to further: sold to join M. Saunders 14,000 gns Newmarket Autumn Sales. *G. Wragg.*

OLD HUBERT 10 ch.g. Gulf Pearl 117 – Wise Counsel (Counsel 118) [1990 15.3g **52** 18g³ 16.5d a16g* a16g 1991 a14g⁴ a16g³ 18s³ 17m] workmanlike gelding: plating-class handicapper: pulled up lame final run in 1991 (April): well suited by extreme test of stamina: acts on any going: effective with or without blinkers or visor: usually wears bandages. *A. Bailey.*

OLD MAN MOSE 2 br.c. (Feb 27) Simply Great (FR) 122 – Wharton Manor 86 **74 p** (Galivanter 131) [1991 7m 7m⁵] 9,800Y: leggy, close-coupled colt: has scope: half-brother to several winners, including 1¼m winner Palace Rebel (by Absalom): dam 1m: 20/1, over 3 lengths fifth of 20 to Modernise in maiden at Newmarket (easily better effort) in October, chasing leaders then staying on well not knocked about: will improve again, particularly at 1m + . *R. W. Armstrong.*

OLD PEG 3 b.f. Reach 122 – Lizarra 74 (High Top 131) [1990 7g 7s a7g a6g⁴ 1991 **55** 8d 7v² 7g⁶ 8d] rather angular filly: plating-class maiden: easily best efforts when in frame: stays 7f: acts on heavy going. *M. H. Easterby.*

OLD SPECKLED HEN 3 ch.f. The Noble Player (USA) 126 – Making Tracks **47** 79 (Sagaro 133) [1990 NR 1991 a7g⁵ a8g* a10g² a10g⁵ 10g 8.2f 10m* 9.7f³ 10.8m a8g] a **55** leggy, rather sparely-made filly: first foal: dam, 7f and 8.2f winner at 2 yrs, became disappointing: won claimer at Lingfield in January and seller (no bid) at Brighton in August: off course over 14 weeks before below form on equitrack final start: stays 1¼m: acts on firm ground. *M. J. Fetherston-Godley.*

OLD STEINE 3 b.g. Elegant Air 119 – Brightelmstone 105 (Prince Regent (FR) — 129) [1990 NR 1991 12m³ 12.3g³ 10g⁵] 62,000Y: quite attractive gelding: good walker and mover: closely related to 2 winners by Shirley Heights, including 1¼m to 11.5f winner Boon Point, and half-brother to 2 winners, including 6f (at 2 yrs) to 1½m winner Golden Torque (by Taufan): dam useful at up to 7f: well beaten in maidens: worth another try at 1½m: sold to join P. Hobbs 13,000 gns Newmarket Autumn Sales. *I. A. Balding.*

OLEJ (USA) 2 b.c. (Mar 5) Danzig Connection (USA) – Smarted (USA) (Smarten **43** (USA)) [1991 8.2f 7g] $130,000Y: smallish colt: first foal: dam won at up to 1¼m: sire won Belmont Stakes: poor form in autumn maidens at Nottingham and Salisbury: bred to be suited by middle distances. *Lord Huntingdon.*

OLETTE 2 b.f. (Jan 31) Rousillon (USA) 133 – Royal Loft 105 (Homing 130) [1991 **67 p** 7m³ 6.1m*] 42,000Y: rather leggy, plain filly: second foal: half-sister to 3-y-o 6.1f winner Desert Ditty (by Green Desert): dam 6f and 7f winner stayed 1m: favourite, won 12-runner maiden at Nottingham in August, leading travelling strongly, then rallying well: should stay 1m: seemed likely to improve again. *G. Wragg.*

OLIFANTSFONTEIN 3 b.c. Thatching 131 – Taplow (Tap On Wood 130) [1990 **70** 7g 1991 6f* 6d² 5m 7d 6g 5m] lengthy, angular colt: modest form: won maiden at Brighton in March: never dangerous in valuable handicaps last 2 outings, in June:

needs further than 5f, and is bred to stay 7f: acts on firm and dead going: sweating fourth start. *R. Simpson.*

OLYMPIC CHALLENGER   7 b.g. Anfield 117 – Calibina 101 (Caliban 123)   — [1990 a7g⁵ a6g 5g 6g³ 6g⁶ 6d⁵ 6g³ 6d 11g³ 1991 8s 11.1s⁶ 8f] lengthy gelding: has a rather round action: plating-class handicapper at 6 yrs: no form in 1991: needs further than 5f and seems to stay 11f: best with give in the ground: usually wears blinkers or visor: tends to get long way behind. *J. H. Johnson.*

OMORSI   4 b.f. Prince Tenderfoot (USA) 126 – Her Name Was Lola (Pitskelly   **35** 122) [1990 a8g⁴ 10.2f 10m 16m 12m² 12f³ 16.2g³ 1991 a12g a13g 12f 12f³ 12d 12g 16.2d⁶ 14.1f⁶ 16m⁶] leggy filly: poor maiden: should stay beyond 1½m: acts on firm ground: visored last 4 starts. *M. J. Fetherston-Godley.*

O MY DARLING (USA)   3 b.f. Mr Prospector (USA) – Midnight Pumpkin   **64** (USA) (Pretense) [1990 7g⁴ 7g 1991 7g⁶ 8m 8m⁶ 8g] good-quartered filly: quite modest maiden: may prove suited by further: sweating third (ran fairly well) start: bandaged last 2 starts. *C. F. Wall.*

ONCE IN MY LIFE (IRE)   3 b.f. Lomond (USA) 128 – No Disgrace (Djakao   **114** (FR) 124) [1990 6d 6g² 8d 6.5g* 1991 6v⁶ 7g⁴ 8d* 8g⁴ 8m* 8g³ 8g⁶ 9d⁵ 9s³ 10f] sturdy, workmanlike filly: closely related to 2 winners in France, notably Poule d'Essai des Poulains winner No Pass No Sale (by Northfields), and half-sister to French 1m winner Belle du Seigneur (by Kings Lake): dam French 2-y-o 7.5f winner on debut: successful in minor event (at 2 yrs) and April listed race at Evry, then Prix de Sandringham at Chantilly in June: good fourth to Shadayid in 1000 Guineas at Newmarket (taken very quietly to post) in between last 2 victories: ran creditably in Prix Jacques le Marois at Deauville, Prix de l'Opera at Longchamp and All Along Stakes at Laurel seventh to ninth starts: stays 9f: acts on good to firm and soft ground: blinkered on debut. *R. Collet, France.*

ONE DOLLAR MORE   3 b.c. Gabitat 119 – Burglars Girl 63 (Burglar 128) [1990   — NR 1991 8g 7d 6.1m] workmanlike colt: sixth foal: brother to fair 4-y-o 1m winner Usa Dollar and half-brother to 7f winner Red Dollar (by Tachypous) and fairly useful 5f and 6f winner Green Dollar (by Tickled Pink): dam sprinter: behind in claimer (pulled hard) and maidens: on toes last 2 starts. *B. Gubby.*

ONE FOR THE CHIEF   3 b.g. Chief Singer 131 – Action Belle (Auction Ring   — (USA) 123) [1990 7m⁵ 7g⁶ 8.2m 8.2g 1991 12.3s 12m 16m 16.2g] rather angular gelding: moderate mover: well beaten facing stiff tasks in handicaps and claimer in first half of 1991: gives impression doesn't stay 2m: visored twice. *R. M. Whitaker.*

ONE FOR THE POT   6 ch.g. Nicholas Bill 125 – Tea-Pot 77 (Ragstone 128)   **71** [1990 11s* 12f* 12.4f* 10v³ 12d4 12g* 13d² 12v* 16.5d⁴ 1991 13d* 18.4d⁶ 14g³ 13.4d⁴ 11.9g⁴ 11.9d³ 16.5d] strong, short-backed gelding: modest handicapper: won at Ayr in April: caught eye last 3 starts after returning from 3-month absence: best form at around 1½m to 2m: acts on any going, but particularly well on easy surface: held up, has turn of foot, and suited by strong gallop: has won for apprentice. *Mrs J. R. Ramsden.*

ONE HEART   6 ch.g. Seven Hearts 98 – Taryn 76 (Crooner 119) [1990 NR 1991   — a6g] compact, workmanlike gelding: poor plater: stays 12.5f: acts on firm going: often blinkered or visored. *R. J. Hodges.*

ONE MAGIC MOMENT (IRE)   3 b.f. Thatching 131 – Debutante 78 (Silly   — Season 127) [1990 a6g⁵ a7g² 6g⁴ 6d* 6m 1991 6g] leggy, workmanlike filly: quite modest winner at 2 yrs: bit backward in handicap in May, 1991: stays 7f: possibly unsuited by top-of-the-ground. *C. A. Cyzer.*

ONENINEFIVE   5 ch.m. Sayyaf 121 – Pink Ribbon (Riboboy (USA) 124) [1990   — 10f⁵ 12f 10f 1991 12f⁵ 17.1d 10.2f] seems of little account. *G. A. Ham.*

ONE TO NOTE   7 br.g. Star Appeal 133 – Town Lady 93 (Town Crier 119) [1990   — 12.2m 8m 1991 16g] smallish, lengthy gelding: moderate mover: quite modest handicapper at 3 yrs, has lost his form: tried blinkered once. *M. P. Muggeridge.*

ONLY FAIR   5 b.h. Prince Tenderfoot (USA) 126 – Lady Green Sleeves (Solinus   — 130) [1990 NR 1991 10v 10d] rangy ex-Irish horse: second foal: dam Irish sprint maiden: very lightly-raced maiden: bandaged and well beaten in 1991. *J. S. Moore.*

ONLY THE LONELY   4 b.g. Mummy's Game 120 – Izobia (Mansingh (USA)   — 120) [1990 7g 10f 1991 7.1d 10.1d] workmanlike gelding: good walker: has markedly round action: poor maiden: blinkered and no promise, including in selling handicaps in 1991: sold 1,650 gns Ascot July Sales. *G. B. Balding.*

ONLY YOURS   3 b.f. Aragon 118 – Welsh Jane 71 (Bold Lad (IRE) 133) [1990   **113** 6m³ 6f* 6m² 6m* 6m 6d⁵ 1991 7.3g⁵ 8g⁵ 8d 8g⁵ 7g 8m* 7g³ 7.3f* 8g⁴ 7m³ 7m² 9f] rangy, workmanlike filly: impresses in appearance: very useful performer: won Child Stakes at Newmarket and Hungerford Stakes (by ¾ length from Jimmy Barnie) at Newbury: ran creditably behind Shadayid in 1000 Guineas (beaten 3½ lengths), Bog Trotter in Kiveton Park Stakes at Doncaster and Mystiko in Challenge Stakes at Newmarket again, second, tenth and eleventh starts: behind in Grade 1 contest at Keeneland, USA, on final one: stays 1m: acts on firm ground: has turn of foot. *R. Hannon.*

ON THE EDGE 3 b.c. Vaigly Great 127 – Final Request 63 (Sharp Edge 123) **75** [1990 6g⁵ 6g 7s 6s 1991 a5g* a5g* a6g² a6g² a7g⁵ 6f⁴ 5m² 5g 5f 6f³ 5m³] quite attractive colt: modest performer: successful at Southwell in handicap and claimer in January: good third in handicaps at Yarmouth and Pontefract last 2 starts: effective at 5f and 6f: acts on good to firm ground, possibly unsuited by soft: has worn tongue strap: unseated rider (saddle slipped) ninth outing: mostly consistent. *T. D. Barron.*

ON THE HOP (IRE) 2 b.f. (Feb 16) Milk of The Barley 115 – Rapid Rhythm 63 — (Free State 125) [1991 5m⁶] 2,500F, 3,000 2-y-o: leggy, close-coupled filly: second foal: dam placed over 5f at 2 yrs, only season to race: 20/1 and green, slow-starting last of 6 in maiden auction at Haydock in August: bit reluctant stalls. *A. P. Stringer.*

ON THE LINE 3 b.c. Belfort (FR) 89 – Queen's Parade (Sovereign Path 125) — [1990 5m⁵ 5s* 1991 7m 7m] close-coupled colt: quite modest form when winner in April at 2 yrs: behind in handicap and claimer in spring as 3-y-o: joined C. Barwell. *M. H. Easterby.*

ON THE SAUCE 4 b.g. Kala Shikari 125 – Kingsfold Flash 50 (Warpath 113) **50** [1990 10.1g 8m 1991 10.8d 12f⁶ 14m 12.3d² 12d⁵ a16g⁴] lengthy, angular gelding: plating-class handicapper at best: stays 1½m: goes well on dead ground: visored final start (below form). *M. J. Haynes.*

ON TIPTOES 3 b.f. Shareef Dancer (USA) 135 – Pennyweight (Troy 137) [1990 **107** 5f* 5g* 5f* 6m⁴ 6m⁶ 1991 6m³ 5m 5.2m* 5m*] big, good-bodied filly: easy mover: useful performer: best efforts to win £6,800 event at Newbury in September by 1½ lengths from Duplicity and listed race at Newmarket in October, chasing leader then going on just inside final 1f, by ¾ length from Blyton Lad: off course 4 months after modest effort (sweating and very edgy) on reappearance: best at 5f: acts on firm ground, yet to race on soft surface. *J. P. Leigh.*

ON Y VA (USA) 4 ch.f. Victorious (USA) – Golden Moony (Northfields (USA)) **72** [1990 10g⁶ 10m 11.5m 10f³ 1991 7d* 7.6g⁴ a7g⁵ 7g² 8.2d⁴ 7v* 8g 7m 7s² 6.9s* a10g a 57 a7g a8g⁵ a7g²] sparely-made, angular filly: modest handicapper: won at Wolverhampton in April, Kempton in June and Folkestone in November: effective at 7f/1m: has form on firm ground, but seems very well suited by a soft surface: acts on fibresand: has drifted right. *R. J. R. Williams.*

OOZLEM (IRE) 2 b.c. (Apr 17) Burslem 123 – Fingers (Lord Gayle (USA) 124) **37** [1991 7g 7g] IR 3,600F, 5,400Y: workmanlike colt: half-brother to several winners, including useful middle-distance stayer Hollow Hand (by Wolver Hollow) and 5f (at 2 yrs) and 1m winner Premier Touch (by Petorius): dam, Irish 1½m winner, is out of sister to very smart sprinter Forlorn River: poor form in October maidens at Goodwood (slowly away) and Salisbury: will stay 1m. *C. A. Horgan.*

Child Stakes, Newmarket—
Only Yours and Trojan Crown beat the odds-on Satin Flower (left);
the other horse is Zigaura

Mrs M. Butcher's "Only Yours"

OPENING RUN (USA)   4 ch.c. Nureyev (USA) 131 – April Run 131 (Run The   —
Gantlet (USA)) [1990 NR 1991 9.7m³ 10.2g 12m] big, close-coupled colt: third
reported foal: half-brother to winners in Ireland at 1½m + by General Assembly and
Cure The Blues: dam well suited by 1½m +: changed hands 2,000 gns Ascot
February (1990) Sales: no show in maiden and amateur events in summer: sold
1,450 gns Newmarket Autumn Sales. *D. A. Wilson.*

OPERA GHOST   5 b.h. Caerleon (USA) 132 – Premier Rose 117 (Sharp Edge   **88**
123) [1990 12f² 12f* 12m* 12m* 12m* 12f 14g 13.3g 1991 11.9d⁴] close-coupled,
quite good-topped horse: carries plenty of condition: fair handicapper: burly on first
run for over a year, very good running-on fourth in moderately-run event at
Haydock in October: suited by 1½m: acts on firm and dead ground: most genuine. *P.
W. Harris.*

OPERA HOUSE   3 b.c. Sadler's Wells (USA) 132 – Colorspin (FR) 118 (High Top **112**
131) [1990 7m* 1991 10m* 10g² 12g⁴] leggy, close-coupled, quite attractive colt:
good walker: has easy action: very useful form: odds on, won 3-runner minor event
at Nottingham in September: beaten neck by Perpendicular in listed race at
Goodwood, 3¼ lengths behind Further Flight in strongly-run St Simon Stakes (led
over 5f out until approaching last) at Newbury: will prove suited by 1½m: can win
races in smart company. *M. R. Stoute.*

OPERATION WOLF   5 ch.g. Adonijah 126 – Sesta (Artaius (USA) 129) [1990 **100**
8m⁵ 9m⁴ 9g 10.2s 1991 10g⁵ 10m* 10g⁶ 10g⁵ 10.1f³ 8g² 10g³ 8m 9m 8d] lengthy,
good-topped gelding: carries plenty of condition: useful handicapper: won £7,800
event at Newmarket in April and ran really well in Royal Hunt Cup at Ascot and
Royal Hong Kong Jockey Club Trophy at Sandown sixth and seventh starts: ran
moderately after: effective over stiff 1m to 1¼m (has given impression worth a try
over 1½m): acts on any going: often bandaged: tough and genuine: sold only 3,000
gns Newmarket Autumn Sales. *C. E. Brittain.*

ORATEL FLYER 4 gr.c. Kirchner 110 – Hyperion Princess (Dragonara Palace **37** (USA) 115) [1990 a5g² 5f⁴ 5m 5m a5g 7f 7m 6g² 5f 7m 6f³ 5m 5.8d a6g⁴ a6g⁴ a5g 1991 5f 5m² 5m 5d⁴ 5d 5f 5m 5.3g a6g a5g a5g⁵ a6g⁶] close-coupled, rather angular colt: moderate mover: poor handicapper, still a maiden: stays 6f: acts on firm going: blinkered once: usually visored nowadays. *R. Thompson.*

ORBA GOLD (USA) 3 br.f. Gold Crest (USA) 120 – Miss Derby (USA) (Master **67** Derby (USA)) [1990 5f³ 5g⁴ 1991 7v⁴ 6d a7g* a7g² a7g⁴] lengthy, rather angular filly: keen walker: moderate mover: quite modest form on all-weather surfaces in summer: ridden by 7-lb claimer, won maiden at Southwell: may well stay 1m: bandaged last 3 starts: wore eyeshield on final one: flashed tail fourth start: sold to join R. Manning 3,400 gns Newmarket Autumn Sales. *P. Kelleway.*

ORCHANDA 3 b.f. Pennine Walk 120 – My Fair Orchid 71 (Roan Rocket 128) **42** [1990 6m 6g a7g⁵ 6m 8.2s⁵ 7d³ a8g⁶ 1991 7v⁴ 8g 8h² 10.5g 11m 9.2s] neat filly: bad mover: poor handicapper: should stay 1¼m: acts on any going: sold to join Mrs A. Knight 2,800 gns Doncaster November Sales. *M. J. Camacho.*

ORCHARD BAY 2 ch.f. (May 18) Formidable (USA) 125 – Green Pool 39 **47** (Whistlefield 118) [1991 5d⁵ 5d² 5f 5f³ 5m* 5m³ 6m² 5g⁵ 6d 7f⁴ 7f 5.7g a7g] 3,400Y: neat filly: second foal: half-sister to 3-y-o Local Dealer (by Scottish Reel): dam half-sister to Rich Charlie: modest plater: no bid after winning at Nottingham in May: stays 7f: best form on top-of-the-ground (well beaten on equitrack): sold out of W. Pearce's stable 1,100 gns Doncaster August Sales after ninth outing. *D. R. Tucker.*

ORCHARD'S PET 5 gr.g. Petong 126 – Toccata (USA) 64 (Mr Leader (USA)) **45** [1990 a6g a6g⁴ a6g a6g² a6g² a6g 8f 8f 7h 6h⁵ 6d² 6f 7m³ 6f⁵ a7g² a7g² 8f 1991 a8g³ a 50 a7g³ 7f⁵ 7g⁴ 8.5g⁵ 8.2d 7m a6g⁴ a7g] leggy, good-topped gelding: has a roundish action: poor handicapper: stays 1m: acts on firm and dead ground: effective with or without blinkers or a visor: suitable mount for apprentice. *W. G. M. Turner.*

ORCHID VALLEY (IRE) 2 b.f. (Apr 2) Cyrano de Bergerac 120 – Dane Valley **— p** (Simbir 130) [1991 7m] IR 1,500Y: close-coupled filly: half-sister to several winners, including 1987 2-y-o 1m winner Valley of Danuata (by Taufan) and 8.2f winner Gordons Dream (by Kafu): dam ran once: 33/1, backward and green, tenth of 13 in October maiden at Redcar, soon in touch after slow start, fading from 2f out and eased: should improve. *R. M. Whitaker.*

OREO COOKIE (IRE) 2 ch.f. (Feb 3) Thatching 131 – Kampai (General **63** Assembly (USA)) [1991 6m² 6m⁴ 8.3g] 12,000F, IR 32,000Y: strong, good-quartered filly: third foal: closely related to 1989 Irish 2-y-o 7f winner Dash of Courage (by Final Straw): dam lightly-raced Irish maiden daughter of smart sprinter Baby Brew: plating-class maiden: ran moderately (tended to hang) final start. *G. Richards.*

ORIEL (USA) 2 gr.f. (Feb 11) Maudlin (USA) – In The Bag (USA) (Lucky **—** Debonair) [1991 6g 5g 6.1m⁶] leggy, rather angular filly: poor mover: half-sister to several winners in North America, including Grade 3 8.5f-placed Debonair Dancer (by Staff Writer): dam winner at up to 1m: sire (by Foolish Pleasure) sprinter: poor maiden: not seen out after July. *J. Wharton.*

ORIENT AIR 3 b.f. Prince Sabo 123 – Chinese Falcon 81 (Skymaster 126) [1990 **66** 5f* 5m 1991 5f² 5m⁵ 5f 5f 6f 7m* 7m 7m 8m 7m] big, lengthy filly: quite modest handicapper: ridden by 7-lb claimer, won at Southwell in August, running on strongly to lead final 1f, flashing tail: needs further than 5f nowadays, and stays 7f: acts on firm going: blinkered fourth outing: sometimes slowly away: inconsistent. *T. D. Barron.*

ORIENTAL DREAM 7 ch.g. Northfields (USA) 132 – Jenny (Red God 128§) **—** [1990 NR 1991 16.2g 21.6f⁴] small gelding: quite modest handicapper on his day: behind in seller at Beverley and handicap (remote fourth, staying on steadily never near to challenge) at Pontefract in spring: best form at 1¼m: suited by the mud: usually visored, wasn't in 1991: possibly needs to dominate: ungenuine hurdler. *F. J. Yardley.*

ORIENTAL MUSIC 3 b.f. Music Boy 124 – Orien (Goldhill 125) [1990 5m⁴ 5g³ **54** 5g⁴ 6d 1991 5g³ 5f⁶ 5f* 7g⁵ 5m 5m 6m 8.2m] strong filly: plating-class performer: below form after winning maiden at Beverley in July: probably doesn't stay 1m, but should be suited by further than 5f: acts on firm going: joined R. Dickin. *J. Etherington.*

ORIENTAL NATIVE (USA) 4 ch.g. Raise A Native – Etoile d'Orient (Targo- **—** wice (USA) 130) [1990 8g 8g 6s 8.2g 1991 a7g 13.8d] strong, workmanlike gelding: no worthwhile form, including in handicaps: unlikely to stay 1m: has been blinkered and worn tongue strap. *P. C. Haslam.*

ORLEANS GIRL   4 b.f. Dixieland Band (USA) – Philassa (USA) (Forli (ARG))   —
[1990 5f² 6f² 6f⁶ 6g² 7m⁵ 10.1m 8g 5m⁴ 5.3f³ 6m 6g* 7g 7d 1991 a6g⁶ a6g] rather
sparely-made filly: moderate mover: quite modest handicapper at 3 yrs: below form
in January 1991: should have proved best at 6f or 7f: acted on firm going: dead. *R. J.
Hodges.*

ORPEN (IRE)   3 gr.c. Caerleon (USA) 132 – Caring (Crowned Prince (USA) 128)   75
[1990 NR 1991 8g⁶ a12g⁵] IR 140,000Y: sixth foal: half-brother to useful 1¼m and
1½m winner Bishop's Ring (by Northfields), later successful in USA: dam unraced
half-sister to Godzilla and dam of Grease: maiden, modest on one run in Ireland:
well-beaten fifth of 15 in claimer at Southwell in December: stays 1m: bought out of
M. V. O'Brien's stable 3,400 gns Newmarket October Sales. *W. A. O'Gorman.*

ORTHORHOMBUS   2 b.c. (May 5) Aragon 118 – Honeybeta 105 (Habitat 134)   91
[1991 5m³ 5m* 5g² 5.2g⁴ 6m⁴ 6.1m² 6.1s³] 11,000Y: workmanlike colt: second
reported living foal: half-brother to a winner in Norway: dam 9f to 1½m winner, is
daughter of Attica Meli: fairly useful performer: won maiden auction at Sandown in
June: best efforts in minor event behind Well Beyond at same course and in
Newbury Sales Super Sprint Trophy (beaten about ½ length by Paris House) next 2
starts: should be better suited at 6f than 5f: acts on good to firm ground, probably on
soft. *G. Lewis.*

ORUJO (IRE)   3 b.c. Try My Best (USA) 130 – Oyace (ITY) (Hogarth (ITY) 116)   80
[1990 8m* 1991 10m⁴ 12m³ 11.4m⁵ 10g] strong, close-coupled colt: fair form: not
seen out until late-August, running well in handicaps at Sandown (2) and Kempton
(£10,600 event) first 3 starts: looking very well, well behind in similar event final
start: will be suited by more strongly-run race at 1½m: sold 26,000 gns Newmarket
Autumn Sales. *Sir Mark Prescott.*

ORYNAC (IRE)   2 b.g. (Feb 15) Cyrano de Bergerac 120 – Flash Donna (USA) 70   —
(Well Decorated (USA)) [1991 7m] 20,000Y: smallish, lengthy gelding: first living
foal: dam modest maiden at 2 yrs well beaten at 3 yrs: 33/1 and very green,
slow-starting ninth of 10 in median auction at Wolverhampton in September: sold
4,800 gns Newmarket Autumn Sales. *B. Hanbury.*

OSARIO   4 b.c. King of Hush 118 – Welsh Jane 71 (Bold Lad (IRE) 133) [1990 7m²   112
7d⁶ 8m⁴ 6s 1991 6g*dis 6m 7.2g⁵ 6m⁵ 6d 6g 5m² 6s⁴ 7g* 7d³ 7v] big, robust,
angular colt: has quick action: impresses in appearance: capable of very useful form,
but difficult to train and none too consistent: first past post in £7,300 event at
Kempton (caused interference at start and placed last) in April and Group 3 event at
Goodwood (gamely by neck from Susurration) in October: very good third to
Danseuse du Soir in Prix de la Foret at Longchamp: behind in Group 3 event at
Milan final start: effective at 6f and 7f: acts on good to firm and soft ground: ran well
when blinkered fourth start: sold 44,000 gns Newmarket Autumn Sales after
penultimate start: reportedly stays in training in Italy. *R. Hannon.*

OSCILANTE   3 b.g. Swing Easy (USA) 126 – Lillylee Lady (USA) (Shecky   —
Greene (USA)) [1990 NR 1991 8g 7m 10m 8.3m] 1,550Y: leggy, lengthy gelding with
scope: moderate mover: second foal: half-brother to poor 1990 3-y-o Cheren Lady
(by Comedy Star): dam unraced daughter of half-sister to smart middle-distance
winner Salt Marsh: no worthwhile form. *R. Akehurst.*

OSGATHORPE   4 ch.g. Dunbeath (USA) 127 – Darlingka 77 (Darling Boy 124)   47
[1990 6m³ 7f³ 6m² 7m* 6m⁵ 6m 8m 6m 6g 7m⁴ 9f 8m⁵ 7d 1991 10d 10d³ 10.9g⁵ 12g]
big, good-bodied gelding: plating-class performer: stays 1¼m: acts on firm and dead
ground: below form when blinkered once: joined G. Richards. *E. Weymes.*

OSHAWA   4 br.f. Alzao (USA) 117 – O'Shaunessy (Charlottesville 135) [1990 8g⁵   88
10m² 10.2f* 12f² 12v 12g* 16.5d* 1991 10d⁴ 20g] rangy filly: fair handicapper:
bandaged, good fourth of 5 at Newbury: tailed-off last in Ascot Stakes later in June,
not seen out again: stays 2m: acts on firm and dead going (stiff task on heavy): has
run creditably for amateur: visits Marju. *B. W. Hills.*

OSSIE   2 b.c. (Apr 16) Nicholas Bill 125 – Ozra 63 (Red Alert 127) [1991 6f 8.1g 8m]   40
5,000Y: close-coupled colt: fluent mover: third foal: brother to 3-y-o Jimlil, fair 6f
winner at 2 yrs, now suited by 1¼m: dam 6f and 7f winner: poor maiden. *B. Palling.*

OUMALDAAYA (USA)   2 b.f. (Apr 3) Nureyev (USA) 131 – Histoire (FR)   84 p
(Riverman (USA) 131) [1991 6.1f⁵ 7m² 7g*] quite attractive filly: good mover: fifth
foal: half-sister to Hispanola (by Kris) 1m and 9f winner in France at 3 yrs and a
minor winner in USA by Touching Wood: dam won over 10.5f is half-sister to Grade
3 winner Hamada: progressive form: well-backed favourite (for third time), won
22-runner maiden at Newmarket in November, soon prominent after slow start and
keeping on really well: will stay 1m: likely to improve further. *J. L. Dunlop.*

Mr J. W. Barrett's "Our Fan"

OUR ACCOUNT (USA) 7 b.h. Private Account (USA) – Our Relation (USA) 83 **113**
(Ribot 142) [1990 12g² 12g* 12g³ 12g 12g⁵ 10s³ 20g³ 11g* 12g³ 1991 12d⁴ 12g³ 12d⁵
15.5g² 12.5g³ 15g 15.5m² 20d⁵ 15.5d] very useful French performer: ran well when
placed in 1991, including when 5 lengths third to Toulon in Prix Maurice de Nieul at
Maisons-Laffitte and 4 lengths second to Victoire Bleue in Prix Gladiateur at
Longchamp on fifth and seventh outings: stays at least 15.5f: probably not at best on
very soft going, but acts on any other: blinkered once: goes well with forcing tactics.
E. Lellouche, France.

OUR AISLING 3 b.f. Blakeney 126 – Mrs Cullumbine 60 (Silly Season 127) [1990 **72**
6m 7d⁵ 1991 9s³ 12m² 14f* 13.8m* 14g³ 13.8g* 16f* 16.2f⁴ 16m⁴ 14m] lengthy,
shallow-girthed filly: modest handicapper: successful, showing progressive form,
at Carlisle in May, Catterick in June and July, and Thirsk in August: suited by test of
stamina: acts on any going: ridden by claimer last 7 outings: bandaged on reappearance. *S. G. Norton.*

OUR AMBER 4 gr.f. Kabour 80 – Amber Vale 98 (Warpath 113) [1990 NR 1991 —
a6g⁶ a12g] second foal: dam, half-sister to very useful chaser Amber Rambler,
stayed 2m: tailed off in NH Flat races: no show in December claimers at Southwell.
D. W. Chapman.

OUR EDDIE 2 ch.g. (May 15) Gabitat 119 – Ragusa Girl (Morston (FR) 125) [1991 **46**
7m a7g] leggy, sparely-made gelding: has a round action: first foal: dam unraced
granddaughter of half-sister to Mr Fluorocarbon and Western Jewel: never a factor
in late-year maidens at Lingfield, slightly better effort on turf. *B. Gubby.*

OUR EMMA   2 b.f. (May 14) Precocious 126 – Miller's Daughter (Mill Reef (USA)   **53**
141) [1991 7m⁶ 6g⁴ 6.1m] 500Y: small, sparely-made filly: third foal: half-sister to
3-y-o Jewel of The Nile (by Glenstal): dam poor half-sister to Goodwood Cup winner
Tug of War: plating-class maiden: bandaged near-hind, ran moderately final start:
stays 7f. *Mrs Barbara Waring.*

OUR FAN   5 b.h. Taufan (USA) 119 – Crufty Wood (Sweet Revenge 129) [1990   **86**
5.8h 5d 5f⁵ 6g³ 6f² 6f² 5m⁶ 6m⁵ 5f² a6g 1991 6d⁶ 6m² 5f² 5f* 5g* 5f³ 6m 5d* 6d³ 6d
5m⁺ 5d* 5m³ 5f⁶ 6g⁶ 6f² 6m 6m] neat, good quartered horse: bad walker: much
improved handicapper in 1991: won at Hamilton and Thirsk in spring and at
Hamilton (2) and Pontefract in summer: claimed £10,010 final start: ideally suited by
5f: acts on any going with possible exception of very soft: ran well when blinkered
once: tough. *J. Berry.*

OUR FREDDIE   7 br.g. Cajun 120 – So Valiant 80 (So Blessed 130) [1990 5m³   **88**
5g³ 5f* 5f* 5m² 5m* 5m² 5g³ 5m⁴ 1991 5m 5s 5g⁶ 5g 5g 5g 5.1m² 5.2f] well-
made, quite attractive gelding: poor mover: useful and vastly improved at 6 yrs:
deteriorated in 1991, only form when neck second of 18 in handicap at Chepstow in
September: very speedy, and best at 5f: acts on any going: wears hood and blinkers:
suited by front-running tactics and tender handling: unbeaten in 4 outings at
Redcar: bandaged near-fore and withdrawn (refused to go down) once at 7 yrs. *W.
Carter.*

OUR JOHN   2 b.c. (May 24) Ballacashtal (CAN) – Ballyreef (Ballymore 123) [1991   **43**
5m 5.9h⁴ 5d 6g⁴ 5f⁴ 6f 8m a8g⁵] 850Y: good-topped colt: has a round action: third
live foal: half-brother to 3-y-o Bally Song (by Song) and middle-distance plater
Derry Reef (by Derrylin): dam poor granddaughter of Prix de Diane winner Belle
Sicambre: poor form in varied events, including sellers: ran respectably on fibresand final start: may stay 1¼m. *Ronald Thompson.*

OUR MAN IN HAVANA   2 ch.c. (Apr 21) Never So Bold 135 – Bellagio 68   **50** p
(Busted 134) [1991 a7g⁴] 18,000F, 19,500Y: fourth foal: brother to 3-y-o 7f winner
Vilany and half-brother to 6f to 1m winner Arany (by Precocious) and 1988 2-y-o 6f
winner Slice (by Sharpo): dam 1¼m winner, stayed 1½m: favourite, around 9
lengths fourth of 13 to Macs Bid in maiden at Southwell in November: should
improve. *P. F. I. Cole.*

OUR MARTHA   3 br.f. Sulaafah (USA) 119 – Before Long (Longleat (USA) 109)   **48**
[1990 8g 7d 7m 1991 7.1d⁵ 10g 8m⁵ a10g] workmanlike filly: poor performer: should
stay beyond 1m: acts on dead ground: not an easy ride: sold 1,150 gns Ascot
September Sales: winning hurdler for J. Roberts. *C. R. Barwell.*

OUR OCCASION   2 b.c. (Mar 15) Sizzling Melody 117 – Skiddaw (USA) (Grey   **72**
Dawn II 132) [1991 6d⁴ 6d³] 12,000F: leggy, close-coupled colt: third foal: half-
brother to 3-y-o Sweet Decree (by Known Fact) and 6f winner Lakeland Beauty (by
Mummy's Pet) later successful in USA: dam never ran: modest form in maidens at
Ascot (slowly away, green, kept on) and Doncaster (favourite, outpaced halfway,
stayed on behind Shujan) in autumn: will probably stay 7f. *R. Hannon.*

OUR PATRICK   3 b.g. Morston (FR) 125 – Sambell 71 (Sammy Davis 129) [1990   —
7f 1991 10g 7g 8.9g⁶] close-coupled gelding: no worthwhile form, slowly away in
handicap in June: bred to stay at least 1m. *K. White.*

OUR SLIMBRIDGE   3 b. or br.g. Top Ville 129 – Bird Point (USA) 87 (Alleged   **56**
(USA) 138) [1990 7m 7d 7g 1991 10.8d 12f 12.2m⁴ 12.5m³ 12.2m⁴ 11g³ 12m 8.2f 11.8g
12.3g³ 10m⁴] plain, rather leggy gelding: moderate mover: plating-class form: in
frame in handicaps, claimer, maiden auction and sellers: should stay beyond 1½m:
acts on good to firm ground. *C. N. Williams.*

OUR TOPSIE   4 b.f. My Dad Tom (USA) 109 – Tops 73 (Club House 110) [1990   **43**
7.2d⁶ 1991 6d⁶ 7g 6g 8m 6g 8.2m] workmanlike filly: poor, lightly-raced maiden:
seems to stay 1m: acts on dead ground, probably on good to firm: trained until after
fourth outing by H. Collingridge. *F. J. O'Mahony.*

OUR VISION   4 b.g. Vision (USA) – Faiblesse (Welsh Saint 126) [1990 7f* 7m   —
8m⁴ 9g 1991 12f⁶ 10.8m a12g] rangy gelding: moderate walker and mover: quite
modest performer at 3 yrs: below form in 1991, tailed off in seller final start: should
stay 1½m: acts on firm going: raced very freely when blinkered: trained reappearance by R. Holder. *L. J. Codd.*

OUT OF FUNDS   5 b.g. Ela-Mana-Mou 132 – Overspent 85 (Busted 134) [1990   **66**
18.4d 1991 12s⁴ 13.4d 16.2g 12g 11.7g] sparely-made gelding: moderate walker:
lightly-raced maiden, fair at 3 yrs but appeared on the downgrade in first half of 1991:
better suited by 1¾m than 1½m: best efforts on firm going: blinkered penultimate
start: joined M. Pipe. *R. Simpson.*

OUT OF STOCK   8 gr. or ro.g. Neltino 97 – Millingdale 65 (Tumble Wind (USA))   **31**
[1990 NR 1991 14d³ 14g] leggy gelding: poor maiden, very lightly raced: virtually
pulled up (reportedly lame) final start: worth a try over 2m: yet to show his form on
very soft going, probably acts on any other: tried blinkered once: has flashed tail
under pressure. *R. J. Hodges.*

OUTSTANDING BILL   5 ch.g. Nicholas Bill 125 – Hardwick Amber 58 (Tan-   —
firion 110) [1990 10.2f⁵ 10v 1991 a11g] leggy, close-coupled gelding: quite modest
maiden at 4 yrs: should have stayed 1½m: seemed to act on any going: was none too
genuine: dead. *J. M. Jefferson.*

OVERATIM (IRE)   3 ch.g. Hatim (USA) 121 – Our Bernie (Continuation 120)   —
[1990 NR 1991 7d 6m a7g⁴ a7g⁵ a10g a14g 6g] IR 5,200F, IR 4,000Y, resold 6,800Y:
sturdy gelding: sixth living foal: half-brother to fairly useful 7-y-o 5f to 7f winner
Tauber (by Taufan) and 2 winners at up to 7f by Ahonoora: dam second 3 times at up
to 1m in Ireland: fourth in maiden at Southwell: tailed off in handicaps last 3 starts:
worth a try at 1m: blinkered last 5 outings: wears bandages. *Mrs N. Macauley.*

OVERPOWER   7 b.g. Try My Best (USA) 130 – Just A Shadow (Laser Light 118)   **64**
[1990 8f⁵ 7.6d 10m² 10g³ 10h³ 10m 9g³ 8f⁶ 1991 8m² 8h³ 9d² 8.5f⁴ 10g 8g² 10m²
10.5g² 8.9g 10.5f³ 10.1f⁶ 10.5g⁵ 8m⁵ 10.1s a10g] sparely-made gelding: quite modest
handicapper: effective at 1m to 1¼m: probably not at his best on soft going, acts on
any other: visored once (below form): has looked none too keen: inconsistent. *M. H.
Tompkins.*

OVER SHARP   2 b.f. (May 28) Beveled (USA) – Over Beyond 78 (Bold Lad (IRE)   **42**
133) [1991 5g³ 5g⁵ 5m² 5m 5m 6m] 3,800Y: leggy filly: has a quick action: half-sister
to 3-y-o Beyond Our Reach (by Reach), successful at 5f (at 2 yrs) and 1m, and
several other winners, including 11.5f winner/successful jumper Tebitto (by
Derrylin): dam, placed at up to 9f in Ireland, is half-sister to good Italian winner
Pipino: sire (by Sharpen Up) 7f to 9f winner: modest plater: best form in spring first
3 starts: should stay at least 7f. *J. Berry.*

OVERT (USA)   6 b.m. Ben Fab (CAN) – Lady More Friendly (USA) (Villamor   —
(USA)) [1990 NR 1991 16.2g a12g] leggy mare: third foal: half-sister to a minor
winner in North America: dam won 3 sprint races: twice raced on flat and tailed off in
poor company. *B. A. McMahon.*

OWER (IRE)   3 b.f. Lomond (USA) 128 – Argon Laser 107 (Kris 135) [1990 7f² 7g   **71**
1991 8d⁵ 10d 7s³ 7m 7.1g² 8.1m 7g* 7d³] sparely-made filly: modest performer: won
maiden at Lingfield in October: effective at 7f and 1m: form as 3-y-o only with some
give in the ground: blinkered last 4 starts: bandaged near-fore first 5: sometimes
sweating: inconsistent. *J. L. Dunlop.*

OWLANDISH   3 b.c. Bold Owl 101 – Whipalash 73 (Stephen George 102) [1990   **39**
8.2s 8g 10.2s 1991 13g⁴ 11.1d⁵ 9f⁵ 8m] workmanlike colt: plating-class form at best,
including in handicaps: may prove best short of 11f: possibly needs a sound surface.
M. O'Neill.

OWLER   3 b.f. Slip Anchor 136 – Strigida 120 (Habitat 134) [1990 NR 1991 12f*   **78 +**
11.5g⁶] close-coupled filly: fourth foal: dam won Ribblesdale Stakes, and is daughter
and granddaughter of winners of that race: 5/4 on, impressive winner of maiden at
Beverley in April: co-favourite, set fair pace but soon left behind over 2f out in listed
race at Lingfield in May: may prove suited by greater test of stamina. *H. R. A. Cecil.*

OWNER'S DREAM (USA)   2 b.c. (Feb 17) Northern Baby (CAN) 127 – Glim   **81**
(USA) (Damascus (USA)) [1991 7d⁴ 7m² 8.1g³ 7d] 130,000Y: compact colt: first foal:
dam unraced half-sister to Glow (by Northern Dancer): fair maiden: well beaten,
pulling hard early on, in 16-runner nursery at Ascot in October final start: better
suited by 1m than 7f. *B. Hanbury.*

OWT ON   4 ch.g. Sweet Monday 122 – Young April 46 (Young Man (FR) 73) [1990   **50**
7f* 8g² 8.2s³ 7m 1991 7.5f 8d 10d 8f a7g a8g³ 10m³ 10.5m⁴ 10.1m* 11m² 12f 8m
10.3d] big, angular gelding: plating-class handicapper: won at Newcastle in August:
best at up to 11f: acts on any going: below form when tried blinkered and in
eyeshield: has flashed tail, and looked none too keen: hard ride: joined J. Fort. *M. W.
Easterby.*

OXBOW   4 b.c. Trojan Fen 118 – Shannon Princess (Connaught 130) [1990 8f 10m³   —
12g 12.3m⁵ 12v⁶ 12g² 10d² 1991 14.6s⁵ 16g] compact colt: good mover: modest
maiden at 3 yrs: no form in spring of 1991, blinkered final start: stays 1½m: acts on
good to firm ground and dead: effective with or without visor: winning hurdler in
March. *R. Akehurst.*

OYSTON'S LIFE   2 b.g. (Apr 7) Be My Guest (USA) 126 – I Don't Mind 97   **60**
(Swing Easy (USA) 126) [1991 6m⁶ 6g 5m* 6m⁵ 7m⁶ 7g] useful-looking gelding: has

plenty of scope: ninth foal: half-brother to fair middle-distance stayer/good hurdler Swingit Saunter (by Gunner B) and 4 sprint winners, including 3-y-o Dokkha Oyston (by Prince Sabo): dam won 10 races at 5f and 6f: won weak maiden at Pontefract in August: well beaten in nurseries subsequently: should stay at least 6f: has twice been bandaged off-hind. *J. Berry.*

<h1 style="text-align:center">P</h1>

PABOUCHE (USA) 2 b.c. (Mar 25) Roberto (USA) 131 – Lady's Slipper (AUS) (Dancer's Image (USA)) [1991 8m*] strong, useful-looking colt: fifth foal: half-brother to 7f winner on only start Aucale (by Nijinsky) and 2 winners in USA: dam good winner in Australia at up to 7f, stayed 1m: favourite but very green and better for race, won 15-runner maiden at Leicester in October by 2½ lengths from stable-companion Pavonis, niggled along vigorously over 2f out then staying on strongly: will improve, particularly over further. *H. R. A. Cecil.*   **78 p**

PACE E SALUTE 2 ch.f. (Apr 14) King Luthier 113 – Sagareina (Sagaro 133) [1991 6m 6m⁶ 6g 6m] small, workmanlike filly: good mover: first reported foal: dam little worthwhile form: fair plater: tailed off final start: will be suited by 7f +. *S. Dow.*   **48**

PACIFIC GEM 4 br.g. Valiyar 129 – Mary Martin (Be My Guest (USA) 126) [1990 7d 8.2f 7m³ 8.2s 10f⁴ 9m⁴ 10d⁵ 9m 8v 1991 10.1s 11.5g 9.7m] medium-sized gelding: modest handicapper at 3 yrs: no show in 1991, off course over 4 months before final start: stays 1¼m: acts on firm and dead going: trained first 2 starts by S. Sherwood. *R. Curtis.*   **—**

PACIFIC RIM 3 ch.g. Absalom 128 – Spare Wheel 67 (Track Spare 125) [1990 a7g² a8g* 1991 a6g* a7g] modest performer: ridden by 5-lb claimer when comfortable winner of claimers at Southwell: last of 7 in similar event at Lingfield in March: effective at 6f and stays 1m. *W. A. O'Gorman.*   **84**

PADDLE STEAMER (USA) 3 ch.c. Riverman (USA) 131 – Lovin' Lass (USA) (Cutlass (USA)) [1990 5g² 5g³ 6.5g⁶ 6g³ 7d⁴ 1991 7s* 7g* 7m⁶ 6g 10.4g⁵] angular, workmanlike colt: sixth foal: half-brother to several winners here and abroad, including fair 1¾m winner Demonstrable (by Alleged): dam stakes-placed winner at 6f and 7f in USA: trained by A. Fabre, successful in minor event at Evry in March and seller (sold 250,555 francs, approx £24,900) at Longchamp in April: seemingly out of depth in £11,900 contest (on toes) at Newmarket, Group 2 event at Rome and listed race at York afterwards: not seen out after June: stays 7f. *C. E. Brittain.*   **91**

PADDY CHALK 5 gr.h. Tina's Pet 121 – Guiletta 63 (Runnymede 123) [1990 NR 1991 6g 6g 6g⁶ 6g 5d 6g] leggy, workmanlike horse: fair handicapper nowadays: faced stiffish tasks in 1991: ideally suited by 6f: probably acts on any going: bandaged: genuine. *L. J. Holt.*   **80**

PADDY'S MATE (IRE) 3 b.c. Never So Bold 135 – Fraulein Tobin (USA) 71 (J O Tobin (USA) 130) [1990 NR 1991 7m⁴ 8.2fʷ⁰] lengthy, unfurnished colt with scope: second foal: half-brother to a winner in Italy by Chief Singer: dam 1m winner out of French 1000 Guineas second Fruhlingstag: 6¾ lengths fourth of 12 to Alfaares in Newmarket maiden, keeping on strongly: walked over in apprentice maiden at Hamilton in May: sold 9,200 gns Doncaster August Sales. *R. Guest.*   **73**

PADDY'S PASSION 2 b.c. (Jan 29) Superlative 118 – Pacific Princess 82 (Dom Racine (FR) 121) [1991 5g a5g⁵ 5s⁵ a5g 5m 7s] 3,100F: strong, deep-girthed colt: second foal: dam 6f (at 2 yrs) and 1m winner: form only when fifth in Folkestone seller: blinkered or visored last 4 starts: not seen out after August. *J. J. Bridger.*   **33**

PADDY TEE 3 b.g. Nicholas Bill 125 – Sabala 93 (Tribal Chief 125) [1990 6g 6g 7f⁴ 7m 1991 10m 10g 8g] leggy gelding: no form in handicap, claimer and seller at 3 yrs: should stay 1m: sold 1,100 gns Doncaster July Sales: won claiming hurdle in October for M. Pipe. *M. R. Channon.*   **—**

PAGEBOY 2 b.c. (Apr 4) Tina's Pet 121 – Edwins' Princess 75 (Owen Dudley 121) [1991 6g 7m 6g² 6m* 7g 6m² 6m⁴ 7m] 3,800F, 6,000Y: small, sturdy, good-bodied colt: second foal: half-brother to poor maiden Four Away (by Valiyar): dam disappointing 2-y-o 5f winner stayed 1m: fair performer: successful in Pontefract nursery in August: ran well in frame in similar events at Doncaster and Newmarket in autumn: below form fifth (reportedly struck into) and final (not knocked about) outings: should stay 7f: acts on good to firm ground. *P. C. Haslam.*   **80**

PAID UP FULL (USA) 2 b.c. (Mar 6) Greek Sky (USA) – Judi's Bobbisox (USA) (National Zenith (USA)) [1991 7f 7m⁵ 7m 8m] $5,000Y: workmanlike colt: **46**

613

second foal: dam unraced: sire (by Nijinsky) French 10.5f winner: poor maiden: best effort (at Chester) second outing: blinkered (tailed off) final one. *Mrs N. Macauley.*

PAINT THE LILY   3 ch.f. Claude Monet (USA) 121 – Screen Goddess 65   **52** (Caliban 123) [1990 6d⁴ 6s a8g³ a8g³ 1991 a8g* a8g⁵ a8g⁵ a10g 10f⁴ 12.2g* 11m 10.2d 10.1d a12g a13g] leggy filly: plating-class performer: won claimer at Southwell in January and seller (gamely, no bid) at Catterick in April: ran moderately last 5 starts, off course over 4 months before penultimate one: stays 1½m: seems to need some give in the ground. *D. C. Jermy.*

PA-JO   4 b.g. Uncle Pokey 116 – Darling June 60 (Midsummer Night II 117) [1990   — NR 1991 9f] leggy, close-coupled gelding: half-brother to 2 minor 2-y-o winners by Coded Scrap: dam won 6f seller at 2 yrs: 50/1, no show in Newcastle maiden in July. *J. H. Johnson.*

PALACEGATE GEM   2 b.f. (Apr 18) Skyliner 117 – Puff Pastry 78 (Reform 132)   **56** [1991 5m 5g* 6m⁴ 6d² 6m 6.1m⁴ 6m³] 3,000Y: angular, workmanlike filly: fourth live foal: half-sister to a prolific winner in Belgium by Daring March: dam 2-y-o 5f winner: fairly useful plater: won 11-runner event (retained 4,800 gns) at Pontefract in June on first run for 2 months: may well prove as effective at 5f as 6f: acts on good to firm and dead ground. *J. Berry.*

PALACEGATE GOLD (IRE)   2 b.c. (Mar 17) Sarab 123 – Habilite 94 (Habitat   **62** 134) [1991 5f⁴ 5m 6g* 7m 6m² 6f⁴ a6g* 6g³ 5m 6g] 5,600F: sturdy colt: has a quick action: half-brother to several winners here and abroad, including 1979 2-y-o 5f winner Primula Girl (by Mount Hagen): dam best at up to 6f: quite modest performer: no bid after winning sellers at Catterick and Lingfield (best effort) in summer: ideally suited by 6f: acts on firm ground: blinkered last 4 starts: sold 6,000 gns Doncaster October Sales. *J. Berry.*

PALACEGATE JEWEL   2 ch.f. (Apr 17) Red Sunset 120 – Choral Park (Music   **57** Boy 124) [1991 5m³ 5m² 5m⁶ 5h* 5f 5d] 2,500Y: smallish, rather leggy filly: second foal: half-sister to 1990 2-y-o 5f winner Warrior Prince (by Prince Sabo): dam poor maiden: plating-class form: has contested sellers: sweating and on toes, won auction event at Carlisle in September: tailed off in Wolverhampton nursery final outing: acts well on hard ground: trained until after penultimate start by J. Berry. *T. P. McGovern.*

PALACEGATE KING   2 ch.c. (Feb 11) King Among Kings 60 – Market Blues   **61** (Porto Bello 118) [1991 6m 7m³ 7m³ 7f⁴ 6f 5s⁵] 3,800Y: sparely-made colt: first reported foal: dam poor: sire 11.7f winner: improving maiden: best effort when fifth of 12 in auction event at Hamilton in November: stays 7f: seems well suited by soft ground. *J. Berry.*

PALACEGATE QUEEN (IRE)   2 br.f. (Mar 28) Milk of The Barley 115 – Up   — And At It 72 (Tamerlane 128) [1991 5f 6d⁶] workmanlike filly: has some scope: half-sister to several winners, including 1986 2-y-o 7f winner Spy Tower (by Tower Walk): dam 7f winner, is half-sister to smart Lordedaw: well beaten in late-season maidens at Beverley and Doncaster. *J. Berry.*

PALACEGATE RACING   2 b. or br.c. (Apr 13) Belfort (FR) 89 – Call Me Kate   **73** 72 (Firestreak 125) [1991 5g 5m⁴ 5m² 5f⁶ 6.1m² a6g² a6g* 6m² 6g 6g* a6g²] 7,200Y: close-coupled colt: eighth foal: brother to 3-y-o Katie Valentine and 2 sprint winners, and half-brother to a winner in Denmark: dam 4-y-o 1¼m winner: modest performer: successful in claimers at Southwell (made all) in August and Catterick in October: ran moderately final start: suited by 6f: possibly unsuited by very firm ground: tends to wander. *J. Berry.*

PALACEGATE ROYALE (IRE)   2 b.c. (May 18) Tender King 123 – Robin   **48** Red Breast 74 (Red Alert 127) [1991 5g 6d⁵] good-topped colt: third known foal: brother to 3-y-o 5f winner Pious Bird: dam 2-y-o 5f winner, is granddaughter of Irish 1000 Guineas winner Princess Trudy: better effort, fading from over 1f out, when fifth in claimer at Warwick in July: may not stay beyond 6f. *J. Berry.*

PALACE LADY   5 b.m. Ballacashtal (CAN) – Belle (DEN) (Comedy Star (USA)   — 121) [1990 11g 6g 7g 6m 7m 5d⁶ 6m 1991 a7g] tall, workmanlike mare: little sign of ability: tried blinkered. *T. Craig.*

PALACE STREET (USA)   4 ch.f. Secreto (USA) 128 – Majestic Street (USA)   **100** (Majestic Prince) [1990 8g² 8m⁵ 8m² 7.2s* 8d⁴ 7m⁴ 7.3g⁶ 8g⁴ 7d² 8m³ 6s 1991 6d* 6m 7g⁶ 7.2g⁶ 6g⁶ 7g 6d] close-coupled, wiry filly: keen walker: shows plenty of knee action: useful performer at best, winning listed event at Doncaster in March and running creditably in Newbury listed event fifth start: off course over 3 months before final one: best form at 6f or 7f with some give in the ground. *G. B. Balding.*

614

Courage Stakes (Limited Handicap), Newbury—Palatial Style laughs at the handicapper

PALATIAL STYLE 4 b.g. Kampala 120 – Stylish Princess (Prince Tenderfoot **111**
(USA) 126) [1990 7f² 8g* 9m 8m² 8g* 8m² 8f³ 10m 9g4 9m² 10.2g* 12s 1991 9m⁶
8.9m4 9m* 8.9g* 10m* 9m] leggy, angular gelding: much improved handicapper
for new trainer in 1991: won at Redcar and York (Andy Capp Handicap, always
prominent) in August and Newbury (£24,400 event, quickened clear in tremendous
style last 1f to beat Bold Bostonian by 7 lengths) in September: heavily-backed
favourite, lack-lustre eighth of 29 in Cambridgeshire at Newmarket: best at around
9f to 1¼m: best form on a sound surface: tough and consistent: joined J. Berry. *M. H.
Easterby.*

PALLIUM (IRE) 3 b.c. Try My Best (USA) 130 – Jungle Gardenia (Nonoalco **79**
(USA) 131) [1990 5g⁵ 6g 5f² 5m² 5m⁶ 1991 5s 5g³ 5g³ 5g³ 5m* 5m³ 5m² 5g 5m* 5g
6m] good-bodied colt: modest handicapper: successful at Wolverhampton in May
and in minor event at Haydock in August: below form last 2 starts: should stay 6f:
best efforts on top-of-the-ground: on toes last 3 starts: visored last 3 at 2 yrs: has
hung right. *M. P. Naughton.*

PALM HOUSE 6 ch.g. Coquelin (USA) 121 – Kew Gift (Faraway Son (USA) 130) —
[1990 NR 1991 12g] lengthy, angular gelding: good mover: lightly raced and no
worthwhile form on flat: should be suited by further than 11f: winning but ungenuine
jumper. *G. Richards.*

PALMION 9 b.g. Dominion 123 – Blessed Palm 76 (St Paddy 133) [1990 a7g 1991 —
a10g] lengthy, attractive gelding: quite modest handicapper in 1987: twice raced
since and no show: best over 7f or easy 1m: yet to show his form on soft going, acts
on any other. *R. Curtis.*

PALM LAGOON (IRE) 2 ch.g. (Mar 20) Thatching 131 – Deepwater Blues 91 **67**
(Gulf Pearl 117) [1991 6g³ 6f4] 48,000F, IR 45,000Y: strong gelding: half-brother to
1988 2-y-o 5f winner Command Bid (by Auction Ring) and a winner in Norway: dam,
2-y-o 5f winner, is sister to top-class sprinter Deep Diver and half-sister to Irish
2000 Guineas winner King's Company: better for race, quite modest form in
maidens at Folkestone in October, edging right latter occasion: moved moderately
to post on debut: sold 5,200 gns Newmarket Autumn Sales. *G. Harwood.*

PALM SWIFT 5 b.m. Rabdan 129 – Swiftsand 65 (Sharpen Up 127) [1990 12m a7g —
1991 11.7m 8f] leggy mare: no worthwhile form, including in handicaps. *A. J.
Chamberlain.*

PALOMELLE (FR) 2 b.f. (Apr 28) Moulin 123 – Pacific Drive (FR) (Kenmare **98**
(FR) 125) [1991 6g 6g* 5.5g⁵ 7.5g 9g* 8g 8s*] third foal: half-sister to French 8.5f
and 11f winner Palata (by Darly): dam French 1m winner: successful in claimers at
Maisons-Laffitte (claimed out of H. Samani's stable £13,600) and Evry in September
and in Prix des Reservoirs (easily best effort, beat Battle Quest a short neck) at
Longchamp in October: will stay 1¼m: acts well on soft ground. *A. Spanu, France.*

PAMIANBE 3 ch.f. Music Boy 124 – City Link Rose (Lochnager 132) [1990 6m —
1991 8.5m 5f 6.1m] big, plain filly: has a round action: no sign of ability: bandaged last
3 starts: sold 1,400 gns Newmarket Autumn Sales. *D. A. Wilson.*

PAMPAS GRASS 2 ch.f. (Apr 20) Primo Dominie 121 – Open Country (Town **44** And Country 124) [1991 5.1d³ a6g⁴ 6m⁴ 5g⁶] neat filly: moderate mover: fifth foal: dam never ran: poor maiden: would probably have stayed 7f: bandaged first 2 starts: dead. *A. N. Lee.*

PANCHELLITA (USA) 2 b.f. (Feb 27) Pancho Villa (USA) – Counselor's Pride **78** (USA) (Good Counsel (USA)) [1991 6g² 6m* 7d³] $150,000Y: workmanlike filly: has plenty of scope: third foal: dam thrice-raced half-sister to 8 winners: sire, good-class sprinter/miler, is half-brother to Royal Academy: modest performer: well-backed second favourite, won maiden at Redcar in August, despite edging noticeably right under pressure: 5/1 and backward, below-form last of 3 in minor event at Chester over 10 weeks later: should stay 7f. *Denys Smith.*

PANCHOS PEARL (USA) 3 b.f. Pancho Villa (USA) – Jackie Pearl (USA) **93** (Ruffled Feathers) [1990 6d³ 6m² 6f* 6m 6m* 6d³ 6m 1991 7m³ 8m⁴ 7.3d³ 6m² 6g 6m⁵ 6m 6m] angular, unfurnished filly: has a fluent, round action: quite useful performer: in frame in £11,900 event, listed race and handicaps: below form last 2 starts: stays 1m: acts on firm and dead ground: consistent. *Mrs J. Cecil.*

PANDESSA 4 b.f. Blue Cashmere 129 – Jeanne du Barry 74 (Dubassoff (USA)) **37** [1990 6m⁶ 8m 1991 12.1f³ 11.8g] lengthy, unfurnished, plain filly: very lightly raced and poor form on flat: stays 12.1f: acts on firm ground: winning hurdler. *Mrs G. R. Reveley.*

PANDY 5 b.g. Thatching 131 – Hot Stone (Hotfoot 126) [1990 10m³ 10.4d 10f⁵ 9m² **73** 10m² 11f* 10.6m³ 10.5g⁴ 1991 10.1g⁵ 12g⁵ 13.3d² 12d] lengthy gelding: has a quick action: modest handicapper: not seen out after June: stays 13f: acts on firm and dead going: well below form for amateur. *G. Thorner.*

PANEL GAME 7 ch.m. Lepanto (GER) – Silly Games 62 (Siliconn 121) [1990 NR — 1991 a12g⁶] leggy, sparely-made mare: bad maiden. *P. Butler.*

PANICO 4 b.c. Superlative 118 – Ex Dancer (USA) (Executioner (USA)) [1990 7g⁶ **44** 6g 8f³ 10m 8f² 8m 7.2d⁴ 1991 8.1g⁶ 9g⁶ 9m] strong colt: poor handicapper, still a maiden: stays 1m well: acts on firm and dead going: effective visored or not: has put head in air. *Miss S. E. Hall.*

PANIC RISING (USA) 3 b.g. Master Willie 129 – Sticky Habit 79 (Habitat 134) **63** [1990 6d 1991 10m 11.5m⁵ 10m a10g³ a12g² a12g] strong, angular gelding: poor mover: quite modest maiden: better at 1½m than shorter: broke leg at Southwell in August: dead. *C. A. Cyzer.*

PANIENKA (POL) 7 b.m. Dom Racine (FR) 121 – Pointe Rousse (FR) (Mar- — gouillat (FR) 133) [1990 16g 1991 16s] good-topped mare: quite modest handicapper as 4-y-o: soundly beaten only 2 subsequent outings, finishing lame on reappearance at 7 yrs: suited by test of stamina: possibly unsuited by firm going and used to act well on soft. *D. W. Chapman.*

PANIKIN 3 gr.g. Red Sunset 120 – Haunting 79 (Lord Gayle (USA) 124) [1990 **99** a7g* a6g⁴ 7s³ 7s 1991 7m⁵ 7.2m* 7.6d³ 6m* 8m⁵ 6g 6g 6m] leggy, close-coupled gelding: fairly useful handicapper: improved to win at Haydock in May and Newmarket (in good style) in July: below form last 2 starts: suited by 6f: yet to race on firm going, probably acts on any other. *J. Wharton.*

PANORAMIC 4 b.c. Rainbow Quest (USA) 134 – Immense (USA) (Roberto **120** (USA) 131) [1990 11s* 12g* 12m⁵ 12g² 12v 1991 10g* 10.5g⁶ 10g³ 12m⁵ 12m² 12f²] very smart French performer: successful at Longchamp in Group 2 Prix d'Harcourt in April to 1½ lengths from Sikeston: ran well final 2 starts behind Splash of Colour in Prix Foy at Longchamp and Sky Classic in Grade 1 Rothmans International at Woodbine: effective at 1¼m to 1½m: seems unsuited by heavy going, acts on any other: consistent. *A. Fabre, France.*

PANSONG 5 b.h. Absalom 128 – Sea Chant (Julio Mariner 127) [1990 8m 5g 8f a7g — 10m 7.6m 10.8f a11g 1991 a7g] leggy horse: poor walker and mover: fair plater at best: has lost his form: stays 1¼m: probably acts on any going: sometimes blinkered or visored. *B. A. McMahon.*

PAPAL LEGATE (USA) 4 ch.c. Deputy Minister (CAN) – Youcanbelieveit **79** (USA) (Hearts of Lettuce (USA)) [1990 8g³ 8g⁶ 9s⁴ 10g⁶ 12m³ 1991 10.8d* 10m] strong, lengthy colt: carries plenty of condition: poor mover: third reported foal: half-brother to a minor winner in the States by Miswaki: dam minor winner at up to 9f in USA: ex-Irish performer: won maiden at Warwick, rallying well despite drifting left: bandaged off-fore, creditable one-paced eighth in £7,800 handicap at New-market later in April: sweating, refused to enter stalls final intended start (May): will prove suited by return to stiffer test of stamina (stays 1½m): acts on good to firm and dead ground: trained at 3 yrs by T. Stack. *P. W. Chapple-Hyam.*

PAPA WESTRAY 2 b.c. (Jun 7) Scottish Reel 123 – Bronze Princess 72 (Hul A **56**
Hul 124) [1991 6m 6m 5f³ 6m] 2,600F: strong colt: has scope: poor mover: half-
brother to 8.2f and 11f winner Normhurst (by Lucky Wednesday) and winners
abroad by Monsanto and Blue Cashmere: dam won twice over 5f at 2 yrs: plating-
class maiden: below form (not knocked about) in Ripon nursery final start (August):
should be suited by further than 5f. *T. D. Barron.*

PAPER CLIP 2 b.f. (Apr 30) Jalmood (USA) 126 – Westonepaperchase (USA) 71 **66**
(Accipiter (USA)) [1991 7g 7g² 8d⁴ a8g² a8g² a8g*] 3,000F: small, sturdy filly: third
foal: dam once-raced (at 2 yrs) daughter of half-sister to smart Prides Profile: quite
modest performer: second in seller second start: didn't need to improve when
winning late-year Lingfield maiden by ¾ length from Mystery Lad: will stay 1¼m. *J.
D. Bethell.*

PAPER DANCE 3 b.g. Mashhor Dancer (USA) – April Days 75 (Silly Season **66**
127) [1990 8m³ 8g 7m 1991 10.2g* 10g³ 12d 10g² 10.2g 11.8m] rangy, shallow-girthed
gelding: turns off-fore out: easy mover: quite modest handicapper: won at Bath in
April: well below form last 2 starts, pulling hard and front rank 9f on final one: suited
by 1¼m: possibly best on a sound surface: has given trouble in preliminaries: gelded
after final outing. *R. J. Holder.*

PAPER DART (USA) 3 b.c. Lear Fan (USA) 130 – Forelie 88 (Formidable **79 d**
(USA) 125) [1990 7m⁶ 6d² 7g 1991 8g² 7g³ 7.6g² 8d² 8.5m 8m 8.9m 8.5f² 7m² 7g³
8m⁴ 8g 7m 6.9f⁵ 8g] modest maiden: placed in 5 handicaps, a maiden auction race
and a maiden in 1991: seems suited by an easy surface: carries head high,
and doesn't find much off bridle: sold 7,200 gns Newmarket Autumn Sales: not one
to trust. *P. T. Walwyn.*

PAPER KNIFE (IRE) 2 b.c. (Feb 11) Sure Blade (USA) 130 – Red Letter Day **62 p**
100 (Crepello 136) [1991 8s⁶ 7g⁵] 92,000F: workmanlike, rather close-coupled colt:
half-brother to 1982 2-y-o 5f winner Holy Day (by Sallust) and useful 3-y-o Redden
Burn (by Green Desert), successful from 6f (at 2 yrs) to 8.9f: dam won over 6f and
1m: quite modest form in maidens at Kempton (eased when beaten) and Warwick
(never a factor) in autumn: should do better when given stiffer test of stamina: sold
12,000 gns Newmarket Autumn Sales. *Major W. R. Hern.*

PAPER SHOES 5 b.m. Workboy 123 – Two Friendly 54 (Be Friendly 130) [1990 **52**
a5g⁴ a6g 5g⁴ a5g 5f² 5g 5d⁵ 5s³ a5g* a5g⁶ 1991 5d² a5g⁶ a5g⁵ a5g³ a5g 5f] leggy
mare: plating-class handicapper: best at 5f: seems to act on any going: effective with
or without blinkers: inconsistent. *R. Earnshaw.*

PAQUERETTE 3 b.f. Crofthall 110 – Bouchette 76 (Current Coin 118) [1990 6m **40 §**
1991 12m⁴ 11m⁴ 9.9m 10d 12d 10f⁴ 10g⁵ 10m] plain filly: moderate mover: poor
maiden: stays 1½m: acts on firm and dead ground: blinkered (found nil and carried
head high) final start: inconsistent and one to be wary of. *A. Smith.*

PARADIGM'S VISION (IRE) 3 b.f. Vision (USA) – Echo Repeating **—**
(Ballymore 123) [1990 7.5g⁶ 7f⁶ 8m 10.6s 1991 12d 12.1d⁵ 12f] leggy, sparely-made
filly: poor mover: poor maiden: well beaten at 3 yrs, including in selling handicaps:
should stay beyond 1m. *A. Harrison.*

PARADISE FORUM 2 ch.f. (Feb 25) Prince Sabo 123 – Sovereign Love 75 (He **78**
Loves Me 120) [1991 5g⁴ 5g⁶ 5m³ 5.1f* 5m³ 5m² 5d³] sparely-made filly: first foal:
dam 1m winner: modest perfomer: won nursery at Nottingham in September: ran
well in similar events afterwards, behind Isaiah at Newmarket final outing: worth a
try at 6f: acts on firm and dead ground: sold to join C. Horgan 14,000 gns Ascot
November Sales. *Lord Huntingdon.*

PARADISE WAY 2 b.f. (Feb 8) Dominion 123 – Remoosh (Glint of Gold 128) **77**
[1991 6m* 7d⁴ 7d⁶] lengthy, good-bodied filly: first foal: dam poor half-sister to
high-class 1985 2-y-o 5f and 6f winner Nomination (by Dominion) out of sister to
very useful stayer and good hurdler Decent Fellow: modest performer: won maiden
at Ascot in June: creditable fourth of 5 to Musicale in Prestige Stakes at Goodwood 2
months later: well beaten in Ascot minor event won by Red Slippers final start: will
stay 1m. *P. F. I. Cole.*

PARBOLD HILL 3 ch.c. Carwhite 127 – Coppice (Pardao 120) [1990 8.2m 8.5m⁶ **—**
8g 1991 10m] leggy, close-coupled colt: well beaten all races, including in handicap
in May. *K. R. Burke.*

PAR DE LUXE 4 b.f. Superlative 118 – Parbold 54 (Sassafras (FR) 135) [1990 7g³ **57 d**
8.5g⁵ 1991 7d⁶ 7.5g 10f 5m² 6d⁴ 5m 8f⁵ 7m 5g 6.1m³ 6m 6m] workmanlike filly:
moderate mover: poor handicapper: none too consistent, and still a maiden: effective at 5f, and probably stays 8.5f: acts on good to firm and dead ground: effective
blinkered or not: twice below form when visored: hard ride. *B. W. Murray.*

PAR

PAREVA (USA) 4 b.c. Pas Seul (USA) – Bare Eva (USA) (Barrera (USA)) [1990 11v a12g 1991 9s 8.5f a11g a8g 9.9f 10m 8.3d 8g 8m] medium-sized colt: seems of little account. *J. S. Wainwright.* —

PARFAIT AMOUR 2 ch.f. (Mar 26) Clantime 101 – Chablisse 69 (Radetzky 123) **68** [1991 6m3 6g3 5.9h* 6m] lengthy, sparely-made filly: first foal: dam won sellers from 1¼m to 1½m: quite modest performer: won maiden at Carlisle in September, running on well after getting bumped 2f out: below form in minor event at Ayr 10 days later: will probably stay 7f: acts on hard ground. *R. M. Whitaker.*

PARFUM D'AUTOMNE (FR) 3 b.f. Sharpen Up 127 – Leaf Fall (FR) **—** (Lyphard (USA) 132) [1990 NR 1991 7g 8g 8g 8.9m 7g] 500,000 francs (approx £46,300) Y: leggy filly: sixth reported foal: dam French 3-y-o 7.5f and 1m winner from useful family: no worthwhile form, including in handicap. *W. J. Haggas.*

PARIOS (FR) 3 ch.c. Sicyos (USA) 126 – Parga (FR) (Gay Mecene (USA) 128) **102** ? [1990 5g4 5m4 5m 5m3 5d2 5g 1991 6m* 6g4 6m6 5g* 5m6 5f5 6m 5g6 5m4] work-manlike colt: made all in maiden at Newmarket in April and handicap (blinkered first time and making all, extremely impressively) at Doncaster in July: 100/1, excellent 2¼ lengths fourth of 10 to On Tiptoes in listed race at Newmarket final start, clear lead long way: very speedy, best at 5f: acts on good to firm and dead going: edgy (below form) sixth and seventh starts: blinkered and taken down early last 6 starts: wears dropped noseband: sold 21,000 gns Newmarket Autumn Sales. *J. W. Payne.*

PARISH CHIMES (IRE) 3 b. or br.f. Dalsaan 125 – Parish Bell (Monseigneur **—** (USA) 127) [1990 6m a6g4 a7g6 1991 a6g] IR 700F: small, good-bodied filly: plating-class maiden: well beaten on all-weather: sold 2,100 gns Ascot May Sales. *R. Guest.*

PARIS HOUSE 2 gr.c. (Mar 20) Petong 126 – Foudroyer (Artaius (USA) **111** 129) [1991 5d* 5d* 5m* 5g* 5m2 5.2g* 5g2 5m* 5d]

Paris House's bold bid to become the first two-year-old since Ennis in 1956 to win the Keeneland Nunthorpe Stakes (two-year-olds were excluded from the race between 1981 and 1985) withered in the final sixty yards. From shortly before halfway, where he'd swept past the American challenger Klassy Briefcase into the lead, Paris House had kept his eight rivals at bay quite comfortably; but as the winning post came up, his stride shortened suddenly and he had nothing in reserve as Sheikh Albadou powered past to take the prize by a length and a half. The participation of Paris House, as well as that of Klassy Briefcase, the Irish colt Title Roll and French filly Divine Danse, compensated in interest for what the race lost in quality through the

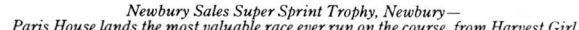

Newbury Sales Super Sprint Trophy, Newbury—
Paris House lands the most valuable race ever run on the course, from Harvest Girl

Flying Childers Stakes, Doncaster—Paris House continues to do connections proud

absence of such as Polish Patriot and Lycius. The presence of the exposed five-year-old Blyton Lad just a neck behind Paris House in third suggests the Nunthorpe was substandard; and furthermore Paris House, in our opinion, was favoured to the tune of approximately 6 lb, or two lengths, by the official scale of weight-for-age. Nonetheless, all credit to Paris House. His was a splendid effort which surpassed anything he'd achieved previously.

Paris House gained the first of Jack Berry's ninety two-year-old successes in a season which saw the trainer break several records, most of which he'd set himself in the preceding two years. Not only did he establish a new mark—for the third successive season—for the number of two-year-old winners trained, he also surpassed his previous best overall total (one hundred and twenty-seven) by sending out one hundred and forty-three winners and for good measure also notched the fastest hundred (which he achieved on July 17th) as well as the fastest fifty. However, his youngsters managed only one success in pattern races, the Flying Childers Stakes at Doncaster in September, between them. Paris House started at short odds to account for four opponents and repeat the stable's success in the race the previous year with Distinctly North, and did so comfortably, without improving on his Nunthorpe form, by two and a half lengths and the same from Power Lake and Colway Bold. Paris House's final run came in the Ciga Prix de l'Abbaye at Longchamp in October. His trainer had expressed worries at Doncaster that the colt might have had enough for the year and although he looked none the worse for his long season in the paddock at Longchamp he came back last of the fourteen runners, eased after weakening a furlong and a half out. Nevertheless, Paris House had given his connections plenty of enjoyment and no little success throughout the year. He had followed up his Doncaster maiden win on Lincoln day with pillar-to-post victories in auction events at Ripon, Pontefract and Newmarket and had bounced back to winning ways in the inaugural running of the valuable Newbury Sales Super Sprint Trophy (a race restricted to horses bought at selected sales for less than 30,000 guineas) after surrendering his unbeaten record to Magic Ring, who was a length and a half too good for him, in an above-average Norfolk Stakes at Royal Ascot.

	Petong	Mansingh	Jaipur
	(gr 1980)	(b 1969)	Tutasi
Paris House		Iridium	Linacre
(gr.c. Mar 20, 1989)		(gr 1969)	Tula Melody
	Foudroyer	Artaius	Round Table
	(ch 1980)	(b 1974)	Stylish Pattern
		Foudre	Petingo
		(b 1975)	Lighted Lamp

In common with most of Jack Berry's two-year-olds, the well-grown, lengthy Paris House, who thrived physically during the year, was acquired

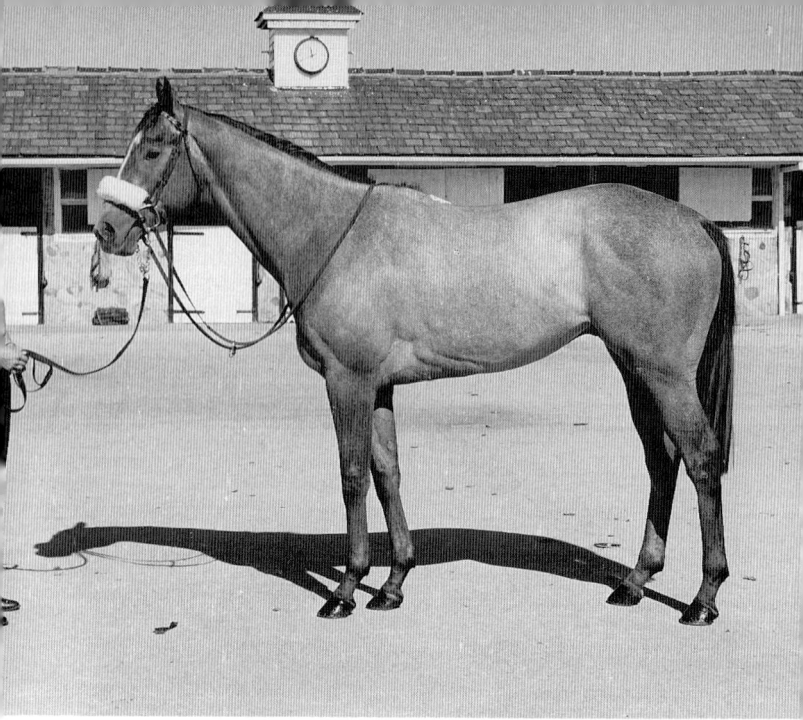

Mr P. E. T. Chandler's "Paris House"

cheaply at public auction, having cost 5,000 guineas at Newmarket's October Sales. He's easily the best winner to date from Petong's five crops of racing age, and is the second winner, following his year-older sprinting sister Petitesse, produced by his twice-raced dam Foudroyer from five foals. Foudroyer is a daughter of the modest mile-and-a-quarter winner Foudre whose only winning offspring is the fair middle-distance stayer Mull House. Foudre's dam Lighted Lamp was a fine broodmare. Her winning sons and daughters are too numerous to mention individually but include the smart middle-distance stayer Torus, the smart French seven-furlong and extended ten-furlong winner Lighted Glory and the useful stayer King Luthier; and besides that trio one of her daughters is also the dam of the Yorkshire Cup winner Mountain Kingdom and the Grade 1 mile-and-a-quarter winner Cool. For all the stamina in his pedigree, Paris House has few pretensions to staying much beyond five furlongs. He acts on good to firm and good to soft ground; he has yet to race on anything firmer or softer. *J. Berry.*

PARISIAN   6 b.g. Shirley Heights 130 – Miss Paris 111 (Sovereign Path 125) [1990   —
NR 1991 13.8f] rangy, deep-girthed gelding: poor mover: twice raced on flat: first run since 2 yrs, soundly beaten in seller. *J. A. Bennett.*

PARISIAN EXPRESS (FR)   3 gr.f. Siberian Express (USA) 125 – Parisana   **48**
(FR) (Gift Card (FR) 124) [1990 7d 9m⁵ 1991 8f⁶ 8.2d 12m 8d* 10g³ 8.3m 8f 8.1s] tall, lengthy filly: poor performer: won claimer at Salisbury in June: ran poorly last 3 starts: unlikely to stay beyond 1¼m: acts on dead ground. *K. O. Cunningham-Brown.*

620

PARISIENNE KING (USA)   2 b.g. (Mar 31) Key To The Kingdom (USA) –   **46**
Paris Dawn (USA) (Mr Redoy (USA)) [1991 6f⁶ 5m⁵ 7g 6g] $9,000F, $22,000Y:
rather leggy, close-coupled gelding: first foal: dam won at up to 9f: poor maiden:
stays 7f: off course 3½ months after second outing. *F. H. Lee.*

PARISIEN SINGER   2 br.f. (Mar 7) Chief Singer 131 – Parisana (FR) (Gift Card   **69**
(FR) 124) [1991 5d⁵ 5m* 5.2f⁶] leggy, rather unfurnished filly: has a quick action:
second foal: half-sister to 3-y-o 1m winner Parisian Express (by Siberian Express):
dam unraced half-sister to Chester Vase winner Palladium and Principia (dam of
Chief Singer) out of Oaks winner Pia: modest form: well-backed favourite, won
maiden at Windsor in July: respectable sixth of 7 in listed race at Newbury following
month: will stay at least 6f: bandaged off-hind, and gave trouble stalls, on debut. *I. A.
Balding.*

PARIS OF TROY   3 b.c. Trojan Fen 118 – Little Loch Broom 60 (Reform 132)   **75** d
[1990 7m³ 7m² 7m 8.2d* 1991 10d⁴ 10g⁵ 9m 9m⁴ 12d⁴ 8m⁶ 10m* 10.5d⁵] leggy,
quite attractive colt: has a long, round action: modest handicapper: didn't have to be
at his best to win claimer at Sandown in August, making virtually all: best at around
1¼m: acts on good to firm ground and dead: joined N. Twiston-Davies. *M. A. Jarvis.*

PARK AVENUE   3 b.c. Grey Desire 115 – Have Form (Haveroid 122) [1990 NR   —
1991 6g 7m 8.1s 7s 12s] 4,500Y, 12,500 2-y-o: tall, workmanlike colt: moderate
mover: second foal: half-brother to 4-y-o 5f performer Shikari's Son (by Kala
Shikari): dam, poor performer, stayed 7f: no sign of ability, including in claimer. *D.
A. Wilson.*

PARKERS JOY   7 b.g. Final Straw 127 – Blakewood 75 (Blakeney 126) [1990 NR   —
1991 10.2g] neat, strong gelding: carries condition: has a markedly round action:
poor plater nowadays: appears to stay 1½m: possibly needs a sound surface. *Miss S.
J. Wilton.*

PARKING BAY   4 b.g. Bay Express 132 – Sophie Avenue (Guillaume Tell (USA)   **77**
121) [1990 8.2f* 9m⁶ 9g⁵ 10g⁵ 10.2g 1991 10.3m² 10.5g* 12d⁵] tall, good-topped
gelding: has scope: modest handicapper: won at Haydock (amateurs) in September:
stays 10.2f: acts on firm ground. *G. A. Pritchard-Gordon.*

PARLEMO (IRE)   2 b.c. (Mar 29) Dance of Life (USA) – Crannog (Habitat 134)   **66**
[1991 7d a7g* a7g4] IR 18,500Y: half-brother to several winners, including 7.5f
winner Gabish (by Try My Best): dam, Irish 6f winner, is sister to very smart
sprinters Bitty Girl and Hot Spark: won late-year maiden at Lingfield, finishing
strongly: will stay 1m. *J. D. Bethell.*

PARLIAMENTARY   3 ch.c. Parliament 117 – Barefoot Contessa (Homeric 133)   **60**
[1990 7m 7m 7f⁵ 6s 1991 a8g* a8g* a8g⁵ 8d⁶ 8.5f⁴ 8.2d³ 8f 8m³ 7g² a8g 7d⁵ 7m]
leggy, sparely-made colt: quite modest performer: won claimers at Southwell in
February and March: ran creditably penultimate start, badly (very steadily to post) 6
days later: effective at 7f and 1m: acts on good to firm and dead going: has given
trouble at stalls: hung badly left at Beverley fifth outing: sold 1,100 gns Doncaster
November Sales. *M. Brittain.*

PARLIAMENT PIECE   5 ch.g. Burslem 123 – Sallywell (Manado 130) [1990 7f³   **95**
8g⁴ 7m 7m⁶ 8m⁴ 7m⁴ 7f² 8f⁴ 8f⁵ 7m 1991 8m³ 8g 7m* 7f* 7g 8g² 7g⁴ 7.1f⁴] big,
lengthy gelding: poor mover: fairly useful handicapper, improved in 1991: won at
Thirsk in May and Epsom (£8,640 event) in June: ran well last 3 starts in Schweppes
Golden Mile at Goodwood, listed event at York and £8,200 contest at Haydock:
suited by 7f/1m: acts on firm ground: visored nowadays: unsuited by Chester track:
suited by forcing tactics. *R. M. Whitaker.*

PARODIA   3 b.f. Glint of Gold 128 – Fox Steep (Habitat 134) [1990 NR 1991 10m]   —
small, sturdy, workmanlike filly: first foal: dam once-raced daughter of half-sister
to Durtal and Detroit: 20/1, slowly away when well beaten in maiden at Redcar in
October. *J. H. M. Gosden.*

PARR (IRE)   3 b.c. Salmon Leap (USA) 131 – Mums 88 (Mummy's Pet 125) [1990   **63**
7g 8g⁶ 1991 7m² 8f] lengthy, workmanlike colt: good walker: quite modest maiden:
hung fire and needed strong pressure to run on when second at Lingfield: tongue
tied down, ran as if something amiss in handicap later in July: probably stays 1m:
worth a try in blinkers: sold 6,800 gns Newmarket Autumn Sales. *M. R. Stoute.*

PARSONSANNCO   3 b.f. Blushing Scribe (USA) 107 – Pink Robber (USA) 85   —
(No Robbery) [1990 5f 6m⁵ 6g 7.5d 7f² a7g³ 7f⁶ a7g⁶ 1991 6g] leggy filly: modest
plater: ran poorly final 2 outings at 2 yrs and on only race (in October) at 3 yrs:
seems suited by 7f: acts on firm ground: sometimes bandaged: looked reluctant
once at 2 yrs. *B. W. Lunness.*

PARTING MOMENT (USA) 4 ch.c. The Minstrel (CAN) 135 – Farewell **104**
Letter (USA) (Arts And Letters) [1990 10g³ 12m² 12d* 16.2f² 14.5g* 15g 15g⁶ 16m⁵
1991 14m³ 16.2s⁴ 14m* 16m⁴ 22.2m³ 16.1m 15s² 16g⁶] rather leggy, attractive colt:
good walker: has round action: useful performer: won handicap at Newmarket in
May: first run for 3½ months, good second of 10, beaten 3 lengths, to Proud Panther
in listed event at Milan in October: effective at 1¾m, and stays extremely well:
probably acts on any going: usually makes running: genuine and consistent. *I. A.
Balding.*

PARTY CITED (USA) 2 b.f. (Feb 17) Alleged (USA) 138 – Dream Play (USA) **100**
(Blushing Groom (FR) 131) [1991 7g 8m 8d³ 7m] 36,000Y: lengthy filly: has scope:
fourth foal: half-sister to 3-y-o 7f winner The Dawn Trader (by Naskra): dam,
winner at up to 9f at 2 yrs, is half-sister to very useful American colt Irish Fighter:
50/1, easily best effort when promoted third of 7, beaten under 5 lengths, to
disqualified Midnight Air in Brent Walker Fillies' Mile at Ascot in September: soon
scrubbed along then kept on when respectable tenth of 30 to Young Senor in
Tattersalls Tiffany Highflyer Stakes at Newmarket 4 days later: will stay at least
1¼m: acts on dead going. *P. A. Kelleway.*

PARTYSECRET 2 b.f. (Mar 28) Tremblant 112 – Party Game 70 (Red Alert 127) —
[1991 a5g 5.1m⁵] tall, leggy, unfurnished filly: third foal: sister to half 3-y-o 5f
handicapper Very Dicey and half-sister to a winner in Belgium by Daring March:
dam 6f winner stayed 7f: no worthwhile form, in claimer at Bath in July second start.
R. V. Smyth.

PARTY'S OVER 3 ch.c. Bairn (USA) 126 – Rose And The Ring (Welsh Pageant **45**
132) [1990 NR 1991 7s⁶ 8.2d⁴ 6m a7g 7.5m 8d⁶ 10g] 4,700F, 4,600Y: leggy, angular
colt: sixth living foal: half-brother to 4 winners, including Irish 1½m/bumpers
winner Rose Appeal (by Star Appeal) and 5f and 1m (seller) winner Electric Rose (by
Electric): dam ran twice: poor maiden: may well stay beyond 1m: best efforts with
plenty of give: has been blinkered: has worn bandages: reared stalls third start: sold
680 gns Doncaster August Sales. *M. Brittain.*

PARTY TREAT (IRE) 3 ch.f. Millfontaine 114 – Party Dancer (Be My Guest — §
(USA) 126) [1990 5m⁴ 5f³ 5f² 5g³ 5m² 5m³ 6d 5d² 6d⁵ 1991 6g 6g 7g 6g 6m 5m 6f⁶ 5f
7g 8f] workmanlike filly: has a round action: reluctant plater: often blinkered, and
has been hooded. *T. Casey.*

PASADENA PET (IRE) 3 b.c. Petorius 117 – Magic Quiz (Quisling 117) **86**
[1990 NR 1991 7.5g² 7g² 5f* 6m² 6g 6m 6m] 11,500F, 18,000Y: quite attractive
colt: moderate mover: half-brother to several winners, including useful 1¼m
performer Nebris (by Nebbiolo) and very useful 1978 Irish 2-y-o 7f winner Magic
North (by Northfields), later winner at up to 10.5f in France: dam Irish 7f winner:
3/1 on, won maiden at Hamilton in May: ran creditably in quite valuable handicaps
next 2 starts, moderately at Ayr (Gold Cup) and York (£12,300 event) afterwards:
should be suited by return to 7f: possibly unsuited by firm going: edged left and
carried head high fourth start: sold 7,600 gns Doncaster November Sales. *J. R.
Fanshawe.*

PAS DE REEF 4 ch.f. Pas de Seul 133 – La Paille 113 (Thatch (USA) 136) [1990 —
9s² 11v 8.2g 9m² 12m² 10m* 11g* 12g² a12g³ a12g⁶ 12m 12s 1991 a14g a12g⁶ 13.8d
16.5m⁶ 16m a14g⁵ 14g⁶ 15.8g⁵] workmanlike filly: poor handicapper: below best in
1991: stays 1½m: acts on good to firm ground and soft. *M. Brittain.*

PASSADINA (USA) 3 b.f. Seattle Slew (USA) – Most Honourable (USA) —
(Exclusive Native (USA)) [1990 NR 1991 8m⁵] leggy, workmanlike filly: third foal:
dam unraced sister to Grade 1 winner My Darling One: 9/2 and green, around 13
lengths fifth of 11 to Celia Brady in maiden at Warwick in August: sold 5,400 gns
Newmarket December Sales. *J. H. M. Gosden.*

PASSAGE HOME 4 b.f. Blakeney 126 – Maze (Silly Season 127) [1990 10f⁵ 11g³ —
12m a12g 1991 12.3s 12d⁶ 12g 10.1m] leggy filly: moderate mover: plating-class
handicapper at best: little show in 1991: stays 11f: blinkered last 2 starts: sold 775
gns Ascot October Sales. *C. W. C. Elsey.*

PASSED PAWN 4 b.g. Blakeney 126 – Miss Millicent (Milesian 125) [1990 **57**
12m² 14g 12m⁴ 12m² 12m⁵ a12g* a11g* a11g³ a14g* 16.2s⁵ 15d* 16.5d 1991
12m 12g 14d² 13m² 15g² 14.1g³ a14g⁶ 11.8m⁶ 13.1m⁵ 12.3g²] small gelding:
plating-class handicapper: effective at 11f and stays 15f: acts on good to firm ground
and dead: usually goes well on fibresand at Southwell, but ran as if something amiss
there seventh start: joined M. Pipe (since successful over hurdles). *M. H.
Tompkins.*

622

PASSING SALE (FR)   4 b.c. No Pass No Sale 120 – Reachout And Touch **125**
(USA) (Youth (USA) 135) [1990 8f 11s² 9.7g* 12g* 12m⁶ 10g² 10g* 12m³ 12g*
1991 10g⁵ 10.5g² 12d² 12m³ 12.5g 10d* 12s* 10v4]

British racegoers might not know a great deal about the French-trained
Passing Sale despite his ending the season as one of the best older middle-
distance performers in Europe, for he's unraced on this side of the Channel.
He'd have been a worthy opponent for any of the British older middle-distance
horses judged on his defeat of Drum Taps and Snurge in the Gran Premio
del Jockey Club at Milan in October where, with a late swoop Passing Sale
collared the always-prominent Drum Taps to win by a neck. The pair were
three and a half lengths clear of a below-par Snurge. This success was Passing
Sale's first in Group 1 company and his first outside France. On home soil,
he's improved with each of his three seasons, gaining five wins along the way.
His victories at three years numbered a Longchamp handicap, listed races at
Maisons-Laffitte and Deauville and the Group 2 Prix du Conseil de Paris at
Longchamp. He found it more difficult to get his head in front in 1991—Milan
aside, his only success came in a muddingly-run Prix du Prince d'Orange at
Longchamp where he got the better of Miss Alleged by a neck in a sprint
finish; but he performed with credit on most occasions. A fifth in the Prix
d'Harcourt at Longchamp on his reappearance was followed by other good
efforts in the Prix Ganay there (beaten only a neck by Kartajana) and the Prix
Jean de Chaudenay (length-and-a-half second to Dear Doctor) and the Grand
Prix de Saint-Cloud (three-and-three-quarter-lengths third to Epervier Bleu),
both at Saint-Cloud. Reasons were forwarded for his two below-par showings:
his trainer reported that Passing Sale had been suffering from heat stroke
before finishing down the field in the Prix Maurice de Nieuil at Maisons-
Laffitte, whilst the horse was encountering very heavy ground for the first
time when a never-nearer fourth in the Premio Roma in November.

			Northfields	Northern Dancer
	No Pass No Sale	(ch 1968)	Little Hut
	(b or br 1982)	No Disgrace	Djakao
Passing Sale (FR)		(b 1976)	Exbury Grace
(b.c. 1987)	Reachout And	Youth	Ack Ack
	Touch (USA)	(b 1973)	Gazala II
	(b 1980)	Everything Nice	Sovereign Path
		(gr 1973)	Emma Canute

Bought for only 65,000 francs as a yearling at the Agence Francaise
August Sales, Passing Sale is the second foal of the unraced Reachout And
Touch. The first foal, Black Touch (by Noir Et Or), never saw the racecourse
but the third, Rancher (by Policeman) has won over a mile in France as well as
twice finishing second in mile-and-a-quarter listed events at Longchamp.
Reachout And Touch is a daughter of the useful Everything Nice. Everything
Nice was successful from five furlongs to ten and a half furlongs and won both
the Cherry Hinton and Musidora Stakes. Like her dam, the fairly useful stayer

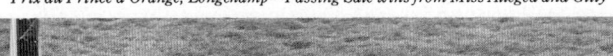

Prix du Prince d'Orange, Longchamp—Passing Sale wins from Miss Alleged and Glity

Emma Canute, she was a game and consistent sort. The name of No Pass No Sale might also be unfamiliar in Britain. His finest hour was in the 1985 French Two Thousand Guineas, which he won on the disqualification of River Mist who hampered another runner. After standing in France for only two seasons, No Pass No Sale was sold to Japan. Passing Sale is his best produce, though he's also sired Masslama, the winner of the latest Prix Vanteaux, a Group 3 race over nine and a half furlongs. A strong colt, Passing Sale is effective at a mile and a quarter and stays a mile and a half well. He's shown his form on good to firm and soft ground but was below his best on the occasions he's encountered anything more extreme. *B. Secly, France.*

PASS THE KEY (IRE)   2 b.g. (Mar 31) Treasure Kay 114 – Piney Pass (Persian   **69**
Bold 123) [1991 6d 6m⁶ 7s* 7m³] 21,000Y: strong gelding: fourth foal: half-brother to 1990 2-y-o 5f winner (stays 7f+) Allinson's Mate (by Fayruz) and two 2-y-o winners by Montekin: dam Irish 2-y-o 8.5f winner: well-backed co-favourite, won median auction maiden at Edinburgh in July: third in Newcastle claimer later same month: better suited by 7f than 6f: has form on good to firm and soft ground: sold 6,000 gns Newmarket Autumn Sales. *N. Tinkler.*

PASTORALE   3 ch.f. Nureyev (USA) 131 – Park Appeal 122 (Ahonoora 122) [1990   **91 +**
NR 1991 7m* 8.2mʷᵒ 8m] leggy, lengthy filly: good mover with a light action: first foal: dam, winner of Cheveley Park at 2 yrs and over 8.5f in USA at 4 yrs, is half-sister to Desirable (dam of Shadayid) and Alydaress: favourite but green, most promising winner of maiden at Newmarket in April, always prominent: walked over in minor event at Nottingham then beaten about 12 lengths, chasing leaders over 6f and not given hard race, in Irish 1000 Guineas at the Curragh following month. *J. H. M. Gosden.*

PATCON   6 b.g. Kafu 120 – Duchess of Howfen 66 (Steel Heart 128) [1990 NR 1991   **64**
a5g² a5g² a5g* a5g⁴ a5g⁴] big, strong, good-topped gelding: carries plenty of condition: bad mover: quite modest handicapper: won at Southwell in February: not seen out after March: suited by 5f: probably unsuited by soft going, acts on any other: tried blinkered: consistent. *T. D. Barron.*

PATER NOSTER (USA)   2 b.c. (Apr 18) Stately Don (USA) 122 – Sainera (USA)   **97 p**
89 (Stop The Music (USA)) [1991 6s*] $85,000Y, resold 58,000Y: half-brother to several winners here and abroad, including useful 1985 2-y-o 6f winner Miscrown (by Miswaki), later 1¼m winner in Italy: dam 2-y-o 7f winner: backed from 14/1 to 7/2, won 13-runner maiden at Yarmouth in October by 7 lengths from Yazaly, soon travelling smoothly behind leaders after slowish start then quickening in fine style over 1f out: will stay 1m: an interesting prospect. *Mrs J. Cecil.*

PATHERO   7 ch.g. Godswalk (USA) 130 – Canoodle 66 (Warpath 113) [1990 13g⁶   **33**
1991 a12g a12g⁴ a14g 16.5m] smallish, sturdy gelding: carries plenty of condition: moderate mover: quite modest as 4-y-o: lightly raced since and below form: stays 2m: used to go extremely well with plenty of give: tried blinkered once. *N. Bycroft.*

PATIENCE CREEK   5 ch.m. Mummy's Game 120 – Brandon Creek 79 (Be My   **51**
Guest (USA) 126) [1990 a8g⁶ 8g 8d a8g⁵ a10g⁵ 1991 a10g* a10g⁵ a10g³ a10g⁶] workmanlike mare: has no action: plating-class handicapper: won at Lingfield in January: not seen out after February: stays 1¼m: acts on firm and dead going. *C. P. Wildman.*

PATRICIAN MAGICIAN   2 b. or br.c. (Apr 12) Lord Ballina (AUS) – Singing   **70**
Witch 71 (Sing Sing 134) [1991 5d² 6f* 6g 7d a6g³ a7g³] leggy colt: half-brother to several winners, including 1985 2-y-o 1m winner My Ton Ton (by Good Times), and fair sprinter Cantoris (by Song): dam half-sister to smart sprinter Vilgora: sire 5f to 7f winner in Australia: modest performer: won minor event at Thirsk in August: best form at 6f: acts on firm ground, and on fibresand. *R. J. R. Williams.*

PATRICIA (USA)   3 ch.f. Assert 134 – Passionist (USA) (Buckpasser) **113**
[1990 7m 1991 9d⁵ 10g* 11.9m* 13.5g* 14.6m* 14d²]
To suggest after her first two runs that Patricia would go on to win three pattern races would have required a bold imagination, though it could be argued that no horse of Cecil's should be written off until the evidence leaves no room for doubt. Patricia had been second favourite for a back-end Leicester maiden at two (as Piggott's second come-back ride), but showed only a hint of ability in finishing down the field. Finishing a well-held fifth of eight, beaten almost fifteen lengths, in a fillies minor event at Wolverhampton on her reappearance hardly augured well. That said, the Watling Street Fillies Stakes

A. F. Budge Park Hill Stakes, Doncaster—Patricia never looks like being pegged back, though Nibbs Point, Always Friendly and Sesame (left to right) stick to their task

was used as an early-season engagement for another Cecil filly Madame Dubois the previous year, and she went on to much better things. Patricia's third outing gave the first indication that she did have plenty of ability. She was stepped up to a mile and a quarter for a maiden at Kempton, and, ridden for stamina, she beat Remaadi by a neck with the sixteen other runners well beaten off. That was the performance of a horse who would improve at a mile and a half and probably beyond. Sure enough, Patricia made considerable progress when stepped up in distance. The Lancashire Oaks tends to attract fillies who have not proved themselves at the top level, and among the eleven who went to post for the latest renewal not one had achieved anything better than useful form. There was open betting with the twice-raced Mohican Girl narrowly preferred at 7/2 to the well-beaten Oaks seventh Ausherra and Cecil's other representative La Sky. Patricia was 11/1, but the race developed into a match between the stable-companions entering the final quarter mile with Patricia wearing down her rival inside the last furlong and running on strongly to have a length and a half in hand at the line. The rest, headed by Ausherra ten lengths away, were well strung out. Once again Patricia's manner of victory left the strong impression that the further she went the better she would be, though she didn't need to improve much, if at all, when justifying favouritism in the Prix de Pomone at Deauville on her next start. Just over five lengths covered the nine-strong field at the finish of this Group 2 event, so in getting up near the line to beat Spendomania a head Patricia probably did well to overcome a sedate early gallop. The pace was a stronger one in her next race, the A. F. Budge Park Hill Stakes at Doncaster, and Patricia, the pick on form despite a penalty for her win in France, completed a four-timer in decisive fashion. She was sent off a strong 11/8 favourite against ten rivals and never looked like being pegged back having quickened ahead under pressure approaching two furlongs out. At the line she was a length and a half clear of Nibbs Point with Sesame, the sole representative from the older generation, a neck further away. There had been talk of Patricia's tackling the Prix Vermeille following her success at Deauville, but it was only after the Park Hill that she was asked to take on Group 1 company for the first time, in the Jefferson Smurfit Memorial Irish St Leger at the Curragh. She was again made favourite but on this occasion found the French challenger Turgeon three lengths too good, running right up to her best in second.

Charles St George's two purchases at the 1989 Keeneland September Yearling Sale, Patricia and Peter Davies, proved rare bargains. They were bought for just 20,000 dollars apiece and a handsome profit was doubtless made on both. A substantial share in Peter Davies was sold to Japanese interests in January, while Patricia became the property of Sheikh Mohammed following her win in France. Patricia's sire Assert was moved to France for the 1991 covering season; he was responsible for just four individual winners in Europe during the latest season with Patricia and Endoli easily the best.

Sheikh Mohammed's "Patricia"

		Assert (b 1979)	Be My Guest (ch 1974)	Northern Dancer What A Treat
Patricia (USA) (ch.f. 1988)			Irish Bird (b or br 1970)	Sea Bird II Irish Lass II
		Passionist (USA) (ch 1976)	Buckpasser (b 1963)	Tom Fool Busanda
			Spa II (b 1963)	Saint Crespin III Pange

This pair are typical of Assert's progeny in that stamina is their strong suit—the average winning distance index of his stock in Britain and Ireland is approximately thirteen furlongs. The useful-looking Patricia is a moderate mover with a quick action who proved her effectiveness on good to firm and dead ground. There's no doubt she would have stayed two miles plus given the chance; it was only in the closing stages that she found her stride in the Irish Leger, having been outpaced early in the straight. She visits Trempolino. *H. R. A. Cecil.*

PATROCLUS 6 b.g. Tyrnavos 129 – Athenia Princess 80 (Athens Wood 126) **38** §
[1990 15.5f⁶ 17m³ 1991 18d⁶ 16m³ 16.2g³ 20g 16.2g⁴ 17.2f* 16g⁴] workmanlike gelding: has a round action: poor handicapper nowadays: won at Bath in July: suited by test of stamina: probably acts on any going: tried blinkered once: has been bandaged: takes a lot of driving, and ungenuine. *R. Voorspuy.*

PAT'S BOY 2 b.g. (Mar 19) Cragador 110 – Mrs Feathers 57 (Pyjama Hunt 126) —
[1991 7f 7g] 5,200F, 3,600Y: leggy gelding: fifth foal: half-brother to fairly useful
1988 2-y-o 5f to 8.5f winner Nightstalker (by Night Shift), later successful in USA:
dam poor maiden: better for race and green, soundly beaten in maidens at Brighton:
sold 775 gns Ascot 2nd November Sales. *M. McCormack.*

PATSY'S PET 3 b.f. Tina's Pet 121 – Emperor Star (King Emperor (USA)) [1990 —
5f 6h² 6v⁵ 7g⁶ 6v⁵ 6d 8d a6g a7g 1991 a7g 8d 9.2d 10m] leggy, rather shallow-
girthed filly: poor maiden: showed signs of retaining a little ability in seller
penultimate start: stays 7f: best form on a sound surface: blinkered (pulled hard)
once at 2 yrs. *T. Fairhurst.*

PAULINES VALENTINE 3 b.f. Aragon 118 – My Haven 77 (Godswalk (USA) —
130) [1990 5m 7f⁴ 7f 8v 1991 8f] leggy, sparely-made filly: poor maiden: well
beaten last 4 starts: stays 7f: sold 900 gns Ascot July Sales. *J. G. FitzGerald.*

PAULINUS 3 b.g. Nomination 125 – New Ribbons 79 (Ribero 126) [1990 NR 1991 —
8s⁶ 8d⁵ 9f⁴ 12.4m 10.1m 9m 10.3d] workmanlike gelding: sixth live foal: half-brother
to three 2-y-o winners, including 1982 1m winner Decorated (by Gunner B), and a
winner in Italy: dam 1½m winner: no worthwhile form. *Denys Smith.*

PAVERS GOOD SHOES 3 b.f. Good Times (ITY) – Windy Sea 105 (Sea Hawk —
II 131) [1990 6g 1991 a7g⁵ a8g⁶ 12f⁵ 10.6m 9m 10.4m 8m] lengthy, angular filly: poor
form at best: should stay at least 1m: has looked headstrong. *M. Brittain.*

PAVONIS 2 b.c. (Apr 14) Kalaglow 132 – Snub (Steel Heart 128) [1991 8m²] **72 p**
7,200Y: leggy colt: fifth foal: brother to 7f and 11.7f winner Heart of Fire and half-
brother to 9f winner Highly Desirable (by High Top) and 3-y-o Hard To Snub (by
Shardari): dam Irish 7f and 9f winner and later in USA: weak 16/1-shot, beaten 2½
lengths by stable-companion Pabouche in maiden at Leicester in October, slowish
start, then disputing lead 2f out: moved moderately to post: likely to stay middle
distances: sure to improve. *H. R. A. Cecil.*

PAY HOMAGE 3 ch.g. Primo Dominie 121 – Embraceable Slew (USA) (Seattle **101**
Slew (USA)) [1990 5d² 5f² 6d5 5.8f³ 7f* 7g⁴ 7g⁶ 8m4 1991 9s² 8g 9m² 8g4 10.6g
8.5f* 7.6g² 8m² 8.3m³ 7g4 7.6m² 9m* 9m] rather leggy, angular gelding: moderate
walker: useful handicapper: successful in 5-runner races at Beverley in July and
Lingfield (apprentice minor event, rallying well) in September: no show in Cambridgeshire at Newmarket final start: will prove ideally suited by further than 7f, and
should stay 1¼m: acts on any going: blinkered once at 2 yrs: hung right fifth and
sixth starts: consistent. *I. A. Balding.*

PAY TO DREAM (IRE) 3 b.g. Runnett 125 – Pursue 78 (Auction Ring (USA) **44**
123) [1990 6g 7s a6g⁵ 1991 8.5m⁵ 7m 8f 8s 8f⁵ 9.7f⁶] compact gelding: poor maiden:
stays 9.7f: acts on firm going: joined R. Weaver. *J. Sutcliffe.*

PEACE FORMULA (IRE) 2 ch.c. (Jan 26) Thatching 131 – Greatest Pleasure **60**
(Be My Guest (USA) 126) [1991 5g 7g⁵ 8m 6m³ 7s 7g a6g³ a7g⁵] IR 26,000Y: rather
unfurnished colt: first foal: dam unraced half-sister to Sing Softly: quite modest
maiden: ran creditably in nurseries final 2 starts: stays 7f: acts on good to firm and
soft ground, and on fibresand: ran moderately for 7-lb claimer sixth outing. *R.
Hollinshead.*

PEACE KING 5 ch.g. Adonijah 126 – Flaming Peace (USA) 64 (Lyphard (USA) —
132) [1990 8f* 12h* 11.5m⁵ 13.3m³ 1991 12.2d] strong, chunky gelding: good walker
and fluent mover: modest performer at 3 yrs: burly, behind in handicap at Warwick
only run in 1991 (April): stays 13.3f: acts on hard ground: winning hurdler. *G.
Harwood.*

PEACE PLANTATION 2 b.c. (Feb 19) Mummy's Game 120 – Dancing Daugh- **64**
ter 79 (Dance In Time (CAN)) [1991 5m⁴ 5g 6d⁶ 7.1d⁶ 8m] compact colt: third live
foal: half-brother to fair 3-y-o miler Take Two (by Jupiter Island), and 7f and 1m
winner Handsome Hotfoot (by Hotfoot): dam 13.4f winner: quite modest maiden:
below best (raced very keenly) final start: should stay 1m: acts on dead ground:
sweating profusely (ran badly after 4-month absence) second outing: twice on toes:
sold 5,000 gns Doncaster November Sales. *R. F. Johnson Houghton.*

PEACH BRANDY 2 ch.f. (May 31) Pharly (FR) 130 – Gin And Lime 75 (Warpath —
113) [1991 6g] small, close-coupled filly: fourth reported foal: dam 14.6f to 2m
winner: 33/1, backward and claimer ridden, always behind and not knocked about in
seller at Yarmouth in July: bred to stay well. *M. H. Tompkins.*

PEACOCK FEATHER 3 b.f. Bustino 136 – Wide of The Mark 91 (Gulf Pearl —
117) [1990 NR 1991 10m⁶ 15.3m⁵ 12d] leggy, unfurnished filly: sixth foal: half-sister
to plating-class 10.2f winner Artistic Champion (by Mummy's Pet) and 6f winner
Audacity (by Zeddaan): dam 1¼m winner: no worthwhile form in minor event,

maiden and claimer: sold to join K. Burke 1,350 gns Ascot 2nd July Sales. *Lord Huntingdon.*

PEAK DISTRICT   5 b.g. Beldale Flutter (USA) 130 – Grand Teton 64 (Bustino   34
136) [1990 10.8m 10.8m 12g 10g 8g 11d 1991 10d⁴ a14g⁵ a12g] small, lengthy gelding:
bad mover: poor maiden handicapper nowadays: stays 1¾m: acts on good to firm
ground and dead: winning hurdler in February: bought for 900 gns Doncaster October Sales. *K. S. Bridgwater.*

PEANUTS PET   6 b.h. Tina's Pet 121 – Sinzinbra 112 (Royal Palace 131) [1990   50
NR 1991 14d 13.8g* 16m* 14g 18.1m²] workmanlike, close-coupled horse: lightly-
raced handicapper on flat: won at Catterick and Nottingham in spring: off course 4½
months before next start (needed run) and very good second on latter course after,
denied clear run throughout last 2½f: stays 2¼m: acts on good to firm going:
winning hurdler/chaser. *B. A. McMahon.*

PEARL ANGEL   2 ch.f. (Mar 8) Superlative 118 – More Or Less 64 (Morston   90
(FR) 125) [1991 6g⁴ 7g* 7m⁴] smallish, sturdy filly: half-sister to several winners,
including 7f to 1¼m winner Goscar (by Vaigly Great) and quite useful 11.1f and 11.7f
winner Queen Angel (by Anfield): dam winning stayer: fairly useful performer: won
7-runner Fay, Richwhite Sweet Solera Stakes at Newmarket in August, quickening
over 1f out and running on very strongly: bit below that form behind Musicale in
Rockfel Stakes at same course over 2 months later, staying on after principals had
gone clear: will stay middle distances. *Miss B. Sanders.*

PEARL ESSENCE (USA)   3 b.f. Conquistador Cielo (USA) – Frau Daruma   54
(ARG) (Frari (ARG)) [1990 6g 7g 1991 8g 12.5m⁴ 11.1d 12g 15.8g⁶ 13.6d* 15.1s³]
workmanlike filly: plating-class form: best effort to win handicap at Redcar in
October, strong late headway: should stay 2m: acts on dead ground, probably on
good to firm. *C. F. Wall.*

PEARL RANSOM   4 ch.f. Durandal 114 – Seed Pearl (Ben Novus 109) [1990 NR   —
1991 9g] non-thoroughbred filly: second foal: dam, quite useful hurdler/fair chaser,
stayed well: 33/1, beaten about 19 lengths when in mid-division for 16-runner ladies
event at Kempton in June, only run. *J. T. Gifford.*

PEARL RUN   10 ch.g. Gulf Pearl 117 – Deep Down (Deep Run 119) [1990 14.8m   50
14.8m⁴ 18f* 16g 14s 20m 16g 14.8m⁶ 1991 14.8g³ 17m 16m 18.4d 14.8m] good-bodied
gelding: moderate mover: poor handicapper nowadays: suited by a test of stamina:
unsuited by soft going nowadays, acts on any other: often bandaged: good mount for
apprentice: has won Heart of England Handicap (now re-named after him) at
Warwick 4 times, and easily best effort of 1991 when third in that event. *E. J. Alston.*

PEARLY WHITE   2 b.f. (Apr 9) Petong 126 – White's Pet (Mummy's Pet 125)   57
[1991 5d 5.7m 6f³ 6m³] 6,800Y: lengthy filly: second foal: sister to 1990 2-y-o 1m
winner Encore Au Bon: dam never ran: plating-class maiden: twice withdrawn after
being very unruly at start: likely to stay 1m: one to treat with caution. *G. B. Balding.*

PEDANTRY (IRE)   3 gr.g. Rusticaro (FR) 124 – Sweet Hostess (Candy Cane   —
125) [1990 5g⁶ 6g 7g 5f 7m 7g⁸ 5m³ 8m 10 6s⁶ 8.2s a7g 1991 a8g⁵ 10d 12m 11g 10m]
leggy gelding: modest plater: modest form below form in non-selling handicaps last 4 starts:
should stay beyond 1m: blinkered once at 2 yrs: sometimes hangs left, and is
difficult ride: sold 1,500 gns Doncaster August Sales. *D. W. Chapman.*

PEERAGE PRINCE   2 b.c. (Apr 22) Thatching 131 – Belle Viking (FR)   71
(Riverman (USA) 131) [1991 6m 6g⁵ 5m 6.1m⁴ 6g* 6m² 5d] 7,400Y: leggy colt: poor
mover: half-brother to several winners, including smart middle-distance performer
Sirk (by Kris), fair 6f/7f handicapper Nordic Brave (by Indian King) and 3-y-o 12.3f
winner Dashing Fellow (by Sure Blade): dam French 1m and 1¼m winner from
family of Vitiges: modest performer: gamely won maiden at Lingfield in October:
good second of 12 for claimer in £11,300 nursery at Newmarket 2 weeks later: will
stay 7f: acts on good to firm ground, not entirely discredited on dead. *Pat Mitchell.*

PEGASUS HEIGHTS   5 ch.g. Air Trooper 115 – Confetti Copse 71 (Town And   —
Country 124) [1990 10.8m 1991 5m 6m] lengthy, plain gelding: no promise in varied
company, including handicap. *R. J. Hodges.*

PEGGOTTY   3 gr.f. Capricorn Line 111 – Silver Empress 63 (Octavo (USA) 115)   39
[1990 6g 6d⁴ 1991 8d 8.3m⁵ 7m 10m] leggy filly: poor maiden: stays 1m (very stiff
task at 1¼m): acts on good to firm ground and dead. *P. Hayward.*

PEGGY MAINWARING   2 b.f. (Feb 19) Petong 126 – Bertrade 75 (Homeboy   50
114) [1991 5m 5g 5m⁶ 6g⁶ 5d] sturdy filly: moderate mover: first foal: dam maiden
stayed 1¼m, is sister to Bertie Wooster: plating-class form in varied events: on
toes, below best final start: should stay 7f. *R. J. Holder.*

PEGGY SPARE 3 b.f. Anfield 117 – Come North 72 (Track Spare 125) [1990 NR **44**
1991 a8g⁶ a10g³ 8f] ninth living foal: half-sister to fair 1983 maiden Rivensky (by
Maystreak): dam best at up to 1m: third of 8 in maiden at Lingfield, only form in the
spring: seemingly better at 1¼m than 1m. *Miss B. Sanders.*

PEGGY SUE 3 ch.f. Hotfoot 126 – Presentable 60 (Sharpen Up 127) [1990 5.1m⁶ —
1991 8.5f 7.5f 5m 6.9m] big, lengthy filly: poor plater: sometimes difficult in
preliminaries: sold 525 gns Ascot 2nd July Sales: dead. *M. J. Camacho.*

PEKING OPERA (IRE) 3 b.c. Sadler's Wells (USA) 132 – Braneakins (Sallust **114** §
134) [1990 7m² 8g² 8d* 1991 12g* 12.3d³ 12g 11.9g⁴] close-coupled, quite attractive
colt: has a quick action: came from rear to win very strongly-run listed event at
Kempton in April by 10 lengths: ran creditably in Dalham Chester Vase (2½ lengths
behind impressive Toulon) next start, poorly afterwards in King Edward VII Stakes
at Royal Ascot and listed race (bandaged off-hind, weakened tamely) at Haydock:
should stay further: very useful, but temperamental and not one to trust: reportedly
sent to C. Clement in USA. *M. R. Stoute.*

PELAGIAN ZEST 6 b.g. Magnolia Lad 102 – Enthusiasm (Abwah 118) [1990 12f —
10m 1991 a8g⁶] of no account. *J. Dooler.*

PELARGONIA 2 ch.f. (Apr 13) Primo Dominie 121 – Pellinora (USA) (King **59**
Pellinore (USA) 127) [1991 6g⁶] 38,000Y: quite attractive filly: sixth foal: half-sister
to 3-y-o 1m (at 2 yrs) and 1¼m winner Prince Russano (by Rousillon) and fairly
useful 1½m winner Peleus (by Irish River): dam, once-raced half-sister to Park Hill
winner I Want To Be, from excellent family: very green sixth of 9 in maiden at
Goodwood in July, drifting right and not knocked about: moved poorly down. *R.
Charlton.*

PELENG (IRE) 3 ch.c. Mille Balles (FR) 124 – Prosodie (FR) (Relko 136) [1990 **71**
7g² 7g⁴ 8m 1991 8m⁴ 12f⁴ 10m a7g* 8d⁴ a8g* a10g² 10g⁶ 11.4m] angular, workman- a **84**
like colt: modest performer: ridden by 7-lb claimer, won maiden at Southwell and
claimer at Lingfield in June: may prove suited to 1m: acts on good to firm and dead
ground: unruly at stalls on intended reappearance: wore net muzzle second start,
eyeshield on all-weather: sold 11,000 gns Newmarket Autumn Sales. *P. A. Kelleway.*

PELORUS 6 b.h. High Top 131 – St Isabel (Saint Crespin III 132) [1990 8m³ 10m **90**
8g 10.2s 1991 9s⁶ 10.1s 8m⁴ 10g² 10m*] leggy horse: usually looks well: fair
handicapper nowadays: off course 4 months before third start and in excellent form
afterwards: comfortably won at Newmarket (apprentices) in October: better suited
by 1¼m than shorter: probably acts on any going: has started slowly, and usually
held up: trained first 2 starts by W. Jarvis. *D. R. C. Elsworth.*

PENANDO 3 b.g. Dreams To Reality (USA) 113 – Pendona 72 (Blue Cashmere —
129) [1990 5f³ a5g⁴ 5m⁵ 5m⁵ 6m² 6m⁶ 7g 6m³ 6d 5f⁶ 5g a5g⁵ a6g² 1991 a6g 6.1m 6g
6m a6g a7g a5g] smallish, workmanlike gelding: has a round action: only a fair plater
on most form, and showed little as 3-y-o: needs further than 5f and stays 7f:
effective with or without blinkers: wore eyeshield fifth and sixth starts: has worn
bandages. *E. A. Wheeler.*

PENDOR DANCER 8 b.g. Piaffer (USA) 113 – Bounding (Forlorn River 124) **53**
[1990 5g 5.8h 5m² 5g 5m⁵ 5m* 5f 5m⁶ 5g 5.8f 5d⁴ 5m 1991 5g 5.3f⁶ 5g⁶ 5m 5d⁴ 5g 5d
5g⁶ 5m 5m⁴ 5g⁶ 5m 5.1d a5g* a5g² a5g] lengthy gelding: poor handicapper
nowadays: won at Lingfield in November: best over 5f: acts on any going: effective
with or without blinkers or visor: sometimes wears crossed noseband: usually
sweating: sold out of W. Carter's stable 2,100 gns Ascot September Sales after
eleventh start. *B. Forsey.*

PENHILL FLAME 5 ch.m. Main Reef 126 – Debian 71 (Relko 136) [1990 6m⁶ —
8.3m⁶ 9f 8f 1991 a6g] close-coupled mare: poor plater. *N. R. Mitchell.*

PENISCOLA STAR 2 br.f. (Feb 5) King of Spain 121 – Octavia (Sallust 134) **52**
[1991 5d⁴ 5g* 5m³ 5g² 5f] leggy filly: half-sister to several minor winners, including
6f to 10.8f winner Neat Style (by Sweet Monday) and to 3-y-o temperamental plater
Kinoko (by Bairn): dam showed a little ability: won seller (retained 6,000 gns) at
Beverley in April: seems suited by an easy surface: subsequently successful in
Austria. *R. Hollinshead.*

PENNINE BOLD 4 b. or br.c. Persian Bold 123 – Tifrums 77 (Thatch (USA) —
136) [1990 8g⁶ 8m 8g 10m 1991 9m⁶] leggy colt: moderate walker and mover: sixth
foal: brother to good-class miler Pennine Walk and quite modest 6f and 7f winner
Kawwas: dam Irish 2-y-o 7f winner: lightly-raced ex-Irish colt: bought out of D.
Weld's stable 1,000 gns Newmarket Autumn (1990) Sales: no worthwhile form,
including in handicap: tailed off in Redcar maiden in August, only run here:
blinkered once. *O. Brennan.*

PENNY DOUBLE (IRE) 3 ch.f. Double Schwartz 128 – Needlewoman 73 —
(Moorestyle 137) [1990 NR 1991 7g⁴ 7g⁵] 8,600Y: leggy filly: first foal: dam maiden
best at 9f and 1¼m: 16/1, slow-starting fourth of 9 in maiden at Goodwood, probably
better effort in the summer: sold 850 gns Newmarket Autumn Sales. *D. R. C.
Elsworth.*

PENNY DROPS 2 b.f. (Mar 5) Sharpo 132 – Darine 114 (Nonoalco (USA) 131) **57**
[1991 5g⁵ 5g⁵ 6m² 5m 6g 7m⁶ 6.1m a7g] 5,800Y: leggy filly: has a very round
action: fifth foal: half-sister to French 3-y-o 9f winner Cast Anchor (by Slip Anchor),
1989 2-y-o 6f winner Albert (by Kings Lake) and a winner in Italy by Caerleon: dam
middle-distance winner, improved greatly at 5 yrs when trained in France:
plating-class maiden: poor form after third outing: seems suited by 6f: usually on
toes: trained first 7 starts by Pat Mitchell. *Lord Huntingdon.*

PENNY HASSET 3 b.f. Lochnager 132 – Bad Payer 72 (Tanfirion 110) [1990 NR —
1991 5m 6f⁵ 5f⁵ 7.5f 6m⁶ 5f 5f] strong, lengthy filly: first foal: dam 2-y-o 5f winner:
plating-class maiden, apparently best effort second start: 3 times never placed to
challenge or knocked about: should prove suited by further than 5f. *M. W. Easterby.*

PENNY MINT 3 ch.f. Mummy's Game 120 – School Road 88 (Great Nephew 126) **79**
[1990 5s 5g² 6g* 6f* 6d 1991 8g⁵ 7g 8m 6m] plain filly: moderate mover: fair winner
in summer at 2 yrs: ran creditably, in handicap second start as 3-y-o: well beaten in
similar events later in summer: stays 7f: possibly unsuited by softish ground. *J. M.
P. Eustace.*

PENNY ORCHID (IRE) 2 b.f. (May 20) Taufan (USA) 119 – Honest Penny **83**
(USA) (Honest Pleasure (USA)) [1991 6g 6g* 6m³ 6m] IR 13,500Y: tall, leggy,
unfurnished filly: has scope: moderate mover: half-sister to 7f to 12.5f winner
Return To Romance (by Trojan Fen) and a winner in Malaysia by Master Dancer:
dam, placed over 5f at 2 yrs in Ireland, from good family: won maiden at Ayr in July,
staying on well: good eighth of 22 to Affair of State in Tattersalls Breeders Stakes at
the Curragh in August: will be suited by 7f+. *W. J. Pearce.*

PENSERAPH 3 br.g. Precocious 126 – Rosalka (ITY) (Relko 136) [1990 5g⁶ 5m⁵ **40**
5.8h⁶ 5f 6g 5m a7g 1991 a5g³ a5g⁶ a6g⁵ a5g⁴ a5g a5g⁶ 5g 6f] leggy, close-coupled
gelding: poor maiden: best efforts at 5f: usually blinkered or visored. *P. Howling.*

PENSHURST 3 ch.g. Adonijah 126 – Jolie Pelouse (USA) (Riverman (USA) 131) —
[1990 NR 1991 6m 7g] leggy, rather close-coupled gelding: first foal: dam
thrice-raced daughter of half-sister to champion filly Chris Evert: behind in maidens
in May: taken early to post and very fractious in stalls before second start:
subsequently gelded. *R. V. Smyth.*

PENTRIDGE 3 ch.f. Pennine Walk 120 – Pennycuick 101 (Celtic Ash) [1990 6m **76**
1991 7g⁶ 6d 6g 8.2m 8.9g² 10g² 12s⁵ 12g² 10g* 11.5m² 8.9g 10m* 10m*] workmanlike filly: moderate mover: progressive handicapper: won at Newmarket in July
then Goodwood (claimer) and Newbury (ladies) in September: needs further than 9f,
and stays 1½m: acts on good to firm ground: sold 16,000 gns Newmarket Autumn
Sales. *G. Lewis.*

PEPLUM (USA) 3 b.f. Nijinsky (CAN) 138 – Chain Store (USA) (Nodouble **108**
(USA) [1990 NR 1991 10m* 11.3d* 12m 12d³ 10.5v4] leggy, quite attractive filly:
half-sister to 3 winners, including Al Bahathri (by Blushing Groom), successful in
Lowther Stakes and Irish 1000 Guineas, and stakes winner at up to 1¼m Geraldine's
Store (by Exclusive Native): dam won at up to 9f: won minor event at Nottingham in
April and Shadwell Stud Cheshire Oaks (green once leading over 1f out, beat Conor
Lily 1½ lengths) in May: well beaten in Oaks at Epsom: ran well in Princess Royal
Stakes at Ascot and Prix de Flore at Saint-Cloud last 2 starts: should have stayed
1¾m: stud. *H. R. A. Cecil.*

PERANG PERCY 5 b.g. Bay Express 132 – Carcosa 103 (Sovereign Lord 120) —
[1990 a7g4 1991 7g2] strong, angular, close-coupled gelding: poor walker: twice raced
and poor form at best: seems to stay 7f. *B. W. Lunness.*

PERCY'S GIRL (IRE) 3 b.f. Blakeney 126 – Laughing Girl 110 (Sassafras (FR) **98**
135) [1990 NR 1991 10.3m* 10m* 12d5] smallish, useful-looking filly: has a fluent,
rather round action: ninth foal: sister to smart but untrustworthy 6f to 11f winner
Percy's Lass and half-sister to several other winners, including good 1m to 11.3f
winner Braiswick (by King of Spain): dam Oaks fourth, is half-sister to Furioso (dam
of Teenoso) and Favoletta: won maiden at Chester in August in good style and
minor event (6/5 on, eventually staying on really well to lead post) at Sandown in
September: bandaged off-fore, around 10 lengths fifth of 8 in Princess Royal Stakes
at Ascot: should prove effective at 1½m: possibly unsuited by dead ground. *G.
Wragg.*

PERESKIA 3 b.f. Petoski 135 – Mytinia 94 (Bustino 136) [1990 6m 7m² 1991   —
a8g⁵ 7g 12f 8.9m] leggy filly: quite modest form second 2-y-o start, virtually none
(including in handicaps) in 1991: bred to be suited by middle distances: wore
eyeshield on reappearance: sold 1,000 gns Newmarket Autumn Sales. *C. E. Brittain.*

PERFAY (USA) 3 ch.c. Nodouble (USA) – Perfect Example (USA) (Far North   86
(CAN) 120) [1990 NR 1991 8d* 8g³ 10m² 9g³] $240,000Y: compact colt: third foal:
brother to 4-y-o 7f winner Perfolia and half-brother to a minor winner in USA: dam
unraced half-sister to Grade 1 winner at up to 1¼m French Charmer (dam of Zilzal)
and to the dam of Polish Precedent: won maiden at Pontefract in April: in frame in
moderately-run autumn minor events: probably stays 1¼m. *H. R. A. Cecil.*

PERFECT CIRCLE 2 b.f. (May 2) Caerleon (USA) 132 – Fair Salinia 125   90 p
(Petingo 135) [1991 6g² 7g* 8d] smallish, sparely-made filly: sixth reported foal:
closely related to 1988 2-y-o 1m winner Horn Dance (by Green Dancer), later stayed
1¾m, and half-sister to fairly useful 1983 2-y-o maiden Fair Habit (by Habitat) and
3-y-o 6f winner Impact (by Green Desert): dam won Oaks and awarded Irish Oaks:
well-backed favourite, won minor event at Kempton in September by 5 lengths,
leading on bridle under 2f out, quickening clear from 1f out: held up and never able to
challenge in Prix Marcel Boussac at Longchamp following month, finishing ninth of
14 to Culture Vulture: should stay 1¼m: looked good prospect at Kempton. *M. R.
Stoute.*

PERFECT LIGHT 2 b.c. (Mar 23) Salmon Leap (USA) 131 – Sheer Gold 92   56 p
(Yankee Gold 115) [1991 8m 8.1g 8.1d] big, workmanlike colt: has scope: second foal:
dam middle-distance stayer in Ireland then smart staying hurdler here: plating-class
form in fair company: gives impression will do better over longer distances. *G. M.
Moore.*

PERFIDY (FR) 3 b. or br.f. Persian Bold 123 – Maiyaasah 75 (Kris 135) [1990 NR   —
1991 7g 7.9g⁵ 6.9f⁶ 8s] leggy, quite attractive filly: poor mover: first foal: dam
lightly-raced maiden, ran only at 1m: no worthwhile form: blinkered final start:
visits Lead On Time. *C. E. Brittain.*

PERFOLIA (USA) 4 ch.f. Nodouble (USA) – Perfect Example (USA) (Far North   104
(CAN) 120) [1990 10g³ 7m* 8v 1991 8m³ 7g 7m* 7m* 7m*] lengthy, angular filly:
has round action: lightly raced and vastly improved after returning from 3-month
lay-off before third start: made virtually all when successful in autumn handicaps at
Doncaster and Newmarket (2), winning easily first 2 occasions and holding on well
by head from Smiling Sun for final win: easily best form at 7f: acts on good to firm
ground: visits Nashwan. *J. H. M. Gosden.*

PERFORATE 2 b.g. (Apr 25) Teenoso (USA) 135 – Bag Lady 86 (Be My Guest   63
(USA) 126) [1991 a7g⁴ 7s⁴ 7m 8g 8.3s a8g] 7,200Y: lengthy, good sort: has plenty of
scope: second foal: half-brother to 3-y-o Carmen's Joy (by Chief Singer), 5f winner
at 2 yrs: dam ungenuine maiden stayed 1m, is out of half-sister to Malinowski,
Gielgud and dam of El Gran Senor: quite modest maiden: ran poorly final 2 starts,
last one on equitrack: will be suited by 1¼m: ran moderately on top-of-the-ground.
Sir Mark Prescott.

PERFORMER 3 gr.f. Green Ruby (USA) 104 – Susie Hall (Gold Rod 129) [1990   —
5m 5m 1991 5f⁶ 7.5f 8.5f⁶ 6d] angular filly: poor plater. *J. Balding.*

PERICOLO (IRE) 2 b.f. (Apr 19) Kris 135 – Wild Abandon (USA) (Graustark)   92 p
[1991 7m³] leggy, unfurnished filly: half-sister to 2 minor winners in USA by Mr
Prospector: dam half-sister to 2 very useful winners, including French 9f and 1½m
winner Mangayah, from family of Shareef Dancer: 14/1 from 8/1, 3 lengths third of 8
to Rose Indien in minor event at Newmarket in October, green over 2f out then
staying on well not knocked about: will improve, and win races. *L. M. Cumani.*

PERJURY (IRE) 3 b.g. Try My Best (USA) 130 – Riverine (FR) (Riverman   60
(USA) 131) [1990 6g⁵ 6m⁶ 6g 1991 8.5m 8d⁴ 8m⁴ 8m*] leggy gelding: quite modest
performer: favourite, won claimer at Newcastle (claimed to join D. Eddy £5,100) in
October, chasing leader and staying on to lead post: should stay beyond 1m: acts on
good to firm ground and dead: blinkered last 2 starts. *D. R. C. Elsworth.*

PERKY DANCER (USA) 3 b.f. Green Dancer (USA) 132 – Pert (USA)   87
(Damascus (USA) 86) [1990 NR 1991 8m² 8m* 8.5m 8m] leggy, quite attractive filly:
fourth foal: half-sister to North American winner Shaker Knit (by Blushing Groom):
dam winner of 8 races, including Grade 3 7f event: won maiden at Newmarket in
May: very disappointing in £10,000 + handicaps at Epsom and (mulish stalls, pulled
very hard) Ascot following month. *L. M. Cumani.*

PERMANENTLY PINK 5 b.g. Auction Ring (USA) 123 – Hawaiian Joss (USA)   —
(Hawaii) [1990 8m³ 12.5f 8.3g 1991 10v⁴] lengthy, angular gelding: moderate mover:

R. O. A. Foundation Stakes, Goodwood—Perpendicular (right) and Opera House fight it out

winning plater at 2 yrs: little form in varied events since: should stay 1¼m: acts on good to firm ground. *R. J. Hodges.*

PERPENDICULAR 3 b.c. Shirley Heights 130 – Pris (Priamos (GER) 123) **113** p [1990 7s* 1991 10s* 10.5g³ 10g*] good-topped colt with scope: moderate mover: successful in smallish fields for £10,700 contest (most impressive) at Ascot in May and listed race (edged right and left in front, beat Opera House a neck) at Goodwood in October: about 5 lengths third of 8 to Environment Friend in William Hill Dante Stakes at York in May: will stay 1½m: flashes tail: will improve again, and is sure to win more races. *H. R. A. Cecil.*

PER QUOD (USA) 6 b.g. Lyllos (FR) – Allegedly (USA) (Sir Ivor 135) [1990 **111** 12g⁵ 10m⁴ 12d² 16m 12g² 12s³ 14g⁵ 12m³ 12g³ 12v² 14s* 12v 1991 15s* 13.4d* 14g⁴ 20g 12g⁴ 13.4m⁵ 15.5m 15g⁴ 16g] leggy, workmanlike gelding: usually looks very well: has a quick, round action: very useful performer nowadays: won Group 3 event at Milan in April and Ormonde Stakes at Chester (by a length from Warm Feeling) in May: ran well in listed events won by Mukddaam at Newmarket and Proud Panther at Milan fifth and eighth starts: ran as though something amiss final one: effective under testing conditions at 1¼m and stays 15f: not at his best on firm going, goes very well on a soft surface: splendidly tough, genuine and consistent: a credit to his trainer. *B. Hanbury.*

PERSIANALLI (IRE) 3 b.c. Persian Bold 123 – Alligatrix (USA) 111 (Alleged **102** (USA) 138) [1990 6m* 6m 1991 6g* 6f* 8g²] tall, rather finely-made, close-coupled colt: impresses in appearance: useful form here in the spring, winning handicap at Kempton and minor event at Folkestone: stays 1m: acts on firm going: taken last and quietly to post here at 3 yrs: sent to USA, winning $60,000 non-graded stakes event over 1m at Del Mar and placed in Grade 3 events. *J. H. M. Gosden.*

PERSIAN BUD (IRE) 3 b. or br.c. Persian Bold 123 – Awakening Rose (Le —
Levanstell 122) [1990 NR 1991 10.1m 10.5g⁶ 12s] 28,000Y: well-made colt: half-brother to Irish 1m and 1½m winner Catherine Clare (by Sallust) and several winners abroad: dam, French 10.5f winner, is half-sister to smart sprinter Rambling Rose and very smart 7f to 10.5f winner Rose Laurel: no worthwhile form, but showed signs of ability in maiden at Haydock second start: sold to join J. Bosley 1,400 gns Ascot November Sales. *P. W. Harris.*

PERSIAN DIPPER 3 b.c. Persian Bold 123 – High Image 79 (High Top 131) —
[1990 NR 1991 a11g a12g] first foal: dam 3-y-o 5f winner out of useful 2-y-o sprint

winner Gay Shadow, herself a half-sister to Honeyblest: no worthwhile form in late-season claimers at Southwell. *R. Bastiman.*

PERSIAN DYNASTY 7 br.h. Persian Bold 123 – Parez 67 (Pardao 120) [1990 8f 45
10f 8f* 9g 8h⁵ 10.8m⁴ 7f* 10m³ 8.2m* 10g⁶ 8f⁵ 9f⁶ 8h 7m 10.2f³ 10.2m 8m 1991 8m²
9m⁶ 7.1m⁴ 8.2f³ 8.1d³ 8.1g* 8f⁵ 8.2m 10m⁶ 8.2f6] small horse: poor handicapper:
won at Chepstow in June: needs at least 7f and stays 1¼m: acts on firm and dead
going: good mount for claimer. *J. M. Bradley.*

PERSIAN EMPRESS (IRE) 2 br.f. (Mar 4) Persian Bold 123 – Route Royale 51
(Roi Soleil 125) [1991 5m⁵ 5.1d³ 6g⁴ 6.1m 7m 7m 7g 6.3s] IR 13,500Y: leggy,
close-coupled filly: sister to 3 winners, including 1983 2-y-o 6f winner Iran Flyer and
Irish 1¾m winner Persian Caprice, and half-sister to 2 winners, including fair miler
Little Big (by Indian King): dam never ran: plating-class maiden: ran well in nursery
at Chester (extremely stiff task) fifth outing, moderately after, in valuable restricted
race at the Curragh final start: stays 7f. *B. A. McMahon.*

PERSIAN FANTASY 2 br.f. (Mar 9) Persian Bold 123 – Gay Fantasy (Troy 72
137) [1991 7g⁴ 7.1m³ 8f⁴ 7d] quite attractive filly: fourth foal: half-sister to useful 9f
and 10.8f winner Lucky Guest (by Be My Guest) and 2 other winners, including fair
7f and 9f winner Trust Troy (by Gorytus): dam unraced half-sister to very useful
middle-distance filly Miss Petard: modest maiden: off course 2 months, creditable
staying-on seventh of 22 in nursery at Doncaster in November: will be suited by
1¼m +. *J. L. Dunlop.*

PERSIAN FLEECE 2 ch.f. (Feb 26) Bold Arrangement 127 – Microcosme 100 44
(Golden Fleece (USA) 133) [1991 5g 7.1d] sparely-made filly: first foal: dam French
2-y-o 6.5f winner, is granddaughter of very smart Mia Pola: never a factor in
maidens at Folkestone (slowly away) and Chepstow in October. *C. A. Austin.*

PERSIAN HAZE (IRE) 2 ch.g. (Apr 5) Bold Arrangement 127 – Crufty Wood 65
(Sweet Revenge 129) [1991 6d 6g 5f 6f 6.9h⁴ 8.3g² 10.5d*] IR 7,400Y, 6,800Y, resold
2,200Y, 7,800 2-y-o: smallish gelding: poor walker: third foal: half-brother to Italian
3-y-o 6f winner Policarpo (by Tumble Wind) and fair sprinter Our Fan (by Taufan):
dam unraced: quite modest form: retained 4,800 gns after winning 20-runner selling
nursery at Haydock in October by 5 lengths, going away, from Wise Move: suited by

*Ormonde EBF Stakes, Chester—
another game performance from the splendid Per Quod (left)
who beats Warm Feeling and Indian Queen*

a thorough test of stamina: acts well on good to soft ground: ran well in visor penultimate start. *Miss S. E. Hall.*

PERSIAN HOUSE   4 ch.g. Persian Bold 123 – Sarissa 105 (Reform 132) [1990   —
12s⁴ 13g³ 12.3m⁴ 10.2g 13d 13.6d² 1991 11.9d 14.6m] big, good-topped gelding: quite modest handicaper: below form in October: should stay beyond 13.6f: acts on good to firm ground and dead: lacks turn of foot, and should prove suited by forcing tactics: winning hurdler in November. *J. M. Jefferson.*

PERSIAN LION   2 br.c. (Apr 17) Reesh 117 – Parijoun (Manado 130) [1991 6.1g⁶   —
7.1d] leggy colt: first living foal: dam of little account: slowly away and always well behind in maidens at Nottingham (6 runners) in August and Chepstow 2½ months later: sold 900 gns Doncaster October Sales. *R. Hollinshead.*

PERSIAN SATAN (IRE)   3 b.f. King Persian 107 – Irish Myth (St Paddy 133)   —
[1990 5g 5f⁵ 5f 7m 7f 8.2g 8m 1991 7m] angular filly: poor mover: poor plater: tailed off in claimer only start in 1991: probably stays 1m. *C. J. Hill.*

PERSIAN SOLDIER   4 b.c. Sandhurst Prince 128 – Persian Case (Upper Case   66
(USA)) [1990 9m 8g⁴ 8m 8d 1991 10f⁵ 12m³ 12m 12g⁶ 12f* 11.9g 11.9m⁵] workmanlike colt: good walker: moderate mover: quite modest handicaper: won at Thirsk in August, allowed to dictate at modest pace: tailed off after: stays 1½m: acts on good to firm ground: below form when visored once: inconsistent. *G. M. Moore.*

PERSIAN SONG   2 b.f. (Apr 27) Persian Bold 123 – Arrangement 72 (Floribunda   45
136) [1991 7f 6s 6m] 10,000Y: leggy filly: sister to Bold Arrangement, a high-class performer at up to 1¼m, and half-sister to several other winners, including winning sprinter Swing Shift (by Swing Easy): dam stayed 7f: poor form in maidens: likely to prove suited by further than 6f. *R. Hannon.*

PERSISTENT GIRL   2 ch.f. (May 30) Superlative 118 – Bushy Top 83 (Thatch-   41
ing 131) [1991 5.2d⁶ 5d] 7,600F, 6,000Y: workmanlike, rather angular filly: third foal: half-sister to a winner in Malaysia: dam 6f winner stayed 7f: poor form in June maidens. *R. Hannon.*

PERSONAL HAZARD   2 ch.g. (Mar 23) Risk Me (FR) 127 – Princess Lily 65   77
(Blakeney 126) [1991 5m⁶ 6g⁴ 7m² 7m³ 7m* 7m 7m 7.6d⁶] 25,000Y: quite good-topped gelding: has scope: first foal: dam, maiden, stayed 1½m, is sister to very useful 1½m winner Believer: modest performer: favourite, won maiden at Chester in August, making all and quickening 2f out: below form afterwards: will be suited by 1m: visored final start. *M. H. Easterby.*

PERSONALITY CLASH   3 b.f. High Top 131 – Five Farthings 90 (Busted 134)   49
[1990 6m 6m 5m 1991 8m 8.5m⁶ 11.5m⁶ 10.5m³ 10f 9.9f 10.5d4] small, sparely-made filly: plating-class maiden: stays 10.5f: best effort on good to firm ground: raced too freely sixth start: sold 2,000 gns Newmarket Autumn Sales. *T. Thomson Jones.*

PERSPECTIVE   3 b.f. Never So Bold 135 – Geopelia 109 (Raffingora 130) [1990   34
a7g 1991 a6g a7g 10m 12m⁴ 11.5m³ 14.1g 12d⁶] plain filly: has a roundish action: poor performer: probably stays 1½m: sold to join B. Stevens 1,500 gns Newmarket July Sales. *M. H. Tompkins.*

PERSUASIUS (IRE)   3 b.g. Petorius 117 – Be A Dancer (Be Friendly 130) [1990   64
6f 6g⁵ 6g³ 1991 5d⁶ 8m 7g² 8f⁵ 9.2f⁵ 10.3d] leggy gelding: quite modest maiden: stays 1m (badly hampered over 9f): acts on firm ground: twice refused to enter stalls in 1991. *W. J. Pearce.*

PERSUASIVE   4 b.f. Sharpo 132 – Queen's Eyot 79 (Grundy 137) [1990 9s* 11v*   —
12h² 12g³ᵈⁱˢ 12m⁵ 10.6g 10d² 10.6d⁶ 10v⁶ 1991 11s³ 15m⁴ 15.1s] lengthy, rather sparely-made filly: has a round action: quite modest performer: off course over 5 months before second start: appears to stay 15f: acts on any going: fair hurdler. *Miss L. A. Perratt.*

PERU   3 b.c. Conquistador Cielo (USA) – Dance Flower (CAN) (Northern Dancer)   73
[1990 7s 1991 7g⁵ 7f* 10f³ 8m⁵ 10m⁴ 10.1m 8h* 8m⁶] compact, attractive colt: has quick action: modest handicaper: won at Redcar (maiden) in May and Carlisle (led final 1f and edged markedly right) in September: looked tremendously well, but well below form and found little final start: stays 1¼m: acts on hard ground: visored last 2 starts: sold 16,000 gns Newmarket Autumn Sales. *J. W. Watts.*

PESIDANAMICH (IRE)   3 b.g. Mummy's Treasure 84 – Bay Supreme (Mar-   68
tinmas 128) [1990 6m⁵ 6f³ 6m⁶ 7f² 6v* 7d a7g⁶ 1991 a7g³ a7g* a7g* a7g² a6g³ a7g*   a 78
a7g² 7g³ 6m 7m 7m 7m a6g a6g²] sturdy gelding: fair performer: successful early on in handicaps at Lingfield and Southwell and claimer at Southwell: below form returned to turf, and when second in claimer at Southwell in December: suited by 7f:

acts on any going: ran creditably when edgy: usually blinkered, first time for 5 outings on final start. *T. D. Barron.*

PETAL GIRL   2 ch.f. (Apr 5) Caerleon (USA) 132 – Amazer (Mincio 127) [1991   **70 p**
7f² 7m⁴] rather leggy filly: has a quick action: half-sister to several winners, notably top-class middle-distance performer Mtoto (by Busted) and very useful middle-distance fillies Button Up (also by Busted) and Astonished (by Connaught): dam won over 6f at 2 yrs in France: in frame in maiden at Salisbury (strong-finishing second) and minor event at Newbury (staying on) in September: will be better suited by 1m: will improve again. *R. F. Johnson Houghton.*

PETANK (IRE)   3 ch.c. Double Schwartz 128 – Hay Knot (Main Reef 126) [1990   —
NR 1991 a7g⁶ 6g 6.1m] lengthy, dipped-backed colt: first foal: dam never ran: no promise in maiden, seller and claimer: blinkered final start. *Pat Mitchell.*

PETASTRA   2 b.f. (Feb 10) Petoski 135 – Star Face (African Sky 124) [1991 7m⁴   **62**
8.1d 8m⁴] angular, rather unfurnished filly: has scope: moderate mover: half-sister to 3-y-o Smasher (by Simply Great) and several winners, including good 7f to 11.3f winner Lord of The Field (by Jalmood) and 6f and 1m winner Torquemada (by Try My Best): dam French 10.5f winner: quite modest maiden: best effort at Ayr (edgy and green, kept on not knocked about) on debut: bred to stay 1¼m: possibly unsuited by dead ground, though also pulled hard second outing. *Mrs J. R. Ramsden.*

PETAURISTA   4 b.f. (May 9) Petong 126 – Lydia Rose 68 (Mummy's Pet 125)   **47**
[1991 5m⁶ 6m 6d] sturdy filly: third reported foal: half-sister to winning sprinter Craft Express (by Bay Express): dam suited by 1¼m: poor maiden: should stay 6f. *M. Johnston.*

PETAVIOUS   6 b.g. Mummy's Pet 125 – Pencuik Jewel (Petingo 135) [1990 a12g²   **61**
a12g³ 12g⁶ 12m² 12m³ 10m⁵ 12m 12g 1991 9s* 10.8m⁴ 12m² 12g⁴ 11.5g 12g⁴ 11.8m* 12m* 10.2g4] leggy gelding: moderate mover: quite modest handicapper: won at Kempton (apprentices, caught eased second on line) in April and Leicester and Southwell in September: stays 1½m: acts on good to firm ground and soft. *Lady Herries.*

PETER DAVIES (USA)   3 ch.c. Bering 136 – French Flick (USA) (Silent **104**
Screen (USA)) [1990 7m* 7m* 8s* 1991 10.5g 8m4] rather leggy colt: very game winner of 4-runner Racing Post Trophy at Doncaster final start at 2 yrs: favourite, set strong pace 7f when tailed off in Dante Stakes at York: 4 lengths fourth of 9 to Collide in minor event at Newbury over 4 months later, leading over 2f out until unable to quicken final 1f: should be suited by middle distances: acts on good to firm ground and soft: lacks a turn of foot: has changed hands: reported to have joined A. Fabre. *H. R. A. Cecil.*

PETE ROSE   2 ch.c. (Apr 20) Nicholas Bill 125 – Hurricane Rose (Windjammer   —
(USA) [1991 5d5] 8,000F, 8,000Y: first foal: dam poor maiden: weak 12/1-shot, tailed-off last of 5 in Catterick maiden in March. *Mrs G. R. Reveley.*

PETER PUMPKIN   3 b.g. Tickled Pink 114 – Wild Pumpkin (Auction Ring   **35**
(USA) 123) [1990 5m 5.3h4 6m 5m6 7f 7f4 7m 6m a7g 1991 a8g5 a5g a6g5 a8g3 10f 7f5 8d4 8f 7g] workmanlike gelding: poor mover: plater: stays 1m: acts on firm and dead going, and on Lingfield equitrack: often blinkered: races freely: rather temperamental. *R. Voorspuy.*

PETER WHIMSEY   2 gr.c. (Mar 7) Petong 126 – Norton Princess 76 (Wolver   **42** §
Hollow 126) [1991 5g 5f 6g4 5.7m 7g 6g] 7,400Y: sturdy, good-bodied colt: fourth foal: half-brother to 1990 2-y-o 5f winner Princess Who (by Lidhame) and 1½m winner Pan E Salam (by Ile de Bourbon): dam 2-y-o 6f winner seemed not to train on: poor maiden: best form at 6f: blinkered final start, usually wears a visor: has unsatisfactory attitude. *M. McCormack.*

PETINATA   2 gr.f. (Mar 21) Petong 126 – Raffinata (Raffingora 130) [1991 7f 8g]   **35**
good-topped filly: has scope: sister to a poor maiden and half-sister to 3 winners, including one-time useful sprinter Peatswood Shooter (by Windjammer): dam never ran: better for race, never dangerous in September maidens at Salisbury and Bath. *R. Charlton.*

PETITE AMIE   3 gr.f. Petoski 135 – Amourette (Crowned Prince (USA) 128)   —
[1990 6s5 6g 7d6 8v 1991 10m 13g 15s] poor form: stiff tasks and well beaten in 1991, including in selling handicap: should stay at least 1m: sold out to join Mrs P. Joynes 1,700 gns Doncaster August Sales. *C. W. Thornton.*

PETITE BELLE   2 b.f. (Apr 27) Legend of France (USA) 124 – Bishah (USA) 86   **50**
(Balzac (USA)) [1991 6m5 7m 8.5f5 7g 8.9m5] compact filly: second foal: half-sister to poor and unsatisfactory 1990 2-y-o Ela-Gorrie (by Valiyar): dam 11f winner, is out

of half-sister to dam of Pawneese: plating-class maiden: will stay 1¼m: acts on good to firm ground. *R. M. Whitaker.*

PETITE-D-ARGENT   2 b.f. (Mar 24) Noalto 120 – Honey To Spare 63 (Track   **69** Spare 125) [1991 5h⁴ 5g² 5m⁵ 6m² 5m² 5.1f³ 5m⁵ 6m*] 680Y: compact filly: moderate mover: half-sister to 1¼m winner My Muszka (by Viking): dam ran only at 2 yrs: modest performer: best effort winning £11,300 nursery at Newmarket by neck from Peerage Prince in October: suited by 6f: yet to race on soft surface: ran well in visor, though wandered badly: bandaged on debut: consistent. *Miss L. A. Perratt.*

PETITE ELITE   4 b.f. Anfield 117 – Gimima 54 (Narrator 127) [1990 12d a8g⁶ a6g   **47 d** 1991 a7g² a6g a5g⁴ a7g a6g⁶ 6d 7f 5m⁴] small, sturdy filly: poor handicapper: stays 7f: acts on good to firm ground: blinkered last 4 outings, wore eyeshield previous six. *J. G. FitzGerald.*

PETITE MELUSINE (IRE)   3 b.f. Fairy King (USA) – Grace de Bois (Tap On   — Wood 130) [1990 5f³ 5m² 5g 6m⁶ 7s a7g a5g 1991 5g 5m 6f 7m a5g] small, angular filly: seems of little account nowadays: blinkered final start: sold to join N. Smith 2,600 gns Doncaster November Sales. *R. Thompson.*

PETITE ROSANNA   5 b.m. Ile de Bourbon (USA) 133 – Let Slip 77 (Busted   **82** 134) [1990 10g 10h* 10g 10g⁶ 10h* 10m⁵ 10m² 10m* 10.2g⁴ 12m³ 12g 1991 15.5f² 14g 16.2f 11.5m 10f³ 10f* 10f² 10.2m² 10m³ 10m] smallish, good-quartered mare: moderate mover: fair handicapper: won at Salisbury in August: below form final start: best efforts at around 1¼m to 1½m: suited by a sound surface: below form when blinkered once: sometimes wears tongue strap: has been bandaged behind. *W. Carter.*

PETITE SIRENE (USA)   2 ch.f. (Apr 24) Storm Bird (CAN) 134 – Santella   — p (USA) (Coastal (USA)) [1991 6g⁵] $77,000Y: rather unfurnished filly: fourth foal: half-sister to 2 minor winners in North America: dam unraced half-sister to dam of Miesque: 4/1, backward and green, 12 lengths last of 5, disputing lead to halfway, to Misterioso in Blue Seal Stakes at Ascot in September: should stay 1m: will improve. *L. M. Cumani.*

PETITE SONNERIE   2 b.f. (Apr 11) Persian Bold 123 – Hiding 84 (So Blessed   **78** 130) [1991 7g⁶ 6g⁶ 6f⁶ 7f⁴ 6s² 7m] 28,000F, 56,000Y: big, good-topped filly: has plenty of scope: half-sister to 3-y-o 7f (at 2 yrs) and 10.2f winner Evading (by Petoski) and 2 sprint winners: dam 2-y-o 5f winner from family of Bassenthwaite: modest maiden: creditable twentieth of 30 behind Young Senor in Tattersalls Tiffany Highflyer Stakes at Newmarket in October: will stay 1m: acts on any going. *G. Lewis.*

PETITESSE   3 gr.f. Petong 126 – Foudroyer (Artaius (USA) 129) [1990 5m 6g 5g⁵   **55** 5.1m² 6g⁴ 5f* 5f² 5f⁵ 6m² 6f⁵ 5f 6m* 6m⁶ 5m 1991 6m⁶ 5s² 6g 6g 6g⁶ 6f⁶ 5d⁵ 5g* 5d* 5f* 5s² 5m 5.3f⁵] small, dipped-backed filly: quite modest handicapper: in excellent form to complete hat-trick at Warwick in the summer: below form last 2 starts: stays 6f: acts on any going: blinkered 3 times: has been mounted on track and often mulish to post, unseating rider and bolting once in July. *G. Blum.*

PETIVARA   4 b.f. Petong 126 – Avahra 108 (Sahib 114) [1990 6f 7m 6f² 6m⁴ 6f⁵ 6m   **42** 6f⁶ 7g 6g⁴ a10g 1991 7m 7.6s⁶ a7g² a7g 9m³ 8.9m a8g] leggy, workmanlike filly: poor handicapper, still a maiden: stays 7f: acts on firm ground: ran well when visored once: has been slowly away. *S. Dow.*

PETMER   4 b.g. Tina's Pet 121 – Merency 75 (Meldrum 112) [1990 10f⁴ 10.1m⁵   **53** 1991 9d⁵ 10.2g⁵ 10.2d* 10g] tall, leggy gelding: plating-class handicapper: edgy, won at Chepstow: well beaten at Windsor later in July: stays 10.2f: acts on firm and dead ground. *G. B. Balding.*

PETOMANIA   2 b.f. (Apr 13) Petong 126 – Placid Pet 65 (Mummy's Pet 125)   **34** [1991 5d³ 5g 5g 5f 5m 5g³ 6f 7m 7.5f] 6,000Y: sparely-made filly: sister to sprint winner Boules and half-sister to 3 winners, 2 of them sprinters: dam 1m winner, is sister to Runnett: poor plater: quite a hard ride: blinkered fourth and fifth starts: difficult stalls second appearance: sold 620 gns Doncaster October Sales. *M. Brittain.*

PETONICA (IRE)   2 b.f. (Apr 24) Petoski 135 – Ivoronica 89 (Targowice (USA)   **77** 130) [1991 7g² 7m⁶] lengthy filly: half-sister to several winners, including useful 6f and 7f winner Lochonica (by Lochnager) and fairly useful 1990 2-y-o 6f winner Ivory Bride (by Domynsky): dam 2-y-o 5f winner: 25/1 and green, neck second of 13 in minor event at York in September, quickening well into contention, run out of it last 50 yds: well-backed favourite, poor sixth of 18, carrying head high, in median auction maiden there month later: will stay 1m. *M. H. Tompkins.*

PETONY (IRE) 3 b.f. Petorius 117 – Norme (FR) (Dark Tiger) [1990 5f² 5m⁴ **43**
1991 7m⁵ 6f⁵ 5m⁶ 7g 5m⁴ 5f 5d 6.1m 5s] leggy filly: plating-class form at best: stays
7f: acts on firm going: blinkered (soundly beaten) fourth outing: refused to enter
stalls on intended reappearance: tail swisher. *C. W. C. Elsey.*

PETOSKI'S CHOICE 3 b.f. Petoski 135 – Elegida 93 (Habitat 134) [1990 NR **69**
1991 8g 8f⁶ 8.3d⁴ 7m⁴ 8m*] 6,800Y: strong filly: seventh foal: half-sister to 1988
2-y-o 7f winner Simascala (by Electric) and French 10.5f winner Height of Elegance
(by Shirley Heights): dam sprinter: quite modest performer: won handicap at
Leicester in July, leading close home despite wandering badly: will prove suited by
1m +: seems unsuited by a soft surface. *M. J. Ryan.*

PETRACO (IRE) 3 b.c. Petorius 117 – Merrie Moira (Bold Lad (IRE) 133) [1990 **83**
6f³ 7d 5d⁵ 1991 6d⁵ 5m 6g* 6m* 7g 6g 6g 5m³ 6m 5d⁶ 6m⁴ 5g] workmanlike colt:
has a quick action: fair handicapper: won at Windsor and York in July: good efforts at
Haydock, Ascot (£16,700 event) and Newmarket (£8,400 contest, favourite and
made most) eighth, tenth and eleventh starts: stays 6f, but best form at 5f: acts on
good to firm ground and dead: blinkered seventh outing: game. *L. J. Codd.*

PETROPOWER (IRE) 3 b.g. Petorius 117 – Gay Honey (Busted 134) [1990 5g³ **46**
5g* 6g³ 5g* 5m⁴ 1991 6d 6f⁵ a5g 6m 6f 9.9f 7m⁴ 6f a6g] lengthy, rather angular
gelding: moderate mover: poor performer: best 3-y-o effort on second start: should
stay 7f: acts on firm going, stiff task on dead: blinkered 3 times, once when
successful at 2 yrs. *M. O'Neill.*

PETRULLO 6 b.h. Electric 126 – My Therape 112 (Jimmy Reppin 131) [1990 9m⁵ **—**
10.5d⁴ 10m⁶ 10m⁴ 1991 10g 10m] strong, rangy horse: usually looks well: has a quick
action: very useful performer in first half of 1990: showed nothing as 6-y-o in pattern
company at Longchamp and Sandown and not seen out after May: suited by 1¼m:
unsuited by firm going, acts on any other: tends to hang, and suited by strong
handling and waiting tactics. *J. R. Fanshawe.*

PET SHOP BOY 3 gr.g. Petong 126 – Moben 73 (Counsel 118) [1990 5m 5m³ 6h **61**
5g² 5m* 6m 1991 7v 8.3m 10g 8.3m 8f² 8f] rather unfurnished gelding: quite modest
handicapper: 25/1-second of 18 at Salisbury in August, always prominent: no
comparable form at 3 yrs: stays 1m: acts on firm going: virtually pulled up on hard
ground: visored last 3 starts: blinkered twice at 2 yrs: bandaged as 3-y-o: sold to join
J. J. O'Neill's stable 3,300 gns Newmarket Autumn Sales. *T. Thomson Jones.*

PETTICOAT POWER 5 b.m. Petorius 117 – Red Realm (Realm 129) [1990 **62**
a7g⁴ a7g² 6f⁵ 6m³ 6d⁴ 6m⁵ 7m* 6f⁶ 7.6m⁴ 7m⁴ 7m³ 7g⁵ 7m³ 7g³ 7d* 1991 7m⁵
8.2g³ 8.1g³ 7f 8.3m 8m⁵ 7s² 8g⁵ 7g 6.9s³] workmanlike, sparely-made mare: quite
modest handicapper: effective from 6f to 1m: probably acts on any going: suitable
mount for inexperienced rider: sometimes bandaged. *Mrs Barbara Waring.*

PETTY CASH 2 b.f. (Apr 21) Midyan (USA) 124 – Money Supply (Brigadier **—**
Gerard 144) [1991 6.9f a8g] 5,200Y: compact filly: half-sister to 3-y-o 1¼m and 11.5f
winner Classic Account (by Pharly) and 2 other winners, including 1988 Irish 2-y-o
6.3f winner Roman Citizen (by Electric): dam unraced sister to very useful Irish 1m
winner Senior Citizen: soundly beaten in maidens at Folkestone and Southwell. *Dr
J. D. Scargill.*

PEURTO DEL CARMEN 2 b.f. (Jan 13) Sweet Monday 122 – On Tour 60 **—**
(Queen's Hussar 124) [1991 6g2] 2,200F, 4,600Y: sturdy filly: second live foal: sister
to 6-y-o 6f (at 2 yrs) to 1¼m winner (stays 13f) Queens Tour: dam out of half-sister
to Coup de Feu and Peleid: 20/1 and backward, always behind in seller at Beverley in
April: moved poorly down. *N. Tinkler.*

PEWTER MAGIC 2 gr.c. (Mar 14) Petong 126 – Infelice (Nishapour (FR) 125) **—**
[1991 5s⁶ 5.7m 7m] 2,800Y: strong, close-coupled colt: quite good mover: fourth
foal: brother to 3-y-o Grey Dancer: dam from family of smart Catherine Wheel: well
beaten in maidens: sweating and unruly start final outing (July): sold 625 gns Ascot
September Sales. *M. R. Channon.*

PFALZ 3 b.f. Pharly (FR) 130 – Leipzig 107 (Relkino 131) [1990 7g² 1991 8m* 8m* **101**
8g] leggy, useful-looking filly: set pace when winning maiden (easily) at Warwick in
April and 6-runner listed race (narrowly from Crystal Path and Trojan Crown) at
Sandown in May: last in Prix d'Astarte at Deauville in August, making most: stays
1m: unsuited by soft. *M. R. Stoute.*

PHALAROPE (IRE) 3 b.g. Petorius 117 – Magee (Weavers' Hall 122) [1990 6f **49 §**
6g 7.5m⁵ 7g⁶ 8m⁶ 1991 8s 8.5f⁶ 10f⁶ 12m⁵ 8d⁵ 9.9f³ 10g* 10.9m⁴ 9m³ 10m 9.9f⁵]
rather leggy, close-coupled gelding: plater: won (bought in 6,400 gns) at Ripon in
July, leading inside final 1f: seems to stay 1½m: acts on firm ground: blinkered

(below form) fifth start: carries head high and probably irresolute: sold 2,100 gns Ascot November Sales. *M. H. Easterby.*

PHARAMINEUX 5 ch.g. Pharly (FR) 130 – Miss Longchamp 94 (Northfields (USA)) [1990 11.7m² 11.7m³ 11.7m³ 14m* 14g* 14g* 16.2m⁶ 16.2s 1991 14g² 14d² 16.2g² 14m* 16.2m⁵ 11.5d* 14s 12m* 12s] strong, workmanlike gelding: has a quick action: modest handicapper: won at Sandown (2) in summer and Goodwood in September: best at 1½m: acts on good to firm and dead ground, unsuited by soft: blinkered final start at 3 yrs: has turn of foot and should do well again at 6 yrs. *R. Akehurst.* **76**

PHARAOH'S DANCER 4 b.c. Fairy King (USA) – Marie Louise 86 (King Emperor (USA)) [1990 NR 1991 9s 8m 8.3m⁶ 8g⁵ 7g³ 8g 7m⁵ 7g²] good-topped colt: has moderate, round action: half-brother to Irish 9f winner Datura (by Simply Great) and Irish 1m to 1¼m winner Spurn The Odds (by Run The Gantlet), and a winner in Brazil: dam 7f and 7.6f winner: plating-class handicapper: should stay 1m: acts on good to firm ground. *E. A. Wheeler.* **57**

PHARGOLD (IRE) 2 ch.g. (May 6) Phardante (FR) 120 – Mallee (Malinowski (USA) 123) [1991 5g 6g 6f a8g] sturdy gelding: of little account. *P. C. Haslam.* —

PHARLANDER (IRE) 2 br.g. (Feb 2) Phardante (FR) 120 – Moll Flanders (ITY) (Maestrale (USA)) [1991 6g⁴ 7g 7f⁴ 7m² 8m] 5,400Y: sparely-made, workmanlike gelding: half-brother to 2 winners in Italy: dam won 6 races in Italy: plating-class maiden: will stay 1¼m: visored or blinkered last 2 starts. *M. H. Easterby.* **56**

PHARLY DANCER 2 b.c. (Apr 13) Pharly (FR) 130 – Martin-Lavell Mail (Dominion 123) [1991 6d] 2,300Y: leggy, angular colt: second foal: half-brother to a winner in Yugoslavia by Petorius: dam unraced: 50/1 and better for race, chased leaders 4f in 21-runner maiden at Ripon in June: seemed likely to improve. *W. W. Haigh.* —

PHARLY STORY 3 b.c. Pharly (FR) 130 – Certain Story (Known Fact (USA) 135) [1990 NR 1991 8d⁴ 7g² 6m³ 10m* 11.8m*] lengthy, rather dipped-backed colt: first foal: dam unraced daughter of useful 5f and 6f winner Epithet (later stayed 1½m): favourite and dropped in class, won seller (sold out of P. Cole's stable 15,500 gns) at Leicester: fairly useful performance when very comfortable winner of handicap at Leicester later in October, making most: suited by 1½m. *M. C. Pipe.* **94 p**

PHAROAH'S GUEST 4 ch.g. Pharly (FR) 130 – Exuberine (FR) 82 (Be My Guest (USA) 126) [1990 8m 10.1g 8g 9g 11.7m 13.1m 10f 10d 1991 a13g² 16.2g* 13.8g⁵] strong, angular gelding: moderate mover: plating-class handicapper: won seller (bought in 6,400 gns) at Beverley in March: not seen out after April: stays 2m: ran well for amateur. *J. Akehurst.* **49**

PHIL-BLAKE 4 br.g. Blakeney 126 – Philogyny 94 (Philip of Spain 126) [1990 10g 8m² 8m⁵ 11m 8d 1991 10f 11.7g 12m 14.8m 9d 12d 10g] leggy, workmanlike gelding: plating-class handicapper at best nowadays: stays 9f: acts on good to firm and dead ground: wears crossed noseband nowadays. *C. Horgan.* —

PHILGUN 2 b.c. (May 18) K-Battery 108 – Andalucia 57 (Rheingold 137) [1991 6m 6g 7m 7m 8.3g⁴] leggy, close-coupled colt: sixth reported living foal: half-brother to 7f seller winner Tokanda (by Record Token) and 7.2f and 9f seller winner Viva Lucia (by Coded Scrap): dam won 1¼m seller: dropped in class, good staying-on fourth of 18 in selling nursery at Hamilton in September: will be suited by further. *C. W. C. Elsey.* **48**

PHILIDOR 2 b.c. (Mar 23) Forzando 122 – Philgwyn 66 (Milford 119) [1991 6f² 6m⁵ 7g*] 28,000Y: smallish, strong colt: first foal: dam maiden stayed 7f, is half-sister to very smart sprinter Primo Dominie: co-favourite, put up best effort to win 18-runner maiden auction at Goodwood in October, always prominent and running on strongly to lead inside final 1f: suited by 7f. *J. M. P. Eustace.* **76**

PHILJOY 5 b.m. Bustino 136 – Formana (Reform 132) [1990 13s² 16f⁴ 18.4d⁶ 14.8m³ 1991 16m 16.2m⁴ 16.1m⁶ 16.9m 15m 13.8m 15.1s] workmanlike mare: poor mover: quite modest maiden at best: lost his form: stays 2m: acts on any going: sold to join R. Juckes's stable 1,500 gns Doncaster November Sales. *C. W. C. Elsey.* —

PHIL-MAN 2 b.c. (Apr 16) Tina's Pet 121 – Pakpao 77 (Mansingh (USA) 120) [1991 7s 7.5f² 7m² 7m³ 7.5f⁶ 7m⁴ 6f 6m a7g] workmanlike colt: half-brother to 3-y-o Pretty Much (by Absalom) and 2-y-o winners by Sparkling Boy and Blue Cashmere: dam 2-y-o 5f winner: fair plater: needs further than 6f, and will stay 1m: seems unsuited by very firm ground, well beaten on fibresand. *T. Fairhurst.* **51**

PHINEAS T BARNUM (IRE) 3 b.c. Godswalk (USA) 130 – Circus Lady (High Top 131) [1990 NR 1991 6m³ a8g] 13,500Y: angular colt: third reported living **— p**

foal: half-brother to a minor winner in USA by Music Boy: dam unraced daughter of Solar, dam also of Desert Sun: showed signs of ability in summer maidens: should do better. *J. J. O'Neill.*

PHONE HOME   2 ch.f. (Apr 9) Norwick (USA) 120 – Gay Amanda 75 (Counsel   **70** 118) [1991 6m⁴ 6.1d* 7g* 7m⁴ 6m 8m] rather unfurnished filly: half-sister to several winners here and abroad, including useful 6f and 7f winner El Mansour (by Tower Walk), later successful in USA: dam stayed 1¼m: successful in maiden at Chepstow and nursery at Lingfield (made virtually all) in mid-summer: ran moderately at best last 3 starts, after unseating rider to post penultimate one: bred to stay 1¼m: seems well suited by give in the ground: sold only 850 gns Ascot November Sales. *J. R. Fanshawe.*

PHOTO CALL   4 b.f. Chief Singer 131 – Photo 83 (Blakeney 126) [1990 10.6f⁶   **41** 8.2s 8g 11f* 11.5m 12f³ 15.5f³ 12f⁵ 16m 1991 12g 12m 16.5m 12.3f 12m³ 11.5f² 12f³] sturdy, angular filly: moderate walker and mover: poor handicapper: stays 1½m: goes well on firm going: blinkered last 4 starts: edged left and swished tail under pressure when successful at 3 yrs. *M. A. Jarvis.*

PHOTO REALISM (IRE)   2 b.f. (Apr 18) Lomond (USA) 128 – Helaplane   **63** (USA) 68 (Super Concorde (USA)) [1991 5.2d² 5d³ 5.7f* 5g² 6.1m⁵] 27,000Y: smallish, workmanlike filly: moderate mover: fourth live foal: half-sister to 3-y-o 2m winner Hello My Darling (by Law Society) and useful miler Strike Force (by Gorytus): dam, maiden, should have stayed 1m: quite modest performer: made most when successful in maiden at Bath in July: stays 6f: sold 2,800 gns Newmarket Autumn Sales. *B. W. Hills.*

PHUSSANDBUSSLE   3 b.f. Pharly (FR) 130 – Sophonisbe (Wollow 132) [1990   **51** 7m 6g 1991 8m⁵ 8d] leggy, dipped-backed filly: keeping-on fifth of 14 in claimer at Salisbury, only worthwhile form: should stay 1¼m: possibly unsuited by a soft surface. *J. L. Dunlop.*

PHYLIEL (USA)   2 ch.f. (Feb 26) Lyphard (USA) 132 – Alydariel (USA) (Alydar   **82** (USA)) [1991 6m* 6m³] $500,000Y: rather unfurnished filly, with scope: first foal: dam minor stakes winner in USA at about 1m, is half-sister to Royal Academy: won 5-runner maiden at Newmarket in July, held up travelling well then quickening on 1½f out: long odds on, 6 lengths last of 3 to Afif in minor event at Folkestone 2 months later, shaken up 2f out, soon beaten: bred to stay 1m: created a favourable impression on debut. *M. R. Stoute.*

PIA BRIDE (USA)   2 b.f. (Mar 31) El Gran Senor (USA) 136 – Beaming Bride **104** p (King Emperor (USA)) [1991 7.5g² 7.5m* 8g⁵ 6.5d²] closely related to 2 winners, notably very useful 1¼m winner Alwuhush (by Nureyev), later Grade 1 winner in USA, and half-sister to 2 winners, including high-class 1m to 1¼m performer Simply Majestic (by Majestic Light): dam, placed at up to 11f in France before winning twice at up to 9f in USA, is half-sister to Oaks third The Dancer: successful in minor event at Deauville in August: better form in Group 3 events at Longchamp (2 lengths fifth to Guislaine) in September and Saint-Cloud (¾-length second of 8 to Cardoun) following month: stays 1m: useful already and may well progress further. *A. Fabre, France.*

PICA   2 ch.f. (Apr 4) Diesis 133 – Barada (USA) (Damascus (USA)) [1991 8m² 8.5f²   **71** 8.9d²] useful-looking filly: third foal: half-sister to fair 5f (at 2 yrs) and 1m winner Amana River (by Raise A Cup): dam lightly-raced half-sister to high-class 2-y-o filly Althea (stayed 9f) and to dam of Green Desert: modest, rather one-paced maiden: narrowly beaten at Beverley and Wolverhampton last 2 starts: will stay at least 1¼m. *H. R. A. Cecil.*

PICASONG   4 b.f. Crooner 119 – Picarosa (Eborneezer 105) [1990 NR 1991 10d   **—** 10.1m⁶ 8.1s⁵ 16m] workmanlike filly: moderate mover: third foal: moderate-to-pointer: no sign of ability, including in handicap: twice mulish to post. *R. Curtis.*

PICK AND CHOOSE   3 br.f. Nomination 125 – Plum Bold 83 (Be My Guest   **—** (USA) 126) [1990 a6g 6d⁵ 6d 1991 a8g 5s⁶ 6m 5g⁶ a5g 7.5m] close-coupled filly: moderate walker: poor maiden: should stay 7f: stiff task on soft ground: visored (below form) fifth start. *J. P. Leigh.*

PICKLES   3 b.g. Petoski 135 – Kashmiri Snow 83 (Shirley Heights 130) [1990 7m⁴   **54** 8g³ 1991 11g 8d 9m 8g⁵ 6.9f] rangy, quite attractive gelding: form as 3-y-o only when fifth of 17 in handicap at Bath, running on well: bred to stay middle distances, but is somewhat headstrong: wore crossed/dropped noseband last 3 outings: sold to join P. Haslam 14,000 gns Newmarket Autumn Sales. *H. Candy.*

PIE HATCH (IRE)   2 b.f. (Feb 23) Huntingdale 132 – Small Is Beautiful   **—** (Condorcet (FR)) [1991 8s a8g a7g] IR 8,000Y: third foal: half-sister to Irish 1m winner Run My Beauty (by Runnett): dam twice-raced granddaughter of Irish 1000 Guineas winner Royal Danseuse: well beaten in maidens. *Sir Mark Prescott.*

PIER DAMIANI (USA) 4 b.c. Shareef Dancer (USA) 135 – All A Lark (General **97** Assembly (USA)) [1990 10m³ 8.5g⁵ 12f⁵ 12g² 12g 12s³ 10g* 14.6g 14s² 1991 12g 12g 13.4d⁴ 12g 10g] deep-girthed colt: quite useful on most form: appeared to run much better on occasions, including when blinkered on second and third starts in slowly-run Group 2 event at Newmarket and Group 3 event at Chester: behind in Group 3 event at Naples final start (July): stays 1¾m: acts on soft ground: hung right and looked ungenuine once. *C. E. Brittain.*

PIGALLE WONDER 3 br.c. Chief Singer 131 – Hi-Tech Girl 93 (Homeboy 114) **52** [1990 5m² 6g⁶ 5d⁶ 6m² 5m⁴ 7m 6g 5g⁶ 6s 1991 6g 7m 6g 7m 6g⁶ 7g 5.1m 6f² 5f² 6g⁴ 5g 5g a5g⁶] chunky colt: good walker: plating-class maiden nowadays: good efforts in frame in handicaps at Thirsk (2) then Leicester: little other form as 3-y-o: effective at 5f and 6f: acts on firm going: possibly unsuited by a soft surface: blinkered last 6 starts. *W. Holden.*

PIGEON LOFT (IRE) 3 gr.f. Bellypha 130 – Dovetail 80 (Brigadier Gerard — 144) [1990 6m 8m⁶ 8f 1991 8g⁶ 7g 7m⁶ 6.9m] leggy filly: poor maiden: well beaten in claimer final start: bred to stay 1¼m but takes keen hold: has given trouble at stalls. *P. Calver.*

PIGEON VOYAGEUR (IRE) 3 b.c. Saint Estephe (FR) 123 – Homing **123** Pigeon (FR) (Habitat 134) [1990 7g 7.5g² 9d* 10s² 1991 11g³ 12.5g² 12.5m³ 12g* 12d⁵ 12g⁶]

Racing is seldom without its hard-luck stories, and the Prix de l'Arc de Triomphe seems to be a regular contributor. The latest running gave us Snurge who apparently banged his head on the stalls and, more typically of the race, Pigeon Voyageur who was badly hampered. In mid-division without much daylight for most of the way, things didn't get any better for Pigeon Voyageur when the field entered the straight and he attempted to get between Miss Alleged and Generous about two furlongs out. He got a bad buffeting for his pains, dropped back to eleventh and then, switched to the outside by Jarnet (who was stood down at a subsequent inquiry into the interference), stayed on to finish fifth of fourteen, six and three quarter lengths behind

P. de Moussac's "Pigeon Voyageur" (T. Jarnet)

Suave Dancer. On the strength of that performance Pigeon Voyageur disputed favouritism in British bookmakers' lists for the Breeders' Cup Turf. William Hill had had him as a 150/1-chance for the Arc. In fact, Pigeon Voyageur had already won a Group 1 race over one and a half miles, only two weeks before the Arc, but that was the weakly-contested Gran Premio d'Italia at Milan. Pigeon Voyageur had won comfortably though, by four and a half lengths from Retinospora in an eleven-runner field which included the British-trained Marcus Thorpe, Jack Lang and Another Bob. Nor was that Pigeon Voyageur's first pattern success as he'd won the nine-furlong Prix Saint-Roman at Long champ before finishing second to Pistolet Bleu in the Criterium de Saint-Cloud on his last two outings as a two-year-old. His three-year-old season before the Gran Premio, however, had been an interrupted one and it was those three outings which seemingly left him with little chance with several of the Arc principals. Pistolet Bleu had beaten him three and three quarter lengths in the Prix Noailles at Longchamp then, after a four-month absence, Pigeon Voyageur was second to all-the-way winner Aelan Hapi in a listed race at Deauville and third, staying on late, to Snurge in the moderately-run Grand Prix de Deauville Lancel. The Arc showed that Pigeon Voyageur was better than that, and that his best was probably still to come, but he could not confirm it in another moderately-run race for the Breeders' Cup Turf at Churchill Downs in November; eighth into the straight he improved only marginally.

Pigeon Voyageur's sire Saint Estephe left stud in France for Japan before any of his offspring had seen the racecourse. French breeders may now be regretting the 1986 Coronation Cup winner's departure as he's since been represented by a number of useful individuals besides Pigeon Voyageur, including the Prix Hubert de Chaudenay winner Justice and listed winners Gravieres and Lady Normandy. Pigeon Voyageur's appearance at the High-flyer Sales didn't engender much excitement and he was purchased for 15,000 guineas. His dam Homing Pigeon ran five times as a three-year-old for Dermot Weld, winning a four-runner minor event over a mile at Navan on her debut. She was a daughter of Come Back, a useful winner from a mile (at two years) to an extended mile and a half in France, and a granddaughter of the 1965 Oaks winner Long Look. Long Look also produced the triple graded stakes winner North Broadway and Homing Pigeon had established a good breeding record before Pigeon Voyageur, her previous six foals yielding four winners, including the very useful French seven-furlong and one-mile winner Ocean Falls (by Wassl) and the Irish Derby fourth Vanvitelli (by Ela-Mana-Mou). Homing Pigeon died the year of Pigeon Voyageur's birth.

			Top Ville	High Top
	Saint Estephe (FR)		(b 1976)	Sega Ville
	(b 1982)		Une Tornade	Traffic
Pigeon Voyageur (IRE)			(ch 1969)	Rough Sea
(b.c. 1988)			Habitat	Sir Gaylord
	Homing Pigeon (FR)		(b 1966)	Little Hut
	(b 1975)		Come Back	Bold Lad
			(ch 1969)	Long Look

Pigeon Voyageur stays a mile and a half well. A round-actioned colt, he has won on soft ground and put up his best effort on dead. The only time he's encountered top-of-the-ground was when chasing home Snurge at Deauville. At the time of writing, the ownership of Pigeon Voyageur is the subject of a legal wrangle, M de Moussac having agreed to sell a half-share in him to the Gerecon Italia Stable before the Gran Premio d'Italia but cancelled the sale after a delay in receiving payment. One thing is for certain, Pigeon Voyageur's fine performance in the Arc won't take any heat out of the argument. *A. Fabre, France.*

PILAR 3 gr.f. Godswalk (USA) 130 – Old Silver (Bold Lad (IRE) 133) [1990 5f 6g 5g **50** 6m 5f4 7f3 7m* 7g3 7m5 8.2g 7f* 6m 6d6 a8g a7g a6g 1991 7d4 6g 7g 8f2 8m 7m6 8.9m 8f] neat filly: poor mover: quite useful plater as 2-y-o: not so good in 1991: should stay 9f: best efforts on firm ground: blinkered fifth start: has worn bandages: inconsistent. *Mrs N. Macauley.*

PIMSBOY 4 b.g. Tender King 123 – Hitopah (Bustino 136) [1990 8.2g3 8.5d 8.2g **61** 8f5 8.2m3 10m 8m 7.5m2 8.2d6 7m 7d4 7d6 1991 a11g6 8g2 8d 7.5g2 7.5f3 8m 10d

8.3g² 8.3m⁵ 7m 8.3m² 8f³ 7m* 8.5f 7g] rather angular gelding: poor mover: quite modest handicapper: won at Southwell in September: severely hampered final start: effective at 7f to 1m: acts on firm and dead ground: usually blinkered nowadays: ran respectably when visored: has flashed tail, and looked none too easy a ride. *P. A. Blockley.*

PIMS CLASSIC 3 gr.g. Absalom 128 – Musical Maiden 76 (Record Token 128) **70** [1990 6m 6g⁴ a7g² a7g² 1991 a6g* 6m 7m 8g a7g a8g] well-made gelding: good mover: modest performer: won maiden at Lingfield in February, making most: well beaten in handicaps after, off course 6 months (gelded) after second start: stays 7f: has been bandaged. *W. J. Haggas.*

PIMS GUNNER (IRE) 3 b.g. Montelimar (USA) 122 – My Sweetie (Bleep- **68** Bleep 134) [1990 5m⁶ 6f* 7g 6m⁴ 8m² 1991 10.1s 8.5m 10.1f⁵ 11m* 12m4] lengthy gelding: has a round action: quite modest performer: best 3-y-o effort to win claimer (claimed out of W. Haggas' stable £9,000) at Southwell in August: should stay 1½m: acts on firm going: winning hurdler. *D. Burchell.*

PINCTADA 9 b.g. Mummy's Pet 125 – Pinaka 69 (Pitcairn 126) [1990 7g⁵ 1991 7d — 7.6d] strong, compact gelding: carried plenty of condition: poor mover: fair handicapper at best: pulled up early final start: suited by 7f: ideally suited by an easy surface: usually held up: excellent mount for inexperienced rider: dead. *R. Simpson.*

PINEAPPLE 3 ch.f. Superlative 118 – Pine Ridge 80 (High Top 131) [1990 6g⁵ **77** 1991 8m⁴ 10.1m⁴ 12f* 11.5g³] lengthy, unfurnished filly: set slow pace when winning 3-runner maiden at Beverley: creditable third of 4 in £10,300 handicap at Lingfield later in July: probably stays 1½m. *M. R. Stoute.*

PINECONE PETER 4 ch.g. Kings Lake (USA) 133 – Cornish Heroine (USA) — 101 (Cornish Prince) [1990 8.2g⁴ 11m* 9g³ 9m 9g 1991 12f] leggy, angular gelding: moderate mover: plating-class handicapper: not seen out after May: needs further than 9f, and stays 11f well: winning hurdler. *O. Brennan.*

PINE GLEN PEPPER 3 ch.g. Aragon 118 – The Ranee (Royal Palace 131) **61** d [1990 5f³ 5g³ 5m² 1991 6f⁴ 6m 7.6g 8.5m 10g 8f 6m 8m] leggy gelding: quite modest maiden at best: below form after reappearance: should be suited by further than 6f: visored last 4 starts: didn't handle descent at Epsom, or turn at Bath: has carried head high: one to avoid. *S. Dow.*

PING PONG 3 br.f. Petong 126 – Conway Bay 74 (Saritamer (USA) 130) [1990 — 5m⁵ 5f³ 5m 6m 5g⁵ 5m³ 5m⁶ 5m 6m⁴ 7f⁶ 5d⁶ a7g² a6g* 1991 a7g⁴ a7g⁴ a6g 7.5g a6g⁶ a6g] compact filly: moderate mover: improved form on fibresand late in 1990: didn't reproduce it: off course 8 months before penultimate start: best at 6f: tried blinkered twice at 2 yrs: sometimes slowly away. *T. Fairhurst.*

PINISI 6 ch.g. Final Straw 127 – Bireme 127 (Grundy 137) [1990 11s 21.6m 1991 — 16.5m 16m³ 18.8f⁵ 16.5g 14.1m 16m] strong, lengthy gelding: no worthwhile form on flat, including in handicaps: winning hurdler. *K. R. Burke.*

PINKJINSKI (IRE) 2 b.g. (Feb 11) Petoski 135 – Winterlude (Wollow 132) **55** [1991 6g 8.2f 8m 8g] 25,000F: sturdy, quite attractive gelding: fifth living foal: half-brother to a winner abroad: dam twice-raced half-sister to smart stayer Hazy Idea, dam of Hittite Glory: plating-class maiden: very stiff task, slowly away and always behind in Redcar nursery final outing: stays 1m. *R. Hannon.*

PINK'N BLACK (IRE) 2 b.f. (May 25) Double Schwartz 128 – Miss Pinkerton **62** (Above Suspicion 127) [1991 5g 5m 5m 7m 6f* 6m² 5g³ 6f* 6.1m] 2,800Y: sparely-made filly: moderate mover: half-sister to several winners, including Tumbledown-wind (by Tumble Wind), smart at up to 1m, and 1987 2-y-o 5f winner Hard To Stop (by Hard Fought): dam won over 1½m in Ireland: useful plater: no bid after winning at Yarmouth in August and September (for 7-lb claimer): suited by sprint distances: acts on firm ground. *G. Blum.*

PINK TURTLE (USA) 3 ch.f. Blushing Groom 131 – Turtle Cove (Dr Fager) **120** [1990 8d⁴ 1991 7g³ 7.5g* 10.5g* 10g² 10m³ 12m² 10.5v] ninth reported foal: half-sister to several winners in North America, notably Great Neck (by Tentam), a graded winner from 9f to 13f on turf in Canada: dam, successful 3 times at up to 1¼m at 3 yrs, is out of high-class 1m to 14.6f winner Sunny Love: progressed very well, winning maiden at Saint-Cloud in June and listed race at Longchamp in July: placed after in Prix de Psyche at Deauville then Prix de la Nonette and Prix Vermeille Escada (coming from towards rear, beaten 1½ lengths by Magic Night) at Longchamp: stays 1½m: acts on good to firm going, seemingly unsuited by heavy: good-class filly. *A. Fabre, France.*

PINTAIL BAY 5 b.g. Buzzards Bay 128§ – Pin Hole 83 (Parthia 132) [1990 12g **51** 10g⁶ 10m 12g³ 10.6d⁴ 12g² 10.6v 11.5g 1991 12m 12g² 9.9g 12s* 10.9g⁴ 14.6m 12m4] big, strong gelding: carries plenty of condition: has a round action: won handicap at Folkestone in July: stays 1½m: acts on good to firm and soft going: inconsistent: joined C. Brooks. *H. J. Collingridge.*

PIOUS BIRD (IRE) 3 b.f. Tender King 123 – Robin Red Breast 74 (Red Alert 127) [1990 NR 1991 5g* 5g5] 5,400Y: sturdy filly: second known foal: dam 2-y-o 5f winner, is granddaughter of Irish 1000 Guineas winner Princess Trudy: won maiden auction race at Wolverhampton in April: would have stayed 6f: bandaged behind on debut, near-hind only final start: dead. *H. Candy.* **65**

PIPE OPENER 3 b.f. Prince Sabo 123 – Bold Polly 67 (Bold Lad (IRE) 133) [1990 NR 1991 7d3 7.1d 8m4 8.1m 8s] 14,500Y: close-coupled filly: fourth foal: half-sister to fair sprinter Viceroy (by Indian King), 7f winner Sir Arnold (by Mummy's Pet) and a winner abroad: dam won twice at 5f: quite modest maiden: best effort on debut: may prove best at 7f: acts on dead ground. *R. Hannon.* **68 d**

PIPERS HILL 4 ch.g. Creative Plan (USA) – Kindle (Firestreak 125) [1990 9m 7m* 5f 6f5 6h2 6m 7d4 7f3 7.6g 7f4 a10g 1991 10.8m] smallish, shallow-girthed gelding: quite modest handicapper as 3-y-o: well beaten only run in 1991 (July): possibly best at 7f: didn't race on soft going, acted on any other: dead. *M. R. Channon.* **—**

PIPING HOT 3 br.g. Daring March 116 – Rosette 91 (Red Alert 127) [1990 6f* 7g 1991 9d 7m 8s4 6m 8.3m] big, lengthy gelding: has a round action: quite modest winner at 2 yrs: bandaged near-fore, no promise in handicaps and claimer in 1991: should stay 7f. *R. V. Smyth.* **—**

PIPISTRELLE 4 b.f. Shareef Dancer (USA) 135 – Latin Melody 109 (Tudor Melody 129) [1990 12m 12f4 13.8m2 13m* 13.8d* 16f2 14f 15m4 13.8f4 16m 1991 16.5m 13.8m 15g4 17.2f2 16.4m2 17.9f 16.9m3 16.2f2 17.2g6 18m2 17.2g] sturdy filly: poor handicapper: stays well: acts on firm and dead ground: visored nowadays: best held up. *Dr J. D. Scargill.* **44**

PIPPA'S DREAM 4 b.f. Doulab (USA) 115 – Chaldea (Tamerlane 128) [1990 8f4 8.5g 7f4 8m 1991 7.9m 8m 10m] workmanlike filly: moderate mover: trained by P. Cole, quite modest handicapper at 3 yrs: no promise in 1991, blinkered final 2 starts: stays 1m: acts on firm ground. *M. P. Muggeridge.* **—**

PIPPA'S PLACE (IRE) 2 b.f. (Feb 18) Gorytus (USA) 132 – Miss Robust (Busted 134) [1991 7f5] IR 5,000Y: small filly: sister to 1¼m winner Bonny Quiver, closely related to a winner by London Bells and half-sister to several winners, including fairly useful 5f (at 2 yrs) to 8.8f (in 1991 in Italy) performer Fair Titania (by Fairy King): dam never ran: 33/1, tailed-off last of 5 in maiden at Yarmouth in August: moved poorly down: sold 3,000 gns Newmarket Autumn Sales. *M. Bell.* **—**

PIP'S OPTIMIST 2 b.g. (Mar 5) Primo Dominie 121 – Great Optimist 55 (Great Nephew 126) [1991 a8g] 5,500Y: brother to 3-y-o Great Design and half-brother to several winners, including 6f winner Matou (by Mummy's Pet): dam in frame over middle distances: 16/1 and ridden by 7-lb claimer, soundly beaten in late-year maiden at Southwell. *P. J. Feilden.* **—**

PIPSQUEAK 3 gr.f. Alleging (USA) 120 – Silver Berry (Lorenzaccio 130) [1990 7m 1991 7g* 8v3 7m 6g* 7.1g2 6d] big, good sort: fairly useful form: successful in maiden at Kempton (by 12 lengths) in June and minor event at Leicester in August: stiff task in listed race at the Curragh final start: should prove ideally suited by further than 6f, and stays 1m: possibly needs an easy surface. *R. Charlton.* **96**

PIQUANT 4 b. or br.g. Sharpo 132 – Asnoura (MOR) (Asandre (FR)) [1990 6f5 6m 6m 6g 7g 6d* 6s 6s4 a7g3 1991 7v 6g3 6m* 8f2 7.6m* 7.3m2 8g 7g] stocky gelding: carries condition: fair handicapper, formerly untrustworthy: won at Newmarket in July and Chester in August: below form final 2 starts: effective at 6f to 1m: acts on any going: twice visored: has swished tail. *Lord Huntingdon.* **84**

PISONE GAIO 2 b.c. (Feb 18) Blakeney 126 – Preobrajenska 93 (Double Form 130) [1991 8m 8s] 10,000Y: sturdy, lengthy colt: third foal: brother to modest 1990 3-y-o maiden Preoblakensky, now successful hurdler: dam won at 5f and 6f at 2 yrs but seemed to go wrong way temperamentally as 3-y-o: no worthwhile form in maidens at Goodwood and Kempton in September. *J. L. Dunlop.* **—**

PISTOLET BLEU (IRE) 3 b.c. Top Ville 129 – Pampa Bella (FR) 115 (Armos) [1990 8g* 9d* 10s* 1991 11g* 12d* 12m2 12d3 12g5] **129**
There was a lot to be settled in the Ciga Prix de l'Arc de Triomphe besides Generous versus Suave Dancer. For a start there was some un-finished business left over from the French Derby, when the then-unbeaten

Prix Noailles, Longchamp—
this French Derby trial goes to the unbeaten Pistolet Bleu from Subotica

Pistolet Bleu, a good-looking colt who would almost certainly have been favourite for that race ahead of Suave Dancer, had had to be withdrawn at the last minute because of injury. Pistolet Bleu had since lost his unbeaten record narrowly to the French Derby second Subotica in the Prix Niel Escada at Longchamp in September on his first run back, but was expected to be better for the outing and he was sent off third favourite for the Arc at 68/10 coupled with his pacemaker Art Bleu. In the end Suave Dancer found far too much foot for him, just as he had for the French Derby opposition. All the same, Pistolet Bleu came out of the encounter with great credit, with enhanced status even: second-best colt in the race in third place behind Suave Dancer and Magic Night, beaten two lengths and a length, three lengths clear of the St Leger winner Toulon. Having tracked the pacemaker, he was allowed a trouble-free run on the inside round the last bend when Art Bleu moved over, and he led the race from the beginning of the straight until the winner quickened by. He kept on stoutly under pressure after that, but was steadily overtaken by the filly. The Arc could not have been run better to suit a staying type like Pistolet Bleu. The same could not be said of his only subsequent race, the Breeders' Cup Turf at Churchill Downs in November, and though he seemed lighter in condition than most in the field we would be inclined to attribute his defeat into fifth to the slow pace and tight track. He raced in the first five throughout, handy from the start, and turned into the short home straight a close third to Itsallgreektome and Sky Classic on the outside of Quest For Fame. Surprisingly, as the leaders quickened it was Quest For Fame who proved the better able to stay with them. Pistolet Bleu dropped back to fourth then fifth as Miss Alleged found her stride, and he looked one paced from there until beginning to run on again near the line. The 28/10 favourite, he finished five lengths down on the long-priced Miss Alleged.

Pistolet Bleu is better than his running at Churchill Downs, on balance of form second behind Suave Dancer among the three-year-olds over middle distances in France in 1991 and about the equal of his year-older stable-companion Epervier Bleu. For a while there seemed a good chance he might be number one. He showed great promise as a staying two-year-old, particularly on the last of his three starts when running away with the Group 1 Criterium de Saint-Cloud. As a result he received a rating of 120 in the International Classification which put him equal-fourth behind a very different sort in Hector Protector. The regard in which he was held in France at the beginning of the latest season can be seen from the fact that he started at 10/1 on for a quite competitive Prix Noailles at Longchamp in April on his re-appearance. He won it comfortably from Subotica by three quarters of a length, having moved through to dictate from early in the straight; third-placed Pigeon Voyageur also went on to make a significant contribution to the season. Pistolet Bleu next went on to the Prix Hocquart at Longchamp in May

Prix Hocquart, Longchamp—Pistolet Bleu and Subotica again, with Beau Sultan

in preparation for the French Derby. On this occasion tougher opposition was expected from Beau Sultan who'd been a four-length second to Suave Dancer in the Greffulhe, but Subotica again turned out to be the main danger. Pistolet Bleu won stylishly. He was ridden differently, being gradually settled down after pulling hard despite a very strong pace early on. It was two thirds of the way up the straight, where Beau Sultan held a slender advantage over Subotica, before Pistolet Bleu was called on for his effort. He soon got the lead, then ran on well under firm hands-and-heels assistance to hold off the battling Subotica by a length and a half. Ground conditions for the latest Arc probably helped Pistolet Bleu. They were on the soft side, so made for more of a test of stamina; and he does seem particularly well suited by give in the ground in any case—his second to Subotica in the Niel on his only outing on good to firm wouldn't be approaching his best though he ran well enough to be able to say he acts on it.

Pistolet Bleu (IRE) (b.c. 1988)	Top Ville (b 1976)	High Top (b 1969)	Derring-Do / Camenae
		Sega Ville (b 1968)	Charlottesville / La Sega
	Pampa Bella (FR) (ch 1981)	Armos (ch 1967)	Mossborough / Ardelle
		Kendie (b 1963)	Klairon / Amagalla

Pistolet Bleu's sire Top Ville is overwhelmingly an influence for stamina. The dam Pampa Bella was never tried beyond ten and a half furlongs, over which distance she won twice in testing conditions. She was by some way the best product of the family in recent times until Pistolet Bleu came along. One of her wins was in the Prix Penelope, and she later finished third in the Prix Saint-Alary and the Prix de Diane. Nine of her dam Kendie's twelve foals won races, some over jumps; Kendie and her dam Amagalla both won in France. *E. Lellouche, France.*

PITCH BLACK (IRE) 2 br.g. (Feb 17) Be My Native (USA) 122 – Turbina (Tudor Melody 129) [1991 6m⁵ 8m 5m4] IR 1,100Y, 6,800 2-y-o: leggy gelding: half-brother to a winner in Ireland over hurdles: dam, placed at up to 17f in France and Ireland, is daughter of half-sister to Bella Paola: best effort under 4 lengths fourth of 11 to Tate Dancer in maiden at Catterick in October, soon towards rear then catching eye running on under tender handling: worth keeping an eye on in modest company, particularly back over further. *M. W. Easterby.* **56 p**

PITT CLUB 3 ch.g. King of Clubs 124 – Clare Bridge (USA) 107 (Little Current (USA)) [1990 NR 1991 8d* 8f4 8.1s 7m 7.1m] rather leggy, quite attractive gelding: second foal: closely related to fairly useful Clare Court (by Glint of Gold), successful at 1m (at 2 yrs) to 1¾m: dam 1m winner stayed 1½m: won apprentice maiden at Warwick in July: failed to reproduce that effort: stays 1m well: mulish third start, **70 d**

blinkered fourth: has twice gone very freely to post: sold to join C. Popham 4,000 gns Ascot October Sales. *I. A. Balding.*

PLACID LADY (IRE) 2 b.f. (May 3) Runnett 125 – Break of Day (On Your Mark 125) [1991 6.1m 5g] IR 3,500Y: lenthy, unfurnished filly: sister to modest 7f and 1m winner Bath and half-sister to 3 winners, 2 in Hong Kong: dam never ran: soundly beaten in maidens at Nottingham (pulled hard) and Redcar in October. *W. Carter.* —

PLAIN FACT 6 b.g. Known Fact (USA) 135 – Plain Tree 71 (Wolver Hollow 126) [1990 6v 6m 6m² 6d 7m³ 6g² 5m² 6s⁵ 6s 1991 5m² 7d 5f* 5m* 5.9m³ 5m* 6g a 5m⁵ 5.6m 5d⁶ 5d a6g* a6g* a6g²] compact, workmanlike gelding: fair performer: successful in claimers at Redcar, Sandown and Wolverhampton in mid-summer and Southwell in December: also won handicap at Southwell in November: effective at 5f and probably stays 7f: acts on any going: has hung right: ran poorly when going much too freely down eighth start. *Sir Mark Prescott.* **81** **89**

PLAN AHEAD 2 ch.f. (Apr 5) King of Clubs 124 – Calametta (Oats 126) [1991 6m 5.3g⁵ 6g² 6g³ 6g² 6g] 5,000Y: sparely-made filly: second foal: dam Irish maiden: modest maiden: ran well when placed in claimers at Goodwood and Catterick and in 18-runner nursery at Newbury: ran badly final start: will be better suited by 7f and 1m: usually claimer ridden. *G. Lewis.* **70 ?**

PLAN MORE ACTION (IRE) 2 ch.g. (Mar 9) Doulab (USA) 115 – Numidia (Sallust 134) [1991 a7g] IR 14,000F, IR 6,000Y: third foal: brother to sprint maiden Diadad and half-brother to 7f winner Premier Choice (by Petorius): dam stayed 9f, is half-sister to very useful French middle-distance winner Dieter: tailed off in late-year maiden at Lingfield. *J. Akehurst.* —

PLANNING AHEAD (IRE) 3 b.g. Lyphard's Special (USA) 122 – Gay Parthia 84 (Gay Fandango (USA) 132) [1990 NR 1991 7g³ 7m³ 7g* 8g] sparely-made gelding: fifth foal: half-brother to winning sprinter Laleston (by Junius): dam ran only at 2 yrs, winning twice at 5f from 2 starts: favourite, appeared to have outstanding chance on debut form when winning seller (retained 9,000 gns) at Leicester in workmanlike style: well-beaten favourite in Newmarket claimer later in June. *P. F. I. Cole.* **74 ?**

PLATINUM ROYALE 4 b.c. Dominion 123 – Zerbinetta 96 (Henry The Seventh 125) [1990 10.1m⁴ 12m³ 12.2m* 1991 14m 18d 12g⁶ 12m 12d³ 14g⁴ 14.6m] strong, good-topped colt: plating-class handicapper: slipped up final start (July): worth another try over 2m+: acts on good to firm ground: sold to join M. Pipe's stable 6,600 gns Newmarket July Sales: won over hurdles in October. *Mrs J. R. Ramsden.* **57**

PLATONIQUE 4 b.f. Dunbeath (USA) 127 – Plato's Retreat 73 (Brigadier Gerard 144) [1990 8f⁴ 12f⁵ 10.2m⁴ 10.2g⁴ 8m 12v 10d 7d⁴ a8g⁵ 1991 8d 9s*] leggy, workmanlike filly: fair performer in 1990: favourite, didn't have to be at best to win claimer (claimed £15,100) at Ripon in April: stays 1¼m: acts on good to firm ground and dead: sent to Sweden, successful there. *Mrs J. R. Ramsden.* **59 +**

PLATOON 4 gr.c. Petong 126 – Shelton Girl 64 (Mummy's Pet 125) [1990 7f 6f 7d* 7g a7g 1991 a6g⁴ a6g⁵ 7d 6g 8g 7m 7g 7f 5g⁴ 5.9m] workmanlike colt: easy mover: plating-class handicapper nowadays: below form after reappearance: stays 7f: acts on any going: sold 2,800 gns Doncaster Summer Sales. *T. D. Barron.* **57 d**

PLAYFUL POET 4 ch.g. The Noble Player (USA) 126 – Phamond 61 (Pharly (FR) 130) [1990 6m 5d 5g² 5m 6s² 5s* 1991 6s⁶ 5g 6m 5d⁵ 5g 5m* 5.1m 5g] deep-girthed, strong-quartered gelding: moderate mover: modest handicapper: below form in 1991, including when winning at Hamilton in July: stays 6f: effective on good to firm ground, but suited by plenty of give: suited by forcing tactics. *M. H. Easterby.* **68**

PLAY GAMES (USA) 3 ch.c. Nijinsky (CAN) 138 – Playful Queen (USA) (Majestic Prince) [1990 NR 1991 12m⁶ 11.7m* 16g 10.2g⁴ 11.7f⁶] $250,000Y: well-made colt: has a short, rather round action: second foal: closely related to 4-y-o Prancing Queen (by Sovereign Dancer): dam, 4-y-o 7f stakes winner, is half-sister to several good winners, notably triple Grade 1 winner (from 1m to 1½m) Fit To Fight: favourite, bumped final 1f and awarded maiden at Bath in July: acted as pacemaker next start and below form in handicaps: suited by 1½m: sweating third and fourth outings: sold 12,000 gns Newmarket Autumn Sales. *G. Harwood.* **72**

PLAY RISKY (IRE) 2 b.c. (Apr 25) Risk Me (FR) 127 – Palucca (GER) (Orsini 124) [1991 7f 10m 8m a6g a8g⁶] sparely-made colt: dam second in German 1000 Guineas and fourth in German Oaks: poor form in varied events, including a seller: twice blinkered: wore eyeshield penultimate start: sold 650 gns Ascot December Sales. *P. A. Kelleway.* **44**

PLAYSAYYAF (IRE)   3 b.c. Sayyaf 121 – Playtime (Primera 131) [1990 5m 7g   —
1991 5g 8d 12m 7d 8m] close-coupled colt: poor plater: visored then blinkered last 2
starts. *B. Gubby.*

PLAY THE ACE   3 b.g. Mansingh (USA) 120 – Boa (Mandrake Major 122) [1990   **54**
5g 5f* 5d* 6f6 5g2 1991 5d 5.7g6 6m3 5f6 6f 6g] big, lengthy, rather angular gelding:
plating-class performer at 3 yrs: soundly beaten last 2 outings: stays 6f: acts on firm
and dead going: has run well when sweating. *P. S. Felgate.*

PLAY THE BLUES   4 gr.f. Cure The Blues (USA) – Casual Pleasure (USA)   —
(What A Pleasure (USA)) [1990 a8g2 8m 6m 8g 1991 8f] leggy, sparely-made filly:
has a round action: second in maiden at Southwell in 1990: well beaten since, in
selling handicap on only outing of 1991 (September): may well prove best at up to
1m: winning hurdler. *R. G. Frost.*

PLAYUP   3 ch.f. High Line 125 – Putupon 89 (Mummy's Pet 125) [1990 6d 7m   —
6d6 1991 10g 14.1g] sparely-made filly: plating-class maiden: never better than mid-
division in summer handicaps: stayed 7f: twice bandaged behind: dead. *Mrs L.
Piggott.*

PLEASANT COMPANY   4 b.f. Alzao (USA) 117 – Keeping Company (King's   —
Company 124) [1990 7g4 8.2g6 8m 8g 7g a12g 8f a6g 1991 a11g a8g] small filly: poor
and lightly-raced maiden: tried blinkered and visored: trained on reappearance by
M. James. *P. A. Blockley.*

PLEASANT EXHIBIT   4 ch.c. Exhibitioner 111 – Miss Fandango 56 (Gay   **71**
Fandango (USA) 132) [1990 5g3 5.3f* 6s4 a6g5 1991 a7g a6g a6g5 7f a7g5 6m* 6g3   a 53
7m6 6d3 5f5 5.8d] good-quartered colt: plating-class handicapper: won at Pontefract
in April: will prove better suited by 6f or 7f than 5f: probably acts on any going:
wears blinkers and severe noseband. *J. D. Bethell.*

PLEASANT TIMES   3 ch.c. Absalom 128 – Lady Warninglid (Ela-Mana-Mou   —
132) [1990 7m 7f 1991 12.2g 12m 12.5m] sparely-made colt: poor mover: well beaten,
including in seller and handicap: bandaged off-fore then blinkered last 2 starts: sold
820 gns Doncaster August Sales. *M. Brittain.*

PLEASE PLEASE ME (IRE)   3 b.f. Tender King 123 – Tacama 64 (Daring   **45**
Display (USA) 129) [1990 8m 6m 1991 5m5 7d5 6m a7g 7f 6m2 6.9m4 5m 8f5 9m 8g
6.1d a8g] smallish, sparely-made filly: plater: always behind in Lingfield claimer
final start: needs further than 5f and stays 1m: acts on firm ground: bandaged on
reappearance: blinkered fifth outing: slowly away first 6 starts: trained until after
fifth by A. Lee. *K. O. Cunningham-Brown.*

PLEASURE AHEAD   4 b.c. Taufan (USA) 119 – Nan's Mill (Milford 119) [1990   **45**
8g 8f 8m 8m3 7f4 8.3m4 7h2 7g 8.3g 8f5 6f3 7m 7f6 1991 a7g6 a6g5 a7g5 a8g2 7d4 8f2
7m 7f3 7g6 7m a10g5 a12g4 a10g4 a12g3] leggy, close-coupled colt: poor mover: poor
handicapper: needs further than 6f and stays 1¼m: acts on hard and dead ground. *M.
R. Channon.*

PLEASURE QUEST   2 b.f. (May 23) Efisio 120 – Eagle's Quest 62 (Legal Eagle   —
126) [1991 5g 6f6 6g] leggy, close-coupled filly: fifth live foal: half-sister to several
winners, including Dumbreck (by Another Realm) winner over 6f (at 2 yrs) and 8.3f:
dam 5f winner: no worthwhile form. *L. J. Holt.*

PLEASURING   2 ch.f. (Feb 27) Good Times (ITY) – Gliding 94 (Tudor Melody   **68**
129) [1991 6g5 6f 5.1g4] workmanlike filly: has scope: closely related to useful 7f and
8.5f winner Bay Street and 1984 2-y-o 7f winner False Lift (both by Grundy) and
half-sister to several winners, including useful 7f winner Rose of Montreaux (by
Habat): dam sprinting half-sister to very smart 1973 2-y-o Splashing (dam of
Bassenthwaite): modest form in maidens at Ascot (won by Sun And Shade) and
Newbury (won by High Sevens) in late-summer: better for race, below best in minor
event at Bath over 6 weeks later: may well stay 1m. *M. McCormack.*

PLECTRUM   3 b.f. Adonijah 126 – Cymbal 80 (Ribero 126) [1990 7m6 1991 10.4g   **52**
a12g2 a10g4] rather leggy, unfurnished filly: plating-class maiden: second in claimer
at Lingfield in November: below form in similar event over 2 weeks later: stays
1½m: changed hands 900 gns Newmarket December Sales before third start: joined
J. Spearing. *B. W. Hills.*

PODRIDA   5 gr.m. Persepolis (FR) 127 – Pot Pourri 97 (Busted 134) [1990 14.8f3   —
14g2 20m a18g 13.8d 1991 14m] good-bodied mare: carries condition: moderate
mover: one-time fair handicapper, not nearly so good nowadays: heavily bandaged,
tailed off only run in 1991 (April): should prove best around 2m: acts on firm going.
B. Stevens.

POD'S DAUGHTER (IRE) 3 b.f. Tender King 123 – Make Your Bid 79 —
(Auction Ring (USA) 123) [1990 5f* 5m⁴ 5g⁶ 5d³ 6g 5f² 6f 1991 6f 7.5f] neat filly:
turns off-fore in: quite modest plater: form only at 5f: acts on firm ground. *C.
Tinkler.*

POETIC LIGHT 3 b.f. Ardross 134 – Sheer Gold 92 (Yankee Gold 115) [1990 NR —
1991 10.5g] strong, lengthy filly: first foal: dam Irish 1½m and 2m winner, later
smart hurdler here: 33/1, backward and very green, soon struggling in maiden at
Haydock in July. *G. M. Moore.*

POETS COVE 3 b.g. Bay Express 132 – Miss Milton (Young Christopher 119) 97 d
[1990 5m² 5m 5f* 5f* 5f* 5g³ 5g⁶ 5m 1991 6f³ 5m⁵ 5g 5f⁶ 5m 5.2m] compact
non-thoroughbred gelding: good walker: has quick action: useful as 2-y-o: easily
best effort in 1991 (including in claimers) when third in minor event at Folkestone:
probably stays 6f: acts on firm going: blinkered final outing: subsequently gelded:
trained until after third by W. Carter. *M. McCormack.*

POINCIANA 2 b.c. (Feb 6) Big Spruce (USA) – Andrushka (USA) (Giboulee 69 p
(CAN)) [1991 6f 7.1m⁴] 11,000Y: strong colt: has scope: first foal: dam won 2 races at
up to 7f: sire, won from 9f to 13f, best at 5 yrs when high class: in need of race, 9
lengths fourth of 11 to Zaahi in maiden at Sandown in September, keeping on well
until last 100 yds: should stay 1m: will improve again. *R. Hannon.*

POIRE DU NORD 3 b.c. Legend of France (USA) 124 – Polly's Pear (USA) 45
(Sassafras (FR) 135) [1990 7m⁴ 7f 7s 1991 a8g 10.8d 8g 10m 14.6g 8m⁴ 8.1s 8.2m 8m]
sturdy colt: plating-class form at best: well beaten last 3 outings: may prove best at
1m: acts on good to firm ground: visored (took strong hold) final start: sold A. Smith
1,800 gns Doncaster November Sales. *R. Hollinshead.*

POLAR FALCON (USA) 4 b. or br.c. Nureyev (USA) 131 – Marie d'Ar- 126
gonne (FR) 104 (Jefferson) [1990 8f* 7g⁴ 9.2g⁴ 8.5m* 8g⁴ 8s³ 8.5s² 8g² 1991
8d* 8d* 6m⁴ 8g⁴ 6f* 8g]

This high-class, versatile and most consistent son of Nureyev will no
doubt be a welcome addition to his owner's Cheveley Park Stud at Newmarket. David Thompson's purchasing of Polar Falcon from Michel Zerolo at
the end of the colt's three-year-old career proved an inspired move, for Polar
Falcon came on in leaps and bounds at four. Stepping up in class as he
improved, he was successful in Group 3 company before Group 2 before his
finest hour in the Ladbrokes Sprint Cup at Haydock; and he ended the season
having a crack at many of the best milers around in the Breeders' Cup Mile at
Churchill Downs. Few could have expected Polar Falcon to scale the heights
he did. Unraced at two, he'd looked fairly well exposed at three, winning an
eight-and-a-half-furlong listed race at Longchamp after getting off the mark in
a maiden there, and in the frame on his six other starts, including a
fourth in the Prix Jean Prat. Even after his length-and-a-half success from
Boxing Day in the Group 3 Prix Edmond Blanc at Evry on his reappearance as
a four-year-old in April, his opposing In The Groove in the Juddmonte Lockinge Stakes at Newbury the following month seemed highly optimistic. But in
a four-horse race run at a crawl for much of the way, In The Groove, sent off at
2/1 on, proved no match for Polar Falcon when the race began from the
two-furlong marker. Despite losing several lengths at the start, Polar Falcon
was soon able to recover and his superior turn of foot over his rivals proved
decisive. He beat In The Groove by two lengths, for trainer Hammond's first
win on English soil. There was no element of farce in Polar Falcon's next win
here in the Ladbroke Sprint Cup in September, which he achieved in a manner
that explained how he could make In The Groove and Candy Glen look so
ordinary in the Lockinge. There were six runners in the field for the Ladbroke

*Juddmonte Lockinge Stakes, Newbury—Polar Falcon wins the sprint,
after they'd crawled for more than half a mile*

Ladbroke Sprint Cup, Haydock—Polar Falcon quickens past Sheikh Albadou

Sprint, and much of the interest centred on how the Guineas winners Shadayid and Mystiko, both bidding for their first victories since Newmarket, would fare back at sprint distances. Shadayid was confidently expected to cope, judging by the betting: she started 13/8 favourite; the Nunthorpe winner Sheikh Albadou came next at 9/4, followed by Mystiko at 9/2 and Polar Falcon at 13/2; Shalford (12/1) and Amigo Menor (20/1) completed the line-up. Sheikh Albadou and Mystiko cut out the early running at a strong pace, closely pursued by Shalford, Amigo Menor and Shadayid. Polar Falcon was held up in last place. It soon became clear that Mystiko, off the bridle at halfway, would be playing no part in the finish, and when Sheikh Albadou set sail for home a furlong later Shadayid's supporters knew their fate for Carson was pumping away for all he was worth on her with little response. Shalford and Amigo Menor soon beat a retreat and it was left to Polar Falcon, yet to be asked for his effort by Asmussen, to throw down a challenge. Some challenge it was. Eased towards the stand rail over a furlong out, Polar Falcon quickened in tremendous style to take it up inside the last half furlong and quickly went a couple of lengths ahead until eased half a length in the dying strides. Shadayid finished third, all of five lengths behind the winner, herself a length and a half to the good of Mystiko who kept on again to shade Shalford for fourth. Polar Falcon's time of 1 min 11.23 seconds knocked 0.41 of a second off the previous course record. There's little doubt that Polar Falcon, who needed to be covered up according to Hammond, had the race tailor-made for him but nothing should be taken away from his performance, one of the best over six furlongs seen all season. A rigid adherence to one set of riding tactics can prove a drawback, however, and this was amply illustrated in Polar Falcon's previous two runs in the Carroll Foundation July Cup and Prix du Haras de Fresnay-le-Buffard Jacques le Marois. On each occasion, the early pace was a sedate one, particularly in the Jacques le Marois, and on each occasion Polar Falcon was plumb last when the tempo quickened appreciably at around the two-furlong pole. In the circumstances then, good fourth places at Newmarket (beaten four lengths by Polish Patriot) and Deauville (beaten less than a length by Hector Protector) are all the more praiseworthy. Sadly, Polar Falcon's fine record of never having finished out of the frame was lost on his final run, in the Breeders' Cup Mile. Set a great deal to do, he was never better than his eleventh-of-fourteen position to Opening Verse and it transpired he'd swallowed some mud. He coughed badly after the race.

Polar Falcon was led out unsold at 425,000 dollars when offered at the 1988 Keeneland July Sales before being purchased by Mr Zerolo. He descends on the dam's side from a highly successful French family. He's the first foal of the useful middle-distance filly Marie d'Argonne, successful in a mile-and-a-quarter Saint-Cloud maiden and third in the Group 3 Prix Penelope there, and later a winner at up to nine furlongs in the USA. Marie d'Argonne is a

Mr David Thompson's "Polar Falcon"

Polar Falcon (USA) (b. or br.c. 1987)	Nureyev (USA) (b 1977)	Northern Dancer (b 1961)	Nearctic
			Natalma
		Special (b 1969)	Forli
			Thong
	Marie d'Argonne (FR) (ch 1981)	Jefferson (ch 1967)	Charlottesville
			Monticella
		Mohair (ch 1974)	Blue Tom
			Imberline

half-sister to Marie de Litz. Very smart at her best from around ten to fifteen furlongs, Marie de Litz won the Prix de Pomone and Prix de Royaumont as well as finishing in the frame in numerous good races, including the Prix Kergorlay, Prix Vermeille and Gran Premio di Milano. Polar Falcon's grandam Mohair is an unraced daughter of Imberline, third in the Epsom Oaks and a half-sister to Shantung. Imberline's record at stud bears the closest inspection. Her seven winners include the smart French performers Corduroy II, Cigaline, Percale (the dam of Prix Vermeille winner Paysanne) and Poile de Chameau. An angular, but nonetheless quite attractive colt, Polar Falcon was a moderate mover in his slower paces. He was effective on ground ranging from firm to soft, at distances between six furlongs and a mile (although he never raced at the minimum trip, he gave the impression he'd have proved effective at it). He possessed a very good turn of foot. His fee to begin with will be £7,500. *J. E. Hammond, France.*

POLAR REGION 5 br.g. Alzao (USA) 117 – Bonny Hollow (Wolver Hollow 126) — [1990 NR 1991 11.8g] leggy, workmanlike gelding: extremely lightly raced and little form on flat since 2 yrs: stays 7f: acts on dead ground: winning hurdler in spring. *J. G. FitzGerald.*

POLEMIC (USA) 3 ch.f. Roberto (USA) 131 – Solartic (CAN) (Briartic (USA)) **114** [1990 6.5g* 6d⁴ 5g² 8g 1991 8d³ 10g² 10.5d⁵ 12m⁶ 10m⁴ 9d³ 9f⁶] very useful performer: second to Treble in Prix Saint-Alary, narrowly-beaten fourth of 7 to

Caerlina in slowly-run Prix de la Nonette and ¾-length third to Martessa in Prix de l'Opera, all at Longchamp: didn't get best of runs in Prix de Diane Hermes at Chantilly third start: modest sixth in Irish Oaks at the Curragh, plenty to do when switched entering straight, keeping on steadily: should stay 1½m: acts on dead ground: to race in USA. *M. Zilber, France.*

POLICIANE (FR) 3 ch.f. Policeman (FR) 124 – Pharlane (FR) (Pharly (FR) 130) — [1990 5m⁶ 6g⁶ 1991 5f 5s 6s] lengthy, unfurnished filly: plating-class maiden: edgy, well beaten in handicaps last 2 starts: bred to stay much further: sold 900 gns Doncaster November Sales. *P. Mitchell.*

POLISH BLUE (USA) 2 b.c. (Apr 10) Danzig (USA) – Office Wife (USA) 75 p (Secretariat (USA)) [1991 7m⁴] $1,250,000Y: compact colt: third foal: half-brother to Irish 3-y-o 1½m and 13f winner Green Marine (by Green Dancer) and a winner in North America: dam winning (and graded-stakes placed) half-sister to Golden Fleece, family also of Be My Guest: 20/1 from 10/1, backward and green, 7 lengths fourth of 6 to Muhtarram in minor event at Leicester in October, held up after slowish start, outpaced 2f out, then staying on strongly not knocked about: will improve and win races. *M. R. Stoute.*

POLISHING 4 ch.g. Touching Wood (USA) 127 – Loveshine (USA) (Gallant 79 Romeo (USA)) [1990 NR 1991 9f⁵ 9.9f⁵ 12.4m* 12f³ 12m⁴ 11.9g⁶ 11.9m] angular, close-coupled gelding: fifth foal: brother to French 7f and 9f winner Touching Love and half-brother to 7f and 12.2f winner Hug Me (by Shareef Dancer): dam, 1m stakes winner, is half-sister to very smart sprinter/miler Clever Trick: modest handicapper: won at Newcastle (maiden) in August: ran poorly in apprentice event final start: should stay beyond 1½m: acts on firm ground, yet to race on a soft surface: winning hurdler. *Mrs P. A. Barker.*

POLISH KING (USA) 3 gr.c. Danzig (USA) – Sintra (USA) (Drone) [1990 8m* 97 1991 8d³ 8d³ 8v⁶ 8v⁴] rather leggy colt: very impressive winner of minor event at Newmarket as 2-y-o: third in £7,400 contest at Thirsk and minor event (visored, well beaten) at Sandown in spring at 3 yrs: left M. Stoute's stable and ran in French listed races late in year, not discredited on final start: disappointing. *N. Clement, France.*

POLISH PATRIOT (USA) 3 b.c. Danzig (USA) – Maria Waleska (Fili- 128 berto (USA) 123) [1990 6m² 6f* 5f² 5f² 6f* 6m⁵ 1991 6m* 6m* 6m*]

The sprint championship was a closely-fought affair ending with none of the leading half-dozen contenders able to establish a clear ascendancy. Things might have been different had the Carroll Foundation July Cup winner

Cork And Orrery Stakes, Ascot—Polish Patriot (far side) rallies to foil Chicarica

Polish Patriot still been around when the likes of Polar Falcon (Ladbroke Sprint Cup), Keen Hunter (Prix de l'Abbaye) and Sheikh Albadou (Breeders' Cup Sprint) were furthering their claims. In the space of a few weeks Polish Patriot shot to the top of the sprinting league through an unbeaten run over six furlongs in a listed race at Lingfield, the Cork And Orrery Stakes at Royal Ascot and the Carroll Foundation July Cup at Newmarket, but on his return from Newmarket was found to have suffered a stress fracture of the off-fore cannon bone and he couldn't race again. However, he is fit to begin stallion duties in 1992 and will stand at the Rathbarry Stud in County Cork at a fee of IR 9,000 guineas.

Polish Patriot booked his Royal Ascot ticket by winning the well-contested Daily Mail Leisure Stakes at Lingfield on his seasonal reappearance in very good style by five lengths from Jimmy Barnie. Both colts had been useful two-year-olds, Polish Patriot out of the first two for the only time when a creditable fifth of nine to Lycius in the Middle Park Stakes. Lingfield showed Polish Patriot on the upgrade. At the same time it confirmed him still head-strong and quite highly strung: he wore a net muzzle in the paddock and to post, and was taken very quietly down by Cochrane. The Cork And Orrery is only on the fringe of the sprint championship. It's Group 3 with conditions that favour a relatively late-developing animal like Polish Patriot. He and ten others in the field of sixteen carried the basic weight for their age and sex while the rest were penalized either 4 lb or 8 lb for their previous success in pattern races. The contest looked wide-open and they bet 5/1 the field, Polish Patriot and Green Line Express sharing favouritism, the former carrying 8-2, 2 lb below Cochrane's day-to-day minimum riding weight. Polish Patriot, who sweated, was held up in a race run at a pace apparently too strong for the leaders' good. He had trouble finding room for a run two furlongs out and had to be switched to the stand rail before mounting a good effort which took him past Chicarica into the lead inside the last hundred yards. The contest wasn't over even then, for the filly rallied and Polish Patriot needed to find more to win by a short head. His jockey wasn't able to pull him up afterwards until reaching the mile start in Swinley Bottom.

At Ascot Chicarica was conceding 1 lb and Jimmy Barnie, under two lengths back in fourth place, was conceding 8 lb; so Polish Patriot obviously had a much stiffer task in the July Cup three weeks later and he started at 6/1. The July Cup is one of only two Group 1 races open to three-year-olds and upwards run over six furlongs in Britain and attracted a field of a similarly high quality to the other, the Ladbroke Sprint Cup at Haydock in September. The future Ladbroke Sprint Cup winner Polar Falcon was in the line-up against him, along with the King's Stand Stakes winner Elbio and the three-year-olds Lycius, Chicarica, Majlood, Exit To Nowhere and Time Gentleman. The Guin-eas winner Mystiko was a late withdrawal, joining other notable absentees in Sheikh Albadou and Divine Danse. Five of the runners were dropping back

Carroll Foundation July Cup, Newmarket—
Polish Patriot (right) looks a top-class sprinter in his final race;
he beats Lycius (noseband) by two lengths with Elbio third,
Polar Falcon (almost hidden by Lycius) fourth and Chicarica fifth

Mr R. A. Kirstein's "Polish Patriot"

in distance, but both second-placed Lycius and fourth-placed Polar Falcon reproduced their mile form, neither being much inconvenienced by the ordinary pace to halfway. As at Royal Ascot, Polish Patriot was settled in behind, though closer up, and again he made his challenge on the inside, this time coming between horses running into the Dip and quickening two lengths clear of Lycius up the hill, ridden out as the second kept on. The favourite Elbio, the one horse stepped up in distance, couldn't match Polish Patriot's acceleration for very long but he seemed to have run right up to his King's Stand form in depriving Polar Falcon of third by a clear margin, only half a length behind Lycius. Chicarica, who handled the extended preliminaries, which included a parade, on a sweltering afternoon less successfully than the winner, came a respectable fifth. Polish Patriot had put up the best performance in a sprint up to this point of the season and, in our opinion, his performance was still marginally the best by the close.

Polish Patriot (USA) (b.c. 1988)	Danzig (USA) (b 1977)	Northern Dancer (b 1961)	Nearctic
			Natalma
		Pas de Nom (b or br 1968)	Admiral's Voyage
			Petitioner
	Maria Waleska (ch 1976)	Filiberto (b 1970)	Ribot
			Fast Line
		Miss Protege (ch 1970)	Successor
			Belle Musique

Whether Polish Patriot would have been capable of reproducing the same level of form over any distance other than six furlongs, we'll never know. His form at six was better than his form at five as a youngster, but none of his form then compared with that as a three-year-old. Given his temperament it's doubtful whether he would have been as effective at much beyond six furlongs, though his dam won the Italian Oaks. Polish Patriot's sire Danzig is building a formidable reputation in Europe as a sprint sire. Dayjur is his best; others include the July Cup winner Green Desert, the Ladbroke Sprint Cup winner Danehill and the Prix de l'Abbaye winner Polonia. The dam Maria Waleska won six races in Italy altogether, another of them the Gran Premio d'Italia. She spent her first eight years at stud in the United States but was brought to Newmarket late on in 1988—her first British foal, Historiette (by Chief's Crown) was in training with Hern in the latest season. Polish Patriot is the last of three successive foals she produced to Danzig. The first of them, Polish Princess, showed modest form in two runs for Cumani as a three-year-old before winning a small race over seven and a half furlongs in Italy as a four-year-old; the second, Big Show, also won a small race—in the States as a two-year-old. Prior to that Maria Waleska produced two winners from four runners, including Roxbury Park (by Mr Prospector), successful at up to a mile and placed in minor stakes. The next dam, a minor winner at three years in the States, is a sister to Sound of Success, dam of the 1978 Benson And Hedges Gold Cup winner Hawaiian Sound on whom Shoemaker made almost all in Shirley Heights' Derby. Polish Patriot, a strong, good-quartered colt, raced only on top-of-the-ground; all his runs in 1991 were on good to firm. A headstrong nature was an important part of his make-up, but so were an excellent turn of foot and gameness in a finish. *G. Harwood.*

POLISH RIDER (USA) 3 ch.c. Danzig Connection (USA) – Missy T (USA) (Lt —
Stevens) [1990 NR 1991 8.1m6] $165,000Y: good-topped, quite attractive colt: twelfth reported foal: half-brother to at least 8 winners, including champion Puerto Rican colt Chef Henry (by Tudor Grey) and 1990 1m stakes winner Tees Prospect (by Tanks Prospect): dam, placed once from 16 starts, from family of Dancing Brave: burly and wearing tongue strap, soon struggling in maiden at Edinburgh in October: sold to join Mrs D. Haine 5,800 gns Newmarket Autumn Sales. *J. H. M. Gosden.*

POLISH STYLE (USA) 2 b.f. (Mar 5) Danzig (USA) – Family Style (USA) ?
(State Dinner (USA)) [1991 7g2 6d*] $1,300,000Y: first foal: dam, half-sister to Grade 1 winner Lost Kitty, was stakes winner from 2 yrs (when champion filly) to 4 yrs at up to 1¼m, including 4 Grade 1 events: successful in 11-runner minor event at Evry in September: will stay 1m: may well prove capable of better. *A. Fabre, France.*

POLISTATIC 4 br.f. Free State 125 – Polyandrist 92 (Polic 126) [1990 8f6 9m5 47
9g6 11.7m7m 10.1g 8m6 1991 11.7g 10.1g 12m3 12f4 12g* 11m* 12s4 12m2 12f 11.8g3
11.8m 11.5s3] smallish filly: poor handicapper: won at Brighton and Redcar (idled) in June: stays 1½m: acts on any going. *C. A. Horgan.*

POLITICAL FACT (USA) 2 ch.c. (Feb 2) Trempolino (USA) 135 – Hire A 100 p
Brain (USA) 92 (Seattle Slew (USA)) [1991 8.5g* 8s3] fourth foal: half-brother to Irish 1m (at 2 yrs) and 1¾m winner Major Inquiry (by The Minstrel), later fairly useful stayer and useful hurdler here: dam Irish 7f winner, is daughter of Grenzen, a high-class winner at up to 9f: favourite, comfortable winner of Galway maiden in August: much better form when running-on 6½ lengths third of 10 to El Prado in Juddmonte EBF Beresford Stakes at the Curragh 10 weeks later: may improve further, especially when granted middle distances. *D. K. Weld, Ireland.*

POLLEN COUNT (USA) 2 b.c. (Mar 20) Diesis 133 – Apalachee Honey (USA) 74 p
(Apalachee (USA) 137) [1991 7g3] $225,000Y: leggy, rather unfurnished colt: has scope: third known foal: half-brother to 1987 2-y-o 7f winner Le Miel (by Lyphard) and a minor winner in USA by Private Account: dam won Grade 1 6f event at 2 yrs: odds on but very green, slow-starting 4 lengths third of 18 to Nan A Buck in maiden at Leicester in September, running on strongly from near under considerate handling: should stay 1m: will improve, and win a similar event. *J. H. M. Gosden.*

POLLY MULDOWNEY 4 ch.f. Precocious 126 – Follow The Stars 86 —
(Sparkler 130) [1990 7m6 7g 7f6 8g6 8g3 8m a7g 1991 a10g a8g a7g 7d 8g 10f6 8g5 8s]
workmanlike filly: moderate mover: quite modest maiden at best: stays 1m: acts on firm ground: tried blinkered: sold 2,100 gns Newmarket July Sales. *R. W. Stubbs.*

POLLY PROCEEDS (USA) 2 b.f. (May 5) Procida (USA) 129 – Polly Daniels 60 p
(USA) 110 (Clever Trick (USA)) [1991 5g5 5m*] $12,000Y: sparely-made filly: second foal: dam useful sprinter: narrowly won 21-runner median auction maiden at Windsor in August, soon prominent, kept on strongly: will stay 6f: seems likely to improve again. *P. F. I. Cole.*

POLONEZ PRIMA 4 ch.c. Thatching 131 – Taiga 69 (Northfields (USA)) [1990 **87**
7f⁴ 8m³ 8m³ 8m³ 9m* 9g² 10d² 10.2s a10g⁶ 1991 10g⁶ 8g 9.9f³ 10.1m³ 7g* 8.1g*
7.9g⁵ 7.1f² 8m 9m 8m³ 8g²] good-bodied colt: fair handicapper: won at Newmarket
and Haydock in August: seems ideally suited by 7f/1m: best form on a sound surface:
below best when sweating once: good mount for apprentice. *J. Banks.*

POLSKI BOY (USA) 3 b. or br.c. Danzig Connection (USA) – Royal Folly **108**
(USA) (Tom Fool (USA)) [1990 6g² 7m* 6g³ 8m⁶ 1991 8s* 8g⁵ 7d* 7m*] $45,000Y:
half-brother to several winners, including Grade 2 9f Louisiana Derby winner
Prince Valiant (by Stage Door Johnny): dam once-raced half-sister to good broodmare Silver Sari: successful in maiden at Saint-Cloud at 2 yrs and in spring as 3-y-o
in minor event at Saint-Cloud then listed race and Prix du Palais Royal at Longchamp (by nose from Murmure): stays 1m: acts on good to firm ground: useful. *R.
Collet, France.*

POLYPLATE 3 b.f. Song 132 – Countless Countess 65 (Morston (FR) 125) [1990 **—**
6g 7f 7m⁶ 8.2g 8m 1991 12.3s 12.2m 10.1f 11.7g] leggy, attractive filly: poor maiden:
well beaten in handicaps at 3 yrs: best effort at 7f: blinkered final outing. *M. J. Ryan.*

POLYROLL 5 b.h. Kampala 120 – Hail To Feathers (USA) (Hail To All) [1990 9g **—**
10g 1991 a8g] big, lengthy horse: moderate mover: fairly useful winner in spring as
3-y-o: generally well below his best subsequently: best up to 8.5f: acts on good to
firm and soft going. *M. R. Channon.*

POLYXENA (USA) 2 b.f. (May 31) Lyphard (USA) 132 – Minstrel Girl (FR) 115 **?**
(Luthier 126) [1991 8v*] fourth reported foal: closely related to a stakes winner
abroad by Northern Dancer: half-sister to a graded stakes-placed winner by Val de
L'Orne: dam, from family of Ma Biche, French 2-y-o 7f winner (stayed 1½m at 3 yrs)
also second in Criterium des Pouliches: 4-length winner of 18-runner newcomers
event at Maisons-Laffitte in November: will be suited by middle distances: should
improve. *Mme C. Head, France.*

PONDERED BID 7 b. or br.g. Auction Ring (USA) 123 – Ponca (Jim French **46**
(USA)) [1990 NR 1991 14d³ 12d 16.5m 14d 14g* 14.6m4] angular gelding: poor
mover: poor handicapper nowadays: won at Nottingham (apprentices) in June:
seems suited by test of stamina nowadays: probably needs give in the ground:
blinkered at 7 yrs: often bandaged: ungenuine hurdler. *I. P. Wardle.*

PONSARDIN 2 b.c. (Apr 11) Petoski 135 – Premiere Cuvee 109 (Formidable **75 p**
(USA) 125) [1991 6m⁴ 5m*] £24,000Y: smallish, stocky colt: second foal: half-brother
to 3-y-o Toulal (by Taufan): dam sprinter, best at 4 yrs when sent to France: confirmed promise of debut when winning maiden at Catterick in October, driven out to
lead inside final 1f: may well improve again, particularly back at 6f. *Sir Mark Prescott.*

PONT AVEN 4 b.f. Try My Best (USA) 130 – Basilea (FR) (Frere Basile (FR) **109**
129) [1990 7m³ 6.5s* 8g² 6g 6d³ 6d⁵ 7g⁶ 1991 5s* 5m 6.5g 6d] useful French
performer: won Group 3 Prix de Saint Georges at Longchamp in May by head from
Luring: below best in pattern company after, in Group 3 event won by Divine Danse
at Maisons-Laffitte final start: probably best at sprint distances: best efforts with
give in the ground: keen sort. *R. Collet, France.*

PONTE CERVO 2 b.g. (Apr 23) Hadeer 118 – Pontevecchio Due 87 (Welsh **35**
Pageant 132) [1991 5g 5g⁶ 6m] 6,800Y: leggy gelding: third foal: dam 6f (at 2 yrs) to
8.5f winner: ran poorly in seller at Nottingham final start
(May): should stay 6f. *G. A. Pritchard-Gordon.*

PONTENUOVO 6 b.g. Kafu 120 – Black Gnat (Typhoon 125) [1990 9f* 8m 8f* **107**
8m 8m* 8m² 7m* 9m 1991 8g 8d 7.6m 8g³ 8d 8m² 7.9g* 8g 7d 7m 8g4] rangy

Bradford & Bingley Handicap, York—Pontenuovo dictates throughout;
Venus Observed pulls well clear of the rest

gelding: has a rather round action: useful handicapper: comfortably won Bradford & Bingley Handicap at York in August: good fourth at Newmarket final start: twice tenderly handled throughout in between: suited by 7f/1m, a sound surface and forcing tactics: goes very well at Ascot: genuine. *D. R. C. Elsworth.*

PONTYNYSWEN 3 b.g. Ballacashtal (CAN) – Tropingay (Cawston's Clown 113) [1990 6g 7m5 a6g a7g 1991 a12g] neat gelding: no worthwhile form in sellers and maidens. *D. Burchell.* —

POOH WEE 3 b.f. Music Boy 124 – Nicoletta 81 (Busted 134) [1990 6m5 6d* 7s 1991 7m4 8m 7.9m 8g* 8m 7.6d 8.1s6] strong, compact filly: poor mover: quite modest performer, best effort in handicaps on reappearance: still well below best when winning claimer at Pontefract in July: stays 1m: acts on good to firm ground and soft: occasionally bandaged behind: sweating and edgy third and fourth starts: sold to join J. J. O'Neill 8,200 gns Doncaster November Sales. *M. J. Camacho.* 70 d

POOLESTA (IRE) 2 b.f. (Mar 17) Hero's Honor (USA) – Radiant (USA) (Foolish Pleasure (USA)) [1991 5m* 6g2 6m3 5d5] IR 60,000F: quite attractive, rather unfurnished filly: third foal: dam, minor winner at around 6f, is half-sister to good middle-distance colt Gold And Ivory: well-backed 11/2-shot and on toes, won maiden at York in May: off course over 3 months before showing fairly useful form in Lowther Stakes at York (staying on behind Culture Vulture) and Moyglare Stud Stakes (won by Twafeaj) at the Curragh in late-summer: fair fifth of 11 to Magic Ring in Cornwallis Stakes at Ascot in October: will stay 7f. *M. W. Easterby.* 96

POPPY CHARM 4 b.f. Star Appeal 133 – Pop Music (FR) (Val de Loir 133) [1990 9f3 12h3 10g3 8f 8m 9m 1991 9.7s] sparely-made filly: plating-class performer at 3 yrs: no show only run in 1991 (November): should stay 1½m: acts on any going. *R. Curtis.* —

POP TO STANS 2 b.g. (May 7) Gold Crest (USA) 120 – Lady of Camelot (FR) (Bolkonski 134) [1991 5g2 5g* 5m4 6.1m3 a6g3 6g] 24,000Y: leggy, good-topped gelding: has scope: sixth foal: brother to fairly useful 1990 2-y-o 5f performer Silken Sailed and half-brother to 3 winners, including 13.8f winner Shawwal (by Shirley Heights): dam 7f and 1m winner in France: modest performer: successful in early-season maiden at Thirsk: looked ungenuine (hung throughout) in York seller on final start: should stay 7f: carries head awkwardly. *T. D. Barron.* 68 §

POPULARITY (USA) 3 ch.f. Blushing Groom (FR) 131 – Populi (USA) (Star Envoy (USA)) [1990 NR 1991 10m4 14m5] leggy, lightly-made filly: seventh reported foal: half-sister to 3 winners in USA, including top-class middle-distance performer Vanlandingham (by Cox's Ridge): dam, winner twice at 2 yrs in claiming company, is half-sister to champion American 1980 middle-distance 3-y-o Temperence Hill: 7½ lengths fourth of 10 to Giventime at Pontefract in August, pushed along after 4f but better effort in maidens: stud. *H. R. A. Cecil.* 58

PORICK 3 b.g. Marching On 101 – Natina-May 59 (Mandrake Major 122) [1990 5m 6m 7f 1991 8d 9.9f 12g] leggy, close-coupled colt: of little account: blinkered/visored once. *D. Moffatt.* —

PORTICO (USA) 2 ch.c. (Feb 3) El Gran Senor (USA) 136 – Thorough 115 (Thatch (USA) 136) [1991 7s*] 60,000Y: fifth foal: brother to Irish 3-y-o 6f (at 2 yrs) and 1m winner Rua d'Oro, also third in Irish 1000 Guineas, and half-brother to fairly useful 7f winner Rah Wan (by Riverman): dam French 1m to 1½m winner: 11/8 on, comfortable winner of 6-runner maiden at the Curragh in October: bred to stay at least 1¼m: will improve. *M. V. O'Brien, Ireland.* 91 p

PORT IN A STORM 2 b.c. (Feb 2) Blakeney 126 – Crusader's Dream (St Paddy 133) [1991 7m4] sixth foal: half-brother to several winners, including 7f and 1m winner Benazir (by High Top) and 1¼m winner Historical Fact (by Reform): dam 2-y-o 6f winner from family of high-class miler Lucyrowe: 20/1 from 10/1, over 3 lengths fourth of 9, always thereabouts, to Fair American in maiden at Lingfield in October: will stay 1¼m: should improve. *W. Jarvis.* 69 p

PORT ISAAC (USA) 3 br.f. Seattle Song (USA) 130 – Key Link (USA) (Bold Ruler) [1990 6m 7m4 1991 8m 10d] lengthy filly: quite modest maiden: visored and well beaten at 3 yrs, in handicap in June: should be better at 1m than shorter. *M. R. Stoute.* —

PORTREE 2 b.f. (Feb 12) Slip Anchor 136 – Rynechra 102 (Blakeney 126) [1991 7g2] second foal: half-sister to smart 1¼m to 13.3f winner Applecross (by Glint of Gold): dam, unraced at 2 yrs, won twice over 1½m and stayed 1¾m well: 6/1, length second of 22 to Oumaldaaya in maiden at Newmarket in November, racing keenly travelling well, green then keeping on strongly: will stay 1¼m: sure to improve and win a race. *H. R. A. Cecil.* 82 p

PORT SODERICK (USA)   4 b.g. Affirmed (USA) – Queen of Cornwall (USA) **35** 109 (Cornish Prince) [1990 10.5g⁴ 10g 10d³ 8m² 11d⁶ 1991 11f 8f 11g⁴ 9m⁶ 11.1f² 10.8m 10m⁶ 12m] lengthy gelding: poor mover: poor handicapper: ran as if something amiss final start: stays 11f: acts on firm and dead ground: has been bandaged off-fore: usually visored nowadays: sold 1,600 gns Doncaster July Sales after third start. *A. Harrison.*

PORT SUNLIGHT (IRE)   3 ch.c. Tate Gallery (USA) 117 – Nana's Girl 109 **90** (Tin Whistle 128) [1990 6m³ 6m⁶ 5m⁵ 8g⁴ 8.2s* 1991 10g 10g⁴ 11 7g⁵ 11.5m³ 12g⁶ 11.7m 10m² 10m³ 9m* 10d⁵ 8.9m 9g] strong, workmanlike colt: carries condition: has a quick action: fairly useful handicapper: ran creditably most outings prior to winning £5,800 event at Newbury in September: below form after, well backed in £30,800 contest final start: effective at 9f and stays 1½m: acts on good to firm ground and soft. *R. Hannon.*

POSITIVE ACCLAIM   3 b.f. Vaigly Great 127 – Acclimatise 116 (Shirley **100** Heights 130) [1990 7m 6g³ 1991 7d* 8g⁶ 8g 10d² 10d³ 11.9m] leggy filly: useful performer: won maiden (edged left) at Brighton in April: placed in Newbury listed races: ran moderately in Lancashire Oaks at Haydock final start: better at 1¼m than shorter: acts on dead going, seems unsuited by top-of-the-ground. *R. Hannon.*

POSITIVE ASPECT   2 ch.f. (Apr 20) Jalmood (USA) 126 – Miss Bunty 70 (Song **37** 132) [1991 6m 8m⁵ 8s] 2,000F, 2,000Y: rather sparely-made filly: has a roundish action: first foal: dam maiden suited by 1m, is sister to very useful Shark Song, successful here and in USA at up to 9f, and half-sister to dam of Prince Sabo: poor maiden: off course all summer after debut: should stay 1¼m. *J. Pearce.*

POSSESSIVE DANCER   3 b.f. Shareef Dancer (USA) 135 – Possessive **118** (Posse (USA) 130) [1990 6m* 1991 8g* 9d* 12g* 12m* 11.9g⁵ 12m]
Possessive Dancer left Britain for two outings in the summer and returned a dual Oaks winner. Like Melodist in 1988, Possessive Dancer followed up her victory in the Oaks d'Italia with one in the much more important Irish equivalent, going one better than Melodist, however, in that she won the

Kildangan Stud Irish Oaks, the Curragh—a close race
between the Italian Oaks winner Possessive Dancer and Epsom winner Jet Ski Lady (rails)

Irish Oaks outright whereas Melodist dead-heated with Diminuendo. Possessive Dancer's improvement from the Oaks d'Italia (in which she beat Imco Lisi two lengths with, more relevantly for British racegoers, Brockette a further two and a quarter lengths back in third) to the Irish Oaks was a marked one in itself, but that pales almost into insignificance besides her long-term progress. Possessive Dancer's two appearances in Britain earlier in 1991 had been in handicap company, modest handicap company at that, when she'd gained impressive wins at Kempton off handicap marks of 73 and 81. Those followed a single run at two years, in a six-runner Newmarket maiden, in which she'd needed almost every yard to get the better of No Comebacks, a filly whose only success to the end of 1991 came in a selling handicap. In the Kildangan Stud Irish Oaks eight and a half months later, Possessive Dancer could be confidently named the winner as early as the home turn. Four of the ten runners were in front of her, all well within striking distance, and they included a weakening early leader and two fillies, Eileen Jenny and Often Ahead, whose latest starts had been in a maiden; with the Ribblesdale winner Third Watch and French challenger Polemic making only laboured progress behind them, the race lay between the 7/4 favourite the Gold Seal Oaks winner Jet Ski Lady and 8/1 fourth-favourite Possessive Dancer. There was never a question of Jet Ski Lady's getting clear on this occasion as Possessive Dancer made smooth headway to challenge approaching the final furlong and although she edged right and didn't go on in the style that seemed possible at

Sheikh Ahmed Al-Maktoum's "Possessive Dancer"

one stage, Possessive Dancer always had the edge, eventually winning by half a length. Progress of this order doesn't come ten-a-penny and for Possessive Dancer it ended with the Irish Oaks. She was made favourite for the Yorkshire Oaks but, she sweated up in the preliminaries and her response to pressure at the two-furlong marker was strictly limited. Possessive Dancer was beaten seven and three quarter lengths behind Magnificent Star and Jet Ski Lady, and after a similarly below-par effort in the Prix Vermeille a month later, connections retired her for the season.

Possessive Dancer (b.f. 1988)	Shareef Dancer (USA) (b 1980)	Northern Dancer (b 1961)	Nearctic
			Natalma
		Sweet Alliance (b 1974)	Sir Ivor
			Mrs Peterkin
	Possessive (b 1982)	Posse (ch 1977)	Forli
			In Hot Pursuit
		Front Row (b 1965)	Epaulette
			Panaview

Possessive Dancer was bred by Walter Swinburn Ltd, the jockey having purchased her dam Possessive for 45,000 guineas in foal to Dara Monarch then sent Possessive to Shareef Dancer whom he'd ridden throughout his five-race career, which, incidentally, also progressed from handicap company (he was second in the Esher Cup) to Irish classic success (in the Irish Derby). The foal by Dara Monarch, Possessive's first, is the dual one-mile claimer winner Possessive Lady while Possessive had a colt foal by Shadeed in 1991 and is now in foal to Green Desert. Until her purchase by Sheikh Ahmed Al-Maktoum shortly before the Oaks d'Italia, Possessive Dancer raced in the name of Swinburn's mother as the filly failed to reach her reserve (the final bid was 20,000 guineas) at the Highflyer Sales. That failure to sell might have had something to do with Possessive's being by an undistinguished sire in Posse and never having raced, but a look a generation back in the pedigree reveals Front Row who was by a far from outstanding stallion (Epaulette) herself but became an excellent broodmare. Front Row bred ten winners in all before being taken out of stud in 1988, the best of them being the smart miler Long Row and Norfolk Stakes winner Colmore Row. Front Row was an Irish classic winner, of the Irish One Thousand Guineas, her dam's second foal Black Satin (later the dam of that good American colt Czaravich) won the same race two years later, and two later siblings were placed in classics, Kingsview into third in a photo finish for the Irish Two Thousand Guineas and Ragapan second in the Irish Derby. April Slipper, a sister to Possessive's grandam Panaview, is the grandam of April Run.

Possessive Dancer is a tall, workmanlike filly. She has now won over six furlongs, a mile, nine furlongs and a mile and a half and shown she acts on good to firm ground and dead, not having raced on anything more extreme. Her career clearly reflects great credit on her trainer. *A. A. Scott.*

POSSESSIVE LADY   4 ch.f. Dara Monarch 128 – Possessive (Posse (USA) 130)   52
[1990 8.2g6 8f* 8g* 10g2 8m4 8g2 8.2m 9m 8.2d 1991 8m5 9m3] leggy, lightly-made filly: plating-class handicapper: not seen out after May: worth another try at 1¼m: acts on firm going, possibly not on dead. *M. Bell.*

POSTAGE STAMP   4 ch.g. The Noble Player (USA) 126 – Takealetter (Wolver   74
Hollow 126) [1990 11d 10.4d4 a11g* 10m 8m3 9m3 10f2 10.6d a12g5 10m6 10d3 1991 12m3 12m4 16.2g* 20g 15.8g6 14s4 16.1g2 15.9m4 16.2g 18m5] rangy, good-topped gelding: good walker: has rather round action: modest handicapper: won at Beverley in June: good fifth to Go South in Tote Cesarewitch at Newmarket, making most at modest pace: subsequently sold to join J. Pearce 23,000 gns Newmarket Autumn Sales: stays well: acts on firm and dead ground: has run creditably for apprentice: largely consistent. *J. W. Hills.*

POST IMPRESSIONIST (IRE)   2 b.f. (Mar 1) Ahonoora 122 – Roblanna 85   54 p
(Roberto (USA) 131) [1991 7m 7g] quite attractive filly: has scope: second foal: half-sister to Irish 3-y-o 1¾m winner Kilcash (by Salmon Leap): dam Irish 2-y-o 9f winner, is out of half-sister to good middle-distance horse Anne's Pretender: bit backward, plating-class form in late-season Newmarket maidens won by Modernise and Oumaldaaya: looks likely to do better, especially over middle distances. *B. W. Hills.*

POTAMOS (USA)   4 b. or br.c. Riverman (USA) 131 – Cautious Bidder (USA)   —
(Bold Bidder) [1990 NR 1991 a12g a7g a8g 8f4] compact colt: closely related to 1984
2-y-o 5f winner Overtrump, later smart stakes winner at around 1m in USA, and
useful 1986 2-y-o 6f winner Mileage Bank (both by J O Tobin) and half-brother to 2
winners in USA: dam best at 2 yrs when very smart winner of 5 races at up to 6f:
behind in maidens: wore eyeshield second outing: sold 2,600 gns Newmarket
September Sales. *C. E. Brittain.*

POTERIUM   3 b.c. Persian Bold 123 – Cryptomeria 86 (Crepello 136) [1990 7g4   **80**
1991 8g3 7g* 8m* 8m 8m 8m 8d 8d4 8.1d6] sturdy, close-coupled colt: fair
performer: justified favouritism in maiden at Lingfield and handicap at Goodwood in
May: easily best efforts in subsequent handicaps on last 2 outings: should stay 1¼m:
acts on good to firm ground and dead: visored and bandaged off-hind final start: sold
16,000 gns Newmarket Autumn Sales, probably to Italy. *J. H. M. Gosden.*

POTTER'S DREAM   4 ch.g. Horage 124 – Sally St Clair (Sallust 134) [1990 8m4   —
7d 8g 8m 7m2 7m5 10d3 10d 9g4 1991 9s5] leggy, workmanlike gelding: modest
maiden: never placed to challenge in claimer (claimed £8,005) only run in
1991 (April): stays 1¼m: acts on good to firm ground and dead: tends to wander:
visored once, hung left and tailed off when blinkered once: sent to Sweden and has
won there. *R. J. R. Williams.*

POWERFUL EDGE   2 ch.c. (May 7) Primo Dominie 121 – Sharp Castan 101   **84** p
(Sharpen Up 127) [1991 6m4 6f*] leggy, attractive colt: seventh foal: closely related
to useful 1985 2-y-o 7f winner Navarzato (by Dominion), later succesful in France,
and half-brother to several winners, notably Dashing Blade (by Elegant Air): dam
best at 2 yrs, when 5f winner and placed in Hoover Fillies' Mile: favourite, made
virtually all in maiden at Salisbury in August, running on strongly final 2f: will stay
7f: likely to improve further. *I. A. Balding.*

POWERFUL PIERRE   3 br.g. Mummy's Game 120 – Harmonious Sound   —
(Auction Ring (USA) 123) [1990 5f 5m 5m4 5f3 5m 5m 1991 6f 5m 7g 5g] strong
gelding: plating-class maiden: no form in 1991: should be suited by further than 5f:
visored (edgy) final start: twice sweating. *L. J. Holt.*

POWER LAKE   2 br.c. (Mar 4) Formidable (USA) 125 – Laugharne (Known Fact   **103**
(USA) 135) [1991 5m* 5m3 6d2 5m2 5g* 5g 5m2 5.3g* 6m4 5d3] 34,000Y: neat,
strong, sprint type: has a quick action: second foal: half-brother to 3-y-o Solfeo (by
Elegant Air): dam once-raced daughter of Boathouse, a half-sister to Bireme and
Buoy: won maiden at Lingfield in June and minor event at Doncaster in July:
reportedly operated on for wind infirmity after following start: subsequently
showed improved form (didn't have to be at best to win minor event at Brighton)
when in frame for Flying Childers Stakes at Doncaster (behind Paris House), then
Middle Park Stakes at Newmarket (won by Rodrigo de Triano) and Cornwallis
Stakes at Ascot (over 3 lengths third to Magic Ring) in autumn: effective at 5f and 6f:
very best efforts on good to firm ground, not at all discredited on dead: wore a
tongue strap last 5 starts, and a crossed noseband last four. *R. Hannon.*

POWER OF PRAYER   4 ch.f. The Noble Player (USA) 126 – Sandra's Choice   **34**
(Sandy Creek 123) [1990 6h 8.3f 1991 10m 9m 8f4 8g] angular filly: poor maiden:
should stay beyond 1m: acts on firm ground. *R. F. Johnson Houghton.*

POWER TAKE OFF   5 b.m. Aragon 118 – Law And Impulse 104 (Roan Rocket   **106**
128) [1990 8g* 8g3 7g 9g3 8g5 1991 10m 8g* 7.9g6 8g5 10m4 8m4 9m4] big, angular,
rather sparely-made mare: good mover: useful performer: won minor event at Ayr
in July: ran well when fourth in Group 3 event at Goodwood won by Filia Ardross and
listed contest won by Rudimentary at Newmarket on fifth and sixth starts: stays
1¼m: acts on good to firm going: trained until after reappearance by D. Elsworth. *P.
J. Makin.*

POYLE GEORGE   6 br.h. Sharpo 132 – Hithermoor Lass 75 (Red Alert 127) **101**
[1990 5f 5d4 5m 5f 5m 1991 5m 5g 5g] smallish, robust horse: has a quick action:
useful performer: good seventh of 15 to Title Roll in King George Stakes at
Goodwood second start: well below that form in Keeneland Nunthorpe Stakes at
York later in August: best at 5f: has won on good to firm going, but possibly needs an
easier surface nowadays: below best when sweating once. *D. R. C. Elsworth.*

PRAIRIE AGENT   6 b.m. Main Reef 126 – Regal Guard 60 (Realm 129) [1990   —
16m4 1991 a14g] rather sparely-made mare: moderate mover: bad plater: seems to
stay 15f: acts on firm going: has given trouble in preliminaries and started slowly. *R.
Ingram.*

PRAIRIE OYSTER   8 ch.g. Northfields (USA) – Huahinee (FR) (Riverman   —
(USA) 131) [1990 NR 1991 14d] poor mover: modest maiden at 3 yrs: tailed off in

handicap in June, first flat run since: probably stays 1¼m: acts on firm and dead going: ungenuine hurdler. *R. Curtis.*

PREAMBLE 2 b.f. (Mar 8) Baillamont (USA) 124 – Luth Celtique (FR) (Thatch **69** (USA) 136) [1991 6f5 7m] 1,000Y: tall, leggy, unfurnished filly: first foal: dam French 1¼m and 10.5f winner, is half-sister to Luth Enchantee: 50/1, keeping-on under 3 lengths fifth of 22, always thereabouts, to Binkhaldoun at Newbury in September, easily better effort in maidens: bred to stay 1¼m: sold to join Mrs J. Ramsden 5,600 gns Newmarket Autumn Sales. *M. D. I. Usher.*

PRECENTOR 5 ro.h. Music Boy 124 – La Magna 104 (Runnymede 123) [1990 6m **64** 5m 5m4 5g2 5m3 6m2 6f4 6m* 6m4 5m4 6g5 5.8d5 1991 6g5 5.8f3 6f5 5f3 6m* 5.7f2 5m* 5m3 6.1d4 a6g a6g2 a7g6] strong, close-coupled horse: moderate mover: plating-class handicapper: successful at Pontefract (2) in September: effective at 5f and 6f: acts on firm and dead going: blinkered: sometimes wears tongue strap: has hung left: has idled in front, and best with waiting tactics: consistent. *J. D. Bethell.*

PRECIOUS AIR (IRE) 3 ch.f. Precocious 126 – Astra Adastra (Mount Hagen **61** (FR) 127) [1990 5m3 5f* 6d3 a6g6 a7g3 1991 7m2 7m* 7g6 7m 7d4 6.9f5 6m a7g6 a6g] rather sparely-made filly: moderate mover: quite modest performer: edgy, won claimer (claimed out of B. Hills's stable £8,551) at Redcar in June, carrying head awkwardly: below form last 6 starts: better at 7f than 6f: acts on good to firm going (well below form on fibresand): visored sixth outing. *Denys Smith.*

PRECIOUS BALLERINA 6 ch.m. Ballacashtal (CAN) – Jenny's Rocket 90 **49** (Roan Rocket 128) [1990 a7g2 9f4 a8g3 a7g 1991 a8g4 a12g6 a8g*] tall mare: plating-class handicapper: won (for first time) amateurs event at Southwell in February: best form at 1m to 1¼m: has sweated: often finds little. *J. Hetherton.*

PRECIOUS CAROLINE (IRE) 3 b.f. The Noble Player (USA) 126 – What A **54** Breeze (Whistling Wind 123) [1990 a6g5 5f a6g2 6m 1991 7.1m 8g5 8d] workmanlike filly: good walker: plating-class maiden, not seen out until September as 3-y-o: ridden by 7-lb claimer, staying-on fifth of 20 in handicap at Wolverhampton: stays 1m: possibly unsuited by top-of-the-ground: slowly away final start. *P. D. Cundell.*

PRECIOUS WONDER 2 b.c. (May 3) Precocious 126 – B M Wonder (Junius **54** (USA) 124) [1991 6g 6.9f 7m6] 500Y, 1,000 2-y-o: workmanlike colt: has round action: fourth foal: dam, granddaughter of Oaks winner Carrozza, well beaten all 3 starts: form only when around 10 lengths sixth of 15 to Deserve in maiden at Lingfield in October: stays 7f. *P. Butler.*

Timeform Handicap, Pontefract—
blinkered Precentor repeats his previous year's success;
the other grey Nevada Mix runs him close

Tote Great St Wilfrid Handicap, Ripon—Premier Touch easily lands a gamble

PREDESTINE 6 b.g. Bold Owl 101 – Combe Grove Lady (Simbir 130) [1990 8m — 11.7g 16.2m 12g* 12m 8.3f 1991 8g] small, leggy gelding: quite modest handicapper at 5 yrs: bandaged and edgy, always behind only run in 1991 (May): best at 1½m: suited by give in the ground. *M. Madgwick.*

PREDICTABLE 5 ch.g. Music Boy 124 – Piccadilly Etta 76 (Floribunda 136) **77 d** [1990 a7g* a7g a6g⁵ 6v 5m⁴ 5g 5m 7m⁵ 6m⁴ 8m* 8d⁴ 8g 8.5f⁵ 8g⁶ 1991 a8g* a8g* a8g* a7g* 8s a7g³ 7m 8f⁶ 8.1d a10g⁴ 8g a7g] lengthy, angular gelding: moderate walker and mover: progressed into fair handicapper in spring, successful at Southwell (2) and Lingfield (2): well below form after sixth outing, off course 4½ months before final start: stays 1m: acts on good to firm and soft going: effective with or without visor. *Mrs A. Knight.*

PREFABRICATE (FR) 5 b.g. Kings Lake (USA) 133 – Celtic Assembly (USA) — 95 (Secretariat (USA)) [1990 NR 1991 9s 10d 8m 9.9m] medium-sized gelding: modest maiden at 3 yrs: no show, including in selling handicap, in 1991: should be suited by further than 1m: possibly best on top-of-the-ground. *J. L. Harris.*

PREMIER CHOICE (IRE) 3 b.g. Petorius 117 – Numidia (Sallust 134) [1990 **52** 5g 6m 6g 5g 1991 8s⁴ 7g* 7m⁶ 6d² a6g³ 7g 6d⁵] smallish, angular gelding: good walker: poor handicapper: won at Catterick in April, hanging right: well below form last 2 starts: should prove best short of 1m: acts on soft ground: sweating second and third starts: blinkered final one: pulls hard: sold 1,050 gns Newmarket Autumn Sales. *W. J. Pearce.*

PREMIER DANCE 4 ch.g. Bairn (USA) 126 – Gigiolina (King Emperor (USA)) **62** [1990 a7g² a8g³ 10m⁵ 12m 7.6m⁵ 8.2s⁴ 7m a8g⁴ 8.2m² 8.2d² 8m 1991 a7g a7g³ a10g* 10.2s² 10d 10g 10.8g³ 10.2g³ 12g a10g³ 8.9g⁵ 10g 10.5d³ a10g⁴ a10g] compact gelding: has quick action: quite modest handicapper: won at Lingfield in March: in-and-out form after: stays 10.5f: probably acts on any going: effective with or without blinkers. *D. Haydn Jones.*

PREMIER ENVELOPE (IRE) 2 b.c. (May 3) King Persian 107 – Kellys Risc **56** (Pitskelly 122) [1991 5d² 5g⁵ 5d⁴ 5g² 5m⁴ 5m⁶ a5g² a5g² 5m* 5m⁴ 5.1m⁵ 5m] 5,600Y: neat colt: moderate mover: third reported live foal: brother to quite modest 1990 2-y-o 5f winner Kellys Kingdom: dam unraced: sweating, won seller (no bid) at Haydock in July: little form in nurseries last 2 starts: will stay 6f: acts on good to firm and dead ground, and on fibresand: ran moderately in blinkers fifth start: usually on toes. *N. Tinkler.*

PREMIER MAJOR (IRE) 2 b.g. (May 2) Bluebird (USA) 125 – Calvino **52** (Relkino 131) [1991 7m 6m 8m⁵] IR 14,000Y: close-coupled gelding: fifth foal: half-brother to 3-y-o Keen Vision (by Vision), 1987 2-y-o 7f winner Y V Tucker (by Valiyar) and temperamental maiden Regal Vine (by Prince Tenderfoot): dam second over 7f at 2 yrs in Ireland: poor maiden: stays 1m. *W. J. Pearce.*

PREMIER PRINCE 5 b.h. King of Spain 121 – Domicile (Dominion 123) [1990 **63** 6m 7g 7m⁴ 7.6m⁶ 7f* 7m⁵ 8d 7m⁶ 7g⁶ 7g 1991 8d 7.6g 7.1m 7g* 7v³ 7.1g 7.1s⁴ 7f*

8g⁵ 7m* 8m 7m⁵ 7g⁶] strong, workmanlike horse: quite modest handicapper: won at Goodwood in June and September (amateurs) and Salisbury in August: ideally suited by 7f: acts on any going: suited by waiting tactics: has ducked right. *L. G. Cottrell.*

PREMIER PRINCESS   5 b.m. Hard Fought 125 – Manntika 77 (Kalamoun 129)   **35** [1990 21.6m⁵ 13.8f 17m⁴ 15.8d* 1991 13.8g 17.2g⁴] workmanlike mare: poor handicapper: stays well: acts on dead going: trained reappearance by W. Bentley: winning hurdler. *G. A. Ham.*

PREMIER ROYALE (IRE)   3 b.g. Indian King (USA) 128 – Rince Si (Mal-   **60** d inowski (USA) 123) [1990 5f⁶ 5f² 5g² 5m² 5m³ 7f⁶ 1991 a7g 8g⁵ 9.2d² 10m 10g⁴ 8.3d² 10.1m a12g³ 10f³ 12m* 15.1g 11m⁶ 12.1m] lengthy, workmanlike gelding: plating-class performer: won claimer at Southwell in September by a head, looking reluctant: stays 1½m: acts on firm and dead ground: blinkered once at 2 yrs: sometimes sweating: headstrong: sold 6,200 gns Newmarket Autumn Sales: ungenuine. *W. J. Pearce.*

PREMIER TOUCH   4 b.c. Petorius 117 – Fingers (Lord Gayle (USA) 124) [1990   **104** 7g 6s² 8m* 7m³ 8m 6g³ 6g⁶ 7.2g⁶ 7d 6s³ 6g 1991 6d⁶ 6m* 6m⁵ 6m 6d⁵ 6g⁶ 6m*] leggy colt: moderate walker and mover: useful handicapper: won at Thirsk in May and Ripon (landed a gamble when easily beating Hinari Televideo by 2½ lengths in Great St Wilfrid Handicap) in August: seems best at 6f or 7f: probably acts on any going: has run well when blinkered: often sweating: has wandered under pressure: joined Miss H. Knight. *T. D. Barron.*

PREMIER VENUES   3 b.g. Gorytus (USA) 132 – Tarnished Image 88 (Targo-   **50** wice (USA) 130) [1990 5f 1991 7f⁵ 7f⁴ 7g⁶ 7f 7m⁴ 10f⁵ 12.1f* 12f⁶] compact gelding: plating-class performer: won handicap at Hamilton in September, improving from rear 2f out: suited by middle distances: acts on firm ground: tends to carry head high. *Mrs G. R. Reveley.*

PRENONAMOSS   3 b.g. Precocious 126 – Nonabella 82 (Nonoalco (USA) 131)   **96** [1990 6g 5m² 5g² 5g⁴ 5m* 6d³ 5g² 1991 5.8m* 6d² 8m 7g² 6m³ 5d 6m] lengthy, rather angular gelding: fairly useful handicapper: won at Bath in May: good third in £16,100 handicap at Ripon: stays 7f: acts on good to firm ground and dead: blinkered 3 times, including when below form last 2 (slowly away final one) outings: sometimes bandaged behind. *D. W. P. Arbuthnot.*

PRE PAINT   2 b.c. (Apr 11) Sizzling Melody 117 – Chalet Girl (Double Form 130)   — [1991 8.2m 6s] 9,200Y: leggy, close-coupled colt: fourth foal: half-brother to 2 winners abroad: dam unraced: well beaten in large fields at Nottingham (seller) and Hamilton (maiden, blinkered) in autumn: sold 1,800 gns Ascot 2nd November Sales. *Miss L. C. Siddall.*

PREPARE (IRE)   3 b.f. Millfontaine 114 – Get Ready 91 (On Your Mark 125)   **56** [1990 7f 5m⁵ 6d 7g 1991 6m⁴ 7g⁵ 6g⁴ 5.1d⁵ 5.7g 5.1f⁵ 5m³ 7f 7m* 7g 7.1m 8g 7g] rather leggy filly: plating-class handicapper: below form after winning at Warwick in August, leading inside final 1f and running on strongly despite flashing tail: finds 5f on sharp side and stays 7f: acts on firm ground and dead: ran creditably when edgy. *R. J. Holder.*

PRESAGE   5 b.h. Petong 126 – Discreet 104 (Jukebox 120) [1990 a7g⁴ a8g a7g³   — a5g a7g a7g a6g 7m 6f⁵ 1991 7f 5f 7m 6f] leggy, close-coupled horse: of little account. *K. B. McCauley.*

PRESENT TIMES   5 b.g. Sayf El Arab (USA) 127 – Coins And Art (USA)   — (Mississipian (USA) 131) [1990 a7g⁶ a7g 10d 1991 12d⁶ 12f] close-coupled, deep-girthed gelding: lightly-raced and poor maiden on flat: shapes as if should stay 1½m: acts on good to firm ground: winning hurdler. *A. Moore.*

PRESET   4 ch.g. Homing 130 – Constanza 94 (Sun Prince 128) [1990 8m³ 8.2m³   — 12.4f³ 12m⁵ 12.3g 14g 1991 a10g 10.8m] workmanlike gelding: quite modest performer: below form in first half of 1991: stays 1½m: acts on good to firm ground: headstrong, has worn crossed noseband: sold 1,700 gns Doncaster Summer Sales. *J. L. Spearing.*

PRESIDENT GEORGE   4 b.g. Be My Native (USA) 122 – Mother White   — (Jukebox 120) [1990 10.2f⁵ 8f⁶ 8g 8m 8g 7.5g 7m 8m 10m 1991 15.8g] leggy gelding: moderate mover: poor plater: stays 1m: has been tried blinkered. *W. Storey.*

PRESQUE NOIR   3 br.c. Latest Model 115 – Orlaith 68 (Final Straw 127) [1990   **67** 6m⁵ 1991 8g 6m 8d³ 7g² 7m 7f 9m 8.1d 9g² 10.3d⁵] good-bodied colt: moderate mover: quite modest maiden: good head second of 20 in handicap at Newmarket penultimate start, running on well from rear: not discredited in ladies event 9 days later: will prove suited by 1m + : acts on firm and dead ground: didn't handle turn at Warwick. *H. Candy.*

PRESSURE GAME 8 b.g. Miami Springs 121 – Cheena (Le Levanstell 122) — [1990 12f 1991 11m6] fourth live foal: dam lightly-raced Irish maiden: ex-Irish gelding: won 1½m handicap as 4-y-o: behind in Southwell claimer (in need of run) in August, first run on flat here: poor hurdler/chaser here as 7-y-o: stays 1½m: acts on firm ground: tried blinkered: formerly trained by J. Byrne. *K. R. Burke.*

PRETONIC 3 b.f. Precocious 126 – Northern Ballerina 52 (Dance In Time **73** (CAN)) [1990 6d 6g4 a6g3 1991 7f 6m* 6d* 6g 5d a6g3 a6g4 a7g] workmanlike filly: modest form: always close up when successful at Hamilton in maiden in May and handicap in June: ran well in handicaps next 3 outings: stays 6f well: acts on good to firm ground and dead. *M. Johnston.*

PRETORIAN GUARD (IRE) 2 b.c. (Mar 10) Petorius 117 – Verthumna **56** (Indian King (USA) 128) [1991 5s4 5g2 5g 5f5 5m5 6g] 7,600F, 5,000Y: workmanlike colt: first foal: dam maiden, ran only at 2 yrs in Ireland: plating-class maiden: visored final outing: sold 820 gns Doncaster October Sales. *D. Moffatt.*

PRETTY POPPY 3 b.f. Song 132 – Moonlight Serenade 66 (Crooner 119) [1990 **52** 5m2 5f* 5d 1991 6v 6d3 5m 5d 7g 7.6m3 8s 7f 7.1m 8.2f a6g a6g6] good-quartered filly: good walker and mover: quite modest performer: below form in handicaps last 6 starts: stays 7.6f: seems best on a sound surface: blinkered fourth start: trained first 4 outings by R. Hannon, next 6 by A. Denson. *P. Mitchell.*

PREVAILING WIND 5 b.g. Night Shift (USA) – Windy Sea 105 (Sea Hawk II — 131) [1990 5sa 5g a7g 5g 5f] sturdy, good-quartered gelding: quite modest handicapper as 3-y-o: well beaten in 1991, still in need of run final start (May): headstrong, unlikely to stay beyond 5f: probably acts on any going: sometimes slowly away. *M. Brittain.*

PRICELESS BOND (USA) 3 ch.f. Blushing Groom (FR) 131 – Pied Princess — (USA) (Tom Fool) [1990 6g3 7m2 8.5m2 9m* 1991 10g 10f4] smallish, angular filly: modest performer: stayed 1¼m: acted on firm ground: in foal to Never So Bold. *J. R. Fanshawe.*

PRICELESS FANTASY 4 ch.f. Dunbeath (USA) 127 – Linda's Fantasy 108 **53** (Raga Navarro (ITY) 119) [1990 7.5d 8d3 9m* 10m2 9g4 10m4 10d2 10.2s a10g 1991 a — a11g 10f 10m 11.7g5 10m 10f6 12g 10g6 10.1g4 10.2f3 10.2g 10.8g* 12f5 9.7s* a12g] small, lengthy filly: good walker: has a round action: won selling events at Warwick (bought in 3,800 gns) in October and Folkestone (no bid, drifted right) in November: stays 1½m: probably acts on any going: trained first 10 starts by I. Wardle, next 4 by J. Roberts. *Pat Mitchell.*

PRICELESS LOOT 3 b.f. Ardross 134 – Pulcinella 95 (Shantung 132) [1990 — 6m6 7.5d 1991 a12g] lengthy, angular filly: poor maiden, best effort on debut. *C. A. Cyzer.*

PRICELESS PET 3 b.f. (Apr 30) Tina's Pet 121 – Spring Lane 85 (Forlorn River — 124) [1991 5g 6m] 2,000F, 500Y: neat filly: fourth foal: closely related to 3-y-o 7f winner Mr Snail (by Petorius) and half-sister to 1m (at 2 yrs) to 11.5f winner Konig (by Jalmood): dam 7f and 1m winner at 2 yrs: no form, slowly away both times, in June seller at Windsor second start. *J. J. Bridger.*

PRIDE OF BRITAIN (CAN) 2 ch.f. (May 29) Linkage (USA) – Witches **55** Alibhai (USA) (Your Alibhai) [1991 6g 5.7f 7.1d] $16,000Y: rather leggy filly: has some scope: sixth foal: half-sister to Restless Julie (by Restless Restless), minor stakes-placed sprint winner at 2 yrs: dam sprint winner: plating-class maiden: below best final start, first for 2½ months. *L. G. Cottrell.*

PRIDE OF PENDLE 2 ro.f. (Mar 5) Grey Desire 115 – Pendle's Secret 73 (Le **53** Johnstan 123) [1991 6d 6m6 6.1m 6m* 6f 7g] leggy, angular filly: sixth reported foal: half-sister to 1986 2-y-o 8.2f winner Rivers Secret (by Young Man): dam 1¼m winner: ridden by 7-lb claimer, narrowly won seller at Redcar (no bid) in August, showing vastly improved form: faced stiff tasks in nurseries afterwards, running fair race in selling event first occasion: stays 6f. *P. Calver.*

PRIDE OF STORM (USA) 3 ch.c. Storm Bird (CAN) 134 – Splendid Pride **86** p (USA) (Exclusive Native (USA)) [1990 NR 1991 8g4 10m] leggy, angular colt: has a long stride: second foal: dam won maiden at around 1m in USA: won maiden at Lingfield in September, setting modest early pace, green then running on strongly: about 5 lengths seventh of 20 in £7,100 apprentice handicap at Newmarket month later, staying on well: should improve. *L. M. Cumani.*

PRIDIAN (IRE) 2 ch.c. (Mar 6) Ahonoora 122 – Priddy Blue (Blue Cashmere **64** p
129) [1991 6s⁴] IR 80,000Y: half-brother to Irish 1988 2-y-o 1m winner Society Glide
(by Solford), later successful in Hong Kong, and 2 winners in USA: dam from family
of Dibidale and Tony Bin: weak 7/1-shot, over 11 lengths fourth of 13 to Pater Noster
in maiden at Yarmouth in October: will improve. *G. Wragg.*

PRIESTGATE 6 ch.g. Stanford 121§ – Change of Luck (Track Spare 125) [1990 —
7f 6m 5d 6g 6d a8g a6g a8g 1991 a8g] lengthy, workmanlike gelding: modest
performer at 4 yrs: lost his form, not seen out in 1991 after January: best at sprint
distances on a sound surface: effective blinkered or not: sold 1,450 gns Doncaster
January Sales. *J. L. Goulding.*

PRIMA AURORA 3 br.f. Primo Dominie 121 – Alumia (Great Nephew 126) —
[1990 NR 1991 6m 6.1m 6.1m⁶ 8d] useful-looking filly: good walker: seventh foal:
half-sister to quite modest maiden Light Your Fire (by Bay Express), apparently
best at 6f: dam unplaced 3 times at 2 yrs: showed signs of a little ability, in selling
handicap final start: may prove best short of 1m. *Lord Huntingdon.*

PRIMA BERGERAC 2 b.f. (Feb 3) Cyrano de Bergerac 120 – La Primavera **51**
(Northfields (USA)) [1991 5m* 5g 5g] 9,000Y: compact filly: sixth foal: half-sister to
3 winners here and abroad, including very smart 1¼m to 1½m winner Highland
Chieftain (by Kampala): dam won over 1½m in Ireland: won maiden at Warwick in
May: below that form in Queen Mary Stakes at Royal Ascot and minor event at
Windsor in July: will stay 6f. *W. Carter.*

PRIMA CAVALLA 3 b.f. Primo Dominie 121 – Highest Tender 56 (Prince **42**
Tenderfoot (USA) 126) [1990 a6g 1991 5f⁴ 6g⁵ 5f⁵ 5m 5m⁵ 5m] good-quartered filly:
poor form, including in handicap: visored final start. *C. Tinkler.*

PRIMA SPERANZA 5 ch.m. Remainder Man 126§ – Rely-on-Pearl (Deep —
Diver 134) [1990 NR 1991 10d 8.1d 7.1s] strong, dipped-backed mare: first reported
foal: dam was none too reliable at start: well beaten in modest company in summer.
B. R. Millman.

PRIMATICE (FR) 4 b.g. Vision (USA) – Rivelina (FR) (Riverman (USA) 131) —
[1990 11g² 10.5g³ 12g³ 1991 a11g a10g 10d 18d 14.6g 12d] rather sparely-made
ex-French gelding: third foal: half-brother to a winner by Melyno: dam unraced: well
beaten, including in handicap, in 1991: stays 1½m: usually blinkered: winner twice
of selling hurdles here, claimed out of M. Pipe's stable 10,000 gns in January: trained
fourth start by N. Mitchell. *D. C. Jermy.*

PRIME BID 2 b.c. (Mar 6) Primo Dominie 121 – Single Bid 68 (Auction Ring **74**
(USA) 123) [1991 5m 5d³ 6m⁵ 6g³ 6d³ 5g² 6g 6m² 6g] 27,000Y: lengthy, good-
topped colt: carries condition: has scope: has a quick action: third foal: half-brother
to 3-y-o 1m and 1¼m winner Bid For Elegance (by Nordance) and a winner abroad
by Music Boy: dam ran only at sprint distances: modest maiden: off course 2
months, ran creditably at York (behind Isaiah) then in nursery at Newbury last 2
starts in October: well worth a try at 7f: sweating (below form) seventh outing: sold
13,000 gns Newmarket Autumn Sales. *R. Hannon.*

PRIME MOVER 3 b.g. Mummy's Game 120 – Feast-Rite (Reform 132) [1990 **72**
6g⁶ 6d a6g* 1991 6m² 6g] tall, quite good-topped gelding: modest form: favourite,
excellent second of 17 in £8,150 handicap at Newmarket in April, running on very
strongly from rear after slow start: second favourite, soon driven along in £25,000
York handicap 2 months later: will prove as effective at 7f: acts on good to firm
ground. *Sir Mark Prescott.*

PRIME PROSPECT 3 b.c. Damister (USA) 123 – Sunningdale Queen 88 (Gay **89**
Fandango (USA) 132) [1990 NR 1991 10f⁴ 10m* 10.6g⁴ 10g* 10g 10m 10m² 9m
10m³] leggy colt: fifth foal: half-brother to Irish 1½m winner Unpaid Member (by
Moorestyle) and to winners in Switzerland and Italy: dam 1½m winner: fairly useful
performer: won maiden at Brighton in May and £7,000 handicap at Newmarket in
June: should stay 1½m: sold 40,000 gns Newmarket Autumn Sales, reportedly to
race in Middle East. *M. A. Jarvis.*

PRIMERA BALLERINA 3 ch.f. Primo Dominie 121 – Yankee Special 60 (Bold —
Lad (IRE) 133) [1990 NR 1991 6.1m⁵ 7g] long-backed filly: second foal: half-sister to
winning hurdler Yankee Flyer (by Henbit): dam plating-class maiden: bandaged,
fifth of 12 in seller at Nottingham, outpaced early: well beaten in Newmarket maiden
9 days later in October: sold to join J. Bosley 1,100 gns Ascot November Sales. *Mrs
L. Piggott.*

PRIMETTA PRINCE 7 ch.g. Morston (FR) 125 – Russian Princess 99 (Henry —
The Seventh 125) [1990 a12g a12g⁵ 1991 a14g] lengthy gelding: modest maiden at 2

yrs: very lightly raced and little subsequent form: tried blinkered once: dead. *W. J. Pearce.*

PRIME WARDEN 5 b.h. Blakeney 126 – Misguided 106 (Homing 130) [1990 12g 42 10g 1991 10s 7m4] strong, compact horse: has a free, rather round action: modest maiden at best: not nearly so good nowadays: should stay beyond 1m: acts on good to firm ground: winning hurdler. *R. J. Holder.*

PRIMITIVE SINGER 3 b.g. Chief Singer 131 – Periquito (USA) (Olden Times) 80 [1990 8s 10.2s5 1991 10g6 12m3 12s*] workmanlike, deep-girthed gelding: carries condition: moderate mover: fair performer: impressively won claimer (claimed to join M. Pipe £16,501) at Goodwood in June: well worth a try at 1¾m: goes well on soft ground: winning hurdler. *Lord Huntingdon.*

PRIMUS 2 b.c. (Mar 21) Primo Dominie 121 – Norpella 95 (Northfields (USA)) 84 [1991 5d3 6m3 6d2 5g4 7m4 7f* 7m2 7f 7m6] leggy, close-coupled colt: good mover: second foal: half-brother to 7f and 8.9f winner Floralia (by Auction Ring): dam 1¼m and 1½m winner stayed 14.8f, is out of half-sister to Teenoso and Topsy: fair performer: showed much improved form to win nursery at Yarmouth in August: unlucky in running in similar event at Chester next start: will be suited by 1m: acts on firm ground. *G. Wragg.*

PRINCE ALDO 4 br.g. Millfontaine 114 – Graunuaile 116 (Proud Chieftain 122) — [1990 10g6 8m4 9f2 8g 1991 a7g a8g a8g a14g] leggy, close-coupled gelding: half-brother to numerous winners here and abroad, notably Merrie Moira (by Bold Lad), 5f and 6f winner at 2 yrs in Ireland later placed in Group 3 company: dam Irish 2-y-o 5f and 1m winner: ex-Irish maiden: in frame in handicaps at Phoenix Park and Tramore (blinkered) in early-summer at 3 yrs: no show in claimers and handicap at Southwell in early part of 1991: stays 9f: blinkered last 2 starts: trained at 3 yrs by A. Redmond. *W. L. Barker.*

PRINCE ALI 2 b.g. (Apr 20) Tina's Pet 121 – Ribbons of Blue 60 (Jimmy Reppin — 131) [1991 5f] 2,000F: second foal: half-brother to modest plater Blue Bell Ribbons (by Music Boy): dam staying mudlark: 25/1, swerved left start, very green and always well behind in seller at Beverley in May. *B. Ellison.*

PRINCE BELFORT 3 b.g. Belfort (FR) 89 – Princess Sharpenup 63 71 (Lochnager 132) [1990 NR 1991 6d 5g 6g4 5f2 5m* 5m6 5f 5m3 a5g] 4,000F: leggy, workmanlike gelding: third foal (all by Belfort): brother to fair sprinter Sharp Anne and 5-y-o 1m winner My Concordia: dam third over 5f at 2 yrs on only outing: quite modest handicapper: won at Catterick in June: may prove best at 5f: acts on firm going: looked unsuited by visor (swerved left stalls, always behind) seventh start: tends to hang, and should prove best with strong handling. *M. P. Naughton.*

PRINCE BOLLINGER 4 b.c. Head For Heights 125 – Almuadiyeh 69 — (Thatching 131) [1990 11d 8g a8g5 12h3 1991 10m 10m 8.3g 8m a10g] strong, lengthy colt: good walker: has a round action: plating-class form as 3-y-o: well beaten in 1991: takes keen hold, and may prove best at around 1¼m: tends to carry head high: hung right second start, blinkered last 2: sold out of D. Arbuthnot's stable 1,050 gns Ascot September Sales after penultimate one. *C. L. Popham.*

PRINCE EMILIO 2 br.c. (Apr 19) Prince Sabo 123 – Rather Warm 103 (Tribal 78 Chief 125) [1991 5m3 5m5 5f4 6g 6d*] 20,000Y: leggy, rather unfurnished colt: sixth foal: half-brother to several winners, including 5f to 7f winner Sparky Lad (by Hot Spark) and 1¼m and 10.4f winner Wodurather (by Touching Wood): dam won at up to 7.6f at 2 yrs: blinkered first time, showed much improved form when winning 23-runner maiden at Haydock in October, making most and running on well: stays 6f: possibly suited by a soft surface: has worn a crossed noseband. *J. Etherington.*

PRINCE FERDINAND 2 b.c. (Feb 11) King of Spain 121 – Greensward Blaze 109 50 (Sagaro 133) [1991 5m* 5f2 6m* 6m5 6g3 6m2 6m2 6g2] 4,000Y: lengthy colt, angular and rather unfurnished: good walker: moderate mover: fifth foal: brother to 3-y-o Prosport: dam won 1m seller: successful in maiden auction at Salisbury in May and £9,300 event at Ascot in June: ran really well last 4 starts, notably when 1½ lengths second of 25, travelling strongly long way, to Casteddu in Racecall Gold Trophy at Redcar final start: will stay 7f: yet to race on a soft surface: consistent. *M. McCormack.*

PRINCE HANNIBAL 4 b.c. High Top 131 – Fluctuate 87 (Sharpen Up 127) 90 [1990 8f4 8.5g3 10f2 10f* 10m* 12f6 12m* 12m 12g 1991 12.2d4 12d4 12g3 11.5m* 12.1d* 11.9m* 11.5g4 11.9m* 11.6m4 12m2 13.3m 12m] rangy colt: fairly useful handicapper, none too consistent: won at Lingfield, Chepstow and Haydock in summer and Brighton (idled) in August: stays 1½m: acts on firm and dead ground:

has worn bandage off-hind: has swished tail and found little, and best with waiting tactics. *J. L. Dunlop.*

PRINCE JAKATOM   4 ch.c. Ballad Rock 122 – Ballysnip (Ballymore 123) [1990   **68**
NR 1991 7g 8m 8d5 8d 10.5f6 11.5g 8.1s5] lengthy, good-quartered colt: has scope:
poor mover: modest handicapper at best nowadays: below form after third start:
gives impression needs at least 1m nowadays and possibly some give in the ground:
usually bandaged: sold 6,200 gns Newmarket Autumn Sales after penultimate start.
D. W. P. Arbuthnot.

PRINCE MERCURY   2 ch.g. (Mar 26) Sharrood (USA) 124 – Princess Zita 90   **67** p
(Manado 130) [1991 7g 7.1s4 7d] 4,400Y: big, good-topped gelding: has a round
action: fourth foal: half-brother to 1½m seller winner Bourbon Prince (by Star
Appeal) and a winner in Brazil: dam, 7f winner, is out of half-sister to smart stayer
Karadar: quite modest maiden: easily best effort second start: will be well suited by
middle distances: has plenty of scope, and looks sort to do better. *J. L. Dunlop.*

PRINCE OF HUTTON   3 b.g. Prince Sabo 123 – Wayward Polly 63 (Lochnager   **41**
132) [1990 5f 5g 1991 a7g 5m5 6d 6g 6d a6g a8g4 8f] robust gelding: moderate mover:
poor maiden: probably stays 1m: best effort on good to firm ground. *M. W. Easterby.*

PRINCE OF IRELAND (IRE)   3 b.c. Anita's Prince 126 – Mooned 64 (Fair   —
Season 120) [1990 5v4 5d5 5g 5g4 6m5 5g4 5d a5g 1991 a6g] IR 3,000Y, resold
1,950Y: workmanlike, dipped-backed colt: has a quick action: poor maiden: off
course 6 months after running poorly in seller as 2-y-o: tailed off in Southwell
handicap in January: best efforts over 5f on good ground: has been tried in blinkers:
sold 520 gns Doncaster January Sales since last start. *N. Bycroft.*

PRINCE OF ROCK (IRE)   3 b.g. Ballad Rock 122 – Prasia (Prince Regent (FR)   —
129) [1990 7g 7m 7m 6d a7g 1991 12d 12g] well-made gelding: moderate mover:
plating-class maiden: showed nothing in claimers in spring as 3-y-o: should stay 1m:
blinkered final start: subsequently gelded: sold 1,300 gns Ascot November Sales. *R.
F. Johnson Houghton.*

PRINCE OF THE SEA (IRE)   3 gr.c. Double Schwartz 128 – Baracuda (FR)   **88**
(Zeddaan 130) [1990 6d2 1991 6d* 6m* 7g] leggy, close-coupled colt: progressed
well in winning auction event at Brighton and 17-runner handicap (running on really
strongly) at Newmarket in April: disappointing in £11,900 handicap at Newmarket
following month, never able to challenge: should stay 7f: wears bandages. *D. W. P.
Arbuthnot.*

Southern Comfort Stakes, Ascot—
Prince Ferdinand wins this graduation race from Langtonian

PRINCE PERICLES (IRE) 2 b.c. (Mar 19) Nordico (USA) – Countess Eileen **71** 111 (Sassafras (FR) 135) [1991 7g⁵ 7d] IR 38,000Y: sturdy, useful-looking colt: good mover: closely related to quite useful 1½m to 13.8f winner Polar Cub (by Northern Baby) and a winner over hurdles and half-brother to 3 winners, including quite modest 1½m winner Les Tamaris (by Red Sunset): dam won over 1m and 1½m and was third in Irish St Leger: 33/1 and very green, modest form, showing up well almost 6f, in maiden at Goodwood won by Mougins: well beaten in similar event at Newmarket later in August: will stay middle distances. *H. Candy.*

PRINCE RODNEY 2 gr.c. (Mar 4) King of Spain 121 – Dancing Diana 82 (Raga **62** Navarro (ITY) 119) [1991 5s⁵ 6m³ 5g³ 7g⁶ 6m 6m] workmanlike colt: first foal: dam 5f (at 2 yrs) to 1m winner: quite modest maiden: looked irresolute when third in seller at Windsor second start: stays 7f: visored (below best) final outing. *R. Hannon.*

PRINCE ROONEY (IRE) 3 b.c. Dayeem (USA) – Fourth Degree (Oats 126) **56** [1990 8d 8.5d 7m³ 6m² 6g⁴ 8g² 7s⁴ 6d⁶ 8d 1991 7v² 7d⁵ 7f⁶ 8m⁴ 7m 7.6d 7g³ 8d² 8.3m 7m⁵] close-coupled colt: has a round action: third reported foal: half-brother to Irish bumpers winner Don Vincento (by Don) and useful hurdler Viking Flagship (by Viking): dam, unraced, out of half-sister to dam of champion U.S. filly Princess Rooney: inconsistent ex-Irish maiden: stays 1m: seems to act on any going, except firm: bandaged fifth to seventh outings: joined M. Pipe. *P. Butler.*

PRINCE RUSSANOR 3 b.c. Rousillon (USA) 133 – Pellinora (USA) (King **102** Pellinore (USA) 127) [1990 8g* 8.2d⁵ 1991 10d* 10g³ 12g] lengthy, rather angular colt: useful form: won minor event (showed quick action) at Nottingham in April: good third in listed Newmarket Stakes: in mid-division for Derby Italiano at Rome in May: should stay 1½m: pulled hard and ran in snatches when disappointing final start at 2 yrs. *J. L. Dunlop.*

PRINCE SECRETO (USA) 2 b.c. (Feb 5) Secreto (USA) 128 – Princess Ivory **81** **?** (USA) (Poison Ivory (USA)) [1991 7g⁵ 7f³ 7m³ 7d² 8g] $25,000Y: smallish, lengthy, attractive colt: carries condition: moderate walker: first foal: dam, won claimer at 4 yrs at up to 1m, is half-sister to Poule d'Essai des Poulains third Glory Forever: fair maiden: looking tremendously well, excellent second of 16 to Louisa Scarlett in nursery at Ascot: ran moderately in similar event at Redcar later in October: will stay 1m: seems well suited by a soft surface. *N. A. Graham.*

PRINCE SOBUR 5 b.g. Jalmood (USA) 126 – Ultra Vires 87 (High Line 125) **60** [1990 16d² 16.2m 14s* 16.2d 17.6g³ 17.4d³ 14d⁵ 18d 1991 16g 16g² 16m³ 16.2g 16.5m² 22.2m 16g² 17.5m³ 16.2g 16.2d] rangy gelding: moderate mover: quite modest handicapper: largely consistent but ran poorly final start: suited by good test of stamina: acts on good to firm, and goes very well with give in the ground (acts on heavy). *M. Blanshard.*

PRINCESS ANNIE 2 br.f. (Mar 22) Prince Sabo 123 – Elaine Ann 66 (Garda's **41** Revenge (USA) 119) [1991 5g 6f 6m 5.2f⁴ 5f] 1,200Y: leggy filly: third foal: dam 6f winner: form only when fourth of 11 in seller at Yarmouth (slowly away) in August: should stay 6f. *G. Blum.*

PRINCESS DECHTRA (IRE) 2 b.f. (Apr 29) Bellypha 130 – Moretta (Artaius **65** (USA) 129) [1991 6.1d⁴ 6d³] IR 5,000Y: sturdy, good-topped filly: poor mover: second foal: dam French maiden half-sister to Zino: quite modest form, staying on, in minor event at Chester and maiden at Doncaster in autumn: will be much better suited by 7f + . *R. Hollinshead.*

PRINCESS EUROLINK 3 gr.f. Be My Guest (USA) 126 – Sweety Grey **—** (Young Emperor 133) [1990 NR 1991 8.3f⁵ 7m⁶ 8m] 8,000F, IR 14,000Y: leggy filly: seventh living foal: half-sister to winning sprinter Al Trui (by Scottish Rifle) and a winner in France by Workboy: dam ran once: plating-class maiden: apparently best effort on debut, trained by J. Berry. *M. C. Pipe.*

PRINCESS EVITA (FR) 2 b.f. (Apr 16) Kings Lake (USA) 133 – Very Bissy **—** (BRZ) (Harken (URU)) [1991 7g] 4,000Y: fourth known foal: dam Grade 1 winner in Brazil: 50/1, bandaged near-hind and backward, last of 22 in maiden at Newmarket in November. *R. Guest.*

PRINCESS JESTINA (IRE) 3 b.f. Jester 119 – Royal Aunt (Martinmas 128) **57** [1990 5f² 5f* 5g 5f⁵ 6f³ 1991 5d⁶ a5g⁵ 5g 8m³ 8f 8g a8g 7g 6g* 6m⁴ 7g⁵ 6f⁴ 7m 6f] leggy, sparely-made filly: plating-class performer: won apprentice handicap at Yarmouth in July: generally well below form afterwards: probably best at 6f: acts on firm going: sold 1,350 gns Ascot October Sales. *Mrs N. Macauley.*

PRINCESS KATIE 3 b.f. Forzando 122 – Jianna 60 (Godswalk (USA) 130) [1990 **53 d** 5f 6m⁴ 7h 6f⁴ 6m⁴ 7f⁴ 6m 7g a8g 1991 7d⁶ 7f⁴ 8m⁵ 7f 10. 1d 7m⁶ 8f 8f⁶ 6.9f 6g] small, sturdy filly: moderate mover: modest plater: should stay 1m: best form on firm ground: blinkered 4 times. *A. Moore.*

PRINCESS MAXINE (IRE) 2 b.f. (Apr 5) Horage 124 – Sallywell (Manado **43** 130) [1991 7f 8.3g] IR 8,200Y: leggy filly: third live foal: half-sister to fairly useful 7f winner Parliament Piece (by Burslem) and winning Irish sprinter Dotrecuig (by Welsh Saint): dam Irish 5f winner at 4 yrs: poor maiden: well beaten over 1m. *Miss L. A. Perratt.*

PRINCESS MOODYSHOE 3 ch.f. Jalmood (USA) 126 – Royal Shoe (Hotfoot **70** 126) [1990 5f³ 6m 6m 6m⁴ 6g 7g⁵ 8d² 1991 11.7f* 12m* 14.1m⁵] plain filly: has round action: favourite, won 7-runner claimers at Bath (maiden) in August and Goodwood (by 6 lengths) in September, making most and running on strongly: fair fifth in handicap at Nottingham: stays 1½m: acts on firm and dead ground. *M. C. Pipe.*

PRINCESS OF ORANGE 2 ch.f. (Apr 30) Master Willie 129 – Outward's Gal **59** (Ashmore (FR) 125) [1991 6g⁵ 7g⁶ 8.1g⁶ 9m³ 8g a8g] lengthy, leggy filly: third foal: half-sister to 1¾m NH Flat race winner Hell of A Guy (by Absalom): dam poor maiden: modest maiden: seems a staying type: well beaten on equitrack. *C. C. Elsey.*

PRINCESS PROUDFOOT 2 b.f. (Mar 20) Hotfoot 126 – Farandella 86 (English Prince 129) [1991 7f] 2,000Y: workmanlike filly: sixth live foal: dam 2-y-o 1m winner later successful in Italy: 12/1 from 5/1, green and in need of race, struggling from halfway in 18-runner claimer at Salisbury in September. *N. A. Graham.*

PRINCESS ROXANNE 4 b.f. Prince Tenderfoot (USA) 126 – Godwyn (Yellow **62** God 129) [1990 8f⁶ 10f⁴ 10m⁵ 10d.4g⁵ a8g⁶ 15d⁵ 9m 12m a12g⁵ 1991 a 11g³ a14g a12g² a10g² a10g⁶ a8g³ a10g⁶ 8d² 9f² 10.4d⁶ 8.2m⁶ 8m 10.5g³ 10.3m* 10.3m⁶ 10.5f⁴ 10.5g 10m⁴ 10.3d* 10.3d 9.7s a10g* a10g³ a10g] lengthy filly: moderate walker: has quick, moderate action: quite modest handicapper: won apprentice events at Chester in August (first win) and October and Lingfield in November: effective at 1m to 1½m: acts on firm and dead going: effective with or without blinkers. *A. Bailey.*

PRINCESS TAMAR 2 gr.f. (Mar 11) Absalom 128 – Alkion (Fordham (USA) **31** 117) [1991 5s⁶ 5m⁶ 7m 7.5f] 4,000F: sturdy filly: third foal: half-sister to a winner in Germany by Stanford: dam once-raced half-sister to very useful sprinter Oscilight: poor maiden: stays 7.5f. *Roy Robinson.*

PRINCESS TARA 3 br.f. Prince Sabo 123 – La Magna 104 (Runnymede 123) **85** [1990 5g 5d² 6m* 6s³ 6f 6m² 6m² 6m⁴ 7m 1991 6g 6d 6g⁴ 8m* 7m³ 8m³ 8g 7.6m 7d] workmanlike, good-quartered filly: fair handicapper: won £11,000 event at Ascot in June, leading 1f out and holding on gamely: well below form last 3 starts, twice in extremely valuable contests: effective at 7f and 1m: seems unsuited by a soft surface: has run well when edgy and sweating: bandaged off-hind second start: sold 29,000 gns Newmarket Autumn Sales. *G. Lewis.*

PRINCE TINO 3 b.g. Bustino 136 – Northern Empress 80 (Northfields (USA)) **—** [1990 NR 1991 8.1d⁵ 7m] good-bodied gelding: has a round action: sixth living foal: half-brother to quite modest 8.2f winner Bold Mac (by Comedy Star), 6f and 7f winner Nevada Mix (by Alias Smith) and a winner in Belgium by Hotfoot: dam ran 3 times: fifth of 11 in maiden at Chepstow, outpaced over 1f out: pulled hard, tailed off in similar event at Lingfield later in July. *N. A. Gaselee.*

PRINCE VAGABOND (IRE) 2 ch.g. (Jan 31) Palace Music (USA) 129 – **44** Mystery Lady (USA) (Vaguely Noble 140) [1991 7m 7g⁶ 8.1g 8m] IR 7,000Y: big, good-topped gelding: has plenty of scope: half-brother to a winner in USA by Smarten Up: dam ran twice: poor maiden: ran very wide into straight on 3 occasions: clearly none too tractable. *Miss L. A. Perratt.*

PRINCIPLE MUSIC (USA) 3 ch.c. Palace Music (USA) 129 – Principle (USA) **89** (Viceregal (CAN)) [1990 NR 1991 10.5m* 12d⁴ 12d] 720,000 francs (approx £66,700) Y: tall, leggy, quite good-topped colt: eighth reported foal: half-brother to fair 1m winner Hold Dear (by Caro) and several winners abroad, including disqualified French 2000 Guineas winner River Mist (by Irish River): dam stakes-placed winner at up to 7f at 2 yrs: won 5-runner maiden at Haydock in August: ran creditably in Newmarket handicap: never dangerous in November Handicap at Doncaster 8 days later: stays 1½m. *A. C. Stewart.*

PRIOLO (USA) 4 b.c. Sovereign Dancer (USA) – Primevere (USA) 91 **126** (Irish River (FR) 131) [1990 8g* 10.5s³ 9g* 9.2g* 10d² 8g* 8g³ 8g³ 1991 8g² 9m² 8g³ 8g⁵ 8m* 8g⁵]

Francois Boutin had good cause to question the truth in J. H. Payne's line 'there's no place like home' after saddling Priolo to win the Emirates Prix du Moulin de Longchamp in September. Priolo's victory, following that of Arazi in the Prix de la Salamandre earlier on the card, gave Boutin a notable Group 1 winning double but some of the crowd didn't see it that way. Boutin was jeered in the winner's enclosure because Priolo had finished ahead of his stable-companion and favourite Hector Protector, and the pair had not been coupled in the betting. A sad note then to end Priolo's career on French soil, a career that had taken in twelve starts, mainly in the highest company, and had seen him finish only once out of the first three. For the record he won six races, notably the Group 1 trio of the Moulin, Jacques le Marois and Jean Prat. Priolo's deserved victory in the Moulin was gained in typical fashion, in that he came with his customary surge having been held up, to deny the always-prominent Mukaddamah, a 33/1-shot who appeared to excel himself, virtually on the line; Lycius came from further back to take third, another length behind. The Moulin had been run at a good gallop, in contrast to many races in France where sprint finishes after an early dawdle often appear the order of the day. This latter style of racing lends itself to bunch finishes and hard-luck stories, and France's other Group 1 event for three-year-olds and upwards over a mile, the Jacques le Marois, was a perfect illustration. Not for the first time in his career, Priolo himself was unlucky. Just over a length covered the first six home at Deauville, Hector Protector nosing out Lycius and Danseuse du Soir for major honours with Priolo fifth after a dreadful run. His jockey chose to make his challenge against the stand rail but Priolo ran into the back of Hector Protector's weakening pacemaker Mousquetaire under two furlongs out when the sprint to the line had just begun. Once switched, Priolo quickened impressively but the damage had been done. Priolo took his revenge on the first three there in the Moulin. Priolo had also looked unfortunate on his second start in the Prix d'Ispahan at Longchamp, short of room for most of the last two furlongs and eventually going down by half a length to Sanglamore. There were no excuses on his two other runs of major consequence—a good third of eight, beaten one and a half lengths, to Second Set in the Sussex Stakes at Goodwood and a fair never-nearer fifth, beaten just under four lengths, to Opening Verse in the Breeders' Cup Mile at Churchill Downs.

Priolo's pedigree details were set out at length in *Racehorses of 1990*. Priolo remains much the best produce of Sovereign Dancer in Europe though the three-year-old pair Supreme Choice, in the frame in the Doncaster and Jockey Club Cup, and Dowland, a useful Irish middle-distance performer, represented him with distinction. Sovereign Dancer remains much more a

Emirates Prix du Moulin de Longchamp—
Priolo (No. 2) is brought with a well-timed run to catch Mukaddamah;
the whips are raised in unison on the next three,
right to left, Lycius, Danseuse du Soir and Sillery

Ecurie Skymarc Farm's "Priolo"

		Northern Dancer (b 1961)	Nearctic
	Sovereign Dancer (USA) (b 1975)		Natalma
		Bold Princess (gr 1960)	Bold Ruler
Priolo (USA) (b.c. 1987)			Grey Flight
	Primevere (USA) (br 1982)	Irish River (ch 1976)	Riverman
			Irish Star
		Spring Is Sprung (b 1973)	Herbager
			Pleasant Flight

force in the States. Itsallgreektome was again his chief standard bearer, helping him to ninth place in 1991 General Sire List. Primevere's second foal, the two-year-old filly Printaniere, also trained and owned by Boutin and Ecurie Skymarc Farm, is a full sister to Priolo. She had two runs in small races at the back-end. A smallish, attractive colt, Priolo showed his best form at a mile. He was effective on ground ranging from good to firm to soft. On occasions he took a keen hold, and, uncharacteristically, flashed his tail under pressure in the Sussex Stakes. Tough, most consistent and possessing a good turn of foot, Priolo was, as in 1990, a worthy contender for the best mile races. He's been retired to stand at the Corbally Stud, Ireland, at a fee of IR 6,000 guineas (October 1st terms). *F. Boutin, France.*

PRIOR CHARGE 4 ch.f. Tender King 123 – Priors Mistress 71 (Sallust 134) [1990 a8g* a10g⁴ 10m 10m a8g⁴ a8g⁶ a10g a8g 1991 a10g 10m 10s 16m⁵] angular, sparely-made filly: has quick action: modest performer at best: stays 1m: trained until after reappearance by Pat Mitchell. *Miss B. Sanders.* —

PRIORY PIPER 2 b.g. (Apr 22) Maris Piper 86 – Priory Girl § (Rugantino 97) [1991 6m 5m] angular gelding: third reported foal: dam of little account: well beaten in sellers in summer at Warwick (sweating) and Wolverhampton. *K. S. Bridgwater.* —

PRIPET (USA) 3 b.f. Alleged (USA) 138 – Smooth Bore (USA) (His Majesty **86** (USA)) [1990 NR 1991 12f 15.8f* 16m* 14m] $700,000Y: angular filly: sixth foal: sister to 1000 Guineas and Oaks winner Midway Lady and half-sister to 3 winners, including 15.8f winner Zabarrjad (by Northern Dancer): dam stakes winner at around 1m as 4-y-o: successful in smallish fields for maiden at Catterick in July and handicap at Thirsk in August: never travelling well in handicap at Sandown: will be suited by return to 2m + : visits In The Wings. *H. R. A. Cecil.*

PRISCILLIAN 7 b.g. Runnett 125 – Douala (GER) (Pentathlon) [1990 NR 1991 — 9s] second foal: dam won at 3 yrs in Germany: successful at 3 yrs in Ireland in 1½m maiden at Limerick and 13f handicap at Leopardstown when trained by J. Oxx: burly, tailed off in claimer, first run on flat after: winning chaser: stays 13f: acts on good to firm ground. *J. A. B. Old.*

PRIVATE ACCESS (USA) 3 b.c. Private Account (USA) – Empress of Canada **76** (CAN) (Accomplish) [1990 7g4 8g2 1991 7.5g4 8.5f2 10m4 8.5f* 8.5m] well-made, good sort: good walker: quite modest performer: 6/4 on, keen to post and in race when making all in maiden at Beverley in May: prominent 6f in £14,200 Epsom handicap 18 days later: effective at 1m and probably at 1¼m: acts on firm going: blinkered last 2 starts: consistent. *I. A. Balding.*

PRIVATE BANK (USA) 2 b.c. (May 30) Private Account (USA) – Lady Ice — p (CAN) (Vice Regent (CAN)) [1991 7m 8.1s] $200,000Y: good-topped colt: has some scope: fourth foal: half-brother to 2 winners in USA by Fappiano, including Surging, Grade 2 winner at around 7f: dam listed winner, was runner-up in Canadian Oaks: poor form in late-season maidens at Doncaster (burly and green) and Edinburgh: looks sort to do better. *A. C. Stewart.*

PRIVATE THOUGHTS 3 b.c. Jupiter Island 126 – Placid Pet 65 (Mummy's — Pet 125) [1990 7m 8.2s 1991 12.2d 8f4dis] leggy colt: staying-on fourth of 9 in claimer (disqualified as rider failed to weigh in) at Carlisle: may well prove suited to 1¼m: sold 1,100 gns Doncaster July Sales. *M. O'Neill.*

PRIVY PURSE (USA) 3 gr.f. Chief's Crown (USA) – Add Mint (USA) (Vigors — (USA)) [1990 NR 1991 10.2g] $300,000Y: sturdy filly: first foal: dam successful 5 times, including in 8.3f stakes at 3 yrs, and placed in 2 Grade 3 handicaps at 4 yrs: second favourite but bit burly, took good hold and prominent 6f when well beaten in maiden at Chepstow in July: sold only 6,400 gns Newmarket December Sales. *H. R. A. Cecil.*

PROBATION 2 b.c. (Feb 8) Nomination 125 – Ballagarrow Girl 66 (North Stoke **43** 130) [1991 5m 5m] 3,400F, 7,000Y: leggy colt: looks weak: fifth foal: brother to quite modest 1990 2-y-o 5f winner Northern Nation and half-brother to temperamental 1988 2-y-o Sky Hill (by Windjammer): dam suited by 1¼m, is half-sister to smart 6f and 7f winner The Quiet Bidder: poor maiden: carrying condition, well beaten in spring: will be much better suited by 6f + . *B. R. Millman.*

PROCURATOR (USA) 5 b.g. Alleged (USA) 138 – Northeastern (USA) (Nor- — thern Dancer) [1990 NR 1991 12.1m] fair maiden as 3-y-o when trained by B. Hills: stayed 1¼m: dead. *D. Moffatt.*

PRODIGAL MISS 3 b.f. Carwhite 127 – Devadara 73 (Royal Levee (USA)) — [1990 NR 1991 8m 12m 12.3g 10.5d] 3,000F: workmanlike filly: half-sister to several winners here and abroad, including 5f to 7f winner Pete Rocket (by Roan Rocket): dam showed some ability at 3 yrs: no form in claimers and sellers: very slowly away first start: reluctant at stalls on third. *W. M. Brisbourne.*

PROFESSIONAL (IRE) 3 b.c. Sadler's Wells (USA) 132 – Miss Allowed **73** (USA) (Alleged (USA) 138) [1990 NR 1991 8m 10.3g2 12.4m4 11.9g3 14.1m3] 135,000F, 580,000Y: workmanlike colt: moderate mover: fifth foal: closely related to 4-y-o 1½m winner Guest Right, Irish 7.9f winner Norquest and a winner in Italy (all by Be My Guest) and 1986 Irish 2-y-o 6f and 7f winner Best Try (by Try My Best): dam unraced daughter of very useful middle-distance filly Miss Toshiba: modest maiden: stays 1¾m: tongue tied down and ran moderately third start: sold E. Pistoletti 7,200 gns Newmarket Autumn Sales. *B. W. Hills.*

PROFILIC 6 b.h. Ballacashtal (CAN) – Sea Charm 70 (Julio Mariner 127) [1990 **83** 6f* 6m 6m 6m 6m3 6f* 7g5 6d 7m 6f3 6f* 6m3 6m 6g 6m 6d 6d 6g 6s6 1991 6d 6m 6g2 6m 6m* 6g 6m 7.1g6 6g 6m* 7m 6f5 6g 7m 6g] big, strong, lengthy horse: usually looks very well: has a long, round stride: fair handicapper: won at Doncaster in May and Newcastle in August: ideally suited by strongly-run race at 6f: acts on any going: has been tried blinkered: usually gets behind and ideally needs strong handling: inconsistent. *Capt. J. Wilson.*

PROFIT A PRENDRE 7 b.g. Tina's Pet 121 – Brave Ballard (Derring-Do 131) **60**
[1990 7g 7m² 9g⁵ 6f* 7m 7m 7f 8m 8g 7m⁶ 8d 8m 7m 6m 6s 1991 a6g 5g 7m 8g 7m
6f* 7.1d* 7m⁶ 8.1g⁶ 9m 8m 7m² 7m 7m³ 8d⁴ 6.1d 6.9s] big, lengthy gelding: has
round action: quite modest handicapper: won amateur events at Redcar (fourth win
there) in May and Chepstow in June: effective at 6f to 1m: acts on any going: carries
head high and sometimes hangs, but goes well for Elaine Bronson: inconsistent. *D.
A. Wilson.*

PROFIT STREAM 2 ch.g. (Mar 12) Adonijah 126 – River Reem (USA) (Irish **52**
River (FR) 131) [1991 7m 6m⁶ 5g a7g a6g⁵] IR 2,500F, IR 2,000Y, 15,500 2-y-o:
workmanlike gelding: poor mover: first foal: dam, unraced, from family of Katies:
plating-class maiden: should be suited by further than 6f. *M. W. Easterby.*

PROFUSION 2 b.c. (Feb 18) Rainbow Quest (USA) 134 – Pauvresse (FR) (Home **79**
Guard (USA) 129) [1991 7g* 7g4] 82,000F: good-bodied colt: half-brother to several
winners in France, including smart middle-distance performer Video Rock (by No
Lute): dam unraced daughter of very useful middle-distance filly Misoptimist:
favourite, won maiden at Newmarket in quite good style, always front rank: looking
very well, soundly-beaten fourth of 5, struggling from 2f out, to Torrey Canyon in
Deploy Acomb Stakes at York later in August: likely to stay 1¼m: looked a fairly
useful prospect on debut. *P. F. I. Cole.*

PROHIBITION 4 b.g. Music Boy 124 – Green Chartreuse 91 (French Beige 127) **78**
[1990 6m* 6f² 6g* 6g³ 6d* 6d 6m 6m² 6m 6f⁵ 6m² 6g* 6d⁴ 5g⁵ 1991 6s⁵ 6d 6m² 6g4
6m* 6m⁶ 6g⁴ 6.1g 6m² 6f 6m 5g² 6m⁵ 5s³] workmanlike gelding: moderate mover:
fair handicapper: won claimer at Newcastle in May: below best last 2 starts, in seller
(odds on) final one: effective at 5f to 6f: acts on good to firm and dead going: twice
below best when blinkered: tends to hang left: trained until after penultimate start
by J. Berry: subsequently sold 6,800 gns Doncaster November Sales. *G. Lewis.*

PROMPTING 2 ch.f. (Feb 7) Primo Dominie 121 – Gentle Persuasion 95 **76**
(Bustino 136) [1991 6m 5g² 5.7f⁴ 5m⁴ 5m⁵ 5m* 5d] lengthy, unfurnished filly: first
foal: dam 2-y-o 6f winner later suited by 1m: modest performer: improved effort to
win nursery at Warwick in October, always prominent: should be suited by further
than 5f: best effort on good to firm ground, ran respectably on dead: sold 8,800 gns
Ascot November Sales. *Lord Huntingdon.*

PRONOBIS 3 ch.g. Niniski (USA) 125 – Protasis (USA) (Native Dancer) [1990 **—**
NR 1991 11.7g 12g] rather leggy gelding: brother to twice-raced 1987 2-y-o Pro
Scania, closely related to a minor winner by Upper Nile and half-sister to 3 winners:
dam won 3 minor races in USA: visored, always ridden along in maidens at Bath
(slowly away, possibly reluctant to race) and Folkestone 6 months later. *J. H. M.
Gosden.*

PROPERS 5 ch.m. Noalto 120 – Budget Queen 101 (Good Bond 122) [1990 7.6m⁵ **—**
6m⁴ 7g 8m³ 8.2g⁶ 7m⁶ 8f³ 10f⁵ 6m 1991 8g 7m] leggy mare: plating-class maiden at 4
yrs: well beaten in early part of 1991: probably best over 7f or 1m: acts on any going.
M. Dods.

PROSEQUENDO (USA) 4 b.g. Robellino (USA) 127 – Allegedly (USA) (Sir **79**
Ivor 135) [1990 NR 1991 8d³ a8g* 10.1f 10g³] tall, leggy, quite good-topped gelding:
has quick action: fourth foal: half-brother to smart middle-distance gelding Per
Quod (by Lyllos) and a winner in North America: dam unraced half-sister to Alleged:
lightly-raced colt: won maiden at Southwell in May: creditable third in Ayr handicap
in June: stays 1¼m: seems quite keen sort: sold to join M. Dixon's stable 3,500 gns
Newmarket Autumn Sales and gelded. *B. Hanbury.*

PROSPORT 3 b.c. King of Spain 121 – Greensward Blaze 50 (Sagaro 133) [1990 **—**
6m⁴ 6g 6g 8d 6v 1991 8.5f⁶ a8g] workmanlike colt: has a round action: poor maiden:
soundly beaten in July at 3 yrs. *N. Bycroft.*

PROUD BRIGADIER (IRE) 3 b.g. Auction Ring (USA) 123 – Naughty One **59**
Gerard (Brigadier Gerard 144) [1990 6f⁶ 5m 5.3f⁶ 1991 8f⁵ 5m 6m⁴ 7m⁶ 7f 6d 6g4
6m⁵ 7m⁴ 7f² 6m 6g* 6m a6g³ a7g4] lengthy, sparely-made gelding: poor mover:
quite modest handicapper: won selling event (no bid) at Brighton in October: ran
well at Lingfield final start: as effective at 6f as 7f: acts on firm going: fell thirteenth
start. *W. Carter.*

PROUD PANTHER (FR) 5 br.h. Blakeney 126 – Pink Panther (Val de Loir **108**
133) [1990 14.5s² 15g 15.5f* 15.5m* 14d⁴ 14m 16g 15.5m⁴ 1991 14s 12d 12.5g 16g4
15m* 15.5m³ 20d² 15s* 12s] sixth foal: half-brother to 2 winners in France: dam
French 9f and 10.5f winner: useful French horse: won handicap at Deauville in
August and listed event at Milan (beat Parting Moment by 3 lengths) in October: ran
well at Longchamp behind impressive Victoire Bleue in Prix Gladiateur and Ciga

Prix du Cadran (stayed on never a threat, beaten 6 lengths) in between: effective at 15f, and stays 2½m: probably acts on any going. *Mme M. Bollack-Badel, France.*

PROVENCE 4 ch.c. Rousillon (USA) 133 – Premier Rose 117 (Sharp Edge 123) **84** [1990 12m⁶ 12g³ 1991 10.8g 14m⁶ 14m³ 16m* 16d 16f 14g 18.2f* 18m] rangy colt with scope: good mover: fair handicapper: won at Redcar in June and Yarmouth (gamely) in September: creditable eighth of 22 in moderately-run Tote Cesarewitch at Newmarket final start: acts on firm ground, possibly unsuited by dead: very much a stayer. *P. W. Harris.*

PROVIDENCE (USA) 2 ch.c. (Feb 17) Diesis 133 – Hotel Street (USA) 93 **81** (Alleged (USA) 138) [1991 6d² 7m* 8m⁵ 8.2m⁴ 7d] smallish, well-made colt: has a long stride: second foal: half-brother to 3-y-o Widyan (by Fappiano), successful at 7f (at 2 yrs) and 11f: dam lightly-raced 1½m winner, is half-sister to stakes winners Royal And Regal and Regal And Royal: fair performer: ran on strongly to win maiden at Newmarket in July: ridden by 5-lb claimer, good fourth of 15 in nursery at Nottingham in September: below form in Goodwood listed event in between and in Ascot nursery final outing: should stay 1¼m: best form on top-of-the-ground. *P. F. I. Cole.*

PRUDENT MANNER 4 ch.c. Cure The Blues (USA) – Prudent Girl 92 **116** (Primera 131) [1990 9m² 7f* 9m* 9g* 9m² 10g³ 1991 8g³ 9m* 7g³ 8g² 8m⁵ 10g⁴ 10d⁶ 10g² 9m²] smart Irish performer: easily landed odds in listed event at Leopardstown in June: good second to Mukaddamah in Group 2 event at the Curragh, George Augustus in listed race at Hoppegarten and River Verdon in Hong Kong Invitation Cup at Sha Tin: best at 1m to 1¼m: acts on firm ground. *D. K. Weld, Ireland.*

PSYCHO SONNY 4 b.g. Aragon 118 – Sunny Reproach (High Top 131) [1990 — a7g* a7g⁴ a7g⁴ a6g⁵ 7m 7m⁵ 8.2g 8m⁵ 7.6m a7g⁴ 7g a7g 10m 8g 7f 1991 a8g⁶ a10g] small, sparely-made gelding: poor walker and mover: poor performer nowadays: probably stays 1m: tried visored, blinkered and in hood: sold 1,400 gns Ascot April Sales. *Mrs A. Knight.*

PUBLIC APPEAL 2 b.c. (Feb 11) Law Society (USA) 130 – Vacherin (USA) **69** (Green Dancer (USA) 132) [1991 7g⁵ 8s⁵ 8.1d⁴ 10m³] 17,000F, 31,000Y: leggy, quite good-topped colt: poor walker: first foal: dam French 11f and 1½m winner: modest maiden: blinkered, best effort when third of 12 at Nottingham: stays 1¼m. *P. F. I. Cole.*

PUCK'S BOSS (IRE) 3 b.g. Fairy King (USA) – Mullaghroe (Tarboosh (USA)) **59** [1990 NR 1991 8f³ 6m* 7m 5.7m] sturdy, lengthy gelding: poor mover: second foal: half-brother to Irish 1m and 1¼m winner Queen of Fins (by Viking): dam never ran: won claimer at Catterick in June by a short head, staying on well: well below form later in summer: should stay 7f. *Sir Mark Prescott.*

PUFF PUFF 5 b.m. All Systems Go 119 – Harmonious Sound (Auction Ring **59** (USA) 123) [1990 7m 6d a10g a12g* a12g² a10g⁴ a12g² 1991 a12g⁴ a12g² 12f* 12f³ a16g* 14f⁴ 14m³ 15.4f 16m⁴ a16g⁶] rather leggy mare: plating-class handicapper: won at Brighton in April and Lingfield (well backed) in August: effective from 1½m to 2m: acts on firm going and equitrack: consistent. *Miss B. Sanders.*

PUFFY 4 ch.g. Wolverlife 115 – Eskaroon (Artaius (USA) 129) [1990 7f 8.5f⁵ 6v² **64** § 7g² 7.5d 7m 8m 8h⁵ 7m 8m 5g 7d* 7d³ 1991 8s 7.5f⁶ 7m² 8h⁴ 8m² 7.1g 10.5d] leggy, rather sparely-made gelding: shows a quick, moderate action: modest handicapper at best: stays 7.5f: acts on any going: effective with or without visor: sometimes blinkered: withdrawn lame fifth intended start: temperamental, one to treat with caution. *G. M. Moore.*

PUNCH N'RUN 3 b.c. Forzando 122 – Wrangbrook (Shirley Heights 130) [1990 **96** 6m³ 6m³ 6f² 7f* 7g⁵ 6d² 6m* 6g* 6d³ 1991 7m 8.5f 6g 6g 6.1m 6s⁵ 6m 7m³ 6m⁶ 6m² 6.5s²] quite attractive colt: moderate mover: useful performer at his best: ran creditably in quite valuable handicaps and French listed race last 4 outings, blinkered last 2 occasions: stays 7f: acts on any going: has tended to hang: often on toes: sold 32,000 gns Newmarket Autumn Sales, reportedly to Italy. *R. Hannon.*

PUNCH THE AIR 3 ch.f. Northjet 136 – Joyfully (FR) (Dilettante II 121) [1990 **58** 7m 8d 1991 a12g⁶ 14.1f* 14.1f* 14.1f* 16m² 17.1m] leggy filly: moderate mover: quite modest handicapper: won at Yarmouth (ridden by 7-lb claimer first occasion, ladies event on second) and Nottingham in space of 3 weeks in August and September: ran moderately final start: stays 2m: acts on firm ground: tends to edge left and not easiest of rides: bandaged near-hind third and fourth starts, off-hind on final one: sold 9,000 gns Newmarket Autumn Sales. *W. J. Haggas.*

PUNKIE 5 b.m. Kinglet 98 – Nelodor 69 (Nelcius 133) [1990 NR 1991 5m 8.2d] —
leggy, plain mare: no worthwhile form, including in handicap. *R. Dickin.*

PURCHASE ORDER (USA) 2 ch.c. (Apr 27) Blushing Groom (FR) 131 – **65**
Sunday Purchase (USA) (T V Lark) [1991 6m 7m4 8.1m4] small colt: moderate
walker: half-brother to several winners, including very smart middle-distance
performer Hatim (by Exclusive Native) and high-class 8.5f to 1¼m winner Bates
Motel and 1979 Horris Hill winner Super Asset (both by Sir Ivor): dam, 1m winner,
is half-sister to high-class 1971 American 2-y-o Rest Your Case: visored and
sweating, best effort 4 lengths fourth of 13 to Cautionary Tale at Edinburgh last
time, hanging right under pressure final 1f: may well stay 1¼m. *J. H. M. Gosden.*

PURE BLISS 4 b.f. Idiot's Delight 115 – Julie Emma (Farm Walk 111) [1990 7d 10s —
12d 1991 16m 6g 7f a7g] lengthy filly: no worthwhile form, though has shown clear
signs of ability. *R. J. Hodges.*

PURE FORMALITY 2 b.f. (Mar 6) Forzando 122 – Sharp Celine (Sharpo 132) **81** p
[1991 6d*] 5,800F: compact, workmanlike filly: first foal: dam unraced daughter of
Irish Oaks winner Celina, family also of Dubian and See You Then: 14/1, won
7-runner maiden at Ascot in October by ½ length from Cloud of Dust, quickening
ahead over 1f out: moved well to post: sure to improve. *D. R. C. Elsworth.*

PURE GREEN (USA) 4 ch.f. Green Forest (USA) 134 – Malakya (Artaius **74**
(USA) 129) [1990 6f3dis 6f2 7m3dis 6m4dis 5m2dis 5f6 5.1m* 5d6 5m 1991 5g2 5g 5m
6f3 5g] strong, lengthy filly: modest handicapper: inconsistent in first half of 1991:
pulls hard, and best at sprint distances: acts on good to firm ground and dead: ran
creditably when blinkered once: difficult ride who has swerved right and hangs: sold
1,300 gns Newmarket September Sales. *M. Moubarak.*

PURSUIT OF LOVE 2 b.c. (Mar 12) Groom Dancer (USA) 128 – Dance Quest **107** p
(FR) 117 (Green Dancer (USA) 132) [1991 6g3 7m* 7m4] strong, good-topped,
attractive colt: has a powerful action: third living foal: half-brother to very useful
French 3-y-o Divine Danse (by Kris), ideally suited by 6f: dam smart French
sprinting half-sister to Noblequest out of good-class pattern-winning sprinter/miler
Polyponder: heavily backed, won 17-runner maiden at Newmarket, soon travelling
strongly and running on in excellent style: 13/2, improved again when around 4
lengths fourth of 9 to Dr Devious in Dewhurst Stakes at Newmarket later in
October, off bridle at halfway then keeping on gamely: will stay 1m. *H. R. A. Cecil.*

PURSUIT OF TRUTH (USA) 2 b.f. (Jan 21) Irish River (FR) 131 – Troyanos **69** p
(Troy 137) [1991 7m*] smallish filly: third foal: dam unraced half-sister to Sun
Princess: 7/1 from 4/1 and bit green, won 6-runner maiden at Yarmouth in July,
quickening to lead 1½f out: will stay at least 1m: seemed likely to improve. *M. R.
Stoute.*

PUSEY STREET BOY 4 ch.c. Vaigly Great 127 – Pusey Street 96 (Native —
Bazaar 122) [1990 8d 8m4 7m* 8.2s5 7f6 8f 7f a7g 1991 10.2s 8g a7g a10g5] leggy,
lengthy, dipped-backed colt: quite modest handicapper at 3 yrs: below form in 1991:
needs strong pace over 7f, and stays 1m: acts on any going. *J. R. Bosley.*

PYARE SQUARE 2 b.c. (Mar 19) Reference Point 139 – Land of Ivory (USA) 109 **75** p
(The Minstrel (CAN) 135) [1991 7f5] sturdy colt: second foal: closely related to 3-y-o
Heart of Darkness (by Glint of Gold),useful 7f winner at 2 yrs: dam 5f (at 2 yrs) and
1m winner, is half-sister to high-class Gold And Ivory: 7/1, slow-starting 8 lengths
last of 5 to Rodrigo de Triano in listed race at Newbury in August, running green
over 2f out and unable to get on terms: moved well to post: likely to stay 1¼m: sure
to improve. *I. A. Balding.*

PYTCHLEY NIGHT 4 b.g. Red Sunset 120 – Lili Bengam (Welsh Saint 126) **72**
[1990 8f6 8f2 7.6d6 7g 8f2 7d 8f 8m 9g a8g* 1991 a8g2 a8g* a10g a8g5 a8g3 8d 7m a **92**
7.6m3 7g 7f5 8.2m 7g* a7g4 a7g* a8g a7g*] lengthy, quite good-topped gelding:
fairly useful handicapper at best: successful in January, November and
December: none too consistent on turf, won at Newmarket in October: best at
7f/1m: acts on firm going and all-weather surfaces (best form on all-weather),
unsuited by dead ground: keen sort: best held up. *D. Morris.*

Q

Q-EIGHT (IRE) 3 b.c. Vision (USA) – Warning Sound (Red Alert 127) [1990 6d **62**
1991 7s 9m 11.1g2 12m2 11m2 10.2s 13.3g] workmanlike colt: has a round action:
modest form when second in 3 handicaps in space of 11 days: off course 4 months

then showed little afterwards: suited by middle distances: acts on good to firm ground: blinkered final outing. *J. D. Czerpak.*

QUACK SECRET (USA) 2 b.f. (Feb 26) Secreto (USA) 128 – Eloquack (USA) — (Elocutionist (USA)) [1991 7g] $65,000Y: workmanlike filly: first foal: dam won 7 races in North America and runner-up in Grade 2 7f event: 33/1, burly and green, slow-starting ninth of 10 in maiden at Goodwood in July. *C. E. Brittain.*

QUADRIREME 2 b.c. (Apr 18) Rousillon (USA) 133 – Bireme 127 (Grundy 137) **67** p [1991 7m] quite attractive colt: half-brother to fairly useful 1989 2-y-o 7f winner Trireme (by Rainbow Quest), later stayed 1¾m, and winning hurdler Dhoni (by Bustino): dam Oaks-winning half-sister to high-class middle-distance stayer Buoy: 11/1, green and better for race, beaten around 8 lengths in mid-division of large-field maiden at Doncaster in October, eased once held: showed quick action to post: will stay middle distances: sure to improve. *Major W. R. Hern.*

QUAGLINO (USA) 3 b.c. Robellino (USA) 127 – Affair 78 (Bold Lad (IRE) 133) **97** [1990 5f³ 7f* 7g 8.2g⁴ 8g² 6g⁵ 1991 7.5g² 8.5f² 9m⁶ 7m* 8d² 8m] workmanlike, good-topped colt: quite good mover: fairly useful performer: won apprentice median auction contest at Lingfield in May: ridden halfway in handicap at Royal Ascot final start: stays 9f: acts on firm and dead going: consistent. *P. T. Walwyn.*

QUALITAIR AVIATOR 5 b.g. Valiyar 129 – Comtec Princess 73 (Gulf Pearl — 117) [1990 a13g* a12g² a16g³ a14g* 12f 12.3d 14g⁵ a14g a16g² a14g⁶ 1991 a13g* a **76** a13g⁴ a14g 12.1g 12m a16g* a14g a16g] close-coupled, workmanlike gelding: moderate mover: modest handicapper: goes extremely well on all-weather, successful at Lingfield in February and November: well beaten last 2 starts: stays 2m: acts on good to firm ground: inconsistent. *J. F. Bottomley.*

QUALITAIR BLAZER 4 ch.f. Blazing Saddles (AUS) – Midfirna (Midsummer — Night II 117) [1990 a7g 7g 10g 10f⁵ 1991 a14g⁴ a12g⁴ a14g⁵ a11g⁴ 9.9m a12g* 14g a **52** a11g²a12g⁴a12g²a14g⁴a11g³a14g²a13g²] compact filly: quite modest handicapper: won at Southwell in June: effective at 11f to 1¾m: twice below form when visored: best form on all-weather surfaces: sold out of J. Bottomley's stable 2,200 gns Doncaster August Sales. *J. R. Jenkins.*

QUALITAIR DREAM 4 b.f. Dreams To Reality (USA) 113 – Maputo Princess **58** (Raga Navarro (ITY) 119) [1990 6g⁵ 6m 6m 7m² 8m 8m 7.2g 7d 6d 6m 6d 7d³ 9g 1991 8s⁵ 8v 7m 7g² 7f a7g] small, workmanlike, good-quartered filly: has a round action: plating-class handicapper: needs testing conditions at 6f, and stays 1m: acts on good to firm ground and soft: ran moderately when blinkered once: inconsistent. *J. F. Bottomley.*

QUALITAIR FLYER 9 b.g. Kampala 120 – Ziobia 78 (Tribal Chief 125) [1990 **35** § NR 1991 8.2d a7g a8g⁴ a8g a11g⁶ a11g² 11m a12g³] small, lengthy gelding: has a round action: poor handicapper nowadays: seems to stay 1½m: acts on any going: has worn blinkers and a visor: tends to hang and a difficult ride: thoroughly unreliable. *J. F. Bottomley.*

QUALITAIR MEMORY (IRE) 2 ch.g. (Feb 9) Don't Forget Me 127 – Whist **35** Awhile (Caerleon (USA) 132) [1991 5m a7g³] 10,000F, 18,000Y: leggy, unfurnished gelding: first foal: dam unraced half-sister to very useful 1983 2-y-o Mahogany: poor form in sellers, at Southwell (bandaged off-hind, better for race after 3½-month absence) in July second occasion. *J. F. Bottomley.*

QUALITAIR PROMISE 3 ch.f. Reach 122 – Maputo Princess (Raga Navarro — (ITY) 119) [1990 6g a7g 6g 8m 1991 10m 10f 9.9m] sparely-made filly: has a round action: little form, including in sellers: retained 740 gns Doncaster January Sales. *J. F. Bottomley.*

QUALITAIR REALITY 3 b.f. Dreams To Reality (USA) 113 – Blushing Nurse — (Saritamer (USA) 130) [1990 6g⁵ 1991 6f 7m 5m⁶ 5.1m 5m 8f] leggy filly: poor mover: poor performer: should be suited by further than 5f: sold out of J. Bottomley's stable 960 gns Doncaster January Sales. *M. F. Barraclough.*

QUALITAIR RHYTHM (IRE) 3 b.f. Drumalis 125 – Abbe's Realm (Realm **54** 129) [1990 NR 1991 10m a8g⁵ 7.9g⁴ 8g 10.5d⁵ a6g³] leggy, close-coupled filly: poor mover: plating-class form: ran well in claimer at Southwell in December, staying on: should stay 1m: possibly needs an easy surface: sold to join J. Bottomley's stable 1,300 gns Doncaster November Sales after fifth start. *J. Hetherton.*

QUALITAIR ROYAL 2 b.g. (Mar 22) Bairn (USA) 126 – Maputo Princess (Raga — Navarro (ITY) 119) [1991 5g] 3,000Y: good-topped gelding: poor walker: fifth foal: half-brother to 1989 2-y-o 6f winner Qualitair Dream (by Dreams To Reality): dam behind in varied company: soon towards rear in maiden auction at Beverley in April: sold 680 gns Doncaster November Sales. *J. F. Bottomley.*

QUALITAIR SOUND (IRE) 3 b.g. Mazaad 106 – A Nice Alert (Red Alert 127) **66**
[1990 8.2m⁴ 8m 6v² 8d 7s 1991 8s 8.2d³ 8g 9m⁵ 12g⁶ 10g⁵ 8m 8g⁵ 8m⁶ 10g 8.9g 8d]
compact, workmanlike gelding: has a poor, round action: quite modest handicapper,
still a maiden: 15 lb out of handicap when running creditably in £11,200 event at
Newmarket ninth start: gelded after following outing and never dangerous subsequently: stays 1¼m: acts on good to firm ground and heavy: winning hurdler. *J. F.
Bottomley.*

QUALITAIR SUPREME 4 ch.f. Exhibitioner 111 – Glendalough (USA) (High **—**
Finance) [1990 7m⁵ 8.2g 10.6s 1991 13d a14g] workmanlike filly: no worthwhile
form, including in handicaps: sold 1,100 gns Doncaster August Sales, resold 1,000
gns Doncaster November Sales. *J. F. Bottomley.*

QUALITAIR SWEETIE 4 ch.g. Sweet Monday 122 – Right Abella 74 (Right **—**
Boy 137) [1990 11g 12m* 12.4m 13g² 12m 12d 13d 13.6d a12g 1991 a11g a12g⁵ a14g]
workmanlike gelding: plating-class handicapper at best as 3-y-o: well beaten at
Southwell in 1991: should stay 1¾m: acts on good to firm going: twice below form
when blinkered. *J. F. Bottomley.*

QUATRE FEMME 4 b.f. Petorius 117 – Irish Kick (Windjammer (USA)) [1990 **74**
5m² 6g² 6f* 6s 6m 1991 6m² 5g⁶ 6f 6g³ 5m⁵ 5f⁴ 6f³ 6m⁵ 7m 6m] leggy, angular filly:
modest handicapper: largely consistent, but below form last 2 starts after returning from 2½-month lay-off: should stay 7f: acts on firm going: has edged left. *M.
Johnston.*

QUATRIA 2 b.f. (Apr 26) Sizzling Melody 117 – Questa Notte 104 (Midsummer **—**
Night II 117) [1991 a6g] sturdy filly: closely related to 2 winners by Song, including
fair sprinter Quaver, and half-sister to several other winners, including 5f winner
Quilting (by Mummy's Pet): dam useful 6f performer: 11/2, slow-starting fourteenth
of 16 in seller at Southwell in July: sold 820 gns Newmarket September Sales. *Sir
Mark Prescott.*

QUAVERING 4 b.c. The Minstrel (CAN) 135 – Flicker Toa Flame (USA) 85 **95**
(Empery (USA) 128) [1990 8g* 1991 8g 8g 8.9m⁶ 7.3m 10.4m* 10m] good-bodied
colt: good mover: lightly raced and fairly useful handicapper: well backed, gamely
won at York in October by 3½ lengths: likely to prove as effective forcing pace at
1m, as at 1¼m: acts on good to firm ground: rather headstrong, and wears a crossed
noseband: has run respectably for apprentice. *J. H. M. Gosden.*

QUEEN OF BEAUFORT 2 gr.f. (Mar 20) Belfort (FR) 89 – Glenfield Portion **51**
86 (Mummy's Pet 125) [1991 5f⁶ 5m⁴ 5m] angular, workmanlike filly: fourth live
foal: half-sister to winning sprinters Glenfield Greta (by Gabitat) and Bernstein
Bette (by Petong): dam 2-y-o 5f winner well beaten at 3 yrs: plating-class maiden:
very troublesome (at stalls) and withdrawn on intended debut and third intended
start (on way to post, jockey injured): temperamental. *P. S. Felgate.*

QUEEN OF DREAMS 3 ch.f. Ti King (FR) 124 – Humeur de Reve (USA) (Lord **—**
Avie (USA)) [1990 a8g⁶ a8g² a8g⁴ 1991 a10g⁶ a10g⁴ 12v] good-topped filly:
plating-class maiden, easily best effort second start at 2 yrs: moved poorly down
before turf handicap in March: stays 1m. *Dr J. D. Scargill.*

QUEEN OF INDIA (USA) 3 gr.f. Chief's Crown (USA) – Queen of Luck **75**
(USA) (Drone) [1990 7m 8d⁴ 1991 7m 10.2f* 8.2g² 8m⁶ 10.3m 10m³ 10m² a10g*]
angular, rather plain filly: modest handicapper: in good heart in the autumn, winning
at Lingfield: also won at Doncaster in May: should prove as effective at 1½m: acts on
firm going. *J. H. M. Gosden.*

QUEEN OF PENDONA 2 b.f. (May 26) King of Spain 121 – Pendona 72 (Blue **37** §
Cashmere 129) [1991 5.3f 6m 5s² 7m 6m 5m 6g 6s⁵ a6g a7g] leggy filly: moderate
mover: ungenuine maiden: stays 6f: well suited by soft ground: usually blinkered,
visored final outing: sometimes edgy: trained first 8 starts by E. Wheeler. *H. A. T.
Whiting.*

QUEEN OF SHANNON (IRE) 3 b.f. Nordico (USA) – Raj Kumari (Vitiges **—**
(FR) 132) [1990 6m 6g² 1991 7m 8d⁶ 7f⁶ a7g³] quite good-topped, angular filly: quite
modest maiden: should be suited by return to 1m: possibly needs an easy surface:
bandaged all round final start, in June: pulls hard. *C. A. Horgan.*

QUEEN OF TOMORROW 3 b.f. Today And Tomorrow 78 – All Glorious 82 **—**
(Crowned Prince (USA) 128) [1990 NR 1991 8g a7g 6d 7g 6.9m] leggy filly: fifth foal:
half-sister to a winner in Malta: dam won over 7f and 1m: poor maiden: 25/1,
worthwhile form only when in mid-division in handicap at Doncaster fourth start:
takes good hold. *P. Burgoyne.*

QUEENSBERRY RULES 2 b.c. (Mar 29) Vaguely Noble 140 – Sorayah 89 **59**
(Persian Bold 123) [1991 6g 7m 8m 7.6m⁶] 17,000Y: quite good-topped colt: has a

very round action: first foal: dam sprinter here subsequently won at up to 11f in USA: plating-class maiden: blinkered first time, creditable sixth of 15 in face of stiff task in nursery at Lingfield: will stay 1¼m: sold 7,200 gns Newmarket Autumn Sales. *J. R. Fanshawe.*

QUEEN'S TICKLE   2 b.f. (Apr 6) Tickled Pink 114 – Queens Pearl (Queens   **57** Hussar 124) [1991 6m* 6g 5.7g² 5d] workmanlike filly: has scope: fourth foal: sister to 5f winner Albert Henry and half-sister to poor sprinter Prince Baccara (by Dublin Taxi): dam of little account: backed at long odds, won 21-runner seller (no bid) at Redcar in September, quickening over 1f out: second of 19 in nursery at Bath, easily best subsequent effort: better suited to 6f than 5f: bandaged near-hind final start. *A. P. Jarvis.*

QUEENS TOUR   6 b.h. Sweet Monday 122 – On Tour 60 (Queen's Hussar 124)   **52 d** [1990 10g 12g⁴ 12m 12g⁶ 12g⁵ 12d⁶ 1991 12s 13d 13d 13m³ 12m⁶ 11.9m⁵ 13d⁴ 13d 13.1m⁶ 10.5d a14g] small, lightly-made horse: poor walker and mover: plating-class handicapper nowadays: below form after fourth start: stays 13f: ideally suited by some give in the ground. *M. Brittain.*

QUESSARD   7 ch.g. Ardross 134 – Marquessa d'Howfen 93 (Pitcairn 126) [1990   — a16g a14g 1991 a14g] strong, lengthy gelding: has shown traces of stringhalt: powerful galloper with a round action: fair maiden at best, but has deteriorated considerably: stays 15f: best with give in the ground: tried visored once. *F. H. Lee.*

QUEST FOR FAME   4 b.c. Rainbow Quest (USA) 134 – Aryenne (FR) 125 **124** (Green Dancer (USA) 132) [1990 11d* 12.3d² 12g* 12g⁵ 1991 12m⁴ 10.4g² 11.1m² 12d 12g³ 12g³]

It is unusual to find an Epsom Derby winner still in training at four. Quest For Fame was only the seventh in twenty years to continue racing, following Mill Reef, Roberto, Snow Knight, Henbit, Teenoso and Slip Anchor. Of these, the greatest successes were enjoyed by Mill Reef, Roberto, Snow Knight and Teenoso. Mill Reef ran away with the Prix Ganay—a victory described in *Racehorses of 1972* as the 'most spectacular we had seen since Sea-Bird II won the Prix de l'Arc de Triomphe'—and then won the Coronation Cup before breaking a leg on the training gallops; Roberto was a most impressive winner of the Coronation Cup, though he was beaten on his two other starts; Snow Knight had a very successful four-year-old campaign in North America; and Teenoso, written off by many as a substandard Derby winner, came back the next season to win the King George VI and Queen Elizabeth Stakes and the Grand Prix de Saint-Cloud. Enterprise wasn't rewarded with either Henbit or Slip Anchor and the decision to persevere with Quest For Fame has so far met with mixed results, though he is to have another season to enhance his racing record after being transferred to Frankel's stable in North America following a good third in the Breeders' Cup Turf at Churchill Downs in November. Quest For Fame filled the same position in the Hollywood Turf Cup the following month on his first start for Frankel and should manage to pick up a good prize as a five-year-old.

Quest For Fame's two performances in the States—Miss Alleged won both races narrowly from North America's 1990 champion turf colt Itsall-greektome—were probably his best of the season. He reversed Ciga Prix de l'Arc de Triomphe form in the Breeders' Cup Turf with Pistolet Bleu, Pigeon Voyageur and In The Groove, who finished fifth, sixth and seventh at Churchill Downs. Quest For Fame had been one of the worst sufferers in scrimmaging that took place early in the home straight in the Prix de l'Arc—he was bumped twice—and he faded into seventh, beaten about eight and a half lengths by the winner Suave Dancer. The Prix de l'Arc was Quest For Fame's long-range target as a four-year-old and he wasn't seen out until the Epsom Derby meeting when he returned in the Hanson Coronation Cup after eleven months off the course, having missed the second half of his three-year-old season with an injury to his near-fore, sustained when fifth in the Budweiser Irish Derby on his only outing after winning the Ever Ready Derby. Quest For Fame was rated below par for a Derby winner, but he had been lightly raced (he ran only three times before the Derby) and looked a progressive type likely to train on. Quest For Fame came fourth in the Coronation Cup, beaten about five lengths by the winner In The Groove after making the running. A sore near-fore shin kept him on the side-lines for three weeks afterwards and he wasn't seen out again until the York August meeting at which he was one of six runners in the Juddmonte International Stakes (sponsored by his owner's stud interests). Controversy surrounded the heavy watering of the York track for the three-day meeting. The policy produced good going in the middle of a dry spell but, unfortunately, horses racing on the far side in the home straight enjoyed an unfair advantage, seemingly supporting criticism that the track's artificial watering system had not irrigated evenly. Some thought the ground was on the soft side and several leading trainers believed it was false, one describing it as 'a joke' and another as 'absolutely outrageous'; but suspicion that the track had been heavily watered to attract certain individual horses, including Quest For Fame (who wouldn't have run on firm), was surely unfounded. In any event, tactics played far and away the biggest part in deciding the outcome of the Juddmonte International. The outsider Terimon and Quest For Fame were at the head of affairs from the start and stole a march on the others early in the straight, stepping up the pace sharply after a fairly steady gallop. Quest For Fame looked to be moving the better entering the last two furlongs but Terimon gradually forged clear to win by two lengths; Quest For Fame had three and a half lengths to spare over third-placed Stagecraft, the odds-on favourite. Quest For Fame had one more outing before the Prix de l'Arc, at Kempton in the BonusPrint September Stakes in which he went down by a neck to Young Buster, conceding 7 lb more than weight for age.

		⎧Blushing Groom	⎧Red God
	⎧Rainbow Quest (USA)	⎨(ch 1974)	⎨Runaway Bride
	⎪(b 1981)	⎩I Will Follow	⎧Herbager
Quest For Fame	⎨	(b 1975)	⎩Where You Lead
(b.c. 1987)	⎪	⎧Green Dancer	⎧Nijinsky
	⎪Aryenne (FR)	⎨(b 1972)	⎩Green Valley
	⎩(br 1977)	⎩Americaine	⎧Cambremont
		(ch 1968)	⎩Alora II

The rangy Quest For Fame, a good mover, made up into a handsome four-year-old and was turned out in magnificent condition in the latest season, a credit to his trainer. His pedigree was covered in detail in last year's Annual. His sire Rainbow Quest showed top-class form at two, three and four (when he won the Prix de l'Arc), and his dam Aryenne won the Poule d'Essai des Pouliches (French Guineas). Aryenne was also represented on the racecourse in the latest season by Quest For Fame's brother Silver Rainbow who won a maiden race at Nottingham over a mile and three quarters in July and wasn't seen out again after coming a close fourth in the Goodwood Cup the following month. Quest For Fame has run his best races at a mile and a half and will stay further. He acts on good to firm and dead ground and is game and genuine. His trainer told us in a *Timeform Interview* that 'from the way the horse works at home we know he is very idle in front' and Quest For Fame is usually waited with. *R. Charlton.*

QUESTING (USA) 2 ch.c. (Feb 27) Diesis 133 – Quest (USA) 90§ (The Minstrel (CAN) 135) [1991 7g] fifth foal: closely related to useful 6f winner Bequest (by Sharpen Up), later Grade 1 winner at 1¼m in USA, and half-brother to 1½m winners Rozinante (by The Minstrel) and Inquirendo (by Roberto): dam, 9f and 1¼m winner, is sister to high-class 1983 French 2-y-o Treizieme and half-sister to Gold Cup second Eastern Mystic: favourite, over 12 lengths seventh of 11 to Khazar in maiden at Salisbury in October, prominent to 2f out: bred to stay 1¼m: should improve.*J. H. M. Gosden.* — p

QUESTION OF DEGREE 5 b.h. Known Fact (USA) 135 – Bernice Clare 68 (Skymaster 126) [1990 NR 1991 8d 8d 8m 10m 8.2f6] small, deep-girthed horse: moderate walker: quite modest form on flat at 3 yrs: behind in handicaps in 1991: brought down third outing: stays 1m well: acts on firm going. *N. Tinkler.* —

QUESTION OF HONOR 3 b.c. Legend of France (USA) 124 – Snow Goose (Santa Claus 133) [1990 7m5 7f3 7g 8m a8g 1991 12s 12.2g] close-coupled colt: poor maiden: well behind in claimer and seller in spring at 3 yrs: should stay at least 1m: best efforts on top-of-the-ground: joined A. Jones. *R. Hollinshead.* —

QUICK GETAWAY 2 ch.f. (Feb 12) Absalom 128 – Pyjama Party 70 (Pyjama Hunt 126) [1991 6g] 4,000Y: stocky filly: first foal: dam, 2m winner, is half-sister to useful 1½m winner Diabolical Liberty: backward and green, pulled up (apparently lame) at halfway in minor event at Windsor (slowly away) in July. *R. Hannon.*

QUICK RANSOM 3 ch.g. Hostage (USA) – Run Amber Run (Run The Gantlet (USA)) [1990 6g 6g a6g⁵ 6g 8.2s 7s² a8g⁴ a8g⁴ a8g² 1991 a10g* a10g a10g³ 10d* 12g³ 12.3d⁶ 12d³ 12g² 12m 12d³ a12g⁵ a14g³] leggy, lengthy gelding: modest handicapper: won at Lingfield (maiden) in January and Ayr in April: fair third at Southwell final start: should stay beyond 1½m: goes well on soft going, below form on top-of-the-ground. *M. Johnston.* **73**

QUICK STEEL 3 b.g. Alleging (USA) 120 – Illiney Girl 66 (Lochnager 132) [1990 a6g 8d 6d 1991 7m 7f 7.1g 6g* 6.1m⁴ 7s* 6.9s⁶] sparely-made gelding: apprentice ridden, won 19-runner handicaps at Folkestone and Yarmouth in October: should prove best at up to 7f: acts on good to firm ground and soft: blinkered last 5 starts. *T. P. McGovern.* **58**

QUIET ACHIEVER (CAN) 6 ch.g. Overskate (CAN) – From Nine To Five (USA) (Secretariat (USA)) [1990 10g 1991 10d] rangy gelding: has a round action: poor handicapper in 1989: twice raced and no show after: best at 1m: acts on firm going: has worn tongue strap: won over hurdles in January. *A. Moore.* **—**

QUIETLY IMPRESSIVE (IRE) 3 b.f. Taufan (USA) 119 – Way Ahead 81 (Sovereign Path 125) [1990 NR 1991 7d⁵ 9s² 8.2d⁵ 8m* 8d⁵ 8.5m 8d³ 10g⁶ 8m* 8.9m* 8.3m⁶ 9m 8g³ 8.1d² 8g⁴] IR 13,500Y: leggy, sparely-made filly: moderate mover: fifth foal: dam Irish 1m winner, is sister to useful 5f to 10.5f winner Everything Nice: quite modest form: won handicap at Salisbury in May and large-field claimers at Newmarket (ridden by 7-lb claimer) and Wolverhampton (well below form, reportedly finished lame) in July: wore tongue strap and back to form in handicaps last 3 starts: should stay 1¼m: acts on good to firm ground and soft. *M. Bell.* **66**

QUIET MISS 2 b.f. (Mar 19) Kind of Hush 118 – Miss Acrow (Comedy Star (USA) 121) [1991 8.9d a8g⁴ a8g³ a7g* a7g*] fifth foal: half-sister to winning stayer Acrow Lord (by Milford): dam, half-sister to smart Hillandale, showed little ability: improving filly: won maiden and nursery at Lingfield late in year: should be well suited by 1m: acts well on equitrack: has worn eyeshield. *D. R. C. Elsworth.* **73**

QUIET VICTORY 4 b.f. Never So Bold 135 – Les Saintes (Kris 135) [1990 8g 5m³ 9g 8m 6m⁶ 1991 8.3g³ 5m² 8g² 6f³ 8.3g 7f 7g³ 7g 6s a8g⁴ a10g] workmanlike ex-Irish filly: plating-class maiden at best: effective at 6f to 1m: acts on firm ground: trained first 4 starts by D. Williams, claimed out of J. White's stable £5,800 after next one. *Miss L. C. Siddall.* **52**

QUINTA ROYALE 4 b.g. Sayyaf 121 – Royal Holly (Royal Buck) [1990 7f* 8m⁶ 8m 8.2m⁶ 8m⁴ 8d 1991 8m⁵ 8.2f³ 11.8g⁴ 9.7m* 11.5g 12f] strong, lengthy gelding: moderate mover: quite modest performer: won seller (no bid) at Folkestone in September: ran moderately after: effective at 1m and probably stays 1½m: acts well on firm going: blinkered last 3 starts: joined J. Jenkins. *R. Akehurst.* **61**

QUINTESSENTIAL 3 b.c. Music Boy 124 – Questa Notte 104 (Midsummer Night II 117) [1990 6d a6g² a6g³ 1991 7g⁴ 8m² 7g⁴ 7g 8f 8m] smallish, workmanlike colt: had a quick action: plating-class maiden: below form in sellers and handicap last 4 starts: stayed 1m: acted on good to firm ground: blinkered or visored in 1991: sold out of Sir Mark Prescott's stable 3,800 gns Ascot 2nd July Sales after fourth start: dead. *C. L. Popham.* **58**

QUINZII MARTIN 3 b.g. Song 132 – Quaranta 83 (Hotfoot 126) [1990 6m 5m² 5m² 5.3h² 5m³ 1991 a6g⁴ 5g⁴ 5f³ 6h³ 5.1d 5m⁴ 8m 6m³ 5.7f 7m a6g a8g⁵] strong, good-bodied gelding: has a quick action: quite modest performer: stays 1m: acts on hard ground: blinkered twice: has run creditably sweating: sold out of Sir Mark Prescott's stable 7,800 gns Newmarket July Sales after seventh start. *D. Haydn Jones.* **60**

QUIP 6 ch.g. High Line 125 – Sans Blague (USA) 108 (The Minstrel (CAN) 135) [1990 12g 12g 12g* 12d 12g* 11d⁴ 12.3g 12f² 15m² 12.2m⁴ 1991 12g 12g³ 12.3d⁵ 11s⁴ 12f² 12.3f⁵ 15.1m³ 12f² 12m²] leggy gelding: has a long stride: poor handicapper: effective at 11f and stays 15f: probably acts on any going: best without visor: sometimes sweats: headstrong and usually allowed to stride on: usually taken down early or very steadily: game and consistent. *M. P. Naughton.* **38**

QUITE SO 7 br.m. Mansingh (USA) 120 – Chiquitita 44 (Reliance II 137) [1990 NR 1991 8m 5g⁴ 5m] small mare: bad performer nowadays: blinkered last 2 starts, bandaged and reluctant to go down final one: ungenuine. *K. White.* **— §**

R

RAAWI 3 b.g. Be My Guest (USA) 126 – Fast Motion 86 (Midsummer Night II 117) **51 §**
[1990 NR 1991 11d3 10g6 10g 10g4 8.1g 12g4 10m5 7.1m4 8.2m 10m5] tall gelding:
brother to high-class middle-distance colt Raami and Scandinavian winner Razeen
and closely related to fair 1½m winner Alanood (by Northfields): dam 2-y-o 6f
winner: plating-class form: probably stays 11f: blinkered final start: twice bandaged
late on: has hung badly, and carried head high: sold to join J. Norton 2,700 gns
Doncaster October Sales: untrustworthy. *R. Boss.*

RABBIT'S FOOT 3 b.f. Touching Wood (USA) 127 – Royal Custody (Reform **45**
132) [1990 7m 1991 a12g 12s 10g 11.8g 10.2g 10m 10m2 10g 10m] small, lightly-made
filly: poor maiden: showed little after second in ladies handicap at Newbury: should
be as effective at 1½m +: acts on good to firm and soft ground: blinkered fourth
outing. *Lady Herries.*

RABSHA (IRE) 3 b.f. Taufan (USA) 119 – Serraj (USA) 57 (Seattle Slew (USA)) **64**
[1990 NR 1991 11d* 10m 16.2g 12s] big, lengthy filly: shows knee action: third foal:
dam third over 1m from 3 starts at 3 yrs: won 4-runner maiden at Ayr in April: well
beaten in varied other events, sweating and on toes before claimer (took keen hold)
final start: sold to join D. McCune 6,000 gns Newmarket Autumn Sales. *B. Hanbury.*

RACECALL GOLD CARD 4 ch.g. Camden Town 125 – Polly Royal 75 (Music **— §**
Boy 124) [1990 10.8m 8f6 7f 7f3 7f 7m 7m 8f4 7h3 7m 1991 a8g] good-topped gelding:
poor handicapper: stays 7f: below form when visored once: probably ungenuine:
sold 2,600 gns Doncaster Summer Sales. *T. Kersey.*

RACE TO TIME (IRE) 3 b.g. Runnett 125 – Plunket's Choice (Home Guard **58**
(USA) 129) [1990 6g6 5g4 7g6 a6g4 a7g4 a8g3 1991 a8g* a10g 8g* 8m 10d5 8d2 8m
a10g6] leggy, quite attractive ex-Irish gelding: plating-class handicapper: won at
Lingfield (maiden) in January and Warwick (bandaged off-hind) in April: ran fairly
well at Lingfield final start, first for over 5 months: best form at 1m: below form on
top-of-the-ground. *R. Akehurst.*

RACHEL'S DANCER (IRE) 3 b.f. Lomond (USA) 128 – Passing Fancy (USA) **—**
(Buckpasser) [1990 6m6 7d* 8.2v4 7d5 1991 9m 12m 8.9g] leggy filly: modest winner
at 2 yrs: behind in handicaps in summer as 3-y-o: should stay 1¼m: possibly unsuited by top-of-the-ground. *B. W. Hills.*

RACHELS EDEN 2 ch.f. (May 13) Ring Bidder 88 – Bundling Bed 69 (Welsh **—**
Pageant 132) [1991 6f] second foal: sister to 1990 2-y-o 5f winner Bidders Love
Lane: dam 2-y-o 6f winner won 9f seller at 4 yrs: 50/1, slow-starting last of 11 in
maiden at Hamilton in August. *R. D. E. Woodhouse.*

RACING RASKAL 4 b.g. Dunphy 124 – Raskaska (Aureole 132) [1990 10g **33**
10.2m 12.3g 12m 15g2 13.8m6 a12g6 15.3m2 16m 18d 1991 12m 14.6m5 17.9f6 15.1g4
13.8m4 a16g3 a14g6] smallish, quite attractive gelding: moderate mover: poor handicapper: stays long distances: acts on firm going. *Capt. J. Wilson.*

RACKETEER (IRE) 3 b.f. Stalker 121 – Splendid Yankee (Yankee Gold 115) **88 d**
[1990 6g 5f2 5f* 5g2 5m4 5f 5g* 5m3 5m 1991 6g 5g6 5d2 5m3 5m 5.1g 5.2g 5g 5.1m
5d 5d 5.2g] leggy, sparely-made filly: moderate walker: fairly useful efforts in
handicaps second to fourth starts, placed in £7,200 contests at Chester (slowly
away) and Epsom: ran moderately after: worth another try at 6f: yet to race on soft
going, acts on any other: reluctant to race when blinkered seventh start: sometimes
mounted on track: sold 2,500 gns Newmarket Autumn Sales. *B. R. Millman.*

RADAR KNIGHT 3 b.c. Beldale Flutter (USA) 130 – Eurynome (Be My Guest **43**
(USA) 126) [1990 5g 7m 7m3 7f2 7f6 8m 1991 8f 10g 10m 12f6 14d 14.1g4* 13.8g4
14.6m4 17.2g] leggy, workmanlike colt: has a roundish action: poor handicapper:
won at Yarmouth in June: off course 3 months before first start: stays 1¾m: acts on
firm going: taken down early as 3-y-o: bandaged fourth start. *R. A. Bennett.*

RADICAL CHIC 3 b.f. Sadler's Wells (USA) 132 – Santa Roseanna 111 (Caracol **77**
(FR)) [1990 7m5 1991 10.2f2 10g*] smallish, rather sparely-made filly: has a fluent,
round action: improved effort to win £10,400 maiden at Ascot in July by 6 lengths,
making all and running on well: will be suited by 1½m. *L. M. Cumani.*

RADIO CAROLINE 3 b.g. All Systems Go 119 – Caroline Lamb 74 (Hotfoot **56**
126) [1990 6g 7m2 6m4 8m6 7f 8d2 8f4 1991 8.2f 8g6 9.2d 11g* 8.5f4 12m3 10f6 9m2
8m 12.2g6] close-coupled, rather sparely-made gelding: plating-class performer:
won maiden auction at Edinburgh in June: probably needs further than 1m but
unlikely to stay beyond 1½m: acts on firm and dead going: visored sixth and last 3
starts: joined M. Tate. *A. Harrison.*

RADWELL 3 b.c. Dunbeath (USA) 127 – Integrity 108 (Reform 132) [1990 6g* **110** 6f* 7g* 1991 8m 8m* 8g5 8g5] workmanlike, good-bodied colt: very useful performer: won 7-runner minor event at Newcastle in June, pushed along towards rear over 3f out then quickening really well to lead inside last: creditable fifth in Prix Messidor at Maisons-Laffitte and Sussex Stakes at Goodwood (facing stiff task, off bridle some way out, kept on to finish 9½ lengths behind Second Set) in July: should stay 1¼m: sold 60,000 gns Newmarket December Sales. *J. R. Fanshawe.*

R A EXPRESS 6 b.g. Bay Express 132 – Pinaka 69 (Pitcairn 126) [1990 5m2 5m3 — 5m2 6f 5d* 5m6 6s3 5g 6f a5g6 5g 5d2 5d3 5m5 6d 1991 5f 5g 5m4 6.1m 5.1m 5m 5g] good-topped gelding: has shown signs of stringhalt: poor mover: quite modest handicapper at 5 yrs: below form in 1991: probably suited by 5f: best form on a soft surface: sometimes bandaged: tries to make running. *B. A. McMahon.*

RAGAMUFFIN ROMEO 2 b.c. (May 4) Niniski (USA) 125 – Interviewme **69 p** (USA) (Olden Times) [1991 7.1d a8g3] lengthy colt: closely related to 3-y-o 7f winner Noelreac Julian (by Caerleon) and 2 other winners and half-brother to 4 winners: dam 2-y-o 6f winner in USA, is half-sister to dam of high-class miler Jaazeiro: 1½ lengths third of 11, finishing well, to Common Council in late-year maiden at Lingfield, better effort: will improve again, particularly over further. *C. E. Brittain.*

RAGE 4 ch.g. Final Straw 127 – Nasty Niece (CAN) (Great Nephew 126) [1990 6f5 6m 5g 7m4 8.5d2 8f* 8g3 11m 1991 11.9g] rangy gelding: good mover: quite modest handicapper at 3 yrs: in need of run and tailed off only run on flat in 1991, first for 14 months: suited by 1m: acts on firm and dead going: winning hurdler. *M. H. Easterby.*

RAGHBAH 3 b.c. Myjinski (USA) – Lady of Saltash (High Award 119) [1990 NR — 1991 7m 10g] lengthy colt: first reported living foal: dam lightly-raced half-sister to very smart 7f and 1m winner Green Girl: showed nothing in maidens in May. *J. White.*

RAGTIME 4 b.g. Pas de Seul 133 – Boldella (Bold Lad (IRE) 133) [1990 8m 10m — 10m 12f 10d 1991 9s6] neat, strong gelding: good walker: plating-class form at best: well beaten only run in 1991 (April): should stay at least 1m: winning hurdler in November. *D. Burchell.*

RAGTIME SONG 2 b.c. (Apr 16) Dunbeath (USA) 127 – Kelowna (USA) (Master Derby (USA)) [1991 7m 7g 7.1s 7.6m] 3,600F: good-bodied colt: half-brother to 3 winners abroad: dam French maiden: no worthwhile form in maidens and a Lingfield nursery. *R. Akehurst.*

RAHEEB 3 br.c. Mansingh (USA) 120 – Spanish Bold 78 (Tower Walk 130) [1990 — NR 1991 9m a8g] 18,500Y: strong colt: second foal: brother to poor maiden Antique Andy: dam 7.6f and 1m winner: no promise in maidens in May. *N. A. Callaghan.*

RAHIF 3 b.c. Shirley Heights 130 – Vaguely 92 (Bold Lad (IRE) 133) [1990 7g4 **85** 1991 8.1m2] well-made colt: 6/1, keen to post and in race, making most, when 3 lengths second of 7 to Kinematic in maiden at Haydock in July: last in listed race at Newbury over 10 months earlier: sold 6,200 gns Newmarket Autumn Sales. *R. W. Armstrong.*

RAINBOW CHASER (IRE) 3 b.f. Rainbow Quest (USA) 134 – Scotia Rose **43** (Tap On Wood 130) [1990 6f3 8m a8g3 1991 a10g5 a8g6] close-coupled, rather angular filly: plating-class maiden: probably stays 1¼m: sold 2,500 gns Ascot April Sales. *P. F. I. Cole.*

RAINBOW CORNER 2 b.c. (Feb 21) Rainbow Quest (USA) 134 – **124 p** Kingscote 118 (Kings Lake 133) [1991 8m* 8m2 8d2]

Readers searching for a horse to follow in France in the coming season could do far worse than enlist Rainbow Corner, a superbly-made individual with a pedigree to match whom we're convinced will develop into a top-class performer, most likely at a mile and a quarter and more. The big, handsome Rainbow Corner, a grand walker, too, made such rapid strides in the autumn that on his third and final outing he finished an excellent second to Arazi in the Grand Criterium at Longchamp in October. Rainbow Corner had made his racecourse debut barely a month earlier, in the seven-runner Prix de Toutevoie for newcomers over the same mile course and distance. If the betting was to be believed, Rainbow Corner was the less-fancied of his stable's two runners, but he emerged comfortably the better in the race and won apparently quite impressively, by a length and a half from his stable-companion after coming from last to first in the two-furlong straight. In his only other

race before the Criterium, the Prix La Rochette at Longchamp, Rainbow Corner forfeited his unbeaten record by decree of the stewards, having been adjudged guilty of hampering the runner-up Steinbeck, whom he'd beaten by a short neck, in the sprint to the line. On the French tote Rainbow Corner was considered to be the most likely danger to Arazi in the Grand Criterium run in early-October. He duly finished second, three lengths down and a short head in front of the subsequent Racing Post Trophy winner Seattle Rhyme, but well though he ran, he never at any stage threatened to overturn the favourite, being pushed along as soon as Arazi eased to the front rounding the final turn then staying on in grand fashion under strong pressure to pip Seattle Rhyme on the line. Considering that Rainbow Corner conceded vital experience to all his five opponents and start to all except Code Breaker, his performance in what was unequivocally the most strongly-contested two-year-old race of the European season bodes well for his prospects. He seems certain to win pattern races as a three-year-old.

Rainbow Corner (b.c. Feb 21, 1989)	Rainbow Quest (USA) (b 1981)	Blushing Groom (ch 1974)	Red God / Runaway Bride
		I Will Follow (b 1975)	Herbager / Where You Lead
	Kingscote (b 1983)	Kings Lake (b 1978)	Nijinsky / Fish-Bar
		Bold Fantasy (b 1974)	Bold Lad / Ribot's Fantasy

Rainbow Corner is from the third crop of the Arc winner Rainbow Quest and is Kingscote's second foal following the three-year-old Kris filly Avowal (she's since had colts by Kris again and Dancing Brave). Kingscote was a very smart sprinter as a two-year-old whose four-length defeat of Northern Eternity in the Lowther Stakes at York was one of the most impressive by her age and sex all season. Kingscote, who ran only once the following season, is a daughter of the lightly-raced but smart and genuine Irish seven-furlong winner Bold Fantasy, second to Lady Capulet in the Irish One Thousand Guineas and to He Loves Me in the Cork And Orrery Stakes. Bold Fantasy, a half-sister to the useful Irish middle-distance mare Ribot's Fantasy, has bred several other winners, among them the Irish five-furlong winner Fantasy Land and the French nine-furlong winner Esna. This is a good family which has had cause to crop up numerous times in *Racehorses*: Rainbow Corner's fourth dam Fantan II bred Ragusa and is a forbear of Sarah Siddons, Seymour Hicks and Princess Pati, among others. *A. Fabre, France.*

RAINBOW FLEET 3 b.f. Nomination 125 – Olderfleet 59 (Steel Heart 128) **49**
[1990 5m 5m² 5m³ 5g² 5f* 6f⁶ 5m 1991 5s s 5g 5.3f⁴ 7m 6.9m 6m⁵] strong,

workmanlike filly: quite modest performer at 2 yrs: best effort in handicaps on final start (in July), never near to challenge: didn't handle turn at Folkestone: stays 6f: acts on firm going. *L. J. Holt.*

RAINBOW STRIPES 4 ch.c. Rainbow Quest (USA) 134 – Pampas Miss (USA) — (Pronto) [1990 10m 10m⁵ 10s 10g⁴ 11.7m 15g³ 12.2m⁴ 14m* 12f⁴ 15.5f 16m* 16d 1991 15.8g] big colt: rather unfurnished: quite modest handicapper at 3 yrs: little promise only run in 1991 (October): suited by test of stamina and a sound surface: below form when blinkered once: not an easy ride, best with strong handling. *B. S. Rothwell.*

RAINBOW TRUST 3 b.c. Rainbow Quest (USA) 134 – Bandit Queen (FR) (Jim **82** French (USA)) [1990 7s⁵ 1991 10g 14m² 14.6f⁴ 16g² 14.6m 16.2m² 16.1m⁶] tall, leggy, close-coupled colt: fair maiden: finished lame final start: stayed 2m: acted on good to firm ground: twice mulish at stalls: seemed one paced: dead. *A. A. Scott.*

RAIN GOD 3 b.g. Lidhame 109 – Rainbow Star (Star Appeal 133) [1990 7f³ 8m 7s **56** 1991 14f³ 16.2g⁶ 14.1g⁴ 14.1f² 13.1f] close-coupled, quite attractive gelding: plating-class maiden: stayed 1¾m: acted on firm going: dead. *Miss A. J. Whitfield.*

RAIN RIDER 2 b.c. (Feb 20) Fools Holme (USA) – Moon Parade 73 (Welsh **64 p** Pageant 132) [1991 8g] 98,000F: leggy, unfurnished colt: has scope: third foal: half-brother to a winner in Italy by Tender King: dam 10.2f winner, is out of sister to very smart middle-distance stayer Castle Keep and half-sister to Gold Cup winner Ragstone, family also of Moon Madness and Sheriff's Star: sire 6f to 1¼m winner: 25/1, green and edgy, tenderly-handled ninth of 16 to Aljadeer in minor event at Newbury in October, held up then outpaced from 2f out: mulish stalls: likely to stay 1¼m: will do better. *J. L. Dunlop.*

RAINRIDGE 2 b.c. (May 15) Rainbow Quest (USA) 134 – Beveridge (USA) 86 **77 p** (Spectacular Bid (USA)) [1991 8m⁴ 8.1d²] well-made, good-quartered colt: has scope: third foal: half-brother to 1990 2-y-o 6f winner (also useful form at 1m and 1¼m) Safa (by Shirley Heights) and 1989 2-y-o 6f winner Between Time (by Elegant Air): dam 2-y-o 7f winner out of half-sister to Formidable and Ajdal: odds on, but better for race and very much on toes, running-on ½-length second of 10 to Trafalgar Boy in maiden at Haydock in October: will stay 1¼m: likely to do better. *J. L. Dunlop.*

RAISE A RUBY 3 b.f. Green Ruby (USA) 104 – Fashion Lover 70 (Shiny Tenth — 120) [1990 6g⁵ 6g⁶ 6g⁴ 5g⁶ 1991 5m a8g] unfurnished filly: poor maiden: blinkered and edgy final start. *M. O'Neill.*

RAISE A STAR 6 b.g. Red Sunset 120 – Hill's Realm (USA) 68 (Key To The **52** Kingdom (USA)) [1990 NR 1991 12m⁵ 12m* 12g 12m⁵ 11.9f* 11.8m 11.9g⁵ 12.5g] quite attractive gelding: lightly raced and plating-class handicapper: won at Folkestone (first win) in July and Brighton in August: stays 1½m: acts on firm and dead going: has been reluctant at stalls: inconsistent: sold 2,000 gns Newmarket Autumn Sales, resold 1,500 gns Ascot December Sales. *R. Akehurst.*

RAISE MEMORIES 5 b.m. Skyliner 117 – Really (Sovereign Gleam 117) [1990 — NR 1991 a12g] angular, good-topped mare: moderate mover: plating-class maiden at 2 yrs: backward in Southwell handicap in January, only run on flat since: best form at 6f: acts on heavy going, possibly not firm: has looked temperamental, and not an easy ride: sold 1,650 gns Ascot May Sales. *B. A. McMahon.*

RAITH PC 2 ch.g. (Apr 16) Aragon 118 – All Fine (Fine Blade (USA) 121) [1991 7d] — 3,600F, 15,000Y: second foal: dam unraced sister to Magnet Cup winner Fine Sun: 50/1, soon behind in maiden at Ayr in July. *G. Richards.*

RAJAI (IRE) 2 br.c. (Mar 16) Last Tycoon 131 – Flame of Tara 124 (Artaius **81 p** (USA) 129) [1991 8.2m²] IR 540,000Y: tall, attractive colt: has plenty of scope: good walker: fourth foal: brother to high-class 3-y-o Marju, successful at 7f (at 2 yrs) and 1m and second in Derby, and half-brother to 2 winners by Sadler's Wells, notably Salsabil: dam best at 3 yrs, winning Pretty Polly Stakes and Coronation Stakes: 5/4, short-head second of 4 to Alphard in maiden at Nottingham in October, finding little initially under 3f out, then running on strongly inside final 1f: showed quick action to post: will improve, and win races. *J. L. Dunlop.*

RAJANPOUR (USA) 6 ch.h. Riverman (USA) 131 – Rajpoura 118 (Kashmir II **59 §** 125) [1990 NR 1991 14d 18d* 16.5m 16.2g* 16m* 20g 16.5m] angular, sturdy horse: type to carry condition: poor mover: plating-class handicapper: won (made most) at Nottingham (first form) in April and Goodwood and Newcastle (by 8 lengths) in May: took little interest and dropped right out once headed otherwise: stays very well: acts on good to firm going: blinkered last 6 starts: thoroughly unreliable. *R. Curtis.*

RAJAYA (USA) 3 b.c. Nureyev (USA) 131 – Don't Sulk (USA) 115 (Graustark) **55** [1990 6m 1991 10m⁴ 10d³ 12.5m 11m] sturdy, quite attractive colt: quite modest form, in frame for maidens: well beaten in summer handicaps: stays 1¼m: gets coltish in preliminaries: sold 6,400 gns Newmarket September Sales. *R. O'Leary.*

RAJPUT RAJAH 4 b.g. Indian King (USA) 128 – Take A Chance (FR) (Baldric II — 131) [1990 7g 7m⁵ 6f 7g 7g 1991 a7g⁴ a7g 7d 10f 7m 10f⁴ 8g 8.3m] lengthy, angular gelding: little worthwhile form: stays 7f: sometimes blinkered. *E. A. Wheeler.*

RAMBO EXPRESS 4 b. or br.c. New Express 95 – Saul Flower (Saulingo 122) **67** d [1990 6m⁶ 6s 6m 6g⁵ 5m⁴ 5.1f⁶ a5g 5.1m 5.3f³ 5d² a6g* a6g⁵ a6g* 1991 a6g⁵ 5g² 5m 5f 6f a5g 6m a6g⁶ a6g a6g⁶ a6g⁵] smallish, workmanlike colt: mostly well beaten in 1991, quite modest form at best: stays 6f: acts on dead going: tried blinkered and visored: needs to be able to dominate: trained first 2 starts by G. Huffer, third one (claimed out of J. Banks's stable £8,501) and next 6 by J. Pearce. *I. Campbell.*

RAMI (USA) 4 br.c. Riverman (USA) 131 – Ancient Regime (USA) 123 (Olden **113** Times) [1990 7g³ 8f 6m* 7m* 7m³ 1991 7g* 6m³ 8g² 7g 7.3f³ 7m 7g⁵] leggy, close-coupled, quite attractive colt: has a quick, moderate action: very useful performer: won listed event at Leicester in April: ran well after when placed, in Queen Anne Stakes at Royal Ascot (head second to Sikeston) and Hungerford Stakes at Newbury (didn't enjoy best of runs) third and fifth starts: stays 1m: acts on firm and dead ground: has been taken quietly to post: ran respectably when visored final start. *P. T. Walwyn.*

RAMPANT GOSSIP 2 gr.g. (Apr 1) Forzando 122 – Trestle 57 (Three Legs **61** 128) [1991 8m 8m 8m 8.3g 8.9m³ 8g] 14,000Y: leggy, angular gelding: has scope: fourth reported living foal: half-brother to 10.8f winner Truss (by Lyphard's Special): dam lightly-raced half-sister to very useful 1975 2-y-o 5f winner Grey Home: quite modest maiden: blinkered second time (ran poorly fourth start), good staying-on third of 19 in claimer at York: ran poorly in Redcar nursery later in October: suited by a good test of stamina: sold 3,600 gns Doncaster November Sales. *M. W. Easterby.*

RAMROD 6 ch.g. Giacometti 130 – Come On Girl (Sheshoon 132) [1990 NR 1991 — 10m] sparely-made gelding: poor and lightly-raced maiden: blinkered when last in seller only run on flat in 1991: stays 13f: acts on firm going: tends to wander. *R. J. Hodges.*

RAMSEY STREET 4 b.f. Mummy's Game 120 – Green Jinks (Hardgreen (USA) — 122) [1990 7d⁵ 8g 10f 1991 11m] rather leggy filly: poor and lightly-raced performer: should stay 1m: best effort on dead going: tried blinkered. *K. S. Bridgwater.*

RANCHO MIRAGE 4 ch.g. Superlative 118 – Que Sera 91 (Music Boy 124) **76** [1990 6m³ 5g* 5g⁶ 5d⁴ 6m 1991 5g 6m 6m² 6g⁵ 6v 6m³ 6m a6g a6g⁵ a6g] robust, a — sprint type: one-time fair handicapper, not nearly so good nowadays: sold out of J. W. Watts's stable 2,800 gns Newmarket Autumn Sales after seventh start: below form at Southwell after, tailed off final start: stays 6f: acts on good to firm and dead (unsuited by heavy) ground. *Mrs N. Macauley.*

RAPIDARIS 5 b.g. Rapid River 127 – Stellaris (Star Appeal 133) [1990 8m 1991 — 7.1d 12m] smallish, lengthy gelding: appears of little account. *B. R. Cambidge.*

RAPID CORACLE (IRE) 3 b.c. Welsh Term 126 – Canoeing (Tap On Wood **98** 130) [1990 6m⁵ 6f² 8g⁶ 7m⁴ 7d² 6d* 1991 8g* 8m² 10g⁵] tall, leggy colt: fairly useful performer: won £18,000 handicap at Sandown in April, tending to idle: ran well in Britannia Handicap at Royal Ascot (5 lengths second to Ajaad) and £53,300 handicap at Sandown (behind You Know The Rules) in summer: stays 1¼m: acts on good to firm ground and dead. *R. Hannon.*

RAPID LAD 13 b.g. Rapid River 127 – Seacona (Espresso 122) [1990 10.8m 10m² **48** 10d⁵ 10f⁴ 1991 10d 10.8m 10f⁶ 10m² 9.9g 9.9f³] compact gelding: good mover: only poor handicapper nowadays: successful 12 times at Beverley, and has not won elsewhere since 1982: best at 1¼m: needs top-of-the-ground: has worn blinkers, but not for long time: held up and suited by strong gallop: particularly well handled by D. Nicholls: tough. *J. L. Spearing.*

RAPID MOVER 4 ch.g. Final Straw 127 – Larive 80 (Blakeney 126) [1990 11m⁴ — 8.2g⁶ 1991 9s 8.3f 15.1g] leggy gelding: poor maiden: soundly beaten, including in handicaps in 1991: tried visored once. *J. K. Kinane.*

RAPID ROSIE 3 ch.f. Noalto 120 – Cora 53 (Current Coin 118) [1990 NR 1991 8m — 8g 7g 10.1d 8.3g 8.1g 8.1s⁶ 8.3m 10m] plain, sparely-made filly: sixth foal: dam won 1m seller at 5 yrs: little form, including in sellers: often pulls hard: sometimes sweats. *P. Hayward.*

RAPPORTEUR (USA) 5 b.g. His Majesty (USA) – Sweet Rapport (USA) **76** (Round Table) [1990 a10g⁶ a10g* a12g³ a10g³ a8g² a10g* a8g⁴ 9g 11.7f² 10.4d 10m² a 92

685

12m⁶ 10g* 10.5m 9m⁴ 9m² 10g³ a10g* a10g* a10g³ a10g* 1991 a12g² a10g* a10g* 10g 10m 10.1f 10d⁴ 10g 11.7m⁴ 10s⁵ 9f⁶ 11.5g* 10m* a10g³ a12g a10g² a10g²] leggy, angular gelding: fairly useful handicapper: successful 11 times at Lingfield (8 of them on equitrack, including in January and February) and hasn't won elsewhere: fair form on turf, winning large-field contests in October: effective at 1¼m to 1½m: usually races prominently: probably acts on any going: has worn bandages: has won for apprentice: splendidly tough and genuine: a great credit to his connections. *C. C. Elsey.*

RAP UP FAST (USA) 2 b.g. (Apr 10) Eskimo (USA) – Naomi's Flash (USA) **48** (Ray Jeter (USA)) [1991 6m 7m 8.1m] $10,000Y: leggy, lengthy gelding: third reported foal: dam won 29 races, at up to 7f, from 2 yrs to 7 yrs: sire (by Northern Dancer) successful at up to 1m: plating-class maiden: best effort (for 7-lb claimer) final start: stays 8.1f. *C. W. Thornton.*

RARE DETAIL (IRE) 3 ch.f. Commanche Run 133 – Sharp Dresser (USA) **78** (Sharpen Up 127) [1990 a8g* 1991 12v* 11.7g² 12g* 12d⁴ 11.8g² 12.1s⁶ 11.8m³ 10.3d] lengthy filly: moderate mover and walker: modest handicapper: won at Folkestone in March and Leicester in June: stays 1½m: acts on equitrack, good to firm and heavy going: bandaged second start: wore eyeshield on all-weather: lacks turn of foot, and should prove best ridden up with pace. *Mrs L. Piggott.*

RARE TASTE (USA) 2 b.c. (Apr 23) Rare Performer (USA) – Tangáta (ARG) **71 p** (Good Manners (USA)) [1991 6g³ 6m² 5f* 5m⁵] $1,800F, $9,700Y, $50,000 2-y-o: tall, rather leggy, useful-looking colt: third reported foal: half-brother to a minor winner: dam sprint-winning sister to champion Argentinian filly Mi Quimera: made all in maiden at Redcar in July: excellent fifth of 7 in nursery at Sandown following month: will prove at least as effective back at 6f. *J. Berry.*

RARFY'S DREAM 3 b.c. Dreams To Reality (USA) 113 – Elbandary (Shirley **69 d** Heights 130) [1990 NR 1991 6f⁵ 8.3d⁵ 6s 7.1s 8f⁵ 7f 10m] 5,600Y: sturdy colt: first foal: dam lightly raced: plating class on most form: easily best effort after debut in handicap at Yarmouth fifth start: stays 1m: seems unsuited by a soft surface: blinkered sixth start: sweating and edgy, pulled hard on final one: joined J. Czerpak. *J. Banks.*

RASAN 4 ch.c. Dominion 123 – Raffle 82 (Balidar 133) [1990 7m 5m⁶ 7m* 7.6m* **94** 7m 7.6m* 7.6f* 1991 7g 7g⁵ 7.6m 7.9g 7.6m²] good-bodied colt: carries condition: moderate mover: fairly useful handicapper: form in 1991 only when good second at Lingfield (goes very well there) in September: stays 7.6f: goes well on firm going. *R. W. Armstrong.*

RASCO 2 gr.g. (Feb 13) Natroun (FR) 128 – Kabylia (FR) (Dancer's Image (USA)) **66 ?** [1991 8m 6.1m 7m² 7g 7d] 9,800Y: leggy, lengthy gelding: half-brother to 6f (at 2 yrs) and 1m winner Schhh You-Know-Who (by Longleat) and several winners abroad: dam useful French sprinting 2-y-o, is sister to Godswalk: easily best effort when second of 8, beaten a head, in maiden at Newcastle in October, stumbling slightly inside last, then running green: apparently well handicapped in nurseries last 2 starts. *J. Etherington.*

RASHEED 4 b.c. Chief Singer 131 – Enchanting Dancer (FR) (Nijinsky (CAN) **57** 138) [1990 11d 8m 10.6s 7m 8.2g 10m⁴ 11.7g⁴ 14d⁵ 12m² 12s 10g⁴ 10g 1991 a10g* a12g⁵ a10g⁴] close-coupled colt: moderate mover: plating-class handicapper: won (for first time) at Lingfield in January by 8 lengths: not seen out after February: best form at 1¼m: yet to race on firm going, unsuited by soft: tried visored once: often bandaged behind: often races freely. *N. A. Callaghan.*

RASHITA 4 b.f. Alzao (USA) 117 – Apapa Port 80 (My Swanee 122) [1990 8.5g **—** 10g⁴ 10.6d 13v⁴ 12.4s⁶ 1991 11.5g 10.2g] lengthy filly: plating-class maiden at best: unseated rider in amateurs event final start: seems to stay 1¼m: tried blinkered once. *R. V. King.*

RASMOOR SONG 3 b.f. Cree Song 99 – Malmo (Free State 125) [1990 7f a7g **—** a6g 1991 a5g a7g] sparely-made filly: no show in maidens and claimers. *D. Lee.*

RATAFIA 3 b.f. Rousillon (USA) 133 – Smageta (High Top 131) [1990 NR 1991 **78 p** 7.5m*] fifth foal: half-sister to fairly useful 10.6f winner Regordes (by Commanche Run) and 2 winners in Italy: dam won 3 times in Italy at 2 yrs: evens, green and bit backward, won 7-runner maiden at Beverley in June, slowly away, leading on bridle 3f out and soon clear despite tending to carry head high: looked sure to do better. *L. M. Cumani.*

RATHAGE 5 b.m. Horage 124 – Rathcoffey Duchy (Faberge II 121) [1990 a14g **—** 10d a12g a12g 1991 17.1m 12g] lengthy, shallow-girthed mare: quite modest handicapper as 3-y-o: little subsequent worthwhile form: suited by 1½m: acts on good to firm and heavy going: tried blinkered once. *G. G. Gracey.*

RATHER GORGEOUS 6 br.m. Billion (USA) 120 – Fair Sara 65 (McIndoe 97) **26** § [1990 12h 12.3g 11m⁶ 16f 18g 13.8f* 13.8d 1991 13.8g⁴ 16m 13.8m³ 12.3f⁶ 13.8m] tall, lengthy, angular mare: temperamental handicapper: seemed reluctant to race final 2 starts: stays 13.8f: acts on firm going: winning hurdler. *Capt. J. Wilson.*

RATIFY 4 br.g. Shirley Heights 130 – Rattle (FR) (Riverman (USA) 131) [1990 NR **97** 1991 11.8g* 12g² 10m 11.9d⁶ 12g] small, sturdy gelding: good walker: has quick action: second foal: dam 7.5f to 1¼m winner: lightly raced and fairly useful performer: won slowly-run minor event at Leicester in June: off course 2½ months, creditable sixth in handicap at Haydock, hanging badly left final 2f: out of depth in St Simon Stakes at Newbury later in October: better suited by 1½m than 1¼m: acts on good to soft ground. *Miss H. C. Knight.*

RAVECINO 2 ch.f. (Mar 22) Ballacashtal (CAN) – Lemelasor 75 (Town Crier **45** d 119) [1991 5f⁵ 5m* 5m⁵ 6m 6f 6f 7m 7.1m] rather plain filly: second foal: dam 5f winner at 2 yrs probably stayed 1m: 25/1-winner of 12-runner seller (no bid) at Thirsk in May: sweating, soundly beaten final start: stays 6f: refused to enter stalls at Redcar in July. *J. S. Haldane.*

RAVENHURST 3 br.g. Bustino 136 – Ravens Peak (High Top 131) [1990 6m 8m **45** d 6d 7f⁶ 8m 1991 9s⁶ 8.5f² 12f 12.2g⁵ 9.9f8f⁶ 12f8m 10f⁵ 12.1f⁴ 11m 8m] smallish, leggy gelding: inconsistent plater: may prove best at 1¼m: acts on firm going: tends to edge left: headstrong: wore net muzzle final start: trained until after tenth start by T. Fairhurst. *J. Hetherton.*

RAVEN RUNNER (USA) 2 b.f. (Jan 25) Storm Bird (CAN) 134 – Simple Taste **84** (USA) 93 (Sharpen Up 127) [1991 7g² 7d³] lengthy, angular filly: first foal: dam 7f winner at 2 yrs (only season to race) from family of Arkadina: fair form in minor events at Kempton (behind Perfect Circle) and Ascot (beaten 7 lengths by Red Slippers) in September: will stay 1m: sure to win a race. *I. A. Balding.*

RAWAABE (USA) 3 ch.f. Nureyev (USA) 131 – Passerine (USA) (Dr Fager) **76** [1990 5m⁴ 5m⁴ 5d* 5g⁴ 1991 5d 5m 5g⁶ 5.1m 5m* 5g] lengthy filly: has a sharp action: good walker: looking really well, confirmed promise of previous start to make all in handicap at Ayr in September, easily best effort at 3 yrs: speedy: acts on good to firm and dead ground: visits Cadeaux Genereux. *H. Thomson Jones.*

RAWAAN (FR) 4 b.g. Labus (FR) – Rose Ness (Charlottesville 135) [1990 — 10.7g³ 11g² 12g* 12g⁵ 14g² 12g⁶ 13v⁶ 12.2d 11d 1991 13.8f] tall ex-French gelding: won maiden at Bordeaux at 3 yrs when trained by A. de Royer-Dupre: well beaten on flat here, in Catterick seller (mulish stalls) only run in 1991: probably stays 1¾m: winning hurdler. *N. Tinkler.*

RAW POWER 2 ch.c. (May 19) Norwick (USA) 120 – Pop Gun 85 (King's Troop — 118) [1991 6m] 1,700Y: lengthy colt: half-brother to 3 winning platers, a winner abroad and temperamental 1987 2-y-o Gunner's Moon (by Relkino): dam best at 5f: tailed-off last in Windsor seller in July. *M. R. Channon.*

RAW TALENT 4 br.g. Gorytus 132 – Welcome Break (Wollow 132) [1990 — 8g⁶ a11g³ 12.2m⁵ 11.5m³ 14g⁶ 1991 a11g⁴ 12s 14.6s] workmanlike gelding: moderate mover: poor handicapper, still a maiden: well beaten in early part of 1991: stays 1¾m: acts on good to firm ground: sold 2,500 gns Doncaster March Sales. *J. R. Jenkins.*

RAYADO (USA) 3 b. or br.c. Shadeed (USA) 135 – Delray Dancer (USA) **66** (Chateaugay) [1990 NR 1991 10.4g 8m² 10m⁶ 9.7s] big, heavy-topped colt: has a markedly round action: half-brother to numerous winners, including outstanding American chaser Zaccio (by Lorenzaccio) and Acomb Stakes winner Kohayalan (by Mr Prospector): dam unraced daughter of half-sister to dam of Arts And Letters: modest maiden: chased leaders 1m and not given hard race in handicap final start: easily best effort at 1m on good to firm ground: sold out of H. Cecil's stable 15,000 gns Newmarket Autumn Sales after third start. *R. Akehurst.*

RAYS MEAD 3 gr.f. Tremblant 112 – Free Range 78 (Birdbrook 110) [1990 5g **53** 1991 5m⁶ 5.1m³ 6g⁵ 5.3f⁴ 5m² 6.1m⁵ 5.3g²] leggy filly: plating-class maiden: stays 6f: below form on firm going: has run well when edgy and on toes: consistent. *L. J. Holt.*

RAZIK (IRE) 3 b.c. Last Tycoon 131 – Warm December (He Loves Me 120) — [1990 NR 1991 7f] 60,000F, IR 140,000Y: third foal: half-brother to useful Irish sprinter St Ame (by Ahonoora) and a winner in USA by Persian Bold: dam Irish 1¼m winner: favourite, broke leg in Salisbury maiden in August. *H. Thomson Jones.*

REACH FOR GLORY   2 b.c. (Apr 10) Reach 122 – Carlton Glory (Blakeney 126)   **54**
[1991 5f⁵ 5g⁴ 6d⁵ 7.5f⁴ 7.5f⁴ 7m³ 7.5f³ 8.3g⁶ 10.5d] 2,600Y: smallish colt: first foal:
dam poor half-sister to smart French miler Gosport: fair plater on his day: stays 1m:
acts on firm ground: visored (looked difficult ride) seventh start: has run creditably
for 7-lb claimer: tends to hang right and one to treat with caution. *R. M. Whitaker.*

REACH FORWARD   2 b.f. (Feb 15) Reach 122 – Good Woman 60 (Good Times   **41**
(ITY)) [1991 5g⁴ 5m 5m⁵ 6.1s⁶ 6g⁵ a7g] 8,000Y: smallish, leggy filly: first foal: dam
maiden probably stayed 6f, is half-sister to smart 1985 2-y-o 5f and 7f winner
Moorgate Man: poor maiden: form only at 5f: sometimes sweating and edgy. *B. R.
Millman.*

REACH ME NOT (IRE)   2 ch.f. (Feb 20) Reach 122 – Injaz (Golden Act (USA))   —
[1991 a8g] 500Y: first foal: dam never ran: well beaten in late-year maiden at
Lingfield. *C. Holmes.*

READY TO DRAW (IRE)   2 ch.c. (Mar 23) On Your Mark 125 – Mitsubishi Art   **58**
(Cure The Blues (USA)) [1991 5d⁶ 5g³ 5m⁵ 6m* 6g² 6d⁴ 6.9m⁴ a6g⁴ a6g⁵ 7f 8m
a6g⁵] IR 3,000F: sparely-made colt: moderate mover: first foal: dam unraced, from
family of Front Row: useful plater: won 13-runner event (no bid) at Nottingham in
May: best form at 6f: below form on fibresand and possibly unsuited by dead ground
on turf. *Ronald Thompson.*

REALISM   6 b.g. Known Fact (USA) 135 – Miss Reasoning (USA) 108 (Bold   —
Reasoning (USA)) [1990 a10g⁵ a12g⁴ a12g* 12f 1991 a12g a13g] lengthy, angular
gelding: has a quick action: plating-class handicapper at 5 yrs: no form in early part
of 1991: stays 1½m: acts on soft going, possibly unsuited by firm: sold 675 gns Ascot
September Sales. *K. O. Cunningham-Brown.*

REAL STUNNER   4 ch.f. Chief Singer 131 – Real Party 68 (Realm 129) [1990 5f*   **78**
6m 5g⁵ 5g 5m⁴ 5m⁶ 6d 6m⁴ 6s 5s 1991 a5g 5d⁴ 5m⁴ 5g 5g² 5g* 5d⁵ 6g 5m⁵ 5f² 5f²
5.6m 6m 5d⁴] big, strong, close-coupled filly: moderate mover: modest handicapper:
won at Catterick in July: stays 6f: acts on firm and dead ground: below form when
visored once. *M. P. Naughton.*

REAPERS REWARD   3 b.f. Oats 126 – Red Ragusa 62 (Homeric 133) [1990 5g   —
8d 1991 6g⁶ 8m⁴ 8g 11m] leggy, rather angular filly: poor maiden: stiff task in selling handicap final start: bred to stay much further than 6f: mounted on track third
outing. *R. Hollinshead.*

RECEPTIONIST   2 b.f. (Feb 15) Reference Point 139 – Ever Genial 117   **56 p**
(Brigadier Gerard 144) [1991 a8g²] second foal: closely related to 3-y-o 1¼m winner
Highly Praised (by Shirley Heights): dam 7f to 1m winner, is granddaughter of smart
middle-distance stayer Guillotina: 11/8, 2 lengths second of 13, staying on, to Grog in
maiden at Southwell: will improve, particularly over further. *H. R. A. Cecil.*

RECOLLECT   9 b.g. Vaigly Great 127 – Archaic 65 (Relic) [1990 NR 1991 6m 8m   —
7.1m 8f 10.2g 10.2f⁶] plating-class performer: no form in 1991: effective at 6f to 1m:
acts on firm and dead going: tried blinkered *Miss J. Thorne.*

RED ARCHER   2 ro.c. (Apr 1) Gorytus (USA) 132 – Carose (Caro 133) [1991   **43 p**
a7g⁶] closely related to several winners on flat and over hurdles, including Italian
pattern winner Rosa de Caerleon (by Caerleon) and 1¼m winner Jason's Quest (by
Golden Fleece): dam half-sister to very smart French colt Noir Et Or: around 13
lengths sixth of 16 to Empeeka in late-year maiden at Southwell: will improve. *P. J.
Makin.*

RED BISHOP (USA)   3 b. or br.c. Silver Hawk (USA) 123 – La Rouquine (Silly   **106**
Season 127) [1990 7m³ 1991 10.5g* 10d* 12g⁵] well-made colt: won maiden at
Haydock in September and £12,100 handicap (easing down from The Glasha, having
quickened in good style to lead 1½f out) at Ascot in October: favourite, every chance
3f out but finished very tired when well beaten in St Simon Stakes at Newbury:
stays 1¼m: goes well on dead ground. *J. H. M. Gosden.*

RED BOMBER   3 b.c. Law Society (USA) 130 – Elodie (USA) (Shecky Greene   —
(USA)) [1990 NR 1991 a12g] 5,000Y: second foal: brother to winning hurdler
Isabeau: dam 11f and 1½m winner: tailed off in claimer at Lingfield in November. *K.
O. Cunningham-Brown.*

RED CRESCENT   3 b.c. Red Sunset 120 – Temple Heights 72 (Shirley Heights   **50**
130) [1990 7g 7g 7s 1991 10.1s 8m 8.5m⁴dis 8g⁶ 10g⁴] compact colt: plating-class
maiden on flat: stays 1¼m: acts on good to firm ground: blinkered last 3 starts: won
claiming hurdle in August: sold 2,300 gns Newmarket Autumn Sales: resold 1,250
gns Ascot December Sales. *J. R. Jenkins.*

REDDEN BURN (IRE)   3 b.c. Green Desert (USA) 127 – Red Letter Day 100 **110**
(Crepello 136) [1990 6g² 6g* 7m* 7m* 1991 8g³ 8.9m* 8d² 8m² 8m⁵ 8.5s*] neat,
attractive colt: has quick action: progressed into a useful performer: won £9,400
handicap at York in June and Group 3 Grosser Preis Von Dusseldorf in October:
beaten narrowly in valuable handicaps and little more than a length in Group 3
contest at Deauville in between: may well stay 1¼m: acts on good to firm ground
and soft: races up with pace: tough and game. *H. R. A. Cecil.*

RED FOR DANGER   2 b.g. (Apr 16) Formidable (USA) 125 – Red Shoes 74   **57** §
(Dance In Time (CAN)) [1991 7d 6g* 6d⁴ 7f⁵ 8m 8f 8g] close-coupled, workmanlike
gelding: moderate mover: second foal: dam stayed 1½m, is daughter of Oaks and St
Leger winner Dunfermline: won maiden claimer (claimed out of I. Balding's stable
£7,200) at Brighton in July: ran poorly last 3 starts, twice looking ungenuine: best
form at 7f on firm ground: ran well when visored, below form in blinkers: tends to
sweat: one to avoid. *A. W. Denson.*

RED INK   2 ch.g. (Mar 11) Blushing Scribe (USA) 107 – Pink Robber (USA) 85 (No   **54**
Robbery) [1991 5g⁴ 6g³ 5.3f 6g] 1,300F, 3,600Y, 5,000 2-y-o: rather unfurnished
gelding: third foal: brother to 3-y-o Parsonsannco: dam 6f winner at 2 yrs:
plating-class maiden: off course 2 months and blinkered, soundly beaten in claimer
final start: stays 6f. *J. Sutcliffe.*

REDISHAM   2 ch.c. (Jan 30) Persian Bold 123 – Barsham 94 (Be My Guest (USA)   **70**
126) [1991 7m⁵ 8m* 8g] IR 28,000Y: first foal: dam 1¼m winner suited by 1½m,
from family of Blakeney and Morston: weak 3/1-shot, won 11-runner maiden at
Redcar in October, making virtually all and staying on strongly despite wandering:
last of 19 in nursery there 13 days later: will be suited by 1¼m+: wears a tongue
strap. *J. H. M. Gosden.*

RED KAY TU   2 ch.c. (Mar 29) Kaytu 112 – Red Penny (Red Alert 127) [1991   **—**
6.1m⁵] small, lengthy colt: second foal: dam never ran: 50/1, tailed-off last of 5 in
maiden at Nottingham in July. *F. Jordan.*

RED KITE   2 ch.g. (Mar 10) Bluebird (USA) 125 – Affirmation (FR) (Affirmed   **64**
(USA)) [1991 5m 5g³ 5d 7g 6g³ 6m 7d³] IR 15,500Y: smallish, workmanlike gelding:
moderate mover: third foal: dam minor French 11f winner at 4 yrs, is from good
family: quite modest maiden: will stay 1m: seems ideally suited by an easy surface:
has run well for 7-lb claimer. *M. Bell.*

Michael Sobell Handicap, York—Redden Burn (No. 4) hangs on resolutely from Charlo

RED MAYDAY 3 b.f. Domynsky 110 – May Kells (Artaius (USA) 129) [1990 5m⁴   — §
5d⁴ 6g⁶ 5g 6g 1991 a7g a8g 6f 5m] leggy, workmanlike filly: moderate mover: poor
maiden: should stay at least 6f: may be temperamentally unsatisfactory and looks
one to avoid. *E. H. Owen jun.*

REDNET 4 b.f. Tender King 123 – Red For Go (Tanfirion 110) [1990 a5g* a5g 5g⁶   —
5g³ 5g* 5f⁶ a5g³ a5g a5g a5g a6g 1991 a6g⁵] tall, good-topped filly: moderate mover:
plating-class handicapper at 3 yrs: lost her form: will prove best at 5f: has worn
tongue strap. *D. W. Chapman.*

RED PADDY 6 ch.g. Red Sunset 120 – Irish Bride (Track Spare 125) [1990 7m⁶   —
7.6m⁵ 8f a10g 1991 8g] sparely-made gelding: fairly useful handicapper at best, but
difficult to train: first run for almost a year, always behind but shaped as if retains
ability at Newmarket in November: stays 9f: acts on firm going: has been slowly
away: has tended to hang, and probably best with waiting tactics. *P. J. Makin.*

RED PENCIL 6 ch.g. Krayyan 117 – Blue Gulf 68 (Gay Fandango (USA) 132)   —
[1990 10.2f 11s² 10f 10m³ 1991 a8g⁵ a11g a8g⁶ 12g 9s] angular gelding: has a quick
action: modest maiden at best: well below form in first half of 1991: stays 11f: acts on
any going: sold 2,200 gns Doncaster October Sales. *R. Hollinshead.*

RED POPPY (IRE) 3 b.f. Coquelin (USA) 121 – Special Thanks (Kampala 120)   **51**
[1990 6g⁴ a6g⁵ 1991 5m⁴ 5m 6g⁵ 6m 7g 6f² 7f⁴ 6.1m 6g² 6.9f] leggy, sparely-made
filly: plater: ridden by 7-lb claimer, in frame at Brighton and Yarmouth, getting
behind after slow start each time and finishing fast when twice second at Brighton:
stays 7f: acts on firm going: blinkered second outing: has hung, carried head high
and found little: not one to rely on. *G. A. Pritchard-Gordon.*

RED PROCESSION 7 ch.g. Red Sunset 120 – Procession 118 (Sovereign Path   —
125) [1990 15g 12g⁶ 1991 12g] leggy, rather angular ex-Irish gelding: bad maiden:
sometimes blinkered. *P. Liddle.*

RED RAINBOW 3 b.c. Rainbow Quest (USA) 134 – Red Berry 115 (Great   **95**
Nephew 126) [1990 6s² 7g⁴ 7m⁴ 8g³ 8.2s* 7.3g² 10v² 1991 11g³ 8v 10g 7.9g 12m²
12m² 16.2d³ 12g 16g] leggy, quite attractive colt: fairly useful performer: very good
second to Surrealist in listed race at Newmarket and ran fairly well in £11,500
handicap at Ascot sixth and seventh starts: ran poorly in Newmarket listed race on
final one: should prove effective at 2m: yet to race on firm ground, acts on any other.
B. Hanbury.

RED RIVER BOY 8 b.g. Latest Model 115 – Count On Me 77 (No Mercy 126)   **52**
[1990 5.8h 8.3m 7g⁴ 6m² 7m² 5.8f⁶ 8f 6m⁵ 7d⁵ a6g⁶ a7g⁵ 1991 a7g* a6g⁴ a7g a5g³
a5g 7g 9g] lengthy gelding: carries plenty of condition: has a round action: plating-
class handicapper: won at Lingfield in January: finds easy 5f on sharp side and stays
1m: acts on any going: has been tried in blinkers: has run well for inexperienced
rider: none too consistent. *R. J. Hodges.*

RED ROSEIN 5 b.m. Red Sunset 120 – Vain Deb 66 (Gay Fandango (USA) 132)   **84**
[1990 6f⁶ 6f⁶ 6m 6d 6f⁴ 6f 5g² 5d 5m 6s 6d 1991 6d 6d 7g 6g⁶ 6m 7.1m⁶ 7f⁵ 6g* 6g*
6f* 6m* 6.1m* 6m 6f* 6g 6m 6g 7m 6.1d] leggy, sparely-made mare: has a quick
action: greatly improved handicapper in 1991: successful at Nottingham in June,
Catterick, Thirsk and Redcar in July, and Nottingham and Ripon in August: suited
by 6f and a sound surface: below form when blinkered: usually bandaged behind:
usually slowly away, and held up: a great credit to her connections. *Capt. J. Wilson.*

RED RUFFIAN 2 b.g. (Feb 10) Red Sunset 120 – Morning Stroll (Tower Walk   **92**
130) [1991 5f⁶ 5d* 5.1m⁶ 6g⁴ 5m* 5g*] 7,200F, 3,000Y: lengthy gelding: has scope:
keen walker: first foal: dam never ran: progressive form: successful in maiden
auction at Salisbury in June and nurseries at Wolverhampton in August and Ayr (in
good style, despite drifting right) following month: should prove as effective at 6f:
ran poorly at Warwick (possibly ill at ease on bend) third start. *R. J. Holder.*

RED SECRET (IRE) 3 br.f. Valiyar 129 – Freeze The Secret (USA) 118 (Nearc-   **49** d
tic) [1990 a7g⁵ a8g⁵ 1991 a10g³ a8g⁴ 10d 12f* 12m 12.5m⁶ 12f⁵ 12g 12m 11.5f 15.4f
16m] sturdy, compact filly: moderate mover: little form after winning handicap at
Folkestone in April: stays 1½m well: acts on firm going: blinkered eighth and tenth
starts: visored (pulled hard) last 2: wore eyeshield on all-weather: has carried head
high: sold out of Mrs L. Piggott's stable 6,200 gns Newmarket July Sales after
eighth start. *G. Blum.*

RED SISTER (IRE) 3 b.f. Gorytus (USA) 132 – Happy Kin (USA) (Bold Hitter   **70**
(USA)) [1990 NR 1991 10.6g³ 10.2f] leggy, rather sparely-made filly: half-sister to 6
winners here and abroad, including William Hill Futurity winner Emmson (by
Ela-Mana-Mou) who later stayed 1½m: dam won from 6f to 8.5f in USA: third in
maiden at Haydock: broke leg at Bath in July: dead. *Major W. R. Hern.*

Kensington Palace Stakes, Ascot—Red Slippers wins hard held

RED SLIPPERS (USA) 2 ch.f. (Apr 12) Nureyev (USA) 131 – Morning **100** p
Devotion (USA) 102 (Affirmed (USA)) [1991 6g² 7d* 8d] strong, lengthy filly: first
reported foal: dam 2-y-o 6f winner stayed 1½m: off course 12 weeks and bit better
for race, heavily-backed winner of 7-runner minor event at Ascot in September,
always travelling well and coming 6 lengths clear of Glacial Moon, hard held: around
4 lengths seventh of 13 finishers to Culture Vulture in Prix Marcel Boussac at
Longchamp 9 days later, racing keenly then unable to quicken: stays 1m: yet to race
on top-of-the-ground: useful already, and may well improve further. *L. M. Cumani.*

RED SOMBRERO 2 ch.g. (Apr 11) Aragon 118 – Hat Hill (Roan Rocket 128) **55**
[1991 5m³ 5g³ 6g⁶ 5.8d⁴ 6.1g² 6.1s⁴ 5.7f³ 7f 6g] 11,000Y: sturdy, close-coupled
gelding: fifth foal: half-brother to 1987 2-y-o 7f seller winner Nore Hill (by Town
And Country), later successful over hurdles, and to a winner in Macau: dam ran 4
times: plating-class maiden: fell penultimate outing: stays 6f: best form on good
ground. *L. G. Cottrell.*

RED SONDU (USA) 3 ch.c. Affirmed (USA) – Sans Pareil (USA) (Quack **76**
(USA)) [1990 NR 1991 10g⁴ 10g⁵ 10f* 12m² 10g 12f⁴] $180,000Y: quite good-topped
colt: has a quick action: half-brother to prolific U.S winner Alabama Gold (by
Yukon): dam lightly-raced half-sister to 1985 2-y-o Grade 3 8.5f winner Mustin
Lake: 11/10 on, won 4-runner maiden at Brighton in August: fair second in claimer at
Goodwood, best subsequent effort: should stay 1½m: lacks turn of foot: sold 13,000
gns Newmarket Autumn Sales. *G. Harwood.*

RED SPRINGS (IRE) 2 b.g. (Apr 7) Red Sunset 120 – French Princess 94 **38**
(Prince Regent (FR) 129) [1991 7m 6s a7g] 25,000Y: angular, close-coupled gelding:
half-brother to several winners, including useful 6f (at 2 yrs) to 9f winner Va
Toujours (by Alzao) and 11.7f winner King Among Kings (by Dara Monarch): dam
stayed well: well beaten late in year in maidens and a seller. *J. G. FitzGerald.*

RED TEMPEST (IRE) 3 b.c. Red Sunset 120 – Msida (Majority Blue 126) **—**
[1990 NR 1991 11d⁴ 11d 11g⁶ 15g 10m⁶ 9.2d⁴ 10m] 13,000Y: compact colt: brother to
1¼m and 14.8f winner Monetary Fund and half-brother to several winners,
including fair miler Jade Ring (by Auction Ring): dam placed over 9f in Ireland: poor
maiden: worth a try at 1m: possibly best on a soft surface: visored last 2 starts. *J. S.
Wilson.*

RED TOTO 4 ch.c. Habitat 134 – Soumana (FR) (Pharly (FR) 130) [1990 8m* 9m³ **99**
8.5d 10m* 10f* 10f⁴ 10m* 9m 1991 10g⁶ 12g² 12g 10f³] rather leggy colt: useful
handicapper: not seen out after fair running-on third at Ripon in July: should prove
better suited by 1½m than shorter: acts on firm ground, seems unsuited by heavy:
sold 32,000 gns Newmarket Autumn Sales. *A. C. Stewart.*

RED VERONA 2 ch.f. (Feb 9) Ballacashtal (CAN) – Chicory (Vaigly Great 127) **48**
[1991 5m² 6m 5.1m 6g] workmanlike filly: fourth foal (previous 3 by Norwick):
half-sister to 17f winner Electric Dancer and a winner in Yugoslavia: dam twice-
raced half-sister to very useful animals Macmillion, winner at 1m and 1½m, and Baz
Bombati, a middle-distance performer: poor maiden stays 6f. *E. A. Wheeler.*

RED VICTOR 4 b.g. Bellman (FR) 123 – Red Sharp (FR) (Sharpman 124) [1990 — a 10g5 8f 8f 10m5 8.5g3 9g6 10m 10f5 10m5 12.5m 12d 1991 8.9m] close-coupled gelding: good walker: moderate mover: plater: stays 1¼m: acts on good to firm ground: usually blinkered. *P. D. Evans.*

REED BED (IRE) 3 b.g. Thatching 131 – Kye-Hye 61 (Habitat 134) [1990 6f5 **59** 6g6 6d* 1991 7g6 6m 7.6m 7m5 8d* 8m3 8m 8.1s3] leggy, good-topped gelding: quite modest performer: favourite, won claimer at Salisbury in June: stays 1m: best efforts on a soft surface: visored seventh start: blinkered previous 3: carries head high: gelded before final start. *R. Hannon.*

REEDLING (USA) 6 b.g. Riverman (USA) 131 – Mary Biz (USA) (T V Lark) — [1990 10m 1991 10g] big, rangy gelding: lightly raced and little worthwhile form on flat, including in seller. *P. Butler.*

REEL OF TULLOCH (IRE) 2 b.g. (Mar 28) Salmon Leap (USA) 131 – Miss **71** Sandman 86 (Manacle 123) [1991 7g*] 17,000Y: quite attractive gelding: half-brother to several winners, including 6f winner Miss Tonilee (by Malinowski) and Spanish Mariner (by Julio Mariner), successful at up to 1½m in Ireland: dam 5f winner at 2 yrs: well-backed 5/2-shot but very green, won 7-runner maiden at Wolverhampton in June, rallying well: subsequently joined P. Haslam: will stay at least 1m. *Lord John FitzGerald.*

REEM ALBARAARI 3 b.f. Sadler's Wells (USA) 132 – Habibti 136 (Habitat **58** 134) [1990 6g3 6m3 1991 7g5 8g 9f4 9m] small, stocky filly: fluent mover, with a sharp action: quite modest maiden: ran poorly in Goodwood handicap final start: stays 9f: acts on firm going: visits Machiavellian. *M. R. Stoute.*

REFERENCE LIGHT (USA) 4 b.c. Diesis 133 – Lulworth Cove 114 (Averof **108** 123) [1990 8m3 8f5 7.6g2 7g2 6d* 1991 6d3 6g3 6m 5g 6s] workmanlike colt: useful performer: best efforts in 1991 when third in £7,400 event at Thirsk and Group 3 event won by Archway at the Curragh: well beaten in Diadem Stakes at Ascot final start, first for nearly 3 months: ideally suited by 6f: acts on dead ground: often gets on edge: hung left and ran moderately for amateur once: sold 21,000 gns Newmarket Autumn Sales. *M. R. Stoute.*

REFERRAL (IRE) 2 b.f. (Feb 11) Reference Point 139 – Happy Kin (USA) (Bold **66** Hitter (USA)) [1991 8.2m4 8.1d 8.9d] lengthy, good-quartered filly: half-sister to several winners here and abroad, including William Hill Futurity winner Emmson (by Ela-Mana-Mou), later stayed 1½m: dam won from 6f to 8.5f in USA: staying-on fourth in minor event at Nottingham in September: didn't show progress expected, racing keenly then finding little off bridle when visored in Wolverhampton maiden final start: should stay middle distances: possibly unsuited by dead ground. *M. R. Stoute.*

REFLECTIVE 4 br.g. Magic Mirror 105 – Thanks Edith (Gratitude 130) [1990 8f — 8g 7m 12m 10f3 12.2d a12g 1991 11f] leggy, sparely-made gelding: plater: stays 1¼m: seems suited by firm going: has run well when blinkered. *M. Avison.*

REGAL CHIMES 2 gr.c. (Mar 8) Another Realm 118 – London Cries (FR) **95** (Bellman (FR) 123) [1991 5d2 5d2 5g2 5d3 5m 5.2g6 5g3 5g3 5f* 5m2 6m 5g5] 5,200Y: leggy, useful-looking colt: first foal: dam showed no sign of ability: fairly useful performer: made all and ran on strongly in minor event at Ripon in August: good second in listed race at Ayr following month, edging right and beaten a neck by Miss Nosey Parker: ran moderately last 2 starts, sweating penultimate one: speedy, and better at 5f than 6f: acts well on firm ground. *B. A. McMahon.*

REGAL CREST (USA) 3 br.g. Gold Crest (USA) 120 – Ambrellita (FR) (Misti **111** IV 132) [1990 5f5 5g* 5d 5g4 5m4 7m5 1991 8d* 8g 6m5 7.2g 7g 9g 8s* 7s*] leggy, light-bodied gelding: moderate mover: useful efforts to win moderately-run listed race at Doncaster in March and when close-up fifth of 9 in similar event over 6f at Haydock: left J. Berry's stable and gelded after fifth outing: returned to form to win £18,000 handicap at the Curragh in October and listed race (improved performance, by length from Blue Daisy) at Leopardstown in November: stays 1m: acts on good to firm ground and soft: sweating second start. *A. J. Maxwell, Ireland.*

REGAL LOVER (IRE) 2 b.c. (Feb 11) Alzao (USA) 117 – King's Chase (King's **73** p Leap 111) [1991 7m6 7m3] 29,000F, 23,000Y: good-topped colt: half-brother to several winners, including 1985 2-y-o 7f winner G G Magic (by Strong Gale), later successful over 1½m and 1¾m: dam twice-raced daughter of half-sister to Irish 1000 Guineas winner Even Star: always-prominent 2¼ lengths third of 9 to White Blade in maiden at Brighton in August: bit coltish on debut: will stay 1m: seemed likely to improve again. *M. Bell.*

REGAL PASSION (IRE) 2 b.g. (Mar 11) Kings Lake (USA) 133 – Bernique 55
(Hello Gorgeous (USA) 128) [1991 5g 6m 7m⁴ 8.2m 8.3g 10m] IR 16,000Y:
workmanlike gelding: has a round action: third foal: half-brother to 3-y-o Tortin (by
Auction Ring) and French winner at up to 1¼m Pas de Panique (by No Pass No
Sale): dam French 1m and 1¼m winner, is half-sister to good 1985 French 2-y-o
stayer Bestebreuje: fair plater on his day: stays 8.3f: blinkered last 3 starts:
sometimes mulish at stalls: sold 4,400 gns Newmarket Autumn Sales. *M. H.
Easterby.*

REGAL RACER ? h g (May 12) Elegant Air 119 Cantico 58 (Green Dancer 64 p
(USA) 132) [1991 7d⁴ 6m] leggy gelding: third foal: half-brother to fair 7f winner
Dauntess (by Formidable): dam staying maiden half-sister to very smart 1m to 1½m
filly Calderina: quite modest form in maiden at Salisbury (green, eased when held)
in June and listed even at Kempton over 2 months later: will be better suited by
1m +: likely to do better. *D. R. C. Elsworth.*

REGAL REFORM 8 b.g. Prince Tenderfoot (USA) 126 – Polly Packer 81 95
(Reform 132) [1990 12m 16.2f* 22d* 16.1f⁴ 18m² 18g³ 16m⁵ 18d⁴ 1991 16g³ 16.2m³
22.2m⁴ 20g] workmanlike, good-bodied gelding: useful performer at best: fair
fourth to Easy To Please in Queen Alexandra Stakes at Royal Ascot: virtually pulled
up (lame off-fore) at Goodwood in July, not seen out again: out-and-out stayer: acts
on firm and dead going: tough, genuine and consistent: a credit to his trainer. *G. M.
Moore.*

REGAL ROMPER (IRE) 3 b.c. Tender King 123 – Fruit of Passion (High Top 36
131) [1990 6d 6g 1991 a8g⁶ 7g 6d³ 6m 6g 5g] rather leggy, good-topped colt: has a
round action: poor performer at best: has looked headstrong, and possibly best at 6f:
best efforts on an easy surface: blinkered (soundly beaten) fifth start: bandaged
reappearance: sold 1,100 gns Doncaster October Sales. *F. H. Lee.*

REGAL SABRE (USA) 3 b.c. Sharpen Up 127 – Royal Heroine 121 (Lypheor 103
118) [1990 6m³ 6m* 6g⁴ 7.3g³ 1991 9m² 10s² 7g* 9m² 8.5f³ 12m⁴ 12.1d 7.9g⁴ 8m⁴
8m⁵ 9m 8d³] strong, good-topped colt: has a powerful action: useful performer: won
minor event at Lingfield in May: placed next 2 starts in listed race at Baden-Baden
and Diomed Stakes at Epsom: ran moderately in apprentice race at Ascot final
outing: stays 1¼m: acts on any going: sometimes on toes. *R. Hannon.*

REGAL SCINTILLA 2 b.f. (Mar 14) King of Spain 121 – Trwyn Cilan 89 (Import 103 ?
127) [1991 5d⁶ 5m² 5.2d⁴ 5d* 5g⁵ 5g⁴ 5.2f⁴ 5m*] 16,000Y: compact filly: good
walker, though turns off-fore in: third foal: half-sister to 1990 2-y-o 5f winner Gone
Savage (by Nomination) and useful sprinter Rivers Rhapsody (by Dominion): dam
best at 5f: appeared to show great improvement in 4-runner Prix d'Arenberg at
Longchamp in September, winning by a short neck from Stormagain: previously
easy winner of maiden at Salisbury by 8 lengths (officially 6) in June: inconsistent
form otherwise: speedy: acts on good to firm and dead ground. *G. B. Balding.*

REGAL VALUE 3 b.g. Nomination 125 – Be Royal 97 (Royal Palm 131) [1990 6m —
6g 1991 10.6g a8g] good-bodied gelding: signs of temperament but little ability:
blinkered final start. *A. Harrison.*

REGENT LAD 7 b.g. Prince Regent (FR) 129 – Red Laser 95 (Red God 128§) 84
[1990 8f 8h 7.5f⁴ 8f⁶ 7.5g² 8m 9m⁴ 8g⁴ 8.5m⁴ 8g 9f² 10m⁵ 8d² 8m³ 7d 1991 8s 7.5g⁴
7m 7.5f² 7.5f² 8m* 8.2g³ 8g 7.9m⁵ 7.5f³ 8m³ 8.9g 8f⁴ 8m 8.5f] leggy gelding: good
walker: fair handicapper: won at Doncaster in May: probably best short of 1¼m: acts
on any going except possibly heavy: best without blinkers: needs extreme waiting
tactics. *Miss L. C. Siddall.*

REGENT'S FOLLY (IRE) 3 ch.f. Touching Wood (USA) 127 – Regent's Fawn 101
(CAN) 72 (Vice Regent (CAN)) [1990 7m 7m* 7g* 1991 10g³ 9m 12g³ 14.6m⁵]
strong, good-bodied filly: carries condition: progressive form: 33/1, third of 19 to
Torchon in King George V Handicap at Royal Ascot third start: 4¾ lengths fifth of 11
to Patricia in Park Hill Stakes at Doncaster 3 months later: stays 14.6f: acts on good
to firm ground: sweating last 3 starts. *W. Jarvis.*

REGINA ROYALE (USA) 4 b.f. Eternal Prince (USA) – Lizzie's Light (USA) —
(Icecapade (USA)) [1990 8g 10.1m⁶ 8.3g 8f 7m⁴ 8m² 8.2s⁵ a6g 1991 8m² 1991 a8g] leggy filly:
has a round action: poor handicapper: stays 1m: acts on good to firm ground and soft:
visored last 4 starts. *C. R. Nelson.*

REHAAN (USA) 3 b.c. Storm Bird (CAN) 134 – Playmate (USA) (Buckpasser) 91
[1990 NR 1991 8g⁴ 7f* 8.1g² 8f³] $700,000Y: rather finely-made, attractive colt:
closely related to 2 winners here by The Minstrel, including very useful but
unreliable Accompanist, and half-brother to 5 winners, including high-class Irish
6.3f and 1m winner Woodman and 1¼m winner Gadabout (both by Mr Prospector):

dam, placed once from 5 starts, is sister to Numbered Account: 4/1 on, easily won maiden at Catterick in July: favourite and edgy, fairly useful performances following month when neck second in handicap at Haydock and last of 3 in minor event at Thirsk: stays 1m. *L. M. Cumani.*

REHEARSAL DINNER (USA) 3 b.c. Alleged (USA) 138 – The Bride (USA) — (Bold Ruler) [1990 NR 1991 11g⁵ 12m] $55,000Y: useful-looking colt: closely related to a graded winner in Argentina by Hoist The Flag, and half-brother to several winners, including 3-y-o 6.5f stakes winner Heavenly Match (by Gallant Romeo): dam sister to Secretariat: well beaten in minor event (visored, wandered under pressure) and maiden: dead. *Lord Huntingdon.*

REINA 3 b.f. Homeboy 114 – Sun Queen 76 (Lucky Sovereign) [1990 NR 1991 6m⁶ — 6.1m] lengthy filly: half-sister to 2 winners, including useful sprinter Swelter (by Tickled Pink): dam sprinter: no worthwhile form in minor event at Kempton (swerved left stalls) and maiden at Nottingham in September. *J. D. Bethell.*

REINE DE THEBES (FR) 4 b. or br.f. Darshaan 133 – Reine d'Egypte (USA) **67** 114 (Val de L'Orne (FR) 130) [1990 NR 1991 8m* 9f⁵ 9f* 10.1f 11s* 13g³ 10g⁴ 18m] leggy, sparely-made filly: first foal: dam, French 1¼m and 1½m winner, is daughter of French Oaks winner Reine de Saba: ex-French, formerly trained by D. Boulard, sold 7,000 gns December, 1990: raced 3 times at 2 yrs, in frame in French Provinces at 1m to 1¼m: modest handicapper here: won seller (bought in 5,000 gns) at Pontefract in April, claimer at Hamilton in May and handicap (improved form) at Edinburgh in July: set lot to do when respectable staying-on eleventh of 22 in Cesarewitch at Newmarket: now needs further than 1¼m, and stays well: acts on firm ground, and clearly goes well on soft: joined C. Allen. *M. H. Tompkins.*

REJOICE (IRE) 3 b.f. Damister (USA) 123 – Rocket Alert 110 (Red Alert 127) **88** [1990 a7g* 1991 a6g* 7m 6g⁴] big, rangy filly: ridden by 5-lb claimer, comfortable winner of January handicap at Southwell: off course over 6 months, better effort in handicaps at Newmarket when fair fourth in August: stays 7f. *W. A. O'Gorman.*

RELATIVELY RISKY 2 ch.f. (Apr 16) Risk Me (FR) 127 – Skelton 70 (Derrylin — 115) [1991 5g 5m 5f 7m] unfurnished filly: second foal: half-sister to 3-y-o Caress (by Godswalk), successful at 5f (at 2 yrs) and 6f: dam 2-y-o 7f and 8.2f sellers winner, is half-sister to very useful stayer Brief Bay: seems of little account. *M. W. Easterby.*

RELENTLESS PURSUIT (IRE) 3 b.c. Thatching 131 – Daring Way (USA) **71** 78 (Alydar (USA)) [1990 6m⁶ 6g a6g* 1991 6m⁴ 7d 7g³ 7d 6g⁵ a6g⁶ 7m] quite attractive colt: modest handicapper: tailed off at halfway when fourth of 23 at Ripon: easily best effort when third at Leicester in June, drifting badly right once leading over 1f out: better at 7f than 6f: seems to need a sound surface: has worn tongue strap: blinkered fourth start: not one to trust implicitly. *P. W. Chapple-Hyam.*

REMAADI (USA) 3 gr.c. Storm Bird (CAN) 134 – Tamanaco Day (USA) (Naskra **100** (USA)) [1990 NR 1991 9m⁶ 10g² 10g² 10d*] $250,000Y: leggy, workmanlike colt: second foal: dam minor winner at 3 yrs in North America, is half-sister to very smart 9f Grade 1 winner Marfa: 11/10, won 10-runner maiden at Brighton in June by 6 lengths from Legal View: stays 1¼m well: looked sort to progress. *J. H. M. Gosden.*

REMANY 2 gr.f. (Apr 1) Bellypha 130 – Moonscape 87 (Ribero 126) [1991 7m 7m] — tall, leggy, workmanlike filly: has a roundish action: half-sister to several winners, including 3-y-o 1½m winner Caithness Cloud (by Lomond), very useful middle-distance stayer Lemhill (by He Loves Me) and useful 6f winner Luna Bid (by Auction Ring): dam staying half-sister to Derby fourth Moon Mountain and Great Wall: beaten around 16 lengths in minor event at Newbury won by Freewheel and 16-runner maiden at Leicester (behind Anlace) in autumn: will stay 1¼m. *M. Blanshard.*

REMTHAT NASER 4 b.f. Sharpo 132 – Warning Sound (Red Alert 127) [1990 — 6m⁵ 7g² 8m* 8m* 7g⁵ 1991 8f 7.6m 8m 8f⁵] neat filly: fairly useful performer at 3 yrs for G. Huffer: below form in handicaps in 1991: stays 1m: acts on good to firm ground and dead: sometimes blinkered, and was when successful: sweating badly second start: keen sort, raced much too freely on reappearance. *J. D. Czerpak.*

REMWOOD GIRL 5 b.m. Remainder Man 126§ – Aliwood Girl 64§ (Broxted **43** 120) [1990 a7g a7g⁶ 10m⁴ 8m 7d 1991 9s 8.1g 10m* 12m⁴ 10.1s] small, plain mare: keen walker: moderate mover: poor handicapper: won at Pontefract in July by 6 lengths: stays 1½m: acts on good to firm and dead ground. *K. S. Bridgwater.*

RENDALLS 3 b.c. Top Ville 129 – On The House (FR) 125 (Be My Guest (USA) **65** 126) [1990 NR 1991 a8g⁴ 10g⁵] leggy, sparely-made colt: fourth foal: half-brother to 7f and 7.6f winner Domus (by Kalaglow) dam, from excellent family, won 1000

Guineas and Sussex Stakes: fourth in maiden at Southwell in September: again bandaged, didn't settle early in similar event at Brighton: sold 2,500 gns Newmarket Autumn Sales. *G. Wragg.*

RENTA KID 2 b.f. (Apr 21) Swing Easy (USA) 126 – Dewberry 68 (Bay Express 132) [1991 6m 5d³ 5.7m³ 5f* 5m⁵ a6g] 800F: leggy, workmanlike filly: half-sister to 2 winners by Monsanto, including 1985 2-y-o 5f winner Monstrosa, and a winner in Macau: dam 6f winner: plating-class form: easily made all in maiden auction at Beverley in July: ran poorly afterwards: should stay 6f: acts on firm ground. *R. Boss.*   **57** d

REPACKER 5 ch.m. Aragon 118 – Golden October 62 (Young Generation 129) [1990 a7g⁵ a10g 1991 a8g] leggy mare: lightly raced and little worthwhile form: stays 7f: usually bandaged: has worn tongue strap. *C. N. Allen.*   —

REPECHAGE 4 b.f. Tina's Pet 121 – Lady's Walk (Pall Mall 132) [1990 9m 12.5g* 12.2d⁵ a12g 1991 10.8g 10.5m 11.8g³ 8.2m 10m 8.9m⁶ 14.6m⁴ 12.3g] sparely-made, angular filly: has round action: poor performer nowadays: better suited by 1½m and 1¾m than shorter: acts on good to firm and dead going. *B. A. McMahon.*   **39**

REPIQUE (USA) 3 ch.f. Sharpen Up 127 – Repetitious 103 (Northfields (USA)) [1990 6m² 1991 6f⁴ 6d* 7.1m* 8m⁵ 7m⁶] smallish, leggy filly: moderate mover: fair performer: under pressure by halfway but got up close home in maiden at Ripon in June and handicap at Sandown in August: ran fairly well in handicaps after: should stay 1m: acts on good to firm ground and dead: visits Ela-Mana-Mou. *L. M. Cumani.*   **73**

REPLEDGE (IRE) 2 b.c. (Apr 16) Alleged (USA) 138 – Repetitious 103 (North-fields (USA)) [1991 8.1m⁴ 8.1s²] 80,000Y: lengthy colt: has scope: half-brother to 3-y-o 6f and 7.1f winner Repique and 1988 2-y-o 1m winner (later one to treat with caution) Sharp 'N Shine (both by Sharpen Up) and 3 other winners, including good French 1¼m performer Sarhoob (by Alydar): dam, 6f to 1m winner, won Stewards' Cup and sister to smart filly Nanticious: staying-on 2½ lengths second of 13 to Valseur in maiden at Edinburgh in November: may stay 1¼m: will improve again. *P. F. I. Cole.*   **68** p

REPLICATE 3 ch.f. Vaigly Great 127 – Remould 83 (Reform 132) [1990 6m 6d³ 6g 1991 7m⁵ 7f 8d⁵ 8m² 10g 8m⁶ 8.2m³ 8.1s 8m⁴ a10g] smallish, lengthy, sparely-made filly: shows quick action: quite modest maiden: placed in claimers: stays 1m well: possibly best on a sound surface (soundly beaten on equitrack): has run well when sweating and edgy: sold out of J. Hills's stable 1,150 gns Ascot November Sales after ninth start. *M. J. Charles.*   **60**

REQUESTED 4 b.g. Rainbow Quest (USA) 134 – Melody Hour 105 (Sing Sing 134) [1990 12.7f³ 12g 12m⁴ 14f* 12m 1991 10.1s⁵ 14g³ a12g⁴ 14m² 13.3d⁴ 16.2m 14.1f⁴ 14f* 14g⁶ 14m⁵ 16.2d*] leggy, sparely-made gelding: moderate mover: half-brother to numerous winners, including very useful middle-distance filly Sing Softly (by Luthier) and fairly useful stayer Military Band (by Sassafras): dam 5f winner at 2 yrs: fair ex-Irish handicapper: won at Salisbury in August and Ascot (£11,450 event, beat Gay Glint by 2½ lengths) in October: stays 2m: probably acts on any going: has found little under pressure: has won when blinkered and for apprentice. *R. Akehurst.*   **75**

RESA GIRL 2 b.f. (Mar 7) Legend of France (USA) 124 – To Oneiro 69 (Absalom 128) [1991 a5g 6f a8g] 920F, 3,500Y: small, lengthy filly: poor mover: fourth foal: half-sister to 3-y-o sprinter Athenian King (by Fairy King) and a winner in Norway: dam 5f and 6f winner: apparently of little account. *J. S. Wainwright.*   —

RESHIFT 3 b.f. Night Shift (USA) – Repoussee (Jimmy Reppin 131) [1990 6g 6g² 6d* 8v 1991 7d⁵ 6g 6d* 7d* 7d] angular, good-topped filly: moderate mover: successful in handicap (made all) at Doncaster, apprentice race at Ripon and 4-runner minor event at Ayr in the spring: never able to challenge in £7,400 handicap at Chester in May: should prove best short of 1m: goes well on dead ground: keen sort: apprentice ridden: game. *M. Bell.*   **94**

RESISTING (USA) 3 b.g. Desert Wine (USA) – Fool's Miss (USA) (Saltville) [1990 8f 8g 9g 1991 10m] lengthy, good-topped gelding: poor form at best: last in selling handicap in October: sold 1,400 gns Newmarket Autumn Sales. *J. H. M. Gosden.*   —

RESOLUTE BAY 5 b.g. Crofthall 110 – Spinner 59 (Blue Cashmere 129) [1990 6g 5m 5m² 6f* 6m 6g⁵ 6m 6m² 6m 5.6g 6g 7g⁴ 6d 7d 1991 5g 7m 6g³ 6m³ 6m 7m² 7m 6.1g* 6m⁶ 7.1m² 7.9g 7.6m 7m⁵ 7.3m⁵ 6g 7m⁵ 6m] lengthy gelding: has a rather round action: fairly useful handicapper: won at Chester (same race for second successive year) in July: effective at stiff 5f to 7f: suited by a sound surface: effective visored, blinkered or not: has started slowly: inconsistent. *R. M. Whitaker.*   **96**

RESOUNDING SUCCESS (IRE) 2 b.f. (Mar 16) Law Society (USA) 130 – **68** p
Dawn Echo (Don (ITY) 123) [1991 6m4] IR 24,000Y: tall, leggy, unfurnished filly:
sister to Irish 3-y-o 7f winner Princess of Zurich and half-sister to 2 winners, including useful 6f and 7f winner Dawn Success (by Caerleon): dam no sign of ability:
weak 5/1-shot, kept on well when over 2 lengths fourth of 6 to Isaiah in maiden at
York in October, green when initially ridden along: will stay 7f: will improve. *B. W.
Hills.*

RESPECTABLE JONES 5 ch.g. Tina's Pet 121 – Jonesee 64 (Dublin Taxi) **77**
[1990 6m5 6g2 6d2 5m* 6m2 5d6 6g4 6m5 6m* 5g3 6s6 a6g* 1991 a5g2 a5g2 a6g2 a 87
a7g* 5d 5g6 6s 6g 6g 5g 6m2 6g 5.7m3 6.1m 5m 5f2 6m 6d 5.1s4 6.1d 5g5 a6g2 a6g*]
leggy, lengthy gelding: fair handicapper: successful as 5-y-o at Lingfield in
December (didn't have to be at best in claimer): inconsistent of turf late in 1991:
effective at 5f to 7f: acts on any going: effective visored or not: good mount for
inexperienced rider: game. *G. B. Balding.*

RESPLENDENT 2 b.f. (Feb 11) Sharrood (USA) 124 – Damaska (USA) **72** p
(Damascus (USA)) [1991 7m4 7d4] 2,500Y: rangy, rather plain filly: third foal: half-
sister to 11f seller winner Taskalady (by Touching Wood): dam unraced: modest
form when fourth in large-field maidens at Doncaster in autumn, behind Berseto
(tongue tied down, sweating) second occasion: will stay 1m: will probably improve
again. *Mrs L. Piggott.*

RESTAPOUR 3 gr.f. Nishapour (FR) 125 – Restive 96 (Relic) [1990 NR 1991 8m —
8m a11g 8m 8g4] angular, workmanlike filly: half-sister to several winners,
including useful sprinters Sharpish (by Sharpen Up) and Respect (by Mummy's Pet)
and 1½m winner Rest (by Dance In Time): dam suited by 7f: well beaten in maidens
and (facing very stiff task) handicap: sold 1,300 gns Newmarket December Sales. *G.
A. Pritchard-Gordon.*

RESTLESS DON 6 b.h. Mandrake Major 122 – La Fille 58 (Crooner 119) [1990 **57**
5f 5d 5g 5f5 5d 6m 5g 5m6 5m 1991 5m 5f 5h5 5g3 5m 5f2 a5g 5f5 5m 5f3 6f5 5m6 5f]
lengthy, dipped-backed horse: plating-class handicapper nowadays: suited by 5f and
a sound surface: has shown tendency to hang: inconsistent: sold 2,500 gns
Doncaster October Sales. *M. H. Easterby.*

RESTLESS NIECE 3 b.f. Uncle Pokey 116 – Lucille Astik (Meldrum 112) [1990 —
NR 1991 6g 6d a8g] strong, workmanlike filly: first foal: dam ran 3 times: no
worthwhile form in maidens, though showed signs of ability after slow start on first
2 starts: off course over 5 months before final one. *T. D. Barron.*

RESTORE 8 ch.g. Habitat 134 – Never So Lovely 87 (Realm 129) [1990 6f6 6m 6f3 **70** d
6d 6d 6m4 6f* 6d 6g 6m5 a7g6 1991 5m* 7g 6m4 6d5 6f5 6f* 7.1m2 7m 6m6 7d 7g
6.9s] useful-looking gelding: hobdayed twice: quite modest performer nowadays:
won claimers at Warwick (drifted left) in April and Ripon in August: best form at 6f
on a sound surface: normally blinkered or visored: often on edge: best with strong
handling: inconsistent. *G. Lewis.*

RETOUCH 5 b.h. Touching Wood (USA) 127 – Nelly Do Da 78 (Derring-Do 131) **97**
[1990 14g4 16m2 20m* 17.6g2 16.2m4 14.6d3 1991 16g 16g2 16g* 20g6 10.1m6 20g2
15.9g2 16.2g5] workmanlike, rather sparely-made horse: good mover: fairly useful
handicapper: won £12,700 event at Kempton in May: ran well most starts after, in
Ascot Gold Cup and Lonsdale Stakes at York fourth and penultimate ones: suited by
thorough test of stamina: acts on good to firm and dead going: most genuine. *P. F. I.
Cole.*

REVARO 5 b.g. Corvaro (USA) 122 – Quick Dream (Crepello 136) [1990 NR 1991 **49**
8d 10d3 10m 12m4] good-bodied gelding: has a round action: plating-class
handicapper nowadays, not seen out after May: effective at 1¼m and stays 1½m:
ideally suited by plenty of give in the ground: wears crossed noseband. *Mrs J. R.
Ramsden.*

REVE DE VALSE (USA) 4 b.c. Conquistador Cielo (USA) – Dancing Vaguely —
(USA) (Vaguely Noble 140) [1990 10.5g4 12g 10v 10.5g4 10.5g2 1991 15m 14.1m5]
workmanlike ex-French colt: first foal: dam French 1½m winner, is daughter of
Dancing Maid: placed over 1m at 2 yrs and 10.5f as 3-y-o when trained by Mme C.
Head: in need of run, well beaten in amateurs event and maiden in autumn as 4-y-o:
stays 10.5f: useful hurdler at best. *Denys Smith.*

REVEL 3 ch.c. Sharpo 132 – Waltz 75 (Jimmy Reppin 131) [1990 5s3 1991 6m2 5f3 **67** d
6m2 6f 7m 6g 9.2s] compact colt: quite modest maiden: no form last 4 starts,
including in claimer: stays 6f, not 9f: acts on good to firm ground: blinkered third and
fourth (bandaged off-hind) outings. *L. Lungo.*

REVERSE THE CHARGE (USA) 2 b.c. (May 13) Phone Trick (USA) – 51
Nona's Hope (USA) (Raja Baba (USA)) [1991 5g⁵ 6d 7g⁴] $75,000Y: small, strong
colt: half-brother to several winners in North America: dam won at up to 9f: sire
very smart sprinter: plating-class maiden: fourth of 6 at Brighton in July: stays 7f:
seemed likely to improve again. *R. Hannon.*

REVIF (FR) 3 gr.c. Kenmare (FR) 125 – Reverente (FR) (Riverman (USA) 131) 84
[1990 6m 1991 8d⁴ 10.6g⁶ 11.8g² 12s] tall, quite leggy, good-topped colt: fair maiden:
good second at Leicester in July, keeping on well: burly, front rank 1m when last in
£70,900 handicap at Ascot over 2 months later: stays 1½m: acts on dead ground. *A.
C. Stewart.*

REVOKE (USA) 4 ro.f. Riverman (USA) 131 – Queens Only (USA) (Marshua's 50
Dancer (USA)) [1990 8m⁵ 8m² 8f⁶ 9m 8m³ 8d³ a8g 1991 8g 7f 10.8g 8.2m⁵ 7g² 8d]
small, sparely-made filly: moderate mover: plating-class maiden: should prove
better suited by 1m than 7f: acts on good to firm going. *C. J. Hill.*

REXY BOY 4 b.g. Dunbeath (USA) 127 – Coca (Levmoss 133) [1990 8f 8v 8m a12g 41
12m a12g 1991 13.8d 8.2d 12.3d 12m⁶ 11.1s³ 13d³ 12.1m* 10m⁶ 12.1f² 12m⁴ 12.1g]
good-bodied gelding: poor handicapper: won at Hamilton in July: probably acts on any going: has worn crossed noseband and blinkers. *W. J. Pearce.*

RHEIN VALLEY (IRE) 3 b.f. Kings Lake (USA) 133 – Rhein Bridge 107 –
(Rheingold 137) [1990 NR 1991 10m] lengthy, good-bodied filly: fifth foal: sister to
Irish St Leger and Ascot Gold Cup runner-up Tyrone Bridge and plating-class
stayer Lakiste: dam, half-sister to very smart middle-distance filly Connaught
Bridge, won Lancashire Oaks: 20/1, green and burly, behind in maiden at Ripon in
April: sold 2,000 gns Newmarket September Sales. *J. W. Watts.*

RHODES 4 ch.g. Pharly (FR) 130 – Beacon Hill 81 (Bustino 136) [1990 10g 13.3m² 85
14.8m³ 16m² 1991 14.6s³ 15.5f* 14g⁴ 17.1m* 16g⁴ 20g 16d⁶ 16.2f⁴ 16m⁵] lengthy
gelding: has a round action: fair handicapper: won at Folkestone (despite looking ill
at ease on bends) and Bath in spring: suited by good test of stamina and
top-of-the-ground: has run fairly well when sweating. *J. Akehurst.*

RHY-BYE 4 b.g. Kabour 80 – Kings Fillet (King's Bench 132) [1990 NR 1991 8d] –
leggy, close-coupled gelding: brother to plating-class but ungenuine 1¼m winner
Precious Memories, also successful over hurdles, and half-brother to 3 other
winners: dam poor plater: 66/1 and wearing crossed noseband, soundly beaten in
maiden at Ayr in April, only run. *R. D. E. Woodhouse.*

RHYTHMIC DANCER 3 b.c. Music Boy 124 – Stepping Gaily 79 (Gay 84
Fandango (USA) 132) [1990 5f³ 5f² 5d² 5f* 5g⁴ 5f* 5m² 5d 1991 5d³ 6m⁶ 6m 5. 1g³ 5g
5.2m] leggy, close-coupled colt: fair performer: not discredited in handicap, listed
race and minor event first, second and fourth starts: speedy: acts on firm and dead
going: keen sort: has worn dropped noseband: often taken down early. *J. Berry.*

RHYTHMIC ECHO 2 b.g. (Feb 27) Sizzling Melody 117 – Calling High (USA) 50
88 (Mountain Call 125) [1991 6g⁶ 6m⁴ 5f⁵] 9,200F: tall, unfurnished gelding:
half-brother to several winners, including middle-distance handicapper Common
Farm (by Tachypous) and 1981 Irish 2-y-o 5f winner Swansea Bay (by Moulton): dam
2-y-o 6f winner: poor form, in Folkestone seller final outing: stays 6f: has joined P.
Howling. *J. Berry.*

RIBBONAIRE (IRE) 2 ch.c. (Mar 22) Mansooj 118 – Bunch of Blue 70
(Martinmas 128) [1991 5m⁴ 6f⁴ 7g⁶ 6m² 6m² 6g⁵ 8m² 7m⁴ 8m⁵ 7g] IR 16,000F:
leggy, workmanlike colt: moderate walker: half-brother to 3-y-o 1m winner Jendee
(by Dara Monarch), 2 winners in Ireland, one of them useful jumper The Musical
Priest (by Baptism), and a winner in South Africa: dam winner at up to 13f in France,
is half-sister to Man o' War winner Czar Alexander: modest maiden: best form at
1m: acts on good to firm ground. *M. H. Tompkins.*

RIBOKEYES BOY 9 b.g. Riboboy (USA) 124 – Molvitesse 75 (Molvedo 137) 49
[1990 a12g² 12f 1991 12f⁵ 10d] close-coupled gelding: plater: probably stays 1½m and
acts on any going: usually bandaged: winning hurdler. *A. R. Davison.*

RICHER SPIRIT 2 b.f. (May 3) Grey Desire 115 – Pokey's Pet (Uncle Pokey –
116) [1991 6m] sparely-made filly: first foal: dam, plater, won at 7f and stayed 1m:
weak 7/1-shot, soon well behind in 9-runner maiden at Pontefract in September. *J.
Berry.*

RICHMOND (IRE) 3 ch.g. Hatim (USA) 121 – On The Road (On Your Mark 60
125) [1990 6f 6g 7m⁴ 7m a7g⁶ 8v² 8d³ 8.2s² a8g² a8g⁵ 1991 7d 8s 8.2d⁴ a8g⁶ 8.3d*
8m³ 9.2d⁵ 8.3s⁵ 8f 8.1g⁴ 8m] sturdy gelding: moderate mover: quite modest
performer: won maiden auction contest at Hamilton in June: should stay beyond 1m:

acts on good to firm ground, and goes well on a soft surface: visored or blinkered nowadays. *J. S. Wainwright.*

RICH PICKINGS 2 b.f. (Jan 31) Dominion 123 – Miss By Miles 91 (Milesian 125) —
[1991 5m 6g] 6,500Y: half-sister to several winners, including smart 6f and 1m winner Missed Blessing (by So Blessed) and useful 1¼m and 1½m winner Buzzbomb (by Bustino): dam game miler: backward, no form in maiden auction at Salisbury in May and claimer at Lingfield in October. *C. A. Cyzer.*

RICKETTY (IRE) 3 b.g. Reasonable (FR) 119 – Kilteelagh Lady (King's Leap 59
111) [1990 5g 7m 5d* 5m3 6d 1991 7d a7g 8g6 a5g3 6g] useful-looking gelding: fairly useful plater: third of 18 in non-selling handicap at Southwell in September: should stay further than 5f: acts on good to firm ground and dead: sold 2,400 gns Doncaster October Sales, to Scandinavia. *M. W. Easterby.*

RICKY'S TORNADO (IRE) 2 ch.c. (Mar 22) Night Shift (USA) – Fodens Eve 82
80 (Dike (USA)) [1991 6m3 5g2 5d] IR 30,000Y: sturdy, quite attractive colt: brother to 5f to 7.1f winner Night Jar and half-brother to several winners here and abroad, including 1m claimer winner Lopski (by Niniski): dam 2-y-o 5f winner: fair form in maidens at Goodwood and Wolverhampton (11/8 on, unable to quicken 1½f out, again edged left then kept on strongly) in September: stiff task, well beaten in Cornwallis Stakes at Ascot following month: better suited by 6f than 5f. *D. R. C. Elsworth.*

RIDGE END (USA) 3 br.f. Cox's Ridge (USA) – Lipika (USA) (Nijinsky (CAN) 40
138) [1990 7m 1991 8m 12m 11.7g5 13.8g5 16.4m3 16m5 16m 12f 12s3] close-coupled, leggy, plain filly: poor performer on balance of form: suited by test of stamina: acts on any going: usually bandaged, mostly on off-fore. *Mrs L. Piggott.*

RIMOUSKI 3 b.c. Sure Blade (USA) 130 – Rimosa's Pet 109 (Petingo 135) [1990 57
NR 1991 10d 11.7m3 12.2f3 9.9f 10m 14.6g5] quite attractive colt: has a markedly round action: fifth living foal: closely related to 6f winner and 1000 Guineas second Kerrera (by Diesis) and half-brother to useful French 1¼m winner Secretariat's Pet (by Secretariat) and to Rock City (by Ballad Rock), a very useful performer at up to 1m: dam 6f to 10.5f winner: quite modest maiden: fair fifth at Wolverhampton, easily best effort in 3 handicaps: ideally suited by around 1½m: tongue tied down second to fourth starts: visored fourth: sold to join B. Cambidge 6,800 gns Newmarket Autumn Sales. *M. R. Stoute.*

RING CYCLE 2 b.f. (Apr 16) Auction Ring (USA) 123 – Absaloute Service 96 64
(Absalom 128) [1991 6d* 6g] workmanlike filly: second foal: dam 2-y-o 5f winner: 5/1, won 9-runner maiden at Goodwood, running on well to lead line: stiffish task, respectable twelfth of 18 in Newbury nursery later in October: stays 6f. *H. Candy.*

RINGLAND (USA) 3 b.c. Gate Dancer (USA) – Tinnitus (USA) (Restless Wind) 77 p
[1990 NR 1991 10.4g 10g3] $135,000Y: compact colt: half-brother to several winners in USA, notably top-class sprinter Groovy (by Norcliffe): dam lightly-raced maiden: 11/2, ¾-length third of 15 to Blue Birds Fly in maiden at Newbury in October: ran in snatches and hung left on debut 8 weeks earlier: sold to join P. Haslam 19,000 gns Newmarket Autumn Sales: will improve again. *G. Harwood.*

RING MY BELL 4 b.g. Auction Ring (USA) 123 – Noon Bells (Ballymore 123) —
[1990 NR 1991 7g 10.5m 12g 8f] good-bodied gelding: first foal: dam Irish 1¼m winner: lightly raced and soundly beaten, including in sellers: tried blinkered. *F. J. Yardley.*

RING OF FORTUNE (FR) 3 b.c. Fast Topaze (USA) 128 – Forgata (FR) 67
(Bolkonski 134) [1990 NR 1991 10m 10.5g6 12.3d3 12m6] strong, good-bodied colt: fourth foal: half-brother to a minor winner in France: dam, in frame over 6f (at 2 yrs) and 1m in France, is half-sister to top-class middle-distance colt Le Marmot: modest maiden: third of 16 in apprentice contest at Ripon, always prominent, edging right and tiring final 1f: form only at 1½m on dead going: winning hurdler for M. Pipe. *M. Moubarak.*

RINGYBOY 6 b.g. Runnett 125 – Graunuaile (Proud Chieftain 122) [1990 NR 1991 —
9g a8g 10.5m 12f] tall gelding: moderate mover: half-brother to numerous winners, from 5f to 2m: dam winner of 3 of her 4 races from 5f to 1m: ex-Irish gelding: won 1¼m apprentice handicap at Navan as 3-y-o: no form, mostly in ladies events, here: tried visored: temperamental hurdler. *J. A. Bennett.*

RINJA (USA) 4 b.c. Robellino (USA) 127 – Dijla 82 (Hittite Glory 125) [1990 10g4 87
8m 8m2 8d 8m6 8.2m4 9g 9m2 1991 8g4 10m2 12g* 10g 14.9m* 13.9g 14g2 13.3m] strong, lengthy colt: carries plenty of condition: usually impresses in appearance: fairly useful handicapper: won at Royal Ascot (Bessborough Stakes, by neck from Local Derby) in June and Warwick (by 4 lengths) in July: ran lack-lustre race in

Bessborough Handicap, Ascot—the finish of a highly competitive race,
left to right, Local Derby (second), Rinja (winner), Hateel (fourth) and First Victory (third)

Newbury Autumn Cup final start: better at around 1¾m than shorter: acts on good to firm ground: often bandaged behind: tough and genuine. *D. W. P. Arbuthnot.*

RIO TRUSKY 2 b.g. (May 6) Ballacashtal (CAN) – Polly's Song 65 (Song 132) **43** [1991 5m 6m⁵ 6g⁵ 8d] 3,600F, 2,200Y: leggy gelding: has scope: first foal: dam, maiden, form only at 5f at 2 yrs: poor maiden: stays 6f: active sort, tends to sweat and get on toes. *J. Hetherton.*

RIPSNORTER (IRE) 2 ch.c. (Mar 20) Rousillon (USA) 133 – Formulate 119 **65 p** (Reform 132) [1991 8m 7.1d 7g²] 25,000F, 20,000Y: big, strong, angular colt: has plenty of scope: half-brother to 3-y-o Colour Quest (by Rainbow Quest) and several winners here and abroad, including smart 1¼m winner Game Plan (by Darshaan) and 15.8f winner Almarreekh (by Glint of Gold): dam top staying 2-y-o filly of 1978, ran only twice afterwards: best effort always-prominent second of 11 to Salisong in maiden at Salisbury in October: will be well suited by 1m +: will do better. *Sir Mark Prescott.*

RISE OVER 5 ch.m. Smackover 107 – Stewart's Rise 52 (Good Bond 122) [1990 **45** 10v⁶ 8f 9g 1991 8m*] big, unfurnished mare: has a round action: poor handicapper: won at Warwick (apprentices) in May: stays 1m: acts on good to firm ground: has worn bandages: often sweats. *K. White.*

RISE UP SINGING 3 ch.g. Noalto 120 – Incarnadine 67 (Hot Spark 126) [1990 **86** 7m 7m 7m⁶ 7.3g 8m* 7.6v 7s* 1991 8m 8g⁴ 8g* 8m* 8m⁴ 7f 10.5f] strong gelding: has scope: moderate mover: fair handicapper: won at Newmarket in June and (£11,200 contest) July: slowly away and always last at Haydock final outing, taking no interest: should stay beyond 1m: acts on any going, except apparently heavy: best blinkered: twice below form sweating: goes well with forcing tactics. *R. Hannon.*

RISHA FLOWER 3 b.f. Kris 135 – Sephira (Luthier 126) [1990 NR 1991 10.3m² **85** 8s* 8m³] workmanlike filly: fifth foal: half-sister to useful 6f to 1m winner Tatsfield and fairly useful 1989 2-y-o 7f winner, later successful in USA, Bartat (both by Habitat) and to 6f and 7f winner Geltser (by Sir Ivor) and a winner in Sweden: dam, French 1m winner, is sister to Sigy and Sonoma: confirmed debut promise when winning maiden at Kempton in September, leading 2f out, edging right, then running on well: fair third in Leicester minor event: seems best with testing conditions at 1m, and should prove fully effective back at 1¼m: sold 15,500 gns Newmarket December Sales. *R. Charlton.*

RISING TEMPO (IRE) 3 b.g. Lomond (USA) 128 – May Hill 124 (Hill Clown **63** (USA)) [1990 NR 1991 a7g² 7d a8g* a7g* 10g⁶ a7g³ 8m a10g⁶ a7g 11.5g] sturdy, heavy-topped gelding: fifth living foal: half-brother to 1989 3-y-o August Climb (by Kings Lake) and fairly useful 1½m and 13f winner Picea (by Mummy's Pet): dam won Yorkshire Oaks and Park Hill Stakes: successful in apprentice maiden and 2-runner apprentice contest in June: ran very well in ladies event at Ascot seventh start, moderately in Lingfield handicaps (under pressure a long way out final start) afterwards: bred to stay further than 1m: has tended to hang. *C. A. Cyzer.*

RISK FACTOR   5 b.g. Auction Ring (USA) 123 – Flying Anna (Roan Rocket 128)   —
[1990 8v⁴ 8f³ 1991 a11g] sturdy, workmanlike gelding: moderate mover: plating-class maiden: no show only run in 1991 (February): stays 1m: acts on heavy going. *D. Moffatt.*

RISK MASTER   2 b.c. (Apr 23) Risk Me (FR) 127 – Trigamy 112 (Tribal Chief   67
125) [1991 6f 7g 6d⁴] 23,000Y: tall, lengthy colt: has scope: half-brother to many winners, including 7f to 1¼m winner New Mexico (by Free State) and 7f winner Mango Manilla (by Martinmas): dam 5f performer: quite modest maiden: stays 6f: may well be suited by give in the ground. *C. A. Horgan.*

RISKMEMAY   2 ch.f. (Apr 7) Risk Me (FR) 127 – Dutch May 109 (Maystreak 118)   —
[1991 5m 5f³ 6.1f] small, stocky filly: sixth reported foal: half-sister to 5f to 7f winner Lucky Dutch (by Lucky Wednesday): dam won 7 sprint races at 2 yrs and 3 yrs: no worthwhile form, including in seller and 3-runner maiden at Beverley. *M. W. Easterby.*

RISK ZONE   2 b.g. (Mar 22) Risk Me (FR) 127 – Gymnopedie (Jaazeiro (USA)   50
127) [1991 5g⁶ 6g⁵ 6g a7g] sturdy gelding: first foal: dam French maiden: poor form in varied races: never dangerous when favourite for fibresand nursery: subsequently gelded. *R. Hannon.*

RISTNA   3 ch.f. Kris 135 – Roussalka 123 (Habitat 134) [1990 NR 1991 8g* 120
10.5m⁴ 8m² 10m* 10m⁴]
Waiting tactics badly misfired in the Dubai Champion Stakes for In The Groove and Ristna. Both fillies were set too much to do in a moderately-run race, having many lengths to make up on the leaders from halfway, and although tremendous late flourishes almost got them there, the post intervened to leave them stranded in third and fourth places respectively when they ought to have been first and second. Ristna was beaten half a length, half a length again and a short head behind Tel Quel, Cruachan and In The Groove. A bold showing had been expected from the supplemented Ristna following a splendid performance over course and distance in the Cheveley Park Sun Chariot Stakes earlier in October. Not a vintage Sun Chariot in face of competition from Arc-weekend, but she really was impressive in coming from behind in another moderately-run affair. Having been held up, she quickened

Cheveley Park Stud Sun Chariot Stakes, Newmarket—
Ristna storms clear of Dartrey (almost hidden), Third Watch (rails),
Filia Ardross (visor) and Sipsi Fach

when the pace quickened three and a half furlongs out, loomed up to challenge on the outside going into the Dip and stormed clear entering the final furlong. She had only four opponents, one of whom, the long-time leader Sipsi Fach, was out of her depth and dropped away to last. The other three, Dartrey, Third Watch and Filia Ardross, crossed the line virtually inseparable, four lengths in Ristna's wake.

Ristna thus shared in the revival of the Gosden stable's fortunes in the autumn after she and some of her stable-companions had been laid low. The Sun Chariot was only her fourth race and she'd been off the course from May to September between the second and third, the Tattersalls Musidora Stakes at York and a graduation race at Doncaster. She caught a tartar in Desert Sun in the last-named. The one-time Guineas favourite ended a disappointing period in his career by beating Ristna at least five lengths, swamping her in the final furlong. Ristna was very well backed that day and there was no good reason to think she would be inconvenienced by the return to a mile, over which distance she'd won a twenty-five-runner maiden at Newbury on her debut. When a close fourth behind Gussy Marlowe, Dartrey and Shamshir in the Musidora, she'd looked less of a stayer than any of the three in front. However, it's true to say now that her best form is at a mile and a quarter. The Americans may well get to know more about her in future for it's said she'll be racing over there as a four-year-old.

Ristna's dam Roussalka was equally effective at a mile and a mile and a quarter: she won the Coronation Stakes and the Nassau Stakes, the latter two years running. One of the few times she failed to make the frame in good company was, incidentally, when favourite for the Sun Chariot. A significant proportion of Roussalka's foals are unraced. The remainder have all shown ability and include Northern Supremo (by Northern Dancer) and High Altar (by High Line), who both stayed a mile and a half, and Gayane (by Nureyev), second to Ajdal in the July Cup in 1987. Good filly though Roussalka was, her dam Oh So Fair produced a better one in Oh So Sharp. Both Ristna and Oh So Sharp are by Kris, so Ristna is very closely related to the fillies' triple crown winner.

		Sharpen Up	Atan
	Kris	(ch 1969)	Rocchetta
	(ch 1976)	Doubly Sure	Reliance II
Ristna		(b 1971)	Soft Angels
(ch.f. 1988)		Habitat	Sir Gaylord
	Roussalka	(b 1966)	Little Hut
	(b 1972)	Oh So Fair	Graustark
		(b 1967)	Chandelle

Gayane we remember as a bit of a handful in the preliminaries and she used to run freely. Ristna is similar. She usually sweats up beforehand, she's keen, and the jockey appeared to skip the parade before the Champion Stakes in order to avoid putting her under unnecessary stress. None of that seems to affect her performance, though. The big, lengthy Ristna may have further improvement in her as a four-year-old; if so, there won't be many better fillies around. *J. H. M. Gosden.*

RISZARD (USA) 2 ch.c. (Mar 28) Danzig Connection (USA) – Tendresse (USA) **76**
(Secretariat (USA)) [1991 6m* 6m] workmanlike colt: second known foal: half-brother to poor maiden Dzet (by Caerleon): dam, unraced, from family of Majestic Prince and Crowned Prince: won 15-runner maiden at Naas in May: weak 4/1-shot, well-beaten eighth of 9 in Chesham Stakes at Royal Ascot: stays 6f: not seen out again. *J. S. Bolger, Ireland.*

RITA'S RISK 2 ch.c. (Mar 8) Risk Me (FR) 127 – Egnoussa 76 (Swing Easy **45**
(USA) 126) [1991 6s a7g 6.1m] leggy, sparely-made colt: has quick action: sixth foal: half-brother to 3-y-o 6f winner Fiorini and a winner in Italy (both by Formidable): dam, half-sister to very smart Devon Ditty, won over 7f: form only on debut (ridden by 7-lb claimer) at Folkestone: blinkered, well beaten in Nottingham claimer in July, looking somewhat irresolute under vigorous riding. *P. A. Kelleway.*

RIVADAVIA (GER) 4 b.f. Athenagoras (GER) – Rita (GER) (Salvo (GER)) **—**
[1990 NR 1991 6g 6m 7g 10m 8g 10g 7m] tall, leggy German-bred filly: won 3 times in Germany at 3 yrs from 7f to 1m: no form in 1991, including in listed races and handicaps. *Lord John FitzGerald.*

RIVAL BID (USA) 3 b.g. Cannonade (USA) – Love Triangle (USA) (Nodouble **68**
(USA)) [1990 7g⁴ 8m 7g² 1991 7f³ 10.2m⁴ 10m³ 9.7m² 10m 8m⁵ 12g⁶] workmanlike,
close-coupled gelding: quite modest maiden: below form last 3 starts, staying-on
steadily from mid-division when sixth of 20 in handicap at Folkestone: may prove
suited by further than 1¼m: possibly unsuited by firm ground: sweating (ran
creditably) second start. *M. A. Jarvis.*

RIVE-JUMELLE (IRE) 3 b.f. M Double M (USA) – Riverwave (USA) **78**
(Riverman (USA) 131) [1990 7m 7m² 7.5m² 1991 10d 10m² 10m* 10.6m² 10.1f⁵
11.7d³ 11.5g³ 10m* 10.5m⁶ 11m³ 9.9f⁶ 10g* 10m²] lengthy, sparely-made filly:
moderate mover: modest performer: successful in claimer at Newmarket (changed
hands £7,200) in May and apprentice handicaps at Windsor in August and Redcar in
September: excellent second in apprentice handicap at Newmarket final start: best
form at 1¼m: acts on good to firm ground. *M. Bell.*

RIVERAIN 3 b.f. Bustino 136 – Gold Rupee 86 (Native Prince) [1990 6g⁶ 7.5d² **47**
7m* 7f³ 7.5g⁶ 9g⁶ a8g² 1991 a8g⁵ a10g⁵ a8g⁶ 10g 11m] workmanlike filly: moderate
mover: poor performer: showed little last 3 starts: should be well suited by further
than 1m: acts on firm going: blinkered third outing: won selling hurdle in October. *T.
D. Barron.*

RIVER CHASE (IRE) 3 ch.f. Salmon Leap (USA) 131 – Amboselli 73 (Raga **61**
Navarro (ITY) 119) [1990 a7g 1991 a8g* 8g* 8f³ 8g³ 8m* 7.1m⁴] big, lengthy filly: a **70**
successful in maiden at Southwell in March, claimer (bandaged) at Ayr in July and
claiming handicap (made all) at Newcastle in October: stays 1m well: acts on firm
ground: game: sold to join K. Bailey 16,000 gns Newmarket Autumn Sales. *Sir Mark
Prescott.*

RIVER DEFENCES (USA) 2 b.c. (Apr 17) Riverman (USA) 131 – Durtal 121 **72 p**
(Lyphard (USA) 132) [1991 7m⁵] tall, useful-looking colt: has scope: brother to
French 7f and 1m winner Lady Isis and half-brother to useful miler True Panache
(by Mr Prospector), Gold Cup winner Gildoran (by Rheingold) and fairly useful but
untrustworthy 10.4f winner Regimental Arms (by Sir Ivor): dam, winner of
Cheveley Park and Fred Darling Stakes, is half-sister to Arc winner Detroit:
well-backed 4/1-shot but very green, over 5 lengths fifth of 11 to Ezzoud in minor
event at Doncaster in September, keeping on steadily not knocked about: gave
trouble stalls: bred to stay beyond 1m: will improve. *P. W. Chapple-Hyam.*

RIVER FALLS 2 b.c. (Mar 5) Aragon 118 – More Fizz (Morston (FR) 125) **113**
[1991 6g² 6m* 6g² 6g* 7m² 6m³]
　　When the *Racing Post* proclaimed on its front page in December,
'Revolution', it wasn't referring to any of the political upheavals on the world
stage but to a speech made by the Senior Steward of the Jockey Club at the
Gimcrack dinner. It usually falls to the owner of the Gimcrack winner to make
the most adventurous speech of the evening, but on this occasion the inven-
tive calls for expanded pool betting and pan-European betting opportunities
by River Falls's owner Tony Budge were overshadowed by Lord Hartington's
plans for a new British Horseracing Board. The impetus for reorganising the
administration of racing increased considerably in the last year. A Home
Affairs Select Committee, inquiring into the Levy on Horserace Betting,
recommended that racing should establish a new body which would more
effectively represent all sections of the racing industry and combine the functions presently exercised by the Jockey Club and the Horseracing Advisory
Council. The HAC responded with proposals which, if accepted, would require the Jockey Club to cede considerable powers to a new authority. Theirs
was a more radical solution than that outlined by Lord Hartington. He proposed reformation not revolution, in an exercise which looks suspiciously like
damage limitation, with representatives of the owners, racecourses and the
HAC (from which the owners and racecourses would withdraw) invited to
share power on a ten-seat British Horseracing Board led by the Senior
Steward. Outside interests were also to be integrated into a number of the
present Jockey Club committees. As the saying goes, expect this one to run
and run.
　　Winning the Gimcrack in its heyday would normally have put a horse in
the forefront of the classic picture but nowadays the race, sponsored by
Scottish Equitable, is of much less consequence than it used to be and you'd
need to look hard to locate River Falls among the ante-post prices for the
classics. The general reaction among the Press to his victory at York in Aug-

Scottish Equitable Gimcrack Stakes, York —
River Falls takes it from Taylor Quigley as Dilum (left) disappoints

		Mummy's Pet	Sing Sing
	Aragon	(b 1968)	Money For Nothing
	(b 1980)	Ica	Great Nephew
River Falls		(gr 1974)	Intent
(b.c. Mar 5, 1989)		Morston	Ragusa
	More Fizz	(ch 1970)	Windmill Girl
	(ch 1983)	Effervescence II	Charlottesville
		(ch 1963)	Vareta

ust seemed to be that he'd emerged the winner not through the extension of his progressive form but by default of the odds-on favourite Dilum; but that's taking credit unfairly from a colt who had improved by leaps and bounds in each of his previous races, so much so that in receipt of 5 lb from Dilum he constituted a genuine threat. River Falls started second favourite at York following three efforts which had seen victory over the course and distance in a two-runner maiden in July on the second outing, and a narrow defeat, seven lengths clear of the remainder, by Rodrigo de Triano in the listed Rose Bowl Stakes at Newbury on the third. River Falls, who looked exceptionally well at York, had made all or most of the running in his earlier races and, in common with plenty of other winners at the August meeting, reaped the benefit of forcing tactics to win by three and a half lengths from the 33/1-shot Taylor Quigley (with Dilum well back in fourth) after quickening the tempo from two furlongs out then running on strongly, despite drifting markedly to his left, inside the last. River Falls again found Rodrigo de Triano too good for him in his last two races. At Doncaster in September in the Laurent-Perrier Champagne Stakes, his first and only attempt at seven furlongs, River Falls couldn't hold on to Rodrigo de Triano from the two-furlong pole and despite running his best race went under by three and a half lengths, edging left once again. Back over six furlongs in the Newgate Stud Middle Park Stakes at Newmarket in October he was readily outpaced when Rodrigo de Triano went on and lost second place to Lion Cavern on the climb to the line, three lengths down.

River Falls is a son of the smart five-furlong to one-mile performer Aragon who was also represented in the latest season by the very useful miler Only Yours. At 80,000 guineas from Newmarket's October Sale, the rangy, good-looking River Falls was by far the most expensive of Aragon's twenty-four yearlings sold at public auction in 1990, most of whom could have been bought for the equivalent of a year's training fees as his steady rather than spectacular record from five crops of racing age suggests. River Falls's dam More Fizz, whose second foal he is following the modest six- and seven-furlong winner Fizz Time (by Good Times), won a maiden race over an extended nine furlongs at Le Croise-Laroche in France where the best of her half-brothers, the smart El Famoso, won three races over middle distances before his export to become a stallion in Scandinavia. Effervescence, a winner twice herself over a mile and a quarter in France, has bred several other winners, including the fairly useful sprinter Cliquot, later the dam of the useful sprinter Premiere Cuvee, and the fairly useful two-year-old five- and six-furlong winner Babycham Sparkle. This is a family which has done very well for the Aga Khan: Effervescence is a half-sister to the top-class sprinter/miler Zeddaan as well as the Poule d'Essai des Pouliches runner-up Gunilla and her less-talented sister Asharaz who later foaled the high-class French stayer Shafaraz. There's enough stamina in River Falls's pedigree to suggest he'll stay a mile, and on the evidence of his best runs at two, which came firstly at six furlongs on good ground then at seven furlongs, he's well worth a try at that distance. So far River Falls has raced only on good or good to firm ground. *R. Hannon.*

RIVER GOD (USA)   4 b.c. Val de L'Orne (FR) 130 – Princess Morvi (USA)   —
(Graustark) [1990 12m* 12g 16.2f* 14.8m* 14m* 14.6g³ 1991 16.2s] well-made, good sort: very smart at 3 yrs (third in St Leger at Doncaster): tailed off in Insulpak Sagaro EBF Stakes at Ascot: withdrawn lame at start at Chester later in May: stayed 2m: acted on firm going, seemed unsuited by soft ground: retired to Blakeley Stud, Shropshire, fee £900 (Oct 1st). *H. R. A. Cecil.*

RIVER ISLAND (USA)   3 b.c. Spend A Buck (USA) – Promising Risk (USA)   **83** d
(Exclusive Native (USA)) [1990 NR 1991 10d* 10f³ 11.8g⁵ 10.8d³ 12.1d⁴] $180,000Y: quite attractive colt: first foal: dam unraced half-sister to Belle's Gold, stakes winner from 6f to 9f, including of Grade 3 events: won maiden at Brighton in April: failed to improve on that in minor events and apprentice race, dropping out tamely and well beaten last 2 outings: stays 1¼m: sold to join J. Old 11,000 gns Newmarket Autumn Sales: best watched. *P. F. I. Cole.*

RIVER NOMAD   4 b.f. Gorytus (USA) 132 – Blue Rider (USA) (Wajima (USA))   —
[1990 7g³ 8m* 8v⁵ 1991 8g] sturdy filly: fairly useful but very lightly-raced performer at 3 yrs: below best in £15,800 handicap at York, only run in 1991 (May): should stay 1¼m: acts on good to firm ground. *P. F. I. Cole.*

RIVER ORCHID   2 b.f. (Mar 24) Mashhor Dancer (USA) – Summer Sky 75   **43**
(Skyliner 117) [1991 5m 6f⁴ 6m⁶ 7s 6m⁵] 1,150Y: smallish, workmanlike filly: first foal: dam 2-y-o 5f winner, is half-sister to very useful 7f to 10.2f winner Lucky Scott, later stakes placed in USA: poor maiden: best effort second start: stays 6f: well beaten on soft ground. *R. J. Hodges.*

RIVER PATROL   3 b.f. Rousillon (USA) 133 – Boathouse 116 (Habitat 134) [1990   **96**
7m³ 7m⁴ 1991 10d⁶ 12g³ 10.2f* 12g² 10.1m² 14.6m] big, rangy, unfurnished filly: fairly useful performer: made all in maiden at Bath in July, tending to wander under pressure: good second of 3 in slowly-run minor event at Newmarket and listed race (won by Gai Bulga) at Newcastle: gave trouble at stalls, stiff task in Group 3 event at Doncaster final start: should be better at 1½m than 1¼m: acts on firm going. *B. W. Hills.*

RIVER RHINE (USA)   3 br.g. Riverman (USA) 131 – Call The Queen (USA)   **77**
(Hail To Reason) [1990 6m³ 1991 8m 7d³ 8g* 9m 8m] rangy gelding: modest performer: ridden by 7-lb claimer, won 6-runner handicap at Doncaster in July, leading 3f out and staying on well: below form in similar events in October: may well stay beyond 1m: left H. Cecil's stable and gelded after third start. *J. W. Watts.*

RIVERS RHAPSODY   4 b.f. Dominion 123 – Trwyn Cilan 89 (Import 127) [1990   **103**
5m* 5d⁴ 5g 5d* 5m³ 6m³ 6m 6m³ 5g* 6m 5m 1991 6g⁴ 5g⁵ 5m³ 5m⁶ 5g 5g³ 6f 5d] smallish, good-quartered filly: useful sprinter: good third to Elbio in U B Group Temple Stakes (hung in early stages) at Sandown in May and Title Roll in King George Stakes at Goodwood in August: below best in Group 3 event in Sweden and

Ciga Prix de l'Abbaye de Longchamp (slowly away) final 2 starts: effective at 5f to 6f: acts on good to firm and dead ground: has turn of foot. *G. B. Balding.*

RIVERTON HEIGHTS (IRE) 3 b.c. Seattle Slew (USA) – Rose Red (USA) 92 (Northern Dancer) [1990 NR 1991 7g] lengthy colt: sixth reported foal (fourth by Seattle Slew): half-brother to the dam of very useful Irish 3-y-o 6f winner Archway: dam, Irish 2-y-o 6f winner unraced at 3 yrs, is half-sister to high-class 1m to 1½m winner Critique: 10/1 from 5/1, carrying condition and tongue tied down, well beaten in Lingfield maiden in October: showed long, round action: should be suited by further: sold 3,200 gns Newmarket Autumn Sales. *J. H. M. Gosden.* —

RIVET 2 gr.g. (Feb 27) Superlative 118 – Moon Charter 45 (Runnymede 123) [1991 5m] 6,600Y: third foal: dam, plater, best run at 7f as 2-y-o: slow-starting last of 21 in median auction maiden at Windsor in August. *M. Blanshard.* —

RIVETER 2 gr.c. (Mar 12) Kalaglow 132 – Lone Galaxie (USA) 69 (Nodouble (USA)) [1991 7m] 1,800Y: lengthy, workmanlike colt: second foal: brother to 3-y-o Galaxy Glow: dam maiden stayed 6f: 50/1, backward and green, slowly away when last of 19 in maiden auction at Leicester in September: showed a very round action. *M. Blanshard.* —

RIVIERA RAINBOW 3 b.c. Rainbow Quest (USA) 134 – Miss Beaulieu 106 (Northfields (USA)) [1990 NR 1991 10g5 8m2 8f2 8m 8m 8m5 8.1m5] smallish, sturdy colt: third foal: half-brother to 1¼m to 1½m winner Riviera Magic (by Niniski) and ungenuine French Riviera (by Teenoso), later winner in Belgium: dam 6f and 1¼m winner: modest maiden at best: well beaten last 4 starts: should be suited by further than 1m: wears bandages: blinkered/visored last 2 starts: sold 10,000 gns Newmarket Autumn Sales: not one to rely on. *G. Wragg.* **74**

RIVIERA VISTA 2 b.c. (Jan 29) Shirley Heights 130 – Miss Beaulieu 106 (Northfields (USA)) [1991 7f4 7g2] tall, quite attractive colt: has scope: fourth foal: half-brother to 3-y-o Riviera Rainbow (by Rainbow Quest), 1¼m to 1½m winner Riviera Magic (by Niniski) and ungenuine French Riviera (by Teenoso), later winner in Belgium: dam 6f and 1¼m winner: fair form, staying on well, in maiden at Yarmouth (in need of race, niggled along at halfway) and 4-runner minor event at Goodwood (1½ lengths behind Bilateral) 11 days later in August: likely to stay 1¼m and win a maiden. *G. Wragg.* **87 p**

RIYADH LIGHTS 6 b.g. Formidable (USA) 125 – Rivers Maid 83 (Rarity 129) [1990 NR 1991 12m 13m6 18g2 17.1d3 22.2m 16.2d a16g6] compact gelding: moderate mover: poor handicapper: seems suited by good test of stamina nowadays: has been blinkered and bandaged behind: still a maiden: unsatisfactory. *M. D. I. Usher.* **41 §**

ROAD TO AU BON (USA) 3 b.c. Strawberry Road (AUS) 128 – Village Lady (USA) (Crimson Satan) [1990 NR 1991 8m5 11.5g5 10g] $22,000Y: lengthy, quite attractive colt: half-brother to 4 minor winners in North America: dam, 3-y-o maiden winner at around 6f from only 2 starts, is half-sister to dam of Grade 1 Travers Stakes winner Willow Hour: well beaten in maidens, off course 3½ months before final start: sold to join J. Baker 15,500 gns Newmarket Autumn Sales. *L. M. Cumani.* —

ROARING BREEZE 2 ch.f. (Apr 29) Roaring Riva 103 – Tree Breeze 111 (Farm Walk 111) [1991 6m3 5.9h6 6.1m 7m] 1,000Y: leggy, sparely-made filly: fifth reported living foal: dam won 9 times at up to 2¼m and was fairly useful staying hurdler: plating-class form in maidens: seems to stay 7f. *Miss S. E. Hall.* **48**

ROARING TRADE 2 ch.f. (Mar 31) Roaring Riva 103 – Crimson Cargo (Import 127) [1991 a5g 5m 5f a5g] 500Y: second foal: dam thrice-raced half-sister to smart 1977 2-y-o sprinter Fire Angel: little worthwhile form, including in sellers. *J. Balding.* —

ROAR ON TOUR 2 b.c. (Mar 15) Dunbeath (USA) 127 – Tickled Trout 70 (Red Alert 127) [1991 5m4 7m5 8.1g6 8m6 7g*] 4,000F, 8,000Y: good-bodied colt: second foal: dam, plater, won at 5f and 6f at 2 yrs: visored first time, won 18-runner nursery at Doncaster in October, showing much improved form: likely to prove at least as effective at 1m as 7f: off course nearly 5 months after debut. *M. H. Easterby.* **67**

ROAVING MONTY (IRE) 3 b.g. Montekin 125 – Monrovia (FR) (Dancer's Image (USA)) [1990 NR 1991 7g 9m 7d] 1,400Y, 2,000Y: workmanlike gelding: fourth foal: half-brother to 1988 Irish 2-y-o 6f winner God's Country (by Burslem): dam placed once in 1m claimer in France: no promise in sellers and claimer. *K. R. Burke.* —

ROBALTO 4 b.g. Ballad Rock 122 – Staritsa (USA) (Alleged (USA) 138) [1990 NR 1991 8f 11.5m 7.6d] close-coupled gelding: third foal: half-brother to temperamental 1987 2-y-o 5f winner Miss Caro Star (by Rusticaro): dam unraced daughter of very —

smart Roussalka (half-sister to Oh So Sharp), and half-sister to Ristna: no show in varied company, twice bandaged: sold 1,150 gns Ascot July Sales. *B. Smart.*

ROBBIE BURNS 5 br.h. Daring March 116 – Gangawayhame 91 (Lochnager — 132) [1990 11.7g 12m 10g⁶ 10s²a 12g 1991 a 10g 12d 12f 10m⁶ 10g] workmanlike horse: poor handicapper at best nowadays: suited by 1¼m: acts on good to firm and soft going. *R. V. Smyth.*

ROBERT DEAR (USA) 5 gr.g. Caro 133 – Marketess (USA) (To Market) [1990 64 8f⁴ 10f² 12g⁵ 8f³ 8.3m* 8m 8.3m 8g 8m 1991 8d³ 8.2m⁵] rangy gelding: quite modest handicapper: not seen out after May: acts on firm and dead going: ran creditably when blinkered once. *M. H. Tompkins.*

ROBERTOLOMY (USA) 2 ch.c. (Feb 28) Roberto (USA) 131 – Respectfully 55 p (USA) (The Minstrel (CAN) 135) [1991 7.1m 8g] 96,000Y: well-grown colt: has scope: second foal: dam, unraced, from family of Be My Guest: better effort, leading over 5f, when beaten around 20 lengths in 1m minor event won by Raja Baba at Newbury in October: green and very slowly away on debut: should stay 1¼m: will improve again. *J. W. Hills.*

ROBERTO RUFO (USA) 2 b.c. (Jan 12) Dactylographer (USA) 119 – Rosy 65 Royal (USA) (Royal And Regal (USA)) [1991 8m 8m 7.1s⁵ 6s] $7,500Y: quite good-topped colt: third reported foal: half-brother to a winner by Irish Escapade: dam unraced: quite modest maiden: ran moderately final outing: will probably stay beyond 1m: acts on soft going. *P. A. Kelleway.*

ROBERTO'S GAL 2 b.f. (Feb 22) Roberto (USA) 131 – Grafitti Gal (USA) 59 (Pronto) [1991 7g 6s⁴ 8m] close-coupled filly: has a quick action: half-sister to winners in North America by Affirmed and Raja Baba: dam, placed in Ireland before winning at up to 11f in USA, is daughter of Grafitti, one of best fillies of her generation: plating-class maiden: best effort second start: bred to stay 1¼m. *J. R. Fanshawe.*

ROBERT'S WAY (USA) 2 b.g. (Feb 27) Al Nasr (FR) 126 – Adalia (Owen 47 Dudley 121) [1991 6g 5m² 6d 6.9m 7.5f⁶ 7.5f⁶ 6m⁴ a7g² 7.5f] lengthy, rather sparely-made gelding: first known foal: dam French 1¼m winner later successful in USA: modest plater: will be suited by 1m+: acts on fibresand: blinkered four of last 5 starts. *M. W. Easterby.*

ROBERTY LEA 3 b.c. Alleging (USA) 120 – Rosy Lee (FR) (Le Haar 126) [1990 79 5m 7g 1991 a8g⁶ a8g* a8g⁶ a8g⁴ 10d 12.3s² 12m 12m* 12g⁴ 11m⁶ 12g² 12d* 11.9m⁶ 14g³ 13.9g² 16.2g 16m 13.3g] close-coupled colt: fair performer: successful in maiden at Southwell in January, claimer at Thirsk in May and handicap at Newbury in July: well beaten after excellent second to Micheletti in £16,600 handicap at York: worth another try at 2m: acts on good to firm ground and soft: blinkered on reappearance: sometimes sweating: game. *T. Fairhurst.*

ROBINGO (IRE) 2 b.c. (Apr 16) Bob Back (USA) 120 – Mill's Girl (Le Lev- 49 p anstell 122) [1991 8f⁴] IR 19,500F, 19,000Y: workmanlike colt: half-brother to 4 winners, including very smart middle-distance colt Quilted (by Patch) and useful 7f to 1¾m winner What A Riot (by Sun Prince): dam Irish 1¾m winner: backed at long odds but green, over 10 lengths fourth of 9 in maiden at Yarmouth in September, staying on from rear final 2f: will improve, particularly over further. *C. E. Brittain.*

ROBINS ARROW 2 gr.c. (Feb 25) Jalmood (USA) 126 – Mainly Dry (The 72 Brianstan 128) [1991 5d³ 5d⁴ 5f³ 5g* 5g* 5m⁴ 5g⁶] 25,000Y: modest colt: good walker: fifth foal: half-brother to 3 sprint winners, including 3-y-o Ellebanna (by Tina's Pet) and useful Tod (by Petorius): dam never ran: modest performer: successful in maiden (making all) at Edinburgh and minor event (on disqualification of Magic Ring) at Goodwood in May: ran poorly final outing (July): speedy: possibly unsuited by very firm ground: keen, active type: trained first 4 starts by J. Berry: sold 6,400 gns Newmarket Autumn Sales. *N. Tinkler.*

ROBINS FIND (IRE) 3 b.g. Reasonable (FR) 119 – Skyway 76 (Skymaster 126) 66 [1990 NR 1991 9g⁶ 11.9g⁶ 12.2m⁴ a14g] IR 10,500Y: workmanlike gelding: half-brother to several winners including Prix Robert Papin winner Maelstrom Lake and Irish 1¼m winner Flying Bid (both by Auction Ring): dam 1¼m winner: quite modest maiden: well beaten in handicap at Southwell in November: stays 1½m: wears severe noseband. *J. G. FitzGerald.*

ROBINS RETURN 3 b.f. Music Boy 124 – Baidedones (Welsh Pageant 132) 41 [1990 5f 6g 5f⁴ 6m⁶ a6g 8.2g 7f⁴ a7g⁶ 1991 8.2f⁵ 7f 9m 8h⁴ 11m⁴ 8m* 8f 10m 8m⁵ 8.1g⁴ 8m 11m] workmanlike filly: poor handicapper: won at Carlisle in June, staying on well: well beaten in selling events last 2 starts: best form at 1m: acts on hard going: sold to join T. Rollingson 1,050 gns Doncaster November Sales. *Denys Smith.*

ROBINS SON 4 b.g. Krayyan 117 – Fleam (Continuation 120) [1990 9m³ 10.5g — 1991 12g⁵] rather angular gelding: sixth foal: half-brother to Irish sprint winner God's Trust (by Green God) and an Irish 1m winner by Red Alert: dam won over 9f in Ireland: poor and lightly-raced gelding: stays 9f. *J. G. FitzGerald.*

ROBSLAD 2 gr.c. (May 6) Hotfoot 126 – Misty Rocket 75 (Roan Rocket 128) — [1991 5f 6m 8f 8.2m] 3,300F, 2,400Y: leggy colt: second foal: dam 1¼m and 1½m sellers winner also won over hurdles: slowly away and no form, in seller final start: blinkered last 2 outings. *Mrs S. M. Austin.*

ROCALITY 2 b.f. (Mar 9) Dreams To Reality (USA) 113 – Rocas 48 (Ile de 75 Bourbon (USA) 133) [1991 5m 6m 6f 7.1m³ 7g* 7m³ 7m*] 700Y: leggy filly: second foal: half-sister to 3-y-o 8.3f winner Homile (by Homing): dam stayer: progressed well throughout season, winning nurseries at Wolverhampton and Leicester in autumn: will stay at least 1m: yet to race on a soft surface: has tended to hang badly and look an awkward ride. *R. Hannon.*

ROCA MURADA (IRE) 2 br.g. (Apr 18) Cyrano de Bergerac 120 – Keppols 56 (Furry Glen 121) [1991 6g⁴ 8m 7d] IR 10,500F, 7,600Y: tall, close-coupled gelding: half-brother to Irish 11.9f winner Keppols Diamond (by Kampala): dam Irish 9f winner placed at up to 1¾m, also won over jumps: consistent, if only plating class, form in late-season maidens: will stay 1¼m. *M. J. Ryan.*

ROCKANGE (IRE) 2 b.f. (Mar 14) Ballad Rock 122 – Ange de Feu (Double — Form 130) [1991 5m] IR 22,000Y: second foal: half-sister to 3-y-o Tumbellina (by Tumble Wind): dam never ran: co-favourite, never dangerous in seller at Thirsk in May: sold 1,200 gns Ascot December Sales. *M. Moubarak.*

ROCKBOURNE 2 b.f. (Mar 4) Midyan (USA) 124 – River Music (Riverman 51 (USA) 131) [1991 5g² 5.2g 5.3m³ 5m⁵ 7m] IR 10,000Y: tall, leggy, light-framed filly: fifth living foal: half-sister to useful sprint winner Time Machine (by Connaught) and useful 1m and 9.1f winner Young Jazz (by Young Generation): dam won over 5f from 3 starts at 2 yrs in Ireland: plating-class maiden: ran moderately in nurseries last 2 starts, off course 2 months in between: worth a try at 6f: sometimes sweats. *J. W. Hills.*

ROCK BREAKER 3 b.c. Green Ruby (USA) 104 – Holloway Wonder 93 (Swing 64 Easy (USA) 126) [1990 5g a6g² a6g⁶ 5d 5m 5g² 5v 1991 5d* 5s³ 6d⁶ 6m⁵ 5m⁴ 5g 5f³] lengthy, good-quartered colt: moderate mover: quite modest performer: made all in handicap at Doncaster in March: best at 5f: acted on firm and dead ground: head-strong: dead. *B. A. McMahon.*

ROCK FACE 4 b.f. Ballad Rock 122 – Misty Halo 93 (High Top 131) [1990 a10g* 69 12.3f⁵ 12.5g 10g⁶ 10g⁴ 11d 12h* 14f* 12f* 14m⁴ 1991 12g³ 16m³ 16f⁵ 14.6m 11.9f³ 12f⁵ 12m* 16m 12g*] leggy, workmanlike filly: quite modest handicapper: won celebrity events at Uttoxeter (straightforward task) and Hexham in autumn: stays 2m: needs a sound surface, and goes very well on firm ground: below form when blinkered: goes well on switchback track. *Sir Mark Prescott.*

ROCK HARD 2 ch.c. (Mar 29) Ballad Rock 122 – Norska 67 (Northfields (USA)) 43 p [1991 7g] 16,000F, 62,000Y: well-grown colt: has scope: half-brother to 1990 2-y-o 7f winner Neroli (by Nishapour), now one not to trust, and to 2 winners in Italy: dam staying maiden at 2 yrs not so good as 3-y-o: green 20/1-shot, raced keenly 4f then handled considerately when twelfth of 13 in minor event at York in September: will improve. *W. Jarvis.*

ROCK HOPPER 4 b.c. Shareef Dancer (USA) 135 – Cormorant Wood 130 124 (Home Guard (USA) 129) [1990 10m² 11.5m* 1991 12g* 12g* 12m³ 12m* 12m² 12m* 12m³ 12g² 12f]

Rock Hopper was one of the many Derby hopefuls to fall by the wayside in 1990—he was co-favourite when sustaining a hairline fracture of a cannon bone after his Calor Derby Trial win at Lingfield—but he repaid handsomely the decision to keep him in training as a four-year-old. He won four of his nine starts, all in pattern company, and finished out of the first three only once, developing into a very smart colt lacking nothing in terms of toughness and consistency.

Rock Hopper quickly made up for lost time, gaining impressive victories in the spring in the Lanes End John Porter Stakes at Newbury, where he beat Warm Feeling with much more in hand than the three-quarters-of-a-length winning margin, and the General Accident Jockey Club Stakes at Newmarket, despite idling, by a neck from Mountain Kingdom. On each occasion Rock Hopper led inside the final furlong and his very good turn of foot proved

General Accident Jockey Club Stakes, Newmarket—Rock Hopper quickens best;
Mountain Kingdom (right) keeps on for second

decisive. The Hanson Coronation Cup provided a much sterner test but that
didn't dissuade punters from siding with him; he was sent off a heavily-backed
15/8 favourite in a field of seven that included Quest For Fame, having his first
run since the Irish Derby, In The Groove and Terimon. Although anything but
discredited, Rock Hopper found In The Groove and Terimon too strong and
went down by half a length and a neck, unable to produce the telling burst of
speed against this stronger opposition. Doubtless those who'd supported
Rock Hopper had envisaged his playing a leading role in the season's top
middle-distance events. It wasn't to be, and comprehensive defeats at the
hands of first Epervier Bleu in the Grand Prix de Saint-Cloud (beaten three

Hardwicke Stakes, Ascot—Topanoora just holds Rock Hopper,
but the stewards reverse the placings; Spritsail is third

lengths) and then Generous in the King George VI and Queen Elizabeth Diamond Stakes (beaten eight lengths into third when tried blinkered) confirmed his part as merely a supporting one. Sandwiched between those placed efforts were other victories in the Hardwicke Stakes at Royal Ascot and Princess of Wales's Stakes at Newmarket. Controversy reigned after the Hardwicke. Irish-trained Topanoora passed the post a short head to the good but the stewards reversed the placings in favour of Rock Hopper—the details are set out in the commentary on Topanoora. The Princess of Wales's Stakes looked easy pickings for Rock Hopper but, unsuited by the slow pace, he struggled to land the odds, rallying splendidly inside the final furlong to beat Mukddaam by a head. It was decided after the King George to rest Rock Hopper and bring him back for an autumn campaign. Rock Hopper was returned to Ascot for his Prix de l'Arc de Triomphe warm-up in the Hoover Cumberland Lodge Stakes and ran a fine race in going down by a head to Drum Taps. It was his first race for over two months and he was carrying plenty of condition. Unfortunately he returned home very sore—he'd pricked a foot a few days before the race—and Arc plans had to be scrapped. Stoute did manage to bring him back for the Japan Cup and, although he finished out of the placings for the first time in the season, his seventh of fifteen to Golden Pheasant, beaten over six lengths, was a fair effort.

Rock Hopper (b.c. 1987)	Shareef Dancer (USA) (b 1980)	Northern Dancer (b 1961)	Nearctic
			Natalma
		Sweet Alliance (b 1974)	Sir Ivor
			Mrs Peterkin
	Cormorant Wood (b 1980)	Home Guard (br 1969)	Forli
			Stay At Home
		Quarry Wood (b 1968)	Super Sam
			Phrygia

Rock Hopper's sire and dam were among the best of their generation. The Irish Derby winner Shareef Dancer enjoyed a good season as a sire. Apart from Rock Hopper, he was also responsible for the winners of the Kildangan Stud Irish Oaks and German One Thousand Guineas winners in Possessive Dancer and Kazoo. The dam Cormorant Wood won the Champion Stakes at three and the Benson and Hedges Gold Cup the following year. Rock Hopper is her second foal and up to now her only offspring to reach the racecourse; the third is a filly called Cliveden Gail (by Law Society). Cormorant Wood didn't stay a mile and a half but there's plenty of stamina in the family. Rock

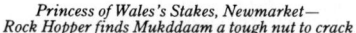

Princess of Wales's Stakes, Newmarket—
Rock Hopper finds Mukddaam a tough nut to crack

Maktoum Al-Maktoum's "Rock Hopper"

Hopper's grandam Quarry Wood was successful at up to a mile and three quarters. She's a half-sister to the very useful hurdler Cullen who won over eighteen furlongs on the flat. Rock Hopper, a well-made colt who's a really good walker, impressed throughout the season in appearance. He shows a quick, fluent action in his slower paces and acts well on a sound surface (he's yet to encounter ground softer than good). Campaigned exclusively at a mile and a half in 1991, he'll stay further given the chance. Held up for a late run, he's shown a tendency to carry his head a bit high and wander under pressure in the finish—he's raced with his tongue tied down since his final start as a three-year-old—but is, without doubt, tough and genuine. He remains in training. *M. R. Stoute.*

ROCKIN' ROSIE   3 b.f. Song 132 – Almarose 79 (Northfields (USA)) [1990 a5g² 58 + 1991 5s* 6m] good-quartered, angular filly: poor mover: won maiden auction at Hamilton on first run for 12 months: good ninth of 17, hampered halfway when travelling comfortably, in handicap at Newmarket later in April: stays 6f. *Dr J. D. Scargill.*

ROCK LEGEND   3 ch.c. Legend of France (USA) 124 – Two Rock 70 (Mill Reef 66 (USA) 141) [1990 NR 1991 7g 10g⁴ 7g⁶ 8.9g⁵ 6s³ 7m⁵ 10g⁵ 11.6m* 12g² 11.5g³ 11.8g⁵ 12.1d] 4,800F: sturdy colt: sixth foal: half-brother to fair 1¼m winner Tracing (by Artaius) and quite modest middle-distance winner Arthurs Stone (by Kings Lake): dam, winner over 13f from 2 starts, is daughter of 1000 Guineas and Oaks runner-up St Pauli Girl: quite modest form: won claimer at Windsor in August: ran very well at Lingfield tenth start, moderately after: well worth a try beyond 1½m: acts on good to firm ground and soft. *M. J. Haynes.*

ROCK OPERA (IRE)   3 ch.c. Ballad Rock 122 – Time For Romance (Cure The 58 Blues (USA)) [1990 NR 1991 5m³ 5m⁶ 6f²] IR 14,000F, IR 8,000Y: quite good-topped colt: first foal: dam French 9.2f and 1¼m winner: placed, showing plating-class form, in maidens at Catterick and Thirsk in late-summer: stays 6f: started slowly first 2 outings. *M. P. Naughton.*

ROCKRIDGE 4 b.g. Chief Singer 131 – Croda Rossa (ITY) (Grey Sovereign 128§) [1990 7f 8m 7g 10m 10g² 10m² 12g 12m³ 12m⁵ 1991 12s 10.8m] rather leggy, attractive gelding: plating-class maiden: behind in handicaps in early part of 1991: suited by 1½m: acts on good to firm ground: sold to join Mrs P. Joynes's stable 3,000 gns Newmarket Autumn Sales, resold 4,000 gns Ascot November Sales. *G. Wragg.* —

ROCK SONG (IRE) 2 ch.g. (Apr 13) Ballad Rock 122 – Mrs Tittlemouse (Nonoalco (USA) 131) [1991 6d 6m 6m 7m 6g 7m4] 26,000F, 9,500Y: tall, rather leggy gelding: has scope: easy mover: fourth foal: brother to maiden Bec Rouge and half-brother to 1990 2-y-o 7f winner Carnbrea Cuddy and to 1m winner Solo Court (both by King of Clubs): dam unraced half-sister to high-class miler Bairn: plating-class maiden: stays 7f: blinkered first time, ducked left stalls and unseated rider third start: ran creditably in them last 2 starts. *P. F. I. Cole.* 49

ROCKY BAY 2 ch.f. (May 5) Bold Owl 101 – Overseas 48 (Sea Hawk II 131) [1991 5m 5g 6m 6g 6g² 6f² a7g² a6g⁵ 7g⁵ 7m] neat filly: has a quick action: sister to 3-y-o Atlantic Way and half-sister to several winners here and abroad, including 1986 2-y-o 6f winner Swallow Bay (by Penmarric): dam poor maiden: quite modest plater: gave impression something amiss final outing: stays 7f: very slowly away once: not particularly consistent. *D. Haydn Jones.* 42

ROCKY HABITAT (IRE) 3 ch.f. Ballad Rock 122 – Little Red Hut (Habitat 134) [1990 5g⁶ 5m⁶ 5m³ 1991 6.9m³ 6g 6m 5d 6m] IR 7,000Y: leggy, lengthy filly: third live foal: dam lightly-raced half-sister to Red Regent: modest form in Ireland in summer at 2 yrs, trained by P. Canty: behind all starts here, including in sellers: blinkered fourth start. *J. R. Jenkins.*

ROCKY ROMANCE 4 b.g. Crooner 119 – Wild Jewel (Great Heron (USA)) [1990 NR 1991 16.2m⁵ 11.5m 10m 16m⁶ 14.1f5] tall, rather close-coupled gelding: good mover: sixth foal: brother to fair 5-y-o winning sprinter Singing Star: dam never ran: lightly-raced gelding: first form in handicap at Nottingham final start: looks staying sort. *R. Curtis.* 34 +

ROCKY WATERS (USA) 2 b. or br.c. (Apr 17) Rocky Marriage (USA) 95 – Running Melody 86 (Rheingold 137) [1991 5f² 6f* 5g⁶ 6m 6m⁶] leggy, lightly-made colt: has a roundish action: second known foal: dam 1m and 1¼m winner, is granddaughter of very smart Fleet Wahine: sire by Riva Ridge: modest performer: easy winner of maiden at Redcar (clear at halfway) in May: ran poorly in minor events afterwards: sweating third (also edgy and on toes) and final (ran as if something amiss) starts: off course 3 months before penultimate one. *Denys Smith.* 71

ROCQUAINE BAY 4 b.f. Morston (FR) 125 – Queen's Royale 80 (Tobrouk (FR)) [1990 NR 1991 7m 8g⁵ 8.3m 10m² 10g⁵ 8g 9.2s5] leggy filly: second foal: dam won from 6f to 1m: poor handicapper: will stay 1½m: acts on good to firm and soft ground: twice below form when sweating. *M. J. Bolton.* 43

ROCTON NORTH (IRE) 3 ch.c. Ballad Rock 122 – Northern Scene 78 (Habitat 134) [1990 5m² 5m² 6d³ 6g* 7s 1991 6g² 6d³ 8m² 7g* 8m³ 7m³ 8m⁶ 7m*] 90

Norwest Holst Trophy, York—a good-class handicap goes to Rocton North (right) by the narrowest of margins from Sheikh Albadou (No. 4); Dominion Gold is third

compact colt: poor mover: fairly useful handicapper: won £19,300 Norwest Holst Trophy at York in May and £7,600 contest (checked 2f out, led post) at Newcastle in June: suited by 1m or stiff 7f: seems best on a sound surface: game and consistent. *R. Hannon.*

RODEO STAR (USA) 5 ch.h. Nodouble (USA) – Roundup Rose (USA) — (Minnesota Mac) [1990 11g³ 8.5d 11d* 12g 11.7g³ 12g³ 10m* 10.6s² 10.4d⁴ 1991 12.3s] workmanlike, plain horse: quite modest handicapper: always behind only run on flat in 1991 (April): stays 1½m: acts on good to firm and soft going: tried visored: has been unruly in stalls: winning hurdler. *N. Tinkler.*

RODMARTON 4 br.g. Durandal 114 – Soulieana 58 (Manado 130) [1990 NR 1991 — a 12g] first foal: dam plating-class maiden: tailed off in Southwell claimer. *A. P. Jarvis.*

RODRIGO DE TRIANO (USA) 2 ch.c. (May 27) El Gran Senor (USA) **120** p 136 – Hot Princess 101 (Hot Spark 126) [1991 6g* 6g* 7f* 7m* 6m*]

In the year in which the five-hundredth anniversary of the discovery of the Americas by the adopted Spanish explorer Columbus will be commemorated by the vast Expo' 92 exhibition in Seville, there could be few horses more aptly named to win the Two Thousand Guineas and embellish the celebrations from afar than Rodrigo de Triano. He takes his name from the Spanish mariner Rodrigo de Triana, Columbus' deck hand who in October 1492 first spotted the island of Guanahani, later renamed San Salvador by Columbus and generally believed to be Watling Island in the Bahamas. Unbeaten in five races, notably the Laurent Perrier Champagne Stakes and the Newgate Stud Middle Park Stakes on his last two outings, Rodrigo de Triano, whose name became mis-spelt somewhere after its initial registration in the supplement to the American Stud Book, has prospects second to none among the home-trained colts and is set to benefit from the expected absence of Arazi who's likely to be aimed at the Kentucky Derby instead. Like those of his French-based contemporary, Rodrigo de Triano's performances have been characterised by a fine turn of foot, and if he gets to Newmarket in May in the same form as he left the racecourse in the autumn he'll take a great deal of beating. At the time of writing he looks a worthy ante-post favourite.

The Champagne-Middle Park double has been achieved only four times in the post-war period and just once, by Bold Lad in 1966, since the Champagne was increased in distance from six furlongs to seven furlongs in 1962. The qualities required to win both events are very different; whereas the Champagne, which always comes first of the pair, is usually contested by later-maturing staying types, the Middle Park, in its heyday a highly prestigious event whose winners regularly topped the Free Handicap, is nowadays contested more often than not by horses with few pretensions to staying beyond sprint distances. The latest renewal of the Champagne, run at Doncaster in September, pitted together five runners among whom the Scottish Equitable Gimcrack winner River Falls and the much-vaunted Artic

Laurent-Perrier Champagne Stakes, Doncaster—
Rodrigo de Triano impresses in beating River Falls and Artic Tracker

Newgate Stud Middle Park Stakes, Newmarket—
Rodrigo de Triano goes through the season undefeated; Lion Cavern does well
to get up for second ahead of River Falls (rails); Power Lake is fourth

Tracker, a close third in the Solario at Sandown last time out, besides Rodrigo de Triano, possessed progressive form of a standard not far short of that usually required to win the race. Rodrigo de Triano, unbeaten in three outings including a narrow defeat of River Falls in a listed race at Newbury in the summer, looked to have the slight edge on form, as the betting suggested, but he emerged an emphatic winner and confirmed that he was very much on the upgrade and as good a colt as had been seen in Britain or Ireland at that stage of the season. Covered up at the back of the field, Rodrigo de Triano had no difficulty in improving his position as the tempo quickened with two furlongs to go, surged to the front a furlong later and, pushed out, forged clear in spite of drifting left to win by three and a half lengths from River Falls; though the early gallop wasn't strong they were well strung out, and Artic Tracker, who held every chance for much of the way, was beaten six lengths into third. As we've said, winning over seven furlongs is one thing; repeating the feat over six furlongs the following month against speedier types under fast conditions in the Middle Park is quite another, but Rodrigo de Triano demonstrated his versatility with an accomplished performance of similar merit to that in the Champagne. Opposed by the Prix Morny third Lion Cavern, the Flying Childers runner-up Power Lake, the highly-regarded Doncaster winner Balla Jidaal, the maiden Eden's Close, and, for the third time, River Falls, this was a more interesting renewal than some of the recent contests that haven't helped the Middle Park's reputation and prestige. Rodrigo de Triano, who didn't look so well as at Doncaster, and became rather edgy beforehand, once again gave his rivals start and a beating in a moderately-run race. Slowly into his stride rather than steadied, Rodrigo de Triano remained at the back of the field until eased to the outside to make his move approaching the Dip, quickened ahead as the eventual runner-up Lion Cavern found his path blocked on the rail and was ridden right out as Lion Cavern came with a late run to deprive River Falls of second place. Lion Cavern was by no means an unlucky loser, however; Rodrigo de Triano looked to be idling in front, a view substantiated subsequently by the riders of the first and second, and had more in hand than the winning margin of a length. Although in terms of form it was a little short of the performance he'd recorded at Doncaster, six furlongs

713

probably doesn't suit Rodrigo de Triano quite so well as seven, at least when the ground is good to firm, and there's no doubt he'll stay the Guineas trip.

The first indications that Rodrigo de Triano would pay to follow in good company came at Newbury in July on his second start when, in a rousing battle with River Falls, he came seven lengths clear of a field containing five previous winners most of whom were, like himself, open to plenty of improvement. Two weeks earlier Rodrigo de Triano had overcome inexperience and a bad start to make a winning first appearance, in the EBF Franklin D. Roosevelt Stakes over six furlongs at Haydock Park; at Newbury, in the listed Manton Rose Bowl Stakes, he looked much nearer the finished article, although once again he gave the impression through the race that he'd win rather more easily than he did. Rodrigo de Triano was sensibly brought along steadily by his promising young trainer and was kept to listed company for his next outing, the Washington Singer Stakes over seven furlongs at Newbury in August. The slowish early gallop didn't make for a true test of stamina, and Rodrigo de Triano, who was conceding 5 lb all round, was able to utilize his turn of foot to excellent effect against four rivals, two of whom subsequently showed themselves to require a much stiffer test of stamina; Rodrigo de Triano swept past the front-running Anchorite with a furlong to run after being given a confident ride to win by a length and a half.

		Northern Dancer (b 1961)	Nearctic
			Natalma
Rodrigo de	El Gran Senor (USA) (b 1981)	Sex Appeal (ch 1970)	Buckpasser
Triano (USA)			Best In Show
(ch.c. May 27, 1989)	Hot Princess (ch 1980)	Hot Spark (ch 1972)	Habitat
			Garvey Girl
		Aspara (gr 1972)	Crimson Satan
			Courtside

When El Gran Senor was retired to stud he possessed everything looked for in a potentially top-class stallion. He was a handsome individual with a pedigree to match, being a son of Northern Dancer out of a mare who'd already produced the top-class two-year-old Try My Best; and, most importantly, he'd been an outstanding racehorse whose finest moment was a convincing victory over the strongest field assembled for the Two Thousand Guineas since 1971. Unfortunately El Gran Senor has been afflicted seriously by fertility problems for which a complete cure hasn't yet been found. Nevertheless his record shows he's a first-rate sire with an Average Earnings Index which places him in the top echelon of the stallion ranks and a high ratio of stakes winners to foals. Following a successful year in 1990, in which he was represented by the King George VI and Queen Elizabeth Stakes winner Belmez, he had four pattern-race winners besides Rodrigo de Triano in 1991 as diverse as the Meadow Meats Flying Five winner Flowing and the Gordon Stakes winner Stylish Senor, as well as Rodrigo de Triano's promising stable-companion El Cortes who's won his only race to date and is said to be rated by his trainer more highly than Dr Devious. Rodrigo de Triano, a late foal who wasn't born until the end of May, isn't anything like so well bred on his dam's side. Hot Princess, who's by the Flying Childers and Palace House winner but modest sire Hot Spark, was fairly useful as a two-year-old when she won a maiden over five furlongs at Leopardstown and a minor event over six furlongs at Navan, and was nearly as good in the following two seasons when she won the Ballycorus Stakes over seven furlongs at Leopardstown at three and three races up to a mile and a quarter in the States at four. Hot Princess, who has been repatriated from Australia by Coolmore, will probably be covered by Sadler's Wells. She had one living foal before Rodrigo de Triano, the 1990 two-year-old seven-furlong winner Cedrela (by Assert). Hot Princess is one of numerous winners from her dam Aspara, a modest maiden who was placed over five furlongs in both Britain and Ireland; all the other four who won here exhibited a shortage of stamina, none of them winning over so far as a mile, although Varuna, a dual winner over Brighton's seven furlongs, later had great success in Scandinavia where he ran placed in the Stockholm Cup, Sweden's top open event over middle distances. The third dam Courtside was a modest and infrequent producer and none of the fourth dam's progeny were particularly noteworthy. Assessed on his pedigree and style of racing, a mile

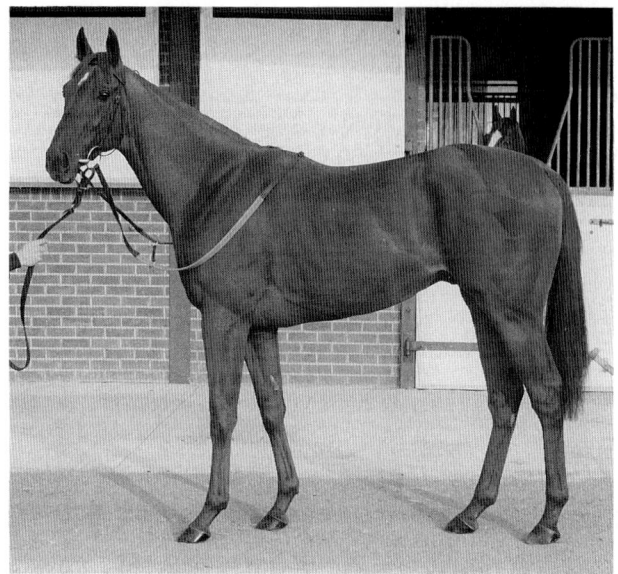

Mr R. E. Sangster's "Rodrigo de Triano"

should suit the quite good-topped Rodrigo de Triano, who has so far raced only on a sound surface. *P. W. Chapple-Hyam.*

ROGER DE BERKSTED (USA)   3 b.c. Topsider (USA) – Liberty Spirit **100** (USA) (Graustark) [1990 6g* 7v* 1991 8g 8m 8m 8g*] leggy, workmanlike colt: useful performer: 16/1, back to 2-y-o form to win 17-runner £8,100 handicap at Newbury in October, always front rank: stays 1m: seems to need give in the ground, and acts on heavy going: sold 21,000 gns Newmarket Autumn Sales. *J. H. M. Gosden.*

ROGERDOR (USA)   3 b.c. Tom Rolfe – Grand Bonheur (USA) (Blushing **93** Groom (FR) 131) [1990 NR 1991 10.6g 14.8f² 14.1f* 14.6m* 16.2f* 18.2f³ 16m] big, good-topped colt: has a long stride: good walker: fifth foal: half-brother to useful 7f and 1m winner Zarbyev (by Nureyev) and useful but disappointing 1988 2-y-o 6f winner Northern Tryst (by Northern Baby): dam won at up to 6f: won maiden at Yarmouth and handicaps (impressive) at Wolverhampton and Haydock in late-summer: bumped early and ran poorly in handicap at Newmarket final outing: stays well: blinkered last 6 starts. *G. Harwood.*

ROGER RABBIT (FR)   2 b.g. (Mar 7) Rusticaro (FR) 124 – Bustelda (FR) **55** (Busted 134) [1991 7g 5s a7g⁶] 4,200Y: sturdy, good-bodied gelding: sixth foal: half-brother to several winners, including 2m winner Bye Bye Baby (by Baby Turk) and 11.7f winner Esprit de Femme (by Esprit du Nord): dam unraced half-sister to good Italian colt Stifelius: plating-class form in maidens: bred to be well suited by at least 1m. *R. Boss.*

ROGER RAMJET (IRE)   3 b.c. Law Society (USA) 130 – Saraday (Northfields **103** (USA)) [1990 7m* 8d² 1991 11g 13m* 14m* 16.2g⁵ 12.3g] IR 32,000F, IR 42,000Y:

rangy, good-topped colt: carries condition: third foal: half-brother to a winner in Germany by Commanche Run: dam Irish staying maiden out of half-sister to Irish 2000 Guineas winner Northern Treasure: won maiden at Leopardstown at 2 yrs and minor events at the Curragh and Leopardstown at 3 yrs: 11/2, 12¾ lengths fifth of 13 to Jendali in Queen's Vase at Royal Ascot: pulled up lame in Ulster Harp Derby at Down Royal in July: stays 1¾m. *J. S. Bolger, Ireland.*

ROGERS NIECE   3 ch.f. Cree Song 99 – R Nancy (Immortal Knight 103) [1990   —
NR 1991 8g 9m 10f 8m] plain, angular filly: first foal: dam, poor maiden on flat, won over hurdles: no sign of ability: wears dropped noseband. *J. Parkes.*

ROKEBY   2 b.c. (Mar 26) Lomond (USA) 128 – Rose Bowl (USA) 131 (Habitat 134)   99
[1991 6d5 6m* 6g3 6m2 7d* 8m2 8d3 8s] smallish, sturdy, rather dipped-backed colt: moderate mover: half-brother to several winners, including very useful 7f and 1½m winner Golden Bowl (by Vaguely Noble) and 7f and 1¼m winner Antigua Rose (by Mill Reef): dam, outstanding 1m to 1¼m performer, is half-sister to top-class Ile de Bourbon: fairly useful performer: successful in maiden at Goodwood in May and listed event at Baden-Baden in August: ran well subsequently, including in Stardom Stakes at Goodwood (beaten 3 lengths by Seattle Rhyme) then Gran Criterium at Milan (won by Alhijaz) in October, final outing: should stay 1¼m: acts on good to firm and soft ground. *I. A. Balding.*

ROLFESON   7 b.h. Rolfe (USA) 77 – Do Something 77 (Pardao 120) [1990 10m3   59
8.2m* 9.1m2 8f* 9g 8g 8m 8g 8.2d 1991 8d 8.3d2 8.3m 8.9g 10m5 10g 8.1s] sturdy, good-quartered horse: good mover: quite modest handicapper: lost his form: effective at 1m to 1¼m: acts on firm and dead going: good mount for apprentice. *B. C. Morgan.*

ROLL A DOLLAR   5 b.g. Spin of A Coin 88 – Handy Dancer 87 (Green God 128)   96   +
[1990 12g 12m3 16m4 22d5 12f3 14g 12m* 11s 1991 12g 12g 13.9g2] tall, workmanlike gelding: good mover: fairly useful handicapper: 33/1, returned to form when third (promoted to second) of 22 to Deposki in Tote Ebor at York, staying on well in straight despite being hampered 1½f out: effective at 1½m to 2m: acts on firm going, probably unsuited by soft. *D. R. C. Elsworth.*

ROLY WALLACE   2 b.c. (Mar 11) Primo Dominie 121 – Ethel Knight (Thatch   60   §
(USA) 136) [1991 6g6 6f2 5m2 6g 5.7m3 6f2 6f* 6m6 7m 6f 7f 5m 6m 6m4] neat colt: second live foal: half-brother to 5f to 7f winner Miss Knight (by Longleat): dam lightly raced: quite modest performer: won maiden auction at Folkestone in August: mostly well below form afterwards but creditable strong-finishing fourth of 15 in Pontefract nursery (looked unco-operative early on) in October: stays 6f: acts on firm ground: has run well in blinkers: bandaged ninth to eleventh outings: one to be bit wary of: sold 2,100 gns Newmarket Autumn Sales. *K. T. Ivory.*

ROMAN FAN (IRE)   3 b.f. Taufan (USA) 119 – Crepe Myrtle 80 (Crepello 136)   —
[1990 5m 1991 6g 7g a10g] sparely-made filly: no sign of ability, in selling handicap final start: bred to stay 1m: bandaged behind penultimate start: sold 725 gns Ascot September Sales. *M. Bell.*

ROMANIAN (IRE)   3 ch.c. Sallust 134 – Cailin d'Or (Roi Soleil 135) [1990 6d5   61
6m5 6d6 1991 8f2 10d 8f3 8m2 8g 9.7m3 12f4 10m] compact colt: quite modest maiden: placed at Brighton (twice), Salisbury (handicap) and Folkestone: should stay 1½m: clearly best efforts on top-of-the-ground: bandaged and on toes fifth start. *A. R. Davison.*

ROMAN PROSE   6 ch.g. Sallust 134 – Mothers Girl (Huntercombe 133) [1990   116
6g* 5.5v3 6g* 6s2 6g3 6d4 6f* 1991 6v4 6g2 6.5g* 6g3 6d5] workmanlike, sparely-made gelding: smart sprinter: won Group 2 Prix Maurice de Gheest at Deauville in August by 2 lengths from Masterclass: length second to Divine Danse in Prix de Ris-Orangis previous month: below form last 2 starts: suited by 6f and a sound surface: tried visored once. *J. E. Pease, France.*

ROMANSH   2 b.c. (Apr 7) Shernazar 131 – Romara 105 (Bold Lad (IRE) 133) [1991   67   p
7m 8m5] tall, angular colt: eighth living foal: closely related to 1m and 1¼m winner Halstead (by Bustino) and 1985 2-y-o 6f winner Bustara (by Busted) and half-brother to several winners, including smart 6f and 1¼m winner Ela Romara (by Ela-Mana-Mou): dam 7f and 1m winner: not fully wound up but shaped well in late-season maidens won by Stani and Pabouche at Leicester: seems likely to be better suited by middle distances: will improve again. *G. Wragg.*

ROMANTIC DANCER   2 b.g. (Feb 14) Lidhame 109 – Good Time Girl 65 (Good   52
Times (ITY)) [1991 6g5 6m 6m 6g 7f6 7g5 10m] leggy gelding: moderate mover: first foal: dam 2-y-o 5f and 6f seller winner: fair plater: suited by 7f: none too easy a ride:

716

races keenly, and usually wears a severe noseband: sold 825 gns Ascot December Sales. *R. Curtis.*

ROMANY RYE 3 ch.c. Nijinsky (CAN) 138 – Zinzara (USA) 119 (Stage Door **101** p Johnny) [1990 NR 1991 12m³ 12m⁴ 14m² 14.6f² 13.9m* 15m* 13.9m² 16g3] big, lengthy colt: has plenty of scope: carries condition: easy mover: third foal: brother to useful 1½m winner Zinsky and closely related to once-raced 1990 3-y-o Romany Marsh (by Lomond): dam 6f and 1¼m winner: successful in smallish fields for maiden at York in June and minor event at Ayr in September: good efforts after, behind Hawait Al Barr in minor event at York and listed race at Newmarket: will prove better suited by 2m than shorter: acts on firm going: useful, and may well improve again at 4 yrs. *G. Wragg.*

ROMOLA NIJINSKY 3 b.f. Bustino 136 – Verchinina 99 (Star Appeal 133) **88** [1990 NR 1991 7m⁵ 7g⁴ 10g⁵ 11.9m 8g5] workmanlike filly: third foal: dam 1m winner: progressive form first 3 starts, making most when fifth of 9 in listed race at Goodwood: last afterwards in Lancashire Oaks at Haydock and minor event at Newmarket: better at 1¼m than shorter: sold to join P. Evans 3,800 gns Newmarket Autumn Sales. *C. E. Brittain.*

RONALD IVOR 5 b.h. Bold Lad (IRE) 133 – Lady Probus 70§ (Shantung 132) — [1990 10f 8m 12d⁶ 8.2m 8g 8f 1991 10s] angular ex-Irish horse: poor mover: won handicaps at Phoenix Park and Galway as 3-y-o: well beaten, including in handicaps after: best form at about 1m: acts on good to firm going. *C. F. C. Jackson.*

RON'S VICTORY (USA) 4 ch.c. General Holme (USA) 128 – Tea And **115** Scandals (USA) (Key To The Kingdom (USA)) [1990 8d⁵ 7m² 5g* 5m² 5d² 6g* 6g⁵ 6m* 6f² 1991 5s³ 6g6] quite attractive colt: high-class performer at 3 yrs, best effort when winning Krug Diadem Stakes at Ascot by 10 lengths: below best in first half of 1991, better effort when ¾-length third to Pont Aven (rec 7 lb) in Prix de Saint-Georges at Longchamp: suited by 6f: went very well on top-of-the-ground: sometimes wore bandages behind: retired to New England Stud, Newmarket, fee £3,000 (Oct 1st terms). *A. J. Falourd, France.*

ROOFING (IRE) 3 b.c. Thatching 131 – Joanne's Joy (Ballymore 123) [1990 7m² **88** 1991 7m⁶ 8m* 8g² 7.1s] sturdy, quite attractive colt: has a quick action: fair performer: won maiden at Doncaster in May: unlikely to stay much beyond 1m: acts on good to firm ground: blinkered final start: sold 13,000 gns Newmarket September Sales, reportedly to race in Scandinavia. *B. W. Hills.*

ROOKERY PARK 2 b.c. (Apr 19) Efisio 120 – Majuba Road (Scottish Rifle 127) — [1991 5f 5m a6g a8g] good-bodied colt: poor mover: first reported foal: dam winning jumper: seems of little account. *J. Ffitch-Heyes.*

ROOM WITH A VIEW (IRE) 2 ch.c. (May 17) Doulab (USA) 115 – Westview **77** 84 (Shirley Heights 130) [1991 6m⁶ 6.1m* 6.3s] 9,000Y: tall, lengthy, angular colt: third foal: dam 13f winner: second favourite after promising debut, narrowly won 23-runner maiden auction at Nottingham in September, staying on strongly from over 2f out: out of his depth in Goffs Premier Challenge Race at the Curragh 19 days later: will be better suited by 7f. *R. M. Whitaker.*

ROSA WHY (IRE) 2 b.f. (Feb 24) Damister (USA) 123 – Fallen Rose (Busted **57** 134) [1991 6g 6m⁴ 7m² 8.2m⁶ a7g] rather finely-made, quite attractive filly: plating-class maiden: likely to stay well: acts on good to firm ground, and on fibresand. *W. Jarvis.*

ROSCOES DINKY 4 br.f. Roscoe Blake 120 – Minibus 77 (John Splendid 116) — [1990 7g 10.2h 1991 a6g a12g 9.7f] leggy filly: no promise, in seller (blinkered) final start. *W. G. M. Turner.*

ROSE ALTO 3 ch.f. Adonijah 126 – Rose Music 86 (Luthier 126) [1990 8g⁵ 1991 **84** 8m⁶ 10g⁴ 9.9m* 9.9f* 10g 10m] leggy, rather close-coupled filly: progressive form to win summer handicaps at Beverley: unimpressive in coat when behind in similar events afterwards, rearing stalls final start: stays 1¼m well: acts on firm going: game. *J. R. Fanshawe.*

ROSEATE LODGE 5 b.g. Habitat 134 – Elegant Tern (USA) 102 (Sea Bird II **89** 145) [1990 9g 8f² 8.2m 8f² 8.2s² 8.3m 9g 8g³ 8g* 8m* 8m² 1991 8g² 8d² 8g⁶ 8m⁴ 8g 10g 8.9g⁶ 8.1m⁶ 9m] compact, workmanlike gelding: fair handicapper: ran moderately final 2 starts: stays 9f: acts on any going. *R. W. Armstrong.*

ROSE CUT (USA) 4 ch.c. Diesis 133 – Sweet Ramblin Rose (USA) (Turn-To) — [1990 8.3f 11.7m 10g⁵ 8g 1991 12d 14.1f6] no worthwhile form, in handicaps in 1991: trained until after reappearance by J. Fanshawe. *P. J. Feilden.*

ROSE D'ETOILE 3 b.f. Jalmood (USA) 126 – Angelic Appeal (Star Appeal 133) —
[1990 5f⁵ 5m⁵ 5m 6d 1991 6f 8f 10g 10g] sparely-made filly: has a moderate, round
action: poor maiden: bred to stay at least 1m. *W. Carter.*

ROSE ELEGANCE 2 ch.f. (Apr 16) Bairn (USA) 126 – Shapina 105 (Sharp Edge **73** p
123) [1991 7.1d⁴] leggy filly: third living foal: half-sister to 1984 2-y-o 6f winner
Thorny Rose (by Tap On Wood), later successful at up to 11.7f, and 6f winner
Elegant Rose (by Noalto): dam won Fred Darling Stakes: 33/1, very green and
ridden by 7-lb claimer, eye-catching fourth of 18 to impressive Never A Care in
maiden at Chepstow in October, travelling smoothly at halfway and keeping on
strongly under considerate handling: sure to improve. *W. R. Muir.*

ROSE GEM (IRE) 2 b.f. (Apr 28) Taufan (USA) 119 – Mombones (Lord Gayle **51**
(USA) 124) [1991 6g 6m³ 7m] IR 8,600F, 13,000Y: rather leggy filly: half-sister to
several winners, including useful 7f to 10.6f winner Hoyer (by Rarity) and 12.3f
winner Doctor Rhythm (by Cure The Blues): dam unraced half-sister to high-class
6f and 7f performer Court Chad: plating-class maiden: well below form in 7f
Newmarket seller in July: races keenly, and wore crossed noseband final 2
starts: sold 2,000 gns Doncaster November Sales. *A. A. Scott.*

ROSE GLEN 5 b.m. Lochnager 132 – Phoenix Rose 85 (Frankincense 120) [1990 **75**
8f⁶ 8g 7m 7g 6m⁶ 7m³ 6g 7d 8d 7m⁴ 7m 1991 a8g 7d⁶ 7m 8m⁵ 10.6g⁴ 9m* 10.3d*
10.5m² 10.9g* 10.9m* 10.5g⁵ 10.5f 10m³ 9m 10.3d³ 9g] big, workmanlike mare: has
a rather round action: modest performer: in excellent form in summer, successful in
claimers at Redcar and Chester and amateurs handicap and claimer at Ayr: effective
at 9f to 11f: acts on firm and dead ground: effective with or without blinkers or visor:
tough and genuine. *A. Bailey.*

ROSEHILL PARK 3 b.c. Nishapour (FR) 125 – Aquarula 88 (Dominion 123) —
[1990 5m 6d 1991 7g 10.1d⁵ 16.2d] small, angular colt: moderate walker: little form,
hampered and unseating rider early on final outing. *D. Marks.*

ROSE INDIEN (FR) 2 br.f. (Feb 21) Crystal Glitters (USA) 127 – Green Rosy **102** p
(USA) (Green Dancer (USA) 132) [1991 6.1f² 6m* 7m*] 480,000 francs (approx
£48,000) Y: leggy, lengthy filly: second foal: dam French 1½m winner: won maiden
at Goodwood in September: followed up in minor event at Newmarket 3 weeks later,
making all and winning by a length from Enaya: will stay 1m: sort to keep improving.
M. Moubarak.

ROSE OF EIRE (USA) 2 b.f. (Feb 10) Irish Tower (USA) – Beautiful You **67**
(USA) (Bold Native (USA)) [1991 6m³ 5g* 5m⁵ 5g² 5g⁵] $52,000Y: close-coupled,
useful-looking filly: sister to 2 winners in USA including a Grade 3 5.3f winner at 2
yrs, and half-sister to 2 others: dam ran 3 times: sire stakes winner from 5f to 1¼m:
odds on, made all in 5-runner maiden at Edinburgh in July: ran as if something amiss
third start, poorly in Ayr nursery final outing: stays 6f: swished tail on debut. *J.
Berry.*

ROSE OF MACMILLION 2 b.f. (Apr 22) Macmillion 110 – Tic-On-Rose **39**
(Celtic Cone 116) [1991 6f 7m] rangy filly: has a round action: third foal: dam, 2m
hurdles winner, is sister to a useful staying hurdler: poor form in autumn maidens:
should stay middle distances. *Mrs Barbara Waring.*

ROSE REVIVED 2 b.f. (Feb 25) Persian Bold 123 – Mums 88 (Mummy's Pet **56**
125) [1991 5m⁴ 6f 6g] small filly: third foal: half-sister to 3-y-o Parr (by Salmon
Leap): dam ran only at 2 yrs, winning at 5f: plating-class maiden: will stay beyond 5f:
sold 2,100 gns Newmarket Autumn Sales. *M. R. Stoute.*

ROSES HAVE THORNS 4 ch.f. Ela-Mana-Mou 132 – Cienaga (Tarboosh **64** d
(USA)) [1990 8m⁵ 10.6s 8.3f* 8g⁶ 9m 1991 10d² 10g 10d 10.4m 10.2g⁵ 10m 12m³
11.5f⁴ 11m⁵ 11.8m⁵ 12m 12m² 10.3g⁵] leggy, rather shallow-girthed filly: has a rather
round action: poor handicapper nowadays: stays 1½m well: acts on firm and dead
ground: effective visored or not: found little penultimate start. *D. Morris.*

ROSGILL 5 ch.g. Mill Reef (USA) 141 – Speedy Rose (On Your Mark 125) [1990 **76**
14f⁴ 13.3m⁶ 11.5m* 11.5m⁴ 12f 11.5m⁴ 15g⁴ 13f² 12f³ 11.5m³ 14g⁴ 16f² 1991 a13g³
a13g³ 11.5m² 12v* 11.5s* 12.2d² 14m 14s 12d² 16m 12d] angular gelding: modest
handicapper: won at Kempton and Lingfield in summer: effective at 1½m to 2m: acts
on any going, but particularly well suited by give: has carried head high: has won for
lady. *P. Mitchell.*

ROSGWEN 4 ch.f. Remainder Man 126§ – Pamkins Hart (Pamroy 99) [1990 12m —
12.5g 1991 a5g a7g 10.3d 10.2g 14.6m] close-coupled filly: seems of little account. *C.
A. Smith.*

ROSIE'S MAC (IRE) 2 b.c. (Feb 8) Petorius 117 – Repicado Rose (USA) **91**
(Repicado (CHI)) [1991 7g* 8s⁶ 7s³] 26,000Y: sixth foal: brother to useful 1990

3-y-o 7f to 1¼m winner Halston Prince (best on top-of-the-ground) and half-brother to 2 other winners: dam placed in USA: comfortable winner of maiden at Fairyhouse in October: fairly useful form subsequently in Juddmonte EBF Beresford Stakes at the Curragh (won by El Prado) and Leopardstown Stakes (beaten 6 lengths by Swing Low) later same month: should stay 1¼m: yet to race on top-of-the-ground. *D. Hanley, Ireland.*

ROSIETOES (USA) 3 b.f. Master Willie 129 – Desrose 74 (Godswalk (USA) 130) [1990 6m² 5.8h² 6g 7d⁵ 1991 7m³ 8g² 8.3m 7m² 9d 8m] leggy, angular filly: quite modest form placed in claimers at Epsom and Newmarket (twice): suited by 1m: below form on dead ground: sold to join G. Cottrell 4,800 gns Newmarket Autumn Sales. *P. J. Makin.* **67**

ROSSANITA (IRE) 3 b.f. Anita's Prince 126 – Chanrossa (High Top 131) [1990 NR 1991 6s³ 6f 5.9h⁴ 7g 6f 8.2m 8m] 2,600Y: lengthy, workmanlike filly: carries condition: moderate mover: third living foal: half-sister to 5f winner Love Prince (by Indian King): dam unraced half-sister to dam of Shady Heights: no worthwhile form: blinkered final outing. *N. Bycroft.* **—**

ROSS GRAHAM 3 gr.g. Macmillion 110 – Play It Sam (Mandamus 120) [1990 NR 1991 8m 12g 14.6d³] lengthy, leggy gelding: first reported living foal: dam lightly raced and of little account over hurdles: 66/1, first worthwhile form when 5 lengths third of 10 to Bean King in minor event at Doncaster in November: gives impression should prove suited by test of stamina. *Mrs Barbara Waring.* **75**

ROSTANDS HERO (IRE) 2 b.g. (Apr 25) Cyrano de Bergerac 120 – Miel (Pall Mall 132) [1991 5m 8m 8d] IR 9,200F, 5,000Y, 5,400 2-y-o: smallish, good-bodied gelding: poor mover: half-brother to several winners, including useful middle-distance stayer Prince of Peace (by Busted) and 1988 2-y-o 1m winner Evanna's Pride (by Main Reef): dam never ran: poor maiden: blinkered second start, visored (best effort) final one. *H. J. Collingridge.* **43**

ROSTHERNE 9 ch.g. Crimson Beau 124 – Correct Approach 77 (Right Tack 131) [1990 13s 1991 a12g 15.8g* 16.2f6] leggy, lengthy gelding: poor handicapper nowadays: enterprisingly ridden to win at Catterick: again blinkered, ran moderately later in July: stays 2m: seems suited by give in the ground: often used to sweat. *R. O'Leary.* **41**

ROSUDGEON 3 ch.g. Undulate (USA) – April Rose (Wollow 132) [1990 5m 6g 7f 5.3h⁴ 1991 10m] sparely-made, close-coupled gelding: poor plater: edgy, well beaten in August, sole 3-y-o start: should stay at least 7f: sold 725 gns Ascot November Sales. *W. G. R. Wightman.* **—**

ROSY SAKER 3 ch.f. Absalom 128 – Anoda (FR) (Amber Rama (USA) 133) [1990 5g⁵ 5m⁶ 5m³ 5f⁴ 5m⁶ 5v² 1991 a5g⁴ 5s⁶ 5g⁶ 6f⁴ 5.1m⁵ 7d] smallish, workmanlike filly: poor walker: has a round action: plater: should stay 6f: acts on any going. *W. G. M. Turner.* **39**

ROUCELLIST BAY 3 ch.g. Rousillon (USA) 133 – Cellist (USA) (Bagdad) [1990 6m 1991 12.2m 13.8f5] leggy, sparely-made, plain gelding: no sign of ability in maiden and claimers: bandaged off-hind on reappearance. *S. E. Kettlewell.* **—**

ROUND BY THE RIVER 2 b.f. (Apr 5) Superlative 118 – Marie Galante 73 (Shirley Heights 130) [1991 5m 7m⁵ 5g⁶] 1,800Y: second foal: dam maiden stayed 14.8f: plating-class maiden: caught eye when slow-starting sixth of 12 at Redcar in October, making late progress under considerate ride: really needs further than 5f, and will stay at least 1m: gives impression capable of winning a seller. *W. W. Haigh.* **59**

ROUSETTE (IRE) 2 b.f. (Feb 2) Rousillon (USA) 133 – Sally Rose 92 (Sallust 134) [1991 6m³ 8g5] small, quite attractive filly: sixth foal: half-sister to 3-y-o 14.1f winner Mountain Bloom (by Shirley Heights), French 1m and 10.5f winner Prairie (by Posse) and 1986 2-y-o 7f winner Trojan Miss (by Troy), later useful over middle distances: dam won 3 times from 1m to 10.2f: weak 11/2-shot and burly, 2 lengths third of 6 to Isaiah in maiden at York, green early then running on well from 2f out: failed to progress in similar event at Bath later in October: should be suited by at least 1m. *Lord Huntingdon.* **68**

ROUSILLON TO BE 4 b.c. Rousillon (USA) 133 – Triple Bar 71 (Jimmy Reppin 131) [1990 11g² 12.3f3 12f² 16f 10g5 a16g 1991 a11g a12g⁶] big, leggy colt: quite modest maiden at best: no form in early part of 1991: should be suited by 1¾m, probably doesn't stay 2m: has carried head high and wandered under pressure: joined J. Davies. *J. D. Bethell.* **—**

ROUSITTO 3 ch.c. Rousillon (USA) 133 – Helenetta 97 (Troy 137) [1990 NR 1991 8d³ 8s⁶ 10.1s* 8g³ 8.2m 10.1g⁴ 9m] 12,000Y: tall, angular colt: moderate mover: second foal: half-brother to 1¼m winner Helen's Guest (by Be My Guest): dam **72**

suited by 1½m, is out of very useful middle-distance performer Lauretta: won median auction contest at Windsor in April and unlucky next start: ran well penultimate outing: never dangerous in Cambridgeshire at Newmarket 4 months later: effective at 1m and 1¼m: may well need give in the ground: carries head rather awkwardly: trained first 6 starts by K. Ivory. *R. Hollinshead.*

ROUTING   3 b.c. Rousillon (USA) 133 – Tura (Northfields (USA)) [1990 6g² 5f   **61** 7d⁴ 7m⁵ 6m 1991 6f⁶ 10f* 10g⁴ 9m⁶ 8g³ 9m⁵ 8.1m³ 9.2f] angular colt: quite modest handicapper: won at Folkestone in May, hanging left: below form final start, leading 6f: effective at 1m and 1¼m: acts on firm going (best 2-y-o effort on dead): has found little and carried head awkwardly: somewhat headstrong: claimed out of M. Bell's stable £8,000 fifth start: not one to trust implicitly. *M. D. Hammond.*

ROUYAN   5 b.g. Akarad (FR) 130 – Rosy Moon (FR) (Sheshoon 132) [1990 14m   **?** 1991 12s³ 14.8m 12g⁶] rangy, good-bodied gelding: fair handicapper as 3-y-o: flattered when third in £14,100 event at Doncaster in March: looked none too keen when tailed off next start: stays 1¾m well: has wandered, and takes keen hold: fairly useful hurdler: temperament under suspicion: joined Mrs J. Pitman. *R. Simpson.*

ROVIRIS   3 b.c. Sir Ivor 135 – Royal Caprice (USA) (Swaps) [1990 10.2s 1991   **—** 15.3m⁶ 10.1f⁵ 14.1f] big, rangy colt: no form in minor event, maidens and handicap. *Mrs L. Piggott.*

ROWANDENE (IRE)   2 gr.g. (Feb 11) Wassl 125 – Hysteria (Prince Bee 128)   **48** [1991 5g⁶] small gelding: first foal: dam unraced daughter of German 7f to 9f winner Kallista, herself daughter of good German mare Kandia: beaten over 3 lengths when keeping-on sixth of 10 in maiden at Thirsk in May. *M. H. Easterby.*

ROWAN GREY   2 gr.f. (Feb 26) Ilium 121 – Little Token (Shack (USA) 118) [1991   **52 d** 5f a6g* 6m⁶ a6g⁵ 5f⁵ 6m⁴ 8m 5m 6m] 1,500Y: small filly: poor mover: first foal: dam ran twice: won seller (retained 3,800 gns) at Southwell in June: well beaten last 3 starts: better suited by 6f than 5f, and should stay further: reluctant stalls fourth start. *A. Smith.*

ROWHEDGE   5 ch.g. Tolomeo 127 – Strident Note 89 (The Minstrel (CAN) 135)   **—** [1990 8.3g 1991 a12g] smallish, lengthy gelding: thrice raced and no form on flat, including in seller: has won over hurdles. *W. M. Perrin.*

ROWLANDSONS GEMS   6 ch.g. Enchantment 115 – Lillicara (FR) (Caraco-   **75** lero (USA) 131) [1990 NR 1991 a10g* a8g] robust gelding: moderate mover: modest handicapper, lightly raced nowadays: won at Lingfield in February by 6 lengths: not seen out after March: better suited by 1¼m than 1m: acts on firm going, possibly unsuited by soft surface: effective blinkered or not: winning hurdler. *D. J. G. Murray-Smith.*

ROWLANDSONS TROPHY   6 b.g. Vaigly Great 127 – Queen's Parade (Sove-   **—** reign Path 125) [1990 NR 1991 14.8g 17.1m] strong, lengthy, dipped-backed gelding: poor handicapper nowadays: best form at 1¼m on soft surface: ran poorly when blinkered. *M. R. Channon.*

ROXY MUSIC (IRE)   2 b.f. (Mar 25) Song 132 – Roxy Hart (High Top 131) [1991   **63** 5m 5m⁴ a5g⁴ 7m⁴ a7g² 7.1m* 9m⁶ 7m⁵] IR 35,000Y: compact filly: sister to modest 7f winner Sawaki and fair 6f and 7.6f winner Farras, and half-sister to 2 winners, including 3-y-o Don't Presume (by Pharly), successful at 6f (at 2 yrs) and 1m: dam unraced half-sister to good sprinter Music Maestro and smart 1985 2-y-o Outer Circle: quite modest performer: apprentice ridden, won selling nursery at Sandown (game winner, bought in 8,000 gns) in August: helped set very fast pace when below form at Sandown (non-seller) penultimate start: stays 7f: acts well on top-of-the-ground. *G. A. Pritchard-Gordon.*

ROYAL ACCLAIM   6 ch.g. Tender King 123 – Glimmer 58 (Hot Spark 126)   **55 d** [1990 7.6m² 7m³ 7.6g 8m 7m² 7.6f³ 7g* 7m² 7m² 8m* 8m 8d 7g³ 1991 7.6g 8d* 8g 8g⁶ 7.6m⁴ 8f 10.1f⁵ 8f⁴ 8m a12g⁶] sturdy gelding: carries condition: quite modest handicapper at best: won at Salisbury in June: stays 1m: yet to race on soft going, acts on any other: usually blinkered or visored: has started slowly: often races with head high: sold out of A. Hide's stable 2,500 gns Ascot October Sales after penultimate start: none too resolute, and best left alone. *J. M. Bradley.*

ROYAL ALASKA   5 br.h. Hotfoot 126 – Snow Damsel (Mandamus 120) [1990 NR   **—** 1991 a14g⁶ 16.2g 14.1f] small, lengthy horse: plating-class maiden at 3 yrs: well beaten after, including in handicaps: stays 1½m: acts on soft going: has been tried visored and blinkered. *P. Burgoyne.*

ROYAL ASTRONAUT (USA)   7 ch.g. Grey Dawn II 132 – Short Stanza (USA)   **—** (Verbatim (USA)) [1990 NR 1991 14.8m] lengthy gelding: modest handicapper at 5 yrs: tailed off at Warwick in April, only subsequent run on flat: will stay beyond 2m: goes very well with plenty of give in the ground: fairly useful hurdler. *R. Akehurst.*

ROYAL BLUE BELL (USA)   3 ch.f. Sharpen Up 127 – Irish Royal (USA) (Irish   79
River (FR) 131) [1990 NR 1991 7g* 7g 8g4] 62,000Y: leggy filly: second reported foal: dam unraced half-sister to very useful American colt T V Series: won 4-runner maiden at Newmarket in August: second favourite, slowly away, headway to chase leaders 2f out, no extra and eased right down in York listed race: 5½ lengths fourth of 5 to Democratic in minor event at Leicester, taking keen hold: stays 1m. *L. M. Cumani.*

ROYAL BOROUGH   6 b.g. Bustino 136 – Lady R B (USA) (Gun Shot) [1990   —
12g* 12g4 14g6 12f 1991 12s 12m 12.3g 11.9m 12d] leggy gelding: has a quick action: fair handicapper at best: no show in first half of 1991, tailed off final start: best form at 1½m: best runs on good ground: has been bandaged off-hind: takes keen hold, and best held up: sold to join M. Naughton's stable 13,000 gns Doncaster August Sales. *J. L. Dunlop.*

ROYAL CIRCUS   2 b.c. (Mar 1) Kris 135 – Circus Ring 122 (High Top 131) [1991   49
6f 8m] 18,000Y: workmanlike colt: fifth live foal: half-brother to very useful 7f (at 2 yrs) and 1¼m winner Lady Shipley (by Shirley Heights) and winning French middle-distance stayer Douglas Fir (by Busted): dam unbeaten at 2 yrs, including in Lowther Stakes, ran once afterwards: form only on debut when slow-starting eighth of 9, never a factor, in maiden at Folkestone in October: should stay 1m. *P. W. Harris.*

ROYAL DARTMOUTH (USA)   6 ch.g. Czaravich (USA) – Blushing Emy   53
(USA) (Blushing Groom (FR) 131) [1990 8m* 8f* 7g 8m2 10g4 8m 8.3m* 8.3f4 8g 1991 7g5 10m 8d6 7.1m3 8.5m2 8g 8g4 8.3g3 8f] tall, lengthy gelding: plating-class handicapper: best at 7f or 1m: acts on any going: often wears dropped noseband: has been slowly away: has found little in front. *B. R. Millman.*

ROYALE ROBINIA (IRE)   3 ch.g. Never So Bold 135 – Ring The Changes 72   78
(Auction Ring (USA) 123) [1990 NR 1991 6m5 6h* 5m2 6d* 6m4 6g 6m 6m] 21,000Y: lengthy, good-quartered gelding: moderate mover and walker: fifth foal: half-brother to useful 6f and 7f winner Bell Tower (by Lyphard's Wish) and a winner in USA by Diamond Prospect: dam 5f winner at 3 yrs: won maiden at Carlisle in May and handicap at Newbury in June: last of 28 in Ayr Gold Cup final start, second in 2 days: may well stay 7f: acts on hard and dead going: sold 5,800 gns Newmarket Autumn Sales. *R. M. Whitaker.*

ROYAL GIRL   4 b.f. Kafu 120 – Royal Aunt (Martinmas 128) [1990 7f 1991 8d]   —
angular filly: very lightly raced and no worthwhile form: not seen after being with-drawn lame in May. *Miss S. E. Hall.*

ROYAL MARRIAGE   3 b.f. King of Spain 121 – Princess Story 64 (Prince de   —
Galles 125) [1990 5f 6m 7m 8d 8.2d a8g a8g4 1991 10.2f5 10.2d 8d6 12g6 12g3 12f6 12g5 10m] leggy filly: poor maiden nowadays: worth a try over further: acts on dead ground: hung right sixth (visored) and seventh starts: joined Mrs J. Retter. *M. D. I. Usher.*

ROYAL MAZI   4 b.f. Kings Lake (USA) 133 – Seven Seas (FR) 78 (Riverman   —
(USA) 131) [1990 11.5g 12g5 14g 14m3 16f* 16s 1991 12d 16.2g 17.1m] angular, workmanlike filly: good walker: moderate mover: plating-class performer at 3 yrs: no form in 1991, blinkered final start, first for 5½ months: stays 2m: best efforts on top-of-the-ground: sold 800 gns Ascot December Sales. *C. R. Beever.*

ROYAL OBERON (IRE)   3 b.c. Fairy King (USA) – Broadway Royal (Royal   69
Match 117) [1990 NR 1991 7d3 7.6d3] IR 60,000Y: leggy, lengthy colt: half-brother to 4 winners, including fair 5f and 6f winner Royal Crofter (by Crofter) and 1989 2-y-o 7f winner Broadway Star (by Alzao): dam never ran: third in newcomers race at Doncaster: blinkered, gave trouble at stalls and soon beaten in 4-runner maiden at Chester in May: dead. *P. F. I. Cole.*

ROYAL OPERA STAR   2 b.c. (Mar 19) King Among Kings 60 – Rojael   —
(Mansingh (USA) 120) [1991 6g] small colt: third living foal: dam never ran: 250/1, slow-starting last-but-one in 25-runner Racecall Gold Trophy at Redcar in October. *Miss H. C. Knight.*

ROYAL PASSION   4 ch.f. Ahonoora 122 – Courtesy Call (Northfields (USA))   60
[1990 8m6 8g 8g 10f 10d* 10.2s* 9g3 1991 10.8m 10g 12v 12m4 10g 10.5d6 10.3g* 10.3d] lengthy filly: shows a quick action: quite modest handicapper: won seller at Doncaster (no bid) in October: stays 1½m: acts on good to firm and soft ground: below form for lady rider: inconsistent. *M. A. Jarvis.*

ROYAL PRINT (IRE)   2 ch.g. (Feb 26) Kings Lake (USA) 133 – Reprint 99   **52 p**
(Kampala 120) [1991 7m 7m5] IR 4,200Y: compact gelding: second foal: dam Irish
1¼m winner: better effort when around 7 lengths fifth of 12 to Casteddu in maiden at
Lingfield in September, prominent from start, one pace under hands and heels
closing stages: likely to stay 1¼m: should improve again. *W. R. Muir.*

ROYAL PRUSSIA (CAN)   2 b.c. (Mar 9) Danzig (USA) – Avowal (CAN)   **83**
(L'Enjoleur (CAN)) [1991 6m4 7f4 6.1m3 7g*] compact, good-quartered, attractive
colt: third reported foal: half-brother to Adarling (by Alleged), minor stakes winner
at about 1m: dam champion 3-y-o and champion sprinter in Canada: fair performer:
improved form when winning maiden at Warwick in October by a neck, clear, from
Green Lane, making all: stays 7f: races keenly. *H. R. A. Cecil.*

ROYAL RESORT   4 b.f. King of Spain 121 – Regency Brighton (Royal Palace   **40**
131) [1990 8f6 10.2f4 10.2f3 10.2f3 10.2f5 10m 10.2f5 8.2v3 a8g 1991 7d8* 8m 5m3 7f5
7m 8.3g4 7m2 7m] leggy, angular filly: poor handicapper: won selling event (no bid)
at Brighton in April: needs further than 5f, and stays 10.2f: acts on firm and dead
going: races keenly: none too consistent. *R. J. Hodges.*

ROYAL RUPERT   4 ro.g. Royal Match 117 – Bidula (Manacle 123) [1990 NR 1991   —
12.5d4] leggy gelding: fifth foal: half-brother to a winning plater: dam never ran:
tailed off in NH Flat race in February: 50/1, showed signs of ability when staying-on
fourth in claimer at Wolverhampton in April. *R. T. Juckes.*

ROYAL SEATON   2 b.c. (Feb 24) Blakeney 126 – Aldbury Girl 79 (Galivanter   **90**
131) [1991 5s* 6m 7g4 7.9g4 7d4 6g] 10,500Y: close-coupled colt: half-brother to
several winners, including fairly useful 6f to 1m winner Absonal (by Absalom): dam
2-y-o 5.9f winner: fairly useful performer: wide-margin winner of Windsor maiden in
April: good seventh of 25 to Casteddu in Racecall Gold Trophy at Redcar final start:
stays 1m: acts on soft ground, well below best on good to firm: has run well when
sweating. *B. R. Millman.*

ROYAL SQUARE (CAN)   5 ch.h. Gregorian (USA) 115 – Dance Crazy (USA)   **86**
(Foolish Pleasure (USA)) [1990 16g 1991 16g 20g 16d 16f2 14m] big, strong horse:
fair handicapper nowadays: good second at Thirsk: unable to dictate pace when well
beaten at Sandown later in August: stays 2m: acts on firm going: suited by a
galloping track: useful hurdler. *G. Harwood.*

ROYAL STANDARD   4 b.c. Sadler's Wells (USA) 132 – Princess Tiara 111   **88**
(Crowned Prince (USA) 128) [1990 10m 12m5 12g 11g2 16m* 14f5 12m* 14d* 1991
12.2d2 14m4 14d4 12m 13m3* 13.1m4 16.2d 16m2 16.5d*] rangy, attractive colt: shows
knee action: fair handicapper: won at Ayr in June and Doncaster (soon in rear) in
November: stays 16.5f: acts on firm and dead going: visored after running in
snatches and carrying head high fourth start at 3 yrs: seemed to take little interest
fourth start in 1991: usually forces pace: joined C. Brooks. *J. Etherington.*

ROYAL STEEL   4 ch.g. Kings Lake (USA) 133 – All Souls 96 (Saint Crespin III   —
132) [1990 10.6d a14g 1991 14m 12.3d] seems of little account. *R. Hollinshead.*

ROYAL SULTAN   2 b.g. (May 8) Destroyer 105 – Hopeful Subject 81   **40**
(Mandamus 120) [1991 7g 8.1s] 3,600Y: strong gelding: half-brother to several
winners here and abroad, including fairly useful 5f to 7.6f winner Paulager (by
Lochnager) and modest 10.8f winner Archipenko (by Milford): dam 2-y-o 1m winner:
well beaten in 7-runner minor event at Catterick (slowly away) in July and maiden at
Edinburgh in November. *Denys Smith.*

ROYAL SUPREME   4 b.g. Another Realm 118 – La Crima 63 (Runnymede 123)   —
[1990 5d 5m 6g 6m 6m 10g 8.3m 8m5 8.2s* 8d 1991 8.2d 11g 9m 7m 8.3d] leggy,
close-coupled gelding: has a quick action: poor handicapper at 3 yrs: no form in 1991:
should stay beyond 1m: seems to need soft ground: blinkered last 4 starts: sold
2,000 gns Doncaster November Sales. *L. Lungo.*

ROYAL VERSE (FR)   4 b.c. Recitation (USA) 124 – Sauce Royale (Royal Palace   —
131) [1990 9m 11.5m2 10m 9m2 10m4 8m 10f 10f 1991 12s 11.5m 10.1f6 a12g 8f]
good-topped colt: fair performer at 3 yrs, has deteriorated considerably: stays 11.5f:
acts well on firm going, possibly unsuited by soft ground: below form when blinkered once: sometimes wears crossed noseband and near-side pricker. *Dr J. D.
Scargill.*

ROYAL WALKABOUT (IRE)   2 b.c. (Mar 2) Pennine Walk 120 – Royal   **62**
Respect 82 (Kings Lake (USA) 133) [1991 5m* 5f5 6g5 7g5 7f5 7g2 7f4 7f3 6m5 6g4
7g] 14,500Y: sturdy, lengthy colt: first foal: dam, maiden stayed 1½m, is half-sister
to useful middle-distance performer Civility and smart 1976 2-y-o 5f performer
Piney Ridge: plating-class performer: won 6-runner maiden at Wolverhampton in

May: rather mixed form in nurseries: will stay 1m: has run well in blinkers: sold 6,200 gns Newmarket Autumn Sales. *Lord John FitzGerald.*

RUADH ADHAR 5 b.m. Heroic Air 96 – Rosemarkie 75 (Goldhill 125) [1990 a8g6 8.2s 6f 1991 8h 6.9m 8s4 9.2d] lengthy mare: no worthwhile form: looked difficult ride when last in seller final start: blinkered last 4 outings. *L. Lungo.* —

RUA D'ORO (USA) 3 b.f. El Gran Senor (USA) 136 – Thorough 115 (Thatch (USA) 136) [1990 6m* 1991 8g* 8m5 7g6 8m3] half-sister to fairly useful 7f winner Rah Wan (by Riverman): dam French 1m to 1½m winner: successful in Derrinstown Stud 1000 Guineas Trial at Leopardstown in May: ran creditably behind Kooyonga at the Curragh in Irish 1000 Guineas (favourite, held up in rear, headway to hold every chance 2f out when 4¾ lengths fifth of 12) and in Matron Stakes (over length third): ran moderately third start: stays 1m: acts on a firm surface. *M. V. O'Brien, Ireland.* **103**

RUBY JAYNE 3 b.f. Green Ruby (USA) 104 – Myna Tyna 85 (Blast 125) [1990 5m 6g 6g6 6g5 5g* 5f3 5m4 5f 5.1m 5g 5v a5g 1991 5.1d] small, leggy filly: has a quick action: poor performer: bit backward in claimer in June, only appearance in 1991: best at 5f: seems unsuited by heavy ground: inconsistent: bought out of A. Bailey's stable 850 gns Doncaster January Sales. *L. J. Barratt.*

RUBY RING 2 b.f. (Apr 19) Formidable (USA) 125 – Red Ruby 113 (Tudor Melody 129) [1991 7.1s6] closely related to useful 7f winner Entrancing (by Posse) and half-sister to several winners, including 1¾m winner Shingle Ridge (by Blakeney): dam very useful miler: sixth of 12 in maiden at Sandown in July: dead. *Lady Herries.* —

RUBY TIGER 4 gr.f. Ahonoora 122 – Hayati 94 (Hotfoot 126) [1990 11.3d2 12d2 12d3 12g5 10g* 10s* 1991 9m3 10v5 11m* 10g* 10g*] **121**

Ruby Tiger's emphatic victory in a six-strong field in the Vodafone Nassau Stakes, which included Oaks runner-up Shamshir and Musidora winner Gussy Marlowe, established her as one of the leading older fillies over middle distances in Europe, arguably second only to In The Groove amongst the British-trained contingent. Ruby Tiger is normally read about, rather than watched, by followers of racing here, for at Goodwood she was having only her fourth race in Britain since winning a minor event at Epsom as a two-year-old. In between she'd taken in trips to Italy, France, Canada, Germany and Ireland, and won in all bar France, most recently capturing Group 2 prizes at Baden-Baden and the Curragh. In the Sea World Pretty Polly Stakes at the Curragh at the end of June she'd dictated the pace and been so much in command that, even though she was allowed to coast the final seventy yards, she still had three lengths to spare over useful handicapper High Pressure and another two over Irish One Thousand Guineas runner-up Julie La Rousse. Ruby Tiger's participation in the Nassau Stakes was in doubt right up to the morning of the race due to a bruised near-fore (she was walked on the grass in the paddock), but her connections were keen to run as she'd apparently sparkled in a gallop with Fly Away Soon that week, and that horse had won the listed Glorious Stakes at the meeting on Friday. Ruby Tiger raced with tremendous enthusiasm as usual, tucked away in third behind Filia Ardross and Gussy Marlowe, and though the three were in a line passing the three-furlong marker, matters didn't stay that way for long; Ruby Tiger quickened

Sea World Pretty Polly Stakes, the Curragh—
the much-travelled Ruby Tiger never looks like being pegged back by High Pressure

Vodafone Nassau Stakes, Goodwood—again no danger to Ruby Tiger

right away in the final quarter mile and, pushed out to the line, came home seven lengths clear of Shamshir, in the process becoming the third four-year-old to win the race, following Roussalka and Free Guest, since it was opened up to older fillies in 1975. North Wind, incidentally, just got up to deprive the below-par Gussy Marlowe of third. Ambitious plans to send Ruby Tiger for the Beverly D Stakes and Japan Cup, amongst other races, had to be shelved when it was discovered she'd cracked a bone in her knee at Goodwood. Happily, she's well on the mend at the time of writing and is to be kept in training another year. Provided she recovers fully, there is every reason to suppose she'll enhance her already considerable reputation still further, both here and abroad, for she's progressed as each season's gone by.

			Lorenzaccio (ch 1965)	Klairon
				Phoenissa
	Ahonoora (ch 1975)		Helen Nichols (ch 1966)	Martial
				Quaker Girl
Ruby Tiger (gr.f. 1987)			Hotfoot (br 1966)	Firestreak
				Pitter Patter
	Hayati (ro or gr 1982)		Silecia (gr 1970)	Sky Gipsy
				Blue Sash

Ruby Tiger is owned by Mrs Philip Blacker, whose husband made a name for himself as a jump jockey, winning the Whitbread and finishing third in the Grand National on Royal Mail, and then as a sculptor—his statues of Red Rum and Desert Orchid can be seen at Liverpool and Kempton respectively. Ruby Tiger failed to reach her reserve as a yearling, luckily for the Blackers, for she's now accrued over £400,000 in prize money. The second Nassau winner sired by the good-class sprinter Ahonoora following Park Express, she's the first foal of Hayati, who won twice at up to a mile and a quarter for Cole. Cole also has charge of Hayati's next two foals, Ambassador Royale (by Pennine Walk), who won a mile-and-a-quarter maiden at Bath in September, and the unraced Sure Blade filly Elminya, both owned by the stable's principal patron Fahd Salman. There's plenty of speed further back in the bottom line of Ruby Tiger's pedigree: her grandam, the unraced Silecia, is a daughter of Sky Gipsy, who won ten times at up to six furlongs as a two-year-old, and Blue Sash, whose dam Star of India was champion two-year-old of 1955, when unbeaten in five starts. This is also the family of another tough, genuine and much-travelled horse trained at Whatcombe in recent years, Beeshi, who won the Prix Foy at Longchamp. Ruby Tiger stays a mile and a half, though she did all her racing in the latest season over shorter distances, and probably acts on any going, though she's yet to encounter very firm. She's splendidly genuine and consistent. *P. F. I. Cole.*

RUDIMENTARY (USA) 3 b.c. Nureyev (USA) 131 – Doubly Sure 59 (Reliance **110** II 137) [1990 NR 1991 10g² 10.1f* 10f³ 10m³ 8m* 8g⁴] strong, good-topped, attractive colt: impresses in appearance: half-brother to Kris, Diesis, smart 6f and 1m winner Keen and fairly useful 1m and 1¼m winner Escrime (all by Sharpen Up), and very smart 1984 2-y-o Presidium (by General Assembly): dam, placed over 1½m, is out of high-class staying 2-y-o Soft Angels: won maiden (13/8 on, unchallenged) at Yarmouth in August and listed race (always front rank, striding out in fine style to beat Cruachan 2 lengths) at Newmarket in October: below best in

Newmarket listed race final start, chasing leaders 6f: at least as effective at 1m as 1¼m: acts on firm going: seems best with forcing tactics. *H. R. A. Cecil.*

RUDJIG (USA) 5 b.h. Secreto (USA) 128 – Chic Belle (USA) (Mr Prospector **101** (USA)) [1990 10.8m* 13.3m² 12g* 14.6d² 16s 1991 10d² 12g³ 12s 13.3d⁵ 13.3d³] good-topped, attractive horse: useful performer: best efforts in first half of 1991 when third in John Porter Stakes and handicap (bandaged behind), both at Newbury: should stay 2m: acts on good to firm and dead (possibly unsuited by soft) going: visored penultimate start: to join D. Hayes in Australia. *J. H. M. Gosden.*

RUE DE FORT 3 gr.g. Belfort (FR) 89 – Royal Huntress (Royal Avenue 123) —
[1990 7m 8f 7g 1991 12m 12m] leggy, close-coupled gelding: has a quick action: poor form: uncertain to stay 1½m: sold 1,750 gns Doncaster October Sales. *B. W. Murray.*

RUE DE REMARQUE 3 ch.f. The Noble Player (USA) 126 – Carolyn- —
christensen 58 (Sweet Revenge 129) [1990 NR 1991 7g] compact filly: second foal: half-sister to 4-y-o 5f winner Maid Welcome (by Mummy's Pet): dam won from 5f to 9.4f, including in sellers: moved poorly down and soon tailed off in Lingfield maiden in October. *M. J. Haynes.*

RUFFINI (IRE) 2 b.g. (Apr 18) Runnett 125 – Pass No Problem (Pas de Seul **63**
133) [1991 6g⁵ 7g³ 7f⁶ 6g⁶ 8g⁴ 7m³] IR 4,200Y: close-coupled gelding: second foal: dam unraced: quite modest maiden: ran creditably in nurseries at Warwick and Leicester (blinkered) last 2 outings: stays 1m: has carried head awkwardly: sold 6,400 gns Newmarket Autumn Sales. *J. R. Fanshawe.*

RUFINA (USA) 3 b.f. Secreto (USA) 128 – Rough Miss (USA) (Poison Ivory **110**
(USA)) [1990 5.5g* 5g* 6g* 6g³ 7g* 6s⁴ 6v* 1991 6v* 6g* 5m⁵ 6v 6v*] $22,000Y: big, leggy, lengthy filly: second foal: dam stakes-placed winner at 2 yrs: leading Italian sprinter: successful in newcomers race, 3 listed contests and a minor event in 1990: won 2 minor contests and Group 2 Premio Melton (very useful perform-ance, second start, by 3 lengths) at Rome in 1991: 7/1 and on toes, led 3f and kept on when 8½ lengths fifth of 10 to Elbio in King's Stand Stakes at Royal Ascot: best form at 6f: acts on heavy going. *L. Brogi, Italy.*

RUHR (IRE) 2 b.c. (Feb 4) Flash of Steel 120 – Astral Way (Hotfoot 126) [1991 **109**
5g⁴ 5g² 7g⁴ 7m* 8.1f⁶ 7m⁴] 37,000F, 30,000Y: strong, lengthy colt: carries con-dition: sixth foal: half-brother to 2 winners in Ireland, including 11f winner Gemini Way (by Pas de Seul): dam French 2-y-o 1m winner: useful performer: narrowly won Newcastle maiden in August: blinkered first time, excellent fourth of 30, beaten under ½ length, to Young Senor in Tattersalls Tiffany Highflyer Stakes at New-market in October, always front rank and battling on really well: best form at 7f, but should prove at least as effective at 1m: acts well on good to firm ground. *B. W. Hills.*

RUIZ MIGUEL 5 br.g. Precocious 126 – Lakshmi 83 (Tribal Chief 125) [1990 **41**
8.3g 8.2d 1991 a7g⁴ a7g⁶ a10g 9s] strong, deep-girthed gelding: poor maiden at best: stays 7f. *L. G. Cottrell.*

RULING DYNASTY 7 br.g. Ile de Bourbon (USA) 133 – Bahariva (FR) (Sir —
Gaylord (USA)) [1990 NR 1991 12.3d] sparely-made gelding: fair winner as 3-y-o: very lightly raced and no subsequent form on flat: stays 1½m: acts on firm going: winning hurdler/chaser. *M. D. I. Usher.*

Main Reef Stakes, Newmarket—Rudimentary beats Cruachan with something in hand

RULLY 2 ch.c. (Feb 17) Rousillon (USA) 133 – Hysterical 68 (High Top 131) [1991 **75** 7.1s³ 7.1m 7.6d* 10g⁶] 13,500Y: strong, well-made colt: has scope: fourth foal: half-brother to useful 7f (at 2 yrs) to 9f winner Comic Talent (by Pharly) and modest 1m winner Courageous Bidder (by Known Fact): dam won over 1½m at 4 yrs, her only season to race: modest performer: off course over 7 weeks before winning maiden at Chester (didn't have to be at best) in October: well beaten though not discredited in Zetland Stakes at Newmarket (pulled hard early) 11 days later: stays 1¼m. *C. E. Brittain.*

RUMBELOW 2 b.c. (Mar 7) Welsh Captain 113 – Romana 72 (Roman Warrior **50** 132) [1991 6d⁶ 7m²] useful-looking colt: first reported foal: dam out-and-out stayer: second in seller at Yarmouth in July, travelling comfortably then keeping on: seemed likely to improve again. *J. R. Jenkins.*

RUMBLED AGAIN (IRE) 2 b.g. (Jan 19) Head For Heights 125 – Gentle **—** Rhythm 67 (Ballad Rock 122) [1991 5f] IR 3,200F: good-bodied gelding: third foal: half-brother to a winner in Belgium: dam, stayed 9f on flat later successful over hurdles, is daughter of sister to On Your Mark: 16/1 and green, slow-starting seventh of 8 in maiden at Redcar in July. *T. D. Barron.*

RUN AND DELIVER (USA) 3 gr.c. Danzig (USA) – Belga (FR) (Le Fabuleux **78** d 133) [1990 NR 1991 8g⁵ 8g² a8g² 10.5g 10m] $325,000Y: tall, leggy, quite good-topped colt: moderate mover: closely related to several winners in France, notably top-class miler Bellypha (by Lyphard) and half-brother to 2 more, notably smart middle-distance colt Bellman (by Riverman): dam French 9f winner: disappointing after fair form in maidens first 2 starts: trained first 3 by M. Stoute: blinkered last 2 starts, looking reluctant to post and in race on final one: sold 13,000 gns Newmarket Autumn Sales: one to avoid. *R. J. R. Williams.*

RUNAWAY LAD (IRE) 3 b.g. Runnett 125 – Kingston Rose (Tudor Music 131) **77** [1990 6m⁴ 6m⁵ 6g* 6d 1991 a7g² 7g³ 7g 7m⁶ a6g²] good-topped gelding: modest performer: creditable second in handicap at Lingfield in June, badly outpaced early and running wide into straight: stays 7f: best efforts on all-weather or with give in the ground: blinkered last 2 starts. *G. A. Pritchard-Gordon.*

RUN DON'T FLY (USA) 5 b.h. Lear Fan (USA) 130 – Gantlette (Run The **115** Gantlet (USA)) [1990 12m² 1991 10g* 12g*] sturdy, quite attractive horse: carries condition: very useful performer, fairly lightly raced: won £11,160 handicap at Newmarket (in good style by ¾ length from Lord Charmer) and Group 2 Premio Ellington at Rome (beat Noble Patriarch by ¾ length) later in May: not seen out again: effective at 1¼m to 1½m: acts on firm going: takes keen hold. *P. F. I. Cole.*

RUN FOR JOYCE 5 br.m. My Dad Tom (USA) 109 – Assel Zawie (Sit In The **—** Corner (USA)) [1990 6g 5f a5g 5d 5m a5g 5m 6g 1991 5g 6d 5m 6.1m 5f 6f 5g] close-coupled mare: carries plenty of condition: bad walker and moderate mover: poor maiden: best at 5f: acts on firm going. *J. Balding.*

RUN FOR NICK (FR) 3 b.g. Nikos 124 – Run For Juliet (USA) (Model Fool) **69** [1990 8g 6g 6d³ 1991 8g² 10s⁶ 8s* 10s 8g³ 8m²] good-topped gelding: modest performer: easily best efforts in Britain when placed in handicaps at Warwick and Carlisle: successful once from 4 starts at Cagnes-sur-Mer in February: stays 1m: acts on good to firm ground and soft: joined Mrs D. Haine. *A. A. Scott.*

RUN HIGH 8 b.g. Thatch (USA) 136 – Fleet Nelly (Vaguely Noble 140) **—** [1990 14g 14m³ 12g² 13g⁴ 14m* 12g³ 13g⁴ 15g³ 14g³ 15.5f* 1991 12f] strong, medium-sized gelding: usually looks well: moderate mover: modest handicapper at 7 yrs: never placed to challenge only run in 1991 (October): needs at least 1½m and stays 2m: acts on any going: good mount for inexperienced rider: splendidly tough, genuine and consistent. *P. Mitchell.*

RUNITAGAIN 4 b.g. Runnett 125 – Staderas (Windjammer (USA)) [1990 6s 6m **—** 1991 a11g 5m 8.3d] tall gelding: lightly raced and no worthwhile form. *K. B. McCauley.*

RUN MILADY 3 b.f. Blakeney 126 – Bewitched 63 (African Sky 124) [1990 6d² **59** d 6d³ 1991 7v² 8m⁶ 11m⁴ 12.1d⁴ 12.3d a12g⁴ 10.9g 9.2s] compact, workmanlike filly: plating-class maiden at best: often contests amateur events: stays 11f: acts on good to firm and heavy ground: joined Mrs S. Austin. *M. Johnston.*

RUNNEL 2 b.c. (Feb 5) Runnett 125 – Ariadne 79 (Bustino 136) [1991 5s 5.3m³ **56** 6g³ a7g² a7g⁵ 7m* 7m⁵ 7g 8m 7m³ 6m⁶ 7m a7g⁵ a6g a6g* a6g² a7g* a8g²] small, a **72** strong-quartered colt: good walker: sixth foal: half-brother to fair sprinter Denham Green (by Dominion) and 1½m winner Cas-En-Bas (by Good Times): dam 2m winner: bought out of J. Dunlop's stable 2,900 gns after winning seller at Southwell in September: much improved on fibresand late in year, twice making all in claimers: stays 7f: twice blinkered. *D. W. Chapman.*

RUNNING FOR COVER (IRE) 2 b.c. (Mar 27) Runnett 125 – North Hut **39** §
(Northfields (USA)) [1991 5d⁶ 5g 6d 5m] 15,000Y: good-quartered colt: has scope:
good walker: half-brother to fairly useful 1990 2-y-o 5f winner The Old Firm (by
Hatim) and very smart 1985 sprinting 2-y-o Dublin Lad (by Dublin Taxi): dam twice-
raced daughter of very useful sprinting 2-y-o Whispering II: poor form: off course
nearly 5 months after debut: blinkered, dropped himself out soon after halfway at
Catterick last time: sold 1,250 gns Doncaster November Sales: may be ungenuine. *J.
J. O'Neill.*

RUNNING GLIMPSE (IRE) 3 br.f. Runnett 125 – One Last Glimpse 73 **63**
(Relko 136) [1990 5g² 5g* 5m⁵ 6m 1991 6g* 5g 5m 6m 6m] smallish filly: quite
modest handicapper: won at Windsor in May, putting head in air when leading over
1f out then running on strongly: below form after: best effort at 6f: sold 2,200 gns
Newmarket Autumn Sales. *Miss B. Sanders.*

RUNNING MONEY 7 b.g. Billion (USA) 120 – Streets Ahead 67 (Ovid 95) **—**
[1990 NR 1991 16m] close-coupled non-thoroughbred gelding: has a round action:
modest handicapper: bandaged at 4 yrs: suited by test of stamina: acts on good to firm ground and a soft surface. *Capt. J. Wilson.*

RUNNING SHADOW (IRE) 3 gr.g. Kalaglow 132 – Regal Flutter (USA) **60**
(Beldale Flutter (USA) 130) [1990 8.2d⁴ 8.2s⁴ 1991 12f³ 12m³ 11m 10f 8.2m⁵ 10m⁵]
tall gelding: quite modest performer: below form third, fourth and final (sweating)
starts: effective at 1m and stays 1½m: acts on any going: sold to Scandinavia 3,600
gns Newmarket Autumn Sales. *J. Etherington.*

RUN RINGS 3 b.c. Commanche Run 133 – Fai La Bella (USA) 85 (Fifth Marine **81**
(USA)) [1990 NR 1991 8g 11.5m* 12g 10m² 10g² 8.9g 8.9g 9m³ 9m 9g] strong,
lengthy colt: has scope: impresses in appearance: has a moderate, quick action:
fourth foal: half-brother to 4-y-o Uninvited (by Be My Guest): dam, out of half-sister
to smart filly Kootenai, showed much improved form at 4 yrs, winning 4 times at
1¼m: won ladies event at Lingfield in June: mostly ran well in valuable handicaps,
always prominent stand side and staying on well when seventh of 29 in
Cambridgeshire at Newmarket penultimate start: favourite, ran poorly in £30,800
Newbury contest 3 weeks later: well worth another try at 1½m. *L. M. Cumani.*

RUNUN 5 br.h. Sharpo 132 – Silent Movie (Shirley Heights 130) [1990 7g 7d **—**
8.2m² 8.2v 16d³ a11g⁵ a11g⁴ 1991 a11g] lengthy, rather sparely-made horse: bad
mover: useful performer at best: pulled up, reportedly with knee injury, only run in
1991 (January): best form at 7f or 1m: acts on firm going: inconsistent. *N. Tinkler.*

RUNWAY ROMANCE (FR) 4 gr.c. Julius Caesar (FR) 115 – Airstrip (Warpath **66**
113) [1990 8.2g* 9f⁵ 7g⁴ 7m 8h³ 1991 11.5m⁵ 10.8g⁴ 17.2f] sparely-made, angular
colt: quite modest handicapper: not seen out after July: stays 11.5f: acts on hard
ground: useful hurdler. *P. J. Hobbs.*

RUN WITH BAILEYS 2 ch.f. (May 21) Baillamont (USA) 124 – Golden Form **—**
(Formidable (USA) 125) [1991 6f 6.1f 8.3g] 5,400Y: sparely-made filly: third foal:
half-sister to a winner in USA at around 1m by Nijinsky: dam fairly useful 9f winner
in Ireland: well beaten in maidens, first an auction: sold 1,150 gns Doncaster
October Sales. *M. Johnston.*

RUNYON (IRE) 3 b.c. Sadler's Wells (USA) 132 – Deadly Serious (USA) 113 **117**
(Queen's Hussar 124) [1990 NR 1991 9v* 9g* 10g* 10g² 11.9g⁴] IR 145,000Y: big,

Derrinstown Stud Derby Trial, Leopardstown—
Runyon is impressive from the blinkered George Augustus and Smooth Performance

Mr M. P. Sissian's "Runyon"

lengthy colt with plenty of scope: has a round action: good walker: sixth living foal: closely related to useful 1m winner Samsova (by Shareef Dancer) and half-brother to 9f winner Sparkling Fire (by Sparkler): dam Galtres Stakes winner out of very smart Joking Apart: very useful Irish colt: successful in maiden at Tipperary and in minor event and Derrinstown Stud Derby Trial at Leopardstown: beaten 4 lengths by Sportsworld in Windfields Farm Gallinule Stakes at the Curragh, 9½ lengths by Corrupt in Great Voltigeur Stakes (pushed along 5f out, keeping on steadily) at York: should prove better at 1½m than shorter. *T. Stack, Ireland.*

RUPERT'S DAUGHTER 8 gr.m. Rupert Bear 105 – Silent Swindler 59 — (Tacitus 124) [1990 NR 1991 6m] leggy, rather plain mare: of little account. *Mrs J. Jordan.*

RUPPLES 4 b.g. Muscatite 122 – Miss Annie 73 (Scottish Rifle 127) [1990 12.5g **38** 14g a12g 11m⁴ 1991 7d³ 9s 8m² 7.6g 8f 8g 7.1d 8.3g 14.1m⁶ 8m] leggy, workmanlike gelding: poor handicapper: seems suited by around 1m: best effort on good to firm ground: usually blinkered, tried visored once. *M. J. Ryan.*

RURIK (USA) 3 b.c. Alydar (USA) – Rukann (USA) (Ruken) [1990 NR 1991 **69** 10.4m⁵ 10m] \$1,400,000Y: big, long-backed colt: ninth reported foal: half-brother to several winners by lesser sires, notably good North American 2-y-o Temperate Sil (by Temperence Hill), later also a Grade One 9f and 1¼m winner: dam won twice from as many starts at 3 yrs: around 7 lengths fifth of 10 to King Athelstan in maiden at York: evens, well beaten in similar event at Leicester later in October: joined F. Brothers in USA. *J. H. M. Gosden.*

RUSHANES 4 ch.c. Millfontaine 114 – Saulonika 94 (Saulingo 122) [1990 6m 5m **54** 6f³ 6h 6m 6m⁵ 6m 6m 6d a7g 1991 a6g² a7g 5g⁵ 6d⁵ 6f a5g 5.3g³ 5m⁴ 5.1s² 5.1d⁵ a **64** a6g* a5g⁶ a6g⁴ a6g⁴ a6g⁴] small, sturdy colt: poor mover: shows traces of stringhalt: quite modest handicapper: won at Lingfield in November: best form at 6f: acts on any going: goes well on all-weather: ran poorly when sweating and edgy. *T. Casey.*

RUSHEY SANDS 3 b.f. Rushmore 92 – Sayida-Shahira (Record Run 127) [1990 —
NR 1991 a10g] first foal: dam never ran: 14/1, well beaten in maiden claimer at
Lingfield in December: sold to join W. G. Turner 1,150 gns Ascot December Sales. *J.
T. Gifford.*

RUSHLUAN 7 gr.g. Kalaglow 132 – Labista 116 (Crowned Prince (USA) 128) **51** +
[1990 10.8m* 12.5m* 12.2m² 11.7f⁴ 14f³ 10g⁵ 1991 12f⁴] leggy, good-topped gelding:
has a quick action: quite modest handicapper in 1990: sole outing at 7 yrs in March:
stays at least 12.5f: acts on firm going, probably unsuited by soft surface: has run
well for amateur: ran creditably in visor. *R. J. Hodges.*

RUSSIAN COURAGE (USA) 2 b. or br.c. (May 15) Nijinsky (CAN) 138 – Bold **?**
Captive (USA) (Boldnesian (USA)) [1991 10s*] brother to French 4-y-o Captor,
successful 3 times at around 11f: half-brother to several winners, most notably
Breeders' Cup Classic victor Skywalker (by Relaunch): dam, sprinter in USA, won
10 races: narrow winner of 17-runner maiden at Deauville in October: stays 1¼m:
should improve. *A. Fabre, France.*

RUSSIAN LIAISON (IRE) 3 br.f. Law Society (USA) 130 – Veruschka 101 **56**
(Lorenzaccio 130) [1990 NR 1991 10g 8g a7g² a7g⁶] 74,000Y: smallish filly: half-
sister to useful Irish sprinter Aberuschka (by Thatching) and a winner in Holland:
dam 2-y-o 6f winner, is half-sister to high-class sprinter Abergwaun: second of 10 at
Southwell, leading 6f and only form in maidens in first half of season. *A. A. Scott.*

RUSSIAN MINK (USA) 3 ch.f. L'Emigrant (USA) 129 – Furry Friend (USA) **64**
(Bold Bidder) [1990 6m 6g² 7d³ 6s* 1991 6g 7d 6d⁵] smallish, angular filly: modest
winner at 2 yrs: sweating and edgy, fair fifth at Newbury in June, best effort in
handicaps: best form at 6f: acts on soft going: gave trouble at stalls penultimate
start: sold 900 gns Ascot November Sales. *Lord Huntingdon.*

RUSSIAN RED 4 ch.c. Kind of Hush 118 – Green Diamond (Green God 128) **56**
[1990 12f⁶ 10f 10m⁶ 10m² 10g⁶ 10h 10g 10d a12g a12g³ a13g² a13g⁴ a12g² 1991 a13g*
a10g* a12g⁵ a10g⁶ a12g² 10f 12f³ a12g³ 12m⁵ a16g] strong, lengthy colt: moderate
mover: plating-class handicapper: won at Lingfield (2) early in 1991: stays 13f: acts
on firm going: inconsistent. *W. G. R. Wightman.*

RUSSLEY 7 b.m. Bay Express 132 – Jendean 68 (Florescence 120) [1990 NR 1991 —
5.1d] tall mare: lightly raced, soundly beaten in modest company. *C. C. Elsey.*

RUSTAKA (USA) 2 b.f. (Mar 2) Riverman (USA) 131 – Katsura (USA) **68** p
(Northern Dancer) [1991 7m] leggy filly: has scope: sixth foal: half-sister to several
winners, including 1990 2-y-o 7f winner (stays 1¼m) Arokat (by Caro) and useful
middle-distance performer Katzina (by Cox's Ridge): dam Irish 7f and 1½m winner,
is out of sister to very smart middle-distance filly Trillionaire: 8/1 and bit backward,
around 12 lengths last of 8, outpaced soon after halfway and very green, to Rose
Indien in minor event at Newmarket in October: showed a round action: will
improve. *B. W. Hills.*

RUSTIC WEDDING 2 b.f. (Apr 14) Red Sunset 120 – Joyful Lass (USA) (Danzig **50**
(USA)) [1991 5.5g 5d 5.1m 6g⁴ 5.3m⁵ 7g* 7.1m 7g⁴ 10.5d a8g] 1,650Y: small, sparely-
made filly: second reported foal: half-sister to a winner in Italy: dam lightly raced:
won selling nursery (bought in 5,000 gns) at Wolverhampton in August: ran well on
equitrack final start: stays 1m: very keen to post fifth start: twice unruly stalls. *G. B.
Balding.*

RUSTIMAN (IRE) 3 br.g. Rusticaro (FR) 124 – Sarsenet (Saritamer (USA) 130) **44**
[1990 6g 8d² a8g 1991 12v⁶ 11.7s 12m 13.1f 11.1d⁴ 11.1d] rather leggy, workmanlike gelding: ran poor maiden, not seen out after June: probably stays 1½m: possibly
unsuited by very soft going. *M. J. Bolton.*

RUTH'S GAMBLE 3 b.g. Kabour 80 – Hilly's Daughter (Hillandale 125) [1990 **72**
5g³ 6g* 6d⁶ 7s⁶ 1991 6f³ 7g⁴ 7g³ 6m⁵ 7g⁴ 6g 6f² 6f³ 7g 6m] lengthy gelding:
modest handicapper: stays 7f: acts on any going: blinkered (appeared mulish) fourth
start: none too consistent. *D. W. Chapman.*

RUTLAND WATER (USA) 4 ch.c. Sharpen Up 127 – Hemlock (USA) (Big **80**
Spruce (USA)) [1990 NR 1991 10.8d³ 12g⁴ 10m⁴ 12g⁵ 11.5d⁵ 10.2g*] strong,
good-bodied colt: moderate mover: third foal: half-brother to 2 winners in USA,
notably Kex (by In Reality), stakes winner at up to 1½m: dam won at up to 1¼m in
USA: fair, lightly-raced handicapper: not seen again after winning at Doncaster
(idled) in July: stays 1½m: acts on good to firm and dead ground: carried head high
second start, sweating final one: sold to join R. Akehurst's stable 15,500 gns
Newmarket Autumn Sales. *P. J. Makin.*

RYECOVE 3 ch.g. Norwick (USA) 120 – Niorkie (FR) (My Swallow 134) [1990 7g **63**
5m² 6d⁴ 6g⁵ 1991 8m a11g³ 12g a12g⁴ 14s² 14m⁵ 16.1g a16g] rangy gelding: quite

modest maiden: second in handicap at Sandown in July: stays 1¾m: acts on good to firm ground and soft: blinkered (led 1m) final start. *R. J. O'Sullivan.*

RYEWATER DREAM 3 b.f. Touching Wood (USA) 127 – Facetious 88 **62** (Malicious) [1990 7m 7m² 8s 1991 10m 12m 10f 11.7f* 12m⁵ 17.2g a12g] smallish, workmanlike filly: modest performer: easily best 3-y-o effort when making all in maiden claimer at Bath in September: tailed off at Lingfield final start: stays 11.7f: acts on firm going. *D. R. C. Elsworth.*

RYTHMIC STYLE 2 b.f. (Feb 13) Swing Easy (USA) 126 – Slick Chick 89 (Shiny **50** Tenth 120) [1991 5g 5f* 5m] 1,800F, 3,000Y: half-sister to 3-y-o Ming Court (by Daring March) and several winners here and abroad, including quite useful 5f to 1¼m winner Basil Boy (by Jimsun): dam won Ribblesdale Stakes: quite modest maiden: 14/1-winner of 18-runner seller (bought in 4,800 gns) at Beverley, chasing leaders and running on well: not discredited in similar event at Thirsk later in May. *T. D. Barron.*

S

SAAFEND 3 b.f. Sayf El Arab (USA) 127 – Gilt Star 92 (Star Appeal 133) [1990 6f⁶ **73** 6m 6g² 6d⁴ 1991 6d³ 7g³ 6g 7g 8m* 8m² 7f⁴ 7m⁶ 7s⁵ 7.6g 9g] sparely-made filly: modest handicapper: won at Yarmouth in July: ran well next 4 starts: some promise penultimate start, little when blinkered in £30,800 contest (brief headway 3f out) at Newbury 23 days later: stays 1m: probably acts on any going. *J. Sutcliffe.*

SABAAH (USA) 3 ch.f. Nureyev (USA) 131 – Dish Dash 118 (Bustino 136) [1990 **65** NR 1991 8.2d² 7f 8g 7.6g] angular filly: fifth foal: sister to 4-y-o White Mantle and half-sister to useful 1986 2-y-o 7f winner Arrasas (by Irish River): dam won Ribblesdale Stakes: quite modest maiden: stiff task on first run for over 3 months, ran fairly well in Lingfield handicap: will be well suited by middle distances: possibly unsuited by firm going: sold 13,000 gns Newmarket December Sales. *R. W. Armstrong.*

SABO'S GIRL 3 b.f. Prince Sabo 123 – Josephine Gibney (High Top 131) [1990 — NR 1991 8s 7.5f] 3,500Y: sparely-made filly: second foal: half-sister to 5f (at 2 yrs) to 1m winner Super One (by Superlative): dam winner in Italy from family of high-class sprinter Green God: behind in maiden and seller (difficult at stalls) in the spring: sold to join T. Kersey 1,250 gns Doncaster August Sales. *P. C. Haslam.*

SABOTAGE (FR) 5 ch.h. Kris 135 – Subject To Change (USA) (Buckpasser) **103** [1990 7m⁴ 8g 9g⁵ 8g⁴ 1991 8m² 8g 8d] leggy, quite good-topped, attractive horse: easy walker: useful handicapper: well beaten in competitive events after excellent second in £17,500 Whitsun Cup at Sandown: not seen after July: stays 9f: acts on good to firm ground: ran creditably when visored once at 4 yrs. *M. R. Stoute.*

SABOTEUR 7 ch.g. Pyjama Hunt 126 – Frondia 76 (Parthia 132) [1990 7g 1991 **36** 7m* 7m 7f⁶ 7m] lengthy, dipped-backed gelding: bad mover: poor handicapper: gamely made all at Yarmouth in July: suited by 7f and a sound surface: tried blinkered once: inconsistent. *M. H. Tompkins.*

SACQUE 3 b.f. Elegant Air 119 – Embroideress 80 (Stanford 121§) [1990 6m⁵ **97** 5.3f² 5m* 5g 1991 5d 6m* 7g⁶ 5m 6s³ 6f* 6f⁴ 6m* 6f² 6m⁴ 6m* 6g] strong, workmanlike filly: good walker: fairly useful handicapper: won at Haydock in May, Ripon in August, Lingfield in September and Newcastle (tending to idle, clearly best effort) in October: suited by 6f: best efforts on top-of-the-ground: bandaged off-hind seventh to ninth starts: tail flasher: consistent: sold 42,000 gns Newmarket Autumn Sales. *D. Morley.*

SACRED NUMBER (USA) 4 ch.c. Irish River (FR) 131 – Disco Girl (FR) **83** (Green Dancer (USA) 132) [1990 11d³ 10m* 1991 12m⁴ 12g⁴ 11.9m 11.9g] rangy, rather sparely-made colt: poor mover: fair handicapper: well beaten last 2 starts: stays 1½m: has given impression will prove suited by some give in the ground: sold only 4,200 gns Newmarket Autumn Sales. *H. R. A. Cecil.*

SADDLEHOME (USA) 2 b.c. (Mar 29) Aragon 118 – Kesarini (USA) 87 (Singh **76** (USA)) [1991 6g 5g² 5f³ 5m³ 5m⁵ 5g³] leggy, short-backed colt: fifth foal: half-brother to 3-y-o Jigging (by Scottish Reel) and 5-y-o 5f (at 2 yrs) and 7f winner That's The One (by Known Fact): dam 2-y-o 5f winner, is out of Coronation Stakes winner Kesar Queen: modest maiden: best effort, keeping on, at Wolverhampton final start: out of depth in Flying Childers Stakes at Doncaster 16 days earlier: worth another try at 6f: capable of winning a modest event in due course. *R. M. Whitaker.*

SADDLERS' HALL (IRE)   3 b.c. Sadler's Wells (USA) 132 – Sunny Val- **123**
ley (Val de Loir 133) [1990 7d⁵ 1991 10g* 10.5g² 12g* 12m⁶ 11.9g² 14.6m² 12g]
    The fate of losers in this game tends to be that they are soon forgotten.
Second-placed Saddlers' Hall's contribution to an entertaining Coalite St
Leger deserves not to be, and should not be since it is the key to understanding him as a racehorse. Although he had previously won the King Edward VII
Stakes over a mile and a half, he is essentially a stayer. He was one of a very
small number in the Leger field able comfortably to stand the searching gallop
as far as the straight; he went on by three lengths between the half-mile and
three-furlong poles, held the lead for another two furlongs and in the course of
his battle with Toulon, which ended in a length-and-a-half defeat, he kept on
so well that he drew at least fifteen lengths clear of the rest. This performance
was Saddlers' Hall's best, no coincidence in its arising on the first opportunity
he had of tackling a mile and three quarters. The return to a mile and a half in
the Breeders' Cup Turf at Churchill Downs in November, when he looked in
superb shape, couldn't have done more to hammer the point home. Pincay
rode him as though under the impression he possessed top-class middle-
distance speed, and declined to take the initiative when the early gallop was
slow. As a consequence Saddlers' Hall was gradually left behind when things
hotted up, dropping back from seventh to tenth in the straight, and was beaten
ten and a half lengths by Miss Alleged. Saddlers' Hall had tackled the top-
class middle-distance horses once before, in the King George VI and Queen
Elizabeth Diamond Stakes, and had been found wanting even though ridden in
the best possible way, second early then taking over from Hailsham half a mile
out in a very strongly-run race. Given a breather before the home turn, he was
made to look slow by Generous and one or two of the others but stuck to his
guns for sixth place, fifteen lengths behind the winner.
    Saddlers' Hall would almost certainly have started shorter than 13/2 for
the Leger had he not been beaten six lengths by Corrupt in the Great Voltigeur Stakes at York. That wasn't his form; nor was his second in a graduation
race on the same course in the spring, when Cruachan had also beaten him by
six lengths, both colts having gone into the race the winners of their only
previous start of the season, Saddlers' Hall in a minor event over a mile and a
quarter at Newmarket. The defeat by Cruachan is much the easier to explain:
holding up Saddlers' Hall in a slowly-run race played right into the winner's
hands, and when it came down to a test of speed from over two furlongs out it
was no contest. Piggott made amends by drastically changing his tactics over
the extra furlong and a half in the King Edward VII Stakes at Royal Ascot.

King Edward VII Stakes, Ascot — Saddlers' Hall looks a Leger prospect

Lord Weinstock's "Saddlers' Hall"

Saddlers' Hall was at the head of affairs for much of the way, setting a strong pace. Most of his seven opponents seemed to be moving more comfortably at various stages of the race, but from around three furlongs out Saddlers' Hall began to get on top; he went a length up as they took the turn, and from early in the straight he drew right away to win most impressively by six lengths from Secret Haunt—unmistakably a staying performance.

		Northern Dancer	Nearctic
Saddlers' Hall (IRE) (b.c. 1988)	Sadler's Wells (USA) (b 1981)	(b 1961)	Natalma
		Fairy Bridge	Bold Reason
		(b 1975)	Special
	Sunny Valley (b 1972)	Val de Loir	Vieux Manoir
		(b 1959)	Vali II
		Sunland	Charlottesville
		(ch 1965)	Sunny Gulf

Saddlers' Hall's half-sister Sun Princess (by English Prince) won the St Leger in 1983; she also ran away with the Oaks to the tune of twelve lengths, the biggest winning margin in the race's history, and finished second in the Prix de l'Arc de Triomphe. Unfortunately, she never recaptured her form as a four-year-old, but connections had far worse misfortune when her first foal, the Dewhurst winner Prince of Dance (by Saddlers' Hall's sire Sadler's Wells) was found to be suffering from cancer of the spine shortly after meeting with his first defeat in the 1989 Derby and had to be put down. The dam Sunny Valley, who produced five winners altogether, died during 1991. A useful winner at up to a mile and a half in France, she was out of the staying mare Sunland, half-sister to, amongst others, the Park Hill winner and Irish Oaks runner-up Sunny Cove.

A win in top mile-and-a-half company would add substantially to Saddlers' Hall's value as a stallion. There seems no doubt that he'll be aimed at such a prize as a four-year-old but from what's been seen of him he'll be chasing shadows. His prospects of winning top races will be infinitely better over distances of a mile and three quarters or more (he'll stay at least two miles). A strong, lengthy, attractive colt, a good walker and mover, Saddlers' Hall acts on good to firm going. The only time he has encountered easier than good was when a close fifth to Junk Bond, heavily backed, in the Houghton Stakes on his two-year-old debut, though some thought that the heavily-watered ground for the Voltigeur bordered on dead. *M. R. Stoute.*

SADLER'S WAY 2 b.c. (Mar 19) Sadler's Wells (USA) 132 – Sophisticated Lady (FR) (Habitat 134) [1991 8g 6s] 50,000Y: tall, leggy colt: has scope: third foal: half-brother to 3-y-o No Big Deal (by Kris): dam, ran once, is sister to Sigy and Sonoma: no worthwhile form in minor event at Newbury (well beaten) then maiden at Folkestone (well behind after slow start, ran on final 2f) in autumn: should stay 1m: looks sort to do better. *G. Lewis.* — p

SAFA 3 b.f. Shirley Heights 130 – Beveridge (USA) 86 (Spectacular Bid (USA)) [1990 6m* 8m2 1991 10f2 10d] leggy, quite good-topped filly: very good walker: quite useful performances when second in Brent Walker Fillies' Mile at Ascot and to Duc de Berry in minor event (bit backward, travelling really well 3½f out and leading briefly close home) at Nottingham in September at 3 yrs: last of 9 in Group 3 event at Maisons-Laffitte, leading 9f: stays 1¼m: possibly unsuited by a soft surface: tail swisher: injured off-fore in March. *A. A. Scott.* 98 +

SAFARI KEEPER 5 b.g. Longleat (USA) 109 – Garden Party 111 (Reform 132) [1990 a7g a10g6 1991 10d 16m 14m4 14d 11.8g 18.1m] workmanlike, angular gelding: moderate walker: worthwhile form only on third outing: no promise after: suited by long distances. *M. J. Wilkinson.* 28

SAFARI PARK 2 ch.f. (May 6) Absalom 128 – Nyeri 104 (Saint Crespin III 132) [1991 6g6 6m 6.1m] 5,000Y: smallish, workmanlike filly: sister to 3-y-o Balsmo, 6f winner at 2 yrs, and winning stayer Grey Gypsy and half-sister to several winners here and abroad, including useful middle-distance stayer Greatham House (by Run The Gantlet): dam stayed 1½m: form only on debut: saddle slipped second start: should be suited by 7f. *B. S. Rothwell.* 43

SAFARI SUNRISE (IRE) 2 b.g. (Mar 31) Precocious 126 – Zebra Grass 85 (Run The Gantlet (USA)) [1991 5m 5f 7m 8m] 12,500Y: leggy, rather close-coupled, unfurnished gelding: half-brother to several winners, including stayer Fedra (by Grundy) and 1989 2-y-o 1m winner Pay The Bank (by High Top): dam 2-y-o 6f and 7f winner from family of Royal Palace: poor form in varied events: favourite, last of 20 in Leicester selling nursery final outing: should be suited by 7f/1m: sold 740 gns Newmarket Autumn Sales. *M. W. Easterby.* 45

SAFAWAN 5 ch.h. Young Generation 129 – Safita 117 (Habitat 134) [1990 8m5 7.2f* 8m* 8m5 8m5 7m5 1991 8g4 8d6 7d3 8m2 7d* 8g] lengthy, robust horse: smart performer at best here at 4 yrs when trained by M. Stoute: sent to France, successful in 1991 in listed race at Longchamp in September by short head from Lady Isis: beaten a nose by Masterclass in Prix Quincey at Deauville previous month: effective at 7f to 1m: acted on firm and dead ground: retired to Wood Farm Stud, Shropshire, fee £2,000 (Oct 1st terms). *J. E. Hammond, France.* 112

SAFE ARRIVAL (USA) 3 gr.f. Shadeed (USA) 135 – Flyingtrip (USA) (Vaguely Noble 140) [1990 7s5 1991 8.5f3 11m2 13m5 10m5 10g 8.1m3 10.5g2 10m] big, lengthy, angular filly: quite modest maiden: disappointing favourite on final start: will prove suited by further than 1m, and stays 11f: probably acts on any going: ran creditably for amateur: sold 18,000 gns Newmarket Autumn Sales. *M. R. Stoute.* 66

SAFE BUILDER (IRE) 2 b.g. (Feb 10) Lord Avie (USA) – Honorine (USA) (Blushing Groom (FR) 131) [1991 8.2f 8f6 8.9m] IR 7,500Y: quite good-topped gelding: fourth foal: half-brother to fairly useful 9f and 1¼m winner Lord Bertie (by Roberto): dam placed at 1m in France: sire champion 2-y-o colt later won 9f Florida Derby: poor form in maidens and a claimer: should stay 1¼m: looked difficult ride when visored final outing. *M. H. Tompkins.* 44

SAFETY TACTIC (IRE) 2 b.c. (Apr 19) Maelstrom Lake 118 – Risky Game (Troy 137) [1991 5d* 5g2 6m* 6g2 5m2 6m4 7m4 6g*] smallish, strong colt: first 97

foal: dam Irish 2-y-o 7f winner out of smart 6f and 7f performer Sweet Mint: fairly useful performer: successful in maiden at the Curragh in April, minor event at Naas in June and Salora EBF Round Tower Stakes (by a length from Night Duty) at the Curragh in September: ran well in pattern company previous 4 starts: stays 7f: acts on good to firm ground, has won on dead: blinkered sixth outing. *D. K. Weld, Ireland.*

SAFETY (USA) 4 b.g. Topsider (USA) – Flare Pass (USA) (Buckpasser) [1990 — 6m5 8f 9g* 8f2 1991 9s 12.5d] lengthy gelding: moderate mover: quite modest handicapper at 3 yrs: stiff tasks in spring of 1991: should prove ideally suited by 1¼m: acts on firm ground: blinkered last 4 outings: sold out of B. Hills's stable 13,000 gns Newmarket July Sales: winning hurdler. *J. White.*

SAFFAAH (USA) 4 ch.c. Secreto (USA) 128 – Somebody Noble (USA) (Vaguely 69 Noble 140) [1990 10g4 10d2 1991 10.8g2 12m5 14g4 12v2 12.2d] strong, round-barrelled colt: lightly raced and modest handicapper: not seen again after running poorly in July: stays 1¾m: acts on heavy ground: has pulled very hard: sold 5,800 gns Newmarket Autumn Sales. *R. W. Armstrong.*

SAGAMAN (GER) 5 b.g. Solo Dancer (GER) – Scholastika (GER) (Alpenkonig 59 (GER)) [1990 12f4 14.8m3 1991 18s* 16g 16s 22.2m6 18.8f2 11.4m3 14m6 16.2d] quite modest handicapper: won at Doncaster in March: stays extremely well: probably acts on any going: ran poorly when visored: also tried blinkered: winning hurdler. *L. J. Codd.*

SAGANECA (USA) 3 b.f. Sagace (FR) 135 – Haglette (USA) (Hagley (USA)) 117 [1990 8d2 7.5g4 8m 1991 10g5 9d2 10.5g5 12g 10g2 10g4 12m3 12m4 12.5d* 12g] $16,000Y, resold $30,000Y: leggy filly: third foal: dam, winner 3 times in USA, is half-sister to smart French 1970 2-y-o 7f winner Round Top, later also successful over 1m: led final 1f to beat Brooklyn's Dance ¾ length in Ciga Prix de Royallieu at Longchamp in October: 56/1, best other effort about 3 lengths fourth of 14 to Magic Night in Prix Vermeille Escada at same course 3 weeks earlier: last of 12 finishers in Breeders' Cup Turf final outing: suited by 1½m: acts on good to firm ground and dead: trained at 2 yrs by G. Collet: changed hands after second 3-y-o start. *A. Spanu, France.*

SAGAUCHE (USA) 3 b.f. Sagace (FR) 135 – Bammell (USA) (Tell (USA)) [1990 — NR 1991 10g 12m 10g] IR 36,000Y: unfurnished filly: second foal: dam unraced half-sister to smart middle-distance colt Free Sweater: no worthwhile form in maidens: sold 860 gns Newmarket July Sales. *R. Hannon.*

SAGEBRUSH ROLLER 3 br.c. Sharpo 132 – Sunita (Owen Dudley 121) [1990 80 § 6d 5d 6d4 1991 7v* 8s2 7g5 7m2 7.1g4 7g 8d 7m] rangy, unfurnished colt: fair handicapper: won at Newcastle in April: below form last 3 starts, looking none too keen at Ayr penultimate one: should be suited by 1m: yet to race on firm going, acts on any other: hangs under pressure and not one to trust implicitly. *J. W. Watts.*

SAHARA STAR 2 b. or br.f. (Feb 17) Green Desert (USA) 127 – Vaigly Star 118 95 (Star Appeal 133) [1991 5g* 5g* 6g3] compact, useful-looking filly: has a quick action: second live foal: half-sister to a winner in Europe: dam, best at 6f, is half-sister to high-class sprinter Vaigly Great: successful in maiden at Sandown in July: followed up in Philip Cornes Molecomb Stakes at Goodwood, improving at halfway then running on well to beat Another Episode by 1½ lengths, going away: over 5 lengths third of 4, finding little off bridle, to Culture Vulture in Lowther Stakes at York later in August: should prove as effective at 6f: fairly useful. *M. R. Stoute.*

SAHEL (IRE) 3 b.c. Green Desert (USA) 127 – Fremanche (FR) (Jim French 80 (USA)) [1990 6g5 1991 7g3] angular, quite good-topped colt: in need of race, 3½ lengths third of 8 to Savoyard in minor event Leicester in May, eventually running on well from rear: should be suited by further. *J. H. M. Gosden.*

SAIF AL ADIL (IRE) 2 b.c. (Jan 24) Reference Point 139 – Hardihostess 104 60 (Be My Guest (USA) 126) [1991 7g 7f] 54,000Y: sturdy, lengthy colt: fifth foal: dam 7f winner at 2 yrs, stayed 1½m: quite modest form in maidens at Newmarket and Newbury (showed up well until 2f out) in August: may do better over middle distances. *B. Hanbury.*

SAIFAN 2 ch.c. (May 24) Beveled (USA) – Superfrost (Tickled Pink 114) [1991 63 5d6 5m3 5m3 5.2f 5m 6m4 6s3] tall, close-coupled colt: has a round action: second foal: half-brother to 3-y-o Almasa (by Faustus), fair 6f winner at 2 yrs: dam 1m seller winner: quite modest maiden: mostly consistent: probably better suited by 6f than 5f: acts on good to firm and soft ground. *J. C. Fox.*

SAILOR BOY 5 b.h. Main Reef 126 – Main Sail 104 (Blakeney 126) [1990 16g 67 16d6 14g 14m2 14m3 17.1f3 13.1h* 14g3 16f5 12d 1991 17.1m 13.1m5 13.1f 14.8s5 11.7f3 14s6 a13g2 a16g a13g3] smallish, quite attractive horse: easy mover, with a

734

light action: quite modest handicapper: below form at Lingfield last 2 starts: effective at 13f to 17f: acts on hard ground, unsuited by soft surface: has run creditably blinkered: has run in snatches: best racing up with pace. *R. Akehurst.*

SAIL PAST (FR)   3 gr.g. No Pass No Sale 120 – All In White (FR) (Carwhite 127)   —
[1990 5m⁵ 6m* 6g³ 7m⁶ 7s 6g 7g 7s 1991 7f 8.5m 9.9f 7g⁶ 7f] leggy, close-coupled gelding: modest form at best, little in 1991: seems to stay 7f: blinkered last 3 starts, also hooded final one: sometimes bandaged behind: sold 1,100 gns Doncaster October Sales. *F. H. Lee.*

SAINT BENE'T (IRE)   3 b.g. Glenstal (USA) 118 – Basilea (FR) (Frere Basile   **65**
(FR) 129) [1990 6m³ 6h³ 6m 7m⁴ 8m 7s 1991 8.2f³ 11.1d⁴ 11.1d² 11.5m 12.1g 12.1s] workmanlike gelding: quite modest maiden: clearly best efforts, set plenty to do, when placed in handicaps at Hamilton: stays 11f: acts on firm and dead going: races freely: trained first 5 starts by W. Pearce. *P. C. Haslam.*

SAINT CALIGULA (IRE)   3 b.g. Petorius 117 – Saint Cynthia (Welsh Saint   **79**
126) [1990 7g² a6g* 6m 6d⁶ a7g* 1991 a6g² a8g³ a7g* a8g⁶ 7m a7g⁴] leggy gelding: fair performer on his day: successful 3 times at Southwell, in claimer in February: favourite, ran poorly in similar events and seller (blinkered) last 3 outings: best form at 7f: often ridden by inexperienced apprentice (not last 2 starts): has looked none too keen, including when successful: sold 5,000 gns Newmarket July Sales. *M. Bell.*

SAINT CIEL (USA)   3 b.c. Skywalker (USA) – Holy Tobin (USA) 83 (J O Tobin   **83**
(USA) 130) [1990 7s² 1991 8s³ 10f* 12d 9.9m³ 10.1d* 10.5m⁵ 10.5f² 10.3m 10.5g*] rather leggy, quite attractive colt: moderate mover: won maiden at Pontefract in April, celebrity sweepstakes at Windsor in June and claimer (claimed by F. Jordan £21,000) at Haydock in September: tailed off in handicap penultimate outing: stays 1¼m: acts on any going: below form in blinkers third and fourth starts: reluctant at stalls twice: retained 24,000 gns Newmarket July Sales after sixth start. *A. A. Scott.*

SAINTLY ARTIST (IRE)   2 b.c. (Apr 23) Tate Gallery (USA) 117 – Saintly   **63**
Angel 87 (So Blessed 130) [1991 6m 6m² 6f⁶ a7g⁴] IR 7,200Y: good-topped colt: half-brother to 3-y-o Blyton Star (by Horage) and several winners, including useful 1983 sprinting 2-y-o African Abandon (by African Sky) and fair 7f and 1m performer Brittania Bell (by Pitskelly): dam lightly-raced 2-y-o 5f winner: quite modest maiden: off course nearly 2 months before final start (July), moving poorly down then running moderately: will stay 1m: sold 1,900 gns Newmarket Autumn Sales. *G. A. Pritchard-Gordon.*

SAINT NAVARRO   6 ch.m. Raga Navarro (ITY) 119 – Saint Motunde 84 (Tyrant   **63**
(USA)) [1990 5f³ 5g³ 5g* 5f⁶ 5f⁶ 5f⁴ 5m* a5g³ 5g⁵ 5d⁵ 5m⁶ 1991 a6g⁵ 5g 5.3f a5g² 5f⁴ 5g 5d 5m³ 6.1m² 5f⁵ 5d⁵ 5m 5g] rather leggy, plain, close-coupled mare: has a round action: quite modest handicapper: best at 5f: probably acts on any going: best in blinkers: ran creditably when visored: goes well at Chester: often starts slowly: sometimes hangs: none too consistent. *C. J. Hill.*

SAINTRY (USA)   2 ch.c. (Apr 19) Groom Dancer (USA) 128 – Sainte Croix   **107**
(USA) (Nijinsky (CAN) 138) [1991 6g⁴ 6g³ 8g* 8g* 8g* 8v³] third foal: half-brother to 4-y-o Waki Gold (by Miswaki), successful at 9f at 3 yrs: dam, French maiden, is sister to smart Irish middle-distance stayer Empire Glory and half-sister to Irish 1000 Guineas winner Gaily and high-class American 6f to 9f winner King's Bishop: successful in minor event then listed contest at Craon in September, then listed event at Lyon following month: 5½ lengths third of 7 to Litron in Prix des Chenes at Evry in November: should stay 1¼m: acts on heavy ground. *Mme C. Head, France.*

SAINT SYSTEMS   5 b.m. Uncle Pokey 116 – Fire Mountain 87 (Dragonara   **53**
Palace (USA) 115) [1990 5m⁵ 5.8f* 5g⁵ 5f³ 5m⁵ 5.8h⁴ 5f³ 5g 5m 5.8f 5.3f 5g 5m* 5d³ 5.8d* a6g² a5g* a6g* a7g⁶ 1991 a5g⁵ 5.3f 6g 6m 5.8f a5g 5d⁶ 5.1g⁶ 5m 5.7m² 5m⁵ 5m² 5d³ 5m⁴ 5m⁴ 5.7f⁵ 5.3g² 5m] angular, sparely-made mare: quite modest handicapper at best: effective at 5f to 6f: acts on firm and dead going: below form in blinkers: has won for apprentice. *C. J. Hill.*

SAINT VENDING   3 br.c. Grey Desire 115 – Girdle Ness 56 (Pitskelly 122)   **43** +
[1990 5m 5v⁵ 5g 6g⁶ 6g² 7.5d* 7.5f 8.2s 1991 12s⁵] sparely-made colt: has a round action: plating-class winner at 2 yrs: below form in claimer in March as 3-y-o, took keen hold and no extra final 2f: should prove at least as effective at 1¼m: possibly unsuited by firm ground: blinkered once. *M. Brittain.*

SAKHAROV   2 b.g. (Apr 28) Bay Express 132 – Supreme Kingdom 85 (Take A   **52**
Reef 127) [1991 5f⁵ 5g⁶ 7g 6m] leggy, unfurnished gelding: first foal: dam 2-y-o 7.2f winner became temperamental as 4-y-o: plating-class form in maidens: lowered in

class, soundly beaten in 21-runner seller at Redcar final start: subsequently gelded: best form at 5f. *F. H. Lee.*

SAKIL (IRE)   3 b.c. Vision (USA) – Sciambola (Great Nephew 126) [1990 7s 1991   —
10g 10.1s 10g 12g⁶ 11.7g 10.1d 12f 12g] good-topped colt: shows quick action: form only when running-on sixth of 14 in handicap at Goodwood: should stay beyond 1½m: sold to join G. Enright 7,000 gns Newmarket Autumn Sales. *C. J. Benstead.*

SAKOSAN   2 gr.f. (May 16) Absalom 128 – River Chimes 43 (Forlorn River 124)   —
[1991 5m 5f 5m⁵] lengthy, sparely-made filly: eighth foal: sister to speedy 1984 2-y-o Absent Chimes and quite modest 1987 2-y-o Rapid Chimes: dam sister to high-class Rapid River: soundly beaten in maidens and a minor event. *N. Chamberlain.*

SALACITY   7 b.g. Sallust 134 – Vera Van Fleet (Cracksman 111) [1990 10v 12s   —
1991 13.8d] close-coupled gelding: bad mover: lightly-raced maiden on flat: tailed off in handicaps last 3 starts. *G. M. Moore.*

SALADAN KNIGHT   6 b.g. Dalsaan 125 – Exciting Times (Windjammer (USA))   57 +
[1990 a8g³ 6m⁵ 6m 6m 5m⁵ 1991 a6g³ 5g 7.5f⁶ 6g] lengthy, good-topped gelding: moderate mover: plating-class handicapper nowadays: best form at 5f and 6f: best on a sound surface: tried blinkered and visored: often on toes: tends to wander. *J. G. FitzGerald.*

SALAZAR   2 b.c. (Apr 10) Pharly (FR) 130 – Scholastika (GER) (Alpenkonig   67
(GER)) [1991 5m 6m⁴ 7m⁶] strong, close-coupled colt: has a round action: fourth known foal: half-brother to 11.5f winner Slipperose (by Persepolis) and winning stayer/fairly useful hurdler Sagaman (by Solo Dancer): dam German bred: quite modest maiden: off course over 4 months after debut: will stay middle distances: sent to Italy. *W. R. Muir.*

SALBYNG   3 b.c. Night Shift (USA) – Hsian (Shantung 132) [1990 7m 7f⁶ 7m 8.2d   65
1991 8.2d* a8g* 8.2m³ 8g* a8g⁶ 8m 10.2g² 10f⁴ 11.4m⁴ 12g 8g⁶ 10.3d] strong colt: carries condition: usually looks well: has a quick action: quite modest handicapper: narrowly successful at Nottingham, Southwell and Bath in first half of season: no show in ladies event final start: probably stays 11.4f: acts on firm and dead going. *J. W. Hills.*

SALDA   2 b.g. (Mar 16) Bustino 136 – Martinova 111 (Martinmas 128) [1991 8m⁵   82
7m 7s] IR 14,500Y: big, lengthy gelding: looks weak: half-brother to 3 winners, notably very useful French sprinter Export Price (by Habitat): dam, third in 1000 Guineas, is half-sister to high-class 1¼m performer Lucky Wednesday: better effort in September maidens at Redcar (green, kept on well) on debut: improved form when ninth of 18 to Fair Crack in Goffs Million at the Curragh following month: likely to stay 1¼m: should win a modest maiden. *R. M. Whitaker.*

SALIC DANCE   3 b.c. Shareef Dancer (USA) 135 – Sandy Island 110 (Mill Reef   —
(USA) 141) [1990 7m³ 8g 7m⁴ 1991 a10g⁵ 10.2g] well-made colt: quite modest maiden: stiffish tasks in handicaps, little promise in visor second start: should stay middle distances: has flashed tail: sold to join G. Ham 3,000 gns Ascot June Sales. *P. T. Walwyn.*

SALISONG   2 gr.c. (Mar 18) Song 132 – Sylvanecte (FR) 70 (Silver Shark 129)   73 p
[1991 7m³ 7g*] 20,000Y: lengthy colt: has scope: brother to several winners, including 6f and 7f winner Band On The Run, and half-brother to useful 6f and 7f winner Silver Lord (by Abwah): dam won over 1¼m: favourite, third in maiden auction at Leicester before comfortably winning maiden at Salisbury in October: will stay 1m: will probably improve further. *P. F. I. Cole.*

SALLY FAY (IRE)   3 b.f. Fayruz 116 – Trust Sally 65 (Sallust 134) [1990 NR 1991   66
6m⁵ 5m⁶ 6d² 5f 7g³ 6d² 6g⁶ 6m* 6m⁵ 6g⁵ 7m⁶ 7g a6g] IR 2,000Y: leggy, workmanlike filly: fifth foal: closely related to modest 1987 2-y-o 5f winner Marley Supalite (by Jester) and half-sister to 6f winner Reasonable Kid (by Reasonable) and a winner in Belgium: dam 5f seller winner: quite modest performer: won maiden at Redcar in August: ran poorly last 2 outings: suited by 6f: acts on good to firm ground and dead, ran poorly on fibresand: sold out of M. H. Easterby's stable 2,500 gns Doncaster October Sales after eleventh start. *T. Kersey.*

SALLY SAAD   3 gr.f. Green Desert (USA) 127 – Biding 97 (Habat 127) [1990 NR   47
1991 7g 7g⁴ 7f³ 6f⁵ 6.1m] 44,000Y: leggy, angular filly: has a quick action: fifth living foal: half-sister to a winner in Italy by Wassl: dam, half-sister to very smart Splashing (dam of Bassenthwaite) won 2 of her 3 races over 5f at 2 yrs: poor maiden: sold 3,600 gns Newmarket December Sales. *B. Hanbury.*

SALLY'S SON   5 b.g. Beldale Flutter (USA) 130 – Sally Chase 101 (Sallust 134)   59
[1990 a7g* a7g³ a8g⁶ 6g³ 5m² 6m³ 6m⁶ 6g 5m⁶ 5. 1f* 5m² a5g² 5m³ 1991 a5g³ a6g*   a 72
a6g⁵ a6g² a7g* a6g² 5m 7f⁶ 5m 5m⁶ 6m 6m⁵ 5.2f⁵ 7g a6g⁵ a6g] strong, good-bodied

gelding: carries plenty of condition: moderate walker: modest handicapper: stays 7f: acts on firm ground and all-weather surfaces: ridden by claimer: effective with or without blinkers or visor: none too consistent on turf. *W. A. O'Gorman.*

SALLYS WON 7 b.g. Free State 125 – Arbatina (Sallust 134) [1990 10.2f 8f 10f⁵ 10m 10f³ 10f 8d 8g 1991 a8g a7g] rangy gelding: moderate mover: poor maiden: no form in handicaps in early part of 1991: stays 1¼m: acts on firm going: withdrawn (broke out of stalls) once at 6 yrs. *R. Curtis.* —

SALLY TADPOLE 2 b.f. (Apr 28) Jester 119 – Sorata (FR) (Sodium 128) [1991 5g²] 2,500Y: half-sister to several winners abroad, including useful Italian miler Mantero (by Derrylin): dam won from 6f to 11f in France: stayed on unable to challenge Nifty Fifty in maiden auction at Edinburgh in April, only outing. *J. Hetherton.* 44

SALMAN (USA) 5 b.h. Nain Bleu (FR) – H M S Pellinore (USA) (King Pellinore (USA) 127) [1990 8f 8m⁶ 9m⁵ 10m⁴ 11d³ 9f 1991 10s² 10s³ 10.4d 8.9g 10m 9m⁶ 9m⁴ 10m⁶ 10m⁶] strong, good-topped horse: has had soft palate operation: plating-class handicapper nowadays: stays 1¼m: acts on any going: has edged right: headstrong, and bolted intended reappearance: had tongue tied down of late: has worn crossed noseband: gives impression none too genuine. *S. G. Norton.* 70 d

SALMINO (IRE) 3 b.c. Salmon Leap (USA) 131 – Amina 80 (Brigadier Gerard 144) [1990 6m 8m* 7m* 1991 7g 8m⁵ 8d³ 7g* 7g⁵ 6m 7m² 7d² 7m] leggy, quite good-topped colt: impresses in appearance: fairly useful handicapper: won at Ayr in July: ran well when second in handicaps within 4 days at same course in September: best form at 7f: acts on good to firm ground and dead: takes keen hold, and has worn crossed noseband: sold 31,000 gns Newmarket Autumn Sales. *Mrs G. R. Reveley.* 96

SALMON DANCER (IRE) 2 b.c. (Mar 12) Salmon Leap (USA) 131 – Welsh Walk (Welsh Saint 126) [1991 6m 7g 8.1g 8.2m 8m] IR 3,000Y, 6,800 2-y-o: leggy, lengthy colt: carries condition: first foal: dam never ran: poor maiden: will probably stay beyond 1m. *M. F. Barraclough.* 37

SALMONID 5 ch.g. Salmon Leap (USA) 131 – Persian Polly 99 (Persian Bold 123) [1990 10g 8m⁵ 10m 10m⁴ 12m* 12m⁶ a12g² a12g* 1991 11.1g⁵ a12g] sturdy, lengthy, rather dipped-backed gelding: carries plenty of condition: quite modest handicapper: not seen again after running as if something amiss at Southwell in June: effective at 1¼m and 1½m: acts on good to firm going: has won 3 times for an amateur. *P. F. I. Cole.* 57

SALT WHISTLE 2 ch.c. (Mar 30) Risk Me (FR) 127 – Marble Moon (Le Moss 135) [1991 5.1m² 6m⁴ 5d 7m* 8.1m⁶ 7.3m⁵ 8g 7m] 9,600Y: lengthy, unfurnished colt: moderate walker: first foal: dam poor half-sister to very useful Irish 1½m and 2m winner Marble Run: favourite but sweating, improved form winning nursery at Newmarket in July: creditable fifth of 9 to stable-companion Beyton in similar event at Newbury 2 months later, easily best subsequent effort: best form at around 7f: acts on good to firm ground: blinkered (very edgy) final start: sold 14,500 gns Newmarket Autumn Sales. *R. Hannon.* 80

SALU 2 br.f. (Mar 29) Ardross 134 – String of Beads 63 (Ile de Bourbon (USA) 133) [1991 7g² 8.9d] leggy, unfurnished filly: second foal: half-sister to 3-y-o Dancing Tudor (by Absalom): dam (of doubtful temperament) stayed 2m, is half-sister to very smart 1983 2-y-o Creag-An-Sgor: 25/1 and better for race, strong-finishing runner-up at Redcar, much better effort in autumn maidens: should stay long distances. *J. Etherington.* 64

SALUTING WALTER (USA) 3 b.c. Verbatim (USA) – Stage Hour (USA) (Stage Director (USA)) [1990 6m⁴ 1991 8m⁶ 8g³ 9m³ 10m² 10.6g² 10m³ 8d* 8m 9d⁶ 7.6g³ 8.9m⁴ 8m 9g³ 7d⁶] leggy, good-topped colt: fair performer: won maiden at Pontefract in July: generally bit below best last 4 outings: worth another try at 1¼m: acts on good to firm ground and dead: occasionally edgy and sweating: sold F. Jordan 20,00 gns Doncaster November Sales. *M. J. Ryan.* 80

SALWAN (USA) 3 ch.c. Sagace (FR) 135 – Sedra 116 (Nebbiolo 125) [1990 7g⁶ 7s⁶ 1991 7g⁵ 10m⁶ 8.3f³ 8f² 10g² 8.1m³ 12s³] angular, leggy colt: shows traces of stringhalt: modest maiden: should stay 1½m: acts on firm going: consistent: sold out of W. Jarvis's stable 12,000 gns Newmarket Autumn Sales after sixth start: winning hurdler. *P. J. Bevan.* 70

SAMAIN (USA) 4 ch.f. Caerleon (USA) 132 – Samarta Dancer (USA) (Marshua's Dancer (USA)) [1990 8m⁵ 10m³ 12.5m 1991 6d 7f⁴ 6m 9m⁵ 10m 11.5s⁵ 8.1g⁵ 10g⁶ 10m] tall, leggy, sparely-made filly: poor handicapper, still a maiden: stays 1¼m: acts on firm ground: has swished tail and hung under pressure: very slowly away final start: sold 2,800 gns Newmarket September Sales. *Pat Mitchell.* 63 d

SAMIR 2 ch.c. (Feb 5) Midyan (USA) 124 – Friths Folly 62 (Good Bond 122) [1991 — 6g] 27,000Y: good-topped colt: fifth foal: half-brother to fair 1985 2-y-o 5f winner Busy Lovie (by Dragonara Palace): dam placed at up to 1½m: 11/1 from 7/2 and bit backward, last of 8 in maiden at Folkestone in October, no danger from 2f out: sold 4,000 gns Newmarket Autumn Sales. *J. L. Dunlop.*

SAMJAMALIFRAN 2 b.f. (Mar 3) Blakeney 126 – Royal Shoe 75 (Hotfoot 126) — [1991 10m] small filly: second foal: half-sister to 3-y-o 11.7f and 1½m winner Princess Moodyshoe (by Jalmood): dam winning jumper: 100/1, burly and very green, slowly away when tailed-off last of 12 in maiden at Nottingham in October. *M. C. Pipe.*

SAMMY NIKA (IRE) 3 b.f. Salmon Leap (USA) 131 – Nikara (FR) (Emerson) — [1990 NR 1991 a7g 5m] 2,000F, 850Y: leggy, lengthy filly: fourth foal: closely related to a winner in Italy by Try My Best and half-sister to 2 winners, notably useful 4-y-o 5f and 6f winner Gilt Throne (by Thatching): dam won over 6f and 7.5f at 2 yrs in France: well behind in maidens in June. *T. Fairhurst.*

SAMMY SLEW (USA) 2 br.c. (Feb 9) Tsunami Slew (USA) – Big Sparkle 64 (USA) (The Big Boss (USA)) [1991 6m⁵ 6g⁵] $50,000Y: lengthy, useful-looking colt: has scope: first foal: dam, minor sprint-stakes winner, won 20 races from 2 yrs to 8 yrs: sire good-class turf performer: quite modest maiden: withdrawn from minor event at Redcar after breaking through stalls: 14 lengths fifth of 7 to Fair Crack in minor event at Windsor later in August: tailed-off last of 5 in Scottish Equitable Gimcrack Stakes at York 9 days later: may stay 1m. *S. G. Norton.*

SAMSOLOM 3 b.g. Absalom 128 – Norfolk Serenade 83 (Blakeney 126) [1990 75 5s⁴ 5m* 5m³ 5g 5g⁵ 5f 6d 5m* 5g⁵ 1991 5f⁴ 5m² 6m³ 6f 5d⁴ 5g² 5m³ 6s⁶ 6m 5f] strong, good-quartered gelding: has round action: modest handicapper: effective at 5f and 6f: acts on any going, except seemingly soft: visored once at 2 yrs: once got loose in preliminaries: sometimes hangs left. *J. A. Glover.*

SAMSON-AGONISTES 5 b.h. Bold Fort 100 – Hello Cuddles 99 (He Loves 71 Me 120) [1990 a5g4 5m* 5m a5g3 5m* 5m² 5g4 5m 1991 5m* 5f* 5f⁶ 5g⁵ 5m] leggy horse: moderate walker and poor mover: modest handicapper: won at Pontefract (apprentices, goes very well there) and Folkestone in September: suited by 5f: acts on firm going. *B. A. McMahon.*

SAM SPADE 3 b.g. Balliol 125 – Song Book 85 (Saintly Song 128) [1990 NR 1991 — 5g 8m 6g 6g⁶ 6m 10.1m 8f 7m] sturdy, angular gelding: sixth living foal: brother to 1m and 9.4f winner Sam Chifney and half-brother to 2 winners: dam 2-y-o 6f seller winner: poor plater: wore crossed noseband first 3 starts. *K. T. Ivory.*

SAM THE MAN 4 b.g. Aragon 118 – First Temptation (USA) 67 (Mr Leader 56 (USA)) [1990 8m 8f 9m 7g 10d⁶ 7d² a10g a7g⁵ 1991 10v* 8.3g] rather sparely-made gelding: plating-class performer: fortunate winner of claimer at Folkestone in March: not knocked about on similar event final start (May): stays 1¼m: acts on heavy going: sold only 925 gns Ascot October Sales. *Miss B. Sanders.*

SAMURAI GOLD (USA) 3 b.c. Golden Act (USA) – Taipan's Lady (USA) 55 § (Bold Hour) [1990 5m⁵ 6f² 6m⁴ 6m⁴ 6d* 1991 5d 8g 6g⁶ 6m 5g⁵ 5m⁴ 6g⁵ 6m 5f 6g⁴ a10g³ a10g⁵] rather leggy colt: plating-class handicapper nowadays: effective at 6f, and stays 1¼m: acts on firm and dead ground: visored last 2 starts, normally blinkered: sometimes edgy: takes keen hold: trained until after tenth start by D. Elsworth: ungenuine. *P. T. Walwyn.*

SANDCASTLE CITY 2 b.c. (Apr 5) Formidable (USA) 125 – Sandstream 72 75 (Sandford Lad 133) [1991 5g³ 5d⁴ 5g² 5d* 5g* 5.2g 6.1g⁶ 6g] 21,000Y: well-made, sturdy colt: eighth foal: half-brother to 3-y-o Swift Stream (by Chief Singer) and several winners here and abroad, including fair 1989 2-y-o 5f winner Between The Sheets (by Pharly): dam 2-y-o 6f winner, is half-sister to Manado: modest performer: successful at Windsor in maiden and minor event (despite hanging left) within a week in mid-summer: below form in Newbury Sales Super Sprint Trophy and nurseries at Chepstow and Kempton afterwards: should be at least as effective at 6f as 5f: acts on dead ground. *R. Hannon.*

SAND-DOLLAR 8 ch.h. Persian Bold 123 – Late Spring 101 (Silly Season 127) 41 [1990 NR 1991 a10g⁴ a10g² a10g⁵ a12g⁶ 8g] leggy, sparely-made horse: poor and lightly-raced handicapper nowadays: stays 1¼m: acts on firm going: sometimes wears crossed noseband. *J. A. B. Old.*

SANDFORD SPRINGS (USA) 4 b.f. Robellino (USA) 127 – Tiger Scout 49 (USA) 86 (Silent Screen (USA)) [1990 10g 14g 11.7m a12g⁵ 13.8m³ 11.7h² 11.7h* 12m⁵ 17.1m 1991 16m⁴ 16.2g 17.1d² 17.2g³ 17.2f⁶ 12.5g⁵ 15.8g 17.2g] good-bodied filly: plating-class handicapper: slipped up final start: stays 17f: acts on hard and dead ground: effective visored or not: tried blinkered once. *R. J. Holder.*

SANDHURST PARK   6 ch.g. Sandhurst Prince 128 – Sandford Lass 87 (Sandford Lad 133) [1990 NR 1991 10.2s⁵ 12m] compact gelding: poor handicapper nowadays: not seen out after May: seems to stay 1¼m: probably acts on any going: has run well when visored. *R. J. Holder.*   —

SANDHURST TYPE (IRE)   3 ch.f. Sandhurst Prince 128 – Double Type (Behistoun 131) [1990 6m⁵ 6g 6g² 7g⁴ 6f⁵ 6f⁵ 6m 1991 8.9g 10.2f6] angular, sparsely-made filly: has a round action: poor maiden: behind facing stiff tasks in summer at 3 yrs: should stay at least 1m: bought 700 gns Ascot February Sales. *A. J. Chamberlain.*   —

SANDICLIFFE WAY (IRE)   3 ch.g. Doulab (USA) 115 – Plainsong (FR) (Amen (FR)) [1990 5f⁵ 7g⁶ 6g³ 6f 8m 8.2d* a8g³ 1991 10.2g 10g⁶ 10g⁵ a10g 16.1g] smallish, lengthy gelding: fair winner at 2 yrs: ran poorly in handicaps at 3 yrs: should stay 1¼m: well suited by dead ground: not the easiest of rides: sold 7,000 gns Newmarket Autumn Sales, probably for Macau. *B. W. Hills.*   —

SANDMOOR DENIM   4 b.g. Red Sunset 120 – Holernzaye 93 (Sallust 134) [1990 6f 7.5d⁵ a11g⁴ 8.5d* 8g a8g² a6g a7g 8m 8.5m 8m 1991 a8g⁵ a7g 6d 8d 10m 7f* a 44 8.2d⁶ 8m* 7f a7g³ 8.2m³ 7m³ 8.2f⁴ 7m² 7m² 7m³ 8m² a8g⁶] close-coupled gelding: quite modest handicapper: won at Catterick and Doncaster in June: ran well after: stays 1m: has form on dead ground, but seems best on top-of-the-ground nowadays: below form when blinkered: had tongue tied down late in year: has sometimes been mounted on track and taken down early: tough and consistent. *S. R. Bowring.*   58

SANDRO   2 b.g. (Apr 7) Niniski (USA) 125 – Miller's Creek (USA) 62 (Star de Naskra (USA)) [1991 7g 8m] 12,000F, 33,000Y: lengthy gelding: third foal: closely related to 3-y-o 6f (at 2 yrs) to 10.2f winner Stone Mill (by Caerleon): dam maiden suited by 1m, is out of half-sister to top Canadian colt Giboulee: bit backward, never better than mid-division in large-field maidens at Leicester and Warwick in autumn: likely to stay middle distances. *J. R. Fanshawe.*   44

SANDY STORM   4 ch.g. Lomond (USA) 128 – Holly Deb (USA) (Xoda (USA)) [1990 a8g a10g 7g a5g a7g a8g⁶ 1991 a8g 7d] smallish, good-bodied gelding: little sign of ability: often blinkered: sold 725 gns Ascot December Sales. *C. N. Williams.*   —

SANGLAMORE (USA)   4 ch.c. Sharpen Up 127 – Ballinderry 112 (Irish **126** River (FR) 131) [1990 10g* 10m² 10.5g* 12m* 1991 9m* 10d³ 12m²]

The latest season underlined that opportunism, allied to judgement of pace, can decide the destination of even the richest prizes. Terimon's all-the-way win in York's International Stakes springs readily to mind, while French racing provided a prime example in the Group 1 Prix d'Ispahan at Chantilly in early-June. With no pace on through the opening quarter-mile, the free-running Sanglamore was wisely allowed to stride on by Pat Eddery and, having settled better in front, there he stayed, running on bravely under pressure in the straight, despite wandering, and warding off several chal-

Prix d'Ispahan, Chantilly—Sanglamore's triumphant return;
Priolo, Zoman and Candy Glen fully extend him

Mr K. Abdulla's "Sanglamore"

Sanglamore (USA) (ch.c. 1987)	Sharpen Up (ch 1969)	Atan (ch 1961)	Native Dancer
			Mixed Marriage
		Rocchetta (ch 1961)	Rockefella
			Chambiges
	Ballinderry (ch 1981)	Irish River (ch 1976)	Riverman
			Irish Star
		Miss Manon (b 1970)	Bon Mot III
			Miss Molly

lengers. The strongest challenge came from Priolo, half a length adrift at the line after being short of room against the rail (the stewards inquired into possible interference between the first two), with only a head and a neck back to Zoman and Candy Glen respectively. Although the contest was arguably unsatisfactory because of the false pace the victory reflected great credit on Sanglamore and his connections. Despite an absence of exactly a year since his victory on the same course in the Prix du Jockey-Club Lancia, the good-topped, attractive Sanglamore was turned out well muscled-up and in magnificent condition, and though appearing to face a stiff task over a much shorter trip against six race-fit rivals, he was in no way neglected by the Parisian crowd who sent him off at 44/10 behind the favourite Zoman (24/10), Priolo (5/2) and Kartajana (34/10); British bookmakers had him as long as 12/1 in their lists. The d'Ispahan was no springboard to further success, however, Sanglamore having to settle for a place, beaten around seven lengths, in the Coral-Eclipse and the King George VI and Queen Elizabeth Diamond Stakes the following month, his only subsequent starts. Sanglamore had every chance in the former, going on from his pacemaker Green's Ferneley entering the final three furlongs but was soon made to look one-paced first by Stagecraft then the winner Environment Friend. He impressed less than usual in appearance before the Eclipse, though it is entirely plausible that the yielding ground was the reason for his below-par effort—he was otherwise campaigned only on a sound surface. Back at probably his optimum distance in the King George, Sanglamore found Generous in a different league, though he ran well, keeping on in typically genuine fashion in a strongly-run race for second, immediately ahead of Rock Hopper, Terimon and Sapience.

Sanglamore was a high-class performer, and we've rated him as good at four as at three, when he progressed rapidly, also winning the William Hill Dante Stakes at York. Unfortunately, he was evidently not the easiest horse to train, and the recurrence of an old ligament injury whilst being prepared for the Breeders' Cup brought about his retirement. Sanglamore will stand at his owner's Juddmonte Farms Stud in Kentucky for a fee of 15,000 dollars live foal, by no means an inflated appraisal for a classic-winning son of Sharpen Up from a proven female line. The now-retired Sharpen Up was also responsible in 1991 in Britain for the Queen Elizabeth II Stakes winner Selkirk and the lightly-raced but already useful Cardinal Point, while the ex-British-trained pair Bequest and Becquerel figured amongst his four stakes winners in the States. Sanglamore was the first live foal of the Ribblesdale Stakes winner Ballinderry. Her second Balliasta (by Lyphard) was unplaced on two outings in France in 1991 while the third Ballindar (by Alydar) is in training in America. Ballinderry is one of five stakes winners produced by the Prix de Diane fourth Miss Manon, another the dual French-classic placed Sharpman being a close relation to Sanglamore. Miss Manon herself remains active, but neither her three-year-old Mangalore with Harwood nor two-year-old Guillem with Cecil has yet made the track; she also has a yearling by the Sharpen Up stallion Diesis. *R. Charlton.*

SAN PIER NICETO   4 b.c. Norwick (USA) 120 – Langton Herring (Nearly A —
Hand 115) [1990 8g⁴ 7.5d⁴ 10g⁴ 8g³ 8g 9f* 7f² 9s³ 10v 1991 11s 10.5g] smallish, lengthy colt: moderate walker and mover: modest handicapper 3 yrs: soundly beaten in 1991, off course nearly 6 months after reappearance: should stay 1¼m: acts on any going, with possible exception of heavy: inconsistent: not easiest of rides: winning hurdler in March. *M. D. Hammond.*

SAN ROQUE   6 b.g. Aragon 118 – Arch Sculptress 85 (Arch Sculptor 123) [1990   27
10f 12g 10g 10m* 10.2f⁴ 10m 11m⁵ 10f8f³ 10f⁴8g 1991 a10g a13g⁶ a10g³ a12g 10.2s 9g 8m 8f 12f⁴ 8f 12g 9d 10s 12g 10m 10s⁴ 12s] sturdy, close-coupled gelding: has a quick action: poor handicapper: effective at 1m and 1¼m: probably acts on any going: usually bandaged nowadays: has worn blinkers and visor: has looked a difficult ride: trained until after penultimate start by D. Wilson. *Miss L. Bower.*

SANS FRAIS   3 b.f. Forzando 122 – Shere Beauty 83 (Mummy's Pet 125) [1990   —
5m³ 5m 6h³ 6f⁵ 5.3h⁵ 6m² 6g 6d 6m 5s³ a6g⁶ 1991 5f a5g 5m] lengthy, sparely-made filly: inconsistent plater: not disgraced in apprentice contest final start, in August: stays 6f: acts on good to firm ground and soft: blinkered once: on toes (well beaten) first 2 outings: often finds little: sold A. Smith 1,000 gns Doncaster November Sales. *R. J. R. Williams.*

SANTANA LADY (IRE)   2 b.f. (Feb 22) Blakeney 126 – Santalina (Relko 136)   57
[1991 7d⁶ a7g⁵] 10,000F, 200,000 francs (approx £20,000) Y: half-sister to several winners, including quite useful 1986 2-y-o 6f winner Sansiya (by Dalsaan) and useful 9f and 1¼m winner Salilia (by Nishapour): dam won over middle distances in France: 33/1, over 15 lengths sixth of 21, staying on when checked 2f out, to Berseto in maiden at Doncaster: well beaten in similar event on fibresand later in month: very stoutly bred. *M. J. Heaton-Ellis.*

SANTARAY   5 ch.h. Formidable (USA) 125 – Stockingful (Santa Claus 133) [1990   —
NR 1991 14.6s 10.8g⁵ 8.1d] big, strong, rangy horse: half-brother to several winners, including useful stayer Wesley (by High Top) and modest middle-distance stayer Velda (by Thatch): dam once-raced half-sister to smart miler Richboy: wearing crossed noseband, stayed on well when fifth in maiden at Warwick: in need of run, stiff task and tenderly handled in Chepstow minor event 7½ months later: won NH Flat race in March: had tongue tied down last 2 starts: winning hurdler. *J. Mackie.*

SANTI SANA   3 b.f. Formidable (USA) 125 – Eldoret 100 (High Top 131) [1990   80
NR 1991 7g⁶ 7d* 8m⁶ 8.1d] strong, stocky filly: sister to very smart 6f to 1m winner Efisio and half-sister to several winners, including 1½m and 2m winner Jinga and 1¼m to 12.3f winner Murango (both by Shirley Heights): dam won at 6f and 1m: won

maiden at Goodwood in August, leading well inside final 1f: very stiff task next start, ran badly in handicap final one: should stay 1m. *Lady Herries*.

SAPIEHA (IRE)   3 b.c. Petorius 117 – Sugarbird 82 (Star Appeal 133) [1990 6m⁵ **111** 7m* 7.3g* 1991 7g⁴ 8d³ 8g² 8g⁵ 7g² 8g 10g³] good-bodied colt: grand walker: moderate mover, with a round action: very useful performer: ran creditably in Poule d'Essai des Poulains at Longchamp (4 lengths third to Hector Protector), St James's Palace Stakes at Royal Ascot (6½ lengths fifth to Marju) and 2 listed races second to fifth outings: fair third of 4 to Perpendicular in moderately-run listed race at Goodwood final one: should stay 1¼m: acts on dead ground: ran poorly when setting pace sixth start. *J. R. Fanshawe*.

SAPIENCE   5 ch.h. Niniski (USA) 125 – Claretta (USA) 82 (Roberto (USA) 131) **117** [1990 8m² 14g² 12m* 12m 1991 12m 12m⁶ 12.5m 10.9m⁶] leggy, rather angular horse: good mover: smart performer at best: well ridden (dictated pace) to win Princess of Wales's Stakes at Newmarket as 4-y-o, generally disappointing since: best effort in 1991 when never-dangerous fifth of 9 to Generous in King George VI and Queen Elizabeth Diamond Stakes at Ascot: never travelling well in Ayr listed event (reportedly finished lame) final start: best at up to 1¾m: acts on any going: has hung: blinkered penultimate start: has joined D. Elsworth. *J. G. FitzGerald*.

SAPPHIRE BREEZE (USA)   3 b.f. Lyphard (USA) 132 – Blue Wind 127 (Lord   — Gayle (USA) 124) [1990 NR 1991 a8g 10f a8g] leggy, narrow filly: third reported foal: dam Oaks winner: bandaged, no promise in spring maidens, very reluctant to go down final start: wore eyeshield at Southwell. *Mrs L. Piggott*.

SAPPHIRINE   4 b.f. Trojan Fen 118 – By Surprise 68 (Young Generation 129)   **64** [1990 a8g² a7g* 7g³ 8d* 7.5f² 8h³ 9f6 9f 1991 8.5g² 7m⁶ 8m⁶ 8m⁴ 10m 12.3f 10m 12f² 12m 9m 12g*] lengthy filly: moderate mover: quite modest handicapper, somewhat inconsistent: won at Doncaster in October: stays 1½m well: acts on hard and dead ground: below form when blinkered once. *R. M. Whitaker*.

SARA ANNE (IRE)   2 b.f. (Mar 27) Sarab 123 – Frans Cap (Captain James 123)   **55** [1991 5m⁴ 5m⁴ 5f⁶ 5m² 6m 5g* 5m² 5m³ 6g 6.1m⁴] leggy, rather sparely-made filly: has a roundish action: first reported foal: dam Irish maiden, fourth twice from 13 starts, including at 1¾m: plating-class performer: won claimer at Nottingham in July: ran at least respectably in nurseries afterwards, moderately in claimer penultimate start: stays 6f: acts on good to firm ground: has run well for 7-lb claimer: sold 5,200 gns Newmarket Autumn Sales. *C. N. Allen*.

SARABAH (IRE)   3 b.f. Ela-Mana-Mou 132 – Be Discreet (Junius (USA) 124)   **83** [1990 6m⁶ 1991 10f³ 10f* 9s 9m² 10m 9g a12g] good-topped filly: fair handicapper at best: won at Folkestone (maiden) in June: easily best subsequent effort when second at Goodwood: better at 1¼m than shorter: acts on firm going. *G. Harwood*.

SARAH-CLARE   3 b.f. Reach 122 – Northern Dynasty 65 (Breeders Dream 116)   **63** [1990 NR 1991 8f 8d 11.5f 10g³ 10g² 11.5m 10g* 10g 10m⁶ 10g 10.3d 11.5s] rangy filly: fifth reported live foal: half-sister to fair middle-distance winners Southern Dynasty (by Gunner B) and Western Dynasty (by Hotfoot) and to 8.2f winner Xai-Tang (by Petong). dam 1m winner. modest form at best: won handicap at Nottingham in August: below form in similar event previous outing and all afterwards: should stay 1½m: best efforts on easy surface. *M. J. Ryan*.

SARAH'S INFLUENCE   5 b.g. Orchestra 118 – Markon (On Your Mark 125)   — [1990 10.6d a6g a11g 1991 a8g] workmanlike gelding: placed in first half of 1989 in maiden at Tipperary and handicap at Mallow: no show in 3 claimers here, blinkered final start: stayed 9f: acted on any going: dead. *D. R. Gandolfo*.

SARALLYN   3 ch.f. Sayf El Arab (USA) 127 – Into Harbour (Right Tack 131) [1990   — NR 1991 6s 6g 6m 8.2f] 8,600F: compact filly: half-sister to several winners, useful 6f winner Jack Tar (by Stanford) and useful 1990 3-y-o sprinter Night At Sea (by Night Shift): dam ran 3 times: no worthwhile form in maidens, seller and claimer: blinkered (somewhat headstrong) last 2 starts. *D. W. P. Arbuthnot*.

SARASOTA BAY   2 b.c. (May 3) Petoski 135 – Be My Queen 84 (Be My Guest   **85** (USA) 126) [1991 7g⁴ 7m² 9s*] unfurnished, workmanlike colt: good walker: moderate mover: fourth foal: brother to 3-y-o Gascoigne Wood: dam 1m winner out of half-sister to Derby second Cavo Doro: fair performer: stayed on strongly when runner-up in median auction maiden at York in October: won listed race at Milan later in month by 2 lengths from Hero's Light: well suited by a test of stamina. *M. Bell*.

SARATOGA SOURCE (USA)   2 ch.f. (Feb 4) Saratoga Six (USA) – Exotic   **82** Source (USA) 79 (The Minstrel (CAN) 135) [1991 7g* 7m³ 7g* 8.5s⁶] $85,000Y: rather leggy, unfurnished filly: first foal: dam 1¼m winner, is half-sister to Alydar's

Best and daughter of sister to Gyr: sire (half-brother to Dunbeath) ran only at 2 yrs, when top-class winner at 6f and 1m: fair performer: favourite, won maiden at Sandown in July and minor event at Warwick (comfortably) in October: well beaten in Grade 3 Selima Stakes at Laurel, USA, 11 days later: will stay at least 1m. *I. A. Balding.*

SARATOGA STAR (USA) 2 ch.f. (Mar 27) Saratoga Six (USA) – Lady Trilby **84**
(USA) (Grenfall (USA)) [1991 5g⁴ 6m⁴ 5.2d³ 6m⁴ 6m 7.5s⁶ 6m 8v] $30,000F, $30,000Y: leggy, rather angular filly: has a roundish action: fourth foal: half-sister to a winner in North America by Caro: dam, winner of 5 races at up to 9f, is half-sister to Nell's Briquette, dam of Love The Groom and Sanquirico: sire (half-brother to Dunbeath) ran only at 2 yrs, when top-class winner at 6f and 1m winner: fair maiden: ran well in Princess Margaret Stakes at Ascot on fifth outing and Tattersalls Cheveley Park Stakes (equal-seventh of 9 to Marling) at Newmarket: blinkered, tailed off in Group 3 race at Milan later in October: should stay 1m: acts on top-of-the-ground and soft. *C. E. Brittain.*

SARAWAT 3 b.c. Slip Anchor 136 – Eljazzi 92 (Artaius (USA) 129) [1990 NR 1991 **86**
12m² 12m* 12g² 12m³ 13.8m*] smallish, workmanlike colt: has a moderate, round action: third foal: half-brother to Prix de Diane winner Rafha (by Kris), also successful at 6f (at 2 yrs) to 11.5f: dam 2-y-o 7f winner stayed 1¼m, is half-sister to Pitcairn and very smart middle-distance stayer Valley Forge: odds on, easily won maiden at Beverley in June and claimer at Catterick in October: stays 1¾m: sold to join Mrs G. Reveley 25,000 gns Newmarket December Sales. *H. R. A. Cecil.*

SARCITA 3 b.f. Primo Dominie 121 – Zinzi (Song 132) [1990 5g⁴ 5g² 5g⁵ 5m **111**
6d* 1991 6m 6m⁴ 5g⁴ 5m* 6m³ 5m 5g* 6f* 5g² 5.6m* 6m* 5d² 5m4]
Sarcita found a rare lease of life in late-summer and early-autumn, contesting six handicaps, winning four and finishing second in the others. It takes an especially progressive sort nowadays to build up a record like that, keeping one step ahead of the handicapper, but in that eight-week spell Mr Gray had hardly any chance of catching up with Sarcita. She lined up for a five-furlong handicap at Goodwood on the last day of July as the winner of two of her eleven starts, seemingly exposed as a modest animal, but went on to such a charge that in the Japan Festival Charity Cup at Ascot on September 27th she put up one of the best performances in a handicap all season. Sarcita met with defeat that day at Ascot, rather unluckily beaten a neck by Gilt Throne after she'd had to race in isolation towards the centre in the closing stages, but connections are unlikely to be fretting too much about that. It was a good prize, £16,570, but after Sarcita's previous five outings that they were already the richer by some £92,000. The two largest contributors to that total were wins in the Tote-Portland Handicap at Doncaster and the Ladbrokes Ayr Gold Cup, a rare double last completed by Jon George in 1977. Sarcita was a gambled-on favourite for the Portland, 13/2 from 11/1 on the day, having won that race at Goodwood (by a head), an apprentice handicap at Newbury and been second at York. The twenty-one-runner contest at Doncaster earned most attention for Farfelu's unseating his rider two furlongs out, recalling the incident two years previously when three horses came down in the same race.

Tote-Portland Handicap, Doncaster—
improving three-year-old filly Sarcita wins going away from Baysham

Ladbrokes (Ayr) Gold Cup—
Sarcita improves again and gives apprentice Brett Doyle an armchair ride;
same-side runners Tbab and Dominuet (rails) finish second and third

Sarcita was produced by Carson from mid-division to catch Baysham in the last fifty yards, for a workmanlike triumph. Workmanlike wasn't a description one could apply to Sarcita's win at Ayr just nine days later. The £52,118 first prize, marginally less than that on offer for Britain's most valuable sprint handicap the William Hill Stewards' Cup, attracted a twenty-eight-strong field but Sarcita won in tremendously impressive style, travelling strongly just behind the leaders from the start and drawing well clear by the furlong marker, eventually beating Tbab three and a half lengths in a course record time. This time Sarcita was 14/1, 5-lb claimer Doyle taking the ride (his first at Ayr) in the absence of Carson, who was at Newbury, and Elsworth's apprentice Hunter who was unwell. Having begun her winning run at Goodwood off an official handicap mark of 74, Sarcita started her final outing of 1991 as favourite for a listed race, the Rous Stakes at Newmarket. Her progress had to come to a halt at some stage, and this was it; driven along going into the Dip, Sarcita was beaten three and three quarter lengths behind Blyton Lad, some way below her best.

		Dominion	Derring-Do
	Primo Dominie	(b 1972)	Picture Palace
	(b 1982)	Swan Ann	My Swanee
Sarcita		(ch 1971)	Anna Barry
(b.f. 1988)		Song	Sing Sing
	Zinzi	(b 1966)	Intent
	(b 1982)	Checkerberry	Connaught
		(gr 1975)	Queensberry

Sarcita was bought for 12,500 guineas as a yearling. Zinzi, whose first foal Sarcita is, ran eleven times in Ireland, winning a five-furlong handicap at Bellewstown on her second run in as many days as a four-year-old. She's from a hitherto minor branch of a well-known family, her grandam being Queensberry, the fastest two-year-old filly of 1959 when she won the Molecomb, Lowther and Cheveley Park Stakes, all by at least four lengths. Having made heavy weather of her Guineas trial, Queensberry was a well-beaten fourth in the first classic, fading up the hill, and wasn't seen out again. At stud Queensberry produced the very useful French sprinter Absalom, useful colts Kingsberry and Queenborough, Silver Berry (the dam of Argentum) and, most importantly, Cranberry Sauce. Several of Queensberry's offspring could be faulted on the count of durability—including Sarcita's grandam Checkerberry, a one-mile Newmarket maiden winner on the first of only four starts—but not Cranberry Sauce who began an ambitious three-year-old campaign with a victory in the Nell Gwyn and ended it with another in the Sun Chariot. She gained distinction as a broodmare as well, with the Child Stakes winner Sauceboat, the Craven Stakes and Prince of Wales's Stakes winner Kind of Hush, and Dusty Dollar who emulated her dam with a win in the Sun Chariot. Sarcita's sire Primo Dominie hasn't set the world alight so far in his stud career but he did have two of the best fillies in Italy in 1991 in Lara's Idea and Arranvanna. His 1991 yearling out of Zinzi sold for 52,000 guineas at the Newmarket October Sales, 22,000 guineas more than his second highest-priced yearling, and is reportedly to be trained by J. W. Payne who had charge of Sarcita for her first three runs as a two-year-old. The lengthy, good-topped Sarcita, who carries condition, is effective at five and six furlongs, has yet to race on soft going but acts on any other. She was tried in blinkers once in the latest season, unsuccessfully, on her sixth start. *D. R. C. Elsworth.*

SARD   3 b.c. Shirley Heights 130 – Jacinth 133 (Red God 128§) [1990 NR 1991   —
14.1m] 2,600Y: big, lengthy, angular colt: half-brother to several winners, including
fairly useful 6f winners Jacquinta (by Habitat) and fair 1½m winners Rubelite (by
Kalaglow) and Spinelle (by Great Nephew): dam best 2-y-o of 1972 and high-class
miler at 3 yrs: blinkered, no sign of ability in maiden at Nottingham in October: sold
1,600 gns Newmarket Autumn Sales. *G. Harwood.*

SARDANIYA (IRE)   3 gr.f. Pharly (FR) 130 – Shanjarina (USA) (Blushing **116**
Groom (FR) 131) [1990 NR 1991 12d* 12m* 12m 10f3] Irish filly: second foal:
half-sister to Irish 1½m winner Shankorak (by Darshaan): dam unraced half-sister
to very useful but somewhat unsatisfactory middle-distance colt Shantaroun: won
maiden at Tipperary in July and Meld Stakes (by ½ length from Zafadola) at the
Curragh in August: good third to Lady Shirl in E P Taylor Stakes at Woodbine: not
disgraced when ninth of 14 in Prix Vermeille at Longchamp: stays 1½m: acts on firm
and dead going: reportedly to be trained by C. Clement in USA. *J. Oxx, Ireland.*

SARDEGNA   4 b.f. Pharly (FR) 130 – Sandy Island 110 (Mill Reef (USA) 141) **105**
[1990 10m* 10.5m2 12s 1991 13.3d2] leggy, angular filly: has a round action: lightly
raced but very useful filly: ran well only run in 1991 when second of 8 to Snurge in
listed event at Newbury in May: stayed 13f: acted on good to firm and dead (ran
badly on soft on first run for over 5 months) ground: stud. *H. R. A. Cecil.*

SAREEN EXPRESS (IRE)   3 gr.g. Siberian Express (USA) 125 – Three   —
Waves (Cure The Blues (USA)) [1990 5m 5m a6g 6m 1991 7g] lengthy, plain gelding:
bad plater: blinkered once. *W. G. M. Turner.*

SARELA (USA)   3 b.f. Danzig (USA) – Santiago Sweetie (USA) (Boldnesian)   —
[1990 NR 1991 7g] lengthy filly: seventh foal: closely related to stakes winner
Flamenco (by Dance Spell), winner of Waterford Candelabra Stakes at 2 yrs, and
half-sister to another: dam, sister to very smart 1975 2-y-o Bold Laddie, won 6f
maiden race at 3 yrs: short-priced favourite and bandaged near-fore, seventh of 14 in
maiden at Kempton in June: visits Darshaan. *J. H. M. Gosden.*

SARIAH   3 ch.f. Kris 135 – Nouvelle Star (AUS) (Luskin Star (AUS)) [1990 6d2   **86**
1991 7g* 7g2 10d5 8.9m5 8g5] leggy, unfurnished filly: has a round action: fair form:
won maiden at Newmarket in May: sweating, respectable fifth in fairly valuable
handicaps at York and Newmarket last 2 starts: stays 9f: visits Polar Falcon. *Major
W. R. Hern.*

SARSTA GRAI   3 b.f. Blakeney 126 – Horton Line 89 (High Line 125) [1990 5f 5g   **57**
6g3 7d4 7f 7m 8v a8g* 1991 8.2f2 8f6 12.2m 12.3g 12f* 12f3 12m a14g2] lengthy,
workmanlike filly: plating-class handicapper: won non-seller at Beverley in July:
stays 1¾m: acts on firm going, unsuited by heavy. *R. Earnshaw.*

SARTIGILA   2 b.f. (Feb 5) Efisio 120 – Ichnusa 83 (Bay Express 132) [1991 5m]   —
close-coupled, good-topped filly: first foal: dam 7f winner appeared to stay 9f: 16/1
from 5/1, backward and green, well-beaten seventh of 8 in maiden at Folkestone in
July: showed poor action to post. *J. W. Payne.*

SARUK (IRE)   2 br.f. (Apr 9) Tate Gallery (USA) 117 – Lovely Kate 104 (Le   —
Levanstell 122) [1991 6s 7g a7g] 6,600F: small, quite attractive filly: half-sister to
several minor winners: dam useful winner in Ireland and second in Irish 1000
Guineas: well beaten in maidens. *D. R. C. Elsworth.*

SARUM   5 b.g. Tina's Pet 121 – Contessa (HUN) (Peleid 125) [1990 a6g a6g* a6g6   **52**
a6g 5f 6f 7f 7f 6g a6g a7g 1991 a7g a10g5 a10g4 a8g* a10g3 a8g2 a7g2 a7g2 7m3
7g3 a7g4 a7g5] tall, leggy, rather narrow gelding: poor mover: quite modest
handicapper: effective at 6f to 1m: acts on good to firm ground: has run well for
apprentice: consistent. *C. P. Wildman.*

SARYAN   8 b.g. Try My Best (USA) 130 – High Fidelyty (FR) (Hautain 128) [1990   **68**
11.1m* 14m 11.7m 14g2 15.5f* 12m 16s 1991 a14g2 12g4] good-bodied gelding: quite
modest handicapper: not seen out after July: better at 1¾m and 2m than shorter:
acts on firm going, seems unsuited by soft: has run moderately in blinkers and for
amateur. *B. J. Curley.*

SASKIA'S REPRIEVE   7 ch.g. Giacometti 130 – Anjamadi (Buff's Own 113)   **38**
[1990 NR 1991 a14g 13.6g2 16.5m3 a14g2 15.1m2 16.1g] leggy, sparely-made gelding: a 29

poor handicapper nowadays: will prove suited by really good test of stamina: acts on good to firm and soft ground: tried blinkered once: visored as 7-y-o: winning hurdler. *J. F. Bottomley.*

SASPARELLA 2 ch.f. (May 16) Sharpo 132 – Palmella (USA) 89 (Grundy 137) **65** [1991 5m* 5g 6g 6m] leggy filly: seventh foal: sister to 5f winner Final Ace and half-sister to 1¼m winner Tino-Ella (by Bustino), fairly useful middle-distance winner Norpella (by Northfields) and 3-y-o 6f winner Furiella (by Formidable): dam 1¼m winner stayed 1½m, is half-sister to Teenoso and Topsy: quite modest performer: easy winner of early-season maiden at Nottingham: around 10 lengths seventh of 14 to Marling in Queen Mary Stakes at Royal Ascot: off course over 2 months, well beaten in face of stiff tasks in nurseries at Newmarket: should stay 6f. *W. Jarvis.*

SASSY LASSY (IRE) 3 b.f. Taufan (USA) 119 – Miss Reasoning (USA) (Bold **64** Reasoning (USA)) [1990 6g4 1991 6m5 6g3 7g* 7g4 7.1m 8m 8d5] leggy, close-coupled filly: quite modest handicapper: won at Leicester in June: should prove better at 1m than shorter: possibly needs an easy surface: sold to join D. Burchell 7,800 gns Newmarket Autumn Sales. *Lord Huntingdon.*

SASTAGO (USA) 2 b.c. (Jan 23) Skywalker (USA) – Sastarda (CHI) (Iram **65** p (ARG)) [1991 8m*] IR 36,000Y: first reported foal: dam won 8 races in Chile and USA: sire won Breeders' Cup Classic: favourite though bit backward, narrowly won maiden at Goodwood in September, pushed along towards rear 3f out, green, then running on strongly final furlong: should stay 1¼m: will improve. *J. H. M. Gosden.*

SATANIC DANCE (FR) 3 b.f. Shareef Dancer 135 – Satanella (GER) **80** (Pentathlon) [1990 7m3 6g5 8g 1991 8g4 10g 7g2] lengthy filly: fair maiden: in frame in £9,000 contest at Kempton (battled on gamely) and handicap at Lingfield in the spring: stays 1m. *C. E. Brittain.*

SATIN FLOWER (USA) 3 b.f. Shadeed (USA) 135 – Sateen (USA) (Round **115** Table) [1990 NR 1991 8d* 10g2 7g* 8m3 7g2 7m2 6s3 9f2 9f6 8.5f3] leggy, attractive filly: fine mover, with a long stride: sixth foal: half-sister to 1988 2-y-o 7f winner Angelic Note (by The Minstrel) and 3 other winners, including 6f and 7f winner Martial Law (by Mr Leader), long-priced Grade 1 1¼m winner in USA at 4 yrs: dam won two 6f stakes races: won maiden at Kempton in May and Jersey Stakes (impressively from Dawson Place) at Royal Ascot: creditable second to Himiko in listed event at Goodwood and Bog Trotter in Group 3 event at Doncaster: ran in USA last 3 outings, beaten nose in Grade 1 Queen Elizabeth II Challenge Cup at Keeneland: stays 9f: acts on good to firm ground and dead: very useful: with C. Whittingham. *J. H. M. Gosden.*

SATIN LAKE (USA) 4 b.f. Well Decorated (USA) – Bunny Lake (Northern **—** Baby (CAN) 127) [1990 8.2g 9s 8.5d 12m4 a11g3 a12g* a14g3 a11g5 a14g5 a12g6 a12g a14g5 a16g a12g2 1991 a14g5 a12g5 12f] smallish, workmanlike filly: plating-class handicapper at 3 yrs: below best in 1991, trained first outing by S. Norton: stays 1½m: acts on good to firm ground: has been tried in blinkers and visor: sold 1,000 gns Doncaster Summer Sales. *D. W. Chapman.*

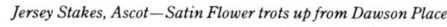

Jersey Stakes, Ascot—Satin Flower trots up from Dawson Place

Sheikh Mohammed's "Satin Flower"

SATIN LOVER 3 ch.g. Tina's Pet 121 – Canoodle 66 (Warpath 113) [1990 6m **86** 1991 12s⁴7g 12d 12m 16g 14.1m* 16.1g* 14m² 14.6m* 16.5d²] workmanlike gelding: vastly improved for new stable in handicaps in autumn: wide-margin winner at Nottingham and Warwick and easily justified favouritism though idled at Doncaster: very good second of 18 at Doncaster final start: effective at 1¾m and 2m: acts on good to firm ground and dead: bandaged first 5 starts when trained by A. Davison. *R. Akehurst.*

SATORIO 7 b.h. Sagaro 133 – Tudor Link 77 (Manacle 123) [1990 NR 1991 a6g] **—** ex-Austrian horse: half-brother to a winner over hurdles by Dominion: dam, in frame in maidens here at 2 yrs, later won in Scandinavia: successful at 3 yrs to 5 yrs in Austria: 50/1, well beaten in claimer at Lingfield in January. *J. E. Long.*

SATURN MOON 6 ch.m. Monsanto (FR) 121 – Ritruda (USA) 95 (Roi Dagobert **—** 128) [1990 NR 1991 10.1s 14.8m] small, sturdy mare: poor mover: poor handicapper: no form in 1991: best form at 1½m on an easy surface: has worn blinkers and visor, including when successful. *Mrs A. Knight.*

SAUVIGNON (IRE) 3 b.f. Alzao (USA) 117 – Romanee Conti (Will Somers **63** 114§) [1990 NR 1991 8d³ 8.1s³ 7g⁴ 7g² 6.9s⁵] IR 19,000F, 90,000Y: sturdy, good-topped filly: half-sister to useful 1979 2-y-o 7f and 1m winner Schwepperusschian (by Take A Reef), later successful at up to 11f in France, fair sprinter Laurie Lorman (by Kampala) and fair 1m winner Taken For Granted (by Martinmas): dam placed at up to 1¼m in Ireland: second in maiden at Newmarket in October: failed to repeat that in Folkestone handicap 11 days later: should prove best at 1m +: sold R. Guest 11,000 gns Newmarket December Sales. *L. M. Cumani.*

SAVAHRA SOUND 6 b.h. Song 132 – Savahra 82 (Free State 125) [1990 6f² 6v* **111** 5m 6m 7f* 6g⁴ 7g 6s 1991 6d⁶ 6d⁵ 7g⁴ 7d 6m 6m⁶ 7m 6g³ 7.1f* 7g] tall, rather dipped-backed horse: has a round action: very useful performer, best effort of 1991

747

when impressive winner of £8,200 handicap at Haydock in September, making all: last of 13 in Group 3 event at Goodwood final start: effective at 6f and 7f: acted on any going: retired to Cobhall Court Stud, Herefordshire. *R. Hannon.*

SAVALARO 2 b.f. (Apr 11) Tinoco 80 – Miss Shifter (Realm 129) [1991 a5g4 **43** 5.3m2 5.3f3 5.3g4 5m a6g a6g5] sparely-made filly: sixth reported foal: dam well beaten all starts: poor sprint maiden. *J. Ffitch-Heyes.*

SAVANGA (USA) 3 b.g. Secreto (USA) 128 – Sun Sprite (USA) (Graustark) **55** [1990 7s a8g5 1991 10.2s 8f3 7m 7.5f* 8f 8g6 7.5f3 8f 7d 8f] smallish, lengthy gelding: fairly useful plater: won at Beverley (no bid) in May: well beaten last 3 starts: well worth another try at 1¼m: acts on firm going: blinkered eighth start: mostly visored otherwise: bandaged seventh start: seemed none too resolute on sixth. *M. McCormack.*

SAVASH (USA) 2 b.g. (Feb 20) Arctic Tern (USA) 126 – Princess Iman (USA) **87** (Seattle Slew (USA)) [1991 7m3 8m4 7f2] leggy, quite attractive gelding: moderate mover: third foal: dam won at around 7f in North America: fair maiden: over 6 lengths fourth of 5, brief effort 2f out, one pace, to Seattle Rhyme in listed race at Goodwood in September: blinkered, well-beaten fourteenth of 18 to Fair Crack in Goffs Million at the Curragh following month: stays 1m. *M. Moubarak.*

SAVILLE WAY 4 ch.g. Gorytus (USA) 132 – Claretta (USA) 82 (Roberto (USA) **33** 131) [1990 9s 8.2g 10m 10m4 10.6d5 12g 10m2 12.5m3 12g 9s 1991 10.8g 10g5 9.9m4 13d 10m* 10m2 12.1g 10m] strong, workmanlike gelding: keen walker: poor handicapper: won at Ayr in July: stays 1½m: acts on good to firm ground and dead: has run well for inexperienced rider: usually bandaged: blinkered last 4 starts. *W. J. Musson.*

SAVINA 3 b.f. Idiot's Delight 115 – Rely-On-Pearl (Deep Diver 134) [1990 NR **—** 1991 8m 10g 8.5m 8g] leggy, unfurnished filly: second foal: dam plater unreliable at start: behind in maidens and handicap: pulled hard last 2 starts: joined M. Pipe. *B. R. Millman.*

SAVOYARD 3 b.c. Sayf El Arab (USA) 127 – Ballad Island 83 (Ballad Rock 122) **103** [1990 NR 1991 7g* 6d2 7g* 7g 7m* 7f4 7d 7m6] 31,000Y: angular, good-topped colt: moderate walker and mover: third foal: half-brother to winning sprinter Hong Kong Girl (by Petong): dam 7f and 1m performer: progressive form: won maiden at Kempton in April, minor event at Leicester in May (made virtually all both times) and £20,170 Ladbroke Bunbury Cup Handicap (held up in very strongly-run race) at Newmarket in July: some promise in £80,000 Ascot handicap penultimate start: should prove at least as effective at 1m: never travelling fluently on very firm ground. *M. A. Jarvis.*

SAVOY FOREVER 3 b.g. Bay Express 132 – My Bushbaby 100 (Hul A Hul 124) **—** [1990 6g 5m3 5s2 1991 5g 5g4 6f 9m] strong, good-topped gelding: quite modest maiden: well beaten in summer as 3-y-o, in handicap and seller last 2 outings: blinkered twice: sold 1,500 gns Ascot September Sales. *Mrs G. R. Reveley.*

SAVOY LADY 4 b.f. Noalto 120 – Pure Perfection (So Blessed 130) [1990 8m4 **—** a11g 12m 1991 10m] workmanlike filly: poor and lightly-raced maiden: should be suited by further than 1m: acts on good to firm ground. *M. Bell.*

SAWAKI 4 br.f. Song 132 – Roxy Hart (High Top 131) [1990 7.6d 8m3 8m3 8g3 7f* **71** 7d 1991 7.1m5 6g5 8d 7f* 7m4] tall, quite attractive filly: has a quick action: modest handicapper: won at Brighton in September: ideally suited by 7f: goes well on top-of-the-ground: sold 30,000 gns Newmarket December Sales. *W. Jarvis.*

SAXON LAD (USA) 5 b.g. Lear Fan (USA) 130 – Presto Youth (USA) (Youth **—** (USA) 135) [1990 6m 1991 10f4 10f3 7m6] leggy, angular gelding: has a poor action: poor handicapper nowadays: stays 7f: acts on firm ground: has hung left. *G. P. Enright.*

SAXON LASS 3 b.f. Martinmas 128 – Khatti Hawk (Hittite Glory 125) [1990 NR **—** 1991 8.9g 12.1g 10.1m] 500Y, 900 2-y-o: smallish filly: first foal: dam, sister to 1¾m and Triumph Hurdle winner Saxon Farm, ran 5 times: no worthwhile form, in seller final start. *A. J. Chamberlain.*

SAYMORE 5 ch.g. Seymour Hicks (FR) 125 – Huahinee (FR) 94 (Riverman **73** (USA) 131) [1990 8g 1991 8m4 8g4 8.3m] leggy, close-coupled gelding: modest and lightly-raced handicapper nowadays: well worth another try at 1¼m: acts on firm and dead ground: takes keen hold: winning hurdler (has broken blood vessel): sold 1,000 gns Ascot November Sales. *C. P. E. Brooks.*

SAYSANA 4 b.f. Sayf El Arab (USA) 127 – Rosana Park 83 (Music Boy 124) [1990 **41** 6f5 5m 5.3h6 7.6m5 6f6 7m5 6f 6h 7h5 6f 5f 7f* 6g6 a5g4 a7g5 a6g6 1991 a7g 8f 10m

7f⁶ 6f⁴ 6g⁶ 9.7m* 10f 9.7g 9.7s] leggy, quite good-topped filly: keen walker: poor performer: won selling handicap (no bid) at Folkestone in August: fell final start: effective at 6f to 9.7f: goes well on top-of-the-ground (acts on hard ground): inconsistent. *A. Moore.*

SAY YOU WILL   7 b.g. Riboboy (USA) 124 – Polita 86 (Constable 119) [1990 7.5d   **41**
7m 7g 7m 7g 6m 6g 7f 7d³ a7g a7g* a8g a7g² 1991 a7g a7g⁴ 7d 7g 7f⁵ 7.6g³ 7m⁶ a **50**
7g⁴ 7f² a7g⁶ 7f 7m 7.1m 7g⁶ a8g² a8g⁶] robust gelding: carries condition: has a quick action: plating-class handicapper: best up to 1m: possibly unsuited by soft going nowadays, acts on any other: has worn blinkers, usually visored: none too consistent, and has looked unenthusiastic. *M. P. Naughton.*

SCALA MILANO   2 b.f. (Mar 26) Music Boy 124 – Song Book 85 (Saintly Song   **53**
128) [1991 6.1f 6m⁶ 5g⁵] leggy filly: has a quick action: half-sister to 3 winners, including modest 1m and 9.4f winner Sam Chifney (by Balliol) and 1982 2-y-o 5f seller winner Song To Singo (by Master Sing): dam 6f seller winner at 2 yrs: progressive form in maidens: apprentice ridden final start. *J. Etherington.*

SCALAMON   4 br.g. Sweet Monday 122 – Mummy's Rascal (Mummy's Pet 125)   **—**
[1990 NR 1991 8h] workmanlike gelding: fourth living foal: dam of no account: blinkered, tailed off in Carlisle claimer in June. *D. Moffatt.*

SCALES OF JUSTICE   5 br.m. Final Straw 127 – Foiled Again 110 (Bold Lad   **83**
(IRE) 133) [1990 10.8m³ 9g³ 11f² 9g* a12g 10m⁵ 9m⁴ 9f* 8m* a10g² 1991 8g 9m 8g 9d 7m 7.3m⁴ 8m* 8m* 8g* a10g] big, rangy mare: fairly useful handicapper: won at Leicester, Doncaster and Newmarket (gamely beat Polonez Prima by ¾ length) at back-end of turf season: below form at Lingfield final start: best form at up to 1¼m: goes very well on a sound surface, possibly unsuited by dead ground: held up, and has turn of foot. *J. W. Hills.*

SCALP 'EM (IRE)   3 b.g. Commanche Run 133 – Supremely Royal (Crowned   **—**
Prince (USA) 128) [1990 NR 1991 16.9g⁶ 15m 12.3g⁶ 15.9d⁶ 15.1s] 17,000Y: rangy gelding: has round action: brother to fair 1¼m winner Amerindian, closely related to winning stayer Elegant Monarch (by Ardross) and half-brother to several winners, including very smart Capricorn Belle (by Nonoalco), successful from 6f to 1m: dam poor maiden from top American family: no worthwhile form, in handicaps last 2 starts. *F. H. Lee.*

SCANDALIZE (IRE)   3 b.f. Dalsaan 125 – Dacani 118 (Polyfoto 124) [1990 5m   **37**
6m⁶ 6g² 7m a7g 1991 a10g⁶ a10g 12v] leggy filly: poor mover: poor form: best effort on reappearance: stays 1¼m: possibly unsuited by top-of-the-ground: sold 2,100 gns Ascot April Sales. *M. J. Fetherston-Godley.*

SCANDALMONGER (USA)   2 b.c. (Apr 12) Foolish Pleasure (USA) – Queen   **69** P
Vega (USA) (Te Vega) [1991 7m 7m⁶] lengthy, useful-looking colt: fluent mover: half-brother to several winners here and abroad, including fair 1987 2-y-o 6f winner Yorkshireman (by Our Native): dam, winner of claimer at around 6f, is half-sister to In Fijar: sire won Kentucky Derby: most promising seventh of 20, beaten over 5 lengths, to Modernise in maiden at Newmarket, held up behind after slow start then catching eye from 2f out making significant progress under very considerate handling: again very weak in market, again left favourable impression in 6-runner minor event won by Muhtarram at Leicester later in October, set plenty to do then eased significantly once held: probably capable of fair bit better, and remains one to keep an eye on in maiden company. *B. W. Hills.*

SCARABEN   3 b.g. Dunbeath (USA) 127 – Varushka 74 (Sharpen Up 127) [1990   **68**
NR 1991 7.6s³ 7m³ 7.9g³ 7.1g⁴ 7m] 2,600Y: strong, lengthy gelding: has a moderate, quick action: second foal: half-brother to quite modest maiden Zanussi Satellite (by Formidable): dam fourth over 5f at 2 yrs on only start: quite modest maiden: below form last 2 starts, travelling strongly to join issue 2f out, edging left and weakening on first of them: stays 1m: acts on good to firm ground and soft. *M. J. Wilkinson.*

SCARBA   3 b.g. Skyliner 117 – Looking For Gold (Goldfella 80) [1990 6d⁵ 1991 5g   **53**
6g 7f² 8m⁴ 9m] big, workmanlike gelding: has a round action: 50/1-second of 6 in maiden at Thirsk, only sign of ability: backward, tailed off in handicap final start: should stay 1m. *D. T. Garraton.*

SCARBOROUGH HILL (IRE)   2 ch.c. (Apr 7) Nashamaa 113 – On The Road   **43**
82 (On Your Mark 125) [1991 7m 6m 6d a7g a6g] IR 3,300Y: leggy, lengthy colt: fifth live foal: half-brother to 3-y-o 8.3f winner Richmond (by Hatim) and quite modest 1m and 8.5f winner Xafu Xafu (by Kafu): dam modest Irish 5f winner at 2 yrs: poor form in varied events, including a seller at Newmarket: sold 600 gns Ascot December Sales. *M. H. Tompkins.*

SCARED STIFF 3 b.f. Electric 126 – Petrify 71 (Air Trooper 115) [1990 7m 7m **48**
7g 1991 8m⁴ 8g 9d⁵ 10g⁶ 10.2d⁶ 12s 10g* 10s 9.7f 11.9f] compact filly: poor
performer: behind after winning claimer (led close home) at Leicester in July: suited
by 1¼m, probably by a sound surface: sold to join D. Burchell 1,000 gns Ascot
October Sales. *G. B. Balding.*

SCARLATINE (IRE) 2 b.f. (Mar 24) Alzao (USA) 117 – The Woman In Red 68 **71** p
(Red Regent 123) [1991 6m⁴ 6.3s] 23,000F, IR 38,000Y: good-bodied filly: second
foal: half-sister to a winner in Italy: dam second at 1m at 2 yrs, is half-sister to 2 good
Italian performers: promising fourth in maiden at Newmarket won by Skimble,
staying on strongly after missing break: favourite, twelfth of 15 to Dedicated Lady in
Goffs Fillies Challenge at the Curragh later in October: should stay 1m: should do
better. *J. H. M. Gosden.*

SCARLET EXPRESS 4 b.g. Precocious 126 – Scarlet Slipper (Gay Mecene **—**
(USA) 128) [1990 a10g⁵ a10g³ 9s² 10g 12d⁴ 11m² 10g⁶ 11g⁵ 12m⁶ 15.5f⁵ 1991 a13g⁴
a11g³ 12m a14g⁶] leggy gelding: poor walker: has a round action: poor maiden: stays
15.5f: acts on firm ground: sometimes blinkered or visored: trained first 2 starts by
P. Kelleway: bandaged final one: winning hurdler. *J. L. Harris.*

SCARLET PRINCESS 3 b.f. Daring March 116 – Noble Mistress 80 (Lord **48**
Gayle (USA) 124) [1990 NR 1991 6m 5g 8m 6g 6d* 5d 6m] smallish, leggy filly: third
reported foal: sister to quite modest 1987 2-y-o maiden Daring Delight: dam 2-y-o 6f
winner: 20/1, worthwhile form only when winning handicap at Nottingham in June,
well drawn and leading final 1f: seems suited by a soft surface: bandaged off-fore
final start, in July. *R. J. Hodges.*

SCATTER 4 b.c. Sharpo 132 – Visitation 84 (Tarqogan 125) [1990 7m² 7.2g⁴ 7m⁴ **99**
8m 1991 9g³ 8g 8m³ 8g³ 8f³ 10m² 8g⁴ 9m 8d*] good-topped colt: poor mover:
quite useful handicapper: won non handicap at Ascot (apprentices) in October:
subsequently sold 30,000 gns Newmarket Autumn Sales: effective at 1m to 1¼m:
acts on firm and dead ground: tends to hang: runs lazily: consistent. *G. Harwood.*

SCATTERPENNY 2 b.f. (Apr 2) Hallgate 127 – Okosan (USA) 72 (Far Out East **39**
(USA)) [1991 5f⁵ 5m 6.1m] small, sparely-made filly: first foal: dam maiden seemed
best at 7f or 1m and at 2 yrs: poor plater: blinkered second outing. *M. W. Easterby.*

SCENIC DANCER 3 b.c. Shareef Dancer (USA) 135 – Bridestowes 92 (Jan **75**
Ekels 122) [1990 6m 7g 8g 8m 7d 1991 9d 10g* 10.1f 12g 11.7m* 12g⁶ 12f⁶ 10.3m
10.3d] small, compact colt: modest handicapper: won at Leicester in May and
Windsor in July: below form last 3 starts, hampered early and never dangerous at
Chester (visored) on final one: better at 1½m than shorter: seems unsuited by firm
ground: often sloppy away, including when tried in blinkers. *A. Hide.*

SCENTED GODDESS (IRE) 3 b.f. Godswalk (USA) 130 – Vivi (Welsh Saint **50**
126) [1990 5.8h² 5.3h³ 5s³ 7m* 7f⁶ a6g² a8g a6g 1991 7d 6f 7g⁵ 8.3g 6m⁴ 8.3m*
8.3g⁶ 8.3m 12f 8f] close-coupled filly: plating-class handicapper: won at Windsor in
July, held up and strong run to lead 1f out: suited by 1m: acts on good to firm ground:
not particularly consistent. *J. S. Moore.*

SCENT OF BATTLE 3 ch.c. Rousillon (USA) 133 – Light O'Battle 97 (Queen's **64** d
Hussar 124) [1990 8g 1991 10v² 10g 10g⁵ 10g 8.3m 9.7m 10m] strong, lengthy colt:
moderate mover: plating-class maiden: should stay 1½m: best effort on heavy
going. *M. J. Haynes.*

SCHILLACHI (IRE) 3 b.c. Flash of Steel 120 – Chalfont Mo 66 (Mummy's Pet **—**
125) [1990 NR 1991 12.1g a12g] IR 80,000Y: good-bodied colt: first foal: dam, quite
modest maiden placed 3 times over sprint distances at 2 yrs, is sister to very useful
5f to 1m winner Teacher's Pet: tailed off in maidens at Chepstow and (blinkered,
edgy) Lingfield. *J. D. Bethell.*

SCHWANTZ 3 b.g. Exhibitioner 111 – Hardirondo 93 (Hardicanute 130) [1990 **—**
6g⁵ 6g 8.2m 1991 a8g 9m⁶ 11.8m] strong, good-bodied gelding: has round action:
poor maiden: probably stays 9f: may prove suited by some give in ground: sold out of
J. Wharton's stable 3,000 gns Ascot February Sales. *W. T. Kemp.*

SCHWARZKOPF 2 ch.c. (Mar 29) Precocious 126 – Wallah Wassl 73 (Great **40**
Nephew 126) [1991 6g 6m] 9,000F, 4,200Y: lengthy, rather sparely-made colt:
second foal: dam, 1½m winner, is daughter of half-sister to high-class stayer
Dakota: poor form in Lingfield maiden (slowly away) and Newmarket seller (never
dangerous) in October. *M. H. Tompkins.*

SCIACCA 4 ch.f. Dalsaan 125 – Hill of Howth (Sassafras (FR) 135) [1990 7s 7d **38**
1991 6v⁵ 7f 8f 10.8m 10m a7g³ a8g² 10m⁴ 8m⁵ a11g⁴ a8g⁶ 10g⁵ 8.9g 10m⁴] small,
lengthy ex-Irish filly: third foal: half-sister to a minor stakes winner in USA by

Welsh Saint: dam won over 11f in Ireland: poor handicapper: stays 11f: acts on good to firm ground. *S. Mellor.*

SCIMITARLIA (USA)   3 ch.f. Diesis 133 – Alia 112 (Sun Prince 128) [1990 NR   **84**
1991 10.1m² 11.9m*] lengthy filly: has a long, rather round stride: fourth live foal: half-sister to fair 1986 middle-distance winner Apply (by Kings Lake): dam won 5 races from 1¼m to 1½m from 7 starts at 3 yrs: favourite, second in maiden at Yarmouth in July and won 3-runner maiden at Haydock 2 weeks later by 8 lengths: stays 1½m: sold 9,600 gns Newmarket December Sales. *H. R. A. Cecil.*

SCORTON (IRE)   2 gr.g. (Apr 24) Standaan (FR) 118 – Shanty (Sea Hawk II 131)   **— p**
[1991 6.1m6] IR 6,400Y, 14,000 2-y-o: leggy, workmanlike gelding: half-brother to winning hurdler Santopadre (by Welsh Saint): dam ran once: 25/1 and backward, well-beaten sixth of 7 in minor event at Nottingham in September: may do better. *Miss S. E. Hall.*

SCOSSA (USA)   3 ch.f. Shadeed (USA) 135 – Scythe 84 (Sharpen Up 127) [1990   **52**
5g 7g6 8g 1991 7d 8.5f5 10m³ 10m6 10.1f4 10f² 8.9m5 10g³ 9.7f 10.1s4] IR 95,000Y: tall, leggy filly: has round action: first foal: dam 9f and 10.4f winner here, later Grade 3 1½m winner in USA: trained at 2 yrs by A. Fabre in France: quite modest form here: unlikely to stay much beyond 1¼m: acts on firm ground: edgy sixth and seventh starts: headstrong: has carried head high: sold J. Spearing 6,000 gns Newmarket December Sales. *J. A. R. Toller.*

SCOTCH IMP   7 ch.m. Imperial Fling (USA) 116 – Bunduq 67 (Scottish Rifle 127)   **35**
[1990 a7g6 a6g4 a7g5 6s 6f 6g 6g* 6m 6m 6s 1991 a5g 6d 6d 6g 6m 7h 7f 7m² 6f6 7m] workmanlike mare: usually dull in coat: poor handicapper: suited by 6f to 7f: acts on any going: sometimes blinkered: inconsistent: sold 2,700 gns Doncaster Summer Sales. *D. W. Chapman.*

SCOTONI   5 ch.g. Final Straw 127 – Damiya (FR) (Direct Flight) [1990 9f 10.8m*   **64**
10.8f5 12f³ 12m 8m5 10.2m 10s 8d³ a7g 1991 a10g³ a10g5 a12g* a12g* a13g² a12g5 12d² 12f 7.6m4 11.5m6 7.6m 11.5g a12g a8g5 a13g* a12g] close-coupled, rather sparely-made gelding: quite modest handicapper: successful at Lingfield in February, March and December: stays 13f: acts on firm and dead going: below form when blinkered once: good mount for apprentice. *R. J. O'Sullivan.*

SCOTS GREY LASSIE   3 gr.f. Absalom 128 – Jose Collins 91 (Singing Bede   **—**
122) [1990 NR 1991 7g 8g 10g 7f] 7,200Y: lengthy, good-topped filly: moderate walker: fourth live foal: half-sister to a winner in Italy: dam best at 5f: no worthwhile form, including in claimer: trained first 3 starts by E. Eldin: joined I. Campbell. *J. Pearce.*

SCOTS LAW   4 b.g. Law Society (USA) 130 – Tweedling (USA) (Sir Ivor 135)   **44**
[1990 a7g 7.5f 8m4 10m4 10f 8f a8g* a8g² a6g³ 1991 a7g³ a8g a7g³ a7g5 7d 8f a7g* a52
a7g 6g 7.6m4 a7g a6g a7g a8g5 a7g] leggy, quite attractive gelding: quite modest handicapper: won at Southwell in May: mainly little form after: stays 1¼m: acts on good to firm ground: tried blinkered once: has carried head awkwardly, appearing rather ungenerous: seems best with forcing tactics. *R. J. O'Sullivan.*

SCOTTIES WIT (IRE)   3 b.g. Lafontaine (USA) 117 – Musical Rock (Sandy   **—**
Creek 123) [1990 NR 1991 7d] IR 2,000Y: plain gelding: third foal (all by Lafontaine): dam Irish maiden: very green, tailed off in maiden at Brighton in April. *J. S. Moore.*

SCOTTISH BAMBI   3 ch.g. Scottish Reel 123 – Bambolona 108 (Bustino 136)   **70**
[1990 NR 1991 7g² 10.2g5 7m4dis 7g² 8.1d 7g] 4,300F: rangy, workmanlike gelding: has a round action: first foal: dam 2-y-o 6f winner: modest maiden: second at Sandown (hung right and put head in air) and Lingfield: suited by 7f: rider failed to weigh in third start. *R. Hannon.*

SCOTTISH CASTLE   3 ch.c. Scottish Reel 123 – Show Home 90 (Music Boy   **89**
124) [1990 7g 7m³ 6d4 7s* 7d* a7g* 7s5 a7g5 1991 7m* 7d4 7g²] strong colt: moderate mover: well backed, impressive winner of £8,000 handicap at Newmarket in April: blinkered, good second in £11,900 handicap (led over 6f) at Newmarket following month: will stay 1m: acts on good to firm ground and soft: also blinkered final start at 2 yrs: suitable mount for a claimer. *W. A. O'Gorman.*

SCOTTISH PARK   2 ch.f. (Mar 5) Scottish Reel 123 – Moss Agate (Alias Smith   **69**
(USA)) [1991 5m 6.1m4 6.1f 7g² 7d] 900F: sturdy, lengthy filly: first foal: dam unraced granddaughter of Park Top: quite modest maiden: runner-up to easy winner Mountain Ash at Catterick in October, easily best effort: stays 7f. *J. P. Leigh.*

SCOTTISH RUBY   2 b.c. (Feb 25) Scottish Reel 123 – Screenable (USA) (Silent   **58**
Screen (USA)) [1991 6m5 6d5 6m 5.9h4 6m6 7d] 5,800F, 11,000Y: close-coupled, angular colt: poor mover: half-brother to 3-y-o Italian 7.5f to 8.8f winner Screen Serenade (by Nordance) and 1½m winner Barrymore (by Robellino), later

successful in USA: dam minor winner at around 1m in North America: plating-class maiden: soundly beaten last 2 starts: will stay 7f. *C. Tinkler.*

SCOTTISH TINA 3 b.f. Scottish Reel 123 – Tina's Melody 80 (Tina's Pet 121) [1990 NR 1991 8f⁶ 7g] 5,400F: leggy, plain filly: first foal: dam, 2-y-o 5f and 6f winner unraced at 3 yrs, is half-sister to Middle Park winner and 2000 Guineas second Mattaboy: no sign of ability in autumn maidens. *A. Moore.* —

SCRAVELS SARAN (IRE) 3 b.f. Indian King (USA) 128 – Persian Royale 94 (Persian Bold 123) [1990 6g 7f³ 7f⁵ 1991 7m 7m 7s⁶ 5.1f 7m 7s] angular filly: plating class at best: needs further than 5f, and should stay 1m: best effort on firm going: flashes tail. *Dr J. D. Scargill.* — §

SCREAMER 3 br.f. Chief Singer 131 – Palumba 100 (Derring-Do 131) [1990 NR 1991 8f] 7,800Y: good-topped filly: fifth foal: sister to plating-class maiden Chief Dancer and half-sister to fair 1985 2-y-o 6f winner C Jam Blues (by Milford) and plating-class miler Victoria Line (by High Line): dam won over 5f at 2 yrs and stayed 1¼m: never able to challenge in claimer at Carlisle in May: moved badly to post: dead. *J. Etherington.* —

SCRUTINEER (USA) 2 b.c. (Feb 21) Danzig Connection (USA) – Script Approval (USA) (Silent Screen (USA)) [1991 8g⁵] $65,000Y: half-brother to several winners, including Raj Waki (by Miswaki) and Agitated Lady (by Agitate), useful at up to 9f: dam ran once: well-backed 4/1-shot, under 13 lengths fifth of 16 to Aljadeer in minor event at Newbury in October, progress 3f out, soon one pace: will improve. *J. H. M. Gosden.* **71 p**

SCRUTINY 2 b.c. (May 30) Primo Dominie 121 – So Precise (FR) (Balidar 133) [1991 5g 5.1m⁵] 10,000Y: strong colt: has scope: half-brother to 11f winner Crystal Park (by Head For Heights) and a winner in Sweden by Elegant Air: dam half-sister to Columnist: quite modest form in minor event at Windsor and maiden auction at Chepstow (still carrying condition) later in May: sold 1,050 gns Newmarket September Sales. *R. Hannon.* **60**

SCULTORE (USA) 2 b.g. (May 17) Leo Castelli (USA) – Glamorous Nell (USA) (Distinctive (USA)) [1991 8m] $6,500Y deep-girthed, plain gelding: half-brother to winners in North America by No Double and Sir Ivor: dam won at up to 7f: sire Grade 2 9f winner: 50/1 and backward, tailed off in 17-runner maiden at Ayr in September. *Denys Smith.* —

SCU'S LADY (IRE) 3 b.f. Mazaad 106 – Lydja 75 (Hethersett 134) [1990 5g³ 5g 6m³ 6g 6m 6g 6d 6m 1991 6d⁶ 6f 10f 12d 9.9f a8g⁴] small, sturdy filly: poor form at 2 yrs: none at 3 yrs: stays 6f: blinkered last 2 starts. *A. Smith.* —

SEABEE 3 ch.c. Adonijah 126 – Fedra 81 (Grundy 137) [1990 7m 7f 7m 10s 1991 12f 12g] small, stocky colt: well beaten, in selling handicap final start. *K. O. Cunningham-Brown.* —

SEA BREAKER (IRE) 3 b.c. Glow (USA) – Surfing 71 (Grundy 137) [1990 NR 1991 12m² 12g³ 11.8g³ 9.7m²] 80,000Y: useful-looking colt with scope: good mover: first foal: dam maiden stayed 7f, is sister to very useful 1981 2-y-o Glancing and half-sister to high-class 1984 sprinting 2-y-o Bassenthwaite: modest maiden: blinkered, second of 3 at Folkestone in July final start, looking none too keen: stays 1½m: carries head awkwardly, and has flashed tail: sold 7,600 gns Newmarket Autumn Sales: probably unsatisfactory. *G. Harwood.* **76 §**

SEA CADET 3 ch.c. Precocious 126 – Sea Power 88 (Welsh Pageant 132) [1990 7m⁶ 1991 10.4d³ 10.5g] stocky colt: modest form: 11½ lengths third of 7 in £7,300 maiden at Chester, soon off bridle: below that form 4½ months later: may well stay 1½m: sold to join K. Bishop 5,800 gns Newmarket Autumn Sales. *Major W. R. Hern.* **68**

SEA CLOUD (USA) 2 b.f. (Feb 17) African Sky 124 – Candle In The Wind 90 (Thatching 131) [1991 6f 6f⁵ 6.1m 6g] 15,500Y: big, close-coupled filly: first foal: dam 6f winner at 2 yrs, is daughter of half-sister to smart miler Long Row: poor maiden: may stay 7f. *M. Blanshard.* **44**

SEA CLOVER (IRE) 2 b.f. (Feb 24) Ela-Mana-Mou 132 – Seattle Siren (USA) 101 (Seattle Slew (USA)) [1991 7m* 7.3g⁵] rather leggy, unfurnished filly: has a roundish action: third live foal: half-sister to 1990 2-y-o 6f winner Chimayo (by Sure Blade) and to Irish 1¼m and 1¾m winner Distant Beat (by Touching Wood): dam 6f winner at 2 yrs, is half-sister to very smart middle-distance winner Pole Position: won maiden at Leicester, quickening over 2f out and keeping on strongly: over 10 lengths fifth of 6 to Soiree in listed race at Newbury later in October, off bridle 3f out, ran green and not knocked about: likely to do better. *Major W. R. Hern.* **77 p**

SEA CRAFT 3 gr.f. Nishapour (FR) 125 – Sea Pageant (Welsh Pageant 132) [1990 —
NR 1991 11.8g a8g 9.9f⁴] workmanlike filly: eighth foal: half-sister to 2 winners over
middle distances, including useful Ocean Ballad (by Grundy): dam unraced half-
sister to high-class Sea Anchor: green, well beaten in maidens: blinkered, made
most 7f then carried head high final start. *N. A. Graham.*

SEA CROWN 2 b.c. (Mar 9) King of Spain 121 – Whip Finish 77 (Be Friendly 130) **59**
[1991 6d 7m 7g 6g 7.1d] 19,000Y: leggy, close-coupled colt: half-brother to several
winners, including very useful sprinter Whipper In (by Bay Express) and Molecomb
winner Hotbee (by Hotfoot): dam won twice over 5f at 2 yrs: plating-class maiden:
best effort at Chepstow final start, hanging persistently left: stays 7f: acts on dead
ground: looks a hard ride: sold 2,200 gns Newmarket Autumn Sales. *M. Blanshard.*

SEA CRUSADER 2 b.c. (Feb 8) Formidable (USA) 125 – Historical Fact 78 **60**
(Reform 132) [1991 5g 6d 6g⁶ 7g 7m⁶ 5.1m⁶ 5f* 5m⁶ 5d] 10,500Y: compact colt: poor
walker and mover: third foal: dam 1¼m winner: made all in 16-runner seller (no bid)
at Folkestone in September: ran moderately in Wolverhampton nursery last time:
probably suited by around 5f and fast conditions: blinkered last 3 starts: sold 8,600
gns Newmarket Autumn Sales. *M. Blanshard.*

SEA DEVIL 5 gr.g. Absalom 128 – Miss Poinciana 78 (Averof 123) [1990 6s* 6g **81**
7.5d⁴ 7m³ 6g³ 6g⁵ 6s² 6s* 6s* 6s* 1991 6m 6m⁵ 6g 6m* 6.1d 6s* 7d] lengthy,
heavy-topped gelding: carries plenty of condition: moderate walker and mover: fair
handicapper: off course 4½ months after second start: won at Redcar (idled) in
October and Hamilton in November: suited by 6f or 7f: acts on good to firm ground
and goes particularly well on soft going: largely consistent. *M. J. Camacho.*

SEA DUNE 2 b.f. (Feb 24) Jupiter Island 126 – Song God 96 (Red God 128§) [1991 **65 p**
6g⁶] workmanlike filly: half-sister to several winners, including French 1m to 9f
winner Rebecca's Song (by Artaius): dam 2-y-o 5f winner: 33/1 and very green,
around 9 lengths sixth of 21 to Katakana in maiden at Newbury in October, held up
then keeping on: will prove suited by further: should improve. *R. Charlton.*

SEA GODDESS 3 b.f. Slip Anchor 136 – Elysian 94 (Northfields (USA)) [1990 7g **78 p**
1991 10.8m³] lengthy, good-topped filly: third foal: 5½ lengths third of 7 to Lucky Guest
in minor event at Warwick in October, leading 3f out until approaching last: should
stay 1½m: can improve again and win a maiden. *W. Jarvis.*

SEAGULL HOLLOW (IRE) 2 b.g. (Mar 29) Taufan (USA) 119 – Marthe **76**
Meynet (Welsh Pageant 132) [1991 6g* 6g³ 7d³] tall, leggy, close-coupled gelding:
looks weak: half-brother to several winners, including fair sprinter Batoni (by
Realm) and 6f and 1m winner/useful jumper Antinous (by Hello Gorgeous): dam
never ran: modest performer: won minor event at Thirsk in May: below form in
4-runner minor event at Chester final start (June): should be better suited by 7f than
6f. *M. H. Easterby.*

SEA LEVEL (FR) 3 b. or br.c. Kind of Hush 118 – Packet 89 (Royal Palace 131) **97**
[1990 7m² 7m* 7g⁴ 8m* 1991 12g³ 10.5g⁶ 16.2g] quite attractive colt: most
progressive colt at 2 yrs: not discredited though well beaten when sixth in Dante
Stakes at York, leading briefly well over 2f out: broke cannon bone (later destroyed)
in Queen's Vase at Royal Ascot: should have been well suited by middle distances:
carried head rather high. *B. W. Hills.*

SEAL INDIGO (IRE) 3 b.f. Glenstal (USA) 118 – Simply Gorgeous (Hello **93 p**
Gorgeous (USA) 128) [1990 5g⁶ 5m³ 8m⁶ 9g⁴ 8m⁴ 9m² 10g 1991 10g 10.2m⁵ 12g*
12m³ 11.7d⁴ 10.2d³ 12f* 10.5f* 10m³ 12.1s*] workmanlike filly: moderate mover:
won claimers at Goodwood in May, Salisbury in August and Haydock (£10,400
event) in September: much improved last 2 starts, leading 1f out when most
impressive winner of handicap at Chepstow in October: seems better at 1½m than
1¼m: goes well on soft ground, and acts on firm: can win more races. *R. Hannon.*

SEA LORD 2 b.c. (Feb 12) Aragon 118 – Floral 82 (Floribunda 136) [1991 7m 6m] —
17,000Y: strong colt: half-brother to several winners, including 5f (at 2 yrs) to 1m
winner Tyrnippy (by Tyrnavos): dam 2-y-o 7f winner: no form, in Lingfield seller
second occasion: sold 700 gns Newmarket Autumn Sales. *M. Blanshard.*

SEAL RING (USA) 2 b.c. (Feb 7) Known Fact (USA) 135 – Royal Graustark **96**
(USA) (Graustark) [1991 5g* 6d⁵ 6g* 6f⁴] good-quartered colt: eighth foal:
half-brother to several winners here and in USA, including fair 1m winner
Holtermann (by Mr Prospector): dam won at up to 7f: fairly useful performer: won
maiden at Salisbury (pulled hard then quickened well) in July and nursery at
Kempton (clear from 1f out) in September: eased when well-beaten fourth of 5 to
Showbrook in Mill Reef Stakes at Newbury 15 days later: will probably stay 7f:

possibly unsuited by dead ground: active type, taken down steadily final start: sold to South Africa. *G. Harwood.*

SEA MEMORY (IRE)   2 b.f. (Apr 23) Don't Forget Me 127 – Top Mouse (High   —
Top 131) [1991 6.1m 7g 7g] 14,000Y: good-bodied filly: fourth living foal: half-sister to 5f winner Idrak (by Young Generation) and a winner in Belgium by Formidable: dam twice-raced sister to smart 5f to 10.5f winner Triple First, herself dam of Maysoon and Three Tails: no worthwhile form, in seller final start: looked ungenuine time before: sold 2,400 gns Newmarket Autumn Sales. *M. Blanshard.*

SEAMERE   8 b.g. Crofter (USA) 124 – Whistling Waltz (Whistler 129) [1990 5g 5g   **86**
5g² 5f* 5f⁶ 5g³ 5m² 5f* 5m⁴ 5m³ 5g³ 5g⁴ 1991 5.9m 5m 5m* 5m* 5f* 5g* 5m² 5g²] workmanlike, deep-bodied gelding: carries plenty of condition: impresses in appearance: moderate mover: much improved handicapper in 1991: successful at Wolverhampton in July, Pontefract, Beverley and Newmarket (idled) in August: suited by 5f on a sound surface: has worn visor, usually blinkered nowadays: excellent mount for inexperienced rider: should prove best with extreme waiting tactics: tough. *B. R. Cambidge.*

SEAN'S SCHOLAR (USA)   4 b.f. Kris S (USA) – Nalees Scholar (USA)   **60**
(Nalees Man (USA)) [1990 NR 1991 10m* 12f² 12m] lengthy filly: half-sister to several winners in USA: dam won 6 races in USA: thrice raced on flat: won seller at Pontefract (bought in 3,500 gns) in September: raced too freely final start: stays 1½m: acts on firm ground. *C. N. Allen.*

SEA PADDY   3 b.g. Reach 122 – Sea Thyme (Persian Bold 123) [1990 NR 1991 8d   **53 §**
7.5f 8g 8d⁴ 9.9f* 9.2d³ 9m 10m 8m 9.7f⁵ 9.9f 10m] 4,000Y: leggy, close-coupled gelding: half-brother to 4-y-o sprint winner Johanna Thyme (by Reesh) and to winners in Hong Kong and Macau: dam never ran: gambled-on favourite, won selling handicap (bought in 6,200 gns) at Beverley in July: disappointing after, again favourite final start: better at 1¼m than shorter: acts on firm going: not ideal ride for 7-lb claimer: wears crossed noseband: headstrong, and not one to trust. *R. Bastiman.*

SEA PLANE   2 gr.c. (May 15) Nishapour (FR) 125 – Pirogue 99 (Reliance II 137)   **56 p**
[1991 8m] leggy, sparely-made colt: half-brother to several winners, including Gold Cup winner Longboat (by Welsh Pageant), useful middle-distance horse Sailors Dance and 11.7f winner Wave Dancer (both by Dance In Time): dam, 1m winner, is closely related to good stayer Torpid: weak 16/1-shot and bit backward, slowly away then kept on into mid-division in maiden at Warwick won by Feminine Wiles in October: sure to improve. *Major W. R. Hern.*

SEA PRODIGY   2 b.c. (Feb 11) Precocious 126 – Aunt Judy (Great Nephew 126)   **58 ?**
[1991 7d 6m 6g² 6m] 2,500Y: workmanlike colt: third foal: half-brother to modest maiden Avuncular (by Rousillon) and quite useful 1988 2-y-o 7f winner Island Mead (by Pharly): dam well-beaten daughter of Juliette Marny: off course 3 months and 50/1, staying-on length second of 8 to Chris Hughton in maiden at Folkestone: well beaten in 27-runner seller at Newmarket later in October: worth another try at 7f. *M. Blanshard.*

SE-AQ   6 b.g. Krayyan 117 – Messie (Linacre 133) [1990 8f 10.2m² 10v 8m* 8.2f⁶   —
8h² 8m 11.5g⁴ 8f 1991 8g] leggy, lengthy gelding: has a quick action: quite modest handicapper: below form only run in 1991 (October): probably best short of 1½m: acts on hard and dead going: has won for amateur. *C. L. Popham.*

SEARCHING STAR   3 b.f. Rainbow Quest (USA) 134 – Little White Star (Mill   **56**
Reef (USA) 141) [1990 6m⁴ 8.2v⁵ 1991 7m 8m a11g⁵ 11.7m³ 10g⁴ 14.1m 12.1d] close-coupled filly: modest mover: plating-class maiden: should stay beyond 11.5f: acts on good to firm ground: sold to join P. Kelleway 5,000 gns Newmarket December Sales. *P. A. Kelleway.*

SEARCY   3 b.g. Good Times (ITY) – Fee 111 (Mandamus 120) [1990 7g 8g 7m⁶   **48**
1991 12g³ 12g 13.1m⁵ 12.3m 12g⁴ 16.2f⁴ 16.9g⁵] workmanlike gelding: good mover: poor performer: probably stays 17f: possibly best on an easy surface: blinkered last 4 starts: sold to join D. Burchell 4,000 gns Ascot October Sales: may be unsatisfactory. *R. F. Johnson Houghton.*

SEASIDE MINSTREL   3 ch.g. Song 132 – Blackpool Belle 70 (The Brianstan   **46**
128) [1990 5m* 5f4 6m³ 6d⁵ 6f³ 5f³ 5g 5m³ 5m⁶ 7f a6g 1991 8g 8.3m 7m² 8f⁴ 8m² 8f⁶ 8g] leggy gelding: modest plater: apparently best effort third start: stays 1m: acts on firm going (below form on fibresand): visored fourth start: blinkered twice at 2 yrs. *C. J. Hill.*

SEATTLE BRAVE   4 b.g. Seattle Song (USA) 130 – Oraston 115 (Morston (FR)   —
125) [1990 14d⁴ 16.2d 13.6m³ 1991 17.1d 17.2g 17.2f⁵] rangy, good-topped gelding:

*EBF Granville Maiden Stakes, Ascot—a field of good-looking newcomers,
and a promising effort from Seattle Rhyme; the colt on the left is Anchorite*

has a round action: modest handicapper: not seen out after July: should prove suited
by thorough test of stamina: acts on good to firm ground. *G. Harwood.*

SEATTLE RHYME (USA)   2 ch.c. (Feb 20) Seattle Dancer (USA) 119 – 124 p
Golden Rhyme 87 (Dom Racine (FR) 121) [1991 6m* 7.1m² 8m* 8d³ 8g*]
   One record that the compilers of the Guinness-sponsored *Horse Racing:
Records, Facts and Champions* are unlikely to need to alter in the foreseeable
future is the 13,100,000 dollars that Robert Sangster and partners paid for
Seattle Dancer as a yearling at Keeneland's July Sale in 1985. In a declining
market the sum paid for the beautifully-bred colt, a Nijinsky half-brother to
the outstanding American Triple Crown winner Seattle Slew and three-parts
brother to the Two Thousand Guineas winner Lomond (by Northern Dancer),
nonetheless exceeded the existing record, paid by Sheikh Mohammed for the
subsequently unraced Snaafi Dancer, by almost 3,000,000 dollars and, incred-
ibly, is almost 10,000,000 dollars more than any yearling has fetched since.
Paying vast amounts of money for a yearling doesn't guarantee success any
more than paying peanuts guarantees failure, as Sangster would be the first to
acknowledge, having seen four of his five previous record-priced yearlings
bought in Europe or North America fail to make much impact as racehorses;
but even though Seattle Dancer somewhat inevitably didn't fulfil the highest
expectations on the track he was still a very useful performer—his five races
brought victories in the Windfield Farms Gallinule Stakes and the Derrinstown Stud Derby Trial, both over a mile and a quarter, as well as second place
in the Grand Prix de Paris and sixth in the Prix du Jockey-Club—and he has
made an auspicious start to his career as a stallion with the highly-impressive
Racing Post Trophy winner Seattle Rhyme leading the way from his first crop.
At 55,000 dollars, Seattle Rhyme cost a fraction of the sum paid for Seattle
Dancer but he's already shown the superior form and on the evidence of his
Doncaster run in particular there's every likelihood of better to come.
   In a year in which most of the top two-year-old races in Britain, thank-
fully, regained a competitive and representative nature that had been absent
for several seasons the Racing Post Trophy, run over a mile at Doncaster in
October, attracted probably the strongest field of all, pitting together eight
experienced and progressive youngsters. Besides Seattle Rhyme, a supple-
mentary entry following his valiant third to Arazi in the Ciga Grand Criterium

*Racing Post Trophy, Doncaster—Seattle Rhyme becomes Derby favourite
by beating Mack The Knife and Assessor decisively*

at Longchamp three weeks earlier, form which just gave him the edge over his rivals, the field contained six others with form useful or better. The pick of these were the highly-regarded Thourios, who'd put a disappointing run at Goodwood behind him when an excellent third to Dr Devious in the Three Chimneys Dewhurst Stakes at Newmarket; the dual winner Ninja Dancer, who'd beaten another Racing Post Trophy runner King's Loch emphatically by three lengths on their latest outing in the Bovis Autumn Stakes; and Mack The Knife, who'd finished just behind Seattle Rhyme when the pair had come second and fourth in the Solario Stakes at Sandown in August and had since run Made of Gold to three quarters of a length in the Royal Lodge William Hill Stakes at Ascot. Nothing was ever travelling so smoothly as Seattle Rhyme, however, and he ran out a highly impressive winner under a supremely confident ride. Seattle Rhyme, who looked really well, wore bandages behind as usual. He was waited with longer than at Longchamp where his connections felt he had burst himself by trying to take on Arazi rounding the home turn, and his rider Asmussen didn't produce him until after Ninja Dancer and Mack The Knife had gone for home past the weakening Thourios with under two furlongs to run. When asked, Seattle Rhyme responded immediately and by the line had drawn three and a half lengths clear of Mack The Knife in second. Ninja Dancer didn't see out the final furlong leaving the proven stayer Assessor, a four-length winner of a well-contested Ascot minor event last time, to stay on into third a length and a half back with the useful Haydock winner Anchorite never dangerous two lengths behind in fourth. Since Reference Point routed his field by eight lengths in the equivalent event in 1986, when it was known as the William Hill Futurity, the race has, with the exception of the Prix du Jockey-Club third Emmson, been won by a collection of disappointing animals but we'll be surprised if Seattle Rhyme doesn't prove himself a high-class colt at three. He's already shown good-class form, possesses a useful turn of foot for one who stays a mile well as a two-year-old,

Mr H. J. Senn's "Seattle Rhyme"

		Nijinsky	Northern Dancer
	Seattle Dancer (USA)	(b 1967)	Flaming Page
	(b 1984)	My Charmer	Poker
Seattle Rhyme (USA)		(b 1969)	Fair Charmer
(ch.c. Feb 20, 1989)		Dom Racine	Kalamoun
	Golden Rhyme	(b or br 1975)	La Ferte Milon
	(ch 1980)	Silly Song	Silly Season
		(b 1972)	Glider

and besides having the physical scope to improve through the winter is
stabled with a trainer whose horses nearly always improve from two to three.
His future looks bright indeed.

Seattle Rhyme has always been held in high regard by his trainer. In
an interview published in *Timeform* after his colt had beaten six other
newcomers in the EBF Granville Stakes over six furlongs at Ascot on King
George day, he revealed 'He's magnificent . . . I don't want to say too much
about Seattle Rhyme's potential because I might jeopardize his chance—I'm
superstitious—but I think he's a good horse'. Seattle Rhyme lost his next
race, the Solario Stakes, largely through inexperience, having come with a
sustained run from last place on the home turn to get within a neck of the
all-the-way winner Chicmond, but in the listed Stardom Stakes at Goodwood
in September he looked much more the complete racehorse. Having been
pushed along to take the lead off the front-running Rokeby two furlongs out,
Seattle Rhyme ran on really strongly, lengthening his stride in excellent
style on the flatter ground in the last furlong. Looking better the further he
went, he passed the post, eased slightly, three lengths to the good. Con-
clusive proof that Seattle Rhyme was exactly what his trainer said he was

came in the Grand Criterium at Longchamp in October. The only English-trained challenger among five attempting to prevent Arazi's completing a six-timer, Seattle Rhyme managed to get closest in the straight but eventually paid for his efforts and lost second place to the promising young stayer Rainbow Corner on the line, three lengths down.

At the time of writing Seattle Rhyme is second or third favourite for the Derby but his pedigree is lighter on stamina than one would expect to see in a potential Derby winner and we shouldn't be certain that he'll be fully effective at the distance. Seattle Dancer showed his best form at a mile and a quarter, and while he can be expected, like Lomond and Seattle Slew, to sire plenty of winners over middle distances, none of the first four dams on the bottom line of Seattle Rhyme's pedigree showed its best form beyond a mile. Indeed, only Silly Song, a well-beaten second in a poor race over a mile and a half at Tramore, was considered to possess any stamina: Golden Rhyme a seven-furlong winner, ran just twice beyond seven, finishing well beaten on each occasion, Glider never ran beyond a mile and Pop Room, Seattle Rhyme's fourth dam, was a five-furlong performer. Furthermore, the only worthwhile winners over middle distances from the quartet are sons of Glider to staying stallions, the White Rose winner Juggernaut, the William Hill Gold Cup winner Aliante and the very useful mile to mile-and-a-half performer Donello; most significantly of all, perhaps, none of Silly Song's six winners has scored beyond nine furlongs and Golden Rhyme's only previous living foal Malhamdale (by Dixieland Band), a fair performer at seven furlongs and a mile, finished well beaten over a mile and a quarter. With so many question marks over his stamina it may well pay to wait until Seattle Rhyme (whom his trainer, in the same interview, described as 'a John Wayne type, big with a relaxed walk'), makes his reappearance, but the indications are that Seattle Rhyme, a strong colt, may well prove best at up to a mile and a quarter. He acts on good to firm and good to soft ground. *D. R. C. Elsworth.*

SEA WAR (IRE)   3 ch.g. Gorytus (USA) 132 – Corinth Canal 77 (Troy 137) [1990   **73**
6m 1991 10g 11.7m² 12.5m* 14m⁵] unfurnished gelding: first past post in maidens at Bath (sweating, edged left and demoted) and Warwick in July: favourite, last of 5 in moderately-run handicap at Haydock following month, held up: should stay 1¾m: sold A. Falourd 10,000 gns Newmarket Autumn Sales. *Major W. R. Hern.*

SEA WATCH   3 b.f. Chief Singer 131 – Brave Advance (USA) 98 (Bold Laddie   —
(USA)) [1990 NR 1991 7m⁵ 6g] 13,000Y: leggy, rather angular filly: moderate walker: fourth foal: dam 2-y-o 5f winner: no worthwhile form in maiden and claimer: sold 600 gns Newmarket July Sales. *J. Etherington.*

SEBOSAN   2 b.c. (Mar 24) Prince Sabo 123 – Ceramic (USA) (Raja Baba (USA))   **76**
[1991 5m² 5g* 6d³ 6g 6f³ 6m 6g] sturdy colt: second foal: half-brother to a winner in Sweden: dam (ran once in Ireland) is granddaughter of top-class 4.5f to 9f winner Furl Sail: modest performer: won maiden at Nottingham in June: in mid-division in Racecall Gold Trophy at Redcar final start: stays 6f: acts on firm ground and dead. *A. Hide.*

SECOND ADVENTURE   3 br.g. Another Realm 118 – Friendly Miss (Be   **58**
Friendly 130) [1990 NR 1991 a6g² a7g⁴ a6g² a5g³ 6g⁶ 7m] 6,400Y, 8,000 2-y-o: half-brother to 1985 Irish 2-y-o 6f winner Tawafan (by London Bells) and a winner in Hong Kong by Noalto: dam 6f winner in Ireland: quite modest form: 3/1 favourite from 14/1, showed nothing in Warwick handicap in May, final start: should be suited by further than 6f: visored last 3 outings. *D. J. G. Murray-Smith.*

SECOND SET (IRE)   3 b.c. Alzao (USA) 117 – Merriment (USA) (Go   **127**
Marching (USA)) [1990 NR 1991 7g* 8.2m* 8g² 8g* 8d⁴ 8g]

After just four races Second Set seemed in reach of the European mile championship. On his third outing he'd done tremendously well for one so in-experienced to run the Derby second Marju to a head in the St James's Palace Stakes at Royal Ascot, and he'd followed up by winning the Sussex Stakes at Goodwood decisively from the One Thousand Guineas winner Shadayid and the leading French four-year-old Priolo. But he was never quite the same again. Possibly the dead ground was against him when he suffered a reverse in the Queen Elizabeth II Stakes at Ascot in September, beaten into fourth place behind Selkirk. Equally, he might have been feeling the strain. Five weeks

Sussex Stakes, Goodwood—Second Set is pressed by the grey Shadayid and Priolo

later he showed nothing whatsoever in the Breeders' Cup Mile at Churchill Downs. In the circumstances it is difficult to be positive about his future, though one would anticipate that a winter's rest and additional experience would benefit him more than most.

The St James's Palace Stakes represented a huge step up for Second Set: as such it pointed to the regard in which he was held at home. A smallish, deep-girthed, quite attractive colt who cost IR 160,000 guineas as a yearling, he lacked the benefit of a run as a two-year-old but you wouldn't have thought so as he came out at Newmarket in May to dictate to the useful maidens Claret and Shaleel in a small field. That three-and-a-half-length victory was followed by another of similar merit at the expense of Claret in a three-runner event at Haydock later in the month. It was with such credentials that Second Set arrived to contest one of Royal Ascot's show-pieces, and started third favourite of seven at 4/1 behind Marju and the Poulains runner-up Acteur Francais. On this occasion Second Set's inexperience showed a little as he lost a place or two in the bunch when the race burst into life round the home turn, but he got right back into things and possibly headed Marju for a stride up front inside the last furlong.

The line-up for the Sussex Stakes was stronger, more evenly matched, than that for the St James's Palace. The three older horses in the line-up, Priolo, the previous two years' second Green Line Express and the Queen Anne Stakes winner Sikeston, were opposed by two Guineas winners (Mystiko and Shadayid), an Irish Guineas second (Star of Gdansk), the apparently-improving Radwell and Second Set, out in the market to 5/1 following reports of widespread coughing in the stable. Dettori gave Second Set a good ride. As expected with Green Line Express and Mystiko present, the pace was a strong one. Star of Gdansk chased them, tracked by the rest who were all held up. Drawn on the rails, Dettori stayed handy there until safely round the turn. Approaching three furlongs out, he dashed his mount between the leaders, seizing an advantage of around three lengths with two furlongs still to go. From there it was a question of whether Second Set could last out. Chased by Shadayid and Priolo, he responded very genuinely to driving, looking much more mature than at Royal Ascot, and, as we said, held on decisively in the end, by a length and a half and a short head from two opponents whom he'd beaten for speed at a critical stage of the race.

Allowing for the fact that the front runners were not at their best, the Sussex Stakes form read well enough to give Second Set a favourite's chance in an international field for the Queen Elizabeth II Stakes. But he was beaten almost five lengths into fourth-of-nine place behind Selkirk, three lengths behind third-placed Shadayid. He was still travelling strongly as they took the home turn, but, in contrast to Goodwood, it was Shadayid not Second Set who quickened the pace. He couldn't lie up; he seemed not to have the same

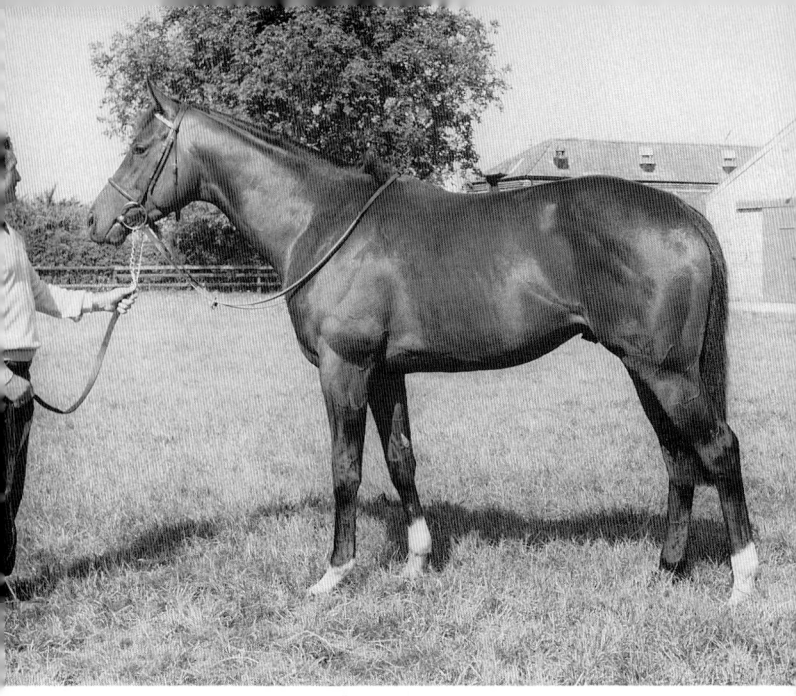

Mr R. L. Duchossois' "Second Set"

sparkle in him and merely kept on at the one speed. The performance couldn't be regarded as disappointing except in that he'd failed to build on Goodwood. However, his Breeders' Cup Mile run certainly was—he never got out of mid-field until fading into twelfth over the last two furlongs, having come under pressure three furlongs out. He was running on medication, bute, reportedly because he'd broken blood vessels in the past. No excuses were made for him afterwards other than he'd been bumped at some stage. He looked in great condition and the ground should have suited him.

Second Set (IRE) (b.c. 1988)	Alzao (USA) (b 1980)	Lyphard (b 1969)	Northern Dancer Goofed
		Lady Rebecca (b 1971)	Sir Ivor Pocahontas II
	Merriment (USA) (b 1975)	Go Marching (b 1965)	Princequillo Leallah
		Tiddlywinks (b 1963)	Court Martial Banri An Oir

Second Set's sale as a yearling was preceded by another as a foal for IR 36,000 guineas. In between time Alzao had continued to show promise as a sire, which might account for some of the added attraction. The dam Merriment had by then produced winners in Belgium and France by Pas de Seul and Trepan respectively; another of her foals, Lake Taupo (by Taufan), had been showing modest form as a two-year-old in Britain, and he has since won races in Malaysia. Merriment's chief claim to fame before Second Set came along was that she's a sister to the high-class French miler Brinkmanship. She showed quite useful form at up to a mile in France but did very little racing and never managed to get her head in front. The next dam is an unraced daughter of the 1953 Irish One Thousand Guineas and Cork And Orrery Stakes third Banri An Oir; another daughter of Banri An Oir, Paris Pike, won the Hollywood Oaks and also produced a Hollywood Oaks winner. There is an Epsom Oaks winner two generations further back on the distaff side of the pedigree —the successful favourite in 1929, Pennycomequick. *L. M. Cumani.*

SECOND TO NONE 4 b.g. Superlative 118 – Matinata (Dike (USA)) [1990 5m³ **60** 6f⁵ 5m² 5m² 5.8f² 1991 5m 5m⁵ 6g] strong gelding: quite modest handicapper: seems best at 5f: acts on firm ground: effective with or without visor or blinkers: sold 760 gns Newmarket Autumn Sales. *D. W. P. Arbuthnot.*

SECRET CONTRACT 6 b.g. Caruso 112 – Sealed Contract 76 (Runnymede **—** 123) [1990 NR 1991 a6g] leggy, light-framed gelding: poor plater. *R. E. Barr.*

SECRET FREEDOM (USA) 3 b.f. Secreto (USA) 128 – Mary Biz (USA) (T V **80** Lark) [1990 6d³ 6g* 6m 7g 8m 1991 11.3d⁵ 11m³ 12g³ 10.1f4] angular filly: fair performer: ran well in Cheshire Oaks and slowly-run race for small-field minor event (held up taking strong hold, never able to challenge) first 2 starts: ran poorly last 2, off course 2 months before each: should prove suited by good pace when at 1½m: acts on good to firm ground and dead. *C. E. Brittain.*

SECRET HAUNT (USA) 3 ch.c. Secreto (USA) 128 – Royal Suite (USA) **111** (Herbager 136) [1990 8m* 1991 8.2m* 12g²] strong, good-bodied colt: moderate mover: won 3-runner minor event at Nottingham in April: 6/1 and looking extremely well, 6 lengths second of 9 to Saddlers' Hall in King Edward VII Stakes at Royal Ascot 2 months later: stays 1½m. *L. M. Cumani.*

Mr G. Sainaghi's "Secret Haunt"

SECRET HAZE 3 ch.f. Absalom 128 – Secret Gill 88 (Most Secret 119) [1990 **82** 6m⁴ 6g² 6d* 1991 6d² 7g²] sturdy filly: carries condition: shows knee action: fair form: beaten head in apprentice race at Ripon and in minor event at Catterick in April: stays 7f: sold to race in USA and won there. *Miss S. E. Hall.*

SECRETILLA (USA) 3 b.f. Secreto (USA) 128 – Satilla (FR) 118 (Targowice **61** (USA) 130) [1990 7f⁶ 1991 7m³ 8f³ 7m* 8f] close-coupled, sparely-made filly: moderate mover: quite modest form: won 3-runner maiden at Redcar: co-favourite, tailed off in handicap at Yarmouth later in August: may well stay beyond 1m: sold 16,500 gns Newmarket December Sales, probably to Italy. *L. M. Cumani.*

SECRET LIASON 5 b.g. Ballacashtal (CAN) – Midnight Mistress (Midsummer — Night II 117) [1990 a7g⁴ a8g³ a8g⁴ a7g a7g 7f 8m⁶ 1991 10g 10g] angular gelding: quite modest handicapper at best, not so good nowadays: stays 1m: acts on firm going: has been tried blinkered: winning hurdler. *W. G. M. Turner.*

SECRET MYTH (IRE) 3 b.c. Secreto (USA) 128 – Mythilene (FR) (Targowice **63** (USA) 130) [1990 NR 1991 10.2m 9g 9f³] IR 50,000Y: good-bodied colt: half-brother to 3 winners in France and Ireland, including Irish 1989 2-y-o 7f winner Ione (by Diesis): dam French 9f and 1¼m winner, is half-sister to very smart French miler Lou Piguet and good 1m and 1¼m performer Chamisene: third in maiden at Newcastle in July: bandaged first 2 starts: dead. *F. H. Lee.*

SECRET SILENCE 3 br.c. Secretariat (USA) – Dame Margot (USA) (Northern — Dancer) [1990 NR 1991 8d 10d] 130,000Y: strong, compact colt: half-brother to 2 winners in USA, including a stakes winner at up to 9f by Lord Avie, and a winner in Japan: dam unraced: better effort seventh of 20 in maiden at Kempton on debut: dead. *I. A. Balding.*

SECRET SOCIETY 4 b. or br.c. Law Society (USA) 130 – Shaara (FR) (Sanctus **95** II 132) [1990 8f* 10.6f⁵ 8m 8g² 8.5m 8m³ 12.3m* 12m⁴ 12m⁴ 12m* 12s⁶ 1991 10g 12.3g* 12m⁴ 13.9g 11.9m* 12s 12m 12d] big, deep-girthed colt: has a rather round action: fairly useful handicapper on his day: won at Ripon in May and Haydock in September: better suited by around 1½m than shorter, and should stay 1¾m: acts on firm going: none too consistent. *M. J. Camacho.*

SECRET SUMMIT (USA) 5 b.g. Diamond Shoal 130 – Ygraine (Blakeney 126) — [1990 NR 1991 12f] ex-Irish gelding: third foal: dam won over 1m in France: poor maiden: first run on flat since 3-y-o, reared stalls and well beaten in claimer at Brighton in March: winning hurdler. *A. Moore.*

SECRET TALENT 3 b.g. Grey Desire 115 – Canty Day 87 (Canadel II 126) [1990 — 7m 7f⁴ 7g 1991 10v⁵ 11m] leggy gelding: soundly beaten, blinkered and looking reluctant in seller final start: dead. *P. Mitchell.*

SECRET THING (USA) 2 b.c. (Feb 28) Secreto (USA) 128 – Nothing Sweeter **102** (USA) (Darby Creek Road (USA)) [1991 5g³ 6.1m² 7d² 8s⁴ 6v] $70,000Y: compact colt: second foal: dam won at up to 1¼m: useful maiden: ¾-length second of 7 to Casteddu in minor event at Ascot, leading briefly over 1f out and staying on well until no extra last 50 yds: excellent fourth of 13, beaten over 3 lengths, to Alhijaz in Gran Criterium at Milan later in October: well below form in all-aged Group 3 event at Rome 3 weeks later: better suited by 1m than less: acts well on soft ground. *C. E. Brittain.*

SECRET WATERS 4 b.f. Pharly (FR) 130 – Idle Waters 116 (Mill Reef (USA) **100** 141) [1990 10g 12m³ 12.5g⁴ 14f⁵ 13.1m* 12.5m* 14f* 12m³ 14.6g⁶ 12m 1991 12.2d 16g³ 12m⁶ 16.2m⁴ 11.9m⁵ 16g 13.9g 13.4m²] leggy, close-coupled filly: moderate mover: useful performer: good second of 6 to Arcadian Heights in listed event at Chester in August: better at 1¾m to 2m than shorter: goes well on top-of-the-ground, possibly unsuited by dead: usually held up: game. *R. F. Johnson Houghton.*

SECURITY ALERT 5 b.g. Head For Heights 125 – Wise Blood (Kalamoun 129) — [1990 NR 1991 a13g] third foal: dam once-raced half-sister to smart middle-distance winner Lafontaine: soundly beaten in claimer at Lingfield in March: sold 825 gns Ascot April Sales. *D. J. G. Murray-Smith.*

SEDUCTRESS 3 ch.f. Known Fact (USA) 135 – Much Too Risky 87 (Bustino — 136) [1990 5m² 5m* 6g* 5m* 5f³ 6m⁵ 1991 6m] small, unfurnished filly: has a quick action: fairly useful winner at 2 yrs: on toes and facing stiff task, disputed lead 3f when soundly beaten in listed race in May, 1991: stays 6f. *M. R. Stoute.*

SEDUISANT 3 b.f. Tina's Pet 121 – Miss Jade 55 (Hardgreen (USA) 122) [1990 — NR 1991 12m] 2,500Y: first foal: dam, plater, stayed 1½m: 50/1, well beaten in maiden at Thirsk in May. *G. R. Oldroyd.*

SEEK A FORTUNE (USA) 2 b.c. (Mar 4) Fortunate Prospect (USA) – **67**
Centerfold Girl (USA) (Decimator (USA)) [1991 5m² 6m⁵] $72,000 2-y-o: leggy,
rather close-coupled colt: half-brother to winners in USA by L'Heureux and Groton:
dam won at up to 7f: sire sprinter: quite modest form in maidens: led almost 4f at
Haydock in May: seemed not to stay at Epsom following month. *J. Berry.*

SEE NOW 6 ch.g. Tumble Wind (USA) – Rosie O'Grady (Barrons Court) [1990 —
NR 1991 9.9m] lengthy gelding: no worthwhile form after winning as 3-y-o: stays 7f:
tried hooded once. *Mrs A. Knight.*

SEIZE THE DAY (IRE) 3 b.c. Lomond (USA) 128 – Cheerful Heart (Petingo **76**
135) [1990 NR 1991 12.3d 14g² 10g² 12f4] IR 44,000Y: good-topped, attractive colt:
moderate mover: half-brother to prolific middle-distance winner/hurdler Suluk (by
Lypheor) and fairly useful 1m and 1¼m winner Momtaaz (by Diesis): dam 1½m
winner in Ireland, is half-sister to Gift Wrapped, dam of Royal Lodge winner Reach:
in frame in maidens (£10,400 event at Ascot third start), then minor event: probably
stays 1¾m: no show on dead ground: sold out of A. Stewart's stable 17,500 gns
Newmarket July Sales after second start. *L. G. Cottrell.*

SELAAH 4 b.c. Rainbow Quest (USA) 134 – Marwell 133 (Habitat 134) [1990 7g* **97**
8m* 8f³ 1991 8d 8g 7.6m 8m 8g* 8d⁵ 8g] leggy, sparely-made colt: fairly useful
handicapper: easily best effort in 1991 when winning £11,350 event at Ascot in
September by 1½ lengths from Nayland: started favourite for Lincoln on first start:
stays 1m: acts on firm ground, possibly unsuited by dead: gave lot of trouble at stalls
once at 3 yrs. *M. R. Stoute.*

SELAGINELLA 2 ch.f. (May 16) Pharly (FR) 130 – Smagiada (Young Genera- **45** p
tion 129) [1991 7g⁶] fourth foal: half-sister to 3-y-o Jack's Croft (by Damister) and to
modest 1988 2-y-o 5f winner Sweet 'N' Sharp (by Sharpo): dam, winner in Italy, is
half-sister to leading 1982 Italian 2-y-o filly Stemegna: 14/1, 15 lengths sixth of 11, no
progress final 2f, to Dance Scene in maiden at Salisbury in October: should improve.
M. R. Channon.

SELDOM IN 5 ch.g. Mummy's Game 120 – Pinzamber (Pinicola 113) [1990 a11g* **42**
a11g a14g³ a14g⁵ a11g⁶ 1991 a14g⁶ 14d⁴ 16.2g⁵ 13.8g³ 16.5m³ a14g³ 14.6g⁶ 16.2f³
16.5g 19m* a18g³ 17.9f] leggy, lengthy gelding: poor handicapper: won at Redcar in
August: suited by thorough test of stamina: acts on firm and dead ground: has
swished tail and tended to carry head awkwardly under pressure. *J. Wharton.*

SELF EXPRESSION 3 b.g. Homing 130 – Subtlety (Grundy 137) [1990 7m* **98**
7m² 7f⁴ 1991 8s 8g 8.2m 9m² 10d 8.5f* 8g* 10g⁴ 8.9g 8.9g 10.3m* 10d] leggy
gelding: fairly useful but inconsistent handicapper: narrowly successful in amateurs
event at Beverley and apprentice contest at Ascot in July and in £7,600 event at
Doncaster in September: stays 1¼m: seems unsuited by a soft surface: carries head
high and tends to hang: gelded after final start: well beaten 3 of last 4 starts, and not
one to trust implicitly. *I. A. Balding.*

SELKIRK (USA) 3 ch.r. Sharpen Up 127 – Annie Edge 118 (Nebbiolo 125) **129**
[1990 8m* 8g⁴ 1991 8g² 11.5g³ 10g³ 8m⁴ 8g* 8d*]
The course of Selkirk's season changed dramatically in the autumn
when, following an operation to remove an undescended testicle, he produced
two impressive winning performances, the second of them in the valuable
and prestigious Queen Elizabeth II Stakes over a mile at Ascot in September.
Until he'd run away with a well-contested listed event at Kempton three
weeks earlier, by five lengths and eight from Susurration and Zonda, the
chances of Selkirk's taking part in the Queen Elizabeth II Stakes, let alone
winning it, had seemed remote. Until then, he'd threatened to become one of
the season's biggest disappointments. Hopes ran high at the beginning that
Selkirk would develop into a classic horse. A big, useful-looking, well-bred
individual, he'd been pitched in against Hector Protector in the Grand Criterium on only his second outing as a two-year-old and had done well to finish
five lengths fourth to that colt. But Selkirk just couldn't seem to win a race at
three. He would have gone close, to say the least, granted a clear run against
Corrupt on his reappearance in the BonusPrint Easter Stakes at Kempton but
was decisively beaten into third place behind Corrupt on better terms in the
Lingfield Derby Trial; he finished third again behind Man From Eldorado in
another Derby trial at Goodwood; then he failed behind Radwell on what
should have been a confidence-boosting exercise in a small race at Newcastle
towards the end of June.

Selkirk had become a real puzzle. He looked most like a strong-running type who found little off the bridle; probably a mile and a half, a mile and a quarter even, was too far for him, yet there'd been no improvement when he'd been brought back to a mile at Newcastle. However, it transpired that he'd shown some discomfort at Newcastle, the cause of which was diagnosed as a pinched testicle, and he underwent surgery to remove it. There was surely no coincidence in the fact that when he returned to the track he put any doubts about his temperament and ability behind. The riding tactics employed on him in the listed race at Kempton—the Milcars Temple Fortune Stakes—were to wait behind the very strong pace. He improved on the bridle through the fourteen-horse field from over three furlongs out, drew clear with Susurration from the two-furlong pole, led entering the last and sprinted away. Naturally, he was covered up again in the Queen Elizabeth II Stakes; and, if anything, he was even more impressive, though against the far stiffer opposition he had much less in hand. The race had an international flavour with runners from California (graded stakes winner Forty Niner Days) and France (Hector Protector, beaten only once over the trip) as well as those from Britain and Ireland. The field might have been stronger but was clearly strong enough for the race to be rated, as it should, one of the biggest tests in the milers' year. The improving Sussex Stakes winner Second Set started favourite at 3/1; he'd probably have gone off shorter if his ability to act on the softish going had not had to be taken on trust. Selkirk, also unproven on the going, started at 10/1. Separating them in the betting came, in order, the classic winners Kooyonga and Hector Protector, Mukaddamah, Sikeston, and another classic winner Shadayid, all of whom had form on the ground, the gambled-on Sikeston being particularly well-known as a mudlark. Forty Niner Days and La Grange Music completed the field of nine. Despite the conditions the race was run at a good gallop, the runners spread out in search of the best ground, Shadayid racing very wide up with the lead until switched towards the inner at the bend, causing the American challenger to check and tightening up Sikeston and Hector Protector in the middle. Selkirk travelled very smoothly in touch at the back, and was still travelling well as he moved up on the outside on the bend. As Shadayid was set alight in the straight, chased by her old rival Kooyonga, she took what seemed like a race-winning advantage, making them all struggle. Selkirk was suddenly left with a fair bit to do, but he put in some good work under firm driving, growing stronger as the race progressed, and went past the two fillies with a wet sail to lead well inside the last furlong and win going away by a length and a half from Kooyonga who narrowly got the

Milcars Temple Fortune Stakes, Kempton—Selkirk sprints clear

Queen Elizabeth II Stakes, Ascot—
Selkirk finishes strongest to win from the fillies Kooyonga and Shadayid (rails)

better of Shadayid, the pair clear of fourth-placed Second Set. Any further opportunity of assessing Selkirk was denied by a minor set-back which cost him a run in the Challenge Stakes and the Breeders' Cup Mile, but he remains in training. On the one performance, just the one performance, he has claims to being the best miler around in what was an ordinary year.

		Atan		Native Dancer
	Sharpen Up	(ch 1961)		Mixed Marriage
	(ch 1969)	Rocchetta		Rockefella
Selkirk (USA)		(ch 1961)		Chambiges
(ch.r. 1988)		Nebbiolo		Yellow God
	Annie Edge	(ch 1974)		Novara
	(ch 1980)	Friendly Court		Be Friendly
		(ch 1971)		No Court

Selkirk was earlier described as well bred. That's perfectly true in that he's by a top-class sire out of a good-class racemare, though it's also true that his dam Annie Edge's pedigree is less distinguished than her racing record. Annie Edge was one of the best fillies of her generation, winner in Britain of the Kiveton Park Stakes from Salieri and placed in numerous races including the Irish One Thousand Guineas, Nell Gwyn Stakes, Lowther Stakes and Queen Mary Stakes, and a multiple stakes winner at up to a mile and a quarter (after being sold as a three-year-old for 330,000 guineas) in North America. Her sire Nebbiolo, a not particularly highly regarded Two Thousand Guineas winner, had a very promising career as a stallion cut short by his death after three years at stud. Her dam, a two-year-old five-furlong winner in Ireland, is out of a mare, No Court, who won over a mile and a half there and also won over hurdles. Both of Annie Edge's other foals of racing age have been in training at Kingsclere. Selkirk's year-older brother Casual Flash won over two miles at Haydock and Beverley for the stable in 1990; his year-younger half-sister Vailmont (by Diesis) picked up a small race over five furlongs at Goodwood in the latest season. The difference in character between the two brothers illustrates the element of chance always present in breeding race-horses. Selkirk would never stay two miles. He may get another chance at a

765

mile and a quarter, though, in the Eclipse or the Champion Stakes perhaps, if he returns in good form as a four-year-old. A long-striding individual he is undoubtedly suited by waiting tactics and a strongly-run race. He acts on dead going; it was good to firm when he disappointed at Newcastle but similar when he beat a small field at Goodwood on his racing debut. *I. A. Balding.*

SELMA (IRE) 2 b.f. (Feb 13) Don't Forget Me 127 – Petite Realm 95 (Realm 129) **61**
[1991 5d² 5g² 5g* 5g 7.5g⁵] IR 17,000Y: closely related to Irish 7f and 9f winner Park Elect (by Ahonoora): dam speedy 2-y-o: modest performer: won auction event at Tipperary in May: twelfth of 14 behind Marling in Queen Mary Stakes at Royal Ascot: fifth of 14 in listed event at Milan in July: should stay 1m: trained until after fourth start by J. Bolger. *O. Pessi, Italy.*

SEME DE LYS (USA) 3 b.f. Slew O' Gold (USA) – Blazon (USA) (Ack Ack **61**
(USA)) [1990 6m⁵ 6g² 7d⁴ 1991 8v⁴ 10v⁵ 11g⁴ 11.1g 10.5d] $225,000Y: ex-Irish filly: half-sister to 1m and 1¼m winner, and winning hurdler, Battalion (by Vaguely Noble): dam minor winner at up to 6f in USA, is half-sister to Exceller: modest ex-Irish maiden: best effort at 3 yrs on reappearance: off course nearly 5 months then well beaten in claimer and seller last 2 outings: stays 1m: acts on heavy going: trained until after third start by J. Oxx: sold 1,800 gns Doncaster October Sales. *G. Richards.*

SENSE OF PRIORITY 2 ch.g. (Mar 22) Primo Dominie 121 – Sense of Pride **91**
(Welsh Pageant 132) [1991 5v² 5g² 5h* 5g* 5m* 7g* 6m³ 7f⁴ 6.9h* 7m* 7g³ 6g²] 6,200F, 2,500Y: rather unfurnished gelding: second foal: dam Irish middle-distance winner: fairly useful performer: successful in maiden at Carlisle, claimer and seller (retained 12,400 gns) at Beverley and minor event at Catterick in summer, then claimer (had simple task) at Carlisle and nursery (in good style) at Catterick in September: odds on though heavily bandaged, only fair second of 11 in claimer at last-named course on final start: seems better suited by 7f than shorter: acts on hard ground: has also worn bandage off-hind: ran creditably, despite wandering, for 7-lb claimer: races prominently. *M. H. Easterby.*

SENTIMENTALITY (IRE) 3 b.c. Reasonable (FR) 119 – Good Reliance **—**
(Good Bond 122) [1990 5m⁵ 5g³ a7g⁶ 6m⁴ 6m³ 5m⁴ 6m⁴ 6m⁴ 5g* 6d 5m⁴ 5.8d 1991 6g a5g 6m] lengthy, good-quartered colt: carries condition: poor mover: useful plater at 2 yrs: well beaten in non-selling handicaps in 1991: stays 6f: possibly unsuited by a soft surface: bandaged reappearance: blinkered last 4 starts at 2 yrs: trained first 2 starts by K. Ivory: sold 950 gns Newmarket Autumn Sales. *R. Hollinshead.*

SEQUEL TWO 3 gr.g. Nishapour (FR) 125 – Roda Haxan 67 (Huntercombe 133) **—**
[1990 7.5d 6g 7g² 7m² 6f⁶ 7m² 7f⁴ 8.2g⁴ 8m² 6s⁵ a7g a7g⁶ 1991 a8g 10g 7g] neat gelding: quite useful plater at 2 yrs: no worthwhile form in summer as 3-y-o: suited by 7f: blinkered 3 times: sometimes races freely: has carried head high. *P. S. Felgate.*

SEQUESTRATOR 8 b.g. African Sky 124 – Miss Redmarshall 80 (Most Secret **—**
119) [1990 NR 1991 7f 8.9m] small, light-framed gelding: poor and lightly-raced handicapper: suited by 7f: acts on firm going: winning hurdler. *P. D. Evans.*

SERENE WOODS (USA) 3 b.f. Woodman (USA) 126 – Serena (SAF) (Jan **—**
Ekels 122) [1990 NR 1991 6m 7g⁵ 7f a7g⁵] sturdy filly: third reported foal: dam winner of South African Oaks: showed a little ability in maidens, but not seen out after June. *J. H. M. Gosden.*

SERENIKI 4 b.f. Dublin Taxi – Highdrive (Ballymore 123) [1990 8m 7m 10f 8h⁶ **—**
a6g⁵ 1991 a7g a6g a8g] leggy, workmanlike filly: poor mover: plater: best effort over 7f: tried blinkered once: has been bandaged behind. *P. Mitchell.*

SERGEANT LEMON 2 ch.g. (Mar 9) Doulab (USA) 115 – Rabuba 65 **33**
(Connaught 130) [1991 6g 7g 10m] 8,000F, 7,000Y: big, strong, plain gelding: poor walker: third foal: dam, placed twice over 1½m, is half-sister to Irish 2000 Guineas second Brother Philips: poor maiden: off course 3½ months and backward, well beaten in seller at Leicester final start. *M. W. Easterby.*

SERGEANT MERYLL 7 b.g. Marching On 101 – Mistress Meryll 61 (Tower **40**
Walk 130) [1990 8m a7g⁶ 8g a8g⁶ 8m⁴ 8m a7g⁴ a8g 8d 7g³ a7g a8g a7g* a7g⁴ 1991 a7g² a8g a8g⁴ a7g⁶ 10.1s 7.6g 7g⁴ 8.1d⁵ 7.6d 7v⁶ 7.6s² 7.1g² 8.3m 8g⁵ 7g 7g a8g] sturdy, quite attractive gelding: moderate mover: poor handicapper: effective at 7f and 1m: best form on an easy surface: tried visored: has won for apprentice. *P. Howling.*

SERIOUS HURRY   3 ch.c. Forzando 122 – Lady Bequick 81 (Sharpen Up 127)   **76**
[1990 5f 5f² 5g² 5d³ a5g* 1991 a5g* 5.3f³ 5f] strong, heavy-topped, sprint type: has
plenty of scope: carries condition: has a quick action: modest handicapper: won at
Lingfield in April: seems unsuited by a soft surface: edgy final start: sold 3,300 gns
Newmarket July Sales. *Sir Mark Prescott.*

SERIOUS TIME   3 ch.g. Good Times (ITY) – Milva 56 (Jellaby 124) [1990 7d a7g   **48**
a7g³ 1991 a8g⁶ a8g⁴ a7g 8.9g4] leggy gelding: plating-class maiden, not seen out
after June: probably stays 9f: wore eyeshield and carried head high final start at 2
yrs. *Sir Mark Prescott.*

SERMIDE (ITY)   3 ch.f. Fire of Life (USA) 113 – Lacey (CAN) (His Majesty   —
(USA)) [1990 NR 1991 10g 14m³ 14.1f⁴ 16.1g] good-topped filly: third reported foal:
half-sister to Italian 4-y-o Nunki (by Clever Trick), maiden here in 1990: dam stakes
winner (at 6f to 7½f) from 2 to 5 yrs in North America: no worthwhile form in
maidens and handicap. *J. H. M. Gosden.*

SESAME   6 b.m. Derrylin 115 – Hot Spice (Hotfoot 126) [1990 12m 13.3m* 12d²   **107**
12g⁴ 12s⁶ 12f² 13.3g² 13.4g² 12m⁴ 12m⁴ 12d* 12s⁴ 12v* 1991 12g⁴ 13.4d⁶ 12m⁶ 12g³
12.5g 14.6m³ 12s⁵ 12g⁶] strong, lengthy mare: carries condition: very useful
performer: ran creditably behind Patricia in Park Hill Stakes at Doncaster and
Topanoora in Group 2 Blandford Stakes at the Curragh sixth and seventh starts:
effective at 1½m and stayed 14.6f: acted on any going, but particularly well suited by
give in the ground: took strong hold and had worn a dropped noseband: tough and
consistent: stud. *M. F. D. Morley.*

SESAME SEED (IRE)   3 b.c. Wassl 125 – Halva (Troy 137) [1990 NR 1991 10m   **76**
12m⁵ 10.6g 12.4f² 14m² 16.1m² 16.1m5] tall, close-coupled, attractive colt: has a
round action: second foal: half-brother to 4-y-o Tauvalera (by Taufan): dam unraced
from good family: modest maiden: narrowly-beaten second in smallish fields for
maiden and handicaps in the North: stays 2m: wandered under pressure fourth
start, pulled hard and hung left on fifth. *J. W. Watts.*

SET ASIDE (IRE)   3 b.c. Petorius 117 – Wollow Princess (Wollow 132) [1990 5f³   **66**
5f⁴ 6g a7g² a6g* 1991 a6g² 6v³ 7m 8g 7f⁴ 6g² 6d³ 5d 7.1g 6g 6.1d] leggy colt: keen a   **78**
walker: good mover: modest form at best: generally below form in handicaps last 4
outings: probably stays 7f: best efforts on all-weather and easy surface on turf: often
blinkered: edgy before eighth (virtually bolted to post) and ninth (sweating)
outings: sold to Scandinavia 4,200 gns Newmarket Autumn Sales. *D. R. C. Elsworth.*

SETO CITY   2 br.c. (Apr 7) Lidhame 109 – Jenny Splendid 101 (John Splendid 116)   **62**
[1991 6m 5m² 5.1m⁵ 5m⁵ 6.1m] leggy colt: has a quick action: sixth foal: half-brother
to quite modest 1984 2-y-o 5f winner Shelley Marie (by Gunner B) and poor winning
sprinter Shari Louise (by Radetsky): dam won from 5f to 7f: quite modest maiden:
better form at 5f than 6f: has edged right: sometimes on toes. *S. Mellor.*

SET THE STANDARDS (IRE)   3 b.g. Mazaad 106 – Jupiter Miss (USA)   **59**
(Hawaii) [1990 6g 6g³ 5f² 6g² 6m⁵ 5d⁵ 5s* 1991 6s³ 5g 6f² 6m] neat gelding: modest
winner at 2 yrs: in frame in handicaps (sweating and on toes third start) as 3-y-o:
worth a try at 7f: probably acts on any going: blinkered second start: sold 1,700 gns
Doncaster July Sales: winning hurdler for A. Whillans. *J. Berry.*

SET UP   3 b.g. Sarab 123 – Gitee (FR) (Carwhite 127) [1990 NR 1991 a8g³ a7g 8f   **42**
7m⁶ 7.1m 6.1m⁶] well-made gelding: first foal: dam never ran: poor maiden: stays 7f:
sold out of M. Bell's stable 1,000 gns Newmarket July Stales after second outing. *D.
Burchell.*

SEVERINE (USA)   2 b.f. (Mar 8) Trempolino (USA) 135 – Sharmila (FR)   **64**
(Blakeney 126) [1991 6g 7f³ 6.3s 7g] IR 70,000Y: close-coupled, sturdy, attractive
filly: second foal: dam once-raced half-sister to Petoski: quite modest maiden: well
beaten after second outing, in Goffs Fillies Challenge at the Curragh penultimate
start: bred to stay well: possibly unsuited by soft ground. *J. L. Dunlop.*

SEXY MOVER   4 ch.g. Coquelin (USA) 121 – Princess Sinna (Sun Prince 128)   —
[1990 10m 1991 12m 8h] leggy gelding: lightly-raced maiden on flat: well beaten in
seller final start (May): should stay 1¼m: visored reappearance: winning hurdler.
W. Storey.

SHAAM (USA)   2 b.c. (May 3) Danzig (USA) – Milliardare (USA) (Alydar (USA))   —
[1991 6d] $800,000Y: small, compact colt: first foal: dam, minor winner in North
America at 4 yrs, is sister to Saratoga Six and half-sister to Dunbeath: weak
5/1-shot, green and tended to hang in 15-runner maiden at Doncaster in November,
finishing well beaten. *A. A. Scott.*

SHAARID (USA)   3 b.c. El Gran Senor (USA) 136 – Summer Silence (USA)   **87**
(Stop The Music (USA)) [1990 NR 1991 9f* 9g4] smallish colt: first foal: dam, 4-y-o

7f winner in North America having shown little here, is out of sister to Mill Reef:
won 4-runner maiden at Redcar in May: fourth of 16 in ladies race at Kempton
following month, taking good hold and always close up: sold 6,500 gns Newmarket
December Sales. *H. Thomson Jones.*

SHAATRA (FR)   2 gr.f. (Feb 2) Siberian Express (USA) 125 – Fowzieh (Sandy   —
Creek 123) [1991 5g] IR 2,000Y: smallish, workmanlike filly: poor walker: third
reported foal (previous 2 by Ya Zaman): dam ran once at 3 yrs: backward, swerved
stalls and soon outpaced in median auction maiden at Thirsk in May: sold 950 gns
Newmarket September Sales. *M. Moubarak.*

SHADAYID (USA)   3 gr.f. Shadeed (USA) 135 – Desirable 119 (Lord Gayle **122**
(USA) 124) [1990 6d* 7m* 8g* 1991 7.3g* 8g* 12m³ 8g² 8g² 6f³ 8d³ 8g]
     You couldn't wish for a tougher or more genuine filly than Shadayid. She
ran eight times as a three-year-old—seven in Group 1 company—over distances ranging from six furlongs to a mile and a half and was only once out of
the first three. She fully deserved her classic victory in the General Accident
One Thousand Guineas and put up three other equally noteworthy performances in defeat in the Coronation Stakes, the Sussex Stakes and the Queen
Elizabeth II Stakes, all over a mile which was undoubtedly her best distance.
She'll be a valuable addition to her owner's growing band of broodmares and
starts her new career with a visit to Nashwan.
     Shadayid gave her owner, trainer and jockey their second successive
victory in the One Thousand Guineas, following that of the versatile Salsabil
whose marvellous campaign (she went on to win the Gold Seal Oaks, the
Budweiser Irish Derby and the Prix Vermeille) almost earned her the official
Horse of the Year award in 1990. Though unrelated to Salsabil, Shadayid
was inevitably compared with her. Both fillies won the Prix Marcel Boussac,
Europe's premier test for two-year-old fillies, and both warmed up for the
Guineas with an impressive victory in the Gainsborough Stud Fred Darling
Stakes at Newbury. Shadayid won the Fred Darling by three lengths with her
jockey easing up, strengthening her winter position as a strong favourite for
the Guineas. Good two-year-old fillies had been thin on the ground and
Shadayid, who hadn't been stretched in three races, had stood out as one of
the few with genuine classic potential. She eventually started at 6/4 on for the
One Thousand Guineas, the shortest-priced favourite for nearly thirty years,
and maintained her unbeaten record with a two-length victory over the Irish-
trained 14/1-shot Kooyonga, hitting the front in the Dip and running on well up
the hill. The Nell Gwyn winner Crystal Gazing, who started second favourite
at 6/1, came out best in a close battle for third with the outsiders Once In My
Life and Only Yours in a fourteen-runner field that lacked strength in depth.
     Shadayid continued in the footsteps of Salsabil in her next race, the Gold
Seal Oaks, raising the difficult question of whether Shadayid possessed the
necessary stamina. 'I think she'll get a mile and a quarter, but a mile and a
half? I don't know. But, then, I said the same last year about Salsabil', was the
opinion of her rider Carson, while her trainer Dunlop parried questions about

Gainsborough Stud Fred Darling Stakes, Newbury—Shadayid shows she's trained on

General Accident One Thousand Guineas, Newmarket—
Shadayid lands the odds from Kooyonga; then come Crystal Gazing (rails),
Once In My Life (hooped cap) and Only Yours

whether she would stay with the reply 'Who knows?'. Sheikh Hamdan takes an active interest in the placing of his best horses and he was understandably keen for Shadayid to attempt to emulate Salsabil. Salsabil's pedigree had provided plenty of encouragement for the view that she would stay a mile and a half, but Shadayid's cast doubts on whether she would get the trip. Shadayid's sire the highly-strung Two Thousand Guineas and Queen Elizabeth II Stakes winner Shadeed almost certainly wouldn't have been effective at much beyond a mile, even though he's by Nijinsky (the only time he ran at a longer distance was when he ran deplorably in the Derby); Shadayid's dam the One Thousand Guineas third Desirable got a mile and a quarter. We doubted Shadayid's proving fully effective over the Oaks trip but she started a hot favourite in a field of nine after two of her supposed main rivals Dartrey and Shamshir were beaten in the Musidora Stakes at York by Gussy Marlowe, a filly not entered at Epsom. The Oaks produced one of the season's biggest shocks when the front-running Irish-trained 50/1-shot Jet Ski Lady romped home by ten lengths. Shadayid was poised on the shoulder of Jet Ski Lady entering the home straight but lack of stamina proved her undoing. She began to make hard work of it entering the last two furlongs and was passed for second by Shamshir close home.

Shadayid was back in action only a week and a half after her hard race at Epsom. The Coronation Stakes at Royal Ascot also attracted the winners of the Irish and French One Thousand Guineas equivalents, Kooyonga (who had followed up her Newmarket performance by winning in good style at the Curragh) and Danseuse du Soir. Kooyonga reversed One Thousand Guineas form with Shadayid after a memorable duel all the way up the home straight. Shadayid never quite looked likely to take the measure of Kooyonga, though she battled on magnificently before going down by three quarters of a length, with Gussy Marlowe just holding off Danseuse du Soir for third. Shadayid performed every bit as well when runner-up again in the Sussex Stakes at Goodwood at the end of July, beaten a length and a half by Second Set in a high-class field. In an adventurous move, Shadayid reverted to six furlongs in her next race, the Ladbroke Sprint Cup at Haydock which also attracted the Two Thousand Guineas winner Mystiko, as well as the Nunthorpe winner Sheikh Albadou and the French-trained four-year-old Polar Falcon, better known as a miler but a good fourth in the July Cup at Newmarket. Shadayid

Hamdan Al-Maktoum's "Shadayid"

Shadayid (USA) (gr.f. 1988)	Shadeed (USA) (b 1982)	Nijinsky (b 1967)	Northern Dancer
			Flaming Page
		Continual (b or br 1976)	Damascus
			Continuation
	Desirable (gr 1981)	Lord Gayle (b 1965)	Sir Gaylord
			Sticky Case
		Balidaress (gr 1973)	Balidar
			Innocence

came third to Polar Falcon and Sheikh Albadou, running very much as though needing further. The Queen Elizabeth II Stakes at Ascot three weeks later gave Shadayid another opportunity to show her worth over her best trip and, deserted on this occasion by her regular rider Carson, who preferred Mukaddamah, she put up at least as good a performance as any previously to finish third to Selkirk and Kooyonga. Normally ridden with restraint, Shadayid was allowed by Eddery on this occasion to bowl along with the leaders. Shadayid kept on gamely under the whip after being sent on in earnest soon after the field straightened out for home. She looked like winning for a moment but Selkirk and Kooyonga both proved too good and Shadayid went down by a length and a half and a neck; Second Set was three lengths further back in fourth. Shadayid ended her racing career in the Breeders' Cup Mile at Churchill Downs in November when, after missing the break and being hampered in the closing stages, she finished a creditable seventh.

The lengthy, good-bodied Shadayid, who is a moderate mover, gained a rather exaggerated reputation for being a nervous and excitable filly. Except for becoming stirred up in the parade for the Queen Elizabeth II Stakes, her behaviour in the preliminaries never gave serious cause for concern, though she was always on her toes. Her natural inclination as a racehorse was to get on with things and she took a strong hold in her races. But she was most reliable and never ran a bad race, showing her form on going ranging from good to firm to dead. Shadayid is the first living foal of Desirable who was also represented on the racecourse in the latest season by the Blushing Groom colt Badie, an impressive winner on his racecourse debut at Kempton in September. Desirable, a Cheveley Park winner, is a half-sister to the Irish Oaks winner Alydaress and to another Cheveley Park winner Park Appeal, and her brother Nashamaa, who was very useful at up to a mile and a half. Their dam Balidaress cost only 2,400 guineas as a yearling and had a fairly modest racing record in Ireland, showing little at two, winning over seven furlongs and a mile at three, and over a mile and a quarter at four as well as being placed over hurdles. Great oaks from little acorns grow! *J. L. Dunlop.*

SHADAYLOU (IRE)   2 ch.f. (Mar 10) Standaan (FR) 118 – Grande Madame 64   **49** (Monseigneur (USA) 127) [1991 7g⁴ 7d³ 7m⁴ 7g 6m⁴] IR 3,200F, 4,000 2-y-o: leggy, rather sparely-made filly: half-sister to Irish 1990 2-y-o 5f winner Classic Player (by The Noble Player) and 2 other winners: dam 2-y-o 8.2f winner, is half-sister to Tumbledownwind, a smart performer at up to 1m: poor maiden: stays 7f: acts on good to firm and dead ground. *Mrs J. Jordan.*

SHADES OF JADE   3 gr.f. General Wade 93 – Gellifawr 80 (Saulingo 122) [1990   **57** 5f 5m 1991 5f 6f⁵ 5s⁶ 5d² 5f⁴ 5.3f⁵ 5m 5m² 5d 5g 5.1m⁵ 5g 5d⁶ 5f] rangy filly: has a very round action: plating-class maiden: second in handicaps at Kempton and Lingfield: below form afterwards: acts on good to firm ground and dead: tends to get on toes. *J. J. Bridger.*

SHADES OF VERA   3 b.f. Precocious 126 – More Reliable (Morston (FR) 125)   **67** [1990 6f 5m⁶ 5m 6m² 6g* 5g 1991 6m⁴ 6g 6.1m⁶ 7g⁵ 6.9m² 7.1s 7f 6m³] angular, unfurnished filly: has quick action: good walker: modest handicapper: blinkered, creditable third of 13 at Lingfield in August: worth a try at 1m: acts on good to firm ground, probably not on soft: sometimes bandaged behind. *G. Lewis.*

SHADHA (USA)   3 ch.f. Devil's Bag (USA) – Treizieme (USA) 121 (The Minstrel   — (CAN) 135) [1990 6f* 7f⁵ 8d 1991 10m⁴ 11.7g 12g 10.1g] good-topped filly: modest winner at 2 yrs: ran with little zest facing stiff tasks in minor event (reared leaving stalls) and handicaps first half of 1991: should stay 1m: seems unsuited by dead ground: visored last 2 starts: bandaged off-hind final one: joined G. Jones in USA. *A. C. Stewart.*

SHADIDEEN (USA)   3 ch.c. Shadeed (USA) 135 – Allegretta 101 (Lombard   **68** (GER) 126) [1990 a8g⁵ 1991 8g 10g 9m 11.7f³] leggy, close-coupled, angular colt: modest form: good third in maiden claimer at Bath on first run for 4 months: may well prove as effective back at 1¼m: acts on firm going: sold to join Miss L. Perratt 9,200 gns Doncaster November Sales. *P. F. I. Cole.*

SHADOW BIRD   4 b.f. Martinmas 128 – In The Shade 89 (Bustino 136) [1990   **59** 10m⁵ 12g² 14g⁶ 13g* 13.3g⁶ 12g a12g5 1991 12d 12m³ 12m⁵ 12g 10.1m⁴ 11.5m² 12g² 11.5f⁶ 10m⁴ 11m 12m* 12d* 12f] leggy, workmanlike filly: moderate mover: quite modest handicapper: won amateur events at Pontefract (hampered and awarded race) and Ascot in autumn: best at around 1½m: acts on firm and dead ground: effective blinkered or not: sold 10,500 gns Newmarket Autumn Sales after final start. *G. A. Pritchard-Gordon.*

SHADOWLAND (IRE)   3 ch.g. Be My Native (USA) 122 – Sunland Park   **59** (Baragoi 115) [1990 7m a7g⁴ a6g 8d 1991 12g 12m² 13.8m⁴ 13.6g⁵ 11.5g] strong gelding: quite modest maiden: came from rear 2 best efforts first half of 1991: stays 13.6f: acts on good to firm ground. *G. A. Pritchard-Gordon.*

SHADY LEAF (IRE)   3 b.f. Glint of Gold 128 – Dancing Shadow 117 (Dancer's   — Image (USA)) [1990 8.2m⁴ 1991 12m⁴ 10f³ 14.1g⁶ 12f 10m] angular, sparely-made filly: modest maiden at best: well beaten after reappearance, in handicaps last 3 starts: stays 1½m: visored (didn't settle) fourth start: sold 3,800 gns Newmarket Autumn Sales, probably to Italy. *M. R. Stoute.*

SHAFAYIF   2 ch.f. (Feb 6) Ela-Mana-Mou 132 – Rare Roberta (USA) 118 (Roberto   — (USA) 131) [1991 6.1m 8m] lengthy filly: fifth foal: half-sister to 1990 2-y-o 5f winner

Beynounah (by Shareef Dancer) and fair 1¼m winner Al Raja (by Kings Lake): dam 6f and 1m winner: bit backward, well beaten in Midlands maidens. *B. Hanbury.*

SHAFFAAF (USA) 3 b.c. Shadeef (USA) 135 – Refill 88 (Mill Reef (USA) 141) — §
[1990 NR 1991 10m 10.6g⁵ 10d 11.7m 10m 10m 11.9g 9m] $410,000F: strong, good-bodied colt: second known foal: half-brother to 1989 2-y-o 7f winner Spurned (by Robellino): dam placed over 6f here later successful at up to 11f in USA: no worthwhile form: often bandaged near-hind: blinkered final start: reared and unseated rider leaving stalls sixth start: sold to join P. Evans 2,400 gns Newmarket Autumn Sales: one to be wary of. *A. A. Scott.*

SHAFOURI (IRE) 3 b.c. Alzao (USA) 117 – Sauntry (Ballad Rock 122) [1990 6g⁴ 92
1991 7f* 7g* 7g 7.1m² 6d 7g 7f² 7g² 8m⁵ 7g² 6.1s² 7g²] rangy colt: poor mover: fairly useful performer: narrow winner of maiden at Folkestone and minor event at Catterick in April: ran creditably in all-aged or mixed-age events at Chepstow and Newmarket last 2 starts: will prove suited by testing conditions at 6f, and stays 1m: acts on any going: usually wears bandages: joined G. Jones in USA. *Mrs L. Piggott.*

SHAGNY (USA) 2 b.c. (Mar 5) Blushing Groom (FR) 131 – South Sea Dancer — p
(USA) (Northern Dancer) [1991 7d] $1,850,000Y: good-quartered colt: third foal: brother to 7f and 8.5f winner Island Wedding and half-brother to 3-y-o 11.9f winner Sijjaal (by Mr Prospector): dam winner at up to 9f at 4 yrs and 5 yrs, is sister to Storm Bird: weak 7/1-shot and very green, tailed-off last of 7 in minor event at Ascot in October: looks sort to do better. *M. R. Stoute.*

SHAH DIAMOND (USA) 3 ch.f. Shahrastani (USA) 135 – Princess Roycraft 84
(USA) (Royal Note) [1990 NR 1991 11g⁴ 12m* 14g* 16.2g 11.9g] workmanlike filly: half-sister to numerous winners, including 1½m winner Hail Caesar and good stakes winner from 9f to 1½m Royal Roberto (both by Roberto): dam very useful winner at up to 1m: neck winner at Salisbury in maiden in May and slowly-run 4-runner minor event in June: well beaten in Queen's Vase at Royal Ascot (wore tongue grip) and handicap (over 3 months later) at Haydock: stays 1¾m: visits Lycius. *J. H. M. Gosden.*

SHAHIMA (USA) 3 b.f. Diesis 133 – Reham 67 (Mill Reef (USA) 141) [1990 NR —
1991 10.5g] big, workmanlike filly: fourth foal: half-sister to modest 1987 2-y-o Fleur de Foret (by Green Forest), later ungenuine: dam placed from 1¼m to 1½m, is half-sister to Smoggy, smart winner at up to 9f in France and USA, and Ribblesdale winner Dish Dash: 16/1, moved moderately down and well beaten in maiden at Haydock in July: sold 2,400 gns Newmarket Autumn Sales. *B. Hanbury.*

SHAHI (USA) 3 ch.c. Shahrastani (USA) 135 – First Kiss 84 (Kris 135) [1990 93
8m³ 1991 16g* 16.2s* 16g 13.9g] good-bodied, workmanlike colt: has a quick action: odds on, easy winner of maiden at Nottingham in June and minor event at Chepstow in July: ninth of 10 in Goodwood Cup, leading briefly 3½f out and eased: ran poorly in Ebor Handicap at York 3 weeks later: stays 2m: reportedly to join D. Hayes in Australia. *H. R. A. Cecil.*

SHAH'S CHOICE 8 b.g. Persian Bold 123 – Royal Display 107 (Right Royal V —
135) [1990 NR 1991 17.1d] fair but ungenuine performer as 4-y-o: twice raced on flat since, tailed off only run in 1991: stays extreme distances: yet to race on soft going, acts on any other: winning hurdler. *C. L. Popham.*

SHAIMA (USA) 3 b.f. Shareef Dancer (USA) 135 – Oh So Sharp 131 (Kris 135) 110
[1990 7m³ 7.3s* 1991 10d⁴ 8v² 8m² 8.1m² 8.9g* 9d 12d*] leggy filly: has a markedly round action: very useful form, winning listed event at York in September and good style by 2½ lengths from St Ninian, quickening to lead under 2f out: beaten only 2 lengths when eighth in Prix de l'Opera at Longchamp next start: won Grade 2 Long Island Handicap at Belmont Park 2 weeks later: stays 1½m: probably suited by some give in the ground: usually on toes: takes keen hold to post, and has been taken down early: to join C. Clement in Florida. *L. M. Cumani.*

SHAKEEL (USA) 3 b.c. Mr Prospector (USA) – Mom's Command (USA) (Top 90
Command (USA)) [1990 NR 1991 8m² 8g⁶ 7m*] $1,800,000Y: sturdy, rather angular colt: second reported foal: dam leading 2-y-o filly in USA and champion 3-y-o filly: best effort second in £7,800 newcomers race at Newmarket in April, making most: 7/1 on, first run for nearly 3 months, not at all impressive in winning 4-runner maiden at Yarmouth in July: stays 1m. *H. R. A. Cecil.*

SHAKELA (USA) 2 ch.f. (Feb 9) Alydar (USA) – Jellatina (Fortino II 120) [1991 — p
6f] $200,000Y: angular filly: half-sister to several winners, including very useful 3-y-o stayer Jendali (by Nijinsky), top-class miler Northjet (by Northfields) and Italian sprinter Madang (by Habitat): dam Irish 9f winner: 11/1, around 12 lengths

fifteenth of 21, never able to challenge, in maiden at Newbury in August: will improve, particularly over 1m +. *B. Hanbury.*

SHAKE TOWN (USA) 3 b.g. Caro 133 – All Dance (USA) (Northern Dancer) 80 [1990 NR 1991 10m 12g 8.1d³ 7m⁴ 7f 7m² 7f⁶ 7m⁴ 8g³ 7g* 7m⁵ 7m* 6.9f⁴ 7g*] $320,000Y: good-bodied gelding: moderate mover: third reported foal: half-brother to Champion Hurdle third Ruling (by Alleged): dam, French 1m winner later placed in USA, is half-sister to Kentucky Derby winner Winning Colors (by Caro): successful, held up, in handicaps at Brighton, Leicester (ridden by 7-lb claimer) and Redcar (£9,700 contest) in October: stays 1m: acts on firm and dead going: tends to hang left, and should prove best with strong handling: sold 29,000 gns Newmarket Autumn Sales. *G. Harwood.*

SHAKINSKI 2 gr.f. (Feb 15) Niniski (USA) 125 – Shakana 91 (Grundy 137) [1991 45 5.2g 6g 7m⁶ 8s a8g⁵] 775Y: leggy, workmanlike filly: first foal: dam, maiden didn't really confirm promise of debut, is out of half-sister to Shergar: plating-class maiden: ran creditably on equitrack final outing: shapes like a stayer. *M. J. Ryan.*

SHAKIRI 2 b.f. (Feb 20) Sizzling Melody 117 – Aspark (Sparkler 130) [1991 5m — a5g a7g] leggy, angular filly: second foal: half-sister to useful 3-y-o sprinter Arturian (by Song): dam little form: soundly beaten in maidens and a minor event. *J. Akehurst.*

SHAKREEN (USA) 2 b.f. (May 5) Alleged (USA) 138 – My Sister 101 (Nonoalco 67 p (USA) 131) [1991 7g 8f² 7.1s³] $150,000Y: workmanlike filly: has a round action: half-sister to a winner in North America by Sharpen Up: dam Irish 7f winner stayed 1½m, is out of half-sister to Yorkshire Cup winner Noble Saint: progressive maiden: bit backward still, over 3 lengths third of 13, travelling strongly 6f, to Gotcha at Chepstow in October: likely to improve further, particularly over middle distances. *Mrs L. Piggott.*

SHALEEL (IRE) 3 b.c. Last Tycoon 131 – Wood Violet (USA) (Riverman (USA) 90 131) [1990 NR 1991 7m² 7g³ 7g⁵ 8g² 10.4g⁴ 10.2m³ 10d* 10g 12d] IR 230,000Y: sturdy, lengthy colt: moderate mover: second foal: half-brother to 4-y-o Sadler's Wood (by Sadler's Wells): dam unraced, from good family: fairly useful performer on his day: favourite, easily won celebrity event at Ascot in September: co-favourite well beaten in handicaps following month: stays 1½m: acts on dead ground: visored last 3 starts: sold 28,000 gns Newmarket Autumn Sales. *P. T. Walwyn.*

SHALFA (USA) 4 b.f. Riverman (USA) 131 – Bon Gout (USA) (Dewan (USA)) 37 [1990 7m⁶ 10.5g⁴ 10m³ 10g⁵ 12m⁵ 9g 8.2d 1991 10f 11f⁶ 10f³ 12m 9.9g 10d⁴ 9f⁶ 9f 9.9f 9.9f* 10.3d] rangy filly: poor handicapper nowadays: won (for first time) at Beverley in September: stays 1¼m: acts on firm ground. *Don Enrico Incisa.*

SHALFORD (IRE) 3 ch.c. Thatching 131 – Enigma 87 (Ahonoora 122) 119 [1990 6m 6m² 5m* 6m* 6f⁵ 7m² 6g² 6g³ 1991 8g⁶ 7g³ 8g 6d* 6m 7g 7.3f⁴ 6f⁵ 6s* 7m⁴]

'A visit to the Bushes', stated one nineteenth century race-reader, 'has many a time brought handsome recompense for the trouble to people whose eyes and wits were not dull.' Such a person would doubtless have been struck by the performance of Shalford in the 1991 Two Thousand Guineas. One doesn't have to go down to the Bushes these days to obtain a good view of the race developing on the Rowley Mile and Shalford's promise was plain to see. Starting at 100/1 in a field of fourteen, Shalford was travelling better than

Diadem Stakes, Ascot—Shalford runs them ragged on the soft ground

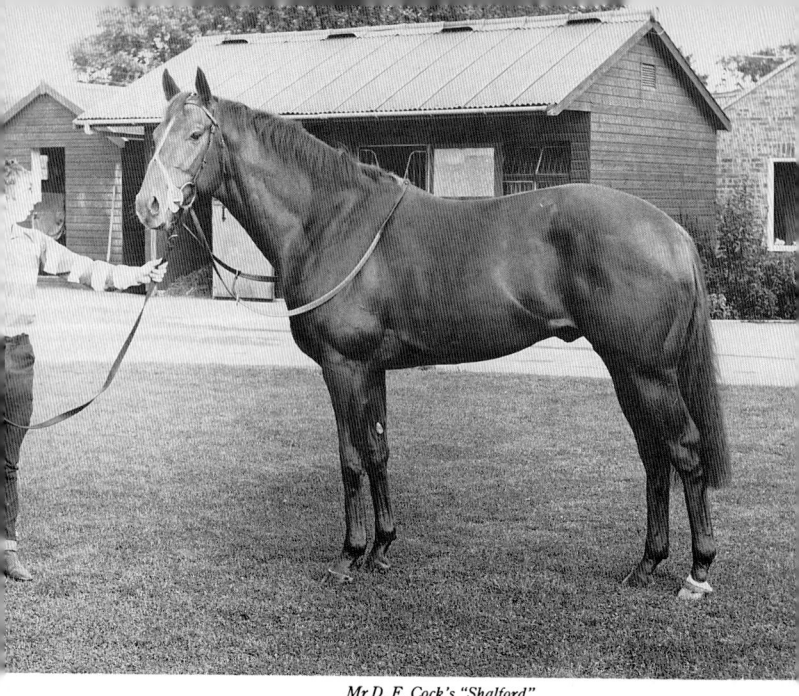

Mr D. F. Cock's "Shalford"

all except perhaps Lycius in the main group as they went into the Dip before fading into tenth—he was very much one to look out for when dropped in distance. The 'handsome recompense', it must be said, took a long time coming. Shalford comfortably won a six-furlong minor event at Newbury next time out but at a short price in what was a weak field, given Chipaya's lack-lustre showing. Simply poor efforts in a listed race at Lingfield and the Jersey Stakes at Royal Ascot were followed by a much more encouraging one, when he made smooth headway to lead below the distance, in the Hungerford Stakes at Newbury, then a short-lived matching of strides up front with Sheikh Albadou in the Ladbroke Sprint Cup at Haydock. The Festival of British Racing at Ascot, almost five months after the Guineas, was Shalford's day, his renaissance spectacular. A 10/1-shot in a field of sixteen in the Diadem Stakes, Shalford was almost immediately taking them all along. The favourite, Bog Trotter, tried to keep tabs on him but to no avail and his early close pursuers Mujadil and Tbab had dropped away well before the furlong marker. In fact, it looked as if they'd all dropped away; Shalford was well and truly out on his own, never in any danger of defeat in the final furlong though the Newmarket listed race winner Montendre and Satin Flower, who'd bolted in herself in the Jersey Stakes, managed some late headway to reduce his final advantage to three and a half lengths and one and a half.

Shalford's dam Enigma was a sprinter of just fair ability: she made the frame four times in maidens and was sold out of Barry Hills's stable for 48,000 guineas at the end of her three-year-old season. She's made a most encouraging start to her career as a broodmare, and was sold for 215,000 guineas (in foal to In The Wings) at the latest Newmarket December Sales, to go to Japan. Shalford is her first foal, the BonusPrint Sirenia Stakes winner Bletchley Park (by Caerleon) her second, and her third was Thatching's fourth highest-priced yearling (at 74,000 guineas) at the 1991 Sales. The fortunes of Enigma's dam Princess Ru took a similar path though she showed even less aptitude for racing in reaching the frame in six maiden races (from a mile to eleven furlongs) in Scotland or the North as a three-year-old before she too was sold at the Newmarket December Sales, for 3,800 guineas. That her record in the paddocks would be very different was apparent as early as her second foal, the smart five-furlong performer Trasi Girl, and she was followed by six other winners including Enigma's sister Princess Tracy, the Ballyogan and Phoenix Sprint Stakes winner who had also done the best of the European challengers in the Breeders' Cup Sprint, finishing fifth, until Dayjur came along. Trasi Girl is the dam of the 1976 Dante winner Trasi's Son.

Shalford (IRE) (ch.c. 1988)	Thatching (b 1975)	Thatch (b 1970)	Forli Thong
		Abella (ch 1968)	Abernant Darrica
	Enigma (b 1983)	Ahonoora (ch 1975)	Lorenzaccio Helen Nichols
		Princess Ru (b 1962)	Princely Gift Chiru

The strong, close-coupled Shalford is a grand walker and has a round action in his faster paces. He usually impresses in his appearance. It's a while since he's had a crack at five furlongs but we know that he's better at six furlongs than longer distances. One must also conclude that, although he has plenty of form on top-of-the-ground, Shalford is best suited by a soft surface. The going was good to soft for his win at Newbury and steady rain had really got into the ground by the time of the Diadem Stakes, the last race on the card at Ascot. Shalford was some way below his best when fourth of fourteen, at 20/1, to Additional Risk in the seven-furlong Hong Kong Invitation Bowl on good to firm ground at Sha Tin in mid-December. *R. Hannon.*

SHALL WE RUN 2 b.f. (Apr 13) Hotfoot 126 – Sirnelta (FR) (Sir Tor) [1991 5m³ **59** 5.2d 5.1g⁵ 6m⁶] leggy, rather sparely-made filly: sister to 3-y-o Love Talk and useful 1m to 10.1f winner Fire Top and half-sister to several other winners, notably smart sprinter Dead Certain (by Absalom): dam won from 1m to 1¼m in France: plating-class maiden: not raced after July: will be better suited by 7f + . *R. F. Johnson Houghton.*

SHALOU 2 b.c. (Feb 21) Forzando 122 – Axe Valley 89 (Royben 125) [1991 7m **67** 6m* 6g] 16,500Y: smallish, lengthy colt: first foal: dam sprinter: modest performer: off course 2 months, won 20-runner seller (retained 8,600 gns) at Lingfield in September, finishing very strongly after seeming to have difficulty going early pace: raced on unfavoured side when well beaten in claimer there 2 weeks later: should stay 7f: may improve. *P. F. I. Cole.*

SHAMBO 4 b.c. Lafontaine (USA) 117 – Lucky Appeal 36 (Star Appeal 133) [1990 **110** 8.2s 11.7f² 11.5m³ 12g 12.3m* 14f² 14g* 12m⁵ 13.3g 1991 16g* 16g* 16.2s² 14g² 15.5m³ 20g 15.9m³ 16g³ 13.9g⁴ 16m³ 15.5d² 14v] strong, quite attractive colt: usually impresses in appearance: moderate walker and mover: much improved in 1991: successful in handicaps at Kempton (Queen's Prize) and Newbury in April: placed in Yorkshire Cup fourth start, Goodwood Cup eighth, Jockey Club Cup at Newmarket tenth and Prix Royal-Oak at Longchamp eleventh: stays 2m: acts on firm going, but ideally suited by some give in the ground: tough, genuine and consistent: credit to his trainer. *C. E. Brittain.*

SHAMPOO 4 ch.c. Sharpo 132 – Wasslaweyeh (USA) 66 (Damascus (USA)) **90** [1990 7m⁵ 6g² 7m 1991 7m⁴ 7d] leggy, quite good-topped colt: has quick action: fairly useful handicapper: off course over a year before good fourth at Ayr: soundly beaten in £80,000 event at Ascot later in September: worth a try at 1m: acts on good to firm ground. *W. J. Haggas.*

SHAMS 2 ch.f. (Jan 26) Dunbeath (USA) 127 – Mawaal Habeebee (Northfields **75** (USA)) [1991 7m² 7m³ 7.6d⁴] sturdy filly: first foal: dam half-sister to Chapel Cottage: modest maiden: placed at Southwell (looked winner 1f out, faltered line) and York (median auction event, edgy) in autumn: below best at Chester (headed 1f out) 13 days later: should stay 1m. *W. J. Haggas.*

Sheikh Mohammed's "Shamshir"

SHAMSHIR 3 ch.f. Kris 135 – Free Guest 125 (Be My Guest (USA) 126) **116**
[1990 7m⁵ 7m* 8g² 8m* 1991 10.5m³ 12m² 12g 10g² 11.9g³ 12m⁶ 12d]
Shamshir failed to register another victory after the Brent Walker
Fillies' Mile on her final start as a two-year-old but added a good deal more
black type to her record. A slight set-back in March combined with cold
weather to prevent her being ready in time for her initial target in 1991, the
One Thousand Guineas. We concluded in *Racehorses of 1990*, however, that
Shamshir was more likely to develop into a leading contender for the Oaks and
after a third in the Tattersalls Musidora Stakes at York, beaten a length as
lack of peak fitness told close home, she duly took her chance at Epsom. It is
difficult to gauge the merit of her performance. She was second to Jet Ski Lady
but beaten ten lengths and didn't travel anything like so fluently through the
race as she had in the Musidora, being ridden along six furlongs out as they
started downhill, before staying on steadily to get second by three quarters of
a length as Shadayid weakened. In the preliminaries Shamshir had sweated
profusely and got very much on edge, something we hadn't seen from her to
anything like that degree before. If that wasn't Shamshir's true form, however, she was given plenty of opportunity to show it afterwards. The Ribblesdale Stakes was a poor effort on her part and she was beaten seven lengths by
Ruby Tiger into second for the Vodafone Nassau Stakes at Goodwood, but she
did better on her next two starts and those are probably the best guides to
Shamshir's merit. She was beaten five lengths into third behind Magnificent
Star in the Aston Upthorpe Yorkshire Oaks at York and just over three
lengths into sixth, staying on well from a more or less hopeless position entering the straight, behind Magic Night in the Prix Vermeille at Longchamp. Our
overall assessment of Shamshir is that she improved for a second season but

776

not by so much as seemed likely at the end of 1990. She was clearly below the best in what was not a vintage year for middle-distance fillies and it came as something of a surprise, to him no doubt as well as to us, when Shamshir turned out to be Sheikh Mohammed's only runner in the Arc. She wasn't discredited in finishing tenth of fourteen.

		⎧ Sharpen Up	⎧ Atan
	⎧ Kris	⎨ (ch 1969)	⎩ Rocchetta
	⎪ (ch 1976)	⎩ Doubly Sure	⎧ Reliance II
Shamshir	⎨	(b 1971)	⎩ Soft Angels
(ch.f. 1988)	⎪	⎧ Be My Guest	⎧ Northern Dancer
	⎪ Free Guest	⎨ (ch 1974)	⎩ What A Treat
	⎩ (ch 1981)	⎩ Fremanche	⎧ Jim French
		(ch 1973)	⎩ La Manche

Shamshir's pedigree was discussed in *Racehorses of 1990*, and in several other none-too-distant previous editions as well, as her dam is that fine middle-distance filly of the mid-'eighties Free Guest. The dam's next foal is another well-above-average performer in Fern (by Shirley Heights) who, like Shamshir, finished runner-up in the May Hill Stakes at Doncaster. They are followed by colts by Shirley Heights and Rousillon. Shamshir stayed a mile and a half and acted on good to firm ground, probably on dead as well. She developed a tendency to sweat and get rather on edge during the preliminaries. A crack at the E. P. Taylor Stakes had to be abandoned after a bout of colic, and Shamshir has been retired. She's to visit Shirley Heights. *L. M. Cumani.*

SHAMSHOM AL ARAB (IRE) 3 gr.c. Glenstal (USA) 118 – Love Locket **46** (Levmoss 133) [1990 6d 7f6 7d 6g 1991 7f5 10m4 10g 9m] lengthy, angular colt: plating-class maiden on flat: stays 1¼m: yet to race on soft ground, has form on any other: blinkered once: winning hurdler. *W. Carter.*

SHANNON EXPRESS 4 gr.g. Magic Mirror 105 – Tatisha (Habitat 134) [1990 **55** 7g 7f 7g4 7m5 7d 8f3 10f2 8f2 10g* 10f2 10d 8m a8g3 a10g2 a11g2 1991 a8g2 a8g* a8g4 a **72** 10.2g 8g6 9.7f* 10f 9.7m2 9.7g] leggy, angular, plain gelding: poor mover: modest and largely consistent handicapper on all-weather surfaces, won at Southwell in February: not so good on turf in 1991, won seller at Folkestone in August: effective at 1m to 11f: acts on firm going, unsuited by dead: ran well when blinkered: trained until after third start by P. Kelleway: has joined M. Hammond. *J. Pearce.*

SHANTI FLYER (IRE) 2 b.f. (Apr 11) Mister Majestic 122 – Dominia **60** (Derring-Do 131) [1991 7m 8g6 8s5] 9,200Y: quite attractive filly: has quick action: eighth foal: half-sister to 3 winners abroad: dam won at around 1m in USA: plating-class maiden: stayed on well (having come off bridle long way out) at Yarmouth last time: may prove suited by further. *A. Hide.*

SHAO LIN 3 b.c. Shirley Heights 130 – Cley 85 (Exbury 138) [1990 NR 1991 12g2 **75 §** 14.1f2 14.1f3 14.1m2 14.1m2 12s3dis] 20,000Y: leggy, unfurnished colt: half-brother to 3 winners, including fair 1½m and 13.3f winner Bodham (by Bustino): dam, 1½m winner, is half-sister to Blakeney and Morston: fair maiden: stays 1¾m: probably acts on firm going: visored, persistently hung left and looked reluctant fourth outing: blinkered (made most) penultimate one: sold out of A. Stewart's stable 10,500 gns Newmarket Autumn Sales after fifth: not one to trust. *R. Akehurst.*

SHAPELY DEB 2 gr.f. (Apr 28) Beveled (USA) – Rustling 68 (Rusticaro (FR) **44** 124) [1991 6m 6.1g6 6m6 7f 6g a8g a6g] 500F: leggy, sparely-made filly: third foal: half-sister to 2 animals by Bairn, including 1¼m winner Neenawn: dam maiden best at 9f or 1¼m: poor maiden: sixth in Folkestone seller on third outing: should stay beyond 6f: blinkered first 2 starts, wore eyeshield final one. *D. R. Laing.*

SHAPING UP (USA) 2 b.f. (Jan 16) Storm Bird (CAN) 134 – Manicure Kit **89** (USA) (J O Tobin (USA) 130) [1991 6g2 7g6 5.7f* 7m] 50,000Y: quite attractive filly: good walker: fourth foal: half-sister to a winner in USA by Flying Paster: dam sprint winner at 2 yrs: progressive filly: favourite, won maiden at Bath in September, running on strongly to lead line: blinkered, excellent eighth of 30 to Young Senor in Tattersalls Tiffany Highflyer Stakes at Newmarket 16 days later, racing keenly in rear then staying on in good style: will stay 1m. *I. A. Balding.*

SHARDELISADA (USA) 3 b.f. Sharpen Up 127 – Flordelisada (USA) (Drone) **85** [1990 NR 1991 8m* 8g3 8d5] lengthy filly: fifth foal: half-sister to very useful 7f (at 2 yrs) and 11.5f winner Duke of Paducah (by Green Dancer), smart miler Dallas (by Blushing Groom) and 2 minor winners in USA: dam successful at up to 1m, is from good family: won maiden at Carlisle in June: beaten 7 lengths in minor event at Newmarket, never able to challenge in slowly-run race: moved moderately down and well beaten in apprentice race at Ascot 3 months later. *L. M. Cumani.*

SHAREEF STAR 3 b.g. Shareef Dancer (USA) 135 – Ultra Vires 87 (High Line — 125) [1990 7g 8m 1991 10g 13.1f] leggy gelding: seems of little account: changed hands 650 gns Doncaster October Sales. *M. Blanshard.*

SHAR EMBLEM 3 b. or br.f. Shardari 134 – Lady's Flag (USA) (Fifth Marine 55 (USA)) [1990 NR 1991 11.5f 10.1f⁶ 12g⁴ a12g⁵ a13g a16g* a13g⁵] 3,100Y: lengthy, rather sparely-made filly: moderate mover: half-sister to 4-y-o 1m seller winner Lady Bunting (by Well Decorated) and 2 winners in USA: dam won twice at up to 9f in USA: plating-class handicapper: won at Lingfield in December: better at 2m than shorter: trained debut (very slowly away) by J. Pearce, next 2 starts (claimed £5,600 last of them) by C. Allen. *S. Dow.*

SHARLIE'S WIMPY 12 ch.g. Tumble Wind (USA) – Sweet Sharlie 77 (Fighting 34 Charlie 127) [1990 5s 6f² 7.6m 7f³ a7g 6m 8m 7d 1991 a6g⁴ a7g 8g³ 6m 8g³ 7m⁴] strong, attractive gelding: carries plenty of condition: good mover: poor handicapper: effective at 6f to 1m: well suited by a sound surface: has worn blinkers: has won for apprentice: finds little and needs waiting tactics. *W. J. Pearce.*

SHARLING 2 gr.f. (Feb 19) Sharrood (USA) 124 – Mrs Darling 70 (Mummy's Pet 50 125) [1991 7m 7m⁶ 5g a7g] 18,000Y: lengthy, workmanlike filly: first foal: dam maiden stayed 6f, is half-sister to 10.2f winner Melodrama out of Portland Handicap winner Matinee: poor maiden: stumbled and unseated rider on debut: fell 2f out when close up at Lingfield on final start. *J. H. M. Gosden.*

SHARON'S RABBIT 3 b.g. Hotfoot 126 – Loving Doll 72 (Godswalk (USA) — 130) [1990 a6g⁵ a7g 1991 a6g a6g⁴ 8s] small gelding: poor maiden: blinkered, looked reluctant to race in selling handicap final start, in April: trained until after reappearance by R. Muddle: sometimes slowly away: one to be wary of. *R. Ingram.*

SHARP AGAIN 2 ch.f. (Mar 10) Beveled (USA) – Albion Polka (Dance In Time — (CAN)) [1991 5s 6m 5.7f 6s] unfurnished filly: first foal: dam unraced: sire (by Sharpen Up) won from 6f to 7f: well beaten in varied events: bandaged near-hind debut: sweating second start: sold 625 gns Ascot December Sales. *D. R. Laing.*

SHARPALTO 4 br.c. Noalto 120 – Sharp Venita 84 (Sharp Edge 123) [1990 7f² 82 6m³ 6m³ 7g* 6m³ 6m² 7f⁴ 7.3g 6d 6g⁴ 6s 1991 8g⁶ 6g⁴ 7m⁴ 7m⁴ 8.2g 6m⁶ 7m⁴ 7g³ 7.1s³ 7g 7g 8m 7d 7m* 7m 7.6d* 8g] workmanlike colt: fair handicapper on his day: won at Warwick (apprentices) and Chester (idled) in October: seems ideally suited by around 7f: probably acts on any going: sometimes slowly away: effective blinkered or not: inconsistent. *E. A. Wheeler.*

SHARP ANNE 4 gr.f. Belfort (FR) 89 – Princess Sharpenup 63 (Lochnager 132) 64 [1990 6m⁴ 6v⁵ 6f 5m² 5g² 5m* 5g* 5g⁴ 5f⁴ 5m⁴ 6m 5m* 5m 6g* 6g 5g⁴ 1991 6m 5f³ 5m⁴ a5g⁵ 6f⁴ 6m⁴] leggy, quite good-topped filly: has a quick action: quite modest handicapper: formerly unreliable, consistent in 1991: stays 6f: suited by a sound surface: effective blinkered or not. *J. Berry.*

SHARP AS YOU LIKE 2 ch.g. (May 14) Risk Me (FR) 127 – Debutina Park 87 59 (Averof 123) [1991 5f* 5.1m⁴ 5f⁵ 7g 5d 5d 8m] 20,000F, 15,500Y: lengthy gelding: moderate walker: has quick action: fifth foal: half-brother to winning sprinters Super Deb (by Superlative) and Avidal Park (by Horage) and to 3-y-o Ivy Cottage (by Damister): dam 2-y-o 6f winner ran only once afterwards: plating-class form in maidens first 3 starts: failed to reproduce that in nurseries, final one a seller: best form on top-of-the-ground at around 5f: blinkered fifth start. *J. Etherington.*

SHARP CHIEF 3 br.f. Chief Singer 131 – Sharp Castan 101 (Sharpen Up 127) 61 [1990 5m³ 5m² 1991 6s 6g* 5m⁵ 6m⁴] leggy, angular filly: quite modest performer: won maiden at Windsor in July, making most: easily best other 3-y-o effort when fourth in minor event (very much on toes) at Kempton: stays at least 6f: steadily to post and wore net muzzle last 3 starts. *I. A. Balding.*

SHARP CIRCLE (IRE) 3 b.f. Sure Blade (USA) 130 – Centre Piece 73 83 (Tompion (USA)) [1990 NR 1991 7g² 8m* 10g 11.5m² 11.7g³ 12.1s] 240,000Y: workmanlike filly: half-sister to several winners, notably very smart sprinter Greenland Park (dam of Fitnah) and Coventry Stakes winner Red Sunset (both by Red God): dam ran 4 times at 2 yrs: won maiden at Edinburgh in June, tending to hang: placed in handicaps at Lingfield and Bath: better at around 11.5f than shorter: acts on good to firm ground: blinkered (ran badly) final start: sold 48,000 gns Newmarket December Sales. *B. W. Hills.*

SHARP COUNSEL (FR) 2 b.c. (Mar 16) Leading Counsel (USA) 122 – Dosha 104 (FR) (Sharpman 124) [1991 7g* 8g 8s* 9d² 8s³] third foal: dam dead-heated in 8.7f event in France at 3 yrs: successful in newcomers event at Bordeaux in August and minor event at Maisons-Laffitte following month: better form when placed in Group 3 events at Longchamp (beaten 1½ lengths by Cristofori) and Saint-Cloud (2¼ lengths behind Code Breaker) in October: will stay 1¼m: yet to race on top-of-the-ground. *E. Lellouche, France.*

SHARP DANCE   2 b.f. (Mar 18) Dance of Life (USA) – Sharp Jose (USA) — p
(Sharpen Up 127) [1991 7g] unfurnished filly: third foal: half-sister to French 3-y-o 9f winner Sharp Dream (by Dominion): dam won at up to 9f in USA: 50/1 and green, showed a little ability in 22-runner maiden at Newmarket in November, racing too freely, losing position over 2f out and eased: will improve. *Miss H. C. Knight.*

SHARPER BLUE   4 b.c. Sharpo 132 – Riverlily (FR) (Green Dancer (USA) 132)   78
[1990 a8g2 10.2s a11g2 1991 a12g2] useful-looking colt: fair and lightly-raced handicapper: not seen out in 1991 after January: stays 1½m: sold only 3,100 gns Newmarket July Sales. *P. J. Makin.*

SHARPGUN (FR)   5 ch.g. Sharpo 132 – Whitegun (FR) (Carwhite 127) [1990 NR   —
1991 11.5g 12g] tall, rather leggy horse: moderate walker: poor mover: modest on most form: should prove best at up to 1m (set too strong a pace over 1½m last time): yet to race on very firm going, probably acts on any other: ran badly in blinkers once. *A. Moore.*

SHARP IMPOSTER (USA)   3 ch.c. Diesis 133 – Informatique (USA) (Quack   99
(USA)) [1990 7d* 1991 11.5d2 11.8m* 12g2 10.3d2 12v5] quite good-topped, attractive colt: has fluent action: contested minor events here as 3-y-o, landing odds in 3-runner race at Leicester in July: second after to Le Corsaire at Newmarket and Knifebox at Doncaster 3½ months later: fifth of 13 in listed race at Bordeaux: stays 1½m: acts on good to firm ground and dead. *H. R. A. Cecil.*

SHARP ISSUE (USA)   3 ch.c. Diesis 133 – Concentrate (USA) (Broadway Forli   —
(USA)) [1990 NR 1991 11m 12m 10.2m a12g a14g 12m a12g a14g6 a16g] 25,000Y: big, lengthy colt: has a markedly round action: second foal: dam unraced half-sister to 3 winners: no sign of ability, including in seller: blinkered twice: bought out of B. Hanbury's stable 1,550 gns Doncaster May Sales after debut. *M. C. Chapman.*

SHARPITOR (IRE)   2 b.c. (May 10) Montelimar (USA) 122 – Flaxen Hair   93 p
(Thatch (USA) 136) [1991 7g3 7.5f* 7m*] 5,000Y: sturdy, close-coupled, quite attractive colt: sixth foal: half-brother to several winners, including smart miler Mirror Black (by Alzao) and 7.5f and 1m winner Colourist (by Petorius): dam unraced: progressive form: successful in maiden at Beverley in September and nursery at York (forged 3½ lengths clear of Thrie-na-Helah) in October: will be suited by 1m + : likely to improve further. *W. Jarvis.*

SHARP MONEY   3 b.f. Sharpo 132 – Pennies To Pounds 80 (Ile de Bourbon   61
(USA) 133) [1990 6m4 6d3 1991 8.1g2 7m4 7m] leggy filly: quite modest form: second in claimer at Edinburgh in September, best effort at 3 yrs: stays 1m: sold A. Smith 1,000 gns Doncaster November Sales. *J. M. P. Eustace.*

SHARP N' EARLY   5 b.h. Runnett 125 – Irish Kick (Windjammer (USA)) [1990   100
6g3 6f* 8g2 6m* 6g 6g2 6d5 1991 6m6 6m] rangy horse: moderate walker and mover: useful performer: fair sixth to Polish Patriot in listed event at Lingfield: not seen again after tailed off in Cork And Orrery Stakes at Royal Ascot later in June: effective at 6f and stays 1m: acts on any going. *J. R. Jenkins.*

SHARP N' EASY   4 b.f. Swing Easy (USA) 126 – Dulcidene 71 (Behistoun 131)   —
[1990 5f4 7m4 8h4 7d2 7d6 7f5 8h2 8f 8f6 7f 8.2s 1991 8g 5f4 6m6 10.2g 7f] rather leggy, angular filly: inconsistent plater: stays 1m: acts on firm and dead ground: sold out of R. Stubbs's stable 1,550 gns Doncaster Spring Sales: has been bandaged behind. *D. R. Tucker.*

SHARP'N SHINE (USA)   5 b.g. Sharpen Up 127 – Repetitious 103 (Northfields   — §
(USA)) [1990 NR 1991 10g] strong, rangy gelding: has a long, rather round stride: fair winner at 2 yrs: twice raced on flat since and no sign of ability: stays 1m: acts on firm ground, possibly unsuited by soft surface: has seemed ungenuine. *C. C. Elsey.*

SHARP N' SMOOTH   4 ch.c. Sharpo 132 – Winning Look 71 (Relko 136) [1990   74
7g 7g2 7m3 7g 7g 6s5 6d3 7g4 a8g2 7d2 a8g* a8g3 1991 a7g6 8s4 6s6 7m3 8d48.2m*
8.5m 8g 7m6 7g 8m5 8.1m* 7d6] close-coupled colt: poor mover: modest hand-icapper: won at Haydock (despite jinking right) in May and Sandown in September: good running-on sixth of 29 in £80,000 event at Ascot final start: should prove better at 1m than shorter: acts on good to firm and soft ground: has run well for apprentice: sold 14,000 gns Newmarket Autumn Sales after final start. *R. Hannon.*

SHARP ORDER   6 ch.g. Sharpo 132 – Cardinal Palace 85 (Royal Palace 131)   —
[1990 NR 1991 8.9m] sparely-made, angular gelding: quite modest performer at best

as 3-y-o: behind in claimer only run in 1991, first run on flat since: stays 9f: acts on a soft surface: has carried head high. *Miss S. J. Wilton.*

SHARP PRINCE 2 ch.c. (May 24) Sharpo 132 – Jungle Queen (Twilight Alley 133) [1991 7.1d*] 11,500Y: closely related to 2 winners by Sharpen Up, notably 1983 Lowther Stakes winner Prickle, and half-brother to 3 winners: dam little form: 8/1, won 20-runner maiden at Chepstow in October by 1½ lengths from Spanish Miner, travelling well and leading just inside final 1f: should stay 1m: should improve. *H. R. A. Cecil.*   **80 p**

SHARP RUNNER (FR) 4 gr.g. Star Appeal 133 – Assembly Day 66 (General Assembly (USA)) [1990 a8g⁵ a7g 6f 7.5d⁶ 8.5d⁶ a8g⁶ 6g 6m 8.5m 11m⁵ 8.2s 12d 12d a8g a10g 1991 a7g a14g 8.2s] robust gelding: bad performer nowadays: should stay 1½m: acts on firm ground: sometimes blinkered: one to be wary of: sold 880 gns Doncaster Summer Sales. *D. W. Chapman.*   **—**

SHARPTHORNE (USA) 3 ch.f. Sharpen Up 127 – Abeer (USA) 115 (Dewan (USA)) [1990 5g³ 5m⁵ 6g* 1991 7.1m⁶ 6m* 5.2m⁵ 6m 6.1s⁴] leggy, sparely-made filly: fairly useful performer: made all in minor event at Kempton in September: ran creditably in £6,800 event at Newbury next start, moderately afterwards in handicap and all-aged minor event: very best form at 6f: acted on good to firm ground: stud. *R. Charlton.*   **91**

SHARP TIMES 8 b.g. Faraway Times (USA) 123 – Sharp Venita 84 (Sharp Edge 123) [1990 5g⁵ 7g⁵ 6g² 6d 6g 5g 6m 6m 6g⁶ 6m 6d 7g a6g 1991 8d⁵ 8m] lengthy, shallow-girthed gelding: poor handicapper nowadays: tubed final start in 1991 (May): effective at 5f to 7f: acts on any going: often bandaged: below form when blinkered: wanders in front: sold 1,400 gns Ascot Summer Sales. *W. J. Musson.*   **—**

SHARP TOP 3 b.f. Sharpo 132 – Two High 89 (High Top 131) [1990 NR 1991 5f⁴ 6.9m 11d 10.1s⁵ a12g³] leggy filly: fourth foal: half-sister to middle-distance winners Needle Light (by Kris) and Diva Madonna (by Chief Singer) and to 1989 2-y-o 6f winner Always Alex (by Final Straw): dam won 4 times over 1½m: poor form, including in claimer on equitrack: probably better at 1½m than shorter: trained first 2 starts by Mrs G. Reveley. *M. J. Ryan.*   **41**

SHARQUIN 4 b.c. Indian King (USA) 128 – Lady of The Land 75 (Wollow 132) [1990 a8g 9s³ 12.3f⁴ 10d⁵ 11.7m² 11g⁵ 10g* 10f* 10f* 10f⁶ 1991 a11g 10.2s⁶ 10s 10m³ 10f⁴ 10d 10m³ 12g² 10m⁵ 12m 10.1m³ 9.9f 12f 10g⁴ 12.3m² 10.1m⁴ 11m⁴ 10.5m 9m] close-coupled colt: carries plenty of condition: poor mover: plating-class handicapper nowadays: effective at 1¼m to 1½m: suited by a sound surface: has been bandaged behind: has run creditably when blinkered: inconsistent. *M. Brittain.*   **55**

SHARRIBA 2 gr.f. (Mar 27) Sharrood (USA) 124 – Alsiba 68 (Northfields (USA)) [1991 7.1s³ 7g⁴ 7.1m² 7.1s² 7.1d²] tall, leggy filly: has scope: second foal: half-sister to fairly useful 3-y-o 1¼m and 1½m winner Smart Blade (by Elegant Air): dam staying daughter of half-sister to Irish 2000 Guineas winner Northern Treasure: modest maiden: 6 lengths second of 18 to impressive newcomer Never A Care at Chepstow final start: will be suited by 1m: acts on good to firm and soft ground. *D. R. C. Elsworth.*   **74**

SHA THA (USA) 3 b. or br.f. Mr Prospector (USA) – Savannah Dancer (USA) (Northern Dancer (USA)) [1990 6.5g³ 7.5g* 8g² 8g³ 1991 8d⁵ 8d² 10.5d⁶ 9g² 8g* 9s* 9f⁴] leggy filly: has plenty of scope: ran as Sabana on debut: won listed race at Deauville in August and All Along Stakes (by ½ length from Julie La Rousse) at Laurel in October: 2 lengths second of 9 to Danseuse du Soir in Dubai Poule d'Essai des Pouliches at Longchamp second start: ran creditably in Grade 1 event at Hollywood Park on final one: stays 9f: acts on any going: with N. Drysdale. *A. Fabre, France.*   **118**

SHATI (IRE) 2 b. or br.c. (May 23) Last Tycoon 131 – Shurooq (USA) 94 (Affirmed (USA)) [1991 6f³ 5f* 5.3g² 6m²] compact colt: third foal: half-brother to fairly useful 3-y-o sprinter Maraatib (by Green Desert) and fair miler Hafhafah (by Shirley Heights): dam 6f and 7f winner at 2 yrs stayed 1½m: heavily-backed favourite, won maiden at Beverley in September: better efforts in minor events at Brighton (ran below-form Power Lake to a head) and Catterick (9/4 on in match, beaten ½ length by Wave Hill) afterwards: stays 6f. *H. Thomson Jones.*   **84**

SHAURNI GIRL 3 ch.f. Precocious 126 – Crockfords Green 73 (Roan Rocket 128) [1990 NR 1991 a8g² a12g a12g⁵] fifth foal: dam 1m winner: best effort in maidens then claimer on all-weather surfaces late in 1991 when second at Southwell: stays 1m. *R. V. King.*   **53**

SHAWINIGA 5 b.m. Lyphard's Wish (FR) 124 – Shining Bright (USA) (Bold **41**
Bidder) [1990 10.2f 10f 8.2f 5s* 6f⁵ 8.2g* 12.3g⁶ 8.5g* 8.2g³ 10f⁵ 9g³ 9s⁴ 10.6d 6m⁴
a8g² 1991 8.2d 12m 5m⁵ 8.2f² 7.1d³ 8.1m⁴ 10m⁴ 7m 8f⁵ 8m⁵ 8m⁴] sparely-made
mare: poor handicapper: stays 1¼m: acts on any going: has run well for amateur:
trained first 8 starts by J. S. Wilson, ninth by Miss L. Perratt: consistent. *J. G.
FitzGerald.*

SHAWWAL (USA) 4 b. or br.c. Shirley Heights 130 – Lady of Camelot (FR) —
(Bolkonski 134) [1990 10g 12m 13.8f* 12m 1991 13.8m 11.1s] lengthy, workmanlike
colt: modest form at best: well beaten in 1991: stays 13.8f: acts on
firm ground. *J. Parkes.*

SHAY 6 b.g. Hays 120 – Barefoot Contessa (Homeric 133) [1990 7g 6m a5g 5d 7g —
5s 1991 5m 8m 5.1m] leggy, rather sparely-made gelding: one-time modest
handicapper: no form for long time: suited by stiff 5f: acts on soft going: tried visored
once. *A. J. Chamberlain.*

SHAYNA MAIDEL 2 ch.f. (Mar 17) Scottish Reel 123 – Revisit 86 (Busted 134) **39**
[1991 7m 7m a8g] sturdy filly: first foal: dam stayer: signs of a little ability, in
October maidens first 2 starts: soundly beaten on fibresand. *W. J. Haggas.*

SHEDAD (USA) 3 ch.c. Diesis 133 – Love's Reward (Nonoalco (USA) 131) [1990 **54**
6m³ 6f⁴ 7g³ 1991 8.2d⁵ 6m 6m 6d³ 5f⁵ 6g 6m⁶ 5g 5s² a5g⁶ a5g⁶ a7g⁴] rangy colt:
has a round action: disappointing maiden: second in seller at Hamilton: stays 7f:
probably acts on any turf going, and ran creditably on fibresand final start: headstrong: has been bandaged: tried blinkered once: sold out of J. L. Dunlop's stable
3,000 gns Newmarket July Sales after fourth start. *T. D. Barron.*

SHEER PRECOCITY 4 b.c. Precocious 126 – Age of Elegance (Troy 137) **107**
[1990 7m⁵ 7g 6f³ 6g 7m 7.6f* 8m³ 7m² 7m 1991 6g⁴ 7f³ 7g 7.1f⁵ 7m*] strong,
useful-looking colt: usually looks very well: has a rather round action: useful
performer: visored, won minor event at Warwick in October by 4 lengths from
Fraar: earlier third to Bold Russian in Beeswing Stakes at Newcastle: sold 50,000
gns Newmarket Autumn Sales: should prove best at up to 7f: acts on firm going:
reportedly to be trained in Italy. *F. H. Lee.*

SHEERWIND 4 b.c. Shernazar 131 – Windy Cheyenne (USA) (Tumble Wind —
(USA)) [1990 11.7m⁵ 10m⁵ 10.1m 10g 1991 17.1g a14g⁵] sturdy, attractive colt: has a
rather round action: no worthwhile form: blinkered in 1991: sold 1,500 gns
Newmarket Autumn Sales. *J. White.*

SHEESHA (USA) 2 ch.f. (Mar 21) Shadeed (USA) 135 – Sedra 116 (Nebbiolo —
125) [1991 6g] close-coupled filly: fourth foal: half-sister to 3-y-o Salwan (by
Sagace), 7f winner Sherjamal (by Raise A Native) and Irish 7f and 1m winner Topper
Up (by Sharpen Up): dam 6f (at 2 yrs) to 1¼m winner: 14/1 and backward, soon well
behind in 9-runner maiden at Nottingham in July. *J. D. Czerpak.*

SHEIKH ALBADOU 3 b.c. Green Desert (USA) 127 – Sanctuary (Welsh **125**
Pageant 132) [1990 6g 1991 6f* 7g² 6g* 7g⁴ 5g* 6f² 5d² a6f*]
'Finished after a half, came into the stretch five wide and was not per-
severed with late when well beaten.' The *Daily Racing Form's* observations
on Green Desert in 1986 seem to sum up the Europeans' unhappy venture to
the first six runnings of the Breeders' Cup Sprint. The transatlantic journey,
the climate, dirt track, tight turn, speed from the stalls and cut-throat early
pace seemed all against them. Princess Tracy did best of those European-
trained horses, coming fifth of eleven in the inaugural running, and she beat as
many of the home team that day as all seven British-trained challengers put
together: Reesh was last in that first edition; Al Sylah twelfth of fourteen in
1985; Double Schwartz eighth and Green Desert ninth and last in 1986; Sylvan
Express eighth, Sharp Romance twelfth and Governor General thirteenth and
last in 1987. We didn't field any runners in 1988 or 1989, and no wonder. Then
came the seventh Breeders' Cup and Dayjur. His performance in the Sprint
served to confirm his brilliance, apparently even converting much of the
American racing world to a similar view, and though he should have done, of
course, Dayjur didn't even win the race. Who would have thought that Dayjur
was just a curtain raiser, a warm-up act for the first European win in the
Breeders' Cup Sprint only twelve months later? Sheikh Albadou, a son of
Green Desert, didn't just win the sprint, he won it by three lengths and very
comfortably at that. Drawn ninth of eleven, Sheikh Albadou travelled
smoothly on the outside in sixth early on, moved to the inside and passed two

opponents going into the turn then to the outside entering the straight. There were two furlongs left to travel. The 5/2-on favourite Housebuster took up the running shortly after but Sheikh Albadou was steadily reeling him in, hit the front himself one furlong out and as Housebuster weakened quickly (he'd broken down) Sheikh Albadou soon went clear, having only to be pushed out.

Sheikh Albadou went off at 263/10 at Churchill Downs but although his chance of winning was not reckoned to be that great in his own country either (14/1 was generally on offer with our bookmakers) one could hardly have wished to be represented by any other of the top European sprinters of 1991. He'd not been out of the first two as a three-year-old over sprint distances, including in three of Europe's four Group 1 sprints for older horses (he didn't run in the July Cup) and this record was built despite, it was said in the first half of the season, his taking his races rather badly, experiencing an abnormal weight loss. Except for when a little coltish on his reappearance, on no occasion could one say that Sheikh Albadou showed anything other than the most commendable attitude on the racecourse, neither in the preliminaries, when he also invariably impressed in his appearance, nor in his races. The most striking feature of Sheikh Albadou's season, however, was his extraordinary rise through the ranks; from a maiden, into handicaps then pattern races. A promising eighth-of-eleven in a six-furlong maiden at Newmarket the previous October was all Sheikh Albadou had to his name going into the latest season but it took just one appearance, breezing in by seven lengths in a Pontefract maiden race in April, before he was being compared to the same stable's Cadeaux Genereux who had begun his rapid progress to the top (for Douieb) with a victory at the same course. Sheikh Albadou met with a short-head defeat off a handicap mark of 99 in the seven-furlong £19,250 Norwest Holst Trophy Handicap at York but that detracted nothing from, in fact rather increased, our enthusiasm for him, so strongly had he travelled through most of the race. Handicaps were still open to him—but not for much longer. Fifteen runners and £25,000 for a handicap should ensure a competitive race but not so with the latest running of the William Hill Golden Spurs Trophy at York. Sheikh Albadou's departure from the ranks of handicappers was a stroll; looming up on the outside, he'd come to the front two furlongs out without being put under pressure, was asked to quicken clear and did so readily. The comparisons with Cadeaux Genereux, the 1988 Golden Spurs winner, were in vogue again, then put aside two weeks later when Sheikh Albadou failed to see out the extra furlong in the Van Geest Criterion Stakes at Newmarket. The Keeneland Nunthorpe Stakes at York, another race Cadeaux Genereux had won (as a four-year-old for Scott, when it was known as the William Hill Sprint Championship), was Sheikh Albadou's second venture into pattern company. An American challenger has much enlivened proceedings at the last two Nunthorpe Stakes, not least (particularly with the bull-like Mr Nickerson in 1990) in their sheer physical presence alongside the home team, but they've soon had to give second best in the race itself. At least the 1991 runner Klassy Briefcase, a winner of four of her five starts earlier in the season who had set an American record for five furlongs in one of them, had some impact on the race. She led the nine-strong field at a tremendous lick over the first one and a half furlongs before the two-year-old Paris House took over and only Sheikh Albadou, Blyton Lad and Poyle George ever got within striking distance. On his first attempt at five furlongs, there was no travelling through the race on the bridle this time for Sheikh Albadou. Paris House still had a clear advantage at the furlong pole but Sheikh Albadou and Blyton Lad were beginning to make inroads into that lead and, with Paris House faltering, Sheikh Albadou led about seventy-five yards out to win by a length and a half, going away. Second and third were separated by a neck with two lengths back to Divine Danse, the favourite, who found her stride much too late. The latest Nunthorpe was slightly below standard judged by the proximity of Blyton Lad, but Sheikh Albadou went on to show that he was no pushover for any of the sprinters around, and more than a match for most. The path for the top sprinters after York is well mapped out, to Haydock for the Ladbroke Sprint Cup (formerly the Vernons) then to Longchamp for the Abbaye, and Sheikh Albadou took in both races, finishing second in both. He made the running in the Ladbroke, at far too strong a pace for sprinting pretenders, the Guineas winners Mystiko and Shadayid, seeing off Shalford as well by halfway but being unable to match Polar Falcon late on. At Longchamp a month later, Sheikh Albadou led briefly before Keen Hunter went on over a furlong out and kept on very bravely to emerge best in a bunch finish for the places.

Keeneland Nunthorpe Stakes, York—
Sheikh Albadou catches Paris House near the finish

Breeders' Cup Sprint, Churchill Downs—
Sheikh Albadou masters the conditions and the locals

With such as Volksraad, Umniyatee, Redden Burn, Himiko, Hawait Al Barr, Elfaslah and Dawson Place in his first crop, Green Desert has emerged as a sire of some distinction. That he'd succeed was hinted at by the 120,320-guinea average paid for his first batch of yearlings. Sheikh Albadou himself fetched 92,000 guineas at the Highflyer. His unraced dam Sanctuary had had three living foals, all runners, prior to him, and two winners in the Known Fact pair Sawlah, who won a five-furlong maiden at Mallow as a two-year-old, and Assignment, a seven-furlong winner in 1989 and successful at five and six furlongs on the Lingfield equitrack in the winter of 1990/1. Both Sanctuary's dam and grandam have outstanding breeding records, twenty-one winners between them. Jojo, a useful sprint handicapper nearly forty years ago, produced amongst others the Sussex Stakes winner Queen's Hussar, the Cheveley Park third Grey Goose, St Hugh's Stakes winner Aunt Audrey and that grand handicapper Scots Fusilier who was still running at the age of twelve having won twenty-two races. Jojo's eighth foal Hiding Place registered four victories as a three-year-old, the Nell Gwyn and three contests at a mile, was sixth in both the One Thousand Guineas and Oaks and fourth in the Sun Chariot. She bred nine winners, all over at least a mile, including Disguise (Horris Hill Stakes), Camouflage (Royal Hunt Cup), Elusive Pimpernel (Hyperion Stakes) and, most memorable of the lot, those genuine and consistent stayers Smuggler and Little Wolf. Regrettably, Little Wolf made the news again in 1991 when, after an unproductive start to his stud career, he was sold for 17,500 guineas at the Newmarket December Sales, it later being reported that he has been returned to the Vowchurch Court Stud in Herefordshire.

	Green Desert (USA)	Danzig	Northern Dancer
	(b 1983)	(b 1977)	Pas de Nom
Sheikh Albadou		Foreign Courier	Sir Ivor
(b.c. 1988)		(b 1979)	Courtly Dee
	Sanctuary	Welsh Pageant	Tudor Melody
	(ch 1979)	(b 1966)	Picture Light
		Hiding Place	Doutelle
		(ch 1963)	Jojo

Sheikh Albadou will be racing in 1992 and we look forward to seeing him again; he was undoubtedly one of the stars of the latest season. Physically, he is an extremely taking individual, strong and good-bodied, and nothing less could be said of his attitude to racing. He tends to be relaxed in the preliminaries when, as we've said, he invariably stands out. By our reckoning, that second in the Ladbroke Sprint was Sheikh Albadou's best performance in

H. Salem's "Sheikh Albadou"

Europe, and his Breeders' Cup triumph lends further credibility to a conclusion that six furlongs is his ideal trip, though clearly there are plenty of races to be won with him at five. He has yet to race on soft ground but acts on firm and dead. As yet, we cannot rate Sheikh Albadou an outstanding sprinter and, though he already has an excellent record, his performances are not quite on a par with what Cadeaux Genereux achieved as a four-year-old. But who is to say that we won't have changed our tune by the time *Racehorses of 1992* comes around? *A. A. Scott.*

SHEIKH PERCY 4 b.g. Busted 134 – Sauhatz (GER) (Alpenkonig (GER)) [1990 a12g 1991 a11g⁴] seventh known foal: dam won at 3 yrs in Germany: 14 lengths fourth of 9 finishers in claimer at Southwell in January (claimed to join T. Bill's stable £4,010). *N. A. Callaghan.* —

SHELBY (ITY) 2 gr.f. (Mar 25) Big Reef 110 – Antartic Sound (Cure The Blues (USA)) [1991 6g⁴ 7f 7.5s² 8v] workmanlike filly: second known foal: dam successful in Italy, including in listed company at 2 yrs: poor form in maidens here for C. Brittain: sent to Italy where second in maiden at Rome in September. *L. Camici, Italy.* **49**

SHELEGAI 3 b.c. Shernazar 131 – Khandjar 77 (Kris 135) [1990 8m⁵ 1991 12m² 14.8g² 14.8f* 13.9g] well-made colt: moderate mover: fair form in maidens: landed odds at Warwick in July by 8 lengths, making most and hanging right under pressure: favourite, well beaten in £16,600 handicap at York, leading over 1¼m: should stay well. *H. R. A. Cecil.* **89**

SHENTIT (FR) 3 b.f. Shirley Heights 130 – Porte des Lilas (FR) (Sharpman 124) **77** p
[1990 8g 9m³ 1991 12m 14.1m⁶ 17.1m* 18.1m* 17.2g] big, rangy filly: successful in
October handicaps at Pontefract and Nottingham: favourite, brought down in similar
event at Bath final start: will prove suited by thorough test of stamina: swishes tail
in paddock: should prove capable of better. *J. L. Dunlop.*

SHERIFF'S BAND 4 ch.g. Posse (USA) 130 – Willis (FR) (Lyphard (USA) 132) **—**
[1990 8f⁵ 8f³ 9f* 8.5d⁵ 1991 12.3s] tall, leggy, sparely-made gelding: shows knee
action: poor handicapper: soundly beaten only run in 1991 (April): stays 9f: probably
acts on any going: suited by forcing tactics: winning hurdler. *M. H. Easterby.*

SHERINGA 2 b.f. (Apr 23) Tout Ensemble – Liza Paul 66 (Ron 103) [1991 7.1s³] **63** p
workmanlike filly: half-sister to 6f and 1m winner Sheer Nectar (by Piaffer) and a
winning plater: dam won 1¼m seller: backward, 5 lengths third of 14 to
Jupiter Moon in maiden at Chepstow in October, soon well behind after slow start,
finished strongly: should improve *G. B. Balding.*

SHERJAMAL (USA) 4 ch.c. Raise A Native – Sedra 116 (Nebbiolo 125) [1990 **50**
6m⁵ 6f⁵ 7m 7f² 9g³ 8.5g⁵ a8g³ 7h² 7m* 7g 6d a7g 1991 a8g a7g a8g⁵ a6g 8m 7f² 7m⁶
8m 8f] sturdy colt: moderate mover: modest performer at 3 yrs: poor form in 1991:
stays 9f: acts on hard ground: bolted at start once. *B. J. Curley.*

SHERNOAKE 6 b.g. Magnolia Lad 102 – Sweet Bush (The Brianstan 128) [1990 **—**
NR 1991 12.2m] plain gelding: bad performer. *B. J. McMath.*

SHEROOG (USA) 3 b.f. Shareef Dancer (USA) 135 – Fall Aspen (USA) **77**
(Pretense) [1990 NR 1991 7m 10m 10.5g² 10s² 8g* 8m 8m 7m³] 240,000Y: tall, leggy
filly: sister to good French middle-distance filly Colorado Dancer, closely related to
smart 1m to 1¼m winner Northern Aspen (by Northern Dancer) and half-sister to 3
winners, including good stayer Mazzacano (by Alleged): dam smart stakes winner at
up to 7f: modest form: made all in maiden at Newmarket in August: appeared to
return to form when third of 5 in minor event at Leicester, setting modest pace:
probably stays 1¼m: acts on good to firm ground: visits Machiavellian. *M. A. Jarvis.*

SHE'S PLEASED (USA) 2 b.f. (Apr 26) Storm Bird (CAN) 134 – Mohair (FR) **79** p
(Blue Tom 127) [1991 6g*] $175,000Y: eighth known foal: half-sister to 3-y-o Elathir
(by Alydar), high-class French 1¼m and 13.5f winner Marie de Litz (by Dictus) and
useful French 1¼m and American winner Marie d'Argonne (by Jefferson): dam
unraced daughter of smart Imberline: weak 10/1-shot, won 7-runner maiden at
Newmarket in October by 3½ lengths from Bunty Boo, held up travelling well,
green when initially asked to quicken, then coming clear in quite good style: may
well stay 1m: will improve. *L. M. Cumani.*

SHE'S SMART 3 gr.f. Absalom 128 – Zeddenosa (Zeddaan 130) [1990 5f⁵ 5m² **88**
5m² 5g* 5m³ 5f⁴ 5f* 6g⁴ 1991 6m³ 5m³ 6g⁶ 5m² 5f* 5.1g⁵ 5m⁵ 5g⁵ 5.6m 5f³ 6m]
small, workmanlike filly: fair handicapper: won at Beverley in July: edgy, back to
form at same course penultimate start: effective at 5f and 6f: acts on firm going:
visored twice at 2 yrs. *M. H. Easterby.*

SHE'S SPECIAL 2 ch.f. (Jan 27) Superlative 118 – Royal Agnes 71 (Royal Palace **72**
131) [1991 5m⁴ 5g 6g a5g⁴ 5m³ 5m³ 5d* 5m³ 5s² 6d³ 7m 6g² 6f 5m⁶ 5g² 5d⁵
6m] 3,800F, 1,600Y: strong, lengthy filly: has a round action: fifth reported foal:
half-sister to ungenuine 1990 2-y-o Active Movement (by Music Boy) and 1m and
1¼m winner Dancing Days (by Glenstal): dam 1¾m winner, is half-sister to smart
1982 2-y-o 6f and 7f winner All Systems Go: quite modest form: won 7-runner
claimer (claimed out of J. Payne's stable £9,100) at Hamilton in June: ran well most
starts afterwards: suited by 6f: acts on good to firm and soft ground: effective with or
without blinkers or visor: trained eighth to eleventh starts by J. S. Wilson. *Miss L. A.
Perratt.*

SHE'S THE TOPS 3 b.f. Shernazar 131 – Troytops 66 (Troy 137) [1990 8.2m³ **83**
1991 10.5g⁵ 12.2m² 12s*] leggy, sparely-made filly: won maiden at Folkestone in
November by 5 lengths, making all: better at 1½m than shorter: best effort on soft
ground: visits Old Vic. *G. Wragg.*

SHEWHOMUSTBEOBEYED 4 ch.f. Miami Springs 121 – Sleepline Promise **§§**
63 (Record Token 128) [1990 5g 5s 5g 5.8d 1991 5g 5g] lengthy, workmanlike filly:
poor and ungenuine maiden: refused to race final start: tried visored: must be
avoided. *A. W. Jones.*

SHIAVONA (IRE) 3 b.f. Sure Blade (USA) 130 – Silent Movie (Shirley Heights **91**
130) [1990 NR 1991 8s⁴ 10m³ 10.5g³ 11.4m² 10m² 10v⁵] close-coupled, workmanlike
filly: moderate mover: third foal: half-sister to one-time fairly useful 7f winner
Runun (by Sharpo): dam, half-sister to very smart 7f to 1¼m performer Noalto,
showed little worthwhile form from 10.6f upwards: second in minor events at

Sandown, making most: far from disgraced in Group 2 event at Rome final start: stays 11.4f. *C. E. Brittain.*

SHIFNAL 6 ch.g. Tower Walk 130 – Leitha (Vienna 127) [1990 NR 1991 14.6m] — leggy gelding: no sign of ability on flat: won selling hurdle in May. *A. P. James.*

SHIHAMA (USA) 3 b.f. Shadeed (USA) 135 – Dubian 120 (High Line 125) [1990 — 6m* 1991 10d 7.3d] sturdy filly: won maiden at Newmarket at 2 yrs: pulled hard when well beaten in listed event and handicap at Newbury in summer of 1991: should stay beyond 6f. *A. A. Scott.*

SHIKARI KID 4 b.g. Kala Shikari 125 – Muffet 75 (Matador 131) [1990 10.2f 7g⁵ **42** 8.2s 7g⁴ 8g⁴ 10.4g² 12.2d³ 12.3f⁴ 10m 10f⁵ 10m⁶ 10m 10m⁴ 11v* 11d³ 1991 10.2s² 11s² 13d 10m 10.3d a11g 12f⁶ 12f³ 11.1s⁴] smallish, angular gelding: has a round action: poor handicapper: stays 1½m: acts on firm going, but ideally suited by very soft: formerly often visored or blinkered, not nowadays: has looked none too keen. *S. G. Norton.*

SHIKARI'S SON 4 br.c. Kala Shikari 125 – Have Form (Haveroid 122) [1990 5g⁵ **58** 5g* 5.3h* 5.8f⁶ 5g² 5d 5f 5g⁵ 5d⁵ 1991 6g 6g 5.8f⁶ 5m⁶ 5f 6m 6g] leggy colt: plating-class handicapper at best nowadays: little form in 1991: suited by 5f: acts on hard and dead ground. *J. White.*

SHILINSKI 4 b.g. Niniski (USA) 125 – Sushila (Petingo 135) [1990 11m⁴ 12.3m² — 12.4m* 1991 16s 16.1m 16m] lengthy gelding: quite modest form at 3 yrs for L. Cumani: well beaten in handicaps in 1991, burly final start: should be suited by further than 1½m: acts on good to firm, possibly unsuited by soft ground: trained reappearance by J. Johnson: winning hurdler. *G. M. Moore.*

SHILTON (USA) 3 gr.g. Topsider (USA) – Save (USA) (Sadair) [1990 NR 1991 **68** 8m 7f* 7g 7m⁶] $92,000Y: robust, lengthy gelding: brother to Put Away, minor stakes winner at up to 1m, and half-brother to several winners, including Grade 2 8.5f winner Save Wild Life (by Quack): dam won 7 races at up to 9f: won maiden at Carlisle in May: ran moderately in handicaps: seemed unsatisfactory and was gelded: dead. *B. W. Hills.*

SHIMMERING SANDS 2 b.f. (Apr 24) Green Desert (USA) 127 – Khaizaraan **68** (CAN) 97 (Sham (USA)) [1991 7m⁶ 6s³] unfurnished filly: fourth living foal: half-sister to a useful winner in Belgium by Miller's Mate: dam won Blue Seal Stakes: quite modest form in maidens at Leicester (odds on but backward and green, front rank 6f) and Yarmouth (weak in market, made much of running) in October: may improve. *M. R. Stoute.*

SHIMMERING SCARLET (IRE) 3 b.f. Glint of Gold 128 – Scarlet Slipper **57** (Gay Mecene (USA) 128) [1990 7m⁴ 8f 7f 1991 7g⁴ 8f² 10.6m⁵ 13.8m⁵ 8.3s⁶ 8.2f 7m* 8m 6f⁴ 7m] close-coupled filly: plating-class handicapper: on toes, won at Catterick in August: effective at 7f and 1m: acts on any going: no show when sweating: very slowly away penultimate start, got well behind on final one: sold 3,800 gns New-market Autumn Sales. *T. D. Barron.*

SHIMMERING SEA 3 b.f. Slip Anchor 136 – Sushila (Petingo 135) [1990 5m* — 7m* 7m⁴ 8m³ 1991 7.6g⁵ 10f] close-coupled filly: fair winner at 2 yrs: ran badly in listed race at Lingfield and minor event (wore net muzzle in preliminaries, took good hold) at Salisbury in summer as 3-y-o: stays 1m. *Major W. R. Hern.*

SHINE ON BRIGHTLY (USA) 3 ch.f. Majestic Light (USA) – Golden **67** Secretariat (USA) (Secretariat (USA)) [1990 NR 1991 10g 10.2g³ 10m a8g* a8g³ 9m⁵ 9g] $8,000Y: good-quartered, rather angular filly: fourth reported living foal: half-sister to very useful 1989 French 2-y-o 1m winner Golden Era (by Hero's Honor): dam ran 5 times: won maiden at Southwell in July: stays 1¼m: found little third start: has worn severe noseband: sold 7,200 gns Newmarket December Sales. *J. A. R. Toller.*

SHINING JEWEL 4 b.c. Exhibitioner 111 – Vaguely Jade (Corvaro (USA) 122) **76** [1990 7g⁴ 8m a8g⁶ 7h² 7m 7g 6m 9m⁵ 8.2v⁴ 8m* 8m³ 9g a7g⁴ a8g* a10g* a8g² a10g 1991 a8g⁴ a10g⁴ a8g² a7g⁶ 8d 8.5g⁶ 7m⁴ 8d³ 8m 8f* 8.2m⁶ 8m] strong, lengthy colt: usually looks well: moderate mover: modest handicapper: considerably ridden, won at Yarmouth in September: effective at 7f to 1¼m: acts on hard and dead ground: has been bandaged: has carried head high. *E. Eldin.*

SHINING WOOD 3 b.f. Touching Wood (USA) 127 – Nihad 76 (Alleged (USA) **56** d 138) [1990 6m 7f7m³ 10s³ 1991 12f⁵ 10m² a11g² 12m⁶ 10.2d a10ga12g³] rather leggy, workmanlike filly: plating-class maiden at best: claimed out of B. Hanbury's stable £6,011 after claimer second start: should prove suited by 1½m+: acts on good to firm ground and soft: has form on both all-weather surfaces: blinkered (first run for 6 months) sixth start: trained third to fifth by Dr J. Scargill. *A. S. Reid.*

SHIPS LANTERN 2 b.f. (May 2) Kalaglow 132 – Sunderland (Dancer's Image — p (USA)) [1991 7g] tall, sparely-made filly: fifth foal: half-sister to fair 1986 2-y-o 7f winner Sannox Bay (by Shirley Heights) and a winner in Italy by Ardross: dam 2-y-o 5f and 6f winner in Ireland: 11/1, around 16 lengths eighth of 22 to Oumaldaaya in maiden at Newmarket in November, losing position then keeping on closing stages: should improve. *C. F. Wall.*

SHIREHALL 3 b.g. Kala Shikari 125 – Portella 78 (Porto Bello 118) [1990 NR — 1991 8m6 8.9m6 8.9m] eighth foal: brother to plating-class maiden Plover, placed at 1m, and half-brother to 1986 2-y-o 6f seller winner Saunders Lass (by Hillandale): dam, placed several times over sprint distances, was very bad at start: no form, tailed off in claimer final start. *P. J. Bevan.*

SHIRL 2 b.f. (Apr 15) Shirley Heights 130 – Bercheba (Bellypha 130) [1991 8m 8m 54 a8g] 47,000Y: sturdy, lengthy filly: showed signs of ability in maidens first 2 starts: no form on fibresand. *W. J. Haggas.*

SHIRLEY BROOK 2 b.f. (May 3) Superlative 118 – Wrangbrook (Shirley 45 Heights 130) [1991 6g 7m5 8.5f4 10.5d] close-coupled, attractive filly: second foal: half-sister to 3-y-o Punch N'Run (by Forzando), useful 6f and 7f winner at 2 yrs: dam little form: poor maiden: soundly beaten in selling nursery final start: stays 8.5f: acts on firm ground: sold 700 gns Doncaster November Sales. *M. J. Camacho.*

SHIRLEY VALENTINE 2 br.f. (May 11) Shirley Heights 130 – Slightly 60 p Dangerous (USA) 122 (Roberto (USA) 131) [1991 8s2] sixth foal: sister to top-class middle-distance colt Deploy and half-sister to champion miler Warning (by Known Fact) and useful 7f to 12.3f winner Timefighter (by Star Appeal): dam, from excellent family, won at 6f and 7f and second in Oaks: odds on, 5 lengths second of 11 to Alight in maiden at Yarmouth in October, always pominent, unable to quicken over 1f out: likely to prove suited by middle distances: will improve. *H. R. A. Cecil.*

SHIRYON 6 b.g. Tickled Pink 114 – Assel Zawie (Sit In The Corner (USA)) [1990 — NR 1991 a8g] quite attractive gelding: poor maiden: tried blinkered once: has worn bandages. *P. J. Bevan.*

SHMOOZY 2 b.f. (Apr 3) Nomination 125 – Myricagale 68 (Wollow 132) [1991 5d] — 2,500F, 5,400Y: lengthy, sparely-made filly: third foal: half-sister to Irish 7f winner Seespotrun (by Bay Express): dam 1½m winner: 20/1, signs of some ability after slow start in auction event at Ripon in April: moved moderately down. *M. W. Easterby.*

SHOCKING 4 ch.f. Dunbeath (USA) 127 – Time For Pleasure (Tower Walk 130) — [1990 a8g a8g 1991 a6g] successful 3 times over sprint distances in Austria: no worthwhile form in claimers here, not seen in 1991 after January: sold 1,000 gns Ascot April Sales. *C. F. Wall.*

SHOCKING TIMES 2 b.f. (Apr 29) Skyliner 117 – Mashin Time 73 (Palm Track 60 122) [1991 7g5 6m2 6g] 1,100Y: sparely-made, close-coupled filly: sixth foal: half-sister to 1m seller winner Tiffin Time (by Lochnager): dam 6f and 1m winner: second in seller at Newmarket in October, making all stand side: well beaten in large-field Newbury maiden final start: capable of winning a seller. *R. Simpson.*

SHOKA (FR) 3 gr.f. Kaldoun (FR) 122 – Sassika (GER) (Arratos (FR)) [1990 7g 86 1991 9d3 10.5g2 10.6g* 11.9m 8g3 10m3 8s4] lengthy, quite attractive filly: has a round action: capable of fair form: made all in maiden at Haydock in June: soon beaten in Lancashire Oaks and last in minor events last 4 starts, off course 3 months before making most last 2: best at around 1¼m: takes good hold: visits Lead On Time. *B. W. Hills.*

SHOOFE (USA) 3 ch.g. L'Emigrant (USA) 129 – Bid For Manners (USA) (Raise 83 A Bid (USA)) [1990 NR 1991 8d 10d 10g 10d 12.3g2 11.5m4 16.9g* 16.9m6 16m* 16m 15.9d*] $30,000F, 50,000Y: good-topped gelding: half-brother to a winner in USA: dam minor winner in USA: won maiden at Wolverhampton in August and handicaps at Nottingham in September and Chester (best effort) in October: suited by test of stamina: acts on good to firm ground and dead: not particularly consistent. *D. Morley.*

SHOOTING LODGE (IRE) 3 b.c. High Line 125 – Heather Croft 79 (Kala 77 Shikari 125) [1990 NR 1991 11.7g6 15.3m2 14m2 13g2 13.8f2] 16,000Y: good-topped, quite attractive colt: second foal: half-brother to 1988 2-y-o 6f seller winner Kinematic (by Montekin): dam sprinting daughter of sister to prolific 1971 2-y-o Sea Music: modest maiden: odds on, led virtually until post in auction contest at Ayr (ridden by 7-lb claimer) penultimate start: suited by test of stamina: possibly unsuited by very firm ground: sold to join J. Jenkins 12,500 gns Newmarket September Sales. *A. C. Stewart.*

SHORT SHOT 5 b.g. Young Generation 129 – Blessed Damsel 99 (So Blessed —
130) [1990 10d 1991 10f] useful-looking gelding: one-time fair performer: has lost his
way: suited by 1¼m: best form on top-of-the-ground: sold 1,550 gns Ascot May
Sales. *A. Moore.*

SHOT STOPPER 3 gr.f. Bellypha 130 – Ideal Home 104 (Home Guard (USA) 71
129) [1990 5m³ 5m 7m 7f³ 7m⁵ 7.3g³ 7m 1991 8g⁵ 8d 8g² 7.1g 10g³ 10m³ 7m³ 7f⁵ 8g]
unfurnished filly: good mover: modest maiden: well beaten last 2 starts: seems
effective at 7f to 1¼m: acts on firm going, possibly unsuited by dead: blinkered
(irresolute) eighth outing: trained until after then by R. Hannon: somewhat inconsistent. *M. C. Pipe.*

SHOUT OUT 4 b.g. Auction Ring (USA) 123 – Manora (USA) (Stop The Music 69
(USA)) [1990 8m 1991 a10g² a8g* 7.5g a7g] rangy gelding, rather dipped-backed:
poor mover: lightly-raced handicapper: won at Southwell (maiden) in April: well
beaten after: stays 1¼m. *C. R. Nelson.*

SHOWACA 3 b.g. Show-A-Leg 107 – Elsaca (Ela-Mana-Mou 132) [1990 6m a7g 34
1991 a6g a5g³ a7g a5g 7d⁶ 8s² 8f a8g 8m] leggy gelding: moderate plater: showed
nothing final start, first for 5 months: stays 1m: acts on soft going: blinkered once:
often apprentice ridden. *R. F. Marvin.*

SHOWBROOK (IRE) 2 gr.c. (Apr 3) Exhibitioner 111 – Aldern Stream **111**
102 (Godswalk (USA) 130) [1991 6g² 6f* 6g⁵ 6m* 5.5g² 6g² 6m* 6f* a8.5f]
For the fourth successive year the Group 3 Anglia Television July Stakes
at Newmarket attracted just four runners, and coming so swiftly after a
combined turn-out of nine for the previous day's listed Chesterfield Stakes
and Group 3 Cherry Hinton Stakes it prompted an understandably strong
outburst from Newmarket's clerk of the course. Quite why the July Stakes
should consistently draw so few runners is not apparent—its penalties aren't
swingeing and the ground at the meeting rarely becomes firm. But the
problem isn't a new one. Since 1900 its eighty-seven runnings have produced
five hundred and thirty-two runners at an average of just over six a year,
which compares unfavourably with those for the Richmond, Gimcrack and
Coventry Stakes, three other races of similar status over six furlongs in
mid-summer, which in the same period have averaged between seven and
twelve runners. What's more, during that time the July Stakes has attracted a
double-figure field on just ten occasions, five of which came in a seven-year

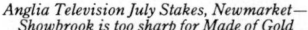

Anglia Television July Stakes, Newmarket—
Showbrook is too sharp for Made of Gold

Rokeby Farms Mill Reef Stakes, Newbury—Showbrook, Jeune (right) and Dilum

period early in the century. Lack of contestants doesn't necessarily mean a lack of quality, however—recent winners of the July Stakes include Superlative, Primo Dominie, Green Desert, Rock City and Mujtahid, for example— but the latest renewal was short on both counts and was little better than might be found for a good graduation event; besides Showbrook, who had won the Woodcote Stakes at Epsom in excellent style by six lengths from Diamond Mine before finishing a never-dangerous fifth to Dilum in the Coventry Stakes at Royal Ascot, the field consisted of the Coventry fourth and seventh Computer Kid and Wilde Rufo, who had accumulated two wins between them from an aggregate of eight starts and Made of Gold, a seven-length winner of a Ripon maiden on good to soft ground the previous month. Showbrook was again an impressive winner, travelling comfortably at the head of affairs passing halfway, quickening approaching the furlong-marker, where only Made of Gold was in a position to catch him, and increasing his advantage under hands-and-heels assistance to three and a half lengths at the line. Made of Gold, who found the distance on the sharp side on the good to firm ground, finished two and a half lengths clear in second.

After the July Stakes, Showbrook maintained a consistent level of form until running moderately in the eight-and-a-half-furlong Breeders' Cup Juvenile at Churchill Downs in November when, wearing goggles and blinkers, he finished last, eased considerably, after holding a prominent position to the end of the back straight. Although Showbrook hadn't shown form good enough to win the Juvenile—he started at 25/1—his pedigree and free-running style lead us to believe he's unlikely to prove so effective at a mile as he is at sprint distances, and it's probably no coincidence that he was never tried beyond six furlongs in his other races. Showbrook had run right up to his best and finished much closer to the Juvenile winner Arazi in the five-and-a-half-furlong Prix Robert Papin at Maisons-Laffitte in July, racing keenly and holding the lead for a while in the second half of the race before being passed comfortably by the length-and-a-half winner. Showbrook is, however, a useful colt to be contesting minor pattern races on the continent and the following month, after proving no match for Dilum and running a little below form in the Scottish Equitable Richmond Stakes at Goodwood, he annexed the Group 2 Moet & Chandon Rennen at Baden-Baden by a length and a half from the German filly Waitowin. Showbrook recorded probably his best performance on his last outing in Britain, in the Rokeby Farms Mill Reef Stakes at Newbury in September. More of the post-race comment focused on Dilum's continued slump in form than on Showbrook's consolidation at the top of the second division; leading after a furlong, Showbrook quickened clear with under two furlongs to run and ran on really well, despite edging quite markedly to his right, to account for the much-vaunted Jeune convincingly by two and a half lengths. Conditions at Newbury were perfect for Showbrook: six furlongs on good to firm or firm ground.

Showbrook, a compact, sprint type on looks who cost IR 15,000 guineas as a foal and 30,000 guineas (at Newmarket's October Sale) as a yearling, doesn't have a fashionable pedigree. His sire Exhibitioner, whose third crop

A. F. Budge (Equine) Ltd's "Showbrook"

Showbrook (IRE) (gr.c. Apr 3, 1989)	Exhibitioner (ch 1982)	Thatching (b 1975)	Thatch
			Abella
		Miss Pudge (b 1975)	Green God
			Carnival Park
	Aldern Stream (gr 1980)	Godswalk (gr 1974)	Dancer's Image
			Kate's Intent
		Betsy Ross (gr 1974)	Petingo
			Clear Path

he's from, was several rungs below the top as a sprinter in Ireland and looks to be heading down the same road as a stallion on the evidence of a succession of moderate runners among whom only the useful Irish sprinter Wicked Polly besides Showbrook stands out. Showbrook's dam Aldern Stream wasn't the most consistent of animals but she won two races, over five furlongs as a two-year-old and seven furlongs, and was capable of useful form at her best. Showbrook is her fifth foal; the previous four, all of whom were by modest stallions, produced just one winner, the fairly useful 1988 Irish two-year-old seven-furlong winner Alpine Spring (by Head For Heights). Aldern Stream's dam Betsy Ross, whose other winners on the Flat and over jumps include the fairly useful middle-distance handicapper Forest of Dean, was a useful race-mare at up to a mile and a quarter in 1977 when she won two races and reached the frame in the Chesterfield Cup and the Irish Sweeps Cambridgeshire;

791

together with the useful Irish middle-distance performer Silvery Blue, she's the best of the three winners from her seven-furlong-winning dam Clear Path.

Showbrook falls into the unfortunate category for which the increased opportunities proposed by the Jockey Club's race-planning department late in the year may not come in soon enough: he's too good to contest all but the best handicaps but isn't good enough to win at the highest level. He seems just the type to find his way abroad and could be campaigned extensively there as a three-year-old. *R. Hannon.*

SHOWGI (USA) 2 ch.c. (Jan 27) Topsider (USA) – Shoag (USA) (Affirmed **80** (USA)) [1991 6g3 6m4 7m* 7d] useful-looking colt: has scope: moderate mover: third foal: dam once-raced half-sister to Prix de Pomone winner Sweet Rhapsody and smart American filly Sisterhood: well-backed favourite, won 16-runner maiden at Redcar in September, off bridle long way out and leading close home: unimpressive in appearance, ran poorly in Ascot nursery following month: will be suited by 1m: possibly unsuited by dead ground. *J. R. Fanshawe.*

SHOWMANSHIP 4 b.g. Shernazar 131 – Melodramatic 112 (Tudor Melody 129) **55** [1990 8f 10.1g 10.6f2 10g 8.2s5 11.5g 10d3 a12g2 a10g 1991 a12g6 10.2s 10g 10m3 12f2 12g* 12h4 12.3d4 12m2 12g 14.1f3 12f5 11.8g 12f2 11.5s] leggy, good-topped gelding: moderate mover: plating-class handicapper: won at Leicester in May: stays 1½m: acts on firm and dead (probably unsuited by very soft) ground: has run well for inexperienced rider: often bandaged: none too consistent. *C. F. Wall.*

SHOW THE FLAG 3 b.g. Beldale Flutter (USA) 130 – Pretty Miss (So Blessed **68** 130) [1990 NR 1991 12m 11.5m2 12g6 10.5d] big, lengthy gelding: fourth foal: half-brother to 7f and 1¼m winner Follow The Drum (by Daring March): dam once-raced half-sister to useful 2-y-o Fair Parrot: quite modest maiden at best: very burly final start: stays 11.5f well: gelded after fourth start: sold to join K. Bailey 10,000 gns Newmarket Autumn Sales. *J. D. Bethell.*

SHREWD GIRL (USA) 3 b.f. Sagace (FR) 135 – Hydahs (USA) (Chieftain II) **79** [1990 NR 1991 10g6 10f2] 58,000Y: leggy filly: shows round action: first reported foal: dam half-sister to Palace Music: second of 8 to Sarabah at Folkestone in June, easily better effort in maidens, outpaced and running green top turn then staying on well: will be well suited by further. *M. R. Stoute.*

SHREWD INVESTMENT 2 ch.c. (Mar 13) Sharrood (USA) 124 – Silverhall **50** (Sparkler 130) [1991 6f 6g 6.9m 7.5f 8m 8m5 8.3g3 10.5d] 7,000Y: workmanlike colt: fourth foal: half-brother to 3-y-o Keep In Trim (by Pharly): dam unraced half-sister to Swiss Maid: modest plater: stays 8.3f: acts on good to firm ground: visored last 4 outings: has been reluctant stalls: tended to hang penultimate start: sold 3,900 gns Newmarket Autumn Sales. *C. Tinkler.*

SHREWD PARTNER (IRE) 2 br.c. (Mar 27) Ahonoora 122 – Practical 95 **72** (Ballymore 123) [1991 7m6 8s* 7d5 8g] workmanlike colt: has scope: has a round action: fifth foal: half-brother to several winners, including Irish 7f winner Pot of Gold (by Rainbow Quest): dam Irish 9f and 1¼m winner, is half-sister to top-class American middle-distance performer Providential and top 1981 2-y-o staying filly Play It Safe and out of half-sister to Hethersett: modest performer: favourite, won maiden at Kempton in September, soon well placed, leading 2f out, keeping on well: ran creditably in nursery at Ascot and minor event at Newbury (seventh of 15 to Aljadeer) afterwards: will stay 1¼m: acts on soft ground. *D. R. C. Elsworth.*

SHUAILAAN (USA) 2 ch.c. (Feb 8) Roberto (USA) 131 – Lassie's Lady (USA) **102** p (Alydar (USA)) [1991 7m*] $750,000Y: leggy, useful-looking colt: has scope: third foal: half-brother to Bite The Bullet (by Spectacular Bid), successful, including in Grade 2 event, at up to 7f: dam, winner at up to 7f, from good family: 7/2 and bit green, won 5-runner Houghton Stakes at Newmarket in October by 1½ lengths from Masad, leading over 1f out and going away near finish: showed fluent action: will stay 1m: sure to improve and likely to make up into smart performer. *A. C. Stewart.*

SHU FLY (NZ) 7 ch.g. Tom's Shu (USA) – Alycone (NZ) (Philoctetes 111) [1990 — 9g 1991 9g4] workmanlike gelding: lightly raced on flat: out of depth only run in 1991: useful hurdler. *Mrs S. Oliver.*

SHUJAN (USA) 2 b.c. (Feb 5) Diesis 133 – Linda's Magic (USA) 114 (Far North **80** p (CAN) 120) [1991 6d*] good-topped colt: first foal: dam 6f and 7f winner, is daughter of unraced half-sister to high-class American turf performer Tiller: 4/1 from 9/4 and backward, had quite a hard race to win 10-runner maiden at Doncaster in November by ½ length from Yazaly, soon ridden along then staying on well from halfway: will be suited by 7f + : should improve. *R. W. Armstrong.*

SHUT UP   2 b.f. (Mar 12) Kind of Hush 118 – Creetown Lady 55 (Creetown 123) [1991 8.1m] 500F: small, plain filly: second foal: dam won 5f and 5.3f sellers at 2 yrs: 66/1, never a factor in maiden at Edinburgh in October: mulish leaving paddock (unseated rider) and at stalls. *R. Allan.*   —

SHYLOU   ? b.f. (Jan 21) Petoski 135 – Lady of The Land 75 (Wollow 132) [1991 5g⁶ 6g⁶ 7f] 5,100Y: angular filly: third foal: half-sister to modest 1¼m winner Sharquin (by Indian King) and a winner in Italy: dam won over 1m and is half-sister to very useful 1976 2-y-o Easy Landing: well beaten in varied events. *Dr J. D. Scargill.*   —

SIANEMA   3 ro.f. Persian Bold 123 – Seriema 72 (Petingo 135) [1990 6m 1991 8g 8m⁵ 8g³ a10g a10g] leggy filly: modest form in maidens in spring: off course over 6 months, behind in handicaps at Lingfield last 2 starts: should be suited by 1¼m. *D. R. Laing.*   **69**

SIANISKI   2 b.f. (May 28) Niniski (USA) 125 – Pagan Queen 83 (Vaguely Noble 140) [1991 8g] workmanlike filly: seventh reported foal: closely related to 1½m winners Green Steps (by Green Dancer) and La Gracile (by Nijinsky): dam won at 1½m and 1¾m: 20/1 and backward, soon well behind when last of 9 in maiden at Wolverhampton in October. *N. A. Graham.*   —

SIBERIAN BREEZE   3 gr.g. Siberian Express (USA) 125 – Zepha 88 (Great Nephew 126) [1990 7g 7m 1991 8.5f 8m 8g⁵ 8.2d 8.3g 8g a7g² 7m] leggy, workmanlike gelding: has a quick action: plating-class handicapper: best effort second at Southwell, staying on strongly: stays 1m: acts on good to firm ground, probably not on dead: blinkered last 4 starts: has run creditably when on toes: crashed through rail and bolted before eighth intended start: winning hurdler. *J. A. Glover.*   **49**

SIBERIAN KING   2 b.g. (Mar 27) Siberian Express (USA) 125 – Fallen Angel 88 (Quiet Fling (USA) 124) [1991 5d 5d 6g⁴ 7.5f 7.5f] 1,900Y: tall, lengthy, dipped-backed gelding: fourth foal: half-brother to 11.7f winner Silvie (by Kind of Hush) and fair 1987 Irish 2-y-o 6f winner Nations Spirit (by Thatching), later successful in North America: dam stayer: poor maiden: sweating profusely last 2 starts. *A. Smith.*   **42**

SIBERIAN SUNSET (IRE)   2 b.c. (Apr 23) Red Sunset 120 – Sabura (Busted 134) [1991 5m⁶ 5g 5m] 7,400F, 8,600Y: good-topped colt: brother to 3-y-o Channon Hill and half-brother to 1¼m seller winner Serious Business (by Sallust) and a winner abroad: dam Irish 5f winner: poor maiden: dead. *R. Hollinshead.*   **48**

SIBERIAN SWING   2 gr.f. (Apr 25) Siberian Express (USA) 125 – Swing Is Back (Busted 134) [1991 6m] workmanlike filly: half-sister to fairly useful 5f to 1m winner Balizara and winning hurdler Tyburn Lad (both by Belfort): dam French 1¼m winner: 66/1, tailed off final 2f in 8-runner maiden at Leicester in October. *J. D. Roberts.*   —

SIBERIAN WINTER (USA)   3 ch.f. Bering 136 – Copperama (AUS) (Comeram (FR)) [1990 NR 1991 9.9f²] sparely-made filly: turns fore feet in: third foal: half-sister to Irish 7f and 1m winner Stormy Exchange (by Storm Bird): dam leading performer in Australia, successful in VATC 1000 Guineas: 7/2 on but green, 3 lengths second of 5 to Flit in maiden at Beverley in September: should do better. *H. R. A. Cecil.*   **66** p

SIBYL O'DONNELL   4 b.f. Durandal 114 – Seersucker (Dolman) [1990 NR 1991 8.1d 10.8m 14.1m] leggy, good-topped filly: first foal: dam unraced: seems of little account. *K. S. Bridgwater.*   —

SIDDINGTON LODGE (IRE)   3 b.g. Wassl 125 – Eloquent Charm (USA) (Private Account (USA)) [1990 NR 1991 8g 10g] 2,000Y, 460 2-y-o, resold 1,050 2-y-o: small, sparely-made gelding: second foal: dam poor maiden out of a winning sister to Ribblesdale winner Nanticious and Stewards' Cup winner Repetitious: tailed off in maidens in the spring. *A. J. Chamberlain.*   —

SIDNEY SMITH (IRE)   3 ch.g. Tate Gallery (USA) 117 – Miss Anna (King's Company 124) [1990 NR 1991 10d 9s⁴ 11.8g 8.3m⁶ 7m²] IR 45,000Y: lengthy, sparely-made gelding: moderate mover: seventh reported foal: half-brother to 3 winners, including quite useful 1980 2-y-o 7f winner Lady Nightingale: dam, half-sister to Providential and Play It Safe, showed no form: 12/1, first form when strong-finishing second of 20 in handicap at Catterick in October, having been outpaced: may prove ideally suited by 1m/1¼m: visored first and final starts: sold to join R. Lee from 10,500 gns Newmarket Autumn Sales. *J. H. M. Gosden.*   **54**

SIE AMATO (IRE)   2 ch.c. (Apr 2) Soughaan (USA) 111 – Wolviston (Wolverlife 115) [1991 7m a6g³ a7g* 7m a7g⁴ a7g a7g] IR 1,700F, IR 3,000Y: sparely-made colt: **55**

fourth foal: dam Irish 2-y-o 5f winner: fair plater: retained 5,600 gns after winning at Southwell in August: ran moderately after fifth start: probably better suited by 7f than 6f. *Capt. J. Wilson.*

SIESTA KEY   6 b.g. Glint of Gold 128 – Petite Hester 85 (Wollow 132) [1990 NR   **79**
1991 16m² 14.6m³] leggy, quite good-topped gelding: usually looks well: modest handicapper: ran poorly and looked awkward ride in claimer final start, first for 4½ months: stays 2m: acts on firm going. *M. Johnston.*

SIFTON'S PRIDE (CAN)   3 b.f. Majesty's Prince (USA) – Original Script   **63 +**
(CAN) (Codex (USA)) [1990 NR 1991 11.4m⁴ 12m² 10g] big, leggy, lengthy filly: first foal: dam, daughter of stakes winner, won sprint maiden at 2 yrs: quite modest maiden: odds-on second of 5 at Folkestone in September, staying on no chance with winner: possibly flattered on debut, and well beaten at Brighton: should prove suited by 1¾m +. *G. Harwood.*

SIGAMA (USA)   5 ch.g. Secretariat (USA) – Lady Speedwell (USA)   **85**
(Secretariat (USA)) [1990 5g 5m* 5f² 5m² 5s³ 5f* 5f² 5m* 5m a5g 1991 5m³ 5g 5g³ 5f² 5f 5g⁴ 5m⁴ 5m 5m 5m² 5g 5m² 5m* 5.2f⁶ 5d] sturdy, dipped-backed gelding: has a quick action: fair handicapper: won at Lingfield in September: best on top-of-the-ground: below form when visored and hooded once, has run fairly well when blinkered: very speedy, best when able to dominate. *F. H. Lee.*

SIGNORE DE ANGLES   2 b.c. (May 16) Sizzling Melody 117 – Lady Lorelei   **38**
105 (Derring-Do 131) [1991 5.3f 6f⁵ 6g⁶ 5g⁶ 6f] 1,100F, 560Y: plain, leggy colt: half-brother to very useful 3-y-o 1¼m and 10.5f winner Gussy Marlowe (by Final Straw) and 6f (at 2 yrs) and 10.5f winner Athene Noctua (by Aragon): dam 5f to 1m winner: poor plater: will stay 7f: blinkered final start (August): bandaged on debut: possibly unsatisfactory: sold 600 gns Newmarket Autumn Sales. *R. W. Stubbs.*

SIGNOR SASSIE (USA)   3 ch.c. The Minstrel (CAN) 135 – Sahsie (USA)   **76**
(Forli (ARG)) [1990 7m 1991 10g² 10m⁶ 12m³] lengthy, heavy-topped colt: good mover: modest maiden: swished tail but stayed on strongly final start: worth a try over further: sold 18,000 gns Newmarket Autumn Sales: winning hurdler for N. Tinkler. *G. Harwood.*

SIGWELLS STEAMER   2 b.g. (Feb 21) King of Spain 121 – Haygate Park 65   **33**
(Final Straw 127) [1991 5d 5m⁶ 5m a5g 7m] 2,600F, 2,600Y: sturdy gelding: first foal: dam 1¼m winner: poor plater: blinkered penultimate start. *W. G. M. Turner.*

SIJJAAL (USA)   3 b. or br.c. Mr Prospector (USA) – South Sea Dancer (USA)   **73**
(Northern Dancer) [1990 NR 1991 8d 9g⁴ 11.8g⁵ 11.9m* 11.6m 11.7f] $800,000?: robust colt: second foal: half-brother to 7f and 8.5f winner Island Wedding (by Blushing Groom): dam winner at up to 9f at 4 yrs and 5 yrs, is sister to Storm Bird: won handicap at Brighton in August: below form in similar events after: may well stay further: sold 22,000 gns Newmarket Autumn Sales. *Major W. R. Hern.*

SIKESTON (USA)   5 b.h. Lear Fan (USA) 130 – Small Timer (USA) (Lyp-   **121**
hard (USA) 132) [1990 8v* 8g 10g² 12g 10d 8v* 10s³ 8v* 1991 10g² 10.5g⁴ 10v* 9m⁶ 8g* 8g⁴ 8m 8d 8v* 8v² 10v*]
    The Brittain-Roberts partnership enjoyed a highly successful season. Mystiko provided them with their first Two Thousand Guineas winner whilst

Queen Anne Stakes, Ascot—
the Royal meeting opens with a win for Sikeston (No. 2) from Rami

Luciano Gaucci's "Sikeston"

the evergreen Terimon finally landed his first Group 1 prize in the Juddmonte International Stakes. Another stalwart to enjoy huge success was Sikeston—indeed, he proved the leading money winner for the stable in 1991. Sikeston again proved a major force when campaigned in Italy. For the second year running he was successful in three pattern events there. He easily accounted for Lara's Idea by two lengths in Europe's final Group 1 contest, the Premio Roma at Rome in November, to add to earlier, narrower Group 1 wins in the Premio Presidente della Republica at Rome in May and the Premio Vittorio di Capua at Milan in October. It's fair to say that part of Sikeston's success in Italy can be attributed to the relative weakness of pattern races in that country and to the fact that he regularly found underfoot conditions there very much in his favour. However, his talent didn't go unrecognized much nearer to home. As heavy rain brought testing conditions for the Queen Elizabeth II Stakes at Ascot in September, the mud-lark Sikeston's odds tumbled from 33/1 in the week leading up to the race to 15/2 at the off. And though confidence in him that day proved misplaced—he never gave his supporters much hope before finishing a remote seventh of nine to Selkirk—clearly all wasn't right. Brittain said after that 'Sikeston couldn't be trained on the firm ground before the race and was 18 kilos overweight'. The horse had shown much more like his true worth here in two other mile races, the Queen Anne Stakes and the Sussex Stakes. Carrying the maximum 6-lb penalty in the Group 2 Queen Anne, Sikeston put up a high-class and gutsy performance to beat Rami by a head, always close up and rallying splendidly inside the last furlong. Remarkably, that was his first win outside Italy. For a horse who stays a mile and a quarter really well—and the stiffer test at a mile the better for him—it was surprising to see him held up by Eddery at Goodwood in the Sussex Stakes (Roberts partnered Mystiko). Badly checked on the home turn, Sikeston ran on really well despite hanging somewhat in the final quarter mile to finish a never-nearer fourth of eight to Second Set, beaten just over four and a half lengths. The remainder of Sikeston's season was spent at Longchamp. He ran well on his first two starts to finish in the frame in the Prix d'Harcourt and Prix Ganay, but found conditions against him in the Prix d'Ispahan and Prix du Moulin and was never able to land a blow.

	Lear Fan (USA) (b 1981)	Roberto (b 1969)	Hail To Reason
Sikeston (USA) (b.h. 1986)			Bramalea
		Wac (b 1969)	Lt Stevens
			Belthazar
	Small Timer (USA) (b 1980)	Lyphard (b 1969)	Northern Dancer
			Goofed
		Watch Fob (b or br 1965)	Tompion
			Pet Child

Sikeston's pedigree details were discussed in *Racehorses of 1990*. As he was bought for 25,000 dollars as a yearling at the Fasig-Tipton Kentucky July Sales, it goes almost without saying that Sikeston has proved a monumental bargain. Sire Lear Fan had a fine year. At the start of the season Sikeston was his only pattern winner in Europe but now Sikeston's been joined by such as Corrupt, Run Don't Fly and French two-year-old Glaieul. Eight months after producing Sikeston, the unraced Small Timer was sold for 57,000 dollars and sent to New Zealand. The foal she was carrying at the time, a daughter of Temperence Hill later named Honeymoon Hill, was returned to Kentucky and sold for only 9,500 dollars. She's won once over a mile in minor company in the States. Sikeston's grandam Watch Fob was a tough and very useful campaigner, winner of eleven of her fifty-six races over five seasons. Her dam Pet Child produced another three stakes winners, including the five-furlong Prix du Bois winner Myosotis. A robust, heavy-topped horse who carries plenty of condition, the tough and genuine Sikeston stays in training. *C. E. Brittain.*

SILCA-CISA 2 ch.f. (Apr 26) Hallgate 127 – Princess Silca Key 61 (Grundy 137) **76**
[1991 5.1g² 5g² 5m³ 5g*] angular, sparely-made filly: moderate mover with quick action: first foal: dam lightly-raced 7f winner, is daughter of half-sister to very speedy 1980 2-y-o Labista: modest performer: well-backed favourite, narrowly won maiden at Redcar in October: speedy. *M. R. Channon.*

SILENT RESPECT (IRE) 2 b.c. (Feb 26) Don't Forget Me 127 – Pallas's Blue **70**
(Pitskelly 122) [1991 6m⁴ 5g³ 6m³ 7g 8m 7g*] IR 26,000Y: good-bodied colt: first foal: dam Irish 2-y-o 1m winner, is out of 1½m-winning half-sister to dam of smart Irish fillies French Score and Ballet Francais: quite modest performer: blinkered, easily made all in maiden at Brighton in October: ran poorly in nurseries previous 2 outings: stays 7f: sold 26,000 gns Newmarket Autumn Sales. *R. Hannon.*

SILENT SISTER 6 gr.m. Kind of Hush 118 – Little Mercy 90 (No Mercy 126) **37**
[1990 NR 1991 a8g⁶ a6g 6f 5g 5m⁵ 6f 7m 8m⁶] lengthy mare: powerful galloper: poor performer nowadays: stays 1m: acts on hard and dead going: not discredited when blinkered. *A. Moore.*

SILICA (USA) 2 ch.f. (Apr 3) Mr Prospector (USA) – Skillful Joy (USA) **66**
(Nodouble (USA)) [1991 7m² 7g] $650,000Y: quite attractive filly: third living foal: dam, very smart at 2 yrs, won 8 races at up to 9f from 2 yrs to 4 yrs: 4 lengths second of 16 to impressive Anlace in maiden at Leicester in October, keeping on unable to challenge: 7/2, showed up to 2f out then eased when beaten behind Oumaldaaya at Newmarket following month: should stay 1m: may do better. *J. H. M. Gosden.*

SILK DEGREES 5 gr.g. Dunbeath (USA) 127 – Bustling Nelly 94 (Bustino 136) **50**
[1990 NR 1991 16m² 15g* 15g⁵ 13g⁴ 16.1m⁶ 15.8g] rather plain gelding: lightly-raced handicapper: won at Edinburgh in June: stays 2m well: acts on good to firm ground: wore near-side pricker fourth start. *W. Storey.*

SILKEN WORDS (USA) 2 b.f. (Apr 11) Alleged (USA) 138 – Tie A Bow (USA) **68**
(Dance Spell (USA)) [1991 6f 7f⁶ 7m³ 8g] $7,500Y: good-topped filly: has a round action: sister to modest stayer Debbie Harry and fair Irish 9f winner Senior Counsel and half-sister to 2 minor winners: dam, placed twice from 2 starts at 2 yrs, is

half-sister to Law Society (by Alleged) and Legal Bid: quite modest maiden: ran badly in Goodwood nursery final outing: should be suited by 1m. *W. R. Muir.*

SILKS DOMINO   6 ch.g. Dominion 123 – Bourgeonette 81 (Mummy's Pet 125)   —
[1990 a13g⁴ a16g² a14g³ a14g⁴ a14g a14g 1991 13.8d] rather plain gelding: has a long stride: poor performer nowadays: seems to stay 2m: best form on a soft surface: sometimes blinkered or visored: best forcing pace: inconsistent: winning hurdler. *O. O'Neill.*

SILKS PRINCESS   5 b.m. Prince Tenderfoot (USA) 126 – Pitlessie 75 (Hook   **54**
Money 124) [1990 a6g 6v 7m 7g 6g 6m⁶ a7g⁴ 6g a7g⁵ a8g* 8.2m 6m* 6m 6m 1991 6m 6.1m 6s 6.9s a7g³ a6g a7g a8g²] lengthy, good-bodied mare: moderate mover: plating-class handicapper: effective at 6f to 1m: acts on good to firm going, best efforts on soft: tried in blinkers and visor. *M. J. Ryan.*

SILK TAPESTRY (USA)   2 b.f. (Mar 28) Tank's Prospect (USA) – Only   **77**
Queens (USA) (Transworld (USA) 121) [1991 7g⁶ a7g⁵ 8.1g* 8g 8g⁵] $85,000Y: leggy filly: fifth foal: half-sister to Grade 1 Beldame Stakes winner Tactile (by Slew O'Gold): dam won Grade 1 Demoiselle Stakes at 2 yrs: sire won Preakness Stakes: modest performer: sweating, much improved to win maiden at Chepstow in August, leading 3f out: ran creditably in nurseries at Goodwood and Redcar: will stay 1¼m: ran poorly on fibresand: sold 27,000 gns Newmarket December Sales. *M. R. Stoute.*

SILK THREAD   8 ch.g. Relkino 131 – Silken Way (FR) 103 (Shantung 132) [1990   **46**
NR 1991 14g 14.1g⁵ a14g* a16g² a16g⁵ a18g] workmanlike gelding: carries plenty of condition: poor handicapper nowadays: won at Southwell in July: stays 2m: suited by an easy surface on turf (goes well in the mud): tried blinkered once: has worn bandages behind. *J. Pearce.*

SILLARS STALKER (IRE)   3 b.g. Stalker 121 – Mittens (Run The Gantlet   **41**
(USA) [1990 5m 5f 5d 6d 1991 10d³ 12.3s³ 14g 12d² 11.8g] workmanlike gelding: poor performer: placed in handicaps, good second in selling event at Pontefract: stays 1½m (in need of race at 1¾m): acts on soft ground: visored once, blinkered 3 times: winning hurdler. *Mrs J. R. Ramsden.*

SILLERY (USA)   3 b.c. Blushing Groom (FR) 131 – Silvermine (FR) 124   **120**
(Bellypha 130) [1990 8d⁴ 8d² 8v* 8s* 1991 9.2g⁶ 9d* 9.2m* 10d² 8g 8m⁴ 10s² 9f] second foal: half-brother to French 1¼m winner Signorelli (by Cox's Ridge): dam French 1000 Guineas winner, is half-sister to Saint Cyrien out of very useful French 7.5f to 9f winner Sevres: successful in listed race at Evry and Prix Jean Prat at Longchamp in May: ran creditably in frame for Grand Prix de Paris Louis Vuitton (raced freely, joining issue over 2f out and caught final strides by Subotica) and Emirates Prix du Moulin (2½ lengths behind Priolo), both at Longchamp, then runner-up to Leariva in Budweiser International at Laurel: effective at 1m and 1¼m, on good to firm ground and heavy: very smart. *Mme C. Head, France.*

SILLY HABIT (USA)   5 b.m. Assert 134 – Habitassa 100 (Habitat 134) [1990   **47**
11.7g³ a14g 12g⁴ 16g 15.3m³ 14g⁵ 17.6m² 18.1m² 17.6g³ 1991 16.2g³ 21.6f²] workmanlike mare: moderate mover: plating-class maiden: stays 2¼m: acts on firm and dead ground. *J. W. Hills.*

SILLY'S BROTHER   5 ch.g. Longleat (USA) 109 – Scilly Isles 54 (Silly Season   **63** d
127) [1990 6s 7f⁴ 7f 7m 6g 8.5g 7g 7.5f⁶ 7f 8g 7.5m³ 7d 8g a6g⁴ a6g⁴ 1991 a8g a7g* a7g⁶ a6g* a6g* a6g³ 7d³ 6m a5g⁴ a5g a6g⁶ a6g 7m 8.1s a7g a6g⁵] heavy-topped gelding: carries plenty of condition: plating-class handicapper: made most when successful at Southwell (3) in 1991: best form at 6f: acts on good to firm and heavy going: below form when blinkered once. *N. Bycroft.*

SILVER BRAID (USA)   3 ch.f. Miswaki (USA) 124 – Chalice of Silver (USA) 74   **101**
(Graustark) [1990 6g 7g* 7g³ 1991 7.3g² 8g 10d⁵ 8g 10m 8m² 8d⁴ 8g⁵] leggy, angular filly: useful on her day: second to Shadayid in Fred Darling Stakes at Newbury and You Know The Rules in moderately-run listed race (headed post having quickened on over 1f out) at Doncaster: suited by 1m: acts on good to firm ground and dead: sometimes sweating and edgy. *D. R. C. Elsworth.*

SILVER CANNON (USA)   9 gr.g. Lot O'Gold (USA) – So High (USA) (Sea   —
Bird II 145) [1990 NR 1991 a10g] lightly raced and modest at best: stays 1¼m: best on an easy surface (used to go very well in the mud): has worn blinkers and a visor: winning chaser. *R. Voorspuy.*

SILVER CONCORD   3 gr.c. Absalom 128 – Boarding House 73 (Shack (USA)   **52**
118) [1990 6m 6g³ 7v³ 6s 1991 7g 6g 8m 7g⁴ 7m³ 7m² 7m 7g] workmanlike colt: plating-class performer, placed in handicaps: soundly beaten last 2 starts: should stay 1m: seems unsuited by soft ground: blinkered, hung badly second start: sold to join G. Moore 5,800 gns Newmarket Autumn Sales. *J. M. P. Eustace.*

SILVERDALE FOX 4 ch.g. Sweet Monday 122 – Its My Turn 80 (Palm Track —
122) [1990 10v² 8.2s⁶ 10.2m² 8.5m⁵ 9g 9.1s⁴ 1991 8d 12m] angular, plain gelding:
modest handicapper: below best in 1991: suited by 1¼m: acts on good to firm ground
and heavy: has given trouble at stalls, once refusing to enter them: has run poorly
when sweating and edgy: of doubtful temperament. *R. Hollinshead.*

SILVERDALE ROSE 2 b.f. (Apr 3) Nomination 125 – Its My Turn 80 (Palm —
Track 122) [1991 6d 6m] unfurnished filly: third foal: half-sister to 3-y-o My Turn
Next (by King of Spain) and fair 1989 2-y-o 6f winner Silverdale Fox (by Sweet
Monday): dam miler: ridden by 7-lb claimer, never a factor in large fields at Haydock
(maiden) and Newmarket (seller) in October. *R. Hollinshead.*

SILVER DILEMMA (USA) 3 b.c. The Minstrel (CAN) 135 – Royal Dilemma **71**
(USA) (Buckpasser) [1990 6m⁴ 6g³ 6g³ 1991 6f² 6d⁴ 6f³ 7m⁵ 6m⁴] well-made colt:
has a quick action: modest maiden: below form last 2 outings and not seen out after
July: should stay 7f: acts on firm going: sweating and edgy third and fourth starts:
below form for apprentice: has wandered under pressure. *I. A. Balding.*

SILVER FANTASY (IRE) 2 gr.f. (Apr 5) Kaldoun (FR) 122 – Gipsy Charmer —
(USA) 69 (Alydar (USA)) [1991 6m] 2,000F, 6,400Y: workmanlike filly: first foal:
dam once-raced half-sister to champion 1982 American 2-y-o colt Roving Boy: 33/1,
tailed off from halfway in 9-runner maiden at Southwell in May: moved badly down:
sold 1,250 gns Ascot November Sales. *J. Balding.*

SILVER HEELS 3 ch.g. Capricorn Line 111 – Balinese Dancer 54 (Moorestyle —
137) [1990 6f⁴ 1991 8g 9g 5m] smallish, plain gelding: soundly beaten, including in
claimers. *J. S. Moore.*

SILVER KITE (USA) 2 b. or br.c. (Mar 2) Silver Hawk (USA) 123 – Strait Lane **111**
(USA) (Chieftain (USA)) [1991 6g* 7g² 7m³ 8d⁶] $650,000Y: strong, medium-sized
colt: brother to French 5.5f (at 2 yrs) to 1m winner (also third in Irish Oaks) Silver
Lane and triple Grade 1 winner (including at 1½m) Hawkster, and half-brother to 3
winners: dam never ran: narrowly won 4-runner listed event at Deauville: best
effort over 5 lengths third of 8 to Arazi in Prix de la Salamandre at Longchamp in
September: below form when last in Grand Criterium there following month: should
stay 1m: very useful. *A. Fabre, France.*

SILVERNESIAN (USA) 2 b. or br.c. (Mar 21) Alleged (USA) 138 – Loot (USA) **69** p
(Boldnesian) [1991 8g⁶] leggy, good-topped colt: has scope: brother to 1984 French
2-y-o 1¼m winner Treasure Map and half-brother to Native Plunder (by Exclusive
Native), fair winner at up to 9f in USA: dam won at up to 9f: 20/1 and very green,
around 13 lengths sixth of 16 to Aljadeer in minor event at Newbury in October,
wandering in rear then staying on well from 2f out: will improve. *J. L. Dunlop.*

SILVER RAINBOW 3 b.c. Rainbow Quest (USA) 134 – Aryenne (FR) 125 **110**
(Green Dancer (USA) 132) [1990 NR 1991 12m² 16.2g² 14g* 16g4] tall, close-
coupled, quite attractive colt: moderate walker: fourth foal: brother to Derby winner
Quest For Fame and half-brother to 1¼m winner In Orbit (by Habitat): dam from
fine family, won French 1000 Guineas: 9/1 on, made all in 4-runner maiden at
Nottingham in July: beaten neck by Jendali and little over length behind Further
Flight in Queen's Vase at Royal Ascot and Goodwood Cup second and final starts:
looks an out-and-out stayer: lazy, and not an easy ride, but game. *G. Harwood.*

SILVER SAMURAI 2 b.c. (Feb 10) Alleging (USA) 120 – Be My Lady (Be My **64**
Guest (USA) 126) [1991 5f⁴ 8m⁴ 6m³ 7d⁴ a7g⁴ a8g⁶] 5,000Y: second live foal:
half-brother to French 4-y-o 12.5f winner Arduous (by Ardross): dam little
worthwhile form: quite modest maiden: ran moderately last 2 starts: stays 1m: has
run creditably for claimer. *R. Hollinshead.*

SILVER SINGING (USA) 4 gr.f. Topsider (USA) – Early Rising (USA) (Grey **94**
Dawn II 132) [1990 5m* 7v⁵ 5.8h 7.3m 5.8m⁴ 5f* 5f* 5f* 5g* 5.6g 5m 5m 1991 5.1g⁵
5m² 5g² 6g 5g⁵ 6g⁴ 6g] leggy, good-topped filly: moderate mover: fairly useful
handicapper: stays 6f: acts on firm going: below form when blinkered once: has run
well when sweating: probably best held up: consistent: reportedly in foal. *I. A.
Balding.*

SILVER STONE BOY 3 gr.c. Another Realm 118 – Elkie Brooks 82 (Relkino **50**
131) [1990 5m 1991 5f 6f⁴ 5m⁴ 5g] workmanlike, good-quartered colt: poor maiden:
last of 16 in handicap final start: should stay beyond 5f: hung left second start. *A.
Smith.*

SILVER STRINGS 11 b.g. Blakeney 126 – Melody Hour 105 (Sing Sing 134) —
[1990 NR 1991 a14g 16m 14m 14g] rangy gelding: poor staying handicapper: acts on
firm going: has been bandaged. *B. Palling.*

SILVER WISP (USA) 2 b.c. (Feb 8) Silver Hawk (USA) 123 – La Ninouchka **102** p
(USA) (Bombay Duck (USA)) [1991 6d⁵ 7d* 7g* 7f*] $28,000F, $65,000Y: strong
colt: progressed well physically: has scope: brother to French 4-y-o 12.3f winner
Mutual Destiny and half-brother to a minor winner in USA: dam winner at up to 9f:
successful in maiden at Salisbury in June and 4-runner minor event at Chester in
July: won 6-runner £5,900 event at former course 5 weeks later by 5 lengths from
Green's Colourist, soon disputing lead, leading 2f out and staying on very well: will
be better suited by 1m: was progressing very well. *G. Lewis.*

SILVIO ALFREDO (USA) 2 b.c. (Mar 2) Groovy (USA) – Magic Glove (USA) **96**
(The Minstrel (CAN) 135) [1991 6g⁴ 6g³ 6m* 6g⁴ 6g⁴ 6m⁵ 7s] 480,000Y: strong
colt: second foal: dam, ran twice, from family of Shareef Dancer: sire top-class
sprinter: fairly useful performer: won maiden at Newmarket in July: faced stiff tasks
afterwards, running really well when fifth of 8, staying on strongly having been
outpaced, in listed race at York, then below form in Group 3 race at Milan: should be
better suited by 7f than 6f: possibly unsuited by very soft ground. *C. E. Brittain.*

SIMMIE'S SPECIAL 3 b.f. Precocious 126 – Zalatia 97 (Music Boy 124) [1990 **75**
5m² 5f² 5d² 1991 5g² 5g* 6m⁵ 5m⁴ 5m⁴ 5m⁶ 5f² 5.1g 5d³ 5d³] angular filly: modest
performer: won maiden at Thirsk in May: ran moderately at Chester eighth start,
creditably afterwards at Haydock and Doncaster: should prove best at 5f: yet to race
on soft ground, probably acts on any other: carries head awkwardly, and tends to
hang. *R. Hollinshead.*

SIMON ELLIS (IRE) 2 ch.g. (Feb 12) Magical Wonder (USA) 125 – Rose In **47**
Time (Hello Gorgeous (USA) 128) [1991 5g⁴ 6g 5.3f 7m 6m 7g a8g⁶] leggy,
sparely-made gelding: second foal: dam never ran: poor form in maidens and sellers:
stays 7f: visored fifth start: trained until after third outing by R. Hannon. *D. R.
Laing.*

SIMONOV 2 br.c. (Mar 21) Rousillon (USA) 133 – Simova (USA) (Vaguely Noble **67** P
140) [1991 8m] quite attractive colt: first foal: dam French maiden, sister to smart
middle distance filly Vidor: weak 25/1-shot, shaped promisingly, running on into
mid-division having been steadied stalls, in 22-runner maiden at Newmarket in
October won by Bold Pursuit: wasn't knocked about, and left impression capable of
considerably better. *G. Harwood.*

SIMPLE TRUTH 4 b.f. Known Fact (USA) 135 – Northern Ballerina 52 (Dance **56**
In Time (CAN)) [1990 5m² 6g² 5s 5d a5g⁵ 1991 a5g⁶ 5.2m⁴ 5f⁶ 5m 5f⁶] small,
lengthy filly: moderate walker and mover: plating-class maiden: stays 6f: acts on
good to firm ground, seems unsuited by soft surface. *M. Johnston.*

SIMPLY AFLAME 3 ch.f. Simply Great (FR) 122 – Grange Fire (Allangrange **70**
126) [1990 NR 1991 10.2s³ 11.9f² 11.4m⁶ 11.7g 16.1g] 5,000Y: workmanlike filly:
seventh foal: half-sister to a winner in Norway: dam unraced sister to smart Irish
1¼m and 1½m winner Abednego and half-sister to Deep Run and to dam of One In A
Million: placed in small-field maidens, best effort but given hard race at Brighton
second start: well beaten in minor event (stiffish task) and handicaps: stays 1½m. *D.
W. P. Arbuthnot.*

SIMPLY DES 4 b.f. Simply Great (FR) 122 – Kashida 68 (Green Dancer (USA) **—** §
132) [1990 12f⁴ 8m³ 12f 10m 10m 12f² 9g 12f² 10f 12g a 12g a 13g 1991 12f⁵ 11.5m⁶ 12m
10m] neat filly: had a round action: poor handicapper: stayed 1½m: acted on firm
going, possibly unsuited by soft: tried visored once: was probably temperamental:
dead. *J. O'Donoghue.*

SIMPLY GEORGE 2 b.c. (May 8) Simply Great (FR) 122 – Grand Occasion 63 **77**
(Great Nephew 126) [1991 5m⁵ 7g² 7g* 7g⁴ 7m⁶ 8m³ 9m* 8g] 13,000Y: leggy,
angular colt: second foal: half-brother to 1¼m and 1½m winner Tiger Shoot (by
Indian King): dam, sometimes bad at start, is out of staying daughter of St Leger
second None Nicer: modest performer: successful in maiden at Brighton in July and
nursery at Sandown in September: ran moderately in Warwick nursery following
month: will be well suited by 1½m: acts on good to firm ground. *R. Boss.*

SIMPLY-H (IRE) 2 b.g. (Feb 19) Simply Great (FR) 122 – Coupe d'Hebe 87 (Ile **65**
de Bourbon (USA) 133) [1991 5g² 5m⁴ 7g² 7m⁶] IR 8,600Y: neat gelding: second
foal: dam won only start, over 1m at 2 yrs: quite modest form when second in minor
event at Windsor and maiden auction (ran on well after troubled run, beaten head) at
Doncaster: otherwise ran moderately, when appearing well handicapped in nursery
at Brighton final start: will be suited by middle distances: best form on good ground,
and on flat tracks. *M. Bell.*

SINCLAIR BOY 5 b.g. Aragon 118 – Amber Flyer 91 (Amber Rama (USA) 133) **65** ?
[1990 10.8f* 8g⁴ 10m 10g² 10f⁴ 10f* 12f⁶ a 12g* 10.2m* a 10g 1991 10m² 10.4d 10.8m⁴

12m 12g 12f⁴ 11.7f] rather leggy, attractive gelding: plating-class handicapper nowadays: effective at 1¼m to 1½m: acts on firm and dead going: usually apprentice ridden: inconsistent: not one to trust. *B. W. Hills.*

SINCLAIR LAD (IRE) 3 ch.c. Muscatite 122 – Kitty Frisk 64 (Prince **67** Tenderfoot (USA) 126) [1990 7m⁶ 6d² 1991 9s³ 8.2d⁵ 10.4d⁶ 8m³ 11m⁴ 9g⁴ 7.6g⁴ 10f⁵ 10g* 11m⁶ 8m] leggy, quite good-topped colt: poor walker and mover: modest performer: won handicap at Pontefract in July, edging left: needs further than 1m, and stays 1¼m: acts on good to firm ground: visored (stiff task, always behind) tenth start. *R. Hollinshead.*

SINCLAIR PRINCE 4 ch.g. Local Suitor (USA) 128 – Mothers Girl — (Huntercombe 133) [1990 6f³ 7m⁴ 8m 7.6g 7g⁶ 8f³ 1991 9s] light-framed gelding: plating-class maiden at best: well beaten only run in 1991 (April): stays 7f: acts on firm ground: sold 1,650 gns Doncaster Spring Sales. *J. Parkes.*

SING ANOTHER 2 ch.f. (May 18) Chief Singer 131 – Another Move 69 (Farm — Walk 111) [1991 6m 7m 8m] 5,200Y: fifth foal: half-sister to 3-y-o 12.4f to 17.9f winner My Desire (by Grey Desire), 1½m and 14.6f winner Tancred Sand (by Nicholas Bill) and 5f and 7f winner Ela-Yianni-Mou (by Anfield): dam 1½m winner, is sister to very useful middle-distance stayer Move Off: poor maiden: should prove suited by 1¼m + . *Mrs G. R. Reveley.*

SINGERS IMAGE 2 br.g. (Apr 8) Chief Singer 131 – Little White Lies 78 **72** (Runnett 125) [1991 5g 6d 6d 6g⁵ 7f 7.3m] workmanlike gelding: easy mover: first foal: dam, maiden stayed 1m, is half-sister to very useful middle-distance filly So True: quite modest maiden: off course 5 weeks, tailed off in nursery at Newbury final outing: better suited by 7f than shorter. *G. B. Balding.*

SINGH HOLME 4 br.g. Mansingh (USA) 120 – Ivy Holme (Silly Season 127) — [1990 5g² 5.3h² 5m 5f 7g a5g a5g⁵ 1991 a7g a7g 5.2f 6g 10.1s] sparely-made gelding: seems of little account nowadays: sold 600 gns Ascot November Sales. *S. T. Harris.*

SINGING DETECTIVE 4 g.g. Absalom 128 – Smoke Creek 67 (Habitat 134) **32** [1990 7f 10g 9f 10g 12g³ a14g² 16g 15v 9s a16g 1991 a14g a8g 8g 10m⁴ a12g 11.8g] rangy, rather angular gelding: moderate walker and mover: has a round action: poor handicapper, still a maiden: stays 1¾m: acts on any going: tried blinkered. *M. Brittain.*

SINGING NELLY 3 b.f. Pharly (FR) 130 – Nelly Do Da 78 (Derring-Do 131) **56** [1990 NR 1991 7.1m³ 8s⁶ a8g⁴ a7g] 7,200Y: rather unfurnished filly: moderate mover: seventh foal: half-sister to several winners, including useful 7f (at 2 yrs) to 2½m winner Retouch (by Touching Wood): dam 2-y-o 5.8f winner: quite modest maiden: favourite but stiff task in Southwell handicap final start: best form at 7f. *B. W. Hills.*

SINGING REPLY (USA) 3 b.f. The Minstrel (CAN) 135 – Bright Reply (USA) **67** (Gleaming (USA)) [1990 NR 1991 8m 10g⁴ 12.3d² 12.2g³ 12.2m⁵ a12g] leggy, unfurnished filly: half-sister to 3 winners in USA: dam ran 3 times: quite modest maiden: bandaged behind, placed at Ripon and (making most) Catterick: ran moderately in Southwell handicap: stays 1½m: acts on dead ground: sold D. Marks 3,800 gns Newmarket December Sales. *J. H. M. Gosden.*

SINGING SARAH 3 b.f. Mansingh (USA) 120 – Fressingfield (Riboboy (USA) — 124) [1990 6m 5m 5m⁶ 1991 7g 11.7m 10.2f 5.1m] workmanlike filly: poor maiden. *J. D. Roberts.*

SINGING STAR 5 b.g. Crooner 119 – Wild Jewel (Great Heron (USA) 126) [1990 **89** 6f* 5f³ 6m 5f⁶ 6m 6f⁵ 5f* 5m⁵ 5g² 5g 5f* 5m² 5m 5m⁴ 5s 1991 5f⁵ 5m* 5g⁵ 5f* 5f 5m³ 5g 5m⁵ 5m 5f⁴ 5m] close-coupled gelding: carries plenty of condition: fair handicapper: won in May at Doncaster and Redcar: ran very well in listed event at Doncaster ninth start: failed to confirm that, last at York final start: worth another try over 6f: best on top-of-the-ground: often slowly away: has worn blinkers, but not when successful: sometimes bandaged. *J. Balding.*

SING OUT (FR) 3 b.c. Auction Ring (USA) 123 – Manora (USA) (Stop The **75** Music (USA)) [1990 6m⁴ 6g² a6g* 6m² 7m 1991 8g⁵ 8g 7f 7.6m 7d] quite good-topped colt: has a quick action: fair performer at best: generally disappointing in handicaps: stays 1m: sold 8,000 gns Newmarket Autumn Sales. *C. R. Nelson.*

SING THE BLUES 7 b.g. Blue Cashmere 129 – Pulcini 61 (Quartette 106) [1990 — a16g³ 15.5f⁵ 17.1f⁵ a16g³ a16g 1991 16.5m] big, lengthy gelding: poor handicapper: not seen out after May: should stay beyond 2m: acts on firm going: winning hurdler in January, 1991. *C. J. Benstead.*

SIOBHAN MARIE 5 b.m. Lochnager 132 – Kilroe's Calin (Be Friendly 130) [1990 NR 1991 a11g a8g] angular mare: first foal: dam soundly beaten on flat, won over hurdles: well beaten in early-season maidens at Southwell. *M. C. Pipe.* —

SIOUX PERFICK 2 b.f. (Feb 1) Blakeney 126 – Siouxsie 90 (Warpath 113) [1991 6g4 7m 7m] half-sister to several winners by Mandrake Major, including 1m winner Last Stand and fairly useful 1983 2-y-o Sajeda, and to unreliable 9f seller winner Pretty Precocious (by Precocious): dam 2-y-o 6f winner: poor maiden: best effort final start: will be suited by further. *C. W. Thornton.* 43

SIPSI FACH 3 br.f. Prince Sabo 123 – Miskin 58 (Star Appeal 133) [1990 6g3 6g* 7m* 7f4 7g* 8g4 7.5g2 1991 8g5 8v5 10g4 10.4g* 11.9m 10.7g 8.9g 10m5] lengthy, angular, rather sparely-made filly: useful performer: won 5-runner listed race at York in June, setting slow early pace: mostly stiff tasks after, returning to form when 6 lengths last of 5 to Ristna in Sun Chariot Stakes (again set modest pace) at Newmarket: suited by 1¼m: possibly unsuited by extremes of going: suitable mount for a claimer: game. *M. Bell.* 100

SIR ALFRED (USA) 6 ch.g. Riverman (USA) 131 – Miss Lilian (FR) (Lyphard (USA) 132) [1990 NR 1991 12f] ex-Irish gelding: second foal: dam won over 11f in France: trained by T. Kinane, placed over 2m at Tipperary and Down Royal as 4-y-o: always behind in Thirsk claimer in September, first run here. *J. K. Kinane.* —

SIR ARTHUR HOBBS 4 b.g. Lyphard's Special (USA) 124 – Song Grove 61 (Song 132) [1990 8v5 7f 7m 6m 6d 6d 8g 7d 6s 7d 1991 6d 6s a7g 6g 8m 8.1m2 8g* 8.1m* 8.2f 8g6 6d 6.1m2 a8g2] strong gelding: moderate mover: quite modest handicapper nowadays: won at Ayr and Haydock in summer: effective at 6f to 1m: acts on good to firm and dead ground and fibresand: has 3 times refused to enter stalls, including when blinkered once at 3 yrs: tried visored. *F. H. Lee.* 62

SIR BANCROFT 3 b.c. Chukaroo 103 – State Romance 67 (Free State 125) [1990 6g4 5m* 7f5 6m 7m5 7d 1991 7d 7m 8g6 8d* 9m2 9m3 8g4 8.9m 8m 10.5g 8g5] lengthy colt: moderate mover: modest handicapper: won at Newbury in May: best effort last 4 starts when fair fifth at Salisbury: stays 9f: acts on good to firm ground and dead: visored (ran moderately) eighth start: genuine. *E. Eldin.* 73

SIR BEDIVERE (USA) 3 ch.c. Northern Baby (CAN) 127 – Foolish Lady (USA) (Foolish Pleasure (USA)) [1990 NR 1991 8.1s2 10m6 9m3 10.2f4 10g] robust colt with scope: second foal: brother to fairly useful but inconsistent 9f winner Scottish Jester: dam maiden half-sister to Dancing Brave: modest maiden on his day: should stay 1¼m +: best effort on soft ground: tongue tied down last 3 starts: looks a hard ride: one to have reservations about. *G. Harwood.* 69

SIR BOUDLE (IRE) 2 b.c. (Feb 6) Double Schwartz 128 – Marqueterie (USA) (Well Decorated (USA)) [1991 5m 6m4 6d*] 14,000F, IR 14,500Y: compact, sprint 68

Daniel Prenn Royal Yorkshire Stakes, York—
Sipsi Fach (rails) is shrewdly ridden in a very slowly-run race;
Cooley's Valve, Flashfoot and Claret are on her outside

type: has a quick action: first foal: dam, no worthwhile form, is daughter of lightly-raced half-sister to high-class Royal Orbit: 11/4, narrowly won 4-runner maiden at Brighton in June, leading halfway and keeping on well. *C. R. Nelson.*

SIR DANCELOT (USA)   3 b.g. Far North (CAN) 120 – Princess Morvi (USA) **77** d
(Graustark) [1990 NR 1991 11.7m² 12f³ 12m⁵ 13.1f 12.1g⁶ 9m] 60,000Y: big gelding: brother to French 9f and 10.5f winner Jolie Spectacle and half-brother to 4 winners, notably Japan Cup winner Pay The Butler and very smart 1½m to 16.2f winner River God (both by Val de L'Orne): dam French 1m and 11f winner: modest maiden, easily best effort on debut: reportedly swallowed tongue second start: wore tongue strap next: trained first 3 starts by G. Harwood. *R. Simpson.*

SIR DANIK (USA)   3 b. or br.c. Danzig Connection (USA) – Miss Hatco (USA) **82**
(Damascus (USA) 86) [1990 NR 1991 8d⁴ 10m⁴ 11.7m 8g³ 10g 8.2f* 8m³ 9f² 8.9g² 9m² 11.9m] IR 60,000Y: good-topped colt with scope: impresses in appearance: carries condition: moderate mover: half-brother to 2 winners in USA: dam unraced: sire won Belmont Stakes: fair handicapper: 20/1, made all at Nottingham in July: mostly ran well afterwards: may well stay 1¼m, doesn't stay 1½m: acts on firm going: ran poorly when sweating: goes well with forcing tactics: sold 19,000 gns Newmarket Autumn Sales. *F. H. Lee.*

SIR GEORGE CHUFFY (IRE)   3 b.g. Welsh Term 126 – Grand Legacy 56 **75**
(Relko 136) [1990 NR 1991 10g³ 10.5m³ 10.4g 13.1m 8d] 5,000F, 5,000Y: leggy, good-topped gelding with scope: fourth foal: brother to a winner in Italy: dam plating-class maiden suited by 1½m+: modest maiden: well beaten, in handicaps last 2 starts: needs further than 1m, and is bred to stay 1½m. *F. H. Lee.*

SIR HARRY HARDMAN   3 b.c. Doulab (USA) 115 – Song Grove 61 (Song 132) **102**
[1990 5f⁴ 5g* 5f² 5g* 5g² 5g² 5d² 6d* 6d 1991 6m⁵ 5g² 6g⁴ 5m 5m⁵ 5g 5g⁴ 5m⁵] strong, good-quartered colt: carries condition: impresses in appearance: moderate mover: useful sprinter: in frame for Palace House Stakes at Newmarket and Duke of York Stakes at York second and third starts: blinkered, creditable fifth in listed race at Doncaster final start, leading over 2f out until hanging markedly left approaching last: stays 6f: acts on firm and dead ground: game and genuine. *F. H. Lee.*

SIRMOOR (IRE)   2 b.c. (Apr 6) Try My Best (USA) 130 – Muted Song (Artaius **45** p
(USA) 129) [1991 6g] IR 7,800Y: tall, close-coupled colt: second living foal: dam unraced half-sister to very useful 1977 2-y-o Royal Harmony: 33/1 and green, around 17 lengths tenth of 21 to Katakana in maiden at Newbury in October, unable to quicken 2f out, not knocked about: looks sort to do better in due course. *R. Hannon.*

SIR NORMAN HOLT (IRE)   2 b.c. (Apr 8) Ela-Mana-Mou 132 – Ploy 87 **—**
(Posse (USA) 130) [1991 8m⁶ 7g] IR 21,000Y: quite good-topped, angular colt: first foal: dam maiden stayed 1½m, is half-sister to Sun Princess and smart 1m to 1¼m winner Dancing Shadow: poor form, soundly beaten, in 6-runner minor event at Newbury and maiden at Salisbury in autumn: bred to stay at least 1¼m. *F. H. Lee.*

SIR OLIVER (IRE)   2 b.g. (Feb 9) Auction Ring (USA) 123 – Euroroe (Busted **03** p
134) [1991 0d³] 1,900Y, 7,000 2-y-o: good-topped gelding: has scope: second foal: dam never ran: 16/1, backward and green, 1½ lengths third of 9, staying on well under very considerate handling, to King Cycle in maiden at Goodwood in October: showed a round action: will improve. *J. Sutcliffe.*

SIR PAGEANT   2 b.c. (Feb 8) Pharly (FR) 130 – National Dress 64 (Welsh **70** p
Pageant 132) [1991 a8g²] 18,000Y: third foal: half-brother to 3-y-o Top It All (by Song) and 1989 2-y-o 6f winner Platinum Dancer (by Petorius), later successful in France: dam, 12.2f winner, is out of half-sister to Connaught: co-favourite, 2 lengths second of 13, staying on dourly, to Citiqueen in maiden at Southwell: will improve. *P. F. I. Cole.*

SIR SLINGSBY   2 b. or br.g. (Mar 30) Lidhame 109 – Susie's Baby (Balidar 133) **50**
[1991 5d⁵ 5m 5.2f] 11,500Y: small gelding: has a quick action: fourth foal: brother to 3-y-o 5f winner Sir Tasker and half-brother to two 2-y-o 5f winners by Kafu: dam lightly raced: poor maiden: sold 525 gns Ascot October Sales. *M. Bell.*

SIR TASKER   3 b.c. Lidhame 109 – Susie's Baby (Balidar 133) [1990 5d³ 5m 5.1g⁵ **60**
1991 5s 5.8m 8m⁶ 7m⁴ 7g 7g⁵ 7f⁴ 7m 6m 6m² 5g³ 6.1m 5d* 5g 5s a6g⁶ a5g* a5g a5g²] compact, quite attractive colt: quite modest handicapper: won at Wolverhampton in October and Lingfield in December: best at sprint distances: acts on firm and dead going: sold out of M. Bell's stable, 1,550 gns Newmarket July Sales after sixth start: suited by forcing tactics: inconsistent. *J. L. Harris.*

SIRTELIMAR (IRE)   2 b.c. (Feb 24) Montelimar (USA) 122 – Sajanjal (Dance **46** p
In Time (CAN)) [1991 7m] 8,000Y: half-brother to 3 winners in USA: dam unraced

half-sister to useful Irish 7f to 1¼m winner Toca Madera: 33/1, prominent 5f then squeezed and dropped right away in 20-runner maiden at Newmarket in October: will do better. *E. Eldin.*

SIR VALID (USA)   2 ch.g. (Jan 29) Valid Appeal (USA) – Asir (USA) (Exclusive   **81** Native (USA)) [1991 5d³ 5g³ 6f⁴ 5.1g* 5.1m³ 5g⁶ 5.3m*] $20,000Y: lengthy, good-quartered gelding: easy mover: first known foal: dam, minor winner at 3 yrs, is out of sister to dam of 6f to 8.5f stakes winner Raise A Man: sire won from 6f to 9f: fair performer: made all in maiden at Bath (for 5-lb claimer) in June and nursery at Brighton (blinkered and edgy, ran on well under very hard riding) in August: should stay 6f. *W. A. O'Gorman.*

SIR VIDAR (IRE)   2 b.c. (Feb 17) Caerleon (USA) 132 – Very Charming (USA)   **62** p (Vaguely Noble 140) [1991 8s⁴ 8.1d⁴] 45,000F, 56,000Y: big colt: has scope: moderate mover: closely related to a winner in France by Green Dancer and half-brother to several winners, notably smart 1¼m winner Theatrical Charmer (by Sadler's Wells): dam, French 10.5f winner, is sister to Dahlia: over 5 lengths fourth of 10, soon off bridle, kept on well, to Trafalgar Boy in maiden at Haydock in October: will improve again, particularly over further. *M. Bell.*

SI SAWAT   4 ch.g. Superlative 118 – Soft Chinook (USA) (Hitting Away) [1990   — a8g⁶ a5g⁵ 6m 8f² 8m* 8m⁵ 9f 8d 1991 7f 8m 8g 7m 8g 7f⁵] strong, deep-girthed gelding: carried condition: quite modest handicapper at 3 yrs: well below best in 1991: stayed 1m: acted on firm going: wore crossed noseband once: tried visored: dead. *M. Avison.*

SISTADARI   3 b.f. Shardari 134 – Sistabelle (Bellypha 130) [1990 NR 1991 10m³   **84** 9g² 10m³ 7m²] angular filly: first foal: dam unraced sister to Bella Colora and half-sister to Colorspin: fair maiden: should prove ideally suited by further than 7f, and stays 1¼m: edged left and swished tail second start. *L. M. Cumani.*

SISTER BRIDGET (IRE)   2 gr.f. (Apr 6) Hawkin's Special (USA) – North   — Spain (USA) (Far North (CAN) 120) [1991 6m 7s⁴ 7m] IR 3,000Y: half-sister to a winner in USA: dam ran 5 times: sire sprinter: no worthwhile form in varied company, when backed at long odds in seller at Lingfield second start: subsequently off course over 10 weeks. *Miss B. Sanders.*

SISTER SAL   4 ch.f. Bairn (USA) 126 – Mercy Cure 81 (No Mercy 126) [1990 6m   — 7m 8f 8.3m 8g⁴ 8g 9m⁴ 10m² 10d a8g⁵ 1991 a10g] lengthy filly: poor handicapper: not seen out after January: stays 1¼m: acts on firm ground: tried visored once: often sweats: sold 2,800 gns Ascot February Sales: inconsistent. *J. Sutcliffe.*

SIXOFUS (IRE)   3 b. or br.g. Glenstal (USA) 118 – Grace Darling (USA)   **58** (Vaguely Noble 140) [1990 6m² 5d⁴ 6m⁶ 6m* 5d⁶ 1991 6v² 6d⁶ 5m⁵ 5.1g³ 6f² 5f 7g² 6m³ 6f⁵ 8m* 8m 9.7s] leggy, rather angular gelding: has a quick action: quite modest performer nowadays: won claimer at Leicester in September, leading 2f out: stays 1m: acts on good to firm ground and dead: joined W. G. M. Turner. *R. Boss.*

SIZZLING AFFAIR   2 b.c. (May 14) Sizzling Melody 117 – Vivchar 80   **37** (Huntercombe 133) [1991 6.1g⁵ 7g 6f] seventh foal: half-brother to a winner in USA by Sallust: dam 2-y-o 5f winner: poor form, well beaten, in maidens: probably stays 7f. *T. Casey.*

SIZZLING ROSE   2 b.f. (Apr 17) Sizzling Melody 117 – Garnette Rose 74   **49** (Floribunda 136) [1991 5m 5g³ 6g⁴ 6g⁵ 5s³ 5g² 6m 5m 7m a6g] 4,100Y: leggy, sparely-made filly: moderate mover: half-sister to several winners here and abroad, including 3-y-o 6f and 7f winner Surrey Racing (by Electric) and fairly useful 1985 2-y-o 5f winner Camilla's Boy (by Faraway Times): dam seemed to stay 1m: poor maiden: good second to Mamma's Too in mid-summer nursery at Leicester: lost form last 3 starts: stays 6f: possibly suited by an easy surface. *W. Carter.*

SIZZLING SAGA (IRE)   3 b. or br.c. Horage 124 – Alsazia (FR) (Bolkonski   **108** 134) [1990 5s⁵ a6g⁶ 5m* 5m* 5g³ 5f³ 5m² 6d* 1991 5g³ 6f² 6d* 6m⁵ 6f* 6m* 6m* 6g² 6.5s* 6s⁴ 6d⁶ 5m] strong, sturdy colt: poor mover: useful performer: successful in minor events (short-priced favourite) at Nottingham, Folkestone and Redcar, £10,900 handicap at Newcastle and listed race at Munich: better at around 6f than 5f: acts on any going: goes well with forcing tactics. *J. Berry.*

SKERRY MEADOW   7 b.g. Anfield 117 – Mi Tia 79 (Great Nephew 126) [1990   — NR 1991 22.2m] compact gelding: out of depth only start in 1991, first on flat since 3-y-o: won hunter chase in May. *W. R. Williams.*

SKI CAPTAIN   7 b.g. Welsh Captain 113 – Miss Nelski 84 (Most Secret 119)   **69** [1990 5f⁴ 5f 5f 5m 5g 5m⁶ 5g⁶ 5m⁴ 5m² 6m 5m 5f² 5m 5d 5m 1991 5g 5m 5m 5g 4g 5m* 5f 5g 5g* 5m³ 5.2g 5m⁶ 5m 5g³ 5.1m 5m² 5g 5.1s 5g a5g] strong, workmanlike gelding: usually looks well: moderate mover: modest handicapper at best nowadays: won at Lingfield in May and Kempton in July: inconsistent after: suited by 5f: acts on any going: has run well when blinkered or visored, but hasn't worn them since 1987: has won for apprentice. *P. Howling.*

SKI CHIEF (USA) 3 b.c. Chief's Crown – Ski Goggle (Royal Ski) [1990 6.5d 7s⁵ **115** 1991 7s² 7m³ 6d5 6s⁶ 6s* 5d*] third foal: half-brother to a winner in USA by Caro: dam won Grade 1 Acorn Stakes at 3 yrs: showed improved form when winning Prix du Petit Couvert at Longchamp in October by ¾ length from demoted Dream Talk: successful also in handicap at Maisons-Laffitte 2 weeks earlier, and placed in spring in maiden at Maisons-Laffitte and Prix du Palais-Royal at Longchamp: off course 3½ months after third start: best form over sprint distances: acts on soft going. *A. Fabre, France.*

SKI DANCER 3 b.c. Dancing Brave (USA) 140 – Ski Sailing (USA) 115 (Royal Ski **75** (USA)) [1990 8s 1991 10.2s 10m 10g⁵ 11.7m⁴ 12f² 12g⁵ 11.9g] tall colt: modest maiden: bandaged and bit backward, no promise on final start, first for 3 months: should stay further: acts on firm going: has hung left, badly so third start: sold 6,000 gns Newmarket Autumn Sales. *D. R. C. Elsworth.*

SKIFFLE 3 b.f. Niniski (USA) 125 – Fleet Girl (Habitat 134) [1990 7m 1991 10.2g **67** 16m² 14m² 17.2g³] lengthy, unfurnished filly: quite modest maiden: creditable third of 14 in handicap (always front rank) at Bath: will prove suited by test of stamina. *B. W. Hills.*

SKIMBLE (USA) 2 ch.f. (Apr 1) Lyphard (USA) 132 – Nimble Folly (USA) **78** p (Cyane) [1991 6m*] useful-looking filly: eighth foal: closely related to several winners, including useful 1989 sprinting 2-y-o Old Alliance and good American 2-y-o Contredance (both by Danzig): dam unraced sister to useful Misgivings: well-backed favourite, won 14-runner maiden at Newmarket in October by ¾ length from Fermoy, leading over 1f out and staying on strongly: moved fluently down: will stay further: will improve. *H. R. A. Cecil.*

SKIP-A-NOTE 3 b.f. Noalto 120 – Hey Skip (USA) (Bold Skipper (USA)) [1990 — NR 1991 10s] 2,000Y: lengthy filly: fifth live foal: half-sister to modest 8.2f and 9f winner Foremast (by Forli): dam won 5 races in USA: 33/1 and in need of race, never dangerous in claimer at Kempton in August. *R. Curtis.*

SKIPLAM WOOD 5 b.m. Cree Song 99 – Mab (Morston (FR) 125) [1990 8m 7m — 1991 8g 11m⁵] compact, plain mare: turns fore-feet in: poor mover: poor maiden at best: stays 7f: keen sort, has worn crossed noseband: not an easy ride: sold 3,900 gns Doncaster October Sales. *D. Lee.*

SKIPPER TO BILGE 4 b.g. Night Shift (USA) – Upper Deck 115 (Sun Prince **75** 128) [1990 8.2s² 8v² 8.2g* 10.6d 10s⁵ 8g4 1991 8g⁵ 8v 8d* 7m 7g 7.6d* 7.6s⁴ 7s* 7d] lengthy, rather angular gelding: modest handicapper: won at Wolverhampton in April, Lingfield (claimer) in June and Kempton in September: effective at 7f, and probably stays 1¼m: goes very well with some give in the ground (acts on heavy going): goes well with forcing tactics: inconsistent. *M. A. Jarvis.*

SKIP TRACER 3 b.g. Balliol 125 – Song To Singo 63 (Master Sing 109) [1990 8g — 7v⁵ 1991 7f⁴ 8g 7f⁵ 10m 8m 8m] close-coupled, angular gelding: poor maiden on

Schweppes Golden Mile (Handicap), Goodwood—
Sky Cloud (No. 12) sustains his run to collar Parliament Piece in the last strides
as Scatter (No. 5) makes ground on both

most form: should stay 1m: acts on firm going: blinkered and wore crossed noseband final start: joined K. Ivory. *J. Etherington.*

SKOLERN 7 b.g. Lochnager 132 – Piethorne 86 (Fine Blade (USA) 121) [1990 8f3   **43**
8h 8f 1991 a8g 9m5 8m] rather leggy, good-topped gelding: quite modest
handicapper at best, not so good nowadays: effective at 7f and 1m: acts on any going:
tried in visor and blinkers: winning hurdler. *A. Harrison.*

SKY CAT 7 b.g. Skyliner 117 – Spring Kitten (Pitcairn 126) [1990 a12g a11g 1991   **55**
12m 8g2 9m2 7m* 7f6 8.2g4 7m5 8.2m 8.3f2 8f] leggy, good-topped gelding: won
selling event (bought in 3,100 gns) at Edinburgh in June: stays 9f: probably acts on
any going: effective blinkered or not: sometimes sweats: keen sort, seems best with
strong handling: has found less than seemed likely, and best with extreme waiting
tactics. *M. H. Easterby.*

SKY CLOUD 5 ch.g. Formidable (USA) 125 – Cloud Nine 97 (Skymaster 126) **104**
[1990 6f 7f4 7f 7g5 6m2 6m* 6m 7.3g6 6d3 6s3 6d* 6s 1991 6d2 7d* 7.6d4 7f5 8g*
8m* 7d2] small, stocky gelding: much improved handicapper in 1991: won Insulpak
Victoria Cup at Ascot in May, Schweppes Golden Mile at Goodwood in August and
£23,300 event at Doncaster (beat Mellottie 2½ lengths) in September: good second
of 29 to Night Jar in £80,000 Tap And Spile (Handicap) at Ascot, leading 1f out but
hanging badly right: best at 7f/1m: acts on good to firm and dead ground: has been
bandaged off-hind: sold 56,000 gns Newmarket Autumn Sales and reportedly to race
in Riyadh: credit to his trainer. *R. Akehurst.*

SKY HUNTER (USA) 2 b. or br.c. (Mar 25) Star de Naskra (USA) – Hunt The   **77**
Thimble (USA) 86 (Turn And Count (USA)) [1991 7m2 7g4 8m5] $100,000Y: tall,
rather leggy colt: brother to useful Irish sprinter Astraeus: dam placed twice at 6f
(at 2 yrs) from 4 starts here and won at up to 1m in USA: modest maiden: off course 7
weeks and bandaged behind, creditable fifth of 19 at Doncaster in September, one
pace final 2f: stays 1m. *R. Hannon.*

SKY PROSPECT 3 b.g. Damister (USA) 123 – November Sky (Martinmas 128)   **72**
[1990 NR 1991 11g 12m3 13.9m3 12.3m2 11.9g 16.1g] leggy, unfurnished gelding:
third foal: half-brother to a winner in Scandinavia by Touching Wood: dam, Irish
1½m winner, is half-sister to very smart 1981 French 2-y-o sprinter Maelstrom
Lake: modest maiden: pulled up lame final start: should have been suited by further
than 1½m: hung left: gelded after running fairly well in blinkers fourth start: dead.
R. Charlton.

SKY SENTRY (USA) 3 b.c. Silver Hawk (USA) 123 – Guardesse (FR) (Home   **70**
Guard (USA) 129) [1990 NR 1991 10m3 10d5 11m3 11.5g3 12.3m3 12s] $90,000Y:
workmanlike colt: second foal: dam winner from 6f to 9f in France and USA: modest
maiden: visored, fair eighth of 19 in apprentice handicap (moved poorly down) final
start: should stay well: acts on good to firm ground. *J. H. M. Gosden.*

SKY TRAIN (IRE) 2 gr.f. (Apr 6) Siberian Express (USA) 125 – Karietta   **68**
(Wollow 132) [1991 7m 7f3 7m5] lengthy filly: has scope: third foal: half-sister to fair
6f and 7f winner Anna Karietta (by Precocious): dam poor half-sister to Karelia, very
useful at up to 1½m: quite modest maiden: sweating and bit backward, easily best
effort when third of 13 at Salisbury, coming from well behind and going on well: edgy
and on toes, readily outpaced from 2f out at Ayr later in September: will probably
stay 1m. *J. L. Dunlop.*

SKYWATCHER 5 b.g. Skyliner 117 – Holernzaye 93 (Sallust 134) [1990 8m 12f   **—**
12.5g 8m 8f 12s a12g 1991 a8g] compact, workmanlike gelding: bad performer
nowadays: stays 1¼m: acts on any going: tried blinkered once. *J. Dooler.*

805

SLADES HILL 4 b.c. Lochnager 132 – Mephisto Waltz 98 (Dancer's Image **62** (USA)) [1990 5f³ 6f* 5m 6m* 6g 6f 1991 6g 6d 5f 6f 5f⁵ 5g⁵ 6g 6d] small, good-quartered colt: moderate mover: quite modest handicapper: best form at 6f: acts on firm going: has twice run fairly well when visored, too free in blinkers: sold 3,000 gns Doncaster October Sales. *Miss S. E. Hall.*

SLANDERINTHESTRAND (IRE) 2 b. or br.g. (Mar 20) Millfontaine 114 – **45** Eccentric Lady (London Bells (CAN) 109) [1991 6d 7m 7g⁵ 6m] 3,800Y, 3,600 2-y-o: good-topped, quite attractive gelding: has plenty of scope: second foal: dam half-sister to one-time fairly useful miler Dr Bulasco: poor maiden: not seen out after August: will probably stay 1m: tended to hang second start. *Denys Smith.*

SLANGI VAH (USA) 8 b.g. Riva Ridge (USA) – La Atrevida (USA) (Bold **46** Bidder) [1990 NR 1991 a7g 10v² 8m] lengthy, deep-bodied gelding: modest handicapper as 5-y-o, not nearly so good nowadays: effective at 9f and stays 1½m: acts on any going: sold 1,600 gns Ascot October Sales. *W. J. Musson.*

SLEEPING CAR (FR) 3 b. or br.c. Dunphy 124 – Lorelta (FR) (Rose Laurel **116 p** 125) [1990 8d* 8m⁴ 1991 10m² 9g* 12s*] 180,000 francs (approx £16,700) Y: third foal: half-brother to French 7.5f winner Sarh (by Deep Roots): dam French 1m winner also successful over jumps: successful in newcomers race at Deauville at 2 yrs: not seen out in 1991 until September, then showed smart form, winning listed race at Evry and beating Deja ½ length in Prix du Conseil de Paris at Longchamp: will stay beyond 1½m: acts on soft going: lightly raced, and is open to further improvement. *P. Bary, France.*

SLEEPLINE FANTASY 6 ch.g. Buzzards Bay 128§ – Sleepline Princess 86 **74** (Royal Palace 131) [1990 8f 7f⁶ 9m 8f⁵ 1991 a7g* 7f* 7g² 7m 8g 8m* 8f 8m] leggy, sparely-made gelding: modest handicapper: won at Southwell and Brighton in March and Ascot (£10,950 event) in July: effective at 7f to 1m: acts on any going: has sweated: none too consistent. *M. R. Channon.*

SLEEPLINE PALACE 4 b.f. Homing 130 – Sleepline Princess 86 (Royal **—** Palace 131) [1990 8d 8g⁵ 10m⁴ 8m⁵ 10m 8f⁵ 10g 7m 7g 7.6m a10g⁶ 1991 a10g a11g⁵ a13g⁵] lengthy, sparely-made filly: quite modest at best: well below form in January of 1991: possibly best short of 1m: acts on hard ground: blinkered (raced freely) once. *M. R. Channon.*

SLENDER 3 b.f. Aragon 118 – Handy Dancer 87 (Green God 128) [1990 6g³ 7m⁴ **63** 6m² 6g² 6f² 6d⁶ 1991 7g² 8m³ 11.1d* 10.1m³ 10g 8.1m² 10m⁵] big, rangy filly: moderate mover: quite modest performer: didn't have to run to best form to win maiden at Hamilton in June: stays 11f: acts on good to firm ground and dead: visored second (ran creditably) and fifth starts: should prove best with strong handling. *Denys Smith.*

SLICK CHERRY 4 b.f. Noalto 120 – Slick Chick 89 (Shiny Tenth 120) [1990 10m **65 d** 8f 8m 10m 10.1m* 10m² 9m³ 9g⁶ 10g 1991 10g⁶ 10.1d* 11.7g⁶ 8.3m 10s 9d³ 9m⁵ 9s] small, good-quartered filly: has a round action: quite modest handicapper: won at Chepstow in June: ran moderately after: stays 10.1f: acts on good to firm and dead ground: has won for claimer: sold 2,000 gns Ascot November Sales. *D. R. C. Elsworth.*

SLICK STYLE (USA) 3 b.f. Barachois (CAN) – Delta Fly (USA) (Delta Flag **—** (USA)) [1990 5m⁶ 7m 1991 8.5m⁴ 10g] lengthy filly: poor maiden: stiff tasks as 3-y-o, tailed off in handicap final start: should be suited by at least 1m: sold 1,400 gns Doncaster August Sales. *J. Etherington.*

SLIGHT RISK 2 b.f. (Mar 5) Risk Me (FR) 127 – Sarah Gillian (USA) (Zen **57** (USA)) [1991 5v⁶ 5m³ 6g⁶ 7g² 7g⁵ 7m⁴ 7m 9m 7d a8g] tall, leggy, unfurnished filly: has a quick action: third foal: half-sister to 3-y-o Gipsy King (by Magic Mirror): dam well beaten all outings: plating-class maiden: soundly beaten, mostly in nurseries, last 4 starts: best form at 7f: wore eyecover on fibresand final outing. *P. A. Kelleway.*

SLIP-A-SNIP 4 b.f. Wolverlife 115 – Stramenta (Thatching 131) [1990 5m* 5f² **78** 5m* 5f 5g⁵ 5f³ 5d² 5g3dis 1991 5d³ 5g⁴ 5g 5m⁵ 5d* 5.2f 5f 5m⁴ 5g 5.2g a5g³ a5g³] lengthy, sparely-made filly: moderate mover: modest handicapper: won at Kempton in August: best at 5f: yet to race on very soft going, acts on any other: trained until after reappearance by R. Akehurst: has won for claimer: inconsistent. *G. B. Balding.*

SLIPRAIL (USA) 4 b.f. Our Native (USA) – Oxslip 106 (Owen Dudley 121) [1990 **79** 10g² 10m⁶ 12.5m² 10.2f* 10m 1991 10g 11d⁴ 10.1f 12v⁶ 8g] big, lengthy filly: fair handicapper: not seen out after July: should stay 1½m: acts on firm and dead ground. *H. Candy.*

SLIPSALOM 3 gr.f. Absalom 128 – Let Slip 77 (Busted 134) [1990 a8g 1991 a10g **39** a8g⁵ 12f² 12f⁴ 12d 10.8m 10m⁴ 10m⁶ 9.7m⁵ 10g⁶] smallish, angular filly: moderate mover: inconsistent plater: stays 1½m: acts on firm going: sold 1,000 gns Ascot November Sales. *W. Carter.*

SLOE BERRY   5 b.m. Sharpo 132 – Native Berry (FR) 76 (Ribero 126) [1990 5f⁵   **75**
5g 5m 5m4 6m⁵ 6g 5f³ 6m⁶ 5m* 5g⁶ 5m* 5d 1991 5d 5g 6g 5g⁵ 5m 7m 5g 5g 5m³ 5d
5d] close-coupled, rather sparely-made mare: moderate walker and mover: modest
and inconsistent handicapper nowadays: stays 6f: acts on firm going: effective with
or without blinkers: trained first 7 starts by C. Brittain. *C. A. Austin.*

SLUMBER THYME (IRE)   2 ch.f. (May 17) Burslem 123 – Chive (St Chad 120)   **36**
[1991 7g 7m] compact filly: seventh foal: half-sister to several winners, including
useful sprinter Amigo Menor (by Whistling Deer) and fair miler Evichstar (by
Jasmine Star): dam never ran: poor form, well beaten, in maidens at Redcar (claimer
ridden) and Leicester in autumn. *J. G. FitzGerald.*

SLY PROSPECT (USA)   3 ch.g. Barachois (CAN) – Miss Sly (USA) (Diamond   **73**
Prospect (USA)) [1990 7s 1991 7f⁴ 8g³ 7f4 8m 7f* 7.5f 7m⁵] strong, lengthy gelding:
has a light action: modest performer: won 5-runner maiden at Thirsk in August,
making most: stays 1m: acts on firm going: blinkered last 4 starts: has hung left: may
well need to dominate: sold to join K. White 2,000 gns Doncaster October Sales. *J.
Etherington.*

SMALL DOUBLE (IRE)   3 b.f. Double Schwartz 128 – Little Cynthia 76   **—**
(Wolver Hollow 126) [1990 6g 6m 5d* 6d a6g a6g⁵ a6g⁵ 1991 7d 8g] leggy filly:
plater: below form in handicaps in April, carrying head awkwardly last time: stays 6f.
N. A. Callaghan.

SMART BLADE   3 gr.g. Elegant Air 119 – Alsiba 68 (Northfields (USA)) [1990   **91**
6m³ 7m4 1991 10g* 10f² 12d* 13.3g4 12.3f² 11m⁶] leggy, good-topped gelding: fair
performer: made most and clear 2f out when winning maiden in May and handicap in
June, both at Salisbury: ran in Ostend final start: suited to 1½m: acts on firm and
dead going: sold 40,000 gns Newmarket Autumn Sales. *I. A. Balding.*

SMART ENDEAVOR   3 b. or br.g. Elegant Air 119 – Good Try 92 (Good Bond   **—**
122) [1990 NR 1991 10.1g 10g a12g 12.3g 11.5m] good-topped gelding: has a round
action: closely related to 1½m winner Castle Heights (by Shirley Heights) and
half-brother to several winners, including quite useful 1984 2-y-o 6f winner
Sergeant Gerard (by Brigadier Gerard) and fairly useful 4-y-o 5f winner Choir
Practice (by Chief Singer): dam 2-y-o 5f winner: no worthwhile form in maidens and
handicaps: sold to join J. Jenkins 1,050 gns Newmarket Autumn Sales. *A. Hide.*

SMARTIE LEE   4 ch.f. Dominion 123 – Nosy Parker (FR) (Kashmir II 125) [1990   **62**
10m³ 12h² 11.7m⁵ 11.5f 11.5g4 10f a12g* a13g a12g 1991 12s² 17.2f 12m² 11.9f² 14m
a12g a16g³] small, close-coupled filly: keen walker: plating-class handicapper: stays
2m: acts on any going and equitrack. *P. F. I. Cole.*

SMART MOVER   2 ch.g. (Apr 1) Vaigly Great 127 – Presentable 60 (Sharpen Up   **—**
127) [1991 6f 5h 6m 8m 10.5d] 1,800Y: angular gelding: moderate mover: brother to
9f and 1¼m winner Blakesware Gold and half-brother to 2 winners, including 1985
2-y-o 1m winner Centrepoint (by Reform): dam placed over 1½m, is half-sister to
Gimcrack winner Wishing Star: well beaten, including in sellers: raced very freely
in visor final start. *N. Bycroft.*

SMART PERFORMER   6 b.g. Formidable (USA) 125 – Brilliant Rosa 91   **— §**
(Luthier 126) [1990 NR 1991 a12g] strong, deep-girthed gelding: moderate mover:
one-time fair performer, no longer genuine. *N. Tinkler.*

SMART REBAL (IRE)   3 b.g. Final Straw 127 – Tomfoolery 73 (Silly Season   **—**
127) [1990 NR 1991 8g 10.1s 7g 7.6m] sturdy, close-coupled gelding: shows high
knee action: half-brother to modest middle-distance stayer Springs Welcome (by
Blakeney), a winning hurdler and 3 winners in Belgium: dam raced only at 2 yrs:
behind in maidens and median auction contest: gelded after third start. *J. Akehurst.*

SMASHER   3 b.f. Simply Great (FR) 122 – Star Face (African Sky 124) [1990 7m   **43**
7d 6d 1991 12f 8.2m⁶ 10.2d 11.5f 12m 12.3g⁶ 15.8g] rather sparely-made filly: poor
maiden: apparently best effort in seller penultimate start: tailed off in handicap 18
days later, leading 1½m: stays 1½m: blinkered last 2 starts. *R. J. R. Williams.*

SMILES AHEAD   3 ch.c. Primo Dominie 121 – Baby's Smile 68 (Shirley Heights   **72**
130) [1990 5f4 6g 8f 6d4 7m 7f² 7m⁶ 8d* a8g4 a8g 1991 12.2g² 10m⁶ 12m² 12g³
12.2m² 13.8m³ 12.2g² 12.3g 12.1d* 12g* 12.3g] lengthy colt: mostly in good form at 3
yrs: clear-cut winner of claimers at Hamilton (claimed out of J. Hetherton's stable
£8,011) in July and Newmarket (best effort) in August, making all: stays 13.8f: has
plenty of form on top-of-the-ground, but seems to go particularly well on an easy
surface: takes keen hold, wears net muzzle and taken to post alone nowadays. *P. J.
Bevan.*

SMILING BEAR (USA) 8 b.g. Nikoli 125 – Share A Smile (USA) (Hagley — (USA)) [1990 NR 1991 10.2s 10.6g 8m 8.5f⁵ 10.2g 12f 16.2f] sparely-made gelding: of no account. *A. W. Potts.*

SMILING CHIEF (IRE) 3 ch.g. Montelimar (USA) 122 – Victa 79 (Northfields **72** d (USA)) [1990 NR 1991 10g³ 10g⁶ a12g 12g a12g] 6,000Y: big, lengthy gelding: half-brother to several winners, including fairly useful stayer Christian's Gold (by Electric) and 6f and 8.5f winner Dalmally (by Sharpen Up): dam, winner twice at 1m who seemed to stay 1½m, is half-sister to dam of Don't Forget Me: easily best effort in maidens and handicap on debut. *C. A. Cyzer.*

SMILING SUN (IRE) 3 ch.g. Thatching 131 – Charites (Red God 128§) [1990 **91** 6g⁴ 6m⁴ 6d* 6m² 7g 8m⁴ 6g a6g⁴ a8g* 1991 8g³ 8g³ 8m 7g⁵ 7d 7m² 7g³] sturdy gelding: poor walker: fairly useful handicapper: inconsistent at 3 yrs, running well on 3 occasions at Newmarket: stays 1m: acts on good to firm ground and dead: blinkered once at 2 yrs. *W. A. O'Gorman.*

SMITH'S PEAK 7 ro.g. Alias Smith (USA) – Sacred Mountain 74 (St Paddy 133) **56** [1990 NR 1991 10m 9m* 10m³ 11.7g⁵ 12g 10g 9m³ 8g⁴ 10m³ a12g a10g⁴] workmanlike gelding: plating-class handicapper: won at Goodwood in May: best form from 1m to 1¼m: acts on good to firm ground: has won for apprentice. *R. J. O'Sullivan.*

SMOKE 5 gr.m. Rusticaro (FR) 124 – Fire-Screen 92 (Roan Rocket 128) [1990 12g **55** 12h⁴ 1991 16.2g 12m 12g 9.9m⁶ 12m* 12.3d² 12f⁴ 12.3f⁶ 12f² 12f* 12.3f*] good-topped ex-Irish mare: poor mover: plating-class handicapper: won at Beverley in June and August and at Ripon in August: stays 1½m well: acts on any going: best without blinkers: changed hands 1,800 gns Doncaster Spring Sales: tough and consistent. *J. Parkes.*

SMOOTH BID (IRE) 2 b.c. (May 10) Auction Ring (USA) 123 – Velvet Breeze — (Windjammer (USA)) [1991 8m 7.1m] good-bodied colt: second foal: dam unraced: last in maiden auctions at Redcar (very green, slowly away) and Chepstow: sold 900 gns Doncaster November Sales. *J. A. C. Edwards.*

SMOOTH FINISH 4 b.g. Welsh Term 126 – Chantry Pearl (Gulf Pearl 117) — [1990 7g 10m 12f³ 12f 12m 1991 8g 12f] sparely-made gelding: poor performer: stays 1½m: acts on firm ground: sold 880 gns Doncaster Summer Sales. *A. Harrison.*

SMUGGLERS GOLD 3 b.f. Gold Claim 90 – Lareda 75 (Burglar 128) [1990 6m — 7m 8m a6g 1991 10d⁴ 11.1d] sparely-made filly: has a round action: well beaten in sellers and handicap: likely to prove suited by middle distances. *M. J. Bolton.*

SNAADEE (USA) 4 br.c. Danzig (USA) – Somfas (USA) (What A Pleasure **109** (USA)) [1990 NR 1991 7m* 7g* 7g⁴ 5m⁶ 6d*] $750,000Y: strong, compact colt: carries condition: fifth foal: brother to very useful 1988 2-y-o 6f winner Russian Bond and closely related to useful 7f winner Adbass (by Northern Dancer) and a winner by Conquistador Cielo: dam, from excellent family, won at up to 7f: very useful colt, lightly raced: won listed event at Doncaster in November by 2 lengths from Gilt Throne: easily landed odds in maiden at Newcastle in May (wore crossed noseband) and apprentice event at Ascot in September: best form at 6f to 7f: has won on good to firm ground, but best efforts with some give. *M. R. Stoute.*

SNAKE EYE 6 b.g. Tina's Pet 121 – Dingle Belle 72 (Dominion 123) [1990 a11g⁶ — § a8g a8g 10.1g² 10.8f³ 11.7g 10m 15.3g* 14.8m⁵ 1991 8.2d] smallish, sturdy gelding: moderate mover: poor handicapper: stays 15f: acts on any going: tried blinkered once: sometimes bandaged: has found little: not one to trust. *W. T. Kemp.*

SNAP BACK 3 b.f. Final Straw 127 – Shalbee 93 (Tachypous 128) [1990 6g a6g — 1991 a5g] stocky filly: tailed off in claimers and maiden. *S. Woodman.*

SNAPIN TIME 2 b.c. (May 27) Domynsky 110 – Baggin Time 91 (Pinsun 108) **31** [1991 5g 6d] angular, sparely-made colt: sixth foal: half-brother to fair 1989 2-y-o 6f and 8.2f winner Laird of Balmoral (by Lochnager) and moderate handicappers Brewin Time and Mashin Time (both by Palm Track), winners from 6f to 1m: dam won from 5f to 1½m: poor form in claimer at Beverley and seller at Ripon (still green) in June. *M. H. Easterby.*

SNAPPY'S BOY JOSH 2 b.c. (Apr 21) Hotfoot 126 – September Snap 46 — (Music Boy 124) [1991 7f 7g] first foal: dam 1m seller winner: slowly away and always well behind in maiden at Yarmouth and 7-runner mixed-aged event at Newmarket in autumn. *R. V. King.*

SNICKERSNEE 3 b.c. Kris 135 – Cat Girl (USA) (Grey Dawn II 132) [1990 NR **72** 1991 12m⁶ 12m 11.5g* 12m] big, strong, rangy colt: fifth foal: half-brother to fairly useful but rather temperamental 7f winner My Sister Ellen (by Lyphard) and 1¼m winner Morasio (by The Minstrel): dam good-class winner at up to 1m in USA: sweating, won amateurs maiden at Yarmouth in July: ran badly starts either side, in amateurs contest at Newmarket final one: sold to join M. Dixon 7,500 gns Newmarket Autumn Sales. *H. R. A. Cecil.*

SNO MARQUE 3 ch.g. Carwhite 127 – Hyacine 43 (High Line 125) [1990 NR **61** 1991 7v 10m³ 12d⁴ 14g 11m* 10g² 11.5m³] 10,000F, 13,000Y: close-coupled gelding: fifth foal: half-brother to winning sprinter Dealers Wheels (by Song) and untrustworthy 1985 2-y-o 6f winner Otter Rock (by Latest Model): dam, placed at up to 1½m, is sister to Capricorn Line: quite modest performer: won claimer at Wolverhampton in July: ran well in similar event (claimed £12,001) next start: lacks turn of foot, and should stay beyond 1½m: visored (no show) fourth start: trained first 5 by R. Boss and sixth by C. Smith. *A. S. Reid.*

SNO SERENADE 5 b.g. Song 132 – When The Saints (Bay Express 132) [1990 **63** 9g 7g 7.6d 9m 10g 8f* 8m⁶ 8h² 8h* 7f³ 8f* a8g* a7g² a8g* a8g³ 1991 10.2m 7m 7.1m 10.1f 8.3d⁶ 8.9m 8g⁴ a6g] tall, leggy, quite attractive gelding: has a quick action: fair handicapper (suited by switchback track) at 4 yrs: little form in 1991: effective at 7f and stays 9f: acts well on very firm going and equitrack, probably unsuited by heavy: below form in visor: trained until after penultimate start by R. Jones. *M. Dods.*

SNOW BLIZZARD 3 gr.c. Petong 126 – Southern Dynasty 81 (Gunner B 126) **50** [1990 7s 1991 10g 7g 10m 10g 9.7m* 10g³ 12f⁴ 11.5s] tall, workmanlike colt: plating-class performer: 50/1, first form when making all in handicap at Folkestone in September: stays 1½m: acts on firm ground: wore tongue strap third outing. *S. Dow.*

SNOW BOARD 2 gr.g. (Feb 20) Niniski (USA) 125 – Troja (Troy 137) [1991 7s — 8.1g] second foal: half-brother to 4-y-o Trojan Steel (by Bellypha): dam, showed a little ability in France, is daughter of Nell Gwyn winner Gently: no worthwhile form in maidens at Kempton and Chepstow in August. *B. W. Hills.*

SNOW FOREST (USA) 2 ch.f. (May 24) Woodman (USA) 126 – Ice Fantasy **97** (USA) (It's Freezing (USA)) [1991 7m* 7m* 7m³ 7.3g² 8f] $200,000Y: close-coupled filly: half-sister to 2 winners in North America, including stakes performer Fighting Fantasy (by Fighting Fit), successful at up to 9f: dam won at up to 7f: fairly useful performer: won maiden at Lingfield and minor event at York (made all and ran on strongly): better efforts in Rockfel Stakes at Newmarket (behind Musicale) and Radley Stakes at Newbury (headstrong to post and in race, beaten 2½ lengths by Soiree) later in autumn: last of 8 in Miesque Stakes (Div.1) at Hollywood Park: should stay 1m: tends to race with head high: with N. Drysdale. *J. H. M. Gosden.*

SNOWGIRL (IRE) 3 gr.f. Mazaad 106 – Rust Free 58 (Free State 125) [1990 **82** 5m² 5f2 5m² 6s 5d⁴ 1991 6g³ 5g* 5m* 5d³ 5m³ 5m⁶ 5m⁴ 6s* 6m³ 6m³ 5d⁵ 6g] good-topped filly: has a quick action: fair performer: won maiden at Edinburgh and minor event (4 days later) at Thirsk in April then handicap at Newmarket (making all) in August: excellent efforts next 3 starts: stays 6f: acts on good to firm ground and soft: tough, game and consistent. *J. Berry.*

SNOW MAIDEN (USA) 3 b.f. Arctic Tern (USA) 126 – Professional Dance **77 ?** (USA) (Nijinsky (CAN) 138) [1990 NR 1991 10.5g⁴ 13.9m⁴ 10.3m⁶] rangy filly: fifth reported foal: sister to modest 1¾m and 2m winner Tartique Twist and half-sister to French 1m and 1½m winner Alliage (by Alleged) and a minor stakes winner in North America: dam unraced half-sister to dam of good French performers L'Emigrant and Salpinx: fourth of 7 in £7,400 contest at York: tailed off after in maidens at same course (edgy and sweating, led over 1¼m) and Chester: sold 12,500 gns Newmarket Autumn Sales: clearly one to treat with caution. *B. Hanbury.*

SNOW PLOUGH (IRE) 3 b.f. Niniski (USA) 125 – River Dancer 118 (Irish **85** River (FR) 131) [1990 6m³ 1991 10f* 10.1g 8g] leggy, rather sparely-made filly: moderate mover: won maiden at Beverley in May, not striding out at all well nor winning so easily as seemed likely 2f out: broke down in handicap final start: middle-distance bred. *M. R. Stoute.*

SNOWY OWL (USA) 3 b.c. Storm Bird (CAN) 134 – Nafees (USA) (Raja Baba **99** (USA)) [1990 6g³ 5d² 6m* 5d* 1991 7m 5m⁴ 6g] sturdy colt: useful performer: 3½ lengths fourth of 7 to Elbio in Group 2 contest at Sandown in May, outpaced until staying on well over 1f out: tended to hang and didn't look keen in listed race at Newbury 8 weeks later: best form at 5f: acts on good to firm ground and dead: visored last 2 starts and final one at 2 yrs: usually had tongue tied down: joined C. Clement in USA. *M. R. Stoute.*

SNUGGLE 4 ch.f. Music Boy 124 – Sinzinbra 112 (Royal Palace 131) [1990 6m⁵ **54 +** 8m⁴ 8.2s² 7m 8.2s⁶ 11.5m 8g 7d 7d 6m 9g 1991 7m 8m⁶] lengthy, workmanlike filly:

plating-class handicapper nowadays: better at around 1m than shorter: acts on any
going, with possible exception of heavy: below form when visored: winning hurdler.
M. H. Tompkins.

SNUGGLE BABY (USA) 3 b.f. Palace Music (USA) 129 – Propitiate (USA) —
(Triple Bend (USA)) [1990 NR 1991 8g] leggy filly: moderate walker: fourth reported
living foal: half-sister to a winner in North America by Youth: dam French 2-y-o 6.5f
winner behind in 1000 Guineas, later second in Grade 3 events at 5 yrs in USA: well
beaten in maiden at Salisbury in June: sold 2,200 gns Newmarket December Sales.
L. M. Cumani.

SNURGE 4 ch.c. Ela-Mana-Mou 132 – Finlandia (FR) (Faraway Son (USA) **125**
130) [1990 12d² 12g² 14.6g* 12g³ 1991 13.3d* 12g* 12.5m* 12d 12s³ 14v*]
Snurge's two-length defeat of Hieroglyphic in the world's richest Group
3 race, the Premio UNIRE Consiglio Europeo Roma Vecchia at Rome in
late-November and worth around £100,000 to the winner, put the seal on a
tremendously successful season for Paul Cole and confirmed his position as
the leading trainer in terms of money won both in Britain and abroad. Cole's
overseas haul of £1,188,180 from ten wins and twelve places was down on his
total in 1990 but was more than enough to secure his second successive
International Racing Bureau award for leading British trainer on foreign
soil—when Brittain's Terimon was beaten in the Japan Cup it left Hannon in
second place with a total of £769,025 which came mainly from a one-two in the
Goffs Million. Notable contributions to Cole's total came from Ruby Tiger,
Culture Vulture, Zoman, Jape, Run Don't Fly and Half A Tick (over £90,000
for third in the Derby Italiano). But the chief contributor was the four-year-old
Snurge who did most of his racing abroad. Snurge was seen only once on a
British racecourse, in fact, when he gave Sardegna a stone and a length
-and-a-half beating in the listed Aston Park Stakes on his reappearance at
Newbury in May, confirming that he'd trained on. After the St Leger winner
doubled his Group 1 winning tally by beating Erdelistan by three quarters of a
length in the Gran Premio di Milano at San Siro the following month he looked
well on course for his first major target of the season, the King George VI

Grand Prix de Deauville Lancel—Snurge (blaze) gives weight all round

and Queen Elizabeth Diamond Stakes, and his bid to become the first Leger winner since Alcide in 1959 to go on to land the race. However, Snurge's tendency to give trouble at the start resurfaced in Milan, with the result that he suffered a cut on his near-hind. The injury was only minor but complications arose and set him back a little in his big-race preparation; that, coupled with the prevailing firm ground, led Cole to pull him out of the Ascot showpiece in the week leading up to the race—'I don't think it's worth risking him'. Snurge would have been an interesting runner, and might have done better against his stable-companion Generous than some expected, given the chance. While Snurge had shown himself to be well suited by an easy surface, his next run—defeating Crnagora and Pigeon Voyageur by a neck and half a length with something in hand in the moderately-run Grand Prix de Deauville Lancel—also showed that he was capable of producing a high-class level of form on top-of-the-ground. Snurge made it to the start for his second major target of the season, the Ciga Prix de l'Arc de Triomphe, but failed to do himself justice. Banging his head leaving the stalls was given as the reason for his trailing the field throughout, but a below-par third behind Passing Sale and Drum Taps next time in the Gran Premio del Jockey Club at Milan suggested, misleadingly as it turned out, that he might have started to train off. However, persistence paid off handsomely in the Roma Vecchia.

Snurge (ch.c. 1987)	Ela-Mana-Mou (b 1976)	Pitcairn (b 1971)	Petingo Border Bounty
		Rose Bertin (ch 1970)	High Hat Wide Awake
	Finlandia (FR) (b 1977)	Faraway Son (b 1967)	Ambiopoise Locust Time
		Musical II (ch 1961)	Prince Chevalier Musidora

Snurge's pedigree was fully documented in *Racehorses of 1990*. His dam Finlandia was also represented here in the latest season by Suomi (by Tate Gallery) and Kajaani (by Simply Great). Suomi proved somewhat disappointing and was sent to the States after finishing well beaten in the Queen Anne Stakes. Two-year-old Kajaani, also with Cole, showed modest form when placed in two maidens. Snurge is effective from around a mile and a half to fourteen furlongs. Whilst his best form has been achieved on an easy surface, he showed himself capable of winning a good prize on good to firm ground. He remains in training and should continue to win his share of good races, especially abroad. *P. F. I. Cole.*

SO APT (IRE) 3 b.c. Taufan (USA) 119 – Anita's Princess (Miami Springs 121) [1990 6m a6g 7m 8v³ 8.2s 1991 12.1m] small, angular colt: has a round action: plating-class maiden: showed little in October seller: should stay 1¼m: best efforts with plenty of give in the ground. *M. H. Tompkins.* —

SOBA GUEST (IRE) 2 ch.g. (Jan 31) Be My Guest (USA) 126 – Brazilian Princess 66 (Absalom 128) [1991 5g³ 5m² 5s⁵ 7d 5f* 5m⁶ 5m⁴ 5d*] 9,200F, 17,000Y: good-bodied gelding: first foal: dam, maiden stayed 1m, is half-sister to Soba: somewhat inconsistent performer: successful in maiden at Catterick (made all) in July and 20-runner nursery at Wolverhampton (easily best effort, quickened to lead over 1f out) in October: saddle slipped fourth start: likely to be as effective at 6f as 5f: acts on dead ground, probably on firm. *J. Berry.* **79**

SO BEGUILING (USA) 2 b. or br.f. (Jan 19) Woodman (USA) 126 – Clint's Sec (USA) (Secretariat (USA)) [1991 6.1d⁵ 7m⁶ 7m* 7.9g 8f 8.2m] $18,000Y: smallish, close-coupled filly: first foal: dam unraced: poor form: won seller at Wolverhampton (bought in 5,000 gns) in July: seems to stay 1m: acts on good to firm ground: bandaged behind fourth (also sweating) and final outings: sold 1,150 gns Ascot 2nd November Sales. *C. R. Nelson.* **49**

SOBERING THOUGHTS 5 ch.g. Be My Guest (USA) 126 – Soba 127 (Most Secret 119) [1990 8.5d 7m⁵ 8g⁵ a8g 6m 6g 6m 6s 6d a6g 1991 a6g a8g a7g⁴ a5g² a5g* a6g* 5g⁴ 7.5g 7g⁶ a7g⁵ a7g⁴ a5g* 6m⁶ a5g⁶ a5g³ a5g a6g] big, plain gelding: moderate mover: poor handicapper: won at Southwell in March and July and Lingfield in between: off course nearly 4 months, below best at Southwell last 2 starts: effective at 5f to 7f: blinkered nowadays: largely consistent. *D. W. Chapman.* **42**

SOBRANIE 3 b.f. High Top 131 – Latakia 80 (Morston (FR) 125) [1990 NR 1991 10m*] quite good-topped filly: seventh foal: half-sister to 11.7f and 13.1f winner **86**

811

Nikatino (by Bustino) and winning plater Jay-Zee-Boy (by Moulton), successful at around 1m: dam 1½m winner: 33/1 and backward, awarded race having been slightly bumped 1f out when ½-length second of 8 to Nibbs Point in maiden at Newmarket in July, green as pace quickened then running on strongly from towards rear: moved moderately to post, showing a roundish action: should be better suited by 1½m. *A. C. Stewart.*

SOBRIETY   6 b.h. Noalcoholic (FR) 128 – Sacred Mountain 74 (St Paddy 133)   **43**
[1990 10.2f² 9f4 10.8m4 10m4 7.6g* 1991 9s 10.8m 8m 10f³ 11.5g a8g² 10s 10m⁵ 10g 8.9g 7d a7g] leggy horse: poor handicapper: good second in amateurs event at Lingfield in June: below form after, tailed off at Southwell final start: best at 1m to 1¾m: acts on hard and dead going: has started slowly: excellent mount for inexperienced rider: trained first 9 starts by G. Balding. *M. B. James.*

SOCIETY BALL   4 b.f. Law Society (USA) 130 – Mariakova (USA) 84 (The   **61**
Minstrel (CAN) 135) [1990 11g4 a12g³ 12.4m a14g³ 14d² 15v² a12g* 1991 12.3d 16.5m 14.1g²] workmanlike filly: modest handicapper at 3 yrs: below form in first half of 1991: will stay 2m: acts on heavy going: looked none too reliable fourth and fifth starts at 3 yrs and usually blinkered after. *N. Tinkler.*

SOCKEM   4 b.g. Nordico (USA) – Floating Petal 90 (Wollow 132) [1990 a6g⁵ a6g4   **46**
7m² 7f* 7f* 7m³ 7g 7g⁶ 7m 7f 7m² 7m4 7g 7m 7d* 7g 1991 a7g 7f 8m 7m 8g³ 7g 7m 8f³ 7g] compact, rather sparely-made gelding: moderate mover: poor handicapper: stays 1m: yet to race on soft ground, acts on any other: ran poorly when blinkered: inconsistent. *C. N. Williams.*

SOCKS AND SHARES   2 ch.c. (Apr 25) Shardari 134 – Lady Tippins (USA)   **74 ?**
(Star de Naskra (USA)) [1991 7g 6.1m4 7g] rather leggy, close-coupled colt: moderate walker: third foal: half-brother to fair but untrustworthy sprinter (useful at 2 yrs) Access Travel (by Auction Ring): dam 6f and 7f winner: quite modest maiden: pulled up at Warwick final start: should be better suited by 7f than 6f: slowly away, but best effort, penultimate start. *P. W. Harris.*

SODA POPINSKI (USA)   3 b.c. Sir Ivor 135 – Four Runs (USA) (Reviewer   **—**
(USA)) [1990 NR 1991 12g⁵ 10.4m] 42,000Y: quite attractive colt: half-brother to 4 minor winners in USA and Italy: dam, lightly raced, won one race at about 6f: fifth of 9 in maiden at Newmarket (apprentices) in June: well beaten in similar event at York (moved badly to post) over 3 months later: sold to join I. Campbell 7,600 gns Newmarket Autumn Sales. *L. M. Cumani.*

SO DISCREET (USA)   3 b.c. Secreto (USA) 128 – I'll Be Around (USA) (Isgala)   **60**
[1990 8g 8.2s⁶ 8d⁶ 1991 10.2g4 13.1f³ 12g 12.1m*] smallish, round-barrelled colt: quite modest performer: won seller (bought in 4,200 gns) at Edinburgh in October, strong run to lead well inside final 1f: reportedly had wind operation after previous start: will prove suited by 1½m+: has form on any going: sold to join J. White 7,400 gns Newmarket Autumn Sales. *J. W. Hills.*

SOHAIL (USA)   8 ch.g. Topsider (USA) – Your Nuts (USA) (Creme Dela Creme)   **—**
[1990 NR 1991 a13g] tall, good-topped gelding: modest handicapper at 4 yrs: never placed to challenge in Lingfield claimer only run in 1991, first run on flat since: stays 1½m: acts on any going: effective with or without blinkers: possibly best with strong handling: winning chaser. *J. White.*

SOHA (USA)   3 b.f. Dancing Brave (USA) 140 – Paris Royal (Mill Reef (USA) 141)   **58**
[1990 NR 1991 12f² 12m 12s] 600,000Y: smallish filly: first foal: dam, half-sister to Irish 2000 Guineas winner Northern Treasure, won Oaks d'Italia: easily best effort in maidens when second at Brighton: sold 30,000 gns Newmarket December Sales, probably to Italy. *A. C. Stewart.*

SOHRAB (IRE)   3 ch.c. Shernazar 131 – On Show 92 (Welsh Pageant 132) [1990   **77**
8d 1991 8g² a7g* 8m 10m³ 8.9g] leggy colt: has scope: moderate walker and mover: modest form: landed odds in maiden at Southwell in July: will prove better at 1¼m than shorter: takes strong hold (made most and well beaten third start), and wore citation bridle final start: sold to join R. Callow 9,500 gns Newmarket Autumn Sales. *G. Wragg.*

SOIREE (IRE)   2 b.f. (Jan 17) Sadler's Wells (USA) 132 – Seminar 113 (Don   **103 p**
(ITY) 123) [1991 6m³ 7m* 7m⁶ 7.3g*]
The progressive Soiree looks just the type to improve into a very useful filly over middle distances as a three-year-old. After making her debut over an inadequate six furlongs, Soiree was kept to around seven furlongs for her three remaining starts, and it augurs well that she was able to maintain her improvement over a distance that was still short of her optimum. After over-

Radley Stakes, Newbury — Soiree beats Snow Forest and Cochabamba despite hanging left

coming race-rustiness and trouble in running to win a maiden at Ayr in September quite readily by a length and a half from Wilsonic, Soiree was thrown in at the deep end in the Tattersalls Tiffany Highflyer Stakes at Newmarket the following month. Although she finished out of the prize money, Soiree ran an excellent race and picked up a £100,000 bonus for her owner by dint of being the first qualifying filly to finish: she was never able to launch a serious challenge but kept running on strongly from mid-division to finish sixth to Young Senor. The greater emphasis that the easier ground placed on stamina in the listed Radley Stakes at Newbury later in October brought the best out of Soiree. Opposed by five previous winners in a six-runner field which included the Rockfel third Snow Forest and the consistent and fairly useful filly Harvest Girl, Soiree emerged a decisive winner, travelling strongly most of the way, leading two furlongs out and running on well to account for Snow Forest by two and a half lengths with Cochabamba two lengths behind in third. It was a useful performance, not far short of those recorded by the best of her female contemporaries, flawed only by slight signs of waywardness: not only did she swerve right leaving the stalls but she hung left when striking the front.

		Northern Dancer	Nearctic
Soiree (IRE) (b.f. Jan 17, 1989)	Sadler's Wells (USA) (b 1981)	(b 1961)	Natalma
		Fairy Bridge	Bold Reason
		(b 1975)	Special
	Seminar (ch 1972)	Don	Grey Sovereign
		(gr 1966)	Diviana II
		Solar Echo	Solar Slipper
		(b 1957)	Eastern Echo

Soiree, probably the best filly seen to date from Sadler's Wells's fourth crop, was purchased for 135,000 guineas at Newmarket's Highflyer Yearling Sale. She's one of numerous winners from her dam Seminar, a very useful two-year-old who won three races over five furlongs and finished fourth in both the Queen Mary and the Lowther Stakes before her transfer to the States where she won over a mile. Most of Seminar's previous winners have also been by sons of Northern Dancer; they include the useful but ungenuine Solaboy (by The Minstrel), successful at six furlongs as a two-year-old but later suited by a mile and a quarter, his sister Sweet Adelaide, a winner over five furlongs as a two-year-old in 1985, and the fair miler Glenroyale (by

Nureyev). Seminar is quite well bred: she's closely related to the smart 1966 Irish two-year-old Sovereign Slipper and half-sister to both the high-class sprinter/miler Boldboy and the dam of the Irish Two Thousand Guineas third and July Cup fourth Prince Echo. Her dam Solar Echo was lightly raced but the third dam, Eastern Echo, was a useful war-time winner. *B. W. Hills.*

SOLAR STAR (USA) 2 b.f. (Apr 28) Lear Fan (USA) 130 – Lajna 88 (Be My 93 Guest (USA) 126) [1991 6m* 6g* 6m⁵] leggy, rather unfurnished filly: has scope: first foal: dam twice-raced daughter of Oaks fourth Shore Line, a sister to Park Hill winner Quay Line: successful in 5-runner maiden at Kempton and 4-runner Ewar Stud Farm Stakes (by a neck from Coffee Ice, pair 6 lengths clear) at Newmarket: sweating and on toes, modest fifth of 6, never a threat, to Musicale in Hillsdown Cherry Hinton Stakes at Newmarket in July: will be suited by 7f + . *M. Bell.*

SOLDE 3 ch.c. Pharly (FR) 130 – Quelle Chance 81 (General Assembly (USA)) 78 [1990 6f2 6g2 7f* 7g4 8.2g5 1991 8g 9.9m4 8d4 7.1m5] angular, unfurnished colt: shows plenty of knee action: modest handicapper: suited by 1m: acts on any going: blinkered final start: takes keen hold. *J. G. FitzGerald.*

SOLE CONTROL 3 b.f. Jupiter Island 126 – Maureen Mhor 70 (Taj Dewan 128) — [1990 NR 1991 12.2d3 14.8f3 12g] 2,500F: angular filly: third reported live foal: dam showed a little ability at 2 yrs: no worthwhile form, beaten 12 lengths plus, when third in Warwick maidens. *H. Candy.*

SOLEIL DANCER (IRE) 3 b.c. Fairy King (USA) – Cooliney Dancer 103 (Dancer's Image (USA)) [1990 6m3 7m5 1991 8s* 8d* 7m2 8g 7.6g4 6s 7g6 8.1d] lengthy, good-quartered colt: good walker: useful performer: won minor event at Kempton and £7,400 contest (making most) at Thirsk in April: good sixth of 13 to Osario in Group 3 contest at Goodwood: struggling when stumbled and rider unseated 2f out in minor event final outing: may prove best at around 1m: acts on good to firm ground and soft: game. *M. McCormack.*

SOLEMN MELODY 4 b.g. Jalmood (USA) 126 – Garganey (USA) (Quack — (USA)) [1990 7f4 10.1m 8g 1991 7.1m] big, angular gelding: lightly raced and no sign of ability. *A. Barrow.*

SOLENT STEEL 6 gr.m. Undulate (USA) – Tavaro (Gustav 121) [1990 NR 1991 — 7.1m 12.1d 16.2g] workmanlike mare: moderate mover: bad handicapper nowadays: stays 1m: acts on a soft surface: often bandaged. *A. J. Chamberlain.*

SOLID (IRE) 3 b.c. Glenstal (USA) 118 – Reine de Chypre (FR) (Habitat 134) 51 [1990 6m 6g 6d 6m a7g4 a8g a6g2 a7g 1991 8.2d 8.2m 8.3g* a8g3 8d4] leggy colt: plating-class handicapper: won selling event at Windsor (no bid) in July: stays 8.3f well: acts on dead ground: has run well on fibresand, but moderately fourth outing (bandaged) at 3 yrs: ran moderately in visor at 2 yrs. *J. R. Jenkins.*

SOLID STEEL (IRE) 3 b.c. Flash of Steel 120 – Bonny Brae (Cure The Blues 51 (USA)) [1990 a8g 1991 a10g3 a8g3 a10g 12g2 11.9g3 11.9m 14m3 12m6 12f6] tall colt: has a round action: plating-class maiden: stays 1¾m: acts on firm going: wore eyeshield on all-weather: subsequently sold out of Mrs L. Piggott's stable 1,500 gns Ascot May Sales. *A. Moore.*

SOLOMONS NEPHEW 4 b.c. Absalom 128 – Strawberry Fields 66 (Song 132) 58 [1990 6m 6f* 7f 7m2 1991 a7g3 a7g 7g5 8d 7m4 7.5g* 8.1d 8g6 7.6m6] lengthy, rather sparely-made colt: plating-class handicapper: won at Beverley in June: better at 7f/1m than shorter: acts on good to firm ground, unsuited by dead: has drifted right. *Dr J. D. Scargill.*

SOLO SAIL 3 b.c. Slip Anchor 136 – Soluce 98 (Junius (USA) 124) [1990 8g 9.5g3 63 1991 12.5v 9d 8f* 9.5m 10s5 10.3g] 50,000Y: second foal: half-brother to fairly useful 1m winner Alfujairah (by Diesis): dam, Irish 7f winner, is half-sister to useful Irish middle-distance filly Cienaga: won claimer at Gowran Park in May: showed little in October seller on first outing on flat here: stays 1m: acts on firm going: blinkered second to fifth starts: trained until after fifth by D. K. Weld in Ireland: claimed out of C. Weedon's stable £8,500 after winning claiming hurdle at Perth in August. *J. H. Johnson.*

SOMEBODY GRAND (USA) 3 ch.c. El Gran Senor (USA) 136 – Somebody — Noble (USA) (Vaguely Noble 140) [1990 NR 1991 8m] leggy, angular, unfurnished colt: fourth foal: closely related to twice-raced 1990 3-y-o Saffaah (by Secreto) and half-brother to 10.2f and 1½m winner Regency Fair (by Assert): dam (unraced) from family of Affirmed: eighth of 13 in £7,800 newcomers race at Newmarket in April: dead. *M. R. Stoute.*

SOMEONE BRAVE 3 b.g. Commanche Run 133 – Someone Special 105   **63**
(Habitat 134) [1990 8f² 8.2d³ 9g⁵ 1991 12d 11.7m⁴ 14m 11.7g 8m] smallish,
sparely-made gelding: moderate walker: quite modest at best at 3 yrs: best effort in
handicaps second start: tailed off final start: stays 11.7f: yet to race on soft ground,
probably acts on any other. *C. A. Horgan.*

SOMERSAULTING (IRE) 3 b.c. Jester 119 – Gwen Somers (Will Somers   **47**
114§) [1990 6g 6g 6m³ 6m 5g³ 6d 5v⁴ 5g 6d⁴ 1991 7v⁵ 8m 6g 8m⁵ 8g⁵ 12s] tall,
angular colt: moderate mover: plater: stiff task in maiden final outing: stays 1m:
suited by an easy surface: blinkered third start, and usually at 2 yrs. *A. R. Davison.*

SOMETHING QUICK (IRE) 3 b.c. Mummy's Treasure 84 – Artillery Row   **78**
(Pals Passage 115) [1990 5f 6m⁵ 7m³ 7g 6m 8m⁴ 7d² 1991 7d⁵ 7g⁴ 8g² 8g* 8s² 8g
8m⁶ 8g² 8f⁴ 9m 8d² 8g² a8g⁵] small, sturdy colt: moderate mover with quick action:
modest handicapper: won at Kempton in June: mostly in good form after, but ran
poorly on equitrack final start: stays 1m well: acts on good to firm and soft ground. *R.
Hannon.*

SONAR 5 b. or br.g. Pitskelly 122 – Diana's Choice (Tudor Music 131) [1990 a13g²   **— §**
14.6f⁶ 1991 a16g a13g] leggy gelding: has a round action: temperamental performer:
stays 13f: acts on good to firm going: sometimes blinkered: one to treat with caution.
Pat Mitchell.

SONDERISE 2 br.c. (Mar 19) Mummy's Game 120 – Demderise 80 (Vaigly Great   **66**
127) [1991 6g 6m 6m 5m² 5m⁶ 5.1m 5d⁴ 5d*] lengthy colt: first foal: dam 2-y-o 5f
winner, is half-sister to useful sprinter Alpine Strings: much improved form when
winning Doncaster nursery in November: should be as effective at 6f as 5f: acts on
good to soft ground: suited by strong handling. *N. Tinkler.*

SONGFEATHER 2 b.f. (Mar 13) Petong 126 – Gay Appeal 76 (Star Appeal 133)   **50**
[1991 5.2g⁵ 7f 7.1m] leggy filly: second foal: dam 1½m winner: plating-class form
when fifth of 8 in maiden at Newbury in July: didn't confirm that in claimers at
Yarmouth and Edinburgh (blinkered, edgy, slowly away) in autumn: sold 2,500 gns
Newmarket Autumn Sales. *B. W. Hills.*

SONGLINES 3 b.f. Night Shift (USA) – Donnas Dream 84 (Young Generation   **78**
129) [1990 6d³ 5m³ 6g³ 6d² a5g* 1991 6f² 5s 5m* 5g⁶ 5g 5.1m⁶ 5g] small, lengthy,
angular filly: modest handicapper: won £7,100 event at Epsom in June: ran fairly
well sixth start, best subsequent effort: best form at 5f: acts on firm ground and
dead: sold 9,000 gns Newmarket December Sales. *R. V. Smyth.*

SONG OF MANULLA 2 b.g. (May 4) Local Suitor (USA) 128 – Heavenly Gaze   **—**
(FR) (Gay Mecene (USA) 128) [1991 5m 7g 7.5f] 2,200F, 5,200Y, resold 1,000Y:
good-bodied gelding: has a round action: third foal: dam never ran: probably of little
account: sold 880 gns Doncaster November Sales. *J. Norton.*

SONG OF SIXPENCE (USA) 7 b.g. The Minstrel (CAN) 135 – Gliding By **101**
(USA) (Tom Rolfe) [1990 13v 10m* 10.2m⁴ 12m⁵ 10m* 10.5m 10f* 10m* 10f* 10.1g*
11.1g³ 10g³ 1991 10g⁵ 10g⁶ 10g⁵ 10.2g* 11.9m⁵ 10m 10g² 10.5g² 10g⁶ 10m⁴
10m⁵ 11g²] big, strong, close-coupled gelding: has a round action: useful
handicapper: won at Doncaster in June: ran well in Group 3 events at Haydock
(behind Lord of Tusmore) and Baden-Baden eighth and ninth starts: suited by
middle distances: probably unsuited by heavy ground, acts on any other: best held
up and suited by good gallop: has run creditably for apprentice: tough and genuine. *I.
A. Balding.*

SONGSTER 2 b.g. (Mar 21) Song 132 – Stedham 84 (Jaazeiro (USA) 127) [1991   **73**
5m⁵ 6m³ 6g⁵ 6m⁴ 6g² 7m³ 6m 7m*] 18,500F, 14,000Y: compact gelding: second
foal: half-brother to 3-y-o Super Spacemate (by Absalom): dam 2-y-o 6f winner:
made all in 19-runner maiden auction at Leicester in September: stays 7f: blinkered
(not discredited) fourth outing. *Lord John FitzGerald.*

SONIC BELLE 2 b.f. (Apr 11) Ballacashtal (CAN) – Concorde Lady 66 (Hotfoot   **—**
126) [1991 7m] 1,100F: tall, angular filly: half-sister to several winners here and
abroad, including fairly useful 1m to 13.3f winner General Concorde (by Radetzky):
dam showed little on flat or over hurdles: 50/1 and ridden by 7-lb claimer, tailed off in
11-runner maiden at Newcastle in August. *B. W. Murray.*

SONIC MUSIC (USA) 4 ch.c. Green Forest (USA) 134 – Laylitna (USA) (Key   **—**
To The Mint (USA)) [1990 NR 1991 7m 7.6d 10.2g 9.7m⁶ 8f] small, chunky colt: fifth
foal: brother to good-class 5-y-o Green Line Express and half-brother to 7f winner
Evening Blush (by Blushing Groom) and a minor winner in USA: dam lightly-raced
daughter of 1967 champion American 3-y-o filly Furl Sail: poor plater: blinkered
once: dead. *T. P. McGovern.*

SONIC SIGNAL 5 b.m. Trojan Fen 118 – Danger Signal 106 (Red God 128§)　**45**
[1990 a10g⁴ 9g⁶ 10g⁴ 10m⁴ 10m 12f⁴ 15.5f⁶ 12m a12g a12g⁶ 1991 10v⁵ a12g 10s 10m
11.5m⁶ 11.6m³ 14.1f² 15.4f² 16.2d 15.8g² 14.6m³ a16g] small, sparely-made mare:
poor handicapper: stays 2m: acts on any going: has worn bandages behind. *M. J.
Haynes.*

SON OF A LADY 4 b.c. Never So Bold 135 – Retort (Reform 132) [1990 NR 1991　—
9s 11f] workmanlike colt: half-brother to a winner abroad by Ebano: dam unraced
sister to Sarissa, dam of Sabre Dance: blinkered, broke leg in 11f claimer: dead. *S. G.
Norton.*

SON OF SCHULA 2 b.c. (May 4) Today And Tomorrow 78 – Schula 81 (Kala　—
Shikari 125) [1991 5.3m⁵] 1,400Y: close-coupled colt: first foal: dam 5f winner: 5/1
and very green, always behind in 5-runner maiden at Brighton in August: moved
poorly down. *J. Berry.*

SONUS (IRE) 2 b.c. (Mar 5) Sadler's Wells (USA) 132 – Sound of Success (USA)　**97 p**
(Successor 85) [1991 8m³ 8m*] good-topped colt: closely related to group-placed
maiden Equator (by Nijinsky) and half-brother to several winners, including Derby
runner-up Hawaiian Sound (by Hawaii) and very useful 1m to 1¾m winner Rapids
(by Head of The River): dam ran twice: co-second favourite but green still, won
14-runner maiden at Leicester in October by 1½ lengths from Alhamad, pair well
clear, leading under 2f out and staying on strongly: has plenty of scope, and gives
impression likely to make a useful colt at 1¼m + . *J. H. M. Gosden.*

SOOTY TERN 4 br.c. Wassl 125 – High Tern 93 (High Line 125) [1990 10.2f*　**49**
12m 8f⁴ 8m⁶ a10g 1991 12.5d⁶ 10.8m 9m* 9f² a8g 11m⁴ 10.2d 8.9m³] compact colt:
plating-class handicapper: won selling event (no bid) at Hamilton in May: stays
1¼m: acts on firm ground, possibly unsuited by dead: inconsistent. *J. M. Bradley.*

SO REFINED 2 b.f. (May 29) Elegant Air 119 – Palumba 100 (Derring-Do 131)　**45**
[1991 6f⁴ 6m⁵ 5m⁶ 6g⁶ 7.5f 7m 8.3g] sturdy filly: sixth foal: half-sister to fair 1985
2-y-o 6f winner C Jam Blues (by Milford) and plating-class miler Victoria Line (by
High Line): dam won over 5f at 2 yrs and stayed 1¼m: poor maiden: soundly beaten
in sellers last 2 starts. *M. H. Easterby.*

SO RHYTHMICAL 7 b.g. Dance In Time (CAN) – So Lyrical 68 (So Blessed　**83**
130) [1990 5f⁶ 5.8f³ 6g⁴ 6m⁵ 6m³ 6m 7g 7m² 6g* 6s² 5s⁴ 1991 5g* 6m 5g⁶ 6d 5g⁴
5.6m 5.2f 7m 6m⁵ 7g] sturdy gelding: carries condition: modest handicapper: won at
Goodwood in June: best subsequent effort on fifth outing: stays 7f: acts on any
going: usually bandaged off-hind: has drifted right: sometimes sweats: sometimes
slowly away. *G. H. Eden.*

SO ROMANTIC (IRE) 3 b.f. Teenoso (USA) 135 – Romara 105 (Bold Lad (IRE)　**97**
133) [1990 7m* 7m 7d² 1991 8g² 10m³ 9d* 8g* 9g] leggy, close-coupled filly: fairly
useful performer: won minor event at Wolverhampton in April and listed race at
Milan in June: stays 1¼m: acts on good to firm ground and dead: consistent: visits
Old Vic. *G. Wragg.*

SO SMUG (USA) 2 b. or br.f. (Mar 11) Nureyev (USA) 131 – Smuggly (USA) 121　**67 p**
(Caro 133) [1991 6g³] $700,000Y: fourth foal: dam won Prix Saint-Alary and from
excellent family: weak 6/1-shot, over 4 lengths third of 7 to She's Pleased in maiden
at Newmarket in October, recovering from slow start, unable to quicken from over
1f out: will improve. *J. H. M. Gosden.*

SO SUPERB 2 b.g. (Feb 7) Superlative 118 – Top And Tail (USA) 81 (Tilt Up　**65**
(USA)) [1991 6g 6m 6g] 16,000F: strong, lengthy gelding: has scope: first foal: dam
sprinting half-sister to very useful French middle-distance stayer Petit Mont-
morency: easily best effort in maidens when around 10 lengths eighth of 21 to
Katakana at Newbury (blinkered) last time, soon fair bit to do then keeping on past
beaten horses: burly previously: will prove suited by further: gelded after final start.
J. L. Dunlop.

SOUGHAAN'S PRIDE (IRE) 3 gr.f. Soughaan (USA) 111 – Divine Apsara　**35**
(Godswalk (USA) 130) [1990 5g 5.8h a7g a7g 1991 a7g a7g 8g 8.3m⁴ 8.3m 11.6m⁶
9.7f] leggy, sparely-made filly: has a round action: poor performer: well beaten last 3
starts: better at 1m than shorter: no form on all-weather. *R. A. Bennett.*

SOUGHT OUT (IRE) 3 b.f. Rainbow Quest (USA) 134 – Edinburgh 117 **106**
(Charlottown 127) [1990 8m² 8g² 1991 10g² 11.3d⁴ 14.1f* 12g³ 14.6m 15d* 14v⁵]
rather leggy filly: useful performer: won maiden at Yarmouth in June and Ciga Prix
de Lutece (gamely made all, despite swishing tail) at Longchamp in October: 7
lengths third to Third Watch in Ribblesdale Stakes at Royal Ascot: well-beaten fifth
of 13 to Snurge in Group 3 event at Rome: suited by test of stamina: acts on firm and
dead going. *M. R. Stoute.*

SOUK (IRE) 3 b.f. Ahonoora 122 – Soumana (FR) (Pharly (FR) 130) [1990 6m⁴ **98**
7f* 1991 7g 7g* 8m³ 8d] smallish, sturdy filly: has a long, round stride: fairly useful
form: won handicap at Newmarket in August: third of 7 in moderately-run race at
Doncaster, easily better effort in listed events after: better at 1m than shorter: acts
on firm going, seemingly not on a soft surface: bandaged near-hind final start. *L. M.
Cumani.*

SOUL INTENT 3 b.f. Lochnager 132 – Tricky 66 (Song 132) [1990 5d 5f 1991 7g —
6f] workmanlike filly: little sign of ability. *W. Bentley.*

SOUL TRADER 2 b.f. (Jan 22) Faustus (USA) 118 – Hot Case 92 (Upper Case **61**
(USA)) [1991 6g⁵ 6f 6.1f] workmanlike filly: sixth foal: half-sister to 7f and 1m winner
Aitch N'Bee (by Northfields) and a winner in Norway: dam best at 7f: quite modest
maiden: best effort on debut: will stay 7f+. *B. W. Hills.*

SOUND INVESTMENT 2 b.c. (Apr 1) Song 132 – Pennies To Pounds 80 (Ile **56**
de Bourbon (USA) 133) [1991 6d⁴ 7g 7m] lengthy colt with plenty of scope: good
walker: third foal: brother to modest 7f winner Platinum Disc and half-brother to
3-y-o Sharp Money (by Sharpo): dam, 8.5f winner, is daughter of sprinting half-
sister to Mummy's Pet: plating-class maiden: failed to confirm promise of debut:
should stay 7f: sold 6,800 gns Newmarket Autumn Sales. *I. A. Balding.*

SOUPCON 5 b.m. King of Spain 121 – Duck Soup 55 (Decoy Boy 129) [1990 7g 7g —
7g⁴ a10g a8g⁴ 1991 a10g⁵ 12s] rather leggy mare: moderate walker: poor performer
nowadays: stays 1m: acts on soft going: often blinkered. *Miss B. Sanders.*

SOUTARI 3 br.c. Scorpio (FR) 127 – Sousocks (Soueida 111) [1990 7m 7m 8d 1991 —
11.7g 12m a12g⁵ a11g a11g 11.7m] good-bodied colt: showed signs of ability making most
in Southwell maiden third start, little otherwise: blinkered last 3 starts. *M.
McCormack.*

SOUTER'S HILL (USA) 4 b.c. Temperence Hill (USA) – Kissapotamus (USA) —
(Illustrious) [1990 7f 10.6f⁶ 12g 15.3m³ 16.2d³ 16g 15.8m⁵ 16m⁵ 15.3m 10f² 1991
14.6s⁴ 11s⁶ 15m 8m] tall, leggy colt: quite modest maiden at best: below form in
1991: stays 2m: acts on good to firm ground and dead. *T. Craig.*

SOUTH AUSTRALIA (CAN) 3 b.c. Shadeed (USA) 135 – Millicent (USA) **75** ?
(Cornish Prince) [1990 7m⁴ 8.2d⁶ 1991 10m² 10.2f² 10.4g 8f⁵] sturdy, lengthy colt:
modest maiden: well below form last 2 starts, dropping himself out 4f out in
apprentice race (reluctant then virtually bolted to post) final one: should stay 1½m:
acts on firm going: wore pricker near side at 3 yrs: sold 4,500 gns Newmarket
Autumn Sales: one to be wary of. *Mrs J. Cecil.*

SOUTH CROFTY (USA) 3 ch.g. Imp Society (USA) – Pia's Estonia (USA) **53**
(Nikoli 125) [1990 5f* 5f² 5m⁵ 5d⁴ 6d a6g⁴ 5s² a6g* 1991 a5g³ a5g³ a6g 5d⁵ 6g⁵]
strong, close-coupled gelding: has markedly round action: quite modest winner at 2
yrs: fair third in Southwell claimer, second and best effort in 1991: effective at 5f and
6f: probably acts on any going. *M. Johnston.*

SOUTH SEA 2 ch.c. (Apr 22) Dunbeath (USA) 127 – Silent Pearl (USA) (Silent **78**
Screen (USA)) [1991 8s 7g 8d* 8g] 16,000Y: big, lengthy colt: has scope: half-
brother to 1m to 1½m winner Silent Girl (by Krayyan) and 6f and 1¼m winner
Always Valiant (by Valiyar): dam, won twice in USA at up to 7f, is daughter of sister
to high-class middle-distance stayer Hopeful Venture: weak 12/1-shot and ridden by
7-lb claimer, comfortably won 11-runner maiden auction at Wolverhampton, leading
3f out: ran moderately (found little off bridle, flashed tail) in nursery at Redcar later
in October: will stay 1¼m. *L. M. Cumani.*

SOUTHWOLD AIR 2 b.c. (Apr 24) Elegant Air 119 – Habutai 70 (Habitat 134) —
[1991 7g] 18,000Y: third foal: half-brother to 3-y-o Bolt of Gold (by Glint of Gold) and
1¼m winner Tislam (by Formidable): dam maiden stayed 7f, is half-sister to
Almaarad: 20/1, always behind in 11-runner maiden at Salisbury in October. *J. L.
Dunlop.*

SOVEREIGN NICHE (IRE) 3 gr.c. Nishapour (FR) 125 – Sovereign Flash **51**
(FR) (Busted 134) [1990 6g 6d 1991 6g 7.5g 8m⁵ 10.2f³ 12g⁵ 10g 12g⁵] sturdy,
lengthy colt: plating-class handicapper, still a maiden: will prove suited by middle
distances: acts on firm going: sold to join N. Miller 3,400 gns Doncaster October
Sales. *Mrs J. R. Ramsden.*

SOVEREIGN PAGE (USA) 2 ch.c. (Apr 29) Caro 133 – Tashinsky (USA) **75** p
(Nijinsky (CAN) 138) [1991 6m] 26,000Y: tall, rather leggy colt: first foal: dam,
showed some ability in France, is closely related to smart 3-y-o Mukaddamah: 12/1,
green and better for race, under 5 lengths seventh of 14 to Yousefia in maiden at
Newmarket in October, keeping on steadily not knocked about: will improve,
probably over further. *B. Hanbury.*

SOVEREIGN ROCK (IRE) 2 ch.c. (Apr 17) Ballad Rock 122 – Sweet Accord 72 (Balidar 133) [1991 5m 5m 6.1m 6m 7d²] IR 14,000Y: compact colt: good walker: moderate mover: brother to useful middle-distance winner Rock Chanteur and half-brother to Irish 1½m winner Heavenly Peace (by Welsh Saint): dam won over 1m and 1¼m in Ireland: easily best effort (blinkered first time) when ½-length second of 22 to Mountain Ash in Doncaster nursery in November: likely to stay middle distances: acts on dead ground. *R. Hannon.*

SPACE TRAVELLER (IRE) 3 ch.g. Tate Gallery (USA) 117 – Parlais 101 — (Pardao 120) [1990 6m 1991 5g 8s] smallish, workmanlike gelding: behind in maiden auction and claimers. *J. S. Haldane.*

SPANIARDS CLOSE 3 b.g. King of Spain 121 – Avon Belle 75 (Balidar 133) 103 [1990 6g 1991 6d⁴ 6m² 6m⁴ 6d* 5.7g³ 5d* 5g* 5d² 5.2g³ 5d*] lengthy, workmanlike gelding: progressive form and finished the season in great heart: won maiden at Lingfield in June, claimers at Sandown in July and Wolverhampton in October, then handicap (carried 10-0) at Doncaster in November: best form at 5f: has form on good to firm ground, though best efforts with some give: has good turn of foot. *P. J. Makin.*

SPANISH EXPRESS 2 br.g. (Apr 30) King of Spain 121 – Pour Moi 73 (Bay 62 Express 132) [1991 5m⁵ 5f⁵ 5g⁵ 5d² 6g⁵] 3,000F, 13,000Y: sturdy gelding: third live foal: half-brother to a poor maiden by Noalto: dam placed over 5f and 6f: quite modest maiden: hung badly left at Haydock final outing (July), having led 4f: better form at 5f than 6f: easily best effort on dead ground. *R. Boss.*

SPANISH GLORY 2 b.f. (Apr 21) King of Spain 121 – Hearten (Hittite Glory 36 125) [1991 6g 7d] leggy, workmanlike filly: has scope: fifth foal: sister to 3-y-o Logarithm and 2 winners, including 1988 2-y-o 5f winner Spanish Oak and half-sister to very useful sprinter Northern Goddess (by Night Shift): dam unraced daughter of very smart middle-distance stayer Nortia: soundly beaten in large-field maidens at Newbury and Doncaster late in season. *I. A. Balding.*

SPANISH GRANDEE (USA) 3 b.g. El Gran Senor (USA) 136 – Stealthy Lady 79 (USA) (J O Tobin (USA) 130) [1990 6d 1991 8g⁴ 10m 8g² 8m* 7.1g² 8m 8f] 40,000Y: sparely-made ex-Irish gelding: poor mover: first foal: dam unraced daughter of Stumped, dam also of Sonic Lady: won handicap at Ayr in June: short-head second in similar event at Haydock, easily best subsequent effort: effective at 7f and 1m: probably doesn't act on firm ground: swished tail third start: seemed unsuited by track at Goodwood: has worn bandages behind. *P. W. Chapple-Hyam.*

SPANISH HARLEM 5 br.g. King of Spain 121 – Luscinia 73 (Sing Sing 134) 51 [1990 6g 6m³ 6f⁴ 5g 6h³ 5f 5m 7m 7d 5s⁶ 1991 6s² 6m 6m⁵ 6g² 6m⁶ 5f³ 6f⁴ 6d⁶] good-bodied gelding: plating-class handicapper: suited by 6f: probably acts on any going: found little third start and may be worth a try in blinkers: sold 1,550 gns Doncaster Summer Sales. *Mrs J. R. Ramsden.*

SPANISH LOVE 5 b. or br.m. Precocious 126 – San Marguerite 80 (Blakeney 37 126) [1990 a10g 10f 8m 8m 8.3g⁴ 8.3m² 8m³ 10m 8f⁴ 9g² 10d 1991 8g⁴ a7g 8.3m⁵ 6.9m* a7g] close-coupled, workmanlike mare: poor mover: poor handicapper: won at Folkestone (apprentices) in August: well beaten at Southwell nearly 4 months later: stays 9f: acts on firm going: trained reappearance by M. Usher. *M. McCormack.*

SPANISH MINER (USA) 2 b.c. (Mar 13) Northern Prospect (USA) – Bo 82 Bolero (USA) (Chieftain II) [1991 6d 7.1d² 8.2g⁵ a7g* a7g³] $50,000Y: compact colt: first foal: dam minor winner in North America: sire very useful sprinter: won maiden at Southwell late in year by 5 lengths, clear, from Big Easy: creditable third in nursery there following month: should stay 1m (last of 5 in listed race at Nantes third start): bandaged near-hind on debut. *A. A. Scott.*

SPANISH PERFORMER 2 b. or br.f. (Apr 21) King of Spain 121 – Dauphiness 53 76 (Supreme Sovereign 119) [1991 5f⁶ 5f² 6g³ 5m² 5f⁴ 6g] 2,000F: leggy, workmanlike filly: moderate walker and mover: half-sister to several winners, including 1½m winner Easy Purchase (by Swing Easy): dam 2-y-o 5f winner: plating-class maiden: blinkered, ran moderately in York seller final outing: likely to stay 7f. *T. Fairhurst.*

SPANISH REALM 4 b.f. King of Spain 121 – Miss Realm 86 (Realm 129) [1990 52 5f 6g 5v 5m 5m 5g 6g 6m 6f 8g 1991 5g a6g⁵ 5.1m a5g⁶ a6g⁶ 6m* 6m 7g 7m] small, sparely-made filly: plating-class handicapper: won at Southwell in September: stays 7f: acts on firm and dead going: tends to hang. *M. Brittain.*

SPANISH RHAPSODY 2 b.f. (Mar 24) King of Spain 121 – My Sweet Melody 34 62 (Music Boy 124) [1991 5g 6m a5g⁶ 7s⁵ 6m a8g] sparely-made filly: second foal:

half-sister to 3-y-o La Cassonade (by Sulaafah): dam poor maiden best at 5f: poor plater: blinkered third outing: sold 460 gns Ascot December Sales. *M. D. I. Usher.*

SPANISH STORM (IRE) 2 b.c. (Apr 6) King of Spain 121 – Storm Crest 80 **92** (Lord Gayle (USA) 124) [1991 5s² 5d* 5g³ 6g* 6g 7g³ 7m* 7m³ 7g⁵] 6,400Y: lengthy, useful-looking colt: has scope: good walker: moderate mover: half-brother to untrustworthy 3-y-o 7f winner Marching Past and 3 other winners here and abroad (all by Daring March), notably very useful sprinter Ongoing Situation: dam won over 5f at 2 yrs and stayed 1½m: fairly useful performer: successful in minor events at Thirsk (landed gamble) in April, Kempton in May and Newmarket (made all in 3-runner event) in August: creditable fifth of 9 in listed race at Craon, France, following month: suited by 7f: acts on good to firm ground and dead. *A. Hide.*

SPANISH VERDICT 4 b.g. King of Spain 121 – Counsel's Verdict (Firestreak **63** 125) [1990 7f⁴ 7h 6f* 7g 6m⁴ 8g 8f² 8.2d⁵ 8m 7d 1991 8g 8m³ 7h³ 7f 8d⁶ 8m² 7d⁴ 8f* 7f³ 7.5f³ 8m⁵ 8f⁶ 8h⁶ 8.5f 7m] sturdy, good-quartered gelding: has a round action: plating-class handicapper: won at Carlisle (apprentices) in July: stays 1m: acts on any going: effective visored or not. *Denys Smith.*

SPANISH WHISPER 4 b.g. Aragon 118 – Whisper Gently 91 (Pitskelly 122) **39** [1990 10f⁶ 8.3g³ 8g⁴ 7m⁶ 7m⁵ 7f 7f³ 8m* 8m a8g⁴ a8g 1991 a10g a10g⁴ 10.2s⁴ 12m⁶ 8.2d 8m² 9.7s⁴ 10m 7m⁶] compact gelding: moderate mover: poor handicapper: stays 1¼m: acts on good to firm and soft going: ran moderately in blinkers: tends to hang under pressure: winning hurdler: inconsistent. *J. R. Bostock.*

SPARE US ALL 7 b.g. Moorestyle 137 – Second Generation 95 (Decoy Boy 129) **38** [1990 6d 1991 a10g²] big, strong, workmanlike gelding: poor and lightly-raced maiden: needs further than 6f, and stays 1¼m. *B. J. Curley.*

SPARKLING VISION 2 b.f. (Apr 16) Vision (USA) – Amina 80 (Brigadier **43** Gerard 144) [1991 6d⁴ 7m⁵ 7m] 14,500Y: smallish, sparely-made filly: half-sister to several winners, including fairly useful 3-y-o 7f and 1m (at 2 yrs) winner Salmino (by Salmon Leap): dam 1¼m winner, is sister to Cheshire and Lancashire Oaks winner Princess Eboli: sire, 8.5f to 1½m winner in USA, including Grade 1 Secretariat Stakes, is brother to Caerleon: poor form: not seen out after August: will stay 1¼m+. *Mrs G. R. Reveley.*

SPARK OF PERSIA (IRE) 3 b.f. Persian Bold 123 – Meg's Pride (Sparkler **39** 130) [1990 NR 1991 10g 10m 10m 10.2d⁴ 12d⁵ 10g⁵] 10,500Y: leggy filly: half-sister to several winners, including 1¼m winner January Don (by Hold Your Peace): dam 1½m winner at 3 yrs in France, is half-sister to very smart French middle-distance colt Coquelin: quite modest plater: should be suited by return to 1½m: acts on dead going: blinkered (ran creditably) final start. *G. A. Pritchard-Gordon.*

SPARTAN SHAREEF (IRE) 2 b.c. (May 1) Shareef Dancer (USA) 135 – **73** p Spartan Helen (Troy 137) [1991 8m] 8,000Y, 12,500C: strong, compact colt: third foal: dam unraced daughter of staying half-sister to Blakeney and Morston: 25/1, around 12 lengths eighth of 22, soon niggled along, stayed on well, to Bold Pursuit in maiden at Newmarket in October: will improve, probably over middle distances. *C. E. Brittain.*

SPEAKER'S HOUSE (USA) 2 b.c. (Mar 21) Lear Fan (USA) 130 – Bring Me **82** Flowers (FR) (Dancer's Image (USA)) [1991 5m* 7d*] $57,000Y: close-coupled, workmanlike colt: has a short action: half-brother to winners in Germany and USA: dam French 2-y-o 6.5f winner later successful in USA: comfortable winner of maiden at Bath in May and 4-runner minor event at Chester following month: will stay 1m. *P. F. I. Cole.*

SPECIAL GALLERY (IRE) 2 b.f. (Feb 25) Tate Gallery (USA) 117 – Salvora **67** (USA) (Spectacular Bid (USA)) [1991 6g³ 6m⁵ 5.9f* 6f 6g 6.3s] IR 10,000Y: smallish, sturdy filly: third foal: half-sister to French 3-y-o 1½m winner Fuente Mayor (by Ti King): dam French 1¼m winner: quite modest performer: wide-margin winner of 2-runner auction event at Carlisle in July: well beaten in face of extremely stiff tasks last 2 outings: will be better suited by 7f. *J. M. P. Eustace.*

SPECIALIST DREAM (IRE) 2 b.c. (May 7) Irish River (FR) 131 – Confiture **—** (USA) (Empery (USA) 128) [1991 6g 6g] rather sparely-made colt: first foal: dam won at 1m and 1¼m (listed race at Bordeaux) at 3 yrs in France: no form in summer, in maiden auction (carrying condition, green, always behind) then seller (went keenly down) in Yorkshire. *L. J. Codd.*

SPECIAL REQUEST 3 b.g. Jalmood (USA) 126 – Legal Sound 85 (Legal Eagle **—** 126) [1990 a7g a6g 7m⁴ 7m 7g 8m 8m 10.6s 1991 7m⁴ 8m 10f 8f 10.1m 14.1m] small gelding: plater: form at 3 yrs only on reappearance: should stay 1m: acts on good to firm ground: blinkered 5 times: visored once: has worn bandages: sold 750 gns Ascot September Sales: resold 700 gns Ascot November Sales. *K. T. Ivory.*

SPECIFIC 2 b.f. (Feb 20) King of Spain 121 – Cut It Fine (USA) (Big Spruce **55** (USA)) [1991 6g 6.1m⁶ 7m* 7g] close-coupled filly: second foal: half-sister to 1989 Irish 2-y-o 6f winner Close The Till (by Formidable): dam poor stayer: fair plater: easily best effort here when winning at Catterick (no bid) in August: will probably stay 1m: slowly away second start: sold 2,500 gns Newmarket September Sales, sent to Denmark and successful twice there. *Sir Mark Prescott.*

SPECIFICITY (USA) 3 b.f. Alleged (USA) 138 – Mandera (USA) 112 (Vaguely **103** Noble 140) [1990 NR 1991 10.5g³ 12.2g* 12s³] leggy filly: eighth reported foal: half-sister to St Leger winner Touching Wood (by Roberto), Irish 1½m winner Mansky (by Nijinsky) and several winners in USA: dam won Princess Royal Stakes: 11/10 on, won 10-runner apprentice race at Catterick in October, always close up and holding Tanz by a neck: good third in listed race at Evry in November: should prove better at 1½m than shorter. *J. H. M. Gosden.*

SPECTACLE JIM 2 b.c. (Feb 24) Mummy's Game 120 – Welsh Blossom 100 **49** (Welsh Saint 126) [1991 6s a5g a6g4] 6,000F, 5,000Y: fourth reported foal: brother to 5f winner Game Features and a winner in Sweden and closely related to smart sprinter Treasure Kay (by Mummy's Pet): dam won 10 times over sprint distances: around 8 lengths fourth of 8 to Battle Colours in late-year maiden at Lingfield, best effort. *J. O'Donoghue.*

SPECTACULAR DAWN 2 gr.f. (Mar 30) Spectacular Bid (USA) – Early Rising **67** p (USA) (Grey Dawn II 132) [1991 7.1m⁶ 7m4] 23,000Y: leggy, unfurnished filly: fifth foal: half-sister to fairly useful sprinter Silver Singing (by Topsider) and a minor winner in USA by Timeless Moment: dam, minor winner in USA at about 1m, is out of half-sister to top-class Key To The Mint: quite modest form in autumn maidens at Sandown (backward and very green, ran wide, stayed on strongly) and Redcar: will be much better suited by 1m +. *J. L. Dunlop.*

SPECTRUM STAR 2 b.f. (Mar 19) Belfort (FR) 89 – Rainbow Trout (Comedy — Star (USA) 121) [1991 a8g] first foal: dam maiden stayed 6f: second favourite, soundly beaten in late-year maiden at Southwell. *A. C. Stewart.*

SPEED OIL 2 br.c. (Mar 6) Java Tiger 79 – Maydrum 50 (Meldrum 112) [1991 **46** 8.3g⁵ 6d] close-coupled colt: second foal: dam lightly-raced maiden: poor form in maidens at Hamilton (slowly away) and Haydock (tailed off) in autumn: withdrawn start on intended debut (unruly) and final intended outing (lame). *R. Bastiman.*

SPEEDO MOVEMENT 2 ch.f. (Feb 17) Scottish Reel 123 – Third Movement **44** 75 (Music Boy 124) [1991 6m⁶ 6.1f 8.1g 7g] 6,800F, 21,000Y: angular filly: fourth foal: half-sister to 11f winner Pleasure Flight (by Jalmood) and a winner in Italy: dam maiden stayed 7f: poor form, well beaten, in maidens: best effort at Catterick (on toes, swishing tail in paddock) final start. *J. Berry.*

SPEEDY SIOUX 2 ch.f. (Mar 11) Mandrake Major 122 – Sioux Be It (Warpath **36** 113) [1991 6m 7m] sparely-made filly: first foal: dam NH Flat race winner: little worthwhile form (never placed to challenge second occasion) in median auction maidens at York almost 3 months apart. *C. W. Thornton.*

SPELL OF THE YUKON (USA) 2 ro.f. (Jan 24) Spectacular Bid (USA) – **81** Winter Words (USA) (Northern Dancer) [1991 5g² 5d* 5m³ 6g* 6g 6g4] compact, quite attractive filly: fifth foal: half-sister to 7.3f (at 2 yrs) to 1½m winner Skazka (by Sir Ivor): dam, winner at up to 1¼m at 3 yrs, is half-sister to Run The Gantlet: fair performer: successful in maiden at Pontefract and nursery at Goodwood in summer, travelling smoothly in small fields then coming clear final furlong: good fourth of 18 in Newbury nursery final outing: will stay 7f: tends to be slowly away. *I. A. Balding.*

SPENDING RECORD (USA) 4 ch.c. Topsider (USA) – Final Figure (USA) **111** (Super Concorde (USA)) [1990 10d² 10m* 11m* 10m* 11g* 1991 10g⁵ 10g4 11m² 9g²] very useful Irish performer: ran well when in frame in 1991 behind Zoman in Group 2 event at the Curragh, Ruby Tiger in Group 2 event at Baden-Baden and George Augustus in listed race at Leopardstown: sent to USA, finishing fourth behind Filago in Grade 1 Oak Tree Invitational at Santa Anita and winning 9f listed River City Handicap at Churchill Downs: will stay 1½m: acts on good to firm ground. *D. K. Weld, Ireland.*

SPHINX 7 b.g. Auction Ring (USA) 123 – The Yellow Girl 102 (Yellow God 129) — [1990 a11g4 a11g⁶ 10m 10.6s 1991 10g 12.2m⁵] lengthy, robust gelding: poor handicapper: stays 11f: probably unsuited by firm going, acts on any other: tried blinkered once. *J. R. Bostock.*

SPICE KING (IRE) 2 ch.g. (Mar 29) Tender King 123 – Soeur Basile (FR) **41** (Belgio (FR) 122) [1991 5f 5f⁵ 6d 6m 5g⁴ 5g⁵ 6f⁴] 9,000 2-y-o: lengthy gelding: moderate mover: second foal: dam unraced close relative of Frere Basile: poor maiden: below best in Ripon selling nursery in August on final start: quite speedy: sold to Scandinavia 2,100 gns Newmarket Autumn Sales. *D. W. Chapman.*

SPIKENARD 2 b.f. (Feb 27) Slip Anchor 136 – Pomade 79 (Luthier 126) [1991 7f **57 p** 8.1g³] good-topped filly: has scope: fifth foal: half-sister to fair 1m winner Face Up (by Top Ville) and winning hurdler Pomatum (by General Assembly): dam disqualified 9f winner on sole outing: bit backward still, much better effort when third of 15 in maiden at Haydock (slowly away, kept on) in September: gives impression very much a staying type: likely to improve further. *P. T. Walwyn.*

SPINAYAB 2 b.f. (May 8) King of Spain 121 – Pallomere 85 (Blue Cashmere 129) — [1991 7g] third live foal: sister to a winner in Germany and half-sister to a winner in Italy by Anfield: dam best at 2 yrs, later 3-y-o 1m winner: 66/1, tailed off in 11-runner maiden at Salisbury in October. *E. A. Wheeler.*

SPINNING 4 b. or br.g. Glint of Gold 128 – Strathspey 105 (Jimmy Reppin 131) **110 §** [1990 12g⁵ 10m³ 10m* 10.8m* 12f² 10m² 10d 12g² 1991 10v⁶ 10.4m⁴ 12g³ 12g² 13.3f² 12m⁶ 10.9m² 12g⁴ 16.5m* 14.6d] tall, rather leggy, useful-looking gelding: good walker: easy mover: very useful performer: first past post in £17,800 handicap at Newmarket (hung left, demoted) in August fourth start and minor event at Doncaster (simple task) in October: mostly ran well in between, including in Group 2 event at Newbury (2½ lengths second to Drum Taps) on fifth outing and Grade 1 Turf Classic at Belmont Park (demoted place after finishing third to Solar Splendour): better at 1½m than shorter and stays 2m: acts on firm going, seems unsuited by a soft surface: has run creditably when blinkered (only near-eye covered penultimate start): has worn net muzzle: tends to hang (markedly so under pressure) and is a most difficult ride: not one to trust: winning hurdler. *I. A. Balding.*

SPIRITED 2 br.g. (Feb 9) Myjinski (USA) – Flying Glory (Flying Mercury) [1991 **34** a5g 5.2g 5m a6g] close-coupled, rather sparely-made gelding: seventh foal: brother to 3-y-o 5f winner Lady of The Fen and half-brother to 7f and 1m seller winner Clipsall (by Petitioner) and a winner abroad: dam unraced: soundly beaten in varied company, including selling: blinkered final start: has been bandaged. *Mrs N. Macauley.*

SPIRIT LEVEL 3 ch.f. Sunley Builds 102 – Tuneful Flutter (Orchestra 118) — [1990 NR 1991 10m 12.3g⁵ 12f a13g] sparely-made filly: first foal: dam twice-raced at 2 yrs: no worthwhile form, including in claimers and minor event. *C. R. Barwell.*

SPIRIT SAM 6 ch.h. Music Boy 124 – Kalia (Wollow 132) [1990 NR 1991 9.7m — a8g] robust horse: moderate mover: poor maiden: often blinkered, not in 1991. *R. V. King.*

SPIRITUALIST 5 ch.g. Simply Great (FR) 122 – Parima 72 (Pardao 120) [1990 — 16.2d 15m⁵ 16m² 16m² 1991 13.8d 16.2g⁶] angular gelding: has a long stride: plating-class handicapper: well beaten in first half of 1991: stays 2m: acts well on top-of-the-ground: sold to join A. Harrison's stable 3,000 gns Doncaster November Sales. *Dr J. Scargill.*

SPITFIRE GIRL 3 b.f. Glint of Gold 128 – Premiere Danseuse 116 (Saritamer **78** (USA) 130) [1990 NR 1991 12m³ 10.5g⁶ 14.1m⁶] leggy filly: half-sister to 11.7f winner Arial Star and 1986 2-y-o 7f winner Bracorina (both by High Line) and a winner in Italy: dam 7f winner, is half-sister to useful sprinters Glenturret and Rollahead: easily best effort in maidens when third at Salisbury in August: sold 2,800 gns Newmarket December Sales. *R. Charlton.*

SPITHEAD 3 b.g. Shareef Dancer (USA) 135 – Britannia's Rule 108 (Blakeney **56** 126) [1990 7g 1991 10g 10m 12f⁶ 12g 12.1s 17.2g a16g] robust gelding: worthwhile form only when sixth of 19 in handicap at Salisbury in September: should be well suited by further than 1½m: acts on firm going: coltish first 2 starts. *H. Candy.*

SPLASH OF COLOUR 4 ch.c. Rainbow Quest (USA) 134 – Cockade 104 **119** (Derring-Do 131) [1990 10g* 12g* 10g⁶ 1991 10g³ 13g² 12m³ 10g⁴ 12m* 12f⁵ 12f] strong colt: smart performer: sustained shin injury early at 3 yrs: returned to his best when winning Group 3 Prix Foy at Longchamp in September by 2 lengths from Panoramic: fair fifth to Sky Classic in Grade 1 Rothmans International at Woodbine following month: behind in Japan Cup (chipped bone in near-fore ankle) final start: suited by 1½m +: acts on good to firm ground: trained first 4 starts in 1991 by M. V. O'Brien: largely consistent: reportedly retired to stud in Japan. *N. Clement, France.*

SPLENDIDLY BOLD (IRE) 2 b.f. (Mar 18) Bold Arrangement 127 – **47 §** Splendidly Gay 80 (Lord Gayle (USA) 124) [1991 5g 6g 7m 6m³ 7f³ 6m⁵ 6m⁴ 6f⁶ 8m]

IR 1,900Y: rather sparely-made filly: has quick action: second living foal: half-sister to Irish 1½m winner Thatch Island (by Burslem): dam, 10.1f and 1¾m winner, is half-sister to very useful miler Tack On: poor maiden: has run in selling nursery: should stay 1¼m: blinkered last 6 starts: has been bandaged off-hind: has run in snatches and found little off bridle, and is one to treat with caution. *M. H. Easterby.*

SPLICE 2 ch.f. (May 19) Sharpo 132 – Soluce 98 (Junius (USA) 124) [1991 5d⁴ 5m² **82** 5m* 5m* 6f⁶ 5m* 5d] rather leggy filly: third foal: half-sister to ex-Irish 3-y-o 1m winner Solo Sail (by Slip Anchor) and 1m winner Alfujairah (by Diesis): dam Irish 7f winner, is half-sister to useful Irish middle-distance filly Cienaga: fair performer: successful in maiden at Folkestone and nurseries at Newcastle (August) and at Newmarket (October): ran respectably (though never able to get near leaders) in face of stiff task in Cornwallis Stakes at Ascot final outing: better form at 5f than 6f: races keenly. *J. R. Fanshawe.*

SPLIT SECOND 2 b.g. (Mar 29) Damister (USA) 123 – Moment In Time 91 **47** (Without Fear (FR) 128) [1991 7m 6m 8.1s] 9,000F, 8,000Y: leggy, rather angular gelding: fifth foal: dam 2-y-o 7f winner: poor form, well beaten, in maidens at Redcar and Edinburgh in autumn. *J. W. Watts.*

SPODE'S BLUE 4 b.f. Sadler's Wells (USA) 132 – Wedgewood Blue (USA) 87 **93** (Sir Ivor 135) [1990 7m⁵ 10g² 7g² 8.5d³ 12d⁴ 10m² 10.6d³ 13.6m* 12.3v* 16.5d³ 1991 16g³ 12m² 16g] rangy filly: moderate walker: fairly useful handicapper: not seen out after May: stays 2m: yet to race on very firm going, acts on any other: genuine and consistent. *B. Hanbury.*

SPOOF 4 b.f. Precocious 126 – Thimblerigger 62 (Sharpen Up 127) [1990 8g⁴ 8g² **52** 7.5d⁴ 8d⁴ 10f⁴ 10m⁴ 10m⁵ 1991 10.2s 12g⁴ 13.8g⁶ 12m⁶ 16m² 15.9m] workmanlike filly: plating-class handicapper nowadays: has taken keen hold, and likely to prove best short of 2m: acts on good to firm ground and dead: tried blinkered once. *M. D. Hammond.*

SPORTING HERITAGE (IRE) 3 b.g. Glenstal (USA) 118 – Sweet Pleasure — 88 (Sweet Revenge 129) [1990 NR 1991 a6g a8g] sixth foal: half-brother to useful 1986 French 2-y-o sprinter Ma Colombine and 1¼m winner Jaaziel (both by Jaazeiro): dam 6f winner at 2 yrs: blinkered, soundly beaten in late-season Southwell claimers. *D. J. G. Murray-Smith.*

SPORTING IDOL 6 b.g. Mummy's Game 120 – Village Idol 74 (Blakeney 126) — [1990 NR 1991 13.1f] leggy, workmanlike gelding: has a round action: winning plater as 4-y-o: no show only run in 1991: probably best at up to 1m: suited by plenty of give in the ground: below form when visored once: often flashes tail: winning hurdler. *C. L. Popham.*

SPORTING LASS 4 br.f. Blakeney 126 – Audela 76 (Sovereign Path 125) [1990 **37** 8m⁶ 10f³ 10.6d 8.2v 1991 a16g³ a12g⁴ a14g] lengthy, good-quartered filly: poor handicapper at best: stays 2m. *P. A. Kelleway.*

SPORTING SIMON 6 ch.g. Vaigly Great 127 – City Link Lass 92 (Double Jump **73** 131) [1990 6f² 6g² 6m* 6f* 7g* 6d 6m² 7m 6m 7m* 8d⁴ 7m 7.6v² 1991 8g 7.6d 7f 6g² 7g³ 7g⁵ 7g⁴ 7s 6m 7g] workmanlike, plain gelding: moderate mover: modest handicapper: effective at 6f to 1m: acts on any going: has been tried in blinkers: genuine: goes very well with forcing tactics: sold 6,000 gns Newmarket October Sales after final start. *B. R. Millman.*

SPORTING WEDNESDAY 6 b.g. Martinmas 128 – Philogyny 94 (Philip of — § Spain 126) [1990 11.7g 11.1m⁶ 10m a8g 8f* 7m 8g a8g 1991 a10g 8f 10.1s 8.1d 7m] leggy gelding: poor handicapper: no form in 1991: stays 1m: acts on firm going: has worn net muzzle and severe noseband: tailed off when blinkered once: not one to rely on. *K. O. Cunningham-Brown.*

SPORT OF FOOLS (IRE) 2 b.f. (Feb 3) Trojan Fen 118 – Senouire (Shirley **58** Heights 130) [1991 5d³ 6f 6f² 7m⁵ 6d² 7m⁶ 6m⁵ 6f 8.3g 8.9d] IR 900F: leggy, sparely-made filly: second foal: dam unraced: plating-class maiden: best form at 6f, though bred to stay much further: seems best with give in the ground: visored fifth (best effort) to seventh starts: trained first 7 outings by J. S. Wilson, next 2 by Miss L. Perratt: sold 700 gns Doncaster October Sales. *A. Bailey.*

SPORTS POST LADY (IRE) 3 ch.f. M Double M (USA) – Pasadena Lady **72** (Captain James 123) [1990 5f² 5f² 5m² 5g* 5g a6g 1991 a5g² 5d 6g 5m* 5f³ 5m* 5g⁴ 5.2f⁶ 5.1m² 5.1m 5g 5.1d 5.1g a5g*] angular, sparely-made filly: modest sprinter: won claimer at Lingfield in June, handicap at Newmarket in July and another claimer at Lingfield in December: best form at 5f: acts on firm going, apparently not on a soft surface: game. *C. J. Hill.*

SPORTS VIEW   2 b.g. (Feb 20) Mashhor Dancer (USA) – Persian Express   **52**
(Persian Bold 123) [1991 6f 8g⁶ 7g⁵] 5,200Y, 8,200 2-y-o: compact, quite attractive
gelding: third live foal: half-brother to 3-y-o In Truth (by Dreams To Reality),
successful at 8.2f (at 2 yrs) and 1½m: dam poor daughter of half-sister to very smart
Tacitus: plating-class maiden: will stay 1¼m. *R. J. Holder.*

SPORTSWORLD (USA)   3 b.c. Alleged (USA) 138 – Gallanta (FR) 112 **121**
(Nureyev (USA) 131) [1990 NR 1991 7d* 10m* 10g* 12g⁴ 8m²] $300,000Y: strong,
full-quartered colt: second foal: half-brother to useful 6f and 7f winner Sundance Kid
(by Fappiano): dam, 5.5f to 1m winner in France, is half-sister to Gay Mecene:
successful at the Curragh in maiden, listed race and Windfields Farm Gallinule
Stakes, making all to beat Runyon 4 lengths in last-named: well-beaten fourth of 6 to
Generous in Budweiser Irish Derby at the Curragh, travelling smoothly long way,
no extra and considerably handled final 2f: 5/4 on, good neck second of 6 to Star of
Gdansk (rec 3 lb) in Desmond Stakes at same course: stays 1¼m: sold to South
Africa. *M. V. O'Brien, Ireland.*

SPOT THE EARLYBIRD (USA)   2 ch.c. (Apr 13) Mertzon (USA) – Cornered   **58**
(USA) (Bold Commander (USA)) [1991 5f⁴ 5g³ 5m² 5d⁴ 5m⁴ 5m 5m⁴ 5m⁵ 7g]
$13,000F, $21,000Y, $42,000 2-y-o: small, sturdy colt: fourth reported foal: half-
brother to a multiple winner in USA by Tarboosh: dam won at up to 7f: sire (by Mr
Prospector) minor 6f winner: plating-class maiden: well beaten in face of stiff task in
Doncaster nursery over 7f: easily best form on a sound surface: visored fourth
outing: sold 6,500 gns Newmarket Autumn Sales. *J. Berry.*

SPOUT HOUSE (IRE)   2 b.f. (May 16) Flash of Steel 120 – Otterhill 67   **45**
(Brigadier Gerard 144) [1991 5g⁶ 6m 5.1d⁴ 7f³ 7.5f⁴ 7.5f² 8m⁴ 8.9m] 13,000Y: small,
leggy filly: good walker: has a roundish action: half-sister to 3 winners here and in
Ireland, including useful miler Ottergayle (by Lord Gayle): dam daughter of very
smart 2-y-o Lowna: poor maiden: fair efforts in northern nurseries fifth to seventh
starts: stays 1m: acts on firm ground: blinkered third to seventh outings. *M. H.
Easterby.*

Classic Thoroughbreds Plc's "Sportsworld"

SPRAY OF ORCHIDS 2 ch.f. (Mar 14) Pennine Walk 120 – Mana (GER) **48**
(Windwurf (GER)) [1991 5f⁵ 5f⁴ 6d 6.9m² 7.5f 7m 7.5f⁴ 7m⁶ 7.1m²] 8,000Y: lengthy
filly: third reported foal: half-sister to 1990 2-y-o 7f winner Losmanar (by Los
Santos): dam won at 2 yrs in Germany: modest plater: has run creditably in selling
nursery: will be better suited by 1m: blinkered (no form) third outing. *J. Etherington.*

SPRINGDALE HALL (USA) 3 ch.f. Bates Motel (USA) – Locksley Hall **50**
(USA) (Raja Baba (USA)) [1990 NR 1991 8.5f⁵ 7m 7.5m⁴ 10d 8.5f⁵ 12m 10.3m]
$28,000Y: big, workmanlike filly: first foal: dam lightly-raced daughter of fairly
useful 7f (at 2 yrs) and 11.7f winner Thoughts of Love: plating-class form: should
prove suited by further than 1m: acts on firm going: sweating and edgy sixth outing:
winning hurdler. *M. W. Easterby.*

SPRINGFIELD GIRL 3 ch.f. Royal Vulcan 83 – Viceroy Lass 42 (Certingo) **—**
[1990 NR 1991 8m 8m 6m] workmanlike filly: first foal: dam maiden, stayed 1¼m:
tailed off in maidens and claimer: blinkered final start. *M. J. Charles.*

SPRINGFIELD PARK 3 gr.g. Belfort (FR) 89 – Crimson Dawn (Manado 130) **—**
[1990 5g 5f⁴ 5m 1991 5f 6g] lengthy, rather shallow-girthed gelding: poor plater:
visored at 3 yrs. *C. J. Hill.*

SPRING FORWARD 7 b.h. Double Form 130 – Forward Princess (USA) **35 §**
(Forward Pass) [1990 18.4d 17.6m* 14s 16g⁵ 15.8d⁶ 18.4f⁴ 16.5f³ 16f⁴ 16g⁴ 17.6f⁵
15.5f⁴ 1991 14m 21.6f 18.4d 17.6m 15s⁴ 16m* 15.1m⁶ 19m 15.9m a14g] small, leggy
horse: usually looks well: poor handicapper: gamely won slowly-run event at Redcar
in July: last after: suited by a test of stamina: acts on any going: sometimes
blinkered, usually visored nowadays: tends to get behind: unreliable. *R. E. Peacock.*

SPRING GUN (USA) 3 ch.c. Mr Prospector (USA) – Seven Springs (USA) 114 **84**
(Irish River (FR) 131) [1990 NR 1991 10g⁴] lengthy, good-topped colt: second
foal: closely related to 8.2f winner Gypsy River (by Alydar): dam, winner of Prix
Morny, is granddaughter of sister to Oaks winner Pia: about 3 lengths fourth of 8 to
Saddlers' Hall in £7,300 contest at Newmarket in May, close up long way. *G.
Harwood.*

SPRING HAY 5 gr.g. Wassl 125 – Spring Silver (Palestine 133) [1990 NR 1991 **—**
12g] leggy, quite good-topped gelding: useful form at best at 3 yrs: well beaten in
handicap only run in 1991 (April): will stay beyond 1½m: acts on any going. *D.
Nicholson.*

SPRING HIGH 4 b.f. Miami Springs 121 – High Voltage 82 (Electrify) [1990 5f **31**
5g 6d 5g a7g a6g a8g 1991 6m 10f 10.1d 7g 8m 8f² 6.9f² a7g² 7m⁶ 6m⁶ 7s a7g⁴ a8g⁴] a45
tall, leggy, lengthy filly: poor handicapper: stays 1m: acts on firm going, seems
unsuited by soft: below form when visored: goes very well blinkered: suited by
forcing tactics. *K. T. Ivory.*

SPRINGLAKE'S LADY 5 b.m. Music Boy 124 – North Pine (Import 127) [1990 **—**
NR 1991 a7g] lengthy mare: fair plater as 3-y-o: blinkered and last in claimer in
March, only run on flat since: stays 9f: acts on firm going. *I. E, Forte.*

SPRING MORN (USA) 6 b.g. Alleged (USA) 138 – Valenciennes (USA) **—**
(Northern Dancer) [1990 8g 8.2s 10g⁵ 12g* 12.3m⁴ 14m 10.6d 1991 16.2g⁴ 21.6f]
lengthy gelding: poor handicapper: seems to stay 2m: best efforts on good ground:
has won when blinkered: often slowly away: has hung badly right. *A. P. Stringer.*

SPRING SAINT 2 ch.c. (Apr 23) Midyan (USA) 124 – Lady of Chalon (USA) **—**
(Young Emperor 133) [1991 7g⁵] 10,000Y: half-brother to several winners, including
smart sprinter Enchantment (by Habitat) and Irish 8.5f and 1¼m winner Emperor
To Be (by Lomond): dam minor winner at up to 6f in USA: 8/1, one-paced 7½ lengths
fifth of 9 to Well Saddled in maiden at Salisbury in October: dead. *M. J. Heaton-Ellis.*

SPRINGS WELCOME 5 b.m. Blakeney 126 – Tomfoolery 73 (Silly Season **70**
127) [1990 12f 10g 12.3d 12ma12g*a12g* 12.3g² 14g 13d 12v⁴a12g³a12g⁴a14g³ 1991 a78
16g⁶ 14d 11.5g* 11.9m⁶ a16g³ 12g a10g* 10m⁴ 14s⁵ 12d² 12g⁵ 12d] workmanlike
mare: fair handicapper: won at Lingfield in May (claimer) and August: effective at
1¼m and stays 2m: acts on good to firm and good going and on all-weather surfaces:
tends to get well behind: has won for 7-lb claimer. *C. A. Cyzer.*

SPRING TERN (USA) 3 ch.c. Arctic Tern (USA) 126 – Date (USA) (What Luck **60**
(USA)) [1990 8g 7m³ 10.2s 1991 9d 10g 10m⁶ 12m* 12f³a11g⁴] sturdy colt: has a
quick action: plating-class handicapper: rallied well to win at Folkestone in August:
below form at Southwell on first run for 3 months: may well stay beyond 1½m: best
efforts on top-of-the-ground: blinkered last 3 outings: sold out of G. Harwood's
stable 7,800 gns Newmarket September Sales before final one. *R. O'Leary.*

SPRING TO GLORY 4 b.g. Teenoso (USA) 135 – English Spring (USA) 116 **42**
(Grey Dawn II 132) [1990 10m⁴ 10.8m⁵ 11.5f⁵ 12m* 14m 16m⁵ 1991 12.3g 10.8g 12f
9.7s⁴] leggy, angular gelding: good mover: poor performer: stays 2m: acts on good
to firm and soft ground: has run creditably when blinkered: flashes tail. *R. J. Hodges.*

SPRING TO THE TOP 4 b.c. Thatching 131 – Queen of The Brush (Averof **69**
123) [1990 8m 8m 7g⁴ 6g 7g 7g* 1991 10m 8d 8f⁴ 8g* 7g 8g² 9g⁶] rather leggy colt:
has a round action: quite modest handicapper: won at Yarmouth in July: worth
another try at 1¼m: acts on good to firm ground, possibly unsuited by dead: seems
suited by galloping track. *J. W. Payne.*

SPRITSAIL 5 b.h. Kalaglow 132 – Set Sail 64 (Alpenkonig (GER)) [1990 11d³ **114**
12m* 12s³ 1991 10g* 12m⁶ 12m³ 12m⁴] tall, rather leggy horse: has a quick action:
very useful performer: won listed event at Goodwood (beat Lord Charmer
comfortably by 2½ lengths) in May: ran creditably after when in frame in Hardwicke
Stakes at Royal Ascot (unseated rider to post, wandered under pressure when 1½
lengths third to subsequently-demoted Topanoora) and Princess of Wales's Stakes
at Newmarket (broke blood vessel): effective at 1¼m to 1½m: best form on a sound
surface: has been retired. *H. R. A. Cecil.*

SPROUTING VENTURE 4 ch.f. Crooner 119 – Two Diamonds (Double Jump **—**
131) [1990 a10g a8g⁵ 11.5g 10d 10m 12d 1991 12m⁶ 16.4m] sparely-made filly: poor
handicapper: seems to stay 1½m: acts on good to firm ground. *R. Curtis.*

SPURNED (USA) 4 b.f. Robellino (USA) 127 – Refill 88 (Mill Reef (USA) 141) **83**
[1990 8.5g² 11.3d 10g 10.1m³ 10m⁶ 10.1g 10g⁵ 11s⁶ 1991 8m² 10f² 11.9g 10.2m⁴]
lengthy, rather angular filly: fair handicapper: stays 1¼m well: acts on firm ground:
raced very freely when visored once. *I. A. Balding.*

Lady Howard de Walden's "Spritsail"

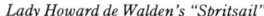

Palan Handicap, Ascot—
Stack Rock hangs on from Mango Manila (left) and Lallapaloosa (rails)

SPY IN THE SKY (BAR) 2 b.c. (Feb 7) Concorde Hero (USA) – Spy Queen 87 **46**
(Quisling 117) [1991 7g 6g 8m a8g] good-topped colt: dam, 2-y-o 6f winner, exported
to Barbados in 1972: poor form, including in sellers: well beaten on equitrack: best
run at 6f. *R. Hannon.*

SRIVIJAYA 4 b.c. Kris 135 – Princess Pati 124 (Top Ville 129) [1990 10.5d² 11g² **76**
11g² 12.5g* 12g 11.8s⁴ 1991 9f³ 10.6g 9m* 8s* 7d² 7m⁴ a8g] good-bodied colt:
usually looks very well: first foal: dam won Irish Oaks: won maiden at
Maisons-Laffite when trained at 3 yrs by A. Fabre: winning hurdler for D.
Nicholson's stable (sold 8,400 gns Doncaster Spring Sales) in February, 1991: won
claimers at Redcar and Edinburgh in summer: claimed out of N. Tinkler's stable
£13,529 penultimate start: effective at 7f, and stays 12.5f: acts on good to firm and
soft going. *Mrs J. Jordan.*

STACK ROCK 4 b.f. Ballad Rock 122 – One Better 77 (Nebbiolo 125) [1990 7.2d **88**
8s⁵ a8g* a7g 1991 10.8m 6m² 7m² 7.1g³ 6g² 7g² 6g* 5g⁶ 6g⁵ 7m⁴ 6m* 6m*] robust
filly: poor mover: improved handicapper in 1991: won at Ascot (£10,100 contest) in
July, Ayr in September and Newmarket in October: seems ideally suited by 6f: acts
on good to firm ground: ran well for claimer: goes very well with forcing tactics:
tough, genuine and consistent. *E. J. Alston.*

STAGECRAFT 4 b.r. Sadler's Wells (USA) 132 – Bella Colora 119 (Belly- **127**
pha 130) [1990 10g³ 10.5g* 10g* 1991 10m* 10g* 10d² 10.4g³ 10d³ 9.7d³ 10m]
    By season's end, the standing ovations that had greeted Stagecraft in
early summer had died away, but while unable to maintain the rate of improvement that had promised to take him right to the top, he kept his form
quite well apart from a lack-lustre race in the Dubai Champion Stakes on his
final appearance in Britain. The improvement Stagecraft showed in May and
June saw him extend his winning sequence to four with clear-cut victories in
the Group 3 Brigadier Gerard Stakes at Sandown and the Group 2 Prince of
Wales's Stakes at Royal Ascot. He'd won a maiden at York and a minor event
at Newmarket at the tail-end of a short season as a three-year-old, being
particularly impressive at Newmarket, where he'd shown a good turn of foot
before beating Philharmonia eased right up. Stronger opposition in an eleven-
runner field at Sandown included Emperor Fountain and Stapleford Manor,
but Stagecraft, who started favourite at 100/30, was every bit as impressive

again, quickening clear in the final two furlongs, having been poised in third from early in the straight. Bold Russian chased him from the distance, but couldn't match Stagecraft's acceleration and was two and a half lengths down at the line. Croupier, who finished the same distance away in third, reopposed Stagecraft in a field of six for the Prince of Wales's Stakes at Royal Ascot. Stagecraft headed the market at 6/4; Terimon, who'd finished second to In The Groove in the Coronation Cup at Epsom on his previous start, shared second favouritism at 5/2 with Zoman, a close third behind Sanglamore and Priolo in the Prix d'Ispahan at Longchamp on his latest outing. Croupier started at 25/1, and another outsider Karinga Bay made the running, tracked by Zoman with Starstreak third on the inside. Stagecraft raced on Starstreak's outside, travelling well within himself, and once shaken up halfway up the straight he lengthened his stride in fine style. Stagecraft drifted across to the rail once in front, but had already put the issue beyond doubt and though eased in the last fifty yards, he still had three lengths to spare over Zoman, who held second by a short head from Terimon.

Stagecraft's Sandown and Royal Ascot performances drew comparisons with that of Mtoto, who'd won the Brigadier Gerard Stakes and the Prince of Wales's as a prelude to success in the Coral-Eclipse in 1987; and Stagecraft was made 2/1 favourite for the latest running at Sandown in July. In a dramatic race, he failed by only a head to complete the hat-trick, cruising up to lead two furlongs out and soon quickening into what looked a winning advantage, but being worn down by the determined rally of the outsider Environment Friend, as the pair drew clear. Stagecraft finished seven lengths ahead of third-placed Sanglamore at Sandown and backers were prepared to give him another chance, but the Eclipse turned out to be the pinnacle of his achievement. He never got in a blow when odds on in the Juddmonte International Stakes at York in August, held up in a race run at a muddling pace on heavily-watered ground, and finished a well-held third behind Terimon and Quest For Fame. The following month, he couldn't match Suave Dancer's scintillating burst—few middle-distance horses could—in the Meadow Meats Irish Champion Stakes at Leopardstown, though he chased the winner hardest for much of the straight before Environment Friend ran on to finish a four-length second, two lengths in front of Stagecraft with Zoman fourth. At Longchamp in October Stagecraft was beaten three quarters of a length and a head by Wiorno and Muroto in the Group 2 Prix Dollar, though on this occasion he came out marginally the best horse at the weights, and ran probably his best race since the Eclipse.

Like Selkirk, Stagecraft raced as a rig in the latest season. He was an entire when making 520,000 guineas at the Newmarket Highflyer Yearling Sales. He's from the second crop of the highly successful Sadler's Wells, and is the first foal of Bella Colora, who was beaten only a short head and the same by Oh So Sharp and Al Bahathri in the One Thousand Guineas. Bella Colora failed to stay a mile and a half in testing conditions when fifth behind Oh So Sharp in the Oaks, and gained her three-year-old successes in the ten-furlong Lupe Stakes at Goodwood and the nine-furlong Prix Dollar at Longchamp. Her dam Reprocolor, who like Bella Colora was trained by Michael Stoute,

Prince of Wales's Stakes, Ascot—Stagecraft puts daylight between himself and, right to left, Terimon, Zoman and Karinga Bay

Sheikh Mohammed's "Stagecraft"

Stagecraft (b.r. 1987)	Sadler's Wells (USA) (b 1981)	Northern Dancer (b 1961)	Nearctic
			Natalma
		Fairy Bridge (b 1975)	Bold Reason
			Special
	Bella Colora (b 1982)	Bellypha (gr 1976)	Lyphard
			Belga
		Reprocolor (ch 1976)	Jimmy Reppin
			Blue Queen

finished fourth at Epsom and later won the Lancashire Oaks. Reprocolor was also responsible for Stoute's Irish Oaks winner Colorspin, the dam of the three-year-old Opera House, but there's plenty of speed further back in the pedigree, and Reprocolor's dam Blue Queen is a half-sister to the top-class sprinter Sandford Lad. Bella Colora's second foal Hyabella (by Shirley Heights) showed very useful form at a mile in 1991; the two-year-old Alum Bay, a colt by Reference Point, made 46,000 guineas as a yearling, and was in training with Henry Cecil in the latest season; the mare also has a yearling filly by Sadler's Wells, and a filly foal by Nashwan. Stagecraft was backed for the Derby before he ever ran, but had just one outing as a two-year-old, being beaten into second at Thirsk. His latest season was his first full one, and he's to continue his career in the United States with trainer Bill Mott. A strong, lengthy sort, usually outstanding in appearance, he was a fine walker, but showed a rather round action in his faster paces. He acted on good to firm ground, showed his best form with some give. It was a shame he was never tried at a mile and a half. *M. R. Stoute.*

STAGE PLAYER 5 b.g. Ile de Bourbon (USA) 133 – Popkins 120 (Romulus 129) —
[1990 NR 1991 18s 17.1m⁵ 17.2f 16.2g⁵] workmanlike, deep-girthed gelding: fair
handicapper at best at 3 yrs: well below best in first half of 1991: best form at around
1¼m: acts on good to firm ground and dead: joined Miss S. Wilton: winning hurdler.
R. Simpson.

STAG NIGHT 2 ch.g. (May 20) Good Times (ITY) – Deer Forest (Huntercombe 51
133) [1991 5f4 6g² 7m² 6m⁶ 7m] 1,200Y: strong, workmanlike gelding: poor mover:
brother to a winner in Hong Kong and half-brother to 3 winners, including 7f and 1m
winner Ballnacarn (by Firestreak): dam no form in 3 outings: plating-class maiden:
runner-up in maiden auction at Pontefract and 17-runner seller (heavily-backed
favourite, well clear of remainder) at Redcar in June: ran moderately afterwards:
will stay 1m. *C. Tinkler.*

STAIRWAY TO HEAVEN (IRE) 3 b.f. Godswalk (USA) 130 – Cathryn's 66
Song (Prince Tenderfoot (USA) 126) [1990 6f* 7m² 6d² 7d* 7s a8g* a8g³ a8g* 1991
a7g² 8.2m³ 7g⁶ 6d³ 6.9m² 7g⁴ 8f³ 7m⁶ 8m* 8m* 8.3f⁶ a8g a7g] angular,
sparely-made filly: smart plater: won handicap (no bid) at Thirsk and claimer at
Newcastle in August: never dangerous last 3 outings: better over 1m than shorter:
acts on firm and dead going: blinkered last 5 outings: suitable ride for apprentice:
genuine: trained until after eleventh start by T. Barron. *C. R. Beever.*

STAMFORD BRIDGE 3 b.c. Dominion 123 – Meadowbank 86 (Northfields 60 d
(USA)) [1990 5f* 6g⁵ 5m³ 5g² 6m⁶ 5m⁶ 6f 6d 1991 5d³ 7g 6g 6m 6m⁴ 6f 8m 7m 6g]
sturdy colt: has a round action: quite modest handicapper who lost his way: stays 6f:
acts on firm and dead ground: bandaged last 4 starts. *M. Brittain.*

STANDARD ROSE 8 b.m. Ile de Bourbon (USA) 133 – Betsy Ross (Petingo —
135) [1990 NR 1991 12f 18m⁴] angular, sparely-made mare: poor and very
lightly-raced performer: seems to stay 18f: best form on soft going: trained
reappearance by M. Madgwick: winning hurdler. *M. R. Channon.*

STAND AT EASE 6 b.g. The Brianstan 128 – Plush 75 (Lombard (GER)) [1990 55 d
NR 1991 12m 8f⁶ 12m 8h* 9m⁶ 8s³ 8g⁵ 8.3f⁴ 8f] workmanlike gelding: poor
performer nowadays: won claimer at Carlisle in June: ran moderately after: stays
1m: acts on any going. *W. Storey.*

STANDING CAST (IRE) 2 ch.c. (Mar 22) Chief Singer 131 – Love For Poetry 87
(Lord Gayle (USA) 124) [1991 7s³ 7s³ 6s*] first reported foal: dam Irish 1m to 9f
winner at 3 yrs: favourite following promising efforts in similar events in October,
won 12-runner maiden at Naas following month, always prominent then drawing
clear final 1f: should stay 1m: may improve. *Mr D. K. Weld.*

STANE STREET (IRE) 3 b.f. Gorytus (USA) 132 – Tumble Ria (Tumble Wind 48
(USA)) [1990 a7g a8g⁶ 1991 a10g³ 11m* 10.8m] second favourite, sold out of P.
Makin's stable 6,000 gns after winning seller at Wolverhampton in May, running on
strongly to lead inside final 1f: last of 17 in selling handicap over 3 months later:
should stay 1½m: sold 1,600 gns Ascot September Sales. *D. C. Jermy.*

STANI (USA) 2 b.c. (Apr 6) Shahrastani (USA) 135 – Shelf Talker (USA) (Tatan 79 p
(ARG)) [1991 7m*] $185,000Y: strong colt: half-brother to numerous winners,
including dual classic-placed Bellotto (by Mr Prospector) and good 1981 American
2-y-o Header Card (by Quack): dam useful winner at up to 9f: 14/1 and backward,
won 16-runner maiden at Leicester in October by a length from Touch Paper,
running green then picking up well from 2f out, pushed out firmly: showed a round
action: will stay 1¼m: will improve. *B. Hanbury.*

STANWAY 4 b.g. Sandhurst Prince 128 – Spring Bride 57 (Auction Ring (USA) 47
123) [1990 10g 10f 8m² 9g⁴ 11.7m⁴ 12m⁵ 10m⁴ 1991 10.8m 8.3g⁶ 10.8g⁵ 9.7s⁵ 16.2d]
strong, good-topped gelding: poor maiden: stays 1½m: best efforts on top-of-the-
ground (acts on hard going): tried blinkered: races keenly: trained first 2 starts by T.
Casey: joined Mrs D. Joynes and is a winning hurdler. *K. S. Bridgwater.*

STAPLEFORD LADY 3 ch.f. Bairn (USA) 126 – Marie Galante (FR) (King of 46
The Castle (USA)) [1990 6g 7m 8d⁵ 1991 12f 14g⁵ 12d⁴ 12f⁴ a12g² 12m³] leggy,
angular filly: plater: creditable second at Southwell: should stay well: acts on dead
ground, below form on very firm: sold to join R. Manning 4,000 gns Newmarket
Autumn Sales. *A. Hide.*

STAPLEFORD MANOR (USA) 4 br.c. Riverman (USA) 131 – Round The 108
Rosie (USA) (Cornish Prince) [1990 8m² 8m* 10.1m* 10m² 12g⁴ 1991 9m⁶ 10g² 10m
12g⁵ 12.1d⁴ 12g⁴] tall, quite attractive colt: good mover: useful performer: ran well
in Group 3 event at Sandown (3 lengths second to Noble Patriarch) and
moderately-run listed race won by Mukddaam at Newmarket second and fourth

starts: effective at 9f, and stays 1½m (at least in moderately-run race): acts on good to firm ground, seems unsuited by dead. *L. M. Cumani.*

STAPLETON (IRE) 2 b.c. (Apr 19) Dance of Life (USA) – Flying Anna (Roan Rocket 128) [1991 6f⁵ 6m² 6m²] IR 40,000F, IR 42,000Y: strong, lengthy, useful-looking colt: has scope: half-brother to 3 winners, including Irish 1½m winner Sotheby Sound (by Auction Ring) and Irish 1m to 9f winner Alianna (by Nebbiolo): dam Irish 5f and 1m winner: sire 7f (at 2 yrs) to 1½m winner, won Grade 1 Man o' War Stakes: progressive colt: didn't handle bend well at Southwell final start, then ran on strongly despite carrying head high: will be better suited by 1m: likely to improve further. *J. W. Watts.*   **65 p**

STARCHY COVE 4 br.f. Starch Reduced 112 – Rosey Covert (Sahib 114) [1990 6m⁶ 5m⁵ 5m⁵ 6g 5g³ 6m* 6g 5f³ 6f² 6m 6g 6g 1991 6m³ 5f 5g 5.9f⁶ 5.1m a5g] leggy filly: plating-class handicapper: well below form after reappearance: stays 6f: probably best on top-of-the-ground: saddle slipped and bolted second start, also bolted (withdrawn) third intended outing. *R. Hollinshead.*   **55 d**

STARCHYS IMAGE 3 b.g. Starch Reduced 112 – Mrs Dumbfounded (Adropejo 114) [1990 8.2m 6g⁴ 7m⁵ 1991 8m 5g⁴ 1.5m 8g³ 7f 8.3m 6.1m⁶ 7m 11d] compact gelding: fair plater: ran moderately last 4 starts: stays 1m: acts on firm going: blinkered seventh outing. *B. Palling.*   **51**

STAR CONNECTION 3 b.f. Faustus (USA) 118 – Emerald Rocket 69 (Green God 128) [1990 5g⁴ 5m² 5m⁴ 5g³ a5g⁴ 1991 8.2d⁴ 8.5f⁴ 7m⁵] workmanlike, good-quartered filly: carries condition: moderate mover: quite modest maiden: ran creditably in handicaps in the spring: stays 8.5f: acts on firm and dead going: ran moderately in blinkers at 2 yrs. *R. M. Whitaker.*   **60**

ST ARILDA 4 b.f. Pas de Seul 133 – St Isabel (Saint Crespin III 132) [1990 8f 10.4g⁴ 12f⁴ 16m 1991 12s² 16g⁵ 16s* 13d⁴ a18g⁶] sparely-made filly: quite modest handicapper: won at Newcastle in April: well beaten final start, first for 4 months: effective at 1½m, and stays well: probably acts on any going. *M. Bell.*   **64**

STAR LEADER 4 b.f. Kafu 120 – Sweet Relief 90 (Sweet Revenge 129) [1990 6f⁶ 8m⁴ 6f⁵ 7g³ 7m* 8m 7m 8.2s 1991 6f⁶ 10m] tall, short-backed filly: moderate mover: plating-class handicapper: no show in 1991: stays 7f: acts on good to firm ground. *R. Hollinshead.*   **—**

STARLIGHT FLYER 4 b.c. In Fijar (USA) 121 – Nareen (USA) (The Minstrel (CAN) 135) [1990 7g 8.2s⁴ 8g² 8m*ᵈⁱˢ 10.5m 10.1g 7g 1991 6s 7m 8m* 8.2m² 8g* 8d* 8.1g³ 7.9g 8.1m 8m] workmanlike, good-bodied colt: carries condition: moderate mover: much improved handicapper in first half of 1991, successful at Thirsk and Sandown (2, £24,900 event second occasion): below form last 3 starts: best at 1m: acts on good to firm but best efforts with some give in the ground (acts on dead): best in blinkers. *M. Moubarak.*   **99**

STARLIGHT WONDER 5 ch.m. Star Appeal 133 – My Lady Muriel (USA) (Visible (USA)) [1990 NR 1991 9g⁴ 14.1m³ 13.6d] lengthy, sparely-made mare: poor maiden: seems to stay 1¾m: acts on good to firm ground: has been unruly at start: winning maiden. *R. E. Barr.*   **39**

STAR LORD 5 b.h. Lord Gayle (USA) 124 – Crack of Light 95 (Salvo 129) [1990 12m³ 14g 12m 1991 12m* 12.3g⁶ 16.1g] angular, sparely-made horse: good mover with a long stride: fairly useful handicapper but clearly difficult to train: won at Salisbury in April, veering sharply left under pressure inside last: ran as if something badly amiss final start: probably stays 1¾m: acts on good to firm and heavy going: takes keen hold: sold only 4,800 gns Newmarket Autumn Sales. *A. C. Stewart.*   **89**

STAR MAESTRO 9 br.g. Music Maestro 119 – Maryland Star 76 (I Say 125) [1990 NR 1991 12g] sparely-made gelding: poor mover: poor plater: best at short of 1½m: suited by give in the ground nowadays: has worn severe bridle. *O. Brennan.*   **—**

STAR MOVER 2 ch.f. (Apr 25) Move Off 112 – Star Attention 91 (Northfields (USA)) [1991 7g⁶ 8.1m⁵ 8.1s] leggy filly: fifth living foal: dam best at sprint distances: poor form in late-season maidens: will stay 1¼m. *W. A. Stephenson.*   **49**

STAR NEWS 3 b.g. Tremblant 112 – Blakesware Saint 74 (Welsh Saint 126) [1990 6m³ 6v⁴ 1991 6m* 7g 7m 8g 10f⁶ 10g⁵ 8m 7m 8m 7m] angular gelding: easily best effort to win maiden at Pontefract in May: should stay 7f: sold 1,900 gns Newmarket Autumn Sales. *M. H. Tompkins.*   **72 d**

STAR NORTH 7 b.h. Star Appeal 133 – Highly Polished 79 (High Top 131) [1990 NR 1991 16g 12d* 12v 12.1d⁶] lengthy, angular horse: fair performer, lightly raced: won handicap at Thirsk in June by 7 lengths: tailed off starts either side, very stiff   **85**

task final one: should stay beyond 1½m: best with give in the ground (acts on heavy ground): trained on reappearance by M. Usher: usually sweating. *M. McCormack.*

STAR OATS 5 ch.g. Oats 126 – Starproof 46 (Comedy Star (USA) 121) [1990 NR 1991 a12g⁶] fourth foal: half-brother to quite modest 1987 2-y-o 5f winner Hollia (by Touch Boy): dam, plater, stayed 7f: 25/1, over 13 lengths sixth of 13 in claimer at Southwell in December: won claiming handicap hurdle in November. *G. Richards.* —

STAR OF ALBION 2 b.f. (May 15) Ajdal (USA) 130 – Beaconaire (USA) (Vaguely Noble 140) [1991 7g.8 1g.7m* 8.2m] rather angular filly: has knee action: closely related to top-class American filly Sabin (by Lyphard) and 1¼m winner Nadma (by Northern Dancer) and half-sister to 2 winners, notably Fatah Flare (by Alydar), dam, winner at up to 1¼m in France, is half-sister to high-class filly Kittiwake, dam of very good American filly Miss Oceana: quite modest performer: favourite, narrowly won maiden at Southwell in September, soon pushed along, stayed on: well beaten in Nottingham nursery (stiff task) 17 days later: pulled hard for 7-lb claimer second start: stays 7f: sold 50,000 gns Newmarket December Sales. *M. R. Stoute.* 61

STAR OF GDANSK (USA) 3 ch.c. Danzig Connection (USA) – Star Empress (USA) (Young Emperor 133) [1990 6g* 7g³ 8g² 1991 7g* 8g² 8g² 12f³ 12g³ 8g⁶ 8m* 8d⁴ 8d 10m⁵ a10f] 121

It may seem a strange thing to say of a horse which finished third in both the Derby and Irish Derby, and in a large field at that at Epsom, but there are doubts as to whether Star of Gdansk truly stays a mile and a half. He's won at six furlongs (at two years), seven furlongs and a mile but never over middle distances. He came much closer to winning a classic in the Airlie/Coolmore Irish Two Thousand Guineas and after his two attempts at a mile and a half he was put back to a mile, and with some success, winning the Desmond Stakes. Anyway, Star of Gdansk lined up for the Irish Two Thousand a 16/1-chance, his win in the Dermot McCalmont Tetrarch Stakes at the Curragh and second in a listed race at Leopardstown earlier in the season leaving him with

Desmond Stakes, the Curragh—Star of Gdansk (left) upsets the odds laid on Sportsworld; Approach The Bench gets third

Henrk de Kwiatkowski's "Star of Gdansk"

something to find. Star of Gdansk tracked the leader, the American challenger Fourstars Allstar, until challenging on his inside and showing in front two furlongs out; he could never extend his advantage decisively and Fourstars Allstar headed him again in the final strides. The step to a mile and a half was a step into the unknown, in pedigree terms as well as on what we'd seen of Star of Gdansk on the racecourse. Star of Gdansk couldn't finish any closer to Generous than eleven lengths in either Derby though one should bear in mind that while the commentator's phrase 'the race is only for third' may give an accurate impression of Star of Gdansk's position in the closing stages at Epsom, it isn't at all true of his performance in the full context of the race. He moved well until encountering some problems with the descent to Tattenham Corner, after which he could only keep on steadily up the straight, conspicuously less inconvenienced by the trip however than rivals such as Hector Protector and Hokusai, and then the distance looked to find him out to a greater degree at the Curragh where he ran rather in snatches on the long turn before quickening well to chase the leaders two and a half furlongs out. Two races stand out in Star of Gdansk's season after the Irish Derby. Of his four efforts back at a mile, beginning with the Sussex Stakes, easily the best was that victory in the Desmond Stakes at the Curragh, gamely seeing off another Irish Derby failure Sportsworld (who gave him 3 lb) by a neck. The last two outings in Star of Gdansk's busy season were in the Champion Stakes at Newmarket and the Breeders' Cup Classic on dirt at Churchill Downs. He chased the leaders for seven furlongs in conditions unlikely to suit in the Breeders' Cup but the Champion Stakes was a good effort; outpaced over three furlongs out after a steady early pace, Star of Gdansk ran on again up the hill to finish two lengths fifth of twelve to Tel Quel.

Star of Gdansk's sire Danzig Connection is one of that small number of good-class performers in the United States which one can safely say stayed a mile and a half. He is the horse most often quoted as the exception to the rule of Danzig's being an influence for speed as, although he was also a leading two-year-old, his greatest triumph came in lifting the Belmont Stakes in game style on sloppy ground. He, like Star of Gdansk, raced in the colours of Henryk de Kwiatkowski. Also in Danzig Connection's first crop is the Prix du Palais Royal winner Polski Boy. Star of Gdansk, who went through the sale-ring for 55,000 dollars as a yearling, is the seventh living foal out of Star Empress following three other winners, two of them stakes winners, including the Grade 3 one-mile Affirmed Handicap winner W D Jacks (by Matsadoon). Star Empress raced only as a three-year-old, winning three races including a six-furlong stakes handicap. Her dam Questar, a winner seven times over four seasons, also bred Royal Rafale, a stakes winner in Puerto Rico who's gone on to greater fame as the grandam of the good-class American sprinter Mt Livermore and the Prix Jean Prat winner Magical Wonder.

Star of Gdansk (USA) (ch.c. 1988)	Danzig Connection (USA) (b 1983)	Danzig (b 1977)	Northern Dancer
			Pas de Nom
		Gdynia (ch 1978)	Sir Ivor
			Classicist
	Star Empress (USA) (ch 1971)	Young Emperor (gr 1963)	Grey Sovereign
			Young Empress
		Questar (b 1955)	Requested
			Albania

The big, lengthy Star of Gdansk stays a mile and a quarter thoroughly; he appears not to act on a soft surface. He's a hard ride and has sometimes given the impression that he'd benefit from blinkers or a visor. He reportedly remains in training. *J. S. Bolger, Ireland.*

STAR OF THE SEA 4 gr.f. Absalom 128 – River Chimes 43 (Forlorn River 124) —
[1990 6m 5m 6g 8m 6m 1991 a6g a5g 8g 8d 13.8m 9.2d] lengthy filly: has a round action: of little account nowadays. *N. Chamberlain.*

STAR PLAYER 5 ch.h. Simply Great (FR) 122 – Star Girl (Sovereign Gleam 117) **91**
[1990 NR 1991 14.6s² 16.2g* 16m* 18.4d* 20g⁴ 16.1m 14.8s⁴ 14s* 18m 16g⁵] close-coupled, medium-sized horse: much improved handicapper: won at Beverley (maiden) and Ripon in April, Chester Cup (idled) in May and Kempton in September: respectable staying-on seventh of 22 in Tote Cesarewitch at Newmarket penultimate start: stiffish task final one: effective at 1¾m to 2½m: acts on good to firm and soft ground: held up, and has good turn of foot. *J. H. Baker.*

STAR QUEST 4 b.c. Rainbow Quest (USA) 134 – Sarah Siddons (FR) 122 (Le **85**
Levanstell 122) [1990 12m⁶ 1991 10.8d² 14g⁵ 12m² 12s 12d] lengthy colt: lightly-raced handicapper: burly on first run for 5 months, ran well when second in moderately-run handicap at Newmarket: behind in Group 1 event in Spain (stiff task) and November Handicap at Doncaster after: better suited by 1½m than shorter, and should stay further: acts on good to firm ground: sold out of R. Charlton's stable 13,000 gns Newmarket July Sales after second start. *J. R. Jenkins.*

STARSTREAK 4 b.c. Comedy Star (USA) 121 – Kochia 54 (Firestreak 125) [1990 **108**
8v* 10m* 10g² 10m⁴ 12m² 10.6m³ 12g⁵ 10d⁶ 1991 10m 10g⁵ 10d⁵ 12f³ 10.9m⁴ 10.3d] rangy, deep-girthed colt: easy mover: very useful performer at 3 yrs: not discredited when fifth in Group 2 event at Royal Ascot (behind Stagecraft, second outing) and third in Swedish Group 3 event: below form after, last (showed little resolution) in minor event final start: stays 1½m: acts on any going: worth a try in blinkers: trained first 5 starts by M. Johnston. *M. C. Pipe.*

STAR SYSTEM (IRE) 3 b.f. Burslem 123 – Wisdom To Know (Bay Express —
132) [1990 6s 1991 7m⁵] smallish, lengthy filly: backward, soundly beaten in maidens. *M. O'Neill.*

STATAJACK (IRE) 3 b.g. King of Clubs 124 – Statira 103 (Skymaster 126) **81**
[1990 a7g⁴ a8g* 1991 a8g* 9s² 8.9m³ 9g] leggy, sparely-made gelding: fair form: won handicap at Southwell in January: placed, staying on well, in claimer at Kempton and handicap (sweating, edgy, pulled hard in rear) at York in the autumn: worth a try at 1¼m: acts on good to firm and soft ground, and all-weather surfaces: broke out of stalls intended second outing. *D. R. C. Elsworth.*

STATE DANCER (USA) 4 b.c. El Gran Senor (USA) 136 – Bimbo Sue (USA) **90**
(Our Michael (USA)) [1990 8m 8f 8f³ 8m* 7m 8m⁵ 1991 8g³ 8m* 8g³ 8g⁵ 7m 8g⁶

7.9m² 8g] angular, lengthy colt: poor mover: fairly useful handicapper: won Thirsk Hunt Cup in May: stays 1m: acts on firm ground: usually ridden up with pace: consistent. *M. Moubarak.*

STATE FLYER   3 ch.g. Flying Tyke 90 – Sunshine State (Roi Soleil 125) [1990   **74** §
6m² 7m³ 7f⁶ 1991 7m 8m⁵ 9m 10d 7g³ 6m² 6d* 6g² 7f³ 8.1g⁶ 7g⁶ 7m 7m] tall, leggy gelding: modest handicapper: won at Hamilton in July: stays 7f: acts on good to firm ground and soft: visored of late: often ridden by 7-lb claimer: soon pushed along and often wanders under pressure: a hard ride and not one to trust. *G. R. Oldroyd.*

STATE GOVERNOR   3 ch.c. Song 132 – Brazilian Beauty (Busted 134) [1990 NR   **74**
1991 8.3d 6m³ 5m⁴ 5.1m² 7m² 7m² a8g* 8f³ a7g a8g⁴] 12,500Y: lengthy colt: closely related to 1m winner Dawn Redwood (by Mummy's Pet): dam unraced close relative of smart stayer Pink Gem: modest performer: second in small-field maidens before making all in 3-runner minor event at Southwell in August: below form on equitrack last 2 starts: stays 1m: has worn bandages: joined D. Chapman. *D. W. Chapman.*

STATELY MARCH   3 b.f. State Trooper 96 – Musical Piece 91 (Song 132) [1990   **63**
5.1m 6d³ 6m* 6m 6d⁶ 6d a5g⁶ a6g 1991 a6g⁵ 6g² 6d 6d² 6f³ 6g* 5.7g⁵ 6g³] small filly: poor mover: quite modest performer: won claimer at Goodwood in May, leading final ½f: stays 6f: acts on dead going, seems unsuited by firm: blinkered once at 2 yrs: bandaged on all-weather. *R. W. Stubbs.*

STATE OF AFFAIRS   4 b.c. Free State 125 – Trigamy 112 (Tribal Chief 125)   **55** d
[1990 8f* 8m* 8m 7g 9g 8g 1991 10.8g³ 10m 10g 10g] strong, sturdy colt: moderate mover: plating-class handicapper: below form after reappearance: stays 11f: acts on firm ground: takes keen hold: wore crossed noseband final 2 starts. *C. A. Horgan.*

STATE VISIT (IRE)   2 b.c. (Mar 29) Be My Guest (USA) 126 – Queen Helen 112   —
(Troy 137) [1991 7m] lengthy, useful-looking colt: second foal: half-brother to 3-y-o 11.1f winner Helen's Bower (by Bellypha): dam 7f (at 2 yrs) and 14.6f winner: 25/1, burly, green and coltish, tailed off in 17-runner maiden at Newmarket in October: sold 2,100 gns Doncaster November Sales. *L. M. Cumani.*

STATIA (IRE)   3 b.f. Slip Anchor 136 – Antilla 87 (Averof 123) [1990 NR 1991 10g   **60** ?
10.2g⁶ 12g⁴ 12g 12.1s 12s²] 26,000Y: leggy, attractive filly: fifth foal: half-sister to 7f winner Sympathy (by Precocious) and 1986 2-y-o 6f winner Uniformity (by Formidable): dam 2-y-o 5f winner, is half-sister to very smart John French and daughter of half-sister to Derrylin: quite modest maiden: well-beaten second at Folkestone final start: may not stay 1½m: possibly unsuited by soft ground: sweating, took good hold third start: sold 5,000 gns Newmarket December Sales. *R. Charlton.*

STATION EXPRESS (IRE)   3 b.g. Rusticaro (FR) 124 – Vallee d'O (FR)   —
(Polyfoto 124) [1990 6g 6g⁵ 7g 7f 7f* 8.2g 7f³ 7d 1991 8m 8m 8f 8.9g 10m 8m] smallish gelding: little worthwhile form in varied company, including sellers, as 3-y-o: stays 7f: acts on firm ground. *R. Hollinshead.*

STATUS FLO   3 b.f. Never So Bold 135 – Ranya's Pet (Busted 134) [1990 NR 1991   **44**
6f 6f a5g 7g⁴ 6g⁴] leggy, sparely-made filly: moderate mover: first foal: dam unraced granddaughter of Irish 1000 Guineas winner Royal Danseuse: first form when running on fourth of 15 in seller at Yarmouth: didn't reproduce that in apprentice handicap day later: needs further than 6f, and should stay 1m: sold 520 gns Newmarket July Sales. *M. H. Tompkins.*

STAUNCH RIVAL (USA)   4 b.g. Sir Ivor 135 – Crystal Bright 75 (Bold Lad   — §
(IRE) 133) [1990 10f⁶ a8g* 9g 10f* 10f 10f⁴ 8.2d 1991 12f] leggy, close-coupled gelding: shows knee action: modest handicapper at 3 yrs: no show only run in 1991: suited by 1¼m: acts on firm going: below form when visored: has hung badly left and looked none too keen: not one to trust. *G. Thorner.*

STAY AWAKE   5 ch.g. Anfield 117 – Djimbaran Bay (Le Levanstell 122) [1990 9s*   **52**
10.6v 1991 8d 8.2d² 8m⁶ 10m] rangy gelding: hobdayed: plating-class handicapper: should stay 1¼m: acts on any going: has won (despite hanging badly left) for apprentice: winning hurdler/chaser. *J. J. O'Neill.*

STEAMY WINDOWS   3 b.f. Dominion 123 – Bahamas Princess 89 (Sharpen Up   — §
127) [1990 NR 1991 8m 8g 7g 12d 10g] 15,000Y: good-bodied filly: fourth foal: sister to very useful 1986 2-y-o sprinter Dominion Royale and half-sister to a winner in Italy by Never So Bold: dam 2-y-o 5f winner, is half-sister to Miner's Lamp, very useful winner at 1m and 9f: bad plater: twice reluctant to race. *R. J. R. Williams.*

STEBECCA   3 b.f. Sparkling Boy 110 – Portalla 72 (Porto Bello 118) [1990 NR   —
1991 8m 5g 8g] compact filly: sixth reported living foal (third by Sparkling Boy): half-sister to poor 5f winner Wesbree Bay (by Kala Shikari): dam, placed at up to 6f at 2 yrs, won twice in Isle of Man: no sign of ability in maiden and sellers: visored final start. *J. S. Moore.*

Sheikh Mohammed's "Steinbeck"

STEEL MIRROR 2 b.c. (Mar 16) Slip Anchor 136 – I'll Try 71 (Try My Best **72** p
(USA) 130) [1991 7d4] 26,000Y: tall, rather leggy colt: second foal: dam 2-y-o 5f
winner later successful in USA, is out of half-sister to Irish 1000 Guineas winner
Katies: 8/1 and green, over 6 lengths fourth of 22, slowly away, finished in good
style, behind For Reg in maiden at Doncaster in November: will improve and win a
race or two. *Mrs J. Cecil.*

STEERFORTH (IRE) 3 b.c. Lomond (USA) 128 – Waffles 100 (Wollow 132) **99**
[1990 7f* 7m 1991 8m 10m* 10g6] strong, useful-looking colt: has scope: very
impressive winner of £14,800 handicap at Newmarket in July by 6 lengths from
Friedland, always close up then leading over 2f out: second favourite, didn't improve
on that but not given hard race when sixth of 16 behind Green Danube in £30,600
Goodwood handicap over 3 weeks later, losing position at top of hill: will stay 1½m:
looked a very useful prospect at Newmarket. *A. C. Stewart.*

STEFANO (USA) 2 ch.c. (Mar 24) Irish Castle (USA) – Parlor Game (USA) **83**
(Stage Door Johnny) [1991 6f* 6f4 6g* 6m4 7g 6g2 8d6 6m] $42,000Y:
good-quartered colt: has a quick action: brother to 2 winners in USA, including 11f
and 2¼m Grade 3 winner Putting Green, and half-brother to several other winners:
dam minor winner at 3 yrs at around 9f: sire very smart at up to 6.5f at 2 yrs: fair
performer: successful in maiden at Carlisle in May and median auction at
Nottingham in June: fair sixth of 8 to Made of Gold in Royal Lodge William Hill
Stakes at Ascot in September: probably stays 1m: appeared not to handle track at
Catterick second outing: suitable mount for a 7-lb claimer. *S. G. Norton.*

STEINBECK (USA) 2 ch.c. (Feb 17) Mr Prospector (USA) – Femme Elite **113**
(USA) 124 (Northjet 136) [1991 5m* 5g2 5.5g3 8m*] first foal: dam won Grand
Criterium, later successful in USA: very useful French colt: met Arazi in small fields

835

on first 3 starts, winning by 2½ lengths in newcomers event at Chantilly in June, then beaten ¾ length in Prix du Bois at Longchamp and 4½ lengths in Prix Robert Papin at Maisons-Laffitte, both in July: awarded Prix La Rochette at Longchamp in September on demotion of short-neck winner Rainbow Corner: suited by 1m: acts on good to firm ground. *A. Fabre, France.*

STELBY 7 ch.h. Stetchworth (USA) 120 – Little Trilby 107 (Tyrant (USA)) [1990 **63** 7g⁴ 6g 6m⁵ 6g⁵ 8.5f⁶ 6h* 6m* 6m 6m 5f⁵ 7m 1991 8.5f⁴ 7m² 7h² 6m 6m 7m 8m] small, quite well-made horse: good mover: quite modest handicapper: caught eye final 2 starts, never placed to challenge or knocked about: effective at 6f to 1m: best on a sound surface: has hung and often got behind, but acts on any track. *O. Brennan.*

STELLA DUCHI 2 gr.f. (May 3) Sharrood (USA) 124 – Ma Petite Lassie 94 (Pas **44** de Seul 133) [1991 6m 5d a6g³ 7g 8.9m] smallish, sparely-made filly: first foal: dam sprinting daughter of sister to 1000 Guineas winner Environment Friend: poor maiden: should stay beyond 6f: acts on equitrack: sold 1,100 gns Newmarket Autumn Sales. *M. E. D. Francis.*

ST ELMO'S FIRE 6 b.g. Electric 126 – Sealady (Seaepic (USA) 100) [1990 NR **58** 1991 a7g* a7g⁴ 10.2s⁴ 12f³] sturdy gelding: quite modest handicapper nowadays: won claimer at Lingfield in March: not seen again after that month: stays 1¼m: acts on soft going, possibly can't take much racing on firm: has run well when blinkered: sold 4,800 gns Ascot April Sales. *C. P. E. Brooks.*

STEP HIGH 3 b.g. Dominion 123 – Short And Sharp 88 (Sharpen Up 127) [1990 **85** d NR 1991 8d 10.2s⁴ 10g³ 10g 8m 7.1m* 8.9g 7.3m⁶ 5d] 35,000Y: lengthy, quite attractive gelding: fourth reported living foal: half-brother to a winner in Italy by Young Generation: dam placed over 6f and 7f at 2 yrs, only season to race: fair form and easily best effort when third in £7,300 event at Newmarket in May, making most: 7/4 on, easily won 3-runner maiden at Sandown in August: gelded after final start: effective at 7f and stays 1¼m. *C. E. Brittain.*

STEPPEY LANE 6 b.m. Tachypous 128 – Alpine Alice 94 (Abwah 118) [1990 12f **65** 13v⁵ 13d 16g⁵ 15v⁴ 16.5d 1991 a14g* a14g* a14g³ 13.8d* 14m* 16m⁶] leggy, workmanlike mare: has a round action: quite modest handicapper: won at Southwell (2), Catterick and Nottingham in first half of 1991: probably stays 2m: acts on any going: has got on edge: has been mounted on track and taken down early. *W. W. Haigh.*

STERLING BUCK (USA) 4 b.c. Buckfinder (USA) – Aged (USA) (Olden **—** Times) [1990 10.1g 10m 12m a 12g⁵ 12m 10d a 13g a 12g 1991 a 10g 12f 7m 10g 9d 10.1m] leggy, close-coupled colt: has a round action: seems of little account: sold to join G. H. Yardley 1,050 gns Ascot September Sales. *M. D. I. Usher.*

STERLING PROSPECT 2 b.g. (Feb 24) Cyrano de Bergerac 120 – Akka **69** (Malacate (USA) 131) [1991 5.8d⁵ 6g 7m 7.1m* 7d 7m] 16,500Y: leggy, rather unfurnished gelding: fourth foal: half-brother to fair 3-y-o maiden Akkazao and a winner in Scandinavia (both by Alzao): dam thrice-raced daughter of half-sister to Oh Winborne and Lady Capulet: modest peformer: 66/1, winner of 15-runner maiden auction at Chepstow in September: tailed off in nurseries (blinkered second occasion) afterwards: stays 7f: acts on good to firm going. *W. Carter.*

STERVIAN 3 b.g. Damister (USA) 123 – Vian (USA) (Far Out East (USA)) [1990 **—** 6d⁶ 1991 8g 6m⁶ 6m 8.9g 10.2g 10g] quite attractive colt: quite modest maiden: easily best efforts at 6f: acts on good to firm ground: has worn dropped noseband: sold out of R. Charlton's stable 4,000 gns Newmarket July Sales after fourth start. *C. C. Elsey.*

STILL SURPRISED 6 ch.g. Nicholas Bill 125 – Noammo (Realm 129) [1990 NR **—** 1991 a8g 9g 6d 8d 7f] big, lengthy, angular gelding: fair winning handicapper at 4 yrs: soundly beaten in first half of 1991: suited by 1m: probably unsuited by soft going, acts on any other: has won when visored: keen sort, who carries head high: has found little: difficult ride. *R. M. Whitaker.*

STINGER 2 ch.c. (Feb 23) Midyan (USA) 124 – Copt Hall Princess 70 (Crowned **66** Prince (USA) 128) [1991 7d² 7.1s 7m 7f⁴ 7d] 41,000F, IR 45,000Y: strong, angular colt: half-brother to several winners here and in Italy, including 1m and 1¼m winner Prince Merandi (by Blakeney) and 1¼m and 1½m winner Dovedon Lady (by Castle Keep): dam 7f winner: quite modest maiden: looked rather irresolute after debut: will probably stay 1m: bandaged behind third start. *C. R. Nelson.*

STINGRAY CITY (USA) 2 b.g. (Feb 16) Raft (USA) 125 – Out of This World 76 **63** (High Top 131) [1991 6f 6d² 7m³ 7.5f³ 8m 7.9g 8m] $31,000Y: good-topped gelding: has scope: half-brother to several winners here and abroad, including 5f (at 2 yrs) to

11.5f winner Amongst The Stars (by Proctor), later successful in USA: dam, stayed 1½m, out of half-sister to May Hill: quite modest maiden: blinkered and on toes, fair seventh of 11 in nursery at Warwick fifth start: well beaten afterwards: probably stays 1m: acts on firm and dead ground. *J. Etherington.*

ST JAMES'S ANTIGUA (IRE) 2 b.f. (Apr 3) Law Society (USA) 130 – Thunderflash (FR) (Northfields (USA)) [1991 7m³ 7m] 27,000F, 40,000Y: lengthy, good-topped filly: has a quick action: sister to useful 1m and 1¼m winner Kawtuban and half-sister to a winner in USA by Naskra: dam, winner at around 1m in USA, is half sister to Chesire Oaks winner Hunston: 33/1 and bit backward, under 2 lengths third of 8, staying on well, to Freewheel in minor event at Newbury in September: chased leaders 5f in Tattersalls Tiffany Highflyer Stakes at Newmarket following month, finishing creditable seventeenth of 30 to Young Senor: will be better suited by 1m. *W. J. Haggas.*   **79 p**

ST JOVITE (USA) 2 b.c. (Mar 11) Pleasant Colony (USA) – Northern Sunset (Northfields (USA)) [1991 7m* 6.3m* 8g* 8d4]   **122**

The letters page of the *Racing Post* has become a lively forum for debate. Towards the end of the latest season the issue of whether horses bred along certain lines are inevitably better suited to racing on turf rather than dirt and vice versa came up there, one reader taking the view that the progeny of American stallions who raced solely on dirt aren't ideally equipped for the demands of turf racing, pointing to what he considered to be their 'lamentable' performance in European pattern races. The paper's bloodstock correspondent Tony Morris, on the other hand, is of the opinion that given the chance most horses are likely to prove 'equally effective (or ineffective) on whatever surface they encounter'. This is a complex subject, one in which statistics aren't always as helpful as they might be, but it's hard to disagree with Morris' point that there's a definite bias against certain American stallions in the minds of many buying for the European turf market. Take Pleasant Colony as an example. On retiring to stud he seemed to have a great deal to recommend

EBF Anglesey Stakes, the Curragh—
nip and tuck between St Jovite and the grey El Prado

Mrs Virginia Kraft Payson's "St Jovite"

him. America's champion three-year-old of 1981, he won the Kentucky Derby and the Preakness Stakes and after defeats in the Belmont and Travers Stakes put up a high-class performance to beat good older horses in the Woodward Stakes. His stock has been popular and successful in America, with more than one in ten of his progeny having won in stakes company, yet European representatives have been few and far between, the majority of them not amounting to much, but St Jovite's achievements in the latest season suggest that buyers on this side of the Atlantic might have been missing something.

St Jovite made his debut in a maiden at Leopardstown in August on the same day the Heinz '57' Phoenix Stakes was run. He ran out a very easy winner and two weeks later was stepped up in class for the Group 3 EBF Anglesey Stakes at the Curragh. With no British-trained runners and a field of only five, the market was dominated by El Prado, unbeaten and conceding 3 lb all round as a result of his win in the John J. Long Memorial Railway Stakes on the same course on his latest start. St Jovite, a 5/2-chance, was never far away and came to take a narrow lead about two furlongs from home. He had to be pushed along firmly to do so then responded gamely to pressure, staying on strongly to beat El Prado by a neck with the three others way back. El Prado went on to justify favouritism in the Group 1 National Stakes at the Curragh a couple of weeks later. St Jovite missed the race, reportedly due to a minor bout of coughing, and instead was sent for the rather less prestigious Panasonic Smurfit EBF Futurity Stakes, again at the Curragh, where the step up to a mile served him well. This time there was an English challenger in the shape of the Sandown winner Tik Fa who made sure St Jovite had to fight all the way again. Tik Fa made the running and had most of the eight-runner field in trouble when his rider increased the pace early in the straight. St Jovite, a shade of odds on, was off the bridle in third at that stage. Driven along firmly to get upsides over a furlong from home, he galloped on strongly, being given a couple of cracks close home to get the better of Tik Fa by a neck with the National Stakes third Mekong two and a half lengths away. The Dewhurst Stakes and the Grand Criterium were announced as possible end-of-season objectives; the French race was eventually chosen and St Jovite put up easily his best effort. His rider Roche adopted sensible tactics, setting a strong gallop in an attempt to blunt Arazi's turn of foot, but all he succeeded in doing was giving that horse a good lead. Arazi cruised past on the home turn, and when first Seattle Rhyme then Rainbow Corner went by entering the straight it looked as if St Jovite might drop right out. However, under strong driving St Jovite lost no further ground in the final furlong and a half. Indeed, he stayed on strongly close home to finish fourth, only three quarters of a length and a short head behind Rainbow Corner and Seattle Rhyme, in doing so establishing himself as one of the top half-dozen two-year-olds in Europe.

Pleasant Colony was responsible for several other good winners in 1991, including the Breeders' Cup Juvenile Fillies winner Pleasant Stage, and there's plenty of interest on the female side of St Jovite's pedigree. Northern Sunset had wins over six and seven furlongs to show from sixteen outings on the Flat and a couple over hurdles in Ireland when sent to the December Sales in 1980. Sold for 10,500 guineas and sent to the States soon after, she's enjoyed tremendous success as a broodmare. All five of her foals who made the racecourse prior to St Jovite are winners, and three of them were very smart. The first was Salem Drive (by Darby Creek Road), who totalled a dozen wins in a long career and won almost a million dollars in prize money; the second Lac Quimet, a brother to St Jovite best at a mile to a mile and a quarter, proved equally durable; his seven stakes victories included five in Grade 2, while Northern Sunset's Roberto colt Norberto finished fourth in the Prix du Jockey-Club and also runner-up in the Grand Prix de Paris. Northern Sunset's dam Moss Greine won over a mile at two. She descends from Carpet Slipper, who produced the Guineas and Oaks winner Godiva as well as Windsor Slipper, winner of the triple crown in Ireland in 1942.

St Jovite (USA) (b.c. Mar 11, 1989)	Pleasant Colony (USA) (b 1978)	His Majesty (b 1968)	Ribot Flower Bowl
		Sun Colony (b 1968)	Sunrise Flight Colonia
	Northern Sunset (ch 1977)	Northfields (ch 1968)	Northern Dancer Little Hut
		Moss Greine (b 1964)	Ballymoss Blaith Na Greine

St Jovite is a tall, attractive colt with plenty of scope and it will come as a surprise if he doesn't train on. As a two-year-old stamina was his forte. It's most unlikely he'll have the pace to make a mark in good races over a mile at three, but over a mile and a quarter or, better still, a mile and a half he should be a force. A powerful galloper with a round action, he races with plenty of enthusiasm and acts on good to firm ground and good to soft. *J. S. Bolger, Ireland.*

ST NINIAN 5 ch.h. Ardross 134 – Caergwrle 115 (Crepello 136) [1990 12m⁶ 10f **103** 9f² 9m³ 10m 8m* 8.2f³ 8m 8g* 8d 8g 1991 8d² 8g* 8d* 8g 8.1g⁶ 8m³ 8.9g² 9m 8g³] useful-looking horse: usually looks really well: improved performer in 1991: impressive when winning handicaps at Newbury (Spring Cup) and Kempton (Jubilee) in spring: returned to best after mid-season break, second to Shaima in listed race at York and third to Hyabella in similar event at Newmarket: suited by 1m/9f: acts on any going: sometimes bandaged near-hind: game and genuine. *M. H. Easterby.*

STOCK HILL LADY 3 b.f. Tina's Pet 121 – Fair Nic (Romancero 100) [1990 NR **35** 1991 8v⁶ 7.1d 6f⁵ 6g] big filly: half-sister to fair sprinter/miler Stock Hill Lass (by Air Trooper): dam runner-up in 3-runner 1½m maiden at 4 yrs on only outing on flat:

fifth of 7 in maiden at Brighton: behind facing stiff task in selling handicap there 5 weeks later. *R. J. Hodges.*

STOCKTINA　4 ch.f. Tina's Pet 121 – Mrewa (Runnymede 123) [1990 5h 5m 6g 5f　**47**
5d 5m 5g 1991 5.1m³ 5f² 5g² 5d³ 6g⁵ 5m a5g 5f⁶ 5.3g* 5g² 5m 5.1d³] smallish filly:
plating-class handicapper: won (for first time) at Brighton in September: best at 5f:
acts on firm and dead ground: below form when blinkered once: ran as if something
amiss penultimate start: suited by forcing tactics. *R. J. Hodges.*

STONECUT (IRE)　2 b.c. (Apr 19) Sure Blade (USA) 130 – Hatta 114 (Realm 129)　**69**
[1991 7f³ 8m³ 8m⁵] rather leggy, close-coupled colt: half-brother to quite modest 6f
and 7f winner Al Amead (by Brigadier Gerard) and a winner in USA: dam won
Molecomb Stakes: quite modest maiden: ran moderately, pulling hard, then
wandering, at Leicester (very free to post) final start: stays 1m: looks a hard ride:
sold 9,000 gns Newmarket Autumn Sales. *G. Harwood.*

STONE FOREST　6 b. or br.g. Thatching 131 – Senta's Girl (Averof 123) [1990　**—**
11.7g 10d 1991 10.6g⁶ 12d] strong, rangy gelding: has a quick action: lightly raced and
little show after winning maiden as 3-y-o: stays 1m: acts on soft going: has been
bandaged. *Miss A. J. Whitfield.*

STONELEIGH ABBEY (IRE)　3 b.g. Sallust 134 – Yellow Creek (Sandy　**—**
Creek 123) [1990 5f⁴ 5g⁴ 5g⁴ 5m⁵ 5f⁵ 6d a6g² a6g a7g² 1991 a6g⁶ 6g⁴ 6m 8d a6g a8g]
sturdy gelding: carried condition: quite modest form at 2 yrs, little in 1991: should be
suited by further than 6f: blinkered last 3 outings: trained first 3 at 3 yrs by R.
Hollinshead. *R. D. E. Woodhouse.*

STONE MILL　3 b.c. Caerleon (USA) 132 – Miller's Creek (USA) 62 (Star de　**102**
Naskra (USA)) [1990 6m² 6m* 6g² 7g³ 8m³ 1991 8d 10g² 12g 8g³ 9m* 8f* 10.2m*
10.1f² 7m⁴] good-bodied, attractive colt: good walker: has a fluent action: useful and
consistent performer: successful in apprentice races (made all) at Ripon and
Chepstow and minor event at Thirsk in between: well beaten in Derby Italiano at
Rome third start: needs further than 7f, and stays 1¼m: possibly needs a sound
surface: blinkered last 5 starts: joined F. Brothers in USA. *B. W. Hills.*

STONE RUN (IRE)　3 ch.g. Commanche Run 133 – Lake Tawa (Cure The Blues　**—**
(USA)) [1990 7f 8f 1991 10m 14f⁶ 14g] unfurnished gelding: no form, backward in
seller and handicaps in 1991: visored final start. *A. P. Stringer.*

STONEWALL JACKSON (IRE)　2 b.c. (Apr 23) Treasure Kay 114 – What A　**69 p**
Friend (What A Guest 119) [1991 5g⁴ 5s²] IR 5,600F, IR 5,600Y: workmanlike colt:
has scope: second foal: half-brother to 3-y-o Chesham Lady (by Fayruz), 5f winner
at 2 yrs: dam unraced: favourite after promising debut 6 weeks earlier, 2 lengths
second to Little Saboteur in maiden auction at Edinburgh in November: will stay 6f:
may improve again. *W. J. Pearce.*

STONYGARTH (IRE)　2 br.c. (Apr 10) Tender King 123 – Auntie Ponny (Last　**44**
Fandango 125) [1991 5.1m 5g 6.1g 7m⁶ 7g 8.3g 10.5d⁶] compact colt: third
foal: dam unraced: quite modest plater: stays 10.5f: has form on good to firm and
dead ground: sold 850 gns Doncaster November Sales: inconsistent. *J. A. C.
Edwards.*

STOPHER　2 br.g. (Mar 3) Lidhame 109 – Snow Tree 86 (Welsh Pageant 132)　**—**
[1991 6m] smallish, quite good-topped gelding: third foal: dam middle-distance
winner out of half-sister to smart stayer Celtic Cone: travelled comfortably to
halfway and eased when beaten over 1f out in 9-runner minor event at Windsor in
July. *J. R. Fanshawe.*

STOPPERS FUTURE　2 b.g. (Apr 10) Midyan (USA) 124 – Rest 70 (Dance In　**—**
Time (CAN)) [1991 6m 5s] 4,800Y: third foal: has markedly round action: half-
brother to 1989 2-y-o 5f seller winner Premier Girl (by Petong): dam 1½m winner:
blinkered, well beaten in late-season claimers: sold 550 gns Ascot December Sales.
G. A. Pritchard-Gordon.

STOP PRESS (USA)　3 b.f. Sharpen Up 127 – Glad Tidings (FR) 85 (Pharly (FR)　**93**
130) [1990 7m⁴ 8m² 1991 10g* 12.3d³ 11.5m² 10.1m* 10.4m³ 10m²] quite attractive
filly: won maiden at Beverley in April and £7,200 handicap (rallying splendidly) at
Epsom in June: best effort neck second to Ijtihaad in £11,600 handicap at Ascot in
July: effective at 1¼m and 1½m: acts on good to firm ground and dead. *M. R. Stoute.*

STOPROVERITATE　2 ch.f. (Apr 8) Scorpio (FR) 127 – Luscinia 73 (Sing Sing　**63**
134) [1991 5f 7m 7.5f⁵ 8.3g 7m⁴ 7m 6s² 5s³ a6g] 9,000F, 1,900Y: workmanlike filly:
has scope: half-sister to several winners on flat and over hurdles, including 5f and 6f
winner Nariz (by Brigadier Gerard): dam won over 1m: quite modest maiden: ran
well third-last start: never a factor in nursery on fibresand: needs further than 5f,

STO

but possibly doesn't stay 1m: acts on top-of-the-ground and soft going: inconsistent. *S. G. Norton.*

STORMAGAIN (USA) 2 ch.f. (Apr 25) Storm Cat (FR) – Encorelle (FR) **102** (Arctic Tern 126) [1991 6d* 5g² 7m² 5m² 6.5d³ 8f²] $52,000Y: fourth foal: closely related to French 3-y-o 1m (at 2 yrs) and 1¼m winner After The Sun (by Storm Bird) and half-sister to a minor winner in North America: dam unraced sister to Escaline: successful in minor event at Evry in June: placed all starts after, on final 2 outings third to Cardoun in Prix Eclipse at Saint-Cloud and second (beaten a neck) in Miesque Stakes at Hollywood Park: stays 1m: acts on firm and dead ground. *F. Boutin, France.*

STORM AT NIGHT (USA) 3 b.c. Storm Bird (CAN) 134 – Nervous Pillow **83** (USA) (Nervous Energy (USA)) [1990 6g² 6g³ 1991 7m³ 8m³ 7f³] strong, lengthy colt: easy mover: fair form: third in listed race (flashed tail) at Kempton and in maidens at Newmarket (2) and Yarmouth: edged right and found little second start, looking one to be wary of: probably stays 1m: reportedly to be trained in USA. *L. M. Cumani.*

STORMBUSTER 2 b.g. (Apr 1) Northern Tempest (USA) 120 – Stolen-Secret **54** (Burglar 128) [1991 6g 6m 5m⁴ 5m] 4,000Y: leggy, lengthy gelding: moderate mover: half-brother to 1986 2-y-o 5f seller winner Five Sixes (by Music Maestro): dam closely related to very smart 5f performer Singing Bede: plating-class maiden: not well treated but ran moderately nonetheless in nursery at Wolverhampton in September: seems suited by 5f: bandaged on debut. *P. S. Felgate.*

STORM CROSSING (USA) 2 ch.c. (Feb 28) Storm Bird (CAN) 134 – Ala **86 p** Mahlik 116 (Ahonoora 122) [1991 7d⁶] strong, good-quartered colt: has scope: first foal: brother and winner later stayed 10.5f, is sister to Negligent and half-sister to out-and-out stayer Ala Hounak: 20/1, backward and green, 7 lengths sixth of 7 to Casteddu in minor event at Ascot in October, pushed along at halfway and never a factor: will stay 1m: will improve. *G. Harwood.*

STORM DOVE (USA) 2 b.f. (May 12) Storm Bird (CAN) 134 – Daeltown (FR) **81** 117 (Dictus (FR) 126) [1991 7s⁶ 6g* 6f³ 6g³] leggy filly: good mover: sister to a minor stakes-placed winner and closely related to 1990 2-y-o 7f winner Littleton (by El Gran Senor): dam French filly stayed 1¼m, much improved at 4 yrs: fair performer: well-backed 11/4-shot following promising debut, won 16-runner maiden at Newmarket in August, rallying well: will probably prove better suited by 7f than 6f: possibly unsuited by firm ground: tail swisher. *R. Charlton.*

STORM DRUM 2 ch.c. (Mar 1) Celestial Storm (USA) 132 – Bushti Music 63 **44** (Bustino 136) [1991 a7g a8g] 17,000Y, 9,000Y: lengthy, quite good-topped colt: fifth foal: half-brother to 3-y-o Mandika (by Flash of Steel) and 1½m (seller) to 16.2f winner Kingsley (by Kings Lake): dam, who stayed 9f, is half-sister to very useful sprinters Hanu and Sanu: poor form, never a factor, in maidens at Lingfield and Southwell late in year. *P. J. Makin.*

STORM MELODY (USA) 2 b.c. (Mar 14) Storm Cat (USA) – Celebration Song **94** (USA) (J O Tobin (USA) 130) [1991 5f* 5g* 5m⁴ 6m 5g⁵] $45,000Y: angular, good-topped colt: has scope: second foal: half-brother to fair 1990 sprinter Rio Tejo (by Tsunami Slew): dam in frame at 6f and 1m in Ireland, and later placed in USA, is half-sister to Seattle Song: sire good class, best at 9f/1m: fairly useful performer: successful in maiden at Doncaster and minor event (in good style) at Beverley in early-summer: didn't progress as anticipated, on final outing (August) over 7 lengths fifth of 11 to Another Episode in listed race at York: bred to stay beyond 5f. *A. A. Scott.*

STORM ORPHAN 4 ch.f. Ballacashtal (CAN) – Grandee Ann (USA) (Cyane) **50** [1990 6f⁵ 5m 7f⁴ 6f⁴ 8m a8g a12g⁶ 1991 10.8g 12f a12g* a13g⁶ a12g] lengthy, good-quartered filly: 20/1, first form when winning claimer at Lingfield in November: below form in handicaps thereafter: probably stays 13f: trained first 2 starts by G. Lewis. *Miss B. Sanders.*

STORM RING (USA) 2 b.f. (Apr 6) Storm Bird (CAN) 134 – Jellapore (CAN) **100** (Raja Baba (USA)) [1991 6m* 6m³ 6m⁴ 6m⁵ 8f²] tall, leggy, quite attractive filly: has scope: fluent mover: fourth foal: closely related to a winner (also graded-stakes placed) in North America by Secreto: dam lightly-raced half-sister to Northern Baby: fairly useful performer: won 4-runner maiden at Haydock in July: never-dangerous ninth of 9 to Marling in Tattersalls Cheveley Park Stakes at Newmarket in October: ½-length second of 8 in Miesque Stakes (Div.2) at Hollywood Park in November: stays 1m. *L. M. Cumani.*

841

STORM RISK 2 ch.c. (Mar 17) Risk Me (FR) 127 – Lightning Legend (Lord 55
Gayle (USA) 124) [1991 6g 6m³ 5m 5m³ 7g] smallish, workmanlike colt: has a quick
action: first foal: dam 2-y-o 7f winner: fair plater: easily best efforts when third:
stays 6f: acts on good to firm ground: has flashed tailed: not seen out after August.
R. Hannon.

STORMSWEPT (USA) 2 b.f. (Jan 27) Storm Bird (CAN) 134 – Kanmary (FR) 74
117 (Kenmare (FR) 125) [1991 5d³ 5m² 5g⁴ 5.1d* 5s⁴ 6.1m⁵ 7g⁵] smallish, quite
attractive filly: first foal: dam French 2-y-o 5f winner stayed 9f: modest performer:
won maiden at Chester in June despite carrying head high and wandering: off course
7 weeks, improved form in minor event at Chester (stiff task) penultimate outing:
ran moderately in Wolverhampton nursery final one: suited by 6f: best form on good
to firm ground, not discredited on soft: blinkered (ran moderately) third start. *J.
Berry.*

STORMY PRAISE (USA) 7 ch.g. Storm Bird (CAN) 134 – Prayers'n Promises 46
(USA) (Foolish Pleasure (USA)) [1990 NR 1991 a6g a6g 8.2s* 8m 8f a8g 9.7s]
lengthy, angular gelding: poor handicapper at best nowadays: won seller (no bid) at
Hamilton in April: effective at 6f to 1m: probably acts on any going: has worn hood,
blinkers and crossed noseband: has run poorly for amateur: headstrong and not an
easy ride. *W. G. M. Turner.*

STORMY WINTER 2 b.c. (Feb 17) Reasonable (FR) 119 – Winter Resort —
(Miami Springs 121) [1991 5m⁶] 7,400Y: quite attractive colt: second reported foal:
half-brother to 6f winner (stays 1m) Masella (by Aragon): dam unraced half-sister to
useful 1¼m winner Power Bender: poor sixth, running on well, in maiden auction at
Salisbury (green) in May: seemed sure to improve. *J. M. P. Eustace.*

STORY OF MY LIFE 2 gr.f. (Apr 25) Sizzling Melody 117 – Friendly Thoughts 35
(USA) (Al Hattab (USA)) [1991 5d 6g⁵ 5m⁶ 6d⁴ 7.1m 6m] 4,000F, 9,000Y:
close-coupled, unfurnished filly: fifth live foal: half-sister to 3-y-o 6f (at 2 yrs) to
11.5f winner Fancy Me (by Dunbeath) and 1¼m seller winner Thanks A Million (by
Simply Great): dam never ran: poor plater: probably stays 7f: sold 700 gns Ascot
October Sales. *G. Lewis.*

STOUR HILL LAD 2 b.c. (Apr 14) Sulaafah (USA) 119 – Miss Kuwait 63 (The —
Brianstan 128) [1991 7m 8g 7.1d] good-bodied colt: moderate mover: third live foal:
half-brother to a winning hurdler: dam, selling hurdler, stayed 2¾m: not fully
wound up, soundly beaten in maidens. *R. J. Hodges.*

ST PATRICK'S DAY 3 ch.g. Night Shift (USA) – Princess Lieven (Royal Palace 73
131) [1990 6m³ 6m⁵ 6g 8m 10g 1991 10.1f³ 10.3m 8m 8d⁶ 8m⁵ 9.7s*] leggy, rather
sparely-made gelding: very good mover: modest performer: won handicap at
Folkestone in November, leading 1f out then edging left: stays 1¼m: acts on good to
firm ground and soft: tends to be slowly away: refused to race and unseated rider at
start third outing: headstrong at 2 yrs, early to post in 1991. *C. E. Brittain.*

STRADBALLY MOUNT 3 gr.c. Carwhite 127 – Marymount (Mount Hagen 67
(FR) 127) [1990 7m⁶ 10s 1991 10.8g 10.1s 10.2f⁶ 8f³ 11.5m³ 12g* 16m³] leggy,
lengthy colt: quite modest performer: led post in claimer at Newmarket in August:
good third in handicap at Nottingham month later, keeping on well: effective at 1½m
and stays 2m: acts on firm going: visored second to fourth starts: trained first 4 by
M. McCormack. *R. Akehurst.*

STRADBROKE 4 b.g. Fairy King (USA) – Mattira (FR) (Rheffic (FR) 129) [1990 36 §
9m² 8g⁶ 10m³ a14g³ 1991 10.8d 8m³ 12.5d 8f⁵ 12g 8h⁴ 8.9m] big, strong, lengthy
gelding: moderate mover: poor maiden: refused to race intended reappearance:
stays 1¼m: acts on good to firm ground: has run creditably when blinkered: has
wandered under pressure. *M. B. James.*

STRADIVARIS FIDDLE 3 ch.f. Music Boy 124 – Stradey Park 103 (Murray- —
field 119) [1990 NR 1991 8f 7g 8m⁶ 7s] sparely-made filly: half-sister to plating-class
1989 2-y-o 5f winner Martin-Lavell Post (by Tina's Pet): dam won over 5f and stayed
1¼m: little promise in maidens, minor event and handicap. *M. J. Ryan.*

STRAIGHT LACED (USA) 4 b. or br.g. Alleged (USA) 138 – Swoonmist 60
(USA) (Never Bend) [1990 13.6m⁶ 1991 a11g a12g* a12g* a12g 11s a11g 9g] lengthy,
angular gelding: quite modest form when winning claimers at Southwell in February
(claimed out of J. Wainwright's stable £4,101, first form) and March (by 8 lengths):
well beaten after in handicaps (took little interest penultimate start) and ladies
event: stays 1½m: seems unsuited by soft ground: often blinkered: trained third to
sixth starts by T. J. Scargill. *J. E. Long.*

STRAIGHT NO CHASER 3 b.g. Norwick (USA) 120 – Pepeke 78 (Mummy's 54
Pet 125) [1990 7d 6g a6g⁶ 1991 9d 10g 6g⁵ 7.5f⁴ 7m] leggy gelding: plating-class

maiden: should have stayed 1¼m: acted on firm going: blinkered final start: dead. *R. Boss.*

STRALDI (IRE) 3 br.c. Ela-Mana-Mou 132 – Cavurina 81§ (Cavo Doro 124) **107** [1990 8d* 1991 12g³ 14m³ 16.2m*] big, workmanlike colt: put up a useful performance to win £10,300 handicap at Ascot in June by a head from Tamarpour, chasing leaders, going on 1½f out then rallying well: stays very well: acts on good to firm ground and dead: rather lazy, but genuine. *H. R. A. Cecil.*

STRANGE KNIGHT (IRE) 2 b.c. (Feb 13) Gorytus (USA) 132 – Parkeen **59** Princess (He Loves Me 120) [1991 5f⁶ 5f² 6m³ a5g³ 5g⁴ 6f² 7g 7g⁵ a6g² 6d* 6f⁶ 6m] 7,000F, 2,700Y: leggy colt: has scope: fourth foal: half-brother to 8.2f and 9f winner Transitional (by Dalsaan) and 2 other winners: dam never ran: quite useful plater on his day: claimed out of P. Haslam's stable £6,300 after third start: retained 5,200 gns after winning at Goodwood in August: will stay 7f: acts on firm ground and dead: has given trouble stalls: tends to wander, and is a difficult ride: sold 8,400 gns Newmarket Autumn Sales after final start. *Mrs L. Stubbs.*

STRANGERSINTHENITE 2 ch.c. (Feb 23) Legend of France (USA) 124 – **52** Angail 89 (Northfields (USA)) [1991 6d 6g³ 6m⁶ 7.9g 6g] 9,200Y: small colt: has a round action: brother to Irish 1¼m winner French Legionnaire and half-brother to useful 1985 2-y-o sprinter Homing Angel (by Homing), later successful in USA: dam 5f performer at 2 yrs: plating-class maiden: ran poorly in nurseries last 2 starts: should be suited by further than 6f. *J. S. Wainwright.*

STRANGER STILL 4 b.f. Cragador 110 – No Relation 94 (Klairon 131) [1990 — 8m⁶ 10.2m 10m² 10g 10.1m⁶ 1991 10.8g] leggy, sparely-made filly: has a quick action: poor maiden: stays 1¼m: acts on good to firm ground. *B. Stevens.*

STRATFORD LADY 2 b.f. (Feb 27) Touching Wood (USA) 127 – Hawks Nest **48** 66 (Moulton 128) [1991 6m 7g] compact filly: sixth foal: half-sister to 1990 2-y-o 6f winner Cheveley Chief (by Chief Singer): dam 6f winner: poor form in claimer at Haydock (late progress under tender handling) and Wolverhampton seller in autumn: will stay well. *J. A. Glover.*

STRATFORD PONDS 6 b.h. High Top 131 – Opinion 71 (Great Nephew 126) — [1990 13.3g 1991 12g⁵] big, angular horse: carried plenty of condition: had a quick action: fairly useful winner at best: best at 1½m: best form on a sound surface: best ridden close to the pace: very useful hurdler: dead. *O. Sherwood.*

STRAT'S LEGACY 4 b.g. Chukaroo 103 – State Romance 67 (Free State 125) **51** [1990 a6g 7m 10f 12h⁵ 12.5m* 1991 10.8m⁶ 8m* 8f 8.2m 8f⁵ 10f² 10.2m⁶ 10g] small, light-framed gelding: poor handicapper: won at Bath in July: effective at 1m to 1½m: acts on firm ground: inconsistent. *D. W. P. Arbuthnot.*

STRAW BABY 3 ch.f. Final Straw 127 – Miss Bretonne (Huntercombe 133) — [1990 NR 1991 8m⁴ 9g 10f 8.1g 10m] 5,000Y: sturdy filly: moderate mover: sixth foal: half-sister to 2 winners in Belgium: dam won in Belgium: little promise, including in seller: sold 660 gns Doncaster October Sales. *R. M. Whitaker.*

STRAW BERET (USA) 3 ch.f. Chief's Crown (USA) – Mostly Sunny (CAN) **80** (Sunny) [1990 7g⁴ 7s³ 1991 10d 8m²] rangy filly: fluent mover: best effort second of 8 in maiden at Newmarket in May, making most: should stay 1¼m: may prove best on a sound surface. *J. H. M. Gosden.*

STRAWBERRY PINK 2 gr.f. (May 25) Absalom 128 – Polly Peachum 123 **89** p (Singing Strand) [1991 6m⁶ 5f* 6f² 5m*] sturdy, rather angular filly: moderate mover: closely related to very useful Able Albert (by Abwah), successful at up to 7f, and half-sister to 5f winner Harry Hull (by Sagaro): dam sprinter: successful in small fields at Redcar in maiden (by 8 lengths) and nursery (looked winner long way out) in summer: stays 6f: acts on firm ground, yet to race on good: bandaged behind last 2 starts: was progressing well. *M. H. Easterby.*

STRAW THATCH 2 b.c. (Feb 1) Thatching 131 – Lashing (USA) 98 (Storm Bird **64** (CAN) 134) [1991 6g 8m 7.9m⁵ 8g] 27,000Y: strong, workmanlike colt: first foal: dam, 6f (at 2 yrs) to 1m winner, is daughter of half-sister to top-class Ack Ack: plating-class maiden: well beaten in Redcar nursery final start: stays 1m. *C. B. B. Booth.*

STREET REBEL (CAN) 3 b.c. Robellino 127 – Street Ballet (Nijinsky 138) **106** [1990 7d⁵ 1991 8v² 7d³ 8g* 8g⁵ 8g³ 10g* 10m⁶ 9g⁴] 12,000Y: sixth reported foal: half-brother to 3 winners in USA: dam champion 3-y-o filly in Canada and placed in Grade 1 events in USA: won maiden at the Curragh in April and minor event at Gowran Park in July: also ran well on former course when 8 lengths fifth of 12 to Fourstars Allstar in Airlie/Coolmore Irish 2000 Guineas then 7 lengths third to

Mukaddamah in John Roarty Memorial International: below form last 2 starts: has won over 1¼m but best form at 1m: blinkered final outing. *N. Meade, Ireland.*

STRENGTH IN DEPTH (IRE) 3 b. or br.f. Strong Gale 116 – Second Service —
(Red Regent 123) [1990 7d⁵ 7d⁵ 6d 1991 7m 12.1s] leggy, workmanlike filly: quite modest form at 2 yrs: behind in autumn handicaps in 1991: should be suited by 1m + . *M. Johnston.*

STRIDE HOME 6 ch.m. Absalom 128 – Another Treat 82 (Derring-Do 131) —
[1990 a10g a16g⁶ 10f³ 10.8m³ 10.1g* 11.5m⁵ 11.7m 10m 1991 9m 12m 10s⁶ 12g 10s 11.6m] sturdy mare: has a quick action: poor handicapper: stays 1½m: seems to act on any going: usually blinkered or visored: joined M. Channon. *M. Madgwick.*

STRIKE FIRE (IRE) 3 b.c. Touching Wood (USA) 127 – Ascot Strike (USA) 85 **94**
(Mr Prospector (USA)) [1990 7.5f* 8g² 9g* 10g⁵ 1991 11.7g³ 11g³ 14.8m³ 12f⁴ 18m³ 16d] lengthy, quite attractive colt: good mover: fairly useful: stays 14.8f: looked unsuited by a soft surface: blinkered (keen hold, ran fairly well) fifth start: sold 10,500 gns Newmarket Autumn Sales, probably to Italy. *P. F. I. Cole.*

STRIKE OIL (FR) 3 ch.c. Fabulous Dancer (USA) 124 – All Found (USA) **111**
(Alleged (USA) 138) [1990 NR 1991 10g 10.5d* 12d* 12.5g⁵ 12.5m] sturdy colt: fourth foal (third by Fabulous Dancer): brother to 11f winner All Dancing: dam 10.5f winner: successful in maiden at Longchamp in April and awarded Prix du Lys at Chantilly in June having been beaten short neck by Glity: fair fifth to Toulon in Prix Maurice de Nieuil at Maisons-Laffitte: not seen out again after finishing tailed off in Grand Prix de Deauville Lancel in August: stays 1½m: acts on dead going: very useful. *J. Cunnington jun, France.*

STRIKING DISTANCE 4 ch.g. Never So Bold 135 – Gallatin Valley (USA) **50**
(Apalachee (USA) 137) [1990 NR 1991 10d 11.5m⁴ 12g⁴] tall gelding: sixth foal: half-brother to 1½m winner Devizes (by Kris) and 7f winner Raja Moulana (by Raja Baba): dam won at up to 1m: first form when fourth in claimer at Newmarket final start (raced keenly): worth another try over 1¼m: joined J. Ffitch-Heyes. *J. Ffitch-Heyes.*

STRIKING IMAGE (IRE) 2 ch.f. (Apr 26) Flash of Steel 120 – Sister Sala **64**
(Double-U-Jay 120) [1991 7m⁶ 7m³ 7.1d] good-bodied, workmanlike filly: has scope: fifth living foal: half-sister to 1985 Irish 2-y-o 1m winner Dalsala (by Dalsaan): dam champion 2-y-o in Norway, is sister to Norsk 2000 Guineas winner Opatia: quite modest maiden: carrying plenty of condition, best effort when third of 16 at Leicester in October, front rank 5f, hung right from over 1f out: likely to stay 1m: possibly unsuited by dead ground. *R. Hannon.*

STRIMMER 3 ch.c. Sharpo 132 – Toppeshamme (USA) 94 (Topsider (USA)) **78**
[1990 NR 1991 6d 7m 6f⁴ 6h⁴ 5f² 6m² 6.1m*] leggy, good-topped colt: moderate mover: first foal: dam 2-y-o 7f and 7.5f winner who showed no form at 3 yrs: modest form: favourite, won claimer at Nottingham in October: should prove at least as effective at 5f as 6f: acts on firm going: tail flasher: sold 13,000 gns Newmarket Autumn Sales. *W. Jarvis.*

STRING PLAYER 9 ch.g. Orchestra 118 – Ghana's Daughter 93 (Sallust 134) —
[1990 a16g a14g 1991 a14g⁵] workmanlike, deep-girthed gelding: has a slightly round action: plating-class handicapper on flat, very lightly raced nowadays: stays 1½m: acts on any going: has been bandaged. *F. H. Lee.*

STRIP CARTOON (IRE) 3 ch.g. Tate Gallery (USA) 117 – Reveal (Pitskelly **41**
122) [1990 6d 6m³ 7f 6m³ 6f⁶ 6m a5g a8g 1991 5m 6d 9.9f a11g a8g a5g 5m⁵ 5f⁴ 5g⁵ 5d⁴ 5m⁵ 6m a5g a5g] smallish, workmanlike gelding: fair plater at 2 yrs: back to near that form seventh to tenth starts in 1991: stays 6f: acts on firm and dead ground: blinkered nowadays: sometimes sweating. *S. R. Bowring.*

STRONG SUIT (IRE) 2 b.c. (Jan 31) King of Clubs 124 – Tumble Dale 88§ **97**
(Tumble Wind (USA)) [1991 6g⁵ 6g² 7.1s⁴ 7g* 7f⁶ 6f* 7m 6g] IR 15,500F: workmanlike colt: second foal: dam ungenuine sprint maiden here at 2 yrs won in USA at 3 yrs: fairly useful performer: won nurseries at Newmarket in August and Haydock (came from well off strong pace) in September: not discredited in face of stiff task in Dewhurst Stakes at Newmarket penultimate outing: never a factor in Racecall Gold Trophy at Redcar final one: will stay 1m: acts on firm ground, possibly unsuited by soft. *R. Hannon.*

STROUBIA (IRE) 3 ch.c. Nordance (USA) – Tatisha (Habitat 134) [1990 NR **57**
1991 12m⁶ 11d 10g a11g³ a11g 10.6g a8g²] IR 7,800F, IR 42,000Y: workmanlike colt: sixth foal: half-brother to 1m to 1¼m winner Shannon Express (by Magic Mirror), 1½m and 2¼m winner Relkisha (by Relkino) and a winner in France: dam, French 1m winner, is half-sister to high-class sprinter Green God: form only when placed in

maiden and handicap at Southwell: stays 11f: blinkered last 3 outings: sold 3,200 gns Newmarket Autumn Sales. *N. A. Callaghan.*

STYLISH DUTCH 2 ch.f. (Apr 30) Risk Me (FR) 127 – Dutch Gold 117 (Goldhill —
125) [1991 6g 6m5] close-coupled filly: fifth living foal: half-sister to 3 winning sprinters: dam sprinter: bit backward, well beaten in seller at York and 7-runner maiden (moved poorly down) at Newcastle in autumn. *M. W. Easterby.*

STYLISH GENT 4 br.g. Vitiges (FR) 132 – Squire's Daughter (Bay Express **74**
132) [1990 8f 9g6 10g 7m6 7d4 1991 7.5v 6.5g 7m5 8m* 8.3m* 8m* 7.6m3 8g 8m] strong, lengthy gelding: modest performer: won claimers at Pontefract in May and Windsor in July and handicap at Pontefract in August: stays 9f: acts on good to firm ground and dead: below form when visored once: not the easiest of rides: sold to join N. Tinkler's stable 11,100 gns Newmarket Autumn Sales: winning hurdler after. *Lord Huntingdon.*

STYLISH GENTLEMAN 2 b.c. (Feb 16) Natroun (FR) 128 – La Gallia 70 **64**
(Welsh Saint 126) [1991 7m 8.3g3 8.1d 7.1m a8g2 a7g6 a7g*] 10,500Y: sturdy colt: half-brother to several winners, including 2 winning 2-y-o sprinters by Lochnager and 5f and 1m winner Gallant Gallois (by Mummy's Game): dam won 3 times over 1½m and also over hurdles: quite modest performer: made most in Southwell nursery late in year: may well stay 1¼m: acts well on fibresand: wore blinkers and eyeshield last 3 outings: claimed £3,550 after fifth outing. *C. Tinkler.*

STYLISH SENOR (USA) 3 ch.c. El Gran Senor (USA) 136 – Gladiolus (USA) **103**
(Watch Your Step) [1990 6m4 7m2 7m6 1991 8d2 10.1g2 12d* 10.1g* 10.4m 12g* 10m5] lengthy, angular colt: moderate walker: useful performer: successful in summer in 3-runner auction contest at Thirsk, graduation event at Windsor and 3-runner Gordon Stakes (beat Trebly ½ length, staying on strongly) at Goodwood: not discredited but readily outpaced in moderately-run Group 3 event at Goodwood final start: will be suited by return to 1½m: yet to race on extremes of going: lazy, and needs firm handling in a finish: visored last 2 starts: tongue tied down third to sixth. *J. R. Fanshawe.*

STYLUS 2 ch.c. (Mar 27) Sharpo 132 – Pine Ridge 80 (High Top 131) [1991 a7g3] **67** p
38,000Y: fifth foal: brother to a winner in USA and half-brother to high-class In The Groove (by Night Shift), Group 1 winner from 1m to 1½m, fairly useful miler Spanish Pine (by King of Spain) and 3-y-o 1½m winner Pineapple (by Superlative): dam 1½m winner: 10/1 from 7/2, always-prominent third of 16, beaten 2½ lengths, to Empeeka in late-year maiden at Southwell: will improve. *M. R. Stoute.*

STYRIAN (USA) 3 b.c. Storm Bird (CAN) 134 – Vachti (FR) 114 (Crystal Palace —
(FR) 132) [1990 7s 1991 10.5g 10.4m] tall, leggy, angular colt: no worthwhile form, pulling very hard in York maiden (wandered and lost place 2f out) final start: sold 1,700 gns Newmarket Autumn Sales. *W. Jarvis.*

SUAVE DANCER (USA) 3 b.c. Green Dancer (USA) 132 – Suavite **136**
(USA) (Alleged (USA) 138) [1990 8s3 1991 10g* 10.5d* 10.5d2 12m* 12g2 10d* 12d*]

'Generous v Suave Dancer. The re-match'. So went the billing for Europe's most valuable race, the Ciga Prix de l'Arc de Triomphe at Longchamp in October. Here was the prospect of an Arc to savour, a second confrontation between the two best middle-distance performers in Europe, one trained in Britain, and the winner of the Ever Ready Derby, the other trained in France and the winner of the French equivalent the Prix du Jockey-Club Lancia, the pair of them head and shoulders above their contemporaries. Generous and Suave Dancer had met in the Budweiser Irish Derby, with Generous the victor, but both had enhanced their reputations with vintage performances since, Generous annihilating the opposition in the King George VI and Queen Elizabeth Diamond Stakes and Suave Dancer brushing aside high-class opposition contemptuously in the Meadow Meats Irish Champion Stakes in September. Suave Dancer's brilliant performance at Leopardstown (the Irish Champion was transferred there after seven years at Phoenix Park) served notice that Generous, off the course since July, would have to be at his best in the Prix de l'Arc. Suave Dancer, who looked to have done very well physically since the Irish Derby, stormed clear of the Coral-Eclipse first and second Environment Friend and Stagecraft in the final stages of the Irish Champion, producing an impressive turn of foot in the home straight after being waited with; Asmussen gave up riding Suave Dancer thirty or forty yards from the post, and eased him close home, but he still had four lengths to spare over

Prix du Jockey-Club Lancia, Chantilly—
Suave Dancer is a clear-cut winner from Subotica (second right) and Cudas (stars)

the runner-up Environment Friend and would have won by at least six, push-ed out. It was a performance which had the connections of Suave Dancer predicting a much closer race with Generous in the Arc. 'Suave Dancer will be on his home ground and that counts for a lot. He was a late-maturing horse and I always believed he would improve through the year and be a better colt at the end of the season,' said trainer John Hammond; while Cash Asmussen, who had ridden Suave Dancer in all his races except the Irish Derby which he'd missed through injury, said 'Suave Dancer is now a much stronger individual and when I got aboard I had to drop my leathers three holes, he had filled out that much. I realise he'll have to be extra special to beat Generous, but I can assure you he is extra special! I've never ridden one better.'

If the Prix de l'Arc went according to the form-book, Generous and Suave Dancer looked almost certain to finish clear, but things are seldom straightforward, especially in the Arc which almost always attracts the strongest and most representative field of the European racing year for a middle-distance event. Half the runners in the latest edition were classic winners, Generous and Suave Dancer being opposed by the Coalite St Leger winner Toulon and the Gold Seal Oaks winner Jet Ski Lady, as well as the previous year's Derby and St Leger winners Quest For Fame and Snurge (also

Meadow Meats Irish Champion Stakes, Leopardstown—
Suave Dancer brushes aside high-class opposition;
Stagecraft and Zoman are the others in the picture

Ciga Prix de l'Arc de Triomphe, Longchamp—under hands-and-heels riding, Suave Dancer wins by two lengths and a length from Magic Night and Pistolet Bleu

third in the 1990 Arc), and the previous year's Irish One Thousand Guineas winner In The Groove who had also won three other Group 1 races, the Juddmonte International, the Dubai Champion and, in 1991, the Coronation Cup. The field was completed by the Prix Vermeille winner Magic Night, the Gran Premio d'Italia winner Pigeon Voyageur, the high-class Pistolet Bleu, who had missed the Prix du Jockey-Club through injury but had been beaten only once in six starts, the Gold Seal Oaks runner-up Shamshir, the 1990 Prix Vermeille runner-up Miss Alleged, the high-class North American seven-year-old El Senor and Pistolet Bleu's pacemaker Art Bleu.

Generous' dismal showing in the Arc—he weakened quickly early in the straight and managed only eighth—robbed the race of a good deal of its significance, but Suave Dancer took his opportunity to add another dazzling victory to his record, winning in such striking style that some questioned whether even a top-form Generous would have been a match for him. Asmussen rode Suave Dancer with tremendous confidence, tucking him in at the back of the field—'I was a little further back than I wanted to be'—as Art Bleu ensured a good gallop, and making no move until approaching the home turn. Brought to the outside early in the straight, Suave Dancer always had a clear passage to make his challenge whenever his rider chose. Asmussen bided his time—'I gave him two hundred yards of fresh air'—before, in his words, 'taking the handbrake off'. The response was immediate and Suave Dancer quickened exceptionally well to make short work of his rivals, cutting them down to lead entering the final furlong and then keeping on under hands-and-heels riding to win by two lengths and one from Magic Night and Pistolet Bleu, with Toulon three lengths further back in fourth, just ahead of Pigeon Voyageur. The first five home were all French-trained three-year-olds; In The Groove (sixth) and Quest For Fame (seventh) led home the British challenge ahead of Generous. Pigeon Voyageur (whose jockey received a suspension for improper riding), Quest For Fame and eleventh-placed Miss Alleged were the worst sufferers in scrimmaging that took place early in the straight, some of it also partly resulting from Art Bleu's rider pulling his mount off the rail rounding the home turn to allow stable-mate Pistolet Bleu to slip through. There was also a hard-luck story for Generous' stable-companion Snurge who trailed in last after hitting his head as the stalls opened. The only blemish on Suave Dancer's performance was that he came off a true line after taking the lead, displaying a by-now predictable tendency to drift to the right, straying all the way to the rail.

Suave Dancer's eccentricity for leaving the straight and narrow has earned him the nickname 'Swerve' Dancer. He had behaved similarly in most of his earlier races, most notably in the Prix du Jockey-Club Lancia at Chantilly in June. In the absence of Pistolet Bleu, Suave Dancer started at odds on in a field of only seven which included Cudas who had beaten Suave Dancer by three quarters of a length in the Prix Lupin the previous month. Suave Dancer had started at 10/1-on in the Lupin to make it three wins from three outings as a three-year-old, having won a maiden race by eight lengths and the Prix Greffulhe by four, both at Longchamp in April. Suave Dancer had come third in a late-season newcomers race at Saint-Cloud on his only start at

Henri Chalhoub's "Suave Dancer"

two. Perhaps the less said about his rider's performance in the Lupin the better. Suffice to report that Cudas was given the more enterprising ride, poaching a decisive advantage early in the straight which served him well as the strong-finishing Suave Dancer came from sixth-of-seven position, ducking right when cracked with the whip in the closing stages. Suave Dancer turned the tables on Cudas in no uncertain manner in the Prix du Jockey Club, winning with a spectacular display by four lengths from Subotica, with Cudas a further length and a half away third, and the Chester Vase and Predominate Stakes runner-up Luchiroverte fourth. Asmussen kept Cudas in his sights all the way and Suave Dancer comprehensively asserted his superiority when given the office, despite swerving right once again after taking the lead. The clash between Suave Dancer and the Derby winner Generous in the Budweiser Irish Derby in July resulted in a clear-cut three-length victory for Generous, though Suave Dancer flattered for a time as he drew up to the front-running Generous in the home straight. But Suave Dancer couldn't get past and began to hang when he had nothing more to give, clearly finding Generous too good on the day.

Generous was retired at the end of the season, so he won't be crossing Suave Dancer's path again. Generous' flawless performances in the Derby, Irish Derby and King George earned him our vote as Horse of the Year, but we have a very high regard for Suave Dancer, too. He'd have dominated the middle-distance scene in Europe in an average year and it's excellent news that he stays in training. There are powerful arguments against racing a three-year-old as good as Suave Dancer for another year. As a top-class middle-distance horse with pace, an enormous sum would have been available to secure him for stud in 1992. And what fields are left to conquer? As we have pointed out many times, the programme of racing in Europe offers the greatest rewards to horses bred and trained to be successful at two and three years. Suave Dancer's reputation and value were established by his successes as a three-year-old, notably in the Prix du Jockey-Club and the Prix de l'Arc. He cannot add materially to his value as a stallion by being raced as a four-year-old, and even if he were to win both the King George and the Prix de l'Arc—announced as his two main targets—the prize money earned would be a fraction of the potential earnings from stud fees. Owners are often criticised for packing good horses off to stud but the commercial pressures on an owner to retire a three-year-old like Suave Dancer are immense. Suave Dancer's owner knows that his decision to keep the horse in training could cost him dear but he explained his philosophy in an interview in *Pacemaker Update* in December. 'Of course there is a risk, but I am a gambler and it would be a crime to hide such a champion . . . Imagine that you are sitting in my place. You have reached your supreme goal—your pleasure is at its maximum. Why give up that pleasure and not see him run again when he will still be at his peak?' Mr Chalhoub said he was most strongly influenced by the belief that Suave Dancer 'will be even better and stronger next season'. Suave Dancer was certainly a progressive three-year-old and looks well-nigh certain to train on. Judged on what Suave Dancer has achieved already, the rising generation of three-year-olds will have their work cut out to prevent his farming the top open-aged middle-distance races in 1992. Although he didn't encounter extremes of going as a three-year-old, Suave Dancer showed his form on good to firm and on dead, so is unlikely to be beholden to the state of the going, as normally found nowadays on King George day and Arc day. And his turn of finishing speed, one of the most valuable assets a top-class racehorse can have, is sure to stand him in excellent stead. We wish him well.

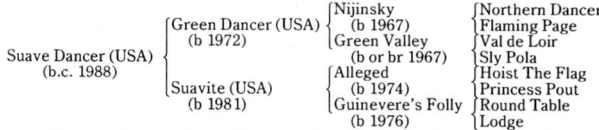

Suave Dancer (USA) (b.c. 1988)
- Green Dancer (USA) (b 1972)
  - Nijinsky (b 1967)
    - Northern Dancer
    - Flaming Page
  - Green Valley (b or br 1967)
    - Val de Loir
    - Sly Pola
- Suavite (USA) (b 1981)
  - Alleged (b 1974)
    - Hoist The Flag
    - Princess Pout
  - Guinevere's Folly (b 1976)
    - Round Table
    - Lodge

The good-looking Suave Dancer, who is a very good mover, should make up into a fine individual as a four-year-old. He has the pedigree to match his looks, too, and was a bargain at only 45,000 dollars as a yearling, bought at the Keeneland September Sale for his owner by Keith Asmussen, father of the jockey. Suave Dancer's sire Green Dancer, like Generous' sire Caerleon, is a son of the triple crown winner Nijinsky. Green Dancer was a member of Nijinsky's first crop and showed high-class form at two and three, winning the Observer Gold Cup (now the Racing Post Trophy), the Poule d'Essai des Poulains (equivalent of the Two Thousand Guineas) and the Prix Lupin. He was a disappointing 6/4 favourite for Grundy's Derby but subsequently ran a very good race over eleven furlongs in the Prix Niel and came a respectable eighth in the Prix de l'Arc. Green Dancer started his stud career in France but has stood most of his time at Gainesway Farm in Kentucky. He's been a useful stallion, though Suave Dancer is, by some way, the best horse he's sired. Suave Dancer's dam Suavite, by the dual Prix de l'Arc winner Alleged out of the fair winning miler Guinevere's Folly, was a 330,000-dollar yearling. Suavite repaid 96,171 dollars of her purchase price during her racing career, winning four races and finishing second in the Grade 3 Comely Stakes over seven furlongs as a three-year-old. Suave Dancer is the second foal of Suavite, a mare who has changed hands twice since foaling Suave Dancer, the first time for 95,000 dollars at the Keeneland November Sale in 1989 and the second time in a private deal before Suave Dancer had started to make a name for himself. Suavite's most recent offspring, a yearling colt by Green Dancer and a colt foal by Arctic Tern, are now owned by Sheikh Mohammed and by Suave Dancer's owner respectively. The Green Dancer yearling is due to go into training with Suave Dancer's trainer; Mr Chalhoub paid 725,000 dollars for the Arctic Tern foal at the Keeneland November Breeding Stock Sale, the highest price paid for a foal at public auction in the States in 1991. Suave

SUB

Dancer's family has already produced two most successful sires in the half-brothers Northfields and Habitat who were both out of Suave Dancer's fourth dam Little Hut. It's a good bet that the major studs have already been falling over themselves to secure an interest in Suave Dancer. He has so much to recommend him as a stallion. *J. E. Hammond, France.*

SUBOTICA (FR) 3 b.c. Pampabird 124 – Terre de Feu (Busted 134) [1990 **121**
7.5g⁴ 8s* 9s* 1991 11g² 12d² 12m² 10d* 10g⁵ 12m*]

Consistency had its reward when Subotica won the Grand Prix de Paris Louis Vuitton at Longchamp in June. That was his fourth race of the season, his seventh all told. Up to then, he hadn't been able to add to wins in a Maisons-Laffitte maiden and an Evry listed event in 1990, but it had taken two of France's best three-year-olds to stop him doing so. Only Pistolet Bleu had come between him and the Prix Noailles and the Prix Hocquart, classic trials at Longchamp; and only Suave Dancer between him and the Prix du Jockey-Club Lancia, the French Derby at Chantilly. Subotica put up a good showing each time, extending Pistolet Bleu rather more on each occasion than Suave Dancer who beat him by four lengths at Chantilly. The absence of Suave Dancer and Pistolet Bleu from the Grand Prix de Paris field left Subotica with an excellent chance in a competitive event which also attracted the Jockey-Club third, the Diane third and fourth and the first two in the Jean Prat—as long as he could reproduce his form over the shorter distance, that was. There seemed a distinct possibility that the drop back to a mile and a quarter would tell against him, for he gave the impression he lacked pace. He had to be scrubbed along when they quickened in the Jockey-Club, and before staying on to finish a clear second he looked to have little chance of even third as the winner went on. However, it's plain now that Suave Dancer would make most middle-distance horses look short of pace. While running in a similar style in the Grand Prix de Paris, Subotica, probably helped by the more testing ground, got up near the finish to win staying on strongly by a neck from Jean Prat winner Sillery, who beat the Group 3 Prix La Force winner Kotashaan by two lengths for second; the favourite, the Jockey-Club third Cudas, came fourth, having had every chance.

Subotica met with a big set-back on his next outing. He looked a good thing for the Piaget d'Or at Deauville in August but the attempt to dictate from the front misfired; the jockey set too slow a pace and some of the others outsprinted him, so he finished only fifth of eight to La Carene. That wasn't his form, obviously. He came back into the Prix de l'Arc de Triomphe reckoning as a lively outsider by turning the tables on Pistolet Bleu in the eight-runner Prix Niel Escada over a mile and a half at Longchamp in September, getting up in the last forty yards from that colt and Arcangues after having plenty to do in the straight. It was a good performance. However, just when he was all set to go for the Arc he developed a rash and had to be withdrawn. It's unlikely that

*Prix Niel Escada, Longchamp—Subotica stays on to lead close home,
accounting for Pistolet Bleu (centre) and Arcangues*

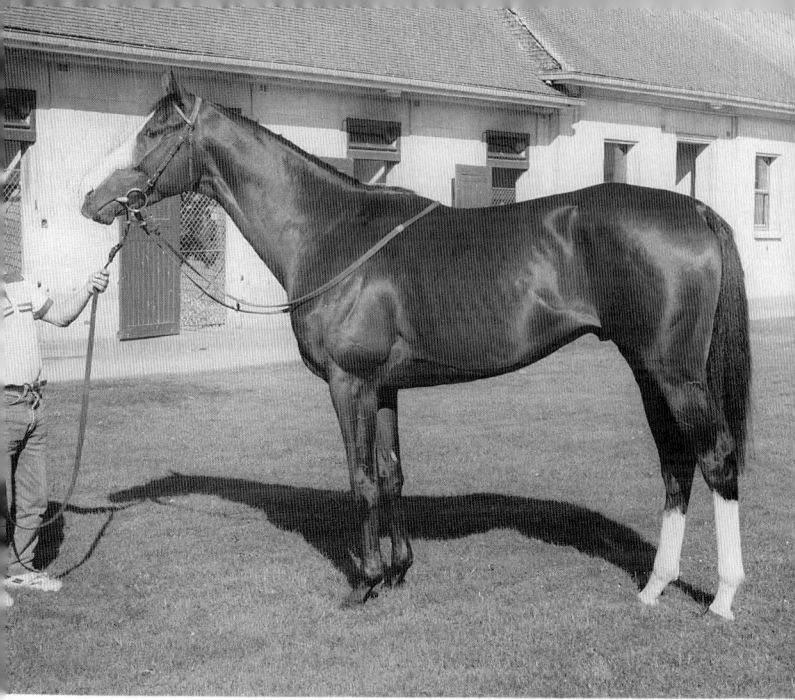

Olivier Lecerf's "Subotica"

he'd have made the first three in the big race, but he would have been an interesting runner, for sure.

	Pampabird (b 1979)	Pampapaul (b 1974)	Yellow God
			Pampalina
		Wood Grouse (ch 1967)	Celtic Ash
Subotica (FR) (b.c. 1988)			French Bird
	Terre de Feu (FR) (b 1983)	Busted (b 1963)	Crepello
			Sans Le Sou
		Ludivine (b 1973)	Luthier
			Tita

Subotica was bought at auction as a yearling in France for the equivalent of around £24,000, sold by his breeder Paul de Moussac in whose colours both sire and dam raced. The sire Pampabird, beset by training troubles in his racing days, was a good-class miler who won the Prix Messidor and the Prix du Rond-Point as a four-year-old. The dam won over a mile at Saint-Cloud and a mile and a quarter at Longchamp from twelve starts. Subotica, her first foal, has been followed by a filly by Antheus called Terre Indienne, sold for around £10,000 at the Deauville Yearling Sales. The next dam Ludivine, dam of at least five other winners counting those over jumps, was a minor winner herself in France. She is out of Tita, who to Diatome threw the top-class middle-distance colt Margouillat, third to Allez France and Comtesse de Loir in the Arc of 1974. Subotica is probably less effective over a mile and a quarter than Margouillat was, but is clearly effective at the distance provided he gets a truer test than he got at Deauville. He stays a mile and a half really well. A big,

851

lengthy colt, he acts on good to firm going and on soft. He sweated up at Chantilly but is genuine and reliable. *A. Fabre, France.*

SUBSONIC (IRE) 3 b.c. Be My Guest (USA) 126 – Broken Wide (Busted 134) **81** p
[1990 7m4 8g 8m 1991 10d6 12f 14g* 12.3d* 14m3 16.1m* 16m* 18m* 16.5d] big, good-bodied colt: has a round action: progressed into a fair handicapper: won at Nottingham and Ripon in June then (looking very well) at Newcastle, Redcar and Pontefract in October: suited by thorough test of stamina: best efforts on top-of-the-ground, though has won on dead: didn't handle turn at Folkestone second outing: rather lazy, and idles in front: can win a good handicap in 1992. *J. L. Dunlop.*

SUBTLE CHANGE (IRE) 3 br.f. Law Society (USA) 130 – Santa Luciana **102**
(GER) (Luciano) [1990 6m2 8m2 8.5m* 8m3 8m5 1991 11.5g3 11.5m2 16.2m6 14g 12g5 14m6 14m* 14d5 16d2 16s* 12d 16s] lengthy, good-topped filly: useful form here, third to Ausherra in listed race at Lingfield: won handicap at Galway in September and listed event at the Curragh (by 6 lengths) in October: stays 2m: acts on good to firm and soft ground: reportedly in season second start: blinkered fifth: trained first 4 by G. Harwood. *L. Browne, Ireland.*

SUDANOR (IRE) 2 b.c. (Apr 10) Khartoum (USA) – Alencon 65 (Northfields **75** p
(USA)) [1991 7d3] IR 10,500F: closely related to a winner by Damascus and half-brother to several other winners: dam won at up to 9f: sire sprinter: 33/1, over 5 lengths third of 22, staying on well, to For Reg in maiden at Doncaster in November: likely to stay 1m: will improve. *M. J. Heaton-Ellis.*

SUDELEY 3 b.f. Dancing Brave (USA) 140 – Peace 113 (Klairon 131) [1990 NR **65**
1991 8m 10g6 11.5m* 11.7m 11.9m] useful-looking filly: has a quick action: closely related to quite modest 1984 3-y-o Flaming Peace and half-sister to numerous winners, including good middle-distance performers Quiet Fling and Peacetime (both by Nijinsky) and Cambridgeshire winner Intermission (by Stage Door Johnny): dam 2-y-o 6f winner: won maiden at Lingfield in June, always close up and green once in front 1½f out: ran badly in handicaps: should have proved better at around 1½m than shorter: stud. *R. Charlton.*

SUEZ CANAL (IRE) 2 b.g. (Mar 23) Commanche Run 133 – Sphinx (GER) **69**
(Alpenkonig (GER)) [1991 7g4 7.1s] leggy, lengthy, angular gelding: fifth reported foal: half-brother to smart 3-y-o 1½m and 12.3f winner Hieroglyphic (by Darshaan) and a winner in Denmark by Pas de Seul: dam German winner from family of Slip Anchor: quite modest maiden: 16/1 and better for race, staying-on 9 lengths fourth of 15 at Salisbury: will be suited by middle distances: possibly unsuited by soft ground. *P. W. Chapple-Hyam.*

SUGEMAR 5 ch.g. Young Generation 129 – Jade Ring 92 (Auction Ring (USA) **62**
123) [1990 7m 8f 10.6s 10m4 9m3 12g 1991 7m6 7m* 8g 7m3 a8g4 8f6 8m] big, strong gelding: poor walker and mover: quite modest handicapper: won (for first time) at Lingfield in May: effective at 7f, and stays 1¼m: acts on good to firm and soft going. *J. A. R. Toller.*

SUIVEZ MOI 7 ch.g. Pas de Seul 133 – Reparata (Jukebox 120) [1990 a16g a14g* —
a14g 18f2 16.5m* 16g 17.6m3 a14g* 16m5 a18g4 17.6f4 15.3m 17.4d 16m* 15.3g3 18d 16.5d a12g6 a16g a14g6 1991 a14g a16g a14g] small, light-framed gelding: poor mover: poor handicapper: no form in early part of 1991: ideally needs further than 1½m and stays well: acts on any going except possibly heavy: raced too freely when visored: suitable mount for apprentice: has sweated: reportedly broke blood vessel once at 6 yrs: genuine: won over hurdles in February. *C. N. Allen.*

SUKEY TAWDRY 5 gr.m. Wassl 125 – Jenny Diver (USA) (Hatchet Man (USA)) —
[1990 12.5f 1991 10s4 12g] leggy mare: poor handicapper: stays 1½m: acts on firm going: tried visored. *P. Butler.*

SULA 3 br.f. Sula Bula 109 – Dusky Damsel 68 (Sahib 114) [1990 5m 5g a7g4 1991 —
8m 12.1f] leggy, sparely-made filly: no worthwhile form, including in a seller. *T. D. Barron.*

SULAAH ROSE 2 b.f. (Jun 12) Sula Bula 109 – Dusky Damsel 68 (Sahib 114) —
[1991 8m] leggy filly: ninth foal: sister to 3-y-o Sula: dam won over 6f at 3 yrs: 50/1, backward and sweating, soundly-beaten last of 11 in maiden at Redcar in October. *Mrs J. Jordan.*

SULCIS 6 ch.g. Castle Keep 121 – Skiboule (BEL) (Boulou) [1990 13g 15g 14d2 —
17g2 a14g 1991 a14g a14g5] well-made gelding: has a fluent action: plating-class handicapper: below form in early 1991: stays 17f: seems to act on any going: has run well when blinkered. *W. Jenks.*

SULLI BOY (NOR) 6 b.g. Sparkling Boy 110 – Lady Sullivan (Pitcairn 126) [1990 10f 6g 8f⁶ 11.7g 1991 10.1g 8g⁶] sturdy, workmanlike gelding: winner 8 times in Scandinavia, including twice over 1m in 1989: never a threat in varied events on flat in Britain: withdrawn lame at start final intended outing (July). *Miss B. Sanders.* —

SULLY'S CHOICE (USA) 10 b.g. King Pellinore (USA) 127 – Salute The Coates (USA) (Solar Salute (USA)) [1990 a5g² a7g² a7g⁵ 5m 5f 6g 5m² 6d 6g 5m⁴ 5f⁶ 5m 6d 1991 6f 5m⁶ 6f⁶ 6f⁵ 6m* 6m* 6f² 6f 6f 6m⁶ 6g 6f* 6g² 5m 6m 7.1m 5s a5g³ a6g] small, sturdy gelding: carries plenty of condition: plating-class handicapper nowadays: won at Pontefract, Thirsk and Yarmouth in autumn: best at 5f or 6f: acts on any going: tried visored: effective with or without blinkers: suitable mount for apprentice: suited by forcing tactics. *D. W. Chapman.* 59

SULTAN'S SON 5 b.h. Kings Lake (USA) 133 – Get Ahead 58 (Silly Season 127) [1990 10f* 12m* 1991 12g 12s⁵ 11d] strong, good-bodied horse: has a round action: fairly useful handicapper at 4 yrs: behind in first half of 1991: suited by 1½m: acts well on top-of-the-ground: joined Mrs A. King. *P. F. I. Cole.* —

SULTRY SINGER 2 b.f. (Mar 7) Sizzling Melody 117 – Maravilla 73 (Mandrake Major 122) [1991 5d* 6.1g⁵ 5g³ 6g³ 5.3f* 6g⁴ 5m² 6.1m³ 6m⁶ 5.7g⁴] 6,000Y: leggy, lightly-made filly: second foal: half-sister to 3-y-o Mu-Arrik (by Aragon): dam, maiden stayed 1m, is half-sister to useful miler Deadly Nightshade: quite modest performer: won maiden auction at Bath and seller (no bid) at Brighton in summer: ran creditably in frame in nurseries afterwards, including for 7-lb claimer: stays 6.1f: yet to race on very soft ground, probably acts on any other: sold 3,200 gns Newmarket Autumn Sales. *G. B. Balding.* 63

SULUK (USA) 6 b.h. Lypheor 118 – Cheerful Heart (Petingo 135) [1990 a12g* a16g³ a14g³ a12g² 13.8m³ 1991 a12g 11.8g 12m⁶ a12g⁵ a14g* a16g] dipped-backed, good-quartered horse: carries condition: plating-class handicapper: gamely won claimer (returned to form) at Southwell in November: ran poorly there following month: stays 1¾m: acts on hard going, goes very well on fibresand: has gone well with forcing tactics: genuine. *R. Hollinshead.* —

SUM MEDE 4 b.g. King Persian 107 – Brun's Toy (FR) (Bruni 132) [1990 10.8m⁶ 10.2f⁶ 9m 10.5g³ 12m 1991 a12g⁵ a12g⁶] leggy, angular gelding: has a quick action: plating-class handicapper: best form at 1¼m: acts on firm going: has been tried blinkered: won over hurdles in January. *B. S. Rothwell.* 54

SUMMER CRUISE 2 b.c. (Mar 15) Slip Anchor 136 – Enthralment (USA) 78 (Sir Ivor 135) [1991 7m³] good-bodied colt: sixth foal: half-brother to a winner in Belgium by Kings Lake: dam, out of sister to Forli, well beaten after winning over 6f on debut at 2 yrs: 9/2 and bit backward, had quite a hard race when over a length third of 16 to Stani in maiden at Leicester in October, front rank throughout: should stay 1¼m: showed a quick action: will improve. *H. R. A. Cecil.* 76 p

SUMMER SANDS 3 ch.f. Mummy's Game 120 – Renira 60 (Relkino 131) [1990 5m 5m* 6g⁴ 5m 6s⁵ 1991 6m 5s 8m 6g⁵ 7g⁴ 7d⁴ 6.9m³ 5d³ 7m² 7d³ 7f 8g] lengthy filly: quite modest performer: below form in seller and handicap last 2 starts: stays 7f: acts on good to firm ground and soft: bandaged off-hind second start: sold out of D. Elsworth's stable 3,600 gns Ascot July Sales after eighth. *J. L. Harris.* 60

SUMMING OAK (IRE) 2 ch.f. (Feb 18) Summing (USA) – Singing Oak (USA) (Tarleton Oak (USA)) [1991 5f] IR 16,000Y, 15,000 2-y-o: leggy, sparely-made filly: half-sister to 2 minor stakes winners in USA: dam won 11 races at up to 9f: sire won Belmont Stakes: 25/1 and better for race, well-beaten last of 7 in minor event at Ripon in August, slowly away and always outpaced: should improve. *C. N. Allen.* — p

SUMMONED BY BELLS 2 ch.f. (Mar 25) Stanford 121§ – Mephisto Waltz 98 (Dancer's Image (USA)) [1991 5m⁴ 5g 6d] workmanlike filly: sixth foal: sister to 2 winning sprinters, including useful Cumbrian Waltzer, and half-sister to 3 other winners here and abroad: dam won over 5f and 6f at 2 yrs: plating-class form in late-season northern maidens: soundly beaten final start: led round paddock by 2 handlers last 2 starts: possibly doesn't have ideal attitude. *M. Johnston.* 55

SUMONDA 3 b.f. Lomond (USA) 128 – Soemba 86 (General Assembly (USA)) [1990 6m² 6m⁴ 7m* 1991 8s* 8g³ 8g 8g² 10g 7f² 7m* 7m³ 8.1d⁵] strong, lengthy filly: has a quick action: useful performer: won minor events at Leicester in March and Ayr (making all and battling on well) in September: below form in minor events last 2 outings: stays 1m: acts on good to firm ground and soft: visored last 4 starts: below form in blinkers (pulled hard) on fifth: swishes tail and carries head high: hasn't ideal attitude: sold 41,000 gns Newmarket December Sales. *G. Wragg.* 95 §

SUN AND SHADE 2 b.f. (Mar 5) Ajdal (USA) 130 – Shadywood 96 (Habitat 134) [1991 6g*] sturdy, quite attractive filly: keen walker: third foal: half-sister to very 93 p smart middle-distance stayer Madame Dubois (by Legend of France) and 3-y-o Be The Best (by Rousillon): dam 1¼m winner stayed 1½m, is half-sister to winner 6f to 1m winner Kashmir Lass and daughter of Cheshire Oaks winner Milly Moss: second favourite but bit green, won 8-runner £9,500 maiden at Ascot in July by 1½ lengths from Mahasin, scrubbed along 2f out, leading 1f out and going away at finish: looked sure to prove capable of considerably better and win more races, but wasn't seen again. *H. R. A. Cecil.*

SUNBURST PRINCESS (IRE) 3 ch.f. Tender King 123 – Rhumb Line (Right Tack 131) [1990 6m 6m 8g 1991 6f⁶ 6g 6m 8g 7m 7m] angular filly: no worthwhile form, in seller and handicaps last 3 starts: sometimes sweating. *J. E. Banks.* —

SUNDAY'S HILL 2 b.c. (Apr 8) Efisio 120 – Elkie Brooks 82 (Relkino 131) [1991 6.1g 6g² 6m* 6g* 6m⁴ 7.3g] good-bodied colt: moderate mover, has a markedly round action: third foal: half-brother to 3-y-o Silver Stone Boy and 1988 2-y-o 6f winner Dolly Bevan (both by Another Realm): dam second over 6f at 2 yrs didn't train on: fairly useful performer: favourite and sweating, won maiden at Newmarket in August and nursery at Ascot (gamely) following month: best effort when fourth, keeping on well having been outpaced, to Misterioso in listed race at York in October: ran moderately in Horris Hill Stakes at Newbury 12 days later: should prove suited by 7f. *M. Blanshard.* 99

SUNDERLAND ECHO 2 br.c. (Feb 25) Daring March 116 – Incarnadine 67 (Hot Spark 126) [1991 6g 7g⁴ 6g 8m] 4,200F, 1,250Y: good-bodied, workmanlike colt: has scope: fifth foal: half-brother to fair 3-y-o 7f (at 2 yrs) and 1m winner Rise Up Singing (by Noalto) and 1987 2-y-o 5f and 6f winner Roedean Honey (by Good Times): dam won over 7f and 1m: off course 2½ months, shaped quite well in face of very stiff task in 1m Pontefract nursery in October, travelling comfortably most of way but having very poor run and not knocked about from 1f out: gives impression will prove suited by 1m: likely to do better. *Mrs G. R. Reveley.* 39 p

SUN ECLIPSE (IRE) 2 ch.f. (May 1) Palace Music (USA) 129 – Sun Breiz (FR) (Boran) [1991 7m 7d] lengthy, unfurnished filly: half-sister to 1990 French 2-y-o 9f winner Synergie (by Dahar) and French 11f winner Gollestan (by Gay Mecene): dam twice raced, from family of Sun Princess: 33/1, always behind in large-field autumn maidens at Leicester (backward) and Doncaster. *M. McCormack.* —

SUNFLOWER SEED 4 b.f. Mummy's Pet 125 – Bright Sun (Mill Reef (USA) 141) [1990 7m 8m⁶ 11m² 11.5g⁵ 10.2m⁵ 12g⁴ 11.5g⁶ a14g 1991 10g 9.7f⁴ 12.1s a12g a10g] lengthy, robust filly: plating-class handicapper, still a maiden: well below form last 3 starts: stays 1½m: acts on firm going: effective visored or not. *P. J. Makin.* 50

SUN GLORY (IRE) 2 b.f. (Feb 22) Glow (USA) – Sun Bed (Habitat 134) [1991 a8g a7g] 21,000F, 8,000Y: neat filly: second foal: sister to 3-y-o Brown As A Berry: dam Irish 2-y-o 5f winner: soundly beaten in claimer at Lingfield and maiden at Southwell late in year. *W. Jarvis.* —

SUNKALA SHINE 3 ch.g. Kalaglow 132 – Allander Girl (Miralgo 130) [1990 NR 1991 16.1m⁴] 5,000F: lengthy, rather unfurnished gelding: half-brother to several winners, including fair sprinter Gaelic Affair (by Irish Love) and fairly useful 1m and 8.5f winner Saynete (by Night Shift): dam unplaced 5 times in Ireland: joint favourite, fourth of 7 to impressive Attadale in maiden at Newcastle in July: went down well. *J. G. FitzGerald.* 53

SUNLEY SENSATION 3 b.f. High Top 131 – Brown Velvet 68 (Mansingh (USA) 120) [1990 NR 1991 a8g⁶ 8d 8m 10.1m] lengthy filly: moderate mover: fourth foal: half-sister to 6f winner Berkeley Hill Boy and French 7f and 1m winner Bartizan (both by Castle Keep): dam, possibly short runner, is half-sister to smart Stumped, dam of Sonic Lady: well beaten in maiden, claimers and a seller. *M. R. Channon.* —

SUNLEY SPARKLE 3 b.f. Sunley Builds 102 – Royal Darwin 69 (Royal Palm 131) [1990 7g 1991 a6g* 8g 7m⁴ 6g⁴ 7m³ 7m* 7.6d⁵ a7g⁴ 6m⁵ a7g 7m⁴ 7g⁶ 8.1s 8.2m] leggy, rather sparely-made filly: won maiden at Lingfield in March and claimer (gamely made all, claimed out of M. Channon's stable £9,205) at Epsom in June: plating class on rest of form: suited by 7f: acts on good to firm going: sold 3,300 gns Doncaster October Sales. *D. R. Gandolfo.* 67 d

SUNNYSIDE ROCK (IRE) 3 ch.g. Ballad Rock 122 – Havana Moon (Ela-Mana-Mou 132) [1990 NR 1991 6g⁴ 6d³ 6m 7m² 7.1g 10.5d 8.1m] 3,000F: workmanlike gelding: first living foal: dam Irish 7f and 1m winner: quite modest form in frame in apprentice claimer and maidens: stays 7f: acts on good to firm ground and dead: wore crossed noseband fourth to sixth outings, tongue strap on final one. *J. Etherington.* 64 d

SUNRAYS (IRE)   2 br.f. (May 25) Vision (USA) – Daybreaker (Thatching 131)   **37**
[1991 6m⁴ 8m 6s a7g] IR 500F, IR 2,000Y: leggy filly: third foal: dam poor daughter
of half-sister to Derby second Cavo Doro: poor maiden: had very stiff task on
fibresand. *C. W. C. Elsey.*

SUNSET DREAMS   4 b.c. Habitat 134 – Pennyweight (Troy 137) [1990 8f 6g³   **64**
7d 1991 6v 6d 6f* 6m 8m 6g 5m* 6f²] angular, good-bodied colt: quite modest
handicapper: won apprentice events at Folkestone and Edinburgh in first half of
1991: effective at 5f, and should stay 7f: goes well on firm ground (faced stiff task on
dead): effective with or without blinkers. *J. D. Czerpak.*

SUNSET REINS FREE   6 b.g. Red Sunset 120 – Free Rein (Sagaro 133) [1990   **48**
12m² 12m a8g² 1991 a8g 8.5f⁴ 10m⁵ 10.5m 12m²] big, good-bodied gelding: carries
plenty of condition: moderate mover: plating-class handicapper: first past post
(drifted left, causing interference) in amateurs event at Pontefract final start
(September): stays 1½m: acts on good to firm ground and dead: effective visored or
not: winning hurdler. *E. J. Alston.*

SUNSET ROSE   4 b.f. Shirley Heights 130 – Rose Bowl (USA) 131 (Habitat 134)   **43**
[1990 8g 10g 12m* 11.7m 12m* 12f⁵ 12s 12m⁴ 12m³ 13.6d 1991 11.7m³ 12g 12s 13.1f]
small, workmanlike filly: has a quick action: poor handicapper: better at 1½m than
shorter: suited by top-of-the-ground: inconsistent. *I. A. Balding.*

SUNSET STREET (IRE)   3 b.c. Bellypha 130 – Sunset Reef (Mill Reef (USA)   **80** d
141) [1990 6d 7d* 7m³ 6m* 7g⁵ 8m⁵ 6m 7.3g 1991 a10g⁶ 8g 11g⁴ 6d 8.5m 8g⁵ 6g
10d 8.1d] lengthy, workmanlike colt: has a quick action: fair winner at 2 yrs:
disappointing in varied events, including listed races and claimers, in 1991: may
need middle distances nowadays: wore eyeshield on reappearance: blinkered twice,
visored once: trained until after sixth start by C. Brittain: sold to join S. Dow 5,400
gns Ascot November Sales. *C. A. Austin.*

SUNWIND   5 b.g. Windjammer (USA) – Mrewa (Runnymede 123) [1990 6f 6m   **—**
7.6m 7f⁶ 8m 8f 1991 a10g] stocky gelding: poor maiden: should stay 1m: acts on firm
and dead going: inconsistent. *R. J. Hodges.*

SUOMI (IRE)   3 b.c. Tate Gallery (USA) 117 – Finlandia (FR) (Faraway Son   **101**
(USA) 130) [1990 7s* 1991 8g⁴ 8g³ 8g] tall, rangy colt: has plenty of scope: won
maiden at Newcastle at 2 yrs by 10 lengths: favourite, in frame in smallish fields for
£6,800 contest (on toes) at Sandown and listed race (made most, narrowly beaten) at
Kempton: sweating, ridden along in mid-division over 3f out when well beaten in
Queen Anne Stakes at Royal Ascot: bred to stay beyond 1m: takes keen hold: joined
N. Drysdale in USA. *L. M. Cumani.*

SUPADUPA   4 ch.f. Superlative 118 – Maysina 76 (Sheshoon 132) [1990 a8g⁵ a6g³   **37**
a8g a5g⁵ 10d a6g 1991 a7g³ a7g³ 7d 10f 8.3g 10g a8g³ a12g⁶] sturdy filly: poor on
most form: appeared to put up much improved effort when third in maiden at
Southwell: well below that form in claimer there after: seems to stay 1m: trained
first 6 outings by J. White. *Mrs Barbara Waring.*

SUPER BEAUTY   2 b.f. (Apr 29) Capricorn Line 111 – Super Lady (Averof 123)   **50**
[1991 5m 7m⁵] smallish, sturdy, rather angular filly: seventh foal: half-sister to
several winners, including fair 6f and 1m winner Super Punk (by Hot Spark) and 6f
(at 2 yrs) to 10.8f winner Super Morning (by Martinmas): dam ran 4 times at 2 yrs:
plating-class form in median auction maidens at Windsor (green, shaped promisingly) and Wolverhampton (stayed on never dangerous) in late-summer: will probably
stay 1¼m. *P. T. Walwyn.*

SUPER BENZ   5 ch.g. Hello Gorgeous (USA) 128 – Investiture 62 (Welsh   **87**
Pageant 132) [1990 6m³ 5f⁶ 7m² 6g 6m⁶ 6g⁶ 7g* 7m* 7m² 7.6g 7d² 7m⁶ 7g 7d⁶ a5g³
a7g a7g⁴ 1991 a6g* a6g⁶ 6d 7g³ 7m⁴ 7m 8d³ 6d 7g² 7.5f⁴ 7g* 7m⁶ 7m* 7g a7g*]
leggy, lengthy gelding: has a roundish action: fair handicapper: successful at
Southwell in February and December and at Goodwood in August and Redcar in
October: effective at 6f to 1m: acts on firm and dead going: occasionally visored: has
won for apprentice: goes very well with forcing tactics: tough and genuine. *T.
Fairhurst.*

SUPERBRAVE   5 b.h. Superlative 118 – Tribal Feast 100 (Tribal Chief 125) [1990   **77**
6f* 6m⁴ 7m 7m⁴ 6m³ 5m* 1991 5g⁶ 6m 5m 6m⁶ 5m⁵ 5g 6m³ 5m⁴ 6g⁴] strong,
lengthy horse: fair handicapper: stays 6f: has raced only on a sound surface: below
form when visored once. *J. Etherington.*

SUPER CHARGE   2 b.g. (May 19) Superlative 118 – Daisy Warwick (USA) 91   **44**
(Ribot 142) [1991 5g 6m 7f 6m] 1,050Y: compact gelding: half-brother to several
winners, including 1982 2-y-o 5.8f winner No Fluke (by Averof) and 13.8f winner

Tranby Croft (by Final Straw): dam placed twice over 5f at 2 yrs: poor form in varied events: should stay 7f: blinkered second and final outings. *M. W. Ellerby.*

SUPER DELIGHT 3 b.f. Norwick (USA) 120 – Super Melody 72 (Song 132) [1990 NR 1991 8d 12g⁵ 16g 11.7f⁶] leggy filly: first foal: dam 2-y-o 5f winner became one to treat with caution: well beaten in maidens and claimer: trained first 3 starts by P. Walwyn. *G. B. Balding.* —

SUPERENDO 3 ch.f. Superlative 118 – Moment In Time 91 (Without Fear (FR) 128) [1990 5g⁴ 5m³ 7f⁴ 6m a8g 1991 8g] smallish, sparely-made filly: poor performer: seemed reluctant to race final outing at 2 yrs: last of 19 in seller only start in 1991: best efforts at 5f: sold 800 gns Ascot September Sales. *D. J. Wintle.* — §

SUPER FLYER (IRE) 2 b.g. (Mar 6) Fayruz 116 – Flying Beauty (Super Concorde (USA) 128) [1991 a6g³ 7f] IR 7,000F, IR 20,000Y: leggy, angular gelding: third foal: half-brother to Irish 1½m winner Master Glaze (by Camden Town): dam showed a little ability at 2 yrs in Ireland: signs of a little ability in seller at Lingfield (soon behind, ran well not knocked about) and claimer at Salisbury (for 7-lb claimer) in late-summer. *C. Weedon.* —

SUPER GUNNER 6 ch.g. Busted 134 – Lunaria (USA) (Twist The Axe (USA)) [1990 a13g* a12g* a13g 12.3d 12g⁵ 16g a12g a12g 1991 15s] lengthy gelding: poor mover: plating-class handicapper at best: tailed off only run in 1991 (July): stays 13f: acts on firm and dead going: sold 1,800 gns Doncaster August Sales. *W. J. Pearce.* —

SUPER HEIGHTS 3 b.g. Superlative 118 – Shadha 57 (Shirley Heights 130) [1990 6m 5f* 6d 7s 1991 8g 8g 10.2g 6f* 6g 6m 7d 5.7m⁵ 6m⁶ 6m³ 6m⁶ 5.7f⁴ 6g⁵ 6m a6g⁵ a7g⁵ a7g³ a7g a6g*] useful-looking gelding: moderate mover: plating-class performer on most form: won handicaps at Redcar in May and Southwell in December: stay 7f: acts on firm and dead going and on equitrack: blinkered seventh to ninth starts: has edged left under pressure: inconsistent and unreliable. *Miss A. J. Whitfield.* 58 §

SUPER LUNAR 7 gr.g. Kalaglow 132 – Roxy Hart (High Top 131) [1990 8f 11m 1991 9g 8g²] strong, close-coupled gelding: modest handicapper: not seen out after running well at Salisbury in May: effective at 1m to 1¼m: seems not at his best on soft going, acts on any other: ran moderately in blinkers: often takes good hold. *L. G. Cottrell.* 66

SUPER MARCO 2 b.c. (Mar 5) Superlative 118 – Sterlonia 96 (Sterling Bay (SWE)) [1991 5g 5.9h² 5m 5g⁶ 5f] 2,800F: close-coupled colt: eighth foal: half-brother to several winners here and abroad, including 3-y-o 6f winner Double Decree (by Sayf El Arab) and useful 1986 2-y-o 5f winner Nutwood Lil (by Vaigly Great): dam won at 7f and 1m: plating-class maiden: best run at 6f: wore crossed noseband first 2 outings: hung right second and third starts: blinkered penultimate one. *W. W. Haigh.* 56

SUPER MORNING 5 b.h. Martinmas 128 – Super Lady (Averof 123) [1990 8g 8g 7g² a8g⁴ 1991 a10g* a10g* a10g² a10g⁶ a10g⁵ 9g 10.8m 10.8m* 8.1d⁴ 8.1g⁵ 10g⁶ 8.3g⁵ 8f³ 9g³ 10.3m* 10m 10.5d 8g² a10g⁶ a8g³ a10g³] tall, good-bodied horse: carries condition: quite modest handicapper: successful at Lingfield (twice) in January, Warwick in May and Doncaster in September: raced wide when very good third of 16 at Lingfield final start: effective at 1m to 10.8f: acts on any going: has run well blinkered or visored, fairly well for amateur. *G. B. Balding.* 68

SUPER ONE 4 b.g. Superlative 118 – Josephine Gibney (High Top 131) [1990 a8g³ a8g* a7g* 9.1m⁶ 7f 7g 7g* 7g⁶ 7g 7m a7g³ 6m a8g² 7f³ 1991 a8g⁴ a7g⁶ a8g⁵ a7g² 7d] compact gelding: moderate mover: quite modest handicapper: not seen out after March: rather headstrong, and should prove best at up to 1m: possibly unsuited by soft going: effective blinkered or not: has worn a tongue strap: inconsistent. *T. D. Barron.* 67

SUPEROO 5 b.g. Superlative 118 – Shirleen (Daring Display (USA)) 129) [1990 7g 8f⁶ 8f⁶ 7.3g 7m 1991 8.5m 8g 7m² 8g⁵ 7.9g³ 7m² 7m] big, workmanlike gelding: carries plenty of condition: has a rather round action: fair handicapper: ran well when second at Newmarket in July (unlucky in Bunbury Cup) and October: ideally suited by strongly-run 7f: acts on firm going. *J. Sutcliffe.* 86

SUPER RITCHART 3 b.g. Starch Reduced 112 – Karousa Girl (Rouser 118) [1990 NR 1991 12.1g⁴ 16.2s² 11.8m 12.1g⁴ 16.1g 12.1d 17.2g] strong gelding: second living foal: brother to 1988 2-y-o 7f seller winner Miss Patdonna: dam never ran: quite modest maiden at best on flat: may prove best short of 2m: possibly unsuited by top-of-the-ground: winning hurdle. *B. Palling.* 67 d

SUPER ROCKY 2 b.g. (Apr 7) Clantime 101 – Starproof 46 (Comedy Star (USA) 121) [1991 5m² 5f* 5m² 5f* 6m² 5m⁴] compact, rather leggy gelding: sixth reported 78

foal: half-brother to 1987 2-y-o 5f winner Hollia (by Touch Paper): dam, plater, stayed 7f: modest sprinter: made all or most in maiden at Hamilton in May and claimer at Ripon in August: ridden by inexperienced apprentice, good second of 4 at Catterick, better effort in nurseries: withdrawn lame at Ayr in September on seventh intended start: suited by 6f: acts well on firm ground: tends to hang left. *J. Berry.*

SUPER SALLY 4 ch.f. Superlative 118 – Sally Chase 101 (Sallust 134) [1990 NR **91** 1991 7m5 8.1d2 7g5 10.3d6 a8g* a8g2 a8g* a10g*] compact filly: second foal: half-sister to quite modest 5-y-o 5f to 7f winner Sally's Son (by Beldale Flutter): dam sprinter, ran only at 2 yrs: fairly useful handicapper: in tremendous form late in 1991, winning at Southwell (maiden) and Lingfield (2): effective at 1m to 1¼m: acts on dead ground. *M. J. Ryan.*

SUPER SARENA (IRE) 2 b.f. (Mar 8) Taufan (USA) 119 – Stop The Cavalry **87** (Relko 136) [1991 6m3 6m 7d3 8m3 8d5] IR 30,000Y: lengthy, rather angular filly: has a quick action: fifth foal: sister to 3-y-o Chew It Over and half-sister to winners abroad by Auction Ring and Try My Best: dam never ran: fair form, staying on, in Prestige Stakes at Goodwood (behind Musicale) and May Hill Stakes at Doncaster (promoted, in race won by Midnight Air) third and fourth starts: hampered 2f out and not knocked about thereafter in Brent Walker Fillies' Mile at Ascot later in September: will be well suited by 1¼m +: acts on good to firm and dead ground: sure to win a race or two. *D. R. C. Elsworth.*

SUPER SERENADE 2 b.c. (May 26) Beldale Flutter (USA) 130 – Super **56** Melody 72 (Song 132) [1991 5.1g4 7m6] compact, quite attractive colt: second foal: half-brother to 3-y-o Super Delight (by Norwick): dam 2-y-o 5f winner became one to treat with caution: plating-class form in maidens at Bath (carrying condition) and Brighton (raced keenly) in summer. *P. T. Walwyn.*

SUPER SPACEMATE 3 gr.g. Absalom 128 – Stedham 84 (Jaazeiro (USA) 127) — [1990 5m3 5f4 5g2 5m3 5m6 6v2 6d4 1991 6s 8m 6m] compact, angular gelding: modest maiden at 2 yrs: well beaten at 3 yrs, including in seller: stays 6f: goes well on heavy ground: sold 1,500 gns Doncaster May Sales. *J. Berry.*

SUPER STAFF (USA) 3 ch.f. Secretariat (USA) – Prodigious (FR) (Pharly **91** (FR) 130) [1990 7m2 1991 10.2m* 12g6 10.4m] leggy, lengthy filly: has a long stride: fair form: won minor event at Doncaster in May: made most at strong pace, tenderly handled once beaten, when 13½ lengths sixth of 14 in Ribblesdale Stakes at Royal Ascot: co-favourite, chased leaders but pushed along vigorously over 5f out when behind in Magnet Cup at York in July: stays 1½m: sent to race in USA. *B. W. Hills.*

SUPERSTRIKE 2 b.g. (May 22) Superlative 118 – Marista (Mansingh (USA) **88** p 120) [1991 a6g*] 25,000Y: sturdy, good-topped gelding: seventh foal: half-brother to 3-y-o Friend of A Friend (by Nishapour) and several winners, including useful 1988 2-y-o 5f winner Four-Legged Friend (by Aragon) and 6f and 1m winner Hanseatic (by Free State): dam lightly-raced half-sister to useful sprinter Cedar Grange, looked temperamental: weak 6/1-shot and carrying condition, won 12-runner maiden at Southwell in July by 7 lengths and the same, quickening clear of Palacegate Racing when shaken up, eased close home: moved moderately to post, fluently in race: looked several notches above the average all-weather debutant, and sure to improve, but wasn't seen again. *W. A. O'Gorman.*

SUPER-SUB 2 b.f. (Mar 30) Formidable (USA) 125 – Charlton Athletic (Bustino **55** 136) [1991 5g6 a6g4 6m 6g 7m2 7m2 a8g6 a7g3 a8g5] 3,200Y: small, sturdy filly: second foal: dam unraced half-sister to Horris Hill Stakes and Challenge Stakes winner Efisio (by Formidable), and a Grade 1 1¼m winner Mountain Bear: quite modest performer: stays 1m: acts on good to firm ground, and on fibresand: gave trouble stalls second appearance: blinkered third. *M. J. Fetherston-Godley.*

SUPER SUMMIT 2 ch.c. (May 18) Superlative 118 – Wollow Maid 73 (Wollow **49** 132) [1991 7d 7m 6.1m 8m] 6,000Y, 6,200Y: compact colt: fourth foal: half-brother to fair sprinter Pinnacle Point (by Lochnager): dam, 1¼m winner, refused to race once: plating-class maiden: best efforts first 2 starts: not knocked about final one: may stay 1m. *J. Pearce.*

SUPERTOP 3 b. or br.c. High Top 131 – Myth 89 (Troy 137) [1990 7g 8g3 1991 **80** 10g4 10.1m 10.2m 10f4] leggy, workmanlike colt: has a round action: fair maiden at best: well beaten last 3 starts: should be better suited by 1½m: probably needs an easy surface. *P. W. Harris.*

SUPER VIRTUOSA 4 b.f. Wassl 125 – Resolve (Reform 132) [1990 7g6 7d **54** 11.7m 12m5 10d5 10.6v 10g* 1991 10g2 10.1d3 11m2 11m2 12.3g* 12f] leggy, lengthy filly: poor mover: plating-class performer: won seller (no bid) at Wolverhampton in

September: stiff task after: stays 1½m well: acts on good to firm and dead ground. *M. C. Pipe.*

SUPER ZOOM   5 ch.g. Ballad Rock 122 – Ruby River (Red God 128§) [1990 5g 6d   —
6m 1991 6m 8m 7.1d 6g] robust, lengthy, dipped-backed gelding: fairly useful 5f
winner as 2-y-o: soundly beaten since: tried visored. *M. R. Channon.*

SUPREME BOY   2 ch.c. (Mar 29) Superlative 118 – Rose And The Ring (Welsh   **67**
Pageant 132) [1991 6f 6f 7g⁴ 7g] 8,800Y: compact colt: half-brother to several
winners, including 5f and 1m winner Electric Rose (by Electric) and 1m and 1¼m
winner Derryring (by Derrylin): dam ran twice: quite modest maiden: best effort
second start: may well stay 1m. *P. W. Harris.*

SUPREME CHOICE (USA)   3 b.c. Sovereign Dancer (USA) – Editor's Choice **114**
(USA) (Sir Ivor 135) [1990 7m 7s 1991 8g⁶ a11g* 11.9m³ 13.3g* 14g² 15.9g* 18m⁴
16m²] lengthy, workmanlike colt: thrived physically: won maiden at Southwell in
May, handicap (wandering badly and reportedly later found to have abscess in
mouth) at Newbury in July and listed race at York in August: in frame last 2 starts
behind Great Marquess in Doncaster Cup (didn't get strong enough pace or best of
runs) and Further Flight in Jockey Club Cup at Newmarket (beaten 1½ lengths):
suited by test of stamina: acts on good to firm ground: very useful and progressive.
B. W. Hills.

SUPREME COURT   4 b.g. Yashgan 126 – My Natalie 64 (Rheingold 137) [1990   —
8.2f³ 7m 10g* 8m² 9m³ 13.8m⁶ a8g 1991 9m 7.5f] sparely-made gelding: plater: best
form at 1¼m: acts on good to firm ground. *M. Dods.*

SUPREME DANCER (FR)   4 b.g. Alzao (USA) 117 – Supreme Solar (Royal   —
Captive 116) [1990 7f⁵ 8m* 8.2g⁵ 7f⁴ 8g 8g 8.3m² 8h³ 7f⁶ 8m⁴ 7d 1991 a7g a8g⁶ 12.1d

Morven Stud Ltd's "Supreme Choice"

12.3d 12m 9.7s 10m 8.5f 7f 10.2g 7m 10m] quite attractive gelding: quite modest performer at 3 yrs: little form in 1991: stays 1m: acts on hard going: has been bandaged: changed hands 5,000 gns Doncaster March Sales: trained first 4 starts by N. Tinkler. *C. Tinkler.*

SUPREME DESIRE 3 gr.f. Grey Desire 115 – Fire Mountain 87 (Dragonara **51** d Palace (USA) 115) [1990 5m⁵ 5g 5m 6d⁴ 6m² 6m 5m 5v 1991 5m² 6f a7g 5m 5f 5h 6.1m] leggy, shallow-girthed filly: plating-class form at best: disappointing after reappearance: best form at 5f: acts on good to firm ground: trained first 5 starts by D. Garraton: very free to post and slowly away final outing. *M. Brittain.*

SUPREME OPTIMIST 7 b.g. Absalom 128 – Cachucha (Gay Fandango (USA) — 132) [1990 NR 1991 a7g 5m 7m 5g 7d a6g a6g⁶ a6g⁴] small, workmanlike gelding: poor handicapper nowadays: stays 7f: acts on any going: usually blinkered. *R. E. Peacock.*

SUPREME WARRIOR 5 b.g. Simply Great (FR) 122 – Sindo 91 (Derring-Do — 131) [1990 NR 1991 12g] workmanlike gelding: has a long stride: quite modest maiden at 3 yrs: no show only run in 1991, first run on flat since: stays 2m: best efforts on firm going: often makes running. *P. J. Hobbs.*

SURCOAT 4 b.c. Bustino 136 – Mullet 75 (Star Appeal 133) [1990 12.3f³ 12g* — 11.5m² 16.2s⁵ 13.6g* 12.4m² 13g⁶ 12.3m* 14g 14d 1991 14f] small, sturdy colt: carries condition: poor mover: modest handicapper at 3 yrs: tailed off only run in 1991: may prove ideally suited by around 1¾m: probably acts on any going: ran well in net muzzle once. *J. H. Baker.*

SUREFOOT SILLARS 4 ch.g. Hotfoot 126 – Make A Signal 76 (Royal Gunner — § (USA)) [1990 7f 8f 7m 8m⁶ 10.2m⁶ 12.2g³ 13m⁴ 12m 15.8m² 16m⁶ 1991 a14g] neat gelding: quite modest handicapper at best: soundly beaten only run in 1991 (January): stays 2m: acts on good to firm and dead ground: has carried head high and wandered under pressure: has run creditably when blinkered: winning hurdler: ungenuine: sold 1,250 gns Ascot May Sales. *O. Brennan.*

SURE HAVEN (IRE) 2 b.c. (Apr 20) Sure Blade (USA) 130 – Tea House 107 **71** p (Sassafras (FR) 135) [1991 7.1s 8.1m²] 34,000Y: rangy colt: has plenty of scope: half-brother to 3 winners, including 1m (at 2 yrs) and 1¼m winner Sybillin (by Henbit), also a good hurdler: dam, Irish 6f and 1m winner, is granddaughter of high-class filly Mesopotamia: 7/2, staying-on 1½ lengths second of 13 to Cautionary Tale at Edinburgh in October, easily better effort in maidens: may well stay 1¼m: likely to make up into better 3-y-o. *Sir Mark Prescott.*

SURE LORD (IRE) 2 ch.c. (Apr 7) Sure Blade (USA) 130 – Lady Graustark **70** (USA) (Graustark) [1991 7.1s⁵ 7m³ 6.9f⁴ 7g³] workmanlike colt: moderate mover: closely related to Irish 3-y-o 1¼m winner Lady Kris (by Kris) and half-brother to several winners, including Siyah Kalem (by Mr Prospector), Milieu (by Habitat) and Bel Bolide (by Bold Bidder), all at least very useful at around 1m: dam won twice at up to 6f at 2 yrs: quite modest maiden: should stay 1m. *W. R. Muir.*

SURELY GIFTED (IRE) 2 b.c. (Apr 26) Sure Blade (USA) 130 – Gift Wrapped **62** 116 (Wolver Hollow 126) [1991 8.1d⁶ a8g⁶] 45,000Y: lengthy, angular, unfurnished colt: closely related to Royal Lodge winner Reach and useful maiden Wrapping (both by Kris) and half-brother to 1¼m seller winner Fusion (by Mill Reef): dam won Lingfield Oaks Trial but best at up to 1¼m: weak 9/1-shot and green, around 9 lengths sixth of 8, outpaced 3f out, not knocked about, to Bonny Scot in maiden (wore a severe noseband) at Haydock in October: no comparable form on equitrack following month. *P. F. I. Cole.*

SURENCHERE (FR) 3 b.g. Maelstrom Lake 118 – Pertinence (FR) (Fiasco — 119) [1990 8m⁵ 8.2d 8.2s³ 1991 11.8g a8g⁴] leggy gelding: modest maiden at 2 yrs: should stay at least 1¼m, but raced too keenly on reappearance: best effort on soft ground: sold 850 gns Doncaster November Sales. *J. G. FitzGerald.*

SURE PRIDE (USA) 3 b.g. Bates Motel (USA) – Coquelicot (CAN) (L'Enjoleur **66** (CAN)) [1990 NR 1991 8g 10d 13g³ 16.2m⁶ a12g⁴ 14.1f 15.4m⁶] 12,500Y: big gelding: has a long stride: sixth reported living foal: brother to 4-y-o Sugar Suite, half-brother to a winner in USA and fair Irish 1½m and 13f winner Snow Plant (both by Snow Knight): dam never ran: quite modest maiden: form only when in frame: tailed off at Folkestone (on toes, didn't handle stand turn) final start: should stay beyond 13f: possibly needs an easy surface: sold to join F. O'Mahony 5,200 gns Ascot October Sales. *P. T. Walwyn.*

SURE SHARP (USA) 4 b.c. Sharpen Up 127 – Double Lock 104 (Home Guard **108** (USA) 129) [1990 8g² 8f 1991 10m 8d³ 8m² 8m² 8g* 8m* 9m⁵] big, good-topped colt: has a fluent, round action: has plenty of scope: very useful performer: narrowly won

Mr Howard Kaskel's "Surrealist"

listed events at Fairyhouse in August and Milan (beat El Dinero by neck) in September: fair staying-on fifth to Susurration in listed event at Newmarket: should prove at least as effective at 1¼m: acts on good to firm ground: has edged right and carried head awkwardly: has run respectably for lady rider. *B. W. Hills.*

SURE SHOT 3 b.f. Sure Blade (USA) 130 – Smeralda (GER) (Dschingis Khan) **62** [1990 NR 1991 12m³ 12m] 230,000Y: very tall, close-coupled filly: half-sister to several winners in Germany, including 2000 Guineas winner Soto-Grande (by Kaiseradler): dam winner in Germany, from family of Slip Anchor: third of 8 in maiden at Beverley: well beaten, having taken keen hold, in similar event at Southwell 3 months later: sold 5,800 gns Newmarket December Sales. *J. H. M. Gosden.*

SURE SHOT NORMAN 2 b.c. (Mar 13) Song 132 – Angel Drummer 59 (Dance **61** In Time (CAN)) [1991 6g 5d 5m⁵ 6g] 11,500F, 23,000Y: quite good-topped colt: good walker: moderate mover: first foal: dam 2-y-o 7f winner later successful over hurdles: quite modest maiden: bandaged near-hind, keeping-on fifth at Windsor in July: seemed to be progressing, but only ninth of 13 when looking really well in Kempton nursery 2 months later: should be suited by 6f + . *J. Sutcliffe.*

SURE SIGN 3 b.f. Sure Blade (USA) 130 – Hyroglyph (USA) (Northern Dancer) **71** [1990 6f a6g³ 1991 a7g³ 7m⁴ a10g* 11m² 12f] leggy filly: modest form: won maiden at Lingfield in July: ran creditably in moderately-run handicap (sweating) next start, badly 6 weeks later: probably stays 11f: hung right on reappearance: sold 3,600 gns Newmarket December Sales. *B. W. Hills.*

SUREST DANCER (USA) 5 b.g. Green Dancer (USA) 132 – Oopsie Daisy **—** (USA) (Dewan) [1990 16.2g⁴ 18m⁵ 18m² 1991 16.2g 21.6f 18g⁵] rather finely-made gelding: has a fluent, slightly round action: quite modest maiden at 4 yrs: well beaten in 1991, including in handicaps: stays 2¼m: acts on firm going: visored on reappearance: blinkered at 4 yrs. *W. L. Barker.*

SURE TO WIN (IRE) 2 ch.c. (May 12) Sure Blade (USA) 130 – Mahabba (USA) **61** 74 (Elocutionist (USA)) [1991 5g* 5m⁶ 7g 8f 8f² a8g²] IR 16,000Y: good-topped colt: has scope: half-brother to useful 3-y-o 11.5f winner Finance Dancer (by Shareef Dancer) and 2 other winners, including Italian Group 3 winner Ready To Dance (by Wassl): dam 1½m winner, is daughter of Lancashire Oaks winner Amphora, a half-sister to Example and Expansive: won maiden at Bath in April: ran well in nurseries last 2 outings, final one (ridden by 7-lb claimer) on fibresand: stays 1m: blinkered fourth and fifth starts: bought out of G. Lewis' stable 11,000 gns Newmarket Autumn Sales. *A. Bailey.*

SURE VICTORY (IRE) 3 ch.f. Stalker 121 – Ultra (Stanford 121§) [1990 6d 1991 **75** 7g⁶ 6d⁵ 7g* 6m* 8m* 8f⁴ 7.1m⁴ 8m 8d] lengthy, plain filly: modest handicapper: improved efforts to win at Ayr, Kempton and Bath in summer: form tailed off steadily afterwards: stays 1m: acts on firm going: has been slowly away. *P. T. Walwyn.*

SURF 2 ch.c. (Feb 3) Sharpen Up 127 – Ebbing Tide (USA) (His Majesty (USA)) **80** p [1991 7g²] 88,000Y: closely related to fairly useful 12.2f winner Tranquil Waters (by Diesis) and half-brother to 2 other winners: dam half-sister to Oh So Fair, dam of Oh So Sharp (by Kris) and Roussalka: bit backward and green, always prominent when keeping-on 2 lengths second of 16 to Mack The Knife in maiden at Newmarket in early-August: seemed sure to improve and win a similar event. *Mrs J. Cecil.*

SURF BOAT 2 ch.f. (Mar 3) Master Willie 129 – Wave Dancer 76 (Dance In Time **66** p (CAN)) [1991 7m 8m] medium-sized, unfurnished filly: second foal: half-sister to French 3-y-o 9f winner Toby Henry (by Jalmood): dam 11.7f winner, is sister to very useful middle-distance horse Sailor's Dance and half-sister to Gold Cup winner Longboat: well beaten in mid-division of October maidens at Newmarket: will do better at 3 yrs. *B. W. Hills.*

SURREALIST (IRE) 3 b.c. Tate Gallery (USA) 117 – Natuschka (Authi 123) **112** [1990 6m 7g* 7d³ 1991 10m* 12m* 12m* 12s⁴] strong colt: fluent mover: not seen out at 3 yrs until August, then progressed well to win minor event at Windsor and, looking very well, listed races at Doncaster and (in good style, despite edging right) Newmarket: creditable 2 lengths fourth of 6 to Topanoora in Group 2 Blandford Stakes at the Curragh 9 days after Newmarket: should stay further: acts on good to firm ground and dead. *B. W. Hills.*

SURREY DANCER 3 b.g. Shareef Dancer (USA) 135 – Juliette Marny 123 **74** (Blakeney 126) [1990 7m 8m 8m 1991 12g² 12.3d⁵ 10g* 10.1m³ 10d³ 10.9m 10d 8.9m 10.3d² 9g] leggy, useful-looking gelding: poor mover: modest handicapper: won at Lingfield in May: easily best effort last 5 starts when second of 17, after smooth headway on outside, at Chester: stays 1½m: acts on good to firm and dead ground: blinkered last 2 outings: retained 14,000 gns Newmarket Autumn Sales in between. *B. Hanbury.*

SURREY RACING 3 b.g. Electric 126 – Garnette Rose 74 (Floribunda 136) **72** [1990 6f 6g 5m 5.8d 1991 6f* 7g* 7g³ 7m³ 7g] neat gelding: has a round action: modest handicapper: won at Brighton in March and Kempton (made virtually all) in April: last of 14 in £8,200 event at Goodwood in August: will stay 1m: acts on firm going, seems unsuited by a soft surface. *G. Lewis.*

SURVIVAL KIT 7 b.m. Homing 130 – Miss Merlin 79 (Manacle 123) [1990 NR **—** 1991 8m 11.5m] workmanlike mare: poor performer, very lightly raced: has been to stud: best effort at 5f: sold 1,650 gns Ascot September Sales. *C. Holmes.*

SUSANNA'S SECRET 4 b.c. Superlative 118 – Queens Welcome 60 **67** (Northfields (USA)) [1990 6f⁵ 7f* 7m* 7m 7m* 7g 1991 6s 7m⁵ 7m² 7m 7m 7.6m 7g 7m 7m 7g* 7m⁶ 7g] strong, close-coupled colt: keen walker: has a quick action: quite modest handicapper: won at Redcar in September: better at 7f than 6f: acts on firm going, possibly unsuited by soft ground: inconsistent. *W. Carter.*

SUSAN'S REEF 6 b.g. Main Reef 126 – Susan's Way (Red God 128§) [1990 6f 6f **32** 8m⁴ 6m⁵ 6f2g 6m 1991 6v³ 8.2s 9m 6m 7m⁵ 8f 8.1g] workmanlike gelding: has a long stride: poor maiden: effective at 6f and stays 1m: acts on good to firm ground and heavy going: below form when visored and blinkered: inconsistent: sold 925 gns Ascot July Sales. *J. M. Bradley.*

SUSURRATION (USA) 4 b.f. Erins Isle 121 – Grease 125 (Filiberto (USA) 123) **116** [1990 8g⁴ 10.5g⁶ 8s* 8v³ 1991 10s⁴ 7g² 7.6m³ 9g² 9v* 8m* 8g² 8m⁶ 7g² 9m* 8v* 9f] tall, angular filly: improved performer in 1991: won ladies events at Kempton and Ascot in summer, listed event at Newmarket (by 3½ lengths from Heart of

Centenary Diamond Stakes, Ascot—
Mrs Pearce on Susurration gains compensation for owner and trainer
after If Memory Serves' controversial disqualification in 1990

Darkness, making most) in October and Group 3 Prix Perth at Saint-Cloud (by 5 lengths from Dolpour) in November: well beaten in Grade 1 The Matriarch Stakes at Hollywood Park final start: best form at 7f to 9f: acts on good to firm and heavy ground: consistent: a credit to her trainer. *J. H. M. Gosden.*

SUZIE SUE (IRE) 2 ch.f. (Apr 30) Ore 116 – Bridal Blush 74 (Coquelin (USA) —
121) [1991 7m] lengthy filly: first foal: dam 2-y-o 5.1f winner out of half-sister to Italian Derby second Teofane: 50/1 and green, soon remote in 12-runner maiden at Lingfield in September. *D. W. P. Arbuthnot.*

SVELTISSIMA 5 b.m. Dunphy 124 – Night Vision 100 (Yellow God 129) [1990 —
NR 1991 a11g] lengthy, workmanlike mare: carries condition: moderate mover: winning plater at 3 yrs: no show only run in 1991, first outing on flat since: effective at 1m and probably stays 11f: acts on any going. *G. R. Oldroyd.*

SWAGMAN (USA) 4 ch.g. Graustark – Mawgrit (USA) (Hoist The Flag (USA)) 47
[1990 7f 10m 10f² 14f5 10f³ 14m⁵ a12g⁶ a12g* 1991 a12g a14g⁴ a12g a12g⁴ a12g²] sparely-made gelding: good mover: poor handicapper: not seen out in 1991 until November, best run when very good second in Southwell claimer: suited by 1½m: best efforts on fibresand: ran moderately when blinkered once. *C. R. Beever.*

SWALE SIDE 2 b.g. (Mar 28) Sayf El Arab (USA) 127 – Onika (Great Nephew 45
126) [1991 a6g⁶ a7g] 1,100F, IR 7,000Y, resold 4,800Y, 7,800 2-y-o: first foal: dam 1m winner at 4 yrs: well beaten (though some late progress) in Southwell claimers won by Runnel late in year. *Mrs G. R. Reveley.*

SWALLOWCLIFFE 2 b.f. (Mar 1) Caerleon (USA) 132 – La Tuerta 96 (Hot 83
Spark 126) [1991 5d⁶ 6g* 6m] unfurnished filly: has scope: good mover: third foal: half-sister to 3-y-o Dominio (by Dominion) and La Cabrilla (by Carwhite), both fairly useful sprint winners at 2 yrs: dam sprinting half-sister to Cadeaux Genereux and quite useful stayer Brightner: fair performer: won maiden at Kempton, headway 2f out and running on well: sweating, respectable eighth of 10 to Bezelle in Princess Margaret Stakes at Ascot later in July: should stay 1m. *P. T. Walwyn.*

SWANSIDE 2 b.f. (Apr 15) Reesh 117 – Azelly 77 (Pitskelly 122) [1991 5m³ 5d 5m 42
6g³ a6g² a6g² a6g² 5g⁴ 5.1f] 580Y: good-topped filly: second foal: dam placed over 5f at 2 yrs, failed to train on: modest plater: mostly ran creditably, including on fibresand: stays 6f: poor efforts on dead ground and when blinkered final start. *M. W. Easterby.*

Prix Perth, Saint-Cloud—
Susurration wins this Group 3 event by five lengths from Dolpour (left)

SWAN STAR 2 br.f. (May 16) Petong 126 – Lewista (Mandrake Major 122) [1991 **36** 5g 6g 6g⁴ 6d 6f⁴ 6m 6g] 1,300Y: tall, leggy filly: first foal: dam of no account: plater: off course over 2 months, visored (well beaten) in claimer final start. *G. Blum.*

SWAN WALK (IRE) 3 gr.g. Godswalk (USA) 130 – Garland Song (My Swanee **58** 122) [1990 6g 10s 7d³ 6d⁵ 1991 a8g⁴ 8d⁴ 8.2f⁴ 8g] close-coupled, quite good-topped gelding: poor mover: modest maiden: may prove bad in maiden at 1m: acts on firm and dead going: blinkered 3 times at 3 yrs: hung left on third. *Mrs N. Macauley.*

SWEEP ALONG (IRE) 3 b.f. Persian Bold 123 – Bristle 96 (Thatch (USA) 136) — [1990 6m 6f6 6.5g 1991 8.2d 7g] smallish, close-coupled filly: quite modest form at best: well beaten in handicaps: should be suited by 7f + : sold to join A. Forbes 2,100 gns Doncaster August Sales. *G. A. Pritchard-Gordon.*

SWEET BUBBLES (IRE) 3 ch.f. Dominion 123 – Regal Decoy (Troy 137) [1990 **61** 6d 1991 a12g* a10g a12g² a12g² a14g³ 11.5m⁵ a12g*] angular filly: quite modest performer: won claimer at Lingfield in April and seller (bought in 7,500 gns) at Southwell in August: stays 1¾m: below form only 3-y-o start on turf. *C. A. Cyzer.*

SWEET DECREE 3 ch.f. Known Fact (USA) 135 – Skiddaw (USA) (Grey Dawn — II 132) [1990 6g 1991 6f a10g 7g] small, sparely-made filly: no form, including in seller: refused to enter stalls intended reappearance: sold 700 gns Newmarket Autumn Sales. *C. A. Cyzer.*

SWEET DRUMALIS (IRE) 2 b.f. (Feb 18) Drumalis 125 – Sauntry (Ballad — Rock 122) [1991 7.1m 7m] IR 7,500F: rangy filly: has scope: fourth foal: half-sister to fairly useful 3-y-o 7f winner Shafouri and fairly useful 5f (at 2 yrs) and 7.6f winner Bollin Zola (both by Alzao): dam unraced daughter of half-sister to good French stayer El Badr: bit backward, soundly beaten in maidens at Sandown (eased considerably) and York (median auction) in autumn: sold 400 gns Ascot December Sales. *Lord Huntingdon.*

SWEET GLEN 3 ch.g. Glenstal (USA) 118 – Quite Sweet 100 (Super Sam 124) — [1990 6m 6g 7g 1991 12f 12.5m] workmanlike gelding: moderate walker: poor maiden: blinkered once. *C. James.*

SWEET GLOW (FR) 4 b.g. Crystal Glitters (USA) 127 – Very Sweet (Bellypha **52** 130) [1990 8d 9d² 9v 10d 8.5g 10d³ 10d³ 9.8g⁴ 8g* 1991 12m³] ex-French gelding: first foal: dam 1¼m winner in France: successful over 1m at 2 and 3 yrs, latter occasion at Saint-Cloud in October 1990 when claimed out of A. Chelet's stable 123,785 francs (approx £12,430): first run on flat after, third in celebrity event at Uttoxeter in September: winning hurdler. *M. C. Pipe.*

SWEETINGS PEARL 3 ro.f. Domynsky 110 – Nellie Bly 80 (Dragonara Palace **52** (USA) 115) [1990 5f 5g³ 5m⁴ 5f² a5g⁶ 5f⁵ 5m⁶ 5f 1991 6g 5g 5m² 5m 5m⁶ 5g 5g⁴ 6f² 5f] leggy non-thoroughbred filly: plating-class sprinter: stays 6f: acts on firm ground: often visored, though not for best 3-y-o efforts: sweating and edgy final start: sometimes bandaged and has tongue tied down: inconsistent. *M. H. Easterby.*

SWEET LIPS 2 ch.f. (Mar 15) Vaigly Great 127 – Kenton's Girl 86 (Record — Token 128) [1991 5f4] sturdy, workmanlike filly: second foal: half-sister to 4-y-o Windy Howe (by Comedy Star): dam, raced only at 2 yrs, won both starts at 5f: backward, fourth of 5 in maiden at Redcar in July, soon remote, then keeping on final 1½f not knocked about: looked one to do better. *J. G. FitzGerald.*

SWEET MIGNONETTE 3 b.f. Tina's Pet 121 – Ixia 91 (I Say 125) [1990 NR 1991 — a11g 8g 10g 12g⁵ a10g] lengthy, rather sparely-made filly: moderate mover: closely related to 1¼m to 13.8f winner Corn Lily (by Aragon) and half-sister to winners, including useful 1m and 1¼m performer Cardinal Flower (by Sharpen Up): dam very game winner at up to 1½m: no worthwhile form in maidens, claimers and selling handicap: sold 2,000 gns Newmarket September Sales. *G. A. Pritchard-Gordon.*

SWEET 'N' LOW 4 b.g. Kampala 120 – Karin Maria 86 (Double Jump 131) [1990 **38** § a8g³ a7g 8.5m 10f² 12m 10f 10f4 1991 a8g⁶ a8g⁴ a10g a10g⁵] angular, rather sparely-made gelding: poor maiden: stays 1¼m: has run fairly well when visored: didn't run on on final start at 3 yrs, and is one to treat with caution. *P. J. Feilden.*

SWEET NOBLE (IRE) 2 ch.g. (Mar 1) The Noble Player (USA) 126 – Penny **56** p Candy (Tamerlane 128) [1991 8m 7m 7.6d³] IR 7,000F, IR 17,000Y: sturdy, close-coupled gelding: half-brother to 2 winners, including Irish 1m and 9f winner Corporal Clinger (by Bruni), later smart jumper here, and to a bumpers winner: dam twice-raced half-sister to Tivola, best 2-y-o filly of 1973 in Italy: easily best effort in maidens when third of 6 at Chester in October, held up by apprentice, taken wide 2f out then staying on not knocked about: will do better in handicaps. *J. G. FitzGerald.*

SWEET N' TWENTY 5 b.m. High Top 131 – Royal Home 69 (Royal Palace 131) **74** [1990 10m⁴ 12f² 12h³ 14g³ 13.8m* 12g³ 11g⁶ 14d 12m² 1991 16.1m⁵] sturdy, lengthy mare: moderate mover: quite modest handicapper at 4 yrs for R. Whitaker: ridden by 5-lb claimer, showed improved form for new stable when fifth of 14 in Northumberland Plate at Newcastle in June: stays 2m (may prove ideally suited by 1¾m): probably acts on any going: consistent: prolific winning hurdler. *M. C. Pipe.*

SWEET PARANG   2 b.f. (Mar 17) Persian Bold 123 – Mystery Ship 105 (Decoy   **37**
Boy 129) [1991 5m⁶ 5g⁴ 5m⁵] 24,000Y: leggy filly: third foal: half-sister to 7f and 1m winner Final Enigma (by Final Straw): dam 2-y-o 5f and 7f winner ideally suited by latter distance: poor maiden: likely to prove suited by around 7f/1m. *C. F. Wall.*

SWEET REQUEST   3 b.c. Rainbow Quest (USA) 134 – Attica Meli 125 (Primera   **—**
131) [1990 NR 1991 11g 14m³ 10.5g⁵ 16.2d 13.3g] tall, leggy colt: half-brother to several winners here and abroad, including useful middle-distance performer Honeybeta (by Habitat) and smart 1979 2-y-o 6f and 7f winner Marathon Gold (by Derring-Do): dam won Yorkshire Oaks and Park Hill Stakes: no worthwhile form: sold 6,400 gns Newmarket Autumn Sales. *A. C. Stewart.*

SWEET REVIVAL   3 b.f. Claude Monet (USA) 121 – Semperflorens (Don 128)   **—**
[1990 NR 1991 8g 12.3f 12f 10.4m] tall filly: first living foal: dam lightly raced: poor form at best, in selling handicap final start. *Mrs S. A. Bramall.*

SWEET SHARPO   3 ch.f. Sharpo 132 – Tumble Judy (Tumble Wind (USA))   **—**
[1990 5m 7g⁵ a6g 1991 a7g⁶] sturdy, good-quartered filly: no worthwhile form: withdrawn after giving plenty of trouble in preliminaries once in 1990. *T. Casey.*

SWEET SOUL DREAM (USA)   3 b.f. Conquistador Cielo (USA) – Minstingu-   **57**
ette (USA) (Boldnesian) [1990 5m³ 8m⁵ 9m⁴ 1991 5f³ 6f² 5.8m³ 7g 5f³ 6g⁴ 5.7m 5m⁶ 7m³ a7g³ 7m⁴ 6f] workmanlike filly: plating-class maiden: stays 7f: acts on firm going (ran creditably on all-weather): sweating fourth start. *D. R. Laing.*

SWEET TASSA   3 b.f. Forzando 122 – Granny's Bank 88 (Music Boy 124) [1990   **51**
6d⁶ 6d 1991 6g 6g 7f² 6g³ 6.9m⁵ 5.1m²] smallish, workmanlike filly: good walker: plating-class maiden: effective at 5f and 7f: acts on firm going: blinkered last 4 starts. *C. F. Wall.*

SWELLEGANT   2 b.f. (Mar 21) Midyan (USA) 124 – Jubilee Song 71 (Song 132)   **84**
[1991 6f² 6m 5g*] 32,000Y: sturdy, well-made filly: good walker and mover: seventh living foal: half-sister to 3 winners, notably 1990 Irish 2-y-o 6f listed winner Bold Jessie (by Never So Bold) and good 5f performer Prince Sabo (by Young Generation): dam 5f winner: fair performer: around 8 lengths equal-seventh of 9 to Marling in Tattersalls Cheveley Park Stakes at Newmarket: evens, well below that form to win 13-runner maiden at Folkestone 6 days later, quickening to lead over 1f out and holding on by neck: stays 6f: bandaged near-hind last 2 starts. *W. J. Haggas.*

SWELL TIME (IRE)   3 b.f. Sadler's Wells (USA) 132 – Amata (USA) (Nodouble   **—**
(USA)) [1990 6m⁶ 6d 1991 9m 12f 11.7g 12.4m 18.1m] poor maiden: trained first 3 starts by R. Hannon: sold 11,000 gns Newmarket December Sales. *C. B. B. Booth.*

SWERVIN MERVIN   3 ch.g. Dominion 123 – Brilliant Rosa 91 (Luthier 126)   **—**
[1990 5m⁶ 6g⁵ 6f 7.5d a7g⁶ a8g⁶ 1991 a10g 12.2g] lengthy gelding: plating-class maiden: stays 1m. *D. Dutton.*

SWIFT ROMANCE (IRE)   3 ch.g. Coquelin (USA) 121 – Douschkina 86 (Dub-   **71**
assoff (USA)) [1990 5m³ 5f⁴ 6d⁴ 6m⁵ 5f³ 5g³ 6m⁴ 6m 1991 7g 8g* 8g 7.6g⁵ 10.1m 8m 5.7m² 7.1g⁵ 7g 6f 7.1m³ 7.6g 8.9m 9g⁶] leggy, workmanlike gelding: moderate walker: modest handicapper: inconsistent after game 33/1-winner at Newbury in April: below-form sixth of 18 in £30,800 event at Newbury (first visit having had a lot to do 3f out): effective at 6f, and should stay 9f: best efforts on sound surface: takes good hold. *B. R. Millman.*

SWIFT SILVER   4 gr.c. Bairn (USA) 126 – Asmalwi 61 (Averof 123) [1990 a8g⁵   **55**
a10g⁵ 9s⁵ 7.5d 7m 8m 1991 a10g³ 10g 10.1d* 11.7g³ 10m⁵ 11.1d² 9g 10.3d²] leggy, sparely-made colt: plating-class handicapper: has round action: won selling event (bought in 7,000 gns, hung left) at Windsor in June: stays 11f: acts on good to firm and dead ground: has been bandaged. *W. J. Musson.*

SWIFT STREAM   3 ch.f. Chief Singer 131 – Sandstream 72 (Sandford Lad 133)   **58**
[1990 6m⁵ 7d 6d 1991 6m 5g⁵ 7g² 8m 8g⁶] tall, lengthy, dipped-backed filly: usually fails to take eye in appearance: plating-class maiden: second in handicap at Doncaster, clearly best effort in summer: suited by 7f: below form on a soft surface: made the running last 3 starts. *R. F. Johnson Houghton.*

SWIFT SWORD   3 gr.g. Sayf El Arab (USA) 127 – Lydiate 77 (Tower Walk 130)   **103**
[1990 5m 5g* 7.5f* 7g⁶ 8m* 8g 8d 1991 8d⁴ 8g⁴ 8m* 8m 10f* 12g⁴ 13.9g 11.9g⁵ 10.9m³] tall, leggy, quite good-topped gelding: moderate walker and mover: useful performer: won auction contest at Redcar and £7,700 handicap at Ripon in summer:

often had stiffish tasks, fourth in £17,800 1½m Newmarket handicap and not at all discredited when third in listed race won by Azzaam at Ayr: stays 1½m: yet to race on soft ground, appears to act on any other: winning hurdler. *Mrs G. R. Reveley.*

SWINGAWAY LADY 3 b.f. Nomination 125 – Partridge Brook 109 (Birdbrook 110) [1990 6m* 7m⁶ 6g⁶ 6d* 7m 7s 1991 6m 6g 7.1g 6g 6d a7g a6g³ a8g] lengthy, unfurnished filly: modest winner at 2 yrs: third of 9 in claimer at Southwell in December at 3 yrs, never nearer: mostly well beaten facing stiff tasks in handicap company: seems to stay 7f: acts on good to firm ground and soft: wore blinkers and eyeshield last 2 starts. *G. Richards.* **50**

SWINGING LADY 3 ch.f. Ballacashtal (CAN) – Parabems 72 (Swing Easy (USA) 126) [1990 NR 1991 6f⁴ 6g⁶ 7m 5f⁴ 7f² 6f⁵ 7f³ a8g⁵ a7g] 800F, 1,600Y: big, leggy, sparely-made filly: third foal: dam sprinter: best effort when second of 5 in maiden at Catterick: bandaged behind in ladies seller next start: best form at 7f. *W. W. Haigh.* **60**

SWING IT OLIVER 3 br.g. Swing Easy (USA) 126 – Citrine 77 (Meldrum 112) [1990 NR 1991 14.6f⁵ 10d 8d⁵ 8.3d² 8f 8.1g] 2,600Y: workmanlike gelding: half-brother to 1984 2-y-o 5f seller winner Lemon Grove, later successful at up to 11f in Italy, and a winning hurdler (both by Move Off): dam second over 6f at 2 yrs: second in maiden median auction at Hamilton, struggling at halfway then running on well: will prove suited by further than 1m: acts on dead ground: visored (very stiff task) final start: sold to join S. Kettlewell 4,400 gns Doncaster October Sales. *G. R. Oldroyd.* **39**

SWING LOW 2 ch.c. (Mar 30) Swing Easy (USA) 126 – Ballaquine 56 (Martinmas 128) [1991 5g⁶ 6m* 6.1s* 6m* 6g* 7s*] 3,700Y: leggy colt: has a quick action: half-brother to a winner abroad: dam won 1¼m seller: progressed considerably with racing: won auction event at Epsom (June) and nurseries at Chepstow (July) and **110**

EBF Leopardstown Stakes—Swing Low is another successful British raider

Newmarket (2, both in good style, second occasion by 5 lengths from Fylde Flyer showing very useful form) in August: successful in Group 3 EBF Leopardstown Stakes by 2 lengths from Irish Memory 2 months later: stays 7f: acts on good to firm and soft ground: goes well for claimer R. Perham. *R. Hannon.*

SWING O'THE KILT 2 b.f. (Apr 24) Hotfoot 126 – La Piccolina 85 (Tudor —
Rhythm 112) [1991 5m 6f a6g 7m a7g] small filly: seems of little account. *P. Calver.*

SWINGTIME BELLE 4 b.f. Swing Easy (USA) 126 – Betbellof 65 (Averof 123) —
[1990 7m 10.2f6 8.3m 10f 10h6 1991 17.2g] workmanlike filly: no sign of ability on flat. *M. P. Muggeridge.*

SWIRLING CLOUD 2 b.f. (Feb 4) Bay Express 132 – High Voltage 82 —
(Electrify) [1991 5d 5g a6g] sparely-made filly: moderate mover: sixth living foal: half-sister to 3 winning sprinters, including one-time useful Dorking Lad (by Cawston's Clown): dam won 3 races at 5f: well beaten in sellers: sold 1,100 gns Ascot July Sales. *K. T. Ivory.*

SWISS AFFAIR (USA) 4 ch.g. Private Account (USA) – Ten Cents A Kiss —
(USA) (Key To The Mint (USA)) [1990 8g 7f 7g 6m5 7f 1991 6m 6g 10.5g6] attractive gelding: shows a quick action: useful winner as 2-y-o: disappointing in varied company since: stays 7f: acts on firm going: below form when visored and blinkered once. *A. A. Scott.*

SWISS BEAUTY 3 b.f. Ballacashtal (CAN) – Cocked Hat Supreme 71 (Uncle 43
Pokey 116) [1990 6m5 6g5 7f3 7.5g5 7.5m 1991 10m5 12.2m5 12g4 12d 9.2f6 12.2m* 11m4] lengthy, good-quartered filly: has a quick action: poor handicapper: on toes, won at Catterick (ladies) in September, leading inside final 1f: needs further than 9f, and stays 1½m: acts on firm ground, probably not on a soft surface: sweating and mulish second and third starts: mounted on track nowadays: sold privately to join Miss Z. Green 5,000 gns Doncaster October Sales: consistent. *Miss S. E. Hall.*

SWORD MASTER 2 b.c. (Feb 23) Sayf El Arab (USA) 127 – Swordlestown Miss 77
(USA) (Apalachee (USA) 137) [1991 7m 7f2 8m3 8g* 10g5] 10,500 2-y-o: strong, workmanlike colt: has scope: fifth foal: brother to a winner abroad: dam Irish 2-y-o 7f winner: modest performer: won maiden at Bath in October: creditable fifth of 9, leading 7f, to Bonny Scot in listed race at Newmarket 5 days later: stays 1¼m. *Bob Jones.*

SWORDSMITH (USA) 4 b.c. Diesis 133 – Lettre d'Amour (USA) (Caro 133) 103
[1990 7g4 8f 7g 7m2 8g2 1991 7g3 8v2 7.2g* 7g6 7.3f 8g 7g 8v5] lengthy colt: carries condition: usually looks very well: has a round action: useful performer: won listed race at Haydock in June (by ½ length from Norton Challenger): good sixth behind La Grange Music in Group 3 event at Newmarket: below form after, in Group 2 event at Rome final start: effective at 7f to 1m: acts on good to firm and heavy ground: to join V. Valiani in Italy. *B. W. Hills.*

SWORD'S POINT 3 ch.g. Sure Blade (USA) 130 – Impudent Miss 105 (Persian 67
Bold 123) [1990 NR 1991 10.1g 12.1g3 12m4 10.1m2 10m 8.9g6 8m4 9m6 7g3 9g] rangy gelding: third foal: half-brother to fairly useful 6f (at 2 yrs) and 7f winner King Al (by Indian King): dam Irish 2-y-o 5f to 1m winner, is half-sister to very smart sprinter Sayyaf: quite modest maiden: seems effective at 7f and 1¼m: blinkered (pulled hard, well beaten) final start: sold 14,500 gns Newmarket Autumn Sales. *I. A. Balding.*

SWORDSTICK 3 b.g. Sure Blade (USA) 130 – Lypharita (FR) 125 (Lightning 83
(FR) 129) [1990 NR 1991 8f* 9d4dis 7.6g* 10m] big, good-topped gelding: has a powerful, round action: first foal: dam, from good family, won French Oaks: bandaged off-hind, won maiden at Ripon in August: easily best effort in handicaps when winning at Lingfield in October, checked over 2f out and leading close home: should stay beyond 1m: seems unsuited by a soft surface: rider failed to weigh in second start: raced freely final one: sold 30,000 gns Newmarket Autumn Sales. *B. W. Hills.*

SYBARITIC SAM (IRE) 2 b.c. (Apr 15) Tate Gallery (USA) 117 – My Natalie 71
64 (Rheingold 137) [1991 7f 7m 8.1d5 a8g* a8g4] 19,000F, 55,000Y: useful-looking colt: seventh foal: half-brother to several winners, including fair 7f/9f performer Ned's Aura (by Dalsaan): dam 1m winner: modest performer: comfortably won maiden at Lingfield in November: will be suited by 1¼m. *N. A. Callaghan.*

SYBILLIN 5 b.g. Henbit (USA) 130 – Tea House 107 (Sassafras (FR) 135) [1990 64
NR 1991 a11g2 10m* 10.1m6 10.3m4 8m2] compact gelding: has a quick action: very lightly-raced handicapper on flat: won at Redcar in August: ran respectably after: keen sort, best at 1m to 1¼m: acts on good to firm ground: smart hurdler. *J. G. FitzGerald.*

SYKE LANE 2 b.f. (Mar 25) Clantime 101 – Redgrave Design 77 (Nebbiolo 125) **44**
[1991 5m³ 5m 6d³ 6g 7g² 7.1m 8m] smallish, sparely-made filly: fourth foal: half-sister to 3-y-o Wotamistakatomaka and 1987 2-y-o 5f winner Arroganza (both by Crofthall): dam 2-y-o 5f winner: easily best effort when neck second of 21 in seller at Newmarket in August: seemed not to handle bend at Catterick fourth start: possibly suited by 7f. *R. M. Whitaker.*

SYLVA HONDA 3 ch.c. Adonijah 126 – Wolverhants 79 (Wolver Hollow 126) **108**
[1990 5g³ 5m⁴ 6g* 5g² 6f³ 6g 6m 1991 7g⁶ 7g 8.5f* 7g 7.6g³ 7.3f⁶ 7m 9m] leggy, lengthy colt: useful performer: won Diomed Stakes at Epsom in June by 2 lengths from Fair Average: ran creditably in listed contest at Lingfield and Hungerford Stakes at Newbury fifth and sixth starts: never dangerous in Group 3 contest and listed race on last 2: stays 8.5f well: yet to race on soft ground, acts on any other. *C. E. Brittain.*

SYLVAN BELLE 2 b.f. (Mar 13) Bellypha 130 – Sylvan Trinket (Moorestyle **40**
137) [1991 a5g³ 6g³ 6g⁵ 5g] close-coupled filly: first living foal: half-sister to quite useful sprinter Singing Sailor: poor maiden: not seen out after August: will probably stay 7f. *P. Mitchell.*

SYLVAN BREEZE 3 b.c. Sulaafah (USA) 119 – Langton Herring (Nearly A **94**
Hand 115) [1990 6m⁶ 6g⁴ 6g² 6d 1991 8g 6m⁴ 6g 6g³ 6m 6d 7g⁶] sturdy, good-quartered colt: has a round action: capable of fairly useful form: little form as 3-y-o other than when in frame in listed races at Newmarket and Baden-Baden: bred to stay beyond 6f, but headstrong: has worn crossed noseband: sometimes taken down early: tends to hang and is a hard ride: not one to trust. *P. Mitchell.*

SYLVANI COTTAGE 6 b.m. Martinmas 128 – Julie Emma (Farm Walk 111) —
[1990 NR 1991 10f 6f] lengthy mare: third foal: dam lightly raced and no sign of ability: no promise, including in seller. *R. J. Hodges.*

SYLVAN (IRE) 2 b. or br.f. (Apr 4) Taufan (USA) 119 – Unspoiled (Tina's Pet **81**
121) [1991 5g³ 6m² 6g* 6m* 6m 6m² 7m] 17,000Y: rangy, useful-looking filly: has scope: has a round action: first foal: dam unraced half-sister to useful middle-distance colt Riberetto: fair form, idling in front, when successful in minor events at Windsor in July: good seventh of 8, beaten around 8 lengths, to Rose Indien in minor event at Newmarket final start: stays 7f: yet to race on dead ground. *C. F. Wall.*

SYLVAN SABRE (IRE) 2 b.c. (Feb 10) Flash of Steel 120 – Flute (FR) (Luthier **88**
126) [1991 5d* 5m² 6g* 6g 6d² 7f³ 6m⁵ 8s 7.3g⁵] 4,000Y: good-bodied, close-coupled colt: has a round action: half-brother to 2 winners in Ireland, including Cambridgeshire winner Any Song (by Bold Lad), later successful in USA: dam showed some ability in France: fair performer: successful in minor events at Doncaster in March and York in May: ran well afterwards when placed and on last 2 starts, behind Lion Cavern in Horris Hill Stakes at Newbury (stiff task) final one: stays 1m: acts on any going. *P. Mitchell.*

SYLVAN SIROCCO 4 b.c. Known Fact (USA) 135 – Juddmonte (Habitat 134) —
[1990 8m 10m⁶ 1991 10m 7m 10m 10.8g] big colt: no worthwhile form: sold 1,300 gns Doncaster November Sales. *P. Mitchell.*

SYLVAN TEMPEST 5 b. or br.g. Strong Gale 116 – Hedwige (African Sky 124) —
[1990 8f 7g² 6g⁵ 7g 8f 10m⁴ 8.3m³ 8m² 10f⁴ 9m⁵ 12g 11.5g 10d 1991 a10g⁵ a10g⁶] leggy gelding: keen walker: poor mover: runner-up in Group 3 event at the Curragh as 3-y-o: generally disappointing since: not seen out after February in 1991: stays 1¼m and acts on firm ground, but easily best form at up to 7f on very soft: tried visored once. *P. Mitchell.*

SYMMETRICAL 2 ch.g. (Jan 25) Kris 135 – Flawless Image (USA) 109 (The **59** p
Minstrel (CAN) 135) [1991 7d] first foal: dam sprinter: 8/1, over 11 lengths seventh of 22 to For Reg in maiden at Doncaster in November, chasing leaders, then fading from 2f out not knocked about: will improve. *B. W. Hills.*

SYRON 3 ch.f. Noalto 120 – Mellow Girl 88 (Mountain Call 125) [1990 NR 1991 9m] —
good-topped, plain filly: moderate walker: seventh foal: half-sister to plating-class 9.4f winner Riva Renald (by Try My Best) and 1¼m winner Daisy Girl (by Main Reef): dam 5f and 6f winner at 2 yrs: backward, never dangerous in seller at Redcar in August. *G. M. Moore.*

SYSTEMATIC 2 b.c. (Mar 24) All Systems Go 119 – Greyburn 85 (Saintly Song **66**
128) [1991 5g⁶ 5g⁶ 6.1g⁴ 7g³ 7d⁶] 4,000F, 6,700Y: good-topped colt: has scope: moderate mover: eighth foal: half-brother to 1m seller winner Cover Inn (by Tachypous) and a winner in Norway by Music Boy: dam 6f to 1m winner: quite modest maiden: off course nearly 4 months, easily best effort when staying-on third of 11 to Khazar

at Salisbury (slowly away) in October: ran moderately in large-field Doncaster nursery following month: will stay 1m: possibly unsuited by dead ground. *R. Hannon.*

T

TACHYON PARK 9 b.h. Frimley Park 109 – Frimley's Alana 73 (Lear Jet 123) **56** d [1990 5f 5m⁵ 5d 6m 5f 1991 5g 5m⁶ 5f⁶ 5.2m⁵ 5.2f³ 5f⁵ 5m³ 5f⁵ 5f⁴ 5.7f 5.2f³ 5g⁵ 5m⁶ a6g a5g⁵ a5g a6g⁵ a6g] strong, good-quartered horse: plating-class handicapper nowadays: best at 5f: well suited by top-of-the-ground: usually blinkered or visored: has hung under pressure. *P. Howling.*

TACTICAL MISSION (IRE) 3 b.g. Rainbow Quest (USA) 134 – Our Village **70** (Ballymore 123) [1990 NR 1991 10g 12d³ 12g² 12d² 12d a12g* 14g 12d] 88,000F, 5,000Y: lengthy, angular gelding: moderate mover: half-brother to 3 winners, including Middle Park winner Mister Majestic (by Tumble Wind): dam well beaten at 3 yrs in France: placed in claimers before landing odds in 4-runner maiden at Southwell in July: edgy, beaten long way in handicaps at Goodwood last 2 starts: should stay beyond 1½m: acts on dead ground: sold to join J. Akehurst 11,000 gns Newmarket Autumn Sales. *C. A. Cyzer.*

TADORA (IRE) 2 ro.g. (May 4) Tate Gallery (USA) 117 – Silbadora 67 (Don **59** (ITY) 123) [1991 6d⁶ 6s⁵ 5m⁴ 6g 6m 5.7g] 15,500Y: tall gelding: has scope: half-brother to several winners, including 1984 Irish 2-y-o 6f winner Upepo (by Kampala) and useful 6f and 7f winner Don Martino (by Martinmas): dam ran only at 2 yrs: plating-class maiden: best effort at 5f: ran poorly afterwards. *C. J. Benstead.*

TAFFY JONES 12 br.g. Welsh Pageant 132 – Shallow Stream 100 (Reliance II — 137) [1990 12m 10f 11.5m 12m 10m 1991 10.8m] big gelding: carries plenty of condition: no longer of much account on flat: winning chaser. *M. McCormack.*

TAGETES 2 br.f. (Mar 2) Chief Singer 131 – Sandford Lady 116 (Will Somers 114§) — [1991 5g⁶] 5,400Y: close-coupled, unfurnished filly: half-sister to several winners, including useful sprinter Gaius (by Sallust) and 1987 2-y-o 1m winner Sandford Prince (by Tap On Wood): dam, half-sister to top-class sprinter Sandford Lad, won 6 times at around 6f: some signs of ability in auction event at Newmarket in May before seemingly losing action 2f out and eased: moved moderately down. *J. Pearce.*

TAHITIAN 2 b.c. (Mar 4) Precocious 126 – Pacificus (USA) 65 (Northern **63** p Dancer) [1991 7m 7g⁶] 22,000Y: smallish, well-made colt: third foal: half-brother to 3-y-o 1m winner Luks Akura (by Dominion) and very useful hurdler Philosophos (by High Top): dam 13f winner: 6½ lengths sixth of 14 to Autocracy at Salisbury in October (pushed along halfway, kept on), easily better effort in maidens: should stay 1m: sold 6,600 gns Doncaster November Sales and has joined Mrs J. Ramsden: will probably improve again. *H. Candy.*

TAIKI TOWN (USA) 2 b.c. (Feb 22) Woodman (USA) 126 – Witching Tempo **51** (CAN) (Danzig (USA)) [1991 5m⁶ a5g 5g⁴ 7g] IR 65,000Y: lengthy, attractive colt: second reported foal: dam unraced: poor form in maidens in mid-summer: always behind in autumn nursery (faced extremely stiff task) at Doncaster: should stay beyond 5f: bolted to post (wore eyeshield) second outing. *D. R. C. Elsworth.*

TAJIGREY 2 gr.f. (Mar 8) Grey Desire 115 – Taj Singh (Mansingh (USA) 120) — [1991 6d] big, lengthy filly: first foal: dam 5f (at 2 yrs) and 7f winner: 50/1, backward and green, soundly beaten in 23-runner maiden at Haydock in October. *B. W. Lunness.*

TAJ VICTORY 4 ch.f. Final Straw 127 – Taj Princess 88 (Taj Dewan 128) [1990 **68** 9m³ 10m⁴ 10g* 12m⁵ 1991 a12g³ a12g² a13g* 12s⁶ 11.6m⁵ 12m* 13.3m⁶ 12d⁵ 12.5g² 10m] compact filly: good walker and mover: modest handicapper: won at Lingfield in March and Kempton in September: stays 13f: acts on good to firm ground. *Lord Huntingdon.*

TAKADDUM (USA) 3 ch.c. Riverman (USA) 131 – Lyphard's Holme (USA) **100** (Lyphard (USA) 132) [1990 6m⁵ 6g 6d* 1991 6g⁵ 7m² 7g* 7g⁴ 8.2m* 7.2g³ 8d⁵ 8g 7.9g 10d] robust, attractive colt: useful performer: won valuable handicaps at Newmarket and Haydock in May: unlucky running-on third (slowly away, not clear run) in listed race at Haydock: below form in valuable handicaps after, in need of race final start: should prove better at 1m than shorter: acts on good to firm ground and dead: has flashed tail: ducked left closing stages third and fourth starts, visored

afterwards: sold 52,000 gns Newmarket Autumn Sales, reportedly to race in Germany. *P. T. Walwyn.*

TAKEALL   4 b.f. Another Realm 118 – Cratloe (African Sky 124) [1990 5f 5d⁶ 5g⁴   **65**
5g 1991 5m³ 5g 5m] well-made filly: modest handicapper at best:
little promise final 2 starts: raced only at 5f: acts on good to firm ground and dead. *B. A. McMahon.*

TAKE ISSUE   6 b.g. Absalom 128 – Abstract 73 (French Beige 127) [1990 14m⁵   **— §**
1991 11.5g] well-made gelding: lightly-raced handicapper nowadays on flat: stays
1¾m: acts on any going: ran poorly when blinkered once: best left alone: winning
hurdler. *J. Sutcliffe.*

TAKE IT IN CASH   2 ch.f. (Mar 25) Ballacashtal (CAN) – Soft Secret (Most   **—**
Secret 119) [1991 7d] angular, rather unfurnished filly: has scope: fourth reported
foal: sister to 5f and 6f winner Ballasecret: dam winner in Belgium: 66/1, slowly
away, pulled hard then faded into last of 21 in maiden at Doncaster in November. *R. Dickin.*

TAKENHALL   6 b.g. Pitskelly 122 – Great Dora (Great Nephew 126) [1990 7m⁴   **71**
7g⁶ 8m³ 8g 6m 6g⁶ 6f 6m 7m⁴ 7m³ 7m* 7g⁶ 7.3g⁴ 7m 7g 10d⁶ 1991 7m⁵ 7g⁴
7m³ 8g 7.9m² 7g* 8m³ 8g⁶ 7g* 7m³ 8d⁶ 7d 8g⁵ 7g] lengthy, workmanlike gelding:
moderate mover: modest handicapper, formerly unreliable: won at Newmarket in
July and York in September: best form at 7f to 1m: acts on firm and dead going: has
been tried in blinkers: usually gets behind: not an easy ride. *M. J. Fetherston-Godley.*

TAKE ONE   5 b.h. Teenoso (USA) 135 – Old Kate 110 (Busted 134) [1990 12f²   **—**
14g* 12m³ 1991 a12g⁴ a13g 16g 14m⁵ 12s⁶ 11.5g] lengthy, robust horse: carries
plenty of condition: moderate walker: poor mover in slower paces: fair handicapper
at 4 yrs for G. Wragg: very much on the downgrade: stays 1¾m: gives impression
will prove best on ground easier than firm. *P. Mitchell.*

TAKE TWO   3 b.g. Jupiter Island 126 – Dancing Daughter 79 (Dance In Time   **86 d**
(CAN)) [1990 7f³ 7m⁵ 7g⁴ 8.2m* 8m* 1991 8.2m² 8.2g* 8m⁴ 10.5m⁶ 10.5f 8.1s 8m]
workmanlike gelding: fair handicapper at his best: won at Haydock in June, leading
close home: disappointing after fourth in Britannia Stakes at Royal Ascot, including
in claimer: stays 1m well: below form on firm and dead ground: blinkered last 2
starts: sweating final one: sold to join J. White 9,200 gns Doncaster November
Sales: best watched. *R. F. Johnson Houghton.*

Timeform Futurity, Pontefract—Tamim wins from Corals Dream and Blake End

TALBERNO BOY (IRE) 2 b.g. (May 11) Cyrano de Bergerac 120 – Tallow Hill **67**
(Dunphy 124) [1991 6f5 5.9h* 7m* 7g5 7f4 8f 7g6 8g] 18,000Y: leggy, attractive
gelding: first foal: dam unraced half-sister to Cheveley Park winner and French
1000 Guineas second Pass The Peace: quite modest performer: successful in
maiden at Carlisle in June: made virtually all when easy winner of nursery at Thirsk
over 2 months later: seems suited by 7f: acts on hard ground: sold 8,800 gns
Newmarket Autumn Sales. *Sir Mark Prescott.*

TALENTED TING (IRE) 2 ch.g. (May 10) Hatim (USA) 121 – An Tig Gaelige **71**
(Thatch (USA) 136) [1991 5f4 7.5f4 8m3 7g4 8.3s6 a7g2 a7g] 6,000 2-y-o: strong,
lengthy gelding: good walker: brother to 3-y-o Tigatim and half-brother
to fair 1986 Irish 2-y-o 7f winner Lyshaan (by Ahonoora): dam, from family of Oaks
winner Long Look, won over 1¾m at 4 yrs in Ireland: modest maiden: ran
particularly well in Southwell nursery penultimate start: will stay beyond 1m: acts
on good to firm and soft ground, and on fibresand. *P. C. Haslam.*

TALENT (USA) 3 b.g. Clever Trick (USA) – Contralto 100 (Busted 134) [1990 **79**
NR 1991 8d5 8d 7g2 7f2 7.1m2 8m4] smallish gelding: has a quick action: seventh
foal: half-brother to 5 winners, including fairly useful 1¾m winner Musical Box (by
Grundy) and very useful pair Enharmonic (by Diesis), successful at 6f to 1m, and
miler Soprano (by Kris): dam 2-y-o 6f and 7f winner, is closely related to smart
Rhyme Royal: fair maiden: second at Lingfield, Newbury (£8,100 handicap) and
(made most) Haydock: best efforts at 7f. *Lord Huntingdon.*

TALES OF WISDOM 2 br.f. (Feb 19) Rousillon (USA) 133 – New Generation **44**
91 (Young Generation 129) [1991 7g 7d a7g] big, strong, plain filly: has plenty of
scope: third foal: half-sister to 3-y-o 1¾m and 2m winner Moving Out (by Slip
Anchor), 1m winner at 2 yrs, and 1988 2-y-o 5f winner Noble Habitat (by
Formidable): dam won at up to 1m: never dangerous in November maidens: final one
on fibresand. *Sir Mark Prescott.*

TALISH 3 br.c. Persian Bold 123 – Baheejah (Northfields (USA)) [1990 6m6 7g **58**
1991 7v6 12m3 11m5 12.3g* 12f4 11.5m3 12f a12g a12g] rather leggy, quite attractive
colt: plating-class handicapper: won at Ripon in July: ran moderately last 3 starts:
stays 1½m: acts on good to firm ground: bought out of C. Brittain's stable 5,400 gns
Newmarket Autumn Sales after seventh outing. *T. D. Barron.*

TALOS (IRE) 3 b.g. Taufan (USA) 119 – Jovial Josie (USA) (Sea Bird II 145) [1990 **97**
7m 7m 1991 8g5 8d* 8d 8m 10g2 10g3 13.9g3 11.9g6 13.3m* 12s] rather leggy
gelding: fairly useful form: won maiden at Ayr in April and Coral Autumn Cup
(improved effort, easing down by 3½ lengths) at Newbury in September: under
pressure when bumped entering straight in £70,900 handicap at Ascot week after
latter: stays 1¾m: has won on dead going, but goes very well on top-of-the-ground.
B. W. Hills.

TAMARPOUR (USA) 4 b.g. Sir Ivor 135 – Tarsila (High Top 131) [1990 12m4 **81**
12f2 11.5m2 10f6 12g 12d6 1991 16.2m2 16.1m* 18m] strong, lengthy gelding: fair
handicapper: won Northumberland Plate at Newcastle in June by 1½ lengths from
Aahsaylad: run best ignored in Tote Cesarewitch at Newmarket 3½ months after
(held up, not clear run, then eased): clearly better suited by 2m than shorter, and
will stay further: acts on firm ground: has run well when sweating and on edge: has
worn crossed noseband: looked none too genuine over hurdles in December. *M. C.
Pipe.*

TAMASHA 2 b.f. (Jun 16) Hotfoot 126 – Polonaise (Takawalk II 125) [1991 6s 6d **64**
8m 7d5] leggy, unfurnished filly: has a quick action: sister to 1m and 1¼m winner Mr
Chris Cakemaker and half-sister to several winners, including fairly useful 7f and
1m winner Wibis Range (by Wolver Hollow): dam won over 9f at 2 yrs in Ireland:
quite modest maiden: will do better over middle distances: sold 3,100 gns Doncaster
November Sales and has joined C. Hill. *J. R. Shaw.*

TAMIM (USA) 2 gr.c. (Feb 7) Topsider (USA) – Passamaquoddy (USA) (Drone) **102**
[1991 5m* 5m⁵ 6m* 6m³ 5m* 5g*] 105,000Y: lengthy colt: has scope: has a quick
action: good walker: half-brother to winners in USA by Alydar and Mr Prospector:
dam, winner at up to 9f, is sister to dam of Dancing Brave: successful in 5-runner
maiden at Haydock in May, then 2 minor events at Pontefract (second when simple
task) and listed event at Doncaster (by 2 lengths from Echo-Logical) in autumn:
stays 6f: yet to race on a soft surface: useful. *H. Thomson Jones.*

TAMISE 4 br.f. Dominion 123 – Miss Thames 105 (Tower Walk 130) [1990 7m 7g² —
a7g⁴ 9g⁶ 1991 a8g a10g 10g] rather leggy filly: has round action: quite modest form
as 3-y-o: below best in 1991: stays 9f: winning hurdler. *J. White.*

TANANA 2 b.f. (Feb 3) Teenoso (USA) 135 – La Nureyeva (USA) (Nureyev (USA) **52**
131) [1991 8.1g⁴ 8.9m 8m⁵ 7d] 3,800Y, 12,500 2-y-o: leggy filly: second foal:
half-sister to 3-y-o 5f winner Very Bold (by Never So Bold): dam maiden stayed 1m,
is half-sister to William Hill Futurity second Cock Robin: plating-class maiden: best
effort on debut: ran moderately when sweating and edgy second start: had stiff task
in Doncaster nursery final one: may stay 1¼m. *J. G. FitzGerald.*

TANCRED GRANGE 2 ch.c. (Mar 4) Prince Sabo 123 – Carpadia (Icecapade **69**
(USA)) [1991 6m⁶ 6g* 7g³ 6m⁵ 7g² 8.9m 8g 7d] 7,000Y: strong, lengthy colt: has
scope: moderate walker: second foal: dam placed once at 3 yrs in France: quite
modest performer: favourite, clear-cut winner of maiden auction at Pontefract in
June: mostly had stiff tasks afterwards, though ran moderately (when 20/1) only on
last 2 starts: probably stays 9f: acts on good to firm ground: sometimes carries head
awkwardly. *Miss S. E. Hall.*

TANCRED WALK 12 b.g. Farm Walk 111 – Darling Do (Derring-Do 131) [1990 —
NR 1991 14m 14d⁶ 12g 14d 16.2g 14.6m] small, sturdy gelding: carries plenty of
condition: moderate mover: modest handicapper at 9 yrs: not nearly so good
nowadays: used to be ideally suited by 1½m to 1¾m and sound surface: sometimes
has tongue tied down: often slowly away and bandaged. *C. F. C. Jackson.*

TANEGRUS 3 b.g. Dunbeath (USA) 127 – Tanagrea (Blakeney 126) [1990 7g³ **72**
7m³ 7m 1991 9g 7g 7d⁴ 7m² 5.1m⁴ 7f³ 7g⁴] compact, good-quartered gelding: good
walker and mover: modest maiden: taken down early before moderate effort final
start, leading 5f: needs further than 5f, and stays 7f: acts on firm ground: has run
well when sweating: gelded after final start. *D. R. C. Elsworth.*

TANEY COMO 2 b.c. (Feb 16) Hadeer 118 – Chase Paperchase 79 (Malinowski **63**
(USA) 123) [1991 a6g⁶ 7m a6g 6.1m 5.2f² 5m³ 6g⁵ 5m⁶] 3,100Y: sturdy colt: second
foal: half-brother to 1990 2-y-o 6f winner Zloty (by Elegant Air): dam maiden stayed
6f: quite modest maiden: ridden by 5-lb claimer, ran well when placed in Yarmouth

Newcastle Brown Ale Northumberland Plate, Newcastle—
Tamarpour lifts this big handicap for the Pipe stable;
Aahsaylad and the grey First Victory fill the minor places

seller and Wolverhampton nursery: stays 6f: acts on firm ground: ran poorly (raced very freely) in visor fourth start: sold 4,800 gns Newmarket Autumn Sales. *W. A. O'Gorman.*

TANFIRION BAY (IRE) 3 b.c. Whistling Deer 117 – Alone All Alone **54** (Tanfirion 110) [1990 6m 5m 7m⁵ a7g 7m 7g⁴ 7m a7g 6d a6g⁴ a7g² a7g 1991 6f³ 7d 6m 8m³ 10d⁴ 9.7m⁴ 12g 11d⁴] rather leggy, close-coupled colt: has a round action: plating-class maiden: should stay 1¼m: acts on good to firm ground: blinkered last 4 starts at 2 yrs: sometimes on toes: not particularly consistent: sold to join P. Hedger 2,100 gns Doncaster November Sales. *P. Mitchell.*

TANFITH (CAN) 4 b.c. Chief's Crown (USA) – Foxy Olympia (USA) (Stage — Door Johnny) [1990 8g⁵ 8m⁵ 1991 7.6d] rather sparely-made colt: useful at 3 yrs: stiff task and pulled very hard in handicap at Chester only run in 1991 (May): will stay 1¼m: acts on good to firm ground: sold to join J. Banks's stable only 4,500 gns Newmarket Autumn Sales. *R. W. Armstrong.*

TANGO TIME 3 ch.g. Music Boy 124 – Liberty Tree 96 (Dominion 123) [1990 **84** NR 1991 6m 7g 8g 6v² 6s* 5.1f* 5s* 5g² 5g³ 5f²] 21,000Y: strong gelding: poor mover: third foal: half-brother to 4-y-o Mood of The Moment (by Jalmood) and 1m claimer winner Take A Liberty (by Aragon): dam 6f to 1m winner: fair handicapper: favourite, won at Lingfield, Bath and Sandown in summer: best efforts last 3 starts: effective at 5f and 6f: acts on any going. *R. Hannon.*

TANODA 5 b.m. Tyrnavos 129 – Anoda (FR) (Amber Rama (USA) 133) [1990 NR **59** 1991 12g* 12.4v³ 12.3s⁶ 10.1g⁶ 12g 10d* 10.2g5 10d⁵ 10.9g² 12.1g 10.5d⁴ 10.3d⁶ 12.1s a12g] leggy mare: poor mover: plating-class handicapper: successful at Carlisle in March and Ripon in June: below form last 2 starts: stays 1½m: needs give in the ground, and goes well on soft: tends to edge left, and has hung badly. *M. Brittain.*

TANZ (IRE) 3 b.f. Sadler's Wells (USA) 132 – Gull Nook 120 (Mill Reef (USA) **79** 141) [1990 NR 1991 12f³ 12.2f² 12.2m* 12.3f³ 12.2g² 11.8m²] leggy, rather sparely-made filly: first foal: dam lightly-raced 10.5f and 1½m winner out of half-sister to Shirley Heights: fair form: simple task in 3-runner maiden at Catterick in August: good second after in apprentice contest and handicap: visits General Holme. *H. R. A. Cecil.*

TAPATCH (IRE) 3 b.c. Thatching 131 – Knees Up (USA) (Dancing Champ **87** (USA)) [1990 6m⁶ 7m* 7g⁴ 8g³ 1991 8.2d⁴ 10f² 12g⁶ 12.3g³ 10.1g⁶ 10g 7.6g 8.1s⁶] compact colt: fair performer: well below form in handicaps and claimer last 3 starts: suited by 1½m: acts on firm going: sold to join G. Moore 14,000 gns Newmarket Autumn Sales. *J. M. P. Eustace.*

TAP DANCING 5 ch.g. Sallust 134 – Amorak 85 (Wolver Hollow 126) [1990 10f⁴ **42** 10m⁴ 12d 1991 10f* 10f] leggy gelding: has a round action: poor handicapper: won at Beverley in April: not seen out after May: gives impression should stay 1½m: acts on firm going: sold 2,500 gns Doncaster Spring Sales. *M. O'Neill.*

TAPESTRY DANCER 3 b.g. Lidhame 109 – Royal Bat 69 (Crowned Prince **45** (USA) 128) [1990 NR 1991 8d 7g 9m 10g 8g 7g² 6g⁴ 6.9m² 7g 7m 6m a8g] close-coupled gelding: third reported foal: half-brother to 5-y-o 1¼m to 1½m winner Crosby Place (by Crooner): dam 6f winner stayed 1m: poor maiden: behind in handicaps last 4 starts, hanging right on first occasion: best form at 7f. *M. J. Haynes.*

TARANGA 8 b.g. Music Boy 124 – Emblazon 91 (Wolver Hollow 126) [1990 a8g — 8g 8.2g³ a12g 1991 7m 10.1s a10g] strong, workmanlike gelding: moderate mover: poor handicapper: suited by 1m: acts on any going: has run creditably when visored: has worn bandages: inconsistent. *J. White.*

TARA'S DELIGHT 4 b.f. Dunbeath (USA) 127 – Tickton Bridge (Grundy 137) **72** [1990 9m³ 10g* 9f⁴ 11f³ 11m⁴ 11.7m 10f* 10g⁵ 11.5m 9f a10g 1991 10f³ 9.7s 8.9m* 8.9g* 9m⁴ 9s* a10g² a8g⁴ a10g²] deep-girthed filly: modest handicapper/claimer: won at Wolverhampton (2) and Kempton at 4 yrs: stays 11f: probably acts on any going: below best when blinkered once and sweating once: tough and consistent. *M. J. Ryan.*

TARA'S GIRL 4 b.f. Touching Wood (USA) 127 – Esquire Lady (Be My Guest **72** (USA) 126) [1990 a6g⁵ a7g⁵ a8g 6g² 6m* 6g 5d 8g³ 7m 6m 7m⁴ 6m 5g³ 5g² 1991 6g⁵ 6.1s⁴ 7m² 7g 7.6m² 6g* 7m 7d] small filly: modest handicapper: won at Salisbury in October: effective at 6f to 1m: acts on good to firm and soft going: effective with or without blinkers or visor. *Mrs Barbara Waring.*

TARDA 4 ch.f. Absalom 128 – Ixia 91 (I Say 125) [1990 8m 10.4d 8m⁴ 7f⁴ 7f⁶ 8f³ **63** 10m 8.2g 1991 9f 10m 8g* 9f* 10m⁴ 9.2f² 9.9f³] angular, shallow-girthed filly: has a round action: quite modest handicapper: won at Ripon in July and August: mostly ran well after but ridden with little enterprise: will prove at least as effective over

1¼m as shorter: acts on firm ground: looked unsuitable mount for inexperienced rider on reappearance. *Mrs G. R. Reveley.*

TARKESHA 5 ch.m. Son of Shaka 119 – Cuddly Toy (Sovereign Lord 120) [1990 NR 1991 6d 6g 7m a7g] sturdy mare: moderate mover: half-sister to 5f to 11f winner Keira (by Keren): dam of little account: no worthwhile form. *D. Morris.* —

TARMON (IRE) 3 ch.g. Whistling Deer 117 – Royal Performance 57 (Klairon 131) [1990 5f5 5.8h3 5f 5.8m 6f6 6m a6g 1991 10g 10.2d 10.2g3 9.7m2 11.5m* 11.9m5 11.8m 11.7f5 9.7m] workmanlike gelding: moderate mover: plater: won at Lingfield in July: acts on good to firm ground: blinkered last 7 starts: sold to join A. Barrow 5,200 gns after winning selling hurdle. *W. R. Muir.* **51**

TAROOB (IRE) 2 ch.f. (Feb 20) Roberto (USA) 131 – Tobira Celeste (USA) (Ribot 142) [1991 8.2m2 8.9d*] leggy, useful-looking filly: sister to top-class middle-distance performer Celestial Storm and half-sister to several winners, including 1½m winner Celestial Guest (by Northjet), and to dam of River Memories: dam winner at up to 9f in France: shaped promisingly, finishing strongly, in Nottingham minor event in September before winning 19-runner Wolverhampton maiden following month from Pica in bunched finish: will improve again, particularly over further. *J. L. Dunlop.* **72 p**

TAROUDANT 4 b.g. Pharly (FR) 130 – Melbourne Miss (Chaparral (FR) 128) [1990 12.3v2 10.2s 1991 a11g2 a12g a12g4 16.2g2 17m* 18d2 18.4d3 18f 16.2d4 18m] rangy gelding: has long stride: modest handicapper: won at Pontefract in April: off course over 4 months before promising fourth at Haydock: set far too much to do when staying-on ninth of 22 in Cesarewitch at Newmarket later in October: suited by good test of stamina: acts on any going except perhaps very firm: has edged left: trained first 8 starts by R. Hollinstead. *R. J. Holder.* **74**

TARRAS MOSS (USA) 3 gr.f. Slew O' Gold (USA) – Kirigen (USA) (J O Tobin (USA) 130) [1990 NR 1991 8g6 10.2g4] $140,000Y: tall, lengthy filly: second reported foal: dam unraced half-sister to very smart Princess Karenda, winner of Hollywood Oaks, and to dam of Thunder Puddles: second favourite, fourth of 11 in maiden at Bath in June: should prove better at 1¼m than shorter: visits Kefaah. *J. H. M. Gosden.* **66**

TARTAN DANCER 2 b.c. (Apr 8) Ballacashtal (CAN) – Waltzing Willow (Swing Easy (USA) 126) [1991 7m] workmanlike, rather angular colt: first foal: dam appeared of little account: 25/1 and very green, slow-starting ninth of 13 in median auction at Wolverhampton in September: may improve. *P. F. I. Cole.* —

TARTAN TINKER (IRE) 3 gr.c. Godswalk (USA) 130 – Travel Away 93 (Tachypous 128) [1990 7m 7m5 8f 9g5 7m 8g6 9g 1991 10g4] leggy colt: moderate mover: quite modest maiden: good fourth at Kempton in April, staying on well: stays 1¼m. *M. Brittain.* **64**

TARTAR'S BOW 4 b.g. Gorytus (USA) 132 – Sweet Eliane (Birdbrook 110) [1990 8.2m5 10g 8.2d 8m* 8d 7d 1991 8g6 10.5d] lengthy, quite attractive gelding: very good walker: quite modest handicapper: stays 1m: seems to need a sound surface: blinkered final start at 3 yrs. *R. J. Holder.* **59**

TARWIYA (IRE) 2 b.f. (Feb 14) Dominion 123 – Touraya (Tap On Wood 130) [1991 6g2 6g2 6g2 5m3 5g* 7g* 6m2 7d*] first foal: dam lightly-raced French 1m **98**

C. L. Weld EBF Park Stakes, the Curragh—
Tarwiya improves again and wins from Market Booster (right) and Via Borghese

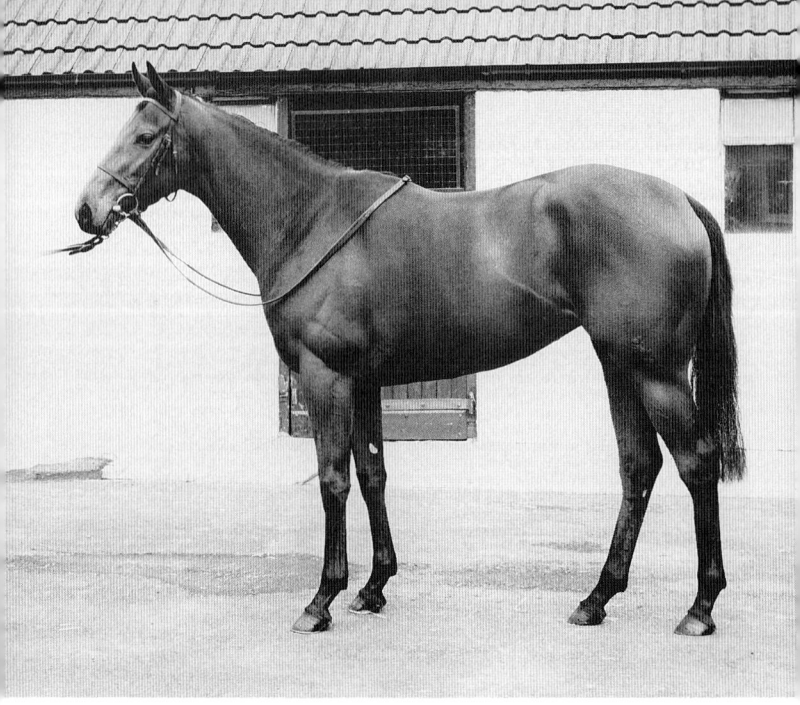

H.H. Aga Khan's "Tarwiya"

winner, from good family: fairly useful performer: showed plenty of promise (including in Group 3 contest) before winning maiden at Naas then listed event at Leopardstown in summer: improved form on last 2 starts, when ½-length second of 8 to Twafeaj in Moyglare Stud Stakes at the Curragh (flashed tail throughout, drifted left under pressure) and winner there in Group 3 event (Via Borghese 2 lengths away third) 20 days later in September: should stay 1m: acts on good to firm and soft ground. *J. Oxx, Ireland.*

TASKING (IRE)   2 ch.f. (May 25) Thatching 131 – Haskeir (Final Straw 127)   54
[1991 5.7f 8g] IR 24,000Y: small, sparely-made filly: second foal: dam unraced daughter of half-sister to St Leger winner Athens Wood: form in September maidens at Bath only when beaten around 5 lengths on debut, headed 3f out and one pace: bred to stay beyond 6f. *B. W. Hills.*

TASMAN OAK (NZ)   5 b.g. Oak Ridge (FR) – Hinemaunga (NZ) (Coolmack 104)   55
[1990 NR 1991 14m⁵ 9g 8.5f³ 14.1f⁶ 14.6m⁶] sturdy, short-backed New Zealand-bred gelding: 50/1, worthwhile form only when third of 6 in slowly-run minor event at Beverley in July: well beaten in handicaps after: should stay beyond 1m: winning hurdler. *Mrs S. Oliver.*

TASMIM   4 b.f. Be My Guest (USA) 126 – Militia Girl (Rarity 129) [1990 8g 7d 1991   —
a11g* a11g² 10.2s 10m 11m 8.5f] tall, sparely-made filly: won maiden (first form) at a 63
Southwell in February, making all: well beaten final 4 starts: stays 11f: has pulled hard: flashes tail: winning hurdler. *P. F. Tulk.*

TATE DANCER (IRE)   2 b.c. (Apr 3) Tate Gallery (USA) 117 – Namatanga   78
(USA) (Foolish Pleasure (USA)) [1991 6m⁵ 5m² 6m³ 6m² 5m* 6g] 30,000F: leggy,

874

sparely-made colt: moderate walker: first foal: dam French maiden daughter of Poule d'Essai des Pouliches second Nonoalca: modest performer: 11/10 on, won 11-runner maiden at Catterick in October, leading under 2f out and keeping on: good twelfth of 25 to Casteddu in Racecall Gold Trophy at Redcar 10 days later: should stay beyond 6f: yet to race on soft surface: twice slowly away: consistent. *R. W. Armstrong.*

TATE EXPRESS (IRE)   2 b.c. (Mar 20) Tate Gallery (USA) 117 – Maryville   **56** Bick (Malacate (USA) 131) [1991 6m 7.5f4 7.5f6] 17,000F, 19,000Y: unfurnished colt: half-brother to 2 Irish maidens: dam Irish middle-distance winner: plating-class maiden: last seen out at Beverley in July: bred to stay middle distances. *N. A. Graham.*

TAUBER   7 b.g. Taufan (USA) 119 – Our Bernie (Continuation 120) [1990 a8g5   **90** d a7g5 6v 7g2 7g3 7m4 7.6g2 7.6m3 6f* 7f6 6m5 6m6 6g* 6m 6m* 6m* 7m4 6g5 6s* a6g a6g2 1991 a5g* a6g* 6d 6g 6g 6g 5m2 5g 5g 5.2f 5g 6m 6m 6m 6g 6d 7m 6m 5s* a6g a5g4 a6g6] rather leggy gelding: has a markedly round action: successful twice at Lingfield (has won there 10 times, 6 of them on turf) in January: best effort after seventh start when winning at Edinburgh: probably ideally needs further than 5f, stays 1m: acts on any going: excellent mount for inexperienced rider. *Pat Mitchell.*

TAUFAN BLU (IRE)   2 b.f. (Apr 5) Taufan (USA) 119 – Engage (Whistling Wind   **76** p 123) [1991 6m5 5g4 5g2] 13,000Y: leggy filly: half-sister to several winners, including useful sprinter African Lady (by African Sky) and Irish 9f winner Cluster of Diamond (by Ballad Rock): dam won from 5f to 1m in Ireland: well-backed 7/2-shot, short-headed by Silca-Cisa in maiden at Redcar in October, keeping on well though drifting left: should prove as effective at 6f: has joined M. Johnston: may improve again. *W. J. Pearce.*

TAURIAN ROYALE   2 b.c. (Mar 25) Aragon 118 – Top Stream 87 (Highland   **56** Melody 112) [1991 5g 5g 6f a6g 7m4 7m 8m4 10m4] 5,600F, 5,600Y: compact colt: moderate mover: half-brother to 2 winners, including useful 6f and 7f winner Kedron (by Absalom): dam won 3 times over 1m at 2 yrs and seemed to stay 1½m: fair plater: probably stays 1¼m: acts on good to firm ground: has raced with head high, and looked not keen: has worn bandages: sold 3,400 gns Newmarket Autumn Sales. *P. F. Tulk.*

TAUTINA (IRE)   3 b.f. Taufan (USA) 119 – Wintina (Tumble Wind (USA)) [1990   **—** NR 1991 7g 8m6] 26,000F, 52,000Y: leggy, workmanlike filly: third foal: sister to fairly useful 1985 Irish 2-y-o 6f winner Ladina and half-sister to useful 8.5f winner Cachondina (by Runnett): dam Irish 6f winner: well beaten in spring maidens: sold 1,300 gns Newmarket Autumn Sales. *A. A. Scott.*

TAWAFIJ (USA)   2 ch.c. (Apr 3) Diesis 133 – Dancing Brownie (USA) (Nijinsky   **—** (CAN) 138) [1991 6m5] $200,000F: good-topped, attractive colt: third foal: dam unraced sister to Nijinsky's Secret: 14/1, burly and green, over 10 lengths fifth of 6 to Prince Ferdinand in £9,300 event at Ascot in June, dropping away over 2f out: will stay 1m: looked capable of better. *H. Thomson Jones.*

TA WARDLE   7 ch.g. Import 127 – Zephyr Lady 59 (Windjammer (USA)) [1990   **35** a12g5 10f* 10f2 9f 12f 11.7g4 17.1f4 16g 12m 17.1d2 1991 18d 16m 13d6 12s4 10.5g] tall, leggy gelding: poor handicapper at best: effective at 1¼m and stays well: probably acts on any going: has got on edge. *M. J. Bolton.*

TAWJIH (USA)   4 b.c. Lyphard's Wish (FR) 124 – Chop Towhee (USA) (Hatchet   **44** Man (USA)) [1990 8g 8f3 10m 8m 1991 8.3g 11.1g4 12g 10.1d5 10.1m 10m] quite attractive, good-topped colt: has round action: poor maiden: probably stays 11f: acts on firm and dead ground. *M. Madgwick.*

TAYLOR QUIGLEY (USA)   2 b.c. (Feb 2) Taylor's Falls (USA) – Heather's   **102** Turn (USA) (Turn To Mars (USA)) [1991 6g2 6f* 6g2 7.1m5 6.3s3 7v6] IR 12,500Y: leggy, quite attractive colt: half-brother to 2 winners in North America: dam smart winner at up to 1½m in Canada at 3 yrs: sire sprinter: useful performer: won maiden auction at Yarmouth in August: better form when placed in Gimcrack Stakes at York (finished strongly behind River Falls) and Goffs Premier Challenge at the Curragh (beaten under ½ length by Colway Bold), and when around 8 lengths sixth of 8 to Cardoun in Criterium de Maisons-Laffitte: stays 7f: easily best form with some give, acts on heavy: ridden by 7-lb claimer first 2 starts. *C. N. Allen.*

TAYLORS PRINCE   4 ch.c. Sandhurst Prince 128 – Maiden's Dance 65   **73** d (Hotfoot 126) [1990 10m5 10g5 9m4 8d6 7m* 7f2 8f 7m5 7m 7.6d 8m3 8d4 1991 8s 7g 8m2 9m* 9m 8.3d4 10.1g* 9m3 10.1m3 10.1m6 11.5m5 10.1f 10.5g 10m 11.5s4] leggy, lengthy, angular colt: moderate mover: quite modest handicapper: won at Wolverhampton in May and Yarmouth in June: ran poorly last 5 starts: probably stays 11.5f:

acts on firm and dead going: has run creditably when visored: has hung right, and seemed none too genuine: difficult ride. *H. J. Collingridge.*

TAYLOR'S REALM   5 gr.m. Another Realm 118 – Sweet Rosina 61 (Sweet   35
Revenge 129) [1990 10f² 12g 10.8m² 11.5g 10f⁵ 11.7m⁴ 12m³ 11.5m⁵ 10f 10f⁵ 12m 1991
10s* 12s 12f] leggy, angular mare: had a quick action: poor handicapper: first run for
new stable, won at Sandown (apprentices) in July: stayed 1½m: probably acted on
any going, but went very well on top-of-the-ground: dead. *R. Akehurst.*

TAZAMISHA   2 b.f. (Jan 29) Blakeney 126 – Ardverikie (Red Alert 127) [1991 5d⁶   40
8.1g⁶ 8.1d⁶ a7g a8g] quite attractive filly: moderate walker: fourth foal: dam lightly
raced and well beaten: poor maiden. *R. Hollinshead.*

TBAB (IRE)   3 b.c. Thatching 131 – Madam Loving 99 (Vaigly Great 127) [1990   97
NR 1991 7d⁴ 6s* 6g 6m² 6s 6m] 16,500F, 47,000Y: useful-looking colt: second foal:
dam 5f and 6f winner, best at 2 yrs: won maiden at Newcastle in May: excellent
second of 28 to Sarcita in Ladbrokes (Ayr) Gold Cup: well beaten in Diadem Stakes
at Ascot (prominent long way) and £12,300 handicap at York (tongue tied down)
afterwards: likely to prove best over sprint distances. *C. E. Brittain.*

TEA AND HONEY   3 ch.f. Night Shift (USA) – Tactless 91 (Romulus 129) [1990   —
6d 5m a7g⁶ a6g 1991 a10g 10d 8m 8g 6g] sturdy filly: seems of little account:
blinkered third start: sold 850 gns Ascot July Sales. *C. A. Cyzer.*

TEACHER'S DRAM   5 b.m. Strong Gale 116 – Top Marks 61 (Breakspear II)   —
[1990 NR 1991 a8g⁴ a10g] lightly raced and little sign of ability. *R. Dickin.*

TEA DUST (IRE)   3 b.f. Pennine Walk 120 – Ridalia 56 (Ridan (USA)) [1990 NR   81 d
1991 7g 8m² 7d² 8g² 7d³ 6.1m³ 8.2m² 8g] 11,500Y: good-topped filly: fifth foal:
half-sister to fair sprinter Powder Blue (by He Loves Me) and French 9f winner
Daring Daphne (by Final Straw): dam showed a little ability: modest maiden: best
effort fourth outing: prominent 5f but kept hanging right, eased down as if saddle
may have slipped, in handicap final start: best efforts at 1m on a sound surface:
sweating and edgy (ran fairly well) seventh start. *P. J. Makin.*

TEAM DECISION (IRE)   2 b.f. (Apr 15) Taufan (USA) 119 – Gratify 65   58
(Grundy 137) [1991 6g⁵ a7g⁴ 7g 7m* 7.1m 7g 10.5d 10m] IR 2,100Y: sturdy filly: has a
round action: second foal: dam ungenuine maiden stayed 2m: fairly useful plater:
won at Wolverhampton in August (retained 5,700 gns): probably stays 1¼m: well
beaten on dead ground: sold 2,100 gns Newmarket Autumn Sales. *Sir Mark Prescott.*

TEAMSTER   5 b.h. Known Fact (USA) 135 – Rosetta Stone 89 (Guillaume Tell   113
(USA) 121) [1990 16g⁴ 16m* 16m* 20d⁴ 16g 18g² 16m⁶ 1991 16.2s* 14g³ 16m³ 20g⁵
15.9m⁶ 20d⁶] good-bodied horse: good mover with a quick action: very useful stayer
on his day: impressive winner from Shambo of Insulpak Sagaro EBF Stakes at Ascot
(for second successive year) in May: fair fifth in Gold Cup at Royal Ascot (badly
hampered): ran poorly after in listed event at York (had foot injury) and Prix du
Cadran at Longchamp (first run for nearly 3 months, weakened quickly 2f out):
suited by test of stamina: acted on any going: had turn of foot: none too reliable:
retired to Forke Farm Stud, Devon, fee £600. *M. R. Stoute.*

TEANARCO (IRE)   3 b.f. Kafu 120 – Lady Kasbah (Lord Gayle (USA) 124) [1990   66
5f³ 5.8m² 5.8h* 5m⁴ 6d* 6d² 1991 7m 8.5m 5.8d 6d 5.7m⁶ 7g⁶ 6g⁵ 6f 6m* 6m 6.1d
7g] leggy filly: quite modest handicapper nowadays: on toes, won at Ayr in September, rallying well: well beaten at Chester and Newmarket (led 5f, hung left) last 2
starts: suited by 6f: acts on good to firm ground and dead: blinkered/visored seventh
and eighth starts: didn't handle track at Epsom: sometimes sweating. *R. J. Holder.*

TEA ROSE (FR)   4 gr.f. Galant Vert (FR) 124 – River Risle (FR) (Kalamoun 129)   63 d
[1990 10s 1991 9.1g 9g* 10g* 9.2g 10.5g 11m⁴ 13.6m⁶ 10m] leggy, close-coupled filly:

Insulpak Sagaro EBF Stakes, Ascot—Teamster wins for the second successive year

moderate mover: fourth foal: half-sister to 2 winners in France, notably useful 1985 2-y-o 9f winner Rivine (by Sharpman): dam 2-y-o 5f winner in France: ex-French filly: successful in minor events at Orleans in April: no worthwhile form on flat in claimers and seller here: worth a try beyond 13f: possibly needs some give in the ground: formerly trained by J. Beguigne: sold 1,250 gns Ascot December Sales. *N. Tinkler.*

TEAZLES LAD 2 b.g. (Apr 11) Belfort (FR) 89 – Dancing Amber (Broxted 120) [1991 5f] quite good-topped gelding: has some scope: fifth reported foal: dam tailed off in novice hurdle: 50/1 and green, soon behind in Beverley claimer in July. *M. W. Ellerby.* —

TEDDY'S PLAY (USA) 2 b.c. (Feb 9) Theatrical 128 – Strictly (ARG) (Dancing Moss 113) [1991 7g5 7d 8g4] $40,000Y: leggy, useful-looking colt: first foal: dam stakes winner in Argentina: modest maiden: off course 2 months, good third to Sword Master at Bath in October: will stay 1¼m: may do better. *J. W. Hills.* 74

TEES GAZETTE GIRL 2 b.f. (Mar 9) Kalaglow 132 – Shadiliya 90 (Red Alert 127) [1991 7g 8m] 4,000Y: half-sister to French 1990 3-y-o 7f winner Larmes de Joie (by Glenstal) and 1989 2-y-o 7f winner Tears of Happiness (by Rousillon) and a winner over hurdles: dam, 7f winner at 2 yrs, is closely related to very useful 5f to 1m winner Shasavaan: slowly away and behind most of way in maiden auctions at Doncaster in June and Redcar in October. *Mrs G. R. Reveley.* —

TEGERE (IRE) 3 ch.f. Thatching 131 – La Duse 66 (Junius (USA) 124) [1990 NR 1991 8m 10.2d] 20,000Y: lengthy filly with scope: first foal: dam, lightly-raced maiden placed at 1½m, is half-sister to smart middle-distance stayer Stetchworth: behind in maiden and maiden claimer at Bath: sold 1,000 gns Newmarket July Sales. *J. W. Hills.* —

TEL-ECHO 7 ch.g. Nishapour (FR) 125 – Rhodante (Busted 134) [1990 NR 1991 10.3m] strong ex-Irish gelding: half-brother to 3 winners abroad, including Rhonda's Ring (by Auction Ring), successful in listed race in USA: dam won twice at up to 1½m in Ireland: useful winning performer on flat as 4-y-o (trained by J. Oxx): no show in Chester claimer in August, only run on flat: will stay beyond 1¾m: acts well on soft going: has been tried in blinkers. *G. B. Balding.* —

TELEGRAPH TOUCH 3 b.c. Cragador 110 – Chanita (Averof 123) [1990 NR 1991 a6g 8.2d 6m 7m5 11f 10g a12g 12d] 2,000Y: workmanlike colt: third foal: brother to 4-y-o April Cracker and half-brother to 5-y-o 6f to 1m winner Merseyside Man (by My Dad Tom): dam unraced: little form, mostly in claimers: often bandaged: sold 720 gns Doncaster July Sales. *M. Brittain.* —

TELETRADER 10 ch.g. Nearly A Hand 115 – Miss Saddler (St Paddy 133) [1990 12f3 13.1h3 10m* 10m6 12m2 10f5 10.2m6 1991 12g6 12.1d5 10g2 10g4dis 9.7f 12f 10.2g6] workmanlike gelding: plating-class handicapper: effective at 1¼m to 1½m: acts on firm going: has given trouble at stalls: has run well for amateur. *R. J. Hodges.* 55

TELLMEABOUTIT 3 b.g. Blushing Scribe (USA) 107 – Orchard Road 74 (Camden Town 125) [1990 6g 6f6 5f a7g 1991 a5g4 a5g6 a6g a8g 6f] leggy gelding: bad maiden: blinkered 4 times, once visored. *Mrs N. Macauley.* —

TELL NO LIES 4 b.f. High Line 125 – No Cards 109 (No Mercy 126) [1990 10m2 10m6 10.6s4 10.6d2 10.5g 8g3 1991 10g 10.1m2 10g4 10.1m* 10g3 10m* 8.9g* 8d 10.4m5] lengthy, rather angular filly: fair handicapper: won at Newcastle in July, Ripon in August and York (quickened really well) in September: below best final 2 starts: stays 1¼m: easily best form on a sound surface (yet to race on very firm ground): trained first 3 starts by Lord John FitzGerald. *M. H. Easterby.* 88

TELLWRIGHT (IRE) 3 b.c. Burslem 123 – Travel Far 53 (Monseigneur (USA) 127) [1990 6m6 1991 8g a7g3 a8g2 a8g] close-coupled colt: quite modest maiden: placed twice at Southwell: ran badly at same course final start: should be suited by 1m + : wore dropped noseband as 3-y-o: bandaged behind last 2 starts: sold 620 gns Newmarket Autumn Sales. *J. A. R. Toller.* 60

TEL QUEL (FR) 3 br.c. Akarad (FR) 130 – Best Girl 108 (Birdbrook 110) [1990 8g* 1991 9.2g2 9d4 10d3 9d* 10d* 10m*] 125

The Dubai Champion Stakes went to France yet again, this time to the fast-improving three-year-old Tel Quel, a 16/1-shot trained by the outstanding Fabre and astutely handled by Thierry Jarnet, an up-and-coming rider who finished second in the French jockeys' table. On his first ride in Britain, Jarnet outshone some of his vastly more experienced colleagues on the difficult straight mile-and-a-quarter course at Newmarket. The modest early pace

Dubai Champion Stakes, Newmarket—
French-trained Tel Quel provides leading owner Sheikh Mohammed
with his only Group 1 winner of the season in Britain;
Cruachan (rails) is a game runner-up with the previous year's winner
In The Groove (far side) a fast-finishing third

set by Terimon, attempting by similar means to repeat his success in the International Stakes at York, posed problems for all the jockeys aiming to hold their mounts up; and, in fact, two of the best of them, Asmussen on the favourite In The Groove and Piggott on the joint-second favourite Ristna, completely misjudged the waiting game. While they sat out of their ground, Jarnet had Tel Quel handily placed and, as things turned out, was perfectly positioned as Cruachan quickened past Terimon with just under four furlongs to go. Tel Quel gradually got into full stride and, sustaining a challenge all the way up the hill, he went on from Cruachan around sixty yards out to win by half a length, the pair of them stealing the honours from the two strong-finishing fillies left with too much to do. In the circumstances it is too soon to go overboard about Tel Quel, who, besides looking somewhat flattered, was opposed by the weakest Champion Stakes field in recent years. However, there's no doubt he was improving at the time. He'd won his two previous races in France, both of them Group 3, the nine-furlong Prix Daphnis at Evry in July and mile and a quarter La Coupe de Maisons-Laffitte in September. He wasn't favourite for either, but having scraped home from Bistro Garden and Funny Baby in the former, he beat the Grand Prix de Paris third Kotashaan by a length and a half, leading fairly late, in a nine-runner race between three-year-olds and upwards in the latter. The ground was dead for both these events; it was good to firm at Newmarket.

Tel Quel (FR) (br.c. 1988)	Akarad (FR) (b or br 1978)	Labus (b or br 1971)	Busted Cordovilla
		Licata (b 1969)	Abdos Gaia
	Best Girl (b 1975)	Birdbrook (gr 1961)	Mossborough Game Bird
		View Mistress (b 1964)	King's Troop My Margaret

A mile and a quarter may be Tel Quel's optimum distance, though most of those sired by the Prix du Jockey-Club runner-up Akarad must be regarded as having good prospects of staying a mile and a half. Tel Quel's sister Vue Cavaliere was best at around a mile and a quarter, at which distance she won the Prix de Psyche at Deauville and came a good fifth of fourteen to Rafha in the Prix de Diane in 1990; she disputed the lead for around the same distance in Salsabil's Prix Vermeille. Best Girl's two previous winners, the modest Irish gelding Fast N'Fabulous (by Le Fabuleux) and the rather better Italian filly Storm On The Beach (by Glint of Gold) were both successful at beyond a mile and a quarter, though the latter seemed better at shorter. Best Girl herself is a sprinting sister to the 1975 One Thousand Guineas second Girl Friend, out of the short-running View Mistress. Girl Friend, by the way, produced one of Brigadier Gerard's more talented runners in the good-class French colt Comrade In Arms who, like Girl Friend, was effective at sprint distances as well as a mile. The third dam My Margaret, a five-furlong winner, was a sister to numerous winners at up to a mile and a half and a half-sister to others, including the Irish Derby winner Charlottown. Physically, Tel Quel has plenty of scope for improvement—he's a tall, leggy sort—and his progress as a four-year-old will be followed with interest. *A. Fabre, France.*

TELSTEAM (IRE)　3 ch.g. King of Clubs 124 – Ridge The Times (USA) 78 (Riva　— Ridge (USA)) [1990 8g 1991 10v 8g 8.2d 5f 8f6 7d 9.7g] angular gelding: has a round action: seems of little account. *W. Carter.*

TEMPELHOF (IRE)　2 b.c. (Apr 25) Alzao (USA) 117 – Konigin Kate (GER)　**59** (Authi 123) [1991 8m 8.1d6 8m] IR 14,000F, 41,000Y: sturdy, quite attractive colt: has a round action: fourth foal: brother to 17f NH Flat race/hurdles winner Hawthorn Blaze: dam 1¼m winner in Ireland: quite modest form in maidens last 2 starts, plugging on at one pace from halfway: likely to be suited by a thorough test of stamina. *J. W. Hills.*

TEMPERING　5 b.g. Kris 135 – Mixed Applause (USA) 101 (Nijinsky (CAN) 138)　**68** d [1990 12m4 14m4 10.6m5 7.5m 7m4 a8g2 a7g a7g5 a11g* a8g5 a10g5 a14g5 1991 a **91** d a12g* a11g* a11g* a10g a11g* a8g a11g 8m6 10f4 12g6 9f3 8m5 9s4 11s6 10.9g3 10f6 12m 12.3f6 11m4 16m a12g3 a14g2 a11g* a8g6 a12g] strong, good-bodied gelding: fairly useful handicapper, much better on all-weather than turf: won at Southwell (4) in January and in November (easily landed odds in claimer): well below best there final start: really needs further than 1m, and stays 1¾m: probably acts on any going: has often sweated: headstrong, and has been taken down early: forces pace. *D. W. Chapman.*

TEMPLE FORTUNE (USA)　2 br.f. (May 3) Ziggy's Boy (USA) – Our Feast　**56** (USA) (Banquet Table (USA)) [1991 5g4 5.2g2 5g4 5.1g6 5.7g] $110,000Y: sturdy filly: quite fluent mover: sister to 3-y-o 7f winner Zigaura and half-sister to 2 minor winners in USA: dam twice-raced half-sister to Our Native: sire (by Danzig) won from 5f to 7f: plating-class maiden: off course 3 months after debut, 2 months after third start: blinkered, raced freely then faded (stiff task) final start: bred to stay beyond 5f. *D. R. C. Elsworth.*

TEMPLE ISLAND (IRE)　3 ch.f. Salmon Leap (USA) 131 – Sainthill (St　— Alphage 119) [1990 NR 1991 10d6 a11g6 a12g] 9,400Y: sturdy filly: ninth reported foal: half-sister to 6f and 9f winner Knockglas (by Hardgreen): dam twice-raced sister to top sprinter Sandford Lad: well beaten in late-season claimers, some late headway first 2 outings. *P. J. Makin.*

TEMPORALE　5 ch.h. Horage 124 – Traminer (Status Seeker) [1990 12m 10m　**41** a11g5 a14g5 1991 a16g4 15.8f 16.2f] close-coupled horse: moderate walker: poor maiden: tried blinkered once: has run creditably when visored. *K. R. Burke.*

TEMPORAL (GER)　3 ch.c. Surumu (GER) – Theresa (Zeddaan 130) [1990 6g3　**117** 6d4 7g 7g* 1991 11g4 10g4 11g4 12g* 12s3 12m2 14g2] 150,000 DM (approx £48,700) Y: fifth foal: brother to 2 winners in Germany, one placed in listed races: dam, successful twice in Germany at 3 yrs and third in 9f listed races, is half-sister to 2 German pattern performers: successful at Hanover in November at 2 yrs and in 19-runner BMW Deutsches Derby (by ½ length from Lomitas) at Hamburg in July at 3 yrs: ran creditably in Aral-Pokal at Gelsenkirchen-Horst and Grosser Preis Von Baden (7 lengths second to Lomitas) fifth and sixth starts: below form in Deutsches St Leger at Dortmund final one: suited by 1½m: acts on good to firm ground and soft: reported in November to have fractured off-hind and unlikely to race in 1992. *B. Schutz, Germany.*

TENACITY　2 b.c. (Mar 16) Primo Dominie 121 – Millaine 69 (Formidable (USA)　**81** 125) [1991 5g4 5m* 6g6 6m3 7m4 7m5 7m 6f2 6.1m3 5m2 6m3] 27,000Y: compact, workmanlike colt: third foal: half-brother to fairly useful 3-y-o sprinter Amber Mill (by Doulab) and a winner in Italy: dam stayed 1½m: fair performer: made all in maiden at Hamilton in May: mostly ran creditably in nurseries and minor events afterwards: stays 7f: acts on firm ground: ran badly at Chester seventh start: subsequently blinkered or visored: flashed tail fifth outing: sold 17,000 gns Newmarket Autumn Sales. *J. Berry.*

Timeform Perspective Handicap, Pontefract—
apprentice-ridden Tendresse gets up for a game win; Munro on runner-up
Double Echo has dropped his whip after striking the winner across the face,
for which he received a six-day suspension

TENDER BID 5 ch.g. Tender King 123 – Princess Biddy 86 (Sun Prince 128)   **46**
[1990 8f* 7f⁵ 9g 8.2m a8g⁵ 8m⁴ a8g a8g 1991 a8g a10g 10v 12d 8.1d⁶] good-topped
gelding: often doesn't take the eye: poor walker and mover: plating-class
handicapper on his day: not seen out after June: seems to stay 1¼m: acts on firm and
dead ground: inconsistent: bought out of J. Long's stable 1,000 gns Ascot May Sales
after penultimate start. *D. Haydn Jones.*

TENDERETTA 4 ch.f. Tender King 123 – Fandetta (Gay Fandango (USA) 132)   **—**
[1990 6m 7m 1991 6s 8g] lengthy, sparely-made filly: half-sister to winning sprinter
Alnashme (by Godswalk): dam unraced: ex-Irish filly: fair form as 2-y-o, winning
over 6f and 7.9f: well beaten since, in listed events in autumn: stays 7f: acts on firm
ground. *J. L. Spearing.*

TENDER KISS (IRE) 3 b.f. Tender King 123 – Nordic Maid 84 (Vent du Nord)   **—**
[1990 5f 5f⁶ 5.3h² 5m 5f 6h⁵ 5m 5m 5f³ 5m a5g⁵ a6g 1991 a5g 6m 8m 5m] strong,
plain filly: has a quick action: fair plater at 2 yrs: ran badly as 3-y-o: should stay 6f:
has hung for apprentice: sometimes bandaged behind. *R. A. Bennett.*

TENDER LOOK (IRE) 2 b.f. (Apr 7) Prince Tenderfoot (USA) 126 – Piercing   **—**
Glances (Patch 129) [1991 7f] third live foal: dam showed a little ability in Ireland,
appearing to stay middle distances: 14/1, always behind in 18-runner claimer at
Salisbury in September. *A. N. Lee.*

TENDER MOMENT (IRE) 3 b.f. Caerleon (USA) 132 – Cannon Boy (USA)   **73**
(Canonero II (USA)) [1990 NR 1991 7m⁶ 8m⁵ a10g⁵] leggy, unfurnished filly: closely
related to winning hurdler Donna Del Largo (by Kings Lake) and half-sister to a
winner in USA by Be My Guest: dam won 9 races in USA, including graded 9f event:
modest maiden: fifth of 8 to Perky Dancer at Newmarket in May: favourite,
well-beaten last at Lingfield 8 weeks later: best effort at 1m. *C. E. Brittain.*

TENDER MONARCH (IRE) 2 br.c. (Apr 9) Tender King 123 – Loving Cup 93   **36**
(He Loves Me 120) [1991 5m³ 5f 5f 5g⁶ a5g 5m 7m 5g 6m] IR 4,100F, 6,600Y:
sparely-made colt: moderate mover: third foal: half-brother to a winner in Italy: dam
2-y-o 6f winner, is out of sister to dam of good animals Good Bond and Roll of
Honour: poor plater: didn't progress from debut, and gave indications of unsatisfactory temperament: sometimes blinkered or visored. *P. J. Bevan.*

TENDER MUSIC 3 ch.f. Music Boy 124 – Sobriquet (Roan Rocket 128) [1990   **—**
5m⁵ 5m³ 5f⁴ 5g 1991 a5g] workmanlike filly: had a round action: poor sprint maiden:
acted on firm going: dead. *Miss L. C. Siddall.*

TENDER REACH 3 b.f. Reach 122 – Betty's Bid (Auction Ring (USA) 123) —
[1990 5.3f⁵ 8m 1991 10d a7g 7f a8g⁵ 9.9f⁶] small filly: poor maiden, not seen out after July: worth a try beyond 1¼m: blinkered fourth start. *R. Voorspuy.*

TENDER TRAIL 4 ch.f. Tender King 123 – Trail (Thatch (USA) 136) [1990 5m —
6m 5.3h⁵ 5m⁴ 5m⁴ 5f⁶ 5.3h² 6m 6f 5.3f a6g 1991 a6g⁶ a5g 7d] small, lengthy filly: has a round action: poor handicapper nowadays: should stay 6f: acts on hard ground: sold 700 gns Newmarket July Sales. *C. J. Benstead.*

TENDER VISION (IRE) 3 b.f. Vision (USA) – Tender Niece 69 (Prince —
Tenderfoot (USA) 126) [1990 NR 1991 10g 9m 8.3d⁵ 7m 10m 11m 10m] IR 4,000Y: sparely-made filly: moderate walker and mover: third living foal: half-sister to 1987 2-y-o 5.3f winner Rendicus (by Red Sunset), subsequently 6f and 7f winner in Italy: dam 1m winner: little sign of ability: may need a soft surface: visored final start: sold 750 gns Doncaster October Sales. *R. M. Whitaker.*

TENDRESSE (IRE) 3 b.f. Tender King 123 – Velinowski (Malinowski (USA) 60
123) [1990 5m⁶ 5m 6m* 5f 6m⁴ 7m 6d 6m⁶ 1991 7g 7g* 7g 8f 7m* 7m² 8m* 8.9m³
8m⁴ 8g 8m 8g 8d²] workmanlike filly: quite modest handicapper: won at Warwick in June, Salisbury (apprentices) in August and Pontefract in September: ran very well in selling contest final start: stays 9f: acts on firm and dead going. *C. J. Hill.*

TEN HIGH (IRE) 2 b.f. (May 15) Leap High (USA) – Another Decade (Daring —
Display (USA)) [1991 6m 8.1g 7m] lengthy, rather sparely-made filly: fourth reported foal: half-sister to a winner in Belgium: dam Irish 2-y-o 5f to 7f winner: well beaten in maidens and a minor event. *B. Ellison.*

TENOFUS 6 ch.g. Crofter (USA) 124 – Valley of Diamonds 74 (Florescence 120) —
[1990 NR 1991 7d] tall, workmanlike gelding: modest handicapper at best as 3-y-o: no show in claimer, only run since: effective at 7f and 1m: acts on any going. *C. D. Broad.*

TENTER CLOSE 5 b.g. Gorytus (USA) 132 – Love Land (FR) (Kautokeino 50
(FR)) [1990 NR 1991 8.2s⁶ 10m 11f⁴ 13m 15.8f* 14.1f⁵] leggy gelding: has a rather round action: won handicap at Catterick in July: stays 15.8f: acts on firm and dead ground: reluctant at stalls and ran badly in visor once: winning hurdler. *M. D. Hammond.*

TEQUILA GOLD 3 b.g. Green Ruby (USA) 104 – Diamante 83 (Sparkler 130) 47
[1990 6g 6g 5s⁵ 1991 10d 9d² 8.2f 10.6g 10m⁴] rather angular gelding: plating-class maiden: below form in summer after second in handicap at Hamilton: stays 9f: may need an easy surface: ran poorly when sweating: visored once at 2 yrs. *J. S. Wilson.*

TERESHENKO 2 b.c. (Apr 8) Persian Bold 123 – Mists of Avalon (USA) 76 35
(Nureyev (USA) 131) [1991 a5g⁶ 5g 5d⁴ 5.2g⁵ 5m] 16,000Y: leggy, close-coupled colt: second foal: dam 2-y-o 1m winner successful at 7f in France as 3-y-o, is half-sister to very useful French miler Private View: poor maiden: blinkered in seller penultimate outing: will be suited by 6f+: trained first 4 starts by N. Callaghan. *B. A. McMahon.*

TERIMON 5 gr.h. Bustino 136 – Nicholas Grey 100 (Track Spare 125) [1990 **124**
9m* 10m⁶ 10m³ 10m² 12m⁶ 10.5g⁴ 10d 1991 9m* 12m² 10g³ 10d⁵ 12m⁴ 10.4g*
10m 12f]

Debate as to who put up the outstanding equine performance of the year will rage on at least until a new season begins to divert everyone's attention. The Generous-Suave Dancer debate and the nomination of Arazi as 'Horse of The Year' in the newly-instituted Cartier Awards will keep the fire burning through the winter, whilst enthusiastic but misinformed letters to the Press, and ill-conceived outbursts from public racing figures serve occasionally to fan the flames. If there existed an award for a feat of jockeyship in the most recent season, the argument would doubtless be just as unremitting, but polemists would be unlikely to deny at least a nomination to the ride of Michael Roberts on Terimon in York's Juddmonte International. Terimon's first Group 1 success in twenty-five starts was due in large part to the tactical awareness of his jockey. Having employed a waiting policy in all the horse's previous races, Roberts quickly took Terimon, a 16/1 chance, to the front this time when no-one else was willing to go on. He set a modest pace, had the two market leaders Stagecraft and Environment Friend toiling when he increased the tempo early in the straight, and had sufficient reserves from the two-furlong pole to repel the challenge of Quest For Fame, eased in the closing stages to beat that rival by two lengths with the odds-on Stagecraft proving a disappointment, three and a half lengths further back in third. The jockey's opportunism notwithstanding, however, Terimon's success was no more than just reward for three seasons' campaigning in the top bracket. Terimon's latest season had begun with a second successive victory in the Group 3 Earl of Sefton Stakes at Newmarket's Craven meeting where Roberts adopted a more familiar strategy, holding him up, gradually making progress towards the stand side from three out, then courageously forcing his way through a briefly-presented gap with under two furlongs to travel and going ahead inside the final hundred yards, holding Emperor Fountain by a neck at the post.

From Newmarket Terimon was sent to Epsom, where he finished a very good second to In The Groove in the Hanson Trust Coronation Cup, showing too much finishing speed for Rock Hopper and Quest For Fame, the latter making his seasonal reappearance, and then to Royal Ascot, where he managed third in the Prince of Wales's Stakes behind Stagecraft. Wearing blinkers for the first time, Terimon was a below-par fifth in the Coral-Eclipse at Sandown, chased along some way from home, then, without the blinkers, acquitted himself with credit in the King George VI and Queen Elizabeth Diamond Stakes, though predictably outclassed by Generous. Having made off with their Group 1 prize at York, Roberts and Terimon again sought to make all in the Champion Stakes, but, after setting a sedate gallop, had no answer to their rivals once pressed from the two-marker, and finished well held in ninth. Finally, Terimon contested the Japan Cup in Tokyo, but could make no impression from mid-division in the straight, and finished twelfth of fifteen. Rock Hopper, the horse he'd already beaten, by the adjudication of an emergency jury, to the title of Cartier 'Older Horse of The Year', finished five places in front of him.

Terimon remains by some way the most successful of Nicholas Grey's progeny. Her first foal, Young Nicholas, finished tailed off in a three-mile handicap chase in December 1990, whilst the four-year-old filly Nidomi (by Dominion) ran only once in 1991, finishing tailed off in an amateur riders'

Juddmonte International Stakes, York —
a first Group 1 success for the five-year-old Terimon who springs a big surprise;
Quest For Fame is second

The Dowager Lady Beaverbrook's "Terimon"

		⎧ Busted	⎧ Crepello
	⎧ Bustino	(b 1963)	⎨ Sans Le Sou
	(b 1971)	⎩ Ship Yard	⎧ Doutelle
Terimon	⎨	(ch 1963)	⎩ Paving Stone
(gr.h. 1986)		⎧ Track Spare	⎧ Sound Track
	⎩ Nicholas Grey	(b 1963)	⎨ Rosy Myth
	(gr 1976)	⎩ Rosy Morn	⎧ Roan Rocket
		(gr 1970)	⎩ Golden Pride

event on the flat. Axioprepis, a three-year-old colt by Formidable, was placed once on the flat in the latest season. Nicholas Grey has also produced a filly by Doulab, due to go into training with Sir Mark Prescott, and a full sister to Terimon. She is now due to visit another of Busted's most successful sons, Mtoto. An admirably tough performer, Terimon had his most successful season so far in 1991, amassing over £477,000 in prize money. Following a change of mind by connections upon his return from Tokyo, Terimon, who was to take his place at stud, is to remain in training. A good-topped horse who displays a round action in his faster paces, Terimon is effective from nine furlongs to a mile and a half, and is best suited by a sound surface. *C. E. Brittain.*

TERNIMUS (USA) 4 ch.c. Arctic Tern (USA) 126 – Lustrious (USA) (Delaware   **70** d
Chief (USA)) [1990 12f* 10.6s⁴ 12g 12.4m* 12f² 13.3m 14f² 12g* 12m 12d 12m⁵ 12s²
12g³ 1991 12d 12f²̇14m⁶ 12d 11.9m 12f 12.3f] leggy, quite attractive colt: moderate

mover: modest handicapper at best: well below form after second start: stays 1¾m: acts on any going: blinkered fourth and fifth starts. *F. H. Lee.*

TERRHARS (IRE)   3 b.c. Anita's Prince 126 – Clodianus (Bay Express 132) **101** [1990 5m* 5m⁵ 6g³ 5m³ 5g 5m 5f 1991 5d² 5m⁶ 5g² 5.8m 5g³ 5m⁴ 6m⁵ 5g* 5m³ 5g⁵ 5.2g* 5g 5.2f4 5.1m 5d⁴ 5.2g* 5g*] leggy colt: progressed into a useful handicapper: successful at Sandown, Newbury (twice) and Salisbury: best at 5f: acts on any going: usually taken alone and quietly to post: usually travels strongly, and is held up: below form after sweating and on toes twelfth start: tough and consistent, a credit to his trainer. *R. Hannon.*

TERTIAN (USA)   2 b.c. (Apr 30) Danzig (USA) – Tertiary (USA) (Vaguely **116** p Noble 140) [1991 8g* 7m* 7v²]

Don't be surprised if Tertian makes up into an even better horse in 1992 than he was in 1991. To begin with, he's by the highly successful American stallion Danzig out of a very well-related mare who's already produced one good horse and a couple of useful ones. He's also a strapping individual, very much the type to go on from two to three, but arguably the most interesting point about him as a two-year-old was the marked improvement he made each time he appeared on a racecourse, progressing into one of the best of his generation. Tertian's debut came in a minor event over a mile at Longchamp in September when he was up against half a dozen other newcomers. After beating them emphatically, Tertian drew some enthusiastic remarks from his rider Eddery, and with connections apparently keen to try him on a galloping track he was sent to Newmarket for the Somerville Tattersall Stakes in early-October. Tertian very much took the eye at Newmarket. A big, strong, good-bodied colt with great scope, he still looked green in the paddock in comparison to several of his more experienced opponents. Moreover, in a race run at a slow early pace he met with plenty of trouble in running, but after pulling hard under restraint early on he quickened well once switched right, heading Mojave inside the final fifty yards and being value for more than the winning margin of a neck. Tertian's third and final appearance came in the Criterium de Maisons-Laffitte four weeks later. The race took place on the same day that Arazi trounced his rivals in the Breeders' Cup Juvenile at Churchill Downs. Needless to say, it didn't generate anywhere near so much publicity as that contest, yet by our reckoning it produced not one but two

Somerville Tattersall Stakes, Newmarket—
French-trained Tertian wins with a shade in hand from Mojave

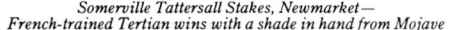

very noteworthy performances. Tertian, coupled with his pacemaker and stable-companion In The News, headed the market at evens in a field of eight with the Cheveley Park runner-up Absurde at 6/4 and the Prix Eclipse winner Cardoun (conceding weight all round) the only other fancied contender, at just over 4/1. Tertian failed to justify favouritism, yet in staying on strongly to run Cardoun to three quarters of a length, the pair five lengths clear of Absurde, Tertian proved that he was already smart.

Tertian (USA) (b.c. Apr 30, 1989)	Danzig (USA) (b 1977)	Northern Dancer (b 1961)	Nearctic Natalma
		Pas de Nom (b or br 1968)	Admiral's Voyage Petitioner
	Tertiary (USA) (ch 1976)	Vaguely Noble (b 1965)	Vienna Noble Lassie
		Goofed (ch 1960)	Court Martial Barra II

Tertian's dam Tertiary, second over an extended mile and a quarter in France, has some illustrious relatives. Her sister Nobiliary won the Prix Saint-Alary and the Washington D. C. International as well as finishing runner-up to Grundy in the Derby, while her half-brother Lyphard, besides being high class on the racecourse, has also proved himself one of the most influential stallions of recent years. All of Tertiary's living offspring have been successful. Her first foal Primary (by Green Dancer) won the Tote-Ebor Handicap in 1986; the second Riverhead (by Riverman) was quite useful on the Flat and over hurdles; while the third Kefaah (by Blushing Groom) wasn't far behind the best three-year-olds of 1988 when his three wins included the Feilden Stakes and the Mecca Bookmakers' Classic; the fourth Ixtapa (by Chief's Crown), and so a close relation to Tertian, won over a mile and a half in France in the latest season. At the time of writing Tertian stands at around 20/1 in the ante-post market for the Two Thousand Guineas. At this point it's not easy to pinpoint his optimum distance. Tertiary's previous winners have all stayed at least a mile and a quarter, but with Danzig generally an influence for speed it shouldn't be taken for granted that Tertian will follow suit. The ground was on the fast side of good for his win at Newmarket. Despite the fact that he didn't stride out well to post he handled it well enough, and his performance in the mud at Maisons-Laffitte suggests that testing conditions don't trouble him at all. He has a high knee action, and also shows a tendency to splay his off-fore leg in his faster paces. *A. Fabre, France.*

TETRADONNA (IRE) 3 b.f. Teenoso (USA) 135 – Miss Bali Beach 88 **102** d (Nonoalco (USA) 131) [1990 7d3 1991 7m2 8g 10.5g6 10g4 10.4m3 10g] rangy filly: has a long stride: ¾-length second of 5 to Crystal Gazing in Shadwell Stud Nell Gwyn Stakes at Newmarket, one pace over 1f out then rallying: well beaten in 1000 Guineas at same course and only modest form at best afterwards: stays 1¼m: blinkered final start. *D. R. C. Elsworth.*

TEXAN CLAMOUR (FR) 3 b.g. Vacarme (USA) 121 – Texan Maid (FR) **66** (Targowice (USA) 130) [1990 7f2 7m 6m2 5.8h 6m2 6m 7f3 6m4 a7g4 a6g3 a8g* a8g a6g6 1991 a7g3 8g6 8g2 8f* 9m2 10g4 8m4 10.3d] small, rather unfurnished gelding: quite modest performer: won seller (bought in 4,600 gns) at Bath in August, leading close home: stays 9f: acts on firm going: blinkered last 2 starts at 2 yrs: sometimes bandaged behind: joined J. Moore. *R. Hannon.*

TEXAN TROOPER 2 b.c. (Jan 31) Tina's Pet 121 – Moorgreen 68 (Green God **37** 128) [1991 6.1g4 6g 8.2f 6f 7m] leggy colt: half-brother to 3 winners over sprint distances: dam placed over 5f: poor plater: blinkered final start: very mulish stalls and withdrawn 6 days later in October: wears bandages: sold 1,100 gns Doncaster November Sales. *Mrs N. Macauley.*

TEXAS SCRAMBLE 2 b.g. (Apr 26) Norwick (USA) 120 – Orange Parade (Dara **53** Monarch 128) [1991 7g2 7g4 7g a7g6 7.1m 10m] tall gelding: has scope: first foal: dam unraced: plating-class maiden: well beaten in sellers last 2 starts, facing stiff task first occasion, backward 6 weeks later: should be suited by further than 7f: sold 900 gns Ascot December Sales. *R. Simpson.*

THARIF 3 b.c. Green Desert (USA) 127 – Mrs Bacon 82 (Balliol 125) [1990 NR **—** 1991 7m3] sturdy, lengthy colt: fifth reported live foal: half-brother to smart sprinter Sizzling Melody (by Song), leading 1984/5 juvenile hurdler Beat The Retreat (by

Town And Country) and another winning hurdler: dam 2-y-o 5f winner didn't train on: in need of race, well beaten after slow start in 3-runner maiden at Redcar in August: sold to join C. Vernon Miller 600 gns Newmarket Autumn Sales. *A. C. Stewart.*

THARSIS 6 ch.g. What A Guest 119 – Grande Promesse (FR) (Sea Hawk II 131) — [1990 12.2d 14.6d 1991 16.2g⁶ 21.6f⁵ a14g] quite modest maiden as 3-y-o: lightly raced on flat and no form since: stays 2m: acts on firm going: usually blinkered at 3 yrs: winning hurdler in January: trained until after penultimate outing by W. Bentley. *R. J. Weaver.*

THATCHABLE 2 ch.f. (Mar 25) Thatching 131 – Crohane (Cracksman 111) [1991 a6g 7.5f] 6,800F, 6,000Y: small, lightly-made filly: half-sister to minor winners in France and Norway: dam from family of To-Agori-Mou: well beaten in claimer on debut. *M. W. Easterby.*

THATCH AND GOLD (IRE) 3 b.c. Thatching 131 – Tuck (Artaius (USA) 129) — [1990 6f 6f⁶ 1991 6m] small colt: has a poor, round action: well beaten in maidens and minor event. *J. Sutcliffe.*

THATCHENNE 6 b.m. Thatching 131 – Enterprisor (Artaius (USA) 129) [1990 53 8m 7g⁶ a6g 6m 1991 6m* 7m 6g² 8.2d 6g* 6g 5.7m⁴ 7m⁵ 6.1m 10.3d] leggy, lengthy mare: plating-class handicapper: made all at Nottingham in May and July: off course nearly 3 months after eighth start and then well beaten: ideally suited by 6f to 7f: acts on firm going: blinkered or visored: often wanders. *M. W. Eckley.*

THATCHER'S DILEMMA 4 b.c. Final Straw 127 – Crane Beach (High Top — 131) [1990 a7g 11.7m 10s 10d⁴ a13g 1991 a10g] workmanlike colt: poor form at best: stays 1¼m: acts on dead ground: sold 1,350 gns Ascot April Sales. *D. W. P. Arbuthnot.*

THAT'LL BE THE DAY (IRE) 2 br.f. (Apr 26) Thatching 131 – Maiden 68 Concert (Condorcet (FR)) [1991 5m* 5g³ 6g³ 6g⁴ 7.5s] IR 42,000Y: leggy, close-coupled filly: fourth foal: half-sister to 3-y-o 1½m winner Green's Van Goyen (by Lyphard's Special) and very smart 5f (at 2 yrs) to 9f winner Candy Glen (by Glenstal): dam once-raced half-sister to dam of Irish 1000 Guineas winner More So: well-backed favourite, won maiden at Newmarket (moved fluently down) in April, leading over 1f out, hanging right then running on well: subsequently in frame in listed races in Italy: last of 7 in similar event there final start: should stay 1m: trained debut only by R. Hannon. *V. Valiani, Italy.*

THAT'S THE ONE 5 br.g. Known Fact (USA) 135 – Kesarini (USA) 87 (Singh 89 (USA)) [1990 6m 6m² 6d 7m² 7m a7g⁴ 6g³ 8m⁴ 6d⁶ 7m 6g 6s⁵ 1991 a7g* 8d] sturdy, close-coupled gelding: moderate walker: poor mover: fairly useful handicapper: won at Southwell: not seen again after below form later in March: best form at 6f and 7f: acts on good to firm and soft going: too free when blinkered: has hung markedly on occasions: consistent. *J. Etherington.*

THE ALIEN (IRE) 3 b.c. Thatching 131 – Anna Carla (GER) (Windwurf (GER)) 66 [1990 NR 1991 1d 10m 11.6m⁵ 12f 16m⁷ 16m⁹ a10g] IR 50,000Y: sturdy colt: second foal: half-brother to lightly-raced 1989 2-y-o 5f winner Priority Paid (by Try My Best): dam won in Germany: quite modest maiden: placed in handicaps at Redcar and Lingfield in October: clearly suited by test of stamina: blinkered (well beaten) final outing: bandaged behind second to fourth starts. *W. Carter.*

THE AUCTION BIDDER 4 b.c. Auction Ring (USA) 123 – Stepping Gaily 79 97 (Gay Fandango (USA) 132) [1990 6f³ 5s* 5d 6s³ 1991 6d⁵ 6g² 7g 6m³ 6m 6m⁶ 6m⁴ 6g 7m 7s] robust, sprint type: carries condition: good walker and mover: quite useful performer: ran well when sixth to Polish Patriot in Cork And Orrery Stakes at Royal Ascot and fourth to Amigo Menor in Group 3 event at Leopardstown: well below best in Group 3 event at Doncaster and listed event at Leopardstown final 2 starts: stays 6f: acts on good to firm and soft going: has hung right. *R. Hollinshead.*

THE BART-MAN 2 b.g. (Apr 6) Myjinski (USA) – Relampego 37 (Monsanto — (FR) 121) [1991 5.2g 6g] close-coupled, angular gelding: first foal: dam probably of little account: green, well beaten in Yarmouth sellers in mid-summer. *E. Eldin.*

THE BLUE BOY (IRE) 3 ch.g. Tate Gallery (USA) 117 – Blue Lookout (Cure 76 The Blues (USA)) [1990 7m 7g 7m 7m³ 1991 8g 10g⁴ 12m⁵ 10g* 11.9m] lengthy gelding, rather unfurnished: modest form on Flat: won claimer (claimed out of J. Dunlop's stable £15,502) at Goodwood in June, tending to wander: stays 1½m: acts on good to firm ground: prolific winning hurdler. *M. C. Pipe.*

THE BOOZY NEWS (USA) 3 ch.f. L'Emigrant (USA) 129 – Zitherplay (USA) 44 (Graustark) [1990 NR 1991 11.7g 10d 10f 9.9f² 10.1m 10.8m⁵ 14.1m a10g] rather unfurnished filly: bad walker: sister to French 7f (at 2 yrs) and 10.5f winner Ark

Ange and half-sister to 2 winners, including Irish 1¼m winner Haunting Harmony (by Nureyev): dam maiden winner at about 1m in USA: plater: best effort second of 19 in handicap at Beverley, staying on from towards rear despite flashing tail: stays 1¼m: blinkered twice: has found little: not one to be too interested in. *W. R. Muir.*

THE BRECKLANDER 3 b.g. Son of Shaka 119 – Clatter 67 (Songedor 116) — [1990 NR 1991 12s] sixth living foal: half-brother to 9f and 1¼m winner Breckland Lady (by Royalty) and 5f winner Burglar Tip (by Burglar): dam placed over 5f at 2 yrs: tailed off in maiden at Folkestone in November. *P. Howling.*

THE CAN CAN MAN 4 b.c. Daring March 116 – Dawn Ditty 100 (Song 132) **81** [1990 8g* 8.2g5 8f* 8f* 8g² 8d 8d 7d* 7d 1991 6s³ 7m* 8m6 7g* 7.6m 8g 7m 8g 7.1m³ 7m² 8f³ 7d 7g 7d] big, rangy colt: turns fore-feet in: fair handicapper: won at Thirsk (drifted markedly right) and Goodwood (set modest pace) in May: inconsistent after: best efforts at 7f and 1m: probably acts on any going: takes keen hold, and best allowed to stride on: has proved awkward at stalls, refusing to enter them once. *M. Johnston.*

THE CUCKOO'S NEST 3 b.c. Precocious 126 – Troy Moon (Troy 137) [1990 **74** 8g 7d³ 1991 a8g 7s* 8g4 7m6 7g 7.2m³ 7m² 7g³ 7g 7g³ 8m 7.6m6] close-coupled colt: modest handicapper: won maiden at Leicester in March: below form last 2 starts and persistently edged left on final one: stays 1m: acts on good to firm ground and soft: wore eyeshield on reappearance: headstrong for 7-lb claimer: has run well when sweating and on toes tenth: ridden up with pace. *C. E. Brittain.*

THE DANDY DON (IRE) 2 ch.g. (Mar 31) On Your Mark 125 – Balacco 70 — (Balidar 133) [1991 5m 6m6] IR 5,800F, IR 4,000Y, 2,500 2-y-o: quite attractive gelding: half-brother to 5f (at 2 yrs) and 8.2f winner Ben Ledi (by Strong Gale), later successful over jumps, and to 2 winners abroad: dam 1¼m winner: little worthwhile form in North in spring. *Denys Smith.*

THE DAWN TRADER (USA) 3 b.f. Naskra (USA) – Dream Play (USA) **70** (Blushing Groom (FR) 131) [1990 6m³ 5m³ 1991 8m² 8f 8g6 7f*dis 7m* 8m5 7f6] rather sparely-made filly: modest performer: first past post in smallish fields for maidens at Thirsk (returning to form but causing interference) and Brighton (comfortably) in summer: stays 1m: acts on firm going: sometimes hangs: sold 9,000 gns Newmarket December Sales. *M. A. Jarvis.*

THE DEVIL'S MUSIC 7 ch.g. Music Boy 124 – Obergurgl 69 (Warpath 113) **47** [1990 5g 5g 7m* 7g6 6f6 6g 6g 7f5 5g 6s 7d² a7g6 a7g5 a7g 1991 6d 6m6 6m 6m 5.9m² 6g4 6g³ 6m6 7m² 7m] robust gelding: carries plenty of condition: turns fore-feet out: shows a quick action: poor handicapper nowadays: stays 7f: not at his best on soft going, acts on any other: has worn blinkers and visor (almost bolted to post and tailed off). *Mrs J. R. Ramsden.*

THE DOMINANT GENE 2 gr.c. (Apr 9) Dominion 123 – Judy's Dowry 80 — (Dragonara Palace (USA) 115) [1991 5d 5g 5g 5g] leggy colt: has a round action: first reported foal: dam 2-y-o 5f winner later won sellers at 1m and 8.2f: no worthwhile form in spring sellers. *J. Wharton.*

THE DREAM MAKER (IRE) 2 b.f. (Mar 18) Cyrano de Bergerac 120 – **40** Bermuda Princess (Lord Gayle (USA) 124) [1991 5m5 5h5 6m5 6m 7.5f] 1,000Y: plain, angular filly: fourth foal: dam Irish maiden: poor form in varied events, including seller: stiff tasks last 2 starts: stays 6f. *Ronald Thompson.*

THE FELTMAKER (IRE) 3 b.c. Shernazar 131 – Miss Siddons (Cure The **85** Blues (USA)) [1990 7m5 1991 10m* 12m6 10d 10m4 11.8m5] small, quite attractive colt: moderate walker, poor mover: fair form: won maiden at Sandown in August: staying-on fourth of 20 in apprentice race at Newmarket, clearly best effort in handicaps last 3 starts: stays 1¼m well: below form on dead ground: sold 14,500 gns Newmarket Autumn Sales. *J. L. Dunlop.*

THE FIVE SISTERS 3 gr.f. Belfort (FR) 89 – La Bleu 67 (Blue Cashmere 129) — [1990 NR 1991 6m] 2,000Y: lengthy, sparely-made filly: first foal: dam won 9f and 1¼m sellers: moved poorly down and no promise in Salisbury maiden in May. *Mrs Barbara Waring.*

THE GLASHA (IRE) 3 ch.c. Jalmood (USA) 126 – Blessed Persian (Persian **106** Bold 123) [1990 NR 1991 9s* 10.1m² 12f6 10d² 10d² 8.1d4] well-made colt: has a long stride: good walker: third foal: dam Irish 7f and 1¼m winner: won maiden at Lingfield in June: good second in quite valuable Ascot handicaps fourth (to Vikron Venture) and fifth (to Red Bishop) starts: favourite and looking very well, ran moderately in minor event on final one: should stay 1½m: seems best on an easy surface (ran as if something amiss third start): useful. *R. Charlton.*

THE GOOFER 4 b.g. Be My Native (USA) 122 – Siliferous (Sandy Creek 123) **70**
[1990 8.2s⁴ 10v⁴ 11g⁵ 9m 10.6d* 11d² 10.6v² 10.4v* 9g⁵ 1991 12.2d⁵ 10s⁶ 12.3d⁴ 12m
11.5s⁴ 12.3g⁵] tall gelding: has a round action: modest handicapper: not seen out
after July: effective at 1¼m to 1½m: very well suited by a soft surface. *A. P. Stringer.*

THE GREEN BOYS (USA) 2 b.c. (Feb 23) Clever Trick (USA) – Indian **81**
Romance (USA) (Raja Baba (USA)) [1991 6d² 7d³ 6m⁵ 6m⁵ 7m* 8g 7g⁶] 135,000Y:
smallish, workmanlike colt: second foal: dam, successful 8 times at up to 1m, is
half-sister to Optimistic Lass, dam of Golden Opinion: sire sprinter/miler: fair
performer: off course 2 months, won nursery at Goodwood in September, coming
through strongly from rear and keeping on really well: should stay 1m: acts on good
to firm ground: sold 14,500 gns Newmarket Autumn Sales. *R. Akehurst.*

THE GREEN GIRLS (USA) 2 b.f. (Apr 5) Distinctive Pro (USA) – Instru- **39**
ment Board (USA) (Instrument Landing (USA)) [1991 6g² 6m] $11,500Y: leggy filly:
first reported foal: dam showed a little ability in USA: sire won from 6f to 7f and
placed in Grade 2 event at 8.5f: ran in sellers at Lingfield (outpaced at halfway then
stayed on well) and Warwick (hampered turn, weakened quickly) in spring: should
stay 1m. *R. Akehurst.*

THE HUYTON LADY 3 ch.f. Brotherly (USA) 80 – The Huyton Girls 67 —
(Master Sing 109) [1990 NR 1991 7.1m 5g 5d] stocky filly: second reported living
foal: dam winning sprinter: last in maiden and claimers: bandaged behind on debut.
M. B. James.

THE JOLLYFRENCHMAN 3 br.g. Macmillion 110 – Willington House —
(Comedy Star (USA) 121) [1990 7m 6d² 6g³ 1991 7.6m 8m 10g] rangy gelding:
modest maiden at 2 yrs: showed nothing in autumn as 3-y-o: should stay 1m: acts
well on dead ground: visored final outing. *Mrs Barbara Waring.*

THE KARAOKE KING 2 b.c. (Mar 19) Sayf El Arab (USA) 127 – Lady **66 p**
Warninglid (Ela-Mana-Mou 132) [1991 7g 7m 8g⁵ 8.9m²] 4,600F: sturdy colt:
moderate walker: good mover: second foal: half-brother to 3-y-o Pleasant Times (by
Absalom): dam, unraced, from family of Rock City and Kerrera: progressive maiden:
length second of 18 to First Right in claimer at York in October: stays 9f: can win a
similar event. *R. Hannon.*

THE LAST EMPRESS (IRE) 3 b.f. Last Tycoon 131 – Beijing (USA) 89 **73**
(Northjet 136) [1990 7m 8.2m⁶ 7m 1991 13.1f 11m³ 14.6g³ 16.2g²* 16m* 16.2f⁵
17.2g⁴] workmanlike filly: moderate walker and mover: modest handicapper: won at
Chepstow and Lingfield in summer: stays 17f: acts on good to firm going. *P. F. I.
Cole.*

THE LAST WASHER (IRE) 2 b.c. (Apr 30) Mazaad 106 – Gigo Jive (Jukebox **40**
120) [1991 7m⁶ 7g 7m 8m] IR 3,600F, 3,000Y: deep-bodied colt: carries condition:
half-brother to a winner in Norway by Cajun: dam never ran: poor plater: stays 7f. *M.
H. Tompkins.*

THE LIGHTER SIDE 5 br.g. Comedy Star (USA) 121 – Moberry 54 (Moss- —
berry 97) [1990 10.2f² 12.5m 8m 12h 11.7m 1991 16.0m] neat, good-bodied gelding:
poor maiden: stays 1¼m: acts on firm going. *B. Preece.*

THE LIQUIDISER 4 ch.g. Connaught 130 – Frivolity 70 (Varano) [1990 12.5g⁴ —
12s* 11m* 14m² 1991 12s⁶ 10d 12.5d] quite good-topped gelding: brother to 2
winners, each over 1½m or more: dam 2m winner, is half-sister to Irish 1000
Guineas and Irish St Leger winner Pidget: fairly useful ex-Irish performer, won
minor events at Tipperary and Killarney as 3-y-o: no form here: not seen out after
April: stays 1¾m: acts on good to firm and soft ground: formerly trained by L.
Browne. *R. Hollinshead.*

THEMAAM 2 b.c. (Mar 21) Night Shift (USA) – Polly's Pear (USA) (Sassafras **70 p**
(FR) 135) [1991 7m 7g³] 10,500F, 66,000Y: useful-looking colt: second foal:
half-brother to 3-y-o Poire du Nord (by Legend of France): dam never ran: easily
better effort in maidens when 4 lengths third of 14 to Autocracy at Salisbury in
October, keeping on well once headed over 2f out: will stay 1m: likely to improve
again. *T. Thomson Jones.*

THE MAGUE 7 br.g. Bold Owl 101 – Silvery Moon (Lorenzaccio 130) [1990 10f **62**
10s 10.8m³ 10m 10.8g#* 10m* 10m 10.2f³ 10f⁶ 10.2m 12g 12f⁴ 13.8f⁵ 1991 10.6g#* 9d³
10.8g 10m⁶] neat gelding: quite modest handicapper: won at Haydock (amateurs) in
June: best at up to 1½m: acts on firm and dead going: often blinkered (also tried in
hood): has found little in front: has won 5 times at Warwick: inconsistent: winning
hurdler: has joined J. Roberts. *R. F. Johnson Houghton.*

THE MARSHALLS LADY (IRE) 3 b.f. Kafu 120 – Miss Redmarshall 80 —
(Most Secret 119) [1990 5m⁴ 5f³ 5f⁴ 6m³ 6m² 1991 6m 7g 6.1m 6g] small,

unfurnished filly: quite modest form at 2 yrs, little in handicaps in 1991: much better at 6f than 5f: bandaged near-hind last 2 starts: sold 3,200 gns Newmarket Autumn Sales. *C. F. Wall.*

THE METROPOLE (IRE) 2 ch.c. (Apr 7) Where To Dance (USA) – Mother 54 Flutter 62 (Gulf Pearl 117) [1991 5s6 6d4 7m2 7f5 8.3g 7m 7g] IR 4,600F, IR 6,400Y: neat colt: half-brother to 1984 2-y-o 5f winner Silent Flutter (by Auction Ring): dam sprint maiden: sire (by Northern Dancer) unraced half-brother to dams of Warning and Rainbow Quest: fair plater: ran poorly last 3 starts, facing stiffish task final one: should stay 1m: blinkered penultimate outing: sold 1,700 gns Doncaster November Sales. *J. H. Johnson.*

THE MINDER (FR) 4 b. or br.g. Miller's Mate 116 – Clarandal 80 (Young 44 d Generation 129) [1990 a10g4 a11g3 1991 a10g5 10f5 12f5 11.5m3 11.5g 12m 9.7m 8f 10f a7g 10.8g a8g] rather leggy gelding: has round action: plating-class performer at best: lost his form: stays 1½m: bought out of Lord Huntingdon's stable 4,500 gns Ascot May Sales. *D. A. Wilson.*

THE NASH 4 ch.c. Joshua 129 – Dawn Affair 77 (Entanglement 118) [1990 NR — 1991 14m 12.2g 11f6] big, workmanlike colt: has round action: sixth living foal: dam maiden: no sign of ability. *J. Mulhall.*

THE NEW GIRL 2 b.f. (Feb 9) Primo Dominie 121 – Try The Duchess 99 (Try 66 My Best (USA) 130) [1991 5.1m 5m5 5d2 5f2 6m 5.7g3] 8,800Y: workmanlike filly: first foal: dam 2-y-o 6f winner: quite modest maiden: good third of 10 in Bath nursery in October: will stay 6f: acts on firm and dead ground. *C. C. Elsey.*

THE NOBLE OAK (IRE) 3 ch.g. The Noble Player (USA) 126 – Sea Palace 45 (Huntercombe 133) [1990 7m 7d 1991 11.7g 12m 10.6g 10.2d 7d 6m* 6m* 5.7m6] small, close-coupled gelding: successful in apprentice selling handicap (bought in 3,200 gns) and handicap (making all for 7-lb claimer) at Windsor in July: stiff task later in month: should prove as effective at 5f: acts on good to firm going: blinkered last 4 starts. *M. McCormack.*

THE OIL BARON 5 gr.g. Absalom 128 – Ruby's Chance 71 (Charlottesville 135) — [1990 a10g 12f4 10m6 10.1m3 12f6 10d2 1991 10v 12m] leggy gelding: poor handicapper, still a maiden: stays 1½m well: acts on hard and dead going. *R. P. C. Hoad.*

THE OLD CHAPEL 2 b.c. (May 10) Lomond (USA) 128 – Chapel Cottage 117 56 (Homing 130) [1991 6g 6d 6d6] 7,400Y: well-grown, quite good-topped colt: third reported foal: dam genuine sprinter: plating-class poor maiden: will probably stay 7f. *B. A. McMahon.*

THE OLD FIRM (IRE) 3 ch.c. Hatim (USA) 121 – North Hut (Northfields 92 (USA)) [1990 6d5 5m* 5d 5d* 5m4 6f3 1991 6f3 6m 7.2g4] small, lengthy colt: moderate mover: fairly useful performer: ran creditably in frame for minor event at Folkestone and listed race (keeping on gamely) at Haydock: stays 7f: acts on firm and dead going: sold 17,000 gns Newmarket July Sales, reportedly to race in Scandinavia. *N. A. Callaghan.*

THE PERFECT LIFE (IRE) 3 b.f. Try My Best (USA) 130 – Mill Princess 106 (Mill Reef (USA) 141) [1990 6d2 5g* 5.5g3 6d 1991 7g* 8d6 6.5g] sister to top-class sprinter/miler Last Tycoon, closely related to very useful sprinter Astronef and French 6f and 6.5f winner Love Boat (both by Be My Guest) and half-sister to 1988 French 2-y-o 6.5f winner Save Me The Waltz (by Kings Lake): dam French 1¼m winner, is half-sister to Irish Derby winner Irish Ball and to dam of Assert, Bikala and Eurobird: successful in Prix du Bois at Longchamp at 2 yrs and in slowly-run Prix Imprudence (making virtually all and rallying well to beat Divine Danse a short head) at Maisons-Laffitte in April at 3 yrs: not disgraced in Poule d'Essai des Pouliches at Longchamp and Prix Maurice de Gheest at Deauville: stays 7f: has been bought by Sheikh Hamdan Al-Maktoum, and visits Nashwan. *R. Collet, France.*

THE POWER OF ONE 2 b.c. (Apr 5) Bellypha 130 – Biding 97 (Habat 127) 70 p [1991 7g 6.9f3] 11,000F: strong, workmanlike colt: sixth living foal: half-brother to 3-y-o filly (by Green Desert) and to a winner in Italy by Wassl: dam, half-sister to very smart Splashing (dam of Bassenthwaite) won 2 of her 3 races over 5f at 2 yrs: better effort in maidens when 2½ lengths third of 12 to Vying Victor at Folkestone (moved moderately down) in October, driven along entering straight then keeping on: should stay 1m: can improve again. *R. Simpson.*

THE PRINCESS OF SPEED 3 b.f. Bay Express 132 – La Jeunesse (Young — Generation 129) [1990 5g4 7g 1991 a8g a6g6] quite modest plater at 2 yrs: tailed off in maidens early in 1991. *R. Thompson.*

THE PRODIGAL 4 b.g. Aragon 118 – Patois (I Say 125) [1990 8m 9m 12m 10m 10g 9g⁴ 10f 1991 10.2s] rangy gelding: has been tubed: modest maiden at 2 yrs, only poor nowadays: stays 9f: possibly needs an easy surface. *P. J. Feilden.* —

THE PRUSSIAN (USA) 5 b.h. Danzig (USA) – Miss Secretariat (USA) (Secretariat (USA)) [1990 10f² 12f³ 10m 1991 10g⁴] compact, rather angular horse: moderate mover: useful handicapper in 1990: bandaged, moderate fourth of 6 to Spritsail in listed event at Goodwood only run in 1991 (May): better suited by 1½m than 1¼m: acts well on firm going. *J. Pearce.* —

THE RIGHT TIME 6 b.g. King of Spain 121 – Noddy Time 97 (Gratitude 130) [1990 7f 5s³ 6f 6f³ 6g 7f⁴ 6m⁴ 6g⁵ 5m³ 6g 5d² 5s 1991 6g 5g⁴ 6m⁵ 6f³ 6g 6d⁵ 6m⁶ 5g² 5f⁵ 6m 5f² a5g 5f* 5f 5f² 5g 6m 5m⁶ 5s] robust gelding: plating-class handicapper: won at Ripon in August: seems ideally suited by 5f: has form on any going but clearly well suited by firm ground nowadays: visored debut, usually blinkered. *J. Parkes.* **61**

THE SHANAHAN BAY 6 b.h. Hays 120 – Tanala Bay (Sterling Bay (SWE)) [1990 a6g* a6g⁶ a5g* a5g⁶ a6g⁵ 5m 5f² a5g 5m³ 5g a5g⁶ a6g 5.1m² 5d* 5g* 1991 5d 5g 5g⁴ 5m 5g a5g⁵ 5m⁵ 5g 5d 5g⁶ a6g a7g³ a8g a6g² a6g] angular horse: poor walker: quite modest handicapper: returned to form late in year: effective at 5f to 7f: acts on any going: usually wears blinkers, has run well when visored: tends to carry head high: goes well with forcing tactics: trained first 11 outings by E. Eldin. *Mrs N. Macauley.* **64**

THE SILENT BIDDER (IRE) 2 b.f. (Mar 11) Auction Ring (USA) 123 – Annais Nin (Dominion 123) [1991 5m⁵] IR 4,000Y: rather leggy filly: has scope: third foal: half-sister to Irish 1m winner/successful hurdler Winston Murphy (by Don): dam unraced: 25/1 and backward, last but one in maiden at York in May. *R. Hollinshead.* —

THE SINGING MAN 5 b.h. Mansingh (USA) 120 – Opalescent 71 (Gulf Pearl 117) [1990 6m 6d 5d 5g⁶ 5m* 5m 5d⁴ 5s 1991 6d 5g 5g 5s³ 5.1m⁶ 5g 5m 5s] lengthy, good-quartered horse: carries condition: poor handicapper: best at 5f: acts on good to firm and soft going: inconsistent: sold 3,400 gns Doncaster November Sales. *J. Balding.* **29**

THETFORD FOREST 4 b.g. Blakeney 126 – Leylandia 69 (Wolver Hollow 126) [1990 10g⁵ 10g* 13g* 12m² 14f* 14g 1991 10g⁴ 16m⁶ 14g³ 14g] well-made, attractive Irish gelding: useful performer: best effort in 1991 when 7 lengths third to Hateel in listed event at the Curragh in June: faded from under 2f out when sixth of 7 in Henry II Stakes at Sandown: suited by 1¾m: probably acts on any going: usually blinkered: usually makes running: has joined D. Nicholson (winning hurdler). *J. Oxx, Ireland.* **106**

THE TITAN GHOST 2 ch.c. (Mar 4) Nicholas Bill 125 – Holloway Wonder 93 (Swing Easy (USA) 126) [1991 7d] big, rangy colt: third foal: half-brother to quite modest 3-y-o 5f winner Rock Breaker (by Green Ruby) and 1989 2-y-o 5f winner Stoneythorpewonder (by Smackover): dam effective at 5f and stayed 1m: 33/1, backward and green, never a threat in 21-runner maiden at Doncaster in November. *B. A. McMahon.* —

THEWAARI (USA) 2 b.f. (Feb 16) Eskimo (USA) – Flying Jester (USA) (Winged T) [1991 6g³ 6d 6.1d] $32,000Y: good-topped filly: has plenty of scope: half-sister to several winners in North America, one in minor stakes: dam, maiden, showed a little ability: plating-class maiden: backward, over 7 lengths third of 5 to Misterioso in Blue Seal Stakes at Ascot: failed to progress at Haydock (favourite, mid-division in large field) and Chester (visored) later in autumn: possibly unsuited by dead ground. *A. A. Scott.* **54**

THE WADKIN 3 b.g. Creetown 123 – Thinkluckybelucky (Maystreak 118) [1990 6g 7d 1991 7.5g 7.5f⁴ 8m 8g 8g⁴] leggy gelding: plater: should have been well suited by further than 1m: seemed to act on firm going: dead. *A. Smith.* **38**

THE WOODEN HUT 8 ch.g. Windjammer (USA) – Bunduq 67 (Scottish Rifle 127) [1990 NR 1991 a12g 12f 14m 11.5g a12g 12d] tall, lengthy gelding: poor mover: poor handicapper nowadays: often bandaged: has been tried blinkered. *R. Voorspuy.* —

THE YELLOW VEST 3 b.g. Superlative 118 – Foolish Things (Song 132) [1990 NR 1991 7d 8.5f³ 8m 7g] sturdy gelding: first foal: dam unraced: poor maiden, not seen out after June: better at 8.5f than shorter. *Mrs J. R. Ramsden.* **45**

THE YOMPER (FR) 9 ch.g. Arctic Tern (USA) 126 – Grundylee (FR) (Grundy 137) [1990 11.7g⁵ 1991 10.1g 11.5m 13.8f³ 11.5g 12v] sturdy gelding: poor and lightly-raced handicapper nowadays: stays 13.8f: acts on firm ground, and goes well on an easy surface: suited by forcing tactics: has won for amateur. *R. Curtis.* —

THIBAAIN (USA) 3 b.c. El Gran Senor (USA) 136 – Catherine's Bet (USA) 78
(Grey Dawn II 132) [1990 8g² 8m⁶ 1991 8f⁵ 8m 8g 12f² 14m² 14g* 16.2d⁵ 14m⁶]
lengthy colt: moderate mover: fair performer: won handicap at Haydock in
September: fair fifth of 16 at same course, weakening final 1f but clearly best effort
in similar events following month: suited by 1¾m: acts on firm ground: takes keen
hold: sold to join J. White 20,000 gns Newmarket Autumn Sales. *H. Thomson Jones.*

THIMBALINA 5 ch.m. Salmon Leap (USA) 131 – Maestrette 77 (Manado 130) 62
[1990 10.2f⁵ 11s³ 11g* 12f³ 10d⁵ 12d* 12g³ 10g* 11.5m* 12d² 12m³ 12d⁴ 10.6s 1991
12s 12d⁴ 12f* 12f² 12g⁵ 12.2f⁴ 12m² 12f³ 11.8m 16.2f⁵ 10.5g] leggy, lightly-made
mare: moderate walker: quite modest handicapper: won at Beverley (for third time)
in May: stays 1½m: unsuited by very soft ground, acts on any other: apprentice
ridden: often on toes: races keenly: has edged badly right: goes well on stiff track:
sold 4,400 gns Newmarket December Sales. *S. G. Norton.*

THINKING TWICE (USA) 2 ch.c. (Apr 7) Kris 135 – Good Thinking (USA) 63
(Raja Baba (USA)) [1991 6d⁶ 6f] strong, compact colt: fourth foal: half-brother to a
winner in North America: dam Irish 2-y-o 7f winner, is half-sister to Treizieme:
quite modest form in maidens at Goodwood (edged right) and Folkestone (bit
coltish, better effort) in October: bred to stay 1m. *P. W. Harris.*

THIN RED LINE 7 b. or br.g. Brigadier Gerard 144 – Golden Keep 77 (Worden 58
II 129) [1990 a12g⁴ a8g⁴ a10g⁶ 10f⁶ 10f³ 10.8m 10.1g 11.7m⁵ 10h² 11.5f² 10h* 10h²
12f² 10m⁵ 12f⁴ 10f* 1991 10f⁴ 12d⁴ 10m 12f 10.1g³ 11.5m⁴ 12g⁴ 10g³ 10m³ 10f² 10.1f³
10f⁶ 10g⁶ 10.1s² 10.3d] leggy gelding: quite modest handicapper: easily best effort in
claimer on penultimate outing: effective at 1¼m to 1½m: acts on any going: usually
visored: often sweating and edgy: best held up: goes particularly well on switchback
track. *J. R. Jenkins.*

THIRD WATCH 3 b.f. Slip Anchor 136 – Triple First 117 (High Top 131) [1990 114
7m* 8m 1991 10g⁶ 12g* 12m 11.9g⁴ 12m 10m³ 12d⁴] deep-girthed, attractive filly:
good mover: 20/1, won Ribblesdale Stakes at Royal Ascot by 7 lengths from Finance
Dancer, running on strongly from rear having carried head high: ran poorly in Irish
Oaks next start, then creditably in Yorkshire Oaks, Prix Vermeille at Longchamp
and Sun Chariot Stakes (moderately-run race, kept on strongly) at Newmarket: ran

Ribblesdale Stakes, Royal Ascot—20/1-shot Third Watch
runs away with this Group 2 event; Finance Dancer (hoops) wins the race for second
with Sought Out (pale colours) and Gai Bulga

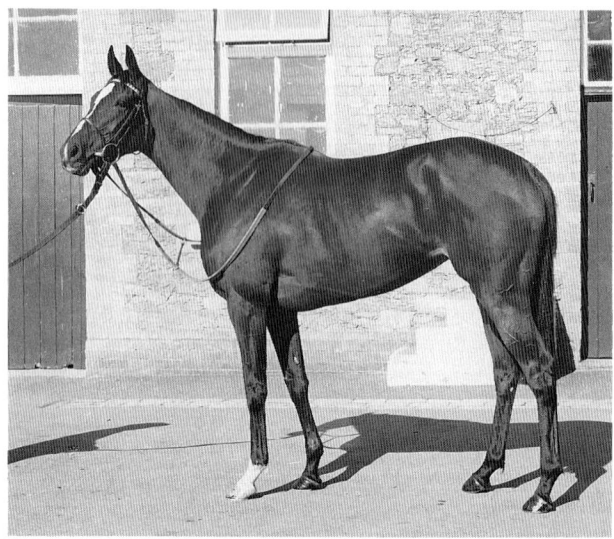

Mr P. G. Goulandris' "Third Watch"

moderately in Princess Royal Stakes at Ascot (raced too freely early on) final start: stays 1½m well: takes keen hold. *J. L. Dunlop.*

THIRKLEBY (IRE)   2 b.g. (May 23) Double Schwartz 128 – Kylemore Abbey — (Junius (USA) 124) [1991 5m 5f⁶ 7m] IR 2,800F, IR 3,600Y, resold 2,300Y. sparely-made gelding: third foal: dam unraced: soundly beaten in seller final start: visored (looked difficult ride) on debut. *J. Hetherton.*

THIRTY FIRST   6 gr.g. Castle Keep 121 – January (FR) (Sigebert 131) [1990 14m — § 14.8m⁴ 12.2g⁵ 16.2f⁴ 17m⁶ 1991 14.6g] lengthy, angular gelding: has a quick action: fairly useful winner as 3-y-o, but has little enthusiasm nowadays: suited by test of stamina: acts on firm going, probably unsuited by soft: tried blinkered once: not genuine. *R. E. Peacock.*

THISTLE GRAND   2 br.c. (Feb 22) Belfort (FR) 89 – Bacchantina (Gulf Pearl — 117) [1991 5d⁴ 5d] 5,200Y, 8,600 2-y-o: smallish colt: moderate walker: seventh foal: brother to 3-y-o Belltina: dam poor plater: soundly beaten in Scottish claimers in April: sold 1,000 gns Doncaster October Sales. *J. S. Wilson.*

THOMAS LENG   6 ch.h. Homing 130 – Fast Asleep (Hotfoot 126) [1990 8.2s   69 10v* 1991 a11g⁵ 10.2s 9g 10.2s⁴ 10d* 10g* 10.4d⁴ 12.3d² 12g 12.4m³ 12.3g³ 11.8g⁶ 13g² 12.1m⁵ 10.9m⁶] leggy, rather sparely-made horse: moderate mover: modest handicapper, one-time unreliable: won at Ayr (apprentices) and Leicester in April: effective at 1¼m to 13f: acts on good to firm ground, but goes particularly well with give in the ground: has worn blinkers and visor: has been bandaged behind. *M. Brittain.*

THOMPSON FLYER   4 b.g. Swing Easy (USA) 126 – Off The Mark (On Your — Mark 125) [1990 7g⁶ 10.1g 10.1m 1991 10m 10s 10g] rangy gelding: has scope: no promise, in handicaps in first half of 1991: sold 2,000 gns Ascot September Sales, resold 1,350 gns Ascot October Sales. *R. V. Smyth.*

THORESBY 4 ch.g. Thatching 131 – Nana's Queen 86 (Ridan (USA)) [1990 8m 8m 6s a8g a8g 1991 6m 6f] workmanlike gelding: poor maiden: best form at 6f: tried visored and blinkered: dead. *J. Norton.* —

THORNBERRY (USA) 3 b.c. Diesis 133 – Oxslip 106 (Owen Dudley 121) [1990 7s² 1991 8d* 8s* 8g* 11g² 10d⁵] fifth foal: brother to quite useful 1¼m and 1¾m winner Sixslip and half-brother to two 1¼m winners by Our Native: dam 7f to 13f winner, is half-sister to very useful stayer Kambalda: successful in maiden at Gowran Park, minor event at Navan and listed race at Leopardstown (by ½ length from Star of Gdansk): subsequently off course 4 months, below best when second to Judicial in listed race at Galway in September: virtually pulled up final outing: best form at 1m. *J. Oxx, Ireland.* 110

THORNFIELD BOY 5 b.g. Homeboy 114 – Pink Blues 103 (Tickled Pink 114) [1990 NR 1991 6g 6g 6m] workmanlike, good-bodied gelding: carries condition: useful handicapper at 3 yrs: shaped as if still retains ability first 2 starts, well beaten (prominent over 4f) in Wokingham Stakes at Royal Ascot final one: stays 6f: probably acts on any going. *R. Akehurst.* —

THORN GODDESS (IRE) 3 br.f. Godswalk (USA) 130 – La Tante (Bold Lad (IRE) 133) [1990 5m 1991 6.9m 5f⁶ 7f 6f 8m 5g] smallish, workmanlike filly: plating-class maiden: showed little last 4 starts: should stay 6f: trained first 5 starts by M. Ellerby: sold 620 gns Doncaster October Sales. *B. S. Rothwell.* —

THORNTON GATE 2 b.g. (Apr 17) Hallgate 127 – Lola Black (FR) (Relkino 131) [1991 5m² 5m 5m 7f* 7m⁵ 6g⁵ 8m⁶ 7m] 3,200Y: leggy gelding: moderate mover: second living foal: dam French 1¼m winner from family of Dominion and Prominent: quite modest performer: off course over 10 weeks, 14/1-winner of 9-runner maiden auction at Thirsk in August, racing keenly then staying on well: below that form subsequently, including in York seller: suited by 7f: ran poorly in blinkers third outing: usually pulls quite hard. *M. H. Easterby.* 64

THORNY FLAT (IRE) 3 b.c. Precocious 126 – Top Bloom (Thatch (USA) 136) [1990 5g² 5d* 5g³ 5f⁴ 5f⁴ 5f⁶ 5m 6v 1991 6g 6m 6d 6m a6g 7m⁶ 10f] small, compact colt: carries condition: moderate mover: plater: well below form in 1991: should stay 6f: seems unsuited by heavy ground: visored final start: blinkered 4 times: has been bandaged behind: very coltish fifth start. *W. J. Pearce.* —

THOR POWER (IRE) 2 b.c. (Feb 1) Auction Ring (USA) 123 – Kitty's Sister (Bustino 136) [1991 7g⁴ 6s 6d a7g⁶ a7g a8g] 11,500Y: lengthy, angular colt: fourth foal: half-brother to 3-y-o 7f handicapper Morgannwg and fairly useful 1989 Irish 2-y-o Mistral's Collette (both by Simply Great), latter successful in 9f listed event in Italy: dam, sister to Lowther winner Kittyhawk (dam of Nomadic Way), very useful at up to 1m: plating-class form in maidens: seems to stay 1m: acts on all-weather surfaces. *D. T. Thom.* 48

THOURIOS 2 b.c. (Feb 7) Green Desert (USA) 127 – Graecia Magna (USA) 109 (Private Account (USA)) [1991 7g* 7g⁵ 7m³ 8g] big, good-topped, attractive colt: has plenty of scope: good walker: has a round action: third foal: half-brother to quite modest 3-y-o Aellopous (seems unreliable) and useful middle-distance performer Akamantis (both by Kris): dam won at 7f and 1½m: very useful performer: wide-margin winner of 18-runner maiden at Salisbury in July: excellent 2½ lengths third of 9 to Dr Devious in Dewhurst Stakes at Newmarket on first run for 11 weeks: around 8 lb below that form when headed well over 1f out and dropping away quickly in Racing Post Trophy at Doncaster 8 days later: races keenly, but should stay 1m: possibly best fresh. *G. Harwood.* 111

THOUSLA ROCK (IRE) 2 ch.c. (Mar 8) Thatching 131 – Resooka (Godswalk (USA) 130) [1991 6g 6f* 5.8d² 6m²] well-grown, quite good-topped colt: usually looks really well: has scope: has a round action: fifth living foal: half-brother to 3 winners, including useful 1990 2-y-o 7f winner Caerdydd (successful in Italy at 3 yrs) and fairly useful 1988 2-y-o 6f winner Gaijin (both by Caerleon): dam unraced daughter of Cheveley Park winner Sookera: fair performer: won maiden auction at Folkestone: runner-up in median auction at Bath and listed event (hanging badly left final 1½f) at Haydock later in mid-summer: stays 6f: was improving well. *P. W. Chapple-Hyam.* 82

THREE LUCKY (IRE) 3 ch.f. Final Straw 127 – Some Dame 72 (Will Somers 114§) [1990 NR 1991 6.1m 6m³] sparely-made filly: half-sister to 3 sprint winners and to winners in France and Belgium: dam, half-sister to high-class Record Run, won over 1¼m: 33/1 and still better for race, staying-on third of 16 to Cash A Million at Warwick in October, easily better effort in maidens: reluctant at stalls on debut: should improve again. *M. D. I. Usher.* 46 p

THREEPENCE 2 b.g. (Feb 2) Sharpo 132 – Penny Blessing 112 (So Blessed 130)   **78**
[1991 5v* 6g3 5m 7m3 6.1s5 6m4] 58,000Y: sturdy gelding: has scope: moderate
mover: half-brother to several winners, including useful 1988 2-y-o 5f winner Song
of Hope (by Chief Singer) and 7f winner Quick Profit (by Formidable): dam, best at 2
yrs when 5f winner, is from family of Mummy's Pet: modest performer: won maiden
at Newcastle in April: 20/1, blinkered and looking really well, put up much improved
performance in face of extremely stiff task when 6 lengths fourth of 6 to Wolfhound
in minor event at Doncaster in October, leading almost 5f: likely to prove best at
sprint distances: easily best effort on good to firm ground, has won on heavy: flashed
tail third start: takes keen hold. *J. Berry.*

THREE WELLS 2 b.c. (Apr 24) Sadler's Wells (USA) 132 – Spring Triple (USA)   **79 p**
(Spring Double) [1991 7g5 7g5 8.1d2] close-coupled, useful-looking colt: closely
related to a winner in North America (by Be My Guest) and half-brother to 2 others:
dam winner of 11 races and second in stakes races at 3, 5 and 6 yrs: led 6f when
flattered 1½ lengths second of 8 to Bonny Scot in maiden at Haydock in October: ran
poorly at Brighton time before: will stay 1¼m: may well do better. *J. L. Dunlop.*

THRESHFIELD (USA) 5 b.h. Northern Prospect (USA) – French Cutie   **72**
(USA) (Vaguely Noble 140) [1990 NR 1991 10.8d6 7g 8m 7f* 6g 8.1g* 8m* 7s3] tall,
quite good-topped horse: modest handicapper: won at Brighton in May, Sandown
(heavily-backed favourite) in July and Pontefract in August: better at 7f and 1m than
shorter: probably acts on any going: sometimes bandaged behind: takes keen hold
and wears crossed noseband. *B. J. Curley.*

THRIE-NA-HELAH (IRE) 2 b.f. (Feb 3) Tender King 123 – Lady Bidder   **80**
(Auction Ring (USA) 123) [1991 6g 6g3 6m4 6m* 7f2 6g* 6f 7m2] IR 3,000Y: lengthy
filly: moderate mover: sixth foal: half-sister to several winners, including 3-y-o My
Alma (by Reasonable), successful at 5f at 2 yrs, and fair miler Classic Suite (by Ya
Zaman): dam unraced daughter of sister to good sprinter Holborn: fair performer:
won maiden auction at Redcar and seller (retained 16,500 gns) at York in summer:
excellent 3½ lengths second of 12 to Sharpitor in £11,200 auction nursery at York
final outing: stays 7f: yet to race on a soft surface: visored last 3 starts. *R. M.
Whitaker.*

THRILL 3 ch.f. Good Times (ITY) – Naughty Party (Parthia 132) [1990 6g4 a7g3   **45**
7g2 7f6 7g 8m 1991 10m a11g3 a12g a12g6 12.3g 11m] stocky filly: carries condition:
good walker: poor maiden: well beaten last 4 starts: will prove suited to middle
distances: visored and blinkered once: sold 850 gns Ascot November Sales. *D.
Haydn Jones.*

THROW AWAY LINE 2 bl.f. (Apr 6) Petorius 117 – Corsage (FR) (Nureyev   **33**
(USA) 131) [1991 5f 5f4] 580Y: tall, leggy, close-coupled filly: third foal: half-sister to
3-y-o 7f seller winner Nishcor (by Nishapour): dam French 1m winner: signs of ability in Beverley maidens in July, edgy second occasion: will stay 6f. *J. Etherington.*

THUNDER BUG (USA) 3 ch.f. Secreto (USA) 128 – Followeveryrainbow   **64**
(USA) (Mehmet (USA)) [1990 7m4 7g4 1991 12.2g5 8g4 8m5 10.1f3 8.3f2 9s5 9.7g*
10.3d] close-coupled filly: quite modest performer: favourite, won seller (sold out of
B. Hanbury's stable £5,800 gns) at Folkestone in October, leading 2f out: may well
prove best at 1¼m: acts on firm ground, seems unsuited by a soft surface. *A. P.
James.*

THUNDERING 6 b.g. Persian Bold 123 – Am Stretchin' (USA) (Ambiorix II 130)   **—**
[1990 a6g a7g5 a7g a8g5 8.2s* 8m 10.6s 8.5g4 8f5 7f 1991 8g6 9f 8.9g 12.3g] lengthy
gelding: has a round action: poor handicapper: below form last 3 starts: stays 1m:
possibly ideally suited by easy surface nowadays: blinkered once. *A. W. Jones.*

THURSLEY 2 ch.g. (Apr 7) Pharly (FR) 130 – Russian Waltz (USA) 75   **52**
(Czaravich (USA)) [1991 6f 6g3 6g2 6g* 7g a7g5] 6,800F, 2,700Y: workmanlike
gelding: first foal: dam, maiden, best at 2 yrs: plating-class performer: won
11-runner maiden auction at Catterick: fair fifth in nursery at Lingfield in December,
first run since July: probably stays 7f. *H. J. Collingridge.*

THYER (USA) 2 b.c. (Apr 25) Nijinsky (CAN) 138 – Qui Royalty (USA) (Native   **83 p**
Royalty (USA)) [1991 8d*] $600,000Y: seventh foal: closely related to 3-y-o
Majlood, very useful 6f winner at 2 yrs, and 1989 2-y-o 6f winner Qui Danzig (both
by Danzig) and half-brother to 2 winners, including Sum (by Spectacular Bid),
successful at up to 1¼m, including in graded stakes: dam very useful stakes-placed
winner at up to 1m: odds on, won 9-runner maiden (apparently quite easily) at
Leopardstown in September by 1½ lengths, with rest well strung out: evidently
highly regarded. *J. S. Bolger, Ireland.*

TIANGAR (IRE)   3 b.c. Last Tycoon 131 – Talaja (Kalamoun 129) [1990 7v* 1991 **110**
7d 7d*] fourth foal: half-brother to 3 winners, including listed race winner
Taboushkan (by Posse): dam very useful winner at up to 7f, out of daughter of Prix
Saint-Alary winner Tonnera: won newcomers race at Maisons-Laffitte in November
at 2 yrs and Prix de la Porte Maillot at Longchamp in June at 3 years, latter by head
from Time Gentlemen: not seen out again: will stay further than 7f: has raced only
on a soft surface. *A. de Royer-Dupre, France.*

TIARNA (IRE)   3 br.f. Thatching 131 – Rosserk (Roan Rocket 128) [1990 5g4 6g   —
1991 7.1g] IR 15,500Y: sixth foal: half-brother to 1989 2-y-o 6f winner Wild Dancer
(by Gorytus): dam, lightly raced in Ireland, is sister to very speedy 1969 Irish 2-y-o
True Rocket, dam of Ballad Rock: trained by T. Stack, fourth of 6 in maiden at
Tipperary in May at 2 yrs: well beaten in maiden at Haydock in September, 1991:
sold 840 gns Doncaster October Sales. *D. Moffatt.*

TIBBS INN   2 ch.g. (Mar 13) Adonijah 126 – Historia 71 (Northfields (USA)) [1991   —
5d5 a6g] 2,600F, 800Y: angular gelding: third foal: half-brother to 3-y-o Dutch
winner Fiaba (by Precocious), quite modest 5f winner at 2 yrs: dam, ran once at 2
yrs, is out of half-sister to high-class Moulton and Derby third Freefoot: well-beaten
last in Midlands maidens in mid-summer. *R. F. Marvin.*

TIBBY HEAD (IRE)   3 b.c. Lyphard's Special (USA) 122 – Deer Park (FR)   **54**
(Faraway Son (USA) 130) [1990 7m 7g5 1991 7m 10g 11.5m 8g3 7.1m] tall, angular
colt: plating-class maiden: staying-on third in claimer at Newmarket, setting
modest early pace: stays 1m: form only on good ground: sold 5,000 gns Newmarket
Autumn Sales. *W. Jarvis.*

TIBRACK (USA)   3 b.c. Lyphard (USA) 132 – Greedy of Gain (Habitat 134) [1990   **95**
NR 1991 7g* 10.1g*] $170,000Y: quite attractive, close-coupled, rather lightly-made
colt: half-brother to several winners abroad, notably high-class 5f and 1m (at 2 yrs)
to 1¼m winner Grease (by Filiberto): dam won 4 times over sprint distances in
Italy: favourite and looking really well, won maiden at Catterick in April and
handicap at Windsor in June: looked one to keep on the right side. *H. R. A. Cecil.*

TIDAL RIVER   2 gr.f. (Mar 26) Absalom 128 – Ebb And Flo 82 (Forlorn River   **31**
124) [1991 5d4 7f4 8.1s] 2,300F, 4,000Y: lengthy filly: moderate mover: half-sister to
several winners, including useful 6f to 1m winner Miss Thames (by Tower Walk)
and fairly useful 1981 2-y-o 7f winner Connaught River (by Connaught): dam, 6f
winner at 2 yrs, stayed 1¼m: poor form in varied events: off course over 3½ months
between starts. *Denys Smith.*

TIDE ECHO   3 b.g. Law Society (USA) 130 – River Goddess (USA) (Northern   **84**
Dancer) [1990 NR 1991 10g3 10.5m2 11.9g 12d5 9d 11s3 9.5v3 12v5 9.5g] leggy
gelding: second foal: brother to French 4-y-o Down By Law, placed at up to 1m: dam
unraced sister to Woodstream and half-sister to Jaazeiro: fair form placed in
maidens, when trained in Britain by R. Charlton: raced in France last 6 outings,
trained first 5 by D. Sepulchre: third in minor event and handicap at Bordeaux. *C. W.
Bartholomew, France.*

TIDEMARK (USA)   4 b.c. Riverman (USA) 131 – Remarkably (USA) (Prince **109**
John) [1990 10g 10.2m* 12d* 12g5 12m2 12m 1991 10m6 10g 12m5 12g5 12g* 12g*
13.9g3 12s* 11d2 12g6] lengthy, good-bodied colt: moderate mover: very useful

*Tote Gold Trophy Stakes (Handicap), Goodwood—
Tidemark has it sewn up entering the closing stages;
Endoli and Spinning (noseband) cut down the winner's advantage before the post is reached*

*Krug Trophy (Handicap), Ascot—Tidemark (left) wins another good prize,
just getting the better of his stable-companion Nibbs Point*

handicapper: won at Goodwood (£28,800 Tote Gold Trophy) and Newmarket
(beaten ½ length by Spinning but hampered and awarded race) in August and
£70,000 Krug Trophy at Ascot (beat Nibbs Point by head) in September: effective at
1½m to 1¾m: acts on good to firm and soft ground: has hung quite noticeably: sent
to USA, second in Grade 2 11f handicap at Belmont Park and just over 8 lengths sixth
of 7 to Miss Alleged in Hollywood Cup. *L. M. Cumani.*

TIEMPO 5 b.m. King of Spain 121 – Noddy Time 97 (Gratitude 130) [1990 6g⁴ 6m⁶ —
5m 1991 a5g⁴ a11g] compact, workmanlike mare: plating-class maiden: likely to
prove best at 6f: acts on a soft surface. *M. H. Tompkins.*

TIFFANY'S CASE (IRE) 2 gr.f. (Jan 21) Thatching 131 – Spindle Berry 92 **51**
(Dance In Time (CAN)) [1991 6m⁵ 7.1m 7g] IR 17,500F, IR 12,000Y: lengthy,
good-topped filly: has scope: fifth foal: half-sister to Irish 3-y-o 1¾m winner Circuit
Court and 7f/1m winner Coalition (both by Law Society) and 1988 2-y-o 6f seller
winner Helen Red (by Trojan Fen): dam, 5f winner at 2 yrs, is daughter of sister to
smart 1½m filly Cranberry Sauce: poor maiden: should stay further than 6f. *C. A.
Horgan.*

TIGANI 5 b.h. Good Times (ITY) – She Who Dares (Bellypha 130) [1990 5m² 5d 5f **96**
6m 5g⁵ 1991 6d² 6g³ 5m 5g] big, good-topped horse: carries condition: smart at his
best, fairly useful nowadays: second in listed race at Doncaster in March, best effort
in 1991: stays 6f: acts on soft ground, but goes particularly well on firm going: often
sweats nowadays: has got on toes: sold to join D. Chapman's stable 12,000 gns
Newmarket Autumn Sales. *D. W. Chapman.*

TIGER CLAW (USA) 5 b.g. Diamond Shoal 130 – Tiger Scout (USA) 86 (Silent **67**
Screen (USA)) [1990 11s9g⁶ 12f* 11.7g² 11.5m² 12g⁴ 12f* 12f³ 11.7m⁵ 10m⁵ 12g⁴ 10d
1991 10f³ 10s⁴ 12f⁴ 10m² 9g² 9m² 10d 10.2d 10g⁴ 10f⁴ 11.9g 10.2s² 9.7f⁶ 9.7s⁵]
good-bodied gelding: quite modest handicapper: stays 1½m: acts on soft ground, but
is suited by a sound surface: best form without blinkers or visor: winning hurdler. *R.
J. Hodges.*

TIGER CUB (USA)   6 b.g. Robellino (USA) 127 – Tiger Scout (USA) 86 (Silent   —
Screen (USA)) [1990 9m 11.7f³ 10f⁵ 9g 12.2f⁴ 10.6s 1991 11.5g 10s 10m] leggy
gelding: poor form, no show in handicaps in 1991: stays 1½m: acts on firm ground. *I.
A. Balding.*

TIGER FLOWER   4 b.f. Sadler's Wells (USA) 132 – Tigresse d'Amour (USA) **103**
108 (Stage Door Johnny) [1990 10m* 12f³ 11m¹ 12g² 12m 11.9g³] big filly: has quick,
moderate action: very lightly raced but useful performer: placed in listed events
won by Mukddaam at Newmarket in June (stayed on really well in moderately-run
race, beaten short head) and Nibbs Point at York in August (favourite, always close
up): very stiff task in between: much better suited by 1½m than 1¼m: best efforts
on good ground: visits Nashwan. *H. R. A. Cecil.*

TIGER SHOOT   4 b.g. Indian King (USA) 128 – Grand Occasion 63 (Great   **65**
Nephew 126) [1990 8.2m⁵ 10.2g⁶ 10f⁶ a12g* 1991 10g* 11.5g² 8m⁴ 9m² 8m 10m⁶
12m] close-coupled, workmanlike gelding: quite modest handicapper: won at
Leicester (landed gamble) in June: excellent seventh in ladies event at Ascot fifth
start: suited by stiff 1m, or 1¼m: acts on good to firm ground: had tongue tied down
first 5 starts: has run well when sweating. *P. J. Feilden.*

TIK FA (USA)   2 b.c. (Feb 27) Timeless Moment (USA) – How Fortunate (USA) **103**
(What Luck (USA)) [1991 7d* 8.1f² 8g² 9s⁵] $65,000Y: rangy, useful-looking colt:
has scope: third reported foal: dam, unraced, is half-sister to dam of very smart 6f to
1¼m winner Carr de Naskra: sire smart sprinter: comfortable winner of maiden at
Sandown in July: improved form when runner-up to Anchorite in minor event at
Haydock and to St Jovite in Panasonic Smurfit EBF Futurity Stakes at the Curragh:
moderate fifth of 7 in Prix Saint-Roman at Evry week later in September: stays 1m:
possibly unsuited by soft ground. *B. Hanbury.*

TILT TECH FLYER   6 b.g. Windjammer (USA) – Queen Kate 52 (Queen's Hus-   —
sar 124) [1990 8f 8.2d 1991 10d] big, leggy, sparely-made gelding: quite modest handicapper as 4-y-o: lightly raced and not nearly so good nowadays: stays 1m: acts on
heavy going, unsuited by top-of-the-ground: winning hurdler in February: formerly
trained by R. Akehurst. *J. Akehurst.*

TIME FOR A BET (USA)   2 b.c. (May 3) Timeless Native (USA) – Betsy Apple   —
(USA) (His Majesty (USA)) [1991 7m] $22,000Y: leggy, angular colt: eighth foal:
brother to Ritter, successful in claimer at around 1m in USA at 3 yrs and half-brother
to 3 other winners, including Diane's Girl (by Relaunch), minor stakes winner at up
to 1¼m: dam lightly-raced half-sister to grandam of Risen Star: 33/1, last of 11 in
minor event at Doncaster in September: showed a round action: sold 3,400 gns
Newmarket Autumn Sales. *T. Thomson Jones.*

TIME GENTLEMEN   3 ch.c. Night Shift (USA) – Final Orders (USA) (Prince **109**
John) [1990 6m* 6m² 6g* 6f⁴ 7m³ 6g* a8.5f⁵ 1991 7g 8v⁶ 7.1m* 7d² 6m 6f 6s]
close-coupled colt: easy mover: capable of very useful form, campaigned mostly in
pattern events: straightforward task to win minor event at Chepstow in May: good
head second to Tiangar in Prix de la Porte Maillot at Longchamp: stays 7f: best
efforts with give in the ground: usually on toes: blinkered and hung right (swerved
sharply once at 2 yrs) final start: may well not have ideal attitude. *J. L. Dunlop.*

TIME LAPSE   2 ch.f. (Apr 22) The Noble Player (USA) 126 – Low Line 66 (High   **62**
Line 125) [1991 a6g² 6m* 6m³ 8m⁶ 8f⁴] 3,600Y: sparely-made filly: first foal: dam,
ran twice at 2 yrs, is sister to Oaks fourth Shore Line and Park Hill winner Quay
Line: quite modest performer: won maiden auction at Pontefract in July: ran well in
nurseries: stays 1m: acts on firm ground. *P. J. Makin.*

TIMELESS TIMES (USA)   3 ch.c. Timeless Moment (USA) – Lovely Hobo   **90**
(USA) (Noholme II) [1990 5m* 5f* 5f* 5f* 6m² 6m* 5m* 5g* 6g* 6m* 6m*
7.3m* 6m* 7.5m* 6m² 5f* 6m³ 6m* 5m³ 8.5f 1991 5g² 7m 7g 6m 8m 6d 7.6g⁵ 5.6m
7m⁵] small, good-quartered colt: moderate walker and mover: remarkably tough
and genuine at 2 yrs, successful in 16 of 21 races: rated 99 then but not quite so good
in 1991, best effort when seventh in Free Handicap at Newmarket second start:
ideally suited by 7f: never raced on a soft surface: blinkered 3 times:
usually looked very well: mostly held up for turn of foot: reportedly retired to
Norton Grove Stud, Malton, fee £1,000 (Oct 1). *W. A. O'Gorman.*

TIME LORD   3 ch.c. Good Times (ITY) – Miss Trilli 89 (Ardoon 124) [1990 5g 6m   **45**
5m⁴ 5f⁵ 6m 6d 1991 5s* 5d⁵ 5.1d a6g] strong colt: won handicap at Leicester in
March: well below that form later in first half of season, stiff tasks last 2 outings:
best form at 5f on soft ground: visored final start: sold 860 gns Newmarket
September Sales. *L. J. Holt.*

TIMES ARE HARD 7 b.g. Bay Express 132 – Raffinrula 75 (Raffingora 130) 42 [1990 a10g* a8g* a10g³ a10g 6g⁶ 8.2s 1991 9s⁴ 8m a10g⁵ 8m a7g² 10.3d] close-coupled gelding: poor handicapper: needs further than 6f and stays 1¼m: acts on good to firm and soft ground: ran creditably when visored. *D. Burchell.*

TIME SLOT (USA) 4 ch.c. Secreto (USA) 128 – Ebbing Tide (USA) (His — Majesty (USA)) [1990 7g⁴ 9f⁵ 10m² 11g 1991 10.1s] close-coupled colt: fifth foal: half-brother to modest 5-y-o 12.2f winner Tranquil Waters (by Diesis), also successful over hurdles, and 1m and 8.5f winner Ice Chocolate (by Icecapade): dam half-sister to Oh So Fair, dam of Oh So Sharp, Roussalka and Our Home: ex-Irish colt: won maiden at the Curragh at 2 yrs and second in handicap at Galway at 3 yrs: bandaged and wearing tongue strap, held up and always behind in claimer at Windsor in April, only run on flat here: stays 1¼m: trained at 3 yrs by M. V. O'Brien: poor hurdler. *B. Stevens.*

TIMID 4 ch.c. Never So Bold 135 – Din Brown (USA) (Tom Rolfe) [1990 8g 6f³ 7f 61 8f³ 8m⁴ 10m² 1991 a11g⁵ a12g² 10.8d⁴ a12g* 11.5g³ 13.8f* 14.6g² 17.2g⁶ 12f] leggy a 69 colt: bad mover: quite modest performer: won claimer at Lingfield in May and seller (bought in 4,300 gns) at Catterick in June: stays 14.6f: acts on firm and dead ground: has drifted left: tried blinkered once: has been bandaged: winning hurdler. *M. C. Pipe.*

TIMIDE ESPION (FR) 5 b.g. Saint Cyrien (FR) 128 – Wind Spring (FR) — (Baldric II 131) [1990 10d 12f⁴ 10.1g 1991 a8g a12g a7g⁵ 8f a7g a7g⁶ 10.5m] big, rangy gelding: won listed race at Le Croise-Laroche as 3-y-o: only plating-class handicapper nowadays: stays 1¼m: has pulled hard and flashed tail: bought out of D. Elsworth's stable 5,600 gns Doncaster January Sales. *D. W. Chapman.*

TIMMINION 9 ch.g. Dominion 123 – My Baby Love 61 (Sovereign Path 125) — [1990 16.2m² 17.4d 16.2s 1991 16.5g⁵ 16f⁶] smallish, lengthy gelding: has a round action: quite modest handicapper: stays 16.5f: best form on sound surface: pulled up final start at 8 yrs: wears bandages: fairly useful hurdler. *R. O'Leary.*

TIMURID (FR) 2 b.c. (May 5) Persian Bold 123 – Kumari (FR) 78 (Luthier 126) 66 p [1991 7m 8m⁶] tall, useful-looking colt: half-brother to very useful stayer Angel City (by Carwhite): dam 1¼m winner: weak in market, improved quite considerably when sixth in Leicester maiden won by Pabouche in October, staying on strongly having been set plenty to do: has more improvement in him, particularly when granted middle distances. *J. L. Dunlop.*

TINA MEENA LISA 2 b.f. (May 28) Kala Shikari 125 – Miss Speak Easy (USA) — (Sea Bird II 145) [1991 5g 5g 5.1m] 5,000Y: sparely-made filly: has a quick action: half-sister to several winners here and abroad, including 1¼m and 1½m winner Sabarab (by Sayf El Arab) and very useful French middle-distance winner Natchitoches (by Pontifex): dam minor French 9f winner: poor maiden: bred to be suited by much further: slowly away first 2 starts. *E. H. Owen jun.*

TINAS LAD 8 b.g. Jellaby 124 – Arbatina (Sallust 134) [1990 12.5m⁴ 14 8m² 12g² 12m² 11.5m⁶ 12m⁵ 11.6m 1991 12.5g 12.1d] big gelding: carries plenty of condition: has a round action: quite modest handicapper at 7 yrs: backward and below form at 8 yrs: ideally suited by 1½m: acts well on top-of-the-ground: has won for amateur: winning chaser. *J. A. C. Edwards.*

TINAZ 4 b.f. Homing 130 – Claironcita 97 (Don Carlos) [1990 8m a10g 1991 a7g a12g a12g] no show, including in handicap. *H. J. Collingridge.*

TINDARI (FR) 3 ch.g. Vacarme (USA) 121 – Yseult (FR) (Olantengy (FR) 122) — p [1990 NR 1991 7.5f 8m] 4,800Y: small, good-bodied gelding: third foal: dam fourth in France at 1m on second of 2 starts: showed signs of ability in claimer at Beverley in July: stumbled badly entering straight and eased considerably in similar event at Newcastle following month: capable of better. *J. M. Jefferson.*

TINO TERE 2 ch.g. (Mar 11) Clantime 101 – Blueit (FR) 101 (Bold Lad (IRE) 133) 94 [1991 5d² 5m* 5d² 5g³ 5m² 5m* 5m² 5m² 5.2f² 5d⁶] 22,000Y: compact, attractive gelding: has scope: good walker: sixth foal: closely related to fairly useful sprinter Blues Indigo (by Music Boy) and half-brother to 2 other winning sprinters, including 3-y-o Indigo (by Primo Dominie): dam 2-y-o 5f winner: progressed into fairly useful performer: made all in maiden at Ripon in April and nursery at York in July: ran very well in nurseries (runner-up), then Cornwallis Stakes (sixth to Magic Ring) at Ascot, afterwards: speedy, and will prove best at 5f: acts on firm and dead ground: flashed tail seventh outing: still on the upgrade. *J. Berry.*

TINTAGEL CASTLE (IRE) 3 br.c. Caerleon (USA) 132 – Merlins Charm — (USA) 113 (Bold Bidder) [1990 6m 1991 8g 8g 8g³] sturdy, lengthy, angular colt: no worthwhile form in maidens: should stay 1m: tail flasher: sold 2,600 gns Newmarket July Sales. *B. W. Hills.*

TINTOMARA (IRE) 3 b.f. Niniski (USA) 125 – Timbale d'Argent (Petingo 135) — [1990 NR 1991 10d 10m] IR 19,000Y: lengthy, good-bodied filly: good walker: closely related to very useful 1¼m and 1½m winner Hajade (by Ile de Bourbon) and French 9f to 13f winner Tambour du Roi (by Green Dancer) and half-sister to 3 winners in France: dam showed a little ability in France: backward, very much caught the eye running on from rear in maiden at Newbury in May: hampered early in similar event at Sandown following month: looked capable of better: sold 3,100 gns Newmarket December Sales. *J. L. Dunlop.*

TIPPLING (USA) 4 b.f. Full Out (USA) – Lady Mellody (USA) (Beat Inflation 41 (USA)) [1990 8m 7m4 8.5m 7m 7g 7g 1991 5m 5m3 6s3 6g a5g 6m3 6m 7.1m 6.1m] smallish, sturdy filly: moderate mover: first foal: dam won at up to 1m in graded-stakes company in USA: ex-Irish maiden: poor handicapper: should prove suited by 7f: acts on good to firm and soft going: trained at 3 yrs by V. Rossiter. *P. Burgoyne.*

TIQUETEEN 4 b.f. Teenoso (USA) 135 – Helvetique (FR) (Val de Loir 133) — [1990 14m4 14g2 16m3 17.6m* 16.5d 1991 16m 17.6m 16.5m] lengthy filly: moderate mover: modest handicapper at 3 yrs: no form in first half of 1991: stays well: acts on good to firm ground and dead. *P. Calver.*

TISBUTASCRATCH (IRE) 2 ch.f. (May 25) On Your Mark 125 – Royal Aunt 40 (Martinmas 128) [1991 6m 5m 5m5 5m 5f 6s] half-sister to 1986 2-y-o 5f seller winner Flag Bearer (by Runnett): dam modest Irish 2-y-o 6f winner: poor plater: has shown her form for 7-lb claimer: carried head awkwardly fourth start. *L. J. Holt.*

TISWA (USA) 3 ch.f. Lyphard (USA) 132 – Happy Bride 116 (Royal Match 117) — [1990 6g 6g* 6m4 6m5 1991 6g6 10f] leggy, quite attractive filly: fair winner at 2 yrs: ran poorly in minor events (bandaged) as 3-y-o: should stay at least 1m: headstrong final start. *B. Hanbury.*

TITCH WIZARD 2 b.g. (Mar 30) Bairn (USA) 126 – Confection (Formidable 82 (USA) 125) [1991 5m* 5d4 5f2 6g2 6m2 5m4 6d* 6.1g* 6g5 6.1g 6f4 5m* 6g* 6m* 6m] 5,000Y: neat gelding: first foal: dam twice-raced daughter of useful middle-distance stayer Mint: fair performer who had very good season: successful 6 times, in maiden at Warwick (April), claimer there and £6,000 3-runner minor event at Chester (July), then when well-backed favourite in claimers at Pontefract, Lingfield and Leicester in autumn: effective over stiff 5f, and will stay 7f: acts on firm and dead ground: tough, game and genuine: sold 13,000 gns Newmarket Autumn Sales. *G. Lewis.*

TITE SPOT 4 ch.f. Muscatite 122 – Luan Causca 70 (Pampapaul 121) [1990 7.5f 6f — 6f 8m a7g* 7m 6s5 6m 7f 6d a6g a6g a6g a5g 1991 a8g 6d] narrow, workmanlike filly: turns off-fore in: plater: lost her form: stays 7f: acts on soft going: tried blinkered once. *N. Tinkler.*

TITIAN GIRL 2 ch.f. (May 3) Faustus (USA) 118 – Redhead 66 (Hotfoot 126) — [1991 5m 6d 7m 8.3g] 4,000Y: sparely-made filly: half-sister to several winners, including 2-y-o sprint winners Lucianaga (by King of Spain) and The Island (by Bairn): dam won 9f seller: seems of little account: withdrawn on intended debut after taking strong hold to post and getting loose: trained first 2 starts by J. S. Wilson. *Miss L. A. Perratt.*

TITIAN RED (CAN) 3 ch.f. Diesis 133 – Carrot Top 112 (High Hat 131) [1990 71 NR 1991 7m4 8m2 8.1m4 10.3m3 10.2f5 10m4 12s4] rather wiry, quite attractive filly: has a quick action: half-sister to several winners, including champion Canadian filly Carotene (by Great Nephew), successful from 6f to 1½m, and Cesarewitch winner Orange Hill (by High Top): dam very useful at up to 1¾m: modest maiden: stayed 1¼m: visits Never So Bold. *B. W. Hills.*

TITLE ROLL (IRE) 3 ch.f. Tate Gallery (USA) 117 – Tough Lady 91 (Bay 104 Express 132) [1990 5g* 6g3 5g* 1991 7g2 8g4 5m5 7g5 5d2 5g* 5g] angular, workmanlike filly: useful performer: contested only listed races and pattern events in 1991, best effort winning 15-runner King George Stakes at Goodwood (despite hanging left) in August, leading ½f out to beat Food of Love by ¾ length: always behind in Nunthorpe Stakes at York 3 weeks later: effective at 5f to 7f: acts on dead ground: blinkered third start. *T. Stack, Ireland.*

TOBACCO ROAD 4 ch.g. Burslem 123 – Ishtar (Dike (USA)) [1990 a8g 10m — 11.7m 8m 8f* 7m 8f 1991 10.1d 8.3g 9.7m] good-bodied gelding: plating-class handicapper at 3 yrs: well beaten in sellers in 1991, found little when blinkered final start: stays 1m: acts on firm ground: sometimes bandaged: unreliable: winning hurdler. *G. A. Ham.*

TO BE FAIR 4 ch.g. Adonijah 126 – Aquarula 88 (Dominion 123) [1990 12f* 12f⁶ **35** 10.2f3 12f 13. 1h3 12m⁶ 12h 12f⁴ 14m 12m 13v 1991 a 12g⁴a 13g⁴a 12ga 12ga 10g 10v 12g 10m⁴ 12m⁵ 12f] workmanlike gelding: poor handicapper nowadays: stays 13f: acts on hard ground, probably not on heavy: tried blinkered (raced freely) and visored: sold out of Dr J. Scargill's stable 950 gns Ascot April Sales: winning hurdler. *P. J. Hobbs.*

TODAY'S FANCY 3 b.g. Today And Tomorrow 78 – Fancy Pages 67 (Touch **29** Paper 113) [1990 6g a6g⁴ a6g⁶ 6g 5f 5g⁶ a5g* 6d a5g 1991 a5g⁵ a5g a5g⁵ a5g 5m] tall, leggy gelding: moderate mover: poor plater on most form: usually blinkered. *Pat Mitchell.*

TOHAMAH 3 b.f. Legend of France (USA) 124 – Abha 117 (Thatching 131) [1990 **61** NR 1991 8f² 8f3 7g⁴ 8m3 8d3] sturdy, lengthy filly: second foal: dam sprinter: quite modest maiden on most form: claimer-ridden third of 20 in selling handicap at Doncaster final start, tending to hang left: needs further: acts on firm and dead going: sold 5,000 gns Newmarket December Sales. *H. R. A. Cecil.*

TOKANDA 7 ch.g. Record Token 128 – Andalucia 57 (Rheingold 137) [1990 a 13g⁴ — 14m3 16f⁵ 16m 1991 16.2g 16.5m 16.2g 14.1f] workmanlike gelding: has a round action: bad handicapper: stays 2m: acts on any going: tried in blinkers and visor. *F. J. Yardley.*

TOLEDO BAY 3 b.f. Flash of Steel 120 – Silk Lady 97 (Tribal Chief 125) [1990 5g — 5g* 5g3 5.8f* 6m3 6f⁶ 6g a6g² a7g a6g⁴ 1991 a8g 8m 7g 8.3g 6m 7g 6.9m 9.7f] sparely-made filly: keen walker: quite modest winner at 2 yrs: ran badly in 1991, often in sellers: suited by 6f: acts on firm going: usually blinkered nowadays: none too keen fourth start: sold out of R. Hannon's stable 1,550 gns Newmarket July Sales after fifth. *G. Lewis.*

TOLL BOOTH 2 b.f. (May 6) Import 127 – Little Hut (Royal Palace 131) [1991 — 5.9h 6m a7g] smallish, workmanlike filly: first reported foal: dam half-sister to 2 winning chasers out of half-sister to Scottish Grand National winner King Con: soundly beaten, slowly away, in maidens and a claimer. *W. Storey.*

TOLLS CHOICE (IRE) 2 ch.g. (Apr 20) Sun Valley 103 – Creativity (Creative **61** Plan (USA)) [1991 5m 5g⁵ 5f 8m² 8m⁵ 8m] IR 4,500Y, 5,200 2-y-o: leggy, unfurnished gelding: first foal: dam Irish maiden half-sister to very useful Irish sprinter Cooleen Jack: sire won from 7f to 1m in Ireland: quite modest maiden: will stay 1¼m. *M. W. Easterby.*

TOMAHAWK 4 ch.g. Be My Guest (USA) 126 – Siouan 78 (So Blessed 130) **72** [1990 8g⁴ 10d² 12.3g* 14g 15d⁶ 1991 15.9g⁶ 13.9g⁵ 12d] leggy, quite good-topped gelding: moderate mover: modest handicapper: best effort in 1991 when very good fifth at York: failed to confirm that in Ascot apprentice event later in September: stays 1¾m: winning hurdler. *R. J. Holder.*

TOMKINS REEF (IRE) 2 b.g. (Mar 10) Hallgate 127 – Lightening Reef (Bon **50** Sang (FR) 126) [1991 7g 7m⁶ 8.2m 7g⁶ 7m] smallish, compact gelding: first foal: dam Irish maiden showed ability at 2 yrs, is granddaughter of National Stakes winner Reap The Wind: poor form: sixth of 16 in seller at Wolverhampton, fourth and best effort: should stay 1m: visored last 2 starts. *J. F. Bottomley.*

TOMMY TARMAC (IRE) 3 b.g. Fairy King (USA) – El-Glaka (Malinowski — (USA) 123) [1990 a7g a6g⁵ 7g⁴ 8m 1991 7.1m] workmanlike gelding: poor mover: moderate plater: stays 7f: visored 3 times, blinkered once: no promise on Flat or over hurdles in 1991. *M. C. Pipe.*

TOM'S APACHE 2 br.g. (Apr 21) Sula Bula 109 – Tom's Nap Hand (Some Hand **53** 119) [1991 6m⁶ 7f 7g] leggy gelding: second foal: half-brother to 3-y-o Tom's Arctic Dream (by Oats): dam poor on flat and over hurdles: withdrawn from maiden at Southwell in July after giving trouble stalls: 33/1, stayed on never dangerous when sixth in maiden at Windsor following month: no form after: fractious sort. *W. R. Williams.*

TOM'S ARCTIC DREAM 3 b.f. Oats 126 – Tom's Nap Hand (Some Hand 119) **50** [1990 7m 8m 7m 1991 a6g3 a5g 8m⁴ 7g 7f⁴ 7.1d a8g3 a6g 6f] sturdy filly: plating-class maiden: below form last 4 starts: better at 1m than shorter: edgy (ran well) third outing: hung left on fifth. *W. R. Williams.*

TOM'S PROSPECT (USA) 3 ch.g. Tank's Prospect (USA) – Snow Pearl **61** (USA) (Boldnesian) [1990 6m 6d 6f⁵ a7g* 7f a8g 6m⁵ 1991 a8g² a7g² a8g² a7g⁵ 8m²] leggy, quite good-topped gelding: moderate mover: plater: ran well most starts in 1991, leading 4f out until post at Brighton in May final start: stays 1m well: visored once at 2 yrs. *C. R. Nelson.*

TOMS VERDICT (USA) 2 ch.g. (Feb 2) Court Trial (USA) – Pleine Lune **74**
(CAN) (Barachois (CAN)) [1991 5g³ 5m* 5m³ 6d⁴] $7,500Y: sturdy gelding: closely
related to 2 winners by Classic Trial and half-brother to 2 winners by Iron
Constitution: sire, brother to champion filly Desert Vixen and smart 6f to 9f winner
Valid Appeal, won at up to 9f: modest performer: won minor event at Pontefract in
May in quite good style: didn't progress as anticipated, finding little and flashing tail
when last of 4 in similar event there (blinkered, sweating and edgy) in July:
subsequently gelded: dead. *W. A. O'Gorman.*

TONGADIN 5 b.g. Petong 126 – River Vixen (Sagaro 133) [1990 8m 8f 12g* 12g⁴ **60**
16.2d⁶ 12g⁶ 15.3m* 14m⁵ 14f³ 15.3m⁶ 13.8f⁶ 10.6s⁶ 13.8d* 12d³ 1991 13.8d 12f⁵
13.8m* 15.8f* 13m⁴ 15.8g⁴] sparely-made, angular gelding: quite modest handicapper: won at Catterick in May (drifted left) and June (by 5 lengths): set too much
to do final start (July): needs further than 1¼m and stays 15.8f: acts on any going:
usually claimer ridden: has worn pricker near side. *M. J. O'Neill.*

TONG-LA-TEE 2 gr.f. (Mar 16) Petong 126 – Donna Pavlova (Don (ITY) 123) **—**
[1991 5m 5f 7f] 9,200Y: half-sister to several winners, including modest 3-y-o 7.5f
winner (at 2 yrs) Hooting Don (by Bold Owl) and 1981 2-y-o 5f winner Little
Ballerina (by Brittany): dam poor maiden: no worthwhile form, in 7f seller at Thirsk
(slowly away, always behind) in August. *C. W. Thornton.*

TONGUE TIED 3 br.f. Petong 126 – Tight (Lochnager 132) [1990 NR 1991 5g⁵ **64**
5f* 5m 6g 6f³ 5m² 5h*ᵈⁱˢ 5m 5m 5m*] rather leggy, close-coupled filly: fifth foal:
dam non-thoroughbred half-sister to sprinters Clantime and Tobermory Boy: quite
modest handicapper: first past post at Hamilton (seller and bought in 5,600 gns,
edging left in front) in May, Carlisle (disqualified for interference) in September and
Pontefract (led post) in October: needs stiff 5f, and may improve back at 6f: acts on
hard ground: slowly away eighth and ninth starts: ridden by 7-lb claimer last 5:
joined J. Wharton. *Mrs J. R. Ramsden.*

TONY SAN (IRE) 2 b.c. (Feb 6) Pennine Walk 120 – Millers Lady (Mill Reef **93**
(USA) 141) [1991 6m 8m⁶ 7m] IR 17,000F: small, quite attractive colt: has a quick
action: fifth foal: half-brother to 1986 Irish 2-y-o 6f winner Rustic Reef (by
Rusticaro) later successful in Italy, and 1988 2-y-o 6f winner Anne's Princess (by
Sandhurst Prince): dam Irish 5f winner at 3 yrs: only modest form in maidens first 2
starts: 100/1, around 10 lengths last of 9 in Dr Devious in Dewhurst Stakes at
Newmarket, slowly away and always behind: better suited by 7f than shorter: will
win a maiden at least. *C. E. Brittain.*

TONY'S FUTURE 3 br.f. King of Spain 121 – Firdale Rosie 78 (Town Crier 119) **—**
[1990 NR 1991 10m⁶ 12g] 9,200Y: leggy, light-framed filly: fifth foal: half-sister to
plating-class 2-y-o's Rosie's Glory (by Hittite Glory) and Decoy Express (by Decoy
Boy): dam 2-y-o 5f winner, appeared not to train on: no worthwhile form in maiden
and claimer in May. *G. A. Pritchard-Gordon.*

TOO CONSPICUOUS (USA) 3 ch.c. Miswaki (USA) 124 – Petit Rond Point **93**
(USA) (Round Table) [1990 6g⁴ 6m* 7d⁴ 6d 1991 6m⁶ 7g² 6m 8m³ 8.1g 7g 8m⁵ 7g⁵
8.1s⁴] lengthy, attractive colt: fluent mover: fair performer but inconsistent: best
efforts in handicaps at Newmarket first and fourth starts: sweating and edgy, led 6f
and found little in claimer on final one: should prove better at 1m than shorter: acts
on good to firm ground and dead: sold 19,000 gns Newmarket Autumn Sales. *N. A.
Callaghan.*

TOO EAGER 5 b.g. Nishapour (FR) 125 – Double Habit (Double Form 130) [1990 **70**
8f 7m 6f 6d* 6g⁴ 5g³ a7g 6m 6m 7d 7m⁶ 7m 6s* 1991 8s 7d* 6s* 6d² 6m 8d⁵ 7m]
lengthy, dipped-backed gelding: modest handicapper: has proved none too
consistent: won at Catterick and Newcastle in spring: suited by 6f or 7f: probably
suited by an easy surface nowadays: best blinkered: often bandaged near-hind. *M.
W. Easterby.*

TOOLEY'S BOY 2 b.c. (Mar 26) Adonijah 126 – Marita 76 (Great Nephew 126) **66**
[1991 6g⁴ 6f 7m 8m 8g] 4,800Y: compact colt: moderate mover: half-brother to
several winners, including very useful 1979 French 2-y-o 5.5f to 7f winner Koboko:
dam won over 9f and 10.5f in France: quite modest maiden: should be well suited by
further than 6f. *Mrs Barbara Waring.*

TOO MUCH CHAMPAGNE (IRE) 3 b.f. Kafu 120 – Nadja 77 (Dancer's **—**
Image (USA)) [1990 6m⁵ 5f⁶ 6g 7g* 7f⁵ 8d 7m⁶ 8m 1991 7v 11g⁵ 9f⁶ 8g⁵ 8f 8m 6f 7f⁴
8.1g 10g 8m⁵] leggy filly: moderate walker: has shown little since winning seller as
2-y-o: best form at 7f: acts on firm ground: trained first 4 starts by J. S. Wilson. *M. P.
Naughton.*

TOOTSIE WOOTSIE 3 b.f. Hotfoot 126 – Hippona (Red God 128§) [1990 5m6 — §
6g 7g 1991 7d] tall, leggy filly: well beaten in maidens and seller: gives trouble at
stalls, extremely temperamental before withdrawn on intended reappearance: one
to avoid. *B. J. McMath.*

TOOWHIT TOWHEE (USA) 3 b.f. Lucky North (USA) – Chop Towhee —
(USA) (Hatchet Man (USA)) [1990 NR 1991 8g6 10s4 14.1m4] $27,000Y: angular,
rather unfurnished filly: fourth foal: half-sister to a winner in USA: dam won twice at
up to 7f in USA: first run for 3 months, 10 lengths fourth of 9 to Doubles at
Nottingham final start, keeping on and best effort in maidens: better at 1¾m than
1¼m: sold 3,800 gns Newmarket Autumn Sales. *J. H. M. Gosden.*

TOP-ANNA (IRE) 3 b.f. Ela-Mana-Mou 132 – Nutshambles (High Top 131) **71**
[1990 NR 1991 a8g a7g3 a7g4 a8g3 9s 7g6 11m3 12m3 12.1d* 12.3d 15g* 15g4 15.8f5
12.1f6 15.1g*] 5,000Y: sparely-made filly: first foal: dam lightly-raced maiden:
modest performer: won amateurs contest at Hamilton and handicap at Edinburgh in
June: improved effort to win handicap at Edinburgh in September final start: should
stay 2m: acts on dead ground and (probably) good to firm: visored last 8 starts:
trained until before penultimate outing by J. Wilson. *Miss L. A. Perratt.*

TOPANOORA 4 b.c. Ahonoora 122 – Topping Girl (Sea Hawk II 131) **118**
[1990 10g* 10g* 11g2 12d2 12v* 10s* 1991 12v* 10g* 10g2 12m2 12.5g2 10.4g4
10d4 12s*]

It's unlikely that many Irish racing fans will remember 1991 as a year of
benevolence so far as British stewarding is concerned. In late-April, their
Cahervillahow, having beaten Docklands Express by three quarters of a
length in the Whitbread Gold Cup, was controversially disqualified and placed
second for causing interference on the run-in. Less than two months later
disqualification also befell the Irish-trained Topanoora, in the Group 2 Hardwicke Stakes at Royal Ascot. Starting at 8/1 in a field of nine which included
Rock Hopper, Spritsail and the French challenger Dear Doctor, Topanoora
was initially settled off the pace towards the inner, made what seemed at
first sight an innocuous move towards the outside once in line for home,
and, having gone to the front inside the last furlong, held on by a short head
from Rock Hopper. However, the announcement of a stewards inquiry and
objection soon after came as no surprise, as Eddery had clearly been forced to

Blandford Stakes, the Curragh—
Topanoora (right) wins this Group 2 race narrowly
from the grey Zafadola and Favoured Nations

Mrs E. McMahon's "Topanoora"

ease up momentarily on Rock Hopper inside the final hundred yards. The wording of Eddery's objection, for 'taking my ground in the last furlong', further sharpened the focus upon the incident that had taken place late on. But, as at Sandown, the stewards saw more to object to than the defeated jockey did. A closer inspection of events from the home turn revealed that in easing his mount to the left once into the straight, Roche, on Topanoora, had checked Eddery's horse slightly, causing sufficient interference to lead the stewards, who accepted that the incident was accidental, to promote Rock Hopper to first place. Eddery's objection was overruled because the interference which had taken place inside the last half furlong had been caused by Spritsail's drifting away from the rail, Carson keeping his whip in his right hand throughout the final stages.

The main difference between the Whitbread and the Hardwicke was the reaction to the stewards' ruling by the deprived connections. Whereas the first went to appeal at Portman Square, Topanoora's trainer adopted a more stoical response, describing the verdict as 'strange', but deciding against an appeal. The lack of an independent tribunal to entertain the hearing was the reason cited by Bolger for his decision. Topanoora didn't go without any success in 1991, however. He landed short odds in minor events at Tipperary and the Curragh in April; and having acquitted himself with credit behind Toulon in the Prix Maurice de Nieiul at Maisons-Laffitte and run well when fourth to Suave Dancer in the Meadow Meats Irish Champion Stakes at Leopardstown, after receiving a less-than-astute ride from Piggott when fourth in York's International Stakes in between, Topanoora ended his season with a Group 2 success, in the Blandford Stakes at the Curragh. Lining up in a six-runner field which included the British contenders Surrealist, Sesame and Hateel, Topanoora, who started the 6/4 favourite, put in a determined challenge from over two furlongs out and kept on well to forge ahead in the closing stages, beating Zafadola half a length. This time a stewards inquiry resulted in his keeping the race, which was a richly-deserved reward for a most consistent colt, out of the first two only twice in his fourteen outings to date.

Topanoora (b.c. 1987)	Ahonoora (ch 1975)	Lorenzaccio (ch 1965)	Klairon Phoenissa
		Helen Nichols (ch 1966)	Martial Quaker Girl
	Topping Girl (br 1972)	Sea Hawk II (gr 1963)	Herbager Sea Nymph
		Round Eye (b 1967)	Round Table All My Eye

Topanoora, a lengthy, attractive colt, is the twelfth foal of Topping Girl, a mare who has produced seven individual winners. The principal winner among these prior to Topanoora was the Royal Match filly Happy Bride, who numbered these a Group 2 and a listed event among her four victories for Bolger, before going on to win a further four times in North America. Topping Girl's other progeny include Daring (by Bold Lad), successful on three occasions in Britain at three, and once in North America at six; Happy Rover (also by Bold Lad), a winner three times on the flat in Ireland in 1991, as well as over hurdles previously; and Happy Smile, a sister to Happy Bride, and also victorious on the flat in Ireland in 1991. The latest of Topping Girl's offspring to race is Happy Bliss (by Vision), placed twice as a two-year-old in Ireland. Both Topping Girl and her dam Round Eye were unraced. Topanoora, who acts on good to firm ground and heavy going, and stays a mile and a half well, remains in training. *J. S. Bolger, Ireland.*

TOPCLASS LADY (IRE) 2 ch.f. (May 19) Burslem 123 – Princess Galicia 82 **47** (Welsh Pageant 132) [1991 5g⁵ 5m⁴ 5m³ 5d⁶ 6m⁵ 5f 6f] 4,000 2-y-o: small, sparely-made filly: fourth foal: half-sister to 3-y-o 7f and 1m (seller) winner Broughton Blues (by Tender King) and 1986 Irish 2-y-o 6f winner Pageant's Pride (by Sallust): dam, maiden, stayed 1m: poor maiden: hung right throughout when facing stiff task in Hamilton nursery final outing: should be better suited by 6f than 5f: ran poorly fourth outing when blinkered, also only start on dead ground: has carried head high: trained first 5 starts by J. S. Wilson. *Miss L. A. Perratt.*

TOPCLIFFE 4 b.f. Top Ville 129 – Sandford Lady 116 (Will Somers 114§) [1990 8f **45** 8f 10m 12.2m³ 10m* 9m⁶ 1991 10g 10g 11m³ 9.9f⁵ 10.9m³ 16m 12f⁶ 11m⁵ 13.8m⁵ 12m* 12.4m²] leggy, lightly-made filly: moderate mover: poor handicapper: won seller (no bid) at Pontefract in October: stays 1¾m: acts on firm going: usually visored nowadays: sold to join Mrs V. Aconley 3,100 gns Doncaster November Sales. *C. W. C. Elsey.*

TOP DREAM 6 br.h. High Top 131 – Pleasant Dream 89 (Sharpen Up 127) [1990 **—** 7f 7g 7.6m⁴ 6d 1991 6d] strong, close-coupled, attractive horse: good walker: has a quick, round action: reportedly chipped bone in knee final start as 3-y-o: fairly useful handicapper on his day, but difficult to train: tailed off only run in 1991 (April): suited by 7f: not suited by firm going and best run on dead: standing at Gyleburn Stud, Dumfriesshire, £200 (Oct 1st). *C. Parker.*

TOPEKA EXPRESS (USA) 8 b.g. Topsider (USA) – Watch Out 99 (Blakeney **—** 126) [1990 10.2m 10m⁵ 10.8m 8m⁴ 8.2f* 9g⁶ 8f⁴ 8g³ 8.5g 8m³ 8.5f³ 8f⁴ 7.5g³ 8.2m² 8g 7.5m⁵ 8m 8m 8m 1991 8.2d 8m 8.2g 8.2m 8m 10m] smallish, sturdy gelding: usually looks well: carries plenty of condition: moderate mover: plating-class handicapper at 7 yrs: below best in 1991: stays 10.8f: acts on firm going, not at his best on soft: effective with or without blinkers or visor: suitable mount for inexperienced rider: winning hurdler. *C. Tinkler.*

TOPHAMS 5 b. or br.h. Good Times (ITY) – Sun Lamp 76 (Pall Mall 132) [1990 **58** d a6g* a5g a6g* a6g 1991 a6g⁵ a6g² a6g⁵ a6g² a7g a6g⁴ 6d 5d 5h⁶ 6g⁶ 6m] big horse: poor mover: plating-class handicapper on all-weather nowadays: no form on turf in 1991, taking little interest penultimate start: suited by 6f: acts on firm ground:

tried visored and blinkered once: trained first 8 starts by R. Hollinshead. *Ronald Thompson.*

TOP IT ALL 3 b.c. Song 132 – National Dress 64 (Welsh Pageant 132) [1990 6m 7m a8g a8g6 1991 a12g4 12.3s 14.1f6 16m] heavy-bodied colt: poor form on flat: seems one paced: winning hurdler. *M. J. Ryan.* —

TOP MILL 3 b.g. High Top 131 – Mill On The Floss 117 (Mill Reef (USA) 141) [1990 NR 1991 10.2g* 12g* 11g] lengthy gelding: first foal: dam 7f (at 2 yrs) and 1½m winner from very good family: won maiden at Chepstow and 2-runner handicap (7/4 on, from Westholme) at Pontefract in July: early to post, chased leaders over 1m when eighth of 14 in handicap at Newbury in October: stays 1½m: sold 44,000 gns Newmarket Autumn Sales. *A. C. Stewart.* 93

TOP OF THE BILL 4 b.c. Star Appeal 133 – Cash Limit 62 (High Top 131) [1990 10g 11.7m3 10f5 10f5 11.5m2 11.7g5 10.6d3 10.2g* 9s 9m6 1991 10m4 12g5 12.3d* 12m6 a12g4 10.1g2 11.5d6 11.5m* 12g 10.3m*] small colt: usually looks well: has a long stride: quite modest handicapper: won £7,400 event at Chester in May and claimers (made most) at Yarmouth in July and Chester in August: effective at 1¼m to 1½m: acts on firm and dead (possibly unsuited by very soft) going: tough and largely consistent. *N. A. Callaghan.* 67

TOP OF THE WORLD 4 b.c. Sallust 133 – Top Ville 129 – Une Florentine (FR) (Pharly (FR) 130) [1990 8m2 8m 10.5g3 12s6 1991 a12g* 16g* 18.4d 16m* 20g 13.3f4] tall colt: useful performer: won maiden at Southwell in March and handicap at Newmarket and Cementone Beaver Henry II Stakes at Sandown (by length from Crack, setting modest gallop) in May: soundly beaten in Gold Cup at Royal Ascot: creditable fourth of 7 to Drum Taps in Ibn Bey Geoffrey Freer Stakes at Newbury: suited by 1½m +, and stayed 2m: seemed best on a sound surface: sold only 4,800 gns Newmarket Autumn Sales: standing at Blackrath Stud, Ireland, fee IR £350. *C. E. Brittain.* 103

TOP ONE 6 ch.g. Sallust 134 – Light Diamond (Florescence 120) [1990 5m3 5m 7m2 8g 1991 6f2 7.6d] close-coupled gelding: quite modest handicapper: below-form second in non-handicap seller at Folkestone in June: stays 7f: acts on any going: often bandaged: finished lame final outing at 5 yrs: pulls hard. *C. J. Hill.* 54

TOP PRIZE 3 b.c. High Top 131 – Raffle 82 (Balidar 133) [1990 NR 1991 a12g] 13,500Y: second-brother to useful 7f to 7.6f winner Rasan (by Dominion): dam, 5.8f winner, is half-sister to Mummy's Pet, Parsimony and Arch Sculptor: 25/1, no show in claimer at Southwell in December. *M. Brittain.* —

TOP REALITY (IRE) 2 b.c. (May 18) Topsider (USA) – My Locket (USA) (Key To The Mint) [1991 7m4 7m* 7s4] IR 15,000Y: fifth foal: half-sister to 2 winners, including Grade 1 9f Milady Handicap victress Seldom Seen Sue (by Lines of 94 p

Cementone Beaver Henry II EBF Stakes, Sandown—
33/1-shot Top of The World makes all to win from Crack and Teamster

Power): dam, placed twice at 3 yrs in Ireland, later successful at up to 9f in USA at 4 yrs: won maiden at Fairyhouse in September: much better form when around 6 lengths fourth of 18 to Fair Crack in Goffs Million at the Curragh following month: will stay 1m: may improve further. *D. Hanley, Ireland.*

TOP REGISTER (USA)   2 b.c. (Apr 17) Dixieland Band (USA) – Contralto 100   **93** p (Busted 134) [1991 8g²] strong, rather angular colt: half-brother to several winners, including smart 6f (at 2 yrs) to 1m winner Enharmonic (by Diesis), very useful miler Soprano (by Kris) and fairly useful 1¾m winner Musical Box (by Grundy): dam 2-y-o 6f and 7f winner, is closely related to smart Rhyme Royal: sire won from 5.5f to 9f, including Grade 2 Pennsylvania Derby: 11/1, burly and green, 3½ lengths second of 16 to Aljadeer in minor event at Newbury in October, leading 2f out and keeping on well when headed: sure to improve, and is certain to win a maiden at least. *Lord Huntingdon.*

TOP ROYAL   2 br.c. (Jan 15) High Top 131 – Maria Isabella (FR) (Young   **58** p Generation 129) [1991 7.1s 7m⁵] 30,000Y: good-bodied colt: quite fluent mover: second reported foal: dam, ran 3 times in France, is half-sister to useful 1986 French 2-y-o 6.5f winner Microcosme: plating-class form in maidens at Sandown in July and Lingfield (slowly away, headway over 2f out, not knocked about once held) 8 weeks later: will stay 1m: may well improve again. *J. L. Dunlop.*

TOP SCALE   5 b.g. Tower Walk 130 – Singing High 87 (Julio Mariner 127) [1990   **51** 7.5d 8.2g² 8f⁴ 9.1m* 10m⁴ 8m² 8.5m⁶ 1991 9f 9.9g* 8.2d 11m³ 10m³ 9f* 9f 8h² 8.5f² 9m² 8m] strong, good-topped gelding: won handicaps at Beverley and Redcar in summer: effective at 1m to 11f: acts on hard ground, possibly unsuited by dead: has run well for inexperienced rider: effective with or without visor and blinkers. *J. Hetherton.*

TOP SHEREEK   3 b.c. High Top 131 – Shereeka 76 (Shergar 140) [1990 6f⁴ 8m⁴   **73** 7m² 1991 7d³ 7m 7m⁵ 7m³ 10.2g⁴ 8m³ 8f⁴ 10g³ 12g⁵ 9.7f⁵] unfurnished colt: modest maiden: takes keen hold, and gives impression will prove best short of 1½m: acts on firm ground and dead: sold A. Falourd 16,500 gns Newmarket Autumn Sales: consistent. *M. A. Jarvis.*

TOP SHIEL   3 b.c. Top Ville 129 – Gelder Shiel (Grundy 137) [1990 NR 1991   **87** p 11.8m⁵ 10m³ 10g*] 40,000Y: big, strong, lengthy colt: has scope: good walker: fourth foal: half-brother to 3 winners here and abroad, including 7f to 1½m winner Takfa Yahmed (by Main Reef) and fairly useful 1m winner Shieling (by Persian Bold): dam unraced daughter of useful 1¼m filly Crofting: favourite, won maiden at Brighton in September easing down by 6 lengths from Northern Trial, held up, shaken up 1f out and soon clear: put head in air and hung right at Sandown previous start: will possibly prove best with some give in the ground: should do well at 4 yrs. *L. M. Cumani.*

TOP SONG   2 br.f. (Mar 4) Noalto 120 – Pounelta 91 (Tachypous 128) [1991 6f   **70** p 7.1m 7f²] tall filly: has a roundish action: second foal: half-sister to untrustworthy 3-y-o 6f (at 2 yrs) and 7f winner Durneltor (by Hard Fought): dam 2-y-o 7f winner, probably stayed 1½m, is half-sister to Dead Certain: best effort when short-head second of 13 to Alto Jane in maiden at Salisbury in September, leading under 2f out until post: stays 7f: likely to progress again. *R. Hannon.*

TOP SPIN   2 b.c. (Feb 23) Niniski (USA) 125 – Spin (High Top 131) [1991 7d 7g   **79** 8.1g⁶ 8f* 7s] IR 34,000Y: leggy, close-coupled, quite attractive colt: fourth live foal: brother to very useful 7f and 12.3f winner Salchow and half-brother to quite useful 1m to 1¼m winner Girotondo (by Young Generation) and 1¼m and 1½m winner Snowspin (by Carwhite): dam never ran: weak 12/1-shot, made all, showing vastly improved form, in 12-runner nursery at Bath in September: had stiff task in Goffs Million at the Curragh following month: will be better suited by 1¼m + . *Major W. R. Hern.*

TOP SPINNER   3 ch.f. Final Straw 127 – Skiboule (BEL) (Boulou) [1990 6g 6g⁵   — 1991 7m 10.2d 11m 12g a12g] workmanlike filly: poor maiden. *D. Haydn Jones.*

TOPSTRIKE   2 b.c. (Mar 14) Sayf El Arab (USA) 127 – Blanche Neige 75 (Forlorn   **76** River 124) [1991 6m 5g a6g* 5m* 5m⁵] 5,000F, 10,500Y: rather leggy, useful-looking colt: progressing physically: fifth foal: dam 2-y-o 5f winner didn't progress, is half-sister to high-class French sprinter Kind Music and very useful 5f performer Boy Trumpeter: modest performer: made most in maiden at Southwell (clear over 1f out, just held on) in July then won 4-runner nursery at Haydock in August, running on strongly: respectable fifth of 9 in Sandown nursery month later: stays 6f: looked extremely well last 2 outings. *W. A. O'Gorman.*

TOP VILLAIN   5 b.g. Top Ville 129 – Swan Ann 84 (My Swanee 122) [1990 8f   **32** 1991 12f⁵ 10m 10m* a11g* 10.6g⁵ a12g² 10m a11g³ 8.9g 10m] rangy gelding: poor a**42**

*King George V Stakes (Handicap), Ascot—Torchon wins with plenty in hand;
Latour and Regent's Folly come next*

handicapper, formerly none too genuine: won in May at Nottingham (first form) and
Southwell: effective at 1½m, but gives impression will prove ideally suited by
around 1¼m: effective blinkered or not: has run fairly well for amateur: winning
hurdler. *Andrew Turnell.*

TORCHON 3 b.c. High Top 131 – Cecilia Bianchi (FR) (Petingo 135) [1990 8g⁵ **110**
1991 8g 10g* 12g* 11.9g* 11.9g 12m³ 12m⁶] rangy colt: very useful performer:
successful in maiden at Leicester in May, King George V Handicap at Royal Ascot
(by 3 lengths from Latour) and listed race at Haydock in July (beat Another Bob 1½
lengths): ran badly in Great Voltigeur Stakes at York fourth start, respectably
afterwards in listed races won by Surrealist at Doncaster and Newmarket: stays
1½m well. *G. Wragg.*

TORGHIA 4 b.f. Taufan (USA) 119 – Brave Louise 76 (Brave Shot) [1990 7f⁵ 7m⁵ **66**
7.3m 7g² 8f⁵ 7m⁴ 9f* 8g² 8m 10d⁶ a10g* 1991 a12g* a10g a12g³ 9g 11.7g³] leggy, a 76
angular filly: has a round action: modest handicapper: won at Lingfield in January:
not seen out after April: stays 1½m: acts on firm going: has run well for 7-lb claimer:
trained first 3 starts by D. Arbuthnot. *T. P. McGovern.*

TORPEDOS LOS (FR) 3 b.c. Baillamont (USA) 124 – Artists Proof (USA) —
(Ribot 142) [1990 7s⁴ 1991 10g⁵ 10m 11.7d] leggy, close-coupled colt: no worthwhile
form: sweating, faced extremely stiff task in handicap in June, final outing: tended to
carry head high on reappearance. *H. R. A. Cecil.*

TORRANCE 7 br.g. Niels 107 – Aurambre (FR) (Sicambre 135) [1990 NR 1991 —
8m] good-topped gelding: tubed: quite modest handicapper: none too reliable, but
goes very well at Brighton (has gained all his 4 wins there): tailed off only run in
1991 (claimer): best at 7f or 1m: best on top-of-the-ground: effective with or without
blinkers: usually wears crossed noseband: has looked reluctant. *W. R. Williams.*

TORREY CANYON (USA) 2 b. or br.c. (May 10) Gone West (USA) – Tovalop **113** p
(USA) (Northern Dancer) [1991 7g* 7g* 8d4] $94,000Y: tall, attractive colt: has
scope: sixth foal: half-brother to Tirana (by Fappiano), winner at 1¼m and 11f in
France at 3 yrs: dam won 3 races at up to 1m: sire, stakes winner at 1m and 9f, won
Grade 1 Dwyer Stakes: successful in maiden at Ascot and 5-runner Deploy Acomb
Stakes at York (by a neck from Niodini) in summer: looking really well, 2 lengths
fourth of 8, staying on gamely, to Made of Gold in Royal Lodge William Hill Stakes at

Mr K. Abdulla's "Torrey Canyon"

Ascot in September: strong-galloping sort, likely to stay 1¼m: very useful already and may well progress further. *R. Charlton.*

TORTIN (IRE) 3 b.f. Auction Ring (USA) 123 – Bernique (Hello Gorgeous (USA) 128) [1990 7f 7m 7f a7g a8g 1991 12.2g 12f 7g a7g 6f 9.2m] workmanlike filly: poor plater: should stay beyond 7f: visored 4 times: trained first 2 starts by J. Hetherton. *G. P. Kelly.* —

TORWADA 8 b.g. Troy 137 – Miss By Miles 91 (Milesian 125) [1990 NR 1991 11.8g 9.7s] strong, stocky gelding: good mover: fairly useful performer at best as 3-y-o for P. Cole: behind in autumn handicaps at Leicester (burly and led 1¼m) and Folkestone (caught eye, running on from rear last 2f not at all knocked about), first runs on flat since: stays 11f well: acts on good to firm ground, but goes very well with plenty of give: fairly useful hurdler. *B. J. Curley.* — p

TOSHIBA COMET 4 b.g. Noalto 120 – Silk Lady 97 (Tribal Chief 125) [1990 6m³ 6m⁴ 7m 5f 5f 6m* 6d* 5g a6g* 1991 a6g* a6g* a6g* a6g* 6g⁵ 6m⁵ 6f* 6m² 6f 6g 6m 6g⁴ 6.1d a6g⁵ a6g³] strong, sturdy gelding: moderate walker: fair handicapper: won at Lingfield (claimers) in January, Southwell in February and Hamilton in May: well below form at Lingfield final start: suited by 6f: probably acts on any going: sometimes wears tongue strap: usually blinkered. *W. J. Pearce.* 87

TOSHIBA COMET STAR (IRE) 2 b.c. (Apr 12) Akarad (FR) 130 – Scuba Diver (Kings Lake (USA) 133) [1991 5d⁵ a5g² 6f³ 5d² 5m* 5s* 6m³ 6f⁴ 8m 6m*] 10,000Y, resold 12,000Y: sturdy colt: has scope: moderate mover: first foal: dam Irish 8.5f winner stayed 1¼m: modest performer: successful in maiden at Carlisle and nursery at Hamilton in summer: sold 15,500 gns after winning 27-runner seller at Newmarket in October: races keenly, but should stay beyond 6f: probably acts on any going. *W. J. Pearce.* 78

TOSHIBA COMET TOO (IRE) 3 ch.g. Gorytus (USA) 132 – No Jargon — (Nonoalco (USA) 131) [1990 6m 7m 7v⁶ 7s a8g* 1991 8m a8g 11m 8d a10g⁶ a12g] big, close-coupled gelding: quite modest winner at 2 yrs: little form in handicap and claimer in 1991: should stay 1¼m: has worn crossed noseband: gelded and off course 5 months after third start, blinkered next. *W. J. Pearce.*

TOSS OF THE COIN 4 ch.g. Rabdan 129 – Cedees 48 (Habat 127) [1990 7m 6f⁶ — 6m 7g⁴ 6m a6g 7m 1991 a8g] sturdy gelding: modest performer as 2-y-o: has lost his form. needs further than 6f, and stays 1m: appears unsuited by soft ground: very slowly away in blinkers once: sometimes hangs. *P. D. Evans.*

TOSS THE DICE 2 ch.c. (Feb 3) Risk Me (FR) 127 – Curfew 76 (Midsummer **48 p** Night II 117) [1991 8m⁵] 30,000F, IR 50,000Y: lengthy colt: has scope: half-brother to 1980 2-y-o 5f winner Goodbye Starter (by Owen Dudley) and 2 winners in Italy: dam placed over 6f at 2 yrs: 5/1, promising fifth of 7 in maiden at Goodwood in September, handy to 2f out, not knocked about when beaten: sure to improve. *M. A. Jarvis.*

TOTAL SHAMBLES (IRE) 3 b.c. Taufan (USA) 119 – Home Bird (Ragusa **44** 137) [1990 a6g 6g 6g⁶ 7f a7g 8m 1991 8.2d 9d a11g 10g 10m 15s 9.2d⁴ 8.3d* 9.2m³ 8m 10m 9.7g] smallish, angular colt: poor mover: poor performer: made all in maiden claimer on second run in 24 hours at Hamilton in July: probably stays 1¼m: acts on dead ground: visored or blinkered in 1991, except for last 5 starts: inconsistent. *J. S. Wainwright.*

TOTAL SPORT (USA) 3 b.f. Taufan (USA) 119 – Miss Habitat (Habitat 134) — [1990 7m 7m 6g 7m⁶ 1991 8m 6f⁶ 10g] leggy, angular filly: poor maiden. *R. Hannon.*

TOUCH ABOVE 5 b.h. Touching Wood (USA) 127 – B A Poundstretcher 82 **61** (Laser Light 118) [1990 8.2s 10f³ 10m* 10.2m⁴ 10d⁶ 10f 10d² a12g² 10f* 10.2f² 10f² 10g⁶ 10.2m³ 12g⁴ 10.2g² 10m* 10.5g⁶ 10m 1991 8m 10f* 10m 9.9g³ 10d 9.9f⁴ 10.2g⁶ 9.9f³ 12m² 9.9f* 10.1m 12f⁶ 9.9f² 9m³ 9m* 10m] leggy horse: good mover: quite modest handicapper: won at Beverley (successful 6 times there) in May and August and Redcar in October: pulled much too hard final start: effective at 9f to 1½m: acts particularly well on a sound surface: has won when sweating: usually set lot to do: tough. *T. D. Barron.*

TOUCHED BY LOVE 3 b.g. Touching Wood (USA) 127 – Secret Valentine 71 **59** (Wollow 132) [1990 NR 1991 10.1m⁴ 10.1f⁴ 14.1f⁶ 12g⁴ 11.5s] neat gelding: second foal: half-brother to 4-y-o 5f and 6f winner Gondo (by Mansingh): dam 6f to 1m winner: quite modest maiden: fourth of 20 in handicap at Folkestone penultimate start, always front rank: stays 1½m: mounted on track second start: joined Miss S. Wilton. *M. J. Ryan.*

TOUCH IN FLIGHT (IRE) 3 b.c. Formidable (USA) 125 – Tilia (ITY) **61** (Dschingis Khan) [1990 8g⁶ 7d 8d⁵ 1991 10d² 11.7m] strong, good-bodied colt: quite modest maiden: bandaged off-fore, second of 5 at Nottingham, easily better effort in spring as 3-y-o: stays 1¼m: best efforts on dead ground. *J. L. Dunlop.*

TOUCHING TIMES 3 b.g. Touching Wood 127 – Pagan Deity 88 (Brigadier **58** Gerard 144) [1990 5m a6g⁴ 6g⁵ 6g⁵ 7m 7g 8.2d³ 1991 12s* 12.3s⁴ 12m⁴ 14f⁵ 12.2m 11.7g³ 12.4m³ 12.3g 13.6m* 12m⁴] angular, sparely-made gelding: won claimers at Leicester in March and Redcar in August: should stay beyond 1½m: acts on good to firm and soft ground: has worn bandages: joined G. Pritchard-Gordon. *G. A. Pritchard-Gordon.*

TOUCHLIN PRIDE 5 b.g. Touch Boy 109 – Lindrake's Pride (Mandrake Major — 122) [1990 8f 8m 10d 7.5d 8.2g 8f 8.5g⁵ 6g 1991 9m] small gelding: quite modest maiden at 3 yrs: not nearly so good nowadays: stays 1m: acts on good to firm ground: tried blinkered once: unseated rider and bolted once: often sweats. *A. Harrison.*

TOUCH 'N' PASS 3 ch.g. Dominion 123 – Hanglands (Bustino 136) [1990 6g 8m — 1991 10m a8g a11g 12f a8g⁶] sparely-made, dipped-backed gelding: no form in maidens and handicaps. *R. O'Leary.*

TOUCH OF WHITE 5 ch.m. Song 132 – Cayla (Tumble Wind (USA)) [1990 5m* — 5g* 5m 5g⁶ 5d⁴ 1991 5g 5g 5g 5m] big, useful-looking mare: fair 5f handicapper: chipped bone in knee in May, 1990: faced stiffish tasks in 1991: acts on dead ground: ran well when blinkered once. *J. Banks.*

TOUCH PAPER (USA) 2 br. or br.c. (May 5) Majestic Light (USA) – Mitey **77 p** Lively (USA) (Olden Times) [1991 7g 6m 7m²] $120,000Y: sturdy, lengthy colt: has a fluent action: half-brother to minor winners in USA by Raise A Native and Nodouble: dam, stakes winner, was runner-up in Acorn Stakes and Kentucky Oaks: weak 7/1-shot, easily best effort when staying-on length second of 16 to Stani in maiden at Leicester in October, having travelled well most of way: will stay 1m: may well progress further, and should win a maiden in due course. *B. W. Hills.*

TOUCH THE CLOUDS 4 b.f. Precocious 126 – Siouxsie 90 (Warpath 113) — [1990 8g 10g 12s 15d³ 16s 1991 12.3d 8.3s 8.3d 13.8m] rather leggy, good-topped filly: moderate mover: poor handicapper, still a maiden: probably stays 15f: acts on heavy going: wears tongue strap nowadays. *C. W. Thornton.*

TOUJOURS LA MUR 3 br.f. Lidhame 109 – Soie Gentille 59 (Shantung 132) — [1990 NR 1991 a8g⁴ a8g⁶] second foal: half-sister to 4-y-o Plain Silk (by Class Distinction): dam needed test of stamina: no worthwhile form in early-season maidens: bought 875 gns Ascot July (1990) Sales. *C. C. Elsey.*

TOULAL 3 b.f. Taufan (USA) 119 – Premiere Cuvee 109 (Formidable (USA) 125) 44 [1990 5d 5d³ 6d⁵ a5g a5g⁵ 1991 6f 5g 5g³ 5m 5d] leggy filly: poor mover: poor maiden: easily best efforts at 5f on easy ground. *M. Johnston.*

TOULON 3 b.c. Top Ville 129 – Green Rock (FR) 86 (Mill Reef (USA) 141) 125 [1990 9g* 1991 10.5d³ 12.3d* 12f 12.5g* 14.6m* 12d⁴]

'(those) who trod Doncaster town moor during race time did not all appear there solely with a view to betting. Very far from it. They delighted in a good horse and a stirring race and in that spirit . . . pour into the main street of Doncaster on the morning of the great race. Anyone desirous of studying the characteristics of the north country folk, as shown in face and form, could find no better place and opportunity for so doing than that afforded by a first floor window, in Hall Gate, let us say, between twelve and one o'clock on the St Leger day. There he will see them of all sorts, from the big-limbed, sturdy sons of the wolds and dales, to the spare, narrow-chested artisans, whose homes are in the great Yorkshire manufacturing towns. There they are, the brawny and the puny, marching along, in the main cheery and good humoured, to one destination, and talking all the time about "t'Leger".' The size of racing crowds and the sociological character of the North may have changed somewhat since *Racing Illustrated* visited Doncaster in 1895, but one thing remains the same—the St Leger is still a race to savour. The latest running saw two colts draw fifteen lengths clear in a gripping trial of strength before the race was decided, Toulon beating Saddlers' Hall. Beforehand, the 1991 St Leger, sponsored for the first time by Coalite, looked an open race, every

Dalham Chester Vase, Chester—usually one of the most informative Derby trials; it is won impressively by the French challenger Toulon

Coalite St Leger Stakes, Doncaster—
Toulon wears down Saddlers' Hall (rails) with the rest well beaten

horse in the field holding a chance of a place. Toulon, Saddlers' Hall and Corrupt had won five pattern races between them at around a mile and a half and were the pick on form, opposed by the Prix du Jockey-Club fourth Luchiroverte and six others who were rising through the ranks in Arcadian Heights, Fly Away Soon, Jahafil and Jendali, who'd all won listed races on their latest starts, and the Old Newton Cup winner Libk and Melrose Handicap winner Micheletti. The last-named—ridden by Piggott—attracted very strong support, eventually starting second favourite to Toulon. Nearly all the field looked in fine shape in the preliminaries. In the race, Arcadian Heights and Jahafil took them along, checking early to avoid a man and child sitting on the track but otherwise striding out at a really good clip as Toulon and Micheletti settled in the rear. The pace was so searching that coming off the turn only Saddlers' Hall, who'd moved up to dispute second, and the first two favourites were still going reasonably well, Saddlers' Hall finding himself in front at the four-furlong marker. As Reid took the race by the scruff of the neck and kicked Saddlers' Hall over three lengths clear in the space of a furlong, Toulon found a gap through mid-field and Micheletti ran into trouble on the rails, never re-emerging with a chance. It made little difference. Saddlers' Hall was in full cry and Toulon the only one who could do anything about it, gradually pulling him back with his powerful, raking stride; he'd got to Saddlers' Hall a furlong out and he kept up the effort to win by a length and a half. The rest were strung out like a Grand National field, though for the record Micheletti finished third.

It was Toulon's third start in Britain and the second time he'd started favourite for one of the classics. He'd shared favouritism with Corrupt in the Ever Ready Derby, the performance that put him at the head of the betting an impressive display in the Dalham Chester Vase. The Chester Vase had a succession of quality winners in the previous ten runnings—Henbit, Shergar, Law Society, Unfuwain, Old Vic and Belmez—and there was no doubting that in Toulon it had another. In a five-runner race, Toulon quickened well to close on the leaders three furlongs out then Eddery had to rein back, with no room

Mr K. Abdulla's "Toulon"

in front of him. Toulon looked a certain winner even at that relatively early stage but entering the straight he couldn't get a run again and was badly bumped before being switched to the outside. Then he quickened again, and in good style with a minimum of effort from the saddle, to beat Luchiroverte a length and a half and Peking Opera another three quarters. The Derby four weeks later, however, was a bitter disappointment. Toulon was never going at all well on the very firm ground and, held up in the rear again, he remained there, finishing tailed off. The ground seemed the most plausible explanation for this dire performance—though, of course, we saw at Doncaster that a galloping track suits him particularly well—and on good going at Maisons-Laffitte in July Toulon was winning again, quickening clear one and a half furlongs out then holding Topanoora by two lengths in the Prix Maurice de Nieuil.

Toulon is by Top Ville who is now back in France, standing at the Haras d'Etreham at a reported 100,000 francs (approximately £10,000), after a spell at Dalham Hall. He is the sire of sixteen pattern or graded winners, Toulon coming very much from the mould, as only one of that sixteen (Norwich) won a pattern race over less than a mile and only one (Pistolet Bleu who won pattern events at nine furlongs and a mile and a quarter in 1990) as a two-year-old. Toulon is the second living foal out of Green Rock, her first being Greenovia (by Ahonoora) who won a mile maiden at Newcastle at two years before reportedly breaking a leg. Toulon is followed by Aquamarine (by Shardari, and therefore a close relation), once-raced for Barry Hills in the autumn, and a 1991 filly by Alzao. Green Rock visited Top Ville again in 1991. She was also trained by Hills. She had her first two races in the Rockfel Stakes and Lupe Stakes but proved only modest, gaining victories at 8/13 and 4/7 in a maiden at Brighton and minor event at Bath, both at around a mile and a half. Green Rock is a sister to the Prix de Psyche winner Green Reef and half-sister to the very smart colt Greensmith and the 1991 Prix Berteux winner Ecologist. Their dam Infra Green had twenty-four starts over three seasons, starting off in Ireland where she won a six-furlong maiden and was given 7-10 in the Irish Free Handicap, and ending her career with a win in the one-and-a-half-mile Gran Premio del Jockey Club at Milan. In between, she'd established herself as one of France's leading middle-distance fillies, her most notable triumph coming, from amongst others Ivanjica and Rose Bowl, in the 1976 Prix Ganay. Infra Green's half-sister North Forland, runner-up in the Ribblesdale Stakes, is dam of the very useful French fillies Libertine and Harmless Albatross and the disqualified 1991 Premio Parioli winner Fortune's Wheel.

Toulon (b.c. 1988)	Top Ville (b 1976)	High Top (b 1969)	Derring-Do Camenae
		Sega Ville (b 1968)	Charlottesville La Sega
	Green Rock (FR) (ch 1981)	Mill Reef (b 1968)	Never Bend Milan Mill
		Infra Green (ch 1972)	Laser Light Greenback II

Toulon is a tall, rangy colt with the physical scope to train on well who was seen out only once as a two-year-old (winning a newcomers race at Longchamp in October) and progressed well as a three-year-old. It may be that his best days are yet to come, but we think he'll struggle against the top horses at a mile and a half, particularly when conditions place the emphasis on finishing speed rather than stamina. That much seemed to be confirmed by his final race of 1991, the Ciga Prix de l'Arc de Triomphe, in which, niggled along at the back of the field some way from home, Toulon stayed on late into fourth, six lengths behind Suave Dancer. Suave Dancer had also beaten Toulon comfortably in the Prix Greffulhe at the same course in April and there is no reason why their relative merits at a mile and a half should change much in 1992. We should like to see both Toulon and Saddlers' Hall over further than a mile and a half again, but then, their owners would probably like to see more worthwhile prizes over staying distances. Toulon acts on good to firm ground and dead. *A. Fabre, France.*

TOURTERELLE 2 br.f. (Mar 8) Alleging (USA) 120 – Frivole 75 (Comedy Star (USA) 121) [1991 7m] smallish filly: first foal: dam 7f winner: 33/1 and better for race, well beaten in large-field maiden at Lingfield in September. *Miss B. Sanders.* —

TOUSSAUD (USA) 2 b. or br.f. (May 6) El Gran Senor (USA) 136 – Image of Reality (USA) (In Reality) [1991 6f²] compact filly: sister to 3-y-o 7f winner Navarra and half-sister to 4 winners, including Canadian Grade 3 7f winner Image of Class (by Codex): dam smart winner at up to 9f at 4 yrs in North America: 11/2 favourite, 1½ lengths second of 21, always thereabouts, to High Sevens in maiden at Newbury in August: will stay at least 7f: will improve, and probably win a maiden. *J. H. M. Gosden.* **75 p**

TOWER BRIDGE (USA) 3 b.c. Riverman (USA) 131 – Linklighter 89 (Busted 134) [1990 NR 1991 8m⁴ 8d² 8m 12g 11.5s] quite good-topped colt: poor mover: fourth foal: dam 6f and 1¼m winner, is granddaughter of Yorkshire Oaks winner Palatch, dam of Patch: quite modest form at best in claimers: showed little after claimed out of R. Smyth's stable £10,003 third (hung right) start: should stay 1¼m: blinkered final outing. *Dr J. D. Scargill.* **57 ?**

TOWNY BOY 5 b.g. Camden Town 125 – Serenesse (Habat 127) [1990 NR 1991 a11g 12g⁵] leggy gelding: poor mover, with a round action: fair handicapper as 3-y-o: no worthwhile form after: suited by 1¼m: probably requires soft ground. *J. M. Jefferson.* —

TRACE OF IRONY (USA) 5 b. or br.m. Cannonade (USA) – Tracy L (USA) (Bold Favorite (USA)) [1990 a8g⁵ a12g⁵ a8g a8g⁶ 10.2f a11g 1991 a8g] quite good-topped mare: has a quick action: quite modest maiden at best, but has deteriorated: probably stays 1m: tried blinkered once: winning selling hurdler in February. *Mrs A. Knight.* —

TRACY'S PRINCE (IRE) 3 ch.g. Be My Guest (USA) 126 – Princess Tracy 111 (Ahonoora 122) [1990 6m 7m³ 8m⁵ 8.2m⁵ 7m 1991 a10g⁴ 7.5m³ 8.5f⁴ 8.5f³] leggy, **61**

sparely-made gelding: moderate mover: quite modest maiden: didn't find much off bridle final start, in July: stays 1m: acts on firm going: sweating third (ran creditably) start: trained until after reappearance by B. Hills. *J. L. Spearing.*

TRADERS DREAM 2 b.c. (May 1) Superlative 118 – Divine Thought 102 **62** (Javelot 124) [1991 6g 6m 7m] IR 8,000Y: good-topped colt: half-brother to 3-y-o Zuhal (by Busted) and 3 winners, including Dee Stakes victor Great Idea (by Great Nephew) and fairly useful stayer Inde Pulse (by Troy): dam, half-sister to high-class 1969 2-y-o Divine Gift, won from 1¼m to 12.5f: quite modest form in listed race at Newbury (behind Rodrigo de Triano) and minor event at Pontefract won by Tamim: ran poorly in Leicester maiden auction week later in September: should stay 7f. *T. Thomson Jones.*

TRADITION 2 b.f. (Feb 23) Last Tycoon 131 – Consolation 95 (Troy 137) [1991 **64** 7m⁴ 8m³] angular, quite attractive filly: has scope: good walker: third foal: half-sister to useful 3-y-o 1m and 1¼m winner Claret (by Rousillon): dam 2-y-o 7f winner stayed 1½m, is half-sister to high-class middle-distance performer Morcon: quite modest form, keeping on, in late-season maidens at Leicester won by Anlace and Pabouche: looked green still and may do better: will stay at least 1¼m. *Major W. R. Hern.*

TRAFALGAR BOY (USA) 2 b.c. (Apr 30) Stalwart (USA) – Emy's A Natural **77** (USA) (Coastal (USA)) [1991 6g⁵ 8m³ 8.1d* 8.3s⁵] $20,000Y: workmanlike colt: third foal: dam won twice at up to 6f at 2 yrs: sire won 4 of 5 races at around 1m at 2 yrs (only season to race), including Grade 1 Norfolk Stakes: modest form: ridden by 7-lb claimer, won maiden at Haydock in October, never far away, kept on well: respectable fifth of 18 in nursery at Hamilton following month: will be better suited by 1¼m. *J. Etherington.*

TRAHIN 3 ch.c. Kris 135 – Mangayah (USA) 115 (Spectacular Bid (USA)) [1990 **—** NR 1991 10g 10.2m⁶] big, useful-looking colt: first foal: dam French 9f and 1½m winner out of half-sister to dam of Shareef Dancer: 4/1, sweating and wearing tongue strap, 12½ lengths sixth of 20 to Mashaallah in maiden at Doncaster in June, never placed to challenge: eased right down 1f out (jockey seemed to think something amiss) on debut. *A. A. Scott.*

TRAINBLEU 3 b.c. Siberian Express (USA) 125 – Skyey 70 (Skymaster 126) **54 §** [1990 6m³ 5.8m³ 6m* 6m 7g 7m 1991 7d 9m 12g 6m 6g² 5m⁶ 6m 6g 6g] strong colt: moderate mover: modest handicapper at best: stays 7f: acts on good to firm ground: sometimes blinkered: retained 3,600 gns Ascot July Sales: inconsistent and one to be wary of. *R. F. Johnson Houghton.*

TRAINEE (USA) 2 b.f. (Mar 20) Danzig Connection (USA) – Rosette (USA) **—** (Military Plume) [1991 7d] $70,000F: half-sister to several minor winners, one stakes placed: dam won 11 races at up to 9f from 2 yrs to 6 yrs: 25/1 and backward, always behind in 21-runner maiden at Doncaster in November. *W. J. Haggas.*

TRAINGLOT 4 ch.c. Dominion 123 – Mary Green 81 (Sahib 114) [1990 12.3d² **110** 14f* 14g⁵ 16g* 18d⁶ 16m? 1991 18.4d 11g* 20g⁴ 15g 18m⁵ 16m⁶] compact colt: very useful performer: won minor event at Beverley: ran well when fourth to Indian Queen in Gold Cup at Royal Ascot later in June: below that form after, fair fifth in Doncaster Cup, modest fifth in Jockey Club Cup at Newmarket: suited by extreme test of stamina: acts on any going. *J. G. FitzGerald.*

TRALEE MAIDEN (IRE) 3 br.f. Persian Bold 123 – Tralee Falcon 82 (Falcon **—** 131) [1990 6g 5f* a7g 1991 a5g 7m] leggy filly: blinkered, quite modest winner at 2 yrs: always behind in claimer and seller in spring as 3-y-o: should be at least as effective at 6f as 5f. *N. A. Callaghan.*

TRANSATLANTICDREAM 3 b.g. Fast Gold (USA) – Proud Miss (USA) **—** (Semi-Pro) [1990 7g 1991 10g] leggy gelding: bit backward, no form in maidens. *I. A. Balding.*

TRANSCRIPT 3 b.f. Transworld (USA) 121 – Lawyer's Wave (USA) (Advocator) **—** [1990 6m 8.2s² 1991 11.5g 10d⁶ 8.1m⁵] rangy filly: modest form at best: showed little in listed races and maiden in 1991: should stay 1¼m: sweating and edged left final start, in July: sold 5,800 gns Newmarket Autumn Sales. *C. E. Brittain.*

TRANSCRIPT (USA) 2 ch.c. (Mar 30) Secretariat (USA) – Devon Ditty 122 **82** (Song 132) [1991 7g⁴ 7.1s 8m²] compact, good-quartered colt: good walker: good mover with light action: half-brother to several winners, including useful 1985 2-y-o 1m winner Ivybridge (by Sir Ivor): dam, best 2-y-o filly in Britain in 1978, subsequently won 9f stakes race in USA: fair maiden: 1½ lengths second of 15 to Aljernaas at Pontefract in October, making most: stays 1m: seems unsuited (well beaten at odds on) by soft ground: sold 24,000 gns Newmarket Autumn Sales. *G. Harwood.*

TRATTORIA (USA) 2 b.f. (Mar 8) Alphabatim (USA) 126 – Falabella (Steel **62** Heart 128) [1991 5m* 5m⁴ 7m⁴ 7.5f 7.6d] leggy, sparely-made filly: moderate walker and mover: half-sister to 1988 Irish 2-y-o 6f winner Botero (by Nasty And Bold) and a winner in North America by Darby Creek Road: dam, maiden here and in USA, is daughter of speedy half-sister to top-class sprinter Matatina and high-class miler Showdown: quite modest performer: won maiden at Thirsk in May: off course over 3 months and on toes, well below form in nursery at Chester final start: better suited by 7f than 5f: possibly unsuited by dead ground. *Denys Smith.*

TRAVELLING BLUES (IRE) 3 gr.g. Ballad Rock 122 – Danielle Delight **50** (Song 132) [1990 5f 5m⁶ 5m* 1991 5d 5m 6g 7m 7f⁴ 8m⁵ 7f² 7f 7m³ 7m] tall, leggy, quite good-topped gelding: plating-class handicapper: placed twice at Catterick: stays 7f: acts on firm going: trained until after penultimate start by Mrs J. Ramsden. *P. A. Blockley.*

TRAVEL MYTH 3 ch.f. Bairn (USA) 126 – Travel Legend 72 (Tap On Wood 130) **60 §** [1990 6f 8g⁴ 7g⁴ 8d⁶ 1991 8.3d⁶ 10g³ 10g] leggy, rather sparely-made filly: quite modest maiden: sweating and edgy, hampered early, hung and found little final start: stays 1¼m: below form on dead going: carries head high, and none too keen. *Mrs G. R. Reveley.*

TRAVEL TOKEN 3 b.g. Tina's Pet 121 – Guiletta 63 (Runnymede 123) [1990 **50** 5m 6g 6d³ 1991 6s 6g⁵ 6m⁴] smallish, rather dipped-backed gelding: has a very round action: plating-class maiden: best 3-y-o effort on final start, in July: stays 6f: acts on good to firm ground and dead. *L. J. Holt.*

TREAD LIKA PRINCE 5 b.h. Prince Tenderfoot (USA) 126 – Flat Refusal **50** (USA) (Ribero 126) [1990 10d 7m a6g⁴ 6d a5g a6g⁵ 5m² a6g³ 6m a6g a6g⁵ 1991 6d*] compact, workmanlike horse: moderate mover: plating-class handicapper: not seen again after winning selling event (bought in 3,500 gns) at Pontefract in April: may well prove best at up to 1m: acts on good to firm ground and soft going: has been visored, blinkered nowadays: has looked a difficult ride: none too reliable at 4 yrs. *Ronald Thompson.*

TREASURE TIME (IRE) 2 b.f. (Mar 20) Treasure Kay 114 – Dowcester 63 **55** (Habitat 134) [1991 6m 6f 6.1f⁶ 5f² 6m] 2,500Y: workmanlike filly: has scope: third foal: dam, placed at 7f from 2 starts at 3 yrs, is out of half-sister to high-class performers Hot Spark and Bitty Girl: plating-class maiden: unlucky favourite in seller at Folkestone in September, running on well after getting checked, beaten a neck: below best in Lingfield seller week later: stays 6f: yet to race on easy ground. *J. White.*

TREASURE TROVE (USA) 2 ch.f. (May 20) The Minstrel (CAN) 135 – River **62** Jig (USA) 98 (Irish River (FR) 131) [1991 5m² 6g⁴ 5d² 7m³ 7m⁵ 8.3s] smallish, sturdy filly: first foal: dam 9f (at 2 yrs) and 1½m winner: plating-class maiden: creditable fifth of 16, staying on well, to Marabella Star in nursery at York in October: stays 7f: acts on good to firm and dead ground: sold 8,000 gns Newmarket December Sales. *M. Bell.*

TREATY STONE LADY 3 b.f. Hotfoot 126 – H R Micro 77 (High Award 119) **—** [1990 5m⁵ 6d 5g 5m⁶ 8m 5m 1991 8m] sturdy filly: poor maiden. *I. Campbell.*

TREBLE (USA) 3 b.f. Riverman (USA) 131 – Trevilla (USA) (Lyphard (USA) **118** 132) [1990 7v⁴ 9v* 1991 9.2g² 10g* 10.5d 9d⁶ 10f⁵] third foal: sister to French maiden Trevillari, second over 1¼m at 2 yrs: dam unraced half-sister to Triptych (by Riverman): won maiden at Maisons-Laffitte in December at 2 yrs and Prix Saint Alary (by ¾ length from Polemic) at Longchamp in May at 3 yrs: ran moderately in Prix de Diane Hermes at Chantilly, creditably (beaten less than 2 lengths) when sixth in Prix de l'Opera at Longchamp 4 months later: 5½ lengths fifth of 8 to Lady Shirl in E P Taylor Stakes at Woodbine: stayed 1¼m: bought by Hamdan Al-Maktoum and visits Caerleon. *Mme C. Head, France.*

TREBLY 3 b.c. Top Ville 129 – Jeema 102 (Thatch (USA) 136) [1990 8.2s 8d⁵ **102 ?** 10.2s⁵ 1991 10.2s² 10d² 10m 10g⁵ 12g² 12g] tall colt: fair form until ½-length second of 3, apparently vastly improved, to Stylish Senor in Gordon Stakes at Goodwood fifth start, rallying gamely: well beaten in Gran Premio d'Italia at Milan 7 weeks later: suited by 1½m: yet to race on firm ground, probably acts on any other: may well have been flattered at Goodwood. *C. E. Brittain.*

TREE FROG (IRE) 2 b.f. (Feb 26) Lomond (USA) 128 – Mountain Lodge 120 **56 p** (Blakeney 126) [1991 7d] fifth foal: half-sister to 3-y-o 12.3f (stays 15f) winner Uluru (by Kris) and 1¼m winner Turbine Blade (by Kings Lake): dam won Cesarewitch and Irish St Leger: 25/1, over 15 lengths seventh of 21 to Berseto in maiden at Doncaster in November, green and behind early, stayed on well from 3f out: swished tail: will improve, particularly granted middle distances. *Lord Huntingdon.*

TREE OWL 2 b.g. (Apr 12) Bold Owl 101 – Jennie's Darling (The Brianstan 128) 37 [1991 5g⁶ 5g 7m 7f] 2,200F, 1,900Y: sparely-made gelding: first reported foal: dam poor maiden: poor plater, last seen out in July. *M. W. Ellerby.*

TREMBALINO 3 b.g. Tremblant 112 – Balinese 86 (Balidar 133) [1990 7m 7f⁵ 61 6g⁵ 1991 7d³ 8f* 12f] good-bodied, rather angular gelding: has high knee action: quite modest form: favourite and ridden by 7-lb claimer, led post in maiden at Brighton in April: never travelling well in handicap 6 weeks later: stays 1m: acts on firm going: sold to join G. Harwood 3,100 gns Ascot September Sales. *R. V. Smyth.*

TRENDY AUCTIONEER (IRE) 3 b.g. Mazaad 106 – Trendy Princess 55 (Prince Tenderfoot (USA) 126) [1990 7m 6g 8f 8m 6d 1991 8m* 8.2m a8g 7g 8f 8.2m 10m 10d²] sturdy, lengthy gelding: easily best efforts when making all in claimer at Salisbury in May and staying-on second of 14 in similar event (burly) at Newmarket in November: stays 1¼m: acts on good to firm ground and dead: blinkered or visored in 1991, except final start: joined M. Pipe. *A. Hide.*

TREVVEETHAN (IRE) 2 ch.g. (May 15) On Your Mark 125 – Carrick Slaney – (Red God 128§) [1991 5m 7m] IR 4,000Y: workmanlike gelding: sixth foal: half-brother to a winner in Italy by Try My Best and winner over hurdles in Ireland by English Prince: dam placed at 2 yrs: soon behind, in 7f seller at Redcar in October. *J. Balding.*

TRIAL TIMES (USA) 2 ch.c. (Apr 8) Court Trial (USA) – Vany (USA) (Lord 77 Vancouver (CAN)) [1991 7g² a7g⁴ a7g* 7g⁵ 8m³] $40,000Y: compact colt: has a moderate, quick action: half-brother to useful 1989 2-y-o Miss Running Vany (by Runaway Groom), successful at up to 9f, and closely related to 2 minor winners by Valid Appeal: dam won at up to 1¼m: sire very useful miler: modest performer: won maiden at Southwell in July: wearing severe noseband and carrying condition, good third of 14 to Batabanoo in nursery at Pontefract in September: better suited by 1m than 7f: acts on good to firm ground and fibresand. *W. A. O'Gorman.*

TRIANGULATION 3 b.g. Tremblant 112 – Gangawayhame 91 (Lochnager 132) – [1990 5m 8g 7f⁶ 7g 1991 12f⁵ 11.7s] tall, unfurnished gelding: plating-class maiden: raced freely in handicaps in spring as 3-y-o: stays 1m: sold 3,500 gns Ascot July Sales. *R. V. Smyth.*

TRIBAL MASCOT (USA) 6 b.g. Our Native (USA) – Little Lady Luck (USA) – (Jacinto) [1990 10m 11.5g 17.1d 1991 14m] tall, close-coupled gelding: quite modest handicapper as 3-y-o: lightly raced subsequently and no worthwhile form: stays 1¼m: acts on good to firm going: tried blinkered. *D. R. Gandolfo.*

TRIBAL WAR (USA) 2 gr.g. (Apr 19) Wind And Wuthering (USA) 132 – – Diamond Oyster 72 (Formidable (USA) 125) [1991 a7g 6m 7f] good-topped gelding: second known foal: dam maiden here at 2 yrs stayed 7f, won at around 6f in North America: no worthwhile form in sellers (slowly away) in July then maiden (blinkered) in August: showed round action to post second start. *C. A. Cyzer.*

TRIBUTE TO DAD 4 b.g. Aragon 118 – Bourienne 58 (Bolkonski 134) [1990 8m – 7m⁶ 8v⁵ 12.5g² 10g 10.1m 10m³ 10m⁶ 15.3f 1991 10.2g] workmanlike gelding: moderate mover: plater: stays 1½m: acts on good to firm ground and heavy: has been bandaged: sold 3,300 gns Doncaster November Sales. *D. J. Wintle.*

TRICKY VERA (IRE) 2 ch.f. (Apr 28) Pennine Walk 120 – Madam Loving 99 – (Vaigly Great 127) [1991 5m⁶] lengthy, sparely-made filly: third foal: closely related to a winner in Scandinavia by Persian Bold and half-sister to 3-y-o 6f winner Tbab (by Thatching): dam 5f and 6f winner, best at 2 yrs: supported at long odds, soon remote in 6-runner £8,000 event at Epsom in June. *T. J. Naughton.*

TRICOTRIC 4 br.f. Electric 126 – Orpheline 76 (Thatch (USA) 136) [1990 8m 42 10m 10.6s 10g 10g⁶ a14g 11m⁴ 12m 1991 12.4v* 12d² 13d⁴ 15m⁶ 12.1g 16.2d] good-topped filly: poor handicapper: won at Newcastle in April: off course 5 months after third start and below form subsequently: stays 13f: goes very well with plenty of give in the ground. *G. M. Moore.*

TRICYCLE (IRE) 2 b.g. (Jan 30) Phardante (FR) 120 – Push Bike (Ballad Rock 42 122) [1991 8m 8m⁶ 8.1m] IR 6,000F, 12,000Y: first foal: poor form: never a threat, in maidens: has given impression will stay well. *J. W. Watts.*

TRICYCLING (IRE) 3 b.g. Flash of Steel 120 – Stradavari (Stradavinsky 121) 51 [1990 a7g 7f⁴ 7f 8m 1991 8v² 11f 10m 10.6g 11.1g² 10.5d⁴ 11d⁵ 12.1m] leggy gelding: plating-class maiden: form only when in frame: stays 11f: possibly best on an easy surface, and acts on heavy going: blinkered last 4 starts: sold to join Miss J. Barclay 3,500 gns Doncaster October Sales. *J. Berry.*

TRING PARK 5 b.g. Niniski (USA) 125 – Habanna 107 (Habitat 134) [1990 a12g³ 12g 12f⁵ 11.7m⁶ 1991 11.4m 17.2g] big, leggy gelding: plating-class handicapper at 4 yrs: no form in 1991: stays 1½m well: acts on firm ground: not the easiest of rides. *R. Curtis.* —

TRIPLE SECRET (USA) 3 b.f. Secreto (USA) 128 – Queen's Banner (USA) (Hoist The Flag (USA)) [1990 7g 1991 10d 10.2f] strong, lengthy filly: shows knee action: behind in minor event and maidens. *R. Hannon.* —

TRIPLE TROUBLE 2 br.c. (Apr 13) Nomination 125 – Be Malicious (Malicious) [1991 6f 7m 7g] 9,400Y: workmanlike colt: poor mover: half-brother to Irish 1m winner Leopoldville (by Record Token) and a winner over jumps abroad: dam thrice-raced half-sister to very useful 5f and 13f winner Costmary: bit backward or sweating, no threat in large-field maiden auctions. *H. J. Collingridge.* **33**

TRIPLICATE 5 b.h. Mill Reef (USA) 141 – Triple First 117 (High Top 131) [1990 8m⁴ 8m 9m⁵ 10.6v 1991 a10g² a10g a12g⁵ 10.8m³ 12f³ 17.1m³ 14.8m² 15.8f⁵ 14g³ 16.2d 12.1g² 15.4f⁵ 16m* 17.2g] small horse: poor walker: quite modest handicapper at best: won at Southwell: tailed off later in September: stays 17f: probably acts on any going: goes well with forcing tactics: effective blinkered or not: often bandaged near-fore: sold 5,200 gns Newmarket Autumn Sales. *J. L. Dunlop.* **66**

TRISETTE 3 ch.f. Adonijah 126 – Canasta Girl 90 (Charlottesville 135) [1990 8g⁴ 10s⁵ 1991 11.5f 13.1m⁴ 12m⁶] quite good-topped filly: modest maiden: may prove suited by test of stamina: sold 4,000 gns Newmarket Autumn Sales. *W. Jarvis.* —

TRISTAN'S COMET 4 br.g. Sayf El Arab (USA) 127 – Gleneagle 91 (Swing Easy (USA) 126) [1990 8m a8g³ 10.2f 8.3m 8m⁶ 10m 1991 a12g] leggy gelding: quite modest at best: no form on flat for some time: stays 1m: winning hurdler on all-weather. *J. L. Harris.* —

TRISTIORUM 4 ch.g. Crofthall 110 – Annie-Jo (Malicious) [1990 7.2d 10.2s a8g³ a12g³ a11g 1991 14.1m⁴ 16.9m 12.1m⁴ 12.1s a12g² a12g] rangy gelding: plating-class a 59 performer: best effort in 1991 when second in claimer at Southwell: tailed off three final start: best form at 1½m: has run well blinkered: best form on all-weather: trained until after penultimate start by J. Etherington. *W. Clay.*

TRIUMPHAL SONG 4 ch.g. Caerleon (USA) 132 – Zither 72 (Vienna 127) [1990 8g 11g⁵ 11.5m* 12.2g⁴ 12.5m⁶ 12m 1991 10g 10d] workmanlike gelding: quite modest handicapper at 3 yrs: no show in first half of 1991: suited by 1½m: acts on firm ground: has won when sweating: joined M. Pipe. *Mrs J. R. Ramsden.* —

TRIVIALITY 3 br.f. Sharpo 132 – Idle Days 80 (Hittite Glory 125) [1990 6g³ 6d* 6g* 5d⁵ 1991 7d³ 6m⁴ 7m⁴ 6m⁶ 6m² 6g²] leggy, quite good-topped filly: useful performer: excellent narrowly-beaten second in large-field handicaps at Newmarket (to Stack Rock) and Doncaster (to Gilt Throne) in October: well below form previous 3 starts: best efforts at 6f: acts on good to firm ground and dead: sold 24,000 gns Newmarket Autumn Sales. *J. H. M. Gosden.* **103**

TROJAN CROWN (IRE) 3 b.f. Trojan Fen 118 – Crown Witness 95 (Crowned Prince (USA) 128) [1990 7f* 7f* 8g³ 8m⁵ 1991 10g⁴ 8m³ 7g⁵ 8m² 8g 9m 7s⁴] rangy filly: good mover and walker: useful form in listed race (sweating) at Sandown, Jersey Stakes at Royal Ascot and Child Stakes (keeping on strongly 1½ lengths behind Only Yours, best effort) at Newmarket second to fourth outings: below form in Prix d'Astarte at Deauville and listed races last 3 starts: should stay beyond 1m: acts on firm ground: blinkered final start. *G. Wragg.* **105**

TROJAN ENVOY 3 br.g. Trojan Fen 118 – Gold Maid (FR) (Green Dancer (USA) 132) [1990 NR 1991 10d 8s 10m 14f⁴ 14f⁴ 14g 16.2g 14.6m 14.1m] 10,500Y: sturdy, close-coupled gelding: second foal: dam 1½m winner in France, raced only at 3 yrs: plating-class form: seems suited by test of stamina: acts on firm going: winning hurdler. *W. Carter.* **49**

TROJAN EXCEL 4 b.f. Trojan Fen 118 – War Ballad (FR) (Green Dancer (USA) 132) [1990 9m² 8.2g² 8.5m² 7h³ 8.2g⁵ 8m⁵ a8g 8.2m 9m 8d a12g a11g 1991 a11g] strong, compact filly: carries condition: good mover: quite modest handicapper at best: has lost her form: should stay 1¼m: acts on firm ground: tried visored, blinkered and with eyeshield: has hung right and found little: sold 1,900 gns Doncaster January Sales. *C. Tinkler.* —

TROJAN LANCER 5 b.h. Trojan Fen 118 – Dunster's Cream 51 (Sharpen Up 127) [1990 11f* 10.2m³ 12m* 12.4m³ 11.5m³ 12m² 13.6d 1991 12m⁵ 12g⁵ 12m⁴ 12m* 11.8g⁵ 11.8g² 12g³ 12d] sturdy, close-coupled horse: carries condition: moderate **63**

walker and mover: quite modest handicapper: won at Carlisle in June: easily best subsequent effort on sixth outing: stays 1½m: ideally suited by top-of-the-ground: suited by waiting tactics. *Dr J. D. Scargill.*

TROJAN STEEL 4 gr.c. Bellypha 130 – Troja (Troy 137) [1990 7m 9f⁵ 12.4s 1991 — 8f 9f] sparely-made colt: plating-class ex-Irish maiden: no form since 2 yrs. *P. Liddle.*

TRONCHETTO (IRE) 2 b.g. (Apr 13) Shernazar 131 – Idle Days 80 (Hittite **65** Glory 125) [1991 8g⁵ 8.1d a7g] strong, workmanlike gelding: has a long, round stride: fifth live foal: half-brother to 3 winners here and abroad, including useful 3-y-o sprinter Triviality (by Sharpo): dam placed from 5f to 10.5f, is out of very useful middle-distance stayer Paresseuse: easily best effort in Wolverhampton minor event on debut: will stay middle distances. *Sir Mark Prescott.*

TROOPING (IRE) 2 b.c. (Apr 2) Auction Ring (USA) 123 – Tunguska 76 **71 p** (Busted 134) [1991 6d⁶] 31,000Y: good-bodied colt: sixth foal: dam 1¼m winner stayed 1½m: 8/1, bit backward and green, over 5 lengths sixth of 7 to Pure Formality in maiden at Ascot in October, chasing leaders over 4f, not knocked about: will improve. *G. Harwood.*

TROPICAL ACE 4 b.f. Final Straw 127 – Rampage 93 (Busted 134) [1990 12f **38** 12m 14f³ 18m⁴ 18d³ 1991 16.2g 16.5m⁴ 16.2f⁴] sturdy filly: has a quick action: plating-class handicapper at best: stays well: acts on good to firm and dead ground: often bandaged. *R. Voorspuy.*

TROPICAL ORCHID 3 b.f. Nomination 125 – Sister Hannah 70 (Monseigneur — (USA) 127) [1990 6m 5m 5f⁶ 5m 5m 1991 5g 6s⁶ 5.1f 6.9m 6m 6f 9.7g] small, stocky filly: poor maiden: probably stays 7f: blinkered final start: sold 900 gns Ascot November Sales. *R. Voorspuy.*

TROTH (USA) 3 ch.f. Blushing Groom (FR) 131 – Suave (USA) (Majestic — Prince) [1990 NR 1991 10.4m] unfurnished filly: fourth reported foal: half-sister to U.S. 1985 2-y-o Grade 3 1m winner Swear (by Believe It) and to 2 winners in North America by Spectacular Bid: dam stakes-placed winner of 5 races: 16/1, bandaged behind and green, well beaten in maiden at York in October, very slowly away then dropping away again early in straight. *J. H. M. Gosden.*

TROUBLEWITHJACK 3 br.f. Sulaafah (USA) 119 – Babe In The Wood **39** (Athens Wood 126) [1990 5m 6m 7d a7g 1991 a10g⁴ a10g⁵ 8m⁴ 10d 11m⁵ 10f] smallish, workmanlike filly: poor mover: plater: stays 11f: acts on good to firm ground. *W. Carter.*

TROUPE 3 b.c. Sadler's Wells (USA) 132 – Lovelight 112 (Bleep-Bleep 134) [1990 **92** 6g² 6g⁵ 1991 7g³ 7.6d* 8m 10m⁶ 10g 8.9g⁵ 8.9g 8m² 9m 9g] lengthy colt: fairly useful form: won maiden at Chester in May: favourite, confirmed earlier promise when head second of 16 to Mudaffar in handicap at Doncaster: disappointing afterwards in Cambridgeshire at Newmarket and £30,800 contest at Newbury: stays 1¼m: acts on good to firm ground and dead: tends to get on edge: bandaged off-hind seventh (sweating) start: is held up. *R. W. Hills.*

TROVE 2 b.c. (Apr 5) Treasure Kay 114 – Old Silver (Bold Lad (IRE) 133) [1991 **88** 5m* 6m* 6m⁵ 6m⁴] 7,200Y, 15,500 2-y-o: leggy colt: fifth foal: half-brother to 3-y-o Pilar (by Godswalk), 7f seller winner at 2 yrs: dam placed over 7.9f at 2 yrs in Ireland: fair performer: showed good turn of foot when winning maiden auction at Haydock and minor event at Windsor in August: improved subsequently in similar contests at Doncaster (behind Balla Jidaal) and Leicester (moved poorly down, behind Distinct Thatcher) in autumn: stays 6f: yet to race on good ground. *Mrs N. Macauley.*

TR TOTO 3 b.g. Final Straw 127 – Trigamy 112 (Tribal Chief 125) [1990 6m 1991 — 6g 6m 5g 7m⁶ 7.6s 6m] good-quartered gelding: poor maiden: stays 7f: has worn crossed noseband and been tubed. *C. A. Horgan.*

TRUBEN (USA) 2 ch.f. (Feb 7) Arctic Tern (USA) 126 – Cadbury Hill (USA) **58 p** (Northern Baby (CAN) 127) [1991 6.1m⁵] $45,000F: lengthy, sturdy filly: first foal: dam, maiden, showed some ability in France at 3 yrs: 12/1 from 6/1, burly and green, under 8 lengths fifth of 18 to stable-companion Mount Helena in maiden at Nottingham in October, green early and plenty to do at halfway, then going on well at finish: will improve and be well suited by at least 1m. *H. R. A. Cecil.*

TRUEBOURNE 2 b.c. (May 21) Precocious 126 – Alpine Alice 94 (Abwah 118) — [1991 5m⁵ 5g 5m⁵ 6m] 500Y: workmanlike colt: half-brother to 3-y-o Hot Sunday Sport (by Star Appeal) and 3 winners, including middle-distance stayer Steppey Lane (by Tachypous): dam 2-y-o 7f winner, is daughter of 1000 Guineas third Alpine

Bloom: poor form, including in seller: not seen out after July: trained until after third start by R. Guest: sold 680 gns Doncaster October Sales. *Pat Mitchell.*

TRUE MOOD 2 b.f. (Mar 9) Jalmood (USA) 126 – Madam Muffin 77 (Sparkler 130) [1991 6s a8g a8g] second foal: half-sister to 3-y-o True March (by Daring March): dam maiden sprinter: soundly beaten in late-year maidens. *J. D. Bethell.* —

TRUE OPTIMIST 4 b. or br.g. Try My Best (USA) 130 – Lenticular 42 (Warpath 113) [1990 10g 6g 8d*dis 8m 12g 7m6 a8g 7d 8s 7d4 10.2s 1991 7m 10s 8.3m5 8f 8.3m5 8f] smallish, good-quartered gelding: first past post in handicap at Gowran Park (swerved left and disqualified) at 3 yrs: form in 1991 only when fifth in Windsor sellers: stays 1m: acts on good to firm and dead ground: tried blinkered and visored: unreliable. *Lord Huntingdon.* 42

TRUE TO KEEP 3 b.f. Castle Keep 121 – Polly's Teahouse 68 (Shack (USA) 118) [1990 NR 1991 8m a11g 8g 8d 6m 6.9m 8.3m a10g5 8.3m] rather leggy, angular filly: first live foal: dam, sprint maiden, daughter of half-sister to Right Tack: poor plater: tailed off final start: possibly doesn't stay 1¼m: blinkered last 2 starts: has sweated. *J. D. Bethell.* —

TRUMPET 2 ch.c. (Feb 27) Dominion 123 – Soprano 112 (Kris 135) [1991 6f6 7f4 7g] angular colt: third foal: dam 7.6f and 1m winner, is out of close relation to smart Rhyme Royal: plating-class maiden: should stay 1m +. *Lord Huntingdon.* 56

TRUSS 4 b.g. Lyphard's Special (USA) 122 – Trestle 57 (Three Legs 128) [1990 NR 1991 10.3d5 10.1m 10.8m* 10g5 10.8m5 11m 14.6m5 12m6 12.3g 10.8g6] angular gelding: moderate mover: poor handicapper: won seller (first form, no bid) at Warwick in July: stays 14.6f: acts on good to firm ground: has been tried in visor and blinkers: winning hurdler: sold 2,400 gns Ascot November Sales. *C. Smith.* 46

TRUST DEED (USA) 3 ch.g. Shadeed (USA) 135 – Karelia (USA) 111 (Sir Ivor 135) [1990 7g 7g3 1991 10g 10g 12d] well-made gelding: modest maiden: below form at 3 yrs, looking none too keen in claimer final start: possibly doesn't stay 1¼m: blinkered last 2 outings: sold to join Mrs A. Knight 2,700 gns Ascot July Sales. *Major W. R. Hern.* —

TRUTHFUL IMAGE 2 b.f. (Feb 27) Reesh 117 – Token of Truth (Record Token 128) [1991 5m2 6m2 6f 5m4 a5g3 7f 6m4 5m3 5d2 5.7g*] 920F, 500Y: good-topped filly: moderate mover: second live foal: dam granddaughter of Cry of Truth, best 2-y-o filly of 1974: showed much improved form in 19-runner nursery at Bath in October, winning by 6 lengths: seems suited by around 6f: possibly ideally suited by some give in the ground: should pay her way in handicaps. *M. J. Ryan.* 77

TRY LEGUARD (IRE) 2 gr.c. (Mar 13) Try My Best (USA) 130 – Crown Coral (Main Reef 126) [1991 5v2 5d* 5d2 5g2 6g3 6g 5d] IR 5,200F: close-coupled colt: modest performer: won maiden at Warwick in April: off course 5 months before facing stiff tasks in nurseries final 2 starts: stays 6f. *W. Carter.* 76

TRY TO BE GOOD 2 b.c. (Jan 28) Crofthall 110 – Bold Gift 61 (Persian Bold 123) [1991 5d3 5d6 5m4 a7g*] 5,700F, 16,500Y: strong, lengthy colt: has plenty of scope: fourth foal: half-brother to 7f and 1m seller winner Mrs Gates (by Good Times): dam, ran only at 2 yrs, stayed 7f: much improved form winning maiden at Southwell in June, running on strongly: will stay 1m. *T. D. Barron.* 67

TRY TRUST (USA) 5 ch.h. Vaguely Noble 140 – Klepto (USA) (No Robbery) [1990 11.7m4 10m3 10m* 12m4 1991 10s5 11.9m6 10m 11.5g* 10m4 10g6 13.4m6 12m 12s] lengthy, good-quartered ex-American horse: has a round action: fair handicapper: won at Lingfield in July: below form last 2 starts: stays 1½m: acts on good to firm ground, possibly unsuited by soft: has taken keen hold: sold 16,000 gns Newmarket Autumn Sales. *C. E. Brittain.* 83

TSAR ALEXIS (USA) 3 br.c. Topsider (USA) – Evening Silk (USA) (Damascus (USA)) [1990 6m 6m 1991 6m 7m6 10.2f a8g2 8.1m a16g] quite attractive colt: has a quick action: quite modest maiden: best efforts at Warwick and Southwell second and fourth starts: tailed off in handicap at Lingfield on final one: stays 1m: sold out of B. Hills's stable 5,000 gns Newmarket Autumn Sales after fifth start. *C. L. Popham.* 66

TSUNAMI 3 b.c. Niniski (USA) 125 – Seasurf 106 (Seaepic (USA)) [1990 NR 1991 10.8g4 12m 14m5 10.4g3 14.1f2 16m] tall, leggy, sparely-made colt: poor mover: brother to 7f to 2m winner Janiski, fair staying maiden Skisurf and a winner abroad, and half-brother to winning hurdler Crested (by Busted): dam 2-y-o 7f winner useful at 1m as 3-y-o: fair maiden: placed at York and Yarmouth: always behind in Newmarket handicap: probably stays 1¾m. *C. E. Brittain.* 80

TUDOR DA SAMBA 2 b.c. (Apr 28) Sizzling Melody 117 – La Belle Princesse 85 (Royal Match 117) [1991 6f5 8g6 8m] 11,000F, 28,000Y: leggy colt: second foal: 58

dam Irish 2-y-o 7f winner, is out of half-sister to smart 7f to 1¾m performer Rocamadour: plating-class maiden: best effort sixth of 8 in minor event at Wolverhampton in September: stays 1m: joined J. R. Fanshawe. *Lord John FitzGerald.*

TUDOREALM (USA) 3 b.f. Palace Music (USA) 129 – Lock's Dream (USA) — (Youth (USA) 135) [1990 NR 1991 7d6 7g 8.5m 8g5 10s] IR 56,000Y: rangy, angular filly: first foal: dam French 9f winner also successful in USA, is out of Princess Royal winner Trillionaire: plating-class maiden: bred to be suited by further than 1m. *D. R. C. Elsworth.*

TUDORGATEWAY 3 b.g. Martinmas 128 – Shikra (Sea Hawk II 131) [1990 6m 65 1991 6f 6d6 6.9s3 6m* 7.6g6 7.1m 8m a6g2] stocky, deep-girthed gelding: won apprentice maiden at Pontefract in July: first outing for almost 3 months and easily best run afterwards when second of 13 in very strongly-run handicap at Southwell in December, soon well behind: should stay 1m: acts on good to firm and soft ground: wears crossed noseband: usually taken steadily to post: sometimes slowly away. *M. H. Tompkins.*

TUDOR GOLD 2 b.f. (Apr 29) Sonnen Gold 121 – Tudari (Mister Tudor) [1991 5f — 5m] 770Y: angular filly: first foal: dam unraced: soon remote in sellers at Beverley in May. *J. Norton.*

TUDOR ISLAND 2 b.c. (Apr 30) Jupiter Island 126 – Catherine Howard 68 51 p (Tower Walk 130) [1991 8m 8m] unfurnished colt: seventh foal: half-brother to several winners, including fair 5f winner Breakaway (by Song) and plating-class stayer Goodtime Hal (by Good Times): dam placed over 1¼m: plating-class form in maidens at Newmarket and Pontefract (still green, always behind, not knocked about) week later in October. *C. E. Brittain.*

TUFF STICK 6 b.g. Welsh Saint 126 – Corr Lady (Lorenzaccio 130) [1990 NR — 1991 a12g6 a8g] ex-Irish gelding: fifth foal: half-brother to 1m and 9f winner Miami Star (by Miami Springs) and 2 winners abroad: dam unraced: won 1¼m maiden at Roscommon in 1988: very lightly raced since: tailed off in claimers early in 1991: has won when blinkered: sold 1,050 gns Doncaster Summer Sales. *Mrs J. Jordan.*

TUFRAJ (USA) 3 ch.c. Kris 135 – Greenland Park 124 (Red God 128§) [1990 6m 58 7f5 7m6 1991 8s6 9d 12m] good-bodied colt: plating-class maiden: best effort at 1m on soft ground: visored, led 7f in claimer final start: sold 2,400 gns Newmarket July Sales. *M. R. Stoute.*

TUGRA (FR) 3 b.f. Baby Turk 120 – Ramsar (Young Emperor 133) [1990 6g 8.2s — 1991 8d 7f 11.7g 11m] rather angular filly: poor maiden. *C. James.*

TULAPET 2 gr.f. (Apr 25) Mansingh (USA) 120 – Iridium 78 (Linacre 133) [1991 — 6m 6m] 8,200Y: compact filly: sister to 4 winners here and abroad, notably Petong, and half-sister to a winner abroad: dam stayed 1¼m: no form, including in auction, in early-summer. *S. Dow.*

TULFARRIS 4 b. or br.g. Glenstal (USA) 118 – Trusted Maiden (Busted 134) — [1990 6s3 9g 8g2 8.2d5 7.2d4 8v 1991 a7g3 a7g4 6s a8g3 6g 7m 9.2s a8g] big, a 55 workmanlike gelding: moderate walker and mover: plating-class maiden: no form on turf in 1991: suited by 7f/1m: acts on dead going: visored last 2 starts. *D. Moffatt.*

TUMBELLINA (IRE) 3 b.f. Tumble Wind (USA) – Ange de Feu (Double Form — 130) [1990 NR 1991 a8g 7m] IR 8,500Y: stocky filly: moderate mover: first foal: dam never ran: no promise in maiden and claimer in the summer. *A. Bailey.*

TUMBLECOMBE 4 b.g. Tumble Wind (USA) – Ching A Ling (Pampapaul 121) — [1990 NR 1991 9s 6.1s] strong, lengthy gelding: no sign of ability. *G. B. Balding.*

TUMBLE TWIST (IRE) 3 b.g. Tumble Wind (USA) – Reshuffle (Sassafras 64 (FR) 135) [1990 7m5 7m 6g* 6g 1991 6g 7g 10g4 7g 7g4 7d] leggy gelding: shows high knee action: modest winner at 2 yrs: best efforts at 3 yrs when fourth in auction race at Nottingham and seller at Leicester: stays 1¼m: well beaten on dead ground: reluctant to post final start: suited by forcing tactics: inconsistent. *B. Hanbury.*

TUNBRIDGE WELLS (IRE) 2 b.c. (Feb 22) Sadler's Wells (USA) 132 – 62 p Tenea (Reform 132) [1991 8m] 320,000Y: strong, good-bodied colt: half-brother to 2 winners in Ireland by Golden Fleece, notably fairly useful 1987 2-y-o 1m winner Gold Discovery: dam once-raced half-sister to Tolmi, Tachypous, Tromos and Tyrnavos among others: 7/1, shaped with promise, having several positions, in 22-runner maiden at Newmarket in October: looks sure to do fair bit better. *J. H. M. Gosden.*

TURBOFAN (IRE) 3 b.c. Taufan (USA) 119 – Timinala 58 (Mansingh (USA) 70 § 120) [1990 7m 7m5 7g2 1991 7m 8.3m 9m2 8.5f3 9m5 9m3 10.2s 10m] angular colt: good mover: modest performer: first past post in handicap at Redcar on third start, idling, edging left and demoted: stays 9f: acts on firm going: visored fifth start: tends to hang, and is hard ride: sold 8,400 gns Newmarket Autumn Sales: irresolute. *J. W. Hills.*

TURBO-R 3 ch.g. Rabdan 129 – Golderama (Golden Dipper 119) [1990 5m⁴ 6g 5g 7m⁵ 5.8m 7m⁴ a7g 8m 10m 8d 1991 12.3g a10g] compact gelding: poor plater: showed nothing in minor event (bandaged) and handicap in autumn: stays 6f: visored or blinkered last 6 starts at 2 yrs: possibly ungenuine. *A. J. Chamberlain.* —

TURBULENT RIVER (USA) 3 b. or br.c. Riverman (USA) 131 – Star Pastures 124 (Northfields (USA)) [1990 NR 1991 8d 7f* 8g 7m 7.6g 7g] lengthy colt: brother to lightly-raced maiden Themaameh and half-brother to useful Irish 7f (at 2 yrs) to 13f winner Esprit d'Etoile (by Spectacular Bid) and middle-distance stayer Lord Justice (by Alleged): dam won from 6f to 1m and stayed 1¼m: 11/4 on, comfortably won maiden at Catterick in June: stiff tasks in handicaps next 3 starts: ran poorly in similar event final one: should stay 1m: sold to join Miss J. Barclay 10,000 gns Newmarket Autumn Sales. *L. M. Cumani.* 71

TURF DANCER 4 b.f. Anfield 117 – Cachucha (Gay Fandango (USA) 132) [1990 6v 8.2g 8.2g⁴ 8.2m⁶ 8.2g 8.2m⁴ 8.2g 11s² 11v 1991 11s 10d 11f 10.6g 12.1d 10g⁶ 11.1s⁴ 9.2d 10.9g⁴ 12.1m] leggy, workmanlike filly: poor handicapper: stays 11f: acts on soft ground: inconsistent. *J. S. Wilson.* 35

TURFKONIG (GER) 5 b.h. Anfield 117 – Thekla (GER) (Prince Ippi (GER)) [1990 11g* 11s* 10g* 12s4 1991 9g* 10s4 10g*] German horse: one of the best horses in his country over the last 3 seasons, winning 11 of 17 starts, including Group 1 Mercedes Benz-Preis at Munich in 1990: successful in pattern races in 1991 at Dortmund and Baden-Baden, latter by short-head and 1¼ lengths from Bin Shaddad and Karinga Bay (both rec 7 lb): 5 lengths fourth to Kartajana in Group 1 event at Munich: stayed 1½m: acted on soft going: reportedly sustained an injury during final race and has been retired to stud in Germany, fee DM 15,000, Oct 1. *Uwe Ostmann, Germany.* 122

TURGEON (USA) 5 gr.h. Caro 133 – Reiko (Targowice (USA) 130) [1990 15.5f² 15.5d* 20g³ 20d⁵ 12s⁶ 12s³ 15.5v³ 1991 14.5s² 15.5m* 12m 15g* 14d* 15.5d* 14v³] 119

It was a case of third time lucky for Turgeon in the Prix Royal-Oak, the French St Leger, at Longchamp in late-October. Second to Top Sunrise in 1989 and third to dead-heaters Indian Queen and Braashee in 1990, he finally managed to add his name to the list of winners when comfortably landing the odds by three quarters of a length from Shambo. Sent to the front turning for home and soon clear of his field, Turgeon never looked like being caught and

Jefferson Smurfit Memorial Irish St Leger, the Curragh—
a deserved victory for five-year-old Turgeon; the three-year-olds
Patricia (far right) and Zafadola (rails) stay on well for the places

Prix Royal-Oak, Longchamp—
Turgeon completes a St Leger double, chased home by older horses Shambo,
Wajd and Michelozzo (there was only one three-year-old in the field of eight)

was eased inside the last furlong. The field for the Royal-Oak, even by its own recent standards, was rather weak (due in no small part to the re-scheduling of the Prix du Cadran from spring to just over three weeks before the Royal-Oak), but Turgeon's success confirmed him as the top French stayer. His victory crowned a tremendous season. After finishing a length second to Mardonius in the Prix de Barbeville at Saint-Cloud on his reappearance, he went on to win the Prix Vicomtesse Vigier at Longchamp for the second successive year later in May, the Prix Kergorlay at Deauville (he was beaten a head by Further Flight conceding him 2 lb but was controversially awarded the race for interference) in August, the Jefferson Smurfit Memorial Irish St Leger at the Curragh in September and then the Royal-Oak. His two other runs saw just fair efforts in the Grand Prix de Saint-Cloud (seventh to Epervier Bleu) and the Premio UNIRE Consigilo Europeo Roma Vecchia at Rome (third to Snurge). Turgeon's victory in the Irish Leger saw him become the first French-trained horse to win the race since Ommeyad in 1957. Improving three-year-old Patricia seemed most people's idea of the winner at the Curragh and was sent off favourite at 15/8. Turgeon, the only five-year-old in the line-up, came next at 3/1 followed by Irish Oaks third Eileen Jenny at 11/2 and Patricia's stable-companion, the Doncaster Cup winner Great Marquess, at 8/1. Few of the others made much appeal. Turgeon won with authority. Always close up travelling smoothly, he took the lead two furlongs out and ran on strongly to beat Patricia by three lengths, with a further three quarters of a length to the Irish three-year-old Zafadola.

Turgeon (USA) (gr.h. 1986)	Caro (gr 1967)	Fortino II (gr 1959)	Grey Sovereign / Ranavalo III
		Chambord (ch 1955)	Chamossaire / Life Hill
	Reiko (FR) (b 1979)	Targowice (b 1970)	Round Table / Matriarch
		Beronaire (ch 1974)	Ribero / No Luck

Turgeon is the first foal of Reiko, a mare who won four times from a mile to eleven furlongs in France and the USA, including in the listed Prix de la Seine. Her next offspring Greenville (by Clever Trick) was successful twice in minor company in the States; her third, Sura (by Northjet), has yet to see a racecourse. Turgeon's grandam Beronaire showed useful form at middle distances. She's a half-sister to the smart Mogami, a son of Lyphard who's since become a leading sire in Japan. Caro has now sired the winners of all the French classics, having been responsible for Siberian Express, Madelia and Crystal Palace. Turgeon, a rather leggy horse, is probably best at around two miles. He acts on any going. He was below his best when blinkered, in the

Mr G. Strawbridge's "Turgeon"

Gold Cup in 1990. A tremendous servant to connections in his three seasons racing up to now—he's been successful seven times in all, six of them in pattern company, and run with credit on the majority of his other starts—he was bought by Sheikh Mohammed before the Prix Royal-Oak, and will continue his career in Saudi Arabia. *J. E. Pease, France.*

TURMERIC 8 ch.g. Alias Smith (USA) – Hot Spice (Hotfoot 126) [1990 13.8m⁶ 13.8m 14g 14g 14f³ 14m³ 14m 13.8f³ 15.3g* 15.8d² 12g⁵ 13.6d³ a16g⁵ 1991 14.1m³ 14.1f 14.1f 14.1f 13.8m 15.8g] leggy, sparely-made gelding: modest handicapper at 7 yrs: no form in 1991: stays 2m: acts on any going: tried visored: bandaged behind: has turn of foot and held up: best with strong handling: has won 8 times at Catterick. *M. F. D. Morley.* —

TURN NOW 4 b. or br.g. Petorius 117 – Millers Lady (Mill Reef (USA) 141) [1990 8m⁶ 7d⁵ 7.9m 9.5f 1991 a8g] IR 8,000Y: ex-Irish colt: half-brother to 2 winners in Ireland, including Rustic Reef (by Rusticaro), later successful in Italy: dam dead-heated over 5f in Ireland: poor ex-Irish maiden: stays 7f: acts on dead ground: tried blinkered once: trained at 3 yrs by P. Finn. *T. B. Hallett.* —

TURTLE BEACH 2 ch.c. (Jan 22) Primo Dominie 121 – Double Finesse 97 (Double Jump 131) [1991 6d⁴] good-topped colt: has scope: half-brother to several winners, including smart 6f to 1m winner Larionov (by Balidar) and smart Irish 5f to 7f performer Mr Brooks (by Blazing Saddles): dam won at up to 1m: 14/1, under 5 lengths fourth of 15 to Beware of Agents in maiden at Doncaster in November, green and soon behind then running on well from halfway: sure to improve. *A. A. Scott.* **65** p

TURTLE WOOD 3 ch.f. Touching Wood (USA) 127 – Turtle Hill 73 (Home Guard (USA) 129) [1990 NR 1991 12.2g 13.8m] 7,800Y: workmanlike filly: fifth foal: half-sister to a winner in Italy by Ile de Bourbon: dam 5f-winning half-sister to high-class 1m to 1¼m performer Gold Rod: burly, tailed off in maiden and (sweating, 3½ months later) claimer: sold 825 gns Ascot December Sales. *J. G. FitzGerald.* —

TUSKY   3 ch.g. Prince Sabo 123 – Butosky 71 (Busted 134) [1990 6f 6g a6g⁵ 6g*   **83** +
6g* 1991 8d 6g] tall, good-topped gelding: moderate walker: fairly useful winner as
2-y-o: 66/1 and visored, seventh of 15 in £25,000 handicap at York in June final start
in 1991: worth a try at 7f: gave considerable trouble at stalls final start and
subsequently gelded. *M. J. Camacho.*

TV PITCH (FR)   3 b.f. Fast Topaze (USA) 128 – Allatum (USA) 81 (Alleged   **66** d
(USA) 138) [1990 7m 1991 12f² 12m³ 16.2f 16m 14.1m] rather leggy filly: modest
form, placed in maidens in the spring: beaten long way in handicaps, off course 8
weeks prior to final start: stays 1½m well: joined D. Lee. *N. A. Graham.*

TWAFEAJ (USA)   2 b.f. (Feb 22) Topsider (USA) – Billy Sue's Rib (USA)   **99**
(Al Hattab (USA)) [1991 5g² 5m² 6m* 6m⁴ 6m² 6m* 6m⁴]
    It was a sad indictment of the level of competition amongst the two-
year-old fillies in Ireland in the latest season that its top race within the
division, the Moyglare Stud Stakes at the Curragh in September, a race the
Irish have at least managed to keep at home more often than not in the
'eighties, should be won by a British-trained filly of no better than useful
merit who wasn't able to win any of the three pattern races she contested at
home. In fact, Twafeaj didn't even need to improve upon the best of her
previous form, which had seen her win just one of her five races, a minor
event over six furlongs at York in June; although she would have had more on
her plate if Bezelle, the pick of the Irish-trained fillies on the evidence of her
length-and-a-half-defeat of Twafeaj in the Princess Margaret Stakes at Ascot
in July, had been able to make the line-up. With Bezelle on the side-lines, the
home defence rested largely on the shoulders of Tarwiya, favourite at 5/2
after fighting off a two-strong British challenge in the listed Rochestown EBF
Stakes at Leopardstown. But she didn't help her cause by flashing her tail
violently and wandering inside the final furlong after coming with a smooth
challenge, and Twafeaj, who'd been bumped two furlongs out, was able to hold
on by half a length. The Moyglare Stud-Cheveley Park double had been
achieved three times in the preceding ten years but there was never any stage

Moyglare Stud Stakes, the Curragh — Twafeaj holds off Tarwiya

in the second half of the Newmarket race at which Twafeaj looked likely to follow in the footsteps of Woodstream, Park Appeal and Capricciosa—all Irish-trained fillies, incidentally—and after making some progress approaching the Dip she couldn't improve her position further and had to give best to the superior speed of Marling, Absurde and Basma, eventually finishing three lengths down in fourth place. Not for the first time Twafeaj looked extremely well, but once again we couldn't help feeling, as we had as early as July when she took fourth place behind Musicale in the Cherry Hinton Stakes at Newmarket, that a seventh furlong, particularly on top-of-the-ground, would have suited her very well, and that distance is likely to be a minimum for her if she's to show to best advantage as a three-year-old. If she's campaigned as a sprinter—she's been raced only on a sound surface to date, incidentally— then she'll probably find her winning opportunities restricted.

Twafeaj (USA) (b.f. Feb 22, 1989)	Topsider (USA) (b 1974)	Northern Dancer (b 1961)	Nearctic Natalma
		Drumtop (b 1966)	Round Table Zonah
	Billy Sue's Rib (USA) (b 1980)	Al Hattab (ro 1966)	The Axe II Abyssinia
		Romeo's Coquette (b 1973)	Gallant Romeo Princess Revoked

Twafeaj, a strong, good-bodied filly, who progressed well physically throughout the season and still has the scope to go on, was purchased for 120,000 dollars at the non-select session of Keeneland's July Yearling Sale. She's by the Northern Dancer sprinter Topsider, an excellent sire of two-year-olds with a high winner-to-runner ratio and such as Salse, Assatis and Doulab among his better representatives, out of the very useful multiple winner Billy Sue's Rib, successful in thirteen races at up to nine furlongs from twenty-two starts. Two of the dam's three foals before Twafeaj were winners, including Elzaeem (by Secreto) who won a three-runner seven-furlong race at Newbury as a two-year-old. Billy Sue's Rib might have been the best of the four winners from her dam Romeo's Coquette, a minor winner twice over sprint distances, but a more familiar name to British racegoers will be her half-brother Green's Sisley, winner of a five-furlong race as a two-year-old at Windsor in 1989 before his export to Italy where he added to his tally. Romeo's Coquette is a half-sister to the well-known broodmare My Bupers, who in a lengthy career at stud has foaled the champion sprinter My Juliet (since the dam of the smart American two-year-old filly Stella Madrid) and the good-class Lyphard's Special as well as the 10,200,000-dollar colt Snaafi Dancer, paradoxically better known than both that pair because he was too slow to make the racecourse. *B. Hanbury.*

TWILIGHT FALLS 6 ch.g. Day Is Done 115 – Grattan Princess (Tumble Wind (USA)) [1990 6s 6g 5d 6s 1991 7d 6m⁴ a6g⁵ 8m 6m⁵ 6.1m*] medium-sized, good-topped gelding: carries plenty of condition: poor mover: poor handicapper: landed gamble (for second time) when winning at Nottingham in October: suited by 6f: acts on good to firm and dead going: often gives trouble at stalls. *M. J. Camacho.* **44**

TWILIGHT FIESTA (IRE) 3 b.g. Burslem 123 – Caithness 78 (Connaught 130) [1990 5m⁴ 5m³ 6g² 5m⁵ 7g 7f* 7g² 8m 7s⁴ 8.2s 1991 8g² 10d 8f* 8g 10m³ 12f³ 11.8g²] smallish, workmanlike gelding: good mover: fairly useful plater: won at Thirsk (bought in 7,200 gns) in July, coming from rear: ran creditably last 3 starts: stays 1½m: acts on any going: often slowly away: sold 5,000 gns Newmarket Autumn Sales. *Mrs J. R. Ramsden.* **62**

TWILIGHT FLAME (IRE) 3 ch.c. Red Sunset 120 – Fleur-de-Luce (Tumble Wind (USA)) [1990 6g 6d 6d a8g a8g² 1991 a10g a10g a8g⁶ 8.3m⁶ 8f 9.7f 8f] rather leggy, close-coupled colt: plater: unruly at stalls, pulled hard but not discredited fourth start: well beaten otherwise in 1991: best efforts at 1m. *M. R. Channon.* **—**

TWILIGHT SECRET 2 b.f. (Apr 15) Vaigly Great 127 – Kristal Air 76 (Kris 135) [1991 7m⁶] workmanlike filly: first foal: dam modest maiden stayed 1m, is half-sister to very useful but temperamental 1977 2-y-o 6f winner Royal Harmony: 33/1 and better for race, around 4 lengths sixth of 18 to Mahool in maiden at Doncaster, held up after slow start then running on steadily: should improve. *J. W. Hills.* **70 p**

TWINKLE BRIGHT (USA) 4 b. or br.f. Star de Naskra (USA) – Lady May **40 +**
(FR) (Luthier 126) [1990 8g 10g 7f 5g 7g² 7m 8.5g 7g 8f 8.5d² 9.5m⁴ 7d* 7.8g 1991
7d⁵] sparely-made ex-Irish filly: fifth reported foal: half-sister to a minor winner in
USA: dam ran 3 times: won handicap at Roscommon in 1990 (trained by K.
Prendergast): staying-on fifth of 20 in seller at Catterick in March, only run in 1991:
stays 9.5f: acts on good to firm ground and dead. *B. J. Curley.*

TWIST AND TURN 2 ch.c. (Feb 26) Groom Dancer (USA) 128 – Twyla 101 **113** p
(Habitat 134) [1991 7m³ 7f* 8.1m* 8d³] good-topped colt: has plenty of scope: fluent
mover: first foal: dam 2-y-o 6f winner, is sister to smart sprinter Defecting Dancer:
very useful performer: impressive winner of maiden at Yarmouth and minor event
at Sandown in August: favourite and in really good shape, improved form when
under 2 lengths third of 8, keeping on well, to Made of Gold in Royal Lodge William
Hill Stakes at Ascot following month: stays 1m: acts on firm and dead going. *H. R. A.
Cecil.*

TWO AND SIXPENCE (USA) 2 b.f. (Jan 29) Chief's Crown (USA) – **— p**
Candlelight Service (USA) (Blushing Groom (FR) 131) [1991 7m] $195,000F: fourth
foal: dam unraced: sire champion 2-y-o in USA, won Travers Stakes at 3 yrs: 25/1
and backward, always behind in 20-runner maiden at Newmarket in October. *B. W.
Hills.*

TWO BADGES (IRE) 3 ch.c. Montekin 125 – Lucy Lacerre 75 (Sallust 134) **—**
[1990 a6g a6g⁴ 1991 8g⁶ a11g⁴ 11m⁶ a12g] smallish, workmanlike colt: poor walker
and mover: showed a little ability first 2 starts in 1991: off course almost 7 months
before final one: probably stays 11f: sometimes wears bandages or boots in front:
has worn tongue strap: sold out of R. Ingram's stable 1,000 gns Doncaster August
Sales after third start. *Mrs A. Knight.*

TWO BIRDS 2 b.f. (May 13) Prince Sabo 123 – Particular Miss 70 (Luthier 126) **39**
[1991 5m 6m⁵ 7g] 2,500Y: workmanlike filly: sixth foal: half-sister to 5f winner
Elder Prince (by Final Straw): dam, 1m winner at 3 yrs, is out of very useful
middle-distance filly One Over Parr, a sister to Polygamy: backward, poor form in
large-field maidens, final one (November) after 5-month break. *C. A. Horgan.*

TWO LEFT FEET 4 b.g. Petorius 117 – Whitstar 93 (Whitstead 125) [1990 8m² **106** d
7f² 11.5m² 10.5m 12f4 7.6v* 8g* 8s⁴ 1991 8d² 8d 10d⁵ 7.6d 8d⁶ 8g 8g] tall, lengthy
gelding: good walker: poor mover: useful performer: best effort in 1991 when
second to Regal Crest in listed event at Doncaster in March: off course over 3
months before well below best in handicap final start: rather headstrong, best form
at around 1m in strongly-run race: seems best with give in the ground and goes
extremely well on heavy: gelded after final start. *Sir Mark Prescott.*

TWO'S AGAINST 3 ch.c. Stanford 121§ – Royal Home 69 (Royal Palace 131) **—**
[1990 NR 1991 10m] 8,000F, 5,200Y: strong, lengthy colt: fifth foal: half-brother to 3
winners, including quite modest 11.7f and 13.8f winner Sweet N' Twenty (by High
Top) and 6-y-o 5f to 7f winner Erris Express (by Bay Express): dam 9f winner: burly
and tubed, tailed off in seller at Ripon in April. *W. J. Pearce.*

TWO-SHOES 2 b. or br.f. (Feb 5) Prince Sabo 123 – Dragusa 61 (Dara Monarch **79**
128) [1991 5m* 5s² 5m² 5m] smallish, workmanlike filly: moderate mover: first foal:
dam 6f and 7f winner, is out of close relation to high-class middle-distance colt
Exdirectory: modest filly: modest performer: retained 9,000 gns after winning
Nottingham seller impressively in April: out of depth in Norfolk Stakes at Royal
Ascot final start: sold 6,400 gns Newmarket Autumn Sales. *M. Bell.*

TWOSIXTYTHREEWEST (FR) 3 gr.f. Kris 135 – Southern Maid (USA) **69**
(Northern Dancer) [1990 NR 1991 7g 8f* 8m] leggy, sparely-made filly: easy mover:
sister to lightly-raced 1990 3-y-o 7f winner Thunderball and half-sister to several
winners in France (at up to 10.5f) and Italy: dam unraced daughter of useful French
7f and 1m performer Midou: 3/1 on, hacked up in bad maiden at Ripon in August on
first run for over 4 months: favourite but edgy, well beaten in Doncaster handicap 13
days later: sold 18,000 gns Newmarket December Sales. *H. R. A. Cecil.*

TWOTIME BID 5 b.g. Taufan (USA) 119 – Avebury Ring (Auction Ring (USA) **70**
123) [1990 8f 10v 8f 8f* 7.5d* 8m³ 8m³ 8.2d³ 8m 7m² 7m* 1991 7m³ 7.1g 8g 7m³]
good-topped gelding: had a round action: modest handicapper: suited by 7f to 1m:
acted on any going: dead. *Miss S. E. Hall.*

TYBURN LAD 4 gr.g. Belfort (FR) 89 – Swing Is Back (Busted 134) [1990 12m **—**
15.3m 8g³ 8f 8f 8.2g⁶ 10.6v⁴ 10s 9s² 1991 8m] lengthy gelding: has a round action:
plater: behind in apprentice handicap (non-seller) on only outing on flat in 1991:
stays 1¼m: best form with some give in ground: usually visored: winning hurdler.
H. J. Collingridge.

TYLERS WOOD 6 br.g. Homing 130 – Beryl's Jewel 86 (Siliconn 121) [1990 a6g⁴ —
a5g³ a5g⁴ 5m³ 5m 5f⁵ 1991 a7g a7g] smallish, compact gelding: quite modest
handicapper at 5 yrs: below form at Lingfield in 1991: stays 6f: yet to race on soft
going, acts on any other. *S. Dow.*

TYNRON DOON 2 b.g. (Feb 20) Cragador 110 – Bel Esprit (Sagaro 133) [1991 5f **58**
7m 6m² 6f 6.9h⁵ 7g⁴ 7m 7.1m³] 3,500F: lengthy, sparely-made gelding: fifth foal:
brother to 6f and 7.3f winner Fille d'Esprit and half-brother to a winner in Germany
and 3-y-o Danse d'Esprit (by Lidhame), 7f winner at 2 yrs: dam no form on flat or
over jumps: stays at least 7f: acts on firm ground: has run well
blinkered: inconsistent. *J. Berry.*

TYRIAN 4 b.f. Elegant Air 119 – Character Builder 92 (African Sky 124) [1990 8f **38** +
a8g 7g⁴ 10.2f 6m² 10.6m 10.6g 8f³ 1991 a7g 8.3g 10g⁴] lengthy filly: moderate mover:
poor handicapper: not seen again after eye-catching fourth in May: stays 1¼m: acts
on firm going: has run well in blinkers. *J. H. Baker.*

TYRIAN PURPLE (IRE) 3 b.c. Wassl 125 – Sabrine (Mount Hagen (FR) 127) **52**
[1990 6f⁵ 6m⁵ 8m² 10s⁵ 1991 10.2s 12.2d⁴ 12g 14f 8.2m 8.5m 8d 8.2f 8g³ 8f² a8g*
8m³ 8m³ 8m 8m] leggy, angular colt: quite modest handicapper: first past post at
Thirsk (apprentices, edged left and demoted) and Southwell in August, making
virtually all: ran moderately last 2 starts: stays 1m: acts on firm ground: wore tongue
strap eighth and ninth starts. *R. Hollinshead.*

TYRNIPPY 5 b.h. Tyrnavos 129 – Floral 82 (Floribunda 136) [1990 8.2g a11g² **58**
a11g⁴ 9g a11g* 8.2d 10v⁴ a12g⁵ 8d⁴ a12g a11g⁶ 1991 a11g* a12g⁴ a12g 11s a11g³]
smallish, sparely-made horse: moderate mover: won claimer at Southwell in
February: below form subsequently, not seen out after May: finds 1m on short side
nowadays, and probably stays 1½m: suited by an easy surface: has been bandaged.
M. Brittain.

TYRONE FLYER 2 b.c. (Apr 3) Celestial Storm (USA) 132 – Dance A Jig (Dance **51**
In Time (CAN)) [1991 8m⁴ 7g 7.1s a8g⁴ a8g] 2,600Y: leggy colt: first foal: dam
once-raced granddaughter of smart Fluke, a half-sister to Bireme and Buoy:
plating-class maiden: will stay middle distances: usually bandaged behind. *T. J.
Naughton.*

TYRONE TURBO (USA) 2 ch.c. (Mar 14) Premiership (USA) – My Go Go **53**
(USA) (Santiago Road) [1991 5m 5g 5m⁵ 6.1m] $20,000Y: sparely-made, rather
angular colt: moderate walker: half-brother to several winners in North America,
one in minor stakes: dam won at up to 7f: easily best effort when around 6 lengths
last of 5, headed over 1f out, to Vailmont in minor event at Goodwood in September:
headstrong, and suited by sharp 5f: wore crossed noseband last 2 starts. *Mrs N.
Macauley.*

TYRWHITT TRYST (IRE) 3 b.g. Prince Regent (FR) 129 – White Goddess 65 —
(Red God 128§) [1990 6f 5m⁵ a8g 1991 a8g] small, stocky gelding: poor mover:
soundly beaten, in handicap in July: sold 1,050 gns Doncaster August Sales. *D. W.
Chapman.*

U

UCCELLO 2 br.c. (Feb 25) Efisio 120 – Silver Berry (Lorenzaccio 130) [1991 5m³ **59**
6m 5g³ 5m² 5m] 32,000Y: lengthy colt: has scope: half-brother to several winners,
including fairly useful 3-y-o 6f and 7f winner Pipsqueak (by Alleging), good sprinter
Argentum (by Aragon) and fair miler Eurodollar (by Sparkler): dam poor half-sister
to very smart 1¼m filly Cranberry Sauce: quite modest maiden: best effort when
½-length second of 7 to Splice at Folkestone in August: ran moderately at Lingfield
(on toes, pulled hard to post) 4 weeks later: should be better suited by 6f than 5f. *L.
J. Holt.*

ULURU (IRE) 3 b.c. Kris 135 – Mountain Lodge 120 (Blakeney 126) [1990 7g⁵ **100**
1991 10g² 13.9m² 14.8g³ 15m² 12.3d*] quite attractive colt: best effort to win
5-runner minor event at Chester in October in fine style by 8 lengths from Ikebana,
leading 4f out and soon clear: placed in maidens and minor event previously:
effective at 1½m, and stays 15f: seems suited by a soft surface: sold 62,000 gns
Newmarket Autumn Sales. *B. W. Hills.*

UMBRIA 2 ch.f. (May 24) Master Willie 129 – Gay Shadow 99 (Northfields (USA)) **38** p
[1991 7f 6m] 3,500Y: leggy, sparely-made filly: half-sister to several winners,
including 11f winner Schweppes Tonic (by Persian Bold) and 7f and 1m winner
Sahara Shadow (by Formidable): dam, winner over 5f and 6f at 2 yrs, is half-sister to

very smart sprinter Honeyblest: ran better than bare results indicate when seventh of 18 in claimer at Salisbury (slow into stride, handy when hampered 2f out) and eighth of 20 in seller at Lingfield (poor draw, not knocked about when unable to reach leaders) in September: likely to stay 1m: an interesting contender for sellers. *C. James.*

UMNIYATEE 3 b.f. Green Desert (USA) 127 – Midway Lady (USA) 126 (Alleged **104** (USA) 138) [1990 NR 1991 7g* 8s* 8m³ 10g⁴ 10.1m³ 8d²] good-topped filly with plenty of scope: shows knee action: moderate walker: first foal: dam won 1000 Guineas and Oaks: useful form: successful in newcomers race at Newbury and £9,000 event (4-runner race, by 15 lengths) at Ascot in the spring: ran well in Goffs Irish 1000 Guineas (4½ lengths third to Kooyonga) and Sea World Pretty Polly Stakes at the Curragh next 2 starts, and when second of 10 to Chipaya in Ascot listed race (made most) on final one: stayed 1¼m: acted on good to firm ground and soft: lacked turn of foot: visits Forty Niner. *B. Hanbury.*

UNANIMOUS (IRE) 3 b.c. Fairy King (USA) – Consensus (Majority Blue 126) **88 d** [1990 6m³ 6m* 6m² 6g⁴ 6m³ 1991 7m 7g* 7g 7.1s⁶ 7m* 8g⁴ 8m* 7m² 8.9m 8m⁵ a7g⁴ a10g] small, close-coupled colt: moderate mover: fair performer at best: won handicap at Lingfield in May and claimers at Newmarket in August and Leicester (set modest pace) in September: stays 1m: acts on good to firm ground: trained until after fourth start by A. Stewart. *N. A. Callaghan.*

UNASSUMING 3 ch.g. Vaigly Great 127 – Petard 112 (Mummy's Pet 125) [1990 **47** 5g⁵ 6m 5m 8.2g 6d 1991 8s* 8d⁴ 12f* 10.6m 12g 10g 10m² 9m³ 10m 8m⁶ 8m 10m³ 10m⁶] workmanlike gelding: won selling handicaps at Ripon (no bid) and Pontefract (bought in 6,000 gns) in April: should prove better at 1½m than shorter: acts on any going: lacks turn of foot: sold to join J. Wainwright 5,200 gns Doncaster October Sales. *Mrs J. R. Ramsden.*

UNCERTAIN 3 ch.c. Noalto 120 – Paridance (Doudance 99) [1990 7s 7s 1991 8g] — rather leggy colt: no worthwhile form in maidens, giving trouble at stalls and hanging right at Thirsk in May. *M. Johnston.*

UNCLE ERNIE 6 b.g. Uncle Pokey 116 – Ladyfold 60 (Never Dwell 89) [1990 — 12g 1991 a11g⁶] leggy, workmanlike gelding: has a round action: modest handicapper at 4 yrs: wearing eyeshield, behind only run on flat in 1991 (February): will stay beyond 1½m: acts on any going: smart chaser. *J. G. FitzGerald.*

UNDER PROTEST (IRE) 2 b.c. (Apr 9) Sarab 123 – Al-Nadda (Be My Guest **43** (USA) 126) [1991 5d 7g 10m] IR 2,800F, IR 3,200Y: good-topped colt: third reported foal: half-brother to Irish 7f winner Revelette (by Runnett): dam second over 1½m in Ireland: poor form: in need of race in sellers last 2 starts: seems to stay 1¼m: mulish stalls final outing: sold 2,200 gns Newmarket Autumn Sales. *R. Hollinshead.*

UNDERWATER (USA) 2 b.c. (Feb 10) Riverman (USA) 131 – Itsamazing **89 p** (USA) (The Minstrel (CAN) 135) [1991 6m²] well-made colt: second foal: dam won 7f listed race at 2 yrs on second of only 3 starts: heavily-backed favourite, 1½ lengths second of 7 to Seattle Rhyme in maiden at Ascot in July, looking likely winner 2f out, running green, then keeping on well towards finish: will stay 1m: seemed sure to improve. *R. Charlton.*

UNFORGIVING MINUTE 2 b.c. (Mar 2) Bellypha 130 – Kindjal 84 (Kris 135) **73 p** [1991 7g 7m³] strong, well-made colt: has a round action: third foal: half-brother to fair 3-y-o maiden Vallance (by Top Ville): dam 1m winner from 3 starts is out of Yorkshire Oaks and Nassau Stakes winner Connaught Bridge: 25/1, under 3 lengths third of 16, prominent, kept on after getting outpaced, to Showgi in maiden at Redcar in September: will improve again, particularly at 1m +. *P. W. Harris.*

UNINVITED 4 b.f. Be My Guest (USA) 126 – Fai La Bella (USA) 85 (Fifth — Marine (USA)) [1990 8g 10m² 8s² 1991 a8g a8g⁴ a13g 10v 9s 8m] leggy, angular filly: modest maiden at 3 yrs: well below form in 1991, off course over 6 months before final start: seems suited by 1¼m: trained first 5 starts by Pat Mitchell: winning hurdler. *J. A. Glover.*

UNJHA 3 br.f. Grey Desire 115 – Comedy Miss (Comedy Star (USA) 121) [1990 NR — 1991 8.9g 10.5g] 4,000Y: leggy, lengthy filly: fourth foal: dam unraced: tailed off in median auction contest and maiden (moved badly to post) in the summer. *E. H. Owen jun.*

UN SOUVERAIN 3 b.c. Kenmare (FR) 125 – Serenita (FR) (Lyphard (USA) 132) — [1990 NR 1991 8f 8d 12m a11g] leggy colt: half-brother to several winners in France, including very useful 8.5f (at 2 yrs) and 11f winner Charlotte Amalie (by Gay Mecene) and 7f winner Sara Lee (by Little Current): dam French 1m winner out of half-sister to top-class middle-distance horse Sigebert: no promise in maidens and claimer: sold out of A. Scott's stable 840 gns Newmarket July Sales after second start. *M. C. Chapman.*

UNTITLED (USA) 4 br.c. Far Out East (USA) – Majestic Gina (USA) **46**
(Ambiopoise) [1990 a8g4 10g a11g2 a12g 1991 a12g a12g5 a13g a13g4 14.6s 8g 12.1d6]
sparely-made colt: poor maiden: stays 11f: bought out of J. Hills's stable 1,800 gns
Ascot May Sales, sold 780 gns Ascot November Sales. *D. J. Wintle.*

UNVEILED 3 ch.f. Sayf El Arab (USA) 127 – Collegian 90 (Stanford 121§) [1990 **76**
6m3 5f* 5d6 6g 5m5 1991 7d* 6m* 8g 5.8m 6g3 5g3 6d 6s4 5.7m3 7.1g6 7m* 6f3 7.1m
5.1m 5g 7m] sturdy, good-quartered filly: moderate mover: modest handicapper:
won claimers at Warwick and Nottingham in April and 5-runner handicap (led close
home) at Brighton in August: below form last 4 starts: needs further than 5f, and
stays 7f: acts on any going except possibly soft: below form when sweating. *R. J.
Hodges.*

UP ALL NIGHT 2 b.f. (Mar 13) Green Desert (USA) 127 – Vielle 123 (Ribero **56 p**
126) [1991 7g4] 30,000Y: sister to fair 8.3f winner Midifina and half-sister to fair
12.2f winner Chevrefeuille (by Ile de Bourbon) and a winner in Belgium: dam very
smart middle-distance filly: 7/1, over 10 lengths fourth of 11, modest progress last 2f,
to Dance Scene in maiden at Salisbury in October: will stay 1m: will improve. *J. W.
Hills.*

UP ANCHOR (IRE) 2 b.f. (Mar 1) Slip Anchor 136 – Pageantry 83 (Welsh **74 p**
Pageant 132) [1991 6g6 8.1g2 8.2m*] rangy, attractive filly: has plenty of scope: third
foal: half-sister to useful 7f and 1m winner Just Class (by Dominion), later graded
winner in USA: dam ran only at 2 yrs when placed over 5f and 6f: favourite, won
minor event at Nottingham in September by 3 lengths from Taroob, soon prominent
travelling well, quickening 3f out then staying on strongly: got loose to post then
pulled hard on debut: very much a staying type: on the upgrade. *P. F. I. Cole.*

UP JENKINS 2 ch.g. (Mar 23) Mummy's Game 120 – Glint of Silver 69 (Sallust **54**
134) [1991 5m5 a6g4 5g 6m] 4,600Y: leggy gelding: third foal: brother to 1989 2-y-o
5f winner Foxtrot Oscar and half-brother to 1988 2-y-o 5f winner Petongs Weeyin
(by Petong): dam placed at 6f: plating-class maiden: hung left and looked unsatisfactory in Redcar maiden auction penultimate outing: blinkered, well beaten in
27-runner Newmarket seller final one: stays 6f: acts on fibresand: sold 2,500 gns
Newmarket Autumn Sales. *G. A. Pritchard-Gordon.*

UPPER HOUSE 2 b.c. (Mar 29) Shirley Heights 130 – On The House (FR) 125 **65 p**
(Be My Guest (USA) 126) [1991 8f 8m6] close-coupled, attractive colt: fluent mover:
fifth foal: half-brother to quite useful 7f winner Domus (by Kalaglow): dam, from
excellent family, won 1000 Guineas and Sussex Stakes: weak in market, sixth of 14
to Sonus in Leicester maiden final start, soon off bridle then staying on steadily:
very backward and green on debut: may well stay 1¼m: will continue improving. *G.
Wragg.*

UP THAT DRIVE 3 gr.g. Kalaglow 132 – Vitry 48 (Vitiges (FR) 132) [1990 6m **—**
a8g 1991 10g] leggy, rather angular gelding: lightly-raced maiden who has shown
ability: bred to stay middle distances. *M. H. Tompkins.*

UP THE PUNJAB 2 br.f. (Feb 22) Daring March 116 – Hunza Water 70 (Relko **70**
136) [1991 6m6 5m 7s2 7g3 6f6 7.1m4 8m* 8f2 8.2m2 8d6 8m4 a7g] 660Y: lengthy,
dipped-backed, plain filly: has a round action: second foal: dam 11.5f winner: modest
performer: won 20-runner selling nursery (no bid) at Leicester in September: well
beaten on fibresand final start: suited by 1m: probably acts on any going: ran
creditably for 7-lb claimer third start: sometimes bandaged near-hind: trained until
after sixth outing by R. Smyth. *S. Dow.*

URARAGSKAL 2 br.f. (Feb 17) Kala Shikari 125 – Seragsbee (Sagaro 133) [1991
5s6 6m 7s 7f a5g] sturdy, plain filly: first foal: dam poor half-sister to smart miler
Fair Season: well beaten in varied events. *J. Akehurst.*

URRAY ON HARRY 7 b.g. Anfield 117 – Noorina (Royal And Regal (USA)) **65**
[1990 8.2s 10v5 8f* 9g5 1991 7.6d6 8m5 8.2g6 8d2 10.2g2 10.5m4 11.8g] smallish,
workmanlike gelding: poor mover: quite modest handicapper: stayed 10.6f: acted on
any going: tended to idle, and was suited by exaggerated waiting tactics: dead. *R.
Hollinshead.*

URSHI-JADE 3 b.f. Pennine Walk 120 – Treeline 59 (High Top 131) [1990 NR **—**
1991 8d 8m5 10.2m] 2,400Y: leggy, lengthy filly: poor mover: fourth foal: half-sister
to fair 1985 2-y-o 7f winner Wryneck (by Niniski) and a winner in Norway by Sharpo:
dam showed some ability over sprint distances at 3 yrs: behind in maidens (very
edgy on debut) and an apprentice race. *K. White.*

USA DOLLAR 4 b.c. Gabitat 119 – Burglars Girl 63 (Burglar 128) [1990 a10g4 **68 §**
12g4 10g5 8g2 8m* 8m* 8m4 8m6 a8g2 8m3 9m 8m 1991 7g 8m 8d6 8g 10g5 8m 10g
8g3 8.9g 8d 8m2 8g3 8g] big, strong colt: modest and untrustworthy handicapper:
failed to go through with effort penultimate start: goes well in strongly-run race at
1m, and should stay further: acts on good to firm ground: blinkered (usually) or
visored nowadays: usually sweating: difficult ride. *B. Gubby.*

USAIDIT 2 b.c. (Mar 7) Commanche Run 133 – Smurfiusa (USA) (Sharpen Up **66**
127) [1991 7m2 7g4] 8,000Y: leggy, angular colt: second foal: dam won in Italy: quite
modest form in maidens at Lingfield (led until inside final 1f) and Salisbury (kept on
behind Autocracy) in autumn: will stay 1m. *W. Carter.*

USHAK 3 b. or br.g. Baby Turk 120 – Persian Carpet (FR) (Kalamoun 129) [1990 **65**
NR 1991 10.1g 11.6m3 a12g 12g] leggy gelding: third foal: dam won 6 races in France
from 3 yrs to 6 yrs at 1¼m to about 11f: third of 7 in minor event at Windsor: well
beaten after in maiden (reported by jockey to be hanging, not knocked about) at
Lingfield and handicap at Goodwood. *H. Candy.*

USHBA (FR) 3 b.f. Head For Heights 125 – Uruguay (GER) 67 (Thatch (USA) **66**
136) [1990 6g 6m4 1991 8g 7g 7g2 6m* 6s] compact filly: moderate walker: quite
modest form in maidens third and fourth starts, making all at Pontefract in October:
effective at 6f and 7f: possibly unsuited by soft ground: often bandaged behind:
trained first 2 starts by M. Usher. *M. McCormack.*

UTRILLO (USA) 2 b.c. (Feb 28) Dahar (USA) 125 – Waltz Me Sue (USA) (Olden **68**
Times) [1991 7f5 7m6] $38,000Y: compact, good sort: half-brother to several minor
winners: dam sprint winner in USA, is half-sister to Imp Society: quite modest form
in maidens at Yarmouth (very slowly away, good late headway) and Lingfield
(reluctant stalls, soon chased along) in autumn. *A. C. Stewart.*

V

VADO VIA 3 b.f. Ardross 134 – Brigado 87 (Brigadier Gerard 144) [1990 NR 1991 **56**
11f2 12m4 10.6g 16.2m5 12g* 12m6 11.8g5] 6,000Y: leggy, workmanlike filly: fourth
foal: half-sister to 1989 2-y-o 7f winner Garscube (by Petong): dam 2-y-o 1m winner:
favourite, won seller (bought in 8,200 gns) at Doncaster in July: rather disappointing
otherwise after debut: will prove suited by 1½m + : claimed to join D. Wintle £7,100
final start: winning selling hurdler. *Mrs J. R. Ramsden.*

VAGUE DANCER 5 b.g. Vaigly Great 127 – Step You Gaily 71 (King's Company **74**
124) [1990 7f 8h 6m 7g5 8.2d6 8m 8d 7m 9.1s6 1991 8s2 8v 10d* 10.2m2 12m6 10.6g3
10g* 12g* 15g3 10m3 10.3m3 10.9m4 9m3] lengthy, rather angular gelding: has a
powerful, roundish action: modest handicapper nowadays: won at Nottingham in
April and Ayr and Doncaster in June: good running-on third of 29 to Mellottie in
Cambridgeshire at Newmarket final start: effective over strongly-run 9f, and stays
1½m: acts on good to firm and soft (possibly unsuited by heavy) going: ran poorly
when blinkered, below form for amateur: sometimes sweats. *Mrs J. R. Ramsden.*

VAGUE NANCY (IRE) 3 b.f. Mazaad 106 – Noble Nancy (Royal And Regal **—**
(USA)) [1990 5m 1991 5g a5g 10g] close-coupled, workmanlike filly: no form in
sellers then claimer. *C. J. Hill.*

VAIGLY MASON 2 b.g. (Apr 17) Vaigly Great 127 – Hunslet 72 (Comedy Star **53**
(USA) 121) [1991 6d6 6g 7g3 7m] lengthy gelding: third foal: dam 7.2f winner, is
sister to useful 1m and 1¼m winner and smart jumper Starfen: best effort
keeping-on third of 7 finishers in maiden at Ayr in July: bandaged off-hind, last of 11
in nursery at Newcastle over a month later: may stay 1m. *M. H. Easterby.*

VAILMONT (USA) 2 ch.f. (Feb 24) Diesis 133 – Annie Edge 118 (Nebbiolo 125) **76**
[1991 6m2 5m* 5.3g3] tall, rather wiry filly: third foal: closely related to high-class
3-y-o miler Selkirk and fairly useful 16.2f winner Casual Flash (both by Sharpen Up):
dam 5f and 7f winner later successful at up to 11f in USA: odds on, though still green
on first start for nearly 3 months, won 5-runner minor event at Goodwood (taken
early down), quickly clear over 1f out: creditable third of 5 to below-form Power
Lake in minor event at Brighton later in September, pulling hard, then giving
impression possibly ill at ease on track: bred to stay 1m. *I. A. Balding.*

VAIN PRINCE 4 b.c. Sandhurst Prince 128 – Vain Deb 66 (Gay Fandango (USA) **51**
132) [1990 9s 10.2f4 12s6 10g4 11.5g2 12.3f* 16d 1991 12s 12.3s 16.5m3 16.5m 13d
14.1f2 15.9m] rangy colt: plating-class handicapper nowadays: stays 2m: acts on any
going: has run creditably in blinkers: inconsistent winning hurdler. *N. Tinkler.*

VAIRAGYA (FR) 4 gr.c. Mendez (FR) 128 – Exigence (USA) (Exclusive Native **49**
(USA)) [1990 8m 11f³ 10m⁶ 11.5g 12d 10d a12g 1991 10.2s 12d 12f⁴ a10g⁴ 12g² 14.1f⁵
14.6g 10g 12g 11.8g] leggy, angular colt: moderate walker: poor maiden: best efforts
at 1½m: acts on firm ground: usually visored or blinkered nowadays: sold out of A.
Hide's stable 1,850 gns Ascot July Sales. *J. R. Jenkins.*

VALATCH 3 ch.c. Valiyar 129 – Love Match (USA) (Affiliate (USA)) [1990 8g **60**
1991 10f 12f⁴ 12m* 16.2g] big, strong, lengthy colt: quite modest performer: won
slowly-run 5-runner maiden auction race at Hamilton in May, leading over 1f out:
ran badly in handicap at Haydock 3 weeks later: should stay beyond 1½m. *Denys
Smith.*

VALIANT DASH 5 b.g. Valiyar 129 – Dame Ashfield 90 (Grundy 137) [1990 **—**
15.8d 1991 16.2f⁵] workmanlike gelding: has a round action: poor handicapper
nowadays: never placed to challenge only run in 1991: should stay well: often
blinkered or visored: winning hurdler. *S. E. Kettlewell.*

VALIANT WARRIOR 3 br.g. Valiyar 129 – Jouvencelle 68 (Rusticaro (FR) **77**
124) [1990 7m 7g⁶ 8d⁶ 1991 8g 8f⁴ 10s⁶ 10m³ 10f⁵ 9m⁵ 11.9g² 11.9m⁵ 12.1d* 12d⁴]
workmanlike gelding: modest performer: won 19-runner handicap at Chepstow in
October, hanging markedly right but leading close home: very good fourth of 22 to
Hieroglyphic in William Hill November Handicap at Doncaster, travelling strongly
long way: stays 1½m well: best efforts on an easy surface: often wears bandages:
best with strong handling: joined D. Nicholson. *H. Candy.*

VALIANT WORDS 4 br.g. Valiyar 129 – Wild Words 76 (Galivanter 131) [1990 **72**
7m⁶ 8f³ 7m* 7.6f⁴ 7g 7g 10g 1991 10d* 10m* 10.2d² 10g 11.5m² 11.4m³ 12g] leggy
gelding: improved handicapper in 1991: won at Lingfield (2) in June: stays 1½m: acts
on firm and dead going: has been bandaged near-fore. *R. Akehurst.*

VALID POINT 3 b.g. Valiyar 129 – Arianna Aldini (Habitat 134) [1990 5f³ 6s* **71**
7g³ 7g 8m 6d 8v⁴ 7.6v² 7s 1991 8g* 8s⁴ 8m 7d 10f⁴ 9.9m] good walker: moderate
mover: modest handicapper: game winner at Carlisle in March: suited by 1m: seems
unsuited by top-of-the-ground, acts well on soft: sometimes gave trouble at stalls,
rearing and getting trapped in them (took no part in race) final appearance, and has
been banned from racing on the flat. *M. Brittain.*

VALKYRIE REEF 2 ch.f. (May 14) Miramar Reef 100§ – Private Sue 61 **38**
(Brigadier Gerard 144) [1991 8f 7g 8m] leggy filly: second foal: dam poor maiden:
poor maiden: ran wide bend at Thirsk on debut: sweating final start. *N. Bycroft.*

VALLANCE 3 b.c. Top Ville 129 – Kindjal 84 (Kris 135) [1990 6m³ 1991 10d² **78**
10.5g⁴] robust colt: has plenty of scope: burly and green, best effort in maidens
when second of 20 at Ripon in June: better for race over 3 months later: will be
better suited by 1½m. *P. W. Harris.*

VALLAURIS 3 b.f. Faustus (USA) 118 – Valeur (Val de Loir 133) [1990 7g 1991 **94**
8g⁵ 8d³ 10.1g³ 10g* 8.1m³ 10.3m⁴ 12d] rangy filly: fairly useful performer: won
moderately-run handicap at Newbury in July, always close up and leading final
strides: apparently very good effort in listed race next start: didn't reproduce that,
running in snatches in apprentice handicap on final one: stays 1¼m: acts on good to
firm ground. *D. R. C. Elsworth.*

VALLEY MILLS 11 ch.g. Red Alert 127 – Haunting 79 (Lord Gayle (USA) 124) **40**
[1990 5g 6g a7g 6g 6f 6g⁵ 6g⁶ 1991 6m⁶ 6m] lengthy, strong gelding: one-time fairly
useful handicapper, only poor nowadays: ideally suited by 7f or testing 6f: acts on
good to firm ground, used to go very well in the mud: tried blinkered: has sweated:
suited by a good gallop: has been bandaged. *T. D. Barron.*

VALLEY OF TIME (FR) 3 br.f. In Fijar (USA) 121 – Vallee Sarthoise (FR) (Val **41**
de Loir 133) [1990 7m² 7d⁶ 7d 1991 7f 7g 8.2m 7g 8.3d³ 11g 8g³ 8.3d⁴ 9.2d 9m⁴ 9.2s⁶]
IR 6,500Y: sturdy filly: sister to a winner in USA and half-sister to 6 winners in
France, including Criterium de Maisons-Laffitte winner Viteric (by Versailles) and
8.5f to 11f winner Prince Sarthois (by Viceregal): dam, French 1m winner, is
half-sister to Grey Dawn II and Right Away: trained by E. O'Grady in Ireland at 2
yrs: poor on most form here: stays 9f: acts on good to firm ground: headstrong in
blinkers sixth start: mulish at stalls final start. *P. Monteith.*

VALSEUR (USA) 2 ch.c. (Mar 15) Lyphard (USA) 132 – Vachti (FR) 114 (Crystal **73** p
Palace (FR) 132) [1991 8.1s*] third foal: closely related to 3-y-o Styrian (by Storm
Bird): dam French 1¼m and 10.5f winner stayed 1½m: well-backed favourite, won
13-runner maiden at Edinburgh in November by 2½ lengths from Repledge,
progress approaching turn after slow start, leading 2f out then staying on well
despite looking green: will stay 1¼m: will improve. *Mrs J. Cecil.*

VALTAKI 6 b.g. Valiyar 129 – Taqa 85 (Blakeney 126) [1990 10.2f⁶ 1991 14.8g⁶ **28**
14m 10.2g⁶ 10.2f⁴] small gelding: poor walker: bad mover: very lightly raced and
poor handicapper nowadays: stays 1¼m: probably acts on any going. *G. A. Ham.*

VALUED FRIEND (USA) 3 b.g. Ziggy's Boy (USA) – Tuvalu (USA) (Our **–**
Native (USA)) [1990 NR 1991 10m 12f⁴ 10m 15.4m a12g⁶] $200,000Y: close-coupled,
angular gelding: half-brother to 3 winners in USA: dam won at around 1m at 2 yrs:
sire won at up to 7f: bought 1,200 gns Newmarket July Sales: little promise in
maidens and claimer after. *J. J. Bridger.*

VA LUTE (FR) 7 b.g. No Lute (FR) 129 – Viverba (FR) (Sanctus II 132) [1990 **44**
10.2f 10m⁵ 1991 12.3g* 12f 12g] leggy, lightly-made gelding: has a round action: 33/1,
easily best effort when winning handicap at Wolverhampton in August: stays 1½m:
winning hurdler. *R. J. Holder.*

VANBOROUGH LAD 2 b.g. (Apr 15) Precocious 126 – Lustrous 73 (Golden **74**
Act (USA)) [1991 5v* 5d³ 6g 6m 6.1g* 5m⁴ 8g 8g² 7d] 5,800F, 1,600Y: lengthy
gelding: has scope: has a round action: third foal: half-brother to a winner at around
1m in Italy by Elegant Air: dam 1½m winner: modest performer: successful in
maiden at Folkestone in March and claimer at Chepstow in July: showed improved
form at 1m, running extremely well, apprentice ridden, when second of 18 to
Bundesbank in Warwick nursery in October: suited by 1m: acts on good to firm and
heavy ground: visored sixth outing: not particularly consistent. *M. J. Haynes.*

VANDA'S GIRL 3 b.f. Noalto 120 – Concorde Lady 66 (Hotfoot 126) [1990 a7g **–**
a8g a7g³ a7g a8g 1991 10d] sparely-made filly: plating-class maiden: burly and
bandaged, tailed off in claimer in November: stays 7f. *A. Bailey.*

VANISKI 4 b.g. Niniski (USA) 125 – Voltigeuse (USA) (Filiberto (USA) 123) **52**
[1990 10m 10g⁶ 12.2d 1991 10f 16m 16m* 16m⁵ 18.1m 17.2g⁶] leggy gelding: easily
best effort when winning seller (no bid) at Lingfield in August: better suited by 2m
than shorter: acts on good to firm ground: visored last 2 starts. *Mrs Barbara Waring.*

VANROY 7 b.g. Formidable (USA) 125 – Princess Tavi (Sea Hawk II 131) [1990 **88** d
8f⁴ 7g⁴ 7m 7g 7g² 7.6m⁵ 8.3m⁵ 11.7m⁵ 8g³ 8g⁵ 9m a8g⁶ a8g² a8g* a7g* 1991 a8g²
a7g* a7g a8g⁴ a8g⁶ 8d 8g 9d⁴ 8m a10g a11g⁵ a8g* a8g] sturdy gelding: carries plenty
of condition: has a rather round action: fairly useful handicapper on all-weather:
successful at Lingfield in January and December (not at best to win claimer): ran
moderately there final start: suited by 7f to 1m: acts on firm and dead ground:
visored nowadays. *J. R. Jenkins.*

VARNISH 4 ch.f. Final Straw 127 – Rainbow's End 83 (My Swallow 134) [1990 7m **73**
8m 1991 8s 10g⁵ 10g] lengthy filly: good walker and mover: lightly raced and modest
handicapper: may prove ideally suited by 1m: acts on good to firm ground. *Lord
Huntingdon.*

VASILIEV 3 b.g. Sadler's Wells (USA) 132 – Poquito Queen (CAN) 113 **81**
(Explodent (USA)) [1990 NR 1991 10m 12g* 13.3g 12d² 11.4m 11.7g⁴ 13.3g²] IR
80,000Y: big gelding: third foal: half-brother to winners in USA and Sweden: dam,
promoted to third place in Oaks, is daughter of very useful staying filly Senorita
Poquito: won maiden at Brighton in June, leading final 1f: visored, very good second
in handicap at Newbury final start: suited by further than 1½m: acts on dead ground:
gelded in autumn. *R. Hannon.*

VA UTU 3 b.g. Balliol 125 – Flame 49 (Firestreak 125) [1990 6g 7m⁶ 10g 1991 10.1s **55**
8m 9m³ 8f⁴ 8g* 7.5m 10g 8m 10m 10.5g 8m⁶] angular gelding: hobdayed at 2 yrs:
won seller (bought in 5,100 gns) at Leicester in June: below form in handicaps and
claimer after, but showed retains ability when never-nearer sixth of 22 final start:
stays 9f: acts on firm going: visored eighth start: trained until after then by M.
Channon. *R. D. E. Woodhouse.*

VAX LADY 4 ch.f. Millfontaine 114 – Opinebo 82 (Nebbiolo 125) [1990 6g⁶ 6f⁴ 5d **–**
5m² 5m⁶ 5f³ 6g* 5g 6g* 6d 6d⁴ 1991 6m 6s 6g 7.3m 7m] small, rather lightly-made
filly: fairly useful sprinter at 3 yrs: well beaten in useful company in 1991: will prove
suited by 6f or stiff 5f: acts on good to firm ground: virtually bolted to post
penultimate start. *J. L. Spearing.*

VAX LASS 2 br.f. (Apr 27) Creetown 123 – Brazilian Beauty (Busted 134) [1991 **–**
5h 5g 5m 7g 10m] 1,000F, 2,900Y: smallish, lengthy filly: poor mover: half-sister to
1m winners Dawn Redwood (by Mummy's Pet) and 3-y-o State Governor (by Song):
dam unraced close relative of smart stayer Pink Gem: no worthwhile form:
blinkered last 2 starts: sold 650 gns Doncaster October Sales. *J. L. Spearing.*

VAYRUA (FR) 6 ch.g. Vayrann 129 – Nabua (FR) (Le Fabuleux 133) [1990 12g⁵ **80**
1991 14g³ 16g⁴] big, good-topped gelding: has round action: fairly useful as 3-y-o:
good third in £7,300 handicap at Sandown in April: well beaten in similar event at

Newmarket following month: should stay 2m: probably acts on any going: useful hurdler at best: sold to join J. Hellens 26,000 gns Ascot June Sales. *G. Harwood.*

VELLANDRUCHA 2 b.f. (Mar 24) Cragador 110 – Shadha 57 (Shirley Heights 130) [1991 5m⁵ 5m] leggy, sparely-made filly: third foal: half-sister to unreliable 3-y-o sprinter Super Heights (by Superlative) and a winner in Italy: dam ran twice at 2 yrs: poor form, beaten around 10 lengths, in maidens at Wolverhampton in late-summer. *J. A. Bennett.* **34**

VELOCE (IRE) 3 b.c. Kafu 120 Joanns Goddess (Godswalk (USA) 130) [1990 6m⁶ a6g 5f 6d³ 5m⁴ 1991 6m 7.5m* 8m 7.1g 7.6g⁶ 7.5f 6.1d] lengthy, robust colt: quite modest handicapper: below form after winning at Beverley in June: better at 7.5f than shorter: acts on good to firm ground and dead: coltish first 2 starts: visored final one. *M. O'Neill.* **62**

VELOCITY 3 b.f. Glint of Gold 128 – Volida 105 (Posse (USA) 130) [1990 NR 1991 6f 7g⁴ 7m³] small filly: first foal: dam, half-sister to Supreme Leader from family of Pebbles, won over 5f at 2 yrs then highly tried at up to 1½m at 3 yrs when appeared suited by 1m: in frame for small-field maidens in the summer: bred to be suited by at least 1m. *W. Jarvis.* **—**

VENICE IN PERIL (IRE) 3 ch.g. Lomond (USA) 128 – Rising Tide 101 (Red Alert 127) [1990 6m 6d 1991 a6g 8.2s 7.5f 6g] workmanlike gelding: behind, including in sellers: bandaged twice. *P. C. Haslam.* **—**

VENT DE MER 5 b.g. Tumble Wind (USA) – Ocean Boulevard (Pitskelly 122) [1990 a5g 7g 1991 7g] strong, lengthy, good-quartered gelding: modest handicapper as 3-y-o: very lightly raced and well beaten subsequently: easily best form over 5f on soft ground. *J. Akehurst.* **—**

VENTURE CAPITALIST 2 ch.g. (Feb 11) Never So Bold 135 – Brave Advance (USA) 98 (Bold Laddie (USA)) [1991 6d³ 6d²] 6,500F: lengthy gelding: moderate mover: fifth foal: dam game 5f winner, raced only at 2 yrs: fair form in maidens at Newmarket (always prominent, faded slightly close home) and Doncaster (beaten head by Beware of Agents) week later in November: will win a modest sprint maiden at least. *R. Hannon.* **79 p**

VENTURE FOURTH 2 b.c. (Jun 10) Hotfoot 126 – Four Lawns 77 (Forlorn River 124) [1991 5m 5m 5m⁵ 7m 8m 7.6d] 2,000Y: neat colt: half-brother to 6f winner Swing Dancer and modest miler Causley (both by Swing Easy): dam 5f winner: poor form in varied events: faced extremely stiff task in Chester nursery final outing: should stay 1m: twice slowly away. *B. A. McMahon.* **41**

VENTURINA (IRE) 2 b.f. (Feb 18) Taufan (USA) 119 – Love Resolved 55 (Dan Cupid 132) [1991 6m⁵ 6m* 7.5f* 7g² 8m] 16,000Y: sturdy filly: half-sister to several winners, including Lingfield Derby Trial winner Riberetto (by Ribero) and fairly useful 5f and 7f winner Tribal Warrior (by Tribal Chief): dam placed over 13f in France: fair performer: successful in maiden at Doncaster and auction event at Beverley in mid-summer: good second of 7, keeping on well, to Pearl Angel in listed race at Newmarket in August: not entirely discredited in May Hill Stakes at Doncaster following month, leading briefly over 2f out: should be well suited by 1m+: sold 25,000 gns Newmarket Autumn Sales. *M. H. Easterby.* **82**

VENTURIST (USA) 4 b.c. Al Nasr (FR) 126 – Sleek Lassie (USA) (Northern Prospect (USA)) [1990 7m 10m³ 10.4m* 10g 11.5m* 11.7m² 12v³ 12.3v⁴ 1991 12m 11.5f² 11.9m* 12g a12g³] big, good-topped colt: fair handicapper: won at York (apprentices) in October: ran well at Lingfield final start: stays 1½m well: acts on firm ground and equitrack, unsuited by heavy (yet to race on dead): often bandaged near-fore: races up with pace: winning hurdler for N. Henderson in February. *J. H. M. Gosden.* **88**

VENT-X-FLYER 3 gr.g. Carwhite 127 – Sophistication (Morston (FR) 125) [1990 a7g 1991 12.2d⁶ a11g⁶ 13.8m] tall, close-coupled gelding: bad maiden: tried to pull himself up on first turn at Catterick final start: subsequently gelded. *W. J. Pearce.* **— §**

VENUS OBSERVED 3 ch.f. Sharpo 132 – Fair And Wise 75 (High Line 125) [1990 5m⁴ 7m* 7m⁶ 1991 8g 7m⁴ 7m⁵ 10m 8m* 7.9g²] leggy, rather angular filly: fairly useful performer: sweating and on toes, won handicap at Newmarket in August, leading inside final 1f: disappointing previous 3 starts: very good second to Pontenuovo in £24,500 handicap at York: suited by 1m: ridden by 7-lb claimer last 2 starts: didn't handle track at Epsom. *H. Candy.* **90**

VERBARIUM (USA) 11 br.g. Verbatim (USA) – Havre (Mister Gus) [1990 10.2f 10m 8m⁶ 10s 10f 1991 10m⁶ 9.9g 12f* 12m] close-coupled, workmanlike gelding: carries condition: poor handicapper nowadays: form in 1991 only when winning **30**

selling event (no bid) at Beverley in July: stays 1½m: acts on any going: sometimes slowly away. *Mrs J. R. Ramsden.*

VERDANT BOY 8 br.g. Green Dancer (USA) 132 – Favorite Prospect (USA) **64** (Mr Prospector (USA)) [1990 8f 8f 8g⁵ 8.2g⁴ 8m 8m a7g⁵ 7m⁴ 7g⁴ 8g 6g² 7d a8g a7g a7g³ 1991 a7g² a7g² a7g a7g³ 7g* 6m² 6m 6g⁵ 8.5m 8d²] quite attractive gelding: carries condition: moderate walker: quite modest handicapper nowadays: won at Edinburgh (hung left) in April: effective at 6f to 1m: acts on firm and dead going: good mount for apprentice: joined H. Whiting. *K. B. McCauley.*

VERDE ALITALIA (IRE) 2 ch.c. (Apr 5) Fayruz 116 – Soul of Discretion **77 p** (Tumble Wind (USA)) [1991 6g 5m³ 5m*] IR 4,200F, 13,000Y, 15,000 2-y-o: sturdy colt: second live foal: dam Irish maiden: progressive colt: easy winner of maiden at Catterick in September: should make a fair sprinter. *J. L. Dunlop.*

VERDON CANYON 7 b.g. African Sky 124 – Windy City (Windjammer (USA)) — [1990 NR 1991 8f 7m] short-backed gelding: appears no longer of much account. *G. A. Pritchard-Gordon.*

VERIGA (USA) 3 b.f. Mr Prospector (USA) – Chain Bracelet (USA) (Lyphard **97 p** (USA) 132) [1990 NR 1991 8s² 8m* 8s*] rangy filly: has plenty of scope: half-sister to French 1¼m winner Zahy (by Alleged) and Irish 1m winner Division (by In Reality): dam good-class winner at up to 1¼m from good family: short-priced favourite, won maiden at Newcastle and 4-runner minor event (by 3 lengths from Andrassy) at Yarmouth in October: should stay further: will improve again. *J. H. M. Gosden.*

VERMONT MAGIC 3 b.g. Elegant Air 119 – Jove's Voodoo (USA) 74 (Northern **79** Jove (CAN)) [1990 7g 7g 7g a8g⁶ 1991 11.7m⁵ 11.9m⁴ 12f 11.7f⁴ 10.4m*] lengthy gelding: modest performer: won selling handicap (bought in 10,000 gns) at York in October in good style, leading 3f out: seems suited by 1¼m: acts on firm going: has worn crossed noseband, including at York: sold to join R. Hodges 15,000 gns Ascot November Sales. *Lord Huntingdon.*

VERNONIA 2 b.f. (Apr 20) Bustino 136 – Neenah 107 (Bold Lad (IRE) 133) [1991 — p 7.1m⁶] 6,000F, 180,000 francs (approx £18,000) Y: leggy, workmanlike filly: second foal: half-sister to 3-y-o Italian winner at around 11f Highland Meeting (by Scottish Reel): dam 2-y-o 5f winner later successful over jumps in France, is half-sister to very smart English and German winner Whip It Quick: 10/1 but green, around 20 lengths sixth of 11 to Zaahi in maiden at Sandown in September, held up and plenty to do 3f out, no progress: likely to prove suited by middle distances: will improve. *J. H. M. Gosden.*

VERRO (USA) 4 ch.c. Irish River (FR) 131 – Royal Rafale (USA) (Reneged) **41** [1990 8m 10f 10m 7g⁵ 7m 8g 1991 a6g⁵ a7g a8g⁴ a6g* a6g⁴ a7g⁴ 6d³ 6m 7m 6.1d a12g a8g⁶] robust, good-quartered colt: carries condition: poor handicapper: won at Southwell in February: stays 7f: acts on dead ground: usually blinkered nowadays: has carried head awkwardly and looked none too easy a ride. *J. A. Bennett.*

VERTEX 3 b.c. Shirley Heights 130 – Rocktest (USA) 104 (Stage Door Johnny) **98** [1990 7s 1991 10g³ 12.2d* 13.3g² 12m* 13.9g 13.3m 11.9d] lengthy, attractive colt: fairly useful form at best: won maiden at Warwick and amateurs event at Newmarket in summer: ran poorly in handicaps after, as if something amiss final start: may well prove suited by 1¾m+: acts on good to firm ground and dead: sold 12,000 gns Newmarket Autumn Sales. *R. Charlton.*

VERVEINE (USA) 2 b.f. (Jan 18) Lear Fan (USA) 130 – Venise (USA) **108 p** (Nureyev (USA) 131) [1991 7g* 7m* 8d³] smallish filly: first foal: dam unraced close relative of Vacarme and half-sister to Vin de France and leading French hurdler Video Tape: successful in newcomers race at Maisons-Laffitte and Prix du Calvados (in good style by ¾ length from Stormagain) at Deauville: length third of 13 finishers to Culture Vulture in Prix Marcel Boussac at Longchamp: will stay 1¼m: likely to improve further. *E. Lellouche, France.*

VERY BOLD 3 b.f. Never So Bold 135 – La Nureyeva (USA) 83 (Nureyev (USA) **57** 131) [1990 NR 1991 5g 5m⁶ 5m⁵ 5f³ 5g 5.3g⁴ 5g* 5m 5d³ 5s a5g² a6g a6g] leggy, lengthy filly: moderate mover: first foal: dam maiden stayed 1m, is half-sister to William Hill Futurity second Cock Robin: made all in handicap at Wolverhampton in October: placed after at same course and Southwell: seems suited by an easy surface (moderately drawn on soft ground). *P. D. Evans.*

VERY DICEY 3 b.g. Tremblant 112 – Party Game 70 (Red Alert 127) [1990 5m⁵ **83** 6m⁵ 6m⁵ 6g⁵ 5m* 5m 5m⁴ 5.8d² 1991 6m 5m⁴ 6g 5g² 5.3f² 5g⁶ 5.7m⁴ 5s⁵ 8.3g 5.3f* 5f* 5d 5d 5g³] strong, workmanlike gelding: fair handicapper: made all at Brighton in August and Salisbury in September: speedy: acts on firm ground and dead: often ridden by 7-lb claimer: has hung: joined S. Dow. *S. Dow.*

VERY EVIDENT (IRE)   2 b.c. (Mar 17) Glenstal (USA) 118 – Royal Daughter   **52 p** (High Top 131) [1991 7g⁶] IR 8,000F, 23,000Y: fourth foal: closely related to 1990 2-y-o 6f winner Love of The Arts (by Tate Gallery): dam, placed over 1½m, is half-sister to Goodwood Cup winner Tug of War: weak 12/1-shot, over 9 lengths sixth of 11 to Salisong in maiden at Salisbury in October, eased when beaten final 1f: bred to stay 1m + : will improve. *B. W. Hills.*

VERY GOOD   2 b.f. (Mar 19) Noalto 120 – Sew Nice 71 (Tower Walk 130) [1991 6g   — 5m] lengthy, good-topped filly: moderate walker: has a quick action: fourth live foal: half-sister to winning sprinter Sew High (by Nicholas Bill): dam sprinter: last in maidens at Brighton (backward, slowly away) and Windsor (led 3f) in mid-summer. *P. Howling.*

VIA BORGHESE (USA)   2 b.f. (Feb 14) Seattle Dancer (USA) 119 – Angela   **93** Serra (Arctic Tern (USA) 126) [1991 6.3m* 7d³] $100,000F: fourth foal: half-sister to 2 winners in North America, one placed in graded stakes: dam won 3 races in Italy, including 6f Premio Legnano: won 11-runner maiden at the Curragh by 3 lengths from Miznah with rest well strung out: 2 lengths third of 5 to Tarwiya in C L Weld EBF Park Stakes there following month: will stay 1m. *M. V. O'Brien, Ireland.*

VIARDOT (IRE)   2 b.c. (Feb 7) Sadler's Wells (USA) 132 – Vive La Reine   **76 p** (Vienna 127) [1991 8d³] 80,000F: rangy, unfurnished colt: closely related to fairly useful 1½m winner De Rivera (by El Gran Senor) and a winner in USA by Storm Bird and half-brother to several winners, including R B Chesne (by Brigadier Gerard) successful in Champagne Stakes: dam, French 1½m winner, is sister to Vaguely Noble: 12/1, 2½ lengths third of 14 to Hill Glitter in minor event at Newmarket in November, chasing leaders then keeping on well not knocked about: sure to improve, particularly over middle distances. *M. R. Stoute.*

VICEROY   4 b.g. Indian King (USA) 128 – Bold Polly 67 (Bold Lad (IRE) 133)   **93** [1990 5d² 5d⁶ 5g 5d 6m⁵ 5g 5m 1991 6m 5f² 5m 5m⁴ 5g³ 5.2f² 5.1m⁴ 5.6m⁶ 5.2f* 5g²] strong, well-made gelding: fairly useful handicapper: ran well most starts and won at Newbury in September: effective at 5f and 6f: yet to race on soft going, acts on any other: effective blinkered or not: sometimes slowly away: has worn crossed noseband and tongue strap: suited by strong handling and exaggerated waiting tactics. *W. J. Pearce.*

VICEROY GEM (IRE)   3 ch.c. Sallust 134 – Gang Plank 84 (Tower Walk 130)   **45** [1990 6m 8g 7g 7g a7g 1991 10g 12f⁶ 10.2g 6.1d 8g⁴ 8f⁶ 7g³ 7m] leggy, workmanlike colt: has a round action: quite modest at best: third in seller at Brighton, best 3-y-o effort: best 3-y-o effort at 7f: selling hurdle winner. *R. J. Holder.*

VICEROY JESTER   6 br.g. Jester 119 – Midnight Patrol (Ashmore (FR) 125)   **58** [1990 8f² 8f⁴ 8f 9g 7f 8m⁵ 10g 10g³ 10f² 12m² 10g³ 12m³ 10.2m³ 10d² 12.2m* 12m² 12d⁴ 1991 12d⁵ 11.7g* 12m 12m 12g⁴ 12.1d] leggy gelding: moderate mover: won handicap at Bath in April: below form after: stays 1½m: acts on any going: has worn blinkers, but not for long time: often sweats: good mount for inexperienced rider: tough and genuine: winning hurdler. *R. J. Holder.*

VICKENDA   6 ch.m. Giacometti 130 – Phlox 101 (Floriana 106) [1990 6f 7.6m⁴ 7m   **35** 7m 1991 a8g a7g² a7g⁶ 7d 7.1d a7g 7.1g] angular, sparely-made mare: poor mover: poor handicapper: hung left and looked none too keen under pressure final start: suited by about 7f: acts on any going: often visored: often slowly away. *C. N. Allen.*

VICTOIRE BLEUE   4 b.f. Legend of France 124 – Vosges 117 (Youth   **114 p** (USA) 135) [1990 10.5d 1991 10.5g 12g 10.5d³ 12g* 16g² 15.5m* 20d*]
    Switching the Prix du Cadran from its traditional May spot in the French stayers' calendar to the Arc-weekend meeting in October was not a resounding success. The event clashed directly with the Jockey Club Cup and attracted yet another weak field, though not so weak as that brushed aside by the filly from the Provinces, Mercale, in 1990. Turgeon's withdrawal at the two-day stage left things looking much easier for Victoire Bleue, a lightly-raced four-year-old filly who'd won for the first time in a mile-and-a-half race for young jockeys at Evry in July and then shown improved form over longer distances in finishing second in the Grand Handicap de la Manche at Deauville and winning the Prix Gladiateur at Longchamp by four lengths. Victoire Bleue started a shade of odds on for the Cadran, opposed by the Gladiateur second and third, Our Account and Proud Panther, their fellow French-trained colt Warfield, Teamster from Britain and the outsiders Elsurimo and Tosca Stella

935

Ciga Prix du Cadran, Longchamp —
odds-on Victoire Bleue slams a weak field in the first running of this race
in its new place on the Arc weekend programme

from Germany. She did the job in good style, striding right away in the last two furlongs to beat Proud Panther by six lengths having experienced no difficulty lying up in a truly-run affair as first Our Account and then Teamster held the lead. Victoire Bleue was pulled out of the Prix Royal-Oak later in the month. In this form she would have given Turgeon a run for his money; all the top stayers will have to look to their laurels in 1992 with her still around and open to further improvement.

Victoire Bleue (b.f. 1987)	Legend of France (USA) (b 1980)	Lyphard (b 1969)	Northern Dancer Goofed
		Lupe (b 1967)	Primera Alcoa
	Vosges (USA) (b 1980)	Youth (b 1973)	Ack Ack Gazala II
		Virunga (b 1970)	Sodium Vale

Victoire Bleue is the second and last foal of the 1983 Prix Vermeille third Vosges; the first, Vison Royal (by Glint of Gold) is a useful jumper in France. M Wildenstein has been a strong supporter of French jumping down the years, and the second dam Virunga produced him a good animal in the Grande Course de Haies des 4 ans winner Video Tape. But breeding jumpers is a secondary consideration. Other winners from this well-known family of his include two very smart milers (Vacarme and Vin de France, both out of Virunga) and a Champion Stakes winner (Vitiges, out of Vale). Virunga showed more stamina than her two sons. One of the exceptional crop of French three-year-old fillies in 1973, she finished third to Allez France and Dahlia in the French Oaks and second to Mysterious in the Yorkshire Oaks; on a later visit to Britain she made the pace for Allez France in the Champion Stakes. Wildenstein runners in Britain are a rarity nowadays, but one can only hope that Victoire Bleue will be trained for the Gold Cup. There won't be many in the field with the combined staying power and turn of foot she clearly possesses. Victoire Bleue, a sparely-made filly, has shown she acts on good to firm and good to soft ground in her relatively short career, never having encountered anything much more extreme. *A. Fabre, France.*

VICTORIA PRINCESS 4 b.f. King of Spain 121 – Renira 60 (Relkino 131) [1990 6m⁵ 6d⁶ 5m 5m⁶ 6m 6g 5m 1991 8d 5d⁶ 5m 6.1s 5.1d⁶] compact, workmanlike filly: moderate walker: poor mover: poor handicapper at best: seems best at 5f: acts on good to firm and dead ground: trained first 4 starts by C. C. Elsey. *L. J. Holt.* —

VICTORIA ROAD (IRE) 3 b.g. Runnett 125 – That's Swiss (Thatching 131) [1990 6g 6d³ 5d 6d 1991 6d⁵ 7.5g³ 7m² 7d² 7m* 7f³ 8.5f³ 7.6g³ 7.6m] lengthy, workmanlike gelding: has a round action: fair performer: won £7,200 handicap at Thirsk in May: ran poorly final start, first for 7 weeks: better at around 7f than shorter: acts on good to firm ground and dead: consistent. *M. H. Easterby.* 80

VICTOR ROMEO 2 b.c. (Jun 1) Nomination 125 – Be My Sweet 78 (Galivanter 131) [1991 5m⁶ 5m 5m⁴ 6g⁴ 6.1m* 7m² 8.2m³ 7m a8g] good-topped colt: good walker: seventh foal: half-brother to modest 1988 2-y-o 6f winner Sola Mia (by Tolomeo) and plating-class 6f and 7f winner Sugar Token (by Record Token): dam, 1m and 1¼m winner, is half-sister to Gunner B: fair plater: retained 4,000 gns after beating Flim Flam Aly by 1½ lengths at Nottingham in August: ran moderately last 2 59 starts, final one on equitrack: stays 1m: acts on good to firm ground: has looked irresolute. *W. J. Pearce.*

VICTORY TORCH (CAN) 6 b.g. Majestic Light (USA) – Victory Songster (USA) (Stratus 122) [1990 8.2s* 8v⁶ 8m² 10s 8.2s 11d⁶ 8g 7d 1991 8.2s 8.2f] close-coupled gelding: hobdayed: moderate mover: poor handicapper nowadays: effective at 1m and stays 1½m: acts on good to firm and soft going: winning hurdler. *K. B. McCauley.* —

VIDEO DEALER 3 b.g. Aragon 118 – Ginnies Pet 106 (Compensation 127) [1990 6m 1991 10.1g 12g] leggy, rather sparely-made gelding: running-on sixth of 18 in median auction contest at Windsor: tailed off in maiden (edgy) and handicap after: not bred to stay middle distances. *C. A. Horgan.* —

VIDEO WALL 3 ch.g. Tremblant 112 – Dawn Ditty 100 (Song 132) [1990 NR 1991 7g 6m 7g 7f³ 6g⁶ 8d 6.9s² 6g³ 6.9m⁵ 6f⁴ 6g a8g⁶ a6g⁵] lengthy, robust gelding: fourth foal: half-brother to 4-y-o 7f and 1m winner The Can Can Man and 5-y-o 5f and 6f winner How's Yer Father (both by Daring March): dam sprinter: quite modest maiden: below form last 4 starts, stiffish tasks in claimers on all-weather surfaces: will prove better at 7f than shorter: acts on any going: visored final start: has wandered markedly, and looks a difficult ride: trained first 11 starts by R. Smyth. *S. Dow.* **56**

VILANIKA (FR) 5 b.m. Top Ville 129 – Kamanika (FR) (Amber Rama (USA) 133) [1990 8f² 8g 7m 8f⁵ 8.2m⁶ 8g* 9m 1991 9g 8g 9m 8m 7s 7m* 7m] tall, leggy mare: modest handicapper at 4 yrs: below that form in 1991, including when winning amateurs event at Redcar in August: stays 1m: acts on any going: has run well when sweating: often pulls hard. *W. Holden.* **50**

VILANY 3 b.f. Never So Bold 135 – Bellagio 68 (Busted 134) [1990 6d⁴ 6m 6g⁶ 1991 6m 8g³ 7d* 7m 7f 7d* 7m 8g] angular filly: moderate mover: fair handicapper: won at Chester (£7,400 contest) in May and Ayr (best effort, led virtually on post) in September: showed little last 2 starts: stays 7f: has form on firm but won only on dead ground: lacks instant turn of foot and should prove best ridden close to pace. *M. H. Tompkins.* **87**

VILCOE BAY 4 b.c. Roscoe Blake 120 – Vilmainder 78 (Remainder 106) [1990 6g 5m 6f 8.2v⁵ 8m 1991 7.5m⁵ a7g 8g 6s] workmanlike colt: poor handicapper: stays 1m. *B. A. McMahon.* —

VILLA BIANCA 5 b.m. Mummy's Game 120 – Belinda (Ragusa 137) [1990 11s⁵ 12g a12g 11d 12s a6g a6g a8g⁵ a12g 1991 a10g] sparely-made, angular mare: poor walker, turns fore-feet in: moderate mover: quite modest handicapper in 1989: little form since: needs further than 6f and stays 11f: needs the mud: tried blinkered. *S. T. Harris.* —

VILLA CAPRI 2 b.f. (Mar 14) Cragador 110 – La Troienne (Henbit (USA) 130) [1991 6d] first foal: dam poor maiden: 12/1, backward and green, soundly beaten in 12-runner maiden at Doncaster in November. *C. E. Brittain.* —

VILLAGE PET 3 b.c. Tina's Pet 121 – Village Lass (No Mercy 126) [1990 5d⁴ 5f² 5f* 6g 5d 5m³ 5m⁶ 5f 5.3f⁵ 5.8d a7g 1991 a5g a6g a5g⁶ 5g³ 5m 5d 5g 5.1g a6g a5g a5g] leggy, angular, plain colt: has a round action: quite modest performer: best at 5f: acts on firm ground: inconsistent, and can't be relied upon. *R. A. Bennett.* **60 d**

VILLANDRY (USA) 3 ch.f. Lyphard's Wish 124 – Valhalla (New Chapter 106) [1990 7g 7.2g⁴ 8g⁴ 1991 10d* 10.5s⁴ 10.5g⁶ 10.5g* 12d⁴ 12.5d⁵] sister to good-class 1m to 1¼m performer Vertige, and half-sister to 2 winners by Far North: dam 1½m winner out of half-sister to Vitiges: won maiden at Evry in February and Prix de Royaumont (by 2 lengths from Darata) at Saint-Cloud in May: ran fairly well after, finishing a place behind Darata, in Prix de Malleret and Ciga Prix de Royallieu at Longchamp, off course 3½ months in between: stays 1½m: has raced only on an easy surface: very useful filly. *A. Fabre, France.* **112**

VINSTAN 5 gr.h. Rabdan 129 – Pretty Fast 52 (Firestreak 125) [1990 NR 1991 a12g] big, lengthy horse: fair form in 2 starts as 3-y-o: no show in Lingfield claimer, first run on flat since: should stay 1½m. *C. A. Smith.* —

VINTAGE 6 b.g. Noalcoholic (FR) 128 – Good To Follow 82 (Wollow 132) [1990 12m³ 12g⁴ 12f 11.7m² 11.7m³ 12g⁴ 12g 12d³ 1991 12m* 11.7m² 12g⁴ 11.6m² 12m⁵ 11.5f*] strong, lengthy gelding: has round action: fairly useful handicapper: won at Kempton in July and Yarmouth in September: better at 1½m than shorter: acts on firm and dead going: bandaged on reappearance: wears tongue strap nowadays: sometimes sweats and gets on toes: usually held up: game. *Major W. R. Hern.* **92**

VINTAGE ONLY 3 b.c. Sayf El Arab (USA) 127 – Bias 108 (Royal Prerogative **100**
119) [1990 5f* 5f3 5d4 5d* 5d2 6m* 6f* 6g2 5g* 5g3 5m3 6d4 1991 7g 6m3 5g 7g6
5m] good-bodied colt: quite good mover: useful sprinter: contested listed races last
4 starts, best effort when third to Lee Artiste at Haydock in May: stiffish task, never
able to challenge at Doncaster final one: stays 6f: possibly ideally suited by a sound
surface: blinkered (front rank 5f) fourth start: tends to hang: usually looks really
well: sold 36,000 gns Newmarket Autumn Sales. *Mrs J. R. Ramsden.*

VINTAGE TYPE 4 b.g. Import 127 – Marock Morley 59 (Most Secret 119) [1990 **59** d
5m6 7m3 a7g 7d4 6m4 7m2 7m* 7m6 7d 6s a7g a6g 1991 a8g3 a8g a7g a7g a8g2 a7g 7f
7f 7m 6m] strong, workmanlike gelding: modest handicapper at 3 yrs: lost his form:
effective at 7f and 1m: acts on good to firm going: has been tried blinkered: rather
headstrong, and has worn a crossed noseband: unreliable: sold 1,500 gns Ascot
October Sales after final start. *D. W. Chapman.*

VINTON VA 6 b.m. Crofter (USA) 124 – Bold Flirt (USA) (Bold Ruler) [1990 10.2f —
10.1g 10.8f 9g 12m a10g5 1991 8.3m 10s a12g] rather leggy, close-coupled mare:
plating-class winner at 4-y-o: little show subsequently: stays 1¼m: suited by give in
the ground: has given trouble at stalls (withdrawn once). *R. A. Bennett.*

VIOLENCE (USA) 3 ch.f. Riverman (USA) 131 – Zolinana (FR) 108 (Sallust 134) **85**
[1990 NR 1991 8.5m4 8.1d* 8g3 8d] 800,000 francs (approx £78,600) Y: leggy filly:
sixth foal: closely related to very smart 1984 French 2-y-o River Drummer (by Irish
River), successful at up to 1m and later stakes winner in USA, and half-sister to
French 10.5f winner Grypstuyver (by Caro): dam, winner of 7f Prix du Calvados at 2
yrs, stayed 1¼m: won maiden at Chepstow in July: ran creditably in minor event
next start, moderately in handicap (chased leaders 6f, eased considerably) at
Goodwood 2 months later: should stay further. *L. M. Cumani.*

VIOLET'S GIRL 3 b.f. Starch Reduced 112 – Otterden (Crooner 119) [1990 NR —
1991 11m] plain filly: second reported foal: dam (non-thoroughbred) winning selling
hurdler: tailed off in Wolverhampton seller in May. *R. T. Juckes.*

VIRGINIA COTTAGE 2 b.f. (Feb 6) Lomond (USA) 128 – Bermuda Classic 98 **45**
(Double Form 130) [1991 6.1f 7m] quite good-topped filly: first foal: dam Irish 2-y-o 5f
and 6f winner stayed 1m: poor form in maidens at Nottingham (better for race and
green, very slowly away then ran on strongly) and Ayr (raced keenly, faded from 2f
out) in September: bred to stay 1m, but will need to settle better. *B. A. McMahon.*

VIRGINIA DANCER (IRE) 2 b.f. (Feb 18) Niniski (USA) 125 – Mirabiliary **36**
(USA) 74 (Crow (FR) 134) [1991 6f6 6.1m 7g] 7,000Y: leggy, lightly-made filly:
second foal: half-sister to 3-y-o Mirror's Image (by Never So Bold): dam 1¼m
winner: poor maiden: bred to stay 1½m: sold 1000 gns Doncaster November Sales.
J. A. C. Edwards.

VIRGINIA STOCK 3 b.f. Swing Easy (USA) 126 – Only Miranda 57 (Typhoon —
125) [1990 7m5 7m 7d 6m 1991 a8g 12g 11.9f] angular filly: little sign of ability. *Dr J.
D. Scargill.*

VIRKON VENTURE (IRE) 3 b.g. Auction Ring (USA) 123 – Madame Fair **83**
(Monseigneur (USA) 127) [1990 NR 1991 10g 8.5f5 8g 9d* 10d* 10d3 9g5] IR
16,000F: leggy, angular gelding: first foal: dam, Irish 1½m winner at 3 to 5 yrs, is
sister to useful Irish middle-distance stayer Maiden Fair: successful in handicaps at
Ayr (gambled on) and Ascot (£9,600 event, on toes) in September: good third to Red
Bishop in £12,100 handicap at Ascot: found 9f on sharp side final outing: acts on dead
ground: bandaged first 2 starts. *M. H. Tompkins.*

VIS-A-VIS 2 gr.c. (May 22) Efisio 120 – River Vixen (Sagaro 133) [1991 5m 5m 6g —
7s 6m] 650Y: tall, workmanlike colt: fourth foal: half-brother to 1m to 15.8f winner
Tongadin (by Petong): dam lightly-raced daughter of half-sister to Oaks second
Mabel: seems of little account: blinkered fourth start. *R. P. C. Hoad.*

VISION OF WONDER 7 b.g. Tyrnavos 129 – Valeur (Val de Loir 133) [1990 **32**
12.5m 18f 17.1f4 16g5 16.5f5 1991 12s6 14.6m] angular gelding: good mover: poor
handicapper: stays very well: acts on any going: has won for apprentice. *J. S. King.*

VISITING ROYALTY (USA) 3 br.f. Riverman (USA) 131 – Noble Lady (USA) —
(Vaguely Noble 140) [1990 NR 1991 a8g 7g4 10.4g] leggy, sparely-made filly: closely
related to James Pride (by Triple Bend), successful 19 times in North America in
course of 10 seasons, and half-sister to several winners, notably high-class 6f to
1¼m winner Noble Nashua (by Nashua): dam lightly raced: well beaten in maidens:
blinkered and sweating final start. *N. A. Graham.*

VITAL CLUE (USA) 4 b.g. Alleged (USA) 138 – Where You Lead (USA) 120 **86**
(Raise A Native) [1990 10.6s2 10.1m2 1991 8m 10d* 10g 12s 10.4m] lengthy gelding:
has quick action: fair handicapper at best: won at Newbury in June: well below best

final 3 starts, blinkered final one: should prove better suited by 1½m+ than 1¼m: acts on good to firm and soft ground: sold to join R. O'Sullivan's stable 20,000 gns Newmarket Autumn Sales. *J. L. Dunlop.*

VITAL VOLTAGE (IRE) 2 ch.g. (Jan 22) Soughaan (USA) 111 – Damariscotta **50** (Ahonoora 122) [1991 5m 6m 7.5f³ 7m³ 7m] IR 3,400F, 1,700Y, resold 1,750Y: leggy, unfurnished gelding: first foal: dam poor Irish maiden: modest plater: will stay at least 1m: acts on firm ground. *M. W. Ellerby.*

VITE VITE 5 ch.g. Kind of Hush 118 – Swiftacre (Bay Express 132) [1990 a10g **45** d a8g 1991 a11g⁵ a10g a8g⁵ a7g³ a8g² a8g⁶ 10s 7.5g 8m 7.6g a7g⁶ 8f 8.2d] strong, workmanlike gelding: modest handicapper as 3-y-o, poor nowadays: finds 7f on sharp side, best form at 1¼m: acts on firm ground: joined R. Spicer. *D. Morrill.*

VITKACY (IRE) 2 b.c. (Apr 26) Tate Gallery (USA) 117 – Treberth 60 (Gay — Fandango (USA) 132) [1991 6f] 9,400Y: third reported foal: half-brother to plating-class 7f winner Bollin Gorgeous (by Hello Gorgeous): dam stayed 1¼m: 8/1 but green, slow-starting last-but-one in 24-runner median auction at Ripon in August: sold 2,200 gns Newmarket Autumn Sales. *J. R. Fanshawe.*

VITTORIA GLENN 3 b.f. Town And Country 124 – Ganadora (Good Times **39** (ITY)) [1990 5m³ 5m³ 5s 5f³ 7f³ 6m 8m⁶ 1991 6f 6m⁶ 5g 5.1m] unfurnished filly: plater: needed further than 5f, and stayed 7f: visored third start: dead. *R. J. Holder.*

VIVA DARLING 2 b.c. (Mar 3) King Luthier 113 – Be My Darling 82 **54** (Windjammer (USA)) [1991 5g⁴ 5m³ 7m] 2,000Y: quite attractive colt: fifth foal: half-brother to 3-y-o Inferring (by Alleging) and French 9f and 9.5f winner Tony's Guest (by Be My Guest): dam 6f winner suited by 1¼m, is out of half-sister to high-class 1969 2-y-o Divine Gift: plating-class maiden: needs further than 5f, and will stay 1m. *B. A. McMahon.*

VIVID CONCERT (IRE) 2 br.f. (Feb 14) Chief Singer 131 – Vive La Difference **73** 86 (Known Fact (USA) 135) [1991 6.1g⁴ 5m² 5m² 5g* 6m²] IR 11,000F, 12,500Y: close-coupled filly: has a quick action: second foal: half-sister to French 3-y-o 11.5f winner Vive L'Empereur (by Northern Fashion): dam, out of half-sister to Val de Loir and Valoris, placed at 6f and 1m here (at 2 yrs) before winning in USA: modest performer: won maiden at Lingfield in August, leading inside final furlong: good second of 10 to Cochabamba in nursery at Ayr following month: will stay 1m. *W. Jarvis.*

VIVITZ (IRE) 2 b.c. (May 7) Alzao (USA) 117 – Stapelea (FR) (Faraway Son **61** (USA) 130) [1991 6d 7.1s⁵ 7s 7m⁵ 8g] IR 15,500F, IR 15,000Y: leggy colt: half-brother to 2 winners in Ireland, including miler Maricica (by Ahonoora), and a winner in Belgium: dam Irish maiden: quite modest maiden: ran moderately in Warwick nursery on final start: has given impression may need stiff test of stamina: has form on good to firm and soft ground. *G. B. Balding.*

VOLCALMEH 3 br.f. Lidhame 109 – Capel Curig 74 (Welsh Pageant 132) [1990 **67** 6m⁶ a6g² 1991 7m* 7f 10.5m⁵ 8g] tall filly: quite modest handicapper: won maiden at Leicester in July, leading close home: ran badly final start: stays 1¼m: well below form on firm going. *P. T. Walwyn.*

VOLCANIC DANCER (USA) 5 b.g. Northern Baby (CAN) 127 – Salva (USA) (Secretariat (USA)) [1990 9.1g⁵ 14g* 14g* 12.5g* 11g* 12.5g 10g 1991 18m⁴] workmanlike gelding: won 4 times in French Provinces in 1990, twice in amateur events: backward, shaped as if retains ability in 5-runner minor event at Pontefract in September: stays 1¾m: sold out of G. Pritchard-Gordon's stable 4,400 gns Doncaster Spring Sales: winning hurdler after. *J. Mackie.*

VOLERIS (FR) 2 b.c. (Jun 4) Kris 135 – Baiser Vole (USA) 123 (Foolish **85** p Pleasure (USA)) [1991 7v*] second foal: brother to French 3-y-o 1m winner I Wich: dam very smart 5.5f (at 2 yrs) to 1m winner, including Poule d'Essai des Pouliches: won maiden at Saint-Cloud in November by 3 lengths: will probably stay 1¼m: will improve. *Mme C. Head, France.*

VOLKSRAAD 3 b.c. Green Desert (USA) 127 – Celtic Assembly (USA) 95 **109** p (Secretariat (USA)) [1990 6m* 1991 7g* 7m³] stocky, powerful colt: type to carry condition: very good mover: half-brother to 1m winner In Unison (by Bellypha): dam 10.6f winner out of Welsh Garden, top 2-y-o filly in Ireland in 1975: operated on for knee injury in the spring: odds on, won minor event at Ascot in September in workmanlike fashion by 1½ lengths from Fairy Flax, leading over 2f out: second favourite, 3½ lengths third of 7 to Mystiko in Challenge Stakes at Newmarket 3 weeks later, soon under pressure but keeping on really well: should be better suited by 1m: will improve again. *H. R. A. Cecil.*

VOLPEDO (USA) 4 ch.g. Secreto (USA) 128 – Votre Altesse (FR) 122 — (Riverman (USA) 131) [1990 10.1m⁴ 10g⁵ 10.6d 16d³ 1991 17.2g] well-made gelding: has round action: no worthwhile form. *R. J. Manning.*

VOODOO RHYTHM 3 ch.c. Be My Guest (USA) 126 – Melody (USA) (Lord **64** d Gayle (USA) 124) [1990 NR 1991 8m 10g³ 10m³ 8d 10.5m⁴ 9.9f] unfurnished colt: eighth foal: brother to 2 winners, including smart 7f filly Guest Performer, closely related to 2 others, including 1988 Irish 2-y-o 6f winner Creole (by Sadler's Wells), and half-brother to 2 more, including useful 1m and 1¼m winner Philharmonia (by Caerleon): dam Irish 7f to 1½m winner: quite modest form in claimers: below form last 3 starts: stays 1¼m: acts on good to firm ground: blinkered fourth outing: bandaged on debut: sold 4,800 gns Newmarket Autumn Sales: resold 1,600 gns Ascot December Sales. *P. W. Chapple-Hyam.*

VOSTOK (IRE) 3 ch.f. The Noble Player (USA) 126 – The Flying Sputnik — (Touch Paper 113) [1990 7m 10s 8g 1991 10m 8f 8g] lengthy, workmanlike filly: well beaten, including in selling handicap: sold 675 gns Ascot October Sales. *G. A. Pritchard-Gordon.*

VUCHTERBACHER 5 b.h. Longleat (USA) 109 – Queensbury Star 76 **50** (Wishing Star 117) [1990 a7g⁵ a7g⁶ a7g² 1991 7.5f 8f⁵ a7g* a7g* 7m² 6m 7f a7g* a **58** 7m* 7m a7g a7g³ a7g*] leggy, close-coupled horse: has a round action: plating-class handicapper: successful in 1991 at Southwell (4 times) and Lingfield: best at 7f: acts on good to firm ground and all-weather surfaces: suited well when visored: sometimes bandaged: excellent mount for an apprentice: tough. *P. F. Tulk.*

VYING VICTOR (USA) 2 b.c. (Apr 15) Flying Paster (USA) – Elegant Victress **82** (CAN) (Sir Ivor 135) [1991 7g 6f³ 6m² 6.9f* 8f] good-topped colt: has scope: good walker: has a round action: eighth foal: brother to useful USA miler Flying Victor, second in Grade 2 1m race at 3 yrs, and half-brother to 3-y-o Desert Victress (by Desert Wine) and several winners, including 1986 2-y-o 7f winner Sharp Victor (by Sharpen Up): dam sprinting half-sister to leading 1983 Canadian 3-y-o Northern Blossom: sire high-class performer from 6f to 1¼m: modest performer: favourite, won 12-runner maiden at Folkestone in October by ½ length from Edgeaway, making most and running on well: ran well in 1m Hoist The Flag Stakes (Div.1) at Hollywood Park in December: yet to race on soft surface: tail swisher. *C. F. Wall.*

W

WAAD (IRE) 3 ch.c. Milk of The Barley 115 – Serena Maria 63 (Dublin Taxi) **69** [1990 5g³ 5f³ 6m⁵ 6g⁵ a6g² a5g³ a6g* 5m* 6m³ 6m* 6m* 6m 7.3g a7g⁵ 1991 6g⁴ 7d⁶ 6d³ 7m⁵ 6m⁴ 7d* a8g 8m³ 7m² 9.7f³] small, sparely-made colt: poor mover: won very strongly-run seller (bought in 4,000 gns) at Warwick in June, coming from rear: ran well in non-selling handicaps last 3 starts: stays 9.7f: acts on firm ground and dead: blinkered 5 times, second to fifth starts in 1991: suitable mount for apprentice: sold 12,500 gns Newmarket Autumn Sales. *N. A. Callaghan.*

WABASH VALLEY (USA) 2 b. or br.c. (Feb 17) Riverman (USA) 131 – **73** Fruhlingstag (FR) 112 (Orsini 124) [1991 7g² 7m⁵ 7m⁵] strong, quite attractive colt: brother to 1988 2-y-o 6f winner River Dove and closely related to 1m winner Fraulein Tobin (by J O Tobin): dam second in Poule d'Essai des Pouliches: modest form in maiden at Salisbury on debut: well below that in Houghton Stakes at Newmarket and maiden at Lingfield: will stay 1m: possibly needs some give in the ground: sold 21,000 gns Ascot 2nd November Sales, to race in Italy. *G. Harwood.*

WADERS DREAM (IRE) 2 b.c. (Feb 2) Doulab (USA) 115 – Sea Mistress **73** (Habitat 134) [1991 6m 5m 6f* 5m] 15,000 2-y-o: leggy colt: first foal: dam, unraced, from family of Pampapaul, Noble Patriarch and He Loves Me: backed at long odds, won 6-runner maiden at Yarmouth in September by 2 lengths: modest seventh of 9, never a factor, in Newmarket nursery following month: much better form at 6f than 5f. *J. E. Banks.*

WAINWRIGHT (USA) 2 ch.c. (Jan 26) Bering 136 – Crystal Bright 75 (Bold **87** p Lad (IRE) 133) [1991 7m²] $115,000Y: quite attractive colt: sixth foal: half-brother to very useful 3-y-o 6f (at 2 yrs) and 7f Group 3 winner Crystal Gazing (by El Gran Senor) and to modest but untrustworthy Staunch Rival (by Sir Ivor), winner at 1m and 1¼m: dam, placed at 5f at 2 yrs, later winner at about 1m in USA: 11/8 on from evens but green, head second of 18 to Mahool in maiden at Doncaster in October, produced to lead inside final 1f then not knocked about unduly as winner rallied: will stay 1m: sure to improve and win a race or two. *J. H. M. Gosden.*

WAJD (USA) 4 ch.f. Northern Dancer (CAN) – Dahlia (USA) 135 (Vaguely Noble **119** 140) [1990 10.5v* 10.5g* 12g* 12g³ 12m⁴ 12f 1991 10.5g 12s* 12m 12m³ 12.5d³ 15.5d³ 12f6] rangy filly: very smart French performer: won Group 2 Grand Prix d'Evry in June by 2 lengths from below-form Epervier Bleu: best efforts after when running creditably behind Saganeca in Ciga Prix de Royallieu at Longchamp and Golden Pheasant in Japan Cup at Tokyo fifth and final starts: stays 1½m: acts on good to firm ground and a soft surface: takes time to quicken: has run well when sweating: visits Mr Prospector. *A. Fabre, France.*

WAKASHAN 3 b.c. Dancing Brave (USA) 140 – Lady Moon 101 (Mill Reef (USA) **99** 141) [1990 8s³ 1991 10m*] lengthy, rather angular colt: has plenty of scope: 6/4 favourite, won 14-runner maiden at Newmarket in April easing up by 2½ lengths from Le Corsaire, taking keen hold and always close up: should be well suited by 1½m: sold to join K. Morgan only 4,000 gns Newmarket Autumn Sales. *H. R. A. Cecil.*

WAKE UP 4 ch.c. Night Shift (USA) – Astonishing (Jolly Good 122) [1990 7g 7f —
10m* 11.7m 10g6 12d 12m 12.2d 12d6 1991 12.3s 17m] sturdy colt: has a long stride: unreliable handicapper: bandaged, well beaten in spring: stays 1¼m: acts on good to firm ground: has worn tongue strap: winning hurdler late in year. *R. O'Leary.*

WAKI GOLD (USA) 4 ch.g. Miswaki (USA) 124 – Sainte Croix (USA) (Nijinsky **78** (CAN) 138) [1990 8m6 10g4 8m2 8m3 8f2 8f6 9m* 12g 9m 1991 11.5m² 12g 10.4m5 9m] rangy gelding: good mover with a long stride: fair handicapper: below form after reappearance: should stay 1½m: acts well on firm going: keen sort, goes well with forcing tactics: sold to join R. Hodges stable 12,000 gns Newmarket Autumn Sales. *P. A. Kelleway.*

WAKIL (IRE) 2 br.c. (Apr 8) Tate Gallery (USA) 117 – Arena 86 (Sallust 134) —
[1991 6g 7d] good-bodied colt: has scope: fifth foal: half-brother to 1m winner Miss Wassl (by Wassl) and a winner abroad by Cure The Blues: dam lightly-raced daughter of very useful 7f and 9f winner Melodramatic: poor form when not fully wound up in late-season maidens at Doncaster and Newbury. *C. J. Benstead.*

WALIM (USA) 3 ch.c. Nijinsky (CAN) 138 – Splendid Girl (USA) (Golden Eagle **105** (FR)) [1990 7f5 8g² 10s* 10g² 1991 10g* 11.5g4 12g6 16.2g] big, rangy colt: useful performer: won listed race at Newmarket in May: 4 lengths sixth to Hailsham in Derby Italiano at Rome: travelled well long way when well beaten in Queen's Vase at Royal Ascot final start: stays 1½m, not 2m: acts on soft ground. *M. R. Stoute.*

WALKERWAY BOY 4 b.c. Muscatite 122 – Hadala (Le Levanstell 122) [1990 —
9m a12g 16m 12m5 10m a8g 1991 a7g5] workmanlike, dipped-backed colt: moderate mover: bad handicapper: should stay at least 1¼m: acts on hard ground: usually blinkered: has looked reluctant to race. *A. Bailey.*

WALKING ON WATER 2 ch.g. (Apr 4) Celestial Storm (USA) 132 – Maiden **78** Pool 85 (Sharpen Up 127) [1991 6m4 6d 6m* 6g² 6s³ 6g 6g] 15,000F, 17,000Y: quite good-topped gelding: half-brother to 3-y-o 5f winner Mazarine Blue (by Bellypha) and several more winners, including very useful sprinter Rich Charlie (by Absalom): dam 5f winner: made all in maiden at Kempton in July: ran well when placed in minor events at Lingfield and Newmarket, respectably (despite hanging left) in Racecall Gold Trophy at Redcar final start: stays 6f: acts on good to firm and soft ground: goes well blinkered or visored: sometimes sweats. *R. F. Johnson Houghton.*

WALKING POSSESSION 2 b.c. (Apr 24) Faustus (USA) 118 – Pepeke 78 **80** (Mummy's Pet 125) [1991 a5g² 7m 5m4 6g 5m* 5d* 5d³ 6s²] 8,000F, 12,000Y: lengthy colt: has scope: moderate mover: second foal: half-brother to 3-y-o Straight No Chaser (by Norwick): dam 7f winner: found his form in autumn nurseries last 4 starts, winning at Redcar and Haydock: effective at 5f and 6f: acts on good to firm and soft ground: off course 3 months after debut on equitrack: effective with or without blinkers. *R. Boss.*

WALKING SAINT 4 b.f. Godswalk (USA) 130 – Saintly Tune (Welsh Saint 126) **57** [1990 8f² 8.5g* 8m³ 8f4 7d5 7g 7.6m6 8m4 7g a8g³ a8g* a8g a10g 1991 9g 8g 8.3m³ 8f 9d5 10m³ 7.9m6 10.3g] close-coupled filly: quite modest handicapper: stays 1¼m: acts on firm ground: none too consistent. *R. Hannon.*

WALKING THE PLANK 2 b.c. (Apr 24) Daring March 116 – Pirate Maid **78** (Auction Ring (USA) 123) [1991 5.7f4 8g* 8d² 8g6] tall, rather unfurnished colt: fourth foal: dam ran once: won maiden at Bath in September: ran creditably in median auction at Wolverhampton and 19-runner nursery (behind Cumbrian Challenge) at Redcar afterwards: stays 1m: acts on dead ground. *P. T. Walwyn.*

WALK IN THE PARK 2 ch.f. (Apr 5) Valiyar 129 – Tripolitaine (FR) (Nonoalco   **82**
(USA) 131) [1991 5.3f⁴ 5g³ 6m⁵ 5.2g* 6m* 6g² 7g³ 6d* 5.7f² 6g⁴ 5g⁴ 6m] small filly:
seventh living foal: half-sister to several winners, including 1989 2-y-o 5f winner
Western Music (by Music Boy): dam won twice at around 11f in France: improved
filly: successful in maiden at Newbury and nurseries at Windsor and Kempton
within 3 weeks in mid-summer: creditable fourth of 8 to Another Episode in minor
event at York on penultimate outing: really needs further than 5f, and stays 7f: acts
on firm and dead ground: tough, raced only between late-May and early-September.
R. Simpson.

WALKONTHEMOON 2 ch.f. (Feb 16) Coquelin (USA) 121 – Lunar Eclipse 95   **35**
(Hot Spark 126) [1991 a5g⁴ a7g⁶] 6,000Y: sister to 1987 2-y-o 5f winner Breeze Up
and half-sister to 3 winners here and abroad, including 1¼m winner Lakh (by Sexton
Blake): dam won twice at up to 6f: well beaten in late-year maidens at Lingfield. *M.
McCormack.*

WALK TALL (IRE) 2 b. or br.c. (Jan 23) Taufan (USA) 119 – Altara (GER)   **58**
(Tarim) [1991 6g³ 7m⁵ 7f] IR 67,000Y: smallish, sturdy colt: moderate mover: fourth
foal: half-brother to a winner in Italy: dam lightly-raced daughter of top German filly
Alaria: plating-class form in maidens at Pontefract and Brighton first 2 starts: ran
moderately at Yarmouth (August) 6 days later: will stay 1m. *J. M. P. Eustace.*

WALK THAT WALK 2 b.f. (Apr 10) Hadeer 118 – Che Gambe (USA) (Lyphard   **61**
(USA) 132) [1991 5m⁴ 5m* 7.6d 7d] leggy, workmanlike filly: first foal: dam unraced:
green, won maiden at Sandown in April: below that form in nurseries (very stiff
tasks) 6 months later: should stay 1m. *C. E. Brittain.*

WALK THIS WAY (IRE) 3 ch.f. Pennine Walk 120 – Tarop (USA) (Dr Fager)   **48**
[1990 NR 1991 8g³ 8.3d² a7g⁴ 8.1g 10.1m⁶ a12g⁴ 11.8g 9.7m³ 9.7g 10m⁴] 11,000Y:
lengthy, workmanlike filly: half-sister to several winners, including very useful
1986 2-y-o 7f winner Tartuffe (by Golden Act): dam, winner over 6f at 3 yrs in USA,
is sister to Amerrico, very useful performer in Britain later stakes winner in USA:
modest plater: stays 1¼m: acts on good to firm ground and dead: blinkered last 4
starts: sometimes bandaged. *A. N. Lee.*

WALLANGRIFF 3 ch.g. Noalto 120 – Concern 63 (Brigadier Gerard 144) [1990   **58**
7g 7m⁶ 6m 8m 1991 a7g a10g a7g² a6g* a6g⁵ 6f⁶ a5g] strong, lengthy gelding: 2/1 on,
made all in maiden at Southwell in February: not seen out after May: stays 7f: often
blinkered, including when successful. *N. A. Callaghan.*

WALLED GARDEN 3 ch.g. Dominion 123 – Last Cutting (Final Straw 127)   **—**
[1990 7s 1991 12d 10.1d⁶ 8.3m] tall, close-coupled, plain gelding: has a round
action: seems of little account. *A. Moore.*

WALSTEAD (IRE) 2 b.c. (Feb 10) Fairy King (USA) – Tecmessa (Home Guard   **68**
(USA) 129) [1991 5m* 6.3s 6g] IR 16,000Y: compact colt: third living foal: brother to
1990 2-y-o 5f winner Lindfield Belle: dam unraced: won maiden at Sandown in April,
leading close home: well beaten 6 months later, facing stiff tasks, in Goffs Premier
Challenge Race at the Curragh and (when not looking so well in himself) Racecall
Gold Trophy at Redcar: will stay 6f +. *W. Jarvis.*

WALTON MELODY 4 ch.f. Kabour 80 – Straight Melody (Highland Melody   **—**
112) [1990 NR 1991 a5g a7g a8g 8g] leggy filly: third reported living foal: dam never
ran: seems of little account. *D. W. Chapman.*

WANDA 4 b.f. Taufan (USA) 119 – Pitaka (Pitskelly 122) [1990 5f² 5v² 5d 7m⁴ 7m   **74**
5m² 5g⁴ 6m 5g 5g* 5d 5g⁶ 5m 1991 5g³ 5f⁶ 6g* 6g⁴ 5d* 5g³ 6.1m 6m 5.1m 5g
5.1s⁵ 5.1d⁴ 5d] close-coupled, angular filly: moderate walker and mover: modest
handicapper: won at Lingfield in May and Ripon (made most) in June: below form
last 7 starts: effective at 5f and 6f: acts on any going, but best efforts on good and
dead ground: often blinkered, not in 1991: has had tongue tied down. *K. R. Burke.*

WANDA'S DREAM (USA) 3 ch.f. Miswaki (USA) 124 – Halo Reply (CAN)   **74**
(Halo (USA)) [1990 5m³ 6f² 5f² 1991 6d³ 5f* 5m 6s²] good-bodied filly: has a quick
action: modest performer: won maiden at Folkestone in April, making virtually all:
very good second in handicap at Lingfield in June, making most and rallying well:
stays 6f: acts on any going. *D. J. G. Murray-Smith.*

WANDERING STRANGER 2 gr.f. (Feb 17) Petong 126 – Doppio 62 (Dublin   **69**
Taxi) [1991 5m² 5m² 5g³] leggy, workmanlike filly: second foal: sister to 1990 2-y-o
5f winner Garth: dam 2-y-o 5f winner out of sister to Runnett: quite modest maiden:
placed in modest company at Windsor (ran on strongly) in August and at Lingfield
and Folkestone in September: should stay 6f. *P. J. Makin.*

WAND (IRE) 2 b.f. (Apr 21) Reference Point 139 – Fairy Dancer (USA) (Nijinsky   **— p**
(CAN) 138) [1991 7g] 230,000Y: sturdy, attractive filly: second foal: half-sister to

Irish 1990 2-y-o 7f winner Adjudicate (by Law Society): dam, once-raced in Ireland at 2 yrs and 3 yrs when 6f winner on debut, is closely related to Sadler's Wells: 20/1 and very green, slow-starting twentieth of 22, showing nothing, in maiden at Newmarket in November: looks capable of much better. *H. R. A. Cecil.*

WANE'S SECRET (IRE)   3 b.g. Horage 124 – Zestino (Shack (USA) 118) [1990 **44** d
5m 5m⁴ 6g⁶ 6m 7f 5s⁵ a5g a7g 1991 a8g a5g² a6g 5g 5f⁵ 6f² 6g 5m 6d⁵ 6d 7m] small, sturdy gelding: moderate mover: plater: well beaten after second at Carlisle in May: seems better at 6f than 5f: has form on any going, best on firm: trained first 9 starts by K. McCauley, tenth by M. Naughton. *H. A. T. Whiting.*

WAR BEAT   3 b.g. Wolver Heights 99 – Branitska (Mummy's Pet 125) [1990 7f⁵ **58**
8m 8m 10.2s 1991 14.1g a12g* 14.1f⁶ 11.9g³ 12.1s a12g] sturdy gelding: has a quick action: quite modest handicapper: won handicap at Lingfield in July: ran well next 2 starts: may prove ideally suited by 1½m: acts on firm ground, not soft: has taken good hold: sold out of C. Brittain's stable 7,200 gns Newmarket Autumn Sales after fifth start. *P. J. Bevan.*

WARFIELD   4 b.c. Glint of Gold 128 – Alys (Blakeney 126) [1990 10.5g⁴ 1991 12g² **108**
14g* 15.5g⁶ 15.5g³ 12.5g 16g² 20d³ 15.5d] second foal: dam French 1m to 1¼m winner: useful French colt: won amateurs event at Angers in May: placed after in listed events at Longchamp in June and Baden-Baden in August and Group 1 Prix du Cadran (6½ lengths behind impressive Victoire Bleue) at Longchamp: well beaten in Prix Royal-Oak there final start: stays 2½m: acts on dead ground (yet to race on top-of-the-ground). *J. Pease, France.*

WARM FEELING   4 b.c. Kalaglow 132 – Height of Passion (Shirley Heights **111**
130) [1990 a10g* a10g* 11g² 12.3d* 12m⁴ 16.2f⁴ 1991 12s* 12g² 13.4d² 16.2m* 20g³] lengthy, workmanlike colt: has quick action: usually impresses in appearance: very useful performer: won quite valuable events at Doncaster in March and Haydock in May (very easily by 6 lengths from Arden): ran very well in John Porter Stakes at Newbury (¾-length second to Rock Hopper), Ormonde Stakes at Chester (beaten a length by Per Quod) and Ascot Gold Cup (4 lengths third to Indian Queen): effective at 1½m to 2½m: acts on good to firm and soft going: tough, genuine and consistent: sent to race in Saudi Arabia. *B. W. Hills.*

WARRIOR PRINCE   3 b.g. Prince Sabo 123 – Choral Park (Music Boy 124) **66** d
[1990 5d⁵ 5m⁴ 5f⁵ 6g 5m* 5m 5v⁶ 6d 1991 5g² 5m 5f 5.9f⁴ 6f 6m 7d 6g 5d⁶ 7m a8g] sturdy, lengthy gelding: poor walker: plating-class performer: mostly well beaten after reappearance: should prove as effective over 6f as 5f: possibly unsuited by heavy ground, acts on any other: blinkered twice: untrustworthy. *R. M. Whitaker.*

WASAIF (IRE)   3 ch.f. Lomond (USA) 128 – Amber Fizz (USA) (Effervescing **79**
(USA)) [1990 NR 1991 8g⁴ 8g³ 6.9f* 7m⁴ 8.1d] strong, lengthy filly: carries condition: moderate mover: third foal: half-sister to poor 1990 maiden Pharly Fizz (by Pharly): dam once-raced half-sister to very smart 1978 American 2-y-o Groton High, from family of Bold Ruler: fair performer: won maiden at Folkestone in September, leading over 1f out: stayed 1m well: seemed to need a sound surface: visits Reprimand. *L. M. Cumani.*

WASEELA (IRE)   2 b.f. (Jan 26) Ahonoora 122 – Wassl's Sister (Troy 137) [1991 **65** p
6f 7m²] rangy filly: has scope: third foal: dam maiden suited by 1½m, is half-sister to Wassl: one-paced 2 lengths second of 13 finishers to Manbaa at Redcar in October, easily better effort in maidens: will probably be suited by 1m: bandaged behind on debut. *A. A. Scott.*

F. H. Lee 25th Anniversary Lymm Stakes, Haydock —
Warm Feeling lands the odds in good style

WASHINGTON RED 2 ch.c. (May 17) Tickled Pink 114 – Apple Queen — (Behistoun 131) [1991 6.1m] 700Y, 2,000 2-y-o: smallish, sturdy colt: half-brother to 1978 2-y-o 5f winner Megan's Girl (by Workboy) and 2 other winners, one over hurdles: dam bad plater: 33/1 and backward, soundly beaten in 23-runner maiden auction at Nottingham in September. *M. F. Barraclough.*

WASHITA 4 b.f. Valiyar 129 – Ardneasken 84 (Right Royal V 135) [1990 8g 8g — 11g⁴ 12g 15v 1991 12d 12m 15.8g 12.1s] workmanlike filly: moderate mover: poor maiden: should stay beyond 11f. *C. W. Thornton.*

WASSELNI 5 br.g. Wassl 125 – Monongelia 98 (Welsh Pageant 132) [1990 16.2m — 1991 16m 14m 13.8f 14.6g 16.5m] angular, sparely-made gelding: moderate mover: of little account: dead. *K. A. Morgan.*

WASSIFA 3 b.f. Sure Blade (USA) 130 – Rye Tops 97 (Ile de Bourbon (USA) 133) **95** [1990 6d 1991 7m³ 7g⁵ 11m* 10d⁵] close-coupled, deep-girthed filly: won 4-runner minor event at Wolverhampton in May, setting very slow early pace: edgy, good fifth of 8 to Ocean Air in listed race at Newbury in June, held up, keeping on never able to challenge: suited by middle distances: sold 25,000 gns Newmarket December Sales. *B. Hanbury.*

WASSL THIS THEN (IRE) 2 b.f. (Apr 19) Wassl 125 – Dancing Decoy 78 **59** (Troy 137) [1991 6.1m 7g⁶ 6d⁵] 7,000F: third foal: half-sister to Irish 3-y-o Taunting, 6f winner at 2 yrs, and Irish 11f winner Catch Twenty Two (both by Taufan): dam placed at 1m and 1¼m, is half-sister to smart sprinter Defecting Dancer: progressive, though quite modest form: should be suited by further than 6f. *D. W. P. Arbuthnot.*

WATCH IT MATEY 3 b.g. Tina's Pet 121 – Mouletta (Moulton 128) [1990 8g⁶ **77** 1991 10.1m³ a12g² 12.3g⁵ a12g 10g² 10.5d 12f*] workmanlike gelding: best effort when impressive winner of claimer (claimed £12,120) at Folkestone in October, always front rank: stays 1½m well: acts on firm ground: visored fifth and sixth outings. *D. Morley.*

WATCH ME GO (IRE) 2 b.c. (May 5) On Your Mark 125 – Nighty Night **68** (Sassafras (FR) 135) [1991 5g 6m⁵ 7g 7.5f⁶ 7g⁵ 7.5f* 8m⁶ 8m 7m 7m] IR 6,800F, 9,800Y: sturdy colt: brother to 1985 Irish 2-y-o 5f winner Fait Dodo and half-brother to several winners, including middle-distance performer Celtic Bhoy (by Red Sunset): dam unraced half-sister to 1969 Criterium des Pouliches winner Vela: easily best effort when winning maiden auction at Beverley in August, quickening clear in good style: will probably stay beyond 1m: acts on firm ground: inconsistent. *Bob Jones.*

WATCH TOWER BAY (IRE) 3 ch.g. Kings Lake (USA) 133 – Noon Bells — (Ballymore 123) [1990 7f 7f⁵ 1991 12g 18.1m] tall gelding: poor form at 2 yrs: in need of race and very stiff tasks in claimer and handicap in autumn of 1991: will prove suited by further than 7f. *R. Boss.*

WATERMILL GIRL 3 b.f. Blakeney 126 – Absurd 60 (Absalom 128) [1990 NR — 1991 8g 10g 7f] smallish filly: second foal: dam 9f winner: always behind, bandaged in seller final start. *D. T. Thom.*

WATERSONG 2 b.f. (Mar 3) Lochnager 132 – Sonoco 61 (Song 132) [1991 a6g **52** a7g³ a6g] first foal: dam sprint maiden: over 6 lengths third of 13 to Macs Bid in maiden at Southwell: broke leg final start: dead. *D. R. Laing.*

WATER WELL 4 b.f. Sadler's Wells (USA) 132 – Soba 127 (Most Secret 119) **95** [1990 7m⁶ 7.6d* 8m⁴ 8f⁶ 8g 6s 1991 8d 6g 8m⁴ 6s] workmanlike, good-quartered filly: fairly useful performer: best effort in 1991 when good fourth to You Know The Rules in listed event at Doncaster: stiff task in Diadem Stakes at Ascot later in September: stays 1m: acts on good to firm ground and dead. *C. E. Brittain.*

WATER WILDERNESS 2 b.c. (Feb 6) Damister (USA) 123 – False Front 85 — (Bustino 136) [1991 6f 7g] angular colt: first live foal: dam 11.7f winner, is grand-daughter of Irish 1000 Guineas winner Lacquer, family also of Bright Finish and Shining Finish: no form in large-field sellers at Yarmouth and Wolverhampton in autumn. *M. H. Tompkins.*

WATTLE SYKE 4 ch.g. King Persian 107 – Sandforgold (Sandford Lad 133) — [1990 10.2f 8f 8g⁶ 8.2g⁴ 7m 8.2m²ᵈⁱˢ 8f³ 7.5g 1991 16.2g a12g a14g³ 16.5m 16.5g 12f⁵] leggy gelding: poor handicapper: best at around 1m: best effort on firm going. *M. C. Chapman.*

WATWICK BAY 3 b.g. Green Ruby (USA) 104 – Jolly Smooth 84 (Jolly Jet 111) — [1990 NR 1991 a8g] half-brother to 7f and 1m winner Well Greased (by Workboy):

dam won at up to 13f: 50/1 and visored, tailed off in maiden at Lingfield in March. *B. Palling.*

WAVEBAND 2 br.f. (Feb 24) Thatching 131 – Waveguide 76 (Double Form 130) **62** [1991 5d* 6m4] 32,000F, IR 10,000Y: neat, quite attractive filly: second foal: dam placed at 5f at 2 yrs, is out of half-sister to Centro, dam of Nicholas Bill, Centroline and Centrocon, herself dam of Time Charter: won maiden at Warwick in July, running green: below that form in minor event at Windsor (moved moderately to post) 12 days later, weakening quickly over 1f out: should stay 6f: possibly unsuited by good to firm ground. *B. W. Hills.*

WAVE HILL 2 b.c. (Feb 24) Sizzling Melody 117 – Trikymia 68 (Final Straw 127) **85** ? [1991 5g2 6f2 5.8d* 7d2 6m2 6m3 6.1m5 6m*] close-coupled colt: first foal: dam third over 5f at 2 yrs on only start, is half-sister to 7 smart or better winners, including Tromos, Tyrnavos and Tachypous: consistently modest on most form: made all in 5-runner median auction at Bath in June: won 2-runner minor event at Catterick in October (on toes, apparently best form) leading inside final 1f to beat 9/2-on shot Shati by ½ length despite drifting slightly left: stays 7f: acts on good to firm and dead ground. *H. R. A. Cecil.*

WAVE MASTER 4 b.g. Chief Singer 131 – Sea Fret 96 (Habat 127) [1990 6m3 6f **52** 6m2 1991 7.1m6 9.7g3 10.3g] sturdy, close-coupled gelding: has a roundish action: plating-class performer nowadays: stays 9.7f: possibly unsuited by very firm ground: below form when blinkered once: sold to join R. Hodges 2,100 gns Ascot November Sales. *P. J. Makin.*

WAVERLEY STAR 6 br.g. Pitskelly 122 – Quelle Blague (Red God 128§) [1990 **57** § a6g4 a6g3 a6g6 5f3 6f 5f3 5g 5m5 6m 5f4 6f4 6g a5g* 5m2 a5g5 6f3 5f2 6m 5m3 6f3 6g 6g 5m* 5m4 5g 1991 a5g4 5d4 6d 5f4 5g 5f5 5m3 6m 5d6 5.9m4 a5g3 5s5 5d3 5.2g 6g5 5m 6m3 5f 5m 5m 6m5 5m3 5m5 6m4] big, workmanlike gelding: poor mover: plating-class handicapper: best at sprint distances: acts on firm and dead ground: often blinkered (has been tried in visor): has edged left: inconsistent. *J. S. Wainwright.*

WAYPOST 3 b. or br.g. Belfort (FR) 89 – Golden Slade 70 (Octavo (USA) 115) — [1990 7m 6g 1991 6m 7.1d 7g 8m] tall, close-coupled gelding: little form, in July claimer final start: stays 7f: probably best effort on dead ground: blinkered third start: sold 1,000 gns Ascot November Sales. *A. Hide.*

WAYWARD SON 2 ro.g. (Mar 9) Risk Me (FR) 127 – Mummy's Chick 77 **45** (Mummy's Pet 125) [1991 6d 5.7f] 14,000Y: small, sparely-made gelding: second foal: dam 2-y-o 5f winner: poor form, always behind, in maidens at Goodwood (showed a round action) in June and Bath 3 months later. *G. Lewis.*

WAYZGOOSE (USA) 3 ch.f. Diesis 133 – Indoor (FR) (Caracolero (USA) 131) **76** [1990 NR 1991 10g3] lengthy, rather sparely-made filly: sixth foal: half-sister to 2 winners in USA: dam won 10.5f Prix de Flore: moderately to post when keeping-on third of 13 in maiden at Leicester in May: sold to join B. Cambidge 4,200 gns Newmarket December Sales. *H. R. A. Cecil.*

WEAREAGRANDMOTHER 4 b.f. Prince Tenderfoot (USA) 126 – Lady — Bettina (Bustino 136) [1990 8g 11m 10m3 12.5g* 12.5m2 10f5 12v 1991 10.2s] workmanlike filly: plating-class handicapper at 3 yrs: well beaten only run in 1991 (March): stays 1½m well: possibly unsuited by extremes of going: has been bandaged behind: winning hurdler in April. *B. A. McMahon.*

WEBSPINNER 3 b.f. Shadeed (USA) 135 – Optimistic Lass (USA) 117 (Mr **61** Prospector (USA)) [1990 NR 1991 7g6 6.9f2 8m2 8.3f4 7.6g] rather unfurnished filly: third foal: closely related to quite modest middle-distance maiden Tsar Maiden (by Nijinsky) and half-sister to Golden Opinion (by Slew O'Gold): dam 6f (at 2 yrs) to 10.5f winner: quite modest maiden: stays 1m: acts on firm going: twice sweating, very edgy before soundly beaten in handicap final start: visits Slew O'Gold. *M. R. Stoute.*

WEDNESDAYS AUCTION (IRE) 3 b.c. Mazaad 106 – Happy Always 48 **52** + (Lucky Wednesday 124) [1990 6g 1991 10g 9m*] workmanlike colt: won claimer at Wolverhampton in May: should stay 1¼m: looked likely to improve again. *B. Hanbury.*

WEEHEBY (USA) 2 ch.c. (Apr 10) Woodman (USA) 126 – Fearless Dame **61** p (USA) (Fearless Knight) [1991 8m] strong, angular colt: good walker: half-brother to several winners: dam minor stakes-winning sprinter: 10/1 from 6/1, always towards rear in 22-runner maiden at Newmarket in October: moved down well: should improve. *A. A. Scott.*

WEEKDAY CROSS (IRE) 3 b.g. Taufan (USA) 119 – Isoldes Tower (Balliol **56**
125) [1990 6g 6d a7g 1991 a10g² 12.2d³ 10g 9.2d³ 8m] good-topped gelding: quite
modest maiden: easily best efforts when placed, edging right in handicap
penultimate start: effective at 9f, and should prove best short of 1½m: acts on dead
ground: blinkered (led over 5f, ran poorly) final start: sold to join J. Jenkins 14,000
gns Newmarket July Sales and gelded. *W. Jarvis.*

WEEKEND GIRL 2 b.f. (Mar 21) Vorvados 118 – Mrs Scattercash (Northfields **—**
(USA)) [1991 6f 6f 7m 10.5d 6.1m] leggy filly: moderate mover: first reported foal:
dam well-beaten third over 1¼m only start on flat: seems of little account. *W. M.
Brisbourne.*

WEE TOSH 2 b.g. (Mar 4) Alleging (USA) 120 – Iron Lass (Thatch (USA) 136) **—**
[1991 5f] smallish, sturdy gelding: first foal: dam once-raced granddaughter of July
Cup winner Merry Madcap: 7/1, last of 16 in claimer at Beverley in May: sold 700 gns
Ascot October Sales. *R. D. E. Woodhouse.*

WELCOMING ARMS 4 b.f. Free State 125 – The Guzzler 69 (Behistoun 131) **50**
[1990 10.6s 10m⁵ 14f⁶ 12.2m² 12.5m⁵ 12d 15v 13.6d 1991 12.3s 13.8g 16.5m a14g*
a12g a14g 12m⁴ 16.1m³ 16.9m* 16m⁵ 18.1m⁶ a14g] angular, workmanlike filly:
plating-class handicapper: won at Southwell (blinkered) in May and Wolverhampton
in September: needs further than 1½m, and stays very well: acts on good to firm
going and fibresand. *P. Calver.*

WELL AND TRULY 4 b.f. Rousillon (USA) 133 – Altana 71 (Grundy 137) [1990 **43**
10m⁶ 10g 10.1m 11.5f⁴ 11.7m 10s⁴ a12g 1991 11.7g 16m 12.1d 16.5m² 14.9m] leggy,
light-framed filly: poor handicapper: stays 2m: acts on any going: ran moderately on
equitrack: inconsistent: sold out of C. C. Elsey's stable after penultimate start 2,200
gns Newmarket July Sales. *P. A. Blockley.*

WELL APPOINTED (IRE) 2 b.g. (Feb 17) Petorius 117 – So Stylish 77 (Great **85**
Nephew 126) [1991 5g⁶ 5g² 6m³ 7m² 7g* 7f² 7m² 7.3m² 7m² 7m 7d²] 10,500Y:
smallish, angular gelding: good mover: first foal: dam, maiden suited by 1½m, is
half-sister to Cesarewitch winner Sir Michael: fair performer: won nursery at
Goodwood in August: runner-up in 4 similar events afterwards, then good second of
3 to West Vermont in minor contest at Chester last time: claimed out of Mrs J.
Ramsden's stable £6,201 after fourth start: will be well suited by 1m: acts on firm
and dead ground: has been bandaged behind: largely consistent. *Mrs L. Stubbs.*

WELL BEYOND (IRE) 2 ch.f. (Feb 24) Don't Forget Me 127 – Mariakova **87**
(USA) 84 (The Minstrel (CAN) 135) [1991 5g* 6m⁵ 6m] IR 8,000F, IR 13,000Y:
lengthy, good-quartered filly: fifth foal: half-sister to 1½m winner Society Ball (by
Law Society): dam, placed on her only 2 starts, seemed suited by 1m: won minor
event at Sandown, running on well to lead near post: creditable fifth of 10, racing
keenly, fading and beaten 6 lengths, to Bezelle in Princess Margaret Stakes at Ascot
later in July: not entirely discredited when seventh of 8 to Twafeaj in Moyglare Stud
Stakes at the Curragh in September: stays 6f. *B. W. Hills.*

WELL DONE RORY 2 b.c. (Apr 10) Homeboy 114 – Star Flower (Star Appeal **—**
133) [1991 5.7f 6.1m] small, good-topped colt: second foal: half-brother to a winner in
Macau: dam poor half-sister to good continental stayer Duky out of half-sister to
Gold Cup winner Shangamuzo: soundly beaten in maidens at Bath and Nottingham
(blinkered, on toes) in September. *R. J. Holder.*

WELL FURNISHED 4 ch.c. Salmon Leap (USA) 131 – Mimicry (Thatch (USA) **87**
136) [1990 8g* 9f* 8g* 9m⁵ 8m 8g⁶ 9m a10g² a10g³ a10g⁵ 1991 9g² 8m⁵ 9g⁴ 8m
8g 8g³ 8.5f³ 8m⁴ 8g⁴ 7.6m⁴ 8m* 8m³ 7m] rangy colt: fair handicapper: won at
Kempton (hasn't won elsewhere) in September: effective at 1m to 1¼m: acts on firm
going: has run well when sweating: sold 30,000 gns Newmarket Autumn Sales,
reportedly to Malaysia. *A. A. Scott.*

WELLINGTON ROCK (USA) 2 ch.c. (Apr 1) Lyphard's Wish (FR) 124 – **74** p
Cuz's Star (USA) (Galaxy Libra 104) [1991 7g⁴ 7d] $52,000Y: tall, useful-looking
colt: shade unfurnished: fluent mover: second foal: dam, ran 5 times unplaced, is
half-sister to joint-second U.S. 2-y-o colt of 1976 Royal Ski: 8/1, 5½ lengths fourth of
11, held up pulling hard, finished well, to Alnasr Alwasheek in minor event at
Kempton: dropped back quickly from 2f out in similar event at Ascot later in
September: will stay 1m: possibly unsuited by dead ground: worth another chance. *J.
A. R. Toller.*

WELL LOG 3 br.f. Reach 122 – Cachucha (Gay Fandango (USA) 132) [1990 6g 6m **—**
6m 8.2g² 1991 10.8g] leggy filly: moderate mover: plater: easily best effort final start
at 2 yrs: well beaten in handicap in October, 1991: should stay 1¼m. *B. Stevens.*

WELL SADDLED (IRE) 2 b.c. (Feb 24) Sadler's Wells (USA) 132 – Ukraine 75 p
Girl 121 (Targowice (USA) 130) [1991 7g*] IR 125,000Y: sixth living foal: brother to
fairly useful middle-distance performer Sadler's Lad, closely related to 2 winners,
including Irish 1¼m winner Ukraine Dancer (by Shareef Dancer) and half-brother to
a winner by Shergar: dam won Poule d'Essai des Pouliches: 6/1, won 9-runner
maiden at Salisbury in October by 2½ lengths from Constructivist, held up in rear
then good progress over 1f out and quickly drawing clear inside last: likely to prove
suited by middle distances: promising. *D. R. C. Elsworth.*

WELLSY LAD (USA) 4 ch.c. El Baba (USA) – Iwishiknew (USA) (Damascus 56
(USA)) [1990 a7g² a8g³ a7g* a6g² a6g* a7g* a7g² a8g³ a7g³ 6f 6m 6g⁵ 6m⁵ 6f⁶ 7g a 74
6m 6g² 6d⁶ 6f 8d* 6s³ a6g³ a6g⁶ 1991 a7g⁵ a8g⁶ a6g⁶ a7g 6d 7.5f a6g* 6g³ 6f a7g
a6g* a6g⁵ 6m a7g 6g 6d 6s² a6g³ a7g a6g* a6g* a6g⁶] leggy, angular colt: moderate
walker: fair handicapper, best on all-weather: won at Southwell in summer (2) and
December (2 claimers): ran very well there final start: effective at 6f and 7f:
probably best with give in the ground on turf: has given trouble in preliminaries and
been slowly away. *D. W. Chapman.*

WELSHMAN 5 ch.g. Final Straw 127 – Joie de Galles 72 (Welsh Pageant 132) 56
[1990 12d 16.2s 1991 14m³ 18.4d⁵ 17.6m⁵ 18f³ 14d* 14g² 16.2g⁵ 14g⁵ 15.9m³ 14m 14g
14.6g²] close-coupled, workmanlike gelding: won handicap at Nottingham (made
all) in June: stays very well: acts on good to firm ground, but goes really well with
give (revels in the mud): goes well with forcing tactics: tough: winning hurdler. *M.
Blanshard.*

WELSH MILL (IRE) 2 b.c. (Apr 30) Caerleon (USA) 132 – Gay Milly (FR) 74 61 p
(Mill Reef (USA) 141) [1991 7.9m⁴] sparely-made, workmanlike colt: sixth living
foal: half-brother to several winners, including very useful 1¼m winner Cocotte (by
Troy) and fairly useful 1984 2-y-o 6f winner Gay Captain (by Ela-Mana-Mou): dam
1m winner out of Irish 1000 Guineas winner Gaily: 14/1 and green, 10 lengths fourth
of 8 to Prince Emilio in maiden at York in October, tracking leaders nearly 5f, not
knocked about when beaten: likely to stay 1¼m: should do better. *Lord Huntingdon.*

WELSH SECRET 3 b.f. Welsh Captain 113 – Bridge of Gold 68 (Balidar 133) 85
[1990 5m 6d 5m 5m² 6g² 6d 1991 6d⁴ 5m* 5g* 6f* 5g* 6m⁵ 6g 6g 6g⁴ 6d 6m] strong,
workmanlike filly: poor mover: fair handicapper: progressed really well when
successful at Pontefract (twice), Catterick (apprentices) then Sandown in the
spring: off course 11 weeks after ninth start then caught eye travelling strongly over
4f both subsequent outings: should be suited by return to 5f: acts on firm going (has
twice shaped well on dead). *Mrs J. R. Ramsden.*

WELSH SIREN 5 b.m. Welsh Saint 126 – Kalonji (Red Alert 127) [1990 8h* 10g 58
10g³ 8m² 10f 8.3m⁵ 8h⁵ 10g⁴ 10.2m⁴ 8d 1991 10.8m² 12g³ 12.3d³ 10g 17.2g]
workmanlike mare: keen walker: moderate mover: plating-class handicapper:
brought down final start, first for 3½ months: better at 1½m than shorter: acts on
hard and dead ground: has edged right: winning hurdler. *K. C. Bailey.*

WE'RE ALL GAME 2 b.f. (Feb 6) Mummy's Game 120 – Swynford's Pride 95 56
(Rapid River 127) [1991 5m 5m⁶ 6g⁵ 6.1m⁶ 5d³] 1,300Y: tall, leggy filly: fourth live
foal: half-sister to fair sprinter Viltash (by Tachypous): dam 5f winner at 2 yrs:
plating-class maiden: best effort (despite tending to hang) in Doncaster nursery in
November on final start: acts on good to soft ground. *B. C. Morgan.*

WESAAM (USA) 2 b.c. (Feb 16) Riverman (USA) 131 – Share The Fantasy 103
(USA) (Exclusive Native (USA)) [1991 6g² 6m² 8m* 8g²] $650,000Y: strong, quite
attractive colt: has plenty of scope: moderate mover: fourth foal: dam smart winner
at up to 7f at 2 yrs: well-backed favourite, won 18-runner maiden at Newmarket in
workmanlike style, leading over 2f out and staying on: very good ½-length second of
19 to Cumbrian Challenge in nursery at Redcar later in month, travelling strongly
most of way but not finding so much as expected: may well stay 1¼m: strong-
running type. *Major W. R. Hern.*

WESAYEM 4 b.f. Shirley Heights 130 – Capital Risk 82 (Bustino 136) [1990 14g⁵ —
14f² 1991 10d 16.2g 12g a14g 15s] angular filly: quite modest form when second in
maiden at Yarmouth for A. Stewart: no form, including in selling handicap, in 1991:
stays 1¾m: has been tried in blinkers. *R. W. Stubbs.*

WESSEX 9 b.h. Free State 125 – Bonandra 82 (Andrea Mantegna) [1990 13v 18m⁴ —
13g 16.5m 20.4m² 18g 1991 18.1m] strong horse: shows traces of stringhalt: poor
handicapper: out-and-out stayer: acts on any going: effective with blinkers or
without. *N. Tinkler.*

WESTCROFT 3 ch.g. Crofthall 110 – Two's Up (Double Jump 131) [1990 NR 1991 —
12.2m 14m 16g 11.1d⁶ 13d] 6,000Y: leggy gelding: fifth foal: brother to 1m to 1½m

winner Burcroft and half-brother to 10.5f seller winner Bob-Double (by Import): dam never ran: no worthwhile form: dead. *R. M. Whitaker.*

WESTERN ACE (IRE) 3 ch.c. On Your Mark 125 – Galva (Gulf Pearl 117) — [1990 7m 7g a8g2 a7g a8g 1991 8f3 a10g5 8g] sturdy colt: quite modest form at best: well beaten in handicaps after last of 3 in minor event at Brighton: should stay 1¼m: sold 3,800 gns Newmarket Autumn Sales. *J. M. P. Eustace.*

WESTERN APPROACH (USA) 2 b.f. (Apr 6) Gone West (USA) – Devon **76 p** Diva (USA) (The Minstrel (CAN) 135) [1991 6m2] strong filly: third foal: closely related to 3-y-o Daki (by Miswaki), successful at 6f (at 2 yrs) and 7f: dam 9f winner at 4 yrs in USA, is daughter of Devon Ditty: sire best at 1m/9f: 9/2, backward and green, length second of 8 to Cloud of Dust in maiden at Leicester in October, travelling strongly long way: bred to stay 7f: sure to improve, and win a similar event. *J. H. M. Gosden.*

WESTERN DANCER 10 b.g. Free State 125 – Polyandrist 92 (Polic 126) [1990 **59** a14g3 14m5 1991 12v4 16g5 16.1g6] lengthy gelding: usually looks well: good mover: ideally suited by good test of stamina: acts on any going: has started slowly: well served by strong gallop. *C. A. Horgan.*

WESTERN DYNASTY 5 ch.g. Hotfoot 126 – Northern Dynasty 65 (Breeders **70** Dream 116) [1990 12g3 14m5 12m4 14g2 12f2 11.5d* 12m* 12g* 12d* 13.3g4 12m 12g6 12s5 1991 12s 12m6 11d6 11.1g3 10m5 11.5s2 10.1g5 11.8m4 12da 12g5a 14g5] big, lengthy gelding: moderate mover: quite modest handicapper nowadays: ideally suited by 1½m: has form on good to firm ground, but very best efforts on an easy surface: game. *M. J. Ryan.*

WESTERN LOCH 4 b.f. Reesh 117 – Westerlake (Blakeney 126) [1990 7.6d 6g **40** 10.1m6 a8g 10m2 9f5 10f* 10d4 8m 8d 10d 1991 7f8g 10.1d 10.2g5 10.2f2 10s 8f6 10f4 9.7s] strong, workmanlike filly: carries condition: poor handicapper nowadays: suited by 1¼m: acts on firm and dead ground: trained first 8 starts by R. Hodges. *R. P. C. Hoad.*

WESTERN WOLF 6 ch.h. Wolverlife 115 – Sweet Kate (Slippered 103) [1990 8f **60** 9g4 8f3 7m2 7.6m 8m2 8f 8.2s 8.2f4 8g 8m6 9m 1991 8g 7.6m 8.3g 8m 7s4 8m] plain horse: usually looks well: fair handicapper at 5 yrs: below form in 1991: best at 7f/1m: acts on soft ground, but goes particularly well on top-of-the-ground: ran poorly in blinkers: bandaged behind once: has broken blood vessel over hurdles. *W. Carter.*

WESTFIELD MOVES (IRE) 3 b.c. Montelimar (USA) 122 – Rathcoffey **66** Daisy (Pampapaul 121) [1990 7f2 7.5g* 8.2g3 7g2 8d4* 7s 1991 10g4 10d6 12d6 10.2f4 9g2 8.9m 9f3 10.3m5 8.9m6 8.1d5 8g 9.7s3] leggy, lengthy colt: fair at 2 yrs, modest handicapper at best in 1991: should prove better at 1¼m than 1m: acts on any going: visored seventh to eleventh starts: mulish at stalls on ninth: rather lazy, but game. *H. J. Collingridge.*

WESTGARTH 2 ch.c. (Apr 19) Tina's Pet 121 – Anse Chastanet (Cavo Doro 124) — [1991 5g 5g] 2,000F, 3,000Y: sturdy colt: first reported foal: dam ran 3 times: well beaten in sprint maidens at Edinburgh: troublesome stalls on ninth: sold to join H. Whiting 700 gns Doncaster October Sales. *K. B. McCauley.*

WESTHOLME (USA) 3 ch.g. Lyphard's Wish (FR) 124 – Shroud (USA) **92** (Vaguely Noble 140) [1990 5f2 6g 7m* 7g* 8d2 1991 10g* 12.3d2 10.6g 11.9m3 11.9m5 12g2 13.9g 10.3m5 11.9d 10.3d] lengthy gelding: won handicap at Beverley in April: fairly useful form in £7,400 handicap at Chester second start: probably best efforts after fourth start in Ebor Handicap at York and £7,600 handicap at Doncaster seventh and eighth: suited by 1½m: acts on good to firm ground and dead: gelded after final start. *M. H. Easterby.*

WEST RIDING (USA) 3 b.g. Topsider (USA) – Kashie West (USA) (Sir Ivor — 135) [1990 6g* 1991 6g5 8g 7d 9m] small, angular gelding: well-backed favourite, rated 83 when making all in maiden at Newbury at 2 yrs: easily best effort since (first run for 5 months), when fair eighth of 15 in handicap at Redcar final start in 1991: should stay 1m: visored (looked none too keen) third start. *J. H. M. Gosden.*

WEST VERMONT (USA) 2 ch.c. (Mar 14) Gone West (USA) – Verria (USA) **90 p** (Blushing Groom (FR) 131) [1991 7m2 7m* 8g3 7d*] $200,000Y: compact, good-bodied colt: has easy action: second foal: half-brother to French 3-y-o Verica (by Diesis), 7f winner at 2 yrs: dam French 1m and 9f winner out of a useful winner at up to 1½m: sire best at 1m/9f: won maiden at Southwell in September and 3-runner minor event at Chester (7/4 on, made all, comfortably, from Well Appointed) in October: will stay beyond 1m: acts on good to firm and dead ground: likely to make up into useful handicapper: joined F. Brothers in USA. *H. R. A. Cecil.*

WEST WITH THE WIND 4 b. or br.g. Glint of Gold 128 – Mighty Fly 117 **63**
(Comedy Star (USA) 121) [1990 10m⁴ 11.5m* 13.3m 12f⁴ 12m⁵ 10g 1991 10.2s 12.1g*
11.9d] leggy, workmanlike gelding: quite modest handicapper: form in 1991 only
when winning at Hamilton in September, first run for almost 6 months: will stay
beyond 1½m: acts on good to firm ground: trained on reappearance by J. Johnson:
winning hurdler. *G. M. Moore.*

WHASSAT 7 b.g. Saher 115 – Whisht (Raise You Ten 125) [1990 9g 9m 10.1m 16m **29**
1991 12m 14m 17.1d⁵ 16.2g 14.6m 10.8m⁶ 10.2g⁵] smallish, good-topped gelding:
carries plenty of condition: poor handicapper: stays 1½m: acts on any going: below
form when blinkered once. *M. P. Muggeridge.*

WHAT A CARD 3 b.f. Myjinski (USA) – Ventrex 95 (Henry The Seventh 125) **—**
[1990 5m⁶ 5g 5g² 6g 7g a8g⁶ 1991 8f 12m 12g⁶ 11m⁶ a12g³ 13d⁶ 12f a11g⁵]
sparely-made filly: poor plater: may well prove best short of 11f: sweating, swished
tail seventh start. *Denys Smith.*

WHATCOMESNATURALLY (USA) 2 ch.f. (Apr 21) Arctic Tern (USA) 126 **46**
– Reina Real (ARG) (Escudo Real) [1991 8.9d 8s] $25,000Y: leggy, angular filly:
half-sister to minor winners in Italy and North America: dam Grade 1 winner in
Argentina: poor form in maidens at Wolverhampton (green, much better effort
though eased when held) and Yarmouth (soundly beaten) in October: will stay 1¼m.
J. W. Hills.

WHAT'S SHE LIKE 2 b.f. (Mar 11) Absalom 128 – Highest Tender 56 (Prince **34**
Tenderfoot (USA) 126) [1991 5g⁵ 6f 6g⁴ a7g 8.2m] 2,000Y: sparely-made filly: fourth
foal: half-sister to winners in Norway and Hong Kong: dam plater: little worthwhile
form, including in sellers: best effort at 6f: looked ill at ease on firm ground second
outing. *M. H. Tompkins.*

WHATS YOURS CALLED 5 ch.m. Windjammer (USA) – Thorganby Melody **—**
(Highland Melody 112) [1990 NR 1991 a8g3) leggy, angular mare: quite modest
performer as 3-y-o, poor nowadays: stays 11f: acts on firm going: blinkered in 1991. *J.
P. Smith.*

WHEELER'S WONDER (IRE) 2 br.f. (Apr 18) Sure Blade (USA) 130 – **55**
Querida (Habitat 134) [1991 8.2m 6m⁶ 7.1d a8g a7g] 21,000Y: leggy, rather angular
filly: half-sister to several winners, including fairly useful 1987 2-y-o 7f winner
Huldine (by Cure The Blues) and Irish 1m winner Quintillon (by Rusticaro), later
successful in USA: dam Irish 2-y-o 7.9f winner, is half-sister to Chief Singer:
plating-class maiden: ran moderately on all-weather surfaces last 2 starts: best
effort at 6f, but should stay further: apparently sold 5,400 gns Newmarket Autumn
Sales. *C. E. Brittain.*

WHEELS OF WEETMAN 4 b.c. Stanford 121§ – Miss Legend (USA) (Bold **—**
Legend) [1990 8g⁵ 8.2m⁶ 6g 1991 6m 6g 5m 6g 7g 5.1g] heavy-topped colt: no
worthwhile form. *B. A. McMahon.*

WHERE'S CAROL 3 gr.f. Anfield 117 – Ludovica (Bustino 136) [1990 5m⁶ 5f⁶ **46**
5m² 5m 5f⁵ 5d³ a6g* a6g* a6g* a8g² 6g 7g 8m a6g³ a6g³ a6g* a6g⁶ a5g⁴ a6g
a6g² a7g 7d⁵ 5g a8g 7m⁵ 6m a6g] lengthy, leggy filly: moderate mover: quite modest
winner at 2 yrs: not so good in 1991, tailed off in Southwell claimer final start: best
form at 6f: best form on all-weather, has won only at Southwell: blinkered once
at 2 yrs: has been unruly at stalls: sometimes has tongue tied down: joined V.
Thompson. *M. Brittain.*

WHERE'S RUTH (IRE) 2 b.f. (Mar 17) Bluebird (USA) 125 – Mannevillette **58**
(USA) (Foolish Pleasure (USA)) [1991 5m 5d³ 6d⁶ a7g* 7g³ 7m] 4,200Y: lengthy
filly: second living foal: dam unraced half-sister to good 1979 French 2-y-o 1m
winner Nice Havrais: retained 8,200 gns after easily winning seller at Southwell in
July: good third in nursery at Leicester following month: got no sort of run at
Newcastle later in August: better suited by 7f than shorter. *M. W. Easterby.*

WHERE'S THE RISK 2 b.g. (May 25) Risk Me (FR) 127 – Sendim On Sam 74 **47**
(Lochnager 132) [1991 5g² 5m² 5g⁴] neat gelding: first foal: dam maiden raced only
at 5f, is granddaughter of smart sprinter Dutch Gold: favourite, poor form when
second in sellers in April: hung left and didn't look easiest of rides later same
month: sold 550 gns Ascot October Sales. *G. Lewis.*

WHIMBREL 3 b.f. Dara Monarch 128 – Lola Sharp (Sharpen Up 127) [1990 5f 7g² **—**
7.5g³ 7m² 7.5g³ 8.5m* 1991 12.2m 9.9f⁵ a12g⁶ 8m] lengthy filly: usually looks dull in
coat: poor walker: plater: should stay 1¼m: acts on good to firm going: blinkered
final start: didn't run on when visored at 2 yrs. *M. H. Easterby.*

WHIPPER IN 7 b.g. Bay Express 132 – Whip Finish 77 (Be Friendly 130) [1990 **—** §
6m⁶ 5f 6g³ a6g³ 6g 7g a7g 6g a7g⁴ a8g 1991 a6g⁴ a8g⁶] tall, good-topped gelding:

carries plenty of condition: poor mover: very useful at best, but has deteriorated considerably: stays 7f: best form on a sound surface: tried blinkered and visored: often slowly away: has worn crossed noseband: not to be trusted. *Mrs N. Macauley.*

WHIPPERS DELIGHT (IRE) 3 ch.g. King Persian 107 – Crashing Juno (Crash Course 128) [1990 5g⁵ 6f³ 7g* 7m* 7f 7g 7f⁴ 7g a8g⁶ 1991 a7g⁴ 8d 9.9f] leggy gelding: twice made all in sellers at 2 yrs: below form in 1991: stays 1m: blinkered penultimate start: sold 2,000 gns Doncaster August Sales: won selling hurdle for G. Charles-Jones. *T. D. Barron.* —

WHIPPET 3 b.h. Sparkler 130 – St Louis Sue (FR) 79 (Nonoalco (USA) 131) [1990 5.5v² 5g⁵ 5m⁴ 6g* 6g³ 6.5g⁴ 6d 5g³ 5v⁵ 5v 1991 5g⁶ 6g 6m⁴ 6m 6g 6s 7d 6d a6g a8g] lengthy, good-quartered horse: bad walker and mover: useful performer at best: has lost his form: suited by sprint distances: acts on any going: has worn visor and blinkers: unseated rider at stalls and withdrawn once at 6 yrs. *C. A. Austin.* **100** d

WHIRLYGIG 7 b.f. (Feb 22) Gorytus (USA) 132 – Avant-Garde (Pas de Seul 133) [1991 5d⁴ 5f³ 6g 5.1g⁶ 7f a8g] smallish filly: first foal: dam ran once at 2 yrs in Ireland: poor maiden: probably stays 7f: has run creditably for apprentice: very free to post final outing. *J. S. Wainwright.* **44**

WHISPER'S SHADOW 2 b.f. (Feb 2) Northern Baby (CAN) 127 – Sir Ivor's Sorrow (USA) (Sir Ivor 135) [1991 8.2m 7m 8s³] 15,000Y: tall, rather angular filly: sister to useful 1¼m performer Splendid Career and half-sister to 2 winners in USA: dam stakes-placed winner in USA: always-prominent under 2 lengths third of 10 to Jasoorah in maiden at Yarmouth in October, easily best effort: will stay 1¼m: seems suited by soft ground. *M. H. Tompkins.* **68**

WHISTLING GALE 4 ch.f. Whistling Deer 117 – Velpol (Polyfoto 124) [1990 8m 1991 a8g] small filly: plater: should stay 1m: acts on soft going. *D. Burchell.* —

WHITE BLADE (USA) 2 b.c. (Feb 13) Diesis 133 – Blanche du Bois (USA) (Green Dancer (USA) 132) [1991 7m* 7m* 8.1m* 7m⁵] $195,000Y: close-coupled, unfurnished colt: first foal: dam, minor winner at up to 9f, is half-sister to dams of Miss Oceana, Larida (herself dam of Magic of Life), Sabin and Fatah Flare: fairly useful performer: successful in maiden at Brighton then nurseries at Salisbury and Sandown (sweating and bit edgy) in summer: last of 5, quickly outpaced 3f out, in Laurent-Perrier Champagne Stakes at Doncaster 2 weeks later: will be better suited by 1¼m: bolted to start on intended debut and taken early to post afterwards: to race in USA. *G. Harwood.* **98**

WHITECHAPEL (USA) 3 br.g. Arctic Tern (USA) 126 – Christchurch (FR) 88 (So Blessed 130) [1990 NR 1991 11g 10g² a12g* 14m 13.3g³] big, lengthy gelding with scope: half-brother to winners, including 4-y-o 1½m winner Church Missionary (by Miswaki), smart 6f to 10.5f winner Church Parade (by Queen's Hussar) and smart middle-distance stayer Castle Rising (by Blakeney): dam, 1½m winner, is half-sister to Highclere: modest form: won maiden at Southwell in June: creditable third in handicap at Newbury in October: lacks turn of foot, and will prove suited by 1¾m + . *Lord Huntingdon.* **69**

WHITE FEN 4 ch.g. Jalmood (USA) 126 – Fotheringay 101 (Right Royal V 135) [1990 NR 1991 14.6s 16.2g] rather sparely-made gelding: brother to a poor animal and half-brother to several winners, notably Ascot Gold Cup winner Ragstone (by Ragusa), very smart middle-distance stayer Castle Keep and Castle Moon (both by Kalamoun), last-named dam of Moon Madness, Sheriff's Star and Lucky Moon: dam won at 1m: well beaten in maidens at Doncaster (green, not knocked about once held) and Beverley in spring. *Lady Herries.* —

WHITE RIVER 5 ch.h. Pharly (FR) 130 – Regain 86 (Relko 136) [1990 12.5f³ 12m 13m² 15.3g* 15.3m⁴ 15.3f* 17.6f⁵ 14m² 14d 1991 14d² 14m⁵ 14.8m³ 14g 13.8m] smallish, lengthy horse: poor mover: plating-class handicapper: well beaten after returning from 4-month lay-off final 2 starts: stays 15.3f: acts on firm ground, goes very well on dead. *D. Haydn Jones.* **52**

WHITE SAPPHIRE 6 b.h. Sparkler 130 – On A Bit 66 (Mummy's Pet 125) [1990 9f⁴ 9m 10.2m⁵ 10g² 10.2m 10m⁶ 1991 a7g a11g] good-topped horse: moderate mover: quite modest handicapper: well beaten in early part of 1991: suited by around 1¼m: possibly suited by easy surface nowadays: tried blinkered: has worn tongue strap: has refused to enter stalls: difficult ride: sold 1,800 gns Newmarket Autumn Sales. *J. G. FitzGerald.* —

WHITE WEDDING 2 ch.f. (Feb 4) Dominion 123 – Sledge 80 (Young Generation 129) [1991 5g³ 7g⁶ 6f] 26,000Y: small, good-quartered filly: fourth foal: half-sister to very useful 1988 2-y-o 6f to 8.5f (in USA) winner Luge (by Lyphard's Special) and a winner by Final Straw, also successful at 2½m over hurdles: dam **56**

third over 1m and 1½m here, won at 9.5f in France: plating-class form in summer maidens: ran poorly final start: stays 7f: possibly needs some give in the ground. *P. F. I. Cole.*

WHITE WITCH (USA) 3 ch.f. Nureyev (USA) 131 – Devil's Sister (USA) **79 ?** (Alleged (USA) 138) [1990 NR 1991 7g 7.6d2 8g 8s3 6m2 7g5 7g4] $500,000Y: close-coupled filly: first foal: dam unraced half-sister to dam of champion Canadian mare Glorious Song (dam of Rahy) and champion U.S. 2-y-o Devil's Bag: fair maiden at best: didn't reproduce that form last 3 starts, odds on first 2 occasions: stays 1m: easily best efforts on a soft surface: may be unsatisfactory. *J. H. M. Gosden.*

WHITTINGHAM (IRE) 2 b.c. (Mar 20) Fayruz 116 – Bohemian Rhapsody 86 **104** (On Your Mark 125) [1991 5g* 5f* 5d* 5g* 6g3 5g2 6g4 6g2 5v* 5d5] 5,400Y: strong, compact colt: sixth foal: half-brother to quite modest sprinter Restless Rhapsody (by Young Generation) and winners in Belgium and Hong Kong: dam best at 5f: successful in auction events at Beverley and listed races at Rome (dead-heated) and Milan in first half of season, and listed event at Rome in September: mostly ran creditably in Italy in between: very good 3 lengths fifth of 8 to Ski Chief in Prix du Petit-Couvert at Longchamp in October: stays 6f: acts on any going: trained first 3 starts by J. Berry. *O. Pessi, Italy.*

WHITTON LAD (IRE) 3 b.c. Anita's Prince 126 – Shuckran Habibi (Thatching — 131) [1990 5m3 5.8m 5f 5m5 a6g3 1991 6m 5m 6f] lengthy, workmanlike colt: poor mover: quite modest form at 2 yrs, none (including in seller) in 1991: easily best effort at 6f on equitrack: ran badly in blinkers at 2 yrs: sold 550 gns Ascot July Sales. *R. Akehurst.*

WHITWORTH GREY 3 gr.g. Marching On 101 – Grey Morley 78 (Pongee 106) — [1990 5m6 6f6 6m3 7f5 7d4 1991 11m 9g 7f 6.9f] leggy, angular gelding: moderate mover: plating-class maiden: soundly beaten in handicaps and claimer (blinkered) in 1991: should stay 1m: acts on firm and dead ground. *G. M. Moore.*

WHO'S TEF (IRE) 3 b.g. Muscatite 122 – Eternal Optimist (Relko 136) [1990 **67** 5f4 5f* 6g4 7.5f 7f5 5f3 6m2 6m 6g 5m5 6g a6g 1991 7g5 6f 7.5f2 8.5m 8g 7f6 8.5f* 8f4 7.5f* 7.5f4 10f* 8f4 8.5f4 8.9m 8m] rather leggy, close-coupled gelding: quite modest handicapper: won at Beverley (twice) and Ripon in summer: stays 1¼m: suited by top-of-the-ground: blinkered twice at 2 yrs: mostly claimer ridden since seventh start in 1991. *M. H. Easterby.*

WHO'S THAT LADY 2 b.f. (Apr 26) Nordance (USA) – Piccadilly Etta 76 **42** (Floribunda 136) [1991 5d6 5f3] 3,500Y: small, leggy filly: sister to 3-y-o 1m (at 2 yrs) and 9f winner Nasab and half-sister to several winners, including 1986 2-y-o 6f winner Einstein (by Mummy's Pet) and fair 1m winner Vitigeson (by Vitiges): dam won from 1½m to 2m: poor form, staying on, in maiden auction at Pontefract in April: backward, slowly away and green on debut: bred to stay 1m + . *M. H. Easterby.*

WICKED THINGS (FR) 3 b.c. Vayrann 133 – Daffodil Walk 91 (Furry Glen — 121) [1990 a8g* 1991 8s 7g 8g 8g5 12d] compact, attractive colt: has a quick action: won maiden at Lingfield late on at 2 yrs: contested minor event and handicaps in 1991, not entirely discredited in 6-runner race at Salisbury fourth start: stays 1m: edgy final start: sold 1,000 gns Newmarket Autumn Sales. *D. R. C. Elsworth.*

WICK POUND 5 b.h. Niniski (USA) 125 – Hors Serie (USA) 103 (Vaguely Noble **55 d** 140) [1990 12.5m 12.2m 12f 13.1h4 14g 1991 a10g 14.8m* 14.8d3 17.2f 18.8f4 14.9m2 13.1f 11.9f] small, lightly-made horse: poor mover: won handicap at Warwick in May: hung and looked none too keen fifth start: stays 1¾m: acts on good to firm and dead going: blinkered nowadays: none too consistent: winning hurdler on equitrack. *J. A. B. Old.*

WIDYAN (USA) 3 b.c. Fappiano (USA) – Hotel Street (USA) 93 (Alleged (USA) **105** 138) [1990 7.3m3 7f* 8g3 10s4 10v3 1991 11g* 12.3d4 12g 10g4 10.5f] rangy, good sort: has a fluent, round action: useful performer: on toes, won minor event at Newbury in April: best effort after (well beaten in pattern events at Chester and the Curragh) when 4 lengths seventh of 20 to Hailsham in Derby Italiano at Rome: very stiff task in handicap final start, first for 3 months: will be suited by return to 1½m: acts on any going: blinkered fourth outing: keen sort. *P. F. I. Cole.*

WIEDNIU (USA) 2 br.f. (May 5) Danzig Connection (USA) – Nicole Mon Amour **72 p** (USA) (Bold Bidder) [1991 6g3] strong filly: has scope: closely related to very useful 5f (at 2 yrs) to 8.5f winner Batzushka (by Danzig) and half-sister to 3 winners by Conquistador Cielo, including useful 7f and 1m winner Cielamour: dam, winner twice at up to 1¼m, is half-sister to Kentucky Derby and Belmont Stakes second Stephan's Odyssey and Grade 1 Acorn Stakes winner Lotka (both by Danzig): 25/1 and very green, 6 lengths third of 21 to Katakana in maiden at Newbury in October, tracking leaders, niggled along halfway, then keeping on well not knocked about: likely to stay 1m + : sure to improve and win a maiden. *Lord Huntingdon.*

WILAYIF (USA) 3 b.f. Danzig (USA) – Kamar (USA) (Key To The Mint (USA)) **75**
[1990 NR 1991 8s² 10d⁴ 8m² 8g² 7m* 7.1s⁵] strong, round-barrelled filly: half-sister to several winners, including very useful 6f to 1m winner Hiaam (by Alydar), 1984 champion Canadian 3-y-o Key To The Moon (by Wajima) and 1990 Kentucky Oaks winner Seaside Attraction (by Seattle Slew): dam and grandam champions in Canada: modest form in maidens: beat sole opponent Bayonne 7 lengths at York: fair fifth of 9 in handicap at Sandown later in July: stays 1¼m: yet to race on firm ground, probably acts on any other. *M. R. Stoute.*

WILCO 2 ch.g. (Mar 4) Bay Express 132 – Solo Singer 66 (Song 132) [1991 5g 5s⁴ **65**
5g⁴ 5m³ 5g 5f⁴ 5d a5g⁴ a6g2] strong, workmanlike gelding: moderate mover: second foal: half-brother to 3-y-o Faustinger (by Faustus): dam maiden suited by 6f, is half-sister to smart French jumper Khorassan: quite modest maiden: ran well on equitrack last 2 starts: better suited by 6f than 5f: acts on good to firm ground. *Andrew Turnell.*

WILD AND LOOSE 3 b.c. Precocious 126 – Regain 86 (Relko 136) [1990 5m **90**
1991 7g⁴ 8g* 10g⁴ 8m³ 10m 8m³ 10d⁶ 8d* 8g⁶] big, lengthy, good-topped colt: moderate mover: fairly useful handicapper: won at Salisbury (maiden) in June and Ascot (£12,000 event) in October: should prove best in strongly-run race when at 1m, and stays 1¼m: acts on good to firm and dead ground: below form when sweating. *D. R. C. Elsworth.*

WILD AT HEART (USA) 2 b.f. (Feb 16) Storm Bird (CAN) 134 – Refinancing **66**
(USA) (Forli (ARG)) [1991 6f⁴ 6m 6f²] leggy, unfurnished filly: first foal: dam once-raced sister to useful Italian 1m to 1¼m performer Lonely Bird out of half-sister to Posse: 10/1 from 6/1, keeping-on neck second of 9 at Folkestone in October, easily best effort in maidens: should stay 1m. *L. M. Cumani.*

WILDE RUFO 2 ro.c. (May 10) Sharrood (USA) – Wanton 106 (Kris 135) **99**
[1991 5g³ 6m* 6g 6m³ 5.2g 7m³ 7m³ 8s] 9,200Y: good-topped colt: second foal: half-brother to 3-y-o Hamoudi (by Miller's Mate): dam sprinter, best at 2 yrs: fairly useful performer: won maiden auction at Newmarket in May: staying-on third of 8, beaten under 3 lengths, to Tertian in slowly-run Somerville Tattersall Stakes at Newmarket penultimate start: creditable eighth of 13 to Alhijaz in Gran Criterium at Milan over 3 weeks later: stays 1m: acts on good to firm and soft ground: inconsistent. *P. A. Kelleway.*

WILD FIRE 2 ch.c. (Apr 18) Kalaglow 132 – Bundu (FR) 88 (Habitat 134) [1991 **75** p
7g⁶ 7f² 8f*] leggy, lengthy colt: fourth foal: half-brother to 3-y-o 1¼m performer Bushy Tailed (by Teenoso) and 1m winner Mbulwa (by Be My Guest): dam 1¼m and 10.6f winner: progressive colt: won maiden at Thirsk in September by 2½ lengths from Naked Truth: will be suited by 1¼m + : likely to improve further. *G. Wragg.*

WILD HONOUR (IRE) 2 b.c. (Apr 1) Fayruz 116 – Hurricane Hazel **82**
(Lorenzaccio 130) [1991 5f² 5.1m⁶ 5d² 5.7m⁵ 6m* 5m² 6m² 5m² 5g* 5m* 6d³ 5.7f*
6g³ 5m* 5g 5m] IR 2,900F, IR 2,800Y, 6,000 2-y-o: compact colt: second reported foal: dam poor Irish maiden: progressed into fair performer: successful in auction contest at Leicester and nurseries at Goodwood, Windsor, Bath (quickened well) and Sandown (held off Arabellajill by a neck) in summer: below form last 2 starts, giving impression feeling effects of hard season: effective at 5f and 6f: best efforts on sound surface: has given trouble stalls. *W. R. Muir.*

WILD JESTER 5 b.g. Jester 119 – Cheap And Sweet (USA) (Rising Market **101**
(USA)) [1990 5g⁴ 5g² 5g 5g* 6.3g⁴ 6d* 5g² 6.3m 5g 6d 8m 5d* 6s⁴ 8d 1991 5m⁶ 5g²
6m* 5.6m⁴ 5d] big, lengthy gelding: brother to a poor Irish maiden: dam unraced: useful Irish handicapper: improved form when narrowly winning minor event at the Curragh in September: respectable fourth of 21 in Tote-Portland at Doncaster (got poor run and finished fast): ran moderately in £16,700 event at Ascot final start: seems best at 5f/6f: acts on good to firm and dead ground. *P. J. Flynn, Ireland.*

WILD PATIENCE (USA) 2 b.f. (Apr 12) Danzig (USA) – Patience Worth **62** P
(USA) (Mr Prospector (USA)) [1991 6.1m³] $425,000F: quite attractive filly: has scope: half-sister to several winners here and abroad, including useful 1986 French 2-y-o 6f winner Savonnerie (by Irish River) and useful 1983 2-y-o 1m winner Girl Friday (by Secretariat), latter second in Lancashire Oaks: dam very useful sprint stakes winner: 5/1 and green, 6 lengths third of 18 to Mount Helena in maiden at Nottingham in October, slowly away and behind at halfway, keeping on strongly final 2f: will stay 1m: will improve considerably. *J. L. Dunlop.*

WILD PERSIAN (IRE) 2 b.f. (Apr 5) Persian Bold 123 – Recapture 58 — (Sassafras (FR) 135) [1991 6g a6g6] IR 1,700Y: leggy filly: sister to Irish 9.5f to 1½m winner Taken By Force and a winner in Norway and half-sister to 2 other winners: dam poor half-sister to Irish 1000 Guineas winner Full Dress II: soundly beaten in 20-runner claimer and 7-runner maiden at Lingfield. *Pat Mitchell.*

WILD PROSPECT 3 b.c. Homing 130 – Cappuccilli 111 (Lorenzaccio 130) [1990 76 6g* 6f5 6g 1991 a8g 7d 8g 7.5g2 7g2 7f2 8m 7f 7f* 7f* 7.5f* 7.6m 7.5f5 7m 8m 7d] smallish, good-quartered colt: has a quick action: modest handicapper: made virtually all when game winner at Catterick (twice) and Beverley in the summer: below form after: best form at around 7f: acts on firm going: goes well on a turning track. *C. Tinkler.*

WILD SABLE (IRE) 3 ch.f. Kris 135 – Fur Hat (Habitat 134) [1990 NR 1991 88 10d* 10.8d2] tall, leggy, rather unfurnished filly: first foal: dam unraced half-sister to Teenoso and sister to Topsy: comfortably won 20-runner maiden at Ripon: 11/10 on, 3 lengths second of 3 to Circus Light in minor event at Warwick 10 days later in June. *M. R. Stoute.*

WILD STRAWBERRY 2 ro.f. (Mar 22) Ballacashtal (CAN) – Pts Fairway 70 (Runnymede 123) [1991 5g6 6d5 6m5 6m* 6m] 3,600F: seventh foal: half-sister to several winners, including 1988 2-y-o 5.8f winner Roheryn (by Enchantment): dam well beaten both starts at 2 yrs: showed vastly improved form, running on strongly, to win £6,700 maiden median auction at York in July: looked to have fine chance in Newmarket nursery 3 weeks later, but sweated up beforehand and ran badly: stays 6f: acts on good to firm ground. *J. M. P. Eustace.*

WILEYS FOLLY 5 ch.m. Krayyan 117 – Friend's Folly (Sweet Revenge 129) 51 [1990 7g3 7g 10g 7s a5g5 7m 1991 a7g a5g5 a5g6 a8g5 7g 6f6 8f6 7f 6m 6f a7g5 8m2 8f* 10f a10g a8g2 a10g4] ex-Irish maiden mare: poor mover: poor handicapper: won (for first time) selling event (no bid) at Brighton in August: best at 1m to 1¼m: acts on firm ground: best without blinkers or visor. *S. Dow.*

WILKINS 2 b.c. (Mar 8) Master Willie 129 – Segos 81 (Runnymede 123) [1991 53 p 7.1d] 13,000F, 24,000Y: strong, angular colt: closely related to a winner over hurdles by High Line and half-brother to useful sprinter Tyrollie (by Balidar): dam ran only at 2 yrs when 1m winner: 20/1, signs of ability, not knocked about, in large-field maiden at Chepstow in October, some late progress from towards rear: likely to stay 1¼m: will do better. *J. R. Fanshawe.*

WILLESDON (USA) 7 ch.h. Master Willie 129 – Dona Maya (USA) (Reviewer 40 (USA)) [1990 12f4 8g 8m 1991 7v 10.2f 8.9m2 10s 12.1g] angular horse: hobdayed: poor handicapper at best nowadays: stays 11f: probably unsuited by soft going, acts on any other: often bandaged: has run well when blinkered. *A. Barrow.*

WILL HE OR WONT HE (IRE) 3 b.c. The Noble Player (USA) 126 – Dusty 59 Highway (High Top 131) [1990 5m6 6s6 7m a6g a6g6 7d 8.2s 10.2s a8g2 1991 a8g* a8g* a7g3 10m 11.6m a8g a8g a10g4 a10g] sturdy, quite attractive colt: has a round action: won 2 claimers early in year at Southwell: off course over 5 months, then behind in handicaps last 6 starts: should stay 1¼m: usually visored: tried blinkered once: very slowly away final start. *C. N. Allen.*

WILLOW BLUE 4 gr.g. Full of Hope 125 – Paddock Princess 80 (Dragonara 67 d Palace (USA) 115) [1990 12f* 12f4 10m3 10g5 12g3 1991 10m3 10m5 8g4 9.5m5 12g 10.8m6 8.1d 10.1s] leggy, close-coupled gelding: second foal: brother to a poor maiden: dam 5f winner ran only at 2 yrs: ex-Irish handicapper: modest form when in frame in apprentice events at Limerick and the Curragh (blinkered): thrice raced here, facing very stiff tasks in minor events then well beaten in Yarmouth claimer: stays 1½m: acts on firm ground: formerly trained by D. J. Murphy. *T. P. McGovern.*

WILL SOON 2 ch.c. (May 15) Nicholas Bill 125 – Henceforth 58 (Full of Hope 60 125) [1991 7m 7g5] 9,800Y: close-coupled, rather sparely-made colt: fifth foal (all by Nicholas Bill): brother to fair sprinter Willbutwhen, 1¼m and 1½m winner William Four and 9f winner Bildad: dam won once over 5f from 3 races at 2 yrs: quite modest form in maidens at Newmarket and Salisbury in October: will stay at least 1m. *H. Candy.*

WILMOTTS 2 b.g. (Apr 23) Petong 126 – Bare Spectacle (Welsh Pageant 132) 45 [1991 5g 5f 5m5 6m 8.2m6 8.3g] first foal: dam poor maiden granddaughter of Cheveley Park second Dame Foolish: modest plater: suited by 1m: best efforts when blinkered. *M. W. Easterby.*

WILSONIC 2 b.f. (Mar 3) Damister (USA) 123 – Cape Chestnut 87 (Bustino 136) 78 [1991 6m2 6f2 7m2] 15,000F, 6,600 2-y-o: leggy, unfurnished filly: has a markedly round action: half-sister to 3-y-o Italian winner at up to 10.5f Cape Heights (by

Bustino), useful 2-y-o 6f winner Moogie (by Young Generation), and to fairly useful 7f (at 2 yrs) and 1¼m winner Dazzling Heights (by Shirley Heights): dam 1m winner: modest maiden: beaten 1½ lengths by Soiree at Ayr final start, having looked likely winner when quickening well ahead 2f out: will stay 1m: should win a run-of-the-mill maiden. *M. Johnston.*

WILTOSKI 3 b.g. Petoski 135 – Cojean (USA) 86 (Prince John) [1990 NR 1991 8m 10g 8f 11.6m 12f] 2,200Y: workmanlike, angular gelding: sixth foal: half-brother to useful 1986 2-y-o 7f winner Iosifa, 11.5f to 2m winner Lothian (both by Top Ville) and a winner in Italy: dam ran only at 2 yrs when successful over 5f: no worthwhile form, though some promise in claimer second start: will prove better at 1¼m than shorter: slowly away first 3 starts: sold to join I. Campbell 5,800 gns Ascot September Sales. *K. T. Ivory.* —

WILY TRICK (USA) 3 b.f. Clever Trick (USA) – Highclere 129 (Queen's Hussar 124) [1990 NR 1991 7g² 8d² 10m⁵ 7.6m² 7g³] tall, leggy, quite attractive filly: half-sister to several winners, including very smart 7f to 1½m winner Height of Fashion (by Bustino), later dam of Nashwan and Unfuwain, and smart middle-distance performer Milford (by Mill Reef): dam won 1000 Guineas and French Oaks: second in maidens at Newbury, Kempton and Lingfield, easily best effort on first 2 occasions: stays 1m. *Lord Huntingdon.* 83

WINDBOUND LASS 8 ch.m. Crofter (USA) 124 – Nevilles Cross (USA) 67 (Nodouble (USA)) [1990 12m⁵ 11.5m 17.1f* 15.3m 17.1m³ 1991 14.8g* 14.8m⁶ 13.1f⁵ 16.1m⁴ 16.9m 13.8m] leggy, plain mare: won handicap at Warwick in April: stays 17f: goes very well on a sound surface. *R. J. Holder.* 60

WINDPOWER (IRE) 2 ch.g. (Apr 28) Sharpo 132 – Night of Wind 101 (Tumble Wind (USA)) [1991 5m* 6g² 6f⁵ 6g 8m] strong gelding: has plenty of scope: poor mover: third foal: half-brother to 3-y-o 6f winner Noble Flutter (by The Noble Player) and 1988 2-y-o 5f winner Howling Gael (by Peterhof): dam won Queen Mary Stakes: won 12-runner maiden at Carlisle in April: well beaten in Ayr nursery final start, first for 3 months: stays 6f: acts on good to firm ground: looked ill at ease on track (though best effort) at Epsom second start. *J. Berry.* 79

WINDSOR HIGHNESS 4 ch.f. Glenstal (USA) 118 – Mrs Simpson (USA) (Windsor Ruler (USA)) [1990 9f 1991 a7g* a7g² a7g 8f 10.1s² 11.5g⁶ 10m⁴ a12g⁵ 11.7m⁴ 10f 7m] lengthy, rather sparely-made ex-Irish filly: suited by 1¼m: goes well on soft ground: blinkered fourth start: often slowly away and soon behind. *M. P. Muggeridge.* 58

WINDSOR PARK (USA) 5 br.g. Bold Forbes (USA) – Round Tower 93 (High Top 131) [1990 10m⁴ 9m⁴ 10m⁵ 11.5g⁵ 10f⁵ a12g a10g⁴ a10g⁶ 1991 a12g⁶ a10g⁴ a10g⁴ a8g⁶ a10g² a12g⁴ a13g² 12s⁶ 12m 10.8m⁵ 11.8g a12g³ a13g³ a14g³] leggy, quite attractive gelding: good walker: plating-class handicapper: stays 1¾m: acts on good to firm going: ran poorly in visor: trained first 8 starts by R. O'Sullivan: none too consistent: winning hurdler. *K. S. Bridgwater.* 57 d

WINDWARD ARIOM 5 ch.g. Pas de Seul 133 – Deja Vu (FR) (Be My Guest (USA) 126) [1990 13.8m⁴ 13.8m² 15.8g⁶ 15m⁶ 15.8m³ 12h⁵ 12f⁶ 13.8f 13.8d⁶ 1991 a37 a14g* a12g³ 16.2f³ 12f⁶ 15.1g] leggy, close-coupled gelding: has a roundish action: poor handicapper: won at Southwell in January: off course 6½ months before next start and below form after: stays 1¾m: acts on good to firm (not firm) and dead going: tried blinkered once: trained reappearance by D. Topley. *N. Bycroft.* 27

WINDY HOWE 4 b.g. Comedy Star (USA) 121 – Kenton's Girl 86 (Record Token 128) [1990 10d 10f⁶ 8.5m⁴ 10d 9s a12g⁵ 1991 a11g⁵ a8g a14g] sparely-made ex-Irish gelding: poor maiden: should stay 1½m: acts on good to firm ground: sometimes blinkered: wore eyeshield final 2 starts: sold 1,000 gns Ascot April Sales. *J. G. FitzGerald.* —

WINGED MONARCH (IRE) 3 gr.g. Kafu 120 – Nuageuse (Prince Regent (FR) 129) [1990 NR 1991 6m 7g 5m 7m] IR 5,000Y: lengthy, robust gelding: half-brother to several winners, including quite modest miler Cloudless Sky (by He Loves Me): dam won 4 times over 5f at 3 yrs in Ireland: last in maidens: visored twice. *M. J. Haynes.* —

WINGED WHISPER (USA) 2 ch.g. (Jan 31) Air Forbes Won (USA) – Soft Reply (Personality (USA)) [1991 5d 5g 5g⁵ 6m⁴ 7.5f* 7m⁴ 7.5f⁴ 8m] $25,000F, $38,000Y: sturdy gelding: carries condition: closely related to a winner by Bold Forbes and half-brother to several minor winners: dam won 5 times at up to 9f, including in stakes: sire won from 6f to 9f: quite modest performer: won nursery at Beverley in July: below that form after, running badly final 2 starts: should stay 61

1m: acts on firm ground: hung badly left second start: blinkered third outing: sometimes bandaged behind: takes keen hold. *C. W. Thornton.*

WINGS OF FREEDOM (IRE)   3 b.g. Fairy King (USA) – Wingau (FR) (Hard   **60** To Beat 132) [1990 7m 8f 8d³ 9g* 10.2s² 1991 8g 8d 11.7d 10g 10s 12.4f⁴ 11.6m³ 12s 12d⁵ 11.8m 14.1m³ 16.1g² 15.8g⁴ 13.8m⁴] rangy gelding: poor mover: quite modest performer, in frame in handicaps and a claimer: stays 2m: acts on soft ground, probably on firm: blinkered 5 times: sold to join J. Jenkins 9,600 gns Newmarket Autumn Sales. *G. Lewis.*

WINNETKA (USA)   2 ch.f. (Apr 17) Theatrical 125 – Zalataia (FR) 124 (Dictus   **?** (FR) 126) [1991 7.5d*] fourth reported foal: dam very smart and genuine middle-distance stayer at 3 yrs and 4 yrs in France, winner of 4 group races: comfortable winner of newcomers race at Saint-Cloud in October: likely to improve, particularly over middle distances. *F. Boutin, France.*

WINOSKI   3 b.g. Petoski 135 – Persevering 95 (Blakeney 126) [1990 NR 1991 a8g   **74** a10g⁴ a10g* 12v² a10g* 12.3d⁴ 10.5m³] 3,800Y: strong, compact gelding: seventh living foal: half-brother to fairly useful sprinter Fair Test (by Fair Season) and 1½m seller winner Crisp Heart (by Dominion): dam winner 4 times at up to 2m, is out of half-sister to very smart middle-distance stayer Petty Officer: successful at Lingfield in maiden in February and handicap in April: not seen out after July: worth a try beyond 1½m: acts on good to firm ground and (probably) heavy: wore eyeshield second and third starts: sold to join D. Williams 4,400 gns Newmarket Autumn Sales. *C. E. Brittain.*

WINSLOW LAD   4 br.g. Horage 124 – Rathcoffey Daisy (Pampapaul 121) [1990   **25** NR 1991 14d⁵ 16.2g 10.2g⁴] angular, sparely-made gelding: moderate mover: poor handicapper: stays 1¾m: acts on good to firm and dead ground: has run well when blinkered: winning hurdler. *T. Casey.*

WINSOME AYR   2 ro.f. (Mar 27) Sharrood (USA) 124 – Iyamski (USA) 86   **32** (Baldski (USA)) [1991 7g 7m 8m] 14,000Y: leggy filly: second foal: half-sister to 3-y-o Ayr Classic (by Local Suitor), 5f and 6f winner at 2 yrs: dam, 7f and 1m winner, is half-sister to smart 1983 Canadian 2-y-o Concorde Prince: little worthwhile form in autumn minor event and maidens: blinkered final start: sold 800 gns Doncaster October Sales. *Miss L. A. Perratt.*

WINTER HAZEL (IRE)   3 b.f. Thatching 131 – Walkyria (Lord Gayle (USA)   **78** d 124) [1990 NR 1991 10d⁴ 11m² 10d 8f⁶ 9.7s] IR 32,000F, IR 50,000Y: leggy filly: has scope: dam Irish middle-distance winner from family of Slip Anchor: fair maiden: well below form last 3 starts, in handicap final one: probably stays 11f: hung left fourth outing: sold to join J. Joseph 2,000 gns Newmarket December Sales. *J. H. M. Gosden.*

WINTER LIGHTNING   2 b.f. (Feb 13) Dominion 123 – Shaft of Sunlight 58   **38** (Sparkler 130) [1991 6g a8g⁵ a8g] sturdy, angular filly: first foal: dam maiden suited by 1½m, is half-sister to Desert Sun: well beaten in maidens, including on fibresand and equitrack. *P. T. Walwyn.*

WINTER PEARL   3 gr.f. Kenmare (FR) 125 – Crillion (USA) (L'Enjoleur   **—** (CAN)) [1990 6m⁶ 1991 7g 8d 8.2m a7g] leggy filly: little form in maidens and handicaps: bred to stay 1m. *R. Hannon.*

WIORNO   3 b.c. Wassl 125 – Just You Wait (Nonoalco (USA) 131) [1990 NR   **123** p 1991 8s* 10g² 10d* 10g⁶ 9.7d*]

We'll be hearing more of Wiorno judged on his performance in the Ciga Prix Dollar at Longchamp in October. His really was an eye-catching display. Held up sixth of the seven runners, he looked a most unlikely winner of the Group 2 prize for eight of the extended nine and a half furlongs, perhaps *the* most unlikely winner as, having been niggled at to improve his position approaching the final straight, he not only failed to do so but dropped back to last after the field had turned for home; there were at least six lengths between Wiorno and the leader Muroto, who was clear. For much of the way Wiorno was unable to make any progress but when he did, he did to some effect, coming with a tremendous run on the inside so that when Muroto passed Longchamp's first winning post, Wiorno was in third, just a length and three quarters behind him. Half a furlong later, at the winning post which mattered, Wiorno was three quarters of a length to the good. The visual impression of what Wiorno accomplished might have been exaggerated somewhat by the leader's tiring but this wasn't a success impressive solely for the manner in which it was achieved; those who failed to catch Muroto were, in finishing order, Stagecraft, Zoman, Approach The Bench, Cudas and Dolpour. Wiorno started an 11/1 fifth-favourite for the Prix Dollar. It was only his fifth chance to recoup part of a 2 10,000-guinea yearling purchase price, and twelve weeks had passed since his previous start. That had been his first venture into pattern company, in the Prix Eugene Adam at Saint-Cloud for which he'd started a short-priced coupled-favourite with the same owner and trainer's Arcangues. Wiorno had done little wrong up until that point, winning a newcomers race at Saint-Cloud on May 1st before being beaten half a length in a listed race at Chantilly and winning a similar event, the Prix Pelleas at Evry (he was always close up in justifying favouritism by three quarters of a length and the same from Audio and another of Fabre's late-maturing stars Tel Quel), in June, but his run in the Eugene Adam was a disappointment. Ridden close to the pace and disputing the lead entering the straight in a moderately-run race, Wiorno was fairly readily outpaced in the final quarter-mile, eased in the last hundred yards in being beaten three and a quarter lengths into sixth of seven behind Arcangues.

		Wassl	Mill Reef	Never Bend
Wiorno (b.c. 1988)		(b 1980)	(b 1968)	Milan Mill
			Hayloft	Tudor Melody
			(b 1973)	Haymaking
		Just You Wait	Nonoalco	Nearctic
		(b 1980)	(b 1971)	Seximee
			Sleat	Santa Claus
			(ch 1969)	Belle of Athens

Many of those in the dark about Wiorno's racing merit before the Dollar would, however, have been familiar with his pedigree. He's a half-brother to the National Stud stallion Reprimand (by Mummy's Pet) who, despite an interrupted career, put up noteworthy performances at two, three and four years, and won the Gimcrack, Earl of Sefton and Trusthouse Forte Mile. He was tried as far as a mile and a quarter only once, finishing a close third in a slowly-run race for the Brigadier Gerard Stakes. Wiorno's unraced dam Just You Wait is half-sister to the fairly useful mile-and-a-quarter winner Kristana (dam of Robert Papin winner Ozone Friendly) and a daughter of Sleat (a half-sister to the St Leger winner Athens Wood) who won the Sun Chariot Stakes. Just You Wait has been given more promising opportunities at stud since Reprimand set foot on the racecourse, producing the now once-raced filly Just A Mirage to Green Desert in 1989 and a colt by Polish Precedent in 1991, having been barren to Salse in between. Wiorno's sire Wassl was sent to Japan before his third crop had reached racing age. In contrast to his experience as a sire, Wassl got off to an auspicious start on each of his three seasons on the racecourse, landing some big bets on his only two-year-old

Ciga Prix Dollar, Longchamp — Wiorno comes from behind to beat Muroto and Stagecraft

start, winning the Greenham at three years and dead-heating with Cormorant Wood for the Lockinge at four, but his twelve other starts produced just one win—in the mud in the Irish Two Thousand Guineas. Wassl stayed a mile and a quarter though not a mile and a half. Wiorno is not certain to get the longer distance on breeding but from what we've seen of him so far, he should be given the chance. Whether he stays a mile and a half or not, Wiorno is likely to progress again; and he's on the verge of high-class form already. *A. Fabre, France.*

WISE FRIEND (USA)　3 b.c. Sagace (FR) 135 – Swalthee (FR) (Sword Dancer 　—
(USA)) [1990 7g 1991 a10g a12g] showed nothing in maiden claimer and maiden at Lingfield in December at 3 yrs. *C. P. Wildman.*

WISE MOVE　2 b.c. (Apr 28) Celestial Storm (USA) 132 – Foston Bridge 68 　**68**
(Relkino 131) [1991 6g 6m⁵ 7m⁵ 8m⁴ 8.2m 10.5d² 8m*] 10,000F, 13,000Y: tall, leggy, rather angular colt: fourth foal: half-brother to 1990 2-y-o 5f winner Sing 'N Swing (by Chief Singer) and 1¼m winner Christmas Hols (by Young Generation): dam placed at 7f from 4 starts at 2 yrs: quite modest performer: favourite and ridden by 7-lb claimer, best effort to win 20-runner selling nursery at Doncaster (bought in 4,800 gns) in October, staying on really strongly to lead close home: stays 1¼m: acts on good to firm and dead ground: twice blinkered, running well first occasion: sold 17,000 gns Newmarket Autumn Sales. *Mrs J. R. Ramsden.*

WISE PORTIA　2 b.f. (Mar 19) Quadratic (USA) – Pervenche (Latest Model 115) 　—
[1991 5.7f⁵] first reported foal: dam, half-sister to 2000 Guineas fourth Cut Throat, ran 3 times here at 2 yrs then went to USA: weak 12/1-shot, well-beaten fifth of 7, losing place after 2f, in maiden at Bath in July: retained 1,300 gns Newmarket Autumn Sales. *H. Candy.*

WISHING WELL　2 ch.f. (Feb 28) Sharpo 132 – Acclimatise 116 (Shirley 　**57**
Heights 130) [1991 5d³] leggy filly: second live foal: half-sister to 3-y-o 7f winner (better at 1¼m) Positive Acclaim (by Vaigly Great): dam 7f (at 2 yrs) to 1¼m winner stayed 1½m: 3/1 and green, plating-class form, keeping on, in maiden at Pontefract in July: seemed sure to improve. *Mrs J. Cecil.*

WISH OF LUCK (USA)　3 ch.f. Diesis 133 – Kesar Queen (USA) 117 (Nashua) 　**76**
[1990 6m² 6d² 7d³ 6m⁴ 1991 8m⁴ 7f² 7g⁵ 7g² 7m⁶ 6.9f² 7.6g] unfurnished filly: has a roundish action: modest maiden: stays 1m: acts on firm ground and dead: blinkered last 2 starts, running creditably though wandering under pressure on first of them: takes keen hold: swishes tail. *H. Thomson Jones.*

WISTFUL (IRE)　2 ch.f. (Mar 30) Glint of Gold 128 – Yen (AUS) (Biscay (AUS)) 　**57**
[1991 5g* 6g³ 7m 8m] angular filly: good mover: third foal: half-sister to poor performer Stock Pile (by Galveston): dam ran without success in Australia: plating-class performer: won seller (retained 4,200 gns) at Leicester in April: off course 3 months and ridden by 7-lb claimer, creditable seventh of 15, never dangerous, kept on well, in nursery at Chester in August: ran poorly in minor event at Doncaster 12 days later: should stay 1m: sold 2,600 gns Doncaster October Sales. *M. Bell.*

WITCHES COVEN　2 gr.f. (Mar 16) Sharrood (USA) 124 – Tricky 66 (Song 132) 　**54**
[1991 7g⁴ 7.5f²] 8,000Y: leggy, rather unfurnished filly: second foal: half-sister to 3-y-o Soul Intent (by Lochnager): dam poor sister to smart sprinter Jester: plating-class form in maiden auctions at Doncaster and Beverley (sweating, still green, stayed on) in summer. *B. W. Hills.*

WITH GUSTO　4 b.c. Taufan (USA) 119 – Finesse 87 (Miralgo 130) [1990 10g 10m 　—
11.7m⁴ a12g a12g⁵ 12d⁵ a13g³ a13g³ a12g⁶ 1991 12s 12g³ a13g⁶] good-topped colt: plating-class maiden at best: well beaten in Lingfield handicap final start: stays 13f: acts on good to firm ground: sometimes bandaged. *K. O. Cunningham-Brown.*

WITNESS BOX (USA)　4 b.c. Lyphard (USA) 132 – Excellent Alibi (USA) 　**93**
(Exceller (USA) 129) [1990 10g 10f* 12m 1991 9g³ 11.8g⁴ 12g 11.5d³ 14g* 16.2g* 13.9g* 13.3m] rangy, workmanlike colt with scope: has fluent, round action: fairly useful handicapper: won at Sandown and Ascot (£10,900 event) in July and York (comfortably made most) in September: well below best in Newbury Autumn Cup final start: much better suited by 1¾m and 2m than shorter: has won on firm ground, but easily best form on an easy surface: races prominently: withdrawn (unseated rider and pulled up lame) penultimate intended outing: should do well at 5 yrs. *J. H. M. Gosden.*

WIZZARD MAGIC　8 ch.h. Ahonoora 122 – Siofra Beag (Steel Heart 128) [1990 　**53** d
7.6m 9m⁶ 10m* 10f⁴ 10.2f³ a8g 9m³ 10m 10f⁴ 10f a8g² a8g³ 1991 a10g² a10g³ a10g

a10g 9s 10.1s a10g a8g 10.2g⁶] good-topped horse: poor mover: plating-class handicapper: lost his form: stays 1¼m: acts on firm going, probably unsuited by soft: best blinkered or visored: suitable mount for inexperienced rider: sometimes sweats. *M. J. Haynes.*

WOLFHOUND (USA) 2 ch.c. (Apr 22) Nureyev (USA) 131 – Lassie Dear (USA) (Buckpasser) [1991 6m* 6m*] angular, good-topped colt: closely related to 3-y-o Deerhound (by Danzig) and a winner in North America by Nijinsky and half-brother to several winners, including useful 1987 2-y-o 6f winner Al Mufti (by Roberto), later stayed 1½m: dam very useful stakes winner at 2 yrs from fine family: favourite, won maiden at Redcar (comfortably, after slow start) and minor event at Doncaster (7/4 on, looked really well, much better effort) 9 days later in October: outpaced and niggled along early on at Doncaster, but quickened well over 1f out to beat Hazm by 1½ lengths, not knocked about: looks very useful colt in the making. *J. H. M. Gosden.*   **94 p**

WOLFSKIN 3 ch.f. Sharpo 132 – Wolverene 114 (Relko 136) [1990 NR 1991 6g] smallish, close-coupled filly: closely related to fair 9f and 10.4f winner Scythe (by Sharpen Up), later Grade 3 1½m winner in USA, and half-sister to several winners, including useful middle-distance winners Shining Tor (by High Top) and Voracity (by Vitiges): dam game stayer: no promise in maiden at Carlisle in March: dead. *J. W. Watts.*   **—**

WOLF WOOD 3 ch.f. Little Wolf 127 – Nightwood 60 (Sparkler 130) [1990 NR 1991 10m] strong filly: fifth foal: half-sister to 7f and 1m winner Night Warrior (by Roman Warrior), later stayed 1½m: dam staying maiden: in need of race, tailed off in Leicester maiden in October. *M. J. Wilkinson.*   **—**

WOODLAND RIDE 2 b.f. (May 20) Northern Tempest (USA) 120 – On A Bit 66 (Mummy's Pet 125) [1991 7g 7m 6g] close-coupled, workmanlike filly: sister to 1990 2-y-o 6f winner Northern Optimist and half-sister to several winners, including 1m and 8.5f winner Wallingfen Lane (by Lochnager) and fair 9f and 1¼m winner White Sapphire (by Sparkler): dam placed at up to 9f: poor form, always behind, in maidens at Redcar and claimer at Catterick in autumn. *J. G. FitzGerald.*   **43**

WOODLANDS CROWN 8 ch.g. Milford 119 – Town Girl 99 (Town Crier 119) [1990 12g 1991 a12g 8f 9d 8.1g⁴ 8.2g 8f 12f² 13.1f] leggy, quite good-topped gelding: poor handicapper: stays 1½m: acts on firm ground. *D. C. Tucker.*   **29**

WOODLANDS GREY 5 gr.g. Nishapour (FR) 125 – Topling 85 (High Top 131) [1990 8m 8m a10g 1991 8.2m 8m a8g] close-coupled, workmanlike gelding: no worthwhile form: has worn bandages behind. *P. A. Pritchard.*   **—**

WOODLANDS LEGEND 2 b.c. (Apr 23) Sayf El Arab (USA) 127 – Vernair (USA) 73 (Super Concorde (USA) 128) [1991 8.1g] 6,000F: second living foal: half-brother to 3-y-o 7f winner Gavin Allen (by Heraldiste): dam 6f winner also successful in Italy: 100/1, backward and ridden by 7-lb claimer, tailed off in 16-runner maiden at Chepstow in August. *D. C. Tucker.*   **—**

WOODMAN'S MOUNT (USA) 3 b.c. Woodman (USA) 126 – Tentamount (USA) (Tentam (USA)) [1990 6f* 7g³ 7f* 7d 9f 1991 8g] angular, quite attractive colt: useful winner at 2 yrs: seventh in Grade 3 event at Aqueduct final 2-y-o start: below form in £18,000 handicap at Sandown in April, 1991: best form at 7f on firm ground. *L. M. Cumani.*

WOODSTOCK LODGE (USA) 3 ch.c. Lyphard's Wish (FR) 124 – Renaissance Queen (USA) (Elocutionist (USA)) [1990 6f⁴ 7m 6m⁶ 8f 1991 a14g] strong, workmanlike colt: good walker: plating-class maiden at best at 2 yrs: tailed off in claimer in November, 1991: should stay 7f. *D. R. Franks.*   **—**

WOODURATHER 5 br.g. Touching Wood (USA) 127 – Rather Warm 103 (Tribal Chief 125) [1990 12d⁵ 12m 10m* 10.4d* 1991 10.2s 10.2g³ 12.5g⁴ 10.3d 10.1s*] small, light-framed gelding: moderate walker: quite modest handicapper: won claimer at Yarmouth in October: stays 1½m: acts on good to firm going, but goes particularly well on soft surface: keen sort, sometimes wears crossed noseband: pulled hard in blinkers penultimate start: winning hurdler. *M. C. Pipe.*   **64**

WOODYARD 2 b.c. (Apr 7) King of Spain 121 – Bustle Along 72 (Bustino 136) [1991 7f 8m] 1,100Y: angular colt: first foal: dam maiden stayed 1½m, is granddaughter of Oaks second Val's Girl: bandaged near-hind, showed little in claimer at Yarmouth and seller at Newmarket in autumn. *Mrs L. Stubbs.*   **40**

WOOLAW BOY 3 b.c. Enchantment 115 – Lightening Blue (Roan Rocket 128) [1990 6g⁶ 7m⁶ 7g 1991 12.1f 12.2g 12.1m] angular colt: poor maiden: tailed off in autumn, in seller final start. *J. S. Haldane.*   **—**

WOOLAW LASS (USA) 3 b.f. Full Extent (USA) 113 – Current River (USA) —
(Little Current (USA)) [1990 5m 5g 1991 7m 10g] smallish filly: no sign of ability, in
selling handicap final start. *J. I. A. Charlton.*

WOOLLAND WANTON 2 ch.c. (Mar 17) Norwick (USA) 120 – Farceuse —
(Comedy Star (USA) 121) [1991 6.1g 6m 7m 7f] neat colt: first foal: dam seemed of
little account: seems of little account too. *C. P. Wildman.*

WOOLLAND WINSOME 2 b. or br.c. (Mar 14) Norwick (USA) 120 – Cygne 44 —
(Piaffer (USA) 113) [1991 7s 8.1g] angular colt: second foal: dam plater, stayed 1m:
carrying condition, soundly beaten in maidens at Kempton and Chepstow in August:
has joined A. Csaky. *C. P. Wildman.*

WORLDBETA (IRE) 3 ch.g. Hatim (USA) 121 – Celestial Star 108 (So Blessed 81 §
130) [1990 6g 6m 5m⁴ 8m 7m² 7g² 7.6v* 8.2s 1991 9.1s* 9m 7f² 7g⁴ 7.6d²] lengthy,
good-bodied gelding: good walker: moderate mover: fair handicapper: won claimer
at Newcastle in April: ran well in frame, but hung and looked none too co-operative
under pressure having led 1½f out at Chester final start, in June: stays 9f: acts on
any going: looks a difficult ride: usually blinkered (wasn't at Newcastle): gelded
after final start. *J. W. Watts.*

WORLD OF TOMORROW 2 b.g. (Apr 19) Today And Tomorrow 78 – Nimble —
Dancer (Northern Wizard 100) [1991 5f 5.1g] 3,400Y: leggy, close-coupled gelding:
moderate mover: fourth reported foal: dam never ran: poor maiden: looked
ungenuine at Bath in June second start, carrying head high and hanging left. *J. Berry.*

WORLD'S CREATION (USA) 3 b.g. Cormorant (USA) – Worlds Fair (USA) 85
(Our Hero (USA)) [1990 5m³ 6s 6g⁶ 8m⁴ 1991 a8g* a8g* a10g² 8g³ 7m] leggy, quite
attractive gelding: odds on, winner at Southwell of maiden in February and handicap
(very keen to post and made all, carried head high) in March: ran well in handicaps
next 2 starts: suited by 1m + : gelded after final start. *B. W. Hills.*

WORTH OF MELTHAM 4 ch.g. What A Guest 119 – Corofin (USA) (Key To 39
The Kingdom (USA)) [1990 11m 12.2m⁵ 12.5g⁴ 18d 11d⁵ 1991 12.2m⁴ 13d* 12.4m⁶
13d² 16m⁴ 17.9f³ 15.1g⁶] big, plain gelding: moderate mover: poor handicapper: won
at Hamilton in June: stays 18f: acts on firm and dead (yet to race on very soft)
ground. *D. Moffatt.*

WOTAMISTAKATOMAKA 3 ch.g. Crofthall 110 – Redgrave Design 77 —
(Nebbiolo 125) [1990 5m 8.5m⁵ 8.2g 10m 7d 1991 10f⁶ 11.1g] lengthy, angular
gelding: quite modest plater at best: stays 8.5f: visored then blinkered last 2 starts
as 2-y-o. *R. M. Whitaker.*

WOTAMONA 3 b.f. Another Realm 118 – Meadow Wood (Meadow Court 129) 48 d
[1990 5m⁵ 7g⁵ 6g 8m 7g 10m² 10s 10.2s 1991 10g 12.2m⁵ 15.3m a12g² a12g 14.1m
14.1f³ 14.1m 10.8g] leggy, sparely-made filly: poor maiden: stays 1¾m: possibly
suited by sound surface: none too consistent. *B. Palling.*

WOTWESHUDDADUN (IRE) 2 b.g. (Apr 21) Cyrano de Bergerac 120 – —
Golden Dividend (Golden Years 94) [1991 5g 6d 7m 7.5f 5f] IR 6,200F, 5,200Y:
angular gelding: moderate walker: half-brother to fairly useful 7f winner (who
stayed 1¾m) Liquid Asset (by Alzao) and a winner abroad: dam unraced half-sister
to very smart middle-distance filly Romantica: no worthwhile form: not seen out
after July: blinkered final outing. *M. W. Easterby.*

WRETS 2 b.g. (Apr 26) Kalaglow 132 – Hayley Warren (Habitat 134) [1991 8s] —
angular, lengthy gelding: sixth foal: half-brother to several winners here and abroad,
including 1m and 1¼m winner Wretham (by Henbit): dam Irish 9f winner: 6/1 and
backward, tailed off in 14-runner maiden at Kempton in September: subsequently
gelded. *M. R. Stoute.*

WRYCREST 2 b.f. (Feb 6) Sharpo 132 – Wryneck 89 (Niniski (USA) 125) [1991 49
6.1f 6f 6g] leggy filly: has quick, moderate action: third foal: sister to 7f to 1m winner
Wrybill: dam won over 7f at 2 yrs on only start: plating-class maiden: best effort final
start: will stay 1m. *R. Charlton.*

WSOM (IRE) 3 b.g. Tate Gallery (USA) 117 – April Bride (USA) (Run The 62
Gantlet (USA)) [1990 7g⁵ 6d 6g 6d² 7d 1991 6m 7m* 7.2m² 7m 7.6d⁴ 8m 7m a7g]
lengthy gelding: quite modest handicapper: won at Warwick in May, staying on very
strongly to lead inside final 1f: below form last 5 starts: may well stay 1m: acts on
good to firm ground and dead: visored final outing: subsequently gelded. *M. O'Neill.*

WYCHWOOD (FR) 2 b.f. (Apr 8) Sayf El Arab (USA) 127 – Hens Grove (Alias —
Smith (USA)) [1991 6f] good-topped filly: second foal: dam plating-class maiden here
later won abroad: beaten 10 lengths, not knocked about, in seller at Yarmouth in
June: sold 600 gns Newmarket September Sales. *W. Jarvis.*

WYCLIFFE 3 ch.g. Dunbeath (USA) 127 – Blakewood 75 (Blakeney 126) [1990 — 6g 5g³ 7m⁵ 6f⁴ 6m 6g 7m 1991 8d 8f] workmanlike gelding: moderate mover: poor maiden: should stay beyond 7f. *Denys Smith.*

WYLAM 4 b.g. What A Guest 119 – Wish You Wow (Wolver Hollow 126) [1990 — 8.5m 12s⁵ 8g 10f 1991 a7g a14g] lengthy, rather sparely-made gelding: modest maiden at best: ran as if something amiss final start at 3 yrs and no promise in early part of 1991: should stay 1¼m: won over hurdles in March. *G. C. Bravery.*

X

XAI-TANG 4 gr.g. Petong 126 – Northern Dynasty 65 (Breeders Dream 116) **42** [1990 8m⁶ 10f 12.5g 9m³ 10g 10g 8g⁴ 9f³ 8.2d* 9g 8m 8m 1991 10s⁵ a11g 10.6g 10.3d 8.3m 8.9m⁴ 8.9g⁴ 8m* 8m* 8m⁶] close-coupled gelding: poor handicapper: won at Pontefract in seller (bought in 5,600 gns) and apprentice event in autumn: effective over stiff 1m and probably stays 1¼m: acts on good to firm and soft ground. *K. White.*

XHAI 9 b.g. Brave Shot – Wild Thyme 63 (Galivanter 131) [1990 10.2f⁴ 10.8m⁴ 9f **41** 12.2m* 12f² 16f⁵ 14f⁶ 12g³ 12m⁶ 1991a 10g 12s⁴ 12f 11.7g 12m⁴ 11.1g⁶ 12.3d 10m³ 10g 10m 11.9f³] angular, workmanlike gelding: poor handicapper: effective at 1¼m, and seems to stay 2m: acts on any going: usually blinkered, faced stiff task when visored: bandaged: suitable mount for apprentice: winning hurdler. *R. Simpson.*

X MY HEART 2 ch.f. (Apr 25) Aragon 118 – Lucky Song 91 (Lucky Wednesday **58** 124) [1991 5g 6m³ 6d* 6m* 6m³ 7g* 7f⁵ 6g⁵ 6g⁴] 7,500Y: narrow, leggy filly: moderate walker: second foal: half-sister to fair 1990 2-y-o 5f and 6f winner Level Xing (by Stanford): dam 5f and 7f winner: fairly useful plater: successful in summer at Goodwood (bought in 4,000 gns) and Newmarket (retained 6,200 gns) and in claimer at Haydock in between: stays 7f well: acts on good to firm and dead ground, below best on firm: sold 6,000 gns Newmarket Autumn Sales. *R. Hannon.*

Y

YAAFOOR (USA) 2 b.g. (Jan 4) Northern Baby (CAN) 127 – Second Glance **62** p (USA) (Big Burn (USA)) [1991 7g⁵ 7d⁵] $260,000Y: third reported foal: dam minor sprint stakes winner in USA: better effort in maidens on second start when staying-on 15 lengths fifth of 21 to Berseto at Doncaster (wore tongue strap, and small bandages behind) in November: will be better suited by 1m +. *A. A. Scott.*

YAAKUM 2 b.c. (Apr 2) Glint of Gold 128 – Nawadder 73 (Kris 135) [1991 7d 8m **58** 8.3g⁴ 10m] robust, angular colt: second foal: dam 7f winner, is out of half-sister to Bruni: plating-class maiden: pulled hard on debut: still burly and lethargic final start: stays 1¼m. *B. Hanbury.*

YAFILL (USA) 2 b. or br.f. (Apr 28) Nureyev (USA) 131 – Taras Charmer (USA) **80** (Majestic Light (USA)) [1991 5g³ 5m² 6f³ 5m⁴ 6.1d*] angular, sparely-made filly: first reported foal: dam minor winner in USA at up to 7f, is half-sister to dams of Zilzal (by Nureyev) and Polish Precedent: fair performer: bandaged near-hind, won minor event at Chester in October by 2½ lengths, going away, from Darling Miss Daisy: will stay 7f: best efforts with some give in the ground: went freely to post, pulled hard and hung right third outing: looks a hard ride and suited by strong handling. *M. R. Stoute.*

YAMAMAH 2 gr.f. (Mar 1) Siberian Express (USA) 125 – Tanouma (USA) 114 **54** (Miswaki (USA) 124) [1991 7m 7m] rangy, unfurnished filly: first foal: dam 6f and 7f winner stayed 1m: plating-class form in large-field October maidens at Newmarket and Lingfield: will stay 1m: sold 3,600 gns Newmarket Autumn Sales. *J. L. Dunlop.*

YAMANOUCHI 7 b.g. Hard Fought 125 – Noreena (Nonoalco (USA) 131) [1990 **50** NR 1991 8.5f⁴ 8h⁵ 8m³ 10.9g* 9m 10.2m⁵ 8m] short-backed ex-Irish gelding: second foal: dam twice-raced daughter of good 1969 French 2-y-o Vela: very lightly raced on flat: won handicap at Ayr in July: below form after: better at around 11f than shorter: acts on good to firm ground: winning hurdler. *D. Moffatt.*

YANKEEDOODLEDANCER 3 b.f. Mashhor Dancer (USA) – Baltimore — Belle 95 (Bold Lad (IRE) 133) [1990 NR 1991 9s 12.2g 12.2m 9.9f] 7,200F, IR 13,000Y: small, sturdy filly: fourth foal: dam winner over 6f (at 2 yrs) to 7.3f, is half-sister to Wollow: seems of little account. *R. M. Whitaker.*

YANKEE FLYER 4 b.f. Henbit (USA) 130 – Yankee Special 60 (Bold Lad (IRE) 133) [1990 7g³ 8g³ 7m³ 8g² 7.6m² 7d³ 8m 1991 7g² 7.6m³ 8g⁴ 8.9m²] sparely-made filly: quite modest maiden: claimed £8,111 final start, finding little off bridle, jinking right and carrying head high: stays 1m: acts on good to firm ground: not one to trust implicitly: winning hurdler for Miss S. J. Wilton. *Lord Huntingdon.* **63 §**

YANKEE SPARKLE 4 br.f. Dara Monarch 128 – Brilleaux 73 (Manado 130) [1990 12.8m 8g³ 12m 1991 8.9m] first foal: dam maiden half-sister to useful miler Welsh Flame, should have stayed 1¼m: ex-Irish filly: poor maiden: best effort at 1m: trained at 3 yrs by L. Browne. *B. R. Cambidge.* **—**

YARRA GLEN 4 ch.f. Known Fact (USA) 135 – Sloane Ranger 84 (Sharpen Up 127) [1990 7g⁶ 10f² 10.2f² 9m 10g 1991 a10g a10g 10f 12f 12f 12g 12g⁵ 12g] lengthy filly: quite modest maiden at best: no form for long time: stays 1¼m: acts on firm going: tried visored once: virtually bolted to post once at 4 yrs: tail flasher. *M. P. Muggeridge.* **—**

YASMEEN VALLEY (USA) 3 b.f. Danzig Connection (USA) – Friendly Circle (USA) (Round Table) [1990 6m² 7m³ 1991 6g 8m² 6m*] tall, rangy, rather angular filly: modest form: made all in maiden at Yarmouth in July: probably stays 1m. *A. C. Stewart.* **69**

YATOO (IRE) 2 ch.c. (Mar 31) Ballad Rock 122 – Phar Lapa 59 (Grundy 137) [1991 5g 6d 6.1m³ 7m⁴ 7.6m] 7,800F, 7,800Y: big, lengthy colt: has scope: third foal: half-brother to 1¼m to 16.1f winner Mrs Barton (by Faustus): dam staying maiden: modest maiden: off course over 4 months, form only when in frame in maiden auction at Nottingham and nursery at York (better effort, behind Sharpitor) in autumn: moderately drawn final start: should stay middle distances. *R. Hannon.* **68**

YAZALY (USA) 2 ch.c. (Mar 3) Blushing Groom (FR) 131 – Capricorn Belle 115 (Nonoalco (USA) 131) [1991 6s² 6d²] strong, lengthy colt: second foal: brother to useful 3-y-o 7f winner Desert Dirham: dam won from 6f (at 2 yrs) to 9f (in USA): runner-up in late-season maidens at Yarmouth in October and Doncaster (looked very well, beaten ½ length by Shujan) 9 days later: will stay 7f: races keenly: likely to win a similar event. *A. A. Scott.* **78 p**

YEAR OF THE DRAGON 3 ch.g. Sharpo 132 – Victory Kingdom (CAN) (Viceregal (CAN)) [1990 NR 1991 a7g² 7v* 7g² 8d4] smallish, sturdy gelding: sixth live foal: half-brother to 4 winners, including French 1m and 9f winner Blushing All Over (by Blushing Groom): dam (stakes placed) won 5 times in USA: won maiden at Folkestone in March: bandaged behind, much better efforts in 17-runner handicaps at Salisbury (apprentices) and Newbury in May: stays 1m: has hung left: gelded after final start. *D. R. C. Elsworth.* **79**

YEARSLEY 5 b.g. Anfield 117 – Mantina (Bustino 136) [1990 7f⁴ 8h* 7.5d⁵ 7m* 8f 8m 8g 1991 8m⁴ 8g 7m⁶ 7m 8f⁶] rangy gelding: usually dull in coat: good walker and mover: fairly useful handicapper at best: effective at 7f to 1m: suited by top-of-the-ground: dead. *M. H. Easterby.* **89**

YELLOW METAL 4 b.c. Reesh 117 – Madame Decoy 67 (Decoy Boy 129) [1990 7m 7h 1991 a7g 8m 9g 9s 10.8m⁶ 10.5g] leggy colt: has round action: bad performer. *A. W. Denson.* **—**

YENOORA (IRE) 2 b.c. (Feb 1) Ahonoora 122 – Beijing (USA) 89 (Northjet 136) [1991 8.2f 8s 10m] lengthy colt: has scope: second foal: half-brother to winning 3-y-o stayer The Last Empress (by Last Tycoon): dam middle-distance staying half-sister to very smart stayer Protection Racket: poor form in autumn maidens: late-developing type, may make his mark in moderate staying handicaps. *P. F. I. Cole.* **48 p**

YEOMAN BID 4 b.g. Longleat (USA) 109 – Bounding (Forlorn River 124) [1990 a7g³ 6f a8g² 8g a7g² a7g³ 7m a8g⁵ 7g a8g⁴ a7g² a7g³ a7g⁵ 1991 a7g⁵ a10g 7g 8.3g a 10f⁵ 10g a7g⁵ a8g] big, angular gelding: has a roundish action: modest form at best: little form in 1991: seems best at 7f: effective with or without blinkers: ran moderately when visored: hung and looked none too keen penultimate start: sold 2,500 gns Doncaster July Sales. *K. T. Ivory.* **— a 49**

YEOMAN BOUND 3 b.g. Norwick (USA) 120 – Bounding (Forlorn River 124) [1990 5m 1991 10.1g 8d] workmanlike gelding: good walker: no promise in minor events and claimer. *K. T. Ivory.* **—**

YEOMAN FORCE 5 b.g. Crofter (USA) 124 – High Voltage 82 (Electrify) [1990 a6g 6f⁶ 5g 5d⁵ 6m 6g* 6m⁶ 6g 6m 1991 7m a6g] tall, angular gelding: has a long stride: quite modest handicapper at best: soundly beaten in 1991: ideally suited by 6f: probably acts on any going: has worn blinkers, often visored. *J. M. Bradley.* **—**

Reference Point Sceptre Stakes, Doncaster—
Piggott brings You Know The Rules from last to first to catch Carson on Silver Braid (rails)

YES 3 b.f. Blakeney 126 – Arrapata (Thatching 131) [1990 a7g 6f⁶ 5f³ 5m² 5m² 6g⁶ **52** 6d 5g³ 5d³ 1991 6g 7g 5g⁵ 6g 6d⁴ 5g³ 5m a5g 6s 6f³ 5.2f² 6g* 6m 7s] compact filly: moderate mover: plating-class handicapper: well beaten after winning claiming handicap at Haydock in September: stays 6f (stiff task at 7f): acts on firm ground and dead: visored twice: usually ridden by claimer: often slowly away. *D. T. Thom.*

YESICAN 5 gr.h. Kalaglow 132 – Geoffrey's Sister 102 (Sparkler 130) [1990 8.3m² **64** a11g⁴ a12g⁵ 1991 a12g³ a16g* a12g* a13g⁵ 13.8m⁶ 12d] lengthy, workmanlike horse: quite modest handicapper: easy winner at Lingfield in January and February: off course 8 months before penultimate start: stays 2m: acts on good to firm ground: often bandaged. *T. Thomson Jones.*

YILDIZ 2 b.f. (Mar 22) Be My Guest (USA) 126 – Yldizlar 77 (Star Appeal 133) **67** P [1991 7m³] rangy, good-topped filly: has plenty of scope: good walker: second foal: dam, twice-raced 2-y-o 7f winner, is half-sister to very useful pair Domynsky and Petrullo: weak 16/1-chance and very green, eye-catching third of 14 to Sea Clover in maiden at Leicester in October, making up plenty of ground final 1½f and beaten under 2 lengths: moved moderately to post: will stay 1¼m: a likeable filly, sure to improve considerably. *B. W. Hills.*

YIMKIN BOOKRA 3 b.g. Nomination 125 – Top Stream 87 (Highland Melody **73** 112) [1990 NR 1991 8d 8m⁴ 8g 10g⁶ 10.2g³ 12f⁵ 10.2g 10.5g] sturdy, lengthy gelding: sixth foal: half-brother to several winners, notably useful 6f and 7f winner Kedron (by Absalom): dam won 3 times over 1m at 2 yrs and seemed to stay 1½m: modest maiden: well beaten in handicaps (amateurs first start) last 2 outings: stays at least 1¼m: acts on good to firm ground. *M. E. D. Francis.*

YONGE TENDER 4 b.f. Tender King 123 – St Clair Star (Sallust 134) [1990 5f⁵ **65** 5g⁴ 5d⁶ 6s⁶ 6m³ 7m³ 6f² a7g² 6m* 6m³ 6d² 6g* 6f a6g⁵ 1991 a6g 6d 7m* 7d³ 7m⁵ 7m² 7.6d 7g* 6m⁴ 6.1m* 7f² 7m* 6f] small, close-coupled filly: carries condition: moderate walker and mover: quite modest performer: won sellers (no bid twice, then bought in 4,600 gns) at Thirsk in April and Yarmouth and Nottingham in July and claimer at Southwell in August: suited by 6f or 7f: acts on firm and dead going: best blinkered: good mount for claimer: has won when sweating and edgy: tough, genuine and consistent. *J. Wharton.*

YORKSHIRE HOLLY 8 br.g. Bivouac 114 – Holly Doon (Doon 124) [1990 16f⁶ **63** d 16f* 18d 1991 18s² 16.1m 15.8g] smallish, workmanlike gelding: quite modest handicapper: off course 6 months and little promise after reappearance: stays 2¼m: probably acts on any going: good mount for claimer: held up, and has turn of foot: trained reappearance by Mrs G. Reveley. *M. Avison.*

YOU ARE A STAR 5 b.g. Persian Bold 123 – Flinging Star (USA) (Northern **80** Fling (USA)) [1990 10m 8m* 8f 8g⁶ 8m* 7m 8m⁶ 8f 9m⁴ 8g 8m* 8g⁵ 1991 8m⁵ 8m*

962

8.2g⁴ 8g 8m 8g 8m4] big, rangy gelding: carries condition: usually looks well: fair handicapper: won at Edinburgh in June despite tending to hang right: suited by 1m: best form on sound surface: ran moderately in visor: has turn of foot, and best held up: winning hurdler. *M. H. Tompkins.*

YOU KNOW THE RULES   4 b.f. Castle Keep 121 – Falls of Lora 107 (Scottish   **101** Rifle 127) [1990 8.5g 7m³ 7f⁵ 8m* 7g⁴ 9g* 12g 8g* 8m 9g 1991 8d 10g⁴ 8d* 8m 10.1f 8g 9s* 10g* 8g³ 11.9g⁵ 8m* 9d 10.5v] sparely-made filly: has a quick action: much improved in 1991: won handicaps at Sandown in May, Goodwood in June, Royal Hong Kong Jockey Club Trophy at Sandown (fourth win there) in July and slowly-run listed event at Doncaster (headed Silver Braid on post) in September: behind in Ciga Prix de l'Opera at Longchamp and Prix de Flore at Saint-Cloud: best at up to 1¼m: acts on good to firm and soft ground: held up and has turn of foot: great credit to her trainer: sold 46,000 gns Newmarket December Sales. *M. R. Channon.*

YOUNG BILL   4 ch.g. Nicholas Bill 125 – Lingdale Lady 66 (Sandford Lad 133)   **37** + [1990 8f 8.2d 6g 1991 7g 8m] close-coupled gelding: lightly-raced maiden: caught eye in handicaps in spring: likely to prove suited by at least 1m: blinkered on reappearance: joined T. Carr. *Mrs J. R. Ramsden.*

YOUNG BUSTER (IRE)   3 b.c. Teenoso (USA) 135 – Bustara 92 (Busted   **120** 134) [1990 7g² 7g² 1991 10d² 12m* 11.5g² 11.1m* 12g³ 10m⁶]

While Sheikh Mohammed's purchase of the White Lodge Stud hasn't yet brought the rewards it might, the familiar chocolate and gold colours of the late Moller brothers, the stud's former owners, continued to be carried with distinction for their executors in the latest season. Young Senor, a 52,000-guinea yearling, won the Tattersalls Tiffany Highflyer Stakes at Newmarket, while a month earlier Young Buster, a White Lodge graduate, took the Group 3 BonusPrint September Stakes at Kempton from the previous year's Derby winner Quest For Fame. Young Buster was himself trained for the Derby in the spring. He hacked up in a mile-and-a-half maiden at Newmarket in April, and started favourite for the Maxims Club Derby Trial at Lingfield the following month, but appeared to have his limitations exposed when beaten four lengths by Corrupt. Intermittent back trouble subsequently kept Young Buster off the track until the September Stakes. Quest For Fame started odds on for the race in a field of five, with Young Buster the only other backed, at 11/4, but the favourite's task didn't look an easy one, conceding the three-year-old 7 lb more than the official weight for age, and Young Buster beat him by a neck. Held up, as he was in all his races as a three-year-old, Young Buster was still going strongly when Quest For Fame took it up from his pacemaker Green's Ferneley early in the straight, quickened to lead over a furlong out

BonusPrint September Stakes, Kempton—
Young Buster has to work hard as Quest For Fame fights back

and held on under pressure as the favourite rallied against the rail; Dolpour ran on to finish one and a half lengths further away in third.

Young Buster failed to add to his tally after Kempton, but in fact put up better performances in defeat in the Cumberland Lodge Stakes at Ascot and the Dubai Champion Stakes at Newmarket. He finished third of five at Ascot, beaten a head and one and a half lengths by the older pair Drum Taps and Rock Hopper, and sixth of twelve at Newmarket, beaten little more than two lengths behind Tel Quel. On form, there's little between the two performances, but in a moderately-run affair at Newmarket Young Buster gave the impression that a return to a mile and a half would suit him ideally. He stays in training and should win more good races. The Ormonde Stakes at Chester could be an early-season target. A rather angular though quite attractive colt, he has a quick action and acts well on top-of-the-ground.

		⎧Youth	⎧Ack Ack
	⎧Teenoso (USA)	⎨ (b 1973)	⎨Gazala II
	⎪ (b or br 1980)	⎪Furioso	⎩Ballymoss
Young Buster (IRE)	⎨	⎩ (b 1971)	⎧Violetta III
(b.c. 1988)	⎪	⎧Busted	⎨Crepello
	⎪Bustara	⎨ (b 1963)	⎩Sans Le Sou
	⎩ (b 1983)	⎪Romara	⎧Bold Lad
		⎩ (ch 1976)	⎩Peaceful

Young Buster is the first foal of Bustara, a mare who won over six furlongs as a two-year-old and finished fourth in the Italian One Thousand Guineas at three, when she also showed she stayed ten furlongs. Bustara's dam Romara, fourth in the Irish One Thousand Guineas, has proved a tremendous success at stud, producing seven winners from her first seven foals, among them the smart Ela Romara, who won the Lowther Stakes at York and the ten-furlong Nassau Stakes at Goodwood in the Moller colours. Romara's two most recent winners, Ile de Roma and So Romantic, were both successful in Sheikh Mohammed's colours, and Sheikh Mohammed also owns Bustara's second foal El Taranda (by Ela-Mana-Mou), who finished fifth of ten in a maiden at Yarmouth on her debut in October. *G. Wragg.*

YOUNG CHRISTOS 4 b.c. Sayf El Arab (USA) 127 – Pahaska 86 (Wolver — Hollow 126) [1990 a10g⁶ 1991 7f] leggy colt: no sign of ability: sold 825 gns Ascot December Sales. *M. Bell.*

YOUNG COMMANDER 7 br.g. Bustino 136 – Bombshell 76 (Le Levanstell 53 122) [1990 8f⁶ 8f⁴ 9g⁴ 8f⁵ 8g* 8m³ 8m 9m 8f³ 8.5m 1991 8g 8g 8.2f⁴ 8.3d 8g² 8s² 7g² 8d⁵ 8f] lengthy gelding: hobdayed: plating-class handicapper: effective at 7f to 9f: acts on any going: usually visored: twice below form when blinkered: best with waiting tactics: none too resolute. *M. P. Naughton.*

YOUNG DUKE (IRE) 3 gr.c. Double Schwartz 128 – Princess Pamela 70 75 (Dragonara Palace (USA) 115) [1990 6m 1991 6m² 6f² 7m* 8m³ 7m³ 8f² 7.1m⁵] leggy colt: modest form: won maiden at Brighton in June: fair fifth of 16 in handicap at Sandown in September, staying on from rear, carrying head awkwardly and wandering when put under pressure: stays 1m: blinkered last 2 starts, visored previous 3: consistent: trained reappearance by M. Usher. *M. McCormack.*

YOUNG FACT 6 b.g. Known Fact (USA) 135 – Yelming 76 (Thatch (USA) 136) — [1990 10.1g³ 11.5m* 11.5m⁵ 10.6s⁴ 10.6s⁵ 10.6m² 10.6g⁵ 12g⁴ 1991 10.2g] sturdy, compact gelding: successful at 2 yrs and 3 yrs in Germany: modest form here: no show in handicap only run in 1991 (June): stays 11.5f: possibly ideally suited to top-of-the-ground. *J. H. Baker.*

YOUNG FREEMAN (USA) 2 b.c. (May 28) Nijinsky (CAN) 138 – Committed 79 p (USA) 128 (Hagley (USA)) [1991 8d²] $450,000Y: big, rangy, good sort: has plenty of scope: third foal: brother to useful Irish 4-y-o 1m (listed) to 9f winner Committed Dancer and closely related to Irish 3-y-o 7f winner Dobie (by Lyphard): dam top-class sprinter, also won over 7.9f: co-favourite but green, strong-finishing length second of 14 to Hill Glitter in minor event at Newmarket in November: moved poorly to post: may stay 1¼m: will improve, and is sure to win a race or two. *G. Harwood.*

YOUNG GEORGE 4 b.g. Camden Town 125 – Young Grace (Young Emperor 60 133) [1990 5s⁴ 8f* 7f⁵ 7g 9m* 10.6m⁵ 10.2m 8g² 9s 9f 1991 8d 10f² 11f⁵ 12m³ 10g 10d² 9.9f² 10f* 10f⁵ 10.1m⁵ 9.9f⁴ 10.9m² 10.5d] good-topped, close-coupled gelding:

carries condition: quite modest handicapper: won at Redcar in July: stays 11f: acts on firm ground, possibly unsuited by very soft: consistent. *M. Dods.*

YOUNG INDIA   4 br.f. Indian King (USA) 128 – Marfisa (Green God 128) [1990   —
6m 5f⁵ 6f 6m 5g 5m 5m 6g⁴ 6f 8.2s³ 8d³ 1991 8m] big, workmanlike filly:
inconsistent handicapper: not seen out after April: probably stays 1m and acts on
any going: tried blinkered once: bandaged occasionally. *D. Burchell.*

YOUNG JAMES   3 ch.g. Hotfoot 126 – Deep Lady 78 (Deep Diver 134) [1990 7f   —
6d 1991 8g 6m 7m⁶ 7g 8d 11.7f⁵ 10g] tall, lengthy gelding: little worthwhile form. *J. H. Baker.*

YOUNG JASON   8 ch.g. Star Appeal 133 – Smarten Up 119 (Sharpen Up 127)   65
[1990 10f⁵ 7.5m 8.2m⁴ 7.5d² 8m² 8g⁵ 10f⁵ 10f⁴ 8m⁵ 8g* 9m 8.5m* 8m 7d 1991 8d
7.6d 8m 8m⁵ 8g⁶ 8f 8m 7.5f* 8f 9m 8m] small, good-bodied gelding: moderate
mover: modest handicapper: inconsistent in 1991: won seller (no bid) at Beverley in
August: ideally suited by a strong gallop at around 1m: acts on any going: tried
blinkered once: goes well with extreme waiting tactics and on a turning track: tends
to carry head high: tough. *F. H. Lee.*

YOUNG MAX   2 b.c. (Feb 11) Nomination 125 – Hollow Heart 89 (Wolver Hollow   58
126) [1991 5m 6m] 66,000Y: deep-girthed colt: fifth foal: half-brother to 3 winners,
including fairly useful 7f to 8.5f winner Aradu (by Posse) and unreliable 6f (at 2 yrs)
to 1m winner Fox Chapel (by Formidable): dam, 5f winner at 2 yrs, is closely related
to smart middle-distance handicapper Royal Match: better for race, signs of ability
in maidens at Sandown (better effort, late progress) and Newcastle (again slowly
away) in autumn: may do better. *D. R. C. Elsworth.*

YOUNG MUSICIAN (IRE)   2 b.g. (Jan 31) Cyrano de Bergerac 120 – Gentalyn   53
(Henbit (USA) 130) [1991 6m 6.1m³] IR 3,000F, IR 15,500Y: big, useful-looking
gelding with plenty of scope: second foal: dam unraced: above himself in
preliminaries, showed plenty of promise when towards rear in maiden median
auction event at York in July: 20/1 from 8/1, didn't improve so much as expected in
5-runner maiden at Nottingham 9 days later, pulling hard until fading 2f out: may do
better. *J. G. FitzGerald.*

YOUNG PITT (IRE)   3 b.g. Pitskelly 122 – Magloire (FR) (Sir Gaylord) [1990 8g   —
8.2s 10s 1991 10g 10g 11.5s] strong gelding: behind in maidens and claimers: has
been slowly away. *T. M. Jones.*

YOUNG RODNEY   2 b.c. (Feb 26) Pharly (FR) 130 – Silent Pool 68 (Relkino 131)   —
[1991 7.1s] 1,500Y: compact colt: fifth foal: half-brother to 9f and 1¼m winner Water
God (by Dominion) and a winner in Austria: dam slow daughter of Park Hill winner
Idle Waters: 33/1, backward and green, soon tailed off in maiden at Chepstow in
October. *J. H. Baker.*

YOUNG SENOR (USA)   2 b.c. (Feb 22) El Gran Senor (USA) 136 – **110**
Liturgism (USA) (Native Charger) [1991 5g² 6g* 6m 7m² 7d³ 7m* 7m]
    Had the Jockey Club had the foresight to allow the inaugural (1990)
Tattersalls Tiffany Highflyer Stakes to be run in October instead of August,
and had Tattersalls had the acumen to combine the separate races for colts
and fillies, then it's quite possible that the beleaguered race would have had a
long life instead of being dropped after just two years. As we predicted in
Racehorses of 1990, the re-siting much later in the season of the Highflyer
Stakes, a £30,000 'open' race for two-year-olds with a bonus scheme restricted to owners of those horses sold at the previous autumn's Highflyer
Yearling Sale, together with alterations to its conditions, resulted in a much
larger field than in 1990; what we didn't anticipate, though, given the reduced
catalogue which the bulk of its runners were drawn from, was its strength in
depth. A maximum field of thirty (thirteen more than in 1990) went to post
headed by the Coventry Stakes runner-up and Lanson Champagne Stakes
winner Dr Devious. The easy Kempton minor event winner Alnasr Alwasheek and the National Stakes winner El Prado, one of two useful challengers
from Ireland, came next in the betting; My Memoirs, from Hannon's stable,
was alone among the runners not purchased at the Highflyer Sale and
therefore didn't qualify for any of the huge bonuses on offer, from £500,000 to
the winner down to £10,000. Young Senor, the winner, started at 14/1, which
seemed a fair reflection of his chance on form that had improved with each
step up in distance. The only blot on his record had come in the Chesham
Stakes at Royal Ascot, where he'd had his head over the side of the adjacent

stall when the doors opened and lost all chance with a very slow start; other than that, he'd run well since a pipe-opener on Two Thousand Guineas day, winning a six-furlong maiden at York in May with some ease (though not before he'd ducked sharply right inside the final furlong), finishing an excellent second to Dr Devious when conceding weight all round in the seven-furlong Krug Superlative Stakes at Newmarket in July, then having around ten weeks off the course (reportedly because he'd been coughing) before returning with a respectable third to Assessor in a well-contested minor event at Ascot. That Ascot run was probably just what Young Senor needed to put him spot on for the Highflyer; back on good to firm ground, he recorded his best performance, tracking the leaders until just inside the two-furlong pole then running on with great determination to hold off the fast-finishing Dr Devious by a head with Alnasr Alwasheek and Ruhr not much further away in third and fourth. Two weeks later, over the same course and distance, Young Senor finished well down the field behind Dr Devious in the Three Chimneys Dewhurst Stakes; possibly the bump he received after a furlong or so was partly to blame, but his finishing effort bore no semblance to that produced under similar conditions in the Highflyer and he faded to finish seventh of the nine runners.

Young Senor (USA) (b.c. Feb 22, 1989)	El Gran Senor (USA) (b 1981)	Northern Dancer (b 1961)	Nearctic Natalma
		Sex Appeal (ch 1970)	Buckpasser Best In Show
	Liturgism (USA) (b 1980)	Native Charger (gr 1962)	Native Dancer Greek Blond
		Cult (b 1974)	Dr Fager Arrangement

The good-bodied Young Senor, a 52,000-guinea purchase, is the latest in the recent stream of useful-or-better winners from his American-based family. His great-grandam Arrangement, a winner of five races of no great importance, began the sequence in the early-'seventies when she foaled the good-class sprinter Lonetree, who frequently carried big weights into the frame (but without success) in graded handicaps as a four- and five-year-old, then followed him with the very smart filly Land Girl, successful in the Grade 3 one-mile Demoiselle Stakes at two and the Grade 2 Gazelle Handicap over nine furlongs at three, and the smart colt Idyll, who finished third in the eight-and-a-half-furlong Norfolk Stakes as a two-year-old and won a Grade 3 event over nine furlongs at four. Young Senor's grandam Cult was the only one of Arrangement's foals not to win—she finished second once and third on five occasions from sixteen attempts—but she's matched her dam at stud by producing three stakes winners, including Coup de Fusil, a multiple winner whose form improved as she got older and who, as a five-year-old, won three Grade 1 Handicaps over nine furlongs or a mile and a quarter, and Young

Senor's dam Liturgism, a winner of seven races at up to nine furlongs from thirty-eight starts. Liturgism bred two winners from three foals of racing age before Young Senor; the fairly useful middle-distance stayer Eastern Diamond (by Diamond Shoal) and the 1990 Irish two-year-old six-furlong winner Brentsville (by Arctic Tern). Young Senor was much better suited by seven furlongs than shorter at two and will almost certainly stay a mile and a quarter at three. A round-actioned colt, he acts on good to soft ground but is probably better suited by good to firm. *G. Wragg.*

YOUNG SHADOWFAX 4 gr.c. Absalom 128 – Miss Twiggy 80 (Tycoon II) 59
[1990 5m⁴ 5m⁴ 6m² 5d 5m 6f* 1991 a6g⁴ a6g³ a8g a6g⁵ 9g 6m⁶ 6g 7d 7m 6f⁴ 6g⁴ 5m⁶ 5g⁵ 5m² a5g 5m] sturdy, good-quartered colt: quite modest handicapper nowadays: stays 6f: best efforts on a sound surface: effective with or without visor: sometimes bandaged near-hind: has had tongue tied down: has run well for apprentice. *C. N. Allen.*

YOUNG VALENTINE 2 ch.g. (Feb 14) Bairn (USA) 126 – Spinner 59 (Blue 59
Cashmere 129) [1991 5m* 5f⁴ 6g⁵] 21,000Y: angular, quite attractive gelding: half-brother to 3 winners, including fairly useful 5f to 7f handicapper Resolute Bay (by Crofter) and 1989 2-y-o 5f winner Another Lane (by Tina's Pet): dam sprinter: plating-class form: game winner of maiden at Newcastle in June: easily better subsequent effort when creditable fifth of 7 in nursery at Goodwood in August: stays 6f: possibly unsuited by firm ground. *R. M. Whitaker.*

YOUNG VALIYAR 2 br.f. (Jan 27) Valiyar 129 – So Generous (Young —
Generation 129) [1991 6m] 2,100F, 1,100Y: neat filly: second foal: half-sister to 1989 2-y-o 5f winner Dalston (by Dalsaan): dam unraced daughter of sister to Yorkshire Oaks winner Outcrop: 50/1, tailed off in 7-runner maiden at Redcar in August: moved poorly down. *B. W. Murray.*

YOUSEFIA (USA) 2 b.f. (Mar 11) Danzig (USA) – Foreign Courier (USA) (Sir 84 p
Ivor 135) [1991 6m⁵ 6m*] leggy filly: lacks substance: has smooth action: sixth foal: sister to high-class sprinter Green Desert and useful 1989 2-y-o 5f winner Kissogram Girl: dam unraced half-sister to top-class filly Althea: 2/1, woolly in appearance and on toes, won 14-runner maiden at Newmarket in October by short head from King Olaf, never far away, leading inside final 1f and just holding on: should improve again. *M. R. Stoute.*

YUKOSAN 4 ch.f. Absalom 128 – K-Sera 95 (Lord Gayle (USA) 124) [1990 a6g* —
a6g³ a6g⁵ 6m⁵ 6v* 7.5g⁶ 7g 6g⁵ a6g a6g⁶ a6g a7g 1991 a6g⁵ 6s 6d⁶ a5g] lengthy filly: quite modest performer at 3 yrs: below form in 1991: should stay beyond 6f: acts on heavy going. *Ronald Thompson.*

YUVRAJ 7 b.g. Final Straw 127 – Never Never Land (Habitat) [1990 NR 1991 —
11.5m⁶ a10g] compact gelding: good mover: modest maiden at 3 yrs: first runs on flat since, well beaten in claimer and seller: stays 1m: acts on any going: effective blinkered or not. *B. J. McMath.*

Z

ZAAGIL (FR) 3 b.c. Crystal Glitters (USA) 127 – La Breloque (Nonoalco (USA) —
131) [1990 NR 1991 8d 8g 7.6s] 400,000 francs (approx £37,000) Y: big, good-topped colt: third foal: half-brother to French 10.5f winner North Code and French 1m to 15f winner Plein d'Esprit (both by Esprit du Nord): dam minor French 1m winner: no worthwhile form in the summer: looked difficult ride final start: sold 1,800 gns Newmarket Autumn Sales. *C. J. Benstead.*

ZAAHI (USA) 2 b. or br.c. (Mar 2) Slew O' Gold (USA) – Alghuzaylah 90 (Habitat **103 p**
134) [1991 7.1m* 7m5] strong, good-bodied colt: third foal: half-brother to useful 6f and 7f (at 2 yrs) winner Kadim (by Diesis) and a winner in USA: dam 2-y-o 5f winner stayed 1m, is half-sister to very smart French 5.5f to 10.5f winner Pitasia: sire top-class middle-distance performer: well-backed favourite, won maiden at Sandown in September in very good style, leading on bridle 2f out and soon clear: 4/1 and looking very well, under 6 lengths fifth of 9 to Dr Devious in Dewhurst Stakes at Newmarket month later, travelling well (though wandering, and bumping rival early on) until fading running down into Dip: will stay 1m: may well be capable of better. *H. Thomson Jones.*

ZABELINA (USA) 3 ch.f. Diesis 133 – Intentional Move (USA) (Tentam (USA)) 57
[1990 NR 1991 8g 9g⁵ 7f⁴ 9.7m⁴] $400,000Y: leggy, sparely-made filly: fourth

reported foal: closely related to smart but lightly-raced 7f and 1m winner Lunar Mover (by Sharpen Up) and half-sister to Dance Teacher (by Smarten), fairly useful 1m winner here at 3 yrs and graded 8.5f and 1¼m winner in USA: dam minor winner at up to 9f in USA: tongue tied down, quite modest form in maidens: stays 1m: acts on firm going. *M. R. Stoute.*

ZAFADOLA (IRE) 3 gr.f. Darshaan 133 – Zarafa (Blushing Groom (Fr) 131) **112** [1990 NR 1991 9d* 7g3 10m5 11g* 12m2 14d3 12s2 14v] Irish filly: first foal: dam unraced granddaughter of Petite Étoile: won maiden race at Mallow and listed race at the Curragh: ran very well on latter course when second to Sardaniya in Meld Stakes and Topanoora in Blandford Stakes and when third to Turgeon in Jefferson Smurfit Memorial Irish St Leger: suited by 1½m+: acts on good to firm and soft going. *J. Oxx, Ireland.*

ZAFRA 3 b.f. Dunbeath (USA) 127 – White's Ferry (Northfields (USA)) [1990 6s — 6g 7g4 7f 8m 8m 8d 1991 16.1g 17.2g] neat filly: has a round action: poor maiden: tailed off in handicaps late at 3 yrs: should stay at least 1m. *C. A. Horgan.*

ZAHR (IRE) 3 b. or br.f. Touching Wood (USA) 127 – Haraabah (USA) 99 (Top- **59** sider (USA)) [1990 NR 1991 8m3 14.1h2 12.2m6] small, sparely-made filly: first foal: dam 5f to 7f winner out of half-sister to high-class 1m to 13f performer Dom Alaric: modest maiden: travelling best taking lead over 2f out when second at Carlisle: ran moderately final start: sold 4,200 gns Newmarket Autumn Sales. *H. Thomson Jones.*

ZAKINTHOS (IRE) 2 b.c. (Mar 18) Reference Point 139 – Ionian Raja (USA) **59** 116 (Raja Baba (USA)) [1991 7m 8m 6.9f] 13,000Y: sturdy, close-coupled colt: carries condition: moderate mover: half-brother to several winners abroad: dam French 7f (at 2 yrs) and 1m winner: plating-class maiden: best effort (though slowly away) second start: edged right and found little final one: will stay 1¼m: sold 6,200 gns Newmarket Autumn Sales. *C. E. Brittain.*

ZALON (IRE) 2 gr.c. (Apr 2) Flash of Steel 120 – Negligence 66 (Roan Rocket **74** p 128) [1991 7m2] IR 95,000Y: half-brother to 3 winners, notably smart 1989 2-y-o 7f winner Negligent (by Ahonoora) and out-and-out stayer Ala Hounak (by Sexton

H.H. Aga Khan's "Zafadola"

968

Blake): dam poor maiden: weak 4/1-shot, running-on 2 lengths second of 9 to Fair American in maiden at Lingfield in October, bit slowly away and soon niggled along: will stay 1m + : will improve. *J. H. M. Gosden.*

ZAMAAN YA ZAMAAN (IRE) 2 b.c. (May 1) Persian Bold 123 – Unbidden Melody (USA) (Chieftain II) [1991 8m] IR 45,000Y: fourth foal: half-brother to 1989 2-y-o 6f winner Ruling Passion (by Bairn): dam half-sister to Faustus: 14/1 from 8/1, burly and green, well beaten in Pontefract maiden in October. *M. A. Jarvis.* —

ZAMIL (USA) 6 b.g. Lyphard (USA) 132 – Wayward Lass (USA) (Hail The Pirates (USA) 126) [1990 14.6d 1991 14.6d] quite good-topped gelding: twice raced on flat and no worthwhile form: winning hurdler. *K. R. Burke.* —

ZAMIRAH (IRE) 2 b.f. (Mar 29) Trojan Fen 118 – Sweet Pleasure 88 (Sweet Revenge 129) [1991 7m* 7g³ 8.1m³] 4,000F, 4,800Y: workmanlike filly: seventh foal: half-sister to useful 1986 French 2-y-o sprinter Ma Colombine and 1¼m winner Jaaziel (both by Jaazeiro): dam 6f winner at 2 yrs: favourite, won maiden auction at Yarmouth in July: ran well in nurseries the following month: may stay 1¼m. *G. Wragg.* **73**

ZANDORA (IRE) 3 b.f. Taufan (USA) 119 – Silver Glimpse 108 (Petingo 135) [1990 NR 1991 8g 6m³ 8s 6m] IR 18,000Y: rather leggy filly: moderate mover: half-sister to 1¼m and 1.5f winner Hintlesham Harry (by Pas de Seul) and 3 winners in France: dam 2-y-o 7f winner in France: tailed off except when third of 6 in maiden at Yarmouth in July, soon driven along in rear: blinkered final start: sold 2,000 gns Newmarket Autumn Sales. *C. E. Brittain.* **48**

ZANDRIL 3 b.c. Forzando 122 – Champ d'Avril 89 (Northfields (USA)) [1990 6m 6m⁴ 5m* 5m* 5g* 5g 1991 5g 6g⁵ 5g 5m 5m 6d³ 5m⁴ 5g² 5.1g⁶ 5m⁵ 5m⁶] lengthy, good-topped colt: poor mover: fair handicapper: suited by 5f: acts on good to firm ground and dead: last when blinkered fifth start: below form at Chester: finds little off bridle, and seems best with waiting tactics. *R. Hannon.* **87**

ZANONI 4 b.c. Mummy's Pet 125 – Princely Maid 71 (King's Troop 118) [1990 6m* 6g⁴ 5m⁵ 5m⁴ 5d* 6d 5s² 5d 1991 5g 8g 6d² 6m 5.1g² 5.2g⁴ 6g 5m 5g 6d⁶ 6m⁴ a6g⁴] leggy, quite attractive colt: has rather round action: quite useful handicapper on his day: odds on, below best in Southwell claimer final start: stays 6f: suited by plenty of give in the ground: has sometimes found little off bridle: inconsistent and hard to win with nowadays. *M. A. Jarvis.* **94**

ZAR-AFSHAN 2 b.f. (Apr 3) Valiyar 129 – Martyrdom (USA) (Exceller (USA) 129) [1991 6g] 500Y: leggy, lightly-made filly: second foal: dam, unraced, from family of Magical Wonder: 33/1 and backward, soon well behind, flashing tail, in maiden at Leicester in May: went very freely to post. *C. Holmes.* —

ZARISSA (USA) 3 b.f. Lyphard (USA) 132 – I Want To Be (USA) 116 (Roberto (USA) 131) [1990 6d⁵ 1991 10g³ 12.2f⁵ 7m³ 8s⁵ 8m] small, lightly-made filly: plating-class maiden on most form: well beaten facing stiff task in handicap final start: bred to be suited by 1m + : acts on any going: visits Never So Bold. *J. L. Dunlop.* **55**

ZARYA 4 b.f. Shelter Half (USA) – Ice Blue (Cure The Blues (USA)) [1990 7f 1991 a8g] twice raced and no show in claimers. *J. Banks.* —

ZAXIS 3 ch.f. Noalto 120 – La Pirouette (USA) 73 (Kennedy Road (CAN)) [1990 8g 8.2v⁶ 8d 1991 12g a11g 8.1g 8m² 8m 8.2f a10g] tall, lengthy filly: poor maiden: second in claimer (claimed out of D. Arbuthnot's stable £3,011) at Leicester, gamely making most: ran poorly afterwards: not bred to stay much beyond 1m: acts on good to firm ground and dead: visored final start, blinkered previous 3: has worn badages behind. *A. S. Reid.* **40**

ZEALOUS 3 ch.f. Hard Fought 125 – Princess Zeddera (English Prince 129) [1990 NR 1991 a12g] 3,300F, 3,000Y: workmanlike filly: fifth reported foal: sister to useful 6f and 7.6f winner Hard Round: dam French 10.5f winner, is half-sister to very useful Home Coming: blinkered, moved poorly down and no promise in claimer at Lingfield in April. *A. N. Lee.* —

ZEALOUS KITTEN (USA) 3 ch.f. The Minstrel (CAN) 135 – Zealous Cat (USA) (Cougar (CHI)) [1990 NR 1991 12d² 12g⁴ 12m⁶ 10.1d⁴ 11.7m 8.9m 12m⁶ 10g⁵ 11.8g 12f a16g] $100,000Y: leggy, close-coupled filly: moderate mover: sixth foal: half-sister to 4 winners in North America, including a prolific winner by Temperence Hill and a stakes-placed colt by Sensitive Prince: dam 3-y-o maiden winner at around 6f in USA out of sister to high-class colt Take Your Place: quite modest maiden at best: stays 1½m: acts on dead ground: visored tenth start: trained first 4 by A. Scott (claimed £6,307 in selling handicap), next one by T. McGovern. *Mrs N. Macauley.* **60 d**

ZEBOIM 5 ch.g. Stanford 121§ – Solarina (Solinus 130) [1990 NR 1991 6f² 6g* 71
6m* 5f 6m* 7f³ 6m⁴ 6m*] big, lengthy, workmanlike gelding: modest and lightly-
raced handicapper: won at Thirsk and Salisbury in May, Yarmouth in July and
Folkestone in September: refused to enter stalls in October: best at 6f or 7f: acts on
firm going: effective with or without blinkers: has won when sweating and for
apprentice. *W. R. Muir.*

ZENISKA (USA) 3 b.g. Cozzene (USA) – Istiska (FR) (Irish River (FR) 131) —
[1990 7s 7s a7g 1991 8d 10d] big, rangy gelding: poor form in maidens and (visored)
handicap: sold 2,400 gns Doncaster May Sales and gelded. *S. G. Norton.*

ZEPHYR FIRE 3 ch.c. Hotfoot 126 – Delta Wind 72 (Tumble Wind (USA)) [1990 —
5m 5f 5f 6g 6g 7f 1991 6m] smallish, compact colt: poor walker: bad plater: blinkered
once. *W. Carter.*

ZEPHYR NIGHTS (USA) 4 b.g. Grey Dawn II 132 – Vaslava (Habitat 134) —
[1990 10f⁶ 12.5g⁵ 13.8m 14m 12f 1991 a13g⁶] leggy, angular gelding: little worthwhile
form: visored only start in 1991 (March): sold to join Grenville Richards' stable
3,400 gns Doncaster Sales later in month: of suspect temperament. *A. Hide.*

ZEPPEKI (IRE) 3 b.g. Taufan (USA) 119 – Avital (Pitskelly 122) [1990 5f⁴ 6m² 70
6m⁴ 6f³ 6s² 7m⁶ 6d 1991 6g³ a7g⁵ 7m³ 8f* 8m*] lengthy, good-quartered gelding:
quite modest performer: favourite, won claimers at Carlisle and Newmarket
(claimed to join M. Hammond £8,725) in May: stays 1m well: probably acts on any
going: has been tried in blinkers. *J. Berry.*

ZIGAURA (USA) 3 b.f. Ziggy's Boy (USA) – Our Feast (USA) (Banquet Table **101** ?
(USA)) [1990 5m² 6m² 6m³ 6m⁴ 6m³ 6m⁶ 1991 7m² 8g 7g* 7g⁶ 8m⁴ 10g⁶ 7g⁴]
lengthy, attractive filly: good mover, with a quick action: 9/4 on and blinkered, won
3-runner maiden at Goodwood in May in workmanlike style: capable of useful form,
second to Mystiko in Free Handicap and fourth to Only Yours in Child Stakes at
Newmarket: stays 1m: acts on good to firm ground: usually held up: finds little off
bridle: looked none too keen and returned home lame penultimate (bandaged) start,
off course 3½ months before running poorly on return: sold 70,000 gns Newmarket
December Sales. *D. R. C. Elsworth.*

ZILLE (GER) 6 b.h. Experte (GER) – Zikade (GER) (Pentathlon) [1990 8g³ 10g² **115**
8g² 8g² 8g* 8.5s* 8s² 8v⁴ 1991 8g* 8d⁴ 8g⁴ 8g 8g⁴ 8g⁵ 8.5s 8v⁴] big, lengthy,
unfurnished horse: German bred: smart performer at best: successful in 1m listed
race at Baden-Baden and 8.5f Group 2 event at Dusseldorf as 5 yrs: also won 1m
listed event at Cologne in April: fourth in Group 3 events in France and Germany
afterwards: seventh in Queen Anne Stakes at Royal Ascot fourth outing: stays 1¼m:
acts on dead ground. *Frau Jutta Schultheis, Germany.*

ZINAAD 2 b.c. (Mar 10) Shirley Heights 130 – Time Charter 131 (Saritamer (USA) 89 p
130) [1991 8m*] 300,000Y: finely-made, quite attractive colt: second foal: brother to
useful 1988 2-y-o 7f winner By Charter: dam tip-top middle-distance performer
(also second in 1000 Guineas) out of sister to Nicholas Bill and Centroline: weak
7/1-shot, won 6-runner minor event at Newbury in September by 2½ lengths from
Grand Master, quickening well to lead inside final 1f, well on top at the finish:
showed a fluent action: will stay middle distances: sure to improve and looks a
useful prospect. *M. R. Stoute.*

ZINBAQ 5 ch.h. Ahonoora 122 – Zaiyundeen (FR) (Exbury 138) [1990 a6g 6m a7g² 53
a7g⁴ 6d 6m³ 7m⁴ 7f⁵ 7m⁵ 7m⁴ 7g⁴ 6m⁴ 6g² 7g⁶ a6g⁵ 1991 a7g⁴ 6v* 6d* 6g 7m³ 7m⁴
6m 6g⁵ 6m⁴ 6v⁴ 6m⁵ 7g⁵ 7g³ 7.1g 7m 7g 7g] quite attractive horse: moderate
mover: won handicaps at Folkestone and Nottingham in spring: effective at 6f and
7f: acts on good to firm and heavy going: suitable mount for inexperienced rider. *C.
J. Benstead.*

ZINGER 3 b.g. Lucky Wednesday 124 – Starkist 81 (So Blessed 130) [1990 a7g* 51
6g a8g⁵ 8.2s 1991 7d* 7m 6d⁶ 6s⁴ 7g⁵ a8g 7m 8m] leggy, quite good-topped gelding:
poor mover: inconsistent plater: led post at Catterick (no bid) in March: should stay
1m: acts on soft going, seems unsuited by top-of-the-ground: has run creditably in
blinkers and visor: sold to join Miss J. Barclay 1,500 gns Doncaster October Sales.
W. J. Pearce.

ZINOVIA (USA) 2 b.f. (Apr 4) Ziggy's Boy (USA) – High Baroque (USA) (Raise 80
A Native) [1991 5g* 5d⁵ 7m³ 5m⁵ 6g⁵ 7m 6g⁶] $8,000Y, resold 11,500Y: leggy,
rather unfurnished filly: second foal: dam ran 6 times: sire (by Danzig) won from 5f
to 7f: modest form at best: won maiden at the Curragh in April: well-beaten second
favourite in 6-runner minor event at Chester next start: mostly out of depth after
running close third in minor event at Naas in July: stays 7f. *K. Prendergast, Ireland.*

ZISKA (USA) 3 gr.f. Danzig (USA) – Heavenly Cause (USA) (Grey Dawn II 132) **87**
[1990 7g³ 1991 8f* 8v⁵ 7m⁶ 7m² 7.6d 8s³] big, lengthy, good-topped filly: moderate
mover: justified favouritism in maiden at Yarmouth in June, edging right: easily best
efforts when placed in handicap at Redcar and minor event at Yarmouth: should
prove better at 1m than shorter: acts on any going: visits Relaunch. *H. R. A. Cecil.*

ZIVANIA (IRE) 3 b.f. Shernazar 131 – Maresca (Mill Reef (USA) 141) [1990 6m³ **101**
6d² 7g² 9.5g* 8d* 8d* 8d* 1991 10g³ 10m² 11g² 12g 11m⁵ 11g⁴ 10s² 11.8g⁴ 13.5g⁶]
IR 12,000Y: lengthy, rather sparely-made filly: closely related to French 1¼m
winners Vanya and Muroto (both by Busted), latter very smart: dam once-raced
half-sister to high-class French middle-distance colts Romildo and Pevero: won
maiden at Dundalk, minor event at Navan and nurseries at Leopardstown and
Gowran Park at 2 yrs: second in listed races at the Curragh in 1991, beaten 3 lengths
by Elfaslah: well beaten in Ribblesdale Stakes at Royal Ascot: ran moderately in
France last 2 outings, trained by N. Clement on first occasion: should stay 1½m:
probably acts on any going: formerly trained by J. S. Bolger in Ireland. *J. Napoli,
France.*

ZLOTY 3 b.c. Elegant Air 119 – Chase Paperchase 79 (Malinowski (USA) 123) —
[1990 5m⁴ 5m³ 6h² 6f² 5g⁶ 6m² 6f* 1991 6m 7g] smallish, sturdy colt: modest
winner at 2 yrs: behind in Newmarket handicaps in spring as 3-y-o, held up pulling
hard on second occasion: should stay 7f: acts on hard ground. *W. Jarvis.*

ZODE 5 b.g. Simply Great (FR) 122 – Star Face (African Sky 124) [1990 8f 8m 8m —
6g⁶ 7g 1991 8g] good-topped, attractive gelding: lightly raced and poor maiden. *G.
Richards.*

ZOMAN (USA) 4 ch.c. Affirmed (USA) – A Little Affection (USA) (King **122**
Emperor (USA)) [1990 8m² 12g 8d* 8f⁵ 8g* 8v³ 1991 8g² 10g* 9m³ 10g² 10d*
10d⁵ 9.7d⁴ 10v³]

Whilst not quite out of the top drawer, Zoman is certainly a good and
most consistent racehorse—there was no more than 7 lb between the best
and the worst of his performances in the latest season, in which he again found
a few too good for him in the top races but managed to pick up pattern events
in Ireland and Scotland, both over a mile and a quarter. Reappearing in the
Trusthouse Forte Mile at Sandown in April, Zoman showed straight away that
he had improved over the winter. Held up initially, he led two furlongs from
home, but, despite running on well, was unable to hold In The Groove in the
last hundred yards, going down by a length. The Group 2 Tattersalls Rogers
Gold Cup at the Curragh three weeks later was only the second occasion on
which Zoman had been asked to race beyond a mile, the other being when he
failed to stay in the Derby. The mile and a quarter proved well within his

*Tattersalls Rogers Gold Cup, the Curragh—
Zoman stays on strongly to win this Group 2 event from Topanoora*

compass as, after leading two and a half furlongs from home, he stayed on strongly to beat Topanoora by four lengths. Zoman ran right up to his best form for minor honours on his next two starts. The Prix d'Ispahan at Chantilly in June is the closest he has come so far to Group 1 success. He finished third to Sanglamore and Priolo, beaten only half a length and a head, having pulled hard when the early pace was modest. Sixteen days later he found Stagecraft three lengths too good in the Prince of Wales's Stakes at Royal Ascot; he moved none too well to post, but that didn't affect his performance as he galloped on resolutely to hold off Terimon for second place. Zoman's second victory came in the fairly weakly-contested Scottish Classic at Ayr in July. Opposed by horses who, in the main, are better over a mile and a half, Zoman set a modest pace, quickened the tempo two furlongs out and comfortably held Corrupt and Karinga Bay, both of whom had swung wide entering the straight. After a two-month break Zoman returned to be campaigned vigorously, being sent far and wide in search of the right opportunity, but a tilt at the Meadow Meats Irish Champion Stakes at Leopardstown proved a bit too ambitious. After leading on the home turn, he was readily outpaced by Suave Dancer, and gradually dropped away to finish fifth of seven. The Ciga Prix Dollar at Longchamp in October offered an easier opportunity, but the race turned out primarily to be a stage for the three-year-old Wiorno. Zoman, awkward at the start, ran respectably to take fourth, two lengths behind third-placed Stagecraft who'd also beaten him at Leopardstown. Zoman's season continued right into November, when, in testing ground at Capannelle in Rome, he finished two and three quarter lengths third of eleven to the mudlark Sikeston in the Premio Roma, the last Group 1 race of the European year.

		Exclusive Native (ch 1965)	Raise A Native
	Affirmed (USA)		Exclusive
	(ch 1975)	Won't Tell You	Crafty Admiral
Zoman (USA)		(b 1962)	Scarlet Ribbon
(ch.c. 1987)		King Emperor	Bold Ruler
	A Little Affection (USA)	(b 1966)	Irish Jay
	(ch 1977)	Chicken Little	Olympia
		(b 1966)	Dashing By

There is little to add to Zoman's pedigree details as described in *Racehorses of 1990*. He is the fourth foal of the smart American sprinter A Little Affection, easily the best of her previous offspring being the Grade 1 Spinaway Stakes runner-up Love And Affection (by Exclusive Era). A tall, lengthy, sparely-made colt, Zoman is effective from a mile to a mile and a quarter, acts on any going with the possible exception of very firm and is effective making the running or held up. Zoman reportedly stays in training and will undoubtedly add to his earnings which already stand at over a quarter of a million pounds. However, if he is to achieve a Group 1 success, it will most likely be gained outside Britain. He would not be out of place in races on turf in North America such as the Arlington Million and the Budweiser International. *P. F. I. Cole.*

ZONDA 3 br.f. Fabulous Dancer (USA) 124 – Oh So Hot (Habitat 134) [1990 6m3 6g* 6m5 1991 8s3 5m* 5.1g2 8g3 8d] leggy, close-coupled filly: tends to look dull in coat: good mover: fairly useful performer: won minor event at Beverley in June: 13 lengths third of 14 to Selkirk in Kempton listed race penultimate start, staying on: stiff task in similar event 5 weeks later: probably stays 1m: acts on good to firm ground: visits Relaunch. *P. F. I. Cole.* **94**

ZONINA (IRE) 3 br.f. Runnett 125 – Captivate 79 (Mansingh (USA) 120) [1990 5g5 5f4 5m2 6m4 5m 6m 1991 5g 5m3 5s 6m2 6g2 6g3 6m 6m2 6m* 5m 6s 6g6 6g 6.1d] well-made filly: plating-class performer: odds on, won 4-runner maiden at Hamilton in July: below form in handicaps last 3 starts: seems better at 6f than 5f: acts on good to firm ground: blinkered 3 times. *R. Hannon.* **54**

ZOOMAR 2 b.f. (May 16) Legend of France (USA) 124 – High Caraval (High Top 131) [1991 5m4 5g 6d a5g] 2,100Y: unfurnished filly: half-sister to several winners, including 2m winner Clwyd Lodge (by Blakeney) and Irish 1¾m winner Carniski (by Nijinsky): dam unraced half-sister to Ribblesdale winner Northern Princess: poor plater: tongue tied down, pulled very hard, hung and ran wide home bend in claimer at Warwick penultimate start: slowly away final one. *B. Palling.* **30**

ZOOM LENS (IRE)   2 ch.f. (Feb 21) Caerleon (USA) 132 – Photo 83 (Blakeney   **61 p**
126) [1991 7m³ 7g⁵] 11,000Y: workmanlike filly: sixth foal: half-sister to 3 winners,
including 3-y-o 11.9f to 14.8f winner Itqan (by Sadler's Wells) and useful sprinter
Quick Snap (by Try My Best): dam 1m and 9f winner, is out of 1000 Guineas second
Photo Flash, a half-sister to Welsh Pageant: promising efforts in large-field maiden
auctions at Leicester (kept on strongly) and Goodwood (6/1 from 7/2, one pace
behind Philidor) in autumn: will improve, particularly at 1m + . *J. L. Dunlop.*

ZOON SAN   2 b.c. (Feb 28) Elegant Air 119 – Linda's Fantasy 108 (Raga Navarro   **58**
(ITY) 119) [1991 5g² 6d³ 7m 7m⁴] smallish, lengthy colt: good mover: fourth foal:
half-brother to fairly useful 3-y-o 9.9f and 1¾m winner Anafi (by Slip Anchor),
winning middle-distance stayer Lindross (by Ardross) and 9f to 10.8f winner
Priceless Fantasy (by Dunbeath): dam won from 6f to 1m: plating-class form in
varied events: badly hampered home turn when keeping-on fourth in nursery at
Thirsk in August final start: will be suited by 1m + : ridden by claimer last 2 starts:
sold 2,800 gns Newmarket Autumn Sales. *J. R. Fanshawe.*

ZUHAL   3 b.f. Busted 134 – Divine Thought 102 (Javelot 124) [1990 NR 1991 9.9f³   **—**
7.1g⁵ 10m⁶ 12.1s] lengthy, angular filly: sister to fair 1¾m winner Field Conqueror
and half-sister to very useful stayer Inde Pulse (by Troy) and Dee Stakes winner
Great Idea (by Great Nephew): dam 1¼m to 12.5f winner, is half-sister to high-class
1969 2-y-o Divine Gift: quite modest maiden: should stay beyond 1¼m: seems not to
act on soft ground: edgy second start: remains in training. *H. Thomson Jones.*

ZUNIL   2 ch.f. (Mar 5) Noalto 120 – Miss Worth 73 (Streak 119) [1991 5g³ 5m* 5g⁴   **56**
5m² a5g³ 5m³ 5d] 1,550Y: neat filly: sixth foal: half-sister to 1m seller winner Inner
Calm (by Jellaby): dam 5f winner: won seller (no bid) at Wolverhampton in May: will
stay 6f: acts on top-of-the-ground and equitrack: sold 1,300 gns Ascot November
Sales. *C. James.*

GENEROUS

TIMEFORM
HORSE OF
THE YEAR

TIMEFORM CHAMPIONS OF 1991

HORSE OF THE YEAR
BEST MIDDLE-DISTANCE HORSE
(RATED AT 139)
GENEROUS (IRE)
3 ch.c. Caerleon – Doff The Derby (Master Derby)
Owner Fahd Salman   Trainer P. Cole

BEST TWO-YEAR-OLD COLT (RATED AT 135)
ARAZI (USA)
2 ch.c. Blushing Groom – Danseur Fabuleux (Northern Dancer)
Owner Mr A. Paulson   Trainer F. Boutin

BEST TWO-YEAR-OLD FILLY (RATED AT 111p)
MIDNIGHT AIR (USA)
2 br.f. Green Dancer – Evening Air (J O Tobin)
Owner Mr M. Poland   Trainer H. Cecil

BEST THREE-YEAR-OLD FILLY (RATED AT 128)
MAGIC NIGHT (FR)
3 b.f. Le Nain Jaune – Pin Up Babe (Prominer)
Owner Hideo Yokoyama   Trainer P. Demercastel

BEST SPRINTER (RATED AT 128)
POLISH PATRIOT (USA)
3 b.c. Danzig – Maria Waleska (Filiberto)
Owner Mr R. Kirstein   Trainer G. Harwood

BEST MILER (RATED AT 129)
SELKIRK (USA)
3 ch.r. Sharpen Up – Annie Edge (Nebbiolo)
Owner Mr G. Strawbridge   Trainer I. Balding

BEST STAYER (RATED AT 125)
TOULON
3 b.c. Top Ville – Green Rock (Mill Reef)
Owner Mr K. Abdulla   Trainer A. Fabre

THE TIMEFORM 'TOP HUNDRED'

Here are listed the 'Top 100' two-year-olds, three-year-olds and older horses in the annual.

Two-Year-Olds

135	Arazi
124p	Rainbow Corner
124p	Seattle Rhyme
122	Cardoun
122	St Jovite
120p	Rodrigo de Triano
119	El Prado
118p	Glaieul
118	Calling Collect
117	Dr Devious
117	Made of Gold
116p	Tertian
116	Litron
116	Mack The Knife
115p	Magic Ring
115	Dilum
114p	Lion Cavern
113p	Bonny Scot
113p	Torrey Canyon
113p	Twist And Turn
113	Captain Horatius
113	River Falls
113	Steinbeck
112	Assessor
111p	Great Palm
111p	Midnight Air
111	Code Breaker
111	Contested Bid
111	Paris House
111	Showbrook
111	Silver Kite
111	Thourios
110p	Hatoof
110	Alhijaz
110	Cristofori
110	Culture Vulture
110	Ninja Dancer
110	Swing Low
110	Young Senor
109p	Alnasr Alwasheek
109p	Casteddu
109p	Marling
109p	Musicale
109	Bradawn Breever
109	Colorific
109	Fair Crack
109	Grand Master
109	Prince Ferdinand
109	Ruhr
108p	Anchorite
108p	Verveine
108	Autocracy
108	Break Bread
108	Mendocino
107p	Pursuit of Love
107	Greek Air
107	Guislaine
107	Mojave
107	Saintry
106p	Aljadeer
106p	Chicmond
106	Jape
106	Kenbu
106	Lady Normandy
105	Governor's Imp
104p	Hypolixo
104p	King's Loch
104p	Mystery Play
104p	Pia Bride
104	Absurde
104	Artic Tracker
104	Basma
104	Bletchley Park
104	Mamma's Too
104	Mougins
104	Sharp Counsel
104	Whittingham
103p	Bezelle
103p	Bold Pursuit
103p	Free Flyer
103p	Lucky Lindy
103p	Soiree
103p	Zaahi
103	Colway Bold
103	Jairzinho
103	Power Lake
103	Tik Fa
103	Wesaam
103?	Regal Scintilla
102p	Rose Indien
102p	Shuailaan
102p	Silver Wisp
102	Secret Thing
102	Stormagain
102	Tamim
102	Taylor Quigley
101	Corals Dream
101	Dedicated Lady
101	Jeune
101	Master of Passion
101	Misaka Togo
101	Nordic Brief
101d	Coffee Ice

Three-Year-Olds

139	Generous
136	Suave Dancer
129	Lomitas
129	Pistolet Bleu
129	Selkirk
128	Environment Friend
128	Magic Night
128	Polish Patriot
127	Marju
127	Second Set
125	Sheikh Albadou
125	Tel Quel
125	Toulon
125?	Mukaddamah
124	Cruachan
124	Hector Protector
124	Lycius
124	Mystiko
123p	Wiorno
123	Kooyonga
123	Pigeon Voyageur
123	Saddlers' Hall
122	Fourstars Allstar
122	Jet Ski Lady
122	Magnificent Star
122	Shadayid
121	Corrupt
121	Danseuse du Soir
121	Eternity Star
121	Sportsworld
121	Star of Gdansk
121	Subotica
120	Caerlina
120	Cudas
120	Desert Sun
120	Martessa
120	Misil
120	Pink Turtle
120	Ristna
120	Sillery
120	Young Buster
120?	Hieroglyphic
119	Arcangues
119	Bog Trotter
119	Brooklyn's Dance
119	Hokusai
119	Shalford
118	Acteur Francais
118	Beau Sultan
118	Divine Danse
118	Gussy Marlowe
118	Lara's Idea
118	Possessive Dancer
118	Sha Tha
118	Treble
117	Crnagora
117	Glity
117	Louve Romaine
117	Runyon
117	Saganeca
117	Temporal
116p	Sleeping Car
116	Approach The Bench
116	Bistro Garden
116	Kotashaan
116	Misty Valley
116	Sardaniya
116	Shamshir
115	Archway
115	Balleroy
115	Deja
115	Dominion Gold
115	Flashfoot
115	Fly Away Soon

115	Ganges	
115	George Augustus	
115	Luchiroverte	
115	Man From Eldorado	
115	Satin Flower	
115	Ski Chief	
114	Crystal Gazing	
114	Favoured Nations	
114	Hundra	
114	Jimmy Barnie	
114	Julie La Rousse	
114	Masslama	
114	Once In My Life	
114	Polemic	
114	Supreme Choice	
114	Third Watch	
114§	Peking Opera	
113p	Perpendicular	
113	Arranvanna	
113	Bright Glow	
113	Fortune's Wheel	
113	Hailsham	
113	La Monalisa	
113	Only Yours	
113	Patricia	
112	Additional Risk	
112	Bufalino	
112	Chicarica	
112	Eileen Jenny	
112	Exit To Nowhere	
112	Irish Shoal	
112	Lady Blessington	
112	Masterclass	
112	Metal Storm	
112	Nine Carat	
112	Opera House	
112	Surrealist	
112	Villandry	
112	Zafadola	

Older Horses

129	Epervier Bleu
127	Stagecraft
126	Polar Falcon
126	Priolo
126	Sanglamore
125	Elbio
125	Miss Alleged
125	Passing Sale
125	Snurge
124	Drum Taps
124	Quest For Fame
124	Rock Hopper
124	Terimon
123	In The Groove
123	Muroto
122p	Keen Hunter
122	Turfkonig
122	Zoman
121	Candy Glen
121	Forty Niner Days
121	Ruby Tiger
121	Sikeston
120	Dear Doctor
120	Kartajana
120	Panoramic

119	Leariva
119	Splash of Colour
119	Turgeon
119	Wajd
118	Further Flight
118	Goofalik
118	Topanoora
117	Bold Russian
117	Colour Chart
117	Erdelistan
117	Green Line Express
117	Sapience
116	Mukddaam
116	Prudent Manner
116	Roman Prose
116	Susurration
115	Arzanni
115	Blyton Lad
115	Boxing Day
115	Dream Talk
115	Feenpark
115	Great Marquess
115	Noble Patriach
115	Ron's Victory
115	Run Don't Fly
115	Zille
114p	Victoire Bleue
114	Antisaar
114	Azzaam
114	Filia Ardross
114	Glorify
114	Karinga Bay
114	Mr Brooks
114	Spritsail
113	Aldbourne
113	Case Law
113	Dolpour
113	Itsabrahma
113	Mardonius
113	Mountain Kingdom
113	Our Account
113	Rami
113	Teamster
112	Echoes
112	Emperor Fountain
112	Hateel
112	Osario
112	Safawan
111+	Morley Street
111	Art Bleu
111	Enharmonic
111	Indian Queen
111	La Grange Music
111	Landyap
111	Montendre
111	Nicholas
111	Norton Challenger
111	Palatial Style
111	Per Quod
111	Savahra Sound
111	Spending Record
111	Warm Feeling
110	Amigo Menor
110	Down The Flag
110	Duke of Paducah
110	Katies First
110	Notley
110	Shambo

110	Trainglot
110§	Spinning
109	Eton Lad
109	Lord Charmer
109	Lucky Guest
109	Pont Aven
109	Snaadee
109	Tidemark

TIMEFORM COMPUTER TIMEFIGURES

Timefigures measure the performance of horses not on their form one against another but in terms of time, in seconds (per five furlongs) faster or slower than a certain fixed standard. The following tables show the best timefigure recorded by the leading horses—judged on time—in each category in 1991. Next to the timefigure is the equivalent timerating in pounds, directly comparable with the Timeform Ratings in this annual volume.

TWO-YEAR-OLDS

1	DR DEVIOUS	−0.79	120
2	CAPTAIN HORATIUS	−0.66	117
3	BONNY SCOT	−0.66	115
4	DILUM	−0.60	115
5	MAGIC RING	−0.60	115
6	RIVER FALLS	−0.53	113
7	GREAT PALM	−0.53	113
8	THOURIOS	−0.53	113
9	LION CAVERN	−0.52	113
10	ANOTHER EPISODE	−0.51	113
11	MIDNIGHT AIR	−0.48	112
12	RODRIGO DE TRIANO	−0.42	111
13	CULTURE VULTURE	−0.40	110
14	YOUNG SENOR	−0.38	110
15	ALJADEER	−0.38	110
16	SHOWBROOK	−0.37	109
17	BASMA	−0.37	109
18	PURSUIT OF LOVE	−0.37	109
19	AUTOCRACY	−0.33	108
20	SONUS	−0.33	108
21	PARIS HOUSE	−0.32	108
22	NINJA DANCER	−0.32	108
23	MUSICALE	−0.31	108
24	TAMIM	−0.28	107
25	MADE OF GOLD	−0.26	107
26	MYSTERY PLAY	−0.23	106
27	ZAAHI	−0.22	106
28	BERSETO	−0.22	106
29	NIFTY FIFTY	−0.21	105
30	LEAD THE DANCE	−0.20	105

THREE-YEAR-OLD SPRINTERS

1	SHEIKH ALBADOU	−0.78	120
2	FOOD OF LOVE	−0.30	108
3	SARCITA	−0.30	108
4	TERRHARS	−0.29	107
5	POLISH PATRIOT	−0.13	103
6	NEVER IN THE RED	−0.11	103
7	SIR HARRY HARDMAN	−0.09	102
8	DIVINE DANSE	−0.06	102
9	DUPLICITY	−0.04	101
10	TRIVIALITY	−0.03	101

THREE-YEAR-OLD MILERS

1	SELKIRK	−0.89	122
2	MYSTIKO	−0.87	122
3	LYCIUS	−0.86	122
4	MARJU	−0.81	120
5	SECOND SET	−0.80	120
6	DESERT SUN	−0.77	119
7	BOG TROTTER	−0.74	119
8	SHADAYID	−0.72	118
9	JIMMY BARNIE	−0.71	118
10	AJAAD	−0.68	117

THREE-YEAR-OLD MIDDLE DISTANCE

1	GENEROUS	−1.41	135
2	ENVIRONMENT FRIEND	−0.92	123
3	SADDLERS' HALL	−0.74	119
4	PEKING OPERA	−0.59	115
5	BROCKETTE	−0.59	115
6	YOUNG BUSTER	−0.59	115
7	CORRUPT	−0.52	113
8	JET SKI LADY	−0.44	111
9	HAILSHAM	−0.42	111
10	JAFFA LINE	−0.42	111

THREE-YEAR-OLD STAYERS

1	TOULON	−0.99	125
2	SADDLERS' HALL	−0.91	123
3	JENDALI	−0.43	111
4	SILVER RAINBOW	−0.41	110
5	LE CORSAIRE	−0.29	107
6	SUPREME CHOICE	−0.25	106
7	PATRICIA	−0.15	104
8	MICHELETTI	−0.12	103
9	MADAGANS GREY	−0.09	102
10	KIYONAGA	0.00	100

OLDER HORSE
SPRINTERS

1	BLYTON LAD	−0.55	114
2	CUMBRIAN WALTZER	−0.51	113
3	ELBIO	−0.35	109
4	POLAR FALCON	−0.35	109
5	BOLD LEZ	−0.27	107
6	NOTLEY	−0.27	107
7	PREMIER TOUCH	−0.26	107
8	LUCEDEO	−0.17	104
9	NORTON CHALLENGER	−0.16	104
10	SNAADEE	−0.16	104

OLDER HORSE
MILERS

1	SIKESTON	−0.86	122
2	TERIMON	−0.72	118
3	RUBY TIGER	−0.65	116
4	NICHOLAS	−0.61	115
5	EMPEROR FOUNTAIN	−0.60	115
6	RAMI	−0.60	115
7	PRIOLO	−0.57	114
8	LANDYAP	−0.56	114
9	DUKE OF PADUCAH	−0.55	114
10	STAPLEFORD MANOR	−0.46	112

OLDER HORSE
MIDDLE DISTANCE

1	SANGLAMORE	−0.98	125
2	STAGECRAFT	−0.96	124
3	ROCK HOPPER	−0.91	123
4	TERIMON	−0.87	122
5	LORD CHARMER	−0.84	121
6	IN THE GROOVE	−0.82	121
7	DRUM TAPS	−0.77	119
8	QUEST FOR FAME	−0.71	118
9	SAPIENCE	−0.67	117
10	TOPANOORA	−0.66	117

OLDER HORSE
STAYERS

1	GREAT MARQUESS	−0.79	120
2	BONDSTONE	−0.47	112
3	TEAMSTER	−0.35	109
4	ARZANNI	−0.34	109
5	SHAMBO	−0.22	106
6	FURTHER FLIGHT	−0.22	106
7	DOUBLE DUTCH	−0.17	104
8	FIRST VICTORY	−0.10	103
9	RETOUCH	−0.09	102
10	SESAME	−0.02	101

1991 STATISTICS (TURF SEASON)

The following tables show the leading owners, trainers, breeders, jockeys, horses and sires of winners during the 1991 turf season, under Jockey Club Rules. The tables are reproduced by permission of *The Sporting Life.*

OWNERS

		Horses	Races Won	Stakes £
1.	Sheikh Mohammed	225	139	1,077,215
2.	Fahd Salman	54	44	982,204
3.	Hamdan Al-Maktoum	162	92	774,215
4.	K. Abdulla	101	71	493,747
5.	Maktoum Al-Maktoum	59	33	467,492
6.	R. E. Sangster	77	54	462,812
7.	The Dowager Lady Beaverbrook	14	11	374,732
8.	George Strawbridge	8	10	312,280
9.	Ecurie Fustok	26	16	288,305
10.	W. J. Gredley	18	4	223,088
11.	David Thompson	21	16	215,209
12.	A. F. Budge (Equine) Limited	36	25	214,081

TRAINERS

		Horses	Races Won	Stakes £
1.	P. F. I. Cole	97	67	1,256,502
2.	R. Hannon	167	126	872,848
3.	M. R. Stoute	123	83	825,838
4.	C. E. Brittain	124	47	717,528
5.	H. R. A. Cecil	126	118	666,918
6.	J. L. Dunlop	105	58	616,645
7.	J. Berry	132	143	602,432
8.	B. W. Hills	119	93	593,593
9.	L. M. Cumani	90	72	574,545
10.	D. R. C. Elsworth	78	37	517,452
11.	J. H. M. Gosden	120	84	452,264
12.	I. A. Balding	79	53	449,789

BREEDERS

		Individ'l Winners	Races Won	Stakes £
1.	Barronstown Stud	8	9	674,665
2.	Swettenham Stud	31	49	396,136
3.	Juddmonte Farms	33	45	394,894
4.	Hesmonds Stud Ltd	13	21	342,183
5.	George Strawbridge	3	5	287,650
6.	Buckram Oak Farm	6	13	271,035
7.	Marystead Farm	3	4	270,278
8.	Stetchworth Park Stud Ltd	5	7	235,652

JOCKEYS

		1st	2nd	3rd	Unpl	Total Mts	Per Cent
1.	Pat Eddery	165	130	76	435	806	20.5
2.	W. Carson	155	130	93	512	890	17.4
3.	M. Roberts	117	109	96	540	862	13.6

		1st	2nd	3rd	Unpl	Total Mts	Per Cent
4.	S. Cauthen	107	79	57	229	472	22.7
5.	A. Munro	103	84	74	478	739	13.9
6.	R. Cochrane	102	103	83	423	711	14.3
7.	L. Dettori	94	91	84	434	703	13.4
8.	J. Carroll	87	75	66	354	582	14.9
9.	T. Quinn	86	78	72	397	633	13.6
10.	D. Holland	79	67	61	339	546	14.5
11.	J. Reid	78	93	74	410	655	11.9
12.	G. Duffield	75	41	59	409	584	12.8

HORSES

		Races Won	Stakes £
1.	Generous 3 ch.c. Caerleon–Doff The Derby	2	631,480
2.	Tel Quel 3 br.c. Akarad–Best Girl	1	262,350
3.	Selkirk 3 ch.r. Sharpen Up–Annie Edge	2	239,605
4.	Environment Friend 3 gr.c. Cozzene–Water Woo	2	217,251
5.	Toulon 3 b.c. Top Ville–Green Rock	2	205,049
6.	Mystiko 3 gr.c. Secreto–Caracciola	3	175,418
7.	Polish Patriot 3 b.c. Danzig–Maria Waleska	3	170,732
8.	Dr Devious 2 ch.c. Ahonoora–Rose of Jericho	4	168,461

SIRES OF WINNERS

		Horses	Races Won	Stakes £
1.	Caerleon (1980) by Nijinsky	15	20	718,301
2.	Green Desert (1983) by Danzig	25	37	330,001
3.	Ahonoora (1975) by Lorenzaccio	18	25	315,772
4.	Night Shift (1980) by Northern Dancer	17	28	303,023
5.	Sharpen Up (1969) by Atan	12	17	292,352
6.	Danzig (1977) by Northern Dancer	18	23	283,629
7.	Sadler's Wells (1981) by Northern Dancer	24	30	267,136
8.	Nureyev (1977) by Northern Dancer	16	26	267,116

FIRST SEASON SIRES OF WINNERS

		Horses	Races Won	Stakes £
1.	Seattle Dancer (1984) by Nijinsky	2	5	161,645
2.	Efisio (1982) by Formidable	5	10	133,796
3.	Tasso (1983) by Fappiano	1	3	82,765
4.	Cyrano de Bergerac (1983) by Bold Lad	9	16	57,138
5.	Midyan (1984) by Miswaki	6	13	42,087
6.	Gone West (1984) by Mr Prospector	2	4	32,200
7.	Risk Me (1984) by Sharpo	7	9	26,830
8.	Sizzling Melody (1984) by Song	4	7	24,759

THE FREE HANDICAPS

TWO-YEAR-OLDS

The following are the weights allotted in the European Free Handicap published on 30th January. The race is to be run over seven furlongs at Newmarket on 15th April, 1992.

	st	lb		st	lb		st	lb
Arazi	9	7	Fair Crack	8	1	Central City	7	11
Rodrigo de Triano	8	13	Guislaine	8	1	Colway Bold	7	11
Cardoun	8	11	Ken de Saron	8	1	Grand Master	7	11
Rainbow Corner	8	11	Lady Normandy	8	1	Harvest Girl	7	11
Seattle Rhyme	8	11	Litron	8	1	Master of Passion	7	11
Dilum	8	9	Mojave	8	1	Poolesta	7	11
El Prado	8	9	Mystery Play	8	1	Red Slippers	7	11
Magic Ring	8	9	Prime Glade	8	1	Regal Scintilla	7	11
Marling	8	9	Prince Ferdinand	8	1	Rose Indien	7	11
St Jovite	8	9	Saintry	8	1	Sahara Star	7	11
Lion Cavern	8	8	Steinbeck	8	1	Balla Jidaal	7	10
Musicale	8	8	Swing Low	8	1	Bit-A-Magic	7	10
River Falls	8	6	Torrey Canyon	8	1	Bletchley Park	7	10
Glaieul	8	6	Twafeaj	8	1	Bobzao	7	10
Made of Gold	8	6	Worldwide	8	1	Feminine Wiles	7	10
Paris House	8	6	Alnasr Alwasheek	8	0	Jape	7	10
Tertian	8	6	Artic Tracker	8	0	Lucky Lindy	7	10
Absurde	8	5	Autocracy	8	0	Mamma's Too	7	10
Calling Collect	8	5	Captain Horatius	8	0	Miss Bluebird	7	10
Culture Vulture	8	5	Casteddu	8	0	Party Cited	7	10
Hatoof	8	5	Colorific	8	0	Rokeby	7	10
Midnight Air	8	5	Freewheel	8	0	Saratoga Source	7	10
Showbrook	8	5	Zinaad	8	0	Sun And Shade	7	10
Silver Kite	8	5	Bonny Scot	7	13	Sunday's Hill	7	10
Basma	8	4	Great Palm	7	13	Whittingham	7	10
Bezelle	8	4	John Rose	7	13	Wilde Rufo	7	10
Code Breaker	8	4	Ninja Dancer	7	13	Bold Pursuit	7	9
Dr Devious	8	4	Power Lake	7	13	Corals Dream	7	9
Kenbu	8	4	Ruhr	7	13	Distinct Thatcher	7	9
Mack The Knife	8	4	Snow Forest	7	13	Enaya	7	9
Cristofori	8	3	Solar Star	7	13	Fern	7	9
Assessor	8	2	Tik Fa	7	13	Kingdom of Spain	7	9
Chicmond	8	2	Cambrian Hills	7	12	Mesaafi	7	9
Twist And Turn	8	2	Coffee Ice	7	12	Night Duty	7	9
Verveine	8	2	Silver Wisp	7	12	Pursuit of Love	7	9
Young Senor	8	2	Storm Ring	7	12	Regal Chimes	7	9
Alhijaz	8	1	Thourios	7	12	Tamim	7	9
Anchorite	8	1	Wolfhound	7	12	Taylor Quigley	7	9
Another Episode	8	1	Aljadeer	7	11			
Fair Cop	8	1	Badie	7	11			

THREE-YEAR-OLDS

5 furlongs plus
126 Polish Patriot
125 Sheikh Albadou
117 Shalford
116 Archway
114 Chicarica
113 Jimmy Barnie
112 Irish Shoal
109 Food of Love
108 Sarcita
108 Sizzling Saga
106 Majlood
106 Persianalli
104 On Tiptoes
104 Title Roll
102 Furajet
102 Haky
102 Medaille d'Or
101 Parios
101 Sir Harry
   Hardman
100 Duplicity
100 Spaniards Close
100 Triviality
100 Vintage Only

7 furlongs plus
128 Selkirk
127 Second Set
125 Mukaddamah
124 Mystiko
123 Kooyonga
123 Lycius
122 Shadayid
118 Bog Trotter
118 Gussy Marlowe
118 Star of Gdansk
115 Hokusai
114 Crystal Gazing
114 Ganges
114 Satin Flower
112 Only Yours
111 Flashfoot

110 Ajaad
110 Desert Sun
110 Dominion Gold
110 Flying Brave
110 Redden Burn
109 Hyabella
109 Radwell
109 Sapieha
109 Volksraad
108 Chipaya
108 Time Gentlemen
107 Fanmore
106 Regal Crest
106 Trojan Crown
105 Cardinal Point
105 Claret
105 Crystal Path
105 Heart of
   Darkness
105 Joli's Princess
105 Sylva Honda
104 Dawson Place
104 Desert Dirham
104 Fair Average
104 Junk Bond
104 Kazoo
104 Pfalz
103 Himiko
103 King Athelstan
103 Rudimentary
103 Suomi
103 Umniyatee
102 Lee Artiste
102 Regal Sabre
102 Zigaura
101 Collide
101 Diamond City
101 Savoyard
100 Green's
   Ferneley
100 Melpomene
100 Soleil
   Dancer

9½ furlongs plus
125 Environment
   Friend
121 Tel Quel
120 Cruachan
117 Young Buster
116 Ristna
112 Perpendicular
111 Man From
   Eldorado
111 Opera House
108 Dartrey
108 Gai Bulga
108 Knifebox
108 Ocean Air
105 Majmu
103 Adversary
103 Hundra
103 Mohican Girl
102 Elfaslah
102 North Wind
102 Prince Russanor
101 Adam Smith
101 Aimaam
101 Jura
101 Red Bishop
101 The Glasha
100 Aptakisic
100 Arokat
100 Circus Light
100 Lovealoch
100 Sharp Imposter
100 Stone Mill

11 furlongs plus
137 Generous
125 Marju
124 Toulon
121 Jet Ski Lady
119 Magnificent Star
117 Corrupt
114 Shaima
113 Shamshir
112 Hailsham

111 Luchiroverte
111 Possessive Dancer
110 Patricia
110 Peking Opera
110 Secret Haunt
110 Surrealist
110 Third Watch
109 Fly Away Soon
109 Jaffa Line
109 Le Corsaire
109 Marcus Thorpe
109 Torchon
107 Always Friendly
107 Half A Tick
107 La Sky
106 Peplum
105 Collins Avenue
104 Brockette
104 Walim
103 Finance Dancer
103 Habaayib
102 Ausherra
102 Conor Lily
102 Kimbers
101 Another Bob
100 Maraakiz
100 Widyan

14 furlongs plus
122 Toulon
119 Saddlers' Hall
108 Supreme Choice
107 Jendali
106 Silver Rainbow
106 Sought Out
105 Jahafil
105 Micheletti
105 Nibbs Point
104 Straldi
103 Arcadian Heights
103 Hieroglyphic
102 Libk

FOUR-YEAR-OLDS AND UPWARDS

5 furlongs plus
124 Polar Falcon
122 Elbio
120 Keen Hunter
116 Green Line
    Express
113 Blyton Lad
112 Case Law
111 Notley
110 Montendre
110 Nicholas
108 Amigo Menor
107 Northern
    Goddess
107 Snaadee
105 Reference Light
102 Gilt Throne
102 Knight of Mercy
102 Premier Touch
101 Rivers Rhapsody
100 Cumbrian
    Waltzer

7 furlongs plus
126 Priolo
120 Zoman
119 Candy Glen
112 Bold Russian

111 La Grange Music
111 Osario
111 Susurration
110 Aldbourne
110 Enharmonic
110 Rami
109 Eton Lad
108 Norton
    Challenger
108 Savahra Sound
107 Landyap
107 Lord Charmer
106 Lifewatch Vision
106 Message Pad
105 Local Lass
104 Sheer Precocity
104 Sky Cloud
103 Sure Sharp
102 Perfolia
102 Swordsmith
101 Military Fashion
101 St Ninian
100 Pontenuovo

9½ furlongs plus
124 Stagecraft
122 Terimon
120 Ruby Tiger

119 Sikeston
116 Goofalik
112 Legal Case
111 Karinga Bay
110 Filia Ardross
108 Palatial Style
107 Emperor
    Fountain
105 Game Plan
103 Northern Hal
102 Power Take Off
100 Lord of Tusmore

11 furlongs plus
124 Sanglamore
123 Quest For Fame
122 Rock Hopper
120 In The Groove
119 Drum Taps
117 Snurge
116 Splash of Colour
116 Topanoora
115 Mukddaam
114 Further Flight
113 Run Don't Fly
113 Spritsail
112 Noble Patriarch
110 Dolpour

110 Tidemark
109 Hateel
108 Azzaam
108 Sesame
105 Spinning
104 Stapleford Manor
102 Sardegna
100 Rudjig
100 Tiger Flower

14 furlongs plus
115 Snurge
113 Arzanni
111 Indian Queen
111 Per Quod
110 Great Marquess
110 Warm Feeling
108 Mountain
    Kingdom
107 Shambo
106 Teamster
103 Morley Street
103 Top of The World
102 Parting Moment
100 Bondstone
100 Nomadic Way
100 Trainglot

INTERNATIONAL CLASSIFICATIONS

The following were published on 9th January, 1992 and contain horses which, during 1991, ran in France, Germany, Great Britain, Ireland or Italy, and were jointly assessed at a rating of 110 or above by the Official Handicappers. Horses racing over different distances and being top rated, are credited with those performances by inclusion in the appropriate division.

TWO-YEAR-OLDS

130 Arazi	115 Glaieul	113 Dr Devious	110 Guislaine
122 Rodrigo de	115 Made of Gold	113 Kenbu	110 Ken de Saron
Triano	115 Paris House	113 Mack The Knife	110 Lady Normandy
120 Cardoun	115 Tertian	112 Cristofori	110 Litron
120 Rainbow Corner	114 Absurde	111 Assessor	110 Mojave
120 Seattle Rhyme	114 Calling Collect	111 Chicmond	110 Mystery Play
118 Dilum	114 Culture Vulture	111 Twist And Turn	110 Prime Glade
118 El Prado	114 Hatoof	111 Verveine	110 Prince Ferdinand
118 Magic Ring	114 Midnight Air	111 Young Senor	110 Saintry
118 Marling	114 Showbrook	110 Alhijaz	110 Steinbeck
118 St Jovite	114 Silver Kite	110 Anchorite	110 Swing Low
117 Lion Cavern	113 Basma	110 Another Episode	110 Torrey Canyon
117 Musicale	113 Bezelle	110 Fair Cop	110 Twafeaj
117 River Falls	113 Code Breaker	110 Fair Crack	110 Worldwide

THREE-YEAR-OLDS

5 furlongs plus	115 Acteur Francais	117 Kotashaan	116 Beau Sultan
126 Polish Patriot	115 Hokusai	117 Sportsworld	116 Sleeping Car
125 Sheikh Albadou	114 Balleroy	117 Young Buster	116 Temporal
117 Shalford	114 Crystal Gazing	116 Louve Romaine	115 Brooklyn's
116 Archway	114 Ganges	116 Ristna	Dance
114 Chicarica	114 Satin Flower	116 Treble	115 Deja
114 Divine Danse	113 Once In My Life	114 Masslama	115 George Augustus
113 Flowing	112 Additional Risk	114 Polemic	115 La Monalisa
113 Jimmy Barnie	112 Julie La Rousse	114 Wiorno	114 Crnagora
112 Irish Shoal	112 Only Yours	113 Lara's Idea	114 Saganeca
111 Exit To Nowhere	111 Flashpoint	112 Perpendicular	114 Shaima
111 Masterclass	111 Gravieres	111 Fabulous	113 Leone
110 Arranvanna	111 Hello Pink	Hostess	113 Shamshir
110 Rufina	111 La Carene	111 Lady Blessington	112 Favoured
110 Ski Chief	111 Nine Carat	111 Man From	Nations
	111 Smooth	Eldorado	112 Hailsham
7 furlongs plus	Performance	111 Opera House	111 Luchiroverte
128 Selkirk	111 Ville d'Amore	110 Fortune's Wheel	111 Possessive
127 Second Set	110 Ajaad	110 Runyon	Dancer
125 Mukaddamah	110 Desert Sun	110 Sardaniya	111 Tao
124 Mystiko	110 Dominion Gold		110 Hondo Mondo
123 Kooyonga	110 Flying Brave	**11 furlongs plus**	110 Patricia
123 Lycius	110 Metal Storm	137 Generous	110 Peking Opera
122 Shadayid	110 Redden Burn	136 Suave Dancer	110 Secret Haunt
121 Hector		131 Lomitas	110 Surrealist
Protector	**9½ furlongs plus**	128 Pistolet Bleu	110 Third Watch
119 Danseuse	132 Suave Dancer	127 Magic Night	110 Villandry
du Soir	125 Environment	125 Marju	110 Zafadola
119 Fourstars Allstar	Friend	124 Toulon	
118 Bog Trotter	121 Subotica	123 Pigeon Voyageur	**14 furlongs plus**
118 Gussy Marlowe	121 Tel Quel	121 Jet Ski Lady	122 Toulon
118 Martessa	120 Cruachan	119 Arcangues	119 Saddlers' Hall
118 Sha Tha	120 Sillery	119 Magnificent Star	
118 Star of Gdansk	118 Caerlina	118 Eternity Star	
117 Misil	118 Glity	117 Corrupt	
116 Bistro Garden	117 Cudas	117 Pink Turtle	

FOUR-YEAR-OLDS AND UPWARDS

5 furlongs plus
124 Polar Falcon
122 Elbio
120 Keen Hunter
116 Green Line
　　Express
114 Roman Prose
113 Blyton Lad
113 Feenpark
112 Case Law
111 Dream Talk
111 Notley
110 Montendre
110 Nicholas
110 Special Power

7 furlongs plus
126 Priolo
120 Zoman
119 Candy Glen
119 Fire The Groom
116 Forty Niner Days
112 Bold Russian
112 Boxing Day
112 Guiza

112 Itsabrahma
112 Mr Brooks
111 La Grange Music
111 Osario
111 Susurration
111 Zille
110 Aldbourne
110 Enharmonic
110 Rami

9½ furlongs plus
124 Stagecraft
122 Terimon
120 Ruby Tiger
119 Kartajana
119 Sikeston
119 Turfkonig
116 Colour Chart
116 Goofalik
116 Leariva
115 Spending Record
114 Muroto
112 Bin Shaddad
112 Legal Case
112 Prudent Manner

111 Karinga Bay
111 Sir Felix
110 Filia Ardross

11 furlongs plus
126 Epervier Bleu
124 Sanglamore
123 Miss Alleged
123 Quest For Fame
122 Rock Hopper
120 In The Groove
120 Passing Sale
119 Dear Doctor
119 Drum Taps
118 Panoramic
118 Wajd
117 Snurge
116 El Senor
116 My Style
116 Splash of Colour
116 Topanoora
115 Mukddaam
114 Erdelistan
114 Further Flight
114 Lights Out

113 Indica
113 Run Don't Fly
113 Spritsail
112 Noble Patriarch
112 Top Waltz
111 Our Account
111 Savoureuse Lady
110 Astico
110 Bateau Rouge
110 Danae de Brule
110 Glorify
110 Silvestro
110 Tidemark

14 furlongs plus
115 Snurge
114 Turgeon
114 Victoire Bleue
113 Arzanni
111 Indian Queen
111 Mardonius
111 Per Quod
110 Great Marquess
110 Warm Feeling

986

IRISH CLASSIFICATIONS

For horses rated 100 or more (95 or more for two-year-olds), which were trained in Ireland in 1991. Horses trained outside Ireland are included if they won, or achieved their rating, in Ireland.

TWO-YEAR-OLDS

118 El Prado	108 Tik Fa	104 Night Duty	98 Portico
118 St Jovite	106 Colway Bold	103 Governor's Imp	97 Affair of State
113 Bezelle	106 Maledetto	103 Mekong	97 Sarastro
110 Fair Crack	106 Poolesta	103 Political Fact	97 Record Sound
110 Swing Low	105 Festive Cheer	103 Via Borghese	97 Top Reality
110 Twafeaj	105 Lucky Lindy	101 Taff's Acre	96 Legal Pressure
109 Autocracy	105 Nordic Brief	100 Fawaayid	96 Misako-Togo
109 Bradawn	105 Safety Tactic	100 Irish Memory	96 Miznah
Breever	105 Thyer	100 Spanish Storm	95 French Flair
109 Colorific	104 Leading Time	99 Northern	95 Ivyanna
108 Fairy Fable	104 Market	Bluebird	95 Rosie's Mac
108 Tarwiya	Booster	98 Cu Na Mara	95 Royal Theatre

THREE-YEAR-OLDS

5 furlongs plus	107 Rimpa	**9½ furlongs plus**	111 Possessive
116 Archway	106 Bufalino	132 Suave Dancer	Dancer
113 Flowing	106 Regal Crest	117 Sportsworld	110 Zafadola
104 Title Roll	106 Thornberry	110 Runyon	108 Retinospora
100 Spring To Light	105 Rinka Das	110 Sardaniya	105 Dowland
	105 Street Rebel	106 Golden Mintage	105 Eileen Jenny
7 furlongs plus	104 Ballyloop	104 Classic Venture	102 Conor Lily
125 Mukaddamah	103 Blue Daisy	102 Elfaslah	101 Often Ahead
123 Kooyonga	103 Umniyatee	102 Sunset Village	100 News Headlines
119 Fourstars Allstar	102 Inishdalla	100 Call Sign	100 Zivania
118 Star of Gdansk	102 Isle of Glass		
112 Additional Risk	102 Rua d'Oro	**11 furlongs plus**	**14 furlongs plus**
112 Julie La Rousse	101 Judicial Wit	137 Generous	102 Muir Station
111 Smooth	101 Nazoo	121 Jet Ski Lady	100 Persian Halo
Performance	100 Gogarty	115 George	100 Roger Ramjet
108 Approach	100 Idle Affair	Augustus	
The Bench	100 Malvernico	112 Favoured	
108 Misty Valley		Nations	

FOUR-YEAR-OLDS AND UPWARDS

5 furlongs plus	115 Spending	**9½ furlongs plus**	**14 furlongs plus**
108 Amigo Menor	Record	120 Ruby Tiger	114 Turgeon
105 Milieu	112 Mr Brooks	112 Prudent Manner	109 Hateel
104 Clean Cut	107 Committed	107 High Pressure	109 Rare Holiday
104 Pharaoh's	Dancer	104 Elementary	103 Coolcullen
Delight	106 Sunset Partner		103 Thetford Forest
103 Anne de	105 Jonjas	**11 furlongs plus**	102 Sleet Skier
Beaujeu	Chudleigh	116 Splash of Colour	101 Breyani
	104 Pre-Eminent	116 Topanoora	
7 furlongs plus	103 Sure Sharp		
120 Zoman	100 Victorious Deed		

SELECTED BIG RACES 1991

Prize money for racing abroad has been converted to £ Sterling at the exchange rate current at the time of the race. The figures are correct to the nearest £.

1   **TRUSTHOUSE FORTE**   1m
    MILE (Gr 2)
£37,818   Sandown   26 April
    In The Groove 4-9-3
      SCauthen **1**
    Zoman (USA) 4-9-4
      TQuinn 1.**2**
    Aldbourne 5-8-11
      LPiggott 2½.**3**
    Bold Russian 4-9-0
      PatEddery 2½.**4**
    Arany 4-9-0 RCochrane 12.5

7/4 Zoman, 15/8 IN THE GROOVE, 10/3 Bold Russian, 13/2 Aldbourne, 50/1 Arany

    Brian Cooper (D. R. C. Elsworth) 5ran
1m42.45 (Good)

2   **PRIX GANAY (Gr 1)**   1¼m 110y
£49,653   Longchamp   28 April
    Kartajana 4-8-13 WMongil ... **1**
    Passing Sale (Fr) 4-9-2
      ELegrix nk.**2**
    Dear Doctor (Fr) 4-9-2
      CAsmussen ¾.**3**
    Sikeston (USA) 5-9-2
      MRoberts ½.4
    Incessant 4-9-2 DBoeuf hd.5
    Panoramic 4-9-2 SCauthen . sh.6
    Muroto 5-9-2 FHead 2.7

9/5 Panoramic, 29/10 KARTAJANA, 31/10 Passing Sale, 36/10 Dear Doctor, 5/1 Sikeston, 16/1 Incessant, 26/1 Muroto

    H. H. Aga Khan (A. de Royer-Dupre)
7ran 2m 18.40 (Good)

3   **GENERAL ACCIDENT**   1m
    1000 GUINEAS STAKES
    (Gr 1) (3y f)
£109,821   Newmarket   2 May
    Shadayid (USA) 9-0
      WCarson **1**
    Kooyonga (Ire) 9-0
      LPiggott 2.**2**
    Crystal Gazing (USA) 9-0
      LDettori 1.**3**
    Once In My Life (Ire) 9-0
      CAsmussen nk.4
    Only Yours 9-0 BRaymond .. hd.5
    Dartrey (Ire) 9-0
      SCauthen 3½.6
    Zigaura (USA) 9-0
      RCochrane 7.7
    Lee Artiste 9-0 TQuinn 3½.8
    Positive Acclaim 9-0
      DNicholls 2½.9
    Cloche d'Or 9-0
      MRoberts ¾.10

Tetradonna (Ire) 9-0 JReid   ½.11
Gentle Aria 9-0
    WRSwinburn 4.12
Silver Braid (USA) 9-0
    JWilliams nk.13
Miranda Jay 9-0 PatEddery 14

4/6 SHADAYID, 6/1 Crystal Gazing, 9/1 Dartrey, 14/1 Kooyonga, 16/1 Zigaura, 18/1 Tetradonna, 20/1 Once In My Life, Silver Braid, 33/1 Miranda Jay, 50/1 Only Yours, 66/1 Lee Artiste, Cloche d'Or, 100/1 Gentle Aria, 150/1 Positive Acclaim

    Hamdan Al-Maktoum (J. L. Dunlop)
14ran 1m38.18 (Good)

4   **GENERAL ACCIDENT**   1m
    2000 GUINEAS STAKES
    (Gr 1) (3y c + f)
£107,994   Newmarket   4 May
    Mystiko (USA) 9-0
      MRoberts **1**
    Lycius (USA) 9-0
      SCauthen hd.**2**
    Ganges (USA) 9-0 FHead 6.**3**
    Generous (Ire) 9-0
      TQuinn 2½.4
    Mukaddamah (USA) 9-0
      LDettori nk.5
    Desert Sun 9-0 PatEddery   1½.6
    Flying Brave 9-0 JReid hd.7
    Hokusai (USA) 9-0
      MKinane 1½.8
    Malvernico (Ire) 9-0
      CRoche 1½.9
    Shalford (Ire) 9-0
      BRaymond sh.10
    Marju (Ire) 9-0 WCarson . 3½ 11
    Bog Trotter (USA) 9-0
      LPiggott 2½.12
    Mujaazif (USA) 9-0
      WRSwinburn 10.13
    Junk Bond 9-0 EMaple 1½.14

6/4 Marju, 13/2 MYSTIKO, 7/1 Desert Sun, 11/1 Bog Trotter, Generous, 14/1 Mukaddamah, 16/1 Ganges, Hokusai, Lycius, 20/1 Mujaazif, 66/1 Flying Brave, Malvernico, 100/1 Junk Bond, Shalford

    The Dowager Lady Beaverbrook (C. E. Brittain) 14ran 1m37.83 (Good)

5   **PRIX HOCQUART (Gr 2)**   1½m
    (3y c + f)
£36,899   Longchamp   5 May
    Pistolet Bleu (Ire) 9-2
      DBoeuf **1**
    Subotica (Fr) 9-2
      TJarnet 1½.**2**

Beau Sultan (USA) 9-2
FHead ¾.3
One To Two (Fr) 9-2
CAsmussen 10.4
Berry (Fr) 9-2 GGuignard ... 10.5
Shotkar (Fr) 9-2 CAubert nk.6

2/5 PISTOLET BLEU and Shotkar, 21/10 Beau Sultan and Berry, 78/10 Subotica, 94/10 One To Two
D. Wildenstein (E. Lellouche) 6ran 2m30.00 (Good to Soft)

6   DUBAI POULE D'ESSAI   1m
      DES POULAINS (Gr 1)
      (3y c)
£100,200   Longchamp   5 May
      Hector Protector (USA) 9-2
      FHead 1
      Acteur Francais (USA) 9-2
      ALequeux hd.2
      Sapieha (Ire) 9-2
      WRSwinburn 4.3
      Orage Noir (USA) 9-2
      TJarnet 5.4
      Crack Regiment (USA) 9-2
      CAsmussen 1.5
      Mousquetaire (USA) 9-2
      CPiccioni 20.6

1/10 HECTOR PROTECTOR and Mousquetaire, 11/2 Crack Regiment, 8/1 Acteur Francais, 12/1 Sapieha, 14/1 Orage Noir
S. Niarchos (F. Boutin) 6ran 1m37.60 (Good to Soft)

7   PRIX LUPIN (Gr 1)   1¼m110y
      (3y c + f)
£49,066   Longchamp   12 May
      Cudas (USA) 9-2 FHead 1
      Suave Dancer (USA) 9-2
      CAsmussen ¾.2
      Bright Glow 9-2
      ALequeux 5.3
      Nine Carat (USA) 9-2
      PatEddery sh.4
      Steamer Duck (USA) 9-2
      GGuignard 2.5
      Arenzano (Fr) 9-2
      DLawniczak 1½.6
      Almendares (USA) 9-2
      LPiggott 5.7

1/10 Suave Dancer, 14/1 Nine Carat, 144/10 CUDAS, 33/1 Steamer Duck, 39/1 Almendares, 40/1 Bright Glow, 58/1 Arenzano
A. E. Paulson (F. Boutin) 7ran 2m11.90 (Good to Soft)

8   DUBAI POULE D'ESSAI   1m
      DES POULICHES (Gr 1)
      (3y f)
£99,404   Longchamp   12 May
      Danseuse du Soir (Ire) 9-2
      DBoeuf 1
      Sha Tha (USA) 9-2
      SCauthen 2.2

Caerlina (Ire) 9-2
LPiggott sh.3
Divine Danse (Fr) 9-2
FHead 2½.4
Zanadiyka (Fr) 9-2
WMongil 3.5
The Perfect Life (Ire) 9-2
CAsmussen 1½.6

3   Only Yours 9-2
      BRaymond nk.7
Isenay (USA) 9-2
AGoldsztejn dist.8
La Carene (Fr) 9-2 ELegrix disq.

La Carene finished fifth, ¾ length behind Divine Danse, but was disqualified and placed last for causing serious interference

2/5 DANSEUSE DU SOIR and Isenay, 74/10 Divine Danse, 77/10 Caerlina, 9/1 The Perfect Life, Zanadiyka, 19/2 Sha Tha, 14/1 La Carene, 24/1 Only Yours
D. Wildenstein (E. Lellouche) 9ran 1m38.60 (Good to Soft)

9   WILLIAM HILL   1¼m110y
      DANTE STAKES (Gr 2)
      (3y)
£69,426   York   15 May
      Environment Friend 9-0
      GDuffield 1
      Hailsham (Can) 9-0
      SCauthen 5.2
      Perpendicular 9-0
      WRyan hd.3
      Commendable (Ire) 9-0
      PatEddery 7.4
      Habaayib 9-0
      WRSwinburn nk.5
      Sea Level (Fr) 9-0 JReid 2½.6
      Peter Davies (USA) 9-0
      LPiggott 10.7
      Bravefoot 9-0 WCarson 8.8

5/2 Peter Davies, 11/4 Perpendicular, 9/2 Hailsham, 6/1 Habaayib, 15/2 Commendable, 11/1 Bravefoot, 20/1 ENVIRONMENT FRIEND, 33/1 Sea Level
W. J. Gredley (J. R. Fanshawe) 8ran 2m12.42 (Good)

10   JUDDMONTE   1m
      LOCKINGE STAKES
      (Gr 2) (3y +)
£40,902   Newbury   17 May
      Polar Falcon (USA) 4-9-0
      LPiggott 1
1*   **In The Groove** 4-9-2
      SCauthen 2.2
      Candy Glen 4-9-5
      EMaple ¾.3
      Air Music (Fr) 4-9-0
      LDettori 4.4

1/2 IN The Groove, 3/1 POLAR FALCON, 7/1 Candy Glen, 20/1 Air Music
D. Thompson (J. E. Hammond) 4ran 1m42.70 (Good to Soft)

11	AIRLIE/COOLMORE	1m
	IRISH 2000 GUINEAS	
	(Gr 1) (3y c + f)	
£121,081	Curragh	18 May

Fourstars Allstar (USA) 9-0
MSmith 1
Star of Gdansk (USA) 9-0
CRoche hd.2
4² **Lycius (USA)** 9-0
SCauthen 6.3
4³ Ganges (USA) 9-0 FHead ¾.4
Street Rebel (Can) 9-0
PVGilson 1.5
Mellaby (USA) 9-0
PatEddery 2.6
Kalahari Prince (Ire) 9-0
LPiggott hd.7
Rinka Das (USA) 9-0
MJKinane ½.8
Approach The Bench (Ire) 9-0
AMunro ¾.9
4 Malvernico (Ire) 9-0
WJSupple 1.10
Golden Mintage (USA) 9-0
PShanahan ½.11
Satrap (Ire) 9-0 SCraine .. 1½.12

Evens Lycius, 6/1 Ganges, 9/1
FOURSTARS ALLSTAR, 10/1 Kalahari
Prince, 12/1 Rinka Das, 14/1 Mellaby,
16/1 Star of Gdansk, 20/1 Golden
Mintage, 25/1 Malvernico, 40/1 Satrap,
50/1 Approach The Bench, Street Rebel
Richard Bomze (L. O'Brien) 12ran
1m38.60 (Good)

12	TATTERSALLS ROGERS	1¼m
	GOLD CUP (Gr 2)	
£38,851	Curragh	18 May
1² **Zoman (USA)** 4-9-1 AMunro . 1
Topanoora 4-8-12 CRoche .. 4.2
2 **Panoramic** 4-9-1
SCauthen 1½.3
Spending Record (USA) 4-8-12
MJKinane 2½.4
Victorious Deed (USA) 4-8-12
SCraine 4.5
Emerald Waters 4-8-9
PShanahan 2.6
Nordic Region 4-8-12
WJSupple 6.7

2/1 ZOMAN, 11/4 Topanoora, 3/1
Panoramic, 8/1 Spending Record,
Victorious Deed, 25/1 Emerald Waters,
33/1 Nordic Region
Fahd Salman (P. F. I. Cole) 7ran
2m07.20 (Good)

13	GOFFS IRISH 1000	1m
	GUINEAS (Gr 1) (3y f)	
£118,446	Curragh	25 May
3² **Kooyonga (Ire)** 9-0
WJO'Connor 1
Julie La Rousse (Ire) 9-0
JPMurtagh 3.2
Umniyatee 9-0 WCarson . 1½.3

Blue Daisy (USA) 9-0
RJGriffiths hd.4
Rua d'Oro (USA) 9-0
LPiggott hd.5
Inishdalla (Ire) 9-0
MJKinane sh.6
Lady Olein (Ire) 9-0
PShanahan 2½.7
Irish Linnet (USA) 9-0
Jean-LucSamyn 2.8
Pastorale 9-0 SCauthen 1½.9
Nordic Soprano (Ire) 9-0
CRoche 5.10
Bold Jessie 9-0
KJManning ¾.11
Himiko (Ire) 9-0
WNewnes sh.12

2/1 Rua d'Oro, 6/1 KOOYONGA, 6/1
Pastorale, Umniyatee, 8/1 Irish Linnet,
11/1 Inishdalla, 16/1 Julie La Rousse, 25/1
Blue Daisy, Himiko, 33/1 Nordic
Soprano, 66/1 Lady Olein, 100/1 Bold
Jessie
Mitsuo Haga (M. Kauntze) 12ran
1m37.20 (Good to Firm)

| 14 | PRIX D'ISPAHAN (Gr 1) | 1m 1f |
| £49,850 | Chantilly | 2 June |
Sanglamore (USA) 4-9-2
PatEddery 1
Priolo (USA) 4-9-2
CAsmussen ½.2
12* **Zoman (USA)** 4-9-2
WCarson hd.3
10³ Candy Glen 4-9-2
LPiggott nk.4
2* Kartajana 4-8-13 WMongil 1.5
2 Sikeston (USA) 5-9-2
MRoberts 2.6
Colour Chart (USA) 4-8-13
SCauthen 2½.7

24/10 Zoman, 5/2 Priolo, 34/10
Kartajana, 44/10 SANGLAMORE, 52/10
Colour Chart, 114/10 Candy Glen, 177/10
Sikeston
K. Abdulla (R. Charlton) 7ran
1m49.90 (Good to Firm)

15	PRIX DU JOCKEY-CLUB	1½m
	LANCIA (Gr 1) (3y c + f)	
£249,252	Chantilly	2 June
7² **Suave Dancer (USA)** 9-2
CAsmussen 1
5² **Subotica (Fr)** 9-2 TJarnet 4.2
7* **Cudas (USA)** 9-2 FHead .. 1½.3
Luchiroverte (Ire) 9-2
MRoberts ¾.4
7³ Bright Glow 9-2 ALequeux ... 1.5
7 Steamer Duck (USA) 9-2
GGuignard sh.6
Justice (Fr) 9-2 PatEddery 3.7

3/5 SUAVE DANCER, 27/10 Cudas,
62/10 Subotica, 10/1 Luchiroverte,
135/10 Justice, 18/1 Steamer Duck, 21/1
Bright Glow

Henri Chalhoub (J. Hammond) 7ran
2m27.40 (Good to Firm)

16	EVER READY DERBY 1½m 10y		
	(Gr 1) (3y c + f)		
£355,000	Epsom	5 June	
4	**Generous (Ire)** 9-0 AMunro ..	**1**	
4	**Marju (Ire)** 9-0 WCarson	**5.2**	
11²	**Star of Gdansk (USA)** 9-0		
	CRoche	7.3	
6*	Hector Protector (USA) 9-0		
	FHead	½.4	
	Hundra (USA) 9-0		
	BRaymond	sh.5	
	Corrupt (USA) 9-0		
	CAsmussen	½.6	
4	Hokusai (USA) 9-0 LPiggott .	4.7	
9²	Hailsham (Can) 9-0		
	SCauthen	6.8	
	Toulon 9-0 PatEddery	½.9	
4*	Mystiko (USA) 9-0		
	MRoberts	7.10	
9*	Environment Friend 9-0		
	GDuffield	10.11	
	Arokat (USA) 9-0		
	PaulEddery	2.12	
4	Mujaazif (USA) 9-0		
	WRSwinburn	30.13	

4/1 Corrupt, Toulon, 5/1 Mystiko, 6/1
Hector Protector, 9/1 GENEROUS, 11/1
Environment Friend, 14/1 Marju, Star of
Gdansk, 25/1 Hokusai, 28/1 Hailsham,
33/1 Mujaazif, 66/1 Hundra, 250/1 Arokat
Fahd Salman (P. F. I. Cole) 13ran
2m34.00 (Firm)

17	HANSON 1½m 10y		
	CORONATION CUP		
	(Gr 1)		
£82,542	Epsom	6 June	
10²	**In The Groove** 4-8-11		
	SCauthen	**1**	
	Terimon 5-9-0 MRoberts ...	**½.2**	
	Rock Hopper 4-9-0		
	WCarson	nk.3	
	Quest For Fame 4-9-0		
	PatEddery	5.4	
	Karinga Bay 4-9-0 BRouse	2.5	
	Spritsail 5-9-0 LPiggott	5.6	
	Sapience 5-9-0		
	WRSwinburn	25.7	

15/8 Rock Hopper, 11/4 Quest For Fame,
7/2 IN THE GROOVE, 6/1 Spritsail, 12/1
Terimon, 33/1 Karinga Bay, Sapience
Brian Cooper (D. R. C. Elsworth) 7ran
2m36.32 (Good to Firm)

18	GOLD SEAL OAKS 1½m 10y		
	(Gr 1) (3y f)		
£147,500	Epsom	8 June	
	Jet Ski Lady (USA) 9-0		
	CRoche	**1**	
	Shamshir 9-0 LDettori	**10.2**	
	Shadayid (USA) 9-0		
	WCarson	¾.3	
	Jaffa Line 9-0 MRoberts	¾.4	

	Magnificent Star (USA) 9-0		
	ASCruz	sh.5	
3	Dartrey (Ire) 9-0 SCauthen ...	2.6	
	Ausherra (USA) 9-0		
	AMunro	7.7	
	Peplum (USA) 9-0		
	PatEddery	3½.8	
	Fragrant Hill 9-0		
	RCochrane	25.9	

Evens Shadayid, 6/1 Shamshir, 7/1
Dartrey, 12/1 Ausherra, Peplum, 14/1
Jaffa Line, 16/1 Magnificent Star, 20/1
Fragrant Hill, 50/1 JET SKI LADY
Maktoum Al-Maktoum (J. S. Bolger)
9ran 2m37.30 (Good to Firm)

19	GRAND PRIX D'EVRY 1½m		
	(Gr 2)		
£34,896	Evry	8 June	
	Wajd (USA) 4-8-8		
	WRSwinburn	**1**	
	Epervier Bleu 4-8-13		
	DBoeuf	2.2	
	Miss Alleged (USA) 4-8-10		
	ELegrix	1½.3	
	Savoureuse Lady 4-8-8		
	TJarnet	nk.4	
	Echoes (Fr) 4-8-8 FHead	½.5	
	Comte du Bourg (Fr) 4-8-13		
	GGuignard	2½.6	
	Franc Bleu Argent (USA) 4-8-9		
	CAubert	15.7	

1/10 Epervier Bleu and Franc Bleu
Argent, 49/10 Miss Alleged, 97/10
WAJD, 138/10 Echoes, 147/10 Comte du
Bourg, 214/10 Savoureuse Lady
Sheikh Mohammed (A. Fabre) 7ran
2m35.59 (Soft)

20	PRIX DE DIANE 1¼m 110y		
	HERMES (Gr 1) (3y f)		
£139,581	Chantilly	9 June	
8³	**Caerlina (Ire)** 9-2 ELegrix	**1**	
	Magic Night (Fr) 9-2		
	ABadel	¾.2	
	Louve Romaine (USA) 9-2		
	DBoeuf	nk.3	
	Masslama (Fr) 9-2		
	WMongil	1½.4	
	Polemic (USA) 9-2		
	PatEddery	½.5	
8²	Sha Tha (USA) 9-2		
	SCauthen	½.6	
	La Monalisa (Fr) 9-2		
	ALequeux	¾.7	
	After The Sun (USA) 9-2		
	ESaint-Martin	½.8	
	Brooklyn's Dance (Fr) 9-2		
	GGuignard	2½.9	
	Kazoo 9-2 WRSwinburn	1.10	
	Treble (USA) 9-2 FHead ...	½.11	
	Gravieres (Fr) 9-2		
	CAsmussen	4.12	
	Ring Beaune (USA) 9-2		
	PBruneau	4.13	

7/5 Brooklyn's Dance and Ring Beaune
and Treble, 21/10 Masslama, 73/10

Gravieres, 87/10 Polemic, 21/2 Kazoo and Sha Tha, 10/1 Louve Romaine, 132/10 CAERLINA, 28/1 La Monalisa, 42/1 After The Sun, 45/1 Magic Night

K. Nitta (J de Roualle) 13ran 2m10.50 (Good to Soft)

21	GRAN PREMIO DI	1½m
	MILANO (Gr 1)	
	(3y + c + f)	
£154,734	Milan	16 June

Snurge 4-9-6 TQuinn 1
Erdelistan (Fr) 4-9-6
  SSoto ¾.2
Bateau Rouge 4-9-6
  OFancera 2½.3
Riverullah (USA) 4-9-6
  ACarboni 1¼.4
Fleeting Wish (USA) 5-9-6
  LSorrentino 2½.5
Teach Dha Mhile 4-9-6
  MBerra 3.6
Kohinoor (Ire) 3-8-6 JCaro .. 12.7
Prorutori (USA) 5-9-6
  AMunro 8
Jung 7-9-6 FJovine 9

1/2 SNURGE, 19/10 Erdelistan, 9/1 Prorutori, 16/1 Fleeting Wish, 23/1 Kohinoor, 26/1 Bateau Rouge, Riverullah, 30/1 Jung, 33/1 Teach Dha Mhile

M. Arbib (P. Cole) 9ran 2m29.80 (Good)

22	QUEEN ANNE STAKES	1m
	(Gr 2) (3y +)	
£54,543	Ascot	18 June

Sikeston (USA) 5-9-8
  MRoberts 1
Rami (USA) 4-9-2
  WCarson hd.2
Fair Average 3-8-6
  WNewnes 3.3
Nayland 5-9-2 SCauthen ... 2½.4
Only Yours 3-8-6
  BRaymond sh.5
Dolpour 5-9-2 TQuinn 1½.6
Zille (Ger) 6-9-5 JReid 3½.7
Bold Russian 4-9-2
  PatEddery 1½.8
Candy Glen 4-9-8 LPiggott ... 1.9
Lord Charmer (USA) 4-9-2
  WRSwinburn 10.10
Suomi (Ire) 3-8-6 LDettori 11

7/2 Bold Russian, Candy Glen, 8/1 Lord Charmer, Rami, 9/1 SIKESTON, Suomi, 10/1 Only Yours, 14/1 Fair Average, 20/1 Nayland, 25/1 Dolpour, 50/1 Zille

Luciano Gaucci (C. E. Brittain) 11ran 1m41.93 (Good)

23	PRINCE OF WALES'S	1¼m
	STAKES (Gr 2) (3y +)	
£58,776	Ascot	18 June

Stagecraft 4-9-3 SCauthen 1
Zoman (USA) 4-9-5
  AMunro 3.2

17² Terimon 5-9-3 MRoberts ... sh.3
17 Karinga Bay 4-9-3
  BRouse 1½.4
Starstreak 4-9-3 TQuinn 3.5
Croupier 4-9-3 RCochrane .. nk.6

6/4 STAGECRAFT, 5/2 Terimon, Zoman, 16/1 Karinga Bay, 33/1 Croupier, 50/1 Starstreak

Sheikh Mohammed (M. R. Stoute) 6ran 2m07.58 (Good)

24	ST JAMES'S PALACE	1m
	STAKES (Gr 1) (3y c + f)	
£121,905	Ascot	18 June

16² Marju (Ire) 9-0 WCarson 1
Second Set (Ire) 9-0
  LDettori hd.2
16 Hokusai (USA) 9-0
  LPiggott 2.3
6² Acteur Francais (USA) 9-0
  SCauthen 1½.4
Sapieha (Ire) 9-0
  WRSwinburn 3.5
Majlood (USA) 9-0
  PatEddery hd.6
Soleil Dancer (Ire) 9-0 JReid . 5.7

7/4 MARJU, 3/1 Acteur Francais, 4/1 Second Set, 9/1 Hokusai, Majlood, 20/1 Sapieha, 33/1 Soleil Dancer

Hamdan Al-Maktoum (J. L. Dunlop) 7ran 1m41.97 (Good)

25	COVENTRY STAKES	6f
	(Gr 3) (2y)	
£27,648	Ascot	18 June

Dilum (USA) 8-13 AMunro 1
Dr Devious (Ire) 8-13
  PatEddery 3.2
Casteddu 8-13 ASCruz 1½.3
Computer Kid 8-13
  KFallon 3½.4
Showbrook (Ire) 8-13
  BRaymond 3.5
Tenacity 8-13 WCarson 2.6
Wilde Rufo 8-13 LDettori 2.7
Combination 8-13
  DeanMcKeown ¾.8
Master Planner 8-13
  TQuinn nk.9
Windpower (Ire) 8-13
  JCarroll 1½.10
Sylvan Sabre (Ire) 8-13
  JWilliams 3.11
Elton Ledger (Ire) 8-13
  LPiggott 2.12
Spanish Storm (Ire) 8-13
  PaulEddery nk.13
Amadeus Aes 8-13 NDay 7.14

11/10 DILUM, 9/2 Dr Devious, 5/1 Showbrook, 12/1 Sylvan Sabre, 16/1 Combination, 25/1 Wilde Rufo, Windpower, 33/1 Spanish Storm, Tenacity, 40/1 Casteddu, 66/1 Amadeus Aes, Computer Kid, Elton Ledger, Master Planner

Fahd Salman (P. F. I. Cole) 14ran
1m15.99 (Good)

26 CORONATION STAKES 1m
(Gr 1) (3y f)

£117,367   Ascot   19 June

13*	**Kooyonga (Ire)** 9-0	
	WJO'Connor	1
	Shadayid (USA) 9-0	
	WCarson	¾.2
	Gussy Marlowe 9-0	
	MRoberts	1½.3
8*	Danseuse du Soir (Ire) 9-0	
	DBoeuf	nk.4
3³	Crystal Gazing (USA) 9-0	
	LDettori	2.5
	Arranvanna 9-0 AMunro ...	3½.6
	Sumonda 9-0 GCarter	4.7
3	Silver Braid (USA) 9-0	
	JWilliams	5.8

9/4 Shadayid, 3/1 KOOYONGA, 10/3
Danseuse du Soir, 6/1 Crystal Gazing,
10/1 Gussy Marlowe, 25/1 Arranvanna,
66/1 Silver Braid, 100/1 Sumonda
    Mitsuo Haga (M. Kauntze) 8ran
1m42.54 (Good)

27 CORK AND ORRERY 6f
STAKES (Gr 3) (3y +)

£39,297   Ascot   20 June

	Polish Patriot (USA) 3-8-2	
	RCochrane	1
	Chicarica (USA) 3-8-3	
	WCarson	sh.2
	Montendre 4-8-10	
	WNewnes	1½.3
	Jimmy Barnie 3-8-10 JReid ..	nk.4
	Osario 4-8-10 BRaymond ..	2½.5
	The Auction Bidder 4-8-10	
	SPerks	1½.6
	Heard A Whisper 3-8-2	
	PaulEddery	¾.7
	La Grange Music 4-8-10	
	WRSwinburn	¾.8
3	Cloche d'Or 3-8-3	
	MRoberts	¾.9
	Anjiz (USA) 3-8-2	
	JFortune	nk.10
13	Inishdalla (Ire) 3-7-13	
	GCarter	nk.11
	Duplicity (Ire) 3-8-2	
	AMcGlone	hd.12
	Green Line Express (USA) 5-9-4	
	ASCruz	nk.13
	Dominio (Ire) 3-7-13	
	AMunro	nk.14
	Reference Light (USA) 4-8-10	
	PatEddery	3½.15
	Sharp N' Early 5-9-4	
	LDettori	7.16

5/1 Green Line Express, POLISH
PATRIOT, 6/1 Chicarica, La Grange
Music, 13/2 Inishdalla, 10/1 Reference
Light, 16/1 Osario, 20/1 Cloche d'Or,
Heard A Whisper, Jimmy Barnie, 25/1
Anjiz, Dominio, 50/1 Duplicity,

Montendre, Sharp N'Early, 100/1 The
Auction Bidder
    R. A. Kirstein (G. Harwood) 16ran
1m13.73 (Good to Firm)

28 GOLD CUP (Gr 1) 2½m

£108,108   Ascot   20 June

	Indian Queen 6-8-13	
	WRSwinburn	1
	Arzanni 4-9-0 LDettori	nk.2
	Warm Feeling 4-9-0	
	MHills	3½.3
	Trainglot 4-9-0 WCarson	nk.4
	Teamster 5-9-2	
	PatEddery	1½.5
	Retouch 5-9-2 TQuinn	hd.6
	Double Dutch 7-8-13	
	WNewnes	2½.7
	Ethan Frome (Fr) 4-9-0	
	ALequeux	2½.8
	Shambo 4-9-0 MRoberts	2.9
	Top of The World 4-9-0	
	AMunro	25.10
	Per Quod (USA) 6-9-2	
	BRaymond	2.11
	Crack 4-9-0 SCauthen	12

13/8 Arzanni, 5/1 Trainglot, 7/1
Teamster, 8/1 Warm Feeling, 12/1
Crack, 14/1 Per Quod, Shambo, 16/1 Top
of The World, 25/1 Double Dutch,
INDIAN QUEEN, Retouch, 66/1 Ethan
Frome
    Sir Gordon Brunton (Lord
Huntingdon) 12ran 4m23.90 (Good)

29 HARDWICKE STAKES 1½m
(Gr 2)

£58,299   Ascot   21 June

17³	**Rock Hopper** 4-8-12	
	PatEddery	1
12²	**Topanoora** 4-8-9 CRoche	2
17	**Spritsail** 5-8-9 WCarson ...	1½.3
2³	Duke of Paducah (USA) 4-8-9	
	RCochrane	3.4
	Dear Doctor (Fr) 4-8-12	
	LPiggott	nk.5
	Sesame 6-8-9 WRSwinburn ..	1.6
22	Dolpour 5-8-9 SCauthen	1.7
	Game Plan 4-8-9 MRoberts ...	6.8
	Down The Flag (USA) 4-8-9	
	BRaymond	½.9

Topanoora finished first, a short head in
front, but was demoted to second for
causing interference to Rock Hopper

5/6 ROCK HOPPER, 7/1 Dear Doctor,
Spritsail, 8/1 Topanoora, 12/1 Down
The Flag, 20/1 Game Plan, 25/1
Dolpour, Duke of Paducah, Sesame
    Maktoum Al-Maktoum (M. R.
Stoute) 9ran 2m30.20 (Good to Firm)

30 KING'S STAND STAKES 5f
(Gr 2) (3y +)

£57,101   Ascot   21 June

	Elbio 4-9-3 SCauthen	1

Irish Shoal (USA) 3-8-10
JReid 3.2
Archway (Ire) 3-8-10
LPiggott ½.3
Furajet (USA) 3-8-7
PatEddery 3.4
Rufina (USA) 3-8-7
LDettori 2.5
Rivers Rhapsody 4-9-0
JWilliams hd.6
Poyle George 6-9-3
WCarson 2.7
Tigani 5-9-3 MRoberts sh.8
Line Engaged (USA) 3-8-10
TQuinn hd.9
Boozy 4-9-0 RFox 3½.10

13/8 ELBIO, 11/4 Archway, 7/1 Rufina,
14/1 Line Engaged, Rivers Rhapsody,
16/1 Furajet, Irish Shoal, 20/1 Boozy,
33/1 Poyle George, Tigani
   Brian Brackpool (P. J. Makin) 10ran
1m01.40 (Good to Firm)

31   GRAND PRIX DE PARIS   1¼m
      LOUIS VUITTON (Gr 1)
      (3y c + f)
£151,363   Longchamp   23 June
15²   **Subotica (Fr)** 9-2 TJarnet 1
      Sillery (USA) 9-2 FHead .. nk.2
      Kotashaan (Fr) 9-2
      GGuignard 2.3
15³   Cudas (USA) 9-2 GMosse ... sn.4
20³   Louve Romaine (USA) 8-13
      PatEddery ¾.5
      Balleroy (USA) 9-2
      ELegrix sh.6
20   Masslama (Fr) 8-13
      WMongil 2.7
5   Shotkar (Fr) 9-2 CAubert 3.8
      Idle Son (USA) 9-2
      PBruneau 20.9

19/10 Cudas, 27/10 SUBOTICA, 42/10
Masslama, 9/2 Idle Son and Sillery, 74/10
Louve Romaine and Shotkar, 10/1
Balleroy, 134/10 Kotashaan
   O. Lecerf (A. Fabre) 9ran 2m05.20
(Good to Soft)

32   BUDWEISER IRISH   1½m
      DERBY (Gr 1) (3y c + f)
£336,239   Curragh   30 June
16*   **Generous (Ire)** 9-0 AMunro .. 1
15*   **Suave Dancer (USA)** 9-0
      WRSwinburn 3.2
16³   Star of Gdansk (USA) 9-0
      CRoche 8.3
      Sportsworld (USA) 9-0
      LPiggott 2.4
      Nordic Admirer (Ire) 9-0
      WJSwinburn dist.5
      Barry's Run (Ire) 9-0
      KJManning dist.6

Evens GENEROUS, 9/4 Suave Dancer,
10/3 Sportsworld, 12/1 Star of Gdansk,
150/1Nordic Admirer, 300/1 Barry's Run

Fahd Salman (P. F. I. Cole) 6ran
2m33.30 (Good)

33   GRAND PRIX DE   1½m
      SAINT-CLOUD (Gr 1)
      (3y + c + f)
£151,057   Saint-Cloud   30 June
19²   **Epervier Bleu** 4-9-8
      DBoeuf 1
29*   **Rock Hopper** 4-9-8
      PatEddery 3.2
2²   **Passing Sale (Fr)** 4-9-8
      GMosse ¾.3
19³   Miss Alleged (USA) 4-9-5
      ELegrix 1.4
12³   Panoramic 4-9-8 TJarnet ns.5
19   Echoes (Fr) 4-9-5 FHead ½.6
      Turgeon (USA) 5-9-8
      ASCruz 2.7
19*   Wajd (USA) 4-9-5
      SCauthen ½.8
      Danae de Brule (Fr) 4-9-5
      GGuignard hd.9
      Wayfaring (Ire) 4-9-8
      SGuillot nk.10
16   Hundra (USA) 3-8-9
      BRaymond 10.11
19   Franc Bleu Argent (USA) 4-9-8
      CAubert 15.12

3/5 EPERVIER BLEU and Franc Bleu
Argent, 3/1 Rock Hopper, 5/1
Panoramic and Wajd and Wayfaring,
10/1 Passing Sale, 13/1 Miss Alleged,
20/1 Turgeon, 42/1 Danae de Brule,
64/1 Echoes
   D. Wildenstein (E. Lellouche) 12ran
2m28.10 (Good to Firm)

34   CORAL-ECLIPSE   1¼m
      STAKES (Gr 1) (3y +)
£147,825   Sandown   6 July
16   **Environment Friend** 3-8-10
      GDuffield 1
23*   **Stagecraft** 4-9-7
      SCauthen hd.2
14*   **Sanglamore (USA)** 4-9-7
      PatEddery 7.3
17*   In The Groove 4-9-4
      RCochrane nk.4
23³   Terimon 5-9-7 MRoberts 2.5
24*   Marju (Ire) 3-8-10
      WCarson 10.6
      Green's Ferneley (Ire) 3-8-10
      WRSwinburn 15.7

2/1 Stagecraft, 3/1 In The Groove,
Marju, 7/2 Sanglamore, 14/1 Terimon,
28/1 ENVIRONMENT FRIEND, 500/1
Green's Ferneley
   W. J. Gredley (J. R. Fanshawe) 7ran
2m07.61(Good to Soft)

35   CARROLL   6f
      FOUNDATION JULY
      CUP (Gr 1) (3y +)
£115,254   Newmarket   11 July
27*   **Polish Patriot (USA)** 3-8-13
      RCochrane 1

994

11³ **Lycius (USA)** 3-8-13
SCauthen 2.2
30* **Elbio** 4-9-6 WRSwinburn ... ½.3
10* Polar Falcon (USA) 4-9-6
LPiggott 1½.4
27² Chicarica (USA) 3-8-10
WCarson 1½.5
Exit To Nowhere (USA) 3-8-13
FHead sh.6
24 Majlood (USA) 3-8-13
PatEddery hd.7
Time Gentlemen 3-8-13
JReid 1½.8

5/2 Elbio, 11/4 Lycius, 6/1 Chicarica,
POLISH PATRIOT, 9/1 Majlood, 12/1
Exit To Nowhere, Polar Falcon, 33/1
Time Gentlemen
R. A. Kirstein (G. Harwood) 8ran
1m 12.98 (Good to Firm)

36   PRIX DE RIS-ORANGIS   6f
    (Gr 3) (3y +)
£20,060   Evry   11 July
8 **Divine Danse (Fr)** 3-8-13
GGuignard 1
Roman Prose 6-9-4
MdeSmyter 1.2
Bourgogne 3-9-0 GMosse ... 2.3
Noble Kara (Fr) 4-8-9
TJarnet 6.4
30³ Archway (Ire) 3-9-0
WMongil 2½.5
Katies First (USA) 4-8-13
GDubroeucq sh.6
30² Irish Shoal (USA) 3-8-11
ELegrix 2½.7
Prebend (USA) 3-8-8
ALequeux nk.8
Luring (USA) 4-8-9
ESaint-Martin sh.9

7/10 DIVINE DANSE, 5/1 Irish Shoal,
72/10 Archway, 87/10 Noble Kara, 9/1
Bourgogne, 129/10 Roman Prose, 168/10
Prebend, 185/10 Luring
Ecurie Aland (Mme C. Head) 9ran
1m 10.40 (Good)

37   KILDANGAN STUD   1½m
    IRISH OAKS (Gr 1) (3y f)
£110,182   Curragh   13 July
Possessive Dancer 9-0
SCauthen 1
18* **Jet Ski Lady (USA)** 9-0
CRoche ½.2
Eileen Jenny (Ire) 9-0
JPMurtagh 3.3
Often Ahead (Ire) 9-0
SCraine 2.4
13² Julie La Rousse (Ire) 9-0
LPiggott nk.5
20 Polemic (USA) 9-0
PatEddery 2.6
18 Jaffa Line 9-0 BRaymond ... 2½.7
Be A Honey 9-0 MJKinane .. ¾.8
Third Watch 9-0 JReid 2.9
Trescalini (Ire) 9-0
WJSupple 5.10

7/4 Jet Ski Lady, 2/1 Third Watch, 11/2
Polemic, 8/1 POSSESSIVE DANCER,
12/1 Eileen Jenny, 16/1 Julie La Rousse,
20/1 Jaffa Line, 100/1 Be A Honey,
Trescalini, 150/1 Often Ahead
Sheikh Ahmed Al-Maktoum (A. A.
Scott) 10ran 2m31.10 (Good to Firm)

38   PRIX ROBERT PAPIN   5f110y
    (Gr 2) (2y c + f)
£34,861   Maisons-Laffitte   21 July
Arazi (USA) 8-11 GMosse 1
25 **Showbrook (Ire)** 8-11
BRaymond 1½.2
Steinbeck (USA) 8-11
SCauthen 3.3
Night Duty (Ire) 8-11
PatEddery 2.4
Palomelle (Fr) 8-9
GDubroeucq 8.5
Mendocino (USA) 8-11
CPiccioni 8.6

4/5 ARAZI and Mendocino, 13/10
Steinbeck, 4/1 Showbrook, 83/10 Night
Duty, 20/1 Palomelle
A. E. Paulson (F. Boutin) 6ran
1m05.50 (Good)

39   PRIX MAURICE DE   1½m 110y
    NIEUIL (Gr 2) (3y +)
£39,840   Maisons-Laffitte   21 July
16 **Toulon** 3-8-5 PatEddery 1
29² **Topanoora** 4-9-0
SCauthen 2.2
Our Account (USA) 7-9-2
DBoeuf 3.3
Top Waltz (Fr) 4-9-4
ELegrix nk.4
Strike Oil (Fr) 3-8-5
ALequeux 3.5
Marcus Thorpe (USA) 3-8-4
BRaymond 10.6
33³ Passing Sale (Fr) 4-9-4
GMosse 4.7
19 Comte du Bourg (Fr) 4-9-4
GGuignard 15.8
29 Sesame 6-9-1 GHind ½.9

6/4 Topanoora, 26/10 Passing Sale, 4 1/10
TOULON, 6/1 Top Waltz, 21/1 Our
Account, Strike Oil, 23/1 Comte du
Bourg, 31/1 Marcus Thorpe, 56/1
Sesame
K. Abdulla (A. Fabre) 9ran 2m30.60
(Good)

40   KING GEORGE VI AND   1½m
    QUEEN ELIZABETH
    DIAMOND STAKES
    (Gr 1) (3y +)
£276,480   Ascot   27 July
32* **Generous (Ire)** 3-8-9
AMunro 1
34³ **Sanglamore (USA)** 4-9-7
PatEddery 7.2
33² **Rock Hopper** 4-9-7
BRaymond 1.3

34	Terimon 5-9-7 MRoberts .. 1½.4
17	Sapience 5-9-7 WCarson 2.5
	Saddlers' Hall (Ire) 3-8-9
	LPiggott 3½.6
15	Luchiroverte (Ire) 3-8-9
	LDettori 10.7
	Tiger Flower 4-9-4
	SCauthen 15.8
16	Hailsham (Can) 3-8-9
	RCochrane 30.9

4/6 GENEROUS, 6/1 Saddlers' Hall, 7/1
Sanglamore, 8/1 Rock Hopper, 18/1
Terimon, 25/1 Tiger Flower, 40/1
Sapience, 66/1 Luchiroverte, 100/1
Hailsham

Fahd Salman (P. F. I. Cole) 9ran
2m28.99 (Good to Firm)

41	SUSSEX STAKES (Gr 1)	1m
	(3y +)	
£108,580	Goodwood	31 July
24²	**Second Set (Ire)** 3-8-13	
	LDettori 1
	Shadayid (USA) 3-8-10	
	WCarson 1½.2
14²	**Priolo (USA)** 4-9-7	
	FHead sh.3
22*	Sikeston (USA) 5-9-7	
	PatEddery 3.4
	Radwell 3-8-13 GDuffield 5.5
32³	Star of Gdansk (USA) 3-8-13	
	CRoche 3.6
27	Green Line Express (USA) 5-9-7	
	ASCruz ½.7
16	Mystiko (USA) 3-8-13	
	MRoberts nk.8

9/4 Shadayid, 9/2 Mystiko, 5/1 SECOND
SET, 6/1 Priolo, 13/2 Star of Gdansk, 12/1
Green Line Express, 14/1 Sikeston, 25/1
Radwell

Richard L. Duchossois (L. M.
Cumani) 8ran 1m40.53 (Good)

42	DICKINS & JONES	2m
	GOODWOOD CUP (Gr 3)	
	(3y +)	
£37,994	Goodwood	1 August
	Further Flight 5-9-0 MHills .. 1
	Great Marquess 4-9-5
	PatEddery 1.2
28	**Shambo** 4-9-0 MRoberts hd.3
	Silver Rainbow 3-7-13
	WCarson sh.4
	Mountain Kingdom (USA) 7-9-7
	SCauthen 4.5
	First Victory 5-9-0
	BRouse 1½.6
	Secret Waters 4-8-11
	JReid 1½.7
	Criminal Law 4-9-0
	SPerks 1½.8
	Shahi (USA) 3-7-13 WRyan ... 2.9
	Play Games (USA) 3-7-13
	PaulEddery 30.10

3/1 Great Marquess, 4/1 Shahi, 9/2
FURTHER FLIGHT, Silver Rainbow,

10/1 Shambo, 11/1 Mountain Kingdom,
12/1 First Victory, 20/1 Secret Waters,
33/1 Criminal Law, 50/1 Play Games

S. Wingfield Digby (B. W. Hills) 10ran
3m28.69 (Good)

43	VODAFONE NASSAU	1¼m
	STAKES (Gr 2)	
	(3y + f + m)	
£50,335	Goodwood	3 August
	Ruby Tiger 4-9-4 TQuinn 1
18²	**Shamshir** 3-8-6 LDettori 7.2
	North Wind (Ire) 3-8-6	
	WCarson 3½.3
26³	Gussy Marlowe 3-8-6	
	RCochrane nk.4
	Filia Ardross 5-9-1 JReid 4.5
	Lilian Bayliss (Ire) 3-8-6	
	PatEddery 8.6

9/4 Gussy Marlowe, 11/4 RUBY TIGER,
6/1 Lilian Bayliss, 12/1 Filia Ardross, 16/1
North Wind

Mrs Phillip Blacker (P. F. I. Cole) 6ran
2m08.71 (Good)

44	PRIX D'ASTARTE (Gr 2)	1m
	(3y + f)	
£25,050	Deauville	3 August
	Leariva (USA) 4-9-3	
	ALequeux 1
	Crystal Path (Fr) 3-8-7	
	ASCruz 1.2
3	**Once In My Life (Ire)** 3-8-10	
	CAsmussen nk.3
14	Colour Chart (USA) 4-9-3	
	SCauthen sh.4
8	La Carene (Fr) 3-8-10	
	ELegrix 1.5
	Belle Bleue 3-8-7 DBoeuf . snk.6
20	Gravieres (Fr) 3-8-7	
	WMongil ½.7
	Trojan Crown (Ire) 3-8-7	
	GCarter 1½.8
	Ville d'Amore (USA) 3-8-7	
	FHead ½.9
	Massaraat (USA) 3-8-7	
	TJarnet 2.0
	Verica (USA) 3-8-7 GMosse 0
	Pfalz 3-8-7 PaulEddery 0

19/10 Colour Chart and Massaraat, 31/10
Ville d'Amore, 33/10 Once In My Life,
7/2 Verica, 73/10 Gravieres, 95/10 La
Carene, 126/10 Belle Bleue, 19/1 Pfalz,
26/1 Crystal Path, 29/1 LEARIVA,
Trojan Crown

Baron T. de Zuylen de Nyevelt (D.
Smaga) 12ran 1m37.20 (Good)

45	PRIX DU HARAS DE	1m
	FRESNAY-LE-BUFFARD	
	JACQUES LE MAROIS	
	(Gr 1) (3y +)	
£100,402	Deauville	11 August
16	**Hector Protector (USA)** 3-8-9
	FHead 1
35²	**Lycius (USA)** 3-8-9
	SCauthen ns.2

26	**Danseuse du Soir (Ire)** 3-8-6	
	DBoeuf	sh.**3**
35	Polar Falcon (USA) 4-9-2	
	CAsmussen	½.4
41[3]	Priolo (USA) 4-9-2	
	ALequeux	sh.5
44[3]	Once In My Life (Ire) 3-8-6	
	ELegrix	¾.6
11	Ganges (USA) 3-8-9	
	GMosse	1.7
31[2]	Sillery (USA) 3-8-9	
	GGuignard	1½.8
24	Acteur Francais (USA) 3-8-9	
	TJarnet	2.9
6	Mousquetaire (USA) 3-8-9	
	PBruneau	20.10

4/5 HECTOR PROTECTOR and Mousquetaire, 36/10 Priolo, 84/10 Lycius, 17/2 Acteur Francais, 9/1 Danseuse du Soir, Polar Falcon, 19/2 Sillery, 13/1 Ganges, 23/1 Once In My Life

S Niarchos (F. Boutin) 10ran 1m39.40 (Good)

46	DESMOND STAKES	1m
	(Gr 3) (3y +)	
£13,068	Curragh	17 August
41	**Star of Gdansk (USA)** 3-8-12	
	CRoche	1
32	**Sportsworld (USA)** 3-9-1	
	LPiggott	nk.2
11	**Approach The Bench (Ire)**	
	3-9-1 MJKinane	2½.3
	Lifewatch Vision 4-9-3	
	KFallon	3.4
	Mubadir (USA) 3-8-8	
	RJGriffiths	nk.5
	Jonjas Chudleigh 4-9-3	
	DVSmith	nk.6

4/5 Sportsworld, 5/2 STAR OF GDANSK, 8/1 Approach The Bench, Lifewatch Vision, 12/1 Mubadir, 16/1 Jonjas Chudleigh

Henryk De Kwiatkowski (J. S. Bolger) 6ran 1m36.30 (Good to Firm)

47	PRIX KERGORLAY	1m7f
	(Gr 2) (3y +)	
£25,100	Deauville	17 August
33	**Turgeon (USA)** 5-9-9	
	CAsmussen	1
42*	**Further Flight** 5-9-7	
	MHills	2
	Le Pommier d'Or 3-8-7	
	MBoutin	1.3
	Sundar 4-9-4 ALequeux	1½.4
	Luynes (USA) 3-8-7	
	TJarnet	1½.5
42	Mountain Kingdom (USA) 7-9-4	
	SCauthen	nk.6
28	Trainglot 4-9-4 WMongil	10.7
42[2]	Great Marquess 4-9-7	
	ELegrix	5.8
28	Ethan Frome (Fr) 4-9-4	
	FHead	1½.9

29	Duke of Paducah (USA) 4-9-4	
	RCochrane	1½.10
39[3]	Our Account (USA) 7-9-7	
	DBoeuf	sh.11
	Diner's Time (Fr) 4-9-4	
	GMosse	10.12

Further Flight finished first, a head in front, but was demoted to second for causing interference to Turgeon

17/10 TURGEON, 48/10 Further Flight, 58/10 Great Marquess, 62/10 Trainglot, 97/10 Luynes, 10/1 Le Pommier d'Or, 135/10 Sundar, 137/10 Diner's Time, Our Account, 14/1 Duke of Paducah, 27/1 Ethan Frome, 29/1 Mountain Kingdom

G. Strawbridge (J. E. Pease) 12ran 3m15.20 (Good)

48	PRIX MORNY AGENCE	6f
	FRANCAISE (Gr 1)	
	(2y c + f)	
£100,402	Deauville	18 August
38*	**Arazi (USA)** 8-11 GMosse	1
	Kenbu (Fr) 8-8 FHead	3.2
	Lion Cavern (USA) 8-11	
	SCauthen	¾.3
	Calling Collect (USA) 8-11	
	DBoeuf	2.4

1/2 ARAZI, 22/10 Lion Cavern, 24/10 Kenbu, 71/10 Calling Collect

A. E. Paulson (F. Boutin) 4ran 1m 13.30 (Good)

49	JUDDMONTE	1¼m85y
	INTERNATIONAL	
	STAKES (Gr 1) (3y +)	
£144,407	York	20 August
40	**Terimon** 5-9-6 MRoberts	1
17	**Quest For Fame** 4-9-6	
	PatEddery	2.2
34[2]	**Stagecraft** 4-9-6	
	SCauthen	3½.3
39[2]	Topanoora 4-9-6 LPiggott	hd.4
34*	Environment Friend 3-8-12	
	GDuffield	8.5
4	Mukaddamah (USA) 3-8-12	
	WCarson	3.6

5/6 Stagecraft, 3/1 Environment Friend, 11/2 Quest For Fame, 14/1 Topanoora, 16/1 Mukaddamah, TERIMON

The Dowager Lady Beaverbrook (C. E. Brittain) 6ran 2m 16.18 (Good)

50	GREAT VOLTIGEUR	1m3f195y
	STAKES (Gr 2) (3y c + g)	
£43,281	York	20 August
16	**Corrupt (USA)** 8-9	
	PatEddery	1
40	**Saddlers' Hall (Ire)** 8-12	
	LPiggott	6.2
	Collins Avenue (USA) 8-9	
	MHills	2.3
	Runyon (Ire) 8-9	
	WCarson	1½.4

Dreams End 8-9
WRSwinburn 10.5
Cooley's Valve (Ire) 8-9
SCauthen 8.6
Torchon 8-9 GCarter 7.7

11/8 Saddlers' Hall, 9/2 Runyon, Torchon, 5/1 CORRUPT, 18/1 Collins Avenue, 25/1 Cooley's Value, Dreams End
F. M. Kalla (N. A. Callaghan) 7ran
2m34.16 (Good)

---

51   ASTON UPTHORPE   1m3f195y
      YORKSHIRE OAKS (Gr 1)
      (3y + f + m)
£75,640   York   21 August

18   **Magnificent Star (USA)**
      3-8-11 ASCruz 1
37²   **Jet Ski Lady (USA)** 3-8-11
      PatEddery sh.2
43²   **Shamshir** 3-8-11
      LDettori 5.3
37   Third Watch 3-8-11
      JReid ¾.4
37*   Possessive Dancer 3-8-11
      SCauthen 2.5
      Fife (Ire) 3-8-11
      WRSwinburn 15.6
43   Gussy Marlowe 3-8-11
      MRoberts 20.7

13/8 Possessive Dancer, 7/4 Jet Ski Lady, 9/1 Gussy Marlowe, Shamshir, Third Watch, 16/1 MAGNIFICENT STAR, 50/1 Fife
Ecurie Fustok (M. Moubarak) 7ran
2m35.92 (Good)

---

52   KEENELAND   5f
      NUNTHORPE STAKES
      (Gr 1) (2y +)
£89,262   York   22 August

      Sheikh Albadou 3-9-3
      PatEddery 1
      Paris House 2-7-10
      DHolland 1½.2
      Blyton Lad 5-9-6
      SWebster nk.3
36*   Divine Danse (Fr) 3-9-0
      FHead 2.4
35³   Elbio 4-9-6 SCauthen nk.5
27   Duplicity (Ire) 3-9-3
      JReid 2.6
30   Poyle George 6-9-6
      LPiggott 4.7
      Title Roll (Ire) 3-9-0
      WCarson ½.8
      Klassy Briefcase (USA)
      6-9-3 JFerrer 2½.9

2/1 Divine Danse, 11/4 Elbio, 6/1 SHEIKH ALBADOU, 7/1 Paris House, 9/1 Klassy Briefcase, Title Roll, 40/1 Blyton Lad, 50/1 Poyle George, 100/1 Duplicity
Hilal Salem (A. A. Scott) 9ran
58.21secs (Good)

---

53   GRAND PRIX DE   1½m 110y
      DEAUVILLE LANCEL
      (Gr 2) (3y +)
£50,201   Deauville   25 August

21*   **Snurge (Ire)** 4-9-8 TQuinn 1
      Crnagora (Fr) 3-8-4
      ESaint-Martin nk.2
      Pigeon Voyageur (Ire) 3-8-7
      TJarnet ½.3
      Sinjar (Fr) 3-8-7 ELegrix sn.4
33   Echoes (Fr) 4-9-1 FHead nk.5
      Spendomania (USA) 4-8-13
      GMosse 1½.6
40   Sapience 5-9-2 PatEddery ... hd.7
      Antisaar (USA) 4-9-2
      SCauthen nk.8
      Farisi (USA) 3-8-7 DBoeuf 3.9
39   Strike Oil (Fr) 3-8-9
      ALequeux 15.10

Evens SNURGE, 11/2 Antisaar, 56/10 Pigeon Voyageur, 19/2 Sinjar, 23/2 Spendomania, 25/2 Sapience, 14/1 Crnagora, Farisi, Strike Oil, 18/1 Echoes
M. Arbib (P. F. I. Cole) 10ran 2m46.30 (Good to Firm)

---

54   GROSSER PREIS VON   1½m
      BADEN (Gr 1) (3y +)
£85,324   Baden-Baden   1 September

      Lomitas 3-8-9 PSchier5en 1
      Temporal (Ger) 3-8-9
      LDettori 7.2
33   **Wajd (USA)** 4-9-2
      SCauthen 4.3
      Krezus (Pol) 5-9-7 DIlic 1½.4
      All Top (Ire) 3-8-9
      MRimmer 2½.5
      Spinning 4-9-7 MHills 2½.6
      Another Bob (USA) 3-8-9
      PaulEddery 7.7
39   Top Waltz (Fr) 3-8-9 LPiggott .. 8
      Mondrian (Ger) 3-8-9 9

6/4 LOMITAS, 26/10 Wajd, 5/1 Mondrian, 13/2 Top Waltz, 9/1 Temporal, 12/1 Spinning, 20/1 All Top, 27/1 Another Bob, 40/1 Krezus
Gestut Fahrhof (A. Wohler) 9ran 2m28.81 (Good to Firm)

---

55   LADBROKE SPRINT   6f
      CUP (Gr 1) (2y +)
£85,837   Haydock   7 September

45   **Polar Falcon (USA)** 4-9-9
      CAsmussen 1
52*   **Sheikh Albadou** 3-9-6
      BRaymond 1½.2
      Shadayid (USA) 3-9-3
      WCarson 3½.3
41   Mystiko (USA) 3-9-6
      MRoberts 1½.4
4   Shalford (Ire) 3-9-6 JReid nk.5
      Amigo Menor 5-9-9
      CRutter 2.6

13/8 Shadayid, 9/4 Sheikh Albadou, 9/2 Mystiko, 13/2 POLAR FALCON, 12/1 Shalford, 20/1 Amigo Menor

David Thompson (J. E. Hammond)
6ran 1m11.23 (Firm)

56 PRIX DE LA SALAMANDRE (Gr 1)   7f
(2y c + f)
£50,151   Longchamp   8 September

48* **Arazi (USA)** 8-11	
GMosse	**1**
Made of Gold (USA) 8-11	
ASCruz	5.**2**
Silver Kite (USA) 8-11	
TJarnet	nk.**3**
Code Breaker (Fr) 8-11	
ELegrix	sn.**4**
Cardoun (Fr) 8-11	
DBoeuf	½.**5**
Guislaine (Fr) 8-8	
GGuignard	1.**6**
Colorific 8-11 PatEddery	nk.**7**
Miss Bluebird (Ire) 8-8	
MRoberts	nk.**8**

1/5 ARAZI, 67/10 Silver Kite, 99/10 Colorific, 13/1 Cardoun, 14/1 Made of Gold, 15/1 Code Breaker, Guislaine, 37/1 Miss Bluebird
  A. E. Paulson (F. Boutin) 8ran 1m20.90 (Good to Firm)

57 EMIRATES PRIX DU MOULIN DE LONGCHAMP (Gr 1)   1m
(3y + c + f)
£90,271   Longchamp   8 September

45 **Priolo (USA)** 4-9-2	
GMosse	**1**
49 **Mukaddamah (USA)** 3-8-12	
WCarson	sh.**2**
45² **Lycius (USA)** 3-8-12	
SCauthen	1.**3**
45 **Sillery (USA)** 3-8-12	
GGuignard	1½.**4**
45³ **Danseuse du Soir (Ire)** 3-8-9	
DBoeuf	nk.**5**
44* **Leariva (USA)** 4-8-13	
ALequeux	4.**6**
41 Sikeston (USA) 5-9-2	
MRoberts	hd.**7**
45* Hector Protector (USA)	
3-8-12 FHead	nk.**8**
22 Bold Russian 4-9-2	
PatEddery	1½.**9**
Primer Amor (Spa) 4-9-2	
RCochrane	ns.**10**
Bague Bleue (Ire) 3-8-9	
WMongil	**11**
45 Mousquetaire (USA) 3-8-12	
PBruneau	**12**

13/10 Hector Protector and Mousquetaire, 33/10 PRIOLO, 42/10 Lycius, 82/10 Bague Bleue and Danseuse du Soir, 15/1 Bold Russian, 29/1 Leariva, Primer Amor, 30/1 Sillery, 33/1 Mukaddamah, 52/1 Sikeston
  Ecurie Skymarc Farm (F. Boutin) 12ran 4m38.40 (Good to Firm)

58 LAURENT-PERRIER CHAMPAGNE STAKES   7f
(Gr 2) (2y c + g)
£41,550   Doncaster   13 September

Rodrigo de Triano (USA)	
8-11 WCarson	**1**
River Falls 9-0	
BRaymond	3½.**2**
Artic Tracker (USA) 8-11	
JReid	2½.**3**
Corals Dream (Ire) 8-11	
KFallon	2½.**4**
White Blade (USA) 8-11	
AClark	3½.**5**

11/8 RODRIGO DE TRIANO, 5/2 Artic Tracker, 3/1 River Falls, 8/1 White Blade, 50/1 Corals Dream
  R. E. Sangster (P. W. Chapple-Hyam) 5ran 1m26.55 (Good to Firm)

59 FLYING CHILDERS STAKES (Gr 2) (2y)   5f
£28,200   Doncaster   14 September

52² **Paris House** 8-11 JCarroll	**1**
Power Lake 8-11	
WCarson	2½.**2**
Colway Bold 8-11	
WRSwinburn	2½.**3**
Diamond Mine (Ire) 8-11	
KDarley	3½.**4**
Saddlehome (USA) 8-11	
JReid	5.**5**

4/6 PARIS HOUSE, 9/4 Colway Bold, 7/1 Power Lake, 16/1 Diamond Mine, 50/1 Saddlehome
  P. E. T. Chandler (J. Berry) 5ran 1m00.19 (Good to Firm)

60 COALITE ST LEGER STAKES (Gr 1) (3y c + f)   1¾m 132y
£175,781   Doncaster   14 September

39* **Toulon** 9-0 PatEddery	**1**
50² **Saddlers' Hall (Ire)** 9-0	
JReid	1½.**2**
Micheletti (USA) 9-0	
LPiggott	15.**3**
40 Luchiroverte (Ire) 9-0	
MRoberts	3.**4**
Fly Away Soon (USA) 9-0	
TQuinn	2.**5**
50* Corrupt (USA) 9-0	
LDettori	5.**6**
Jendali (USA) 9-0 ASCruz	3.**7**
Arcadian Heights 9-0	
WRSwinburn	1½.**8**
Libk 9-0 RHills	10.**9**
Jahafil 9-0 WCarson	dist.**10**

5/2 TOULON, 6/1 Micheletti, 13/2 Corrupt, Saddlers' Hall, 7/1 Fly Away Soon, 11/1 Jahafil, 12/1 Arcadian Heights, Luchiroverte, 15/1 Jendali, 25/1 Libk
  K. Abdulla (A. Fabre) 10ran 3m03.12 (Good to Firm)

61 MEADOW MEATS IRISH CHAMPION STAKES (Gr 1) (3y + c + f) 1¼m
£92,300 Leopardstown 14 September

32^2 **Suave Dancer (USA)** 3-8-11 CAsmussen 1
49 **Environment Friend** 3-8-11 GDuffield 4.2
49^3 **Stagecraft** 4-9-6 SCauthen .. 2.3
49 Topanoora 4-9-6 CRoche 1.4
23^2 Zoman (USA) 4-9-6 BRaymond ¾.5
Prudent Manner 4-9-6 MJKinane 8.6
Gogarty (Ire) 3-8-11 WJSupple dist.7

4/6 SUAVE DANCER, 5/1 Stagecraft, 7/1 Zoman, 8/1 Environment Friend, Topanoora, 50/1 Prudent Manner, 200/1 Gogarty

Henri Chalhoub (J. E. Hammond) 7ran 2m06.80 (Good to Soft)

62 PRIX NIEL ESCADA (Gr 2) (3y c + f) 1½m
£40,241 Longchamp 15 September

31* **Subotica (Fr)** 9-2 TJarnet 1
5* **Pistolet Bleu (Ire)** 9-2 DBoeuf nk.2
Arcangues (USA) 9-2 PatEddery ½.3
George Augustus (USA) 9-2 SCauthen 2.4
47^3 Le Pommier d'Or 9-2 MBoutin 8.5
47 Luynes (USA) 9-2 PBodin . 2½.6
53 Sinjar (Fr) 9-2 ELegrix 6.7
31 Shotkar (Fr) 9-2 CAubert 5.8

3/10 Arcangues and Luynes and Pistolet Bleu and Shotkar, 62/10 George Augustus, 115/10 Sinjar, 14/1 Le Pommier d'Or

O. Lecerf (A. Fabre) 8ran 2m28.50 (Good to Firm)

63 PRIX VERMEILLE ESCADA (Gr 1) (3y f) 1½m
£100,604 Longchamp 15 September

20^2 **Magic Night (Fr)** 9-2 ABadel 1
Pink Turtle (USA) 9-2 TJarnet 1½.2
53^2 **Crnagora (Fr)** 9-2 ESaint-Martin 1½.3
Saganeca (USA) 9-2 WMongil hd.4
51* Magnificent Star (USA) 9-2 ASCruz hd.5
51^3 Shamshir 9-2 LDettori sn.6
20* Caerlina (Ire) 9-2 ELegrix . 2½.7
51 Third Watch 9-2 JReid nk.8
Sardaniya (Ire) 9-2 MJKinane ¾.9
51 Possessive Dancer 9-2 SCauthen ½.10
Lady Blessington (Fr) 9-2 DBoeuf ¾.11
Sagace's Choice (USA) 9-2 CAsmussen 1½.12
Lorymaya (Fr) 9-2 FHead ... 5.13
L'Amour Fou (Ire) 9-2 DBouland 15.14

22/10 Magnificent Star, 3/1 MAGIC NIGHT, 53/10 Caerlina, 71/10 Possessive Dancer, 116/10 Pink Turtle, 136/10 Sardaniya, 17/1 Sagace's Choice, 18/1 Lorymaya, 20/1 Crnagora, 27/1 Lady Blessington, 32/1 Third Watch, 35/1 Shamshir, 56/1 Saganeca, 67/1 L'Amour Fou

Mme P. Demercastel (P. Demercastel) 14ran 2m27.80 (Good to Firm)

64 JEFFERSON SMURFIT MEMORIAL IRISH ST LEGER (Gr 1) (3y +) 1¾m
£83,119 Curragh 21 September

47* **Turgeon (USA)** 5-9-8 ACruz . 1
Patricia (USA) 3-8-9 SCauthen 3.2
Zafadola (Ire) 3-8-9 JPMurtagh ¾.3
Muir Station (USA) 3-8-12 CRoche 3.4
37^3 Eileen Jenny (Ire) 3-8-9 LPiggott hd.5
47 Great Marquess 4-9-8 PaulEddery 10.6
Arcane (USA) 4-9-8 JFEgan ½.7
Super Flame (Can) 4-9-8 PShanahan 12.8
Persian Halo (Ire) 3-8-12 WJO'Connor sh.9
Dowland (USA) 3-8-12 MJKinane hd.10

15/8 Patricia, 3/1 TURGEON, 11/2 Eileen Jenny, 8/1 Great Marquess, 9/1 Zafadola, 16/1 Persian Halo, 20/1 Dowland, 25/1 Muir Station, 40/1 Super Flame, 100/1 Arcane

George Strawbridge (J. E. Pease) 10ran 3m05.30 (Good to Soft)

65 GENO EUROPA PREIS (Gr 1) (3yo +) 1½m
£89,041 Cologne 22 September

54* **Lomitas** 3-8-10 PSchiergen ... 1
Indica (Ger) 4-9-2 KWoodburn 8.2
Leone (Ger) 3-8-10 GBocskai 5.3
53 Spendomania (USA) 4-9-2 MPhilipperon 1½.4
Highness Lady (Ger) 4-9-2 MRimmer ½.5
54 Krezus (Pol) 5-9-7 DIlic dist.6
Dancing Point (Swi) 4-9-7 ManfredHofer dist.7

Gestut Fahrhof (A. Wohler) 7ran 2m27.65 (Good)

66   HOOVER   1½m
      CUMBERLAND LODGE
      STAKES (Gr 3) (3yo +)
£31,239   Ascot   26 September
      Drum Taps (USA) 5-9-5
          LDettori 1
40³   **Rock Hopper** 4-9-5
          PatEddery hd.2
      Young Buster (Ire) 3-8-9
          WRSwinburn 1½.3
      Azzaam (USA) 4-9-0
          WCarson 1.4
      Hateel 5-9-0 RCochrane 12.5

9/4 Rock Hopper, 5/2 Azzaam, 11/4
Young Buster, 13/2 DRUM TAPS, 10/1
Hateel
    Lord Carnarvon (Lord Huntingdon)
5ran 2m34.73 (Good)

67   ROYAL LODGE   1m
      WILLIAM HILL STAKES
      (Gr 2) (2y c + g)
£86,328   Ascot   28 September
56²   **Made of Gold (USA)** 8-10
          ASCruz 1
      Mack The Knife 8-10
          WCarson ¾.2
      Twist And Turn 8-10
          SCauthen 1.3
      Torrey Canyon (USA) 8-10
          PatEddery hd.4
      Grand Master (Ire) 8-10
          AMunro 10.5
      Stefano (USA) 8-10
          RCochrane 8.6
      Nan A Buck (USA) 8-10
          LPiggott ½.7
      Ler Cru (Ire) 8-10
          MRoberts 10.8

7/4 Twist And Turn, 4/1 MADE OF
GOLD, Torrey Canyon, 6/1 Mack The
Knife, 9/1 Grand Master, 14/1 Nan A
Buck, 33/1 Ler Cru, 66/1 Stefano
    Ecurie Fustok (M. Moubarak) 8ran
1m46.66 (Good to Soft)

68   QUEEN ELIZABETH II   1m
      STAKES (Gr 1) (3y +)
£228,135   Ascot   28 September
      Selkirk (USA) 3-9-0
          RCochrane 1
26*   **Kooyonga (Ire)** 3-8-11
          WJO'Connor 1½.2
      Shadayid (USA) 3-8-11
          PatEddery nk.3
41*   Second Set (Ire) 3-9-0
          LDettori 3.4
      Forty Niner Days (USA) 4-9-4
          PValenzuela 2½.5
57   Hector Protector (USA) 3-9-0
          FHead 1½.6
57   Sikeston (USA) 5-9-4
          MRoberts 10.7
27   La Grange Music 4-9-4
          WRSwinburn 20.8

57²   Mukaddamah (USA) 3-9-0
          WCarson 1½.9

3/1 Second Set, 7/2 Kooyonga, 11/2
Hector Protector, 15/2 Mukaddamah,
Sikeston, 9/1 Shadayid, 10/1 SELKIRK,
20/1 Forty Niner Days, 50/1 La Grange
Music
    George Strawbridge (I. A. Balding)
9ran 1m44.34 (Good to Soft)

69   BRENT WALKER   1m
      FILLIES' MILE (Gr 1)
      (2y)
£91,125   Ascot   28 September
      Culture Vulture (USA) 8-10
          TQuinn 1
      Mystery Play (Ire) 8-10
          SCauthen 2.2
      Party Cited (USA) 8-10
          DHolland 2.3
      Fern 8-10 LDettori 8.4
      Super Sarena (Ire) 8-10
          WCarson 12.5
      Baharlilys 8-10 MRoberts 7.6
      Midnight Air (USA) 8-10
          PatEddery 7

Midnight Air finished first, ¾ length in
front of Culture Vulture, but was
disqualified and placed last for causing
serious interference
5/2 CULTURE VULTURE, 11/4
Midnight Air, 3/1 Fern, 4/1 Mystery
Play, 12/1 Super Sarena, 50/1 Party
Cited, 100/1 Baharlilys
    C. Wright (P. F. I. Cole) 7ran 1m46.11
(Good to Soft)

70   TATTERSALLS   6f
      CHEVELEY PARK
      STAKES (Gr 1) (2y f)
£91,651   Newmarket   2 October
      Marling (Ire) 8-11
          WRSwinburn 1
      Absurde (Fr) 8-11
          FHead 1½.2
      Basma (USA) 8-11
          WCarson hd.3
      Twafeaj (USA) 8-11
          PatEddery 1½.4
      Storm Ring (USA) 8-11
          LDettori 3.5
      Nimble Deer 8-11
          DHolland 2.6
      Swellegant 8-11 MHills ½.7
      Saratoga Star (USA) 8-11
          MRoberts dh.7
      Affair of State (Ire) 8-11
          TQuinn 2½.9

15/8 MARLING, 5/2 Absurde, 5/1
Basma, Twafeaj, 12/1 Affair of State,
20/1 Storm Ring, Swellegant, 50/1
Saratoga Star, 100/1 Nimble Deer
    E. J. Loder (G. Wragg) 9ran 1m11.17
(Good to Firm)

71   NEWGATE STUD   6f
      MIDDLE PARK STAKES
      (Gr 1) (2y c)
£77,644   Newmarket   3 October
58*   **Rodrigo de Triano (USA)** 9-0
      WCarson 1
48³   **Lion Cavern (USA)** 9-0
      SCauthen 1.2
58²   **River Falls** 9-0 BRaymond .. 2.3
59²   Power Lake 9-0 JReid 1½.4
      Balla Jidaal (USA) 9-0
      PatEddery 1½.5
      Eden's Close 9-0 RHills 3½.6

Evens RODRIGO DE TRIANO, 4/1
Balla Jidaal, 9/2 River Falls, 7/1 Lion
Cavern, 25/1 Power Lake, 66/1 Eden's
Close
      R. E. Sangster (P. W. Chapple-Hyam)
6ran 1m11.11 (Good to Firm)

72   CIGA GRAND   1m
      CRITERIUM (Gr 1)
      (2y c + f)
£120,846   Longchamp   5 October
56*   **Arazi (USA)** 8-11 GMosse 1
      Rainbow Corner 8-11
      PatEddery 3.2
      Seattle Rhyme (USA) 8-11
      CAsmussen sh.3
      St Jovite (USA) 8-11
      CRoche ¾.4
56   Code Breaker (Fr) 8-11
      ELegrix 5.5
56³   Silver Kite (USA) 8-11
      TJarnet nk.6

1/5 ARAZI, 48/10 Rainbow Corner, 58/10
Seattle Rhyme, 12/1 St Jovite, 24/1 Silver
Kite, 26/1 Code Breaker
      A. E. Paulson (F. Boutin) 6ran
1m41.40 (Good to Soft)

73   CIGA PRIX DOLLAR   1m 1f160y
      (Gr 2) (3y +)
£30,212   Longchamp   5 October
      Wiorno 3-8-9 TJarnet 1
2   **Muroto** 5-9-2 FHead ¾.2
61³   **Stagecraft** 4-9-4
      SCauthen hd.3
61   Zoman (USA) 4-9-4 AMunro . 2.4
46³   Approach The Bench (Ire)
      3-8-9 CAsmussen 1.5
31   Cudas (USA) 3-9-2
      GMosse 2½.6
29   Dolpour 5-9-0 PatEddery .. 1½.7

9/10 Stagecraft, 7/2 Muroto, 4/1 Zoman,
58/10 Cudas, 11/1 WIORNO, 14/1
Dolpour, 20/1 Approach The Bench
      D. Wildenstein (A. Fabre) 7ran
2m04.00 (Good to Soft)

74   PRIX MARCEL   1m
      BOUSSAC
      (Gr 1) (2y f)
£80,564   Longchamp   6 October
69*   **Culture Vulture (USA)** 8-11
      TQuinn 1

      Hatoof (USA) 8-11
      PatEddery sh.2
      Verveine (USA) 8-11
      DBoeuf 1.3
56   Guislaine (Fr) 8-11
      ELegrix ½.4
48²   Kenbu (Fr) 8-11 FHead 2½.5
      La Piaf (Fr) 8-11
      CAsmussen ½.6
      Red Slippers (USA) 8-11
      LDettori hd.7
      Urban Sky (Fr) 8-11
      MBoutin 5.8
      Perfect Circle 8-11
      WRSwinburn 2.9
      Waitowin (Ire) 8-11
      LPiggott 3.10
      Maratha (USA) 8-11
      GGuignard 5.11
      Alzarina (Ire) 8-11
      ALequeux ¾.12
      Wizzy (USA) 8-11
      ESaint-Martin 10.13
      Lady Normandy 8-11
      TJarnet .... pu

36/10 Red Slippers, Verveine, 37/10
Kenbu, 4/1 CULTURE VULTURE,
74/10 Hatoof, 144/10 La Piaf, Wizzy, 15/1
Perfect Circle, 20/1 Lady Normandy,
26/1 Guislaine, 27/1 Maratha, 36/1
Waitowin, 74/1 Urban Sky, 94/1
Alzarina
      C. Wright (P. Cole) 14ran 1m40.60
(Good to Soft)

75   CIGA PRIX DE   5f
      L'ABBAYE DE
      LONGCHAMP (Gr 1)
      (2y +)
£70,493   Longchamp   6 October
      Keen Hunter (USA) 4-9-11
      SCauthen 1
55²   **Sheikh Albadou** 3-9-11
      BRaymond 1.2
      Magic Ring (Ire) 2-8-8
      AMunro hd.3
35   Archway (Ire) 3-9-11
      WRSwinburn sn.4
      Flowing (USA) 3-9-8
      MJKinane hd.5
52   Divine Danse (Fr) 3-9-8
      FHead ½.6
36   Katies First (USA) 4-9-8
      DBoeuf 1½.7
      Special Power (Ire) 4-9-11
      CAsmussen hd.8
      Bradawn Breever (Ire) 2-8-8
      RGriffiths hd.9
30   Rivers Rhapsody 4-9-8
      JWilliams 2½.10
      Danzante (USA) 3-9-8
      PatEddery ¾.11
36   Noble Kara (Fr) 4-9-8
      ESaint-Martin nk.12
36   Luring (USA) 4-9-8
      GMosse nk.13
59*   Paris House 2-8-8
      JCarroll 1½.14

21/10 Magic Ring, 3/1 Sheikh Albadou,
37/10 Divine Danse, 52/10 Paris House,
115/10 Katies First, KEEN HUNTER,
17/1 Danzante, 19/1 Special Power, 21/1
Flowing, 41/1 Bradawn Breever, 43/1
Archway, 46/1 Noble Kara, 72/1 Luring,
91/1 Rivers Rhapsody
  Sheikh Mohammed (J. Gosden) 14ran
59.40secs (Good to Soft)

76	CIGA PRIX DE L'ARC DE	1½m
	TRIOMPHE (Gr 1)	
	(3y + c + f)	
£503,525	Longchamp	6 October

61*	**Suave Dancer (USA)** 3-8-11	
	CAsmussen 1
63*	**Magic Night (Fr)** 3-8-8	
	ABadel 2.2
63³	**Pistolet Bleu (Ire)** 3-8-11	
	DBoeuf 1.3
60*	Toulon 3-8-11 PatEddery 3.4
53³	Pigeon Voyageur (Ire) 3-8-11	
	TJarnet ¾.5
34	In The Groove 4-9-1	
	SCauthen hd.6
49²	Quest For Fame 4-9-4	
	WRSwinburn 1½.7
40*	Generous (Ire) 3-8-11	
	AMunro ¾.8
	El Senor (USA) 7-9-4	
	MJKinane ns.9
63	Shamshir 3-8-8 LDettori 2.10
33	Miss Alleged (USA) 4-9-1	
	ELegrix ½.11
	Art Bleu 4-9-4 CAubert 6. 12
51²	Jet Ski Lady (USA) 3-8-8	
	CRoche 5.13
53*	Snurge 4-9-4 TQuinn 6.14

9/10 Generous, 37/10 SUAVE DANCER,
68/10 Art Bleu and Pistolet Bleu, 8/1
Snurge, 95/10 Quest For Fame and
Toulon, 102/10 Magic Night, 26/1 Pigeon
Voyageur, 32/1 In The Groove, 40/1 Jet
Ski Lady, 43/1 Miss Alleged, 48/1 El
Senor, 91/1 Shamshir
  Henri Chalhoub (J. Hammond)
14ran 2m31.40 (Good to Soft)

77	CIGA PRIX DE L'OPERA	1m 1f
	(Gr 2) (3y + f + m)	
£40,282	Longchamp	6 October

	Martessa (Ger) 3-8-13	
	THellier 1
44	**Colour Chart (USA)** 4-9-2	
	SCauthen ¾.2
37	**Polemic (USA)** 3-8-9	
	PatEddery sn.3
	Fire The Groom (USA) 4-9-6	
	GStevens nk.4
45	Once In My Life (Ire) 3-8-11	
	CAsmussen nk.5
20	Treble (USA) 3-9-2 FHead .. nk.6
57	Leariva (USA) 4-9-4	
	ALequeux nk.7
	Shaima (USA) 3-8-9	
	LDettori sn.8

44	Massaraat (USA) 3-8-9	
	TJarnet ½.9
	Vanya 4-8-13	
	WRSwinburn ns.10
	You Know The Rules 4-8-13	
	LPiggott 2½.11
63	Lorymaya (Fr) 3-8-11	
	GMosse 2.12
	Olden Rijn (USA) 3-8-9	
	DBoeuf nk.13

2/1 Polemic, 22/10 Colour Chart and
Massaraat and Shaima, 52/10 Fire The
Groom, 99/10 You Know The Rules, 10/1
Once In My Life, 106/10 Treble, 12/1
Leariva, 20/1 Lorymaya, 34/1 Olden Rijn,
38/1 Vanya, 664/10 MARTESSA
  Stall Hof Heidendom (A. Wohler)
13ran 1m56.30 (Good to Soft)

78	CORNWALLIS STAKES	5f
	(Gr 3) (2y)	
£29,484	Ascot	12 October

75³	**Magic Ring (Ire)** 9-2	
	AMunro 1
	Harvest Girl (Ire) 8-9	
	SCauthen 2½.2
71	**Power Lake** 8-13	
	BRaymond 1.3
	Mamma's Too 8-8	
	JCarroll 1½.4
	Poolesta (Ire) 8-8	
	LDettori nk.5
	Tino Tere 8-13 NDay 1.6
	Cindora (Ire) 8-8	
	SWhitworth 2½.7
	Splice 8-8 GDuffield 2½.8
	Allthruthenight (Ire) 8-13	
	WRyan hd.9
38	Night Duty (Ire) 8-13	
	PaulEddery nk.10
	Ricky's Tornado (Ire) 8-13	
	JWilliams 7.11

10/11 MAGIC RING, 11/2 Mamma's Too,
8/1 Poolesta, 9/1 Power Lake, 10/1
Harvest Girl, 16/1 Night Duty, Splice,
33/1 Ricky's Tornado, Tino Tere, 50/1
Cindora, 100/1 Allthruthenight
  Fahd Salman (P. F. I. Cole) 11ran
1m02.42 (Good to Soft)

79	JUDDMONTE EBF	1m
	BERESFORD STAKES	
	(Gr 2) (2y)	
£26,376	Curragh	12 October

	El Prado (Ire) 9-2 LPiggott ... 1
56	**Colorific** 8-11 DHolland ... 2½.2
	Political Fact (USA) 8-11	
	MJKinane 4.3
	Governor's Imp (USA) 8-11	
	MHills sh.4
	Mekong (USA) 8-11	
	JPMurtagh ½.5
	Rosie's Mac (Ire) 8-11	
	RHughes 3½.6
	Bryan Station (USA) 8-11	
	CRoche ¾.7

25	Sylvan Sabre (Ire) 8-11	
	GHind	1.8
	Pollys Glow (Ire) 8-8	
	KJManning	hd.9
	Blackwater Pearl (USA) 8-11	
	PShanahan	nk.10

5/2 EL PRADO, 4/1 Colorific, 11/2 Governor's Imp, 6/1 Mekong, 8/1 Bryan Station, 9/1 Political Fact, 12/1 Pollys Glow, Rosie's Mac, 20/1 Blackwater Pearl, Sylvan Sabre

R. E. Sangster (M. V. O'Brien) 10ran 1m43.80 (Soft)

80	PRIX DE LA FORET	7f
	(Gr 1) (2y + c + f)	
£50,455	Longchamp	13 October

57	Danseuse du Soir (Ire) 3-9-6	
	DBoeuf	1
	Itsabrahma 5-9-12	
	GNordling	2.2
27	Osario 4-9-12 MBirch	½.3
	Hello Pink (Fr) 3-9-10	
	ABadel	hd.4
57³	Lycius (USA) 3-9-10	
	SCauthen	sn.5
	Silicon Bavaria (Fr) 4-9-8	
	ELegrix	1.6
45	Ganges (USA) 3-9-10	
	FHead	sh.7

3/5 Lycius, 26/10 DANSEUSE DU SOIR, 87/10 Hello Pink, 103/10 Ganges, 111/10 Itsabrahma, 131/10 Silicon Bavaria, 172/10 Osario

D. Wildenstein (E. Lellouche) 7ran 1m22.80 (Good to Soft)

81	PREMIO VITTORIO DI	1m
	CAPUA (Gr 1) (3y + c + f)	
£69,167	Milan	13 October

68	Sikeston (USA) 5-8-11	
	MRoberts	1
	Misil (USA) 3-8-9 GDettori	1.2
	Dominatus 5-8-11	
	MBerra	5½.3
11	Golden Mintage (USA) 3-8-9	
	SDettori	5.4
26	Arranvanna 3-8-6	
	VMezzatesta	2.5
	Prospective Ruler (USA) 3-8-9	
	GPucciatti	¾.6
	El Dinero (Ire) 3-8-9	
	GCarter	5.7
	Akeem (USA) 3-8-9 SSoto	8.8
	Dordone (Ity) 6-8-11	
	SLandi	14.9
	Magikrem (USA) 5-8-11	
	ADiNardo	dist.0

Allevamento White Star (C. Brittain) 10ran 1m43.30 (Heavy)

82	CHALLENGE STAKES	7f
	(Gr 2) (3y +)	
£42,192	Newmarket	17 October

| 55 | Mystiko (USA) 3-9-0 | |
| | MRoberts | 1 |

22	Only Yours 3-8-11	
	WCarson	2.2
	Volksraad 3-8-11	
	PatEddery	1½.3
13	Himiko (Ire) 3-8-8	
	MHills	1½.4
4	Bog Trotter (USA) 3-8-11	
	LPiggott	hd.5
68	La Grange Music 4-9-0	
	GDuffield	10.6
20	Kazoo 3-8-11 BRaymond	nk.7

9/4 MYSTIKO, 7/2 Bog Trotter, Volksraad, 7/1 Only Yours, 10/1 La Grange Music, 12/1 Kazoo, 16/1 Himiko

The Dowager Lady Beaverbrook (C. E. Brittain) 7ran 1m22.77 (Good to Firm)

83	ROCKFEL STAKES	7f
	(Gr 3) (2y f)	
£20,640	Newmarket	18 October

	Musicale (USA) 8-11	
	PatEddery	1
69²	Mystery Play (Ire) 8-8	
	SCauthen	1½.2
	Snow Forest (USA) 8-8	
	DHolland	¾.3
	Pearl Angel 8-8	
	MRoberts	6.4
	Mathaayl (USA) 8-8	
	RHills	2½.5
	Be My Everything (Ire) 8-8	
	WRyan	8.6

7/4 MUSICALE, 15/8 Mystery Play, 4/1 Mathaayl, 9/1 Snow Forest, 12/1 Pearl Angel, 100/1 Be My Everything

R. E. Sangster (H. R. A. Cecil) 6ran 1m23.92 (Good to Firm)

84	THREE CHIMNEYS	7f
	DEWHURST STAKES	
	(Gr 1) (2y c + f)	
£130,195	Newmarket	18 October

25²	Dr Devious (Ire) 9-0	
	WCarson	1
	Great Palm (USA) 9-0	
	AMunro	2½.2
	Thourios 9-0 RCochrane	sh.3
	Pursuit of Love 9-0	
	PatEddery	1½.4
	Zaahi (USA) 9-0 RHills	1½.5
	Free Flyer (Ire) 9-0	
	ASCruz	hd.6
	Young Senor (USA) 9-0	
	JReid	2½.7
	Strong Suit (Ire) 9-0	
	BRaymond	2.8
	Tony San (Ire) 9-0	
	MRoberts	hd.9

3/1 DR DEVIOUS, 7/2 Great Palm, 4/1 Zaahi, 6/1 Young Senor, 13/2 Pursuit of Love, 8/1 Thourios, 20/1 Free Flyer, 33/1 Strong Suit, 100/1 Tony San

Luciano Gaucci (P. W. Chapple-Hyam) 9ran 1m23.45 (Good to Firm)

85   DUBAI CHAMPION   1¼m
     STAKES (Gr 1) (3y +)
£262,350   Newmarket   19 October

Tel Quel (Fr) 3-8-12 TJarnet .	**1**
Cruachan (USA) 3-8-12		
RCochrane	½.2
76	**In The Groove** 4-9-0	
	CAsmussen	½.3
	Ristna 3-8-9 LPiggott	sh.4
46*	Star of Gdansk (USA) 3-8-12	
	CRoche	1.5
66³	Young Buster (Ire) 3-8-12	
	JReid	nk.6
73³	Stagecraft 4-9-3	
	SCauthen	3½.7
73	Dolpour 5-9-3 LDettori	2½.8
49*	Terimon 5-9-3 MRoberts	hd.9
61²	Environment Friend 3-8-12	
	GDuffield	2½.10
	Glity (USA) 3-8-12	
	ALequeux	3½.11
34	Marju (Fr) 3-8-12	
	WCarson	12.12

4/1 In The Groove, 11/2 Marju, Ristna,
15/2 Young Buster, 8/1 Cruachan,
Environment Friend, 10/1 Terimon, 12/1
Stagecraft, 16/1 TEL QUEL, 33/1 Star of
Gdansk, 50/1 Glity, 100/1 Dolpour
   Sheikh Mohammed (A. Fabre) 12ran
2m01.93 (Good to Firm)

86   GRAN PREMIO DEL   1½m
     JOCKEY CLUB (Gr 1)
     (3y +)
£223,633   Milan   20 October

39	**Passing Sale (Fr)** 4-9-3	
	ALequeux	**1**
66*	**Drum Taps (USA)** 5-9-3	
	MRoberts	nk.2
76	**Snurge** 4-9-3 TQuinn	3½.3
21	Fleeting Wish (USA) 5-9-3	
	JHeloury	5.4
21³	Bateau Rouge 4-9-3	
	MJerome	3.5
39	Marcus Thorpe (USA) 3-8-11	
	AMunro	5½.6
	Green Senor (USA) 3-8-11	
	MPlanard	nk.7
	Tarvisio 4-9-3 SDettori	½.8
	Retinospora (Ire) 3-8-11	
	LPiggott	sh.9
21	Riverullah (USA) 4-9-3	
	FJovine	1½.10

   A. Boutboul (B. Secly) 10ran 2m33.90
(Soft)

87   VODAFONE HORRIS   7f64y
     HILL STAKES (Gr 3)
     (2y c + g)
£26,732   Newbury   24 October

71²	**Lion Cavern (USA)** 8-12	
	SCauthen	**1**
	Autocracy (Ire) 8-12	
	JReid	2.2

	Muharib (USA) 8-12	
	BRaymond	3½.3
	Jeune 8-12 PatEddery	hd.4
79	Sylvan Sabre (Ire) 8-12	
	JWilliams	3½.5
	Jitterbugging 8-12	
	DHolland	2½.6
	Sunday's Hill 8-12	
	WNewnes	12.7

4/9 LION CAVERN, 11/2 Autocracy, 9/1
Jeune, 10/1 Jitterbugging, 20/1 Sunday's
Hill, 25/1 Muharib, 66/1 Sylvan Sabre
   Sheikh Mohammed (A. Fabre) 7ran
1m31.46 (Good)

88   RACING POST TROPHY   1m
     (Gr 1) (2y c + f)
£135,994   Doncaster   26 October

72³	**Seattle Rhyme (USA)** 9-0	
	CAsmussen	**1**
67²	**Mack The Knife** 9-0	
	WCarson	3½.2
	Assessor (Ire) 9-0 JReid ..	1½.3
	Anchorite 9-0 MBirch	2.4
	Ninja Dancer (USA) 9-0	
	BRaymond	1½.5
	King's Loch (Ire) 9-0	
	WRyan	nk.6
84³	Thourios 9-0 RCochrane	hd.7
	Beldi (USA) 9-0 GDuffield	8.8

2/1 SEATTLE RHYME, 4/1 Thourios,
5/1 Mack The Knife, 11/2 Ninja Dancer,
7/1 King's Loch, 9/1 Anchorite, 14/1
Assessor, 66/1 Beldi
   H. J. Senn (D. R. C. Elsworth) 8ran
1m39.58 (Good)

89   ST SIMON STAKES   1½m5y
     (Gr 3) (3yo +)
£21,987   Newbury   26 October

47³	**Further Flight** 5-9-3 MHills ..	**1**
43	**Filia Ardross** 5-9-0	
	MRoberts	nk.2
	Always Friendly 3-8-7	
	AMunro	2½.3
	Opera House 3-8-7	
	DHolland	½.4
	Red Bishop (USA) 3-8-7	
	SCauthen	12.5
39	Sesame 6-8-11 SWhitworth ..	1.6
	Red Rainbow 3-8-7	
	ASCruz	1½.7
60³	Micheletti (USA) 3-8-7	
	PaulEddery	nk.8
	Finance Dancer (Ire) 3-8-4	
	LDettori	12.9
	Oh So Risky 4-9-0	
	JWilliams	sh.10
	Ratify 4-9-0 ATucker	10.11

5/2 Red Bishop, 9/2 Opera House, 11/2
Always Friendly, 6/1 FURTHER
FLIGHT, 8/1 Micheletti, 9/1 Filia
Ardross, 11/1 Finance Dancer, 12/1
Sesame, 25/1 Red Rainbow, 33/1 Oh So
Risky, 40/1 Ratify

S. Wingfield Digby (B. W. Hills) 11ran
2m38.18 (Good)

90	PRIX ROYAL-OAK	1m7f110y
	(Gr 1) (3y +)	
£40,363	Longchamp	27 October

64*	**Turgeon (USA)** 5-9-3	
	ASCruz	1
42³	**Shambo** 4-9-3 MRoberts	¾.2
54³	**Wajd (USA)** 4-9-0	
	SCauthen	1.3
	Michelozzo (USA) 5-9-3	
	CAsmussen	1.4
	Elsurimo (Ger) 4-9-3	
	MRimmer	4.5
	Kashan (Ire) 3-8-11 PBodin ..	6.6
	Warfield 4-9-3 ELegrix	1.7
47	Our Account (USA) 7-9-3	
	DBoeuf	1.8

3/5 TURGEON, 24/10 Kashan and Wajd,
53/10 Michelozzo, 10/1 Shambo, 13/1 Our
Account, 14/1 Warfield, 21/1 Elsurimo
  G. Strawbridge (J. Pease) 8ran
3m23.40 (Good to Soft)

| 91 | BREEDERS' CUP | 6f (Dirt) |
| | SPRINT (Grade 1) (3y +) | |
| £304,094 Churchill Downs 2 November |

75²	**Sheikh Albadou** 3-8-12	
	PatEddery	1
	Pleasant Tap (USA) 4-9-0	
	EDelahoussaye	3.2
	Robyn Dancer (USA) 4-9-0	
	LPincayJnr	½.3
	Senor Speedy (USA) 4-9-0	
	JFChavez	nk.4
	Media Plan (USA) 3-8-12	
	PValenzuela	¾.5
	Clever Trevor (USA) 5-9-0	
	DPettinger	nk.6
	Take Me Out (USA) 3-8-12	
	MSmith	¾.7
	Polish Numbers (USA) 4-9-0	
	ACorderoJnr	2.8
	Housebuster (USA) 4-9-0	
	CPerret	1½.9
	Deposit Ticket (USA) 3-8-12	
	PDay	1½.10
	Key Spirit (Can) 5-9-0	
	MWalls	¾.11

2/5 Housebuster, 88/10 Pleasant Tap,
12/1 Polish Numbers, 16/1 Clever
Trevor, 18/1 Deposit Ticket, 19/1 Senor
Speedy, 22/1 Robyn Dancer, Take Me
Out, 263/10 SHEIKH ALBADOU, 38/1
Key Spirit, 65/1 Media Plan
  H. Salem (A. Scott) 11ran 1m09.20
(Fast)

| 92 | BREEDERS' CUP MILE | 1m |
| | (Gr 1) (3y +) | |
| £304,094 Churchill Downs 2 November |

	Opening Verse (USA) 5-9-0	
	PValenzuela	1
	Val des Bois (Fr) 5-9-0	
	CMcCarron	1¼.2

	Star of Cozzene (USA) 3-8-11	
	PDay	ns.3
80*	Danseuse du Soir (Ire) 3-8-8	
	DBoeuf	2¼.4
57*	Priolo (USA) 4-9-0 FHead ...	nk.5
	Jolie's Halo (USA) 4-9-0	
	CPerret	1.6
	Shadayid (USA) 3-8-8	
	WCarson	ns.7
	Scan (USA) 3-8-11	
	JASantos	½.8
	In Excess 4-9-0 GStevens ...	¾.9
	Tight Spot (USA) 4-9-0	
	LPincayJnr	dh.9
55*	Polar Falcon (USA) 4-9-0	
	CAsmussen	ns.11
68	Second Set (Ire) 3-8-11	
	LDettori	2¼.12
68²	Kooyonga (Ire) 3-8-8	
	WJO'Connor	3.13
	Sultry Song (USA) 3-8-11	
	JBailey	4.14

22/10 In Excess, 28/10 Tight Spot, 64/10
Priolo, 89/10 Polar Falcon, 114/10
Kooyonga, 15/1 Scan, 16/1 Jolie's Halo
and Sultry Song and Val des Bois, 19/1
Star of Cozzene, 22/1 Shadayid, 267/10
OPENING VERSE, 28/1 Second Set,
41/1 Danseuse du Soir
  A. E. Paulson (R. J. Lundy) 14ran
1m37.40 (Good)

93	BREEDERS' CUP 1m110y (Dirt)
	JUVENILE (Gr 1)
	(2y c + g)
£304,094 Churchill Downs 2 November

72*	**Arazi (USA)** 8-10	
	PValenzuela	1
	Bertrando (USA) 8-10	
	ASolis	5.2
	Snappy Landing (USA) 8-10	
	GStevens	3½.3
	Offbeat (USA) 8-10	
	MSmith	hd.4
	Agincourt (USA) 8-10	
	JFChavez	1¾.5
	Dance Floor (USA) 8-10	
	PDay	3¼.6
	Pine Bluff (USA) 8-10	
	CPerret	ns.7
	Tri To Watch (USA) 8-10	
	ACorderoJnr	3.8
	Star Recruit (USA) 8-10	
	LPincayJnr	5.9
	Devil On Ice (USA) 8-10	
	JASantos	3.10
	Big Sur (USA) 8-10	
	CMcCarron	1½.11
	Onlooker (USA) 8-10	
	JBailey	6.12
	Bag (USA) 8-10 DFlores ...	hd.13
38²	Showbrook (Ire) 8-10	
	LPiggott	14

21/10 ARAZI, 5/2 Bertrando, 37/10
Dance Floor, 5/1 Tri To Watch, 19/1
Devil On Ice and Onlooker and Offbeat,
25/1 Showbrook, 28/1 Pine Bluff, 37/1

Star Recruit, 48/1 Bag, 61/1 Snappy Landing, 62/1 Agincourt, 69/1 Big Sur
A. E. Paulson (F. Boutin) 14ran 1m44.60 (Fast)

94 BREEDERS' CUP TURF (Gr 1) (3y+) 1½m
£608,187 Churchill Downs 2 November

76 **Miss Alleged (USA)** 4-8-11 ELegrix **1**
Itsallgreektome (USA) 4-9-0 JVelasquez ½.**2**
76 **Quest For Fame** 4-9-0 PatEddery 2.**3**
Sky Classic (Can) 4-9-0 PDay 2.4
76³ Pistolet Bleu (Ire) 3-8-10 DBoeuf ½.5
76 Pigeon Voyageur (Ire) 3-8-10 GStevens 2¾.6
85³ In The Groove 4-8-11 SCauthen 2.7
14 Kartajana 4-8-11 EDelahoussaye nk.8
76 El Senor (USA) 7-9-0 JASantos ns.9
60² Saddlers' Hall (Ire) 3-8-10 LPincayJnr ½.10
29 Dear Doctor (Fr) 4-9-0 CAsmussen 8.11
63 Saganeca (USA) 3-8-7 ACorderoJnr ns.12
Filago (USA) 4-9-0 PValenzuela .... pu

28/10 Pistolet Bleu, 33/10 Sky Classic, 47/10 Itsallgreektome, 69/10 Kartajana, 15/2 In The Groove, 78/10 Filago, 19/1 Pigeon Voyageur, 20/1 Dear Doctor, 31/1 El Senor, 421/10 MISS ALLEGED and Saddlers' Hall and Saganeca, 58/1 Quest For Fame
Fares Farm (P. Bary) 13ran 2m30.80 (Good)

95 CRITERIUM DE MAISONS-LAFFITTE (Gr 2) (2y c+f) 7f
£35,212 Maisons-Laffitte 2 November

56 **Cardoun (Fr)** 8-12 ALequeux **1**
Tertian (USA) 8-9 TJarnet ¾.**2**
70² **Absurde (Fr)** 8-6 ESaint-Martin 5.**3**
In The News (USA) 8-9 SGuillot ¾.4
Shivaree (Fr) 8-9 MdeSmyter ns.5
Taylor Quigley (USA) 8-9 MTebbutt 1½.6
Martial du Berlais (Fr) 8-9 WMongil 1½.7
Je Ne Suis Pas La (Fr) 8-6 GDubroeucq nk.8

Evens In The News and Tertian, 6/4 Absurde, 41/10 CARDOUN, 104/10 Martial du Berlais, 147/10 Je Ne Suis Pas La, 177/10 Shivaree, 29/1 Taylor Quigley
E. Zorbibe (E. Lellouche) 8ran 1m29.70 (Heavy)

96 CRITERIUM DE SAINT-CLOUD (Gr 1) (2y c+f) 1¼m
£50,302 Saint-Cloud 3 November

Glaieul (USA) 8-11 DBoeuf ... **1**
48 **Calling Collect (USA)** 8-11 CAsmussen sh.**2**
Contested Bid (USA) 8-11 PatEddery 5.**3**
67 Grand Master (Ire) 8-11 AMunro sn.4
Soiree Mondaine (Fr) 8-8 DBouland 4.5
Apple Tree (Fr) 8-11 TJarnet 1½.6
Philippin (Fr) 8-11 ELegrix ... 6.7
Ca Alors (Fr) 8-8 JGuerin .. 1½.8
Rasmussen (Fr) 8-11 GGuignard nk.9

Evens Calling Collect, 37/10 GLAIEUL, 47/10 Apple Tree, 51/10 Contested Bid, 9/1 Philppin, 19/1 Grand Master, 23/1 Soiree Mondaine, 29/1 Rasmussen, 33/1 Ca Alors
D. Wildenstein (E. Lellouche) 9ran 2m20.30 (Heavy)

97 PREMIO RIBOT (Gr 2) (3y+) 1m
£35,305 Rome 3 November

81² **Misil (USA)** 3-8-11 GDettori . **1**
81* **Sikeston (USA)** 5-8-11 MRoberts 3½.**2**
Art Sebal (USA) 3-8-11 VMezzatesta 5.**3**
Irgaim 6-8-11 JacquelineFreda 2.4
Swordsmith (USA) 4-8-11 DHolland 4.5
81 El Dinero (Ire) 3-8-11 LSorrentino ¾.6
Highly Praised 3-8-11 MJerome 15.7
Audio (Ger) 3-8-11 MJKinane 2½.8

Scuderia Laghi (V. Caruso) 8ran 1m42.70 (Heavy)

98 PREMIO ROMA (Gr 1) (3y+) 1¼m
£106,045 Rome 10 November

97² **Sikeston (USA)** 5-8-12 MRoberts **1**
Lara's Idea 3-8-8 GDettori .. 2.**2**
73 **Zoman (USA)** 4-8-12 AMunro ¾.**3**
86* Passing Sale (Fr) 4-8-12 ALequeux 5.4
Legal Case 5-8-12 LDettori 2½.5
66 Azzaam (USA) 4-8-12 WCarson 4.6

Fortune's Wheel (Ire) 3-8-11
ELegrix 3.7
97³ Art Sebal (USA) 3-8-11
VMezzatesta 2.8
73² Muroto 5-8-12 FHead 4.9
86 Retinospora (Ire) 3-8-11
LFicuciello 7.10
Optimist 5-8-12 BJovine 11

Allevamento White Star (C. Brittain)
11ran 2m06.50 (Heavy)

99 JAPAN CUP (Gr 1) (3y +) 1½m
£678,261   Tokyo   24 November
Golden Pheasant (USA) 5-8-13
GStevens 1
76² **Magic Night (Fr)** 3-8-5
ABadel 1½.2
Shaftesbury Avenue (Aus)
5-8-13 DGauci 1½.3
Mejiro McQueen 4-8-13
YTake 1½.4
Rough Habit (NZ) 5-8-13
JCassidy ½.5
90³ Wajd (USA) 4-8-9 TJarnet . 1¼.6
66² Rock Hopper 4-8-13
PatEddery ns.7
Fujiyama Kenzan 3-8-9
SKojima 1¾.8
Main Caster 5-8-9 KMinai ... ½.9
Carib Song 5-8-13
MShibata ½.10
86² Drum Taps (USA) 5-8-13
LDettori nk.11
85 Terimon 5-8-13
MRoberts 1½.12
Splash of Colour 4-8-13
FHead nk.13
Mejiro Ardan 6-8-13
MTamura 6.14
George Monarch 5-8-13
SHayata 2½.15

9/10 Mejiro McQueen, 5/1 Magic Night,
86/10 Drum Taps, 99/10 Rock Hopper,
126/10 Terimon, 141/10 Shaftesbury
Avenue, 172/10 GOLDEN PHEASANT,
24/1 Rough Habit, 25/1 Carib Song, 35/1
Wajd, 42/1 Fujiyama Kensan, 46/1
Mejiro Ardan, 55/1 Splash of Colour, 97/1
George Monarch, 126/1 Main Caster
    W. Gretzky and Summa Stable (C.
Whittingham) 15ran 2m24.70 (Firm)

100 PREMIO UNIRE   1¾m
CONSIGILO EUROPEO
ROMA VECCHIA (Gr 3)
(3y +)
£99,908   Rome   24 November
86³ **Snurge (Ire)** 4-9-3 TQuinn 1
Hieroglyphic (Ire) 3-8-8
WCarson 2.2
90* **Turgeon (USA)** 5-9-3
CAsmussen 4.3
Riverullah (USA) 4-8-13
FJovine 1¾.4
Sought Out (Ire) 3-8-5
BRaymond 9.5

Goldline Seeker 3-8-8
BJovine 5½.6
90² Shambo 4-8-13 JReid 2¾.7
86 Fleeting Wish (USA) 5-8-13
JHeloury 12.8
Jack Lang 3-8-8 GDettori nk.9
Bernasco 5-8-13
JacquelineFreda 15.10
54 Another Bob (USA) 3-8-8
VMezzatesta 2.11
64³ Zafadola (Ire) 3-8-5
JPMurtagh 2½.12
Imco Lisi 3-8-5 GDiChio 6.13

M. Arbib (P. Cole) 13ran 3m15.69
(Heavy)

1008

1011

TRAINERS

The figures in brackets are the number of winners each trainer has had on the flat (turf and all-weather) in Britain over the past five years from 1987 to 1991 inclusive. The trainers' telephone numbers are given after.

Aconley, Mrs V. A. (—:—:—:0:1)
Westow (065381) 594 and
(0653) 695042 (home)
Akehurst, J. (—:—:—:4:13)
Lambourn (0488) 72688
Akehurst, R. P. J. (27:25:33:34:42)
Epsom (0372) 748800 and
fax (0372) 739410
Allan, A. R. (1:1:1:1:1)
Cornhill-on-Tweed (089082) 581
Allen, C. N. (2:7:8:19:16)
Newmarket (0638) 667870 and
76767 and mobilephone (0831) 349629
Alston, E. J. (1:10:1:6:12)
Preston (0772) 612120
Arbuthnot, D. W. P. (17:3:10:20:12)
Newbury (0635) 578427
Armstrong, R. W. (25:36:21:26:10)
Newmarket (0638) 663333 or 663334
Austin, C. A. (0:0:1:0:2)
Wokingham (0734) 786 425
Austin, Mrs S. M. (—:—:—:0:0)
Malton (065385) 200
Avison, M. (—:1:0:4:0)
Nawton (0439) 71672

Bailey, A. (30:21:12:10:11)
Bailey, K. C. (0:0:1:0:2)
Lambourn (0488) 71483
Baker, J. H. (0:2:0:3:6)
Tiverton (03985) 317 and
mobilephone (0831) 500767
Balding, G. B. (13:7:15:18:18)
Whitcombe (0305) 260724
Balding, I. A. (31:43:41:48:53)
Kingsclere (0635) 298210
Balding, J. (1:2:5:7:4)
Doncaster (0302) 710096 and
(0777) 818407 (stable)
Banks, J. E. (—:—:—:—:3)
(0638) 667997 (office) and
661472 (home)
Barker, Mrs P. A. (—:—:—:0:1)
Wetherby (0937) 582151
Barker, W. L. (—:—:—:—:0)
Scorton (0325) 378266 and
mobilephone (0836) 260149
Barons, D. H. (0:0:0:0:0)
Kingsbridge (0548) 550326 and
550411
Barr, R. E. (—:—:—:—:0)
Stokesley (0642) 710687
Barraclough, M. F. (—:—:—:—:0)
Claverdon (092684) 3332
Barratt, L. J. (0:4:0:0:1)
Oswestry (069188) 209
Barron, T. D. (19:18:24:58:39)
Thirsk (0845) 587 435
Barrow, A. K. (—:—:0:0:0)
Bridgwater (0278) 732522

Barwell, C. R. (—:—:—:0:0)
Tiverton (03985) 537 and 224
Bastiman, R. (1:3:7:12:14)
Wetherby (0937) 583050
Beaumont, P. (—:0:0:0:0)
Brandsby (03475) 208
Beever, C. R. (—:—:0:1:1)
Grantham (0476) 870177
Bell, M. L. W. (—:—:18:21:43)
Newmarket (0638) 666567
Bennett, J. A. (0:0:0:0:2)
Sparsholt (023559) 635
Bennett, R. A. (—:0:1:4:1)
Maidenhead (0628) 30290
Benstead, C. J. (12:14:9:6:5)
Epsom (037 22) 73152
Bentley, W. (8:0:1:1:0)
Middleham (0969) 22289
Berry, J. (31:70:92:127:143)
Lancaster (0524) 791179
Bethell, J. D. W. (2:4:11:10:11)
Didcot (0235) 834333
Bevan, P. J. (4:0:0:0:1)
Kingstone (0889) 500647 (yard) or
500670 (home)
Bishop, K. S. (0:0:0:0:0)
Bridgwater (0278) 671437
Blanshard, M. T. W. (5:3:8:5:6)
Lambourn (0488) 71091
Blockley, P. A. (0:3:2:3:1)
Hednesford (0543) 425499 and
422420
Blum, G. (2:3:1:2:6)
Newmarket (0638) 713916
Bolton, M. J. (0:0:0:2:1)
East Grinstead (0980) 621059
Booth, C. B. B. (6:7:4:4:5)
Flaxton (065 381) 586
Bosley, J. R. (1:0:0:0:0)
Bampton (0993) 850 212
Boss, R. (19:23:23:36:18)
Newmarket (0638) 661335
Bostock, J. R. (—:—:—:1:3)
Swaffham (0366) 47870
Bottomley, J. F. (—:—:4:5:4)
Malton (0653) 694597 (stable)
Bower, Miss L. J. (0:0:0:0:0)
Alresford (0962) 771552
Bowring, S. R. (2:7:2:4:2)
Mansfield (0623) 822451
Bradley, J. M. (2:2:1:4:2)
Chepstow (0291) 622486
Bradstock, M. F. (—:0:0:0:0)
East Garston (048839) 8801
Bramall, Mrs S. A. (—:—:—:—:0)
Hutton Sessay (0845) 401333
Bravery, C. V. (—:0:1:0:0)
Jevington (03212) 3662
Bravery, G. C. (—:—:—:—:0)
Newmarket (0638) 661680

1013

Brazington, R. G. (0:0:0:0:0)
  Redmarley, Glos. (0452) 840384
Brennan, O. (1:2:0:2:0)
  Newark (063 686) 332
Bridger, J. J. (0:0:0:2:0)
  Chichester (0428) 722528
Bridgwater, K. S. (0:1:0:0:2)
  Solihull (056478) 2895
Brisbourne, M. W. (—:—:—:—:0)
  Shrewsbury (074381) 536 and 360
Brittain, C. E. (38:40:36:42:53)
  Newmarket (0638) 663739 and
  664347
Brittain, M. A. (57:44:26:27:21)
  Warthill (0759) 71472
Broad, C. D. (—:—:—:—:1)
  Westbury-upon-Severn, Gloucester
  (0452) 76835 (office) and
  830015 (home)
Brooks, C. P. E. (—:0:1:0:1)
  Lambourn (0488) 72077 (office) and
  72909 (home)
Burchell, W. D. (0:0:1:7:4)
  Ebbw Vale (0495) 302551
Burgoyne, P. V. J. P. (3:0:0:0:0)
  Sparsholt (023 559) 688
Burke, K. R. (—:—:—:—:0:2)
  Broadway (0386) 858153 and 858489
Butler, N. (0:0:0:0:0)
  Lewes (0273) 890124
Bycroft, N. (10:10:2:2:6)
  Brandsby (034 75) 641

Caldwell, T. H. (—:—:0:0:0)
  Warrington (0565) 777275
Callaghan, N. A. (20:27:32:31:30)
  Newmarket (0638) 664040
Calver, P. (7:7:7:18:8)
  Ripon (0765) 600313
Camacho, M. J. C. (6:8:12:20:15)
  Malton (0653) 694901
Cambidge, B. R. (0:2:1:2:4)
  Shifnal (095 276) 249
Campbell, I. (1:4:3:7:1)
  Newmarket (0638) 660829
Candy, H. D. N. B. (33:20:16:23:16)
  Wantage (0367) 820276
Carter, W. Y. (—:2:23:20:15)
  Leatherhead (0372) 377209
Casey, W. T. (1:3:1:4:5)
  Lambourn (0488) 73004
Cecil, H. R. A. (180:112:117:111:119)
  Newmarket (0638) 662192 or
  662387 (home)
Cecil, Mrs J. (—:—:—:—:19)
  Newmarket (0638) 560634 (office) and
  662420 (home) and fax (0638) 560636
Chamberlain, A. J. (—:—:—:—:0:0)
  Swindon (0285) 861347
Chamberlain, N. (1:0:0:0:0)
  West Auckland (0388) 832 465
Champion, R. (0:0:1:0:0)
  Newmarket (0638) 666546
Channon, M. R. (—:—:—:16:22)
  Lambourn (0264) 810225 and
  (0488) 71149 (stable)
Chapman, D. W. (13:36:29:22:24)
  Stillington (0347) 21683

Chapman, M. C. (0:0:0:1:7)
  Market Rasen (0673) 843663
Chapple-Hyam, P. W. (—:—:—:—:27)
  Manton (0672) 514901
Charles, M. J. (0:0:0:1:0)
  Warwick (0926) 493878
Charlton, J. I. A. (0:0:0:0:0)
  Stocksfield (0661) 843 247
Charlton, R. J. (—:—:—:37:26)
  Beckhampton (06723) 533 (office) and
  330 (home)
Christian, S. P. L. (1:1:0:0:0)
  Kinnersley (0905) 371233
Clay, W. (0:0:0:0:0)
  Fulford (0782) 392 131
Codd, L. J. (—:—:3:0:3)
  Nantwich (0270) 610172
Cole, P. F. I. (55:43:51:53:73)
  Whatcombe (04882) 433 or 434
Collingridge, H. J. (6:7:12:7:9)
  Newmarket (0638) 665454
Cottrell, L. G. (23:19:12:4:10)
  Cullompton (088 46) 320
Craig, T. (6:1:4:1:1)
  Dunbar (0368) 62583
Cumani, L. M. (83:73:88:109:72)
  Newmarket (0638) 665432
Cundell, P. D. (8:5:1:0:1)
  Newbury (0635) 578267
Cunningham, T. W. (0:0:0:0:0)
  Northallerton (0609082) 695
Cunningham-Brown, K. O.
  (1:0:7:4:2)
  Stockbridge (0264) 781611
Curley, B. J. (0:1:0:3:3)
  Newmarket (0638) 508251
Curtis, R. (—:3:3:4:3)
  Epsom (0372) 277645
Cyzer, C. A. (—:—:14:9:20)
  Horsham (0403) 730255
Czerpak, J. D. (—:—:0:2:4)
  Newmarket (025125) 3505

Davison, A. R. (0:2:0:0:0)
  Caterham (0883) 344523
Denson, A. W. (0:0:1:0:0)
  Epsom (03727) 29398
Dickin, R. (0:0:0:1:5)
  Dymock (053185) 644
Dixon, M. (—:—:—:—:0)
  Epsom (0372) 279308
Dods, M. J. K. (—:—:—:—:3)
  Darlington (0325) 374270
Donnelly, T. W. (—:—:—:—:0)
  Hartshorne (0283) 226046 and
  216965 (office)
Dooler, J. (—:—:0:0:0)
  Goole (0405) 861903
Dow, S. L. (0:6:7:5:17)
  Epsom (03722) 75878 (home)
Dunlop, J. L. (61:66:66:78:58)
  Arundel (0903) 882194 (office) or
  882106 (home)

Earnshaw, R. (0:0:3:4:2)
  Harrogate (0423) 567790
Easterby, M. H. (68:64:57:61:58)
  Malton (065 386) 566

1014

Easterby, M. W. (12:25:19:25:14)
Sheriff Hutton (03477) 368
Eckley, M. W. (5:4:1:1:2)
Ludlow (058472) 372
Eden, G. H. (—:—:—:2:4)
Newmarket (0638) 667938
Edwards, J. A. C. (5:6:1:0:0)
Ross-on-Wye (098987) 259 and
639 (home)
Eldin, E. (6:10:10:10:3)
Newmarket (0638) 662036 or 663217
Ellerby, M. W. (0:0:1:0:0)
Pickering (0751) 74092
Ellison, B. (—:—:—:0:3)
Burythorpe (0653) 600158
Elsey, C. C. (—:—:3:8:7)
Lambourn (0488) 71242
Elsey, C. W. C. (13:10:10:9:4)
Malton (0653) 693149
Elsworth, D. R. C. (31:28:35:44:40)
Fordingbridge (07253) 220 (home) or
528 (office)
Enright, G. P. (—:0:1:0:0)
Haywards Heath (0273) 479183
Etherington, J. (11:11:18:17:9)
Malton (0653) 692842
Eustace, J. M. P. (—:—:0:6:10)
Newmarket (0638) 664277
Evans, P. D. (—:—:0:0:3)
Welshpool (093874) 288

Fairhurst, T. (8:10:11:12:15)
Middleham (0969) 23362
Fanshawe, J. R. (—:—:0:18:22)
Newmarket (0638) 660153 and
664525
Feilden, P. J. (0:1:7:6:5)
Newmarket (0638) 577637
Felgate, P. S. (8:17:12:10:6)
Melton Mowbray (0664) 812019
Fetherston-Godley, M. J. (6:10:2:7:13)
East Ilsley (063528) 250
Ffitch-Heyes, J. R. (2:0:0:1:2)
Lewes (0273) 480804
Fisher, R. F. (4:2:1:0:0)
Ulverston (0229) 55664 and
55819 (office)
FitzGerald, J. G. (7:20:22:21:12)
Malton (0653) 692718
Forsey, B. (0:1:0:0:1)
Crowcombe (09848) 270
Forster, T. A. (0:0:0:0:0)
Letcombe Bassett (02357) 3092
Fox, J. C. (0:1:3:2:0) Fyfield
Francis, M. E. D. (8:8:4:3:0)
Lambourn (0488) 71700
Franks, D. R. (—:—:—:—:0)
Esh 091-373 5460 (office) and
091-3840989
Frost, R. G. (1:0:0:0:0)
Buckfastleigh (03644) 2267

Gandolfo, D. R. (0:0:0:0:0)
Wantage (02357) 3242
Garraton, D. T. (—:—:—:0:0)
Rillington (N. Yorks) (09442) 506
Gaselee, N. A. D. C. (1:3:2:0:0)
Lambourn (0488) 71503

Gifford, J. T. (0:0:0:3:0)
Findon (0903) 872226
Glover, J. A. (8:12:3:5:4)
Worksop (0909) 475962 or
475425 (stable)
Gosden, J. H. M. (—:—:28:87:86)
Newmarket (0638) 669944
Graham, N. A. (—:11:—:6:7)
Newmarket (0638) 665202 (office) and
667851 (home)
Grissell, D. M. (0:—:0:0:0)
Heathfield (042482) 241
Gubby, B. (0:1:0:7:0)
Bagshot (0276) 63282 and
71030 (evenings)
Guest, R. (—:—:7:7:5)
Newmarket (0638) 661508

Haggas, W. J. (17:14:16:21:27)
Newmarket (0638) 667013
Haigh, W. W. (7:3:3:5:6)
Malton (0653) 694428
Haine, Mrs D. E. S. (—:0:1:0:0)
Newmarket (0638) 561001
Haldane, J. S. (1:1:0:0:1)
Kelso (0573) 24956
Hall, Miss S. E. (9:7:6:12:6)
Middleham (0969) 40223
Hallett, T. B. (0:0:0:0:0)
Saltash (0752) 846829
Ham, G. A. (—:—:—:0:1)
Axbridge (0934) 750331
Hammond, M. D. (—:—:—:5:1)
Middleham (0969) 40228
Hanbury, B. (31:40:42:36:36)
Newmarket (0638) 663193 (stable) and
(0440) 820396 (home)
Hannon, R. M. (33:43:55:73:126)
Marlborough (0264) 850254
Harris, J. L. (0:0:0:6:8)
Melton Mowbray (0949) 60671
Harris, P. W. (0:0:2:8:3)
Berkhamsted (0442) 842480
Harris, S. T. (0:0:0:2:0)
Amersham (0494) 715446
Harrison, R. A. (—:—:—:7:4)
Middleham (0969) 23788
Harwood, G. (67:73:109:69:55)
Pulborough (0798) 873011 or
873012
Haslam, P. C. (23:22:—:—:14)
Middleham (0969) 24351
Haynes, M. J. (10:11:6:9:9)
Epsom (07373) 51140
Hayward, P. A. (2:0:1:1:0)
Netheravon (0980) 70585
Heaton-Ellis, M. J. B. (—:—:—:—:0)
Wroughton (0793) 815009
Henderson, N. J. (0:0:0:0:0)
Lambourn (0488) 72259
Hern, W. R. (36:30:45:30:23)
Lambourn (0488) 73300 (office) and
(063528) 251 (home) and
fax (0488) 71728
Herries, Lady (6:6:9:4:14)
Arundel (090674) 421
Hetherton, J. (—:—:2:4:10)
Malton (0653) 696778

1015

Hide, A. G. (8:8:11:10:15)
Newmarket (0638) 662063
Hill, C. J. (2:5:3:11:16)
Barnstaple (0271) 42048
Hills, B. W. (96:93:73:113:99)
Lambourn (0488) 71548 and
fax (0488) 72823
Hills, J. W. (13:14:16:28:20)
Lambourn (0488) 73144 and
fax (0488) 73099
Hoad, R. P. C. (0:1:0:2:0)
Lewes (0273) 477124
Hobbs, P. J. (0:0:0:0:0)
Watchet (0984) 40366
Hodges, R. J. (2:8:12:25:27)
Somerton (045822) 3922
Holden, W. (5:4:3:1:3)
Newmarket (0638) 577384
Holder, R. J. (13:8:17:16:18)
Portbury (0275) 372192 and
fax (0275) 374185
Hollinshead, R. (28:33:30:41:31)
Upper Longdon (0543) 490298 and
490490
Holmes, C. J. (0:0:0:0:0)
Gerrards Cross (02407) 5964
Holt, L. J. (9:6:13:6:4)
Tunworth (0256) 463376
Horgan, C. A. (1:6:9:3:4)
Billingbear (0344) 425382
Houghton, R. F. J. (26:36:24:25:13)
Blewbury (0235) 850480
Howling, P. (5:9:5:6:6)
Brook (042868) 4065
Huntingdon, Lord (15:31:26:20:36)
West Ilsley (0635) 28747 or
28725 (stable)

Incisa, D. E. (1:2:0:2:4)
Leyburn (0969) 40653
Ivory, K. T. (18:7:7:7:5)
Radlett (0923) 855337

Jackson, C. F. C. (3:2:0:0:0)
Malvern (0886) 880463
James, A. P. (0:0:0:0:0)
Evesbatch (0885) 410240
James, C. J. (4:6:1:1:3)
Newbury (048 839) 280
James, M. B. C. (0:2:0:0:0)
Whitchurch (0948) 4067
Jarvis, A. P. (—:—:—:—:1)
Abingdon (0235) 851341
Jarvis, M. A. (19:31:28:28:24)
Newmarket (0638) 661702 and 662519
Jarvis, W. (27:26:32:31:29)
Newmarket (0638) 669873 (office) or
662677 (home)
Jefferson, J. M. (5:4:1:0:0)
Malton (0653) 697225
Jenkins, J. R. (8:15:10:13:12)
Royston (0763) 241141 (office) and
246611 (home)
Jermy, D. C. (0:0:0:0:1)
Warminster (0985) 213155
Johnson, J. H. (0:0:0:1:0)
Bishop Auckland (0388) 762113 and
730872

Johnston, M. S. (1:5:15:28:31)
Middleham (0969) 22237
Jones, A. P. (—:—:—:—:0)
Lambourn (0488) 72637
Jones, A. W. (1:0:1:1:0)
Oswestry (0691) 659720
Jones, D. H. (4:6:3:7:2)
Pontypridd (0443) 202515
Jones, Mrs G. E. (—:0:0:0:0)
Upton-on-Severn (0684) 592691
Jones, G. H. (0:0:0:0:0)
Tenbury Wells (056887) 676 and 305
(stable)
Jones, H. Thomson (30:41:37:34:37)
Newmarket (0638) 664884
Jones, P. J. (0:0:0:0:0)
Marlborough (067286) 427
Jones, R. W. (—:—:—:—:3)
Wickhambrook (0440) 820342
Jones, T. M. (0:4:0:2:0)
Guildford (048 641) 2604
Jones, T. Thomson (—:—:—:7:8:7)
Lambourn (0488) 71596
and 72933
Jordan, F. T. J. (3:1:3:1:0)
Leominster (056 882) 281
Jordan, Mrs J. (—:—:—:—:3)
Middleham (0969) 24421
Juckes, R. T. (0:0:0:0:0)
Abberley, Worcs. (0299) 896471

Kelleway, P. A. (12:16:13:8:13)
Newmarket (0638) 661461
Kelly, G. P. (0:0:0:0:0)
Sheriff Hutton (03477) 518
Kemp, W. T. (0:0:0:0:0)
Duns (03615) 242
Kernick, N. (0:0:0:0:0)
Kingsteignton (0364) 42755
Kersey, T. (0:0:1:0:2)
West Melton (0709) 873166
Kettlewell, S. E. (1:0:0:1:2)
Middleham (0969) 40295
Kinane, J. K. (—:—:—:—:0)
Selkirk (0835) 23814
King, Mrs A. L. M. (3:0:0:1:3)
Stratford-on-Avon (0789) 205087
King, J. S. (2:0:4:2:0)
Swindon (0793) 731481
King, R. V. C. (—:—:—:0:0)
Exning (0638) 77592 and
77754 or 77248
Knight, Mrs A. J. (0:0:0:0:4)
Cullompton (0823) 680959
Knight, Miss H. C. (—:—:—:—:0:1)
Wantage (0235) 833535

Laing, D. R. (15:19:—:—:4)
Lambourn (0488) 72381
Leach, M. R. (0:1:0:0:0)
Newark (0636) 626518
Leach, P. S. (—:—:0:1:0)
Taunton (0823) 433249
Leadbetter, S. J. (0:0:0:0:0)
Ladykirk (0289) 382519
Lee, A. N. (—:2:8:7:4)
Newmarket (0638) 662734 (home) and
669783 (stable)

Lee, D. (0:0:0:0:0)
Pickering (0751) 32425
Lee, F. H. (2:8:27:25:30)
Wilmslow (0625) 529672 and
533250 (stud)
Lee, R. A. (0:0:0:0:2)
Presteigne (0544) 267672 and
mobilephone (0836) 537145
Leigh, J. P. (3:3:1:4:5)
Willoughton, Lincs. (042 773) 210
Lewis, G. (25:32:23:26:41)
Epsom (037 22) 77662 or 77366
Liddle, P. (—:—:0:0:0)
Chester-le-Street 091-410-2072
Long, J. E. (1:0:0:0:0)
Plumpton (0273) 890244
Lungo, L. (—:—:—:—:0:1)
Carrutherstown (0387) 84691
Lunness, B. W. (—:—:—:—:0)
Hilton (0283) 732436

Macauley, Mrs N. J. (7:6:14:24:21)
Sproxton (0476) 860578 and
860090 (office)
Mackie, W. J. W. (0:9:6:8:3)
Derby (0283) 585604
Madgwick, M. J. (1:2:3:5:0)
Denmead (0705) 258313
Makin, P. J. (18:24:29:27:23)
Ogbourne Maisey (0672) 512973
Manning, R. J. (—:—:—:0:0)
Winterbourne, Avon (0454) 773274
Marks, D. (3:1:2:1:0)
Lambourn (0488) 71767
Marvin, R. F. (—:—:—:—:0:0)
Newark (0623) 822714
McCain, D. (0:0:0:0:0)
Cholmondeley (0829) 720352
McConnochie, J. C. (—:—:0:0:0)
Stratford-on-Avon (0789) 450607
McCormack, M. (7:4:12:5:16)
Wantage (023 559) 433
McCourt, M. (4:1:3:2:1)
Letcombe Regis (023 57) 4456
McGovern, T. P. (—:—:—:0:2)
Haywards Heath (0444) 881594
McKie, Mrs V. J. (—:—:—:—:0)
Buckingham (0296) 730707
McLean, B. (0:0:0:0:0)
Morpeth (0670) 787478 and
787314 (home)
McMahon, B. A. (6:20:21:22:14)
Tamworth (0827) 62901
McMath, B. J. (—:—:—:0:0)
Newmarket (0638) 665868
Mellor, S. T. E. (3:2:2:0:0)
Wanborough (0793) 790230
Millman, B. R. (—:—:—:12:9)
Cullompton (0884) 6620 and
carphone (0860) 661854
Mitchell, N. R. (0:0:0:0:0)
Piddletrenthide (0300) 4739
Mitchell, P. (5:12:15:13:8)
Epsom (037 22) 73729
Mitchell, P. (Pat) K. (6:2:6:11:5)
Newmarket (0638) 660013
Moffatt, D. (2:0:2:1:7)
Cartmel (05395) 36689

Monteith, P. (2:3:1:2:2)
Rosewell (031-440) 2309
Moore, A. (1:0:4:3:1)
Woodingdean (0273) 681679
Moore, G. M. (18:12:18:10:7)
Middleham (0969) 23823
Moore, J. S. (—:—:—:0:1)
Thruxton (0264) 88538 (office) and
(0380) 728526 (home) and
mobilephone (0831) 256532
Morgan, B. C. (6:6:3:2:0)
Barton-under-Needwood (028 375)
304
Morgan, K. A. (0:0:0:0:0)
Waltham-on-the-Wolds (066478) 711
Morley, M. F. D. (19:30:26:25:20)
Newmarket (0638) 667175
Morris, D. (—:—:—:2:6)
Newmarket (0638) 667959
Moubarak, M. Y. (—:1:1:15:18)
Newmarket (0638) 666553
Muggeridge, M. P. (—:—:—:1:3)
Fyfield (0264) 850872
Muir, W. R. (—:—:—:—:13)
Chaddleworth (04882) 463
Mulhall, J. L. (0:0:0:0:0)
York (0904) 706321
Murphy, M. P. F. (—:—:0:0:0)
Bury St Edmunds (028484) 8980 and
(0638) 665328
Murray, B. W. (—:—:—:0:1)
Malton (0653) 692879
Murray-Smith, D. J. G. (2:9:8:9:7)
Upper Lambourn (0488) 71041
Musson, W. J. (14:10:6:4:9)
Newmarket (0638) 663371

Nash, C. T. (—:—:—:—:0)
Wantage (0367) 820510
Naughton, M. P. (7:8:19:12:21)
Richmond, N. Yorks (0748) 822803
and mobilephone (0831) 414217
Naughton, T. J. (—:—:—:—:6)
Epsom (0372) 745112
Nelson, C. R. (26:22:19:30:11)
Lambourn (0488) 71391
Nicholson, D. (0:0:0:0:0)
Condicote (0451) 30417
Norton, J. (0:2:0:0:0)
Barnsley (0226) 387633
Norton, S. G. (33:33:11:20:19)
Barnsley (0924) 830450 and
830406 (office)

O'Donoghue, J. (0:0:0:0:1)
Reigate (073 72) 45241
O'Gorman, W. A. (10:24:10:51:29)
Newmarket (0638) 663330
Old, J. A. B. (1:1:0:1:1)
Barbury Castle (0793) 845200 or
845900
Oldroyd, G. R. (1:2:0:1:5)
Malton (065385) 224 (stable)
O'Leary, R. M. (0:1:2:0:1)
Malton (065386) 684 and 404
Oliver, Mrs S. (1:0:1:0:0)
Himley (0902) 892648 (stable) and
892017 (home)

1017

O'Mahony, F. J. (—:—:—:0:0)
   Dormansland (0342) 833278
O'Neill, J. J. (0:1:0:8:2)
   Penrith (08534) 555
O'Neill, M. J. (—:—:9:12:13)
   Lydiate 051-531 9616 (office),
   6887 (home) and 526 9115 (evening)
O'Neill, O. (0:1:0:2:1)
   Cheltenham (024 267) 3275
O'Shea, J. G. M. (0:0:0:0:0)
   Kidderminster (0789) 750536
O'Sullivan, R. J. (—:0:7:6:11)
   Bognor (02432) 67563
Owen, E. H. (0:0:1:0:0)
   Denbigh (08244) 264 and 356

Palling, B. (1:1:4:4:1)
   Cowbridge (0446) 772089
Parker, C. (0:0:0:0:0)
   Lockerbie (05765) 232
Parkes, J. E. (0:1:6:2:4)
   Malton (0653) 697570
Parrott, Mrs H. K. (—:—:—:0:0)
   Deerhurst (0684) 292214
Payne, J. W. (9:9:5:4:12)
   Newmarket (0638) 668675
Payne, S. G. (—:—:0:0:0)
   Carlisle (06973) 20010
Peacock, R. E. (0:2:3:1:3)
   Tarporley (0829) 732716
Pearce, J. N. (3:3:5:13:11)
   Newmarket (0638) 664669
Pearce, W. J. (8:18:24:21:29)
   Hambleton (0845) 597373
Perratt, Miss L. A. (—:—:—:—:6)
   Ayr (0292) 266232
Perrin, W. M. (—:—:—:0:0)
   Buntingford (076 384) 8113
Piggott, Mrs S. E. (1:17:34:13:15)
   Newmarket (0638) 662584
Pipe, M. C. (16:5:2:10:17)
   Wellington, Somerset (0884) 840715
Pitman, Mrs J. S. (0:2:2:1:0)
   Lambourn (0488) 71714
Popham, C. L. (0:0:0:0:0)
   Bishop's Lydeard (0823) 432769
Potts, A. W. (0:0:0:0:0)
   Barton-on-Humber (065 261) 750
Preece, W. G. (1:2:0:0:0)
   Telford (095 286) 249
Prescott, Sir Mark (26:34:40:48:48)
   Newmarket (0638) 662117
Pritchard, P. A. (—:0:0:0:0)
   Shipston-on-Stour (029588) 689
Pritchard-Gordon, G. A.
   (35:20:16:18:14)
   Newmarket (0638) 662824

Ramsden, Mrs L. E. (11:14:32:26:38)
   Sandhutton (0845) 587226
Rees, Miss G. M. (—:—:—:0:0)
   Scunthorpe (0724) 863347
Reid, A. S. (—:—:—:—:0)
   Thurleigh 071-723 1824
Reveley, Mrs M. (20:12:15:15:34)
   Saltburn (0287) 650456
Richards, G. W. (1:1:0:2:0)
   Greystoke (07684) 83392

Richmond, B. A. (1:0:0:0:0)
   Wellingore (0522) 810578
Ringer, D. J. (—:0:0:0:0)
   Newmarket (0638) 662653 and
   666021 (home)
Roberts, J. D. (0:0:1:0:3)
   Tiverton (0398) 31626
Robinson, M. H. B. (1:0:0:0:0)
   Wantage (0235) 835050
Robinson, W. R. (0:0:0:0:0)
   Scarborough (0723) 862162
Roe, C. G. A. M. (0:0:0:0:0)
   Chalford (0453) 885487
Rothwell, B. S. (—:—:—:—:0)
   Catwick (0964) 542583
Ryan, M. J. (29:22:13:32:23)
   Newmarket (0638) 664172

Sanders, Miss B. V. J. (5:14:7:4:7)
   Epsom (03722) 78453
Scargill, Dr J. D. (—:9:8:18:7)
   Newmarket (0638) 663254
Scott, A. A. (—:—:24:29:23)
   Newmarket (0638) 661998
Scudamore, M. J. (0:0:0:0:0)
   Hoarwithy (043 270) 253
Sharpe, Mrs N. S. A. (0:0:0:0:0:0)
   Leominster (0568) 2673
Shaw, D. (—:—:—:—:0)
   Ashington
Shaw, J. R. (4:1:2:2:0)
   Newmarket (0638) 661680
Sherwood, O. M. C. (0:2:0:0:0)
   Upper Lambourn (0488) 71411
Sherwood, S. E. H. (—:—:—:0:0)
   East Ilsley (063528) 678
Siddall, Miss L. C. (2:9:8:4:2)
   York (090 484) 291
Simpson, R. (14:8:7:6:5)
   Swindon (0793) 791149
Smart, B. (0:0:0:0:0)
   Lambourn (0488) 71632
Smith, A. (1:3:1:1:1)
   Beverley (0482) 882520
Smith, C. A. (—:—:—:—:2)
   Malvern (06845) 5900
Smith, D. (16:14:15:8:9)
   Bishop Auckland (0388) 603317 and
   606180
Smith, J. P. (2:0:1:0:0)
   Rugeley (054 36) 6587
Smith, N. A. (—:—:—:0:0)
   Evesham (0386) 793263
Smith, Mrs S. J. (—:—:—:—:0)
   Bingley (0274) 564930
Spearing, J. L. (5:3:8:13:12)
   Alcester (0789) 772639
Stephenson, W. A. (1:0:0:0:0)
   Bishop Auckland (0388) 720213 and
   720432 (hostel)
Stevens, B. (1:0:2:0:0)
   Winchester (0962) 883030
Stewart, A. C. (37:40:30:41:29)
   Newmarket (0638) 667323
Storey, W. L. (1:0:0:0:2)
   Consett (0207) 55259
Stoute, M. R. (105:99:116:78:83)
   Newmarket (0638) 663801

1018

Stringer, A. P. (—:—:2:5:4)
Carlton Husthwaite (0845) 40 13 29
Stubbs, Mrs L. (—:—:—:—:0)
Newmarket (0638) 56 00 14
Sutcliffe, J. R. E. (13:12:18:17:3)
Epsom (037 22) 7 28 25

Tate, F. M. (0:0:0:0:0)
Kidderminster (056 283) 243
Thom, D. T. (12.10.6:11:3)
Newmarket (063 877) 288
Thompson, R. (2:0:4:1:0)
Grantham (0780) 4 108 12
Thompson, Ronald (8:7:5:7:4)
Doncaster (0302) 842 857,
845904 and 840174
Thompson, V. (0:0:0:0:0)
Alnwick (0665) 576272
Thorne, Miss J. C. (0:0:1:0:0)
Bridgwater (027 874) 588
Thorner, G. E. (0:0:0:—:0)
Letcombe Regis (02357) 3003
Thornton, C. W. (14:15:12:12:9)
Middleham (0969) 23350
Tinkler, C. H. (31:24:35:29:15)
Malton (0653) 695981
Tinkler, N. D. (31:24:24:17:13)
Malton (065385) 245 and 5 12
Toller, J. A. R. (15:6:7:7:4)
Newmarket (0638) 668503
Tompkins, M. H. (24:16:44:46:42)
Newmarket (0638) 661434
Trietline, C. C. (0:0:0:0:0)
Welford-on-Avon (0789) 750 294
Tucker, D. C. (0:0:0:0:0)
Frome (0373) 62383
Tucker, D. R. (1:0:0:0:0)
Cullompton (0823) 680159
Tulk, P. F. (—:—:—:—:6)
Newmarket (0638) 663209
Turnell, A. (1:2:4:2:5)
East Hendred (0235 833) 297
Turner, W. G. (—:0:0:0:0)
Tavistock (082 281) 237
Turner, W. (Bill) G. M. (5:3:6:2:2)
Corton Denham (096322) 523
Twiston-Davies, N. A. (—:—:0:0:0)
Cheltenham (0451) 850278

Upson, J. R. (—:—:—:—:0)
Towcester (0327) 860043
Usher, M. D. I. (15:8:14:12:4)
East Garston (0488) 398953/4 (office)
and 7 1307 (home)

Voorspuy, R. (3:2:0:1:5)
Polegate (032 12) 7133

Wainwright, J. S. (2:2:4:3:5)
Malton (065385) 537
Wall, C. F. (9:13:9:15:7)
Newmarket (0638) 66 1999
Walwyn, P. T. (36:30:36:48:24)
Lambourn (0488) 7 1347
Waring, Mrs B. H. (0:2:1:5:6)
Malmesbury (0225) 742044
Watson, F. (0:0:1:0:0)
Sedgefield (0740) 20582

Watts, J. W. (32:23:25:27:14)
Richmond (0748) 850444
Weaver, R. J. (0:—:0:0:0)
Leicester (0530) 243105
Webber, J. H. (0:0:0:0:0)
Banbury (0295) 750226 and
750466 (stable) and
mobilephone (0836) 580129
Weedon, C. V. (—:—:—:0:1)
Chiddingfold (0428) 683344
Weymes, E. (4:10:6:5:2)
Leyburn (0969) 40229
Wharton, J. (—:9:13:15:11)
Melton Mowbray
(0664) 78334 (stable)
and 65225 (home)
Wheeler, E. A. (3:4:2:7:8)
Lambourn (0488) 71650 and
carphone (0836) 201356
Whitaker, R. M. (33:49:29:36:24)
Wetherby (0532) 892265 and
(0937) 582122
White, J. R. (—:0:5:2:5)
Wendover (0296) 623387
White, K. B. (2:1:0:1:3)
Craven Arms (058 476) 200
Whitfield, Miss A. J. (—:—:0:4:3)
Lambourn (0488) 72342
Whiting, H. A. T. (1:—:—:0:3)
Melsonby (0325) 718008
Wigham, P. (0:0:0:1:1)
Malton (094 42) 332
Wightman, W. G. R. (7:3:8:3:5)
Upham (0489) 892565
Wildman, C. P. (3:1:3:3:3)
Salisbury (0980) 52226
Wilkinson, B. E. (0:0:0:0:0)
Middleham (0969) 23385
Wilkinson, M. J. (0:0:0:0:0)
Chipping Warden (029586) 713
Williams, C. N. (1:1:2:4:2)
Newmarket (0638) 665 116
Williams, D. L. (0:0:0:0:0)
Lower Broadheath (0527) 33731
and (0905) 640074
and (0836) 547942
Williams, R. J. R. (26:18:17:15:20)
Newmarket (0638) 663 218
Williams, W. R. (0:0:—:0:0)
Idestone (0392) 8 1558
Wilson, A. J. (0:0:0:0:0)
Cheltenham (0242) 244713
Wilson, D. A. (9:7:15:19:11)
Headley (03722) 78327 (office) and
73839 (home)
Wilson, Capt. J. H. (5:11:8:7:12)
Preston (0772) 8 12780
Wilton, Miss S. J. (—:0:0:0:1)
Stoke-on-Trent (0782) 550861
Wintle, D. J. (1:0:0:0:1)
Westbury-on-Severn (045 276) 459
and 825
Woodhouse, R. D. E. (0:0:0:0:2)
York (065 381) 637
Woodman, S. (2:0:0:0:0)
Chichester (0243) 527136
Wragg, G. (27:31:25:32:51)
Newmarket (0638) 662328

Yardley, F. J. (1:1:1:1:0)
  Ombersley (0905) 620477

The following relinquished their
licence during the season

Armytage, Mrs S. (—:0:1:1:2)
Bailey, P. G. (2:2:0:0:0)
Durr, F. (10:2:10:5:3)
Dutton, D. (—:—:—:0:0)
FitzGerald, Lord J. (11:9:11:5:6)
Gracey, G. G. (0:0:0:0:0)
Huffer, G. A. (23:12:16:21:0)
McCauley, K. B. (—:—:—:6:2)
Morrill, D. (—:—:—:0:0)

Radbourne, Miss D. J. (—:—:—:0:0)
Redmond, J. V. (—:—:—:0:0)
Smyth, R. V. (6:12:10:11:5)
Stubbs, R. W. (9:12:8:9:8)
Topley, D. H. (—:—:1:0:1)
Wardle, I. P. (0:1:0:1:1)
Wilson, J. S. (7:8:13:22:9)
Wilson, W. T. J. (—:2:0:0:0)
Wingrove, K. G. (—:—:0:0:0)
Yeoman, D. (1:0:0:0:0)

The following had their licence
withdrawn
Ingram, R. (—:—:—:—:2)

JOCKEYS

The figures in brackets show the number of winners each jockey has
ridden on the flat (turf and all-weather) in Britain during the past five years
from 1987 to 1991 inclusive. Also included are telephone numbers and riding
weights.

Adams, N. M. (21:17:23:36:15) 7   8
  (0488) 72004 and
  carphone (0836) 787881
Austin, G. P. (—:—:—:0:0) 7   8
  (0638) 663857 and
  661357

Bacon, A. E. (6:8:8:0:0) 7 13
  071-2516666 and
  (0402) 229168 (agent)
Bardwell, G. S. (27:39:10:26:17) . 7   7
  (0638) 660621 (home) and
  (agent) 668484 or (0860) 864864 and
  fax (0638) 660946
Baxter, G. E. (22:19:21:30:24) 8   2
  (0903) 873780 (agent)
Birch, M. (92:95:91:61:55) 8   4
  (0653) 628578 and 628683 and
  carphone (0860) 245768
Bowker, Miss J. (1:3:3:1:0) 7   7
  (0638) 660013
Bradshaw, K. (10:7:4:0:0) 8   3
  (0638) 666709
Brette, P. (1:0:2:0:0) 7 12
  c/o (0638) 661508
Brown, J. H. (3:3:3:0:0) 8   2
  (0653) 697768

Carlisle, N. A. (6:9:17:20:27) 7   8
  (0638) 663863 and
  (agent) (0638) 666431 and 667336
Carr, J. M. (4:8:5:0:0) 8   2
  (0653) 692695 and 693356
Carroll, J. (24:49:62:50:87) 8   2
  (0524) 791697 and
  carphone (0831) 801770
Carson, W. F. H.
  (100:130:138:187:155) 7 10

  (0638) 660947, (0285) 658919 and
  (agent) 081-748-9746 or (0836) 315000
Carter, G. A. (50:42:49:89:75) 7 12
  (0638) 665950 (home) and
  (agent) 668484 or (0860) 864864 and
  fax (0638) 660946
Carter, Miss W. J. (2:—:0:—:0) ... 8   0
  (0653) 693522
Cauthen, S. M.
  (197:104:164:142:107) 8   7
  (02357) 2450 and
  (0860) 407107 (agent's mobile) and
  fax (02357) 72141
Charnock, L. (24:18:15:18:17) 7   9
  (0653) 695004
Clark, A. S. (18:20:38:23:20) 8   2
  (07982) 3028 and
  (agent) (0793) 870606
Cochrane, R.
  (111:120:120:109:102) 8   4
  (0638) 743045 and
  mobilephone (0831) 300934
Connorton, N. B.
  (46:34:21:26:26) 8   0
  (0748) 824059 (home) and (0850)
  707330 and (agent) (0964) 551135 and
  (0860) 233041
Craggs, G. (0:—:—:—:0) 8   0
  c/o (0653) 692842
Crealock, G. A. (—:—:—:—:6) ... 7 12
  (0638) 560657
Crossley, B. G. (12:9:16:20:11) ... 7 10
  (0638) 751367 (home) and
  agent (0347) 22410 and
  mobilephone (0836) 326084
Cruz, A. (4:1:2:4:43) 8   2
  (0638) 662299 and
  (agent) (0733) 263816

1020

Culhane, P. A. (24:38:24:20:29) ... 8   0
(0937) 836171 and
mobilephone (0831) 201425 and
(agent) (0423) 887097 or
mobilephone (0860) 311357
Curant, J. A. (2:2:2:1:0) 7   12
(01876) 0250 and (0638) 780027
Curant, R. D. (16:5:0:0:0) 8   3
(0672) 40717

D'Arcy, P. W. (4:7:5:6:3) 8   2
(0638) 750005 and
(agent) (0273) 23889 or
(0850) 725039
Darley, K. P. (55:38:70:83:66) ... 8   0
(0347) 22588 and
mobilephone (0860) 926556
Dawson, S. (15:14:16:12:11) 7   9
(0488) 72261 (home) and
(0903) 873780 (agent)
Day, N. P. (17:26:22:39:28) 8   3
agent (0638) 730012 and
(0831) 336611
Dettori, L. (8:22:75:141:94) 8   4
(0638) 666431 and 667336 (agent)
Dicks, A. C. (1:1:0:0:1) 8   4
(0272) 519184 and (027581) 2192
Duffield, G. P. (64:77:87:84:88) ... 8   0
(0638) 668484 or (0860) 864864 or
fax (0638) 660946 (agent) and
76544 (home)
Dwyer, C. A. (6:3:3:1:2) 8   8
(0638) 660663

Eddery, J. D. (—:—:—:4:1:2) 8   0
(0748) 5640 (agent)
Eddery, P. J. J.
(195:183:171:209:165) 8   4
(0844) 290282 and 201427
Elliott, R. P. (8:10:19:22:14) 8   0
(0969) 22884

Fallon, K. F. (—:31:28:39:29) 8   1
(0904) 647213 and
fax (0904) 634127 (agent) and
(0653) 693087 (home)
Findlay, Mrs J. M.
(—:—:—:—:0) 8   0
(0434) 681849
Forte, A. M. (—:—:—:—:0) 8   4
(0626) 779006
Fortune, J. J. (—:8:29:46:32) 7   10
(0793) 870606 (agent)
Foster, G. N. (6:3:0:4:0) 7   11
(090674) 531
Fox, R. D. S. (20:16:11:6:13) 7   7
(0638) 778188 and
(0733) 263816 (agent)

Gibson, D. (13:16:30:30:22) 7   9
(0235) 835184 and
mobilephone (0831) 103354
Giles, M. A. (3:3:4:12:0) 7   7
(0904) 647213 and
fax (0904)634127 (agent)
Greaves, Miss A. A.
(—:—:3:49:34) 8   1
(0845) 587435

Guest, E. J. (0:—:1:5:0) 8   7
(0638) 721183 and
(0253) 812194 (agent)

Harley, P. M. (—:—:—:—:0) 8   8
(0932) 243913 and
carphone (0860) 234342 (agent)
Hill, P. D. (10:0:—:0:0) 7   7
(05435) 78213 and (0347) 810825
Hillis, R. P. (—:40:7:11:4) 8   2
carphone (0831) 236748 and
(agent) (0733) 263816
Hills, M. P. (75:76:77:61:65) 8   2
(0364) 42332 and
mobilephone (0860) 235151 (agent)
Hills, R. J. (46:52:63:56:67) 8   0
(0364) 42332 and
mobilephone (0860) 235151 (agent)
Hind, G. E. P. (5:2:23:28:26) 7   12
Hood, W. (2:1:4:7:5) 8   5
(0638) 778366
Horsfall, S. S. (3:0:0:3:0) 8   6
c/o (0302) 710096
Houston, Miss J. (3:0:3:4:1) 7   7
(0638) 669839 and 668503
Howe, N. J. (7:5:4:8:7) 8   2
(02357) 68227 (home) and
(agent) 071 2516666 and (0402) 229168

Johnson, E. (5:10:4:4:1) 7   8
(0285) 655020 and
mobile (0831) 345360

Keightley, S. L. (4:3:6:0:2) 8   11
(0638) 666070
Kennedy, J. B. (0:0:0:—:0) 8   11
(0488) 72734

Lang, T. L. (0:0:1:0:2) 8   4
(0296) 625310
Lappin, R. T. (13:6:4:22:8) 7   12
(0964) 551135 and (0860) 233041
Lowe, J. J. (60:41:36:45:54) 7   8
(0904) 708871 (home) and
mobilephone (0860) 244284 or
(agent) (0609) 748241 and
mobilephone (0836) 229366 and
fax (0609) 748749
Lucas, T. G. (15:—:—:—:1) 8   6

Mackay, A. (21:36:10:14:18) 7   8
(0638) 560464 and
(agent) (0932) 243913 and
mobilephone (0860) 234342
McAndrew, M. A. (0:0:0:0:1) 7   12
(0845) 587226 (office) and
524309 (home)
McGhin, R. (0:1:2:1:0) 8   5
(0638) 660920
McGlone, A. D. (9:16:15:25:24) ... 7   12
(0264) 790421 and carphone (0836)
242788 and (agent) (0423) 871624 or
mobilephone (0860) 401683
McKay, D. J. (9:5:3:3:0) 7   8
(0488) 684993 and
carphone (0860) 889007
McKeown, D. R.
(20:59:86:87:72) 8   2

(0977) 681247 and
mobilephone (0860) 685439 and
(agent) (0306) 888318 and
mobile (0860) 243068
McLaughlin, J. F. S.
(—:—:—:—:1) 8 7
(0638) 668115
Mellor, Miss. A. D. (9:11:7:3:2) ... 7 7
(0793) 790230 and
carphone (0836) 278602
Mercer, A. (6:2:5:3:1) 7 12
(0748) 811103
Morris, A. (0:1:3:1:1) 8 0
(0403) 891339
Morris, Mrs C. L. (1:0:—:1:0) 8 8
(0273) 681679
Morris, S. D. (2:7:2:1:0) 8 0
(0653) 692098
Muggeridge, R. J.
(—:—:—:—:0) 8 7
(0264) 850652 and 850872
Munro, A. K. (6:33:38:95:110) 7 12
(0954) 781783 (home) and
mobilephone (0831) 364757 and
(agent) (0536) 412144 and
(0831) 630363
Murray, J. G. (0:4:3:0:3) 8 3
c/o (0403) 730255 and (09442) 419 and
8879 (agent)

Newnes, W. A. P.
(48:44:40:53:30) 8 2
(023559) 272 and
mobilephone (0831) 171809 and
Fax (023559) 611 and
(agent) 071 240 2963 and
(0850) 369112
Nicholls, D. (33:32:28:26:30) 8 6
(0347) 23094,
mobilephone (0831) 238088 and
(agent) (0904) 647213 and
fax (0904) 634127
Nutter, C. (2:1:2:5:2) 8 0
(0638) 668153

Peate, Mrs A. J. (—:—:—:2:0) 7 7
(0638) 666758
Perks, S. J. (18:18:34:29:23) 8 5
(0543) 491594
Piggott, L. K. (—:—:—:3:48) 8 6
(0638) 662584 and
mobilephone (0836) 222269
Price, R. W. (0:2:10:6:6) 7 8
(0638) 669712 and
(agent) (0932) 243913 and
carphone (0860) 234342
Procter, B. T. (2:2:4:1:2) 8 2
(063528) 596
Proud, A. (10:12:7:4:7) 7 10
(0949) 43350 (home) and
50099 (office) and
mobilephone (0860) 913063

Quinn, J. A. (14:23:19:31:32) 7 7
(0638) 730445
mobilephone (0831) 321813 and
(agent) (0904) 647213 and
fax (0904) 634127

Quinn, T. R. (55:46:63:90:99) 8 2
(0635) 200530 and
carphone (0860) 287172 and
fax (0635) 202051 and
(agent) (0788) 832958 and
mobile (0831) 821100

Raymond, B. H.
(45:77:66:75:74) 8 5
(0638) 730387 (home) and
(agent) 666431 and 667336
Raymont, S. J. (2:1:1:5:7) 8 0
(06723) 533 and (0249) 817007
Reid, J. A. (81:79:84:67:80) 8 6
(0367) 820214 (agent)
Riding, A. (3:4:3:1:0) 7 13
(0638) 660212 (agent)
Roberts, M. L.
(74:121:107:128:118) 7 13
(0638) 661026 (home) and
(063528) 331 (agent)
Rogers, T. (—:—:—:0:5) 8 7
(0635) 64853
Rouse, B. A. (50:51:56:36:13) 8 2
(0293) 871547
Rutter, C. L. P. (27:15:14:28:24) . 7 12
023 559 614 and
(0836) 760769 (mobile)
Ryan, W. (69:58:49:59:72) 8 2
(0423) 871624 or
mobilephone (0860) 401683 (agent)
and (0638) 717236 (home)

Sedgwick, P. (—:—:0:3:2) 8 0
c/o (0759) 71472
Shoults, A. F. (11:4:4:7:2) 7 12
(0638) 731238 and
(agent) (0604) 414710
Skingle, A. T. (—:—:—:—:0) 8 4
c/o (0638) 668675
Smith, V. (1:3:0:1:3) 8 6
(0638) 668972 and (agent) 668974 or
(0831) 865974
Sofley, J. A. (—:—:—:0:0) 7 10
(0638) 661331
Sprake, T. J. (4:4:8:12:17) 7 11
(0793) 870606 (agent)
Street, R. (8:6:3:0:2) 7 8
(0488) 71412 and 71548 and
(agent) (0273) 23889 or
(0850) 725039
Swinburn, W. R. J.
(92:88:93:112:68) 8 6
(0440) 820277 (home) and
(0638) 660811 and 660258 (agent)

Tebbutt, M. J. (0:2:8:23:15) 8 4
(0638) 668484 and
mobilephone (0860) 864864 and
fax (0638) 660946
Tinkler, Mrs K. A.
(21:16:12:13:8) 7 7
(065385) 245 and 512
Turner, H. E. (0:—:—:—:0) 8 2
(0292) 283399
Turner, S. (—:—:—:3:5) 9 1
(0937) 582690 and
(0831) 502899 mobilephone

Vincent, Miss L. J.
(—:—:—:—:1) 8   7
(0488) 73385 and
mobilephone (0831) 532068

Webster, S. G. (3:19:23:19:12) 8   2
(0904) 608458

Wernham, R. A. (3:12:6:7:0) 8   4
(0235) 833754

Wharton, W. J. (0:0:1:0:0) 8   6
(0638) 70280

Whitehall, A. J. (3:8:0:0:0) 7 11
(0635) 298598 and
(03727) 24018 (agent)

Whitworth, S. J.
(22:31:24:34:26) 8   0
(0672) 40961 (home),
carphone (0860) 676696 and
(agent) (0932) 243913 and
(0860) 234342 (mobile)

Wigham, M. (28:23:33:27:9) 8   4
(02357) 70098 and
carphone (0831) 456426

Williams, J. A. N.
(15:25:35:62:64) 7 12
(0454) 218622 and
carphone (0836) 520252

Williams, T. L. (53:28:38:27:19) .. 7   9
(0488) 72734 (home) and
carphone (0860) 589885 and
(agent) (0932) 243913 and
(0860) 234342

Wood, M. (10:1:2:1:4) 8   0
(065385) 412

Wood, S. (9:17:12:15:23) 7   7
(0347) 22410 and
mobilephone (0836) 326084 (agent)

The following relinquished their licence
during the season:

Bleasdale, J. (13:11:6:8:9)
Burke, P. A. (4:23:14:12:8)
Eddery, Paul A. (37:52:44:50:72)
McGiff, B. C. (—:—:—:—:2)
Walsh, M. P. (—:1:2:4:0)

APPRENTICES

The following list shows the employer and riding weight of every apprentice who holds a current licence to ride on the flat, and the number of winners he or she has ridden in Britain, wins in apprentice races being recorded separately.

Apprentices may claim 7 lb until they have won 15 races, 5 lb until they have won 50 races and 3 lb until they have won 85 races. Apprentice races are excepted in all these cases. The allowance each apprentice is entitled to claim is shown in brackets. The claim may be exercised in all handicaps and selling races, and in all other races with guaranteed prize money of not more than £8,000.

Ahern, Miss K. (7) 7   7
(J. Dunlop)

Aldwincle, W. J. (7) 7   7
(Mrs S. Piggott)

Allen, Miss M. (7) 8   0
(W. Carter)

Armes, Miss A. C. (7) 4 + 5 ap 7   0
(H. Candy)

Arrowsmith, F. P. (7) 4 + 9 ap 8   5
(I. Balding)

Avery, C. M. (7) 3 + 3 ap 7   7
(L. Holt)

Baker, C. J. (7) 7 12
(O. Brennan)

Balding, Miss Claire. (7) 1 ap 7   0
(J. Balding)
(0302) 710096 (agent) and
(0777) 818407

Bastiman, H. J. (7) 5 + 1 ap 7   8
(R. Bastiman)

Bates, A. (7) 5 7   7
(P. Kelleway) (0638) 560464 and
mobilephone (0831) 390708

Bedford, Miss J. M. (7) 7 12
(Mrs G. Reveley)

Beeching, Miss K. F. (7) 2 .... 7 10
(S. Bowring)

Benney, Miss S. J. (7) 7   7
(C. Cyzer)

Bentley, E. (7) 2 + 2 ap 7 12
(M. Morley)

Berry, R. K. (7) 7   7
(D. Elsworth)

Biggs, D. D. (3) 56 + 12 ap 7   8
(M. Ryan) (0638) 561287 and
(agent) (0638) 664172 and
660829

Biggs, Miss D. D. M. (7) 2 + 1 ap .. 7   7
(P. Howling)

Bott, R. P. (7) 7   0
(G. Blum)

Bovingdon, Miss S. K. (7) 8   2
(G. Balding)

Bowe, P. D. P. (7) 1 ap 7 10
(W. Musson)

Boxer, Miss E. J. (7) 8   0
(R. Bennett)

Bradley, Michael (7) 7 12
  (J. Bradley)
Bradley, M. P. (7) 8 5
  (I. Balding)
Bramhill, J. A. (7) 1 .... 7 7
  (B. McMahon)
Bray, V. (7) 2 ap 7 7
  (M. Stoute)
Brett, Miss. B. N. (7) 7 7
  (Mrs S. Piggott)
Bridger, Miss R. J. (7) 8 2
  (J. Bridger)
Brown, G. (7) 7 10
  (G. Eden)
Brown, K. (7) 7 2
  (D. Wintle)
Busfield, S. M. (7) 7 11
  (B. Hills)

Cairns, A. (7) 2 .... 7 10
  (A. Lee)
Carroll, Miss B. S. (7) 8 0
  (G. Pritchard-Gordon)
Carson, D. A. (7) 1 + 1 ap 7 0
  (R. Hollinshead)
Carter, L. A. (7) 8 0
  (R. Akehurst)
Chandler, G. (7) 7 12
  (Miss G. Reveley)
Clark, Miss C. M. M. (7) 1 ap 8 0
  (A. Hide)
Cogley, Miss K. (7) 7 7
  (G. Pritchard-Gordon)
Collingwood, Miss G. A. (7) 1 ap . 7 7
  (D. Smith)
Cripps, Miss C. L. (7) 8 4
  (R. Hollinshead)
Cripps, D. (7) 7 7
  (P. Mitchell)
Curran, L. A. (7) 8 2
  (M. O'Neill)
Currie, W. A. (7) 8 5
  (Mrs J. Pitman)

D'Arcy, T. (7) 7 7
  (B. Curley)
Darmanin, N. (7) 7 12
  (J. Spearing)
Darmanin, P. (7) 8 7
  (R. Hollinshead)
Davies, S. G. (7) 6 + 5 ap 7 10
  (H. Cecil) (0638) 662192 and
  663079 (agent)
Denaro, Mark (7) 1 ap 7 12
  (R. Hannon)
Denaro, M. J. (7) 8 + 3 ap 8 1
  (C. Allen) (0964) 551135 and
  (0860) 233041 (agent)
Dennis, J. P. (7) 7 0
  (R. Hollinshead)
Doran, Miss V. T. (7) 8 0
  (W. Pearce)
Dovey, Miss K. (7) 7 0
  (J. Bethell)
Doyle, B. (5) 20 + 4 ap 7 0
  (C. Brittain)
Drowne, S. J. (7) 2 + 3 ap 7 10
  (R. Holder)

Edmunds, J. P. (7) 7 12
  (J. Balding)
Eiffert, S. (7) 8 0
  (R. Guest)
Elwell, Miss A. M. (7) 7 7
  (E. Owen)

Fallon, G. J. (7) 8 0
  (I. Balding)
Fanning, J. K. (3) 59 + 3 ap 7 5
  (T. Fairhurst) (09442) 419
Fifield, D. G. A (7) 7 8
  (C. Horgan)
Fordham, J. R. (7) 7 7
  (R. Hollinshead)
Forletta, Miss E. (7) 8 2
  (A. Stewart)
Forster, G. (7) 8 + 4 ap 7 12
  (C. Allen)
Fothergill, S. P. (7) 7 7
  (N. Tinkler)
Frost, W. D. (7) 1 ap 7 8
  (M. O'Neill)

Garth, A. R. (7) 1 + 3 ap 7 4
  (R. Hollinshead)
Gibbs, D. (7) 1 + 1 ap 7 7
  (R. Hannon)
Giles, S. M. (7) 4 + 9 ap 8 2
  (J. Berry)
Godsafe, M. S. B. (7) 2 ap 7 13
  (M. Tompkins) (0327) 349700
Griffiths, Miss C. E. (7) 1 ap 8 5
  (Lady Herries)
Griffiths, D. C. (7) 7 7
  (I. Balding)
Griffiths, M. E. P. (7) 7 2
  (I. Campbell)
Gwilliams, N. L. (5) 16 + 1 ap 7 8
  (W. Carter) (0372) 377209 and 377240

Hall, N. V. (7) 1 + 1 ap 7 10
  (G. Wragg) (0638) 577457 (agent)
Halliday, V. (7) 4 .... 7 6
  (T. Barron)
Harris, J. C. (7) 7 10
  (L. Cumani)
Harrison, D. P. (7) 11 + 4 ap 7 0
  (Lord Huntingdon)
Havlin, R. (7) 2 + 1 ap 7 5
  (Miss L. Perratt)
Hawkes, S. R. (7) 7 0
  (A. Jarvis)
Hawksley, C. L. (7) 3 + 1 ap 7 0
  (H. Cecil) (0638) 577238 and
  (0831) 865974 (agent)
Haworth, S. M. (7) 2 + 5 ap 7 12
  (J. Berry)
Herrington, M. (7) 8 4
  (R. Whitaker)
Hodgson, C. A. (5) 30 + 10 ap 7 13
  (M. Tompkins)
  (0638) 661434 and
  (agent) (0327) 349700
Holland, D. P. 101 + 8 ap 7 10
  (B. Hills) (0488) 71548 and
  (agent) (0403) 59345 or
  mobilephone (0850) 300449

Hollick, W. J. (7) 7 12
(J. Berry)
Holmes, Miss M. B. (7) 7 9
(D. Arbuthnot)
Houghton, P. (7) 1 .... 8 7
(G. Harwood)
Howarth, Miss N. (7) 1ap 7 4
(P. Haslam)
Humphries, M. B. (7) 1 .... 7 7
(R. Hollinshead)
Hunt, Michael (7) 1ap 7 0
(J. FitzGerald)
Hunter, J. J. (7) 3 + 4 ap 7 5
(D. Elsworth)
Husband, E. L. (7) 1 + 5 ap 7 10
(R. Hollinshead)
Hutton, P. (5) 20 + 2 ap 7 13
(J. Fanshawe)

Jermy, M. (7) 1 + 1 ap 7 10
(S. Dow)
Johnson, P. A. (7) 1 + 3 ap 8 2
(M. Easterby)
Jones, Miss W. J. (7) 7 2
(R. Hannon)
Joyce, Miss D. P. (7) 7 7
(A. Davison)

Knott, S. T. (7) 7 10
(E. Alston)

Lanigan, S. (7) 1ap 7 7
(L. Cumani)
Lejeune, A. J. (7) 2 + 1 ap 8 10
(G. Balding)
Lidgard, Miss H. V. (7) 7 10
(B. Hanbury)
Liggins, A. (7) 7 0
(J. Pearce)

Madden, Miss F. M. (7) 7 7
(H. Thomson Jones)
Maher, W. (7) 7 7
(D. Chapman)
Maloney, S. J. (5) 33 + 4 ap 7 5
(M. Brittain)
Marsden, T. (7) 1 + 1 ap 7 12
(J. Berry)
Marshall, J. (7) 4 + 3 ap 7 10
(Mrs N. Macauley)
Mason, Miss K. L. (7) 7 4
(J. Czerpak)
Mayne, Miss T. M. (7) 7 10
(D. Tucker)
McDonnell, Miss K. S.
(7) 3 + 4 ap 7 0
(W. Muir)
McGoldrick, M. (7) 7 0
(J. Kinane)
McKeon, J. J. (7) 7 7
(M. O'Neill)
McLaughlin T. G. (7) 6 + 3 ap 7 7
(C. Cyzer)
Meredith, D. (7) 3 .... 8 5
(R. Dickin)
Middleton, D. J. (7) 8 0
(J. Czerpak)

Milligan, G. E. H. (7) 1 + 1 ap 7 0
(Mrs S. Piggott)
Mitchell, G. C. (7) 2 ap 7 10
(R. Williams)
Mitchell, R. P. (7) 7 7
(J. White)
Moffat, D. (7) 1 .... 6 10
(D. Moffat)
Moogan, R. M. (7) 7 5
(A. Moore)
Moorhouse, Miss P. J. T. (7) 7 12
(S. Norton)
Morris, P. J. (7) 7 10
(J. Jenkins)
Mulvey, S. (7) 1ap 7 10
(M. Tompkins) (0327) 349700 (agent)
Munday, C. J. A. (7) 6 + 4 ap 7 10
(B. Hills)

Neill, Miss A. G. (7) 8 2
(E. Alston)
Newton, L. (5) 15 + 3 ap 7 5
(A. Scott) (0638) 661998 and
agent (0638) 660021 (evenings only)
Norton, F. (5) 41 + 7 ap 7 5
(G. Wragg) (0904) 647213 and
fax (0904) 634127 (agent)

O'Dwyer, J. J. (7) 3 .... 7 12
(M. Bell)
O'Gorman, Miss E. S. (5) 37 + 2
ap 7 8
(W. O'Gorman)
O'Gorman, S. M. (3) 59 + 4 ap 7 8
(I. Balding)

Parkin, G. (7) 1 + 3 ap 7 10
(R. Hollinshead)
Parkin, P. A. (7) 8 0
(J. Balding)
Pattinson, K. (7) 8 2
(M. Stoute)
Pears, O. J. (7) 7 + 1 ap 7 12
(S. Norton)
(0924) 830450 and
(0977) 620264 (agent)
Perham, R. (5) 47 + 6 ap 8 0
(R. Hannon)
Plowright, Miss M. (7) 7 7
(Miss J. Thorne)
Pollard, C. (7) 2 .... 7 9
(M. Bell)
Powell, Miss D. J. (7) 7 0
(C. Williams)
Procter, A. R. (7) 8 + 6 ap 8 7
(D. Elsworth)
Prys-Jones, Miss B. L. (7) 7 10
(J. Berry)
Purseglove, Miss T. N. (7) 2 + 1
ap 8 0
(G. Balding)

Ramshaw, T. M. (7) 8 4
(R. Johnson Houghton)
Reed, Miss H. J. (7) 7 7
(M. Camacho)
Roberts, P. B. (7) 7 0
(J. Berry)

Rogers, D. (7) 8 0
  (H. Candy)
Rogers, I. M. (7) 1 ap 8 2
  (W. Hern)
Rolfe, Miss H. S. (7) 7 0
  (N. Tinkler)
Roxburgh, P. C. (7) 7 2
  (R. Charlton)
Russell, B. J. (7) 1 .... 7 7
  (W. Holden)
Rutter, K. (7) 11 + 5 ap 7 13
  (M. Jarvis)
  (0638) 577238 and
  (0831) 865974 (agent)

Sanders, S. (7) 1 + 4 ap 7 4
  (B. McMahon)
Scally, C. (7) 1 ap 7 12
  (K. Ivory)
Scott, Miss F. J. (7) 8 0
  (M. Naughton)
Scott, M. A. (7) 1 ap 7 0
  (Miss B. Sanders)
Simpson, A. J. (7) 1 + 2 ap 8 8
  (P. Cole)
Simpson, M. (7) 1 + 1 ap 8 0
  (A. Stewart)
Sked, K. P. (7) 7 0
  (C. Thornton)
Slater, Miss H. (7) 7 13
  (L. Cumani)
Slattery, J. V. (7) 1 .... 8 10
  (O. O'Neill)
Smith, J. D. (7) 2 + 2 ap 6 12
  (G. Harwood)
Smith, Miss M. J. (7) 1 ap 7 7
  (N. Macauley)
Stather, D. M. (7) 4 ap 8 2
  (R. Charlton)
Swift, C. J. (7) 7 12
  (A. Stewart)
Swinnerton, J. (7) 7 0
  (J. Banks)

Tate, J. D. (7) 2 + 1 ap 7 7
  (N. Callaghan)
Thomas, B. (7) 3 + 3 ap 7 5
  (E. Wheeler)
Thompson, D. R. (7) 1 .... 8 0
  (H. Candy)
Tierney, D. P. (7) 1 ap 7 10
  (G. Balding)
Todd, A. W. (7) 7 9
  (Ronald Thompson)
Toole, D. J. (7) 6 9
  (M. Haynes)

Tucker, A. P. (5) 23 + 15 ap 7 10
  (M. McCourt) (0932) 243913 and
  carphone (0860) 234342 (agent) and
  mobile (0831) 855741
Turner, P. J. (7) 6 + 6 ap 7 2
  (M. Bell)

Varley, N. G. (7) 7 5
  (I. Balding)
Vickers, Miss S. P. (7) 7 12
  (G. Pritchard-Gordon)

Waterfield, R. J. (7) 7 7
  (R. Holder)
Weaver, J. C. (7) 8 + 11 ap 7 12
  (L. Cumani) (0423) 871624 and
  (0860) 401683 (mobile)
Webb, C. (7) 7 7
  (W. Hern)
Williams, David (7) 1 .... 7 0
  (M. Tompkins) (0327) 349700 (agent)
Williams, Miss S. (7) 7 0
  (D. Haydn Jones)
Williams, S. D. (7) 8 + 5 ap 8 9
  (J. Glover)
  (0709) 886276 and
  (0831) 300935 (agent)
Wilson, T. G. A. (7) 3 + 3 ap 7 3
  (C. Wall)
Wright, D. T. (7) 1 ap 6 12
  (M. Brittain)
Wright, M. G. (7) 7 4
  (F. Lee) (0733) 333252 (agent)

The following winning apprentices
relinquished their licence during
the season:

Brislen, P. (7) 1
Cairns, S. (7) 1 + 3 ap
Campbell, C. (7) 2 + 1 ap
Faulkner, Miss G. (7) 1 + 1 ap
Granger, R. Y. (7) 1 ap
Hunt, M. R. (7) 2 ap
Husband, G. I. (5) 42 + 10 ap
Kennedy, N. A. (5) 23 + 2 ap
Lane, B. B. (7) 6 + 7 ap
Lees, D. W. (7) 1 + 3 ap
Litwin, W. B. (7) 1 + 4 ap
Mahoney, L. D. (7) 1 + 1 ap
Marshall, M. (5) 15 + 10 ap
Martinez, A. L. (7) 1 + 1 ap
McCabe, D. R. (7) 1
McGrath, G. J. (7) 1 ap
O'Neill, G. J. (7) 1 ap
Spence, A. J. (7) 2 ap

1992 FLAT RACING FIXTURES

March

3 Tue.	Lingfield (a)
6 Fri.	Southwell (a)
7 Sat.	Lingfield (a)
10 Tue.	Lingfield (a)
14 Sat.	Southwell (a)
18 Wed.	Southwell (a)
19 Thu.	Doncaster
20 Fri.	Doncaster
21 Sat.	Doncaster, Lingfield (a)
23 Mon.	Folkestone
24 Tue.	Leicester
25 Wed.	Catterick
26 Thu.	Brighton, Wolverhampton
27 Fri.	Beverley
28 Sat.	Beverley, Warwick
30 Mon.	Folkestone, Newcastle
31 Tue.	Leicester

April

1 Wed.	Hamilton
2 Thu.	Brighton
3 Fri.	Kempton
4 Sat.	Lingfield
6 Mon.	Wolverhampton
7 Tue.	Pontefract
8 Wed.	Ripon
9 Thu.	Hamilton
10 Fri.	Newbury, Thirsk
11 Sat.	Newbury, Thirsk
13 Mon.	Brighton, Edinburgh, Nottingham
14 Tue.	Newmarket
15 Wed.	Newmarket, Pontefract
16 Thu.	Newmarket, Ripon
18 Sat.	Haydock, Kempton, Newcastle
20 Mon.	Kempton, Newcastle, Nottingham, Warwick
21 Tue.	Warwick
22 Wed.	Catterick, Folkestone
23 Thu.	Beverley
24 Fri.	Carlisle, Sandown
25 Sat.	Leicester, Ripon, Sandown (mixed)
27 Mon.	Pontefract, Windsor*, Wolverhampton
28 Tue.	Bath, Nottingham
29 Wed.	Ascot
30 Thu.	Newmarket, Redcar, Salisbury

May

1 Fri.	Hamilton, Newmarket
2 Sat.	Haydock, Newmarket, Thirsk
4 Mon.	Haydock (mixed), Kempton, Pontefract, Warwick
5 Tue.	Chester, Sandown*
6 Wed.	Chester, Salisbury
7 Thu.	Brighton, Carlisle, Chester

8 Fri.	Beverley, Carlisle, Lingfield
9 Sat.	Bath, Beverley, Lingfield
11 Mon.	Hamilton, Windsor*, Wolverhampton
12 Tue.	York
13 Wed.	Kempton*, York
14 Thu.	York
15 Fri.	Newbury, Newmarket, Thirsk
16 Sat.	Hamilton*, Lingfield*, Newbury, Newmarket, Southwell*, Thirsk
18 Mon.	Bath, Edinburgh
19 Tue.	Beverley, Goodwood
20 Wed.	Goodwood
21 Thu.	Catterick, Goodwood
22 Fri.	Haydock, Pontefract*, Salisbury
23 Sat.	Doncaster, Haydock, Kempton, Lingfield*, Southwell*, Warwick*
25 Mon.	Chepstow, Doncaster, Leicester, Redcar, Sandown
26 Tue.	Leicester, Redcar, Sandown*
27 Wed.	Brighton, Ripon*
28 Thu.	Brighton, Carlisle
29 Fri.	Goodwood*, Hamilton, Newcastle, Nottingham
30 Sat.	Edinburgh, Lingfield, Wolverhampton*

June

1 Mon.	Leicester, Redcar
2 Tue.	Folkestone, Newbury*, Yarmouth
3 Wed.	Beverley*, Epsom, Yarmouth
4 Thu.	Beverley, Epsom
5 Fri.	Catterick, Epsom, Goodwood*, Haydock*, Southwell
6 Sat.	Carlisle*, Catterick, Epsom, Haydock, Leicester*
8 Mon.	Nottingham, Pontefract
9 Tue.	Pontefract, Salisbury
10 Wed.	Beverley, Hamilton*, Kempton*, Southwell
11 Thu.	Chepstow*, Hamilton, Newbury
12 Fri.	Doncaster*, Goodwood*, Sandown, Southwell, York
13 Sat.	Bath, Lingfield*, Nottingham*, Sandown, Wolverhampton*, York
15 Mon.	Brighton, Edinburgh, Windsor*
16 Tue.	Royal Ascot, Thirsk
17 Wed.	Ripon, Royal Ascot
18 Thu.	Ripon, Royal Ascot
19 Fri.	Ayr, Newmarket*, Redcar, Royal Ascot
20 Sat.	Ascot, Ayr, Lingfield*, Redcar, Southwell*, Warwick*

22 Mon.	Edinburgh, Nottingham, Windsor*, Wolverhampton*
23 Tue.	Brighton, Newbury*, Yarmouth
24 Wed.	Carlisle, Chester*, Kempton*, Salisbury
25 Thu.	Carlisle, Salisbury
26 Fri.	Bath*, Doncaster, Goodwood*, Lingfield, Newcastle*, Newmarket
27 Sat.	Chepstow, Doncaster*, Lingfield*, Newcastle, Newmarket, Warwick*
29 Mon.	Hamilton*, Pontefract, Windsor*, Wolverhampton
30 Tue.	Chepstow, Folkestone

July

1 Wed.	Catterick*, Epsom*, Warwick, Yarmouth
2 Thu.	Brighton*, Catterick, Haydock*, Yarmouth
3 Fri.	Beverley*, Haydock, Sandown, Southwell
4 Sat.	Bath, Beverley, Haydock, Nottingham*, Sandown
6 Mon.	Edinburgh, Leicester, Ripon*, Windsor*
7 Tue.	Newmarket, Pontefract
8 Wed.	Bath, Kempton*, Newmarket, Redcar*
9 Thu.	Chepstow*, Newmarket, Redcar
10 Fri.	Chester*, Lingfield, Warwick, York
11 Sat.	Chester, Lingfield, Salisbury, Southwell*, York
13 Mon.	Beverley*, Edinburgh, Windsor*, Wolverhampton
14 Tue.	Beverley, Folkestone, Leicester*
15 Wed.	Catterick, Sandown*, Southwell, Yarmouth*
16 Thu.	Catterick, Chepstow*, Hamilton*, Sandown
17 Fri.	Hamilton*, Newbury, Newmarket*, Southwell, Thirsk
18 Sat.	Ayr, Lingfield*, Newbury, Newmarket, Ripon, Wolverhampton*
20 Mon.	Ayr, Bath, Nottingham*, Windsor*
21 Tue.	Ayr, Folkestone
22 Wed.	Doncaster, Hamilton*, Redcar*, Sandown*, Yarmouth
23 Thu.	Brighton, Doncaster*, Hamilton*, Yarmouth
24 Fri.	Ascot, Ayr*, Carlisle, Pontefract*, Yarmouth
25 Sat.	Ascot, Ayr, Newcastle, Southwell*, Warwick*
27 Mon.	Lingfield, Newcastle, Windsor*, Wolverhampton*
28 Tue.	Beverley, Goodwood, Leicester*
29 Wed.	Catterick, Epsom*, Goodwood, Southwell*
30 Thu.	Goodwood, Salisbury*, Yarmouth

| 31 Fri. | Edinburgh*, Goodwood, Newmarket*, Thirsk |

August

1 Sat.	Goodwood, Newmarket, Thirsk, Windsor*
3 Mon.	Nottingham*, Ripon
4 Tue.	Brighton, Nottingham*, Redcar
5 Wed.	Brighton, Kempton*, Pontefract
6 Thu.	Brighton, Pontefract
7 Fri.	Haydock*, Newmarket*, Redcar, Wolverhampton*
8 Sat.	Haydock, Lingfield*, Newmarket, Redcar, Southwell*
10 Mon.	Leicester*, Thirsk*, Windsor
11 Tue.	Bath, Catterick*, Yarmouth
12 Wed.	Beverley, Salisbury
13 Thu.	Beverley, Salisbury
14 Fri.	Folkestone, Haydock*, Newbury, Southwell
15 Sat.	Lingfield*, Newbury, Ripon, Wolverhampton
17 Mon.	Hamilton, Windsor
18 Tue.	Folkestone, York
19 Wed.	Kempton*, Yarmouth, York
20 Thu.	Salisbury*, Yarmouth, York
21 Fri.	Chester, Sandown
22 Sat.	Chester, Ripon, Sandown
24 Mon.	Nottingham
25 Tue.	Brighton, Pontefract
26 Wed.	Brighton, Redcar
27 Thu.	Lingfield
28 Fri.	Edinburgh*, Goodwood, Newmarket, Thirsk
29 Sat.	Goodwood, Newcastle, Newmarket, Windsor*
31 Mon.	Chepstow, Epsom, Newcastle, Ripon, Warwick, Wolverhampton

September

1 Tue.	Epsom, Ripon
2 Wed.	York
3 Thu.	Salisbury, York
4 Fri.	Haydock, Kempton
5 Sat.	Haydock, Kempton, Thirsk
7 Mon.	Hamilton, Wolverhampton
8 Tue.	Carlisle, Leicester, Lingfield
9 Wed.	Doncaster
10 Thu.	Doncaster, Folkestone
11 Fri.	Doncaster, Goodwood
12 Sat.	Chepstow, Doncaster, Goodwood
14 Mon.	Bath, Leicester
15 Tue.	Sandown, Yarmouth
16 Wed.	Ayr, Sandown, Yarmouth
17 Thu.	Ayr, Lingfield, Yarmouth
18 Fri.	Ayr, Newbury, Southwell
19 Sat.	Ayr, Newbury
21 Mon.	Edinburgh, Folkestone, Nottingham, Pontefract
22 Tue.	Kempton, Nottingham
23 Wed.	Brighton
24 Thu.	Ascot
25 Fri.	Ascot, Haydock, Redcar
26 Sat.	Ascot, Haydock, Redcar

28 Mon.	Bath, Hamilton,
	Wolverhampton
29 Tue.	Brighton, Newcastle
30 Wed.	Newmarket, Salisbury

October

1 Thu.	Lingfield, Newmarket
2 Fri.	Goodwood, Newmarket
3 Sat.	Goodwood, Newmarket
5 Mon.	Pontefract, Warwick
6 Tue.	Folkestone, Redcar, Warwick
7 Wed.	Haydock, York
8 Thu.	Haydock, York
9 Fri.	Ascot
10 Sat.	Ascot, York
12 Mon.	Leicester
13 Tue.	Chepstow, Leicester
14 Wed.	Redcar
15 Thu.	Newmarket
16 Fri.	Catterick, Newmarket
17 Sat.	Catterick, Newmarket
19 Mon.	Edinburgh, Folkestone,
	Nottingham
20 Tue.	Chepstow, Chester
21 Wed.	Chester
22 Thu.	Newbury, Pontefract
23 Fri.	Doncaster
24 Sat.	Doncaster, Newbury
26 Mon.	Leicester, Lingfield
27 Tue.	Leicester, Redcar
28 Wed.	Yarmouth
29 Thu.	Nottingham
30 Fri.	Newmarket
31 Sat.	Newmarket

November

2 Mon.	Newcastle
3 Tue.	Hamilton
5 Thu.	Edinburgh, Lingfield (a)
6 Fri.	Doncaster
7 Sat.	Doncaster
9 Mon.	Folkestone
10 Tue.	Southwell (a)
14 Sat.	Lingfield (a)
17 Tue.	Southwell (a)
27 Fri.	Southwell (a)
28 Sat.	Lingfield (a)

December

2 Wed.	Southwell (a)
3 Thu.	Lingfield (a)
10 Thu.	Southwell (a)
15 Tue.	Southwell (a)
16 Wed.	Lingfield (a)
19 Sat.	Lingfield (a)
22 Tue.	Lingfield (a)
28 Mon.	Southwell (a)
31 Thu.	Lingfield (a)

CHARACTERISTICS OF RACECOURSES

ASCOT—The Ascot round course is a right-handed, triangular circuit of 1m 6f and 34 yds, with a run-in of 2½f. There is a straight mile course, over which the Royal Hunt Cup is run, and the Old mile course which joins the round course in Swinley Bottom. All races shorter than a mile are decided on the straight course. From the 1½-mile starting gate the round course runs downhill to the bend in Swinley Bottom, where it is level, then rises steadily to the turn into the straight, from where it is uphill until less than a furlong from the winning post, the last hundred yards being more or less level. The straight mile is slightly downhill from the start and then rises to the 5f gate, after which there is a slight fall before the junction with the round course. Despite the downhill run into Swinley Bottom and the relatively short run-in from the final turn, the Ascot course is galloping in character; the turns are easy, there are no minor surface undulations to throw a long-striding horse off balance, and all races are very much against the collar over the last half-mile. The course is, in fact, quite a testing one, and very much so in soft going, when there is a heavy premium on stamina. In such circumstances races over 2 miles to 2¾ miles are very severe tests.
DRAW: The draw seems of little consequence nowadays.

AYR—The Ayr round course is a left-handed, oval track, about twelve furlongs in extent, with a run-in of half a mile. Eleven-furlong races start on a chute, which joins the round course after about a furlong. There is a straight six-furlong course of considerable width. The course is relatively flat, but there are gentle undulations throughout, perhaps more marked in the straight. It has a good surface and well-graded turns, and is a fine and very fair track, on the whole galloping in character.
DRAW: On the straight course a low draw is an advantage in big fields, particularly when the ground is soft.

BATH—The Bath round course is a left-handed, oval track, just over a mile and a half in extent, with a run-in of nearly half a mile. There is an extension for races over five furlongs and five furlongs and 161 yards. The run-in bends to the left, and is on the rise all the way. The mile and the mile-and-a-quarter courses have been designed to give over a quarter of a mile straight at the start, and the track generally is galloping rather than sharp.
DRAW: The draw seems of little consequence nowadays.

BEVERLEY—The Beverley round course is a right-handed, oval track, just over a mile and three furlongs in extent, with a run-in of two and a half furlongs. The five-furlong track bends right at halfway. The general galloping nature of the track is modified by the downhill turn into the straight and the relatively short run-in. The five-furlong course is on the rise throughout, and so is rather testing even in normal conditions; in soft going it takes some getting, particularly for two-year-olds early in the season.
DRAW: High numbers have an advantage over the five-furlong course.

BRIGHTON—The Brighton course takes the shape of an extended 'U' and is 1½ miles in length. The first three furlongs are uphill, following which there is a slight descent followed by a slight rise to about four furlongs from home; the track then runs more sharply downhill until a quarter of a mile out, from where it rises to the last hundred yards, the finish being level. The run-in is about 3½ furlongs, and there is no straight course. This is essentially a sharp track. While the turns are easy enough, the pronounced gradients make Brighton an unsuitable course for big, long-striding horses, resolute gallopers or round-actioned horses. Handy, medium-sized, fluent movers, and quick-actioned horses are much more at home on the course. There are no opportunities for long-distance plodders at Brighton.
DRAW: In sprint races a low number is advantageous, and speed out of the gate even more so.

CARLISLE—Carlisle is a right-handed, pear-shaped course, just over a mile and a half in extent, with a run-in of a little more than three furlongs. The six-furlong course, of which the five-furlong course is a part, the mile course, and the mile-and-a-half course start on three separate off-shoot extensions. For the first three furlongs or so the course runs downhill, then rises for a short distance,

levelling out just beyond the mile post. From there until the turn into the straight the course is flat, apart from minor undulations. The six-furlong course, which bears right soon after the start, and again at the turn into the straight, is level for two furlongs, then rises fairly steeply until the distance, from which point it is practically level. The track is galloping in character, and the six-furlong course is a stiff test of stamina for a two-year-old.
DRAW: High numbers have an advantage which is more marked in the shorter races.

CATTERICK—The Catterick round course is a left-handed, oval track, measuring just under nine furlongs, with a run-in of three furlongs. The five-furlong course bears left before and at the junction with the round course. From the seven-furlong starting gate the round course is downhill almost all the way, and there is a sharp turn on the falling gradient into the straight. The five-furlong course is downhill throughout, quite steeply to start with, and less so thereafter. Catterick is an exceedingly sharp track with pronounced undulations of surface, and it is therefore an impossible course for a big, long-striding animal. Experience of the track counts for a great deal, and jockeyship is of the utmost importance.
DRAW: A low number gives a slight advantage over five furlongs, but in races over six furlongs and seven furlongs a slow beginner on the inside is almost certain to be cut off.

CHEPSTOW—The Chepstow round course is a left-handed, oval track, about two miles in extent, with a run-in of five furlongs. There is a straight mile course, over which all races up to a mile are run. The round course has well-marked undulations, and the straight course is generally downhill and level alternately as far as the run-in, thereafter rising sharply for over two furlongs, and then gradually levelling out to the winning post. Notwithstanding the long run-in and general rise over the last five furlongs, this is not an ideal galloping track because of the changing gradients.
DRAW: Of little consequence nowadays.

CHESTER—Chester is a left-handed, circular course, only a few yards over a mile round, the smallest circuit of any flat-race course in Great Britain. It is quite flat and on the turn almost throughout, and although the run-in is nearly straight, it is less than two furlongs in length. Apart from extreme distance events, such as the Chester Cup and other 2¼m races, the course is against the long-striding, resolute galloper and greatly favours the handy, medium-sized, sharp-actioned horse.
DRAW: Given a good start, the draw is of little consequence. A slow start is virtually impossible to overcome in sprint races.

DONCASTER—Doncaster is a left-handed, pear-shaped course, over 15 furlongs round and quite flat, except for a slight hill about 1¼ miles from the finish. There is a perfectly straight mile, and a round mile starting on an off-shoot of the round course. The run-in from the turn is about 4½ furlongs. This is one of the fairest courses in the country, but its flat surface and great width, its sweeping turn into the straight, and long run-in, make it galloping in character, and ideal for the big, long-striding stayer.
DRAW: The draw is of no importance on the round course. On the straight course high numbers have an advantage, particularly in big fields.

EDINBURGH—The Edinburgh round course is a right-handed oval track, nearly a mile and a quarter in extent, with a run-in of half a mile. There is a straight five-furlong course. The track is flat, with slight undulations and a gentle rise from the distance to the winning post. The turns at the top end of the course and into the straight are very sharp, and handiness and adaptability to negotiate the bends is of the utmost importance. The big, long-striding, cumbersome horse is at a distinct disadvantage on the round track, especially in races at up to a mile and three furlongs, but to a lesser extent in races over longer distances.
DRAW: Over five furlongs low numbers have a considerable advantage when the stalls are on the stand side and high numbers have a slight advantage when the stalls are on the far side. High numbers have an advantage in seven-furlong and mile races.

EPSOM—Epsom is a left-handed, U-shaped course, 1½ miles in extent. The Derby course is decidedly uphill for the first half-mile, level for nearly two furlongs and then quite sharply downhill round the bend to Tattenham Corner and all the way up the straight until approaching the final furlong, from where there is a fairish rise to the winning post. The run-in is less than four furlongs. The 7f and 6f courses start on tangential extensions. The 5f course is quite straight and sharply downhill to the junction with the round course. Races over 1½ miles can be testing if the pace over the first uphill four furlongs is strong, as it frequently is in the Derby. Otherwise the track is not really testing in itself, and races up to 8½ furlongs are very sharp indeed, the sprint courses being the fastest in the world. Owing to its bends and pronounced downhill gradients, Epsom favours the handy, fluent-actioned, medium-sized horse: big horses sometimes handle the course well enough, but cumbersome horses, long-striding gallopers, or those with pronounced 'knee-action' are not suited by it and are frequently quite unable to act upon it, especially when the going is firm or hard. Any hesitation at the start or slowness into stride results in considerable loss of ground over the first furlong in sprint races. For this reason Epsom is no course for a green and inexperienced two-year-old, slow to realise what is required.

DRAW: Nowadays a high draw is a considerable advantage over five furlongs and a slight advantage over six. A low number is an advantage over distances of seven furlongs to a mile and a quarter. A quick start is desirable at up to seven furlongs at least.

FOLKESTONE—The Folkestone round course is a right-handed, pear-shaped track, about ten and a half furlongs in extent, with a run-in of two and a half furlongs. There is a straight six-furlong course. The course is undulating, with the last part slightly on the rise, but notwithstanding its width, the easy turns, and the uphill finish, it is by no means a galloping track.

DRAW: No advantage on the straight course. Middle to high numbers have a slight advantage over seven furlongs. High numbers seem to have an advantage over a mile and a quarter and a mile and a half.

GOODWOOD—The Goodwood track consists of a nearly straight six-furlong course, with a triangular right-handed loop circuit. Races over two and a half miles start near the winning post: the horses run the reverse way of the straight, branch left at the first or lower bend, go right-handed round the loop and return to the straight course via the top bend. Races over two miles, one and three quarter miles and one and a half miles are also run on this course. Over distances between seven furlongs and a mile and a quarter all running is done in the direction of the finish, with all but the mile and a quarter races using the lower bend. Although there is a five-furlong run-in from the top bend, the turns and, more specially, the pronounced downhill gradients from the turn, make Goodwood essentially a sharp track, favouring the active, handy, fluent-mover rather than the big, long-striding horse. This is of lesser importance in long-distance races, where the emphasis is on sound stamina, and of great importance in the shorter-distance races, particularly in sprints and especially when the going is on top. The five-furlong course is one of the fastest in the country.

DRAW: A low number is regarded as advantageous in sprint races when the ground is soft. Alacrity out of the gate is certainly of importance in five-furlong races.

HAMILTON—The Hamilton track is a perfectly straight six-furlong course, with a pear-shaped, right-handed loop, the whole being a mile and five furlongs in extent from a start in front of the stands, round the loop and back to the winning post. The run-in is five furlongs. The turns are very easy, and the course is undulating for the most part, but just over three furlongs from the winning post there are steep gradients into and out of a pronounced hollow, followed by a severe hill to the finish.

DRAW: Middle to high numbers have an advantage in races over the straight course.

HAYDOCK PARK—Haydock Park is a left-handed, oval-shaped course, about thirteen furlongs round, with a run-in of 4½ furlongs, and a straight 6-furlong course. The alternative 6-furlong course and all races of 1½ miles start on tangential extensions to the round course. Haydock is rather galloping in character.

DRAW: When conditions are testing there is a considerable advantage in racing close to the stand rail in the straight. Whatever the conditions, in races over 7 furlongs and a mile a good start and a handy position on the home turn are important.

FLAT RACING FIXTURES 1992

Sat	Apr 18	Beamish Handicap
		Field Marshal Stakes
Sat	May 2	Fairey Spring Trophy
Mon	May 4	Swinton Insurance Hurdle
Fri	May 22	Spinal Injuries Association Raceday
Sat	May 23	Tote Credit Silver Bowl
		Sandy Lane Stakes
Fri	June 5	Burtonwood Brewery Handicap
Sat	June 6	Hazlewood Foods John of Gaunt Stakes
Thu	July 2	July Trophy
Fri	July 3	Johnny Osborne Handicap
Sat	July 4	Lancashire Oaks
		Old Newton Cup
		Cock of the North Stakes
Fri	Aug 7	Ormskirk Handicap
Sat	Aug 8	Burtonwood Brewery Rose of Lancaster Stakes
		Coral Bookmakers Handicap
Fri	Aug 14	Claude Harrison Handicap
Fri	Sep 4	Castle Club Handicap
Sat	Sep 5	The Sprint Cup
Fri	Sep 25	Stanley Leisure Dream Mile
Sat	Sep 26	Vaux Handicap
Wed	Oct 7	Fonseca Port Handicap
Thu	Oct 8	Hawthorn Handicap

N.B. The details given above are correct at the time of going to press, but factors outside the control of the Haydock Park Executive may result in alterations having to be made.

For enquiries and special group prices please contact:
HAYDOCK PARK RACECOURSE, NEWTON-LE-WILLOWS,
MERSEYSIDE WA12 0HQ
Phone: Ashton-in-Makerfield (0942) 725963

HAYDOCK PARK .... LEADING THE FIELD

KEMPTON—Kempton is a right-handed, triangular course, just over 13 furlongs round. The ten-furlong Jubilee Course starts on an extension to the round course. Sprint races are run over a separate diagonal course. The Kempton track is perfectly flat with normal characteristics, being neither a sharp track nor a galloping one.
DRAW: On the sprint course a draw near the rails is advantageous when the ground is soft; when the stalls are placed on the far side a high draw is an enormous advantage nowadays whatever the going.

LEICESTER—The Leicester round course is a right-handed, oval track, about a mile and three quarters in extent, with a run-in of four and a half furlongs. The straight mile course, on which all races of up to a mile are run, is mainly downhill to halfway, then rises gradually for over two furlongs, finishing on the level. The course is well-drained, the bends into the straight and beyond the winning post have been eased and cambered, and the track is galloping. For two-year-olds early in the season it poses quite a test of stamina.
DRAW: Low numbers have an advantage in races at up to a mile and the advantage seems to be more marked when the going is on the soft side.

LINGFIELD (Turf)—The Lingfield Park round course is a left-handed loop, which intersects the straight of seven furlongs and 140 yards nearly half a mile out. For nearly half its length the round course is quite flat, then rises with easy gradients to the summit of a slight hill, after which there is a downhill turn to the straight. The straight course has a considerable downhill gradient to halfway, and is slightly downhill for the rest of the way. The straight course is very easy, and the track as a whole is sharp, putting a premium on speed and adaptability, and making relatively small demands upon stamina, though this does not, of course, apply to races over two miles. The mile and a half course, over which the Derby Trial is run, bears quite close resemblance to the Epsom Derby course.
DRAW: On the straight course high numbers have a big advantage, usually the higher the number the bigger the advantage.

LINGFIELD (All-Weather)—The all-weather track is laid out inside the turf track, following much the same line in the straight and the back straight then turning sharply for home at the top corner, so that it is only a mile and a quarter in extent, a chute in the straight providing a thirteen-furlong start. There is no straight sprint course, the fields at five furlongs and six furlongs having two bends to negotiate. The surface is Equitrack, whereas Southwell's is Fibresand.
DRAW: A low number seems an advantage in sprints, but the ability to lie handy is probably even more important.

NEWBURY—The Newbury round course is a left-handed, oval track, about a mile and seven furlongs in extent, with a run-in of nearly five furlongs. There is a straight mile course, which is slightly undulating throughout. Races on the round mile and over the extended seven furlongs start on an extension from the round course. Notwithstanding the undulations this is a good galloping track.
DRAW: A high number used to be a fairly considerable advantage over the straight course, but since the narrowing of the track the advantage seems to have disappeared.

NEWCASTLE—Newcastle is a left-handed, oval-shaped course of a mile and six furlongs in circumference. There is also a straight course, over which all races of seven furlongs or less are run. The course is decidedly galloping in character, and a steady climb from the turn into the straight makes Newcastle a testing track, particularly for two-year-olds early in the season. Ability to see the journey out thoroughly is most important.
DRAW: On the straight course, the softer the ground the bigger the advantage the lower numbers enjoy. On a sound surface, horses racing up the middle seem to be at a disadvantage with those racing towards either rail.

NEWMARKET ROWLEY MILE COURSE—The Cesarewitch course is two and a quarter miles in extent, with a right-handed bend after a mile, the last mile and a quarter being the straight Across the Flat. From the Cesarewitch start the course runs generally downhill to a sharp rise just before the turn. There are undulations throughout the first mile of the straight, then the course runs downhill for a furlong to the Dip, and uphill for the last furlong to the winning post. This is an exceedingly wide, galloping track, without minor irregularities of surface, so it is ideal for the big, long-striding horse, except for the descent into the Dip, which is more than counterbalanced by the final hill.

1034

NEWMARKET SUMMER (JULY) COURSE—The Newmarket Summer Course is two miles and a furlong in extent, with a right-handed bend at halfway, the first mile being part of the Cesarewitch course, and the last the straight Bunbury Mile. The course runs generally downhill to a sharp rise just before the turn. There are undulations for the first three quarters of a mile of the straight, then the course runs downhill for a furlong to a dip and uphill for the last furlong to the winning post. This is an exceedingly wide, galloping track, ideal for the big, long-striding horse, except for the descent into the dip, which is more than counterbalanced by the final hill.
DRAW: The draw confers little advantage.

NOTTINGHAM—The Nottingham round course is a left-handed, oval track, about a mile and a half in extent, with a run-in of four and a half furlongs. There is a straight 6f course, but no longer a straight mile. The course is flat and the turns are easy.
DRAW: In sprints when the stalls are placed on the stand side high numbers have a clear advantage, increasing as the ground softens. With the stalls on the far side low numbers are preferred.

PONTEFRACT—Pontefract is a left-handed, oval track, about two miles in extent. There is no straight course, and the run-in is only just over two furlongs. There are considerable gradients and a testing hill over the last three furlongs. The undulations, the sharp bend into the straight, and the short run-in disqualify it from being described as a galloping track, but there is a premium on stamina.
DRAW: A low number is advantageous particularly over five furlongs but it becomes a decided disadvantage if a horse fails to jump off well.

REDCAR—Redcar is a narrow, left-handed, oval track, about a mile and three quarters in extent, with a run-in of five furlongs, which is part of the straight mile course. The course is perfectly flat with normal characteristics, and provides an excellent gallop.
DRAW: Middle to high numbers have a big advantage on the straight course.

RIPON—The Ripon course is a right-handed, oval circuit of 13 furlongs, with a run-in of 5f, and a straight 6f course. Owing to the rather cramped bends and the surface undulations in the straight, the Ripon track is rather sharp in character.
DRAW: On the straight course the draw is of no importance but in races on the mile course, horses drawn in the high numbers seem to have an advantage.

SALISBURY—The Salisbury track is a right-handed loop course, with a run-in of seven furlongs, which, however, is not straight, for the mile course, of which it is a part, has a right-handed elbow after three furlongs. For races over a mile and three quarters horses start opposite the Club Enclosure, and running away from the stands, bear to the left, and go round the loop. The course, which is uphill throughout the last half-mile, is galloping and rather testing.
DRAW: Low numbers are favoured in sprints when the going is soft.

SANDOWN—Sandown is a right-handed, oval-shaped course of 13 furlongs, with a straight run-in of 4f. There is a separate straight course which runs across the main circuit over which all 5f races are decided. From the 1¼m starting gate, the Eclipse Stakes course, the track is level to the turn into the straight, from where it is uphill until less than a furlong from the winning post, the last hundred yards being more or less level. The 5f track is perfectly straight and rises steadily throughout. Apart from the minor gradients between the main winning post and the 1¼m starting gate, there are no undulations to throw a long-striding horse off balance, and all races over the round course are very much against the collar from the turn into the straight. The course is, in fact, a testing one, and over all distances the ability to see the trip out well is of the utmost importance.
DRAW: On the five-furlong course high numbers have a considerable advantage in big fields when the ground is soft, and high numbers are favoured when the stalls are placed on the far side whatever the ground. Low numbers are favoured when the stalls are on the stand side.

SOUTHWELL—The left-handed course is laid out in a tight, level, mile-and-a-quarter oval, a spur to the three-furlong run-in providing a straight five furlongs.

There are two types of surface, the all-weather track on the outside of the turf track. Nearly all races here are truly run. The all-weather surface is Fibresand, whereas Lingfield's is Equitrack.
DRAW: No advantage on the straight five furlongs. Over six and seven furlongs on the round course a low draw is probably advantageous, a quick beginning definitely so.

THIRSK—The Thirsk round course is a left-handed, oval track, just over a mile and a quarter in extent, with a run-in of half a mile. There is a straight six-furlong course, which is slightly undulating throughout. The round course itself is almost perfectly flat, but though the turns are relatively easy and the ground well levelled all round, the track is on the sharp side and by no means ideal for a horse that requires time to settle down, and time and space to get down to work in the straight.
DRAW: High numbers have a big advantage on the straight course.

WARWICK—Warwick is a broad, left-handed, oval track, just over a mile and three quarters in extent, with a run-in of about three and a half furlongs. There is no straight course, the five-furlong course having a left-hand elbow at the junction with the round course. Mile races start on an extension from the round course, the first four and a half furlongs being perfectly straight. This is a sharp track, with the emphasis on speed and adaptability rather than stamina. The laboured galloper is at a disadvantage, especially in races at up to a mile.
DRAW: A high number is advantageous in races up to a mile when the ground is soft, but a quick beginning is also important.

WINDSOR—Windsor racecourse, laid out in the form of a figure eight, is 12½ furlongs in extent. In races of around 1½ miles both left-handed and right-handed turns are met. The last five furlongs of the course are straight, except for a slight bend to the right three furlongs from the finish. The six-furlong start is now on an extension of the straight. Although perfectly flat throughout, the bends make this track rather sharp in character. However, as there is a nearly straight 5f run-in the relative sharpness of the track is of no consequence in the longer races. Big, long-striding horses which normally require a more galloping course are at little or no disadvantage over these trips.
DRAW: No material advantage.

WOLVERHAMPTON—The Wolverhampton round course is a left-handed, pear-shaped or triangular track, just over a mile and a half in extent, with a run-in of five furlongs. There is a straight course of five furlongs. The course is level throughout, with normal characteristics.
DRAW: The draw confers no advantage.

YARMOUTH—The Yarmouth round course is a narrow, left-handed, oval track, about thirteen furlongs in extent, with a run-in of five furlongs. There is a straight mile course. Apart from a slight fall just before the run-in, the track is perfectly flat, with normal characteristics.
DRAW: Middle to high numbers have an advantage on the straight course.

YORK—York is a left-handed, U-shaped course, 2 miles in extent, and quite flat throughout. There is also a perfectly flat straight course, over which all 5f and 6f races are run. 7f races start on a spur which joins the round course after about two furlongs. The run-in from the turn is nearly 5 furlongs. This is one of the best courses in the country, of great width throughout and with a sweeping turn into the long straight. The entire absence of surface undulations makes it ideal for a long-striding, resolute galloper, but it is really a splendid track, bestowing no great favours on any type of horse.
DRAW: The draw has usually been of significance on the straight course in recent seasons but the advantage hasn't remained constant, low numbers being favoured at some meetings, high numbers at others. At the last meeting in 1991 the draw seemed to bestow no material advantage.

York

1992 Fixtures

Great Races Great Racing

MAY
TUESDAY 12th●WEDNESDAY 13th●THURSDAY 14th

JUNE
FRIDAY 12th●SATURDAY 13th

JULY
FRIDAY 10th●SATURDAY 11th

AUGUST
TUESDAY 18th●WEDNESDAY 19th●THURSDAY 20th

SEPTEMBER
WEDNESDAY 2nd●THURSDAY 3rd

OCTOBER
WEDNESDAY 7th●THURSDAY 8th●SATURDAY 10th

Fifteen Days Racing

See it Live . . .

York Race Committee, The Racecourse, York YO2 1EX

Telephone: (0904) 620911   Fax: (0904) 611071

ERRATA & ADDENDA

'RACEHORSES OF 1990'

Arzanni	dam won over 7f and 11.5f
Church Missionary (USA)	All Saints Day is by Alydar
Dayjur (USA)	is a bay
Eastern Sunset	is brother to Easter Rambler
Ganges (USA)	is a grey, as are dam and maternal grandam
Hector Protector (USA)	is a chestnut. Also (Page 391) Nonoalco won Salamandre in 1973
Kaikoura	dam top-rated filly in New Zealand, 1973/4
Lycius (USA)	Page 532 won Middle Park by half a length
Matter of Law	is a bay
Regal Crest (USA)	Peter Davies won Somerville Tattersall Stakes
Roger Ramjet (Ire)	IR 32,000F
Shadayid (USA)	Page 828 Shadeed ran in Derby (well beaten)
Shaikh Safi	El Dalsad won a nursery
Shamshom Al Arab (Ire)	Allez Au Bon is by Alzao
Star of Gdansk (USA)	sire of dam is Young Emperor
Sun Surfer (Fr)	later won French Provincial maiden (9.2f*) for J. Hammond
Volksraad	half-brother to In Unison

'RACEHORSES OF 1989'

Learycal (USA)	rating should be 108

Standing at Thornton Stud

KRIS

chesnut 1976 by SHARPEN UP - DOUBLY SURE by Reliance

CHAMPION EUROPEAN MILER
in 1979 and 1980
CHAMPION SIRE of Group 1 winners:

OH SO SHARP, COMMON GROUNDS, UNITE, FITNAH, FLASH OF
STEEL, SUDDEN LOVE, RAFHA, SHAVIAN, SHAMSHIR,
LEADING SIRE of BLACK TYPE PERFORMERS to Runners

Fee:£25,000 + £25,000 Oct 1st (Limited to 51 mares)

John Day, Thornton-le-Street, Thirsk, Yorkshire.
Telephone: (0845) 522522.
Enquiries to:
LONDON THOROUGHBRED SERVICES LTD.,
44 St Leonard's Terrace, London SW3 4QH.
Telephone: 071 - 351 - 2181. Fax: 071 - 352 - 8958.

Standing at Woodland Stud

PHARLY

chesnut 1974 by Lyphard - Comely by Boran
Winner of 3 Group 1 races at 2 and 3 years

Highly Successful Sire

with Lifetime Earnings of £4,500,000

including

33 Group / Stakes Winners

His First 10 crops have produced
53% Winners to Foals

Fee: £5,000 October 1st NFNF (Limited to 48 mares)

Woodland Stud, Snailwell Road, Newmarket, Suffolk.
Telephone: Newmarket (0638) 663081.

Enquiries to:
LONDON THOROUGHBRED SERVICES LTD.,
44 St Leonard's Terrace, London SW3 4QH.
Telephone: 071 - 351 - 2181. Fax: 071 - 352 - 8958.

Standing at Littleton Stud

ROBELLINO

bay 1979 by Roberto - Isobelline by Pronto
Dual Group Winner, broke course record at Ascot at 2

Champion First Season Sire
in England 1985 (when standing in USA)

Sire of 53% winners to Foals
from his first 6 crops

FIRST ENGLISH CROP of 2-year-olds in 1992
Fee: £5,000 October 1st NFNF

Jeff Smith or Ted Voute, Littleton Stud, Winchester, Hants. S021 2QF.
Telephone: Winchester (0962) 880210.

Enquiries to:
LONDON THOROUGHBRED SERVICES LTD.,
44 St Leonard's Terrace, London SW3 4QH.
Telephone: 071 - 351 - 2181. Fax: 071 - 352 - 8958.

Standing at Woodland Stud

SHARPO

chesnut 1977 by SHARPEN UP - MOIETY BIRD by Falcon

EUROPE's LEADING SIRE

of 2-year-olds in 1991

with 15 individual Winners

Lifetime Earnings over £2,000,000
including 10 Group/Stakes winners

Fee: £5,000 October 1st NFNF (Limited to 50 mares)

Woodland Stud, Snailwell Road, Newmarket, Suffolk.
Telephone: Newmarket (0638) 663081.
Enquiries to:
LONDON THOROUGHBRED SERVICES LTD.,
44 St Leonard's Terrace, London SW3 4QH.
Telephone: 071 - 351 - 2181. Fax: 071 - 352 - 8958.

Standing at Highclere Stud

SHARROOD

grey 1983 by CARO - ANGEL ISLAND by Cougar II

Good Looking (1.2 Million Dollar Yearling)
Dual Group 2 Winner, Classic Placed, Winner of 4 races at 2

Very Successful First Season Sire in 1991
Sire of 7 Winners of 9 races, 9 others placed and £134,367

40 Two-Year-Olds in 1992
39 Yearlings in 1992

Fee: £5,000 October 1st NFNF

Carolyn Warren, Highclere Stud, Newbury, Berks RG15 9LT.
Telephone: (0635) 253212.

Enquiries to:
LONDON THOROUGHBRED SERVICES LTD.,
44 St Leonard's Terrace, London SW3 4QH.
Telephone: 071 - 351 - 2181. Fax: 071 - 352 - 8958.

Standing at Brook Stud

SHAVIAN

bay 1987 by KRIS - MIXED APPLAUSE by Nijinsky

Winner at Ascot at 2

A LEADING MILER at 3 in 1990
including:
**St James's Palace Stakes Gr.1 at Royal Ascot
Beefeater Gin Celebration Mile Gr.2 at Goodwood**

rated 125 in Racehorses of 1990

Fee: £6,000 October 1st NFNF (Limited to 51 mares)

Will Edmeades, Brook Stud, Cheveley, Newmarket, Suffolk CB8 9DG
Telephone: Newmarket (0638) 730212. Fax: (0638) 730819.

**Enquiries to:
LONDON THOROUGHBRED SERVICES LTD.,
44 St Leonard's Terrace, London SW3 4QH.
Telephone: 071 - 351 - 2181. Fax: 071 - 352 - 8958.**

1046

Standing at Plantation Stud

SLIP ANCHOR

bay 1982 by SHIRLEY HEIGHTS - SAYONARA by Birkhahn

Champion European 3-year-old in 1985

One of the Leading British Based Sires
59% winners to 3yo runners in 1991
(10 or more runners)

Fee: £15,000 October 1st NFNF (Limited to 50 mares)

Leslie Harrison, Exning, Newmarket, Suffolk CB8 7LJ.
Telephone: Exning (0638) 577341. Fax: (0638) 578474.
Enquiries to:
LONDON THOROUGHBRED SERVICES LTD.,
44 St Leonard's Terrace, London SW3 4QH.
Telephone: 071 - 351 - 2181. Fax: 071 - 352 - 8958.

STALLIONS FOR 1992

AL HAREB (El Gran Senor - Icing)

ALZAO (Lyphard - Lady Rebecca)

ARCHWAY (Thatching - Rose of Jericho)

BE MY GUEST (Northern Dancer - What a Treat)

BLUEBIRD (Storm Bird - Ivory Dawn)

CAERLEON (Nijinsky - Foreseer)

CLASSIC MUSIC (Northern Dancer - Fairy Bridge)

DANEHILL (Danzig - Razyana)

DON'T FORGET ME (Ahonoora - African Doll)

EL GRAN SENOR (Northern Dancer - Sex Appeal)

GLENSTAL (Northern Dancer - Cloonlara)

HIGH ESTATE (Shirley Heights - Regal Beauty)

COOLMORE

CONTACT: COOLMORE STUD, FETHARD, CO. TIPPERARY, IRELAND.
TEL: 353-52-31298. TELEX: 80695. FAX: 353-52-31382.
BOB LANIGAN: 353-52-31298. CHRISTY GRASSICK: 353-52-31313.

LAST TYCOON (Try My Best - Mill Princess)

LAW SOCIETY (Alleged - Bold Bikini)

LOMOND (Northern Dancer - My Charmer)

PERSIAN HEIGHTS (Persian Bold - Ready & Willing)

ROYAL ACADEMY (Nijinsky - Crimson Saint)

SADLER'S WELLS (Northern Dancer - Fairy Bridge)

SCENIC (Sadler's Wells - Idyllic)

SEATTLE DANCER (Nijinsky - My Charmer)

STORM BIRD (Northern Dancer - South Ocean)

THATCHING (Thatch - Abella)

TIROL (Thatching - Alpine Niece)

TRY MY BEST (Northern Dancer - Sex Appeal)

WAAJIB (Try My Best - Coryana)

WOODMAN (Mr. Prospector - Playmate)

Airlie

A Quality Source of International Bloodlines

STALLIONS FOR 1992

Ballad Rock

Champion Irish Sprinter and now one of Europe's most reliable sires of speedy two-year-olds who also train on – **ROCK CITY** (**Gr.2** Gimcrack Stakes and 5 other **Gr.** wins); **BALLA COVE** (**Gr.1** Middle Park Stakes and dual **SW** in USA); **CHIEF SINGER** (4 **Gr.** wins and Classic placed) and **FLAMING ROCK** (3 **Gr.1**'s; Champion in S. Africa).

Salt Dome

Gr.2 winning sprinter in USA by **BLUSHING GROOM** and brother in blood to **MT LIVERMORE** (himself sire of **HOUSE-BUSTER**, 14 **Gr.** and Stakes wins in the USA, incl. the 1991 Vosburgh Stakes, **Gr.1**). **SALT DOME's** first crop yearlings averaged **6,929 gns** (23 sold) and his 1991 foals made up to **12,500 gns**.

Ela-Mana-Mou

European Champion Racehorse and now a leading International Sire with Classic winners **SNURGE** (**Gr.1** St Leger, **Gr.1** Gran Premio di Milano, 1991 etc.; and third **Gr.1** Prix de l'Arc de Triomphe 1990); **TRIVIAL PURSUIT** (in Sweden) and **EUROBIRD** (in Ireland). Also sire of **Gr.1** winners **ALMAARAD** and **NATSKI** (in Australia); **EMMSON** and **SUMAYR** (in France). 1991 yearlings averaged **18,047 gns**.

Standaan

Brilliantly fast sprinter from top French and Italian families. Defeated Champion Sharpo by over 3 lengths in **Gr.3** Palace House Stakes. Was **Champion First Crop Sire** in N.Z., siring a Classic winner. First Irish crop foals made up to **40,000 gns** and now siring 2-y-o winners in Europe including the useful **TRACK TWENTY NINE**.

Glow

Grade 2 winning miler by the great **NORTHERN DANCER**, and closely related to Champion sire **CAERLEON** (sire of **GENEROUS**) and to **Gr.** sire **VISION**. Over 73% of his runners have won or have been placed in 1991, incl. **DANCE PARTOUT** (4 wins), **SPARKLING SOLO** (2 wins, £17,336) and Stakes-placed winning 2-y-o **POLLY'S GLOW**.

Airlie

Lucan, Co. Dublin.
Tel: 01 6280267/6281548/6280597.
Fax: 01 6283109.

DARLEY STUD MANAGEMENT STALLIONS FOR 1992

Standing at Dalham Hall Stud, Newmarket

LYCIUS 1988 by Mr Prospector - Lypatia by Lyphard
Record breaking Group 1 winner at 2 and placed in 5 G.1 races at 3, defeated the winners of 15 G.1 races. Retired to stud in 1992.

MACHIAVELLIAN 1987 by Mr Prospector - Coup de Folie by Halo
Unbeaten Champion European 2yo in 1989. The best son of Mr Prospector to stand in Europe, grandam half sister to **NORTHERN DANCER**. 1st Foals 1992.

OLD VIC 1986 by Sadler's Wells - Cockade by Derring-Do
Champion European 3yo in 1989, winner of French and Irish Derbies **G.1.** 1st Foals 1992.

POLISH PRECEDENT 1986 by Danzig - Past Example by Buckpasser
Winner of 7 consecutive races in 1989 including 2 Group 1 races. 1st Yearlings 1992

SHAREEF DANCER 1980 by Northern Dancer - Sweet Alliance by Sir Ivor
A Leading Sire in 1991 with **POSSESSIVE DANCER** (dual Oaks winner), **ROCK HOPPER, KAZOO, GLEN JORDAN, NEDIYM** etc.

SOVIET STAR 1984 by Nureyev - Veruschka by Venture VII
Champion European Sprinter 1988. Winner of 5 Group 1 races. 2-y-olds 1992

Standing at Aston Upthorpe Stud, Oxfordshire

MTOTO 1983 by Busted - Amazer by Mincio
Champion European 4-year-old in 1987. Winner of King George VI & Queen Elizabeth Diamond S. **G.1**, Coral-Eclipse S. **G.1** (twice), Prince of Wales's S. **G.2** (twice). 2-y-olds 1992

Standing at Kildangan Stud, Co. Kildare.

IN THE WINGS 1986 by Sadler's Wells - High Hawk by Shirley Heights
G.1 winner in USA, England and France of Breeders' Cup Turf **G.1**, Hanson Coronation Cup **G.1**, Grand Prix de Saint-Cloud **G.1**. 1st Foals 1992

SHAADI 1986 by Danzig - Unfurled by Hoist the Flag
Unbeaten 2-y-old, winner at 3 of Airlie/Coolmore Irish 2000 Guineas **G.1**, St James's Palace S. **G.1**, Charles Heidsieck Champagne Craven S. **G.3**. 1st Yearlings 1992

Enquiries to:
Mrs Notman or Mrs Blackwell, **Darley Stud Management Company Ltd.,** Dalham Hall Stud, Duchess Drive, Newmarket, Suffolk. Telephone: Newmarket (0638) 730070. Fax: (0638) 730167.

51 Lansdowne Road
Ballsbridge
Dublin 4

Telephone: 686222
Telex: 93850 BBA EI
Fax: 685634

BBA Ireland Ltd

The oldest and
most experienced
Bloodstock Agency
group in the world

Stallion and
Broodmare
Management

Insurance

Shipping

Representation
at Public Sales
Worldwide

Negotiation of
Private Sales
and Purchases

Syndication

Directors:

J.H.N.D. Irwin
Chairman

T.N. O'Callaghan
Managing

A.M.V. Nicoll

Major C.R. Philipson

J.F. Harvey-Barnes

M.J. Dowling

F.A. McNulty
Financial

E. McGarry
Secretary

Executive:

C. Wilson
Insurance

Allow us to make you a part of our history.

Horses remain at owners risk while in charge of the agency

Timeform

The Champions

from the 'Racehorses' series

Horse of the Year

1969	Levmoss	**133**
1970	Nijinsky	**138**
1971	Brigadier Gerard	**141**
	Mill Reef	**141**
1972	Brigadier Gerard	**144**
1973	Apalachee	**137**
	Rheingold	**137**
1974	Allez France	**136**
1975	Grundy	**137**
1976	Youth	**135**
1977	Alleged	**137**
1978	Alleged	**138**
1979	Troy	**137**
1980	Moorestyle	**137**
1981	Shergar	**140**
1982	Ardross	**134**
1983	Habibti	**136**
1984	Provideo	**112**
1985	Pebbles	**135**
1986	Dancing Brave	**140**
1987	Reference Point	**139**
1988	Warning	**136**
1989	Zilzal	**137**
1990	Dayjur	**137**
1991	Generous	**139**

Best Two-Year-Old Colt

1969	Nijinsky	131		1981	Wind & Wuthering	132
1970	My Swallow	134		1982	Diesis	133
1971	Deep Diver	134		1983	El Gran Senor	131
1972	The Go-Between	129		1984	Kala Dancer	129
1973	Apalachee	137		1985	Huntingdale	132
1974	Grundy	134		1986	Reference Point	132
1975	Manado	130		1987	Warning	127p
1976	Blushing Groom	131		1988	Prince of Dance	128
1977	Try My Best	130p			Scenic	128
1978	Tromos	134		1989	Be My Chief	123p
1979	Monteverdi	129		1990	Hector Protector	122p
1980	Storm Bird	134		1991	Arazi	135

Best Two-Year-Old Filly

1969	Mange Tout	125		1981	Circus Ring	122
1970	Cawston's Pride	131		1982	Ma Biche	123
1971	Rose Dubarry	127		1983	Treizieme	121
1972	Jacinth	133		1984	Triptych	125
1973	Melchbourne	125		1985	Femme Elite	124
1974	Cry of Truth	129		1986	Forest Flower	127
1975	Theia	128		1987	Ravinella	121p
1976	Cloonlara	130		1988	Tessla	116p
1977	Cherry Hinton	125			Pass The Peace	116p
1978	Sigy	132		1989	Negligent	118p
1979	Aryenne	120		1990	Shadayid	117p
1980	Marwell	124		1991	Midnight Air	111p

Best Sprinter

1969	Song	132		1981	Marwell	133
1970	Amber Rama	133		1982	Sharpo	130
1971	Joshua	129		1983	Habibti	136
1972	Deep Diver	134		1984	Chief Singer	131
1973	Sandford Lad	133		1985	Never So Bold	135
1974	Saritamer	130		1986	Last Tycoon	131
1975	Flirting Around	134		1987	Ajdal	130
1976	Lochnager	132		1988	Soviet Star	128
1977	Gentilhombre	131		1989	Cadeaux Genereux	131
1978	Solinus	130		1990	Dayjur	137
1979	Thatching	131		1991	Polish Patriot	128
1980	Moorestyle	137				

Best Miler

Year	Horse	Rating	Year	Horse	Rating
1969	Habitat	**134**	1981	Northjet	**136**
1970	Welsh Pageant	**130**	1982	Green Forest	**134**
1971	Brigadier Gerard	**141**	1983	Luth Enchantee	**130**
1972	Brigadier Gerard	**144**	1984	El Gran Senor	**136**
1973	Thatch	**136**	1985	Shadeed	**135**
1974	Nonoalco	**131**	1986	Dancing Brave	**140**
1975	Bolkonski	**134**	1987	Miesque	**131**
1976	Wollow	**132**	1988	Warning	**136**
1977	Blushing Groom	**131**	1989	Zilzal	**137**
1978	Homing	**130**	1990	Markofdistinction	**130**
1979	Kris	**135**		Royal Academy	**130**
1980	Known Fact	**135**	1991	Selkirk	**129**

Best Middle-Distance Horse

Year	Horse	Rating	Year	Horse	Rating
1969	Park Top	**131**	1982	Assert	**134**
1970	Nijinsky	**138**	1983	Shareef Dancer	**135**
1971	Mill Reef	**141**	1984	Teenoso	**135**
1972	Mill Reef	**141**		Sagace	**135**
1973	Rheingold	**137**	1985	Slip Anchor	**136**
1974	Allez France	**136**	1986	Dancing Brave	**140**
1975	Grundy	**137**	1987	Reference Point	**139**
1976	Youth	**135**	1988	Mtoto	**134**
1977	Alleged	**137**		Tony Bin	**134**
1978	Alleged	**138**	1989	Old Vic	**136**
1979	Troy	**137**	1990	Saumarez	**132**
1980	Argument	**133**	1991	Generous	**139**
1981	Shergar	**140**			

Best Stayer

Year	Horse	Rating	Year	Horse	Rating
1969	Levmoss	**133**	1980	Le Moss	**135**
1970	High Line	**125**	1981	Ardross	**131**
1971	Rock Roi	**127**	1982	Ardross	**134**
1972	Rock Roi	**127**	1983	Little Wolf	**127**
1973	Parnell	**130**	1984	Commanche Run	**129**
1974	Ragstone	**128**	1985	Oh So Sharp	**131**
1975	Bruni	**132**	1986	Moon Madness	**128**
1976	Sagaro	**129**	1987	Reference Point	**139**
1977	Dunfermline	**133**	1988	Minster Son	**130**
	Sagaro	**133**	1989	Michelozzo	**127p**
1978	Buckskin	**133**	1990	Snurge	**130**
1979	Buckskin	**131**	1991	Toulon	**125**
	Le Moss	**131**